CROSSWORD PUZZLE DICTIONARY

CROSSWORD PUZZLE DICTIONARY

6TH EDITION

ANDREW SWANFELDT

HarperPerennial

A Division of HarperCollinsPublishers

A hardcover edition of this book was published in 1994 by HarperCollins Publishers, Inc.

The sixth edition was compiled by the staff of Dictionary & Reference Specialists:
Editor: Frank R. Abate
Associate Editors: Jacquelyn S. Goodwin, Elizabeth J. Jewell
Editorial Assistants: Ellen Cavanagh, Terri Finkeldey, Ruth Manley, Julie Marsh, Daniel Partner

HarperCollins books may be purchased for educational, business, or sales promotional use. For information, please write to: Special Markets Department, HarperCollins Publishers, Inc., 10 East 53rd Street, New York, N.Y. 10022.

FIRST HARPERPERENNIAL EDITION PUBLISHED 1995.

Designed by Jessica Shatan

Editor's Preface

This thoroughly revised and expanded Sixth Edition of *The Crossword Puzzle Dictionary*, originally compiled by the late Andrew Swanfeldt, reflects the many significant changes in language, politics, society, history, and culture since the previous edition.

Geopolitical entries have been completely reworked and substantially expanded. Coverage of larger and more established countries has been increased and brought up-to-date. Among the additional entries are those for the new nations of Eastern Europe and for nations established as a consequence of the breakup of the Soviet Union. Major cities of the world, all 50 states of the United States, and major U.S. cities all receive fuller coverage. Information about each of the continents is also revised and updated.

This edition also includes new entries for prominent authors, composers, artists, dramatists, playwrights, and architects, entered under the country of their birth or fame. Another new feature is the inclusion of Nobel and Pulitzer prize recipients, plus winners of the Academy Awards. Coverage of noted figures in science and technology is considerably expanded. Sports entries are updated with names of prominent athletes and new teams.

Coverage of the general language, including synonyms and terms closely related to clues used in crossword puzzles, has also been carefully reviewed and enhanced. The heart of this dictionary, its coverage of answer words for common crossword puzzle clues, has also been much enhanced. Those familiar with previous editions will find this new "Swanfeldt" still as easy to use as always, while newcomers will value its thoroughness and precision.

Abbreviations Used in this Book

abbr.	abbreviation	her.	heraldic
anc.	ancient	Ind.	Indian
Afr.	African	Ir.	Irish
anat.	anatomical	It.	Italian
Ar.	Arabic	Jap.	Japanese
Austr.	Australian	L.	Latin
bot.	botanical	mas.	masculine
Br.	British	Mex.	Mexican
c.	capital	N.Y.	New York
Cal.	California	O.T.	Old Testament
Ch.	Chinese	pert. to	pertaining to
comb. form	combining form	P.I.	Philippine Islands
D.	Dutch	pl.	plural
Dan.	Danish	Russ.	Russian
F.	French	Sc.	Scottish
fem.	feminine	Sgt.	sergeant
FL.	Florida	Sp.	Spanish
G.	German	W.	Welsh
Gr.	Greek	Yid.	Yiddish
Heb.	Hebrew		

A

aa: 4 lava 9 aphrolite

aal, al: 8 mulberry
   dye: 8 morindin

aalii: 4 tree, wood

aardvark: 8 anteater, earth pig, edentate

Aaron: 10 high priest
   associate: Hur
   brother: 5 Moses
   builder of: 10 golden calf
   burial place: Hor
   father: 5 Amram
   sister: 6 Miriam
   son: 5 Abihu, Nadab 7 Eleazar, Ithamar

Aaron's rod: 7 mullein

aba: 4 robe 5 cloth 6 fabric 7 garment

abaca: 4 hemp 5 fiber, lupis

aback: 6 behind 8 unawares 10 by surprise

abaculus: 4 tile 7 tessera

abacus: 4 slab 10 calculator
   Chinese: 7 suan pan

abaddon: pit 4 hell 5 hades

Abadite, Ibidite: 6 Muslim

abaft: 4 back 5 arear 6 astern, behind 8 rearward

abalone: 5 awabi, ormer, shell 6 sea ear 7 mollusk

abandon: 4 drop, flee, junk, quit 5 ditch, leave, scrap, waive, yield 6 abjure, desert, disuse, give up, maroon, reject, resign, vacate 7 discard, forsake 8 abdicate, forswear, rashness, renounce 9 surrender 10 enthusiasm, exuberance, relinquish

abandoned: bad 4 left, lost 6 wanton 7 corrupt, forlorn 8 derelict, flagrant, forsaken, stranded 9 desolated, destitute, dissolute, shameless, unbridled 10 dissipated, profligate 12 unrestrained

abandonment instrument: 6 waiver

abase: 5 shame 6 defame, demean, demote, grovel, humble, lessen, reduce 7 degrade, put down 9 denigrate, humiliate 10 depreciate

abash: 5 shame, upset 6 dismay, put out 7 chagrin, mortify 8 bewilder, confound 9 discomfit, embarrass, humiliate 10 disconcert

abashed: 7 ashamed 8 red-faced, sheepish

abate: ebb, end 4 ease, fall, omit, slow, void, wane 5 allay, annul, let up, lower, quash, relax, remit, slake 6 deduct, lessen, recede, reduce 7 abolish, assuage, die down, nullify, slacken, subside 8 decrease, diminish, mitigate, moderate 9 alleviate

abatement: 6 rebate 8 decrease 9 allowance, deduction, reduction 10 diminution, relaxation, subsidence

abatis: 8 obstacle 9 barricade 13 fortification

abba: 6 father

abbey: 6 priory 7 convent, nunnery 8 cloister 9 monastery, sanctuary
   assistant: 5 prior 8 prioress
   head: 5 abbot 6 abbess
   pert. to: 8 abbatial

abbreviate: cut 4 clip, dock 5 prune 6 digest 7 abridge, curtail, cut back, shorten 8 condense, contract, truncate 9 make brief

ABCs: 6 basics 8 alphabet 9 rudiments

abdicate: 4 cede, quit 5 demit, leave 6 disown, forego, resign, retire, vacate 7 abandon, lay down 8 disclaim, renounce 9 surrender 10 relinquish

abdomen: gut, pot 5 belly 6 paunch 7 midriff, stomach 9 bay window
   crustacean: 5 pleon
   pert. to: 6 gastric, ventral 8 visceral

abduct: 5 seize 6 kidnap, snatch

abecedarian: 4 tyro 6 novice 7 learner 8 beginner, neophyte 9 fledgling 10 tenderfoot 12 alphabetical

abecedarium: 6 primer 12 alphabet book
   relative: 8 acrostic

abed: 4 sick 7 resting, retired 8 sleeping

Abel: *brother:* 4 Cain, Seth
   parent: Eve 4 Adam
   slayer: 4 Cain

Abelard's beloved: 7 Heloise

abele: 6 poplar

aberrant: odd 5 weird 7 deviant, unusual 8 abnormal, atypical, peculiar, straying 9 unnatural, wandering

aberration: 4 slip 5 error, fault, lapse, mania, quirk 8 delusion, illusion, insanity 9 deviation 10 divergence 11 abnormality 12 eccentricity 13 hallucination

abet: aid 4 back, goad, help 5 egg on 6 assist, foment, incite, second, uphold 7 espouse, further, support, sustain 8 befriend 9 encourage, instigate 11 countenance

abettor: 6 patron 8 advocate, promoter 9 accessory, auxiliary, supporter 10 accomplice **11** confederate, conspirator

abeyance: **4** stay **5** break, letup, pause **7** respite **10** on the shelf, suspension

abhor: **4** hate, shun **6** detest, loathe **7** despise, dislike **8** execrate **9** abominate

abhorrence: **5** odium **6** hatred **7** disgust **8** aversion **9** antipathy, revulsion **10** repugnance **11** detestation

Abi: *father:* **9** Zechariah
husband: **4** Ahaz
mother: **8** Hezekiah

abide: **4** bear, last, live, stay **5** await, brook, delay, dwell, exist, pause, stand, tarry **6** accept, endure, linger, remain, reside, submit, suffer **7** sojourn, sustain **8** continue, tolerate **9** acquiesce, withstand

Abiel's son: Ner

à bientot (F.): **6** so long

abies: **4** firs **5** trees **10** evergreens

Abigail: *husband:* **5** David, Nabal
son: **5** Amasa

ability: **5** force, knack, power, skill **6** energy, talent **7** caliber, faculty, know-how, prowess **8** aptitude, capacity, facility, strength **9** dexterity, ingenuity **10** capability, competence, efficiency **11** proficiency

abject: low **4** base, mean, meek, poor **6** humble, paltry, sordid **7** hangdog, ignoble, servile, slavish **8** beggarly, contrite, cringing, degraded, wretched **9** miserable **10** submissive

abjure: **4** deny **5** avoid, spurn **6** eschew, give up, recall, recant, reject, resign, revoke **7** abandon, disavow, retract **8** abnegate, disclaim, forswear, renounce, take back, withdraw **9** repudiate

ablate: **8** melt away, vaporize **12** disintegrate

ablation: **7** erosion, removal **11** evaporation

ablaze: **5** afire, lit up **6** aflame, ardent **7** burning, glowing, ignited, radiant **8** inflamed

able: apt, fit **4** up to **5** adept, smart **6** au fait, clever, facile, strong, suited **7** capable **8** dextrous, skillful, suitable, talented, vigorous **9** competent, dexterous, effective, efficient, qualified, versatile **10** proficient

ablution: **4** bath **7** washing **9** cleansing **10** church rite

abnegate: **4** deny **5** forgo **6** abjure, forego, refuse, reject **7** disavow **8** disclaim, forswear, renounce **10** relinquish

Abner: *cousin:* **4** Saul
father: Ner

abnormal: **5** queer **7** deviant, erratic, offbeat, unusual **8** aberrant, uncommon **9** anomalous, eccentric, irregular, out-of-line, unnatural **10** exorbitant **11** exceptional **13** extraordinary

aboard: **4** onto **6** on deck **7** astride, present **9** alongside

abode: **4** flat, home **5** condo, house, manor **6** estate **7** cottage, mansion **8** domicile, dwelling, tenement **9** apartment, residence **10** habitation **11** condominium
animal: zoo **9** menagerie
of Dead: Dar **4** Aaru, Hell **5** Aralu, Hades, Orcus, Sheol **6** Heaven **8** Valhalla **9** Purgatory
of gods: **4** Meru **6** Asgard **7** Asgarth, Olympus **8** Asgardhr

abolish: end **4** kill **5** abate, annul, erase, quash **6** cancel, repeal, revoke, vacate **7** destroy, nullify, rescind, wipe out **8** abrogate **9** eradicate **10** annihilate, do away with, invalidate **11** discontinue, exterminate

aboma: boa **6** python **8** anaconda

abominable: **4** vile **6** horrid, odious **9** atrocious, execrable, loathsome, revolting **10** unpleasant **12** disagreeable

abominable snowman: **4** yeti **7** monster
habitat: **9** Himalayas

abominate: **4** hate **5** abhor **6** detest, loathe **8** execrate

abomination: **4** evil **5** crime, curse **6** horror, infamy, plague **7** outrage **8** anathema, atrocity, disgrace **9** antipathy **10** abhorrence, odiousness, repugnance **11** detestation

à bon marché (F.): **5** cheap

aboriginal: **5** early, first **6** native **7** endemic **8** primeval **9** primitive **10** indigenous, primordial

aborigine: **6** Indian, native, savage **8** earliest, original **10** autochthon **13** autochthonous

abortion: **7** failure **8** misbirth **11** miscarriage, monstrosity

abortive: **4** idle, vain **6** futile, no good **8** bootless **9** fruitless **11** ineffectual **12** unproductive, unsuccessful

abound: **4** teem **5** crawl, swarm **8** overflow

abounding: **4** rife **5** alive, flush **6** full of, jammed, packed **7** replete, teeming **8** abundant, thronged **9** plentiful

about: **4** as to, in re, near, some **5** anent, astir, circa **6** active, almost, around **7** apropos, close to **9** as regards **10** concerning, relative to, respecting, throughout **11** surrounding **13** approximately

about-face: **6** switch **8** flip-flop, reversal **9** turnabout, volte-face **12** change of mind

above: oer **4** atop, over, past, upon **5** aloft **6** beyond, higher, on high **7** on top of **8** overhead, superior **9** exceeding **12** transcendent

above all: **6** indeed, mostly **7** chiefly **9** in the main, primarily

aboveboard: **4** open **5** frank, overt **6** honest, square **8** bona fide **9** in the open **10** on the level

above water: **4** safe **5** clear **7** solvent **9** out of debt

abracadabra: 5 charm, spell 6 jargon 10 hocus-pocus 11 incantation

abrade: rub 4 file, fret, gall, rasp, sand, wear 5 chafe, erode, grate, grind 6 scrape 7 corrode, eat away 8 irritate 9 excoriate

Abraham: 9 patriarch
bosom: 6 heaven 8 paradise
brother: 5 Haran, Nahor
concubine: 5 Hagar
father: 5 Terah
grandfather: 5 Nahor
grandson: 4 Esau
nephew: Lot
shrine: 5 Caaba, Kaaba
son: 5 Isaac, Medan, Shuah 6 Midian, Zimran 7 Ishmael
wife: 4 Sara 5 Hagar, Sarah 7 Keturah

abrasive: 4 sand 5 emery 6 pumice, quartz 8 annoying, corundum 9 provoking, sandpaper

abraxas: gem 5 charm

abreast: 4 even, up to 5 abeam 6 beside 8 parallel 9 alongside 10 side by side
of the times: 6 modern 7 popular 8 up to date 9 au courant (F.), cognizant 12 contemporary

abri: 6 dugout 7 shelter

abridge: cut 5 limit 6 reduce, shrink 7 capsule, curtail, cut back, shorten 8 compress, condense, contract, diminish, retrench 9 encapsule, summarize 10 abbreviate

abridgement: 5 brief 6 digest, precis, sketch 7 epitome, summary 8 abstract, synopsis 9 lessening 10 compendium, diminution

abroad: 4 asea, away 5 astir 6 afield, astray 7 distant 8 outre mer (Fr.), overseas

abrogate: 4 undo, void 5 annul, quash, remit 6 cancel, repeal, revoke 7 abolish, nullify, rescind 8 overrule, set aside

abrupt: 4 curt, fast, rude 5 bluff, blunt, brief, brisk, gruff, hasty, jerky, quick, sharp, sheer, short, steep, terse 6 sudden 7 brusque 8 headlong, vertical 9 impetuous 10 unexpected 11 precipitous 13 unceremonious

Absalom: *captain:* 5 Amasa
father: 5 David
sister: 5 Tamar
slayer: 4 Joab

abscess: 4 boil 5 ulcer 6 fester, lesion

abscond: fly, run 4 bolt, flee, quit, skip 5 scram 6 decamp, escape 7 make off 8 clear out 12 absquatulate

absence: 4 lack, void, want 5 leave 6 vacuum 7 truancy 8 furlough, omission 10 deficiency, withdrawal 13 nonappearance, nonattendance

absent: off, out 4 away, gone 7 lacking, missing 10 not present

absent-minded: 7 bemused, far away 8 distrait, dreaming, unseeing 9 oblivious 10 abstracted 11 inattentive

absent without leave: 4 AWOL

absolute: 4 pure, rank, real, true 5 sheer, stark, total, utter, whole 6 actual, entire, simple 7 perfect, plenary 8 complete, despotic, explicit, implicit, outright, positive 9 arbitrary, downright, out and out, undoubted 10 autocratic, peremptory 11 categorical, unalienable, unqualified 13 unadulterated, unconditional

absolutely: yea, yes 4 amen 5 quite, truly 6 wholly 7 for sure, utterly 8 of course 9 certainly, perfectly 10 positively, thoroughly 13 unequivocally

absolution: 6 pardon 7 amnesty 9 acquittal, cleansing, remission 11 exculpation, forgiveness

absolve: 4 free 5 clear, remit 6 acquit, excuse, exempt, let off, pardon, shrive 7 forgive, release 8 dispense, liberate, overlook 9 discharge, exculpate, exonerate, vindicate

absorb: 5 merge, unite 6 engage, imbibe, soak up, take in 7 combine, consume, drink in, engross, immerse, occlude 8 take over 10 assimilate 11 incorporate

absorbed: 4 rapt 6 intent, lost in 7 riveted 8 immersed, involved 9 engrossed, wrapped up 10 abstracted 11 preoccupied

absquatulate: 4 flee, scat 5 scoot, scram 6 decamp 7 abscond

abstain: 4 deny, fast 5 forgo, spurn, waive 6 desist, eschew, forego, pass up, refuse, reject 7 forbear, refrain 8 hold back, keep from, let alone, teetotal 9 do without

abstemious: 5 sober 7 ascetic, austere, sparing 8 moderate 9 abstinent, temperate

abstinence: 8 sobriety 10 self-denial 12 renunciation

abstract: 4 cull, deed, pure 5 brief, ideal, steal 6 deduct, divert, precis, remove 7 abridge, excerpt, purloin, summary 8 abstruse, detached, separate, synopsis, withdraw 9 difficult, epitomize, recondite, summarize 10 compendium 11 theoretical
art: 6 unreal 12 non-objective 13 expressionist
being: ens 4 esse 5 entia (pl.)

abstracted: 7 bemused, far away, pensive 8 absorbed 9 engrossed 11 preoccupied 12 absent-minded

abstruse: 4 deep 6 mystic, remote, subtle 7 obscure 8 abstract, esoteric, profound 9 recondite 10 mysterious 11 hard to grasp

absurd: 4 wild 5 crazy, droll, inane, inept, silly, wacky 6 stupid 7 asinine, foolish 9 fantastic, ludicrous, senseless 10 irrational, ridiculous 11 meaningless, nonsensical 12 inconsistent, preposterous

abundance

abundance: 4 lots 5 store 6 oodles, plenty, riches, wealth 8 fullness, opulence, plethora 9 affluence, amplitude, plenitude, profusion 10 quantities 13 plenteousness

abundant: 4 lush, much, rich, rife 5 ample, thick 6 common, lavish 7 copious, fertile, profuse, replete, riotous, teeming 8 fruitful, generous, numerous, prolific 9 abounding, bountiful, luxuriant, plenteous, plentiful, prevalent 11 overflowing

abuse: mar, tax 4 flay, harm, hurt, maul 5 curse, fault, scold, wrong 6 berate, defile, injure, insult, misuse, punish, revile 7 affront, bedevil, calumny, exploit, obloquy, outrage, pervert, slander, upbraid, violate 8 maltreat, misapply, mistreat 9 blaspheme, contumely, desecrate, disparage, invective, objurgate 10 impose upon, manipulate, opprobrium, scurrility 12 vituperation

abusive: 4 foul 5 rough 6 savage 7 corrupt, profane 8 insolent, libelous 9 offensive, perverted 10 calumnious, scurrilous 11 blasphemous 12 vituperative

abut: 4 join 5 touch 6 adjoin, border, rest on 10 end against

abysmal: 4 deep 6 dreary 8 profound, unending, wretched 10 bottomless

abyss: pit 4 deep, gulf, hell, void 5 chasm, Hades 6 bottom, depths, vorago 7 gehenna, inferno 8 infinite 9 perdition

Abyssinia: See **Ethiopia**

acacia: 4 tree 5 babul, boree, cooba, myall 6 locust, wattle 7 catechu 9 boobyalla, gum arabic

academic: 5 rigid 6 formal, unreal 7 bookish, classic, erudite, learned 8 pedantic 9 professor, scholarly 11 quodlibetic, theoretical 12 conventional

division: 4 term 7 quarter 8 semester 9 trimester

academy: 5 ecole 6 lyceum, manege, school 7 college, society 8 seminary 9 institute 10 university

---

Academy Awards: 5 Oscar

1927
- *picture:* 5 Wings
- *actor:* 8 Jannings
- *actress:* 6 Gaynor

1928
- *picture:* 14 Broadway Melody
- *actor:* 6 Baxter
- *actress:* 8 Pickford

1929
- *picture:* 25 All Quiet on the Western Front
- *actor:* 6 Arliss
- *actress:* 7 Shearer

1930
- *picture:* 8 Cimarron
- *actor:* 9 Barrymore
- *actress:* 8 Dressler

1931
- *picture:* 10 Grand Hotel
- *actor:* 5 Beery, March
- *actress:* 5 Hayes

1932
- *picture:* 9 Cavalcade
- *actor:* 8 Laughton
- *actress:* 7 Hepburn

1934
- *picture:* 18 It Happened One Night
- *actor:* 5 Gable
- *actress:* 7 Colbert

1935
- *picture:* 17 Mutiny on the Bounty

- *actor:* 8 McLaglen
- *actress:* 5 Davis

1936
- *picture:* 13 Great Ziegfeld
- *actor:* 4 Muni
- *actress:* 6 Rainer

1937
- *picture:* 15 Life of Emile Zola
- *actor:* 5 Tracy
- *actress:* 6 Rainer

1938
- *picture:* 20 You Can't Take It With You
- *actor:* 5 Tracy
- *actress:* 5 Davis

1939
- *picture:* 15 Gone With the Wind
- *actor:* 5 Donat
- *actress:* 5 Leigh

1940
- *picture:* 7 Rebecca
- *actor:* 7 Stewart
- *actress:* 6 Rogers

1941
- *picture:* 19 How Green Was My Valley
- *actor:* 6 Cooper
- *actress:* 8 Fontaine

1942
- *picture:* 10 Mrs. Miniver
- *actor:* 6 Cagney
- *actress:* 6 Garson

1943
- *picture:* 10 Casablanca *(cont.)*

Academy Awards *(cont.)*
  actor: **5** Lukas
  actress: **5** Jones
1944
  picture: **10** Going My Way
  actor: **6** Crosby
  actress: **7** Bergman
1945
  picture: **11** Lost Weekend
  actor: **7** Milland
  actress: **8** Crawford
1946
  picture: **19** Best Years of Our Lives
  actor: **5** March
  actress: **11** de Havilland
1947
  picture: **19** Gentleman's Agreement
  actor: **6** Colman
  actress: **5** Young
1948
  picture: **6** Hamlet
  actor: **7** Olivier
  actress: **5** Wyman
1949
  picture: **14** All the King's Men
  actor: **8** Crawford
  actress: **11** de Havilland
1950
  picture: **11** All About Eve
  actor: **6** Ferrer
  actress: **8** Holliday
1951
  picture: **15** American in Paris
  actor: **6** Bogart
  actress: **5** Leigh
1952
  picture: **19** Greatest Show on Earth
  actor: **6** Cooper
  actress: **5** Booth
1953
  picture: **18** From Here to Eternity
  actor: **6** Holden
  actress: **7** Hepburn
1954
  picture: **15** On the Waterfront
  actor: **6** Brando
  actress: **5** Kelly
1955
  picture: **5** Marty
  actor: **8** Borgnine
  actress: **7** Magnani
1956
  picture: **22** Around the World in 80 Days
  actor: **7** Brynner
  actress: **7** Bergman

1957
  picture: **20** Bridge on the River Kwai
  actor: **8** Guinness
  actress: **8** Woodward
1958
  picture: **4** Gigi
  actor: **5** Niven
  actress: **7** Hayward
1959
  picture: **6** Ben-Hur
  actor: **6** Heston
  actress: **8** Signoret
1960
  picture: **9** Apartment
  actor: **9** Lancaster
  actress: **6** Taylor
1961
  picture: **13** West Side Story
  actor: **6** Schell
  actress: **5** Loren
1962
  picture: **16** Lawrence of Arabia
  actor: **4** Peck
  actress: **8** Bancroft
1963
  picture: **8** Tom Jones
  actor: **7** Poitier
  actress: **4** Neal
1964
  picture: **10** My Fair Lady
  actor: **8** Harrison
  actress: **7** Andrews
1965
  picture: **12** Sound of Music
  actor: **6** Marvin
  actress: **8** Christie
1966
  picture: **16** Man for All Seasons
  actor: **8** Scofield
  actress: **6** Taylor
1967
  picture: **19** In the Heat of the Night
  actor: **7** Steiger
  actress: **7** Hepburn
1968
  picture: **6** Oliver
  actor: **9** Robertson
  actress: **7** Hepburn **9** Streisand
1969
  picture: **14** Midnight Cowboy
  actor: **5** Wayne
  actress: **5** Smith
1970
  picture: **6** Patton
  actor: **5** Scott *(cont.)*

Academy Awards (cont.)
  actress: **7** Jackson
1971
  picture: **16** French Connection
  actor: **7** Hackman
  actress: **5** Fonda
1972
  picture: **9** Godfather
  actor: **6** Brando
  actress: **8** Minnelli
1973
  picture: **5** Sting
  actor: **6** Lemmon
  actress: **7** Jackson
1974
  picture: **16** The Godfather, Part II
  actor: **6** Carney
  actress: **7** Burstyn
1975
  picture: **25** One Flew Over the Cuckoo's Nest
  actor: **9** Nicholson
  actress: **8** Fletcher
1976
  picture: **5** Rocky
  actor: **5** Finch
  actress: **7** Dunaway
1977
  picture: **9** Annie Hall
  actor: **8** Dreyfuss
  actress: **6** Keaton
1978
  picture: **10** Deer Hunter
  actor: **6** Voight
  actress: **5** Fonda
1979
  picture: **14** Kramer vs. Kramer
  actor: **7** Hoffman
  actress: **5** Field
1980
  picture: **14** Ordinary People
  actor: **6** DeNiro
  actress: **6** Spacek
1981
  picture: **14** Chariots of Fire
  actor: **5** Fonda

  actress: **7** Hepburn
1982
  picture: **6** Gandhi
  actor: **8** Kingsley
  actress: **6** Streep
1983
  picture: **17** Terms of Endearment
  actor: **6** Duvall
  actress: **8** MacLaine
1984
  picture: **7** Amadeus
  actor: **7** Abraham
  actress: **5** Field
1985
  picture: **11** Out of Africa
  actor: **4** Hurt
  actress: **4** Page
1986
  picture: **7** Platoon
  actor: **6** Newman
  actress: **6** Matlin
1987
  picture: **11** Last Emperor
  actor: **7** Douglas
  actress: **4** Cher
1988
  picture: **7** Rain Man
  actor: **7** Hoffman
  actress: **6** Foster
1989
  picture: **16** Driving Miss Daisy
  actor: **8** Day-Lewis
  actress: **5** Tandy
1990
  picture: **16** Dances With Wolves
  actor: **5** Irons
  actress: **5** Bates
1991
  picture: **17** Silence of the Lambs
  actor: **7** Hopkins
  actress: **6** Foster
1992
  picture: **10** Unforgiven
  actor: **6** Pacino
  actress: **8** Thompson

Acadian: 5 Cajun
acajou: 6 cashew **8** mahogany **9** laurel oak
acaleph: 9 jellyfish
acarid: 4 mite, tick **6** insect
acaudal: 7 anurous **8** tailless
accede: let **5** agree, allow, grant, yield **6** assent, attain, comply, concur, give in **7** approve, consent **9** acquiesce **10** take office **11** acknowledge

accelerate: gun, rev **4** race **5** hurry **6** hasten **7** advance, forward, further, quicken, speed up **8** dispatch, expedite, go faster, increase, step on it **9** move ahead, stimulate **11** precipitate
accelerator: 8 throttle **9** activator, cyclotron
accent: 4 beat, burr, mark, tone **5** drawl, ictus, pitch, pulse, sound, throb, twang **6** brogue, rhythm, stress **7** cadence **8** emphasis **9**

underline **10** inflection, intonation
mark: **5** acute, breve, grave **6** macron, umlaut **10** circumflex

accented: **7** marcato
syllable: **5** arsis

accentuate: **6** set off **7** sharpen **8** bring out **9** emphasize, intensify

accept: buy, see **4** take **5** admit, adopt, agree, allow, bow to, grant, honor **6** assent, endure, take in **7** approve, believe, embrace, espouse, receive **8** tolerate **9** acquiesce **10** understand **11** acknowledge

acceptable: **6** decent, not bad, viable **7** average, welcome **8** adequate, all right, pleasant, suitable **9** palatable **10** good enough **12** satisfactory

accepted: **5** valid **6** proper **7** correct, popular, routine **8** credited, orthodox, standard **9** canonical, customary, prevalent **10** sanctioned **12** conventional, countenanced

access: way **4** adit, door, gate, path, road **5** entry, onset, route, spell **6** attack, avenue, entree, portal, street **7** flare-up **8** approach, entrance, eruption, increase, outburst, paroxysm **9** admission **10** admittance, passageway, right of way

accessible: **4** near, open **5** handy **6** at hand, patent, public **8** pervious **9** available, reachable **10** attainable, convenient, easy to meet, obtainable, procurable **12** approachable, unrestricted

accession: **5** enter **7** arrival **8** addition, approach, increase **9** adherence, agreement, inaugural, increment, induction **11** acquisition **12** installation

accessory: **4** aide, ally, tool **5** extra **6** helper **7** abettor, adjunct **8** a party to, addition, additive, trapping **9** appendage, assistant, auxiliary, secondary **10** accomplice, additional, attachment, incidental, subsidiary, supplement **11** concomitant, confederate, contingency, subordinate, subservient, unessential **12** appurtenance, contributory **13** accompaniment

accident: hap **4** case, fate, luck **5** event, fluke, wreck **6** chance, hazard, mishap **7** fortune **8** calamity, disaster, incident **9** mischance **10** misfortune **11** catastrophe, contingency, contretemps **12** happenstance, misadventure

accidental: **6** casual, chance, random **9** extrinsic, haphazard, secondary, unplanned, unwitting **10** extraneous, fortuitous, incidental, unexpected, unforeseen, unintended **11** conditional, inadvertent, subordinate **12** adventitious, nonessential **13** unintentional **14** unpremeditated

acclaim: **4** clap, fame, hail, laud **5** cheer, eclat, extol, honor, kudos **6** praise, repute, salute **7** applaud, approve, commend, glorify, ovation, root for **8** plaudits **9** pay homage **10** compliment **11** approbation

acclimate: **5** enure, inure **6** harden, season **7** toughen **8** accustom **9** condition, habituate

acclivity: **4** hill, rise **7** incline **11** upward slope

accolade: **5** award, honor, medal **6** eulogy, salute **7** laurels, tribute **8** ceremony, citation, encomium **9** laudation, panegyric **10** decoration, salutation **11** distinction

accommodate: aid, fit **4** give, hold, lend, suit **5** adapt, board, defer, favor, house, lodge, put up, serve, yield **6** adjust, attune, billet, change, comply, oblige, orient, settle **7** conform, contain, quarter **9** make agree, reconcile

accompany: **4** join, lead **5** add to, pilot **6** assist, attend, convey, convoy, escort, follow, go with, squire **7** coexist, conduct **8** chaperon **9** chaperone **10** supplement

accomplice: **4** aide **6** cohort, helper **7** abettor, partner **9** accessory, assistant, associate, colleague **11** confederate **12** participator **13** co-conspirator

accomplish: **4** end, win **5** reach **6** attain, effect, finish, fulfil, make it, manage **7** achieve, execute, fulfill, furnish, perfect, perform, produce, realize, succeed **8** bring off, complete, dispatch, engineer **9** put across **10** consummate

accomplished: apt **4** able, done **5** adept, ended **6** expert **7** skilled **8** finished, talented **9** versatile **10** proficient

accomplishment: art **4** deed, feat **5** craft, skill **7** success **8** learning **10** attainment **11** achievement, performance

accord: **4** jibe **5** agree, allot, award, grant, tally, unity **6** accede, adjust, bestow, concur, treaty **7** concede, concert, consent, entente, rapport **8** affinity, volition **9** give as due, harmonize, reconcile **10** compliance, conformity, correspond

accordant: **7** attuned **8** agreeing, coherent, suitable **9** congruous, consonant **10** compatible, consistent, harmonious **11** conformable **13** correspondent

accordingly: **4** ergo, then, thus **5** hence **9** therefore, thereupon, wherefore **12** consequently, in the same way

accost: **4** hail, meet **5** greet, speak **6** call to, halloo, salute, waylay **7** address, solicit, speak to **8** approach, bid hello, confront **9** encounter **10** button-hole

account: IOU, tab, use **4** bill, chit, deem, item, rate, tale, view **5** basis, score, story, value, worth **6** client, detail, esteem, profit, reason, record, report, repute **7** history, invoice, recital **8** business, customer, estimate **9** advantage, chronicle, discourse,

inventory, narrative, reckoning, statement **10** commentary, importance, recitation **11** description, explanation
book: **6** ledger

accountable: **6** liable **10** answerable, explicable **11** responsible **12** attributable

accountant: CPA **5** clerk **7** auditor **8** reckoner **10** bookkeeper, controller **11** comptroller

accoutre, accouter: arm, rig **4** gird **5** array, dress, equip **6** attire, clothe, outfit **7** costume, furnish, turn out **8** decorate

accoutrements, accouterments: **4** gear **7** regalia **8** fittings, materiel **9** equipment, trappings

accredit: **4** okay **6** ratify **7** approve, ascribe, certify, confirm, empower, endorse, license **8** deputize, notarize, sanction, validate, vouch for **9** attribute, authorize **10** commission

accretion: **4** gain **6** growth **8** addition, increase **9** coherence, increment **11** enlargement **12** accumulation

accrue: add **4** earn, gain, grow **5** amass, right, swell **6** demand **7** collect, fall due, redound **8** cumulate, increase, multiply, snowball **10** accumulate

accumulate: **4** grow, save **5** amass, hoard, lay in **6** accrue, garner, gather, muster, pile up **7** collect, compile, store up **8** assemble, increase **9** stockpile

accumulation: **4** bank, fund, heap, mass, pile **5** stack, store **7** backlog, cumulus, nest egg **8** dividend, interest, treasure **9** inventory **10** acervation **11** aggregation

accurate: **4** true **5** exact, right **7** certain, correct, precise **8** reliable **9** authentic, errorless, on the nose, veridical **10** dependable

accursed: fey (Sc.) **6** damned, doomed **7** hellish **8** damnable, ill-fated **9** abhorrent, execrable **10** abominable, detestable

accuse: tax **4** cite **5** blame **6** allege, attack, charge, defame, finger, indict **7** arraign, censure, impeach **8** denounce, reproach **9** inculpate **10** calumniate **11** bring to book, incriminate, recriminate
falsely: **5** libel **7** slander

accuser: **7** charger, delator **8** libelant **9** plaintiff **10** prosecutor **11** complainant

accustom: use **5** adapt, drill, enure, inure, train **6** orient, season **7** toughen **9** acclimate, condition, get used to, habituate **11** familiarize

ace: jot, one, pip **4** a-one, atom, card, hero, mark, star, tops, unit **5** adept, basto, flyer, point **6** expert **7** aviator **8** particle, topnotch **9** first-rate, hole-in-one **11** crackerjack, hairbreadth, tennis score

acerbic: **4** acid, sour, tart **5** acrid, harsh, sharp **6** bitter, severe **7** caustic **9** corrosive, sar-

castic **10** astringent **11** acrimonious

acerbate: vex **7** envenom **8** embitter, irritate **9** infuriate **10** exasperate

acetaldehyde: **5** ethyl **7** ethanol

acetic acid: **7** vinegar
salt: **7** acetate

acetylene: **5** tolan **6** alkyne, ethyne, tolane

ache: **4** hurt, long, pain, pang, pine **5** bleed, smart, throb, throe **6** desire, grieve, hunger, stitch, suffer, twinge **7** anguish **8** soreness, yearn for

achieve: get, win **4** earn, gain **5** reach **6** afford, attain, effect, finish, obtain **7** compass, execute, fulfill, produce, realize, succeed, triumph **8** complete, conclude, contrive **9** terminate **10** accomplish, consummate

achievement: act **4** coup, deed, feat **6** action **7** exploit **9** execution **11** performance, tour de force **14** accomplishment

Achilles: *advisor:* **6** Nestor
  charioteer: **9** Automedon
  father: **6** Peleus
  fought in: **9** Trojan War
  friend: **9** Patroclus
  hero of: **5** Iliad
  horse: **7** Xanthus
  lover and captive: **7** Briseis
  mother: **6** Thetis
  slayer: **5** Paris
  soldier: **8** Myrmidon
  teacher: **6** Chiron **7** Centaur
  victim: **6** Hector
  vulnerable part: **4** heel

achromatic: **7** neutral **8** diatonic **9** colorless

acid: dry, LSD **4** keen, sour, tart **5** acerb, acrid, harsh, sharp **6** biting, bitter **7** acetose, acetous, pungent, vinegar **8** vinegary **9** corrosive **10** vinegarish **11** acrimonious
  in fruit: **5** malic **6** citric **8** tartaric
  kind of: **5** amino, boric, iodic, oleic **6** acetic, cyanic, formic **7** stearic **8** carbolic
  neutralizer: **6** alkali
  nitric: **10** aquafortis
  radical: **4** acyl **6** acetyl **7** benzoyl, malonyl
  used in dyeing: **6** citric, oxalic **7** benzoic
  used in tanning: **6** lactic, tannic

acid rain: **7** fallout **12** air pollutant

Acis: *father:* **6** Faunus
  lover: **7** Galatea
  slayer: **10** Polyphemus

acknowledge: bow, nod, own **4** aver, avow **5** admit, allow, grant, thank, yield **6** accept, affirm, answer, avouch, reveal **7** concede, confess, declare, divulge, own up to, profess 8 disclose 9 recognize

acme: cap, top 4 apex, peak 5 crest 6 apogee, climax, crisis, height, heyday, summit, vertex, zenith 8 pinnacle 11 culmination

acolyte: 6 helper, novice, server 8 altar boy, follower 9 attendant

aconite: 9 monkshood, wolfsbane
poison from: 4 bikh

acorn: 4 mast 6 oak nut
dried: 6 camata 8 camatina
edible: 7 ballote, bellote

acouchi: 5 elemi, resin

acquaint: 4 tell 5 teach 6 advise, clue in, fill in, inform, notify 7 apprise, present 8 disclose 9 enlighten, introduce

acquaintance: 4 kith 6 friend 9 associate, companion, knowledge 11 familiarity

acquainted: 4 know, up on 6 au fait, versed 8 informed 9 in the know

acquiesce: bow 5 abide, agree, yield 6 accede, accept, assent, comply, concur, submit 7 concede, conform, consent

acquire: add, buy, get, win 4 earn, gain, grab, reap 5 amass, learn, reach 6 garner, gather, obtain, pick up, secure, take on 7 collect, develop, procure 8 contract 9 cultivate

acquisitive: 4 avid 6 greedy 8 covetous, grasping 10 avaricious

acquit: 4 bear, free 5 clear 6 behave, excuse, let off, pardon, parole 7 absolve, amnesty, comport, conduct, release 8 liberate 9 discharge, exculpate, exonerate, vindicate

acreage: 4 land 5 tract 6 realty 7 grounds 8 property 11 landholding

acrid: 4 sour 5 harsh, rough, sharp 6 biting, bitter 7 caustic, pungent, reeking 8 unsavory, virulent 9 acidulous, corrosive 10 astringent, irritating

acrimonious: mad 5 angry, gruff, harsh, irate, sharp, surly, testy, wroth 6 bitter, cranky 7 caustic 8 stinging 9 rancorous, resentful 11 contentious, quarrelsome

acroamatic: 4 oral 8 esoteric

acrobat: 7 gymnast, tumbler 8 balancer, stuntman 9 aerialist, trapezist 13 contortionist
garment: 6 tights 7 leotard

acrogen: 4 fern, moss 9 liverwort

acropolis: 4 fort, hill 7 citadel

across: 4 over 6 beyond, facing 7 athwart 8 opposite 9 astraddle 10 transverse
the board: all 5 total 6 in toto, wholly 8 sweeping 10 altogether

acrostic: 4 game 6 phrase, puzzle 7 acronym 11 composition

act: law 4 bill, deed, fake, feat, move, skit, turn, work 5 doing, edict, emote, feign, put-on, serve, stunt 6 behave, bestir, decide, decree 7 comport, exploit, perform,

portray, pretend, statute 8 function, play part 9 dissemble, ordinance, represent 10 observance 11 impersonate, performance 12 have an effect
by turns: 9 alternate
for: 5 front, spell 7 relieve, stand in 8 pinch-hit 9 represent
like: ape 4 copy, echo, mime 5 mimic 7 imitate 8 simulate
on: 4 rule 6 affect 9 influence, take steps
up: 7 carry on, show off 9 misbehave

action: fun 4 case, deed, fray, step, work 5 cause, fight, means 6 affair, battle 7 conduct, process 8 behavior, conflict, function, goings-on, maneuver, movement 9 animation 10 deportment, enterprise, proceeding 11 transaction
field of: 4 bowl, lane 5 alley, arena, court, stage 7 stadium
legal: res 4 suit 6 trover 8 replevin 10 litigation
out of: 6 broken, unused 7 dormant 8 disabled 9 sidelined 10 broken down, on the bench, on the blink 11 inoperative

activate: 6 arouse, charge 7 start up 8 energize, mobilize, vitalize

active: 4 busy, spry 5 agile, alert, brisk, in use, quick, zippy 6 hearty, lively, moving, nimble 7 dynamic, kinetic, working 8 animated, athletic, spirited, vigorous 9 energetic, sprightly 10 productive, up and about 11 functioning, industrious

activity: ado 4 life, stir, work 6 bustle, doings 8 business, exercise, function, movement 10 occupation

actor: 4 doer, mime 5 mimic 6 mummer, player 7 artiste, histrio, trouper 8 comedian, stroller, thespian 9 performer, tragedian 11 barnstormer, entertainer
cue: 4 hint, word 6 prompt
group of: 4 cast 6 troupe 7 company
incompetent: ham 6 emoter
lines: 4 role, side
part: 4 hero, lead, role, star 5 cameo, heavy 7 heroine, ingenue, villain 8 juvenile
substitute: 7 stand-in 10 understudy
supporting: bit 5 extra, super 6 walk-on

actress: 4 diva 7 ingenue 9 soubrette 10 comedienne

actual: 4 real, true 6 extant 7 current, genuine 8 bona fide, concrete, existing, material, physical, positive, tangible 9 authentic, veritable 11 substantial

actuality: 4 fact 5 being 6 verity 7 reality 9 existence, substance

actuate: 4 move, stir 5 drive, enact, impel, spark, start 6 arouse, bestir, incite, set off 7 agitate, animate, enliven, inspire, provoke, trigger 8 motivate 9 instigate 11 put in motion

acumen: wit **7** insight **8** keenness, sagacity **9** acuteness, sharpness **10** astuteness, perception, shrewdness **11** discernment **12** perspicacity **14** discrimination

acuminate: **5** taper

acupuncture: **7** therapy **9** procedure **11** anaesthesia, perforation

acute: **4** dire, keen **5** quick, sharp, smart **6** astute, severe, shrewd, shrill, subtle, urgent **7** crucial, extreme, intense, pointed **8** critical, incisive, piercing **9** ingenious, sensitive **10** discerning, perceptive **11** high-pitched, intelligent, penetrating, quick-witted **13** perspicacious

adage: saw **5** axiom, maxim, motto **6** by-word, dictum, homily, saying, truism **7** bromide, precept, proverb **8** aphorism, apothegm

Adah: *husband:* **4** Esau **6** Lamech
son: **5** Jabal, Jubal

Adam: *grandson:* **4** Enos **5** Enoch
rib: Eve
son: **4** Abel, Cain, Seth
teacher: **6** Raisel
wife, first: **6** Lilith

Adam-and-Eve: **9** puttyroot

adamant: **4** firm, hard **5** rigid, stony **8** obdurate **9** immovable, unbending **10** inflexible, relentless, unyielding

Adam Bede author: **5** Eliot

adapt: fit **4** suit **5** alter, enure, inure, shape **6** adjust, change, comply, gear to, modify, tailor, temper **7** arrange, conform, convert, qualify **8** attemper **9** acclimate, harmonize, reconcile **11** accommodate

adaptable: **6** pliant, supple **8** bendable, flexible **9** all-around, malleable, resilient, tractable, versatile **10** adjustable, changeable **11** conformable **12** reconcilable

add: sum, tot **4** fuse, join, tote **5** affix, annex, put in, tally, total, unite **6** append, attach, figure, reckon **7** augment, combine, compile, compute, connect, say more, subjoin **9** calculate
to: **5** annex, mix in **6** blow up, expand, tack on **7** amplify, augment **8** increase **10** strengthen, supplement
up: **5** recap **6** be okay, go over **8** ring true **9** summarize

adda: **5** skink **6** lizard

adder: **5** krait, snake, viper **7** serpent

addict: fan **4** buff, user **5** hound, slave **6** votary, zealot **7** deliver, devotee, fanatic, habitue, hophead, pothead **8** acidhead **9** crackhead, mainliner **10** aficionado, enthusiast

addiction: **5** habit **9** surrender **10** attachment **11** disposition, enslavement

addition: ell **4** plus, wing **5** annex, rider **6** prefix, suburb, suffix **7** adjunct, codicil, joining **8** addendum, increase **9** accession, accretion, amendment, appendage, expansion, extension

in: too **4** also, else **7** besides, further **11** furthermore

additional: new **4** else, more **5** extra, fresh, other **9** auxiliary **12** supplemental

addled: **4** asea **5** at sea, dizzy, giddy, upset **7** mixed up **8** confused **9** befuddled, flustered **10** bewildered

address: aim, sue, woo **4** call, hail, home, tact, talk **5** abode, court, greet, poise, skill **6** accost, adjust, aplomb, appeal, eulogy, manner, salute, speech **7** lecture, oration, speak to **8** approach, dispatch, harangue, mail drop, petition, presence **9** dexterity, discourse, residence, statement **10** allocution, peroration **11** take a stance

adduce: **4** cite, name **5** offer, quote **6** allege, submit, tender **7** advance, mention, present, suggest **11** give as proof

adeps: fat **4** lard

adept: ace, apt **4** A-one, able, deft, up on, whiz **5** handy, sharp **6** adroit, artist, expert, good at, master **7** capable **8** skillful **9** dexterous, masterful, tolerable **10** acceptable, consummate, proficient

adequate: **4** fair, okay, so-so **5** ample **6** decent, enough, not bad, plenty **8** all right, possible, suitable **9** competent, effective **10** answerable, sufficient **12** commensurate, satisfactory

à deux: **6** for two **8** intimate

adhere: **5** cling, stick **6** cleave, cohere **8** hold fast **12** stay together

adherence: **7** loyalty **8** devotion, fidelity **9** constancy **10** allegiance, attachment

adherent: **4** ally **6** votary **8** believer, disciple, follower, henchman, partisan, servitor, upholder **9** supporter

adhesive: gum, wax **4** bond, glue, tape **5** epoxy, paste **6** cement, gluten, mastic, sticky, viscum **7** stickum **8** birdlime, mucilage **9** tenacious

adhibit: **5** admit, affix, let in **6** attach

adieu: **4** ciao, ta-ta **5** adios, aloha **6** good-by, so long **7** good-bye **8** à bientot (F.) au revoir, farewell **11** leave-taking, valediction **13** auf wiedersehn (G.)

adipose: fat **4** suet **5** fatty **6** tallow

adit: **5** stulm **6** access, tunnel **7** opening, passage **8** approach, entrance **9** admission, mine entry **10** passageway

adjacent: **4** near, next, nigh **5** close, handy **6** beside, hard by **7** against, meeting **8** abutting, touching **9** adjoining, bordering **10** contiguous, juxtaposed **11** coterminous, neighboring **12** conterminous

adjective: **8** modifier **9** dependent, qualifier
demonstrative: **4** that, this **5** these, those
limiting: the
verbal: **9** gerundive

adjoin: add **4** abut **5** touch, verge **6** append,

attach, border, butt on **7** contact **8** be next to, neighbor **9** juxtapose

adjourn: end **4** stay **5** close, defer, delay **6** put off, recess **7** disband, suspend **8** dissolve, hold over, postpone, prorogue **9** terminate **11** discontinue

adjudge: **4** deem, find, rule **5** award, grant **6** decide, decree, settle **7** referee **9** arbitrate, determine

adjunct: **4** aide, part **5** annex **6** helper **7** quality **8** addition, appanage, appendix **9** accessory, appendage, associate, auxiliary, colleague **10** complement **11** subordinate **12** appurtenance

adjure: ask, beg, bid **5** plead **6** appeal, charge **7** beseech, command, entreat, implore

adjust: fit, fix, set **4** bend, suit, trim, true, tune **5** adapt, align, aline **6** attune, change, line up, settle, temper, tune up **7** address, arrange, balance, conform, correct, justify, rectify, work out **8** modulate, regulate, set right **9** harmonize **10** concinnate, coordinate, straighten **11** accommodate, systematize

adjutage: **4** tube **5** spout **6** nozzle

adjutant: **4** aide **6** helper **7** officer **9** assistant, auxiliary **10** aide-de-camp
bird: **5** crane, stork **6** argala **7** marabou

ad-lib: **9** improvise **11** extemporize

admeasure: **5** allot **7** mete out **9** apportion

Admetus' wife: **8** Alcestis

administer: run **4** dose, rule **5** apply, issue, treat **6** direct, give to, govern, manage **7** conduct, control, deal out, execute, furnish **8** carry out, dispense **9** look after, supervise **10** distribute **11** superintend

administrator: **7** manager, officer, trustee **8** director, executor **9** executrix

admirable: **5** brave, great **6** worthy **7** capital **8** laudable, splendid **9** deserving, estimable, excellent
name meaning: **7** Miranda

Admiralty Island: **5** Manus
capital: **8** Lorengau

admire: **4** like **5** adore, honor, prize, value **6** esteem, regard, revere **7** approve, idolize, respect **8** look up to, venerate **11** think well of

admirer: fan **4** beau, buff **5** lover **6** backer, patron **7** booster, devotee, fancier **9** patroness

admission: fee **4** adit, cost **5** price **6** access, charge, entree, ticket **7** ingress **8** entrance **10** admittance, concession, confession, disclosure **15** acknowledgement
receipts: **4** gate, take **9** box-office

admit: own **4** avow **5** agree, allow, enter, grant, let in, own up **6** accept, avouch, enroll, induct, permit, take in **7** adhibit, concede, confess, include, profess, receive **8** initiate **9** come clean, recognize **11** acknowledge

admonish: **4** warn **5** alert, chide, scold **6** advise, enjoin, exhort, notify, rebuke, remind **7** caution, counsel, lecture, monitor, reprove **8** reproach **9** reprehend, reprimand, sermonize

ado: **4** fuss, stir, to-do **6** bother, bustle, flurry, hassle, hubbub, pother, ruckus **7** trouble, turmoil **9** commotion, confusion **10** excitement, hullabaloo

adobe: **4** clay **5** brick, house **6** mudcap

adolescence: **5** teens, youth **6** nonage **7** puberty **8** minority **9** salad days

adolescent: lad **4** girl, lass, teen **5** green, minor, young **6** subdeb **8** immature, juvenile, teenager, youthful **9** pubescent

Adonis: *beloved:* **9** Aphrodite
slayer of: **4** boar

adopt: **4** pass **5** enact **6** accept, assume, borrow, choose, employ, take up **7** approve, embrace, espouse, receive, support **8** advocate, maintain, practice **9** affiliate **10** naturalize **11** appropriate

adorable: **4** cute **5** sweet **6** lovely **7** angelic, lovable, winsome **8** charming, kissable **9** appealing **10** cuddlesome, delightful

adoration: **6** homage **7** worship **8** devotion, idolatry **9** reverence

adore: **4** love **5** honor **6** admire, dote on, esteem, praise, revere **7** cherish, glorify, idolize, respect, worship **8** hold dear, venerate **9** delight in

adorn: **4** deck, gild, trim **5** array, begem, grace, primp, prink **6** bedeck, doll up, emboss, enrich, set off **7** bedizen, dignify, dress up, enhance, furbish, garnish **8** beautify, decorate, emblazon, ornament, trick out **9** bespangle, caparison, embellish, glamorize

ad patres: **4** dead **8** deceased

ad rem: **8** relevant **9** pertinent **10** to the point

Adriana's servant: **4** Luce

Adriatic: *city:* **6** Venice
island: Bua, Eso **7** Lagosta, Lastovo
peninsula: **6** Istria
port: **4** Bari, Pola **5** Fiume **6** Ancona, Rimini **7** Trieste
resort: **4** Lido **5** Split
river into: **4** Reno **5** Adige, Bosna, Drini, Kerka, Piave
wind: **4** bora **10** tramontana, tramontane (pl.)

adrift: **4** asea, lost **5** loose **6** afloat, astray, aweigh **8** derelict, homeless, unmoored **9** wandering **10** unanchored

adroit: apt **4** deft **5** adept, handy, sharp, smart **6** artful, brainy, clever, expert, facile, habile **7** cunning **8** dextrous, skillful **9** dexterous, ingenious, masterful **10** proficient **11** quick-witted, resourceful

adulate: **4** fawn **7** idolize, lionize **8** enshrine, fawn upon, soft-soap **10** overpraise, slaver over

adulator: fan **5** toady **6** yes-man **9** flatterer, sycophant **10** bootlicker, brown-noser

adult: **4** aged, ripe **5** imago **6** mature, nubile **7** grown-up **8** seasoned, tempered **9** developed, full-blown

adulterate: cut, mix **5** alloy, alter, spike **6** debase, dilute, doctor, weaken **7** falsify, thin out **8** denature **10** tamper with

adulterated: cut **5** mixed **6** impure **8** spurious **11** counterfeit, watered down

adumbrate: **4** bode **5** augur **6** darken, hint at, sketch **7** obscure, outline, portend, presage, suggest **8** indicate, intimate, rough out **10** foreshadow

adust: **6** burned, gloomy, sallow **7** parched **8** scorched **9** sunburned

advance: aid **4** cite, help, lend, loan, rise **5** boost, get on, raise, serve **6** adduce, allege, assign, better, foster, hasten, move up, prepay **7** bring up, elevate, forward, further, improve, proceed, promote, propose, upgrade **8** increase, overture, progress, put forth **9** encourage, get nearer, push ahead **10** accelerate, aggrandize, appreciate **11** improvement, make headway
guard: van **6** patrol **7** outpost **8** point man
slowly: **4** inch, worm **5** crawl, creep

advanced: **5** ahead, early **7** liberal **8** tolerant **9** premature **10** avant-garde, precocious **11** enlightened, progressive
equally: **4** even **5** equal **7** abreast
most: **8** farthest, foremost, headmost

advantage: use **4** boot, edge, gain, odds **5** asset, favor, start, stead **6** behalf, behoof, profit **7** account, benefit **8** handicap, interest, leverage, overplus **9** upper hand **11** opportunity, superiority

advantageous: **6** useful **9** expedient, favorable, strategic **10** auspicious, beneficial, commodious, profitable, propitious **11** encouraging

advent: **5** onset, start **6** coming **7** arrival **8** approach

adventitious: **6** casual **7** foreign **8** acquired, episodic **9** extrinsic **10** accidental, fortuitous, incidental **12** nonessential

adventure: **4** feat, lark, risk **5** event, geste, quest **6** chance, danger, hazard **7** exploit **8** escapade **10** enterprise, experience **11** undertaking

adventurer: **7** gambler **9** daredevil, mercenary **13** fortune hunter

adventurous: **4** bold, rash **5** brash **6** daring, errant **8** intrepid, reckless **9** audacious, foolhardy, hazardous, imprudent

adversaria: ana **5** memos, notes **10** miscellany **12** commentaries

adversary: foe **5** enemy, rival **8** opponent **9** assailant **10** antagonist, competitor

adverse: con **4** anti **7** against, counter, harmful, hostile **8** contrary, critical, inimical, negative, opposing, opposite, untoward **9** diametric **11** conflicting, detrimental, disinclined, unfavorable **12** inauspicious, unpropitious

adversity: woe **5** trial **6** misery, sorrow **7** setback, tragedy, trouble **8** calamity, distress, hardship **9** suffering **10** affliction, ill-fortune, misfortune

advert: **4** note **5** refer **6** allude, attend **7** bring up, observe **8** consider, point out

advertise: **4** plug, puff, push **5** bruit **6** blazon, inform, notify, report **7** build up, declare, display, exploit, promote, publish **8** announce, ballyhoo, proclaim **9** broadcast, publicize **10** promulgate

advertisement: **4** bill, sign, spot **6** dodger, insert, notice, teaser **7** affiche, handout, leaflet, placard, release, stuffer **8** circular, handbill **9** broadside, throw-away **10** commercial
book jacket: **5** blurb **11** testimonial
outdoor: **5** flyer **6** banner, poster **9** billboard **10** skywriting **11** marquee sign

advice: tip **4** news, word **6** notice **7** caution, counsel, opinion, pointer, tidings **8** guidance **9** direction **10** admonition, suggestion **11** instruction **12** intelligence **13** word to the wise **14** recommendation
seek: **6** confer, huddle **7** consult

advisable: **4** wise **6** proper **7** politic, prudent **9** befitting, desirable, expedient

advise: **4** post, read, tell, warn **5** coach, guide **6** inform, notify **7** apprise, caution, counsel, suggest **8** acquaint, admonish, advocate, disclose **9** encourage, recommend

adviser, advisor: **4** tout **5** coach, guide **6** nestor **7** monitor, tipster **9** confidant, counselor **10** admonisher, consultant, Dutch uncle, instructor

advisory: **6** notice, report **7** warning **9** hortatory
body: **5** board, panel **7** cabinet, council **9** committee, think tank **10** brain trust

advocate: pro **4** abet, back, urge **5** favor, plead **6** advise, defend, friend, lawyer **7** endorse, espouse, promote, support **8** argue for, champion, hold with, partisan **9** counselor, paraclete, proponent, recommend **11** intercessor
of new laws: **9** neonomian

adytum: **6** shrine **7** sanctum **9** sanctuary

adz, adze: axe **7** hatchet
relative: **6** pickax

Aeacus: *father:* 4 Zeus
  son: 6 Peleus 7 Telamon
Aeetes: *daughter:* 5 Medea
  keeper of: 12 Golden Fleece
  kingdom: 7 Colchis
Aegean Sea: *ancient peoples:* 5 Psara, Psyra 6
  Samian 7 Leleges, Samiote
  gulf: 5 Saros 7 Argolis, Corinth, Saronic
  island group: 8 Cyclades, Sporades 10
  Dodecanese
  river into: 6 Struma, Vardar 7 Marista
  rock: Aex
Aegeon's wife: 7 Aemilia
Aegir's wife: Ran
aegis, egis: 6 shield 7 backing, control,
  defense 8 auspices, guidance 9 patronage
  10 protection 11 sponsorship
Aegisthus: *father:* 8 Thyestes
  mother: 7 Pelopia
  slayer: 7 Orestes
  victim: 6 Atreus 9 Agamemnon
Aegyptus: *brother:* 6 Danaus
  father: 5 Belus
  mother: 8 Anchinoe
Aello: 5 Harpy
Aeneas: *beloved:* 4 Dido
  companion: 7 Achates
  father: 8 Anchises
  grandfather: 5 Capys
  great-grandson: 4 Brut
  mother: 9 Aphrodite
  rival: 6 Turnus
  son: 5 Iulus 8 Ascanius
  wife: 6 Creusa 7 Lavinia
Aeneid: *archer:* 7 Acestes
  author: 6 Vergil, Virgil
  first word: 4 arma
  hero: 6 Aeneas
  king slain by Aeneas: 6 Turnus
  second word: 8 virumque
  steersman: 9 Palinurus
  third word: 4 cano
Aengus' mother: 5 Boann
Aeolian lyricist: 6 Sappho
Aeolus' daughter: 6 Canace 8 Halcyone
aeon, eon: age 5 kalpa (Ind.) 8 eternity 12
  billion years 14 geologic period
aeonian, eonian: 7 eternal, forever 8 infinite
  11 everlasting
aerate: 6 add air, aerify, charge 7 inflate 9
  oxygenate, ventilate 11 expose to air
aerial: 4 aery, airy 5 lofty 6 high up, unreal 7
  antenna 8 antennae (pl.), ethereal 9 imaginary 10 light as air 11 atmospheric 13
  unsubstantial
aerie, eyrie: 4 nest 5 brood 9 penthouse 10
  cliff house
aeriform: 6 unreal 7 gaseous 10 intangible
aerobatics: 4 loop, roll 5 feats, stunt 11 flying feats

aerolite: 10 brontolite, meterorite
aeronaut: 5 pilot 7 aviator 10 balloonist
aerose: 6 brassy
aerostat: 5 blimp 7 airship, balloon 8 zeppelin 9 dirigible
aerugo: 4 rust 9 verdigris
aes: 4 coin 6 bronze
Aesculapius' teacher: 6 Chiron
Aeson: *brother:* 6 Pelias
  son: 5 Jason
Aesop work: 6 Fables
  character: ox; ant, ass, dog, fox 4 frog,
  hare, lion 5 eagle, mouse 8 tortoise 11
  grasshopper
aesthete: 8 virtuoso 10 dilettante 11
  cognoscente, connoisseur
aesthetic, esthetic: 8 artistic, pleasing, tasteful 9 beautiful 12 well-composed
aet, aetat (L.): 7 of an age
Aeta: Ita 8 Filipino 10 Philippino
Aether's father: 6 Erebus
Aetolian prince: 6 Tydeus
afar: off 4 away 6 remote 7 distant
affable: 4 open 5 civil 6 benign, genial,
  urbane 7 amiable, cordial, likable 8 charming, friendly, gracious, pleasant, sociable 9
  agreeable, convivial, courteous 10 accessible 11 complaisant, good-natured 12 easy
  to talk to
affair: 5 event, issue, thing 6 action, matter 7
  concern, lookout 8 business, endeavor,
  interest, intrigue, occasion 10 engagement,
  proceeding 11 transaction 12 circumstance
  love: 5 amour, tryst 7 liaison, romance 8
  intrigue 10 attachment
  social: 4 ball, gala 5 party 6 at home, soiree
  7 blowout, shindig 9 gathering 11 get
  together
affect: hit 4 move, stir, sway 5 act on, alter,
  fancy, feign, touch 6 assume, change, strike
  7 concern, impress, operate, pretend, profess 8 bear upon, frequent, interest, simulate, soften up 9 cultivate, influence 11
  counterfeit, hypothecate
affectation: 4 airs, pose, sham 5 put-on 6
  facade, fakery 7 pietism 8 artifice, pretense
  9 hypocrisy, mannerism 10 false front
affected: 5 moved, stagy 6 chi-chi, too-too 7
  mincing, stilted, studied, touched 8 disposed, involved, mannered, precious 9
  unnatural 10 artificial, influenced 11 pretentious 13 grandiloquent
affection: 4 love 5 amour, fancy 6 esteem, liking, malady, regard 7 ailment, emotion,
  feeling 8 fondness, weakness 10 attachment, friendship, propensity, tenderness
affectionate: 4 fond, warm 6 ardent, doting,
  loving, soft on, tender 7 amorous, devoted
  8 attached 11 sentimental

affianced: 7 engaged 8 intended, plighted, promised 9 betrothed, bride-to-be, groom-to-be 10 set to marry

affiant: 8 deponent

affidavit: 9 statement 10 deposition 11 attestation

affiliate: 4 ally, join 5 merge, unite 6 attach, branch, relate 7 chapter, connect 9 associate, tie up with 10 subsidiary 11 combine with, group member

affinity: 4 bias 6 accord, liking 7 kinship, rapport 8 relation, sympathy 10 attraction, connection, fellowship, preference, similarity 11 propinquity, resemblance 12 predilection

affirm: 4 aver, avow 5 posit, swear 6 allege, assert, attest, avouch, depose, ratify, uphold, verify 7 declare, profess, testify 8 maintain, validate 9 predicate, pronounce 10 asseverate 11 state as true

affirmative: aye, nod, yea, yep, yes 4 amen, yeah 7 hopeful 8 dogmatic, positive, thumbs up 9 assertive 10 optimistic 11 declarative, predicative

affix: add 4 join, nail, seal 5 annex, pin on, stamp, unite 6 anchor, append, attach, clip to, fasten, staple 7 adhibit, connect, impress, subjoin

afflatus: 6 vision 10 creativity 11 inspiration

afflict: try, vex 4 hurt, pain, rack 5 beset, grill, gripe, harry, wound 6 burden, grieve, harass, pester, plague 7 oppress, torment, trouble 8 distress

afflicted: sad 6 ailing, woeful 7 doleful, grieved, put-upon 8 impaired, stricken, troubled 9 depressed, lacerated, suffering 10 in distress

affliction: rue, woe 4 care, evil, loss, pain 5 cross, grief, trial 6 duress, misery, ordeal, sorrow 7 anguish, disease, illness, scourge, trouble 8 calamity, distress, hardship, sickness 9 adversity, martyrdom 10 heartbreak, misfortune 11 tribulation 12 wretchedness

affluence: 4 flow 6 afflux, influx, riches, wealth 7 fortune 8 opulence 9 abundance, plenitude, profusion, substance 10 prosperity

affluent: fat 4 rich 5 flush, river 6 loaded, stream 7 copious, well off 8 in clover, well-to-do 9 flowing to, tributary 10 in the money, well-heeled 12 on easy street

afford: 4 bear, give, lend, risk 5 grant, incur, spare, stand, yield 6 manage, supply 7 furnish, provide 10 pay the cost

affray: row 4 feud, riot 5 brawl, clash, fight, melee 6 attack, battle, fracas, ruckus, strife, tumult 7 assault, contest, quarrel, scuffle 9 encounter 10 donnybrook, free-for-all 11 disturbance

affright: awe, cow 5 alarm, daunt, dread, scare, spook 7 startle, terrify 8 frighten 10 intimidate

affront: cut 4 defy, slap, snub 5 abuse, beard 6 insult, jeer at, nettle, offend, slight 7 outrage, provoke, put down 8 disgrace, illtreat, irritate 9 humiliate, indignity, stand up to 10 defamation

afghan: dog 5 hound, shawl, throw 7 blanket 8 coverlet

Afghan fox: 6 corsac

Afghanistan: *capital:* 5 Kabul
city: 5 Herat, Qalat, Tagab, Tigri 6 Gardez, Ghazni, Kunduz, Maidan 7 Baghlan, Qala Nau 8 Charikar, Kandahar 11 Chaghcharan
currency: pul 7 afghani
language: 4 Dari 6 Pashai, Pashto, Pushtu, Turkic 7 Balochi, Persian
mountain pass: 6 Khyber, Peiwar
mountain peak: 7 Nowshak, Sikaram 10 Shah Fuladi
mountain range: 8 Koh-i-Baba, Safed Koh 9 Hindu Kush
people: 5 Tajik, Uzbek 6 Baloch, Hazara, Pathan 7 Pushtun, Sistani 8 Pashtoon
river: 4 Panj 5 Kabul, Kunar 6 Qonduz 7 Hari Rud, Helmand 8 Amu Darya

aficionado: fan 4 buff 5 freak 7 admirer, devotee 8 follower 10 enthusiast

afield: 4 away 6 abroad, astray, beyond 11 at a distance

afire: 5 aglow, eager 6 ablaze, alight, ardent 7 burning, flaming, ignited

afloat: 4 asea 5 awash 6 adrift, buoyed, natant 7 flooded, rumored 9 operating 10 above water, going about 11 circulating

afoot: 5 about, a pied, astir 6 abroad 7 brewing, walking 8 under way 9 happening 10 in the works, shanks mare

aforesaid: 5 ditto 10 prior named 13 last mentioned

aforethought: 7 planned 10 deliberate 12 premeditated

afraid: rad (Sc.) 4 wary 5 loath, timid 6 aghast, averse, craven, scared 7 alarmed, anxious, fearful 8 cowardly, hesitant, skittish 9 concerned, reluctant, terrified 10 frightened 12 apprehensive, fainthearted 13 pusillanimous

afreet, afrit, afrite: jin 4 djin, jinn, ogre 5 demon, djinn, giant, jinni 6 djinni 7 monster

afresh: 4 anew, over 5 again, newly 6 de novo

Africa (see also individual countries): *city:* **4** Giza, Oran **5** Accra, Cairo, Dakar, Lagos, Rabat, Tunis **6** Bangui, Durban, Harare, Ibadan, Luanda, Lusaka, Maputo **7** Abidjan, Algiers, Conakry, Conakry, Kampala, Mombasa, Nairobi, Tripoli, Yaounde **8** Cape Town, Freetown, Khartoum, Kinshasa, Monrovia, Pretoria **9** Mogadishu, Salisbury, Timbuctoo **10** Addis Ababa, Alexandria, Casablanca **11** Brazzaville, Dar es Salaam, Ouagadougou **12** Johannesburg, Leopoldville **14** Elisabethville
country: **4** Chad, Mali, Togo **5** Benin, Congo, Egypt, Gabon, Ghana, Kenya, Libya, Niger, Sudan, Venda, Zaire **6** Angola, Ciskei, Gambia, Guinea, Malawi, Rwanda, Uganda, Zambia **7** Algeria, Burundi, Cabinda, Comoros, Lesotho, Liberia, Morocco, Namibia, Nigeria, Senegal, Somalia, Tunisia **8** Botswana, Cameroon, Djibouti, Ethiopia, Tanzania, Transkei, Zimbabwe **9** Cape Verde, Mauritius, Swaziland **10** Ivory Coast, Madagascar, Mauritania, Mozambique, Seychelles, Upper Volta **11** Burkina Faso, Cote d'Ivoire, Sierra Leona, South Africa **12** Guinea-Bissau **16** Equatorial Guinea
dam: **5** Aswan
desert: **5** Namib **6** Libyan, Nubian, Sahara **8** Kalahari
former kingdoms: **4** Kush **5** Aksum, Nubia
gulf: **4** Aden **5** Gabes, Sidra **6** Guinea
island: **6** Azores, Djerba **7** Aldabra, Comoros, Madeira, Reunion, Sao Tome **8** Canaries, Principe, St. Helena **9** Ascension, Cape Verde, Mauritius **10** Fernando Po, Madagascar, Seychelles
lake: **4** Chad, Tana **5** Abaya, Assal, Kyoga, Mweru, Ngami, Nyasa, Tumba, Volta **6** Albert, Chilwa, Dilolo, Kariba, Malawi, Moeris, Nasser, Rudolf, Shirwa **7** Leopold, Turkana **8** Victoria **9** Bangweulu, Mai Ndombe **10** Tanganyika
language: Gur, Ibo, Kwa, Twi **4** Akan, Geez, Igbo, Saho, Taal **5** Bantu, Dinka, Fanti, Galla, Hausa, Tigre **6** Arabic, Berber, Gurage, Yoruba **7** Amharic, Argobba, Khoisan, Swahili **8** Cushitic, Kingwana, Malagasy, Tigrinya **9** Afrikaans
mountain peak: **5** Elgon, Kenya **7** Cathkin, Tibesti **8** Cameroon **11** Kilimanjaro
mountain range: **4** Pare **5** Atlas **9** Ruwenzori **11** Drakensberg
park: **9** Serengeti **15** Kalahari Gemsbok
people: Dan, Edo, Ewe, Fon, Ibo, Ijo, Kru, Vai, Vei, Yao **4** Agau, Agni, Akim, Akka, Akra, Alur, Arab, Asha, Bari, Beja, Boer, Boni, Copt, Efik, Egba, Ekoi, Fula, Hutu, Igbo, Kafa, Lozi, Luri, Madi, Moor, Nama, Nuba, Nupe, Qung, Riff, Saho, Sara, Yaka, Zulu **5** Bantu, Bassa, Batwa, Dinka, Dogon, Fanti, Felup, Galla, Grebo, Gurma, Hausa, Inkra, Kafir, Mande, Masai, Mossi, Pygmy, Rundi, Shluh, Songe, Temne, Tutsi **6** Bariba, Basuto, Berber, Damara, Dorobo, Dyerma, Fulani, Hamite, Harari, Herero, Kabyle, Kikuyu, Nilote, Nubian, Senufo, Somali, Tuareg, Ubangi, Watusi, Yoruba, Zenaga **7** Akwapim, Ashango, Ashanti, Bedouin, Bushmen, Dahoman, Khoisan, Malinke, Sandawe, Songhai, Swahili **8** Khoikhoi, Mandingo **9** Hottentot
river: Nun, Omo **4** Athi, Geba, Nile, Ruvu, Tana, Uele **5** Benue, Binue, Chari, Chobe, Congo, Niger, Shari, Volta **6** Atbara, Bafing, Gambia, Joliba, Orange, Ruvuma, Sabaki, Ubangi **7** Limpopo, Lualaba, Luapula, Salabar, Semliki, Senegal, Zambezi **9** Crocodile

---

(L.), encore **8** once more **10** repeatedly **11** from scratch
Africa: (see box)
Afrikaans: **4** Boer, Taal
afrite: See **afreet**
Afro: **6** hair-do
aft: **4** back **6** astern, behind **9** posterior, to the rear
opposite of: **4** fore
after: for **4** next, past **5** apres (F.), since **6** behind, beyond, hinder **8** in back of, rearward **9** following, in spite of **10** concerning, looking for, subsequent
a fashion: **6** in a way, partly **7** somehow **9** to a degree
all: but, yet **5** still **6** though **7** besides, however **9** in any case **11** just the same, nonetheless
awhile: **4** anon, soon **5** later
after-dinner: **12** postprandial
aftermath: **5** issue **6** effect, payoff, result, sequel, upshot **7** outcome **8** follow-up **11** consequence
afternoon nap: **6** siesta

afternoon performance: 7 matinee
afterthought: 9 added idea 10 double-take 15 late inspiration
in letter: 10 postscript
afterwards: 4 then 5 later 7 by and by 9 thereupon 11 in the future 12 subsequently
aga, agha: 4 lord 5 chief, title 6 leader 8 official 9 commander
wife: 5 begum
agacella: 8 antelope
Agag's slayer: 6 Samuel
again: bis (F.) 4 anew, more, over 6 afresh, de novo (L.), encore 7 besides, further 8 moreover, once more 12 additionally
against: con 4 anti, from, near, upon 6 beside, facing, next to, versus 7 opposed, vis-a-vis 9 counter to, in spite of 10 concerning, respecting
against the law: 7 illegal, illicit 12 unauthorized
agal: 4 cord, rope
agalloch: 5 garoo 7 incense 8 calambac 9 aloeswood, calambour, eaglewood
agama: 9 chameleon
Agamemnon: *avenger:* 7 Orestes
brother: 8 Menelaus
daughter: 7 Electra 9 Iphigenia
father: 6 Atreus
rival: 9 Aegisthus
son: 7 Orestes
wife: 12 Clytemnestra
agape: 4 agog, ajar, open 6 amazed 7 yawning 9 awestruck 10 bewildered, confounded, slackjawed 11 dumbfounded, open-mouthed
agar, agar-agar: 6 gelose 12 algae extract 13 culture medium
agate: mib, taw 4 ruby 6 achate, marble, quartz 8 type size 10 chalcedony
agave: 4 aloe 5 amole, datil 6 maguey, mescal, pulque 9 amaryllis
fiber: 4 pita 5 istle, sisal
age: eld, eon, era 4 aeon, grow, time 5 cycle, epoch, ripen, years 6 mature, mellow, period, siecle (F.), wither 7 century, develop 8 blue moon, duration, eternity, lifetime, majority 10 generation
geological: See **geology: age**
of one's age: 5 aetat (L.)
same: 4 peer 6 coeval
aged: old 4 ripe 5 anile, dated, hoary, passe 6 feeble, infirm, mature, senile 7 ancient, elderly 8 seasoned, timeworn 9 senescent, up in years, venerable 10 antiquated
ageless: 7 eternal 8 enduring, timeless
agency: 4 firm, hand 5 cause, force, lever, means, proxy 6 bureau, medium, office 7 company, vehicle 9 influence, operation 10 instrument
agenda: 4 card, list 5 slate 6 docket, record 7

program 8 calendar, schedule 10 memorandum
Agenor: *daughter:* 6 Europa
father: 7 Antenor
son: 6 Cadmus
agent: fed, spy 4 doer, G-man, T-man 5 actor, buyer, cause, envoy, force, means, organ, proxy 6 broker, dealer, deputy, factor, medium, seller 7 bailiff, channel, facient, steward 8 assignee, emissary, executor, operator, promoter, salesman 9 go-between 10 commissary, instrument 11 facilitator 12 intermediary 14 representative
appoint: 6 depute 8 deputize
drug: 4 nark
insurance: 11 underwriter
agger: 4 road, tide 5 mound 7 rampart 9 earthwork 10 prominence
agglomerate: 4 heap, lump, mass, pile 7 cluster 9 aggregate 10 collection 12 volcanic rock
agglutination: 5 union 8 adhesion
aggrandize: 4 lift 5 boost, exalt, raise 7 advance, augment, build up, dignify, elevate, enlarge, ennoble, glorify, magnify, promote 8 increase
aggravate: irk, nag, vex 4 gall, rile 5 anger, annoy, peeve 6 nettle, pester, worsen 7 enhance, enlarge, incense, magnify, provoke 8 aggrieve, heighten, increase, irritate 9 intensify, make acute 10 exacerbate, exasperate 11 fan the flame, get one's goat
aggregate: all, sum 4 bulk, mass 5 add up, bunch, gross, total, unite, whole 6 amount, volume 9 accretion, composite 10 accumulate 11 agglomerate
aggregation: 4 herd 5 flock, group, hoard 7 cluster, company 8 quantity 9 congeries, gathering 10 assemblage, collection, cumulation 11 association, combination
aggression: war 4 raid 6 attack, injury 7 assault, offense 8 invasion 9 intrusion 10 initiative 11 provocation 12 encroachment
aggressive: 4 bold 5 pushy 7 scrappy 8 militant 9 bellicose 10 pugnacious 11 hard-hitting 12 enterprising
aggressor: 7 invader 8 attacker 9 assailant
aggrieve: try 4 harm, hurt, pain 5 harry, wrong 6 injure, offend 7 afflict, oppress, trouble 8 distress 9 aggravate, persecute
aghast: 6 afraid 7 shocked, stunned 8 appalled 9 horrified, petrified, stupefied, terrified 11 scared stiff
agile: 4 deft, fast, spry, wiry 5 alert, brisk, light, lithe, quick 6 active, adroit, limber, lively, nimble, supple, valant 7 lissome, springy 8 dextrous
agio: 7 premium 10 banking fee

agitate: fan, irk, jar, vex **4** move, rile, rock, roil, seek **5** alarm, churn, drive, harry, rouse, shake, upset **6** debate, excite, foment, harass, incite, rattle, ruffle **7** discuss, disturb, fluster, inflame, perturb, provoke, push for, trouble **8** activate, convulse, disquiet, distress **9** make waves **10** discompose

agitation: **4** flap, stew **5** furor, storm **6** bustle, energy, flurry, tumult, unrest, uproar **7** ferment, flutter, rampage, tempest, turmoil **8** paroxysm, upheaval, violence **9** commotion, confusion **10** excitement, turbulence **11** trepidation
prone to: **9** emotional

Aglaia: **5** Grace

aglet, aiglet: pin, tag **8** metal tip **9** fancy stud **11** shoelace tip

agley: **4** awry **5** askew, wrong **6** aslant

agnate: **4** akin **6** allied **7** connate, kindred **8** paternal

agnomen: **5** alias **7** epithet **8** nickname

agnostic: **7** doubter, infidel, skeptic **8** nescient **10** unbeliever **11** freethinker

agnus dei: **4** hymn, lamb **6** prayer **8** mass part

ago: **4** back, erst, past, syne (Sc.), yore **5** since

agog: **4** avid, keen **5** eager **6** lively **7** all eyes, excited, popeyed **8** bursting, worked up **9** expectant, impatient **10** breathless

agon: **6** debate **7** contest **8** conflict, struggle **11** competition

agonize: **4** bear, rack **6** strain, writhe **10** excruciate

agony: **4** hell, pain **5** dolor, grief, throe, trial **6** misery **7** anguish, despair, torment, torture, travail **8** distress **9** heartache, nightmare, suffering **11** tribulation

agora: **8** assembly **11** market place

agouti, agouty: **6** rodent
relative: **4** paca **9** guinea pig

Agra tomb: **8** Taj Mahal

agrafe, agraffe: **4** hook **5** clamp, clasp **6** eyelet **9** fastening, sculpture

agrarian: **5** rural **8** agrestic, pastoral **10** campestral **12** agricultural, land reformer

agree: fit **4** jibe, side, suit **5** admit, allow, grant, match, tally, unite, yield **6** accede, accord, assent, comply, concur, square, submit **7** arrange, comport, concede, conform, consent, promise **8** check out, coincide, get along, quadrate **9** acquiesce, be willing, congruous, cooperate, harmonize, reconcile **10** correspond, homologate

agreeable: **4** nice **5** ready, sweet **7** amiable, welcome, willing **8** amenable, charming, pleasant, pleasing, sociable, suitable **9** appealing, compliant, consonant **10** acceptable, compatible, convenient **11** consentient
render: **7** dulcify

agreement: nod **4** bond, deal, pact **5** lease **6** treaty, unison **7** bargain, compact, consent, entente, harmony, rapport **8** contract, covenant **9** concordat, indenture **10** accordance **11** arrangement, concordance, concurrence **13** understanding **15** entente cordiale
in opinion: **9** consensus, unanimity
secret: **5** covin **9** collusion **10** conspiracy
written: **6** cartel **8** contract

agremens, agrements: **6** graces **8** niceties **9** amenities

agrestic: **5** rural **6** rustic **7** bucolic **10** unpolished

agriculture: **7** farming, tillage **8** agronomy **9** husbandry
area: **11** breadbasket
college student: **5** aggie
establishment: **4** farm **5** grove, ranch **7** orchard **8** vineyard
god: **4** Nabu, Nebo, Thor **6** Faunus, Tammuz **8** Amaethon
goddess: Ops **5** Ceres **7** Demeter
machine: **4** disk, plow **5** baler, drill, mower **6** binder, harrow, header, reaper, seeder, tedder **7** combine, tractor **8** thrasher, thresher **9** separator **10** cultivator **11** caterpillar
pert to: **7** georgic **8** geoponic
science: **8** agrology **11** arviculture

agriculturist: **6** farmer, grower **7** planter, rancher **10** husbandman, orchardist

Agrippina: *brother:* **8** Caligula
husband: **8** Claudius
son: **4** Nero

aground: **6** ashore **7** beached **8** stranded

agrypnia: **8** insomnia **13** sleeplessness

agua: **4** bufo, toad

aguacate (Sp.): **7** avocado

ague: **5** chill, fever **7** malaria

ague tree: **9** sassafras

agueweed: **7** boneset, comfrey, gentian **10** eupatorium

Ahab: *daughter:* Athalia, Athaliah
father: **4** Omri
wife: **7** Jezebel

Ahasuerus: *minister:* **5** Haman
wife: **6** Vashti

Ahaz: *son:* **8** Hezekiah
wife: Abi

Ahaziah's sister: **9** Jehosheba **11** Jehosobeath

ahead: **4** fore **5** early **6** before, onward **7** betimes, forward, in front, leading, one up on **8** advanced, anterior **9** in the lead, preceding **10** beforehand

Ahinoam: *husband:* **4** Saul **5** David
son: **5** Ammon

Aholibamah's husband: **4** Esau

Ahriman's angel: div **4** deev, deva

ahu: 5 mound 7 gazelle 8 boundary, memorial 9 stone heap

ahuehuete: 5 cedar 6 sabino 7 cypress

ai: 5 sloth 8 edentate

aid: 4 abet, back, help 5 allay, boost, coach, favor, grant, serve, treat 6 assist, relief, remedy, rescue, succor, uphold 7 advance, be of use, forward, further, subsidy, support 8 befriend 9 alleviate, auxiliary, give a hand 10 facilitate, go to bat for 11 collaborate

Aida: *composer:* 5 Verdi
father: 8 Amonasro
lover: 7 Radames
rival: 7 Amneris

aide: 6 deputy, second 7 officer, orderly 8 adjutant 9 assistant, attendant, man Friday 10 girl Friday 11 subordinate

aigrette: 5 egret, heron, plume, spray 8 feathers

ail: 4 ache, fail, pain 6 affect, bother, falter, sicken, suffer 7 decline, feel ill 8 take sick 10 feel poorly

ailment (see also **disease**): 6 malady 7 disease, illness 8 disorder, sickness, weakness 9 affection, complaint, infirmity 10 affliction, disability 13 indisposition

aim: end, try 4 bent, goal, head, plan 5 essay, level, point, sight, train 6 aspire, design, direct, intend, intent, scheme, strive, target 7 address, attempt, go after, propose, purpose, resolve 8 ambition, consider, endeavor, estimate, shoot for, zero in on 9 calculate, intention, objective 11 destination

aimless: 4 idle 5 blind 6 chance, random 7 erratic 8 drifting 9 desultory, haphazard, hit-or-miss, senseless 10 undirected 11 to no purpose

aimlessness: 8 flanerie (F.)

aine (F.): 5 elder 6 senior

air: sky 4 aria, aura, lilt, mien, pose, song, tell, tune, vent 5 ether, ozone, style, voice 6 aerate, aerify, allure, aspect, broach, cachet, expose, manner, melody, regard, vanity, welkin 7 bearing, display, exhibit, publish 8 attitude, behavior, carriage, demeanor, proclaim 9 broadcast, semblance 10 appearance, atmosphere, deportment 11 affectation, haughtiness
containing: 9 pneumatic
current: 4 wind 5 draft 6 breeze 7 draught
downward motion (pert. to): 9 katabatic
element: 4 neon 5 argon, xenon 6 helium, oxygen 7 krypton 8 nitrogen
overcast: 4 haze, smog 5 smaze 7 pea soup 10 cloudiness

aircraft: 4 kite 5 blimp, plane 6 copter, glider 7 balloon, chopper 8 aerostat, airplane, autogyro, zeppelin 9 dirigible 10 helicopter
carrier: flattop
fleet formation: 7 echelon

group: 4 wing 5 fleet 6 flight 10 escadrille
manufacturer: 4 Lear, Vega 5 Astra, Piper 6 Bendix, Boeing, Cessna, Hughes, United, Vultee, Wright 7 Convair, Curtiss, Douglas, Grumman, Tupolev 8 Ilyushin, Lockheed, Northrop, Republic 9 McDonnell 11 DeHavilland
motorless: 6 glider
part: fin 4 keel, tail, wing 5 cabin 6 cabane 7 aileron, cockpit, nacelle 8 fusilage 9 empennage
pilotless: 5 drone
route: 6 skyway
route marker: 5 pylon
shelter: 6 hangar
vapor: 8 contrail

airing: 4 walk 6 pasear 8 exposure

airplane: jet 4 gyro 5 avion, drone, liner 6 bomber, glider, tanker 7 biplane, fighter 8 autogyro, triplane 9 transport 10 flying boat, gyrocopter 11 clipper ship
atomic bomb: 8 Enola Gay
battle: 8 dogfight
inventor: 6 Wright 7 Bleriot
maneuver: dip 4 bank, buzz, dive, loop, roll 8 hedgehop, nosedive, sideslip, tailspin 9 Immelmann 10 barrel roll
operator: 5 flier, flyer, pilot 7 aviator 8 aeronaut 11 barnstormer
supersonic transport: SST 8 Concorde

air plant: 8 epiphyte

airport: 5 drome 8 airdrome, airfield 9 aerodrome
area: 5 apron, tower 6 runway 7 taxiway

airports, noted: *Amsterdam:* 8 Schiphol
Atlanta: 10 Hartsfield
Berlin: 5 Gatow, Tegel 9 Tempelhof
Boston: 5 Logan
Chicago: 5 O'Hare 6 Midway
Denver: 9 Stapleton
Dublin: 7 Shannon
Geneva: 8 Cointrin
London: 7 Gatwick 8 Heathrow
Los Angeles: LAX
Moscow: 12 Sheremetyevo
New York: JFK 6 Newark 7 Kennedy 9 La Guardia
Newfoundland: 6 Gander
Paris: 4 Orly 8 De Gaulle 9 Le Bourget
Rome: 7 Da Vinci 8 Ciampino 9 Fiumicino
Tel Aviv: 9 Ben Gurion
Tokyo: 6 Atsugi, Haneda, Narita
Toronto: 7 Pearson
Washington: 6 Dulles 8 National

air pressure: 5 baric

air propeller: fan

airs: 4 show 7 hauteur 8 pretense 9 arrogance 10 uppishness 11 affectation

air spirit: 5 Ariel, sylph

airtight: 6 sealed 8 hermetic 9 foolproof 12 impenetrable, invulnerable

airy: gay 4 cool, rare, thin 5 empty, light, lofty, merry 6 aerial, breezy, jaunty, jocund, lively 7 haughty 8 affected, animated, debonair, delicate, ethereal, flippant, graceful, trifling, volatile 9 sprightly, visionary, vivacious 11 atmospheric 13 insubstantial, unsubstantial

aisle: way 4 lane, path, walk 5 alley 7 passage 8 corridor 10 passageway

ait: oat (Sc.) 4 eyot, holm, isle 5 islet

ajar: 4 open 10 discordant

Ajax's father: 7 Telamon

ajonjoli: 6 sesame

akia: 5 shrub 6 poison

akimbo: 4 bent 6 angled 7 crooked

akin: sib 4 near 5 alike, close 6 agnate, allied 7 cognate, connate, related, similar 9 analogous 10 comparable, correlated 11 consanguine

aku: 6 bonito 10 victorfish

akule: 4 fish, scad 7 goggler

ala: 4 axil, drum, wing 6 axilla, recess

Alabama: *capital:* 10 Montgomery
city: Opp 4 Elba, Troy 5 Ozark, Piper, Selma 6 Dothan, Jasper, Mobile 7 Cullman, Gadsden, Opelika 8 Anniston 10 Birmingham, Huntsville, Tuscaloosa
explorer: 6 De Soto
Indian tribe: 5 Creek 6 Tohome 7 Choctaw, Koasati 8 Cherokee 9 Chickasaw
motto: 26 Audemus Jura Nostra Defendere (We dare defend our rights)
mountain: 6 Cheaha 11 Appalachian, Beaver Creek
nickname: 12 Heart of Dixie, Yellowhammer
river: Pea 5 Coosa 6 Cahaba, Mobile, Sipsey, Tensaw 7 Alabama, Conecuh, Sepulga 9 Tennessee, Tombigbee
state bird: 12 yellowhammer
state fish: 6 tarpon
state flower: 8 camellia
state tree: 4 pine

---

alabaster: 6 gypsum 7 calcite 9 aragonite

alacrity: 4 zest 5 haste, speed 8 celerity, dispatch, rapidity 9 briskness, eagerness, readiness 10 enthusiasm, promptness 11 willingness

Aladdin's lamp spirits: 4 jinn 5 genni

à la diable (F.): 7 deviled 8 seasoned

alameda: 4 mall, walk 9 promenade

Alamo: 4 fort 5 aspen 6 battle, poplar, shrine 7 mission 10 cottonwood
hero: 5 Bowie 8 Crockett

à la mode (F.): 4 chic 7 stylish 11 fashionable

alant: 10 sneezeweed

alar: 6 pteric, winged 8 axillary, winglike 10 wing-shaped
opposite of: 7 apteral

alarm: din, SOS 4 bell, fear 5 alert, clock, noise, panic, scare, siren, upset 6 alarum,

---

Alaska: *capital:* 6 Juneau
city: Eek 4 Nome 5 Sitka 6 Barrow, Bethel, Chevak, Kodiak, Naknek, Seward 9 Anchorage, Fairbanks, Ketchikan
discoverer: 6 Bering
glacier: 4 Muir 8 Columbia 10 Mendenhall
highway: 5 Alcan 6 Marine
island: 4 Adak, Atka, Attu 5 Amlia, Kiska, Umnak 6 Agattu, Kodiak, Shuyak 7 Afognak, Baronof, Diomede, Nunivak
island group: Fox, Rat 4 Near 7 Fur Seal, Trinity 8 Aleutian, Pribilof, Shumagin 9 Alexander, Andreanof 13 Four Mountains
mountain peak: 4 Bona 5 Hayes, Spurr 6 Alapah, Katmai, Miller, Oratia 7 Foraker, Kennedy, St. Elias 8 Hamilton, McKinley, Vsevidof 9 Blackburn, Michelson 10 Bendeleben, Chamberlin, Veniaminof 11 Fairweather
mountain range: 5 Baird 6 Brooks, De Long 7 Chugach, Rockies, St. Elias 8 Aleutian, Wrangell 9 West Point 10 Richardson
peninsula: 5 Kenai 6 Seward
people: Auk 4 Dene, Tena 5 Aleut, Inuit 6 Ahtena, Eskimo, Innuit 7 Ingalik, Khotana, Koyukon, Tlingit
river: 4 Taku 5 Alsek, Chena, Kobuk, Yukon 6 Copper, Innoko, Noatak, Tanana 7 Koyukuk, Stikine, Susitna 8 Colville 9 Kuskokwim, Matanuska, Porcupine
sea: 6 Bering 7 Chukchi
state bird: 9 ptarmigan
state fish: 6 salmon
state flower: 11 forget-me-not
state tree: 6 spruce
strait: 6 Bering, Etolin 8 Shelikof
volcano: 5 Kukak 6 Griggs, Mageik, Pavlof, Seguam 7 Korovin, Redoubt, Torbert 8 Makushin 10 Shishaldin

appall, buzzer, dismay, excite, outcry, signal, tocsin **7** disturb, startle, warning **8** frighten, surprise **9** commotion **11** disturbance, trepidation **13** consternation

alarmist: **9** Cassandra, pessimist, worrywart **11** scaremonger **13** prophet of doom

alas: ach, woe **5** alack **6** ochone (Sc.) **8** welladay, wellaway **9** alackaday **12** interjection

Alaska: (see box)

alate: ant **5** aphid **6** insect, winged

alb, albe: **7** camisia **8** vestment

albacore: **4** tuna **5** tunny **6** germon

Albania: **8** Shqiperi
  capital: **6** Tirana, Tirane
  city: **4** Fier **5** Berat, Vlore **6** Avlona, Durres, Valona **7** Chimara, Coritza, Durazzo, Elbasan, Koritza, Prevesa, Scutari, Shkoder **8** Tepeleni
  currency: lek **4** leke **6** qintar
  dialect: Geg **4** Cham, Gheg, Tosc, Tosk **7** Ghegish, Toskish
  former king: Zog **4** Zogu
  lake: **5** Ohrid **6** Prespa **7** Scutari, Skhodra
  mountain: **4** Alps **6** Pindus **7** Korabit
  people: **4** Gheg, Tosk
  river: **4** Arta, Drin, Osum **5** Buene, Erzen, Seman **6** Devoll, Vijose **7** Shkumbi **8** Shkumbin

---

albatross: **4** bird **5** nelly **6** fabric, gooney **9** hindrance, mallemuck **11** encumbrance

albeit: but, tho **5** altho, while **6** though **8** although **10** for all that **15** notwithstanding

Alberta: *capital:* **8** Edmonton
  city: **4** Olds **5** Banff, Edson **7** Calgary **10** Lethbridge **11** Medicine Hat
  lake: **4** Cold **5** Slave **6** Legend, Louise, Pigeon **8** Peerless
  mountain peak: **5** Trout **6** Robson **7** Wallace **8** Columbia **10** Eisenhower
  mountain range: **7** Rockies
  province of: **6** Canada
  provincial bird: **9** horned owl
  provincial flower: **8** wild rose
  resort: **5** Banff **6** Jasper **10** Lake Louise
  river: Bow **4** Milk **5** Peace, Smoky **6** Battle, Oldman, Wapiti **7** Red Deer, Wabasca **9** Athabasca

Albion: **6** Anglia **7** England

albula: **5** chiro **8** bonefish

album: ana **4** book **6** record **8** register **9** anthology, scrapbook **10** collection

albumen: egg white

albuminoid: **7** elastin, keratin, protein **8** collagen

alburnum: **7** sapwood

alcazar: **6** castle, palace **8** fortress

Alcestis: *father:* **6** Pelias
  husband: **7** Admetus
  rescuer: **8** Heracles, Hercules

alchemy: art **5** magic **7** sorcery **11** thaumaturgy **13** transmutation
  god: **6** Hermes

Alcidice: *daughter:* **4** Tyro
  husband: **9** Salmoneus

Alcinous: *daughter:* **8** Nausicaa
  wife: **5** Arete

Alcmaeon: *father:* **10** Amphiaraus
  wife: **10** Callirrhoe

Alcmene's husband: **10** Amphitryon

alcohol: **5** booze, ethyl, vinyl **6** liquor, methyl **7** ethanol, spirits **8** methanol
  aromatic: **8** farnesol, geraniol, linalool
  crystalline: **6** guaiol **7** menthol, talitol **8** mannitol
  liquid: **5** allyl, butyl **6** pentyl **7** butanol **8** glycerol
  radical: **4** amyl
  solid: **5** cetyl **6** sterol **11** cholesterol
  standard: **5** proof

alcoholic: **4** wino **6** addict **9** spiritous **11** dipsomaniac **12** intoxicating

alcoholic drink: ale, bub, dew, gin, nog, rum, rye **4** arak, bang, beer, beno, bosa, boza, brew, chia, grog, nipa, raki, sake, sake, saki, soma, wine **5** airah, bhang, bombo, booze, bozah, bubud, budge, bumbo, drink, hooch, julep, lager, negus, pisco, posca, stout, toddy, vodka **6** arrack, brandy, caudle, cognac, kumiss, liquor, mescal, porter, posset, pottle, Scotch, stingo, strunt, tipple, whisky **7** bitters, bourbon, guarapo, liqueur, lowball, sloe gin, tequila, whiskey **8** absinthe, aperitif, cocktail, highball, vermouth **9** applejack, aqua vitae, hard cider, moonshine **10** intoxicant **11** mountain dew
  add to: **4** lace **5** spike
  measure: **4** dash, dram, gill, pony, shot **5** fifth, rouse **6** double, jigger, pottle **7** snifter **10** two fingers
  server: **7** barman, barmaid, skinker, tapster **9** barkeeper, bartender, sommelier, barkeep
  shop: bar, pub **5** local **6** saloon, tavern **7** shebeen **12** watering hole

Alcott heroine: Jo, Amy, Meg **4** Beth

alcove: bay **4** nook **5** arbor, bower, niche, oriel **6** cranny, gazebo, recess **7** cubicle, dinette, pergola **8** alhacena (Sp.) **11** compartment

al dente: **13** firm to the bite, not overcooked

alder: arn (Sc.) **4** tree **5** shrub
  genus: **5** alnus

ale: mum **4** beer, bock, brew **5** lager, nappy (Sc.), stout **6** porter, stingo **8** beverage
  mixed with sweetener: **4** flip **7** bragget

ale mug: 4 toby 5 stein
Alea: 6 Athena
alee: 5 ahead 7 leeward
opposite of: 5 stoss 8 windward
alehouse: bar, pub 4 cafe 6 bistro, saloon, tavern 7 taproom 8 grogshop 10 beer garden 11 rathskeller
alembic: 5 still 6 retort, vessel 7 refiner 9 distiller
Alençon product: 4 lace
alert: 4 gleg (Sc.), warn, wary 5 agile, alarm, alive, awake, brisk, eager, ready, sharp, siren 6 active, bright, lively, nimble, tocsin 7 wakeful 8 vigilant, watchful 9 observant, wide-awake 11 circumspect
alette: 4 wing 8 abutment
Aleut: See **Eskimo**
Aleutian Island (see also **Alaska**): 4 Adak, Atka, Attu 5 Amlia, Kiska, Umnak 6 Akutan, Amukta, Kodiak, Seguam 7 Kagamil 8 Amchitka, Unalaska
group: Fox, Rat 4 Near 9 Andreanof
alewife: 4 fish 6 allice 7 herring, pompano, walleye
Alexander: *birthplace:* 5 Pella
cut: 11 Gordian Knot
father: 6 Philip
horse: 10 Bucephalus
kingdom: 9 Macedonia
mistress: 8 Campaspe
mother: 8 Olympias
tutor: 9 Aristotle
victory: 4 Gaza, Tyre 5 Egypt, Issus 6 Arbela, Persia 7 Babylon
Alexandria: *bishop:* 10 Athanasius
magistrate: 8 alabarch
patriarch: 4 papa
theologian: 5 Arius
Alexandria Quartet: *author:* 7 Durrell
books: 4 Clea 7 Justine 9 Balthazar 10 Mountolive
narrator: 6 Darley

Algeria: *capital:* 7 Algiers
city: 4 Oran 5 Blida, Medea, Setif 6 Biskra 7 Tlemcen 11 Constantine
currency: 5 dinar 7 centime
desert: 6 Sahara
measure: pik 5 rebis, tarri 6 termin
mountain: 5 Tahat 7 Ahaggar 9 Tell Atlas 11 Sahara Atlas
national anthem: 8 Kassaman (We Pledge)
people: 4 Arab 6 Berber 7 Kabyles
river: 7 Cheliff, Sheliff
weight: 4 rotl

---

alfalfa: hay 6 fodder, lucern 7 lucerne
alforja: bag 5 pouch 6 wallet 9 saddlebag
algae: 4 kelp, nori 6 desmid, diatom, lichen 7 seaweed 8 plankton, rockweed 9 stonewort
genus: 5 dasya 6 alaria, nostoc, padina
study: 8 algology
algarroba: 5 carob 8 mesquite, raintree
Algeria: *(see box)*
algid: 4 cold, cool 6 chilly, clammy
Alhambra: 6 palace 7 citadel
site: 5 Spain 7 Granada
Ali: *descendant:* 7 fatimid 8 fatimite
wife: 6 Fatima
Ali Baba: *brother:* 6 Cassim
password: 6 sesame
slave: 8 Morgiana 10 woodcutter
alias: AKA 7 epithet, pen name 9 pseudonym 10 nom de plume (F.) 11 assumed name, nom de guerre (F.)
alibi: 4 plea 6 excuse 7 pretext 10 offer an out
Alice in Wonderland: *author:* 7 Carroll
cat of Alice: 5 Dinah
character: 5 Queen 6 Walrus 7 Duchess 8 Dormouse 9 Carpenter, Mad Hatter, March Hare 11 Cheshire cat, White Rabbit
alien: 5 fremd 6 exotic 7 foreign, hostile, invader, opposed, strange 8 outsider, stranger 9 brought-on, different, extrinsic, foreigner, immigrant, outlander, unrelated
alienate: 4 part, wean 6 convey, devest 8 disunite, estrange, separate, transfer 9 disaffect 10 cause a rift
alienist: 6 shrink 9 therapist 12 psychiatrist
aliform: 8 winglike 10 wing-shaped
alight: sit 4 land, rest 5 aglow, lodge, perch, roost 6 arrive, bright, settle 7 deplane, descend, lighted, radiant 8 dismount 9 disembark, touch down
align, aline: 4 true 5 array, level 6 adjust, even up 7 marshal 8 regulate 10 join up with, straighten
alike: 4 akin, same 5 equal, twins 7 similar, uniform 8 of a piece 9 congruent, duplicate, identical 10 comparable
aliment: pap 4 food 6 viands 7 pabulum, rations 8 victuals 9 nutriment, substance 10 sustenance 11 nourishment
alimony: 4 keep 9 allowance 10 settlement 11 maintenance 12 support money
aline: See **align**
alive: 4 keen, spry, vive (F.) 5 alert, astir, aware, brisk, quick, vital, vivid 6 active, extant, living 7 dynamic, vibrant 8 animated, existent, swarming 9 breathing, sprightly, unexpired 10 not out of it 11 unforgotten
alkali: lye, reh 4 kali, salt, soda, usar
volatile: 7 ammonia
alkaline: *remedy:* 7 antacid
salt: 5 borax

alkaloid: **6** conine, eserin, heroin **7** caffein, cocaine, codeine, quinine **8** atropine, caffeine, morphine **10** strychnine

all: sum **5** gross, quite, total, whole **6** entire, in toto, solely, wholly **7** plenary **8** entirely, everyone, totality **9** aggregate, everybody **10** altogether, completely, everything, thoroughly **11** exclusively

all-fired: **7** extreme **9** excessive **10** inordinate

all in: **4** beat **5** tired, weary **6** bushed, pooped **7** worn out **9** exhausted

all-knowing: **10** omniscient

all out: **7** utterly **9** full scale **10** unreserved

all over: **4** done **5** ended **8** finished **9** universal **10** everywhere, throughout

all right: yes **4** okay **6** agreed **9** hunky-dory

all there: **4** sane

allay: **4** calm, cool, ease, lull **5** abate, quell, quiet, still **6** pacify, reduce, soften, soothe, temper **7** appease, assuage, comfort, compose, lighten, mollify, relieve **8** mitigate, palliate **9** alleviate

allege: **4** aver, avow, cite **5** claim, offer, plead, state **6** affirm, assert, charge **7** advance, ascribe, declare, present, profess **8** maintain **9** attribute **10** asseverate

allegiance: tie **4** duty **5** honor **6** fealty, homage **7** loyalty, tribute **8** devotion, fidelity **9** constancy, obedience **10** obligation

violation of: **7** treason **9** defection

allegory: **4** myth, tale **5** fable, story **7** parable **8** apologue

alleviate: aid **4** ease, help **5** abate, allay, salve, slake **6** lenify, lessen, soften **7** assuage, lighten, relieve **8** diminish, mitigate, moderate, palliate

alley: via, way **4** lane, mall, path, walk **5** byway **6** vennel (Sc.) **7** passage

alliance: **4** pact **5** union **6** accord, fusion, league, treaty **7** compact, entente, society **8** affinity, agnation, covenant **9** coalition **10** federation, fellowship **11** affiliation, association, confederacy, partnership

allice, allis: **4** shad

allied: **4** akin **6** agnate, in with, joined, linked, united **7** cognate, connate, germane, kindred, related, similar **9** analogous, connected

alligator: **6** caiman, cayman, jacare, yacare **9** crocodile

alligator pear: **7** avocado **8** aguacate (Sp.)

allium: **4** leek **5** onion **6** chives, garlic

allmouth: **6** angler

allocate: **5** allot, allow, award, share **6** assign **7** earmark, mete out **8** set aside **9** apportion **10** distribute

allonge: **5** rider **12** ballet stance

allot: tag **4** give **5** award, grant, share **6** accord, assign, bestow, design, ordain, ration **7** deal out, dole out, let have, present, pro-rate, reserve, specify **8** allocate **9** apportion, parcel out, prescribe **10** distribute

allow: let **4** bear, lend **5** admit, defer, grant, stand, yield **6** accept, assign, endure, permit, suffer **7** approve, concede, confess, own up to, suppose **8** consider, sanction, tolerate **9** authorize, give leave **11** acknowledge

allowance: fee **4** agio, edge, gift, odds, part **5** leave, quota, share **6** bounty, margin, salary **7** aliment, alimony, measure, pension, per diem, portion, stipend **8** discount, handicap, quantity, sanction **9** advantage, allotment, deduction, reduction, tolerance **10** concession, permission

short: **6** ration **9** scrimping

traveling: **7** mileage

weight: **4** tare, tret **7** scalage

alloy: mix **4** fuse **5** blend **7** mixture **8** compound **9** composite **10** adulterate, amalgamate

carbon and iron: **5** steel

Chinese: **7** paktong **8** packtong

copper and aluminum: **9** duralumin

copper and tin: **6** bronze, oreide, ormolu, oroide, pewter

copper and zinc: **5** brass **6** tombac **8** arsedine

copper, iron and zinc: **4** aich **7** rheotan

costume jewelry: **4** aich **6** oreide, ormolu, oroide, tombac **8** arsedine

fusible: **6** solder

gold and silver: **4** asem **8** electrum

gold-like: **4** aich **6** oreide, ormolu, oroide **8** arsedine

heat resistant: **6** cermet **7** ceramal

Japanese: **5** mokum

lead and tin: **5** calin, terne **6** pewter

mercurial: **7** amalgam

nickel and iron: **7** elinvar

nickel and silver: **8** alfenide

nonferrous: **4** tula

pewter-like: **5** bidri

silver with copper or tin: **6** billon

sulfuric: **6** niello

All's Well That Ends Well character: **5** Diana, Lafeu **7** Bertram

allspice tree: **7** pimento

allude to: **5** imply, infer **6** advert, hint at, relate **7** bring up, connote, mention, refer to, suggest, touch on **8** indicate, intimate, point out **9** insinuate

allure: air, woo **4** bait, draw, lead, lure, move, sway **5** angle, bribe, charm, court, decoy, snare, tempt **6** entice, entrap, glamor, induce, seduce **7** attract, beguile, ensnare **8** blandish, inveigle, persuade **9** captivate, fascinate, influence

allusion: **4** hint **7** mention **8** innuendo, instance **9** quotation, reference **10** intimation

alluvial: *clay:* **5** adobe

deposit: mud **4** sand, silt, wash **5** delta, drift, geest **6** gravel, placer

fan: **5** delta

alluvion: **4** flow, wash **5** flood **10** inundation

ally: pal **4** aide, join **5** unite **6** backer, friend, helper **7** connect, partner **8** adherent, relate to **9** affiliate, assistant, associate, auxiliary, colleague, supporter, take sides **10** accomplice **11** confederate

almanac: **4** ordo **8** calendar, yearbook **9** chronicle, ephemeris

almandine: **6** garnet, spinel

almighty: **5** great **7** extreme **8** powerful, puissant **10** omnipotent **12** irresistible

Almighty: God **6** Father, Yahweh **7** Creator, Jehovah **12** Supreme Being

almond: nut **5** badam **6** kanari

paste: **8** marzipan

pert. to: **10** amygdaline

served with: **8** amandine

syrup: **6** orgeat

almost: **4** nigh **5** about, close **6** all but, feckly (Sc.), nearly **8** as good as, not quite **9** virtually **13** approximately

alms: **4** dole, gift **6** aumous (Sc.) **7** charity, handout **8** donation, offering, pittance **11** benefaction **12** contribution

chest: **4** arca **7** poor box

dispenser: **7** almoner, almsman **11** eleemosynar

almsman: **6** beggar, pauper

almuce: **4** hood **6** tippet **9** headdress

aloe: **4** pita **5** agave **6** maguey

compound: **5** aloin

extract: **5** orcin **7** orcinol

powder: **5** picra

aloes: **5** tonic **8** agalloch **10** agallochum

aloft: **4** high **5** above **6** upward **7** skyward **8** airborne, in the air, overhead

aloha: **4** love **5** hello **7** goodbye **8** farewell, greeting, kindness **9** affection **10** salutation

alone: **4** bare, lorn, only, sole, solo **5** aloof, apart, solus **6** single, unique **8** desolate, detached, isolated, separate, solitary **9** matchless **11** exclusively **12** incomparable, unparalleled **13** unaccompanied

along: **4** near, with **5** ahead **6** as well, beside, onward **7** forward, in a line **8** advanced, on the way, together **10** lengthwise **11** approaching **12** in accord with

alongside: **6** beside, next to **7** abreast, against, close by **8** parallel

Alonso's son: **9** Ferdinand

aloof: shy **4** cold, cool **5** alone, apart, proud **6** frosty, remote, silent, social **7** distant, removed **8** detached, reserved, reticent **9** withdrawn **11** at a distance, indifferent, standoffish

alopecia: **8** baldness **11** phalacrosis

alopecoid: **7** foxlike, vulpine

alouatte: **6** monkey

aloud: **4** oral **5** vocal **7** audible

alp: **4** peak **5** mount **8** mountain

alpaca: **4** paco, wool **5** cloth

habitat: **4** Peru **5** Andes **7** Bolivia

relative of: **5** llama **7** guanaco

alpha: **5** chief, first, start **11** Greek letter

and omega: all **5** whole **6** entire **15** beginning and end

alphabet (see also **Anglo-Saxon, Arabic, Greek, Hebrew, letter**): **4** ABCs **5** order **6** basics, primer **7** letters **9** rudiments **11** abecedarium

character: **4** ogam, ogum, rune **5** ogham

pert. to: **11** abecedarian

Runic: **7** futharc, futhork

alpha rhythm: **9** brain wave

Alpine: *antelope:* **7** chamois

climber: **10** alpestrian

dance: **5** gavot

dog: **9** St. Bernard

dress: **6** dirndl **10** lederhosen

dwelling: **6** chalet

herdsman: **4** senn

pass: col **7** Brenner, Splugen **10** St. Gotthard **14** Great St. Bernard

peak: **5** Blanc **8** Jungfrau **10** Matterhorn

tunnel: **5** Blanc **7** Arlberg, Simplon **10** St. Gotthard

wind: **4** bise, bora **5** foehn

Alps: *Austrian:* **5** Tirol, Tyrol

Italian: **9** Dolomites

Yugoslav: **6** Julian **7** Dinarid

already: now **6** before **7** earlier **8** even then, formerly **10** beforehand, by this time, previously

also: and, too, yet **4** erst, more, plus **5** again, ditto **6** as well **7** besides, further **8** likewise, moreover **9** similarly **10** in addition

also-ran: dud **5** loser **7** failure, washout

altar: **5** table **6** shrine **7** chantry **9** sanctuary

area: **4** apse **7** chancel

boy: **6** server **7** acolyte

cloth: **4** pall **7** frontal

curtain: **6** riddel, riddle

enclosure: **4** bema

hanging: **6** dorsal, dossal, dossel

ledge: **6** gradin **7** retable

platform: **8** predella

portable: **10** superaltar

screen: **7** reredos

top: **5** mensa
vessel: pyx **5** cruet, paten **7** chalice, piscina **8** ciborium **10** monstrance

alter: **4** geld, redo, spay, turn, vary, veer **5** adapt, amend, emend, reset, shift **6** adjust, change, modify, mutate, neuter, revamp, revise, temper **7** convert **9** transform

altercation: row **4** spat, tiff **5** brawl, fight, scrap, set-to **6** strife, tussel **7** dispute, quarrel, wrangle **8** argument, squabble **10** contention, falling out **11** controversy

alter ego: **5** agent **6** friend **8** henchman **9** confidant, other self **12** doppelganger, doubleganger

alternate: sub **4** else, sway, vary **5** other, proxy, recur, shift **6** change, deputy, rotate, seesaw **8** intermit **9** oscillate, take turns **11** interchange, reciprocate

alternative: **6** choice, either, option, way out **8** elective, loophole **10** preference

Althaea's husband: **6** Oeneus

although: **5** while **6** albeit **7** despite, whereas **11** granted that **15** notwithstanding

altitude: **6** height **7** ceiling **9** elevation, loftiness
measuring device: **8** orometer **9** altimeter

altitude sickness: **7** soroche

alto: **4** part **6** singer **7** althorn, saxhorn **8** vocalist

altogether: **5** quite **6** in toto, wholly **7** en masse, totally, utterly **8** all in all, entirely **10** by and large, completely, thoroughly **12** collectively
in the: **4** bare, nude **5** naked **8** stripped **9** au naturel

altruism: **7** charity **10** generosity **11** benevolence **12** philanthropy **13** unselfishness

alum: **4** grad **7** styptic **10** astringent
rock: **7** alunite

alumina: **4** clay **5** argil **8** corundum

aluminum: *calcium silicate:* **7** epidote
discoverers: **4** Davy **6** Wohler
hydrousphosphate: **9** wavellite
oxide: **7** alumina
sulfate: **4** alum

alumnus: **4** grad **5** pupil **8** graduate

alveolate: **6** pitted **11** having holes, honeycombed

always: e'er **4** ever **6** semper (L.) **7** for good, forever **8** evermore **9** eternally, uniformly **10** constantly, habitually, invariably **11** continually, perpetually, unceasingly **12** till doomsday **13** everlastingly

ama: **5** amula **9** candlenut

Amadis' beloved: **6** Oriana

amadou: **4** fuse, punk **6** tinder **9** touchwood

amah: **5** nurse **7** servant

amain: **7** greatly **8** forcibly, speedily **9** violently **10** vigorously **11** exceedingly

Amalekite king: **4** Agag

amalgamate: mix **4** fuse, join **5** alloy, blend, merge, unite **6** mingle **7** combine **8** coalesce, compound **11** consolidate

Amaltheia: **4** goat
horn: **10** cornucopia
nursling: **4** Zeus

amanita: **6** agaric, fungus

amanuensis: **6** penman, scribe, typist **8** recorder **9** scrivener, secretary **11** transcriber **12** stenographer

Amasa's father: **6** Jether

amass: **4** save **5** gross, hoard, stack, store **6** gather, heap up, pile up **7** collect, compile **8** assemble **9** stockpile **10** accumulate

amateur: ham **4** tiro, tyro **6** novice, votary **7** admirer, dabbler, devotee, fancier **8** beginner, neophyte **9** greenhorn **10** aficionado, dilettante **15** nonprofessional

Amati: **6** violin **11** violin maker
birthplace: **7** Cremona

amative: **6** ardent, erotic, loving **7** amorous **10** passionate

amaze: awe **4** stun **7** astound, stagger, stupefy **8** astonish, bowl over, confound, surprise **9** dumbfound, overwhelm **11** flabbergast

amazement: **6** wonder **8** unbelief **12** astonishment **13** consternation

amazon: ant **5** harpy, shrew, vixen **6** parrot, virago **11** hummingbird

Amazon River: *discoverer:* **6** Pinzon
early explorer: **8** Orellana, Teixeira
estuary: **4** Para
headwater: **7** Maranon, Ucayali **8** Apurimac
tributary: Ica **4** Napo, Paru **5** Jurua, Jutai, Negro, Purus, Xingu **6** Japura **7** Madeira, Tapajos

Amazons: *country:* **9** Asia Minor **10** Cappadocia
queen: **9** Hippolyta **12** Penthesileia

ambari: **4** hemp **5** fiber **7** cordage

ambassador: **5** agent, envoy **6** deputy, legate, nuncio **8** diplomat, emissary, minister **9** messenger **12** intermediary **14** representative **15** plenipotentiary
pert. to: **8** legatine

amber: **5** resin **6** yellow **8** amberoid

amberfish: **6** kahala **10** yellowtail

ambiance, ambience: **6** milieu **10** atmosphere **11** environment **12** surroundings

ambiguity: **7** duality, evasion, paradox **9** duplexity, duplicity, looseness, obscurity **10** hesitation **12** doubtfulness **13** inconsistency

ambiguous: **4** dark **5** vague **6** unsure **7** cryptic, dubious, unclear **8** doubtful **9** equivocal, uncertain, unsettled **10** indefinite, indistinct **11** problematic **12** questionable **13** indeterminate

ambit: **5** limit, scope, space **6** bounds, extent,

sphere **7** circuit, compass **8** boundary, precinct **13** circumference

ambition: aim **4** goal, hope, mark, wish **5** dream, drive **6** desire **7** purpose **9** intention, objective **10** aspiration

ambitious: **4** avid, bold, keen **5** eager, showy **7** emulous **8** aspiring **9** energetic, on the make **10** aggressive **11** power-hungry **12** enterprising

amble: **5** mosey **6** dawdle, stroll **7** meander, saunter **9** poke along

ambo: **4** desk **6** pulpit

Amboina button: **4** yaws

ambrosia: **5** honey **6** nectar **7** dessert **8** red-brown

ambrosial: **5** sweet, tasty **6** divine **8** fragrant, heavenly, luscious, perfumed **9** delicious **13** fit for the gods

ambry: **4** safe **5** chest, niche **6** closet, recess **10** repository

ambulatory: **7** movable, walking

ambush: mug **4** lurk, trap **5** await, blind, snare **6** lay for, waylay **7** assault **8** surprise **12** take unawares

ameliorate: **4** ease, help, mend **6** better, uplift **7** improve, promote **8** mitigate

amen: yea, yes **5** truly **6** assent, so-be-it, verily **7** exactly **8** approval, response, sanction **9** assuredly, certainly **10** that's right

Amen-Ra's wife: Mut

amenable: **4** open **6** docile, liable, pliant **7** willing **9** receptive, tractable **10** responsive **11** accountable **12** in the mood for

amend: **4** edit **5** alter **6** better, change, reform, remedy, repair, revise **7** correct, improve, rectify, redress **8** put right, work over

amends: **7** apology, redress **8** atonement, expiation **10** recompense, reparation **11** restitution **12** compensation **13** peace offering

amenities: **7** manners **8** agremens, comforts, niceties **9** agrements, etiquette **10** civilities, courtesies **11** formalities **12** conveniences, pleasantries

ament: **5** idiot, moron **6** catkin **7** cachrys, cat-tail, gosling **8** imbecile, nucament

amerce: **4** fine **6** punish **8** penalize

American (see also **United States**): **4** Yank **6** Gringo, Yankee, Yanqui

American Indian: See **Indian (Americas)**

amethyst: gem **7** onegite

Amfortas' father: **7** Titurel

ami (F.): **5** lover **6** friend

amiable: **4** kind, warm **6** genial **7** affable, cordial, lovable, winsome **8** charming, engaging, friendly, gracious, sociable **9** agreeable, courteous **11** good-humored, good-natured, kind-hearted

amicable: **8** friendly **9** peaceable **10** harmo-nious, neighborly **12** well-disposed

amice: **4** cape, cowl, hood **5** ephod **6** almuce, tippet, vakass **8** vestment

amid: **5** among, midst **6** during **7** between **10** surrounded **11** encompassed

amino acid: **7** protein

amino compound: **7** diamide, diamine **8** tri-amine

amiss: ill **4** awry, bias **5** agley, askew, wrong **6** astray, faulty **7** haywire **8** improper **9** erroneous, incorrect **10** inaccurate

amity: **5** peace **6** accord **7** concord, harmony **8** goodwill **10** friendship **12** friendliness

ammonia: **9** hartshorn **11** refrigerant
  derivative: **5** amide, amine **6** anilid **7** anilide, diamine

ammoniac: **8** gum resin

ammunition: **4** ammo, arms, shot **5** bombs **6** powder, shells **7** bullets, rockets, weapons **8** grenades, materiel, missiles, ordnance, shrapnel **9** artillery, resources
  case: **9** bandolier
  depot: **4** dump **6** armory **7** arsenal **8** magazine

amnesia: **5** fugue **8** blackout **11** memory lapse **13** forgetfulness

amnesty: **6** pardon **10** absolution **11** forgiveness

amoeba, ameba: olm **7** proteus **8** organism **9** protozoon

amok, amuck: mad **5** crazy **6** crazed **7** violent **8** frenzied **12** uncontrolled

amole: **4** salt, soap **5** agave, plant

Amon's son: **6** Josiah

among: **4** amid, with **5** midst **7** between, betwixt **8** to each of **12** in the thick of

amor: **4** Eros, love **5** Cupid

amoral: **7** neutral **9** objective, shameless, unethical

amorous: **4** fond **6** ardent, erotic, loving, tender **7** amatory, fervent **10** passionate **12** affectionate

amorphous: **5** vague **8** formless, inchoate **9** irregular, shapeless, undefined **12** lacking unity **14** uncrystallized

amortize: **6** pay off **8** alienate, settle up, write off **9** liquidate **12** pay gradually

Amos: **6** O.T. book **7** prophet

amotion: **7** ousting, removal **11** deprivation

amount (see also **quantity**): gob, sum, tab **4** bulk, cost, dose, part, unit **5** add up, chunk, equal, price, reach, stack, store, tally, total, whole **6** extent, number **7** measure, portion, signify **8** comprise, quantity **9** aggregate
  fixed: **4** rate **8** set price **11** fixed charge
  indefinite: any **4** some
  made: lot **5** batch
  relative: **5** ratio **6** degree
  small: bit, jot, tot **4** dash, drop, iota, lick,

mite, whit, wisp **5** grain, pinch, shred, speck, taste, trace **6** morsel, trifle **7** dribble, driblet, modicum, smidgen **8** fragment, molecule, particle

amour propre: **5** pride **6** egoism, vanity **7** conceit **8** self-love **10** narcissism

ampere unit: **4** volt, watt

ampersand: and **4** also, plus **9** character

amphetamine: **5** benny, upper **7** pep pill **8** inhalant **9** nose spray, stimulant

amphibian: eft, olm **4** frog, hyla, newt, rana, toad **7** caudate, proteus **8** tree toad **9** caecilian **10** salamander **14** land-water craft
family: **7** Hylidae, Pipidae, Ranidae **9** Bufonidae, Proteidae, Sirenidae
order of: **5** anura **6** eryops **7** aglossa, caudata **9** salientia
young: **7** tadpole **8** polliwog

amphibole: **7** edenite, oralite, uralite **9** tremolite **10** hornblende

Amphion: *father:* **4** Zeus **5** Iasus
mother: **7** Antiope
twin brother: **6** Zethus
wife: **5** Niobe

amphitheater: **4** bowl, oval **5** arena, cavea **6** circus **7** stadium **10** auditorium

Amphitrite: *father:* **6** Nereus
husband: **8** Poseidon
mother: **5** Doris
son: **6** Triton

Amphitryon's wife: **7** Alcmena, Alcmene

amphora: jar, urn **4** vase **6** pelike

ample: **4** full, good, much, rich, wide **5** broad, great, large, roomy **6** enough, plenty **7** copious, liberal, opulent **8** abundant, adequate, generous, handsome, spacious **9** bounteous, bountiful, capacious, extensive, plentiful, unstinted **10** munificent, sufficient

amplify: pad **5** swell, widen **6** dilate, expand, extend, stress **7** augment, enlarge **8** increase, lengthen, multiply **9** add detail **10** exaggerate

amputate: cut, lop **5** prune, sever **6** excise, remove **7** chop off, curtail **9** eliminate

amuck: See **amok**

amula: ama **6** vessel **7** wine cup

amulet: gem **4** juju, mojo **5** charm, saffi, token **6** fetish, grigri, saphie **7** periapt **8** greegree, ornament, talisman **10** lucky piece, protection

Amulius' brother: **7** Numitor

amuse: wow **6** divert, engage, please, regale, tickle **7** beguile, delight, disport, enliven, gratify **8** distract **9** entertain, knock dead **10** exhilarate **11** play the fool

amusement: fun **4** game, jest, play **5** mirth, sport **7** pastime **8** pleasure **9** avocation, diversion, merriment **10** recreation, relaxation **13** divertisement, entertainment
place: **4** fair, park **5** movie **6** casino, cinema, circus, midway **7** theater **8** carnival

amusing: **5** droll, funny **7** comical, risible **8** humorous, pleasant **9** laughable, ludicrous, priceless, quizzical **10** ridiculous **11** rib-tickling

Amy's sisters: Jo, Meg **4** Beth

Amycus: *enemy:* **5** Lycus **8** Dascylus
father: **8** Poseidon
friend: **8** Hercules
mother: **5** Melie

amyl: **6** pentyl, starch **7** alcohol

an: one **7** article

ana: **6** events **7** sayings **9** anecdotes, anthology **10** collection, miscellany **11** memorabilia

anabasis: **7** advance, headway, on-going **8** progress **10** expedition **12** forward march

anabatic: **9** ascending **12** upward moving

anaconda: boa **5** snake

Anacreon's birthplace: **4** Teos

anadem: **5** crown **6** diadem, fillet, wreath **7** chaplet, coronet, garland

anagogic: **6** occult **8** abstruse, mystical

anagram: **4** game **5** rebus **6** puzzle **9** logogriph

analgesic: **5** opium **6** codein **7** anodyne, aspirin, codeine **8** sedative **10** anesthetic, pain-killer

analogous: **4** akin, like **5** alike **6** allied **7** cognate, related, similar **8** parallel **10** comparable, equivalent **11** correlative **13** correspondent

analogy: **8** metaphor **10** comparison, congruence, similarity, similitude **11** resemblance

analysis: **4** test **5** audit, study **8** exegesis **9** breakdown, criticism, reduction, titration **10** dissection **11** examination **14** interpretation

analyze: **4** sift **5** assay, parse, study, weigh **7** break up, dissect, examine **8** diagnose, separate **9** determine, reason out, subdivide, take apart

ananas: **7** pinguin **9** pineapple

Ananias: **4** liar **6** fibber **12** prevaricator
wife: **8** Sapphira

anarchist: **5** rebel **7** radical **8** mutineer, nihilist **9** insurgent **13** revolutionary

anarchy: **4** riot **5** chaos **6** revolt **7** license, misrule, mob rule **8** disorder, lynch law, nihilism **9** confusion **11** lawlessness

anathema: ban **4** oath **5** curse **6** pariah, phobia **7** censure, outcast **9** bete noire (F.) **10** abhorrence, hated thing **11** imprecation, malediction **12** denunciation

anatomy: **4** body **8** analysis, skeleton **9** structure **10** dissection, morphology
animal: **7** zootomy
cell: **8** cytology

microscopic: **9** histology
plant: **9** phytotomy
research: **11** vivisection

Anaximander's principle: **7** apeiron

ancestor: Eve **4** Adam **8** forebear **9** matriarch, patriarch, precursor, prototype **10** forefather, forerunner, progenitor **11** predecessor
having common: **14** consanguineous
of a family branch: **6** stirps
worship: **6** manism

ancestry: **4** race **5** stock **6** family, origin **7** descent, lineage **8** breeding, heredity, pedigree **9** genealogy **10** bloodlines, extraction, family tree **11** antecedents
relating to: **6** atavic **9** atavistic

Anchises' son: **6** Aeneas

anchor: fix **4** bind, hook, moor **5** berth, bower, kedge, rivet **6** attach, drogue, secure **7** chaplet, connect, grapnel, killick, support **8** make fast **10** come to rest
bill: **4** peak
hoist: cat **7** capstan
part: arm **4** palm **5** fluke, shank, stock
position: **5** atrip
rest: **9** billboard
shaped: **8** ankyroid
timber: **7** grouser

anchorage: **4** dock, port, rade (Sc.) **5** haven **6** harbor, refuge **7** mooring **8** mainstay

anchorite: nun **4** monk **6** hermit **7** ascetic, eremite, recluse, stylite **8** anchoret

anchorman: key **5** emcee **8** mainstay **11** commentator

anchovy: **5** sprat **7** herring

ancient: old **4** aged, auld (Sc.) **5** hoary **6** bygone **7** antique, archaic, classic, elderly **8** historic, Noachian, obsolete, primeval **9** primitive **10** antiquated **11** patriarchal **12** along in years

ancilla: aid **6** helper **7** adjunct **8** handmaid **9** accessory

ancillary: **7** related **9** auxiliary **10** subsidiary **11** subordinate **13** supplementary

ancon: **5** elbow **6** corbel **7** console **9** olecranon

and: too **4** also, plus **7** besides, further **8** moreover **10** connective **11** furthermore

and so forth: etc **4** more **6** others **8** etcetera

Andean: **5** grand, lofty **8** Peruvian

andiron: dog **7** firedog, hessian

Andorra: *capital:* **14** Andorra la Vella
currency: **5** franc **6** peseta **7** centime, centimo
language: **7** Catalan
mountain: **8** Pyrenees **11** Coma Pedrosa
river: **6** Madriu, Valira

andradite: **6** aplome, garnet

android: **5** robot **9** automaton
in Star Trek: **4** Data

Andromache's husband: **6** Hector

Andromeda: **5** heath, plant **13** constellation
father: **7** Cepheus
husband: **7** Perseus
mother: **10** Cassiopeia

ane (Sc.): one **4** once

anecdote: **4** joke, tale, yarn **5** story **6** sketch **9** narrative
collection: ana

anele: **5** bless **6** anoint, shrive

anemia: **4** fern **9** emptiness **11** lack of blood

anemic: wan **4** pale, weak **6** watery **8** lifeless, listless **10** exsanguine **12** without vigor

anemone: **9** buttercup **10** windflower

anent: **4** in re **5** about, as for **7** apropos **9** regarding **10** concerning **13** in reference to

aneroid: **9** barometer

anesthetic: gas **5** ether **6** obtuse, opiate **7** anodyne, cocaine, dulling, menthol **8** morphine, sedative **9** analgesic, novocaine **10** chloroform, palliative **12** unperceptive

anew: **4** over **5** again **6** afresh **8** once more, recently

anfractuous: **6** spiral **7** sinuous, turning, winding **8** tortuous

angel: **4** dear, lamb **6** backer, cherub, patron, seraph, spirit **7** sponsor **8** guardian **9** harbinger, messenger **13** heavenly being
apostate prince: **5** Eblis **7** Lucifer
biblical: **5** Uriel **7** Chamuel, Gabriel, Jophiel, Michael, Raphael, Zadkiel
bottomless pit: **7** Abaddon **8** Apollyon
hierarchy: **6** Powers **7** Thrones, Virtues **8** Cherubim, Seraphim **9** Dominions
of death: **6** Azrael **7** Sammael
Paradise Lost: **5** Uriel **6** Belial **7** Ariocha
worship: **5** dulia

angelic: **4** pure **7** saintly **8** cherubic, heavenly, innocent **9** celestial, spiritual

angelus: **4** bell **6** prayer **8** devotion
painter: **6** Millet

anger: ire, irk, vex **4** bile, fury, gall, rile, roil **5** annoy, pique, wrath **6** choler, dander, enrage, nettle, offend, rancor, spleen, stir up, temper **7** burning, dudgeon, incense, inflame, passion, provoke **8** acrimony, irritate, vexation **9** aggravate, infuriate **10** antagonize, exasperate, resentment **11** displeasure, indignation

Angevin: **11** Plantagenet

angle: aim, ell, tee **4** bend, bias, fish, fork, hook **5** bevel, crook, facet, phase, point, quoin, slant, twist **6** aspect, jockey, scheme, zigzag **7** gimmick, perigon **8** fishhook, intrigue, position **10** standpoint
equal (pert. to): **8** isogonal, isogonic
external: **4** cant
having no: **6** agonic
mathematical: **5** acute, right **6** obtuse **7** oblique

measuring device: **6** octant **7** sextant **10** semicircle

of branch and leaf: **4** axil

of keel and bowsprit: **6** steeve

of ore vein: **4** hade

salient: **5** arris

angler: **7** lophiid, rodster, schemer, troller **8** allmouth, piscator **9** fisherman, goosefish, trickster

The Compleat: **11** Izaak Walton

Anglo Saxon: *armor:* **7** hauberk **9** habergeon

army: **4** fyrd

assembly: **4** moot **5** gemot **6** gemote

coin: ora **5** sceat, styca **6** mancus

confederacy: **9** heptarchy

deity: Ing **4** Frey, Wyrd **5** Freyr

epic: **7** Beowulf

freeman: **5** thane, thegn **8** Ethelred

king: Ine **4** Edwy **5** Edred **6** Alfred, Egbert, Harold

king's council: **5** witan **11** witenagemot

letter: edh, eth, wyn **4** wynn **5** thorn

nobleman: **4** earl **8** atheling

poet: **4** scop

sheriff: **5** reeve **6** gerefa

slave: **4** esne

tax: **4** geld

village: ham

writer: **4** Bede

Angola: *capital:* **6** Luanda

city: **7** Lubango, Malange **8** Benguela

currency: **4** lwei **6** kwanza

people: **5** Bantu, Kongo **6** Mbundu **7** Bakongo **8** Kimbundu **9** Ovimbundu **12** Luanda-Chokwe

river: **5** Congo, Cuito, Kasai **6** Cuando, Cuanza, Cunene, Kwango **7** Zambezi

---

angora: cat **4** goat, hair, wool, yarn **6** mohair, rabbit

angry: mad **4** grim, sore **5** cross, huffy, irate, livid, vexed, wroth **6** fuming, ireful, put out **7** furious, painful, teed off, uptight **8** burned up, choleric, inflamed **9** in a temper, indignant, irascible, resentful **11** exasperated, fit to be tied

anguilla: eel

anguish: rue, woe **4** ache, pain, pang **5** agony, dolor, grief, throe **6** misery, sorrow **7** torment, torture **8** distress **10** heartbreak

angular: **4** bony, lank, lean, thin **5** gaunt, sharp **6** abrupt **7** jutting, pointed, scraggy, scrawny **8** rawboned **13** sharp-cornered

ani: **6** cuckoo **9** blackbird

anil: dye **6** indigo

anile: old **5** silly **6** doting, feeble, infirm, senile, simple **7** flighty, foolish **9** doddering **11** old-womanish

anima: **4** life, soul **6** psyche **9** inner self **10** vital force

animadversion: rap **4** slur **5** blame, knock **7** censure, obloquy, reproof **8** reproach **9** aspersion, criticism **10** perception, raking over **11** observation **12** faultfinding

animal: **5** beast, biped, brute, gross, lusty **6** carnal, fleshy, mammal, rodent **7** sensual **8** creature, organism, physical **9** marsupial, quadruped

arboreal: **4** unau **5** chimp, koala, lemur, sloth **6** gibbon, marten, monkey **7** dasyure, opossum, raccoon, tarsier **8** kinkajou, marmoset, squirrel **9** orangutan

Biblical: **4** reem **8** behemoth **9** leviathan

burrowing: **4** mole **6** badger, gopher, marmot, rabbit, wombat **7** echidna **9** armadillo, groundhog, woodchuck

coat: fur **4** fell, hair, hide, pelt, skin, wool **6** pelage

collection: zoo **9** menagerie

crawling: **4** worm **5** snake

cross-bred: **4** mule **5** hinny **6** hybrid

doctor: vet **12** veterinarian

draft: **4** mule, oxen (pl.) **5** horse **8** elephant

enclosure: pen, run, sty **4** barn, cage, coop, cote, fold, yard **5** hutch, kraal, stall **6** corral **7** paddock, pasture

equine: ass **5** horse, zebra

extinct: **4** dodo, urus **8** dinosaur, mastodon

fat: **4** lard, suet **5** cetin **6** tallow **7** lanolin

feline: cat **4** lion, lynx, puma **5** tiger **6** jaguar, ocelot **7** cheetah, leopard, panther

female: cow, dam, doe, ewe, gyp, hen, roe, sow **4** hind, mare, slut **5** bitch, filly, jenny, nanny, vixen **6** heifer **7** lioness, tigress

footless: **5** apoda

group: pod **4** herd, pack **5** drove, flock, pride, swarm **6** gaggle, school

hibernating: **4** bear **9** groundhog, woodchuck

life: **4** bios **5** fauna

life (god of): **6** Faunus

lover: **8** zoophile **10** zoophilist

lupine: **4** wolf

male: cob, ram, tom **4** boar, buck, bull, cock, jack, stag, stud **5** billy, steer **6** gander **7** rooster **8** stallion

many-footed: **7** decapod, hexapod **8** multiped **9** centipede, millipede

marine: orc **4** brit, fish, inia, seal **5** coral, otter, polyp, salpa, whale **6** dugong, walrus **7** dolphin, manatee, rotifer **9** jellyfish **10** ctenophore, ctenophran

meat-eating: **9** carnivore

microscopic: **5** ameba, monad **6** acarid,

amoeba **8** rhizopod **9** protozoan **10** animalcule

monkey-like: **5** lemur, loris

mythical: **4** faun, yeti **5** Hydra, snark **6** bagwyn, bunyip, dragon, garuda, Geryon, kraken, sphinx **7** centaur, griffin, mermaid, phoenix, unicorn **8** basilisk, Cerberus, Loch Ness, Minotaur **10** cockatrice

nocturnal: bat, owl **4** coon **5** lemur, ratel, tapir **6** possum **7** opossum, raccoon **9** armadillo

one-celled: **5** ameba, monad **6** amoeba **9** protozoan

ovine: **5** sheep **6** argali

pack: ass **4** mule **5** burro, camel, horse, llama **6** donkey

parasitic: **8** entozoon

plant-eating: **9** herbivore

porcine: hog, pig, sow **4** boar

pouched: **5** koala **6** possum **7** opossum, wallaby **8** kangaroo **9** marsupial

rabbit-like: **4** pika **6** marmot

ruminant: cow **4** deer, goat **5** camel, sheep **6** alpaca, vicuña **7** guanaco **8** antelope

science: **7** zoology **8** ethology

symbol: **5** totem

track: pug **4** slot **5** spoor

undersized: **4** runt

ursine: **4** bear

vulpine: fox

young: cub, kid, pup **4** brit, calf, colt, fawn, foal, lamb, parr **5** bruin, chick, filly, puppy, shoat, whelp **6** cygnet, heifer, kitten **7** gosling **8** suckling, yearling **9** fledgling

animal and plant life: **5** biota

Animal Farm author: **6** Orwell

animalcule: **5** ameba, monad **6** amoeba **7** microbe, no-see-um, rotifer **9** protozoan

animate: **4** move, perk, stir **5** liven, rouse **6** ensoul, excite, fire up, living, vivify **7** actuate, enliven, inspire, quicken **8** activate, energize, vitalize **9** stimulate **10** exhilarate, invigorate **12** give motion to

animated: gay **5** brisk, peppy, vital, vivid **6** active, blithe, lively **7** buoyant, jocular **8** spirited, vigorous **9** sprightly, vivacious **10** full of zest **12** enthusiastic

animation: vim **4** dash, elan, life, zing **5** verve **6** esprit, spirit

anime: **5** copal, elemi, resin **9** oleoresin

animism: **8** naturism

animosity: **4** hate **6** enmity, malice, rancor **7** dislike **9** antipathy, hostility **10** antagonism, resentment

animus: **4** mind, soul **6** effort, rancor, spirit, temper **7** ill will **8** attitude **9** intention, objective **10** antagonism **11** disposition, inclination

anion: ion **8** particle
opposed to: **6** cation

anisette: **7** cordial, liqueur

Anius' daughter: **5** Elais

ankle: **4** coot (Sc.) **5** talus **6** tarsus
pert. to: **6** tarsal

anlage: **4** base **6** embryo, source **8** blastema, rudiment **10** primordium

anna: **9** Hindu coin

annals: **5** diary **6** record **7** history **8** archives **10** chronicles **11** publication **13** year by year log

annalist: **6** writer **7** diarist **8** recorder **9** historian **12** chronologist

Annapolis student: **4** pleb **5** plebe **10** midshipman

annatto, annotto, arnatto: dye **4** tree **5** urucu **6** salmon **7** achiote
derivative: **5** bixin **7** orellin

anneal: **4** bake, fuse, heat **5** smelt **6** temper **7** toughen **10** strengthen

annelid: **4** worm
fresh water: **4** naid
marine: **9** autolytus

annex: add, ell **4** wing **5** affix, seize, unite **6** append, attach, fasten, obtain, pick up, secure **7** acquire, preempt, procure **8** addition, arrogate, take over **9** extension **11** appropriate

Annie Oakley: **4** pass **6** ticket **7** freebie **12** sharpshooter

annihilate: end **4** kill, raze, rout, slay **5** crush, erase, wreck **6** devour, murder, negate, squash **7** abolish, destroy, expunge, nullify, wipe out **8** decimate, demolish, massacre **9** eradicate, extirpate **10** extinguish, obliterate **11** exterminate **12** reduce to ruin

anniversary: **4** fete **7** jubilee **8** birthday, ceremony **11** celebration **13** commemoration
hundredth: **10** centennial
one hundred fiftieth: **16** sesquicentennial
tenth: **9** decennial
thousandth: **10** millennial **11** millenniary
wedding: see **wedding:** *anniversary*

annotate: **4** edit, note **5** gloss **6** remark **7** comment, explain **9** elucidate **10** illustrate

announce: bid, cry **4** call, tell **5** bruit, state **6** assert, blazon, herald, inform, report, reveal **7** declare, divulge, publish, usher in **8** foretell, proclaim **9** advertise, broadcast, enunciate, introduce, make known **10** promulgate **11** give the word

announcement: **5** blurb, edict **6** decree, dictum, notice **7** message **8** bulletin **9** broadcast, manifesto, statement **11** declaration **12** notification, proclamation
of marriage: **5** banns

announcer: **4** page **5** crier, emcee
of coming events: **4** seer **6** herald **7** prophet **9** harbinger

annoy

annoy: bug, dun, ire, irk, nag, try, vex **4** bait, bore, fret, gall, nark, pain, rile **5** chafe, harry, peeve, pique, spite, tease, upset, worry **6** badger, harass, heckle, molest, needle, nettle, offend, pester, rattle **7** bedevil, disturb, provoke, trouble **8** distress, irritate **9** aggravate, displease, embarrass **10** exasperate **13** inconvenience

annoyance: **4** drag, pain, pest **5** thorn, trial, worry **8** headache, nuisance, vexation **11** disturbance **13** inconvenience

annual: **4** book **5** plant **6** flower, yearly **7** etesian **8** yearbook **11** publication

annul: **4** undo, void **5** blank, elide, erase, quash, remit **6** cancel, negate, recall, repeal, revoke **7** abolish, blot out, nullify, rescind **8** abrogate, derogate, dissolve, overrule **9** disaffirm **10** annihilate, extinguish, invalidate, neutralize, obliterate **11** countermand

annular: **6** banded, cyclic, ringed **8** cingular, circular

annulet: **4** ring **5** ridge **6** fillet **7** molding

anoa: **6** wild ox **8** sapiutan
  relative: **7** buffalo

anode: **5** plate **8** terminal **9** electrode
  deposit: **5** anion

anodic: **9** ascending

anodyne: **4** balm **6** opiate **7** soother **8** narcotic, sedative **9** analgesic **10** anesthetic, painkiller, palliative

anoesia, anoia: **6** idiocy

anoint: oil **5** anele **6** grease **9** apply balm **10** consecrate

anole: **6** lizard **9** chameleon

anomalous: odd **6** off-key **7** deviant, foreign, strange, unusual **8** aberrant, abnormal, atypical, peculiar **9** eccentric, irregular **11** incongruous **12** out of keeping **13** contradictory

anomy: **7** miracle

anon: **4** soon, then **5** again, later **6** afresh **7** by and by, shortly **8** in a while **9** afterward, presently

anonym: **5** alias **10** nom-de-plume

anonymous: **7** unknown **8** nameless, unavowed, unsigned **9** incognito

anorexia: **7** fasting **14** self-starvation

another: new **4** more **5** fresh **6** second **7** further, one more **9** different **10** additional, not the same

anserine: **5** silly **6** stupid **7** foolish **9** gooselike

answer: **4** meet, plea, suit **5** avail, react, reply, serve **6** refute, result, retort, return **7** defense, fulfill, riposte, satisfy **8** rebuttal, repartee, response, solution **9** conform to, rejoinder **11** acknowledge
  opposite of: ask **7** inquire **8** question

answerable: **6** liable **8** amenable **9** obligated **10** reponsible **11** accountable

ant: **5** emmet **7** pismire, termite

  genus: **6** eciton **7** formica **8** myrmecia
  kind: **4** army **6** amazon, driver **7** soldier **9** carpenter
  leaf-cutting: **4** atta
  male: **8** micraner **9** ergataner
  nest: **4** hill **5** mound **6** colony **9** formicary
  nonworker: **5** drone
  queen: **4** gyne
  stinging: **5** kelep **8** ponerine
  worker: **6** ergate

ant bear: **8** aardvark, edentate, tamanoir

ant cow: **5** aphid

anta: **4** pier **5** tapir **8** pedestal, pilaster

Antaeus: *enemy:* **8** Hercules
  father: **8** Poseidon
  mother: **4** Gaea

antagonism: **6** animus, enmity, rancor **7** dislike **8** friction **9** animosity, antipathy, hostility **10** opposition

antagonist: foe **5** enemy, rival **7** battler, warrior **8** opponent **9** adversary **10** competitor

antagonistic: **4** anti **6** at odds **7** counter, hostile, opposed **8** contrary, inimical **9** dissonant **11** dead against

Antarctica: *explorer:* **4** Byrd, Cook, Ross **5** Ronne, Scott **6** Mawson **7** Wilkins **8** Amundsen
  land areas: **5** Coats, Oates **6** Adelie, Graham, Wilkes **7** Enderby **8** Victoria **9** Ellsworth, Queen Maud
  mountain: **5** Siple **9** Admiralty, Ellsworth, Pensacola
  sea: **4** Ross **5** Davis **7** Weddell **8** Amundsen
  seal: **4** Ross **9** sterrinck

ante: pay **5** price **9** poker term **10** come up with **11** initial cost

anteater: **5** tapir **6** animal **7** antbear, echidna **8** aardvark, aardwolf, edentate, tamandua, tamanoir
  scaly: **5** manis **8** pangolin

antecedent: **4** fore **5** cause, prior **6** former, reason **7** premise **8** ancestor, anterior, previous **9** foregoing, precursor, prototype **10** forerunner **11** predecessor

antedate: **7** precede **10** come before **11** make earlier

antediluvian: **10** antiquated **12** old-fashioned **14** before the Flood

antelope: gnu **4** puku **5** eland, takin, yakin **6** dik-dik, impala **7** gazelle **8** steenbok **9** pronghorn **10** hartebeest
  brown: **5** nagor
  extinct: **7** blaubok
  female: doe
  forest: **5** bongo
  four-horned: **6** chouka **7** chikara **10** chousingha
  gazelle-like: **5** beira **7** gerenuk
  genus: **4** oryx
  goat-like: **5** goral, serow **7** chamois

golden: **6** impala
harnessed: **4** guib
male: **4** buck
mountain: **7** chamois
mythical: **4** yale
pied: **8** bontebok
pronghorn: **6** cabret, cabrie, cabrit **7** cabrree
reddish: **7** grysbok
royal: **5** ipete **9** kleeneboc
sheep-like: **5** saiga
short-maned: gnu **6** nilgau
tawny: **5** oribi
tiger-like: **8** agacella
young: kid
antenna: **4** palp **6** aerial, feeler, lead-in
insect: **5** clava
radar: **7** scanner
Antenor: *father:* **8** Aesyetes
son: **6** Agenor **11** Archelochus
wife: **6** Theano
anterior: **5** front, prior **6** atloid, before, former **7** earlier, ventral **8** atlantal, previous **9** foregoing, preceding **10** antecedent
anteroom: **4** hall **5** foyer, lobby **8** entrance **9** vestibule **11** antechamber
anthelion: **4** halo **6** nimbus **7** antisun, aureole **10** countersun
anthem: **4** hymn, song **5** motet, psalm **6** choral **9** antiphony, offertory **10** responsory
anther: **10** stamen part
anthesis: **9** full bloom **13** efflorescence
anthill: **4** bank **5** mound **9** formicary
anthology: ana **4** book **5** album **6** corpus **7** garland **8** excerpts **9** potpourri **10** collection, miscellany **11** compilation
Anthony Adverse author: **5** Allen
anthozoan: **5** coral, polyp **7** anemone
anthropoid: ape **5** orang **6** gibbon, monkey, simian **7** gorilla, primate, siamang **9** orangutan **10** chimpanzee, troglodyte
anthropophagite: **8** cannibal
anti: con, foe **6** contra **7** against, opposed
anti-aircraft: *fire:* **5** flack
gun: **5** archy **6** pom-pom
antic: **4** dido, lark **5** caper, comic, droll, prank, stunt **6** gambol **7** caprice, gambado **9** ludicrous **10** frolicsome, shenanigan, tomfoolery **11** monkeyshine
anticipate: **4** balk, hope **5** augur, await **6** divine, expect, prepay, thwart **7** counter, foresee, obviate, portend, prepare, presage, prevent **8** do before, forecast, outguess **9** apprehend, forestall, foretaste **10** enjoy ahead **11** precipitate **13** look forward to
anticipation: **6** augury **9** foresight, intuition **10** expectancy **12** presentiment
anticipating: **8** pregnant
antidote: **4** cure **6** remedy **10** corrective, preventive **11** neutralizer, restorative
Antigone: *father:* **7** Oedipus

mother: **7** Jocasta
sister: **6** Ismene
Antilles: *god:* **4** Zeme
native: **5** Ineri
pearl of the: **4** Cuba
antimacassar: **4** tidy **5** doily
antimony: **4** kohl **7** stibium
pert. to: **7** stibial
Antioch proselyte: **7** Nicolas
antipasto: **6** relish **9** appetizer **11** hors d'oeuvre
antipathy: **6** enmity, hatred, nausea, rancor **7** allergy, dislike **8** aversion, distaste, loathing **9** animosity, hostility **10** abhorrence, antagonism, repugnance
antipodal: **7** opposed **8** contrary, opposite **9** diametric **10** across from
antiquated: old **4** aged **5** fusty, hoary, passe **6** old hat **7** ancient, archaic **8** obsolete, outdated, outmoded **9** primitive **12** antediluvian **13** superannuated
antique: old **5** relic, virtu **7** classic, has-been **8** artifact, heirloom, type face **9** out of date, venerable **12** old-fashioned
antiseptic: **4** dull **5** clean, vapid **6** iodine, phenol **7** alcohol, camphor, sterile **8** creosote, hygienic, peroxide, sanitary **9** boric acid, germicide, purifying **10** overly neat **12** disinfectant
powder: **6** formin
antisocial: **7** hostile **8** solitary **9** reclusive **11** anarchistic, stand-offish **12** misanthropic
antithesis: **7** reverse **8** antipode, contrast **10** opposition **13** exact opposite
antitoxin: **4** sera (pl.) **5** serum
antler: **4** horn
branch: bay **4** brow, snag, tine **5** crown, royal **7** speller **8** surroyal, trestine **9** bezantler
knob: **6** croche
main stem: **4** beam
skin surrounding: **6** velvet
unbranched: dag **5** spike **7** pricket **9** greenhorn
Antony and Cleopatra character: **4** Eros, Iras **5** Menas, Philo **6** Gallus, Taurus **7** Agrippa
Anubis: *associate of:* **5** Thoth **6** Osiris
center of worship: **7** Dog City **9** Kynopolis
country: **5** Egypt
form: dog **6** jackal
god of: **5** tombs **10** underworld
anuran: **4** toad **10** salientian
anurous: **8** tailless
Anu's consort: **4** Anat
anvil: **5** forge **6** smithy, stithy **7** bickern **8** beakiron
bone: **4** amos **5** incus **7** incudes (pl.)
point: **4** beak, horn
tinsmith's: **5** teest
anxiety: **4** care, fear **5** alarm, anger, doubt, dread, panic, worry **7** caution, chagrin, con-

cern, scruple, trouble **8** disquiet, suspense **9** misgiving **10** foreboding, perplexity, solicitude, uneasiness **12** apprehension

anxious: **4** agog **5** eager **6** uneasy **7** carking, unquiet **8** desirous, restless, watchful **9** disturbed, expectant, impatient

any: **4** much, part, some **8** quantity, whatever **9** one or more

anybody: one **7** someone

anyway: **11** at all events **12** nevertheless

Anzac: **10** Australian **12** New Zealander

A-one: **4** tops **5** prime **8** superior **9** first rate, top-drawer

aorist: **9** verb tense

aoristic: **10** indefinite **12** undetermined **13** indeterminate

aorta: **6** artery

aoudad: **4** auri **5** sheep

apa: **4** tree **7** wallaba

apace: **4** fast **7** quickly, rapidly, swiftly **8** speedily

Apache: **4** Yuma **6** Indian **9** Jicarilla, Mescalero **10** Chiricahua
  beverage: **6** tiswin
  chief: **7** Cochise **8** Geronimo
  jacket: **6** bietle

apar: **9** armadillo

apart: **4** away **5** alone, aloof, aside, riven, solus, split **7** asunder, enisled, removed **8** detached, divorced, in pieces, isolated, reserved, secluded, separate **9** divergent **10** abstracted **11** dissociated **12** individually
  from: **6** but for **7** barring, save for **9** excepting, excluding, outside of

apartment: **4** digs, flat **5** abode, condo, rooms, suite **6** rental, walk-up **7** chamber **8** building, dwelling, tenement
  upper: **5** solar **6** sollar

apathetic: **4** dull, limp, logy **5** inert, stoic **6** supine, torpid **7** unmoved **8** listless, sluggish **9** impassive, incurious, unfeeling **10** insensible, phlegmatic **11** indifferent, unemotional **12** uninterested **13** dispassionate

apathy: **6** acedia, phlegm, torpor **7** languor **8** doldrums, lethargy **9** lassitude, unconcern **12** indifference

ape (see also **anthropoid**): **4** boor, copy, lout, mime **5** magot, mimic **6** baboon, gelada, gibbon, monkey, parrot, simian **7** emulate, imitate, portray, primate, take off **9** orangutan **10** chimpanzee **11** impersonate
  family: **8** pongidae
  largest: **7** gorilla

apeak: **8** vertical

apeman: **6** Tarzan

aper: **4** boar, mime **5** mimic **7** buffoon, copycat

apercu: **6** digest, precis, sketch **7** insight, outline **10** conspectus **11** brief survey

aperitif: **4** whet **5** drink **8** cocktail **9** appetizer

aperture: gap **4** hole, leak, pore, rima, slit,

slot, vent **5** chasm, cleft, crack, stoma **6** window **7** fissure, opening, orifice, ostiole **8** loophole, spiracle **11** perforation

apex: tip, top **4** acme, cusp, noon, peak **5** crest, crown, point, spire **6** apogee, climax, summit, vertex, zenith **8** meridian, pinnacle **9** fastigium **11** culmination, ne plus ultra (L.) **12** quintessence
  covering: epi **6** finial
  elbow: **5** ancon
  pert. to: **6** apical
  rounded: **6** retuse

Aphareus: *brother:* **7** Lynceus
  son: **4** Idas

aphid: **5** louse **8** parasite

aphorism: saw **5** adage, axiom, gnome, maxim, motto **6** dictum, saying **7** epigram, precept, proverb **8** apothegm

Aphrodite: **5** Venus **8** Cytherea **9** butterfly
  consort: **4** Ares
  father: **4** Zeus
  mother: **5** Dione
  priestess: **4** Hero
  son: **4** Eros **5** Eneas **6** Aeneas
  temple site: **6** Paphos

apiary: **4** hive, skep **8** beehouse

apiece: per **4** each **6** singly **8** one by one **9** severally **11** for every one **12** individually, respectively

apish: **5** silly **7** foppish, slavish **8** affected

apishamore: **7** blanket

aplomb: **4** ease, elan, tact **5** nerve, poise **6** surety **8** coolness **9** assurance, composure, sangfroid **10** confidence, equanimity **11** nonchalance, savoir faire

apocalypse: **6** vision **8** prophecy **10** prediction, revelation

apocopate: **5** elide **7** shorten

apocryphal: **4** sham **5** false **6** unreal, untrue **7** dubious **8** doubtful, spurious **10** fictitious, not genuine **11** counterfeit, unauthentic, uncanonical

Apocryphal book: **5** Tobit **6** Baruch, Esdras, Judith **9** Maccabees

apodal: **8** footless

apogee: **4** acme, apex, peak **6** climax, summit, zenith **12** highest point

apograph: **4** copy **10** transcript

Apollo: **6** Delius **7** Phoebus
  abode of: **7** Helicon
  beloved of: **6** Cyrene, Daphne **8** Calliope
  birthplace: **5** Delos
  father: **4** Zeus **7** Jupiter
  festival: **5** Delia **6** Carnea
  instrument: **4** lute, lyre
  mother: **4** Leto **6** Latona
  oracle site: **6** Delphi
  priest: **7** Calchas
  sacred vale: **5** Tempe

sister: **5** Diana **7** Artemis
son: Ion **7** Orpheus
traveler: **6** Abaris
twin: **5** Diana

Apollyon: 5 devil, Satan **7** Abaddon, Lucifer **9** archfiend, Beelzebub
evil spirit of: **16** Pilgrim s Progress
vanquished by: **9** Christian

apologetic: 5 sorry **8** contrite, penitent **9** defensive, regretful **10** remorseful

apologue: 4 myth **5** fable, story **7** parable **8** allegory

apology: 4 plea **5** alibi **6** excuse, regret **7** defense **8** mea culpa **9** penitence **11** explanation, vindication **13** justification **14** acknowledgment

apostate: 7 seceder, traitor **8** deserter, disloyal, recreant, renegade, turncoat **9** faithless **10** recidivist

apostle: 4 John, Jude, Paul **5** James, Peter, Silas, Simon **6** Andrew, Philip, Thomas **7** Matthew, teacher **8** Barnabas, disciple, follower, Matthias, preacher, Thaddeus **9** messenger **10** evangelist, missionary **11** Bartholomew
of Indies: **6** Xavier
pert. to: **7** petrine
to Franks: **4** Remi
to Gauls: **5** Denis
to Gentiles: **4** Paul
to Goths: **7** Ulfilas
to Ireland: **7** Patrick

apothecary: 7 chemist **8** druggist, gallipot **10** pharmacist
weight: **4** dram **5** grain, pound **7** scruple

apothegm: saw **5** adage, axiom, gnome, maxim **6** dictum, saying, truism **7** proverb **8** aphorism

apotheosize: 5 deify, exalt **7** ennoble, glorify, idolize **8** enshrine, idealize **10** consecrate

Appalachians: *range:* **6** Ramapo **7** Taconic **8** Catskill **9** Allegheny, Blue Ridge **10** Berkshires, Cumberland, Great Smoky

appall, appal: awe **4** stun **5** daunt, shock **6** dismay **7** depress, horrify, terrify **8** frighten **10** scare stiff **11** make shudder **13** give the creeps

appalling: 5 awful **7** awesome, fearful **8** alarming, dreadful, terrible **9** frightful, unearthly **10** petrifying

appanage: 5 grant **7** adjunct **9** allowance, endowment, privilege **10** perquisite **11** prerogative

apparatus (see also **device, instrument**): rig **4** gear, tool **5** gizmo **6** dingus, gadget, outfit, system **7** utensil **8** material **9** appliance, equipment, machinery, mechanism, trappings **10** furnishing **11** contrivance **12** appurtenance

apparel (see also **dress, vestment**): **4** duds, garb, gear, robe, togs, wear **5** adorn, array, dress, equip **6** attire, clothe, outfit **7** costume, deck out, garment, raiment, vesture **8** clothing, wardrobe **9** embellish **11** furnishings, habiliments

apparent: 4 open **5** clear, overt, plain ·**6** patent **7** evident, glaring, obvious, seeming, visible **8** distinct, manifest, palpable, probable **9** easy to see **10** noticeable, ostensible, plain as day **11** discernible, perceptible, unconcealed **12** unmistakable

apparition: 5 ghost, haunt, shade, spook **6** shadow, spirit, sprite, wraith **7** eidolon, fantasy, phantom, specter, spectre **8** illusion, phantasm, revenant **9** hobgoblin **10** appearance, phenomenon **13** hallucination

appeal: ask, beg **4** call, plea, seek, suit **5** charm, plead **6** adjure, allure, prayer, summon, turn to **7** address, beseech, entreat, glamour, implore, request, solicit **8** approach, petition **9** importune **10** attraction, supplicate

appealing: 4 cute **6** catchy **7** winsome **8** engaging, fetching, pleading, pleasant **9** agreeable, imploring **10** attractive, entrancing

appear: 4 come, look, loom, seem **5** arise, enter, issue, occur **6** arrive, emerge, show up **7** compear (Sc.), develop, emanate **11** materialize

appearance: air, hue **4** form, idea, look, mien, show, view **5** front, guise, sight **6** aspect, facade, manner **7** arrival, bearing, display **8** demeanor, illusion, presence, pretense **9** semblance **10** disclosure, phenomenon **11** countenance **13** manifestation
first: **5** debut **8** premiere **9** unveiling

appease: 4 calm, ease, hush **5** allay, mease (Sc.), quiet, slake **6** buy off, pacify, please, soften, soothe **7** assuage, content, gratify, mollify, placate, satisfy **8** mitigate **9** sweettalk **10** conciliate, propitiate **11** tranquilize

appellation: nom (F.), tag **4** name **5** label, title **7** epithet, moniker **8** cognomen, nickname **9** sobriquet **11** designation

appellee: 9 defendant **10** respondent

append: add **4** clip, hang **5** affix, annex, pin to, tag on **6** attach **7** subjoin **8** fasten to

appendage: arm, awn, ear, fin, leg, tab, tag **4** aril, barb, flap, limb, palp, tail, wing **5** canda, extra, rider **6** branch, suffix **7** adjunct, antenna, codicil **8** addition, hanger-on, offshoot, parasite, tentacle **9** accessory **10** dependency

appendix: 5 organ **7** addenda (pl.) **8** addendum, epilogue **10** supplement

appertain: 6 bear on, belong **7** apply to, concern, refer to **8** relate to **12** have to do with

appetite: yen **4** lust, urge, zest **5** gusto, taste **6**

desire, hunger, liking, orexis, relish **7** craving, longing, passion, wanting **8** cupidity, penchant, tendency **10** preference, propensity
abnormal: **4** pica **7** bulimia
excessive: **5** greed **8** gluttony, gulosity **10** polyphagia
pert. to: **6** oretic
voracious: **7** edacity **8** rapacity

appetizer: **5** snack **6** canape, relish, savory, tidbit **8** aperitif, cocktail **9** antipasto **11** hors d'oeuvre

applaud: **4** clap, hail **5** cheer, extol **6** praise **7** acclaim, approve, commend, endorse, root for **10** compliment

applauders: **6** claque

applause: **4** hand **5** eclat, kudos **6** bravos, cheers, huzzas, salvos **7** hurrahs, ovation **8** clapping, plaudits **11** approbation

apple: **4** crab, pome **6** Esopus, pippin, russet **7** Baldwin, Fameuse, Wealthy, Winesap **8** Ben Davis, Cortland, Greening, Jonathan, McIntosh **9** Delicious, Oldenberg **10** Rome Beauty **11** Granny Smith, Gravenstein, Northern Spy, Spitzenburg **12** Yellow Newton, York Imperial **17** Yellow Transparent
acid: **5** malic
blight: **5** aphid **8** eriosoma
crushed pulp: **6** pomace
drink: **5** cider **8** Calvados
genus: **5** malus
immature: **6** codlin **7** codling
pastry: **7** strudel
ribbed: **7** costard
seed: pip
wild: **4** crab

apple knocker: **4** hick **5** yokel **6** rustic **7** bumpkin, hayseed **9** greenhorn

apple of one's eye: **7** darling **8** favorite

apple-polish: **4** fawn **5** toady **7** flatter **8** kowtow to **10** curry favor

applesauce: **4** bunk, pulp **5** hokum, hooey **6** relish **7** baloney, dessert, rubbish **8** nonsense **9** poppycock

appliance (see also **tool**): **4** gear **6** device, gadget **7** utensil **9** implement **10** instrument **11** contrivance

applicable: apt, fit **4** meet **5** ad rem (L.) **6** proper, useful **7** apropos, fitting, germane **8** apposite, relative, relevant, suitable **9** pertinent **10** to the point **11** appropriate

applicant: **8** prospect **9** candidate, solicitor

application: use **4** form **5** study **6** appeal, effort **7** request **8** dressing, industry, petition, sedulity **9** diligence, relevance **11** mental labor **12** perseverance

applique: **6** design **7** overlay **8** ornament, trimming **10** decoration

apply: ask, fit, use **5** put on, rub on **6** appeal,

bear on, bestow, betake, devote, direct, employ, impose, relate **7** conform, overlay, pertain, request, solicit, utilize **8** carry out, petition, put in for, spread on **9** persevere **10** administer **11** superimpose **13** put into effect

appoggiatura: **9** grace note

appoint: fix, set **4** name **5** allot, elect, equip **6** assign, decree, detail, direct, outfit **7** confirm, furnish, mark out **8** delegate, nominate **9** authorize, designate, prescribe **10** commission
as agent: **6** depute **8** delegate, deputize

appointment: **4** date, post **5** berth, tryst **6** billet, office **7** meeting, station **8** position **9** selection **10** assignment, engagement, rendezvous **11** assignation

apportion: **5** allot, award, grant, share, split **6** assess, assign, divide, parcel, ration **7** divvy up, dole out, mete out, prorate **8** allocate **10** distribute

apportionment: **4** deal **8** dividend, division **9** allowance **12** distribution

appose: **9** place near **11** put opposite **13** put side by side

apposite: apt **6** timely **7** germane **8** relevant, suitable **9** pertinent **11** appropriate

appraise: **4** rate **5** assay, gauge, judge **6** assess, survey **7** analyze, examine **8** estimate, evaluate **10** adjudicate **11** put a price on

appreciable: **7** evident, obvious **8** apparent, palpable, tangible **10** noticeable **11** discernible, perceptible

appreciate: **4** feel, love **5** judge, prize, value **6** admire, esteem **7** advance, cherish, realize, respect **8** increase, treasure **9** be aware of **10** understand **11** go up in worth

appreciation: **5** gusto **6** thanks **7** tribute **8** judgment **9** enjoyment, gratitude **11** recognition, testimonial **12** gratefulness

apprehend: nab, see **4** know, view **5** catch, grasp, seize **6** arrest, detain, divine, fathom, wise up **7** capture, foresee, make out, realize **8** conceive, perceive **9** recognize **10** anticipate, comprehend

apprehensible: **5** lucid **6** noetic **7** sensate **8** knowable **12** intelligible

apprehension: **4** fear, idea **5** doubt, dread, worry **6** arrest, dismay, notion **7** anxiety, capture, concern **8** distrust, mistrust, suspense **9** misgiving, suspicion **10** conception, foreboding, perception, solicitude, uneasiness **11** premonition **12** anticipation, intellection, presentiment **13** understanding

apprehensive: apt **5** aware, jumpy **6** morbid **7** fearful, nervous **9** cognizant, conscious **10** discerning

apprentice: **4** tyro **6** novice, rookie **7** learner, trainee **8** beginner, neophyte **9** greenhorn, novitiate **10** tenderfoot

apprise, apprize: **4** tell, warn **5** value **6**

advise, inform, notify, reveal **8** acquaint, disclose **10** appreciate

apprised: 5 aware **7** knowing

approach: try **4** loom, near **5** essay, verge **6** access, accost, advent, coming, impend **7** address, advance, close in, get warm, landing, solicit **8** overture **9** draw close, procedure **11** approximate, break the ice **12** narrow the gap

approbation: 4 okay **5** favor **6** assent, esteem, praise, regard, repute **7** plaudit, respect **8** applause, approval, blessing, sanction **10** admiration **12** commendation

appropriate: apt, due, use **4** grab, meet, take **5** annex, claim, right, steal, usurp **6** assign, assume, borrow, pilfer, pirate, proper, timely, worthy **7** apropos, condign, convert, fitting, germane, impound, preempt, purloin, related **8** accroach, arrogate, becoming, deserved, relevant, suitable **9** pertinent **10** applicable, confiscate, convenient, felicitous, plagiarize **11** set apart for

appropriation: 5 grant **7** stipend, subsidy **9** allotment, allowance **11** special fund

approval: 4 amen **5** eclat **6** assent **7** go ahead, support **8** blessing, sanction **10** imprimatur **11** approbation, benediction

approve: 4 back, like, okay, pass **5** adopt, allow, clear, favor, value **6** accept, admire, concur, ratify **7** applaud, certify, commend, confirm, consent, endorse, initial, vote for **8** accredit, sanction **9** authorize **10** compliment **11** countenance, think well of

approximate: 4 near **5** about, circa, close **8** approach, estimate, resemble **9** come close

approximately: 4 nigh **5** about **6** almost, around, nearly **7** roughly **9** virtually **10** more or less **11** practically

appurtenance: 4 gear **5** annex **7** adjunct **8** appendix **9** accessory, apparatus, appendage, appliance, belonging

après (F.): 5 after **10** afterwards

apricot: ume **4** ansu, tree **5** color, fruit **8** Blenheim
confection: **5** mebos **6** meebos
cordial: **7** perisco **8** periscot
vine: **6** maypop

a priori: 9 deductive **11** conditional, inferential, presumptive, reasoned out

apron: bib **4** tier **5** cover, smock **6** runway, shield, tarmac **8** pinafore **10** protection
leather: **4** dick **8** barmskin, lambskin **9** forestage

apropos: apt **4** as to, in re, meet **5** about, anent **6** timely **7** fitting, germane **8** by the way, relevant, suitable **9** opportune, pertinent **10** to the point **11** appropriate, in respect to

apse: 5 niche **6** recess **10** orbit point, projection

apt: fit, pat **4** able, deft, keen **5** adept, alert, prone, quick, ready **6** clever, liable, likely **7** apropos, capable, fitting **8** apposite, dextrous, disposed, inclined, skillful, suitable, tendency **9** competent, consonant, dexterous, pertinent **10** proficient **11** appropriate

apteral: 8 wingless
opposite of: **4** alar **5** alate

apteryx: 4 bird, kiwi

aptitude: art **4** bent, gift, turn **5** craft, flair, knack **6** genius, talent **7** ability, faculty, leaning **8** instinct **10** propensity **11** disposition

aquamarine: gem **4** blue **5** beryl, color

aquarium: 4 bowl, pond, pool, tank **5** globe

aquatic plant: 4 lily **5** coral, lotus **6** enalid, sugamo **7** elatine, seaweed **10** hydrophyte

aqueduct: 5 canal **7** channel, conduit, passage **9** conductor, water pipe
of Sylvius: **4** iter

aquila: 5 eagle

Aquilo: 4 wind **7** norther

aquiline: 6 hooked **7** curving **9** eagle-like, prominent

Aquinas: *nickname:* **13** Angelic Doctor
work: **5** Summa

aquosity: 7 wetness **8** moisture **10** wateriness

ara: 5 macaw

arab: 4 waif **5** gamin, nomad **6** urchin **8** wanderer

araba: cab **5** coach **6** monkey **8** carriage

Arabian (see also individual countries): *abode:* dar **4** tent
alphabet: See **Arabic:** *alphabet*
antelope: **5** addax
author: **6** lokman
banquet: **5** diffa
bazaar: suq
bird: **7** phoenix
caliph: Ali **6** sharif, sherif **7** shareef, shereef
caravan: **6** cafila
cloak: aba
clothing: aba **4** haik **6** cabaan **7** burnous **8** burnoose, keffiyeh
coffee: **5** mocha
cosmetic: **4** kohl
countries: **4** Aden, Iraq, Oman, Sana **5** Egypt, Libya, Qatar, Sudan, Syria, Yemen **6** Jordan, Kuwait **7** Algeria, Bahrain, Lebanon, Morocco, Tunisia **10** Mauritania **11** Saudi Arabia
currency: **4** lari **5** carat, dinar, kabik, riyal
demon: **4** jinn **5** afrit, genie, jinni **6** afreet, jinnee
dish: **8** couscous
drink: **4** bosa, boza **5** bozah **6** lebban
drum: **9** tara-booka
fabric: aba **4** haik
father: abu **4** abba, abou
flour source: **4** samh
gazelle: **4** cora **5** ariel
goddess: **5** Allat

grammar: **7** ajrumya
horse: **6** anezeh **8** kadischi, palomino
infantryman: **5** askar
jasmine: **4** bela **10** sampaquita
judge: **4** cadi
land: **6** feddan
measure: den, saa **4** ferk, foot, kist **5** achir, barid, cadba, cafiz, covid, cuddy, makuk, mille, qasab, teman, woibe, zudda **6** artaba, assbaa, covido, feddan, gariba, ghalva **7** caphite, farsakh, farsang, kiladja, marhale, nusfiah
palm: **4** doom, doum
peasant: **6** fellah
philosopher: **6** Farabi **8** Averroes
plant: kat **5** retem
prince (see also *ruler* below): **6** sherif **7** shereef
raiders: **8** fedayeen
religion: **5** Islam **12** Christianity
river bed: **4** wadi, wady
romance: **5** antar **6** antara
ruler: **4** amir, emir **5** ameer, emeer, sheik **6** sultan
shrub: kat **5** alhaj, retem
tambourine: **4** taar **5** daira
tea shrub: kat
tent encampment: **5** douar
vessel: **4** dhow **6** boutre, sambuk
weight: **4** rotl **5** cheki, kella, nasch, nevat, ocque, oukia, ratel, toman, vakia **6** bokard, dirhem, miskal, tomand **8** farsalah
wind: **6** simoom, simoon
Arabian Nights: *bird:* roc **4** aqib
    character: Ali **4** Sidi **5** Amina **7** Zobeide
    dervish: **4** Agib
    merchant: **7** Sindbad
    poet: Kab **5** Antar
    prince: **7** Alasnam
    sailor: **6** Sinbad **7** Sindbad
    sorceress: **5** Amine
    youth: **7** Aladdin
Arabic: *alphabet:* ayn, dad, dal, jim, kaf, kha, lam, mim, nun, qaf, sad, sin, tha, waw, zay **4** alif, dhal, shin **5** ghayn
    script: **5** cufic, kufic, neski **6** neshki
arable: **7** fertile **8** plowable, tillable
aracanga: **5** macaw
aracari: **6** toucan
arachnid: **4** crab, mite, tick **6** acarus, spider **8** scorpion **9** tarantula
Aram: **12** ancient Syria
Aramaic: **6** Syriac **9** Samaritan
araneous: **4** thin **8** delicate, gossamer **9** arachnoid **10** cobweblike
araphorostic: **7** unsewed **8** seamless
araponga: **8** bellbird
Arawakan: *Indian:* **4** Uran **5** Araua, Bares, Guana, Moxos, Piros **6** Campas **7** Atorais, Banivas, Jucunas, Lucayos, Tacanan, Ticunan **8** Lorenzan

language: **5** Taino
    spirit: **4** zemi
arbiter: **5** judge **6** umpire **7** referee **8** dictator **9** moderator **11** adjudicator
arbitrary: **4** rash **6** random, thetic **7** willful **8** absolute, despotic **9** imperious **10** autocratic, capricious, highhanded, peremptory, tyrannical **11** dictatorial **12** unreasonable **13** irresponsible
arbitrate: **6** decide, settle **7** adjudge, mediate **9** determine, intercede
arbitrator: **8** mediator **9** ombudsman **11** conciliator
arbor: bar, rod **4** axle, beam, tree **5** bower, shaft **6** garden, gazebo **7** mandrel, pergola, retreat, spindle, trellis
arbustum: **5** copse **7** orchard **10** plantation
arc: bow **4** bend, halo **5** curve, orbit **7** rainbow **9** spotlight **10** circle part
    chord of: **4** sine
    horizon: **7** azimuth
arca: box **5** chest, paten **9** reliquary
arcade: **6** loggia **7** gallery, portico **8** arcature **9** colonnade **10** passageway
Arcadia: **4** Eden **6** Arcady **8** paradise
    huntress: **8** Atalanta
    princess: **4** Auge
    town: **4** Alea
    woodland spirit: Pan
arcadian: **5** ideal, rural **6** rustic, simple **7** bucolic, idyllic **8** pastoral, shepherd
arcane: **6** hidden, occult **8** esoteric **10** cabalistic, mysterious
arcanum: **6** elixir, remedy, secret **7** mystery
Arcas: *father:* **4** Zeus
    mother: **8** Callisto
    son: **4** Azan **8** Apheidas
arch: bow, coy, sly **4** bend, hump, span **5** chief, curve, great, prime, saucy, vault **6** camber, clever, fornix, impish, instep **7** cunning, eminent, roguish, support, waggish **9** principal **11** mischievous
    inner curve of: **8** intrados
    kind of: **4** flat **5** Roman, round, Tudor **6** lancet **7** rampant, trefoil **9** horseshoe, primitive, segmental **10** shouldered **11** equilateral **12** basket-handle, four-centered **13** three-cornered
    memorial: **6** pailoo, pailou, pailow
    molding: **9** accoclade
    part: **8** keystone, springer, voussoir
    pointed: **4** ogee **5** ogive **6** Gothic
archaic: old **7** ancient **8** historic, obsolete **9** venerable **10** antiquated **12** old-fashioned
archangel: **5** Satan, Uriel **7** Gabriel, Michael, Raphael
arch-enemy: **5** devil, Satan
archer: **4** Clym, Egil, Tell **5** cupid **6** bowman **9** Robin Hood **11** Sagittarius
archery: *deity:* **6** Apollo **7** Artemis

locker: **6** ascham
lover: **11** toxophilite
target: **4** wand **5** clout
archetype: **4** idea **5** ideal, model **7** example, paragon, pattern **8** exemplar, original, paradigm **9** prototype **10** pilot model
architect: **5** maker **6** artist, author **7** artisan, builder, creator, planner **8** designer **9** draftsman
architectural: **8** tectonic
architecture: *convexity:* **7** entasis
order: **5** Doric, Ionic **10** Corinthian
ornament: ove **5** gutta **6** dentil, rosace **7** rosette
style: **5** Doric, Greek, Ionic, Tudor **6** Gothic, Lancet, Norman **7** Baroque, Bauhaus, Cape Cod, Moorish **8** Academic, Colonial, Egyptian, Georgian **9** Byzantine, Palladian **10** Corinthian, Romanesque **11** Carolingian, Renaissance
archive: **5** annal **6** museum, record **7** library **8** document, register **9** chronicle
archon: **5** ruler **8** dictator, official **10** magistrate
arc lamp rod: **6** carbon
Arctic: *animal:* **6** narwal, walrus **7** caribou, lemming **8** narwhale, reindeer
base: **4** Etah
bay: **6** Baffin
bird: auk **9** ptarmigan
canoe: **5** kayak, umiak **6** oomiak
current: **8** Labrador
dog: **5** husky **7** samoyed **8** malamute
explorer: Nay, Rae **4** Byrd, Eric, Kane, Ross **5** Davis, Peary **6** Baffin, Bering, Button, Greely, Hearne, Hudson, Nansen, Nobile **7** McClure, Wilkins, Wrangel **9** Amundsend, Frobisher, Rasmussen **10** Stefansson, Willoughby
forest: **5** taiga
frozen soil: **10** permafrost
gulf: **8** Amundsen
gull (genus): **4** xema
headland: **5** Odden
island: **5** Banks, Devon **6** Baffin **7** Wrangel **8** Bathurst **9** Greenland
jacket: **5** parka **6** anorak
musk ox: **6** ovibos
peninsula: **4** Kola **6** Taymyr
people: **4** Lapp **5** Aleut, Inuit, Yakut **6** Eskimo, Koryak, Nenetz **7** Chukchi **9** Kamchadal, Laplander
plain: **6** tundra
plant: **5** sedum, poppy **8** bluebell **9** saxifrage
sea: **4** Kara **6** Laptev **7** Barents, Chukchi, Lincoln **8** Beaufort, Victoria **9** Greenland
snowstorm: **5** purge
arctic: icy **4** cold, cool, shoe **5** gelid, polar **6** boreal, chilly, frigid, galosh **8** northern, overshoe
Arcturus: **4** star

arcuate: **4** bent **5** bowed **6** arched, curved, hooked
ardent: hot **4** avid, fond, keen, warm **5** eager, fiery, rethe (Sc.) **6** ablaze, fervid **7** amorous, earnest, feeling, fervent, flaming, intense, shining, zealous **8** desirous, vehement **9** impetuous, perfervid **11** inflammable **12** enthusiastic
ardor: **4** dash, elan, glow, heat, love, zest **5** gusto, verve **6** desire, fervor, mettle, spirit **7** passion **8** devotion, vivacity **9** animation, calenture **10** enthusiasm
arduous: **4** hard **5** lofty, steep **6** trying **7** onerous **8** exacting, tiresome, toilsome **9** difficult, laborious, strenuous **10** exhausting
area: **4** belt, size, zone **5** field, range, realm, scene, scope, space, tract **6** extent, locale, region, sector, sphere **7** expanse, purlieu **8** district, province **9** bailiwick, territory **12** neighborhood
measure: are **4** acre, rod **6** orpent **7** hectare
pert. to: **7** spatial

Argentina: *capital:* **11** Buenos Aires
city: **4** Azul, Goya **5** Jujuy, Salta **6** Parana **7** Cordoba, La Rioja, Mendoza, Posadas, Rosario, San Juan, Santa Fe, Tucuman, Ushuaia **8** Santiago **10** Corrientes **11** Mar del Plata
cowboy: **6** gaucho
currency: **4** peso **7** austral, centavo
dance: **5** tango
estuary: **7** La Plata
explored by: **5** Cabot **11** Juan de Solis
measure: **4** sino, vara **5** legua **6** cuadra, fanega **7** manzana
mountain pass: **9** Uspallata
mountain peak: **4** Mayo **5** Cachi, Laudo **6** Bonete, Pissis, Rincon **9** Aconcagua, Incahuasi, Tupungato
mountain range: **5** Andes
people: **4** Lule **7** Guarani
plain: **6** pampas
port: **6** Rawson, Viedma **7** La Plata, Rosario **8** Gallegos **11** Bahia Blanca
ranch: **8** estancia
river: **4** Coig **5** Atuel, Chico, Dulce, Limay, Negro, Teuco **6** Chubut, Parana, Quinto, Salado **7** bermejo, Uruguay **8** Colorado, Gallegos **9** Rio Grande
southern steppes: **9** Patagonia
volcano: **5** Lanin, Maipo **6** Domuyo **7** Peteroa
weight: **4** last **5** grano **7** quintal **8** tonelada

38

areca: 4 palm 5 betel

arena: pit 4 bowl, oval, ring, rink 5 court, field, stage 6 sphere 7 stadium, theater 8 coliseum, province 10 hippodrome 12 amphitheater
sports: see **field:** *athletic*

arenaceous: 5 sandy 6 gritty 8 sabulous

areola: pit 4 area, ring, spot 5 space 9 periphery 10 interstice

areometer: 10 hydrometer

Ares: 4 Mars
father: 4 Zeus
mother: 4 Enyo, Hera
sister: 4 Eris
son: 6 Cycnus

arete: 4 crag 5 crest, ridge, valor 6 virtue 9 manliness 10 excellence

argali: 5 sheep 6 aoudad

argent: 4 coin 5 money, white 6 silver 7 shining, silvery 9 whiteness

Argentina: (see box)

argil: 4 clay 7 alumina

argillaceous: 5 loamy 6 clayey, doughy, earthy, spongy

Argonaut: 5 Jason 8 wanderer 10 adventurer

Argos: *king:* 4 Abas 6 Danaus 7 Lynceus 8 Acrisius, Adrastus
princess: 5 Danae

argosy: 4 boat, ship 5 craft, fleet 6 supply, vessel 7 galleon 10 storehouse

argot: 4 cant 5 flash, lingo, slang 6 jargon, patois 7 dialect

argue: 4 moot, show, spar 5 cavil, claim, clash 6 bicker, debate, induce, reason 7 contend, contest, discuss, dispute, quarrel, wrangle 8 indicate, maintain, persuade 11 expostulate, remonstrate

argument: row 4 case, fuss, idea, plea, plot, text 5 set to, theme 6 combat, debate, hassle, reason 7 defense, polemic, rhubarb, summary 8 abstract 9 discourse, statement 10 difference 11 altercation, controversy
conclusive: 6 corker 7 crusher 8 clincher 9 knockdown 11 sockdolager, sockdologer
fallacious: 7 sophism
negative side: con
positive side: pro
specious: rot 8 claptrap, nonsense 9 sophistry 10 paralogism
starting point: 7 premise

argumentative: 7 eristic 8 forensic 10 indicative, rhetorical 11 contentious, presumptive 12 disputatious 13 controversial

Argus-eyed: 8 vigilant 10 on the alert

argute: 5 acute, sharp 6 shrewd, shrill 8 sawedged 9 sagacious

arhat: 4 monk 5 lohan, saint

aria: air 4 solo, song, tune 6 melody 7 sortita

arid: dry 4 bald, bare, dull, lean 6 barren, jejune, meager 7 parched, sterile 8 withered 9 unfertile, waterless 10 desiccated, siccaneous 12 moistureless 13 uninteresting

ariel: 7 gazelle

Aries: ram 4 goat 6 zodiac 13 constellation
mother: 4 Enyo

Arikara: Ree

aril: pod 7 coating 8 covering 9 appendage 10 integument

ariose: 7 melodic 8 songlike 9 melodious

arise: 4 flow, lift, rear, soar 5 begin, get up, issue, mount, raise, stand, surge, tower, waken 6 accrue, amount, appear, ascend, come up, derive, emerge, happen, spring 7 develop, emanate, proceed 8 stem from 9 come about, originate, take place

arista: awn 5 beard 9 appendage

aristocracy: 5 elite 8 nobility 9 oligarchy 10 upper crust 11 ruling class

aristocrat: 4 peer 7 Brahmin 8 nobleman 9 blue-blood, patrician 12 thoroughbred

Aristophanes work: 5 Birds, Frogs 6 Clouds, Plutus

Arizona: *capital:* 7 Phoenix
city: Ajo 4 Mesa, Yuma 5 Tempe 6 Bisbee, Tucson 7 Kingman, Nogales 8 Prescott 9 Flagstaff
dam: 6 Hoover, Parker 7 Boulder 8 Coolidge, Tailings 9 Roosevelt 10 Glen Canyon
desert: 7 Painted
early explorer: 6 De Niza 8 Coronado
forest: 6 Kaibab 9 Petrified
gorge: 6 Chelly 11 Grand Canyon
Indian: 4 Hopi, Pima, Yuma 6 Apache, Navaho, Navajo, Papago
Indian war chiefs: 7 Cochise 8 Geronimo
lake: 4 Mead 6 Havasu, Mohave, Powell 9 Roosevelt, San Carlos
mountain peak: 5 Lemon 6 Graham 7 Hualpai, Pastora 8 Mazatzal 9 Humphreys
mountain range: 5 Black 7 Hualapi 8 Gila Bend, Huachuca, Pinaleno 9 Santa Rita 10 Chiricahua 12 San Francisco, Superstition 13 Santa Catalina
river: 4 Gila, Salt 5 Verde 8 Colorado, San Pedro 9 San Carlos
site of noted battle: 8 O.K. Corral (Tombstone)
state bird: 10 cactus wren
state flower: 7 saguaro
state motto: 9 Ditat Deus (God enriches)
state nickname: 11 Grand Canyon
state tree: 9 paloverde

Aristotle: 5 Greek 11 philosopher
 birthplace: 6 Thrace 7 Stagira
 category: 4 time 5 place 6 action 7 quality
 8 position, quantity, relation 9 passivity,
 substance 10 possession
 disciple: 11 Peripatetic
 father: 10 Nicomachus
 guardian: 8 Proxenus
 school: 6 Lyceum
 student: 9 Alexander
 teacher: 5 Plato
 wife: 7 Pithias
 works: 7 De Anima, Organon, Poetics 8
 Politics, Rhetoric
Arizona: (see box)
ark: bin, box 4 boat, ship 5 barge, chest, hutch
 6 basket, coffer, refuge, wangan 7 retreat,
 shelter, wanigan 8 flatboat
 builder: Noe 4 Noah
 resting place: 6 Ararat

Arkansas: *capital:* 10 Little Rock
 city: 4 Hope, Mena 5 Salem, Wynne
 6 Des Arc 7 De Queen 8 El Dorado 9
 Fort Smith, Jonesboro, Pine Bluff 10
 Hot Springs 11 Fayetteville
 Indians: 5 Caddo, Osage 6 Quapaw
 lake: 6 Chicot 7 Greeson, Norfork
 motto: 13 Regnat Populus (The people rule)
 mountain: 4 Blue 5 Ozark 6 Boston,
 Walker 8 Magazine
 river: Red 5 Black, White 6 Saline 8
 Arkansas, Cimarron, Ouachita 9 St.
 Francis 11 Mississippi
 spa: 10 Hot Springs
 state bird: 11 mockingbird
 state flower: 12 apple blossom
 state tree: 4 pine
 U.S. president: 7 Clinton

---

arkose: 9 sandstone
arm: bay, fin 4 limb, spur, wing 5 bough,
 equip, fiord, firth, fjord, force, inlet, might,
 power 6 branch, energy, member, outfit,
 sleeve, weapon 7 flipper, fortify, furnish,
 prepare, protect, provide, support 8
 strength 9 appendage, extension 10 instrument, projection
 bone: 4 ulna 6 radius 7 humerus
 hollow at bend: 8 chelidon
 joint: 4 ares 5 elbow, wrist
 muscle: 6 biceps 7 triceps
 part: 4 ares 5 elbow, wrist
 pert. to: 8 brachial
armada: 4 navy 5 fleet 8 flotilla, squadron,
 warships 9 task force

armadillo: 5 poyou 6 mulita 7 tatouay 8 pangolin 10 pichiciago
 giant: 4 tatu 5 tatou 6 peludo
 small: 4 peba 11 quirquincho
 three banded: 4 apar 5 apara 6 mataco
armament: 7 defense 8 ordnance, security,
 weaponry 9 munitions, safeguard 12 military gear
armamentarium: 4 data 5 store 6 armory 7
 arsenal 9 apparatus, equipment 10 collection
armband: 7 maniple 8 brassard
Armenia: *ancient name:* 5 Minni 8 Anatolia
 capital: 7 Yerevan
 lake: 5 Sevan
 mountain: 7 Aragats
 river: 4 Aras
armet: 6 helmet
armistice: 4 lull 5 peace, truce 9 cessation 10
 suspension
armoire: 8 cupboard, wardrobe 12 clothespress
armor: 4 egis, mail 5 guard, plate 6 byrnie,
 sheath, shield 7 cuirass, defense, hauberk 8
 covering 10 protection
 arm: 8 brassard, brassart 9 gardebras
 armpit: 8 pallette
 bearer: 6 squire 7 armiger, custrel
 cap: 10 cerveliere
 elbow guard: 9 cubitiere
 face: 6 beaver 7 ventail 8 aventail
 foot: 8 sabbaton, solleret
 hand: 8 gauntlet
 head: 4 coif 6 helmet 7 basinet
 horse: 5 barde 6 crinet 7 peytrel, poitrel 8
 chamfron
 knee: 11 genouillere
 leg: 4 boot, jamb 5 jambe 6 greave 7
 chausse, jambeau
 shoulder: 7 ailette 8 pauldron, pouldron 9
 epauliere
 skirt: 4 tace 5 tasse 6 taslet, tasset 11 bra-
 conniere
 thigh: 5 cuish 6 cuisse, tuille 8 cuissard
 throat: 6 camail, gorget
armored: 6 mailed, plated 8 ironclad,
 shielded 9 panoplied, protected 11
 encuirassed
armpit: ala (L.) 5 oxter (Sc.) 6 axilla 7 axi-
 llae (pl.)
 pert. to: 7 axillar
armory: 4 dump 5 depot 7 arsenal 8 magazine 9 warehouse
army: 4 here, host 5 array, crowd, force,
 horde 6 cohort, legion, number, throng,
 troops 7 militia 8 soldiers, warriors 9 multitude
 chaplain: 5 padre
 commission: 6 brevet

engineer: **6** sapper **7** pioneer

enlisted man: NCO **5** GI Joe **7** private **8** doughboy

mascot: **4** mule

meal: **4** chow, mess

NCO: PFC **8** corporal, sergeant

officer: **5** major **7** captain, colonel, general **10** lieutenant

pert. to: **7** martial **8** military

post: **4** base, camp, fort

postal abbreviation: APO, FPO

school: OCS, OTS **7** academy **9** West Point

storehouse: **5** depot **6** armory **7** arsenal

unit: **5** corps, squad, troop **6** detail, outfit **7** brigade, company, platoon **8** division, regiment **9** battalion, task force **10** detachment

vehicle: **4** jeep, tank **9** half-track

army ant: **6** driver **9** legionary

arnatto: See **annatto**

aroid: **4** taro **5** apium, tania **6** tanier **8** araceous

aroma: **4** odor **5** nidor, savor, scent, smell **6** flavor **7** bouquet, perfume **9** fragrance, redolence

aromatic: **5** balmy, spicy, sweet **6** fruity, savory **7** odorous, piquant, pungent **9** ambrosial

gum: **5** myrrh

herb: **4** dill, mint, nard **5** anise, basil, clary, nondo, thyme **8** lavender, rosemary

seed: **5** anise, cumin **6** nutmeg

spice: **4** mace **5** clove **8** cinnamon

tree: **6** balsam, laurel **8** huisache **9** sassafras

weed: **5** tansy

around: **4** near **5** about, alive, circa **6** in turn **7** close by, through **10** encircling, enveloping, everywhere, on all sides **12** here and there

around-the-clock: **8** constant, unending **9** incessant, perpetual **10** continuous **11** day and night

arouse: **4** call, fire, move, spur, stir, whet **5** alarm, awake, evoke, pique, raise, rally, rouse **6** excite, foment, incite, kindle, revive, summon, thrill, work up **7** actuate, agitate, animate, enliven, incense, inflame **9** stimulate

arpeggio: **7** roulade **8** flourish **10** musical run

arraign: try **4** cite **6** accuse, charge, indict **7** impeach **8** denounce **9** challenge **11** incriminate **13** call to account

arrange: fix, set **4** edit, file, form, plan, sort **5** adapt, align, array, drape, frame, grade, group, score, space **6** adjust, codify, design, devise, settle **7** catalog, compose, dispose, gradate, marshal, prepare, seriate, work out **8** classify, conclude, organize, regulate, tabulate **9** collocate **10** put in order **11** alphabetize, orchestrate

mutually: **5** agree **7** concert

arrangement: **4** deal **5** index, order, setup **6** format, layout, scheme, system, treaty **7** pattern **8** contract, sequence **9** direction, structure **10** allocation **11** composition, disposition **12** dispensation

arrant: bad **5** utter **6** brazen **7** blatant, vagrant **8** rascally **9** confirmed, downright, itinerant, notorious, out and out, shameless **11** unmitigated **13** thoroughgoing

arras: **7** drapery, hanging **8** tapestry

array: **4** garb, host, robe, show **5** adorn, align, dress, habit, order **6** attire, bedeck, clothe, draw up, finery, series **7** apparel, arrange, company, deck out, display, furnish, marshal **8** accouter, grouping **10** assemblage

arrears: **4** IOUs **9** liability **11** unpaid bills **12** indebtedness

arrest: nab **4** curb, grab, halt, hold, jail, stay, stop **5** catch, check, delay, pinch, seize **6** collar, detain, hinder, lock up, retard, thwart **7** capture, custody, suspend **8** imprison, obstruct, restrain, slow down **9** apprehend, intercept, interrupt **11** incarcerate

arresting: **8** gripping, pleasing, striking **10** impressive, noticeable

arret: **5** edict **6** decree **8** decision, judgment

arrie: auk **5** murre **9** guillemot, razorbill

arris, aris: **4** pien **5** angle, piend

arrive: **4** come, land, show **5** reach **6** appear, attain, make it, turn up **7** prosper, succeed **8** get there

arrogance: **5** pride **6** hubris, hybris **7** conceit, disdain, egotism, hauteur **9** insolence **10** effrontery **11** affectation

arrogant: **5** lofty, proud **6** lordly, uppish **7** haughty **8** affected, assuming, cavalier, fastuous, insolent, superior **9** conceited, insulting, presuming **10** disdainful, hoity-toity **11** dictatorial, domineering, highfalutin, impertinent, overbearing **12** contemptuous, contumelious, presumptuous, supercilious

arrogate: **4** grab, take **5** claim, seize, usurp **6** assume **7** preempt **8** take over **10** commandeer, confiscate

arrondissement: **4** ward **8** division

arrow: pin, rod **4** bolt, dart, reed **5** shaft **6** sprite, weapon **7** missile, pointer **9** indicator

case: **6** quiver

feathered: **4** vire

maker: **6** bowyer **8** fletcher

part: **4** barb, butt, head, nock **5** shaft, stele **7** feather

point: neb **4** barb

poison: **4** haya, inee, upas **5** urali **6** antiar, curare, sumpit, wagogo **7** woorali

rotating: **4** vire

arrow-shaped: 6 beloid 8 sagittal 9 sagittate

Arrowsmith author: 5 Lewis

arrowstone: 9 belemnite

arrowwood: 5 alder 9 buckthorn 10 burro-brush

arroyo: 5 brook, creek, gulch, gully, hondo, zanja 6 ravine, stream 7 channel 11 watercourse

ars artium (L.): 5 logic

arsenal: 6 armory, supply 8 dockyard, magazine 10 storehouse 13 armamentarium

arsenate: *copper:* 7 erinite
 hydrous zinc: 7 adamite
 red manganese: 9 sarkinite

arsenic: 6 poison 8 chemical
 antimony: 10 allemonite
 sulfide: 7 realgar
 trisulfide: 8 orpiment

arsenillo: 9 atacamite

arsenopyrite: 7 danaite

arsis: 4 beat 5 ictus 6 accent, rhythm
 opposed to: 6 thesis

arson: 12 incendiarism

arsonist: 7 firebug 10 pyromaniac

art: ars (L.) 4 wile 5 craft, knack, magic, skill, trade 7 calling, cunning, faculty, finesse, science 8 business, learning 9 dexterity, duplicity, ingenuity 10 profession 11 contrivance, cultivation
 black: 5 magic 7 alchemy 8 wizardry 9 diablerie 10 demonology, necromancy 11 conjuration
 fancier of: 6 votary 7 devotee, esthete 10 dilettante 11 connoisseur
 gallery: 5 salon 6 museum
 manual: 5 craft, sloid, slojd, sloyd
 school: 4 Dada 5 Dutch 6 ashcan, French, Paduan 7 Bauhaus, Flemish, Italian, Lombard, Umbrian 8 American, eclectic, Milanese, Scottish 9 Bolognese 10 Raphaelite
 style: pop 4 Dada 5 genre 6 cubism 7 baroque, fauvism, realism 10 surrealism 11 objectivism, primitivism, romanticism 13 impressionism 14 abstractionism

Artemis: 5 Diana
 birthplace: 5 Delos
 brother: 6 Apollo
 father: 4 Zeus
 mother: 4 Leto
 priestess: 9 Iphigenia

artel: 5 union 11 association, cooperative

artery: way 4 path, road 5 route 6 course, street, vessel 7 anonyma, conduit, highway 9 maxillary
 head: 7 carotid
 heart: 8 coronary
 pulsation: 5 ictus
 trunk: 5 aorta 6 aortae (pl.)

artful: apt, sly 4 foxy, wily 5 suave 6 adroit, clever, crafty, facile, shrewd, smooth, tricky 7 crooked, cunning, politic, vulpine 8 slippery, stealthy 9 deceitful, deceptive, designing, dexterous, practical

Artful Dodger: 7 Dawkins (Jack)

artfulness: 8 subtlety 9 diplomacy, duplicity, strategem 10 refinement

arthritis: 4 gout

arthron: 5 joint 12 articulation

Arthur: See **King Arthur**

artichoke: 5 plant 6 Cynara 7 chorogi
 leafstalk: 5 chard
 relative: 7 cardoon

article: one, the 4 item, term 5 essay, paper, piece, plank, point, story, theme, thing 6 clause, detail, object, report 7 feature 8 causerie, doctrine 9 condition, statement 10 particular 11 composition, stipulation
 French: la, le, les, une
 German: das, der, die, ein 4 eine
 Italian: la, gli, una, uno
 Spanish: el, la, las, los, una, uno 4 unas, unos

articulate: say 5 speak, utter, vocal 6 fluent, verbal 7 express, jointed 8 distinct 9 enunciate, pronounce, talkative 10 formulated, meaningful, say clearly 12 intelligible

artificer: 4 hoax, plot, ploy, ruse, wile 5 blind, cheat, dodge, feint, fraud, guile, skill, trick 6 deceit, device, gambit 7 cunning, evasion, finesse 8 intrigue, maneuver, pretense 9 deception, expedient, ingenuity, invention, stratagem 10 subterfuge 11 machination

artificial: 4 mock, sham 5 bogus, faked, false 6 ersatz, forced, pseudo, unreal 7 assumed, feigned 8 affected, falsetto, spurious 9 insincere, pretended, simulated, synthetic, unnatural 10 factitious, fictitious, theatrical 11 counterfeit

artillery: 4 arms, guns 6 cannon 7 rockets 8 missiles, ordnance
 emplacement: 7 battery
 fire: 5 salvo 6 rafale 7 barrage
 wagon: 6 camion 7 caisson

artilleryman: 6 gunner, lascar 8 topechee 9 cannoneer 10 bombardier

artiodactyl: ox, pig 4 deer, goat 5 camel, sheep 6 artiad 7 giraffe 8 antelope 12 hippopotamus

artisan: 6 expert 9 craftsman 12 professional 13 skilled worker

artist: 4 star 5 actor 6 dancer, expert, master, singer, wizard 7 painter 8 designer, musician, sculptor, virtuoso 9 performer 12 professional

artless: 4 naif, open 5 frank, naive, plain 6 candid, rustic, simple 7 natural 8 innocent, trusting 9 childlike, guileless, ingenuous, untutored **10** unaffected **11** undesigning **15** unsophisticated

arty: **5** showy **9** imitative, overblown **11** pretentious, superficial

Aruba: **6** island
 sea: **9** Caribbean

arui: **5** sheep **6** aoudad

arum: **4** taro **5** aroid, plant **10** cuckoopint
 family: **7** araceae
 water: **5** calla

arundinaceous: **5** reedy

Aryan: **11** Indo-Iranian **12** Indo-European
 deity: **6** Ormazd, Ormuzd
 god of fire: **4** Agni
 language: **5** Farsi, Latin **7** Persian **8** Sanskrit
 of India: **5** Hindu

as: for, qua **4** like, that, thus, when **5** equal, since, while **7** because, equally, similar **9** therefore
 a rule: **7** usually **8** commonly **9** generally **10** ordinarily
 good as: **5** about **6** all but, almost, nearly
 if: **5** quasi **9** seemingly
 long as: **5** since **7** because **10** seeing that **11** considering

As You Like It: *character:* **5** Celia, Phebe **6** Jaques, Oliver **7** Charles, Orlando **8** Rosalind
 clown: **10** Touchstone
 forest: **5** Arden
 Rosalind's alias: **8** Ganymede

Asa: **6** healer **9** physician
 father: **4** Abia
 son: **11** Jehoshaphat

asafetida: **4** hing **6** ferula **8** gum resin

ascend: **4** rise, soar **5** climb, mount, scale, tower **7** clamber **8** escalate, progress **12** gain altitude

ascendancy: **4** sway **5** power **7** control, mastery, success **8** dominion, prestige, whip hand **9** authority, dominance, influence, supremacy **11** sovereignty, superiority

ascent: **4** hill, ramp, rise **5** slope **6** stairs **7** incline, upgrade, upswing **8** eminence, gradient, progress **9** acclivity, elevation **11** advancement

ascertain: get **5** learn **6** dig out **7** find out, seek out, unearth **8** discover **9** determine

ascetic: nun **4** monk, yogi **5** fakir, stark, stoic, Yogin **6** Essene, severe, strict **7** austere, eremite, recluse, stylite **8** anchoret **9** abstinent, anchorite **10** abstemious **11** disciplined, self-denying
 Buddhist: **7** bhikshu

ascot: tie **5** scarf **6** cravat **7** necktie **9** racetrack
 relative: bib **6** choker **7** bolo tie

ascribe: lay **4** cite **5** blame, infer, refer **6** accuse, allege, assign, attach, charge, credit, impute **8** accredit **9** attribute

ascription: **6** prayer **11** declaration
 of praise: **6** gloria
 popular: **6** repute

ascus: bag, sac

asea: **4** lost **6** addled, adrift, in a fog **7** puzzled, sailing **8** confused **9** befuddled, uncertain **10** bewildered, ocean-going

aseptic: **4** cold **5** clean **6** barren **7** sterile **8** detached, lifeless **9** purifying

Asgard: *bridge to:* **7** Bifrost
 watchman: **8** Heimdall

Asia: (see also individual countries): **6** Orient **7** Far East, Mideast **8** Near East **9** continent **10** Middle East
 country: **4** Iran, Iraq, Laos, Oman **5** Burma, China, India, Japan, Korea (North; South), Nepal, Qatar, Syria, Yemen **6** Bhutan, Brunei, Cyprus, Israel, Jordan, Kuwait, Russia (part), Taiwan, Turkey (part) **7** Armenia, Bahrain, Georgia, Lebanon, Vietnam **8** Malaysia, Maldives, Mongolia, Pakistan, Sri Lanka, Thailand **9** Indonesia (part), Kampuchea, Singapore **10** Azerbaijan, Bangladesh, Kazakhstan, Kyrgyzstan, Tajikistan, Uzbekistan **11** Afghanistan, Philippines, Saudi Arabia **12** Turkmenistan **18** United Arab Emirates
 desert: **4** Gobi, Thar **6** Syrian **7** Arabian, Kara Kum **8** Kyzyl Kum **10** Rub al Khali, Taklimakan
 lake: **4** Aral (Sea) **6** Baikal **7** Caspian (Sea) **8** Balkhash, Tungting
 mountain range: **5** Altai, Kumon, Sayan **6** Elburz, Kunlun, Pamirs, Qilian, Zagros **7** Khingan, Kumgang, Qin Ling **8** Stanovoy, Tien Shan **9** Himalayas, Hindu Kush, Karakoram **10** Tablonovyy
 people: Han, Lao, Mon, Tai **4** Arab, Kurd, Shan, Thai, Turk **5** Aryan, Karen, Khmer, Malay, Tajik, Tamil, Uzbek **6** Indian, Lepcha, Manchu, Mongol, Semite, Sindhi **7** Baluchi, bedouin, Bengali, Persian, Punjabi, Tibetan **8** Armenian, Kanarese **9** Chungchia, Dravidian, Indo-Aryan, Sinhalese
 river: Hsi, Ili **4** Amur, Lena, Onon, Ural, Yalu **5** Huang, Indus, Menam **6** Ganges, Irtysh, Mekong, Tigris, Yellow **7** Salween, Yangtze, Yenisey **9** Euphrates, Irrawaddy **11** Brahmaputra

ash: ase (Sc.) **4** coke, tree **5** ember, rowan **6** cinder **7** clinker, residue
receptacle: bin, box, urn
reduce to: **7** cremate
tobacco: **6** dottel, dottle

ashamed: **7** abashed, hangdog **8** contrite, redfaced **9** mortified **10** humiliated, remorseful **11** embarrassed

Ashanti pepper: **5** cubeb

ashen: wan **4** gray, grey, pale **5** waxen **6** pallid **7** ghastly **8** blanched **9** cinereous

Asher: *daughter:* **5** Serah **6** Beriah
father: **5** Jacob
son: **4** Usui **6** Jimnah

ashkoko: **4** cony, hare **5** daman, hyrax

Asia: (see box)

Asia Minor (see also **Asia**): **6** Turkey **8** Anatolia **9** peninsula
ancient city: **4** Myra, Myus, Teos, Troy **5** Issus, Perga **6** Mylasa, Patara, Priene, Sardis, Tarsus **7** Ephesus, Miletus **8** Colophon
ancient kingdom: **5** Caria, Ionia, Lydia, Mysia, Troad, Troas **6** Pontus **7** Cilicia, Hittite, Phrygia, Pisidia **8** Bithynia, Pergamum
mountain: Ida
mountain range: **6** Sultan, Taurus
river: **5** Halys **8** Monderez
sea: **5** Black **6** Aegean **7** Marmara **13** Mediterranean

aside: off **4** away, gone **5** aloof, apart **6** aslant **7** private, whisper **8** reserved, secretly, separate **9** obliquely, stage ploy **10** digression **11** parenthesis

aside from: **4** save **7** barring, besides **9** except for, excluding, outside of

asinine: **4** dull **5** crass, dense, inept, silly **6** absurd, obtuse, simple, stupid **7** doltish, fatuous, foolish, idiotic **9** gooselike, senseless

ask: beg, bid, sue **4** pray, quiz, seek **5** claim, crave, exact, plead, query, speer (Sc.), utter **6** adjure, demand, expect, invite **7** beseech, consult, entreat, implore, inquire, request, require, solicit **8** petition, question **11** interrogate

askance: **4** awry **5** askew **7** crooked **8** sideways **9** obliquely **10** doubtfully **11** skeptically **13** distrustfully, with suspicion

askew: **4** alop, awry **5** agley, amiss, atilt **6** aslant **7** asquint, crooked **8** cockeyed **9** distorted, out of line, to one side

asleep: out **4** dead, idle **6** dozing, latent, numbed **7** dormant, napping, unaware **8** off-guard **9** unfeeling **10** motionless, slumbering **11** not on the job, unconscious

asomatous: **10** immaterial **11** incorporeal

asp: **5** adder, aspen, snake, viper **7** serpent **8** ophidian
representative headdress: **6** uraeus

asparagus: **5** sprue

aspect: air **4** face, look, mien, side, view **5** angle, facet, guise, phase **6** manner, visage **7** bearing, feature, outlook **8** carriage, prospect **9** semblance **10** appearance **11** countenance

aspen: **4** tree **6** poplar **7** quaking **9** quivering, trembling, tremulous

asperity: ire **5** rigor **8** acerbity, acrimony, hardness, severity, sourness, tartness **9** briskness, harshness, roughness **10** bitterness, difficulty, unevenness **11** crabbedness **16** disagreeableness

asperse: **4** slur **5** abuse, decry, libel **6** defame, malign, revile **7** baptize, detract, slander, traduce **8** besmirch, christen, sprinkle **9** denigrate, discredit, disparage

aspersion: **7** baptism, calumny **8** innuendo **9** invective **12** vituperation

aspersorium: **4** font **5** basin, stoup

asphalt: **7** bitumen **8** blacktop, uintaite **10** wurtzilite

asphyxia: **5** apnea **6** apnoea **11** suffocation

aspic: gel **4** mold **5** jelly **7** gelatin **8** lavender

aspirant: **7** hopeful **9** applicant, candidate

aspiration: aim **4** goal, hope **5** ideal **8** ambition

aspire: try **4** hope, long, rise, seek, soar, wish **5** tower, yearn **6** ascend, desire **11** be ambitious

ass: **4** dolt, duff, fool **5** burro, chump, dunce, idiot, kiang, kulan **6** donkey, koulan, onager, quagga **8** imbecile **9** blockhead, simpleton **10** nincompoop
female: **5** jenny
male: **4** jack

assail: **4** beat, pelt **5** assay, beset, stone, storm, whack **6** accuse, attack, impugn, invade, malign, molest, scathe **7** assault, belabor, bombard **8** fall upon **9** encounter

assailant: **6** mugger **8** attacker **9** aggressor

Assam: **11** Indian state
capital: **8** Shillong
city: **4** Ledo **7** Gauhati, Nowgong
hills: **4** Abor, Garo, Miri, Naga **5** Khasi **6** Lushai
rubber: **7** rambong
silkworm: eri **4** eria
tribesman: Aka **4** Ahom, Garo, Naga **5** Lhota

assassin: gun **5** bravo, ninja **6** hit man, killer, slayer **8** murderer **9** cut-throat **10** hatchet man
of Abel: **4** Cain
of Archduke Ferdinand: **7** Princip
of Gandhi: **5** Godse
of Garfield: **7** Guiteau
of J. F. Kennedy: **6** Oswald
of R. F. Kennedy: **6** Sirhan

of Martin Luther King: Ray

of John Lennon: **7** Chapman

of Lincoln: **5** Booth

of McKinley: **8** Czolgosz

of Lee Harvey Oswald: **4** Ruby

assault: mug **4** beat, raid, slug **5** beset, onset, pound, smite, storm **6** affray, assail, attack, breach, buffet, charge, fall on, invade **7** bombard, violate **8** outburst **9** incursion, onslaught **10** aggression **11** impinge upon

assay: try **4** test **5** prove **6** try out **7** analyze, examine **8** analysis, appraise, evaluate **9** determine **10** experiment

assemblage: **4** army, crew, herd, host, mass, pack **5** bunch, crowd, drove, flock, swarm **6** convoy, galaxy, hookup, throng **7** cluster, turnout **9** community **11** aggregation **12** congregation

art: **7** collage

assemble: fit **4** call, mass, meet **5** amass, piece, rally, unite **6** couple, gather, huddle, muster, summon **7** collect, convene, convoke, recruit **10** foregather **11** put together

assembly: hui **4** bevy, diet, feis, moot, raad **5** forum, group, junta, party, press, setup, troop **6** gemote, pow-wow, senate **7** comitia, company, council, husting, meeting, session, society **8** audience, conclave, congress, tribunal **10** convention, parliament **11** convocation, legislature

ecclesiastical: **5** synod **10** consistory **11** convocation

full: **5** plena

of witches: **5** coven

place: **5** agora

room: **4** hall **10** auditorium

assent: aye, bow, nod, yea, yes **4** amen **5** admit, agree, yield **6** accede, accept, accord, chorus, comply, concur, submit **7** approve, concede, conform, consent **8** adhesion, sanction **9** acquiesce, subscribe **10** compliance, condescend **11** acknowledge

assert: say **4** aver, avow, cite **5** claim, plead, posit, state, utter, vaunt, voice **6** affirm, allege, assure, avouch, defend, depone, depose, uphold **7** advance, betoken, contend, declare, protest, support **8** advocate, champion, maintain **9** predicate, vindicate

positively: **5** swear **10** asseverate

assertive: **8** cock-sure, dogmatic, forceful, positive **9** defensive, pragmatic **10** aggressive **11** affirmatory

assess: tax **4** cess, levy, rate, scot, toll **5** price, value **6** charge, impose **7** measure **8** appraise, estimate **9** apportion

assessment: fee, tax **4** duty, levy **5** tithe **6** impost, surtax, tariff **7** scutage **9** valuation

assessor: **5** judge **11** adjudicator

asset: **9** advantage **11** distinction, strong point

assets: **5** goods, means, money, worth **6** credit, wealth **7** capital, effects **8** accounts, property **9** resources, valuables

assiduous: **4** busy **6** active **7** devoted **8** diligent, sedulous, studious **9** laborious, unwearied **10** persistent **11** hardworking, industrious, painstaking, persevering, unremitting **13** indefatigable

assign: fix, set **4** cede, give, rate, seal, sign **5** allot, allow, award, endow, order, refer **6** adduce, affect, allege, charge, convey, depute, detail, reckon, select, settle **7** adjudge, advance, appoint, ascribe, consign, dispose, mete out, specify, tribute **8** allocate, delegate, transfer **9** apportion, attribute, designate, determine **10** commission, distribute **11** appropriate

assignation: **4** date **5** tryst **7** meeting **10** rendezvous **11** appointment

assignment: job **4** duty, task **5** chore, stint **6** lesson **11** appointment

assimilate: **4** fuse **5** alter, blend, learn, liken, merge **6** absorb, digest, imbibe, take in **7** compare **8** resemble **9** transform **10** comprehend, metabolize, understand **11** appropriate, incorporate

assist: aid **4** abet, back, help **5** avail, boost, coach **6** back up, succor **7** be of use, benefit, relieve, support, sustain **8** befriend **9** give a hand **10** facilitate

assistant: **4** aide, ally, hand, zany **5** valet **6** deputy, lackey, minion, second **7** abettor, orderly, partner **8** adjutant, adjuvant, henchman, servitor **9** associate, auxiliary, secretary **10** accomplice **11** confederate, subordinate

to pastor: **6** curate, deacon, verger

assistants: **4** crew **5** staff

assize: **4** rate, rule **5** court, edict, trial **6** decree **7** hearing, inquest, measure, precept, session, sitting, statute **8** assembly, standard, tribunal **9** enactment, ordinance **10** regulation

associate: mix, pal **4** aide, ally, chum, join, link, mate, peer, yoke **5** buddy, crony **6** cohort, fellow, friend, helper, hobnob, mingle, relate, spouse **7** adjunct, bracket, comrade, connect, consort, partner **8** copemate, federate, identify, intimate **9** affiliate, assistant, attendant, coadjutor, colleague, companion, secondary, socialize **10** fraternize **11** concomitant

in crime: **10** accomplice

association: **4** body, bond, clan, club, coop, tong **5** artel **6** cartel, league, pledge **7** company, consort, society **8** alliance, converse, intimacy, overtone, sodality **9** coalition, syndicate **10** assemblage, connection, fellowship, sisterhood **11** aggregation, brotherhood, combination, confederacy, conjunction, connotation, partnership

criminal: mob **4** gang, ring

literary: **6** lyceum **9** athenaeum
merchants': **5** hanse
political: **4** axis, bund **5** junta, party **7** machine
secret: **5** cabal, lodge
student: **7** council **8** sorority **10** fraternity
workers': **5** guild, union

assonance: pun **5** rhyme · **8** paragram **11** resemblance

assort: **4** file, rank, type **5** group **8** classify **10** put in order

assortment: lot, set **4** olio **5** batch, group, suite **6** medley **7** melange, mixture, variety **8** pastiche **9** potpourri **10** collection, miscellany

assuage: **4** calm, ease **5** abate, allay, slake **6** lessen, modify, pacify, quench, reduce, soften, solace, soothe, temper **7** appease, comfort, mollify, relieve, satisfy **8** diminish, mitigate, moderate **9** alleviate **11** tranquilize

assuasive: **7** calming **8** soothing

as such: **5** per se **8** in itself **9** basically, in the main **11** in its own way

assume: don **4** dare, mask, sham **5** adopt, cloak, elect, feign, indue, infer, put on, raise, seize, usurp **6** accept, affect, clothe **7** believe, pretend, receive, suppose, surmise **8** accroach, arrogate, simulate, take over **9** undertake **11** appropriate, counterfeit

assumed: **5** alias, false **8** affected, supposed **9** fictional, uncertain **10** artificial, fictitious **12** hypothetical, supposititious

assumed name: **5** alias **6** anonym **9** pseudonym **10** nom de plume (F.) **11** nom de guerre (F.)

assuming: **5** lofty **8** arrogant, superior **11** pretentious **12** presumptuous
different form: **7** protean

Assyria: **5** Ashur, Assur **6** Asshur
capital: **5** Calah **7** Nineveh
city: **4** Hara, Opis **5** Al Sur, Kalhu **6** Arbela, Kalakh **7** Nineveh **9** Dur Sargon
god: El, Zu, Ira, Sin **4** Adad, Anet, Nabu, Nebo **5** Ashur, Hadad, Ninip **6** Asshur, Nergal, Shamas **7** Ninurta
goddess: **4** Nana, Nine **5** Istar **6** Allatu, Ishtar **9** Sarpanitu
king: Pul **5** Belus **6** Sargon **10** Esarhaddon **11** Sennacherib, Shalmaneser **12** Ashurbanipal
measure: **4** cane, foot **5** gasab, makuk **6** artaba, gariba, ghalva **7** mansion
queen: **9** Semiramis
river: **6** Tigris

assurance: **4** word **5** brass, faith, nerve **6** aplomb, belief, credit, pledge, safety, surety **7** courage, promise **8** audacity, boldness, coolness, security **9** certainty, certitude, cockiness, guarantee, impudence **10** confidence, effrontery **12** self-reliance

assure: **4** aver **6** assert, avouch, secure **7** confirm, declare, hearten **8** convince, embolden **9** encourage, vouchsafe **10** asseverate, certiorate, strengthen, underwrite **13** say positively

assuredly: **4** amen **6** surely, verily **10** truthfully **11** indubitably, undoubtedly

Assyria: (see box)

astart: **8** suddenly

asterisk: **4** star **13** reference mark

Asterius: **8** argonaut, minotaur
father: **10** Hyperasius
mother: **8** Pasiphae
wife: **6** Europa

astern: aft **4** back **6** behind **9** in the rear

asteroid: **4** Eros, Hebe, Iris, Juno **5** Ceres, Flora, Irene, Metis, Vesta **6** Apollo, Astrea, Egeria, Europa, Hygeia, Icarus, Pallas, planet, Psyche, Thetis **7** Eunomia, Fortuna, Lutetia **8** Massalia, starfish, starlike, Victoria **9** Melpomene, planetoid **10** Parthenope, star-shaped
first and largest: **5** Ceres
nearest earth: **4** Eros

asthmatic: **5** pursy **6** wheezy **7** panting, puffing

astir: **5** about, afoot, alert **6** active, moving, roused **8** out of bed **10** up and doing

Astolat's Lily Maid: **6** Elaine

astonish: awe **4** daze **5** amaze **7** astound, impress, startle **8** bewilder, confound, surprise **11** flabbergast

astonished: **5** agape **9** awestruck

astonishing: **8** fabulous **9** wonderful **10** incredible, stupendous **11** spectacular

astound: **5** amaze, appal, shock **6** appall **7** stagger, terrify **8** astonish, confound **9** overwhelm

astragalus: **5** talus **9** anklebone

astrakhan: **5** cloth **7** caracul, karakul

astral: **6** remote, starry **7** stellar **8** sidereal, starlike **9** visionary

astray: **4** awry, lost **5** agley, amiss, aside, wrong **6** abroad, afield, errant, erring, faulty **7** sinning **8** mistaken **9** wandering

astride: **4** atop **7** à cheval (F.), mounted **8** bridging, spanning **9** astraddle **10** straddling

astringent: **4** acid, alum, sour, tart **5** acerb, harsh, stern **6** severe, tannin **7** austere, binding, styptic **11** acrimonious, compressive, contracting **12** constrictive
extract: **7** catechu
gum: **4** kino

astrologer: **4** Josh **6** Merlin **7** diviner **10** star reader **11** Nostradamus

astronaut: 9 cosmonaut
  American: 4 Bean, Duke, Ride 5 Irwin, Roosa, Scott, White, Young 6 Aldrin, Anders, Borman, Cernan, Conrad, Kerwin, Lousma, Lovell, Worden 7 Collins, Schirra 8 McDivitt, Mitchell, Stafford 9 Armstrong, Mattingly 10 Cunningham
  first American: 7 Shepard
  first American woman: 4 Ride
  first Canadian: 7 Garneau
  first in orbit: 7 Gagarin
  first on moon: 9 Armstrong
  first space walker: 6 Leonov
  first woman: 10 Tereshkova
astronomer: 10 Hipparchus
astronomical: far 4 huge 5 great 6 uranic 7 distant, immense 8 colossal, infinite
  instrument: aba 9 telescope 10 equatorial
  measurement: 5 apsis 7 azimuth
  Muse: 4 Clio 6 Urania
astute: sly 4 foxy, keen, wily 5 acute, canny, quick, sharp, smart 6 clever, crafty, shrewd 7 cunning, skilled 9 sagacious 10 discerning 14 discriminating
asunder: 5 apart, split 7 divided 8 divorced 9 separated
asylum: ark 4 home 5 altar, cover, haven 6 bedlam, harbor, refuge 7 alsatia, hospice, retreat, shelter 9 sanctuary 11 institution
asymmetric: 4 skew 9 distorted 10 unbalanced
asymmetry: 13 disproportion
at: 5 there 7 located
  at all: 4 ever 5 aught, nohow 6 anyway
  at hand: 4 near, nigh 7 close by, present
at last: 7 finally 10 ultimately
at once: now, PDQ 4 anon 5 amain 6 presto 9 forthwith, instantly, right away 11 immediately
Ata, Aeta: Ita 7 Negrito
Atahualpa: 4 Inca 6 Indian
ataman: 5 chief, judge 6 hetman 7 Cossack, headman
atap: 8 nipa palm
atavism: 9 reversion
atavus: 8 ancestor 11 grandfather
atelier: 6 studio 7 bottega 8 workshop
ates: 8 sweetsop
Athamas: *daughter:* 5 Helle
  son: 7 Phrixos, Phrixus 8 Learchus
  wife: Ino
athanor: 4 oven 7 furnace
Athapascan Indian: 4 Dene, Hupa 5 Hoopa
atheist: 7 doubter 8 agnostic 11 nonbeliever
Athena, Athene: 4 Alea, Auge, Nike 5 Areia 6 Ergane, Hippia, Hygeia, Itonia, Pallas, Polias 7 Minerva 8 Apaturia, Athenaia 9 Parthenos, Poliuchos, Promachos 10 Chalinitis

  pert. to: 9 Palladian
  temple: 9 Parthenon
Athens: *alien resident:* 5 metic
  ancient capital of: 6 Attica
  assembly: 4 pnyx 5 boule
  assembly platform: 4 bema
  astronomer: 5 Meton
  clan: obe
  coin: 5 oboli 6 obolus 7 chalcus, chalkos
  festival: 8 Apaturia, Athenaea 11 Scirophoria
  founder: 7 Cecrops
  general: 6 Nicias 7 Phocion 8 Zenophon
  hill: 9 Acropolis 10 Lycabettus
  hill where Paul preached: 9 Areopagus
  historian: 8 Xenophon
  king: 6 Codrus 7 Cecrops, Pandion
  lawgiver: 5 Draco, Solon
  magistrate: 5 draco 6 archon, dicast
  marketplace: 5 agora
  mountain: 6 Parnes
  orator: 9 Isocrates
  philosopher: 5 Plato 8 Socrates 9 Aristotle
  platform: 4 bema 6 bemata (pl.)
  rival: 6 Sparta
  sculptor: 7 Phidias 10 Praxiteles
  seaport: 7 Piraeus
  statesman: 8 Pericles 9 Aristides
  temple: 4 Nike 9 Parthenon
  theater: 5 Odeon, Odeum 8 Dionysus
  youth center: 6 Lyceum
athlete: pro 4 jock, star 5 boxer 7 acrobat, amateur, gymnast, tumbler 8 wrestler 9 aerialist
  athlete's foot: 8 ringworm 10 skin fungus
athletic: 5 agile, burly, lusty, vital 6 brawny, robust, sinewy, strong 8 muscular, powerful, vigorous 9 acrobatic, energetic, strapping
  contest: 4 agon, game, meet, race 5 match 8 Olympics
  field: 4 oval, ring, rink 5 arena, court, green 6 course 7 diamond, stadium 8 gridiron
  prize: cup 5 medal, purse 6 ribbon, trophy
athletics: 5 games, sport 8 exercise
athwart: 4 over 6 across, aslant 7 against, oblique 9 crosswise 10 perversely
Atlanta: *baseball team:* 6 Braves
  football team: 7 Falcons
  street: 9 Peachtree
atlantal: 6 atloid 8 anterior, cephalic
Atlantides: 8 Pleiades 10 Hesperides
atlas: 4 bone, book, list, maps, tome 5 titan 8 mainstay
Atlas: *daughter:* 4 Maia 6 Merope 7 Alcyone, Calypso, Electra, Kelaine, Taygete 8 Asterope, Pleiades
  mother: 7 Clymeme
atmosphere: air 4 aura, mood, tone 5 ether 6 miasma, nimbus, welkin 7 climate, feeling 8 ambiance 10 background 11 environment

disturbance: **5** storm **6** static
gas: **5** argon **6** oxygen **8** nitrogen
phenomenon: **6** aurora, meteor
pressure: **10** barometric

atole: **4** mush **5** gruel **8** corn meal, porridge

atoll: **4** reef, ring **5** coral **6** island
Pacific: **4** Beru, Ebon, Mili **5** Makin, Wotho **6** Bikini, Canton, Jaluit, Likiep, Majuro, Tarawa **8** Eniwetok

atom: ace, bit, jot **4** iota, mite, mote, whit **5** monad, shade, speck, tinge **8** molecule, particle, quantity **9** corpuscle, scintilla
electrically charged: ion **5** anion **6** cation
nucleus: **6** proton **7** neutron

atomic: **4** tiny **6** minute **7** nuclear **9** molecular **13** infinitesimal
particle: **4** beta, pion **5** alpha, meson, quark **6** photon, proton **7** neutron **8** electron
physicist: **4** Bohr, Rabi **5** Fermi, Pauli **6** Dalton **7** Compton, Meitner, Thomson **8** Einstein
pile: **7** reactor
submarine: **5** Sargo, Skate **6** Triton **8** Nautilus
theory originator: **6** Dalton

atomize: **5** grate, spray **6** reduce **8** nebulize, vaporize **9** devastate, pulverize

atomy: **4** atom, mite, mote **5** pygmy **8** skeleton

atone: **6** repent **7** expiate **10** compensate, make amends

atonement: **7** penance **10** reparation **12** satisfaction

atonic: **7** unheard **9** voiceless **10** unaccented

atrabilious: **4** glum **6** gloomy, morose, sullen **10** melancholy

atramentous: **4** ebon, inky **5** black

Atreus: *brother:* **8** Thyestes
father: **6** Pelops
half brother: **10** Chrysippus
mother: **10** Hippodamia
slayer: **9** Aegisthus
son: **8** Menelaus **9** Agamemnon **11** Pleisthenes
wife: **6** Aerope

atrio: **6** valley **10** depression

atrip: **6** aweigh

atrium: **4** hall **5** court **6** cavity **7** auricle, chamber, passage **8** entrance

atrocha: **5** larva

atrocious: bad **4** dark, rank, vile **5** awful, black, cruel, gross **6** brutal, odious, savage, wicked **7** heinous, ungodly, violent **8** grevious, horrible, terrible **9** execrable, frightful, nefarious **10** abominable, villainous

atrophy: **6** shrink, starve, wither **9** waste away **10** emaciation **11** deteriorate

Atropos: **4** Fate

attach: add, fix, tag, tie **4** bind, glue, join, link, take, vest, weld **5** affix, annex, hitch, paste, seize, unite **6** accuse, addict, adhere, adjoin, append, arrest, cement, fasten, indict **7** adhibit, appoint, ascribe, connect, subjoin **9** affiliate, associate, garnishee

attaché: **4** aide **8** diplomat

attached: **4** fond **6** doting
at base: **7** sessile
to the land: **8** agrarian, praedial

attachment: **4** love **8** devotion, fondness **9** accessory, addiction, adherence, affection **10** engagement, friendship **11** inclination

attack: fit **4** bout, fray, pang, raid, rush **5** assay, begin, beset, blitz, drive, fight, foray, ictus, onset, sally, spasm, storm **6** accuse, action, affray, assail, battle, charge, invade, onrush, pounce, sortie, strike, stroke, thrust **7** assault, besiege, censure, offense, potshot, seizure **8** paroxysm **9** incursion, onslaught **10** aggression
deceptive: **5** feint **9** diversion
suicidal: **8** kamikaze

attain: get, hit, win **4** earn, gain, rise **5** reach, touch **6** accede, amount, arrive, aspire, effect, secure, strike **7** achieve, acquire, compass, procure, succeed **8** overtake **10** accomplish, comprehend

attainment: **4** feat **5** skill **6** wisdom **14** accomplishment

attar: oil **7** essence, perfume

attempt: try **4** dare, seek, shot, stab, wage **5** assay, begin, essay, frame, start **6** effort **7** venture **8** endeavor, exertion **9** undertake **10** enterprise, experiment

attend: see **4** go to, hear, heed, mind, tend, wait **5** await, guard, nurse, serve, treat, visit, watch **6** assist, convoy, follow, harken, listen, shadow **7** care for, consort **8** champion, chaperon, minister **9** accompany

attendance: **4** gate **6** number, regard **8** presence **9** attention **11** application, expectation

attendant: aid **4** maid, page, zany **5** guide, usher, valet **6** escort, helper, minion, porter, squire, waiter **7** courier, equerry, orderly, pageboy **8** chasseur, follower, henchman **9** assistant, associate, attentive, companion **10** consequent, subsequent **11** chamberlain, concomitant **12** accompanying **13** lady in waiting

attendants: **5** suite, train **7** cortege, retinue **9** entourage

attention: ear **4** care, heed, hist, note **5** study **6** notice, regard **7** achtung (G.), respect **8** courtesy **9** diligence, obedience, vigilance **10** observance **11** observation **13** concentration, consideration

attentive: **4** wary **5** alert, awake, civil **6** intent, polite **7** careful, gallant, mindful **8** studious, watchful **9** advertent, assiduous, courteous, listening **10** interested **11** circumspect

attenuate: sap **4** thin **5** water **6** dilute, lessen, rarefy, reduce, weaken **7** slender **8** decrease, diminish, enfeeble, tapering **9** subtilize

attest: 5 prove, swear, vouch **6** adjure, affirm, invoke **7** certify, confirm, testify, witness **9** subscribe **12** authenticate

attic: 4 loft **6** garret **8** cockloft

Attic: 5 Greek **8** Athenian

Attic salt: wit

Attila: Hun **5** Etzel

attire: See **dress**

attitude: air, set **4** bias, mien, mood, pose **5** angle, phase, slant, stand **6** action, aspect, manner **7** bearing, feeling, posture **8** behavior, position **11** disposition

attorney: 5 agent, proxy **6** deputy, factor, lawyer **7** proctor **8** advocate **9** barrister, counselor, solicitor **10** counsellor

attract: 4 bait, draw, lure, pull **5** catch, charm, court, fetch, tempt **6** allure, engage, entice, invite, seduce **8** interest **9** captivate, fascinate, influence, magnetize

attraction: 4 card **6** magnet **7** gravity **8** affinity, penchant, witchery

attractive: 4 chic, cute, fair **5** bonny **6** lovely, pretty, taking **7** winning, winsome **8** alluring, charming, fetching, graceful **9** beautiful

attribute: fix, owe **4** mark, sign, type **5** badge, blame, place, power, refer **6** allege, allude, assert, assign, bestow, charge, impute, symbol **7** ascribe, pertain, quality **8** accredit, property **10** reputation **11** peculiarity **14** characteristic

attribution: 6 theory **8** etiology

attrition: 4 wear **5** grief **6** regret, sorrow **7** penance, remorse **8** abrasion, friction **9** weakening

attune: key **4** tune **5** adapt, agree **6** accord, adjust, temper **7** prepare **9** harmonize

atua: 5 being, demon **6** spirit

auberge: inn **6** hostel **7** albergo

aubergine: 6 purple **8** eggplant

auction: 4 cant, roup (Sc.), sale, sell, vend **5** trade **6** barter, bridge **8** disposal

hammer: **5** gavel

platform: **5** block

price: bid **5** upset

audacious: 4 bold **5** brash, hardy, saucy **6** brazen, cheeky, daring **7** forward **8** arrogant, fearless, impudent, insolent, intrepid, spirited **9** barefaced, imprudent, shameless **10** courageous **11** adventurous, impertinent, venturesome **12** presumptuous

audacity: 4 gall, grit, guts **5** brass, cheek, nerve, spunk, valor **7** courage **8** boldness, temerity **9** assurance, cockiness, derring-do, hardihood, impudence, insolence, sauciness **10** effrontery **12** impertinence

audible: 5 aloud, clear, heard **8** distinct

audience: 4 fans **5** house **6** public **7** gallery, hearing **8** assembly, audition, tribunal **9** following, interview, reception **10** spectators

audio-visual aid: 4 film, tape **5** slide, video **10** television

audit: 4 scan **5** check, probe **6** reckon, survey, verify **7** examine, inquire, inspect **8** analysis, estimate **10** accounting **11** investigate

audition: 4 test **5** trial **6** tryout **7** hearing

auditor: CPA **6** censor, hearer **8** listener **10** accountant, bookkeeper **11** comptroller

auditorium: 4 hall, room **5** cavea, odeum **7** theater

auditory: 4 otic **5** aural **8** acoustic

au fait (F.): 6 expert, versed **8** informed **9** competent, in the know **10** proficient

au fond (F.): 8 at bottom **9** basically **10** thoroughly

auger: bit **4** bore, tool **5** grill **6** gimlet, wimble

aught: 4 nil **4** zero **5** zilch **6** cipher **7** nothing **8** anything, goose egg

Augie March creator: 6 Bellow

augite: 8 pyroxene

augment: add, eke **4** grow **5** exalt, swell **6** append, dilate, expand, extend **7** amplify, enhance, enlarge, improve, magnify **8** heighten, increase, multiply **9** increment **10** aggrandize

augur: 4 bode, omen, seer, talk **5** argue **6** auspex, divine **7** betoken, foresee, portend, predict, presage, promise, prophet, signify **8** forebode, foreshow, foretell, forewarn, indicate, official, prophesy **9** auspicate **10** anticipate, conjecture, foreshadow, soothsayer **13** prognosticate

augury: 4 rite, sign **5** token **6** herald, ritual **7** warning **8** ceremony, forecast **9** harbinger, sortilege **10** divination, foreboding, forerunner

august: 5 awful, grand, noble **6** solemn **7** exalted, stately **8** imposing, majestic **9** dignified, venerable **11** magisterial

Augustus: 5 Roman **7** emperor

death place: **4** Nola

enemy: **9** Cleopatra **10** Mark Antony

sister: **7** Octavia

auk: 4 loom (Br.) **5** arrie, lemot, murre, noddy **6** puffin, rotche **7** dovekey, dovekie **9** guillemot

extinct: **5** great **8** garefowl

family: **7** alcidae

genus: **4** alca, alle

razorbill: **4** falk **5** murre

aula: 4 hall, room **5** court **6** emblic

aumildar (Ind.): 5 agent **6** factor **7** manager **9** collector

au naturel (F.): raw **4** nude **5** naked **6** unclad **8** stripped, uncooked **9** in the buff

aura: air **4** glow, halo, mood, odor **5** aroma **6** nimbus **7** essence, feeling, quality **8** mystique **9** emanation **10** atmosphere, exhalation

aura pura: 5 ozone

aural: 4 otic **7** audible **9** auricular

appendage: ear

aureate: **6** gilded, golden, ornate, rococo, yellow **8** splendid **9** brilliant

aureole: **4** halo **5** crown, glory, light **6** corona, nimbus **8** gloriole

auricle: ear **5** pinna **6** atrium, earlet **7** trumpet *part:* **7** earlobe

---

Australia (see also **Queensland**): **7** country **9** continent

capital: **8** Canberra

city: Ayr **4** Yass **5** Dubbo, Perth, Weipa **6** Casino, Hobart, Mackay, Sydney **7** Kogarah, Mildura **8** Adelaide, Brisbane, Toowomba **9** Melbourne, Newcastle **10** Wagga Wagga

currency: **4** cent **6** dollar

desert: **6** Gibson **7** Simpson **10** Great Sandy **13** Great Victoria

greeting: **4** g'day

horse: **4** prad

island: **5** Heard **6** Fraser **7** Ashmore, Cartier, Norfolk **8** Bathurst, Kangaroo, Thursday **9** Christmas

island groups: **5** Cocos **7** Keeling **8** Coral Sea, McDonald

lake: **4** Eyre **5** Carey, Cowan, Frome **6** Austin, Barlee, Mackay **7** Amadeus, Eyerard, Torrens **8** Carnegie

landmark: **5** Uluru **9** Ayers Rock

mountain peak: **4** Hale **5** Bruce **6** Bogong, Cradle, Morgan **7** Painter **9** Kosciusko

mountain range: **5** Snowy **6** Stuart **7** Darling, Gregory **8** Flinders, Musgrave, St. George **9** Petermann **14** Australian Alps

national flower: **12** golden wattle

national song: **15** Waltzing Matilda

people: **6** Binghi **9** aborigine

river: Ord **4** Avon, Daly, Swan **5** Namoi, Paroo, Roper, Yarra **6** Barwon, Bulloo, Calgoa, Hunter, Isaacs, Murray **7** Darling, Fitzroy, Lachlan, Staaten **8** Burdekin, Flinders, Gascoyne, Georgina, Goulburn

sea: **5** Coral, Timor **6** Tasman **7** Arafura

state: **8** Tasmania (Van Diemen's Land), Victoria **10** Queensland **13** New South Wales

strait: **4** Bass **6** Torres

---

auricular: **4** otic **7** hearsay **12** confidential

aurochs: **4** urus **5** bison **6** wisent

Aurora: Eos **4** dawn **7** morning, sunrise

auroral: **4** eoan, rosy **7** eastern, radiant

aurum: **4** gold

auscultate: **6** listen

auspex: **5** augur **7** diviner, prophet **10** forecaster, soothsayer

auspicate: **5** augur **7** portend, predict **8** initiate **10** inaugurate

auspices: **4** care, egis, sign **5** aegis **7** backing, support **8** guidance **9** patronage **10** protection **11** sponsorship

auspicious: **4** fair, good **6** dexter **9** favorable, fortunate, opportune **10** propitious, prosperous **12** advantageous

Aussie: **5** Ozzie **10** Australian

austere: **4** cold, grim, hard **5** bleak, grave, gruff, harsh, rigid, rough, sharp, stern, stiff **6** bitter, formal, severe, simple, somber, strict **7** ascetic, earnest, serious, spartan **8** rigorous **9** unadorned, unsmiling **10** astringent, forbidding, relentless **13** unembellished

Australia (see box)

Australian: *animal:* **4** tait **5** koala, panda **6** bunyip, cuscus, wombat **7** dasqure, wallaby **8** duckbill, kangaroo, platypus **9** bandicoot, phalanger

apple: **6** colane

badger: **6** wombat

bag: **5** dilli

bear: **5** koala

beefwood: **5** belar

beverage: **4** kava

bird: emu **4** emeu, lory **5** arara, crake, grebe, stint **6** gannet, leipoa **7** bittern, boobook, bustard, figbird **8** berigora, dabchick, dotterel, lorikeet, lyrebird, morepork, whimbrel **9** bower-bird, cassowary, coachwhip, friarbird, stipiture **10** paradalote, partincole, sanderling

boomerang: **5** kiley, kilie

brushwood: **6** millee

bush: ake

bustard: **7** bebilya

cake: **6** damper **7** brownie

call: **5** cooee, cooey

cat: **7** dasyure

catfish: **6** tandan

cattle stealer: **6** duffer

cedar: **4** toon

clover fern: **6** nardoo

cockatoo: **5** galah

coin: **4** dump

colonist: **8** sterling

composer: **5** Meale **6** Antill **8** Grainger

countryman: **8** Billijim

crayfish: **5** yabby **6** yabbie

cycad: **5** banga

dog: **5** dingo **6** Kelpie

dry lake: **5** playa

duckbill: **8** platypus

eucalyptus: **6** bimbil, mallee **7** carbeen
fern: **5** nardu **6** nardoo
fish: **4** dart, mado, mako **5** yabby **6** tandan, yabbie
fruit: **5** nonda
golf star: **6** Norman (Greg)
gum tree: **4** kari **6** tewart, tooart, touart
herb: **8** piripiri
horse: **7** brumbee **8** yarraman
horse race: **12** Melbourne Cup
hut: **6** miamia
insect: **4** laap, lerp
kangaroo: **4** joey **5** tungo **7** bettong
kiwi: roa
lizard: **6** goanna
lorikeet: **6** parrot, warrin
mahogany: **6** jarrah **7** gunning
marsupial: **4** tait **5** koala **6** wombat **8** kangaroo
measure: **4** saum
mile: **4** naut
moth: **6** bogong
no: **4** baal, bail, bale
opera star: **5** Melba **10** Sutherland
owl: **7** boobook **8** morepoke, morepork
palm: **8** bangalow
parakeet: **6** budgie **7** corella **10** budgerigar
parrot: **4** lory **7** corella, lorilet **8** lorikeet **9** cockateel, cockatiel
pepper: **4** arva, kava, yava **6** ava-ava
petrel: **4** titi
phalanger: **5** ariel
pine: **5** kauri, kaury
plant: **5** lakea **6** acacia, correa, wattle **7** calomba, waratah **8** eucalypt, warratau
pond: **9** billabong
rat: **8** hapalote **9** hapalotis
ratite: **4** emeu
rifleman: **5** yager

rustler: **6** duffer
shark: **4** mako
shield: **8** heelaman, heilaman, hielaman, yeelaman
snake: **6** elapid
soldier: **5** Anzac **6** digger, swaddy **8** Billijim
sorcerer: **5** boyla **6** boolya
spear: **7** wommera, woomera
talk: **6** yabber
tennis star: **5** Laver, Smith **8** Newcombe **9** Goolagong
thicket: **6** mallee
throwing stick: **5** kiley, kylie **7** wommera, woomera **9** boomerang
toy: **8** weet-weet
tree: gum **4** toon **5** belah, belar, boree, gidya, penda **6** gidgea, gidgee, gidyea, marara **7** alipata **8** beefwood, curajong, flindosa, flindosy, ironbark **9** koorajong **10** bunya-bunya
tulip: **7** waratah **8** warratau
war club: **5** waddy
weapon: **5** hulla, waddy **6** hullah **7** leangle, liangle **10** hullanulla
wilderness: **7** outback
wood: emu
woombat: **5** koala
workman: **8** Billijim
writer: **4** West **5** White
austringer: **8** falconer
Austronesian language: **4** Niue **7** Tagalog
autarch: **6** despot **8** autocrat
auteur: **8** director, virtuoso **9** film-maker
authentic: **4** pure, real, sure, true **5** exact, right, valid **6** actual, proper **7** correct, genuine **8** bonafide, credible, official, original, reliable **9** veritable **10** authorized **11** trustworthy **13** authoritative
authenticate: **4** seal **5** prove **6** attest, verify **7**

Austria: *artist:* **5** Klimt **9** Kokoschka
capital: **4** Wien **6** Vienna
city: **4** Graz, Linz, Wels **5** Steyr **7** Bregenz **8** Salzburg **9** Innsbruck **10** Klagenfurt
clothing: **6** dirndl
composer: **4** Berg **5** Haydn **6** Mahler, Mozart, Webern **7** Strauss **8** Bruckner Schubert
currency: **5** ducat, krone **6** florin, heller, zehner **8** groschen **9** schilling
dance: **5** waltz **6** dreher
food: **7** strudel **15** Wiener schnitzel
measure: **4** fass, fuss, joch, mass, muth, yoke **5** halbe, linie, meile, metze, pfiff, punkt **6** achtel, becher, seidel **7** klafter, viertel **8** dreiling **10** muthmassel **12** futtermassel

mountain pass: **5** Loibl **7** Brenner, Plocken **9** Semmering
mountain peak: **9** Hochstuhl, Hochvogel **10** Hochfeiler, Wildspitze **13** Grossglockner
mountain range: **4** Alps **6** Allgau, Carnic **8** Bavarian, Otztaler **10** Hohe Tauern
national flower: **9** edelweiss
nobility: **6** Ritter **9** Esterhazy
painter: **5** Klimt **7** Schiele **9** Kokoschka
psychiatrist: **5** Adler, Freud
river: Inn, Mur **4** Enns, Lech, Murz, Raba **5** Drava, Steyr, Traun **6** Danube **7** Salzach
weight: **4** marc, saum, unze **5** denat, karch, pfund, stein **7** centner, pfennig **8** vierling **9** quentchen

bear out, confirm, endorse **8** validate, vouch for

author: 4 doer **5** maker **6** father, framer, parent, source, writer **7** creator, founder **8** ancestor, begetter, compiler, composer, inventor, novelist, producer **9** architect, initiator **10** instigator, originator, playwright

authoritative: 5 sound **7** factual, learned **8** dogmatic, official, oracular, positive **9** authentic, canonical, effectual, imperious, masterful, scholarly **10** conclusive, convincing, ex cathedra, legitimate, peremptory **11** dictatorial, magisterial

authority: 4 rule, sway **5** force, might, power, right **6** artist, expert, source, weight **7** command, control, warrant **8** dominion, prestige, sanction **9** influence **10** competence, importance, specialist **12** jurisdiction **13** justification

judicial: **4** banc

preponderant: **8** hegemony

symbol: **7** scepter

woman's: **7** distaff

authorize: let **4** vest **5** allow **6** clothe, permit, ratify **7** approve, empower, endorse, entitle, indorse, justify, license, warrant **8** accredit, delegate, legalize, sanction **10** commission, legitimize

authorless: 8 unsigned **9** anonymous

autobiography: 4 vita **5** diary **6** memoir

autochthonous: 6 native **7** edaphic, endemic **10** aboriginal, indigenous

auto court: inn **5** motel

autocrat: 4 czar, tsar, tzar **5** mogul **6** Caesar, despot, kaiser, tyrant **7** autarch, monarch **8** dictator **9** sovereign

autocratic: 8 absolute, arrogant, despotic **9** arbitrary **10** tyrannical

autograph: ink **4** name, sign **9** signature **11** John Hancock

automatic: 7 routine **8** habitual **10** mechanical, push-button, self-acting **11** instinctive, involuntary, spontaneous

automation: 5 golem, robot **7** android, machine

automobile: car **4** heap, jeep **5** coupe, crate, racer, sedan **6** jalopy **7** Berline, flivver, machine, phaeton, steamer **8** brougham, roadster, runabout **9** cabriolet **11** convertible

army: **4** jeep

British: AC, MG **5** Alvis, Riley, Rover **6** Allard, Anglia, Austin, Consul, Humber, Jaguar, Jowett, Morgan, Morris, Rapier, Singer, Zephyr **7** Bentley, Daimler, Hillman, Sunbeam, Triumph **8** Berkeley, Vauxhall **10** Rolls-Royce **11** Austin-Healy, Hillman-Minx, Morris-Minor **12** Metropolitan **13** Sunbeam-Talbot

Czech: **5** Skoda

early: EMF, Reo **4** Alco, Benz, Cord, Knox, Moon, Olds, Sear, Star **5** Brush, Regal,

Riker, Roper **6** Auburn, Dupont, Duryea, Graham, Haynes, Kissel, Mercer, Model T, Saxson, Thomas, Winton **7** Autocar, Bugatti, La Salle, Maxwell, Oakland, Premier, Rambler, Simplex, Stevens, Tourist **8** Apperson, Chalmers, Chandler, Franklin, Mercedes, National, Overland, Peerless **9** Hupmobile **10** Cunningham, Duesenberg, Jackrabbit, Locomobile **11** Graham-Paige, Pierce-Arrow **12** Crane-Simplex, Hispano-Suiza, Lozier Marmon, Owen-Magnetic, Pope-Hartford, Stutz Bearcat **13** Baker-Electric, Ofeldt-Steamer, Stevens-Duryea, White-Streamer, Wills-St. Claire **14** Cugnot's steamer, Stanley-Steamer **15** Isotta-Fraschini **16** Columbia-Electric

French: **5** Simca **7** Citroen, Panhard, Peugeot, Renault **8** Dauphine

German: BMW, DKW **4** Opel **6** Taunus **7** Goliath, Porsche, Weidner **8** Borgward, Rometsch, Wartburg **10** Golomobile, Lloyd-Wagon, Volkswagen **12** Mercedes-Benz

Italian: **4** Fiat **6** Lancia **7** Bugatti, Ferrari **8** Maserati **9** Alfa-Romeo

Japanese: **5** Honda, Mazda **6** Datsun, Nissan, Subaru, Toyota **10** Mitsubishi

Korean: **8** Hyundai

part: **4** hood **5** motor, trunk **6** engine **7** chassis **8** ignition

Russian: Zim **6** Pobeda **9** Moskvitch

supercharged: **6** hot rod

Swedish: **4** Saab **5** Volvo

United States: **4** Ford, Jeep **5** Buick, Capri, Dodge, Pinto **6** Cougar, Saturn, Impala, LeMans, Torino **7** Caprice, Lincoln, Mercury, Montego, Mustang, Pontiac, Ventura **8** Cadillac, Chrysler, Corvette, Imperial, Plymouth **9** Chevrolet **10** Oldsmobile **11** Continental, Thunderbird

autonomous: 4 free **8** separate **9** sovereign **11** independent **12** self-governed

autopsy: 8 necropsy **10** dissection **11** examination

auto race: 4 drag **5** rally

driver: **4** Foyt **5** Mears, Petty, Senna, Sneva, Unser **6** Fangio **7** Garlits, Guthrie, Stewart **8** Andretti **9** Muldowney **10** Rutherford, Yarborough

kind: **4** drag, Indy, kart, road **6** NASCAR, sports, street **8** funny car, stock car **9** endurance, Grand Prix **10** Formula One

notable: **6** Le Mans, Monaco **7** Daytona, Indy 500, Trans-Am **12** Indianapolis

autumn: 4 fall **6** season **8** maturity **11** harvest-time

auxiliary: aid, sub **4** aide, ally **6** backup, branch, helper **7** abetter, abettor, adjunct, partner, reserve **8** adjutant **9** accessory, adminicle, ancillary, assistant, coadjutor, secondary, tributary **10** additional, subsidiary, supporting **11** subordinate, subservient **13** supplementary

ava: **4** kava **5** shrub **6** pepper

avail: aid, use **4** help **5** serve, stead, value **6** profit **7** account, benefit, purpose, service, success, suffice, utilize **9** advantage **10** assistance

available: fit **4** free, open **5** handy, on tap, ready **6** usable **7** present **9** effectual, practical **10** accessible, attainable, convenient, obtainable, up for grabs **11** efficacious

avalanche: **4** heap, mass, pile **5** flood, slide **6** deluge **7** torrent **9** landslide, snowslide **10** inundation

Avalon, Avilion: **4** isle **6** island
tomb: **6** Arthur

avant-garde: new **7** leaders, offbeat **8** advanced, original, pioneers, vanguard **10** innovative **12** trailblazing, trendsetting

avarice: **7** avidity **8** cupidity, rapacity, venality **9** money-lust
spirit of: **6** Mammon

avaricious: **5** close **6** greedy, hungry, stingy **7** miserly **8** covetous, grasping **9** niggardly, penurious **12** parsimonious

avast: **4** halt, hold, stay, stop **5** cease

avatar: **8** epiphany **10** embodiment **11** incarnation

ave: **4** hail **8** farewell, greeting **10** salutation

Ave Maria: **6** prayer **8** Hail Mary **10** rosary bead

avenge: **5** repay **6** injure, punish **7** pay back, redress, requite, revenge **8** chastise **9** retaliate, vindicate **10** get even for

avenger: **7** nemesis **10** vindicator

avenue: rue (F.), way **4** gate, mall, pike, road **5** drive, entry **6** access, arcade, artery, course, outlet, street **7** opening **9** boulevard **10** passageway **12** thoroughfare

aver: say **5** claim, prove, state, swear **6** affirm, allege, assert, assure, avouch, depose, insist, verify **7** certify, contend, declare, justify, protest **8** maintain, proclaim **9** predicate **10** asseverate **11** acknowledge

average: par, sum **4** fair, mean, norm, so-so **5** ratio, usual **6** common, medial, median, medium, middle, normal, not bad **7** typical **8** mediocre, moderate, ordinary, standard **10** proportion **12** run-of-the-mill **13** approximation

averse: **5** balky, loath **7** against, opposed **8** hesitant, inimical **9** reluctant, unwilling **11** disinclined, ill-disposed, unfavorable **12** recalcitrant

aversion: **4** hate **5** odium **6** enmity, hatred, horror **7** disdain, disgust, dislike **8** distaste **9** antipathy **10** repugnance **11** abomination **12** estrangement **14** disinclination

avert: **4** bend, fend, foil **5** avoid, deter, dodge,

evade, parry, twist **6** thwart **7** deflect, prevent, ward off **8** preclude, stave off **9** forestall, frustrate, keep at bay, turn aside

aviary: **4** cage **6** volary **8** dovecote, ornithon **9** birdhouse, columbary
keeper: **8** aviarist

aviation: **6** flying **10** airplaning **11** aeronautics

aviator: (see also **aircraft, airplane**): ace **5** flier, flyer, pilot **6** airman, fly-boy **7** birdman
notable: **4** Byrd, Post **6** Yaeger **7** Bennett, Cochran, Earhart **8** Corrigan **9** Chennault, Doolittle, Lindbergh **10** Richthofen (Red Baron) **12** Rickenbacker
signal: out **4** over **5** roger

avid: **4** agog, keen, warm **5** eager, rabid **6** ardent, greedy, hungry **7** anxious, athirst, devoted **8** covetous, desirous, grasping **9** impatient, voracious

avidity: **7** avarice, craving, longing **8** cupidity **10** greediness

avifauna: **5** birds, ornis

avocado: **4** coyo, pear, tree **5** palta **6** chinin **13** alligator pear
dish: **9** guacamole

avocation: **5** hobby **7** pastime **8** sideline **9** amusement, diversion **10** recreation

avocet: **4** bird **5** stilt **6** godwit

avoid: **4** duck, shun **5** annul, avert, dodge, elude, evade, hedge, parry, shirk, skirt, spair (Sc.) **6** bypass, escape, eschew **7** abstain, boycott, forbear, forsake, refrain **8** keep from, sidestep **10** fight shy of, steer clear

avoidance: **8** escapism **9** annulment **10** withdrawal

avoirdupois weight: ton **4** dram **5** ounce, pound **7** long ton

a votre sante (F.): **5** skoal, toast **6** prosit (G.) **12** to your health

avow: own **5** admit, state, swear **6** affirm, assert, avouch, depose **7** confess, declare, justify, profess **8** maintain, proclaim **11** acknowledge

avowal: **4** word **8** averment **9** assurance **10** profession **14** representation

awa: **4** kava **8** milkfish

awabi: **7** abalone

await: **4** bide, pend **5** abide, tarry **6** attend, expect, impend **8** mark time, watch for **10** anticipate, be ready for

awake: **5** alert, alive, astir, aware, rouse **6** active, arouse, excite, revive **7** careful, heedful **8** open-eyed, vigilant **9** attentive, conscious **10** up and about

awakening: **7** letdown **9** debunking, eye-opener **13** enlightenment

award: **4** give, mete **5** allot, grant, honor, medal, prize **6** accord, assign, bestow, confer **7** adjudge, appoint, mete out, present, tribute **8** accolade, judgment, sentence **9** apportion, determine **10** decoration

academic: **6** degree **7** diploma **8** cum laude **9** sheepskin **12** Phi Beta Kappa **13** magna cum laude, summa cum laude

broadcasting: **7** Peabody

cinema: **5** Oscar

detective story: **5** Edgar

Off-Broadway: **4** Obie

recording: **6** Grammy

science fiction: **4** Hugo

television: **4** Emmy

theater: **4** Tony

aware: hep, hip **4** wary **5** alert, alive **7** knowing, mindful **8** apprised, apprized, informed, sensible, vigilant, watchful **9** au courant, cognizant, conscious **11** intelligent

away: awa (Sc.), fro, off, out, via **4** gone **5** along, apart, aside, forth, hence **6** abroad, absent, at once, begone, onward, thence **7** distant **8** directly, right off **9** elsewhere, forthwith

awe: cow **4** fear **5** alarm, amaze, daunt, scare **6** fright, regard, terror, wonder **7** buffalo, respect **8** astonish, bewilder, overcome **9** fascinate, overpower, reverence **10** intimidate, veneration

aweigh: **5** atrip

awesome: **4** eery **5** awful, eerie, weird **6** solemn **7** dreaded, ghostly, uncanny **8** imposing, terrible **9** appalling, unearthly **12** spell-binding

awful: bad **4** dire, ugly **6** august, horrid **7** awesome, fearful **8** dreadful, majestic, shocking, terrible **9** appalling, frightful **10** impressive, tremendous

awfully: **4** very **5** quite **7** greatly **9** extremely

awkward: **5** gawky, inapt, inept **6** clumsy, gauche, rustic, uneasy **7** boorish, loutish, stilted, uncouth, unhandy **8** bungling, lubberly, ungainly, untoward, unwieldy **9** difficult, graceless, ill at ease, inelegant, lumbering, maladroit, ponderous **10** backhanded, blundering, cumbersome, ungraceful, unskillful **11** heavyhanded **12** embarrassing, inconvenient

awl: **4** tool **5** punch **6** gimlet

awn: ear **4** barb **5** beard **6** arista **7** bristle **9** appendage

awning: **4** hood **6** canopy, screen, shield **7** shelter **8** velarium

fastening: **6** earing

relative: **7** marquee

awry: **5** agley (Sc.), amiss, askew, wrong **6** faulty, uneven **7** askance, asquint, crooked, haywire, oblique **8** cockeyed **9** distorted **11** out of kilter

ax: adz, axe **4** adze, fire, sack **6** twibil **7** cleaver, dismiss, hatchet, kick out, twibill **8** battle-ax, tomahawk **9** discharge

blade: bit

butt: **4** poll

handle: **5** helve

axial: **7** central, midmost, pivotal

axilla: **6** armpit **8** shoulder

axiom: saw **5** adage, dicta (pl.), maxim, motto **6** byword, dictum, saying, truism **7** precept, proverb **8** aphorism, apothegm, sentence **9** principle **11** proposition

axis: **4** axle, deer, stem **5** pivot **6** chitra **7** fulcrum, spindle **8** alliance

axle: bar, cod, pin **4** axis **5** arbor, shaft **7** mandrel, spindel

axolotl: **4** newt **10** salamander

ayah: **4** maid **5** nurse **9** nursemaid

aye, ay: pro, yea, yes **4** aver, ever, okay, vote **6** always, assent **7** forever **11** affirmative, continually

aye-aye: **5** lemur **6** will do **10** understood

Azerbaijan: *capital:* **4** Baku, Baky

language: **5** Azeri

people: **5** Azeri **10** Daghestani

Azores: *city:* **5** Horta **12** Ponta Delgada

island: **4** Pico **5** Corvo, Faial **6** Flores **8** Graciosa, Sao Jorge, Terceira **9** Sao Miguel **10** Santa Maria

volcano: **4** Pico

Aztec: *ball game:* **8** tlachtli

emperor: **9** Moctezuma, Montezuma

god: **4** Xipe **9** Xipetotic **11** Xiuhtecutli

language: **7** Nahuatl

myth: **4** Nana, Nata

stone: **9** temelactl **12** chalchihuitl

temple: **6** teopan **8** teocalli

azure: **4** bice, blue **8** cerulean **9** cloudless, unclouded

azygous: odd **6** single

B

baa: 5 bleat

baahling: 4 lamb

Baal: 4 idol 5 deity 8 false god
consort: 6 Baltis

baba: 5 child (Ind.) 7 rumcake

babacoote: 5 lemur

babassu: oil 4 palm, soap

Babbitt: 5 alloy, metal 9 bourgeois 10 philistine 11 materialist
author: 5 Lewis

babblative: 7 verbose 9 garrulous, talkative 10 loquacious

babble: yak 4 chat 5 prate, run on 6 cackle, drivel, gibber, gossip, murmur 7 blabber, blather, chatter, clatter, prattle, twaddle 8 nonsense 11 stultiloquy

babel: din 5 clang, tower 6 hubbub, jargon, medley, racket, tumult, uproar 7 discord 9 charivari, confusion 10 hullabaloo

babiche: 6 lacing, thongs

babillard: 4 bird 11 whitethroat

baboon: ape 4 papa 5 drill 6 chaema 7 babuina 8 mandrill

babul: gum, lac 4 tree, wood 6 acacia, mimosa
pod: 5 garad

babushka: 5 scarf 8 kerchief 11 grandmother
relative of: 8 bandanna

baby: tot 4 baba, babe, doll, nene (Sp.) 5 bairn (Sc.), child, humor, spoil 6 coddle, fondle, infant, moppet, pamper, weanie (Sc.) 7 bambino (It.), indulge, papoose 9 youngster
bed: 4 crib 6 cradle 8 bassinet
carriage: 4 pram 5 buggy 6 gocart 8 stroller 12 perambulator
christening robe: 7 chrisom, chrysom
cry: mew 6 squall
food: pap 4 milk 6 pablum 7 formula
outfit: 7 layette
shoe: 6 bootee

babyish: 6 simple 7 puerile 8 childish

Babylonia: *abode of the dead:* 5 Aralu
building: 8 ziggurat
capital: 7 Babylon
city: 5 Erech, Larsa 6 Calneh, Cunaxa, Cuthah, Lagash, Nippur, Sippar
conqueror: 6 Persia, Sargon, Semite 8 Seleucus, Sumerian 9 Alexander
cycle of moon: sar 5 saros
divison: 5 Akkad, Sumer
epic of: 9 Gilgamesh

god: Anu, Aya, Bel, Hea, Hes, Ira, Ler, Sin, Utu 4 Adad, Anat, Apsu, Baal, Gula, Irra, Nebo, Utug 5 Alala, Alalu, Dagan, Enlil, Etana, Ninib, Nusku, Siris, Urash 6 Ishtar, Marduk, Nergal, Oannes, Tammuz 7 Ninurta, Shamash 8 Merodach 10 Adramelech 11 Adrammelech
goddess: Aya 4 Erua, Nana, Nina 5 Belit, Istar 6 Belili, Beltis, Ishtar 7 Mylitta
hero of myth: 5 Adapa, Etana 9 Gilgamesh
Jewish exile ruler: 8 Exilarch
language: 8 Akkadian, Sumerian
mountain: 6 Ararat
New: 7 Chaldea
priestess: 5 Entum
river: 6 Tigris 9 Euphrates
ruler: 5 Cyrus, Gudea 6 Sargon 8 Naram-Sin 9 Alexander, Hammurabi 14 Nebuchadnezzar
sun god's attendant: 6 Bunene
tower: 5 Babel 7 zikurat 8 ziggurat
waters: 4 Apsu
weight: 4 mina 5 maneh

Babylonian: 6 lavish, wicked 7 opulent

bacalao: 5 murre 7 codfish, grouper 9 guillemot

bacca: 5 berry

baccalaureate: 6 degree, sermon 7 address, service 14 bachelor of arts

baccarat: 4 game
player: 6 punter
term: 5 banco
variety of: 11 chemin-de-fer

baccate: 5 pulpy 7 berried

bacchanal: 4 orgy 7 debauch, reveler 8 carouser

Bacchanal's cry: 4 evoe 5 evohe

bacchante: 6 maenad 9 priestess

Bacchus: 8 Dionysus
father: 4 Zeus 7 Jupiter
mother: 6 Semele
son: 7 Priapus

bachelor: 7 unmated 8 celibate 9 unmarried
recently married: 8 benedict

bachelor button: 8 milkwort 10 bluebottle

bacillus: 4 germ 5 virus 7 microbe

back: aid, tub, vat 4 abet, hind, nata, rear, tail 5 angel, bet on, dorsa (pl.), notum, spine, splat, stern 6 assist, dorsum, second, uphold, verify 7 endorse, finance, sponsor,

support, sustain **8** bankroll, rearward **9** encourage, posterior, reinforce **10** strengthen
at the: aft **5** abaft, arear **6** astern **7** postern
lower part of: **4** loin
of neck: **4** nape **6** scruff
pain: **7** lumbago
pert. to: **6** dorsal, lumbar, tergal

backbite: **5** abuse **6** defame, vilify **7** asperse, slander

backbone: **4** grit, guts **5** nerve, pluck, spine, spunk **6** mettle, spirit **7** stamina, support **8** mainstay, vertebra

backer: **5** angel **6** patron **7** sponsor **8** investor, promoter

backgammon: *old relative:* **7** pachisi **8** parchesi, parchisi
term: **4** blot **6** double
variation: **10** acey-deucey

background: **4** rear **6** offing **7** scenery, setting **8** distance, training **9** education

backing: aid **6** lining, refuse **7** support **9** financing **10** embankment **11** endorsement

backlash: **6** recoil **8** reaction

backlog: **7** reserve, surplus **12** accumulation

back off: ebb **6** recede, retire **7** retreat, reverse **10** give ground, retrograde

back out: **4** funk **5** welsh **6** renege **8** crawfish, withdraw

back scratcher: **7** strigil

backslide: **4** fall **5** lapse **6** desert, revert **7** relapse **11** deteriorate

back-street: **6** secret **8** on the sly **13** surreptitious

Back Street author: **5** Hurst

back talk: lip **4** guff, sass **9** insolence

backup: **4** help **5** spare **9** alternate **10** substitute, supporting

backward: shy **4** dull, slow **5** arear, loath **6** astern, averse, behind, bygone, stupid **7** bashful, laggard, lagging, reverse **8** dilatory, hesitant **9** recessive, reluctant, to the rear, unwilling **10** behindhand, hesitating **11** into the past **13** retrogressive, retrospective

backwater: ebb **5** bayou **7** retract, retreat

backwoodsman: **4** hick **9** hillbilly

backwort: **7** comfrey

bacon: pig **4** pork **5** prize
Canadian: **4** loin
fat: **5** speck
side: **6** flitch, gammon
slice: **6** collop, rasher

Bacon work: **6** Essays **11** New Atlantis **12** Novum Organum

bacteria, bacterium: **4** germ **6** aerobe **7** microbe **8** organism **10** aerobacter
chain: **6** torula **7** torulae (pl.)
culture: **4** agar **8** agar-agar
dissolver: **5** lysin

free from harmful: **7** asepsis, aseptic
rod-shaped: **7** bacilli (pl.) **8** bacillus
spherical: **5** cocci (pl.) **6** coccus
spiral: **8** spirilla (pl.) **9** spirillum
vaccine: **8** bacterin

Bactrian: **5** camel

bad: big, ill, sad **4** evil, full, lewd, poor, sick, vile **5** nasty, sorry, wrong **6** arrant, faulty, rotten, severe, sinful, wicked **7** baleful, baneful, corrupt, harmful, hurtful, immoral, inutile, naughty, spoiled, tainted, unlucky, unsound, vicious **8** annoying, criminal, depraved, flagrant, inferior, unsuited **9** abandoned, atrocious, blemished, dangerous, defective, incorrect, injurious, offensive, perverted, worthless **10** aggravated, distressed, inadequate, iniquitous, pernicious **11** deleterious, displeasing, inopportune, unfavorable **12** disagreeable, inauspicious
blood: **4** hate **5** anger **6** enmity **10** bitterness, ill-feeling, resentment
debt: **7** default
habit: **4** vice **5** fault **7** frailty **8** weakness
luck: **7** ill wind **9** adversity **10** misfortune, tough break

badderlocks: **4** kelp **6** murlin **7** henware, seaweed

badge: pin **4** mark, sign **5** token **6** emblem, ensign, symbol **8** insignia **10** cognizance

badger: nag **4** bait **5** annoy, brock, chivy, hound, tease, worry **6** bother, chivvy, harass, heckle, pester, teledu, wombat **7** torment **8** carcajou, huckster, irritate **9** bandicoot, mistonusk
group: **4** cete

Badger State: **9** Wisconsin

badigeon: **5** paste **6** cement **11** composition

badinage: **6** banter **7** joshing, kidding, teasing **8** raillery, repartee **11** give and take

badly: **4** illy **6** poorly, unwell **7** harshly **8** faultily, severely **9** seriously **10** shamefully **11** imperfectly **12** unskillfully **13** unfortunately

badminton: **5** poona (Ind.)
equipment: **10** battledore **11** shuttle cock

bad-mouth: **4** slur **7** run down **9** criticize, disparage

Baedeker: **9** guidebook **10** tourist aid

baffle: **4** balk, foil, pose **5** elude, evade, fling, stump **6** defeat, delude, outwit, puzzle, thwart **7** confuse, deceive, grating, mystify, nonplus **8** bewilder, confound **9** confusion, deflector, discomfit, frustrate **10** circumvent, disconcert

bag: cod, net, pod, pot **4** gain, poke, sack, trap **5** bulse, catch, forte, pouch, purse, seize, snare, steal **6** budget, cavity, entrap, hangup, pocket, sachet, wallet **7** alforja, balloon,

capture, reticle, satchel **8** reticule **9** cartridge, container, gladstone, haversack, specialty, way of life **10** collection, pocketbook **11** portmanteau
botanic: sac **4** asci **5** ascus, spore
canvas: **7** musette
fishing net: **4** bunt, fyke
hop: **7** sarpler
muslin: **6** tillot
traveling: **4** grip **6** valise **8** backpack, knapsack, suitcase

bagatelle: **4** game **5** verse **6** trifle

baggage: **4** arms, gear, minx **5** hussy, huzzy, nasty, tents, trash, wench **6** harlot, refuse, trashy, trunks **7** clothes, effects, luggage, rubbish, valises **8** carriage, rubbishy, suitcase, utensils **9** munitions, viaticals, worthless **10** prostitute **11** impedimenta

baggy: **5** loose **6** flabby, puffed

Baghdad (see also **Iraq**): *capital of:* **4** Iraq
district: **5** Karkh **7** Rusafah
merchant: **6** Sinbad **7** Sindbad
river: **6** Tigris

bagnio: **4** bath **5** bagne **6** prison **7** brothel **8** bordello, hothouse

bagpipe: **5** drone **7** musette **8** zampogna **10** doodlesack, sordellina
mouthpiece: **4** muse
pipe: **6** drones **7** chanter
play: **5** skirl
player: **5** piper **7** doodler
sound: **5** skirl
tune: **4** port

bah: foh, pah, rot **5** faugh, pshaw **6** humbug **8** nonsense

Bahamas: *capital:* **6** Nassau
discoverer: **8** Columbus
Indian: **6** Lucayo
islands: Cat **4** Long **5** Abaco, Exuma, Grand, Turks **6** Andros, Bimini, Caicos, Inagua **7** Acklins, Crooked **9** Eleuthera, Mayaguana **11** San Salvador
national anthem: **17** March On Bahamaland

bahia: bay

Bahrain: **11** archipelago
capital: **6** Manama
currency: **4** fils **5** dinar
gulf: **7** Arabian, Persian
island: **5** Sitra **6** Sitrah **7** Bahrain **8** Muharraq, Umm Nasan

bail: dip **4** bond, hoop, lade, lave, ring, rynd, yoke **5** ladle, scoop, throw, vouch **6** bucket, handle, secure, surety **7** custody, deliver, release **8** bailsman, bulwarks, security **9** guarantee

bailiff: **5** agent **6** deputy **7** steward **8** overseer **9** constable **10** magistrate **12** court officer

bailiwick: **4** area **6** domain, office **8** home base, province **9** territory **12** jurisdiction

bairn: **5** child

bait: bad **4** bite, chum, feed, halt, iron, lure **5** decoy, tempt, worry **6** allure, attack, badger, entice, harass, repast **7** fulcrum, gudgeon, provoke, torment **8** crawlers **9** persecute **10** allurement, enticement, exasperate, inducement, temptation **11** refreshment
artificial: **9** hackle fly

baize: **6** fabric **7** drapery

bake: dry **4** cook, fire **5** batch, broil, grill, parch, roast **6** anneal, harden **7** biscuit

baker: **4** kiln, oast, oven **6** baxter **7** furnace, roaster, utensil
sheet: pan
shovel: **4** pale, peel

baker's dozen: **8** thirteen

baker's itch: **4** rash **9** psoriasis

baking chamber: **4** kiln, oast, oven

baking dish: **7** cocotte, ramekin

baking soda: **9** saleratus

Bakongo goddess: **6** Nyambe, Nzambi

baksheesh: tip **5** favor **7** present **8** gratuity

Balaam's beast: ass **6** donkey

balance: **4** even, rest **5** poise, scale, weigh **6** adjust, equate, offset, sanity, stasis **7** residue **8** equality, equalize, serenity **9** composure, equipoise, remainder, stability **10** neutralize, steadiness **11** equilibrium **12** counterpoise
lose: **4** trip **7** stagger
weighing: **6** auncel

balancer: **7** acrobat, athlete, gymnast

balcony: **5** oriel, porch, solar **6** piazza, sollar **7** balagan, gallery, mirador, pergola, terrace **8** brattice, verandah
church singer: **8** cantoria
projecting: **6** gazabo, gazebo

bald: **4** bare, base **5** crude, naked, plain, stark **6** callow, paltry, pilled, shaven, smooth **7** epilose, literal, sheared **8** glabrous, hairless **9** unadorned, uncovered **11** undisguised, unvarnished

Balder, Baldur: *father:* **4** Odin
mother: **5** Frigg
murder weapon: **9** mistletoe
slayer: **4** Hoth, Loke **5** Hothr
son: **7** Forsete, Forseti
wife: **5** Nanna

balderdash: rot **5** bilge, trash **6** drivel, jargon **7** baloney **8** claptrap, malarkey, nonsense **9** rigmarole **10** flumdiddle

baldicoot: **4** coot, monk

baldmoney: **7** gentian **8** spicknel

baldness: **8** alopecia **11** phalacrosis

baldric, baldrick: **4** belt **6** girdle, zodiac **7** balteus, support **8** baltheus, necklace

bale: woe **4** evil, harm **5** crate, death **6** bundle, sorrow **7** package **8** compress, disaster **9** influence, suffering *of wool:* **7** sarpler

Balearic Islands: **5** Ibiza **7** Cabrera, Majorca, Minorca **8** Mallorca **10** Formentera
capital: **5** Palma
language: **7** Catalan
measure: **5** palmo **6** misura, quarta, quarte **7** quartin **8** barcella, quartera
port: **5** Palma
weight: **5** artal, artel, cargo, corta, libra, mayor, ratel, rotel **8** quartano

baleen: **5** whale **9** whalebone

baleful: bad **6** evil **6** deadly, malign **7** noxious, ruinous **8** sinister, wretched **10** calamitous, malevolent, pernicious **11** destructive

balk: jib, shy **4** beam, bilk, foil, loft **5** block, check, demur, hunch, rebel, reest (Sc.), ridge, waver **6** baffle, defeat, falter, hinder, impede, outwit, rafter, recoil, refuse, thwart **7** quibble **8** hang back **9** discomfit, frustrate, stop short **14** disappointment

Balkans: **9** mountains, peninsula
countries: **6** Greece, Serbia **7** Albania, Croatia **8** Bulgaria **9** Macedonia **10** Montenegro, Yugoslavia (formerly) **17** Bosnia-Herzegovina
mountain: **6** Pindus **7** Rhodope **11** Dinaric Alps **12** Albanian Alps
people: **4** Serb, Slav **5** Croat **7** Slovene **10** Macedonian **11** Montenegrin

balky: **6** mulish **8** stubborn **9** obstinate

ball: bal (F.), bob, orb, toy **4** bead, pill **5** dance, globe, glome **6** bullet, muddle, pellet, pompon, rundle, sphere **7** confuse, mandrel, ridotto **8** spheroid **11** glomeration
and chain: **4** wife **6** burden
club: **4** nine, team **6** eleven
game: cat **4** golf, polo, pool **5** bocce, bocci, rugby **6** pelota, soccer, tennis **7** cricket, croquet, snooker **8** baseball, football, lacrosse **9** billiards
lofted: fly, lob
low: **5** liner
minced meat: **5** pinda **7** rissole
of fire: **4** whiz **6** dynamo, genius **7** hustler **8** go-getter, live wire **11** eager beaver
up: **5** snarl **6** foul up **7** confuse, perplex
wooden: **4** knur

ballad: lai (F.), lay **4** lied, lilt, poem, song **5** derry **6** sonnet **7** canzone

ballast: **4** load, trim **5** poise, stone **6** burden, gravel, weight **7** balance **9** saburrate

ballerina: **6** dancer **8** coryphee, danseuse

ballet: **4** Agon **5** dance, drama, Rodeo **7** Giselle **8** Firebird, Panorama, Swan Lake **9** Fancy Free, pantomime **10** Le Sylphide, Nutcracker, Petrouchka **12** choreography, Pillar of Fire **13** Vienna Waltzes **14** Sleeping Beauty
choreographer: **5** Ailey, Bruhn, Tudor **6** Alonso, Ashton, Bejart, Fokine, Graham, Petipa, Taylor, Tharpe **7** DeMille, Joffrey, Massine, Robbins, St. Denis **9** MacMillan **10** Cunningham **11** Ballanchine, Baryshnikov **12** Bournonville
composers: **5** Ravel **7** Copland, Delibes **9** Prokofiev **10** Stravinsky **11** Tchaikovsky
dance for two: **9** pas de deux
exercise rod: **5** barre
knee bend: **4** plie
leap: **4** jete **9** entrechat, pas de chat
movement: pas **5** brise **8** glissade
pose: **6** pointe **9** arabesque
wear: **4** tutu **6** tights **7** leotard **8** toe shoes
whirl: **9** pirouette

ballistic missile: **4** ICBM, IRBM, MIRV, MRBM, SLBM

balloon: bag **5** blimp **6** expand, gasbag **7** airship, distend, inflate **8** aerostat **9** dirigible
basket: car **7** gondola, nacelle

ballot: **4** poll, vote **5** elect, voice **6** billet, choice, ticket

ballyhoo: **4** plug, tout **6** hoopla, puff up **7** promote, trumpet **9** publicity

balm: oil **5** salve **6** lotion, relief, solace **7** anodyne, comfort, perfume, soother, unguent **8** ointment **9** fragrance
horse: **10** citronella
of Gilead: **6** balsam, poplar **11** Balsam Mecca

balmy: **4** mild, soft **5** bland, daffy, moony, spicy, sunny, sweet **6** gentle, insane **7** healing, lenient **8** aromatic, fragrant, soothing **9** assuaging **10** refreshing **11** odoriferous

baloney: **4** bunk **5** hooey **6** humbug **8** nonsense

balsa: **4** raft, tree, wood **5** float

balsam: **4** riga, tolu, tree **5** resin **6** annual, storay **7** copaiba **8** bdellium, ointment
apple: **4** vine **7** creeper **8** amargosa, amargoso, ampalaya

Baltic native: **4** Lett **7** Latvian **8** Estonian **10** Lithuanian

Baltic Sea: *canal:* **4** Gota, Kiel
gulf: **4** Riga **6** Danzig **7** Bothnia, Finland
island: **4** Dago **5** Faron, Oland, Visby **6** Karlso, Sarema **7** Gotland **8** Bornholm
port: Abo **4** Kiel, Riga **6** Gdansk, Gdynia **7** Tallinn **8** Klaipeda **9** Stockholm **10** Copenhagen
river: **4** Oder, Odra **5** Dvina, Neman **7** Vistula

Baltic States: **6** Latvia **7** Estonia **9** Lithuania

Baltimore: (see box)

balustrade: **7** barrier, parapet, railing **8** banister

Balzac character: **4** Nana **6** Goriot

Bambi: **4** deer **6** animal
aunt: Ena

bambino: **4** baby **5** child **6** infant

bamboo: 4 cane, reed, tree
  sacred: 6 nandin
  sprouts: 5 achar
  sugar: 9 tabasheer
  woven: 6 sawali

> **Baltimore:** *river:* 8 Patapsco
>   *bay:* 10 Chesapeake
>   *baseball team:* 7 Orioles
>   *race track:* 7 Pimlico
>   *horse race:* 9 Preakness
>   *founding family:* 7 Calvert

---

bamboozle: 4 dupe, fool, hoax 5 cheat, cozen, grill, trick 6 cajole, humbug 7 buffalo, deceive, defraud, mystify, perplex 8 hoodwink 11 hornswoggle
ban: bar 4 tabu, veto 5 block, taboo 6 enjoin, forbid, hinder, invoke, outlaw 7 condemn, exclude 8 anathema, denounce, execrate, prohibit 9 proscribe 11 malediction 12 denunciation, interdiction 15 excommunication
Bana: *conqueror:* 7 Krishna
  daughter: 4 Usha
banal: 4 flat 5 corny, inane, silly, stale, trite, vapid 6 jejune 7 insipid, trivial 9 hackneyed 10 pedestrian 11 commonplace 13 platitudinous
  phrase: 6 cliche
banana: 4 musa 6 ensete 7 platano (Sp.) 8 plantain
  bunch: 4 hand, stem
  family: 4 musa 6 pesang 8 musaceae
  leaf: 5 frond
  spider: 9 tarantula
  wild: fei
banana fish: 6 albula 8 ladyfish
banana oil: 7 blarney 8 soft soap
bananas: mad 5 batty, crazy
band: tie 4 belt, cord, crew, fess, gang, girt, hoop, ring, zone 5 group, label, strap, strip, tribe, unite 6 armlet, bundle, collar, collet, fillet, girdle, streak, string, stripe, team up, troupe 7 binding, circlet, company, garland, orphrey 8 bracelet, cincture, ligament, symphony, tressure (her.) 9 aggregate, orchestra 10 collection
  armed: 5 posse
  armor: 6 tonlet
  brain: 6 ligula 7 ligulae (pl.)
  narrow: 4 tape 5 stria 6 striae (pl.)
  small: 5 combo
bandage: 4 bind, tape 5 blind, clout, dress, sling, truss 6 fettle, fillet, ligate, swathe 8 cincture, ligature 9 blindfold

fastener: 7 ligator
nose: 9 accipiter
surgical: 5 spica 6 spicae (pl.) 7 fasciae (pl.), fascial
bandeau: 5 strip 6 fillet 9 brassiere 10 hair ribbon
bandicoot: rat 6 badger 7 molerat
bandikai: okra
bandit: 4 caco 5 bravo, thief 6 banish, outlaw, robber 7 bandido, brigand, ladrone 8 marauder, picaroon 10 highwayman
bandleader: 6 master 7 choragi, maestro 8 choragus 9 conductor
bandmaster: 5 Sousa
bandy: 4 cart, swap 5 bowed, trade 6 banter 7 chaffer, discuss 8 carriage, exchange 9 toss about, use glibly 11 give and take 12 treat lightly
bane: woe 4 evil, harm, kill, pest, ruin 5 curse, death, venom 6 injury, murder, poison, slayer 7 bugbear, nemesis, scourge 8 bete noir, mischief, murderer, nuisance
baneful: bad, ill 4 evil, vile 7 harmful, hurtful, noxious, ruinous 8 venomous 9 sinistral 10 malevolent, pernicious
bang: rap 4 beat, blow, dash, dock, drub, slam 5 clash, drive, excel, force, impel, pound, sound, thump, whack, whang 6 bounce, cudgel, energy, strike, thrash, thwack 7 sardine, surpass 8 forelock 9 explosion
  into: hit 5 crash 7 collide

> **Bangladesh:** *bay:* 6 Bengal
>   *capital:* 5 Dacca, Dhaka
>   *city:* 5 Bogra 6 Khulna, Mungla, Sylhet 7 Barisal 8 Chandput 10 Chittagong
>   *governor:* 5 nawab
>   *language:* 6 Bangla
>   *mountain:* 10 Keokradong
>   *national anthem:* 15 Amar Sonar Bangla (My Golden Bengal)
>   *people:* 7 Bengali, Biharis
>   *poet:* 6 Tagore
>   *river:* 5 Padma, Tista 6 Ganges, Jamuna (Brahmaputra), Meghna

---

bangle: 4 flap, roam 5 droop, waste 7 circlet, fritter, trinket 8 bracelet, ornament
bang-up: 5 crack 6 tiptop 9 first-rate
Bani's son: Uel 4 Amzi 5 Amram
banish: ban 5 expel, exile, expel, fleme 6 bandit, deport, dispel, forsay, outlaw 7 abandon, condemn, dismiss, exclude 8 displace, relegate 9 ostracize, proscribe, transport 10 expatriate, repatriate

banister: 7 railing 10 balustrade

bank: bar, bay, cop, rim, row 4 bink, brae, brew, caja, dike, dune, dyke, edge, hill, mass, pile, ramp, rive, sand, seat, tier, weir 5 banco, bench, bluff, brink, fence, levee, marge, mound, ridge, share, shelf, shoal, shore, slope, stack, stage, trust 6 causey, degree, depend, margin, reckon, rivage, strand 7 anthill, deposit, pottery, shallow 8 barranca, barranco, platform 9 acclivity, elevation, exchequer 10 depository, embankment
 clerk: 6 teller
 examiner: CPA 10 accountant
 requirement: 5 funds, money 6 assets 7 surplus 8 deposits
 river: 4 ripa

bankroll: wad 4 back 5 funds 7 finance 8 currency 9 grubstake, subsidize

bankrupt: sap 4 bung 5 broke, drain, smash, strip 6 busted, devour, quisby, ruined 7 failure 8 beggarly, depleted 9 destitute, insolvent 12 impoverished

banner: 4 fane, flag, jack 5 color 6 ensign, fannon, pennon 7 leading, pennant, salient 8 banderol, foremost, gonfalon, standard, vexillum 9 banderole, exemplary, oriflamme 10 surpassing

banns: 6 notice 12 proclamation

banquet: 4 fete, meal 5 feast 6 dinner, junket, regale, repast 8 carousal, festival
 room: 8 cenacula (pl.) 9 cenaculum

banquette: way 4 seat 5 shelf 7 footway 8 platform, sidewalk 10 embankment

banshee: fay 5 fairy, sidhe 6 goblin, spirit

bantam: 4 cock 5 saucy, small 6 little 7 chicken, rooster 9 combative 10 diminutive
 breed: 8 Sebright

banter: kid, rag, rib 4 fool, jest, joke, josh, mock 5 chaff, jolly, tease 8 badinage, raillery 10 persiflage, pleasantry 11 give and take, playfulness

Bantingize: 4 diet

bantling: 5 child 6 infant

Bantu: *dialect:* 6 Chwana 8 Sechuana
 language: Ila 4 Suto 5 Ronga 6 Thonga 7 Nyanaja 8 Nyamwezi 10 Wanymawezi
 people: 4 Baya, Bihe, Bule, Fang, Gogo, Gola, Guha, Hehe, Jaga, Luba, Maka, Nama, Vira, Yaka, Zulu 5 Duala, Kongo, Lunda, Nyoro 6 Banyai, Damara, Kaffir, Kikuyu, Rwanda, Waguha, Yakala 7 Swahili, Wachaga 8 Bechuana 10 Ganda Kafir

banxring: 6 mammal, tupaya 7 pentail 9 tree shrew
 genus: 4 tana
 look-alike: 8 squirrel

banzai: cry 6 attack

baobab: 4 tree 7 tebeldi

baptism: 7 rebirth 9 aspersion, cleansing, immersion, sacrament 10 initiation 11 christening
 robe: 7 chrisom
 vessel: 4 font 6 fontal, spring 7 piscina
 water: 5 laver

baptize: dip 4 full, name 5 heave 6 purify 7 cleanse 8 christen, sprinkle

bar: ban, dam, fid, gad, law, rod 4 axle, band, bank, beam, bolt, cake, gate, hide, joke, lock, oust, pole, rail, reef, save, shut, stop 5 arbor, bench, bilco, block, close, court, deter, estop, fence, hedge, lever, perch, shade, shaft, strap, strip 6 billet, bistro, brooch, except, fasten, grille, hinder, meagre, saloon, stripe 7 barrage, barrier, confine, counter, exclude, prevent 8 conclude, handicap, leave out, obstacle, obstruct, pass over, preclude, prohibit, restrain, restrict, surround, tribunal 9 barricade, fastening, gatehouse, hindrance, interpose, ostracize 10 crosspiece, difficulty, impediment, inhibition, portcullis 11 obstruction
 acrobat: 7 trapeze
 bullion: 5 ingot
 millstone: 4 rynd
 resisting pressure: 5 strut
 supporting: fid, rod 9 stanchion
 tamping: 7 stemmer
 window: 5 jemmy, jimmy 7 forcing

barb: awn, bur, jag, mow 4 burr, clip, file, flue, hair, herl, hook, jagg 5 beard, horse, point, ridge, shaft 6 pigeon 7 bristle, kingish 9 appendage 10 projection
 anchor: 4 flue
 feather: 4 harl, herl 5 ramus 7 pinnula, pinnule 8 pinnulae

Barbados: *capital:* 10 Bridgetown
 former Indian: 5 Carib 6 Arawak
 liquor: rum
 mountain: 9 Mt. Hillaby
 native: Bim

barbarian: Hun 4 boor, Goth, rude, wild 5 alien, brute 6 savage, vandal 7 ruffian 9 foreigner, untutored 10 Philistine, unlettered 11 uncivilized

barbarism: 4 cant 8 savagism, solecism 10 savageness

barbarity: 6 ferity 7 cruelty 8 ferocity, rudeness, savagery 9 brutality 10 inhumanity

barbarous: 4 fell, rude, wild 5 crude, cruel 6 brutal, savage 7 foreign, Hunnish, inhuman, slavish, uncivil 8 ignorant 9 ferocious, primitive 10 illiterate, outlandish, tramontane, unpolished **11** uncivilized **12** uncultivated

Barbary ape: **5** magot **6** monkey

Barbary Coast States: **5** Tunis **7** Algeria, Morocco, Tripoli

barbecue: **4** bake **5** broil, grill
rod: **4** spit **6** skewer

barbed: **4** bent **6** hooked **8** uncinate

barber: **6** Figaro, poller, shaver, tonsor **7** scraper, tonsure **11** chirotonsor

barber's itch: **8** ringworm

Barcelona: *sea:* **13** Mediterranean
founder: **5** Barca (Hamilcar)

bard: **4** poet, scop **5** druid, runer, scald **6** singer **8** minstrel, musician **10** troubadour
India: **4** bhat

Bard of Avon: **11** Shakespeare

bare: **4** bald, mere, nude **5** alone, crude, empty, naked, plain, stark, strip **6** barren, callow, denude, divert, divest, expose, histie, meager, meagre, paltry, pilled, reveal, simple **7** divulge, exposed, unarmed, uncover **8** desolate, disclose, stripped **9** in the buff, unadorned, uncovered, worthless **10** threadbare **11** defenseless, unconcealed, unfurnished **13** unaccompanied

barefaced: **4** bold **6** brazen **7** blatant, glaring **8** impudent **9** audacious, out-and-out, shameless **11** undisguised

barefooted: **6** unshod **9** discalced

barely: **4** only **5** faint **6** hardly, merely, poorly **8** scantily, scarcely, slightly **13** unqualifiedly **14** insufficiently

barf: **5** vomit **7** upchuck

barfly: **5** drunk, stiff **8** carouser

bargain: **4** deal, huck, pact, sale **5** cheap, steal **6** barter, dicker, haggle, palter **7** chaffer, compact, contend, contest **8** contract, covenant, giveaway, struggle **9** agreement, negotiate, situation, stipulate **10** engagement **11** come to terms, transaction

bargain-basement: **5** cheap **6** tawdry

bargain for: **6** expect **7** count on

barge: **4** ark, tow **4** bark, boat, raft, scow **5** lunge, lurch **6** barque, lumber, tender, thrust, vessel **7** lighter **8** flagship, flatboat **9** intrude on **12** move clumsily
charge: **10** lighterage
coal: **4** keel

bark: **4** bag, bay, rub, wap, yap, yip **4** boat, coat, howl, husk, peel, pelt, pill, rind, ross, ship, skin, yawp **5** balat, barca, barge, cough, shell, shout, strip **6** abrade, cortex, girdle, vessel **7** solicit, tanbark **8** cortices, covering
aromatic: **6** sintoc **9** sassafras
at: **5** scold **6** rebuke
cloth: **4** tapa **5** tappa **8** mulberry
covered with: **9** corticate **10** corticated

medicinal: **4** coto **5** casca, madar, niepa, nudar **7** quinine **8** cinchona **9** sassafras
outer: **8** periderm
pert. to: **8** cortical
remove: **4** ross **5** scale
resembling: **8** cortical
rough: **4** ross
tanning: **5** alder
up the wrong tree: err **5** stray

barker: dog **4** tout **7** spieler **8** pitchman **9** solicitor

barking deer: **7** muntjac, muntjak

barley: **5** grain
ground: **6** tsamba
pert. to: **11** hordeaceous
steep: **4** malt
variety: big **4** bere, bigg

barmy: **5** foamy, kooky, silly **6** frothy, screwy, yeasty **7** flighty, foolish, idiotic

barn: **4** byre **6** stable **10** storehouse
part: bay, mow **4** loft **5** stall **7** hayloft

barn dance: **7** hoedown
official: **6** caller

barnacle: **5** leech **8** hanger-on, parasite **9** appendage, shellfish **11** encumbrance

barnstorm: **4** tour **5** stump **6** troupe

barometer: **9** rainglass

barometric line: **6** isobar

baron: **4** peer **5** mogul **6** tycoon, vassal (Br.) **7** magnate **13** double sirloin (Br.)

baroque: **6** ornate, rococo **9** grotesque, irregular **11** extravagant **13** overdecorated

barrack: **4** camp **6** casern **7** cuartel (Sp.) **8** quarters

barracuda: **4** fish, kaku, spet **5** barry, pelon **6** becuna, picuda, sennet **10** guaguanche **12** guanchepelon

barrage: **4** hail **5** burst, salvo **6** attack, volley **7** barrier **9** broadside, cannonade, fusillade **10** obtruction, outpouring **11** bombardment

barranca, barranco: **4** bank **5** bluff **6** ravine

barrel: fat, keg, tun, vat **4** butt, cade, cask, drum, knag **6** runlet, tierce, vessel **7** cistern, hogshed, rundlet **8** cylinder **9** container, kilderkin
herring: **4** cade
maker: **6** cooper
part: **4** hoop, side **5** stave
raising device: **9** parbuckle
stopper: **4** bung
support: **4** hoop **6** gantry **7** gauntry

barren: dry **4** arid, bare, dull **5** empty, gaunt, stark, stern **6** desert, effete, fallow, jejune, meager **7** sterile **8** desolate, devoid of, impotent, treeless **9** childless, exhausted, fruitless, infertile **10** unfruitful **12** unproductive, unprofitable

barren oak: **9** blackjack

barren privet: **7** alatern **9** houseleek

barrette: bar **8** ornament

Barrie character: **5** Peter, Wendy **9** Tiger Lily **10** Tinker Bell **11** Captain Hook
nurse: **4** Nana

barrier: bar, dam **4** door, gate, line, moat, wall, weir **5** bound, chain, fence, hedge, limit **6** abatis, hurdle, screen **7** barrage, defense, parapet, railing **8** boundary, fortress, frontier, stockade **9** barricade, palisades, restraint, roadblock **10** difficulty **11** obstruction
movable: **4** bars, door **5** blind, shade **6** screen **7** curtain **8** shutters **10** portcullis

barring: **7** save for **9** aside from, excepting, outside of

barrio: **4** slum **6** ghetto **7** village **8** district

barrister: **6** barman, lawyer **7** counsel **8** advocate, attorney **9** solicitor

barroom: pub **4** cafe **6** lounge, saloon, tavern **7** cantina (Sp.), doggery, taproom **8** dramshop

barrow: hod, hog **4** bank, dune, hill, mote **5** grave, gurry, mound **6** tumuli **7** hillock, trolley, tumulus **8** mountain

barter: **4** chap, chop, cope, coup, hawk, sell, swap, vend **5** corse, trade, troke, truck **6**
dicker **7** bargain, cambium, permute, traffic **8** commerce, exchange **9** excambion **11** reciprocate

Bartered Bride composer: **7** Smetana

bas: low

bas-relief: **9** plaquette

basal: **5** basic **7** basilar **11** fundamental

basalt: **6** marble, navite **7** pottery

base: bed, low **4** clam, evil, foot, foul, lewd, mean, poor, root, stem, step, vile **5** basis, cheap, dirty, muddy, petty, snide **6** abject, bottom, common, ground, menial, paltry, podium, shabby, sordid, vulgar **7** bastard, bedrock, caitiff, comical, hangdog, housing, ignoble, lowdown, servile, slavish, support **8** degraded, infamous, inferior, pedestal, scullion, shameful, stepping, unworthy, wretched **9** absorbent, degrading, establish, predicate, worthless **10** despicable, foundation, villainous **11** ignominious **12** contemptible, dishonorable, disreputable **13** dishonourable
architectural: **5** socle **6** plinth
attached by: **7** sessile
military: HDQ **4** camp **5** depot **12** headquarters
structural: **6** plinth

baseball: *field:* **7** diamond
founder: **9** Doubleday
glove: **4** mitt
Hall of Fame site: **11** Cooperstown
hit: **4** bunt
official: ump **5** coach **6** umpire **7** manager
players: Ott **4** Cobb, Dean, Ford, Foxx, Mays, Rose, Ruth, Ryan **5** Aaron, Banks, Bench, Berra, Brock, Carew, Grove, Kiner, Maris, Perry, Spahn, Young **6** Feller, Gehrig, Gibson, Hunter, Koufax, Mantle, Morgan, Musial, Palmer, Seaver, Wagner **7** Hornsby, Hubbell, Jackson, Jenkins, Johnson, Speaker **8** Clemente, DiMaggio, Robinson, Williams **9** Alexander, Killebrew **10** Campanella **11** Yastrzemski
team: **4** nine
teams (American League): **5** Twins (Minnesota) **6** Angels (Cal.), Red Sox (Boston), Royals (Kansas City), Tigers (Detroit) **7** Brewers (Milwaukee), Indians (Cleveland), Orioles (Baltimore), Rangers (Texas), Yankees (N.Y.) **8** Blue Jays (Toronto), Mariners (Seattle), White Sox (Chicago) **9** Athletics (Oakland)
teams (National League): **4** Cubs (Chicago), Mets (N.Y.), Reds (Cincinnati) **5** Expos (Montreal) **6** Astros (Houston), Braves (Atlanta), Giants (San Francisco), Padres (San Diego) **7** Dodgers (Los Angeles), Marlins (Florida), Pirates (Pittsburgh), Rockies (Colorado) **8** Phillies (Philadelphia) **9** Cardinals (St. Louis)
term: bag, bat, box, ERA, fan, fly, hit, out, peg, RBI, run, tap **4** balk, ball, bean, bunt, burn, deck, foul, hill, home, hook, pill, sack, save, turn, walk, wild **5** alley, apple, bench, booth, clout, count, curve, drive, error, flied, force, frame, glove, homer, lined, mound, pitch, plate, popup, score, slide, swing **6** assist, batter, clutch, double, dugout, groove, hitter, lumber, popout, putout, rubber, runner, screen, series, single, sinker, slider, stance, strike, string, target, triple, windup **7** arbiter, battery, blooper, bullpen, circuit, cleanup, diamond, fielder, floater, infield, pitcher, side-arm, squeeze, stretch **8** delivery, fork ball, grounded, grounder, knuckler, outfield, pinch-hit, spitball **9** full-count, hot corner, sacrifice, strikeout, two-bagger **10** double-play, scratch-hit, triple-play **11** squeeze play, three-bagger

basketball: *coach:* Iba **4** Rupp **5** Smith **6** Knight, Wooden **8** Auerbach
inventor: **8** Naismith
official: ref **7** referee **12** striped shirt
players: **4** Bird, Reed, West **5** Cousy **6** Baylor, Cowens, Erving, Jordan, Pettit, Walton **7** Bellamy, Frazier, Johnson, Russell **8** Havlicek **9** Archibald, Robertson **11** Abdul-Jabbar, Chamberlain
positions: **5** cager, guard **6** center **7** forward hoopster, swing man
pro teams (NBA): **4** Heat (Miami), Jazz (Utah), Nets (New Jersey), Suns (Phoenix) **5** 76ers (Philadelphia), Bucks (Milwaukee), Bulls (Chicago), Hawks (Atlanta), Kings (Kansas City), Spurs (San Antonio) **6** Knicks (New York), Lakers (Los Angeles), Magics (Orlando), Pacers (Indiana) **7** Bullets (Washington), Celtics (Boston), Hornets (Charlotte), Nuggets (Denver), Pistons (Detroit), Rockets (Houston) **8** Clippers (Los Angeles), Warriors (Golden State) **9** Cavaliers (Cleveland), Mavericks (Dallas) **11** Supersonics (Seattle) **12** Timberwolves (Minnesota), Trail Blazers (Portland)
team: **4** five **7** cagemen, quintet
term: gun, jam, key **4** cage, dunk, foul, hook, hoop, pass, zone **5** block, bonus, glass, lay-up, stuff, tip-in **6** bucket, charge, freeze, tap-off, tip-off, travel **7** dribble, foul out, matchup, rebound, time-out **8** jump ball, man-to-man, slam dunk, turnover **9** backboard, backcourt, field goal, free throw **11** ball control **14** three-point shot

baseless: **4** idle **9** unfounded, untenable **10** gratuitous, groundless **11** unsupported
base on balls: **4** pass, walk
bash: bat, lam **4** beat, blow, dent, mash, swat, wham, whop **5** party, smash **6** bruise, strike, wallop **7** blowout, hit hard **8** wingding
Bashemath's husband: **4** Esau
bashful: coy, shy **5** blate (Sc.), mousy, timid **6** demure, modest **7** daunted **8** backward, blushing, dismayed, retiring, sheepish **9** diffident, shrinking
Bashkir capital: Ufa
basic: **5** chief, vital **7** central, primary **9** elemental, principal **10** elementary, underlying **11** fundamental, rudimentary **13** indispensable
basically: **8** at bottom **9** in essence, primarily **11** essentially
basil (see also **bezel**): **4** herb **5** plant, royal **6** fetter
basilica: **6** church, shrine, temple **7** Lateran
part of: **4** apse, nave
basin: cwm, pan 4 bowl, dish, dock, ewer, font, sink, tank **5** laver, stoup **6** cirque, crater, marina, valley, vessel **7** cuvette, piscina **8** lavatory, receptor, washbowl **9** reservoir **10** depression **11** aspersorium
geological: **4** tala
basis: **4** root **5** axiom **6** bottom, ground, reason **7** essence, footing, premise, support **10** foundation, groundwork
bask: sun **4** beek (Sc.), warm **5** acrid, bathe, enjoy, revel **6** bitter **7** rejoice **9** luxuriate
basket: ark, fan, ped **4** kipe, trug **5** cassy (Sc.), cesta (Sp.), chest, crate, creel, scull **6** cassie (Sc.), dosser, hamper, hoppet, panier **7** canasta, hanaper, pannier, scuttle **9** container **10** receptacle
coal mine: **4** corf
eel: **4** buck
fig: **4** caba **5** frail **6** tapnet
fire: **5** grate **7** cresset
fish: pot **4** caul, cawl, corf, hask, skip, weel **5** crate, creel, maund **6** courge
fruit: **6** pottle **7** prickle
jai-alai: **5** cesta
material: **4** cane, rush **5** osier, otate **6** willow
twig: **6** wattle
water-tight: **7** wattape
wicker: cob **4** cobb, coop **5** willy **6** hamper **7** hanaper **8** bassinet
work: **4** caba **5** cabas, slath **6** slarth
basketball: (see box)
Basques: *bay:* **6** Biscay
cap: **5** beret
city: **4** Irun **5** Eibar **6** Bermeo, Bilbao, Sestao, Tolosa **7** Vitoria
dance: **8** zortzico
game: **6** pelota **7** jai alai
language: **7** Euskera
mountains: **8** Pyrenees **10** Cantabrian
petticoat: **8** basquine
province: **5** Alava **7** Vizcaya **9** Guipuzcoa
bass: low **4** deep, fish **5** voice **6** singer **7** achigan, jewfish
bassinet: **4** crib **6** cradle **7** baby bed
basswood: lin **4** bast **5** tilia **6** linden
bast: **4** bark, flax, hemp, jute **5** fiber, ramie **6** phloem **8** piassava
bastard: **4** base **5** false **6** cannon, galley, hybrid, impure **7** byspell, lowbred, mongrel **8** bantling, spurious **10** artificial **11** adulterated **12** illegitimate
baste: sew **4** beat, cane, cook, drub, lard, tack **6** cudgel, punish, stitch, thrash

bastion: 5 tower 7 bulwark, citadel, rampart 8 fortress 10 stronghold
defensive: 4 fort 13 fortification
shoulder: 6 epaule

bat: hit, wad 4 bate, beat, blow, club, gait, lump, mass, swat, toot, wink 5 binge, brick, piece, speed, spree, stick 6 aliped, backie (Sc.), baston, beetle, cudgel, racket, strike, stroke, wander 7 flutter, noctule, vampire 8 bludgeon, serotine 9 reremouse 10 battledore, chiroptera, packsaddle 11 rattlemouse 12 chauvesouris, flittermouse
around: 4 roam 6 debate, ponder
European: 9 barbastel 11 barbastelle
species: 9 pipistrel 11 pipistrelle

Bataan: 9 peninsula
bay: 5 Subic 6 Manila
city: 7 Balanga
island: 5 Luzon

batch: lot 4 mass, mess, sort 5 group 6 bundle 7 mixture 8 quantity 10 collection

bate: 6 deduct, except 7 exclude 8 decrease

bateau: 4 boat

batfish: 6 diablo

bath: dip 4 bate, pert 5 therm 6 plunge, shower 7 balneum 8 ablution 10 natatorium
pert. to: 7 balneal
public: 7 piscine
sponge: 5 luffa 6 loofah
treatment by: 13 balneotherapy

Bath river: 4 Avon

bathe: bay, tub 4 bask, lave, stew, wash 5 embay 6 enwrap 7 immerse, pervade, suffuse 8 permeate

bathhouse: 6 cabana 8 balneary

bathing suit: bikini, trunks 7 maillot

bathos: 8 comedown 10 anticlimax

bathroom: W.C. (abbr.), loo 4 head, john 6 hammam, toilet 7 latrine 8 facility, lavatory, outhouse, restroom, sudatory 10 sudatorium 11 water closet

Bathsheba: *husband:* 5 David, Uriah
son: 7 Solomon

baton: rod 4 bend 5 staff, stick 6 baston, cudgel 7 bourdon, scepter, sceptre 9 truncheon

batrachian: 4 frog, toad

batten: 6 enrich, fatten, thrive 9 fertilize

batter: ram 4 beat, dent, maim 5 clour, dinge, frush, paste, pound 6 bruise, hammer, hitter, pummel 7 bombard, cripple, destroy, shatter, striker 8 demolish

battery: *floating:* 4 cell 5 praam 7 parapet 9 artillery 11 bombardment
plate: 4 grid
terminal: 5 anode 7 cathode

battle: war 4 duel, fray, meet, tilt 5 brush, fight, joust, onset 6 action, affray, combat 7 bombard, contend, contest, hosting, warfare 8 conflict, skirmish, struggle 9 encounter 10 engagement, tournament 11 competition, hostilities
area: 4 zone 5 arena, front 6 sector 7 terrain, theater
cry: 6 slogan 9 catchword
formation: 5 herse 6 deploy
line: 5 front
order: 7 regalia 8 battalia
royal: 5 melee 9 scrimmage
site: 5 Bulge, Crecy, Marne, Somme 6 Midway, Shiloh 7 Britain, Bull Run, Dunkirk, Jutland, Okinawa 8 Antietam, Manassas, Waterloo, Yorktown 9 Agincourt, Gallipoli 10 Armageddon, Gettysburg 11 Belleau Wood 12 Pork Chop Hill
trophy: 5 medal, scalp 6 ribbon

Battle Hymn of the Republic author: 4 Howe

battleship: 11 dreadnaught 16 superdreadnaught

batty: 5 crazy, silly 7 foolish

bauble: bow, toy 4 bead 6 button, gewgaw, trifle 7 trinket 8 gimcrack 9 plaything 10 knickknack

bauxite derivative: 8 aluminum

Bavaria: 6 Bayern (G.)
capital: 6 Munich
city: Hof 5 Furth 6 Passau 8 Augsburg, Bayreuth, Nurnberg, Wurzburg 9 Nuremberg 10 Regensburg
lake: 5 Ammer, Chiem 9 Starnberg
mountain: 10 Allgau Alps 11 Wetterstein 14 Bohemian Forest
peak: 5 Arber 9 Zugspitze
river: Alz, Ilz, Inn, Nab 4 Eger, Isar, Lech, Main 5 Amper, Iller, Regen, Saale 6 Danube 7 Altmuhl, Regnitz
Wagner festival site: 8 Bayreuth

bawd: 4 aunt, hare 5 dirty, madam 6 defile 7 commode 8 procurer 9 procuress 10 fruitwoman, prostitute

bawdy: 4 foul, lewd 5 dirty 7 obscene 8 unchaste

bawl: cry 4 howl 5 golly, shout 6 bellow, boohoo, outcry 8 glaister 10 vociferate
out: 5 scold 9 reprimand

bay (see also individual states and countries): dam, ria, voe 4 bank, bark, cove, gulf, hole, hope, howl, loch (Sc.), roan, tree, yaup, yawp 5 bahia (Sp.), berry, bight, color, creek, fiord, fjord, fleet, Fundy, haven, horse, oriel, sinus 6 Baffin, Bengal, Biscay, Hudson, laurel, recess, window 7 enclose, estuary, silanga, ululate 8 Delaware 10 Chesapeake 11 compartment, indentation
bird: 5 snipe 6 curlew, godwit, plover

camphor: **6** laurin
Bayard: 5 horse
Baylor University site: 4 Waco **5** Texas
Bay of Biscay: *island:* Yeu **5** Belle, Groix **6** Oleron
   resort: **7** Hendaye **8** Biarritz
   river to: **5** Adour, Loire **7** Garonne **8** Charente
bayonet: 4 stab **5** knife **6** pierce, weapon
bayou: 5 brook, creek, inlet, river **6** outlet, stream **7** rivulet **9** backwater
Bayou State: 9 Louisiana
Bay State: 13 Massachusetts
bazaar, bazar: 4 fair, fete, sale **5** agora, burse **6** market **7** canteen **8** emporium **9** bezesteen **10** exposition
bazoo: 4 talk **5** kazoo, mouth
be: are **4** esse (L.), être (F.), live **5** abide, exist, occur **6** remain **7** breathe, subsist **8** continue
beach: 4 bank, moor, ripa, sand **5** coast, plage (F.), playa (Sp.), shore **6** ground, shilla, strand **7** hardway, seaside, shingle
beachcomber: 7 vagrant **8** vagabond
beachhead: van **7** landing **8** foothold
beacon: 4 mark, sign **5** baken, fanal, guide, phare **6** ensign, pharos, signal **7** cresset, seamark, warning **8** signpost **10** lighthouse, watchtower
   light: **7** cresset, lantern
Beaconsfield, Earl of: 8 Disraeli
bead: 4 drop, foam **5** sewan, sight **6** bauble, bubble, prayer, wampum **7** globule, molding, sparkle, trinket
   string: **6** rosary **7** chaplet **8** necklace
beady: 5 round, small **8** globular **10** glistening
beak: neb, nib **4** bill, nose, peak **5** snout, spout **7** rostrum **8** mandible **9** proboscis, schnozzle **10** promontory
   ship's: bow, ram **4** prow
   without: **9** erostrate
beaker: cup **4** tass **5** bocal, bouse, glass **6** bareca, bareka, vessel
be-all and end-all: 4 A to Z, acme **7** epitome **8** entirety, sum total, ultimate, whole bit **9** aggregate **10** everything **11** ne plus ultra (L.) **13** alpha and omega
beam: bar, ray **4** balk, emit, glow, I-bar, sile (Sc.), stud, T-bar **5** arbor, caber, flash, gleam, gleed, joist, light, shaft, shine, smile **6** binder, girder, rafter, timber, walker **7** bumpkin, chevron, radiate, support, trimmer **10** architrave
beaming: gay **4** rosy **6** bright, joyous, lucent **7** radiant, shining **8** all aglow, cheerful
beamy: 5 broad **7** massive **8** mirthful
bean: urd **4** chap, gram, head **5** brain, skull **6** caster, collar, fellow, frijol (Sp.), kidney, lentil, nipple, noggin, strike, thrash, trifle **7** calabar, frijole (Sp.) **11** castigation
   Asian: **4** gram, mung
   climbing: **4** lima, pole
   cluster: **4** guar
   curd: **4** tofu
   eye: **4** hila **5** hilum
   kind: **4** goa, soy, wax **4** lima, navy, snap **5** black, cacao, green, jelly, pinto **6** castor, coffee, kidney, string **7** calabar, jumping **8** hyacinth **13** scarlet runner
   lima: **4** haba **5** sieva
   locust: **5** carob
   lubricant: ben
   Mexican: **6** frijol **7** frijole, jumping
   poisonous: **4** loco **7** calabar
bean shooter: 8 catapult **9** slingshot
Beantown: 6 Boston
bear: cub, lug, sun **4** gest, tote **5** abide, allow, beget, breed, bring, brook, brown, bruin, carry, drive, geste, honey, koala, panda, polar, press, sloth, stand, yield **6** afford, behave, endure, pierce, render, suffer, thrust, uphold **7** comport, conduct, forbear, glacier, grizzly, Kermode, produce, support, sustain, undergo **8** cinnamon, forebear, tolerate **9** carnivore, Himalayan, transport **10** silvertips, spectacled **13** constellation
   Alaskan: **6** Kodiak
   female: sow **7** she-bear
   genus: **5** Ursus
   male: **4** boar **6** he-bear
   smallest: sun **7** Malayan
   South American: **10** spectacled
   young: cub
bear bush: 8 inkberry
bear cat: 4 paud **9** binturong
beard: 4 barb, defy **5** brave **6** arista, goatee **7** Vandyke **8** confront, face up to, hair tuft, whiskers **9** challenge **11** mutton chops
bearded: 5 hairy **6** barbed **7** barbate, hirsute **9** whiskered **11** barbigerous
bearing: aim, air **4** gest, mien, port **5** birth, front, geste, habit, poise, trend **6** allure, apport, aspect, course, gerent, manner, orient, thrust **7** address, conduct, meaning, posture, purport, support **8** amenance, attitude, behavior, carriage, demeanor, pressure, relation, tendency, yielding **9** direction, gestation, influence, personage, producing **10** cognizance, deportment **11** comportment, countenance **12** significance
   fine: **6** belair
   heraldic: **4** ente, orle **5** pheon
   plate: gib
bear down: 5 exert, press **6** stress **8** approach
beardless: 5 young **6** callow
bear-shaped: 8 ursiform

bear upon: 6 affect 7 concern
 grain: awn 6 arista
 grain: rye 5 awned, wheat 8 aristate
beast: 4 bete (F.) 5 brute 6 animal, savage 7
 monster 8 blighter 9 quadruped
 mythical: roc 4 yeti 5 harpy, Hydra 6
 dragon, Garuda, Geryon, gorgon, Kraken,
 Orthos, Scylla, Sphinx, Triton 7 centaur,
 chimera, Echidna, figfaun, griffin, griffon,
 Midgard, phoenix 8 Cerberus, chimaera,
 Minotaur 9 Charybdis, Sasquatch 10 Jabberwock
 pertaining to: 7 leonine
 royal: 4 lion
beast of burden: ass, yak 4 oxen (pl.) 5
 burro, camel, horse, llama 6 donkey,
 onager
beastly: 5 feral, gross 6 animal, brutal 7 bestial, brutish, inhuman, swinish 9 offensive
 10 abominable, disgusting
beat: bat, cob, dad (Sc.), fan, fib, tap, taw, tew
 4 baff, bang, bash, bate, belt, best, blow,
 bolt, bray, cane, chap, club, daud, ding,
 dint, drub, dump, dunt, fell, flap, flax, flog,
 frat, haze, lash, lump, maul, mill, pant, pelt,
 prat, rout, scat, slam, tack, tick, whip, whop
 5 baste, berry, churn, clink, douse, fight,
 filch, flail, knock, pound, pulse, round,
 scoop, strap, throb, thump, trump, whang,
 worst 6 accent, batter, beetle, buffet, cotton, cudgel, defeat, fettle, hammer, hamper, larrup, outrun, pummel, raddle,
 rhythm, squash, strike, stroke, swinge,
 switch, thrash, threap (Sc.), thresh 7
 assault, battuta, belabor, blister, cadence,
 canvass, conquer, contuse, exhaust, fatigue,
 pulsate, shellac, surpass, trounce, vibrate 8
 belabour, fatigued, lambaste, overcome,
 shellack, vanquish 9 exhausted, pulsation,
 throbbing 10 assignment
 back: 5 repel 7 repulse 8 drive off
 down: 5 crush 7 wear out 8 dispirit, suppress 10 make abject
 into plate: 8 malleate
beater: rab 4 maul, seal 5 caner, lacer 6
 dasher, mallet 8 thresher 9 scrutcher
beatify: 6 hallow 7 glorify 8 sanctify
beat it: 4 scat 5 scram 7 vamoose
beatitude: joy 5 bliss 7 benison 9 happiness
 11 blessedness
beau: 5 beaux (pl.), blade, dandy, flame,
 lover, spark, swell 6 escort, fellow, garcon, steady, suitor 7 admirer, bravery,
 courter, coxcomb, cupidon, gallant 8 follower 9 boyfriend
Beau Brummell: fop 5 dandy 7 coxcomb
beau geste: 5 favor 7 gesture
beau ideal: 5 model 8 paradigm 14 shining
 example

beau monde (F.): 7 fashion, society
beaut: 4 lulu
beautician: 10 beautifier, cosmetiste (F.) 11
 cosmetician
beautifier: 8 cosmetic
beautiful: 4 fair, fine, glad, mear, meer, mere
 5 belle, bonny 6 blithe, bonnie, choice,
 comely, decore, lovely, poetic, pretty 7 elegant 8 charming, delicate, fairsome, gorgeous, graceful, handsome, stunning 9
 exquisite 11 good-looking
 people: 5 elite 6 jet set 9 haut monde 10
 haute monde 11 high society
beautify: 4 gild 5 adorn, grace, hight, preen,
 primp, prune 6 bedeck 7 adonize, garnish
 8 decorate 9 embellish, glamorize
beauty: 5 belle, charm, grace 6 eyeful, looker,
 polish 8 knockout 10 comeliness, goodliness, loveliness 11 pulchritude
 goddess: Sri 5 Freya, Venus 6 Freyja 7 Lakshmi 9 Aphrodite
 lover: 7 esthete 8 aesthete
beaver: hat 4 coin 6 castor, rodent
 cloth: 6 kersey
 eater: 9 wolverine
 skin: 4 plew
Beaver State: 6 Oregon
because: for 4 that 5 since 8 as long as, inasmuch
because of that: 7 thereby 9 therefore
becken: 7 cymbals
beckon: bow, nod 4 wave 6 curtsy, summon 7
 bidding, command, curtsey, gesture 10
 salutation
becloud: 4 hide 5 bedim 6 darken, puzzle 7
 confuse, mystify, obscure, perplex 8 befuddle, overcast
become: get, wax 4 grow, pass, suit 5 adorn,
 befit, grace 6 accord, befall, beseem,
 betide, change 7 behoove, flatter
becoming: 4 good 5 right 6 comely, gainly 7
 decorum, farrand, farrant 8 decorous,
 handsome, suitable, tasteful 10 attractive,
 convenient, flattering 11 appropriate
becscie: 9 merganser
becuna: 9 barracuda
bed: cot, pad 4 base, bunk, doss, lair, plot 5
 basis, berth, couch, layer 6 bottom, couche
 (F.), cradle, litter, matrix, pallet, strata, tuck
 in 7 channel, lodging, stratum 8 matrices,
 plancher, rollaway 9 basegrave, stretcher
 10 apishamore, foundation
 feather: tye
 small: cot 4 crib 6 cradle, pallet 7 hammock, truckle, trundle 8 bassinet
 straw: 9 shakedown
bed stay: 4 slat
bedbug: 5 cimex 6 chinch, cimice (pl.) 8
 conenose

bedding: 5 duvet 6 linens, quilts, sheets 8 blankets 9 comforter 10 bedclothes

bedeck: gem 4 lard, trim 5 adorn, array, dight, grace 7 dress up 8 ornament 9 embellish

bedevil: 5 abuse, annoy, worry 6 muddle, pester 7 bewitch, confuse, torment

bedim: fog 4 mist 5 cloud 6 darken 7 becloud, obscure

bedizen: 4 daub 5 adorn, array, dizen 6 bedaub 9 overdress

bedlam: 4 riot 5 chaos, noise, rudas (Sc.) 6 asylum, madman, tumult, uproar 7 lunatic, madness 8 madhouse 9 confusion

Bedouin: 4 Arab, Moor 5 nomad
head cord: 4 agal
official: 4 cadi 5 sheik
religion: 5 Islam
tribe: 4 Harb

bedridden: ill 6 ailing, laid up 8 confined 13 incapacitated

bedrock: 5 basis, nadir 6 bottom

bedroll: 6 bindle

bedroom: 4 flat 5 berth, cabin 7 boudoir, chamber 11 compartment

bee: dor, fly 4 apis, idea, ring 5 party 6 dingar, insect, notion, torque 7 caprice, stinger 9 gathering 11 hymenoptera 12 hymenopteron
colony of: 5 swarm, yeast
family: 5 apina 6 apidae
female: 5 queen
genus: 4 apis
girl named for: 7 Melissa
house: gum 4 butt, hive, scap, skep 6 apiary 7 alveary, bee-butt 9 alvearium
house covering: 6 hackle
male: 5 drone
nose: 4 lora (pl.) 5 lorum
pert. to: 8 apiarian
pollen brush: 5 scopa 6 scopae (pl.) 9 sarothrum

beebread: 8 ambrosia

beech: 4 buck, tree 6 myrtle
genus: 5 fagus

beechnut: 4 mast

beef: 4 meat 5 gripe 8 complain
cut: 4 loin, rump, side 5 baron, chine, chuck, filet, flank, roast, round, shank, steak 6 cutlet, fillet, muscle, saddle 7 brisket, knuckle, quarrel, quarter, sirloin 8 short-rib, shoulder 9 aitchbone, rattleran 11 filet mignon, porterhouse 13 Chateaubriand
dried: 5 bucan, jerky, vifda, vivda 6 buccan 7 charqui
pickled: 5 bully
salted: 4 junk
spiced: 8 pastrami, pastroma, pastromi

beefeater: 6 warder, yeoman

beefy: 5 heavy, hefty, husky 6 brawny, fleshy, stolid

Beehive State: 4 Utah

beekeeper: 8 apiarist, skeppist 12 apiculturist

beep: 4 tone, toot 6 signal

beer: ale, mum 4 bock, brew, grog, scud (Sc.) 5 kvass, lager, stout 6 liquor, porter, stingo, swanky 8 beverage
barley: 5 chang
cask: 4 butt
ingredient: 4 hops, malt 5 yeast 6 barley
king: 9 Gambrinus
maize: 5 chica 6 chicha
maker: 6 brewer
mug: see *vessel* below
Russian: 5 kvass
shop: pub 6 saloon, tavern
unfermented: 4 wort
vessel: mug 4 Toby 5 stein 6 flagon, seidel, tanker 8 schooner 9 blackjack

beer and skittles: fun 4 play

beery: 7 maudlin, muddled

beeswax substitute: 7 ceresin

beet: 5 chard, sugar 6 mangel 8 beetrave 9 vegetable 12 mangel-wurzel
genus: 4 beta
soup: 7 borscht

Beethoven: *birthplace:* 4 Bonn
opera: 7 Fidelio
sonata: 6 Spring 8 Kreutzer 9 Moonlight, Waldstein 10 Pathetique 12 Appassionata
symphony: 5 fifth, first, ninth, sixth, third 6 Choral, eighth, Eroica, fourth, second 7 seventh 8 Pastoral

beetle: bat, bug, jut, ram 4 beat, dung, goga, gogo, hang, maul, stag 5 amara, bulge, click, drive, gogga, hispa, meloe 6 chafer, golach, goloch, jutout, mallet, pestle, scarab, weevil 7 firefly, June bug, prinoid, project 8 Hercules, lowering, overhang 9 prioninae (pl.) 10 battle-dore, projecting
bark: 5 borer
bright: 7 ladybug
family: 10 elateridae 11 clavicornes, clavicornia
fire: 6 cucuyo
genus: 5 fidia
grain: 7 cadelle
grapevine: 6 thrips
ground: 5 amara
horny substance of: 6 chitin
mustard: 9 blackjack
rhinoceros: 4 uang
sacred: 6 scarab
wing cover: 5 shard
wood: 6 sawyer

beetle-browed: 6 morose 8 scowling

beetle-head: 5 dunce 6 plover 9 blockhead

befall: hap 4 come 5 occur 6 astart, become, betide, happen 7 come off, pertain 8 bechance

67

beholden

befit: dow 4 suit 5 beset 6 become, behove, beseem, betide 7 behoove 9 agree with 10 go together

befog: 5 cloud 6 obsane, puzzle 7 confuse, mystify, obscure

before: ere 4 ante, said, up to 5 afore, ahead, avant, coram (L.), first, forby, front, prior 6 facing, forbye, former, rather, sooner 7 already, earlier, forward 8 anterior, hitherto 9 in advance 10 previously

before long: 4 anon, soon 9 presently

before now: ere 4 gone, over 6 erenow

befoul: 4 soil 5 dirty 6 bemire, defile, malign 7 pollute 8 entangle

befriend: aid 4 abet, help 5 favor 6 assist, favour, foster, succor 7 benefit, support, sustain 11 countenance

befuddle: 4 daze 5 addle, besot 6 muddle 7 becloud, confuse, fluster, mystify, stupefy

beg: ask, bid, sue, woo 4 coax, pray, sorn (Sc.) 5 cadge, crave, mooch, plead 6 adjure, appeal 7 beseech, entreat, implore, request, solicit 8 petition 9 importune, panhandle 10 supplicate

beget: ean 4 bear, sire 5 breed, yield 6 author, create, father 7 acquire, engraff 8 engender, generate 9 germinate, procreate

begetter: 4 sire 6 author, father, mother, parent

beggar: 4 ruin 5 asker, randy, rogue 6 bacach (Ir.), bidder, canter, devour, mumper, pariah, pauper, wretch 7 almsman 8 palliard, stroller 9 maunderer, mendicant, schnorrer, suppliant 10 impoverish, panhandler, petitioner, starveling, supplicant 12 hallan-shaker
saint: 5 Giles
speech: 4 cant

beggarly: 4 mean, poor 5 cheap, petty, sorry 6 abject, paltry 8 bankrupt, indigent, wretched 10 despicable 12 contemptible

Beggar's Opera author: Gay 6 Brecht

begin: 4 fang, lead, open, rise 5 arise, enter, start 6 attack, get off, spring 8 commence, embark on, inchoate, initiate 9 institute, introduce, originate 10 embark upon, inaugurate

begin again: 4 anew, over 5 renew 6 resume 7 restart

beginner: 4 boot, tiro, tyro 5 rooky 6 novice, rookie 7 amateur, entrant, noviate, recruit, student, trainee 8 freshman, neophyte 9 candidate, debutante, novitiate, postulate 10 apprentice

beginning: egg 4 dawn, edge, germ, rise, root, seed 5 alpha, birth, debut, start 6 outset, setout, source 7 geneses (pl.), genesis, initial, nascent 8 entrance, exordium, inchoate, rudiment 9 day spring, embryonic, inception, incipient, the word go 10 conception, elementary, foundation, incunabula (pl.), initiation, opening gun 11 incunabulum 12 commencement

begone: off, out 4 away, scat, shoo 5 scoot, scram 6 aroint, avaunt, depart, get out 7 vamoose

begrudging: 6 grudge, loathe 7 envious, grumble 9 reluctant

beguile: fox 4 coax, foil, gull, lure 5 amuse, charm, cheat, cozen, elude, evade, trick 6 brique, delude, divert, entrap, seduce 7 deceive, ensnare, flatter, mislead 9 entertain 10 manipulate

behalf: 4 part, sake, side 5 stead 6 affair, matter, profit 7 benefit, defence, defense, support 8 interest 9 advantage

behave: act 4 bear, go on, quit, work 5 carry, react, treat 6 acquit, demean, deport, handle 7 comport, conduct, gesture, manager 8 function, regulate, restrain

behavior, behaviour: air 4 mien, port 5 guise, tenue 6 action, manner 7 bearing, conduct, decorum 8 amenance, breeding, carriage 9 demeanour 10 deportment, governance 11 comportment

behead: 9 decollate 10 decapitate, guillotine

Belarus: *capital:* 5 Mensk, Minsk
city: 5 Mozyr, Orsha, Pinsk
currency: 5 kopek, ruble
leader: 6 Kebich 7 Poznyak 11 Shushkevich
province: 5 Brest, Gomel, Minsk 6 Grodno, oblast 7 Mogilev, Vitebsk

---

behemoth: 4 huge 5 beast, giant, hippo 7 monster

behest: bid, law 4 hest, rule 5 order 6 decree, demand 7 bidding, command, mandate 9 prompting 10 injunction 12 solicitation

behind: aft 4 past, rear, rump, ward 5 abaff, abaft, after, ahind (Sc.), arear, later, passe, tardy 6 arrear, astern 8 backward, buttocks, derriere (F.), dilatory 9 posterior 10 afterwards

behold: eye, see, spy 4 ecce (L.), espy, gaze, hold, keep, look, scan, stop, view, wait 5 sight, voila, watch 6 descry, regard, retain 7 discern, observe, witness 8 consider, maintain, perceive

beholden: 7 obliged 8 indebted

behoof: use **6** profit **7** benefit **8** interest **9** advantage

behoove: dow, fit **4** need, suit **5** befit, ought **6** belong, proper **7** require **8** suitable **9** incumbent

---

Belgium: **7** Flemish, Walloon
  artist: **5** Bouts **6** Massys, Rubens **7** Bruegel, Gossart, Mabusse, Memling, Patinir, Van Dyck, Van Eyck **8** Gossaert, Magritte, van Cleve **12** van der Weyden
  author: **11** Maeterlinck
  canal: **5** Union **6** Albert **7** Campine
  capital: **8** Brussels **9** Bruxelles
  city: Ans, Huy, Spa **4** Gand, Mons **5** Alost, Ciney, Eupen, Ghent, Ieper, Jumet, Liege, Namur, Ypres **6** Bruges, Brugge, Deurne, Lierre, Ostend, Turnai **7** Antwerp, Berchem, Herstal, Hoboken, Ixelles, Louvain, Malmedy, Mechlin, Muscron, Roulers, Seraing **8** Bastogne, Courtrai, Turnhout, Verviers, Waterloo
  commune: Ath, Ely, Hal, Mol, Spa **4** Aath, Boom, Geel, Genk, Lier, Niel, Roux, Zele **5** Aalst, Evere, Genck, Halle, Jette, Ronse, Uccle, Ukkel
  composer: **6** Franck (Cesar)
  dog: **7** griffon **9** Brabancon
  forest: **8** Ardennes
  Gaul tribe: **4** Remi **6** Belgae, Nervii
  geographer: **8** Mercator
  king: **6** Albert **7** Leopold **8** Baudouin
  lowland: **7** polders
  marble: **5** rance
  measure: vat **4** aune, last, pied **5** carat **6** perche **8** boisseau
  mountain: **8** Botrange
  people: **7** Fleming, Walloon
  port: **4** Gent **5** Ghent **6** Brugge, Ostend **7** Antwerp
  province: **5** Liege, Namur **7** Antwerp, Brabant, Hainaut, Limburg **8** Flanders **9** Luxemburg
  queen: **7** Fabiola
  region: **7** Campine, Famenne **8** Ardennes **10** Kempenland
  river: Lys **4** Dyle, Leie, Maas, Yser **5** Demer, Dijle, Lesse, Meuse, Nethe, Rupel, Senne **6** Dender, Ourthe, Sambre **7** Ambieve, Schelde, Scheldt
  tribe: **9** Bellovaci
  violinist: **5** Ysaye
  weight: **4** last **5** carat, livre, pound **6** charge **7** chariot **8** esterlin

---

beige: tan **4** ecru **5** color, grege (F.) **10** unbleached

Beijing (Peking): *square:* **9** Tienanmen
  alley: **6** hutong

being: ens **4** etre (F.), self **5** entia, gnome, human, thing, troll **6** animal, entity, extant, living, mortal, person **7** because, essence, present, reality **8** creature, ontology, standing **9** actuality, existence **11** subsistence **12** constitution
  abstract: ens **5** entia
  actual: **4** esse
  celestial: **5** angel **6** cherub, seraph **8** divinity
  in front: **6** anteal
  physiological: **4** bion
  science of: **8** ontology

Bela's son: Ard, Iri **4** Uzzi **5** Ezbon

Bel's wife: **5** Belit **6** Beltis

belabor, belabour: ply **4** beat, drub, lash, work **6** assail, batter, buffet, cudgel, hammer, hamper, rehash, repeat, thrash, thwack **7** dwell on

---

Belize: *bay:* **8** Amatique
  capital: **8** Belmopan
  city: **7** Corozal **10** Belize City, Punta Gorda
  district: **4** Cayo **6** Belize, Toledo **7** Corozal **10** Orange Walk, Stann Creek
  gulf: **8** Honduras
  mountain: **4** Maya **8** Victoria
  people: **4** Maya **5** Carib **6** Creole **7** mestizo **8** Garifuna
  river: New **5** Sibun **6** Belize

Belarus: (see box)

belated: **5** tardy **7** delayed, overdue **12** old-fashioned

belay: **4** stop **5** beset, cease **6** invest, secure, waylay **7** besiege **8** encircle

belaying pin: **5** kevel **7** bollard

belch: **4** boke, bolk, burp, galp, rasp **5** eruct **8** eructate **10** eructation

beldam, beldame: hag **4** fury **5** crone, jixen **6** Alecto, Erinys, virago **7** Jezebel **8** ancestor **9** Tisiphone **11** grandmother

beleaguer: **5** belay, beset **6** invest **7** assault, besiege **8** blockade, surround **9** encompass

belfry: **4** shed **5** tower **7** clocher **9** campanile

Belgium: (see box)

Belial: **5** devil, Satan

belie: **4** hide **6** belong, defame **7** besiege, falsify, pertain, slander, traduce **8** disguise, negative, strumpet, surround **9** encompass **10** calumniate, contradict, contravene **11** counterfeit **12** misrepresent

belief: fay, ism **4** mind, sect, view **5** credo, creed, dogma, faith, tenet, troth, trust **6** credit **7** opinion **8** credence, doctrine, reliance, religion **9** assurance, certainty, principle **10** confidence, conviction, persuasion
liable to: **7** credent **9** credulous

believe: buy, wis **4** deem, trow, ween **5** judge, think, trust **6** accept, credit **7** suppose, swallow **8** accredit, consider, credence

believer: ist **8** adherent, advocate, disciple, partisan
in all religions: **6** omnist
in God: **5** deist **6** theist
in predestination: **13** particularist

Belili's brother: **6** Tammuz

belittle: **5** decry, dwarf, sneer **6** slight **7** detract **8** minimize **9** criticize, denigrate, discredit, disparage **10** depreciate **13** underestimate

Belize: (see box)

bell: **4** call, fair, gong, peal, ring, roar, toll **5** chime, cloak, codon, flare, knell, swell **6** bellow, bubble (Sc.), crotal, curfew, tocsin **7** blossom, campana, campane, corolla **8** carillon **9** beautiful **13** tintinnabulum
alarm: **6** tocsin
axle bearing: cod
clapper: **6** tongue
kind of: **4** door, gong, hand **5** ship's **6** church, jingle, school **8** electric
ringer: **6** sexton, toller **12** carillonneur
ringer of fiction: **9** Quasimodo
shaped: **10** campanular **11** campanulate
sound: **4** ding, dong, toll **5** knell **6** tinkle
tower: **6** belfry **9** campanile

belladonna: **5** dwale, plant **6** remedy **7** manicon **8** narcotic **9** dwayberry **10** nightshade
extract: **7** atropin **8** atropine

bellbird: **6** shrike **8** arapunga

bellboy: **4** page **6** porter, redcap

bell ear: **6** cannon

Bellerophon: *father:* **7** Glaucus
horse: **7** Pegasus
spring: **7** Pelrene
victim: **7** Chimera

belles-lettres (F.): **10** literature

Bell for Adano author: **6** Hersey

bell, book, and candle: **15** excommunication

bellicose: mad **5** irate **7** hostile, warlike **8** militant **10** pugnacious **11** belligerent

belligerent: hot **7** hostile, warlike **8** choleric, fighting, jingoist **9** bellicose, combative, irascible, litigious, wrangling **10** pugnacious **11** contentious, hot-tempered, quarrelsome **12** antagonistic, disputatious

Bellini: *opera:* **5** Norma **8** Il Pirata **9** I Puritani **12** La Sonnambula
sleepwalker: **5** Amina

bellow: cry, low, moo, yap **4** bawl, beal, bell, roar, rout, yaup, yawp **5** belve, blart, croon, roust (Sc.), shout **6** buller, clamor **7** bluster, ululate **10** vociferate

bellwether: **5** sheep **6** leader

belly: bag, cod, gie (Sc.), gut, pod **4** bouk, kyte (Sc.) **5** bingy, bulge, pleon, tummy **6** hunger, paunch **7** abdomen, stomach **8** appetite

belong: fit, set **4** bear, vest **5** apply, belie **6** inhere, relate **7** pertain **9** appertain

belongings: **4** gear **5** goods, traps **6** assets, estate **7** effects **8** chattels, property **9** household **10** appendages **11** possessions **13** appurtenances

beloved: **4** dear, idol **5** cheri (F.) **6** adored, cherie (F.) **7** darling, dearest **8** precious **9** boy friend, inamorata, valentine **10** girl friend, sweetheart

below: **4** down **5** infra, sotto (It.), under **7** beneath **8** downward, inferior **10** downstairs, underneath

belt: **4** area, band, beat, blow, cest, faja, gird, mark, ring, sash, zone **5** cinch, girth, strap, strip, tract, whack, zonar **6** bodice, cestus, cingle, fettle, girdle, invest, region, strait, stripe, zonnar, zonule **7** baldric, circuit, passage **8** ceinture, cincture, encircle, surround **9** bandoleer, encompass **10** cummerbund
conveyor: **5** apron
ecclesiastical: **7** baldric, balteus **8** baldrick, baltheus
non-Muslim: **5** zonar

belted: **6** zonate **7** girdled **9** cinctured

bema: **4** pace, step **7** chancel

bemired: **5** dirty, muddy, stuck **10** bogged down

bemoan: rue **4** wail **6** bewail, grieve, lament, regret, sorrow **7** deplore

bemuse: **5** addle **7** confuse **8** distract

bench: bar, pew **4** banc, seat **5** board, judge, ledge, stool **6** settee **7** discard
church: pew, pue **6** sedile (L.)

bench hook: **5** clamp

benchmark: **5** gauge, model **7** measure **8** standard **13** comparison aid

bend: bow, nid, ply, sag **4** arch, flex, kink, turn **5** angle, baton, bulge, crimp, crook, curve, stoop, twist **6** buckle, cotice, cotise, crouch, direct, divert, fasten, inflex, submit **7** bendlet, incline, refract **9** genuflect
backward: **6** retort
in timber: sny

bender: leg **5** binge, drunk, spree **7** whopper **8** guzzling, sixpence

---

Benin: *capital:* **9** Porto Novo
city: **6** Abomey, Ouidah **7** Parakou **10** Natitingou
clothing: **6** agbade
former inhabitants: Edo **4** Bini
former name: **7** Dahomey
gulf: **6** Guinea
leader: **5** Soglo **7** Kerekou
mountain: **7** Atakora
people: Fon **4** Adja, Mahi **6** Bariba **7** Yorubas
port: **7** Cotonou
province: Zou **4** Mono **5** Queme **6** Borgou **7** Atakora **10** Atlantique
river: **4** Mono **5** Niger

---

bending: **5** lithe **6** pliant, supple **7** anfract, crooked, flexion **8** flection
beneath: **5** below, lower, under **11** underground
Benedictine: **4** monk **7** Cluniac, liqueur
title: dom
benediction: **4** amen **5** grace **6** prayer **7** benison **8** approval, blessing **10** invocation
benefaction: **4** alms, boon, gift **5** grant **7** charity, present **8** donation, gratuity **11** approbation
benefactor: **5** agent, angel, donor **6** friend, helper, patron, savior **8** promoter **14** philanthropist
beneficience: **6** bounty **7** charity **8** donation, goodness, kindness
beneficial: **4** good **6** useful **7** helpful **8** salutary **9** desirable, enjoyable, favorable, healthful, lucrative, wholesome **10** profitable, salubrious **11** serviceable **12** advantageous, remunerative
beneficiary: **4** heir, user **5** donee **6** vassal **7** heiress, legatee **9** feudatory
benefit: **4** aid, use **6** boon, boot, gain, gift, help, prow, sake **5** avail, boost **6** assist, behalf, behoof, better, profit, usance **7** advance, bespeak, concert, deserve, improve, service, utility, welfare **8** befriend, interest **9** advantage, charity do, emolument **11** performance **12** contribute to
benevolent: **4** good, kind **6** benign, loving **7** amiable, liberal **8** generous **10** altruistic, charitable, munificent **13** philanthropic, tenderhearted
benign: **4** boon, good, kind, mild **5** bland **6** genial, gentle **7** affable **8** benedict, gra-

cious, harmless, salutary **9** benignant, favorable, wholesome **10** benevolent, charitable, favourable, propitious, salubrious
Benin: (see box)
benison: **8** blessing **9** beatitude **10** invocation **11** benediction
Benjamin: *descendant:* **4** Aher
grandson: Iri
son: Ehi **4** Gera, Rosh
benne: **6** sesame
bent: aim, bow, set **4** bias, gift, turn **5** bound, bowed, crank, crump, flair, knack, prone, taste, trend **6** akimbo, biased, braced, courbe, course, curved, energy, genius, hooked, swayed, talent **7** crooked, curvant, decided, flexion, flexure, impetus, leaning, leveled, pronate, purpose, stooped, tension **8** aptitude, declined, flection, penchant, tendency **9** curvature, direction, prejudice **10** determined, proclivity, propensity **11** disposition, inclination **13** prepossession **14** predisposition
benthonic plant: **6** enalid
benthos: **5** fauna, flora
benumb: nip **4** daze, dunt, numb, stun **5** daver (Sc.) **6** cumber, deaden **7** fretish, fretize, stupefy
benzine derivative: **6** phenol
Beowulf: **4** epic, poem
monster: **7** Grendel
bequeath: **4** give, will **5** endow, leave, offer **6** bestow, commit, demise, devise, legate, quethe **7** bequest, commend **8** hand down, transmit **9** testament
bequest: **4** gift, will **6** legacy **8** bequeath, heritage, pittance **9** endowment
berate: jaw, nag **4** lash, rail **5** abuse, chide, scold, score **6** revile **7** censure, reprove, upbraid **8** chastise **10** vituperate
Berber: **4** Moor **6** Hamite, Kabyle **7** Haratin
chief: **4** caid, qaid
dialect: **6** Tuareg
empire: **7** Almohad **9** Almoravid
tribe: **4** Daza, Riff, Tibu **6** Tuareg
bereave: rob **5** strip **6** divest, sadden **7** deprive, despoil **10** dispossess
bereft: orb **4** lorn, lost, poor **6** robbed **7** forlorn **8** bereaved **9** destitute **12** dispossessed
beret: cap, hat, tam **7** biretta, chapeau **8** birretta, chapeaux (pl.), headgear
berg: ice **4** floe **6** barrow **8** eminence, mountain
bergamot: **4** bose, mint, pear **5** snuff **6** citrus, orange **7** Bergama, essence, Monarda, perfume
Berlin: *boulevard:* **14** Kurfurstendamm, Unter den Linden
districts: **6** Dahlem **9** Grunewald **12** Hansa Quarter

gate: 11 Brandenburg
park: 10 Tiergarten
river: 5 Havel, Spree
berm, berme: 4 bank, edge, path 5 ledge, shelf 7 terrace
Bermuda: 11 archipelago 12 coral islands
capital: 8 Hamilton
discoverer: 8 Bermudez (Juan de)
former name: 13 Somers Islands
parish: 5 Paget 6 Sandys, Smiths 7 Warwick 8 Hamilton, Pembroke 9 St. George's 10 Devonshire 11 Southampton
pond: 10 Devils Hole
port: 8 Freeport, Hamilton, St. George
Bermuda cedar: 7 juniper
Bermuda grass: 4 doob
Bermuda Triangle: 6 Devils
boundaries: 7 Bermuda 9 Melbourne (FL) 10 Puerto Rico
berretta: See **biretta**
berry: bay, dew, haw 4 beat, cran, lime, rasp 5 acini, bacca, black, fruit, goose, grape, guava, mound, salal, savin 6 acinus, baccae, banana, burrow, lingon, orange, pepper, sabine, thresh, tomato 7 currant, hillock 9 muskmelon, tangerine 10 watermelon
disease: 8 bluestem
medicinal: 5 cubeb
berry-like: 7 baccate
berserk: mad 5 bravo 6 pirate 7 enraged, warrior 8 frenzied, maniacal
berth: bed, job 4 bunk, dock, slip 5 place, wharf 6 billet, office 7 lodging, mooring 8 position 9 anchorage, situation 11 appointment
bertha: 4 cape 6 cannon, collar
beryl: gem 5 jewel 7 emerald 10 aquamarine
green: 11 davidsonite
yellow: 8 heliodor
beseech: ask, beg, sue 4 pray 5 crave, plead 6 adjure, appeal, obtest 7 entreat, implore, solicit 9 impetrate, obsecrate 10 supplicate
beseeching: 9 precative
beset: ply 4 sail, stud 5 allot, belay, harry, siege, spend 6 assail, attack, harass, infest 7 arrange, bejewel, besiege, perplex 8 blockade, encumber, obstruct, surround 9 beleaguer
beside: by 4 hear 5 along, aside 6 next to 7 abreast 8 adjacent
comb. form: 4 para 5 juxta
besides: by, and, but, too, yet 4 also, else, over, then 6 beyond, except, withal 8 moreover 10 additional 11 furthermore
besiege: 4 gird, girt 5 belay, belie, beset, siege, storm 6 attack, invest, pester, plague 7 solicit 8 blockade, surround 9 beleaguer

besmirch: 4 soil 5 smear, sully, taint 7 asperse, blacken 8 discolor
besom: mop 4 drab (Sc.) 5 broom, erica, heath, sweep 6 sloven (Sc.) 7 heather
besot: 4 dull 6 muddle, stupid 7 stupefy 8 befuddle 9 infatuate
besotted: 5 drunk 8 enamored 10 infatuated
bespangle: dot 4 star, stud 5 adorn 8 sprinkle
bespatter: 4 blot, dash, soil, spot 5 muddy, plash, stain, sully 6 malign, sparge 7 asperse, scatter 8 reproach, sprinkle
bespeak: ask 4 cite, hint, show 5 argue, imply, order, speak 6 accost, attest, engage, steven 7 address, arrange, benefit, betoken, discuss, exclaim, reserve 8 foretell, indicate, put in for 9 stipulate
best: ace 4 a-one, beat, most, oner, pick, tops, wale 5 cream, elite, excel, worst 6 choice, defeat, finest, flower, outwit, utmost 7 conquer, largest, optimum, paragon, surpass 8 greatest, nonesuch, outmatch, outstrip, peerless, vanquish 9 excellent, nonpareil, overmatch 11 superlative
bestial: low 4 vile, wild 5 feral 6 brutal, filthy 7 brutish, inhuman 8 depraved
bestir: 5 rouse
bestow: add, put, use 4 deal, dote, give 5 allot, allow, apply, award, beset, grant, lodge, place 6 accord, beteem, confer, demise, devote, divide, donate, employ, entail, extend, harbor, impart, render 7 collate, dispose, instate, present, quarter, tribute 8 bequeath 11 communicate
bestride: 5 mount 6 stride 8 straddle
bet: lay, pot 4 ante, gage, play, plot, risk, wage 5 hedge, stake, wager 6 gamble, pledge
broker: 6 bookie 9 bookmaker
fail to pay: 5 welch, welsh
faro: 7 sleeper
horse racing: 6 exacta 7 pick six 8 perfecta, quinella, quiniela
roulette: bas 4 noir 5 carre, rouge 6 milieu 7 dernier, encarre, enplein
betake: hie 4 move 5 apply, catch, grant 6 assume, commit, remove, repair, resort 7 commend, journey
bete noire: 4 bane, hate 5 dread 6 terror 7 bugaboo, bugbear 10 black beast 11 abomination
betel: 4 ikmo, itmo, siri 6 pupulo
leaf: pan 4 buyo
betel palm: 5 areca
extract: 7 catechu
masticatory: pan 4 buyo
Betelgeuse: 4 star
bethel: 6 chapel 9 sanctuary
Bethesda: 4 pool 6 chapel
bethink: 5 think 6 devise, recall 7 reflect 8 consider, remember 9 recollect 10 deliberate

Bethlehemite: 4 Boaz
Beth's sister: Jo, Amy, Meg
Bethuel's son: 5 Laban
betide: hap 5 befit, occur, trite 6 become, befall, chance, happen 7 betoken, presage
betimes: 4 anon, rath, soon 5 early, rathe 8 speedily 9 forthwith, sometimes 10 seasonably 11 prematurely 12 occasionally
betise: 5 folly 9 silliness, stupidity
betoken: 4 mark, note, show 5 augur 6 assert, betide, denote, evince, import 7 bespeak, express, oblique, portend, presage, signify 8 forebode, foreshow, indicate 9 symbolize 10 foreshadow 13 prognosticate
betray: 4 blab, blow, boil, gull, sell, sile, sing, tell, undo, wray 5 peach, snare, spill 6 accuse, delude, descry, reveal, seduce, snitch, squeal, turn in 7 beguile, deceive, falsify, mislead, sell out 8 disclose, discover 11 double-cross
betrayer: rat 5 Judas, skunk 7 seducer, traitor 8 derelict, informer
betroth: 4 affy 6 assure, engage, ensure, pledge, plight 7 espouse, promise 8 affiance, contract, handfast
better: aid, top 4 good, mend, more 5 amend, emend, excel, safer, wiser 6 bigger, choice, exceed, reform 7 advance, choicer, correct, greater, improve, promote, rectify, relieve, support, surpass 8 increase, superior 9 desirable, meliorate, upper hand 10 ameliorate, preferable
better half: 4 wife 6 spouse
betting: *adviser:* 4 tout
between: 4 amid 5 amell, among, entre (F.) 7 average, betwixt 12 intermediate
   law: 5 mesne
between the lines: 6 latent, secret
bevel: 4 blow (Sc.), cant, edge, push (Sc.) 5 angle, bezel, miter, mitre, slant, slope 6 aslant 7 chamfer, incline, oblique 8 diagonal
   corners: 5 splay
   end of timber: 5 snape
   out: 4 ream
beverage: ade, ale, nog, pop, tea 4 beer, grog, mead, milk, soda, wine 5 cider, cocoa, draft, drink, juice, lager, leban, morat, negus, punch, treat, water 6 coffee, eggnog, liquid, liquor, nectar, posset 7 cordial, potable, spirits 8 cocktail, libation, potation 9 metheglin 10 melicratum
   alcoholic: See **alcoholic drink**
   container: vat 5 flask 6 kettle 7 canteen, charger 9 separator
   extract: 4 kola
   malted wheat: 6 zythem, zythum
   mixed: 5 negus, punch, smash 6 bishop
   mulberry and honey: 5 morat

   Oriental: rak 4 sake 5 rakee 6 arrack
   pepper: 4 kava
   Polynesian: 4 kava
   South American: 4 mate 9 yerba mate
bevy: 4 herd, pack 5 covey, drove, flock, group, swarm 6 flight, school 7 company 8 assembly 9 gathering, multitude 10 collection

Bhutan: *animal:* yak
   assembly: 7 Tsongdu
   butter: 4 ghee
   capital: 6 Thimbu 7 Thimphu
   city: 12 Phuntsholing
   currency: 5 paise, rupee 7 chetrum 8 ngultrum
   district: 4 Daga, Paro 6 Mongar, Samchi, Tongsa, Wangdi 7 Chhukha, Chirang, Punakha, Thimphu 8 Bumthang, Lhuntshi, Phodrang, Shemgang 9 dzongkhag, Tashigang 10 Geylegphug, Pemegatsel 15 Samdrup Jongkhar
   first king: 5 Ugyen
   language: 6 Nepali 8 Dzongkha
   leader: 4 king 5 Dorji 6 Singye 9 Wangchuck
   monastery, fortified: 5 dzong
   people: 5 Bhote 6 Lepcha
   plain: 4 Duar
   river: 4 Kuru 5 Torsa 7 Bumtang, Sankosh, Wong Chu

bewail: cry, rue 4 keen, moan, sigh, wail, weep 5 mourn 6 bemoan, grieve, lament, plaint, sorrow 7 deplore 8 complain
beware: 4 cave, heed, shun 5 avoid, spend 6 eschew 7 look out, warning 8 take care, watch out
bewilder: fog 4 daze, foil, gaum 5 abash, addle, amaze, amuse, deave 6 baffle, bemist, bother, dazzle, fuddle, muddle, puzzle 7 buffalo, confuse, mystify, perplex, stagger, stupefy 8 astonish, confound, distract, entangle, surprise 9 embarrass, obfuscate 10 spifflicate 11 spifflicate
bewildered: 4 asea, lost, mang 5 agape, dazed 8 confused, helpless 9 perplexed
bewilderment: awe, fog 4 daze 9 amazement, confusion 10 perplexity
bewitch: hex 5 charm, fasci, spell, trick 6 enamor, entice, glamor, grigri, hoodoo, thrill, voodoo 7 attract, bedevil, delight, enchant, glamour 8 ensorcel, forspeak, greegree 9 captivate, ensorcell, fascinate
Beyle's penname: 8 Stendhal
beyond: 4 free, over, past 5 above, after,

aside, forby, ultra **6** forbye, yonder **7**
besides, further, outside **8** superior **9** hereafter **10** too deep for
the sea: **11** ultramarine
the threshold: **12** ultraliminal
bezel, basil: rim **4** edge, ouch, seal **5** bevil,
crown, facet **6** chaton, flange **8** template
bhagavat: **7** blessed
bhakta: **7** devotee **9** worshiper
bhalu: **4** bear
bhang, bang: **4** hemp **5** ramie **7** hashish **8**
narcotic **9** marijuana **10** intoxicant
product of: **6** majoon
bhangi: **6** mehtar **7** sweeper **9** scavenger
bharal: tur **5** sheep **6** nahoor
bhat: **4** bard **8** minstrel
bhikku, bhikshu: **4** monk **5** friar **6** priest **7**
ascetic **9** mendicant
bhoosa: **5** chaff, husks, straw
b'hoy: **5** rowdy **8** gangster
bhut: **5** demon, ghost **6** goblin, spirit
Bhutan: (see box)
bias: **4** awry, bent, sway **5** amiss, color, slant,
slope **7** bigotry, incline, leaning, oblique **8**
clinamen, diagonal, tendency **9** clinamina
(pl.), prejudice, procedure **10** favoritism,
partiality, prepossess, propensity **11** declination, disposition, favouritism, inclination
12 predetermine, predilection **13** prepossession
biased: **6** warped **7** partial **8** one-sided **9** jaundiced **10** prejudiced **11** tendentious
bib: sip **4** brat, fish **5** apron, drink **6** tipple,
tucker **7** bavette (F.) **9** neckpiece **10** protection
bibelot: **5** curio **7** trinket **8** ornament **9** objet
d'art (F.) **10** knickknack
Bible: (see box)
Bible society: **6** Gideon
Biblical: **10** scriptural
bicker: war **4** bowl, spar, tiff **5** argue, brawl,
cavil, fight **6** assail, attack, battle, rattle **7**
contend, dispute, quarrel, wrangle **8** pettifog, skirmish, squabble **10** contention
bicycle: **4** bike **5** wheel **10** two-wheeler
for two: **6** tandem
rider: **7** cyclist
ten-speed: **10** derailleur
bid: beg **4** call, hist, pray **5** clepe, offer, order
6 adjure, charge, direct, enjoin, invite,
reveal, summon, tender **7** command,
declare, entreat, proffer, request **8**
announce, proclaim, proposal
biddable: **6** docile **8** obedient
biddy: hen **7** chicken
bide: **4** face, stay, wait **5** abide, await, dwell,
tarry **6** endure, remain, reside, suffer **7**
sojourn **8** continue, tolerate **9** encounter,
withstand

bidonville: **10** shantytown
bier: **4** pyre **5** frame, grave **6** coffin, hearse,
litter **7** support **10** catafalque, handbarrow
biff: **4** blow **6** strike
bifid: **6** forked
bifocal: **4** lens
bifold: **6** double **7** twofold
bifurcation: wye **4** fork **5** split **6** branch **8**
division
big: **4** bold, huge, vast **5** bulky, chief, grand,
great, gross, hefty, large **6** mighty **7** bumping, eminent, leading, massive, pompous,
violent **8** boastful, bouncing, enormous, generous, gigantic, imposing, pregnant **9** notorious **10** tremendous **11** magnanimous, outstanding, pretentious, threatening
shot: VIP **5** mogul, titan, wheel **6** tycoon **7**
notable **8** brass hat **9** celebrity **11** heavy-
weight **13** high-muck-a-muck
Big Dipper: *constellation:* **9** Ursa Major
star: **5** Alcor, Dubhe, Merak, Mizar **6**
Alioth, Alkoid, Megrez, Phecda
bigener: **4** mule **6** hybrid
bigfoot: **4** omah **9** sasquatch
bighorn: **5** sheep **6** aoudad, argali **8** cimarron
bight: bay **4** bend, coil, gulf, loop **5** angle,
curve, inlet, noose **6** corner, hollow
bignou, biniou: **7** bagpipe
bigot: **6** cafard, racist, zealot **7** fanatic **9** hypocrite
bigoted: **6** biased, narrow **9** hidebound, illiberal, sectarian **10** intolerant, prejudiced **12**
narrow-minded
big toe: **6** hallux
bijou: **5** jewel **7** trinket
bile: **4** boil, gall, hump **5** venom **6** choler,
growth
bilge: **4** scum **5** bouge, bulge **8** nonsense
bilingual: **6** diglot
bilk: gyp **4** balk, hoax **5** cheat, cozen, dodge,
shake, trick **6** delude, escape, fleece **7**
deceive, defraud, swindle **9** frustrate **10**
disappoint
bill: act, dun, law, neb, nib, tab **4** beak, note,
peck, rise **5** libel, score, visor **6** caress,
charge, indict, pecker, pickax, poster, strike
7 invoice, lampoon, mattock, placard,
statute **8** billhook, document, headland,
petition **9** memoranda (pl.), reckoning,
statement **10** broadsword, memorandum,
promontory **13** advertisement
anchor: pee
five dollar: fin, vee
one dollar: **4** buck **8** frogskin
ten dollar: **7** sawbuck
billet: bar, gad, job, log **4** bunk, loop, note,
pass, post **5** berth, enrol, house, lodge,
order, put up, stick, strap **6** ballot, canton,
enroll, harbor, letter, notice, ticket **7** bear-

Bible (see also **apostle**): *angel:* **5** Micah **7** Gabriel, Raphael
animal: **4** reem **5** daman **6** hydrax **8** behemoth **9** leviathan
apocrypha: Bel **5** Tobit **6** Baruch, Daniel, Esdras, Esther, Jeremy, Judith, Syriac, Wisdom **7** Azariah, Susanna **8** Jeremiah, Manasses **9** Maccabees **14** Ecclesiasticus
ascetic order: **6** Essene
battle scene: **10** Armageddon
betrayer: **5** Judas **7** Delilah
book: Job **4** Acts, Amos, Ezra, Joel, John, Jude, Luke, Mark, Osee, Ruth **5** Abdia, Aggai, Hosea, James, Jonah, Josue, Kings, Micah, Nahum, Peter, Titus **6** Baruch, Daniel, Esdras, Esther, Exodus, Haggai, Isaiah, Joshua, Judges, Michea, Psalms, Romans, Samuel, Sirach **7** Ezekiel, Genesis, Habacuc, Hebrews, Malachi, Matthew, Numbers, Obadiah, Timothy **8** Habakkuk, Jeremiah, Malachia, Nehemiah, Philemon, Proverbs, Sophonia **9** Ephesians, Galatians, Leviticus, Machabees, Zechariah, Zephaniah **10** Chronicles, Colossians, Revelation **11** Corinthians, Deuteronomy, Philippians, Song of Songs **12** Ecclesiastes, Lamentations **13** Paralipomenon, Song of Solomon, Thessalonians
character: see *name* below
charioteer: **4** Jehu
city: Ain, Dan **4** Arad, Aven, Cana, Elim, Elon, Gath, Gaza, Geba, Maon, Rome, Tyre, Zoar **5** Akkad, Arvad, Ashur, Assur, Jaffa, Joppa, Petra, Sidon, Sodom **6** Bethel, Biblos, Emmaus, Gadara, Jerico, Tarsus **7** Babylon, Bethany, Nineveh, Samaria **8** Gomorrah, Nazareth **9** Beersheba, Bethlehem, Bethsaida, Jerusalem
clan: **6** Shelah
country: Nod, Pul **4** Aram, Bela, Edam, Elam, Gath, Hali, Moab, Seba, Seir **5** Ammon, Judah **6** Canaan, Israel **7** Galilee, Samaria
currency: **4** beka, mina **5** bekah, daric, gerah, pound **6** shekel, talent **7** drachma **8** denarius
desert: **5** Sinai
first five books: **5** Torah **10** Pentateuch
garden: **4** Eden **8** Paradise **10** Gethsemane
giant: **4** Anak, Emim **7** Goliath
giant killer: **5** David
group: **6** Essene, Scribe **8** Herodian, Pharisee, Sadducee **10** Messianist
hill: **4** Zion

hunter: **6** Nimrod
judge: **4** Agog, Elon **6** Gideon, Samson **8** Jephthah
king: Asa, Gog, Iva **4** Agag, Ahab, Ahaz, Amon, Bera, Jehu, Omri, Reba, Saul **5** David, Herod, Hiram, Joram, Nadab, Rezin, Tidal, Zimri **6** Birsha, Hezion, Japhia, Jotham, Uzziah **7** Jehoram, Solomon
kingdom: **4** Elam, Moab **5** Judah, Judea **6** Israel **8** Chaldeae
land of plenty: **6** Goshen
liar: **7** Ananias
measure: hin, kab, kor, log **4** bath, omer, seah **5** ephah, homer
mountain: Hor **4** Ebal, Nebo, Peor, Sina, Sion, Zion **5** Heres, Horeb, Sinai, Tabor **6** Ararat, Carmel, Gilead, Moriah, Olivet, Pisgah
name: Ahi, Asa, Eri, Eve, Evi, Hor, Iri, Koa, Lot, Ner, Ono, Reu, Toi, Uel, Uri **4** Abel, Acan, Acub, Adam, Ader, Adna, Ador, Agee, Aher, Aman, Anak, Anam, Aner, Aram, Arem, Arie, Asan, Asom, Ater, Aven, Azal, Cain, Cana, Dura, Edar, Edec, Edes, Eker, Enan, Enos, Eran, Esau, Etam, Gera, Irad, Iram, Isac, Mary, Neri, Obal, Omar, Oreb, Oren, Paul, Reba, Sami, Sara, Seth, Suba, Ucal, Vale **5** Ahlab, Alian, Amasa, Aroer, Bedan, Besai, Caleb, Elias, Ephai, Esrom, Hadad, Hanes, Isaac, Mered, Nahum, Oseas, Peleg, Rahad, Tarah, Vania **6** Naaman, Pilate, Ramath **7** Abadias, Abigail, Antioch, Elmodam, Idithum, Sidrach, Tabitha
navigator: **4** Noah
Old Testament version: **10** Septuagint
ornament: **4** urim **7** thummin
patriarch: Noe, Reu **4** Adam, Ezra, Noah, Saul, Seth, Shem **5** Aaron, David, Isaac, Jacob, Jacob, Josue, Moses, Nahor, Peleg **6** Gideon, Israel, Lamech, Samuel **7** Abraham, Solomon **8** Nehemiah
people: **4** Moab, Phut, Seba **5** Ammon **6** Hamite, Hivite, Kenite, Levite **7** Amorite, Dodanim, Moabite
plain: **4** Maab **5** Mamre **7** Jericho
plotter: **5** Haman
poem: **5** psalm **8** canticle
pool: **6** Siloam
priest: Eli **5** Aaron **6** Levite
pronoun: thy **4** thee, thou **5** thine
prophet: **4** Amos, Ezra, Joel, Osee **5** Abdia, Elias, Hosea, Jonah, Micah, Nahum **6** Daniel, Elijah, Haggai, Isaiah *(cont.)*

Bible (*cont.*)
   7 Ezekial 8 Jeremiah, Malachia, Sophonia, Zacharia, Zephania
   queen: Abi 5 Sheba 6 Esther, Vashti 7 Jezebel
   region: 4 Enon 5 Ophir, Perea 6 Bashan
   reproach: 4 raca
   river: Zab 4 Nile 5 Abana, Arnon 6 Jordan, Kishon
   ruler: see *king* above
   sacred place: 10 tabernacle
   scholar: 7 Biblist 9 Biblicist
   sea: Red 4 Dead 7 Galilee 8 Tiberias 10 Gennesaret
   shepherd: 4 Abel 5 David

   spice: 5 myrrh 6 cassia, stacte 12 frankincense
   spy: 5 Caleb
   stone: 4 ezel 6 ligure
   strong man: 6 Samson
   tower: 4 Edar 5 Babel
   town: see *city* above
   tree: 5 cedar
   tribe: see *people* above
   valley: 4 Baca, Elah 6 Shaveh, Siddim
   version: 4 Geez 5 Douay, Itala 6 Geneva, Syriac 7 Bishops, Vulgate 8 Bohairic 9 King James 10 New English, Septuagint 15 Revised Standard
   weed: 4 tare
   witch's home: 5 Endor

ing, epistle, harbour, lodging, missive, pollack, quarter 8 coalfish, document, firewood, ornament, position, quarters 11 appointment, requisition
billet-doux: 8 mash note 10 love letter
billiards: 4 game, pool 5 carom 7 snooker
   player's turn: 6 inning
   play to open: lag 6 string
   shot: run 4 miss 5 break, carom, masse 6 cannon 7 bricole, cushion, scratch
   stick: cue
   term: 4 rack, spot 5 chalk 6 bridge, pocket 7 cue ball, English 8 balkline, rotation 9 eight ball 10 object ball 12 straight-rail
billibi: 10 mussel soup
   relative: 12 bouillabaise
billingsgate: 5 abuse 7 obloquy 8 ribaldry 12 vituperation
bill of fare: 4 card, menu 5 carte
billow: sea 4 wave 5 bulge, float, surge, swell 6 ripple, roller 7 breaker 8 undulate
billowing: 5 tidal 7 surging
billy: caw 4 chap, club, goat, mate 6 cudgel, fellow 7 brother, comrade 8 billikin, bludgeon 9 blackjack
billycock: 5 derby 6 bowler
bin: ark, box, cub 4 bing, cart, crib, vina 5 frame, hutch, pungi, stall, store, wagon 6 basket, bunker, hamper, manger, trough, within 9 container 10 receptacle
   coal: 6 bunker
   fish: 5 canch, kench
binary: 6 double, hybrid 7 twofold
binate: 4 dual 6 double, paired 7 coupled, twofold
bind: jam, tie 4 gird, hold, tape 5 stick 6 cement, fetter, secure 7 confine 9 constrict, indenture, make stick 11 predicament

   tightly: 4 frap
   to secrecy: 4 tile, tyle
   wings of a bird: 5 truss 6 pinion, skewer
binder: 4 band, beam, bond, cord, rope 5 baler, cover, frame, lever 6 fillet, folder, girder, header 9 bondstone
binding: 4 band, cord, rope, tape 5 valid 6 edging, ribbon 7 galloon, mousing, webbing 9 stringent 10 astringent, obligatory 11 restraining, restrictive
   limp: 4 yapp
bindle stiff: 4 hobo 5 tramp 8 vagabond
binge: bat, bow, hit 4 blow, bust, soak, toot 5 beano, drunk, party, spree 6 bender, cringe 7 indulge 8 carousal 9 obeisance (Sc.) 10 indulgence
bingo: 4 game, keno 5 lotto 6 brandy
biniou: See **bignou**
bioclean: 7 aseptic 8 germ-free
biography: 4 life, vita (It.) 6 memoir 7 account, history, memoire (F.), recount
   saint's: 11 hagiography
biological class: 5 genus, order, phyla (pl.) 6 family, genera (pl.), phylum 7 species
bionomics: 7 ecology
biota: 13 flora and fauna
biotic community: 5 biome
biotite: 4 mica 7 anomite
birch: 4 cane, flog, tree, whip 5 canoe 6 betula 7 hickory
bird: ani, auk, daw, nun, pie, tit 4 avis (L.), crow, hawk, kite, lark, ruff, tern, wren 5 brant, egret, finch, hobby, pewee, pewit, quail, raven, robin, snipe, terek, vireo 6 bulbul, condor, dipper, dunlin, falcon, hoopoe, linnet, magpie, marten, mocker, oriole, phoebe, plover, shrike, thrush 7 bluejay, bustard, buzzard, catbird, flicker,

halcyon, irrisor, jackdaw, kinglet, ortolan, peacock, redwing, skylark, sparrow, swallow, tanager, warbler, waxwing **8** airplane, bluebird, boatbill, bobolink, bobwhite, chicadee, grosbeak, kingbird, pheasant, redstart, starling, thrasher **9** blackbird, blackcock, brambling, bullfinch, goldfinch, partridge, phalarope, ptarmigan, sandpiper **10** bufflehead, flycatcher, meadowlark, roadrunner, tropicbird, woodpecker **11** butcherbird, hummingbird **12** yellowhammer **13** whooping crane

adjutant: **5** stork **6** argala **7** hurgila, marabou

African: **4** taha **6** cuckoo, quelea **7** touraco **8** shoebill, umbrette **9** secretary **10** weaverbird

American: **4** sora **5** robin, vireo **6** darter, fulmar, turkey **7** grackle, tanager **8** cardinal **10** bufflehead

Antarctic: **4** skua **5** booby **6** petrel **7** penguin **11** frigatebird

aquatic: **4** duck, gull, loon, swan, tern **5** goose, grebe, small, terne **7** penguin **8** dabchick, flamingo

aquiline: **5** eagle

Arabian Nights: roc

Arctic: auk **4** tern **6** fulmar, jaeger, plover **9** phalarope

Asiatic: **4** mine, myna **5** monal, pitta **7** hilltit **8** dotterel, hornbill **9** brambling, feng-huang, fenghwang, fruit dove

Attic: **11** nightingale

Australian: emu, roa **4** emeu, kiwi, lory, nene, wren **5** arara **6** leipoa **7** boobook, bustard, waybung **8** bellbird, lorikeet, lyrebird, manucode **9** cassowary, coachwhip, friarbird, pardalote **10** kookaburra **11** butcherbird

black: ani, ano, daw, pie **4** crow **5** merle, raven **6** oriole **7** jackdaw **8** starling

brilliant plumage: **4** tody **5** jalep **6** oriole, trogon **7** jacamar, tanager **8** pheasant

Central American: daw **4** crow, rave, rook **5** raven **6** magpie **7** corvine, jacamar, quetzal **8** puffbird

crane-like: **5** wader **6** chunga

crocodile: **9** trochilus

crow-family: daw, jay, pie **4** craw **5** raven **6** magpie **7** jackdaw

crying: **6** ramage **7** limpkin

diving: auk **4** loon **5** grebe

dressing of feathers: **5** preen

emu-like: **9** cassowary

European: ani, daw, emu, mew, qua **4** cirl, darr, emeu, gled, kite, mall, moro, osel, rook, stag, whim, yite **5** amsel, boonk, glede, mavis, merle, ousel, ouzel, sacer, saker, serin, stork, tarin, terek, terin, whaup

6 avocet, avoset, cushat, gaylag, godwit, linnet, loriot, marten, merlin, missel, redcap, whewer, windle, winnel, wranny **7** bittern, bustard, harrier, haybird, kestrel, motacil, ortolan, sakeret, starnel, wagtail, whiskey, winnard, witwall **8** bargoose, bee-eater, chepster, dotterel, garganey, redstart, wheybird, whimbrel, wrannock, yoldring **9** brambling, gallinule, goldfinch, goosander, peregrine, swinepipe, wheybeard **10** chiffchaff, lammegeyer, turtledove, whitterick **11** capercailie, lammergeier, nightingale **12** capercailzie

extinct: moa **4** dodo, jibi, mamo **7** offbird

finch-like: **7** chewink, tanager

fish-catching: **6** osprey **9** cormorant

flightless: emu, moa **4** dodo, emeu, kiwi, rhea **7** apteryx, ostrich, penguin, ratitae **9** cassowary, solitaire

fly-catching: **8** redstart **9** solitaire

flying backwards: **7** humming, swallow

food: hen **5** capon **6** pullet, turkey **7** chicken, rooster

frigate: ioa, iwa **6** tropic

gallinaceous: **6** peahen **7** peacock, peafowl

game: **5** quail, snipe **6** grouse, turkey **8** curassow, pheasant, woodcock **9** merganser

genus: **4** alca, crax, otis **7** certhia **9** apatornis

gull-like: **4** tern **6** jaeger

Hawaiian: ava, ioa, iwa **4** iiwi, koae, mamo, moho, nene **7** apapane **12** honeycreeper

heron family: **4** benu, ibis **5** egret **7** bittern

honey eater: **4** moho

humming: ava **5** carib **7** colibri

insectivorous: owl **5** vireo

jay: gae **6** magpie

large: emu **4** emeu, guan, rhea **5** eagle **6** curlew, willet **7** bustard, megapod, ostrich, pelican, seriema **8** curassow, shoebill **11** lammergeier

largest: **7** ostrich

lark-like: **5** pipit

long-billed: **5** snipe **7** pelican

long-legged: io **4** sora **5** heron, snipe, stilt, wader **6** avocet, avoset, curlew **7** seriema **8** flamingo

long-necked: **4** swan **5** agami, crane, geese (pl.), goose, stork **7** anhinga, ostrich

male: cob, tom **4** cock **5** drake **6** gander **7** peacock, rooster **11** chanticleer

marsh: **4** sora **5** snipe, stilt

meadow: **8** bobolink

Mexican: **6** jacana, towhee **7** jacamar

mythological: roc **5** hansa **6** simurg **7** phoenix, simurgh

New Zealand: kea, moa **4** kaka, kiwi, kulu, ruru, titi, weka **6** kakapo **7** apterix, apteryx **8** morepork, notornis **10** blightbird

nonpasserine: **4** tody **6** hoopoe, motmot **8**

hornbill **10** kingfisher
Northern: auk **6** gannet, puffin
of Athena: owl
of Juno: **7** peacock
of paradise: **8** manucode
of peace: **4** dove
of prey: owl **4** hawk, kite **5** eagle, elant, owlet **6** eaglet, elanet **7** goshawk, vulture **9** accipeter
of Zeus: **5** eagle
oldest known: **13** archaeopteryx
oscine: **4** chat **6** dronge, oriole **7** tanager
ostrich-like: emu, moa **4** emeu, rhea **10** cassowarie
parrot-like: **4** lory **8** parakeet **11** budgeree-gah, budggerygah
parson: poe, tue, tui
parts of body: neb, nib **4** bill, cere, crop, knee, lora, mala **5** lores **6** covert, pecten, pileum, pinion, rostra, syrinx **7** ambiens **8** pectines (pl.), scapular
passerine: **5** finch **7** sparrow, starnel **9** chat-terer, coachwhip
pert. to: **5** avian, avine **8** ornithic **9** volu-crine
pink: **8** flamingo
plover-like: **5** drome **7** lapwing
Poe's: **5** raven
predatory: owl **4** kite **5** yager **6** falcon, shrike **9** cormorant
protuberance at base of bill: **4** cere
rare: **8** rara avis
ratite: emu, moa **4** emeu **7** ostrich **9** cas-sowary
red-tailed: **4** koae
sacred: **4** ibis
sea: auk, ern **4** erne, gony, gull, skua, smew, tern **5** eider, murre, solan **6** gannet, petrel, puffin **7** pelagic, pelican **9** albatross **10** shearwater, tropicbird
shore: ree **4** rail, sora **5** snipe, stilt, wader **6** avocet, avoset, curlew, plover, willet
Sindbad's: roc **4** rock, rukh
singing: **4** lark, wren **5** finch, mavis, robin, shama, veery, vireo **6** canary, linnet, mocker, oriole, oscine, thrush **7** mocking, robinet **8** bobolink, redstart **12** whippoor-will
small: tit **4** tody, wren **5** dicky, pipit, vireo **6** dickey, linnet, siskin, todies (pl.), tomtit **7** creeper, humming, sparrow, titlark, wheater **8** starling **9** didappers
South American: **4** guan, ibis, mina, myna **5** chaja, macaw, mynah **6** barbet, becard, shrike, toucan **7** cariama, oilbird **8** bellbird, boatbill, caracara, curassow, guacharo, hoactzin, puffbird
swallow-like: **4** cran **5** swift
swimming: **4** loon **5** grebe

talking: **4** crow, mina, mino, myna **5** mynah **6** parrot
tall: **6** avocet, avoset
tropical: ani **4** koae, tody **6** barbet, motmot, toucan, trogon
underwater: **6** dipper
unfledged: gor **4** eyas **6** gorlin **8** bubbling, nestling
Vishnu's: **6** Garuda
wading: **4** ibis, rail, sora **5** crane, heron, snipe, stilt, stork **6** avocet, jacana **8** flamingo, shoebill **9** sandpiper, spoonbill
web-footed: **4** duck, loon, swan **5** drake, goose, grebe **6** avocet, avoset, gander, wigeon **7** anhinga, pelican, skimmer **8** flamingo **9** snakebird
West Indies: ani **4** tody
white-tailed: ern **4** erne **5** egret
woodcock: **5** pewee
young: eya **4** gull **5** piper **7** flapper, nestler **8** birdikin, nestling **9** fledgling
bird cage: **6** aviary, pinjra, volary, volery **7** paddock
bird clapper: **9** scarecrow
bird crest: **4** tuft
bird eye: **12** cuckoo flower
birdman (see also **pilot**): **5** pilot **6** airman **7** aviator **13** ornithologist
bird nest: **4** aery, eyry **5** aerie, eyrie
bird of passage: **8** wanderer **9** transient
bird route: **6** flyway
birds: **4** aves
collective: **4** fowl
domesticated: **7** poultry
bird's-eye view: **6** apercu
bird-witted: **5** giddy
birdwoman: **5** pilot **8** aviatrix **9** aviatress, avi-atrice **13** ornithologist
biretta, berretta: cap **5** beret **8** skullcap **13** clergyman's cap
biri: **9** cigarette
birl: **4** spin, toss, whir **5** whirr **6** rattle, rotate **7** revolve
birma: **6** calaba
birr: bur **4** blow, burr, push, rush, wind **5** force, storm, vigor **6** energy, onrush, thrust **7** impetus
birth: **4** bear **5** onset, start **6** burden, origin, spring **7** descent, genesis, lineage **8** ances-try, delivery, geniture, nascency, nativity **9** beginning, naissance, parentage **10** extrac-tion
after: **9** postnatal
assists at: **7** midwife **10** accoucheur **12** obstetrician
before: **8** prenatal
born as: nee
goddess: **5** Parca
lying-in: **12** accouchement

new: **10** renascence **11** Renaissance
nobleness: **6** eugeny
pert. to: **5** natal **13** primogenitive
birth control: **7** the pill **9** diaphragm, vasectomy **10** spermicide **13** contraception
   leader: **5** Baird **6** Sanger
birthday: **11** anniversary, celebration
   ode: **12** genethliacon
   pert. to: **10** genethliac **12** genethliacal
birth flower: *April:* **5** daisy
   August: **9** gladiolus
   December: **10** poinsettia
   February: **8** primrose
   January: **9** carnation
   July: **8** sweet pea
   June: **4** rose
   March: **6** violet
   May: **15** lily of the valley
   November: **13** chrysanthemum
   October: **6** dahlia
   September: **5** aster
birthmark: **4** mole **5** naeve, nevus **6** naveus **7** blemish, feature, spiloma **13** port-wine stain **14** characteristic
   pert. to: **7** naevoid
birthplace: **10** incunabula (pl.;L.) **11** incunabulum (L.)
birthrate: **8** natality
birthright: **8** heritage
birth stone: *April:* **7** diamond **8** sapphire
   August: **7** peridot **8** sardonyx **9** carnelian
   December: **6** zircon **9** turquoise
   February: **8** amethyst
   January: **6** garnet
   July: **4** ruby
   June: **5** agate, pearl **9** moonstone **11** alexandrite
   March: **6** jasper **10** aquamarine, bloodstone
   May: **7** emerald
   November: **5** topaz
   October: **4** opal **5** beryl **10** tourmaline
   September: **8** sapphire **10** chrysolite
bis: **5** again, twice **6** encore, repeat **7** replica **9** duplicate
biscuit: bun **4** bake (Sc.), roll, rush, snap **5** scone, wafer **6** cookie **7** cracker, pentile, pretzel **8** hardtack **9** porcelain **11** earthenware
bisect: **4** fork **5** cross, halve, split **6** cleave, divide **8** separate
bisexual: **13** hermaphrodite
bishop (see also *ecclesiastic*): **4** bird, pope **5** angel **6** archer, bustle, priest **7** pontiff, prelate, primate **8** beverage, director, overseer **9** clergyman, inspector **13** administrator **14** superintendent
   apron: **7** gremial
   assistant: **6** verger **9** coadjutor

buskin: **6** caliga **7** caligae (pl.)
cap: **4** hura **5** miter, mitre **7** biretta **8** berretta, mitrella
first year revenue: **5** annat **6** annate
jurisdiction: see **bishopric, diocese, episcopate, episcopacy**
private room: **9** accubitus
robe: **6** chimar, chimer **7** chimere
staff: **7** crosier
stave: **6** baculi (pl.) **7** baculus
throne: **4** apse **8** cathedra
title: **4** abba, anba **7** prelate, primate
vestment: alb **4** cope **6** chimer, rochet **7** gremial, tunicle **8** dalmatic **10** omophorion **11** epigonation, epimanikion
bishop's weed: **4** ammi **6** ammeos **8** bolewort, goutweed
bison: **6** bovine **7** aurochs, bonasus, buffalo
bisque: **4** soup, turn **5** china, color, point **8** ceramics, ice cream
bistro: bar **4** cafe **6** tavern **9** nightclub **10** restaurant
bisulcate: **6** cloven
bit: ace, end, jot, ort, wee **4** atom, bite, curb, doit, food, iota, item, mite, mote, part, snap, tool, whit **5** blade, check, crumb, drill, pezzo, piece, scrap, shred, speck, while **6** bridle, cannon, eating, morsel, smidge, splice, tittle, trifle **7** morceau (F.), portion, scatche, smidgen, smidgin, smigeon, snaffle **8** fraction, fragment, particle, quantity, restrain, smitchin, victuals **9** restraint
   horse's curb: **6** pelham
   Irish: **7** traneen
bit by bit: **9** gradually
bite: bit, cut, eat, nip **4** bait, cham, chew, food, gash, gnap, gnaw, hold, knap, meal, snap **5** chack, chamm, champ, cheat, chomp, pinch, seize, share, smart, snack, sting, trick **6** crunch, morsel, nibble, pierce **7** cheater, corrode, impress, partake, sharper, slander **8** lacerate, puncture, victuals **9** denticate, masticate
bite one's tongue: rue **6** regret
bite the bullet: **8** face up to **10** meet head-on **14** do it regardless
biting: **4** acid, hoar, keen **5** acrid, sharp, snell **6** bitter, rodent, severe **7** caustic, cutting, mordant, nipping, pungent **8** clear-cut, incisive, poignant, scathing, stinging **9** corrosive, sarcastic, trenchant, vitriolic
biting dragon: **8** tarragon
biting of nails: **12** phaneromania
bito: **4** balm, tree **7** hajilij
   oil: **6** zachun
bit part: **5** cameo **6** walk-on
bitt: **4** post **5** block
bitter: bad **4** acid, bask, gall, keen, sore, sour,

tart **5** acerb, acrid, amara, bleak, harsh, irate, sharp **6** biting, picric, severe **7** austere, caustic, crabbed, cutting, galling, hostile, painful, pungent, satiric **8** grievous, poignant, stinging, virulent **9** malicious, offensive **10** afflictive **11** acrimonious, distressful **12** antagonistic

bitter apple: **9** colocynth

bitter bush: **9** snakeroot

bitter-ender: **7** diehard

bitter gentian: **9** baldmoney

bitter grass: **9** colicroot

bitterly: **4** hard, sour **8** cursedly

bittern: **4** bump **5** boonk, heron, least **6** kakkak

bitterness: rue **4** acor, bile, fell, gall **5** atter **6** enmity, malice, rancor **7** amarity **8** acerbity, acrimony, severity **9** amaritude, hostility, poignancy, virulence **11** malevolence

bitter oak: **6** cerris

bitters: **4** amer (F.) **5** tonic **6** liquor **7** gentian **8** camomile, cinchona **9** Angostura
pert. to: **9** amaroidal

bitter spar: **8** dolomite

bittersweet: **7** climber **10** confection, nightshade

bitter vetch: ers **5** vicia

bitterweed: **7** ragweed **9** horseweed **10** sneezeweed

bitter wintergreen: **10** pipsissewa

bitterwort: **7** felwort **9** dandelion

bitumen: tar **5** pitch **7** asphalt, naphtha **8** alkitran **9** alchitran, elaterite, petroleum

bivalve: **4** clam, spat **6** cockle, diatom, mussel, oyster **7** mollusk, Pandora, scallop **9** brachipod
genus: **5** pinna **6** anomia **7** toheroa **12** gastrochaena

bivocal: **9** diphthong

bivouac: **4** camp **5** etape, watch **6** encamp **7** shelter **10** encampment

biwa: **6** loquat

bizarre: odd **5** antic, dedal, outre, queer **6** quaint **7** curious, strange **8** fanciful **9** eccentric, fantastic, grotesque **10** ridiculous **11** extravagant

Bizet opera: **6** Carmen

blab: **4** chat **5** blart, blate, clack **6** babble, betray, gossip, reveal, tattle **7** blabber, chatter **8** telltale

black: jet **4** calo, dark, ebon, evil, foul, inky, onyx **5** dirty, dusky, ebony, murky, Negro, noire (F.), raven, sable, slate, sooty **6** atrous, dismal, gloomy, pitchy, sullen **7** melanic, Negrito, piceous, swarthy, unclean **8** charcoal, mournful **9** atrocious **10** blackamoor, calamitous, forbidding
and white: **11** chiaroscuro

black and blue: **5** livid

spot: **6** bruise, shiner **10** ecchymosis

black art: **5** magic **7** alchemy **8** wizardry **10** necromancy **11** conjuration

blackball: **4** pill, veto **6** ballot **7** boycott, exclude, heeball **9** ostracize

blackberry: **6** agawam **8** dewberry

blackbird: ani, daw, pie **4** crow, merl **5** amsel, colly, merle, ousel, ouzel, raven **6** colley **7** jackdaw

blackboard: **5** slate

blackcap: **4** gull **7** warbler **8** chicadee, titmouse **9** raspberry

black cod: **6** beshow **9** sablefish

blackdamp: **9** chokedamp

black death: **6** plague

black diamond: oil **4** coal **8** hematite

black earth: **4** mold **9** chernozem

black elder: **9** hackberry

blacken: ink, tar **4** char, soot **5** bleck, cloud, japan, sully **6** darken, defame, malign, vilify **7** asperse, slander, traduce **8** besmirch **10** calumniate

black eye: **5** mouse, shame **6** bruise, shiner, stigma **7** scandal **9** contusion

black-eyed Susan: **5** daisy **6** ketmia **9** Rudbeckia **10** coneflower

blackface: **5** actor, comic, sheep **8** boldface, minstrel

blackfin: **4** fish **5** cisco, sesis

blackfish: **5** whale **6** tautog **10** nigrescent
school: **5** grind

black grunt: **10** tripletail

blackguard: **4** shag **5** devil, gamin, guard, rogue, scamp, snuff **6** rascal **7** vagrant, villain **8** criminal, hanger-on, vagabond **9** scoundrel

blackhead: **4** clam **6** comedo, mussel

black hole: **4** cell **7** dungeon **8** solitary **13** collapsed star

blackjack: oak **4** club, duck, flag, game, jack **5** billy **6** beetle, jerkin, vessel, weapon **7** tankard

blackleg: **4** scab, snob **7** disease, gambler **8** apostate, swindler **13** strikebreaker

blacklist: ban, bar **4** shun, veto

blackmail: **5** bribe **6** coerce, extort **7** payment, tribute

blackmailer: **5** ghoul **7** leecher

blackmailing: **8** chantage **9** extortion

Blackmore heroine: **10** Lorna Doone

blackout: **5** faint **6** darken **8** darkness, scrounge **11** suppression

black plague: **7** bubonic

Black Sea: *ancient name:* **6** Pontus **13** Pontus Euxinus
arms: **9** Sea of Azov **12** Sea of Marmara
connecting straits: **5** Kerch **8** Bosporus **11** Dardanelles
peninsula: **6** Crimea

ports: **5** Varna **6** Batumi, Burgas, Odessa, Samsun **7** Trabzon **9** Constanta **10** Sevastopol

river to: Bug, Don **4** Rion **5** Kuban, Rioni **6** Danube **7** Dnieper, Sakarya **8** Dniester

black sheep: **7** deviate **9** reprobate

blacksmith: gow **5** shoer, smith **6** plover, smithy, stithy **7** farrier, striker **10** horseshoer

shop: **5** anvil, stith **6** smithy, stithy **8** smithery

blacksnake: **4** whip **5** quirt, racer

blackthorn: haw **4** sloe, tree

black widow: **6** spider **7** pokomoo

blackwort: **7** comfrey

bladder: sac **7** blister, inflate, vesicle
comb. form: **4** asco

blade: bit, fop, oar **4** blow, bone, edge, leaf, shiv **5** blood, dandy, fluke, grain, knife, spark, spear, spire, sword **6** cutter, lamina, scythe, sickle **7** gallant, laminae (pl.), scapula **9** propeller

blague: lie **4** hoax **6** humbug **8** claptrap, nonsense, raillery

blah: **4** bunk, dull **8** nonsense

blahs: **5** dumps, ennui **7** boredom, malaise **8** doldrums

Blake's symbol: **4** Zoas

blamable: **6** faulty **8** culpable **11** blameworthy **13** reprehensible

blame: **4** call, hurt, onus, twit **5** chide, fault, guilt, odium, shend **6** accuse, charge, dirdum, impute, rebuke, revile, scance **7** ascribe, censure, condemn, obloquy, reproof, reprove, upbraid **8** reproach **9** challenge, criticism, inculpate, liability **10** accusation **11** culpability, reprobation **12** reprehension **13** animadversion
deserving: **8** culpable

blameless: **4** good **7** perfect **8** innocent, spotless **9** faultless, righteous **13** unimpeachable **14** irreproachable

blanch: **4** fade, pale **5** chalk, scald, white **6** argent, bleach, blench, whiten **8** etiolate **9** whitewash

bland: **4** kind, mild, oily, open, soft **5** suave **6** benign, genial, gentle, smooth, urbane **7** affable, amiable, insipid, lenient **8** gracious **9** benignant, courteous **10** wishy-washy **11** good-natured **12** ingratiating

blandish: **4** coax **5** charm **6** allure, blanch, cajole **7** beguile, flatter, wheedle **10** compliment

blank: **4** bare, flan, form, shot, void **5** annul, blind, break, clean, empty, range, space **6** vacant **7** nonplus, unmixed, vacuous **8** omission, unfilled **9** colorless, downright, fruitless, frustrate

blanket: **4** brot, wrap **5** cotta, cover, layer, manta, quilt, sheet, throw **6** afghan, poncho, serape **8** coverlet **10** barraclade
cowboy: **5** sugan **6** soogan, sougan, sugann
goat's hair: **6** cumbly
horse: **5** manta
Indian: **6** stroud

blare: **4** peal **5** blast, blaze, noise **6** blazon, scream **7** fanfare, tantara, trumpet **11** flamboyance

blarney: **4** coax **5** stone **6** butter, cajole **7** flatter, wheedle **8** flattery, soft soap

blasé: **5** bored, jaded, sated, weary **8** satiated **9** surfeited **11** indifferent

blasphemy: **7** calumny, cursing, impiety **8** anathema, swearing **9** profanity, sacrilege **10** execration **11** imprecation, irreverence, malediction **12** vilification

blast: bub, nip, wap **4** bang, blow, gale, gust, ruin, wind **5** party, split, stunt **6** attack, blight, wither **7** blowout, bluster, explode, shatter, shindig, shrivel **8** dynamite, outburst, proclaim **9** criticize, discharge, explosion **10** detonation

blast furnace: *lower part:* **4** bosh
nozzle: **6** tuyere

blat: **5** bleat, blurt **7** exclaim

blatant: **4** glib, loud **5** gaudy, gross, noisy, silly, vocal **6** coarse, vulgar **8** brawling **9** bellowing, clamorous, inelegant, obtrusive, shameless **10** vociferous

blather: **4** stir **5** bleat **6** babble **7** blither, prattle **8** nonsense **9** commotion

blaubok: **5** etaac **8** antelope

blaze: **4** burn, fire, glow, mark, shot **5** flame, flare, flash, glare, gleam, glory, shine, torch **6** bleeze **7** bonfire, declare, pioneer, sparkle **8** splendor **9** firebrand **10** effulgence, illuminate **11** coruscation **13** conflagration

blazer: **6** jacket

blazon: **4** deck, show **5** adorn, blare, boast **6** depict, shield **7** declare, display, exhibit, publish **8** emblazon, inscribe **9** delineate, embellish **11** description, publication **14** representation

bleach: sun **5** chalk **6** blanch, blench, chlore, purify, whiten **7** decolor, lighten **8** etiolate

bleachers: **5** seats, stand **8** scaffold **10** grandstand

bleaching vat: **4** keir, kier

bleak: dim, raw **4** blae, blay, cold, gray, grim, pale **5** sprat **6** bitter, bleach, dismal, dreary, frigid, gloomy, pallid **7** cutting **8** desolate, **9** cheerless **10** depressing
fish: **4** blay, bley **5** sprat

blear: dim **4** blur, dull **5** faint **6** darken **7** deceive, mislead **8** hoodwink, protrude

bleared: **4** inky **5** dusky **6** rheumy

bleat: baa **4** blat, blea **5** blart, gripe **7** blather, bluster, whicker

bleb: 4 blob 5 bulla 6 bubble 7 blister, pustule, vesicle 8 swelling

bleed: 4 flow, leak, shed 5 exude 6 escape, extort, fleece 7 agonize 9 blackmail

bleeding heart: 8 dicentra

blemish: mar 4 blot, blur, dent, flaw, gall, lack, mark, rift, scar, slur, spot, vice, want, wart 5 blame, breck, crack, fault, mulct, speck, sully, tache, taint 6 blotch, breach, defame, defect, impair, injure, macula, macule, smirch, stigma 7 blister, default, failing, fissure, maculae (pl.) 8 pockmark 9 birthmark, deformity, discredit, disfigure 10 defacement, deficiency 12 imperfection 13 disfigurement
wood: 4 mote
wound: 4 scar 8 cicatrix 9 cicatrice

blend: mix 4 blot, fuse, join, meng 5 blind, cream, merge, shade, spoil, stain, tinge, unite 6 commix, dazzle, mingle 7 combine, confuse, corrupt, deceive, mixture, pollute 8 coalesce, tincture 9 admixture, associate, commingle, harmonize, integrate 10 amalgamate 11 incorporate

blended: 5 fondu, mixed 6 merged 7 mingled 9 confluent

blesbok: 5 nunni 8 antelope

bless: 4 keep, sain, wave 5 adore, anele, bensh (Yid.), extol, favor, guard, thank, wound 6 favour, hallow, praise, thrash 7 approve, beatify, glorify, protect 8 dedicate, macarize, preserve, sanctify 10 consecrate, felicitate

blessed: 4 holy 5 happy 6 divine, joyful, sacred 8 benedict, bhagavat, blissful, hallowed 9 beatified, benedight 11 consecrated

blessing: 4 boon, gift 5 bliss, grace 6 praise 7 benison, worship 8 felicity 9 beatitude 10 benedicite, beneficent 11 benediction

blight: nip 4 ruin, rust, smut 5 blast, frost 6 mildew, wither 7 destroy 9 frustrate

blimp: 7 airship, balloon, Colonel 8 zeppelin 9 dirigible

blind: bet, pot 4 ante, dark, daze, dull, hood 5 blank, blend, decoy, dunch, front, shade, stake, wager 6 ambush, bisson, dazzle, screen, secret 7 aimless, bandage, benight, eclipse, execate, eyeless, obscure, pretext, shutter 8 abortive, artifice, bayardly, blinding, hoodwink, ignorant, involved, jalousie, outshine, purblind, unseeing 9 benighted, concealed, deceitful, defective, insensate, intricate, senseless, sightless 10 incomplete, misleading, subterfuge 11 intoxicated 12 shortsighted
as a hawk: 4 seel
part of: 4 slat
printing for: 7 braille

blind alley: 7 dead end, impasse 8 cul-de-sac

blind god: 4 Hoth 5 Hoder, Hothr

blind spot: 6 hang-up 7 bigotry

blind staggers: gid 7 vertigo

blind worm: 5 orvet

blinder: 4 flap 5 bluff 7 blinker 8 hoodwink 9 blindfold 11 obstruction

blindfold: 4 dark 5 blink, bluff 7 bandage, blinder, obscure 8 heedless, hoodwink, reckless 9 concealed

blindness: 6 bisson, cecity 7 ablepsy, anopsia 8 oblepsia 9 ignorance
color: 13 achromatopsia 14 monochromatism
day: 11 hemeralopia
partial: 7 meropia 10 cecutiency
snow: 13 chiona-blepsia

blink: 4 shun, wink 5 blush, cheat, flash, gleam, shine, trick 6 glance, ignore, obtuse 7 blinter, condone, flicker, glimmer, glimpse, neglect, nictate, sparkle, twinkle 9 blindfold
at: 7 condone 8 overlook
on the: 7 haywire 10 out of order, out of whack 11 in disrepair, inoperative

blinker: eye 5 bluff, light 6 signal 7 blinder, goggles 8 coquette, hoodwink, mackerel

blinking: 5 utter 6 damned 8 blooming, complete

blintze: 5 crepe 7 pancake

bliss: joy 4 Eden, kaif, seil (Sc.) 5 glory 6 heaven 7 delight, ecstasy, gladden, rapture 8 felicity, gladness, paradise, pleasure 9 happiness 11 contentment
place of: 4 Eden 6 Utopia 7 Elysium 8 Paradise

blissful: 4 holy 5 happy 6 blithe, elated 7 blessed, Elysian, Utopian 8 ecstatic, euphoric 9 beatified, glorified

blister: 4 beat, bleb, blob, lash 5 blain, bulge 6 bubble, scorch 7 vesicle 8 lambaste, vesicate 10 vesicatory

blithe: gay 4 glad 5 bonny, happy, jolly, merry 6 bonnie, jovial, joyous, lively 7 gaysome, jocular, winsome 8 cheerful, gladsome 9 sprightly

blitzkrieg: 4 raid 6 attack 11 bombardment 12 lightning war

blizzard: 4 blow, gale, wind 5 purga 6 retort 9 snowstorm, squelcher

bloat: 5 puffy, swell 6 expand, tumefy 7 distend, ferment, inflate 8 drunkard

bloated: 5 bloat, cured 6 sodden, turgid 7 pompous

blob: lip, wen 4 bleb, blot, boil, daub, drop, lump, mark, mass 6 bubble, pimple, splash 7 blemish, blister, blossom, globule, pustule, splotch 8 globular

bloc: 4 ring 5 cabal, party, union 6 cartel, clique 7 faction 11 combination

block: ame, bar, cob, dam, hob, nog, row, vol 4 bloc, cake, clog, cube, fill, foil, head, mass, stop 5 annex, check, chump, deter, nudge, parry, shape, spike, stump 6 hamper, hinder, impede, oppose, outwit, square, street, stymie, taplet, thwart 7 buckler, inhibit, outline, prevent 8 blockade, obstacle, obstruct, stoppage 9 barricade, blockhead, frustrate, hindrance, intercept 11 obstruction
architectural: 6 dentil, mutule
electrically insulated: 6 taplet
football: 4 clip
for shaping metal objects: ame
ice: 4 cube 5 serac
mechanical: 6 pulley
metal type: 4 quad, quod
nautical: 7 deadeye
perforated: nut
small: 7 tessera

blockade: bar, dam 5 beset, block, siege 6 whisky 7 embargo 8 obstruct 9 beleaguer, moonshine 11 obstruction, restriction

blockhead: ass, oaf 4 bust, coof, dolt, fool, mome 5 block, chump, cuddy, dunce, idiot, ninny 6 noodle 7 dizzard, halfwit, tomfool 8 beefhead, clodpate, gamphrel, hardhead 9 blockpate, grouthead, hoddy-peak, numbskull, screwball, simpleton 10 beetlehead, dunderhead, hoddy-doddy

blockhouse: 4 fort 8 garrison

bloke: guy, man 4 chap, toff 6 fellow 9 personage

blonde: 4 fair 5 light, straw 6 flaxen, golden, yellow 9 towheaded

blood: kin, sap 4 gore, life, mood, race 5 blade, fluid, serum, stock 6 claret, indred 7 gallant, kinship, kinsman, lineage, youstir (Sc.) 8 relation 9 lifeblood 14 consanguineous
cell: réd 5 white 8 hemocyte, monocyte 9 leukocyte 10 hemoglobin, lymphocyte 11 erythrocyte
clot: 7 embolus 8 thrombus
deficiency: 6 anemia 7 anaemia
disease: 8 leukemia
fluid part: 5 serum 6 plasma 7 opsonin
mixed: See **hybrid**
of the gods: 4 icor 5 ichor
particle in: 7 embolus
parts of: 4 cell 6 plasma 8 platelet
poisoning: 6 pyemia 7 pyaemia, toxemia 10 septicemia
pressure: 8 systolic 9 diastolic
serum: 6 plasma
stagnation: 4 clot 5 cruor, grume 6 stases, stasis
strain: 4 race 5 stock 6 family
testing instrument: 13 hemabarometer 14 haemabarometer

blood and thunder: 6 uproar 8 violence 9 melodrama 13 Sturm und Drang

bloodbath: 7 carnage 8 massacre 9 slaughter

blood brother: 6 friend 8 intimate

bloodcurdling: 4 gory 8 horrible 10 terrifying

blooded: 9 pedigreed 12 thoroughbred

blood feud: 8 vendetta

blood fine: cro (Sc.) 4 eric 7 galanas, wergild 9 bloodwite

bloodhound: 4 lyam, lyme

blood horse: 12 thoroughbred

bloodless: 4 dead, pale 6 anemic 7 anaemic, inhuman 8 lifeless 9 colorless, unfeeling 10 exsanguine

blood money: cro 7 breaghe 12 compensation

blood pudding: 7 sausage

blood relationship: 7 kinsman 8 relative 13 consanguinity

bloodroot: 7 puccoon 10 tetterwort

bloodshed: 5 death 7 carnage 8 violence 9 slaughter

bloodshot: red 8 inflamed

bloodstone: 10 chalcedony

bloodsucker: 5 leech 7 sponger, vampire 11 extortioner

bloodthirsty: 6 bloody, carnal 9 ferocious, homicidal, murderous 10 sanguinary

blood vessel (see also **blood**): 4 vein 5 hemad 6 artery, venule 9 arteriole, capillary
comb. form: vas
rupture: 6 rhexis

bloody: 4 gory, grim 5 cruel 6 cruent 7 imbrued 8 bleeding, hematose, infamous 9 cruentous, ferocious, haematose, merciless, murderous, red-handed 10 sanguinary 11 ensanguined 12 bloodstained, bloodthirsty, contemptible

bloom (see also **flower**): bar, dew 4 blow, film, glow, lump, slab 5 flush 7 blossom, blowing 8 floreate, flourish 13 efflorescence

bloomer: 5 error 6 blower 7 blunder, failure

blooming: 4 rosy 5 flush, fresh, green 6 abloom, damned, florid 7 healthy

blooper: 4 goof, slip 5 error, radio 7 blowing, blunder, faux pas, roseate 8 blinking 10 prospering

blossom (see also **flower**): bud 4 blob, blow, open 5 bloom 6 flower 7 burgeon, prosper 8 flourish 9 effloresce 13 efflorescence
small: 8 floweret

blot: mar 4 blob, blue, daub, flaw, soil, spot 5 blend, erase, smear, speck, stain, sully 6 blotch, cancel, damage, defect, efface, impair, macula, shadow, smirch, smudge, smutch, stigma 7 blemish, eclipse, expunge, maculae (pl.), obscure, tarnish 8 disgrace, reproach 9 bespatter 10 obliterate, stigmatize 12 obliteration 13 disfigurement *out:* **5** annul, erase **6** efface **7** abolish **10** annihilate, obliterate

blotch: dab **4** blot, gout, spot **5** patch, smear, stain **6** macula, mottle, smirch, stigma **7** blemish, maculae (pl.), pustule, splotch **8** eruption, maculate

blouse: **5** shell, shirt, smock, tunic **7** casaque, chemise **10** shirtwaist

bushman's: **5** bluey

blow: bob, cob, cop, dub, fan, jab, pat, rap, tap, wap **4** ande, baff, bang, bash, beat, belt, biff, birr, blad, blaw, brag, buff, bump, chap, conk, crig, cuff, daud, dint, dird, drub, dunt, dush, fleg, gale, gowf, huff, jolt, knap, lash, mint, oner, pant, plug, puff, scud, slam, slap, slug, sock, wind **5** binge, blade, blast, blizz, bloom, boast, botch, break, brunt, burst, clink, clour, clout, clump, crump, curse, douse, dowse, filip, flack, flick, gowff, ictus, impel, knock, peise, shock, skite, slipe, sound, spend, storm, swipe, thump, treat, waste, whack, whang **6** bensel, bensil, betray, bounce, buffet, depart, dirdum, expand, fillip, flower, frolic, larrup, wallop **7** assault, attaint, bensail, bensall, bensell, blossom, blowout, bluster, boaster, destroy, inflate, publish, shatter, whample **8** boasting, calamity, confound, disaster, disclose **9** bastinado

in: **4** come **5** enter **6** arrive

mock: **5** feint

over: end **4** pass **7** subside

up: **4** bomb **5** scene **7** explode, inflate **8** dynamite, outburst

blow-by-blow: **8** detailed, itemized, thorough **10** particular

blower: fan **5** whale **6** puffer **7** bloomer **8** braggart **9** swellfish **11** sacheverell

blowfish: **6** puffer

blowfly: **10** bluebottle

blowgun: **10** peashooter

blowhard: **7** boaster **8** braggart

blowhole: **7** nostril **8** spiracle

blown: **5** stale, tired **6** opened **7** blossom, swollen, tainted **8** betrayed, flyblown, inflated **9** distended, exhausted, worthless

blowzy: **5** dowdy **6** frowzy **10** disheveled, slatternly

blub: **4** bulb **5** dwell **6** puffed **7** blubber, swollen

blubber: cry, fat **4** blub, foam, wail, weep **5** swell, thick, whine **6** bubble, flitch, medusa, nettle, seethe **7** blobber, bluster, swollen, whimper **9** disfigure

remove: **6** flense

whale: **5** fenks, speck **6** muktuk

blubbery: fat **5** obese **7** swollen **9** quivering **10** gelatinous **11** protuberant

bludgeon: bat, hit **4** club, mace **5** billy, stick **6** coerce, cudgel, weapon

blue: low, sad, sky **4** aqua, bice, cyan, glum, navy, teal **5** Alice, azure, Copen, livid, ocean, perse, small **6** cobalt, gloomy, indigo, marine, risqué, severe **7** celeste, gentian, learned, lobelia **8** cerulean, cynanine, dejected, downcast, electric, literary **9** turquoise **10** despondent, melancholy

asbestos: **11** crocidolite

gray: **5** merle, pearl, slate **7** cesious **8** caesious

green: **4** aqua, bice, teal **5** beryl **8** calamine **9** turquoise

red: **5** smalt **6** mallow **7** fuschia **8** gridelin, mazarine **9** gris-de-lin

sheep: **6** bharal

sky: **5** azure **8** cerulean

Bluebeard's wife: **6** Fatima

blue blood: **5** noble **9** gentleman **10** aristocrat **12** bluestocking

blue boneset: **4** Scot **6** lupine **10** cornflower, mistflower

bluebonnet: cap **4** Scot **7** bluecap **8** Scotsman **10** cornflower

bluebottle: **5** bluet **7** barbeau, blowfly **8** hyacinth

bluecap: **4** Scot **10** bluebonnet

blue catalpa: **9** paulownia

blue-chip: **5** solid **9** exemplary **11** prestigious

blue dandelion: **7** chicory

blue dye herb: **4** woad **6** indigo

Blue Eagle agency: NRA

blue earth: **10** kimberlite

bluefish: **4** bass, tuna **5** saury **8** weakfish

bluegill: **7** sunfish

Bluegrass State: **8** Kentucky

Blue Grotto site: **5** Capri (Italy)

blue gum: **4** tree **10** eucalyptus

Blue Hen State: **8** Delaware

blue huckleberry: **11** tangleberry

bluejacket: gob, tar **6** sailor

blue jaundice: **8** cyanosis

blue jeans: **5** Levis **6** denims

blue Joe: **8** bluegill

blue John: **4** milk

bluejoint: **6** redtop

Blue Law State: **11** Connecticut

bluenose: **4** boat, snob **5** prude **7** puritan **8** moralist **11** Nova Scotian

blue-pencil: **4** edit **6** delete, redact, revise

blue peter: **4** coot, flag **9** gallinule

bluepoint: **6** oyster

blueprint: map **4** plan, plot **5** chart, draft, trace **6** sketch **7** diagram, outline **8** game plan, strategy **9** cyanotype

bluer: **4** anil

blue-ribbon: top **4** best **6** Grade A **7** supreme **8** top-notch

blue rocket: 9 monkshood 10 delphinium

blues: 4 song 5 dumps 6 cafard, police 7 megrims, sadness 10 melancholy, mulligrubs 11 despondency

bluestocking: 5 woman 6 avocet, pedant 12 intellectual

bluet: 5 cloth, plant 9 Houstonia, innocence 10 bluebottle 11 farkleberry 12 quaker-ladies

bluethroat: 7 warbler

bluff: 4 bank, brag, curt, dupe, fool, rude 5 blunt, burly, cliff, frank, gruff, short, surly, trick 6 abrupt, assume, crusty, delude 7 blinder, blinker, brusque, deceive, uncivil 8 barranca, barranco, churlish, hoodwink, impolite 9 blindfold, outspoken, precipice 13 unceremonious

Bluff King Hal: 5 Henry

blunder: err, mix 4 balk, bull, flub, gaff, roil, slip, stir 5 boner, botch, break, error, fault, lapse, misdo 6 blotch, boggle, bumble, bungle, gazabo, gazebo, mingle, muddle, wallow 7 bloomer, confuse, derange, failure, faux pas, mistake, stumble 8 solecism 9 confusion, mismanage 11 disturbance

blunderbuss: gun 9 espingole 10 stumblebum

blunge: mix 5 blend 10 amalgamate

blunt: 4 bald, curt, damp, dull, flat 5 bluff, brusk, inert, plain, plump, stunt 6 clumsy, deaden, obtund, obtuse, stupid, weaken 7 brusque 8 hebetate 9 depressed, downright 10 point-blank 11 insensitive 13 unceremonious
mentally: 8 hebitate

blur: dim, hum 4 blob, blot, mist, soil, spot 5 blear, cloud, smear, stain, sully, taint 6 mackle, macule, smudge, stigma 7 blemish, confuse, obscure 9 disfigure

blurb: ad 4 puff, rove 5 brief 6 notice 7 writeup 10 commercial 12 announcement, commendation 13 advertisement

blush: 4 glow, look, rose 5 blink, color, flush, gleam, rouge, tinge 6 glance, mantle, redden 7 crimson 8 likeness 10 appearance, rubescence

blushing: red 4 rosy 5 ruddy 7 roseate 8 flushing 9 rosaceous 10 erubescent 11 embarrassed

bluster: 4 blow, huff, rage, rant, roar 5 blast, bleat, boast, bully, noise, storm, swank, swash 6 babble, bellow, bounce, hector, huffle, tumult 7 blubber, bravado, gauster, roister, swagger 8 boasting, bullying, threaten 9 confusion, gasconade 10 intimidate, swaggering, turbulence 11 fanfaronade, rodomontade

boa: 5 aboma, scarf, snake 6 giboia, python 8 anaconda 9 neckpiece 11 constrictor

Boadicea's people: 5 Iceni

boar: hog 4 aper, male 5 swine 6 barrow, hogget 8 sanglier 9 hoggaster
genus: sus
head: 4 hure
wound: 4 gore 5 ganch

board: 4 deal, diet, eats, fare, food, keep, lath, slat 5 enter, found, get on, house, lodge, meals, panel, plank, stage, table 6 accost, embark, planch, shield 7 cabinet, council, duoviri, emplane, enplane, entrain, planche 8 approach, tribunal 9 authority, shipboard 10 commission, management, provisions 11 switchboard 13 entertainment

boast: gab 4 blaw, blow, brag, crow, pomp, rave 5 brave, extol, exult, glory, prate, roose, scold, skite, vapor, vaunt 6 bounce, clamor, extoll, flaunt, menace (Sc.), outcry, splore 7 bluster, clamour, display, glorify, show off, swagger 8 flourish, threaten 9 gasconade 11 rodomontade

boaster: 5 skite 6 crower, gascon, pedant 7 bouncer, bravado, cracker, ruffler 8 blowhard, braggart, cacofogo, fanfaron, glorioso, jingoist, rodomont 9 cacafuego 11 braggadocio

boastful: big 6 parado 8 fanfaron 9 cock-a-hoop, gasconade, kompology 11 rodomontade, swellheaded, thrasonical

boat (see also **canoe, sailboat, ship, vessel**): ark, cat, cot, gig, tub, tug 4 bark, brig, carv, cory, junk, proa, raft, saic, scow, ship, skag, tack, trow, yawl 5 aviso, barca, barge, bully, canoe, coble, craft, dingy, ferry, ketch, knorr, liner, shell, skiff, skift, sloop, smack, xebec, yacht, zebec 6 baidak, bateau, carvel, chebec, cruise, cutter, dinghy, dugout, galley, garvey, packet, vessel, zebeck 7 chebeck, coracle, cruiser, gondola, lighter, nacelle, pinnace, scooter, steamer 8 pessoner, runabout, schooner, trimaran 9 houseboat, hydrofoil, submarine, transport 10 hydroplane, watercraft
Arab: 4 dhow
Chinese: 4 junk 6 sampan
coal cargo: 7 collier
deck: 4 poop 5 orlop
dispatch: 5 aviso
fishing: 8 bracozzo, skipjack
flat-bottomed: arc, bac 4 dory, keel, punt, scow 5 barge 6 bateau
freight: 7 lighter
front: bow 4 prow
garbage: 6 hopper
harbor: tug 5 barge 7 bumboat
Italian: 7 gondola
joint: 4 jerl
merchant: 6 argosy, holcad
military: LST 6 PT-boat

New Guinea: **7** lakatoi
ornamental: **9** navicella
part: bow **4** beam, deck, helm, hold, hull, keel, mast, prow **5** bilge, cabin, stern, wheel **6** bridge, galley, gunnel, kelson, rudder, saloon, thwart, tiller **7** capstan, gangway, gunwale, keelson **12** companionway
pin: **5** thole
post: poy **4** biff **7** bollard, capstan **9** sternpost
propellant: oar, row **4** pole, sail, wind **5** motor, scull **8** outboard
racing: gig **5** scull
ride: row **4** sail **6** cruise
round: **4** gufa **5** goofa **6** goofah
sailing: See **sailboat**
triple-hulled: **8** trimaran
twin-hulled: **9** catamaran
undersea: sub **9** submarine **11** submersible
Viking: **5** knorr
boatman: **5** poler **6** barger, Charon **7** hobbler, hoveler, huffler, oarsman, sculler **8** hoveller **9** gondolier **10** barcajuolo
boatswain: **5** bosun **6** serang
whistle: **4** pipe
Boaz: *son:* **4** Obed
wife: **4** Ruth
bob: bow, cut, dab, job, rap, tap **4** ball, blow, buff, calf, clip, coin, cork, duck, grub, jeer, jerk, jest, knob, mock, worm **5** bunch, cheat, dance, filch, float, flout, shake, taunt, trick **6** bingle, buffet, curtsy, delude, pommel, strike, weight **7** bobsled, bobtail, cluster, curtsey, haircut, pendant, refrain **8** shilling **9** bobsleigh
bobac: **6** marmot
bobber: **4** cork, duck **5** float **6** bobfly **7** dropper **8** deadhead
bobbery: row **4** fray **5** brawl, fight, melee **6** hubbub, tumult **8** squabble **9** commotion **11** disturbance
bobbie, bobby: cop **4** bull **6** copper, peeler **7** officer **9** policeman
bobbin: pin **4** cord, pirn, reel **5** braid, quill, spool **7** ratchet, spindle **8** cylinder **10** cuckoopint
frame: **5** creel
pin: **7** spindle
bobble: dib **4** mess **5** gum up **6** fumble
bobby: See **bobbie**
bobcat: **4** lynx
bobolink: **4** bird, reed **7** bunting, ortolan **10** butterbird
bobsled: bob **6** ripper
bobtail: bob, cur **4** dock **6** rabble, strunt (Sc.) **7** curtail **8** sheepdog **9** deficient **11** abbreviated
bobwhite: **4** bird **5** colin, quail **9** partridge
bocardo: **6** dokhma **7** bokardo

Boccaccio work: **9** Decameron
bode: **4** omen, stop **5** augur, offer **6** herald **7** message, portend, presage **8** forebode, forecast, foreshow, foretell, indicate **9** messenger **10** inaugurate **13** foreshadowing, prognosticate
bodice: **4** jupe **5** choli, gilet, waist **6** basque, corset
bodiless: **9** trunkless **10** immaterial **11** incorporeal
bodily: **5** solid **6** actual, carnal **7** fleshly, sensual, somatic **8** corporal, entirely, material, physical **9** corporeal **10** completely **11** corporeally, substantial
bodily motion: **5** shrug **7** gesture
boding: **7** ominous **9** foretoken **10** foreboding, prediction, prognostic
bodkin: awl, pin **6** dagger, needle **7** hairpin, poniard **8** stiletto **9** eyeleteer
body: **4** bole, bouk, bulk, form, mass, nave, rupa, soma, stem **5** flesh, group, stiff, torso, trunk **6** corpse, corpus, extent, licham, object, person **7** cadaver, carcass, company **8** extensum, majority **9** aggregate, curcurbit, substance **10** assemblage, foundation **11** association, corporation
anterior part of: **7** prosoma
armor: **4** tace **6** corium
away from center: **6** distal
cavity: **5** sinus **6** coelom, pelvis **7** coelome
fluid: **5** blood, lymph, serum **6** plasma, saliva
heavenly: sun **4** luna, moon, star **5** comet **6** meteor, planet **8** asteroid, luminary
joint: hip, jaw, toe **4** knee **5** ankle, elbow, wrist **7** knuckle **8** shoulder
of persons: **5** corps, posse
of water: bay, sea **4** gulf, lake, pond, pool **5** ocean **6** lagoon, sealet **9** reservoir
path: **5** orbit
pert. to: **5** somal **8** physical, systemic
wagon: box
wall: **6** paries, septum
bodyguard: **5** thane **6** escort **7** retinue, trabant **9** attendant, lifeguard, protector
body politic: **4** weal **5** state **6** nation **9** community
Boeotia: *capital:* **6** Thebes
region: **5** Ionia
boeotian: **10** philistine
Boer: **5** Dutch **6** farmer
dialect: **4** Taal
enemy: **9** uitlander
general: **5** Botha
bog: bug, car, fen, gog, hag **4** bold, carr, cess, mire, moor, moss, ooze, sink, slew, slue, syrt **5** marsh, saucy, swamp **6** morass, muskeg, slough **7** forward **8** quagmire **9** conceited

bog down: 4 mire 5 delay, stall 6 bemire

bogey: bug, cow, hag 5 bogie, bogle, devil, ghost, gnome, shade, spook 6 boggle, booger, goblin, spirit, wraith 7 boggard, boggart, bugaboo, bugbear, gnomide, specter, spectre 9 hobgoblin, scarecrow 10 bullbeggar

boggle: jib, shy 4 balk, foil, stop 5 alarm, botch, demur, scare, start 6 baffle, bungle, goblin, shrink 7 bauchle, blunder, perplex, scruple, stagger 8 frighten, hesitate 9 dissemble, dumbfound, embarrass

boggy: wet 4 miry, soft 5 fenny, gouty, haggy, mossy 6 quaggy, swampy 7 boggish, queachy

bogus: 4 fake, sham 5 false, phony 6 forged 8 spurious 9 imitation 10 fictitious 11 counterfeit

bogy: See **bogey**

Bohemian: 4 arty 5 gipsy, gypsy 6 Picard 7 beatnik 8 maverick 13 nonconformist
dance: 6 redowa

boil: sty 4 bile, blob, buck, coct, cook, rage, sore, stew, stye, teem 5 anger, botch, brede, poach, steam 6 betray, bubble, buller, burble, decoct, seethe, simmer 7 anthrax, estuate, inflame 8 aestuate, ebullate 10 ebbulliate, effervesce
almost: 5 scald
down: 6 decoct 8 simplify 10 streamline

boiler: 4 reef 6 copper, heater, kettle, retort 7 alembic, caldron, furnace 8 cauldron
plate: 4 sput
tube scaler: 6 sooter

boisterous: 4 gurl, loud, rude 5 burly, gurly, noisy, rough, windy 6 coarse, stormy, strong, unruly 7 furious, massive, roaring, violent 8 cumbrous, strident, vehement 9 clamorous, excessive, excitable, turbulent 10 blustering, tumultuous, unyielding, vociferous

bold: big, bog, yep 4 derf, pert, rash, rude, wise, yepe 5 bardy, bield, brash, brave, brent, frack, freak, freck, gally, hardy, large, manly, nervy, peart, saucy, steep, stout 6 abrupt, audace, brassy, brazen, crouse, daring, fierce, heroic, strong 7 assured, dashing, defiant, forward, grivois, haughty, massive, valiant 8 arrogant, familiar, fearless, grivoise, immodest, impudent, insolent, intrepid, malapert, powerful, resolute 9 audacious, bodacious, confident, dauntless, imprudent, undaunted 10 courageous, forritsome 11 venturesome 12 enterprising, overassuming, presumptuous, stouthearted 13 overconfident

boldness: 4 brow 5 bield, nerve, vigor 6 daring 7 bravery, chutzpa, courage 8 audacity, chutzpah, temerity 9 assurance, hardiesse, hardihood, hardiness 10 brazenness, confidence, effrontery 11 intrepidity, presumption 13 dauntlessness

bole: 4 clay, dose, stem 5 bolus, crypt, trunk 7 opening

bolero: 5 dance, waist 6 jacket

Bolero composer: 5 Ravel

bolide: 6 meteor 7 missile

Bolivia: *capitals:* 5 La Paz, Sucre
city: 5 Oruro, Uyuni 6 Camiri, Potosi, Robore, Viacha 8 Trinidad 9 Santa Cruz
department: 4 Beni 5 La Paz, Oruro, Pando 6 Elbeni, Potosi, Tarija 9 Santa Cruz 10 Chuquisaca, Cochabamba
food: 5 chuno 6 humita, quinoa 7 saltena
lake: 5 Poopo 8 Titicaca
language: 6 Aymara 7 Quechua, Spanish
liberator: 5 Sucre 7 Bolivar
measure: 6 league 7 celemin
people: Uro, Uru 4 Iten, Moxo, Uran 6 Arawak, Aymara, Charca, Chicha, Tacana 7 Aymaran, Puquina, Quechua, Sirione 10 Chiriguano
plateau: 9 Altiplano
region: 6 Valles, Yungas 7 Oriente
river: 4 Beni 5 Abuna, Orton 6 Baures, Mamore, Yacuma 7 Guapore, Madeira 9 Pilcomayo, San Miguel 11 Madre de Dios
weight: 5 libra, macro

boll: pod 4 bulb, grow, knob 5 onion 6 bubble 7 capsule, measure 8 pericarp 12 protuberance

boll weevil: 6 picudo

bollard: 4 bitt, post

bollix: 4 flub, mess 5 botch, gum up 6 bungle

bolo: 5 knife 7 machete, sundang 8 pacifist 9 defeatist

Bolshevik: 7 radical, Russian 9 anarchist, socialist
leader: 5 Lenin

bolster: aid, pad 6 pillow 7 cushion, support 8 compress, maintain 9 reinforce 10 strengthen

bolt: bar, pen, pin, rod, run 4 beat, dart, flee, gulp, lock, pawl, rush, sift 5 arrow, bilbo, close, elope, flash, gorge, latch, rivet, shaft 6 assort, decamp, desert, fasten, flight, garble, pintle, purify, refine, secure, strong, toggle, winnow 7 missile, shackle, thunder 8 fastener, separate, stampede 9 lightning

bolus: cud **4** bole, clop, lump, mass, pill, rock

bomb: dud, egg **4** flop, mine **5** blare, shell **6** ashcan **7** bombard, failure, grenade, marmite **8** fall flat **9** pineapple **10** projectile **11** blockbuster

bombard: **4** bomb **5** blitz, crump, shell **6** batter, bottle, strafe, vessel

bombardier: **6** gunner **12** artilleryman

bombardment: **5** blitz, siege **6** attack, rafale, strafe **7** barrage **9** cannonade

bombardon: **4** oboe, tuba **7** bassoon

bombast: gas, pad **4** rage, rant, rave **5** stuff **6** padded **7** bluster, stuffed, tympany **8** boasting, rhetoric **9** turgidity **11** rodomontade **12** altiloquence **14** grandiloquence

bombastic: **5** tumid, vocal **6** fluent, heroic, turgid **7** bombast, flowery, fustian, orotund, pompous, ranting, stilted **8** inflated **9** expansive, flatulent, grandiose, plethoric **10** lexiphanic, rhetorical **12** magniloquent

bombinate: hum **4** boom **5** drone

bombproof chamber: **8** casemate

bombyx: eri **4** eria, moth **8** silkworm

bonafide: **4** real, true **7** genuine **9** authentic, veritable

bon ami (F.): **5** lover **6** friend **10** sweetheart

bonanza: **4** mint **6** eureka **7** jackpot **8** eldorado, Golconda, gold mine

Bonanza State: **7** Montana

bonbon: **5** candy, cream **6** dainty **7** caramel **8** confetti, confetto **9** sugarplum

bond: tie, vow **4** bail, band, duty, glue, knot, link, note, yoke **5** bound, chain, nexus **6** binder, cement, connex, engage, escrow, fetter, league, pledge **7** husband, manacle, shackle **8** adhesive, contract, covenant, guaranty, ligament, ligature, mortgage, security, vinculum **9** agreement, composure, guarantee **10** constraint, husbandman, obligation **11** association, householder

chemical: **5** diene **7** valence

bondage: **4** yoke **7** helotry, peonage, serfdom, slavery **9** captivity, restraint, servitude, thralldom

bondsman: **4** carl, esne, peon, serf **5** churl, Helot, slave **6** stooge, surety, thrall, vassal **7** chattel, peasant, servant, villein

bone: rib **4** core, cram, ossa (pl.) **5** blade, study **6** fillet, radius **7** humerus, utterly

ankle: **5** talus **6** tarsus

anvil: **5** incus **7** incudes (pl.)

arm: **4** ulna **6** radius **7** humerus

back: **5** spine **8** vertebra

breast: **6** sterna (pl.) **7** sternum

cartilage: **6** ossein

cavity: **5** antra (pl.), sinus **6** antrum

cell: **10** osteoblast

change into: **6** ossify

collar: **8** clavicle

dorsal: **4** ilia (pl.) **5** ilium

elbow: **4** ulna

formation: **7** ostosis **10** parostosis

girdle: **12** sphenethmoid

manipulator: **9** osteopath **12** chiropractor

pert. to: **6** osteal **7** osseous

scraper: **6** xyster

thigh: **5** femur

bonefish: **8** ladyfish

bonelet: **7** ossicle

boner: **5** error **7** blooper, blunder, faux pas, mistake

bones: **4** dice, ossa **8** skeleton

boneset: **7** comfrey **8** hempweek **12** thoroughwort

bongo: **4** drum **8** antelope

boniata: yam

boniface: **8** landlord, publican **9** barkeeper, innkeeper **12** saloonkeeper

bonito: aku, atu **4** fish, nice **5** cobia **6** bonita, pretty, robalo **8** albacore, mackerel, skipjack

bonkers: mad **5** crazy **6** insane

bon mot: pun **4** jest, quip **9** witticism

bonne: **5** nurse **9** nursemaid **11** maidservant

bonnet: cap, hat **4** hood **5** cover, decoy, toque **6** capote, slouch **7** chapeau, coronet **8** headgear **9** headdress **10** accomplice, chinquapin

brim: **4** poke

string: **5** bride

bonnet monkey: **4** zati **5** munga

bonny, bonnie: gay **4** fine **5** merry, plump **6** blithe, pretty, strong **7** healthy **8** budgeree, handsome **9** beautiful **11** goodlooking

bonus: tip **4** gift, meed **5** award, bribe, bunce, pilon, prize, spiff **6** reward **7** cumshaw, premium, subsidy **8** dividend, lagnappe **9** allowance, lagniappe **12** compensation

bon vivant: **5** sport **7** epicure, gourmet

bony: **4** hard, lank, lean, thin **5** stiff, tough **6** osteal, skinny **7** osseous **8** skeletal

boo: **4** hoot, jeer **5** decry, grass **9** marijuana

boob: ass **4** fool **5** dunce, goony, neddy **6** nitwit

boobook: owl **6** cuckoo

booby: **5** dunce, idiot, loser, prize **6** sleigh, stupid **8** goosecap **9** simpleton

boodle: **4** loot, swag **5** cheat, crowd, graft **6** noodle **7** plunder **8** caboodle

boohoo: sob **4** hoot, weep **5** shout **8** sailfish

boojum: **5** snark

book: log, mss. **4** opus, text, tome **5** Bible, canto, diary, divan, enter, folio, liber, libri (pl.) **6** arrest, manual, record, volume **7** blotter, catalog, writing **8** brochure, document, libretto, register **9** catalogue, potboiler

accounts: day **5** bilan, liber **6** ledger **7** journal
alphabet: **9** abecedary
back: **5** spine
best selling: **5** Bible
binding material: **5** cloth, paper **6** canvas **7** buckram, leather
blank: **5** album, diary **6** tablet
church music: **6** hymnal
collector: **12** bibliomaniac
covering: **6** jacket **7** binding **9** dust cover
cover ornamentation: **7** tooling
design: **6** format, layout
destroyer: **11** biblioclast
devotional: **5** Bible **6** gospel, missal **7** diurnal, psalter **8** breviary
division: **7** chapter
elementary reading: **6** primer
fiction: **5** novel **7** mystery, western
group: **7** trilogy
Islam: **5** kitab, Koran **6** Hadith, Khabar
jacket notice: **5** blurb
kept in print: **8** backlist
large: **4** tome **5** folio
lover: **11** bibliophile
make-up: **6** format
manuscript: **5** codex, draft **7** codices (pl.)
map: **5** atlas
mass: **6** missal
navigator's: log **7** logbook **9** portolano
obscene: **11** pornography
of hours: **4** Hora **5** Horae (pl.)
of masses: **6** missal
of nobility: **6** Burke's **7** peerage
of psalms: **7** psalter
of rules: **5** Hoyle
page: **5** folio
palm: **4** tara **7** taliera
part: **4** leaf, page **5** cover, spine **7** binding, chapter, section **9** signature
pert to: **13** bibliographic
sacred : **4** Veda (Hindu) **5** Akdas (Bahai), Kitab; Koran (Islam) **6** Agarna (Jainist), Kojiki (Shinto), Lao Tzu (Taoist), Avesta (Zoroastrian) **9** Adi Granth (Sikh), Tripitaka (Buddhist)
school: **4** text **6** primer, reader **7** grammar, speller **9** geography **10** arithmetic
size: **6** octavo, quarto **8** twelvemo **9** duodecimo
title page: **6** rubric
translation: **4** pony
words of opera: **8** libretto
bookbinder: 12 bibliopegist
bookcase: 5 forel **6** forrel
book dealer: 10 bibliopole **11** bouguiniste
bookish: 8 highbrow, pedantic
bookkeeper: 7 auditor **10** accountant

bookkeeping term: 4 loss, post **5** audit, debit, entry **6** credit **9** statement
booklet: 8 brochure **10** literature
bookman: 6 bookie, dealer **7** scholar **9** publisher **11** litterateur
bookplate: 8 exlibris
bookworm: 6 reader **7** scholar **11** bibliophile
boom: jib **4** bang, bump, crib, pole, roar, spar **5** croon **7** bumpkin, resound, support **8** bowsprit, flourish **9** bombilate, bombinate **10** prosperity
boomerang: 5 kalie, kiley **6** recoil **7** rebound **8** backfire, ricochet
boon: gay **4** bene, gift, good, kind **5** favor, grant, merry, order **6** benign, bounty, favour, goodly, jovial, prayer **7** benefit, command, present **8** blessing, intimate, petition **9** congenial, convivial, favorable **10** concession, prosperous **11** benefaction
boon companion: cob, pal **4** chum **5** buddy **6** cobber
boondocks: 6 sticks **9** backwoods **10** hinterland, wilderness
boondoggle: 6 trifle **7** deceive, goof off **9** goldbrick
boor: cad, oaf **4** boob, carl, lout, pill **5** chuff, churl, clown, looby, slave, yokel **6** carlot, clunch, hoblob, lubber, lummox, rustic **7** cauboge, grobian, peasant, villein **8** bosthoon **9** barbarian, roughneck, vulgarian **10** clodhopper, countryman, husbandman, philistine, tramontane
boorish: 4 rude **5** gawky, rough, surly **6** clumsy, coarse, rustic, sullen, vulgar **7** awkward, crabbed, hoblike, ill-bred, loutish, roister, uncouth **8** churlish, cloddish, clownish, lubberly, ungainly **9** bourgeois **10** uncultured, unmannerly
boost: aid **4** abet, back, help, lift, plug, push, rise **5** coach, exalt, hoist, raise **6** assist, rear up **7** advance, commend, elevate, endorse, indorse, promote **8** increase **9** encourage **10** assistance **12** commendation
booster: 4 shot **9** injection **10** enthusiast
boot: pac, use **4** cure, gain, help, kick, shoe, sock **5** avail, booty, eject, jemmy, kamik, spoil, start **6** bootee, buskin, casing, crakow, enrich, fumble, galosh, novice, sheath, thrill **7** benefit, dismiss, recruit **8** chassure (F.), covering **9** advantage, discharge, dismissal
half: pac **4** pack **6** buskin, cocker **7** blucher, bottine **8** cothurni (pl.) **9** cothurnus
heavy: pac **5** stogy **6** brogan **8** Balmoral
high-water: **5** wader
loose-topped: **10** wellington
riding: **5** jemmy **7** gambado, jodhpur
small: **7** bottine **8** bottekin

booted: 4 shod 7 ocreate

booth: 4 loge, shed, shop, sook, souk 5 bothy, cabin, crame, house, kiosk, stall, stand 6 tienda (Sp.) 7 balagan

bootleg: 7 illegal, illicit, smuggle 11 clandestine 12 illegitimate 13 surreptitious

bootless: 6 futile 7 useless 9 incurable, worthless 10 remediless, unavailing 12 unprofitable

bootlick: 4 fawn 5 toady 7 flatter 9 brownnose 11 apple-polish

booty: 4 gain, loot, pelf, prey, swag 5 cheat, graft, prize 6 spoils 7 despoil, pillage, plunder 10 chevisance

booze (see also **alcoholic drink**): 4 bout 5 budge, drink, spree 6 fuddle, liquor 7 alcohol

boozer: pub 5 toper 6 bouser 8 drunkard

bora: 4 wind

borax: 6 tincal

border: hem, rim 4 abut, brim, dado, eave, edge, line, nark, orle, rand, roon, rund (Sc.), side, trim 5 bound, braid, brink, coast, costa, flank, forel, frame, limit, march, marge, plait, skirt, strip, touch, verge 6 adjoin, costae, edging, forrel, fringe, impale, margin, purfle, set off, stripe 7 bordure, confine, outline, selvage 8 boundary, frontier, neighbor, surround, tressour, tressure 9 extremity, periphery 10 sidepieces 11 come close to
fluted: 5 frill
ornamental: 4 dado 5 frame 6 fringe
wall: 4 dado, ogee 7 cornice

bordering: 6 edging 8 abutting, adjacent

bore: bit, irk, tap 4 drag, gaze, hole, pall, poke, push, ream, size, tide, tire, tool 5 annoy, augur, chink, drill, eagre, ennui, gauge, prick, punch, tewel, trick, weary 6 befool, gimlet, pierce, thrust, tunnel 7 caliber, calibre, carried, crevice, opening 8 aiguille, diameter 9 annoyance, penetrate, perforate, terebrate 10 put to sleep 11 perforation 12 buttonholder

Boreas: 4 wind 7 norther
son: 5 Butes 6 Calais

borecole: 4 kail, kale

bored: 7 ennuyee (F.)

boredom: 5 ennui 6 tedium 7 fatigue 9 weariness

borer: 6 insect 7 hagfish, termite 8 shipworm

boring: dry 4 dull, flat 5 banal, trite 6 broach, tiring 7 irksome, tedious 8 piercing, tiresome 9 wearisome 11 displeasing, penetrating 13 uninteresting

boring tool: bit 5 auger, drill 6 gimlet, wimble

born: nee (F.) 6 innate 7 nascent, natural 8 inherent 9 delivered

dead: 9 stillborn
prematurely: 8 abortive
well: 4 free 5 noble 7 eugenic

borne (see also **bear**): 4 rode 6 narrow 7 carried, endured
by the wind: 6 eolian

Borneo (see also **Brunei, Malaysia, Indonesia**): *Indonesian name:* 10 Kalimantan
people: 4 Dyak
river: 6 Barito, Kapuas, Rajang 7 Mahakam
sea: 4 Java, Sulu 7 Celebes 10 South China

boron: 5 borax, boric 7 ulexite

borough: 4 burg, town 5 brush, burgh 6 burgus, castle 7 citadel, village 8 fortress, township

borrow: 4 copy, loan, take 5 adopt, steal 6 pledge, surety 7 chevise, hostage, tithing 11 frankpledge

bosc: 4 pear

boscage: 4 wood 5 grove 7 thicket

bosh: end, rot 4 joke, show, talk, tosh 5 trash 6 bushwa, figure, flaunt, humbug, trivia 8 nonsense 9 poppycock

bosky: 5 bushy, shady, tipsy, woody 7 fuddled 11 intoxicated

Bosnia and Herzegovina: *alphabet:* 8 Cyrillic
capital: 8 Sarajevo
currency: 5 dinar
sea: 8 Adriatic

---

bosom: 4 barm (Sc.) 5 close, heart, sinus 6 breast, cavity, desire, recess 7 beloved, embrace, inclose 8 intimate 9 cherished 11 inclination, indentation

boss: bur, guv (Br.), pad 4 baas, buhr, burr, head, knob, stud 5 bully, chief, empty, knosp, order, owner 6 brooch, button, direct, emboss, hollow, leader, manage, master, shield 7 capataz, cushion, foreman, hassock, headman, manager, phalera 8 director, domineer, overseer 9 supervise 10 politician, supervisor
African: 5 bwana
French: 6 patron
Italian: 7 padrone
logging camp: 5 bully
political: 7 cacique
shield: 4 umbo
Spanish: 4 jefe

bossy: cow 4 calf 9 imperious, masterful 11 dictatorial, domineering

Boston: (see box)

bot: 5 larva

botany: *angle:* 4 axil

cell: **5** spore
depression: **5** fovea **7** variole

Boston: *author:* **6** Alcott **7** Emerson **9** Hawthorne **10** Longfellow
baseball field: **10** Fenway Park
baseball team: **6** Red Sox
basketball team: **7** Celtics
district: **7** Back Bay, Roxbury, Southie **8** Hyde Park, Mattapan, North End, South End **10** Beacon Hill, Dorchester
hockey team: **6** Bruins
landmark: **6** Common **11** Faneuil Hall, King's Chapel **12** Copley Square, Old Ironsides **13** Old State House, Trinity Church **14** Old North Church **15** U.S.S. Constitution
nickname: **8** Beantown **15** Athens of America, Cradle of Liberty **16** Hub of the Universe
park: **8** Franklin **12** Boston Common, Public Garden **15** Arnold Arboretum
respected class: **7** Brahmin
river: **6** Mystic **7** Charles, Chelsea **8** Neponset
site of: **8** Marathon, Massacre, Tea Party **10** Bunker Hill **12** Freedom Trail

---

botch: dub, mar, mux **4** boil, mend, mess, ruin, sore **5** bitch, bodge, spoil **6** boggle, bumble, bungle, cobble, jumble, muck up, repair **7** blunder, louse up **8** swelling **10** hodge-podge
botcher: **6** grilse, salmon **7** bungler, butcher, clouter, cobbler
both: two **7** equally
handed: **12** ambidextrous
bother: ado, ail, nag, vex **4** fuss **5** annoy, deave, tease, worry **6** badger, bustle, dither, flurry, gravel, harass, meddle, moider, molest, pester, pother, puzzle, tamper **7** confuse, disturb, perplex, trouble **8** bewilder, irritate, nuisance **10** discompose **13** inconvenience
Botswana: (see box)
bottle: jug **4** vial **5** cruet, cruse, flask, glass, gourd, house, phial **6** bundle, carafe, carboy, corner, fiasco, flacon, flagon, magnum, vessel **7** canteen, costrel **8** building, decanter, demijohn, jeroboam, preserve, restrain **9** aryballos, aryballus, container
size: **4** pint, pipe **5** fifth, quart **6** magnum **8** jeroboam
small: **4** vial **5** ampul, cruet, phial **6** doruck, flacon **7** ampoule, costrel **8** decanter **11** vinaigrette

bottleneck: **7** barrier **8** blockade
bottom: bed **4** base, dale, foot, fund, holm, lees, root **5** abyss, basis, belly, dregs, floor, nadir **6** ground **7** bedrock, essence, grounds, lowland, support, surface **8** buttocks, sediment **10** foundation, groundwork **11** fundamental
boudoir: **4** room **5** cabin **7** bedroom, cabinet **11** sitting room

---

Botswana: *capital:* **8** Gaborone
city: **5** Kanye **7** Lobatse, Mochudi **8** Tsetseng **11** Francistown
currency: **4** pula **5** thebe
desert: **8** Kalahari
district: **5** Chobe **6** Ghanzi **7** Central, Kweneng **8** Kgatleng **9** Kgalagadi, Ngamiland
park: **5** Chobe **7** Gemsbok, Nsai Pan
people: **5** Bantu **6** Tswana **7** Basarwa, Bushmen, Kalanga **8** Batswana **9** Kgalagadi **10** Bamangwato
river: **4** Okwa **5** Sashe **6** Botete **7** Limpopo **8** Okavango

---

bouffant, bouffante: **4** full **6** puffed, teased **7** bulging
bough: arm, leg **4** limb, twig **5** shoot, spray, sprig **6** branch, ramage **7** gallows **8** offshoot, shoulder
bouillabaisse: **4** stew **7** chowder
bouillon: **4** soup **5** broth **8** consomme
boulder: **4** rock **5** stone
monument: **8** megalith
transported by ice: **7** erratic
boulevard: way **6** avenue, street **7** highway **12** thoroughfare
boulevardier: **4** roue **5** dandy, idler
bounce: **4** bang, blow, brag, bump, fire, jump, leap, sack **5** boast, bound, bully, carom, chuck, eject, knock, scold, thump, verve **6** spirit, spring, strike **7** address, bluster, dismiss, rebound, swagger **8** proclaim, ricochet **9** discharge, explosion, expulsion, terminate **10** resilience
bouncing: big **5** buxom, lusty, stout **7** healthy **9** excessive
bound: dap, end, hop **4** bent, bind, bond, brow, butt, dart, girt, jump, leap, mere, ramp, scud, skip, stem **5** ambit, bourn, going, limit, ready, stend, sting, tiled, vault, verge **6** border, bounce, bourne, curvet, define, domain, finish, finite, hurdle, oblige, prance, spring **7** barrier, certain,

chained, closure, confine, costive, delimit, dressed, rebound, saltate, secured, trussed **8** boundary, confined, destined, enclosed, frontier, handfast, landmark, precinct, prepared, shackled **9** compelled, inhibited, obligated **10** borderland, indentured **11** apprenticed, constrained, termination
back: **5** carom **6** resile
by a vow: **6** votary

boundary: ahu, end, rim **4** dole, dool, edge, line, mear, meer, mere, meta, mete, term, wall **5** ambit, bourn, fence, hedge, limit, march, metae, mound, verge **6** border, bourne, define, limits **7** barrier, bounder, termini (pl.) **8** environs, frontier, precinct, terminus **9** demarcate, perimeter

bounder: cad, cur **4** boor, rake, roue

boundless: **4** vast **6** untold **7** endless, eternal **8** infinite **9** limitless, unlimited **10** immoderate, unconfined, unmeasured **11** illimitable, measureless **12** immeasurable, interminable

bountiful: **4** good, lush, rich **5** ample **6** freely, lavish **7** liberal, profuse **8** abundant, generous **9** bounteous, plenteous, plentiful **10** munificent

bounty: **4** boon, gift, meed **5** award, bonus, grant, valor, worth **6** reward, virtue **7** largess, premium, present, prowess, subsidy **8** goodness, gratuity, kindness **9** allowance **10** generosity, liberality, recompense **11** beneficence, munificence

bouquet: **4** aura, odor, posy **5** aroma, cigar, posey, spray **7** corsage, nosegay **9** fragrance **10** compliment **11** arrangement, boutonniere

bourgeois: **6** common, stupid **7** boorish, burgher **8** mediocre **9** hidebound **11** middle class

bourn, bourne: **5** brook **6** stream **7** rivulet

bout: job **4** turn **5** booze, essay, fight, match, round, set-to, siege, spell, trial **6** attack, fracas **7** attempt, carouse, circuit, contest, debauch, outside, without **8** conflict **10** knobkerrie
drinking: bat **4** bust, toot **5** binge, spree **6** bender **7** carouse

bovine: bos, cow **4** bull, calf, dull, kudu, neat, slow, zebu **5** bison, steer **6** oxlike, stolid **7** buffalo, patient, taurine **8** longhorn, sluggish
genus: bos
hybrid: **6** catalo

bow: arc, nod, tie **4** arch, beck, bend, bent, duck, fold, knot, prow, stem, turn, wend **5** binge, conge, crush, curve, defer, kneel, noued, stoop, yield **6** archer, assent, bauble, buckle, curtsy, fiddle, ribbon, salaam, submit, swerve, weapon **7** depress, incline, inflict,

rainbow **8** crescent, greeting **9** obeisance, prostrate **10** capitulate **11** buckle under
facing sea: **4** atry
of ship: **4** beak, prow, stem
oriental: **5** salam **6** salaam
toward: **5** afore
wood for: yew

bowdlerize: **6** censor, screen **9** expurgate

bowed: **4** bent **5** kneed **6** arcate, curved **7** bulging

bowels: gut **5** belly, colon **8** entrails **9** intestine **10** compassion **11** disembowels, eviscerates

bower: **4** jack, nook **5** abode, arbor, joker, knave **6** anchor **7** berceau, chamber, cottage, embower, enclose, pergola, retreat, shelter

bowfin: **4** amia **6** lawyer **7** grindle, mudfish

bowie: tub **4** bowl, cask, pail **5** knife

bowl: cap, cup, pan **4** coup **5** arena, basin, bowie, depas, phila, rogan **6** beaker, crater, syphus, tureen, vessel **7** stadium, whiskin

bowlegged: **5** bandy **6** curved **9** misshapen

bowler: hat **5** derby **6** kegler **8** trundler

bowling: **5** bocci **7** tenpins **8** duckpins, fivepins, ninepins **10** candlepins
division: **5** frame
pin: **4** duck **7** ninepin, skittle
place: **4** lane, lawn, rink **5** alley
score: **5** spare **6** strike
terms: tap **4** loft **5** split **6** cherry, turkey **8** Brooklyn, railroad

bowman: **5** cupid **6** archer

bow-shaped: **6** arcate

box: bin, lug, pix, pyx **4** arca, cage, caja, case, cist, crib, cuff, cyst, loge, pack, scob, seat, slap, slug, spar, stow, till, tray **5** barge, boist, buist, buxus, caddy, chest, clout, crate, fight, hutch, punch, shrub, stall, trunk, TV set **6** arcana (pl.), buffet, bunker, carton, casket, coffin, hopper, shrine, strike **7** arcanum, cabinet, caisson, casquet, cassone, confine, enclose, fostell, hanaper, package, trummel **9** container, fisticuff **10** receptacle
alms: **4** arca
ammunition: **7** caisson **9** bandoleer, bandolier
document: **7** hanaper

boxcar: **7** carrier

boxer: dog, hat, pug **5** champ **7** bruiser, fighter, sparrer **8** pugilist **12** prizefighter
"Brown Bomber": **5** Louis (Joe)
champion: Ali (Muhammad) **5** Tyson (Mike) **6** Tunney (Gene) **7** Dempsey (Jack), Foreman (George), Frazier (Joe) **8** Graziano (Rocky), Marciano (Rocky) **9** Patterson (Floyd), Schmeling (Max)
hand covering: **5** cesti, glove **6** cestus
weight class: fly **5** heavy, light, straw **6** bantam, middle, welter **7** cruiser, feather

boxing: 4 bout 5 match 8 pugilism 10 fisticuffs 13 prize-fighting
blow: jab 5 feint, punch
knockout: TKO
rules: 11 Queensberry

box office: 4 gate 6 income 8 receipts

boxwood: 4 tree 5 seron

boy: bub, lad, son, tad 4 chap, nino (Sp.), page, puer (L.) 5 buddy, chabo, child, gamin, knave, rogue, valet, youth 6 garcon (F.), nipper, rascal, shaver, urchin 7 gossoon, servant 8 henchboy 9 shaveling, stripling, youngster

boycott: 4 shun 5 avoid, debar 9 blackball 10 ostracized

boyfriend: 4 beau 5 beaux (pl.), lover 6 steady 8 paramour 9 inamorato 10 sweetheart

brabble: 5 argue 7 chatter, quarrel

brace: leg, tie, two 4 bind, case, frap, gird, mark, pair, prop, stay 5 nerve, strut 6 clench, couple, crutch, fasten, fathom, splint 7 embrace, refresh, stiffen, support 8 buttress, encircle 9 reinforce, stimulate, suspender 10 strengthen 11 mantelpiece

bracelet: 4 band, ring 5 chain, charm, slave 6 armlet, bangle, grivna 7 armilla, circlet, manacle, poignet 8 handcuff 10 calombigas

bracer: 5 drink, tonic 6 breeze 9 stimulant

brachyuran: 4 crab 10 crustacean

bracing: 5 crisp, quick, tonic 10 salubrious 11 stimulating 12 invigorating

bracken: 4 fern 5 plaid

bracket: 4 join 5 brace, class, level, shelf, strut 6 corbel, couple, sconce 7 console, fixture, spotted 8 category, speckled 9 merganser

brackish: 5 foist, salty 6 bracky, saline 7 saltish 8 nauseous 11 distasteful

bract: 4 leaf 5 glume, palea, palet 6 spadix, spathe

brad: pin 4 nail 5 rivet, sprig

brag: 4 blaw, blow, crow, defy, huff, yelp 5 bluff, boast, flird, preen, strut, vaunt 6 bounce, splore 7 display, gauster, roister, swagger 8 braggart, flourish, pretense, threaten 9 gasconade 11 rodomontade

braggadocio: 7 boaster 8 braggart, rodomont 9 swaggerer 10 cockalorum, pretension

braggart: 4 brag 5 boast 6 blower, crower, gasbag, gascon, potgun 7 boaster, cracker, ruffler, windbag 8 bangster, blowhard, fanfaron, rodomont 9 loudmouth, renommist 10 burgullian 11 braggadocio, rodomontade

Bragi's wife: 4 Idun 6 Ithunn

Brahma: 5 Hindu 7 creator
first woman created by: 6 Ahalya

Brahman: 5 Aryan, Hindu 6 cattle, priest, pundit

land grant: 5 sasan
precept: 5 sutra, sutta
title: aya

Brahmin: 7 egghead 8 highbrow 9 Bostonian 10 aristocrat 12 intellectual

braid: cue 4 band, jerk, lace, plat, trim 5 brede, fancy, freak, jiffy, lacet, onset, plait, pleat, queue, start, tress, trick, twine, vomit, weave 6 bobbin, border, cordon, moment, plight, ribbon, sennet, snatch, string 7 caprice, entwine, upbraid 8 brandish, ornament, reproach, soutache, trimming 9 deceitful, interlace 10 interweave
gold and silver: 5 orris
hemp: 5 tagal
knotted: 5 lacet

brain: 4 bean, harn (Sc.), kill, mind, utac, wits 5 skull 6 psyche 7 furious 8 cerebrum (L.), computer 9 intellect
box: pan 5 skull 7 cranium
disease of: 6 chorea 10 meningitis 12 encephalitis
layer: 4 obex 6 cortex
membrane: 4 tela 8 meninges
operate on: 6 trepan
orifice: 4 lura
part: 4 aula, stem 7 medulla 8 cerebrum 10 cerebellum, encephalon, gray matter 11 pericranium 14 corpus callosum
passage: 4 iter
pert. to: 8 cerebral 10 cerebellar, encephalic
tumor: 6 glioma
white matter: pia 4 alba, dura

brainchild: 4 opus, work 9 invention

brainless: 5 silly 6 stupid 7 foolish, witless 11 thoughtless

brainstorm: 4 idea 11 inspiration

brain trust: 5 panel 7 council 8 advisers

brake: 4 cage, curb, drag, fern, rack, slow, stop, trap 5 block, check, copse, delay, deter, snare, vomit 6 bridle, harrow, hinder, retard 7 dilemma, thicket 9 brushwood

bramble: 5 brier, thorn 6 bumble 10 cloudberry

brambly: 5 spiny 6 thorny 7 prickly

bran: 5 treat 6 cereal, chisel

branch: arm, bow 4 brog, bush, chat, fork, limb, part, rame, rami, snag, spur, stem, twig 5 bough, creek, ramus, shoot, spray, sprig, vimen, withe 6 divide, member, outlet, raddle, ramage, ramify, stolon, stream 7 diverge, tendril 8 district, offshoot 10 department 11 bifurcation 12 ramification
angle of: 4 axil
of nerves: 4 rami (pl.) 5 ramus

branched: 6 forked, ramate, ramose 7 cladose

branchia: 4 gill

brand: 4 birn, blot, burn, flaw, kind, mark, sear, smit, sort 5 buist, stain, stamp, sword, taint, torch 6 stigma 8 flambeau 9 cauter-

Brazil: *bay:* **9** Guanabara, Sao Marcos **13** Todos os Santos

beach: **5** praia **7** Ipanema **10** Copacabana

capital: **8** Brasilia

city: **5** Belem, Natal **6** Cuiaba, Macapa, Maceio, Manaus, Santos **7** Aracaju, Goiania, Sao Luis **8** Boa Vista, Curitiba, Sao Paulo **10** Pernambuco **12** Rio de Janeiro

currency: **4** reis **5** conto, dolra **7** centavo, cruzado, milreis **8** cruzeiro **11** cruzado real

dance: **5** samba **6** maxixe **7** lambada **9** bossa nova

drink: **4** mate **5** assai **6** batida

export: **6** coffee **7** iron ore **11** orange juice

fiber: **4** imbe

fish: **8** arapaima

forest: **5** matta, selva

holiday: **8** carneval, carnival

Indian: **4** Anta **5** Arara, Bravo, Carib, Guana **6** Arawak, Bororo, Caraja, Kayapo, Tupian **7** Guarani, Tariana **8** Araquaju, Botocudo

island: **6** Maraca, Marajo **7** Caviana, Mexiana

measure: **4** moio, pipa, sack, vara **5** braca, fanga, legoa, milha, palmo, passo, tonel **6** canada, covado, cuarta, league, quarto, tarefa **7** alquier, garrafa **8** alqueire **9** pollegada, quartilho

monkey: sai **6** miriki **9** belzebuth

mountain: Mar **5** Geral **6** Acarai, Orgaos, Parima **7** Parecis **8** Estrondo, Roncador, Tombador **9** Espinhaco **10** Tumuc-Humac **13** Pico da Neblina

palm: **4** jara **5** assai, inaja, tucum **6** babaca, jupati **7** babassu, cassava **9** barriguda

plant: **4** imbe, para, yage, yaje **5** caroa **7** ayapana, seringa **9** jaborandi

plateau: **8** planalto

promontory: **4** frio

ranch: **7** fazenda

religion: **7** macumba **9** candomble **13** Roman Catholic

river: **4** Para, Paru **5** Negro, Purus, Verde, Xingu **6** Amazon, Parana **7** Madeira, Tapajos, Uruguay **8** Paraguay, Parnaiba **9** Tocantins **12** Sao Francisco

rubber: ule

slum: **6** favela

swampy area: **8** Pantanal

tree: apa, ule **4** anda, assu, uhle **5** araca, tingi **6** biriba, brauna, satine **7** araroba, becuiba, gomavel, paraiba, seringa, wallaba **8** bakupari **10** barbatimao, dal guarabu

weight: bag **4** onca **5** libra **6** arroba, oitava **7** arratel, quilate, quintal **8** tonelada

wood: **6** embuia **8** kingwood

ize, character, trademark **10** stigmatize

on stolen cattle: **4** duff

sheep: **4** smit

brandish: **4** dart, show, wave **5** bless, braid, shake, swing, wield **6** flaunt, hurtle **7** flutter, glitter, swagger, trot out, vibrate **8** flourish **9** coruscate, irradiate

brandling: **4** parr **9** earthworm

brandy: **4** marc **5** bingo **6** cognac **11** aguardiente (Sp.)

and soda: peg

cocktail: **7** cobbler, sidecar, stinger **9** alexander

mastic: **4** raki **5** rakee

plum: **9** slivovitz

brannigan: **5** brawl, spree **6** bender, ruckus **10** falling out **11** altercation

brant: **4** rout **5** erect, goose, proud, quink, sheer, steep **7** steeply **8** straight

brash: **4** bold, rash **5** hasty, saucy, storm **6** attack, brazen **7** brittle, forward **8** cocksure, impudent, tactless **9** irascible **11** thoughtless **12** presumptuous

brass: **4** cash, gall **5** alloy, money, nerve **6** brazen **7** officer **8** temerity **9** impudence, insolence **10** effrontery

brassard, brassart: **5** badge **6** bracer **7** armband

brassbound: set **5** rigid **10** inflexible

brass hat: **7** general, officer **8** superior

brassica: **4** cole, kale, rabe, rape **6** turnip **7** cabbage, mustard **8** broccoli **11** cauliflower

brass tacks: **5** facts **6** basics **10** essentials

brassy: **4** bold **6** aerose, brazen **8** impudent

brat: bib, imp **4** film, scum **5** apron, bairn, bilsh, child, cloak **6** infant, mantle, urchin **7** garment **8** clothing **9** offspring

bravado: **4** pomp **5** brave, pride, storm **6** bravor, hector **7** bluster, bombast, bravade, bravery, bravura, swagger **9** gasconade

brave: **4** bold, braw (Sc.), dare, defy, face, fine, game, good, prow **5** adorn, boast, bravo, bully, gutsy, hardy, manly, Roman, stout, vaunt **6** breast, chin-up, daring, heroic, manful, plucky **7** bravado, gallant, soldier, swagger, valiant, venture, warrior **8**

cavalier, defiance, embolden, fearless, intrepid, stalwart, superior, valorous, virtuous **9** challenge, dauntless, excellent, undaunted **10** courageous **11** venturesome **12** stouthearted

Brave New World author: **6** Huxley

bravery: **4** grit **5** valor **6** daring, mettle, spirit, valour **7** bravado, bravura, courage, heroism **8** boldness **9** fortitude, gallantry, gentleman, hardihood

bravo: ole (Sp.), rah **4** thug, viva **5** brave, bully **6** bandit, Indian **7** bravado, villain **8** applause, assassin **9** cutthroat, desperado

brawl: din, row **4** clem, fray, riot **5** broil, fight, melee, revel, scold **6** affray, bicker, fracas, habble, revile, rumpus, shindy, strife, tumult, uproar **7** brabble, discord, dispute, quarrel, scuffle, wrangle **8** complain, squabble **10** contention, donnybrook, free-for-all **11** altercation, disturbance

brawling: **5** noisy **7** blatant **9** clamorous **10** clamourous, vociferous **11** quarrelsome

brawn: **4** boar **5** flesh **6** fatten, muscle **8** strength **10** headcheese

brawny: **5** beefy **6** fleshy, robust, sinewy, strong, sturdy **7** callous **8** muscular, powerful, stalwart

bray: cry, mix, rub **4** beat, rout, tool **5** grind, noise, pound **6** bruise, heehaw, outcry, pestle, thrash, whinny

brazen: **4** bold, pert **5** brass, harsh, sassy **6** brassy **7** callous, forward **8** immodest, impudent, insolent, metallic **9** shameless

Brazil: (see box)

breach: gap **4** chap, flaw, gool, rent, rift **5** brack, breck, chasm, cleft, crack, pause, split, wound **6** bruise, harbor, hernia, hiatus, inroad, schism **7** assault, blemish, dispute, fissure, opening, quarrel, rupture **8** breaking, fraction, fracture, interval, trespass **9** violation **10** disruption, infraction **12** infringement, interruption **14** nonfulfillment **16** misunderstanding
  of etiquette: **5** gaffe **8** solecism

breach pin: **4** tige

bread: bun **4** diet, fare, food, loaf, pone, roll **5** dough, money **6** staple **7** aliment, bannock (Sc.) **10** livelihood, sustenance
  boiled: **4** cush **6** panada
  browned: **4** toast **6** sippet **7** crouton
  communion: **4** azym, host **5** azyme, wafer
  crust: **4** rind
  dry and crisp: **4** rusk **8** zwieback **10** melba toast
  kind: rye **4** corn, pita **5** rolls **6** French, pocket, sticks **7** biscuit, Italian **8** baguette, chapatty, grissini, kouloura, tortilla **9** croissant, kugelhupf, sourdough **12** pumpernickel

  leavened: **5** kisra **6** cocket
  Passover: **5** matzo **6** matzoh, matzos (pl.), matzot (pl.) **7** matzoth (pl.)
  pert. to: **6** panary
  unleavened: **4** azym **5** azyme **6** matzos **7** bannock, matzoth **8** afikomen

bread-and-butter: **5** basic **8** everyday, ordinary
  pert. to: **6** living **7** support **8** daily job **10** livelihood **12** note of thanks

bread spread: jam **4** oleo **5** jelly **6** butter **9** margarine, marmalade, preserves **13** oleomargarine

breadth: **4** span **5** brede, range, scope, width **6** extent **8** diameter, distance, latitude **9** amplitude, dimension

break: gap **4** boon, bust, dash, hint, knap, pick, plow, rend, rent, rift, rive, ruin, rush, slip, snap, stop, tame, tear **5** alter, blank, burst, cleft, crack, craze, frush, lapse, pluck, sever, smash, wound **6** bruise, change, cleave, defeat, hiatus, impair, lacuna, pierce **7** blunder, caesura, crackle, crevice, crumble, destroy, disable, dispart, disrupt, exhaust, fissure, lacunae (pl.), opening, respite, rupture, shatter **8** caesurae, fraction, fracture, interval, separate **9** interrupt, penetrate **10** invalidate **12** interruption
  down: **7** debacle, failure **8** collapse **9** cataclysm **10** catabolism
  in: **5** stave, train **7** intrude **8** initiate **9** interrupt **13** enter forcibly
  of day: **4** dawn, morn **5** sunup **7** morning
  out: **5** erupt **6** escape **10** bring forth
  up: **4** part **5** split **7** disband, disrupt **8** disperse, dissolve, separate **9** take apart **10** put a stop to

breakable: **7** brittle, bruckle, friable **8** delicate

breakbone fever: **6** dengue

breaker: **4** surf, wave **6** billow, comber, roller

breakwater: cob, dam **4** cobb, dike, mole, pier, pile, quay **5** jetty **6** refuge **11** obstruction

bream: tai **4** fish, scup **5** broom **7** sunfish
  sea: **4** shad **5** porgy **6** sargus

breast: **4** bust, crop **5** bosom, brave, chest, heart **6** thorax **9** encounter
  ornament: **8** pectoral

breastbone: **6** sterna (pl.) **7** sternum, xiphoid **9** gladiolus
  pert to: **7** sternal

breastplate: *armor:* **4** urim **6** gorget, lorica, shield **7** poitrel, thummin **8** poitrail
  ecclesiastical: **4** urim

breastwork: **4** fort **5** redan **7** brattle, bulwark, parapet, rampart **10** forecastle

breath: **4** ande, gasp, hint, huff, life, pant, pech, puff, sigh, wind **5** pause, scent, smell, vapor, whiff **6** breeze, pneuma **7** halitus, instant, respite **10** exhalation

breathe: **4** ande, live, pant, pech, puff, sigh **5** exist, speak, utter **6** aspire, exhale, inhale, wheeze **7** afflate, emanate, respire, suspire
hard: **4** gasp, pant

breather: **4** rest **5** break, pause, truce **6** recess **7** respite **9** armistice

breathing: **5** alive **7** gasping **9** spiration **11** respiration
difficult: **7** dyspnea **8** dyspnoea
harsh: **4** rale
impairment of: **9** emphysema
orifice: **4** nose, pore **5** mouth, nares **7** nostril **8** spiracle
smooth: **4** lene
sound: **4** rale **5** snore, snort **7** stridor

breathless: **4** dead **5** stale, tense **6** stuffy **10** motionless

breech: **4** bore, butt, doup **5** block **7** droddum **8** buttocks, derriere **9** posterior

breeches: **5** chaps, jeans, levis **8** jodhpurs, knickers, trousers **10** pantaloons

breeching: **4** rope **7** harness

breed: ilk **4** bear, kind, race, rear, sort, type **5** beget, brood, caste, cause, class, hatch, raise, stock, train **6** create, strain **7** educate, nourish, produce, progeny, species, variety **8** engender, instruct, multiply **9** offspring, originate, propagate **10** generation

breeding: **6** origin **7** culture, descent **8** behavior, civility, training **9** education, gestation **10** deportment, extraction **11** development, instruction
science: **8** eugenics

breeze: air, zip **4** aura, blow, easy, flaw, gale, gust, pirr, stir, wind **5** blast, cinch, rumor, waltz **6** breath, report, zephyr **7** freshen, quarrel, whisper **10** effortless **11** disturbance
land: **6** terral

breezy: **4** airy **5** brisk, fresh, windy **6** airish **9** easygoing, vivacious

bressumer: **4** beam **6** girder, lintel **7** support

breve: **4** bird, mark, note, writ **5** brief, order **6** letter **7** compose, precept **8** syllable

brevet: **6** confer **9** promotion **10** commission

breviary: **4** ordo **6** digest, portas **7** coucher, epitome, summary **8** abstract **10** compendium, prayer book **11** abridgement

brevity: **8** laconism **9** briefness, shortness, terseness **11** conciseness **12** succinctness

brew: ale, mix **4** beer, boil, loom, make, plot, pour **5** hatch **6** devise, dilute, foment, gather, liquor, seethe **7** concoct, incline, prepare **9** beverage, contrive **9** potpourri **10** miscellany

brewer: *grain:* rye **4** corn, malt **6** barley
vat: tun

yeast: **4** barm **6** leaven

briar: see **brier**

bribe: fee, fix, oil, rob, sop, tip **4** bait, gift, hire, meed **5** bonus, cuddy, graft, offer, steal, sugar, tempt **6** buy off, extort, grease, payola, suborn **7** corrupt **8** gratuity **10** allurement

bric-a-brac: **5** curio, vertu, virtu **7** bibelot **8** trinkets **11** knickknacks

brick: **4** pave, tile **5** block, quarl, stone **6** fellow, quarle
handler: **6** hacker
oven: **4** kiln
sun-baked: bat **5** adobe
tray: hod
vitrified: **7** clinker
wood: nog **4** dook **6** scutch

bridal: **7** nuptial, wedding **8** espousal, marriage

bride: bar, leg, tie **4** loop, rein, rose **5** woman **6** bridle, kallah

bridge: way **4** game, link, pons, pont, span **5** cross, truss **6** ponton **7** auction, bascule, connect, pontoon, trestle, viaduct **8** contract, traverse **9** alcantara, gang-plank
combination: **6** tenace
forerunner: **5** whist
lever: **4** draw **5** swing **7** bascule
of musical instrument: **5** magas **10** ponticello
part: **4** arch, deck, pier **5** cable, pylon **7** caisson **8** spandrel
player: **4** east, west **5** north, south
pontoon plank: **5** chess
score: leg
support: **4** pier **5** truss
term: bid, bye, leg, set **4** book, game, pass, ruff, slam, suit, void **5** dummy, raise, trick, trump **6** double, renege, revoke, rubber **7** finesse, jump bid, no-trump, overbid **8** contract, redouble **9** duplicate, grand slam, overtrick, part score, singleton **10** little slam, vulnerable

bridle: bit, gag **4** curb, rein, rule **5** brake, brank, bride, check, guard, guide, strut **6** direct, govern, halter, master, muzzle, simper, subdue **7** blinder, control, harness, repress, snaffle, swagger **8** restrain, suppress **9** restraint
noseband: **6** musrol **8** cavesson

brief: few **4** curt, list, rife, writ **5** blurb, breve, charm, pithy, quick, short, terse **6** abrupt, common, letter **7** abridge, compact, compose, concise, invoice, laconic, mandate, outline, precept, summary **8** breviate, condense, fleeting, succinct, syllabus **9** catalogue, condensed, ephemeral, memoranda (pl.), prevalent **10** abridgment, compendium, memorandum, transitory **11**

compendious **12** condensation
brier, briar: **4** barb, pipe **5** erica, thorn **6** smilax
briery: **5** sharp, spiny **6** thorny **7** prickly
brig: **4** boat, jail **6** prison, vessel **8** stockade **10** guardhouse
brigand: **5** thief **6** bandit, pirate, robber **7** cateran, ladrone, soldier **8** marauder, picaroon **10** highwayman
bright: apt, gay **4** fine, glad, rosy **5** acute, aglow, alert, anime, beamy, clear, fresh, gemmy, light, lucid, nitid, quick, riant, sharp, smart, sunny, vivid, witty **6** cheery, clever, florid, garish, limpid, lively, lucent, orient **7** forward, fulgent, radiant, ringing, shining **8** animated, cheerful, colorful, flashing, gleaming, luminous, lustrous, splendid, splendor **9** brilliant, cloudless, effulgent, favorable, refulgent, sparkling **10** epiphanous, glistening, glittering, precocious **11** intelligent
brighten: **4** gild **5** cheer, clear, light, liven, shine **6** cantle, engild, polish **7** animate, burnish, enliven, furbish, lighten **8** illumine **9** irradiate
brightness: **5** eclat, flame, gleam, gloss, nitor, sheen **6** acumen, bright, fulgor, luster **7** clarity, fulgour, sparkle **8** splendor **9** clearness **10** brilliance, effulgence
brilliance: **4** fame **5** eclat, flame, glory **6** acuity, dazzle, genius, luster **8** keenness, radiance, splendor **10** brightness, effulgence
brilliant: gay **4** good, keen, neon, sage, wise **5** breme **6** bright, clever, signal **7** eminent, erudite, flaming, learned, radiant, shining **8** dazzling, glorious, luminous **9** effective, prismatic, refulgent, sparkling **10** glittering **11** prismatical, resplendent **13** distinguished
brim: lip, rim, rut, sea **4** edge **5** bluff, brink, marge, ocean, verge, water **6** border, margin **8** copulate, strumpet **9** periphery
brimstone: **5** shrew **6** sulfur, virago **7** sulphur **8** spitfire
brindled: **5** tawny **7** branded, flecked **8** streaked
brine: sea **4** main, salt **5** ocean, tears **6** pickle **8** marinade
preserve in: **4** corn, cure, salt
brine shrimp: **7** artemia
bring: **4** bear, sell, take **5** carry, fetch **6** convey, deduce **7** conduce, convert, procure, produce **9** accompany, transport
about: **5** cause **6** create, effect **7** achieve **10** accomplish
back: **6** effect, recall, return, revive **7** produce, restore **8** occasion, retrieve, transact **9** instigate **10** consummate
forth: ean (Sc.) **4** bear **5** educe, hatch, incur **6** adduce, beteem **7** produce

forward: **7** present **9** introduce
in: **4** earn, reap **5** usher, yield **6** import, report, return **9** introduce
near to: **6** appose
off: **7** achieve, succeed **8** complete
on: **5** cause **6** induce
out: **7** display, publish
to: **6** revive **11** resuscitate
to earth: **4** land
together: **4** join **5** match, unite **7** compile **11** consolidate
to light: **6** elicit, reveal **7** unearth **8** disclose, discover
to naught: **4** dash **6** negate **7** confute **9** frustrate
up: **4** rear, stop **5** nurse, raise, refer, train, vomit **6** broach **7** educate **11** regurgitate
up to date: **4** post **5** brief **6** inform
brink: end, eve, lip, rim, sea **4** bank, brim, edge, foss **5** marge, shore, verge **6** border, margin
briny: **5** brack, ocean, salty **6** saline
brioche: bun **4** roll **6** stitch **7** cushion, pudding, savarin
Briseis' lover: **8** Achilles
brisk: gay **4** busy, fast, keen, pert, racy, spry, yern **5** agile, alert, alive, budge, crisp, fresh, frisk, peart, perky, quick, sharp, smart, yerne **6** active, adroit, breezy, cocket, crouse, lively, nimble, snappy **7** allegro **8** animated, friskful, spirited **9** energetic, sprightly, vivacious **11** stimulating **12** effervescing
bristle: awn **4** barb, hair, seta, tela **5** anger, birse, brush, parch, preen, setae, strut, toast **6** chaeta, palpus, ruffle, setula **7** chaetae, setulae, stubble, whisker
surgical: **4** seta **5** seton
bristled: **7** horrent **8** echinate
bristlelike: **5** setal **8** setiform
bristling: **5** rough **6** hispid, horrid, setose, thorny **7** horrent, scrubby
brit, britt: **5** sprat **7** herring **10** crustacean
Britain: See **England, Ireland, Scotland, Wales**
British (see also **England**): **5** Welsh **7** English **8** Scottish **13** Northern Irish
actor/actress: **4** Gwyn, Tree **5** Caine, Donat, Leigh, Moore, Niven, Smith, Terry **6** Arliss, Coward, Harris, Irving, Lillie, Whitty **7** Burbage, Connery, Garrick, Gielgud, Langtry, Langtry, Olivier, Siddons **8** Anderson, Campbell, Fontanne, Guinness, Harrison, Redgrave, Williams
architect: **4** Adam, Wren **5** Jones **7** Lutyens
artist: **4** Byrd, Opie **5** Blake, Holst, Moore **6** Turner **7** Hogarth, Millais, Poynter **8** Reynolds **9** Constable **12** Gainsborough
composer: **4** Arne **5** Elgar **6** Delius, Handel

7 Britten, Purcell, Stainer **8** Sullivan **15** Vaughan Williams

conductor: **7** Beecham **10** Barbirolli

dramatist: Fry **4** Hare **5** Eliot, Wilde **6** Barrie, Coward, Dryden, Jonson, Pinero, Pinter **7** Marlowe, Osborne, Shaffer **8** Congreve, Sheridan, Stoppard **9** Middleton **10** Galsworthy **11** Shakespeare

poet: **4** Gray, Lear, Pope **5** Auden, Blake, Burns, Byron, Donne, Eliot, Keats, Noyes, Scott, Wilde **6** Brooke, Cowper, Dryden, Graves, Jonson, Milton, Thomas **7** Chaucer, Hopkins, Housman, Kipling, Marlowe, Shelley, Sitwell, Spenser **8** Browning, Macaulay, Rossetti, Tennyson **9** Coleridge, Masefield, Stevenson, Swinburne **10** Wordsworth **11** Shakespeare

songwriter: **6** Lennon, Webber **9** McCartney

British Columbia: *capital:* **8** Victoria

city: **6** Duncan **7** Kitimat, Nanaimo, Quesnel **8** Kamloops, Smithers **9** Vancouver

Indian: **5** Haida **7** Shuswap

island: **6** Graham **7** Moresby **9** Vancouver **14** Queen Charlotte

lake: **6** Babine, Chilko, Fraser, Muncho, Stuart **7** Thutade

mountain: **5** Coast, Rocky **7** Cariboo, Purcell, Selkirk **8** Monashee

river: **4** Nass **5** Liard, Peace **6** Fraser, Skeena **7** Parsnip **8** Columbia

strait: **6** Hecate

Britomartis: **7** Artemis **8** Dictynna

mother: **5** Carme

brittle: **4** frow, weak **5** brash, candy, crisp, crump, eager, frail, frowy, frush, short **6** crispy, crumpy, feeble, fickle, frough, infirm, slight **7** brickle, bruckle, fragile, friable, froughy **8** delicate, snappish **9** breakable, crumbling, frangible, irritable **10** perishable

broach: air, awl, cut, pin, rod, tap **4** open, ouch, shed, spit, spur, stab, veer, vent **5** begin, dress, drift, prick, rimer, spool, voice **6** boring, brooch, gimlet, launch, pierce, reamer, submit **7** advance, bring up, enlarge, mention, propose, publish, spindle, suggest, violate **8** approach, broacher, deflower, incision **9** introduce **11** perforation

broad: **4** deep, free, vast, wide **5** ample, beamy, large, plain, roomy, thick, woman **6** coarse, risqué **7** evident, general, grivois, liberal, obvious, platoid **8** grivoise, spacious, tolerant **9** capacious, expansive, extensive, outspoken **12** unrestrained **13** comprehensive

broadbill: **4** bird, gaya, raya **5** scaup **8** shoveler **9** swordfish

broadcast: sow **4** seed, send, show **5** radio, strew **6** spread **7** declare, program, publish, scatter **8** announce, televise, transmit **9** advertise

broad-footed: **8** platypod

broad-minded: **7** lenient, liberal **8** catholic, tolerant

broadside: **4** bill **5** salvo **7** barrage **8** circular

broadsword: **4** bill, kris **6** glaive, spatha **7** cutlass, Ferrara **8** claymore, scimitar

brobdingnagian: big **4** huge **5** giant **8** colossal, gigantic

brocade: **5** cloth **6** broche, kincab **8** baudekin **9** baldachin

brocard: **4** gibe, rule **5** maxim, moral **6** speech **7** sarcasm **8** aphorism **9** principle

brochure: **4** book **5** tract **8** pamphlet, treatise

brocket: **4** deer, pita, stag **5** brock **7** spitter

brogue: **4** hose, shoe **5** fraud, trick **6** accent, brogan **7** dialect **8** trousers

broil: row **4** burn, char, feud, fray, heat **5** alarm, brawl, grill, melee, scrap **6** affray, birsle, braise, splore, tumult **7** brulyie (Sc.), contest, discord, dispute, embroil, garboil, quarrel **8** conflict, grillade **10** contention, dissension **11** altercation, disturbance

broiling: hot **6** torrid **8** sizzling, steaming **9** scorching **10** sweltering

broke: **4** poor **8** bankrupt **9** insolvent, penniless

broken: **4** rent, torn **5** burst, gappy, rompu (F.), rough, tamed **6** hackly, ruined, shaken **7** crushed, fracted, reduced, subdued **8** outlawed, ruptured, weakened **9** cashiered, dispersed, fractured, shattered **10** incoherent, incomplete **11** fragmentary **12** disconnected, intermittent

down: **6** shabby **7** haywire

broker: **5** agent **6** corser, dealer, factor, jobber **7** brogger, changer, courser, peddler, realtor, scalper **8** broacher, huckster, merchant **9** go-between **10** pawnbroker

brokerage: fee **4** agio **10** commission

brolly: **8** umbrella

bromide: **5** trite **8** compound, sedative **9** platitude **11** commonplace

bronco: **5** horse **6** cayuse **7** broncho, mustang **9** estrapade (Sp.)

bronco buster: **6** cowboy, ginete

Bronte: **4** Anne **5** Emily **9** Charlotte

brother: **8** Branwell

hero: **9** Rochester **10** Heathcliff

novels: **8** Jane Eyre, Villette **9** Agnes Grey **16** Wuthering Heights

Bronx cheer: boo **9** raspberry

bronze: aes (L.), tan **4** bust **5** alloy, brown **6** statue

film: **6** patina

gilded: **6** ormolu

nickel: **11** cupronickel

pert. to: **7** aeneous

brooch: bar, pin **4** boss, clip, ouch **5** cameo, clasp **6** fibula, plaque, shield **8** ornament **9** brochette

brood: fry, nye, set, sit **4** mope, nest, nide, race, weep **5** aerie, breed, covey, flock, group, hatch, issue, sedge, worry, young **6** cletch, clutch, family, litter, ponder **7** progeny, species **8** cogitate, incubate, meditate **9** multitude, offspring **11** contemplate

brook: run **4** bear, beck, burn, ghyl, gill, rill, rush, sike **5** abide, bayou, bourn, creek, stand **6** arroyo (Sp.), bourne, canada, endure, gutter, rindle, rivose, runlet, stream, suffer **7** comport **8** quebrada, tolerate **11** watercourse

brooklet: **4** beck, rill **6** rillet, runnel **7** rillock, rivulet **9** arroyuelo (Sp.)

broom: mop **4** fray, swab **5** besom, bream, brush, spart, sweep, whisk **8** splinter

broom plant: **5** hirse, shrub, spart, whisk **7** cyticus, genista, heather **8** deerweed

broomcorn millet: **5** hirse **7** sorghum

broth: **4** bree, broo, soup **5** stock **6** brewis, jussal, jussel **7** pottage **8** bouillon, consomme, jusshell

brothel: **4** crib, stew **6** bagnio, bordel **8** bordello **10** bawdy house

brother: bub, fra, kin, pal, sib **4** mate, monk, peer **5** billy, buddy, cadet, frere (F.), friar **6** fellow, fraile, frater (L.) **7** comrade, sibling *pert. to:* **9** fraternal

brotherhood: **4** club, gild **5** guild, lodge **6** friary **8** bratstro, sodality **10** fellowship, fraternity **11** association

brotherly: **4** kind **6** tender **9** fraternal **12** affectionate

brougham: **8** carriage **9** limousine

brought up: **4** cade

brouhaha: din **4** fuss **5** babel, furor **6** clamor, furore, racket, ruckus, rumpus, tumult **9** commotion **10** hullabaloo **11** pandemonium

brow: top **4** brae, bree, edge, mien, snab (Sc.) **5** bound, brink, crest, front, ridge, slope **8** boldness, forehead **9** acclivity, gangplank **10** effrontery **11** countenance

browbeat: **5** abash, bully **6** hector **7** depress **10** disconcert, intimidate

brown: dun, tan **4** coin, cook, dark, sear **5** dusky, penny, sedge, sepia, taupe, tawny, tenne, toast, umber **6** gloomy, russet, sennet, tanned **9** half-penny
cocoa: **6** sahara
dark: **5** sepia, umber **6** bister, bistre **9** chocolate
light: tan **4** ecru, fawn **5** beige, khaki, tenne
purple: **4** puce
red: bay **4** cuba, roan **5** henna, sepia **6**

auburn, russet, sorrel, Titian **8** chestnut
yellow: **6** almond, bronze **12** butterscotch

brown Betty: **7** pudding **10** coneflower

brown study: **7** reverie **10** absorption **11** abstraction

brownie: elf, nis **4** cake, puck **5** cooky, fairy, nisse, pixie, urisk **6** goblin, sprite, uruisg (Sc.) **9** sandpiper **10** leprechaun

brownnose: **9** sycophant

browse: **4** brut, crop, feed, scan, skim **5** graze **6** forage, nibble, peruse **7** dip into, pasture

bruin: **4** bear

bruise: **4** bash, bray, dent, dunt, hurt, maim, maul **5** black, break, crush, curry, delve, dinge, pound **6** batter, breach, damage, hatter, injury, mangle, shiner **7** contuse, dammish, disable **9** pulverize, triturate

bruiser: **5** boxer **8** pugilist

bruit: din **4** fame, hint, rale, tell **5** noise, rumor, sound **6** blazon, clamor, report **7** declare, hearsay **8** intimate

brume: fog **4** haze, mist, smog **5** vapor

brumous: **5** foggy, misty **6** hiemal, sleety **7** wintery

Brunei: *capital:* **17** Bandar Seri Begawan
city: **5** Seria **6** Bangar, Tutong
district: **6** Belait, daerah, Tutong **9** Temburong
port: **5** Muara **11** Kuala Belait

brunette: **4** dark **5** brown, brune, gipsy, gypsy **7** swarthy

brunt: jar **4** blow, jolt **5** clash, force, onset, shock **6** attack, effort, impact **7** assault **8** outburst

brush: **4** comb, fray, skim **5** broom, clash, clean, copse, fight, graze, sweep, touch **6** badger, battle, brosse (F.), stroke **7** thicket **8** skirmish **9** brushwood, encounter, sideswipe **11** undergrowth

brushwood: **4** rone **5** brake, brush, copse, frith, scrog, scrub **6** rammel **7** coppice, thicket

brusque: **4** curt, rude **5** bluff, blunt, brusk **6** gruff, hasty, rough, short **6** abrupt **7** violent **8** cavalier, impolite **12** discourteous

brut: dry **6** browse

brutal: **5** cruel, feral, gross **6** carnal, coarse, savage, severe **7** beastly, bestial, brutish, caddish, inhuman **8** ruthless **9** atrocious, barbarous, ferocious, insensate

brute: **5** beast, yahoo **6** animal, savage **7** ruffian **9** scoundrel

bryophyte: **4** moss **5** plant **9** liverwort

Brython (see also **Wales**): **4** Celt **5** Welsh **6** Briton **7** Cornish
god: Dea, Ler **5** Brian, Dylan, Lludd **8** Amaethon
goddess: Don **8** Rhiannon **9** Arianrhod

bubal: 4 topi 8 antelope
bubble: air, bub 4 bead, bell (Sc.), bleb, blob, boil, boll, dupe, foam, glob, seed, suds 5 caper, cheat, empty, slosh 6 burble, delude, seethe, trifle 7 blister, blubber, deceive, globule 8 delusive 9 pipe dream 10 effervesce 11 speculation
bubbling: gay 8 effusive 9 sparkling
buccal: 4 oral
buccaneer: 6 pirate, rifler, robber, viking 7 corsair, mariner, spoiler 8 Picaroon 10 freebooter
  standard: 5 roger 10 Jolly Roger
Bucephalus: 5 horse, steed 7 charger
  owner: 9 Alexander
buck: fob, ram 4 boil, butt, deer, dude, male, pass, prig, rear, soak, stag, toff, wash 5 carry, dandy, steep 6 basket, dollar, oppose, resist 7 sawbuck 8 antelope, prickett, sawhorse 9 buckwheat, pulverize
  first year: 4 fawn
  fourth year: 4 sore
buckaroo: 6 cowboy 8 horseman
buckboard: 8 carriage
bucket: tub 4 bail, bowk, cage, pail 5 cheat, hurry, scoop, skeel 6 bailer, barrel, drench, hoppet, situla (L.), vessel 7 swindle 8 cannikin
  handle: 4 bail
  molten glass: 7 cuvette
Buckeye State: 4 Ohio
buckle: bow 4 bend, curl, hook, kink, tach, warp 5 clasp, marry, twist, yield 6 couple, fasten, fibula (L.), secure 7 contend, fermail, fibulae (L.pl.), grapple 8 fastener, struggle 10 distortion
  down: 5 set to 7 address, pitch in
  part: 5 chape 6 tongue
  under: bow 5 yield 6 cave in 10 capitulate
buckler: 4 crab 5 block 6 shield 7 rotella, roundel, shutter
buckram: 6 fabric 7 precise 10 cuckoopint, stiffening 11 muscle-bound
buckthorn: 5 rhamn 7 alatern, cascara 8 lotebush 9 alaternus, chaparral
buck up: 5 brace 7 comfort
buckwheat: 4 buck 8 sarrazin
buckwheat tree: 4 titi 6 teetee
bucolic: 4 idyl 5 local, naive, rural 6 farmer, rustic, simple 7 cowherd 8 agrestic, ecologue, herdsman, pastoral
bud: eye, gem, imp, pip 4 bulb, cion, germ, girl, grow, knop, seed 5 child, graft, scion, shoot, youth 6 button, flower, germin, sprout 7 blossom, brother, gemmule 8 bourgeon 9 germinate
  arrangement: 11 aestivation
  social: deb 8 debutant 9 debutante

Buddha: Foh 7 Gautama 10 Shakyamuni, Siddhartha
  cause of infinite existence: 6 nidana
  center: 5 Lassa, Lhasa
  chant: 6 mantra
  church: 4 Terá
  column: lat
  disciple: 6 Ananda
  doctrine: 7 trikaya
  dryad: 6 Yaksha, Yakshi
  enlightenment: 5 bodhi
  evil spirit: 4 Mara
  fate: 5 karma
  father: 11 Suddhodhana
  fertility spirit: 6 Yaksha, Yakshi
  festival: bon 5 Bodhi, Poson, Varsa, Vesak 9 Buart Nark
  final beatitude: 4 raga 7 nirvana
  for justice: 6 dharna, dhurna
  gateway: 5 toran, torii 6 torana
  god: 4 Deva
  greater: 8 Mahayana
  hatred: 4 dosa
  hell: 6 Naraka
  holy city: 8 Varanasi
  holy person: 11 bodhisattva
  Japanese image: 8 Daibutsu
  language: 4 Pali
  lesser: 8 Hinayana
  life cycle: 6 anicca
  mendicant: 6 bhikku 7 bhikshu
  monastery: 4 Tera 6 Vihara
  monk: 4 lama 5 arhat, yahan 7 bhikshu, poongee 8 poonghee, poonghie, talapoin
  monument: 5 stupa
  mother: 5 Maya
  paradise: 4 Jodo
  passion: 4 raga
  Path: 14 Noble Eightfold
  prayer: 4 mani
  priest: 4 lama 7 mahatma
  rebirth: 7 samsara
  relic mound: 5 stupa
  religious community: 6 sangha
  retribution: 5 karma
  rock temple: 4 rath 5 ratha
  sacred city: 5 Lassa, Lhasa
  school: 5 ritsu
  scripture: 5 sutra 9 Tripitaka
  sect: Zen 6 tendai 7 Jodo-shu 8 Mahayana 9 Theravada 10 Mantrayana
  shrine: 4 tope 5 stupa 6 dagoba, pagoda 7 chorten
  son: 6 Rahula
  spiritual leader: 4 guru 9 Dalai Lama
  stupa site: 9 Amaravati
  teaching: 6 dharma
  throne: 5 asana

title: **7** Mahatma
tree: **5** bodhi, pipal **6** botree
wife: **9** Yasodhara
will to live: **5** Tanha
buddy: boy, cob, pal **4** chum, mate **5** crony **6** cobber **7** brother, comrade **9** companion
buddy-buddy: **4** cozy **5** close **8** intimate
budge: fur **4** move, stir **5** booze, brisk, stiff, thief **6** jocund, liquor **8** movement **11** nervousness
budget: bag **4** body, boot, pack, plan, roll **5** batch, bunch, stock, store **6** bottle, bundle, parcel, socket, wallet **7** program **12** accumulation
buds: **8** burgeons, dehisces
pickled: **6** capers
buff: fan, rub, tan **4** coat **5** shine **6** addict, polish **7** leather **8** nonsense **10** enthusiast
in the: **4** nude **5** naked
buffalo: ox **4** anoa, buff, Cape, stag **5** bison, bugle, water **6** buffle, hamper **7** carabao, caribou, gazelle, nonplus, overawe, tamarau, zamouse **8** bewilder **9** bamboozle, frustrate
crossbreed: **7** beefalo, cattalo
European: **6** wisent
large: **4** arna, arni **5** arnee
meat: **7** biltong
wild: **4** arna, arni **5** arnee **8** seladang
buffalo gourd: **11** calabazilla
buffalo tree: **10** rabbitwood
buffer: dog, pad **6** bumper, fender, pistol **7** cushion
buffet: bar, bob, box, hit **4** beat, blow, buff, cuff, slap, toss **5** filip, smite, stool **6** abacus, batter, fillip, strike, strive, thrash, wallop **7** contend, counter, hassock **8** credence, credenza, cupboard, lambaste **9** footstool, sideboard **10** affliction
bufflehead: **4** duck, fool **5** clown, dunce **6** buffle **9** merrywing
buffleheaded: **4** dull **6** simple, stupid
buffoon: dor, wag, wit **4** aper, fool, jape, mime, mome **5** actor, antic, buffo, clown, comic, drole, droll, mimer **6** harlot, jester, mummer, stooge **7** playboy **8** balatron, gracioso, humorist, merryman, ridicule **9** harlequin **10** harlequina, hobby-horse **11** merry-andrew, Punchinello
bug: bog, dor **4** flaw, germ, idea, mite, wire **5** annoy, bogey, bulge, roach, stink **6** bedbug, beetle, chinch, elater, insect, scheme **7** bellied, bugbear, forward, pompous, wiretap **8** hemipter, hobbyist **9** conceited, hide a mike, hobgoblin, prominent **10** enthusiast, flashlight **11** hunchbacked
genus: **9** Hemiptera
June: **3** dor **6** beetle

lightning: **7** firefly
needle: **7** ranatra
bugaboo: **4** bogy, fear, goga, gogo, ogre, **5** alarm, bogey, bogie, gogga **6** bodach, goblin **7** bugbear, specter, spectre **8** worricow (Sc.) **9** hobgoblin, scarecrow, worriecow (Sc.) **10** mumbo-jumbo
bugbane: **4** herb **9** hellebore **10** rattleroot
bugger: **4** chap **5** scamp **6** fellow, rascal
buggy (see also **carriage**): **4** cart, shay, trap **5** nutty **7** caboose, foolish, vehicle **8** demented, infested, stanhope **9** gladstone
bughouse: **5** crazy, nutty **6** asylum, bedlam, insane
bugle: **4** bead, horn **5** black **6** flugel **7** buffalo, bullock, clarion, trumpet **10** mellophone
blare: **8** tanatara
call: **4** taps **6** alerte (F.), sennet, tattoo **7** retreat **8** reveille
note: mot
yellow: iva
bugleweed: **4** mint **6** indigo
bug off: **5** leave, scram **6** go away **7** buzz off, get lost
build: big **4** bigg, form, make, rear **5** edify, erect, found, frame, raise, set up, shape **6** create, graith **7** fashion **8** assemble, increase, physique **9** construct, establish, fabricate
nest: **6** nidify
up: **5** erect **7** enhance **8** increase **9** publicity **10** strengthen
builder: **5** maker **7** erector **8** tectonic **9** carpenter **10** contractor **11** constructor
labyrinth: **8** Daedalus
of wooden horse: **5** Epeus **6** Epeius
building: hut **4** casa (Sp.), pile **5** aedes, hotel, house **6** biggin, bottle, chalet, fabric **7** edifice, factory **8** dwelling **9** apartment, structure **10** storehouse **11** edification
addition to: ell **4** apse, wing **5** annex **6** lean-to
dilapidated: **7** rookery **8** firetrap, tenement
exhibition: **6** museum
farm: **4** barn, crib, shed, silo
gateway: **5** pylon
material: **4** iron, wood **5** adobe, brick, glass, steel, stone **6** cement, stucco **8** concrete
medieval: **6** castle
part: ell **4** apse
projection: bay, ell **4** apse, wing **5** annex **6** dormer, lean-to **7** cornice
public: **5** edile **6** aedile, casino, church, museum, temple **7** capitol, library, theater **10** auditorium
rib: **9** tierceron
round: **7** rotunda

sacred: **4** fane **6** church, mosque, pagoda, shrine, temple **7** edicule **8** pantheon **9** cathedral, synagogue
triangular: **6** A-frame

bulb: bud **4** blub, corm, knob, lamp, root, seed **5** globe, onion, swell, tuber **6** bulbus, crocus **9** expansion **12** protuberance
edible: yam **4** sego, taro **5** onion **6** garlic, potato
segment: **5** clove

bulbous: **5** round **7** swollen

bulbul: **4** bird, kala

Bulgaria: *capital:* **5** Sofia
city: **4** Ruse **5** Varna **6** Burgas, Pleven, Sliven **7** Plovdiv **11** Stara Zagora
currency: lev **4** leva **8** stotinka
former empire: **7** Ottoman **9** Byzantine
mountain: **6** Musala **7** Balkans, Rhodope **8** Rila Dagh **12** Transitional
port: Lom **4** Ruse **5** Varna, Vidin **6** Burgas
religion: **15** Eastern Orthodox
river: **4** Arda **5** Mesta **6** Danube, Struma, Yantra **7** Maritsa, Tundzha
sea: **5** Black
weight: oka, oke **5** tovar

bulge: bag, bug, jut **4** bump, cask, hump, knob, lump **5** belly, bilge, bloat, bouge, flask, pouch, swell **6** billow, cockle, dilate, extend, pucker, wallet **7** blister, distend **8** protrude, swelling **9** convexity, gibbosity **10** projection

bulging: **4** full **5** bombe, bowed, pudgy **6** convex **7** gibbous **8** bouffant

bulk: **4** body, heap, hold, hulk, hull, lump, mass, pile, size **5** cargo, gross, might, power, stall, swell **6** expand, extent, figure, volume **7** bigness **8** majority, quantity **9** aggregate, dimension, largeness, magnitude **11** massiveness

bulkhead: **4** wall **5** check **7** battery **9** partition, structure

bulky: big **5** burly, gross, large, stody, stout **6** clumsy **7** hulking, massive, weighty **8** unwieldy **9** corpulent, policeman, ponderous

bull: cop **4** apis, jest, male, seal, slip, toro (Sp.), zebu **5** bobby, boner, drink, edict, error **6** bovine, letter, peeler, taurus (L.) **8** cajolery, document, flattery, nonsense **9** detective, policeman, quadruped **10** zapaterito (Sp.)
angry: **5** gorer
castrated: **4** stot **5** steer **7** bullock
half man: **8** minotaur
hornless: **5** doddy **6** doddie
pert. to: **7** taurine
sacred: Hap **4** Apis, Hapi
young: **4** stot (Sc.) **5** stirk **7** bullock

bulla: **4** bleb, case, seal **5** blain **7** vesicle

bullate: **8** puckered **9** blistered

bulldoze: cow, dig, ram **4** push **5** bully, force, scoop **6** coerce, menace, pistol **8** browbeat, restrain, threaten **10** intimidate

bulldozer: **5** bully **6** grader **7** machine

bullet: **4** ball, lead, shot, slug **5** hurry **6** pellet, sinker, tracer **7** missile
diameter: **7** caliber
fake: **6** pellet

bulletin: **4** memo **6** notice, poster, report **7** program **9** statement **11** publication **12** announcement

bullfight: **7** corrida **9** novillada
bullring: **12** plaza de toros
cheer: ole
entrance: **5** toril
fence: **7** barrera
final act: **5** faena
lance: **4** vara
parade: **5** paseo

bullfighter: **6** torero **7** matador, picador, **8** capeador, toreador **12** banderillero
famous: **8** Cordobes, Manolete **9** Dominguin
foot: **6** torero
mounted: **8** toreador
suit: **12** traje de luces

bullfinch: alp, olp **4** monk, nope, olph, pope **5** hedge

bullheaded: **6** stupid **8** stubborn **9** obstinate **10** headstrong

bullion: bar **4** gold **5** ingot, metal **6** billot, silver

bull-like: **7** taurine

bullock: **4** stot **5** bugle, steer, stirk **6** bovine **9** quadruped

bull's eye: **6** center, target

bully: **4** boat, boss, fine, good, huff, mate, punk **5** brave, bravo, great, tough **6** bounce, harass, hector, jovial, menace, tyrant **7** bluster, bouncer, bullock, darling, dashing, gallant, gauster, huffcap, roister, ruffian **8** bangster, barrater, barrator, browbeat, bulldoze, domineer, frampler, harasser **9** blusterer, bulldozer, companion, excellent, scrimmage **10** burgullian, intimidate, sweetheart

bulrush: **4** reed, rush, tule **5** sedge **6** bumble **7** cattail, papyrus, scirpus

bulwark: **4** bail, fort, wall **5** fence, mound **6** defend, shield **7** bastion, defence, defense, parapet, protect, rampart **10** breakwater, stronghold

bum: beg, din **4** hobo, idle **5** cadge, drink, drone, idler, mooch, tramp **6** borrow, frolic, guzzle, sponge **7** guzzler **8** vagaband

bumble: bee **4** veil **5** botch, drone, idler **6** beadle, bungle, jumble, muffle **7** bittern, blunder, bramble, bulrush, bungler

bump: hit, jar **4** bang, blow, bust, jolt, lump, oust, thud, whop **5** bulge, clash, knock, thump **6** bounce, demote, nodule, strike **7** collide, pothole, replace **8** swelling **9** downgrade, hip thrust **12** protuberance

bumper: **4** fine **5** glass, guard, large **6** buffer, fender, goblet **8** carangid, doorstop **10** successful

bump into: **4** meet **7** collide **8** come upon **9** encounter, run across, sideswipe

bumpkin: oak, yap **4** clod, gawk, hick, lout, rube **5** churl, yahoo, yokel **6** lummox, rustic **7** hayseed **9** chawbacon

bump off: **4** do in, kill **6** murder, rub out **7** put away **9** liquidate

bumptious: **5** cocky **8** insolent **9** obtrusive

bumpy: **5** rough **6** uneven **7** jolting

bun: jag **4** buzz, roll **7** biscuit, chignon **8** hair knot

bunch: lot, set **4** body, crew, herd, lump, pack, tuft **5** batch, clump, crowd, flock, group **6** bundle, circle **7** cluster **8** assemble, quantity, swelling **9** aggregate **10** collection

bunco: con, gyp **5** cheat, trick **7** defraud, swindle

bund: **4** band **6** league **7** society **10** embankment, federation **11** confederacy

bundle: lot, pot, wad **4** band, hank, pack, pile, roll **5** bunch, group **6** bindle, packet, parcel, wrap up **7** package **10** collection
arrows: **5** sheaf **6** quiver
grain: **5** sheaf, shock
hay: **4** bale
sticks: **5** fagot **6** faggot **7** fascine
straw: **4** bolt

bung: **4** cork, plug **5** spile **7** stopper, stopple, tampion

bungle: err **4** flub, goof, muff **5** botch, fluff, gum up, spoil **6** boggle, bumble, foozle, fumble, mess up **7** blunder, louse up **9** mismanage **10** pull a boner

bungling: **6** clumsy **7** awkward **8** slipshod **9** maladroit, unskilled **10** blundering

bunk: bed, cot **5** berth, hokum, hooey, lodge, put up, sleep **6** billet, trough **7** baloney, twaddle **8** log truck, nonsense

bunker: bin **4** crib, hold **6** dugout, hazard **7** shelter **8** obstacle, sandtrap **10** difficulty **11** compartment

bunkum: rot **4** jazz **6** drivel, humbug **7** hogwash **8** buncombe **9** poppycock **10** balderdash, doubletalk

bunt: tap **4** butt, push **5** shove **6** strike **8** sail part **9** spearhead, wheat smut

bunting: **4** bird, flag, pape **5** finch **6** fabric, towhee **7** cowbird, garment, ortolan **8** bobolink

Bunyan's blue ox: **4** Babe

Burma: **6** Myanma **7** Myanmar
archipelago: **6** Mergui
canopy: **8** tauzaung
capital: **6** Yangon **7** Rangoon
city: **4** Paan, Pegu **5** Falam, Manle, Prome **6** Lashio, Loikaw, Sittwe **7** Henzada **8** Mandalay, Moulmein
currency: pya **4** kyat
dagger: dah, dao, dow **4** dout
deer: **6** thamin **7** thameng
demon: nat
division: yin **6** yin-mya (pl.) **8** Mandalay **9** Irrawaddy **10** Tenasserim
garment: **6** tamein
gate: **5** toran
gibbon: lar
girl: **4** mima
hill dweller: Lai
island: **6** Ramree **7** Cheduba
language: Lai **4** Chin, Pegu **6** Kachin **7** Burmese
measure: dha, lan, tha **4** byee, dain, seit, taim, teng **6** palgat
musical instrument: **4** turr **5** tarau
official: wun **4** woon **6** sawbwa
peak: **4** Popa **8** Nattaung, Victoria **11** Hkakabo Razi
people: Lai, Mon, Tai **4** Chin, Kadu, Naga, Shan **5** Karen, Lhota **6** Burman, Kachin, Khamti, Peguan **7** Karenni **8** Chingpaw
river: Uyu **4** Mali, Nmai, Pegu **6** Salwin, Shweli **7** Kaladan, Myitnge, Salween, Sittang **8** Chindwin **9** Irrawaddy **10** Tenasserim
robber: **6** dacoit
ruined city: Ava
sash: **7** tubbeck
sea: **7** Andaman
sport: **7** chinlon
state: Mon **4** Chin, Shan **5** Karan, Kayah, pyine **6** Kachin **7** Rakhine **8** pyine-mya (pl.)
traveler's shed: **5** zayat
tree: **4** acle **7** yamanai
weight: mat, moo, vis **4** kait, ruay, viss **5** candy, tical, ticul

buoy: dan **5** elate, float, raise **6** hold up, marker, signal, support, sustain **8** deadhead
mooring: **7** dolphin

buoyant: gay **5** happy, light, on air **6** blithe, lively **7** elastic, hopeful, lilting, springy **8** animated, cheerful, floating, sanguine, spirited, volatile

burble: yak **4** boil, gush **5** run on **6** bubble, gurgle, jabber **7** chatter, prattle

burbot: **4** fish, ling **6** lawyer **7** ellpout
genus: **4** lota
relative: cod

burden: tax, try, vex **4** birn (Sc.), care, cark, clog, crux, duty, idea, load, onus **5** cargo, theme, worry **6** charge, grieve, hamper, impose, lading, plague, saddle, weight **7** afflict, ballast, essence, freight, message, nucleus, oppress, perturb, refrain, trouble **8** capacity, encumber, handicap, overhead **9** aggravate, grievance **10** imposition
of complaint: **8** gravamen

burden bearer: **5** Atlas **9** worry wart

burdensome: **5** heavy **7** arduous, irksome, onerous, weighty **8** cumbrous, grievous, grinding **9** demanding, difficult **10** oppressive **11** importunate, troublesome

bureau: **4** desk **5** chest **6** agency, office **7** dresser **10** chiffonier, department, escritoire

bureaucrat: **8** official, stickler **9** penpusher **10** politician **11** functionary **12** civil servant **13** petty official

bureaucratese: **4** cant **6** jargon **12** gobbledygook

burg: **4** city, town **6** hamlet **7** village **8** hick town **11** whistle-stop

burgeon: bud **4** grow **5** bloom **6** expand, flower, sprout **7** shoot up **8** increase, put forth

burglar: **4** yegg **5** crook, thief **6** cat man, robber **8** peterman

burglary: **5** caper, heist, theft **7** break-in, larceny, robbery **8** stealage

burgomaster: **4** gull **5** mayor **7** alcalde **10** magistrate

burgoo: **4** soup, stew **5** gruel **6** picnic **8** porridge

burial: **9** interment **10** deposition
case: box, urn **6** casket, coffin **11** sarcophagus
ceremony: **7** funeral
litter: **4** bier **10** catafalque
mound: low **6** barrow **7** tumulus
pile: **4** pyre
place: **4** tomb **5** grave **7** pyramid **8** catacomb, cemetery, golgotha **9** graveyard, mausoleum, sepulcher **10** necropolis **12** potter's field

burin **4** tool **6** graver

Burkina Faso: *capital:* **11** Ouagadougou
city: Leo **4** Kaya **9** Koudougou
people: **4** Bobo, Lobi, Samo **5** Mande, Marka, Mossi **6** Fulani, Senufo, Tuareg **7** Gurunsi, Voltaic **9** Boussance
river: **5** Volta

burl: **4** knot, lump **5** bulge **6** growth, veneer **11** excrescence

in mahogany: **3** roe

burlap: **5** gunny **6** fabric **7** bagging, sacking **8** wrapping
fiber: **4** hemp, jute

burlesque: ape **4** mime, mock **5** farce, mimic, revue **6** comedy, overdo, parody, satire **7** ham it up, lampoon, overact, takeoff **8** comedian, ridicule, travesty **9** slapstick, top banana **10** caricature, exaggerate
serenade: **8** shivaree **9** charivari

burly: big **5** beefy, bulky, heavy, hefty, husky **6** brawny, hearty, stocky, sturdy **8** muscular, thickset **9** strapping

Burma: (see box)

burn: **4** brew, char, fire, plot, raze, rill, sear, sere **5** adust, anger, blaze, broil, brook, cense, flame, parch, scald, singe, waste, water **6** scorch, stream, tingle **7** combure, combust, consume, cremate, flicker, oxidize, rivulet, smolder **8** squander **9** cauterize **10** incinerate
midnight oil: **6** stay up **9** lucubrate
surface: **5** singe **6** scorch **7** blister
up the road: **5** speed

burned: **5** baked **6** seared **7** charred **8** ustulate

burner: **6** Bunsen, censer **8** thurible

burning: hot **4** fire **5** afire, angry, blaze, calid, eager, fiery, flame, gledy **6** ablaze, ardent, fervid, torrid, urgent **7** caustic, cautery, fervent, flaming, glaring, glowing, mordant, shining **8** ardurous, exciting, inustion **9** consuming, cremating, inflaming **10** combustion, phlogistic **13** conflagration
bush: **5** wahoo
malicious: **5** arson

burnish: rub **4** buff **5** glaze, gloss, shine **6** luster, patina, polish **7** furbish

burnisher: **4** tool **5** agate **6** buffer **7** frottom **8** polisher

burnoose, burnous: **5** cloak **6** mantle **7** garment **8** albornoz

burnsides: **5** beard **7** general **8** whiskers

burnt work: **10** pyrography

burr: nut, pad, rib **4** barb, birr, boss, buzz, halo, knob, ring, whir **5** briar, whirr **6** banyan, circle, corona, tunnel, washer **7** sticker **8** parasite **9** whetstone **10** sweetbread

burro: ass **6** donkey **9** quadruped **10** pack animal

burrow: **3** den, dig **4** heap, hole, mine, mole, root, tube **5** berry, couch, mound **6** furrow, tunnel **7** passage, shelter **8** excavate

bursa: sac **4** hall, sack **5** pouch **6** cavity **9** residence

bursar: **6** purser, terrar **7** cashier **9** paymaster, treasurer **10** controller

burst: pop **4** blow, bust, loss, rend, scat **5** blast, break, erupt, flash, go off, salvo, split **6** broken, damage, injury, volley **7** explode, flare up, rupture, shatter **8** outbreak, sundered **9** interrupt
forth: **5** erupt, sally **7** blasted
inward: **7** implode
out: **5** blurt **7** exclaim **9** ejaculate
bursting: **8** erupting **10** dehiscence

Burundi: *capital:* **9** Bujumbura
king: **5** mwami
lake: **7** Rugwero **10** Cyohoha-Sud, Tanganyika
language: **6** French **7** Kirundi, Swahili
people: Twa **4** Hutu **5** Bantu, Pygmy, Tutsi **6** Bahutu, Watusi **7** Hamitic

---

bury: **4** hide, sink **5** cover, inter, inurn **6** entomb, inhume, shroud **7** conceal, engross, immerse, repress, secrete **8** inundate, submerge **9** overwhelm, stash away
bus: **6** jitney, travel **7** circuit, omnibus, vehicle **9** charabanc
busby: cap, wig **6** fur hat **8** bearskin **9** headdress
bush tod **4** buss, butt **5** bosch, clump, grove, shrub **6** branch, tavern **7** boscage, cluster, thicket **11** advertising
bushed: **4** beat, worn **5** spent **8** dog-tired **9** exhausted
bushel: foo (Sc.), gob, lot **4** full
forty: wey
quarter of: **4** peck
bushing: **5** drill **6** collet, lining **7** padding
machine: **6** sleeve
bush-league: **6** non-pro **7** amateur **8** inferior **10** second-rate
bushman (see also **Africa**): san (pl.) **4** gung, saan (pl.) **5** bushy **6** Abatoa, Abatua, Abatwa, rustic **8** woodsman
blanket: **5** bluey
language: **7** Khoisan
bushmaster: **5** snake, viper
bushwa: **4** bosh, bull, bunk **5** hooey, trash **7** baloney, hogwash, rubbish **8** nonsense
bushwacker: **5** papaw **6** pawpaw, scythe, sniper **8** guerilla
bushy: **5** bosky **6** dumose, dumous **7** bushman, queachy
hair: **4** shag
heap: tod
business: ado, art, job **4** care, firm, fuss, game, line, task, work **5** cause, trade **6** affair, custom, matter, metier, office **7** calling, concern, trading, traffic **8** activity, commerce,

industry, vocation **9** diligence, following, patronage, rickmatic **10** employment, enterprise, occupation, solicitude **11** disturbance, importunity, intercourse, transaction **13** attentiveness, establishment
custom: **9** patronage
place of: **4** mart, shop, store **6** market, office, shoppe **8** emporium
businessman: **9** executive
buskin: **4** boot, shoe **7** bottine, tragedy **8** cothurni (L.pl.), half-boot, stocking **9** brodequin, cothurnus (L.)
buss: **4** boat, bush, calf, deck, kiss **5** dress, smack **6** vessel **9** transport
bussu: **4** palm **7** troolie
bust: **4** fail, raid, ruin, tame **5** bosom, break, burst, chest, flunk, lemon, loser, spree **6** arrest, breast, bronze, demote, reduce, statue **7** degrade, dismiss, failure **8** bankrupt **9** blockhead, sculpture **10** depression
bustard: **4** bird, kori **5** crane, paauw **7** bebilya, houbara **8** gompaauw
genus: **4** otis **6** otidae
buster: **4** crab, wind **5** blade, child **6** fellow
bustle: ado **4** fuss, stir, to-do, whir **5** frisk, haste, whirr **6** clamor, fistle, flurry, hubbub, hustle, pother, racket, tumult, unrest, uproar **7** clatter, turmoil **8** activity, tournure **9** agitation, commotion, whirlwind **10** hurly-burly
woman's: **6** bishop
busy: **4** nosy **5** brisk **6** active, at work, intent, lively, occupy **7** engaged, humming, on the go, operose **8** diligent, employed, occupied, sedulous, tireless, untiring **9** assiduous, attentive, detective, laborious, officious **11** distracting, industrious
busybody: **5** snoop, yenta (Yid.) **6** gossip **7** marplot, meddler, snooper **8** factotum, quidnunc
but sed (L.), yet **4** mere, only, save **5** still **6** except, unless **7** besides, howbeit, however **11** nonetheless **12** nevertheless
butcher: **4** kill, slay **5** botch, spoil **6** bungle, murder **8** mutilate **9** slaughter **10** meat vendor **11** executioner
hook: **7** gambrel
rabbi: **8** shochtim
tool: saw **5** knife, steel **7** cleaver
butcher-bird: **6** shrike
butchery: **6** murder **7** carnage **8** abattoir, massacre, shambles **9** bloodbath, slaughter
butler: **7** servant, spencer, steward **8** factotum, retainer **9** major-domo **10** manservant
butt: end, jut, pit, ram, tun **4** buck, bunt, cart, cask, fool, goad, goat, jolt, push, rump, stub **5** hinge, joint, mound, stump **6** adjoin, breech, target, thrust **7** fall guy, project **8**

derriere, flatfish, flounder **13** laughing stock
cigar or cigarette: **5** snipe
in: **6** meddle **7** intrude **9** interfere, interrupt, intervene

butte: **4** hill **7** picacho **8** mountain

butter: fat, oil **4** food **6** beurre (F.), cajole, spread **7** blarney, flatter
artificial: **4** oleo **9** butterine, margarine **13** oleomargarine
pert. to: **7** butyric
semifluid: ghi **4** ghee
serving of: pat
shea: **5** galam **6** bambui, bambuk **7** bambara
tree: **4** shea **5** fulwa **8** phulwara
tub: **6** firkin
without solids: **5** drawn **9** clarified

butter-and-eggs: **6** clover **7** ransted **8** ramstead, ranstead, toadflax

buttercup: **6** flower **7** anemone **8** crow-foot, reindeer **10** butter-rose
fruit: **6** achene

butterfingered: **6** clumsy **7** awkward **9** all-thumbs

butterfish: **5** coney **6** blenny, gunnel

butterfly: **4** kiho **5** satyr **6** idalia, morpho, ursula **7** admiral, buckeye, monarch, skipper, vanessa, viceroy **8** arthemis, cecropia, grayling **9** aphrodite, underwing **10** fritillary, lepidopter, swim stroke
expert: **13** lepidopterist
fish: **6** blenny, chiton **7** gurnard
genus: **8** melitaea **10** heliconius
larva: **11** caterpillar
lily: **4** sego **8** mariposa

butterwort: **9** steepweed

buttery: **6** larder, pantry, spence **9** storeroom, wheedling **10** flattering

button: bud **4** boss, chin, hook, knob, knop **5** badge, catch, pearl **6** bauble, buckle **8** fastener, lapel pin
ornamental: **4** stud
part: **4** hole **5** shank
three jewel: **6** troche

button-down: **6** proper, square **8** orthodox, straight **10** unoriginal **12** conservative, conventional

buttonhole: **4** loop, slit **6** accost, detain, eyelet **11** boutonniere, get the ear of

buttress: **4** pier, pile, prop, stay **5** brace **7** support **8** abutment

buxom: **5** busty, hefty, jolly, plump, prone, sonsy **6** bosomy, florid, sonsie **7** shapely **8** bouncing **10** curvaceous **11** full-figured

buy: **4** chap, coff (Sc.), coup, deal, gain, shop **5** bribe, trade **6** market, obtain, ransom, redeem, secure **7** acquire **8** purchase
back: **6** redeem
cheaply: **5** steal **7** bargain
to sell at a profit: **7** regrate

buyer: **5** agent **6** client, patron **7** shopper **8** customer, prospect **9** purchaser
beware: **12** caveat emptor
stolen property: **5** fence

buzz: hum **4** burr, call, hiss, ring, whir **5** fancy, fling, phone, rumor **6** notion **7** whisper **9** bombinate, telephone

buzzard: **4** aura, hawk **5** buteo, harpy **6** condor, curlew **7** vulture **9** senseless
bald: **6** osprey
honey: **4** pern

buzzer: bee **4** bell **5** alarm, badge **6** signal

buzz off: **5** leave, scram **6** depart **7** pull out

by: ago, per, via **4** near, past **5** apart, aside, close **6** beside, nearby, next to, toward **7** besides, through **9** alongside **10** concerning **11** according to
and by: **4** anon, soon **5** later **7** shortly
means of: per **4** from, with **7** through
mouth: **4** oral

bygone: **4** past, yore **5** olden **6** former **7** ancient, elapsed **8** backward, departed

byname: **6** byword **7** surname **8** cognomen, nickname **9** sobriquet

bypass: **4** miss, shun **5** evade, shunt, skirt **6** detour **7** circuit **8** sidestep

Byron character: **4** Inez, Lara **6** Haidee **7** Don Juan, Manfred **12** Childe Harold

bystander: **7** witness **9** spectator

byway: **4** lane, path **5** alley

byword: saw **5** axiom, motto **6** byname, phrase, saying **7** epithet, proverb **8** nickname **9** catchword

Byzantine: **6** tricky **7** complex, devious, empire, **8** involved **9** intricate

C

C: 7 hundred
Caaba: 6 shrine
caama: fox 4 asse 10 hartebeest
cab: 4 hack, taxi 6 hansom
cab driver: 5 cabby 6 cabbie, cocher (F.) 7 cochero (Sp.)
cabal: 4 camp, plot, ring 5 junta, party 6 brigue, circle, clique, scheme 7 coterie, council, faction, in group 8 intrigue 10 conspiracy 11 machination
  pert. to: 9 factional
cabalistic: 6 arcane, mystic, occult 10 mysterious
caballero: 6 escort, knight 8 cavalier, horseman 9 chevalier, gentleman
cabana: 5 cabin 7 cottage, shelter 9 bathhouse
cabaret: 4 cafe, club 6 tavern 8 late spot 9 floor show (Br.), nightclub 10 liquor shop, restaurant, supper club, tea service
cabbage: 4 chou (F.), crib, kale, kohl 5 filch, steal 6 pilfer 7 bowkail (Sc.), purloin 8 borecole, colewort
  daisy: 11 globeflower
  fermented: 10 choucroute (F.), sauerkraut
  salad: 4 slaw 8 coleslaw
  seed: 5 colza
  soup: 4 kale (Sc.) 7 borscht
  tree: 7 angelin 8 palmetto
  variety: 4 cale, kale 5 colza, savoy 8 colewort, kohlrabi
cabbagehead: 5 dunce 9 screwball
cabbageworm: 6 looper 7 cutworm
cabin: cot, den, hut 4 cell, shed 5 berth, booth, coach, hovel, lodge, shack 6 cabana, shanty 7 cockpit, cottage 9 stateroom
cabin boy: 7 grummet
cabin car: 7 caboose
cabinet: box 4 case 5 board, chest, habut 6 bureau, closet, vanity 7 almirah (Ind.), armoire, commode, console, council, etagere, whatnot 8 cellaret, cupboard, ministry, vargueno 10 chiffonier 11 summerhouse
cable: 4 boom, link, rope, wire 5 chain 6 stitch 8 telegram
  lifter: 7 wildcat
  post: 4 bitt
cable car: 4 tram 6 telfer 7 telpher
cable TV: 13 shared antenna

cabochon: gem 5 stone 8 ornament 9 unfaceted 10 style of cut
caboodle: kit, lot 10 collection
caboose: cab, car 5 buggy 6 galley
cabotin: 5 actor 9 charlatan
cabotinage: 7 emoting 9 ham acting, theatrics
cabrilla: 4 bass 7 grouper
cacao: 4 bean, seed, tree 5 broma, cocoa 6 arriba 9 chocolate
cache: 4 bury, hide 5 store 7 conceal, secrete 8 treasure 10 storehouse 11 hiding place
cachepot: jar, urn 7 planter
cachet: 4 seal 5 stamp, wafer 6 status 8 prestige 11 distinction
cachexia: 7 illness, wasting 9 morbidity 12 malnutrition
cacholong: 4 opal
cackle: gab, jaw 4 blab, chat 5 clack, laugh 6 babble, gabble, giggle, gossip, titter 7 chackle, chatter, prattle, twaddle 8 laughter
cacoethes: 4 itch 5 mania 6 desire
cacography: 11 misspelling
  opposite: 11 orthography
cacophonous: 5 harsh 7 raucous 8 jangling, strident 9 dissonant 10 discordant 11 unmelodious
cactus: 4 bleo 5 dildo, nopal, plant 6 barrel, cereus, chaute, chende, cholla, mescal, old man 7 airampo, opuntia, saguaro 8 chichipe 9 organ pipe 11 prickly pear
  drug: 6 peyote
  fruit: 6 cochal
  plantation: 7 nopalry
  stem lump: 6 areole
cad: cur 4 boor, heel 5 churl, creep 6 rascal, rotter 7 bounder, dastard 9 scoundrel
cadaver: 4 body 5 stiff 6 corpse 7 carcass 8 skeleton
cadaverous: 4 pale 5 gaunt 6 wasted 7 ghastly, haggard 9 emaciated
caddie: 5 gofer 11 club carrier
caddow: 5 quilt 7 jackdaw 8 coverlet
caddy: box, can 4 case 5 chest 9 container
cade: keg, pet 4 cask, lamb 6 barrel, coddle 7 indulge, juniper
cadence: 4 beat, lilt, pace, tone 5 meter, metre, pulse, sound, swing, throb 6 rhythm 8 clausula 10 inflection, modulation
cadet: 5 plebe, youth 6 embryo, junior 7 student 10 midshipman 11 West Pointer

cadew: 4 worm

cadge: beg, bum 4 bind, hawk 5 carry, mooch 6 borrow, peddle, sponge 8 scrounge 9 panhandle

Cadmus: *city:* 6 Thebes
daughter: Ino 5 Agave 6 Semele 7 Autonoe
father: 6 Agenor
sister: 6 Europa
wife: 8 Harmonia

cadre: 4 cell, core, unit 5 frame, group 6 scheme 7 nucleus 9 framework

caduceus: 4 wand 5 staff 6 emblem, symbol 7 insigne, scepter, sceptre

caducity: 5 lapse 8 senility 10 feebleness 14 perishableness

Caesar (Julius): 6 tyrant 7 emperor
assassin: 6 Brutus 7 Cassius
capital: 4 Roma
colleague: 7 Bibulus
country conquered by: 4 Gaul
daughter: 5 Julia
eulogist: 6 Antony
fatal day: 4 Ides
message: 4 veni, vici, vidi
place of victory: 9 Pharsalus
river crossed by: 7 Rubicon
sister: 4 Atia
site of famous message: 4 Zela
son-in-law: 6 Pompey
wife: 7 Pompeia 8 Cornelia 9 Calpurnia

caesura: 4 rest, stop 5 break, pause 8 interval 10 verse break 12 interruption

cafard: 5 blues 6 apathy 7 boredom 10 depression 12 listlessness

cafe: 5 diner 6 saloon 7 barroom, cabaret 8 teahouse 9 nightclub 10 restaurant 11 coffeehouse

caffeine: 5 thein 6 theine 8 alkaloid 9 stimulant

cage: box, car, mew, pen 4 coop, jail 5 brake 6 aviary, basket, bucket, chapel, prison, shut in 7 chantry, confine 8 imprison, scaffold, strainer 9 enclosure, inclosure 11 incarcerate
hawk's: mew 5 meute

cagey, cagy: sly 4 foxy, wary, wily 6 astute, shrewd 7 cunning

cahoots: 6 league 9 collusion 11 partnership

caiman: 6 cayman, jacare (Sp.) 9 alligator, crocodile

Cain: 8 murderer 10 fratricide
brother: Pur 4 Abel, Seth
descendant: 6 Lamech
father: 4 Adam
killer of: 4 Abel
land: Nod
mother: Eve
nephew: 4 Enos
son: 5 Enoch

Caine Mutiny: *author:* 4 Wouk
character: 5 Queeg
ship: 11 mine sweeper

cairn: 8 landmark, monument 9 stone heap 11 trail marker

cairngorm: 6 quartz

Cairo: *river:* 4 Nile
fortress: 7 Citadel
people: 7 Cairene
Christian: 4 Copt

caisson: box 5 chest, float, wagon 7 chamber, pontoon
disease: 5 bends

caitiff: 4 base, mean, vile 6 wicked 8 cowardly 10 despicable

cajole: con 4 coax 5 jolly, tease 6 entice, whilly (Sc.) 7 beguile, flatter, wheedle 8 blandish, butter up 9 sweet talk

cake (see also **cookie, pastry, pie**): bar, bun, set 4 lump, mass 5 block, crust, patty, wedge 6 harden, nacket (Sc.), pastry 7 bannock 8 meringue, solidify 9 coagulate
almond: 8 macaroon
boiled in honey: 8 teiglech
cholesterol free: 9 angel food
coffee: 6 kuchen
corn: 4 pone 7 fritter 8 tortilla
custard: 4 flan 6 eclair 9 creampuff
dough: 6 batter
filled: 4 tart 9 enchilada
fried: 7 cruller 8 doughnut
griddle: 7 bannock (Sc.), crumpet, hotcake, oatcake, pancake 11 flannel cake
rich: 5 torte 7 stollen 8 madeline 9 madeleine
rum: 4 baba
sacrificial: 6 hallah 7 challah
seed: wig 4 wiff
small: bun 4 tart 6 cookie, muffin 7 cupcake
tea: 5 scone
thin: 5 scone, wafer 10 shortbread
topping: 5 icing 8 frosting
unleavened: 5 matzo 6 damper 8 tortilla

cakewalk: 5 dance, march, strut 6 prance

calaba: 4 tree 5 birma

calabash: 5 gourd 6 curuba

calaboose: can, jug 4 brig, gaol, jail 5 clink 6 cooler, lockup, prison 8 hoosegow

caladium: 4 taro

calamanco: 6 fabric 7 garment

calamitous: sad 4 dire, evil 5 black, fatal 6 bitter, dismal, tragic, woeful 7 adverse, baleful, direful, hapless, ruinous, unhappy, unlucky 8 grievous, wretched 9 miserable 10 afflictive, deplorable, disastrous 11 distressful, unfortunate

calami: pen 5 quill 9 sweetflag

calamity: 4 blow, evil, ruin 5 storm 6 misery,

sorrow **7** scourge, tragedy **8** accident, disaster, fatality **9** adversity, cataclysm **10** affliction, misfortune **11** catastrophe **12** misadventure, wretchedness

calangay: **8** cockatoo

calash: **6** calesa, sailor **8** carriage **10** woman's hood **11** Asian seaman

calcar: **4** oven, spur **7** furnace

calced: **4** shod

calcite: *animal:* **8** skeleton
deposit: **4** spar, tufa **5** tatar **10** stalactite, stalagmite
soil with: **4** marl

calcium: *carbonate:* **4** tufa
oxide: **9** quicklime
sulfate: **6** gypsum **14** plaster of paris

calculate: aim **4** plan, rate, tell **5** count, think **6** assess, expect, figure, number, reckon **7** average, compute, prepare **8** consider, estimate, evaluate **9** determine, enumerate

calculation: **4** care **7** caution **8** forecast, prudence **9** deduction, logistics, reckoning **10** adjustment, estimation **11** computation

calculating: sly **4** wily **6** crafty, shrewd **7** cunning, guarded **8** cautious, scheming

calculator: **5** table **6** abacus **7** soroban **8** computer **10** accountant

Calcutta:
part: **6** Maidan
prison: **9** Black Hole
river: **7** Hooghly
slum: **6** bustee

caldron, cauldron: pot, vat **6** boiler, kettle, vessel **8** red color

Caleb's son: Hru, Hur

Caledonia: **8** Scotland

calefy: **4** heat, warm

calembour: pun

calendar: log **4** card **5** diary, slate **6** agenda, docket **7** almanac, journal, program **8** menology, register, schedule
church: **4** ordo
former: **6** Julian
French revolution: **6** Nivose **7** Floreal, Ventose **8** Brumaire, Fervidor, Gernubak, Messidor, Pluviose, Prairial **9** Fructidor, Thermidor **11** Vendemiaire
kind: **5** lunar, solar
modern: **9** Gregorian

calenture: **4** fire, glow, zeal **5** ardor, fever **7** passion **9** sunstroke

calf: boy, leg **4** dolt **5** bobby, bossy, youth **6** bovine, muscle **7** fatling
flesh: **4** veal, veau (F.)
hide: kip
motherless: **4** dogy **5** dogie
muscle: **9** plantaris
pert. to: **5** sural
unbranded: **8** maverick

Caliban: **5** beast, slave
adversary of: **8** Prospero
deity of: **7** Setebos
witch mother: **7** Sycorax

caliber: **4** bore, rank **5** class, value, worth **6** degree, talent **7** ability, breadth, compass, quality, stature **8** capacity, diameter

calibrate: **5** grade **7** measure **11** standardize

calico: **4** girl **5** cloth, woman **7** disease, spotted **8** goldfish **9** womankind **12** multicolored
bass: **7** crappie
bird: **6** plover **9** turnstone
horse: **5** pinto **7** piebald
wood: **7** Halesia **14** silverbell tree

California *capital:* **10** Sacramento
city: **6** Carmel **7** Anaheim, Burbank, Oakland, San Jose **8** Palo Alto, Pasadena, San Diego **9** Long Beach **10** Los Angeles **11** Palm Springs **12** Beverly Hills, San Francisco, Santa Barbara
desert: **6** Mojave **8** Colorado
fault zone: **10** San Andreas
film center: **9** Hollywood
Indian: **4** Hupa, Juma, Pomo, Seri **5** Hoopa, Modoc, Yorok **6** Mohave
island: **8** Alcatraz **13** Santa Catalina
motto: **6** Eureka (I Have Found It)
mountain pass: **6** Donner, Sonora
mountain peak: **6** Shasta **7** Whitney
national park: **7** Redwood, Sequoia **8** Yosemite
prison: **6** Folsom **8** Alcatraz **9** Tehachepi **10** San Quentin
sites: **9** Queen Mary **10** Disneyland **11** Death Valley **16** Golden Gate Bridge
state bird: **11** valley quail
state fish: **5** trout
state flower: **11** golden poppy
state tree: **7** redwood
U.S. president: **5** Nixon **6** Reagan
wine area: **4** Napa

caliginous: dim **4** dark **5** murky **7** obscure

Caligula: *adopted by:* **8** Tiberius
father: **10** Germanicus
horse: **9** Incitatus
mother: **9** Agrippina
other name: **5** Gaius

caliph, calif: Abu, Ali **4** Bakr, Imam, Omar **6** Othman **7** Muawiya **9** caliphate

descendant: 4 Alid 7 Abbasid, Fatamid, Omayyad 8 Fatamite
fourth: Ali

calix: cup 7 chalice

calk (see also **caulk**): 9 shoe plate

call: bid, cry, dub 4 cite, dial, hail, name, page, stop, term, yell 5 claim, clepe, clock, elect, phone, rouse, shout, style, utter, visit, waken, yodel, yodle 6 accuse, appeal, arouse, demand, invite, invoke, muster, quethe, summon 7 address, appoint, collect, command, convene, convoke, entitle, impeach 8 announce, assemble, nominate, proclaim, vocation 9 challenge, reprimand, telephone, terminate 10 denominate
back: 6 revoke 8 retrieve 10 phone again 11 ask to return
distress: PAN, S.O.S. 6 Mayday
down: 5 scold 6 berate, invoke, rebuke 7 censure, reprove 8 denounce, execrate 9 reprimand
for: 4 page 5 exact 6 demand 7 predict, request, require
forth: 5 evoke 6 arouse, elicit, invoke, signal, summon 7 evocate
off: end 4 kill 5 count 6 cancel
on: ask, bid 4 urge 5 visit 6 drop in 8 appeal to
out: 5 ascry, shout 6 holler, muster 11 give voice to
to: 4 hail 5 ascry 6 accost, halloo 7 address
to attention: hop 6 remind
together: 6 muster 7 convene, convoke
to mind: 4 cite 6 recall 8 remember

calligrapher: 6 penman, writer 7 copyist 9 engrosser

calling: art, job 4 rank 5 trade 6 career, metier, naming, outcry 7 pursuit, station, summons 8 business, function, position, shouting, vocation 9 condition, summoning, utterance 10 employment, invitation, occupation, profession 11 appellation, convocation, undertaking 13 circumstances

Calliope's son: 7 Orpheus

Callisto's son: 5 Arcas

Call of the Wild author: 6 London (Jack)

callous: 4 hard 5 horny, tough 6 brawny, obtuse, torpid 8 obdurate 9 indurated, unfeeling 11 hardhearted, indifferent 14 pachydermatous

callow: raw 4 bald, bare 5 crude, green 6 marshy 7 meadow 8 immature, juvenile, unformed, youthful 9 unfledged 13 inexperienced 15 unsophisticated

calm: lee 4 cool, dill, easy, fair, hush, lull, mees (Sc.), mild, rest 5 abate, allay, charm, mease, peace, quell, quiet, sober, still, stoic 6 defuse, docile, gentle, irenic, pacify, placid, sedate, serene, smooth, soothe, steady 7 appease, assuage, halcyon, mollify, pacific, patient, placate, restful, unmoved 8 composed, decorous, peaceful, restrain, tranquil 9 collected, impassive, temperate, unexcited, unruffled 10 halcyonian, phlegmatic, unconfused 11 complacence, tranquilize, undisturbed 13 dispassionate, imperturbable 15 undemonstrative

calmness: 5 poise 6 repose 8 ataraxia, serenity 9 composure, placidity, quietness, sangfroid, stillness 10 equanimity 11 self-control, tranquility 12 peacefulness 13 impassiveness

calorie, calory: 5 therm 10 energy unit

calotte: 6 ice cap 7 glacier 8 skull cap 11 snowy summit

calumet: 4 pipe

calumniate: 4 slur 5 belie, libel, smear 6 accuse, attack, defame, malign, revile, vilify 7 asperse, blacken, slander, traduce 9 blaspheme

calyx: 4 leaf 5 sepal
helmet-shaped: 5 galea
of flower: 8 perianth

cam: cog 4 awry, lobe 5 askew, catch, wiper 6 tappet 7 crooked, trippet 8 perverse

camalig (P.I.): hut 5 cabin 10 storehouse

camaraderie: 7 jollity 9 good cheer 10 fellowship 11 sociability 12 friendliness

camarilla: 4 cell, ring 5 cabal, junta 6 clique

Cambodia (Kampuchea):   *capital:* 9 Phnom Penh
city: 6 Angkor, Kratie 8 Siem Reap 10 Battambang
currency: sen 4 riel
lake: 8 Tonle Sap
province: 5 khetf
river: 6 Mekong
temple: 9 Angkor Wat

Cambria: See **Wales**

cambric: 5 linen 6 fabric 7 batiste

Cambridge (Eng.): 11 University
boat races: 4 Lent
college official: 6 bedell
council: 5 caput
first college: 10 Peterhouse
honor examination: 6 tripos
river: Cam
student: 5 sizar, spoon 6 optime

Cambridge (U.S.): *college:* 6 Lesley 9 Radcliffe
river: 7 Charles
state: 13 Massachusetts

university: MIT **7** Harvard
camel: 6 mehari **8** ruminant **9** dromedary
   driver: **6** sarwan **8** cameleer
   female: cow
   male: **4** bull
   nickname: **15** ship of the desert
   relative: **5** llama **6** alpaca, vicuna **7** guanaco
   two-humped: **8** Bactrian
   young: **4** calf, foal
camellia: 8 japonica
camelopard: 7 giraffe
Camelot: *lord:* **6** Arthur
   magician: **6** Merlin
camel's hair: aba **5** cloth **6** camlet **8** cameline
   garment: aba
cameo: gem 7 carving, phalera, relievo, rilievo
   8 anaglyph **9** sculpture
   cutting tool: **5** spade
   stone: **4** onyx **5** agate **8** sardonyx **10** chalcedony
camera: 7 chamber **10** department, instrument
   part: **4** lens **5** prism **6** finder, mirror **7** bellows, shutter **9** diaphragm **10** viewfinder
   12 aperture ring
   platform: **5** dolly **6** tripod
cameraman: 8 camerist, operator **12** photographer **13** projectionist
Cameroon: *capital:* **7** Yaounde
   city: **4** Buea, Edea **5** Kribi **6** Douala
   currency: **5** franc **7** centime
   people: **5** Bantu **6** Fulani **7** Hamitic
camion: bus **4** dray **5** truck, wagon **8** motor-
   bus
camlet: 6 Angora, fabric, mohair **9** camelteen,
   camletine
Camorra: 5 Mafia
camouflage: 4 fake, hide, mask **6** muffle,
   screen **7** conceal **8** disguise **9** deception
camp: 4 pest, tent **5** etape (F.), horde, siege,
   tabor **7** barrack, bivouac, shelter **8** quarters
   10 settlement
   follower: **5** bidar (Ind.) **6** gudget (Sc.)
   pert. to: **7** castral
   provision seller: **6** sutler
campaign: 5 drive, plain, stump **7** canvass,
   crusade, solicit **9** champaign, operation
campanero: 8 arapunga, bellbird
campanile: 5 tower **6** belfry **7** clocher, steeple
camphol: 7 borneol
camphor: 7 asarone, menthol
campus: 4 quad **5** field **7** college, grounds **10**
   university
campy: 5 outre **7** extreme **8** affected **11** exaggerated
Camus work: 5 Rebel **6** Plague **8** Caligula,
   Stranger **12** State of Siege
can: cup, jug, may, tin **4** able, fire, jail **5** caddy,
   could, eshin, skill **6** toilet, vessel **7** ability,

capable, dismiss **8** conserve, preserve **9**
competent, container, discharge, knowledge **10** cleverness, receptacle

Canada (see also **Quebec**): *architect:* **8**
Erickson
   capital: **6** Ottawa
   city: **5** Banff **6** London, Oshawa, Quebec, Regina **7** Calgary, Halifax, St.
   John's, Toronto, Windsor **8** Edmonton,
   Hamilton, Montreal, Victoria, Winnipeg **9** Carstairs, Saskatoon, Vancouver **10** Thunder Bay
   currency: **4** cent **6** dollar
   early explorer: **5** Cabot, Davis **6** Baffin,
   Hudson **7** Cartier, Erikson
   language: **6** French **7** English
   measure: ton **5** minot, perch, point **6**
   arpent **7** chainon
   mountain: **5** Logan **6** Selwyn **7** Cascade, Rockies **8** Columbia **9** Mackenzie
   10 Laurentian, Shickshock **11**
   Appalachian
   national anthem: **7** O Canada
   national emblem: **6** beaver **9** maple leaf
   province: **6** Quebec **7** Alberta, Ontario
   8 Manitoba **10** Nova Scotia **12** New
   Brunswick, Newfoundland, Saskatchewan **15** British Columbia **18** Prince
   Edward Island
   river: Red **5** Yukon **6** Nelson, Ottawa **8**
   Columbia **9** Churchill, Mackenzie **10**
   St. Lawrence
   sport: **6** hockey **8** lacrosse
   territory (see also individual entries): **5**
   Yukon **9** Northwest
   waterfall: **7** Niagara **9** Horseshoe,
   Reversing **11** Montmorency

Canadian: 6 Canuck
canadine: 8 alkaloid
canaille: mob **5** flour **6** rabble **8** riffraff
canal: cut **4** cano, duct, pipe, tube **5** ditch,
   drain, fossa (L.), graff, zanje **6** fossae (L.pl.),
   groove, sea arm, strait, trench **7** acequia
   (Sp.), channel, conduit, raceway, towpath **8**
   aqueduct **10** waterspout **11** watercourse
   anatomical: **6** Alcock, Hering **7** Schlemm **9**
   Haversian **10** alimentary
   dredging machine: **7** couloir
   famous: Soo **4** Erie, Kiel, Lynn, Suez **6**
   Morris, Panama **7** Welland
   footpath: **7** towpath
canape: 4 tapa **6** relish **9** appetizer **11** hors
   d'oeuvre

canard: lie 4 duck (F.), hoax 9 grapevine 11 fabrication

canary: 4 bird, fink 5 dance 6 singer, snitch 7 stoolie 8 informer, squealer
forerunner of: 5 serin
wild: 7 warbler 9 goldfinch

canary broom: 7 genista

Canary Islands: 5 Lobos, Palma 6 Gomera, Hierro 8 Graciosa, Tenerife 9 Alegranza, Lanzarote 11 Gran Canaria 13 Fuerteventura
city: 5 Telde 6 Laguna, Llanos, Palmas 7 Orotava 8 Arrecife 9 Santa Cruz 11 Guía de Isora
commune: 4 Icod
measure: 8 fanegada
mountain: 5 Teide 6 La Cruz 8 El Cumbre, Tenerife 9 Teneriffe 11 Gran Canaria

canary yellow: 6 meline

canasta: 4 game 5 cards, crate 6 basket, hamper
play: 4 meld

cancel: 4 blot, dele, omit, void 5 annul, erase, quash, remit 6 delete, efface, recall, remove, revoke 7 abolish, call off, destroy, expunge, nullify, rescind, retract, scratch 8 abrogate 10 obliterate 11 countermand

cancer: 4 Crab 5 tumor 6 blight 7 sarcoma 9 carcinoma
kind: 8 Hodgkins, leukemia

Cancer: 4 crab 6 zodiac 13 constellation

cancion: 4 song 5 lyric

candent: hot 7 fervent, glowing

candescent: 7 glowing 8 dazzling 11 luminescent

Candia: 5 Crete 8 Iraklion 9 Heracleum 10 Herakleion

candid: 4 fair, just, open, pure 5 blunt, clear, frank, naive 7 artless, sincere 8 splendid 9 guileless, honorable, impartial, ingenuous, outspoken 10 aboveboard, immaculate 11 unconcealed 15 straightforward

candidate: 7 nominee 8 aspirant, prospect 9 applicant
list: 4 leet 5 slate 6 roster
religious: 9 postulant
winning: 7 electee

Candiot, Candiote: 6 Cretan

candle: dip, wax 5 light, taper 6 cierge (F.) 9 chandelle
holder (see also **candlestick**): 6 lampad, sconce, sconse, spider 7 menorah 9 girandole 10 candelabra 11 candelabrum, candlestick
kind of: 8 bayberry
place of keeping: 9 chandlery
wax: 5 taper 6 bougie

candlelight: 4 dusk 8 twilight 9 nightfall

candlelighter: 5 spill 7 acolyte

candlenut tree: ama 5 kukui 6 bankul

candlestick: 6 lampad, sconce 8 flambeau, standard 9 flambeaux (pl.)
bracket: 6 sconce, sconse
branched: 5 jesse 8 dicerion, dikerion 9 girandole, tricerion, trikerion 10 chandelier 11 candelabrum

candlewood: 4 tree 5 shrub 9 coachwhip

candor, candour: 6 purity 7 honesty 8 fairness, kindness, openness 9 frankness, innocence, integrity, unreserve, whiteness 10 brightness, brilliance, kindliness 12 impartiality 13 outspokenness

candy: 4 corn, kiss, mint 5 fudge, gundy, lolly, penny, sweet, taffy 6 bonbon, comfit, cotton, nougat, toffee 7 brittle, caramel, congeal, flatter, fondate, jellies, sweeten 8 licorice, lollipop, sourball 9 chocolate, granulate, jelly bean, sweetmeat 10 confection 11 crystallize 12 Jordan almond
almond: 8 marzipan
base: 7 fondant
medicated: 7 lozenge 9 cough drop
mixture: 6 fourre
nut: 7 praline 13 peanut brittle
pulled sugar: 5 taffy 6 penide
sugar: 7 fondant 8 alphenic

candy striper: 10 nurse's aide

candytuft: 5 plant 6 flower, iberis

cane: rod 4 beat, dart, flog, pipe, reed, stem, tube, whip 5 birch, lance, staff, stick 6 bamboo, punish, rattan 7 calamus, hickory, malacca, scourge 9 crabstick
dense growth: 9 canebrake
knife: 7 machete
part: 7 ferrule
sugar: 7 sucrose

Canfield: 8 Klondike 9 solitaire

cangle: 7 dispute, quarrel, wrangle

canine (see also **dog**): cur, dog, fox, pup 4 fisc, wolf 5 canis (L.), hound, pooch 7 doglike
tooth: 7 laniary

caning: 6 rattan, wicker 8 birching, whipping

canister: box 9 container

canker: 4 rust 5 stain 6 infect 7 consume, corrode, corrupt, pervert, tarnish 9 verdigris

cannabis: 4 hemp
drug: 5 bhang 7 hashish 9 marijuana

Cannery Row author: 9 Steinbeck (John)

cannibal: 6 savage 15 anthropophagite

cannikin: can, cup 4 pail 6 bucket

cannon: bit, gun 5 crack, thief 6 mortar, pompom 7 bastard 8 howitzer, ordnance 9 artillery 10 pickpocket
breech-end knob: 8 cascabel
early: 5 aspic, saker 7 robinet
fire: 7 barrage

firing stick: **8** linstock
fodder: **8** infantry
handle: **4** anse
muzzle plug: **7** tampion
part: **4** bore **5** chase **6** breech, muzzle **7** chamber, rimbase **8** cascabel, trunnion
shot: **5** grape
support: **8** trunnion
cannonade: 5 blitz, burst, salvo **6** volley **7** barrage
cannoneer: 12 artilleryman
cannon fodder: 8 infantry, soldiers
cannot: 6 unable
cannular: 6 hollow **7** tubular
canny: sly **4** cozy, snug, wary, wily, wise **5** lucky, pawky, quiet **6** clever, frugal, gentle, shrewd **7** careful, cunning, knowing, prudent, quietly, thrifty **8** cautious, skillful, watchful **9** carefully, dexterous, fortunate, sagacious **10** cautiously **11** comfortable, sharpwitted
canoe: 4 boat, kiak, pahi, proa, waka **5** birch, kayak, prahu, skiff, umiak, waapa **6** ballam, dugout, oomiak, pitpan **7** almadia, bidarka, coracle, currane, pirogue
bark: **5** birch **7** cascara
carry: **7** portage
dugout: **5** banca **6** baroto, corial **7** pirogue, piroque **12** pambanmanche
large: **5** pah **5** bungo
sailing: **4** proa **5** prahu
skin-covered: **4** kiak **5** bidar, kayak **7** baidara
war: **4** proa
canon: law **4** code, hymn, laud, list, rule, song, type **5** axiom, Bible, gorge, gulch, model, monks, table, tenet **6** decree **7** precept, statute, tribute **8** canticle, decision, quitrent, standard **9** catalogue, clergyman, criterion **10** regulation **11** sacred books **12** constitution
Alexandrian: **10** Septuagint
enigmatical: **4** nodi (pl.) **5** nodus
musical: **11** composition
Old Testament: **11** Palestinian
resident: **8** stagiary
canonical: 8 accepted, orthodox **10** sanctioned **13** authoritative
hour: **4** laud, none, sext **5** matin, prime **6** tierce **7** vespers **8** compline
canonicals: alb **4** cope, cowl, hood, robe **5** amice, stole **6** chimer, rochet, tippet **7** maniple, tunicle **8** chasuble, cincture, dalmatic **9** vestments
canopy: sky **4** ceil, cope, dais, hood **5** shade, vault **6** awning, celure, finial, tester **7** marquee, shelter **8** covering **9** baldachin, baldaquin, pavillion **11** baldacchino
altar: **7** ciboria (pl.) **8** baldakin, ciborium **9** baldachin, baldaquin **10** baldachino **11** baldacchino
bed: **6** tester **7** sparver
canorous: 5 clear **7** musical **8** sonorous **9** melodious **10** euphonious
cant: tip **4** coax, heel, lean, list, nook, sing, tilt, turn **5** argot, bevel, chant, hield, idiom, lingo, lusty, merry, niche, pitch, share, slang, slant, slope, whine **6** careen, corner, herald, intone, jargon, lively, patois, patter, snivel **7** auction, incline, portion, singing, wheedle **8** cheerful, pretense, vigorous **9** barbarism, hypocrisy, vulgarism **10** intonation, vernacular **13** colloquialism **17** sanctimoniousness
cantabank: 6 singer **7** chanter
cantaloupe: muskmelon
cantankerous: 6 ornery **7** grouchy, peevish **8** perverse **9** irritable, malicious **10** brabagious **11** contentious **12** crossgrained, curmudgeonly
cantata: 4 mote, poem **8** serenata **11** composition
cantatrice: 6 singer **9** chanteuse
canteen: K.T., P.X., bar **5** bazar, flask **6** bazaar **7** cantina
canter: jog, run **4** gait, lope, pace, rack **5** rogue **6** beggar, whiner **8** vagabond **10** street arab
Canterbury: *archbishop:* Odo **4** Lang **6** Anselm, Becket **7** Cranmer, Dunstan **9** Augustine
gallop: **5** aubin
canticle: ode **4** hymn, laud, song **5** canto **6** anthem, hirmos **7** bravura **11** Song of Songs **13** Song of Solomon
church: **6** Te Deum, Venite **10** Benedicite, Benedictus, Magnificat **12** Nunc Dimittis
cantilena: 6 legato, melody **8** graceful
cantillate: hum **5** chant **6** intone, recite
cantina: bar, pub **5** pouch, store **6** pocket, pommel, saloon, tavern **7** canteen, gin mill **8** groggery
canting: 5 atrip, pious **12** hypocritical
cantle: 4 join, nook, part **5** cheer, piece, raise, slice **6** corner **7** portion, segment **8** brighten, fragment **11** cornerpiece
canto: air, fit **4** book, pace, song **5** verse **6** melody, passus
canton: 4 part **5** angle **6** billet, corner **7** portion, quarter, section **8** district, division
cantor: 5 hazan **6** leader, singer **7** chanter, chazzan, soloist **9** precentor
cantoria: 7 balcony, gallery
cantrip: 5 charm, spell, trick
cantus: 4 song **5** chant
canty: 6 lively **8** cheerful **9** sprightly
Canuck: 8 Canadian
canvas: 4 duck, sail, tarp, tent, tewk **5** scrim **6**

burlap **7** picture, poldavy **8** painting
waterproof: **9** tarpaulin
canvasback: **4** duck **6** cheval
canvass: **4** beat, hawk, poll, sift **5** randy, study **6** debate, peddle, search **7** agitate, discuss, examine, solicit, trounce **8** campaign, consider **10** scrutinize **11** electioneer, investigate
canvasser: **5** agent **6** poller, rodman **7** counter **8** salesman
canyon: gap **4** pass **5** cajon, cañon, chasm, gorge, gulch, gully **6** arroyo, coulee, ravine, valley
  mouth: **4** abra
  small: **6** canada
canzonet: air **4** song **5** canto **6** ballad **7** canzona, canzone **8** madrigal
caoba: **5** quira **8** mahogany, muskwood
caoutchouc: **6** rubber
  source: ule **6** caucho
cap (see also **hat, head covering**): fez, hat, lid, taj, tam, tip, top **4** acme, beam, best, coif, cork, dome, eton, hood, hure, mate, pass, topi **5** beret, chief, cover, crown, excel, match, outdo, plate, seize, topee, trump **6** arrest, beanie, bonnet, climax, cornet, helmet, mobcap, puzzle, summit, top off, turban **7** commode, ferrule, fitting, overlie, overtop, perplex, retread, surpass **8** calyptra, complete, headgear, surprise, tarboosh **9** detonator, headpiece **10** noisemaker **11** mortarboard
  child's: **5** mutch, toque **6** biggin, bonnet
  close-fitting: **4** coif **5** toque **6** cloche **7** calotte
  covering: **8** havelock
  ecclesiastical: **5** beret, miter **6** barret **7** biretta, galerum, galerus **8** barretta **9** zucchetto
  hunter's: **7** montero
  knitted: **5** toque
  military: **4** kepi **5** busby, shako
  muslin: **5** mutch
  part: **4** bill, peak **5** visor
  Roman: **6** pileus
  Scotch: tam **8** balmoral **9** glengarry **11** tamoshanter
  set one's: **6** pursue
  sheepskin: **6** calpac **7** calpack
  skull: **5** beame **6** callot, pileus **7** calotte, yamilke **8** yarmulka
  steel: **10** cerveliere
capa: **5** cloak **6** mantle
capability: art **5** craft, skill **6** stroil **7** ability **8** capacity **9** potential **10** competence, efficiency
capable: apt, can, fit **4** able **5** adept **6** expert **7** skilled **9** competent, effective, efficient, qualified **10** proficient **12** accomplished

  of being cut: **7** sectile **8** scissile
  of being defended: **7** tenable
  of being heard: **7** audible
  of being molded: **7** plastic
  of being touched: **8** tangible
  of endurance: **4** wiry **5** tough
  of extension: **7** tensile
  of flying: **6** volant
  of suffering: **8** passible **9** sensitive
  render: **6** enable
capacious: **4** full, wide **5** ample, broad, large, roomy **6** goodly **8** captious, spacious **9** extensive **10** commodious **12** considerable
capacitate: **7** qualify
capacity: **4** bent, gift, size, turn **5** knack, power, skill, space **6** burden, extent, spread, talent, volume **7** ability, caliber, calibre, content, faculty, fitness **8** aptitude, strength **9** continent, endowment, intellect **10** capability, competence
Capaneus: *father:* **9** Hipponous
  mother: **8** Astynome
  slayer: **4** Zeus
  son: **9** Sthenelus
  wife: **6** Evadne
cap-a-pie: **7** utterly **10** head to foot, throughout
caparison: **4** deck, trap **8** clothing, covering **9** adornment, decoration, trappings
cape: ras **4** cope, gape, head, look, neck, ness, writ **5** amice, cappa, cloak, fanon, fichu, orale, point, sagum, stare, stole, talma **6** bertha, chapel, mantle, sontag, tabard, tippet **7** leather, manteel **8** headland, lambskin, mantilla, pelerine **9** inverness, peninsula, sheepskin **10** projection, promontory
  crocheted: **6** sontag
  lace: **5** fichu **6** bertha **8** collaret
Cape anteater: **8** aardvark
Cape armadillo: **8** pangolin
Cape Colony plateau: **5** karoo **6** karroo
Cape Dutch: **9** Afrikaans
Cape elk: **5** eland
Cape gooseberry: **4** poha **12** ground cherry
Cape jasmine: **8** gardenia
Cape lancewood: **7** assagai
cape merchant: **10** supercargo
Cape polecat: **5** zoril **8** muishond
Cape Province: *people:* **4** Xosa **5** Pondo
Cape ruby: **6** garnet, pyrope
Capek: *creature:* **5** robot
  play: RUR
capel: **4** rock, wall **5** horse **6** quartz
capelin: **5** smelt **7** ice fish
caper: hop **4** dido, jump, lark, leap, romp, skip, skit **5** antic, brank, dance, flisk, frisk, prank, sauce, shrub **6** cavort, frisco, frolic, gambol, gamond, prance, spring, tittup, vagary **7** corsair, courant, friscal, gambado **8** capricci (pl.), capriole, marigold **9** capric-

cio, condiment, devilment, privateer **11** monkeyshine, waggishness
family: **13** capparidaceae

capercaillie: **4** cock **6** grouse
courtship: lak

capernoited: **7** crabbed, peevish **9** irritable **11** intoxicated **12** muddleheaded

capernoitie: **4** head **6** noddle

capeskin: **7** leather **9** sheepskin

capful: **4** puff **8** quantity

capias: **4** writ **7** process

capillary: **6** minute **7** slender **8** filiform, hairlike **11** blood vessel

capillus: **4** hair

capilotade: **4** stew **5** sauce **6** ragout

capital: cap, top **4** cash, city, good, main, rare, seat **5** basic, chief, fatal, great, major, money, stock, vital **6** deadly, letter, mortal, primal, wealth **7** central, chattel, leading, radical, serious, weighty **9** copacetic, excellent, paramount, principal **10** prominent first-class, pre-eminent **11** scrumptious
ancient: **4** Roma
gambler's: **5** stake
impairment of: **7** deficit **9** depletion
inadequate: **10** shoestring
provide: **4** back **5** angel **7** finance

capital punishment: **7** hanging **8** shooting **9** injection **12** death penalty **13** electrocution

capitalist: **6** banker **8** investor **9** financier, plutocrat

capitalize: **4** back, fund, help **5** stake **7** finance, sponsor **8** bankroll **9** subsidize

capitano: **5** chief **7** captain, headman, soldier

capitate: **8** headlike **10** headshaped

Capitol Hill group: **5** House **6** Senate **8** Congress

Capitoline triad: **4** Juno **7** Jupiter, Minerva

capitulate: **4** fall **5** agree, title, yield **8** headline **9** enumerate, surrender **11** buckle under

caporal: **7** foreman, tobacco **8** overseer

capote: **4** hood **5** cloak **6** bonnet, mantle, topper **8** overcoat

cappuccino: **14** espresso coffee

capric acid salt: **6** rutate

caprice: fad **4** kink, mood, whim **5** antic, braid, fancy, freak, humor, quirk **6** maggot, notion, temper, vagary, whimsy **7** boutade, conceit, crochet, impulse, whimsey **9** capriccio **12** inconsistent

capricious: **5** dizzy, doddy, fluky, moody **6** fickle **7** comical, erratic, flighty, wayward **8** fanciful, freakish, humorous, unsteady, volatile **9** arbitrary, crotchety, fantastic, humorsome, whimsical **10** changeable, inconstant

Capricorn: **4** Goat **6** beetle, Zodiac **13** constellation
star within: **5** Deneb

capriole: **4** leap **5** caper **6** spring **9** headdress

capripede: **4** goat **5** satyr

caprylate: **4** acid, salt **5** ester **7** octoate

capsize: **4** coup, keel **5** upset **8** overturn

capstan: **4** drum **5** hoist, lever **8** cylinder, windlass
catch: **4** pawl

capstone: **4** acme, apex, peak **6** apogee, climax **8** pinnacle **11** culmination

capsule: pod **4** boll, case, pill **5** shell, theco, wafer **6** ampule, sheath **7** ampoule **8** pericarp **9** cartridge, detonator **10** repository

captain: boh **4** capo, head **5** chief, pilot **6** leader, master **7** captian, foreman, headman, manager, skipper **8** capitano, governor **9** centurion, commander, principal **14** superintendent
boat: gig
fictional: **4** Ahab, Nemo **5** Bligh, Queeg
pirate: **4** Kidd

caption: **5** title **6** leader, legend **7** cutline, heading **8** headline, overline, subtitle **9** underline

captious: **5** testy **6** crafty, severe **7** carping, cynical, fretful, peevish **8** alluring, caviling, contrary, critical, perverse, petulant **9** capacious, insidious, irascible **10** capricious, censorious **12** faultfinding **13** hypercritical

captivate: win **4** take **5** catch, charm **6** allure, enamor, please, ravish, subdue **7** attract, bewitch, capture, enamour, enchant **8** enthrall, overtake **9** enrapture, fascinate, infatuate

captive: **5** slave **6** enamor **7** caitiff, hostage **8** prisoner

captivity: **4** bond **6** duress **7** bondage, serfdom, slavery **9** servitude, thralldom **10** subjection **11** confinement **12** imprisonment

captor: **5** taker **6** victor **7** catcher

capture: bag, cop, get, nab, net, win **4** fang, grab, hook, land, prey, take, trap, tree **5** catch, prize, raven, seize **6** arrest, collar, obtain **9** apprehend, captivate **10** circumvent **12** apprehension

capuche: **4** cowl, hood

Capuchin: **4** monk **5** friar **6** monkey, pigeon

caput: top **4** head **7** chapter, council, section **8** division **9** paragraph

capybara: **6** rodent

car (see also **automobile**): box, bus, van **4** auto, jeep, rath **5** buggy, coach, coupe, hutch, ratha, sedan, train, wrong **6** basket, hotrod **7** awkward, chariot, touring, trailer, trolley, vehicle **8** roadster, sinister **10** automobile, left-handed **11** convertible **12** station wagon
aerial cable: **6** telfer **7** telpher
armored: **4** tank
railroad: box, oil **4** club, flat, mail, tank **5**

chair, coach, diner **6** buffet, dining, hopper, parlor **7** baggage, caboose, express, freight, gondola, pullman, sleeper, tourist **9** furniture, passenger **12** refrigerator

carabao: **5** mango **7** buffalo

caracara: **4** hawk

carack: See **carrack**

caract: See **character**

carafe: **6** bottle **7** thermos

caramel: **5** candy, sweet **6** bonbon **9** flavoring **10** confection

carapace: **5** crust, shell **6** lorica

carara: **9** coronopus

caravan: van **4** trek, trip **5** fleet, group **6** cafila, convoy, safari, travel **7** journey, trailer (Br.), vehicle **9** motor home (Br.)
slave: **6** coffle

caravansary: inn **4** chan, khan **5** hotel, serai **6** hostel, imaret **8** choultry, hostelry **9** resthouse

car barn: **5** depot

carbine: gun **5** rifle **6** musket, weapon **7** escopet **9** escopette

carbohydrate: **5** sugar **6** starch **8** dextrose **9** cellulose

carbon: **4** coal, coke, copy, soot **6** crayon **7** replica **8** graphite
deposit: **4** soot
point: **6** crayon

carbonate: **4** burn, char, fizz **6** aerate, alkali **7** enliven **9** carbonize, energizer

carborundum: **5** emery **8** abrasive

carboy: jug **6** bottle

carbuncle: **4** boil **5** jewel **6** garnet **7** abscess, pustule

carcajou: **4** lynx **6** badger, cougar **9** wolverine

carcanet: **5** chain **6** collar **8** headband, necklace

carcass: **4** body **6** corpse **7** carrion

carcoon: **5** clerk **7** manager

card: map, pam, wag, wit **4** comb, menu, plan **5** chart, fiche, joker, tease **6** cartel, ticket **7** program **8** schedule **9** character, eccentric **10** attraction, pasteboard
spot: pip
wool: tum **4** comb, rove, toom

card game: lu, gin, hoc, loo, pam **4** bank, faro, hock, keno, ruff, skat, slam, snap, solo, spin, vint **5** beast, chico, cinch, comet, crimp, decoy, gilet, gleek, monte, omber, ombre, pedro, pique, pitch, poker, rummy, stuss, trump, two-up, waist, whist **6** basset, boston, bridge, casino, commit, ecarte, euchre, fantan, flinch, hearts, masset, piquet, rounce, sledge, smudge **7** baccara, bezique, canasta, cayenne, Chicago, cooncan, old maid, sevenup **8** baccarat, commerce, conquian, contract, cribbage, handicap, Napoleon, patience, pinochle, tresillo,

vederuff **9** Newmarket, old sledge, panguinui, solitaire **10** blackstone **11** everlasting, high-low-jack, speculation **14** spite and malice
bid: **4** slam **6** misere
fortune-telling: **5** tarot
holding: **6** tenace
old: hoc, loo, pam **4** brag, ruff **5** comet, gilet, omber, ombre, trump **7** primero, reversi **8** penneech, penneeck
player who cuts: **4** pone
playing card: ace, pam, ten **4** jack, king, trey **5** basto (Sp.), deuce, joker, knave, queen, taroc, tarot
term: bid, bue, cat, pic **4** ante, book, card, deal, hand, meld, pair, pass, suit **5** dummy, flush, raise, trump **6** renege, tenace, tricon **8** sequence, straight **9** doubleton, singleton **10** Yarborough
widow: **4** skat
wild: **5** joker

cardigan: **6** fabric, jacket, wampus **7** sweater

cardinal: red **4** bird, main **5** basic, chief, cloak, color, vital **6** cleric **7** radical **9** principal **10** underlying
assembly at Rome: **7** college
hat: **8** gallerum
notification of elevation: **9** biglietto
office: hat **6** datary **7** dataria
title: **8** eminence

cards (see also **card game**): **4** deck, pack, suit

care: **4** cark, cure, duty, fret, heed, mind, reck, soin (F.), tend, wish, yeme **5** grief, guard, nurse, pains, worry **6** burden, desire, grieve, lament, regard, sorrow **7** anxiety, auspice, caution, cherish, concern, keeping, scruple, thought, tuition **8** business **9** attention, diligence, direction, oversight **10** management, solicitude **11** calculation, heedfulness **12** watchfulness **14** responsibility
for: **4** like, mind, tend **5** guard, nurse, treat **6** foster, relish **7** nurture
requiring: **7** fragile **8** ticklish
under another's: **4** ward **6** charge **7** protege **10** apprentice

careen: tip **4** cant, heel, keel, list, sway, tilt, veer **5** lurch, slope, swing, weave **7** incline

career: run, way **4** life, road **5** trade **6** charge, course, gallop **7** calling, pursuit, running **8** business, vocation **10** occupation, profession, racecourse **11** achievement

carefree: **4** easy **5** frank, happy **6** blithe, breezy, secure **8** reckless **10** insouciant **12** happy-go-lucky, lighthearted

careful: **4** wary **5** canny, chary, exact **6** frugal, intent **7** anxious, guarded, heedful, prudent, thrifty **8** accurate, cautious, diligent, discreet, dreadful, gingerly, mournful, troubled, vigilant, watchful **9** advertent, attentive, exquisite, observant, provident **10** economical, meticulous, respectful, respective, scrupulous, solicitous, thoughtful **11** circumspect, considerate, painstaking, punctilious

carefully: **7** charily **8** gingerly

careless: lax **4** cool, easy, lash, rash **5** slack **6** casual, overly, remiss, supine, untidy, unwary **7** languid **8** heedless, listless, reckless, slattern, slipshod, slovenly **9** forgetful, haphazard, negligent, unheeding, unmindful **10** delinquent, neglectful, nonchalant, regardless **11** inadvertent, inattentive, indifferent, perfunctory, spontaneous, thoughtless, unconcerned **13** irresponsible

caress: coy, hug, pat, pet **4** bill, dant (Sc.), kiss, neck **6** coddle, cosset, fondle, pamper, stroke **7** cherish, embrace **10** endearment

caretaker: **6** keeper **7** curator, janitor **9** custodian **11** housekeeper, housesitter

Carew's love: **5** Celia

careworn: **5** jaded, lined **7** haggard, pinched **8** troubled **9** exhausted **10** distressed

carfuffle: **6** flurry, ruffle **8** disorder **9** agitation **10** disarrange

cargador: **6** porter **7** carrier **9** stevedore

cargo: **4** bulk, load **6** burden, lading **7** freight, payload **8** property, shipment **10** freightage
discarded: **6** jetsam
loader: **9** stevedore
space in ship: **4** hold
stabilizer: **7** ballast
take on: **4** lade, load
wrecked ship: **7** flotsam

caribe: **4** fish **6** pirana, piraya **7** piranha

Caribbean: sea **6** region
bird: **4** tody
Indian: **5** Carib
island: **4** Cuba **5** Aruba **6** Nassau, Tobago **7** Antigua, Barbuda, Bonaire, Curacao, Grenada, Jamaica **8** Dominica, Trinidad **10** Hispaniola, Puerto Rico
island group: **6** Cayman, Virgin **7** Leeward **8** Antilles, Windward **10** West Indies

caribou: **4** deer **8** reindeer

carica: **4** tree **6** papaya, pawpaw

caricature: ape **4** copy, mock, skit **5** farce, libel, mimic, squib **6** overdo, parody, satire **7** cartoon, lampoon **8** travesty **9** burlesque **12** exaggeration

caries: **5** decay **6** cavity **10** ulceration **11** saprodontia

carillon: **5** bells **6** chimes **9** bell tower, organ stop **12** glockenspiel

cark: ail, vex **4** care, heed, load, stew **5** cavil, pains, worry **6** burden, charge, harass **7** anxiety, perplex, trouble **8** distress

carling: **6** rafter **7** support

Carmelite: **4** monk **5** friar **10** White Friar
barefoot: **8** Teresian **9** discalced
reformer: **7** Theresa **14** John of the Cross

carmen: **4** poem, song **11** incantation

Carmen composer: **5** Bizet

carmine: red **7** crimson, scarlet **8** coloring

carnage: **6** murder, pogrom **8** butchery, massacre **9** bloodshed, slaughter

carnal: **4** crow, lewd **6** animal, bodily, sexual **7** brutish, earthly, fleshly, lustful, secular, sensual, worldly **8** material, temporal **9** corporeal **11** unspiritual **12** bloodthirsty, unregenerate

carnation: **4** pink, self **5** flake **6** flower **7** bizarre, picotee **8** Dianthus **9** flesh tint, grenadine (F.)

carnelian: **4** sard **10** chalcedony

carnival: **4** fair, fete **7** revelry **8** festival **9** Mardi Gras **11** merrymaking
attraction: **4** ride **6** midway **8** sideshow **10** concession
performer: **4** geek **5** carny

carnivore: cat, dog, fox **4** bear, coon, lion, lynx, mink, puma, seal, wolf **5** civet, coati, genet, hyena, otter, panda, pekah, ratel, sable, stoat, tiger **6** cougar, ermine, feline, ferret, jackal, jaguar, marten, ocelot, possum, serval, weasel **7** dasyure, genette, glutton, leopard, opossum, polecat, raccoon, tigress **8** mongoose **9** ichneumon

carnose: **6** fleshy

carob: **4** tree **9** algarroba, chocolate, evergreen **10** locust bean **12** St. John's bread

carol: lay **4** noel, sing, song **5** ditty, yodel, yodle **6** alcove, ballad, warble **8** madrigal

Caroline island: Yap **4** Truk **5** Palau **6** Kosrae, Kusaie, Ponape **7** Pohnpei

carom: **4** shot **6** bounce, glance, strike **7** rebound **8** ricochet

carousal: **4** lark, orgy, riot, romp, toot **5** binge, drunk, feast, randy, revel, spree **6** frolic, shindy, splore **7** banquet, carouse, revelry, wassail **8** festival, jamboree **9** bacchanal

carouse: **4** bout, hell, riot **5** birle (Sc.), bouse, drink, quaff, revel, spree, toast **7** wassail **8** carousal **9** celebrate

carp: nag **4** fish, sing, snag, talk, yerk **5** cavil, prate, scold, speak **6** censor, nibble, peck at, recite **7** censure, chatter, henpeck, quibble **8** complain, goldfish **9** criticize, discourse

carpel: **9** carpophyl **10** carpophyll

carpenter: ant, bee **6** framer, joiner, wright **7** artisan, builder **8** tectonic **9** artificer **10** woodworker **12** cabinetmaker
machine: saw **5** lathe **6** planer, shaper
ship: **5** chips
tool: adz, awl, saw **4** adze, file, rule, vise **5** auger, level, miter, plane **6** chisel, clamps,

gimlet, hammer, pliers, square **7** hatchet **9** plumb line **11** screwdriver

carpet: mat, rug **4** kali **5** tapet, tapis **6** fabric **8** covering **10** wall-to-wall
design: **9** medallion
earliest pile fabric: **10** Pazyryk rug
on the: **7** scolded **11** reprimanded
top: **4** pile
variety: rag **4** Agra, shag **5** kilim, plush, sisal **6** hooked, prayer, saxony, Wilton **7** braided, dhurrie, ingrain, Persian, Turkish **8** moquette, Oriental, Turkoman **9** Axminster, broadloom

carping: **6** jawing **7** blaming **8** captious, caviling, critical **10** censorious **12** faultfinding **13** hypercritical

carplike fish: **4** dace, rudd

carpus: **5** wrist

carr, car (Br.): bog, fen **4** pool **5** grove

carrack, carack: **4** boat **7** galleon

carrageen: **4** alga, moss **7** seaweed

carriage (see also **cart**): air, gig **4** gait, garb, hack, load, mien, shay **5** bandy, brake, break, buggy, coach, drain, front, midge, poise, wagon **6** burden, convoy, furrow, landau, manner, surrey **7** baggage, bearing, conduct, gesture, hackney, phaeton, vecture, vehicle **8** barouche, behavior, demeanor, dormeuse, equipage, portance **9** behaviour, execution, framework **10** conveyance, deportment, management **14** administration
baby: **4** pram **5** buggy **6** gocart **8** stroller **12** perambulator
closed: cab **4** hack, taxi **6** calash **7** caleche **8** brougham, clarence
covered: **6** Berlin, landau **7** ricksha **8** carryall, dearborn, stanhope
driver: **4** hack **5** cabby **8** coachman
four-wheeled: **5** coupe **6** surrey, whisky **7** phaeton, whiskey **8** barouche, clarence, rockaway, victoria **9** chariotee, gladstone
French: **6** fiacre
one-horse: fly, gig **4** ekka (Ind.), shay, trap **5** sulky **6** dennet **7** cariole, dogcart **8** carriole
open: **7** dogcart, dos-a-dos **8** sociable
portable: **5** sedan
three-horse: **6** troika
two-seated: **6** tandem
two-wheeled: gig **4** shay, trap **5** essed, sulky, tonga **6** chaise, cisium, esseda, hansom **7** carreta, chariot, tilbury **8** carretta **9** caretella, carromata **11** jinrickshaw

carriage trade: **5** elite **7** society

carried: **5** borne, giddy, toted **6** carted, lugged, wafted **8** drifting, ravished **10** abstracted **11** transported

carrier (see also **conveyance**): hod **4** ship **5** hamal, macer, plane **6** bearer, cadger,

hamaul, hammal, khamal, porter **7** airline, courier, drayman, flattop, hammaul, postman, remover **8** cargador, portator, railroad, teamster **9** messenger

carrion: **4** vile **6** corpse, refuse, rotten **7** carcass, corrupt **9** loathsome

Carroll character: **5** Alice, Bruno, snark **6** hatter, rabbit, Sylvie, walrus **7** duchess **8** Dormouse **9** Carpenter, Mad Hatter, March Hare **10** Jabberwock, Mock Turtle, Tweedledee, Tweedledum **11** Cheshire Cat, White Rabbit **12** Humpty Dumpty **13** Queen of Hearts

carrot: **4** root **5** plant **6** daucus **10** enticement
deadly: **5** drias
family: **7** parsley **8** ammaicea **12** umbelliferae
genus: **5** carum
top: **7** red-head
type: **6** Nantes **7** Danvers **9** Chantenay, Imperator
wild: **8** hilltrot **10** laceflower

carrousel: **4** ride **12** merry-go-round

carry: hug, jag, lug **4** bear, cart, gest, hold, lead, take, tote, tump **5** bring, cadge, geste, guide, poise **6** behave, convey, convoy, delate, derive, extend **7** conduct, contain, produce, support, sustain, undergo **8** continue, transfer, transmit **9** prosecute, transport **11** comportment
away: **4** kill, take **5** eloin, reave, steal **6** eloign, remove **9** transport
off: win **4** kill **6** kidnap **7** succeed
on: **4** rant, rave, wage **6** manage **7** conduct, perform, proceed **8** continue, maintain, transact **9** misbehave, prosecute
out: **6** effect **7** execute, perform, sustain **9** complete
over: **4** tide **5** table **6** extend, shelve **8** contango, postpone, transfer
the day: win **7** prevail

carryall: bag, bus **4** case, tote **8** carriage

carrying: **6** gerent **9** gestation

cart (see also **carriage**): **4** butt, char, dray, haul, tote, wain **5** araba, bandy, bogie, carry, sulky, tonga, wagon **6** charet, convey **7** chariot, hackery, trolley, trundle, tumbler, tumbrel, tumbril, vehicle **8** charette
farmer: **7** morfrey **8** morphrey
freight: **8** carreton
horse: **8** cartaver (Sc.)
license: **6** caroon **7** caroome, carroon
racing: **5** sulky
rope: **5** wanty (Sc.)
strong: **4** dray
two-wheeled: bin, gig **4** shay **5** dandy, sulky, tonga **6** reckla **7** tumbril **8** carretta (Sp.)

cartage: **7** drayage, haulage

carte: map **4** card, list, menu **5** chart **7** charter, diagram

carte du jour: 4 menu

cartel: 4 card, defy, pact, pool, ship 5 paper, trust 6 corner, letter, treaty 8 contract 9 agreement, challenge, syndicate 10 convention

carter: 7 drayman, trucker 8 horseman, teamster

Carthage: *citadel:* 5 Bursa, Byrsa
 emblem: 4 palm
 founder: 4 Dido 11 Phoenicians
 general: 5 Hanno 8 Hannibal
 god: 6 Moloch
 goddess: 5 Tanit 6 Tanith
 magistrate: 5 sufet 7 suffete
 pert. to: 5 Punic
 queen: 4 Dido
 victor at Zama: 6 Scipio

Carthusian: nun 4 monk 7 eremite
 founder: 5 Bruno
 monastery: 5 Pavia 7 Certosa
 noted: 4 Hugh
 product: 10 Chartreuse
 superior: 5 prior

cartilage: 6 tissue 7 gristle
 ossified: 4 bone

cartload: 6 fother

cartograph: map 4 plat 5 chart

carton: box 4 case 9 container 10 receptacle

cartoon: 10 caricature

cartoonist: 4 Arno, Capp, Ding, Hart, Nast, Szep 5 Gould, Kelly, Young 6 Addams, Disney, Schulz 7 Feiffer, Keppler, Ketcham, Mauldin, Thurber, Trudeau 8 Goldberg, Herblock

cartouche: box 4 case, mesa

cartridge: bag 4 case 5 shell 7 capsule 8 cylinder
 holder: 4 clip

cartwheel: 4 coin 6 tumble 10 handspring

carucate: 4 hide, land 5 carve, field

caruncle: 4 comb, gill 6 growth, wattle

carve: cut, hew 5 sculp, sever, slice, split 6 chisel, create, sunder 7 dissect 9 sculpture

carving: *in stone:* 5 cameo 8 intaglio 10 engrailing
 in wood: 9 whittling
 pert. to: 7 glyphic, glyptic
 relief: 5 cameo

carya: 5 pecan 6 pignut 9 bitternut

caryatid: 6 column, figure 7 support 9 priestess
 male: cap 5 atlas 7 telamon

casa (Sp.): 5 house 8 building, dwelling

casaba: 5 gourd, melon 9 muskmelon

Casanova: 4 rake, roue, wolf 5 lover, Romeo 6 chaser 7 Don Juan 8 lothario, paramour 9 ladies' man

cascade: 5 falls, force (Sc.), spout 8 cataract 9 waterfall

case: bag, box, hap, pod 4 bunk, burr, deed, file, pack, pair, suit 5 brace, bulla, burse, casus, cover, crate, event, folio, state, theca, trial 6 action, affair, binder, carton, chance, coffin, couple, matter, quiver, sheath, survey 7 cabinet, capcase, capsule, enclose, envelop, example, holster, inclose, lawsuit, oddball, satchel 8 accident, argument, cupboard, envelope, instance, pomander, situated 9 cartouche, cartridge, condition, container, happening 10 occurrence, receptacle, sabretache 11 contingency
 cigar: 7 humidor
 cosmetic: 7 compact
 document: 7 hanaper
 explosive: 5 shell 6 petard 11 firecracker
 grammatical: 6 dative 8 ablative, genitive, vocative 9 objective 10 accusative, nominative
 small: tye 4 etui 5 bulla, etwee 6 trouse
 toiletries: 4 etui 5 etwee

case history: 5 story 6 record 7 example 12 illustration

casement: 4 sash 6 window 8 covering

cash: 4 coin, cush, dump, dust, jack, jake 5 blunt, brass, bread, clink, darby, dough, funds, money 6 specie 7 capital, hemlock 8 currency 10 ready money, spondulics
 keeper: 6 bursar, teller 7 cashier 9 treasurer

cashbox: 4 till 6 coffer

cashew: nut 4 tree 7 maranon

cashier: 6 purser, reject 7 destroy, discard, dismiss, kick out 8 throw out 9 terminate, treasurer 10 cashkeeper

casing: 4 boot, shoe, tire 5 gaine 6 coffin, collet, lining, sheath 8 covering 9 framework

cask: keg, tub, tun, vat 4 butt, cade, cowl, knag, pipe 5 bowie, bulge, foist 6 bareca, bareka, barrel, cardel, casque, firkin, tierce 7 barrico, fostell 8 cassette, hogshead, puncheon 9 kilderkin
 bulge: 5 bilge
 oil: 4 rier
 orifice: 8 bunghole
 rim: 5 chimb, chime
 stave: lag
 wine: fat, tun 4 butt, fust, pipe 6 tierce

casket: box, pix, tye 4 case, cask, cist, till, tomb 5 chest 6 Accera, chasse, coffer, coffin 7 casquet, fostell 8 cassette 9 reliquary 11 sarcophagus

Caspian Sea: 4 lake 5 Tates
 ancient name: 11 Caspium Mare 12 Hyrcanium Mare
 canal: 8 Volga-Don
 river to: 4 Emba, Kura, Ural 5 Terek, Volga

casque: hat 4 cask 5 armor 6 helmet 9 headdress

Cassandra: 7 prophet, seeress
 country: 4 Troy
 father: 5 Priam

lover: **9** Agamemnon
mother: **6** Hecuba
prophet of: **4** doom
slayer: **9** Aegisthus **12** Clytemnestra
cassation: **8** quashing **9** annulling, canceling **10** abrogation
cassava: **4** aipi, juca, yuca **5** aipim **6** casiri, manioc **7** tapioca **8** mandioca
casserole: **4** dish **6** tureen
cassette: **4** tape **6** casket, holder, sagger **9** cartridge **10** tape holder
cassia: **4** drug, herb, tree **5** senna, shrub
bark: **8** cinnamon
cassie: **6** basket **8** huisache
Cassiopeia: **13** constellation
daughter: **9** Andromeda
husband: **7** Cepheus
kingdom: **8** Ethiopia
cassock: **4** gown **5** gippo **6** priest **7** pelisse, soutane **9** clergyman
cassone: box **5** chest
cassowary: emu **4** bird **5** murup **6** moorup
cast: **4** emit, fish, hurl, lose, mold, molt, shed, spew, tint, toss **5** eject, fling, found, heave, mould, pitch, shade, sling, throw, tinge, vomit **6** bestow, confer, tailor **7** cashier, deposit, discard
about: **4** hunt, seek **9** ferret out, search out
aside, away: **4** jilt, junk, shed **5** scrap, wreck **6** maroon, reject **7** abandon, discard, dismiss **8** squander **9** shipwreck
down: **5** abase **6** abattu, deject, sadden **7** abattue, depress, destroy **8** demolish, dispirit **9** woebegone **10** discourage, dispirited **11** crestfallen **12** disconsolate
lots: **4** draw **5** cavel
off: **4** free **5** untie **6** disown, unmoor **7** discard **9** eliminate
out: **5** eject, expel **6** banish
up: add **5** total, vomit **6** reckon **7** compute, measure **8** reproach
castaway: **4** waif **5** tramp **6** pariah, reject **7** outcast **8** derelict, stranded **9** shipwreck
caste: **4** jati, rank **5** breed, class, grade, order **6** degree, status
group: **5** Sudra, varna **6** Vaisya **7** Brahman **8** outcaste, panchama **9** Kshatriya **11** untouchable
merchant: **6** banian, banyan
priestly: **4** magi (pl.) **5** magus
caster: **4** vial **5** cruet, cruse, phial, wheel **6** castor, hurler, roller **7** pitcher, trundle
castigate: **4** lash **5** emend, scare, scold **6** berate, punish, rebuke, revise, strafe, subdue **7** censure, chasten, correct, reprove **8** chastise, lambaste **9** criticize **10** tongue-lash
castigatory: **5** penal **8** punitive **10** corrective
Castile: *hero:* **5** El Cid

province: **5** Avila, Soria
river: **4** Ebro, Esla **5** Douro, Duero
Castilian: **7** Spanish
casting: *mold:* die **6** matrix **7** matrice
rough: pig
castle: **4** fort, rock, rook **5** abode, morro **7** alcazar (Sp.), bastile, chateau, citadel **8** bastille, castillo, fastness, fortress **10** stronghold **13** fortification
gate: **10** portcullis
in the air: **5** dream **6** vision **7** fantasy **8** daydream **9** imagining
ledge: **7** rampart
Norman: **5** motte **6** bailey
part: **4** bawn, keep, moat **6** donjon, merlon **7** rampart **9** embrasure **10** drawbridge
tower: **4** keep **6** turret **9** gatehouse
wall: **6** bailey **10** battlement
walled court: **6** bailey
warden: **6** disdar, dizdar **9** castellan
castor: hat **4** bean, star **6** beaver **7** leather
Castor: *and Pollux:* **5** twins **6** Gemini **8** Dioscuri
brother: **6** Pollux **10** Polydeuces
father: **4** Zeus **9** Tyndareus
horse: **8** Cyllaros
mother: **4** Leda
patron of: **7** sailors **8** athletes
sister: **11** Helen of Troy **12** Clytemnestra
slayer: **4** Idas
castor oil: **9** cathartic
castrate: gib **4** geld, spay, swig **5** alter, capon, prune **6** eunuch, neuter **7** evirate **8** caponize, mutilate **10** emasculate
casual: **5** stray **6** chance, random **7** cursory, natural, offhand **8** informal **9** easy-going, haphazard, uncertain **10** accidental, contingent, fortuitous, incidental, nonchalant, occasional **11** indifferent, low-pressure **14** unconventional, unpremeditated
casualty: **4** loss **5** death **6** chance, hazard, injury, mishap **8** accident, disaster **9** mischance **10** misfortune **11** contingency **12** misadventure
casus: **4** case **5** event **8** occasion
cat: tom **4** boat, chat (F.), flog, gato (Sp.), lion, lynx, pard, puma, puss **5** civet, felid, kitty, moggy, ounce, pussy, tiger **6** calico, cougar, feline, jaguar, malkin, mawkin, ocelot, tibert, tipcat **7** caracal, cheetah, leopard, panther, tigress, wildcat **8** baudrons (Sc.) **9** carnivore, catamount, grimalkin **11** caterpillar **12** double tripod, mountain lion
breed: Aby, Rex, Van **4** Manx **5** alley, Korat, tabby **6** Angora, Birman, Calico, Cymric, Somali, sphynx **7** bobtail, Burmese, Maltese, Persian, Siamese **8** Balinese **9** Chartreux, Himalayan, Maine coon **10** Abyssinian **11** Egyptian Mau, Russian blue

12 Scottish fold

civetlike: **5** genet

cry: mew **4** hiss, meow, miau, purr, wail **5** miaou, miaow, miaul **9** caterwaul

disease: **6** rabies **8** leukemia **9** distemper, enteritis

Eugene Field's: **6** calico

female: **9** grimalkin

genus: **5** felis **7** felidae (pl.)

cat-o-nine-tails: **4** lash, whip **7** cattail

catachresis: **10** word misuse

cataclysm: **5** flood **6** deluge **7** debacle **8** disaster, overflow, upheaval **11** catastrophe

catacomb: **4** tomb **5** crypt, vault **8** cemetery

catafalque: **4** bier **6** coffin

cataian: **5** thief **7** sharper **9** scoundrel

catalepsy: **6** trance **7** seizure

catalog, catalogue: **4** book, list, roll, rota **5** brief, canon, flyer, index **6** record, roster **7** arrange, itemize **8** classify, register, schedule **9** enumerate, repertory **10** prospectus **11** systematize

bookseller's: **11** bibliotheca

of goods: **9** inventory

of saints: **9** hagiology

Catalonia: *dance:* **7** sardana

marble: **8** brocatel **10** brocatelle

catalyst: **4** goad, spur **7** impetus **8** stimulus **9** incentive **10** motivation

catamaran: **4** boat, raft, trow **5** balsa, float **6** vessel **8** auntsary **10** double hull

catamount: **4** lynx, puma **6** cougar **12** mountain lion

cataplasm: **8** poultice

catapult: **5** throw **6** launch, onager **7** bricole **8** ballista, crossbow **9** slingshot

cataract: lin **4** linn **5** falls, flood **6** deluge **7** cascade, Niagara **8** Victoria **9** waterfall **10** eye disease

cataria: **6** catnip

catarrh: **4** cold **5** rheum

catastrophe (see also **cataclysm**): **8** accident, calamity, disaster, fatality **10** denouement, misfortune

catbird: **7** mimidae

catcall: boo **4** hoot, razz **6** deride **8** pooh-pooh **10** Bronx cheer, strawberry

catch: bag, cop, get, nab, net **4** draw, hasp, haul, hawk, hold, hook, land, nail, pawl, snap, stop, trap, tree **5** grasp, hitch, ketch, knack, seize, snare, trick **6** button, clutch, corner, detect, detent, engage, enmesh, entrap, snatch **7** attract, capture, ensnare, grapnel **8** entangle, overtake, surprise **9** intercept **12** come down with

fire: **6** ignite, kindle

one's breath: **4** gasp **5** chink

sight of: **4** espy, spot **6** descry

up with: **8** overtake

catchall: bag **6** basket **10** receptacle

catchfly: **5** plant **7** campion, silence

catching: **6** taking **8** alluring **10** contagious, entrapping, infectious **11** captivating

catchword: cue, tag **5** motto **6** byword, phrase, slogan

catchy: **6** fitful, tricky **9** appealing

cate: **4** food **6** viands **8** dainties **10** delicacies, provisions

catechism: **5** guide **6** manual **8** carritch **9** questions **10** carritches (Sc.)

catechumen: **5** pupil **7** audient, auditor, convert, student **8** beginner, neophyte

categorical: **8** absolute, explicit **11** dictatorial, unequivocal, unqualified

category: **4** rank **5** class, genre (pl.), genus, order **6** family **7** species **8** division **12** denomination **14** classification

catena: **4** link **5** chain **6** series **7** excerpt

cater: **4** feed **5** humor, serve, treat **6** pander, purvey, supply **7** provide **8** diagonal

cateran: **7** brigand **8** marauder **10** freebooter

catercousin: pal **8** intimate

caterpillar: cat **4** muga **5** aweto, eruca, larva **6** canker, erucae (pl.), risper, woubit **7** tractor

caterwaul: cry **4** wail **5** miaul

catface: **4** scar **10** depression

catfish: mud **4** cusk, elod, pout, raad, shal **5** bagre, raash **6** docmac, hassar, raasch, tandau **7** candiru **8** bullhead **9** sheatfish

genus: **13** saccobranchus

catgut: **4** cord, rope **5** tharm **6** string, violin

cathartic: **8** lapactic, laxative **9** cleansing, purgative

cathedral: dom **4** seat **5** duomo **6** church

famous: **5** Reims **6** Amiens **7** Seville **8** Chartres, Coventry, National **9** Notre Dame **10** St. Patrick's, Strasbourg **11** Hagia Sophia **15** St. John the Divine

part: **4** apse, nave **5** porch, tower **6** chapel **8** transept **10** ambulatory

passage: **5** aisle, slype

cathode: **9** electrode

catholic: **5** broad, papal **6** cosmic, global **7** general, liberal **8** orthodox, tolerant **9** universal **10** ecumenical

Catholic: See **Roman Catholic**

catkin: **5** ament, spike

catlike: **6** feline **8** stealthy **9** noiseless

catmint: nep, nip **4** herb **6** catnip, Nepeta

catnap: nap **4** doze **6** siesta, snooze **10** forty winks

catnip: nep **6** catnep **7** cataria, catwort

Catoism: **9** austerity, harshness

Catreus: *daughter:* **6** Aerope **7** Clymene **9** Apemosyne

father: **5** Minos

mother: **8** Pasiphae

cat's-cradle: **4** game **7** ribwort

cat's-paw: 4 dupe, gull, pawn, tool 5 cully

cattail: 4 flag, musk, reed, rush, tule 5 ament, cloud, reree 6 catkin 7 bulrush, matreed 9 down raupo
English name: 16 Cossack asparagus
family: 9 Typhaceae

cattle: 4 cows, dhan (Ind.), kine, neat, oxen 5 beefs, bulls, stock 6 beasts, beeves, calves, steers 7 bovines, heifers 9 ruminants
assemblage: 4 herd 5 drove
brand: 4 duff 5 buist
breed: 4 Nata, Zobo 5 Angus, Devon, Dutch, Niata (dwarf), Saler 6 Belted, Durham, Jersey, Sussex 7 Brahman, Brangus, Kerries 8 Aberdeen, Ayrshire, Bradford, Charbray, Friesian, Galloway, Gelbvieh, Guernsey, Hereford, Holstein, Limousin, Longhorn, Normandy 9 Charolais, Red Polled, Shorthorn, Teeswater 10 Beefmaster, Brown Swiss, Maine-Anjou, Murray Grey, Simmenthal, Tareutaise
call: 4 sook
castrated: 5 steer
dealer: 6 drover, herder
dehorned: 5 muley 6 mulley, polled
female: cow
genus: bos
goddess: 6 Bubona
group: 4 herd 5 drove 7 creaght (Ir.)
male: 4 bull
plague: 10 rinderpest
shelter: 4 byre 5 barth
sound: low, moo
tick: 8 carapato
yard: 6 cancha
young cow: 6 heifer
young heifer: 4 calf

cattleman: 6 cowboy 7 byreman, rancher 8 stockman

catty: 4 mean 8 spiteful 9 malicious

catwalk: 7 footway, walkway

catwort: 6 catnip

Caucasian: *goat:* tur
ibex: zac
language: Laz, Udi 4 Andi, Avar, Laze, Lazi, Udic 5 Udish 7 Semitic 9 Itranican
race: 5 Aryan, Osset 6 Ossete
rug: 4 baku, kuba 5 chila 7 derbend
tribe: 4 Imer, Kurd, Laze, Lazi, Svan 5 Pshav 7 Kubachi

caucho: ule 4 tree 6 rubber

caucus: 7 council, meeting, primary 8 election

caudal: 4 rear 9 posterior
appendage: 4 tail

caudata: 4 newt 5 snake 10 salamander

cauk: 4 spar 5 chalk 6 barite 9 limestone

caul: web 4 cawl, trug, veil 5 creel 7 network, omentum 8 membrane, tressour, tressure

cauldron: See **caldron**

cauliflower: 7 cabbage 8 brassica, broccoli 9 disfigure
head: 4 curd

caulk, calk: nap 4 cork, fill, flag 5 putty 6 chinse 7 chintze, occlude 9 stop leaks 14 make watertight

caulking: 5 oakum

cause: aim, gar (Sc.), key 4 case, chat, move, root, spur, suit 5 agent, basis, breed 6 create, effect, gossip, ground, induce, malady, motive, object, origin, reason, source, spring 7 concern, disease, lawsuit, produce, provoke 8 business, engender, movement, occasion 9 originate, wherefore 10 bring about, mainspring, prime mover

causerie: 4 chat, plea, talk 6 debate 10 discussion 12 conversation

causes, science of: 8 etiology

causeuse: 4 sofa 6 settee 8 loveseat 9 tete-a-tete

causeway: way 4 dike, road 7 chausse (F.), highway

causey: dam, way 4 bank, pave, road 5 mound 6 street 7 highway 8 sidewalk

caustic: lye 4 tart 5 acerb, acrid, sharp 6 biting, bitter, severe 7 burning, cutting, erodent, mordant, pungent, satiric 8 alkaline, scathing, snappish, stinging 9 corrosive, sarcastic, satirical, vitriolic 10 malevolent 11 acrimonious
agent: 7 cautery, erodent

cauterize: 4 burn, char, fire, sear 5 brand, inust, singe 9 sterilize

caution: 4 care, heed, warn 6 advice, cautel, caveat, exhort 7 anxiety, counsel, precept, proviso 8 admonish, forecast, monition, prudence, wariness 9 diligence, vigilance 10 admonition, precaution, providence 11 calculation, forethought, reservation 12 watchfulness

cautious: 4 wary 5 alert, canny, chary, siker 6 fabian, sicker 7 careful, guarded, prudent 8 discreet, vigilant 10 scrupulous 11 circumspect

cavalcade: 4 raid, ride 5 march 6 parade, safari 7 journey, pageant 10 procession

cavalier: gay 4 curt, easy, fine 5 brave, frank, lofty, proud, rider 6 escort, knight 7 brusque, gallant, haughty, offhand, soldier 8 Royalist 9 caballero, chevalier 10 disdainful 12 high-spirited, supercilious 13 high-and-mighty

Cavalleria Rusticana: *character:* 4 Lola 5 Alfio 7 Turiddu
composer: 8 Mascagni

cavalry: 6 horses, troops 8 horsemen 10 knighthood
horse: 6 lancer
tactic: 6 charge
weapon: 5 lance, saber

cavalryman: 5 spahi 6 hussar, lancer, spahee 7 courier, dragoon, soldier, trooper 8 gendarme, horseman

cavatina: air

cave: den, tip 4 café, cove, grot, hole, lair, rear, sink, toss, weem 5 antre, cavea, croft, crypt, speos, store, upset 6 antrum, beware, cavern, cavity, cellar, forgou, grotto, hollow, larder, luster, pantry, plunge, winnow 7 reserve, spelunk 8 collapse, overturn 9 storeroom 10 wine cellar
  dweller: 10 troglobite, troglodyte
  famous: 5 Luray (VA) 7 Lascaux (F.), Mammoth (KY), Waitomo (NZ) 8 Carlsbad (NM)
  formation in: 7 drapery 9 flowstone, helictite 10 stalactite, stalagmite 12 gypsum flower
  researcher: 9 spelunker 12 speleologist
  science of researching: 10 speleology

caveat: 6 beware, notice 7 caution, warning

cave in: 5 stove, yield 6 submit 8 collapse

cavern: See **cave**

cavernous: 4 vast 6 gaping, hollow 10 sepulchral 11 reverberant

cavetto: 5 gorge 7 molding

caviar: ova, roe 4 eggs, ikra 5 ikary 6 relish 8 delicacy
  source: 6 beluga 7 sterlet 8 sturgeon

cavie (Sc.): 4 cage, coop 7 hencoop

cavil: 4 cark, carp, haft 6 haggle 7 quibble 9 criticise, criticize, exception, objection

caviling: 4 mean 5 fussy, small 8 captious, picayune

cavity: bag, pit, sac 4 abri, cave, dalk, dent, hole, mine, vein, void 5 antra (pl.), atria (pl.), fossa, geode, lumen, mouth, sinus 6 antrum, atrium, camera, cavern, fossae (pl.), grotto, hollow, vacuum 7 cistern, vesicle 8 cul-de-sac 10 depression, excavation
  anatomical: 5 antra (pl.), fossa 6 antrum, fossae (pl.)
  brain: 6 coelia
  gun: 4 bore
  heart: 7 auricle 9 ventricle
  lode: vug 4 voog, vugg, vugh
  pert. to: 5 sinal 6 atrial, geodic
  sac-like: 5 bursa 6 bursae (pl.)
  skull: 4 aula 5 fossa, sinus
  stone: 5 geode

cavort: 4 play, romp 5 bound, caper, cut up 6 curvet, gambol, prance 11 horse around

cavy: 4 mara, moco, paca, pony 6 agouti, aperea, cayuse, rodent 8 capybara 9 guinea pig

caw: cry 4 call, cawl 5 croak, quark, quawk 6 squall, squawk

cawl: 4 trug 6 basket

caxi: 4 fish 7 snapper

cay: See **key**

cayenne: 5 whist 6 canary, pepper 7 copepod 8 capsicum

cayuse: 4 cavy, pony, wind 6 bronco 7 broncho

cease: end 4 halt, liss, quit, rest, stop 5 avast, douse, dowse, lisse, pause, peter 6 desist, devall, finish 7 abstain, refrain 8 intermit, knock off, leave off 9 terminate 11 discontinue

cease-fire: 5 truce 7 detente 9 armistice

ceaseless: 4 ever 7 endless, eternal 8 unending 9 continual, incessant, unceasing 11 never-ending

ceasing: 9 cessation

Cecrops' daughter: 5 Herse 8 Aglauros

cecum: pit 4 pore 6 cavity

cedar: 4 toon, tree 5 savin 6 deodar, sabina, sabine, savine 7 cypress 10 arborvitae
  bird: 7 waxwing
  camphor: 6 cedrol
  green: 5 cedre (F.), color
  moss: 8 hornwort

cede: 4 cess, give 5 award, grant, leave, waive, yield 6 assign, resign, submit 8 hand over, renounce, sign over, transfer 9 surrender 10 relinquish

cedula (Sp.): IOU, tax 6 permit 8 document, schedule, security 11 certificate

ceil: 4 line 7 overlay 8 wainscot

ceiling: 6 lining, screen, soffit 7 curtain, testudo 8 covering, paneling 10 testudines (pl.) 11 wainscoting
  covering: tin 9 calcimine, kalsomine
  decorated: 7 plafond
  division: 5 trave
  mine: 5 astel
  wooden: 8 plancher

Celebes: *bovine:* ox 4 anoa
  island: 4 Muna
  people: 6 toraja 7 toradja

celebrate: 4 keep, sing 5 extol, honor, revel 6 extoll, praise 7 glorify, observe 8 emblazon, eulogize, proclaim 9 solemnize 11 commemorate

celebrated: 4 kept 5 famed, noted 6 famous 7 eminent, feasted, renomme 8 glorious, observed, renowned 9 distingue, prominent 10 solemnized 11 conspicuous, illustrious 13 distinguished

celebration: 4 fete, gala, rite 6 renown 7 jubilee 8 jamboree 9 celebrity, festivity

celebrity: VIP 4 fame, lion, name, star 5 eclat 6 renown, repute 9 superstar 11 celebration

celerity: 5 haste, hurry, speed 8 dispatch, rapidity, velocity 9 prestezza, quickness, swiftness

celery: *family:* 6 pascal
  relative of: 6 carrot 7 parsnip
  wild: 8 smallage

celestial: 4 holy 6 divine, uranic 7 angelic, Chinese, ethered 8 beatific, empyreal, ethereal, heavenly, Olympian
  being: 5 angel 6 cherub, seraph 8 cherubim (pl.), seraphim (pl.)
  body: sun 4 moon, star 5 comet 6 meteor, nebula, planet 8 asteroid 9 satellite
  elevation of mind: 7 anagoge
  hierarchy: 6 angels, powers 7 thrones, virtues 10 archangels 11 dominations 14 principalities
  matter: 6 nebula
celibacy: 8 chastity
celibate: 6 chaste, single 8 bachelor, spinster 9 unmarried
cell: egg 4 cage, germ, jail 5 cabin, crypt, group, vault 6 cytode, prison 7 cellule, chamber, cubicle, dungeon 9 hermitage 10 ergastulum 11 compartment
  blood: red 5 white 8 hemocyte 9 leukocyte 11 erythrocyte
  bull: 5 toril 7 toriles (pl.)
  coloring: 10 endochrome
  colorless: 10 achroacyte, lymphocyte
  connecting: 10 heterocyst
  division: 7 meiosis, mitosis, spireme
  generative: 6 gamete
  group: 6 ceptor 7 cascade 8 blastema
  layer: 8 blastula 10 blastoderm
  lens-shaped: 8 lenticel
  migratory: 9 leucocyte
  pert. to: 6 cytoid
  photoelectric: eye
  star-shaped: 10 astroblast
  structural unit: 7 energid, nucleus 10 protoplast
  study of: 8 cytology
  substance: 5 linin
cell-like: 6 cytoid
cella: 4 naos
cellar: 4 cave 5 vault 7 hypogee 8 basement 9 storeroom
cellaret: 4 case 7 cabinet 9 sideboard
cellophane: 7 wrapper 9 packaging
cellular: 6 porous 7 areolar 9 alveolate
celluloid: 4 film 7 plastic 8 xylonite
cellulose: 12 carbohydrate
  acetate: 7 acetose
  elastic: 5 rayon
Celsius: 10 centigrade 11 thermometer
Celt: 4 Gael, Gaul, Manx, Scot 5 Irish, Welsh 6 Breton, Briton, Eolith 7 Cornish
Celtic: 4 Erse, Gael 8 Scottish
  abbot: 5 coarb
  chariot: 5 essed
  chieftain: 6 tanist
  divinity: 7 Taranis
  foot soldier: 4 kern
  giant: 5 Fomor

  god: Ler 4 Leir, Llyr
  harp: 5 telyn 11 clairschach
  hero: 5 Fionn
  language: 4 Erse, Manx 5 Irish, Welsh 6 Breton, Celtic, Cymric, Gaelic 9 Brythonic
  peasant: 4 kern
  priest: 5 Druid
  primitive writing: 4 ogam
  sword: sax 4 seax
cembalo: 8 dulcimer 11 harpsichord
cement: fix 4 glue, join, knit, lime, lute 5 imbed, paste, putty, stick, unify, unite 6 cohere, fasten, gulgul (Ind.), mortar, solder 7 asphalt 8 adhesive, concrete, hadigeon (F.), solidify 11 agglutinate
  hydraulic: 4 paar
  infusible substance: 4 lute
  mixer: 8 temperer
  plastic: 8 albolite, albolith
  quick-drying: 6 mastic
  substance: 6 celite
  window glass: 5 putty
cemetery: 6 litten 7 charnel 8 catacomb, Golgotha 9 graveyard 10 necropolis 11 polyandrium
  underground: 8 catacomb
cenchrus: 5 grass 6 millet
cenobite: nun 4 monk 5 friar 6 essene, hermit 7 recluse 8 monastic 9 anchorite
cenoby: 5 abbey 6 priory 7 convent
cense: 4 rank 6 assess, rating 7 perfume, thurify 8 estimate, position
censer: 8 thurible, thurifer
censor: 4 blip, edit 6 critic, cut out 7 clean up 8 restrict, suppress 9 detractor, expurgate 10 blue pencil, bowdlerize
censorious: 6 severe 7 carping 8 blameful, captious, critical 9 satirical 10 denouncing 11 reproachful 12 fault finding
censurable: 5 amiss, wrong 8 blamable, culpable 13 reprehensible
censure: 4 carp, flay 5 blame, chide, decry, judge, slate 6 accuse, berate, charge, rebuff, rebuke, remord, targue (Scot.), tirade 7 chasten, condemn, impeach, inveigh, reprove 8 disallow, reproach 9 challenge, criticize, reprimand 10 animadvert, exprobrate, vituperate 11 disapproval 12 reprehension 13 animadversion 15 discommendation
census: 4 list, poll 5 count 6 survey 11 enumeration
cent: 4 coin 5 penny 6 copper
centaur: 6 Chiron, Nessus 8 horse-man
  father: 5 Ixion
Centennial State: 8 Colorado
center, centre: cor, hub, mid 4 axis, core, foci (pl.), nave, seat 5 focus, heart, mecca, midst, pivot, spine 6 middle 7 lineman,

nucleus **8** centrate **10** focal point **12** headquarters
away from: **6** distal
toward: **4** orad **5** entad **10** centerward
centerpiece: **7** epergne
centigrade: **5** scale **7** Celsius **11** thermometer
centipede: **4** veri **6** earwig, golach, goloch **8** chilopod, myriapod **9** arthropod, geophilus
central: key, mid **5** axial, basic, chief, focal, prime **6** median, middle, tarete **7** capital, centric, leading, pivotal, primary **8** dominant **9** clustered **11** cylindrical, equidistant **12** all-absorbing, concentrated
Central African Republic: *capital:* **6** Bangui
city: **5** Bouar **7** Bambari **9** Berberati
currency: **5** franc **7** centime
language: **5** Sango
people: **4** Baya **5** Banda

Central America: **6** Belize, Panama **8** Honduras **9** Costa Rica, Guatemala, Nicaragua **10** El Salvador
agave: **5** sisal
ant: **5** kelep
bird: **7** jacamar **8** puffbird
canoe: **6** pitpan
Indian: **4** Maya **5** Carib
language: **7** Nahuatl, Spanish **10** Papimiento
measure: **7** cantaro, manzana
monkey: **4** mono
mullet: **4** bobo
rodent: **4** paca
snake: **10** bushmaster
stockade: **4** boma
tragon: **4** bird **6** quezal **7** quetzal
tree: ebo, ule **4** eboe **5** amate **9** sapodilla
village: **4** boma **6** pueblo
weight: **4** kilo **5** libra

---

centrifugal: **8** efferent **9** radiating
centripetal: **6** inward **8** afferent, unifying **12** centralizing
century: age **6** siecle (F.) **7** hundred **9** type style
ten: **7** chiliad **10** millennium
century plant: **4** aloe **5** agave **6** maguey
beverage from: **6** mescal, pulque **7** tequila
fiber: **4** pita, pito
ceorl: **5** churl, thane **7** freeman, villein
cepa: **5** onion
cephalagia: **8** headache
cephalic: **8** atlantal, cerebral

cephalopod: **5** squid **7** inkfish, octopus **10** cuttlefish
secretion: ink
Cepheus: *daughter:* **9** Andromeda
wife: **10** Cassiopeia
ceral: **4** waxy **7** waxlike
ceramics: **5** tiles **7** pottery **9** abrasives, stoneware **10** dinnerware
coating: **5** glaze
oven: **4** kiln
shape: **5** press **6** jigger **7** extrude **8** slip cast
sieve: **4** laun
cerate: wax **4** lard **5** salve **8** ointment
ceratoid: **5** horny
Cerberus: dog **7** monster **8** guardian **9** custodian
guarded: **5** Hades
offspring of: **6** Typhon **7** Echidna
overcome by: **5** Sibyl **6** Aeneas **7** Orpheus **8** Hercules
cere: wax **4** sere, wrap **6** anoint, embalm
cereal: rye **4** bean, bran, corn, mush, oats, rice **5** grain, maize, spelt, wheat **6** barley, farina, hominy **7** oatmeal, soybean **8** porridge **9** buckwheat
coating: **4** bran
grass: oat, rye **4** ragi, rice **5** grain, wheat **6** barley, raggee
seed: **6** kernel
spike: ear
cereal grass genus: **6** secale
cerebral: **6** mental **7** psychic **8** highbrow
cerebration: **7** thought **9** brainwork **10** reflection
cerement: **6** shroud **9** cerecloth
ceremonial fuss: **10** panjandrum
ceremonious: **5** grand, lofty, stiff **6** formal, proper, solemn **7** precise, stately, studied **10** respectful **11** punctilious **12** conventional
ceremony: **4** fete, form, pomp, rite, show, sign **5** state **6** augury, parade, powwow, review, ritual **7** display, pageant, portent, prodigy **8** accolade, function, marriage, occasion **9** formality, solemnity **10** observance **11** celebration
Ceres: **7** Demeter
daughter: **10** Persephone, Proserpina
father: **6** Cronus, Saturn
festival: **8** cerealia
goddess of: **5** grain **7** harvest **11** agriculture
mother: Ops **4** Rhea
cerise: red **6** cherry
cerite: **7** mineral **8** allanite
cernuous: **7** nodding **8** drooping **9** pendulous
cero: **4** fish **6** sierra **7** cavallo, pintado **8** mackerel
certain: **4** firm, real, sure, true **5** bound, clear, exact, fixed, plain, siker (Sc.) **6** actual, sicker, stated **7** assured, precise, settled **8**

absolute, apparent, constant, official, positive, reliable, resolved, unerring **9** confident, steadfast, undoubted **10** dependable, inevitable, infallible, undeniable **11** determinate, indubitable, trustworthy **12** indisputable **13** incontestable **14** unquestionable **16** incontrovertible

certainly: **4** amen, ywis **5** iwiss, truly **6** certes, indeed, verily **7** hardily **8** forsooth

certainty: **8** firmness, sureness **9** assurance, dogmatism **10** confidence, conviction

certificate: **4** bond **5** check, libel, scrip **6** attest, ticket, verify **7** diploma, voucher **9** statement, testimony **10** credential **11** attestation, declaration, testimonial **13** certification

cargo: **8** navicert

debt: IOU **9** debenture

land: **6** amparo (Sp.)

medical, for ill student: **8** aegrotat

money owed: **9** debenture

certify: **4** avow, vise **5** swear **6** affirm, assure, depose, evince, verify **7** endorse, license, testify **9** determine, guarantee

under oath: **6** attest

certiorari: **4** writ **6** review

cerulean: **4** blue **5** azure **6** coelin **7** sky blue

cervine: elk **4** deer, stag **5** moose **6** cervid **8** cervidae (pl.), reindeer

cervix: **4** neck

cespitose: **6** matted, tufted **7** tangled

cess: bog, tax **4** cede, duty, levy, luck, rate, tyrf **5** slope, yield **6** impost **7** measure **9** surrender **10** assessment, estimation

cessation: end **4** halt, liss, lull, rest, stay, stop **5** death, letup, lisse, pause, truce **6** recess **7** ceasing, respite **8** interval, stoppage, surcease **9** armistice, remission **10** conclusion **11** termination **12** intermission, interruption **14** discontinuance

of being: **5** death **8** desition

cession: **6** ceding **8** yielding **9** surrender **10** compliance, concession

cesspool: den, sty **4** sump **5** sewer **7** cistern

cetacean: orc **4** cete, orca **5** whale **6** beluga **7** dolphin, grampus **8** porpoise

blind: **4** susu

genus: **4** inia

cete: **5** whale **7** cetacea

Ceylon: See **Sri Lanka**

Chablis: **4** wine **8** Burgundy

chack: **4** bite, snap **5** clack, snack **8** wheatear

chackle: **6** cackle, rattle **7** chatter

chacma: **6** baboon

chacra: **4** farm **5** milpa, ranch

Chad, Tchad: *capital:* **8** N'Djamena

currency: **5** franc **7** centime

language: **4** Sara **5** Sango **6** Arabic, French

people: **4** Sara

chaeta: **4** seta **5** spine **7** bristle

chafe: irk, rub, vex **4** fret, frig, frot, fume, gall, heat, josh, rage, warm, wear **5** anger, annoy, grind, scold **6** abrade, banter, excite, fridge, harass, injury, nettle **7** incense, inflame **8** friction, irritate, raillery

chaff: guy, hay, kid, pug **4** bran, caff (Sc.), guff, joke, josh, quiz, twit **5** borak, chyak, dross, glume, hulls, husks, straw, tease, trash **6** banter, bhoosa, chyack, refuse **7** tailing **8** raillery, ridicule

chaffer: **5** bandy, sieve, wares **6** buying, dicker, haggle, higgle, market **7** bargain, chatter, selling, traffic **8** exchange **9** negotiate **11** merchandise

chaffinch: **7** robinet

chaffy: **5** scaly **7** acerose, acerous, paleate, trivial **9** bantering, worthless **10** paleaceous

Chaillot resident: **8** madwoman

chain: guy, row, set, tew, tie, tye **4** bind, bond, file, gyve, join, link **5** cable, leash, suite, train **6** catena, chigon, collar, fasten, fetter, hobble, secure, series, string, tether **7** bobstay, catenae (pl.), connect, embrace, enslave, manacle, network, shackle **8** bracelet, restrain **9** constrain **10** chatelaine **13** concatenation

collar: **4** tore **6** torque

key: **10** chatelaine

of islands: **11** archipelago

of quotations: **6** catena

of rocks: **4** reef

ornamental: **10** chatelaine

pert. to: **8** catenary

set with precious stones: **7** sautoir

chain-like: **8** catenate

chains: **7** bondage, serfdom

lady in: **9** Andromeda

chair: **4** seat **5** Eames, sedan, stool **6** Breuer, chaise, office, rocker, throne **7** preside **8** electric **9** Barcelona **12** chaise longue

back: **5** splat

bishop's official: **8** cathedra

cover: **4** tidy **5** doily **12** antimacassar

decoration: **8** claw foot

easy: **6** morris, rocker **8** recliner

folding: **9** faldstool

litterlike: **4** kago

occupy: **7** preside

portable: **5** sedan **6** howdah

type: **4** club, easy **6** morris **7** rocking **8** captain's **9** reclining

chairperson: **4** head **5** emcee **7** speaker **8** director **9** moderator **10** supervisor

chaise: gig **4** shay **8** carriage, curricle

chaise longue: **6** daybed

chalcedony: **4** onyx, opal, sard **5** agate, flint **6** jasper, quartz **7** opaline **9** carnelian **10** bloodstone **11** chrysoprase

green spotted with red: **10** bloodstone
orange: **4** sard
Chalcodon: *father:* **4** Abas
   son: **9** Elephenor
Chaldea, Chaldaea: *measure:* **4** cane, foot **5** makuk, qasab **6** artaba, gariba, ghalva **7** mansion
   part of: **9** Babylonia
   people: **6** Semite
   river: **6** Tigris **9** Euphrates
   ruler: **12** Nabopolassar **14** Nebuchadnez-zar
chalet: hut **5** cabin, house **7** cottage **8** lavatory
chalice: ama, cup **4** bowl **5** calix, grail **6** goblet **7** calices (pl.)
   cover: **4** pall **8** animetta
chalk: **4** cauk, pale, scar, talc, tick **5** creta, score **6** blanch, bleach, crayon, credit, rubble, whiten **7** account **9** limestone, reckoning
   out: **6** sketch **8** block out, rough out **11** skeletonize
   up: get, win **6** pick up **7** acquire
challenge: **4** call, dare, defy, gage **5** blame, brave, claim, query, stump **6** accuse, appeal, cartel, charge, dacker, daiker, demand, forbid, impugn, invite, take on **7** arraign, censure, impeach, provoke, reprove, summons **8** question, reproach **9** exception, objection **10** controvert **11** impeachment
   judge: **6** recuse
   to a duel: **6** cartel
challenger: **5** rival **7** duelist **8** pugilist **9** adversary, contender **10** competitor
chamber: oda **4** cell, flat, hall, kiva, room **5** atria (pl.), bower, solar, soler **6** atrium, bridal, camara, camera, hollow, sollar **7** bedroom, boudoir, caisson, cubicle, lochlus **9** apartment, camarilla, vestibule **11** compartment
   annealing: **4** leer
   bombproof: **8** casemate
   council: **10** consistory
   drying: **4** kiln, oven
   judge's: **6** camera
   pert. to: **7** cameral
   private: **5** adyta (pl.) **6** adytum **7** sanctum **8** conclave
   underground: **4** cave **5** crypt **6** cavern **7** hypogee
chamberlain: **6** factor **7** officer, servant, steward **9** attendant, chamberer, treasurer **10** camerlengo **14** superintendent
   papal: **10** camerlengo, camerlingo
chambray: **5** cloth **6** fabric **7** gingham
chameleon: **5** anole, anoli **6** lizard
chameleonic: **6** fickle **10** changeable, inconstant
chamfer: **5** bevel, flute **6** furrow, groove **7**

   channel **11** countersink
chamois: **4** gems, skin **5** cloth, gemse **6** chammy, shammy, shamoy **7** leather **8** antelope, ruminant
   Biblical: **6** aoudad
   male: **7** gemsbok
champ: **4** bite, chaw, firm, hard, mash **5** field, gnash **7** trample **8** ruminate **9** masticate **11** battlefield
champagne: **4** wine **5** color, fizzy **6** bubbly
   bottle: **6** magnum **8** jeroboam, rehoboam **9** balthazar **10** methuselah, salmanazar
champignon: **6** fungus **8** mushroom
champion: ace, aid **4** a-one, abet, back, defy, hero **6** assert, attend, defend, squire, victor **7** espouse, fighter, protect **8** advocate, defender **9** challenge, combatant, firstrate **10** blue-ribbon, unexcelled **11** outstanding, titleholder
championship: **5** crown, title **7** defense, pennant **8** advocacy **9** supremacy **10** leadership
champleve: **6** enamel, inlaid
chance: die, hap, lot **4** case, dint, fate, luck, odds, risk, tide **5** ettle, stake **6** betide, casual, gamble, happen, hazard, mishap, random **7** aimless, fortune, stumble, venture **8** accident, casualty, fortuity **9** adventure, haphazard, happening, mischance **10** contingent **11** contingency, opportunity, probability
   by: **5** haply
   even: **6** tossup **10** fifty-fifty
   favorable: **4** odds
chancellor: **5** judge **7** adviser, officer **8** minister
chancery: **5** court **6** office **8** headhold, registry **14** chancellorship
   in: **8** helpless
chandelier: **6** pharos **7** fixture, parapet **9** lampstand **11** candelabrum
chandler: **6** dealer **8** merchant, provider **9** tradesman
change: mew **4** move, swap, turn, vary, veer **5** adapt, alter, amend, break, coins, shift **6** modify, mutate, remove, revamp, revise, switch **7** commute, convert, deviate **8** castrate, revision, transfer **9** diversity, permutate, rearrange, transform, transmute, transpose, variation **10** alteration, correction, difference, transition **11** desexualize, vicissitude **13** metamorphosis **15** diversification
   appearance: **6** obvert
   back: **6** return, revert
   character of: **8** denature
   color: dye **5** blush **6** redden
   course: **4** tack, turn, veer **5** sheer
   into: **6** become
   music: **4** muta
   subject to: **7** mutable **8** amenable, variable

sudden: **8** peripety

changeable: **5** eemis, giddy, immis **6** fickle, fitful, mobile **7** bruckle, erratic, mutable, protean, variant **8** amenable, catching, unstable, volatile **9** alterable, irregular, mercurial, uncertain, unsettled **10** capricious, inconstant, irresolute **11** chameleonic
in form: **9** metabolic

changeless: **5** fixed **6** steady **8** constant **9** steadfast **10** invariable

changeling: oaf **4** dolt, fool **5** child, dunce, idiot **7** waverer **8** imbecile, renegade, turncoat **9** simpleton **10** substitute

changeover: **5** shift **10** alteration, conversion

changing: *color:* **11** allochrous
pattern and color: **13** kaleidoscopic

channel: gat, ree, ria, rut **4** cano, cava, dike, duct, dyke, gool, gote, gout, pipe, vein, wadi, wady **5** canal, chase, ditch, drain, drill, flume, flute, glyph, media (pl.), regal, rigol, river, sinus, stria **6** arroyo, artery, furrow, groove, gutter, medium, rabbet, rivose, sluice, strait, stream, striae (pl.), trough **7** conduct, conduit, passage, rivulet, silanga, tideway **8** aqueduct, guideway **10** instrument **11** watercourse
artificial: gat **4** leat **5** canal, drain, flume **6** sluice **7** drainer
brain: **4** iter
formed by cutting: **5** scarf
longitudinal: **6** rabbet
marker: can, nun **4** buoy
narrow: **6** furrow, strait
near port: **5** deeps
river: bed **6** alveni (pl.) **7** alvenus
ship: gat
vertical: **5** glyph
vital: **5** aorta **6** artery
water: gat **4** gote, gurt, leat, pipe, race **5** canal, drain, flume **6** sluice **7** conduit **8** aqueduct, millrace, tailrace

Channel Islands: **4** Sark **6** Jersey **8** Alderney, Guernsey
measure: **4** cade **5** cabot
seaweed: **5** vraic

channelbill: **8** rainfowl

channeled: **6** fluted **7** voluted **8** furrowed **9** chamfered

channels: **5** media **6** striae

chanson: **4** song **5** lyric **6** ballad **7** refrain

chant: **4** cant, sing, song, tune **5** carol, psalm **6** anthem, cantus, intone, warble **7** introit, worship **8** vocalize **9** plainsong **10** cantillate, intonation **12** cantus firmus
Jewish: **6** Hallel
type: **8** Anglican **9** Ambrosian, Gregorian

chantage: **9** extortion **12** blackmailing

chanter: **6** cantor, singer **7** bagpipe **8** songster

9 chorister

chanteuse: **6** singer **10** cantatrice

chantey, chanty: **4** song

chanticleer: **4** cock **7** rooster

Chantilly: **4** lace **12** whipped cream

chantry: **4** cage **5** altar **6** chapel, shrine **9** endowment **11** incantation

chaos: pie **4** gulf, mess, void **5** abyss, babel, chasm **6** jumble **7** anarchy, mixture **8** disorder, shambles **9** confusion **10** unruliness **11** lawlessness
primordial: **4** Apsu
utter: **6** tophet **7** topheth

Chaos: *Babylonian:* **4** Apsu
daughter: Nox, Nyx
Maori: **4** kore
son: **6** Erebus

chaotic: **5** snafu **7** muddled **8** confused, formless

chap: boy, buy, man, rap **4** bean, beat, blow, chip, chop, cove, duck, gent, kibe, mash **5** billy, bloke, bully, buyer, chink, cleft, crack, knock, lover, split, trade, youth **6** barter, breach, bugger, callan, choose, fellow, redden, shaver, strike, stroke **7** callant, chapman, chappie, fissure, husband, roughen **8** blighter, customer, division
old: **6** geezer
young: **6** gaffer

chaparral: **7** thicket **9** buckthorn

chapel: **4** cage, cape, cope, cowl, hood **5** choir, cloak **6** bethel, church, shrine **7** chantry, service **8** bethesda **9** reliquary, sanctuary
private: **7** oratory
sailor's: bethel

chaperon: **4** hood **6** attend, duenna (Sp.), escort, matron **7** oversee, protect **8** guardian, trapping **10** escutcheon **11** gouvernante (F.)

chaplain: nun **5** padre **8** sky pilot **9** clergyman

chaplet: **4** bead, orle **5** crown **6** anadem, anchor, circle, fillet, rosary, trophy, wreath **7** coronal, coronet, garland **8** moulding, necklace, ornament

chapman: **5** buyer **6** dealer, hawker, trader **7** peddler **8** customer, merchant

chaps: **4** boys, jaws, lads **5** flews **8** breeches, leggings, overalls

chapter: **4** body, cell, post **5** caput, lodge **6** branch **7** correct, meeting, section **8** assembly **9** reprimand **10** contingent

char (see also **chare**): **4** burn, cart, sear **5** broil, chark, chore, singe, trout **6** scorch **7** blacken, chariot **8** sandbank **9** carbonize

charabanc: bus **5** coach **7** vehicle

character: **4** bent, card, kind, mark, mold, note, part, role, rune, sign, sort, tone **5** brand, fiber, stamp, tenor, token, trait,

write **6** caract, emblem, figure, letter, mad-cap, mettle, nature, oddity, repute, stripe, symbol **7** edition, engrave, essence, impress, quality **8** inscribe **9** agreement, ampersand, eccentric, integrity **10** reputation **11** disposition, personality
assumed: **4** role **9** incognito
bad: **5** drole (F.)
chief: **4** hero, lead, star **7** heroine **11** protagonist
group: **5** ethos
of a people: **5** ethos
vein: **6** streak
word-representing: **8** logogram **9** logograph
characteristic: **4** cast, mark, mien **5** trait **6** nature **7** feature, impress, quality, typical **8** property, symbolic **9** attribute, lineament **11** distinctive, pathognomic, peculiarity
individual: **9** idiopathy
characterize: **4** mark **6** define, depict **7** engrave, entitle, imprint, portray **8** describe, indicate, inscribe **9** delineate, designate, represent **11** distinguish
charade: **6** enigma, puzzle, riddle **7** pageant, picture, tableau **8** disguise, pretense **11** make-believe
charcoal: **5** carbo, chark **6** carbon, fusain, pencil **7** blacken, drawing
animal: **9** boneblack
reduce to: **4** char
chard: **4** beet **5** Swiss **7** thistle **9** artichoke
chare, char: job **4** lane, task, turn **5** alley, chore **6** finish, street **7** perform
charge: fee **4** bill, cark, cost, duty, fill, lien, load, onus, rate, rush, toll, ward **5** debit, onset, order, price, refer **6** accuse, adjure, allege, assess, attack, burden, career, credit, defame, demand, enjoin, impute, indict, tariff, weight **7** arraign, ascribe, assault, average, censure, command, concern, custody, expense, impeach, keeping, mandate, mission **8** chastise, overload, price tag **9** challenge, oversight **10** commission, impetition, impregnate, injunction, management **11** arraignment, encumbrance, incriminate, instruction **14** responsibility
customary: **4** dues
grazing: **5** agist
with gas: **6** aerate
chargeable: **6** costly, liable **7** weighty **9** expensive, important, momentous **10** burdensome **11** responsible, troublesome
charged: **5** tense **9** emotional, on the cuff **10** purposeful
with electricity: **4** live
chargeman: **7** blaster, foreman **10** battery man
charger: **4** dish **5** horse, mount, plate, steed **6** vessel **7** accuser, courser, platter **8** warhorse
charges: *boat carrying:* **7** boatage

legal: **4** dues, fees **5** costs **9** retainers
outdoor storage: **7** yardage
repairs to barrister's quarters: **9** detriment
charily: **8** frugally, gingerly **9** carefully, sparingly **10** cautiously, watchfully
chariness: **7** caution **8** prudence **9** frugality, integrity **11** heedfulness, sparingness **14** circumspection
chariot: car **4** cart, char, wain **5** buggy, essed, wagon **6** charet, esseda, essede **7** vehicle **8** carriage, charette **9** chariotee
for carrying image of god: **4** rath **5** ratha
Greek four-horse: **8** quadriga
Greek two-horse: **4** biga
Roman: **5** essed **6** esseda, essede
charioteer: **5** pilot **6** auriga, Ben-Hur, driver **7** wagoner **9** charioter
charisma: **5** charm, grace, power **6** allure, appeal, glamor, impact **8** urtchery **9** magnetism **11** fascination
charitable: **4** kind **6** benign, humane **7** lenient, liberal **8** generous **9** favorable, forgiving, indulgent **10** beneficent, benevolent **12** eleemosynary **13** compassionate, philanthropic
charity: **4** alms, dole, gift, love, pity, ruth **5** mercy **6** bounty **7** handout, largess **8** lenience **9** affection **10** almsgiving, generosity, liberality, tenderness **12** eleemosynary, philanthropy
dispenser: **7** almoner **14** philanthropist
charivari: **4** jest **5** babel **6** medley **8** serenade, shivaree **10** callithump **11** celebration
chark: **5** cup **4** burn, char, coal, coke **5** glass **6** cinder, noggin **8** charcoal
charlatan: **4** sham **5** cheat, faker, fraud, quack **6** con man **7** cabotin, empiric **8** imposter, magician **9** pretender **10** medicaster, mountebank
Charlemagne: *brother:* **8** Carloman
conquest: **5** Avars **6** Saxons
court hero: **6** Roland
father: **5** Pepin
knight: **4** Gano **7** Ganelon, Paladin
nephew: **6** Roland **7** Orlando
peer: **6** Oliver **7** Paladin
pert. to: **8** Caroline
sword: **7** Joyeuse
Charles' Wain: **4** Bear, Ursa **9** Big Dipper
Charlie Chan creator: **7** Biggers
charlock: **4** weed **5** kraut **7** mustard, yellows
charlotte: **7** custard, dessert
Charlotte Corday's victim: **5** Marat
charm: obi **4** calm, juju, jynx, mojo, play, song **5** allay, freet, freit, grace, magic, obeah, saffi, safie, spell, weird **6** allure, amulet, beauty, caract, enamor, entice, fetich, fetish, glamor, grigri, melody, please, saphie, scarab, soothe, subdue, summon **7** assuage, attract, beguile, bewitch, cantrip,

conjure, control, delight, enamour, enchant, enthral, flatter, glamour, periapt, singing, sorcery **8** breloque, enthrall, entrance, greegree, practice, talisman **9** agreeable, captivate, fascinate, seduction **10** attraction, demonifuge **11** incantation

extra: **5** add-on

protective: **6** amulet

charmer: **5** Circe, siren **8** exorcist, magician, sorcerer **9** sorceress **11** spellbinder

charming: **7** amiable, eyesome, winning, winsome **8** adorable, delicate **9** agreeable, beautiful, glamorous **10** attractive, glamourous **11** considerate

charnel: **7** ghastly **8** cemetery **10** sepulchral

house: **7** ossuary **8** mortuary

Charon: **7** boatman **8** ferryman **9** satellite

father: **6** Erebus

home: **5** Hades **10** underworld

mother: Nox, Nyx

payment to: **4** obol **6** obolus

river: **4** Styx

Charpentier opera: **6** Louise

charqui: **4** beef, meat **5** jerky **6** xarque

chart: map **4** card, plan, plat, plot **5** carte, graph **6** design, devise, record, scheme **7** diagram, dope out, explore, outline, project **8** document, platform **9** blueprint **10** cartograph

charter: let **4** deed, hire, rent **5** carte, chart, grant, lease **6** charta, permit **9** privilege **10** commission, conveyance

chary: shy **4** dear, safe, wary **5** chere, scant **6** frugal, prized, skimpy **7** careful, guarded, sparing **8** cautious, hesitant, precious, reserved, vigilant **9** diffident, reluctant, treasured **10** economical, fastidious, scrupulous **11** circumspect

Charybdis rock: **6** Scylla

chase: **4** hunt, shag, sick **5** annoy, catch, chevy, chivy, harry, score **6** chivvy, emboss, follow, frieze, furrow, gallop, groove, harass, hollow, indent, pursue, quarry, scorse, trench **7** channel, engrave, kick out, pursuit **8** ornament

away: **4** rout, shoo **5** drive

goddess: **4** Dian **5** Diana **7** Artemis

chaser: gun, ram **4** beer, tool, wolf **5** drink **6** hunter, masher **7** Don Juan **8** airplane, engraver

chasm: gap, pit **4** gulf, rift **5** abyss, blank, canon, chaos, cleft, gorge **6** breach, canyon, hiatus **7** fissure **8** aperture, crevasse, interval

glacial: **7** crevass **8** crevasse

chasse: **4** slip, step **5** glide **6** liquor, sashay, shrine **7** dismiss **9** reliquary

chassepot: **5** rifle

chasseur: **6** hunter **7** footman **8** huntsman **9** attendant

chassis: **5** frame

chaste: **4** neat, pure **5** clean, moral **6** decent, honest, modest, proper, severe, vestal, virgin **7** classic, elegant, refined **8** celibate, elevated, innocent, virtuous **9** continent, unadorned, undefiled, unsullied **10** immaculate, unaffected

chasten: **4** rate **5** abase, smite, smote, sober **6** humble, punish, purify, refine, subdue, temper **7** afflict, censure, correct **8** chastise, moderate, restrain, simplify **9** castigate, humiliate, reprimand **10** discipline

chastise: **4** beat, flog, lash, slap, trim, whip **5** amend, blame, scold, spank, strap, taunt **6** accuse, anoint, berate, charge, punish, purify, rebuke, refine, swinge, temper, thrash **7** chasten, correct, reprove, scourge, suspect **9** castigate **10** discipline

chastity: **5** honor **6** purity, virtue **7** modesty **8** celibacy, goodness **9** innocence

chasuble: **6** deacon, planet **8** vestment

form: **6** Gothic **10** fiddleback

ornament: **7** orphrey

Orthodox: **9** phelonion

chat: gab, mag **4** bird, chin, cone, coze, gist, talk, tove, twig **5** ament, cause, dally, point, prate, speak, spike **6** babble, branch, catkin, confab, gabble, gibber, gossip, jabber, potato, samara **7** chatter, prattle **8** causerie, converse, spikelet, strobile **9** dalliance **11** confabulate **12** conversation

chateau: **5** house, manor, villa **6** castle **7** mansion **8** fortress

Chateaubriand work: **4** René **5** Atala **10** Les Natchez

chatelaine: pin **4** etui, hook **5** chain, clasp, etwee, purse **6** brooch **8** mistress **9** keyholder **11** housekeeper, watchholder

chaton: **5** basil, bezel, bezil **7** setting

chattel: **4** gear **5** goods, money, slave, wares **7** capital **8** bondsman, property **9** livestock, principal

chatter: gab, jaw, mag, yap **4** blab, carp, chat, hack, rick, talk, tear, yirr **5** cabal, clack, garre, haver, prate, shake **6** babble, gabble, gibber, gossip, jabber, palter, rattle, shiver, tattle, yammer, yatter **7** blabber, brabble, chackle, chaffer, chipper, chitter, clitter, nashgob, prabble, prattle, shatter **8** schmoose, verbiage **9** small talk **11** goosecackle

conjurer's: **10** hanky-panky

chatterbox: jay, mag **4** piet **5** clack **6** gossip, magpie **8** quidnunc **10** chatterbag, chattermag **12** blabbermouth **13** chatterbasket

chattering: **8** babbling **9** prattling, talkative **10** loquacious

chauffeur: **5** cabby, drive **6** driver **8** operator **9** transport

chaussee: **4** road **6** street **7** highway **8** causeway

chaussure: 4 boot, shoe 7 slipper 8 footgear
chauvinism: 4 zeal 8 jingoism 11 nationalism
chaw: jaw, vex 4 chew, envy, mull 5 champ, grind 6 ponder 7 portion 8 ruminate 9 chawbacon, masticate
chawbacon: 4 chaw, lout 5 yokel 6 rustic 7 bumpkin
cheap: low 4 base, poor, vile 5 close, dirty, gaudy, kitch, price, tacky, tight, tinny, value 6 abject, common, kitsch, plenty, shoddy, sordid, stingy, tawdry, trashy 7 bargain, dealing 8 inferior, purchase 9 innkeeper, low-priced 10 despicable 11 depreciated, inexpensive 12 contemptible
cheap jack: 6 hawker, monger, pedlar, pedler, vendor 7 peddler 8 huckster 9 Cheap-John 11 underhanded 12 unprincipled
cheat: do, bam, bob, cog, con, fob, gip, gum, gyp, nip 4 bilk, bite, clip, dupe, fake, flam, geck, gull, hoax, jilt, jouk, liar, mump, rook, sell, sham, skin 5 bunco, bunko, cozen, cully, dodge, faker, fling, foist, fraud, gouge, guile, knave, mulct, rogue, scamp, spoil, trick, welsh 6 baffle, chiaus, chisel, daddle, delude, deride, doodle, duffer, fiddle, fleece, grease, humbug, illude, jockey, outwit, raddle, renege, shaver 7 abusion, beguile, deceive, defraud, escheat, finesse, foister, gudgeon, juggler, mislead, plunder, quibble, sharper, swindle 8 artifice, delusion, dry-shave, hood-wink, imposter 9 bamboozle, hypocrite, imposture, scoundrel, strategem, victimize 10 highbinder, mountebank 15 prestidigitator
cheater: 4 bite, gull 5 knave 6 bilker, topper 7 sharper 9 trickster
check: bit, dam, nab, nip, tab 4 balk, curb, damp, rein, snub, stay, stem, stop, stub, test, twit, were 5 abort, allay, block, brake, catch, chide, chink, choke, crack, daunt, delay, deter, draft, limit, quell, repel, stall, still, stunt, tally, taunt, token 6 arrest, attack, baffle, bridle, defeat, detain, detent, gravel, hinder, impede, oppose, outwit, quench, rabbet, rebate, rebuff, rebuke, scotch, stifle, ticket, verify 7 backset, command, control, inhibit, monitor, refrain, repress, reproof, reprove, repulse, setback 8 bulkhead, encumber, obstruct, restrain, withhold 9 constrain, frustrate, interrupt, overpower, reprimand, restraint, supervise 10 difficulty 11 certificate, counterfoil, examination
growth of: 5 stunt 7 shorten
in: 6 arrive 8 register
out: die 5 leave 6 depart 7 confirm 11 investigate
over: 4 pore 5 study 7 examine, inspect 10 scrutinize
checkerboard: 7 dambrod 8 damboard 12 draught board
marked like: 10 tessellate

checkered: 4 pied, vair 5 diced, plaid 6 motley, seesaw, uneven, varied 7 suspect 9 irregular 10 changeable, variegated 11 diversified
checkers: 4 game 6 damrod, drafts 8 chequers, draughts
move: 4 dyke, fife, huff 5 cross 7 bristol
opening: 6 souter
term: 4 king 5 block, crown
checkerwork: 7 tessera 8 tesserae (pl.)
inlay: 6 mosaic
checklist: 7 catalog 9 catalogue, inventory
checkmate: 4 gain, lick, stop, undo 6 baffle, corner, defeat, outwit, stymie, thwart 9 frustrate
checkrein: 4 curb 7 saccade
cheddar: 6 cheese
cheek: 4 chap, gall, gena, jole, jowl, leer, sass 5 bucca, chyak, crust, genae (pl.), nerve, sauce 6 chyack, haffet, haffit 8 audacity, temerity 9 brashness, impudence
bone: 5 malar 6 zygoma
distended: 7 buccate
muscle: 10 buccinator
pert. to: 5 genal, malar 6 buccal
cheep: pip, yap, yip 4 hint (Sc.), peep, pule 5 chirp, creak (Sc.), tweet 6 squeak, tattle 7 chirrup, twitter
cheer: ole (Sp.), rah 4 fare, food, root, viva, yell 5 bravo, elate, feast, heart, huzza, mirth, shout, whoop 6 cantle, gaiety, hurrah, huzzah, solace, viands 7 acclaim, animate, applaud, cherish, comfort, console, enliven, gladden, hearten, jollity, refresh, rejoice 8 applause, brighten, inspirit, pheasant, vivacity 9 animation, encourage, merriment 10 exhilarate, invigorate 11 acclamation, hospitality 13 entertainment, hospitality
burst: 5 salvo
cheerful: gay 4 cant, glad, gleg (Sc.), rosy 5 cadgy, canty (Sc.), chirk, douce, happy, jolly, merry, peart, ready, sunny 6 blithe, bright, cheery, chirpy, crouse, genial, hearty, hilary, jocund, lively 7 buoyant, chipper 8 cheering, gladsome, homelike, sanguine 9 contented, lightsome, sprightly 10 enlivening 11 comfortable 12 lighthearted
cheerless: sad 4 cold, drab, glum, gray 5 bleak, drear 6 dismal, dreary, gloomy 7 forlorn, joyless 8 dejected 10 dispirited, melancholy 11 comfortless 12 disconsolate
cheerio: 5 adieu 6 bye-bye 7 good-bye
cheese: 4 Brie, Edam, feta, Jack 5 brick, Colby, cream, Gouda, Swiss, Ziega 6 Asiago, Barrie, Dunlop, Glarus, mysost, romano, Zieger 7 Cheddar, cottage, Gruyere, Munster, ricotta, sapsago, Stilton 8 American, Bel Paese, Muenster, Parme-

san **9** Camembert, Emmenthal, Gammelost, Jarlsberg, Limburger, provolone, Roquefort **10** Emmentaler, Gorgonzola, mozzarella, Neufchatel **11** Liederkranz, Port du Salut
brown: **6** mysost
curdy: **4** trip
dish: **4** cake **6** fondue, omelet **7** rarebit, souffle
green: **7** sapsago
large: **7** kebbock, kebbuck
milk whey: **5** ziega **6** zieger
Normandy: **7** angelot
pert. to: **6** caseic **7** caseous
poached: **10** gnocchetti
white: **10** Neufchatel
cheesecake: **6** leg art **7** dessert **10** photograph
cheese maggot: **7** skipper
cheeseparing: **6** penury **9** parsimony **10** stinginess
cheesy: **4** fine, poor **5** cheap, smart **6** shabby, sleazy **7** caseous **8** inferior **9** excellent, worthless
cheetah: cat **5** youse, youze **7** guepard **8** gueparde
chef: **4** cook **7** saucier **9** cuisinier **10** cuisiniere
chef d'oeuvre: **7** classic **9** showpiece, work of art **11** masterpiece, tour de force
chela: **4** claw **5** slave **6** pincer **7** servant **8** disciple
chelicera: **8** mandible **9** appendage
chelonian: **6** turtle **8** tortoise
chemical: **4** acid, salt **6** alkali **8** catalyst **10** alchemical **13** iatrochemical
agent: **8** catalyst
compound: **4** acid, base, diol, imin **5** amide, azine, ceria, diene, ester, imine, purin **6** boride **7** inosite, leucine, metamer
element: See **element:** *chemical*
measure: **4** dram, gram **5** liter, titer
salt: sal
chemise: **5** shift, shirt, smock **6** camisa **8** lingerie
chemisette: **4** sham **6** guimpe
chemist: **7** analyst **8** druggist **9** alchemist **10** apothecary, pharmacist
vessel: **4** vial **5** ampul, cupel, flask, phial **6** aludel, ampule, beaker, retort **7** ampoule **8** bolt head, test tube
workroom: lab **10** laboratory
cheri, cherie: **4** dear **7** beloved, darling **9** cherished **10** sweetheart
cherish: aid, hug, pet **4** dote, hope, like, love, save **5** adore, cheer, cling, enjoy, nurse, prize, value **6** caress, esteem, faddle, fondle, foster, harbor, nestle, pamper, pettle, revere **7** comfort, embosom, embrace, indulge, nourish, nurture, protect, support,

sustain **8** enshrine, inspirit, preserve, treasure **9** cultivate, encourage, entertain
cheroot: **5** cigar
cherry: **4** bing, duke, gean **5** morel **7** capulin, chapman, lambert, morello, oxheart **8** amarelle, napoleon **9** bigarreau
acid: **7** cerasin
color: red **6** cerise
extract: **8** cerasein
sour: **8** amarelle
sweet: **4** bing **7** lambert, oxheart
wild: **4** gean **7** marasca, mazzard **10** maraschino
cherry finch: **8** hawfinch
cherry holly: **5** islay
cherry laurel: **7** cerasus
cherry orange: **7** kumquat
cherrystone: **4** clam **6** quahog
cherub: **5** angel, putti (pl.), putto **6** seraph, spirit **8** seraphim (pl.)
chervil: bun **4** herb
Cheshire district: **4** Hale **5** Hoole **6** Marple
chess: *draw game:* **9** stalemate
finish: **4** draw, mate **7** endgame **9** checkmate, stalemate
Japanese: **5** shogi
move: **5** debut **6** castle, fidate, gambit **10** fianchetto
opening: **5** debut **6** gambit **10** fianchetto
pert. to: **8** scacchic
piece: man **4** king, pawn, rook **5** queen **6** bishop, knight
chest: ark, box, kit **4** arca, bust, cist, cyst, fund, safe **5** ambry, bahut, front, hoard, hutch, trunk **6** basket, breast, bunker (Sc.), bureau, casket, coffer, coffin, hamper, locker, shrine, stripe, thorax **7** caisson, capcase, cassone (It.), commode, deposit, dresser, enclose, highboy **8** cupboard, treasury **9** container, strongbox **10** chiffonier, contention, receptacle, repository **11** controversy, gardeviance
alms: **6** almoin **7** almoign
animal: **7** brisket
bone: **5** costa
human: **6** breast, thorax
meal: **6** girnal, girnel
pert. to: **8** thoracic
sacred: ark **4** arca, cist
sound: **4** rale **7** rhonchi (pl.) **8** rhonchus
stone: **4** cist, kist
supply: **6** wangan, wangun **7** wanigan **8** wannigan
chesterfield: **4** coat, sofa **5** divan **8** overcoat **9** davenport
chestnut: **4** joke, ling, rata, tree **5** brown, horse **6** cliche, marron (F.), sativa **7** crenata, dentata
and gray: **4** roan
dwarf: **9** chincapin **10** chinquapin

genus of: **8** castanea
water: **4** ling **5** trapa

chevalier: **5** noble **6** knight **7** gallant **8** cavalier, horseman **9** caballero (Sp.), gentleman **10** greenshank

cheverel, cheveril: **6** pliant **7** elastic, kidskin **8** flexible

chevet: **4** apse **11** termination

chevisance: **5** booty, issue, spoil **6** remedy, supply **8** chivalry, resource **9** expedient, substance **10** enterprise, provisions **11** achievement, transaction

chevron: **4** beam, mark **5** glove **6** rafter, stripe, zigzag **7** molding **10** gravystain

chevrotain: **4** napu **7** deerlet, kanchil, tragule

chew: cud **4** bite, cham, chaw, gnaw, quid **5** chamm, grind, munch, rumen **6** mumble **8** meditate, ruminate **9** denticate, manducate, masticate
inability to: **8** amasesis
on: **8** consider
out: jaw **5** scold **7** bawl out, tell off **10** tongue-lash
the rag: **6** gossip **7** chatter

chewing gum base: **6** chicle

chewink: **4** bird **5** finch, joree **6** towhee

chiastolite: **5** macle **10** andalusite

chiaus: **5** cheat **8** sergeant, swindler **9** messenger

Chibcha: **4** zipa **5** zaque **6** Indian, muisca, zacqua

chic: **4** pert, posh, trig, trim **5** natty, nifty, smart **6** dapper, modish **7** elegant, soignee, stylish

---

Chicago: *airport:* **5** O'Hare **6** Midway
baseball field: **7** Wrigley **8** Comiskey
county: **4** Cook
district: **4** Loop **8** West Side **9** Gold Coast, North Side, South Side
fire origin: **11** O'Leary's barn
football field: **7** Soldier
lake: **4** Wolf **7** Calumet **8** Michigan
nickname: **9** Windy City **10** Second City
shopping area: **15** Magnificent Mile

---

chicanery: **4** ruse, wile **5** feint, trick **8** artifice, intrigue, trickery **9** deception, duplicity, sophistry, stratagem

chichi: **5** showy, swank **7** splashy **8** affected **11** pretentious

chick: **4** girl, tick **5** child, natty **6** moppet, screen, sequin, sprout **7** chicken **8** young one

chickadee, chicadee: **8** titmouse

chickaree: **8** squirrel

chicken: hen **4** cock, fowl **5** biddy, capon, chick, child, chuck, fryer, layer, manoc, poult **6** bantam, chicky, pullet **7** broiler,

rooster **8** cockerel **11** chickabiddy
breed: **4** Java **7** Dorking, Hamburg, Leghorn **9** Wyandotte **10** mille fleur **14** Rhode Island Red
castrated: **5** capon
cooking: **4** fowl **5** fryer **7** broiler, roaster
pen: **4** coop
raising device: **7** brooder
young: **5** chick, fryer, poult **6** pullet **7** broiler

chickenhearted: **5** timid **8** cowardly

chicken out: **4** quit **6** renege

chicken snake: **4** boba

chick-pea: **4** gram, herb **5** chich, cicer **8** garbanzo, garvance, garvanzo **9** garavance

chickweed genus: **6** alsine

chicle: gum **5** latex

chicory: **4** bunk, root **5** plant **6** endive **7** succory, witloof
family: **12** cichoriaceae

chide: **4** rail, rate **5** blame, check, flite, flyte, scold **6** berate, rebuff, rebuke, threap, threep, threpe **7** censure, reprove, upbraid, wrangle **8** admonish, call down, reproach **9** objurgate, reprehend, reprimand

chief: aga, big, boh, cap, cob, dux, mir **4** agha, arch, boss, duce, duke, head, high, jefe, khan, main, rais, raja, reis, tyee **5** alder, elder, first, great, major, prime, rajah, ruler, thane, titan, vital **6** adalid, cabeza, leader, master, rector, sachem, staple **7** capital, captain, central, eminent, foreman, overman, palmary, prelate, premier, supreme **8** big wheel, dominant, especial, foremost, intimate, sagamore **9** chieftain, commander, number one, paramount, principal, prominent **11** predominant

chiffonier: **5** chest **6** bureau **7** cabinet, commode, dresser

chigger: **4** mite **6** chigoe, insect, jigger, red-bug

chignon: bun **4** knot **5** chain, twist

chigoe: **4** flea **7** chigger

chilblain: **4** kibe, mule (F.), sore **5** blain **6** pernio **8** swelling **12** inflammation

child (see also **children**): ben (Heb.), boy, bud, imp, kid, son, tad, tot **4** baba, babe, baby, bata, brat, chit, girl, nino (Sp.), page, tike, tyke **5** bairn (Sc.), chick, chiel (Sc.), gamin, issue, minor, youth **6** cherub, enfant (F.), filius (L.), infant, moppet, urchin **7** bambino (It.), progeny **8** bantling, chiseler (Ir.), daughter **9** firstling, offspring, youngster **10** adolescent, descendant **11** chickabiddy
advancement: **9** precocity
chubby: **8** rolypoly **10** butterball
dainty: elf **5** fairy
gifted: **7** prodigy
homeless: **4** waif
illegitimate: **6** by-blow **7** bastard
killer: **11** infanticide

parentless: **6** orphan
patron saint: **8** Nicholas
pert. to: **6** filial
puckish: imp
roguish: **6** urchin
spoiled: **4** brat **5** mardy **7** cockney
street: **4** Turk **5** gamin
tiny: tot **4** babe, baby, tyke **6** infant, peewee
unmannerly: **4** brat **7** smatche (Sc.)

childbirth: **5** labor **7** lying-in, travail **11** confinement, parturition
goddess: **4** Apet, Auge, Upis **5** Damia **6** Lucina **7** Auxesia

childish: **4** slow, weak **5** naive, petty, silly, young **6** puling, simple, weanly (Sc.) **7** asinine, babyish, foolish, kiddish, puerile, unmanly **8** bairnish, brattish, immature, juvenile **9** childlike, credulous, infantile, kittenish
talk: **7** prattle
walk: **6** toddle

childless: **6** barren **7** sterile **9** infertile
childlike: **4** meek **6** docile, filial **7** babyish, dutiful **8** childish, innocent, trusting **9** confiding, frivolous **10** submissive

children: **4** kids **5** heirs, young **7** progeny **9** offspring
dislike of: **9** misopedia **10** misopaedia
medical science: **10** pediatrics **11** paediatrics
room: **7** nursery
study: **8** pedology **9** paedology
tender of: **4** amah **5** nanny **6** sitter **9** governess, nursemaid

Chile: *(see box)*
chill: ice, raw **4** ague, cold, cool, dazy (Sc.) **5** algor, gelid, rigor, shake **6** frappe, freeze, frigid, frosty, shiver **7** depress, frisson, glacial, malaria **8** coldness **11** refrigerate
chiller: **7** shocker **8** thriller
chilling: **4** eery **5** eerie **6** wintry **7** glacial
chills and fever: **4** ague **7** malaria

chilly: raw **4** cold, cool, lash **5** algid, bleak, hunch **6** arctic, frosty **9** cauldrife
Chimaera: **7** monster, ratfish **11** holocephali
chime: din, rim **4** bell, edge, peal, ring, suit, ting **5** agree, prate **6** accord, cymbal, jingle, melody **7** concord, harmony **8** singsong
in: **4** tell **5** offer, state **6** chip in **9** interrupt
chimera: **5** dream, fancy **6** mirage **8** illusion **16** pipe dream fantasy
chimerical: **4** vain, wild **6** absurd, unreal **7** utopian **8** delusive, fanciful, romantic **9** fantastic, imaginary, unfounded, visionary
chimes: **5** bells **8** carillon
chimney: lum **4** flue, pipe, tube, vent **5** gully, stack, tewel **6** funnel **7** fissure, opening, orifice **10** smokestack
cover: **4** cowl **7** turncap
deposit: **4** soot
piece: **5** parel **6** mantel
post: **5** speer
chimney corner: **8** fireside **9** inglenook
chimpanzee: ape **5** jacko, pigmy **6** baboon, monkey **10** anthropoid, troglodyte
chin: jaw, rap **4** chat **5** menta (pl.) **6** mentum
double: **4** fold **7** buccula
china: **4** ware **6** dishes **7** ceramic, pottery **8** Cinchona, crockery **9** porcelain **11** earthenware
fine: **5** Spode **6** Sevres **7** Dresden, Limoges, Meissen **8** Wedgwood
China: (see box)
China Sea: *gulf:* **4** Siam **6** Tonkin **8** Thailand
island: **6** Hainan, Ryukyu **7** Formosa **11** Philippines
chinaberry: **5** lilac **9** soapberry
chinch: **6** bedbug
chine: **4** back, grow **5** chink, crack, crest, ridge, spine **6** cleave, ravine, sprout **7** crevice, fissure **8** backbone
Chinese: **5** Cerai, Seres, Seric, Sinic **6** Mongol, Sinico **7** Asiatic, Cataian, Sangley **9** Celestial
pert. to: **5** Seric **6** Serian **7** Sinitic **8** Senesian

---

Chile: *capital:* **8** Santiago
city: **5** Arica **6** Arauco, Cobija, Serena **7** Caldera, Copiapo, Iquique **8** Coquimbo, Valdivia **10** Concepcion, Talcahuano, Valparaiso, Vina del Mar **11** Antofagasta, Punta Arenas
currency: **4** peso **5** libra **6** condor, escudo
Indian: Ona **4** Auca, Inca, Onan **6** Arauca, Aymara, Chango **7** Quechua
island: **5** Byron, Guafo, Hoste **6** Chiloe, Easter **13** Juan Fernandez **14** Tierra del Fuego
measure: **4** vara **5** legua, linea **6** cuadra, fanega

mountain: **4** Maco, Toro **5** Andes, Maipu, Pular, Torre, Yogan **13** Ojos del Salado
mountain range: **5** Andes
river: Loa **5** Itata, Maipu, Maule **6** Bio-Bio, Chuapa, Lontue **7** Illapel, Mapocho **8** Valdivia **9** Aconcagua
rodent: **10** chinchilla
shrub: **5** lithi **6** pepino
tree: **4** brea, pelu, ulmo **5** coleu, rauli, roble **6** alerce, alerse, coigue, muermo
volcano: **5** Lanin, Maipo **6** Antuco, Lascar, Llaima **7** Calbuco
weight: **4** kilo **5** gramo, grano, libra **7** quintal
workman: **4** roto **9** inquilino

China: 8 Zhongguo
aborigine: Yao **4** Mans, Miao **6** Mantzu, Yaomin **7** Miaotse, Miaotze
alloy: **7** paktong **8** packtong
ancient name: **4** Tsao **5** Seres **6** Cathay
antelope: **6** dzeren
arch: **6** pailoo, pailou, pailow
artichoke: **7** chorogi
bamboo: **7** whangee
banker: **6** shroff
bean: soy **6** cowpea
black tea: **6** oolong
boat: **4** bark, junk **6** sampan
brigand: **9** hunghutze, hunghutzu
Buddha: Fo, Foh
Buddhist paradise: **7** Chingtu
cabbage: **7** bok choy, pakchoi, wong bok **8** Michihli
calculator: **6** abacus **7** suan pan, swan pan
canton: Fu **5** Hsein
capital: **6** Peking **7** Beijing
city: Nom, Ude **4** Amoy, Luda, Luta, Tsin, Wuhu **5** Jehol, Macao, Macau, Pekin, Wuhan **6** Canton, Fachan, Fuchau, Hankau, Hankow, Harbin, Huchau, Kalgan, Mukden, Nankin, Ningpo, Peking, Suchau, Swatow, Tsinan, Yunnan **7** Beijing, Chengdu, Chengte, Chengtu, Chingtu, Fatshan, Foochow, Hanyang, Kaifeng, Lanchau, Nanjing, Nanking, Paoting, Taiyuen, Tianjin, Tunkuan, Wenchau, Wuchang, Yenping **8** Changsha, Chaochau, Fancheng, Hangchau, Hangchow, Kiaochau, Nanchang, Quingdao, Shanghai, Shaohing, Shenyang, Siangtan, Tengchau, Tientsin, Tsingtao, Tungchau, Tunghwan, Yanphing **9** Changchau, Chinkiang, Chongqing, Chungking, Guangzhou, Lienkiang **10** Chingkiang, Kingtechen
civet: **5** rasse
clay: **6** kaolin
cloth: sha **4** moxa, pulo, silk **6** nankin **7** nankeen
cloth-stiffening gelatin: **7** haitsai
cooking style: **5** Hunan **6** Fukien, Peking **8** Szechuan **9** Cantonese
cosmic order: tao
currency: le, pu, fan, fen, neu, sen, yen **4** cash, cent, jiao, mace, tael, tiao, yuan **5** liang, sycee, tsien **6** dollar, ticket **9** candareen **10** Kupingtael **11** Haikwantael
customs collector: **5** hoppo
deer: **8** elaphure
desert: **4** Gobi, Mu Us **5** Ordos **10** Taklimakan
dialect: **4** Amoy **5** Hakka **6** Canton, Ningpo, Swatow **7** Foochow, Wenchow
dog: **4** chow, peke **7** Shar-Pei **8** pekinese
dragon: **6** chilin
drink: **6** samshu
duck eggs: **5** pidan
dulcimer: **7** yang-kin
dynasty: Han, Sui, Wei, Yin **4** Chin, Chou, Hsia, Ming, Sung, Tang, Tsin, Yuan **5** Shang **6** Manchu
exchange medium: **5** sycee
factory: **4** hong
feudal state: Wei
figurine: **5** magot
fir: **5** nikko
fish: **7** trepang
flute: che **4** tche
fruit: **6** lichee, litchi
ginger: **9** galingale
god: **4** Ghos, Joss, Shen **5** Kuant
gong: **6** tamtam
gooseberry: **9** carambola
grass: bon **5** ramie
grass linen: **8** barandos
gruel: **6** congee, conjee
herb: tea **7** ginseng
herb genus: **7** nandina
houseboat: **5** tanka
idol: **4** joss **6** pagoda
indigo: **6** isatis
isinglass: **4** agar **8** agar-agar
island: **4** Amoy **5** Macao **6** Hainan, Taiwan **7** Formosa
jute: **7** chingma
laborer: **6** coolie
lake: **6** Po-yang **7** Qing Hai **8** Dongting, Tung-ting
language: Wu, Yue **4** Shan **8** Mandarin **9** Cantonese, Putonghua
largest city: **8** Shanghai
magistrate: **8** mandarin
magnolia: **5** yulan
mandarin's residence: **6** oyamen
measure: cho, fen, tou, yan, yin **4** chih, fang, kish, quei, shih, teke, tsan, tsun **5** chang, ching, sheng, shing **6** kung ho, kung li, kung mu, tching, tchung **7** kung fen **8** kung chih, kung shih **9** kung ching, kung sheng
medical technique: **11** acupuncture
mountain: Omi **4** Omei, Sung **5** Altai, Tsins **6** Inshan, Kunlun, Pamirs, Pu-ling **7** Alashan, Everest, Hinggan, Kuliang, Qin Ling **8** Himalaya
musical instrument: di, kin **4** pipa, xiao **5** cheng, sheng **7** samisen
Nationalist Party: **10** Kuomintang
(cont.)

China (*cont.*)
noodles: 4 mein
nurse: ama 4 amah
official: 4 kuan, kwan 5 amban
oil: 4 tung
old name: 6 Cathay
orange: 7 kumquat 8 mandarin
ox: 4 zebu
pagoda: taa 4 taag
parasol tree: 6 aogiri
peony: 6 moutan
people: Yi, Han, Hui 4 Buyi, Miao 5 Uygur 6 Manchu, Mongol, Zhuang
pert. to: 4 Sino
philosopher: 4 Moti 5 Motzu 6 Laotse, Laotzu 9 Confucius
plant: tea, udo 4 rice, tche 5 ramie 7 ginseng
poet: 4 Li Po 5 Laozi 7 Li Tai-Po
pony: 7 griffin
porcelain: 7 Celadon, Nankeen
porcelain glaze: 7 eelskin
porgy: tai
positive principle: 4 yang
pottery: 4 Kuan, Ming, Ting 5 Chien 7 boccaro, Tzuchou
provincial chief: 6 taoyin
puzzle: 7 tangram
race: 4 Lolo 5 Sinic, Soyot 6 Mongol
religion: 6 Taoism 12 Confucianism
river: Han, Hsi, Ili, Kan, Min, Pei, Wei 4 Amur, Hwai, Liao, Tung, Yuan, Yuen 5 Hwang, Peiho, Tarim 6 Mekong, Yellow 7 Hoangho, Huang He, Sikiang, Yangtze 12 Yangtsekiang
roller: 7 sirgang
salutation: bow 6 kowtow
sauce: soy

secret society: hui 4 tong
sedge: 4 mati
silk: sha 5 pekin, tasar 6 pongee, tussah 7 taysaam, tsatlee 8 shantung
silkworm: 4 sina 6 tussah, tusser 9 ailanthus
silver: 5 sycee
sky: 4 tien
sleeping platform: 4 kang
society: 4 Hoey, Huey, Hung, Tong 5 Triad
squash: 6 cushaw
stocks: 6 cangue
street: 6 hutung
student: 9 sinologue
sugar cane: 5 sorgo
taa: 6 pagoda
Tartar tribe: 4 Toda
tax: 5 likin
tea: cha 4 Tsia 5 bohea, congo, congu, Emesa, hyson 6 oolong
temple: taa 6 pagoda
tree: 5 nikko 6 gingko, kinkan, litchi 7 hagbush, kumquat 9 bandoline, soapberry
tribe: 4 Shan, Toba
vegetable: udo
vine: 5 kudzu 7 yangtao
walking stick: 7 whangee
warehouse: 4 hong
wax: 4 cere, pela
weight: fen, hao, kin, ssu, tan, yin 4 chee, chin, mace, shih, tael 5 catty, chien, liang, picul, tsien 6 kung li 7 haikwan, kung fen, kung ssu, kung tun 8 king chin 9 candareen 10 kuping tael 11 haikwan tael
wind instrument: 5 cheng, sheng
wormwood: 4 moxa

chink: gap 4 bore, cash, coin, kink, rent, rift, rime 5 boore, check, chine, cleft, crack, grike, money 6 cranny, jingle, rimose, rimous, sprain 7 chinkle, crevice, fissure 8 aperture 9 chaffinch 10 interstice
chinky: 5 rifty 6 rimose
Chinook: 4 wind 6 Indian 8 Flathead
chief: 4 Tyee
god: 8 tamanoas
people: 7 tilikum 8 tillicum
powwow: 4 wawa
salmon: 7 quinnat
woman: 10 klootchman
Chinook State: 10 Washington
chinquapin: oak 6 bonnet 8 chestnut, wankapin 9 rattlenut
chintzy: 4 mean 5 cheap, petty 6 stingy 7 miserly

chip: bit, cut, hew, nig 4 chap, clip, knap, nick, pare 5 crack, flake, piece, scrap, spale, spalt, waste 6 chisel 7 counter 8 fragment, splinter
in: 5 share 10 contribute 11 come through
of stone: 5 spall 6 gallet
chipmunk: 6 backee, chippy, rodent 8 squirrel
chipper: gay 4 spry 5 chirp, perky 6 babble, cockey, lively 7 chatter, chirrup, twitter 8 cheerful
chirk: gay 6 lively 7 chirrup 8 cheerful, embolden 9 encourage
chirm: din, hum 5 chirp, croon, noise 6 clamor
chirography: 6 script 7 writing 10 engrossing 11 handwriting
chiromancy: 9 palmistry 10 chirognomy

chirp 136

chirp: pip **4** peek, peep, pipe **5** cheep, chelp, chirk, chirl, chirm, chirt, tweet **7** chipper, chirrup, chitter, rejoice, twitter, wheetle
chirrup: 5 chirk, chirp, tweet **7** chitter, twitter
chisel: cut, gad, gyp **4** chip, form, pare, tool **5** burin, carve, cheat, gouge, hardy **6** gravel, haggle **7** bargain, defraud, engrave, quarrel, shingle **9** sculpture
ancient stone: **4** celt
engraving: **7** scooper, scorper
mine: gad **6** peeker
sculpture: **7** gradine **9** ebauchoir
stonemason's: **5** drove
toothed: **6** jagger
chiseler: 5 cheat, crook **6** gouger **9** bargainer
chiselled: 8 clearcut
chiselly: 6 gritty **8** gravelly **10** unpleasant **12** disagreable
chit: dab, IOU, kid **4** bill, girl, mind, note, rice **5** child, draft, shoot **6** infant, letter, moppet, sprout **7** voucher **8** young one **9** offspring **10** memorandum
chitchat: 4 talk **6** banter, gossip **9** small talk **12** conversation
chiton: 4 gown, robe **5** tunic **7** mollusk **9** sea cradle
chitter: 4 peep **5** chirp **6** shiver **7** chatter, twitter
chivalrous: 5 brave, civil, noble **6** gentle, polite **7** courtly, gallant, genteel, valiant, warlike **8** knightly **9** courteous, honorable
chive: cut **4** stab **5** clout, clove, knive, onion **6** bulbet
chivy, chivvy: run, vex **4** hunt, race **5** chase, tease **6** badger, flight, harass, pursue **7** pursuit, scamper, torment **8** maneuver **9** confusion
chlamys: 5 cloak **6** mantle **7** garment
Chloe: 11 shepherdess
beloved: **7** Daphnis
chloride: 4 salt **5** ester **7** calomel, muriate **8** compound
chlorine: 6 bleach
chloroform: 4 kill **10** anesthetic
discoverer: **6** Liebig **7** Guthrie **9** Soubeiran
ingredient: **7** acetone
liquid used: **7** acetone
chobdar: 5 usher **9** attendant
chock: 5 block, chuck, cleat, wedge
chocolate: bar **5** candy, cocoa **8** beverage
family: **13** sterculiaceae
machine: **6** conche
powder: **5** cocoa **6** pinola
seed: **5** cacao
stick for mixing: **7** molinet
substitute: **9** carob bean
tree: **4** cola **5** cacao
choice: 4 a-one, best, fine, pick, rare, wale, weal, will **5** cream, elite, prime, voice **6**
chosen, dainty, flower, option, picked, select, superb **8** delicate, druthers, election, eximious, uncommon, volition **9** excellent, exquisite, recherche **10** preferable, preference **11** alternative
choicy: 5 fussy, picky **6** choosy **7** finicky **10** fastidious **11** persnickety
choir: 4 band **5** quire **6** chorus **7** chorale, kapelle
leader: **6** cantor **9** precentor **11** choirmaster
member: **4** alto, bass **5** basso, tenor **7** songman, soprano **8** baritone **9** chorister, contralto **12** mezzo-soprano
vestment: **4** gown, robe **5** cotta **8** surplice
choke: dam, gag **4** clog, fill, plug, quar **5** check, close, grane **6** hinder, impede, stifle **7** congest, querken, repress, silence, smother **8** obstruct, stoppage, strangle, suppress, throttle **9** constrict, neckcloth, suffocate **10** asphyxiate, extinguish
choler: ire **4** fury, rage **5** anger, wrath **6** spleen, temper **9** distemper, ill temper **10** resentment **11** biliousness **12** irascibility
choleric: mad **5** angry, cross, fiery, huffy, testy **6** fumish, touchy **7** bilious, enraged, iracund, peevish, peppery, waspish **8** wrathful **9** impatient, irascible **10** passionate **11** belligerent, hot-tempered, quarrelsome **13** quick-tempered
render: **6** enrage
chomp: 4 bite, chew **5** munch **6** crunch **8** ruminate **9** masticate
choose: opt **4** chap, cull, pick, vote, wale, weal **5** adopt, chuse, elect **6** prefer, select **7** embrace, espouse **9** single out
choosy, choosey: 7 finical, finicky **9** selective **10** fastidious
chop: cut, hew, jaw, lop **4** chap, dice, gash, hack, hash, jowl, rive, slit **5** carve, cleft, crack, knock, mince, slash, stamp, trade, truck, whang **6** barter, change, cleave, incise **8** exchange **9** cotolette
down: **4** fell, raze **5** level
off: lop **4** drib **5** prune **8** amputate
chop-chop: 7 quickly **8** promptly **9** posthaste **12** lickety-split
chophouse: 10 restaurant
Chopin: 7 pianist **8** composer
birthplace: **6** Poland
lover: **4** Sand (George)
chopping block: 7 hacklog
chopping tool: axe **7** cleaver, hatchet
choppy: 5 rough
choragus: 6 leader **10** bandleader
chord: 4 cord, tone **5** nerve, triad **6** string, tendon **7** harmony **8** filament **9** harmonize
arc: **4** sine
harplike: **8** arpeggio
musical: **5** major, minor

ninth: 4 none
seventh: 6 tetrad
succession: 7 cadence
chore: job 4 duty, task 5 stint 6 errand 9 housework 10 assignment
choreography: 7 dancing
chorister: 6 singer 7 chanter 8 choirboy
chorography: 9 map-making
chortle: 5 laugh, snort 7 chuckle
chorus: 4 song 5 choir 6 accord, assent, unison 7 concert, concord, harmony, refrain, singers 8 response
girl: 6 dancer, singer 7 chorine
leader: 7 choragi (pl.) 8 choragus 9 conductor
chosen: 5 elect, elite 7 elected 8 selected
Chosen: 5 Korea
chosen people: 10 Israelites
chough: 4 bird, crow
chouse: 4 dupe, gull, sham 5 chase, cheat, trick 6 harass 7 defraud, swindle 8 swindler 10 imposition
chow: dog 4 eats, food, grub, meal 6 fodder
chowchow: dog 4 bird, hash, olio 7 mixture 8 mishmash 10 hodgepodge, miscellany
chowderhead: 4 dope 5 dunce 6 noodle 7 schnook 9 lame-brain
Christ (see also **Jesus**): 4 Lord 7 Messiah, Saviour
Christian: 7 Gentile 8 Nazarene
denomination: 6 Quaker 7 Baptist 8 Anglican, Lutheran, Orthodox 9 Calvinist, Methodist 10 Protestant 12 Episcopalian, Presbyterian 13 Roman Catholic
early: 8 Galilean
Eastern: 6 Uniate 8 Orthodox
Egyptian: 4 Copt
christen: 4 name 7 baptize 10 denominate
Christmas: 4 noel, yule 7 holiday 8 festival, nativity, yuletide
carol: 4 noel 5 nowel
crib: 6 creche, manger
decoration: 5 holly 6 tinsel 9 mistletoe
midnight Mass supper: 9 reveillon
Christmas Carol: *author:* 7 Dickens
character: Tim 6 Marley 7 Scrooge 8 Cratchit, Fezziwig
Christmas rose: 9 hellebore
Christ's thorn: 4 nabk, nubk 5 shrub 6 jujube
chromium: 7 element, mineral
group element: 7 uranium 8 tungsten 10 molybdenum
chromolithograph: 7 picture
chronic: 5 fixed, usual 6 severe 7 intense, routine 8 constant 9 confirmed, continual, customary, lingering, prolonged 10 continuous, inveterate 12 disagreeable
chronicle: 5 annal, diary, story 6 record 7 account, archive, history, recital 8 register 9 narrative

chronicler: 5 Pepys 6 writer 7 Boswell 8 compiler, recorder, reporter 9 historian 10 biographer 11 memorialist
chronology: 6 record 8 time line 11 arrangement 14 classification
according to: 5 datal
error in: 9 prolepsis 11 anachronism
chronometer: 4 dial 5 clock, watch 9 metronome, timepiece 10 timekeeper
chrysalis: 4 kell, pupa 5 pupae (pl.)
chrysolite: 7 olivine, peridot
chrysoprase: 10 chalcedony
chthonian: 6 Hadean 8 infernal, plutonic 10 sulphurous
chub: 4 dace, dolt, fool, lout 5 chopa 6 chevin, shiner 8 fallfish, mackerel 9 hornyhead, squawfish
chubby: 5 chuff, fubsy, plump, pudgy, round, tubby 6 choaty, rotund, zaftig (Yid.) 8 roly-poly
chuck: hen, log, pig 4 beef, cast, food, fowl, grub, hurl, jerk, lump, shed, toss 5 chock, cluck, ditch, pitch, throw 6 bounce 7 chicken, discard 9 dismissal
chuckle: 5 cluck, exult, laugh 6 giggle, titter 7 chortle
chuff: fat 4 boor, glum, ugly 5 brick, churl, cross, miser, proud, sound, sulky, surly 6 chubby, elated, rustic 7 swollen 9 conceited 11 ill-tempered
chug: 4 puff
chum: cad, cob, pal 4 bait, mate, pard 5 amigo, buddy, butty, crony 6 cobber, copain, friend 8 roommate 9 associate, companion
around: 6 hobnob
chump: ass, oaf, sap 4 boob, dolt, head, jerk 5 block 7 fall guy 8 lunkhead 9 blockhead, schlemiel, schlemihl
chunk: dab, gob, pat, wad 4 junk, slug 5 claut, piece, throw, whang
chunky: 4 game 5 hefty, lumpy, plump, squat, stout, thick
church (see also **cathedral**): 4 cult, sect, tera (Jap.) 5 creed, faith 6 temple 7 edifice 9 sanctuary, structure 10 house of God 13 house of prayer
adjunct: 6 belfry 7 steeple 9 bell tower
altar end: 4 apse
altar offering: 8 altarage
attendant: 6 server 7 acolyte 8 altarboy 9 altargirl
balcony: 8 cantoria
bench: pew, pue 4 seat
bishopric: see 7 diocese 10 episcopacy, episcopate
body of: 4 nave
calendar: 4 ordo
caretaker: 6 sexton

chapel: **7** oratory
congregation: **7** synaxis
council: **5** synod, Trent **6** Nicene **7** Ephesus, Vatican **14** Constantinople
court: **4** Rota
deputy: **5** vicar **6** curate
dignitary: **4** dean, pope **5** abbot, canon **6** bishop **7** prelate, primate **8** cardinal **9** monsignor
dissenter: **7** sectary
district: **6** parish **7** diocese, mission
dominion of: **11** sacerdotium
doorkeeper: **7** ostiary
early Christian: **8** basilica
endowed: **8** benefice
entrance chapel: **7** galilee
episcopacy: **7** prelacy
government: **9** hierarchy
home: **5** manse **7** deanery, rectory **8** convento **9** parsonage
law: **5** canon
member: **11** communicant
morning service: **6** matins
officer: **5** elder, vicar **6** beadle, deacon, lector, sexton, warden **7** prelate, sacrist **8** reverend **9** clergyman, moderator, presbyter, sacristan **11** headborough
part of: **4** apse, bema, loft, nave **5** aisle, altar, solea **6** vestry **7** chancel, narthex **8** cantoria, sacristy, transept **9** sanctuary
pert. to: **9** ecclesial **14** ecclesiastical
prayer: **5** kyrie **12** kyrie eleison
property: **5** glebe
reader: **6** lector
recess: **4** apse
revenue: **5** tithe **8** benefice
Roman: **7** lateran **8** basilica
room: **6** vestry **7** galilee **8** sacristy
seat: pew, pue **5** bench **6** sedile **7** sedilia (pl.)
service: **4** Mass, rite **6** matins **7** nocturn, vespers **8** compline, evensong **9** communion **13** Morning Prayer
stand: **4** ambo
stipend: **7** prebend
vault: **5** crypt
vessel: ama, pyx **4** font **5** amula, paten **7** chalice, columba, piscina **8** ciborium **9** colymbion **10** monstrance
vestry room: **8** sacristy
wall: **6** cashel
warden's aide: **7** hoggler
wing: **5** aisle
churchgoer: **11** communicant
churchly: **9** religious, spiritual
churchyard: **6** litten **8** cemetery **9** graveyard
churl: cad, man **4** boor, carl, gnof, hind, lout, serf **5** carle, ceorl, chuff, gnoff, knave, miser **6** bodach, carlot, lubber, rustic, vassal, yeoman **7** bondman, freeman, haskard, husband, niggard, peasant, villain, villein **10** countryman, curmudgeon
churlish: **4** mean **5** bluff, gruff, rough, surly **6** crabby, rustic, sordid, sulky, sullen, vulgar **7** boorish, crabbed, uncivil, violent **9** illiberal **10** ungracious, unyielding **12** cross-grained
churn: **4** beat, kirn (Sc.), stir **5** drill, shake **7** agitate
part: **6** dasher
chute: **4** rush, tube **5** flume, hurry, rapid, shoot, slide **6** hopper, trough **7** cascade, decline, descent **8** downfall, stampede **9** waterfall
cibol: **5** onion **7** shallot
ciborium: pix, pyx **6** canopy, coffer, vessel
cicada: **6** cagale, cigala, locust **11** grasshopper
noise: **5** chirr
cicatrix: eye **4** mark, scab, scar, seam
cicatrization: **8** scarring
cicely: **5** myrrh (Sc.) **7** chervil
Cicero: **5** Roman **6** orator **9** statesman
speech: **10** Philippics
target: **8** Catiline **10** Mark Antony
cicerone: **5** guide, pilot **6** mentor, orator **7** courier **9** conductor
Cid, el: Ruy **4** epic, hero, poem **5** Bivar, chief, title **7** Spanish **9** commander
sword of: **6** colada, tizona
cider: **5** perry **6** perkin, swanky **8** beverage
fermented: **9** apple jack
pulp: **6** pomace
cigar: **4** toby, weed **5** claro, smoke, stogy **6** corona, maduro, stogie **7** bouquet, cheroot, culebra **8** perfecto **9** Belvedere
case: **7** humidor
crude: **7** cheroot, culebra
thin: **8** panatela, panetela **9** cigarillo, panatella, panetella
cigarette: fag **4** biri, butt, pill **5** cubeb, smoke **6** gasper, reefer **9** cigarillo **10** coffin nail
cigarfish: **4** scad **8** quiaquia
cilium: **4** hair, lash **7** eyelash **8** barbicel
cima: See **cyma**
cimarron: **5** slave **6** maroon **7** bighorn, wild dog
cimbia: **4** band **6** fillet
cimex: **6** bedbug, insect
Cimmerian: **4** inky **5** black, nomad **6** gloomy **7** stygian **8** infernal **9** plutonian
cinch: **4** belt, bind, easy, gird, grip, hold, pipe, snap **5** girth **6** fasten **8** card game, sinecure **9** certainty
cinchona: **4** bark, tree
extract: **7** quinine
cinct: **4** girt **9** encircled
cincture: **4** band, belt, gird, halo, list, ring **5** girth **6** cestus, collar, fillet, girdle **7** baldric,

compass 8 encircle 9 enclosure 11 environment, surrounding

cinder: ash 4 gray, slag 5 chark, dross, ember 6 scoria 7 clinker, lapilla, residue

cinders: 5 gleed, track

cinema (see also **motion picture**): 4 film, show 5 flick, movie 6 screen 7 picture 13 motion picture

cinerarium: urn 9 columbary 11 columbarium

cinerator: 6 ashery 9 crematory 11 incinerator

cinerous: 4 gray 5 ashen

cingular: 7 annular 8 circular

cingulum: 4 band 5 ridge 6 girdle

cinnabar: ore 7 mineral 9 vermilion
color: red
derivative: 11 quicksilver

cinnamic acid derivative: 7 sinapic

cinnamon: 4 tree 5 canel, spice 6 canela, canell, canelo, cassia 7 canella, canelle 8 barbasco

cinnamon apple: 8 sweetsop

cinnamon oak: 8 bluejack

cinnamon stone: 6 garnet 8 essonite

cinquefoil: 6 clover 7 frasier 8 cowberry

cion (see also **scion**): bud 5 graft, scion, shoot, uvula 10 descendant

Cipango: 5 Japan 6 Nippon

cipher: key, nil 4 code, null, zero 5 aught, ought 6 decode, device, figure, letter, naught, nought, number, symbol 8 goose egg 9 nonentity 10 cryptogram

cippus: 6 pillar 8 landmark 10 gravestone

circa: 5 about 6 around 13 approximately

Circassian: *dialect:* 6 Adighe 8 Cherkess 9 Abkhasian, Kabardian
king: 9 Sacripant

Circe: 5 siren 9 sorceress, temptress 11 enchantress
brother: 6 Aeetes
father: Sol 6 Helios
island: 5 Aeaea
lover: 7 Ulysses 8 Odysseus
niece: 5 Medea
son: 5 Comus 9 Telegonus

circle: cwm, lap, set 4 disk, gyre, halo, hoop, loop, maru (Jap.), orbe, ring, rink, turn 5 class, crown, cycle, frame, group, monde, realm, rhomb, rigol, round, swirl, twirl 6 bezant, cirque, clique, collet, cordon, corona, diadem, girdle, rotate, rundle, spiral, system 7 chukkar, chukker, circlet, circuit, company, compass, coronet, coterie, enclose, revolve, ringlet 8 encircle, surround 9 circulate, encompass 10 associates, companions 13 circumference
around sun or moon: 6 corona, nimbus
geographic: 6 tropic
graph: 8 pie chart

heraldry: 7 annulet
inner: 5 bosom
longest chord: 8 diameter
luminous: 4 aura, halo 6 corona, nimbus 7 aureole
part of: arc 5 chord 6 degree, radius, secant, sector 13 circumference 15 segment diameter

circlet: 4 band, hoop, ring 6 bangle, cirque 7 circuit 8 bracelet, headband
of light: 7 aureola, aureole

circuit: lap 4 area, bout, iter, loop, tour, zone 5 ambit, cycle, orbit, round, route 6 ambage, circle, detour 7 compass, itinera (pl.) 8 district 10 revolution 13 circumference
auxiliary: 5 relay
court: 4 eyre

circuitous: 4 mazy 6 curved 7 crooked, devious, oblique, sinuous, twisted, vagrant, winding 8 circular, flexuous, indirect, rambling, tortuous 9 ambagious, ambiguous, deceitful, underhand, wandering 10 roundabout, serpentine 12 disingenuous, labyrinthine

circular: 4 bill 5 libel, orbed, round 6 ringed 7 annular, cycloid, discoid, perfect 8 cingular, complete, encyclic, globular, pamphlet 9 orbicular 10 circuitous, roundabout 11 publication
indicator: 4 dial
motion: 4 eddy, gyre 5 whirl 8 gyration
plate: 4 disc, disk

circulate: air, mix 4 move, turn 6 rotate, spread 7 diffuse, publish 9 propagate 10 promulgate 11 disseminate
publicly: 6 report 9 broadcast

circumference: arc, rim 4 ambi 5 girth 6 border, bounds, limits 7 circuit 8 boundary, surround 9 dimension, perimeter, periphery

circumlocution: 6 ambage 7 winding 8 rambling, verbiage 9 prolixity, verbosity 10 meandering, periphrase, redundancy, roundabout

circumscribe: 5 bound, fence, limit 6 define 7 confine, enclose, environ 8 encircle, restrain, restrict, surround 9 encompass

circumscribed: 6 narrow 7 insular, limited

circumspect: 4 wary, wise 5 alert, chary 7 careful, guarded, prudent 8 cautious, discreet, watchful 9 attentive 10 deliberate

circumstance: fix 4 fact, item 5 event, phase, state 6 affair, detail, factor, pickle 7 element, episode 8 incident, position 9 condition, situation 10 occurrence, particular 11 environment, opportunity 12 surroundings

circumstantial: 5 exact 6 minute 7 precise 8 detailed, thorough 9 pertinent 10 incidental, particular **11** inferential **12** nonessential

circumstantiate: **7** support **8** evidence

circumvent: **4** balk, dupe, foil **5** cheat, check, cozen, evade, trick **6** baffle, delude, entrap, escape, outwit, thwart **7** capture, deceive, defraud, ensnare, prevent **8** encircle, surround **9** encompass, frustrate, overreach, underfong

circus: **4** ring **5** arena **6** big top, circle, cirque **9** spectacle **10** hippodrome **12** amphitheater **13** entertainment
   arena wall: **5** spina
   attraction: **5** freak **8** sideshow **9** menagerie
   column: **4** meta
   employee: **10** roustabout
   gear: **4** tent **5** rings **7** trapeze
   performer: **5** clown, flyer, tamer **7** juggler **9** aerialist
   rider: **8** desultor

cirque: **5** basin **6** circle, circus, corrie, recess **7** circlet, erosion

cirrus: **5** cloud **7** tendril **8** filament

cisco: **8** blackfin, whitefin

cist: box **4** tomb **5** chest **6** casket **7** chamber **9** cistavaen

Cistercian: nun **4** monk
   founder: **6** Robert (of Molesme)
   popular name: **8** Trappist **11** Trappistine

cistern: sac, tub, vat **4** tank, well **6** cavity **7** cuvette **8** cisterna **9** impluvium, reservoir

cit: **8** townsman **9** tradesman **10** shopkeeper

citadel: arx **4** fort, hall **5** Alamo, tower **6** castle **7** borough **8** fastness, fortress **10** stronghold **13** fortification
   of Athens: **9** Acropolis
   of Carthage: **5** Bursa, Byrsa
   of Corinth: **11** Acrocorinth
   of Moscow: **7** Kremlin

citation: **6** notice **7** mention, summons **8** encomium, monition **9** quotation, reference **10** allegation **11** enumeration

cite: **4** call, tell **5** allay, quote, refer **6** accite, accuse, adduce, allege, arouse, avouch, excite, notify, repeat, summon **7** arraign, bespeak, excerpt, extract, mention **8** indicate

citizen: cit **5** voter **6** member, native **7** burgess, burgher, citoyen (F.), denizen, elector, freeman, oppidan **8** civilian, commoner, occupant, resident **9** citoyenne (F.) **10** inhabitant

citizenship: *admission to:* **14** naturalization **15** enfranchisement
   pert. to: **5** civic

citrine: **5** color **7** rhubarb

citron: **5** etrog **6** cedrat, yellow

citrullus: **7** pumpkin **10** watermelon

citrus: *belt:* **5** Texas **7** Florida **10** California
   disease: **8** buckskin

drink: ade **5** juice
family: rue
fruit: **4** lime, ugli **5** lemon **6** citron, orange, tangor **7** kumquat, tangelo **8** bergamot, mandarin, shaddock **9** tangerine **10** grapefruit
pest: **7** red mite

city: **4** burg, dorp, town, urbs (L.) **5** ville **6** ciudad, staple **9** community **10** metropolis **12** municipality
   celestial: **4** Zion
   eternal: **4** Roma, Rome
   hanging gardens: **7** Babylon
   holy: **5** Mecca **6** Medina **9** Jerusalem
   leaning tower: **4** Pisa
   official: **5** mayor **7** manager, marshal **8** alderman **10** councilman
   oldest inhabited: **8** Damascus
   part: **4** slum, ward **5** block, plaza **6** barrio, ghetto, square, uptown **8** business, downtown, red light **11** residential **12** neighborhood
   pert. to: **5** civic, urban **7** oppidan **9** municipal **12** metropolitan
   planner: **8** urbanist
   problem: **4** riot, slum, smog **5** crime **6** ghetto **7** poverty, traffic
   slicker: **4** dude
   wicked: **5** Sodom **8** Gomorrah

City: *of Bells:* **9** Strasburg **10** Strasbourg
   of Bridges: **6** Bruges
   of Brotherly Love: **12** Philadelphia
   of Churches: **8** Brooklyn
   of David: **9** Jerusalem
   of Dreaming Spires: **6** Oxford (Eng.)
   of God: **6** church, heaven **8** Paradise **10** civitas dei **12** New Jerusalem
   of Hundred Towers: **5** Pavia
   of Kings: **4** Lima (Peru)
   of Lights: **5** Paris, Perth
   of Lilies: **8** Florence
   of Masts: **6** London
   of Rams: **6** Canton (OH)
   of Refuge: **5** Bezer, Golan **6** Hebron, Kedesh, Medina **7** Shechem **12** Ramoth-Gilead
   of Saints: **8** Montreal
   of Seven Hills: **4** Rome
   of Victory: **5** Cairo
   of Violet Crown: **6** Athens

city-state: **4** Rome **5** Genoa, Milan, polis **6** Athens, Bremen, Lübeck, Sparta **7** civitas, Hamburg **8** Florence

Cius: **6** Gemlik

civet: cat, cit **5** rasse, zibet **6** bondar, musang, zibeth **7** fossane, nandine

civet-like animal: **5** genet

civic: lay **5** civil, suave, urban **6** polite, public, urbane **7** secular

civil: 4 hend 5 hende, suave 6 polite, urbane 7 affable, courtly, elegant, politic, refined 8 discreet, gracious, obliging, polished, well-bred 9 civilized, courteous 10 cultivated, respectful 11 complaisant 13 condescending

civilian: cit 5 civvy 7 citizen, teacher 12 non-combatant, practitioner
dress: 5 mufti

civility: 6 comity 7 amenity, decorum 8 courtesy 9 propriety 10 affability, compliance, politeness 11 complacence 12 complaisance

civilization: 6 kultur (G.) 7 culture 10 refinement 11 cultivation

civilize: 4 tame 5 teach, train 6 polish, refine 7 educate 8 humanize, urbanize 9 cultivate 11 domesticate

civil rights (extinction of): 9 attainder
Civil War: *admiral:* 8 Farragut
battle: 6 Shiloh 7 Bull Run 8 Antietam 9 Vicksburg 10 Gettysburg 11 Chattanooga 12 Spotsylvania
commander: Lee 4 Hood, Pope 5 Ewell, Grant, Meade, Sykes 6 Custer, Hooker, Stuart 7 Forrest, Jackson, Sherman 8 Burnside, Sheridan 9 McClellan

civil wrong: 4 tort
clabber: mud 4 mire 6 curdle, lopper 12 bonnyclabber

clack: gab, jaw, yak 4 blab 5 chack, cluck, crack 6 cackle, gossip, rattle, tongue 7 chatter, clacket, clatter, prattle 10 chatterbox

clad: 5 drest, robed 6 beseen, decked, garbed 7 adorned, arrayed, attired, clothed, covered, dressed 8 sheathed

cladose: 6 ramose 8 branched
clag: mud 4 clog, clot, daub, mire 5 fault, stick 6 adhere, burden

claggum: 5 taffy 7 treacle 8 molasses 9 sweetmeat

claim: ask 4 aver, call, case, lien, mine, name 5 exact, right, shout, title 6 assert, demand, elicit 7 acclaim, derecho, pretend, profess, require 8 maintain, pretence, pretense, proclaim 9 challenge, homestead, postulate, vindicate 11 encumbrance

claimant: 7 usurper 9 arrogator, pretender
clairvoyance: ESP 7 insight 8 sagacity 10 divination 11 discernment, penetration

clairvoyant: 4 seer 6 omener 7 prophet, psychic, seeress

clam: 4 base, clog, daub, glam, hush, mean 5 clamp, crash, glaum, grasp, grope, smear, stick 6 adhere, clutch, sticky 7 bivalve, clangor, mollusk, steamer 8 adhesive
genus of: mya
kinds of: 4 mega 5 blunt, chama, giant, razor, solen 6 gweduc, quahog 7 geoduck,

quahaug 9 hard-shell, soft-shell 10 little neck

clamant: 4 dire, loud 6 crying, urgent 9 clamorous 10 imperative

clamber: 5 climb, scale 6 claver 7 rammack 8 scramble, struggle

clamjamfry: mob 5 crowd 6 rabble 7 rubbish
clammy: 4 damp, dank, soft, wack 5 moist, sammy 6 sticky, waughy

clamor: cry, din, hue 4 bere, bunk, roar, rout, to-do, wail 5 blare, boast, bruit, noise, shout 6 bellow, hubbub, outcry, racket, tumult, uproar 7 stashie 10 hullabaloo, hurly-burly, vociferate

clamorous: 4 loud 5 noisy 7 blatant, clamant, yelling 8 brawling, decrying 9 clamatory, turbulent 10 boisterous 11 openmouthed

clamp: lug, nip, pin 4 bolt, glam, grip, hold, nail, vise 5 block, clasp, glaum 6 fasten 7 grapple 8 fastener, holdfast 10 clothespin

clan: set, sib 4 cult, race, sect, sept, unit 5 class, group, horde, party, tribe 6 clique, family 7 coterie, society 8 division 10 collection, fraternity
emblem: xat 5 totem 6 tartan
head of: 5 chief, elder, thane
pert. to: 6 tribal

clancular: 6 secret 11 clandestine
clandestine: bye, sly 4 foxy 5 privy 6 artful, covert, hidden, secret 7 bootleg, furtive, illicit 8 phratria, stealthy 9 clancular, concealed 10 fraudulent 12 hugger-mugger 13 surreptitious, under-the-table

clang: din 4 ding, peal, ring 5 clank, clash, noise 6 jangle, timbre

clangor: din 4 clam, roar 5 clang 6 hubbub, uproar

clank: 4 ring 5 sound 6 rackle
clannish: 5 close 6 secret, tribal, united
clap: 4 bang, flap, peal, slap 5 cheer, clink, crack 6 poster, strike, stroke 7 applaud, chatter, plaudit 9 explosion 11 thunderpeal

clapper: 6 rattle, tongue 7 knacker, knocker
support: 7 baldric 8 baldrick

claptrap: 4 bull 5 hokum, trash 6 blague, device, drivel, humbug 7 fustian 8 malarkey, nonsense, trickery 10 pretension 11 insincerity

clarify: 5 clean, clear 6 purify, refine, render, settle 7 cleanse, explain, glorify 8 depurate, eliquate, simplify 10 illuminate 11 transfigure 13 straighten out

clarinet: 4 reed 14 wind instrument
mouthpiece: 4 birn
snake charmer's: 4 been

clarion: 5 clear, sharp 7 ringing, trumpet
clarity: 5 glory 8 accuracy, literacy, splendor 9 clearness 10 brightness, brilliance 11 pellucidity

claro: 4 mild 5 cigar 12 light-colored

clash: jar 4 bang, bolt, dash, news, slam 5 brawl, brunt, crash, fight, occur, prate, shock 6 affray, differ, gossip, hurtle, impact, strife, strike, tattle 7 collide, discord, scandal 8 argument, conflict 9 collision, interfere

clasp: hug, pin 4 fold, grab, grip, hasp, hold, hook, hoop, ouch, tach 5 cling, grasp, morse, preen, seize, tache 6 agrafe, brooch, buckle, clench, clutch, enfold, enwrap, fasten, fibula, gimmer, gimmor, infold 7 agraffe, amplect, barette, embrace, entwine, fermail, tendril 8 fastener, surround 9 constrain, safety-pin 10 chatelaine

class: ilk, set 4 clan, kind, race, rank, sect, sort, type 5 breed, caste, genre, genus, grace, grade, group, order, tribe, varna 6 circle, family, gender, period, rating 7 dignity, meeting, seminar, species, variety 8 category, division 9 abteilung 10 collection, excellence 11 description 12 denomination

biological: 5 genus 6 genera (pl.)

caste: see **Hindu**

member: 4 coed 6 junior, senior 8 freshman 9 sophomore

middle: 11 bourgeoisie

pert. to: 7 generic

working: 11 proletariat

classic: top 4 book 5 model 7 ancient, vintage 8 standard, top-notch 9 venerable 11 composition, masterpiece, tour de force

classical: 4 pure 5 Attic, Greek, Latin, Roman 6 chaste 8 academic, masterly 9 firstrate

academics: 8 sciences 10 humanities

economics: 4 Mill 5 Smith 7 Malthus, Ricardo

literature: 5 Greek, Roman

music: 5 opera 6 lieder, sonata 8 symphony 9 song cycle

classification: 4 file, rank, rate, sort 5 genra (pl.), genre, genus, grade, order, taxis 6 genera (pl.), rating, system 8 analysis, category, division, taxonomy 12 confidential, distribution

classify: 4 list, rank, rate, size, sort, type 5 grade, group, label, range 6 assort, codify, divide, ticket 7 arrange, catalog, dispose, marshal 8 register 9 catalogue, segregate 10 categorize, distribute, pigeonhole

classy: 4 chic, tony 5 nifty, slick, smart 7 elegant, stylish 11 fashionable

clatter: din, jar 5 clack, noise, rumor 6 babble, gabble, gossip, rackle, rattle, tattle, uproar 7 blatter, chatter, clutter, prattle, reeshie 9 commotion 10 hurly-burly 11 disturbance

Claudia's husband: 6 Pilate

claudicant: 4 lame 7 limping

Claudius: 4 King (*Hamlet*) 7 emperor

nephew: 6 Hamlet

slayer: 6 Hamlet 9 Agrippina

successor: 4 Nero

wife: 8 Gertrude 9 Messalina

clause: 4 part 5 close, plank, rider 6 phrase 7 article, passage, proviso 8 sentence 9 condition, provision 10 conclusion 11 stipulation

additional: 5 rider

claut: 4 hand, lump, rake, tear 5 chunk 6 clutch, scrape 7 handful, scratch

clavecin: 11 harpsichord

claver: 5 prate 6 clover, gossip 7 chamber, chatter

clavichord: 6 spinet

clavicle: 4 bone 10 collarbone

clavis: key 8 glossary

clavus: 4 band, corn 5 strip 6 bunion, callus

claw: dig 4 clee, fawn, hand, hook, nail, pull, sere, tear, unce 5 chela, cloof, clufe, court, grasp, griff, seize, talon, uncus 6 clutch, nipper, scrape, ungula 7 crubeen, flatter, scratch, wheedle 8 lacerate

clay: cob, pug 4 bole, galt, loam, lute, marl, mire 5 argil, brick, cloam, earth, gault, loess, ochre, rabat, tasco 6 cledge, clunch, kaolin 8 lifeless 9 inanimate

bed: 5 gault

box: 6 saggar, sagger

building: 5 adobe, tapia

casting: 4 slip

constituent: 7 alumina

covered with: 6 lutose

deposit: 4 marl

fragment: bat

friable: 4 bole

layer: 4 lias 5 sloam

lump: 4 clag, clod

made of: 7 fictile

mineral: 7 nacrite

mold: dod

musical instrument: 7 ocarina

pert. to: 5 bolar

piece: 4 tile

pottery: 6 kaolin 7 ceramic, kaoline

tropical: 8 laterite

claybrained: 4 dull 6 stupid

clayey: 5 bolar, heavy, malmy, marly 6 cledgy, lutose 9 argillous 12 argillaceous

clay pigeon: 6 target

clead: 6 attire, clothe

clean: fay, fey, hoe, mop 4 dust, fair, pure, smug, swab, trim, wash, wipe 5 bream, clear, curry, empty, feigh, grave, scour, scrub, smart 6 chaste, clever, kosher, purify 7 apinoid, cleanse, clearly, furbish, perfect 8 absterge, brightly, dextrous, entirely, renovate, spotless, unsoiled 9 destitute, dexter-

ous, guiltless, speckless, undefiled **10** immaculate **11** butterworth, untarnished **12** spick-and-span, straighten up **13** unadulterated
clean slate: **10** tabula rasa

cleaner: **4** soap **5** borax, purer **6** ramrod **8** cleanser **9** detergent **10** dentifrice, toothpaste
fish: **6** scaler

cleaning implement: mop **4** swab **5** broom, brush **6** loofah, ramrod, sponge, vacuum **7** chamois, sweeper

cleanly: **4** neat, pure **6** adroit, artful, chaste **7** correct, elegant **8** innocent, skillful **9** dexterous

cleanse: **4** farm, heal, soap, wash **5** brush, clean, dight, purge, rinse, scour, scrub **6** purify, refine **7** baptize, clarify, deterge, sweeten **8** renovate **9** disinfect, expurgate, sterilize

cleanser: lye **9** detergent **10** clarifiant

cleansing: **4** bath **7** abluent, clysmic, washing **8** ablution, lavation **9** acquittal, cathartic, purgation **10** emundation **12** purification

cleansing process: **4** bath **6** shower **7** washing

clear: net, rid **4** free, gain, open, over, pure, quit **5** atrip, breme, brent, clean, erase, lucid, plain, prune, sharp, vivid **6** acquit, assoil, bright, candid, clever, exempt, fluted, limpid, lucent, patent, purify, settle, smooth **7** absolve, clarify, clarion, crystal, deliver, evident, glaring, graphic, lighten, obvious, release, rule out **8** apparent, brighten, definite, distinct, explicit, manifest, pellucid, relevant, scot-free, shake off **9** cloudless, discharge, disengage, elucidate, enigmatic, exculpate, exonerate, extricate, vindicate **10** see-through, unconfused **11** disentangle, open-and-shut, perspicuous, transparent **12** intelligible
away: fay, fey **5** feigh **6** dispel **8** evacuate **9** eliminate, expurgate
out: **4** scat **5** scram **6** decamp, desert, skidoo **7** take off
up: **5** solve **6** settle **9** elucidate

clear-cut: **5** exact, lucid, sharp **7** concise **8** chiseled, definite, distinct, incisive **9** chiselled **10** unconfused **11** categorical **12** unquestioned

clear-headed: **10** perceptive

clearing: *in woods:* **5** glade, tract **8** slashing
of land: **4** sart **6** assart

clear-sighted: **10** discerning **13** perspicacious

cleat: **4** bitt **5** block, chock, kevel, wedge **6** batten **7** bollard, coxcomb, support **9** butterbur

cleavage: **5** chasm, cleft, split **6** schism **7** fission, fissure **8** division **9** partition **10** separation

cleave: cut, rip **4** chop, hold, join, link, part, rely, rend, rift, rive, slit, tear **5** break, carve, chawn, chine, clave, cleft, cling, clove, crack, sever, shear, split, stick **6** adhere, bisect, cohere, divide, pierce, sunder **7** dispart, fissure **8** separate

cleaver: axe **4** froe, frow

cleche: **4** urde **5** urdee **11** cross-shaped

cleek: **4** club, hook, link **5** crook, pluck, seize **6** clutch, snatch **8** fishhook, golf club

clef: key **9** character
bass: eff
treble: gee

cleft: gap **4** chap, chop, fent, flow, reft, rift, rima, rive **5** break, chasm, chawn, chink, clove, crack, crena, riven, split **6** breach, cleave, cloven, cranny, crotch, divide, recess **7** crevice, divided, fissure, opening **8** aperture, fracture

cleft-lip: **7** harelip

Cleite: *father:* **6** Merops
husband: **7** Cyzicus

clemency: **4** pity **5** mercy **6** lenity, pardon **7** quarter **8** kindness, leniency, mildness **10** compassion, indulgence

Clemens, Samuel: **5** Twain (Mark)

clement: **4** easy, kind, mild, soft, warm **6** gentle **7** lenient **8** merciful **9** forgiving, indulgent **10** benevolent **13** compassionate

clench: **4** fist, grip, grit, hold **5** brace, clasp, clint, close, grasp **6** clinch, clutch **9** interlock **10** strengthen

cleome: **5** caper **6** flower **11** spider plant

Cleopatra: **5** Egypt, queen
attendant: **4** Iras **8** Charmian
killer: asp
lover: **6** Antony, Caesar **10** Mark Antony
river: **4** Nile
sister: **7** Arsinoe

Cleopatra's Needle: **7** obelisk

clepsydra: **9** timepiece **10** water clock

clergy: **5** cloth **8** ministry
body of: **6** pulpit **7** college

clergyman: **4** abba, abbe, dean, Papa **5** canon, clerk, padre, pilot, prior, rabbi, vicar **6** bishop, cleric, curate, deacon, divine, domine, father, parson, pastor, priest, rector **7** cassock, prelate, primate **8** cardinal, chaplain, minister, preacher, reverend **9** blackcoat, dignitary, monsignor, presbyter **10** archbishop **12** ecclesiastic
office: **4** cure **6** curacy **8** ministry **9** pastorate, priorship, rectorate
residence: **5** manse **6** priory **7** rectory **8** vicarage **9** parsonage
traveling: **12** circuit rider

clergywoman: nun **6** sister **8** rectress **9** priestess **10** religieuse

cleric: See **clergyman**

clerical: 10 of the cloth

clerical clothing: alb 5 amice, cloth, fanon, orale, rabat, stole 6 collar 7 biretta

clerk: nun 4 monk 5 agent, steno, write 6 cleric, commis, hermit, layman, priest, scribe, teller, yeoman 7 carcoon, compose, gomasta, scholar 8 employee, greffier (F.), recorder, salesman 9 assistant, clergyman, registrar, secretary 10 accountant 11 salesperson 12 ecclesiastic, stenographer
court: 11 protonotary 12 prothonotary
hotel: 7 deskman
passenger ship: 6 purser

clerkly: 7 learned, scribal 9 scholarly

clever: apt, sly 4 able, cute, deft, fine, gnib, hend, keen 5 agile, alert, clean, clear, handy, hende, lithe, quick, slick, smart, witty 6 active, adroit, artful, astute, bright, expert, habile, heppen, neatly, nimble, pretty, shrewd 7 amiable, cunning, parlous 8 dextrous, handsome, obliging, skillful, talented 9 dexterous, ingenious 10 well-shaped 11 clean-limbed, dexterously, intelligent, quick-witted 13 scintillating

cleverness: can 4 tact 5 skill 6 esprit 9 dexterity, ingenuity 10 adroitness, astuteness

clevis: 4 hake 5 copse 6 muzzle 7 fitting 10 connection

clew (see also **clue**): bag, tip 4 ball, coil 5 blome, globe, raise, skein 6 hurdle, secure, thread 10 sail corner

cliche: 6 truism 7 bromide 8 banality 9 hackneyed, platitude 11 stereotyped

click: 4 pawl, tick 5 agree, catch 6 detent 7 come off, ratchet

click beetle: 6 elater

client: 5 ceile 6 patron 7 patient 8 customer, henchman, retainer 9 dependent

clientele: 6 public 9 following

cliff: hoe 4 crag, hill, rock, scar 5 bluff, cleve, heuch, heugh, scarp, shore, slope 6 cleeve, height 7 clogwyn 8 hillside, palisade 9 precipice

cliff-hanger: 8 suspense 9 melodrama

climate: 4 mood 5 clime 6 region, temper 7 weather 8 attitude 9 condition 10 atmosphere
control chamber: 7 biotrin

climax: cap, top 4 acme, apex, near, peak, shut 5 mount, scale, tight 6 apogee, ascend, finish, opogee, summit, zenith 9 gradation 11 culmination

climb: gad 4 ramp, rise, shin 5 creep, grimp, mount, scale, speed (Sc.), twine 6 ascend, ascent, shinny 7 clamber
down: 6 alight 7 descend 8 dismount
on: 5 mount, scale

climber: 6 rigger, scaler 11 mountaineer 12 alpenstocker

climbing device: 6 ladder

climbing plant: ivy 4 vine 5 liana, liane 7 creeper 8 clematis 11 honeysuckle, trumpet vine

clime: See **climate**

clinch: fix, get, hug 4 bind, grip, nail, seal 5 clamp, cling, clink, clint, grasp, rivet, seize 6 clench, clutch, fasten, secure, snatch 7 confirm, embrace, grapple, scuffle 8 complete, conclude, holdfast 9 establish

cling: hug 4 bank, hang, hold, rely 5 clasp, stick, trust 6 adhere, cleave, clinch, cohere, depend, fasten, shrink, wither 7 cherish, embrace, shrivel 8 contract 9 persevere

clingfish: 6 testar

clink: ale, jug, put, rap 4 beat, blow, brig, cash, clap, coin, jail, move, ring, slap 5 latch, money, rhyme, seize 6 clinch, jingle, lockup, moment, prison, strike, tinkle 7 instant 8 hoosegow 9 assonance, calaboose 10 guardhouse

clinker: 4 slag 5 waste 9 wonderful (Br.)

clinquant: 5 clink, showy 6 tinsel 8 tinseled 10 glittering

Clio: See **Muse**

clip: bob, cut, dod, hug, lip, lop, mow, nip 4 barb, chip, coll, crop, dock, dodd, hold, pace, pare, poll, snip, trim 5 clasp, force, prune, shear 6 clutch, fasten, hinder, holder 7 curtail, curtain, cut down, embrace, scissor, shorten 8 diminish, encircle, mark down 9 encompass 10 abbreviate, overcharge

clipper: 4 boat, ship 6 shears, vessel 7 shearer, workman

clique: cot, mob, set 4 bloc, clan, club, gang, ring 5 cabal, group, junta, write 6 circle, cletch 7 coterie, faction, in-group 8 conclave, sodality 9 camarilla 11 combination

clitter: 5 noise 6 rattle 7 chatter 10 stridulate

cloak: aba 4 brat, capa, cape, coat, hide, mant, mask, pall, rail, robe, veil, wrap 5 capot, cover, guise, manta, manto, sagum 6 assume, bautta, capote, caster, chapel, dolman, mantle, mantua, pharos, screen, serape, shield, shroud, tabard, visite 7 bavaroy, chlamys, conceal, garment, manteau, manteel, pelisse, pretext, shelter, zimarra 8 albornoz, burnoose, disguise, intrigue, mantilla, palliate 9 dissemble 10 camouflage, roquelaure 11 portmanteau
African: 5 jelab 6 jellab
Arabian: 7 feridgi, ferigee, ferijee 8 feridjee
baptismal: 7 chrisom
bishop's: 10 mantelleta
ecclesiastical: 4 cope
Greek: 6 abolla 7 chlamys
hooded: 6 camail 8 burnoose
Indian: 5 choga

Jewish: **6** kittle **9** gaberdine
large-sleeved: **10** witzchoura
loose: **5** palla
monk's: **8** analabos
Punjabi: **5** choga
Roman: **5** sagum **7** alicula, paenula
Roman military: **10** paludament **11** paludamenta (pl.) **12** paludamentum
sleeveless: aba **6** dolman **7** paenula
Spanish: **4** capa **5** manta **6** mantle
Turkish: **6** dolman
waterproof: **6** poncho
worn over armor: **6** tabard

clobber: **4** beat, belt, slug **5** patch, pound, smear **6** cobble, defeat, strike, wallop
cloche: hat, jar **4** bell **5** cover
clocher: **6** belfry **9** bell tower, campanile
clock: nef **4** bell, call, dial, gong, time **5** cluck, hatch, hurry, meter, watch **6** beetle, Big Ben, crouch **7** digital **8** horologe, incubate, ornament, recorder **9** clepsydra, hourglass, indicator, taximeter, timepiece **11** chronometer, speedometer
ancient water: **9** clepsydra
astronomical: **8** sidereal
maker: **9** horologer **10** horologist
part of: **4** dial, drum, face **5** alarm, bundy, hands, verge **6** detent, foliot, weight **7** crystal, display **8** pendulum, recorder **10** escapement, mainspring
regulating body: **6** quartz **8** pendulum **10** escapement
ship-shaped: nef
water: **9** clepsydra
weight: **5** peise
clocker: **5** timer **8** railbird **11** embroiderer
clockwise: **6** deasil, dessil **7** deiseal **8** positive
clod: sod **4** clat, clot, dolt, dull, lout, lump, turf **5** clout, clown, divot, earth, glebe, gross, knoll, yokel **6** dimwit, ground, stupid **7** bumpkin **9** blockhead, coagulate **10** clodhopper
cloddish: **5** gross **6** stupid **7** boorish, illbred
clodhopper: **4** boor, clod, shoe **6** rustic **7** bumpkin, plowman
clodpate: **4** clot, dolt, fool **7** ramhead **8** clodpole, clodpoll, imbecile **9** blockhead
clog: gum, jam, log **4** clag, clam, cloy, curb, load, lump, shoe, skid, stop **5** block, check, choke, dance, sabot **6** adhere, burden, chopin, fetter, galosh, hamper, hobble, hogtie, impede, remora, sandal, secque, weight **7** galoshe, pattern, perplex, shackle, trammel **8** coalesce, encumber, obstruct, overshoe, restrain **9** embarrass, hindrance, restraint **10** difficulty **11** encumbrance
with mud: **4** daub **6** daggle
cloggy: **5** heavy, lumpy **6** sticky
clogwyn: **5** cliff **9** precipice

cloister: **4** hall, stoa **5** abbey, aisle, stoae (pl.) **6** arcade, friary, immure, piazza, priory **7** closter, convent, nunnery, seclude **9** cloistral, enclosure, hermitage, monastery, sanctuary, sequester **11** ambulatoria (pl.) **12** ambulatorium
pert. to: **9** claustral, cloistral
Cloister and the Hearth author: **5** Reade
cloistered: **7** recluse **8** shut away **11** sequestered
clone: **4** copy, dupe **6** double **7** replica **9** duplicate **13** identical twin
cloof, clufe: **4** claw, hoof **6** cleave
clop: **4** limp **5** sound **6** hobble
close: cap, end, hot **4** clit, firm, hard, hide, near, nigh, quit, seal, shut, slam, snug, stop **5** anear, block, cease, cheap, dense, finis, garth, gross, muggy, thick, tight **6** clause, clench, effect, expiry, finale, finish, narrow, nearby, period, stingy, strait **7** adjourn, compact, context, extreme, miserly, occlude, similar **8** accurate, adjacent, complete, conclude, familiar, imminent, intimate, taper off **9** barricade, extremity, niggardly, terminate **10** avaricious, conclusion, nip-and-tuck **11** termination **12** parsimonious
a hawk's eyes: **4** seel
firmly: bar **4** lock, seal **5** tight **6** batten, cement
closefisted: **4** near **6** stingy **7** miserly **8** handfast **9** niggardly
closely: **4** just **6** almost, barely, narrow, nearly **7** by a hair **9** carefully, compactly
closemouthed: **5** quiet **6** secret, silent
closeness: **7** secrecy **8** fidelity, intimacy **9** parsimony, proximity **10** stinginess, strictness **11** conciseness, literalness **14** oppressiveness
closest: **4** next **7** nearest **9** proximate
closet: **4** ewry, room, safe **5** ambry, cubby, cuddy **6** armary, locker, pantry, secret **7** cabinet, conceal, private **8** conclave, cupboard, gardevin, wardrobe **9** gardevine **12** confidential
closing device: pin **4** lock, snap **6** button, velcro, zipper **7** gripper **10** hook and eye
closure: end, gag **5** bound, limit **7** cloture **8** clausure **9** agreement, enclosure **10** conclusion **11** confinement, containment **12** entrenchment
clot: dot, gel **4** clag, clat, clod, gout, jell, lump, mass **5** clart, group, grume **6** balter, cotter **7** clodder, congeal, embolus, thicken **8** coagulum, concrete, solidify **9** blockhead, clodplate, coagulate **12** crassamentum
cloth: rag **5** bluet, toile (F.), tweed, twill **6** canvas, clergy, drapet, fabric, livery, napkin **7** acetate, drapery, garment, raiment, textile,

worsted **8** dwelling, material, sheeting **10** cassinette

baptismal: **7** chrisom

bark: **4** tapa **9** tapa cloth

blemish: yaw **4** pull, snag, tear **5** amper

camel's hair: aba **6** camlet

coarse: **4** duck **5** crash, gunny **6** burlap, linsey

crinkled: **5** crape, crepe **10** seersucker

dealer: **6** draper, mercer

dryer: **6** tenter

dye method: tie **5** batik

fine-textured: **4** mull, pima, silk **7** percale

finisher: **7** beetler

flaw in: **4** rase

flaxen: **5** linen

glazed: **5** tammy

goat's hair: **5** tibet **6** camlet, mohair

heavy: **9** petersham

hemp: **4** jute **5** gunny **6** baline, burlap, canamo

homespun: **4** kelt

instrument: **8** ringhead

knitted: **6** jersey, tricot

light: **4** silk **6** tissue **7** challis, chiffon, etamine

lining: **5** serge **8** sarcenet, sarsenet

measure: ell **4** nail

mesh: net **5** super, tulle **11** cheesecloth

metallic: **4** acca, tash

mourning: **5** crape, crepe

muslin: **5** adati

narrow: **4** tape **5** braid **6** edging, ribbon

old kind: **4** acca, tuke **5** tewke **6** samite

ornamental: **4** gimp, lace **6** lampas, riband **8** tapestry

poplin: **7** tabinet **8** tabbinet

print: **5** batik **6** calico **7** challis, percale

printer: **7** candroy

raised design: **7** brocade

remnant: **4** fent

ridge in: **4** wale

roll: **4** bolt

rug: mat **6** canvas **7** matting

satin: See **fabric:** *satin*

shop: **7** mercery

silk: See **fabric:** *silk*

soft: **5** panne, plush, surah **6** fleece, velvet **7** flannel **9** montagnac

stiff: **7** taffeta **9** crinoline

stretcher: **6** tenter

synthetic: **5** nylon, rayon **6** dacron **7** acetate

toweling: **5** terry

twilled: rep **4** jean **5** denim, serge

used as a dressing: **5** stupe

velvet: **5** panne

weatherproof: **4** tarp **6** canvas

woolen: **6** kersey

clothe: don, dub, rig, tog **4** deck, garb, gird, gown, robe, vest **5** adorn, array, clead, cleed, dress, dress, endow, endue, frock, habit **6** attire, enrobe, invest, swathe **7** apparel, vesture **8** accouter, accoutre **9** authorize, represent

clothes: **4** duds, garb, gear, suit, tack, togs, wear **5** get-up, habit **6** attire **7** apparel, baggage, costume, raiment, regalia, threads, toggery, vesture **8** clothing, frippery, garments **9** vestments **10** bedclothes **11** habiliments

basket: **6** hamper

civilian: **5** mufti

collection: **8** wardrobe

dealer: **6** ragman **7** fripper **9** fripperer

informal: **5** jeans, smock **6** halter, shorts, slacks, sweats, trunks **9** sweat suit

pert. to: **8** vestiary **10** habilatory

presser: **7** sadiron

clothesmoth: **5** tinea

clothespress: kas **5** chest **7** armoire, dresser **8** wardrobe

clothing: **4** wear **6** attire **7** apparel **8** wardrobe

coarse: **4** brat **5** burel

protective: **5** armor

woman's: **6** fardel

cloud: fog, nue (F.) **4** blur, dust, haze, hide, mist **5** bedim, befog, gloom, nubia, stain, sully, swarm, taint, vapor **6** cirrus, damage, darken, deepen, defame, nebula, nimbus, screen, shadow, stigma **7** blacken, confuse, cumulus, eclipse, obscure, perplex, tarnish **8** befuddle, overcast **9** obfuscate **11** thunderhead

form: **6** cirrus, nebule **7** cumulus, stratus **9** mare's tail

morning: **4** velo

pert. to: **7** nebular **12** nephological

study of: **9** nephology

wind-driven: **4** rack, scud

cloudburst: **6** deluge **9** rainstorm **11** cats and dogs **12** gully whomper

cloudless: **5** azure, clear **6** bright

cloudy: dim **4** dark, dull, hazy **5** filmy, murky, shady **6** gloomy, lowery, opaque **8** overcast **10** indistinct, lackluster

clough: **5** cleft **6** ravine, valley

clour: **4** blow, bump, dint **5** thump **6** batter

clout: bat, box, hit **4** beat, blow, bump, clod, club, cuff, join, mend, nail, pull, slap, slug, swat **5** patch, power, smite **6** strike, target, thrash, washer **7** bandage **8** bosthoon **9** influence **11** what it takes **12** handkerchief

clouter: **7** botcher, cobbler

clove: bud **4** bulb, tree **5** spice **6** ravine

cloven: **5** cleft, split **9** bisulcate

cloven-footed: **8** fissiped

clover: red **5** lotus, medic, nardu **6** alsike,

legume, luxury, nardoo **7** alfalfa, comfort, lucerne, melilot, trefoil **10** prosperity

cloverleaf: fan **7** freeway **8** crossway **11** interchange

clown: hob, oaf **4** aper, boor, fool, goff, joey, lout, mime, mome, zany **5** churl, comic, mimer, punch, zanni (It.) **6** august, bodach, hobbil, jester, lubber, rustic, stooge **7** buffoon, bumpkin, peasant, playboy **8** merryman **9** harlequin, joculator **10** bufflehead, countryman, Emmet Kelly, harlequina **11** merry-andrew, punchinello **13** pickle-herring

clownish: raw **4** rude, zany **5** gawky, rough **6** clumsy, coarse, rustic **7** awkward, boorish, hoblike, ill-bred, loutish, uncivil **8** ungainly **9** untutored

cloy: **4** clog, glut, nail, pall, sate **5** gorge, prick **6** pierce **7** satiate, satisfy, surfeit

club: bat, hit, set **4** beat, cane, join, mace, maul, polt, team **5** billy, bunch, clout, kebby, lodge, order, staff, stick, unite, yokel **6** clique, cudgel, kebbie, menage, weapon **8** bludgeon, sorority, spontoon **9** blackjack, truncheon **10** fraternity, knobkerrie, shillelagh **11** association
famous: **5** Lambs **6** Friars **7** Century, Garrick, Grolier **9** Explorers
golf: **4** iron, wood **5** wedge **6** putter **9** sand wedge

clubfoot: **7** talipes **9** deformity

clubfooted: **7** taliped

club moss: **8** buckhorn

clubs: **4** suit **5** basto, cards

club-shaped: **7** clavate

clubstart: **5** stoat

cluck: hen **4** call, fuss **5** chuck, clack, click, clock, sound **9** dumb bunny **13** featherweight

clue (see also **clew**): key **4** clew, hint, idea, mark, sign **5** guide, trace **7** inkling **8** innuendo **10** indication, intimation, suggestion **11** fingerprint

clufe: See **cloof**

clump: tod **4** blow, bush, heap, lump, mass, mott, tope, tuft **5** bunch, group, grove, patch, tread **6** clunch, dollop **7** cluster, thicket **10** hodgepodge

clumsy: **4** rude **5** blunt, bulky, gawky, hulky, inapt, inept, stiff **6** gauche **7** awkward, boorish, ill-made, unhandy **8** bungling, tactless, ungainly, unwieldy **9** all thumbs, lumbering, maladroit **10** cumbersome **11** heavy-handed **13** inappropriate

Cluny product: **4** lace

cluster: bog **4** bush, cyme, knot, lump, tuft **5** bunch, clump, group **7** bourock, cluther, package **8** fascicle **9** glomerule **10** collection **11** agglomerate, aggregation

fern spore: **4** sori (pl.) **5** sorus
fiber: nep
flower: **4** cime, cyme **5** ament, umbel **6** raceme **7** panicle **8** anthemia
flower-like: **7** rosette
growing in: **8** acervate
of seven stars: **8** Pleiades

clustered: **6** tufted **8** racemose **9** aciniform, aggregate, glomerate **10** coacervate

clutch: nab **4** clam, claw, clem, clip, fist, glam, grab, grip, nest **5** brood, catch, clasp, claut, cleek, cling, glaum, grasp, gripe, hatch, lever, power, seize, talon **6** cleach, clench, cletch, clinch, retain, snatch **7** control **8** coupling

clutter: **4** mess **6** bustle **7** clatter **8** disorder **9** confusion **10** disarrange, hodgepodge

Clymene: *father:* **7** Oceanus
husband: **7** Iapetus
mother: **6** Tethys
son: **5** Atlas **10** Prometheus

Clytemnestra: *daughter:* **7** Electra **9** Iphigenia **12** Chrysothemis
father: **9** Tyndareus
half-sister: **5** Helen
husband: **9** Agamemnon
mother: **4** Leda
paramour: **9** Aegisthus
son: **7** Orestes
victim: **9** Agamemnon, Cassandra

cnemis: **4** shin **5** tibia **7** legging

coach: bus, car **4** hack, help **5** araba, cabin, prime, teach, train, tutor **6** advise, direct, fiacre (F.), mentor, saloon **7** adviser, omnibus, prepare, tallyho **8** carriage, dormeuse, instruct **10** instructor, stagecoach
railway: **5** diner **6** dining **7** Pullman, sleeper

coach dog: **9** Dalmatian

coachman: fly **4** fish, jehu, whip **5** pilot **6** driver **7** coachee, coacher **8** yemschik
assistant: **10** postillion
Russian: **7** yamshik **8** yemschik **9** yamstchik

coadjutor: **4** aide **6** bishop **7** partner **8** coworker **9** assistant, associate, successor

coagulant: **4** curd **6** rennet, rennin **7** styptic **8** gelatine

coagulate: gel, set **4** cake, clod, clot, curd, jell **5** quail **6** cotter, curdle, posset **7** clabber, congeal, thicken **8** solidify

coagulation: **4** gout **7** clotter

coal: **4** bass, fuel **5** chark, ember, gleed, stoke **6** carbon, cinder **10** fossil fuel
agent: **6** fitter
bed: **4** seam, vein
bin: **6** bunker
block: jud
carrying box: hod **7** scuttle
constituent: **4** goaf **6** carbon, ethene, phe-

nol, pyrene **7** benzene **8** creosote **11** naphthalene

distillate: tar

dust: **4** coom, culm, smut, soot, swad **5** coomb

gas: **7** methane **14** carbon monoxide

immature form of: **7** lignite

kind of: jud **4** dant, hard, soft **5** brown **6** cannel, coking **7** lignite **9** tasmanite **10** anthracite, bituminous **13** subbituminous

lump: cob

mine explosive: **9** Bobbinite

miner: **7** collier

miner's disease: **9** black lung **11** anthrocosis **14** pneumoconiosis

mining implement: **7** breaker

oil: **8** kerosene

refuse: **4** coke, dust, slag **6** cinder **7** backing, clinker

size: cob, egg, nut, pea **4** lump **5** slack, stove **6** broken **8** chestnut **9** buckwheat

wagon: **4** carf, corb, tram

worker: **7** collier, geordie **8** chaffman

coalesce: mix **4** fuse, join **5** blend, merge, unite **6** embody **7** combine **10** amalgamate

coalescence: **5** union **6** fusion, league **11** combination

coalfish: sey **4** parr **5** cuddy **6** beshow, billet, cudden, podler, sarthe **7** baddock, glashan, pollack

coalition: **4** bloc **5** trust, union **6** fusion, league, merger **8** alliance **11** combination, confederacy, conjunction **13** confederation

coarse: low, raw **4** dank, hard, hask, lewd, loud, rank, rude, vile **5** bawdy, broad, crass, crude, dirty, gross, harsh, heavy, loose, randy, routh, thick **6** brutal, callow, common, earthy, impure, ribald, rustic, vulgar **7** blatant, fulsome, goatish, obscene, raucous, sensual **8** clownish, homespun, immodest, indecent, unchaste **9** inelegant, offensive, unrefined **10** boisterous, indelicate, unpolished **12** scatological

food: **6** fodder

coast: **4** bank, land, ripa **5** beach, blide, shore, slide **6** adjoin, border, rivage, strand **7** seaside **8** approach, littoral, seaboard, seashore

area: **7** seaside **8** seacoast **9** coastline, shoreline

dweller: **7** orarian

pert. to: **7** coastal, orarian **8** littoral, riparian

projection: **4** cape, ness **8** headland **9** peninsula

Coast Guard: *boat:* **6** cutter

service-woman: **4** Spar

training ship: **5** Eagle

coaster: mat **4** sled **5** trout **8** toboggan **9** container

coat (see also **cloak**): **4** bark, daub, husk, rind,

zinc **5** cloth, cover, crust, glaze, habit, layer, paint, plate, shell, terve **6** enamel, jacket, mantle, parget, pelage, veneer **7** garment, incrust, overlay, plaster, vesture **8** membrane, tegument **9** petticoat **10** integument

animal: fur **4** hair, hide, pelt, wool **6** pelage

arctic: **5** parka

fastener: **4** frog **6** button, zipper

Irish: **9** coatamore

kind of: car, pea **4** cape, jupe, mail, robe, sack, toga **5** armor, parka, simar, tails **6** coatie, duster, jerkin, kirtle, mantle, reefer, rocket, topper **7** cassock, cutaway, haubeck, morning, paletot, pelisse, surcoat, surcote, surtout **8** benjamin, mackinaw, overcoat **9** gaberdine, newmarket, redingote **12** chesterfield

neck: **6** george

part: **4** cuff **5** lapel, skirt **6** collar, george, pocket, sleeve

seaman's: pea **5** grego

soldier's: **5** tunic

pert to: **8** heraldic

coati: **5** nasua **6** animal, narica **10** coatimundi

coating: **4** aril, film **6** patina, veneer **8** mucilage

coat of arms: **5** crest

coax: beg, coy, pet **4** cant, dupe, fawn, lure, urge **5** tease **6** cajole, cuitle, entice **7** beguile, cuittle, flatter, implore, wheedle **8** blandish, butter up, collogue, inveigle, persuade, soft soap **9** influence **10** manipulate

cob: ear, mew **4** beat, blow, gull, loaf, lump, mole, mule, pier, pony, swan, toss **5** block, break, chief, excel, horse, outdo, piece, stump, throw, thump **6** basket, cobnut, leader, muffin, peapod, spider, strike **7** beating, seagull, surpass, threash **8** dumpling **10** breakwater

cobble: **4** darn, make, mend, pave **5** botch, patch, stone **6** bungle, repair **7** clobber, snarl up **11** cobblestone

cobbler: pie **4** snob **5** sheep, soler, sutor **6** souter **7** botcher, catfish, crispin, dessert, pompano, saddler **8** chuckler, scorpion **9** killifish, shoemaker

pitch: **4** code

cobia: **4** fish **6** bonito

cobra: asp, nag **4** naga, naja **5** snake, viper **6** uraeus

enemy: **8** mongoose

genus: **4** naja

tree: **5** mamba

cobweb: net **4** trap **5** snare, wevet **8** gossamer **9** intricacy

cocaine: **4** snow **5** crack **8** alkaloid, narcotic **9** stimulant **10** anesthetic

source: **4** coca

coccyx: **8** tailbone

cochleate: 6 spiral 11 shell-shaped

cock: tap 4 bank, fowl, heap, kora, pile, rick 5 fight, fugie, gallo, shock, stack, strut, valve, yowle 6 faucet, leader 7 chicken, contend, gorcock, rooster, swagger 8 gamecock, malemass 10 cockalorum 11 chanticleer
gun: nab
of the walk: 8 kingfish
weather: 4 vane

cockade: 4 knot 5 badge 7 rosette

cock-a-hoop: 4 awry 5 askew 6 elated, lively 8 boastful, cockeyed

Cockaigne: 6 utopia 8 paradise

cock-and-bull story: lie 6 canard 7 untruth 8 tall tale 9 falsehood

cockatoo: ara 5 arara, cocky, galah, macaw 6 abacay, cockie, parrot 8 calangay, ganggang
genus: 7 cacatua, kakatoe

cockatrice: 7 serpent 8 basilisk

cockboat: cog 7 rowboat

cockchafer: 6 beetle

cocker: dog, pet 4 shoe 6 coddle, fondle, pamper, quiver, reaper 7 cater to, fighter, indulge, legging, nurture, spaniel

cockerel: 4 cock, slip 6 bantam

cockeyed: 4 alop, awry 5 askew, drunk 10 inebriated 11 intoxicated

cockfight: 4 game, spar 5 match 7 contest

cockfighting: 13 alectryomachy

cockhorse: 5 lofty, proud 7 astride, upstart 8 exultant

cockle: 4 boat, gall, gith, kiln, oast 5 bulge, shell, stove 6 darnel, pucker, ripple, wabble 7 mollusk, wrinkle 9 whimsical

cocklebur: 5 plant 7 burdock, clotbur 8 Xanthium

cockpit: pit 4 ring, rink, well 5 arena, cabin, field 7 gallera

cocksure: 4 sure 5 cocky 7 certain 8 positive 9 confident

cocky: 4 pert 6 crouse, farmer, jaunty 8 arrogant, insolent 9 conceited 11 smart alecky

cocoa, coco: 4 head, palm, tary 5 broma 6 yuntia 9 chocolate

coconut: 7 coquito
dried meat: 5 copra
fiber: 4 coir, kyar

cocoon: pod 4 clew, clue 5 shell 11 incunabulum

cod: bag, cor, pod 4 axle, bank, cusk, fish, fool, hoax, husk, rock 5 belly, pouch, scrod, torsk 6 burbot, codger, cultus, fellow, pillow 7 bacaloa, cushion
cod-like: bib 4 hake, ling 5 gadus
family: 7 gadidae
genus: 5 gadus
related fish: 7 rattail 9 grenadier
young: 5 scrod, sprag 7 codling

coda: 4 part 5 rondo 6 finale 10 conclusion

coddle: pet 4 baby, cade, cook 5 humor, nurse, spoil 6 caress, cocker, cosset, cotton, fondle, pamper 7 cater to, indulge, parboil

code: law 4 flag 5 canon, codex 6 cipher, digest, secret, signal 7 precept
inventor: 5 Morse
message: 6 cipher 10 cryptogram
type: ZIP 4 area 5 civil 6 postal 8 Napoleon 9 Hammurabi, Justinian

coded message: 10 cryptogram

codex: 4 code 5 annal 9 formulary 10 manuscript

codger: cod 5 churl, crank, miser 6 fellow 7 niggard

codicil: 5 rider 6 sequel 8 appendix 10 supplement

codify: 5 index 6 digest 8 classify 11 systematize

coerce: cow 4 curb, make, urge 5 bully, check, drive, force 6 compel, menace 7 concuss, enforce, repress 8 bludgeon, bulldoze, restrain, restrict 9 blackmail, constrain, terrorize 10 intimidate

coercion: 5 force 6 duress

coeval: 4 peer 12 contemporary

coffee: *after dinner:* 9 demitasse
alkaloid: 7 caffein
bean: nib
beverage: Rio 4 Java, Kona 5 Milds, Mocha 6 Bogota, Brazil, Santos 7 Sumatra 8 Medellin 9 Maracaibo
cake: 6 kuchen
French: 4 café
grinder: 4 mill
kind: 4 drip, java 5 decaf, mocha, Sanka 7 arabica, instant 8 espresso 11 freeze-dried 13 decaffeinated
maker: pot, urn 5 silex 10 percolator
refuse: 6 triage
with milk: 10 café au lait

coffee shop: 5 diner 7 tea room 8 snack bar 9 lunchroom 12 luncheonette

coffeeberry: 6 jojoba 7 cascara, soybean 8 peaberry 9 buckthorn, chaparral

coffeepot: urn 6 biggin 9 cafetiere

coffer: ark, box, dam 5 chest, hutch, trunk 6 casket, forcer, trench 7 caisson 8 ciborium, standard

coffin: 4 bier, case, cist, mold 6 basket, casing, casket 11 sarcophagus
cloth: 4 pall 5 cloak
support: 4 bier

cog: cam, lie 4 gear, jest 5 catch, cheat, cozen, tenon, tooth, trick, wedge, wheel 6 cajole 7 deceive, produce, quibble, wheedle 8 cockboat 9 fabricate, falsehood

cogent: 5 pithy, valid 6 potent, strong 7 telling 8 forcible, powerful 9 trenchant 10 conclusive, convincing, legitimate, persuasive

cogitate: 4 mull, muse, plan 5 think 6 ponder 7 connate, reflect 8 consider, meditate

cognate: kin 4 akin 5 alike 6 allied 7 kindred, related, similar 8 bandhava, relative

cognizance: ken 4 heed, mark 5 badge, crest 6 emblem, notice 7 bearing, cockade 9 knowledge 11 observation, recognition 12 apprehension

cognizant: 4 onto, ware 5 awake, aware 8 sensible 9 conscious 10 conversant 11 intelligent 12 apprehensive

cognize: 4 know 5 grasp 6 fathom 8 perceive 9 apprehend, recognize 10 appreciate, understand

cognomen (see also **name**): 4 name 5 style, title 6 byname 7 agnomen, moniker, surname 8 nickname, patronym 11 appellation

cognoscente: 5 judge 6 critic, expert 9 authority 10 specialist

cohabit: 4 live 5 dwell 6 occupy 8 accustom 9 accompany

cohere: fit 4 glue, suit 5 agree, cling, stick, unite 6 adhere, cement, cleave 7 connect 8 coincide 9 glutinate

coherence: 5 union 8 cohesion 9 congruity 10 accordance, connection, continuity 11 consistency

cohort: 4 band, mate 6 fellow 7 company 9 associate

coif, coiffe: cap 4 hood 6 beggin, burlet, hairdo 7 arrange 8 skullcap 9 headdress

coiffure: 6 hairdo 9 headdress

coign: 5 wedge 6 corner 8 position 10 projection

coil: ado, wip 4 ansa, clew, curl, fuss, hank, loop, roll, wind 5 helix, querl, tense, twine, twist 6 rundle, spiral, tumult, windup 7 haycock, ringlet, trouble 8 encircle 9 confusion, encounter 10 difficulty 11 convolution
electric: 6 teaser

coin: die, ori 4 cash, dime, make, mint 5 angle, brown, chink, clink, metal, money, quoin, shape, stamp, token, wedge 6 change, corner, create, invent, specie, strike 7 convert 8 currency 9 fabricate, neologize, originate 11 cornerstone
box: pyx 4 till 5 meter 8 register
collector: 11 numismatist
copper: 4 cent 5 bodle, brown, penny
counterfeit: 9 brummagem
difference: 5 value 11 seigniorage
edge corrugation: 7 reeding
front: 4 head 7 obverse
imperfectly minted: 8 brockage
kind of: lap, ora 4 dime, doit, mite, rial, rosa 5 cuyne, daric, disme, ducat, eagle, groat 6 bawbee, beaver, besant, bezant, cunzie 7 bezzant, carolus, crocard, louleau

8 bezantee, crockard 10 castellano
pert. to: 10 numismatic 12 numismatical
reverse side: 4 tail 5 verso
roll: 7 rouleau
science: 11 numismatics
silver: 4 batz, dime, dump, pina, tara 5 bezzo 6 tester, teston
stamper: 4 mill
weight: 6 shekel

coinage: 7 fiction, mintage 9 invention, neologism
collector: 11 numismatist

coincide: gee 4 jibe 5 agree, tally 6 concur 9 harmonize 10 correspond

coincidence: 9 concourse 11 concurrence 12 concomitance, simultaneity

coincident: 4 even 8 together 9 consonant 10 concurrent 11 concomitant 12 contemporary 15 contemporaneous

coiner of new words: 9 neologian, neologist

coition: 7 meeting 10 attraction 11 conjunction

coke: aks 4 coal, core, dope 5 chark 7 cocaine

col: 4 pass 10 depression

colander: 5 sieve 7 utensil 8 strainer

Colchis: *king:* 6 Aeetes
princess: 5 Medea

cold: flu 4 ague, dead, dull 5 algid, bleak, frore, gelid, rheum, virus 6 arctic, chilly, frigid, frosty, wintry 7 catarrh, chilled, distant, glacial 8 reserved, rhigosis, unheated 9 apathetic, cheerless 10 insensible, spiritless 11 hyperborean, indifferent, unemotional 12 unresponsive 13 dispassionate, marblehearted 15 undemonstrative
instrument to apply: 9 cryoprobe
pert. to: icy 5 gelid 6 frigid, frozen 10 frigorific
remedy: 8 vitamin C 12 decongestant 13 antihistamine

cold and damp: raw 4 dank 5 bleak

cold-blooded: 7 callous 9 unfeeling

colder: 4 husk 6 refuse 7 rubbish

cold feet: 4 fear 5 alarm, doubt 9 cowardice 12 apprehension

cold mist: 4 drow

cold-shoulder: cut 4 snub 6 ignore, rebuff

cold steel: 5 sword 6 dagger 7 bayonet

cold sweat: 4 fear 5 shock 11 trepidation

coleoptera insect: 6 beetle, insect, weevil

Coleridge's sacred river: 4 Alph

Colette: 8 novelist
characters: 4 Gigi 5 Cheri 8 Claudine

colewort: 4 cole, kale 7 cabbage

colic: 5 gripe 9 bellyache 10 mulligrubs

coliseum: 4 bowl, hall 5 arena 7 stadium, theater 8 building 12 amphitheater

collaborate: aid 9 cooperate

collagen: 7 protein 10 albuminoid

collapse: 4 cave, fall, fold 5 crash, slump, wreck 6 bust-up 7 crumple, debacle, deflate, failure, flummox, smashup 8 contract, downfall 9 breakdown, telescope 11 prostration

collar: nab 4 band, eton, gill, grab, ring, ruff 5 chain, fichu, ruche, seize 6 bertha, gorget, tackle, torque 7 capture, chignon, circlet, shackle 8 cincture, neckband, necklace 9 neckpiece
horse: 6 hounce
jeweled: 8 carcanet
kind of: 4 cowl, ruff 5 fanon, jabot, orale, phano, rabat, Roman, ruche, V-neck 6 cangue, carcan, rabato, rebato 7 bargham, panuelo 8 carcanet, Peter Pan 10 chevesaile, turtleneck

collarbone: 8 clavicle

collate: 5 order 6 bestow, confer, verify 7 arrange, bracket, compare, emamine 9 integrate

collateral: 4 side 8 indirect, parallel, security 9 ancillary 10 subsidiary 11 concomitant, subordinate

collation: tea 4 meal 5 lunch 6 repast, sermon 7 address, reading 8 dejeuner, parallel, treatise 10 collection, comparison, conference 12 consultation, contribution

colleague: 4 aide, ally 6 deputy 7 adjunct, consort, partner 8 confrere 9 assistant, associate

collect: tax 4 call, heap, levy, pile, pool, save 5 amass, glean, group, hoard, raise 6 accoil, accrue, confer, garner, gather, muster, prayer, sheave 7 compile, engross, impound, round up 8 assemble, contract 9 aggregate 10 accumulate, congregate, simmer down 11 agglomerate

collected: 4 calm, cool 5 sober 6 serene 8 composed 9 aggregate, clustered 10 coacervate 11 agglomerate, unflappable 13 dispassionate

collection: ana 4 bevy, clan, olio 5 batch, group, store, suite 6 bundle, conger, sorite 8 assembly, caboodle 9 aggregate, anthology, collation, repertory 10 assemblage, assortment, cancionero
animals: zoo 9 menagerie
clothes: 8 wardrobe
facts: 4 data
literary: ana 7 library 8 analects 11 florilegium
miscellaneous: 4 olio 6 fardel, jumble, medley
poems: 5 divan, sylva 9 anthology 10 cancionero
proper names: 11 onomasticon

collector: *bird egg:* 8 oologist
book: 11 bibliophile

coin: 11 numismatist
item: 5 curio 11 collectible
stamp: 11 philatelist

colleen: 4 girl, lass, miss 5 belle 6 damsel, lassie, maiden

college: 5 lycee 6 school 7 academy 8 seminary 9 electoral 10 assemblage, university 11 institution 12 organization
accounts: 6 battel
building: gym, lab 4 dorm, hall 9 dormitory
campus: 4 quad 10 quadrangle
course: 5 major, minor 7 seminar
court: 4 quad
degree: B.L.S., B.Sc., LL.B., LL.D., M.Sc., Ph.D., S.C.B. 5 Litt.D.
female: 4 coed
graduate: 4 alum 6 alumna, alumni (pl.), doctor, master 7 alumnae (pl.), alumnus 8 bachelor
living quarters: 4 dorm, hall 9 dormitory
official: 4 dean 5 prexy 6 beadle, bursar, regent 7 proctor, provost 9 president, registrar 10 chancellor
pert. to: 8 academic 10 collegiate
professor: don 6 docent, doctor
session: lab 5 class 7 lecture, seminar 8 tutorial
song: 9 alma mater
student group: 4 frat 8 sorority 10 fraternity
term: 7 quarter 8 semester 9 trimester
treasurer: 6 bursar
U.S. oldest: 7 Harvard
U.S. woman's oldest: 9 Mt. Holyoke

collet: 4 band, ring 5 chuck 6 casing, circle, collar, flange, socket 7 bushing, ferrule 8 neckband

collide: hit, ram 4 bump, dash, hurt 5 carom, clash, crash, wreck 6 hurtle, strike

collier: fly 4 boat 5 miner 6 plover, vessel 7 geordie
boy: 6 hodder
lung disease: 11 anthracosis

colliery: 4 mine

collision: 5 clash, crash, shock 7 crackup, smashup 8 clashing 9 encounter 10 opposition, percussion 12 interference

collocate: set 5 place 7 arrange 8 position

colloquial: 6 patois 8 familiar, informal 9 unstudied 10 vernacular 14 conversational

colloquy: 4 chat, talk 6 parley 8 dialogue 9 discourse 10 conference 12 conversation

colluctation: 8 struggle 10 contention

collude: 4 plot 6 scheme 7 connive 8 collogue, conspire

collusion: 6 deceit 7 cahoots, secrecy 9 agreement 10 complicity, connivance
law: 5 covin

collusive: 9 convinous 10 fraudulent

Cologne: *German spelling:* **4** Koln
  king: **6** Caspar, Jaspar

Colombia: *capital:* **6** Bogota
  city: **4** Cali **5** Neiva, Pasto, Tunja **6**
  Cucuta, Ibaque, Quibdo **7** Leticia,
  Popayan **8** Medellin **9** Cartagena,
  Manizales, San Andres **10** Santa Maria
  12 Barranquilla **15** Barrancabermeja
  currency: **4** peso, real **6** condor, peseta
  7 centavo
  export: **6** coffee **7** cocaine **8** emeralds **9**
  petroleum
  Indian: **5** Boros, Chita **6** Betoya,
  Tahami, Tunebo, Yahuna **7** Chibcha
  mahogany: **7** albarco
  measure: **4** vara **7** celemin
  mountain: **5** Andes
  river: **4** Sinu, Tomo **5** Cauca **6** Atrato,
  Atroto, Pattia, Yapura **7** Orinoco **9**
  Magdalena
  volcano: **5** Huila, Pasto **6** Purace
  weight: bag **4** kilo, saco **5** gramo, libra
  6 carga **7** quilate, quintal

colon: **4** coin, mark, sign **6** farmer **7** planter **8**
  colonist **9** intestine **10** husbandman
Colonel Blimp: **9** blusterer **10** fuddy-duddy
  12 stuffed shirt
colonial teak: **8** flindosa
colonist: **7** pioneer, settler **8** emigrant
colonize: **5** found **6** gather, settle **7** migrate **9**
  establish
colonizer: ant **6** oecist **7** settler
colonnade: row **4** stoa **7** pergola, portico, terrace **9** peristyle
colony: **5** swarm **9** community **10** dependency, settlement
colophon: **6** device, emblem
colophonite: **6** garnet **9** andradite
colophony: **5** resin, rosin
color: dye, hue **4** blee, cast, flag, tint, tone **5**
  badge, blush, paint, shade, stain, tenne,
  tinge **6** banner, ensign, redden **7** distort,
  pennant, pigment **8** standard, tincture **10**
  complexion
  achromatic: **4** gray **5** black, white
  change: **8** iridesce, opalesce
  dull: dun **4** drab **5** terne
  full of: **9** chromatic
  graduation: **5** shade
  healthy: tan
  light: **4** tint
  line of: **6** streak
  malachite: **4** bice

  mat white: **9** alabaster
  mulberry: **7** morello
  neutral: **4** ecru, gray **5** beige, black, white
  painter: **6** Titian
  pale: **6** pastel
  primary: red **4** blue **5** black, white **6** yellow
  quality: **4** tone
  secondary: **5** green **6** orange, purple
  shade of difference: **6** nuance
  unhealthy: sallow
  uniform in: **4** flot
  value: see *quality* above
  varying: **10** iridescent, opalescent
color: For colors see their names: **red, green,
  purple**, etc.; for shades see main color.
  EXAMPLES, "reddish brown" see **brown**;
  "grayish green" see **green**.
color bar: **9** apartheid **10** Jim Crow law **11**
  segregation **14** discrimination
color blindness: **9** Daltonism **13** achromatopsia **14** monochromatism
color organ: **8** clavilux
color photography inventor: **4** Ives

Colorado: *capital:* **6** Denver
  city: **5** Aspen, Delta **6** Arvada, Aurora,
  Pueblo **7** Boulder, Greeley, Manassa **8**
  Lakewood, Trinidad **11** Fort Collins **15**
  Colorado Springs
  early explorer: **4** Pike
  Indian: Ute **4** Iowa **6** Pawnee **8** Arapa-
  hoe, Cheyenne, Comanche
  motto: **13** Nil sine Numine (Nothing
  Without Providence)
  mountain: **5** Longs **6** Elbert **7** Rockies
  9 Pikes Peak
  resort: **4** Vail **5** Aspen
  river: **4** Bear **5** Green, White **6** Platte **7**
  Laramie **8** Arkansas, Colorado **9** Rio
  Grande **10** Republican
  state bird: **11** lark bunting
  state flower: **9** columbine
  state tree: **10** blue spruce

colorant: dye **4** anil **7** pigment
coloratura: **6** singer **7** soprano **8** vocalist
colored: **6** biased **9** distorted, prismatic **14**
  misrepresented
  partly: **4** pied **6** motley **7** piebald **10** variegated
colorful: gay **5** vivid **9** brilliant
colorimeter: **10** tintometer
coloring: *cell:* **10** endochrome
  matter: dye **5** morin **7** pigment **8** clorofil
  10 endochrome **11** chlorophyll

colorless: wan **4** drab, dull, pale **5** ashen, blake, blank, plain **6** pallid **7** hueless, neutral **8** blanched **9** impartial **10** achromatic **11** transparent **13** uninteresting

colors, set of: 7 palette

colossal: big **4** huge, vast **5** great, large **7** immense, mammoth, titanic **8** enormous, gigantic **9** monstrous

colossus: 5 giant, titan **6** statue **7** monster, prodigy

colporteur: 6 hawker **7** apostle, peddler **10** evangelist, missionary **11** distributor

colt: gun **4** foal, tyro **5** filly **6** pistol **8** beginner, neophyte **9** quadruped, youngster

coluber: 5 snake **7** serpent

colubrine: 6 crafty **7** cunning **9** snakelike

columbine: 4 bird, dodo **5** plant **6** flower **8** dovelike

Columbus: *birthplace:* **5** Genoa
burial place: **7** Seville
companion: **5** Ojeda
embarkation port: **5** Palos
patron: **8** Isabella **9** Ferdinand
ship: **4** Nina **5** Pinta **10** Santa Maria
son: **5** Diego

column: lat, row **4** file, line, post **5** shaft, stela, stele **6** pillar **7** support **8** cylinder, pilaster **9** formation
arrange in: **8** tabulate
base: **6** plinth **9** stylobate
female figure: **8** caryatid
male figure: **5** Atlas **7** telamon **8** atlantes (pl.)
part: **4** anta, fust **5** galbe, scape, shank, socle **6** plinth **7** capital, entasis **8** pilaster
pert. to: **8** columnar
small: **5** stele
support: **5** socle
type of: **5** Doric, Ionic **10** Corinthian

columnar: 6 terete **7** stelene **8** vertical

columnist: 6 writer **7** analyst

columns: *series of:* **9** colonnade
set in: **7** tabular
without: **7** astylar

coma: 4 tuft **5** bunch, carus, sleep **6** stupor, torpor, trance **7** cluster **8** lethargy **13** insensibility

comate: 5 hairy

comatose: out **6** drowsy **9** lethargic **10** insensible

comb: 4 card, lash, rake **5** brush, clean, crest, curry, tease **6** smooth **11** disentangle
flax: **6** hackle, heckle **7** hatchel
horse: **5** curry

comb-like: 8 pectinal **9** pectinate

combat: war **4** bout, cope, duel, fray, meet, rush, tilt **5** clash, fight, joust, repel, set-to **6** action, battle, oppose, resist, strife **7** contend, contest, counter, scuffle **8** argument, conflict, struggle **9** encounter, withstand **10** antagonize, contention
challenge to single: **6** cartel
code: **6** duello
place: **5** arena

combatant: 6 dueler **7** battler, fighter **8** champion **10** contestant

combative: 8 militant **9** agonistic, bellicose **10** pugnacious **11** agonistical, belligerent

comber: 4 wave **7** breaker **11** beachcomber

combination: key **4** bloc, gang, pact, pool, ring **5** cabal, junto, party, trust, union **6** cartel, clique, corner, merger **7** combine, consort, coterie, faction **8** alliance, ensemble **9** aggregate, camarilla, coalition, composite, composure, synthesis **10** concoction, conspiracy **11** association, coalescence, composition, confederacy, conjunction, corporation, unification **12** undergarment **13** incorporation

combine: add, mix, wed **4** bloc, join, pool **5** blend, marry, merge, total, unite **6** absorb, concur, embody, merger, mingle, splice **7** conjoin, conjure, machine **8** coalesce, compound, concrete, condense, contract, federate **9** construct, cooperate **10** amalgamate **11** combination, consolidate **12** conglomerate

combining form: See list at back

comboy: 6 sarong

combust: 4 burn **5** burnt **8** consumed **10** incinerate

combustible: 4 fuel, peat **5** fiery **9** irascible **10** accendible **11** inflammable
material: gas, oil **4** coal, coke, peat **6** tinder

combustion: 4 fire, heat **5** therm **6** tumult **7** burning **8** volatile **9** agitation, confusion, consuming, cremation, oxidation **12** inflammation
residue: ash, gas **7** clinker

come: 4 grow **5** arise, issue, occur, reach **6** accrue, appear, arrive, befall, emerge, happen, spring **7** advance, develop, emanate **8** approach, practice **9** eventuate
a cropper: **4** fail, fall
across: **4** find, meet **9** encounter **10** contribute
after: **5** ensue **6** follow **7** succeed
again: **6** return
along: **4** fare **7** improve **8** progress
apart: **5** break **12** disintegrate
at: **6** attack
before: **7** precede, prevene **8** antecede
between: **8** alienate **9** interpose
by: get **4** gain **6** obtain **7** acquire, inherit
clean: **7** confess
down with: **5** catch **8** contract
forth: **6** appear, emerge
from: **5** ensue **6** derive, result

in: **5** crash, enter **6** arrive **7** intrude

into view: **4** loom **6** appear, emerge

of age: **6** mature

off: **5** break, click, occur **6** go over, pan out **7** develop, succeed

on: **4** bait, lure **5** decoy, snare

out: **5** debut **6** appear, emerge, emerse, extend **8** protrude

to: **5** total **6** arrive, awaken, revive **7** recover

to a head: **6** climax **9** suppurate

to nothing: end **4** stop **5** cease **8** fall flat

to terms: **4** join **5** agree **6** assent, settle **7** approve, consent **8** coincide **9** acquiesce

together: **4** bump, join, meet **5** clash, merge **7** collide, convene **8** assemble, converge

under: **7** subvene

up: **5** arise, occur **6** appear

comeback: **5** rally **6** answer, retort, return **7** rebound **8** recovery, repartee

comedian: wag, wit **4** card **5** actor, antic, clown, comic **6** jester **7** buffoon

comedown: **4** fall, land **5** crash **6** alight, bathos **7** descend **8** collapse

comedy: **5** drama, farce, revue **8** comoedia (L.), travesty **9** burlesque, slapstick

muse: **6** Thalia

symbol: **4** sock

comely: **4** fair, hend, pert **5** bonny, hende **6** decent, goodly, liking, lovely, pretty, proper **7** farrant **8** becoming, decorous, graceful, handsome, pleasing, suitable **9** agreeable, beautiful **10** gratifying, personable **11** good-looking

comestible: **4** food **5** manna, viand **6** edible **7** eatable, victual **8** esculent

comet: **6** meteor

discoverer: **5** Biela, Encke, Swift **6** Donati, Halley, Olbers **8** Kohoutek

part: **4** coma

tail: **8** streamer

comeuppance: due **6** rebuke **7** deserts **12** chastisement

comfit: **5** candy **7** confect, praline **8** conserve, preserve **9** sweetmeat **10** confection

comfort: aid **4** ease, rest **5** bield (Sc.), cheer **6** buck up, endure, relief, repose, solace, soothe, succor **7** animate, assuage, cherish, confirm, console, enliven, gladden, refresh, relieve, support, sustain **8** inspirit, nepenthe, pleasure, reassure **9** encourage, well-being **10** strengthen **11** consolation

comfortable: **4** bein, bien, cosh, cozy, easy, like, snug, trig **5** comfy, homey **7** relaxed **8** cheerful, euphoric, well-to-do **9** contented **10** acceptable, commodious, complacent, gratifying **11** consolatory, encouraging

comforter: **4** puff **5** cover, quilt, scarf **6** tippet **7** cheerer **8** pacifier

comfortless: **7** forlorn **8** desolate **9** cheerless **12** inconsolable

comfrey: **5** daisy **9** blackwort

comic: wag, wit **5** droll, funny **8** comedian, farcical **9** burlesque, laughable, ludicrous

strip: **7** funnies

comical: low **4** base, zany **5** droll, funny, queer, witty **7** amusing, jocular, risible, strange, trivial **8** humorous, ticklish **9** diverting, laughable, ludicrous, quizzical, whimsical **10** capricious

coming: due **4** next **6** advent, future **7** arrival, forward **8** deserved **9** impending **11** approaching

coming out: **5** debut **8** issuance

comma: **4** lull, sign **5** pause **8** interval

command: bid **4** beck, bode, boon, call, fiat, hest, rule, sway **5** beken, check, edict, exact, force, hight, order, power, ukase **6** adjure, beckon, behest, charge, compel, degree, demand, direct, enjoin, govern, impose, master, ordain **7** appoint, behight, bidding, control, dictate, mandate, officer, precept, require **8** domineer, restrain **9** authority, direction, influence, ordinance, prescribe **10** commission **11** appointment

supreme: **8** hegemony

to a horse: gee, haw, hup **4** whoa **6** giddap

to a sled dog: **4** mush **6** begone

to stop: **4** whoa **5** avast

commander: cid, cio **4** head **5** chief **6** leader, master, rammer **7** captain, drungar, emperor, general, officer **10** commandant **11** commendador (Sp.) **13** generalissimo

of a thousand men: **9** chiliarch

commanding: **8** dominant, imposing **9** imperious, masterful **10** imperative **13** authoritative

commandment: law **4** rule **5** edict, order **7** precept

commando: **4** seal **6** raider, ranger

comme il faut (F.): **6** proper **7** fitting

commemorate: **7** observe **9** celebrate, solemnize **11** memorialize

commemoration: **5** award, medal **6** plaque **7** service **8** memorial **11** celebration **13** solemnization

commence: **4** fall, open **5** arise, begin, found, start **6** incept, spring **7** kick off, lead off, take off **8** initiate **9** institute, originate

commencement: **4** dawn **5** alpha, birth, onset, start **7** genesis, opening **9** beginning **10** graduation **13** baccalaureate

commencer: **4** tyro **6** novice **8** beginner, neophyte

commencing: **7** initial, nascent **9** incipient

commend: pat **4** give, laud **5** adorn, boost, extol, grace, offer **6** bestow, betake, commit, praise, resign **7** applaud, approve, bespeak, deliver, entrust, intrust **8**

bequeath **9** predicate, recommend **10** compliment, ingratiate
highly: **5** extol **8** eulogize **10** panegyrize
to favor: **10** ingratiate

commendable: **4** good **6** worthy **8** laudable **9** exemplary, honorable **12** praiseworthy

commensurate: **4** even **5** equal **6** enough **8** adequate **10** answerable, convenient **11** appropriate **12** proportional **13** corresponding, proportionate

comment: **4** note, talk, word **5** aside, gloss, gloze **6** notate, postil, remark **7** descant, discuss, explain, expound, observe **9** criticise, criticism, criticize, discourse **10** animadvert, annotation, commentary **12** obiter dictum **13** animadversion

commentary: **5** gloss **6** memoir **7** account **8** glossary, treatise

commentator: **6** critic, glozer **7** analyst **9** annotator, expositor, glossator, scholiast **10** glossarist **13** glossographer

commerce: **5** trade **6** barter **7** traffic **8** business, exchange **10** connection **11** interchange
vehicle: **5** truck

commercial: **9** mercature **10** mercantile **13** advertisement

commination: **6** threat

commingle: mix **4** fuse, join **5** blend, merge, unite **7** combine, embroil **10** amalgamate

comminute: **4** mill **5** crush, grind **9** pulverize, triturate

commiseration: **4** pity **7** empathy **8** sympathy **10** compassion, condolence

commission: **4** send, task **5** board, trust **6** brevit, charge, demand, depute, errand, office, ordain, permit **7** command, consign, empower, mandate, mission, warrant **8** delegate, encharge **9** allowance, authority, authorize, brokerage, establish **10** constitute **11** instruction **12** compensation, dispensation, perpetration **13** authorization

commissioner: **5** envoy **7** officer **8** delegate

commissure: **4** seam **5** joint, miter, mitre **8** juncture **10** miter joint

commit: **4** give **5** allot, refer **6** assign, betake, remand **7** command, confide, consign, deposit, entrust, intrust **8** bequeath, delegate, imprison, relegate, turn over **9** recommend **10** perpetrate

committee: **4** body **5** board, group, junta **7** council **9** executors, guardians

commixture: **6** fusion **7** mixture **8** compound **9** composite

commode: cap **5** chest **8** cupboard **10** chiffonier

commodious: fit **5** ample, roomy **6** proper, useful **8** spacious, suitable **9** capacious **10** beneficial, convenient **11** comfortable, serviceable **12** advantageous

commodity: **4** item, ware **5** goods **6** staple **7** article

common: low **4** base **5** banal, brief, cheap, joint, stale, trite, usual **6** coarse, mutual, ornery, vulgar **7** average, current, general, generic, natural, popular, regular, trivial, unnoble **8** all right, familiar, frequent, habitual, mediocre, ordinary, pandemic, plebeian, trifling **9** bourgeois, customary, defective, hackneyed, prevalent, universal, unrefined **10** second-rate **11** commonplace **12** matter-of-fact

common effort: **8** teamwork

commoner: **5** ceorl, plebe **7** burgess, citizen, student **8**

common fund: pot **4** pool **5** purse

common law: **6** custom **9** tradition

commonly: *accepted:* **7** popular, vulgate
thought: **7** reputed **8** putative

common man: **4** pleb **8** plebeian

commonplace: **4** dull, fade, worn **5** banal, daily, plain, prose, stale, trite, usual **6** common, garden, truism **7** humdrum, prosaic, tedious, trivial **8** ordinary **9** hackneyed **11** stereotyped, unimportant **13** unexceptional
remark: **6** cliche, truism **9** platitude

common sense: **6** wisdom **8** gumption, judgment

common stock: **5** share **8** security
roturier **12** participator

commonwealth: **5** state **6** public **9** community **10** federation, res publica

commotion: ado, din **4** bree, fray, fuss, heat, riot, stir, to-do, whir **5** alarm, flare, hurry **6** bustle, cathro (Sc.), flurry, fracas, garray, mutiny, pother, tumult, unrest, welter **7** clatter, tempest, turmoil **8** brouhaha, disorder, upheaval, uprising **9** agitation, confusion **10** concussion, convulsion, ebullition, excitement, turbulence **11** disturbance, pandemonium **12** perturbation

commune: **4** area, talk **5** argue, realm, share, treat **6** advise, confer, debate, import, parley, reveal **7** consult, discuss, divulge **8** converse, district, township **11** communicate, intercourse, participate **12** conversation
Israeli: **7** kibbutz
Russian: mir **7** kolkhoz

communicable: **4** open **5** frank **8** catching, sociable **9** expansive, garrulous, talkative **10** contagious, diffusible, infectious **13** communicative

communicant: **6** member **8** adherent, receiver **9** celebrant, informant

communicate (see also **commune**): **4** tell **5** speak **6** bestow, convey, impart, inform, reveal, signal **7** declare, dictate, divulge **8** converse

communication: 4 note 5 favor 6 favour, letter 7 message 8 telegram 9 directive 10 communique, connection 11 interchange 12 conversation
means: fax 4 drum, flag, note, post 5 cable, modem, phone, radio, smoke 6 letter, movies, speech, tomtom 9 broadcast, satellite, telegraph, telephone 10 television

communion: 4 cult, host, Mass, sect, talk 5 bread, creed, faith, share, unity, water 6 church, homily 7 concord 8 antiphon, converse, viaticum 9 agreement, eucharist, sacrament 10 confession, fellowship 11 intercourse 12 conversation, denomination 13 communication, participation
case: 5 burse
cloth: 8 corporal 9 corporale 11 purificator
cup: ama 7 chalice
plate: 5 paten
table: 5 altar 8 credence
vessel: pyx 6 lavabo 8 ciborium

communique: 6 report 7 message 12 announcement 13 communication

communism: 8 Leninism 10 Bolshevism

communist: Red 5 pinko 6 Soviet 7 comrade, Marxist

community: mir 4 body, burg, city 5 firca, state, thorp 6 cenoby, colony, hamlet, nation, polity, public 7 enclave, society, village 8 district, likeness, province, township 9 frequency 10 commonness 12 commonwealth, neighborhood
pert. to: 8 societal

commute: 5 alter 6 change, travel 7 convert 8 exchange 10 substitute 11 interchange

comose: 5 hairy 6 tufted

compact: 4 bond, case, firm, hard, knit, pact, plot, snug, trim 5 brief, close, dense, gross, pithy, solid, terse, thick 6 vanity 7 bargain, concise, concord, serried 8 alliance, condense, contract, covenant, solidify, succinct 9 agreement, concordat 10 compaction, compressed, conspiracy, federation 11 compendious, concentrate, confederacy, consolidate, sententious 13 understanding

compadre: pal 5 amigo, buddy 6 friend 9 companion

companion: pal 4 chum, fere, mate, peer, twin, wife 5 buddy, bully, butty, crony, cully, matey 6 comate, escort, fellow, friend, spouse 7 compeer, comrade, consort, husband, partner 8 compadre, helpmate 9 associate, attendant 11 concomitant 12 acquaintance
constant: 6 shadow
equal: 4 peer 7 compeer
faithful: dog 7 Achates

companionable: 6 social 7 amiable, cordial 8 friendly, gracious, sociable 9 agreeable

company: mob, set 4 band, bevy, body, core, crew, fare, fere, firm, gang, gest, ging, host, rout, team 5 coven, covey, crowd, flock, geste, group, guest, horde, party, squad, troop 6 actors, circle, clique, cohort, covine, curney (Sc.), throng, troupe 7 battery, college, consort, society, visitor 8 assembly 9 camarilla, cavalcade, concourse, gathering 10 fellowship 11 association, partnership 13 companionship

comparable: 4 like 7 similar 8 parallel 9 analogous

comparative: 4 than 5 equal, rival 7 compeer 8 relative 11 approximate

compare: vie 4 even 5 apply, liken, match, scale 6 confer, relate 7 collate, examine, senible 8 contrast, estimate 10 assimilate

comparison: 6 simile 7 analogy, parable 8 likeness, likening, metaphor 9 collation 10 conference, similitude 11 examination

compartment: bay, bin 4 cell, part 5 abode, stall 6 alcove, bunker, region 7 cellule, chamber, section 8 division 9 apartment 10 pigeonhole
granary: 8 grintern

compass: 4 area, gain, room, size 5 field, gamut, range, reach, scope 6 arrive, attain, bounds, circle, degree, device, effect, extent, sphere 7 achieve, caliber, circuit, confine, divider, enclose, environ, go round, horizon, pelorus 8 boundary, cincture, circuity, surround 10 accomplish, comprehend
beam: 7 trammel
card: 4 rose
housing: 8 binnacle
ink leg: pen
kind of: sun 4 gyro 5 solar
part: pen 4 airt, vane 5 rhumb 6 gimbal, needle 7 gimbals, trammel 8 trammels
pocket: 6 diacle
point: airt 5 airth, rhumb 7 azimuth
sight: 4 vane
suspender: 6 gimbal

compassion: rue 4 pity, ruth 5 grace, heart, mercy, sorry 6 lenity 7 remorse 8 clemency, humanity, sympathy 10 condolence 12 misericordia 13 commiseration

compatible: 8 suitable 9 accordant, agreeable, congenial, congruous, consonant 10 consistent, harmonious 16 noncontradictory

compatriot: 9 associate, colleague 10 countryman

compeer: 4 mate, peer, rank 5 equal, match 7 comrade 9 colleague, companion 11 comparative

compel: gar (Sc.) 4 make, move, urge 5 cause, drive, exact, force, impel, press 6 coerce, enjoin, extort, incite, oblige **7** actuate, command, dragoon, enforce, require **9** constrain, influence, instigate, overpower **11** necessitate, subjudicate

compelled: has **4** must **5** bound

compelling: **6** cogent **7** telling **8** forceful **9** demanding **10** conclusive, convincing, persuasive

compendious: **5** brief, short, terse **6** direct **7** compact, concise **8** succinct **9** condensed **11** expeditious **13** comprehensive, short and sweet

compendium: **4** list **5** brief **6** apercu, digest, precis, sketch **7** catalog, compend, epitome, medulla, outline, summary **8** abstract, breviary, syllabus, synopsis **10** abridgment **11** compilation, composition, contraction **12** abbreviation

compensate: pay **4** jibe **5** agree, atone, repay, tally **6** recoup, reward, square **7** correct, redress, requite, restore, satisfy **9** indemnify **10** contervail, recompense, remunerate **12** counterpoise **14** counterbalance

compensation: fee, pay, utu **4** hire **5** bonus, wages **6** amends, angild, gersum, offset, reward, salary **7** damages, payment, redress, stipend **8** pittance, requital **9** emolument, indemnity **10** recompense **11** restitution, counterpoise, remuneration, satisfaction **15** indemnification

compete: pit, vie **4** cope, tend **5** match, rival **6** strive **7** contend, contest, emulate

competent: apt, can, fit **4** able, good, meet, sane **5** adept, capax, smart **6** worthy **7** capable, endowed, skilled **8** adequate, suitable **9** effective, efficient, qualified **10** proficient, sufficient

competition: **4** game, heat **5** match, trial **7** contest, rivalry **8** conflict, tug-of-war **9** emulation **10** contention, free-for-all, opposition

competitor: foe **5** enemy, rival **6** player **7** entrant **8** opponent **9** adversary, candidate, combatant **10** antagonist, contestant

Compiegne's river: **4** Oise **5** Aisne

compilation: ana **4** book, code **5** cento **6** digest **9** accretion **10** collection, compendium, confection

compile: add **4** edit **5** amass **6** gather, select **7** arrange, collect, compose, prepare **8** assemble **11** anthologize

compiler: **6** author, editor

complacent: **4** calm, smug **7** fatuous **9** satisfied **11** comfortable **13** self-satisfied

complain: ail, yip **4** beef, carp, fret, fuss, kick, moan, rule, wail, yelp, yirn **5** brawl, croak, croon, gripe, whine **6** bewail, charge, cotter, grieve, grizze, grouse, murmur, repine, yammer **7** deplore, grumble, protest **9** bellyache **11** expostulate

complainant: **5** asker **7** accuser, querent, relator **9** plaintiff

complaining: **9** plaintive, querulous

complaint: ill **6** lament, malady, plaint **7** ailment, disease, illness, protest **8** disorder, gravamen, jeremiad **9** exception, grievance **10** accusation **11** lamentation

complaisant: **4** able, easy, kind **5** buxom, civil, suave **6** polite, smooth, urbane **7** affable, amiable, lenient, willing **8** gracious, obliging, pleasing **9** compliant, courteous, favorable **10** favourable **12** ingratiating

complement: **4** crew, gang **5** force **6** amount **7** adjunct, obverse **10** completion, supplement **11** counterpart **13** accompaniment

complete: all, end **4** dead, deep, fill, full **5** close, every, plumb, quite, ripen, total, utter, whole **6** effect, entire, finish, intact, mature **7** achieve, execute, germane, perfect, plenary, realize **8** absolute, blinking, circular, conclude, fullfill, implicit, thorough **9** implement, surfeited, terminate **10** accomplish, consummate, effectuate **11** unqualified **12** wholehearted

completely: all **5** quite

completeness: **5** depth **9** entelechy

completion: end **6** finish **9** plenitude

complex: **4** hard, mazy **5** mixed **6** knotty **7** network, tangled, twisted **8** involved, manifold, syndrome **9** composite, difficult, entangled, intricate, perplexed **10** interlaced **11** complicated **12** labyrinthine **13** heterogeneous, sophisticated

complexion: hue **4** blee, look, rudd, tint **5** color, humor, state, tenor, tinge **6** aspect, temper **10** appearance

compliance: **7** harmony **8** civility **9** obedience **10** concession, submission **11** application **12** acquiescence, complaisance, tractability

compliant: **4** easy, oily **6** pliant, supple **7** ductile, dutiful, willing **9** indulgent **10** applicable, manageable, obsequious, sequacious **11** complaisant

complicate: **5** mix up **6** intort, muddle, puzzle, tangle **7** confuse, involve, perplex **8** bewilder

complicated: **4** hard **6** knotty, prolix **7** complex, gordian, snarled, tangled **8** involved **9** difficult, elaborate, embroiled, intricate, plexiform **10** disordered

complication: **4** node, plot **5** hitch, nodus, snarl **7** dilemma, problem **9** complexus, confusion, intricacy **10** difficulty, perplexity

compliment: **4** gift, laud **5** extol **6** boquet, eulogy, praise **7** adulate, applaud, bouquet, commend, flatter, tribute **8** encomium, flummery, gratuity **9** adulation, panegyric **12** blandishment, commendation, congratulate

comply

comply: 4 cede, mind, obey 5 abide, adapt, agree, apply, yield 6 accede, accord, assent, enfold, submit 7 conform, embrace, observe 9 acquiesce 11 accommodate

component: 4 item, part, unit 6 factor, member 7 element 8 integral 10 compounder, ingredient 11 constituent

comport: act 4 bear, jibe, suit 5 agree, brook, carry, tally 6 accord, acquit, behave, demean, endure, square 7 conduct 9 behaviour, harmonize 10 correspond, deportment 11 comportance

comportable: 8 suitable 9 endurable, tolerable 10 consistent

comportment: 4 mien 7 conduct, dealing 8 behavior, demeanor 9 behaviour, demeanour 10 deportment

compose: pen, set 4 calm, dite, form, lull, make 5 allay, brief, clerk, dight, order, write 6 accord, adjust, create, design, indite, settle, soothe 7 arrange, compone, concoct, conform, dispose, fashion, produce 8 compound, comprise, comprize, regulate 9 alleviate, construct, formulate 10 constitute 11 tranquilize

compose type: set

composed: 4 calm, cool 5 quiet, sober, wrote 6 demure, placid, sedate, serene 7 written 8 compound, decorous, tranquil 9 collected, composite, unruffled 11 unflappable 13 dispassionate, self-possessed

composer: 4 bard, poet 5 odist 6 author, writer 7 elegist 8 monodist, musician 10 compositor, typesetter

group: 6 Les Six

composition (see also **musical composition**): ana 4 mass, opus, work 5 cento, ditty, drama, essay, paper, piece, poesy, theme 6 accord, lesson, make-up, thesis 7 article, compost, mixture, picture, writing 8 acrostic, compound, fantasia 9 admixture, aggregate, composure, congruity, formation, invention, structure, synthesis 10 adjustment, compendium, composture, confection, manuscript 11 arrangement, combination, compositure, conjunction 12 constitution, construction

art of: 8 rhetoric

for two: 4 duet 6 duetto

literary: 4 book 5 cento, drama, essay, novel, theme 6 satire, thesis 7 tragedy 8 treatise

metrical: 4 poem, rime 5 poesy, rhyme

mournful: 5 dirge, elegy

compositor: 7 caseman, printer 10 type setter

compos mentis: 4 sane 5 lucid 6 normal 11 sound-minded

compost: 4 soil 6 mingle 7 compote, mixture 8 compound 10 fertilizer 11 composition

composure: 4 bond, mien 5 quiet, union 6 repose 7 balance, posture 8 calmness, serenity 9 sangfroid 10 composture, equanimity, sedateness 11 combination, composition, tranquility

compote, compot: 4 bowl 5 fruit 7 dessert

compound: 4 fill, join 5 alloy, blend, ester, unite 6 adjust, jumble, medley, settle 7 amalgam, combine, complex, compone, compose, compost 8 ceromide 9 admixture, aggregate, composite, enclosure 10 amalgamate, commixture, compromise, concoction, confection, constitute, hodgepodge, settlement

alkaline: 4 soda

amorphous: 7 phenose

chemical: 4 amid, amin, azin, imid, imin 5 amide, amine, azine, azola, borid, ceria, ester, imide, imine, osone 6 borids 7 inosite, leucine, metamer 8 chloride

containing double bonds: 5 diene 6 triene

containing two hydroxyl groups: 4 diol

crystalline: 5 aloin, oscin 6 amarin, anisil, phenol 7 tropine

hypnotic: 7 trional

organic: 4 amin 5 amine, ester, ketol 6 ketole, ketone

compound interest: 9 anatocism

comprehend: get, see 4 know 5 grasp, imply, savvy, seize, sense 6 attain, digest, embody, fathom, follow, take in, uptake 7 contain, discern, embrace, enclose, imagine, include, involve, realize 8 comprise, comprize, conceive, conclude, perceive 9 apprehend 10 appreciate, understand

comprehensible: 8 exoteric, included 9 comprised, scrutable 11 conceivable 12 intelligible

comprehension: 4 hold 5 grasp 6 noesis 7 epitome, knowing, summary 9 inclusion, intension 10 conception 11 connotation

comprehensive: big 4 full, wide 5 broad, grand, large 7 concise, generic 8 encyclic, spacious 9 all-around, expansive, extensive, panoramic 11 compendious 12 all-inclusive, encyclopedic

compress: nip, tie 4 bale, bind, firm, wrap 5 cling, cramp, crowd, crush, press 6 gather, shrink 7 abridge, bolster, compact, curtail, deflate, embrace, flatten, repress, squeeze 8 astringe, condense, contract, restrain 9 constrain, epitomize 11 consolidate

medical: 5 stupe 7 bandage, pledget

compressor: 4 pump 6 device 7 machine 9 condenser

comprise, comprize: 4 hold 5 cover, imply, seize 6 attach, confer, embody 7 compose, contain, embrace, enclose, include, involve 8 conceive, perceive 10 comprehend, constitute

comprised: 4 rapt 8 included 9 engrossed 14 comprehensible

compromise: 6 settle 7 concede 8 compound, endanger 9 surrender 10 concession 12 middle ground
opposition to: 13 intransigence

comptroller: 7 auditor, officer 10 controller

compulsion: 4 need, urge 5 force 6 duress, stress 7 impulse 8 coaction, coercion 9 necessity 10 constraint

compulsory: 8 coercive, forcible 10 imperative, obligatory

compulsory service: 5 draft 6 angary 7 angaria, slavery

compunction: 5 qualm 6 regret, sorrow 7 remorse, scruple 9 misgiving 10 conscience, contrition, repentance

compute: add, sum 4 cast, rate 5 count, tally 6 assess, figure, number, reckon 7 account 8 estimate 9 calculate, enumerate

computer: 5 brain, Eniac 6 abacus, univac 7 machine 10 calculator 13 adding machine
bank: 6 memory
character set: 5 ASCII
component: CPU, CRT, VDT 4 chip, disk 5 cable, CD-ROM, modem, mouse 7 monitor 8 keyboard
correct: 5 debug 8 beta test
data: 4 file 6 folder 8 printout, software 9 directory
developer: 4 Jobs 6 Turing 7 Babbage 9 Hollerith 10 Von Neumann
information: 4 data 5 input 6 output
language: Ada 4 LISP, LOGO 5 ALGOL, Basic, COBOL 6 Pascal, PROLOG 7 Fortran, Modula-Z
memory: RAM, ROM 4 bank, card, core 5 board, flash 6 bubble
monitor: EGA, CGA, RGB, VGA 4 SVGA 7 backlit 9 plasma-jet 10 monochrome
operating system: CP/M, DOS, OS2 4 Unix
printer: 5 laser 6 impact, ink-jet 9 dot-matrix 10 daisy-wheel 13 letter-quality
software: 4 game 8 database, graphics 10 integrated 11 spreadsheet 14 communications, word-processing
storage medium: 5 CD-ROM 8 hard disk 9 paper tape, punch card, tape drive 10 floppy disk
term: bit, GUI, key, LAN 4 byte 7 network, program 8 database, hardware, keypunch, kilobyte, megabyte, software, terminal 9 interface 10 file server 11 binary digit 14 microprocessor
type: PC, pen 4 mini 5 micro 6 analog, laptop 7 digital, palmtop 8 notebook, personal 9 Macintosh, mainframe 11 workstation
worker: 10 keyboarder, keypuncher, programmer 13 system analyst

comrade: pal 4 ally, chum, mate, peer 5 billy, buddy, crony 6 copain (F.), digger, fellow, frater, friend, hearty 7 brother 8 copemate 9 associate, companion

comte (F.): 5 count

comtesse (F.): 8 countess

con: rap 4 anti, know, lead, look, pore, read, scan 5 cheat, guide, knock, learn, steer, study 6 direct, peruse, regard, versus 7 against, deceive, examine, inspect, opposed, swindle 10 understand

conation: 4 will 8 tendency, volition 11 inclination

concatenate: 4 join, link 5 chain, unite 7 connect

concave: 4 void 6 arched, dished, hollow 7 bowlike, vaulted 8 incurved 9 depressed

concavity: dip, pit 4 bowl, dent, hole 6 crater, hollow 10 depression

conceal: 4 bury, hide, mask, sile, veil 5 cache, cloak, couch, cover, feign 6 closet, emboss, pocket, screen, shroud 7 secrete 8 bescreen, disguise, ensconce, withhold 9 dissemble 10 camouflage
goods: 5 cache, eloin 6 eloign

concealed: 4 dern (Sc.) 5 blind 6 buried, covert, hidden, latent, occult, perdue, secret, veiled 7 covered, larvate 8 abstruse 9 blindfold, disguised, insidious, recondite, withdrawn 11 clandestine

concealing: 9 designing 10 obvelation

concede: own 4 cede 5 admit, agree, allow, grant, own up, waive, yield 6 accord, assent 7 confess 9 surrender, vouchsafe 10 condescend 11 acknowledge

conceit: ego 4 idea 5 fancy, pride 6 notion, vagary, vanity 7 caprice, egotism, tympany 9 arrogance, conundrum 10 conception, self-esteem 11 swelled head

conceited: bug 4 fess, vain 5 chuff, cocky, flory, huggy, proud 6 clever 8 arrogant, dogmatic, priggish, snobbish 9 pragmatic, whimsical 11 coxcombical, egotistical, opinionated 12 narcissistic

conceive: 4 form, make, plan, ween 5 begin, brain, dream, fancy, frame, think 6 devise, ideate, ponder 7 imagine, realize, suppose, suspect 8 comprise, comprize, contrive 9 apprehend, formulate 10 comprehend, understand

concent: 7 concord, harmony 9 agreement, harmonize 10 accordance 11 consistency

concentrate: aim, fix 4 mass, pile 5 coact, exalt, focus, unify 6 arrest, attend, center, gather 7 compact, essence, thicken 8 approach, assemble, condense, contract 9 intensify 10 centralize 11 consolidate 12 conglomerate

concentration: 7 extract 8 fixation 10 absorption 11 application

concentration camp: 6 prison, stalag

concept: 4 idea 5 fancy, image 7 opinion, thought 11 disposition

conception: ens 4 idea 5 fancy, fetus, image, start 6 belief, design, embryo 7 conceit, purpose 8 notation 9 beginning 10 cogitation, impression 12 apprehension 13 comprehension

conceptual: 5 ideal 8 abstract

concern: 4 bear, care, firm, reck, sake 5 apply, cause, event, grief, touch, worry 6 affair, affect, behold, charge, employ, matter, regard 7 anxiety, article, company, disturb, involve, pertain, respect, trouble 8 business, interest 9 implicate, rickmatic 10 solicitude 11 corporation, distinguish 12 apprehension 13 consideration, establishment

concerned: 6 intent 7 anxious, worried 8 affected, bothered, involved

concerning: for 4 in re 5 about, anent, as for 7 apropos 9 regarding

concert: 4 plan, tune 5 unite 6 accord, chorus, concur, devise 7 arrange, benefit, concent, concord, consort, consult, harmony, recital 9 agreement 11 performance 13 entertainment

concert hall: 5 odeon, odeum 10 auditorium

concertina: 9 accordion, bandonion

concession: 4 boon 5 favor, grant, lease 6 assent, favour, gambit 7 cession 9 admission, allowance, privilege 10 compliance, compromise 12 acquiescence 13 condescension 15 acknowledgement

conch: 5 shell 6 cockle, mussel 7 mollusk

concierge: 6 porter, warden 7 doorman, janitor 9 attendant 10 doorkeeper

conciliate: get 4 calm, ease 5 atone 6 adjust, pacify, soothe 7 acquire, appease, concile, mollify, placate, satisfy 9 reconcile 10 propitiate 11 tranquilize

conciliatory: 4 mild, soft 6 gentle, giving, irenic 7 lenient, pacific, winning 8 irenical, lenitive 9 forgiving 10 mollifying 12 propitiating

concilium: 7 council

concise: 4 curt, neat 5 brief, crisp, pithy, short, terse 7 compact, laconic, pointed, precise, serried 8 mutilate, pregnant, succinct 9 condensed 10 contracted 11 compendious, sententious 12 epigrammatic 13 comprehensive, short and sweet

concision: 6 schism 7 faction 8 division 10 cutting off, mutilation

conclave: 6 closet 7 chamber, meeting 8 assembly 13 secret meeting

conclude: bar, end 4 rest 5 close, estop, infer, judge, limit 6 clinch, deduce, figure, finish, gather, reason, settle, wrap up 7 achieve, arrange, confine, embrace, enclose, resolve, suppose 8 complete, dispatch, graduate, restrain 9 determine, speculate, terminate 10 comprehend

conclusion: end 4 amen, coda, last 5 finis 6 finale, finish, period, result, upshot 7 finding, outcome 8 epilogue, judgment 9 diagnosis, inference 10 conjecture, settlement 11 probability, termination

conclusive: 4 last 5 final, valid 6 cogent 7 certain, extreme, telling 8 decisive, definite, ultimate 10 convincing, peremptory 11 irrefutable 12 unanswerable 13 determinative

concoct: mix 4 brew, cook, fame, plan, plot, vamp 5 hatch 6 decoct, devise, digest, invent, refine, scheme 7 compose, dream up, perfect, prepare 8 compound, intrigue 9 fabricate, originate 10 assimilate

concomitant: 4 mate 6 fellow, joined, linked 7 consort 9 accessory, associate, attendant, attending, companion, conjoined, cooperant 10 associated, coincident, concurrent 11 synchronous 12 accompanying 13 accompaniment, supplementary

concord: 4 pact 5 agree, amity, peace, union, unity 6 treaty, unison 7 compact, concert, consent, harmony, oneness 8 covenant 9 agreement, communion, congruity 10 accordance, consonance

concordant: 8 unisonal 9 agreeable, congruous, consonant 10 harmonious 13 correspondent

concourse: 5 crowd, place, point 6 throng 7 company 8 assembly 9 affluence, frequency, gathering 10 assemblage, confluence 11 coincidence, concurrence, conjunction, cooperation

concrete: 4 clot, firm, hard, knot, mess, real 5 beton, solid, unite 6 actual 7 combine, congeal, special 8 coalesce, compound, solidify, tangible 9 concresce 10 particular
component: 4 sand 5 water 6 gravel
construction: 6 tremie 7 caisson

concretion: 4 clot, mess 5 pearl 6 nodule 8 calculus

concubine: 5 woman 7 adalisk 8 mistress 9 odalisque

concur: 4 jibe, join 5 agree, chime, unite 6 accede, accord, assent 7 approve, combine, consent, go along 8 coincide, converge 9 acquiesce, cooperate 10 correspond

concurrence: 5 union 6 assent, bestow 7 consent, consort, meeting 8 adhesion 9 adherence, agreement, concourse 10 conspiracy 11 coincidence, conjunction

concurrent: 6 coeval, united 7 meeting 10 associated, coincident 11 concomitant, synchronous 12 accompanying, simultaneous

concuss: jar 4 jolt 5 clash, force, shake, shock 6 coerce 7 agitate

condalia: 9 chaparral

condemn: ban 4 damn, doom, file, fine 5 blame, decry, judge 6 amerce, attain, awreak, banish, detest 7 adjudge, censure, convict 8 denounce, reproach, sentence 10 confiscate, disapprove

condemnation: 4 doom 5 blame 7 censure, decrial 11 reprobation 13 animadversion 14 disapprobation

condense: cut 5 brief, unite 6 decoct, digest, harden, lessen, narrow, reduce, shrink 7 abridge, combine, compact, deflate, distill, shorten, thicken 8 compress, diminish, solidify 9 constrict, epitomize, evaporate, intensify 11 concentrate, consolidate

condensed: 4 curt 5 brief 7 compact, concise 8 abridged, absorbed 11 compendious

condenser: 4 cric 6 aludel

condescend: 5 deign, favor, grant, stoop 6 assent, oblige, submit, unbend 7 concede, descend 9 patronize, vouchsafe

condescension: 7 disdain 8 courtesy 10 affability, concession 12 complaisance

condiment (see also **spice**): rea, soy 4 herb, kari, mace, sage, salt 5 caper, curry, salsa, sauce, spice, thyme 6 catsup, cloves, pepper, relish 7 chutney, cuminos, ketchup, mustard, paprika, vinegar 8 allspice, turmeric 9 appetizer, seasoning 10 mayonnaise, piccalilli

container: 5 cruet

stand: 6 caster

condisciple: 7 student 12 schoolfellow

condition: 4 case, mode, rank, rote, term 5 angle, birth, cause, class, estre, facet, place, stage, state 6 estate, fettle, gentry, morale, plight, status 7 article, calling, premise, proviso, station 8 covenant, occasion, position 9 agreement, exception, provision, requisite, situation 10 limitation, sine qua non 11 predicament, stipulation 13 circumstances

critical: 9 emergency

favorable: 4 odds

conditional: 4 iffy 9 qualified, tentative 10 accidental

conditioned: 6 finite 7 limited

condolence: 4 pity, ruth 7 empathy 8 sympathy 10 compassion 13 commiseration

condone: 5 blink, remit 6 acquit, excuse, forget, ignore, pardon 7 absolve, forgive 8 overlook

condor: 4 coin 6 tiffin 7 vulture 8 gymnogyp

conduce: aid 4 help, hire, lead, tend 5 bring, guide 6 confer, effect, engage 7 advance, conduct, further, redound 10 contribute

conduct: act, run 4 bear, deed, gest, lead, mien, rule, wage 5 carry, geste, guard, guide, usher 6 action, attend, behave, convey, convoy, demean, deport, direct, escort, govern, manage, squire 7 bearing, channel, comport, conduce, conduit, control, execute, officer, operate 8 behavior, carriage, chaplain, demeanor, guidance, regulate, transact 9 accompany, behaviour, demeanour, supervise 10 administer, deportment, governance, government, proceeding 11 comportment, countenance, superintend

scandalous: 9 esclandre (F.)

conductor: cad 4 gude 5 guard 6 convoy, copper, escort, leader 7 cathode, maestro 8 aqueduct, cicerone, conveyor, director 10 impresario

stick: 5 baton

conduit: 4 duct, main, pipe, tube, wire 5 cable, canal, sewer 6 trough 7 channel, conduct, culvert, passage 8 aqueduct, pipeline

cone: 4 chat 5 crack, solid, spire 6 bobbin, object 7 cluster, fissure, strobil 8 strobile 9 container

section: 8 parabola

cone-shaped: 5 conic 6 pineal 7 conical

conenose: 6 bedbug

coney: See **cony**

confab: 4 chat, talk 6 powwow 7 prattle 10 conference 11 confabulate 12 conversation

confect: mix 4 form, make 6 pickle 7 prepare 8 preserve 9 construct

confection: 5 candy, dulce, sweet 6 bonbon, cimbal, comfit, dainty, nougat 7 caramel, confect, fondant, mixture, praline, sherbet, succade 8 compound, delicacy, marzipan, preserve, sherbert 9 confiture, marmalade, sweetmeat 10 concoction 11 bittersweet, compilation, composition, preparation

Confederacy: *banknote:* 8 blueback

capital: 8 Richmond

general: Lee 4 Hill, Hood 5 Bragg, Price 6 Morgan 7 Hampton, Jackson, Pickett 10 Beauregard, Longstreet

guerrilla: 11 bushwhacker

president: 5 Davis

soldier: reb

vice-president: 8 Stephens

victory: 7 Bull Run 11 Chickamauga 16 Chancellorsville

confederate: aid, pal, reb 4 ally 5 rebel, stall, unite 6 league 7 abetter, abettor, conjure, fedarie, federal, partner 8 conspire, federate 9 accessory, assistant, associate, auxiliary 10 accomplice 12 collaborator

confederation: 4 band, body 5 union 6 league 7 compact, society 8 alliance, covenant 9 coalition 10 conspiracy, federation 11 association

confer: dub 4 give, meet, talk 5 award,

endow, grant, treat **6** advise, bestow, donate, impart, invest, parley, powwow **7** commune, compare, conduce, consult, counsel, discuss, instate, present **8** comprise, converge **10** contribute, deliberate

conference: rap **4** talk **5** synod, trust **6** confab, huddle, parley, powwow **7** council, meeting, palaver **8** colloque, colloquy, congress **9** collation, comparing, discourse, interview **10** comparison, discussion **11** association **12** consultation, conversation
technique: **13** brainstorming

confess: own **4** avow, sing **5** admit, grant **6** attest, avouch, beknow, recant, reveal, shrive **7** concede, divulge **8** disclose, discover, manifest **11** acknowledge

confession: **5** credo, creed **6** avowal, shrift, shrive **9** admission, communion, statement **10** profession

confetti: **4** tape **5** candy **7** bonbons **9** sweetmeat **10** confection
container: **8** cascaron

confidant: **6** friend **8** intimate

confide: **4** rely, tell **5** trust **6** commit, depend **7** believe, consign, entrust, intrust **8** turn over

confidence: **4** hope **5** bield, faith, trust **6** aplomb, belief, credit, mettle, morale, secret, spirit **7** courage **8** affiance, boldness, credence, reliance, sureness **9** assurance, certitude, hardihood, hardiness **10** effrontery **11** presumption **12** impertinence
game: **4** scam **5** bunco, bunko, sting **7** swindle
lack: **8** insecure **9** diffident **10** diffidence, insecurity

confident: **4** bold, smug, sure **5** hardy, siker **6** crouse, secure, sicker **7** assured, certain, hopeful, reliant **8** constant, fearless, impudent, sanguine, trustful **9** dependent, undaunted **10** dogmatical **11** trustworthy **12** presumptuous **13** self-possessed

confidential: **5** bosom, privy **6** covert, secret **7** private, subrosa **8** esoteric, intimate **9** auricular **11** trustworthy
law: **9** fiduciary

configuration: **4** cast, form **5** shape **6** figure **7** contour, outline **10** topography

confine: bar, box, dam, hem, new, pen, pin, sty, tie **4** bind, cage, coop, hasp, jail, keep, lock, seal **5** bound, cramp, delay, impen, limit, pinch, stint **6** border, corral, fetter, forbar, hamper, hurdle, immure, impale, intern, pinion, pocket, tether **7** astrict, compass, impound **8** boundary, conclude, imprison, restrain, straiten **9** carcerate, constrain, restraint **11** incarcerate **12** circumscribe

confined: ill **4** pent **5** bound, caged **6** sealed **7** cramped, cribbed, limited **8** impended, interned **9** impounded **10** cloistered **13** incommunicado
to select group: **8** esoteric

confinement: mew **7** lying-in **8** clausure, firmance **9** captivity, restraint **10** childbirth, constraint, internment **11** contraction **12** accouchement, imprisonment
place of: mew, pen **4** brig, cage, coop, goal, jail, stir **5** limbo **6** asylum, corral, prison **7** dungeon **9** calaboose **12** penitentiary

confirm: fix, set **4** firm, seal **5** prove **6** affirm, assent, assure, attest, avouch, clinch, ratify, settle, verify **7** approve, comfort, endorse, fortify, sustain **8** accredit, convince, sanction, validate **9** approbate, establish **10** comprobate, strengthen **11** corroborate, countersign **12** adminiculate, authenticate, substantiate

confirmed: set **5** fixed **6** arrant, stable **7** chronic **8** habitual, ratified **9** fortified, initiated **10** encouraged, inveterate **11** established

confiscate: **4** grab **5** seize, usurp **7** condemn, preempt **8** arrogate **9** sequester **11** appropriate

conflagration: **4** fire **5** blaze, fever **7** burning, inferno **9** holocaust **10** combustion **12** inflammation

conflict: war **4** bout, duel, fray, rift **5** broil, brush, clash, fight, grips, mix-up **6** action, battle, combat, mutiny, oppose, strife **7** contend, contest, discord, warfare **8** disagree, militate, struggle, tug-of-war **9** collision, encounter, rebellion **10** contention **11** competition, controversy
final: **10** Armageddon

conflicting: **7** adverse, warring **8** clashing **10** contending **12** incompatible, inharmonious

confluence: **5** crowd **7** conflux, meeting **8** junction **9** concourse **12** assimilation

conform: fit **4** lean, obey, suit **5** adapt, agree, apply, yield **6** accede, adjust, assent, comply, settle, submit **7** compose **9** acquiesce, harmonize, reconcile **10** correspond **11** accommodate

conformist: **6** pedant **7** babbitt **9** precisian **10** philistine **11** reactionary

conformity: **7** decorum, harmony **8** affinity, likeness, symmetry **9** agreement, congruity, obedience **10** accordance, compliance, similarity, submission **11** affirmative **12** acquiescence, complaisance
to law: **6** dharma **8** legality

confound: mix **4** blow, dash, maze, rout, stam, stun **5** abash, addle, amaze, spend, spoil, waste **6** baffle, dismay, muddle, rattle **7** astound, confuse, confute, corrupt, destroy, flummox, perplex, stupefy **8** astonish, bewilder, distract, surprise **9** discomfit, dumbfound, embarrass, frustrate, overthrow **10** disconcert **11** intermingle

confraternity: **4** body **5** union **7** society **11** brotherhood

confrere: **6** fellow **7** comrade **9** colleague

confront: **4** defy, face, meet **5** beard, brave **6** oppose, resist **7** affront, compare **8** envisage, face up to, threaten **9** challenge, encounter

confuse: mix **4** dash, daze, maze, muss, rout **5** abash, addle, amaze, befog, blend, cloud, snarl **6** baffle, bemuse, bother, burble, caddle, flurry, fuddle, jumble, muddle, puzzle, rattle **7** bedevil, blunder, derange, fluster, mystify, nonplus, perplex, stupefy **8** befuddle, bewilder, confound, distract **9** barbulyie, discomfit, dumbfound, obfuscate **10** demoralize, disarrange, discompose, disconcert

confused: **4** asea, lost **5** foggy, muddy, vague **6** doiled, doited **7** chaotic, mixed up, obscure **8** deranged **9** chagrined **10** bewildered, hurly-burly, topsy-turvy, tumultuous **13** helter-skelter

confusion: din **4** coil, dust, fuss, harl, mess, moil, riot **5** babel, chaos, chevy, chivy, deray, mix-up, snafu, snarl, strow **6** babble, bedlam, caddle, chivvy, habble, hubbub, huddle, jabble, jumble, muddle, pother, rabble, rumpus, tophet, tumult, uproar, welter **7** blunder, bluster, clutter, farrage, flutter, garboil, topheth, turmoil, widdrim **8** disarray, disorder **9** agitation, commotion **10** hullabaloo, hurly-burly **11** disturbance, trepidation **12** hugger-mugger, perturbation, razzle-dazzle **13** embarrassment

confute: **4** deny **5** rebut **6** expose, refute **7** silence **8** confound, convince, disprove, infringe, overcome **9** overwhelm

conge: bow **5** adieu **6** curtsy **7** license, molding **8** farewell, passport **9** clearance, dismissal **10** permission **11** leave-taking

congeal: gel, ice, set **4** jell **5** candy **6** cotter, curdle, freeze, harden **7** stiffen, thicken **8** concrete, solidify **9** coagulate **10** gelatinize **11** crystallize

congealing agent: **6** pectin **8** gelatine

congee: **9** departure **11** leave-taking

congener: **4** kind, race **5** class, genus

congenial: **4** boon **5** natal **6** native **7** connate, kindred **10** compatible **11** sympathetic

conger: eel **4** pike

congeries: **4** mass, ruck **5** group **6** muster **8** assembly **9** gathering **10** collection

congestion: jam **4** heap **8** crowding, stoppage **9** gathering **12** accumulation

conglobation: **4** ball

conglomerate: **4** heap, mass, pile, rock **5** stack **6** cartel **7** combine **9** clustered **10** assemblage **11** agglomerate **12** concentrated

Congo: *capital:* **11** Brazzaville
currency: **5** franc **7** centime

Congo River: *tributary:* **4** Uele **6** Ubangi **7** Aruwima

congou: tea

congratulate: **4** laud **5** greet **6** salute **8** macarize **10** compliment, felicitate

congregate: **4** herd, mass, meet, teem **5** group, swarm, troop **6** gather, muster **7** collect, convene **8** assemble

congregation: **4** body, fold, host, mass **5** flock, swarm **6** church, parish **7** meeting, synaxes **8** assembly, brethren **9** gathering **10** collection **11** convocation

congress: **4** dail, diet **5** synod **7** council, meeting **8** assembly, conclave **10** conference, convention, parliament **11** convocation, legislature

Congress: *building:* **7** Capitol
member: **7** senator **14** representative
upper house: **6** Senate

congruity: **6** accord **7** concord, fitness, harmony **8** symmetry **9** agreement, coherence **10** conformity, consonance **11** composition, consistency, correctness, suitability **13** compatibility **14** correspondence

conical: **8** tapering

conifer: fir, yew **4** pine, tree **5** cedar, larch, pinon **6** spruce **7** cypress, hemlock, juniper, pinacle, pinales, redwood, sequoia **10** arborvitae

conium: **7** hemlock

conjecture: aim **4** plot, shot, view **5** augur, ettle, fancy, guess, opine **6** belief, divine, theory **7** imagine, opinion, presume, suppose, surmise, suspect **9** inference, speculate, suspicion **10** conclusion, estimation **11** contrivance, speculation, supposition

conjoined: wed **6** joined, linked, united **7** related **8** conjunct, touching **11** concomitant

conjoint: **6** mutual, shared **8** combined **9** conjoined **10** associated **11** correlative **12** simultaneous

conjugal: **6** wedded **7** marital, nuptial **9** connubial **11** matrimonial

conjugate: **5** yoked **6** joined, united **7** coupled, display, inflect

conjunction: and, but, nor, tie **4** than **5** joint, since, union **6** either, hookup **7** coition, consort, neither **9** coalition, concourse **10** connection **11** association, combination, composition, concurrence

conjuration: art **4** rune **5** charm, magic, spell, trick **6** voodoo **10** necromancy **11** incantation, legerdemain

conjure: beg **4** pray **5** charm, crave, halse **6** adjure, invent, invoke **7** beseech, combine, entreat, imagine **8** conspire, contrive, exorcise, exorcize **9** importune **10** supplicate **11** confederate

conjuror: **4** mage, sear **5** Circe **6** merlin, pellar, shaman, wizard **7** juggler, warlock **8** magician, sorcerer **9** coswearer, enchanter **15** prestidigitator

conk: die, hit **4** fail, head, nose, swat **5** faint, knock, stall **7** decease **8** pass away

Conlaech: *father:* **10** Cuchulainn
mother: **5** Aoife

connate: **4** akin, born **5** fused **6** allied, inborn, innate **7** cognate, kindred, related **9** congenial **10** congenital, deep-seated

connect: tie, wed **4** ally, bind, glue, join, knit, link **5** affix, chain, marry, unite **6** attach, bridge, cement, cohere, connex, couple, fasten, relate **7** combine **8** continue **9** affiliate, associate, correlate, interlock **11** communicate

---

Connecticut: *capital:* **8** Hartford
city: **4** Avon **6** Bethel, Darien, Groton **7** Meriden, Norwalk **8** New Haven, Stamford **9** Greenwich, New London, Waterbury **10** Bridgeport
motto: **21** Qui Transtulit Sustinet (He Who Transplanted Still Sustains)
river: **6** Thames **10** Housatonic
state bird: **5** robin
state flower: **14** mountain laurel
state tree: oak

---

connection: tie **4** bond, link **5** nexus, union **6** family **7** contact, kinship **8** affinity, alliance, commerce, intimacy, junction, relative, syndetic **9** coherence, reference, relevance **10** catenation, continuity **11** affiliation, association, conjunction, intercourse **12** articulation, relationship **13** communication

connective: and, nor **6** either **7** neither **8** syndetic **11** conjunction

connective tissue: **6** fascia

conniption fit: **7** tantrum

connive: **4** abet, plot, wink **5** blink, cabal **6** assent, foment, incite, scheme **7** collude **8** intrigue, overlook **9** machinate

connoisseur: **5** judge **6** critic, expert **7** epicure, gourmet **8** gourmand **9** collector **11** cognoscente

connotation: **4** hint **6** intent **7** meaning **10** denotation **13** comprehension, signification

connote: **5** imply **7** add up to **8** indicate

connubial: **6** wedded **7** marital **8** conjugal, domestic **11** matrimonial

conquer: get, win **4** beat, best, down, gain, lick, rout, tame **5** crush, daunt **6** defeat, evince, humble, master, reduce, subdue, victor **7** acquire, prevail, subject, triumph **8** overcome, surmount, vanquish **9** checkmate, discomfit, overpower, overthrow, overwhelm, subjugate

conqueror: **4** hero **6** victor, winner **7** William **12** conquistador

conquest: **7** mastery, triumph, victory

conquistador: **6** Cortez **9** conqueror

consanguineous: **4** akin **6** carnal **7** kindred, related

consanguinity: **5** blood, nasab **7** kinship **8** affinity **12** relationship

conscience: **5** grace, heart, inwit, qualm, sense **6** erinys, psyche, virtue **7** monitor, probity, scruple, thought **9** casuistry, punctilio **11** compunction

conscienceless: **6** amoral, shifty, tricky, unfair **7** devious **12** unprincipled

conscientious: **4** fair, just **5** exact, rigid **6** honest, strict **7** dutiful, upright **8** faithful **9** honorable **10** scrupulous **11** punctilious

conscious: **4** keen **5** alive, awake, aware **7** feeling, knowing **8** rational, sensible, sentient **9** attentive, cognizant, concerned **10** perceptive **12** apprehensive

consciousness: **9** awareness
loss of: **4** coma **5** faint **8** apoplexy

consciousness-altering: **11** psychedelic

conscript: **5** draft, enrol **6** enlist, muster **7** recruit

consecrate: vow **4** fain, seal **5** bless, deify **6** anoint, devote, hallow, ordain **8** dedicate, sanctify **10** inaugurate **11** apotheosize

consecrated: **4** holy **5** blest **6** oblate, sacred, votive **7** blessed **8** hallowed
cloth: **11** antimension
oil: **6** chrism
thing: **6** sacrum

consent: let **5** agree, allow, grant, yield **6** accede, accord, assent, beteem, comply, permit **7** approve **9** recognize **10** permission **11** concurrence **12** acquiescence **13** authorization

consequence: end **4** bore **5** event, fruit, issue, worth **6** effect, import, moment, repute, result, sequel, weight **7** concern, outcome **8** aftering, interest, occasion **9** aftermath, emanation, inference **10** importance **11** aftereffect, consecution **13** consideration

consequently: **4** ergo, then, thus **5** hence, later **8** pursuant **9** therefore **11** accordingly **12** subsequently **13** consecutively

conservative: **4** safe, Tory **5** staid **6** stable **7** diehard **8** moderate, old-liner **9** bourgeois

11 reactionary, right-winger **12** preservative

conservatory: **6** school **7** academy **10** glasshouse, greenhouse

conserve: can, jam **4** save **5** guard, jelly **6** defend, keep up, secure, shield, uphold **7** husband, protect, sustain **8** maintain, preserve **9** confiture, sweetmeat

consider: see **4** deem, heed, mull, muse, rate **5** ettle, judge, study, think, weigh **6** behold, debate, expend, impute, ponder, reason, reckon, regard **7** account, believe, canvass, examine, inspect, reflect, suppose **8** cogitate, estimate, look upon, meditate, ruminate **9** calculate, entertain, speculate **10** adjudicate, deliberate, think about **11** contemplate

considerable: **5** geyan (Sc.), large, smart **7** notable, several **9** capacious, important **10** cognizable, noteworthy, remarkable **11** perceptible, significant

considerate: **4** kind, mild **6** gentle **7** careful, heedful, prudent, serious **8** delicate **9** attentive, observant, regardful **10** deliberate, reflective, respectful, thoughtful **11** sympathetic, warm-hearted

consideration: **4** sake **5** price, topic **6** aspect, esteem, motive, notice, reason, regard **7** respect, thought **9** attention, deference, incentive, influence **10** importance, inducement, recompense, reputation **11** consequence

considering: for **5** since **6** seeing

consign: **4** doom, give, mail, send, ship **5** allot, award, dight, remit, shift, yield **6** assign, commit, devote, remand, resign **7** address, confide, deliver, deposit, entrust, intrust **8** delegate, relegate, transfer, turn over **9** recommend **10** commission

consignee: **5** agent **8** receiver

consist: lie **4** hold **5** exist, stand **6** inhere, reside **7** contain, embrace **8** comprise, dovetail **9** harmonize

consistency: **4** body **5** union **6** degree **7** concord, harmony **8** firmness, solidity, symmetry **9** adherence, coherence, congruity **10** consonance, uniformity **11** composition, persistency **14** correspondence, substantiality

consistent: **4** firm **7** durable, logical, uniform **8** coherent, enduring, suitable **9** accordant, congruous, consonant, unfailing, unvarying **10** changeless, compatible, persisting

consociate: **9** associate **11** confederate

consolation: sop **4** fine **6** relief, solace **7** comfort **10** booby prize

console: **4** calm **5** allay, ancon, cheer, organ, table **6** buck up, solace, soothe **7** bracket, cabinet, comfort, relieve, support, sustain **9** alleviate, encourage

consolidate: mix **4** fuse, knit, mass, pool, weld **5** blend, merge, unify, unite **6** harden, mingle **7** combine, compact **8** coalesce, compress, condense, organize, solidify **10** amalgamate, strengthen **11** concentrate

consomme: **4** soup

consonance: **6** accord **7** harmony **9** agreement, resonance

consonant: **6** dental, fortis, letter, sonant **7** palatal, phoneme, spirant, unified **8** harmonic, in accord, suitable **9** accordant, agreeable, congruous **10** coincident, compatible, concordant, consistent, harmonious
hard: **6** fortis
hissing: **8** sibilant
smooth: **4** lene **5** lenis
voiceless: **4** lene, surd **6** atonic **7** spirate

consort: cot **4** aide, ally, join, mate, wife **5** agree, group, tally, unite **6** accord, attend, escort, mingle, spouse **7** company, concert, husband, partner **8** accustom, assembly **9** accompany, associate, colleague, companion, forgather **10** foregather **11** association, combination, concurrence, conjunction

consortium: **5** group, guild, order, union **6** cartel **8** alliance, congress

conspectus: **4** list **5** brief **6** survey **7** outline **8** synopsis **11** abridgement

conspicuous: **5** clear, famed, plain **6** extant, famous, marked, patent, signal **7** eminent, glaring, notable, obvious, pointed, salient, visible **8** apparent, manifest, striking **9** egregious, prominent **10** celebrated, noticeable **11** discernible, distinctive, illustrious, outstanding, perspicuous **13** distinguished

conspiracy: **4** coup, plan, plot, ring **5** cabal, covin, junto **6** scheme **7** compact **8** intrigue **9** agreement, champerty **11** combination, concurrence, confederacy, machination

conspire: **4** abet, plot **5** unite **6** league, scheme **7** collude, complot, conjure **8** contrive **9** cooperate **11** confederate

constable: cop **4** bull **5** bobby **6** beadle, harman, keeper, police, warden **7** bailiff, officer **8** tipstaff **9** policeman **13** police officer

constancy: **4** zeal **5** ardor **6** fealty **7** loyalty **8** devotion, fidelity **9** adherence, diligence, eagerness, integrity, stability **10** allegiance, attachment **11** earnestness **12** perseverance
symbol of: **6** garnet

constant: set **4** even, fast, firm, leal, true **5** fixed, loyal, solid, still, tried **6** stable, steady **7** certain, chronic, durable, forever, lasting, regular, staunch, uniform **8** enduring, faithful, positive, resolute **9** confident, continual, immovable, incessant, permanent, perpetual, steadfast, unvarying **10** consistent, continuous, invariable, persistent, unwavering

Constantine: *birthplace:* 4 Nish 6 Naissa
mother: 6 Helena
son: 7 Crispus
victim: 6 Fausta 7 Crispus
wife: 6 Fausta

Constantinople: See **Istanbul**

constantly: 4 ever 6 always 10 invariably 11 perpetually 12 continuously

constate: 6 assert 9 establish

constellation: 5 group 6 dipper 7 cluster, pattern 10 assemblage 13 configuration
altar: Ara
archer: 11 Sagittarius
Argo division: 4 Vela
arrow: 7 Sagitta
balance: 5 Libra
Big Dipper: 9 Ursa Major
bird of paradise: 4 Apus
bull: 6 Taurus
Champion: 7 Perseus
charioteer: 6 Auriga
Charles' Wain: 6 Dipper
clock: 10 Horologium
compass: 5 Pyxis 8 Circinus
crab: 6 Cancer
crane: 4 Grus
cross: 4 Cruz
crow: 6 Corvus
crown: 6 Corona
dog: 5 Canis
dolphin: 9 Delphinus
dove: 7 Columba
dragon: 5 Draco
eagle: 6 Aquila
fish: 6 Pisces
goat: 9 Capricorn
herdsman: 6 Bootes
hunter: 5 Orion
lady in the chair: 10 Cassiopeia
lady, chained: 9 Andromeda
lion: Leo
Little Dipper: 9 Ursa Minor
lyre: 4 Lyra
maiden: 5 Virgo
northern: Leo 4 Coma, Lynx, Lyra, Ursa 5 Aries, Canes, Draco 6 Aquila, Auriga, Bootes, Cancer, Cygnus, Gemini, Taurus 7 Cepheus, Lacerta, Pegasus, Sagitta 8 Hercules 9 Andromeda, Delphinus, Vulpecula 10 Cassiopeia
peacock: 4 Pavo
rabbit: 5 Lepus
ram: 5 Aries
sails: 4 Vela
southern: Ara 4 Apus, Argo, Crux, Grus, Pavo, Vela 5 Canis, Cetus, Hydra, Indus, Lepus, Libra, Mensa, Musca, Norma, Virgo

6 Antlia, Carina, Corvus, Crater, Dorado, Fornax, Pictor, Pisces, Puppis, Tucana, Volans 7 Columba, Phoenix, Sextans 8 Aquarius, Circinus, Scorpius, Sculptor 9 Centaurus, Chameleon, Monoceros, Reticulum 10 Horologium 11 Capricornus, Sagittarius 12 Microscopium
stern: 6 Puppis
swan: 6 Cygnus
twins: 6 Gemini
water bearer: 8 Aquarius
whale: 5 Cetus
winged horse: 7 Pegasus
wolf: 5 Lupus

consternation: 4 fear 5 alarm, dread, panic 6 dismay, fright, horror, terror 9 amazement, confusion, trepidity 11 distraction, trepidation 12 befuddlement

constituent: 4 item, part 5 piece, voter 6 detail, factor, matter, member 7 elector, element 9 component 10 ingredient

constitute: fix, set 4 form, make 5 enact, forge, found, set up, shape 6 depute, graith, ordain 7 appoint, compose, station 8 compound, comprise 9 determine, establish 10 commission

constitution: law 4 code 5 being, canon, humor, state 6 custom, health, nature, temper 7 charter 8 physique 9 enactment, ordinance, structure 11 composition, disposition 12 organization 13 establishment

constitutional: 4 walk 6 inborn, innate 8 exercise 9 essential, organical 10 congenital, deep-seated

Constitution State: 11 Connecticut

Constitution, U.S.S.: 12 Old Ironsides

constrain: 4 bend, bind, curb, fain, urge 5 chain, check, clasp, cramp, deter, drive, force, impel, limit, press 6 coerce, compel, hold in, oblige, ravish, secure 7 astrict, confine, enforce, oppress, repress, violate 8 compress, distress, hold down, restrain 9 constrict 10 constringe 11 necessitate

constraint: 4 bond 5 force 6 duress, stress 7 reserve 8 coercion, distress, pressure 9 captivity, restraint, stiffness 10 compulsion, obligation 11 compression, confinement

constrict: tie 4 bind, curb, grip 5 choke, cramp, limit 6 hamper, shrink, strait 7 astrict, deflate, squeeze, tighten 8 astringe, compress, condense, contract, restrict 9 constrain 10 constipate, constringe
breath: 8 strangle

constrictor: boa 5 snake 6 muscle, python 8 anaconda 9 sphincter, strangler

construct: 4 form, make, rear 5 build, dight, erect, frame, model, set up 6 devise 7 arrange, combine, compose, confect, fashion **8** construe, engineer **9** fabricate, originate **11** put together

construction: **6** design, makeup **7** synesis **8** building, erection

constructive: **7** helpful **8** creative, implicit, inferred

construe: **5** infer, parse **6** render **7** analyze, dissect, explain, expound, resolve **8** spell out **9** construct, interpret, translate

consuetude: use **4** wont **5** habit, usage **6** custom **8** practice

consul's recognition: **9** exequatur

consult: ask **5** cabal, refer **6** advise, confer, decree, devise **7** concert, counsel, discuss, meeting **8** consider, contrive, decision **9** agreement, determine **10** deliberate

consultant: **6** expert **7** adviser, counsel

consultation: **6** advice **7** council, counsel **9** collation, interview **10** conference, discussion **12** deliberation

consume: eat, use **4** burn, fret, rust, wear **5** drink, raven, spend, use up, waste **6** absorb, absume, bezzle, canker, devour, engage, expend, feed on, perish **7** corrode, destroy, dwindle, engross, exhaust, swallow **8** gobble up, squander **9** dissipate **10** incinerate, monopolize

consumer: **4** usee, user **5** buyer

consummate: end **4** fine, full, ripe **5** ideal, sheer, utter **6** arrant, effect, finish, wind up, wrap up **7** achieve, consume, crowned, perfect, perform **8** absolute, complete **9** culminate, exquisite, out-and-out **10** accomplish

consumption: use **5** decay, waste **7** expense **8** phthisis **11** destruction, expenditure, white plague **12** tuberculosis

contact: **4** abut, join, meet **5** touch, union **6** arrive, impact, syzygy **7** meeting, rapport, taction **8** junction, tangency, touching **10** connection, contiguity **11** contingency **13** juxtaposition

contagion: pox **5** taint, virus **6** miasma, poison **7** disease **9** infection **13** contamination
preventative: **4** shot **7** vaccine **8** antidote **10** alexiteric **11** prophylaxis

contagious: **7** noxious **8** catching **9** pestilent, spreading **10** infectious **12** communicable

contain: **4** have, hold, keep **5** carry, check, cover, house **6** embody, retain, take in **7** embrace, enclose, include, subsume, sustain **8** comprise, restrain **10** comprehend, simmer down

container: bag, bin, box, can, cup, jug, keg, pan, pod, pot, tin, tub, urn, vat **4** cage, case, cask, crib, ewer, sack, silo, tank, vase **5** crate, cruet, gourd, pouch **6** barrel, basket, bottle, carboy, carton, hamper, hatbox, holder, shaker **7** bandbox, capsule, hanaper, inkwell **8** canister, decanter, demijohn, hogshead, puncheon **10** receptacle

containing: For all phrases beginning with this word, see under the main word or phrase. EXAMPLE "containing air": see **air:** *containing.*

contaminate: **4** foul, harm, slur, soil **5** stain, sully, taint **6** befoul, debase, defile, infect, injure, poison **7** corrupt, debauch, pollute, tarnish, vitiate **8** dishonor **9** desecrate **10** adulterate

conte (F.): **4** tale **5** story **9** narrative, novelette

conte (It.): **5** count

contemn: **4** hate **5** flout, scorn, spurn **6** reject, slight **7** despise, disdain **8** contempt, look down

contemplate: **4** muse, plan, scan, view **5** deign, study, think, weigh **6** look at, ponder, regard, survey **7** propose, reflect **8** consider, meditate **9** speculate, think over

contemplation: **5** study **6** musing, prayer, regard, theory **7** request **8** petition **9** intention **10** meditation **11** speculation **12** deliberation **13** consideration

contemporaneous: **6** coeval, living, modern **7** current **8** existing, up-to-date **10** coincident **12** contemporary, simultaneous

contemporary: **6** coeval **7** current **10** coexistent, concurrent **12** simultaneous

contempt: **5** scorn, shame, sneer **6** slight **7** contemn, disdain, mockery **8** derision, disgrace **9** contumacy, contumely **10** disrespect **11** indignation

contemptible: low **4** base, mean, vile **5** cheap, petty, sorry **6** abject, paltry, scurvy, shabby, sordid, yellow **7** pitiful, scorned **8** beggarly, infamous, inferior, sneaking, unworthy, wretched **9** groveling, worthless **10** despicable **11** ignominious **12** dishonorable **13** insignificant

contemptuous: **7** haughty **8** arrogant, flouting, insolent, scornful **9** hubristic, insulting **10** despicable, disdainful **12** contemptible, supercilious

contend: say, vie, war **4** cope, race, wage **5** argue, bandy, brawl, claim, fight **6** assert, battle, bicker, buffet, bustle, combat, debate, oppose, reason, strive **7** bargain, compete, contest, dispute, quarrel **8** conflict, contrive, cope with, maintain, militate, squabble, struggle

contender: **7** entrant **10** contestant **11** protagonist

content: **4** calm, ease, gist, paid **5** happy **6** amount, at ease, please **7** appease, gratify, replete, satiate, satisfy, suffice, willing **8** capacity **9** satisfied **12** satisfaction

contented: **4** cozy **5** sated **8** cheerful **9** satisfied

contention: war **4** bait, bate, feud, riot, tiff **5** broil **6** combat, debate, strife **7** contest, discord, dispute, opinion, quarrel, rivalry, wrangle **8** argument, conflict, squabble, struggle, variance **9** rebellion **10** dissension, litigation **11** altercation, competition, controversy **12** disagreement

contentious: **7** carping, peevish **8** perverse **9** bellicose, litigious, wrangling **10** pugnacious **11** belligerent, quarrelsome **12** cantankerous, disputatious

contentment: **4** ease **5** bliss **8** pleasure **9** happiness **11** complacence **12** satisfaction **13** gratification

conterminous: **4** next **8** adjacent, proximal, touching **9** adjoining, bordering

contest: bee, sue, try, vie **4** agon, bout, cope, duel, feud, fray, game, pitt, race, spar, tiff, tilt **5** broil, clash, fight, set-to, trial **6** action, adjure, affray, battle, combat, debate, defend, oppose, resist, strife, strive **7** bargain, brabble, compete, contend, dispute, protest, tourney, warfare **8** argument, conflict, skirmish, struggle, tug-of-war **9** champerty, encounter **10** controvert, tournament **11** altercation
kind of: **6** tryout **7** lawsuit **10** litigation
narrowly won: **8** squeaker

contestant: **4** vier **5** rival **6** player **7** agonist, entrant **8** finalist, prospect **9** candidate, combatant, contender, defendant, plaintiff **10** competitor **12** participator

contiguous: **4** next, nigh **6** nearby **7** close by **8** abutting, adjacent, touching **9** adjoining, immediate, proximate **10** contacting, near-at-hand **11** neighboring

continence: **6** virtue **8** chastity, sobriety **10** abstinence, moderation, temperance **13** self-restraint

continent: **4** Asia, land, mass **5** sober **6** Africa, chaste, Europe **7** content **8** capacity, mainland, moderate **9** Australia, temperate **10** Antarctica, controlled, restrained **12** North America, South America
hypothetical: **7** Pangaea **8** Cascadia, Laurasia **12** Gondwanaland
lost: **8** Atlantis

contingency: **4** case **5** event **6** chance **7** adjunct, contact **8** fortuity, incident, prospect **9** accessory, emergency **10** crossroads **11** possibility, uncertainty

contingent: **6** casual, chance **8** doubtful, touching **9** dependent **10** accidental, fortuitous **11** provisional

continual: **7** endless, lasting, regular, undying, uniform **8** constant, enduring, unbroken **9** ceaseless, connected, incessant, perennial, permanent, unceasing **10** continuous, invariable **11** everlasting, unremitting **12** imperishable **13** unintermitted, uninterrupted

continually: aye **4** ever **6** always, hourly,

steady **7** endless, eternal, forever **9** perpetual **10** constantly **11** incessantly, unceasingly

continuance: **4** stay **5** delay **6** sequel **8** duration **9** endurance, procedure **10** continuity **11** adjournment **12** perseverance, postponement

continue: be **4** bide, dure, go on, last, live, stay **5** abide, carry, exist, unite **6** beleve, endure, extend, remain, resume, take up **7** beleave, carry on, connect, persist, proceed, prolong, sustain **8** protract **9** persevere

continued: **5** still **6** serial **7** chronic **8** constant **9** extending **10** protracted

continuity: **6** script **8** cohesion, scenario **9** coherence **10** connection

contort: wry **4** bend, coil, turn, warp **5** gnarl, screw, twist, wrest **6** deform, writhe **7** distort, pervert **8** obvolute **9** convolute

contortionist: **7** acrobat

contour: **4** form, line **5** curve, graph, shape **6** figure **7** outline, profile **9** lineament **10** appearance, silhouette **13** configuration

contra: **6** offset **7** against, counter, opposed **8** opposite **9** opposed to, vice versa **11** contrasting **12** contrariwise

contraband: **6** banned **7** illegal, illicit **8** hot goods, smuggled, unlawful

contract: get **4** bond, knit, pact **5** agree, catch, cramp, incur, lease, limit **6** cartel, engage, lessen, narrow, pledge, pucker, reduce, shrink, treaty **7** abridge, bargain, compact, crumple, curtail, promise, shorten, shrivel, wrinkle **8** condense, covenant, restrict **9** agreement, betrothal, constrict, indenture **10** abbreviate, constringe, convention, obligation, sicken with **11** arrangement, concentrate, stipulation **12** come down with
addition to: **5** rider **7** codicil **9** amendment
furnishing slaves: **8** assiento
maritime: **8** bottomry
part: **6** clause **7** article, proviso
unlawful: **10** chevisance

contraction: tic **5** cramp, spasm **6** intake, twitch **7** elision, epitome **9** gathering, reduction, shrinkage, stricture **10** abridgment, compendium, limitation **11** conciseness, confinement **12** abbreviation
common: een, eer, oer, oft, tis **5** arent, shant
heart: **8** systolic

contractor: **7** builder, remover **8** supplier

contradict: **4** deny **5** belie, rebut **6** forbid, impugn, negate, oppose, recant, refute **7** counter, dispute, gainsay **8** disprove **9** disaffirm **10** contravene, controvert

contradiction: **6** denial **7** paradox **8** antilogy, negation **10** gainsaying

contradictory: **6** oppose **8** antipode, contrary **9** dissonant **12** incompatible, inconsistent

contraption: rig 4 tool 6 device, gadget 7 machine 11 contrivance

contrary: 5 balky, polar, snivy 6 averse, contra, ornery, snivey 7 adverse, counter, hostile, opposed, reverse, wayward 8 captious, contrair, inimical, opposite, perverse, petulant 9 repugnant, unpopular, vexatious 10 discordant, discrepant, refractory 11 prejudicial, unfavorable 12 antagonistic, cantankerous, cross-grained 13 insubordinate
to fact: 5 false
to law: 7 illegal 16 unconstitutional
to reason: 6 absurd

contrast: 6 strife 7 compare, contend 8 opposite 9 diversity 10 difference, divergence

contravene: 4 defy, deny 6 hinder, oppose, thwart 7 dispute, violate 8 infringe, obstruct 9 disregard, repudiate 10 contradict, transgress

contravention: sin 4 vice 5 crime 6 breach 7 offense 9 violation 13 contradiction, transgression

contretemps: 4 slip 5 boner, hitch 6 mishap, scrape 8 accident 9 mischance 10 occurrence
music: 11 syncopation

contribute: aid 4 ante, give, help, tend 5 cause, grout 6 assist, bestow, chip in, concur, confer, donate, supply, tender 7 conduce, further, pitch in 9 cooperate, subscribe

contribution: sum, tax 4 alms, boon, gift 5 essay, share 6 impost 7 article, largess, payment, present, renewal, writing 8 donation, offering 9 collation 10 imposition

contrite: 4 worn 5 sorry 6 humble, rueful 8 penitent 9 repentant, sorrowful 10 apologetic, remorseful

contrition: 7 penance, remorse

contrivance: art, gin 4 gear, plan, tool 5 shift 6 deceit, design, device, gadget, scheme 7 fiction, machine, project 8 adaption, artifice, resource 9 apparatus, appliance, doohickey, invention 10 conjecture, instrument 11 contraption

contrive: 4 brew, make, plan, plot 5 frame, fudge, hatch, weave 6 afford, design, devise, divine, invent, make up, manage, scheme, wangle 7 achieve, agitate, concoct, consult, contend, dream up, fashion, procure, project, work out 8 conspire, engineer, intrigue 9 fabricate, machinate 10 accomplish

contrived: pat 5 hokey 10 artificial

contriver: 8 Daedalus 9 architect 10 originator

control: law, run 4 curb, hold, rein, rule, sway 5 charm, check, grasp, gripe, guide, power, skill, steer 6 bridle, direct, empire, govern, handle, manage, regime, subdue 7 command, conduct, mastery, preside 8 attemper, dominate, dominion, hegemony, regulate, restrain 9 influence, ordinance, prescribe 10 ascendancy, discipline, domination, manipulate, moderation, possession, regulation 11 predominate, superintend 12 jurisdiction

controversial: 7 eristic 9 debatable, polemical 12 disputatious 13 argumentative

controversy: row 4 spat, suit, tiff 5 chest 6 debate, strife 7 dispute, quarrel, wrangle 8 argument 10 contention, difference, difficulty, discussion, falling-out, litigation 11 altercation 12 disagreement

controvert: 4 deny, face, moot 5 argue 6 debate, oppose, oppugn, refute 7 contest, dispute, gainsay 9 challenge 10 contradict

contumacious: 6 unruly 7 riotous 8 insolent, mutinous, perverse, stubborn 9 obstinate, seditious 10 disdainful, headstrong, rebellious, refractory, unyielding 11 disobedient, intractable 13 insubordinate

contumely: 5 abuse, scorn 6 contek, insult 7 conteck, contemn, disdain 8 contempt, rudeness 9 arrogance 10 opprobrium 11 humiliation

contuse: 4 beat 5 pound 6 bruise, injure 7 squeeze

contusion: 4 blow, bump 6 bruise

conundrum: pun 4 whim 6 enigma, puzzle, riddle 7 conceit 8 crotchet

convalesce: 4 mend 7 improve, recover 10 recuperate

convene: sit 4 call, meet, open 5 unite 6 gather, muster, summon 7 convoke 8 assemble, converge 10 congregate, foregather

convenience: 4 ease 6 toilet 7 benefit, comfort 8 plumbing 9 appliance

convenient: fit 5 handy, ready 6 proper, useful 7 adapted, close-by, helpful 8 becoming, suitable 9 agreeable, available, congruous, favorable, opportune 10 accessible, commodious, near-at-hand 11 appropriate 12 commensurate

convent: 5 abbey 6 priory 7 meeting, nunnery 8 cloister 9 community, monastery, sanctuary
head: 5 abbot 6 abbess, mother 8 hegumene, superior 10 hegumeness
member: nun 4 monk 5 friar 6 sister 7 brother 8 cenobite 9 anchorite, religeuse, religious
pert. to: 6 friary
reception room: 8 arlatory
room: 9 parlatory

convention: 4 diet, feis, mise, rule 5 synod, usage 6 cartel, caucus, custom, treaty 7 decorum, meeting **8** assembly, congress, contract, covenant, practice **9** agreement, gathering, tradition **10** conference **11** convocation

conventional: **4** more **5** nomic, right, trite, usual **6** decent, formal, modish, proper **7** correct, regular **8** academic, accepted **9** customary, hidebound **10** ceremonial, stipulated **11** contractual

conventionalize: **5** adapt **7** conform, stylize

converge: **4** join, meet **5** focus **6** concur **8** approach, focalize

conversant: **5** adept, awake, aware **6** busied, expert, versed **7** skilled **8** familiar, occupied, up-to-date **9** concerned, practiced **10** acquainted, proficient

conversation: **4** chat, talk **6** confab, parley **7** conduct, palaver **8** behavior, chitchat, colloquy, dialogue, parlance **9** discourse, tete-a-tete **10** conference **11** association, interchange, intercourse **13** communication, interlocution
of three: **7** trialog **9** trialogue
private: **6** celidh (Sc.) **8** collogue **9** tete-a-tete

converse: **4** chat, chin, live, move, talk **5** dwell, speak **6** confer, homily, parley **7** commune, obverse, reverse **8** colloque, exchange, opposite **9** discourse **11** association, confabulate

convert: **4** turn **5** alter, amend, apply, renew **6** change, decode, direct, novice **7** restore, reverse **8** converse, neophyte, persuade **9** acetalize, proselyte, transform, translate, transmute, transpose **10** regenerate **11** proselytize **12** metamorphose, transmogrify

convertible: **4** auto **7** soft-top **10** automobile, changeable, equivalent, reciprocal, synonymous **15** interchangeable

convex: **5** bowed **6** arched, camber, curved **7** bulging, gibbous, rounded **9** cymbiform **11** protuberant
molding: **5** ovolo, torus

convey: **4** bear, cart, cede, deed, lead, mean, pass, send, take, tote, will **5** bring, carry, ferry, grant, guide, hurry, steal **6** assign, convoy, delate, demise, devise, eloign, impart, import, pass on, remove **7** auction, conduct, deliver, dispone, dispose **8** alienate, bequeath, transfer, transmit **9** accompany, transport **11** communicate

conveyance: bus, car, sak **4** auto, cart, deed, sled, taxi, tram **5** grant, stage, theft, train, wagon **6** demise **7** charter, conduct, rattler, trailer, trolley, vecture, vehicle, waftage **8** carriage, carrying, stealing, transfer **9** transport **10** automobile **11** transmittal
public: bus, cab, car **4** taxi, tram **5** train **6** subway **7** omnibus, ricksha, steamer, trolley

8 airplane, cable car, elevated, railroad, rickshaw **9** streetcar **10** jinricksha, jinrikisha

convict: **4** find **5** argue, felon, lifer, prove **6** attain, termer, trusty **7** attaint, captive, condemn, culprit **8** criminal, jailbird, prisoner, sentence **10** malefactor

conviction: **4** mind, view **5** creed, dogma, faith, tenet **6** belief, credit **7** opinion **8** sentence **9** assurance **10** confidence

convince: get **4** draw **6** assure, prompt **7** win over **8** talk into **9** prevail on **11** bring around

convinced: **4** sold, sure **6** assure, subdue **7** certain **8** absolute, positive **9** persuaded

convincing: **5** sound, valid **6** cogent, potent **7** telling **8** forcible **10** conclusive, persuasive

convivial: gay **4** boon **6** festal, genial, jovial, lively, social **7** festive, jocular **8** reveling **9** vivacious

convocation: **4** diet **5** synod **7** calling, council, meeting **8** assembly, congress **9** gathering **10** convention, graduation **12** congregation

convoke: bid, sit **4** call, cite, meet **6** gather, muster, summon **7** convene **8** assemble **10** congregate

convolute: **4** coil, roll, wind **5** twist **6** tangle, writhe **7** contort **8** obvolute

convolution: **4** coil, curl, fold **5** gyrus, whorl **9** sinuosity
of brain: **5** gyrus

convolve: **5** twist **6** enfold, enwrap, infold, writhe

convolvulus: **4** vine **12** morning glory

convoy: **4** lead **5** carry, guard, guide, pilot, watch **6** attend, convey, escort, manage **7** caravan, conduct **9** accompany, conductor, safeguard

convulse: **4** rock, stir **5** shake **6** excite **7** agitate, disturb

convulsion: fit **5** shrug, spasm, throe **6** attack, tumult, uproar **8** laughter, paroxysm **9** agitation, commotion **11** disturbance

cony, coney: das **4** hare, pika **5** daman, dassy, ganam, hutia, hyrax, lapin **6** burbot, dassie, gazabo, gazebo, rabbit **7** ashkoko
catcher: **5** cheat **7** sharper **8** swindler

coo: **4** curr (Sc.), woot **6** murmur

cook: fix, fry **4** bake, boil, chef, make, sear, stew **5** broil, grill, poach, roast, saute, shirr, steam **6** braise, decoct, seethe, simmer **7** dream up, prepare, process, servant **8** barbecue, cocinero, contrive, cusinero, magirist **9** cuisinier
in simmering liquid: **5** poach
one's goose: **4** do in **5** spoil **6** defeat
partially: **6** blanch **7** parboil

cooked: **4** done

cookery: **7** cuisine, science **8** magirics

cookie, cooky: 4 cake, snap 6 hermit 7 biscuit (Br.), brownie, oatcake 8 seedcake 9 Toll House 10 confection, gingersnap, shortbread 13 chocolate chip

cooking: *art:* 7 cuisine 8 magirics
device: Aga 4 etna 5 grill, range, stove 7 brazier, griddle, hibachi 10 rotisserie
odor: 5 nidor
pert. to: 8 culinary
room: 5 cuddy 6 galley 7 kitchen
vessel: pan, pot, wok 4 etna, olla 5 fryer 6 caster, chafer, fry pan, spider, tureen 7 broiler, griddle, roaster, skillet, steamer 8 colander, fleshpot 9 autoclave, bain marie 12 double boiler

cool: air, fan, ice 4 calm, cold 5 algid, allay, chill, fresh, gelid, nervy, sober, staid, whole 6 chilly, go easy, placid, quench, sedate, serene 7 unmoved 8 careless, cautious, composed, moderate, tranquil 9 collected, temperate, unruffled 10 deliberate, nonchalant, unfriendly 11 indifferent, refrigerate, unconcerned 12 unresponsive 13 dispassionate, imperturbable, self-possessed
one's heels: 4 wait

cooled: 6 frappe

cooler: fan 4 icer, jail, olla 5 drink 6 icebox, lockup, prison 11 refrigerant 12 refrigerator

coolie: 7 changar

cooling device: fan 7 freezer 12 refrigerator 14 air-conditioner

coolness: 5 nerve 6 aplomb 8 serenity 9 assurance 10 equanimity

coony: sly 4 cute, foxy 6 clever, crafty

coop: cot, cub, mew, pen, pot 4 cage, cote, jail 5 cramp, hutch 6 basket, corral 7 confine 9 enclosure 11 cooperative

cooperate: 4 tend 5 agree, coact, unite 6 concur 7 combine, conduce, connive 8 coadjute, conspire 10 contribute 11 collaborate

cooperation: 8 teamwork

cooperator: 9 auxiliary, colleague 10 accomplice

coordinate: 5 adapt, equal 6 adjust 7 arrange, syntony 8 classify 9 harmonize, integrate, reconcile 10 concurrent

coordination: 4 bond 5 skill 7 harmony, liaison 12 relationship
inability: 6 abasia
lack: 8 asynergy

coot: 4 duck, fowl, rail 5 smyth 6 beltie, henbil, person, scoter 13 phalacrocorax

cooter: 4 idle 6 loiter, turtle 8 tortoise

cootie: nit 4 bowl, game 5 louse 6 vessel 8 grayback

cop: bag, nab, rob 4 bank, blow, bull, head, heap, lift, pile, trap, tube 5 bobby, catch, crest, filch, mount, quill, shock, snare, steal, stock, swipe 6 copper, peeler, spider, strike 7 capture 9 patrolman, policeman 13 police officer
cop-out: 6 excuse 7 retreat 9 defection

copacetic: 4 fine 5 dandy, prime 6 snappy 7 capital 12 satisfactory

copaiba: 4 tree 6 balsam 9 oleoresin

copal: 5 anime, resin

cope: vie, war 4 cape, duty, face 5 cappa, cloak, cover, dress, equal, match, notch, rival, vault, wield 6 barter, canopy, chapel, combat, flight, make do, mantel, muzzle, oppose, strike, strive 7 contend, contest 8 complete, deal with, exchange, struggle, vestment 9 encounter

Copenhagen: *park:* 6 Tivoli
shopping district: 7 Stroget

copestone: 5 crown, stone 6 coping 11 culmination

copier: fax 4 stat 5 Xerox 6 scribe 9 photostat

copious: 4 full, good, lush, rich 5 ample, large 6 fluent, lavish, plenty 7 diffuse, flowing, fulsome, profuse, replete, teeming, uberous 8 abundant, affluent, numerous 9 exuberant, plenteous, plentiful, redundant 11 overflowing

copper: cop 4 bull, cent 5 bobby, metal, penny 6 cuprum, peeler 9 butterfly, policeman
alloy: 5 brass 6 oroide 7 rheotan
arsenic sulfide: 8 enargite
coin: 4 cent 5 brown, penny
engraving: 9 mezzotint
sulfate: 7 vitriol

copperhead: 5 snake, viper

coppice: 4 bosk, wood 5 copse, firth, grove 6 forest, growth 7 thicket 9 brushwood, underwood

Corpreus: *father:* 6 Pelops
son: 10 Periphetes
victim: 7 Iphitus

copse: cut, hag 4 hasp, trim, wood 6 clevis 7 coppice, shackle, thicket

Copt: 8 Egyptian 9 Christian 11 Monophysite
language: 6 Arabic 8 Bohairic
monastic founder: 15 Anthony of Thebes
title: 4 anba

copula: 4 band, link 5 union 7 coupler

copy: ape 4 echo, edit, mime 5 dummy, image, mimic 6 ectype, effigy, follow, record 7 emulate, estreat, imitate, redraft, replica, reprint, tracing 8 apograph, likeness 9 abundance, antigraph, duplicate, imitation, reproduce 10 transcribe, transcript 11 counterpart 12 reproduction
exact: 5 tenor
kind of: 6 carbon, ectype 7 estreat, extract, pattern, replica 9 duplicate, facsimile
true: 7 estreat

copying: 7 mimicry 8 mimetism
copyist: 6 scribe 7 copycat 10 plagiarist 12 calligrapher
pert. to: 8 clerical
copyread: 4 edit
copyright: *infringe:* 6 pirate 10 plagiarize
coque: bow 4 loop 8 trimming
coquet: toy 5 dally, flirt 6 lead on 11 string along
coquette: toy 4 vamp 5 dally, flirt 6 trifle 9 philander 11 hummingbird
coquettish: coy 4 arch 7 roguish
cora: 7 gazelle
coral: red 4 pink 5 polyp 6 palule 8 skeleton, zoophyte 9 limestone, madrepore, mille-pore 10 stalactite
division: 7 aporosa
formation: 5 palus
island: key 4 reef 5 atoll
corbel: 4 knot 5 ancon 6 timber 10 projection
corbie: 4 crow 5 raven
cord: rib 4 band, bind, bond, welt 5 nerve, twine 6 bobbin, sennet, string, tendon, thread 7 amentum, measure 10 aiguilette, cordeliere
drapery: 7 torsade
goat's hair: 4 agal
parachute: 7 ripcord
twisted: 7 torsade
cordage: 4 coir, eruc, feru, hemp, imbe, jute, rope 5 fiber 6 sennit 7 rigging
Corday's victim: 5 Marat
corded: 4 tied 6 repped, ribbed, welted 7 stacked, twilled
Cordelia: *father:* 4 Lear
sister: 5 Regan 7 Goneril
cordelle: tow 4 cord, rope 7 towline, towrope
cordial: 4 real, warm 5 shrub 6 ardent, elixir, genial, hearty 7 liqueur, sincere, zealous 8 anisette, friendly, gracious, vigorous 9 courteous, unfeigned 10 hospitable
cordiality: 5 ardor 6 regard, warmth 10 friendship, heartiness
cordon: 4 lace 5 braid, group, guard 6 ribbon
bleu: 4 chef, cook 6 ribbon 10 decoration
sanitary: 10 quarantine
core: cob, hub, nut 4 coke, gist, nave, pith 5 focus, heart, nowse, spool 6 center, centre, kernel, matrix, middle, nodule 7 company, corncob, essence, nucleus 9 substance
corge: 5 score 6 twenty
coriander: 4 herb 8 cilantro 14 Chinese parsley
corinne: 7 gazelle
corium: 5 layer 6 dermis
cork: oak 4 plug, seal, stop 5 float, shive 6 bobber 7 soberin, stopper, stopple
pert. to: 7 suberic
tissue: 5 suber
wax: 5 cerin

corker: 4 lulu 5 dandy 8 knockout 9 humdinger
corking: 4 fine 8 pleasing 9 excellent
corkscrew: 4 coil, wind 5 twist 6 spiral
corkwood: 5 balsa 6 blolly 8 harefoot
cormorant: 4 bird, shag 5 norie, scart 6 gor-maw, scarth 7 glutton 8 ravenous 13 phalacrocorax
young: 7 shaglet
corn: zea 4 salt, samp 5 grain, maize, mealy 6 clavis, heloma, kernel 7 callous 8 preserve 9 granulate
bread: 4 pone 7 hoecake 8 tortilla 9 hush puppy 10 johnnycake
dealer: 10 cornmonger
ear: cob 5 mealy 6 mealie, nubbin
food: 6 hominy
ground: 4 meal 5 grist
hulled: 4 samp 6 hominy
Indian: zea
knife: 7 machete
spike: cob, ear
Corncracker State: 8 Kentucky
corndodger: 4 pone 5 bread 8 dumpling
corned: 6 salted
cornel: 4 tree 6 cherry 7 dogwood 8 redbrush
corner: box, get, wro 4 bend, cant, coin, nook, pool, trap, tree 5 angle, bight, catch, coign, elbow, herne, ingle, niche, quoin, trust 6 cantle, canton, coigne, cranny, recess 8 monopoly
cornerpiece: 6 bumper, cantle
cornerstone: 5 basis, coign 6 coigne 7 support 9 curbstone 10 foundation
cornet: 4 horn 8 woodwind 10 instrument
cornflower: 7 barbeau 10 bluebonnet, bluebottle
cornhouse: 7 granary 8 corncrib
Cornhusker State: 8 Nebraska
cornice: cap 4 band, drip, eave 5 crown 6 geison 7 molding 8 astragal
basket: 4 caul
diamond: 6 quartz
support: 5 ancon
underside: 6 soffit 8 plancier
wolframite: cal
cornmeal: 4 masa, samp 5 atole 7 hoecake 10 johnnycake
cornsilk: 5 floss
cornucopia: 4 horn 9 abundance 12 horn of plenty
Cornwall: *castle* 8 Tintagel
mine: bal 5 wheal
ore: 5 whits
Cornwallis: *adversary:* 6 Greene 10 Washington
surrender site: 8 Yorktown
corny: 5 banal, stale, trite 6 old hat 11 sentimental

corolla: 4 bell 8 perianth
part: 5 galea, petal
corollary: 5 dogma 6 result, truism 7 adjunct,
theorem 9 deduction, inference 10 end
product 11 consequence, proposition
geometric: 6 porism
corona: 4 halo 5 cigar, crown, glory 6 circle,
fillet, rosary, wreath 7 aureole, circlet, garland, scyphus
coronation: 9 inaugural
stone: 5 Scone
coroner: 6 elisor 7 officer 8 examiner
coronet: 4 band, burr 5 crown, tiara 6 anadem, circle, diadem, timbre, wreath 7
chaplet
coronopus: 4 herb 6 carara
corporal: NCO 4 fano 5 fanon, fanum, phano
6 bodily
corporal punishment: 5 death 7 penalty 8
spanking, whipping
corporate: 6 united 8 combined 9 aggregate
corporation: 4 body, firm 5 trust 10 fellowship, foundation 11 association, combination
corporeal: 4 real 5 hylic, somal 6 actual, bodily, carnal 7 somatic 8 material, physical,
tangible 11 substantial
corpse: DOA 4 body 5 mummy, relic, stiff 7
cadaver, carcass, carrion
fat of: 9 adipocere
pert. to: 7 deathly 10 cadaverous
corpulent: fat 5 bulky, burly, husky, obese,
plump, stout 6 fleshy, portly, rotund 7 adipose, bellied, weighty 8 rolypoly 10 overweight
corpus: 4 body, bulk, mass 8 writings 10 literature
corpuscle: 4 cell 9 leucocyte
lack of red: 6 anemia
red blood: 7 hematid 8 haematid 11 polk-
ilocyte, schistocyte
corral: pen, sty 4 coop 5 atajo, pound 7 confine, enclose 8 stockage, surround 9 enclosure, inclosure
correct: due, fit, fix 4 edit, lean, nice, okay,
smug, true 5 amend, check, emend, exact,
right 6 adjust, better, change, inform,
proper, punish, rebuke, reform, remedy,
repair, revamp, revise, strict 7 chasten,
improve, perfect, precise, rectify, redress,
reprove 8 accurate, chastise, definite,
emendate, make over, regulate, rigorous,
truthful 9 castigate, faultless 10 immaculate, particular, scrupulous 11 comme il
faut, punctilious 12 conventional
correctable: 10 corrigible
correction: 10 discipline, punishment 11 castigation
correlated: 4 akin 7 matched, related

correlative: nor 4 then 5 equal, still 6 either,
mutual 7 neither 8 analogue, conjoint 9
analogous 10 reciprocal 13 correspondent
correspond: fit, gee 4 jibe, suit 5 agree,
match, tally, write 6 accord, concur, square
7 comport, respond 8 coincide, parallel,
quadrate 9 analogous, harmonize 11 communicate
correspondence: 4 mail 7 analogy, letters,
traffic 8 homology 9 assonance, congruity
10 similarity
correspondent: 5 match 6 pen pal, writer 8
quadrate, suitable 9 accordant, analogous,
congruous 10 accomplice, concordant,
equivalent 11 conformable, contributor,
correlative
corresponding: 4 akin 5 alike 7 similar
in sound: 5 rimic 6 rhymic
part: 7 isomere
corrida: 9 bullfight
shout: olé
corridor: 4 hall 5 aisle, oriel 6 arcade 7
couloir, gallery 8 coulisse 10 passageway
corrie: 6 cirque, hollow
corrigible: 8 amenable 10 corrective, punish-
able 11 correctable
corroborant: 5 tonic 10 supporting 12 invigorating 13 strengthening
corroborate: 5 prove 7 bear out, confirm,
support, sustain 8 validate 9 establish 11
countersign 12 substantiate
corrode: eat 4 bite, burn, etch, gnaw, rust 5
decay, erode, waste 6 be-gnaw, canker,
impair 7 consume, eat away 8 wear away
corrosive: 4 acid 6 ardent, biting 7 caustic,
erosive, fretful, mordant 9 sarcastic 11
destructive 14 disintegrating
corrugate: 5 crimp 6 furrow, rumple 7 crinkle, crumple, wrinkle
corrugation: 4 fold 6 crease, pucker 7 wrinkle
corrupt: bad, low, rot 4 evil, vile 5 blend, bribe,
spoil, stain, sully, taint, venal 6 augean,
canker, debase, impure, poison, putrid, ravish, rotten 7 abusive, attaint, carrion, crooked,
defiled, degrade, deprave, envenom, falsify,
immoral, pervert, pollute, putrefy, violate,
vitiate 8 confound, empoison, two-faced 9
abandoned, dishonest 10 adulterate, demoralize, flagitious, profligate 11 contaminate,
purchasable 13 double-dealing
corsage: 5 waist 6 bodice 7 bouquet, flowers
corsair: bug 6 pirate, robber 8 picaroon, rockfish 9 buccaneer, sea robber 10 freebooter
body: 5 armor, cover
corset: 4 belt, busk 6 bodice, girdle 7 support
covering: 8 camisole
strip: 4 bone, busk
Corsica: *birthplace of:* 8 Napoleon
capital: 7 Ajaccio

corslet: 6 bodice 8 corselet 11 breastplate

cortege: 4 pomp 5 suite, train 6 parade 7 funeral, retinue 10 procession

cortex: 4 bark, peel, rind 8 peridium

corundum: 4 ruby, sand 5 emeru, emery 7 alumina 8 abrasive, sapphire

coruscate: 5 blaze, flash, gleam, shine 7 glisten, glitter, radiate, sparkle, twinkle 8 brandish 11 scintillate

corviform: 7 corvine 8 crowlike

corvine bird: daw 4 crow, rook 5 raven

coryza: 4 cold
  symptom: 6 sneeze

cos: 7 lettuce, romaine

cosa nostra: 5 Mafia 9 syndicate

cosen: See **cozen**

cosh: 4 neat, snug, tidy 5 happy, quiet, still 6 attack, lively, strike, weapon 7 assault 8 familiar, friendly 11 comfortable

cosher: pet 4 chat 5 feast, visit 6 pamper, sponge

cosmetic: 5 blush, cream, henna, liner, paint, rouge 6 enamel, make-up, pomade, powder 7 blusher, mascara 8 eye liner, lipgloss, lipstick 9 eye shadow 10 foundation, nail polish
  medicated: 6 lotion
  paste: 4 pack
  white lead: 6 ceruse

cosmic: 4 vast 6 global 7 orderly 8 catholic, infinite 9 universal 10 harmonious 12 cosmopolitan

cosmonaut: See **astronaut**

cosmopolitan: 6 global, smooth, urbane 8 ecumenic 10 ecumenical 13 sophisticated

cosmos: 5 earth, globe, order, realm, world 6 flower, nature 7 harmony 8 creation, universe
  opposed to: 5 Chaos

Cossack: 4 Slav 5 tatar 6 ataman, hetman, tartar 7 Russian, soldier 10 cavalryman
  captain: 6 Sotnik
  chief: 6 ataman, hetman
  district: 6 voisko
  mount: 5 steed 7 charger
  regiment: 4 polk, pulk
  squadron: 6 sotnia, sotnya
  village: 8 stanitza
  whip: 5 knout

cosset: pet 4 baby, love 6 caress, coddle, cuddle, fondle, pamper

cossette: 4 chip 5 slice, strip 9 schnitzel

cossid: 9 messenger

cost: 4 loss, pain 5 price, value 6 charge, outlay 7 expense 8 estimate 9 detriment, sacrifice, suffering 11 deprivation, expenditure 14 characteristic
  business: 8 overhead

costa: rib 4 side, vein 5 ridge 6 border, mid-rib

Costa Rica: *capital:* 7 San Jose
  city: 7 Cartago, Heredia 8 Alajuela 9 Guadalupe
  currency: 5 colon 7 centimo
  export: 6 coffee 7 bananas
  people: 6 Guaymi
  volcano: 5 Barba, Irazu
  weight: 4 caja

costate: 6 ribbed

costly: 4 dear, fine, high, rich 6 lavish 8 gorgeous, precious, prodigal, splendid 9 dearthful, expensive, priceless, sumptuous 10 exorbitant, invaluable 11 extravagant

costmary: 4 herb 5 plant, tansy 7 alecost 12 mint geranium

costume (see also **dress, vestment**): rig 4 garb, robe, sari, suit 5 dress, getup, habit 6 attire, outfit 7 apparel, clothes, raiment, uniform 8 clothing, ensemble 10 habiliment

costus root: 4 herb 6 pachak, pochok

cot: bed, hut, mat, pen 4 boat, coop, cote, fold 5 abode, cabin, couch, cover, house, stall 6 pallet, sheath, tangle 7 charpai, charpoy, cottage, shelter 8 bedstead, dwelling 9 sheepfold, stretcher 11 fingerstall

cote: cot, hut 4 coop, fold, shed, wine 5 house, quote 7 cottage, shelter 8 hillside, outstrip, vineyard 9 inclosure, sheepfold

Cote d'Azur: 7 Riviera

Cote d'Ivoire: See **Ivory Coast**

coterie: set 4 ring 5 junto, monde 6 circle, clique, galaxy 7 platoon, society 9 camarilla, entourage

cothamore: 8 overcoat 9 greatcoat

cothurnus: 4 boot 6 buskin

cotillion: 5 dance 9 quadrille, solitaire

cotta: 5 stole 6 mantle 7 blanket 8 surplice, vestment

cottage: hut 4 bari, cosh 5 bower, cabin, house, lodge, shack 6 bohawn, cabana, chalet, shanty 7 shelter 8 bungalow 9 hosthouse 10 guesthouse
  partition: 5 speer 6 hallan
  Russian: 5 dacha
  Swiss: 6 chalet

cottage cheese: 9 pot cheese, smearcase 10 curd cheese 12 farmer cheese

cotter, cottar: mat, pin, vex 4 clot 6 fasten, potter, pucker, shrink, toggle, wither 7 congeal, cottier, peasant, shrivel, villein 8 cottager, cotterel, entangle 9 coagulate

cotton: 4 beat, flog 5 agree, fiber, toady 6 coddle, combed, fabric 7 algodon, garment, succeed 8 perceive 9 harmonize 10 fraternize, understand

and linen: **7** fustian

cleaner: **5** willy **6** willow

cloth: **4** baft, jean, lawn, leno, susi **5** bafta, bluet, denim, doria, khaki, lisle, manta, surat, terry, vichy, wigan **6** baline, calico, cangan, hum-hum **7** camboye, cotonia, flannel, galatea, jaconet, nankeen, percale, silesia

cloth blemish: nit

Egyptian: sak **4** Pima **5** sakel

extraction: **5** bolly

fiber: **4** lint, noil **6** stapel

flowered: **6** chintz

fuzz remover: **6** linter

gauze: **4** leno

handkerchief: **7** malabar

knot in: nep **4** slub

lawn: **7** batiste

light: **7** etamine

long-staple: **4** maco

measure: lea **4** bolt, hank

printed: **6** calico

refuse: **8** grabbots

seed pod: **4** boll **5** bolly

seed remover: gin

sheeting: **5** manta **6** muslin **7** percale **8** drilling

striped: **5** bezan **7** express, ticking

strong: **4** duck **5** scrim **6** canvas

thread: **5** lisle

twilled: **4** jean **7** silesia

up to: **10** ingratiate

waste: **4** noil **6** linter

cotton gin inventor: **10** Eli Whitney

Cotton State: **7** Alabama

cottonseed kernel: **4** meat **7** oil cake

cottontail: **4** hare **7** leveret

cottonwood: **4** tree **5** alamo **6** poplar

couch: bed, cot, lie, put **4** hide, lair, lurk, sofa **5** divan, inlay, lodge, press, skulk, slink, sneak, squat, stoop, utter **6** burrow, litter, pallet, settee **7** conceal, express, overlay, recline **8** disguise **9** accubitus (L.), davenport, embroider

couch grass: **5** quack, quick **6** quitch, scutch

couchant: **4** abed **5** prone **6** supine **7** lurking **9** crouching, squatting

cougar: cat **4** puma **7** panther **9** catamount **12** mountain lion

cough: **4** bark, hack **5** hoast **6** tussis **9** pertussis
pert. to: **7** tussive

cough drop: **6** pastil, troche **7** lozenge **8** pastille

cough up: **4** ante **5** yield **10** contribute

coulee: **4** lava **5** gorge, gulch **6** cooley, ravine

couloir: **5** gorge, gully **7** hallway, passage **8** corridor

council: **4** body, dail, diet, rede **5** board, boule, cabal, divan, junta, junto, synod **6** senate **7** cabinet, consult, husting, meeting **8** assembly, conclave, congress, ministry **10** conference, consistory, federation **11** convocation **12** consultation
church: **5** synod **10** consistory
pert. to: **7** cameral
political: **5** cabal, junta
table cover: **5** tapis

counsel: **4** lore, rede, rule, urge, warn **5** chide **6** advice, advise, confer **7** caution, suggest **8** admonish, advocate, attorney, prudence **9** barrister, counselor, recommend **10** counsellor **11** exhortation, instruction **12** consultation, deliberation

counselor, counsellor: **4** sage **6** lawyer, mentor, nestor **7** adviser, advisor, counsel, proctor **8** attorney **9** barrister

counselor-at-law: **9** barrister

count: add, sum, tot **4** bank, cast, earl, foot, graf, name, rely, tell, tote **5** comte (F.), judge, score, tally **6** census, depend, esteem, figure, impute, number, reckon, rely on **7** account, ascribe, compute, trust in **8** numerate, sanction **9** ascertain, calculate, enumerate **10** depend upon

countenance: aid, mug **4** abet, brow, face, mien, puss, show, vult **5** favor, front **6** aspect, favour, visage **7** approve, bearing, conduct, endorse, feature, proffer, support **8** befriend, demeanor, hold with, sanction **9** demeanour, encourage, semblance **10** appearance **11** physiognomy

counter: bar, vie **4** chip, dump, eddy, pawn **5** shelf, stand, table **6** combat, marker, oppose **7** adverse, contend, current **8** contrary, opposite **10** contradict **12** football play **13** contradictory

counteract: **5** annul, check **6** oppose, resist, thwart **7** balance, correct, destroy, nullify **8** antidote, negative **9** frustrate **10** compensate, neutralize **11** countermand **12** counterpoise

counterattack: **6** answer, charge

countercurrent: **4** eddy **5** swirl **7** backset **9** whirlpool

counterfeit: tin **4** base, coin, copy, duff, fake, mock, sham **5** belie, bogus, dummy, false, feign, forge, fudge, phony, queer **6** affect, assume, forged, pseudo, tinsel **7** falsify, feigned, imitate **8** deformed, simulate, spurious **9** brummagem, disguised, dissemble **10** adulterate, artificial, fictitious, fraudulent

counterfoil: **4** stub **5** check

counter-irritant: **4** moxa **5** seton, stupe **6** arnica, ginger, iodine, pepper **7** mustard **8** liniment

countermand: **4** stop **5** annul **6** cancel, forbid, recall, revoke **7** abolish, rescind, reverse **8** abrogate, prohibit **9** frustrate **10** counteract

counterpane: **6** spread **8** bedcover, coverlet **9** bedspread

counterpart: **4** copy, like, mate, twin **5** image, match **6** double **7** obverse, vis-à-vis **8** parallel **9** duplicate, facsimile **10** complement, equivalent, similitude

counterpoint: **4** foil **7** descant **8** contrast **11** arrangement **13** juxtaposition

counterpoise: **6** make up, offset, set off **7** balance **8** equalize **10** compensate, counteract **13** counterweight **14** counterbalance

countersign: **4** mark, seal, sign **6** signal **7** confirm, endorse **8** consigne, password, sanction **9** signature, watchword **11** corroborate

countersink: **4** ream **5** bevel **7** chamfer

countertenor: **4** alto **8** falsetto

counting frame: **6** abacus

countless: **8** infinite **10** numberless **12** incalculable

Count of Monte Cristo: **6** Dantes
   author: **5** Dumas (pere)

count on: **4** lean, rely **6** depend, expect

count out: bar **6** except **7** rule out **9** eliminate

country: **4** home, land, pais (Sp.), pays (F.) **5** realm, rural, state, tract, weald **6** ground, nation, people, region, sticks **7** bucolic, outland **8** district, homeland **9** champaign, territory **10** fatherland **12** commonwealth
   ancient: **4** Aram, Elam, Elis **5** Sheba
   dance: **4** reel **6** square
   home: **5** manor, ranch, villa **7** cottage **8** hacienda
   man: **4** jake, rube **5** swain, yokel **6** farmer, rustic **7** bumpkin, hayseed, plowman **10** compatriot, inhabitant
   mythical: **6** Utopia
   open: **4** moor, wold **5** heath, weald
   pert. to: **5** rural **6** rustic **7** predial **8** agrestic, pastoral, praedial
   place: **4** farm, peat **5** ranch, villa
   reside in: **9** rusticate
   road: **4** lane, path **5** byway

county: **4** seat **5** shire **6** domain, parish **7** borough **8** district

coup: buy **4** blow, plan, play **5** scoop, upset **6** attack, barter, putsch, strike, stroke **7** capsize, traffic **8** overturn, takeover **9** stratagem

coup de grace: end **7** quietus **9** deathblow

coup d'etat: **9** stratagem **10** revolution

couple: duo, tie, two **4** bond, case, dyad, join, link, mate, pair, span, team, twin, yoke **5** brace, leash, marry, twain, unite **7** bracket, connect **8** assemble

coupled: **5** yoked **6** joined, wedded **7** gemalad **8** geminate **9** conjugate

coupler: **4** link, ring **7** drawbar, shackle, tirasse

couplet: **4** pair, poem **5** brace **7** distich

coupon: **4** form, slip, stub **5** check, stamp **7** portion

courage: **4** grit, guts, prow, sand, soul **5** heart, nerve, pluck, spine, spunk, valor **6** daring, mettle, spirit **7** bravery, heroism, prowess **8** audacity, backbone, boldness, firmness, tenacity **9** assurance, fortitude, gallantry, hardihood **10** resolution
   symbol of: **10** bloodstone

courageous: **4** bold, game **5** brave, hardy, manly, stout **6** daring, heroic, manful, plucky **7** gallant, spartan, staunch, valiant **8** fearless, intrepid, valorous **9** undaunted **11** adventurous **12** enterprising, high-spirited

courante: **4** romp **5** caper, dance, music **6** letter **7** current, gazette, running **9** messenger, newspaper

courier: **4** post **5** envoy, guide, scout **7** estafet, orderly, postboy, soilage **8** cicerone, dragoman, estafeet, horseman **9** attendant, go-between, messenger **10** cavalryman

courlan: **4** bird **7** limpkin

course: lap, run, way **4** bent, flow, game, heat, line, mode, path, race, rill, rink, road, rote, went **5** cycle, drift, orbit, route, tenor, track, trail, trend **6** artery, career, cursus, gallop, manner, method, series, stream, street, system **7** beeline, conduct, highway, passage, pathway, process, routine, running, subject, traject **8** curricle, progress, sequence, tendency **9** direction **10** curriculum, proceeding, racecourse, succession **11** watercourse
   alter: **4** veer **6** detour
   dinner: **5** salad **6** entrée **7** dessert **9** blue plate
   easy: **4** pipe, snap **5** cinch **8** sinecure
   habitual: rut, way **4** rote **7** regimen, routine
   of action: **6** career **8** demarche **9** procedure
   of study: **5** major **7** seminar **8** syllabus **10** curriculum
   roundabout: **6** detour **11** indirection

courser: **5** horse, racer, steed **7** charger **8** warhorse

court: bar, bid, see, sue, woo **4** area, body, quad, rota, seek, yard **5** arena, curea, curry, favor, forum, judge, patio, space, spark, tempt, train **6** allure, atrium, gemote, homage, invite, palace **7** address, attract, retinue, solicit **8** hustings, serenade, tribunal **9** attention, enclosure **10** quadrangle
   action: **4** case, suit **5** trial

attendant: **5** staff **6** elisor, staves
bring into: sue **4** sist **6** arrest
calendar: **6** docket
call to: **7** summons **8** subpoena **11** arraignment
circuit: **4** eyre, iter
crier: **6** beadle
cry: **4** oyes, oyez
decision: **6** assize **7** finding, verdict **8** judgment
ecclesiastical: **5** Curia **10** consistory
exemption: **6** essoin
hearing: **4** oyer, suit **5** trial **6** action
inner: **5** patio
Mikado's: **5** dairi
minutes: **4** acta **10** transcript
of equity: **8** chancery
official: **5** clerk, crier, macer (Sc.) **7** bailiff
old: **4** leet **5** gemot **6** gemote **8** woodmote
order: **4** nisi, rule, writ **6** decree
panel: **4** jury
participant: **4** jury **5** crier, judge **6** elisor, lawyer **7** pleader, witness **8** advocate, talesman **9** defendant, plaintiff
pert. to: **5** aulic **10** fornaneous
session: set **4** oyer **6** assize **7** sitting **8** sederunt **11** downsitting
writ: **6** capias **7** summons **8** subpoena
court game: **6** squash, tennis **8** racquets **9** badminton **11** racquetball
court-martial: **8** drumhead
courteous: **4** fair **5** buxom, civil, suave **6** polite, urbane **7** affable, cordial, gallant, genteel, gentile, refined **8** debonair, gracious **9** attentive **10** respectful **11** complaisant, considerate, gentlemanly **12** well mannered
courtesan: **5** whore **6** geisha, madame **10** prostitute
courtier: **4** beau **5** beaux (pl.), wooer **7** courter **8** courtman **9** attendant, courtling, flatterer
courtly: **4** hend, prim **5** aulic, civil, hende, lofty **6** polite **7** elegant, refined, stately **8** gracious, polished **9** dignified
courtship: **4** suit **7** romance **8** sparking
courtyard: **4** area, quad **5** patio **7** cortile **9** curtilage **10** quadrangle
cousin: coz, kin **4** akin **6** allied **8** relative
couthie: **4** smug **6** kindly, smooth **8** friendly, pleasant **9** agreeable **11** comfortable
couturier, couturiere: **8** designer **10** dressmaker
cove: bay, den **4** cave, chap, gill, hole, nook, pass **5** basin, bight, creek, inlet **6** fellow, hollow, recess, valley **7** molding
covenant: **4** bind, bond, mise, pact **5** agree **6** accord, cartel, engage, pledge, treaty **7** bargain, compact, concord, promise **8** alliance, contract, document **9** agreement, concordat, condition, stipulate, testament, undertake **10** convention **11** confederacy, stipulation, transaction
cover: cap, lid **4** coat, hide, mask, pave, roof, span, veil **5** drape, hatch, put-on **6** mantle, screen, shield **7** obscure, overlay, shelter
a bet: **4** fade
a fire: **4** bank
a hatch: **6** batten
ground: **5** speed **7** advance
the eyes: **9** blindfold
up: **4** hide **7** conceal
up for: **6** shield **7** protect
with mud: **6** belute
with straw: **6** thatch
with strips of bacon: **4** lard
coverall: **4** gown **6** jumper **10** boiler suit
covered: **4** clad, shod **5** mossy **6** covert, hidden **7** encased **8** screened **9** cleithral, concealed, panoplied, sheltered
covering: fur, hap **4** aril, bark, boot, case, hood, hull, husk, mask, pall, roof, tarp, tile **5** apron, armor, crust, quilt, shell, testa **6** awning, canopy, drapet, facing, heling, helmet, jacket, pelage, screen, sheath, shroud **7** capsule, ceiling, healing, overlay, pericap, wrapper **8** casement, clothing, coverlet, umbrella **9** coverture, operculum **10** integument **11** smokescreen
defensive: **5** armor **6** helmet **10** camouflage **11** smokescreen
seed: **4** aril
thin: **4** film **6** veneer
coverlet: **5** quilt, rezai, throw **6** afghan, caddow, spread **7** blanket **8** coverlid **9** comforter **11** counterpane
covert: den, lie, sly **4** lair **5** niche, privy **6** asylum, harbor, hidden, latent, masked, refuge, secret **7** covered, defense, harbour, private, shelter, subrosa, thicket **8** hushhush **9** concealed, disguised, insidious, shrubbery **10** underbrush **12** confidential **13** under-the-table
covet: sin **4** ache, envy, pant, want, wish **5** crave, yearn **6** desire, grudge, hanker
covetous: **4** avid, gair, gare, keen **5** eager, itchy **6** frugal, greedy, stingy **7** miserly **8** desirous, grasping **9** mercenary **10** avaricious **12** parsimonious
covey: **4** bevy **5** brood, bunch, flock, hatch **7** company **8** assembly
cow: awe **4** beef, bogy, cowl, cush, faze, kine, vaca **5** abash, alarm, bossy, brock, bully, daunt, dompt, moggy, scare **6** bovine, female, goblin, heifer, subdue **7** bluster,

bugbear, depress, dragoon, overtop, squelch, terrify **8** browbeat, dispirit, frighten, threaten **9** quadruped, strongarm **10** intimidate

barn: **4** byre **7** vaccary

barren: **5** drape

cud: **5** rumen

dung: **4** upla

French: **5** vache

group: **4** herd, kine **6** cattle

hornless: not **4** moil **5** doddy, muley **6** doddie, mulley, polled **7** pollard

hybrid: **7** cattabu, cattalo

pasture: **7** vaccary

pen: **6** corral

sound: low, moo

Spanish: **4** vaca

young: **4** calf **5** stirk **6** heifer

coward: **6** craven **7** caitiff, chicken **9** jellyfish **10** scaredy-cat

cowardly: shy **4** argh **5** timid **6** afraid, cowish, craven, yellow **7** caitiff, chicken **11** lily-livered **12** fainthearted **13** pusillanimous

cowbird: **7** bunting **9** blackbird

cowboy: **5** rider, roper, waddi **6** drover, gaucho, herder **7** llanero, puncher, vaquero **8** buckaroo, buckayro, herdsman, wrangler **9** cattleman **10** cowpuncher **12** broncobuster

breeches: **5** chaps, levis **8** jodhpurs

contest: **5** rodeo

rope: **5** lasso, riata **6** lariat

cowcatcher: **5** guard, pilot

cowed: **8** downcast **11** crestfallen

cower: **4** fawn **5** quail, stoop, toady, wince **6** coorie, cringe, crouch, hurkle, shrink **11** apple-polish

cowfish: **4** toro **7** grampus, manatee, sirenia

cow-headed deity: **4** Isis

cowherd: **8** herdsman, neatherd

cowl: cap, lid, tub **4** hood, monk **6** bonnet, vessel **7** capuche

cowled: **6** hooded **9** cucullate

cowpea: **5** sitao **9** black-eyed

cow pilot: **4** fish **9** chirivita **10** damselfish

cowpuncher: See **cowboy**

cowslip: **8** auricula, cyclamen, primrose **12** shooting star **13** marsh marigold **16** Virginia bluebell

coxa: hip **6** haunch

coxcomb: fop, nob **4** beau, buck, dude, fool, toff **5** cleat, dandy, hinge **7** princox **8** popinjay **12** lounge lizard

coy: pal, shy **4** arch, coax, nice **5** aloof, chary, decoy, quiet, still **6** allure, caress, demure, modest, proper **7** bashful, distant **8** reserved **9** diffident **10** coquettish, disdainful, hesitating **12** self-effacing

Coyote State: **11** South Dakota

coypu: **6** nutria, rodent

coze: **4** chat, talk **6** gossip **8** converse

cozen, cosen: cog, con, gyp **4** bilk, gull **5** cheat, trick **6** chisel **7** beguile, deceive, defraud, swindle **8** hoodwink **9** bamboozle **11** double-cross

cozy: **4** easy, safe, snug **5** bield, homey **6** chatty, secure, toasty **8** covering, familiar, homelike, sociable **9** contented, gemutlich, talkative **10** buddy-buddy, palsy-walsy **11** comfortable

cozy retreat: den **4** lair, nest, nook **5** ingle

crab: gin **4** beef, fuss, yawp **5** anger, gripe, maian, racer, winch **6** buster, cancer, grouse, hermit, peeler **7** buckler, fiddler, grumble **8** arachnid, irritate, windlass **9** horseshoe **10** crosspatch, crustacean, curmudgeon

abdomen: **5** apron

claw: **5** chela **6** nipper

constellation: **6** Cancer

fiddler: uca

genus: uca **6** birgus **7** limulus, squilla

resembling: **8** cancroid

suborder: **9** brachyura

crab apple: **5** malus, scrog

crabbed: **4** dour, glum, ugly **5** cabby, cross, testy **6** bitter, cranky, crusty, morose, rugged, sullen, trying **7** boorish, cornish, cramped, crooked, gnarled, knotted, obscure, peevish **8** churlish, contrary, petulant, vinegary **9** difficult, fractious, intricate, irregular **10** perplexing **11** intractable

crabgrass: **4** weed **9** digitaria

crabstick: **4** cane **5** crank, stick **6** cudgel

crabwood: **8** andiroba

crack: gag, pop **4** a-one, bang, blow, chap, chip, chop, clap, cone, flaw, jest, jibe, joke, kibe, leak, quip, rend, rift, rime, snap, yerk **5** brack, break, check, chine, chink, clack, cleft, craze, split **6** cleave, cranny **7** blemish, cocaine, crackle, crevice, crevise, fissure **8** fracture **9** witticism **10** proficient

down on: **5** quash **6** attack **7** repress **10** discipline

up: **5** amuse, crash, extol, smash **8** collapse **9** break down

crackbrain: **8** crackpot **9** ding-a-ling, screwball

crackbrained: **5** crazy, kooky, nutty **7** erratic **12** unreasonable

cracker: **4** bake, liar **5** wafer **7** biscuit, boaster, breaker, burster, redneck, saltine, snapper **8** braggart, Georgian **11** firecracker

Cracker State: **7** Georgia

crackhead: **6** addict

crackle: **4** snap **5** break, crack **7** brustle, crinkle, sparkle, sputter **9** crackling, crepitate

crackpot: nut **4** kook, loon **5** crank **7** erratic, lunatic **9** screwball

cracksman: 4 yegg 7 burglar, peteman

cradle: bed, cot 4 crib, rest, rock 5 cader, frame 6 creche 7 berceau, shelter 8 bassinet, cunabula 9 framework 11 incunabulum
song: 7 lullaby 8 berceuse

craft (see also **boat**): art, job 4 boat 5 fraud, guile, skill, trade 6 deceit, metier, talent, vessel 7 ability, know-how 8 aptitude, artifice, vocation 9 dexterity 10 employment, occupation 12 skillfulness

craftsman: 4 hand 5 navvy 6 artist, potter, weaver, writer 7 artisan, builder, workman 8 mechanic 9 artificer, carpenter

crafty: sly 4 arch, foxy, wily 5 adept 6 adroit, astute, callid, shrewd, subtle, tricky 7 cunning, vulpine 8 captious, fetching 9 cautelous, deceitful, ingenious 10 fallacious, fraudulent 13 Machiavellian 15 Mephistophelean

crag: tor 4 craw, neck, rock, scar, spur 5 arete, brack, cliff 6 throat 9 precipice

craggy: 5 harsh, rough 6 abrupt, knotty, rugged

crake: 4 bird, crow, rail, rook 5 raven 8 railbird

cram: wad 4 bone, fill, glut, pack, stow, urge 5 crowd, crush, drive, force, gorge, grind, learn, press, study, stuff, teach 6 bone up, review 7 jam-pack, squeeze

cramp: 4 coop, kink, pain 5 crick, crowd, pinch, stunt 6 hamper, hinder, knotty 7 confine 8 compress, contract, restrain, restrict 9 constrict, difficult 11 contraction
one's style: 5 queer 9 frustrate

cranberry: 7 pembina 8 bilberry, foxberry 9 mossberry, sourberry
habitat: bog

crane: job 4 bird, grus 5 davit, heron, jenny, raise, wader 6 sarsus 7 derrick, stretch 9 cormorant 10 wading bird
arm: gib, jib 6 gibbet 7 ramhead
charges: 7 cranage
genus: 4 grus
Malayan: 5 sarus
neck: 4 gaze 5 stare
pert. to: 6 gruine
ship: 5 davit
small: 10 demoiselle
traveling: 5 jenny, titan 7 goliath

crane fly: 6 tipula

cranial nerve: 4 vagi (pl.) 5 vagus
root: 5 radix 7 radices (pl.)

cranium: pan 4 head 5 skull 8 brainpan
nerve root: 5 radix
part: 7 calotte 8 calvaria
pert. to: 7 cranial

crank: wit 4 bent, crab, kook, sick, weak, whim, wind 5 brace, loose, rogue, shaky,

winch 6 ailing, boldly, grouch, handle, infirm 7 awkward, bracket, fanatic, lustily 8 crackpot, grumbler, sourpuss 9 distorted, eccentric, sprightly

cranky: 4 ugly 5 crazy, cross, lusty, shaky, testy 6 ailing, infirm, sickly 7 crooked, grouchy 8 tortuous 9 crotchety, difficult, irritable 10 ill-humored 11 hot-tempered 12 disagreeable

cranny: 4 hole, nook 5 chink, cleft, crack, niche 6 corner 7 crevice, fissure

crap: 5 dregs, money 7 gallows, greaves, rubbish 8 nonsense, sediment

crape: 4 band, curl, friz 5 crepe, crimp, drape, gauze 6 shroud 8 mourning

crapehanger: 7 killjoy 10 spoilsport

crapulence: 7 surfeit 8 gluttony 11 overfeeding 12 intemperance, intoxication

crash: 4 fail, fall 5 blast, burst, cloth, crush, shock, smash, sound, wreck 6 fiasco, impact 7 failure, intrude, shatter, smashup 8 collapse, splinter 9 collision

crass: raw 4 dull, rude 5 crude, dense, gross, rough, thick 6 coarse, obtuse, stupid 9 unrefined

crate: box, car 4 case, crib 5 plane, seron 6 basket, cradle, encase, hamper, hurdle 7 canasta, vehicle 9 container 10 receptacle
bar: 4 slat

crater: cup, pit 4 cone, hole 5 fovea 6 cavity, hollow 7 caldera 10 depression

cravat: tie 4 neck 5 ascot, scarf, stock 7 bandage, necktie, overlay 8 crumpler 9 neckcloth 10 fourinhand 11 neckerchief

crave: ask, beg 4 long, need, pray, seek 5 covet, yearn 6 desire, hanker, hunger, thirst 7 beseech, entreat, implore, request, require, solicit 10 supplicate

craven: 6 afraid, coward, scared 7 dastard 8 cowardly, defeated, overcome, poltroon, recreant, sneaking 10 vanquished 11 lily-livered 12 fainthearted

craw: maw 4 crop 7 stomach 9 ingluvies

crawl: lag 4 drag, fawn, inch, ramp, swim 5 creep, kraal 6 cringe, grovel, scride 7 slither

crayfish: 4 crab 5 yabby 6 yabbie 7 crawdad, lobster 8 cambarus, crawfish 9 ecrevisse 10 crustacean

crayon: 4 plan 5 chalk 6 pastel, pencil, sketch 7 drawing

craze: fad 4 flaw, mode, rage 5 break, crack, crush, furor, mania, vogue 6 defect, impair, madden, weaken, whimsy 7 derange, destroy, fashion, shatter, whimsey 8 distract 9 bedlamize, infirmity 10 dernier cri 11 infatuation

crazed: mad, ree 4 amok, loco, wild, wood, zany 5 balmy, batty, daffy, dotty, manic, nutty, potty, wacky **6** coocoo, dottle, insane, looney **7** lunatic **8** deleerit, delieret, demented, deranged **10** crackbrain, distraught

crazy: mad **4** gaga, luny, nuts **5** batty, daffy, goofy, silly, wacky **6** absurd, cuckoo, insane, looney, maniac, teched **7** bananas, bonkers, cracked, lunatic **8** crackpot, demented **9** possessed **10** crackbrain, unbalanced **11** harebrained **12** preposterous

creak: gig **4** rasp, yirr **5** cheep (Sc.), croak, grind, groan **6** squeak **8** complain

cream: **4** beat, best, pick, whip **5** creme, elite, froth, sauce **6** bonbon **8** emulsion, ointment

creamery: **5** dairy

cream of tartar: **5** argol

cream puff: **6** pastry **8** weakling

creamy: **4** rich **5** reamy **6** smooth **8** luscious

crease: **4** fold, lirk, ruck, ruga, seam **5** crimp, pleat **6** furrow, rimple **7** crumple, wrinkle

create: **4** coin, form, make, plan **5** build, cause, forge, shape, write **6** design, invent **7** compose, fashion, imagine, produce **8** generate **9** establish, originate

creation: **5** world **6** cosmos, effect **7** fashion, product **8** creature, universe **9** macrocosm **10** production **11** masterpiece

creative: **9** demiurgic, inventive **10** innovative, productive **12** constructive

creativity: **6** genius

creator: God **5** maker **6** author **7** founder **8** designer **9** architect **10** originator

creature (see also **animal**): man **4** tool **5** beast, being, slave, thing **6** animal, minion, person, wretch **8** hellicat (Sc.) **9** dependent **10** animalcule, individual
  fabled: elf **4** puck, yeti **5** gnome, troll **6** dragon, merman **7** centaur, mermaid, unicorn

creche: **4** crib **6** manger **7** nursery (Br.)

credence: **5** faith, trust **6** belief, buffet, credit **8** credenza **10** acceptance, confidence **11** reliability **15** trustworthiness

credential: **7** voucher **8** credence **11** certificate, testimonial

credenza: **5** niche, shelf, table **6** buffet **8** credence, cupboard **9** sideboard

credible: **6** likely **7** credent **8** probable **9** authentic, plausible, reputable **11** trustworthy **12** satisfactory

credit: **4** deem, feel, loan **5** asset, chalk, faith, honor, merit, tenet, trust **6** belief, charge, esteem, impute, renown, repute, weight **7** ascribe, believe **8** accredit, credence **10** estimation **11** recognition

credulous: **4** fond **5** naive **6** unwary **8** credible, gullible

creed: ism **4** cult, sect **5** credo, dogma, faith, tenet **6** belief **7** trowing **8** doctrine **10** confession
  Christian: **6** Nicene **8** Apostle's

creek: bay, ria, rio **4** burn (Sc.), cove, kill, pill, rill, slue **5** bayou, bight, bogue, brook, crick, fleet, inlet, zanja **6** arroyo, estero, Indian, slough, stream **7** estuary, freshet, rivulet **11** watercourse

creel: **4** caul, cawl, rack, trap **6** basket, junket

creep: **4** fawn, inch, ramp **5** crawl, prowl, skulk, slink, steal **6** cringe, dawdle, grovel, scride **7** cramble, gumshoe **9** pussyfoot

creeper: ivy **4** shoe, vine, worm **5** snake **6** ipecac, romper, tecoma

creeping: **4** slow **7** reptant, servile **9** reptilian **11** reptatorial

creese: **4** kris, stab **5** sword **6** dagger, weapon

cremate: **4** burn **9** incremate **10** incinerate

Cremona: **5** Amati **6** violin

crena: **5** cleft, notch **7** scallop **11** indentation

crenic acid salt: **7** crenate

creole: **6** patois **7** mestizo

Creole State: **9** Louisiana

crepe: **6** blintz, fabric **7** frizzed, pancake **8** crinkled, wrinkled

crepey cloth: **6** plissé

crepitate: **4** snap **6** rattle **7** crackle

crepuscule: **8** twilight

crescent: **4** horn, lune, moon, rool **5** curve, lunar, lunule **7** lunette, menisci (pl.) **8** meniscus **10** semicircle
  point: **4** cusp

crescent-shaped: **6** bicorn, lunate **7** lunated, lunular **9** semilunar

crescive: **7** growing **10** increasing

cresset: **5** torch **6** basket, beacon, signal **7** furnace **8** flambeau

crest: cop, tip, top **4** acme, apex, comb, edge, knap, peak, seal, tuft **5** chine, crown, plume, ridge **6** apogee, climax, copple, crista, finial, height, helmet, summit **7** bearing **8** pinnacle, whitecap **10** cognizance **11** culmination
  rugged: **5** arete

crested: **6** muffed **7** crisate, crowned **8** pileated **9** coronated

crestfallen: low **4** blue, down **5** cowed **8** dejected **10** dispirited **11** downhearted **12** disconsolate

creta: **5** chalk

cretaceous: **6** chalky

Crete: (see box)

Cretheus: *son:* **8** Amythaon
  wife: **7** Biadice

cretin: **5** idiot

Creusa: *father:* **5** Priam
  husband: **6** Aeneas
  mother: **6** Hecuba
  son: **8** Ascanius

Crete: 6 Candia
  cape: 4 krio 5 krios
  capital: 5 Canea 6 Khania
  city: Hag 5 Khora 6 Kisamo, Malemi, Mallia, Meleme, Retimo 7 Kasteli 8 Iraklion, Nikolacs, Sphakion 9 Heraclion, Tympakion 11 Palaiokhora
  earth spirit: 6 Curete
  flier: 6 Icarus
  goddess: 8 Dictynna 11 Britomartis
  king: 5 Minos 9 Idomeneus
  language: 5 Greek 6 Minoan (ancient)
  man of brass: 5 Talos
  maze: 9 labyrinth
  monster: 8 Minotaur
  mountain: Ida 5 Dikte 9 Psiloriti
  princess: 7 Ariadne

crevasse: 5 chasm, split 8 cleavage
crevice: 4 bore, leak, nook, seam, vein 5 break, chine, chink, cleft, crack, grike 6 cranny 7 fissure, opening 8 cleavage, crevasse, peephole 10 interstice
crew: men, mob, set 4 band, gang, herd, oars, team 5 covey, group, hands, party, squad, staff 6 seamen, throng 7 company, faculty, members, retinue 8 equipage, mariners 10 assemblage, complement
crewel: 6 caddis 7 caddice 10 crewelwork, embroidery
crib: bed, bin, box, cab, cot, cub, hut, key 4 boom, dive, pony, rack, raft, trot 5 boose, boosy, cheat, crate, frame, hovel, stall, steal 6 bunker, cratch, creche, manger, pilfer 7 purloin 8 cribbage 9 enclosure 10 plagiarize, storehouse
cribbage score: nob, peg
crick: 4 kink 5 creek, hitch, spasm, twist
cricket: 4 game, grig 6 insect
  genus: 7 gryllus
  run: bye
  side: ons
  sound: 5 chirp 12 stridulation
  team: 6 eleven
  term: off, ons, rot 4 over 5 smick 6 yorker
crier: 4 huer 5 cryer 6 beadle, herald, wailer 7 muezzin
crime: act, sin 4 evil, rape 5 abuse, arson, blame, theft, wrong 6 felony, murder, piacle 7 misdeed, offense 8 iniquity 9 violation 10 wickedness 11 abomination, malefaction, misdemeanor 13 transgression
  ecclesiastical: 6 simony
  goddess of: Ate
  organized: 10 underworld
  scene of: 5 venue
Crimea: 4 Krym 9 peninsula

  city: 5 Kerch, Yalta 10 Sevastopol
  people: 5 Tauri
  river: 4 Alma
  sea: 4 Azof, Azov 5 Black
criminal: bad 4 yegg 5 crook, felon 6 guilty, inmate, nocent, slayer, wicked 7 convict, culprit, illegal 8 culpable, gangster 9 desperado, wrongdoer 10 blackguard, deplorable, flagitious, malefactor, malfeasant 11 blameworthy, disgraceful 13 reprehensible
  habitual: 8 repeater 10 recidivist
  refuge: 7 Alsatia 11 Whitefriars
criminology branch: 8 penology
crimp: bit, rub 4 bend, curl, fold, friz, pote, wave, weak 5 cramp, flute, frizz, pinch, plait 6 goffer, hold in, ruffle 7 crinkle, friable, gauffer, wrinkle 8 hold back, obstacle 9 corrugate 12 inconsistent
crimson: dye, lac, red 4 pink, rose 5 blush, color, rouge 6 bloody, maroon, modena 7 carmine, scarlet
crine: 4 hair, mane 6 shrink 7 shrivel
cringe: bow 4 bend, fawn, jouk 5 binge, cower, crawl, quail, sneak, stoop, toady, wince, yield 6 crouch, grovel, shrink, submit 7 crinkle, distort, truckle 8 bootlick 11 apple-polish
cringing: 6 abject 7 hangdog
cringle: orb 4 disk 6 eyelet, terret 7 grommet
crinite: 5 hairy 6 fossil
crinitory: 5 hairy 7 crinose
crinkle: 4 bend, curl, kink, turn, wind 5 crimp, plica, ridge 6 pucker, ripple, ruck up, rumple, rustle 7 crackle, wrinkle 9 corrugate 11 convolution
cripple: mar 4 halt, harm, hurt, lame, main, wing 6 bacach, hobble, impair, injure, scotch, spavin, weaken 7 crapple, crumpet, disable, lamiter (Sc.) 8 enfeeble, handicap, mutilate, paralyze 9 hamstring 12 incapacitate
crisis: 4 acme, crux, pass, turn 5 panic, peril, pinch, trial 6 strait 8 decision, juncture 9 criterion, emergency 10 crossroads 11 conjunction 12 turning point
crisp: new 4 cold 5 brisk, clear, curly, fresh, nippy, pithy, sharp, short, stiff, terse 6 biting, bright, lively 7 bracing, brittle, concise, cutting, friable 8 clearcut 9 crackling, trenchant
crispin: 4 coat 9 shoemaker
crisscross: 4 awry 7 network 8 confused 9 intersect
cristate: 6 ridged, tufted 7 crested
criterion: low 4 norm, rule, test, type 5 axiom, canon, gauge, nodel, proof 6 metric 7 measure 8 standard 9 yardstick 10 indication, touchstone

critic: **5** booer, judge, momus **6** carper, censor, expert, slater **8** collator, reviewer **9** detractor, literator, muckraker, nitpicker **11** connoisseur, criticaster, faultfinder

critical: **4** dire, edge **5** acute, exact **6** urgent **7** carping, exigent **8** captious, decisive, exacting **10** censorious, fastidious **12** faultfinding **14** discriminating
mark: **6** obelus **7** obelisk
study: **6** examen **8** exegesis

criticism: **5** blame **6** review **7** comment **8** critique, diatribe, judgment **9** stricture **10** assessment, commentary **13** animadversion

criticize: hit, pan, rap, rip **4** carp, flay, slam, slur, yelp **5** blame, blast, cavil, judge, knock, roast **6** jeer at, rebuke, review **7** censure, comment, examine **8** critique **9** castigate **10** animadvert

Crius: *father:* **6** Uranus
mother: **4** Gaea, Gaia
sister: **7** Eurybia
son: **8** Astraeus

croak: caw, die **4** gasp, kill **5** creak, quark, speak **6** grouch, grouse **7** forbode, grumble **8** complain

Croatia: *capital:* **6** Zagreb
city: **5** Fiume, Rieka, Split **6** Osijek, Rijeka **9** Dubrovnik
currency: **5** dinar
mountain: **6** Kapela **11** Dinaric Alps

crochet: **4** hoot, lace **5** braid, plait, weave **11** Orvieto lace

crock: jar, pig, pot **4** bull, smut, soil, soot **5** stool **6** critch, smudge **8** potsherd **11** earthenware

crockery: **5** china, cloam **6** dishes, plates **11** earthenware

crocodile: goa **5** gator **6** cayman, gavial, jacare, mugger **7** reptile **9** alligator
genus: **11** goniopholis

crocus: **4** irid, lily **7** saffron **9** colchicum **12** pasqueflower

Croesus: **4** king **9** moneybags, plutocrat
capital: **6** Sardis
country: **5** Lydia
father: **8** Alyattes

croft: **4** farm **5** crypt, field, garth, vault **6** bleach, cavern

cromlech: **5** quoit **6** circle, dolmen **7** gorsedd **9** cyclolith

Cromwell: **4** Noll **6** Oliver
regiment: **9** Ironsides
son: **7** Richard
son-in-law: **6** Ireton
victory site: **6** Naseby

crone: hag **4** cive **5** biddy, witch **6** beldam **7**

beldame **9** cailleach, cailliach

Cronus: **5** Titan
daughter: **4** Hera **6** Hestia **7** Demeter
father: **6** Uranus
mother: **4** Gaea
sister: **4** Rhea **6** Cybele, Tethys
son: **4** Zeus **5** Hades **7** Jupiter, Neptune **8** Poseidon
wife: **4** Rhea **6** Cybele

crony: pal **4** chum **9** associate, companion

crook: **4** bend, turn, warp **5** cheat, cleek, crump, curve, pedum, staff, thief, trick **6** robber **7** crosier, crozier **8** artifice, swindler **10** camshachle (Sc.)

crooked: cam **4** agee, awry, bent **5** agley (Sc.), askew, false, gleed, lying, snaky, snide **6** akimbo, artful, aslant, crabby, crafty, curved, errant, shifty, tricky, zigzag **7** askance, asquint, corrupt, crabbed, oblique, turning, twisted, winding **8** tortuous **9** dishonest, distorted, irregular **10** circuitous, fraudulent, misleading **12** dishonorable, unscrupulous

croon: hum, low **4** boom, lull, sing, wail **5** chirm, whine **6** lament, murmur **8** complain

crop: cut, maw, top **4** clip, craw, knap, reap, trim, whip **5** fruit, quirt, shear **6** gather, gebbie, silage **7** curtail, harvest, tillage **8** gleaning, ingulies
goddess of: **6** Annona
second growth: **5** rowen
year's: **6** annona

cropper: **8** collapse, disaster

croquet: **5** roque

croquette: **5** cecil **6** oyster

crosier, crozier: **5** crook, cross, staff

cross: go, mix **4** ford, rood, span **5** angry, testy, trial **6** bisect, crabby, cranky, crouch, emblem, gibbet, grumpy, outwit, signum, sullen, symbol, thwart, touchy **7** athwart, crabbed, fretful, froward, oblique, peevish, pettish, potence, sell out **8** crotched, crucifix, petulant, snappish, suastica, swastika, traverse, vexillum **9** frustrate, half-breed, intersect, irritable, plaintive **10** affliction, ill-humored, transverse **12** disagreeable **13** quick-tempered
barred: **11** trabeculate
fiery: **8** crantara **9** crostarie
Greek: **6** fylfot
stroke: **5** serif **6** ceriph
swords: **4** duel **5** fight **6** combat
tau: **4** crux **5** ankh
type: **5** Greek, Latin, Papal **6** Celtic, fleuré, formée, moline **7** Maltese **8** Egyptian, Lorraine

crossbar: **4** axle, rung **5** round **10** horizontal

crossbeam: bar **5** trave **6** girder

crossbow: **6** weapon **8** arbalest

crossbreed: 5 husky 6 hybrid 9 hybridize

cross-examine: 5 grill 8 question 11 interrogate

cross-eye: 6 squint 9 esotropia 10 strabismus

cross-grained: 7 gnarled 8 churlish, perverse 9 irascible 12 cantankerous

crosshatch: 7 engrave

crossing: 7 passage 8 opposing

cross out: 4 dele 5 blank, erase 6 cancel, delete 9 eliminate

crosspatch: 4 bear, crab 6 grouch

crosspiece: bar 4 spar, yoke 5 grill 8 crossarm 10 doubletree

cross-rib: 4 arch 6 lierne

crossroads: 4 pass 5 pinch 6 crisis 8 zero hour 9 carrefour 11 interaction 12 turning point
  goddess: 6 Hecate, Hekate, Trivia

crossruff: 6 seesaw 9 alternate

cross section: 4 part 5 slice 6 sample 14 representation

crosswise: 6 across 7 athwart 8 acrostic, diagonal

crotch: 4 fork, pole, post 5 cleft, notch, stake 9 stanchion

crotchet: fad 4 hook, kink, whim 5 fancy 6 vagary 9 conundrum 11 peculiarity 12 eccentricity

crotchety: 6 cranky 10 capricious

crouch: 4 bend, fawn, ruck 5 cower, hunch, squat, stoop 6 cringe 7 scrooch

crouching: 8 couchant

crouton: bit 5 toast 7 garnish

crow: aga, caw, cry, daw, jay 4 bird, brag, rook 5 boast, exult, raven, vaunt 6 carnal, corvas, magpie 7 grapnel, jackdaw, swagger 9 blackbird
  colony: 7 rookery
  cry: caw
  pert. to: 7 corvine

crow-like: 7 corvine

crowbar: pry 5 jemmy, jimmy, lever 7 gablock 8 gavelock

crowd: jam, mob, set 4 bike, cram, herd, host, pack, push, rock, rout, stow, swad 5 bunch, cramp, crush, drove, flock, group, horde, posse, press, serry, shoal, swarm, three, wedge 6 boodle, clique, hubble, huddle, jostle, rabble, throng 7 bourock (Sc.), company, squeeze 10 multitude 10 assemblage, clamjamfry (Sc.), confluence
  penetrate: 5 elbow 6 needle

crowded: 4 full 5 close, dense, thick 6 filled, jammed, loaded, packed 7 bunched, compact, serried, stipate, stuffed, teeming 9 chock-full, congested

crowder: 6 loader 7 fiddler 8 thatcher

crown: cap, top 4 coin, pate, peak, poll 5 adorn, basil, bezel, bezil, crest, miter, mitre, tiara 6 anadem, circle, climax, corona (L.), diadem, fillet, invest, laurel, potong, reward, summit, trophy, wreath 7 aureole, chaplet, coronet, garland, install 8 coronate, enthrone, pinnacle, surmount 9 finish off, headdress, sovereign
  pert. to: 7 coronal

crown prince: 4 heir 7 dauphin (F.) 8 atheling

crozier: See **crosier**

cru: 8 vineyard

crucial: 4 dire 5 acute, vital 6 severe, trying 7 pivotal, telling 8 critical, decisive 9 important, necessary

crucible: pot 4 dish, etna, test 6 cruset, ordeal, retort 7 furnace 10 affliction 11 climacteric

crucifix: pax 4 rood 5 cross

crucify: vex 4 hang, kill 5 harry 6 martyr 7 mortify, torment, torture 8 cruciate 9 persecute

crud: goo 4 curd, gook, gunk, junk 5 filth, slime, trash 6 refuse 7 thicken

crude: raw 4 bald, bare, rude 5 crass, green, harsh, rough 6 callow, coarse, savage, unripe, vulgar 7 uncouth 8 immature, impolite 9 primitive, unglossed, unrefined, untrained 10 incomplete, unpolished 11 undeveloped 13 inexperienced

cruel: 4 fell, hard 5 harsh 6 bloody, brutal, fierce, savage, severe, unjust, unkind 7 bestial, brutish, inhuman, neronic 8 barbaric, diabolic, fiendish, inhumane, pitiless, ruthless, sadistic, tyrannic 9 atrocious, draconian, ferocious, heartless, merciless, rapacious, unfeeling 10 diabolical, sanguinary, vindictive 11 hardhearted

cruet: ama, jar, jug 4 vial 5 cruse 6 bottle, caster, guttus, vessel 7 ampulla, burette 9 container

cruise: 4 boat, sail, trip 6 voyage 9 excursion

cruiser: 4 ship 6 vessel 7 warship 9 patrol car, powerboat

cruising: 4 asea

cruller: 7 olycook, olykoek 8 doughnut 9 friedcake

crumb: bit, ort 5 piece, scrap, shred 6 little, morsel 7 remnant, smidgen, smidgin 8 fragment, particle

crumb covered: 7 breaded

crumble: rot 5 break, crush, decay, slake, spoil 6 molder, perish 7 moulder 9 break down, decompose, pulverize 12 disintegrate

crumbly: 7 friable

crumpet: 4 cake 6 muffin 7 pikelet

crumple: 4 fold, muss 5 crush 6 crease, furrow, raffle, rumple 7 crunkle, wrinkle 8 collapse, contract 9 corrugate

crunch: 4 bite, chew 5 chomp, crump, crush, gnash, grind, munch, press 6 cranch 7 craunch, scrunch 8 ruminate 9 masticate

cruor: 4 gore 5 blood

crural joint: 4 knee

crus: 5 shank

crusade: war **5** jehad, jihad **8** campaign **10** expedition

crusader: **7** pilgrim, Templar **8** reformer
enemy: **7** Saladin, Saracen
port: **4** Acre

crush: bow, jam **4** cram, dash, mash, mill, mull **5** brake, break, crash, craze, crowd, force, grind, press, quash, quell, smash, tread, unman **6** bruise, burden, crunch, squash, subdue, thwack **7** conquer, crumple, depress, destroy, oppress, overrun, repress, scrunch, scrunge, shatter, squeeze, squelch **8** bear down, compress, demolish, overcome, suppress **9** overpower, overwhelm, pulverize **10** annihilate, obliterate

crust: **4** cake, hull, rind **5** shell **6** eschar, harden **7** coating **8** pellicle

crustacean: **4** crab, flea, scud **5** louse, prawn **6** endite, isopod, shrimp **7** lobster, squilla **8** barnacle **9** water flea **10** whale louse
appendage: **5** exite **6** endite **7** pleopod
claw: **5** chela **6** pincer
feeler: **7** antenna
genus: **5** eryon, hippa **6** tripos
group: **7** caridea
larva: **5** alima **8** nauplius
limb: **6** podite **8** podomere
small: **6** isopod **7** copepod **8** barnacle
ten-footed: **4** crab

crusty: **4** curt **5** bluff, blunt, crisp, gruff, surly, testy **6** morose **7** crabbed, peevish, pettish **8** choleric, snappish **11** ill-tempered

crux: nub **4** ankh, core, gist, pith **5** cross, point **6** kernel, puzzle, riddle **7** problem **9** substance **10** difficulty

cry: boo, caw, cri (F.), fad, hue, ole, sob, yip **4** bawl, bump, call, evoe, hawk, hoot, howl, keen, mewl, pule, rage, scry, wail, weep, yell, yelp **5** clepe, crede, greet, groan, rumor, shout, sound, utter, vogue, whewl, whine **6** bellow, boohoo, clamor, demand, lament, outcry, quethe, scream, shriek, slogan, snivel, squall, squeal, wimick, yammer **7** clamour, exclaim, fashion, screech **8** proclaim **11** acclamation, lamentation
court: **4** oyes, oyez
derisive: bah, boo **4** hiss, hoot **6** phooey **7** catcall **9** razzberry **10** Bronx cheer
for: **4** need **6** demand, desire
for help: PAN **6** Mayday
gang's signal: **4** whyo
havoc: **8** mobilize
of approval: ole, rah **5** bravo
of pain: **4** ouch
of relief: **4** phew, whew
of sorrow: woe **4** alas **5** alack
of triumph: aha **6** hurrah
out: bay **4** bawl, hoot, howl **5** blame, crake, deery **7** censure, exclaim, protest **8** complain, denounce

political: **6** slogan **10** shibboleth

crying: **4** dire **6** urgent **7** burning, clamant, heinous **8** pressing, recreant **9** notorious **11** exclamatory

crying bird: **7** limpkin

crying hare: **4** pika

crying out: **10** childbirth **11** confinement

crypt: pit **4** cave, cell, tomb **5** croft, vault **6** cavern, grotto, recess **7** chamber **8** follicle **9** mausoleum **10** depression

cryptic: **4** dark **5** murky, vague **6** hidden, occult, secret **7** obscure **9** enigmatic, recondite **10** mysterious **12** hieroglyphic

cryptogram: **4** code **6** cipher **11** cryptograph

crystal: ice **4** dial, hard **5** clear, glass, lucid **6** limpid, pebble **7** acicula, diamond **8** clearcut, pellucid **11** crystalline, transparent
gazer: **4** seer **7** seeress
ice: **6** frazil
twin: **5** macle

crystalline: **4** pure **7** crystal **8** pellucid **11** transparent
acid: **7** alanine
compound: **5** alban **6** anisil, oscine **7** aconite, amarine **8** atropine
mineral: **4** mica, spar **6** quartz **7** apatite **8** boracite, elaterin
phenol: **5** orcin **6** orcine
pine tar: **6** retene
salt: **5** borax **8** analgene, racemate
structure: **6** sparry **8** siderite

Cuba: *bay:* **4** Nipe, Pigs **10** Guantanamo
bird: **6** trogon **8** tocororo
capital: **6** Havana
carriage: **7** volante
castle: **5** Morro
city: **6** Guines **7** Palmira **8** Camaguey, Matanzas, Santiago **10** Cienfuegos, Santa Clara **14** Puerto Principe
currency: **4** peso **6** gourde **7** centavo **8** cuarenta
dance: **5** conga, mambo, rumba **6** danzon **9** cha-cha-cha
fish: **6** diablo **7** viajaca
measure: **4** vara **5** bocoy, tarea **6** cordel, fanega **10** caballeria
national anthem: **10** La Bayamesa
rodent: **5** hutia **6** pilori
root: **7** malanga
rum: ron **7** Bacardi
secret police: **5** porra
snake: **4** juba
storm: **6** bayamo
tobacco: **4** capa **6** vuelta
U.S. naval base: **10** Guantanamo
ward: **6** barrio
weapon: **7** machete
weight: **5** libra **6** tercio

substance: 4 urea 6 dulcin 9 scopoline

crystallize: 5 candy, sugar 7 congeal 8 solidify 9 granulate

Cry the Beloved Country author: 5 Paton

cub: fry, pen 4 bear, coop, shed 5 stall, whelp 6 lionet, novice 7 codling 8 reporter 9 youngster

Cuba: (see box)

cubbyhole: 4 nook

cube: cut, die 4 dice 5 block, solid 10 hexahedron

cube spar: 9 anhydrite

cubic: 5 solid 9 isometric

decimeter: 5 liter, litre

meter: 5 stere

shape: 6 cuboid

cubicle: bay 4 cell, room 5 booth, niche 6 alcove, office

cubitus: 4 ulna 7 forearm

Cuchulain, Cuchullin: 4 hero 7 warrior

father: Lug

foe: 5 Maeve

kingdom: 6 Ulster

mother: 8 Dechtire

son: 8 Conlaoch

wife: 4 Emer 5 Eimer

cuckoo: ani 4 bird, fool, gowk, koel 5 clock, crazy, silly 7 boobook 8 rainfowl 10 road runner

kind: 6 coucal, kobird 7 dowbird, wryneck 8 coccyzus

cuckoopint: 4 arum 5 aaron, plant 6 bobbin, dragon 7 buckram 8 mandrake 9 wakerobin

cucullate: 6 cowled, hooded 7 covered 10 hood-shaped

cucumber: 4 cuke, pepo 5 gourd 6 conger, pepino (Sp.), pickle 7 gherkin 9 elaterium

cud: 4 chew, quid 5 bolus, rumen 6 cudgel

cuddle: hug, pet 6 caress, cosset, fondle, nestle 7 embrace, snuggle

cuddy: ass 4 lout 5 bribe, cabin 6 donkey, galley, pantry 9 blockhead

cudgel: bat 4 beat, cane, club, drub, rack 5 baste, drive, kebby, kevel, staff, stave, stick 6 alpeen, ballow, baston, kebbie, thrash, weapon 7 belabor, bourdon 8 bludgeon, shillala 9 bastinado, blackjack, crabstick, fustigate, truncheon 10 nightstick, shillelagh

cue: nod, tip 4 ball, hint, mast, tail, wink 5 braid, cluff, plait, queue, stick, twist 6 prompt, signal 7 pigtail 9 catchword 10 intimation

cuff: box 4 bank, blow, gowf, slam, slap, slug, swat 5 clout, fight, gowff, miser, smite, spank 6 buffet, codger, mitten, strike, wallop 7 scuffle 8 gauntlet, handcuff

cuirass: 4 mail 5 armor, loric, plate 6 lorica, thorax

cuisine: 4 food, menu 5 table 7 cookery

cul-de-sac: 6 pocket, strait 7 deadend, impasse 10 blind alley, difficulty

culicid: 8 mosquito

cull: opt 4 dupe, gull, pick, sift, sort 5 elect, glean, pluck 6 assort, choose, gather, remove, select 8 separate 9 single out

culm: 5 slack 6 refuse 7 deposit

culmen: top 4 acme 5 ridge

culmination: end 4 acme, apex, noon, peak 5 crown 6 apogee, climax, summit, vertex, zenith 10 completion 11 ne plus ultra 12 consummation

culpa: 5 fault, guilt 10 negligence 12 carelessness

culpable: 6 faulty, guilty, laches 7 immoral 8 criminal 10 censurable 11 blameworthy 13 reprehensible

culprit: 5 felon 7 convict 8 criminal, offender 10 malefactor

cult: 4 clan, sect 5 creed, faith 6 church, ritual, school 7 worship 8 religion 12 denomination

cultivate: ear, hoe 4 disk, farm, grow, plow, rear, tend, till, work 5 nurse, raise, study, train 6 affect, foster, harrow, plough 7 acquire, cherish, educate, husband, improve, nourish, prepare 8 civilize 9 encourage

cultivated: 5 civil 6 polite 7 genteel, refined 8 cultured, well-bred 12 domesticated

land: 4 farm 5 arada, tilth

cultivation: 6 polish 7 culture, farming, tillage 9 culturing, husbandry 10 refinement 12 civilization

art: 9 geoponics

cultivator: 4 plow 6 farmer, harrow, plough, tiller 7 grubber, husband 10 husbandman

culture: art 4 agar 5 taste 6 polish 7 tillage 9 knowledge 10 discipline, refinement 11 savoir faire 12 civilization 13 enlightenment

medium: 4 agar

culver: 4 dove 6 pigeon

culvert: 5 drain, sluit 6 bridge 7 conduit 8 overpass

cumbersome: 5 heavy 6 clumsy 7 awkward, onerous, weighty 8 cumbrous, unwieldy 10 burdensome

cumbrous: 8 clogging, unwieldy 9 difficult, vexatious 10 burdensome, cumbersome

cumin: 5 anise, cumic 7 parsley

cummerbund: obi 4 band, belt, faja, sash

cumshaw: tip 5 bonus 6 thanks 7 present 8 gratuity

cumulate: 4 heap 5 amass, lay up 6 gather 7 combine 9 stockpile 10 accumulate

cunabula: 6 cradle

cuneal: 7 cuneate 11 wedge-shaped

cuneiform: 4 bone 6 wedged 7 writing 8 sphenoid

cunner: 5 canoe 6 nipper, wrasse

cunning: sly, wit 4 arch, cute, foxy, keen, wily 5 downy, guile, sharp, smart 6 adroit, artful, astute, callid, clever, crafty, deadal, deceit, shrewd, subtle, tricky, wisdom 7 curious, finesse, know-how, politic, vulpine 8 dextrous, skillful, stealthy 9 chicanery, colubrine, designing, dexterity, ingenious, knowledge, sagacious 10 fraudulent 10 witchcraft 13 Machiavellian

cup: ama, dop, mug, tyg 4 tass, toby 5 bouse, calix, cruse, glass, grail, phial, stein, tazza 6 beaker, crater, goblet, noggin, potion, vessel 7 chalice, stirrup, tankard
  assay: 4 test 5 cupel 6 beaker
  Communion: 7 chalice
  cup-shaped: 8 pezizoid 9 scypliate 10 cyathiform
  diamond cutting: dop
  eared: 6 quaich, quaigh
  earthenware: mug
  fungus: 6 aecium
  handle: ear, lug
  holder: 4 zarf
  horn-shaped: 6 holmos
  large: 5 grail, jorum
  looped handles: 5 kylix 9 cantharus, kantharos
  loving: tyg 5 award, prize
  of tea: 5 forte, thing 6 metier
  pastry: 7 dariole
  resembling: 9 oalicular
  small: 4 shot 5 chark, cruse 6 noggin 8 cannikin 9 demitasse
  sports: 5 Davis, Ryder, World 6 Curtis 7 Stanley 8 America's, Wightman
  two-handled: tig, tyg 5 depas

cupbearer of the gods: 4 Hebe 8 Ganymede

cupboard: kas 4 case, safe 5 ambry, cuddy 6 buffet, closet, larder, pantry 7 armoire, cabinet, dresser 8 credenza 9 sideboard

cupel: 4 burn, test 6 refine

Cupid: Dan 4 Amor, Eros, love 7 Amorino
  beloved of: 6 Psyche
  mother: 5 Venus
  weapon: 5 arrow

cupidity: 4 lust 5 greed 6 desire 7 avarice, avidity, longing 8 appetite 12 covetousness
  demon of: 6 Mammon

cupola: 4 dome, kiln 5 vault 6 turret 7 furnace, lantern, lookout

cur: cad, dog, yap 4 fice, mutt, tike, toad, tyke 5 feist 6 canine, messan, messin, rotter 7 bobtail, mongrel 9 goldeneye, yellow dog

curacao: 7 liqueur

Curacao: 6 island 7 liqueur
  city: 10 Willemstad
  sea: 9 Caribbean

curare: 5 urare, urari 6 oorali, poison

curassow: 4 crax, mitu 8 game bird

curate: cur 4 abbe 5 agent 7 dominie, vicaire 8 minister 9 assistant, clergyman

curative: 7 healing 8 remedial, salutary, sanative 9 medicinal 11 restorative, therapeutic 12 invigorating

curator: 6 keeper 7 manager, steward 8 guardian, overseer 9 custodian 14 superintendent

curb: bit 4 foil, rein 5 brake, check, curve, guard, limit 6 arrest, bridle, govern, hamper, thwart 7 control, inhibit, repress, shackle 8 hold back, hold down, moderate, restrain, restrict, withhold 9 constrain, hindrance 10 hamshackle

curculio: 4 turk 6 weevil

curd: See curdle

curdle: 4 clot, earn (Sc.), leep, quar, sour, yern 5 quail, quarl, spoil 6 posset, quarle 7 clabber, congeal, thicken 8 condense 9 coagulate
  agent causing: 6 rennet

cure: age, tan 4 boot, care, heal, heed, help, jerk, salt, save 5 reest, smoke 6 charge, curacy, physic, remedy, season 7 restore, therapy 8 antidote, preserve
  by smoking: 6 gammon, smudge
  in sun: 6 rizzar
  skins: 5 dress

cure-all: 4 balm 5 avens 6 elixir, remedy 7 nostrum, panacea 10 catholicon

curfew: 4 bell 6 signal

curio: 5 relic, virtu 6 bauble, gewgaw 7 bibelot 8 keepsake, souvenir 9 bric-a-brac, curiosity, objet d'art 10 knickknack

curious: odd 4 nosy, rare 5 queer 6 prying, quaint 7 cunning, strange, unusual 8 freakish, meddling, peculiar, singular 9 intrusive, wondering 11 inquisitive

curl: 4 bend, coil, kink, lock, roll, wave, wind 5 acker, crisp, tress, twist 6 buckle, frowse, ripple, spiral, writhe 7 crimple, flexure, ringlet, tendril 11 convolution 12 heartbreaker

curled: 5 fuzzy, kinky 7 savoyed

curlew: 4 bird, fute 5 kioea, snipe, whaup 6 marlin, smoker 7 bustard

curlicue: ess, tag 5 caper, curve 6 paraph, squirl 7 souggle 8 flourish, purlicue, squiggle

curling mark: tee

curly: 4 wavy 5 crisp 7 rippled 8 crinkled

curmudgeon: 4 crab 5 churl, miser 6 grouch 7 niggard

currant: 5 berry 6 raisin, rizzar
  genus: 5 ribes

currency: 4 cash, coin 5 bills, lucre, money, scrip 6 specie 10 greenbacks 11 legal tender

current: now, way 4 eddy, flow, flux, ford, rife, tide 5 drift, going, rapid, tenor, trend, usual

6 coeval, common, course, living, motion, moving, recent, stream **7** counter, flowing, general, ongoing, present, running, thermal, torrent **8** frequent **9** prevalent **10** prevailing **11** electricity **15** contemporaneous
generator: **12** electromotor
measuring device: **7** ammeter
ocean: **7** riptide **8** undertow **9** maelstrom, whirlpool
pert. to: **7** voltaic

currish: **4** base **7** cynical, ignoble **8** snarling **12** mean-spirited

curry: **4** comb, drub **5** clean, dress, groom **6** bruise, cajole, powder **7** prepare **9** condiment, seasoning
favor: **4** fawn **6** cajole, smooge

curse: ban **4** bane, blow, damn, oath **5** spell, swear **6** malign **7** beshrew, malison **8** anathema **9** blaspheme, imprecate **10** execration, vituperate **11** deprecation, malediction **12** anathematize **13** excommunicate

cursed: bad **6** damned, odious **8** blighted, virulent **9** execrable **13** blankety-blank

cursory: **4** fast **5** brief, hasty, quick, short **6** fitful, speedy **7** passing, shallow, sketchy **8** careless, rambling **9** desultory, irregular, transient **10** discursive, evanescent **11** superficial

curt: **4** rude, tart **5** bluff, blunt, brief, brusk, short, terse **6** abrupt **7** brusque, concise **8** cavalier, succinct **9** condensed

curtail: cut, lop **4** clip, crop, dock, pare, stop **5** abate, short, slash, stunt **6** lessen, reduce, teaser **7** abridge, bobtail, shorten **8** diminish, minorate, retrench **9** decurtate, epitomize **10** abbreviate

curtain: end **4** boom, drop, mask, veil, wall **5** blind, drape, shade **6** purdah, screen, shroud **7** ceiling, conceal, drapery **8** portiere
half: **4** bise, cafe **5** brise
holder: rod
raiser: **9** forepiece

curtains: end **5** death **6** demise **7** decease, drapery

curtilage: **4** quad, yard **5** court **9** enclosure **10** fenced area

curtsy, curtsey: bob, bow **4** beck **5** conge **9** obeisance

curvaceous: **7** endowed, rounded, shapely, stacked **9** well-built

curvature: arc **4** bool, curl **8** kyphosis, lordosis **9** arcuation, scoliosis
center locus: **7** evolute
convex: **6** camber
surface: **5** plane

curve: arc, bow, ess **4** arch, bend, curb, ogee, turn, veer **5** ambit, bight, crook, crump, swirl, twist **6** bought, spiral **7** circuit, concave, contour, curvity, ellipse, flexure, inflect, sinuate **8** parabola, sinusaid, twisting **9** convexity, curvature
cusp: **7** spinode
double point of: **6** acnode
kind: **9** parabolic **10** memniscate
mathematical plane: **5** polar
parallel to an ellipse: **6** toroid
S-shaped: ess **4** ogee **7** sigmoid

curved: **4** bent **5** round, wound **6** convex, hamate, turned **7** arcuate, arrondi, crooked, curvant **8** anchoral, aquiline, arciform
inward: **5** adunc **6** hooked **8** aduncous

curvet: hop **4** leap, turn **5** bound, caper, frisk **6** cavort, frolic, gambol, gyrate, prance **8** corvetta (F.) **9** courbette, horse leap

Cush: *father:* Ham
son: **4** Seba **6** Nimrod

cushat: **4** bird, dove **6** pigeon

cushion: bag, cod, mat, pad **4** boss, seat **5** gaddi, squab **6** buffer, insole, jockey, pillow, sachet **7** bolster, hassock **9** upholster
stuffing: **4** baru, down **5** kapok **8** feathers

cusk: **4** fish, tusk **5** torsk **6** burbot

cusp: tip **4** apex, horn, peak **5** angle, point, tooth **6** corner **8** paracone **10** projection

cuspid: **11** canine tooth

custard: **4** flan **5** flawn **6** doucet, dowcet, dowset **8** flummery **9** charlotte

custard apple: **5** anona **6** annona, pawpaw **8** sweetsop

custodian: **5** guard **6** bailee, keeper, warden **7** curator, janitor **8** cerberus, guardian **9** caretaker, protector **10** supervisor

custody: **4** care, ward **5** trust **6** charge **7** control, durance, keeping, tuition **11** safekeeping **12** guardianship

custom: fad, law, mos (L.), tax, use **4** duty, form, garb, mode, more, rite, rote, rule, toll, wont **5** habit, haunt, usage, vogue **6** dastur, impost, ritual **7** costume, fashion, tribute **8** business, practice **9** costumbre, patronage **10** consuetude, convention, observance, tailor-made **12** constitution
of peoples: **5** mores
with force of law: mos

customary: **5** nomic, usual **6** common **7** general **8** familiar, habitual, orthodox **10** accustomed **11** traditional **12** conventional **14** consuetudinary

customer: **4** chap **5** buyer **6** client, patron **7** callant, patient, shopper **8** consumer, prospect **9** purchaser
group: **9** clientele
steady: **7** habitue, regular

customs: tax **4** cess, duty, levy, rate, toll **5** mores **6** impost, tariff **7** trewage
officer: **8** douanier

cut: bob, hew, lop, mow, nip, rip **4** bite, chip,

chop, clip, crop, dock, fell, gash, hack, knap, mode, nick, pare, raze, slit, snee, snip, snub, trim **5** carve, flick, knife, lance, mince, notch, piece, prune, razee, scarp, sever, share, shear, shorn, slash, slice, snick, split **6** ablate, bisect, broach, chisel, cleave, dilute, divide, excise, haggle, ignore, incise, lessen, mangle, reduce, slight, swinge **7** affront, curtail, shorten, whittle **8** lacerate, mark down, retrench **9** engraving

a melon: **5** allot **8** dispense

a rug: **5** dance

across: **5** slice **8** transect **9** intersect, transcend

along: go **5** speed

back: **4** clip, pare, trim **5** lower, shave, slash **6** reduce **8** mark down

capable of being: **7** sectile

down: **4** pare **5** clear, slash **9** economize

in: mix **6** horn in **7** intrude **9** interpose, interrupt, introduce

in half: **5** halve **6** bisect, secant **8** dimidate

in small pieces: **4** dice, hash **5** mince **6** sliver

off: lop, nig **4** clip, crop, drib, poll **5** elide, roach, shave **7** deprive, divorce, exscind **8** amputate, truncate **9** apocopate, intercept **10** disinherit

out: **4** dele **5** elide **6** exsect, remove **7** exscind **9** eliminate

roughly: jag **4** hack, snag **7** butcher

short: bob **4** clip, crop, dock, poll **5** abort, check, clipt **6** arrest **7** curtail

slanting: **4** bias **5** bevel, miter, mitre

with die: **4** dink

with shears: **4** snip **5** shirl

wool: dod **4** dodd **5** shear

cut and dried: 5 trite **7** routine **8** foregone

cutaneous: 6 dermal

cutaway: 4 coat

cute: coy **4** keen **5** coony, dinky, sharp **6** clever, pretty, shrewd **7** cunning **8** affected **10** attractive

cuticle: 4 hide, skin **8** membrane, pellicle **9** epidermis **10** integument

blister: **4** bleb **5** bulla

ingredient: **5** cutin

cutis: 4 skin **6** corium, dermis

cutlass: 5 sword **6** dusack, tesack **7** machete

cutout: 9 decoupage

cutpurse: 5 thief **10** pickpocket

cutter: 4 beef, boat, sled **5** bravo, sloop, smack **6** cotter, editor, sleigh, slicer **7** clipper, incisor, ruffian **9** cutthroat, foretooth

cutthroat: 5 bravo, cruel **6** hit man **7** ruffian **8** ruthless

cutting: hag, raw **4** curt, keen, kerf, slip, tart, twig **5** acute, bleak, crisp, scion, scrap, scrow, sharp **6** biting, bitter, secant, severe **7** caustic, mordant, painful, satiric **8** chill-

ing, incisive, piercing, poignant, wounding **9** sarcastic, trenchant **10** blustering **11** abridgment, curtailment **12** adulteration

edge: **5** blade

implement: ax, axe, bit, hob, saw **4** adze **5** burin, knife, lathe, mower, plane, razor **6** chisel, reaper, scythe, shears **8** scissors

of last letter: **7** apocope

remark: dig **4** gibe **5** taunt **7** put-down

cuttlefish: 5 sepia, squid **7** octopus, scuttle

ink: **5** sepia

cutup: wag **5** devil, scamp **7** show off **9** prankster

cuvette: pot, tub **4** tank **5** basin **6** bucket, trench **7** cistern

Cybele: 4 Rhea

brother: **6** Cronus

father: **6** Uranus

mother: **4** Gaea

son: **4** Zeus **7** Jupiter, Neptune **8** Poseidon

sweetheart: **5** Attis

Cyclades Island: Ios, Zea **4** Keos, Milo, Nios, Sira, Syra **5** Delos, Melos, Naxia, Naxos, Paros, Syros, Tenos, Tinos **6** Andros **7** Amorgos

cycle: age, eon, era **4** aeon, bike **5** chain, epoch, pedal, round, saros, wheel **6** circle, course, period, series **7** bicycle, circuit, vehicle **8** tricycle, unicycle **10** motorcycle, revolution, two-wheeler

cyclone: 4 gale, gust, wind **5** blast, storm **6** baguio **7** tornado, twister, typhoon **9** hurricane, whirlwind, windstorm

cyclopean: 4 huge, vast **6** strong **7** massive, titanic **8** colossal, gigantic **9** herculean

Cyclopes: 5 Arges **7** Brontes **8** Steropes

father: **6** Uranus **8** Poseidon

mother: **4** Gaea

Cyclops: 5 giant **7** monster **10** Polyphemus

feature: **6** one eye

cyclostome: 7 hagfish, lamprey

cygnet: pen **4** fowl, swan

cylinder: 4 beam, drum, pipe, tube **6** barrel, bobbin, gabian, piston, platen, roller **8** lock part

cylindrical: 5 round **6** terete **7** centric, tubular

cyma: 4 gola, gula, ogee **7** molding

cymar (see also **simar**): **4** robe **5** shift

cymbal: tal, zel **8** doughnut **10** brass plate

cymbals: 6 becken, piatti

Cymbeline's daughter: 6 Imogen

Cymric: 5 Welsh

god of dead: **5** Pwyll

god of sky: **7** Gwydion

god of sun: **4** Lleu, Llew

god of underworld: **4** Gwyn

cynic: 5 Timon **7** doubter, knocker **9** pessimist **11** misanthrope

cynical: 6 ironic, sullen **7** currish, doglike **8** cap-

tious, downbeat, negative, sardonic, snarling
cynosure: **4** hero, star **5** focus **8** lodestar, polestar **9** celebrity
cypress: **9** belvedere

Cyprus: *capital:* **7** Nicosia
  city: **6** Paphos **7** Limasol **9** Famagusta
  currency: **4** para **5** pound **7** piaster
  measure: oka, oke, pik **4** cass **5** donum, kouza **6** gomari, kartos **7** medimno
  mountain: **7** Kyrenia, Olympus, Troodos

Cyrano de Bergerac: **4** poet **6** author **7** duelist
  author: **7** Rostand
  beloved: **6** Roxane
  feature: **4** nose
cyrenaic: **7** hedonic **10** hedonistic
Cyrus: *daughter:* **6** Atossa
  treasurer: **10** Mithredath
cyst: bag, sac, wen **5** pouch **6** ranula **7** vesicle
Cyzicus: *mother:* **6** Aenete
  slayer: **5** Jason
  wife: **6** Cleite

Czech Republic (see also **Slovak Republic**): *author:* **5** Capek, Havel, Kafka
  capital: **5** Praha **6** Prague
  city: **4** Brno **5** Opava, Plzen **6** Pilsen **7** Ostrava
  composer: **6** Dvorak (Antonin) **7** Janacek (Leos), Smetana (Bedrich)
  currency: **5** ducat, haler **6** haleru, heller, koruna, koruny (pl.)
  munitions plant: **5** Skoda
  river: Vah **4** Eger, Elbe, Gran, Isar, Iser, Labe, Oder, Ohre, Waag **5** Nitra **6** Moldau, Morava, Vltava

---

czar: **4** Ivan, king, Paul, tsar **5** baron, noble, Peter **6** kaiser, prince, tycoon **7** emperor **8** Nicholas
  daughter: **8** czarevna, tsarevna
  son: **10** czarevitch, tsarevitch
  wife: **7** czarina, tsarina
Czech Republic: (see box)
Czechoslovakia: See **Czech Republic, Slovak Republic**
czigany: **5** gypsy

D

dab: hit, pat **4** blow, chit, lump, peck, spot **5** clout, smear **6** blotch, strike **7** portion, splotch **8** flatfish, flounder

dabble: dib **4** mess **5** dally **6** dibble, meddle, paddle, potter, splash, tamper, trifle **7** moisten, spatter **8** sprinkle

dabbler: **7** amateur **10** dilettante

dabchick: **5** grebe **9** helldiver

dace: **4** chub

dacoit: **6** robber **8** criminal **9** plunderer

dactyl: toe **6** finger **10** metric foot

dactylogram: **11** fingerprint

dactylopodite: **5** thumb **6** pollex

Dadaism: **14** artistic revolt
   followers: Arp **4** Ball **5** Ernst, Tzara **6** Aragon, Breton **7** Duchamp
   forerunner of: **10** surrealism

daddy longlegs: **5** stilt **7** spinner, tipulid **8** arachnid, crane fly (Br.) **10** harvestman

dado: **6** groove **7** solidum **11** wall molding

daedal: **4** rich **6** varied **7** bizarre **8** artistic, skillful **9** ingenious, intricate **10** variegated

Daedalus: *constructor of:* **9** labyrinth
   monster: **8** Minotaur
   son: **6** Icarus
   victim: **5** Talos **6** Perdix

daffodil: **5** dilly **7** jonquil **9** narcissus

daft: mad **4** luny, wild **5** balmy, barmy (Br.), crazy, giddy, potty, silly **6** cuckoo, insane, looney **7** cracked, foolish, idiotic **8** imbecile

Dag's horse: **8** Hrimfaxi **9** Skinfaksi

Dagda's kin: **5** Boann **6** Aengus, Brigit

dagger: **4** dirk, itac (P.I.), kris (Malay), snee **5** crise, katar (Ind.), skean (Ir.) **6** anlace, bodkin, coutel, creese, diesis, kreese, stylet, weapon **7** dudgeon, poniard **8** stiletto **10** misericord
   Burmese: dah, dow
   handle: **4** hilt
   stroke: **4** stab **8** stoccado

daily: **4** a day **7** diurnal, per diem **9** circadian, hodiernal, newspaper, quotidian

daintily: **8** gingerly

dainty: **4** cate, nice, rare **5** acate, denty **6** bonbon, choice, costly, friand, mignon, minion, picked, scarce **7** elegant, finicky, minikin **8** delicacy, delicate, migniard **9** exquisite, squeamish **10** confection, fastidious

dairy: **7** vaccary **8** creamery

   food: **4** milk **5** cream **6** butter, cheese, yogurt
   tool: **9** separator

dais: **4** seat **5** bench, podia (pl.), stage, table **6** canopy, podium, settle **7** estrade, terrace **8** chabutra, platform

daisy: **5** gowan, oxeye **6** shasta **7** comfrey **10** moonflower

dak: **4** post

Dakota Indian: **4** Crow **5** Omaha, Osage, Sioux, Teton **6** Lakota, Mandan, Oglala, Santee **7** Arikara, Yankton **8** Arikaree

Daksha's father: **6** Brahma

Dalai Lama: **5** ruler **13** reincarnation
   country: **5** Tibet
   religion: **8** Buddhism

dale: **4** dell, dene, glen, vale **5** spout **6** bottom, dingle, trough, valley

Dallas: *basketball team:* **9** Mavericks
   football team: **7** Cowboys
   nickname: **4** Big D
   river: **7** Trinity
   stadium: **10** Cotton Bowl
   university: SMU

dalles: **6** rapids

dally: toy **4** chat, fool, idle, play, wait **5** delay, flirt, sport, tarry **6** dabble, dawdle, lead on, linger, loiter **10** trifle with **11** string along

dam: bar, bay **4** mare, stay, stem, stop, weir **5** block, check, choke, garth, mound **6** anicut, causey **7** annicut, barrier **8** blockade, obstacle, obstruct, restrain

dama: **5** addra **7** gazelle

damage: mar **4** blot, cost, harm, hurt, loss, ruin, tear **5** burst, cloud, spoil, wound **6** charge, deface, defect, impair, injure, scathe **7** expense, scratch **8** accident, disserve, mischief, sabotage **9** detriment, disprofit, vandalism
   pert. to: **5** noxal

damages: **5** award **7** payment

daman: **5** hyrax

damask: **5** color **6** fabric **8** deep pink

dame: **4** lady **5** title, woman **6** matron
   correlative: **4** sire

dammar: **5** resin, rosin

damn: **4** ruin **5** curse **7** condemn, swear at

damnable: **6** odious **8** infernal **9** execrable **10** detestable, outrageous

damnation: 9 perdition
damned: 4 lost 6 doomed 8 accursed
damnum: 4 harm, loss 9 detriment
damourite: 4 mica 9 muscovite
damp: deg, fog, wet 4 dank, dewy, dull, mist, roky 5 dabby, humid, moist, muggy, musty, rafty, rainy, soggy 6 clammy, deaden, muffle, quench, stupor 7 depress 8 dejected, dispirit 10 discourage
damper: 5 bread 7 checker 8 register
damsel: 4 girl, lass, miss 6 maiden 8 donzella, princess 10 demoiselle
Dan: *prince:* 7 Ahiezer
town: 4 Elon
Danae's kin: 4 Zeus 7 Perseus 8 Acrisius
dance: bal (F.), bob, hop, jig 4 ball, clog, frug, haka, hoof, prom, rock, shag 5 baile (Sp.), caper, frisk, stomp, tread, twist 6 Boston, masque, monkey 7 saltate 9 cotillion 10 roundabout
Argentine: 5 tango
Balinese: 6 barong
ballroom: 5 polka, rumba, waltz 6 chacha 7 foxtrot, mazurka, Peabody, twostep 10 Charleston, Turkey Trot 11 black bottom
Brazilian: 5 samba 6 maxixe 7 lambada 9 bossa nova
Burmese: pwe
ceremonial: 6 areito
chorus: 5 strut 6 cancan, kordax
college: 4 prom
country: hay 6 morris, square 7 hoedown 8 haymaker 10 villanella
designer: 13 choreographer
drama: 6 ballet
English: 6 althea, morris
exhibition: tap 6 apache
fads: 4 frug, pony, shag, slam 5 break, dirty, Lindy, twist, vogue 6 hustle, monkey 7 lambada 10 Charleston 12 mashed potato
formal: 4 prom 5 pavan 6 minuet 7 mazurka 9 farandole
German: 9 allemande
gypsy: 7 farruca 8 flamenco 10 zingaresca
Hawaiian: 4 hula
Hebrew: 4 hora
India: 6 nautch
Italian: 8 courante 9 rigoletto 10 tarantella
Japanese: No 6 kabuki
Latin American: 5 conga, mambo, rumba, samba, tango 6 chacha, maxixe 7 carioca, criolla 8 merengue
lively: jig 4 juba, reel, trot 5 fling, galop, gavot, polka 6 bolero, branle, canary 8 galliard, rigadoon 9 cotillion, farandole, jitterbug, shakedown, tambourin 10 corybantic 11 schottische
masked: 7 ridotto

Muse: 11 Terpsichore
nineteenth-century: 7 tempete
old: 5 loure, rondo 6 bource, carole, cebell, corant, minuet 7 boutade, coranto, furlana, lavolta 8 chaconne 9 horedance, sarabande 10 tarantella
Peruvian: 5 cueca
shoes: 4 taps 5 pumps 8 slippers, toeshoes
slow: 6 adagio, minuet, valeta
Spanish: 4 jota 8 fandango, flamenco 9 paso doble
square: 7 argeers, lancers 9 quadrille
strut: 8 cakewalk
sword: 8 matachin 11 Flamborough
voluptuous: 5 belly 8 habanera
dance of death: 7 macabre
dancer: 6 artist, hoofer 7 danseur 9 chorus boy 11 terpsichore
Biblical: 6 Salome
female: 4 pony 7 artiste, chorine 8 bayadere, coryphee, danseuse, devadasi 9 ballerina
dandelion: 7 chicory 10 bitterwort
stalk: 5 scape
dander: 5 anger, scurf 6 stroll, temper, wander 7 passion, saunter
dandle: pet 4 love 6 caress, fondle, pamper 9 knee-swing
dandruff: 5 flake, scurf 6 furfur
dandy: fop 4 beau, buck, dude, fine, jake, prig, toff, yawl 5 nifty, swell 7 capstan, coxcomb, foppish, jessamy 8 popinjay, sailboat 9 exquisite, first-rate 12 Beau Brummell
danger: 4 fear, risk 5 doubt, peril 6 hazard 7 pitfall, venture 8 distress, jeopardy 9 adventure
signal: 4 bell 5 alarm, siren 6 tocsin
dangerous: bad, rum 5 nasty, risky 6 unsafe 7 parlous 8 insecure 9 hazardous 10 precarious
dangle: lop 4 hang, loll 5 droop, swing 7 shoggle, suspend
Danish: 4 roll 6 pastry
anatomist: 5 Steno
astronomer: 5 Brahe
author: 8 Andersen
physicist: 4 Bohr
dank: wet 4 damp 5 humid, moist 6 clammy, coarse 7 drizzle
danta: 5 tapir
Dante: (see box)
Danube: *ancient name:* 5 Ister 8 Danubius
begins: 11 Black Forest
city on: Lom, Ulm 4 Baja, Linz, Ruse 6 Braila, Mohacs, Passau, Vienna 8 Belgrade, Budapest
dam: 8 Iron Gate
delta: 8 Black Sea
German name: 5 Donau

Dante: *beloved:* **8** Beatrice
birthplace: **8** Florence
circle of hell: **5** Caina
illustrator: **4** Dore
patron: **5** Scala
verse form: **7** sestina
work: **7** Inferno **8** Commedia, Convivio, Eclogues, Epistles, Paradise **9** Purgatory, Vita Nuova **12** Divine Comedy

tributary: Inn, Olt, Vah **4** Enns, Hrow, Isar, Lech, Naab, Prut, Raba, Sava **5** Arges, Drava, Iller, Iskur, Nitra, Tisza, Traun **6** Leitha, Morava, Velika **7** Altmuhl, Siretul

Danzig: *city in:* **6** Poland
coin: **6** gulden **7** pfennig
liqueur: **7** ratafia
Polish name: **6** Gdansk

dap: dab, dib, dip **4** skip **6** bounce, dibble **7** rebound

Daphne: **5** nymph **8** Mezereon
father: **5** Ladon **6** Peneus
mother: **6** Creusa
pursued by: **6** Apollo
turned into: **10** laurel tree

Daphnis' lover: **5** Chloe

dapper: **4** neat, trim **5** natty **6** spruce **7** finical, foppish

dappled: **6** dotted **7** flecked, mottled, spotted **8** freckled **10** variegated

darbies: **8** manacles **9** handcuffs

Dardanelles: **6** strait **10** Hellespont
part: **8** Bosporus
sea: **6** Aegean **7** Marmara

dare: **4** dast, defy, face, osse, risk **5** brave **6** assume **7** attempt, venture **9** challenge, undertake

daredevil: **6** madcap **12** swashbuckler

daresay: **5** agree **7** believe, presume, suppose

dargah, durgah (Ind.): **4** tomb **5** court **6** mosque, shrine

daring: **4** bold, rash **5** brave, hardy, manly, nerve **6** heroic **7** courage **8** devilish, fearless **9** audacious **10** courageous **11** adventurous, venturesome

dariole: cup **5** shell

Darius: *conqueror:* **9** Alexander
father: **9** Ahasuerus
prince: **6** Daniel

dark: dim, sad, wan **4** ebon **5** black, blind, brown, dingy, dusky, faint, murky, shady, sooty, unlit, vague **6** brunet, closed, cloudy, dismal, gloomy, opaque, wicked **7** melanic, obscure, rayless, stygian, swarthy **8** abstruse, ignorant, lowering, sinister **9** ambiguous, Cimmerian, infuscate, recondite, secretive, shuttered, tenebrous, uncertain **10** caliginous, indistinct, mysterious

dark-complexioned: **5** dusky **7** swarthy

darken: dim **4** dull **5** bedim, shade, sully, umber **6** deepen, shadow **7** becloud, benight, blacken, eclipse, obscure, opacate, tarnish **8** overcast **9** obfuscate, overcloud **10** overshadow

darkness: **4** dusk, murk **5** gloom, night, shade **6** shadow **7** dimness, privacy, secrecy **8** gloaming, iniquity, twilight **9** blackness **10** wickedness
realm: Po **6** Erebus

darling: joe (Sc.), pet **4** cute, dear, duck **5** aroon (Ir.), deary, honey, sweet **6** cherie, cuddly, moppet **7** beloved **8** adorable, favorite **10** attractive, delightful, sweetheart

darn: **4** mend **5** patch **6** cussed, damned, repair **7** blasted, doggone

darnel: **4** tare, weed **5** grass **6** cockle

darner: **6** needle

dart: **4** bolt, flit, leap **5** bound, fling, scoot, shaft, speed, start **6** scurry, spring, sprint **7** missile **9** flechette
barbed: **10** banderilla

D'Artagnan: *companion:* **5** Athos **6** Aramis **7** Porthos
creator: **9** Dumas pere

dart-like: **8** spicular

Dartmouth College location: **7** Hanover

Darwin: **10** naturalist
ship: **6** Beagle
teacher in evolution trial: **6** Scopes
theory: **9** evolution
work: **12** Descent of Man **15** Origin of Species

das: **4** fish **6** dassie **9** blacktail **12** Hindu servant

Das Kapital author: **4** Marx

dash: pep **4** bang, ding, elan, gift, hurl, line, pelt, race, ruin, rush, show, slam **5** abash, ardor, break, clash, crash, crush, fling, knock, smash, speed, spice, style, swash, throw **6** energy, hurtle, hyphen, shiver, spirit, splash, sprint, stroke, thrust **7** bravura, collide, depress, display, shatter, spatter, splotch **8** confound, gratuity, splinter **9** animation, bespatter, frustrate, overthrow

dasheen: **4** taro

dashiki: **7** garment **12** African shift
relative: **6** muu-muu

dashing: gay **4** bold, chic **5** bully, showy **6** jaunty, lively, swanky, veloce **7** stylish **8** spirited **11** fashionable

dastard: cad, sot **5** sneak **6** coward, craven **7** dullard **8** poltroon

dastardly: 4 base, foul, mean 5 nasty 6 rotten 10 despicable

data: 5 facts 8 material 11 information

date: age, day, era, woo 5 epoch, fruit 6 escort 7 take out 9 originate 10 engagement, extend from, rendezvous 11 anniversary, appointment
erroneous: 11 anachronism
on coin: 7 exergue

dated: 5 passe 6 demode, old hat 7 archaic 8 outmoded 12 old-fashioned 13 unfashionable

dateless: 8 timeless 10 immemorial

dating: 6 timing 8 courting

daub: 4 blob, blot, clag, clam, clat, coat, gaum, soil 5 clart, cleam, cover, paint, slake, smear 6 bedaub, grease 7 besmear, plaster, splotch 8 slaister

daughter: 4 bint, hija (Sp.) 5 child, fille (F.), filly 6 alumna 7 cadette
pert. to: 6 filial

Daughter of Moon: 7 Nokomis

daunt: awe, cow, daw 4 daze, faze, stun, tame 5 abash, break, check, deter 6 dismay, subdue 7 conquer, control, overawe, repress, stupefy, terrify 8 dispirit, overcome 10 disconcert, discourage, dishearten, intimidate

dauntless: 4 bold, good 5 brave, gutsy 7 aweless 8 fearless, intrepid, unafraid 10 courageous 11 indomitable, lionhearted

davenport: 4 desk, sofa 5 couch, divan 12 chesterfield
small: 8 love seat

David: 4 king, poet 7 warrior 8 musician
chief ruler: Ira
companion: 6 Hushai
daughter: 5 Tamar
employer: 5 Nabal
father: 5 Jesse
favorite son: 7 Absalom
friend: 5 Ittai 8 Jonathan
killed: 5 Uriah 7 Goliath
kin: 6 Michal 7 Abigail
king of: 5 Judah 6 Israel
man of: Ira 4 Igal 7 Shammah
musician: 5 Asaph
prophet: 6 Nathan
scribe: 7 Shavsha
son: 7 Absalom, Solomon
traitor: 10 Ahithophel
valley of Goliath's death: 4 Elah
wife: 9 Bathsheba

David Copperfield character: 4 Dora 5 Agnes, James 6 Barkis, Betsey, Dartle 8 Micawber, Peggotty, Traddles 9 Uriah Heep, Wickfield 10 Steerforth

Davy: 4 lamp

dawdle: lag 4 idle, loaf, poke 5 dally 6 diddle, linger, loiter, putter, trifle 8 lollygag 9 waste time 10 fool around

dawn: 4 morn 5 sunup 6 aurora 7 morning, sunrise 8 daybreak 9 beginning
goddess: Eos 5 Ushas 6 Aurora
pert. to: 4 eoan 7 auroral
symbol: dew

day: yom (Heb.) 4 date, time 5 epoch 6 period 8 lifetime
before: eve 9 yesterday
father of: 6 Erebus
god of: 5 Horus
hot: 8 scorcher
joyful: 8 festival
judgment: 8 doomsday
of Atonement: 9 Yom Kippur
pert. to: 6 ferial

day blindness: 11 hemeralopia

daydream: 4 muse 6 vision 7 fantasy, reverie

days: *fateful:* 4 Ides
fifty: 13 quinquagesima
fourteen: 9 fortnight
gone by: 4 yore 7 long ago 8 old times 9 antiquity 10 yesteryear

daze: fog 4 stun 5 daunt 6 bemuse, benumb, dazzle, muddle, trance 7 confuse, stupefy 8 befuddle, bewilder 9 dumbfound

dazed: 4 asea 5 dizzy, dopey, woozy 6 addled, groggy 7 stunned 9 in a stupor 10 punchdrunk

dazzle: 4 daze 5 blind, shine 7 eclipse 8 bewilder, outshine, surprise

dazzling: 5 vivid 6 bright, garish 7 fulgent, glaring, radiant 8 gorgeous 9 brilliant, sparkling 10 candescent, foudroyant 11 pyrotechnic

deaccession: 10 museum sale

deacon: 5 adept 6 cleric, doctor, layman, master 10 adulterate
prayers: 6 ectene
stole: 7 orarion

dead: 4 cold, dull, flat, gone, mort (F.), numb, tame 5 amort, inert, quiet, slain 6 asleep, lapsed, muerto (Sp.) 7 defunct, expired, extinct, sterile, tedious 8 absolute, complete, deceased, departed, inactive, lifeless, moribund, obsolete 9 apathetic, bloodless, inanimate, nerveless, unfeeling, unsalable 10 breathless, lusterless, monotonous, motionless, spiritless, unexciting 11 indifferent, ineffectual, inoperative 12 extinguished, unproductive, unprofitable
house of: 4 tomb 5 grave 6 morgue 7 ossuary 8 mortuary 9 crematory, ossuarium
Mass for: 7 requiem
region of: Po 5 Hades 6 Erebus

dead duck: 5 goner 9 sure loser 13 hopeless cause

Dead Souls author: 5 Gogol

deadbeat: bum 7 sponger 8 parasite 10 freeloader

deaden: 4 dull, kill, mute, numb, stun 5 blunt
6 benumb, dampen, muffle, obtund, opiate, retard, weaken 7 petrify, repress, stupefy 8 paralyze 10 devitalize

dead end: 4 stop 7 impasse 8 cul-de-sac 9
blank wall 10 blind alley

deadfall: 4 trap 9 brush pile

deadhead: 6 bobber 8 non-payer 12 lacking
cargo
band: 12 Grateful Dead

deadline: 5 limit 8 boundary

deadlock: tie 4 draw 7 impasse 9 stalemate
10 standstill

deadly: 4 dire, fell 5 fatal 6 lethal, mortal 7
capital, fateful, ruinous 8 venomous, virulent 9 pestilent 10 implacable, pernicious
11 destructive, internecine

deadpan: 5 blank 6 vacant 9 impassive

deaf: 8 heedless 9 unhearing, unmindful

deal: 4 dole, part, sale 5 allot, board, plank,
sever, share, trade, wield 6 bestow, divide,
handle, parcel 7 bargain, deliver, inflict,
portion, scatter, wrestle 8 dispense, separate 9 apportion, negotiate 10 administer,
distribute 11 transaction
great: 4 lots 5 loads, steal 6 oodles 7 bargain 8 very much 9 big amount
with: 4 cope 6 handle 10 take care of

dealer: 5 agent 6 badger, broker, cadger, jobber, monger, seller, trader 8 merchant,
operator 9 middleman, tradesman 10
negotiator, trafficker 11 distributor
secondhand goods: 10 pawnbroker

dealing: 7 trading, traffic 8 exchange 11
intercourse
shrewd: 6 deceit 9 chicanery

dean: 5 doyen 6 senior, verger 8 official

dear: pet 4 agra (Ir.), cara (It.), cher (F.), fond,
high, lief, near 5 honey, loved 6 costly,
scarce, worthy 7 beloved, darling, lovable 8
esteemed, glorious, precious, valuable 9
cherished, expensive, heartfelt, honorable,
important 10 sweetheart 12 affectionate

dearly: 6 deeply, keenly, richly 8 heartily 9
earnestly

dearth: 4 lack, want 6 famine 7 paucity,
poverty 8 scarcity 10 deficiency

death: end 4 bale, bane, doom, mort (F.) 5
decay 6 demise, muerte (Sp.) 7 decease,
quietus 8 biolysis, curtains, rawbones 9
bloodshed, departure 10 expiration, extinction, grim reaper
after: 10 posthumous
angel of: 6 Azrael
aware of portending: fey
bringing: 6 funest
goddess: Hel 4 Dana, Danu
march: 7 cortege, funeral
meditation: 11 thanatopsis

mercy: 10 euthanasia
notice: 4 obit 8 obituary
personification: 4 Mors 5 Ankou 6 Charos,
Charus
put to: gas 4 hang, kill, slay 5 choke, lynch
6 murder, starve, stifle 7 garrote 8 strangle
9 suffocate 11 assassinate, electrocute
rate: 9 mortality
rattle: 4 rale
register: 9 necrology
song: 5 dirge, elegy 8 threnody
symbol of: 5 orant

death-defying: 4 bold, rash 6 heroic 9 audacious, imprudent

deathless: 7 abiding, eternal, undying 8
immortal 12 imperishable

deathly: 5 fatal 6 deadly, grisly, lethal, mortal
7 ghastly, macabre 8 gruesome, moribund
10 cadaverous 11 destructive

debacle: 4 rout 5 wreck 6 defeat 7 beating,
failure 8 collapse 9 breakdown, cataclysm

debar: 4 deny, tabu 5 estop, taboo 6 forbid,
hinder, refuse 7 boycott, deprive, exclude,
prevent, suspend 8 preclude, prohibit 9
foreclose, interdict 10 disqualify

debase: 5 alloy, lower, stoop 6 defile, demean,
humble, impair, reduce, revile, vilify 7
cheapen, degrade, deprave, devalue, pervert, traduce, vitiate 8 dishonor 9 brutalize
10 adulterate, degenerate, depreciate 11
deteriorate

debased: low 4 vile 7 corrupt

debatable: 4 moot 8 arguable 9 uncertain 10
in question

debate: 4 agon, moot 5 argue, fight 6 reason,
strife 7 agitate, canvass, contend, contest,
discuss, dispute, examine, palaver, quarrel,
wrangle 8 argument, consider, militate, question 9 dialectic, quodlibet 10 contention,
deliberate 11 controversy 12 dissertation
pert. to: 8 forensic
place of: 5 forum 6 Lyceum
stoppage of: 7 cloture

debauch: 4 bout, orgy 5 spree, taint 6 defile,
guzzle, seduce 7 corrupt, deprave, mislead,
pollute, violate 9 bacchanal, dissipate 10
hellbender, lead astray, saturnalia 11 contaminate

debauched: 4 lewd 6 wanton 9 dissolute

debauchee: rip 4 rake, roue 6 lecher 8 rakehell 9 libertine

debilitated: 4 weak 5 seedy 6 feeble, infirm,
sapped 9 burned out, enervated

debility: 5 atony 7 languor, malaise 8 weakness 9 infirmity, lassitude 10 feebleness

debit: 4 loss 6 charge

debonair: 4 airy 6 jaunty, polite, urbane 7
affable 8 graceful, gracious

Deborah's husband: 8 Lapidoth

debouche: 4 exit 5 mouth 6 outlet 7 opening, passage 9 emergence

debris: 5 scree, talus, trash, waste 6 refuse, rubble 7 rubbish 8 detritus

debt: sin 5 debit, fault 7 arrears 8 trespass 9 arrearage, liability 10 obligation
acknowledgment: IOU 4 bill, note
without: 7 solvent 11 unobligated

debunk: 6 expose, show up, unmask 8 disabuse 11 disillusion, set straight

debut: 7 opening 8 entrance, premiere 9 beginning, coming out 12 introduction

decad: ten

decade: 9 decennium

decadent: 6 effete, rotten, sinful, wicked 7 decayed 9 declining 10 degenerate, iniquitous, retrograde 12 deteriorated 13 retrogressive

decamp: 4 bolt 5 elope, scoot 6 depart, levant, mizzle 7 abscond, run away, take off, vamoose 8 clear out 9 skedaddle 10 hightail it

decant: 4 emit, pour 6 unload 8 transfer

decanter: 6 carafe

decapitate: 6 behead 10 guillotine

decapod: 4 crab 5 prawn, squid 7 lobster 10 crustacean

decay: ebb, rot 4 conk, dote, doze, fade, fail, ruin 5 death, spoil, waste 6 caries, mildew, wither 7 decline, failure 8 decrease 9 adversity, decadence, decompose 11 destruction, deteriorate, dissolution 12 dilapidation, disintegrate, putrefaction
dental: 6 caries
in fruit: 4 blet

deceased: 4 dead 7 defunct 8 departed

deceitful: sly 4 foxy 5 false, lying 6 fickle, hollow, shifty, sneaky 7 sirenic 8 tortuous 9 dishonest, faithless, insidious, insincere 10 circuitous, fallacious, mendacious 11 underhanded 13 machiavellian

deceivable: 8 gullible

deceive: con, lie 4 bilk, dupe, fool, gaff, gull, hoax, jilt 5 abuse, blind, bluff, catch, cheat, cozen, dodge, hocus, trick 6 baffle, betray, delude, humbug, illude 7 beguile, defraud, mislead 8 filmflam, hoodwink 9 bamboozle, frustrate 11 doublecross 12 misrepresent

deceiver: 6 trepan 7 juggler, sharper, warlock 8 magician

decelerate: 4 slow 5 brake 11 reduce speed

decency: 7 decorum 8 goodness 9 propriety

decennium: 6 decade

decent: 4 fair, good, pure 5 clean 6 chaste, comely, honest, modest, proper, seemly 7 correct, fitting, shapely 8 adequate, decorous 10 acceptable, conforming, sufficient 11 appropriate, respectable

deception: gyp 4 gaff, ruse, scam, sham, wile 5 cheat, covin, craft, fraud, guile, magic, trick 6 cautel, deceit, humbug 7 blaflum (Sc.), cunning, evasion, fallacy, fiction, knavery, pretext, sleight, slyness 8 artifice, falsedad (Sp.), intrigue, prestige, subtlety, trickery, trumpery 9 chicanery, collusion, duplicity, falsehood, hypocrisy, imposture, mendacity, sophistry, treachery 10 artfulness, camouflage, dishonesty, subterfuge 11 contrivance, counterfeit, dissembling 13 deceitfulness, dissimulation

deceptive: 5 false 8 delusive, illusory 10 fallacious, misleading

decided: 4 firm, flat, sure 5 fixed 6 all set, formed 7 certain, settled 8 clear-cut, decisive, definite, resolved 10 determined 11 established 14 unquestionable

decima: 5 tenth, tithe

decimal base: ten

decimate: 5 wreck 7 destroy, wipe out 8 demolish, massacre 9 slaughter 10 annihilate

decipher: 4 read 5 break, solve 6 decode, detect, reveal 7 analyze, unravel 8 discover, indicate 9 translate

decision: 4 fiat 5 arret, canon 6 crisis, decree, ruling 7 verdict 8 finality, judgment, sentence 9 precedent 10 conclusion, resolution 12 adjudication 13 determination
maker: 5 judge 6 umpire 7 referee 9 executive
sudden: 4 whim 7 impulse

decisive: 5 final 6 crisic 7 crucial 8 critical 10 conclusive, peremptory

deck: hit, tog 4 buss, dink, heap, pink, trig 5 adorn, array, cover, dress, equip, floor, prink, punch, store 6 blazon, clothe, fettle 7 apparel, balcony, bedight, bedizen, feather, terrace 8 beautify, decorate, platform 9 embellish 11 pack of cards
high: 4 poop
kind: gun 4 boat, main, spar 5 berth, upper 6 bridge 7 shelter 8 platform, splinter 9 hurricane, promenade 10 forecastle
lowest: 5 orlop
part: 7 scupper

deckle-edged: 5 erose

declaim: 4 rant, rave 5 orate, speak, spout 6 recite 7 elocute, inveigh 8 denounce, harangue, perorate 9 discourse

declaration: 4 word 6 oracle, placet 9 affidavit, assertion, statement 10 allegation, deposition, disclosure, exposition 11 affirmation 12 announcement, asseveration, proclamation 13 advertisement, pronouncement

declare: bid, say, vow 4 aver, avow, deny, tell 5 posit, state, voice 6 affirm, allege, assert, assure, avouch, blazon, depone, herald,

indict, notify, relate **7** behight, express, profess, protest, signify, testify **8** announce, denounce, describe, indicate, maintain, manifest, proclaim **9** advertise, nuncupate, pronounce **10** annunciate, asseverate, promulgate **11** acknowledge, communicate
in cards: bid **4** meld

declination: 4 bias **5** slope **7** descent **8** swerving **9** deviation

decline: dip, ebb, set **4** bend, fade, fail, fall, flag, sink, turn, wane **5** chute, droop, lower, repel, slope, slump, stoop, stray **6** debase, refuse, reject, weaken **7** descend, descent, deviate, disavow, dwindle, failure, forbear **8** decrease, languish, withdraw **9** decadence, declivity, recadence, repudiate **10** retrograde **13** deterioration

declivity: dip **4** drop, fall **5** cliff, scarp, slope **6** calade **7** decline, descent **8** gradient **9** precipice

decoct: 5 smelt, steep **6** reduce, refine **7** extract **8** boil down, condense

decoction: 7 essence, extract

decode: 5 crack **8** decipher **9** figure out

decompose: rot **5** decay, spoil **7** putrefy

decor: 5 motif **7** setting **10** background, design plan **11** furnishings, style scheme

decorate: 4 bind, cite, deck, pink, trim **5** adorn, dress, inlay, panel **6** emboss, parget **7** festoon, garnish, miniate **8** ornament, titivate **9** embellish

decorated: 6 ornate **7** damasse, honored, wrought **9** sigillate **10** beribboned

decoration: 4 bahl, bulb **5** medal **6** frieze, plaque, tinsel **7** epergne, garnish, regalis **8** applique, fretwork, ornament **9** furniture **10** chambranle, decorament
metalware: **4** tole
military: DSC, DSM, DSO **5** medal **6** ribbon
pert. to: **8** medallic

decorous: 4 calm, good, prim **5** grave, quiet, sober, staid **6** decent, demure, modest, polite, proper, sedate, seemly, serene, steady **7** fitting, orderly, regular, settled **8** becoming, composed, mannerly **9** befitting, dignified, unruffled **11** appropriate

decorticate: 4 flay, hull, husk, pare, peel, pill, skin **5** strip **6** denude **9** excoriate

decorum: 7 decency **9** etiquette, propriety **10** convention

decoy: 4 bait, lure, tole **5** drill, plant, shill, tempt **6** allure, entice, entrap, pigeon **8** inveigle **9** shillaber

decrease: ebb **4** drop, fall, loss, sink, wane **5** abate, decay, taper, waste **6** impair, lessen, shrink **7** decline, dwindle, slacken, subside **8** diminish, moderate, retrench **9** decession, decrement **10** diminution

decree: act, law **4** rule, will **5** edict, enact, order, tenet, ukase **6** arrest, assize, decern (Sc.), dictum, indict, ordain **7** adjudge, appoint, command, mandate, statute **8** decision, rescript, sentence **9** determine, enactment, ordinance **10** adjudicate, plebiscite **12** adjudication, announcement
authoritative: **5** arret, canon
imperial: **4** fiat
Oriental: **5** irade **6** firman
papal: **4** bull

decrement: 4 loss **5** waste **8** decrease **10** diminution

decrepit: 4 lame, weak **6** feeble, infirm, senile, shabby **7** failing, invalid, rundown, unsound **9** bedridden **10** broken down **11** in disrepair

decretum: 4 rule **5** canon **7** precept **10** regulation

decry: boo **4** slur **5** lower **6** lessen **7** asperse, censure, condemn, degrade, detract **8** belittle, derogate **9** deprecate, discredit, disparage, down-grade, underrate **10** depreciate, undervalue

decuple: 7 tenfold

decussate: 5 cross **7** form an X **9** intersect

dedicate: vow **6** devote, direct, hallow, oblate **7** ascribe **8** inscribe **9** nuncupate **10** consecrate

deduce: 4 draw, lead **5** bring, drive, infer, trace **6** derive, elicit, evolve, gather **7** extract, make out **8** conclude

deduct: 4 bate, dock, take **5** abate, allow **6** defalk, remove **7** curtail **8** abstract, discount, separate, subtract, take away

deduction: 4 agio **6** rebate **7** reprise **8** illation, write-off **9** inference **10** conclusion

deed: act **4** case, fact, feat, fiat, gest **5** chart, doing, title **6** action, convey, escrow, pottah, remise **7** charter, exploit **8** contract, document, transfer **9** adventure **10** instrument **11** achievement, performance, tour de force **14** accomplishment
benevolent: **4** boon **5** favor **8** benefice
evil: sin **11** malefaction

deeds: 4 acta **9** res gestae

deem: say **4** hope, reck, tell **5** judge, opine, think **6** esteem, expect, ordain, reckon, regard **7** account, adjudge, believe, surmise **8** announce, consider, judgment, proclaim **10** adjudicate

deep: low, sea **4** howe, rapt **5** abyss, grave, great, gruff, heavy, ocean **6** hollow, intent **7** abysmal, intense, serious, unmixed **8** absorbed, abstruse, complete, powerful, profound, thorough **9** entangled, insidious, recondite **11** far-reaching

deep-dyed: 6 rooted **7** long-set, old-line **9** colorfast, confirmed, hard-shell, indelible, ingrained **10** inveterate

deepen: 5 cloud **6** darken **7** enhance, thicken **9** intensify **10** strengthen

deep-seated: 6 inbred, innate, primal 8 inherent 9 intrinsic 10 congenital, entrenched, in the blood 11 instinctive

deer: 4 hind 6 animal, cervid, mammal 8 ruminant
Asian: 4 axis, maha, napu, shou, sika 5 maral 6 chitra, hangul, sambar 10 barasingha, chevrotain
barking: 7 muntjac, muntjak
cry: 4 bell
European: red 6 fallow 9 white-tail
fallow: 4 dama
family: 8 cervidae
female: doe 4 hind
genus of: 6 cervus
large: elk 5 moose 6 wapiti 7 caribou
male: 4 buck, hart, spay, stag 7 roebuck
meat: 5 jerky 7 charqui, venison
North American: elk 5 moose 6 wapiti
path: run 4 slot 5 trail
pert. to: 6 damine 7 cervine
small: roe 7 roebuck
South American: 4 pudu 6 guemal, vanada 7 brocket
young: kid 4 fawn, spay 7 spitter

de-escalate: 6 weaken 8 decrease, diminish, slow down

deface: mar 4 foul, ruin, scar 5 spoil 6 damage, defoil, deform, injure 7 blemish, detract, distort 8 mutilate 9 disfigure, vandalize

de facto: 7 in being 8 existing 10 unofficial

defalcation: 5 theft 9 pilferage 10 peculation 12 embezzlement

defame: 4 foul 5 abase, cloud, libel, smear 6 injure, malign, vilify 7 asperse, blacken, blemish, detract, slander, traduce 8 dishonor 9 denigrate, discredit 10 calumniate

default: 4 fail, flaw, lack, omit, want 7 blemish, failure, forfeit, mistake, neglect 8 omission 10 negligence 11 delinquency, dereliction 12 imperfection 13 nonappearance

defeasance: 6 defeat 7 undoing 9 annulment, overthrow

defeat: win 4 balk, beat, best, drub, foil, loss, rout, ruin, undo 5 break, check, floor, skunk, worst 6 baffle, cumber, master, thwack 7 conquer, deprive, destroy, preempt, reverse, shellac 8 overcome, vanquish, Waterloo 9 discomfit, frustrate, overpower, overthrow, overwhelm 10 defeasance, disappoint 12 discomfiture
at chess: 4 mate 9 checkmate
narrowly: nip 4 edge 7 nose out

defeatist: 7 kill-joy 8 fatalist 9 Cassandra, pessimist

defect: 4 flaw, lack, vice, want 5 craze, fault, minus 6 damage, desert, injury 7 blemish, failing, forsake 8 drawback, renounce,

weakness 10 deficiency 11 shortcoming 12 imperfection
in timber: 4 knot
without: 5 sound 7 perfect 8 flawless

defective: bad, ill 4 poor 6 faulty 7 halting, unsound 8 impaired, vitiated 9 deficient, imperfect

defector: 6 bolter 8 apostate, deserter, renegade 9 turnabout 10 repudiator

defend: 4 back, hold, save, wear 5 guard, watch 6 assert, forbid, screen, secure, shield, uphold 7 contest, espouse, justify, prevent, protect, shelter 8 advocate, champion, conserve, maintain, preserve, prohibit 9 exculpate, vindicate

defendant: 7 accused 8 appellee
answer: 4 plea 14 nolo contendere

defender: 8 advocate, champion, guardian, upholder 9 proponent, protector
of the people: 7 tribune 9 ombudsman

defense (see also **fortification**): 4 egis, fort 5 aegis, alibi, fence, grith 6 answer, behalf, covert, excuse, sconce 7 bulwark, shelter 8 apologia, boundary, security 9 coverture, safeguard 10 protection
position: 7 rampart 10 bridgehead
unit: AAF 4 army, NATO, navy, SEAL 5 SEATO 7 marines, Rangers 8 air force 13 Special Forces

defenseless: 4 bare 5 naked 7 unarmed 8 helpless 9 unguarded

defensible: 7 tenable 9 excusable

defer: bow 4 wait 5 delay, yield 6 put off, shelve, submit 7 suspend 8 lay aside, postpone, prorogue, protract 9 hold off on 10 capitulate 12 knuckle under 13 procrastinate

deference: 6 homage, regard 7 respect 8 courtesy 9 obeisance

defiant: 4 bold 5 brave 6 daring 8 insolent 11 challenging

deficiency: 4 lack, want 5 fault, minus 6 dearth, defect 7 absence 8 scarcity, shortage 10 inadequacy, scantiness 13 insufficiency

deficient: 5 short 6 meager 7 bobtail

deficit: 8 shortage 9 arrearage, income gap 11 debit excess 12 business loss

defile: 4 pass, soil 5 abuse, dirty, gorge, smear, sully, taint 6 debase, infect, ravish 7 corrupt, deprave, passage, pollute, tarnish, violate 8 dishonor, maculate 9 desecrate 11 contaminate

defiled: 6 impure 7 unclean 8 maculate

definable: 6 finite

define: end, fix, set 4 mere, term 5 bound, limit 6 decide 7 clarify, delimit, explain, expound 8 describe, discover 9 demarcate, determine, interpret, prescribe 11 distinguish 12 characterize, circumscribe

definite: 4 sure 5 clear, final, fixed, sharp 7 certain, limited, precise 8 distinct, explicit, limiting 10 conclusive 11 determinate, determining, unequivocal 12 determinable, unmistakable

definitive: 5 final 8 clear-cut, explicit, specific 10 conclusive

deflect: 4 bend, warp 5 parry 6 divert, swerve 7 deviate, refract 8 turn away

deflower: 6 ravage, ravish 7 despoil, violate

Defoe character: 4 Moll, Xury 6 Crusoe, Friday, Roxana 7 Mrs. Veal

deform: mar 4 maim, warp 6 deface 7 contort, cripple, distort 8 misshape 9 disfigure 10 disarrange

deformed: 7 crooked, hideous 8 formless 9 amorphous, loathsome, monstrous, shapeless, unshapely 11 counterfeit

deformity: 4 flaw 6 defect 7 blemish 13 disfigurement
of foot: 5 varus 7 talipes

defraud: rob 4 bilk, fake, gull, rook, trim 5 cheat, cozen, gouge, mulct, trick 6 chouse, fleece 7 swindle 9 bamboozle

defray: pay 6 expend, prepay 7 finance 10 stand treat 11 foot the bill, pay expenses 12 pick up the tab

deft: 4 neat, trim 5 agile, handy, quick 6 adroit, expert, nimble, spruce 8 dextrous, skillful 9 dexterous

defunct: 4 dead 7 extinct 8 deceased, departed, finished

defy: 4 dare, face 5 beard, brave, flout, scorn, stump 6 oppose, resist 7 affront, outface 8 champion 9 stand up to

dégagé: 6 casual 7 relaxed 8 detached, informal 10 uninvolved 11 free and easy 13 unconstrained

degenerate: rot 6 debase, effete, worsen 7 corrupt 8 decadent, depraved 10 go downhill 11 deteriorate

degradation: 7 descent 8 ignominy

degrade: 4 bust 5 abase, decry, lower, shame, strip 6 debase, demean, demote, depose, humble, reduce, vilify 7 corrupt, decline, depress 8 disgrace, dishonor 9 disparage, humiliate 10 degenerate, depreciate 11 deteriorate

degraded: 5 seamy 6 abject, fallen 7 debased 10 degenerate, diminished

degrading: 4 base 6 menial 8 shameful

degree: 4 bank, heat, rank, rate, rung, step, term, tier 5 class, grade, honor, order, pitch, point, stage, stair 6 extent, medium, soever 7 Celsius, diploma, measure, station 8 quantity, standing 9 gradation 10 attainment, Fahrenheit
academic: B.L.S., B.Sc., L.L.B., L.L.D., M.Sc., Ph.D. 4 D.Lit. 5 Litt.D.
honorary: 8 laureate

kind of: nth 5 third
of academic excellence: 8 cum laude 13 magna cum laude, summa cum laude
seeker: 9 candidate
slight: ace, nth 4 hair, inch 5 shade 8 slightly 9 gradation

degust, degustate: 5 savor, taste 6 relish

dehydrate: dry 9 desiccate, evaporate

deific: 6 divine 7 godlike

deification: 10 apotheosis

deify: 5 exalt 7 glorify, idolize 10 consecrate 11 apotheosize

deign: 5 stoop 9 vouchsafe 10 condescend

deigning: 11 patronizing

deity (see also **god** and **goddess** under appropriate country or function): god 4 deva, idol, muse 6 genius 7 creator, demigod, godhead, godling 8 Almighty, divinity 12 supreme being
half-fish: 6 Oannes
half-goat: 4 faun
hawk-eyed: 5 Horus 6 Sokari 7 Sokaris
jackal-headed: 6 Anubis
tutelary: 5 genie, lares, numen 7 Hershef, penates

deja vu: 8 illusion 10 paramnesia, seen before

de jure: 7 by right 8 lawfully

deject: 5 abase, lower 6 humble, lessen 7 flatten 8 dispirit 9 overthrow 10 demoralize, discourage, dishearten

dejected: low, sad 4 blue, down, glum, sunk 6 abased, gloomy, pining 7 humbled, unhappy 8 repining, wretched 9 cheerless, depressed, prostrate, woebegone 10 despondent, spiritless 11 crestfallen, downhearted 12 disconsolate, disheartened, fainthearted

dejection: 5 dumps 7 despair 10 melancholy

dejeuner: 5 lunch 9 breakfast, collation

Delaware: *bay:* 8 Delaware, Rehoboth 11 Indian River
cape: 8 Henlopen
capital: 5 Dover
city: 5 Dover, Lewes 6 Newark, Smyrna 7 Chester, Milford, Seaford 9 New Castle 10 Wilmington
Indian: 6 Lenape 8 Delaware 9 Nanticoke 11 Lenni-Lenape
island: 4 Kent 5 Kelly, Reedy 8 Pea Patch
peninsula: 8 Delmarva
river: 6 Indian 7 Leipsic 8 Delaware 9 Broadkill, Christina, Nanticoke
state bird: 7 blue hen
state flower: 12 peach blossom
state insect: 7 ladybug
state tree: 5 holly

delay: lag **4** slow, stay, stop, wait **5** allay, check, dally, defer, demur, deter, dwell, stall, tarry **6** arrest, dawdle, detain, hinder, impede, linger, loiter, put off, retard, temper, weaken **7** assuage, prolong, respite **8** demurral, hesitate, macerate, mitigate, obstruct, postpone, reprieve, stoppage **9** detention, hindrance, lingering **10** cunctation, moratorium, suspension **13** procrastinate

delayed: **4** late **5** tardy **7** belated, overdue

delaying: **8** dilatory

dele: **4** omit **5** erase **6** cancel, delete, efface, remove **7** expunge **9** eradicate, extirpate **10** blue pencil, obliterate

delectable: **5** tasty **8** pleasing **9** delicious, desirable, diverting, enjoyable **10** delightful **11** pleasurable

delegate: **4** name, send **6** assign, commit, depute, deputy, legate, nuncio **7** appoint, consign, empower, entrust **8** emissary, transfer **9** authorize, surrogate **10** commission **12** commissioner **14** representative

delegation: **7** mission **9** committee **10** deputation

delete: **4** dele, omit **5** erase, purge **6** cancel, remove **7** destroy, expunge **9** eliminate, eradicate **10** obliterate
opposite of: **4** stet **7** put back, restore

deleterious: bad **7** harmful, hurtful, noxious **8** damaging **9** injurious, malignant **10** pernicious **11** destructive, detrimental, prejudicial

Delian god: **6** Apollo

deliberate: **4** cool, pore **5** study, think, weigh **6** advise, confer, debate, ponder **7** consult, planned, reflect, resolve **8** consider, measured, meditate, mull over **9** determine, leisurely, speculate, voluntary **10** purposeful, thought out **11** circumspect, intentional **12** premeditated **13** dispassionate

deliberation: **7** counsel **10** reflection
without: **4** rash **8** headlong **9** on impulse

Delibes ballet: **5** Naila **6** Kassya, Sylvia **8** Coppelia, La Source

delible: **10** eradicable

delicacy: roe **4** cate, ease, tact **5** taste **6** caviar, dainty, luxury, nicety **7** finesse **8** niceness, pleasure, subtlety **9** exactness, precision **10** daintiness, femininity, refinement **11** savoir faire
lacking: **5** gross **7** boorish **9** unrefined

delicate: **4** airy, fine, lacy, nice **5** frail, light, silky **6** dainty, minion, petite, puling, queasy, slight, tender **7** elegant, finical, fragile, minikin, refined, subtile, tenuous **8** araneose, araneous, charming, ethereal, graceful, luscious, migniard, pleasant **9** agreeable, beautiful, exquisite, sensitive **10** delightful, fastidious **11** comfortable, considerate

delicatessen: **11** charcuterie

delicious: **5** tasty, yummy **6** savory **8** heavenly **9** ambrosial, exquisite, luxurious, nectarous, toothsome **10** delectable, delightful **11** scrumptious

delight: joy **4** glee, love **5** bliss, charm, feast, mirth, revel **6** admire, divert, liking, please, ravish, regale **7** ecstasy, enchant, gladden, gratify, rapture, rejoice **8** entrance, gladness, pleasure, savoring **9** delectate, enjoyment, enrapture, happiness **11** delectation
in: **6** relish

delightful: **4** nice **6** dreamy **7** elysian **8** adorable, delicate, glorious **9** delicious **10** delectable, enchanting, entrancing **11** pleasureful

Delilah's paramour: **6** Samson

delimit: See **define**

delineate: map **4** draw, limn, line **5** trace **6** blazon, depict, design, sketch, survey **7** outline, picture, portray **8** describe **9** represent **12** characterize

delineation: **5** image **7** account **10** expression

delinquency: **7** default, failure, misdeed, offense **8** omission **9** violation **10** misconduct **11** dereliction, malfeasance, misdemeanor

delinquent: lax **6** remiss **7** overdue **8** behind in **9** negligent **12** teen offender

deliquesce: **4** melt, thaw **7** liquefy **8** dissolve

delirious: **4** mad **5** wild **6** manic **6** insane, raving **7** frantic, lunatic **8** deranged, ecstatic, frenetic, frenzied **9** rapturous **10** irrational **11** lightheaded

delirium: **5** fever, mania **10** aberration **13** hallucination

delirium tremens: **6** shakes **7** horrors

delitescent: **6** latent **10** obfuscated

deliver: rid **4** bail, deal, free, give, save, tell **5** bring, serve, speak, utter **6** commit, convey, redeem, render, rescue, resign, succor, unbind **7** consign, declaim, dictate, present, release, relieve **8** dispatch, hand over, liberate **9** enunciate, pronounce, surrender **10** bring forth, emancipate **11** come through

delivery: **5** birth **6** rescue **7** address **8** shipment **9** rendition **11** deliverance, parturition **12** accouchement

dell: **4** dale, glen, vale **6** dingle, ravine, valley

Delphi: **6** oracle, shrine, temple **9** sanctuary
god: **6** Apollo
mountain: **9** Parnassus
priestess: **6** Pythia

Delphic: **5** vague **7** cryptic, obscure **8** oracular **9** ambiguous, enigmatic

delphinium: **8** larkspur

delta: **5** mouth **8** alluvium, triangle

delude: **4** bilk, dupe, fool **5** cheat, evade, trick **6** take in **7** beguile, deceive, mislead **8** hoodwink **10** circumvent, lead astray

deluge: sea **4** flow **5** flood, swamp **6** engulf **7** niagara, torrent **8** downpour, inundate, overflow, submerge **9** cataclysm, overpower, overwhelm **10** cloudburst

delusion: **5** dream, trick **6** mirage, vision **7** chimera, fallacy, fantasy **8** illusion, phantasm **9** deception **13** appersonation, hallucination
Buddhist: **4** moha
of grandeur: **11** megalomania
partner of: **5** snare

delusive: **5** false **6** unreal **7** seeming **8** fanciful, illusory **9** deceiving, imaginary

deluxe: **5** plush, super **6** choice **7** elegant, opulent **8** palatial **9** extra fine, luxurious, sumptuous

delve: dig, dip **4** mine, seek **5** plumb, probe **6** search **7** dig into, explore **11** investigate

demagogic: **8** factious

demagogue, demagog: **6** leader **8** agitator, fomenter **10** instigator **12** rabble rouser

demand: ask, cry **4** call, need **5** claim, exact, order, query **6** charge, elicit, expect, summon **7** command, inquire, mandate, request, require **8** question **9** challenge **10** commission **11** requisition

demarcate: **5** bound, limit **6** define **7** mark off **8** separate **12** circumscribe, discriminate

demean: **5** abase, lower **6** debase, deride **7** degrade **8** belittle, maltreat **9** disparage, humiliate

demeanor: **4** mien **5** habit **6** action **7** bearing, conduct **8** behavior, carriage, portance **9** treatment **10** deportment, management **11** comportment, countenance

demented: mad **4** luny **5** buggy, crazy, nutty **6** insane, looney **7** fatuous **8** deranged

demerit: **5** fault **7** bad mark **11** shortcoming **12** imperfection

Demeter: **5** Ceres
daughter: **4** Kore **10** Persephone, Proserpina, Proserpine
goddess of: **5** crops, grain
headdress: **5** polos
mother: **4** Rhea
shrine: **9** anaktoron

demigod: **4** hero **7** godling
pert. to: **7** satyric
sylvan: **4** faun **5** satyr

demirep: **11** adventuress

demise: **5** death **7** decease **8** bequeath **13** pass by descent

demit: **5** lower **6** resign **8** abdicate, withdraw **10** relinquish **11** resignation

demiurgic: **8** creative **9** formative

demo: car **5** model **7** display, protest **13** show of feeling, test recording

demobilize: **7** break up, disband **9** muster out **12** demilitarize

democratic: **7** popular **10** self-ruling **11** egalitarian, not snobbish

demode: **5** passe **8** outdated **12** old-fashioned

demoiselle: **5** crane **7** kaikara

demolish: **4** raze, ruin **5** demon, level, waste, wreck **6** batter **7** destroy **9** devastate, overthrow

demon, daemon: hag, imp, nat **4** aitu, atua, ogre **5** devil, fiend, genie, lamia, Satan, witch **6** Abigor, afreet **7** shaitan, villain, warlock **10** evil spirit **11** poltergeist
assembly of: **6** sabbat
drive out: **8** exorcize
female: **8** succubus
Hebrew: **8** Asmodeus
Iroquois: **5** otkon
male: **7** incubus
person possessed by: **9** energumen
prince of: **9** Beelzebub
worship of: **9** diabolism
Zoroastrian: **5** daeva

demoniac: **7** satanic **8** devilish, diabolic, fiendish, infernal **10** diabolical

demonstrate: **4** show **5** prove **7** display, explain, portray **8** manifest

demonstration: **4** show, sign **5** proof **9** portrayal **10** apparition **11** mass protest **12** illustration **13** manifestation

demonstrative: **4** that, this **5** these, those **8** effusive, outgoing **9** emotional, expansive, ostensive **11** unrestrained

demoralize: **6** weaken **7** confuse, corrupt, deprave, pervert, unnerve **9** disspirit, undermine **10** discourage, dishearten **11** disorganize

Demosthenes: **6** orator
follower: **5** Bryan
oration: **9** philippic

demote: **4** bust **6** reduce **9** downgrade

demotic: **6** common **7** popular

demulcent: **8** soothing **9** softening **10** mollifying

demur: **4** stay **5** delay, doubt, pause **6** boggle, linger, object **7** protest, scruple **8** hesitate, question **9** challenge **12** irresolution

demure: coy, shy **4** prim **5** grave, staid **6** modest, sedate **8** composed, decorous

den: mew **4** cave, cove, dell, dive, glen, hole, lair, nest, room **5** bield, cabin, couch, haunt, study **6** burrow, cavern, covert, grotto, hollow, ravine **7** retreat **8** hideaway, snuggery, workroom

denary: **7** tenfold

dendroid: **8** tree-like **11** arborescent

dendrophilous: **8** arboreal

denial: See **deny**

denigrate: **5** libel **6** defame, malign **7** disdain, put down, slander **8** ridicule **9** deprecate, disparage **10** speak ill of

Denmark (see also **Copenhagen, Danish, Scandinavian**): *author:* 7 Dinesen 8 Anderson
bay: 4 Fano, Kiel 6 Alborg, Nissum
capital: 10 Copenhagen
city: 5 Arhus 6 Alborg, Odense 7 Esbjerg 8 Elsinore, Gentofte
fjord: Ise, Lim 8 Mariager, Roskilde
island: Als, Fyn 4 Aero 5 Samso 7 Falster, Lolland 8 Bornholm 9 Langeland
king: 8 Frederik, Waldemar 9 Christian
lake: 6 Arreso
measure: ell, fod, mil, pot 4 alen, favn, rode 5 album, kande, linje, paegl, tomme 6 achtel, paegel, paegle, skeppe 7 landmil, oltonde, skieppe, viertel 8 fjerding 9 korntonde, ottingkar
parliament: 9 Folketing
peninsula: 7 Jutland
philosopher: 11 Kierkegaard
pirate: 6 Viking
queen: 9 Margrethe
river: 4 Omme, Stor 5 Guden, Varde
sea inlet: 8 Kattegat 9 Skagerrak
territory: 9 Greenland 13 Faeroe Islands
weight: es, lod, ort, vog 4 eser(pl.), last, mark, pund, unze 5 carat, kvint, pound, quint, tonde 6 toende 7 centner, lispund, quintin 8 lispound, skippund 9 ship pound, skibslast 10 bismerpund

denizen: 6 native 7 citizen, dweller, habitué 8 resident 10 inhabitant
Denmark: (see box)
dennet: gig 8 carriage
denominate: 4 call, name 5 title 6 denote 8 christen, indicate, nominate 9 designate
denomination: 4 cult, sect 5 class, title, value 6 church 7 society 8 category 9 communion 10 persuasion 11 appellation
  religious: 7 Baptist 8 Lutheran 9 Methodist, Unitarian 12 Episcopalian, Presbyterian 14 Congregational
denotation: 4 sign 5 token
denote: 4 give, mark, mean, name, show 6 import 7 betoken, express 8 indicate 9 designate, recommend, represent 10 denominate
denouement: end 6 answer, result 7 outcome 8 solution 11 explanation
denounce: 6 accuse, delate, descry, menace, scathe 7 arraign, condemn, upbraid 8 threaten 9 fulminate 10 stigmatize 13 inform against

de novo: 4 anew 5 again, newly 6 afresh 8 once more 12 from the start
dense: 4 firm 5 close, foggy, gross, heavy, murky, silly, solid, thick 6 obtuse, stupid 7 compact, crowded, serried 11 thickheaded 12 impenetrable
density: 4 mass 11 compactness
dent: 4 bash, dint, nick 5 dinge, notch, tooth 6 batter, hallow, indent 7 blemish, depress 10 depression, impression 11 indentation
dentate: 6 jagged 7 serrate, toothed
dentil: 5 block
dentin, dentine: 5 ivory 6 enamel
dentistry: *appliance:* dam 4 burr
  branch: 9 exodontia 11 orthodontia 12 orthodontics
  plastic: 6 cement
  tool: 6 scaler 7 forceps
denture: 5 plate 10 set of teeth
denude: 4 bare 5 scalp, strip 6 divest 11 decorticate
denunciation (see also **denounce**): 7 censure 8 diatribe 9 philippic 10 accusation 12 condemnation 18 malediction
deny: nay 5 debar, repel 6 abjure, disown, forbid, impugn, negate, refuse, refute, reject, renege 7 confute, deprive, disavow, dispute, forsake, gainsay, protest 8 abnegate, disclaim, forswear, renounce, withhold 9 disaffirm 10 contradict, contravene, controvert
deodar: 5 cedar
depart: die 4 blow, exit, pass, quit, vary 5 found, leave, mosey, sever 6 begone, decamp, demise, desist, divide, perish, recede, retire, sunder 7 abscond, deviate, forsake, get away, pull out, retreat, take off, vamoose 8 farewell, separate, withdraw
department: 4 part 5 realm 6 branch, bureau, sphere 7 portion 8 division, province 11 subdivision
departure: 4 exit 5 death, going, twist 6 egress, exodus 7 decease 9 deviation 10 difference, divergence 11 abandonment, leavetaking
  words of: 4 ta-ta 5 aloha 6 so long 7 goodbye 8 farewell
depend: 4 bank, hang, lean, rely, rest, turn 5 count, hinge, trust 7 confide
dependable: 4 sure 5 loyal, solid 6 secure, steady 7 certain 8 faithful, reliable 11 responsible, trustworthy
dependency: 6 colony 7 apanage, mandate 8 appanage 9 addiction
dependent: 4 ward 5 child 6 client, minion, vassal 7 subject 8 clinging, follower 9 reliant on 10 contingent, sequacious 11 conditional, provisional, subordinate
depict: 4 draw, limn 5 paint 6 blazon 7 pic-

ture, portray **8** describe **9** delineate, represent **12** characterize

depilate: **4** husk **5** shave

depilatory: **5** rusma

depilous: **8** hairless

deplete: **5** drain, empty, use up **6** reduce, unload **7** exhaust **8** diminish **10** impoverish

deplorable: sad **8** grievous, terrible, wretched **10** calamitous, lamentable **11** distressing, unfortunate

deplore: rue **4** moan, sigh, wail **5** mourn **6** bemoan, bewail, grieve, lament, regret **10** disapprove

deploy: **6** unfold **7** display **9** spread out

deplume: **5** pluck, strip

depone: **5** swear **7** testify **11** bear witness

deport: **5** evict, exile, expel **6** banish, behave, demean **7** bearing, conduct **8** send away **9** transport

deportment: air **4** gest, mien **5** geste, habit **6** action, manner **7** address, bearing, conduct **8** behavior, breeding, carriage, demeanor

depose: **4** aver, oust **5** abase **6** affirm, assert, divest, remove **7** degrade, dismiss, testify **8** dethrone, displace **10** dispossess

deposit: lay, set **4** bank, cast, dump, fund, hock, pawn **5** chest, lodge, place, store **6** entomb, pledge, repose, settle **7** consign, entrust, put down **8** security **11** part payment **12** accumulation
alluvial: **5** delta, geest
black: **4** soot
earthy: **4** gobi, marl, sand, silt **5** loess, trona **6** sludge **8** alluvium
geyser: **6** sinter **10** travertine
glacial: **4** kame **5** eskar, esker **7** moraine
gold-containing: **6** placer
gravel: **5** apron
marine: **5** coral
mineral: bed **4** lode, vein **5** manto
roric: dew
teeth: **6** tartar
wine cask: **4** lees **6** tartar

deposition: **6** burial **7** deposit, opinion **8** sediment **9** affidavit, statement, testimony **10** allegation **11** declaration **12** displacement **13** precipitation

depository: **4** bank, safe **5** attic, chest, vault **6** locker **7** ossuary **9** strongbox

depot: **4** base, gare (F.) **6** aurang (Ind.), aurung **7** arsenal, station **8** magazine, terminal, terminus **9** warehouse **10** storehouse

deprave: **5** taint **6** debase, defile, malign, revile **7** corrupt, pervert, vitiate **10** degenerate, depreciate

depraved: bad **4** evil, ugly, vile **6** rotten, wicked **7** bestial, immoral, vicious **9** abandoned, graceless **10** profligate **11** demoralized **12** incorrigible

depravity: **4** vice **8** villainy

deprecate: **8** play down **9** denigrate, underrate **10** depreciate, disapprove

depreciate: **4** fall **5** abase, decry, slump **6** lessen, reduce, shrink **7** cheapen, degrade, depress, detract, devalue **8** belittle, derogate, diminish, minimize **9** disparage, dispraise, downgrade **10** undervalue

depredate: rob **4** prey, raze, sack **5** spoil **6** ravage, thieve **7** despoil, destroy, pillage, plunder **8** lay waste, prey upon

depress: bow, cow **4** dash, dent, fall, sink **5** abase, appal, chill, crush, lower, slump **6** appall, dampen, dismay, humble, indent, lessen, sadden, weaken **7** degrade, flatten **8** browbeat, diminish, dispirit, enfeeble **9** subjugate **10** depreciate, discourage, dishearten

depressed: low, sad **4** blue, down, glum **6** gloomy, hollow, lonely, oblate, somber, triste **8** dejected, downcast **9** afflicted, heartsore **10** in the dumps, spiritless **11** downhearted, melancholic

depressing: **5** bleak **6** dismal, dreary

depression: dip, pit **4** fall, foss, howe (Sc.) **5** atrio, basin, cowal, crypt, dinge, fossa, fosse, nadir **6** cafard, cavity, crater, dismay, gulley, ravine, valley **7** alveola, blowout **8** doldrums **9** dejection **11** despondency
between mountains: col
pert. to: **6** bathic

deprivation: **4** loss, want **6** penury **7** amotion, poverty **8** hardship **11** destitution

deprive: rob **4** deny **5** strip **6** depose, divest, hinder, remove **7** bereave, cashier, despoil **9** dismantle, relieve of **10** dispossess

deprived: **4** reft **5** needy **12** impoverished

depth: **5** abyss **8** deepness, strength **9** abundance, intensity **10** profundity **11** perspective **12** abstruseness, completeness, profoundness
in: **8** thorough **13** comprehensive
without: **4** thin **7** cursory, shallow, sketchy **11** superficial

depth charge: **4** bomb, mine **10** projectile

depths: **5** heart **7** lowness **10** inmost part

deputation: **7** mission **10** delegation

depute: **4** send **5** allot, assign **6** devote **7** appoint **8** delegate **10** commission, constitute

deputy: **4** aide **5** agent, envoy, proxy, vicar **6** commis, legate **7** bailiff **8** delegate **9** assistant, surrogate, vigilante **10** substitute

deracinate: **6** uproot **9** eradicate, extirpate

derange: **5** upset **7** confuse, disturb, perturb **8** disorder, displace, unsettle **9** interrupt **10** discompose **11** disorganize

deranged: mad **5** crazy **6** insane **8** demented, maniacal **10** distraught, unbalanced

derby: hat 4 race, town 5 shire 6 bowler

deregulate: 8 end curbs 9 decontrol 11 free of rules

derelict: bum, lax 4 hobo, wino 5 dingy, seedy, tramp 6 remiss, shabby 7 drifter, run down, vagrant 8 castaway, deserted, forsaken 9 abandoned 10 delinquent, neglectful

deride: 4 geck (Sc.), gibe, hoot, jape, jeer, mock, twit 5 fleer, rally, scoff, scorn, taunt 6 illude 8 ridicule 9 make fun of

de rigueur: 5 right 6 proper 7 correct 8 required 11 fashionable

derision: 8 contempt
sound of: boo 4 hiss 5 snort

derivation: 6 origin, source 9 etymology 10 wellspring

derivative: 7 spin-off 8 offshoot 9 outgrowth, traceable 10 unoriginal

derive: get 4 draw, stem 5 carry, infer, trace 6 deduce, evolve, gather, obtain 7 extract, proceed, receive 9 originate

derm: 4 skin 7 cuticle

dermal filament: 4 hair

dernier cri: 4 mode, rage 5 craze, style, vogue 7 fashion 8 last word

derogate: 5 annul, decry 6 lessen, repeal 7 detract, slander 8 restrict, withdraw 9 disparage 10 depreciate

derrick: rig 4 lift, spar 5 crane, davit, hoist 6 steeve, tackle
part: jib, leg 4 boom

derring-do: 7 bravado, courage 8 audacity

derringer: 6 pistol, weapon

dervish: 5 fakir 9 mendicant
cap: taj
of Arabian Nights: 4 Agib
practice: 7 dancing, howling 8 whirling

descant: 4 sing, song 6 melody, remark, warble 7 comment 9 discourse 11 observation 12 counterpoint, dissertation 13 accompaniment

descend: 4 fall, sink 5 avale, lower, stoop 6 alight, derive, go down 7 decline 9 originate 10 spring from
by rope: 6 rappel

descendant: son 4 cion, heir, seed 5 child, scion 7 spin-off 8 daughter, offshoot 9 offspring

descendants: 4 seed 5 issue 7 progeny 9 posterity 10 generation

descended from same mother: 5 enate 6 enatic

descent: 4 drop, fall 5 birth, chute, issue, scarp, slope, stock 6 escarp, strain 7 assault, decline, lineage 8 ancestry, breeding, downfall, pedigree 9 avalanche, declivity, onslaught 10 declension, derivation, extraction, generation 11 declination, degradation, inclination

airplane: 8 approach

skier's: 6 schuss

describe: 4 tell 6 define, depict, relate, report 7 declare, explain, express, narrate, outline, picture, portray, recount 9 delineate, designate, discourse, enumerate, represent 10 illustrate 12 characterize

description: ilk 4 kind, sort, type 7 account, recital, variety, version 9 chronicle 12 presentation

descry: see, spy 4 espy 5 sight 6 behold, detect, reveal, turn up 7 discern, display 8 disclose, discover, perceive 9 determine 11 distinguish

Desdemona: *husband:* 7 Othello
servant: 6 Emilia
slayer: 7 Othello
traducer: 4 Iago

desecrate: 5 abuse 6 defile 7 pollute, profane, violate 8 unhallow 11 contaminate

desecration: 9 blasphemy, sacrilege

desert: due, erg, rat 4 bolt, fail, flee, sand 5 merit, waste 6 decamp, defect, go AWOL, renege, reward 7 abandon, abscond, badland, demerit, forsake, hornada 8 renounce 9 backslide, wasteland 10 punishment, relinquish, wilderness
animal: 5 addax 6 fennec, lizard 7 courser 8 tortoise 10 chuckwalla 11 kangaroo rat
area: 4 Gobi, Thar 5 Negev, Sahel 6 Libyan, Mohave, Nubian, Sahara, Syrian 7 Arabian, Atacama, Kara Kum, Painted 8 Colorado, Kalahari, Kyzyl Kum 10 Australian, Great Basin, Patagonian 11 Death Valley 13 Great Salt Lake, Great Victoria
area of shifting sand: erg
beast: 5 camel 9 dromedary
dry lake bed: 5 playa
dweller: 4 Arab 5 nomad 7 Bedouin
hallucination: 6 mirage
pert. to: 6 eremic
rat: 10 prospector
science: 9 eremology
ship: 5 camel
shrub: 4 palm 5 retem 6 alhagi, cactus, raetam 7 had bush 8 creosote, mesquite 9 sagebrush, succulent 10 camel thorn
traveling group: 7 caravan
valley: 6 bolson
vehicle: 9 dune buggy
watering spot: 5 oasis
wind: 6 samiel, simoom 7 sirocco 9 harmattan

desert candle: 5 plant 8 ocotillo

deserted: 6 lonely 7 forlorn 8 desolate, forsaken 9 abandoned 11 uninhabited

deserter: rat 6 bolter 8 apostate, defector, fugitive, recreant, renegade

desert-like: dry 4 arid, sere

deserve: 4 earn, rate 5 merit 10 be worthy of

desiccate: dry 4 sear 5 drain, parch 6 wither 7 shrivel 9 dehydrate

desideratum: 4 need 6 desire

design: aim, end, map 4 draw, goal, idea, mean, plan, plot 5 allot, decor, drift, ettle, model, motif, shape 6 device, intend, intent, invent, layout, object, sketch 7 destine, diagram, fashion, outline, pattern, project, propose, purpose 8 contrive 9 calculate, delineate, intention 10 conception 11 contemplate, contrivance

inlaid: 6 mosaic 8 intarsia

of scattered objects: 4 seme

open: 8 filigree, fretwork

perforated: 7 stencil

raised: 8 repousse 9 bas relief

skin: 6 tattoo

sunken: 8 intaglio

designate: set 4 mark, mean, name, show 5 label, style, title 6 assign, choose, denote, intend, settle 7 appoint, entitle, specify 8 describe, identify, indicate 9 appellate, nuncupate 10 denominate 11 distinguish 12 characterize

designed: 8 prepense 10 thought out 11 intentional 12 premeditated

designer: 7 planner, plotter, schemer 8 engineer 9 architect, couturier

designing: 6 artful, crafty 7 cunning 8 planning, plotting, scheming 10 foreseeing, fraudulent

desinential: 8 terminal

desipient: 5 silly 7 foolish

desirable: 7 welcome 8 eligible, pleasing, salutary 9 agreeable, excellent 10 attractive, beneficial, worthwhile

desire: yen 4 care, hope, itch, lust, need, urge, want, will, wish 5 ardor, covet, crave, mania, yearn 6 affect, aspire, hanker, hunger, prefer, thirst, yammer 7 craving, fantasy, inkling, longing, passion 8 appetite, cupidity 9 appetency, cacoethes 10 desiderium

want of: 11 inappetence

desirous: 4 fain, fond 5 eager 6 ardent, greedy 7 envious, wishful 8 covetous 10 solicitous 11 acquisitive

desist: 4 ease, halt, quit, stop 5 cease 7 abstain, forbear, hold off 11 discontinue, refrain from

desk: pew 4 ambo 5 board, table 6 pulpit 7 lectern 8 prie-dieu 9 davenport, monocleid, secretary 10 escritoire, monocleide

desman: 4 mole 7 muskrat

Desmanthus: 5 Acuan

desmid: 4 alga 5 algae (pl.)

desolate: sad 4 bare, lorn, ruin, sack, sole 5 alone, bleak, gaunt 6 dreary, gloomy, lonely, ravage 7 destroy, forlorn, lacking 8 deprived, deserted, forsaken, solitary 9 abandoned, destitute, dissolute, woebegone 11 comfortless, uninhabited 12 disconsolate

desolation: woe 5 grief, havoc 6 sorrow 7 sadness 10 melancholy 11 destruction, devastation

area of: 5 waste 6 desert

Desmodium: 7 trefoil

despair: 5 gloom, grief 6 give up, sorrow 8 lose hope 10 melancholy 11 despondency 12 hopelessness

desperado: 6 bandit, outlaw 7 ruffian 8 criminal 10 lawbreaker

desperate: mad 4 rash 7 extreme, frantic 8 headlong, hopeless, perilous, reckless 9 dangerous 10 despairing, despondent, infuriated, outrageous 11 precipitate 13 irretrievable

despicable: low 4 base, mean, vile 5 cheap, dirty 6 abject, paltry, scurvy, shabby, sordid 7 caitiff, ignoble 8 unworthy, wretched 9 loathsome, miserable 11 ignominious 12 contemptible, contemptuous

despise: 4 defy, hate 5 scorn, scout, spurn 6 detest, loathe, slight 7 contemn, disdain 8 misprize, vilipend 9 abominate, disregard 10 look down on

despite: 4 hate, snub 6 injury, insult, malice 7 ill will 8 aversion, contempt 12 regardless of

despoil: rob 4 raid, ruin, sack 5 harry, reave, rifle, strip 6 divest, fleece, ravage, ravish, remove 7 bereave, deprive, disrobe, pillage, plunder 8 deflower, disarray, unclothe 9 depredate

Despoina: 4 Kore 10 Persephone

despondency: 6 misery 7 despair 10 depression, melancholy 11 desperation

despondent: sad 4 blue 8 dejected, downcast, hopeless 9 woebegone 10 dispirited 11 discouraged 12 disconsolate, heavyhearted

despot: 4 czar, tsar, tzar 6 satrap, tyrant 7 autarch, monarch 8 autocrat, dictator 9 strong man

despotic: 6 lordly 8 absolute, dominant 9 arbitrary 10 tyrannical

dessert (see also **cake, pastry, pie**): ice, pie 4 cake 5 fruit, glace (Fr.) 6 eclair, mousse, pastry, sorbet, sweets 7 pudding, sherbet, strudel 8 ice cream, Napoleon, sillabub, syllabub 9 pound cake, sweetmeat 10 blanc-mange, zabaglione 11 baked Alaska, creme brulee

destination: aim, end 4 fate, goal 7 address 8 terminus 9 objective

destine: 6 decree, direct, doom to, intend 9 devise for, fix before, preordain 11 assign ahead, set aside for **12** predetermine

destiny: lot **4** doom, fate **5** karma **6** future, kismet **7** fortune **8** God s will **13** inevitability

destitute: **4** poor **5** clean, needy **6** bereft, devoid, wasted **7** forlorn, lacking, wanting **8** bankrupt, beggared, defeated, deprived, desolate, forsaken, helpless, indigent **9** abandoned, defaulted, driftless **10** devastated, frustrated **12** disappointed, impoverished

destroy: eat, end, gut **4** blow, full, raze, ruin, rush, slay, undo **5** break, craze, erase, erode, quell, smash, smite, spoil, wrack, wreck **6** blight, cumber, deface, defeat, efface, famish, ravage **7** abolish, consume, expunge, overrun **8** amortize, confound, decimate, demolish, desolate, dissolve, mutilate, overturn, sabotage **9** depredate, devastate, dismantle, eradicate, extirpate, liquidate, overthrow **10** annihilate, counteract, extinguish **11** assassinate, exterminate

destroyer: hun **6** vandal **7** warship **8** saboteur

Destroyer: **4** Siva

Destroying Angel: *fungus:* **7** amanita
Mormon: **6** Danite

destruction: end **4** bane, doom, loss, ruin **5** decay, havoc, waste **7** Abaddon (Heb.) **8** downfall, excision, shambles **9** holocaust, perdition **10** extinction, subversion
god: **4** Siva
goddess: Ara
of species: **8** genocide

destructive: **4** fell **5** fatal **6** deadly, mortal **7** baleful, deathly, fateful, harmful, hurtful, noisome, noxious, ruinous **8** wasteful **9** poisonous, truculent **10** catawampus, pernicious **11** deleterious, internecine

desuetude: **6** disuse **7** neglect **12** obsolescence

desultory: **4** idle **5** hasty, loose **6** casual, fitful, random, roving **7** aimless, cursory **8** rambling, unsteady, wavering **9** irregular, unsettled **10** discursive, incidental, inconstant **12** disconnected

detach: **5** sever **6** cut off **7** disjoin, divorce, isolate **8** disunite, separate, unfasten, withdraw **9** disengage **10** disconnect

detached: **4** free **5** alone, aloof, apart **7** neutral, removed **8** taken off, unbiased **10** impersonal **11** unconcerned, unconnected **13** disinterested, dispassionate

detail: **4** item **6** assign, nicety, relate **7** account, appoint, article, itemize, minutia, narrate, specify **8** rehearse, salience, spell out **9** enumerate, narrative **10** particular **11** stipulation **12** circumstance

detailed: **4** full **6** minute, prolix **8** itemized, thorough, tiresome **9** wearisome **10** meticulous, protracted

detain: **4** hold, keep, stay, stop **5** check, delay **6** arrest, hinder, retard **8** imprison, restrain, withhold
in time of war: **6** intern

detect: see, spy **4** espy, find, spot **5** catch **6** descry, divine, expose, reveal **7** develop, discern, nose out, uncover **8** decipher, discover

detection device: **5** radar, sonar **6** dowser **11** divining rod

detective: PI, tec **4** bull, dick **5** Morse, Pasco **6** Gideon, sleuth, tracer **7** Dalziel, gumshoe, Maigret, scenter, Spenser, spotter, Wexford **8** flatfoot, operator, Sam Spade, The Saint **9** James Bond, Nero Wolfe **10** Luke Thanet, Martin Kane, Miss Marple, Nick Carter, Perry Mason, Peter Salem, Philo Vance, private eye **11** Charlie Chan, Ellery Queen, Father Brown, Green Hornet, John Appleby, Nick Charles, Peter Wimsey, Travis McGee **12** investigator, Simon Templar **13** Adam Dalgleish, Albert Campion, C. Auguste Dupin, Hercule Poirot, Michael Shayne, Philip Marlowe **14** Roderick Alleyn, Sherlock Holmes
story writer: **7** P.D. James **8** Ed McBain, Rex Stout **9** S.S. Van Dine **10** Emma Lathen, Ian Fleming, Ngaio Marsh **11** Colin Dexter, Dick Francis, Ellery Queen, John Creasey, Ruth Rendell **12** G.K. Chesterton, Michael Innes, Reginald Hill, Robert Parker **13** Dorothy Sayers, Edgar Allen Poe, Ross Macdonald, Wilkie Collins **14** Agatha Christie, Dorothy Simpson, Georges Simenon, John D. MacDonald **15** Dashiell Hammett, J. Van der Wetering, John Dickson Carr, Raymond Chandler **16** Arthur Conan Doyle, Margery Allingham **18** Erle Stanley Gardner

detector: **7** reagent
storm: **7** sferics
weather change: **9** barometer

detent: dog **4** pawl **5** catch, click

detente: **8** easement **14** rapprochement

detention: **5** delay **7** capture **9** hindrance, restraint **10** arrestment

deter: bar **5** block, check, delay **6** hinder, retard **7** prevent **8** dissuade, keep from, restrain **9** constrain **10** discourage, dishearten, intimidate

detergent: **4** soap **7** purging, smectic, solvent **8** cleanser **9** cleansing

deteriorate: **4** fail **5** decay, spoil **6** debase, impair, weaken **7** decline, wear out **9** backslide **10** degenerate

determinable: **5** fixed **8** definite **9** judicable **10** mensurable

determinate: **7** certain **8** definite, resolute, resolved, specific **9** arbitrary **10** invariable **11** established

determinative: **5** final **7** shaping **8** limiting **9** directing **10** conclusive **13** authoritative

determine: end, fix, get **4** test **5** assay, award **6** assess, assign, decide, decree, define, descry, settle **7** adjudge, analyze, appoint, arrange, dispose, resolve **8** conclude **9** admeasure, arbitrate, ascertain, calculate **10** adjudicate, constitute, deliberate, predestine

determined: set **4** bent, firm **6** dogged, intent, mulish, sturdy **7** decided, settled **8** foregone, perverse, resolute, resolved, stubborn **9** obstinate, pigheaded **10** persistent, unyielding

deterrent: **5** block **6** hurdle **8** obstacle **9** hindrance **14** discouragement

detest: **4** damn, hate **5** abhor, curse **6** loathe **7** condemn, despise, dislike **8** denounce, execrate **9** abominate

detestable: **4** foul, vile **6** horrid, odious **7** heinous **8** infamous **9** nefarious **10** despicable **12** antipathetic

dethrone: **6** depose, divest

detonate: **4** fire **5** blast **6** blow up, set off **7** explode **9** fulminate

detonator: cap **7** torpedo **9** explosive

detour: **5** avoid, skirt **6** bypass **7** circuit **8** go around **9** deviation

detract: **5** decry **6** defame, divert, vilify **7** asperse, traduce **8** belittle, derogate, minimize **9** disparage **10** depreciate

detraction: **7** calumny, scandal, slander

detriment: **4** cost, hurt, loss **5** damna (pl.), wound **6** damage, injury **8** mischief **9** disprofit **10** impediment **12** disadvantage

detrimental: **7** adverse, harmful, hurtful **9** injurious **10** pernicious **11** deleterious

detritus: **4** tuff **5** chaff, scree, waste **6** debris **7** garbage, rubbish

Detroit: *baseball team:* **6** Tigers
basketball team: **7** Pistons
football team: **5** Lions

de trop: **6** excess **7** surplus, too much **8** in the way, unwanted **11** superfluous

deva: **5** angel, deity

Devaki's son: **7** Krishna

devalue: See **depreciate**

devastate: **6** ravage **7** destroy, pillage, plunder, scourge **8** demolish, lay waste **10** depopulate

develop: **4** form, grow **5** arise, ripen **6** appear, detect, evolve, expand, flower, mature, reveal, unfold, unfurl **7** educate, enlarge, expound, uncover **8** disclose, discover, engender, generate, manifest **9** elaborate, germinate, transpire

development: **6** growth **7** stature **8** breeding, increase **9** evolution, expansion, formation, unfolding **11** elaboration
arrested: **7** aplasia
full: **8** maturity, ripeness
going back: **13** retrogression

Devi: *beneficent:* **5** Guari
consort: **4** Siva
fierce: **4** Kali
light: Uma
malignant: **5** Durga
riding a tiger: **6** Chandi

deviate: err, yaw **4** lean, miss, vary, veer **5** drift, lapse, sheer, stray **6** change, depart, detour, recede, squint, swerve, wander **7** decline, deflect, digress, diverge
from the norm: **6** mutate
from the vertical: **4** hade **5** angle, slant **10** out of plumb

deviation: **7** anomaly **11** declination

device: gin, mot **4** tool **5** drift, meter, motto, shift **6** design, emblem, gadget, scheme **7** compass, fiction, impresa, imprese, project, vehicle **8** artifice, fastener, gimcrack **9** apparatus, appliance, doohickey, expedient, invention, regulator, stratagem **10** concoction, instrument **11** contraption, contrivance
curve measuring: **9** rotameter
holding: **4** vise **5** clamp

devil (see also **evil**, **Satan**): imp **4** Deil (Sc.), haze, mahu **5** annoy, bogey, demon, fiend, Satan, tease **6** dybbuk, pester **7** Amaimon, clootie, dickens, gremlin, Lucifer, Old Nick, torment, warlock **8** Apollyon, diabolus, Mephisto **9** archfiend, Beelzebub, cacodemon, scoundrel **14** Mephistopheles
Dante's: **8** Cagnazzo
pert. to: **7** satanic **10** diabolical
printer's: **10** apprentice
ruler: **10** diabolarch
tree: **4** dita
worship: **8** satanism

deviled: **9** a la diable

devilfish: ray **5** manta

devilish: **6** daring, rakish, wicked **7** demonic, extreme, hellish, inhuman, satanic **8** demoniac, diabolic, fiendish, infernal **9** excessive **10** diabolical **15** Mephistophelian

devil-may-care: gay **4** fast, rash **5** blasé **6** madcap **7** raffish **8** heedless, reckless **9** imprudent **10** nonchalant **11** harum-scarum

devil's bones: **4** dice

devious: sly **4** foxy **6** crafty, errant, roving, shifty, tricky **7** vagrant, winding **8** indirect, rambling, tortuous **9** eccentric, irregular **10** circuitous, farfetched, roundabout

devise: **4** plan, plot, will **5** array, forge, frame, weave **6** convey, cook up, design, invent, scheme **7** appoint, arrange, bethink, concoct, consult, dream up, prepare **8** bequeath, contrive **9** construct, fabricate, formulate **11** put together

devitalize: **6** deaden **10** eviscerate

devoid: **4** bare **5** empty **6** barren, free of, vacant **7** lacking, wanting **9** destitute

devoir: **4** duty, task **6** effort

devolve: **4** pass **8** overturn, transfer, transmit **11** change hands

devote: vow **4** ally, avow, doom, give **5** apply **6** addict, attach, bestow, depute, resign **7** address, consign, destine **8** dedicate, venerate **10** consecrate **11** appropriate

devoted: **4** true **5** liege, loyal, pious **6** devout, fervid **7** adoring, arduous, zealous **8** attached, constant, faithful **9** assiduous, religious **10** obsequious, venerating

devotee: fan, nun **4** buff, monk **6** votary, zealot **7** admirer, amateur, fanatic **8** follower, partisan **9** supporter **10** aficionado, enthusiast

devotion: **4** aves (pl.) **6** fealty, prayer **7** loyalty, passion, worship **8** fidelity **9** adoration, reverence **10** allegiance
excessive: **13** ecclesiolatry
object of: **4** idol **5** totem **6** fetich, fetish
period of: **4** Lent **6** novena

devour: eat **4** fret **5** raven, waste **6** engulf **7** consume, engorge **10** annihilate

devout: **4** good, holy, warm **5** godly, pious **6** hearty, solemn **7** cordial, devoted, godlike, saintly, sincere **8** reverent **9** religious, righteous, spiritual

dew: **4** rime **8** moisture **9** hoarfrost

dewlap: **4** jowl **7** wattles

dewy: **4** damp **5** moist, roric **6** gentle **9** sparkling **10** glistening, refreshing

dexter: **5** right **6** honest **9** fortunate **10** auspicious **15** straightforward

dexterity: art **5** craft, knack, skill **7** ability, address, agility, aptness, cunning, finesse, sleight **8** aptitude, deftness, facility **9** adeptness, diplomacy, quickness, readiness **10** adroitness, cleverness, expertness, nimbleness

dextral: **10** auspicious **11** right-handed

dey: **5** pasha, ruler

dhan: **6** cattle, wealth **8** property

diabetes remedy: **7** insulin

diablerie: **7** devilry, sorcery **8** mischief **10** black magic, demonology, witchcraft

diabolical, diabolic: **5** cruel **6** wicked **7** hellish, inhuman, satanic, violent **8** demoniac, devilish, fiendish, infernal

diacritic: **4** mark **5** tilde **6** umlaut **11** distinctive

diadem: **5** crown, tiara **6** anadem, circle, emblem, fillet **7** coronet **8** headband

diagnose: **7** analyze **8** identify, pinpoint

diagonal: **4** bias **7** slanted **13** catercornered

diagram: map **4** plan **5** chart, epure (F.), graph **6** design, schema **7** outline **9** blueprint

dial: **4** disk, face **6** tune in **7** control, crystal **8** horologe **9** indicator, telephone

dialect: **5** argot, idiom, lingo **6** brogue, debate, patois, patter, speech **8** language **10** vernacular **11** phraseology
Georgia: **6** Gullah
London: **7** cockney
Louisiana: **5** Cajun
most prestigious: **8** acrolect

dialogue: **4** chat, talk **6** parley **10** discussion **12** conversation
having nature of: **13** interlocutory

diameter: **4** bore **14** circle bisector
half: **5** radii (pl.) **6** radius

diametric: **7** counter **8** contrary, opposite

diamond: gem, ice **4** rock **5** field, jager, jewel **7** lozenge **8** corundum **9** brilliant, briolette, sparkling
crystal: **7** glassie
cutter: **12** brilliandeer
element: **6** carbon
famous: See **stone:** *famous*
fragments: **5** chips
glazier's: **6** emeril
holding device: dop **4** dopp
imitation: **5** paste **6** spinel, zircon **9** schlenter **13** cubic zirconia
industrial: **4** bort **5** bortz
necklace: **7** riviere (F.)
surface: **5** facet
unit of weight: **5** carat

diamond-hard: **7** adamant

Diamond State: **8** Delaware

Diana: **7** Artemis
father: **7** Jupiter
mother: **6** Latona
twin: **6** Apollo

diana monkey: **7** roloway

diaphanous: **5** filmy, gauzy, sheer **8** gossamer **11** transparent

diaphragm: **7** midriff
pert. to: **7** phrenic

diary: log **6** record **7** journal **8** register **9** ephemeris

diaskeuast: **6** editor **7** reviser

diastase: **4** malt **6** enzyme

diatribe: **6** tirade **8** harangue **9** criticism, invective, philippic **12** denunciation

Diaz de Bivar's title: **5** El Cid

dibble: dib **7** dip bait **10** garden tool

dibs: **5** claim, share, syrup **6** rights

dice: **4** cube **5** bones **6** gamble **7** checker
game: **5** craps

losing throw: **5** three **7** boxcars **9** snake eyes

throw of six: **4** sice

dicey: **5** risky **6** chancy **9** uncertain

dichotomize: **4** part **5** sever **6** divide **7** break up **8** separate **10** split in two

dick: tec **6** copper **8** flatfoot **9** detective, policeman

Dickens: *character:* Pip, Tim **4** Dora, Nell **5** Fagin, Krook, Lucie, Nancy, Pross, Sikes, Smike **6** Carton, Cuttle, Darnay, Dartle, Dombey, Jarley, Merdle, Wardle, Weller **7** Defarge, Dorritt, Estella, Gargery, Jaggers, Jellyby, Manette, Peggoty, Podsnap, Scrooge, Snagsby, Spenlow, Squeers, Stryver, Tiny Tim, Trotter **8** Cratchit, Havisham, Jarndyce, Micawber, Nickleby, Pickwick **9** Bill Sikes, Uriah Heep **11** Oliver Twist **12** Artful Dodger

pen name: Boz

dicker: **4** deal, swap **5** daker **6** barter, haggle **7** bargain, chaffer **8** exchange **9** agreement, negotiate

dickey: **4** weak **5** shaky **10** shirt front

dictate: say **4** tell **5** order, utter **6** decree, enjoin, impose, ordain **7** command, deliver, mandate, require **9** prescribe, principle **11** communicate

dictatorial: **6** lordly **7** pompous **8** arrogant, despotic, dogmatic, positive **9** imperious, masterful **10** autocratic, peremptory, tyrannical **11** doctrinaire, domineering, magisterial, opinionated, overbearing **13** authoritative

diction: **5** style **6** phrase **7** wording **8** language, parlance, verbiage **10** vocabulary **11** enunciation, phraseology

dictionary: **7** lexicon **8** wordbook **9** thesaurus **10** vocabulary **11** onomasticon

compiler: **7** Johnson, Webster **13** lexicographer

geographical: **9** gazetteer

poet's: **6** gradus

dictum: **5** adage, axiom, edict **6** decree, saying **7** opinion **8** apothegm **9** principle, statement **13** pronouncement

Dictynna: **11** Britomartis

didactic: dry **7** preachy **8** pedantic **10** moralistic **11** instructive

didacticism: **6** homily **8** pedantry

diddle: gyp **4** hoax **5** cheat **6** befool, dawdle, jiggle, loiter, trifle **7** swindle **9** waste time

dido: **5** antic, caper, frill, prank, trick **6** gewgaw **7** trinket **8** furbelow, gimcrack

Dido: *father:* **5** Belus

founder of: **8** Carthage

husband: **7** Acerbas

other name: **6** Elissa

sister: **4** Anna

wooer: **6** Aeneas

die: ebb **4** cube, dado, dice (pl.), fade, mold, seal, wane **5** abate, croak, stamp, yearn **6** chance, depart, expire, finish, perish, vanish, wither **7** decease, succumb **8** languish, puncheon **9** grow faint

loaded: **6** fulham, fullam

symbol: ace

die-hard: **4** Tory **7** old fogy **8** hardnose, mossback, rightist, stubborn **9** dogmatist, obstinate, pigheaded **11** reactionary **12** conservative

Dies Irae (L.): **4** hymn **8** Mass part **10** day of wrath

diet: **4** fare, fast, food **5** board **6** reduce, viands **7** regimen **8** congress, victuals **10** bantingize, convention **11** convocation, legislature

difference: **5** clash **6** change **7** discord, dispute **8** conflict, division, variance **10** alteration, dissension, unlikeness **11** controversy, discrepancy, distinction **12** disagreement

different: **5** other **6** divers, sundry, unlike **7** diverse, several, unalike, unusual, variant, various **8** distinct, manifold, separate **9** disparate, divergent **10** dissimilar, variegated **11** diversified

differentiate: **8** contrast **11** distinguish **12** discriminate

difficult: **4** hard **5** fussy, rough, tough **6** crabby, cranky, knotty, rugged, uphill **7** arduous, labored, not easy, obscure, painful, practic **8** abstract, puzzling, stubborn **9** intricate, laborious **11** complicated, troublesome

difficulty: ado, fix, jam, rub **4** snag **5** fight, nodus **6** hassle, pickle, plight, scrape, strait **7** barrier, dilemma, dispute, pitfall, problem, quarrel, trouble **8** asperity, obstacle, severity, struggle **9** hindrance, objection **10** impediment **11** controversy, obstruction, vicissitude **12** complication, disagreement

diffidence: **5** doubt **7** modesty, reserve, shyness **8** distrust, humility, timidity **9** suspicion **10** hesitation **11** bashfulness **12** apprehension

diffuse: **4** full, shed **5** strew, wordy **6** divide, expand, extend, prolix, spread **7** copious, pervade, pour out, publish, radiate, scatter, verbose **8** disperse **9** circulate, dissipate, expatiate, garrulous, irradiate, propagate **10** widespread **11** disseminate

diffusion: **7** osmosis **10** outpouring

dig: get, hoe **4** claw, gibe, grub, hole, like, mine, poke, root **5** delve, nudge, probe, spade, taunt **6** burrow, exhume, plunge, quarry, shovel, thrust **7** approve, unearth **8** excavate, scoop out

dig out: **6** go into **7** uncover **10** do research **11** investigate

digest: 4 code 5 ripen 6 absorb, codify, mature, precis 7 concoct, epitome, pandect, summary 8 condense, synopsis 10 abridgment, assimilate, compendium, comprehend

digestion: 7 eupepsy 8 eupepsia
agent: 6 pepsin, rennin 7 maltase
ailment: 5 colic 6 gripes 7 pyrosis 9 dyspepsia 12 constipation
having good: 8 eupeptic

digging, fitted for: 7 fodient

digit: toe 4 unit 5 thumb 6 figure, finger, number 7 integer, numeral
podal: toe
shield for: cot 5 stall 7 thimble
vestigial: 7 dewclaw

diglot: 9 bilingual

dignified: 5 grand, lofty, noble, staid 6 august, sedate, solemn 7 courtly, stately 8 majestic 11 magisterial

dignify: 5 adorn, exalt, grace, honor 7 elevate, ennoble, promote

dignitary: VIP 5 nabob 6 big gun, leader 7 notable 8 brass hat, luminary, official

dignity: 4 rank 5 honor, pride, worth 6 repute 7 bearing, decorum, fitness, gravity, majesty, station 8 elegance, prestige, standing 9 nobleness 10 excellence

digress: 4 veer 5 drift, stray 6 swerve, wander 7 deviate, diverge 8 divagate 10 depart from

digression: 5 aside 7 episode 8 excursus 9 excursion

dike, dyke: 4 bank, pond, pool 5 digue, ditch, levee 7 channel 8 causeway 10 embankment 11 watercourse

dilapidated: 5 dingy 6 beat-up, shabby 7 damaged, run-down 10 threadbare 12 falling apart

dilapidation: 4 ruin 5 decay 9 disrepair 10 raggedness 14 disintegration

dilate: 5 swell, widen 6 expand, extend 7 amplify, broaden, distend, enlarge, inflate, prolong, stretch 8 increase, lengthen, protract 9 discourse, expatiate

dilatory: 4 slow 5 slack, tardy 6 fabian, remiss 8 backward, delaying, inactive, sluggish 10 behindhand 15 procrastinating

dilemma: fix 4 node 5 poser 7 problem 8 quandary 10 perplexity 11 predicament 12 complication 13 Hobson's choice

dilettante: 5 lover 7 admirer, amateur, dabbler, dabster, esthete 8 aesthete

diligence: 4 heed 6 effort 7 caution 8 carriage, industry 9 constancy 10 stagecoach 11 application, earnestness, heedfulness

diligent: 4 busy 6 active, eident, steady 7 careful, earnest, heedful, operose 8 sedulous 9 assiduous 11 hardworking, industrious, painstaking, persevering

dill: 4 herb 6 pickle 9 flavoring, seasoning

dilly: pip 4 darb, lulu 5 beaut, dandy 9 humdinger

dillydally: lag, toy 4 loaf 5 stall 6 loiter, trifle 9 vacillate

dilute: cut 4 thin 5 alter 6 debase, modify, reduce, weaken 8 diminish 9 attenuate, water down

dim: wan 4 blur, dark, dull, fade, gray, hazy, mist, pale, veil 5 bleak, blear, dusky, faint, foggy, misty 6 cloudy, darken, gloomy, obtuse 7 eclipse, obscure, shadowy, tarnish 8 overcast 9 obfuscate 10 indistinct, mysterious 11 crepuscular

dime: 4 coin 5 disme

dimension: 4 bulk, size 5 scope 6 aspect, extent, height, length 7 breadth, quality 9 magnitude, thickness 10 importance, proportion
fourth: 4 time

diminish: ebb 4 ease, fade, melt, pare, sink, wane, wear 5 abate, lower 6 dilute, lessen, reduce, subdue, wither 7 abridge, assuage, curtail, deplete, dwindle, subside 8 condense, decrease, derogate, minimize, moderate, peter out, retrench, taper off 9 alleviate, epitomize, extenuate

diminution: 8 decrease 9 abatement, decrement, lessening 10 attenuation, curtailment

diminutive: wee 4 tiny 5 dwarf, petty, runty, small 6 bantam, little, petite 9 miniature, minuscule 11 lilliputian 12 teensy-weensy

dimness: 5 gloom 8 darkness 9 obscurity

dimple: 6 hollow, ripple 11 indentation

dim-witted: 4 dull, slow 5 dopey 6 obtuse 8 backward 11 thick-headed

din: bum 4 riot 5 alarm, bruit, clang, noise 6 clamor, hubbub, racket, rattle, steven, tumult, uproar 7 clangor, clatter, discord, turmoil 9 commotion, confusion 10 hullabaloo

dine: eat, sup 5 feast 6 regale

diner: 4 cafe 6 eatery 8 train car 10 coffee shop, restaurant 11 greasy spoon 12 luncheonette

dinette: 6 alcove 10 kitchen set

ding: 4 beat, dash, push, ring 5 clang, drive, excel, fling, knock, pound, thump 6 stroke, thrash, thrust

dingbat: 4 fool 5 dunce 6 dimwit 9 dumb cluck 12 featherbrain

dinge: 4 dent, dint 6 batter, bruise 10 depression

dinghy: 4 boat 5 skiff 7 rowboat, shallop

dingle: 4 dale, dell, glen, vale 6 valley

dingo: 7 wild dog

dingus: 5 gizmo 6 gadget 9 doohickey 11 thingamajig

dingy: dun 4 dark, drab, mean 5 dirty, dusky,

grimy, seedy, smoky, tacky **6** gloomy, shabby **7** run-down, squalid **8** smirched **11** dilapidated

dinky: **4** cute, neat, poor **5** small **8** trifling **13** insignificant

dinner: **4** meal **5** feast **6** repast **7** banquet
after: **12** postprandial
course: **4** nuts, soup **5** fruit, salad **6** entree **7** dessert **9** appetizer
pert. to: **8** cenatory

dint: **4** beat, blow, dent, nick **5** clour, delve, dinge, force, notch, onset, power, press, shock **6** attack, chance, effort, strain, strike, stroke **7** imprint **8** efficacy, exertion, striking, struggle **10** impression **11** indentation

diocese: see **8** district **9** bishopric
division: **6** parish **7** mission

Dione: *consort:* **4** Zeus
daughter: **9** Aphrodite

Dionysus: **7** Bacchus
attendant: **6** Maenad
festival: **7** Agrania **8** Agrionia
mother: **6** Semele
pert. to: **7** Bromian

diopside: **7** alalite **8** pyroxene

diorite: **7** diabase

Dioscuri: **5** twins **6** Anaces, Castor, Gemini, Pollux
father: **4** Zeus **9** Tyndareus
mother: **4** Leda
sister: **5** Helen **12** Clytemnestra

dip: sag, sop **4** bail, drop, dunk, lade, sink, soak **5** delve, ladle, lower, sauce, slope **6** candle, go down, hollow, plunge **7** decline, immerse, moisten **8** decrease, downturn, submerge **10** depression, pickpocket
in water: **5** douse, rinse, souse

diploma: **6** degree **7** charter **9** sheepskin **11** certificate

diplomacy: **4** tact **5** poise **7** finesse **8** delicacy **9** dexterity **10** artfulness

diplomat: **4** dean **6** consul **7** attache **8** minister **10** ambassador
office of: **7** embassy

dipody: **6** syzygy

dipper: **5** ladle, scoop **8** songbird

dippy: mad **5** silly, wacky **6** absurd **7** foolish **9** screwball

dipsomania: **9** potomania **10** alcoholism

dipteran: fly **4** gnat **8** mosquito
lobe of wing: **5** alula

dire: **4** dern, evil **5** awful, fatal **6** deadly, dismal, funest, tragic, woeful **7** doleful, drastic, fearful **8** dreadful, horrible, terrible, ultimate **10** calamitous, oppressive, portentous **12** overpowering

direct: aim, bid, con **4** airt, bain, bend, boss, edit, even, flat, head, helm, lead, open, rein, sway, turn **5** apply, blank, coach, frank,

guide, order, point, refer, steer, teach, train, utter, write **6** ensign, govern, handle, honest, impart, lineal, manage **7** address, appoint, command, conduct, control, convert, execute, express, officer, preside **8** dedicate, instruct, marshall, regulate, straight **9** categoric, downright, immediate **10** administer, forthright, point-blank **11** categorical, compendious, superintend, superscribe **15** straightforward

direction (see also **compass**): way **4** bent, care, duct, east, road, rule, west **5** north, route, south, trend **6** course **7** address, bearing, command, control, mandate, precept **8** guidance, tendency **10** management, regulation **11** arrangement, inclination, information, instruction **13** determination
biblical: **5** selah
court: **5** order
line of: **5** range
pole to pole: **5** axial
printer's: **4** dele, stet
without: **7** astatic

direction finder: **7** compass

directive: **5** edict, order **6** decree, ruling **10** injunction, memorandum **13** pronouncement

directly: now **6** at once **8** promptly **9** instantly, presently, right away **11** immediately, straightway **12** straightaway

director: **4** boss, head **5** coach, guide, pilot **6** archon, bishop, leader, rector **7** manager, prefect, trainer **8** governor, producer **9** conductor **10** supervisor **13** administrator **14** superintendent

directory: **4** list, ordo **5** guide, index **9** phonebook

dirge: **4** keen, song **5** elegy **6** lament **7** epicede, requiem **8** epicedia (pl.), threnody **9** epicedium

dirigible: **5** blimp **7** airship **8** zeppelin

dirk: **4** snee, stab **5** skean, sword **6** dagger, weapon

dirndl: **5** dress, skirt

dirt: fen, mud **4** dust, gore, muck, nast, smut, soil **5** earth, filth, grime, trash **6** gossip, gravel, ground, refuse **7** lowdown, mullock, squalor **11** scuttlebutt

dirty: low **4** base, clat, foul **5** bawdy, cabby, dingy, foggy, grimy, gusty, horry, muddy, nasty, stain, sully **6** bemire, clarty, defile, filthy, greasy, grubby, impure, mussed, smutty, soiled, sordid, stormy **7** begrime, brookie, bruckle, clouded, muddied, obscene, squalid, sullied, tarnish, unclean **10** despicable

dirty dig: **4** gibe **5** taunt

dirty look: **5** frown, glare, scowl

dirty pool: **5** trick **8** foul play **9** chicanery, duplicity 10 unfairness 13 double-dealing

Dis: 5 Hades, Pluto 8 Dis Pater

disability: 8 drawback, handicap 10 limitation 12 disadvantage

disable: 4 lame, maim 5 break, wreck 6 bruise, dismay, weaken 7 cripple 9 hamstring 10 disqualify 12 incapacitate

disabuse: 4 free 6 debunk, expose, show up 8 set right 9 enlighten

disaccharide: 5 biose 7 lactose, maltose, sucrose 10 saccharose

disadvantage: 4 hurt, loss, risk 6 damage, injury 7 penalty 8 handicap 9 detriment

disadvantageous: 7 adverse, hurtful 11 detrimental, prejudicial, unfavorable

disaffected: 5 false 6 untrue 8 disloyal, forsworn, mutinous, perjured, recreant 9 estranged, faithless, insidious 10 perfidious, traitorous 11 treacherous

disaffection: 6 deceit 7 disease, disgust, dislike 8 disorder 9 distemper, hostility 10 alienation, discontent, disloyalty 13 indisposition 14 disinclination

disaffirm: 4 deny 5 annul 6 negate 7 reverse 9 repudiate 10 contradict

disagree: 4 vary 5 argue, clash, fight 6 differ 7 dissent, quarrel 8 conflict

disagreeable: bad 4 sour, vile 5 cross, harsh, nasty 6 cranky 7 hateful, peevish 8 annoying, petulant 9 invidious, irritable, offensive, repugnant 10 forbidding, unpleasant 11 displeasing, distasteful

disagreement: 5 clash, fight 7 discord, dispute, dissent, wrangle 8 argument, variance 9 diversity 10 contention, difference, difficulty, dissension, divergence, unlikeness 11 contrariety, controversy, discrepancy, displeasure, incongruity 16 misunderstanding

disallow: 4 deny, veto 6 forbid, refuse, reject 7 censure 8 disclaim, prohibit 10 disapprove

disappear: fly 4 fade, flee 6 vanish 7 evanish 8 evanesce

disappoint: 4 balk, bilk, fail, fall, mock, undo 6 baffle, defeat, delude, outwit, thwart 7 deceive, destroy, let down, nullify 9 frustrate

disapproval: 7 censure, dislike, dissent 9 disliking 10 opposition 14 disapprobation
sound of: boo 4 hiss, hoot 7 catcall 9 raspberry 10 Bronx cheer

disapprove: 4 veto 6 reject, resent 7 condemn, protest 8 disallow, turn down 9 deprecate

disarm: 5 charm 6 defuse, subdue 7 win over 12 demilitarize, make harmless

disarming: 4 glib 5 suave 8 smooth 8 unctuous 10 soft-spoken 12 ingratiating

disarrange: 4 muss 5 upset 6 deform, ruffle 7

clutter, confuse, disturb 8 dishevel, unsettle 9 dislocate 10 discompose, disconcert 11 disorganize

disarray: 4 mess 5 strip 6 jumble, muddle 8 disorder 9 confusion 10 dishabille

disassociate: 4 part 7 break up, pull out 8 separate 11 cut ties with 12 withdraw from 14 sever relations

disaster: woe 4 bale, blow, evil, ruin 6 mishap 7 tragedy 8 accident, calamity, casualty, fatality 9 cataclysm, extremity, mischance 10 misfortune 11 catastrophe 12 misadventure

disavow: 4 deny 6 abjure, disown, recant, refuse, reject 7 decline, retract 8 abnegate, disclaim, renounce 9 repudiate

disband: 4 part 7 break up, dismiss, release, scatter 8 disperse, dissolve, separate 9 discharge 12 disintegrate

disbelieve: 5 doubt 6 reject 7 suspect 8 question 9 discredit

disbeliever: 5 cynic 7 atheist, heretic, skeptic

disburden: rid 4 ease 7 relieve 8 get rid of, jettison 9 exonerate 11 disencumber

disburse: 5 spend 6 defray, expend, lay out, pay out 8 dispense 10 distribute

discalced: 6 unshod 8 barefoot

discard: 4 dump, jilt, junk, omit, oust, shed 5 chuck, ditch, scrap, shuck, sluff 6 disuse, divest, reject, slough 7 abandon, cashier, dismiss, forsake 8 cast aside, eliminate, repudiate, throw away
pile: 4 heap 5 trash 8 boneyard

discern: see 4 espy, read 5 judge 6 behold, descry, detect, notice 7 observe 8 discover, perceive 10 understand 11 distinguish

discernible: 7 evident, visible 8 apparent, manifest 11 conspicuous, perceptible 15 distinguishable

discerning: 4 wise

discernment: 4 tact 5 flair, taste 6 acumen 7 insight 8 sagacity 9 sharpness 10 astuteness, divination, perception, shrewdness 11 penetration 12 clairvoyance, perspicacity 14 discrimination

discharge: can 4 boot, dump, emit, fire, free, pour, sack 5 eject, empty, expel, exude, shoot 6 acquit, bounce, defray, effect, exempt, let out, unlade, unload 7 absolve, cashier, disband, dismiss, execute, give off, release, relieve 8 disgorge, displace, evacuate 9 exculpate, exonerate, explosion, liquidate, muster out 10 liberation

disciple: ite 4 John, Jude, Mark 5 James, Judas, Peter, Simon 6 Andrew, Philip, Thomas 7 apostle, Matthew, scholar, student 8 adherent, believer, follower

disciplinarian: 4 czar, tsar, tzar 6 tyrant 7 trainer 8 martinet 10 taskmaster

discipline: 4 cane, whip 5 birch, drill, inure, spank, teach, train 6 punish, school 7 chasten, control, scourge 8 chastise, instruct, regiment, regulate, restrain, training 9 obedience 10 keep in line, strictness 11 hold in check, self-control

disclaim: 4 deny 6 abjure, disown, refuse 7 disavow 8 abdicate, abnegate, disallow, renounce 9 repudiate

disclose: 4 bare, blow, open, tell 5 admit, utter 6 betray, descry, expose, impart, reveal, shrive, unseal, unveil 7 confess, develop, display, divulge, exhibit, uncover 8 discover, indicate 9 make known

disclosure: 6 expose 10 revelation

discolor: run 4 fade, spot 5 smear, stain, tinge 6 streak 7 tarnish 8 besmirch

discoloration: 4 mark, spot 5 stain

discomfit: irk, vex 4 rout 5 abash, annoy, upset 6 baffle, defeat, rattle 7 confuse, disturb, perturb 8 confound 9 embarrass, frustrate 10 disconcert

discomfort: 4 pain 6 dismay, grieve, sorrow, unease 7 disturb 8 distress 9 annoyance, embarrass 10 discourage, uneasiness 11 displeasure 13 inconvenience 14 discouragement

discommode: 5 upset 6 bother, put out 7 trouble 13 inconvenience

discompose: 4 fret 5 upset 6 flurry, ruffle 7 agitate, confuse, derange, disturb, fluster, perturb 8 disorder, displace, disquiet, unsettle 9 discharge 10 disarrange, disconcert

disconcert: 4 faze 5 abash, daunt, feeze, upset, worry 6 baffle, blench, rattle 7 confuse, disturb, nonplus, perplex, perturb 8 bewilder, confound 9 discomfit, embarrass 10 disarrange, discompose

disconnect: 4 undo 5 sever 6 unplug 7 disjoin 8 dissolve, disunite, separate, uncouple

disconnected: 6 abrupt, broken 7 cursory 8 rambling 9 desultory, scattered 10 abstracted, disjointed, incoherent

disconsolate: sad 6 gloomy, woeful 7 forlorn 8 dejected, desolate, hopeless 9 cheerless, miserable, sorrowful 10 dispirited, melancholy

discontent: 8 disquiet 9 dysphoria 10 uneasiness 11 displeasure, unhappiness 12 restlessness

discontinue: end 4 drop, quit, stop 5 break, cease, let up 6 desist, disuse, give up 9 terminate

discord: din, jar 5 clash 6 strife 7 faction 8 conflict, variance 9 cacophony, diversity 10 contention, difference, dissension, dissonance 12 disagreement
goddess of: Ate 4 Eris

discordant: 5 harsh 6 hoarse 7 jarring 8 contrary, jangling 10 discrepant, mismatched 11 incongruous, quarrelsome 12 antagonistic, incompatible, inconsistent, inharmonious
musically: 8 scordato
serenade: 9 charivari

Discordia: 4 Eris

discotheque: 4 club 5 disco 7 cabaret 9 nightclub

discount: 4 agio 5 batta (Ind.) 6 ignore, rebate 7 dismiss 8 minimize 9 allowance, deduction, disregard, reduction 10 brush aside, disbelieve

discourage: 4 carp 5 daunt, deter 6 dampen, deject, hinder 7 depress, inhibit, prevent 8 dispirit, dissuade, restrain 10 discomfort, dishearten

discourse: 4 talk, tell 5 orate, paper, speak, tract 6 eulogy, homily, parley, preach, sermon 7 account, address, comment, declaim, discuss, dissert, lecture, oration, prelect 8 argument, colloquy, converse, parlance, treatise 9 expatiate, narration, panegyric, soliloquy 10 commentate 11 description 12 conversation, dissertation
art of: 8 rhetoric
long: 6 screed, tirade 7 descant 9 philippic

discourteous: 4 rude 6 scurvy 7 ill-bred, uncivil 8 impolite, ungentle 10 unmannerly 11 ill-mannered 13 disrespectful

discover: see, spy 4 espy, find 5 learn 6 define, descry, detect, expose, invent, locate, reveal 7 confess, discern, display, divulge, explore, find out, uncover, unearth 8 decipher, disclose, manifest, perceive 9 apprehend, ascertain

discoverer: spy 5 scout 8 explorer, inventor 10 originator

discovery: 4 find 5 trove 6 espial, strike 10 disclosure, revelation

discredit: 5 decry, doubt 6 damage, expose, show up 7 asperse, blemish, impeach, scandal, suspect 8 belittle, disgrace, dishonor, distrust, ignominy 9 disparage, disrepute 10 disbelieve

discreet: 4 wary 5 civil 6 polite, silent 7 careful, guarded, politic, prudent 8 cautious, reserved, reticent 11 circumspect

discrepant: 8 contrary 9 different, divergent 10 discordant 11 conflicting, disagreeing 12 inconsistent

discrete: 8 detached, distinct, separate 9 unrelated

discretion: 4 tact 6 wisdom 7 caution 8 judgment, prudence 9 restraint 13 secretiveness

discriminate: 5 favor 8 perceive, show bias 9 demarcate, segregate 10 place apart 11 distinguish 13 differentiate, play favorites

discriminating: 6 astute 7 careful, choosey 8 critical 9 selective 10 discerning, prejudiced

discrimination: 5 taste 6 acumen 8 inequity 10 partiality 11 discernment

discursive: 6 roving 7 cursory 8 rambling 9 desultory 10 digressive

discus: 4 disk 5 quoit
  thrower: 10 discobolus

discuss: air 4 moot 5 argue, bandy 6 confer, debate, parley 7 agitate, bespeak, consult, dispute, examine 8 talk over 9 discourse 10 deliberate

discussion: rap 4 talk 6 confab, huddle, parley, powwow 8 causerie 10 conference 11 bull session
  group: 5 class, panel 7 seminar 10 round table
  medium of: 5 forum
  open to: 4 moot 9 debatable

disdain: 5 flout, scorn, spurn 7 contemn, despise, put down, sneer at 8 contempt, derision, ridicule 9 arrogance 11 haughtiness

disease: bug 4 harm 5 virus 6 malady 7 ailment, illness, trouble 8 debility, distress, sickness 9 complaint, infirmity 10 discomfort, pestilence, uneasiness
  animal: coe, pip 5 braxy, colic, farcy, hoose, hooze, mange 6 amoeba, garget, rabies 7 spavins 8 glanders, sacbrood 9 distemper, tularemia
  contagious: 4 cold 5 mumps 7 measles, rubella 9 hepatitis, influenza 10 chicken pox, diphtheria 12 tuberculosis 13 German measles, whooping cough
  local: 7 endemic
  plant: fen 4 bunt, rust, scab, smut 5 ergot, speck 6 calico, coleur, mildew, mosaic 7 erinose, viruela, walloon 8 brindled, melanose
  prediction about: 9 prognosis
  recognition of: 9 diagnosis
  skin: 4 acne, rash 5 favus, hives, psora, tinea 6 dartre, eczema, herpes, lichen, tetter 7 scabies 8 impetigo, ringworm 9 psoriasis, xeroderma 11 scleroderma
  wide-spreading: 8 epidemic, pandemic

disembark: 4 land 6 alight 8 go ashore

disembodiment: 4 soul 6 spirit

disembowel: gut 4 hulk 6 paunch 8 gralloch 10 eviscerate

disembroil: 6 free of 8 untangle 9 extricate

disenchanted: 5 blase 7 knowing, let down, unhappy 9 turned off 11 enlightened, put straight, worldly-wise 13 disillusioned

disencumber: rid 4 ease 7 lighten, relieve 8 unburden 9 disengage

disengage: 4 free 5 clear, untie 6 detach,

loosen 7 release, retreat, unravel 8 liberate, uncouple, unfasten 9 extricate

disentangle: 4 comb 5 clear, loose 6 evolve 7 unravel 8 separate 9 extricate 13 straighten out

disfavor: 5 odium 7 dislike, umbrage 9 bad repute, disesteem 11 displeasure

disfigure: mar 4 scar 5 spoil 6 deface, deform, injure, mangle 7 blemish 8 mutilate

disgorge: 4 spew, vent 5 eject, empty, expel, vomit 7 bring up 9 discharge 10 relinquish

disgrace: 4 blot, slur, soil, spot 5 abase, crime, odium, shame, stain 6 infamy, stigma 7 affront, attaint, degrade, scandal, slander 8 contempt, dishonor, ignominy, reproach 9 discredit, disesteem, humiliate 10 opprobrium 11 humiliation

disgruntled: 4 sore 5 upset 7 peevish

disguise: 4 hide, mask, veil 5 belie, cloak, feign 6 facade, masque 7 conceal, obscure, pretend 8 artifice, pretense 9 coverture, dissemble, incognito 10 camouflage, false front, masquerade 11 dissimulate

disgust: 5 repel, shock 6 degout (F.), horror, nausea, offend, revolt, sicken 8 aversion, distaste, loathing, nauseate 9 antipathy 10 abhorrence, repugnance

disgusting: 4 foul, vile 5 gross, nasty 6 filthy 7 beastly, fulsome, hateful, noisome, obscene 8 shocking

dish (see also **food**): cup 4 bowl, food 5 basin, nappy, paten, plate 6 critch, looker, patera, saucer, tureen 7 charger, plateau, platter, ramekin 8 favorite 9 casserole, container 10 preference
  gravy: 4 boat
  main: 6 entree

dishabille: 8 disarray, disorder 10 deshabille 13 partly dressed

Dishan's son: 4 Aran

dishearten: 5 daunt 6 deject 7 depress, flatten, unnerve 8 dispirit 10 demoralize, discourage

disheartened: 6 gloomy 8 downcast 10 despondent 11 discouraged

disheveled: 5 messy 6 sloppy, untidy 7 ruffled, rumpled, tousled, unkempt 8 mussed up, slovenly, uncombed 10 disorderly, in disarray 11 disarranged

dishonest: 5 false, lying 7 corrupt, crooked, knavish 8 cheating, two-faced 9 deceitful 10 fraudulent, perfidious, untruthful 13 untrustworthy

dishonor: 5 shame, stain 6 defame, defile 7 degrade, obloquy, violate 8 disgrace, ignominy 9 discredit, disparage, disrepute 10 opprobrium

dishonorable: 4 base, foul 5 shady 7 corrupt,

ignoble **8** infamous, shameful, unsavory **9** unethical **12** unscrupulous

disinclination: 7 dislike **8** aversion, distaste **9** antipathy **10** reluctance, repugnance **12** disaffection

disinclined: 6 averse **9** reluctant, unwilling **10** indisposed

disinfect: 7 cleanse **8** sanitize **9** sterilize

disinfectant: 5 iodin **6** iodine, phenol **9** germicide **10** antiseptic

disingenuous: 4 wily **5** false **6** artful, tricky **7** devious **8** indirect, specious **9** insincere **10** circuitous

disinherit: 6 cut off, disown **7** deprive **10** exheredate

disintegrate: 4 melt **5** decay, erode **7** crumble, disband **8** dissolve, separate **9** decompose

disinter: 5 dig up **6** exhume **7** unearth

disinterested: 4 fair **8** unbiased, uncaring **9** apathetic, impartial **11** unconcerned

disjoin: 4 part, undo **5** sever **6** detach, sunder **7** break up **8** dissolve, disunite, separate **10** disconnect, dissociate

disjointed: 7 muddled **8** inchoate, unhinged **10** disordered, incoherent **12** disconnected, lacking unity

disk: CD **4** chip, dial, hard **5** cakra, medal, paten, plate, sabot, wheel **6** bezant, chakra, floppy, harrow, record, washer **7** medalet, phalera **9** cultivate, faceplate, floptical, medallion, millstone
hockey: **4** puck
metal: **4** flan, gong **6** ghurry, sequin **8** zecchino
pert. to: **6** discal **7** discoid
solar: **4** Aten

dislike: 4 loth, mind **6** detest, loathe **8** aversion, distaste **9** antipathy, disrelish, prejudice **10** repugnance **11** displeasure **12** disaffection
object of: **8** anathema
of children: **9** misopedia

dislocate: 5 splay **7** disrupt **8** disjoint, displace **10** disarrange

dislodge: 5 expel **6** remove **8** force out

disloyal: 5 false **6** untrue **9** faithless **10** inconstant, perfidious, traitorous, unfaithful **11** disaffected, treacherous

dismal: sad, wan **4** dark, dire, dull, glum, gray **5** black, bleak, drear, sorry **6** dreary, gloomy, triste **7** doleful, ghastly, joyless, ominous, unhappy **8** dolorous, funereal, lonesome **9** cheerless, sorrowful **10** acherontic, calamitous, lugubrious, melancholy **11** unfortunate

dismantle: 4 rase, raze **5** annul, strip **6** divest **7** deprive, destroy, rescind, uncloak **8** dismount, take down **10** do away with

dismay: 4 fear, ruin **5** alarm, appal, daunt, dread **6** appall, fright, subdue, terror **7** depress, deprive, horrify, terrify **8** affright, confound **9** dejection **10** depression, discomfort, discourage **11** trepidation **12** apprehension **13** consternation

dismember: 4 maim, part, rend **5** sever **6** mangle **7** dissect **8** disjoint, mutilate

dismiss: can **4** boot, bust, drop, oust **5** chuck, eject **6** banish, bounce, reject, remove **7** cashier, disband, discard **8** relegate **9** discharge, overthrow

dismissal: 5 conge **6** ouster **7** removal **9** discharge

dismount: 6 alight, get off **9** dismantle, take apart

Disney (Walt): 10 cartoonist
character: **4** Huey, Puff **5** Daisy, Dewey, Dumbo, Goofy, Louie, Pluto **6** Donald, Mickey, Minnie
film classic: **5** Bambi **7** Aladdin **8** Fantasia **9** Pinocchio, Snow White **10** Cinderella, Jungle Book **13** 101 Dalmations, Little Mermaid **15** Lady and the Tramp, Reluctant Dragon, Steamboat Willie

disobedient: 6 unruly **7** forward, naughty, wayward, willful **8** mutinous **10** rebellious, refractory **11** intractable **12** contumacious **13** insubordinate

disoblige: 6 offend **7** affront

disorder: 4 mess, muss, riot **5** chaos, snafu **6** burble, jumble, litter, malady, mucker, muddle, ruffle, tousle, tumult **7** ailment, clutter, confuse, derange, disturb, embroil, flutter, illness, misdeed, perturb, trouble **8** disarray, dishevel **9** commotion, complaint, confusion, distemper **10** disarrange, discompose, disconcert, misconduct **11** disorganize, misdemeanor **13** indisposition
visual: **10** strabismus

disorderly: 5 randy **6** unruly **8** slipshod, slovenly **10** topsy-turvy **12** hugger-mugger, ungovernable, unmanageable

disorganize: 5 upset **7** confuse, derange, disband, disrupt **8** disorder, dissolve **10** disarrange

disown: 4 deny **6** reject **7** disavow, retract **8** abdicate, disclaim, renounce **9** repudiate **10** disinherit

disparage: 4 slur **5** abuse, decry, lower **6** slight **7** degrade, depress, detract, impeach **8** belittle, derogate, dishonor, disprize, minimize **9** discredit **10** depreciate

disparate: 7 unequal **8** separate **9** different **10** dissimilar **16** disproportionate

dispassionate: 4 calm, cool, fair **5** stoic **6** sedate, serene **8** composed, moderate **9** collected, impartial, temperate, unruffled **10** deliberate, unimpaired **12** unprejudiced

dispatch: rid 4 free, kill, mail, note, post, send 5 haste, hurry, speed 6 hasten 7 deliver, depeche (F.), dispose 8 celerity, conclude, expedite 9 quickness 10 accelerate, accomplish, promptness

dispatch boat: 5 aviso 6 packet

dispel: 7 scatter 8 disperse 9 dissipate

dispendious: 6 costly 9 expensive 11 extravagant

dispensation: 4 plan 6 scheme 7 license, release 9 allotment, exemption 10 indulgence 12 distribution

dispense: 4 deal 5 forgo 6 effuse, excuse, exempt, forego, manage 7 absolve, arrange, dole out, hand out, provide 9 apportion 10 administer, distribute
with: 5 chuck, scrap 7 discard 8 get rid of 9 eliminate, toss aside

disperse: sow 4 rout 5 strew 6 dispel, spread, vanish 7 break up, diffuse, scatter 8 separate, squander 9 dissipate 10 distribute 11 disseminate

dispirit: cow 4 damp 5 daunt 6 deject 7 depress, flatten 10 discourage, dishearten, intimidate

dispirited: low, sad 4 blue 6 abattu (F.) 8 abbattue (F.), downcast 9 cheerless, woebegone 11 crestfallen 12 disconsolate

displace: 6 banish, depose, mislay, remove 7 push out 8 dislodge, supplant, take over 9 discharge, dislocate, supersede

display: air 4 pomp, show, wear 5 boast, scene, sight, sport 6 blazon, evince, expose, extend, flaunt, parade, reveal, unfold, unveil 7 etalage, exhibit, pageant, trot out, uncover 8 ceremony, disclose, discover, emblazon, exercise, flourish, indicate, manifest, splendor 9 spectacle, spread out 10 exhibition 11 affectation 13 demonstration

displease: vex 4 miff 5 anger, annoy, pique 6 offend 7 provoke 8 irritate 10 discontent, dissatisfy

displeasing: bad 7 irksome 9 offensive 10 unpleasant 11 distasteful 12 disagreeable

displeasure: ire 5 anger 6 injury 7 dislike, offense, umbrage 8 disfavor, distaste, vexation 10 discomfort, discontent, resentment, uneasiness 11 indignation
show: cry 4 pout 5 frown, scowl

disport: 4 play 5 amuse, frisk 6 divert, frolic, gambol

disposal: 4 sale 8 riddance 9 clearance 11 arrangement, transferral

dispose: set 4 bend, give, mind 5 array, order, place 6 adjust, attire, bestow, settle 7 appoint, arrange, prepare 8 dispatch, organize, regulate 9 determine 10 distribute

disposed: apt 5 fixed, prone, ready 7 tending 8 arranged, inclined

disposition: 4 bent, bias, mood, turn 5 humor 6 affect, animus, health, nature, temper 7 concept 8 aptitude, attitude, disposal 9 affection, character, diathesis 10 adjustment, management, proclivity, propensity 11 arrangement, inclination, temperament 12 constitution, distribution, organization

dispossess: 4 oust 5 eject, evict, expel, strip 6 depose, divest 7 bereave, deprive

dispraise: 5 blame 7 censure 9 disparage 10 depreciate 11 detract from

disproportion: 9 disparity 10 inequality

disproportionate: 6 uneven 7 unequal 8 lopsided 9 irregular, overblown 10 asymmetric, unbalanced

disprove: 5 rebut 6 negate, refute 7 confute, explode 8 overturn 9 discredit 10 controvert

disputable: 4 moot 5 vague 6 unsure 7 dubious 8 doubtful, fallible, insecure 9 uncertain 10 indefinite, precarious

disputant: 6 arguer 7 debater

disputation: 7 polemic 8 argument 9 dialectic 10 discussion 11 controversy

dispute: 4 deny, feud, fuss, moot, spat 5 argue, brawl, cabal 6 barney, bicker, debate, differ, haggle 7 brabble, contend, contest, faction, gainsay, quarrel, wrangle 8 argument, question, squabble 9 argy-bargy, encounter 10 contravene, controvert, litigation 11 altercation, controversy 12 disagreement

disqualify: 5 debar 6 outlaw 7 disable, rule out 8 prohibit 9 indispose 10 invalidate 12 incapacitate

disquiet: vex 4 fear, fret, pain 6 excite, stir up, unease, unrest 7 agitate, anxiety, disturb, fluster, trouble, turmoil 10 discompose, discontent 12 restlessness 13 inconvenience

disquisition: 5 essay 8 treatise 10 discussion

disregard: 4 omit 5 waive 6 forget, ignore, pass by, slight 7 neglect 8 discount, overlook 9 pretermit 10 contravene 11 inattention 12 indifference

disrelish: 7 dislike 8 distaste 9 antipathy

disreputable: low 4 base, hard 5 seamy, shady 7 raffish 8 shameful, unsavory 9 notorious 13 discreditable

disrepute: 5 odium 7 bad name 8 disgrace, dishonor, ignominy, reproach 9 disesteem

disrespect: 8 rudeness 9 insolence 10 incivility 11 discourtesy

disrespectful: 5 fresh, sassy 7 uncivil 8 impolite, impudent 10 irreverent 11 impertinent

disrobe: 4 bare 5 strip 6 divest 7 take off, undress

disrupt: 4 rend, tear 5 break 7 disrump 11 discontinue, disorganize

dissatisfaction: 5 ennui 6 unrest 8 distaste 9 annoyance 10 discontent 11 displeasure

dissect: 5 carve, cut up 7 analyze 9 anatomize, dismember

dissemble: 4 hide, mask 5 cloak, feign 6 boggle 7 conceal, pretend 8 disguise, simulate 11 counterfeit, dissimulate

dissembler: 5 actor 9 hypocrite

disseminate: sow 5 strew, teach 6 effuse, spread 7 diffuse, publish, scatter, send out 8 disperse 9 broadcast, circulate, propagate 10 distribute

dissent: 4 vary 6 differ, oppose 7 protest 8 disagree 9 exception, objection 10 dissidence 12 disagreement 13 nonconformity 14 nonconcurrence
signal of: nay

dissenter: 7 heretic, sectary 8 recusant 9 protestor 10 Protestant, schismatic, separatist, unbeliever 13 nonconformist

dissentious: 8 factious 11 contentious

dissert: 7 discuss 9 discourse

dissertation: 5 essay, theme, tract 6 debate, theses (pl.), thesis 7 descant, lecture 8 treatise 9 discourse 10 discussion

Dissertation on a Roast Pig author: 11 Charles Lamb

disservice: 4 harm 5 wrong 6 damage, injury 8 mischief

dissever: 4 part 6 sunder 8 disunite

dissidence: 6 schism, strife 7 dissent 8 conflict 10 contention 12 disagreement 13 nonconformity

dissimilar: 6 unlike 7 difform, diverse 9 anomalous, different, disparate 13 heterogeneous

dissimulate: 5 feign 7 deceive, pretend 8 disguise 9 dissemble

dissipate: 5 spend, waste 6 dispel, expend 7 diffuse, scatter, shatter 8 disperse, dissolve, evanesce, squander 9 evaporate 11 fritter away, overindulge

dissocial: 10 unfriendly 11 standoffish

dissociate: 5 sever 7 disjoin 8 disunite, separate

dissolute: lax 4 wild 5 loose, slack 6 rakish, wanton 7 immoral, lawless 8 uncurbed 9 abandoned, debauched, unbridled 10 licentious, profligate 12 unrestrained

dissolution: end 4 ruin 5 decay 6 bust-up, demise 7 breakup, decease, divorce 10 abrogation 11 adjournment, termination 14 disintegration
comb. form: lys

dissolve: 4 fade, fuse, melt, thaw, void 5 annul 6 relent, unbind 7 adjourn, destroy, disband, disjoin, divorce, liquefy 8 discandy, disunite, separate 9 decompose, dissipate 10 deliquesce 12 disintegrate

dissolved: 6 solute

dissolving: 7 diluent

dissonant: 5 harsh 7 grating, jarring 8 jangling 10 discordant 11 cacophonous, incongruous, unmelodious 12 inconsistent, inharmonious

dissuade: 5 deter 6 dehort, divert 10 discourage, disincline

distaff: 5 woman 6 female 12 maternal side

distal: 6 remote 7 distant 8 terminal
angle: 4 axil
opposite of: 8 proximal

distance: 4 step 5 depth, range, space 7 farness, mileage, reserve, yardage 8 interval, outstrip 10 background, remoteness
measuring device: 6 stadia 8 odograph, odometer, viameter 9 pedometer, telemeter
on earth's surface: 8 latitude 9 longitude

distant: far, off 4 afar, away, cold 5 aloof 6 remote, yonder 7 faraway, foreign, removed 8 reserved 9 separated 10 discrepant

distaste: 7 disgust, dislike 8 aversion 9 disrelish 11 displeasure 14 disinclination

distasteful: 7 hateful 8 brackish, nauseous, unsavory 9 loathsome, offensive, repugnant, repulsive 10 unpleasant 11 unpalatable 12 disagreeable

distemper: 4 soak 5 steep 6 choler, dilute, malady 7 ailment, disease, illness 8 disorder, sickness, unsettle

distend: 4 fill, grow 5 bloat, plump, swell, widen 6 dilate, expand, extend, spread 7 balloon, enlarge, inflate, stretch

distended: 4 wide 5 blown 7 swollen 8 patulous

distich: 7 couplet

distill, distil: 4 emit 6 infuse 7 extract, ferment, trickle

distillation: 7 essence 10 refinement
device: 5 still 6 retort 7 alembic, matrass

distinct: 5 clear, plain, vivid 7 diverse, legible, obvious, special 8 apparent, separate 9 different 10 articulate, individual

distinction: 4 note, rank 5 glory, honor 6 laurel, luster, renown 9 variation 10 prominence, reputation, separation 14 discrimination 15 differentiation

distinctive: 8 peculiar, talented 9 prominent 11 conspicuous, outstanding 14 characteristic, discriminating
air: 6 cachet

distingué: 6 urbane 7 eminent 8 cultured, polished 10 cultivated

distinguish: 6 define, descry 7 discern 8 perceive, separate 9 designate, punctuate 10 discrepate 12 characterize, discriminate 13 differentiate

distinguished: 5 noted 6 famous, marked 7

eminent, notable, special **8** distinct, laureate, renowned **9** brilliant, prominent **10** celebrated **11** conspicuous, illustrious **13** extraordinary

distort: **4** warp **5** slant, twist **6** deform, garble **7** falsify, pervert **8** misstate **10** disfeature **12** misrepresent

distorted: **4** awry **5** askew **7** colored, crooked, deviant, gnarled **9** misshapen **10** anamorphic **11** anamorphous

distract: **5** addle, amuse, mix up **6** bemuse, divert, harass, puzzle **7** agitate, confuse, disturb, embroil, perplex **8** bewilder, confound

distraught: mad **6** crazed **7** frantic, worried **8** deranged, harassed

distress: ail **4** hurt, need, pain **5** agony, anger, annoy, dolor, grief, gripe, worry, wound **6** danger, grieve, harass, harrow, misery, sorrow **7** afflict, anguish, anxiety, oppress, perplex, torture, trouble **8** aggrieve, calamity, straiten **9** adversity, constrain, martyrdom, necessity **10** affliction, constraint, discomfort **11** tribulation
call: Pan, SOS **6** mayday
signal: **5** alarm, flare, siren

distressing: sad **6** woeful **7** fearful, painful **9** sorrowful **10** deplorable, lamentable **11** troublesome

distribute: **4** deal, dole, mete, sort **5** allot, issue, share **6** assign, assort, divide, expend, impart, parcel **7** arrange, dispose, prorate **8** allocate, classify, dispense, disperse, separate **9** apportion, partition **10** administer **11** disseminate

distributively: **4** each **6** apiece **9** severally **10** separately **12** individually, respectively

distributor: **6** dealer, jobber **8** auto part **10** colporteur

district: **4** area, slum, ward **5** tract, vicus (L.) **6** canton, parish, region **7** circuit, country, demesne, diocese, quarter **8** locality, precinct, province **9** community, territory **12** neighborhood
theater: **6** rialto

District of Columbia: See **Washington, DC**

distrust: **4** fear **5** doubt **7** suspect **8** be wary of **9** suspicion **12** apprehension

distrustfully: **7** askance **11** skeptically

disturb: vex **4** rile, roil **5** alarm, annoy, rouse, upset **6** freeze, harass, molest, ruffle **7** agitate, derange, perturb, trouble **8** disquiet, distract, unsettle **9** discomfit, interfere, interrupt, make waves **10** disarrange, discompose, disconcert

disturbance: **4** riot, rout **5** alarm, brawl **6** affray, bother, fracas, hubbub, pother, rumpus, tumult, uproar **7** clatter, ferment, trouble, turmoil **8** disorder **9** agitation, annoy-

ance, commotion, confusion **10** excitement **11** derangement, distraction, trepidation **12** discomposure, interruption, perturbation **13** collie-shangie (Sc.), inconvenience
atmospheric: **5** storm **7** cyclone, thunder, tornado **9** hurricane, lightning
emotional: **8** neurosis
ocean: **7** tsunami

disunite: **4** part **5** sever, untie **6** detach, divide, sunder **7** disband, disjoin, dissent, divorce, split up, unravel **8** alienate, dissever, dissolve, estrange, separate **10** disconnect, dissociate

disuse: **7** abandon, discard **9** desuetude **12** obsolescence

disyllabic foot: **4** iamb **7** spondee, trochee

ditch: rut **4** dike, junk, moat **5** canal, scarp **6** gutter, trench **7** abandon, channel **8** get rid of, jettison **9** throw away **10** excavation
side: **5** scarp

dither: **4** flap **5** hissy, panic, shake, tizzy, waver **6** babble, shiver **7** tremble, twitter **9** vacillate **10** act nervous **12** shilly-shally

dithyrambic: **4** wild **10** boisterous

ditto: **4** same **6** repeat **8** likewise **9** duplicate

ditty: lay **4** poem, song **6** melody

diurnal: **5** daily **9** ephemeral
opposite: **9** nocturnal

divagate: **5** drift, stray **6** wander **7** digress

divan: **4** sofa **5** couch **6** lounge, settee **9** davenport **13** Muslim council

divaricate: **6** forked **7** diverge **11** spread apart

dive: den **4** dump, fall, jump, leap **5** joint, lunge, swoop **6** plunge **7** descend, hangout **8** submerge, tailspin
kind of: **4** swan **6** gainer **9** jackknife

dive into: try **5** begin, start

diver: **4** loon **7** pearler, plunger **9** submarine
disease: **5** bends **12** aeroembolism
gear: **4** mask, tank **5** scuba **7** flipper, snorkel, wet suit

diverge: **6** branch, differ, divide, ramify, spread **7** deviate, digress **8** disagree

divers: **4** many **6** sundry **7** several, various

diverse: **6** motley, sundry, unlike, varied **8** distinct, separate **9** different, multiform **10** dissimilar **13** heterogeneous

diversion: jeu (F.) **4** game, play **5** feint, hobby, sport **7** pastime **9** amusement, avocation, merriment **10** deflection, digression, recreation, relaxation **11** distraction **13** divertisement, entertainment

diversity: **6** change **7** variety **10** difference, unlikeness **11** variegation

divert: **5** amuse, relax **7** beguile, deflect, delight **8** dissuade, distract **9** entertain, turn aside

diverting: **5** droll **8** pleasant **9** laughable

divest 218

divest: 4 bare, doff 5 spoil, strip 6 denude, depose 7 bereave, deprive, despoil, disrobe, uncover 8 denature, dethrone, take away, unclothe 9 dismantle 10 dispossess
of sham: 6 debunk

divide: cut, lot 4 deal, fork, part, rift, zone 5 cleft, divvy, ridge, sever, share, slice, space, split 6 branch, cleave, differ, parcel, ramify, sunder 7 aliquot, diverge, fissure, prorate 8 alienate, allocate, classify, disunite, graduate, separate 9 apportion, dismember, intersect, multisect, partition, watershed 10 distribute
into feet: 4 scan
into parts: 4 paly 6 bisect, gobbet 7 quarter, trisect 9 bifurcate, septinate

divided: 4 reft, rent 5 apart, split 6 halved, parted 7 fissate, partite 8 areolate, camerate 10 incomplete

dividend: 5 bonus, yield 6 return, reward 12 extra portion

divider: 6 screen 7 compass 9 partition

divination: 4 omen 6 augury 8 prophecy 9 good guess 11 discernment 12 clairvoyance
ability: ESP
by dreams: 11 oneiromancy
by figures: 8 geomancy
by fire: 9 pyromancy
by lots: 9 sortilege
by numbers: 10 numerology
by rods: 7 dowsing
by stars: 9 astrology
by the hands: 9 palmistry
manual: 6 I Ching

divine: 4 holy 5 guess, pious 6 detect, devise, priest, sacred 7 blessed, foresee, godlike, portend, predict, presage 8 adorable, forebode, foreknow, foretell, heavenly, immortal, minister, perceive 9 ambrosial, celestial, clergyman, religious 10 anticipate, conjecture, superhuman, theologian 12 supernatural
artificer: 8 tvashtar, tvashtri
being: 4 deva
communication: 6 oracle
gift: 5 grace
messenger: 7 apostle
render: 5 deify
Sarah: 9 Bernhardt
spirit: 5 numen
word: 5 logos
work: 7 theurgy

Divine Comedy author: 5 Dante

diviner: 4 seer 5 augur, sibyl 6 oracle 7 prophet 8 haruspex 10 soothsayer 11 clairvoyant 14 prognosticator

diving: 8 plunging 10 acrobatics, submerging
bird: 4 auk 5 loon 5 grebe 6 osprey 7 pelican

divinity (see also **god, goddess**): 5 candy, deity 7 godhood 8 theology

division: 4 chap, clan, dole, neat, part, rift 5 group, realm, share 6 canton, schism, sector 7 roulade, section 8 arpeggio, category, cleavage 9 Abteilung, allotment, concision, departure, partition 10 department 11 bifurcation, compartment, disjunction
athletic contest: lap, set 4 half, heat 5 round 6 inning, period 7 chukker, quarter
Bible: 4 book 5 verse 9 Apocrypha, Testament
play: act 5 scene
poem: 5 canto 6 stanza
political: 4 city, ward 5 state 6 county, parish 7 borough 8 district, province
religious: 4 cult, sect 6 schism
result: 8 fraction, quotient
social: 4 clan 5 caste, class, tribe
time: age, day, eon, era 4 aeon, hour, week, year 5 month, night 6 decade, minute, moment, second 7 century, weekend 9 fortnight
word: 8 syllable

divorce: 5 sever 6 sunder 7 break up 8 dissolve, disunion, disunite, separate 10 separation 11 dissolution
Jewish law: get 4 gett
mill: 4 Reno

divot: sod 4 clod, turf 10 lump of turf

divulge: 4 bare, show, tell 5 voice 6 impart, reveal, spread, unfold 7 publish, uncover 8 disclose, discover, give away, proclaim

divvy: 5 share 6 divide 7 portion

Dixie Land: 5 South

dizziness: 6 megrim 7 vertigo 9 giddiness
with headache: 10 scotodinia

dizzy: 4 daze 5 crazy, faint, giddy 6 fickle, stupid 7 foolish 8 swimming, unsteady 10 capricious 11 lightheaded, vertiginous

DNA: 4 gene 11 nucleic acid
segment: 7 cistron
shape: 11 double helix

Dnieper/Dnepr: *cities on:* 4 Kiev 5 Orsha 7 Kherson, Mogilev, Nikopol 8 Smolensk
tributary: 4 Psel, Sozh, Sula 5 Desna, Psiol 7 Pripyat 8 Berezina, Ingulets

do: act 4 bilk, dost, make, suit 5 avail, cheat, guise, serve, trick 6 answer, finish, render, wind up, work at 7 achieve, arrange, clean up, execute, perform, produce, satisfy, suffice 8 carry out, transact 10 accomplish, administer
away with: rid 4 drop 7 abolish 8 dissolve 9 liquidate 11 discontinue
in: 4 kill, ruin 6 defeat, finish, murder 7 destroy, exhaust, wear out 9 liquidate
out of: 5 cheat, cozen 7 defraud
up: tie 4 wrap 5 clean 7 arrange, prepare
well: 7 prosper, succeed
without: 5 forgo 6 forego, pass up, refuse

dobbin: 4 mare

docent: 5 guide 7 teacher 8 lecturer

docile: 4 calm, meek, tame 6 gentle 7 ductile, dutiful 8 biddable 9 tractable 10 manageable

dock: cut 4 bang, clip, moor, pier, quay 5 basin, wharf 6 marina 7 bobtail, curtail, shorten 12 prisoner's box
post: 4 pile 7 bollard
ship's: 4 slip 5 basin, berth
worker: 9 stevedore
yard: 7 arsenal

docket: 4 card 6 agenda 7 program 8 calendar, schedule 13 police blotter

doctor: 4 dose 5 fix up, treat 6 healer, medico, repair 7 dentist, scholar 8 sawbones 9 internist, physician 10 adulterate 11 aesculapian
aide: 5 nurse
oath of: 11 hippocratic
specialist: 7 oculist, surgeon 9 internist, osteopath, otologist, urologist 10 oncologist, podiatrist 11 chiropodist, neurologist, optometrist, orthopedist, radiologist 12 chiropractor, gynecologist, nephrologist, obstetrician, orthodontist, pediatrician, proctologist, psychiatrist 13 dermatologist, gerontologist 14 opthalmologist 15 endocrinologist

doctrine: ism 4 doxy, lear, rule 5 credo, creed, dogma, maxim, tenet 6 belief, gospel, theory 7 article, opinion, precept 8 position 9 principle 10 discipline
pert. to: 10 dogmatical 12 teleological
secret: 7 esotery
single principle: 6 henism, monism
specific: 6 cabala, heresy, malism, Mishna 7 Mishnah 8 fatalism, hedonism 10 agathology, pragmatism 13 monarchianism
spreader: 12 propagandist

document: 4 bill, book, cite, deed, writ 5 lease, paper 6 record, verify 7 bear out, confirm, missive, precept, writing 8 contract, covenant, mortgage, validate 9 indenture 10 manuscript 11 corroborate
addition: 5 rider 7 codicil 9 amendment
file: 7 dossier
original record: 8 protocol
permissive: 7 license
provisional: 5 scrip
receptacle: 7 hanaper
signed by all parties: 8 syngraph
storehouse: 8 archives
travel: 8 passport
true copy: 7 estreat

Dodecanese Island: Kos 4 Syme 5 Kasos, Leros, Telos 6 Khalke, Lipsos, Patmos, Rhodes 7 Nisyros, Piscopi 8 Kalymnos 9 Karpathos
part of: 6 Greece

dodder: 5 shake 6 totter 7 tremble

doddering: old 5 inane 6 infirm, senile 7 foolish

dodge: 4 duck, jink, ruse 5 avoid, cheat, elude, evade, parry, shift, shirk, trick 6 escape 7 deceive, evasion 8 artifice, sidestep 9 expedient 10 equivocate

dodger: 6 shield 7 haggler, portion 8 circular, handbill 13 advertisement
corn: 4 pone

dodo: 7 old fogy 8 mossback 10 back number, fuddy-duddy 11 extinct bird

doe: roe, teg 4 deer, fawn, hind 6 female

doer: 6 dynamo, worker 7 hustler 8 activist, go-getter, live wire 9 performer 10 ball of fire

doff: 5 douse 6 remove 7 discard 8 put aside

dog: cur, mut, pug, pup 4 mutt, tyke 5 bitch, canis (L.), frank, lemon, pooch, puppy, trail, whelp 6 bowwow, canine, detent, rascal, shadow, wiener 7 mongrel 9 carnivore
African: 7 basenji
Australian: 5 dingo
breed: pug 4 Dane, puli 5 boxer, hound, Husky, spitz 6 Afghan, basset, beagle, borzoi, Briard, collie, Eskimo, poodle, Saluki, setter 7 Basenji, bulldog, griffon, harrier, Maltese, mastiff, pointer, Samoyed, Scottie, Shar-Pei, Shih Tzu, spaniel, terrier, whippet 8 Airedale, Alsatian, chow chow, coach dog, Doberman, elkhound, foxhound, keeshond, Labrador, Malamute, Malemute, Malinois, papillon, Pekinese, Pyrenees, Samoyede, Sealyham, shepherd, springer 9 Chihuahua, coonhound, dachshund, Dalmatian, deerhound, Great Dane, greyhound, kerry blue, Lhasa apso, schnauzer, St. Bernard, wolfhound, Yorkshire 10 Bedlington, bloodhound, Boston bull, Chesapeake, Manchester, otter hound, Pomeranian, Rottweiler, schipperke, weimaraner 11 bull terrier, Groenendael, ruby spaniel, Skye terrier 12 cairn terrier, Gordon setter, Newfoundland, water spaniel, Welsh terrier 13 Boston terrier, cocker spaniel, Great Pyrenees, Prince Charles 15 Brussels griffon, highland terrier, Riesenschnauzer 17 Bouvier de Flandres
close-haired: pug 5 boxer
Dorothy's: 4 Toto
Eskimo: 5 husky 7 Samoyed 8 Malamute, Malemute, Samoyede
famous: 4 Asta, Fala, King, Nana, Tige, Toby 5 Balto, Benji, Devil 6 Feller, Lassie 8 Checkers 9 Beethoven, Old Yeller, Rin-Tin-Tin 11 Strongheart
FDR's: 4 Fala
female: 5 bitch
fox-like: 6 colpeo

genus: **5** canis
German origin: **5** boxer **8** Doberman **9** Drahthaar **10** Weimaraner
group of puppies: **6** litter
hauling: **5** husky **7** Samoyed **8** Malamute, Malemute, Samoyede **9** Dalmatian
house: **6** kennel
howling of: **9** ululation
hunting: **5** hound, toler **6** basset, beagle, borzoi, saluki, setter, talbot **7** courser, harrier, pointer **8** elkhound **9** retriever, wolfhound **10** bloodhound
iron: **7** firedog
large: **4** Dane **5** boxer **6** briard, collie, police **7** mastiff **9** wolfhound **12** Newfoundland
long-haired: **4** alco, chow **7** spaniel
lover of: **11** cynophilist
Orphan Annie's: **5** Sandy
register: **8** studbook
small: Pom, pug, pup **4** alco, Peke **8** Pekinese **9** Chihuahua, Pekingese **10** Pomeranian
space traveler: **5** Leika
Ulysses's: **5** Argos, Argus
underworld: **8** Cerberus
upper lip: **5** flews
Welsh: **5** corgi **8** Sealyham
wild: **5** adjag, dhole, dingo **6** jackal **7** agouara **8** cimarron
dog days: **8** canicule
dogfight: **5** brawl, melee, scrap **9** air battle **10** free-for-all
dogfish: **5** shark **6** bowfin
dogged: **8** stubborn **9** obstinate, tenacious **10** determined, persistent, purposeful **11** persevering
doggerel: **4** poem **5** rhyme **6** jingle **10** light verse
doggish: **5** showy, sulky **7** stylish **8** snappish, snarling
doggone: **4** damn, darn, drat **5** blast **6** shucks **9** son of a gun
dogie: **9** stray calf
dogma: **5** canon, credo, creed, tenet **6** belief, dictum **8** doctrine **10** conviction, philosophy
dogmatic: **6** biased **7** a priori **9** arbitrary, assertive, doctrinal **10** intolerant, peremptory, pontifical, prejudiced **11** dictatorial, opinionated
do-gooder: **8** altruist, idealist **9** soul saver **10** fixer-upper **13** bleeding heart
Dogpatch depicter: **4** Capp (Al)
dog rose: **9** eglantine
fruit: hip
dogs: **4** feet
dog star: **6** Sirius
constellation: **10** Canis Major
dogwood: **5** osier, sumac **6** cornel

flowering: **7** boxwood
genus: **6** cornus
doily: mat **6** napkin
kin: **7** coaster **12** antimacassar
doings: **5** deeds **6** events **7** actions **9** functions **10** activities
doldrums: **5** blues, dumps, ennui **6** apathy, tedium **7** boredom **10** depression, low spirits, ocean calms
dole: **4** alms **5** allot **6** relief **7** charity, deal out, handout, mete out, welfare **8** dispense **9** apportion **10** distribute
doleful: sad **5** drear, heavy **6** dismal, dreary, rueful **7** flebile **8** downcast, mournful **9** plaintive, sorrowful **10** lugubrious, melancholy **12** disconsolate
dolent: **9** sorrowful
doll: toy **4** babe, baby **5** array, puppe (G.) **6** maumet, moppet, muneca (Sp.), poupee (F.), puppet **8** mistress **9** golliwogg **10** sweetheart
up: **5** adorn, dress **11** put on the dog
dollar: one **4** buck **8** frogskin, simoleon
dollop: bit, tot **4** blob, dash, lump **5** snort **6** jigger, splash **10** tiny amount
Doll's House heroine: **4** Nora
dolly: car **4** cart **5** truck **7** carrier
dolor: **5** grief **6** sorrow **7** anguish, sadness **8** distress, mourning **11** lamentation
dolorous: sad **6** dismal **7** doleful **8** grievous **9** sorrowful
dolphin: **4** fish **6** dorado **7** bollard **8** moor spar, porpoise **10** bottlenose
famous: **7** Flipper
river: **5** bouto
dolt: ass, oaf **4** clod, fool **5** chump, dummy, dunce, idiot **7** bluntie (Sc.), dullard, halfwit **8** imbecile, numskull **9** blockhead, ignoramus, simpleton **10** dunderhead
doltish: **4** dull **5** dense, thick **6** stupid **7** foolish **8** blockish **11** thickheaded
domain: **4** area **5** realm, world **6** empire, estate, sphere **7** demesne **8** dominion, province **9** bailiwick, territory
Dombey and Son author: **7** Dickens
character: **4** Paul **5** Edith, Toots **6** Carker, Cuttle, Nipper **7** Blimber **8** Bagstock **9** Walter Gay
dome: cap **4** cima **6** cupola **7** calotte, edifice
domed: **7** vaulted
domestic: **4** cook, maid **6** native **7** servant **8** homebred, homemade **9** home-grown **11** housewifely
establishment: **6** menage
domesticate: **4** tame **5** train **6** master **7** reclaim **8** civilize **10** housebreak
domicile: **4** home **5** abode, house **6** menage **8** dwelling **9** residence **10** habitation
identification: **9** doorplate

dominant: 5 bossy, chief 6 ruling 7 central, regnant, supreme 8 superior 9 ascendant, imperious, paramount, prevalent, principal 10 commanding, preeminent, prevailing 11 outweighing 12 preponderant 13 overbalancing

dominate: 4 rule 5 reign 6 govern 7 control 8 stand out 9 tower over

domination: 4 sway 5 power 7 command, control, mastery 9 supremacy 11 sovereignty

domineer: cow 4 boss, rule 5 bully 7 command, oppress 8 bulldoze, ride over, walk over 12 crack the whip

domineering: 5 bossy 6 lordly 7 haughty 8 arrogant 9 imperious, masterful 10 tyrannical 11 dictatorial, magisterial, overbearing

Dominican: 4 monk 9 Predicant

Dominican Republic: *agricultural area:* 5 Cibao
bay: 4 Ocoa, Yuma 5 Neiba 6 Samana 7 Isabela, Riuncon 8 Escocesa
cape: 5 Beata, Falso, Viejo 6 Engano
capital: 12 Santo Domingo
city: 4 Bani, Moca 5 Neiba 8 Barahona, La Romana, Santiago
dance: 8 merengue
Indian: 5 Carib 6 Arawak
island: 5 Beata, Saona 8 Catalina 10 Hispaniola
lake: 10 Enriquillo
mountain: 4 Tina 5 Gallo 10 cordillera, Pico Duarte
peninsula: 6 Samana
plain: 8 Vega Real
river: 4 Yuna 5 Yaque

---

dominie: 6 pastor 9 clergyman, pedagogue 12 schoolmaster

dominion: 4 rule, sway 5 realm, reign 6 domain, empire 7 control, dynasty, regency 9 authority, hierarchy, ownership, supremacy 10 ascendancy 11 sovereignty 12 jurisdiction
church: 11 sacerdotium
joint: 11 condominium

domino: die 4 mask

dominoes: 4 game 5 bones 7 ivories

domus: 4 home 5 house

don: 4 wear 5 array, dress, put on 6 assume, clothe, invest 7 get into 8 nobleman 9 gentleman, professor 10 instructor

Donar: 4 Thor

donate: gie (Sc.) 4 give 6 bestow 7 hand out, present, provide 10 contribute

donation: 4 gift 5 grant 7 bequest, present 8 offering 11 benefaction 12 contribution

Don Carlos: *author:* 8 Schiller
opera composer: 5 Verdi

done: 4 over 5 baked, ended 6 cooked 7 through 8 finished 9 completed, exhausted 12 accomplished

done for: 4 dead 5 goner, kaput 6 licked, ruined 7 wrecked 8 bankrupt 10 on the ropes

done in: 4 beat 5 spent 6 pooped, used up 7 worn out 8 frazzled 9 played out

donee: 7 heritor 8 receiver 9 recipient 11 beneficiary

Don Giovanni composer: 6 Mozart

Don Juan: 4 rake 6 masher 7 seducer 9 libertine 10 lady-killer, profligate

donkey: ass 4 fool 5 burro, jenny, neddy 6 onager 8 imbecile, numskull
cry: 4 bray 6 heehaw

donkey engine: 6 yarder 10 locomotive 11 cargo lifter

donna: 4 lady, wife 5 madam, woman 8 mistress

donor: 5 giver 10 benefactor 11 contributor 14 philanthropist

Don Quixote: *author:* 9 Cervantes
beloved: 8 Dulcinea
companion: 11 Sancho Panza
steed: 9 Rosinante, Rozinante

doodle: 4 dolt, draw 5 cheat 6 putter 7 cartoon, trifler 8 scribble 10 nincompoop

doodlesack: 7 bagpipe

doohickey: 6 doodad, gadget 11 thingamabob

dooly, doolie: 6 litter 9 palanquin

doom: law, lot 4 damn, fate, ruin 5 death 6 decree, kismet 7 condemn, destine, destiny, fortune, statute 8 calamity, decision, judgment, sentence 9 ordinance, preordain 10 adjudicate, predestine

doomed: fey 5 fatal 8 accursed 9 sentenced

door: 4 exit, gate 5 entry, hatch 6 portal 7 barrier, opening, passage 11 entranceway
back: 7 postern
crosspiece: 6 lintel
fastener: bar 4 bolt, hasp, lock 5 catch, latch
holder: 5 hinge
holy: 11 amphithyron
part: 4 jamb, knob, sill 5 panel 6 alette
storm: 6 dingle
trap: 4 drop

doorkeeper: 5 guard 6 porter, warden 7 ostiary 9 concierge (F.)

doormat: rug 8 weakling 10 pantywaist

dope: hop 4 drug 5 crack, dunce, opium, paste 6 heroin, opiate 7 cocaine, hashish, predict, stupefy 8 narcotic 9 marijuana
out: 5 crack, solve 6 decode, fathom 7 clear up 10 unscramble 12 get the answer

doped: 4 high 6 stoned 7 drugged 8 hopped-up 9 spaced out

dopester: 4 tout 7 tipster 10 forecaster

dopey, dopy: 4 dull 5 dazed, woozy 6 groggy, torpid 8 sluggish 9 lethargic 10 punch drunk

doppelganger: 6 double, spirit, wraith 10 apparition 11 counterpart

dor: bee 6 beetle 11 drumbledore

dorcas: 7 gazelle

do-re-mi: 4 song 5 money

dorian: 6 simple

Dorian festival: 6 Carnea 7 Carneia

doric: 6 rustic

Doric: *frieze bottom:* 6 taenia
　　frieze slab: 6 metope

Doris' king: 8 Aegimius

dormancy: 6 torpor 8 abeyance 10 quiescence

dormant: 5 fixed, quiet 6 asleep, latent, torpid 7 resting 8 inactive, sleeping 9 unaroused 10 stationary

dormer: 6 window 7 lucarne

dormitory: 12 sleeping room 13 residence hall
　　monastery: 6 dorter 7 dortour

dormouse: 4 loir 5 lerot
　　pert. to: 7 myoxine

dornick: 5 linen 6 damask

dorsal: 5 notal 6 aboral, tergal 7 abaxial 9 posterior
　　opposed to: 7 ventral

dorsum: 4 back

dose: 4 bole 5 draft, treat 6 doctor, drench, potion 7 draught 8 medicate, quantity

doss: 7 bed down 12 lodging house

dot: 4 clot, lump, mote, peck 5 dowry, point, speck 6 period 7 speckle, stipple 8 particle, sprinkle 9 bespangle 10 besprinkle, distribute
　　over the letter i: 6 tittle

dotage: 6 old age 7 anility 8 senility 10 feebleness 11 senectitude

dote on: 5 adore, fancy, spoil 6 pamper, revere 7 idolize, worship

doting: 4 fond 6 loving 7 devoted, doddery, fatuous 8 overfond 13 overindulgent

dotterel: 6 plover 7 lapwing 9 turnstone

dotty: 5 crazy, wacky 6 spotty 8 obsessed 9 eccentric 12 feebleminded

Douay Bible: 4 Aree

double: ply 4 dual, fold, twin 5 duple, fetch, twice 6 binary, binate, clench, duplex 7 twofold 8 geminate 9 ambiguous, duplicate, look-alike 11 counterpart

double-cross: 5 cheat 6 betray 7 deceive, sell out, swindle 9 treachery

doubled: 5 gemel 6 paired 7 twinned

double dagger: 6 diesis

double dealing: 6 deceit 8 trickery 9 duplicity

double-edged: 9 ancipital

doublespeak: 9 ambiguity, vague talk 12 equivocation 13 foggy language

double-talk: 5 hokum 7 twaddle 8 nonsense 9 gibberish 12 gobbledygook

doubt: 4 fear 5 demur, dread, qualm, query, waver 7 scruple, suspect 8 distrust, hesitate, mistrust, question 9 discredit, misgiving, suspicion 10 diffidence, disbelieve, indecision 11 uncertainty 12 apprehension

doubter: 5 cynic 6 Thomas 7 skeptic 10 unbeliever

doubtful: 4 iffy 6 unsure 7 dubious, fearful 8 wavering 9 ambiguous, diffident, equivocal, uncertain, undecided 10 apocryphal, hesitating, irresolute, suspicious 11 distrustful, vacillating 12 apprehensive, questionable, undetermined 13 problematical

douceur: sop, tip 4 gift 5 bonus 7 present 8 gratuity 9 pourboire

dough: 4 cash, loot 5 money, moola, paste 7 cabbage 10 green stuff

doughnut: 6 sinker 7 cruller
　　relative: 7 fritter 9 friedcake

doughty: 4 fell 5 brave 7 valiant 8 intrepid

doughy: 4 ashy, soft 5 pasty 6 flabby, pallid 7 viscous

dour: 4 glum, grim, hard, sour 5 rough, stern 6 gloomy, morose, severe, strong, sullen 7 ominous 9 obstinate 10 inflexible

douse, dowse: 4 doff, duck, dunk, stow 5 rinse, slosh 6 drench, plunge, put out, strike 7 immerse 8 downpour 9 drenching 10 extinguish

douzepers: 4 Ivon 5 Gerin, Ivory, Ogier, Otton, peers 6 Anseis, Gerier, nobles, Oliver, Roland, Samson, Turpin 7 knights 8 Engelier, paladins 9 Berengier 17 Gerard de Rousillon

dove: 5 color 6 culver, pigeon 7 namaqua 8 pacifist 11 conciliator
　　home: 4 cote 9 columbary
　　pert. to: 9 columbine
　　political opposite: 4 hawk
　　sound: coo 4 curr

dovekey, dovekie: auk 9 guillemot

dovelike: 4 pure 6 gentle 7 lovable 9 columbine

dovetail: fit 4 jibe, mesh 5 agree, tally, tenon 6 go with 8 check out 10 correspond

dovish: 7 antiwar 9 peaceable 10 nonviolent

dowager: 6 matron 9 matriarch 10 grande dame

dowdy: 4 drab 5 seedy, tacky 6 blowzy, shabby, untidy 8 slovenly 9 unstylish 10 slatternly
　　woman: 5 frump

dowel: peg, pin **4** coak **6** pintle

dower: dot **5** dowry, endow **6** talent **9** endowment **13** bride's portion

dowitcher: **5** snipe

down: **4** dowl, fell, flix, flue, fuzz, hill, lint **5** below, dowle, floor, fluff **7** hillock, plumage **9** overthrow
at the heel: **5** seamy, seedy
in the mouth: **4** glum **7** unhappy **8** dejected **9** depressed **11** discouraged
under: **8** Tasmania **9** antipodes, Australia **10** New Zealand
with: **4** a bas

downbeat: **4** grim **5** bleak **6** dismal, gloomy **8** negative **11** pessimistic

downcast: sad **6** abject, gloomy, morose **7** forlorn **8** hopeless **10** despondent, dispirited, melancholy **11** discouraged **12** disheartened

downer: **6** bummer **7** bad trip **10** depressant **11** barbiturate

downfall: pit **4** fate, ruin, trap **5** abyss **7** descent, undoing **8** collapse **9** precipice, ruination **11** destruction, ecroulement

downgrade: dip **4** bust, drop **5** lower **6** debase, demote, lessen, reduce **7** decline, descent, devalue **9** declivity

downpour: **4** rain **6** deluge **7** torrent **10** cloudburst

downright: **4** flat, pure, rank **5** blank, blunt, plain, plumb, sheer, stark **6** arrant, direct **8** absolute, complete, positive, thorough **9** out-and-out **10** forthright **11** unmitigated

downstairs: **5** below

downtrend: dip, sag **4** drop, fall, slip **5** slide, slump **7** decline

downwind: **7** leeward

downy: **4** soft **5** mossy, nappy, pilar, quiet **6** fluffy, placid **7** cunning, knowing **8** soothing

dowry: See **dower**

dowse: See **douse**

doxy: ism **5** wench **6** harlot **7** opinion **8** doctrine

doyen: **4** dean **6** expert **8** virtuoso **9** authority **10** past master

doze: nap, nod **5** decay, sleep **6** catnap, drowse, snooze **7** slumber, snoozle

drab: **4** bawd, dull **5** dingy, mousy, wench, whore **6** dreary **7** prosaic **8** lifeless **9** colorless **10** monotonous, prostitute **13** uninteresting

drachma: **4** coin, dram
one-sixth: **4** obol

draconian: **5** cruel **6** severe, strict

Dracula author: **10** Bram Stoker

draff: **4** lees **5** dregs, drink **6** refuse **7** hogwash

draft: nip, sip **4** dose, dram, gust, levy, plan, swig, toot **5** drink, epure, swipe **6** call up, devise, drench, potion, redact, scroll, sketch **7** draught, drawing, outline, pattern, project **8** beverage **9** conscript **10** air current
evader: **6** dodger

draftsman, draughtsman: **6** drawer **7** tippler **9** architect

drag: lug, tow, tug **4** bore, draw, haul, pull, swig, tear, tump **5** brake, delay, drawl, trail, trawl **6** anchor, burden, linger, taigle (Sc.) **7** grapnel **9** lag behind **10** wet blanket
out: **6** elicit, extend **7** prolong **8** protract

dragnet: **5** trawl **7** grapnel

dragoman: **5** agent, guide **11** interpreter

dragon: **7** monster **8** basilisk
biblical: **5** Rahab
biting: **8** tarragon
Chinese: **4** lung
French: **8** Tarasque
killer: **6** Cadmus, Sigurd **7** Beowulf, Perseus **8** St. George, St. Martha
Norse: **6** Fafner, Fafnir
Vedic: Ahi

dragonfly order: **7** odonata

dragoon: **6** coerce **9** force into **10** cavalryman

drain: dry, gaw, sap **4** fade, milk, pump, sink, tire, tube **5** canal, empty, gully, sewer, spout **6** burden, furrow, guzzle, outlet, siphon, trench **7** acequia, channel, deplete, draw off, exhaust **9** drink down, undermine **11** watercourse
arched: **7** culvert

drainage: **11** waste system
area: **5** basin

drained: **5** all in, spent **6** used up **7** worn out **8** depleted

drainpipe: **6** leader

dram: nip **4** mite, slug **5** draft, drink **6** drachm **7** snifter **8** potation, quantity

drama: **4** play **5** farce, opera **6** comedy, heroic, masque **7** theater, tragedy **8** conflict, pastoral, the stage **9** melodrama **10** intermezzo **11** composition, Elizabethan, tragicomedy **16** commedia dell arte
Chinese: **11** Peking opera **12** Beijing opera
court: **5** trial
father of: **7** Thespis
Japanese: No, Noh **6** kabuki
main act: **8** epitasis
muse: **6** Thalia **9** Melpomene
Spanish: **15** auto sacramental
television: **9** soap opera
unspoken: **9** pantomime

dramatic: **4** wild **5** vivid **6** scenic **10** theatrical **12** melodramatic
expression system: **8** delsarte

dramatist: **5** actor **7** actress **10** playwright

drape: **4** hang **5** adorn, cover **6** sprawl, swathe

7 curtain, hanging, valance **8** spraddle **10** wrap around **11** fall in folds

drapeau: **4** flag **8** standard

draper: **6** tailor

drastic: **4** dire **5** harsh **6** severe **7** extreme, radical **8** rigorous

draught: See **draft**

Dravidian (see also **India**): *language:* **4** Gond, Kota, Toda, Tulu **5** Arava, Gondi, Khond, Malto, Oraon, Tamil **6** Andhra, Brahui, Kodagu, Kurukh, Telegu, Telugu **7** Kannada **8** Kanarese **9** Malayalam
demon: **4** bhut
tribe: **6** Badaga **7** Collery

draw: lug, tie, tow, tug **4** drag, duct, hale, haul, lade, limn, lure, pull **5** catch, educe, train **6** allure, deduce, depict, derive, design, elicit, entice, induce, inhale, select, sketch **7** attract, detract, extract, inspire, portray **8** inveigle, standoff **9** allowance, delineate, reproduce, statement
again: **5** remap **6** replat
back: **5** wince **6** cringe, recede, recoil, resile, retire, shrink **7** retract, retreat
close: **4** near **8** approach, come nigh
finely: **4** etch
forth: **5** educe, evoke **6** elicit **7** pull out
off: sap **5** drain **6** siphon **7** extract **8** abstract
out: **4** pump **5** educe **6** elicit, extend **7** extract, prolong **8** lengthen, protract **11** interrogate **12** cross-examine
tight: **4** frap, furl, lace **5** brace, cinch
up: **4** halt, stop **5** frame **7** prepare **9** formulate

drawback: **6** defect **8** handicap **9** detriment, hindrance **12** disadvantage

drawer: **4** till

drawers: **5** pants **6** shorts **7** panties **9** long johns, underwear
chest of: **6** bureau **7** commode, dresser **9** semainier **10** chiffonier

draw game: **9** stalemate

drawing: **4** plan, plat **5** draft, epure **7** hauling, picture, pulling **10** attracting, extracting **11** centripetal, delineation
absent-minded: **8** doodling
by number: **7** lottery
exaggerated: **7** cartoon **10** caricature
instrument: **9** eidograph **10** pantograph
watercolor: **4** wash

drawing room: **4** sala (Sp.) **5** salon **6** parlor, saloon

drawl: **5** drant **6** loiter

drawn: wan **4** worn **6** peaked **7** haggard

drawstring: tie **4** cord **5** latch

dray: **4** cart **5** wagon **6** camion

drayage: **7** cartage, haulage

drayman: **6** carter **7** carrier, wagoner

dread: awe **4** fear **5** alarm **6** dismay, horror, terror **7** anguish, anxiety **8** affright **12** apprehension

dreadful: **4** dire **5** awful **6** grisly, horrid **7** direful, fearful, ghastly, grimful, hideous **8** doubtful, horrible, shocking, terrible **9** frightful **10** formidable

dreadnaught, dreadnought: **4** tank **7** warship **8** fearless **10** battleship

dream: **4** hope, muse, reve (F.) **5** fancy **6** vision **7** chimera, fantasy, imagine, reverie, romance **8** illusion, phantasm **9** nightmare **10** apparition, aspiration
god of: **8** Morpheus
pert. to: **7** oneiric, somnial **9** oneirotic

dreamer: **4** poet **6** mystic **7** fantast **8** idealist **9** visionary **10** ideologist

dreaminess: **7** languor **8** euphoria

dreamy: kef **4** soft **5** great, super, vague **6** divine, groovy **7** faraway, pensive **8** fanciful, soothing **9** beautiful, marvelous **11** imaginative

dreary: sad **4** dire, dull, flat **5** bleak, cruel, ourie (Sc.) **6** boring, deadly, dismal, gloomy, lonely, somber **7** doleful **8** grievous **9** cheerless, sorrowful **10** depressing, monotonous, oppressive, pedestrian **11** distressful

dredge: dig, mop **4** coat, sift **5** scoop **6** deepen **8** excavate **9** search for

dredger: **6** duster **9** sprinkler

dregs: **4** lees, scum **5** draff, dross **6** bottom, dunder, rabble, refuse **7** deposit, grounds, residue **8** remnants, riffraff, sediment, settling **10** subsidence **12** crassamentum

drench: **4** dose, hose, sink, soak **5** douse, draft, drink, drown, souse, steep **6** imbrue **7** immerse **8** permeate, saturate, submerge

drenched: wet **4** asop **6** soaked **7** sopping

dress: don, dub, fig, ray, rig, tog **4** duds, garb, gear, gown, hone, knap, mill, rail, robe, suit, tire, trim, wear **5** adorn, array, curry, equip, fix up, frock, groom, guise, habit, prink, prune, treat **6** attire, clothe, enrobe, invest, outfit, revest, toilet **7** apparel, bandage, clothes, costume, deck out, garment, garnish, raiment, toggery, vesture **8** clothing, decorate, ornament, vestment **9** embellish, equipment, vestiture **10** habiliment **12** accouterment
clerical: **5** cloth
court: **4** robe
feathers: **5** preen
gaudily: **5** primp, prink **7** bedizen
in full armor: **7** panoply
informal: **5** jeans, Levis **6** shorts, slacks **8** negligee **9** blue-jeans
kind of: alb **4** huke **5** crape, crepe, ephod, mufti, tails, tenue, tunic, weeds **6** dirndl,

finery, gaiter, kirtle, livery, tuxedo **7** regalia
8 lava-lava, peignoir **9** canonical, decollete,
polonaise
leather: tan, taw, tew **5** curry
mean: **4** rags
odd: rig **5** getup
ornament: **4** frog, lace **5** jabot, ruche **6**
sequin, zequin **7** ruching **8** chequeen,
zecchino **10** embroidery
riding: **5** habit **8** breeches, jodhpurs
stone: nig **5** nidge, spall **7** scabble
dress down: **5** scold **6** berate **7** bawl out, tell
off **9** castigate **10** tongue-lash
dressed: **4** clad **5** bound **7** habited
well: **4** braw, chic **5** smart **6** modish **7**
soignee, stylish **9** spruced-up
dresser: **5** chest, rober **6** bureau **7** commode,
modiste **8** cupboard **9** semainier **10** chiffonier
leather: **6** tanner **7** currier **8** levanter
scrupulous: fop **4** dude **5** dandy **8** macaroni
12 Beau Brummell
dressing: **5** sauce **7** bandage **8** stuffing
dressing stone: **9** scotching
dressmaker: **5** sewer **7** modiste **8** stitcher **9**
couturier **10** couturiere, seamstress
form: **7** manikin **8** mannikin **9** mannequin
dribble: **4** drip, drop **5** drool **6** bounce **7** slobber, trickle **11** fritter away
driblet: bit **6** trifle **8** pittance, small sum
drift: sag **4** dene, dune, ford, herd, plot, tide,
till **5** drove, fleet, float, flock, tenor, trend **6**
broach, course, design, device, scheme,
tunnel **7** impetus, impulse, pasture, purport **8** tendency **9** deviation **10** propulsion
along: **4** tide **5** float **10** move slowly
sidewise: **4** crab **8** crescent
driftage: **6** jetsam **7** flotsam **8** wreckage
drifter: bum **4** hobo **5** tramp **7** floater, vagrant
8 vagabond, wanderer **12** rolling stone
drill: gad, saw, tap **4** bore, spud **5** auger, borer,
churn, decoy, train, tutor, twirl, whirl **6**
allure, entice, furrow, pierce, school,
seeder, stoper **7** channel **8** exercise,
instruct, practice **9** perforate
drilling: **5** denim
drink (see also **alcoholic drink, beverage**):
bib, lap, sip, tea **4** brew, grog, horn, swig, tiff,
tope **5** booze, draft, punch, quaff, toast **6**
absorb, bracer, chaser, coffee, drench, guzzle, hooker, imbibe, liquid, potion, tipple **7**
draught, potable, swallow **8** beverage, cocktail, highball, libation, potation **10** intoxicant
carbonated: pop **4** cola, fizz, soda **9** ginger
ale
Christmas: nog **6** eggnog **7** wassail
drugged: **6** mickey
farinaceous: **6** ptisan
frozen: **6** frappe

fruit: ade **5** assai, bland, julep, morat **6**
rickey **7** ratafia
honey: **4** mead
hot: **5** cocoa, negus, toddy **6** caudle
magic: **8** nepenthe
molasses and vinegar: **6** swanky
of gods: **6** nectar
Oriental: **4** sake
portion: **4** gill, shot **5** ounce **6** dollop, jigger
Russian: **5** vodka
sassafras: **6** saloop
small: nip, peg, tot **4** dram, pony, shot, slug
5 snort **6** chaser, jigger **7** snifter
Tatar: **6** kumiss
drinker (see also **drunkard**): sot **4** lush **5**
toper **7** imbiber, intaker, quaffer **8** drunkard **9** alcoholic, inebriate
drinking: **8** guzzling, tippling **9** carousing
bout: bum **4** orgy, toot **5** binge, spree **6**
bender
horn: **6** rhyton
salutation: **5** skoal **6** prosit **7** wassail **11** a
votre sante
vessel: cup, mug **4** bowl, tass (Sc.) **5** glass,
gourd, hanap, jorum, stein **6** beaker, cappie
(Sc.), dipper, goblet, noggin, patera **7**
canikin, snifter, tankard **8** cannikin,
schooner
drip: sie **4** bore, drop, jerk, leak, pill **5** creep,
eaves **7** dribble, trickle **10** wet blanket
frozen: **6** icicle
drippy: **5** soupy **6** slushy **7** drizzly, insipid,
maudlin **10** unpleasant **11** sentimental
drive: hit, run **4** bang, bear, butt, goad, herd,
push, ride, send, spur, urge **5** chase, crowd,
force, hurry, impel, press, shove, sweep,
vigor **6** attack, compel, cudgel, hasten,
plunge, propel **7** impulse, operate, overtax
9 constrain
away: **4** shoo **5** chase, repel **6** banish, dispel **7** repulse
down: **4** tamp
frantic: **7** bedevil
out: **4** rout **5** exile, expel **8** exorcise **9** eradicate
public: **9** esplanade
too close: **8** tailgate
drive-in: **7** open-air, theater **10** restaurant
drivel: **4** dote **5** drool **6** dotage, slaver **7** twaddle **8** claptrap, nonsense
driver: **4** jehu **5** drabi (Ind.) **6** cabbie, caller,
hackie, hammer, jarvey, mallet **7** catcher,
spanker **8** coachman, engineer, golf club,
motorist, overseer, teamster **9** chauffeur,
propeller **10** charioteer, taskmaster
of golden chariot: **6** Helios
drizzle: **8** sprinkle **9** misty rain
droll: odd **5** comic, funny, merry, queer **6**
jocose **7** amusing, comical, jocular, strange

8 farcical, humorous 9 diverting, laughable, ludicrous, whimsical 10 ridiculous

drollery: wit 4 jest 5 farce, humor 6 japery 10 buffoonery 11 waggishness

dromedary: 5 camel

dromond: 6 galley 7 warship

drone: bee, bum, hum 4 drum, slug 5 drant, idler, snail 6 bumble, draunt, lubber 7 bagpipe, humming, shirker, sleeper, speaker 8 loiterer, sluggard 9 bombilate

dronish: 4 slow 8 indolent, sluggish

drool: 6 drivel, slaver 7 slobber

droop: sag 4 bend, drop, flag, hang, loll, pine, sink, wilt 5 slump 6 slouch, wither 7 decline 8 languish

drooping: 4 lank, limp, weak 5 baggy, saggy, tired, weary 6 flaggy, floppy 7 languid, nodding, sagging 8 dejected, downcast 10 dispirited
of eyelid: 6 ptosis
on one side: 4 alop

drop: dap 4 bead, blob, drib, drip, fall, omit, shed, sink, stop 5 droop, lower, plump, plunk, slump 6 plunge 7 abandon, curtain, descent, dismiss, dribble, forsake, globule, plummet, release 8 decrease, quantity 10 relinquish 11 discontinue
in: 5 enter, visit 6 arrive, call on, stop by 8 surprise
lachrymal: 4 tear
off: nap 4 doze 5 sleep 8 decrease
syllable: 5 elide 7 elision

droplet: 7 globule

dropout: 6 misfit 8 maverick

dropped: 6 fallen 7 left off, lowered 8 released, went down 11 had done with

dropper: 7 pipette

dropsy: 5 edema

dross: 4 lees, scum, slag 5 chaff, dregs, sprue, waste 6 garble, refuse, scoria, sinter 7 cinders 8 leavings 9 recrement
iron: 6 sinter

drought, drouth: 6 thirst 7 aridity, dryness

drought plant: 9 xerophyte

drove (see also **drive**): mob 4 herd 5 atajo (Sp.), crowd, flock, horde 6 chisel, pushed, throng 7 steered 10 assemblage

drown: 5 flood 6 drench 8 get rid of, inundate 9 overwhelm

drowse: nod 4 doze 5 sleep 6 catnap, snooze 7 slumber

drowsiness: 8 dullness, lethargy 9 oscitancy 10 sleepiness 12 sluggishness

drowsy: 4 dull, logy 5 noddy 6 sleepy, stupid, supine 7 lulling 8 comatose, indolent, oscitant, sluggish 9 somnolent, soporific 11 heavy-headed

drub: tap 4 bang, beat, drum, lick, trim, whip 5 pound, stamp 6 berate, cudgel, pummel,

thrash 7 belabor, shellac 8 lambaste

drubbing: 4 rout 7 debacle 9 thrashing, trouncing, walloping

drudge: 4 grub, moil, plod, toil 5 grind, scrub, slave 6 digger, endure, slavey, suffer 7 plodder 9 workhorse
literary: 4 hack

drudgery: 4 moil, toil, work 5 labor

drug: LSD, pot 4 dope, dull, numb 5 crack, hocus, opium, upper 6 downer, heroin, opiate 7 cocaine, hashish, stupefy 8 medicine, narcotic, sedative 9 analgesic, marijuana 10 pain killer, put to sleep 11 barbiturate
addict: 6 junkie 7 sniffer 8 snowbird 9 acid freak, crackhead, mainliner
and ship: 8 shanghai
container: bag 4 deck 6 packet 7 capsule
depressant: 6 downer, heroin 7 codeine 8 atropine, morphine
emetic: 5 senna 6 ipecac
hallucinogenic: LSD 4 hemp 6 mescal, peyote 7 cocaine 9 marijuana
of forgetfulness: 5 lotus, opium 7 hashish 8 nepenthe
stimulant: 5 upper 7 cocaine, pep pill, zedoary 9 digitalis 11 amphetamine

drugged: 4 high 5 hyped 6 stoned, wasted, zonked 7 freaked, on a trip 8 turned on 9 spaced out 10 insensible

drugget: 10 mat, rug

druggist: 10 apothecary, pharmacist
bible: USP

drugstore: 8 pharmacy

druid: 6 priest
priestess of opera: 5 Norma
stone: 6 sarsen
symbol: 9 mistletoe

drum: 4 cask, drub 5 bongo, drone, gumbe, gumby, tabor 6 barrel, tambor, tom-tom, tympan 7 capstan, tambour, timbrel 8 bamboula, cylinder 9 reiterate, tambourin 10 tambourine
kettle: 5 naker 6 atabal, nagara, timbal 7 timpani (pl.), tympani (pl.) 9 darabukka 10 tambourone
string: 5 snare
tighten cords: 4 frap

drumbeat: 6 ruffle 8 berloque
at hour for sleep: 6 tattoo

drumbeater: 8 advocate, promoter 9 supporter 10 press agent, tub-thumper

drumfire: 5 salvo 6 volley 7 barrage 9 fusillade 11 bombardment

drummer: 8 salesman 13 percussionist

drumstick: 6 tampon

drunkard: sot 4 soak 5 dipso, rummy, souse, toper 6 boozer 7 fuddler, tippler, tosspot 8 borracho 9 alcoholic, inebriate 11 dipsomaniac

drunken: **4** gone **5** tight, tipsy **6** blotto, loaded **7** pickled, pie-eyed, sottish **8** squiffed **10** inebriated **11** intoxicated

drupelet: **5** acini (pl.) **6** acinus, kernel

dry: sec, ted **4** arid, brut, dull, sere, wipe **5** baked, drain, prosy, vapid, wizen **6** barren, boring, jejune **7** insipid, parched, sapless, sterile, sub-arid, thirsty, xerotic **8** tiresome **9** dehydrate, drinkless, exsuccous, fruitless, pointless, sarcastic, waterless **10** evaporated, siccaneous, teetotaler **11** displeasing **12** moistureless, unprofitable **13** uninteresting

goods: **4** wear **6** linens, napery **7** fabrics **8** clothing, textiles

grass: hay

leather: sam

out: **5** steam, toast **6** rizzar (Sc.) **7** sober up **8** detoxify

run: try **8** maneuver **9** rehearsal

shave: **5** cheat **7** defraud

spell: **7** drought

up: **6** shrink, wither **7** shrivel **9** dehydrate, desiccate, evaporate, exsiccate, keep quiet **10** dehumidify

dryad: **5** nymph **6** yaksha, yakshi

dual: **4** twin **6** binary, double **7** twofold

dub: **4** rub **4** call, flub, muff, name, poke **5** botch, fluff **6** duffer, goof up, thrust **7** entitle **8** add sound, beginner, nickname, rerecord **9** schlemiel

dubious: **8** doubtful **9** ambiguous, equivocal, uncertain, unsettled **10** disputable, precarious **12** questionable, undetermined

ducal: **5** noble

ducat: **4** coin **6** sequin, ticket

duck: bob, bow, pet **4** dive, dunk, fowl, jouk **5** avoid, dodge, douse, evade, shirk, souse **6** plunge **7** darling, odd chap **8** sidestep **11** shy away from

Asiatic: **8** mandarin

black: **9** blackjack

bluebill: **5** scaup

brood: **4** team

dead: **5** goner

diving: **4** smew **9** goldeneye **10** bufflehead, butterball

eating: **5** Pekin **6** Peking

eggs in brine: **5** pidan

eider: **4** colk, wamp

freshwater: **4** teal

freshwater genus: aix

genus: **4** anas **7** nettion

group: **4** sord, team **5** skein

heraldic: **6** canne **8** cannette

hooked-bill: **9** merganser

hunter's screen: **5** blind

male: **5** drake

Muscovy: **4** pato

old squaw: **6** quandy

Old World: **7** pochard **9** sheldrake

out: **4** flee **6** escape **9** disappear **10** go suddenly **11** take a powder

pert. to: **7** anatine

pintail: **4** smee, smew **8** piketail **11** querquedule

rare: **5** merse

ring-necked: **5** bunty

river: **4** smee, teal **7** pintail, widgeon **8** piketail, shoveler **9** greenwing

ruddy: **6** bobber **9** blackjack

sea: **4** coot **5** eider, scaup **6** scoter **7** scooter **9** harlequin

soup: **4** snap **5** cinch **6** breeze **8** pushover **9** easy as pie **10** child's play

tree: **7** yaguaza

wild: **4** teal **5** scaup **7** gadwall, mallard **10** canvasback

wooden: **5** decoy

yellow-billed: **7** geelbec **8** geelbeck

duckbill: **8** platypus **10** mallangong

duckweed: **5** lemna

duct: **vas 4** main, pipe, tube, vasa (pl.) **5** canal **7** channel, conduit, passage, trachea **8** aqueduct

ductile: **4** soft **6** docile, facile, pliant **7** plastic, pliable, tensile **8** flexible, tractile **9** compliant, malleable, tractable **10** manageable, sequacious

ductless gland: **6** pineal, thymus

dud: **4** bomb, bust, flop **5** lemon **6** fizzle, turkey **7** failure, washout

dude: fop **5** dandy, swell **7** coxcomb, peacock **8** macaroni **12** Beau Brummell, clotheshorse, fashion plate

rancher: **9** Easterner **10** tenderfoot

dudeen: **8** clay pipe

dudgeon: ire **4** fury, huff, rage **5** anger, pique, wrath **7** umbrage **8** ill humor **10** resentment

duds: **4** togs **6** attire **7** apparel, clothes **8** garments **10** belongings

due: **4** debt, just, meed, meet, owed **5** merit, owing **6** extent, lawful, mature, proper, unpaid **7** deserts, exactly, fitting, payable **8** adequate, deserved, directly, rightful, suitable **9** scheduled **10** sufficient **11** appropriate **12** attributable

duel: **4** tilt **5** fence, fight **6** combat **7** contest, dispute **8** conflict **13** affair of honor

duelist: **9** combatant, principal

aide: **6** second

duende: **5** charm **6** allure **9** magnetism

duenna: **8** chaperon **9** governess

dues: **4** fees **5** taxes, tolls **7** charges **8** payments **11** assessments

duet: duo **4** pair **11** piece for two

ballet: **6** adagio

lower part: **7** secondo
upper part: **5** primo

duff: **5** humus, slack **7** pudding **8** coal dust

duffer: dub **4** dope **5** dunce **6** geezer **10** stumblebum **11** incompetent

dugong: **6** sea cow **7** manatee

dugout: **4** abri, boat, cave **5** banca, banka, canoe **6** cayuca, cayuco **7** foxhole, pirogue, shelter **10** excavation

dulcet: **5** sweet **8** pleasing, soothing **9** agreeable, melodious, organ stop **10** harmonious

dulcimer: **7** cembalo **9** pantaleon **10** instrument
Chinese: **7** yang-kin
gypsy: **8** cimbalom
Persian: **6** santir

dull: dim, dry, dun, sad **4** blah, dead, drab, dumb, flat, gray, logy, mopy, numb, poky, slow, tame **5** blear, blind, blunt, dingy, foggy, heavy, inert, mopey, murky, muted, prosy, stale, vapid **6** boring, cloudy, dampen, darken, deaden, dismal, dreary, drowsy, gloomy, leaden, lessen, muffle, obtund, obtuse, somber, stodgy, stolid, stuffy, stupid, torpid, weaken **7** doltish, humdrum, insipid, prosaic, tedious, vacuous **8** boeotian, lifeless, listless, overcast, sluggish, tiresome **9** apathetic, colorless, inanimate, lethargic, pointless **10** indistinct, insensible, lackluster, monotonous, pedestrian, slow-witted, uninspired **11** thick-headed **13** unimaginative
become: **4** fade, pall, rust **7** cloud up, tarnish **8** hebetate
finish: mat **5** matte
noise: **4** klop, thud

dullard: **4** clod, dolt, dope **5** dunce, idiot, moron **6** dimwit **8** dumbbell **9** lamebrain, simpleton

dullness: **6** apathy, torpor **7** languor **8** hebetude, lethargy, monotony **9** bluntness **10** mediocrity

dulse: **5** algae **7** seaweed

duly: **7** rightly **8** properly **9** fittingly, regularly **13** appropriately

Dumas fils: *character:* **7** Camille

Dumas père: *character:* **5** Athos **6** Aramis, Dantes **7** Porthos **9** D'Artagnan, musketeer

dumb: mum **4** dull, mute **6** silent, stupid **7** asinine, idiotic **8** ignorant **9** senseless **10** speechless, tongue-tied **11** meaningless **12** inarticulate

dumbbell: **4** boob, dope, fool **6** nitwit **7** dullard, fathead **9** exerciser

dumbfound: **4** daze, stun **5** amaze **6** boggle **7** nonplus, stagger **8** astonish, surprise **11** flabbergast

dummy: **4** copy, dolt, fake, sham **5** dunce,

front **6** effigy, layout **9** ignoramus, imitation, simpleton **10** fictitious, figurehead, substitute
in bridge: **11** exposed hand
magazine: **7** paste-up
window: **7** manikin **9** mannequin

dump: **4** beat, coin, drop, fire, junk **5** chuck, ditch, empty, hovel, let go, scrap **6** pigsty, unload **7** deposit **8** get rid of, jettison **11** storage area

dumpling: **5** blimp, knish **6** dim sum **7** darling, gnocchi (pl.) **8** doughboy, quenelle **10** butterball

dumps: **5** blues **8** doldrums, the blahs **9** dejection **10** depression, melancholy **11** despondency

dumpy: **5** pudgy, squat **6** stubby **8** thickset **9** shapeless

dun: tan **4** dark, drab, dull **5** annoy, brown, dingy, sepia **6** pester, plague **8** pressure **9** importune **13** demand payment

dunce: ass, oaf **4** boob, dodo, dope, fool **5** chump, idiot, moron **6** dimwit **7** jackass **8** bonehead, dumbbell, imbecile, lunkhead, numskull **10** dunderhead, nincompoop

dune: **5** ridge **7** barchan, barkhan **8** sand hill

dungarees: **5** jeans, pants **6** slacks **8** overalls, trousers
fabric: **5** denim

dungeon: **4** cell, jail **5** vault **6** donjon, prison **9** oubliette **10** ergastulum (L.)
of Calcutta: **9** Black Hole

dunk: dip, sop **4** soak **5** douse, steep **6** drench **7** immerse, moisten **8** saturate

dunlin: **4** stib **9** sandpiper

duo: **4** duet, dyad, pair **6** couple **7** twosome

dupe: con, fob, mug **4** bilk, fool, gull, hoax, tool **5** cheat, patsy, trick **6** delude, outwit, pigeon, sucker, victim **7** cat's-paw, deceive, defraud, mislead, swindle **8** flimflam, hoodwink **9** bamboozle

duple: **4** dual **6** binary, double **7** twofold

duplicate: **4** copy, mate, same **5** alike, ditto, spare **6** carbon, double, repeat **7** do again, estreat, replica **9** facsimile, identical, reproduce **10** bridge game, transcript **11** counterpart
genetic: **5** clone

duplicity: **5** fraud, guile **6** deceit **7** cunning, perfidy **8** trickery **9** deception, falsehood, treachery **13** dissimulation, double-dealing

durable: **4** firm **5** hardy, stout, tough **6** stable, staple, strong **7** lasting **8** constant, enduring **9** long-lived, permanent **10** consistent

duration: age, run **4** span, term, time **5** space **6** length, period **8** lifetime **9** longevity
denoting: **4** time **5** clock, timer **9** stopwatch
of ministerial charge: **9** pastorate

of position: **6** tenure
without beginning or end: **8** eternity
D'Urberville lass: **4** Tess
duress: **5** force **8** coercion, hardship, pressure **9** necessity **10** compulsion, constraint
durgah: See **dargah**
during: **4** amid **5** while **7** pending **10** throughout **11** at the time of
durra: **4** corn **6** millet **7** sorghum
durst: **5** dared **8** ventured
dusk: eve **5** gloom **6** darken **7** dimness **8** darkness, gloaming, twilight
dusky: dim **4** dark **5** brown, murky, tawny **6** gloomy, somber **7** obscure, shadowy, swarthy, unclear **8** blackish, blue-gray **11** dark-skinned
dust: ash **4** coat, dirt, smut, soot **5** clean, earth, flour, pouce, stive (Sc.), strew **6** pollen, powder **7** eburine, fall-out, remains, turmoil, wipe off **8** levigate, sprinkle **9** commotion, confusion
  measuring device: **9** koniscope
  reduce to: **4** mull **9** pulverize
  speck: **4** mote
dust off: **4** redo **8** renovate **9** bring back, refurbish
dustup: row **4** tiff **7** quarrel **8** argument
dusty: dim, dry **4** arid **7** clouded, powdery
Dutch: See **Netherlands**
Dutch uncle: oom **6** mentor **7** adviser
Dutch ware: **5** delft
dutiful: **5** loyal **6** docile **7** willing **8** faithful, obedient, reverent **9** compliant **10** respectful, submissive **11** reverential **13** conscientious
duty: job, lot, tax **4** care, onus, role, task, toll **5** chore, stint, trust **6** burden, charge, devoir, exitus (L.), impost, office, tariff **7** purpose, respect, service, station, tribute **8** function **10** allegiance, obligation
  on commodities: **6** excise
  shirk: **6** truant **7** goof off **9** goldbrick
  tour of: **4** turn **5** hitch, hours, shift, trick, watch
dwarf: elf **4** grig, runt, tiny **5** crowl (Sc.), gnome, midge, pigmy, pygmy, scrub, stunt, troll **6** midget, peewee **7** manikin **8** belittle, decrease, diminish, minimize, Tom Thumb **9** make small, tower over **10** diminutive, homunculus, overshadow **11** lilliputian
  in Snow White: Doc **5** Dopey, Happy **6** Grumpy, Sleepy, Sneezy **7** Bashful
  king: **8** Alberich
  male: **9** nannander
  race: **8** Nibelung
dwarfish: **4** tiny **5** elfin, runty, small, squat **6** nanoid **7** stunted
dwarfishness: **6** nanism

dwell: lie **4** bide, live, stay **5** abide, delay, exist, lodge, pause, tarry **6** remain, reside **7** inhabit
  on: **5** brood, nurse **6** repeat **7** belabor, prolong **10** linger over
dweller: **5** liver **6** tenant **7** denizen **8** habitant, occupant, resident **9** addressee **10** inhabitant
  around city: **11** suburbanite
  cave: **10** troglodyte
  city: **7** slicker **8** townsman, urbanite
  desert: **4** Arab **5** nomad **7** Bedouin
  earth: **9** tellurian
  institutional: **6** inmate
  lone: **6** hermit **7** eremite, recluse
  monastic: nun **4** monk **5** abbot **6** abbess **8** cenobite
  temporary: **6** lodger, roomer **7** boarder **9** transient
dwelling: hut **4** casa, digs, flat, home, slum, tent **5** abode, cabin, condo, hotel, house, hovel, motel, villa **6** castle, chalet, duplex, palace, shanty **7** chateau, cottage, lodging, mansion, trailer, triplex **8** building, bungalow, domicile, tenement **9** apartment, residence **10** habitation, pied-a-terre
dwindle: ebb **4** melt, pine, wane **5** abate, waste **6** lessen, shrink **7** decline **8** decrease, diminish, peter out, taper off
dye: aal, azo **4** anil, tint **5** color, eosin, fucus, imbue, stain, tinge **6** litmus, madder **7** aniline, pigment, toluene **8** colorant
  blue: **4** anil, woad **6** indigo
  brown: **5** sumac **6** sumach
  coal-tar: **7** magenta
  hair: **5** henna **6** rastik
  purple: **6** archil, orchil **8** murexide
  quercitron bark: **6** flavin
  red: **5** aurin, eosin **7** annatto, magenta **8** rhodamin **9** rhodamine **10** orseilline
  red-brown: **5** henna
  red-orange: **5** chica **7** fuchsin **8** morindin
  source: **5** murex
  violet: **7** gallein **8** thionine
  yellow: **4** woad **5** arusa
  yellow-red: **7** annatto
dyeing apparatus: vat **4** ager
  scrape: **6** harass
dying: moribund
dyke: See **dike**
dynamic: **5** vital **6** active, potent **7** driving, intense **8** forceful, spirited, vigorous **9** energetic
dynamite: TNT **5** blast **6** blow up **9** explosive
  inventor: **5** Nobel
  kind of: **6** dualin **7** dualine **9** fulgurite **10** kieselguhr
dynamo: **7** hustler **8** go-getter, live wire **9** generator

    in distributing system: **7** booster
    inventor: **7** Faraday
    part: **5** rotor **7** brushes **8** armature **10** commutator
dynast: **5** ruler **6** prince **8** governor
dynasty: **5** realm **8** dominion **10** line of rule

dyspeptic: **6** crabby **7** grouchy **10** ill-humored **11** bad-tempered
dysphoria: **7** anxiety **10** discomfort, discontent
dystopia: **10** living hell **13** dreadful place

E

each: all, per **5** every **6** apiece **8** everyone

eager: hot **4** agog, avid, keen, sour, warm, wave **5** afire, agasp, itchy, ready, sharp **6** ardent, greedy, intent **7** anxious, athirst, brittle, burning, excited, fervent **8** desirous, spirited, vigorous, yearning **9** desireful, impatient, impetuous, strenuous **12** enthusiastic, forereaching

eagerness: **4** elan, zeal **5** ardor **6** fervor **7** ardency, avidity **8** alacrity, cupidity, fervency **9** alertness, constancy, readiness **10** enthusiasm, impatience **13** impetuousness

eagle: **6** aquila **8** allerion, bateleur, berghaan, insignia, U.S. emblem **9** golf score
biblical: **4** gier
constellation: **6** Aquila
genus of: **10** Haliaeetus
nest: **4** aery, eyry **5** aerie, eyrie
relative: **4** hawk **6** falcon
sea: ern **4** erne

eaglestone: **7** aetites

eagre: **4** bore, wave

ear: lug (Sc.) **4** hear, heed, obey, plow, till **5** auris (L.), spike **6** listen **7** auricle, hearing **8** audience **9** attention, cultivate
absence of: **6** anotia
bone: **5** ambos, incus **6** stapes **7** malleus, stirrup
canal: **5** scala
cavity: **6** meatus **7** cochlea
cleaning device: **8** aurilave
covering: lap **4** flap, muff
doctor: **9** otologist
inflammation of: **6** otitis
middle: **4** drum **8** tympanum
near: **7** parotic
part of: **4** burr, lobe **5** helix, pinna **6** tragus
pert. to: **4** otic **5** aural **7** entotic **9** auricular
plug: **7** stopple
science of: **7** otology

earache: **7** otalgia

eardrop: **7** earring, pendant

eared seal: **5** otary

earl: **4** peer **8** nobleman
wife of: **8** countess

earlier: ere **4** erst **5** elder, first **6** before, former, sooner **8** formerly, previous

early: old **5** prior **6** timely **7** ancient, betimes, too soon **9** in advance, matutinal, premature **10** beforehand

earmark: tag **5** allot, label, stamp, trait **7** feature **8** set aside **10** reserve for **14** identification

earn: get, win **4** gain, rate **5** gross, merit **6** obtain **7** achieve, acquire, deserve, realize **8** drag down

earner: **6** worker **11** breadwinner

earnest: **4** hard **5** grave, sober, staid **6** ardent, hearty, intent, sedate, solemn **7** engaged, forward, serious, sincere, zealous **8** diligent, emphatic **9** heartfelt **10** expressive, thoughtful **12** affectionate, wholehearted

earnest money: **5** token **6** pledge **7** deposit **8** security

earnings: pay **5** wages **6** income, salary **7** profits, returns **9** dividends

earring: **4** grip **8** ornament **9** girandole

ear shell: **7** abalone

earshot: **5** sound **7** hearing

earsplitting: **4** loud **6** shrill **8** piercing

earth: erd (Sc.), orb **4** bury, clay, dirt, fill, grit, land, loam, marl, muck, soil, turf **5** glebe, globe, loess, terra (L.), world **6** ground, planet **7** topsoil **10** terra firma
compound: **7** tierras
crust constituent: **6** silica
deposit: **4** marl, silt **5** loess **8** alluvium
dweller: **9** tellurian
god: Geg, Keb, Seb **5** Dagan
goddess: **4** Gaea, Gaia **5** Ceres, Terra **6** Semele **7** Demeter
layer of: **5** sloam
lump of: **4** clod
metallic: ore
opposite side of: **9** Antipodes
pert. to: **4** geal **5** terra **8** telluric **9** planetary **11** terrestrial
pigment: **5** ochre, umber
ridge of: **4** kame **6** rideau
science: **7** geodesy, geology **9** geography

earth bob: **4** grub **6** maggot

earthdrake: **6** dragon

earthenware: **4** delf **5** china, delft **7** biscuit, ceramic, faience, pottery **8** crockery **9** porcelain **10** terra-cotta
maker: **6** potter
piece of: **5** shard

earthfall: 9 landslide

earth hog: 8 aardvark

earthling: 5 human 6 mortal

earth lodge: 5 hogan

earthly: 6 carnal 7 mundane, secular, terrene, worldly 8 material, physical, possible, temporal 11 conceivable, terrestrial

earthnut: 5 arnot, chufa 6 peanut 7 truffle

earthquake: 5 seism, shock 6 tremor 7 temblor 10 aftershock
  intensity scale: 7 mercali, Richter
  measuring device: 10 seisometer
  pert. to: 7 seismic
  point directly above: 9 epicenter
  science: 10 seismology

earthstar: 6 fungus 7 geaster

earthwork: 5 agger 7 rampart 10 breastwork, embankment 13 fortification

earthworm: ess 7 annelid, ipomoea

earthy: low 5 gross, salty 6 coarse, fleshy 7 sensual 9 practical, realistic, unrefined 11 terrestrial

earwax: 7 cerumen

earwig: 6 golach (Sc.) 9 centipede 12 eavesdropper

Ea's daughter: 4 Nina

ease: 4 calm, rest 5 allay, knack, peace, quiet, relax 6 loosen, pacify, reduce, relief, repose, smooth, soften, soothe 7 appease, assuage, comfort, faculty, freedom, leisure, liberty, lighten, relieve, slacken 8 diminish, facility, mitigate, moderate, palliate, pleasure, security, unburden 9 alleviate, disburden, enjoyment 10 ameliorate, facilitate, relaxation, solicitude 11 contentment, naturalness, tranquility 12 satisfaction
  at: 6 degage, otiose 7 relaxed, resting
  off: 4 slow 5 slack

easel: 5 frame 7 support

easily: 6 gently, glibly 7 handily, readily 8 smoothly 13 without effort

east: 4 Asia 6 Levant, Orient
  pert. to: 4 eoan 8 oriental

Easter: 5 Pasch 6 Eostre, Pascha
  first Sunday after: 9 Quasimodo
  pert. to: 7 paschal
  Sunday before: 4 Palm

Easter Island: 7 Rapa Nui

Eastern Church: 8 Orthodox
  bishop: 4 abba
  choir platform: 5 solea
  convent head: 8 hegumene
  festival day: 8 apodosis
  monk: 7 caloyer
  prayer: 6 ectene, ektene

East Indies: See **Indonesia**

easy: 4 calm, cozy, glib, mild 5 cushy, light, suave 6 facile, gentle, secure, simple 7 lenient, natural 8 carefree, careless, familiar, graceful, homelike, moderate, tranquil, unforced 9 compliant, indulgent, tractable, unhurried 10 manageable, unaffected 11 comfortable, complaisant, susceptible, unconcerned 13 unconstrained

easygoing: 4 calm 5 homey 6 casual, placid 7 relaxed 8 carefree, informal 10 unaffected 11 low-pressure 12 happy-go-lucky

easy job: 4 pipe, snap 5 cinch 8 sinecure

easy mark: 4 dupe 5 chump 6 pigeon, sucker 7 fall guy 9 soft touch

eat: sup 4 bite, dine, fare, feed, fret, gnaw, grub, rust 5 erode, feast, lunch, munch, taste 6 absorb, devour, ingest, ravage 7 consume, corrode, destroy, swallow 8 wear away 9 breakfast, partake of
  between meals: 5 snack
  by regimen: 4 diet
  grass: 5 graze 6 forage 7 pasture
  greedily: 4 cram, wolf 5 binge, gorge, raven, stuff 6 gobble 10 gormandize
  sumptuously: 5 feast 6 regale 7 banquet

eatable: 6 edible 8 esculent 10 comestible

eater: 8 consumer
  big: 7 glutton 8 gourmand 11 trencherman
  fastidious: 7 epicure, gourmet 8 Lucullus 10 gastronome

eating-place: inn 4 cafe 5 diner, grill, hotel 6 tavern 7 automat, beanery, tearoom 8 grubbery 9 cafeteria, chophouse, lunchroom 10 restaurant 11 greasy spoon 12 luncheonette
  institutional: 9 cafeteria, refectory 10 dining hall
  military: 8 mess hall

eave: 7 cornice

ebb: 4 fail, sink, wane 5 abate, decay 6 recede, reflux, retire 7 decline, subside 8 decrease, diminish 9 backwater

ebb and flow: 5 estus 6 aestus

Eber's son: 6 Joktan

Eblis: 5 Devil, Satan
  before the fall: 6 Azazel
  son: Sut, Tir 4 Awar 5 Dasim 8 Zalambur

ebon: 4 dark, inky 5 black, raven, sable

ebony: 5 black 8 hard wood

eboulement: 9 landslide

ebullience: 4 zest 6 gaiety 8 vitality 9 animation 10 enthusiasm, exuberance 11 high spirits

ebullient: 5 brash 6 lively 7 boiling 8 agitated 12 effervescent

ebullition: 7 ferment 8 outburst 9 agitation, commotion 10 excitement 12 fermentation 13 effervescence

ecaudate: 8 tailless

ecce (L.): 4 look 6 behold

eccentric: odd **4** card, kook **5** crank, queer, weird **7** bizarre, devious, erratic, strange **8** abnormal, peculiar, singular **9** anomalous, character, irregular, quizzical, screwball

eccentricity: 5 quirk **6** foible, oddity **7** caprice **8** crotchet **9** queerness **10** aberration **11** peculiarity, strangeness **12** idiosyncrasy

ecclesiastic: 4 abbe **5** abbot, clerk **6** divine, parson, pastor, priest **7** prelate **8** minister, reverend **9** clergyman

  belt: **7** balteus **8** baltheus

  council: **5** synod

  court: **4** rota

  garment: alb **4** cope **5** amice, cappa, fanon, orale, rabat, stole **6** callot **7** biretta, calotte, cassock **8** berretta

  head: **6** rector

  land: **5** glebe

  living: **8** benefice

  military: **5** padre **8** chaplain

  ruler: **8** hierarch

  service: see **canonical**: *hour*

  unit: **6** parish

ecdysiast: 6 peeler **8** stripper **11** stripteaser

echelon: 4 rank **5** level **6** lineup **8** maneuver **9** formation

echidna: 8 anteater

  three-toed: **6** nodiak

echinate: 5 spiny **7** bristly, prickly

echinoderm: 8 starfish **9** sea urchin

echo: 4 ring **6** repeat, second **7** imitate, iterate, resound, respond, revoice **8** response **9** imitation **10** repetition **11** reverberate **13** reverberation

eciton: ant

eclat: 4 fame, pomp **5** glory, kudos **6** praise, renown, repute **7** acclaim **8** applause, facility, splendor **9** notoriety **10** brilliancy **11** distinction, ostentation

eclectic: 5 broad, mixed **6** choosy, varied **7** blended, diverse, jumbled **8** catholic, combined **9** many-sided, selective

eclipse: dim **4** bind, blot, hide **5** blind, block, cloud, cover, shade, sully **6** darken, dazzle, exceed **7** conceal, obscure, travail **8** outrival **10** extinguish, overshadow **11** obscuration, occultation

  demon of: **4** Rahu

  shadow: **8** penumbra **9** penumbrae (pl.)

eclogue: 4 idyl, poem **5** idyll **7** bucolic

ecology, oecology: 9 bionomics

economical: 5 chary **6** frugal, saving **7** careful, prudent, thrifty **9** provident

economics: *element:* **9** commodity

  theoretical: **9** plutology

economize: 4 save **5** skimp, stint **6** scrimp **7** husband, utilize **8** retrench

ecostate: 7 ribless

ecru: 5 beige, linen **10** unbleached

ecstasy: joy **5** bliss **6** heaven, trance **7** delight, emotion, madness, rapture **8** euphoria, paradise **9** happiness **10** exaltation

ecstatic: **4** rapt **8** glorious **9** enchanted, entranced, rhapsodic **10** enraptured

ectad: 5 outer **7** outward **8** exterior

  opposite of: **5** entad

ectype: 9 imitation

ecu: 4 coin **6** shield

Ecuador: *bay:* **8** Caraquez, Sardinas

  capital: **5** Quito, Sucre

  city: **4** Loja, Nono, Puyo, Tena **5** Chone, Daule, Guano **6** Ambato, Cuenca, Ibarra, Pujili, Tulcan **7** Azogues, Cayambe, Machala, Pelileo, Pillaro **8** Babahoyo, Guaranda, Riobamba

  conqueror: **7** Pizarro

  currency: **5** sucre **7** centavo

  Indian: **4** Cara, Inca **5** Palta **6** Canelo, Jibaro

  island: **4** Puna **9** Galapagos

  language: **7** Quechua, Spanish

  measure: **5** libra **6** cuadra, fanega

  mountain: **5** Altar, Andes **6** Sangay **7** Cayambe **8** Cotopaxi, Illiniza

  volcano: **8** Antisana, Cotopaxi **10** Chimborazo

---

ecumenical: 6 global **7** liberal **8** catholic, tolerant, unifying **9** universal, worldwide **12** all-inclusive, cosmopolitan

ecumenical council: 4 Lyon **5** Lyons, Trent **6** Nicaea **7** Vatican **9** Chalcedon

eczema: 6 herpes, tetter **9** malanders **10** dermatitis

edacity: **8** appetite, gluttony, voracity **12** ravenousness

Edda: 4 saga

Eddaic god: 4 Odin

eddo: 4 taro

eddy: 4 purl, weel (Sc.) **5** gurge, shift, swirl, whirl **6** vortex **7** backset **9** maelstrom, whirlpool **12** contrary flow **14** countercurrent

edema: 5 tumor **6** dropsy **8** swelling **9** puffiness **12** intumescence

Eden: 6 garden, heaven, utopia **7** arcadia, elysium **8** paradise

edentate: 5 sloth **7** ant bear **8** aardvark, anteater, pangolin, tamandua **9** armadillo, toothless

Edessa's king: 5 Abgar

edge: hem, jag, lip, rim 4 bank, bite, brim, brow, hone, rand, side, trim, whet 5 arris, bevel, blade, brink, crest, frill, ruler, sidle, splay, sting, verge 6 adjoin, border, flange, fringe, impale, margin 7 nose out, selvage, sharpen 8 boundary, keenness, selvedge 9 advantage, beginning, perimeter, periphery, sharpness 10 escarpment
run along: 5 skirt
sharp: 5 beard
uneven: 4 wany 5 waney

edged: 5 erose, sharp 7 crenate, cutting, trimmed

edge in: 7 intrude, sneak by 9 gain entry 10 infiltrate 11 slip through

edging: hem 4 lace 5 frill, picot 6 border, fringe 7 binding 8 rickrack 10 embroidery
loop: 5 picot

edgy: 5 sharp, tense 6 touchy 7 angular, jittery, nervous, uptight 8 critical, snappish 9 irritable

edible: 7 eatable 8 esculent 9 palatable 10 comestible
arum: 4 taro
fungus: 5 morel 7 truffle
gallingale: 5 chufa
mollusk: 4 clam 6 oyster 7 scallop
parts of fruit: 4 pulp
rush: 5 chufa
seaweed: 4 agar 5 dulse, laver 6 delisk 8 agaragar
seed: nut, pea 4 bean 7 pumpkin
tuber root: oca, uva, yam 4 beet, eddo, taro 6 turnip 7 parsnip 8 rutabaga

edict: act, ban, law 4 bull, fiat 5 arret, bando, bulla, irade, order, ukase 6 decree, dictum, notice 7 command, embargo, program, statute 9 ordinance, programma 12 announcement, proclamation
papal: 4 bull

edifice: 4 dome 6 church 8 building 9 structure
kind: 6 castle, museum, palace, temple 7 capitol, mansion 8 monument 9 cathedral 10 tabernacle

edify: 5 teach 6 better, inform 7 educate, improve 8 instruct 9 enlighten, make clear 10 illuminate

edile: 10 magistrate

edit: 5 alter, emend 6 direct, redact, review, revise 7 arrange, compile, correct, prepare, publish, rewrite 8 copyread 9 supervise 10 blue-pencil

edition: 4 kind 5 issue, print, stamp 6 source 7 version 9 character 10 extraction

editor: 8 redactor 9 emendator, publisher, redacteur 10 diaskeuast, journalist
room: 7 sanctum

Edom: 7 Idumaea
capital: 5 Petra
chieftain: 4 Iram
conquered by: 6 Israel 9 Nabateans 10 Hasmoneans
descendants of: 4 Esau
king: 5 Hadad
mountain: Hor
new territory: 6 Idumea

Edomite's ancestor: 4 Esau

educate: 4 rear 5 coach, drill, teach, train, tutor 6 inform, school 7 develop, nurture 8 instruct 9 cultivate, enlighten 10 discipline, strengthen 12 indoctrinate

educated: 4 bred 6 taught 7 learned, trained 8 lettered, literate, schooled, well-read 11 experienced 13 knowledgeable

education: 7 nurture 8 breeding, learning, pedagogy, training 9 erudition 10 background, discipline 11 scholarship
institution: 6 school 7 college 8 seminary 10 university
organization: NEA, PTA 6 lyceum

educator: don 5 tutor 7 teacher 9 pedagogue, professor 10 instructor

educe: 5 evoke 6 elicit, evolve 7 extract 9 eliminate

eel: 4 grig 5 elver, moray, siren 6 conger 7 lamprey, muraena 8 anguilla, wriggler 9 snipefish
cut and cooked: 10 spitchcock
fish for: 7 sniggle
marine: 6 conger
migration: 7 eelfare
sand: 6 launce
young: 5 elver

eelboat: 6 schuit

eel-like: 10 anguilloid

eelpot: 4 trap

eelpout: 6 burbot, guffer, yowler 10 muttonfish

eel-shaped: 12 anguilliform

eelworm: 4 nema

eely: 7 elusive, evasive, wriggly 8 slippery, slithery 9 wriggling

eerie, eery: 5 scary, timid, weird 6 dismal, gloomy, spooky 7 awesome, ghostly, macabre, strange, uncanny 8 eldritch, ghoulish 9 unearthly, unnatural, unworldly 10 frightened 11 phantom-like

efface: 4 dele, raze 5 erase 6 cancel, rub out 7 blot out, destroy, expunge 9 eradicate, extirpate 10 obliterate

effacement: 7 erasure 10 withdrawal

effect: 4 make 5 cause, close, eclat, enact 6 intent, result, sequel 7 achieve, acquire, compass, conduce, emotion, execute, fulfill, operate, outcome, perform, produce, purport, realize 8 complete 9 influence 10 accomplish, bring about, consummate, expression, impression **11** consequence **13** manifestation

of past experience: **5** mneme

effective: **4** able, real **5** sound **6** active, actual, causal, potent **7** capable, telling **8** adequate, forceful, powerful, striking, vigorous **9** brilliant, competent, effectual, efficient **10** perficient **11** efficacious, influential

effectiveness: **5** force, power, punch **8** strength, validity **10** efficiency

effects: **5** goods **7** baggage **8** chattels, movables, property **10** belongings **11** possessions

effectual: **5** valid **6** useful **7** capable **8** adequate, workable **9** effective, efficient **10** does the job, functional, productive **13** authoritative

effeminate: **4** weak **5** timid **6** chichi, prissy **7** unmanly **8** oversoft, womanish **9** emolliate, not virile, sissified **12** nicenellyish, overdelicate **13** overemotional

effervesce: **4** fizz, foam, huff **6** bubble **7** enthuse, ferment, sparkle **8** rave over

effervescent: gay **4** airy **6** breezy, bubbly, frothy, lively, snappy, yeasty **7** buoyant **8** animated, bouncing, spirited, volatile **9** ebullient, exuberant, full of pep, vivacious

effete: **4** sere, soft, weak **5** spent **6** barren **8** decadent, moribund **9** exhausted

efficacious: **5** valid **6** mighty, potent **8** forcible, powerful, vigorous, virtuous **9** available, effective, officious, prevalent **10** legitimate **11** efficiently

efficient: **4** able **5** adept **6** expert **7** capable **8** powerful, skillful **9** competent, effective, effectual **11** efficacious

effigy: **5** dummy, image **8** likeness **9** jackstraw

efflorescence: **8** anthesis, blooming **9** flowering **10** burgeoning **11** fulfillment

effluvium: **4** aura, odor **5** vapor **9** emanation **10** exhalation

efflux: **7** outflow **8** effusion **9** effluence, emanation

effort: try **4** task, toil, work **5** chore, drive, essay, force, labor, nisus, pains, power, trial **6** energy, strain, stress **7** attempt, trouble **8** endeavor, exertion, struggle **9** diligence **11** application, undertaking

effortless: **4** easy **6** facile, simple, smooth **8** painless

effrontery: **4** gall **5** brass, cheek, nerve **7** chutzpa **8** audacity, boldness, temerity **9** hardihood, impudence, insolence, sauciness **10** confidence, incivility **11** presumption **12** impertinence

effulgence: **5** blaze, glory **8** radiance, splendor **10** brightness, brilliance

effulgent: **6** bright **7** radiant **8** luminous

effuse: **4** flow, gush, shed **7** emanate **9** pour forth, spread out **11** disseminate

effusive: **5** gushy **6** smarmy **7** cloying, profuse **8** bubbling **9** exuberant, rhapsodic **12** unrestrained **13** demonstrative

eft: **4** newt **6** lizard, triton **10** salamander

egad: **8** mild oath **9** expletive

egeran: **8** idocrase **11** vesuvianite

egeria: **12** woman adviser

egest: **4** void **7** excrete

egg: ova (pl.) **4** abet, goad, ovum, prod, seed, spur, urge **5** ovule, spore **6** incite **7** actuate **9** instigate

before maturation: **6** oocyte

case: **5** shell **6** ovisac **7** ootheca

collector: **8** oologist

fertilized: **6** zygote **7** oosperm, oospore

fish: roe **5** berry **6** caviar

insect: nit

measuring device: **7** oometer

nest: **6** clutch

part of: **4** yolk **5** shell, white **7** albumen, latebra

Philippine duck: **5** balut

small: **5** ovule

tested: **7** candled

unfertilized: **8** oosphere

white of: **5** glair **7** albumen

yolk: **6** yellow **8** vitellus

egger: **4** moth

egghead: **7** Brahmin **8** highbrow **12** intellectual

eggnog: nog **8** beverage

eggplant: **7** brinjal **8** brinjaul **9** aubergine

egg-shaped: **4** ooid, oval **5** ovate, ovoid **6** ooidal **7** obovoid, ovaloid, oviform

eggshell: *confetti-filled:* **8** cascaron

Egil's brother: **6** Volund

egis: See **aegis**

Eglah: *husband:* **5** David

son: **7** Ithream

eglantine: **8** woodbine **10** sweetbrier **11** honeysuckle

Eglon's king: **5** Debir

ego: **4** self **6** psyche **7** conceit **9** number one **11** personality, selfishness

egotism: **5** pride **6** vanity **7** conceit **8** self-love **9** arrogance **10** narcissism, self-esteem

egotistic: **4** smug, vain **5** cocky **7** selfish, stuck-up **8** boastful, superior **9** conceited **11** swell-headed **12** self-centered, vainglorious **13** self-important

egregious: **4** rank **5** gross **7** blatant, glaring, heinous **8** flagrant, shocking **10** deplorable, outrageous

egress: **4** exit **5** issue **6** outlet **7** outgate, passage **9** departure

egret: **5** heron, plume **6** gaulin **8** gaulding

Egypt (see also **Egyptian**): *ancient ruler:*
7 pharaoh
capital: 5 Cairo
city: 4 Giza, Qena, Suez 5 Asyut,
Benha, Luxor, Tanta 7 Al Arish 8 Port
Said 9 El Mansura 10 Alexandria
currency: 5 pound 7 piaster
desert: 6 Libyan, Sahara 7 Arabian
food: ful 4 fool
gulf: 4 Suez 5 Aqaba
mountain: 5 Sinai 6 Gharib, Nugrus 9
Gebel Musa, Katherina
peasant: 8 fellahin
peninsula: 5 Sinai
people: 4 Arab 6 Nubian 7 Bedouin,
Hamitic
religion: 4 Copt 11 Sunni Muslim
river: 4 Nile, Qena 7 Rosetta 8 Dami-
etta
sea: Red 13 Mediterranean
waterway: 9 Suez Canal

Egyptian: 4 Arab, Copt 5 Nilot
air god: Shu
animal: fox 4 adda, lynx 5 genet, hyena 6
jackal, jerboa 7 gazelle 9 ichneumon
antelope: 5 bubal
army chieftain: 6 sirdar
beer: 6 zythum
beetle: 6 scarab
bird: 6 sicsac
boat: 5 baris 8 dahabeah
bottle: 6 doruck
bull: 4 apis
burial jar: 7 Canopus
calendar: 4 Ahet, Apap, Tybi 5 Choik,
Payni, Shemu, Thoth 6 Hathor, Mechir,
Mesore, Paophi 7 Pachons 9 Phamenoth,
Pharmuthi
cap: fez
cat-headed goddess: 4 Bast 5 Pakht
Christian: 4 Copt
civilization: 6 Tasian
clover: 7 berseem
cobra: 4 haje
concubine: 5 Hagar
cosmetic: 4 kohl
cotton: Sak 4 pima
crocodile-headed god: 4 Sobk 5 Sebek
cross: 4 ankh
crown: 4 atef
dam: 4 sudd
dancers: 7 ghawazi 8 ghawazee
deity: Hor, Mut, Nut 4 Anta, Apet, Bast,
Isis, Maat, Sati 5 Anaka 6 Hathor, Seshat,

Tefnut 7 Nepthys 8 Nechebit
descendant: 4 Copt 6 fellah
dog: 6 saluki
drink: 4 bosa, boza 5 bozah
drug: 8 nepenthe
elysium: 4 Aalu
emblem: 4 aten 5 lotus
gateway: 5 pylon
god: Set 4 Ptah, Seth 5 Thoth 6 Anubis 7
Serapis
goddess: Mut, Nut 4 Bast, Isis 5 Pakht 6
Sekhet 8 Nekhebet
guard: 6 ghafir 7 ghaffir
guide: 8 dragoman
hawk-headed god: 5 Horus
herb: 5 anise
instrument: 7 arghool, arghoul, sistrum
judge of the dead: 6 Osiris
king: Tut 4 Fuad, Mena 5 Menes 6
Cheops, Farouk, Ramses 7 Ptolemy, Rame-
ses 9 Akhenatem, Amenhotep 11
Tutankhamen
laborer: 5 aperu
lighthouse: 6 pharos
lily: 5 calla, lotos, lotus
lion-headed goddess: 4 Bast 5 Pakht 6
Sekhet
lizard: 4 adda 5 scink, skink
love goddess: 6 Hathor
lute: 5 nabla
maternity goddess: 4 Apet
measure: apt, dra, hen, rob 4 dira, draa,
kada, khet, ocha, roub, theb 5 abdat, ardab,
ardeb, cubit, farde, keleh, kilah, sahme 6
artaba, aurure, baladi, kantar, kedlah, rob-
hah, schene 7 choryos, daribah, malouah,
roubouh, toumnah 8 kassabah, kharouba
10 dira baladi, dira mimari, kerat kamel,
nief keddah 11 feddan nasri
monarch: 7 Pharaoh
monument: 6 Sphinx 7 obelisk, pyramid
official: 5 mudir
paper: 6 papyri 7 papyrus
peasant: 6 fellah
Pharaoh's headdress: 7 pschent
plant: 5 cumin 6 cummin, lentil
pyramids at Giza: 6 Cheops (Khufu),
Khafre 7 Menkure
queen: 9 Cleopatra, Nefertiti, Nofretete 10
Hatshepsut
relic: 5 mummy
ruined cities: 5 Tanis 6 Abydos, Karnak,
Thebes 7 Memphis
sacred bird: 4 ibis
sacred bull: 4 apis
sacred flower: 5 lotos, lotus
sanctuary: 5 secos, sekos
seal: 6 scarab
serpent: 5 apepi

shrub: kat
solar disk: **4** Aten
stone: **7** Rosetta
sun god: Tem, Tum **4** Atmu, Atum
symbol: uta **4** ankh **6** scarab
talisman: **5** angle
temple: **4** Idfu **5** Luxor **6** Abydos, Karnak, Osiris **7** Dendera
tomb: **7** mastaba, pyramid
underworld: **4** Aaru, Duat **6** Amenti
vase: **7** canopic
viper: **8** cerastes
vulture-headed goddess: Mut **8** Nekhebet
weight: ket, oka, oke **4** dera, heml, khar, okia, rotl **5** artal, artel, deben, kerat, okieh, ratel, uckia **6** hamlah, kantar **7** drachma, quintal
wind: **6** kamsin **7** chamsin, kamseen, khamsin **8** khamseen

Ehud's son: **6** Naaman
eider duck: **4** colk
eidetic: **5** vivid
eidolon: **4** icon **5** ghost, image **7** phantom **10** apparition
eight: eta (Gr.) **6** ogdoad
    group of: **5** octad, octet **6** octave **7** octette
eighth: *circle:* **6** octant
    day after nones: **4** ides
    note: **6** quaver
    order: **5** octic
eight-sided: **9** octagonal
eighty: **9** fourscore
Eire: **4** Erin **5** Ierne **7** Ireland **8** Hibernia
Eireannach: **8** Irishman
ejaculate: **5** blurt, eject **7** exclaim
ejaculation: **7** begorra **8** uttering **11** exclamation
eject: **4** boot, cast, emit, oust, spat, spew, spit, void **5** erupt, evict, expel, spout, spurt, vomit **6** banish, bounce **7** dismiss, exclude, extrude, obtrude **8** disgorge **9** discharge, ejaculate **10** disembogue, dispossess
ejection: **6** ouster **8** eviction **9** expulsion
eke: **7** augment, enlarge, husband, stretch **8** increase, lengthen **10** supplement
el: **4** bend
elaborate: **5** fancy **6** expand, ornate **7** amplify, develop, enlarge, explain **8** detailed **9** embellish, intricate **11** complicated, extravagant, painstaking
Elam: *capital:* **4** Susa
    king: **12** Chedorlaomer
elan: **4** dash **5** ardor, gusto, style, verve **6** spirit, warmth **7** potency **9** eagerness **10** enthusiasm
elanet: **4** kite
elapse: **4** pass, slip **6** expire
elasmobranch fish: ray
elastic: **6** garter, spongy **7** buoyant, springy **8**

cheverel, cheveril, flexible, stretchy **9** expansive, resilient **10** propulsive
    fluid: gas
    material from whales: **6** baleen
elastin: **10** albuminoid
elate: **4** buoy **5** cheer, exalt, exult, flush, lofty, raise **6** excite, please, thrill **7** elevate, gladden, inflate, success **8** elevated, heighten, inspirit **9** stimulate **10** exhilarate
elated: **5** happy, vogie (Sc.) **6** jovial **7** excited, jocular **8** exultant, jubilant **9** cock-a-hoop, overjoyed
elater: **6** beetle **8** skipjack
elaterite: **7** bitumen
Elatha's son: **4** Bres
Elatus' daughter: **6** Caenis **7** Caeneus
Elbe: **4** Labe
    city: **6** Melnik **7** Dresden, Hamburg **9** Magdeburg
    tributary: **4** Eger, Elde, Iser **5** Havel, Mulde, Saale **6** Elster, Vetava
elbow: **4** bend **5** ancon, joint, nudge, shove **6** jostle
    bend an: **5** drink **6** imbibe
    bone: **4** ulna **5** ulnae (pl.)
    pert. to: **5** ulnar **8** anconeal
elbowroom: **6** leeway **10** ample space
elcaja: **6** mafura
eld: **9** antiquity
elder: iva **4** aine (F.) **5** prior **6** senior **7** oldster **8** ancestor, danewort, superior **9** presbyter **10** forefather
elderly: old **4** aged, gray **6** senile **7** ancient **9** up in years, venerable **11** over the hill
eldritch: **4** eery **5** eerie, weird **7** uncanny **9** frightful
Eleanor's husband: **7** Henry II
elect: **4** call, pick **6** assume, choose, chosen, decide, opt for, prefer, select, vote in **7** embrace, espouse, pick out **9** legislate
election: **6** choice **9** balloting **10** plebiscite **11** alternative
    majority of votes: **9** plurality
    nominating: **7** primary
    to break the: **6** runoff
electioneer: **5** stump **8** campaign, politick **9** seek votes
elective: **8** optional **9** voluntary
elector: **5** voter **6** elisor **7** chooser **11** constituent
Electra: *brother:* **7** Orestes
    father: **9** Agamemnon
    husband: **7** Thaumas
    mother: **12** Clytemnestra
    sister: **9** Iphegenia
    son: **8** Dardanus
electric: **6** static **8** magnetic
    carrier: **9** conductor
    circuit regulator: **7** booster

coil: **5** tesla
current: **6** direct **11** alternating
current meter: **7** ammeter **9** voltmeter
current moderator: **5** coder **9** rheometer **10** attenuator
generator: **6** dynamo
light: arc **4** neon **12** incandescent
measuring unit: amp, ohm, rel **4** volt, watt **5** barad, farad, henry, joule **6** ampere, proton **7** coulomb **8** kilowatt
motor part: **10** commutator
particle: ion
pole: **5** anode **7** cathode
power: **7** wattage
resistance: **6** ohmage
safety device: **4** fuse
strength: **8** amperage
transmission: **5** radio
wave meter: **9** ondometer

electrify: jar **4** jolt **5** amaze **6** dazzle, fire up, thrill **7** astound, stagger, startle **8** astonish **9** galvanize

electronic tube: **6** triode **7** tetrode **8** klystron

electrum: **5** amber

Electryon: *brother:* **6** Mestor
daughter: **7** Alcmene
father: **7** Perseus
grandson: **8** Heracles, Hercules
mother: **9** Andromeda
wife: **5** Anaxo

eleemosynary: **4** free **9** dependent **10** charitable, gratuitous

elegance: **4** chic **5** grace, style, taste **6** finery, luxury, polish **7** dignity **8** courtesy, grandeur, richness, splendor **9** propriety **10** concinnity, refinement **12** gracefulness

elegant: **4** chic, fine, posh **5** swank **6** dainty, dressy, superb, urbane **7** courtly, genteel, refined, stately **8** delicate, graceful, handsome, polished, tasteful **9** admirable, beautiful, excellent, exquisite, recherche, sumptuous **10** concinnous, fastidious

elegiac: sad **8** mournful **9** plaintive

elegist: **4** Gray, poet **6** Milton **10** Propertius

elegit: **4** writ

elegy: **4** poem, song **5** dirge **6** lament **7** epicede **9** epicedium **11** lamentation

element: air **4** fire **5** basic, earth, group, metal, water **6** matter **7** essence, quality **8** rudiment **9** component **10** ingredient **11** constituent, environment, fundamental
chemical: tin (Sn) **4** gold (Au), Iron (Fe), lead (Pb), neon (Ne), zinc (Zn) **5** argon (Ar), boron (B), radon (Rn), xenon (Xe) **6** barium (Ba), carbon (C), cerium (Ce), cesium (Cs), cobalt (Co), copper (Cu), curium (Cm), helium (He), indium (In), iodine (I), nickel (Ni), osmium (Os), oxygen

(O), radium (Ra), silver (Ag), sodium (Na), sulfur (S) **7** arsenic (As), bismuth (Bi), bromine (Br), cadmium (Cd), calcium (Ca), cerbium (Er), fermium (Fm), gallium (Ga), hafnium (Hf), hahnium (Ha), holmium (Ho), iridium (Ir), krypton (Kr), lithium (Li), mercury (Hg), niobium (Nb), rhenium (Re), rhodium (Rh), silicon (Si), terbium (Tb), thorium (Th), thulium (Tm), uranium (U), Wolfram (W), yttrium (Y) **8** actinium (Ac), aluminum (Al), antimony (Sb), astatine (At), chlorine (Cl), chromium (Cr), Europium (Eu), fluorine (F), francium (Fr), hydrogen (H), illinium (Il), lutecium (Lu), masurium (Ma), nitrogen (N), nobelium (No), platinum (Pt), polonium (Po), rubidium (Rb), samarium (Sm), scandium (Sc), selenium (Se), tantalum (Ta), thallium (Tl), titanium (Ti), tungsten (W), vanadium (V) **9** americium (Am), berkelium (Bk), beryllium (Be), columbium (Cb), germanium (Ge), lanthanum (La), magnesium (Mg), manganese (Mn), neodymium (Nd), neptunium (Np), palladium (Pd), plutonium (Pu), potassium (K), ruthenium (Ru), strontium (Sr), tellurium (Te), virginium (Vi), ytterbium (Yb), zirconium (Zr) **10** dysprosium (Dy), gadolinium (Gd), lawrencium (Lr), molybdenum (Mo), phosphorus (P), promethium (Pm), technetium (Tc) **11** californium (Cf), einsteinium (Es), mendelevium (Md) **12** praseodymium (Pr) **13** protoactinium (Pa)
combining power: **7** valence
decomposed: **5** anion
different weight: **7** isotope
even valence: **6** artiad
family: **7** halogen
minute: **5** monad
nonmetallic: **5** boron **6** bromin, iodine **7** bromine, silicon
nonvolatile: **6** barium
of air: **5** argon **6** oxygen **8** nitrogen
rare earth: **6** erbium

elemental spirit: **5** genie

elementary: **5** basic, crude, plain **6** simple **7** initial, primary **8** inchoate, original **9** primitive **10** rudimental, uncombined **11** fundamental, rudimentary
organism: **5** monad
reader: **6** primer

elemi: **5** anime, resin **9** oleoresin

elephant: **5** hathi **6** muckna, tusker **7** mammoth **8** mastodon **9** pachyderm
call: **4** barr **7** trumpet
dentin: **5** ivory
driver: **6** mahout
ear: **4** taro

enclosure: 5 kraal
extinct: 8 mastodon
famous: 5 Babar, Dumbo
female: cow
goad: 5 ankus
group: 4 herd
male: 4 bull
maverick: 5 rogue
pert. to: 11 pachydermic
seat: 6 howdah
trap: 6 keddah
trappings for: 5 jhool
trunk: 9 proboscis
tusk: 5 ivory 9 scrivello

elephant boy: 4 Sabu
elephantine: 4 huge 6 clumsy 8 colossal, enormous, gigantic, ungainly 9 ponderous
goddess: 4 Sati
elevate: 4 lift, rear, rise 5 elate, erect, exalt, extol, heave, hoist, raise, setup, tower 6 uplift 7 advance, dignify, enhance, ennoble, glorify, promote 8 heighten, inspirit 10 exhilarate
elevated: 4 high 5 great, lofty, noble, risen, steep 6 elated, raised 7 boosted, exalted, moved up 8 majestic, towering, uplifted 9 dignified 10 high-minded
elevation: 4 bank, hill, rise 5 mound, ridge 6 ascent, height 8 altitude, eminence, highness, mountain 9 acclivity 10 exaltation, prominence 11 advancement
of mind: 7 anagoge
reference point: 9 benchmark
to sainthood: 12 canonization
elevator: bin 4 cage, lift, silo 5 hoist 9 ascenseur
elf: fay, hob, imp, pug 4 peri, pixy 5 dwarf, fairy, gnome, ouphe, pixie 6 goblin, sprite 7 brownie, incubus, succubi 8 succubus 10 changeling, leprechaun
elfin: 4 tiny 6 impish 7 puckish, tricksy 8 delicate, prankish 9 fairylike
elfwort: 10 elecampane
Elgin marbles: 7 friezes 10 sculptures
Eli: 4 Yale
son: 6 Hophni 8 Phinehas
Elia: 11 Charles Lamb
Eliam's daughter: 9 Bathsheba
Elian: 8 Eretrian
elicit: 4 draw, milk, pump 5 claim, educe, evoke, exact, wrest, wring 6 deduce, demand, entice, extort, induce 7 extract 8 bring out 9 call forth
elide: 4 omit, skip 5 annul 6 ignore 7 nullify 8 slur over, suppress 9 apocopate
eligible: fit 6 proper, worthy 8 suitable 9 available, desirable, qualified 10 acceptable
Elijah: 5 Elias 7 prophet 8 Tishbite

eliminate: 4 drop, kill, oust 5 erase, expel, purge 6 cut out, delete, except, ignore, remove 7 abolish, exclude, silence, weed out 8 get rid of 9 eradicate
Eliot, George: 12 Mary Ann Evans
hero: 6 Marner
heroine: 6 Romola
novel: 8 Adam Bede 11 Middlemarch, Silas Marner 14 Mill on the Floss
Eliot, T.S.: 6 author
work: 9 East Coker, Gerontion, Hollow Men 11 Burnt Norton, Dry Salvages 12 Ash Wednesday, Four Quartets, The Waste Land 13 Little Gidding, The Sacred Wood
Elisha: *father:* 7 Shaphat
home: 11 Abelmeholah
servant: 6 Gehazi
elision mark: 10 apostrophe
Elissa: See Dido
elite: 4 best 6 choice, flower, gentry, select 7 quality, society 9 haut monde, top drawer 10 blue bloods, uppercrust 11 aristocracy 12 quintessence
gathering: 6 galaxy
elixir: 6 potion, spirit 7 arcanum, cordial, cure-all, nostrum, panacea
of life: 6 amrita 7 amreeta
Elizabeth I: 4 Bess 5 Tudor 6 Oriana
mother: 6 Boleyn
elk: 4 deer 5 eland, moose 6 sambar, wapiti
genus of: 5 Alces
ell: 4 wing 5 annex 8 addition 9 extension
ellipse: 4 oval
elliptical: 4 oval 5 ovate 7 concise 8 abridged, cut short 10 contracted
elm: *family of:* 8 Ulmaceae
fruit of: 6 samara
rock: 5 wahoo
elocute: 7 declaim
elocution: 7 oratory 9 eloquence
elocutionist: 6 reader 7 reciter, speaker
eloge: 6 eulogy 7 oration 8 encomium 9 panegyric
elongate: 6 extend 7 draw out, stretch 8 lengthen, protract
elongated: 4 lank 6 linear 7 prolate, slender 9 stretched, strung out
elope: 4 flee 6 decamp 7 run away
eloquence: 7 fluency, oratory 8 rhetoric 9 elocution, facundity, loftiness
eloquent: 5 vivid 6 fervid, moving, poetic 8 stirring 10 expressive, meaningful, oratorical, persuasive 11 impassioned
else: 4 more 5 other 7 besides, further, instead 9 otherwise 10 additional
elsewhere: 4 away 7 not here 12 another place
elucidate: 5 clear 7 clarify, explain 8 simplify,

spell out **9** interpret **10** illustrate

elude: **4** duck, flee, foil **5** avoid, dodge, evade **6** baffle, befool, delude, escape **7** beguile, deceive **9** frustrate

elusive: **4** eely **5** cagey **6** subtle, tricky **7** evasive **8** baffling **10** impalpable, lubricious **11** hard to grasp

elute: **5** rinse **7** cleanse, soak out **8** dissolve **10** use solvent

elver: eel

Elysian: **8** beatific, blissful **10** delightful

Elysium: **4** Eden **8** Paradise

elytrum of beetle: **4** wing **5** shard

emaciated: **4** lean, thin **5** gaunt **6** peaked, skinny, wasted **7** scrawny, wizened **8** starving, underfed **10** cadaverous

emanate: **4** flow **5** arise, issue **6** effuse **7** breathe, give off, proceed, radiate **8** stem from **9** come forth, originate

emanation: **4** aura **5** radon **6** efflux **7** outcome **8** emission **9** ectoplasm, effluence **10** exhalation **11** consequence

emancipate: **4** free **5** loose **6** unbind **7** manumit, release **8** liberate, unfetter **11** enfranchise

emancipator: **5** freer, Moses **7** Lincoln **9** deliverer

emasculate: **4** geld **6** soften, weaken **8** castrate, enervate **10** devitalize **12** make impotent

embalm: **7** mummify, perfume **8** preserve

embankment: **4** bund, dike, fill, quay **5** digue, levee, mound, revet **6** staith **7** backing **9** banquette

embargo: ban **5** edict, order **8** blockade, stoppage **9** restraint **10** impediment, inhibition **11** prohibition, restriction

embark: **5** begin, board, start **6** take up **7** enter on **8** commence, engage in **11** venture upon

embarras de richesses (F.): **13** overabundance

embarrass: **4** faze **5** abash, annoy, shame, upset **6** hamper, hinder, impede **7** confuse, flummox, nonplus **8** bewilder, confound, dumfound, encumber, entangle, handicap, obstruct, straiten **9** discomfit, dumbfound **10** complicate, disconcert

embarrassment: fix **5** shame **6** unease **7** chagrin **8** distress **9** confusion **10** discomfort, perplexity **11** humiliation **12** bewilderment, discomposure, entanglement **13** inconvenience, mortification

embassy: **5** envoy **7** mission **8** legation **10** ambassador **13** foreign office

embattled: **8** fighting **9** embroiled, fortified **10** crenelated **11** hardpressed

embattlement: **7** parapet

embay: **7** shelter **8** encircle, surround

embed: **5** infix, inlay, set in **7** implant, ingrain **8** entrench

embellish: **4** deck, gild, trim **5** add to, adorn, dress, grace **6** bedeck, blazon, emboss, enrich, flower **7** apparel, bedrape, garnish, magnify **8** beautify, decorate, ornament **9** elaborate, embroider **10** exaggerate

embellished: **6** florid, gested, ornate

ember: ash **4** coal, slag **6** cinder **7** clinker

embezzle: **4** rook **5** steal **6** thieve **7** defraud, swindle **8** peculate **11** appropriate

embitter: **4** sour **7** acidify, envenom **8** acerbate **9** acidulate **10** exacerbate, exasperate

emblaze: **5** adorn, honor **6** kindle **9** embellish

emblazon: **4** laud **5** adorn, extol **7** deck out, display, exhibit, glorify **9** celebrate

emblem: bar **4** mace, orle, sign, star, type **5** badge, crest, image, token **6** device, figure, shield, symbol **7** scepter **8** allegory, colophon, insignia **9** character **10** coat of arms, escutcheon
of authority: **4** mace
of Christianity: **5** cross
of clan: **5** totem
of Islam: **8** crescent
of Judaism: **11** Star of David
of U.S.: **5** eagle

emblematic: **7** typical **8** symbolic **10** figurative

emblic: **4** aula **5** aulae (pl.)

embodiment: map **6** avatar **7** epitome **11** incarnation **15** personification
of Ptah: **4** Apis

embody: **4** fuse **5** blend, merge, unite **6** mirror, take in, typify **7** contain, embrace, include **8** coalesce, organize **9** incarnate, personify, represent **10** comprehend **11** incorporate

embolden: **4** abet **5** brave, nerve **6** assure, buck up **7** bolster, hearten, inspire, support **9** encourage, enhearten

embolism: **8** stoppage **9** occlusion **11** obstruction **13** intercalation

embolus: **4** clot

embosom: **6** foster **7** cherish, embrace, enclose, shelter **8** surround

emboss: **5** adorn, chase **6** indent **8** ornament **9** embellish, embroider **10** do in relief

embossing: **8** celature

embouchure: **10** mouthpiece, river mouth

embowed: **6** arched **7** vaulted

embower: **7** enclose **9** shelter in

embrace: hug **4** clip, fold, love, neck, side **5** adopt, bosom, chain, clasp, cling, enarm, grasp **6** accept, caress, clinch, comply, cradle, cuddle, embody, enfold, huddle, inclip, infold, plight **7** cherish, contain, enclose, espouse, include, involve, welcome **8** comprise, encircle **9** encompass **10** comprehend **11** incorporate

embrangle: **7** confuse, perplex

embrocation: **6** arnica **8** liniment

embroider: tat **4** lace **5** couch, panel **6** emboss, frieze, pad out, stitch **7** build up **8** ornament **9** elaborate, embellish **10** exaggerate

embroidery: **4** lace **6** bonnaz, edging, hedebo **7** orphrey **8** arrasene **10** needlework
figure: **6** etoile
frame: **7** taboret
hole: **6** eyelet
machine-made: **6** bonnaz
thread: **5** floss

embroil: **5** mix up **6** muddle **7** confuse, involve **8** distract, entangle **9** commingle, implicate **12** get in trouble

embroilment: **4** spat, tiff **5** fight **6** fracas **7** dispute, quarrel **8** argument, squabble **11** altercation

embrown: tan **6** darken

embryo: **4** germ, seed **5** fetus, ovule **6** foetus **9** peritroch
young: **8** blastula

emcee: **4** host **8** director **9** moderator **10** run the show

eme (Sc.): **5** uncle **6** friend **8** relative

emeer: See **emir**

emend: **4** edit **5** alter **6** better, reform, repeal, revise **7** correct, improve, rectify, redress

emendator: **6** editor

emerald: gem **5** beryl, green **7** smaragd

Emerald Isle: **4** Eire, Erin **7** Ireland

emerge: **4** loom, rise **5** issue **6** appear, evolve **7** develop **9** come forth **10** come in view **11** materialize

emergence: **4** need **8** debouche, exigence **9** outgrowth **10** occurrence

emergency: fix **5** pinch **6** crises (pl.), crisis, crunch, strait **8** exigency, juncture **11** contingency
money: **5** scrip **8** reserves
signal: SOS **5** flare, siren

emergent: **6** rising

Emerson: *friend:* **7** Thoreau
philosophy: **17** transcendentalism
work: **5** essay **6** Brahma, Merlin **8** Threnody **12** Self-Reliance

emery: **8** abrasive, corundum **11** carborundum

emetic holly: **6** yaupon

emeute: **4** riot **6** tumult **8** outbreak, uprising

emigrant: **7** exodist, settler **8** colonist, stranger

emigre: **5** alien, exile **7** evacuee, refugee **10** expatriate

eminence: **4** hill, note, rank, rise **5** knoll **6** ascent, esteem, height, renown, repute **8** standing **9** elevation, loftiness **10** projection, promontory **11** distinction

eminent: big **4** high **5** great, lofty, noble, noted **6** famous, marked, signal **8** glorious, renowned, singular, towering **9** egregious **10** celebrated, noteworthy **11** conspicuous, illustrious, outstanding **13** distinguished

emir, emeer: **5** noble, ruler, title **6** leader, prince **8** governor **9** chieftain, commander
province: **7** emirate

emissary: spy **5** agent, envoy, scout **6** deputy, legate **7** courier **8** delegate **14** representative

emission: **4** flow **8** ejection, issuance **9** discharge, radiation

emissive: **8** exhalant

emit: **4** beam, cast, give, pour, send, shed, vent **5** eject, exude, fling, issue, utter **6** exhale, expire, let out **7** give off, radiate, release **8** throw off, transmit **9** discharge **10** disembogue
heat: **4** glow
light: **4** glow **9** luminesce
offensive odors: **4** reek

emmer: **5** spelt, wheat

emmet: ant **7** pismire **8** formicid

emolliate: **6** soften, weaken

emollient: **4** balm **5** salve **6** lotion **8** lenitive, ointment, soothing

emolument: **4** fees **5** wages **6** income, profit, salary **7** benefit, stipend **9** advantage **12** compensation

emote: act, mug **4** gush, rant **7** ham it up, overact **12** be theatrical

emotion: ire, joy **4** fear, hate, love **5** agony, anger, grief, heart **6** relief, sorrow **7** ecstasy, feeling, passion **8** jealousy, movement, surprise **9** affection, agitation, sensation, sentiment **11** disturbance, sensibility **14** susceptibility
without: **9** apathetic

emotional: **6** moving **8** stirring, touching **9** rhapsodic, sensitive **10** hysterical, passionate, responsive

emotionless: **4** cold **5** staid **6** frigid, torpid **7** deadpan, distant **8** reserved **9** apathetic, impassive, unfeeling **11** coldblooded

empathy: **4** pity, ruth **6** accord **7** rapport **8** affinity, sympathy **13** understanding

emperor: **4** czar, king, tsar, tzar **5** ruler **6** caesar, kaiser, sultan **7** monarch **9** imperator, sovereign

emphasis: **5** focus **6** accent, stress, weight **8** salience

emphasize: **6** play up **7** dwell on, feature **8** pinpoint, point out **9** highlight, punctuate **10** accentuate, underscore

emphatic: 7 certain, decided, earnest, marcato 8 absolute, decisive, definite, distinct, enfatico, forcible, positive 9 energetic

empire: 4 rule, sway 5 power, realm, reign, state 6 domain 7 control, kingdom 8 dominion 11 sovereignty

Empire State: 7 New York

empirical: 7 factual 12 experimental 13 observational, trial-and-error

emplacement: 7 battery 8 platform

employ: use 4 hire 5 apply 6 bestow, engage, occupy, retain, supply, take on 7 concern, enclose, involve, service, utilize 8 exercise

employed: 4 busy 6 unidle 7 engaged, working

employee: 4 hand, help 6 worker 8 hireling 9 jobholder 10 wage earner
bank: 5 clerk, guard 6 teller 7 cashier 8 watchman 10 bookkeeper
minor: cog 6 helper, minion 7 servant 9 assistant, underling
slaughterhouse: 5 sider

employer: 4 boss, user 6 gaffer 7 manager 12 entrepreneur

employment: job, use 4 task, toil, work 5 craft, trade, usage 7 calling, purpose 8 business, vocation 10 engagement, occupation, profession

empoison: 7 envenom 10 make bitter

emporium: 4 mart, shop 5 bazar, store 6 bazaar, market

empower: 6 enable 7 entitle, license 8 accredit, delegate, deputize, sanction 9 authorize 10 commission

empress: 5 queen, ruler
Austrian: 12 Maria Theresa
Byzantine: 5 Irene 7 Endocia 8 Theodora
French: 7 Eugenie 9 Josephine
of India: 8 Victoria
Russian: 4 Anna 7 czarina, tsarina, tzarina 9 Catherine, Elizabeth

empress tree: 9 paulownia

emptiness: 4 void 6 hunger, vacuum 7 inanity, vacancy, vacuity

empty: rid 4 bare, dump, free, idle, pour, toom (Sc.), void 5 blank, drain, expel 6 barren, devoid, hollow, unload, vacant, vacate 7 deplete, exhaust, untaken 8 disgorge, evacuate, unfilled 9 discharge 10 unburdened, unoccupied

empty-headed: 5 silly, vapid 6 jejune, simple, stupid 7 fatuous, moronic, witless 8 ignorant 11 bird-brained

Empusa: 7 specter 9 hobgoblin

empyreal: 7 sublime 9 celestial

empyrean: 5 ether 7 heavens 9 firmament

emu: 4 rhea 6 ratite 9 cassowary
relative: 7 ostrich

emulate: ape, vie 4 copy 5 equal, excel, rival 7 compete, imitate

emulation: 6 strife 7 contest 10 contention 11 competition

emulsive: 9 softening

emyd: 6 turtle

enable: let 5 allow 6 permit 7 empower, entitle, qualify 9 authorize 12 make possible

enact: 4 pass 6 decree, effect, ordain 7 actuate, appoint, execute, perform, portray 9 legislate, personate, represent 10 bring about, constitute

enactment: law 6 assize, decree 7 passage, statute 9 ordinance 14 representation

enamel: 5 glaze, gloss, paint 6 aumail 7 dentine, schmelz 8 cosmetic, schmelze

enameled: 6 inlaid 10 variegated

enamored: 6 soft on 7 charmed, smitten 9 bewitched, entranced 10 captivated, crazy about, fascinated, in love with, infatuated

Enan's son: 5 Ahira

en bloc: 5 as one 8 as a whole 11 all together

en brochette: 8 skewered

encamp: 4 tent 5 lodge 7 bivouac

encase: box 5 cover 7 inclose

enceinte: 8 pregnant 9 expectant, with child

enchain: 4 bind 5 tie up 6 fetter

enchant: 5 charm 6 delude 7 bewitch, delight 8 ensorcel, enthrall 9 captivate, enrapture, fascinate, hypnotize, mesmerize, spellbind

enchantment: hex 5 charm, magic, spell 7 gramary, sorcery 8 gramarye, wizardry 10 necromancy, witchcraft 11 fascination, incantation

enchantress: hag 5 Circe, fairy, Medea, siren, witch 9 sorceress 11 Morgan le Fay

encharge: 7 entrust 10 commission

enchase: 5 inlay 7 engrave 8 decorate, ornament

enchiridion: 6 manual 8 handbook

enchorial: 6 native 7 demotic 8 domestic 11 of the people

encina: oak

encipher: 4 code

encircle: 4 band, belt, gird, girt, ring 5 embay, embow, hem in, inorb, orbit 6 emball, engirt, enlace, girdle 7 embrace, enclose, environ, wreathe 8 cincture, ensphere, surround 9 encompass, loop about 10 wrap around 12 circumscribe 13 circumference

encircling band: 4 halo, ring, zone 6 choker 8 bracelet, necklace

enclose: box, hem, mew, pen, rim 4 cage, gird, pale 5 bound, bower, fence, hedge, house 6 circle, corral, encase, encyst, enfold, enlock, enwrap, picket, pocket, shut in 7 contain, embosom, embrace, envelop, harness **8** comprise, conclude, encircle, imprison, palisade, surround **9** encompass, put inside **12** circumscribe

enclosure: haw, mew, pen, sty **4** bawn, cage, cell, coop, cote, fold, wall, weir, yair, yard **5** atajo, booly, court, crawl, fence, kraal, pound, stall **6** aviary, corral, cowpen, garden, hurdle, kennel, paling, prison, runway **7** paddock **8** cincture, cloister, sepiment, stockade **9** cofferdam **10** quadrangle

encomiast: **8** eulogist **10** panegyrist

encomium: **5** eloge **6** eulogy, praise **7** plaudit, tribute **8** accolade, citation **9** panegyric **10** compliment, salutation **12** commendation

encompass: **4** be-go, belt, clip, gird, ring, wall **5** belie, beset **6** begird, circle, embody, engird, take in **7** contain, embrace, enclose, environ, include **8** comprise, encircle, engirdle, surround **9** beleaguer, circulate **10** circumvent **12** circumscribe

encore: bis **5** again **6** recall, repeat **10** repetition
anti: boo **4** hiss **7** catcall

encounter: **4** bout, espy, face, meet **5** brush, fight, force, incur, onset, run-in **6** accost, affray, assail, attack, battle, breast, combat, oppose **7** address, affront, contest, dispute, hosting, run into **8** come upon, conflict, confront, skirmish **9** collision, forgather, interview **10** engagement, foregather, occurrence, tournament
courageously: **5** beard, brave **7** weather
group: **12** therapy sit-in **13** confrontation

encourage: **4** abet, back **5** boost, cheer, egg on, impel, nerve **6** advise, assure, buck up, exhort, foment, foster, incite, induce, second, uphold **7** advance, animate, cherish, comfort, confirm, console, enliven, forward, further, hearten, inspire, promote, support, sustain **8** embolden, inspirit, reassure **9** instigate, stimulate **10** give hope to, strengthen **11** countenance

encouragement: **4** lift, push **5** boost **6** praise **7** support **8** approval **9** incentive, patronage **12** pat on the back

encouraging: **4** good, rosy **6** likely **7** helping, hopeful **9** favorable, promising **11** comfortable, inspiriting **12** advantageous

encroach: **5** poach **6** invade **7** impinge, intrude, presume **8** entrench, infringe, overstep, trespass

encroachment: **6** inroad **9** intrusion **10** aggression, infraction

encuirassed: **7** armored **8** loricate

encumber: tax **4** clog, load **5** beset, check **6** burden, hamper, hinder, impede, retard, saddle **7** involve, oppress **8** entangle, handicap, obstruct, overcome, overload, slow down **9** embarrass, weigh down **10** overburden

encumbrance: **4** clog, lien, load **5** claim **6** burden, charge **7** trouble **8** handicap, hardship, mortgage **9** albatross **10** impediment **13** embarrassment, inconvenience

encyclic: **8** circular **13** comprehensive

encyclopedic: **7** erudite **8** complete **9** extensive, scholarly **10** exhaustive **11** wide-ranging **12** all-inclusive **13** comprehensive

end: aim, tip **4** fate, goal, heel, stop, tail **5** amend, cease, close, death, ensue, finis, issue, limit, napoo, omega, raise, scrap, stash **6** define, design, expire, finale, finish, napooh, object, period, upshot, windup **7** abolish, achieve, closure, destroy, lineman, purpose, remnant **8** boundary, complete, conclude, dissolve, finality, surcease, terminal, terminus **9** cessation, determine, extremity, intention, objective, terminate **10** completion, conclusion, denouement, expiration **11** consequence, destruction, discontinue, termination **12** consummation **14** accomplishment
loose: tag **6** thread
musical: **4** coda, fine
on: **7** upright **8** vertical
remove: tip **4** clip
tending to: **5** telic
upper: tip **4** apex, head

end-all: **6** killer **7** quietus **8** clincher **9** last straw **11** coup de grace

endanger: **4** risk **6** hazard, menace **7** imperil **10** compromise, jeopardize

endearing: **5** sweet **7** lovable

endearment: **6** caress **9** sweet talk **10** loving word
term of: hon, pet **4** dear **5** angel, honey, lover, sugar **7** darling, sweetie **8** baby doll, precious **10** sweetheart

endeavor: aim, job, try **4** best, seek, work **5** assay, essay, exert, labor, study, trial **6** affair, effort, strife, strive **7** afforce, attempt **8** exertion, interest, struggle **9** undertake **10** enterprise

ended: **4** done, over, past **8** finished

endemic: **5** local

endive: **7** chicory, witloof **8** escarole

endless: **7** eternal, forever, undying **8** immortal, infinite **9** boundless, ceaseless, continual, incessant, perpetual, unceasing **10** continuous **11** everlasting, measureless **12** interminable **13** uninterrupted

endlong: **10** lengthwise **14** longitudinally

endmost: **4** last **8** farthest, remotest

End of World: **8** doomsday **10** Armageddon **15** Gotterdammerung

endorse: **4** back, okay, sign **5** boost **6** second

7 approve, certify, indorse, stand by, support **8** advocate, sanction, vouch for **9** authorize, guarantee **11** countenance

endorsement: 4 fiat, visa **5** rider **7** backing **8** approval, sanction **9** signature

endow: 4 fund, give, will **5** award, bless, endue, equip, found, grace, grant, leave **6** clothe, enrich, invest, supply **7** furnish, provide **8** bequeath
with bodily form: **11** materialize
with power: **8** energize

endowment: 4 gift **5** dower, dowry **6** talent **7** ability, chantry **8** appanage, dotation **9** mentality **10** foundation

end result: 7 outcome, product

endue: 5 endow, teach **6** clothe, invest **8** instruct

endurable: 7 livable **8** bearable **9** tolerable **10** sufferable **11** supportable

endurance: 5 pluck **7** stamina **8** gameness, patience, strength, tenacity **9** fortitude, hardihood, suffering **10** resolution **11** continuance, persistence, resignation **12** perseverance

endure: 4 bear, bide, last, live, wear **5** abide, allow, brook, stand **6** drudge, harden, remain, suffer **7** comfort, forbear, persist, prevail, sustain, toughen, undergo, weather **8** continue, forebear, tolerate **9** withstand **10** strengthen **11** bear up under

endured: 5 borne

enduring: 4 fast **6** biding **7** durable, eternal, lasting, staunch **8** immortal **9** continual, perennial, permanent **11** everlasting **12** imperishable

Endymion: *loved by:* **6** Selene
mother: **6** Calyce
son: **7** Aetolus

enemy: fae, foe **4** Axis, feid **5** devil, fiend, Satan **6** foeman **7** hostile **8** opponent **9** adversary, ill-wisher **10** antagonist, backfriend

energetic: 4 fast, hard, spry **5** brisk, peppy **6** active, hearty, lively **7** arduous **8** emphatic, forceful, forcible, full of go, vigorous **9** dynamical, strenuous **10** expressive **11** hardworking **12** enterprising

energize: 7 animate **8** activate **10** invigorate

energumen: 7 fanatic **8** demoniac **10** enthusiast

energy: pep, vim, zip **4** bang, bent, birr, life **5** drive, force, might, nerve, power, steam, vigor **6** effort, intake, output, spirit **7** potency **8** activity, strength, vitality **9** animation
lack: **5** atony **7** inertia **9** lassitude
measuring device: **11** dynamometer
unit: erg **4** dyne **5** joule **7** quantum **8** watt hour **10** horsepower

enervate: sap **6** weaken **7** exhaust, tire out, unnerve **8** enfeeble **10** debilitate, devitalize

enfant terrible: 4 brat **5** devil, scamp, whelp **6** terror **7** hellion **12** trouble-maker

enfeeble: 4 numb **5** drain **6** deaden, impair, soften, weaken **7** deplete **8** enervate **9** attenuate, undermine **10** debilitate

enfilade: 4 rake

enfold: hug **4** wrap **5** clasp, cover **6** cuddle, enlace, enwrap, infold, swathe **7** embrace, enclose, envelop, squeeze **8** encircle, surround

enforce: 5 exact **6** coerce, compel **7** execute, implant **8** carry out, insist on **9** constrain, prosecute **10** administer

enfranchise: 4 free **7** let vote, manumit, release **8** liberate **10** emancipate

engage: 4 book, hire, join, mesh, rent, sign **5** agree, catch, enter, lease, trade **6** absorb, arrest, embark, employ, enlist, induce, oblige, occupy, pledge, take on **7** bespeak, betroth, conduce, engross, involve, promise **8** contract, covenant, entangle, interest, persuade, set about **9** interlock, undertake

engaged: 4 busy **5** hired **6** bonded, meshed **7** assured, earnest, entered, pledged, versant **8** employed, involved, occupied, promised **9** affianced, betrothed

engagement: job **4** aval, date **5** fight **6** affair, battle, escrow **7** booking, contest, meeting **8** skirmish **9** betrothal, encounter **10** attachment, employment **11** appointment, involvement

engager: 6 surety

engaging: 5 sapid **6** taking **7** winning **10** attractive **11** interesting

engender: 5 beget, breed, cause **6** excite **7** develop, produce **8** generate, occasion **9** procreate, propagate

engine: gas **5** motor, steam **7** turbine **8** gasoline **10** locomotive
covering: **4** cowl
kind of: gin, jet, ram **4** goat **5** dinky, mogul **6** diesel, helper, mallet, piston, pusher, rotary, wankel **7** turbine **8** dollbeer **10** locomotive
military: ram **4** tank **6** onager **7** robinet **8** ballista, helepole **9** espringal **11** ribaudequin
part: cam **4** gear, plug, pump **5** choke **6** boiler, piston, stator **8** cylinder, manifold, throttle **9** crankcase **10** carburetor **12** differential, transmission
speed up: rev

engineer: 4 plan **6** driver, manage **7** planner, plotter **8** contrive, designer, inventor, maneuver **9** construct **10** accomplish **11** constructor, superintend

engirdle: 8 surround **9** encompass

engirt: 7 envelop **8** encircle

England: *alcoholic drink:* ale **4** mead **5** stout **6** bitter, porter, squash
city: **5** Leeds **6** Oxford **7** Bristol, Norwick **8** Brighton, Coventry, Plymouth **9** Cambridge, Leicester, Liverpool, Newcastle, Sheffield **10** Birmingham, Manchester, Nottingham, Portsmouth **11** Southampton
dialect: U, RP **4** non-U **7** Cockney **9** Yorkshire **13** Queen's English
dynasty: **4** York **5** Tudor **6** Stuart **7** Hanover, Windsor **9** Lancaster **11** Plantagenet
elevator: **4** lift
export: **4** coal **5** china, steel
fish: **9** Dover sole
gasoline: **6** petrol
holiday: **4** bank **9** Boxing Day **12** Guy Fawke's Day
invader: **4** Celt, Dane, Jute, Pict **5** Angle, Roman, Saxon **6** Norman, Viking
island: Man **5** Wight **6** Scilly
king: **5** Henry, James **6** Alfred, Canute, Edward, George, Harold **7** Charles, Richard, William **8** Ethelred
king, first: **6** Egbert
lake: **10** Windermere
lord protector: **8** Cromwell
measure: ell, pin, rod, ton, tun, vat **4** acre, bind, boll, comb, cran, foot, gill, goad, hand, hide, inch, last, line, mile, once, palm, peek, pint, pipe, pole, pool, rood, sack, span, trug, wist, yard, yoke **5** bodge, carat, chain, coomb, cubit, digit, float, floor, fluid, hutch, minim, perch, point, prime, quart, skein, stack, truss **6** barrel, bovate, bushel, cranne, fathom, firkin, gallon, hobbet, jugrum, league, manent, oxgang, pottle, runlet, strike, sulung, thread, tieree **7** furlong, hobbitt, quarten, quarter, rundlet, spindle, tertian, virgate **8** carucate, chaldron, hogshead, landyard, puncheon, quadrant, standard **9** shaftamt, shaftmont **10** barleycorn, barn gallon, kilderskin, winchester **13** tablespoonful
region: **8** Midlands **9** Cotswolds **11** West Country
religion: **8** Anglican
resort: **8** Brighton **9** Blackpool **12** Lake district
river: Wye **4** Avon, Eden, Ouse, Tees, Tyne **5** Trent, Tweed **6** Humber, Severn, Thames
school: **4** Eton **5** Rugby **6** Harrow, Rodean **7** St. Paul's **11** Gordonstoun **12** Charterhouse
sport: **5** bowls, rugby **7** cricket **11** lawn bowling
strait: **5** Dover
symbol: **8** John Bull
Tower of London guard: **6** yeoman **9** beefeater
truck: **5** lorry
university: **5** Leeds **6** Exeter, London, Oxford **9** Cambridge **10** Manchester
weight: **5** stone

English (see also **England; British**):   **7** British
aborigine: **4** Pict
actor/actress: See **British**
admiral: **6** Nelson, Ramsey, Rodney, Vernon
admirer of: **10** anglophile
air force: RAF
Antarctic explorer: **5** Scott
antenna: **6** aerial
apartment: **4** flat
apple: **6** beefin, biffin, coling, rennet **7** beaufin, costard **8** coccagee **9** guarenden, guarender
apron: **8** barmskin
archbishop: **4** Lang, Laud **6** Becket **7** Cranmer
architect: See **British**
artist: See **British**
bailiff: **5** reeve
bed: **4** doss
biologist: **6** Huxley
boat: **7** coracle
car fender: **4** wing
car hood: **6** bonnet
car trunk: **4** boot
cattle tender: **7** byreman
charity school scholar: **8** blue coat
cheese: **7** cheddar, Stilton, truckle
chinaware: **5** Spode **8** Wedgwood
church caretaker: **6** verger
church officer: **6** beadle
circuit court: **4** eyre
class: **4** form
clergyman: **4** Inge **5** Donne, Oates **6** Becket, Newman **7** Cranmer, Latimer
conductor: **5** Boult **7** Beecham **10** Barbirolli
conservative: **4** Tory
conspirator: **6** Fawkes
court: **4** eyre, leet **5** gemot **6** gemote **8** hustling **9** Old Bailey

cricket field: **5** Lord's **7** the Oval
crown tax: **4** geld
dance: **6** morris
dandy: **4** toff
diarist: **5** Pepys **6** Evelyn
dramatist: See **British**
early conqueror: **5** Horsa **7** Hengist
economist: **4** Mill **6** Angell, Keynes **7** Gresham, Malthus, Ricardo
elevator: **4** lift
emblem: **4** lion
entertainment: **4** busk **7** ridotto
essayist: **4** Elia, Lamb, Lang **5** Bacon **6** Steele **7** Addison
estate: **4** este
explorer: **4** Cook, Ross **5** Cabot, Drake, Scott **6** Hudson
field: **5** croft
food dealer: **12** costermonger
forest: **5** Arden **8** Sherwood
freeman: **5** ceorl, churl
game: **5** darts, rugby **6** soccer **7** cricket, snooker
gasoline: **6** petrol
generator: **6** dynamo
gold: **4** rial, ryal
gun carrier: **4** bren
historian: **4** Bede **5** Acton, Grote **7** Toynbee **8** Macaulay
humorist: **4** Lear
jacket: **4** Eton
jail: **4** gaol, nick
laborer: **5** navvy
land: **5** laine
law: **4** soke **6** esnecy **7** danelaw
lawyer: **7** bencher **9** barrister, solicitor
liberal: **4** Whig
lunch: **6** tiffin
machine gun: **4** Bren, Sten
magistrate: **4** beak
man: **6** Briton **8** John Bull **9** Britisher
molasses: **7** treacle
monk: **4** Beda, Bede **5** Baeda
news agency: **7** Reuters
officer's civilian dress: **5** mufti
old letter: wen **5** thorn
order: **6** Garter
painter: see **British:** *artist*
pamphleteer: **5** Defoe, Swift
Parliament houses: **5** Lords **7** Commons
Parliament proceedings: **7** Hansard
party member: **4** Tory, Whig **7** Liberal **8** Laborite **9** Labourite **12** Conservative
patron saint: **6** George
peasant: **5** churl
pert. to: **8** Anglican **10** Anglo-Saxon
philosopher: **4** Hume **5** Bacon, Locke **6** Hobbes **7** Russell, Spencer **9** Whitehead

pirate: **4** Kidd **5** Drake **6** Morgan **7** Hawkins
policeman: **5** bobby **6** copper, peeler
prairie: **4** moor **5** heath
prime minister: **4** Eden, Grey, Peel, Pitt **5** Bevin, Major **6** Attlee **7** Asquith, Baldwin **8** Disraeli, Thatcher **9** Churchill, Gladstone, MacDonald, Macmillan **11** Chamberlain, Lloyd George
printer: **6** Caxton
prison: **4** gaol
public school: **4** Eton **5** Rugby **6** Harrow **7** Roedean **9** Sandhurst
queen: **4** Anne, Mary **8** Victoria **9** Elizabeth
racing town: **5** Ascot **10** Epsom Downs
rebel: **5** Essex, Tyler **8** Cromwell **10** Washington
resort: **4** Bath **8** Brighton **9** Blackpool
rifle: **7** Enfield
royal house: **4** York **5** Tudor **6** Stuart **7** Hanover, Windsor **9** Lancaster **11** Plantagenet
royal household officer: **7** equerry
royal residence: **7** Windsor
scientist: **6** Darwin, Huxley **7** Boyd-Orr, Hawking
seaman: **5** limey **6** rating
serf: **6** thrall
settler: **4** Jute, Pict **5** Angle, Saxon **6** Norman
sheep: **8** Cotswold
shoemaker: **4** snob
sixpence: **5** sprat
slave: **4** esne
socialist: **6** Fabian
soldier: **5** tommy **7** redcoat **8** fusileer, fusilier
spy: **5** Andre **7** Philbin
stable: **4** mews
statesman: **5** Simon **10** Walsingham
stone monument: **8** cromlech
streetcar: **4** tram
tavern: pub
tea muffin: **5** scone **7** crumpet
theater: **5** Globe **6** Old Vic **8** National **9** Palladium
thicket: **7** spinney
thrush: **5** mavis
title: **4** dame, duke, earl, king, lady, lord, peer **5** baron, noble, queen **6** knight, prince **7** baronet, duchess, marquis **8** baroness, countess, marquess, princess, viscount **11** marchioness, viscountess
tourist: **7** tripper
traitor: **5** Blunt **6** Philby **7** Burgess, Maclean
tribe: **5** Iceni
truck: **5** lorry

tutor: don
uplands: **5** downs
windshield: **10** wind screen
wrench: **7** spanner

engorge: 4 glut **5** gorge **6** devour

engrave: cut **4** etch **5** carve, chase, print, sculp **6** chisel, incise **7** enchase, impress, imprint, stipple **8** inscribe, ornament **9** character, sculpture
by dots: **7** stipple

engraver: 6 chaser, etcher **7** artisan **13** siderographer
notable: **5** Durer **7** Hogarth
tool of: **5** burin

engraving: *instrument:* **6** stylet
pert. to: **7** glyphic, glyptic
wax: **8** intaglio **9** cerograph, xylograph **11** glyptograph

engross: 4 bury, grip, hold **6** absorb, engage, occupy **7** immerse **8** enthrall **9** fascinate, overwhelm, preoccupy

engrossed: 4 rapt **6** intent

engrosser: 7 copyist **12** calligrapher

engulf: 5 flood, swamp, whelm **6** deluge, devour **7** swallow **8** inundate, submerge **9** overwhelm

enhance: 4 lift **5** enarm, exalt, raise **6** deepen **7** augment, elevate, enlarge, greaten, improve, sharpen **8** heighten, increase **9** aggravate, intensify **10** exaggerate

enhearten: 8 embolden

enigma: 5 rebus **6** puzzle, riddle, sphinx **7** mystery, problem **9** conundrum

enigmatic: 6 mystic **7** cryptic, elusive, obscure **8** baffling, mystical, puzzling **9** equivocal **12** inexplicable

enisle: 6 cut off **7** isolate **8** separate

enisled: 5 alone, apart **8** solitary

enjoin: bid **5** order **6** charge, decree, forbid **7** command, dictate, require **8** admonish, prohibit

enjoy: own **4** have, like **5** eat up, fancy, savor **7** command, possess **10** appreciate **11** think well of

enjoyment: fun, use **4** ease, zest **5** gusto **6** liking, relish **7** delight **8** felicity, pleasure **9** happiness **11** delectation **12** satisfaction **13** gratification

enkindle: 5 light **6** arouse, excite, ignite, stir up **7** incense, inflame **9** set on fire

enlace: tie **5** twine, twist, weave **6** enfold **7** entwine **8** encircle, entangle **10** interweave

enlarge: add, eke (Sc.) **4** grow, huff, ream **5** add to, swell, widen **6** broach, dilate, expand, extend, spread **7** amplify, augment, broaden, build up, develop, distend, enhance, greaten, magnify, stretch **8** increase, lengthen **9** elaborate, expatiate,

intumesce **10** aggrandize, exaggerate, make bigger

enlarged: 8 varicose

enlargement: 6 growth **8** addition, swelling **9** accretion, expansion, inflation **13** magnification

enlarging gradually: 5 evase

enlighten: 5 edify, teach **6** inform **7** apprise, educate **8** acquaint, instruct **9** irradiate **10** illuminate **11** disillusion

enlightened person: 10 illuminato **11** bodhisattva

enlightenment: 5 bodhi **6** wisdom

enlist: 4 join **5** enter **6** embark, engage, enroll, induct, sign up **7** impress, recruit **8** register **9** volunteer

enlisted man: GI

enlistment: 4 tour **5** hitch **11** service time

enliven: 4 warm **5** cheer, pep up, rouse **6** revive **7** animate, comfort, inspire, refresh **8** brighten, inspirit **9** encourage, stimulate **10** exhilarate, invigorate

enlivening: 5 vital **6** genial **9** sprightly

enlock: 7 enclose

en masse: 5 as one **8** as a whole, in a group **11** all together

enmesh: 4 trap **5** catch **7** ensnare **8** entangle

enmity: 5 spite **6** hatred, malice, rancor **7** dislike, ill will **8** aversion, bad blood **9** animosity, antipathy, hostility **10** antagonism, repugnance, resentment **11** malevolence

ennead: 4 nine **8** ninefold

ennoble: 5 exalt, honor, raise **6** uplift **7** dignify, elevate, glorify

ennui: 6 apathy, tedium **7** boredom, languor **8** doldrums **9** lassitude, weariness **12** indifference, listlessness

Enoch: *father:* **4** Cain **5** Jared
son: **4** Irad **10** Methuselah

enormous: big **4** huge, vast **5** great, large **6** heroic, mighty **7** immense, mammoth, massive **8** abnormal, colossal, gigantic **9** excessive, monstrous **10** gargantuan, prodigious, stupendous, tremendous **11** elephantine

Enos: *father:* **4** Seth
grandfather: **4** Adam
grandmother: Eve
uncle: **4** Abel, Cain

enough: 4 enow **5** ample, basta **6** fairly, plenty **8** adequate, passably **9** tolerably **10** sufficient **12** satisfactory

enounce: say **5** state, utter **8** proclaim **9** enunciate

enrage: 5 anger **6** grieve, madden **7** incense, inflame **9** infuriate **10** exasperate

enraged: 5 irate **7** berserk **8** choleric, maddened, wrathful

enrapture: 5 charm **6** ravish, thrill **7** beguile,

bewitch, delight, enchant **8** enravish, enthrall, entrance **9** captivate, fascinate, transport

enrich: 5 adorn, endow **6** fatten **7** enhance, fortify, improve **8** decorate, ornament **9** embellish, fertilize **10** make better **11** add vitamins

enrobe: 6 attire, clothe

enroll, enrol: 4 join, list **5** enter, write **6** enfold, enlist, induct, record, sign up **7** impanel, recruit **8** inscribe, register **11** matriculate

enroot: 7 implant

en route: 8 on the way **9** in transit

ens: 5 being **6** entity **9** existence

ensconce: 4 hide **5** cover **6** settle **7** conceal, shelter **9** establish **11** place snugly

enscribe: See **inscribe**

ensemble: 4 cast **5** decor, getup, whole **6** outfit, troupe **7** company, costume **9** aggregate **11** combination

enshrine: 7 cherish **10** hold sacred

enshroud: 4 hide, veil, wrap **5** cloak **7** conceal, obscure **8** envelope

ensiform: 6 ensate **7** xiphoid

ensign: 4 flag, sign **5** badge **6** banner, signal, symbol **7** officer, pennant **8** gonfalon, standard **9** oriflamme
  of Othello: **4** Iago
  of sovereignty: **7** regalia
  papal: **8** gonfalon

ensilage: 4 feed **6** fodder

enslave: 5 chain **7** shackle **8** enthrall **9** subjugate

enslavement: 7 bondage, serfdom **9** addiction, servitude, thralldom

ensnare: net, web **4** mesh, trap **5** benet, catch, noose, snarl **6** allure, enmesh, entoil, entrap **7** beguile, springe **8** entangle **10** intertwine

ensorcell, ensorcel: 5 charm **7** bewitch, enchant **9** fascinate

ensoul, insoul: 7 animate

ensuing: 4 next **9** following, resulting **10** subsequent, succeeding

ensure: 5 guard **6** clinch, secure **7** protect, warrant **8** make safe **9** guarantee

entad: 6 inward
  opposite of: **5** ectad

entail: 6 demand, impose **7** call for, include, involve, require **11** necessitate

ental: 5 inner
  opposite of: **5** ectal

entangle: 4 knot, mesh, mire, trap **5** catch, ravel, snafu, snare **6** engage, enlace, enmesh, entrap, foul up, muddle, puzzle **7** confuse, embroil, ensnarl, involve, perplex **8** bewilder, encumber **9** embarrass, implicate **10** intertwine, interweave

entangled: 7 complex **9** intricate, twisted up **10** interwoven **11** complicated

entanglement: web **4** knot **6** affair **7** liaison **8** obstacle **13** embarrassment

entellus: 6 monkey **7** hanuman

entente: 6 treaty **8** alliance **9** agreement, coalition **13** understanding

enter: 4 join, post **5** admit, share **6** appear, arrive, engage, enlist, enroll, entrer (F.), pierce, record **7** get into, intrude **8** initiate, inscribe, register **9** introduce, penetrate, sign up for **11** matriculate
  into: **8** take part **11** participate
  militarily: **6** invade
  upon: **5** begin **6** embark

enteric: 10 intestinal

enterprise: job **4** firm, push, task, zeal **5** drive, essay, vigor **6** action, effort, spirit **7** attempt, project, venture **8** business, endeavor, gumption **9** adventure, operation **10** initiative, management **11** undertaking

enterpriser: 12 entrepreneur

enterprising: 4 bold **5** alert **6** active, daring **7** driving **8** hustling **9** ambitious, energetic, wide-awake **10** aggressive, courageous **11** hardworking, industrious, progressive

entertain: 5 amuse, treat **6** divert, harbor, regale **7** beguile, cherish **8** consider, interest, play host **10** think about **11** contemplate

entertainer: 4 host, mime **5** actor, comic **6** amuser, dancer, singer **7** actress, hostess, regaler, showman, speaker, trouper **8** comedian, magician, minstrel **9** performer, soubrette (F.) **10** comedienne, songstress **11** pantomimist

entertainment: fun **4** fair, fete, gala, play **5** cheer, feast, opera, revue, sport, treat **6** kermis, shivvo **7** banquet, ceilidh (Ir.), concert, pastime, ridotto **8** function, musicale **9** amusement, diversion, enjoyment, festivity, reception **10** recreation

enthrall: 4 grip **5** charm **6** absorb **7** engross, enslave **8** intrigue **9** captivate, fascinate, spellbind

enthrone: 5 crown, exalt

enthusiasm: 4 elan, fire, zeal, zest **5** ardor, mania, verve **6** fervor, spirit **7** ardency, passion **9** animation, eagerness **10** ebullience, fanaticism

enthusiast: bug, fan, nut **4** buff **5** freak, lover **6** addict, maniac, rooter, zealot **7** devotee, fanatic **8** follower **9** supporter **10** aficionado

enthusiastic: 4 keen **5** rabid **6** ardent, gung ho **8** hipped on **10** forthgoing

enthymeme: 8 argument **9** syllogism

entice: 4 bait, coax, draw, lure, tole, wile **5** charm, decoy, tempt **6** allure, cajole, incite, induce, invite, seduce **7** attract, bewitch, wheedle **8** inveigle, persuade

entire: all **4** full **5** every, gross, sound, total, utter, whole **6** choate, intact **7** perfect, plenary **8** absolute, complete, integral, unbroken **9** undivided **10** unimpaired **11** unqualified **12** all-inclusive, undiminished

entirely: **4** only **5** alone, quite **6** solely, wholly **7** utterly **10** altogether, thoroughly **11** exclusively

entitle: dub **4** call, name, term **5** allow **6** enable, permit **7** empower, qualify **8** nominate **9** authorize, designate **10** denominate **12** characterize, make eligible

entity: ens **4** body, unit **5** being, thing **7** essence, integer **9** existence, structure **10** individual

entomb: **4** bury **5** inter, inurn **6** inhume

entourage: **5** court, staff, train **7** retinue **9** following, retainers **10** associates, attendants, sycophants

entracte: **8** interval **9** interlude **12** intermission

entrails: **6** vitals **7** giblets, innards, insides, viscera

entrain: **5** board

entrance: **4** adit, boca (Sp.), door, gate, hall **5** charm, debut, entry, foyer, mouth, stulm, toran, way in **6** access, atrium (L.), entree, portal, ravish, zaguan **7** delight, gateway, hallway, ingress, postern **9** admission, beginning, enrapture, fascinate, incursion, induction, overpower, threshold, vestibule **10** admittance, appearance **12** introduction

entranced: **4** rapt **8** ecstatic **10** mesmerized

entrant: **7** starter **8** beginner **10** competitor, contestant **11** participant

entrap: bag, net **5** catch, decoy, snare **6** allure, ambush, taigle (Sc.), trepan **7** beguile **8** entangle, inveigle

entre (F.): **7** between

entreat: ask, beg, bid, sue **4** pray, seek, urge **5** crave, plead **6** adjure, appeal, exhort, invoke **7** beseech, conjure, implore, prevail, request, solicit **8** persuade, petition **9** impetrate, importune **10** supplicate

entreaty: **4** plea, suit **8** petition **9** treatment **11** importunity, negotiation

entree: **5** entry **6** access **8** entrance **9** admission **10** acceptance, main course, permission

entrench, intrench: fix, set **5** dig in, embed **6** anchor, invade **7** implant **8** encroach, infringe, trespass **9** establish

entrenchment: **5** ditch **7** closure, foxhole

entrepot: **5** depot **9** warehouse **10** storehouse

entrepreneur: **7** manager **8** employer, operator **10** impresario **11** enterpriser

entresol: **9** mezzanine

entrust: **4** give **6** assign, commit **7** address, commend, confide, consign, deposit, intrust **8** delegate, encharge, hand over **11** give custody

entry: **4** adit, hall, item, memo, note **5** debit **6** credit, entree, postea, record **7** ingress, passage **8** entrance, notandum, register **9** vestibule **10** adjustment, contestant, enlistment, enrollment

entwine: **4** coil, lace **5** braid, twist, weave **6** enlace **7** wreathe **9** interlace **10** interweave

enumerate: **4** tell **5** add up, count **6** detail, number, recite, reckon, relate **7** compute, itemize, recount, tick off **8** estimate **9** calculate **13** particularize

enumeration: **4** list **5** tally **6** census **7** account, catalog **9** catalogue

enunciate: say **5** state, utter, voice **7** declare, enounce **8** announce, proclaim **9** pronounce **10** articulate

enure: See **inure**

envelop: **4** hide, mask, veil **5** cloak, cover **6** bemist, encase, enfold, engirt, enwrap, invest, muffle, sheath, shroud, swathe **7** blanket, conceal, enclose, environ, obscure **8** surround **9** encompass

envelope: **4** coma, husk, rind **5** shell **6** jacket **7** wrapper **8** covering **10** integument

envenom: **6** poison **7** corrupt, vitiate **8** embitter **12** fill with hate

envious: **7** jealous **8** covetous **9** invidious, resentful **10** begrudging

environ: hem **4** gird **5** limit **6** girdle **7** envelop, inclose **8** encircle, surround **9** encompass **12** circumscribe

environment: **6** medium, milieu **7** climate, element, habitat, setting **8** ambiance, ambience **10** background **12** surroundings

environs: **7** suburbs **8** vicinity **9** outskirts **10** nearby area

envisage: **4** face **8** confront **9** visualize

envision: **5** dream **7** imagine, picture **8** conceive **9** conjure up **11** bring to mind

envoy: **5** agent, envoi (F.) **6** deputy, legate **7** courier **8** emissary **9** messenger **10** ambassador **12** commissioner **14** representative **15** plenipotentiary

envy: **5** covet **6** grudge **8** begrudge, jealousy

enwrap: **4** roll **5** clasp **6** enfold **7** enclose, envelop

enzyme: **6** cytase, lipase, olease, papain, pepsin, rennin, urease **7** adenase, amylase, casease, diatase, erepsin, guanase, inulase, maltase, pectase, pepsine, tannase **8** catalase, cytolist, eraptase, esterase, protease **9** biogenase, deamidase, deaminase, invertase, trehalase **10** amygdalase

leather-making: **7** tannase

opposite of: **5** azyme

eoan: 7 auroral

eolith: 4 celt 5 flint

eon: age 5 epoch 8 eternity

eonic: 4 eral

epee: 4 foil 5 blade, sword

epergne: 5 stand 11 centerpiece

ephah: 7 measure
  one-tenth: 4 omer
  ten: 5 homer

ephelis: 7 freckle

ephemeral: 5 brief, vague 7 passing 8 fleeting 9 temporary, transient 10 evanescent, short-lived, transitory 11 impermanent

Ephialtes' slayer: 6 Apollo 8 Hercules

Ephraim's descendant: 7 Resheph

epi: 6 finial

epic: Cid 4 Edda, epos, saga 5 grand, Iliad, noble 6 Aeneid, epopee, heroic 7 Beowulf, Odyssey 8 epyllion, imposing, majestic, Ramayana 9 narrative 12 Song of Roland

epicarp: 4 husk, rind

epicede: ode

epicedium: ode 4 song 5 dirge, elegy

epicene: 7 sexless, unmanly 10 effeminate

epichoric: 5 local

Epictetus: 5 Stoic 11 philosopher
  birthplace: 10 Hierapolis
  expelled from: 4 Rome
  home: 6 Epirus

epicure: 7 gourmet 8 gourmand 9 bon vivant, epicurean, high liver 10 gastronome, sensualist, voluptuary 11 connoisseur

epicurean: 4 rich 6 lavish 7 Apician, sensual 8 hedonist, Lucullan 9 libertine, luxurious, sybaritic 10 voluptuous

epidemic: 4 rash 6 plague 8 outbreak 10 pestilence, widespread

epiderm appendage: 4 horn

epidermis: 4 skin 7 cuticle

epigram: 4 poem 6 bon mot, saying

epigramatic: 5 terse, witty 7 concise, piquant, pointed

epigraph: 5 motto 7 imprint 9 quotation 11 inscription

epilogue, epilog: 8 appendix, follow-up, postlude 10 conclusion

Epimetheus: *daughter:* 6 Pyrrha
  wife: 7 Pandora

epinard: 7 spinach

Epiphany: 10 Twelfth Day

episcopacy: 9 bishopric

Episcopal parish head: 6 rector

episode: 5 event, scene, story 8 incident 9 happening 10 occurrence

episperm: 5 testa

epistaxis: 9 nosebleed

epistle: 4 note 6 letter 7 message, missive

epitaph: 8 hicjacet 11 inscription

epithet: 4 name, oath, term 5 curse, title 6 insult, phrase 7 agnomen 9 expletive, sobriquet 11 abusive word, appellation

epitome: 5 brief 6 digest, precis, resume 7 summary 8 abstract, synopsis, ultimate 10 abridgment 12 condensation, quintessence

epitomize: 5 sum up 6 embody, typify 8 boil down, compress, condense 9 exemplify, summarize 10 abbreviate

epoch: age, era 4 date, time 5 event 6 period

epochal: 4 eral

epopee: 4 epic, epos

epoptic: 6 mystic, secret

epure: 5 draft 7 diagram, drawing, pattern

equable: 4 calm, even, just 6 placid, serene, smooth, stable, steady 7 regular, uniform 8 constant, tranquil, unvaried 9 easygoing, unruffled

equal: tie 4 cope, egal (F.), even, isos (Gr.), like, meet, peer, same 5 alike, match, rival 7 abreast, compeer, emulate, uniform 8 adequate 9 identical 10 equivalent, tantamount 11 comparative, counterpart 12 commensurate, counterpoise

equal-angled figure: 6 isogon

equality: par 6 equity, parity 7 balance, egality 8 evenness, fairness 12 impartiality
  legal: 7 isonomy

Equality State: 7 Wyoming

equally: 5 alike 6 evenly, justly 8 likewise 9 similarly 10 fifty-fifty

equanimity: 4 cool 5 poise 6 aplomb 7 egality 8 calmness, evenness, serenity 9 composure 11 tranquility

equate: 5 match 7 balance, compare, even out 8 equalize

equatorial: 8 tropical

equestrian: 5 rider 6 jockey 7 vaquero (Sp.) 8 horseman

equidistant: 7 central, halfway

equilibrium: 5 poise 7 balance 9 equipoise

equine: 4 colt, foal, mare 5 filly, horse, steed, zebra

equine water sprite: 5 kelpy 6 kelpie

equip: arm, rig 4 deck, gear, gird, heel 5 array, dress, enarm, endow 6 attire, fit out, outfit 7 apparel, appoint, furnish, prepare, qualify, turn out 8 accouter, accoutre 10 habilitate

equipment: 4 gear 5 goods 6 attire, tackle 7 harness, panoply 8 armament, materiel 10 provisions 12 appointments 13 paraphernalia

equipoise: 7 balance 13 counterweight

equitable: 4 even, fair, just 5 equal, right 6 honest 7 upright 9 impartial, objective, righteous 10 reasonable

equitation: 12 horsemanship

equity: law 7 honesty, justice 8 equality, fairness 9 cash value, rectitude 10 investment 11 uprightness

equivalent: 4 akin, same 5 alike, match 8 of a piece, parallel 9 identical, the same as 10 comparable, synonymous, tantamount

equivocal: 4 hazy 5 vague 7 dubious, obscure 8 doubtful 9 ambiguous, enigmatic, uncertain 10 ambivalent, indecisive 11 problematic 12 questionable, undetermined 13 indeterminate, problematical

equivocate: fib, lie 5 dodge, evade, hedge, parry, shift, stall 6 escape, palter, weasel 7 quibble, shuffle 8 sidestep 9 pussyfoot 10 mince words 11 prevaricate

equivoque: mot, pun 4 quip 9 witticism 11 paronomasia

era: age 4 aeon, date, time 5 epoch, stage 6 period

eradicate: 4 dele, raze 5 erase 6 delete, remove, uproot 7 abolish, destroy, wipe out 8 demolish 9 extirpate 10 annihilate, deracinate 11 exterminate

eral: 7 epochal

erase: 4 blot, dele 5 annul 6 cancel, delete, efface, excise, remove, rub out 7 destroy, expunge, scratch 9 eliminate, eradicate 10 obliterate

ere: 5 prior 6 before 10 rather than, sooner than

Erebus: *parent:* 5 Chaos
  sister: Nox
  son: 6 Charon

erect: 4 make, rear, step 5 build, exalt, put up, raise, set up 6 unbent 7 elevate, upended, upright 8 standing, straight, vertical 9 construct, establish, fabricate, institute 10 upstanding 13 perpendicular

erelong: 4 anon, soon

eremite: 6 hermit 7 ascetic, recluse 8 anchoret 9 anchorite
  hut: 4 cell

Erewhon: 6 utopia
  author: 6 Butler

ergo: 5 hence 9 as a result, therefore

ergot: 6 fungus 12 grain disease

Erin: 4 Eire 7 Ireland 8 Hibernia 9 Innisfail

Erinys: 4 Fury 6 Alecto 7 Megaera 9 Tisiphone

Eriphyle: *brother:* 8 Adrastus
  daughter: 8 Eurydice
  father: 6 Talaus
  son: 7 Alcmeon

Eris: *brother:* 4 Ares
  daughter: Ate
  goddess of: 6 strife 7 discord
  missile: 5 apple

eristic: 12 disputatious 13 controversial

Eritrea: *capital:* 6 Asmara
  city: 7 Mitsiwa
  formerly part of: 8 Ethiopia
  sea: Red

ermine: fur 5 stoat 6 weasel 7 miniver
  relative: 4 mink

erode: 4 rust 5 decay 6 abrade 7 corrode, destroy, eat into 8 wear away 9 undermine 11 deteriorate 12 disintegrate

Eros: 4 Amor 5 Cupid
  beloved: 6 Psyche
  brother: 7 Anteros
  father: 6 Hermes 7 Mercury
  mother: 5 Venus 9 Aphrodite

erose: 6 uneven 9 irregular

erotic: 4 lewd, sexy 5 bawdy 6 ardent, carnal, loving, ribald 7 amatory, amorous, sensual 8 immodest, indecent, prurient 9 salacious

err: sin 4 miss, slip 5 lapse, stray 6 bungle, wander 7 blunder, deviate, misplay, mistake 8 misjudge 10 transgress 12 miscalculate, misinterpret

errand: 5 chore 7 journey, mission

errand boy: 4 page 5 gofer 7 bellhop, courier 9 messenger

errant: 6 astray 8 shifting 9 deviating, itinerant, wandering 10 journeying 11 adventurous

erratic: odd 4 wild 5 queer, wacky 6 fitful 7 strange, vagrant, wayward 8 aberrant, peculiar, unstable, variable 9 eccentric, irregular, wandering 10 capricious, changeable 12 inconsistent 13 unpredictable

erratum: 5 error 7 mistake

errhine: 6 sneeze

erroneous: 5 amiss, false, wrong 6 faulty, untrue 7 unsound 8 mistaken 9 incorrect, misguided 10 fallacious, inaccurate

error: sin 4 bull, flub, muff, slip 5 bevue, boner, fault, fluff, lapse 6 fumble, miscue 7 bloomer, blunder, default, erratum, fallacy, falsity, misplay, misstep, mistake, offense, rhubarb 8 solecism 9 violation 10 inaccuracy 12 irregularity, malformation
  measuring device: 11 aberrometer

ers: 5 vetch 9 kersenneh

ersatz: 4 fake, sham 5 phony 9 imitation, synthetic 10 artificial, substitute 11 replacement

Erse: 5 Irish 6 Celtic, Gaelic 8 Scottish

erstwhile: 6 former, whilom 7 one-time 8 formerly 10 heretofore

eruca: 11 caterpillar

eruct: 4 burp, emit, spew 5 belch 8 disgorge

erudition: 4 lore 6 wisdom 7 letters 8 learning, literacy 9 education, knowledge 11 instruction, scholarship

erupt: 4 emit, gush, spew 5 burst, eject, expel, spout 6 blow up 7 cast out, explode 8 throw off 9 discharge, pour forth

eruption: 4 rush 5 storm 7 flare-up 8 outbreak, outburst 9 commotion, explosion
  skin: 4 acne, rash 5 rupia 6 blotch, pimple 9 festering

Eryx: *father:* **5** Butes
  mother: **5** Venus **9** Aphrodite
Esau: **4** Edom
  brother: **5** Jacob
  country: **4** Edom
  descendant: **7** Edomite
  father: **5** Isaac
  father-in-law: **4** Elon
  grandson: **6** Amalek
  mother: **7** Rebekah
  son: **5** Korha, Reuel **7** Eliphaz
  wife: **4** Adah **10** Aholibamah
escalate: **4** go up, grow, rise **5** climb, mount, swell **6** expand, extend, step up **7** advance, broaden **8** increase **9** intensify
escapade: **4** lark **5** antic, caper, fling, prank, sally **9** adventure, excursion
escape: lam **4** bolt, flee, jink (Sc.), miss, skip, slip **5** avoid, break, dodge, elope, elude, evade, issue, spill **6** eschew, outlet **7** abscond, get away, leakage, outflow, take off **8** break out, get loose **9** disappear, diversion, evaporate **10** fly the coop **11** distraction
  means: **8** loophole
escargot: **5** snail
escarole: **6** endive
escarp: **5** cliff, slope
eschalot: **5** onion
eschar: **4** scab **5** crust
eschew: **4** shun **5** avoid **6** escape **7** abstain
escolar: **8** mackerel
escort: see **4** beau, lead, show **5** guard, usher **6** attend, convoy, squire **7** conduct, consort, gallant **8** cavalier, chaperon **9** accompany, attendant, bodyguard, safeguard
escritoire: **4** desk **6** bureau **9** secretary
escrow: **4** bond, deed, fund **7** deposit
esculent: **6** edible **7** eatable **10** comestible
escutcheon: **6** shield
  band: **4** fess **5** fesse
  cord: **10** cordeliere
Esdras' angel: **5** Uriel
esker, eskar: **4** kame **5** mound, ridge
Eskimo: Ita **4** Yuit **5** Aleut, Yupik **6** Innuit **7** Inupiat
  bird: **4** fute
  boot: **5** kamik
  canoe: **5** cayak, kayak, umiak **6** oomiac, oomiak **7** oomiack
  coat: **5** parka **6** parkee, temiak
  dog: **5** husky **8** malamute, malemute
  dwelling: **4** iglu **5** igloo, topek, tupek, tupik **9** barrabora
  goddess: **5** Sedna
  knife: ulu
  medicine man: **7** angakok, angakut, angekok, angekut **8** angekkok
  mountain: **7** nunatak

  plain: **6** tundra
  settlement: **4** Etah
  sledge: **7** komatik
esne: **4** serf **7** bondman **8** hireling
esodic: **8** afferent
esophagus: **6** gullet **7** pharynx
esoteric: **5** inner **6** arcane, mystic, secret **7** private **8** abstruse **9** recondite **10** acroamatic, mysterious **12** confidential
esoteric doctrine: **6** cabala
esoteric knowledge: **6** gnosis
ESP: **9** foresight, intuition **11** premonition **12** clairvoyance
espadon: **9** swordfish
espalier: **7** lattice, railing, trellis
Español: **7** Spanish
espantoon: **4** club **8** spontoon
esparto: **4** alfa **5** grass
especial: **4** dear **5** chief, close **8** intimate, peculiar, specific, uncommon **10** particular **11** exceptional, outstanding
especially: **6** mainly, really **7** notably **8** uniquely **9** expressly, primarily **10** singularly **11** exclusively
espial: **6** notice **9** discovery **11** observation
espionage: **6** spying **12** surveillance
esplanade: **4** walk **5** drive **6** maidan **7** roadway **9** promenade
espouse: wed **4** back, mate, tout **5** adopt, boost, marry **6** defend, take up **7** betroth, embrace, further, husband, promote, support **8** advocate, champion, maintain
esprit: wit **4** elan, zing **5** verve **6** spirit **10** cleverness **12** intelligence
esprit de corps: **9** team unity **10** fellowship, group pride, solidarity
espy: see **4** spot **5** sight, watch **6** behold, descry, detect, locate, notice **7** discern, observe **8** discover
esquire: **7** armiger
ess: **4** worm **5** curve, sigma **7** sigmoid **8** curlicue, curlycue
essay: try **4** seek **5** chria (L.), paper, theme, tract, trail **6** effort, satire, take on, thesis **7** article, attempt, venture, writing **8** endeavor, exertion, treatise **9** undertake **10** enterprise, experiment **11** make a stab at **12** disquisition, dissertation
essayist: **4** Elia, Lamb **5** Paine **6** Holmes, Steele **7** Addison, Emerson
esse: **5** being **9** existence
essence: ens **4** core, crux, gist, odor, pith, soul **5** attar, being, heart, ousia (G.) **6** entity, nature, spirit **7** element, extract, meaning, perfume **9** existence, principle, substance **10** extraction **11** concentrate
Essene: **6** mystic **7** ascetic **8** celibate
essential: key **4** main **5** basic, vital **7** crucial, leading, needful **8** cardinal, inherent **9**

intrinsic, necessary, principal, requisite **10** sine qua non **11** fundamental **13** indispensable

essonite: 6 garnet

establish: fix, set **4** base, rear, rest, show **5** build, erect, found, plant, prove, setup, start **6** avouch, clinch, create, ground, locate, ordain, ratify, settle, verify **7** appoint, approve, confirm, install, instate, justify, provide, situate, sustain **8** colonize, constate, ensconce, identify, initiate, organize, radicate, regulate, validate **9** determine, institute, originate **10** accomplish, constitute **11** corroborate

established: 4 fast, firm, sure **7** certain

establishment: 4 mill **5** elite, house, plant **6** ecesis, menage **7** company, concern, dounset (Sc.), factory **8** business, Old Guard **10** enterprise **11** institution, ruling class **12** control group

estancia (Sp.): 4 farm **5** ranch

estate: 4 fief, home, rank **5** acres, class, finca, manor, order, taluk **6** assets, domain, ground, legacy, status **7** demesne, dignity, fortune **8** allodium, freehold, hacienda, position, property, standing **9** condition, situation **10** belongings, plantation **11** latifundium
  fourth: **5** press **9** newspaper
  manager: **7** steward **8** executor, guardian

esteem: 4 deem **5** adore, count, favor, honor, pride, prize, value, worth **6** credit, regard, repute **7** account, cherish, opinion, respect **8** approval, venerate **9** deference, reckoning, reverence **10** admiration, appreciate, estimation **13** consideration

ester: 6 oleate **7** acetate, tropate **8** compound, stearate

estero: 5 inlet **7** channel, estuary

Esther: 8 Hadassah
  enemy: **5** Haman
  festival: **5** Purim
  foster father: **8** Mordecai
  husband: **6** Xerxes **9** Ahasuerus

esthesiometer: 10 tactometer

esthetic: See **aesthetic**

estimable: 4 good **5** solid **6** decent, honest, worthy **8** laudable **9** admirable, honorable **10** worthwhile **11** meritorious, respectable

estimate: set **4** rank, rate **5** assay, gauge, guess, judge, prize, think, value **6** assess, figure, reckon **7** average, believe, surmise **8** appraise, consider, evaluate **9** calculate **11** computation

estimation: 4 fame, view **5** honor **6** belief, regard, repute **7** opinion **8** judgment

estivate: 6 summer
  opposite of: **9** hibernate

estoc: 5 sword

Estonia: *capital:* **7** Tallinn
  city: **5** Tartu **11** Kohtla-Jarve
  currency: **5** kroon
  river: **5** Narva
  sea: **6** Baltic

estop: bar **5** debar **6** hinder, impede **7** prevent **8** preclude, prohibit

estrade: 4 dais **8** platform

estrange: 4 part, wean **6** divert **7** break up **8** alienate, disunite **9** disaffect **10** antagonize, drive apart

estrangement: 6 schism **7** divorce **10** falling out, separation

estray: 4 waif **5** dogie

estreat: 4 copy, fine **5** exact **6** record **7** extract **9** duplicate

estuary: ria **5** firth, frith, inlet **6** estero **10** river mouth, tidal basin

esurient: 6 greedy, hungry **9** voracious

etaac: 7 blaubok **8** antelope

etagere: 7 whatnot **12** display stand

et al: 6 others **9** elsewhere

etat: 5 state

etch: 6 incise **7** engrave, impress **8** inscribe

Eteocles: *father:* **7** Oedipus
  kingdom: **6** Thebes
  mother: **7** Jocasta
  son: **8** Laodamas

eternal: 6 eterne **7** ageless, endless, lasting, undying **8** constant, enduring, immortal, timeless **9** boundless, continual, deathless, immutable, perpetual, unceasing **10** perdurable **11** everlasting **12** imperishable, interminable, unchangeable **13** uninterrupted

Eternal City: 4 Rome

eternally: 6 always **7** forever **11** in perpetuum

eternity: age, eon **4** aeon **8** infinity **9** afterlife **12** the hereafter

etesian: 6 annual **8** periodic, seasonal
  pert. to: **4** wind

ethanol: 7 alcohol

etheostomoid: 4 fish **6** darter

ether: air, gas, sky **5** ozone **7** heavens, solvent **8** empyrean **10** anesthetic, atmosphere

ethereal: 4 aery, airy **5** filmy **6** aerial **7** fragile, slender **8** delicate, gossamer, heavenly **9** celestial, unearthly **10** spiritlike

ethical: 5 moral **7** upright **8** virtuous **9** righteous **10** aboveboard

ethics: 6 morals, values **9** moral code, standards **10** conscience, principles

etiolate: 4 pale **6** bleach, weaken

Ethiopia: 9 Abyssinia
  capital: **10** Addis Ababa
  currency: **4** birr **6** santim
  measure: tat **4** cubi, kuba **5** derah, messe **6** cabaho, sinjer, sinzer, tanica **7** entelam, farsakh, farsang, ghebeta

mountain peak: **9** Ras Dashan
mountain range: **5** Simen
river: Omo **4** Abay (Blue Nile) **5** Awash **6** Tekeze

etiquette: **4** form, Post **5** usage **6** custom **7** conduct, decorum, manners **8** courtesy, protocol **9** amenities, propriety **10** civilities **12** good behavior
breach of: **8** solecism

etna: **4** lamp **7** volcano

Etruria: *city:* **4** Veii
god: **5** Tinia **8** Acheloos
goddess: Uni **6** Menfra
king: **4** Lars **7** Porsena
pert. to: **8** Etruscan
pottery: **8** bucchero

etui, etwee: **4** case **8** reticule **10** needlecase

etymology: **10** word change, word origin **11** word history

etymon: **4** root **5** radix **7** radical

eucalyptus: **4** yate **6** jarrah **7** blue gum **8** iron bark, messmate
eater: **5** koala
family: **6** myrtle
gum: **4** kino
insect secretion: **4** laap, lerp

Eucharist: **4** Host **9** communion, sacrament **11** Lord's Supper
box: pix, pyx
bread plate: **5** paten
cloth: **4** fano **5** fanon
cup: **5** calix **7** chalice
wafer vessel: **8** ciborium
wine vessel: ama **5** amula

Euclid: **5** Greek **8** geometer **13** mathematician
work: **8** Elements

eugenic: **8** wellborn **10** hereditary

eulogistic: **9** laudatory **11** encomiastic, panegyrical **12** commendatory

eulogize: **4** laud **5** extol **7** glorify **9** celebrate

eulogy: **5** eloge, paean **6** hesped (Heb.), homage, praise **7** address, oration, tribute **8** encomium **9** panegyric **11** composition

eunuch: **5** spado **7** gelding **8** castrato

euphonium: **4** tuba

euphony: **5** meter **6** melody **7** harmony

euphorbia: **5** plant **6** spurge

euphoria: **4** ease **7** comfort, elation **9** well-being **12** exhilaration

Euphrates tributary: **6** Balikh, Khabur

euplexoptera: **6** earwig

Eurasia: *range:* **4** Ural **5** Urals

eureka red: **4** puce

Euripides: *play:* Ion **5** Helen, Medea **6** Hecuba **7** Electra, Orestes **8** Alcestis **10** Andromache, Hippolytus **11** Trojan Women

euripus: **6** strait **7** channel

Europa: *brother:* **6** Cadmus
father: **6** Agenor
husband: **8** Asterius
sons: **5** Minos **8** Sarpedon **12** Rhadamanthys

Europe (see also individual countries): *countries:* **5** Italy, Malta, Spain **6** Cyprus, France, Greece, Latvia, Monaco, Norway, Poland, Russia (part), Sweden, Turkey (part) **7** Albania, Andorra, Armenia, Austria, Belarus, Belgium, Denmark, Estonia, Finland, Georgia, Germany, Hungary, Iceland, Ireland, Romania, Ukraine **8** Bulgaria, Moldavia, Portugal, Slovenia **9** Lithuania, Macedonia, San Marino **10** Azerbaijan, Luxembourg, Yugoslavia **11** Netherlands, Switzerland, Vatican City **12** Great Britain **13** Czech Republic, Liechtenstein **14** Slovak Republic

European Community (EC): **12** Common Market
Court of Justice site: **10** Luxembourg
executive site: **8** Brussels
legislative site: **8** Brussels **10** Luxembourg
member: **5** Italy, Spain **6** France, Greece **7** Belgium, Denmark, Germany, Ireland **8** Portugal **10** Luxembourg **11** Netherlands **13** United Kingdom
Parliament site: **10** Strasbourg (France)

Eurydice's husband: **7** Orpheus

Eurytus's daughter: **4** Iole

eutaxy: **4** form **8** dispatch, tidiness **9** good order **10** management

Euterpe: **4** Muse
lover: **7** Strymon
son: **6** Rhesus

evacuant: **6** emetic **8** diuretic, emptying **9** cathartic, purgative

evacuate: **4** quit, void **5** empty, expel, leave **6** desert, remove, vacate **7** abandon, move out **12** withdraw from

evade: gee **4** bilk, duck, foil, shun **5** avert, avoid, dodge, elude, hedge, parry, shirk **6** baffle, escape, eschew **7** fend off **10** equivocate

evaluate: **4** rank, rate **5** class, grade, judge **6** assess, ponder **8** appraise

evaluation: **5** assay, worth **8** critique, judgment **9** appraisal **10** estimation

evanesce: **4** fade **5** empty **6** vanish **9** disappear, dissipate, evaporate

evanescent: **7** cursory, evasive **8** fleeting, fugitive **9** ephemeral, fugacious, transient, vanishing **11** impermanent

evangel: **6** gospel

Evangeline's home: **6** Acadia

evangelist: **4** John, Luke, Mark **6** Graham, Sunday, writer **7** apostle, Edwards, Matthew, Roberts **8** crusader, disciple **9**

McPherson, patriarch **10** missionary, revivalist

evaporate: **5** dry up **8** condense, evanesce, fade away **9** dehydrate, disappear

evasion: **5** dodge, shift **6** escape **9** avoidance **10** subterfuge **12** equivocation

evasive: sly **4** eely **5** dodgy **6** shifty **7** devious, elusive, elusory, unclear **8** slippery **9** deceitful **12** tergiversate

eve: **4** dusk **6** sunset **7** sundown **9** threshold

Eve: rib **5** woman **6** female

even: een, tie **4** fair, just **5** aline, equal, exact, flush, grade, level, match, plain, rival, suant **6** direct, placid, smooth, square, steady **7** abreast, balance, equable, flatten, regular, uniform **8** moderate, parallel **9** equitable, impartial **10** coincident **15** straightforward

even if: tho **8** although

even-tempered: **4** calm, mild **6** placid, serene **11** slow to anger, unflappable

evener: **7** leveler **9** equalizer **10** double-tree

evening: eve **4** ereb (Heb.), sera (It.), soir (F.) **5** abend (G.), noche (Sp.) **6** sunset **8** eventide, twilight

dress: tux **4** gown **5** tails **6** formal, tuxedo **7** smoking **8** black tie, white tie **12** dinner jacket

party: **6** soiree

pert. to: **11** crepuscular

prayer: **7** vespers

primrose: **7** fuchsia **9** oenothera

song: **8** serenade

star: **5** Venus **6** Hesper, Vesper **8** Hesperus

evenness: **7** balance **8** equality **10** equanimity, uniformity **11** consistency

event: hap **4** case, fact, fate, feat, tilt **5** casus (L.), doing, match **6** factum (L.), result **7** contest, episode **8** incident, landmark, occasion **9** adventure, happening, milestone **10** experience, occurrence, phenomenon **11** competition, consequence **12** circumstance

first: **5** debut **6** opener, prelim **8** premiere

eventful: **7** notable **8** historic **9** important, memorable, momentous **11** significant

eventide: **4** dusk **6** vesper **7** evening **8** twilight

eventual: **4** last **5** final, later **6** future **7** ensuing **8** ultimate

eventually: **6** one day **7** finally **8** in the end, sometime **10** ultimately **13** sooner or later

eventuate: **5** occur **6** happen, result

ever: aye, eer **6** always **7** forever **8** in any way **9** at any time **10** constantly **11** continually, perpetually

Everglades: **5** marsh, swamp

evergreen (see also **conifer**): fir, ivy **4** ilex **5** galax, heath, holly, savin **6** laurel, savine **7** jasmine **9** mistletoe **12** rhododendron

genus of: **4** Olax **9** Cupressus **11** Pittosporum

tree: fir, yew **4** pine **5** carob, cedar, larch **6** balsam, calaba, spruce

Evergreen State: **10** Washington

everlasting: **6** eterne **7** durable, endless, eternal, forever, lasting, tedious, undying **8** constant, enduring, immortal, infinite, timeless **9** continual, incessant, perpetual, unceasing, wearisome **10** perdurable **12** imperishable **13** uninterrupted

everlasting flower: **6** orpine **8** amaranth **10** immortelle **11** strawflower

evermore: **6** always **9** eternally **10** constantly

every: all, ilk (Sc.) **4** each **6** entire **8** complete

everybody: all **8** everyone

everyday: **5** usual **6** common **7** mundane, prosaic, routine **8** ordinary **11** commonplace

everything: all

evict: **4** oust **5** eject, expel **6** remove **7** kick out **10** dispossess

evidence: **4** show **5** proof, token, trace **6** attest, reveal **7** display, exhibit, support **8** argument, indicate, manifest, muniment **9** testimony **10** illustrate

evident: **5** broad, clear, plain **6** patent **7** glaring, obvious, visible **8** apparent, manifest, palpable **10** noticeable **11** discernible, indubitable, transparent **12** demonstrable

evil (see also **devil**): bad, ill, sin **4** base, foul, harm, vice, vile **5** crime, malum (L.), wrong **6** menace, wicked **7** adverse, baleful, corrupt, heinous, hurtful, immoral, misdeed, noxious, satanic, vicious **8** calamity, depraved, devilish, disaster, iniquity, mischief, sinister **9** injurious, malicious, malignant, malignity, nefarious, offensive, worthless **10** malevolent, misfortune, pernicious **11** malefaction

incarnation of: **5** Satan **7** Lucifer **8** Mephisto **9** Beelzebub **10** Old Scratch **14** Mephistopheles

evildoer: **5** cheat, crook, felon **6** sinner **7** culprit, villain **8** criminal **9** miscreant **10** malefactor

evil eye: hex **4** jinx **5** curse, Jonah **6** hoodoo, whammy **11** malediction

evil spirit: imp **5** demon, devil, fiend

evince: **4** show **5** prove **6** subdue **7** conquer, display, exhibit **8** indicate, manifest

eviscerate: gut **10** devitalize, disembowel, exenterate

evocative: **6** moving **8** stirring **9** remindful **10** suggestive **11** reminiscent, stimulating

evoke: **5** educe, waken **6** arouse, elicit, excite, summon **9** stimulate **10** bring forth

evolution: **6** change, growth **7** biogeny **8** progress **10** biogenesis **11** development

evolve: 4 emit, grow 5 ripen 6 derive, expand, mature 7 develop, enlarge 8 increase 10 show change 11 disentangle

ewe: teg 5 sheep
old: 5 crone

ewer: jug 5 basin 7 pitcher 9 container

ewest: 4 next 7 nearest

ex: 6 former 9 strike out

exacerbate: irk 5 tease 6 enrage, excite, worsen 7 provoke 8 embitter, increase, irritate 9 aggravate, infuriate 10 exasperate

exact: ask 4 even, fine, levy, true 5 wreak, wrest 6 compel, demand, elicit, extort, formal, minute, square, strict 7 careful, certain, command, correct, enforce, estreat, extract, literal, precise, regular, require 8 accurate, critical, explicit, rigorous, specific 9 identical 10 methodical, meticulous, scrupulous 11 painstaking, punctilious 13 hypercritical

exacting: 5 fussy 6 severe, strict, trying 7 arduous, exigent, finicky, onerous 8 pressing, rigorous 9 demanding, stringent 10 burdensome

exactly: 4 just 5 fully, quite, spang, truly 6 evenly, just so, wholly 7 totally 8 entirely, of course 9 assuredly, certainly, on the nose 10 absolutely, altogether, positively

exactness: 8 accuracy 9 precision, rightness

exaggerate: 6 extend, overdo 7 amplify, enhance, enlarge, magnify, romance, stretch 8 increase 9 aggravate, embroider, overstate

exaggerated: 5 outre 6 padded 7 blown up, extreme 8 inflated, prodigal 11 extravagant

exaggeration: 7 puffery 9 hyperbole 10 caricature, embroidery 13 embellishment, overstatement

exalt: 4 laud 5 extol, honor, raise 6 praise, uplift 7 acclaim, advance, dignify, elevate, enhance, ennoble, glorify, inspire, magnify, promote 8 enthrone, heighten 9 intensify 10 aggrandize

exaltation: 5 bliss 7 ecstasy, elation, rapture 9 elevation, transport 10 apotheosis 11 deification

exalted: 4 high 5 grand, noble 6 august, lordly 7 haughty, sublime 8 glorious 11 high-ranking, illustrious

examen: 7 inquiry 11 examination 13 investigation

examination: 4 exam, oral, quiz, test 5 assay, audit, check, trial 6 examen, review, survey 7 autopsy, inquest, inquiry 8 research, scrutiny 10 comparison, inspection 11 exploration, inquisition 13 consideration, investigation 14 reconnaissance

examine: con, try 4 feel, scan, sift, view 5 assay, probe, quest 6 candle, ponder 7 ana-

lyze, canvass, explore, inspect, observe, palpate 8 look over, overhaul 10 scrutinize 11 inquire into, interrogate, reconnoiter

examiner: 6 censor, conner 7 analyst, auditor, coroner 9 inspector 10 inquisitor

example: 4 case 5 ideal, model 6 sample 7 pattern 8 exemplar, foregoer, instance, paradigm, specimen 9 precedent 11 case history, description 12 illustration 15 exemplification

exanimate: 4 dead 8 lifeless 10 spiritless

exasperate: ire, irk 4 bait, gall, rile 5 annoy 6 enrage, excite, nettle, stir up 7 agitate, inflame, provoke, roughen 8 irritate 9 aggravate

exasperated: 5 fed up, wroth 9 indignant

ex cathedra: 8 official 13 authoritative

excavate: dig 4 mine, mole 5 dig up, scoop 6 burrow, dredge, tunnel 9 hollow out

excavation: cut, pit 4 hole 5 grave 6 cavity, groove, trench
for ore: 4 mine 5 stope 6 quarry

exceed: top 4 best, pass 5 excel, outdo, outgo 6 better, outrun, outvie, overdo 7 eclipse, overtax, surpass 8 go beyond, outstrip, overstep, surmount 9 overshoot, transcend 11 predominate

exceedingly: 4 tres (F.), very 5 amain 7 parlous 9 extremely 10 remarkably, strikingly

excel: cap, top 4 best 5 outdo, shine 6 better, exceed 7 surpass 8 outclass, outrival 10 be expert at, tower above

excellence: 5 arete (Gr.), merit, worth 6 virtue 7 quality 8 goodness 10 perfection 11 distinction, superiority

excellent: 4 braw (Sc.), fine, good, tops 5 brave, bully, great, prime, super 6 choice, famous, grade A, select, spiffy, worthy 7 capital, corking, elegant 8 generous, peerless, sterling, superior, top-notch, valuable 9 admirable, first-rate 10 inimitable, preeminent, sans pareil 12 transcendent

except: bar, but 4 bate, omit, only, save 6 exempt, unless 7 besides, exclude, rule out 9 eliminate, other than

exception: 5 demur 7 dissent, offense 9 complaint, condition, objection

exceptional: 4 rare 7 notable, special, unusual 8 singular, superior, uncommon 9 wonderful 10 remarkable 11 outstanding 13 extraordinary

excerpt: 4 cite 5 quote, scrap 7 extract, pick out, portion, section 10 select from

excess: 4 glut, over, plus, riot 5 flood 7 nimiety, overage, surfeit, surplus 8 overmuch, plethora 9 profusion 10 exuberance, redundancy 11 prodigality, superfluity 12 intemperance 13 over-abundance

excessive: too 4 over 5 enorm (Sc.), undue 6

de trop (F.) **7** extreme, nimious **8** enormous, overmuch **9** exuberant **10** exorbitant, immoderate, inordinate **11** extravagant, intemperate **12** extortionate, unreasonable

exchange: set **4** mart, swap **5** bandy, store, trade, truck **6** barter, bourse, dicker, excamb (Sc.), market, rialto, switch **7** commute, traffic **9** tit for tat, transpose **10** quid pro quo, substitute **11** reciprocate **12** headquarters

exchequer: **5** funds, money **6** coffer **8** finances, treasury

excise: tax **4** duty, toll **6** cut out, impost, remove, resect **7** exscind, extract **8** alcabala (Sp.) **9** extirpate, surcharge

officer: **8** revenuer

excision: cut **7** erasure, removal **9** exsection **10** amputation, rooting out **11** eradication, extirpation

excite: **4** fire, spur, stir, whet **5** elate, impel, pique, rouse **6** arouse, awaken, foment, incite, kindle, thrill, turn on **7** agitate, animate, inflame, provoke **8** disquiet **9** electrify, galvanize, stimulate, titillate

excited: hot **4** agog, avid **5** eager, moved **6** heated **7** fevered, frantic **8** atwitter, worked up **9** steamed up **11** carried away

excitement: ado **4** stir, to-do **5** fever, furor **6** hubbub, warmth **7** turmoil **8** hysteria **9** commotion **10** hullabaloo **11** disturbance

exclaim: **6** cry out **8** burst out **9** ejaculate **10** vociferate **12** say violently

exclamation: aha, aie, bah, boo, fie, foh, hep, hey, hic, huh, och, oho, pah, poh, suz, tut, ugh, wow, yah **4** adad, ahem, alas, arra (Ir.), darn, drat, egad, evoe, garn, gosh, hech, heck, hein (F.), hist, hoch (G.), hola, phew, pish, psha, pugh, rats, rivo, tush, wugg **5** alack, arrah (Ir.), bravo, faugh, feigh, heigh, holla, humph, ohone (Ir.), pshaw **6** clamor, hurrah, indeed, ochone (Ir.), outcry **7** hosanna **9** alackaday, expletive **12** interjection

of contempt: foh, pah

of disgust: ugh **4** rats, yech

of exhilaration: **4** evoe

of pain: **4** ouch

of reproach: fie

of sorrow: **4** alas **9** alackaday

of surprise: aha, gee, oho, wow

exclude: ban, bar **5** debar, eject, expel **6** banish, except, exempt, reject **7** keep out **8** prohibit **9** blackball, eliminate, ostracize **13** excommunicate

exclusive: **4** only, rare, sole **5** alone, aloof, elite, scoop, whole **6** entire, select, single **7** private **8** cliquish, complete, snobbish **10** restricted

excommunicate: **5** curse **6** banish **8** unchurch **9** ostracize

excoriate: **4** flay, gall **5** chafe, score, strip **6** abrade **8** denounce, lambaste **9** lash out at **11** decorticate

excrescence: **4** burl, lump, wart **6** pimple **8** tubercle **9** outgrowth

excruciating: **5** acute **6** fierce, severe **7** extreme, intense, painful, racking **9** agonizing, torturous **10** tormenting, unbearable **12** insufferable

exculpate: **4** free **5** clear, remit **6** acquit, excuse, pardon **7** absolve, forgive, justify, release **8** palliate **9** discharge, exonerate, vindicate

excursion: row **4** ride, sail, tour, trek, trip **5** jaunt, sally, tramp **6** cruise, junket, outing, ramble, safari, sortie, voyage **7** journey **8** campaign, escapade **10** digression, expedition

excusable: **6** venial **7** tenable **9** allowable **10** defensible, pardonable **11** justifiable

excuse: **4** plea **5** alibi, remit **6** acquit, copout, defend, let off, pardon **7** absolve, apology, condone, forgive, indulge, pretext **8** dispense, occasion, overlook, pass over **9** exculpate, exonerate, extenuate, vindicate, whitewash

execrable: bad **4** base, foul, vile **8** accursed, damnable, wretched **9** atrocious, monstrous, revolting **10** abominable, detestable, horrifying

execrate: **4** damn, hate **5** abhor, curse **6** detest, loathe, revile **8** denounce **9** imprecate, objurgate **12** anathematize

execute: act, gas **4** hang, kill, obey, play, slay **5** lynch **6** direct, effect, finish, manage **7** conduct, enforce, perform **8** carry out, complete **9** discharge **10** accomplish, administer **11** electrocute

execution: **7** garrote, killing **8** garrotte **9** rendition, technique **10** completion **11** achievement, fulfillment, transaction

executive: CEO **4** dean **5** mayor **7** manager, officer, premier **8** director, governor, official, overseer **9** president **10** supervisor **12** entrepreneur **13** administrator

executor: **4** doer **5** agent **8** enforcer **9** performer **13** administrator

exegesis: **10** exposition **11** explanation **14** interpretation

exegete: **6** critic **11** interpreter

exemplar: **5** model **7** example, pattern **9** archetype **12** illustration

exemplary: **5** ideal, model **6** worthy **7** typical **8** laudable, sterling **9** admirable, emulative **11** commendable **12** praiseworthy

exemplify: **6** embody, typify **9** epitomize, represent, symbolize **10** illustrate

exempt: 4 free 5 clear, spare 6 excuse, fidate 7 exclude, release, relieve 8 excepted 9 discharge 12 not subject to

exemption: 7 freedom 8 immunity 9 exception 12 dispensation

exequy: 4 rite 7 obsequy 8 ceremony 10 procession

exercise: ply, use, vex 5 drill, etude, exert, train, wield 6 employ, harass, lesson, parade, praxis, push-up, school 7 aufgabe, display, prepare, problem, provoke, utilize, work out 8 activity, maneuver, practice 9 athletics 10 exhibition, gymnastics, recitation 12 calisthenics 14 constitutional

exerciser: 5 groom

exert: try, use 5 apply, wield 6 employ, strain 8 exercise, put forth

exertion: 4 toil, work 5 essay, labor, trial 6 action, effort, energy 7 trouble 8 endeavor, industry, strength, struggle 11 elbow grease

exfoliate: 5 scale 8 flake off 10 desquamate

exhalation: 5 steam 8 effuvium 9 breathing, emanation 10 expiration 11 evaporation

exhale: 4 emit 6 expire 7 blow out, respire 10 breathe out

exhaust: sap 5 drain, empty, use up 6 expend, overdo, weaken 7 deplete, fatigue, wear out 8 enervate 9 discharge 10 impoverish

exhausted: 4 beat, dead, done, worn 5 all in, spent, tired, weary 6 barren, beaten, bushed, effete, pooped 7 emptied 8 consumed, dog-tired 9 washed out

exhausting: 7 arduous

exhaustion: 7 fatigue 8 collapse 9 depletion, inanition, lassitude 11 prostration

exhaustive: 6 all-out 8 complete, sweeping, thorough 9 intensive 13 comprehensive

exheridate: 10 disinherit

exhibit: air 4 fair, show 5 stage 6 evince, expose, ostend, parade, reveal 7 display, perform, produce, trot out 8 disclose, evidence, manifest 9 represent 11 demonstrate

exhibition: 4 fair, show 5 sight 7 display, pageant 8 showcase 9 cosmorama, spectacle 10 exposition 12 presentation 13 demonstration

exhilarate: 5 cheer, elate, pep up 6 excite, uplift 7 animate, enliven, gladden 10 invigorate

exhilaration: 6 gaiety 7 jollity 8 gladness, hilarity 9 merriment 10 joyousness

exhort: bid 4 goad, prod, spur, urge, warn 5 egg on, plead 6 advise, incite, preach 7 beseech, caution 8 admonish, appeal to 9 encourage

exhume: dig 5 delve, dig up 7 unearth 8 disinter

exigency: fix, jam 4 need, want 5 pinch 6 cri-

sis, plight 7 urgency 8 juncture, pressure, quandary 10 difficulty 11 requirement

exigent: 5 vital 8 critical, exacting, pressing 9 demanding, necessary 10 imperative 13 indispensable

exiguity: 7 paucity

exiguous: 4 tiny 5 scant, small, spare 6 meager, sparse 7 slender 10 diminutive

exile: 4 oust 5 eject, expel 6 deport, outlaw, pariah 7 outcast, refugee 8 drive out, fugitive 9 nonperson, ostracize 10 banishment, expatriate 12 proscription

exist: am, are 4 live 6 endure, remain 7 breathe, survive
passively: 7 subsist 8 vegetate

existence: ens 4 esse, life 5 being 6 entity, inesse 7 essence, reality 9 actuality
beginning of: 5 birth 6 origin 8 nascency
having no: 4 dead, null, void 7 defunct
pert. to: 5 ontic 8 ontology

existent: 4 real 5 alive, being 6 extant 7 present 9 living now
at same time: 15 contemporaneous
in name only: 7 nominal, titular

Existentialist: 5 Buber, Camus 6 Marcel, Sartre 7 Jaspers 9 Heidegger 11 Kierkegaard

exit: 4 door, gate 5 going, leave, split 6 egress, exodus, outlet, way out 7 buzz off, outgate, passage, pull out, retreat 8 debouche 9 departure 10 withdrawal
area without: 8 cul-de-sac 10 blind alley

exode: 5 farce 8 travesty 10 afterpiece

exodus: 9 migration 10 mass flight

Exodus author: 4 Uris (Leon)

exonerate: 4 free 5 clear 6 acquit, excuse 7 absolve, relieve 9 disburden, discharge, exculpate, vindicate 12 find innocent

exorbitant: 5 undue 8 abnormal 9 excessive, expensive, out of line 10 immoderate, outrageous, overpriced 11 extravagant 12 extortionate, unreasonable

exorcism: 5 charm, spell 9 expulsion 11 incantation

exordium: 7 preface, prelude 8 foreword, preamble, prologue 9 beginning 12 introduction

exoteric: 6 layman 7 popular 8 external, outsider 13 easily grasped

exotic: 5 alien 7 foreign, strange, unusual 8 enticing, striking 9 different, glamorous 10 extraneous, outlandish

expand: wax 4 grow, open 5 splay, swell, widen 6 dilate, extend, unfold, unfurl 7 amplify, augment, balloon, broaden, develop, distend, enlarge, inflate, magnify, stretch 8 increase, lengthen 9 expatiate, explicate, intumesce, spread out 10 make bigger

expanded: 8 patulous

expanse: 4 area, room 5 range, reach, space, sweep, tract 6 extent, spread 7 stretch 8 distance 9 magnitude
vast: 5 ocean 6 desert, empire

expansion: 6 growth 8 increase 9 extension 10 dilatation, distention 11 development, enlargement

expansive: 4 free, wide 5 ample, broad, large 6 genial 7 elastic, liberal 8 effusive, outgoing, spacious 9 bombastic, extensive, grandiose 11 extroverted 13 demonstrative

expatiate: 6 expand, wander 7 amplify, descant, discuss, dwell on, enlarge 11 elaborate on 12 talk at length

expatriation: 5 exile 10 banishment

expect: 4 deem, hope 5 await, guess 6 assume, plan on, reckon 7 believe, foresee, look for, presume, suppose 8 envision 9 calculate 10 anticipate

expectant: 4 agog 5 alert, eager 7 hopeful, waiting 8 pregnant, sanguine 11 watching for

expectation: 4 hope 6 belief 7 surmise 8 prospect 10 confidence 12 anticipation

expectorate: 4 spit

expedient: 4 wise 5 dodge 6 proper 7 politic, stopgap 9 advisable, makeshift 10 profitable 12 advantageous

expedite: 4 hie 4 free 5 hurry, speed 6 hasten 7 quicken 8 dispatch 10 accelerate, facilitate 11 move quickly

expedition: 4 trek, trip 5 drave (Sc.), haste, hurry, jaunt 6 safari, voyage 7 crusade, journey, mission 8 alacrity, progress 9 excursion

expeditious: 4 fast 5 hasty, quick, rapid, ready, swift 6 prompt, speedy 9 effective, immediate

expel: 4 oust 5 eject, evict, exile 6 banish, deport 7 cast out, exclude 8 dislodge, forjudge 9 discharge, eliminate, forejudge 10 dispossess, expatriate

expend: 5 spend, use up, waste 6 pay out 7 consume 8 disburse, dispense, shell out, squander 9 dissipate 10 distribute

expenditure: 4 cost 5 outgo 6 outlay 11 consumption 12 disbursement

expense: 4 cost, loss 5 batta (Ind.), price 6 charge, outlay 8 overhead 11 consumption, expenditure 12 disbursement

expensive: 4 dear, high 6 costly, lavish 10 high-priced 11 dispendious, extravagant

experience: see 4 feel, have, know, live, meet, view 5 assay, event, skill, taste, trial 6 affair, endure, ordeal, suffer 7 calvary, feeling, know-how, undergo 8 training 9 adventure, encounter, go through, knowledge 10 background

experienced: met 4 able, wise 6 expert 7 capable, trained, veteran 8 seasoned 9 practiced, qualified, underwent

experiment: try 4 test 5 assay, essay, trial 7 analyze 8 research

experimental: 9 empirical, tentative

expert: ace, pro 4 deft, good 5 adept 6 adroit, artist, au fait, clever, habile 7 artiste (F.), capable, skilled 9 authority 10 proficient 11 experienced 12 professional

expertness: 5 knack, savvy, skill 7 ability, mastery 8 facility 9 dexterity

expiate: 5 atone, avert 7 redress 10 make amends, propitiate

expiatory: 8 piacular 9 purgative

expiration: end 5 death 10 exhalation, extinction 11 termination

expire: die, end 5 cease, expel, lapse 6 perish, run out

expiry: 5 close, death 10 extinction 11 termination

explain: 5 solve 6 define, expand, unfold 7 clarify, expound, justify, unravel 8 describe, manifest, spell out 9 elucidate, explicate, interpret, make clear 10 account for, illuminate

explanation: key 5 cause 6 answer, motive, reason 7 account, apology, meaning 8 exegesis 9 rationale 10 exposition 11 description 13 clarification

expletive: 4 oath 5 curse 9 swear word 11 exclamation

explicate: 6 expand, unfold 7 amplify, explain, expound 9 interpret

explicit: 4 open 5 clear, exact, fixed, plain 7 express, obvious, precise 8 absolute, clearcut, definite, positive, specific 9 categoric, outspoken 10 plain to see 11 categorical, unambiguous, unequivocal 13 unconditional

explode: 4 fire 5 blast, burst, erupt, go off 6 blow up, refute 7 deflate 8 detonate, disprove, dynamite 9 fulminate

exploding meteor: 6 bolide

exploding star: 4 nova

exploit: act 4 deed, feat, gest, milk 5 abuse, geste, stunt 6 misuse 7 utilize 8 impose on, profit by, put to use 9 adventure, heroic act 10 manipulate 11 achievement, tour de force

exploration: 5 probe 6 search 11 examination 13 investigation

explore: map, try 4 test 5 chart, probe, scout 6 search 7 examine, feel out 8 look into 9 range over 11 investigate

explorer: 4 Byrd, Cook, Eric 5 Bruce, Cabot, Clark, Davis, diver, Drake, Lewis, Scott 6 Baffin, Balboa, Burton, Carter, Cortes, Cortez, DaGama, De Soto, DeLeon,

Hearne, Hudson **7** pioneer, Pizarro, Raleigh, Stanley **8** Amundsen, Columbus, Magellan, Vespucci **9** Champlain, Frobisher **10** Chancellor, discoverer

explosion: pop **5** blast **6** blow-up, report **8** outburst **10** detonation

explosive: TNT **4** bomb, mine **5** tense **6** amatol, powder, tonite **7** ammonal, lyddite, melnite **8** cheddite, critical, dynamite, eruptive, unstable, volatile **9** fulminate, guncotton, plastique **10** ammunition, detonative **11** hot-tempered **13** nitroglycerin **15** trinitrotoluene
coal mine: **9** Bobbinite
device: cap **6** petard **9** initiator
high: TNT **7** cordite
igniter: **4** fuse
picric acid: **7** lyddite
projectile: **5** shell **6** rocket **7** grenade, missile **9** cartridge
sound: **4** bang, boom, chug **5** pluff, vroom

exponent: **6** backer **8** advocate, champion, promoter **9** expounder, supporter

expose: **4** bare, open, risk **5** strip **6** betray, detect, reveal, unmask **7** display, exhibit, pillory, publish, uncover, unearth **8** disclose, discover, muckrake, ridicule, satirize, unclothe **10** jeopardize

exposed: **6** unsafe **11** unprotected

exposition: **4** fair, mart, show **5** tract **6** bazaar **7** account **8** analysis, exegesis, treatise **10** exhibition **11** declaration, explanation **14** interpretation

ex post facto: **5** later **9** done after **10** subsequent **11** retroactive **12** after the fact

expostulate: **5** argue **6** object, oppose **7** discuss, dispute, examine, protest **8** complain **11** remonstrate

exposure: **5** vista **7** outlook **9** discovery, publicity, unmasking **10** divulgence, laying bare **11** orientation **12** helplessness

expound: **5** state, treat **6** define **7** develop, explain, exposit, express **8** construe **9** elucidate, explicate, hold forth, interpret

express: **4** vent **5** emote, opine, rapid, speak, state, utter, voice **6** convey, denote, direct, phrase, reveal **7** declare, dictate, expound, nonstop, testify **8** definite, describe, explicit, manifest **9** expatiate, high-speed **10** articulate, particular, peremptory
appreciation: **5** thank
approval: **6** praise **7** applaud
pity: **6** bemoan
regret: **9** apologize

expression: **4** form, pose, show, sign, term, word **5** idiom, token, voice **6** byword, oracle, phrase, symbol **8** laconism **9** euphemism, statement, utterance **10** holophrase **11** delineation, holophrasis **13** manifestation **14** representation
facial: **4** grin, leer, ogle **5** frown, scowl, smile, sneer, wince **7** grimace
hackneyed: **6** cliche **7** bromide **8** banality
mathematical: **8** equation
metaphorical: **6** figure
of approval: **4** clap **5** smile **7** ovation **8** applause
of assent: aye, nod, yea, yes **4** amen, okay **6** placet, righto, so be it **8** of course **9** sure thing
of contempt: bah, fie **4** geck, hiss **5** pshaw, sneer
of gratitude: **12** thanksgiving
of incredulity: **6** indeed, really
of opinion: **4** poll, vote
of sorrow: ay **4** alas **11** lamentation
of weariness: **4** sigh

expressionless: **5** stony **6** vacant **7** deadpan **9** impassive **11** inscrutable

expressive: **5** vivid **6** poetic **7** graphic **8** eloquent, emphatic **10** indicative **11** significant

expressly: **4** just **6** namely **7** clearly, plainly **9** specially

expressway: **4** road **7** freeway, highway, parkway **18** interstate turnpike
German: **8** autobahn

expropriate: **4** take **5** seize **7** preempt **10** commandeer, confiscate

expulsion: **5** exile **7** ousting, removal **8** ejection, eviction **9** debarment, discharge **10** banishment

expunge: **4** dele **5** erase **6** cancel, delete, efface, excise **7** blot out, destroy, scratch **9** eradicate **10** annihilate, obliterate

expurgate: cut **4** blip **5** purge **6** censor, remove **10** blue-pencil, bowdlerize

exquisite: fop **4** dude, nice **5** dandy, exact **6** choice, dainty **7** careful, elegant, refined **8** affected, delicate **9** beautiful, delicious, excellent, matchless, perfected, recherche **10** consummate, fastidious **12** accomplished **14** discriminating

exsanguine: **6** anemic **9** bloodless

exscind: **6** cut out, excise **9** extirpate

exsert: **8** protrude, stick out **11** thrust forth

exsiccate: dry **4** sear **5** parch **9** dehydrate

exsuccous: **7** dried up, sapless **8** withered **9** juiceless

extant: **5** alive, being **6** living **8** existent, existing, manifest

extemporaneous: **5** ad-lib **6** casual **7** offhand **9** impromptu **10** improvised, off-the-cuff **11** unrehearsed **14** unpremeditated

extend: eke, lie, run **4** grow, rise, span **5** bulge, cover, offer, range, reach, renew, widen **6** accord, deepen, dilate, expand, spread, strain **7** amplify, broaden, display, distend, draw out, enlarge, overlap, overrun, proffer, prolong, radiate, stretch **8** continue, increase, lengthen, protract, protrude **10** exaggerate, generalize, outstretch

extension: **4** area **5** scope **8** addendum, addition, duration, increase **9** expansion **11** enlargement **12** augmentation **13** amplification
building: ell **4** wing **5** annex **6** lean-to
of time: **4** stay **7** respite **8** reprieve
trench: sap

extensive: **4** vast, wide **5** ample, broad, large **7** immense **8** expanded **9** capacious **10** widespread **11** far-reaching, wide-ranging **13** comprehensive

extent: due, tax **4** area, body, bulk, levy, size, writ **5** ambit, limit, range, reach, scope, space, sweep **6** amount, degree, spread **7** acreage, breadth, compass, expanse **8** duration, increase, latitude **9** dimension, extension, magnitude, territory, valuation **10** assessment

extenuate: **4** thin **5** gloze **6** excuse, lessen, temper, weaken **7** justify **8** diminish, mitigate, palliate **9** alleviate, gloss over, whitewash **10** depreciate

exterior: **5** ectad, ectal, outer, shell **6** facade **7** outside, outward, surface **8** external

exterminate: **4** kill **6** uproot **7** abolish, destroy, wipe out **9** eradicate, extirpate **10** annihilate, extinguish

external: out **5** alien, outer **7** foreign, outside, outward **8** exterior **9** extrinsic **10** peripheral **11** superficial

extinct: **4** dead, gone, lost **7** defunct **8** quenched, vanished **11** disappeared, nonexistent **12** extinguished

extinction: **5** death **6** expiry **9** abolition **10** expiration **11** destruction **12** annihilation, obliteration

extinguish: end **5** choke, douse, quash, quell **6** cancel, put out, quench, stifle **7** destroy, expunge, smother **8** snuff out, suppress **9** suffocate **10** annihilate

extirpate: **4** dele **5** erase, expel **6** excise, uproot **7** destroy, exscind **8** demolish **9** eradicate **10** annihilate, deracinate **11** exterminate

extol: **4** laud **5** bless, exalt **6** praise **7** applaud, commend, elevate, enhance, glorify **8** emblazon, eulogize **9** celebrate

extort: **5** bleed, exact, force, wrest, wring **6** compel, demand, elicit, wrench **7** extract, squeeze **9** blackmail

extortion: **5** fraud, theft **6** racket, ransom **7** tribute **8** chantage, coercion, exaction **9** shakedown **10** overcharge

extortionate: **9** excessive **10** exorbitant

extra: odd **4** more, orra (Sc.), over, plus **5** added, bonus, spare **7** adjunct, special, surplus **8** superior **9** accessory, lagniappe, unusually **10** additional, uncommonly **12** supplemental

extract: dig, pry **4** cite, draw **5** educe, exact, quote, steep, wring **6** decoct, deduce, derive, elicit, evulse, extort, obtain, remove, render **7** essence, estreat, excerpt, exhaust, pull out **8** separate, withdraw **9** decoction, quotation **11** concentrate
information: **4** pump **5** grill **8** question

extraction: **5** birth, stock **6** origin **7** descent, essence **8** breeding, tincture **9** parentage

extraneous: **5** outer **6** exotic **7** foreign **9** extrinsic, unrelated **10** accidental, immaterial, irrelevant

extraordinary: odd **4** rare **6** signal **7** amazing, notable, special, strange, unusual **8** abnormal, singular, uncommon **9** irregular, monstrous, unheard of, wonderful **10** additional, incredible, phenomenal, remarkable, surprising, tremendous **11** exceptional **13** distinguished

extravagant: **4** wild **5** outre **6** costly, heroic, lavish **7** baroque, bizarre, fanatic, nimious, profuse, vagrant **8** prodigal, reckless, romantic, wanderer, wasteful **9** excessive, expensive, fantastic, luxurious **10** exorbitant, thriftless **11** dispendious **12** preposterous, unreasonable, unrestrained

extreme: end **4** last **5** final, great, limit, ultra, undue, utter **6** far out, heroic, severe, utmost **7** drastic, forward, howling, intense, outward, violent **8** advanced, devilish, farthest, greatest, terrible, terrific **9** desperate, excessive, nth degree, outermost, stringent, uttermost **10** avant-garde, conclusive, immoderate

extremely: **4** very **6** mighty **8** terribly **9** unusually **11** exceedingly

extremist: **5** basic **7** fanatic, radical **11** fundamental **13** revolutionary

extremity: arm, end, leg, tip, toe **4** foot, hand, limb, need, tail **5** limit, verge **6** border, finger, margin **8** boundary, disaster, terminus **9** bitter end

extricate: **4** free **5** clear, loose **6** rescue **8** liberate, untangle **9** disengage **10** disembroil **11** disentangle **12** wriggle out of

extrinsic: **5** alien **7** foreign, outward **8** external **10** accidental, extraneous, incidental **11** unessential **12** adventitious, nonessential

extroverted: **7** affable **8** friendly, outgoing, sociable **10** gregarious

extrude: **4** spew **5** eject, expel **7** project **8** force out

exuberance: 4 life, zest 5 vigor 6 energy, spirit 8 buoyancy, vivacity 9 animation 10 enthusiasm

exuberant: 6 lavish, lively 7 copious, fertile 8 effusive 9 abounding, excessive, luxuriant, plentiful, vivacious 10 flamboyant 11 uninhibited 12 unrestrained

exudation: gum, lac, sap, tar 5 pitch, resin, rosin 9 discharge, secretion

exude: 4 emit, ooze, seep, weep 5 sweat 7 give off, secrete 8 perspire 9 discharge, percolate

exult: 4 brag, crow, leap 5 boast, gloat, glory 7 rejoice

exultant: 6 elated, joyous 8 jubilant 10 triumphant

exuviate: 4 molt, shed 5 moult 6 slough

eyas: 4 bird 8 nestling

eye (see also **sight, vision**): ee (Sc.); orb 4 disc, gaze, glim, lamp, loop, mien, ogle, scan, view 5 glare, watch 6 behold, goggle, oculus (L.), peeper, regard, vision 7 blinker, observe, witness 10 scrutinize 11 contemplate

black: 5 mouse 6 shiner
cavity: 5 orbit
colored portion: 4 iris
cosmetic: 4 kohl, kuhl 5 liner 6 shadow 7 mascara
covering: 6 eyelid 9 blindfold
defect: 4 cast 6 anopia, myopia 11 astigmatism
disease: 6 iritis 8 cataract, glaucoma, trachoma 14 conjunctivitis
doctor: 15 ophthalmologist
hollow: 5 orbit 6 socket
instrument for examining: 8 otoscope 14 ophthalmoscope
opening in: 5 pupil
part: 4 disc, iris, uvea 5 pupil 6 areola, cornea, retina
pert. to: 5 irian, optic 7 areolar, corneal, retinal 9 ocellated
protector: 5 patch, visor 7 blinker, goggles
pupil dilater: 8 atropine 10 belladonna
simple: 6 ocelli (pl.) 7 ocellus

eyebrow: 4 bree (Sc.) 11 supercilium

eye-catching: 6 marked 9 prominent 10 noticeable 11 conspicuous

eyedropper: 7 pipette

eyeglasses: 5 specs 6 lenses 7 lorgnon, nippers 8 monocles, pince-nez 9 lorgnette

eyelash: 5 cilia (pl.) 6 cilium
dye: 7 mascara
loss: 9 madarosis

eyeless: 5 blind 9 sightless

eyelet: 6 agrafe, gromet, oillet 7 agraffe 8 peephole 10 buttonhole 11 perforation

eyeleteer: 6 bodkin

eyelid: *drooping of:* 6 ptosis
pert. to: 9 blepharal

eye-popping: 7 amazing 8 exciting, stirring 9 thrilling 11 astonishing

eyer: 8 beholder 9 spectator

eyeshot: 5 range, reach

eyesight: 4 view 5 sight 11 observation

eyesore: 4 mess 6 defect 7 blemish

eyetooth: 6 cuspid

eyewash: rot 5 bilge 6 bunkum, drivel, excuse 8 claptrap, flattery

eyot: ait 5 islet

eyra: 7 wildcat

eyrie: See **aerie**

Ezekiel: *father:* 4 Buzi
four beasts: 5 Aniel 6 Azriel, Haniel 7 Kafziel

F

fabian: 4 Shaw 8 cautious, dilatory 9 socialist
fabiform: 10 bean-shaped
fable: lie 4 myth, tale 5 story 6 legend 7 fiction, parable, untruth 8 allegory, apologue 9 falsehood, narrative
  animal of: 6 dragon 7 centaur, unicorn
  being of: 4 ogre 5 dwarf, giant, troll
  bird of: roc 7 phoenix
  collection: 8 bestiary
  serpent of: 8 basilisk
fabric (see also **cloth** and individual fabrics, **cotton, linen, silk, etc.**): rep, web 4 felt, repp 5 baize, beige, build, crepe, frame, lisle, rayon, serge, terry, tulle 6 creton, etoile 7 bunting, etamine, texture 8 cretonne, material 9 construct, cottonade, framework, structure
  calico: 5 sallo 6 sallco
  coarse: mat 5 crash 6 burlap
  corded: rep 4 repp 5 pique
  cotton: 4 duck, lawn, pima, susi 5 baize, chino, denim, khaki, lisle, pique, wigan 6 burrah, calico, canvas, chintz, dimity, madras, muslin, oxford 7 batiste, buckram, cambric, flannel, galatea, gingham, hickory, percale 8 bourette
  cotton knit: 10 balbriggan
  cotton mixture: 6 mashru 7 delaine, satinet, zanella 9 bombasine, bombazine, grusaille
  cotton of light quality: 4 leno 7 jaconet, organza 9 silkaline
  cotton print: 5 batik 6 calico 7 percale 8 cretonne
  cotton twilled: 5 denim, sallo 6 salico 7 fustian, silesia
  cotton with silk embroidery: 8 agabanea
  curtain material: 4 leno 5 ninon, scrim 6 chintz, moreen, velvet 7 silesia
  dealer: 6 draper, mercer
  finisher: 6 beetle
  flag material: 7 buntine, bunting
  heavy: 5 denim 6 canvas 9 petersham
  linen: 4 crea (Sp.), ecru 5 carde, crash 6 barras 7 buckram, drabbet, sinelon
  linen and cotton: 9 huckaback
  linen of light quality: 4 lawn 5 scrim
  lustrous: 5 satin 6 poplin, sateen
  medieval: 4 acca 6 samite
  metallic: 4 acca, lamé, tash
  old: 9 ciclatoun

  plaid: 6 tartan
  printed: 5 batik 6 calico 7 challis, percale
  satin: 5 pekin 6 etoile
  satin imitation: 6 sateen
  sheer: 4 lawn 5 gauze, voile 6 dimity 7 batiste, chiffon, organdy
  silk: 4 alma, gimp, gros, ikat, soie 5 caffa, carde, crepe, moire, ninon, rumal, satin, surah, tulle 6 blatta, camaka, faille, mantua, patola, piquet, pongee, samite 7 alamode, chiffon, foulard, organza, taffeta 8 barathea, bourette, sarcenet, sarsenet 9 charmeuse, grosgrain, levantine, matelasse 10 bombay-cine
  silk (thin): 4 moff 5 tulle 6 pongee 7 hernani 8 eolienne
  silk and cotton: 6 crepon, gloria 9 bombasine, bombazine
  silk and linen: 8 brocatel 10 brocatelle
  silk and wool: 6 crepon, gloria 7 challie, challis 8 eolienne
  silk imitation: 5 rayon 7 satinet
  silk mixture: kin 4 acca 5 balda 6 mashru 7 grogram 8 marocain 9 baldachin, baldaquin, farandine
  silk-ribbed: rep 4 repp 6 faille 7 epingle
  silk yarn: 7 schappe
  straw: mat 7 matting
  striped: aba 7 galatea, ticking
  suiting: 6 dacron 7 acrilan, acrylic
  surface: nap
  synthetic: 5 nylon, orlon, rayon 6 dacron 7 acetate, acrilan, acrylic, plastic 9 polyester
  textile: rep 5 moire 7 etamine
  texture: 4 woof
  thin: 5 gauze 8 gossamer, tarlatan 9 grenadine
  towel: 4 huck 5 terry
  Turkish: 6 agaric 7 chekmak 8 cottonee 10 terry cloth
  twilled: rep 4 alma, jean 5 denim, sallo, serge, surah 6 coburg, sallco 8 corduroy, dungaree, shalloon, whipcord 9 bombasine, bombazine, gabardine, levantine, messaline, tricotine 10 broadcloth, kerseymere
  unbleached: 5 beige 6 muslin
  upholstery: rep 4 repp 6 frieze 7 tabaret
  velvet-like: 5 panne 6 velure 8 duvetine 9 velveteen
  waste material: 5 mungo

watered silk: **5** moire
waterproof: **8** burberry
white: **8** coteline
wide: **6** cotele
wool: **5** baize, beige, casha, serge, tweed **6** afghan, alpaca, angora, burnet, frisca, melton, merino, mohair, moreen, tartan, vicuna **7** bolivia, debeige, delaine, droguet, frisado, frizado, hernani, worsted **8** burberry, cashmere, cataloon, harateen, rattinet, shetland, zibeline, zibeline **9** astra khan, catalowne, gabardine, grenadine, harrateen, montagnac
wool (coarse): **6** djersa, duffel, kersey, witney **8** blocking
wool dress: **5** beige **7** delaine **8** wildbore **9** grenadine
wool mixture: **7** delaine, zanella **9** grisaille
wool-ribbed: rep **4** repp **8** marocain
worsted: **7** etamine
woven: **4** lamé **5** tweed, twill **6** tissue, tricot **7** blanket, damasse, textile
fabricate: **4** coin, form, make, mint **5** build, frame **6** devise, invent, make up **7** concoct, fashion, produce **8** contrive **9** construct **11** manufacture
fabrication: lie **7** fiction, forgery, untruth **8** pretense **9** falsehood
fabricator: **4** liar **6** forger **12** manufacturer
fabula: **5** story
fabulist: **4** liar **5** Aesop, Grimm **6** fabler **8** Andersen **10** parabolist
fabulous: **7** amazing, feigned **8** mythical, romantic **9** legendary **10** apocryphal, fictitious, incredible, phenomenal, remarkable **11** astonishing
facade: **4** face, mask **5** front, put-on **8** pretense
face: map, mug, pan **4** dare, defy, dial, leer, line, meet, moue **5** cover, front, stand **6** facade, oppose, veneer, visage **7** feature, grimace, surface **8** confront, envisage **9** encounter, semblance, stand up to **11** countenance, physiognomy
artery: **9** maxillary
bone: **5** malar **6** zygoma **7** maxilia **8** mandible
covering: **4** mask, veil
defect: **7** harelip
false: **4** mask
guard: **6** beaver
ornament: **4** veil **5** jewel, patch **9** cosmetics
paint: **4** fard **6** parget
part: eye, jaw, lid, lip **4** brow, chin, nose **5** cheek
with masonry: **5** revet
face eastward: **9** orientate
face-off: **8** showdown **13** confrontation

facer: **4** blow **6** bumper, defeat, enigma, puzzle **7** dilemma, tankard
facet: **4** side **5** angle, bezel, culet, phase **6** aspect
facetious: **5** comic, droll, funny, witty **6** jocose **7** amusing, jocular **8** humorous, polished **9** laughable **12** wisecracking
face-to-face: **7** affront, vis-a-vis
face value: par
facia: **5** plate **6** tablet
facient: **4** doer **5** agent
facile: **4** able, easy, glib **5** adept, quick, ready, slick **6** expert, fluent **7** shallow
facilitate: aid **4** ease, help **5** speed **6** assist **8** expedite
facility: art **4** ease **5** eclat, knack, skill **7** address, freedom **9** dexterity, readiness **10** adroitness, expertness, pliability
facing: **5** front, panel **6** veneer **7** surface **8** covering, opposite
downward: **5** prone
inward: **8** introrse
outward: **8** extrorse
upward: **6** supine
facsimile: fax **4** copy **5** model **7** replica, telefax **9** duplicate, imitation **10** similitude **11** counterpart
fact: **4** data (pl.), deed, fait (F.) **5** datum, event, truth **6** verity **7** keynote, lowdown, reality **9** actuality, certainty, thing done **12** circumstance
support: **15** circumstantiate
faction: **4** bloc, sect, side **5** cabal, junto, party **6** circle, clique, schism **7** coterie, dispute, quarrel **8** intrigue, offshoot **9** concision **11** combination
factious: **7** warring **8** fighting **9** seditious **11** dissentious, quarrelsome
factitious: **4** sham **5** false **9** unnatural **10** artificial
factor: gen **4** doer, gene **5** agent, cause, maker **6** author, detail **7** bailiff, steward **8** adherent, aumildar, gomashta, gomastah **11** chamberlain, constituent
factory: **4** mill, shop **5** plant **6** aurang, aurung **8** building, fabrique (F.), officina (Sp.), workshop **11** manufactory **13** establishment
book: **7** bindery
factotum: **5** agent **7** servant **8** handyman
factual: **4** real, true **7** genuine, literal
faculty: wit **4** ease, gift **5** flair, knack, power, skill, staff **6** talent **7** ability **8** aptitude, capacity
fad: **4** rage, whim **5** craze, fancy, hobby **7** crochet, fashion **9** amusement
faddle: **6** trifle **8** nonsense
fade: die, dim **4** dull, pale, wilt **5** decay **6** per-

ish, vanish, wither **7** decline, lighten **8** diminish, discolor, dissolve, evanesce, languish **9** lose color **11** become faint
camera device: **4** iris **9** diaphragm

Faerie Queen: *author:* **7** Spenser
character: ate, Una **4** Alma **5** Guyon **6** Amoret **7** Artegal **8** Calidore, Florimel, Gloriana **11** Britomartis

Fafnir: *brother:* **5** Regin
slayer: **6** Sigurd **7** Sigurth **9** Siegfried

fag: **4** flag, tire, toil **5** droop, weary **6** drudge, menial **7** exhaust, fatigue, frazzle **9** cigarette

faik (Sc.): **6** lessen

fail: ebb **4** flag, fold, lose, sink, wane **5** flunk **6** desert, falter **7** exhaust, flicker, founder **8** languish, peter out

failing: **5** fault **6** foible **7** blemish, frailty **8** weakness **9** infirmity **10** deficiency **11** delinquency, diminishing **12** imperfection

fail-safe: **8** riskless **9** foolproof **10** error-proof

failure: dud **4** bust, flop, lack, loss, miss **5** bilge, decay, fault, lapse, lemon **6** fiasco, fizzle **7** bloomer, debacle, decline, default, neglect **8** abortion, collapse, omission **10** bankruptcy, deficiency **11** delinquency, miscarriage, shortcoming **13** deterioration **14** disappointment

fain: **4** fond, glad **5** eager **7** pleased, willing **8** desirous, inclined **11** constrained

faineant: **4** idle, lazy **5** idler **8** inactive, sluggard

faint: dim **4** dark, pale, pall, soft, weak **5** fuzzy, swoon, vague **6** evanid, feeble, hushed, sickly **7** blurred, languid, obscure, syncope **8** delicate, languish, listless, sluggish **9** simulated **10** indistinct

fainthearted: **5** timid **6** afraid, craven **8** cowardly, timorous

fair: **4** calm, even, just, mart **5** bazar, belle, blond, clear, feria (L.), right **6** bazaar, blonde, comely, decent, honest, kermis, lovely, pretty **7** exhibit, kermess **8** distinct, middling, unbiased **9** beautiful, equitable, impartial **10** auspicious, exhibition, reasonable **12** unprejudiced **13** disinterested, dispassionate

fair game: **4** butt, dupe **6** victim

fair-haired: pet **5** blond **6** blonde **8** favorite

fairest: **6** flower

fairly: **4** well **7** plainly **8** properly, suitably **9** favorably, tolerably **10** handsomely **12** legitimately

fairness: **6** equity **7** honesty, justice **8** equality **12** impartiality

fairy: elf, fay, hob, imp **4** peri, perl, pixy, puck **5** dwarf, gnome, pixie **6** goblin, spirit, sprite, yaksha, yakshi **7** banshee, gremlin,

sylphid **10** leprechaun **11** enchantress
abode: **4** shee **5** sidhe
air: **5** sylph
chief: **4** Puck
king: **6** Oberon
of the Tempest: **5** Ariel
queen: Mab, Una **7** Titania
shoemaker: **10** leprechaun
spirit of death: **7** banshee
tricky: **4** Puck

fairy-like: fey **5** elfin

fait: **4** deed, fact

faith: **4** cult, sect **5** certy (Sc.), creed, troth, trust **6** belief, certie (Sc.), church, credit, pledge **7** promise **8** affiance, reliance, religion **9** bona fides **10** confidence, conviction
article: **5** tenet **9** credendum

faithful: **4** fast, feal, firm, leal, true **5** liege, loyal, pious, tried **6** honest, steady, trusty **7** devoted, sincere **8** accurate, constant **9** steadfast, veracious **13** conscientious

faithfulness: **8** fidelity

faithless: **5** false, punic **6** fickle, hollow, unjust, untrue **7** atheist **8** apostate, delusive, disloyal, shifting, unstable **9** deceptive, mercurial **10** inconstant, perfidious **11** disaffected, incredulous, treacherous **12** unsatisfying

faithlessness: **7** falsity, perfidy, untruth **8** betrayal **10** infidelity

faja: **4** band, belt, sash **5** strip

fake: **4** hoax, sham **5** bogus, cheat, dummy, false, feign, fudge, phony **7** falsify, furbish, pretend, swindle, trump up **8** simulate, spurious **9** imitation **10** fictitious, fraudulent **11** counterfeit, manufacture

faker: **5** quack **6** humbug **7** peddler **9** charlatan, pretender

fakir: **4** monk, yogi **7** ascetic, dervish **9** mendicant

falbala: **7** flounce **8** furbelow, trimming

falcon: **4** hawk **5** hobby, saker **6** lanner, luggar, lugger, merlin, musket, tercel **7** kestrel **9** peregrine
bait: **4** lure
blind: **4** seel
genus: **5** Falco
male: **6** tercel **7** tiercel
nestling: **4** eyas
strap for: **4** jess

falconer: **6** hawker **8** ostreger **10** austringer

falderal: See **folderol**

fall: sag **4** drip, drop, flop, plop, ruin, ruse, sile, sink, slip **5** abate, cloit (Sc.), crash, hance, lapse, plump, rapid, shoot, slump **6** autumn, happen, perish, recede, season, topple, tumble **7** cascade, decline, degrade, depress, descend, devolve, dribble, escheat, plummet, retreat, stumble, subside **8** cataract, collapse, commence, decrease **9** backslide, prostrate, surrender **10** capitulate, depreciate, disappoint **11** precipitate

back: **6** recede **7** relapse, retreat

behind: lag **5** lapse, trail **6** follow **8** straggle **10** lose ground

flat: die **4** fail, goof **6** bungle **7** misfire **9** fizzle out

guy: **4** butt, dupe, gull **5** chump, patsy **6** pigeon, sucker **9** scapegoat

in: **4** cave **5** agree **6** concur, line up **9** terminate

out: row **4** spat, tiff **5** scrap **6** bicker, differ **7** quarrel, wrangle **8** disagree

short: shy **4** fail, lack, miss

fallacious: sly **6** untrue **8** delusive, guileful, illusory **9** deceitful, deceptive, insidious **10** fraudulent, misleading **11** treacherous

fallacy: **4** flaw **5** error **6** idolum **7** mistake, pitfall **11** false notion

fallal: **4** ruff **6** finery, gewgaw

fallen: **5** loose, slain **6** ousted, sinful **7** debased, deposed, immoral

fallfish: **4** chub

fallible: **5** human **6** faulty, unsure **7** errable **9** imperfect **10** unreliable

falling: **6** cadent **8** prolapse, windfall **10** subsidence

fallout: **9** by-product, radiation **12** chance result

fallow: **4** pale **6** barren **9** yellow-red, yellowish **12** uncultivated

fallow deer: **6** damine

false: **4** fake, sham **5** bogus, fause (Sc.), paste, phony, wrong **6** fickle, hollow, pseudo, untrue **7** bastard, crooked, feigned **8** disloyal, illusive, recreant, spurious **9** deceitful, deceptive, dishonest, erroneous, faithless, incorrect, insincere, irregular, pretended **10** apocryphal, artificial, calumnious, fictitious, groundless, mendacious, misleading, perfidious, traitorous, untruthful **11** counterfeit, disaffected, treacherous, unveracious **12** hypocritical

falsehood: cog, fib, lie **4** flam, tale **5** fable, story **6** canard **7** fiction, perfidy, romance, untruth **8** roorback **9** deception, duplicity, imposture, mendacity, treachery **10** pseudology **11** fabrication

falsify: lie **4** fake **5** belie, feint, forge **6** betray, doctor **7** violate **9** dissemble **10** adulterate **11** counterfeit

Falstaff: *ancient:* **6** Pistol

follower: Nym

opera composer: **5** Verdi

play: **7** Henry IV

playwright: **11** Shakespeare

prince: Hal

falter: **4** fail **5** pause, waver **6** boggle, flinch, totter **7** fribble, stumble, tremble **8** hesitate

Fama: **5** rumor

fame: **4** name, note **5** bruit, glory, honor, kudos, rumor **6** esteem, renown, report, repute **7** acclaim, hearsay **8** eminence, prestige **9** celebrity **10** prominence, reputation

familiar: **4** bold, cozy, easy, free, tosh **5** usual **6** common, friend, homely, versed **7** affable **8** frequent, habitual, intimate, sociable **9** customary, household, presuming, well-known **10** accustomed, conversant **12** acquaintance **13** unconstrained

familiarize: **4** haft **8** accustom **9** habituate, make known **10** naturalize

family: kin **4** clan **5** class, flesh, group, house **6** cletch **7** kindred, lineage, progeny **8** category **9** household **10** generation

head: **4** wife **6** father, mother **7** goodman, husband **9** matriarch, patriarch **11** householder **13** pater familias (L.)

pert. to: **7** nepotic **12** genealogical

famine: **6** dearth, hunger **8** scarcity **10** starvation **11** destitution

famished: **6** hungry **7** starved **8** ravenous

famous: **5** grand, known, noted **6** namely **7** eminent, namable, notable **8** renowned **9** excellent, notorious, prominent **10** celebrated **11** conspicuous, illustrious, outstanding **13** distinguished

famulus: **7** servant **9** attendant

fan: **4** beat, buff, cool **5** punka **6** basket, blower, colmar, punkah, rooter, shovel, spread, winnow **7** admirer, devotee, groupie **8** follower **9** flabellum, propeller **10** enthusiast

alluvial: **5** delta

form of: **7** plicate

fanatic: mad **5** bigot, crazy, rabid, ultra **6** zealot **7** devotee **8** frenetic **9** energumen, extremist, phrenetic **10** enthusiast, monomaniac **11** extravagant

fancied: **6** unreal **7** dreamed **9** imaginary **10** fictitious

fanciful: odd **5** ideal, queer **6** dreamy, quaint, unreal **7** bizarre, strange **8** romantic **9** conceited, fantastic, grotesque, visionary, whimsical **10** capricious, chimerical, notionable **11** imaginative, unrealistic

fancy: fad **4** idea, love, maze, ween, whim **5** dream, freak, guess, humor **6** deluxe, ideate, liking, megrim, notion, ornate, vagary, vision, whimsy **7** caprice, chimera, conceit, elegant, fantasy, romance, suspect **8** conceive, illusion, phantasm, phantasy **9** capriccio **10** conception, conjecture, decorative, impression, ornamental **11** hanker after, imagination, inclination

fandango: 4 ball, tune 5 dance

fanfare: 4 pomp, show 5 salvo 7 display, panoply, tantara 8 ceremony, flourish

fanfaronade: 7 bluster 8 boasting, bragging 10 swaggering 11 ostentation

fanfoot: 5 gecko 6 lizard

fang: 4 earn, take, tusk, vang 5 begin, seize, snare, tooth 6 assume, obtain 7 capture, procure 9 undertake

fanion: 4 flag 6 banner, guidon

fanlight: 7 transom

fanon: 4 cape 5 orale 7 maniple

fan-shaped: 10 flabellate

fantast: 7 dreamer 9 visionary

fantastic: odd 5 queer, weird 6 absurd, quaint, unreal 7 bizarre 8 fanciful, freakish, romantic, singular 9 grotesque, whimsical 10 capricious, chimerical, ridiculous 11 extravagant, imaginative 12 unbelievable

fantasy: 4 idea, whim 5 dream, fancy 6 desire, vision 7 caprice, chimera, imagery, phantom, romance 8 illusion, phantasm 9 odd notion 10 apparition 11 imagination, inclination 13 hallucination

fantocinni: 5 shows 7 puppets

fantod: pet 4 fuss 6 fidget 7 anxiety

far: 4 long 6 remote 7 distant
across: 4 wide
down: 4 deep

faraway: 6 dreamy, remote 7 distant, removed 9 oblivious 10 abstracted, stargazing

farce: 4 mime 5 stuff 6 comedy, satire 7 mockery 8 drollery, pretense, travesty 9 burlesque, forcemeat

farceur: wag 5 joker

farcical: 5 comic, droll, funny 6 absurd 7 Atellan 9 ludicrous 10 ridiculous

fare: eat 4 diet, food, path, rate, wend 5 cheer, going, price, track, viand 6 happen, travel 7 journey, passage, proceed, prosper 8 progress 9 equipment, passenger, provision, sagaciate 10 expedition 11 nourishment 13 entertainment

farer: 8 traveler

farewell: ave (L.) 4 vale (L.) 5 adieu, adios, aloha, conge, final 7 goodbye, leaving, parting 8 à bientot 9 bon voyage, departure 11 valedictory

farfetched: 6 forced 7 devious, dubious 8 doubtful, strained, unlikely 9 recherche 10 improbable, roundabout

farina: 4 meal 5 flour 6 starch

farinaceous food: oat, rye 4 meal 5 flour, grain, salep, spelt, wheat 6 barley, cereal 7 pudding 10 cornstarch

farm: 4 grow, till 5 croft, raise, ranch, range 6 garden, grange, rancho, spread 7 hennery, potrero 8 estancia, hacienda, hatchery 9 cultivate, farmstead 10 plantation

building: 4 barn, crib, shed, silo
Israeli collective: 7 kibbutz
Soviet collective: 7 kolkhoz

farmer: 4 tate 6 grower, tiller, yeoman 7 granger, hayseed, planter, plowman, rancher 8 producer 9 hacendero (Sp.), ploughman 10 cultivator, husbandman 13 agriculturist
Egyptian: 6 fellah 8 fellahin (pl.)
migratory: 4 Okie
South African: 4 Boer
tenant: 6 cotter 7 cottier 12 sharecropper

farming: 9 husbandry 11 agriculture

farm out: let 4 hire

farnesol: 7 alcohol

faro: 5 monte
bet: 7 sleeper
card: 4 soda
card combination: 5 split 6 cathop
player: 6 punter

farouche: 4 wild 5 surly 6 fierce, savage 7 boorish 10 unsociable

far-out: 7 extreme, radical 8 advanced 10 avant-garde, unorthodox 11 in left field

farrago: 6 medley 7 mixture 10 hodgepodge

far-reaching: 4 deep, vast 7 intense 8 profound

farrier: 5 shoer, smith 10 blacksmith, horseshoer 12 veterinarian

farrow: 9 pig litter

farseeing: 10 telescopic

farsighted: 6 astute, shrewd 9 hyperopia, provident, sagacious 13 hypermetropic

farther: 6 longer 7 remoter 10 in addition

farthest: 7 endmost, extreme, farmost, longest, outmost 8 remotest

farthing: 4 coin 8 quadrans

fascia: 4 band, sash 6 fillet 7 molding

fascicle: 6 bundle 7 cluster

fascinate: 5 charm 6 allure, enamor 7 attract, bewitch, enchant, engross 8 entrance, interest, intrigue 9 captivate, enrapture, spellbind

fascinating: 9 glamorous 10 attractive

fascination: 5 charm, spell 6 allure

Fascism: 6 Nazism 7 Falange 12 dictatorship
leaders of: 6 Franco, Hitler 9 Mussolini

fashion: fad, ton (F.) 4 form, make, mode, mold, rage 5 craze, forge, frame, guise, model, mould, shape, style, vogue 6 create, custom, design, fangle, invent, manner, method 7 compose, portray 8 contrive 9 construct, fabricate

fashionable: 4 chic 5 smart 6 modish, with it 7 a la mode, dashing, stylish 9 au courant

fashioned: 4 made 6 carved 7 wrought

fast: 4 diet, firm 5 agile, apace, bawdy, brisk, fixed, fleet, hasty, loose, quick, rapid, stuck, swift 6 lively, secure, speedy, stable, starve

7 abiding, settled **8** enduring, faithful, reckless **9** immovable, indelible, lecherous, steadfast, unfadable, velocious **10** abstinence, stationary, unyielding **11** expeditious
day of: **5** Ember **6** Friday
period of: **4** Lent **6** Advent

fasten: bar, fix, pen, pin, tag, tie **4** bend, bind, bolt, clip, gird, girt, glue, knit, lace, lash, link, lock, moor, nail, rope, seal, snib, soud, weld, wire **5** affix, annex, belay, brace, chain, clamp, clasp, cling, latch, paste, rivet, seize, strap, truss **6** anchor, attach, batten, cement, clinch, picket, secure, solder, staple, tether **7** connect, padlock **8** transfix

fastener: bar, big, nut, pin **4** agal, bolt, frog, hasp, lock, nail, snap **5** catch, clamp, clasp, latch, rivet, screw, strap, thong **6** buckle, button, hatpin, staple, zipper **7** latchet, padlock **8** staylace

fastidious: **4** fine, nice **5** chary, fussy, natty **6** choicy, choosy, dainty **7** choosey, elegant, finical, finicky, haughty, refined **8** critical, delicate, exacting, overnice, scornful **9** exquisite, squeamish **10** meticulous, particular

fastigate: **7** conical, pointed

fastness: **4** fort **6** castle **7** citadel, sanctum **8** fortress **10** stronghold

fastuous: **5** lofty **7** haughty **8** arrogant **11** pretentious **12** ostentatious

fat: oil, tub **4** lard, lipa, rich, suet **5** adeps, brosy, cetin, chuff, ester, fleck, gross, lipid, lipin, obese, plump, podgy, pudgy, pursy, squab, stout, thick **6** fleshy, grease, lipide, oleate, portly, pubble, stocky, tallow **7** adipose, blubber, fertile, fulsome, lanolin, opulent, pinguid, stearin **8** extended, fruitful, lanoline, stearate, stearine, unctuous **9** corpulent **10** profitable **11** flourishing
hard: **4** suet
liquid: **5** olein **6** oleine
wool: **7** lanolin **8** lanoline

fatal: fey **4** dire **6** deadly, doomed, lethal, mortal **7** ominous, ruinous **8** destined **9** condemned, prophetic **10** calamitous, disastrous, pernicious, portentous **11** destructive

fatality: **5** death **8** calamity, disaster

fata morgana: **6** mirage

fatback: **8** menhaden, salt pork, sowbelly

fatbird: **8** guacharo

fate: end, lot **4** doom, ruin **5** event, karma **6** chance, kismet **7** destiny, fortune, outcome **8** downfall **14** predestination
goddess: Ker **4** Nona, Norn **5** Morta, Tyche **8** Adrastea **9** Adrasteia

fated: **6** doomed **7** decreed **8** destined **10** inevitable

fateful: **7** crucial **8** critical, decisive **9** momentous, prophetic **10** inevitable, portentous **11** destructive, predestined

Fates: *Greek:* **5** Moera, Moira **6** Clotho, Moerae, Moirai **7** Atropos **8** Lachesis
Roman: **4** Nona **5** Decum, Morta, Parca **6** Parcae

fat farm: **9** health spa **10** diet resort

fathead: oaf **4** boob, dolt **5** chump, dunce **6** dimwit **8** numskull

father: abu (Ar.), ama, dad, pop **4** abba, abou (Ar.), baba (Ar.), bapu, dada, papa, pere (F.), sire **5** adopt, babbo, beget, daddy, friar, padre (Sp.), pater (L.), vader (Dan.) **6** author, create, old man, parent, priest **7** founder, tatinek (Czech.) **8** generate, inventor **9** confessor, originate, paternity, procreate **11** acknowledge
of English learning: **4** Bede
of geometry: **6** Euclid
of gods and men: **4** Zeus
of human race: **4** Adam
of plenty: **8** Abiathar
pert. to: **6** agnate **8** paternal

fatherhood: **9** paternity

fatherly: **6** kindly **8** paternal **10** protective

Father of Waters: **11** Mississippi

Father Time: *implements:* **6** scythe **9** hourglass
personified: **6** old man

fathom: **5** brace, delve, solve **7** measure **9** ferret out, penetrate **10** understand

fathomless: **7** abysmal **16** incomprehensible

fatidic: **9** prophetic

fatigue: fag **4** jade, tire **5** spend, weary **6** overdo, taigle (Sc.) **7** exhaust, wear out

fatigued: **4** beat **5** spent, tired, weary **6** bushed, pooped **7** drained, worn out **9** exhausted **11** tuckered out

Fatima: *descendant:* **7** Fatimid **8** Fatimite
husband: Ali **9** Bluebeard
sister: **4** Anne
stepbrother: Ali

fat person: **4** lump **5** blimp, squab, tubby **8** roly-poly **12** humpty-dumpty

fatten: **4** lard **6** batten, enrich, thrive

fatty: **4** oily **5** suety **6** greasy **7** adipose **8** blubbery

fatuous: **5** inane, silly **6** stupid, unreal **7** foolish, idiotic, witless **8** demented, illusory, imbecile **9** frivolous, insensate

faucet: tap **4** cock **5** valve **6** spigot **7** hydrant

faugh: bah, fie, ugh

Faulkner: *character:* **4** Anse, Cash, Darl **5** Addie, Caddy, Jason, Jewel **6** Bayard, Dilsey, Popeye, Sutpen **7** Quentin **9** Dewey Dell
family: **6** Snopes **7** Bundren, Compson **8** Sartoris

trilogy: **7** The Town **9** The Hamlet **10** The Mansion

work: **5** Pylon **6** A Fable **8** Sartoris **9** Sanctuary **11** As I Lay Dying **14** Absalom Absalom

fault: sin **4** debt, flaw, flub, lack, slip, vice **5** abuse, blame, culpa (L.), error, guilt, lapse, tache (Sc.) **6** defect, foible, vitium (L.) **7** blemish, blunder, default, demerit, failure, frailty, mistake, neglect, offense **10** peccadillo **11** culpability, delinquency, misdemeanor **12** imperfection **13** transgression
in mining: **4** hade

faultfinder: **5** momus **6** carper, critic **7** caption, knocker, nagster

faultless: **4** pure **5** right **7** correct, perfect, precise **8** flawless **9** blameless **10** impeccable **13** unimpeachable **14** irreproachable

faulty: bad, ill **5** amiss, unfit, wrong **6** flawed, marred **8** fallible, specious **9** defective, incorrect **10** inaccurate

faun: **5** satyr
of Praxiteles: **6** marble

fauna and flora: **5** biota

Faunus: *grandfather:* **6** Saturn
son: **4** Acis

Faust: *author:* **6** Goethe **7** Marlowe
composer: **6** Gounod

faux pas: **4** bull, slip **5** boner, error, gaffe, lapse **6** boo-boo, bungle **7** blooper, misstep, mistake

faveolate: **9** alveolate **11** honeycombed

favonian: **4** mild **6** gentle

favor: aid, for, pro **4** boon, face, gree, help **5** bless, grace, leave, spare **6** esteem, letter, uphold **7** advance, feature, forward, support **8** advocacy, befriend, goodwill, kindness, resemble **9** party gift, patronage, privilege, subscribe **10** assistance, concession, indulgence, permission **11** accommodate, approbation, countenance **13** communication
pay: woo **5** court

favorable: **4** good, kind, rosy **5** clear **6** benign **7** benefic, optimal, popular **8** friendly, gracious, pleasing **9** approving, opportune **10** auspicious, charitable, convenient, propitious **12** advantageous

favored: **6** gifted **9** fortunate, preferred

favorite: pet **6** minion **7** darling, popular

favoritism: **4** bias **8** nepotism **9** prejudice

fawn: **4** buck, deer, jouk **5** color, cower, crawl, kotow, toady, whelp **6** cringe, grovel, kowtow, shrink **7** adulate, flatter, hangdog, servile, truckle **9** parasitic, sycophant **10** ingratiate
skin: **6** nebris

fay: elf **5** fairy, pixie **6** sprite

faze: **5** abash, daunt, worry **6** bother, rattle **7** confuse, nonplus, perplex **8** irritate **9** embarrass **10** disconcert

fealty: **6** homage **7** loyalty **8** fidelity **9** constancy, obeisance **10** allegiance

fear: awe **5** alarm, doubt, dread, panic **6** danger, dismay, fright, horror, phobia, terror **7** anxiety, suspect **8** affright, disquiet, distrust, venerate **9** agitation, reverence, revulsion **10** solicitude **12** apprehension **13** consternation
of animals: **9** zoophobia
of being alone: **10** monophobia
of blood: **10** hemophobia
of burial alive: **11** taphephobia
of cats: **12** aelurophobia, ailurophobia
of darkness: **11** nyctophobia
of death: **11** necrophobia **13** thanatophobia
of dirt: **10** mysophobia
of dogs: **10** cynophobia
of drafts: **10** aerophobia
of enclosed places: **14** claustrophobia
of fire: **10** pyrophobia
of heights: **10** acrophobia
of night: **11** nyctophobia
of open spaces: **11** agoraphobia
of pain: **10** algophobia
of poisons: **10** toxiphobia
of strangers: **10** xenophobia
of thunder: **11** astraphobia **12** brontophobia **13** tonitrophobia
of water: **11** hydrophobia

fearful: **4** dire **5** awful, timid **6** afraid **7** ghastly, nervous, panicky, worried **8** cautious, doubtful, dreadful, grewsome, gruesome, horrible, horrific, shocking, terrible, timorous **9** appalling, frightful, trembling **10** formidable, horrendous, meticulous **11** distressing **12** apprehensive

fearless: **4** bold **5** brave **6** daring, heroic **8** intrepid **9** audacious, confident, dauntless, undaunted **10** courageous

feasible: **6** doable, likely, viable **8** possible, probable, suitable **9** practical, realistic **10** reasonable

feast: eat, foy (Sc.), sup **4** dine, fete, luau, meal **5** festa, treat **6** regale, repast, spread **7** banquet, delight, festino, gratify **8** festival, potlatch **10** burrakhana
January 6: **8** Epiphany
of lanterns: Bon
of lights: **7** Hanukka **8** Chanukah, Hanukkah
of lots: **5** Purim
of nativity: **9** Christmas
of tabernacles: **7** Succoth
of weeks: **8** Shabuoth
Passover: **5** seder

feasting: **9** epulation
companion: **7** convive

feat: act **4** deed, gest **5** geste, stunt, trick **7** exploit, miracle, venture **11** achievement, performance, tour de force **14** accomplishment

feather: **4** deck, down, vane **5** adorn, penna, pinna (L.), pluma (L.), plume, quill **6** clothe, fledge, fletch, hackle, pinion
barb: **4** harl, herl **7** pinnula
down: **4** dowl **5** dowle **7** plumule
mature: **10** teleoptile
quill: **5** remex **7** calamus
shaft: **5** scape
shank: **4** boot
shoulder: **4** cape

featherbrained: **5** giddy, silly **7** flighty, foolish **9** frivolous **11** empty-headed

feathered: **7** pennate, pinnate

feather key: **6** spline

feathers: **5** dress **6** attire **7** plumage
shed: **4** molt **5** moult

feather star: **8** comatula **9** comatulae (pl.), comatulid

featherweight: **5** dunce, light **7** trivial **10** of no matter

feathery: **4** soft **5** light **6** fluffy

featly: **6** neatly, nimbly **8** properly

feature: **4** face **5** favor, motif, token, trait **6** aspect, detail, play up, stress **7** amenity, element, outline **8** salience **9** attribute, character, emphasize, lineament **11** countenance **14** characteristic
natural: **9** geography

febris: **5** fever

feckless: **4** weak **8** careless **9** shiftless, worthless **10** unreliable **11** ineffective, thoughtless **13** irresponsible

fecund: **7** fertile **8** fruitful, prolific

fecundate: **9** fertilize, pollinate **10** impregnate

fed up: **5** bored **7** wearied **8** satiated **9** disgusted, surfeited

federation: **5** union **6** league **8** alliance **9** coalition **11** association, confederacy

fedora: hat

fee: **4** cost, dues, feal, feul (Sc.), fier, hire, rate, wage **5** price **6** charge, reward, salary **7** expense, payment, stipend, tribute, tuition **8** gratuity, malikana, retainer **9** allowance, bienvenne, emolument, pourboire **10** assessment, honorarium, perquisite, recompense **12** compensation
bridge: **4** toll
money-changing: **4** agio
outdoor storage: **7** yardage
trucking: **7** cartage
wharf: **7** quayage

feeble: **4** lame, mean, poor, puny, weak **5** faint, frail **6** flabby, flimsy, infirm, scanty, sickly, weakly **7** fragile, invalid, languid **8** decrepit, impotent, inferior, thewless (Sc.), yielding **9** miserable **10** inadequate, indistinct **11** debilitated

feebleminded: **5** anile, dotty **7** moronic **10** irresolute **11** vacillating

feed: eat, hay **4** bait, bran, fill, grub, meal, oats, sate **5** grass, graze, nurse **6** fodder, foster, repast, suckle, supply **7** blowout, furnish, gratify, herbage, indulge, nourish, nurture, satiate, satisfy, sustain **9** replenish
the kitty: **4** ante
to excess: **4** glut **5** binge, gorge, stuff **7** surfeit **8** overfill **9** crapulate

feeder: **6** branch **9** tributary
fire: **6** stoker

feel: paw **4** deem **5** grope, probe, sense, touch **6** finger, fumble, handle **7** believe, examine, explore, texture **8** perceive **9** be moved by **10** appreciate, experience

feeler: **4** palp **6** palpus **7** antenna, smeller **8** proposal, tentacle **12** trial balloon

feeling: **4** mood, pity, tact, view **5** humor, sense, touch **6** morale **7** emotion, opinion, passion **8** attitude **9** affection, sensation, sentiment **10** atmosphere, experience, perception **11** sensibility **13** consciousness **14** susceptibility
capable of: **8** sentient
evocative of: **7** emotive
lack of: **4** cold **6** apathy **8** numbness, uncaring **9** unconcern **10** anesthesia **13** insensibility

feet (see also **foot**): **4** dogs

feign: act **4** fake, seem, sham **5** avoid, fable, shape, shirk **6** affect, assume, invent **7** conceal, fashion, imagine, pretend, romance **8** disguise, simulate **9** dissemble, personate **11** counterfeit, dissimulate, make-believe
ignorance: **7** connive
sickness: **8** malinger

feigned: **5** false, put on **6** pseudo **9** insincere **10** artificial, fictitious

feint: **4** hoax, ploy, ruse, wile **5** bluff, dodge, shift, trick **6** gambit **8** pretense **9** diversion
in fencing: **5** appel

feis: **8** assembly, festival **10** convention

feisty: **6** lively **8** snappish, spirited **9** energetic **10** aggressive **11** belligerent, quarrelsome

feldspar: **6** albite, gneiss **7** odinite, syenite **9** anorthite **11** labradorite
yield: **6** kaolin

felicitate: **6** salute **12** congratulate

felicitous: apt **5** happy **6** joyous **7** apropos, fitting **8** pleasing **11** appropriate

felicity: joy **9** happiness, well-being

felid: cat

feline: cat, sly, tom **4** lion, lynx, pard, puma **5** civet, tiger **6** jaguar **7** cheetah, leonine,

leopard, sinuous, wildcat **8** stealthy **9** grimalkin **11** treacherous
breathing: **4** purr

fell: cut, fen, hew **4** down, hide, hill, moor, pelt, ruin, skin, very **5** cruel, eager, field, great, sharp **6** deadly, fierce, fleece, intent, mighty, savage, shrewd **7** brutish, crashed, doughty, hideous, inhuman, tumbled **8** mountain, spirited **9** barbarous, ferocious, marshland, momentous, prostrate **11** destructive

fellah: **7** peasant

fellow (see also **man, person**): guy, lad, man **4** bean, beau, bozo, chap, cove, dick, duck, hind, mate, peer **5** billy, bloke, match **6** bugger, codger, hombre (Sp.), person, sirrah **7** chappie, comrade, partner **8** neighbor **9** associate, companion **10** sweetheart **12** contemporary
awkward: oaf **4** lout **5** booby, clown **6** galoot **7** bumpkin **11** hobble-de-hoy
brutish: **5** yahoo
conceited: **7** egotist **8** braggart **9** know-it-all
craven: **6** coward
dissolute: **4** rake, roue **9** debaucher
dull: **4** clod, drip, fogy **5** dunce, fogey
fat: **7** glutton
fine: **5** brick, bully **8** bonhomme (F.)
funny: wag, wit **4** card **5** clown, comic
honest: **6** trusty
lazy: bum **6** loafer **9** drawlatch
little: bub **5** caddy **6** birkie, caddie, shaver **9** dandiprat
mean: cad **4** boor **5** bucko, churl **8** blighter
old: **6** codger, geezer, gleyde
old-fashioned: **4** fogy
queer old: **6** geezer **10** curmudgeon
ragged: **10** ragamuffin **14** tatterdemalion
reckless: **4** buck **5** blade **9** daredevil, hell-raker
rowdy: **6** roarer **7** hellion **8** larrikin
shrewd: **6** gazabo, gazebo
silly: **8** dotterel
stupid: ass **4** clod, dolt, simp **5** dunce, moron **9** blockhead
tricky: **5** knave, scamp **6** rascal
vain: fop
worthless: bum, cur **5** rogue, scamp **7** brothel **9** schlemiel (Yid.), scoundrel

fellowship: **5** guild, union **7** company **8** alliance **9** communion **10** fraternity, membership **11** association, brotherhood, camaraderie, comradeship, corporation, familiarity, intercourse, partnership **12** friendliness **13** companionship

felly: **7** cruelly **8** savagely **11** barbarously **13** destructively

felo-de-se: **7** suicide

felon: **4** base **5** cruel **6** wicked **7** convict, culprit, whitlow **8** criminal, offender **10** lawbreaker, malefactor

felony: **5** crime **7** offense

felt: hat **6** fabric, sensed

felwort: **7** gentian

female: **4** girl, lass **5** woman **7** womanly **8** feminine, ladylike, womanish **9** womanlike **10** effeminate
animal: cow, dam, doe, ewe, hen, sow **4** mare, slut **5** bitch, filly, jenny, tabby **6** heifer **7** lioness, tigress
assistant: **8** adjutrix **9** adjutrice **10** girl friday
camel: **4** naga
figure: **5** orant **8** caryatid
fish: **4** raun
fox: **5** vixen
monster: **6** gorgon
principle: **5** Sakti
red deer: **4** hind
sandpiper: **5** reeve
sheep: ewe
slave: **7** odalisk **9** odalisque
spirit: **7** banshee
warrior: **6** Amazon

feminine: **4** soft, weak **6** female, tender **8** womanish **10** effeminate

femme fatale: **5** siren **7** Lorelei **8** Mata Hari **9** temptress **10** seductress

femoral: **6** crural

femur: **9** thighbone

fen: bog **4** carr, fowl, moor **5** marsh, snipe, swamp **6** morass **8** quagmire

fence: bar **4** cage, coop, duel, gird, rail, wall **5** dodge, guard, hedge, parry, pen in **6** paling, picket, rasper **7** barrier, bulwark, defense **8** encircle, palisade, surround **9** enclosure **12** circumscribe, dealer in loot **14** buy stolen goods
fish: net **4** weir
interwoven: **6** raddle
mending: **11** politicking
on the: **9** undecided **11** uncommitted
picket: **6** paling
sunken: **4** ha-ha

fencer: **7** duelist, parrier **9** gladiator, swordsman
cry of: **6** touche **7** en garde

fencing: **9** swordplay
attack: **5** lunge **6** thrust **7** reprise
breastplate: **8** plastron
cry: **4** sasa
hit: **5** punto
maneuver: **5** appel
movement: **4** volt
position: **5** carte, prime, sixte, terce **6** octave, quarte, quinte, tierce **7** seconde, septime
position of hands: **9** pronation **10** supination

redoubling of attack: 7 reprise
term: 4 bind 5 lunge, parry 6 thrust, touche
thrust: 7 riposte
weapon: 4 epee, foil 5 blade, saber, sabre, sword 6 rapier

fend: 4 ward 5 avert, avoid, parry 6 defend, manage, resist 7 keep off, provide, support 8 push away 10 take care of

fender: 5 guard 6 buffer, bumper, shield 8 mudguard 11 splashboard

fenestra: 6 window 7 foramen, opening 8 aperture, fontanel

fennec: fox

fennel: 4 herb 9 seasoning
relative: 7 parsley

feracious: 8 fruitful

feral, ferine: 4 wild 6 deadly, savage 7 bestial, untamed 8 unbroken 11 uncivilized 14 undomesticated

fer-de-lance: 5 snake, viper

Ferdinand's wife: 8 Isabella

feria: 4 fair 6 fiesta 7 holiday

fermail: 5 clasp 6 buckle

ferment: 4 barm, heat, turn, work, zyme 5 fever, yeast 6 enzyme, seethe, tumult, uproar 7 agitate 8 disorder 10 ebullition, exacerbate, excitement, turbulence

fermenting mixtue: bub 4 wort

fern: 4 lady, tara, tree, weki 5 brake, sword 6 clover 7 Asiatic, bracken, woodsia 8 polypody, tropical 10 maidenhair 12 adder's-tongue
climbing: 4 nito
edible: roi 4 tara
genus: 7 Onoclea, Osmunda 8 Psilotum
leaf: 5 frond
royal: 6 osmund
scale: 7 ramenta (pl.) 8 ramentum
stalk: 5 stipe

fern-like: 7 pteroid

ferocious: 4 fell, grim, wild 5 cruel, feral 6 bloody, brutal, fierce, raging, savage 7 inhuman, ominous, violent 8 pitiless, ravenous, ruthless 9 barbarous, malignant, merciless, murderous, rapacious, truculent 10 implacable, malevolent, relentless, sanguinary 11 remorseless 12 bloodthirsty

ferret: 4 tape 6 mammal, weasel 7 polecat
male: hob

ferret out: 4 hunt, seek 5 probe 6 elicit 7 uncover 9 search for

ferric oxide: 5 rouge 6 powder

ferrotype: 7 tintype

ferrule: cap 4 ring, virl (Sc.) 6 collet, pulley, verrel 7 bushing, verrell

ferry: 4 pont, scow 7 traject

ferryman: 6 Charon

fertile: fat 4 rank, rich 5 gleby 6 fecund, hearty 7 teeming 8 abundant, fruitful, generous, prolific 9 exuberant, feracious, inventive, luxuriant, plenteous, plentiful 10 productive, profitable
render: 6 enrich

fertilize: 6 batten, enrich 8 fructify 9 fecundate 10 impregnate, inseminate

fertilizer: 4 marl 5 guano, humus 6 alinit, manure, pollen, potash 7 compost, nitrate 8 nitrogen 11 phosphorous 14 superphosphate

ferule: rod 5 ruler 6 fennel 10 discipline

fervent: hot 4 keen, warm 5 eager, fiery 6 ardent, bitter, fierce, raging, savage 7 boiling, burning, glowing, intense 8 vehement 9 impetuous, religious 10 passionate 11 impassioned

fervor: 4 fire, heat, love, rage, zeal 5 ardor 7 ecstasy, feeling, passion 8 candency 9 eagerness, vehemence 10 enthusiasm, excitement 11 earnestness

fess: bar 4 band

fester: rot 4 grow 6 rankle 7 blister, inflame, pustule, putrefy, smolder 8 embitter, ulcerate

festival: bee 4 fair, fete, gala 5 feast, feria, festa, revel 6 fiesta 7 banquet, holiday 8 carnival, carousal, jamboree 11 celebration
church: 6 Easter 9 Christmas
Epiphany: 7 uphelya (Sc.)

festive: gay 4 gala 5 merry 6 festal, genial, joyous 7 jocular, playful 8 mirthful, sportive 9 convivial 10 frolicsome 11 celebratory

festivity: 4 gala 5 mirth, randy, revel 6 gaiety, splore 7 jollity, jubilee, whoopee 8 function 10 joyfulness 11 celebration, merrymaking 12 conviviality 13 entertainment, glorification
god: 5 Comus 7 Bacchus 8 Dionysus

festoon: 4 loop, swag 6 wreath 7 garland 8 decorate

fetch: get 4 gasp, tack, take 5 bring, sweep, trick 6 double, elicit, obtain, wraith 7 achieve, attract, go after, realize, sell for 8 artifice, interest, retrieve 9 stratagem
round: 6 revive 8 convince, persuade

fetching: 4 cute 8 alluring, charming, pleasing 10 attractive 11 fascinating

fete: 4 fair, gala 5 bazar, feast 6 bazaar, fiesta, regale 7 banquet, holiday 8 ceremony, festival 9 entertain 11 celebration

fetid: 4 foul, olid, rank 5 fusty, musty 6 putrid, rancid, rotten, virose 7 miasmic, noisome, noxious 8 mephitic, stinking 9 offensive 10 malodorous

fetish, fetich: obi 4 idol, joss, juju, obia 5 charm, huaca, image, obeah, obiah, totem 6 amulet, grigri, voodoo 7 sorcery 8 fixation, greegree, idee fixe, talisman 10 mumbo jumbo

fetter: **4** band, bind, bond, gyve, iron **5** basil, chain, tie up **6** anklet, garter, hamper, hobble, hog-tie, hopple, impede **7** confine, enchain, manacle, shackle, trammel **8** handcuff, restrain **9** restraint

fettle: **4** mend, trim **5** dress, groom, order, shape **6** repair, strike **7** fitness, harness, spirits **9** condition

feud: **4** fief, fray **5** broil **6** affray, enmity, strife **7** contest, dispute, quarrel **8** conflict **9** hostility **10** contention
blood: **8** vendetta

feudal: **6** lordly **8** manorial, medieval **9** imperious **10** oligarchic
estate: **4** fief **5** feoff
jurisdiction: soc **4** soke
lord: **5** liege **7** vavasor **8** suzerain, vavasour
penalty: **7** sursise
pert. to: **5** banal
tenant: **6** vassal **7** homager
tenure: **6** socage

fever: **4** fire **6** febris (L.) **7** ferment **9** calenture **10** excitement **11** temperature **13** conflagration
kind of: **4** ague **5** octan, swamp **6** dengue, sextan, sodoku **7** malaria, quartan, scarlet, spotted **8** undulant
without: **8** apyretic

feverish: **5** fiery **6** hectic **7** excited, febrile, flushed, frantic, parched **8** inflamed, restless **9** overeager **11** impassioned

few: **4** less, some, thin **5** scant **6** scarce, skimpy **7** limited, not many, several **8** exiguous

fewness: **7** paucity

fey: odd **5** elfin, queer **7** puckish **9** eccentric, visionary, whimsical **12** otherworldly

fez: hat **8** tarboosh

fiacre: **4** hack **5** coach **8** carriage

fiance: **8** intended **9** betrothed

fiasco: **4** bomb, flop, mess **6** fizzle **7** debacle, failure, washout **8** disaster

fiat: **5** edict, order **6** decree **7** command **8** decision, sanction **9** ordinance **12** announcement, proclamation

fib: lie **5** hedge, story **7** untruth **9** falsehood **10** equivocate **11** prevaricate

fiber, fibre: **4** root **5** grain **6** nature, thread, tissue **7** quality **9** character
band: **6** fillet
bark: **5** olona, terap
hat: **5** datil
kind of: nap, nep, tal, tow **4** adad, aloe, bast, buri, coir, eruc, feru, flax, hemp, ixle, jute, kyar, lint, marl, noil, pita, silk, sola, wool **5** abaca, civil, erizo, floss, istle, istli, ixtle, kapok, linen, mudar, oakum, ramee, ramie, sisal **6** amiray, cotton, manila, raffia, staple **7** castuli, haurizo, sabutan **8** fibrilla,

filament, keratose **9** gamelotte **10** anodendron, escobadura
knot: nep
palm: **4** eruc **6** raffia **7** coquita, coquito
synthetic: **5** nylon, orlon, rayon **6** dacron **7** acetate, acrilan **9** polyester
yarn: **6** strand

fibril: **4** hair **8** filament

fibrin: **6** gluten

fibrous: **4** ropy, wiry **6** sinewy **7** stringy

fibula: **5** clasp **6** brooch, buckle **7** leg bone

fickle: **5** dizzy, giddy **6** shifty **7** erratic, flighty **8** unstable, unsteady, variable, volatile, wavering **9** faithless, frivolous, mercurial, unsettled **10** capricious, changeable, inconstant, irresolute **11** vacillating **12** inconsistent

fictile: **6** molded **7** plastic

fiction: **4** tale, yarn **5** fable, novel **6** deceit, device, fabula, legend **7** coinage, fantasy, figment, forgery, romance **9** falsehood, invention **10** concoction, pretending **11** contrivance, dissembling, fabrication **14** counterfeiting

fictitious: **4** fake, sham **5** bogus, dummy, false, phony **6** untrue **7** assumed, feigned **8** fabulous, fanciful, mythical, spurious **9** imaginary, imitative, pretended, trumped up **10** apocryphal, artificial, not genuine **11** counterfeit

fid: **9** splice pin **10** topmast bar

fiddle: bow **4** viol **5** cheat **6** doodle, fidget, putter, tinker, trifle, violin **7** swindle **10** fool around

fiddler: **4** crab **7** scraper **8** sixpence **9** violinist

fiddler crab: uca

fiddlesticks: **4** bosh **5** pshaw **8** nonsense

Fidelio: *composer:* **9** Beethoven
hero: **9** Florestan
heroine: **7** Leonora

fidelity: **5** troth, truth **6** fealty **7** honesty **8** adhesion, devotion, veracity **9** adherence, closeness, constancy **10** allegiance **12** faithfulness
symbol of: **5** topaz **7** diamond

fidgety: **5** fussy, jumpy **6** uneasy **7** jittery, nervous, restive, twitchy, unquiet **8** restless **9** impatient, irritable

fiducial: **4** firm **7** trusted **8** reliable **9** confident **11** trustworthy **12** solid as a rock

fiduciary: **7** trustee

field: lea, lot **4** acre, area, mead, pale, plot **5** campo, croft, paddy, plain, range, realm, rowen, sawah, scope **6** campus, domain, ground, meadow, sphere **7** compass, entries, paddock, pasture, terrain **8** clearing, vocation **9** grassland **10** department
athletic: **4** oval, ring, rink **5** arena, court, green **6** course, stadia (pl.) **7** diamond, stadium **8** gridiron

common share: **4** dale
extensive: **7** savanna **8** savannah
god: **4** Faun
goddess: **5** Fauna
hand: **4** hoer **5** sower **6** picker, plower **7** laborer
pert. to: **8** agrarian, agrestic **10** campestral
questions: **11** reply glibly
Roman: **4** ager
stubble: **5** rowen
field mouse: **4** vole
field of blood: **8** Aceldama
fieldwork: **5** redan **7** lunette **13** fortification
fiend: **5** beast, brute, demon, devil, Satan **6** addict, expert, maniac, wizard **7** fanatic, monster **8** succubus **10** evil spirit
fiendish: **5** cruel **6** wicked **7** demonic, inhuman, vicious **8** demoniac, devilish, diabolic, infernal **9** barbarous **10** diabolical
fierce: **4** bold, fell, grim, wild **5** cruel **6** ardent, gothic, raging, savage **7** brutish, fervent, furious, intense, violent **9** ferocious, impetuous, truculent **10** catawampus, forbidding, passionate **12** disagreeable, uncontrolled
fiery: hot, red **5** adust **6** ablaze, ardent, fervid, torrid **7** burning, fervent, flaming, furious, glowing, igneous, parched, peppery, violent **8** choleric, feverish, inflamed, spirited, vehement **9** excitable, hotheaded, impetuous, irascible, irritable **10** mettlesome, passionate **11** combustible, inflammable
fiesta: **4** fete **5** feria, party **7** holiday **8** festival **9** festivity
fife: **4** pipe **5** flute
fifty-fifty: **4** even **7** equally **11** half and half
fig: rig **5** array, dress, fruit, shape **6** trifle **7** furbish **9** condition, little bit **10** tinker's dam
basket: **5** cabas
crate: **5** seron
family tree: **8** mulberry
genus: **5** ficus
sacred: **5** pipal
Smyrna: **5** eleme, elemi
Figaro: **6** barber
author: **12** Beaumarchais
character: **6** Rosina **7** Susanna **8** Almaviva **9** Dr. Bartolo **10** Don Basilio
opera composers: **6** Mozart **7** Rossini
fight: box, war **4** bout, duel, fray, grit, spat, tiff, tilt **5** argue, brawl, clash, melee, pluck, scrap, set-to **6** affair, affray, battle, bicker, combat, debate, fracas, mettle, oppose, resist, spirit, strife, tussle **7** contend, contest, dispute, quarrel, ruction, scuffle, wrangle **8** conflict, militate, skirmish, squabble, struggle **9** encounter, pugnacity **11** altercation **12** disagreement
against the gods: **9** theomachy
fighter: pug **4** vamp **5** boxer **6** cocker **7** battler, duelist, soldier, warrior **8** andabata, barrater, barrator, champion, guerilla, pugilist, scrapper **9** combatant
fighting: **7** warlike **8** militant **10** pugnacious **11** belligerent
street: **4** riot **5** brawl **10** free-for-all
fighting fish: **5** betta
figment: **5** dream, fable, fancy **7** fiction **9** invention **11** fabrication
fig-shaped: **8** ficiform
figuration: **4** form **5** shape **7** outline **9** symbolism **10** appearance
figurative: **6** florid **7** flowery **8** symbolic **9** allegoric **10** not literal, rhetorical **12** metaphorical
use of words: **5** trope
figure: sum **4** body, cost, form, rate **5** add up, build, digit, guess, image, judge, motif, price, shape, total, value **6** amount, design, emblem, number, reckon, symbol **7** chiffer, compute, contour, notable, numeral, outline **8** likeness **9** calculate, character, personage, play a part, quotation **13** configuration
geometrical: **4** cone, cube, lune **5** prism, rhomb, solid **6** circle, gnomon, oblong, sector, square **7** ellipse, lozenge, rhombus **8** crescent, pentacle, triangle **9** rectangle
human form: **4** nude **5** atlas, dummy **6** statue **7** manikin, telamon **8** atlantes, caryatid **9** mannequin
many-sided: **4** cube **6** isogon **7** decagon, hexagon, nonagon, octagon, polygon **8** pentagon, tetragon **10** hexahedron, octahedron **12** dodecahedron
of speech: **5** trope **6** aporia, simile **7** imagery **8** metaphor, metonymy
ornamental: **7** topiary **8** gargoyle
praying: **5** orant
symbolic: **6** emblem
figured: **7** adorned, faconne (Fr.) **8** computed **9** patterned
figurehead: **4** tool **5** dummy, front **6** puppet, stooge **7** stand-in
figure out: **4** dope **5** crack, solve **6** decode **7** clear up, resolve, unravel **10** unscramble **12** get the answer
figurine: **7** tanagra **9** statuette
motion picture: **5** Oscar
filament: **4** hair, harl, wire **5** fiber, fibre **6** mantle, strand, thread
lamp: **8** tungsten
filbert: **8** hazelnut
filch: bob, nim, rob **4** lift **5** pinch, steal, swipe **6** pilfer **7** purloin

file: row 4 line, rank, rasp, tool 5 index, label, queue 6 folder, record, smooth 7 arrange, cabinet, dossier 8 apply for, register 9 grind down 10 procession
combmaker's: 6 carlet
document: 7 dossier
nail: 10 emery board
filet: net 4 lace
filial: 9 childlike 10 respectful
filibeg: 4 kilt 5 skirt
filibuster: 5 block, delay, stall 6 hinder 9 talkathon 14 political stall 15 talk against time
filigree: 4 mesh 7 network, tracery 8 fretwork, lacelike
filing: 5 lemel 8 limation
Filipino: See **Philippines**
fill: pad 4 cram, feed, glut, heap, load, pack, sate 5 earth, gorge 6 blow up, charge, occupy, supply 7 distend, enlarge, execute, fraught, inflate, perfect, perform, pervade, satiate, satisfy, suffuse 8 complete, compound, permeate 9 replenish 10 accomplish, embankment, take care of 11 sufficiency
cracks: 4 calk, plug, shim 5 caulk, putty
in: 5 brief, spell 6 inform 7 put wise 8 acquaint 10 substitute 13 bring up to date
with zeal: 7 enthuse
fille (F.): 4 girl 8 daughter
filled: SRO 4 full 5 sated, solid 6 loaded, packed 7 replete 9 saturated 10 carried out
fillet: 4 band, bone, orle, orlo, tape 5 crown, miter, snood, stria, strip, tiara 6 anadem, binder, diadem, ribbon, striae (pl.), turban, wreath 7 bandeau, chaplet, garland, molding 8 headband, tressure 9 sphendone
architectural: 6 cimbia, fascia, listel, quadra, reglet, regula, taenia 8 bandelet, cincture
filling: *dental:* 5 inlay
fabric: 4 weft, woof
fillip: tap 4 blow, flip, snap 5 boost, twist 6 buffet, charge, jazz up 8 stimulus 9 extra dash, stimulate
filly: tap 4 colt, foal, girl, mare 9 youngster
film (see also **motion picture**): 4 blur, brat (Sc.), haze, mist, scum, skin, veil 5 flake, layer 6 lamina, patina 7 coating 8 beeswing, negative, pellicle 10 photograph
filmy: 4 hazy 5 gauzy, misty, wispy 6 cloudy 7 clouded 8 gossamer 13 unsubstantial
filter: 4 sift 5 drain, sieve 6 purify, refine, screen, strain 8 strainer 9 percolate
sugar: 4 clay
filth: 4 dirt, dung, muck, slop, smut 5 offal 6 ordure, refuse, vermin 7 garbage, squalor 9 obscenity

filthy: low 4 foul, miry, vile 5 dirty, gross, nasty 6 impure, rotten, sordid 7 bestial, immoral, obscene, raunchy, squalid, unclean 8 indecent, sluttish 9 polluting, repulsive, revolting 10 disgusting, licentious 11 disgraceful
fimbriate: 7 fringed
fin: arm 4 hand 5 fiver, pinna 7 acantha, airfoil, flipper 10 stabilizer
finagle: 5 cheat, trick 6 wangle 7 connive, deceive 9 machinate
final: 4 exam, last, test 6 latter 7 dernier, extreme, outmost 8 decisive, definite, eventual, farewell, ultimate 9 uttermost 10 concluding, conclusive, definitive 11 terminating 13 determinating
final outcome: 5 issue 6 payoff, upshot
finale: end 4 coda 5 close, finis 6 ending, windup 7 closing 8 swan song 9 cessation 10 conclusion 11 termination
finally: 8 at length, in the end 10 ultimately 11 irrevocably 12 in conclusion 13 once and for all
finance: tax 4 back 5 endow, stake 6 pay for 7 banking 8 bankroll 9 subsidize 10 underwrite
finances: 5 funds, money 8 accounts, supports 9 economics, exchequer
financial: 6 fiscal 8 monetary 9 pecuniary
finch: 4 fink, moro, pape 5 serin, terin 6 burion, citril, linnet, siskin, towhee 7 chewink, redpoll, senegal, tanager 8 amadavat 9 snowflake
find: get 5 catch 6 locate 8 discover
by keen search: 5 probe 6 ferret
find fault: nag 4 carp, crab, fret 5 blame, cavil, scold 7 grumble 8 complain 9 bellyache, criticize
find guilty: 7 convict
find out: 4 hear 5 learn 6 detect 7 unearth 8 discover 9 ascertain, determine
fine: rum, tax 4 good, jake, levy, nice, pure, thin 5 bonny, brave, bully, clear, dandy, frail, nifty, noble, sharp, sheer, silky, swell 6 amerce, bonnie, bright, choice, finish, ornate, proper, slight, spiffy, subtle, tender 7 elegant, forfeit, fragile, penalty, perfect, precise, tenuous 8 absolute, all right, delicate, handsome, penalize, pleasant, skillful, splendid, superior, top-grade, very well 9 beautiful, excellent, ingenious, sensitive 10 assessment, consummate, fastidious, pulverized, punishment, surpassing
for misdemeanor: 5 mulct
record of: 7 estreat
finery: 6 frills 7 clothes, gaudery, gewgaws, panoply, regalia 8 frippery, glad rags 9

showiness, trappings **10** fancy dress, Sunday best

finesse: art **4** tact **5** guile, skill, taste **6** outwit **7** cunning **8** artifice, delicacy, subtlety **9** dexterity, stratagem **10** artfulness, bridge play, manipulate, refinement, shrewdness **11** sensitivity **12** one-up-manship

fin-footed: **8** pinniped

Fingal's cave: *island:* **6** Staffa
kingdom: **6** Morven

fingent: **7** pliable **8** flexible, yielding

finger: paw, tap, toy **4** feel **5** digit, index, pinky, thumb, touch **6** handle, pilfer, pinkie **7** purloin **8** identify, indicate, inform on, point out
bone: **7** phalanx
guard for: cot **5** stall **7** thimble
inflammation of: **5** felon **7** whitlow
little: **7** minimus
pert. to: **7** digital **8** digitate
snap with: **6** fillip

finger board: **4** fret

Finger Lakes: **5** Keuka **6** Cayuga, Otisko, Owasco, Seneca **7** Conesus, Hemlock, Honeoye **8** Canadice **11** Canandaigua, Skaneateles

fingerlike: **6** dactyl

fingerling: **4** parr **8** troutlet

fingernail moon: **6** lunule

fingerprint: **11** dactylogram
mark: **4** arch, loop **5** whorl **9** composite
science: **12** dactyloscopy

finial: epi **5** crest **8** ornament, pinnacle

finical: **4** nice **5** fussy **6** choosy, dainty, dapper, jaunty, prissy, spruce **7** choosey, finicky, foppish, mincing **8** delicate **9** squeamish **10** fastidious, meticulous **11** overprecise **14** overscrupulous

finis: end **4** goal **5** close **10** conclusion

finish: die, end **4** char, kill, mill **5** bound, cease, chare, cheve, close, enden (G.), glaze, limit **6** fulfil, windup **7** achieve, execute, fulfill, perfect, surface **8** complete, conclude, terminal **9** erudition, terminate **10** accomplish, completion, conclusion, consummate, perfection
dull: mat **5** matte
glossy: **6** enamel

finished: did, oer, pau **4** done, fine, gone, over, ripe **5** ended, kaput **6** closed, ornate **7** refined, stopped **8** climaxed, lustered, polished **9** completed, concluded, perfected, performed **10** terminated **11** consummated **12** professional

finisher: **4** eyer **5** ender **7** beetler **8** enameler

finishing line: **4** tape

finite: **5** fixed **7** limited **9** definable **10** restricted, terminable **11** conditioned

fink: **8** informer, squealer **13** strikebreaker

Finland: **5** Suomi
bathhouse: **5** sauna
capital: **8** Helsinki
city: **4** Oulu **5** Espoo, Lahti, Turku **7** Tampere
composer: **8** Sibelius (Jean)
currency: **5** penni **6** markka
god: **5** Tapio **6** Jumala
harp: **7** kantele
island: **5** Aland, Karlo **6** Kimito **9** Vallgrund
isthmus: **7** Karelia
language: **4** Avar, Lapp **5** Ugric **6** Magyar, Ostyak, Tarast **7** Finnish, Samoyed
measure: **5** kannu, tunna, verst **6** fathom, sjomil **7** tunland **8** ottinger, skalpund, tunnland
mountain: **6** Haltia
river: **4** Kemi Oulu

Finlandia composer: **8** Sibelius

Finnegan's Wake author: **5** Joyce

fiord, fjord: arm, bay, ise **5** firth **12** sealoch inlet

fir: **9** evergreen
genus: **5** abies
type: red **6** balsam, Canada, Fraser **7** Douglas

Firbolg queen: **6** Tailte **7** Talitiu

fire: can, feu (F.) **4** bale, burn, heat, zeal **5** ardor, arson, fever, gleed, light, shoot, stoke **6** arouse, excite, fervor, ignite, incite, kindle, spirit **7** animate, burning, dismiss, explode, fervour, glimmer, inflame, inspire **8** detonate, illumine, irritate, vivacity **9** calenture, cauterize, discharge, holocaust, terminate **10** combustion, enthusiasm, illuminate **12** inflammation **13** conflagration
artillery: **5** salvo **7** barrage
basket: **5** grate **7** cresset
containing: **7** igneous
fighter: **4** vamp
god: **4** Agni, Loki **6** Vulcan **10** Hephaestus
military: **4** flak **5** salvo **6** rafale **7** barrage
particle: arc **5** spark
pert. to: **7** igneous
sacrificial: **4** agni
set: **6** accend, ignite, kindle **7** inflame **8** enkindle, irritate
worshiper: **5** Parsi **6** Parsee **9** pyrolater **10** ignicolist

firearm: gun **5** piece, rifle **6** musket, pistol **7** demihag **8** revolver

fireback: **7** reredos **8** pheasant

fireboat: **8** palander

firebrand: **5** blaze **6** bleery

firebug: **10** incendiary, pyromaniac

firecracker: 5 squib 6 petard 7 cracker, snapper 9 skyrocket

firedamp: gas 7 methane

firedog: 7 andiron

fireman: 4 vamp 6 stoker, tizeur 9 fire-eater

fireplace: 5 focus, fogon, forge, foyer, heath, ingle 8 cheminee
part: hob 6 mantel 9 ingleside 11 hearthstone

fireplug: 7 hydrant

firer: 6 stoker 10 incendiary

fireside: 9 ingleside 11 hearthstone

firestone: 5 flint

firewood: 4 lena 5 fagot 6 billet, billot

fireworks: 4 gerb 5 gerbe 7 fizgigs, rockets 9 sparklers 10 girandoles 11 tour-billion 12 pyrotechnics
resembling: 11 pyrotechnic

firing: 4 fuel

firm: hui 4 buff, fast, hard, sure, trig 5 champ, dense, exact, firma, fixed, hardy, house, loyal, rigid, solid, sound, stith, stout, tight 6 hearty, secure, settle, sinewy, stable, stanch, steady, stolid, strong 7 adamant, certain, compact, company, confirm, context, decided, durable, staunch, unmoved 8 constant, faithful, fiducial, obdurate, resolute, unshaken 9 backboned, establish, immovable, immutable, standfast, steadfast 10 consistent, determined, unslipping, unwavering, unyielding 11 established, partnership, substantial, substantive, well-founded 13 establishment

firmament: sky 7 heavens 8 empyrean

firmly fixed: 6 rooted, stable

firmness: 4 iron 7 courage, resolve 8 solidity, strength, tenacity 9 constancy, stability 10 immobility, steadiness 11 consistency 13 determination 15 indissolubility

firn: ice 4 neve, snow

first: 4 erst, head, high, main 5 alpha, chief, forme, nieve, prime 6 primal, primus 7 highest, initial, leading, primary 8 earliest, foremost, original 9 primitive, principal 10 aboriginal, primordial
appearance: 5 debut 8 premiere

firstborn: 4 heir 5 eigne 6 eldest

first class: 5 prime 9 excellent, topdrawer 10 first-cabin

first-rate: 4 A-one, good, jake 5 prime 6 tiptop 7 skookum 8 clipping, top-notch 9 admirable, excellent

firth: 4 kyle 5 fiord, fjord, frith, inlet 7 coppice, estuary

Firth of Clyde island: 4 Bute 5 Arran

fiscal: 8 monetary 9 financial

fiscus: 8 treasury

fish: net 4 cast, quab 5 angle, drail, seine, troll 7 poisson (F.)

African: 6 anabis

Alaska: 6 iconnu

ascending river from sea: 7 anadrom

Atlantic Coast: 4 opah, pogy 6 bunker, salema 7 alewife, bugfish, bughead, fatback, oldwife 8 bonyfish, menhaden 9 greentail 10 mossbunker

Australian: 4 mado 6 groper 7 grouper

bait: 5 killy 9 killifish

barbed tail: 8 stingray 9 stingaree

California: 4 rena 5 reina 6 rasher 8 bocaccio 9 garibaldi

carangold: 4 scad 5 jurel

carp: id, ide, orf

catfish: 6 hassar 9 sheatfish

caviar-yielding: 7 sterlet 8 sturgeon

climbing perch: 6 anabas

cod: bib 4 cusk, hake, ling 5 torsk 6 gadoid 7 bacalao, beardie

colorful: 4 opah

cyprinoid: id, ide 4 dace

devil: ray 5 manta

eel-like: 4 link, opah 6 conger, cuchia 7 eelpout, lamprey

electric: 4 raad 7 torpedo

elongated: eel, gar 6 saurel

European: id, ide, rud 4 boce, dace, rudd, spet 5 alose, bleak, bream, sprat 6 angler, barbel, braice, meagre, plaice 7 gudgeon, lavaret, picarel

female: 4 raun 7 henfish

flat: dab, ray 4 butt, dace, sole 5 bream, fluke, skate 6 plaice, turbot 7 halibut, sanddab, sunfish, torpedo 8 flounder

Florida: 5 crunt 6 atinga, salema 7 burfish, tomtate 8 burrfish

flying: 7 hatchet

food: cod, eel, gar, iki, sey 4 bass, boga, carp, haik, hake, scup, shad, sole, stew, tile, tuna 5 bolti, cisco, hilsa, jurel, siera, skate, smelt, trout 6 baleen, groupa, hilsah, mullet, pompon, salema, salmon, tautog, wahoon, weever, wrasse 7 alewife, escolar, garlopa, halibut, herring, pompano, pompoon, sardine, snapper 8 mackerel, sea trout 9 barracuda 10 barracouta

four-eyed: 8 anableps

freshwater: id, gar, ide, orf 4 bass, carp, chub, dace, orfe, pike, rudd 5 bream, loach, roach, tench 6 darter, redeye, sucker 7 crappie, mooneye

game: 4 bass, cero, pike, tuna 5 perch, trout 6 grilse, marlin, salmon, tarpon 8 grayling 9 swordfish

grunt: 5 ronco 10 bluestripe

Hawaiian: aku 4 ulua 5 akule, lania

herring: 4 brit, shad 5 sprat, sprot 7 alewife 8 pilchard

Japanese: ayu, tai

kind of: cat, cod, dab, eel, gar, ide, orf **4** bass, carp, chub, dace, dorn, hake, hiku, jocu, lant, lija, ling, mado, masu, meat, mero, mola, opah, orfe, pega, peto, pike, pogy, pout, rena, roud, rudd, ruff, scad, scup, shad, sier, skil, sole, spet, spot, tope, ulua **5** bream, lance, midge, otter, perch, pogie, porgy, prane, roach, ruffe, scrod, seine, skate, smelt, trout, umbra, wahoo **6** anabas, barbel, blenny, caribe, dugong, launce, mullet, porgie, sauger, saurel, shiner, timcod, turbot, wrasse **7** alewife, grampus, grunion, haddock, machete, pegador, pintado, piranha, poisson **8** gourhead, hardhead, John Dory, pilchard, sturgeon **9** teleostei **10** candlefish

large: **4** cusk, opah **5** chiro, sargo, shark **6** bichir, tarpon **7** escolar, gourami, jewfish, sennett **8** arapaima, sturgeon **10** blanquillo, maskalonge, maskinonge, whale shark **11** muskellunge

little: see *small* below

long: eel, gar **7** lamprey

mackerel-like: **4** cero **5** tunny **6** coelho **7** escolar, pintado

Mediterranean: **5** porgy, sargo **6** chivey **9** menominee

nest-building: **5** acara **11** stickleback

New England: **4** hake

New Zealand: ihi **5** hikus

newly hatched: fry

Nile: **4** erse **5** saide

olive green: **7** lutfisk **8** ludefisk

one-horned: **9** monoceros

parasitic: **6** remora

pert. to: **7** piscine **8** ichthyic **9** piscatory

pike: gar **4** lude

pilot: **6** romero

poisonous: **8** lionfish

raw: **7** sashimi

ray-like: **5** skate

river: **8** arapaima **10** barramunda

rock: **4** rena **5** reina **8** buccacio

scaleless: **9** alepidote

seaweed: **9** sargassum

serpentine: eel

shark-eating: som **4** pega **7** catfish

shell: **7** abalone

small: fry, ide, ihi **4** brit, dace, goby, spet **5** saury, sprat **6** blenny, cunner, limpet, minnow, riggle, sennet, shiner **7** sardine **8** halfbeak, seahorse, spearing

small bait: **5** killy **8** killfish

South American: **4** gogy, mapo **5** acara **6** acoupa, aimara, almara, caribe **7** piranha

sparoid: tai **5** porgy, sargo

spear-snouted: gar **6** marlin **7** sawfish **8** chimaera, sailfish **9** swordfish

spined: **9** porcupine, stonefish **12** demon stinger

spitting: **10** archerfish

star: **7** asteria

sucking: **6** remora

teleost: eel **6** iniomi

toad: **4** sapo **6** slimer

toothed: **5** shark **7** piranha **8** moray eel

total haul: **4** mess **5** catch

tree-climbing: **6** anabas

tropical: **8** coachman

tunny: **4** tuna

voracious: **4** pike **5** shark **6** caribe **9** barracuda

West Indies: **4** Boga, cero, sier **5** chopa **6** Blanco **7** guapena **12** walleyed pike

young: fry **4** parr **6** alevin

fish basket: pot **4** caul **5** creel, slath

fisher: **5** eeler, pecan **6** seiner, wejack **7** trawler, troller

fisherman: **5** eeler **6** angler, seiner **7** prawner, trawler **8** peterman, piscator **9** harpooner **11** Izaak Walton

fishery: **7** piscary **9** piscation

fish gig: **5** spear

fish handler: **4** icer

fish hawk: **6** osprey

fish hide: **7** eelskin

fishhook: gig **5** angle, Kirby **6** Sproat **7** Kendall **8** Aberdeen, barbless, Carlisle, limerick

feathered: fly **5** sedge **6** hackle

fishing duck: **9** merganser

fishing gear: lam, net, rod, tew **4** cork, flew, flue, gaff, gimp, hook, line, reel, trot **5** cadar, cader, float, sedge, seine, shood, snell **8** trotline

fishing ground: **4** haaf

fishing vessel: **4** dory, scow **5** smack **6** seiner **7** trawler **8** skipjack

fishlike: **8** ichthyic

fish limb: fin

fishline: **5** snell **7** boulter

fish lure: fly, jig **4** plug **5** spoon **7** spinner

fishmonger: **7** peddler **8** pessoner

fishnet: **4** bunt **5** seine, trawl **6** sagene

fishnet line: **5** meter

fishnet mender: **8** beatster

fish peddler: **6** ripier, ripper **7** rippier **10** fishmonger (Br.)

fish pole: pew

fishpond: **7** piscina

fish preserve: **6** warren

fish relish: **7** botargo

fish roe: **6** caviar **7** caviare

fish sauce: **4** alec **5** garum

fish spear: gig **7** trident

fish trap: **4** coop, fyke, weel, weir **5** willy **6** eelpot

fishwife: **9** buttwoman

fishy: **4** dull **6** vacant **10** improbable, lusterless, suspicious, unreliable **11** extravagant

fissile rock: **5** shale

fission: 8 breaking, cleavage, cleaving 9 splitting 12 reproduction

fissure: gap 4 chap, cone, flaw, gool, leak, lode, rent, rift, rima, rime, seam, vein, vent 5 break, chasm, chine, chink, cleft, crack 6 cleave, cranny, divide, lesion 7 blemish, crevice, opening 8 aperture, cleavage, coloboma, crevasse, quebrada

fissured: 6 rimate 7 fissate, rimosed

fist: job 4 nave 5 grasp, nieve 6 clench, clutch, daddle, effort, strike 7 attempt 8 puffball, tightwad 11 handwriting

fistic: 10 pugilistic

fisticuffs: 4 ring 6 boxing 8 pugilism 13 prize-fighting

fistula: 4 pipe, reed, tube 5 sinus 6 cavity

fit: apt, fay, gee, pan, rig 4 able, ague, good, hard, meet, ripe, suit, well, whim 5 adapt, adept, besit, chink, fancy, ictus, ready, right, spasm 6 adjust, attack, become, behove, besort, go with, habile, heppen, proper, seemly, stroke, strong, suited 7 adapted, behoove, capable, condign, conform, correct, healthy, prepare, qualify, tantrum 8 adequate, apoplexy, becoming, dovetail, eligible, glooming, idoneous (L.), outbreak, paroxysm, passable, suitable, syncopes 9 befitting, competent, congruous, opportune, pertinent, qualified 10 applicable, commodious, convenable, convenient, correspond, go together 11 accommodate, appropriate
  out: 6 outfit 7 habille, prepare 9 equipment
  together: fay 4 mesh, nest 5 panel 8 dovetail

fitful: 4 gery 7 cursory, flighty 8 restless, unstable, variable 9 impulsive, irregular, spasmodic, uncertain 10 capricious, convulsive 12 intermittent

fitly: pat 4 duly 6 gladly, meetly 7 happily 8 properly, suitably

fitness: 7 aptness, decency, decorum, dignity 8 aptitude, capacity, justness 9 rectitude 10 competence 11 suitability

fitout: 4 outfit 9 equipment

fitted: apt 4 able 6 geared, suited 7 adapted 8 adjusted, equipped 9 qualified 10 convenient
  for digging: 7 fodient, laniary

fitting: apt, due, pat 4 meet 5 happy, right 6 become, proper, seemly 8 decorous, graceful, suitable 9 befitting 10 adjustment, answerable, habiliment 11 appropriate

five: 4 cinq (F.), funf (G.) 5 cinco (Sp.) 6 cinque (It.) 7 epsilon (Gr.), quinque (L.)
  group of: 6 pentad

five-dollar bill: V, fin, vee

five-finger: 4 fish 5 oxlip, plant 10 cinquefoil

fivefold: 9 quintuple

Five Nations: 7 Cayugas, Mohawks, Oneidas, Senecas 9 Onondagas
  founder: 8 Hiawatha

five-year period: 6 pentad 7 lustrum

fix: peg, pin, set 4 bind, glue, mend, moor, nail, seal 5 affix, allot, found, imbed, limit, lodge, place, rivet, tryst 6 adjust, anchor, arrest, assign, assize, attach, buy off, cement, clinch, define, fasten, ficche, freeze, make up, pickle, plight, repair, revamp, settle, temper 7 appoint, arrange, confirm, delimit, dilemma, impress, imprint, prepare, station, trouble 8 renovate, transfix 9 determine, establish, stabilize 10 constitute 11 predicament, recondition, reconstruct 13 embarrassment
  firmly: set 4 moor 5 brace, grave, imbed, stamp 6 anchor, cement, enroot 7 engraff

fixed: pat, set 4 fast, firm 5 siker, staid 6 frozen, intent, mended, sicker, stable 7 certain, dormant, settled, statary 8 arranged, attached, constant, definite, explicit, fastened, immobile, moveless, resolute, stubborn 9 immovable, indelible, inerratic, permanent 10 stationary 12 determinable, refrigerated
  amount: 4 rate 6 ration 7 stipend 10 remittance
  star: 4 Vega

fixer: 8 handyman

fixture: 5 annex 7 bracket, shelves 8 counters, shelving 10 furnishing

fizgig: 9 fireworks, whirligig

fizzle: 4 fuss 6 barney 7 failure, flivver, hissing 9 agitation

fjord: See **fiord**

flabby: lax 4 fozy, lash, limp, weak 5 frush 6 feeble 7 flaccid

flabellate: 9 fan-shaped

flaccid: 4 limp 6 flabby, flaggy 8 yielding

flack: 4 blow, flap 5 throb 6 stroke 7 flutter

flag: fag, sag, sod 4 fail, fane, pine, tire, turf, waif, wilt 5 droop, woman 6 banner, colors, ensign, flower, pennon, signal 7 ancient, cattail, decline, drapeau, pennant 8 banderol, brattach, languish, standard, streamer, vexillum 9 banderole, flagstone, fourpence
  designer: 14 vexillographer
  kind of: 5 Roger 6 burgee, colors, danger, ensign, fanion, guidon, muleta 7 calamus, curtain, pennant 8 banderol, brattach, masthead, standard, streamer, vexillum 9 banderole, blackjack 10 Jolly Roger

flagellants: 4 albi

flagellate: 4 beat, flog, lash, whip 5 throw 6 thrash 7 flutter, scourge

flagellum: 4 whip 5 shoot 6 runner 7 scourge

flageolet: 4 pipe 6 zufolo 7 basaree, zuffolo
  Hindu: 7 basaree

flagging: 4 weak 7 languid 10 spiritless

flagitious: 6 rotten, sinful, wicked 7 corrupt,

heinous **8** criminal, flagrant, grievous **10** scandalous, villainous

flagon: cup, mug **5** stoup **6** bottle, vessel **7** flacket

flagrant: bad **4** rank **5** gross **6** odious, wanton, wicked **7** glaring, hateful, heinous, scarlet, violent **8** shameful **9** abandoned, atrocious, egregious, monstrous, nefarious, notorious **10** flagitious, outrageous, profligate, villainous

flagstone: **5** shale, slate

flagstone layer: **5** paver

flail: **4** beat, flog, whip **6** thrash, thresh
part: **7** swingle

flair: ray **4** bent, odor **5** skate, smell, taste **6** talent **7** leaning **8** aptitude **11** discernment

flak: **9** criticism **10** opposition

flake: nut **4** chip, film, flaw, rack, snow **5** fleck, flock, scale, strip **6** hurdle, lamina, paling **7** flaught **8** dandruff, fragment **9** screwball

flaky: **5** scaly **7** laminar **8** laminose

flam: **4** whim **5** cheat, false, freak, trick **6** cajole, humbug, untrue **7** deceive, pretext, rubbish **8** drumbeat, illusory, nonsense, pretense **9** deception, deceptive, falsehood

flambeau: **5** torch **6** kettle **11** candlestick

flamboyant: **5** showy, swank **6** florid, ornate **7** flaming **9** flamelike **11** extravagant, resplendent

flame: **4** beau, fire, glow **5** ardor, blaze, flare, flash, glare, gleed, light **7** burning **9** affection **10** brightness, brilliance, sweetheart
fire without: **4** punk
movement: **4** dart, lick

flaming: **5** afire, fiery, vivid **6** ardent, flambe **7** blazing, burning, flaring **9** brilliant, consuming, flamelike **10** flamboyant, passionate **12** illuminating

Flanders capital: **5** Ghent

flanerie: **6** stroll **7** loafing **8** idleness **9** aimlessly, strolling **10** pillowcase

flaneur: **6** loafer **7** trifler

flank: **4** leer, side **5** thigh **6** border

flannel: **4** lana **6** stamin **9** washcloth

flap: rob, tab, tag, wap **4** clap, flip, fuss, loma, slam, slap, waff **5** alarm, flack, flaff, flipe, lapel, skirt **6** bangle, faffle, lappet, strike, tongue **7** aileron, blinder, flounce, flutter, swindle **8** hang down **9** appendage, operculum **10** epiglottis
furnished with: **5** lobed

flapper: **7** snicket **9** backfisch **10** backfische

flare: **4** bell, flue **5** blaze, flame, flash, fleck, fusee, light, torch **6** signal, spread **7** flicker **8** outburst **10** illuminate **11** ostentation

flaring: **4** bell, flue **5** evase (F.), gaudy **7** flaming, glaring **8** dazzling

flash: **4** pool, rush **5** blash, blaze, burst, flame, flare, fluff, glaik, gleam, glent, glint, marsh, spark **6** bottle, fillip, glance **7** fouldre, glim-

mer, glimpse, glisten, glitter, instant, shimmer, sparkle **11** coruscation, fulguration, scintillate

flashing: **6** bright, flashy **7** forward **8** meteoric, snapping **9** fulgurant, fulgurous

flashy: gay **4** flat, gaud, loud **5** fiery, gaudy, showy **6** frothy, garish, ornate, slangy, sporty **7** insipid, tinhorn **8** dazzling, vehement **9** impetuous **10** spiritless

flask: **4** olpe **5** betty, bulge, girba **6** bottle, fiasco, flacon, guttus **7** ampulla, canteen, matrass **8** cucurbit **9** aryballos

flask-shaped: **10** lageniform

flat: **4** dead, dull, even, fade, plat, tame **5** abode, aflat, banal, bland, blunt, level, molle, plane, prone, vapid **6** boring, dreary, flashy **7** decided, insipid, platoid, prosaic, uniform **8** directly, dwelling, lifeless, unbroken **9** apartment, downright, prostrate, tasteless **10** homaloidal, horizontal, monotonous, unanimated **12** unmistakable **13** uninteresting

flatboat: ark **4** scow **5** barge

flatfish: dab, ray **4** butt, dace, sole **5** bream, fluke **6** acedia, plaice, turbot **7** sanddab, sunfish, torpedo **8** flounder

flatiron: **7** sadiron

flat-nosed: **6** simous

flatten: **4** even **5** level **6** deject, smooth **7** depress **8** compress, dispirit **9** prostrate **10** complanate, discourage, dishearten

flattened: **6** oblate **7** planate

flatter: **4** bull, claw, coax, fage, fume, palp **5** charm, float, gloze, honey, smalm **6** become, cajole, fickle, fleech, fraise, glaver, smooge, soothe **7** adulate, beguile, blarney, flether, flutter, wheedle **8** blandish, bootlick, butter up, collogue **10** compliment, ingratiate

flatterer: **5** toady **6** cogger, glozer **7** soother **8** courtier **9** sycophant **10** assentator, greasehorn

flattering: **7** buttery, candied **11** assentatory

flattery: **4** bull, bunk **5** fraik, gloze, salve, taffy **6** butter, fleech, praise **7** blarney, fawning, flether, palaver **8** cajolery **9** adulation **10** compliment **14** obsequiousness

flatulent: **5** gassy, windy **6** turgid **7** pompous, ventose **8** inflated **9** bombastic

flaunt: **4** bosh, show, wave **5** boast, vaunt **6** expose, parade, trapes **7** display, exhibit, flutter, traipse **8** brandish

flavor: **4** gamy, odor, rasa, salt, tang, zest **5** aroma, devil, sapid, sapor, sauce, savor, scent, taste, tinge **6** asarum, relish, season **7** perfume **8** hautgout, piquancy **9** fragrance

flavorable: **5** sapid, sipid, tasty **6** savory **9** palatable

flavoring material: **4** mint, sage **5** spice **6** orgeat **7** cumarin **8** coumarin, cumarone **9** coumarone

flavorless: 5 stale, vapid 9 tasteless

flaw: fib, gap, lie, mar 4 gall, hole, rase, rift, spot, wind 5 brack, cleft, crack, craze, fault, flake 6 breach, defect 7 blemish, default, fissure, nullify, whitlow 8 fracture, fragment, gendarme 10 intoxicate 12 imperfection

flawless: 5 sound 7 perfect 9 faultless

flax: pob, tow 4 card, harl, lint 5 hards, hurds, linen, linin, pouce 6 bobbin
filament: 4 harl
holder: 7 distaff
prepare: ret
refuse: pob
remove seed: 6 ribble
tool: 7 hatchel, swingle

flaxen: 5 blond, straw 6 blonde, golden

flaxen-haired: 4 bawn

flaxseed: 7 linseed

flay: 4 skin 5 slash, strip 6 assail, attack, fleece 7 censure, pillage, reprove 9 excoriate 11 decorticate

flea: 6 chigoe 10 sandhopper
genus: 5 pulex

fleck: fat 4 flea, flit, spot, tuft 5 flake, flare 6 dapple, streak, stripe 7 flutter, speckle 8 particle 9 variegate

fledgling, fledgeling: 5 squab

flee: fly, lam, run 4 bolt, fleg, loup, shun 5 elude, speed 6 escape, vanish 7 abandon, abscond, forsake 8 liberate 9 disappear, skedaddle

fleece: abb, jib, teg 4 bilk, fell, flay, gaff, wool 5 cheat, fleck, pluck, shear 6 toison 7 despoil

fleecy: 5 wooly 6 linten, woolly

fleeing: 7 fugient 8 fugitive

fleer: 4 gibe, grin, jeer, leer, mock 5 flout, laugh, scoff, sneer, taunt 7 grimace 8 derision

fleet: bay 4 fast, flit, navy, sail, skim, swim 5 creek, drain, drift, evand, float, flote, hasty, inlet, quick, rapid, swift 6 abound, argosy, armada, hasten, nimble, speedy 7 estuary 8 flotilla 10 evanescent, transitory

fleeting: 5 brief 6 caduke, volage 7 flighty, passing 8 caducous, fugitive, volatile 9 ephemeral, fugacious, transient 10 evanescent, short-lived, transitory 11 impermanent

Flemish: 8 geographer: 8 Mercator
painter: 5 Bouts 6 Mabuse, Massys, Rubens 7 Gossart, Memling, Patinir, van Eyck 8 Breughel, Brueghel, Gossaert, van Cleve 12 van der Weyden

flesh: kin 4 body, meat, race 5 stock 6 family, muscle 7 kindred, mankind 8 humanity 9 mortality 10 sensuality
appendage: 5 palpi (pl.) 6 palpus
colored mineral: 9 sarcoline
formation: 8 sarcosis
kind of: 5 brawn 6 chevon, chiver 7 carrion
pert. to: 7 sarcoid

resembling: 7 sarcoid

fleshbrush: 7 strigil

flesh-eating: 11 carnivorous

fleshy: fat 5 beefy, gross, human, obese, plump, pulpy, stout 6 animal, bodily, brawny, carnal 9 corpulent
fruit: 4 pear, pome 5 berry, drupe, melon 6 tomato

fleur-de-lis: lis, lys 4 iris, liss, luce, lucy

fleuret: 4 epee 5 sword 6 flower

flex: 4 bend 5 tense

flexible: 4 limp, lush, soft 5 buxom, lithe, withy 6 limber, pliant, supple 7 ductile, elastic, flexile, lissome, plastic, pliable, springy, willowy 8 cheverel, cheveril, yielding 9 tractable, versatile 10 manageable
shoot: 4 bine
tube: 4 hose

flexuous: 5 snaky 6 zigzag 7 relaxed, sinuous, winding 8 softened, tortuous, wavering 9 adaptable 10 circuitous, flickering, serpentine, undulating

flexure: 4 bend, bent, curl, fold 5 curve

flick (see also **motion picture**): cut, hit 4 blow, flip, flit, snap, toss, whip 5 flisk, throw 6 flitch, propel 7 flutter

flicker: 4 fail, flit 5 flare, flunk, waver 6 fitter, shiver, yucker 7 blinter, flimmer, flitter, flutter, tremble, twinkle 8 flichter 9 flaughter, palpitate 10 woodpecker

flickering: 7 flabent, lambent 8 flexuous, unsteady

flier: ace 5 pilot 6 airman 7 aviator 8 operator
female: 8 aviatrix 9 aviatress, aviatrice

flight: hop, lam 4 bolt, rout 5 chevy, chivy, flock, floor, scrap, story, volee 6 chivvy, escape, exodus, hegira, hejira 7 flaught, getaway, migrate, mission, scamper 8 stampede, swarming 9 agitation, migration 12 perturbation
in: 8 on the lam
of fancy: 5 sally
of steps: 4 rise 5 stoop 6 perron, stairs
of wild fowl: 5 skein
pert. to: 5 volar
put to: 4 rout

flightiness: 9 lightness

flightless bird: emu, moa 4 dodo, kiwi, weka 7 ostrich, penguin

flighty: 5 barmy, giddy, swift 6 fitful, nimshi, volage, whisky 7 foolish, giggish 8 fleeting, freakish 9 transient 10 capricious 11 harum-scarum 13 shuttlewitted

flim-flam: fob 4 hoax 5 freak, trick 6 humbug, tricky, trifle 7 swindle 8 nonsense, trifling 9 deception, deceptive 11 nonsensical

flimmer: 7 flicker, glimmer

flimsy: 4 limp, vain, weak 5 frail, gaudy 6 feeble, paltry, sleazy, slight 7 shallow, tenuous 10 gossamered 11 superficial 13 insubstantial, unsubstantial

flinch: 4 funk, game 5 feign, start, wince 6 blench, falter, flense, recoil, shrink

fling: 4 buzz, cast, dart, dash, ding, emit, fleg, gibe, hurl, kick, toss 5 cheat, dance, flirt, pitch, sling, sneer, throw, whang 6 baffle, effuse, hurtle, plunge, rebuff, spirit 7 flounce, repulse, sarcasm, scatter, swindle 9 overthrow

flint: 5 chert, miser, silex 6 quartz 9 firestone, skinflint

flintlock: 6 musket

flinty: 4 hard 5 cruel 8 obdurate

flip: tap 4 flap, glib, pert, snap, toss, trip 5 flick, flirt, slirt 6 fillip, limber, nimble, pliant, propel 7 journey 10 somersault

flippant: 4 airy, glib 6 fluent, limber, nimble 9 talkative

flipper: arm, fin, paw 4 hand

flip through: 4 scan 6 browse 7 dip into 8 glance at

flirt: tap, toy 4 dart, fike, flip, gibe, jeer, jest, joke, mash, mock, play, toss, wink 5 dally, flick, fling, throw 6 coquet, fillip, lead on, masher, spring, trifle 7 trifler 8 coquette 9 philander

flirtatious: coy 4 arch 10 coquettish

flit: 4 dart, flow, scud 5 fleck, fleet, flick, float, flurr, hover, quick, scoot, swift 6 nimble 7 flicker, flutter, migrate

flitter: rag 5 droop, hover, piece, waver 6 tatter 7 flicker, flutter, shuffle 8 fragment

flittermouse: bat 10 fledermaus

float: bob, fly, sea 4 buoy, cork, flow, flux, hove, pont, raft, ride, sail, scow, soar, swim, waft, wave 5 balsa, drift, fleet, flood, hover, ladle 6 billow, bobber, bungey, ponton 7 flatter, flotter, pontoon 8 overflow 9 catamaran, negotiate, podoscaph
aloft: 4 soar

floating: 4 free 5 awash, loose 6 adrift, afloat, flying, natant 7 movable 8 drifting, fluitant, shifting, variable 9 wandering

flocculent: 6 woolly

flock: mob 4 bevy, fold, herd, pack 5 brood, bunch, charm, covey, crowd, drift, drove, flake, fleck, group, sedge, shoal, swarm 6 flight, hirsel 7 company 9 multitude 10 assemblage 11 aggregation
kind of: nid, nye, pod 4 nide, sord 5 covey, sedge, tribe
of geese: 6 gaggle
of lions: 5 pride
pert. to: 6 gregal

flocks (god of): Pan

floe: 4 raft 7 iceberg

flog: cat, tan 4 beat, cane, hide, lash, toco, toko, wale, whip 5 birch, excel, fight, flail, linge, quilt, skeeg 6 cotton, larrup, strike, switch, thrash 7 baleise, belabor, scourge, sjambok, surpass, trounce 8 slaister 10 flagellate

flood: sea 4 bore, flow, flux 5 eagre, float, spate 6 deluge, excess 7 debacle, freshet, torrent 8 alluvion, inundate, overflow 9 cataclysm 10 inundation, outpouring 14 superabundance
before: 12 antediluvian

flooded: 5 awash 6 afloat 10 surrounded

floodgate: 5 hatch 6 sluice

floodlight: 5 klieg

floor: 4 drop, flat 5 level, story 6 defeat, ground, lay low 7 planche 8 bowl over 9 knock down

floor covering: mat, rug 4 tile, wood 5 tapis (Fr.), vinyl 6 carpet, marble, planks 7 parquet 8 linoleum, oilcloth, terrazzo

flop: dud 4 bomb, bust, fail, fall, whop 5 lemon, loser 6 fizzle 7 failure

flora: 6 plants 9 florilege 10 vegetation 11 florilegium

flora and fauna: 5 biota

floreate: 5 bloom

Florence: 7 Firenza
bridge: 12 Ponte Vecchio
cathedral: 5 Duomo
coin: 6 florin 7 ruspone
family: 6 Medici
gallery: 5 Pitti 6 Uffizi
iris: 5 ireos, orris
palace: 5 Pitti 6 Uffizi 7 palazzo, Vecchio

Florentine (see also **Florence**): 4 gold 6 finish

floret bract: 5 palea, palet

florid: red 5 buxom, fresh, ruddy 6 ornate 7 flowery 8 blooming, rubicund, vigorous 10 figurative, flamboyant, rhetorical 11 embellished, full-blooded

Florida: *capital:* 11 Tallahassee
city: 5 Miami, Ocala, Tampa 7 Hialeah, Key West, Orlando, Palatka, Pompano 8 Sarasota 9 Pensacola 12 Daytona Beach, Jacksonville, St. Petersburg 14 Fort Lauderdale
discoverer: 11 Ponce de Leon
Indian: 6 Calusa 8 Seminole, Tequesta
island (see also *key* below): 4 Pine 7 Sanibel 8 St. George 11 Dry Tortugas
key: 4 Long, West 5 Largo 8 Longboat, Marathon 10 Islamorada
resort: 7 Key West 8 Sea World 10 Clearwater, Miami Beach 11 Disney World, Epcot Center 12 Daytona Beach 13 Captiva Island, Sanibel Island
space center: 7 Kennedy 9 Canaveral
state bird: 11 mockingbird
state flower: 13 orange blossom
state tree: 9 sabal palm

floss: 5 fluff, skein, waste 6 sleave, stream

flotage: 8 buoyancy

flotilla: 5 fleet 6 armada

Flotow opera: 6 Martha

flotsam: 6 jetsam 8 driftage, wreckage 9 drift-wood

flounce: 4 flap, slam 5 fling, frill 6 ruffle 7 falbala, falbelo 8 flounder, furbelow, struggle

flounder: dab 4 butt, keel, roll, toss 5 bream, fluke, megin 6 grovel, muddle, plaice, turbot, wallow 7 flounce, plounce, stumble, sunfish, topknot, vaagmar, vaagmer 8 flatfish, struggle, vaagmaer

flour: 4 atta, meal 5 clear 6 patent, powder, red dog
bleach: 5 agene
diabetic: 9 aleuronat
maker: 6 miller
sifter: 6 bolter
sprinkle with: 6 dredge
testing device: 11 farinometer
wheat: 4 atta

flourish: 4 boom, brag, grow, riot, rise, show, wave 5 adorn, bloom, boast, cheve, gloss, quirk, vaunt 6 parade, paraph, thrive 7 blossom, display, enlarge, fanfare, prosper, roulade 8 arpeggio, brandish, curlicue, curlycue, increase, ornament 9 embellish 10 decoration 11 ostentation

flourishing: fat 4 frim 5 green, palmy 7 florent 8 thriving 10 prosperous, successful

floury: 4 meal

flout: bob 4 gibe, jeer, mock 5 fleer, flite, flyte, frump, scoff, scorn, sneer, taunt 6 deride, insult, quip at, scount 7 jeering, mockery 8 betongue

flow: ebb, jet, run 4 bore, flit, flux, fuse, gush, hale, lava, lave, melt, pour, roll, shed, sile, teem, well 5 avale, drain, eagre, exude, fleam, float, flood, glide, issue, river, spill, spurt 6 abound, afflux, deluge, recede, stream 7 current, emanate, flutter, meander, spurtle 8 alluvion, inundate 9 streaming 10 menstruate, outpouring 12 menstruation

flower: bud 4 best, blow, flag, iris, ixia, pink, posy, rose 5 aster, bloom, cream, elite, lilac, pansy, tulip 6 azalia, crocus, dahlia, orchid, posies (pl.), unfold 7 blethia, blossom, develop, fairest, gentian 8 camellia, choicest, daffodil, freshest, gardenia, geranium, hyacinth, ornament 9 carnation, embellish, gladiolus 10 upper class, upper crust 13 chrysanthemum
appendage: 5 bract
artificial: 7 rosette 8 gloxinia
band: 6 wreath
bell-shaped: 4 lily 5 tulip
blooming for a year: 6 annual
blue: 6 lupine 8 harebell

bud: 5 ament, caper 6 spadix
bulb: 4 iris, lily 5 tulip 6 crocus, dahlia, scilla, squill 7 anemone, begonia, jonquil, muscari 8 daffodil, hyacinth 9 gladiolus, narcissus 10 chionodoxa 11 fritillaria
cluster: 4 cime, cyme 5 ament, bract, umbel 6 corymb, raceme 7 panicle 9 glomerule
desert: 4 lily 5 poppy 6 cactus, mallow 7 chicory
extract: 4 atar, otto 5 attar, ottar
fall: 5 aster 6 cosmos 13 chrysanthemum
garden: 4 iris, ixia, lily, pink, rose 5 aster, canna, daisy, lilac, pansy, peony, phlox, tulip 6 asalia, olivia, orchid, violet 7 freesia, petunia, verbena 8 bletilla, camellia, daffodil, gloxinia, hyacinth, primrose 9 buttercup, carnation, gladiolus, narcissus 10 heliotrope, ranunculus 11 honeysuckle
goddess: 5 Flora
imaginary: 7 amarant 8 amaranth
large: 5 canna, peony
late-blooming: 5 aster
mass: 8 anthemia
meadow: 5 bluet
modest: 6 violet 10 Quaker Lady
obsolete: 5 pense
of death: 8 asphodel
of forgetfulness: 5 lotus
part: 5 bract, calyx, ovary, petal, sepal, style 6 anther, pistil, spathe, stamen, stigma 7 corolla, nectary, petiole 8 filament, peduncle, perianth, pericarp
passion: 6 maypop
pink: 4 rose 7 rhodora
prickly: 4 burr
purple: 5 lilac, pense
receptacle: 4 vase 5 torus
spring: 4 iris 5 lilac, peony, tulip 6 crocus 7 arbutus 8 daffodil, hepatica
stand: 7 epergne
stylized: lis
unfading: 7 amarant 8 amaranth
unknown kind: 8 belamour
white: 5 gowan
wild: 4 sage 5 bluet, daisy 6 lupine 7 anemone, arbutus 8 bluebell, hepatica 9 buttercup, innocence
wind: 7 anemone
yellow: 5 daisy, gowan, pense 7 jonquil 8 daffodil, marigold 9 buttercup

flower holder: pot 4 frog, vase 5 lapel

flowering: 7 flowery 8 anthesis, blooming 11 florescence

flowering plant: rue 4 arum 5 avens, calla, canna, orpin, phlox, yucca, zamia 6 azalea, bareta, cosmos, oxalis, spirea, teasel 7 barreta, gentian, lobelia, pavonia, petunia, rhodora, spiraea, tamarix, torenia, waratah 8 acanthus, ageratum, damewort, gera-

flowerless plant: 4 fern, moss 6 lichen 7 acrogen

nium, gerardia, valerian 9 candytuft, coreopsis, gloxinias, goldenrod, hollyhock, monkshood 10 pulsatilla, snapdragon

flowerlike: 7 anthoid

flowerpot: 8 cache pot 10 jardiniere

flowery: 5 fancy, wordy 6 florid, ornate, prolix 7 florent, verbose 8 eloquent 9 bombastic, flowering 10 figurative, flosculous, rhetorical

flowing: 4 flux 5 fluid, fluor, tidal 6 afflux, fluent 7 copious, current, cursive, emanent, fluxing 9 affluxion, emanation 10 transitive
together: 9 confluent

flu: 6 grippe 9 influenza

flub: 4 muff 5 boner, botch, error 6 bollix, bungle, goof up 7 blunder

fluctuate: 4 sway, vary, veer, wave 5 shift, waver 7 vibrate 8 undulate, unsteady 9 oscillate, vacillate 10 irresolute 12 undetermined

fluctuating: 8 unstable, unsteady

flue: net 4 barb, down, open, pipe, thin 5 flare, fluff, fluke, stack 6 expand, feeble, funnel, sickly, tunnel 7 chimney, flaring, passage, shallow

fluency: 9 eloquence, profusion 10 smoothness

fluent: 4 glib 5 fluid, ready 6 facile, liquid, smooth, stream 7 copious, flowing, fluidic, renable, verbose, voluble 8 eloquent, flippant 9 talkative 12 smooth-spoken 13 talkativeness

fluff: nap 4 down, flue, lint, puff 5 flash, floss, whiff

fluffy: 4 soft 5 downy, drunk, fluey, fuzzy 6 linten 8 feathery, unsteady 12 undependable

fluid: ink 4 rasa 5 water 6 fluent, liquid, watery 7 flowing, fluible, fluxile, gaseous 8 floating, fluxible
kind of: gas, ink, oil, sap, tar 4 bile, icor, milk 5 blood, ether, grume, ichor, latex, nerol, plasm, serum, water 7 acetone, coal oil, naphtha, tearlet 8 gasoline, kerosene
measure: rhe
pert. to: 7 humoral
without: 7 aneroid

fluidity unit: rhe

fluke: 4 fish, flue 5 blade 8 flounder

fluky: 8 unsteady 9 uncertain 10 capricious

flume: 4 leat 5 chute, gorge, water 6 ravine, sluice, stream 7 channel

flummox: 4 fail 7 confuse, perplex 8 confound 9 embarrass 10 disconcert

flunk: 4 bust, fail 7 flicker

flunky: flunkey: 4 snob 5 toady 6 cookee, lackey, menial 7 footman, servant, steward

flurry: ado 4 gust, stir 5 haste, skirl 6 bother, bustle, scurry, squall 7 confuse, flusker, fluster, flutter, footster 9 agitation, carfuffle 10 discompose

flush: 4 even, glow, pool, rose 5 blush, elate, rouge, vigor 6 aflush, excite, lavish, mantle, morass, redden, thrill 7 animate 8 abundant, affluent, prodigal, rosiness 9 abounding, encourage 10 prosperous

flushed: red 4 ruby 5 aglow 6 florid 7 scarlet 8 vigorous 10 prosperous

flushing: 8 blushing 9 rubescent

fluster: 5 shake 6 flurry, fuddle, muddle, pother, rattle 7 confuse, flusker, footster 8 befuddle, flustrum 10 discompose

flute: nay 4 fife 5 crimp 6 flauto, goffer, zufolo 7 chamfer, channel, gauffer, magadis, piccolo, zuffolo 8 flautino
ancient: 5 tibia
Hindu: bin 5 pungi
player: 5 piper 6 aulete 7 flutist, tootler 8 auletris, flautist
stop: 7 ventage
wood for: 5 kokra

fluting: 5 strix 7 gadroon, godroon, strigil 10 gadroonage, godroonage

flux: 4 flow, fuse, melt 5 float, flood, resin, rosin, smear, smelt 6 fusion, stream 7 euripus, flowing, outflow

fly: bee, hop 4 flee, fleg, flit, leap, melt, scud, soar, solo, whir, whiz, wing 5 agile, alert, float, midge, pilot, quick, sharp, whirr 6 aviate, insect, nimble, spring, vanish 7 avigate, avolate, knowing 8 coachman 9 disappear
African: 4 zimb 5 zebub 6 tsetse
enemy: 6 spider
fishing: bee 4 lure 5 nymph, sedge 6 Cahill, huzard 7 Babcock, grannom 8 coachman, Ferguson, hare's ear 9 alexandra 10 Barrington
genus: 5 Dacus
kind of: bee, bot, fag, mau, plu 4 gnat, kivu, zimb 5 alder, cadew, horse, midge, whame 6 breeze, gadfly, seroot, tsetse 7 butcher, collier, tachina 8 housefly 9 shoemaker 10 bluebottle 11 caterpillar, trichoptera
small: 4 gnat 5 midge
two-winged: 8 dipteron

flyaway: 5 giddy 7 flighty 8 restless 12 unrestrained

flybane: 12 cinnamonroot

flyblow: 5 larva

fly-by-night: 6 shifty, unsure 7 dubious 10 unreliable 12 undependable, unscrupulous 13 untrustworthy

flycatcher: 4 tody 5 pewee 6 phoebe, yetapa 7 fielder, grignet, grinder

flyer: ace 5 pilot 7 aviator, Pegasus 8 aeronaut, operator

flying: **5** awing **6** flight, volant, waving **8** aviation, floating **9** fugacious
pert. to: **7** aviatic
adder: **9** dragonfly
boat: **8** seaplane **9** amphibian
body: **6** meteor
device: **4** kite **6** glider
expert: ace
fish: **5** saury **7** gurnard
machine: **5** plane **8** aerostat **9** gyroplane **10** helicopter
mammal: bat
ship: SST **5** blimp **7** aeronat, biplane, shuttle **8** airplane **9** amphibian, dirigible, monoplane, transport **10** helicopter

Flying Dutchman heroine: **5** Senta

Fo: **6** Buddha

foal: **4** colt **5** filly

foam: fob, sud **4** fume, head, scud, scum **5** frost, froth, spume, yeast **6** bubble, freath, lather **7** blubber

foaming: **5** nappy **6** yeasty **7** spumous

foamy: **5** barmy, spumy, sudsy **6** frothy

fob: **4** buck, foam **5** cheat, froth, trick **6** impose, pocket **8** flimflam, imposter, ornament, swindler

focal: **7** central, centric, nuclear, nucleus **13** concentrative

focus: **4** foci (pl.) **5** point, train **6** center, hearth **8** converge, polestar **9** fireplace **11** concentrate, nerve center

fodder: hay **4** feed, food, vert **5** mange **6** forage, silage **9** provender
kind of: ers, oat, rye **4** corn, rape **5** batad, maize, vetch, wheat **6** barley, clover, millet **7** alfalfa **8** deerweed **11** bitter vetch
storing place: **4** silo **5** bakie **6** haymow, silage **8** ensilage
trough for: **6** manger

foe: **5** enemy, fiend, rival **7** adverse, hostile, opposer, saracen **8** opponent **9** adversary, ill-wisher **10** antagonist

fog: dag, rag **4** damp, daze, haar, haze, mist, moke, moss, murk, prig, roke, smog **5** bedim, brume, cloud, grass, vapor **6** nebula, salmon, stupor **7** obscure, pogonip **8** bewilder, moisture **10** aftergrass **12** bewilderment

foggy: dim **4** dull, hazy, moky, roky **5** dense, dirty, misky, misty, murky, rooky **6** cloudy, marshy **7** brumous, muddled, obscure **8** confused, nubilous **9** beclouded

foghorn: **5** siren

fogy: **6** foozle

foible: fad **4** weak **5** fault, ferly **6** feeble **7** frailty **8** weakness **9** infirmity **11** shortcoming **12** imperfection

foil: **4** balk, soil, tain **5** blade, blunt, elude, evade, stain, stump, sword, track, trail **6** baffle, blench, boggle, defeat, defile, outwit, stigma, stooge, thwart **7** beguile, failure, pollute, repulse, trample **8** disgrace **9** frustrate, overthrow **11** frustration

foist: fob **4** cask, dupe, gull **5** barge, cheat, fudge, fusty **6** galley, impose, suborn, thrust **7** palm off, swindle **8** brackish, hoodwink **9** rascality **11** interpolate

fold: bow, lap, pen, ply, wap **4** bend, cote, fail, flap, furl, loop, plie, ruga, tuck **5** clasp, crimp, drape, flipe, flock, layer, plait, pleat, plica, prank, sinus, yield **6** bought, crease, double, hurdle, infold, plight, pucker, rimple **7** crumple, embrace, flexure, placate, plicate **8** surround **9** enclosure, overthrow, plicature
kind of: **4** loop **5** bight, lapel, plica, quire **6** bought, dewlap, octavo **7** plicate **9** replicate
of skin: **4** ruga **5** plica

folded: **4** shut **6** closed **7** plicate

folder: **5** cover, folio **6** binder **7** leaflet **8** pamphlet

folderol, falderal: **8** nonsense

foliage: **6** leaves **7** leafage **8** greenery

foliated: **5** lobed **7** spathic

folio: fo **4** case, leaf, page **6** number

folk: **6** daoine, people **7** friends **9** intimates, relatives

folklore: **4** myth **6** custom, legend **7** history **9** tradition **12** superstition
genie of: **7** sandman

folks: kin **6** people **7** parents **9** relatives

folkway: mos **5** mores (pl.) **6** custom **7** pattern

folletto: imp **5** fairy **6** goblin, spirit

follicle: sac **5** crypt

follow: ape, dog, see, tag **4** copy, hunt, next, seek, shag, tail **5** adopt, after, chase, ensue, snake, spoor, trace, track, trail **6** attend, pursue, result, shadow **7** imitate, observe, replace, succeed **8** practice, supplant **9** accompany, alternate, supervene **10** comprehend, understand

follow behind: dog, lag, tag **4** heel, hunt, nose, tail **5** hound, trace, trail **6** shadow **7** draggle **9** supervene

follower: fan, ist, ite, son **4** aper, beau, zany **5** gilly **6** bildar, ensuer, gillie, gudget, lackey, minion, sequel, sulter, vassal, votary **7** acolyte, devotee, grifter, pursuer, retinue, spaniel **8** adherent, courtier, disciple, henchman, partisan, retainer, servitor **9** attendant, caudatory, caudrilla, dependent, satellite, sequacer, sycophant **10** aficionado, sweetheart **11** cuadrillero

following: **4** next, sect **5** after, below, suant, train **6** sequel **7** devotee, ensuing, sequent **8** business, trailing, vocation **9** clientele, supporter **10** posthumous, profession,

sequential, subsequent, succeeding, successive **12** subsequent to
exact words: **7** literal **8** verbatim
laws of arithmetical algebra: **6** scalor
follow-up: 6 sequel
folly: sin 4 whim **6** betise, dotage, lunacy **7** daffery, daffing, foolery, foppery, madness, mistake **8** fondness, idleness, lewdness, morology, nonsense, rashness **9** silliness **10** imprudence, wantonness **11** foolishness, witlessness **12** indiscretion
foment: 4 abet, brew, spur **5** rouse, stupe **6** arouse, excite, incite **7** agitate, ferment, provoke **9** encourage, instigate
fond: tid 4 dear, dote, fain, fool, fund, warm, weak **5** silly, stock, store **6** ardent, befool, caress, dearly, doting, loving, simple, tender **7** amatory, amorous, beguile, browden, devoted, foolish, insipid **8** desirous, enamored, sanguine, trifling, uxorious **9** credulous, enamoured, indulgent, savorless **10** curcuddoch, infatuated, passionate **12** affectionate
of dainties: **6** friand **9** friandise
of drink: **8** bibulous
of hunting: **7** venatic
fonda: inn 5 hotel
fondle: hug, pet 4 baby, coax, love, neck, waly **5** clasp, daunt, wally **6** caress, cocker, coddle, cosset, dandle, pamper, stroke **7** cherish, embrace **8** blandish, canoodle
fondly: 6 dearly **7** foolish **8** tenderly **9** foolishly **14** affectionately
fondness: gra 4 love **5** folly, taste **6** liking **8** dearness, soft spot, weakness **9** affection **10** attachment, tenderness **11** affectation, foolishness **12** predilection **15** Philotherianism
fondu: 6 cheese **7** souffle
fons: 6 origin, source **8** fountain
font: 4 pila **5** basin **6** source, spring **7** piscina **8** delubrum, fountain **10** aspersoria (pl.) **11** aspersorium
fontal: 6 source **8** original **9** baptismal
food: bit, pap 4 bit., cate, chow, diet, eats, fare, farm, gear, grub, meat, peck, prog **5** bread, broma, cheer, foray, scaff, tripe **6** fodder, foster, morsel, viands, wraith **7** aliment, edibles, handout, pabulum, vittles **8** flummery, grubbery, victuals **9** nutriment, provender **10** provisions, sustenance **11** comestibles, nourishment
animal: **4** feed **5** grain, grass **6** fodder, forage **9** provender
choice: **4** cake **6** pastry **8** ambrosia
container: jar **4** bowl, dish, olla **5** crock, plate **6** saucer
craving for: **4** pica **7** bulimia
devotee: **7** epicure, gourmet

dislike of: **6** asitia **9** sitomania **10** cibophobia
dressing: **5** sauce **7** garnish
element: fat **6** gluten **7** mineral, protein, vitamin **12** carbohydrate
farinaceous: **4** sago
garnish: **5** sauce **7** parsley **8** dressing
heavenly: **5** manna
invalid: pap **5** broth **7** gelatin **14** calf's foot jelly
kind of: pap, poi, sop **4** ants, chum, crum, mess, mush, sago **5** acate, balut, bread, broma, cates, gruel, jelly, manna, puree, salep, scaff, souse, tripe **6** cagmag, cereal, farina, forage, hominy, vivres **7** abalone, boscage, pemican, tapioca **8** ambrosia, aperient, beebread, pemmican **9** aperitive, rechauffe **10** rechauffee
list: **4** diet, menu **5** carte
of gods: **6** amrita **7** amreeta **8** ambrosia
pert. to: **8** cibarial **9** cibarious
protein: **4** fish, meat **5** dairy **6** cheese **7** legumes
provision of: **4** mess **6** ration **8** catering
scarcity: **6** famine
seller: **6** grocer **7** viander
semidigested: **5** chyme
soft: pap
southern: **4** okra, pone **5** grits, gumbo **6** greens, hominy **7** chitlin, hoecake **9** hushpuppy **11** chitterling
special dish: **4** hogo, olla, stew **5** bredi, pilaf, pilau, pilaw, pizza **6** haslet, hominy, majoon, omelet, paella, panada, pilaff, ragout, salmis, scouse, sundae, zimmis **7** chowder, custard, rarebit, ravioli, souffle **8** cabeliau, hautgout, omelette, sillabub, sukiyaki, tournedo **9** cabilliau, colcannon, galantine, succotash **10** salmagundi, shishkebab
storage pit: **4** cist
foofaraw: ado
fool: ass, cod, cow, fop, fox, kid, mug, oaf, sap 4 boob, butt, dolt, dupe, gowk, gull, hoax, jape, jest, joke, simp, zany **5** bluff, clown, dunce, goose, idiot, moron, ninny, noddy, silly, spoof, trick **6** cuckoo, delude, dotard, gammon, jester, motley, nitwit, outwit, take in, tamper **7** buffoon, coxcomb, deceive, mislead, witling **8** hoodwink, imbecile, surprise **9** blockhead, simpleton **10** nincompoop
around: **4** play **5** cut up, dally **6** trifle **7** have fun, skylark, toy with **8** lallygag **9** philander, waste time
foolable: 5 naive **8** gullible
foolhardy: 4 rash **6** daring **8** headlong, heedless, reckless **11** adventurous **12** presumptuous

foolish: mad **4** daft, rash, zany **5** anile, barmy, batty, buggy, crazy, dizzy, goofy, goosy, inane, inept, silly **6** absurd, harish, simple, stupid, unwise **7** asinine, fatuous, flighty, foppish, gullish, idiotic, puerile, witless **8** anserine, cockeyed, heedless **9** brainless, childlike, desipient, doddering, imprudent, insensate, ludicrous, senseless **10** half-witted, indiscreet, irrational **11** nonsensical **12** preposterous

foolishness: **5** folly **6** levity **9** absurdity, horseplay, stupidity **10** insipience

foolproof: **4** sure **7** certain **8** risk free **10** infallible

fool's gold: **6** pyrite

fool's paradise: **7** chimera **8** illusion

fool's stitch: **6** tricot

foot: dog, pes **4** base **5** meter, speed **6** bottom, pay for, tootsy, trilby **7** measure **9** extremity
animal: pad, paw **4** hoof **7** fetlock, pastern
armor: **8** solleret
lever: **5** pedal **7** treadle
metric: **4** iamb **5** arsis, paeon **6** dactyl, iambus **7** anapest, pyrrhic, spondee, triseme, trochee **8** bacchius, epitrite, molossus, tribrach
pain: **8** talalgia
part: toe **4** arch, ball, heel, sole **6** instep, thenar
pert. to: **5** pedal, podal **6** pedate

foot bone: **6** cuboid, tarsus **7** phalanx **8** scaphoid **10** astragulus, metatarsus

foot doctor: **10** podiatrist **11** chiropodist

foot soldier: **4** kern (Sc.), peon **6** Zouave **7** dogface **8** doughboy **11** infantryman

football: **5** rugby **6** rugger, soccer **7** pigskin
famous coach: **4** Yost **5** Brown, Halas, Hayes, Jones, Leahy, Shula, Walsh **6** Bryant, Devine, Ewbank, Landry, Layden, Rockne **7** Paterno **8** Lombardi, Robinson **9** Wilkinson **10** Gibbs Stagg, Parseghian
field: **8** gridiron
kick: **4** drop, punt **5** place **6** spiral **10** conversion, extra point
pass: **4** bomb, jump **5** flare **6** screen, shovel **7** forward, lateral **9** square out **11** flea-flicker
position: end **4** back **5** guard **6** center, safety, tackle **8** fullback, halfback, receiver, split end, tailback, tight end **10** cornerback, linebacker **11** quarterback, running back
pro teams (NFL): **4** Jets (New York), Rams (Los Angeles) **5** Bears (Chicago), Bills (Buffalo), Colts (Indianapolis), Lions (Detroit) **6** Browns (Cleveland), Chiefs (Kansas City), Eagles (Philadelphia), Giants (New York), Oilers (Houston), Saints (New Orleans) **7** Bengals (Cincinnati), Broncos (Denver), Cowboys (Dallas), Falcons (Atlanta), Packers (Green Bay), Raiders (Los Angeles), Vikings (Minnesota) **8** Chargers (San Diego), Dolphins (Miami), Panthers (Carolina), Patriots (New England), Redskins (Washington, D.C.), Seahawks (Seattle), Steelers (Pittsburgh) **9** Cardinals (Phoenix) **10** Buccaneers (Tampa Bay) **11** Forty-Niners (San Francisco)
score: **4** goal **6** safety **9** field goal, touchdown **10** conversion, extra point
team: **6** eleven (see *pro teams* above)
term: **4** down, sack, yard **5** blitz, block, drive, flank **6** fumble, huddle **7** defense, end zone, holding, kick-off, offense, offside, rushing **8** clipping, goal post, uprights **9** scrimmage, secondary **12** interception, interference
trophy: **7** Heisman (college)

footer: **6** walker **10** pedestrian

footfall: pad **4** step **5** tread **7** vestige

footing: **4** base, lace, rank **5** basis, track **6** status **7** balance, support, surface, toe-hold **8** standing **9** condition **12** relationship

footless: **4** aped **5** inept **6** apodal, clumsy, futile, stupid **7** awkward, useless **13** unsubstantial

footloose: **4** free **7** nomadic **9** wandering **10** unattached

footman: **6** flunky, lackey, menial **7** servant **8** chasseur **9** attendant

footnote: **9** reference **11** explanation

footpad: **4** thug **5** thief **6** mugger, robber **9** holdup man **10** stickup man

footpath: **4** lane **5** trail **8** side-walk, trottoir **9** banquette

footprint: **5** trace, track, tread
fossil: **9** ichnolite
rabbit: **5** prick

footrest: **4** pouf, rail **5** stool **7** cricket, hassock, ottoman

footstalk: **7** pedicel, petiole **8** peduncle

footwear (see also *shoe*): pac, ped **4** boot, hose, pack, shoe, sock **5** kamik, sabot **6** arctic, galosh, kamika (pl.), patten, rubber, tights **7** Wellies **8** stocking **11** Wellingtons

fop: **4** buck, dude, dupe, fool **5** dandy **7** coxcomb, jessamy **8** gimcrack, popinjay **9** exquisite **11** Beau Brummel **12** fashion plate, lounge lizard, man-about-town

foppery: **9** absurdity

foppish: **5** apish, dandy, silly **6** dapper, spruce, stupid **7** fangled, finical, foolish **8** dandyish

foppishness: **13** dandification

for: pro **7** because **8** favoring **9** favouring, in favor of **10** concerning
all voices: **5** tutti
cash: **9** al contado (Sp.)
each: per
fear that: **4** lest

nothing: **6** gratis, lanyap **8** gratuity **9** lagniappe

shame: fie

temporary use: **4** jury

that reason: **4** ergo (L.) **9** therefore

which reason: **6** whence

forage: ers, oat, rye **4** corn, mast, raid, rape **5** grass, maize, raven, spoil, wheat **6** barley, browse, clover, fodder, millet, ravage, russud **7** alfalfa **8** deerweed **9** pasturage **10** provisions **11** bitter vetch

foramen: **4** pore

foray: **4** rade, raid **5** melee **6** ravage, sortie **7** chappow, hership, pillage **9** incursion

forbear, forebear: **4** bear, help, shun, sire **5** avoid, forgo, spare **6** desist, endure, forego, parent **7** abstain, decline, refrain **8** ancestor **10** ancestress, forefather, foreparent

forbearance: **5** mercy **6** lenity **8** mildness, patience **9** tolerance **10** abstinence, self-denial **13** self-restraint

forbearing: **4** easy, mild **7** lenient, patient **8** tolerant **9** desisting, restraint

forbid: ban **4** defy, deny, fend, tabu, veto **5** debar, taboo **6** defend, enjoin, impede, refuse **7** forfend, forwarn, gainsay, inhibit **8** disallow, forefend, forspeak, preclude, prohibit **9** challenge, interdict, proscribe **10** contradict **11** countermand

forbiddance: ban **4** veto **12** interdiction, proscription

forbidden: **4** tabu **5** taboo **6** banned, denied **8** verboten **10** prohibited

Jewish law: **4** tref

Forbidden City: **5** Lhasa

forbidding: **4** grim **5** black, gaunt, stern **6** fierce, odious, strict **9** offensive, repellent **10** unpleasant **11** displeasing, prohibiting **12** disagreeable, interdicting

forbode: See **forebode**

forboding: See **foreboding**

force: gar, gut, vim, vis **4** bang, birr, clip, cram, dint, feck, make **5** coact, drive, exert, farce, impel, might, peise, poach, power, press, repel, shear, stuff, wrest **6** coerce, compel, cudgel, energy, extort, oblige, ravish, stithy **7** ability, afforce, cascade, impetus, impulse, potency, require, violate **8** coaction, coercion, efficacy, momentum, pressure, strength, validity, violence, virility **9** constrain, influence, puissance, restraint, waterfall **10** compulsion, constraint, constringe **11** necessitate

air upon: **4** blow

down: **4** tamp **5** stuff

into smaller space: **8** compress

kind of: **4** army, birr, dyne, elod, soul, task **5** agent, cadre, dynam, enemy, fohat, nerve,

posse, steam, tonal **6** nature **7** voltage **8** battalia, sanction **9** bioenergy **11** centrifugal **13** reinforcement

onward: **4** urge **6** propel

out: **5** evict **6** banish, unseat

producing rotation: **6** torque

to do without: **7** deprive

with full: **5** amain

forced: **5** rigid, stiff **7** labored **8** spurious, strained **9** reluctant **10** artificial, compulsory, farfetched **11** constrained, involuntary, spontaneous **12** artificially

contribution: tax **4** duty, levy, toll **6** demand, excise, impost **7** tribute **8** exaction **10** assessment

feeding: **6** gavage

forceful: **6** mighty, strong, virile **7** dynamic, violent **8** eloquent, enfatico, forcible, vigorous **9** effective, energetic

forcemeat: **5** farce

forceps: **7** pincers **8** dentagra

forces: **4** army **6** troops

forcible: **5** stout, valid **6** cogent, mighty, potent **7** intense, violent, weighty **8** emphatic, forceful, powerful, puissant, vigorous **9** energetic, impetuous, necessary **10** compulsory, convincing, impressive, obligatory **11** efficacious, influential

forcibly: **5** amain **6** hardly **9** violently **10** vigorously

ford: **4** wade, wath **5** drift **6** stream **7** current **8** crossing **9** wathstead

Fordham's team: **4** Rams

fore: van, way **5** afore, ahead, front, prior, track **6** former **7** earlier, further, journey **8** advanced, formerly **10** antecedent, previously

forearm: arm

bone: **4** ulna

pert. to: **7** cubital

forebear: See **forbear**

forebode, forbode: **4** bode, omen **5** augur, croak **6** divine **7** betoken, portend, predict, presage **8** foretell, prophesy **10** foreboding **13** prognosticate **15** prognostication

foreboding, forboding: **4** omen **5** black **6** augury, boding, gloomy **7** anxiety **8** bodement, sinister **10** prediction **11** pessimistic, presagement **12** apprehension, presentiment

forecast: **4** bode **5** guess, infer **6** scheme **7** caution, foresee, fortune, predict, surmise **8** foredeem, foretell, prophesy **9** calculate, foregleam, forepoint, forescent, foretoken, prognosis **10** conjecture, foreordain, prediction, prognostic **11** calculation, foredestiny **12** predetermine **15** prognostication

forecaster: **4** seer **6** oracle **7** prophet **8** dopester **11** nostradamus **13** meteorologist

foreclose: 5 debar 6 hinder 7 prevent 8 preclude 10 dispossess

foredoom: 7 destiny 10 predestine

forefather: 4 sire 5 elder 6 parent 7 forbear 8 ancestor 9 grandsire 10 forerunner, progenitor

forefend: See **forfend**

forefinger: 5 index

forefoot: paw, pud

forefront: van 5 front

foregather: 4 meet 7 consort, convene 8 assemble 9 encounter 10 fraternize

forego: See **forgo**

foregoer: 7 example 8 ancestor 10 forerunner 11 predecessor

foregoing: 4 past 5 above 8 anterior, previous 9 preceding 10 antecedent

foregone: 4 past 8 previous
conclusion: 9 certainty

forehanded: 5 early 6 timely 7 prudent, thrifty

forehead: 4 brow 5 frons, front 7 frontes 8 sinciput
pert. to: 7 metopic
prominence: 8 glabella
strap: 4 tump

foreign: 5 alien, fremd 6 exiled, exotic, forane, remote 7 distant, ecdemic, exclude, strange 8 barbaric, peregrin 9 barbarous, extrinsic, peregrine 10 extraneous, irrelevant, outlandish, tramontane 12 adventitious, exallotriote, exterraneous, incompatible, inconsistent
geology: 7 epigene

foreigner: 5 alien, haole 6 gringo, pakeha 7 greener, pardesi 8 outsider, stranger 9 barbarian, estranger, outlander 10 tramontane 12 ultramontane

foreign quarter: 6 barrio, ghetto 7 enclave

foreign service: *official:* 4 aide 6 consul 7 attache 8 diplomat 10 ambassador
residence: 7 embassy 9 consulate

foreign to: 6 dehors

foreknow: 5 infer 6 divine 7 foresee 8 conclude, prophesy 9 prescient 11 preconceive

foreknowledge: 10 prescience

forel: 4 case 6 border, sheath 7 selvage 8 slipcase

foreland: 8 headland 10 promontory

forelock: 4 bang 6 cotter 8 linchpin

foreman: 4 boss 5 chief 6 gaffer, ganger, leader 7 capataz, captain, headman, manager, steward 8 overseer 9 chargeman 10 supervisor

foremost: 4 head, high, main 5 chief, first, forme, front, grand 6 banner 7 leading, supreme 9 principal
part: van 5 front

forenoon: 7 morning

forensic: 6 debate 8 rhetoric 11 disputation 13 argumentative

foreordain: 7 destine, foresay, predoom 8 forecast 9 preordain 10 predestine 12 predestinate, predetermine

forepart: 5 front 9 stomacher
of horse's hoof: toe

forerun: 6 herald, outrun 7 precede, prelude 8 announce 9 forestall, introduce, precourse, prefigure 10 anticipate, foreshadow

forerunner: 4 omen, sign 5 usher 6 augury, herald 8 ancestor, foregoer, fourrier 9 harbinger, messenger, precedent, precursor 10 forefather, foreganger, progenitor, prognostic 11 predecessor

foresee: 4 read 6 divine 8 forecast, foreknow 10 anticipate

foreshadow: 7 forerun 9 adumbrate, prefigure

foreshank: 4 shin

foreshow: 4 bode 5 abode, augur 7 betoken 8 foretell, prophesy 9 auspicate, foretoken 13 prognosticate

foresight: 6 vision 8 prudence 9 prevision 10 prescience, prevoyance, providence 11 forethought 12 anticipation, clairvoyance 14 farsightedness

foresighted: 9 prescient, provident 10 farsighted 11 clairvoyant

forest: 4 gapo, wood 5 Arden, glade, gubat, silva, sylva (L.), taiga, waste 6 jungle, timber 7 boscage 8 caatinga, woodland 10 wilderness
deity: 4 faun 5 dryad, satyr 7 Aegipan 8 Silvanus, Sylvanus
glade: 5 camas 6 camass, cammas 7 quamash
god: Pan 5 Tapio
love of: 9 hemophily
open place: 5 glade
pert. to: 6 sylvan 7 nemoral 9 forestral
road: 4 path, ride 5 trail
subarctic: 5 taiga
treeless: 4 wold
warden: 6 ranger

Forest City: 8 Portland, Savannah 9 Cleveland

forest fire locator: 7 alidade

forestall: 5 avert, deter 7 rule out 8 preclude, stave off

forester: 6 ranger 7 montero, treeman, woodman 8 woodsman 10 lumberjack

foretaste: 4 gust 6 teaser 8 prospect 12 anticipation

foretell: 4 bode, erst, read, spae 5 augur, insee, weird 6 divine 7 bespeak, foresay,

foretelling

portend, predict, presage **8** forebode, forecast, foreshow, forewarn, prophesy, soothsay **9** predicate, prefigure, prophetic **10** vaticinate **13** prognosticate

foretelling: **9** fatidical, prophetic

forethought: **7** caution **8** prepense, prudence **9** foresight, provident **12** aforethought, anticipation **13** premeditation

foretoken: **4** omen **7** promise **8** forecast, foreshow, foresign **9** auspicate **10** presignify **13** prognosticate

foretold: **10** annunciate

foretooth: **5** biter **6** cutter **7** incisor

forever: aye **4** ever **5** etern **6** always, eterne, semper (L.) **7** endless **8** eternity **9** endlessly, eternally, perpetual **10** constantly, invariably **11** ceaselessly, continually, everlasting, incessantly, perpetually, unceasingly **12** interminably, unchangeably **13** everlastingly

forewarn (see also **foretell**): **5** augur

forewarning: **4** hint, omen **7** portent **11** premonition

foreword: **5** proem **7** preface **8** preamble **12** introduction

for example: e.g. **6** such as

forfeit: **4** fine, lose **5** crime, dedit, forgo **6** forego **7** escheat, misdeed, penalty **8** forfault
law: **7** abandum

forfeiture: **4** fine **5** mulct **7** penalty **9** decheance **10** amercement

forfend, forefend: **5** avert **6** secure **7** prevent, protect **8** preserve

forge: **4** mint **5** feign **6** smithy, swinge **7** falsify, fashion **8** bloomery **9** fabricate **11** counterfeit, fabrication, manufacture
nozzle: tew **5** tewel
on: **5** drive
tongs: tew
waste: **5** dross, sprue
wrought iron: **8** bloomery

forged: **10** artificial **11** counterfeit

forger: **5** smith **9** falsifier **10** coachsmith, fabricator **13** counterfeiter

forgery: **4** fake, sham **7** fiction **8** bloomery **11** counterfeit, fabrication **13** falsification

forget: **4** omit **5** fluff **6** ignore **7** neglect **8** overlook **9** disregard **10** draw a blank **11** disremember
one's lines: **5** fluff

forgetful: **6** remiss **7** bemused **8** careless, heedless **9** negligent, oblivious **10** neglectful **11** inattentive

forgetfulness: **7** amnesia, amnesty **8** oblivion
fruit of: **5** lotus
river of: **5** Lethe

forgivable: **6** venial

forgive: **5** remit, spare **6** excuse, pardon **7** absolve, condone **8** overlook **9** exculpate

forgiven: **7** excused

forgiveness: **6** pardon **9** remission **10** absolution **11** condonation

forgiving: **6** humane **7** clement **8** merciful, placable **9** remissive **10** charitable

forgo, forego: **4** quit **5** leave, waive **7** abstain, forbear, forfeit, forsake, neglect, precede, refrain **8** abnegate, dispense, forebear, overlook, renounce **9** sacrifice, surrender **10** relinquish

forgoing: **5** above

fork: **4** tine **5** prong **6** bisect, branch, crotch, divide **7** fourche **10** divaricate, fourchette
kind of: **4** croc, evil **5** glack, graip, pikle **7** biprong **9** tormentor

forked: **5** bifid **6** furcal **7** divided, furcate **8** branched **9** furciform **10** bifurcated **11** forficulate

forlorn: **4** lorn, lost, reft **5** alone, stray **6** abject, bereft, ruined **7** forfare **8** deserted, desolate, forsaken, helpless, hopeless, pitiable, wretched **9** abandoned, cheerless, desperate, destitute, miserable **10** friendless **11** comfortless **12** disconsolate

form: ame **4** blee, body, make, mode, mold, plan, rite, thew **5** bench, build, frame, guise, image, model, shape **6** adjust, create, figure, invent, manner, ritual, schema, sponge **7** arrange, compose, confect, contour, develop, fashion, outline, pattern, portray, produce, profile **8** ceremony, conceive, likeness, organize, schemata (pl.) **9** construct, etiquette, fabricate, formation, structure **10** appearance, constitute, expression, figuration, observance, similitude **12** conformation **13** configuration, questionnaire
carved: **8** statuary
display: **4** rack **7** manikin **9** mannequin
geometrical: See **figure**: *geometrical*
into arc: **5** embow
into ball: **8** conglobe
into chain: **8** catenate
into fabric: **4** felt, knit **5** weave
into network: **10** reticulate
literary: ode **5** novel, poesy **6** satire, sonnet **7** romance
liturgical: **4** rite **6** litany **7** service
lyrical: **6** rondel **7** sestina, sestine (pl.)
of government: **6** polity
of greeting: bow **4** wave **5** hello, salam **6** salaam, salute **7** curtsey
pert. to: **5** modal

formal: set, tux **4** gown, prim **5** exact, stiff **6** solemn **7** nominal, orderly, precise, regular, solward, starchy, stilted **8** academic,

affected, formular, reserved, starched **9**
essential, officious **10** ceremonial, methodical, systematic **11** ceremonious, punctilious, superficial **12** conventional

formality: **4** form, rite **6** ritual **8** ceremony **9**
punctilio **15** conventionality

format: **4** size **5** shape, style **6** makeup **7** pattern

formation: **4** form, rank **6** spread **9** structure
10 procession **11** composition, development **12** construction
bone: **7** ostosis **10** parostosis
cell: **6** tissue
ecological: **5** biome
flesh: **8** sarcosis
geological: lia **4** ione **5** atoll, ledge **6** schist
7 tapeats, terrain, terrane
military: **4** line **5** herse, snail **6** flight **7** echelon
sand: **4** dene, dune

formative: **7** plastic

formed: **5** built **6** shaped **7** decided, matured,
settled, wrought **10** constitute
at foot of mountain: **8** piedmont
by law: **9** corporate
crudely: **9** roughhewn
from above: **8** catogene
ingeniously: **5** dedal **6** daedal
of clustered grains (bot.): **7** grumose
on earth's surface: **7** epigene

former: die, nee, old **4** erst, fore, late, once,
past **5** forme, gauge, guide, maker, prior **6**
whilom **7** ancient, creator, earlier, further,
pattern, quondam, templet **8** previous,
sometime **9** aforetime, erstwhile **10**
antecedent

formerly: ere, nee **4** erst, fore, once, then **5**
grave **6** before **7** onetime **8** sometime **9**
aforetime, anciently, erstwhile **10** heretofore

formicary: ant **7** anthill, dweller

formicid: ant

formidable: **5** awful, tough **6** fierce **7** fearful
8 alarming, dreadful, menacing, terrible **11**
redoubtable, threatening

formless: raw **5** arupa **7** anidian, chaotic **8**
deformed, unshaped **9** amorphous, shape-
less **13** indeterminate

Formosa: See **Taiwan**

formula: law **4** rule **6** method, recipe, theory
7 receipt **8** equation

formular: **5** model **6** formal, proper **7** regular

formulate: put **5** draft, frame **6** cook up,
devise, draw up, make up **7** dream up,
hatch up

formulated: **6** stated **7** created, written

forsake: **4** deny, drop, flee, quit, shun **5** avoid,
forgo, leave, waive **6** beleve, defect, depart,

desert, forego, refuse, reject **7** abandon,
beleave, discard **8** renounce, withdraw **9**
surrender, throw over **10** relinquish

forsaken: **4** lorn **7** forlorn **8** deserted, desolate **9** abandoned, destitute

forswear: **4** deny **6** abjure, reject **7** abandon,
perjure **8** abnegate, renounce, take back

forsworn: **8** perjured **11** disaffected

fort: dun, lis, pah **4** liss, shee **5** gotta, redan,
sidhe **6** castle, strong **7** bastile, bastion, bulwark, citadel, fortify **8** bastille, castillo, fastness, fortress **10** blockhouse, protection,
stronghold
sloping bank of: **6** glacis

forte: bag **4** bent **5** knack, skill, thing **6** metier,
talent **7** calling **8** long suit, strength **9** specialty **10** excellence **11** strong point

forth: out **4** away **6** abroad, manage, onward **7**
forward **8** outdoors **10** accomplish

forthright: **5** blunt, frank, plain **6** candid **7**
brusque, frankly **9** downright **11** straightway **13** straightforth **15** straightforward

forthwith: now **6** bedene, direct **7** believe,
betimes **8** directly **9** extempore, presently,
therewith **11** immediately

fortification (see also **defense**): **4** boma,
moat, wall **5** redan, tower **6** abatis, castle,
glacis, shield **7** bastion, bulwark, citadel,
parapet, rampart, ravelin, redoubt **8**
fortress, palisade **9** barricade **10** stronghold
12 machiolation
kind of: **4** fort **5** redan **6** abatis, sconce **7**
lunette, parados, ravelin, redoubt **8** ceinture, demilune, estacade **9** bastionet, fortal-
ice
part: **5** redan **7** bastion, ravelin **8** barbette

fortify: arm, man **4** fort **5** spike **6** abatis,
picket **7** bastile, confirm **8** bastille, embat-
tle, fortress, palisade **9** barricade **10** invigorate, strengthen, stronghold

fortitude: **6** mettle **7** bravery, courage, heroism, stamina **8** strength **9** endurance **10**
resolution **12** resoluteness **14** impregnabil-
ity

fortress: **4** fort, keep **5** rocca **6** castle **7**
alcazar, barrier, bastile, borough, castlet,
castrum, chateau, citadel, fortify **8** alcalzar,
alcazava, bastille, chateaux (pl.), fastness **10**
stronghold **13** fortification, propugnaculum
outwork of: **6** tenail **8** tenaille

fortuitous: **5** happy, lucky **6** casual, chance,
random **9** hazardous **10** accidental, contingent, incidental **12** adventitious **13**
serendipitous

fortuity: **4** luck **6** chance **9** accidence **11**
serendipity

fortunate: edi, hap, sri **4** good, shri, well **5**
faust, happy, lucky, shree **6** dexter **7**

favored **8** gracious **9** favorable **10** auspicious, prosperous, successful

fortune: hap, lot **4** bahi, doom, fate, hail, luck **5** weird, worth **6** boodle, bundle, chance, estate, mishap, riches, wealth **7** destiny, portion, success, tidy sum **8** accident, hacienda **9** adventure **10** prosperity **11** king's ransom **13** circumstances
goddess: **5** Tyche

fortune teller: **4** seer **5** gypsy, sibyl, sybil **7** diviner, palmist, psychic **11** clairvoyant **12** phrenologist

forty: **13** quadragesimal

forty days: **4** Lent

forty-five-degree angle: **6** octant

forty-five inches: ell

forty-third asteroid: **4** Eros

43,560 square feet: **4** acre

forty winks: nap **6** siesta, snooze

forum: **5** court **8** tribunal

forward: on, bog, bug **4** abet, bain, bold, free, help, pert, send, ship, step **5** ahead, along, brash, eager, favor, forth, frack, freck, front, hasty, ready, relay, remit, saucy, serve, spack, ultra **6** afford, ardent, avaunt, before, bright, coming, favour, forthy, hasten, onward, prompt, send on, to; aid **7** advance, earnest, extreme, further, promote, radical, support **8** adelante, arrogant, champion, immodest, impudent, perverse, petulant, transmit **9** audacious, encourage, forthward, obtrusive, overready **10** accelerate, forritsome, precocious **11** disobedient, progressive

fossa: pit **4** foss, moat **5** canal, ditch, fosse, fovea, graff, grave **6** cavity, trench **10** depression

fossil: **4** fogy, mark **5** mummy **6** dolite **7** antique, lituite, remains **8** calamite, conodont **10** antiquated
egg: **7** ovulite
footprint: **7** ichnite
fuel: oil **4** coal, peat **9** petroleum
mollusk: **6** dolite
resin: **5** amber **8** retinite
science: **12** paleontology
shell: **6** dolite
toothlike: **8** conodont
worm track: **7** nereite

fossorial: **9** burrowing

foster: **4** feed, food, help, rear **5** nurse **6** harbor **7** cherish, embosom, gratify, imbosom, indulge, nourish, nursing, nurture, promote, sustain **8** befriend, forester **9** cultivate, encourage, fosterage, offspring **11** nourishment

foster child: **5** nurry **7** stepson **12** stepdaughter

foudroyant: **8** dazzling, stunning **10** thundering

fougue: **5** ardor **11** impetuosity

foul: **4** base, hory, roil, vile **5** bawdy, black, dirty, grimy, horry, muddy, nasty, sully, weedy **6** clarty, defame, dirten, filthy, impure, malign, odious, putrid, rotten, soiled, unfair **7** abusive, defaced, fulsome, hateful, illegal, noisome, obscene, profane, smeared, squalid, unclean, vicious **8** entangle, indecent, polluted, stinking, wretched **9** dastardly, dishonest, loathsome, nastiness, obnoxious, offensive **10** detestable, disgusting, scurrilous **11** contaminate, unfavorable **12** dishonorable, inauspicious, scatalogical

foulard: tie **11** neckerchief **12** handkerchief

foulmouthed: **7** abusive, obscene, profane **10** scurrilous **11** opprobrious

foulness: **9** feculence

foul play: **5** crime **6** murder **7** killing **8** violence

found: fix, try **4** base, cast, rest **5** board, build, endow, erect **6** attach, create, depart **8** equipped, practice, provided, supplied **9** establish, institute, originate, supported **10** foundation

foundation: bed **4** base, body, fund, gist, sill **5** bases (pl.), basis, found, stock **6** bottom, legacy, reseau, riprap **7** bedding, bedrock, chantry, roadbed **8** donation, pedestal **9** beginning, endowment **11** corporation **12** substructure

founder: **4** fail, sink **6** author, caster, dismay, dynast, falter **7** stumble **8** collapse, inventor, miscarry **9** architect, patriarch, supporter, undermine **10** maintainer, originator **11** dumbfounder, establisher
metal: **5** yeter **6** yetter

founding: **8** settling

foundling: oaf **4** waif **6** infant, orphan **8** nursling

fount: **4** fons **6** source **8** fountain **9** reservoir

fountain: jet **4** fond, head, syke, well **5** fount **6** phiale, pirene, source, spring **7** bubbler **8** aganippe **9** reservoir **10** wellspring
god of: **4** Fons
nymph: **5** naiad

fountainhead: **6** origin, source

Fountain of Youth site: **6** Bimini

fountain pen: **5** stick, stylo

four: **6** tetrad **7** quartet

fourchette: **4** fork **8** wishbone

fourflusher: **9** pretender

four-footed: **9** quadruped

fourgon: van **4** cart **5** wagon **7** tumbril

Four Horsemen: war **5** death **6** famine **8** conquest
book: **5** Bible **10** Apocalypse **11** Revelations

four hundred: 5 creme, elect, elite 6 select 7 society

four inches: 4 hand 7 measure

four-in-hand: 7 necktie

fourpence: 5 groat

fourscore: 6 eighty

four-sided: 13 quadrilateral

foursome: 6 tetrad 7 quartet

foursquare: 7 solidly 8 quadrate 10 forthright

fourth: 5 quart 6 fardel 7 quarter 8 quadrant

fourth estate: 5 media, press 10 newspapers

foveate: 6 pitted

fowl: hen 4 bird, cock, duck 5 chick, chuck, goose, manoc, quail 6 grouse, pigeon, turkey 7 chicken, poultry, rooster 8 pheasant, volaille 9 partridge 10 guinea fowl
kind of: 4 coot, keel 5 banty, brant, malay, poult, snipe 6 bantam, Houdan, rumkin, Sussex 7 galeeny, minorca

fox: tod 4 fool 5 trick 6 baffle, canine, outwit 7 beguile, confuse, stupefy, vulpine 10 intoxicate, perplexity
cape: 4 asse
female: 5 vixen
foot: pad
genus: 6 Vulpes
home: den
hunter's cry: 4 soho 5 yoick 7 tally-ho
kind of: kit, red 4 asse, gray, stag 5 vixen, zorro 6 Arctic, corsac, fennec 7 karagan, reynard 8 bat-eared 9 maned wolf 10 raccoon dog
male: dog
scent of: 4 drag
young: cub, pup

foxglove: 7 popdock
leaf poison: 9 digitalis

foxlike: 7 vulpine 9 alopecoid

foxtail: 5 brush, grass

fox-trot: 5 dance

foxy: sly 4 wily 5 coony 6 artful, astute, clever, crafty, shrewd, tricky 7 cunning, vulpine 10 fraudulent

foyer: 5 lobby 6 hearth 7 narthex 8 anteroom, entrance 9 fireplace, greenroom

fra: 4 monk 5 friar 6 priest 7 brother

fracas: 4 bout 5 brawl, fight, melee, set-to 6 rumpus, uproar 7 quarrel 8 fraction 9 commotion 11 disturbance

fraction: bit 4 part 5 break, piece, scrap 6 breach, fracas, little 7 ruction, rupture 8 breaking, fracture, fragment

fractional: 7 partial

fractious: 4 ugly 5 cross 6 unruly 7 crabbed, peevish, waspish 8 perverse, snappish 9 irritable

fracture: 4 flaw, rend 5 break, cleft, crack 6 breach 7 rupture 8 fraction

Fra Diavolo composer: 5 Auber

fragile: 4 fine, frow, weak 5 frail, frowy, light 6 feeble, frough, infirm, slight 7 brickle, brittle, froughy, slender 8 delicate, ethereal 9 frangible

fragility: 8 delicacy 12 delicateness

fragment: bit, ort 4 blad, chip, flaw, grot, part, snip, wisp 5 broke, crumb, flake, groat, piece, relic, scrap, shard, sherd, shred, spall 6 gobbet, morsel, parcel, screed, sheard, sippet, sliver 7 cantlet, flinder, flitter, fritter, oddment, portion, remnant 8 fraction 10 smithereen
biographical: 8 anecdote
diamond: 4 bort
ice afloat: 5 brash

fragmentary: 5 hashy 6 broken

fragments: 5 frush 7 gubbins
literary: ana 7 analect

Fragonard painting: 7 Bathers 8 The Swing 14 Progress of Love

fragrance: 4 odor 5 aroma, scent, smell 6 flavor, parfum (F.) 7 cologne, flavour, incense, perfume 9 perfumery, redolence

fragrant: 5 balmy, olent, spicy 7 odorant, odorous, perfumy, scented 8 aromatic, redolent 9 ambrosial 11 odoriferous

fragrant ointment: 4 balm, nard

fragrant wood: 5 aloes, cedar

frail: 4 fine, puny, weak 5 crazy 6 basket, flimsy, infirm, sickly 7 brittle, bruckle, fragile 8 delicate 12 destructible 13 insubstantial

frailty: sin 4 vice 5 fault 6 foible 7 failing 8 weakness 9 frailness, infirmity 10 peccadillo 12 imperfection

fraise: 4 fray, fuss, ream, ruff 6 cajole, defend, praise 7 defense, enlarge, flatter, pancake 8 cajolery 10 strawberry

frame (see also **framework**): bin 4 bunk, form, mold, plan, plot, sill 5 build, cadre, easel, panel, serve, shape, trave 6 abacus, adjust, binder, border, cook up, devise, fabric, invent, manage, profit, redact, resort, tenter 7 arrange, attempt, chassis, fashion, furnish, hatch up, outline, portray, prepare, proceed, prosper 8 contrive, regulate 9 calculate, construct, fabricate, structure
kinds of: ame, mat 4 bier, calm, caum, gill, sash, sess, sime, sley 5 airer, cadar, cader, dekle, easel, grate, herse, knape, scray, trave 6 abacus, deckel, deckle, tenter 7 drosser, hayrack, taboret

frame of mind: 4 bent, mood 5 humor

frame-up: 4 plot 10 conspiracy

framework: 4 rack, sill 5 cadge, cadre, racke 6 replum, stroma 7 chassis, nacelle, trestle 8 skeleton 9 structure

franc: *piece of twenty:* 5 louis
twentieth part of: 7 centime

France: 4 Gaul 6 Gallia

actor/actress: 5 Boyer 6 Bardot 8 Signoret 9 Bernhardt, Chevalier

airplane: 5 avion

among: 5 entre

and: et

annuity: 5 rente

appellation: nom

architect: 7 Garnier, L'Enfant, LeNotre 11 Le Corbusier

article: la, le, un, les, une

artist: Arp 4 Dore, Dufy 5 Corot, Degas, Manet, Monet 6 Braque, Cormon, Ingres, Legros, Millet, Renoir, Seurat, Vernet 7 Bonnard, Cezanne, Chardin, Daumier, Deveria, Duchamp, Gauguin, Lorrain, Matisse, Rouault , Utrillo, Watteau 8 Dubuffet, Pissarro, Rousseau, Steinlen 9 Deschamps 15 Toulouse-Lautrec

author: 4 Gide, Hugo, Sand, Zola 5 Camus, Dumas, Sagan, Verne 6 Balzac, Proust, Racine, Sartre 7 Colette, Moliere, Mérimée, Rimbaud 8 Flaubert, Rabelais, Stendhal, Voltaire 10 Baudelaire

axe: 5 hache

baby: 4 bébé 6 enfant

bachelor: 6 garcon

bacteriologist: 7 Pasteur

ball: bal

ballad: lai 7 virelai

bay: 5 Seine 6 Biscay

beach: 5 plage

beast: 4 bête

bed: lit 6 couche

beef: 5 boeuf

billiards: 7 bouchon

bitters: 4 amer

blessed: 4 beni 5 sacré

boat: 6 bateau 8 chaloupe

bond: 5 rente

boxing: 6 savate

boy: 6 garçon

brandy: 6 cognac 8 armagnac, Calvados, eau de vie

brewery: 9 brasserie

brush: 6 brosse

butcher shop: 11 charcuterie

cafe: 9 estaminet

cape: 5 talma

capital: 5 Paris

card game: 6 ecarte 7 baccara 8 baccarat

cardinal: 7 Mazarin 9 Richelieu

care: 4 soin

castle: 7 chateau

cathedral city: 5 Reims, Rouen 6 Nantes, Rheims 8 Chartres

chanteuse: 4 Piaf

chaperon: 11 gouvernante

cheese: 4 Brie 7 fromage 9 Camembert, Roquefort

chemist: 5 Curie 7 Pasteur

chestnut: 6 marone, maroon

citizen: 7 citoyen

city: Aix, Pau 4 Caen, Metz, Nice, Vimy 5 Aries, Arles, Arras, Brest, Dijon, Havre, Lille, Lisle, Lyons, Nancy, Nerac, Nesle, Nîmes, Paris, Reims, Rouen, Tours, Tulle, Vichy 6 Amiens, Angers, Calais, Cannes, Lemans, Nantes, Pantin, Perret, Rennes, Rheims, Senlis, Sèvres, Tarare, Toulon 7 Limoges, Orléans, Valence 8 Bordeaux, Clermont, Mulhouse, Rochelle, Toulouse 9 Levallois, Marseille 10 Marseilles

cleric: 4 abbé

cloth: ras 5 toile 8 blancard

cloud: nue

coffeehouse: 9 estaminet

composer: 4 Lalo 5 Bizet, Faure, Ravel, Satie, Thome 6 Boulez, Chopin , Franck, Gounod, Halevy 7 Berlioz, Debussy, Delibes, Milhaud, Poulenc 8 Massenet 9 Massaiaen , Offenbach 10 Saint-Saens

comrade: ami

concrete: 5 béton

conjunction: 4 mais

cordial: see *liqueur* below

cotton: 7 jasmine

couturier: 4 Dior 5 Patou 6 Chanel 7 Balmain 8 Givenchy 9 Courreges, St. Laurent

cowardly: 5 lâche

cowboy: 6 baille 7 gardian

creamcake: 7 dariole

crown: écu

currency: ecu, sol, sou 4 gros 5 agnel, blanc, blank, franc, franc, livre, obole 6 besant, denier, dizain, teston 7 centime, centime, dizaine, testoon 8 cavalier, Louis d'or, Napoleon

custom: 9 Gallicism

daffodil: 10 polyanthus

daisy: 10 marguerite

dance: bal 5 gavot 6 branle, canary, cancan 7 bourrée, boutade

dash: 4 élan

daughter: 5 fille

dead: 4 mort

dean: 5 doyen

dear: 4 cher

delicatessen: 11 charcuterie

devil: 6 diable

directory: 10 directoire

doorkeeper: 9 concierge

dramatist: 4 Hugo 5 Genet, Piron 6 Racine, Sartre 7 Anouilh, Beckett, *(cont.)*

France (*cont.*)

Cocteau, Ionesco, Moliere, Rostand **9** Corneille, Giraudoux **11** Maeterlinck

dressmaker: **9** couturier **10** couturiere

duke: duc

dungeon: **6** cachot

dynasty: **5** Capet **6** Valois **7** Bourbon, Orleans **11** Carolingian, Merovingian

ecclesiastic: **4** abbé

egg: **4** oeuf

empress: **7** Eugénie **15** Marie Antoinette

essayist: **4** Gide **9** Montaigne

evening: **4** soir

exclamation: **4** hein

export: **4** wine **8** clothing

FBI: **15** Sûreté Nationale

finally: **5** enfin

food: **4** pâté **5** crêpe **6** quiche **8** escargot, truffles **9** cassoulet **13** bouillabaisse

friar: **5** frère

friend: ami **4** amie (fem.), amis (pl.) **5** amies (pl.)

gala: **4** fête

game: jeu **4** jeux (pl.)

god: **4** dieu

good: bon

goodbye: **5** adieu **8** à bientôt, au revoir

green: **4** vert

hairdresser: **7** friseur **8** coiffeur

hat: **5** beret **7** chapeau **8** chapeaux

health: **5** santé

heaven: **4** ciel

here: ici

high school: **5** lycée

high: **4** haut

horse stable: **6** ecurie

husband: **4** mari

income: **5** rente

inn: **5** hotel **7** auberge

island: ile, yeu **4** Elba **6** Hyeres, Oleron, Ushant **7** Corsica **8** Belle-Ile

judgment: **5** arrêt

king: roi **5** Capet, Louis, Pepin **11** Charlemagne

knife: **7** couteau

lace: **10** colberteen, colbertine **12** Valenciennes

laugh: ris **4** rire

laundry: **13** blanchisserie

leather: **4** cuir

lenten season: **6** Careme

library: **12** bibliothèque

line of defense: **7** Maginot

liqueur: **8** anisette **9** Cointreau **10** chartreuse **12** creme de cacao, Grand Marnier **13** creme de menthe

lord: **8** seigneur

lover: **5** amant

lyric: **6** rondel **7** descort, rondeau

magistrate: **7** echevin

maidservant: **5** bonne **7** lisette

marshal: Ney **4** Foch, Saxe **5** Murat **6** Pétain

mask: **5** loups

mathematician: **5** Borel

me: moi

measure: pot **4** aune, line, mile, mine, muid, pied, sack, velt **5** arpen, carat, lieue, ligne, minot, perch, pinte, point, pouce, toise, velte **6** arpent, hemine, league, perche, quarte, setier **7** chopine, heminée, poisson, septier **8** boisseau, quartaut, roquille **9** decillion, quarteron **12** tonneau de mer

milk: **4** lait

mine: **4** à moi

money: see *currency* above

month: Mai **4** Août, Juin, Mars, mois **5** Avril **7** Février, Janvier, Juillet, Octobre **8** Decembre, Novembre **9** Septembre

mountain: **4** Alps, Jura **6** Vosges **7** Cote d'Or **8** Auvergne, Cevennes, Pyrenees **9** Mont Blanc, Puy de Dôme, Vignemale **10** Puy de Sancy

museum: **5** musée, Orsay **6** Louvre

nail: **4** clou

name: nom

national anthem: **12** Marseillaise

national flower: **4** lily **10** fleur de lis

national motto: **24** Liberté, Égalité, Fraternité (Liberty, Equality, Fraternity)

no: non

noon: **4** midi

nose: nez

nothing: **4** rien

novelist: see *author* above

nursemaid: **5** bonne

of: de

officer: **6** préfet

old money: **6** besant

one: un, une

opera: **5** Faust, Lakmé, Manon **6** Carmen, Mignon **7** La Juive

painter: see *artist* above

palace: **6** palais **10** Versailles

pancake: **5** crêpe

parish priest: **4** curé

Parliament chamber: **5** senat

party: bal

pastry shop: **10** patisserie

patron saint: **5** Denis, Denys **6** Martin

philosopher: **4** Caro **5** Camus **6** Pascal, Sartre **8** Rousseau **9** Descartes

physicist: **5** Arago, Binet **6** Ampère

pocket: **5** poche

poem: dit, lai **7** rondeau

(*cont.*)

France (*cont.*)
police: 4 flic 6 Sûreté 8 gendarme
porcelain: 7 Limoges
port: see *seaport* below
preposition: de
president's residence: 6 elysee
pretty: 4 joli 5 jolie
priest: 4 abbé, curé, père
pronoun: ils, lui, mes, moi 4 elle, nous, vous 6 tienne
psychologist: 5 Binet
pupil: 5 élève
queen: 5 reine
rabbit: 5 lapin
race course: 7 Auteuil
railroad: 11 chemin de fer
railroad station: 4 gare
read: 4 lire
rear: 7 arrière
Republic calendar: 6 Nivôse 7 Floréal, Ventôse 8 Brumaire, Fervidor, Frimaire, Germinal, Messidor, Pluviôse, Prairial 9 Fructidor, Thermidor 11 Vendémiaire
resort: Pau 4 Nice 5 Vichy 6 Cannes, Menton 7 Riviera 8 Biarritz, Chamonix 9 Deauville
rest: 5 repos
restaurant: 6 bistro
Revolutionary hero: 6 Danton
Revolutionary leader: 5 Marat 11 Robespierre
Revolutionary radical: 7 Jacobin
river: Ain, Ill, Lot, Lys 4 Aire, Aude, Cher, Eure, Gard, Gers, Loir, Oise, Orne, Saar, Tarn, Yser 5 Adour, Aisne, Drôme, Indre, Isère, Loire, Maine, Marne, Meuse, Rance, Rhône, Saône, Sarre, Seine, Seyre, Somme, Veste, Yonne 6 Allier, Ariège, Escaut, Loiret, Nièvre, Sambre, Scarpe, Vienne 7 Ardèche, Durance, Garonne, Gironde, Moselle, Scheldt 8 Charente, Dordogne, Nantaise
roast: 4 rôti 5 rotir
room: 5 salle
royal family: 5 Capet 6 Valois
saint: 5 Denîs, Denys 6 Martin
savant: 7 Diderot
school: 5 ecole, lycée 8 Barbison, Barbizon
scientist: 5 Curie 7 Pasteur
sculptor: 5 Barye, Rodin 6 Houdon 7 Maillol 9 Bartholdi
sea: mer
shelter: 4 abri

shield: ecu 5 targe
shoe: 9 chaussure
shopgirl: 9 midinette
sister: 5 soeur
slang: 5 argot
soldier: 5 assis, poilu 6 Zouave 8 chasseur
son: 4 fils
song: 5 caira, chant 6 aubade 7 ballade, chanson, Madelon, virelai, virelay
soul: âme
south: sud 4 Midi
spirit: âme 4 élan 6 esprit
stable: 6 écurie
star: 6 étoile
state: 4 état
stock exchange: 6 bourse
store: 8 boutique
story: 5 conte
street: rue
stupid: 4 bête
summer: été
sun king: 8 Louis XIV
symbol: 4 lily 10 Fleur-de-lis
theater: 5 odeon
then: 5 alors
ticket window: 7 guichet
title: duc 5 comte
tobacco: 5 tabac
true: 4 vrai
Verdun battle: 4 Vaux
verse: 4 vers
verse form: lai 4 alba 6 rondel 7 ballade, virelay
very: 4 très
vessel: 7 navette
vinegar: 8 vinaigre
vineyard: cru 5 vigne
waiter: 6 garçon
wall: mur
water: eau 4 eaux (pl.)
weight: 4 gros, marc, once 5 carat, livre, pound, tonne, uckia 7 tonneau 8 esterlin 9 esterling
who: qui
wicket: 7 guichet
wife: 5 femme
wine: vin
wine district: 5 Médoc 8 Bordeaux, Burgundy, Provence 9 Champagne
wine shop: 6 bistro
wing: 4 aile
woman: 5 femme
world: 5 monde
you: 4 vous

Franciscan: 8 Capuchin, Minorite 9 Cordelier 10 Poor Clares 11 Friars Minor
nun: 5 Clare

franchise: soc 5 grant 6 patent 7 license 8 freelage, suffrage 9 privilege
old English: soc 4 soke

francolin: 4 bird 5 titar 9 partridge

frangible: 7 brittle, fragile 9 breakable

frank: 4 free, open, rank 5 bluff, lusty, naive, plain 6 candid, direct, honest 7 artless, genuine, liberal, profuse, sincere 8 carefree, cavalier, generous, vigorous 9 ingenuous, luxuriant, outspoken 10 licentious, unreserved 15 straightforward, unsophisticated

frankincense: 8 olibanum

Frankish hero: 6 Roland

Franklin: *invention:* 5 stove 8 bifocals
pen name: 11 Poor Richard

frankly: 6 freely, openly 7 plainly 8 candidly 9 artlessly, liberally, sincerely, willingly 10 forthright 11 ingenuously 12 unreservedly 13 undisguisedly

frankness: 6 candor 7 freedom 8 openness 9 telltruth, unreserve

Franks: 7 Salians
hero: 6 Oliver, Roland
king: 5 Pepin 6 Clovis 11 Charlemagne
law of: 5 Salic
peasant: 4 liti (pl.) 5 litus
vassal: 4 leud

frantic: mad 5 rabid 6 insane 7 furious, lunatic, violent 8 deranged, feverish, frenetic, frenzied 9 delirious, desperate, phrenetic 10 distracted, distraught

frap: 5 brace 6 secure, strike 7 tighten 10 strengthen

frappe: ice 4 iced 5 chill 6 cooled, freeze, frozen 9 milk shake

frat: 11 brotherhood

frater: 7 brother, comrade

fraternal: 9 brotherly

fraternity: 4 club 8 sorority 10 sisterhood 11 brotherhood

fraternize: 6 cotton, hobnob, mingle 9 affiliate, associate, forgather 10 foregather

fraud: 4 dole, fake, gaff, gaud, gull, jape, ruse, sham, wile 5 cheat, craft, faker, guile, hocus, quack, trick 6 brogue, deceit, humbug 7 defraud, knavery, roguery, swindle 8 artifice, impostor, subtlety, trickery, trumpery 9 collusion, deception, imposture, stratagem 10 imposition 11 fraudulency 13 bamboozlement, circumvention

fraudulent: 4 fake, wily 5 snide 6 crafty, quacky 7 abusive, crooked, cunning 8 cheating, covinous, guileful, spurious 9 deceitful, deceiving, deceptive, designing, dishonest, horsefair, insidious, underhand

10 fallacious, misleading 11 clandestine, counterfeit, treacherous

fraught: 4 fill, lade, load 5 cargo, equip, laden 6 burden, supply 7 freight 9 freighted, transport

fraxinus: ash 4 tree

fray: 4 feud, fret, riot 5 alarm, brawl, broil, broom, clash, dread, feaze, fight, melee, panic, ravel 6 affray, assail, attack, battle, bustle, combat, fraise, fridge, fright, inroad, terror, tumult 7 contest, frazzle, ruction, terrify 8 disperse, frighten 9 commotion, dissipate 12 apprehension

frayed: 4 worn 7 raveled 10 threadbare

frazzle: 5 upset 7 exhaust, wear out 9 prostrate

freak: 4 bold, flam, lune, mood, whim 5 braid, fancy, fleck, humor, prank, sport 6 frolic, greedy, humour, megrim, mosaic, streak, vagary, whimsy 7 caprice, checker, chimera, crochet, monster, whimsey 8 capricci (pl.), flimflam 9 capriccio, variegate 10 enthusiast 11 monstrosity 12 whimsicality

freakish: odd 4 flam 5 screwy 7 curious, flighty 9 arbitrary, fantastic, whimsical 10 capricious

fream: 4 roar

freckle: 4 mark, spot 7 blemish, ephelis, frecken, lentigo, speckle
remover: 6 adarce

Frederick I's nickname: 10 Barbarossa

Frederick the Great: 6 Alaric

free: lax, rid 4 liss, open, quit, void 5 broad, clear, enode, frank, lisse, loose, ready, siker, slake, spare, untie 6 acquit, adjust, beyond, degage, devoid, exempt, gratis, immune, lavish, loosen, remove, rescue, sicker, unbind 7 absolve, deliver, forward, grivois, inexact, leisure, liberal, manumit, outside, release, relieve, unbound, willing 8 abundant, detached, dispatch, distinct, expedite, familiar, floating, generous, grivoise, indigent, innocent, liberate, overfree, separate, unfasten, unhamper, unleased 9 at liberty, discharge, disengage, exculpate, exonerate, expansive, extricate, footloose, guiltless, ingenuous, outspoken, separated, unbridled, unchecked, unimpeded 10 autonomous, emancipate, gratuitous, immoderate, licentious, openhanded, self-ruling, unattached, uncombined, unconfined, unfettered, unimpaired, unreserved 11 disencumber, disentangle, independent, magnanimous, spontaneous, untrammeled 12 uncontrolled, unencumbered, unrestrained, unrestricted 13 communicative, self-directing, unconstrained
from bacteria: 7 aseptic, sterile
from blame: 5 clear 6 acquit 7 absolve, relieve 8 innocent 9 exonerate

from bondage: **7** manumit **10** emancipate **11** affranchise

from dirt: **5** clean **7** apinoid

from discount: net

from moisture: dry **9** dehydrate

from restraint: **5** loose, untie

from suspicion: **5** clear, purge **6** acquit **7** absolve **9** exculpate, exonerate

freebooter: **5** rider **6** pirate **7** cateran, corsair **8** pillager **9** buccaneer, plunderer **10** filibuster

freed: **8** absolute **13** disencumbered

freedom: **4** ease **7** abandon, content, leisure, liberty, license, release **8** facility, freelage, immunity, latitude, openness **9** exemption, frankness, readiness **10** generosity, liberality, liberation **11** manumission, willingness **12** emancipation, independence **13** outspokenness **14** unreservedness

from activity: **4** rest **6** recess **7** respite **14** dolce far niente (It.)

from fraud: **7** honesty **9** bonafides

from pain: **6** aponia

from strife: **5** peace

of access: **6** entree

free-for-all: **4** race **5** brawl, fight, melee **6** barney **11** competition

freehold: **4** alod **5** allod **6** estate, tenure **7** alodium **8** allodium

freeholder: **6** yeoman

freeing: **9** acquittal **11** manumission

freeloader: **5** leech **6** sponge **8** hanger-on, parasite **12** lounge lizard

freely: **4** lief **5** noble, nobly **6** gratis **7** frankly, largely, readily **8** heartily **9** beautiful, bounteous, bountiful, copiously, excellent, liberally, voluntary, willingly **10** abundantly, generously **11** beautifully, bounteously, bountifully, excellently, plenteously, plentifully, voluntarily **12** munificently **13** spontaneously **14** unobstructedly **15** unconditionally

freeman: **4** aire **5** ceorl, churl, thane, thegn **6** yeoman **7** burgess, burgher, citizen

free of charge: **8** buckshee

Freestone State: **11** Connecticut

freethinker: **7** infidel, skeptic **8** agnostic **10** espritfort, unbeliever

free time: **4** rest **6** recess **7** leisure

freeze: ice **4** rime **5** chill **6** frappe, harden **7** chilled, congeal, impound **11** conglaciate, refrigerate

freezer: **4** icer

freezing: icy **4** cold **5** gelid, nippy **6** frigid, frosty

freight: **4** load **5** cargo, laden **6** lading **7** fraught **9** transport **10** freightage

freightage: **5** cargo **6** lading **7** freight

freighted: **5** laden **7** fraught

French: See **France**

French-Belgian river: Lys **4** Yser

Frenchman: **4** Gaul **6** Picard **8** Parisian

frenetic, phrenetic: mad **4** wild **5** crazy, fresh, rabid **6** insane, madman **7** fanatic, madness, violent, zealous **9** delirious **10** distracted, ornamental, passionate **12** absentminded

frenzied: **4** amok, mang **5** amoke, amuck, rabid **6** ramage **7** berserk, enraged, frantic, furious **8** frenetic, furibund, maddened **9** delirious

frenzy: mad **4** amok, fury, rage **5** amoke, amuck, furor, mania **7** frantic, madness, oestrus **8** delirium, insanity, maniacal **9** amazement **11** distraction

frequency: **5** crowd **6** throng **7** crebity **9** community, concourse **11** familiarity

unit: **7** fresnel

frequent: **5** haunt, howff, often, usual, visit **6** affect, common, effect, hourly, sundry **7** current, enhaunt, prevail **8** familiar, habitual **9** assiduous, crebrouse, habituate **10** persistent

frequented place: **4** dive **5** haunt **6** resort

frequenter: **7** denizen, habitue

frequently: oft **5** often **6** hourly **8** ofttimes **10** repeatedly

fresco: **5** mural, shade **8** coolness, painting

fresh: new **4** cool, good, pert, pure, racy **5** brisk, green, ruddy, sassy, saucy, sound, sweet, vivid **6** breezy, bright, caller, florid, lively, recent, strong, unused **7** unfaded, untired, untried **8** flippant **9** obtrusive, unspoiled **10** additional, meddlesome, refreshing, unimpaired **11** smart-alecky **12** invigorating, presumptuous

and lively: **4** racy

freshen: **5** renew **6** breeze, revive **7** refresh, sweeten

freshet: **5** flood, spate **6** stream **9** streamlet **10** inundation

freshly: **5** again

freshman: **4** colt, tyro **5** bejan, frosh, plebe **6** bejant, novice, rookie **8** neophyte, newcomer **10** apprentice

freshness: **4** verd **5** youth **8** verdancy **9** fraicheur

lose: dry **4** fade, wilt **6** wither

fret: nag, rub, vex **4** care, fray, gall, gnaw, pout, rage, stew **5** chafe, grate, pique, tease, worry **6** abrade, devour, harass, murmur, nettle, plague, rankle, ripple, ruffle, strait **7** agitate, consume, disturb, grizzle, roughen **8** diminish, disquiet, irritate, vexation

fretful: **5** angry, cross **6** repine, sullen **7** carking, frecket, gnawing, peevish, pettish **8** captious, corroded, fretsome, petulant, restless **9** corrosive, impatient, irascible, irritable, plaintive, querulous **10** ill-humored, ill-natured

Freudian term: **6** id; ego **8** superego

Frey: *father:* **5** Njord **6** Njorth
sister: **5** Freya **6** Freyja
wife: **4** Gerd

Freya's husband: **4** Oder

friable: **5** crimp, crisp, crump, loamy, mealy
clay: **4** bole

friar: fra **4** fish, monk **5** frere **6** Bhikku, fraile, frater **7** Bhikshu, brother **8** Capuchin, monastic **9** Carmelite, mendicant **10** Franciscan **11** Augustinian **12** Austin Friars
black: **9** Dominican
gray: **11** Franciscans, Friars Minor
house: **6** friary
mendicant: **7** Servite
white: **9** Carmelite

friary: **8** cloister **9** monastery **11** brotherhood

fribble: **4** fool **6** falter, totter, trifle **7** stammer **8** trifling **9** frivolity, frivolous

fricassee: **4** stew **6** potpie **10** blanquette

fricative: *Anglo-Saxon:* edh

friction: rub **5** chafe **7** discord **8** conflict **9** attrition **10** dissension
air: **7** windage

fridge: rub **4** fray **5** chafe **6** fidget, icebox **8** irritate **12** refrigerator

fried: **4** frit (F.) **5** drunk **7** sauteed

fried cake: **7** cruller **8** doughnut

friend: ami (F.), amy, cob, eme, pal **4** ally, amie (F.), chum, kith **5** amiga (Sp.), amigo (Sp.), buddy, crony **6** bon ami (F.), cobber, cummer, gimmer, kimmer **7** comrade, gremial, kinsman **8** cockmate, compadre, paramour, relative **9** associate, attendant, bonne amie (F.), broadbrim, companion, confidant **10** confidante **12** acquaintance

Friend: **6** Quaker
church founder: **9** George Fox

friendless: **7** forlorn

friendliness: **5** amity **8** affinity, amicable, goodwill **10** fellowship **13** companionship

friendly: sib **4** cosh, good, kind **5** chief, howdy **6** blithe, chummy, genial, homely, howdie **7** affable, amiable, amicous, cordial **8** amicable, homelike, intimate, sociable **9** favorable **10** favourable, hospitable **11** warm-hearted **12** well-disposed

Friendly island: **5** Tonga

friendship: **5** amity **6** accord **8** relation **9** affection **10** attachment

Friendship author: **6** Cicero

frieze: **4** kelt (Sc.) **5** adorn, chase **8** trimming **9** embroider **10** decoration
band: **6** taenia

frigate (see also **boat, ship**): **5** zabra (Sp.)

frigate bird: iwa **8** alcatras **12** man-of-war bird

Frigg: *husband:* **4** Odin
son: **6** Balder

fright: awe, cow **4** fear, fray, funk, gast **5** alarm, gliff, panic, shock **6** affray, dismay, horror, scarce, schrik, terror **7** startle **11** trepidation **13** consternation

frighten: awe, cow **4** fray, funk, hare, haze, shoo **5** afear, alarm, appal, gliff, hazen, scare **6** affray, appall, ascare, boggle **7** frecken, startle, terrify **8** affright **10** intimidate

frightened: **4** awed, eery, gast **5** eerie, timid **6** afraid **8** skittish

frightful: **4** grim **5** awful, ferly, scary **6** horrid, ugsome **7** affreux, fearful, gashful, ghastly, hideous **8** alarming, dreadful, fearsome, horrible, horrific, shocking, terrible, terrific **10** horrendous, tremendous

frightfulness: **13** atrociousness **15** schrecklichkeit (G.)

frigid: icy **4** cold **5** acold, aloof, bleak **6** arctic, chilly, frosty, frozen **7** glacial **8** freezing

frill: **4** purl **5** jabot, ruche **6** ruffle **7** flounce **8** furbelow **9** balayeuse **11** chitterling

fringe: hem, rim **4** loma **6** border, edging, margin **8** ciliella, trimming

fringed: **9** laciniate **10** frimbriate

frippery: **6** finery **7** regalia **9** full dress **10** Sunday best

frisk: pat **4** leap, skip, whid **5** brisk, caper, dance, flisk **6** curvet, frisco, frolic, gambol, lively, search **7** disport, friscal **8** caracole **9** shake down **10** frolicsome

frisky: gay **4** pert **6** lively **7** playful **8** frisking, sportive **9** kittenish **10** frolicsome

frisson: **5** chill **6** quiver, shiver, thrill **7** shudder

frith: **4** help **5** firth, hedge **6** hurdle, wattle **7** coppice, estuary, freedom **8** liberate, security **9** brushwood, copsewood, underwood **10** protection

fritter: **5** shred, spend, waste **6** bangle **7** pancake, scatter **8** fragment, squander

frivol: **6** trifle **9** frivolous

frivolity: **6** levity **7** fribble, inanity **8** nonsense **9** lightness

frivolous: gay **5** giddy, inane, petty **6** frivol, futile **7** fatuous, fribble, shallow, trivial **8** gossamer **9** childlike, worthless **11** empty-headed, light-headed **14** featherbrained

frizzed: **5** crepe **6** crispy

fro: **4** away, back, from **5** hence, since **8** backward

frock (see also **dress**): jam **4** gown, slip, wrap **5** tunic **6** cleric, jersey, mantle **7** workman **9** gaberdine

frog: **4** toad **5** frosh, frosk, jakie **6** peeper **7**

paddock, quilkin **8** ferreiro **9** amphibian
pert. to: **6** ranine
rearing place: **7** ranaria (pl.) **8** ranarium
zoological order: **5** anura **6** anoura **9** salientia
frogman: **5** diver **7** swimmer
gear: **4** mask **5** scuba
frohlich: gay **5** happy **6** joyous
frolic: bum, gay **4** blow, game, gell, jink, lark, orgy, play, ramp, romp **5** caper, freak, frisk, merry, prank, randy, sport, spree **6** curvet, gambol, plisky, prance, rollix, shindy, splore **7** disport, gammock, pliskie, scamper, stashie, wassail **8** carousal **9** gilravage **10** masquerade
frolicsome: gay **4** roid **5** gilpy **6** frisky, gilpey **7** jocular, waggish **8** espiegle, friskful, gamesome, sportive
from: fro
beginning to end: **4** A to Z, over **7** through **10** soup to nuts
head to foot: **7** capapie
here: **5** hence
that time: **6** thence
the egg: **5** ab ovo
the time that: **5** since
this time: **5** hence
front: bow, van **4** brow, face, fore, head, prow **5** afore **6** before, facade, facing, oppose, sector **7** forward, further, obverse **8** forehead, foremost, forepart, foreside **9** forefront **10** appearance, effrontery **11** countenance
toward the: **8** anterior
frontal: **6** sindon **7** metopic
frontier: **4** face **5** bound, march **6** border, oppose **7** barrier, defense **8** boundary
frontiersman: **4** Cody **5** Boone, Clark **6** Carson **7** pioneer, settler **8** Crockett
fronton: **7** jai-alai
frore: **4** cold **6** frosty, frozen
frost: ice, nip **4** foam, hoar, rime **7** failure
frosted: **4** iced **5** glace **6** frozen
frostfish: **5** smelt **6** tomcod **9** whitefish
frosting: ice, mat **5** icing
frosty: icy **4** cold, rimy **5** chill, frore, gelid, glary **6** frigid, froren, frozen **8** chilling, freezing
froth: fob **4** barm, foam, scum, suds **5** spume **6** freath, lather
frow: **4** frau, froe, wife **5** vrouw, woman
froward: **5** balky, cross **7** adverse, awkward, peevish, wayward **8** contrary, perverse, petulant, untoward **9** obstinate **10** refractory, unyielding **11** disobedient, unfavorable **12** ungovernable
frown: **4** lour, pout, sulk **5** gloom, glout, lower, scowl **6** glower, glunch **7** frounce
frowsy, frowzy: **5** musty **6** blowzy **7** raffish, unkempt **8** slovenly **10** disordered

frozen: **4** hard **5** fixed, frore, gelid, glary **6** chilly, frappe, froren **7** chilled, frosted **8** hardened, immobile **9** congealed **10** unyielding **11** coldhearted **12** refrigerated **13** unsympathetic
fructify: **9** fertilize **10** impregnate
frugal: **4** mild **5** chary, roman, spare, tight **6** saving **7** careful, sparing, thrifty **9** economize, provident **10** economical, unwasteful **12** parsimonious **13** penny-pinching
frugality: **6** thrift **7** economy **8** prudence **9** chariness
fruit (see also **berry, melon**): fig **4** date, kiwi, lime, pear, plum, pome **5** apple, berry, drupe, grape, issue, lemon, melon, olive, peach, young **6** almond, casaba, cherry, orange, quince, result **7** apricot, avocado, azarole, current, product, progeny **8** dewberry **9** blueberry, nectarine, offspring, persimmon, pineapple, tangerine **10** grapefruit, production, watermelon
aggregate: **5** berry **7** etaerio
apple-like: **4** pome **6** quince
astringent: **4** sloe
baccate: **5** berry
beverage: ade **4** wine **5** cider, juice, punch
blackthorn: **4** sloe
buttercup: **5** akene **6** achene **7** achenia (pl.) **8** achenium
citrus: **4** lime **5** lemon **6** citron, orange, pomelo, tangor **7** kumquat, tangelo **8** bergamot, mandarin, minneola, shaddock **9** tangerine **10** grapefruit
collective: **7** syncarp **10** syncarpium
cooked in syrup: **7** compote
decay: **4** blet
desert region: **5** terfa **6** terfez
dish: **7** compote **8** ambrosia
dried: **5** prune **6** orejon, raisin
drink: see *beverage* above
dry: **5** regma **6** achene, samara
early maturing: **8** rareripe
elm tree: **6** samara
fleshy: **4** pear, plum, pome **5** berry, drupe, melon **6** tomato
fleshy part: **9** sarcocarp
goddess of: **6** Pomona
gourd family: **4** pepo
horseradish tree: ben
husk: **5** lemma
hybrid: **7** tangelo
imperfect: **6** nubbin
juicy: **4** lime, pear, plum **5** grape, lemon, peach **6** orange **7** apricot **9** pineapple **10** grapefruit
layer: **7** epicarp
less: **8** acarpous
lime & lemon: **6** citron
many-seeded: **10** watermelon **11**

pomegranate
maple: **6** samara
mild acid: **5** guava
multiple: fig **4** cone **8** mulberry **9** pineapple
of cactus: **5** sabra
of rose: **11** cynorrhodon
of strawberry: **7** etaerio
oily: **5** olive
one-seeded: **5** akene **6** achene, samara **7** achenis (pl.) **8** achenium
palm tree: **4** date **7** coconut
peach-like: **7** apricot **9** nectarine
pear-shaped: fig **7** avocado
plum-like: **4** sloe **6** loquat **7** carissa
pome: **4** pear **5** apple **7** azarole
preserving: **6** medlar
pulp: pap
pulpy: uva **4** pome **5** berry, drupe, grape
red: **4** plum **5** apple **6** cherry **9** raspberry **10** strawberry **11** pomegranate
refuse: **4** marc
rind: **7** epicarp
rosebush: hip
science of: **8** pomology
seed: pip, pit
spicy: **5** cubeb
spore: **6** aecium
stalk: **8** peduncle
stone: **4** paip, plum **5** drupe, peach, prune **6** cherry **7** apricot **9** nectarine
strawberry-family: **7** etaerio
study of: **8** pomology **9** carpology
sugar: **7** glucose **8** fructose
tropical: fig **4** date **5** gourd, guava, mango **6** banana, litchi, papaya, pawpaw **8** tamarind **9** cheri moya, pineapple, sapodilla **10** mangosteen
vine: **5** grape
winged: **6** samara
withered: **6** nubbin
yellowish: **5** papaw **6** quince
fruit basket: **6** pottel, pottle
fruit bats: **8** pteropid **10** pteropidae
fruit dealer: **9** frontsman, fruiterer **11** greengrocer
fruitful: fat **6** fecund, gravid **7** fertile **8** abundant, prolific **9** feracious, plenteous, plentiful, procreant **10** productive
fruitgrower: **8** fruitist **10** orchardist, pomologist **14** horticulturist
fruition: joy **8** pleasure **9** enjoyment **11** achievement, fulfillment, realization
fruitless: dry **4** geld, vain **5** addle, blank **6** barren, futile **7** sterile, useless **8** abortive **10** profitless **11** ineffectual **12** unprofitable, unsuccessful
fruit of Jove: **9** persimmon
fruit of paradise: **6** pomelo **10** grapefruit
fruit stone: pit **4** paip **6** pyrene **7** putamen

frump: vex **4** drab, mock, snub, sulk **5** dowdy, flout **6** gossip **7** provoke **8** irritate
frustrate: **4** balk, bilk, dash, foil, null, vain, void **5** baulk, blank, block, check, cross, crush, elude **6** baffle, blight, defeat, delude, hamper, impede, outwit, scotch, thwart **7** deceive, nullify, prevent, useless **8** confound, infringe, nugatory **9** cancel out, checkmate, discomfit **10** circumvent, counteract, disappoint, disconcert, neutralize **11** countermand, ineffectual **12** unprofitable
frustration: **6** fiasco **12** discomfiture **15** disillusionment
fry: **4** sile **5** brook, roast, saute, young **6** sizzle **9** offspring
fryer: **6** pullet **7** chicken
frying pan: **6** spider **7** griddle, skillet
fuddle: **5** booze **6** muddle, tipple **7** fluster
fuddled: fap, ree **5** bosky, tipsy **7** muddled
fudge: pad **4** fake **5** candy, cheat, foist, hunch, welsh **6** devise, humbug **8** contrive, nonsense **9** interlope, makeshift **10** exaggerate, substitute **11** counterfeit
fuel: gas, oil **4** coal, coke, peat, wood **5** argal, argol, argul, stoke **6** acetol, elding, firing, petrol **8** charcoal, gasoline, kerosene, kerosine **9** petroleum **10** exaggerate **11** combustible
fugacious: **6** flying **8** fleeting, volatile **10** evanescent
fuggy: **5** musty **6** smelly, stuffy
fugitive: **5** exile, fleme **6** emigre, exiled, outlaw **7** fleeing, refugee, roaming, runaway **8** banished, deserter, fleeting, runagate, unstable, vagabond, volatile **9** fugacious, strolling, transient, uncertain **10** evanescent
fugue: **4** fuga **9** ricercare
exponent: **4** Bach **6** Handel
Führer, der: **6** Hitler, leader
Fukien river: Min
fulcrum: **4** bait, prop **5** thole **7** support
fulfill: **4** fill, full, meet **6** effect, finish, occupy **7** achieve, execute, perform, satisfy **8** complete **9** implement **10** accomplish, effectuate
fulfillment, fulfilment: **6** effect **9** execution **10** completion **11** contentment, performance, realization **13** gratification **14** accomplishment
fulgent: **6** bright **7** shining **8** dazzling, luminous **9** effulgent
full: bad, big **4** good **5** ample, round, sated, solid, total **6** entire, fulfil, honest, loaded **7** baptize, copious, destroy, diffuse, fulfill, fulsome, maximum, orotund, perform, plenary, replete, teeming, trample **8** adequate, bouffant, brimming, complete, entirely, resonant **9** bouffante, capacious, plentiful

10 consecrate, exhaustive, unabridged **12** well-supplied **13** comprehensive
cloth: **4** felt **7** cleanse, compact, thicken
skirt: **7** pleated **8** gathered

full-blooded: **5** flush, ruddy **6** florid **8** rubicund **12** thoroughbred

full-blown: **4** lush, ripe **5** adult **6** all-out, mature **7** grown-up

fuller: **4** tool **6** groove, hammer **7** creaser

fuller's earth: **4** clay **6** filter, powder

fuller's grass: **8** soapwort

full force: **5** brunt

full-grown: **6** mature **9** developed

fullness, fulness: **5** fulth **6** plenty **7** satiety **8** pleonasm **9** abundance, amplitude, plumpness, repletion **10** fleshiness, perfection **12** completeness

full of: *cracks:* **6** rimose
glands: **7** adenose
hollows: **8** lacunose
minute openings: **6** porous
sand: **7** arenose
sap or juice: **7** succous **9** succulent
thorns: **6** briary
twists: **5** kinky **7** sinuous, winding **8** tortuous
wrinkles: **6** rugose

fully: **5** amply **6** wholly **7** clearly, largely, utterly **8** entirely, maturely **9** perfectly **10** abundantly, completely, distinctly **11** plenteously, plentifully

fulmar: **4** bird **5** nelly **7** malduck

fulminate: **7** explode, inveigh **8** detonate

fulsome: fat **4** foul, full **5** gross, plump, suave **6** coarse, wanton **7** copious, lustful, overfed **8** abundant, nauseous **9** offensive, overgrown, repulsive, satiating, sickening **10** disgusting, indelicate, nauseating

fumble: paw **4** boot **5** abase, botch, error, grope **6** bobble, bungle, faffle, haffle, huddle, mumble

fume: **4** emit, foam, odor, rage, rant, reek **5** ewder, fumet, smoke, storm, vapor **6** exhale **7** flatter, fumette **8** fumigate, outburst **10** exhalation

fun: gag, gig **4** game, gell, glee, hoax, jest, joke, play **5** mirth, sport **6** frolic, gaiety, gayety **9** amusement, diversion, horseplay, merriment **10** pleasantry **13** entertainment

function: act, run, use **4** duty, role, work **5** doing **6** action, office **7** calling, operate, service **8** activity, business, ceremony, occasion **9** festivity, gathering, operating, operation **10** occupation, profession, providence **11** performance **13** entertainment
social: tea **4** ball, gala **5** party, roast **6** dinner, soiree **8** luncheon **9** reception
trigonometrical: **4** sine **6** cosine, secant **7** tangent

fund: **4** fond, pool **5** basis, endow, stock, store **6** bottom, ground, supply **7** deposit, reserve **10** foundation, groundwork **12** accumulation

fundamental: **5** basal, basic, vital **7** basilar, organic, primary, radical **8** original, rudiment **9** elemental, essential, important, necessary, paramount, principle **10** elementary

funds: **4** caja, cash **5** money **9** resources

funeral: **6** burial, dismal, exequy **7** cortege, funebre **8** exequial, funereal **9** forthfare, obsequies **10** sepulchral
bell: **5** knell
director: **8** embalmer **9** mortician **10** undertaker
oration: **5** eloge **6** eulogy **8** encomium **9** panegyric
pile: **4** pyre
song: **5** dirge, elegy, elogy, nenia **6** elegie **7** elogium, epicede **8** threnody **9** epicedium
structure: **10** catafalque

funereal: **5** feral, grave **6** dismal, gloomy, solemn **7** funebre, funeral **8** mournful **9** funebrial, funebrous **10** funebrious

funest: sad **4** dire **5** fatal **7** doleful

fungus: **4** bunt, cepe, mold, rust, smut **5** ergot, fungi (pl.), fungo, morel, moril, uredo, yeast **6** agaric, fungal, lichen, mildew, oidium, telium **7** agarics, amanita, blewits, fungoid, fungous, geaster, truffle **8** amanitin, mushroom, parasite, puffball **9** stinkhorn, toadstool **10** fungaceous
disease: rot **5** tinea **6** thrush **8** lumpy jaw
edible: **4** cepe **5** morel **6** mycena **7** boletes, parasol, truffle, waxy cap **8** mushroom **9** fairy ring **10** shaggy mane **11** chanterelle
lack: **4** leaf, root, stem **11** chlorophyll
parasitic: **5** ergot
scientist: **10** mycologist

fungus-like: **6** agaric

funk: **4** kick, odor, rage **5** shirk, smell, spark **6** coward, flinch, fright, recoil, shrink **8** frighten **9** cowardice, touchwood

funnel: **4** pipe **6** hopper **7** conduct **8** transmit

funny: odd **5** comic, droll, queer **7** amusing, bizarre, comical, jocular, risible, strange **8** humorous, peculiar **9** laughable, ludicrous

funny bone: **9** olecranon

funnyman: wit **8** comedian

fur: **4** flix, pell, pelt **5** budge, stole **6** furrow, pelage
coat: **6** pelage
collection of: **5** pelts **6** peltry
kind of: fox **4** mink, paen, scut, seal, vair, woom **5** budge, civet, coney, fitch, lapin, otter, sable **6** ermine, galyac, galyak, marten, martin, moutin, nutria **7** calabar, calaber, caracul, karakul, miniver, platina,

sealine **8** karakule, ragondin **9** silver fox
piece: **5** stole
refuse: **4** kemp

fur-bearing animal: fox **4** lynx, mink, mole, seal **5** genet, otter, sable, skunk **6** beaver, coyote, ermine, fisher, marten, martin, nutria, rabbit **7** muskrat, opossum, raccoon **8** squirrel **10** chinchilla **11** Persian lamb

furbelow: **5** frill **6** ruffle **7** falbala, falbelo, flounce **8** trimming

furbish: fig, rub **4** fake, vamp **5** clean, scour **6** polish **7** burnish **8** renovate

Furies: **5** Dirae **7** Erinyes
individual: **6** Alecto, Erinys **7** Erinnys, Erinyes, Megaera **9** Tisiphone

furious: mad **5** angry, brain, irate, rabid **6** fierce, furied, insane, stormy **7** frantic, mankind, rushing, violent **8** frenzied, vehement, wrathful **9** impetuous, turbulent **10** boisterous, tumultuous, uproarious

furl: **4** fold, roll, wrap **5** frese **6** enfold, fardel, furdel

furlana: **5** dance, music

furlong: **4** shot **5** stade **6** furrow **7** stadium **10** quarentene

furlough: **5** leave **6** permit **8** passport

furnace: **4** bosh, dome, kiln, oven **5** stove, tisar **6** calcar, cupola, heater **7** athanor, howells, rotator, smelter **8** bloomery, bruckner **9** scorifier **11** incinerator
part: **4** bosh, flue **5** grate

furnish: arm **4** feed, give, lend **5** array, endow, equip, frame, indue **6** afford, graith, insure, render, supply **7** apparel, appoint, garnish, provide **8** hand over, minister, palisade **10** accomplish, administer
crew: man
with battlements: **9** crenelate
with meals: **5** board, cater

furnished: **5** boden, garni **8** equipped, provided, supplied **9** garnished

furnishing: **5** stuff **7** fitment **8** fixtures, muniment, ornament **9** adornment, apparatus, furniture **10** enrichment, habiliment

furniture: **6** graith, outfit **7** fitment, tallboy **8** equipage **9** equipment **10** decoration, encoignure, furnishing **13** embellishment
designer: **5** Aalto, Eames **6** Brever, Morris, Wright **8** Saarinen **10** van der Rohe **11** Duncan Phyfe
style: **6** Empire, Shaker **8** Colonial, Louis XIV, Louis XVI, Sheraton **11** Biedermeier, Chippendale, Hepplewhite, Renaissance

furor: ado, cry, fad **4** fury, rage, to-do **5** craze, mania **6** frenzy **7** madness **10** dernier cri

furrow: fur, rut **4** grip, plow, rout **5** chase, drain, drill, field, rigol, score, stria **6**

groove, sulcus, trench **7** channel, crumple, windrow, wrinkle

furrowed: **7** porcate, sulcate **8** porcated **10** corrugated **12** rivose rugose

furry: **5** hairy

further: aid, and, new, yet **4** abet, also, fore, help, more **5** again, front, serve **6** afford, beyond, former **7** advance, earlier, forward, promote, remoter **8** moreover **9** advantage **10** accelerate, additional, in addition

furtherance: **6** assist **8** facility, progress **9** promotion **10** assistance **11** advancement

furthermore: and **4** also **7** besides **8** more-over

furthersome: **4** rash **7** helpful **11** venture-some **12** advantageous

furtive: sly **4** wary, wily **6** secret, sneaky **7** hangdog **8** mystical, sneaking, stealthy **10** creepmouse **11** clandestine **13** under-the-table

fury: ire **4** rage **5** anger, breth, furor, rigor, vixen, wrath **6** beldam, choler, frenzy **7** beldame, madness, oestrus **8** delirium, violence **9** furiosity, vehemence **10** fierceness, turbulence **11** indignation

fuse: **4** flux, frit, melt, weld **5** blend, smelt, unite **6** anneal, mingle, solder **7** liquefy **8** dissolve **10** amalgamate **11** incorporate

fusee: **5** flare, torch **6** signal

fusion: **4** flux **6** fusure, merger **8** alliance, blending **9** coalition **11** coalescence

fuss: ado, row, tew, vex **4** busk, fike, rout, spat, stir, to-do **5** bearm, touse, whaup, worry **6** bother, bustle, caddle, fantad, fantod, fettle, fidget, fissle, fistle, fizzle, fraise, fuffle, fustle, pother, potter, tumult **7** dispute, friggle, fussock, nitpick, quarrel, sputter, trouble **8** business **9** confusion **10** disconcert

fussy: **4** anal **5** picky **6** bustle, fidfad, spruce **7** fidgety, finical, fretful **8** overnice **9** irritable **10** fastidious, meticulous **14** overparticular

fustanella: **5** skirt **9** petticoat

fustian: **4** rant **5** tumid **7** bombast, pompous **8** claptrap, inflated **9** bombastic, worthless

fustigate: **4** beat, whip **6** strike

futile: **4** idle, vain **5** empty **6** otiose **7** useless **8** hopeless, trifling **9** frivolous, worthless **11** ineffectual

futility: **11** uselessness **13** frivolousness

future: **5** later **6** coming, onward **9** hereafter

fuzz: nap **4** down, lint, pile **5** fluff **8** puff-ball

fyke: **7** fishnet **8** fishtrap

fylfot: **5** cross **6** emblem **8** swastika

G

Gaal's father: 4 Ebed

gab: lie, yap 4 talk 5 boast, mouth, prate, scoff 6 gossip 7 chatter, deceive, prattle

Gabael's son: 5 Aduel

gabardine, gaberdine: 4 coat, gown 5 cloth, frock, smock 6 fabric, mantle 7 garment 8 pinafore

gabbard, gabbart: 4 scow 5 barge 6 vessel 7 lighter

gabble: rai (Sc.), yap 4 cank, chat, talk 6 babble, cackle, gossip, habble, jabber, yabble 7 chatter, clatter, twaddle

gabbro: 4 rock 6 norite

gabelle: tax 4 duty 6 excise, impost

gabi: 4 taro

gabirit: 4 mold 5 gauge, model

gable: 4 wall 6 dormer, pinion

Gabriel's instrument: 4 horn 7 trumpet

gad: 4 band, oath, roam, rope, rove 5 prowl, stray 6 ramble, wander 7 traipse 9 gallivant

Gad: *chieftain:* Ahi
    descendant: Zia
    father: 5 Jacob
    mother: 6 Zilpah
    son: Eri 5 Ezbon
    tribe of: 6 Erites

gadfly: 4 pest 6 bother, critic 7 annoyer 8 busybody

gadget: 4 tool 5 gibbe (Sc.), gismo 6 device, doodad, jigger, widget 9 doohickey 11 contrivance

gadus: 7 codfish

gadwall: 4 duck

gadzooks: 4 egad

Gaea: 5 Earth 6 Tellus
    consort: 6 Uranus
    offspring: 5 Titan 6 Pontus, Titans, Uranus
    parent: 5 Chaos

Gaelic (see also **Irish**): 4 Erse 6 Celtic 8 Highland
    clan: 4 Sept
    hero: 6 Ossian
    John: Ian
    land distribution: 7 rundale
    poem: 4 Duan
    spirit: 5 kelpy 6 kelpie 7 banshee
    warrior: 5 Dagda 6 Fenian

gaff: 4 hoax, hook, pick, spar, spur, talk 5 fraud, laugh, spear, trick 6 clamor, deceit, fleece, outcry 7 prating 8 raillery

gaffe: 4 goof 5 boner, error 7 blooper, blunder, faux pas, mistake

gag: 4 hoax, hush, joke, 5 choke, heave, retch, 6 be sick, muffle, muzzle 7 prevent, silence 8 obstruct, suppress, throttle 9 wisecrack 13 interpolation

gage (see also **gauge**): bet 4 pawn, risk 5 stake, wager 6 pledge 8 appraise, defiance, security 9 challenge

gaiety: fun, joy 4 glee 5 mirth 7 jollity 8 hilarity 9 festivity, good humor, merriment

gain: buy, get, net, win 4 boot, earn, good, pelf, reap 5 clear, lucre, reach 6 attain, effect, income, obtain, profit, secure 7 achieve, acquire, advance, benefit, conquer, prevail, procure, realize 8 increase 9 accretion, advantage, increment 12 appreciation
    ill-gotten: 4 pelf 5 graft, lucre 6 payola

gainsay: 4 deny 6 forbid, impugn, negate, oppose, refute, resist 7 dispute 10 contradict, controvert

Gainsborough painting: 7 Blue Boy

gait: run 4 lope, pace, rack, step, trip, trot, walk 5 amble, strut, tread 6 canter, gallop 7 journey, shamble

gaiter: 4 boot, spat 6 puttee 7 cutikin (Sc.), legging 8 overshoe

gala: gay 4 fete 5 merry, party 6 festal, fiesta 8 festival 9 glamorous 11 celebration

galago: 5 lemur 6 monkey 7 primate 8 bush baby

Galahad: 4 pure 6 knight 10 Round Table
    father: 8 Lancelot
    mother: 6 Elaine
    quest: 9 Holy Grail

Galapagos Islands resident: 6 iguana 8 tortoise

Galatea: *lover:* 4 Acis
    suitor: 10 Polyphemus

galaxy: 6 nebula

gale: 4 blow, gust, wind 5 blast, storm 7 cyclone, tempest, tornado, twister, typhoon 8 outburst 9 hurricane, windstorm 11 northeaster, northwester, southeaster, southwester

galea: cap 6 helmet

Galen: 9 physician

galilee: 5 porch 7 portico

Galilee: *ruler:* 5 Herod

town: 4 Cana, Nain 8 Nazareth, Tiberias 9 Capernaum

Galileo: *birthplace:* 4 Pisa

galimatias: 6 jargon 8 nonsense 9 gibberish

galipot, gallipot: sap 5 rosin 6 barras 10 turpentine

gall: vex 4 bile, fell, flaw, fret 5 annoy, chafe, cheek, spite 6 abrade, harass, injure, poison, rancor 7 blemish 8 acerbity, cecidium, irritate, parasite, temerity 9 excoriate, impudence 10 bitterness, effrontery, exasperate

Gallagher's partner: 5 Shean

gallant: gay 4 beau, prow 5 blade, brave, bully, lover, noble, showy, swain 6 escort, polite, suitor 7 amatory, conduct, stately 8 cavalier, handsome, polished, splendid 9 attentive, chevalier, courteous 10 chivalrous, courageous 11 fashionable 12 high-spirited

gallantry: 7 bravery, courage, heroism 8 courtesy 9 attention 11 intrepidity

galled: mad, raw 4 sore 6 peeved

galleon: 4 ship 6 carack, vessel 7 carrack
cargo: oro 4 gold

gallery: 5 porch, salon 6 arcade, loggia, piazza 7 balcony, portico, terrace, veranda 8 audience, catacomb, corridor 9 promenade

galley: 4 boat, ship, tray 5 cuddy, proof 6 bireme, galiot, hearth 7 birling, birlinn, galliot, kitchen, trireme, unireme 8 cookroom, galleass 10 triaconter

galliard: 5 dance

Gallic: 4 Gaul 6 French

gallimaufry: 4 hash 6 jumble, medley, ragout 7 melange, mixture 8 pastiche 9 potpourri 10 hodgepodge

gallinae: 4 hens 6 grouse, quails 7 rasores, turkeys 8 chickens, peafowls 9 curassows, partridge, pheasants

gallinule: hen 4 coot, fowl, rail 7 moor hen 8 water hen

gallivant: gad 4 flit, roam, rove 6 travel, wander 7 traipse

galloon: 4 lace 5 braid 6 ribbon 8 trimming

gallop: run 4 gait, pelt 5 chase, speed 6 hasten, sprint 7 mad dash 8 fast clip

galloping dominoes: 4 dice

gallows: 5 bough 6 gibbet 7 potence 8 scaffold

galluses: 10 suspenders

galoot: guy 6 fellow, person 9 screwball, simpleton

galore: 7 profuse 8 abundant 9 plentiful

galosh: 4 boot 6 arctic, rubber 8 overshoe

galvanize: 4 coat, stir 6 excite 7 startle 9 electrify, stimulate 12 move to action

Galway Bay islands: 4 Aran

galyak: fur 7 kidskin 8 lambskin

gam, gamb, gambe: leg 4 chat 5 visit

gambado: 4 boot 5 antic, caper, prank 6 spring 7 legging

Gambia, The: *capital:* 6 Banjul
city: 5 Basse 6 Fatoto 7 Kuntaur 10 Georgetown
currency: 5 butut 6 dalasi
people: 4 Fula 5 Wolof 8 Mandinga
village in "Roots": 7 Juffura

gambit: 4 move, ploy, ruse 5 trick 7 gimmick, opening 8 maneuver 9 strategem

gamble: bet 4 dice, gaff, game, risk, spec 5 stake, wager 6 chance, hazard, plunge 9 speculate 11 uncertainty

gambler: 5 dicer 6 carrow (Ir.), player 7 plunger, sharper 8 blackleg, gamester 10 speculator
accomplice: 5 shill

gambling (see also **game:** *gambling*): *pert. to:* 8 aleatory
place: 4 Reno 6 casino, Nevada 8 Foxwoods, Las Vegas 10 Monte Carlo 12 Atlantic City
stake: pot 4 pool

gambol: hop 4 play 5 caper, frisk, prank 6 cavort, frolic

game (see also **sport**): fun, jeu (F.) 4 food, lame, lark, plan, play, prey 5 brave, dodge, prank, sport, trick 6 course, frolic, gamble, gritty, plucky, quarry, racket, spunky 7 contest, foolery, pastime, project 8 enduring, resolute 9 amusement, diversion 10 courageous
ball: cat, tut 4 golf, polo, pool 5 bocci, fives, rugby 6 hockey, pelota, soccer, squash, tennis, tipcat 7 bowling, cricket, croquet, jai alai 8 baseball, football, handball, ping-pong, softball 9 billiards 10 basketball, volleyball 11 lawn bowling
bird: 4 duck 5 quail 6 turkey 7 bustard 8 pheasant 9 partridge
board: go 4 keno 5 bingo, chess, Halma, lotto, Ouija, salta, weigi (Ch.) 7 Pachisi, squails 8 checkers, cribbage, dominoes, Mah-jongg, Monopoly, Parchesi, Parchisi, Scrabble 9 crokinole, Parcheesi 10 backgammon
card: gin, hoc, loo, nap, pam, war 4 bank, brag, faro, hock, jass, ruff, skat, slam, snap, solo, spin, vint 5 beast, chico, cinch, comet, crimp, decoy, gilet, gleek, monte, omber, ombre, pedro, pique, pitch, poker, rummy, stuss, trump, two-up, waist, whist 6 basset, birkie, boston, bridge, casino, commit, ecarte, flinch, hearts, loadum, masset, piquet, rounce, sledge, smudge 7 bezique, canasta, cayenne, Chicago, cooncan, hundred, old maid, primero, reversi, seven-up 8 baccarat (F.), Canfield, commerce, conquian, contract, cribbage, handicap, Michi-

gan, napoleon, patience, penneeck, pinochle **9** cinq-cents, montebank, new market, solitaire, tredrille **11** speculation **14** spite and malice

carnival: **5** darts **6** hoopla

child's: tag **7** marbles **8** leapfrog **9** hopscotch **11** hide and seek **13** tiddledy winks

confidence: **4** scam **5** bunco, bunko, sting **6** racket

court: **5** roque **6** pelota, squash, tennis **7** jai alai **8** handball **9** badminton **10** basketball, volleyball

dice: **4** ludo **5** craps **7** pachisi **8** dominoes, trey-trip

gambling: **4** beno, faro, keno, pico **5** beano, bingo, boule, craps, keeno, lotto, monte, pique, pitch, poker, rondo, stuss **6** brelan (F.), fan-tan (Ch.), piquet, policy **7** baccara, barbudi, primero, rondeau (F.) **8** baccarat, crackloo, roulette **9** black-jack, crackaloo, montebank, twenty-one, vingt-et-un (F.) **10** panguingui (Phil. Is.)

goal: run **4** home **5** first, score, spare, tally **6** basket, strike **9** touchdown

kind of: **4** mora (It.) **5** board, video **6** merels, morris, quoits **7** diabolo, loggats, loggets, marbles **8** computer **9** philopena **10** electronic, jackstraws, spillikins

official: **5** judge, timer **6** umpire **7** referee, starter **8** linesman **10** timekeeper

outdoor: **4** polo **6** tennis **7** cricket, croquet **9** badminton **10** horseshoes

parlor: **5** jacks **7** matador **8** charades

pin: **7** bowling, kegling, tenpins **8** ninepins, skittles

plan: **8** strategy

racket: **5** bandy **6** squash, tennis **8** lacrosse **9** badminton

rule authority: **5** Hoyle

stewed in wine: **5** salmi **6** ragout

war: **10** kriegspiel

word: **5** ghost, rebus **6** crambo **8** acrostic, Scrabble **9** crossword **15** anagram charades

gamekeeper: **8** warrener

gamester: **5** dicer **6** player **7** gambler

gamete: egg **4** ovum **5** sperm **6** zygote **8** oosphere

gamin: imp, tad **6** urchin

domain: **6** street

gaming cube: die **4** dice (pl.)

gammon: leg **4** bosh, dupe, foot, gull **5** bacon, cozen, feign, thigh **6** delude, humbug **7** beguile, deceive, mislead, pretend

gamp: **8** umbrella

gamut: **4** A to Z **5** orbit, range, reach, scale **6** extent, series **7** compass **10** soup to nuts

gamy: **5** spicy **6** smelly **7** lustful **8** spirited **10** malodorous **12** disreputable

ganch: **4** kill **6** impale **7** execute

gander: **4** look **5** goose **6** glance **9** simpleton

Gandhi: *name:* Aba, Abu **4** Abba, Abou, Bapu **5** Rajiv **6** Indira **7** Mahatma **8** Mohandas

publication: **7** Harijan

ganef: **5** crook, gonif, thief **6** goniff, rascal **8** swindler

gang: mob, set **4** band, crew, pack, ring, team **5** crowd, group, horde, shift **6** clique, outfit, travel **7** company

member of: **4** b'hoy **5** crook, rowdy, tough

Ganges River city: **7** Benares **8** Calcutta, Varanasi **9** Allahabad

gangling: **4** bony **5** lanky **6** skinny **7** awkward **9** spindling

ganglion: **5** tumor

gangplank: **6** bridge **8** platform

gangrene: rot **7** mortify **8** necrosis **9** sphacelus

gangster: **4** goon, hood, thug, yegg **5** crook, rough, thief **6** bandit, gunman **7** mobster, ruffian **8** criminal, hireling

female companion: **4** moll

gangway: **7** couloir, walkway **8** corridor **9** gangplank **10** passageway

gannet: **4** bird, fowl **5** goose, solan

family: **4** sula

ganoid fish: gar **6** bowfin **8** sturgeon

gaol: **4** brig, jail, nick **6** prison

gaoler: **5** guard **6** jailer, matron, warden

gap: col **4** flaw, pass, rent **5** break, breck, chasm, chawn, cleft, clove, meuse, notch, space **6** breach, hiatus, lacuna, ravine **7** fissure, lacunae (pl.), opening **8** aperture, interval, quebrada **10** interstice **12** interruption **13** discontinuity

gape: ope **4** gasp, gawk, gaze, pant, rent, yawn **5** chawn, stare **6** rictus **7** dehisce **8** oscitate **10** rubberneck

gaping: **4** open **7** cracked, yawning **9** cavernous, separated

of plant capsule: **10** dehiscence

garage: **6** hangar, siding **7** carport **8** building

garb: **5** array, dress, habit, style **6** attire, bundle, clothe, custom, method **7** apparel, clothes, costume, fashion, raiment, vesture **8** carriage, clothing, vestment **10** appearance, habiliment

garbage: **5** offal, trash, waste **6** debris, litter, refuse, scraps **7** rubbish

garble: **4** sift **5** twist **6** jumble, mangle, refine, refuse, select **7** distort, pervert **8** disguise, mutilate

garcon (F.): boy, lad **6** waiter

garden: **4** Eden, hall, park, yard **5** arbor, patch, tract **6** jardin (F., Sp.) **8** outfield **9** arboretum, cultivate, enclosure **11** commonplace

cover: **5** mulch **7** compost **8** peat moss

implement: hoe **4** fork, hose, rake **5** edger, mower, spade **6** dibble, duster, scythe, shovel, sickle, trowel, weeder **7** loppers, sprayer **9** secateurs **13** pruning shears *kind of:* **4** herb, rock **5** oasis, truck, water **6** cactus, flower, formal, indoor **7** kitchen, organic **8** chinampa **9** botanical, container, terrarium, vegetable **10** wild flower, zoological

protector: **7** Priapus

Garden State: 9 New Jersey

gardener: 7 yardman **9** topiarist **14** horticulturist

garfish: 8 hornbeak, hornfish

Gargantua's son: 10 Pantagruel

gargantuan: 4 huge, vast **5** giant **7** titanic **8** enormous, gigantic **9** monstrous

gargle: 9 mouthwash **11** collutorium

garish: 4 loud **5** cheap, gaudy, showy **6** bright, tawdry **8** dazzling **9** offensive

garland: bay, lei **4** band **5** crown, glory, **6** anadem, corona, crants, diadem, laurel, rosary, wreath **7** chaplet, coronal, festoon **9** anthology

garlic: 4 moly, ramp **5** chive, clove

garment (see also **undergarment**): **4** brat, cape, coat, gear, gown, jupe, rail, robe, sari, vest **5** cloak, dress, habit, pulea **6** attire, kimono **7** apparel, leotard, raiment **8** vestment **10** investment

ancient: **4** toga **5** palla, stola **6** chiton **7** chlamys **8** himation

ecclesiastical: See **vestment**

infant's: **6** diaper, woolly **7** bunting, sleeper **9** Dr. Dentons

Malay: **6** cabaya, kabaya, sarong

medieval: **5** simar **6** kirtle, rochet, tabard **8** chausses

mourning: **5** weeds **9** sackcloth

protective: bib **4** brat **5** apron, armor, chaps, smock **7** cuculla **8** overalls, pinafore **9** coveralls

rain: **6** poncho **7** oilskin, slicker

sleeveless: aba **4** cape, vest **5** tunic **6** mantle **7** sweater **8** slip-over

South Seas: **5** pareu **6** sarong **8** lavalava

upper: **4** coat, vest **5** jupon, shirt, tunic, waist **6** blouse, jersey, peplos, peplus **7** sweater **8** cardigan, guernsey, pullover, slip-over

garner: 4 reap **5** store **6** gather **7** collect, granary **10** accumulate

garnet: 5 jewel, stone **8** essonite

black: **8** melanite

deep-red: **6** pyrope **9** almandine, almandite

green: **7** olivine

garnish: 4 trim **5** adorn, dress, equip **6** set off **7** furnish, parsley **8** decorate, ornament **9** embellish

garret: 4 loft **5** attic, solar **6** soller, turret **7** mansard **8** cockloft **10** upper floor, watchtower

garrote, garrotte: 4 kill **7** execute **8** strangle, throttle

garrulous: 5 gabby, talky, wordy **6** prolix **7** gossipy, verbose, voluble **8** fanfaron **9** talkative **10** longwinded, loquacious

garter: 4 belt **5** snake **7** elastic **9** supporter

garth: dam **4** weir

garvey: 4 boat, scow

gas: 4 fuel, fume, reek, talk **5** steam, vapor **6** gossip, petrol **7** bombast **10** anesthetic, asphyxiate, illuminant

air: **4** neon **5** argon, ozone, xenon **6** oxygen **7** ammonia, krypton, sulfate **8** nitrogen **13** carbon dioxide

balloon: **6** helium

blue: **5** ozone

charcoal: **5** oxane

charge with: **6** aerate

colorless: **5** keten, ozone **6** arsine, ethane **7** ammonia

flammable: **6** butane, ethane **7** methane, propane **8** hydrogen

inert: **5** argon, radon, xenon **6** helium **8** nitrogen

marsh: **7** methane

mustard: **7** yperite

nitrogen and carbon: **8** cyanogen

oxygen: **5** ozone

poisonous: **6** arsine **7** mustard, stibine

gasbag: 7 balloon, boaster, windbag

gascon: 7 boaster **8** braggart **10** swaggering **12** swashbuckler

gasconade: 7 bluster, bravado **8** boasting

gaseous: 4 thin **5** fluid, light **7** tenuous **8** aeriform, gasiform, volatile **13** unsubstantial

gash: cut **4** bite, chop, slit **5** cleft, gorge, slash, wound **6** pierce **8** incision

gasket: 4 ring, seal

gasoline: gas **6** petrol

gasp: 4 gulp, huff, pant **5** croak **6** wheeze **9** suck in air **13** inhale sharply

gassy: 5 windy **8** inflated **9** flatulent

gastronome: 7 epicure, gourmet **8** gourmand **11** connoisseur

gastropod: 4 slug **5** harpa, oliva, snail **6** nerita, nerite, volute **7** mollusk **8** pteropod

ear-shaped: **7** abalone

marine: **5** cowry, murex **6** cowrie, limpet, tethys **7** aplysia

gat: gun **6** pistol **7** channel, passage **8** revolver

gata: 5 shark

gate: bar, way **4** door, exit, hole, pass, take **5** hatch, valve **6** defile, escape, method, portal, spigot, wicket **7** barrier, opening, postern **8** entrance, receipts **9** box office, threshold, turnstile

flood: **6** sluice

gate money: fee **5** price **9** admission

Gates of Hercules: 9 Gibraltar

gatehouse: bar **5** lodge

gatekeeper: 6 porter, warden **8** Cerberus, guardian, watchman **9** concierge

gateway: 4 arch **5** pylon, toran, torii (Jap.) **6** portal, torana **8** entrance

gather: 4 bale, brew, cull, furl, herd, mass, meet, pick, rake, reap 5 amass, bunch, flock, glean, group, infer, pleat, pluck, raise, shirr 6 bundle, deduce, derive, garner, muster, scrape, summon 7 collect, compile, convene, convoke, harvest, recruit 8 assemble, colonize, compress, conclude, contract, increase 10 accumulate, congregate 11 agglomerate, concentrate 12 conglomerate

gatherer: 5 miser 7 gleaner 9 collector

gathering: bee, tea 4 bevy, fest, stag 5 crowd, party, troop 6 galaxy, plisse, shivoo, smoker 7 company, klatsch, meeting, turnout 8 assembly, function 9 concourse 10 assemblage, collection, congestion, convention 11 convocation 12 accumulation, congregation

gauche: 5 crude, inept 6 clumsy 7 awkward, uncouth 8 bumbling, plebeian, tactless 9 maladroit 10 left-handed

gaucho: 6 cowboy 8 herdsman 9 Argentine
  lariat: 5 riata
  weapon: 4 bola 7 machete

gaud: 4 bead 6 bauble, gewgaw 7 trinket 8 artifice, ornament

gaudy: 4 loud 5 cheap, feast, showy 6 flashy, garish, tawdry, tinsel 7 brankie (Sc.), glaring 8 festival 9 tasteless 11 pretentious 12 meretricious, ostentatious

gaufre: 5 wafer 6 waffle

gauge, gage: 4 size 5 judge, meter, scale 7 measure 8 estimate, standard 9 criterion, indicator, yardstick
  pressure: 9 manometer
  rain: 8 udometer
  wind: 10 anemometer

Gauguin: *autobiography:* 6 Noa Noa
  island: 6 Tahiti

Gaul: 6 France, Gallia (L.)
  chariot: 5 esses 6 esseda, essede
  god of thunder and rain: 7 Taranis
  god of vegetation: 4 Esus
  magistrate: 9 vergobret
  people: 4 Remi 6 Belgae, Celtae 8 Aquitani
  priest: 5 druid
  river goddess: 8 Belisama
  seer: 5 vates

gaulding: 4 bird 5 egret, heron

gaunt: 4 bony, grim, lank, lean, slim, thin 5 spare 6 barren, hollow, meager, wasted 7 haggard, scraggy, scrawny, slender 8 desolate, rawboned 9 emaciated 10 attenuated, cadaverous, forbidding

gauntlet: 4 dare, test 5 glove 6 ordeal 9 challenge, cross fire
  to run: 6 ordeal, suffer
  to take up: 4 defy
  to throw down: 9 challenge

Gautama: 6 Buddha 10 Siddhartha
  wife: 6 Ahalya

gauze: 4 film, leno 5 crepe, lisse, tulle 6 fabric, tissue 7 bandage, chiffon 11 cheesecloth

gavel: 4 maul 6 hammer, mallet 9 grain pile

gavial: 9 crocodile

Gawain: *brother:* 6 Gareth 7 Gaheris
  father: Lot
  slayer: 8 Lancelot
  son: 5 Lovel 8 Florence, Gyngalyn
  uncle: 6 Arthur

gawk: 4 gape, gaze, lout 5 stare 7 bumpkin 9 simpleton 10 rubberneck

gawky: 6 clumsy 7 awkward 8 bumbling, ungainly 9 lumbering

gay: 4 airy, boon, daft, glad, gleg 5 bawdy, bonny, brisk, happy, jolly, loose, merry, riant, showy 6 blithe, bonnie, bright, flashy, frisky, garish, jocund, jovial, joyful, lively, wanton 7 festive, gleeful, jocular 8 cavalier, cheerful, colorful, mirthful, sportive 9 brilliant, convivial, sprightly, vivacious 10 brilliante, frolicsome, homosexual, licentious 12 lighthearted

gazabo: boy, guy, man 6 fellow, person

gaze: eye 4 gape, gawk, leer, look, moon, ogle, peer, pore, scan, view 5 glare, gloat, sight, stare 6 behold, glower, regard

gazebo: 6 pagoda 8 pavilion 9 belvedere 11 summerhouse

gazelle: ahu, goa 4 admi, cora, dama, kudu, mohr, oryx 5 ariel, mhorr 6 dorcas, Grant's, Loder's 7 buffalo, chikara, corinne 8 antelope, Thomson's 9 springbok
  kin: 6 impala

gazelle hound: 6 saluki

gazette: 7 courant, journal 9 newspaper

gazetteer: 5 atlas, guide 10 dictionary

gazump: 5 cheat 7 swindle

Ge: See **Gaea**

gean: 6 cherry

gear: cam, cog, rig 4 duds, togs 5 dress, equip, goods, stuff, tools 6 doings, graith (Sc.), outfit, pinion, tackle, things 7 apparel, harness, rigging 8 clothing, cogwheel, garments, materiel, property 9 apparatus, equipment, mechanism, trappings, vestments 10 appliances, belongings, implements 12 appurtenance 13 accoutrements, paraphernalia

Geb: *daughter:* 4 Isis 8 Nephthys
  father: Shu
  son: Set 6 Osiris
  wife: Nut

gecko: 6 lizard 7 tarente

gee: 4 jibe 5 agree 7 command 9 turn right

Gehenna: pit 4 hell 5 hades 7 inferno 10 underworld

geige: 6 fiddle, violin

gel: set 6 harden 7 congeal, thicken 8 solidify 9 coagulate

gelatin, gelatine: 5 jelly 6 medium, pectin 7 protein, sericin 8 agaragar

geld: fix 4 spay 5 alter, prune 6 neuter 8 castrate, mutilate 9 expurgate 10 emasculate

gelid: icy 4 cold, iced 6 frozen

gelt: 4 gold 5 money

gem: bud 4 jade, keas, naif, onyx, opal, ruby, sard 5 agate, amber, beryl, cameo, jewel, paste, pearl, stone, topaz 6 amulet, bedeck, garnet, muffin, scarab, spinel 7 diamond, emerald, mineral, paragon 8 intaglio, sapphire, tigereye 9 carnelian, germinate 10 aquamarine 11 masterpiece

bishop's: 8 amethyst

black: jet 4 onyx 8 obsidian

blue: 6 zircon 8 sapphire 9 turquoise 10 aquamarine 11 lapis lazuli

cut: 7 navette 8 baguette, cabochon, marquise 9 brilliant

face: 5 facet

green: 4 jade 7 emerald, peridot 10 chrysolite

imperfect: 5 loupe

iridescent: 4 opal 5 pearl 7 cat's-eye 8 tigereye 9 moonstone

measure of weight: 5 carat

of fidelity: 5 topaz

of immortality: 7 emerald

of law: 4 ruby

of love: 8 amethyst

of peace: 7 diamond

of purity: 5 pearl

of truth: 8 sapphire

paste: 6 strass

purple: 8 amethyst

rectangular: 6 baguet 8 baguette

red: 4 ruby, sard 5 avena 6 garnet, pyrope 9 carnelian

relief-carved: 5 cameo

setting for: 4 ouch, pave 6 chaton

support: 7 setting

surface: 5 bezel, bezil, facet

Gem State: 5 Idaho

gemel: 4 twin 6 hinged, paired

geminate: 6 binate, double 7 coupled

Gemini: 5 twins 6 Castor, Pollux, zodiac 13 constellation

gemmule: bud 5 ovule

gemsbok: 4 oryx 8 antelope

gemutlich: 4 cozy 6 genial, kindly 8 cheerful 9 agreeable 11 comfortable, good-natured

gendarme: 7 soldier 9 policeman 10 cavalryman

gender: sex 4 male 5 class, genus 6 female, neuter

genealogy: 7 lineage 8 ancestry, heredity, pedigree 10 family tree 12 descent chart, family record

general: 5 broad, gross 6 common, leader 7 average, officer 8 catholic 9 commander, customary, prevalent, universal 10 prevailing, widespread

Civil War: Lee 4 Hood 5 Grant, Meade 6 Custer, Hooker, Stuart 7 Jackson, Pickett, Sherman 8 Burnside, Sheridan 9 McClellan

generalize: 5 widen 6 extend, spread 7 broaden

generate: 4 make 5 beget, breed, steam 6 create 7 develop, produce 8 engender 9 originate, procreate, propagate

generation: age, era 4 kind, race 5 breed, stock 6 family 7 descent, progeny 8 creation 9 genealogy, offspring, posterity 11 descendants, procreation

generative: 8 prolific 10 productive

generator: 6 dynamo, engine 7 creator 8 auto part 10 alternator

generic: 6 common 9 universal 12 encompassing 13 comprehensive

generosity: 7 charity, largess 8 largesse

generous: big 4 free, good, kind, rich 5 ample, frank, noble 6 honest 7 fertile, liberal 8 abundant, gracious, handsome, highborn, spirited 9 bountiful, excellent, honorable, plenteous, unselfish, unstinted 10 altruistic, benevolent, big-hearted, charitable, courageous, free-handed, munificent, openhanded 11 magnanimous, stimulating, warmhearted

genesis: 4 dawn 5 birth, start 6 origin 9 beginning 11 origination

genet: 5 berbe, horse 8 civet fur

genial: 4 bein, bien, warm 5 douce 6 benign, forthy, inborn, jovial, kindly, native 7 cordial, festive 8 cheerful, friendly, pleasant 9 benignant, expansive, gemutlich 10 enlivening

genie: 5 demon, jinni 6 spirit

genitor: 6 parent 7 creator 10 procreator

geniture: 5 birth 8 nativity 9 offspring 10 generation

genius: 4 gift 5 flair, knack 6 brains, talent, wizard 7 ability, mastery, prodigy 8 aptitude 9 intellect 10 brilliance, creativity 12 intelligence

genouillere: 7 kneelet 9 kneepiece

genre: 4 kind, sort, type 5 class, style 7 species 8 category 11 description 14 classification

gens: 4 clan 5 tribe 6 family

genteel: 4 nice 6 polite 7 refined, stylish 8 graceful, lady-like, well-bred 10 cultivated 11 fashionable

gentian: 6 flower 7 felwort 9 baldmoney

Gentile: 5 pagan 7 heathen 9 Christian, non-Jewish

gentility: 8 breeding 10 refinement

gentle: moy 4 calm, deft, dewy, easy, fair, kind, meek, mild, soft, tame 5 bland, light, milky, quiet, sweet, tamed 6 benign, docile, facile, placid, polite, tender 7 amabile, bonaire, clement, gradual, lenient 8 amenable, dovelike, lenitive, maidenly, mansuete, moderate, peaceful, soothing, tranquil, well-born **9** courteous, excellent, honorable, tractable **10** chivalrous **11** considerate **13** compassionate

gentleman: don, rye, sir **5** sahib, senor **6** bayard, mister, squire, esquire **7** younker **8** cavalier **9** caballero

Gentlemen Prefer Blondes author: 4 Loos

gentlewoman: 4 lady

gentry: 5 elite **7** quality, society **10** gentlefolk, upper class

gentry: 5 noble **7** genteel **8** graceful **9** courteous

genu: 4 knee **5** joint

genuflect: 5 kneel **6** kowtow **11** bend the knee

genuine: 4 pure, real, true, vrai (F.) **5** frank, plain, pucka, pukka **6** actual, dinkum, honest **7** germane, gradely, sincere **8** bonafide **9** authentic, heartfelt, intrinsic, simon-pure, true-penny, unalloyed, unfeigned, veridical, veritable **10** legitimate **13** unadulterated **15** unsophisticated

genus: 4 kind, sort **5** class, order **6** gender **8** category **14** classification

   pert. to: **7** generic

geode: 5 druse **6** cavity, nodule

geology: 12 earth science

   division: age, era **4** lias, lyas **5** epoch, trias

   epoch: **6** Eocene **7** Miocene **8** Pliocene **9** Oligocene, Paleocene **11** Pleistocene

   era: **8** Cenozoic, Mesozoic **9** Paleozoic **11** Precambrian

   period: **7** Permian **8** Cambrian, Devonian, Jurassic, Silurian, Tertiary, Triassic **10** Archeozoic, Cretaceous, Ordovician, Quaternary **11** Proterozoic **12** Mississipian **13** Pennsylvanian

   remains: **7** fossils

   science: **9** hydrology **12** paleontology, oceanography **13** palaeontology, sedimentology

geometric: 8 analytic **9** algebraic **10** arithmetic

geometry: *angle:* **9** incidence

   curve: **6** spiral **7** ellipse, evolute **8** parabola, sinusoid

   father: **6** Euclid

   figure: **4** cone, lune **5** prism, rhomb **6** circle, gnomon, oblong, sphere, square **7** ellipse, hexagon, octagon, polygon, rhombus **8** heptagon, pentagon, rhomboid, spheroid, triangle **9** rectangle

   proposition: **7** theorem

   solid: **4** cube **5** prism **6** sphere **7** pyramid

   surface: **5** nappe, torus

geoponic: 5 rural **12** agricultural

Georgia (Eurasian): *capital:* **7** T'bilisi

   currency: **5** ruble

   mountain: **8** Caucasus

Georgia (U.S.): *capital:* **7** Atlanta

   city: **5** Macon **6** Albany, Athens, Dalton **7** Augusta **8** Columbus, Savannah

   early explorer: **6** de Soto

   island: Sea **6** Amelia, Jekyll, Sapelo **7** Ossabaw, St. Simon **10** Cumberland **11** St. Catherine

   mountain range: **9** Blue Ridge **11** Appalachian

   Pres. Carter's birthplace: **6** Plains

   river: **5** Flint **6** Oconee **8** Altamaha, Ocmulgee, Savannah **12** Apalachicola **13** Chattahoochee

   state bird: **8** thrasher

   state flower: **12** Cherokee rose

   state tree: **7** live oak

   swamp: **10** Okefenokee

   U.S. president: **6** Carter

Geraint's wife: 4 Enid

germ: bud, bug **4** seed **5** spore, virus **6** embryo, sprout **7** microbe **8** rudiment **9** bacterium, beginning

germ cell: egg **4** ovum **5** sperm

German: 4 Goth **5** Boche, Saxon **6** Teuton

   ancient tribesman: **4** Jute **6** Teuton **9** Ostrogoth

   angry: **4** bose

   animal: **4** tier

   article: das, der, die, ein **4** eine

   beautiful: **5** schon

   blue: **4** blau

   bread: **4** brot

   bright: **4** hell

   but: **4** aber

   cake: **5** torte **9** lebkuchen **11** pfeffernuss

   canal: **4** Kiel

   castle: **7** schloss

   cheese: **4** kase

   chicken: **4** huhn

   child: **4** kind **6** kinder(pl.)

   Christmas: **11** Weihnachten

   clever: **4** klug

   clock: uhr

   code: **5** Salic

   cold: **4** kalt

   daughter: **7** tochter

   day: tag

   dead: tot

   dear: **4** lieb **8** liebchen

   deep: **4** tief

   dog: **4** hund

   door: tur

   early: **4** fruh

earth: **4** erde
eight: **4** acht
evening: **5** abend
eye: **4** auge
field: **4** feld
five: **4** funf
forest: **4** wald
forest-keeper: **9** waldgrave
four: **4** vier
gnome: **6** kobold
good: gut
hair: **4** haar
hall: **4** saal **5** diele, halle
happy: **4** froh
head: **4** kopf
heart: **4** herz
highway: **8** autobahn
house: **4** haus
home: **4** heim
knight: **6** ritter
lancer: **4** ulan
language: **7** Deutsch
leaf: **5** blatt
letter: **5** brief
measles: **6** masern
Miss: **8** fraulein
mister: **4** herr
moon: **4** mond
Mrs.: **4** frau
never: nie
nine: **4** neun
no: **4** nein
nobleman: **4** graf **5** adlig **6** junker, ritter **7** younker
one: **4** eins
overture: **8** vorspiel
pronunciation mark: **6** umlaut
school: **10** realschule, volkschule **14** oberrealschule
seven: **6** sieben
shoe: **5** schuh
singing festival: **10** sangerfest **11** saengerfest
six: **5** sechs
society: **4** bund **6** verein **10** turnverein **12** gesellschaft
son: **4** sohn
song: **4** lied
star: **5** stern
stone: **5** stein
sun: **5** sonne
teacher: **6** lehrer
ten: **4** zehn
three: **4** drei
tooth: **4** zahn
tower: **4** turm
two: **4** zwei
village: **4** dorf
white: **5** weiss
wine: **4** hock, wein **5** Rhine **7** Moselle
woman: **4** frau, frow

world: **4** welt
year: **4** jahr
yes: ja **6** jawohl
young: **4** jung
germane: **4** akin, true **5** ad rem **6** allied **7** apropos, genuine, related **8** relevant **9** pertinent **11** appropriate

Germany: *architect:* **7** Gropius **14** Mies van der Rohe
artist: **5** Durer, Ernst, Grosz **7** Holbein **9** Grunewald
bacteriologist: **4** Koch
canal: **4** Kiel
capital: **4** Bonn **6** Berlin
city: **4** Koln **5** Essen, Halle **6** Munich **7** Cologne, Leipzig, Munchen **8** Dortmund, Mannheim **9** Frankfurt, Magdeburg, Nuremberg, Stuttgart, Wiesbaden **10** Dusseldorf
cheese: **4** kase **7** Munster **8** Tilsiter **9** Limburger
composer: **4** Bach **5** Weber, Weill **6** Brahms, Handel, Wagner **7** Strauss **8** Schumann **9** Beethoven, Hindemith, Meyerbeer **11** Humperdinck, Mendelssohn
currency: **4** mark **6** kronen, thaler **7** pfennig **8** groschen **12** deutsche mark
dramatist: **4** Mann **5** Grass **6** Brecht, Goethe **7** Buchner **8** Schiller **10** Durrenmatt
dynasty: **5** Saxon **8** Habsburg **10** Hohenstauf **12** Hohenzollern
Kaiser: **7** Wilhelm
league: **9** Hanseatic
measure: aam, imi **4** last, sack, stab **5** carat, eimer, kanne, kette, maass **6** strich **7** klafter **8** scheffel, schoppen, stubchen **9** masskanne
mountain: **4** Harz
national anthem: **15** Deutschland-Lied (Song of Germany)
Nazi anthem: **15** Horst Wessel song
Nazi government: **10** Third Reich
Nazi leader: **6** Hitler (Adolf) **9** der Fuhrer
philosopher: **4** Kant **5** Hegel **9** Nietzsche **12** Schopenhauer
poet: **5** Heine, Rilke **6** Goethe **8** Schiller
river: Ems, Inn **4** Elbe, Main, Oder, Ruhr **5** Donau, Fulda, Mosel, Rhine, Saale, Spree, Werra, Weser **6** Danube, Neckar, Neisse **7** Moselle
weight: lot

germicide: 5 iodin 6 iodine 10 antiseptic 11 bactericide 12 disinfectant

germinate: bud, gem 6 evolve, sprout 7 develop 10 effloresce

gerontological: 6 senile

geryon: 7 monster

gesso: 5 paste 6 gypsum 7 plaster

gest, geste: 4 deed, feat, tale 7 exploit, romance 9 adventure

gestation: 7 bearing 8 breeding, carrying 9 pregnancy

gesture: act, nod 4 sign, wave 6 beckon, motion, salute 8 courtesy 9 formality 10 empty offer 11 gesticulate

get: pen, win 4 earn, find, gain, take, trap 5 annoy, beget, catch, child, fetch, learn, reach, seize 6 appear, attain, baffle, become, corner, derive, induce, obtain, puzzle, secure, suffer 7 achieve, acquire, capture, conquer, possess, prepare, procure, realize, receive, recover 8 contract, irritate, overcome, persuade, retrieve, vanquish 9 ascertain, determine 10 comprehend, conciliate, understand
  along: 4 fare 5 agree, hurry 7 advance, prosper, succeed 8 progress
  away: lam 4 flee, scat, shoo 6 depart, escape
  back: 6 recoup, redeem, regain 7 recover
  on: 5 board 6 embark 7 prosper, succeed
  out: 4 exit 5 leave, scram 6 elicit, escape, reveal 7 publish, take off 8 evacuate
  up: 5 arise, array, dress, style 6 invent 7 arrange, costume, prepare 9 construct
  well: 4 heal 10 recuperate

get-together: bee 4 stag 5 party 6 social 7 meeting

gewgaw: toy 4 gaud 6 bauble, fangle, fegary, trifle 7 trinket 8 gimcrack 10 knickknack

geyersite: 4 opal

Ghana: *capital:* 5 Accra
  city: 6 Elmina, Kumasi, Tamale 7 Sunyani 9 Cape Coast, Koforidus 10 Bolgatanga
  currency: 4 cedi 6 pesewa
  people: Ga, Ewe 4 Akan 5 Fante 7 Akwapim, Ashanti, Dagomba
  river: 5 Volta

ghastly: wan 4 grim, pale 5 lurid 6 dismal, grisly, pallid 7 charnel, deathly, fearful, hideous, macabre 8 dreadful, gruesome, horrible, shocking, terrible 9 frightful

ghat: 4 pass 5 range 7 landing 8 mountain

gherkin: 6 pickle 8 cucumber

ghost: hag 4 bhut, hant 5 duppy, shade, shape, spook 6 daemon, shadow, spirit, wraith 7 banshee, boggart, eidolon, haunter, lemures (pl.), phantom, specter 8 guytrash, phantasm, revenant 10 apparition, glimmering 11 poltergeist

ghostly: 4 eery 5 eerie, scary, weird 6 spooky 7 shadowy, uncanny 8 spectral 9 spiritual

ghoul: 4 ogre 5 fiend 7 monster, vampire 11 grave robber

ghoulish: 9 loathsome

ghyl: See **gill**

giant: 4 Bara, eten, huge, ogre, rahu, Ymir 5 Argus, Cacus, jumbo, titan, troll 6 ogress 7 Antaeus, Cyclops, Goliath, mammoth, monster 8 behemoth, Bellerus, colossus 9 cyclopean, Gargantua, leviathan, monstrous 10 gargantuan, prodigious, tremendous

gibber: 5 stone 6 pebble 7 boulder, chatter

gibberish: 6 jabber, jargon 7 blather, twaddle 8 claptrap 9 rigmarole 10 double-talk, mumbo jumbo

gibbet: 4 hang 5 noose 7 gallows 8 string up

gibbon: ape, lar 6 monkey, wou-wou 7 hoolock, siamang 10 anthropoid

gibbous: 6 convex, humped 7 hunched, rounded 11 hunchbacked, protuberant

gibe: 4 gird, jape, jeer, mock, quip, twit 5 fleer, fling, flirt, flout, gleek, scoff, sneer, taunt 6 deride, heckle 7 laugh at, poke fun, sarcasm 8 ridicule

giddy: 4 daft 5 dizzy, faint, silly 6 fickle, volage 7 erratic, flighty, reeling, heedless 9 befuddled, frivolous 11 harebrained 13 featherheaded

gift: sop 4 bent, boon, dash, dole 5 bonus, bribe, dower, dowry, favor, grant, knack, pilon, power, token 6 bounty, donary, genius, gersum, hansel, legacy, talent 7 aptness, benefit, faculty, handsel, largess, present, subsidy 8 aptitude, bestowal, blessing, donation, gratuity, largesse, offering, pittance, potlatch 9 endowment, gratitude, lagniappe, readiness 10 compliment 11 benefaction, beneficence, serendipity 12 contribution

gifted: 4 deft 5 smart 6 bright, clever 8 talented 9 brilliant, ingenious

gig: job 4 boat, goad, spur 5 rouse, spear, stint 6 chaise 7 demerit, provoke 8 carriage

gigantic: big 4 huge, vast 5 giant, large 7 immense, mammoth, titanic 8 colossal, enormous 9 cyclopean, gigantean, monstrous 10 gargantuan, prodigious

giggle: 5 laugh, tehee 6 teehee, titter 7 snicker, snigger

gila: 5 trout 6 lizard 7 monster, reptile 10 woodpecker

Gilbert and Sullivan opera: 7 Thespis 8 Iolanthe, Patience 9 Ruddigore, The Mikado 10 Gondoliers 11 H.M.S. Pinafore

Gilbert island: 5 Makin 6 Tarawa

gild: 5 adorn, paint, tinge 7 overlay 8 brighten, decorate, inaurate 9 embellish

Gilda's father: 9 Rigoletto

gilet: 4 vest 6 bodice 9 waistcoat

gill, ghyl: ivy 4 cove, girl, lass 5 brook 6 collar, ravine, stream, tipple, valley, wattle 10 sweetheart
four: 4 pint

gilt: hog, pig, sow 4 gold 5 money 6 gilded, golden

gimcrack: fop, toy 6 bauble, flimsy, gew-gaw, trifle 7 trinket, trivial 8 ornament, trumpery 9 frivolous 10 knickknack 13 unsubstantial

gimlet: 4 tool 8 cocktail

gimme: 6 greedy 11 acquisitive

gimmick: 4 ploy, ruse 5 trick 6 device, gadget 8 maneuver

gimp: vim 4 trim 5 orris 6 spirit 7 cripple 8 lame walk, trimming

gin: net 4 crab, grin, rack, sloe, trap 5 snare, trick 6 device, diddle, liquor, scheme 7 springe 8 artifice, beverage, schnapps 10 intoxicant 11 contrivance

ginger: pep, vim 5 spice, vigor 6 mettle, revive, spirit 8 piquancy, spirited
genus: 8 zingiber
wild: 6 asarum

gingerbread: 4 cake 5 money 6 wealth 8 trimming 13 pfefferkuchen (G.)

ginger cookie: 4 snap

gingerly: 6 warily 7 charily 8 daintily 9 carefully, elegantly, finically, guardedly, mincingly 10 cautiously 12 fastidiously

ginger root: 4 race

gingham: 8 chambray

ginseng: 4 herb 5 panax 6 aralia

Gioconda, La: 8 Mona Lisa
painter: 7 da Vinci

gipsy: See **gypsy**

giraffe: 5 piano 6 animal, spinet 10 camelopard

girandole: 7 pendant 8 water jet 11 candelabrum

girasol, girasole: 4 opal 5 thorn 9 artichoke

gird, girt: 4 belt, bind, gibe, hasp, hoop, jerk, mock 5 brace, equip, scoff, sneer 6 clothe, fasten, secure 7 besiege, enclose, prepare, provide 8 encircle, surround 9 encompass

girder: 4 beam 6 binder

girdle: obi 4 band, bark, belt, bind, cest, ring, sash, zone 5 girth 6 bodice, cestus, circle, corset, moocha 7 baldric, balteus, environ, equator 8 cincture, cingulum, encircle

girl: gal, sis 4 chit, coed, gill, jill, lass, maid, minx 5 fille, filly, quean (Sc.), skirt, sylph, wench 6 amoret, calico, damsel, female, hoyden, tomboy 7 colleen, flapper, ingenue 9 backfisch, debutante 10 jeune fille, sweetheart 11 maidservant
of song: Amy, Ida, Sue 4 Lucy, Lulu, Mary 5 Daisy, Dinah, Dolly, Laura, Molly, Sally, Susie, Tammy 6 Louise, Margie 7 Adeline, Jeannie, Mary Lou, Rosalie, Susanna

girlish: 5 sissy 7 artless 8 immature, maidenly, youthful

girth: 4 band, belt, hoop 5 cinch, cinct, strap, width 6 girdle 7 measure 8 cincture, encircle 13 circumference

gist: nub 4 core, crux, pith 5 heart, point 7 essence, meaning 10 foundation

gitano, gitana (Sp.): 5 gipsy, gypsy 6 gitane (F.)

give: gie (Sc.) 4 cede, dole, emit, hand, mete 5 apply, endow, grant, serve, yield 6 accord, afford, bestow, commit, confer, denote, devote, donate, impart, render, supply 7 consign, dispose, furnish, intrust, present, proffer, propose, provide, stretch 8 bequeath 9 vouchsafe 10 administer, contribute, deliquesce, elasticity
a hand: aid 4 abet, help 6 assist
away: 4 dump 6 betray 7 divulge 8 disclose, get rid of, part with, telltale 9 sacrifice
back: 4 echo 6 recede, remise, retire, return 7 replace, restore 8 make good
forth: 4 emit 6 exhale 8 eradiate
in: 5 bow to, yield 6 relent, submit 7 succumb 8 back down 9 surrender 10 capitulate
off: 4 emit 5 cease, exude, issue 7 publish
out: 4 deal, emit, mete 5 exude, issue, print 6 weaken 7 publish, release 9 circulate
rise: 6 gender 7 produce 8 engender, occasion 9 originate
up: 4 cede, drop, quit, stop 5 cease, demit, forgo, spare, waive, yield 6 devote, forego, resign, retire, reveal, vacate 7 abandon, deliver, despair, present, succumb 8 abdicate, renounce, swear off 9 lose heart, sacrifice, surrender 10 have no idea, relinquish

given: 5 fixed 6 stated 7 donated, granted 8 addicted, disposed, inclined 9 specified

givey: 4 soft

glabrous: 4 bald 6 smooth

glace: ice 6 glazed 8 polished

glacial: icy 4 cold 5 gelid 6 arctic, frigid, frosty, frozen, wintry 7 hostile

glacier: 6 icecap 8 ice sheet
deposit: 5 eskar, esker 6 placer 7 moraine 8 diluvium
direction: 5 stoss
fissure: 8 crevasse
fragment: 7 serac 8 iceberg
hill: 4 paha 7 drumlin
ridge: 4 kame, osar (pl.) 5 eskar, esker
snow: 4 neve
snow field: 4 firn, neve

glacis: 5 slope 7 incline

glad: gay **4** fain **5** eager, happy, merry, sunny **6** blithe, bright, cheery, elated, genial, jocund, jovial, joyous **7** pleased, willing **8** cheerful **9** delighted, gratified, satisfied **11** exhilarated, tickled pink **12** lighthearted

gladden: **5** cheer, elate **6** please **7** delight, gratify, rejoice

glade: **4** vale **5** marsh **8** clearing

gladiator: **5** boxer **6** fencer **7** fighter
competition: **5** ludus
trainer: **7** lanista

gladness: joy **5** bliss, mirth **8** pleasure **9** happiness **12** cheerfulness, exhilaration

glamor, glamour: **5** charm, magic **6** allure **7** glitter, romance **8** illusion, witchery **9** magnetism **11** enchantment

glamorous, glamourous: **6** exotic **8** alluring, charming, romantic **11** fascinating

glance: **4** look, peek, peep, scan, skim **5** brush, flash, graze **6** careen, squint **7** glimpse, rebound **9** quick look

gland: **5** liver, lymph **6** carnel, pineal, thymus **7** adrenal, parotid, thyroid **8** exocrine, pancreas, salivary **9** endocrine, pituitary **12** hypothalamus
edible: **5** liver **6** thymus
enlargement: **6** goiter **7** adenoma
secretion: **5** sebum **7** hormone
swelling: **4** bubo **5** mumps

glandular: **7** adenoid

glare: **4** gaze **5** blaze, flame, scowl, stare **6** glower **7** glitter **8** radiance **9** showiness

glaring: **4** rank **5** clear, gaudy, gross, plain, vivid **6** brazen, bright, strong **7** blatant, burning, evident, obvious, staring, visible **8** apparent, flagrant, manifest **9** barefaced **11** conspicuous

glary: **6** frosty, frozen **7** intense, shining **8** slippery

glass: **4** lens, pane **6** beaker, bottle, cloche, cullet, goblet, mirror **7** crystal, monocle, tumbler **9** barometer, telescope **11** thermometer
alcohol: mug **4** pony **5** stein **6** jigger, rummer, seidel **7** Pilsner, snifter **8** schooner
colored: **5** smalt **7** opaline **10** aventurine
container: jar **6** bottle **7** matrass
design: **4** etch
gem: **5** paste **6** strass
molten: **5** metal **7** parison
pert. to: **6** vitric
remove bubbles: **5** plane

glasses: **5** specs **6** shades **7** goggles **8** bifocals, pince-nez **10** binoculars, spectacles

glassmaking: *device:* **7** ironman
frame: **7** drosser
material: **4** frit
oven: **4** lehr

glassworker: **6** blower, teaser **7** glazier

glasswort: **4** kali **5** plant

glassy: **4** hard **5** sharp **6** shrill **8** strident **9** apathetic **10** forbidding, lackluster, unwavering, unyielding

Glaucus: *father:* **8** Sisyphus
son: **11** Bellerophon

glaze: **4** blur, coat, size **5** cover, glare, sheen, shine **6** enamel, finish, polish, veneer **7** burnish, grow dim, incrust, overlay, vitrify **8** film over

glazier: **11** glassworker

gleam: ray **4** beam, glow **5** blink, blush, flash, glint, sheen, shine **7** glimmer, glitter, shimmer, sparkle **8** radiance, splendor **9** coruscate **10** brightness **11** coruscation, scintillate

gleaming: **6** ablaze, bright **7** shining

glean: **4** cull, reap **6** garner, gather **7** collect, extract

gleaning: **4** crop

glee: joy **4** song **5** mirth, sport **6** gaiety **7** delight, elation **8** hilarity **9** happiness, merriment **10** minstrelsy **12** cheerfulness **13** entertainment

gleeful: gay **5** happy, merry **6** joyous **7** jocular

gleeman: **8** minstrel, musician

glen: **4** dale, dell, vale **5** heuch (Sc.) **6** dingle, valley **10** depression

glib: pat **4** easy, oily **5** quick, ready, slick **6** casual, facile, fluent, smooth **7** offhand, shallow, voluble **8** flippant, slippery, unforced **9** impromptu, insincere, talkative **10** nonchalant, unthinking **11** superficial

glide: **4** flow, sail, sile, skim, slip, soar **5** coast, creep, merge, slide, steal **6** glance **7** slither **8** glissade

gliding over: **6** labile **7** eliding

glim: bit, eye **5** light, watch **12** illumination

glimmer: **4** fire, glow **5** blink, flash, gleam **7** glimpse, glitter, shimmer, sparkle

glimmering: **5** flash, ghost **7** inkling

glimpse: **4** espy, peek **5** trace **6** glance **7** glimmer **11** view briefly **12** fleeting look

glint: **5** flash, gleam, shine **6** luster **7** glisten, glitter, sparkle **10** brightness

glitch: **5** error **6** defect, mishap **11** malfunction

glitter: **4** fire, glow, pomp, show **5** flash, gleam, sheen, shine **6** glamor, tinsel **7** glamour, glimmer, glisten, spangle, sparkle, twinkle **8** radiance **9** coruscate **10** brilliancy **11** coruscation, scintillate

glittering: **5** gaudy, gemmy **6** bright, fulgid **7** radiant **8** lustrous **9** brilliant, clinquant, sparkling, twinkling

gloaming: eve **4** dusk **8** twilight

gloat: **4** brag **5** exult, vaunt **7** revel in **8** crow over

global: **6** all-out, cosmic **7** general **9** universal, worldwide

globe: orb **4** ball, clew **5** earth, world **6** planet, sphere
half: **10** hemisphere
pert. to: **7** spheric

globular: **5** beady, round **9** orbicular, spherical

globule: **4** bead, blob, drop **6** bubble **7** droplet **8** particle, spherule

glockenspiel: **4** lyra **8** carillon **9** xylophone

glom (Sc.): **4** take **5** steal, swipe, watch **10** understand

gloom: **4** dark, dusk, murk **5** cloud, drear, frown **7** despair, dimness, sadness **8** darkness **9** dejection, heaviness, obscurity **10** cloudiness, depression, desolation, melancholy

gloomy: dim, sad, wan **4** blue, dark, dour, eery, glum **5** black, brown, dusky, eerie, heavy, moody, murky, stern **6** cloudy, dismal, dreary, morose, somber, sullen **7** clouded, obscure, stygian **8** darkling, darksome, dejected, desolate, downcast, overcast **9** cheerless, darkening, depressed, saturnine, tenebrous **10** depressing, despondent, foreboding, lusterless, melancholy, sepulchral, tenebrific **11** pessimistic **12** disconsolate, disheartened

glop: goo **4** guck, muck **11** thick liquid

glorify: **4** hery, laud **5** adore, adorn, bless, boast, exalt, extol, glory, honor, vaunt **6** praise **7** clarify, elevate, ennoble, magnify **8** emblazon, eulogize **9** celebrate **11** apotheosize

gloriole: **4** aura, halo **7** aureole

glorious: **5** grand, noble **6** bright **7** eminent, haughty, radiant **8** boastful, ecstatic, gorgeous, renowned, splendid **9** wonderful **10** celebrated, delightful **11** illustrious, magnificent, resplendent

glory: **4** fame, halo **5** boast, eclat, exult, honor, kudos, pride **6** beauty, praise, renown **7** aureole **8** ambition, splendor **9** greatness **10** admiration, brilliancy, effulgence, reputation **11** distinction **12** magnificence

gloss: **4** glow **5** dodge, gloze, sheen, shine **6** blanch, enamel, excuse, luster, polish, remark, veneer **7** burnish **8** annotate, flourish, palliate, pretense **9** semblance, sleekness **10** brightness, commentary **14** interpretation
over: **5** blink **6** excuse, ignore, wink at **7** neglect **9** extenuate, whitewash

glossal: **7** lingual

glossary: **4** list **7** lexicon **8** word list **10** dictionary

glossy: **5** nitid, silky, sleek **6** bright, smooth **7** shining **8** lustrous, polished, specious **9** plausible

glove: **4** cuff, mitt **6** mitten, sheath **7** chevron, dannock, gantlet **8** gauntlet

fabric: **4** silk, wool **5** nylon **6** cotton
leather: kid **4** napa **5** mocha, suede **7** pigskin **8** deerskin
shape: **5** trank

glow: **4** beam, halo **5** ardor, blush, flame, flush, gleam, gloss, shine **6** warmth **7** glimmer **13** incandescence

glower: **4** sulk **5** frown, scowl, stare **9** look black

glowing: hot, red **5** fiery, vivid **6** ardent **7** burning, candent, fervent, radiant, shining **10** candescent

Gluck opera: **5** Orfeo **7** Alceste **16** Iphigenia in Aulis

glucose: **5** sugar **6** starch **7** sucrose **8** dextrose

glue: **4** fix **5** mount, paste, stick **6** adhere, attach, cement, fasten, gluten, sizing **7** sericin **8** adhesive, mucilage

glum: **4** dour **5** moody, surly **6** dismal, gloomy, morose, sullen **8** dejected, frowning, overcast **10** melancholy **11** threatening

glume: **4** leaf **5** bract

glut: **4** cloy, fill, gulp, sate **5** draft, gorge **6** englut, excess, pamper **7** engorge, satiate, surfeit, swallow **8** overfeed, overload, plethora, saturate

gluten: gum **4** glue **6** fibrin **8** adhesive

glutethimide: **8** sedative **13** phenobarbitol

glutinous: **4** ropy, sizy **5** gluey, gummy **6** sticky **7** viscous

glutton: hog, pig **8** gourmand **9** overeater, wolverine

gluttonous: **6** greedy **7** hoggish **9** voracious

glyph: **6** symbol **7** channel

gnar, gnarr: **5** growl, snarl

gnarl: **4** gnar, knot **5** growl, knurl, snarl, twist **6** tangle **7** contort

gnarled: **6** knotty, rugged, sinewy **7** crabbed, twisted **8** hardened **9** roughened

gnash: **4** bite **5** chomp, grind

gnat: fly **4** pest **5** midge **6** insect

gnaw: eat **4** bite, chew, fret **5** erode **6** harass, nibble **7** corrode, torment **8** wear away

gnome: elf, saw **5** adage, bogey, dwarf, elves (pl.), maxim, motto, pigmy, troll **6** goblin, kobold, sprite **8** aphorism, apothegm
king of: Gob

gnomon: **9** indicator **10** sundial pin

gnostic: **4** wise **6** clever, shrewd **7** knowing **12** intellectual
evil being: **8** Demiurge

gnu: **5** takin **6** mammal **8** antelope **10** wildebeast

go: act, bet, bid, die, gae, mog, run **4** fall, fare, gang, lead, move, pass, read, ride, turn, walk, wane, wend, work **5** break, elope, leave, mosey, occur, set-to, steal, visit **6** amount, attain, become, belong, betake, depart, elapse, follow, happen, intend, resort, result, retire, travel **7** conduce, operate, proceed, succeed **8** diminish, traverse, withdraw **9** circulate, harmonize, undertake

aboard: **6** embark **7** entrain

ahead: **7** proceed **8** continue, progress

along: **5** agree **6** concur

around: **5** avoid **6** detour **10** circumvent

ashore: **4** land **6** debark **9** disembark

astray: err, sin **8** aberrate, miscarry

away: **4** exit, scat, shoo **5** leave, scram **6** begone, depart, retire

back: ebb **6** recede, return, revert **7** regress, retreat **10** retrogress

back on: **6** betray, renege **7** abandon **10** break faith

before: **4** lead **7** precede **8** antecede

between: **7** mediate **9** interpose

down: sag **4** fall, sink **5** lower **7** decline, descend, founder **8** decrease **11** deteriorate

forward: **4** fare **7** advance **8** progress

into: **5** audit, delve, enter, probe **7** examine

mad: **4** rage, rave, roar **5** erupt

on: **5** enter **7** proceed **8** continue

over: **5** renew **7** retrace **9** backtrack

swiftly: run **5** scoot, speed

through: **6** endure, suffer **9** penetrate **10** experience

to and fro: **5** waver **6** totter, wig-wag **7** stagger **9** fluctuate, vacillate **11** shuttlecock

to pot: die **4** fail **7** decline **11** deteriorate

up: **4** rise **5** arise, raise **6** ascend

with: fit **4** date, suit **5** agree **6** escort **9** accompany, harmonize

goa: **6** mugger (Ind.) **7** gazelle

goad: egg, gad, rod **4** brod, dice, edge, move, prod, spur, urge, yerk **5** ankus, decoy, impel, pique, prick, sting, thorn **6** incite **7** inflame **8** irritate, stimulus **9** incentive, instigate, stimulate **10** incitement

go-ahead: **4** okay **8** all clear **10** green light **13** authorization

goal: aim, end **4** base, butt, dole, hail, mark, mete **5** bourn, finis, score, tally **6** object **7** purpose **8** ambition **9** intention, objective **10** aspiration **11** destination **12** consummation

goat: kid, ram, tur **4** ibex, tahr **5** beden, billy, goral, nanny **6** alpaca, chamal, pasang, victim **7** fall guy, markhor **8** aegagrus, ruminant **9** bouquetin, stambecco, steinbock

constellation: **9** Capricorn

disease: **7** takosis

flesh: **6** chevon

genus: **5** capra

god of: Pan

kind: **6** Angora, Saanen **8** Cashmere **10** Nubian Boer, Toggenburg

male: **4** buck **5** billy

pert. to: **6** capric **7** caprine, hircine

wild: **4** ibex **6** bezoar **7** markhor **9** Daghestan

wool: **6** mohair **8** cashmere

goatee: **5** beard **7** Vandyke

goatherd: **5** Damon

goatish: **4** lewd **6** coarse **7** caprine, hircine, lustful **9** salacious **10** lascivious

goatskin: kid **9** chevrette

goatsucker: **4** bird **8** nightjar **9** nighthawk **12** whippoorwill

gob: tar (Br.) **4** hunk, lump, mass **5** chunk **6** sailor, seaman **7** mariner **8** quantity

gobbet: **4** drip, drop **5** piece **6** morsel **7** driblet, portion **8** fragment, mouthful

gobble: **4** gulp **6** snatch **7** swallow

go-between: **5** agent, envoy **6** broker **7** arbiter **8** mediator **10** mouthpiece **11** internuncio **12** intermediary

Gobi Desert site: **4** Asia

goblet: cup **5** glass, hanap **6** beaker, vessel **7** chalice **8** standard

goblin: elf, hag, nis **4** bhut **5** bogey, bogle, bucca, gnome, nisse, ouphe, pooka, troll **6** booger, churel, kobold, sprite **7** brownie

gobs: **4** lots **5** heaps, loads, scads **6** oodles, plenty

go-cart: **4** pram **5** wagon **12** perambulator

god (see also **deity, goddess**): Ada, Ani, Asa, Bel, Bes, Geb, Keb, Ler, Min, Pan, Ran, Seb, Tiu, Tyr, Ull, Van **4** Abba, aitu, Amen, Amon, Aten, Aton, Baal, deus (L.), deva, dieu (F.), dios (Sp.), Frey, Hler, idol, Kama, Loke, Loki, lord, Nora, Odin, Orra, Ptah, Rama, Surt, Thor, Vali, Yama, Zeus **5** Aeger, Aegir, Asura, Baldr, Brage, Brama, Donar, Freyr, Hades, image, maker, Othin, Pluto, Shiva, Surtr, Woden **6** Apollo, Brahma, Christ, Cronus, Elohim, Ganesa, Hermes, Hoenir, Kronus, Marduk, Njorth, Osiris, Saturn, Vulcan, Yahweh **7** Bacchus, creator, Forsete, godhead, Heimdal, Jehovah, Jupiter, Krishna, Mercury, Serapis, Vitharr **8** Almighty, Dionysus, divinity **9** Heindallr, Hlorrithi **10** Hephaestus **11** Ramachandra

false: **4** Baal, idol **6** Mammon **10** golden calf

love for: **5** piety **6** amadis, bhakti

God be with you: **5** adieu, adios **7** goodbye **11** vaya con Dios

goddess: Bau, Dis, Eir, Eos, Hel, Mut, Nut, Uma **4** Anta, Bast, Devi, Gaia, Hela, Hera, Isis, Juno, Kali, Nina, Norn, Saga, Urth, Wyrd **5** Belit, Ceres, Diana, Durga, Freya, Frigg, Gauri, Nanna, Venus **6** Athena, Aurora, Chandi, Freyja, Frigga, Hecate, Hestia, Shakti, Tiamat **7** Artemis, Asynjur, Demeter, Mylitta, Parvati **9** Aphrodite,

Haimavati **10** Persephone, Proserpina

godfather: don **7** padrino, sponsor

god-fearing: **5** pious **6** devout **9** religious

godforsaken: **6** dismal **8** desolate, wretched **9** miserable, neglected

god-horse: **6** mantis

godless: **6** unholy, wicked **7** heathen, impious, profane **9** atheistic

god-like: **5** pious **6** deific, devout, divine **8** immortal **9** religious

godliness: **5** piety **13** righteousness

godly: **4** holy **5** pious **6** devout **7** saintly **8** gracious **9** religious, righteous

gods: For gods of specific localities, religions or functions, see under the specific locality, religion or function. EXAMPLES: "Hindu god": see **Hindu:** *god/goddess*; "god of war": see **war:** *god of*.

gods' abode: **6** heaven **7** Olympus **8** Valhalla

godsend: **4** boon **8** blessing **9** life saver

Goethe drama: **5** Faust **6** Egmont, Stella **7** Clavigo

gofer: **9** errand boy, messenger

goffer: **4** iron **5** crimp, pleat

go-getter: **6** dynamo **7** hustler **8** live wire

goggle: bug, eye **4** roll **5** stare **6** squint

goggler: **4** scad **5** akule

goggles: **5** specs **7** glasses **8** blinkers

going: run, way **4** exit, fare, gait, gate, path, road **5** bound **6** access **7** current **8** behavior **9** departure **10** passageway

goiter: **6** struma **7** strumae (pl.)

gola: **4** cyma **7** granary **9** storeroom

gold: or (F.), oro (Sp.) **4** gelt, gilt **5** aurum (L.), metal **6** riches, wealth **7** bullion **9** clinquant
bar: **5** ingot
black: oil
California prospector: **10** forty-niner
deposit: **6** placer
fool's: **6** pyrite
gold rush site: **8** Klondike **9** Pike's Peak **11** Sutter's Mill
imitation: **6** ormolu, oroide
measure of weight: **5** carat, karat
pert. to: **4** dore **6** aurous
process: **7** alchemy
symbol: Au
thin sheet of: **4** foil, leaf **6** latten
uncoined: **7** bullion
yielding: **10** auriferous

gold braid: **5** orris

goldbrick: **4** loaf **5** shirk **7** swindle

Gold Bug author: Poe

golden: **4** gilt, rich **5** auric, blest, blond **6** blonde, mellow, yellow **7** aureate, halcyon, shining **8** precious **9** favorable, Pactolian, yellowish **10** propitious

golden age: **9** siecle d'or (F.)

golden ager: **7** oldster **13** elderly person, senior citizen

golden apple giver: **5** Paris

golden bough: **9** mistletoe

golden chain: **8** laburnum

Golden Fleece: *keeper of:* **6** Aeetes
land of: **7** Colchis
seeker: **5** Jason **8** Argonaut
ship used: **4** Argo

golden oriole: **5** pirol **6** loriot

Golden State: **10** California

goldeneye: cur **9** merrywing

goldenrod: **8** solidago

goldfinch: **8** graypate, greypate **10** wild canary **12** yellow-hammer

goldfish: **4** carp **6** calico, popeye **8** lionhead **9** garibaldi, shubunkin
crucible: **6** cruset

gold-plate: **4** gild, gilt

goldsmith: **7** artisan **9** artificer

golem: **5** robot **9** automaton, blockhead

golf: *assistant:* **5** caddy **6** caddie
club: **4** iron, wood **5** baffy, cleek, mashy, spoon, wedge **6** brassy, driver, jigger, mashie, putter **7** brassie, midiron, niblick
conceded putt: **5** gimme
course: **5** links
cry: **4** fore
cup: **5** Ryder **6** Walker
hazard: **4** trap **5** stymy, water **6** bunker, stymie
mound: tee
mulligan: **9** free drive
score: par **5** bogey, bogie, eagle **6** birdie, Nassau **8** handicap
stroke: **4** hook, loft, putt **5** drive, slice
target: cup **4** flag **5** green
term: ace, lie, par, tee **4** baff, putt, shot **5** divot, dormy, green, round **6** dormie, stroke **7** gallery **9** hole-in-one

golfer: **8** linksman
notable men: **4** Ford, Kite, Pate **5** Boros, Hagen, Hogen, Irwin, Jones, Shute, Smith, Snead **6** Casper, Miller, Nelson, Norman, Ouimet, Palmer, Player, Rogers, Watson **7** Couples, Sarazen, Stadler, Stewart, Strange, Trevino, Wadkins **8** Crenshaw, Nicklaus, Weiskopf **10** Middlecoff **11** Ballesteros
notable women: **4** Berg, King **5** Lopez, Suggs **6** Alcott, Caponi, Carner, Daniel, Rankin, Turner, Wright **7** Bradley, Okamoto, Sheehan **8** Zaharias **9** Didrikson, Whitworth

Goliath: **5** giant
home: **4** Gath
place of death: **4** Elah
slayer: **5** David

golly: **4** oath, yell

Gomer: *father:* **7** Japheth
   husband: **5** Hosea
gondola: car **4** boat **5** barge, coach
gone: **4** away, left, lost **6** absent **7** missing **8**
   absorbed, departed, finished, vanished
gone by: ago, o'er **4** over, past
Goneril: *father:* **4** Lear
   sister: **5** Regan **8** Cordelia
gonfalon: **4** flag **6** banner, ensign **7** pennant **8**
   standard
goober: **6** peanut
good: bon (F.), fit **4** able, bein, bien (F.),
   boon, braw, fine, full, gain, kind, nice, prow
   5 ample, brave, bueno (Sp.), bully, moral,
   nifty, pious, sound, valid **6** benign, devout,
   expert, profit, proper **7** copious, gradely,
   helpful, liberal, trained, upright **8** becoming, budgeree, decorous, friendly, gracious,
   interest, orthodox, pleasant, pleasing, salutary, skillful, suitable, virtuous **9** agreeable,
   bountiful, competent, dauntless, enjoyable,
   estimable, excellent, favorable, fortunate,
   indulgent, reputable, righteous, well-being
   10 auspicious, beneficial, benevolent,
   courageous, gratifying, profitable, sufficient
   11 pleasurable, respectable, responsible,
   well-behaved **12** considerable, satisfactory,
   stouthearted, well-disposed
good-bye, good-by: **4** tata **5** adieu (F.), adios
   (Sp.), aloha, ciaou (It.) **6** see you, so-long **7**
   cheerio **8** farewell
Good Earth author: **4** Buck
good-for-nothing: **4** orra **7** useless, wastrel **8**
   spalpeen (Ir.) **9** worthless **10** ne'er-do-well
   11 rapscallion
good health: **5** skoal **6** prosit **7** slainte
goodliness: **5** grace **6** beauty **8** goodness,
   kindness **10** comeliness, excellence
good-looking: **4** fair **5** bonny **6** comely, pretty
   7 eyesome, winsome **8** handsome **9** beautiful **10** attractive, personable
good luck: **7** fortune
   image: **6** alraun
goodly: **4** kind **5** large **6** comely, portly **8** gracious, handsome & capacious, excellent **12**
   considerable
good-natured: **6** genial, jovial **7** amiable **8**
   cheerful, obliging **9** easy-going, gemutlich
goodness: **5** honor, merit, worth **6** bounty,
   purity, virtue **8** chastity, kindness **9** integrity
   10 excellence, generosity, goodliness **11**
   beneficence, benevolence
goods: **4** gear **5** stock, wares **7** chattel, effects
   8 property **11** commodities, merchandise,
   possessions
   cast overboard: **5** lagan, ligan **6** jetsam,
   lagend
   lost in shipwreck: **7** flotsam
   smuggled: **10** contraband

stolen: **4** loot, pelf **5** booty **6** spoils
good spirit: **8** eudaemon
goodwill: **4** love **5** amity, favor **8** kindness,
   sympathy **9** readiness **10** friendship, heartiness **11** benevolence **12** friendliness
goody: **5** candy **6** bonbon, tidbit **8** goodwife **9**
   sweetmeat
goof: err **5** gum up, spoil **7** blunder
goofy: **5** silly **6** insane **7** foolish **8** gullible
gook: **4** muck **5** bilge, hooey, trash **6** drivel
goon: sap **4** boob, dope, thug **6** mugger **7**
   hoodlum
gooney bird: **9** albatross
goosander: **9** merganser
goose: **4** bird **5** ninny, solan **7** widgeon **9**
   screwball, simpleton
   cry: **4** honk, yang **5** cronk
   flock: **4** raft **6** gaggle
   genus: **4** chen **5** anser **6** branta
   kind: **4** snow, swan **5** brant **6** Canada,
   Embden **7** gray lag **8** Toulouse **10**
   Sebastopol
   mackerel: **9** phalarope
   male: **6** gander
   pert. to: **8** anserine **9** grossular
   snow: **4** chen **5** wavey **9** whitehead
   tailor's: **8** flatiron
   wild: **5** brant **7** gray-lag **8** barnacle
   young: **7** gosling
goose egg: zip **4** zero **5** zilch **6** cipher, naught
   7 nothing
gooseflesh: **5** bumps **7** pimples
goosefoot: **5** blite, plant, shrub
gopher: **4** tuza **6** rodent **8** squirrel, tortoise
Gopher State: **9** Minnesota
Gorboduc's son: **6** Porrex
Gordian: **9** intricate **11** complicated
gore: **4** stab **5** blood, filth, inset, slime **6** gusset, insert, pierce **7** carnage **9** penetrate
gorge: **4** fill, gaum, glut, pass, sate **5** cajon,
   canon, chasm, flume, gulch, gully, kloof,
   strid **6** canyon, coulee, defile, englut, nullah, ravine, valley **7** couloir, overeat,
   pitcher, satiate **8** quebrada **10** gluttonize
gorgeous: **4** vain **5** grand, showy **6** costly **8**
   dazzling, glorious, splendid **9** beautiful, luxurious **11** magnificent, resplendent
Gorgon: **6** Medusa, Stheno **7** Euryale
   father: **7** Phorcys
   hair: **6** snakes
   mother: **4** Ceto
   slayer of Medusa: **7** Perseus
   watcher for: **4** Enyo **5** Deino **6** Graeae (pl.)
   8 Pephredo
gorilla: ape **7** primate **10** anthropoid
gorse: **4** whin **5** furze **7** juniper
gory: **6** bloody **9** murderous **10** sanguinary **12**
   bloodstained
goshawk: **7** tiercel

keeper: **8** ostreger **10** austringer

gospel: **4** book **5** creed, truth **7** tidings **8** doctrine, good news, last word, teaching
four: **4** John, Luke, Mark **7** Matthew
harmony of the four: **11** diatessaron

gossamer: **4** airy **5** filmy, gauzy, sheer **10** diaphanous

gossip: gab **4** blab, chat, dirt **5** clack, rumor, snoop **6** babble, gabble, magpie, tattle **7** chatter, hearsay, prattle, scandal **8** busybody, idle talk, informer, quidnunc **9** chatterer **10** newsmonger, talebearer, tattletale **11** scuttlebutt

Goth: **8** Visigoth **9** barbarian, Ostrogoth
hero: **5** Wudga
last: **8** Roderick

Gothamite: **9** New Yorker

Gothic: **4** rude **5** rough **6** fierce **8** barbaric, medieval, Teutonic

Gouda: **6** cheese
kin of: **4** Edam

gouge: **4** tool **5** cheat, fraud **6** cavity, chisel, groove **7** defraud **9** extortion **10** overcharge

goulash: **4** stew **6** jumble **7** mixture **8** mishmash

Gounod opera: **5** Faust

gourd: **4** hole, pepo **5** melon, pepos **6** bottle, vessel **7** anguria **8** calabash, cucurbit **9** colocynth **11** chilacayote
rattle: **6** maraca
sponge: **5** loofa, luffa

gourmand: **7** glutton **8** big eater **11** trencherman

gourmet: **7** epicure **9** bon vivant **10** gastronome **11** connoisseur

gout: **4** clot, drop **5** taste **6** blotch **7** podagra **9** arthritis **11** coagulation, discernment

govern: run **4** curb, rein, rule, sway **5** guide, regle, steer **6** bridle, direct, manage, police **7** command, conduct, control, preside, refrain **8** dominate, regulate, restrain **9** influence, supervise **10** administer, discipline

governance: **7** control **10** government, management

governess: **5** nanny, tutor **6** abbess **7** teacher **8** mistress **9** nursemaid

government: law **4** rule **5** power **6** regime **7** conduct, fascism, regency, regimen, tyrany **8** guidance, monarchy, republic **9** authority, autocracy, democracy, despotism, hierarchy, oligarchy **10** governance, management, regulation **11** aristocracy **15** totalitarianism
agent: **5** envoy **6** consul **8** diplomat, minister **10** ambassador
art of: **8** politics **13** statesmanship
by a few: **9** oligarchy
by church: **9** hierarchy, theocracy **10** hierocracy

by one: **8** monarchy **9** autocracy **12** dictatorship
by people: **9** democracy
by rich: **10** plutocracy
by three: **8** triarchy **11** triumvirate
by women: **8** gynarchy **11** gynecocracy
by worst men: **12** kakistocracy
head: **4** czar, king, tsar **5** queen **6** caesar, kaiser **7** emperor, empress, premier **8** dictator **9** president **10** presidente
official: **6** syndic **10** bureaucrat
opposition to: **10** antarchism
without: **6** acracy **7** anarchy

governor: bey **4** lord **5** deity, nabob, pilot, ruler **6** rector, regent **7** captain, control, manager, viceroy **8** director **9** president, regulator **10** gubernator, magistrate
castle: **6** alcaid **7** alcaide **9** castellan

gown: **4** robe, toga **5** frock, habit, manto, toosh, tunic **6** clothe, invest, mantua **7** garment **11** formal dress
dressing: **4** robe **6** kimono **8** peignoir
loose: **5** smock **6** banian, camise, chimer **7** cassock, chemise
Moslem: **4** jama **5** jamah

Goya figure: **4** Maja

grab: nab **4** boat, hold, take **5** catch, clasp, grasp, seize **6** arrest, clutch, collar, snatch **7** capture, grapple **11** appropriate

grabble: **5** grope, seize **6** snatch, sprawl **7** grapple **11** appropriate

grace: **4** ease **5** adorn, charm, favor, leave, mercy **6** beauty, become, bedeck, polish, prayer, virtue **7** commend, dignify, gratify **8** beautify, easiness, efficacy, elegance, kindness **9** embellish, privilege **10** comeliness, goodliness, permission, refinement, seemliness **12** dispensation **14** attractiveness

graceful: **4** airy, easy **6** comely, gainly, mignon, seemly **7** elegant, fitting, genteel, tactful **8** charming, debonair, delicate **9** beautiful **11** appropriate

graceless: **4** ugly **5** cruel **7** awkward **8** depraved **9** abandoned, inelegent, merciless **10** ungracious **11** unfortunate

gracenote: **12** appoggiatura

graces: **8** agremens **9** agrements

Graces: **6** Aglaia, Charis, Thalia **10** Euphrosyne
father: **4** Zeus
mother: **5** Aegle

gracile: **4** thin **6** slight **7** slender **8** graceful

gracious: **4** good, kind, mild **5** civil, godly, happy, lucky, suave **6** benign, goodly, kindly **7** affable **8** benedict, debonair, generous, handsome, merciful, pleasing **9** benignant, courteous

grackle: **9** blackbird

gradation: **4** rank, step **5** scale, stage **6**

degree, series **8** position **10** difference

grade: peg **4** mark, rank, rate, size, sort **5** class, level, order, stage **6** ascent, assort, degree, rating, select **7** incline, inspect **8** classify, gradient, graduate **14** classification

grader: 9 bulldozer

gradient: 4 ramp **5** grade, slope

gradine, gradin: 5 shelf **7** retable

gradual: 4 easy, slow **6** gentle **9** leisurely **10** step by step

graduate: 6 alumna **7** alumnus **9** calibrate

Graeae, Graiae: 4 Enyo **5** Deino **8** Pephredo
  father: **7** Phorcus, Phorcys
  sister: **6** Gorgon, Medusa **7** Gorgons

graff: 5 canal, ditch, fosse **6** trench

graft: dig **4** cion, toil, work **5** bribe, ditch, gravy, labor, scion, trade **6** boodle, inarch, payoff, payola, trench **7** bribery

grafted: 6 united **8** attached
  heraldry: **4** ente

grail: ama, cup **4** bowl **6** vessel **7** chalice, platter **8** sangraal, sangreal
  knight of: **4** Bors **7** Galahad **8** Parsifal, Percival

grain: jot, rye **4** corn, grit, meal, oats, rice, seed, wale, whit **5** fiber, grist, maize, scrap, spark, speck, trace, wheat **6** barley, cereal, kernel, russud (Russ.) **7** granule, modicum, texture **8** particle **9** granulate
  beard: awn
  brewing: **4** malt
  bundle: **5** sheaf
  chaff: **4** bran, grit
  coating: **4** bran
  disease: **4** smut **5** ergot
  dried: **5** straw **6** groats, rissom, rizzom
  ear of: **5** spike **6** ressum
  foodstuff: **6** cereal
  fungus: **5** ergot
  funnel: **6** hopper
  goddess of: **5** Ceres **7** Demeter
  ground: **4** meal **5** flour, grist
  line: **5** swath
  measure: **6** thrave
  mixture: **6** fodder **7** farrage **9** bullimong
  outer membrane: **6** extine
  parched: **7** graddan
  price: **4** fiar (Sc.)
  receptacle: bin **4** silo **8** elevator
  refuse: pug **5** chaff
  scoop: **5** shaul
  spike: ear
  stack: **4** rick
  tool: **5** flail
  warehouse: **8** elevator

grainy: 6 coarse **8** granular, textured

gram: 6 weight
  one-tenth: **8** decigram
  molecule: mol **4** mole

grammar: 6 syntax **9** accidence **11** linguistics
  case: **6** dative **8** ablative, genitive, locative, vocative **9** objective **10** accusative, nominative, possessive
  describe: **5** parse
  direct address: **8** vocative
  example: **8** paradigm
  term: **5** tense **6** active, gender, gerund, number, person, phrase, simile **7** article, passive **8** metaphor **10** declension, infinitive, inflection **11** conjugation

grammary: 5 magic **10** necromancy **11** enchantment

grampus: orc **4** orca **5** whale **7** cetacea, dolphin **8** cetacean, scorpion

granada: 11 pomegranate

granary: bin **4** gola **6** garnel, garner, girnal, girnel, grange **8** cornloft **9** cornhouse **10** repository, storehouse

grand: 4 epic, main **5** chief, great, lofty, noble, showy **6** august, epical, famous, superb, swanky **7** exalted, immense, stately, sublime **8** foremost, glorious, gorgeous, majestic, splendid **9** dignified, grandiose, principal, sumptuous **10** impressive, preeminent **11** ceremonious, illustrious, magnificent **13** comprehensive

Grand Canyon State: 7 Arizona

Grand Duke of Hell: 6 Abogor

grand slam: 4 vole **5** homer **7** home run

grandee: 5 pasha **6** bashaw **7** magnate **8** nobleman **10** clarissimo (It.)

grandeur: 4 pomp **5** state **6** parade **7** majesty **8** elegance, splendor, vastness **9** greatness, immensity, loftiness, nobleness, sublimity **10** augustness **12** magnificence

grandfather: 6 atavus, exempt **7** founder **8** grandfer, gudesire (Sc.) **10** forefather
  pert. to: **4** aval

grandiloquent: 6 heroic, turgid **7** pompous **9** bombastic

grandiose: 4 epic **5** grand **6** turgid **7** pompous **8** imposing **9** bombastic, expansive, flaunting **10** impressive

grandmother: 4 yaya (Gr.) **6** granny, gudame (Sc.) **7** grannie **8** babushka (Russ.)
  Devil's: **4** Baba

grange: 4 farm **7** granary **9** farmhouse

granger: 6 farmer

granite: 6 aplite **7** haplite, syenite **8** alaskite

Granite State: 12 New Hampshire

granitic: 4 hard **7** austere **10** inflexible

grant: aid **4** boon, cede, gift, give, lend, loan, mise **5** admit, allot, allow, bonus, chart, cowle, spare, yette, yield **6** accede, accord, afford, assent, bestow, betake, beteem, bounty, confer, octroi, patent, permit, remise **7** adjudge, concede, consent, promise, subsidy, tribute **8** bestowal, donation, transfer **9** franchise, undertake **10** concession, permission, relinquish **11** acknowledge

granular: 5 sandy **6** coarse, grainy

granule: 4 pill **5** grain **6** nodule, pellet **8** particle

grape: uva **5** Pinot, Tokay **6** Agawam, Lalang, Malaga, Malage, Muscat **7** Catawba, Concord, Hamburg, Mission, Niagara **8** Delaware, Riesling, Thompson **9** muscadine **11** Scuppernong
acid: **7** racemic
cluster: **10** racemation
conserve: **5** jelly, uvate
cultivation: **11** viniculture, viticulture
dried: **6** raisin
drink: **4** dibs, sapa, wine
fermentation: **6** cuvage (F.)
gatherer: **8** vintager
genus of: **5** vitis
juice: **4** dibs, must, sapa, stum
pert. to: **4** uval **10** botryoidal
refuse: **4** marc
residue: **4** marc, rape **6** pomace
seed: **6** acinus
spirit: **4** marc
sugar: **8** dextrose, fructose

grapefruit: 6 pomelo **8** shaddock

Grapes of Wrath: *author:* **9** Steinbeck
family: **4** Joad
people: **5** Okies

grapevine: 4 caro **5** rumor **6** gossip, report

graph: map **5** chart **6** sketch **7** diagram, outline

graphic: 5 lucid, vivid **6** visual **7** precise **8** explicit, incisive **9** pictorial, realistic, well drawn **11** picturesque

graphite: 4 lead **6** carbon

grapnel: 4 drag, hook **6** anchor

grapple: 4 grab, hold **5** grasp **6** clinch, tackle **7** contend, grapnel, seizing, seizure, wrestle **8** struggle

grasp: nab, see **4** clam, fist, grab, grip, hold, take **5** catch, clasp, seize, snare **6** clench, clinch, clutch, snatch **7** control, embrace, grapple **8** handfast **9** apprehend **10** comprehend, understand **13** comprehension

grasping: 4 avid, hard **6** greedy, grippy **7** miserly **8** covetous **9** mercenary **10** avaricious **12** apprehension, parsimonious
adapted for: **10** prehensile, prehensive

grass (see also **cereal**): pot **4** lawn, reed, turf **6** darnel **7** hassock, herbage, pasture **9** colieroot, marijuana, vetiveria **10** greensward
blade of: **7** traneen
dried: hay **6** fodder
fiber: **4** flax **5** istle, ramee,' ramie **6** bhabar
fodder: **4** dura, gama **6** millet
forage: **7** setaria
genus of: **4** aira **5** stipa **6** clover, lygeum **7** setaria
kinds of: eel, fog, hay, poa **4** alfa, bent, cane, diss, leaf, reed **5** avena, brome, grama, sedge, spart, spike, stipa, sudan **6** enalid, marram, quitch, redtop, sesame, sorrel **7** Bermuda, buffalo, esparto, orchard, timothy, traneen **8** bluestem, calfkill **9** bluegrass, bouteloua
tuft: **7** tussock

grasshopper: 4 grig **6** locust
relative: **7** katydid

grassland: lea **4** lawn, rakh (Ind.), vale **5** field, range, veldt **6** meadow, pampas **7** pasture, prairie, savanna

grate: jar **4** fret, grid, grit, rasp **5** grill, grind **6** abrade, basket, offend, prison, scrape **7** grating **8** imprison, irritate

grateful: 8 thankful **9** agreeable **12** appreciative

gratification: 4 gust **6** reward **8** delicacy, gratuity, pleasure **9** enjoyment **10** recompense **11** contentment **12** satisfaction

gratified: 4 glad **5** proud **7** pleased **9** delighted

gratify: 4 feed, sate **5** adorn, amuse, feast, grace, grant, humor, wreak **6** arride, foster, pamper, please **7** appease, content, delight, flatter, gladden, indulge, requite, satisfy

grating: 4 grid, rasp **5** grill, harsh, raspy, rough **6** grille, hoarse **8** gridiron, grinding, strident **9** dissonant **11** latticework

gratitude: 6 thanks **7** tribute **12** appreciation, gratefulness, thankfulness

gratuitous: 4 free **6** gratis, wanton **7** unasked **8** baseless, needless **9** voluntary **10** groundless **11** superfluous, unwarranted

gratuity: fee, tip **4** dole, gift **5** bonus, bribe, pilon **6** bounty **7** cumshaw, pension, present **9** baksheesh, lagniappe, pourboire **10** compliment **11** benefaction

grave: 4 tomb **5** carve, crypt, sober, staid, vault **6** sedate, solemn, somber **7** austere, earnest, engrave, serious **8** decorous **9** important, mausoleum, momentous, sepulcher
cloth: **8** cerement
robber: **5** ghoul

gravel: 4 dirt, grit **6** bother **7** perplex **8** alluvium **9** embarrass

gravelly: 5 harsh **6** coarse **7** rasping

graven: 6 carved, etched **8** engraved **10** sculptured

graver: 5 burin **8** engraver, sculptor

gravestone: 5 stela, stele **6** cippus, marker **8** monument **9** headstone, tombstone

graveyard: 8 cemetery **10** churchyard

graveyard of the Atlantic: 12 Cape Hatteras

gravid: 8 pregnant

graviers: 4 dice
graving tool: 5 burin
gravity: 4 pull 7 dignity 8 enormity, sobriety 9 heaviness, influence, solemnity 10 attraction, importance 11 earnestness, seriousness, weightiness 12 significance 13 momentousness 17 authoritativeness
  law discoverer: 6 Newton
  without: 7 agravic
gravy: jus (F.) 5 graft, juice, sauce 8 windfall
gravy dish: 9 sauceboat
gray, grey: dim 4 ashy, dull, gris, hoar 5 ashen, bleak, hoary 6 dismal, leaden 7 grizzly, hueless, neutral 9 cheerless 10 achromatic
  bluish: 7 cesious
  dark: 5 slate, taupe 6 Oxford 8 charcoal 10 battleship
  light: 4 ashy 5 pearl
  Quaker: 5 acier
graylag: 5 goose
grayling: 4 fish 9 butterfly
gray matter: 4 head, mind, obex 5 brain 9 intellect 11 thinking cap
Gray's churchyard opus: 5 Elegy
gray whale: 7 ripsack
graze: 4 crop, feed, rase, skim 5 brush, shave, touch 6 browse, scrape 7 pasture
grazing ground: 4 colp 5 range 6 collop, meadow 7 pasture
grease: fat, oil 4 lard, soil 5 bribe, cheat, cozen, smear 6 creesh (Sc.) 7 lanolin 9 lubricate
greaser: 6 stoker
greasewood: 4 sage 5 chico 6 orache 7 chamiso, hopsage 10 iodine bush
greasy: fat 4 oily, rich 5 dirty, fatty, gross, porky 7 smeared 8 indecent, slippery, unctuous 10 indelicate 11 threatening
great: big 4 deep, fell, huge, much, rial, unco, vast 5 ample, chief, grand, large, yeder 6 grande (F., Sp.), heroic, mickle 7 capital, eminent, extreme, howling, immense, intense, titanic, violent 8 almighty, elevated, enormous, favorite, horrible 9 elaborate, excellent, important, prolonged 10 delightful, omnipotent 11 magnificent
great albacore: 5 tunny 7 bluefin
Great Barrier island: 4 Otea
Great Bear: 9 Big Dipper, Ursa Major
great blue heron: 5 crane
Great Britain: See **England, Scotland, Wales**
great deal: 4 gobs, lots
Great Divide: 7 Rockies
greaten: 5 exalt 7 enhance, enlarge, magnify 8 increase
greater: 6 better, higher 8 mightier, superior
greatest: 4 arch, best, most 6 utmost 7 extreme, noblest, supreme
Great Expectations hero: Pip

greathearted: 5 brave 7 gallant 8 fearless, generous 9 unselfish 10 courageous
Great Lake: 4 Erie 5 Huron 7 Ontario 8 Michigan, Superior
greatly: 4 much 6 vastly 8 markedly 9 immensely 10 infinitely
great many: lac 4 lakh
greatness: 8 grandeur 9 magnitude 11 magnanimity
grebe: 8 dabchick 10 diving bird
Grecia: 6 Greece
Grecian: 5 Greek 9 Hellenist

Greece (see also **Athens, Greek**):
  capital: 6 Athens
  city: 4 Elis 6 Candia, Delphi, Nikhia, Patras, Sparta 7 Piraeus 8 Salonika 9 Peristeri
  cheese: 4 feta
  currency: 6 lepton 7 drachma
  gulf: 7 Argolis, Corinth, Laconia, Saronic 8 Messenia, Salonika, Toronaic 9 Strymonic
  island: Ios, Kos 4 Keos, Milo 5 Chios, Corfu, Crete, Delos, Melos, Naxos, Paros, Paxos, Psara, Samos, Syros, Tenos, Thira, Zante 6 Andros, Candia, Cerigo, Ikaria, Ithaca, Lemnos, Lesbos, Leukas, Limnos, Patmus, Rhodes, Skyros 7 Amorgos, Kythnos, Mykonos, Simolus, Siphnos 10 Cephalonia, Samothrace
  island group: 6 Aegean, Ionian 8 Cyclades, Sporades 10 Dodecanese
  mountain: Ida 4 Oeta, Ossa 5 Athos 6 Othrys, Pelion, Pindus 7 Cyllene, Helicon, Olympus, Rhodope 8 Hymettus, Taygetus 9 Cambunian, Cithaeron, Parnassus 10 Erymanthus 11 Hagios Elias
  river: 4 Arta 6 Peneus, Struma 7 Alpheus 8 Achelous, Cephisus 9 Arakhthos, Vistritsa
  weight: mna, oka, oke 4 mina 5 litra, maneh, minah, obole, pound 6 diobol, dramme, kantar, obolos, obolus, stater, talent 7 chalcon, chalque, drachma 8 diobolon, talanton 12 tetradrachma
  wine: 7 retsina

---

greed: 7 avarice 8 cupidity, voracity 11 selfishness
greedy: 4 avid 5 eager 6 grabby 7 miserly 8 covetous, grasping 9 rapacious 10 avaricious, gluttonous, insatiable
Greek: 6 Argive 7 Hellene

abode of gods: **7** Olympus
actor: **7** Thespis
administrator: **10** amphodarch
altar: **7** eschara
army corps: **6** evzone
avenging spirit: **4** Fury **6** Erinys
basin: **6** louter
beauty: **4** Lais
bondman: **6** penest
castanet: **8** crotalum
Catholic: **5** Uniat **6** Uniate
chamber: **12** bouleuterion
church: **8** Orthodox
citadel: **9** Acropolis
clan: **4** obes **5** genos
cloak: **6** abolla **7** chlamys
column: **5** Doric, Ionic **10** Corinthian
contest: **4** agon
council: **9** Areopagus
counselor: **6** Nestor
courtesan: **5** Thais **7** Aspasia
cup: **5** depas
currency: **4** mine, obol **5** hecte, nomas **6** lepton, phenix, stater **7** diobolo, drachma
dialect: **5** Doric, Elean, Eolic, Ionic **6** Aeolic
dirge: **5** linos
doom: ker
dramatist: **7** Thespis **8** Menander **9** Aeschylus, Euripides, Sophocles **12** Aristophanes
enchantress: **5** Circe, Medea
epic: **5** Iliad **7** Odyssey
essence: **5** ousia
fabulist: **5** Aesop
Fate: **6** Clotho **7** Atropos **8** Lachesis
festival: **5** delia, haloa **8** Apaturia
flask: **4** olpe
fleet commander: **7** navarch
flute: **7** hemiope
folk dance: **7** romaika
foot-race course: **6** stadia (pl.) **7** diaulos, stadium
foot soldier: **7** hoplite
Fury: **6** Alecto, Erinys **7** Erinyes, Megaera **9** Tisiphone
galley: **6** bireme **7** trireme, unireme
garment: **5** tunic **6** abolla, chiton, peplos, peplus **7** chlamys
giant: **4** Otus **5** Mimas **7** Aloadae **9** Enceladus, Ephialtes
gift: **6** xenium
god: Dis, Pan **4** Ares, Eros, Zeus **5** Hades, Momus, Pluto, satyr **6** Aeolus, Apollo, Cronus, Hermes, Kronos, Nereus, Triton **7** Bacchus **8** Dionysus, Poseidon
goddess: Ara, Ate, Eos, Not, Nyx, Ops **4** Alea, Dice, Dike, Enyo, Gaea, Gaia, Hebe, Hera, Leto, Nike **5** Horae, Irene, Metis, Moera, Niobe, Vesta **6** Athena, Eirene,

Hecate, Hekate, Hestia, Selena, Selene, Semele **7** Ariadne, Artemis, Astarte, Demeter, Eunomia, Nemesis **9** Aphrodite **10** Persephone
Gorgon: **4** Enyo **5** Deino **6** Graeae, Graiae, Medusa, Stheno **7** Euryale **8** Pephredo
governor: **6** eparch
gymnasium: **4** xyst **9** palaestra
hero: **4** Aias, Ajax, Idas **5** Jason **7** Cecrops, Perseus, Theseus **8** Achilles, Heracles, Odysseus
historian: **7** Ctesias **8** Polybius, Xenophon **9** Herodotus **10** Thucydides
hobgoblin: **6** Empusa
hunter: **5** Orion
huntress: **7** Artemis **8** Atalanta
instrument: **5** aulos **8** barbiton
jar: **7** amphora
judge: **6** dikast **7** heliast
jug: **5** ascos
king: **5** Minos **6** Nestor **9** Agamemnon
lawgiver: **5** Draco, Minos, Solon
legislative council: **5** boule
letters: chi, eta, phi, psi, rho, tau **4** beta, iota, zeta **5** alpha, delta, gamma, kappa, omega, sigma, theta **6** lambda **7** epsilon, omicron, upsilon
lover: **7** Rhoecus
lyre player: **5** Arion **6** Apollo
man of brass: **5** Talos
marker: **5** stela, stele
market place: **5** agora
marriage: **5** gamos
mathematician: **6** Euclid **10** Archimedes
measure: pik **4** bema, piki, pous **5** baril, cados, chous, cubit, diote, doron, pekhe, pygon, xylon **6** acaena, bachel, bacile, barile, cotula, dichas, hemina, koilon, lichas, milion, orgyia, palame, pechys, schene, xestes **7** amphora, choemix, cyathos, diaulos, hekteus, metreta, stadion, stadium, stremma **8** condylos, daktylos, dekapode, dolichos, medimnys, palaiste, plethron, spithame, stathmos **9** hemiekton, oxybaphon
monster: **5** Hydra
musical interval: **6** ditone, meseme
musical note: **4** mese, nete
musical system: **5** neume
mustard: **6** sinapi
nymph: **5** Oread **8** Arethusa
official: **6** archon
overseer: **5** ephor
paradise: **7** Elysium
patriarch: **5** Arius
patriot: **6** klepht
people: **5** demos **6** Argive, Cretan, Ionian **7** Hellene, Spartan **8** Athenian
philosopher: **4** Zeno **5** Galen, Plato **6** Thales **8** Diogenes, Socrates **9** Aristotle **10** Pythagoras

physician: **5** Galen **11** Hippocrates

pilaster: **4** anta

pillar: **5** stela, stele

pitcher: **4** olla, olpe **8** oenochoe

platform: **4** bema **6** logeum

poem: **5** Iliad **7** Odyssey

poet: Ion **5** Arion, Homer **6** Pindar **9** Aeschylus, Euripides, Simonides, Sophocles

poetess: **5** Sapho **6** Sappho **7** Corinna

portico: **4** stoa, xyst

precinct: **7** temenos

priest: **4** papa **5** pater

priestess: **4** Auge, Hero, Iole **8** Caryatid

promontory: **6** Actium

province: **4** nome **5** nomos **7** eparchy

rose: glaieul

sacred place: **6** abaton

sage: **5** Solon **6** Thales **8** Socrates

sanctuary: **5** hiera

sculptor: **5** Myron **7** Phidias

senate: **5** boule

serpent: **4** seps

settler: **5** metic

shield: **5** pelta

ship: **4** saic **5** diota **6** bireme, galley **7** trireme, unireme

shrine: **5** secos, sekos

skeptic: **5** Timon

slave: **5** helot **6** penest

slave woman: **5** Baubo, Iambe

soldier: **5** evzon **7** hoplite, palikar

song: ode **5** melos, paeon

soothsayer: **7** Calchas

sorceress: **5** Circe, Siren

speech: **6** rhesis

statesman: **8** Pericles **9** Aristides **12** Themistocles

statue: **6** xoanon

storm wind: **6** lelaps **7** lealaps

subdivision: **5** phyle

temple: **4** naos **5** cella

theater: **5** odeon, odeum

time: **7** chronos

township: **4** deme

tribal division: **7** phratry

underworld: Dis **5** Hades

vase: **5** dinos

verse: **6** Alcaic

village: obe

wine pitcher: **4** olpe

word: **5** logos

green: new, raw **4** bice, live, verd, vert (F.) **5** cedre, crude, fresh, mossy, verde (Sp.), virid, young **6** callow, recent, unripe **7** untried, verdant **8** blooming, gullible, ignorant, immature, inexpert **9** malachite, undecayed, unskilled, untrained **11** flourishing **13** inexperienced **15** unsophisticated

blue: **4** cyan, saxe **7** sistine **9** turquoise

gray: **5** olive

pale: **7** celadon

shade: **4** lime, nile **5** apple, kelly **6** bottle **7** emerald

woodbine: **7** peridot

yellow: **7** opaline

greenback: **6** dollar **8** frogskin **10** paper money

greenery: **7** verdure

greengage: **4** plum

greenhorn: **4** hick, jake, rube, tyro **6** novice **8** beginner **9** cheechaco, cheechako **10** tenderfoot **12** apple knocker

Greenland: *base:* **4** Etah

discoverer: **10** Eric the Red

Eskimo: Ita

greenlet: **5** vireo

green light: **4** okay **7** go-ahead **8** approval

Green Mansions author: **6** Hudson

Green Mountain Boys' leader: **10** Ethan Allen

Green Mountain State: **7** Vermont

green peak: **10** woodpecker

greenroom: **5** foyer **6** lounge

greens: **5** salad

greenstone: **4** jade **7** diorite **8** nephrite **9** malachite

greensward: **4** turf **5** grass

greet: cry **4** hail **6** accost, salute **7** address, embrace, receive, welcome

greeting: ave, bow **4** hail **5** aloha, hello, salut (Fr.) **6** salute **7** address, welcome **9** reception **10** salutation

gregarious: **6** social **8** friendly, outgoing, sociable **9** convivial, talkative **11** extroverted

gremlin: imp **5** devil, gnome

Grenada: *capital:* **9** St. Georges

currency: **4** cent **6** dollar

Indian: **5** Carib

island: Hog **9** Calivigny, Carriacou **16** Petite Martinique

mountain: **11** St. Catherine

grenade: **4** bomb **5** shell **9** explosive

grenadier: **4** fish **7** rattail, soldier

grenadine: **5** cloth, syrup **6** fabric **9** flavoring

gres: **8** ceramics **9** stoneware

Gretna Green visitor: **6** eloper

Greya's husband: **4** Oder

grid: **5** grate **6** buccan **7** grating, network **8** gridiron

griddle: **5** grill

griddle-cake: **7** crumpet, pancake **8** flapjack

gridiron: **5** field, grill **7** brander, grating, network

grief: woe **4** care, harm, hurt, pain **5** agony, dolor, tears, trial, wrong **6** mishap, regret, sorrow **7** anguish, chagrin, emotion, failure, offense, sadness, trouble **8** disaster, distress, hardship **9** grievance, suffering **10** affliction, desolation **11** lamentation

Grieg: *dancer:* **6** Anitra
work: **8** Peer Gynt

grievance: **4** beef **5** wrong **6** burden, injury **8** gravamen, hardship **9** complaint, injustice **10** affliction, oppression **11** displeasure

grieve: rue **4** pain, pine, sigh, wail, weep **5** mourn, wound **6** bemoan, lament, sadden, sorrow **7** afflict **8** complain, distress

grievous: sad **4** sore **5** heavy, sorry **6** bitter, severe, tragic, woeful **7** heinous, intense, very bad **8** dolorous, shocking **9** atrocious **10** burdensome, calamitous, deplorable, oppressive **11** distressing

griffon: **7** monster **8** Dutch dog

grifter: **5** thief **6** con man **8** swindler **12** rip-off artist
henchman: **5** shill **6** come-on

grigri, gris-gris: **5** charm **6** amulet, fetish **8** talisman

grill, grille: **5** broil, grate **7** grating, griddle **8** gridiron, question **11** interrogate, third-degree **12** cross-examine

grilse: **5** trout **6** salmon **7** botcher

grim: **4** dour, sour **5** angry, bleak, cruel, gaunt, harsh, stern **6** fierce, grisly, horrid, savage, severe, sullen **7** austere, furious, ghastly, hideous, ominous, ragging **8** horrible, pitiless, ruthless, sinister **9** ferocious, frightful, merciless, repellent **10** forbidding, inexorable, relentless, unyielding

grimace: mop, mow, mug **4** face, mock, moue **5** fleer, scowl, smirk, sneer **6** glower **9** make a face

grimalkin: cat, hag **6** feline, she-cat

grime: **4** dirt, smut, soil, soot **5** filth, sully

grimp: **5** climb

grimy: **4** foul **5** dingy, dirty **6** grubby, soiled **7** swarthy

grin: **5** fleer, smile, smirk

grind: rut **4** chaw, chew, grit, mill, mull, whet **5** chafe, chore, crush, gnash, grate, study **6** abrade, crunch, drudge, harass, polish, powder **7** oppress, sharpen **8** bookworm **9** blackfish, comminute, pulverize, triturate

grinder: **4** hero **5** hoagy, molar, tooth **8** sandwich **9** submarine **10** flycatcher

grinding: **7** grating, wearing **10** burdensome, oppressive **12** excruciating

grindle: **6** bowfin

grip: bag **4** hold, vise **5** cinch, clamp, clasp, cleat, grasp, rivet, seize **6** clench, clutch, handle, valise **7** control, grapple, handbag, mastery, satchel **8** handfast, take hold **9** constrict **12** scene-shifter

gripe: **4** beef, carp, fret, kick, rail **5** annoy **6** grouse, harass, squawk **7** grumble, protest **8** complain **9** bellyache

grippe, grip: **4** flue **9** influenza

gripper: **6** nipper

gripping device: dog **4** hand, vise **5** tongs **6** pliers

gripsack: **7** handbag

gris-gris: See grigri

grisly: **4** grim **7** ghastly, hideous **8** dreadful, gruesome, horrible, terrible **10** terrifying

grison: **5** huron **6** weasel

grist: lot **4** malt **5** grain, stint **6** output **8** quantity **9** provision

gristle: **9** cartilage

grit: **4** dirt, guts, sand, soil, soot **5** earth, nerve, pluck **6** gravel **7** bravery, courage **8** backbone, decision, tenacity **12** perseverance

grits: **5** grain **6** hominy

gritty: **4** game **5** sandy **6** plucky **7** arenose, arenous **8** resolute, sabulous **10** persistent

grivet: **6** monkey

grivois: **4** bold, free **5** broad **8** indecent

grizzly: **4** bear **7** grayish

groan: **4** moan **5** creak **6** lament **7** whimper

grog: rum **5** drink **6** liquor **8** beverage

groggery: pub **6** saloon, tavern **7** barroom **8** alehouse

groggy: **5** dazed, foggy, shaky, tipsy, tired **6** sleepy **7** muddled **8** unsteady, wavering **9** tottering

groom: **4** comb, mafu, syce, tend, tidy **5** brush, clean, curry, dress, mafoo, train **7** hostler, marshal, prepare, servant **8** benedict **9** assistant **11** horsekeeper

grooming: **8** toilette

groove: rut **4** dado, rake, slot **5** canal, chase, flute, glyph, regal, rigol, scarf, shaft, stria, sulci(pl.) **6** furrow, gutter, hollow, rabbet, raglet, scrobe, striae(pl.), sulcus **7** channel, striate **10** excavation

groovy: **6** modern **9** excellent, marvelous

grope: **4** feel, poke, test **5** probe **6** fumble, handle **7** examine, fish for, grabble **11** move blindly

grosbeak: **7** warbler **8** hawfinch

gross: big, fat, low, sum **4** bulk, clod, dull, mass, rank, rude **5** amass, broad, brute, bulky, burly, close, crass, crude, dense, heavy, plain, rough, thick, total, whole **6** animal, brutal, coarse, earthy, entire, filthy, greasy, impure, vulgar **7** beastly, brutish, compact, fulsome, general, glaring, massive, obscene, obvious, sensual, swinish, witless **8** cloddish, flagrant, indecent **9** egregious, unlearned, unrefined **10** disgusting, indefinite, indelicate, scurrilous

grotesque: **5** antic, eerie, weird **7** baroque, bizarre **8** fanciful **9** fantastic, ludicrous, whimsical **11** incongruous **12** preposterous

grotto: den **4** cave, grot, hole **5** crypt, speos, vault **6** cavern, recess

grouch: **4** crab, sulk **5** crank, scold **6** grouse **7** grumble **8** complain, sourpuss **10** crosspatch

ground: **4** base, dirt, fund, land, root, soil **5** earth, field, train **6** bottom, estate, reason **7** country, premise, terrain **8** initiate **9** establish, territory **10** foundation, fundamenta (pl.) **11** fundamentum
break: dig **4** plow **8** excavate **12** start to build
gain: **8** progress **9** move ahead
give: **5** yield **7** retreat
kinds of: bog, lot **4** acre, farm, moor, park, plat **5** arada, glebe, marsh, patch, range, swale, tilth **6** calade, maiden, meadow, reseau **7** cripple, curragh, pasture
raised: **5** ridge **7** hillock, hummock

groundhog: **6** marmot **9** woodchuck

Groundhog Day: **9** Candlemas

groundless: **4** idle **5** false **8** baseless **9** unfounded **10** gratuitous **11** unwarranted

groundnut: **5** chufa, gobbe **6** goober, peanut

ground pine: iva

grounds: **4** lees **5** basis, dregs, grout **6** bottom **8** sediment **9** settlings
college: **6** campus
military: **4** base, camp, fort **8** presidio **11** reservation

ground squirrel: **6** gopher, marmot **8** chipmunk **9** woodchuck **10** prairie dog

groundwork: **4** base, root **5** basis **6** bottom, fundus **7** support **8** planning, practice, training **10** foundation **11** preparation **12** underpinning

group: lot, mob, set **4** bevy, gang, herd, mass, ring, sect, team **5** batch, brood, cabal, class, clump, drove, firca, flock, genus, horde, party, squad, suite, tribe **6** bundle, clique, family, galaxy, gather, nation **7** arrange, cluster, collect, company, consort **8** assemble, assembly, classify, division **10** assemblage, assortment, collection, congregate **11** aggregation
pert. to: **7** generic

grouper: **4** fish, hind, mero **5** guasa

groupies: **4** fans **9** followers, hangers-on

group together: **4** band, meet **7** cluster **8** assemble

grouse: **5** gripe, quail **6** gorhen, grouch, repine **7** cheeper, gorcock, grumble **8** complain, pheasant, squealer **9** gelinotte, ptarmigan **10** whitebelly **12** capercaillie

grout: **5** dregs **6** mortar **7** grounds, plaster

grouty: **5** cross, sulky **6** sullen

grove: **4** bush, tope, wood **5** copse, hurst, lucus (L.) **6** pinery **7** boscage, boskage, coppice, thicket
pert. to: **7** nemoral

grovel: **4** fawn **5** crawl, toady **6** cringe, kowtow, wallow **7** truckle **9** be servile

groveling: **6** abject **7** hangdog **12** contemptible

grow: age, bud, get, wax **4** come, eche, rise **5** edify, raise, swell **6** accrue, batten, become, expand, extend, thrive **7** augment, develop, distend, enlarge, improve, nourish **8** develope, flourish, increase **9** cultivate **10** accumulate
old: age **5** ripen **6** mature **7** senesce

grower: **6** farmer, raiser **7** rancher **10** orchardist **13** agriculturist **15** arboriculturist

growl: **4** gnar, gurr **5** gnarl, snarl **6** mutter, rumble **7** grumble

grown: **5** adult, risen **6** mature **8** expanded

grownup: man **5** adult, woman

growth: wen **4** cyst, mole, rise, wart **5** swell, tumor **7** stature **8** increase, swelling **9** accretion, expansion, heterosis, keratosis **11** development, enlargement **12** augmentation
in clusters: **8** racemose
on another: **8** parasite
on surface: **9** epigenous
organic: **9** accretion
promoting: **8** nutrient **9** nutriment
retarding: **9** paratonic

grub: bob, dig, eat **4** chow, feed, food, moot, plod, root **5** dwarf, larva, stump **6** drudge, larvae(pl.), maggot, search **7** plodder **8** victuals

grubby: **5** dirty, grimy, small **8** dwarfish, slovenly

grudge: **4** envy **5** pique, spite **6** malice, rancor **10** resentment

grue: **6** shiver **7** shudder

gruel: **4** mush **5** atole **6** burgoo, crowdy **8** porridge

grueling: **4** hard **6** brutal, tiring **7** racking **9** fatiguing, punishing

gruesome: **4** ugly **6** grisly, horrid, sordid **7** fearful, ghastly, hideous, macabre **8** horrible

gruff: **4** curt, rude, sour **5** bluff, harsh, rough, short, surly **6** abrupt, hoarse, morose, severe, sullen **7** brusque, crabbed **8** churlish

grumble: **4** crab, fuss, kick **5** bitch, croak, growl, snarl **6** grouch, grouse, repine, rumble, squawk, yammer **8** begrudge, complain

grumpy: **5** cross, moody, surly

grungy: **5** dirty **10** uncared for

grunt: **4** fish **5** groan, snork, snort

guacharo: **7** fatbird, oilbird

guaiol: **7** alcohol

Guam: *capital:* **5** Agana
people: **8** Chamorro
port: **4** Apra

guanay: 9 cormorant
guanaco: 5 llama 6 alpaca
  relative: 5 camel
guar: 4 bean
guarantee: 4 bail, band, bond, seal 6 assure, avouch, ensure, insure, surety 7 certify, endorse, hostage, warrant 8 guaranty, security, warranty 9 assurance, vouchsafe
guarantor: 5 angel 6 backer, patron 7 sponsor 11 underwriter
guarapucu: 4 fish, peto 5 wahoo
guard: 4 care, curb, herd, hold, keep, rail, tend, ward 5 bless, fence, hedge, watch 6 bantay, bridle, convey, custos, defend, dragon, escort, fender, gaoler, jailer, keeper, patrol, police, sentry, shield, warden 7 keeping, lineman, protect 8 conserve, preserve, restrain, security, sentinel, watchman 9 attention, custodian, protector 10 cowcatcher, protection
  foil: 6 button
  line of: 6 cordon
  on: 4 wary 5 alert, ready 8 vigilant, watchful 9 observant
guarded: 4 wary 6 manned 7 careful 8 cautious, defended, discreet 9 protected 11 circumspect
guardhouse: 4 brig 5 clink 6 prison 8 hoosegow
guardian: 6 keeper, parent, pastor, patron, warden 7 curator 8 defender, watchdog 9 custodian, protector
  church relics: 10 mystagogue
  heavenly: 5 angel
  legal: 7 trustee
  pert. to: 7 tutelar 8 tutelary
  subject of: 4 ward
  watchful: 5 Argus 8 Cerberus
guardianship: 4 care 5 trust 7 custody, keeping, tuition 8 tutelage
guasa: 7 grouper, jewfish

Guatemala: *capital:* 13 Guatemala City
  city: 5 Coban 6 Flores, Jalapa, Salama, Solola 7 Antigua, Jutiapa 9 Escuintla, Tiquisate 16 Chichicastenango
  currency: 7 centavo, quetzal
  Indian: 4 Itza, Ixil, Maya 5 Xinca
  measure: 4 vara 6 fanega 7 manzana
  river: 5 Dulce 7 Motagua 8 Polochic, Sarstoon 10 Usumacinta
  volcano: 4 Agua 5 Fuego 7 Atitlan

Guaycuruan Indian: 4 Toba
gudgeon: pin 4 bait, fish, lure 5 pivot 6 burbot, socket
Gudrun: *brother:* 6 Gunnar
  husband: 4 Atli

guenon: 4 mona 6 grivet, monkey
guerdon: 6 reward 8 requital 10 recompense
guerrilla: 8 partisan 11 bush fighter
guess: aim 4 shot 5 fancy, infer, think 6 assume, deduce, divine 7 believe, imagine, opinion, presume, surmise, suspect 8 estimate 9 speculate 10 conjecture
guest: 6 caller, inmate, lodger, patron, roomer 7 boarder, visitor
guesthouse: inn 5 hotel, motel 11 caravansary
guff: lip 4 sass 5 hooey 6 humbug 7 hogwash 8 backtalk, claptrap, nonsense 10 balderdash
guffaw: 4 howl 6 heehaw 10 belly laugh, horselaugh
guidance: 4 helm, help 6 advice 7 auspice, conduct, counsel 8 steerage 9 direction 10 leadership, management 11 instruction
guide: 4 airt, buoy, clue, lead, pole, rein, rule, show 5 model, pilot, reign, steer, teach, treat, tutor, usher 6 beacon, bridle, convey, convoy, direct, escort, govern, leader, manage 7 conduce, conduct, control, marshal, teacher 8 director, instruct, landmark, polestar, regulate, shepherd, textbook 9 catechism, conductor, itinerary, prescribe, regulator 10 instructor 11 superintend 12 show the way to
guidebook: 8 baedeker 9 itinerary 11 tourist's aid
guided missile: V1, V2, AAM, ABM, ASM, ATA, Bat, SAM, SSM, TOW 4 Azon, Hawk, ICBM, IRBM, Lark, Loki, Loon, Nike, SLBM, Thor, Zuni 5 Atlas, drone, Snark, Titan 6 Ariane, Bomarc, Exocet, Falcon, Redeye, Viking 7 Bullpup, Patriot, Polaris, Terrier, Tiny Tim, Trident 8 Hellfire, Redstone, Silkworm, Tomahawk 9 Minuteman 10 Copperhead, Sidewinder
guideway: 4 slot 5 track 7 channel
Guido: *fifth note:* sol
  first note: ut
  fourth note: fa
  high note: la
  highest note: 4 ela
  second note: re
  third note: mi
guild: 4 club 5 order, union 6 league 7 society 8 alliance, sodality 10 fellowship 11 association, brotherhood
guile: 4 wile 5 cheat, craft, fraud 6 deceit, humbug 7 cunning 9 duplicity, treachery
guileful: 4 foxy, wily 6 crafty, shifty, tricky 7 cunning, devious 9 deceitful, insidious 10 fallacious, fraudulent 13 Machiavellian
guileless: 5 naive 6 candid, honest 7 artless 8 innocent 9 ingenuous
guillemot: auk 4 loon, quet 5 murre 7 dovekey, dovekie

guillotine: 6 behead 10 decapitate
wagon for: 7 tumbrel, tumbril
guilt: sin 5 blame, culpa, fault, shame 6 piacle 7 offense 8 iniquity 10 wickedness 11 criminality, culpability
guiltless: 4 pure 5 clean 8 innocent 9 blameless, righteous
guilty: 6 nocent, wicked 7 correal 8 culpable
guinea fowl: 4 keet
guinea pig: 4 cavy
Guinea, Republic of: *capital:* 7 Conakry
city: 4 Boke, Labe, Pita 5 Fouta 6 Kankan 7 Dubreka
currency: 4 kori, syli
people: 4 Fula, Peul 5 Sopso 7 Malinke
river: 4 Milo 5 Niger 6 Bafing, Gambia 7 Senegal 8 Konkoure
Guinevere's husband: 6 Arthur
guise: hue 4 form, garb, mask, mien 5 cloak, cover, dress, habit, shape 6 aspect, attire, deceit, manner 7 arrange, fashion 8 behavior, likeness, practice 9 semblance 10 appearance, masquerade
guitar: uke 5 sitar, tiple 6 sancho 7 cittern, ukulele 8 chitarra 10 calascione
guitarlike instrument: 4 lute, rota 6 citole 7 bandore, pandora, samisen 8 mandolin
half step in pitch: 5 dital
key: 5 dital
of India: 4 vina 5 sitar
part: 4 fret 6 bridge, pickup, string 7 peg head 9 sound hole, tuning key 11 finger board
pick: 8 plectrum
play: 5 pluck, strum
small: 7 ukulele
style of playing: 10 bottleneck
guitguit: 4 bird 6 pitpit
gula, gulae (pl.): 4 cyma, ogee 6 gullet, throat 7 molding
gulch: 5 gorge, gully 6 arroyo, canyon, coulee, ravine, valley
gulf: arm, bay, gap 4 cove, eddy 5 abyss, bayou, chasm, firth, inlet 6 vorago 9 barathrum, whirlpool 10 separation
noted: 4 Aden, Oman, Riga 5 Maine 6 Alaska, Guinea, Mexico, Tonkin 7 Arabian, Bothnia, Finland, Persian 8 Amundsen, Thailand 10 California 13 Saint Lawrence
Gulf States: 5 Texas 7 Alabama, Florida 9 Louisiana 11 Mississippi
gull: mew 4 dupe, fool, tern 5 cheat, larid 6 sucker, teaser, victim 7 cheater, deceive, defraud, fall guy, mislead 8 dotterel, hoodwink 9 bamboozle, kittiwake 10 mountebank
kinds of: cob 4 skua 5 allan, annet, pewit 6 larine, teaser, waggel 11 burgomaster
pert. to: 6 larine, laroid

gullet: maw 6 throat 9 esophagus
gullible: 5 green, naive 9 credulous
Gulliver's Travels: *author:* 5 Swift
flying island: 6 Laputa
human beast: 5 Yahoo
island kingdom: 8 Lilliput
gully: 5 gorge, gulch 6 arroyo, gutter, ravine, valley 7 couloir 11 watercourse, knife (Sc.)
gulp: 4 bolt, glut, swig 5 swill 6 gobble, guzzle 7 swallow
gum: 4 clog, hive, kino 5 cheat, nyssa, stick, trick 6 chicle, gluten, hashab, humbug, impede, tissue, tupelo 7 bilsted, gingiva 8 mucilage 10 eucalyptus 11 masticatory
derivative: 8 bassorin 10 tragacanth, traganthin 12 tragacanthin
kinds of: 4 guar 5 tuart 6 acacia, acacin, arabic, balata, touart 7 acacine, dextrin
resin: 5 elemi, gugal, myrrh 6 salban 9 sagapenum 12 frankincense
gum tree: 5 xylan
gumbo: 4 ocra, okra, soup 7 melange
gumma: 5 tumor
gummy: 6 mastic, sticky 7 viscous 8 adhesive
gumption: 7 courage 8 boldness 10 enterprise, initiative, shrewdness
gums: ula 7 alveoli
pain in: 7 ulalgia
pert. to: 6 uletic 8 gingival
gumshoe: PI, cop, tec 4 dick 5 skulk, sneak 6 sleuth 9 detective, pussyfoot 10 private eye
gun: gat, rod 5 rifle, tommy 6 cannon, heater, pistol, weapon 7 carbine, shotgun 8 revolver 9 matchlock, surfboard 11 blunderbuss
ammunition carrier: 7 caisson
barrel cleaner: 6 ramrod
barrel groove: 7 rifling
kinds of: Uzi 4 bore, bren, roer, sten 5 baril 6 ack-ack, archie, barker, mortar 7 aerogun, bazooka 8 amusette 9 automatic
large: 6 cannon 9 artillery
mount: 6 tripod, turret
part: pin 4 bolt, bore, butt, grip, lock 5 frame, sight, stock 6 barrel, breech, hammer, muzzle, rammer, safety 7 trigger
platform: 11 emplacement
science: 10 ballistics
size: 7 caliber
gunfire: 4 rake, shot 5 salvo 6 strafe, volley 7 barrage 8 enfilade 9 fusillade
gunman: 6 killer 7 torpedo 8 assassin
gunner: 6 sniper 7 shooter 8 marksman, rifleman 9 cannoneer 10 bombardier 12 artilleryman
gunny: tat 4 jute 6 burlap
Gunther's uncle: 5 Hagen
gurgle: 5 plash 6 babble, burble 7 sputter
Gurkha's sword: 5 kukri

gurnard: 4 fish 8 dragonet, sea robin
guru: 5 guide 7 teacher 9 maharishi
gush: 4 flow, pour, teem 5 issue, smarm, spate, spout, spurt 6 effuse, stream 10 outpouring
gushing: 7 mawkish, prating 8 effusive, unctuous 10 blabbering, flattering
gusset: 4 gore 5 brace 6 insert
gust: 4 puff, scud, waft, wind 5 blast, draft, whiff 6 flurry, squall 8 outburst, paroxysm 9 explosion
gusto: 4 elan, zest 5 taste 6 fervor, liking, relish 7 delight, passion 8 pleasure 9 enjoyment 12 appreciation
gusty: 5 windy 6 savory, stormy 7 squally 8 agitated 11 tempestuous
gut: 5 belly, clean 6 paunch, ravage 7 plunder, stamina, stomach 9 bay window 10 disembowel, eviscerate
gutsy: 4 bold 5 brave, nervy 6 spunky 8 fearless, intrepid 9 audacious 10 courageous
gutta: 8 ornament
gutta-percha: 5 latex 6 balata
gutter: 5 ditch, gully, siver (Sc.) 6 groove, trench, trough 7 channel, scupper 11 watercourse
guttural: 4 deep 5 burry, harsh, velar 7 rasping, throaty
guy: kid, man, rod 4 josh, rope, stay, twit 5 cable, chain, guide, spoof, tease 6 decamp, fellow, gazabo, gazebo, person 8 ridicule
  give the guy to (Br.): 4 jeer 6 escape 8 ridicule
guy rope: 4 stay, vang
Guyana: *capital:* 10 Georgetown
  city: 6 Enmore, Linden, Suddie 7 Bartica, Charity 9 Mackenzie 10 Enterprise 12 New Amsterdam
  currency: 4 cent 6 dollar
  river: 6 Cuyuni, Potaro 7 Berbice 8 Demerara, Mazaruni 9 Essequibo 10 Courantyne

guzzle: 4 bolt, gulp, swig 5 drink, quaff, swill 6 devour, tipple 7 toss off
gymnast: 6 turner 7 acrobat, athlete, tumbler 8 balancer
gymnastic: *equipment:* mat 4 bars 5 rings 11 balance beam, pommel horse
  stunt: kip 4 flip 5 vault 9 handstand, headstand 10 handspring, headspring
  swing 7 trapeze
gyp: 5 cheat, steal, sting 6 diddle, rip off 7 defraud, sharper, swindle 8 swindler 9 trickster 10 overcharge
gypsum: 4 geso 6 parget 8 selenite 9 alabaster
  resembling: 11 alabastrine
gypsy, gipsy: 4 calo 5 caird, nomad 6 gitana, gitano, roamer 7 cziqany, tzigany, zincala, zincalo, zingana, zingano, zingara, zingaro 8 Bohemian, brunette, wanderer, zigeuner
  ancestral home: 5 India
  boy: 4 chal
  camp: tan
  dance: 10 zingaresca
  devil: 4 beng
  dialect: 6 Romany 7 Rommany
  fortune: 4 bahi
  gentleman: rye
  girl: chi 4 chai
  horse: gri, gry
  husband: rom
  nongypsy: 4 gajo
  paper: lil
  Syrian: 5 Aptal
  thief: 4 chor
  village: gav
  wife: 4 romi
gyrate: 4 spin, turn 5 twirl, whirl 6 rotate 7 revolve
gyrator: top
gyre: 4 ring 6 circle, vortex 7 circuit 10 revolution
gyrfalcon: 6 jerkin
gyve: 4 iron 5 chain 6 fetter 7 shackle

H

H: 5 aitch 8 aspirate
   sound of: 8 aspirate
H-shaped: 5 zygal
habeas corpus: 4 writ
haberdashery: hat 5 shirt, socks 6 gloves 7 necktie 8 menswear
habile: 4 able 6 adroit, clever, expert 8 skillful
habiliment (see also **dress, gown**): 4 garb 5 habit 6 attire 7 apparel, clothes, costume, raiment 8 clothing, equipage, fittings, ornament, vestment 9 billiment, equipment, faculties 11 furnishings
habilitate: 5 dress, equip, train 6 clothe, outfit 7 educate
habit (see also **dress**): rut, use 4 coat, garb, gown, suit, vice, wont 5 array, guise, haunt, thews, usage 6 attire, clothe, custom, estate, groove 7 bearing, clothes, costume, garment, pattern, routine 8 demeanor, practice, tendency 9 addiction 10 consuetude 11 disposition
habitant: 7 dweller 10 inhabitant
habitat: 4 home 5 abode, house, range 6 patria 7 station 8 locality 11 environment
habitation: 4 home, tent 5 abode, house, hovel, igloo 6 colony, harbor, warren 7 lodging, domicile 8 dwelling, lodgings, quarters, tenement 9 community, chaumiere (F.), occupancy, residence 10 settlement
habitual: 5 usual 6 common, hectic 7 regular, routine 8 familiar, frequent, ordinary 9 customary 10 accustomed, inveterate
habituate: use 5 enure, inure 6 addict, season 8 accustom, frequent 9 acclimate 11 acclimatize, familiarize
habitude: 5 habit 6 custom 11 familiarity
habitué: 6 patron 7 denizen 8 customer 10 frequenter
hachure: 4 line, mark 7 shading
hacienda: 4 farm 5 ranch 6 estate 10 plantation 13 establishment
   proprietor: 9 hacendado
hack: cab, cut, hag, hew 4 chop, taxi 5 coach, cough 6 drudge, fiacre, haggle, mangle 7 butcher, chatter, stammer, stutter 8 carriage, mutilate 9 mercenary
hackee: 8 chipmunk
hackle: 4 bait, comb 6 mangle 7 plumage 8 feathers

hackly: 5 rough 6 broken, jagged
hackney: nag 4 hack, pony 5 horse, noddy 8 carriage
hackneyed: old 4 worn 5 banal, stale, trite 6 cliché, common 7 worn out 8 outdated 10 threadbare 11 commonplace, stereotyped

---

Hades: Dis, pit 4 hell 5 Orcus, Sheol 7 Gehenna, inferno 8 Tartarus 11 netherworld
   god: 5 Pluto
   guard: 8 Cerberus
   inhabitant of: 7 hellion
   lake to: 7 Avernus
   mother: 4 Rhea
   pert. to: 7 sheolic 8 infernal
   river: 4 Styx 5 Lethe 7 Acheron

---

hadj, hajj: 10 pilgrimage
haff: 6 lagoon
haft: 6 handle
hag: bog, cut 4 bogy, hack, wood 5 copse, crone, demon, ghost, marsh, notch, rudas (Sc.), witch 6 beldam, goblin, harass, spirit 7 beldame, fatigue, pasture, terrify 8 harridan, quagmire 9 cailleach, cailliach, enclosure, hobgoblin
Hagar's son: 7 Ishmael
hagdon: 6 fulmar 7 seabird 10 shearwater
hagfish: 5 borer
haggard: 4 bony, lank, lean, pale, thin, wild, worn 5 drawn, gaunt, spare 6 wasted 7 anxious, untamed 8 careworn, harrowed 9 exhausted, suffering 10 cadaverous
Haggard novel: She
   heroine: 6 Ayesha
haggle: cut, hew 4 deal, hack, prig 5 cavil 6 badger, barter, chisel, dicker, higgle, huckle, palter, scotch 7 bargain, chaffer, dispute, stickle, wrangle 8 beat down
haggler: 6 dodger 8 huckster
hagioscope: 6 squint 7 opening
hagride: 6 harass, obsess 7 oppress, torment
hail: ave 4 ahoy, call, goal 5 greet, sleet, sound, whole 6 accost, health, salute 7 address, fortune, graupel 8 greeting 10 salutation 13 precipitation
hailer: 8 bullhorn

hair: fax, fur **4** barb, coma, mane, shag **5** crine, tress **6** crinet, nicety, trifle **7** bristle, whisker **8** capillus, filament, finespun **9** chevelure
accessory: **8** barrette
Angora goat: **6** mohair
braid: **5** plait, queue **7** pigtail
coarse: **4** kemp, seta, shag **7** bristle
curl: **4** lock **7** ringlet
disease: **8** dandruff, psilosis
dye: **5** henna
excessive: **7** pilosis
facial: **5** beard **6** goatee **7** Vandyke **8** whiskers **9** moustache, sideburns
false: rat, wig **6** peruke, switch, toupee **7** periwig
fringe: **5** bangs **8** frisette, frizette
grooming aid: **4** comb **5** brush **6** pomade
having: **6** pilose **7** barbate, hirsute, villous **8** crinated
horse: **4** mane **5** seton **7** fetlock
intestinal: **6** villus
knot: bun **7** chignon
lock: **4** curl **5** tress **7** cowlick
loss: **8** alopecia, baldness
ornament: bow **4** comb **5** tiara **6** ribbon **7** coronet **8** barrette
pert. to: **6** crinal
plant: **6** villus
remover: **5** razor **6** shaver **8** epilator **9** depilator, epilatory **10** depilatory
roll: **4** puff **5** twist **7** chignon **9** pompadour
short: **6** setula, setule
soft: **4** down **6** villus
unruly: mop **6** tousle **7** cowlick
white: **4** snow
hairbrained: **5** giddy **7** foolish **8** heedless, volatile
hairbreadth: ace **5** close **10** very narrow
haircloth: aba **6** cilice
haircut: **7** tonsure
hairdo: DA, bob **4** afro, glib (Ir.), perm **5** braid, plait, wedge **6** bubble, marcel **7** beehive, crew cut, page-boy, pigtail, shingle **8** bouffant, coiffeur, duck-tail, ponytail **9** pompadour
hairdresser: **6** barber **7** friseur **8** coiffeur **9** coiffeuse **10** beautician **13** cosmetologist
hairless: **4** bald **8** depilous
hairnet: **5** snood
hairpin: **4** bend **6** bodkin **8** bobbypin
hair-raising: **4** eery **5** eerie, scary, weird **10** terrifying
hairy: **5** bushy **6** comate, comous, pilose, shaggy **7** bristly, crinite, hirsute **9** dangerous, difficult, harrowing
Haiti: *capital:* **12** Port-au-Prince
city: **5** Cayes **8** Gonaives **10** Port-de-Paix
currency: **6** gourde **7** centime

discoverer: **8** Columbus
liberator: **9** Toussaint **10** Dessalines
location: **10** Hispaniola
river: **10** Artibonite
hajj: See **hadj**
hake: **4** fish, idle **5** tramp **6** loiter, trudge
halberd: **6** weapon **8** battle-ax
halcyon: **4** bird, calm **5** happy, quiet **6** golden **8** affluent, peaceful, tranquil **9** unruffled **10** kingfisher, prosperous
Halcyone: *father:* **6** Aeolus
husband: **4** Ceyx
hale: **5** sound **6** hearty, robust, strong, summon **7** healthy **8** vigorous
Halevy opera: **5** Juive
half: **6** moiety **7** partial, portion
halfbeak: ihi **5** balao
half breed: **5** metis **6** mustee **7** mestiza, mestizo, mulatta, mulatto **8** octoroon, quadroon
half circumference: **10** semicircle
half diameter: **6** radius
halfhearted: **4** cold, cool, tame **5** faint, tepid **8** listless, lukewarm **10** spiritless **11** indifferent
half-man: **4** faun **6** garuda **7** centaur **8** minotaur
half mask: **4** loup **6** domino
half-month: **9** fortnight
half-moon: **8** crescent **9** semilunar
figure: **4** lune
half-turn: **8** caracole
halfway: mid **6** almost, middle, nearly **7** midmost, partial **8** midpoint **9** partially **11** equidistant
half-wit: **4** dolt **5** dunce, idiot, moron **8** imbecile **9** blockhead
half-witted: **4** dull **5** dotty, silly **7** foolish **9** senseless
Halicarnassian: **9** Dionysius, Herodotus
halicore: **6** dugong, sea cow **7** manatee
Halifax citizen: **10** Haligonian
halite: **4** salt **8** rock salt
hall: **4** aula, room, saal (G.) **5** entry, foyer, lobby, manor, odeon, odeum, salle **6** atrium, durbar, saloon **7** chamber, gallery, hallway, passage **8** anteroom, corridor **9** vestibule **10** auditorium, misericord, passageway **11** misericorde
music: **4** gaff **5** odeon, odeum
reception: **5** salon **6** parlor
student residence: **4** dorm **5** bursa **9** dormitory
halloo: **5** greet, shout **6** accost
hallow: **5** bless **8** dedicate **10** consecrate
hallowed: **4** holy **6** sacred **7** blessed
hallowed place: **4** fane **5** altar **6** bethel, chapel, church, shrine, temple **9** cathedral, sanctuary, synagogue
hallucination: d.t.s **5** dream **6** mirage, vision

7 chimera, fantasy **8** delirium, delusion, illusion **10** apparition

hallux: 6 big toe

halo: arc **4** glow, nimb **5** glory **6** areola, areole, brough (Sc.), circle, corona, nimbus **7** areola, aureole **8** cincture, gloriole

halogen: 6 iodine **7** bromine **8** chlorine, cyanogen, fluorine

haloperidal: 10 depressant **12** tranquilizer

halothane: 10 anesthetic

halt: hop **4** bait, lame, limp, stem, stop **5** cease, hilch, hitch, pause, stand, **6** arrest, desist, docked, **7** limping **8** lameness, stoppage **9** cessation, mutilated, terminate

halter: 4 rope **5** leash, noose, strap, widdy **6** bridle, hamper **8** cavesson, restrain **9** hackamore

halting: 4 lame **7** limping **8** spavined **9** defective **10** hesitating **11** vacillating

ham: pig **4** hock, pork **5** actor, thigh **7** amateur, overact

Ham: *brother:* **4** Shem **7** Japheth
  father: **4** Noah
  son: **4** Cush **6** Canaan
  son's land: **8** Ethiopia

hamadryad: 5 nymph **6** baboon

hamate: 6 curved, hooked **7** hamular **8** hamiform

Hamilcar: 5 Barca **7** general **12** Carthaginian
  conquest: **5** Spain
  home: **8** Carthage
  son: **8** Hannibal

Hamite: *father:* **4** Abel
  language: **4** Afar, Agao, Beja **5** Belin, Galla **6** Berber, Kabyle, Shilha, Somali, Zenaga **8** Cushitic, Numidian, Tamashek **9** Ethiopian, Gaetulian **11** Mauretanian
  people: **4** Beja, Bogo **5** Fulah, Oromo **6** Berber, Fulani, Gallas, Somali

hamlet: 4 dorp, town **5** aldea (Sp.), casal, hamel, moray, vicus (L.) **6** bustee, casale (It.), thorpe **7** clachan (Sc.), village **10** settlement

Hamlet: *beloved:* **7** Ophelia
  castle: **8** Elsinore
  character: **7** Laertes, Ophelia **8** Gertrude, Polonius **11** Rosencrantz **12** Guildenstern
  country: **7** Denmark
  dramatist: **11** Shakespeare
  friend: **7** Horatio
  mother: **8** Gertrude
  slayer: **7** Laertes
  uncle: **8** Claudius
  victim: **7** Laertes **8** Claudius, Polonius

hammer: bit, hit, tup **4** beat, claw, jack, maul, mell, reel, tack, tamp **5** gavel **6** batter, beetle, mallet, martel, pummel, sledge, strike, swinge **7** belabor **8** malleate **11** doorknocker

blacksmith's: **6** fuller, oliver
bricklayer's: **6** scutch
face: **4** trip
firearm: **4** cock **7** doghead
half-round: **6** fuller
head: **4** peen, poll
medical: **6** plexor **7** plessor
stone: **5** kevel, spall
type: air **4** claw, tack **6** sledge **8** ball peen **9** pneumatic

hammerhead: 5 shark **8** numskull **9** hog sucker

hammock: 5 swing **7** machila

hamper: bin, ped **4** beat, clog, curb, load, slow **5** block, cramp, crate, rusky (Sc.), seron (Sp.) **6** basket, burden, fetter, halter, hinder, hopple, impede, panier **7** buffalo, confine, hanaper, manacle, pannier, perplex, shackle, trammel **8** encumber, entangle, obstruct, restrain, restrict **9** container, embarrass

hamstring: hox **4** hock, lame **5** hough **6** hinder, impair **7** cripple, disable

Hananiah: *father:* **4** Azur
  son: **8** Zedekiah

hand: fin, paw, pud **4** claw, give, mano, mitt, neif, pass **5** claut (Sc.), grasp, nieve, power, share **6** clunch, daddle, famble, pledge, worker **7** ability, flipper, forepaw, laborer, proffer, workman **8** applause, bestowal, transmit **9** betrothal, craftsman, indicator, operative, signature **11** handwriting
  back: **10** opisthenar
  by: **8** manually
  clenched: **4** fist
  covering: **4** mitt, muff **5** glove **6** cestus (L.), mitten **7** gantlet **8** gauntlet
  deformity: **11** talipomanus
  down: **8** bequeath
  hollow: **6** gowpen, gowpin
  on hip: **6** akimbo
  palm: **6** thenar
  part: **4** nail, palm **5** digit, thumb, wrist **7** cuticle, fingers, knuckle
  pert. to: **6** manual
  poker: **4** pair **5** flush **8** straight **9** full house **10** royal flush
  without: **7** amanous

handbag: bag **4** etui, grip **5** cabas, etwee, pouch, purse **6** clutch, valise **7** satchel **8** gripsack, pochette, reticule **10** minaudiere, pocketbook

handball: *game:* **6** pelota **7** jai alai
  point: ace

handbarrow: 4 bier **8** hand cart

handbill: 5 flyer, libel **6** dodger, notice, poster **7** leaflet **8** circular, pamphlet **13** advertisement

handbook: 6 manual **9** guidebook **11** enchiridion

handcar: 6 gocart 7 go-devil

handcloth: 5 towel 6 napkin 12 handkerchief

handcuff: 4 cuff, iron 5 darby 6 nipper 7 manacle, shackle 8 bracelet, handbolt, handlock, restrain

Handel: *composition:* 5 Largo
opera: 4 Nero 6 Almira, Xerxes 7 Rodrigo 8 Berenice 9 Agrippina
oratorio: 4 Saul 6 Esther 7 Jephtha, Messiah

handful: 4 grip, wisp 5 claut, gripe 6 gowpen, gowpin, yaffle 7 maniple, problem 8 quantity

handicap: bar, law 4 edge, even, lame, lisp, odds 6 burden, hinder, impede 7 stammer, stutter 8 drawback, encumber 9 advantage, embarrass, head start 12 disadvantage

handicapper: 5 rater

handicraft: art 5 trade 6 metier 8 vocation

handicraft goddess: 7 Minerva

handicraftsman: 6 carver, potter, weaver 7 artisan, workman 9 craftsman

handiwork: tat 7 sampler 10 embroidery

handjar: 5 knife 6 dagger 7 khanjar

handkerchief: 5 clout, fogle, hanky 6 madras 7 bandana, belcher, sneezer 9 barcelona, handcloth, muckender, neckcloth 11 neckerchief

handle: ear, fan, lug, nob, paw, ply, use 4 ansa, bail, bool, deal, feel, gaum, grip, haft, hank, hilt, knob, name 5 gripe, grope, helve, lever, shaft, swipe, touch, treat, wield 6 behave, direct, finger, manage 7 act upon, control 8 doorknob, handgrip 10 manipulate
ancient: 4 ansa
bucket: 4 bail, bale
cup: ear
equipped with: 6 ansate
pail: 4 bail
printing press: 6 rounce
pump: 5 brake
scythe: 5 snath, snead, thole 6 snathe
shaped: 6 ansate
sword: 4 haft, hilt
whip: 4 crop

handled: 5 dealt 6 ansate 7 managed

handling: use 4 care 7 control, running 9 treatment 10 management 11 supervision

hand-me-down: 4 used 5 cheap 9 ready-made 10 secondhand

hand mill: 5 quern 7 grinder

hand out: 6 donate 7 present 8 give away 10 administer, distribute

handout: aid 4 alms, dole, food, gift, meal, mete 5 snack 7 charity 8 donation

hand over: 4 ante, cede 5 yield 8 transfer

hand-picked: 5 elite 8 selected

handreading: 9 palmistry

hands: men 4 crew 7 workers 8 pointers

hands off: 4 tabu 5 taboo

handsome: 4 braw (Sc.), fair, fine, pert 5 ample, belle, bonny, handy, ready 6 bonnie, clever, comely, goodly, heppen, limber 7 elegant, gallant, liberal 8 becoming, budgeree, generous, gracious, suitable 9 beautiful, dexterous 10 attractive, convenient, manageable 11 appropriate, good-looking 12 considerable

handspring: 6 tumble 9 cartwheel

handwriting: 4 fist, hand 5 ronde 6 scrawl, script 9 autograph 10 griffonage, manuscript 11 calligraphy, chirography
on the wall: 4 mene 5 tekel 8 graffiti, upharsin
study of: 10 graphology

handy: apt 4 deft, near 5 adept, ready 6 adroit, clever, heppen 7 close-by 8 adjacent, handsome, skillful 9 available, dexterous, versatile 10 accessible, convenient

Handy Andy's catch: 5 Oonah

handyman: 5 fixer 8 factotum, repairer 15 Jack-of-all-trades

hang: lag, lop, sag 4 kilt, loll, pend, rest 5 drape, droop, hinge, knack, lynch, slope, swing 6 append, dangle, depend, gibbet, talter 7 crucify, execute, stretch, suspend 9 declivity 11 inclination
around: 4 loaf 5 hover 6 loiter 8 frequent
back: lag 6 falter 8 hesitate
down: 5 droop 6 dangle 7 suspend
fire: 4 pend 8 hesitate, postpone 13 procrastinate
onto: 5 cling

hangar: 4 shed 6 garage, stable 7 shelter 9 penthouse

hangdog: 4 base 5 cowed 6 shifty 7 ashamed, fawning, furtive 8 cringing, sneaking 9 groveling

hanger-on: bur 5 leech, toady 6 hangby, heeler, sponge 7 adjunct, dangler, slinger, sponger 8 bottomer, loiterer, onsetter, parasite 9 appendage, dependent, sycophant 10 blackguard, free-loader

hanging: 5 arras, drape 6 celure, tippet 7 pendent, pensile, valance 8 inclined 9 declivity, execution, suspended 11 inclination

Hanging Gardens site: 7 Babylon

hangman: 6 hangie 9 Jack Ketch 11 executioner

hangout: bar, pub 4 dive 5 joint 10 rendezvous

hangover: 8 residuum 11 aftereffect 12 katzenjammer (G.)

hang-up: 5 block 6 phobia 8 fixation 9 obsession

hank: 4 coil, loop 5 skein 6 bundle, handle 7 control 9 influence

hanker: yen **4** ache, long **5** crave, yearn **6** desire, hunger, thirst
Hannibal: **7** general
   conqueror: **4** Scipio
   father: **13** Hamilcar Barca
   home: **8** Carthage
   place of victory: **6** Cannae
hansom: cab
hap: lot **4** luck **5** check, occur, seize **6** befall, chance, snatch **7** fortune, venture **9** happening **10** occurrence, prosperity
haphazard: **6** casual, chance, random **8** careless **10** accidental **11** any which way **13** helter-skelter
hapless: **4** poor **7** unlucky **11** starcrossed, unfortunate
happen: **4** come, fall, fare **5** evene, occur **6** arrive, befall, betide, chance, mayhap **7** come off, perhaps, stumble **9** eventuate, transpire
happen again: **5** recur **7** reoccur
happening: hap **4** case, fact **5** event, thing **6** chance, faring **7** episode **8** incident, occasion **10** occurrence
happily: **5** fitly, haply **6** gladly **7** luckily **8** joyously **10** gracefully **11** contendedly, fortunately, opportunely **12** felicitously, peradventure, prosperously, successfully **13** appropriately
happiness: joy **4** glee, sele (Sc.), weal **5** bliss, cheer, mirth **6** felice, gaiety **7** delight, ecstasy, elation, felicia, rapture **8** felicity, gladness, hilarity **9** beatitude, enjoyment, eudaemony, transport, well-being **10** exaltation, jubilation, prosperity **11** blessedness
   god: **5** Ebisu
   incapacity for: **9** anhedonia
happy: apt, gay **4** cosh, glad, gleg **5** blest, lucky, merry, ready, seely, sonsy, sunny **6** elated, sonsie **7** blessed, content, fitting, halcyon, radiant **8** carefree, frohlich, gracious, mirthful **9** contented, fortunate **10** felicitous, propitious, prosperous
happy-go-lucky: **6** casual **8** carefree **9** easygoing
happy hour: **12** cocktail time
happy hunting ground: **6** heaven **8** paradise
Haran: *brother:* **7** Abraham
   daughter: **5** Iscah **6** Milcah
   father: **5** Terah
   son: Lot
harangue: nag **4** rant, rave **5** orate, scold, spiel **6** screed, sermon, speech, tirade **7** address, declaim, oration **8** diatribe, jeremiad, perorate **10** concionate
harass: fag, hag, nag, try, vex **4** bait, fret, gall, hake, hale, haze, jade, rack, raid, tire **5** annoy, beset, bully, chafe, chase, grind, gripe, harry, herry (Sc.), hurry, pique, tease,

weary, worry **6** badger, bother, bucket, cumber, hatter, heckle, impede, molest, obsess, pester, plague, pother, scrape **7** afflict, affront, agitate, disturb, exhaust, fatigue, hagride, oppress, perplex, provoke, scourge, torment, trouble **8** distract, distress, irritate **9** exagitate, persecute, tantalize
harbinger: **4** camp, host, omen, sign **5** usher **6** herald, symbol **7** presage, shelter **8** fourrier, harborer **9** messenger, precursor **10** forerunner
   spring: **5** robin **6** crocus
harbor, harbour: bay, inn **4** cove, gulf, hide, hold, port **5** basin, bayou, haven, inlet **6** asylum, billet, breach, bunder, covert, foster, refuge **7** fairway, lodging, quarter, retreat, seaport, shelter **9** harborage
   entrance: **4** boca
   fee: **7** keelage
   harbor master: **7** havener
hard: fit **4** acid, cold, dear, dere, dure, firm, iron, mean, oaky, sour **5** champ, close, cruel, hardy, harsh, horny, rigid, rocky, rough, solid, stern, stiff, stony **6** coarse, frozen, knotty, marble, robust, severe, steely, strict, strong **7** adamant, arduous, austere, callous, compact, earnest, intense, onerous, scleral **8** diligent, granitic, grasping, hardened, obdurate, renitent, rigorous, scleroid, toilsome **9** difficult, energetic, fatiguing, inclement, intricate, laborious, petrified, repelling, reprobate, resistant, strenuous, stringent, unfeeling, wearisome **10** inflexible, oppressive, perplexing, persistent, relentless, ungraceful, unyielding **11** at close hand, complicated, distressing, down-to-earth, impregnable, persevering, unremitting **12** blood-and-guts, disreputable, extortionate, impenetrable, incorrigible, unalleviated **13** unsympathetic
   to please: **7** finicky
   coal: **10** anthracite
   core: **7** obscene **12** intransigent, pornographic **13** dyed-in-the-wool
   corn: rye **5** wheat
   drawn: **4** taut **5** tense
hard-boiled: **5** rough, tough **7** callous **8** obdurate, seasoned **11** down-to-earth **13** unsympathetic
harden: gel, set **4** bake, cake, salt, sear **5** beath, enure, inure, steel **6** endure, freeze, ossify, temper **7** congeal, petrify, stiffen, thicken, toughen **8** concrete, condense, indurate, solidify **9** habituate **10** strengthen **11** acclimatize
hardened: **4** hard **5** caked **6** frozen, gelled, inured **7** callous, steeled **8** obdurate **9** abandoned, reprobate **10** impenitent,

impervious, inveterate, solidified **12** impenetrable

hardhat: **6** worker **7** builder **12** conservative

hardhead: **4** fish **5** whale **7** ribwort **8** knapweed, mackerel, menhaden **9** blockhead **10** niggerhead

hardheaded: **4** keen **6** shrewd **7** willful **8** stubborn **9** sagacious **10** longheaded **11** down-to-earth, sharp-witted **12** matter-of-fact

hardhearted: **4** cold, mean **5** cruel, stern, stony, tough **7** callous **8** obdurate, pitiless **9** unfeeling **13** marblehearted, unsympathetic

hardihood: **5** pluck, vigor **7** bravery, courage **8** audacity, boldness, temerity **9** hardiness, impudence, stoutness **10** confidence, effrontery, imprudence, resolution, robustness **11** intrepidity **13** audaciousness

hard line: **4** firm **5** fixed **10** determined, inflexible

hardly: **6** barely **7** faintly, hardily, harshly, roughly **8** forcibly, scarcely, severely, unfairly **11** unfavorably

hardness: **6** durity **8** asperity, severity, solidity **9** substance
measuring device: **9** durometer
scale: **4** Mohs

hardpan: **7** bedrock **8** ortstein

hard-shell: **9** confirmed, extremist **14** fundamentalist

hardship: **5** assay, peril, rigor, trial **6** injury **7** penalty **8** asperity, hardness **9** adversity, endurance, grievance, injustice, privation **10** affliction, difficulty

hardtack: biscuit, galette (F.), pantile

hard times: **9** recession **10** depression

hardwood: ash, oak **4** pelu, teak **5** maple **6** walnut **7** hickory **8** mahogany
genus: **7** quercus

hardy: **4** bold, firm, hale, hard, rash, wiry **5** brave, lusty, manly, stout, tough **6** chisel, daring, robust, rugged, strong, sturdy **7** compact, healthy, spartan **8** galliard, intrepid, resolute, stubborn, vigorous **9** audacious, confident **10** courageous

Hardy heroine: **4** Tess

hare: dol **4** bawd (Sc.), pika **5** harry, lepus, tease, worry **6** malkin, rabbit **7** leporid, leveret **8** frighten, leporide **10** jack rabbit
female: doe
genus of: **5** lepus
male: **4** buck
pert. to: **8** leporine
tail: **4** scut
track: **4** file, slot
young: **7** leveret

harem: oda **4** odah **5** serai **6** serail, zenana **8** seraglio
male attendant: **6** eunuch
room: oda
slave: **9** odalisque

haricot: **4** stew **6** ragout **7** halicot **9** green bean **10** kidney bean

hark: **4** hear, heed, hist **6** attend, listen, notice **7** whisper

harken: See **hearken**

harlequin: **5** clown **7** buffoon **9** fantastic **11** masquerader

harm: hob, ill, mar, sap **4** bale, bane, evil, hurt, pain, teen **5** abuse, annoy, grief, shend, wound, wrong **6** damage, damnum, injure, injury, scathe, sorrow, **7** disease, impeach, **8** disserve, endamage, nuisance, **10** disservice, misfortune, wickedness **11** impeachment

harmful: bad **4** evil **5** nasty, toxic **6** nocent **7** baneful, hurtful, malefic, noisome, noxious **8** damaging, sinister **9** injurious **10** pernicious **11** contrarious, deleterious, detrimental, mischievous

harmless: **4** safe **6** dovish **8** innocent, nontoxic **9** innocuous **11** inoffensive

harmonica: **10** mouth organ
relative of: **7** panpipe

Harmonia: *father:* **4** Ares, Mars
husband: **6** Cadmus
mother: **5** Venus **9** Aphrodite

harmonious: **6** cosmic, dulcet **7** cordial, musical, spheral, tuneful **8** amicable, peaceful **9** accordant, agreeable, congruous, consonant, harmonial, melodious, peaceable **10** compatible, concentive, concordant **11** harmoniacal, symmetrical **12** proportional

harmonize: gee, key **4** jibe, sing, tone, tune **5** adapt, agree, blend, chime, hitch, rhyme **6** accord, adjust, attune, cotton **7** concent, concord, consist, consort **9** reconcile **10** correspond, sympathize

harmony: **4** tune **5** amity, music, peace **6** cosmos, melody **7** concert, concord, rapport **9** agreement **10** accordance, atmosphere, conformity, congruence, consonance **11** cooperation **12** togetherness
bring into: **6** attune
lack: **7** discord

harness: **4** gear, tack, yoke **5** heald, hitch **6** fettle, halter, tackle **7** enclose, hitch-up **9** equipment, trappings
marker: **7** knacker, lorimer
part: bit, tug **4** hame, rein **5** blind, trace **6** billet, bridle, collar, saddle, terret **7** crouper **9** breeching, circingle, martingal, ridgeband, surcingle **10** breastband, crownpiece, martingale

harp: **4** arpa, koto, lyre **6** trigon **8** bedlamer **10** instrument **11** clairschach

harper: coin, **8** minstrel, musician

harpoon: **5** spear **7** javelin

harpsichord: 6 spinet 8 clavecin, virginal 12 clavicembalo

harpy: 4 bird 5 eagle, leech, scold, vixen 6 virago 8 fishwife, swindler 11 extortioner

Harpy: 5 Aello 7 Celaneo, monster, Ocypete, Podarge

harridan: hag 5 crone, horse, vixen, woman 8 strumpet

harrier: dog 4 hawk 5 bully 8 harasser

harrow: vex 4 disk, drag 5 brake, harry, wound 6 spader 7 oppress, torment 8 distress, lacerate 9 cultivate 10 cultivator

harrowed: 6 pained 7 haggard 8 tortured

harry: rob, vex 4 sack 5 annoy, hound, hurry, spoil, steal, worry 6 harass, harrow, hector, plague, ravage 7 agitate, bedevil, despoil, pillage, plunder, torment 9 persecute

harsh: raw 4 grim, hard, hask 5 acerb, acrid, asper, brute, crude, cruel, grill, gruff, raspy, rough, sharp, stern, stiff 6 bitter, brazen, coarse, severe, strict, sullen, unkind 7 austere, braying, drastic, grating, rasping, raucous 8 acerbate, catonian, clashing, croaking, district, guttural, jangling, rigorous, strident, ungentle 9 dissonant, inclement, insensate, repellent, squawking, truculent, unfeeling 10 astringent, discordant, oppressive, relentless 11 acrimonious, disagreeing 12 disagreeable

harshness: 5 rigor 6 duress 7 crudity, raucity 8 acerbity, acrimony, asperity, severity

hart: roe 4 deer, stag 7 red deer, venison
mate: 4 hind

hartebeest: 4 asse, tora 5 caama, kaama 6 lecama 7 bubalis 8 antelope

hartshorn: 6 antler 7 ammonia 11 sal volatile

harum-scarum: 4 rash, wild 7 flighty 8 reckless 11 thoughtless 13 irresponsible

Harun-Al-Rashid's wife: 7 Zobeide

haruspex: 4 seer 5 augur 7 diviner, prophet 8 foreseer 9 predictor 10 soothsayer 14 prognosticator

harvest: 4 bind, crop, reap 5 amass, cache, hoard 6 foison, gather 8 ingather, stow away
festival: 6 Opalia
fly: 6 cicada
god: 6 Cronus
goddess: Ops 4 Rhea 5 Ceres 7 Demeter

harvest home: 4 kern, kirn (Sc.)

harvester: 8 spalpeen

hash: 4 chop 5 mince, mix-up 6 jumble 7 mixture 9 talk about 11 gallimaufry, olla podrida (Sp.)

hashish: 4 hemp 5 bhang 8 cannabis, narcotic

hashmark: 6 stripe

hasp: 4 gird 5 catch, clasp 7 confine 8 fastener

hassle: row, try 4 talk 5 annoy 6 bother, hustle 7 quarrel, wrestle 8 argument, squabble 9 commotion 10 discussion 11 altercation, controversy

hassock: 4 boss, pess 5 grass, sedge 6 buffet 7 cushion, ottoman, tussock 8 footrest 9 footstool

haste: hie 4 rush 5 hurry, speed 6 bustle, flurry 7 urgency 8 dispatch, rapidity 9 quickness, swiftness 10 expedition, nimbleness 11 festination, impetuosity 12 precipitance 13 impetuousness, precipitation

hasten: hie, run 4 pell, race, rush, trot 5 crowd, drive, fleet, hurry, speed 6 ex-pede, gallop, scurry 7 advance, scamper 8 dispatch, expedite 9 festinate 10 accelerate 11 precipitate

hastily: 6 nimbly 8 speedily 11 impatiently 13 precipitately

hasty: 4 fast, rash 5 brash, fleet, quick, swift 6 abrupt, daring, nimble, speedy, sudden 7 cursory, forward, hurried 8 headlong, pell-mell, succinct 9 hotheaded, hurrisome, impatient, impetuous 10 indiscreet 11 expeditious, precipitate, precipitous

hasty pudding: 4 mush 6 supawn 9 stirabout

hat: cap, dip, fez, lid, nab, tam, wig 4 baku, barb, felt, topi 5 beany, benjy, benny, beret, boxer, cordy, derby, dicer, kelly, terai, topee, toque 6 Alpine, beaver, boater, bonnet, bowler, castor, claque, cloche, coolie, fedora, panama, shovel, turban 7 biretta, caubeen, chapeau, homburg, petasus, salacot, shallow 8 capeline, copatain, headgear, sombrero 9 Dunstable, stovepipe, wideawake 10 belltopper 11 mortarboard
brimless: 7 pillbox
close fitting: 5 toque 6 turban
covering: 8 havelock
crown: 4 poll
ecclesastic: 5 miter 7 biretta
fiber: 4 felt, sola 5 straw
fur used in: 4 mink 5 coney 6 beaver, ermine 8 coonskin
lady's: 5 caddy, cooie 6 bonnet, Breton, caddie, slouch 7 leghorn 8 duckbill 9 harlequin 12 Gainsborough
maker: 8 milliner
medieval: 6 abacot 7 bycoket
military: 5 shako
oilskin: 5 squam 9 sou'wester
opera: 5 crush, gibus 6 claque, topper
palm-leaf: 7 salacot
pert. to: 9 castorial
pith: 4 topi 5 topee
Quaker: 9 broadbrim
silk: lum (Sc.) 4 tile 5 opera 6 topper 7 catskin 8 gossamer
soft: 6 fedora
straw: 6 boater
tall: 9 stovepipe
three-cornered: 7 tricorn

ventilated: **5** terai
wide-brimmed: **9** sou'wester

hatch: 4 brew, door, gate, sire, vent **5** breed, cleck, clock, cover **6** clutch, wicket **7** concoct **8** contrive, hatchway **9** floodgate
covering: **4** tarp

hatchel: 5 tease, worry **6** heckle **7** torment

hatchet: adz, axe **4** adze, mogo **8** tomahawk

hatchet man: 4 tool **6** critic, killer, stooge **8** assassin, henchman

hatching: 6 cletch **8** breeding

hatchway: 7 scuttle

hate: 4 teen **5** abhor, scorn **6** detest, enmity, loathe, malice, rancor, revile **7** contemn, despise, dislike, ill will **8** aversion, execrate, loathing **9** abominate, animosity, hostility, malignity **11** detestation

hateful: 4 evil, foul **5** black, nasty **6** odious **7** heinous **8** flagrant, infamous **9** abhorrent, invidious, loathsome, malignant, obnoxious, offensive, revolting **10** abominable, detestable, disgusting, malevolent **11** distasteful **12** disagreeable

hatful: 4 lots, many, much **8** quantity

hatred (see also **fear**): **5** odium, spite **6** enmity, rancor **8** aversion **9** animosity, hostility, malignity **10** abhorrence, repugnance **11** abomination, detestation, malevolence
of argument: **8** misology
of children: **9** misopedia **10** misopaedia
of mankind: **11** misanthropy
of marriage: **8** misogamy
of strangers: **10** xenophobia

hatter: 8 milliner

haughtiness: 4 airs **5** pride **6** morgue **7** hauteur **9** arrogance, insolence

haughty: 4 airy, bold, high **5** aloof, dorty, lofty, noble, proud **6** lordly, snooty **7** distant, exalted, fatuous, hontish, paughty, stately **8** arrogant, cavalier, glorious, scornful **9** egotistic, imperious, masterful **10** disdainful, fastidious **11** domineering, magisterial, overbearing **12** contemptuous, presumptuous, supercilious

haul: lug, tow, tug **4** cart, drag, draw, hurl, move, pull, tote **5** bouse, catch, heave, shift, trice **8** cordelle **9** transport

haulage: 6 towage **7** cartage, drayage

hauler: 7 tractor

haulm: 4 culm, stem **5** straw **6** stalks

haunch: hip **4** huck **5** hance **12** hindquarters

haunt: den, **4** dive, howf, lair, nest **5** ghost, habit, howff, skill **6** custom, infest, linger, obsess, resort, spirit, wraith **7** hangout, phantom, specter, terrify **8** frequent, practice **9** companion **10** fellowship, hang around

haunted: 6 filled, spooky **8** infested

hautboy, hautbois: 4 oboe **9** organ stop **10** strawberry

hauteur: 5 pride **9** arrogance **11** haughtiness

haut monde: 5 elite **11** high society

have: hae (Sc.), own **4** hold **5** enjoy, ought **6** retain **7** carry on, contain, possess, undergo **10** experience
at: **6** attack
done: **5** cease **6** finish
had it: **7** given up **8** defeated **9** disgusted
it coming: **4** earn **5** merit **7** deserve
it out: **7** discuss
on: **4** wear **5** tease
to do with: **4** deal

haven: bay, lee **4** hope, port **5** hotel, inlet **6** asylum, harbor, recess, refuge **7** retreat, shelter **9** anchorage, roadstead, sanctuary

haversack: bag

havoc: hob **4** loss, ruin **5** waste **6** ravage **7** destroy **9** devastate **10** desolation **11** destruction, devastation

haw: 4 sloe, yard **5** fence, hedge **6** falter **8** hawthorn

---

Hawaii: *ballad:* **4** mele
beach: **7** Waikiki
beverage: **4** kava
breechcloth: **4** malo
bush: see *shrub* below
canoe: **5** waapa
capital: **8** Honolulu
channel: **4** Auau
chant: **4** mele
city: **4** Aiea, Hilo **5** Lihue **6** Kailua **7** Kameohe, Kanache, Wailuku **9** Pearl City
cloak: **4** mamo **6** ahuula
cloth: **4** kapa, tapa **5** tappa
cookout: **4** luau
cord: aea
crater: **7** Kilauea
dance: **4** hula
discoverer: **4** Cook
farewell, hello: **5** aloha
feast: **4** luau **7** ahaaina
fern: **4** heii **5** ekaha, uluhi **6** iwaiwa **7** amaumau
fiber: **4** pulu
first settler: **10** Polynesian
fish poison: **4** hola **6** auhuhu
fish: ahi **4** ulua **5** akule **8** mahimahi
flower: pua **5** ilima
food: poi **4** kalo, taro **6** kaukau, laulau
garland: lei
garment: **6** holoku, muumuu **7** holomuu
god: **4** Kane **5** Wakea
goddess: **4** Pele (*cont.*)

hawfinch

Hawaii (cont.)
- *goose:* 4 nene
- *grass:* 6 emoloa
- *harbor:* 5 Pearl
- *hawk:* io
- *herb:* ape, pia 4 hola 5 awiwi 6 auhuhu
- *instrument:* uke 7 ukalele, ukelele, ukulele
- *island:* 4 Maui, Oahu 5 Kauai, Lanai 6 Hawaii, Niihau 7 Molokai 9 Kahoolawe
- *lava:* aa 8 pahoehoe
- *loincloth:* 4 malo, maro
- *lomilomi:* rub 7 massage, shampoo
- *love:* 5 aloha
- *man:* 4 kane
- *massage:* 8 lomilomi
- *morning glory:* 5 koali
- *mountain:* 5 Kaala 7 Waianae 8 Mauna Kea, Mauna Loa
- *native:* 6 Kanaka 10 Polynesian
- *naval base:* 11 Pearl Harbor
- *nickname:* 10 Aloha State
- *octopus:* hee
- *pantheon:* 4 Kane
- *parrot fish:* 5 lauia
- *partnership:* hui
- *pepper:* ava
- *pit for baking:* imu
- *plant:* pia 4 hala, taro 5 olona 8 pandanus
- *poem:* 4 mele
- *porch:* 5 lanai
- *precipice:* 4 pali
- *priest:* 6 Kahuna
- *raven:* 5 alala
- *root:* 4 taro
- *root paste:* poi
- *seaweed:* 4 limu
- *shaman:* 6 Kahuna
- *shrub:* 4 akia 5 akala, olona 6 aupaka
- *song:* 4 mele
- *staple:* poi 4 taro
- *starch plant:* pia
- *starch root:* pia 4 taro
- *state bird:* 4 nene 5 goose
- *state flower:* 8 hibiscus
- *state song:* 11 Hawaii Ponoi
- *state tree:* 5 kukui 9 candlenut
- *temple:* 5 heiau
- *thanks:* 6 mahalo
- *thrush:* 4 amao 6 olomao
- *valley:* 5 Manoa
- *volcano:* 7 Kilauea 8 Mauna Kea, Mauna Loa 9 Haleakala
- *white man:* 5 haole
- *wind:* 4 kona
- *windstorm:* 4 kona
- *woman:* 6 wahine
- *yam:* hoi

hawfinch: 4 kate 8 grosbeak

hawk: io, cry, gos 4 eyas, kite, sell, vend 5 astur, cadge 6 falcon, osprey, peddle 7 buzzard, haggard, harrier, kestrel, puttock, vulture 8 caracara, jingoist, militant, swindler 9 accipiter, warmonger 11 mortar-board
- *cage:* mew
- *leash:* 4 jess, lune
- *male:* 6 musket, tercel 7 tiercel
- *nest:* 5 aerie
- *nestling:* 4 eyas
- *pinion feather:* 6 sarcel

hawker: 6 badger, cadger, coster, duffer, pedlar, vendor 7 chapman, mercury, packman, peddler 8 falconer, huckster, pitchman 9 colporter 10 colporteur 12 costermonger

hawk-eyed: 12 sharp-sighted

Hawkeye State: 4 Iowa

hawklike: 9 bellicose 11 accipitrine, belligerent

hawser: 4 line, rope
- *post:* 4 bitt 7 bollard

hawthorn: haw, may 5 aglet 6 aiglet 8 cockspur, maybloom, quickset

hay: bed, net 4 park 5 chaff, fence, grass, hedge 9 provender
- *bundle:* mow 4 bale, rick, wisp 5 gavel, stack, truss 7 hayrick
- *kind of:* 6 clover 7 alfalfa, timothy
- *line:* 5 swath 7 windrow
- *second cutting:* 5 rowen
- *spreader:* 6 tedder
- *storage:* mow 4 loft

haycock: 4 coil

hayfork: 4 pike 5 pikel 9 pitchfork

haymaker: 8 farm hand 10 boxing blow

hayseed: 4 hick, rube 5 yokel 6 farmer, rustic 10 countryman

hazard: bet, die, lay, lot 4 risk 5 peril, stake, wager 6 chance, danger, gamble, menace 7 imperil, venture 8 accident, casualty, endanger, jeopardy 9 adventure 10 jeopardize

hazardous: 5 risky 6 chance, chancy, queasy, unsafe 8 insecure, perilous 9 dangerous, uncertain 10 fortuitous, jeopardous, precarious 11 adventurous

haze: fog 4 beat, film, mist, smog 5 cloud, devil, scold, smoke, vapor 6 harass, vapour 7 drizzle, obscure, reverie 8 frighten

hazel: nut 4 bush 6 cobnut 7 filbert 8 noisette 12 reddish brown

Hazor king: 5 Jabin

hazy: dim 5 filmy, foggy, misty, smoky, thick, vague 7 clouded, nebular, obscure, unclear 8 nebulous 9 uncertain 10 indistinct

head: aim, cop, mir, nab, nob, top 4 bean, boro, cape, capo (It.), coco, conk, crop, kopf (G.), lead, mind, pate, poll, tete (F.), turn 5 caput (L.), chief, chump, first, front,

338

froth, start, testa (It.), tibby **6** cabeza (Sp.), cobbra, direct, garret, leader, manage, noggin, noodle, person, sconce, source, spring **7** captain, coconut, costrel, cranium, crumpet, leading, prelate **8** director, foremost, fountain, headland, initiate **9** intercept, president, principal **10** caper-nutie, drug addict, headmaster, promontory **11** capernoitie **12** intelligence

army camp: **10** commandant

back part: **7** occiput

bald: **9** pilgarlic

boar: **4** hure

bone: **5** skull **7** cranium **8** parietal

crown: **6** cantle

muscle: **11** occipitalis

nautical: **6** toilet **8** lavatory

ornament: hat, wig **4** hair, veil **5** tiara **7** coronet

part: **4** pate **5** scalp **6** earlap, temple **7** cranium

pert. to: **8** cephalic

shaven: **7** tonsure

shrunken: **7** tsantsa

side of: **4** lore **5** lorum **6** temple

skin: **5** scalp

top: **4** pate **5** crown, scalp **7** coxcomb

headache: **6** megrim **8** headwark, migraine **10** cephalagia

headband: **5** miter, mitre, vitta **6** diadem, fillet, infula **7** circlet, coronet **8** frontlet **9** sphendone

headcheese: **5** brawn

head cook: **4** chef

head covering (see also **headdress**): **4** caul **5** scalp

headdress: **4** caul, coif, pouf, veil **5** ampyx, crown, cupee, miter, mitre, tiara, toque **6** almuce, bonnet, coiffe, faille, hennin, mobcap, pinner, turban **7** bandore, bycoket, coronet, topknot **8** biliment, binnogue, capriole, coiffure, stephane, tressure **9** rigolette **10** fascinator

medieval: **5** barbe **6** abacot

military: **5** busby, shako **6** casque, helmet

royal: **5** crown, tiara **6** diadem

sacred: **6** uraeus

Spanish woman's: **8** mantilla

widow's: **7** bandore

headgear: See **headdress**

headily: **6** rashly **9** violently

heading: **5** title, topic **7** caption **8** headline

topical: **5** trope

headland: ras **4** bill, cape, head, nase, naze, ness, peak **5** Morro, ridge, strip **8** foreland **10** promontory

headless: **4** rash **6** stupid **7** foolish, topless **8** beheaded **10** acephalous, leaderless

headline: **6** banner **7** feature **8** streamer

headliner: **4** star **11** personality

headlong: **4** rash **5** hasty, steep **6** abrupt, sudden **8** reckless **9** desperate, foolhardy, headfirst, impetuous, impulsive **11** precipitate, precipitous

headman: **4** boss, jefe (Sp.) **5** chief **6** ataman, cabeza, hetman **7** capitan, captain, foreman **8** alderman, caboceer, capitano **11** executioner

headmaster: **9** principal **11** gymnasiarch

headpiece: See **headdress**

headquarters: **4** base, seat **5** depot, yamen **6** center **8** exchange, precinct **9** battalion

head-shaped: **8** capitate

headstall: **5** noose

headstone: **8** memorial, monument **11** grave marker

headstrong: **4** rash **5** cobby **6** mulish, unruly **7** hotspur, violent, willful **8** stubborn **9** obstinate **10** bullheaded **11** forthright **10** hotspurred, self-willed **11** intractable, stiffnecked **12** contumacious, ungovernable

head to foot: **7** cap-a-pie

heady: **4** rash **7** huffcap, violent, willful **9** impetuous **11** exhilarated, intoxicated, precipitate **12** intoxicating

heal: **4** cure, hale, knit, mend **5** amend **6** remedy, repair **7** recover, restore **10** recuperate

heal-all: **4** balm **7** figwort, panacea

healer: asa **4** balm **6** doctor **9** naprapath, physician **12** practitioner

healing: **5** balmy **8** covering, curative, remedial, sanative

agent: **6** balsam

goddess: Eir

pert. to: **7** medical **9** medicinal

science: **8** medicine **9** iatrology, latrology

health: **4** hail, hale **5** sante (F.), toast **7** fitness, slainte, stamina **8** eucrasia, euphoria, haleness, vitality **9** well-being **11** disposition

goddess: **7** Minerva

poor: **4** sick **7** illness

resort: spa

healthy: fit **4** hale, sane, well **5** bonny, hoddy **6** bonnie, hearty, robust **8** salutary, vigorous **9** wholesome **10** healthsome, salubrious

heap: ahu, cob, cop, mow **4** balk, bing, bulk, deck, dess (Sc.), gobs, hill, lump, mass, much, pile, pyre, raft, rick, ruck **5** amass, cairn, clump, crowd, spire, stack **6** burrow, hipple, jumble, plenty, throng **7** bourock, cumulus, hurrock **9** congeries, multitude **10** accumulate, collection, congestion, cumulation

hear: ear, see **4** feel, hark, heed, obey **5** learn **6** attend, harken, listen **7** hearken **8** perceive **10** adjudicate

hear ye: **4** oyes, oyez

hearer: **7** audient, auditor **8** disciple, listener

hearing: ear **4** test **5** sound, trial **6** assize, report **7** earshot, lecture, meeting **8** audience, audition, scolding **9** attention, audiencia, interview, knowledge **10** attendance, conference, discussion

court: **4** oyer

distance: **7** earshot

judicial: **5** trial **7** retrial

pert. to: **8** acoustic

hearken, harken: **4** hark, hear, heed, wait **6** attend, listen **7** inquire, whisper

hearsay: **4** buzz, fame, talk **5** on-dit, rumor **6** report **9** grapevine **11** scuttlebutt

hearse **4** bier, bury, tomb **5** dirge, grave **6** coffin **8** monument, threnody **10** catafalque

heart: cor, hub **4** core, gist, hati, love **5** cheer, focus **6** center, centre, depths, middle, ticker **7** courage, emotion, essence, feeling **9** affection, character **10** compassion

cavity: **6** atrium

chamber: **7** auricle **9** ventricle

contraction: **7** systole

covering: **11** pericardium

disease: **7** cardiac

expansion: **8** diastole

record: **17** electrocardiogram

shaped: **7** cordate

stimulant: **8** thialdin **9** digitalis, thialdine **10** adrenaline, epinephrin **11** epinephrine

heartache: rue, woe **4** pang **5** grief **6** sorrow **7** anguish **10** affliction, cardialgia

heartbeat: **5** pulse, throb **7** systole **9** pulsation

irregular: **10** arrhythmia

quivering: **12** fibrillation

heartbreak: **5** grief **6** sorrow **7** tragedy

heartbroken: **12** inconsolable **13** grief-stricken

heartburn: **4** envy **6** enmity **7** pyrosis **8** jealousy **10** cardialgia, discontent, heartscald, heartscaud **11** indigestion

hearten: **5** cheer **6** arouse, spirit **7** cheer up, refresh **8** embolden, inspirit, reassure **9** encourage

heartfelt: **4** dear, deep, real, true **6** honest **7** earnest, genuine, sincere **8** bona fide, profound

hearth: **5** cupel, focus, fogon, foyer **8** bloomery, fireside

goddess: **5** Vesta **6** Hestia

line: **6** fettle

heartily: **6** dearly, freely, warmly **8** actively, strongly **9** cordially, earnestly, profusely, sincerely, zealously, zestfully **10** abundantly, completely, vigorously **14** wholeheartedly

heartiness: **4** soul **8** goodwill, strength **9** soundness **10** cordiality

heartless: **4** cold **5** cruel **7** callous **8** hopeless, listless, ruthless **9** merciless, unfeeling **10** despairing, despondent, hard-boiled, spiritless **13** unsympathetic

heartsease, heartease: **5** pansy, peace **11** peace of mind **12** tranquillity

heartthrob: **4** dunt, idol, love **5** flame, honey, sweet

heartwood: **4** dura **7** duramen

hearty: **4** firm, hale, real, rich, warm, well **5** cobby, heavy, sound **6** active, cheery, devout, robust, sailor, stanch **7** comrade, cordial, earnest, fertile, healthy, sincere, staunch **8** abundant, cheerful, heartful, vigorous **9** energetic, unfeigned, wholesome **10** full-bodied, nourishing **11** substantial, warmhearted **12** enthusiastic

heat: ire **4** fire, mull, rage, warm, zeal **5** ardor, cauma, chafe, fever, roast, tepor **6** anneal, choler, degree, warmth **7** caloric, ferment, hotness, inflame, passion **8** fervency **9** agitation, animation, chauffage, commotion, vehemence **10** excitement, hot weather **11** temperature **12** exasperation **14** passionateness

measure: **5** therm **6** calory, kelvin, therme **7** calorie, celsius **10** centigrade, fahrenheit **11** calorimeter, pyronometer

pert. to: **7** thermic

quantity: **6** degree **11** temperature

unit of: BTU **5** therm **7** calorie

white: **13** incandescence

heated: **6** ardent **7** excited **8** sizzling, vehement **10** phlogistic **11** acrimonious

heater: **4** etna, oven **5** stove **6** boiler **7** choffer (Sc.), furnace **8** radiator

heath: **4** ling, moor **5** besom, erica, plain, heather

family: **7** calluna **8** ericacea

scrub: **9** chaparral

tree: **5** briar, brier

heathen: **5** pagan **6** ethnic, paynim **7** gentile, saracen **8** idolater, paganist **11** irreligious

deity: **4** idol

non-Jewish: **6** ethnic

non-Muslim: **7** infidel

heather: **4** grig, ling **5** erica

family: **9** ericaceae

heatless: **4** cold **8** athermic

heautarit: **7** mercury **11** quicksilver

heave: gag **4** cast, haul, heft, hurl, keck, lift, pant, pull, push, quap, toss **5** hoist, pitch, raise, retch, scend, throw, vomit **7** elevate, estuate **8** struggle

heaven: sky **4** Zion **5** dyaus, ether, glory **6** Himmel (G.), utopia, welkin, zodiac **7** Elysium, Nirvana, Valhall **8** devaloka, empyrean, paradise, Valhalla **9** firmament **12** promised land

pert. to: **6** uranic **9** celestial

queen: **4** Mary **7** Astarte

heavenly: **4** lush **5** yummy **6** divine, sacred **7** angelic, olympic, sublime, uranian **8** ethereal, supernal **9** angelical, celestial, celestine *being* (see also **angel**): **5** angel **6** cherub, seraph

belt: way **6** galaxy, nebula, zodiac

body: sun **4** luna, moon, star **5** comet **6** planet **8** asteroid, luminary **9** satellite

city: **4** Sion, Zion

twins: **6** Castor, Gemini, Pollux **8** Dioscuri

heaviness 5 gloom **6** weight **7** gravity, sadness **10** oppression **12** sluggishness

heavy: **4** clit, deep, dull, logy, loud **5** actor, beefy, burly, dense, grave, gross, hefty, hoggy, massy, thick **6** clayey, cloggy, coarse, gloomy, hearty, leaden, stodgy, strong, stupid **7** big shot, doleful, intense, massive, onerous, porcine, serious, villain, violent, weighty **8** burdened, grievous, inactive, lifeless, lowering, overcast, pregnant, profound, sluggish **9** heavisome, laborious, lethargic, ponderous, saturnine **10** afflictive, burdensome, cumbersome, encumbered, oppressive **13** consequential

heavy-headed: **4** dull **5** inept **6** drowsy, gauche, stupid **8** bumbling **9** maladroit, ponderous **10** uninspired

heavy-hearted: sad **10** despondent, melancholy

hebdomad: **4** week **5** seven

hebetate: **4** dull **5** blunt

Hebrew: Jew **6** Semite **7** Semitic **8** Hebraean **9** Israelite

acrostic: **4** agla

alphabet: Mem, Nun, Sin, Taf, Tav, Tet, Vav, Yod, Yud **4** Alef, Ayin, Beth, Caph, Kaph, Koph, Ooph, Resh, Shin **5** Aleph, Cheth, Gimel, Lamed, Sadhe, Tsade, Zayin **6** Daleth, Samekh

ancestor: **4** Eber

clean: **6** kosher

dance: **4** hora

day: yom

eternity: **4** olam

gentile: goi, goy **5** goyim (pl.)

God, names of: El **5** Eloah **6** Adonai, Elohim, Yahweh **7** Jehovah, Jehovah

greeting:: **6** shalom

high priest: Eli **5** Aaron

infinity: **6** adalam

Jehovah: **5** Jahve, Yahve, Yahwe **6** Jahvah, Jahveh, Yahveh, Yahweh **7** Jahaveh

juniper: **4** ezel

lawbreaking: **6** averah

lesson: **9** Haphtarah

man: rab **5** bahur, hakam

measure: cab, hin, kab, kor **4** epha, ezba, omer, reed, seah **5** cubit, ephah, homer

month: Ab **4** Adar, Elul **5** Iyyar, Nisan, Tebet **6** Kislew, Shebat, Tammuz, Tishri, Veadar **7** Heshwan

parchment: **6** mezuza **7** mezuzah

school: **5** heder, schul

scriptures: **4** Tora **5** Torah

son: ben

teacher: **5** rabbi

thief: **5** ganef, ganof, gonof **6** gonoph

title: rab **4** abba

unclean: **4** tref

weight: **4** beka, reba

Hebrides island: **4** Mull, Skye **5** Islay

hecatomb: **9** sacrifice, slaughter

heckle: nag **4** bait, gibe **5** chivy, hound, tease **6** badger, hackle, harass, hector, needle **7** torment **8** bullyrag

hectic: **4** busy **6** fervid **8** exciting, feverish, habitual, restless **11** consumptive **14** constitutional

hector: nag **4** bait **5** bully, harry, worry **6** harass, heckle, plague **7** bluster, dragoon, torment **8** bludgeon, braggart, browbeat, irritate **9** roisterer, swaggerer **10** intimidate

Hector: *companion:* **8** Diomedes

father: **5** Priam

mother: **6** Hecuba

rescuer: **6** Agenor

slayer: **8** Achilles

wife: **10** Andromache

Hecuba: *daughter:* **6** Creusa **8** Polyxena **9** Cassandra

husband: **5** Priam

son: **5** Paris **6** Hector **7** Helenus, Troilus **9** Deiphobus, Polydorus

victim: **10** Polymestor

hedenbergite: **8** pyroxene

hedge: bar, haw, hem **4** boma, cage, coop **5** beard, evade, fence, frith, guard, skulk **6** hinder, hurdle, privet, weasel **7** barrier, enclose, protect **8** boundary, obstruct, quickset, separate, sepiment, sidestep, straddle, surround **14** counter-balance

hedgehog: **6** urchin **7** echinus **8** herisson, hurcheon **9** porcupine

hedonic: **8** cyrenaic

hedonist: **4** rake **7** epicure **8** sybarite **9** bon vivant **13** pleasure lover

heed: ear **4** care, cark, cure, gaum, hark, hear, mind, note, obey, reck **5** await, watch **6** attend, beware, harken, listen, notice, regard, remark **7** caution, hearken, observe, respect **8** consider **9** attention, diligence **10** cognizance, solicitude **11** observation

heedful: **4** wary **5** alert, chary **6** attent **7** careful, mindful **8** diligent, watchful **9** advertent, attendant, attentive, observant **10** meticulous, respectful **11** considerate

heedless: **4** rash **5** giddy **6** remiss, unwary **7** languid, witless **8** careless, reckless **9** blindfold, forgetful, negligent, oblivious **10** incautious, indiscreet, insouciant, regardless, unthinking **11** hairbrained, inadvertent, inattentive, indifferent, lightheaded, thoughtless, unobservant

heehaw: 4 bray 5 laugh 6 giggle, guffaw 10 horselaugh

heel: cad, end, tip 4 calx, cant, knob, lean, list, tilt 5 knave, rogue, slant, talon 6 careen, rascal 7 incline 12 protuberance
bone: 9 calcaneus

heft: 5 heave, hoist, raise 6 strain, weight 8 exertion 9 heaviness, influence 13 ponderousness

hefty: big 5 beefy, burly, heavy, rough 6 rugged 7 massive, weighty 8 powerful, vehement, vigorous

hegemony: 9 authority, dominance, influence 10 leadership

hegira, hejira: 6 exodus, flight 9 migration

heifer: 4 calf, quey 5 stirk 10 colpindach (Sc.)

height: 4 acme, apex, mote 5 crest 6 climax, summit, zenith 7 stature 8 altitude, eminence, pinnacle 9 celsitude, dimension, elevation, procerity, steepness 11 magnanimity
fear of: 10 acrophobia

heighten: 4 lift 5 elate, exalt, raise 6 accent, bolster 7 advance, augment, elevate, enhance 8 increase 9 aggravate, intensify 10 aggrandize

heinous: 4 evil 6 crying, malign, odious, wicked 7 hateful 8 flagrant, grievous, shocking 9 atrocious, execrable, malicious, nefarious 10 abominable, flagitious, outrageous

heir: son 5 heres, scion 7 heritor, legatee 9 firstborn, inheritor, successor 11 beneficiary

heiress: 5 begum 8 daughter, heretrix, heritrix

Hejaz city: 5 Mecca

Hel: *dog:* 4 Garm
father: 4 Loki
mother: 9 Angurboda
realm: 7 Niflhel 8 Niflheim

held: See **hold**

Helen of Troy: *abductor:* 5 Paris
brother-in-law: 9 Agamemnon
daughter: 8 Hermione
half-sister: 12 Clytemnestra
13 Clytaemnestra
husband: 8 Menelaus
mother: 4 Leda

heliacal: 5 solar

helical: 6 spiral

helicon: 4 tuba

helicopter: 4 gyro 7 chopper 8 autogiro 9 eggbeater 10 rotor plane, spiral wing, whirlybird

Helios: 6 Apollo
daughter: 5 Circe 8 Heliadae, Heliades
father: 8 Hyperion
son: 8 Phaethon

heliotrope: 6 borage, flower 8 turnsole 10 bloodstone

heliport: 10 landing pad

helix: 4 coil 6 spiral

hell: 5 hades, limbo, sheol 6 prison, tophet 7 dungeon, Gehenna, inferno 9 barathrum, purgatory

hell-bent: 8 reckless 10 determined

hellebore: 5 plant 7 bugbane 8 crowfoot 10 Indian poke 13 Christmas rose

Hellen: *father:* 9 Deucalion
mother: 6 Pyrrha
son: 5 Dorus 6 Aeolus, Xuthus

Hellene: See **Greece**

Hellenistic school: 9 Pergamene

Hellespont: 11 Dardanelles
swimmer: 7 Leander

hellgrammite: 6 dobson 8 fish bait, sialidae

hellish: 6 wicked 7 avernal, stygian 8 devilish, diabolic, infernal, plutonic 9 malignant 10 detestable, diabolical

hello: 8 greeting 10 salutation

helm: 5 helve, steer, wheel 6 direct, tiller 8 guidance
position: 4 alee 5 aport

helmet: cap 4 sola, topi 5 armet, galea, topee 6 casque, heaume, morion, salade, sallet 7 basinet 8 schapska 9 casquetel, headpiece
part: 4 bell 5 crest, plume, visor 7 ventail 8 aventail 9 chin strap

helmet-shaped: 7 galeate

helmsman: 5 pilot 9 steersman

Heloise's lover: 7 Abelard

helot: 4 serf 5 slave 6 vassal 7 bondman

help: aid, bot, S.O.S., use 4 abet, boot, bote, cure, lift, mend, rede, tide 5 avail, boost, favor, frith, heeze, serve, speed, stead 6 assist, favour, relief, remedy, repair, succor 7 advance, benefit, forbear, forward, further, improve, promote, relieve, support, sustain 8 befriend, champion, facility 9 adminicle, alleviate, forestall 10 assistance, contribute, facilitate, strengthen 11 cooperation

helper: aid 4 ally 5 aider 6 deputy, server 7 abetter, abettor, ancella, servant, striker 8 adjutant, adjutrix, employee, helpmate 9 adjutrice, assistant, samaritan 10 apprentice, benefactor 11 subordinate

helpful: 4 good 6 aidant, useful 8 adjuvant, helpsome, salutary 9 auxiliary 10 beneficial, profitable 11 furthersome, serviceable 12 advantageous, constructive

helpless: 4 numb, weak 6 feeble, futile, unable 7 forlorn 8 impotent, unaiding 9 destitute, powerless 10 bewildered, unsupplied 11 defenseless, incompetent, unprotected 12 irremediable

helpmate: 4 wife 6 helper 8 helpmeet 9 companion

helter-skelter: **6** random **7** flighty, hotfoot, turmoil **8** pellmell **9** hit-or-miss **11** any which way

helve: **4** haft **5** lever **6** handle

Helvetian: **5** Swiss **6** Suisse

hem: **4** edge, seam **5** hedge **6** border, edging, margin, stitch **7** confine, enclose, environ, inclose **8** surround **9** fimbriate
  in: **5** beset, limit **6** impale **7** enclose, inclose **8** surround

hematite: **7** iron ore **10** bloodstone **12** black diamond

hemeralopia: **6** defect **9** blindness

hemi: **4** half

hemlock: **4** bunk, herb, pine, tree **5** tsuga **6** conium **7** conifer
  drinker: **8** Socrates
  poison: **6** conium

hemoglobin: **10** sickle cell

hemophiliac: **7** bleeder

hemp: ife, kef, kif, pua, tow **4** bang, carl, flax, harl, jute, rine, sunn **5** abaca, bhang, istle, ramie, sisal, sizal **6** ambary, banana, cabuja, fennel, manila **7** hashish **8** cannabis, nepenthe **9** marijuana

hen: pea **4** fowl, rail, wife **5** biddy, chick, woman **6** gorhen, nester, pullet, towdie **7** chicken **9** gallinule
  broody: **6** sitter
  coop: **5** caire
  spayed: **7** poulard
  young: **6** pullet

henbane: **4** herb **10** nightshade

hence: fro **4** away, ergo (L.), thus **5** since **7** hereout, thither **9** therefore **11** accordingly

henceforth: **9** from now on, hereafter

henchman: **4** page **6** flunky, gillie, lackey, minion, squire **7** mobster **8** adherent, disciple, follower **9** attendant, supporter

Hengist: *brother:* **5** Horsa
  daughter: **6** Rowena
  kingdom: **4** Kent
  people: **5** Jutes

henna: dye **6** alcana **7** alcanna

henpeck: nag **4** carp

Henry II: *adversary:* **6** Becket
  drama about: **15** The Lion in Winter
  surname: **5** Anjou **11** Plantagenet
  wife: **7** Eleanor

Henry IV: **9** Lancaster **11** Bolingbroke

Henry V: Hal
  victor at: **9** Agincourt

Henry VIII: *daughter:* **4** Mary **9** Elizabeth
  fifth wife: **9** Catherine
  first wife: **9** Catherine
  fourth wife: **4** Anne
  second wife: **4** Anne
  sixth wife: **9** Catherine
  son: **6** Edward

  surname: **5** Tudor
  third wife: **4** Jane

Henry of Portugal: **9** navigator

hepatitis: **8** jaundice

Hephaestus: **6** Vulcan
  father: **4** Zeus **7** Jupiter
  mother: **4** Hera, Juno
  wife: **5** Venus **6** Charis **8** Charites **9** Aphrodite

heptad: **5** seven **11** septivalent

Hera: **4** Juno
  brother: **4** Zeus
  husband: **4** Zeus
  mother: **4** Rhea
  son: **4** Ares

Heracles: See **Hercules**

herald: **4** bode **5** crier, greet, usher **6** beadle, Hermes, signal **7** declare, forerun, trumpet **8** announce, blazoner, foretell, outrider, proclaim **9** harbinger, introduce, messenger, precursor **10** forerunner, foreshadow

heraldry: **6** armory **9** pageantry
  band: **4** fess **5** fesse
  bastardy mark: **4** bend **5** baton **7** bendlet **8** sinister
  bearing: **4** orle
  bell: **7** compane **10** campanella
  blood-red: **6** murrey
  chaplet: **4** orle
  charge: vol **7** boterol, saltier, saltire **8** boteroll, tressour, tressure
  circle: **6** bezant
  cross: **4** paty **5** patee, patte **6** ermine, moline, pattee **7** erminee, patonce, saltier, saltire
  device: **4** ente, orle **5** crest **6** altier
  fleur-de-lis: lis, lys
  gold: or
  grafted: **4** ente
  green: **4** vert
  keylike: **4** urde
  knot: **4** Lacy, Wake **5** Bowen, Dacre **7** Heneage **8** Stafford **9** Bourchier **10** Harrington
  leg: **4** gamb, jamb **5** gambe, jambe
  line: **4** unde
  scattered: **4** seme
  shield: **10** escutcheon
  tincture: or **5** tenne **6** argent
  triangle: **5** giron
  winged: **4** aile
  wreath: **4** orle **5** torse

herb: iva **4** anet, balm, dill, leek, mint, moly, sage, wort **5** anise, basil, chive, plant, sedge, thyme **6** annual, borage, catnip, clover, lovage, sesame, yarrow **7** caraway, ginseng, oregano, parsley **8** marjoram, tarragon **9** coriander
  aromatic: **4** anet, balm, dill, hemp, mint,

nard, sage **5** anise, basil, clary, nondo, tansy, thyme **6** catnip, fennel, hyssop **7** chervil, cudweed, gentian, mustard, saffron, vetiver **8** lavender, rosemary, wormseed **9** basilmint, coriander, spearmint **11** everlasting

bitter: rue **4** aloe, woad **7** aletris, boneset **8** centaury **10** turtlehead

bog: **5** calla **9** steepweed, steepwort

climbing: **4** faba **5** vicia

coarse: **5** tansy **6** eringo, eryngo **7** leafcup **8** pokeweed

flowering: **7** anemone, dittany **8** stapelia **9** calendula, celandine

genus: iva **4** ruta **5** ajuga, canna, cicer, cruca, galax, gavra, inula, lemna, loasa, rheum **6** aralia, asarum, cassia, dondia, isatis, mentha, nerine **7** alyssum, anemone, cirsium, hedeoma, torenia **8** psoralea **9** grindelia

medicinal: rue **4** aloe **5** senna, sumac, tansy **6** arnica, lovage, tutsan **7** aconite, boneset **9** horehound

mythical: **4** moly

narcotic: **4** hemp

perennial: pia **4** balm, irid **5** sedum **6** fennel, madder, yarrow **7** bugbane, lopweed **8** sainfoin, soapwort **9** digitalis

poisonous: **4** loco **6** conium **7** hemlock, henbane **8** mandrake **9** hellebore

salad: **6** chives, endive **7** chicory **10** watercress

shoot: udo

sweet-scented: **6** cicely **8** woodruff

trinity: **8** hepatica

woody: rue

herbage: 5 grass **7** foliage, pasture

herbicide: 10 weed killer

herculean: 4 huge, vast **5** giant **7** immense, mammoth, titanic **8** colossal, enormous, gigantic **10** superhuman **12** overwhelming

Hercules: 8 Heracles

captive: **4** Iole

companion: **5** Hylas

friend: **6** Iolaus

lion's home: **5** Nemea

mother: **7** Alcmene

stone: **9** loadstone

sweetheart: **4** Iole

victim: **5** Hydra

wife: **4** Hebe **6** Megara **8** Deianira

herd: mob **4** crew, lead, ruck **5** bunch, crowd, drift, drive, drove, flock, group, guard **6** corral, gather, hirsel, masses, pastor, rabble **7** creaght, shelter **8** guardian **9** associate **10** assemblage, congregate **11** aggregation

herdsman: 5 booly **6** booley, cowboy, drover, gaucho **8** bucolic, vaquero **9** garthman, ranchero (Sp.), wrangler

god: **5** Pales

here: aca (Sp.), ici (F.) **4** aqui (Sp.) **5** ready **6** hither **7** on earth, present

hereafter: 5 after, later **6** beyond, future

hereditary: 6 inborn, innate, lineal **8** heirship **9** ancestral, descended **10** congenital **11** inheritable, patrimonial

heredity: 4 line **5** birth **8** genetics **11** inheritance

factor: **4** gene

heresy: 6 schism **7** dissent **8** Arianism **9** defection, misbelief **10** Gnosticism, infidelity, radicalism **11** unorthodoxy **13** nonconformism

heretic: 5 Arian **6** bugger **7** gnostic, infidel, Patarin **8** apostate **9** dissenter, miscreant, sectarian **10** schismatic, unbeliever **13** nonconformist

heretofore: 4 erst **6** before **8** erewhile, formerly, hitherto, previous **9** erstwhile

heritage: 6 legacy **9** patrimony, tradition **10** birthright **11** inheritance

heritor: 4 heir **5** donee **9** inheritor

heritrix, heretrix: 7 heiress

herl: fly **4** barb

hermaphrodite: 5 scrat **9** androgyne **10** androgynous

Hermes: 7 Mercury

birthplace: **7** Cyllene

father: **4** Zeus

mother: **4** Maia

son: **7** Evander **9** Autolycus

staff: **8** caduceus

winged cap: **7** petasos, petasus

winged shoes: **7** talaria

hermetic: 6 sealed, secret **8** airtight **9** alchemist, resistant

Hermione: *father:* **8** Menelaus

husband: **7** Orestes **11** Neoptolemus

mother: **5** Helen

hermit: 4 monk **5** clerk, loner **6** anchor **7** ascetic, eremite, inclusa, incluse, recluse, stylite **8** anchoret, beadsman, bedesman, inclusus, marabout **9** anchorite

hut: **4** cell

hermit crab: 8 pagurian

hermitage: 7 ashrama, retreat **8** cloister, hideaway **9** monastery, reclusery

hernia: 6 breach **7** rupture **10** protrusion

hero: ace **4** idol **5** darer **6** knight **7** demigod **8** champion **9** conqueror **10** topnotcher **11** protagonist

deified: **7** demigod

legendary: **6** Amadis, Roland **7** Paladin

Hero's lover: 7 Leander

Herodias: *daughter:* **6** Salome

husband: **5** Herod

heroic: 4 bold, epic, huge **5** brave, great, large, noble **6** daring, epical, mighty **7** extreme, gallant, spartan, valiant **8** colossal, enormous, fearless, intrepid, powerful **9** bombastic **10** courageous **11** extravagant, illustrious, magnanimous, outstanding, venturesome **13** grandiloquent

heroin: **4** drug, junk **5** horse, smack **8** narcotic

heroine: **8** lead role **11** demigoddess, leading lady

heroism: **5** valor **6** daring, valour **7** bravery, courage **8** chivalry, nobility **9** fortitude **13** unselfishness

heron: **4** hern, rail, soco **5** crane, egret, herne, quawk, wader **7** bittern, hernser, quabird **8** aigrette, gaulding, heronsew **9** cormorant, herneshaw, heronsewe, heronshaw
genus: **5** ardea

herpes: **5** fever, virus **6** eczema **7** blister **8** cold sore, shingles **10** chicken pox **11** Epstein-Barr **12** encephalitis **13** mononucleosis

herpetologist's concern: **8** reptiles

herring: **4** raun **7** alewife, anchovy **8** scuddawn
barrel: **4** cade, cran
catch: **4** tack
family: **8** pilchard
female: **4** raun
fry: **4** sile
genus: **6** clupea
head: cob
lake: **5** cisco
young: **4** brit **5** matie, sprat, sprot

Hersey setting: **5** Adano

Hertha: **4** Erda **7** Nerthus

Hesiod: **4** poet **5** Greek
heroine: **7** Pandora
work: **8** Theogony **12** Works and Days

hesitancy: **10** hesitation, indecision, reluctance

hesitant: shy **4** loth **5** chary, loath, timid **6** averse, wobbly **7** bashful, halting **8** timorous, wavering **9** reluctant

hesitate: **4** balk, wait **5** delay, demur, doubt, pause, stall, waver **6** boggle, falter, loiter, scotch **7** stammer **8** hang back **9** vacillate **10** dillydally **12** shilly-shally, wiggle-waggle **13** procrastinate

hesitating: coy **4** hink **7** halting **8** backward, doubtful **9** ambiguous **10** indecisive **11** vacillating

Hesperia: **5** Italy, Spain

Hesperides: **5** Aegle **6** Hestia **7** Hespera **8** Arethusa, Erytheia, Erytheis

Hesperus: **5** Venus **11** evening star
father: **8** Astraeus
mother: Eos

hessonite: **6** garnet

Hestia: *father:* **6** Cronus
mother: **4** Rhea

hetaera, hetaira: **8** mistress, paramour **9** companion, concubine, courtesan **12** demimondaine

heterogeneous: **5** mixed **6** motley, unlike **7** diverse **9** different **10** dissimilar **13** miscellaneous **14** indiscriminate

Heteroousian: **5** Arian

hetman: **6** ataman **7** Cossack, headman

hew: cut **4** chip, chop, fell, hack **5** carve, wound **6** haggle, strike, stroke

hex: **4** jinx **6** voodoo **7** bewitch

hexad: **6** sextet

hexadecene: **6** cetene

hexastich: **6** sestet, stanza **7** strophe

heyday: joy, May **4** acme **5** prime **6** height, spring, zenith **8** wildness **14** frolicsomeness

Hezekiah: *father:* **4** Ahaz **7** Neariah
kingdom: **5** Judah
mother: Abi
son: **8** Manasseh
wife: **9** Hephzibah

hiatus: gap **5** break, chasm, pause **6** breach, lacuna **7** opening **8** interval, vacation **12** interruption

Hiawatha: *author:* **10** Longfellow
grandmother: **7** Nokomis
mother: **7** Wenonah
wife: **9** Minnehaha

Hibernia: **4** Eire, Erin **7** Ireland

hiccup, hiccough: **4** burp **5** spasm **9** singultus

hick: **4** jake, rube **5** yokel **6** hiccup, rustic **7** bumpkin, hayseed **8** cornball

hickey: **6** pimple **7** pustule

hickory: **5** pecan **9** bitternut, shellbark

hidden: **4** lost **5** inner, perdu **6** arcane, buried, cached, closed, covert, innate, latent, masked, occult, secret, veiled **7** arcanum, covered, cryptic, obscure, recluse **8** screened, secluded, secreted **9** concealed, invisible, recondite **10** mysterious **11** clandestine, delitescent, undisclosed **12** subterranean

hide: bar, fur, kip, lie **4** bury, coat, dern, fell, hill, hood, lurk, pelt, skin, stow, veil **5** cache, cloak, cloud, couch, cover, derne (Sc.), skulk **6** huddle, screen, shroud **7** abscond, conceal, cover up, eclipse, leather, secrete, shelter **8** carucate, disguise, ensconce, hoodwink, palliate, suppress, withhold **9** dissemble **10** camouflage, flagellate
cleaning instrument: **6** slater
measured in: **8** hidation
remove hair from: **4** moon
undressed: kip **4** pelt
worker: **6** tanner

hidebound: **6** narrow **7** bigoted, miserly **9** barkbound, bourgeois, illiberal, niggardly **10** restrained **12** conventional

hideous: 4 fell, grim, ugly 5 awful 6 grisly, horrid, odius, ogrish 7 ghastly, ogreish 8 deformed, dreadful, grewsome, gruesome, horrible, shocking, terrible 9 dismaying, frightful, revolting 10 detestable, discordant, terrifying

hideout: den, mew 4 cave, lair 5 cache 7 retreat 8 hideaway

hides: 4 furs 5 skins 6 peltry

hiding: 7 secrecy 8 flogging 9 coverture

hie: 5 haste, hurry, speed 6 betake, hasten, scurry, strive 8 expedite

hiemal: 6 wintry

hierarch: 4 boss, head 5 chief 6 leader, master, satrap 10 high priest

hieroglyphic: 7 cryptic 9 illegible

hieroglyphics key: 12 Rosetta stone

higgle: 6 haggle 7 bargain, chaffer

high: alt 4 dear, haut (F.), main, much, tall 5 acute, chief, drunk, first, lofty, sharp, steep 6 costly, shrill, stoned, wasted 7 eminent, exalted, haughty, violent 8 elevated, foremost, hopped up, piercing, towering, turned on 9 admirable, expensive, important, principal, turbulent 10 tripped out, tumultuous 11 mountainous

high and dry: 8 marooned, stranded

high-and-mighty: 8 arrogant, insolent, superior 9 imperious 11 overbearing

highbinder: 5 cheat, rowdy 6 conman 7 ruffian 8 swindler

highborn: 5 noble 8 generous 12 aristocratic

highbred: 7 genteel, refined

highbrow: 7 egghead 10 doubledome 12 intellectual 14 intelligentsia

high-class: 6 classy 10 first-class

higher: 7 greater 8 superior

highest: top 5 first 6 upmost 7 extreme, maximal, supreme 8 bunemost, greatest, overmost

highest point: 4 acme 6 zenith

high-flying: 7 icarian 11 pretentious

high-handed: 6 lordly 8 arrogant, cavalier, despotic 9 arbitrary 11 dictatorial, domineering, overbearing

high-hat: 4 snub 8 snobbish 12 aristocratic

Highlander (see also **Scotland**): 4 Celt, Gael, Kelt, Scot 6 Tartan 8 clansman 16 Gluneamie
dance: 4 reel 5 fling
language: 4 Erse
pouch: 6 sporan 7 sporran
weapon: 8 claymore, skeandhu

Highland war cry: 6 slogan

highlight: 6 accent, stress 7 feature 9 emphasize, underline

high-pitched: 6 shrill 7 shrieky 8 agitated

high-pressure: 8 forceful, pressing 9 insistent 10 aggressive

high-priced: 4 dear 6 costly 9 expensive

high priest: Eli

high rise: 4 tall 5 lofty 10 multistory, skyscraper

highroad: 7 highway

high-sea: 4 main

high-sounding: 4 arty 7 fustian, pompous 8 imposing 9 bombastic, overblown 10 altisonant

high-spirited: 5 fiery, jolly, merry 6 lively 7 gallant, gingery, peppery 8 cavalier 10 mettlesome

high-strung: 5 tense 7 nervous, uptight 9 excitable

high-toned: 7 stylish 8 elevated 9 dignified 11 fashionable

highway: way 4 bahn (G.), iter (L.), path, pike, road 5 Alcan 6 Appian, artery, causey, course, rumpad, street 7 Lincoln, parkway 8 autobahn, causeway, chaussee (F.), highroad, speedway, turnpike 9 boulevard 10 expressway, interstate, throughway 12 thoroughfare

highwayman: pad 5 rider, thief 6 bandit, padder, robber 7 brigand, footpad, ladrone 8 hightoby 9 bandolero

Highwayman: *author:* 5 Noyes

hijack: rob 6 coerce

hike: 4 jerk, toss, walk 5 march, raise, throw, tramp 6 ramble

hilarious: mad 5 funny, merry, noisy 6 jovial 7 jocular 8 mirthful 9 ludicrous

hilarity: fun, gig, joy 4 glee 5 cheer, mirth 6 gaiety 7 jollity, whoopee 9 happiness, joviality, laughter, merriment 10 joyousness 12 cheerfulness, exhilaration

hill: ben, hoe, kop, pap, tor 4 bank, brae, bult, dagh, dune, fell, heap, hide, knap, knob, loma, mesa, pile 5 bargh, butte, cerro (Sp.), cliff, cover, hurst, morro, mound, mount 6 ascent, barrow, copple, djebel 7 colline, picacho 9 acclivity, elevation, monadnock
D.C.: 7 Capitol
glacial: 4 kame, paha 7 drumlin
Jerusalem: 6 Olivet
range: 5 ridge
sand: 4 dene, dune
top of: tor 4 peak 6 summit

hillbilly: 4 rube 5 yokel 6 rustic 7 bumpkin, hayseed 12 backwoodsman

hillock: 4 tump 5 croft, hurst, knoll, kopje, mound, toman (Sc.) 6 coppet 7 hummock 8 molehill
over grave: 7 tumulus

hillside: 4 brae, cote 5 cleve, cliff, falda (Sp.), slade, slope 6 cleeve

hilly: 5 steep

hilt: 6 handle 8 handgrip

hilum: 4 scar 5 porta 7 nucleus

Himalaya: *animal, bear-like:* **5** panda
 antelope: **5** goral, serow
 bear: **5** bhalu
 bearcat: **5** panda
 cedar: **6** deodar
 cypress: **6** bhutan
 dweller: **6** Sherpa **8** Nepalese
 goat: **4** kras, tahr, tair, thar
 oxen: yak
 peak: Ka, Api **6** Kailas **7** Everest **12**
 Kanchenjunga
 pheasant: **5** monal
 sheep: **6** bharal, nahoor
 swamp: **5** Terai
 tableland: **5** Tibet
Himavat's daughter: 4 Devi
himene, himine: 4 hymn, song
himself: 4 ipse (L.)
Himyarite: 4 Arab **7** Axumite, Sabaean
Hinayana Buddhism: 5 shojo **6** lesser
hind: doe, lad, roe **4** back, chap, rear, stag **5**
 coney **6** fellow, rustic, worker **7** bailiff,
 peasant, servant, steward, venison **8**
 cabrilla, domestic **9** posterior **11** hindquar-
 ter
hinder: bar, let **4** slow **5** after, block, cheat,
 check, choke, cramp, debar, delay, deter,
 embar, estop, hedge **6** arrest, detain, hamper, harass, impede, impend, injure, retard,
 scotch **7** bog down, deprive, forelay,
 impeach, inhibit, prevent **8** encumber,
 handicap, obstruct, preclude, prohibit **9**
 embarrass, foreclose, forestall, frustrate,
 hamstring, interrupt, posterior
hindmost: 4 last, rear **9** aftermost
hindrance: bar, rub **4** clog, curb, snag, stop **5**
 block, check, delay, hitch **6** arrest **7** barrier
 8 drawback, obstacle **9** detention, deterrent, restraint **10** difficulty, impediment **11**
 encumbrance, impeachment, obstruction
 12 interruption
Hindu (see also **Rama, Indian**): **4** Babu,
 Koli, Sikh **5** Tamil **6** Gentoo, Hindoo **8**
 Kolarian
 abode of gods: **4** Meru
 adherent: Sik **4** Jain, Seik, Sikh **5** Jaina,
 Seikh
 age of world: **4** yuga
 alphabet: **6** Sarada
 ancestral race: **5** Aryan
 apartment: **5** mahal
 Aryan race: **4** Swat
 ascetic: **4** jogi, sadh, yati, yogi **5** sadhu
 atheist: **7** nastika
 book: **4** Veda **6** Tantra **11** Yajna-valkya
 calendar: Pus **4** Asin, Jeth, Kaur, Magh **5**
 Aghan, Asarh, Chait, Katik, Sawan **6**
 Bhadon, Kartik, Phagun **7** Baisakh, Phal-
 gun, Sarawan

 call to prayer: **4** azan
 caste: Dom, Mal, Meo **4** Dasi, Gola, Koli,
 Kori, Mali, Pasi, Teli **5** Goala, Palli, Sudra,
 Varna **6** Babhan, Soodra **7** Brahman **11**
 untouchable
 caste member: Jat **4** Jain **6** Banian, Banyan,
 Rajput, Vaisya **7** Harijan, Rajpoot **9** Kshatriya, Vakkaliga
 charm: **6** mantra
 chief: mir **6** sirdar
 coin: ana, pai, pie **4** anna, pice **5** paisa,
 rupee
 congregation: **5** samaj, somaj
 convert to Islam: **6** shaikh
 cremation: **4** sati **6** suttee
 dancer: **8** devadasi
 deity: Dev **4** Deva, Dewa, Maya, Rama,
 Yama **5** Ganesa, Varuna, Vishnu **7** Ganesha,
 Krishna **9** Jagannath **10** Jagannatha, Juggernaut **11** Ramachandra
 demon: **4** Bali, Bhut, Ketu, Rahu **5** Asura **6**
 Daitya
 devotee: **4** yati
 disciple: **4** sikh
 divine being: dev **4** deva
 doctrine: **5** Karma **6** dharma
 drink: **4** soma
 duty: **6** dharma
 essence: **4** rasa, rata **5** atman **6** amrita
 family: **5** gotra
 female energy: **5** Sakti **6** Shakti
 festival: Tij **4** Hola, Holi, mela **5** Durga **6**
 Dewali, Divali, Hoolee **16** Thaipusam
 Dashara
 flute: bin **5** pungi
 garment: **4** sari **5** saree
 gentleman: **4** babu **5** baboo, sahib
 god (see also *deity* above): **4** Agni, Deva,
 Kama, Siva, Vayu, Yama **5** Asura, Shiva,
 Simia **6** Brahma, Ganesa, Skanda, Varuna **7**
 Ganesha
 goddess: Sri, Uma, Vac **4** Devi, Kali, Shri,
 Vach **5** Durga, Gauri, Sakti, Shree, Ushas **6**
 Chandi, Shakti **7** Parvati **9** Haimavati
 guitar: **5** sitar
 headdress: **5** rumal
 heaven: **5** dyaus
 hermitage: **7** ashrama
 hero: **4** Nala, Rama
 holy book: **4** Veda **6** Sastra
 holy sage: **4** rishi
 hymn: **6** mantra
 idol worship: **5** arati
 incarnation: **6** avatar
 Indra: **5** Sakka, Sakra
 king: **4** Nala **5** Sesha **6** Shesha
 lady: **4** devi, rani **5** ranee
 law: **5** Karma
 lawgiver: **4** Manu

life principle: 4 jiva 5 atman, prana
literature: 4 Veda 5 sruti 6 shruti
loincloth: 5 dhoti
magic: 4 jadu, maya 5 jadoo
magician: 5 fakir 6 fakeer
mantra: om, um
master: 5 sahib
mendicant: 4 naga 7 bairagi, vairagi 8 sannyasi
mental discipline: 4 yoga
monastery: 4 math
monkey god: 7 Hanuman
mystic: 4 yogi
noble: 5 rajah 8 maharaja
non-violence: 6 ahimsa
offering: 4 bali, lepa 5 pinda
paradise: 7 Nirvana
patriarch: 5 pitri
philosophy: 4 yoga 5 tamas
poem: 6 Purana 8 Ramayana 11 Mahabharata 12 Bhagavad-Gita
prayer rug: 4 asan 5 asana
priest: 5 hotar
prince: 4 raja, rana 5 rajah 8 maharaja 9 maharajah
pundit: 5 swami
queen: 4 rani 5 ranee 8 maharani 9 maharanee
rebirth: 13 reincarnation
religion: 5 Prana 7 Jainism, Sivaism 8 Shivaism
rice: 4 boro
rite: 4 puja 5 achar, pooja
ruler: 5 rajah
saint: 4 guru, yogi
scripture: Li, rig 4 Veda 5 Sruti 6 Purana, Sastra, Smriti, Tantra 7 Samhita, Shastra 8 Brahmana 9 Upanishad
sect: 4 Sikh, siva 6 Aghori
social division: 5 caste, varna
soldier: 4 Sikh 5 sepoy
soul: 4 atma 5 atman
spirit: 4 Jiva, Mara 5 Asura, Atman, Prana 7 Muktama
supreme being: 6 Vishnu
teacher: pir 4 guru
temple: 4 deul 6 vimana
term of respect: 5 sahib
title: aya, sri 4 mian, raja, shri, sidi 5 rajah, sahib, shree, swami 7 bahadur
tower: 5 stupa
triad god: 4 Siva
tunic: 4 jama 5 jamah
unknown god: Ka
unorthodox: 4 Jain 5 Jaina
Upanishad: 4 Isha, Veda 7 Vedanta
worship: 4 puja 5 pooja
Hindustan: Ind 5 India
language: 4 Urdu 5 Hindi

tribesman: 4 toda
hinge: har 4 butt, hang, turn 5 gemel, joint, mount, pivot, stand 6 depend, gimmer, gimmor, hingle, lamina, pintle
Hinnom Valley: 7 Gehenna
hinny (see also **mule**): *dam:* ass 5 jenny
sire: 5 horse 8 stallion
hint: cue, tip 4 clew, clue, time, turn 5 cheep (Sc.), imply, infer, trace 6 allude, moment 7 inkling, mention, suggest 8 allusion, innuendo, intimate, occasion 9 catchword, insinuate 10 indication, intimation, suggestion 11 insinuation
hip: hop 4 coxa, huck, limp, miss, skip 6 haunch, huckle
pert. to: 7 sciatic
hip boots: 6 waders
hipbone: 5 ileum, ilium
hippie: mod 5 freak, rebel 6 copout 8 bohemian, longhair
Hippocrates: *birthplace:* Kos
drug: 5 mecon, opium
hippodrome: 5 arena 6 circus 7 contest
Hippolytus: 9 Greek hero
father: 7 Theseus
mother: 7 Antiope 9 Hippolyne
stepmother: 7 Phaedra
hippopotamus: 6 seacow 8 behemoth 9 pachyderm
hire: buy, fee, let, use 4 rent, sign, wage 5 bribe, lease, price, put on, wages 6 employ, engage, retain, reward, salary 7 charter, conduce, recruit, stipend 9 allowance 12 compensation
hireling: 4 esne, grub, hack, serf 5 slave 8 gangster 9 mercenary
hirsute: 5 hairy, rough 6 coarse, shaggy 7 pileous
hispid: 5 rough, spiny 7 bristly 8 strigose, strigous
hiss: boo 4 hish, sizz, whiz 5 whizz 6 fissle, fistle 8 goose cry, pooh-pooh 9 raspberry 10 assibilate
hissing: 6 fizzle 8 sibilant 9 sibilance
hist: 4 hark, hush 7 be quiet
historian: 8 annalist 10 chronicler
history: 4 tale 5 drama, story 6 annals, memoir, record 7 account 8 relation 9 biography, chronicle, genealogy, narrative
muse: 4 Clio
histrio: 5 actor
histrionics: 6 acting 9 dramatics 11 theatricals 13 theatricality
hit: bat, lam, lob, ram, rap, tap 4 bump, bunt, cast, club, slog, slug, sock, swat, wham 5 clout, flick, knock, smack, smite, smote, throw, touch 6 attain, batted, bingle, strike 7 collide, success 8 bludgeon 10 production, succession

baseball: **4** bunt **5** homer, liner **6** double, single, triple **7** home run **8** grounder **9** line drive

golf: **4** chip **5** drive, shank, slice

hit-or-miss: **6** casual, chance, habnab, random **7** aimless **8** careless **9** haphazard

hitter: **6** batter **7** batsman, slugger

hitch: hop, tie, tug **4** halt, hook, join, knot, limp, pull **5** agree, catch, crick, hotch, marry, thumb, unite **6** attach, enlist, hobble **8** obstacle, stoppage **9** harmonize, hindrance **10** enlistment, impediment **11** contretemps, obstruction

hither: **4** here **6** nearer **11** to this place

hitherto: ago, yet **5** as yet **6** before **7** thus far

Hitler: **6** Führer

aerie: **13** Berchtesgaden

follower: **4** Nazi

Hittite: *ancestor:* **4** Heth

capital: **6** Pteria

storm god: **6** Teshub, Teshup

hive: **5** store, swarm **6** apiary **7** store up **9** multitude

hives: **5** uredo **7** allergy **9** urticaria

hoagie, hoagy: **4** hero **9** submarine **13** large sandwich

hoar: **4** cold, gray, rime **5** frost, hoary, musty, stale **6** biting **7** ancient **9** antiquity, venerable **13** venerableness

hoard: **4** save **5** amass, chest, hutch, lay up, stash, stock, store **6** supply **7** husband, reserve **8** quantity, treasure, treasury **10** accumulate, collection

hoarder: **5** miser **6** storer **9** treasurer

hoarfrost: rag **4** rime, rind **9** cranreuch (Sc.)

hoarse: dry, raw **5** gruff, harsh, rocky, rough **7** grating, raucous **10** discordant

hoarseness: **4** frog **5** croup

hoary: old **4** aged, gray, hoar **5** moldy, mossy, musty **7** ancient, hoarish, whitish **9** canescent, venerable

hoax: bam, cod, fun, gyp, hex, kid **4** bilk, dupe, fake, fool, gaff, gegg, gull, gunk, joke, ruse, sell, sham **5** bluff, cheat, spoof, trick **6** canard, diddle, humbug, string **7** deceive **8** artifice **9** bamboozle, deception **11** hornswoggle

hob: elf, peg, pin, tap **4** game, mark, nail **5** clown, fairy, ledge **6** ferret, rustic, sprite **7** mandrel **8** mischief **10** countryman, projection

hobble: tie **4** clog, clop, gimp, limp **5** bunch, cramp, hitch, leash **6** fetter, hamper, hogtie, hopple **7** cramble, perplex, shackle, spancel **9** embarrass **10** difficulty, perplexity **13** embarrassment

hobbledehoy: lad **5** youth

hobbler: **5** pilot **7** boatman, hoveler, laborer **8** retainer **12** longshoreman

hobby: fad **5** horse **6** falcon **7** pastime **9** avocation, diversion

hobgoblin: bug, elf, hag, imp **4** bogy, Puck **5** bogey, bogie, bugan, poker, spook **6** boodie (Sc.), sprite **7** bugaboo **8** bogglebo, worricow (Sc.) **9** coltpixie **10** apparition

hobo: boe, bum **5** tramp **7** drifter, floater, vagrant **8** vagabond

hock: ham, hox **4** pawn **5** ankle, hough, thigh **6** mallow, pledge **8** mortgage **9** hamstring **10** houghsinew

hocket: **6** hiccup **8** obstacle **12** interruption

hockey: **5** bandy **6** shinny

arena: **4** rink

cup: **6** Calder, Canada **7** Stanley

disk: **4** puck

goal: net

official: **7** referee **8** linesman

penalty: **7** hooking **8** boarding, fighting, roughing, slashing, spearing, tripping **12** high-sticking, interference

players: Orr **4** Hull **5** Bucyk **6** Mikita, Parent **7** Gretzky, Lemieux, Ratelle, Richard **8** Beliveau, Esposito **9** Mahovlich **10** Delvecchio

positions: **4** wing **6** center, goalie **7** forward **10** defenseman, goaltender

pro teams (NHL): **4** Jets (Winnipeg) **5** Blues (St. Louis), Kings (Los Angeles) **6** Bruins (Boston), Devils (New Jersey), Flames (Calgary), Flyers (Philadelphia), Oilers (Edmonton), Sabres (Buffalo), Sharks (San Jose) **7** Canucks (Vancouver), Rangers (New York), Whalers (Hartford) **8** Capitals (Washington), Penguins (Pittsburgh), Red Wings (Detroit) **9** Canadiens (Montreal), Islanders (New York), Lightning (Tampa Bay), Nordiques (Quebec) **10** Black Hawks (Chicago), Maple Leafs (Toronto), North Stars (Minnesota) Senators (Ottawa)

stick: **6** burley **7** cammock (Sc.)

terms: **4** deke, save, slot **5** icing **6** boards, chippy **7** face-off, red line **8** blue line, empty net, offsides **9** backcheck, bodycheck, center ice, forecheck, power play **10** center line, penalty box **11** shorthanded **12** box formation **14** penalty killing

hocus: **4** drug **5** cheat, fraud **7** deceive **8** cheating, deceiver, trickery **10** adulterate

hocus-pocus: **5** cheat, trick **6** humbug **7** juggler **8** flimflam, quackery **9** trickster **12** charlatanism

hod: 4 soil, tray 6 barrow 7 scuttle 11 coal scuttle

hodgepodge: ana 4 hash, mess, olio, stew 5 cento 6 jumble, medley 7 mixture 8 mishmash 10 hotchpotch, miscellany 11 gallimaufry, olla podrida 12 mingle-mangle

hoe: dig 4 brod, hill, till 5 clean, cliff, padle, worry 6 sarcle, scrape 7 dogfish, trouble 8 griffaun 9 cultivate 10 promontory

hog: sow 4 bene, boar, dime, galt, gilt, take 5 shoat, shote, swine 6 barrow 7 glutton, hogling 8 shilling 9 boschvark 10 backfatter, locomotive, motorcycle 11 appropriate
breed: 5 Essex 9 Hampshire
food: 4 mash 5 slops, swill 6 acorns
genus: sus
young: pig 5 shoat

hog peanut: 8 earthpea

hog plum: 4 amra

hogfish: 8 scorpene

hoggish: 5 hoggy 7 selfish, swinish 10 gluttonous

hognut: 5 ouabe 6 pignut 8 earthnut

hogshead: 4 cask 6 barrel, hogget, vessel

hogtie: 4 bind, clog, curb 5 leash 6 fetter, hamper 8 obstruct, restrain

hogwash: 4 slop 5 draff, swill 6 drivel 7 baloney, pigwash 8 nonsense 10 balderdash 13 horsefeathers

hoiden: See **hoyden**

hoi polloi: mob 6 masses, rabble 8 populace, riffraff

hoist: cat, gin 4 jack, lift 5 boost, crane, davit, heave, heeze, horse, lewis, raise, setup, winch 7 derrick, elevate 8 elevator, windlass

hoist sail: 4 swig

hoity-toity: 5 dizzy, giddy, proud 6 snooty 7 flighty, haughty, pompous 8 arrogant 11 harum-scarum, patronizing, thoughtless 13 irresponsible

hokum: 4 blaa, blah, bunk 11 foolishness

hold: own 4 bind, bite, bulk, clip, fill, have, hook, keep, rely, seat, stow, tend 5 avast, carry, catch, grasp, guard, rivet 6 adhere, arrest, behold, cleave, clench, clutch, decree, defend, detain, harbor, occupy, retain 7 adjudge, contain, control, support, sustain 8 consider, interest, maintain, thurrock 9 entertain, mesmerize, spellbind 10 possession, stronghold 11 catch hold of
a brief for: 6 defend 8 advocate
back: dam 4 curb, halt, stem, stop 5 check, deter 6 detain, retard 7 inhibit, repress 8 restrain 9 hindrance
fast: hug 4 hook, nail 5 cling, stick 6 clinch, cohere
forth: 5 offer, orate, speak 7 exhibit, expound 8 continue, maintain, propound 9 discourse
in custody: 4 jail 6 detain, intern
off: 5 avert 7 refrain
on: 4 stop, wait 7 forbear 8 continue
out: 4 last 6 endure 7 exclude, protend 8 continue
up: rob 4 halt, lift, rein 5 boost, check, delay, raise 6 hijack 7 display, exhibit, robbery, stick-up, support, sustain 8 stoppage 10 overcharge
water: 5 sound 10 consistent

holder: 5 haver 6 tenant, vessel 9 container 10 receptacle

holding: 4 land 5 asset 6 estate, tenure 8 property
adapted for: 10 prehensile

hole: bay, den, gap, pit 4 bore, cave, cove, deep, dump, flaw, gate, gulf, leak, mine, nook, peck, rent, vent 5 abyss, chasm, inlet, shaft 6 burrow, cavern, cavity, cranny, crater, defect, eyelet, grotto, hollow, pierce, prison, recess 7 dungeon, mortise, opening, orifice, ostiole 8 aperture, bunghole, peephole 9 perforate 10 excavation 11 perforation, predicament
instrument for making: awl 4 bore 5 drill 8 stiletto
wall: 4 muse 5 meuse, niche

Holi, Hoolee: 5 Hindu 8 festival

holia: 4 fish 6 salmon

holiday (see also individual religions and countries): 4 fete 5 feria, festa, merry 6 fiesta, jovial, outing 7 festive, playday 8 festival, vacation 9 convivial, Mardi Gras

holiness: 4 pope 5 piety 7 halidom 8 divinity, halidome, sanctity 9 sanctuary 11 saintliness 12 consecration 13 righteousness

Holland: See **Netherlands**

holler: 4 yell 5 shout 6 shriek 7 protest

hollow: den, dip 4 boss, cave, cove, deep, dent, doke, glen, hole, holl, howe, huck, lean, thin, vain, void 5 bight, chase, cuppy, empty, false, gaunt, goyal, goyle, heugh, scoop, sinus, stria 6 cavern, cavity, cirque, groove, hungry, socket, sunken, vacant, valley 7 concave, muffled, unsound 8 alveolus, fossette, not solid, specious 9 cavernous, deceitful, deeply set, depressed, faithless, worthless 10 depression, sepulchral 11 treacherous 12 unsatisfying
out: cut, dig 4 bore 6 excise
hollow-eyed: 7 haggard

hollowed: 7 concave, glenoid, spouted

hollowed out: 6 cavate

hollowness: 6 vanity 7 vacuity

holly: 4 assi, holm, ilex 5 shrub, yapon, yupon 6 hulver, yaupon, youpon
pert to: 6 ilicic

holm oak: 4 ilex 5 holly

Holmes' word: **10** elementary

holobaptist: **12** immersionist

holocaust: **7** inferno **9** sacrifice **11** destruction

holster: **4** case **7** housing **8** scabbard **10** pistol case

holt: den **4** grip, hill, hold, lair, wood **5** copse, grasp **7** retreat **10** wooded hill

holy: Ste. (F.) **5** pious, sacre (F.), saint, santo (Sp.), santa (Sp.) **6** devout, divine, hallow, sacred **7** blessed, perfect, sainted, saintly, sinless **8** blissful, hallowed **9** inviolate, sanctuary, spiritual **10** sacrosanct **11** consecrated **13** sanctimonious

Holy City: Qom, Qum **4** Kiev, Rome, Zion **5** Lhasa, Mecca **6** Medina, Moscow **7** Benares **9** Allahabad, Jerusalem

Holy Grail: **8** Sangraal, Sangreal
 castle: **9** Monsalvat
 knight: **7** Galahad

Holy Joe: **9** clergyman

Holy Land: **9** Palestine
 pilgrim: **6** palmer

holy oil: **6** chrism

Holy One: God **6** Christ **7** Jehovah **8** Mohammed **12** Supreme Being

Holy Roman emperor: **4** Otho, Otto

Holy Rood: **5** cross **8** crucifix

holy statue: **4** icon, ikon **5** ikono

holy water receptacle: **4** font **5** stoup
 sprinkler: **11** aspergillum

homage: **5** honor **6** eulogy, fealty, regard **7** loyalty, manrent, ovation, respect **9** adoration, deference, obeisance, reverence **10** allegiance

homager: **6** tenant, vassal

homaloidal: **4** even, flat

hombre: guy, man **6** fellow

homburg: hat **4** felt

home: den **4** nest **5** abode, being, domus, house **6** asylum, estate, maison (F.) **7** habitat, hospice, village **8** domestic, domicile, dwelling **9** homestead, orphanage, residence **10** habitation **11** hearthstone
 at: **4** chez (F.)
 country: **7** cottage **8** bungalow
 wheeled: RV **7** trailer

home base: den **5** plate

homeborn: **6** native **10** indigenous

homelike: **4** cozy **5** homey **6** homely, homish **8** cheerful, friendly, homesome **11** comfortable

homely: **4** rude, ugly **5** plain **6** hameil, hamelt, hamilt, kindly, simple **7** plainly **8** domestic, familiar, friendly, homelike, intimate **9** unsightly **10** intimately **12** unpretending, unpretentious

homemade: **5** plain **6** simple **8** domestic

Homer: *birthplace:* **5** Chios

character: **4** Ajax **5** Helen, Paris, Priam **6** Hector, Nestor **7** Ulysses **8** Achilles, Menelaus, Odysseus
 poem: **5** Iliad **7** Odyssey

Homeric: **4** epic **6** epical

homesickness: **9** nostalgia

homespun: **4** kelt (Sc.), rude **5** plain **6** coarse, folksy **13** unpretentious

homestead: **4** farm, toft, tref (W.) **7** onstead

homicide: **6** murder

homilist: **8** preacher

homily: **5** adage **6** sermon **8** assembly **9** communion, discourse **11** exhortation

hominy: **4** bran, corn, samp **5** grits

Homo sapiens: man **10** human being

homogeneous: **4** like **5** equal, solid **6** entire **7** similar **10** comparable, compatible, consistent

homologous: **9** identical

homonym: **8** namesake **10** soundalike

homunculus: **5** dwarf **7** manikin

honcho: **4** boss **6** leader **8** in charge

Honduras: *capital:* **11** Tegucigalpa
 city: **7** Gracias, La Ceiba **8** Yuscaran **9** Choluteca, Comayagua, Juticalpa, Santa Rosa **12** San Pedro Sula
 currency: **7** centavo, lempira
 Indian: **4** Maya, Ulua, Ulva **5** Lenca **8** Misquito
 island: **5** Utila **6** Rostan **7** Guanaja
 measure: **4** vara **5** milla **6** mecate, tercia **7** cajuela, manzana **10** caballeria
 river: **4** Coco, Sico, Ulua **5** Aguan, Wanks **6** Patuca **9** Choluteca **10** Chamelecon
 weight: **4** caja

---

hone: **4** long, pine, whet **5** delay, dress, strop **6** lament **7** grumble, sharpen **8** oilstone **9** whetstone

honest: **4** fair, full, just, open, pure **5** frank, roman **6** candid, chaste, decent, dexter, dinkum, proper, rustic, square **7** genuine, sincere, upright **8** bonafide, faithful, reliable, rightful, straight, suitable, truthful, upright, virtuous **9** equitable, guileless, honorable, ingenuous, veracious **10** creditable, forthright **11** trustworthy **13** conscientious, dispassionate, incorruptible, unadulterated **15** straightforward

honestly: **5** truly **6** dinkum, justly **8** directly **9** telltruth

honesty: **5** honor **6** equity **7** decency, justice, probity **8** fairness, fidelity, veracity **9** constancy, integrity **10** generosity, liberality **11**

uprightness 12 incorruption, suitableness, truthfulness **13** honorableness **15** trustworthiness **19** straightforwardness

honesty plant: 7 lunaria **8** moonwort

honey: mel **4** dear, miel (F., Sp.) **5** sweet **6** nectar **7** darling, flatter **8** precious
fermented drink: **4** mead
source: bee **6** nectar

honey badger: 5 ratel

honey bear: 8 kinkajou

honeybee: 7 deseret **8** angelito
disease: **8** sacbrood

honeyberry: 4 tree **5** genep, genip

honey buzzard: 4 hawk, pern

honeycomb cell: 7 alveola **8** alveolus

honeycombed: 6 favose, pitted **8** alveolar

honeydew: 5 melon **6** mildew, orange

honey eater: iao **6** manuao **9** sugarbird

honeyed: 5 sweet **6** sugary **7** candied **10** flattering **11** mellifluous

honeysuckle: 6 azalea, widbin **8** lonicera, woodbine **9** columbine

Hong Kong: *bay:* **4** Mirs **5** Sheko **7** Repulse
capital: **8** Victoria
currency: **4** cent **6** dollar **13** British dollar **14** Hong Kong dollar
peak: **8** Victoria
peninsula: **7** Kowloon

Honolulu: *island:* **4** Oahu
landmark: **11** Diamond Head

honor: 4 fame, fete, prow **5** adore, award, exalt, glory, grace, izzat, medal **6** credit, decore, esteem, homage, laurel, praise, regard, repute, revere **7** dignify, dignity, emblaze, ennoble, glorify, honesty, respect, worship **8** accolade **9** celebrate, deference, obeisance, reverence **10** estimation, reputation
pledge: **6** parole

honorable: 4 dear, just, true **5** moral, noble, white **6** gentle, honest **7** upright **8** generous, honorary, sterling **9** dearworth, estimable, reputable **10** creditable **11** commendable, illustrious, magnanimous, meritorious, respectable

honorarium: fee, tip **6** reward, salary **7** douceur, payment **8** gratuity

Honshu: *bay:* Ise
port: **4** Kobe

hooch: See **hootch**

hood: cap **4** coif, cowl, hide, thug **5** amice, blind **6** biggin, bonnet, burlet, camail, canopy, chapel, tippet **7** calotte, capuche, hoodlum, surtout **8** capsheaf, caputium, chaperon, covering
academic: **8** liripipe, liripoop
monk's: **4** atis, cowl **5** atees
saddle: **8** tapadera, tapadero
vehicle: **6** bonnet, capote

hooded: 9 cucullate **10** capistrate

hoodlum: yap **4** goon, thug **5** rowdy **6** goonda **7** mobster, ruffian **8** hooligan

hoodoo: 4 jinx **5** Jonah **6** voodoo **7** bad luck, bewitch, unlucky

hoodwink: 4 dupe, fool, hide, wile **5** blear, blind, bluff, cheat, cosen, cover, cozen, trick **6** befool, delude **7** blinder, blinker, deceive, mislead **9** blindfold

hooey: 4 bunk **6** bunkum **7** baloney, boloney, bushwah **8** buncombe, nonsense

hoof: 4 clee, foot, walk **5** cloof, cloot, cluif, dance, tramp **6** ungula

hoofer: 6 dancer, walker

hook: 4 barb, gaff, gore, hake, hock, hold, huck, trap **5** catch, cleek, curve, hamus, hitch, larin, seize, snare, steal **6** agrafe, anchor, fasten, larree,' pilfer, tenter **7** agraffe, capture, grunter, hamulus, hitcher **8** crotchet **10** chatelaine

hooka, hookah: 4 pipe **7** nargile **8** narghile **9** narghileh

hooked: 6 hamate **7** hamular, uncinal **8** addicted, ankyroid, aquiline, uncinate

hooker: 10 prostitute **12** street walker

hooky player: 6 truant

hooligan: 6 loafer **7** hoodlum, ruffian

hoop: 4 bail, band, ring, tire **5** clasp, garth, girth, shout **6** basket, circle, frette **7** circlet, trundle **8** encircle, surround **10** basketball, finger ring

hoopskirt: 9 crinoline

hoosegow: jug **4** jail **6** lockup, prison **10** guardhouse

Hoosier State: 7 Indiana

hoot: boo **4** jeer, whoo **5** shout, whoop **6** boohoo **7** ululate

hootch, hooch: 5 booze, drink, house **6** liquor **8** barracks, dwelling **11** thatched hut

Hoover Dam lake: 4 Mead

hop: fly, hip **4** dope, halt, jump, leap, limp, skip **5** bound, dance, hitch **6** flight, gambol, spring **8** jump over **11** supercharge

hopbush: 6 akeake

hope: 4 deem, spes (L.), want, wish **5** dream, faith, haven, trust **6** aspire, desire, expect, morale **7** cherish, confide **8** prospect, reliance **9** esperance **10** aspiration **11** expectation **12** anticipation
goddess of: **4** Spes
lack of: **7** despair
symbol of: **4** opal

hopeful: 8 sanguine **9** confident, expectant **10** optimistic

hopeless: 4 gone, vain **6** futile **7** forlorn, useless **8** downcast **9** desperate, heartless, incurable **10** despairing, despondent, desponding, remediless **11** ineffectual **12** disconsolate, irremediable **13** irrecoverable, irretrievable

hophead: **6** addict
Hophni: *brother:* **8** Phinehas
   father: Eli
Hopi Indian: **4** Moki **5** Moqui **6** Pueblo
   god: **7** Kachina, Katcina **8** Katchina
   prayer stick: **4** paho
hop kiln: **4** oast
hoplite: **7** soldier
hop-o'-my-thumb: **5** dwarf, fairy **6** midget
hopped up: **4** high **6** stoned, zonked **7**
   drugged
hopper: box **4** tank **5** chute **6** dancer, leaper
   10 freight car, receptacle
hopple: See **hobble**
hopscotch: **7** pallall
   stone: **5** potsy **6** peever
Horae: **4** Dike **6** Eirene **7** Euromia
horde: **4** army, camp, clan, pack **5** crowd,
   group, swarm **6** legion, throng **9** multitude
horehound: **4** mint **6** henbit
Horite chief: **4** Seir
horizon: rim **4** edge, goal **8** prospect
horizontal: **4** flat **5** level
hormigo: **5** quira **7** ant tree
hormone: **8** autacoid **13** cell secretion
   female: **8** estrogen **12** progesterone
   male: **8** androgen **12** testosterone
horn: **4** scur, tuba **5** brass, bugle, cornu,
   drone, siren **6** antler, cornet, French, rhyton **7** antenna, trumpet **8** oliphant, trombone **9** alpenhorn, saxophone **10** cornucopia, flugelhorn
   blast: **4** mort, toot **7** fanfare, tantara **9** tantarara
   crescent moon: **4** cusp
   deer: **4** tine **5** prong **6** antler
   drinking: **6** rhyton
   Hebrew: **6** shofar **7** shophar
   player: **6** bugler **9** cornetist, trumpeter
   without: **5** doddy **6** doddie, polled **7** acerous
hornbill: **4** bird, tock **6** homrai
   genus of: **7** buceros
hornet: **4** wasp
hornpipe: **4** tune **5** dance **8** matelote
hornswoggle: **4** hoax **5** cheat, trick **7** swindle
   9 bamboozle
horny: **4** hard **8** ceratoid **9** calloused, toughened **10** semiopaque **15** sexually aroused
hornyhead: **4** chub
horologe: **4** dial **5** clock, watch **9** hourglass,
   timepiece
horoscope: **4** dial **7** diagram **8** forecast **10**
   prediction
horrendous: **7** fearful **8** horrible **9** frightful
horrible: **4** dire, grim, ugly **5** great **6** grisly,
   horrid **7** fearful, ghastly, hideous, horrent,
   very bad **8** atrocius, dreadful, gruesome,
   horrific, shocking, terrible **9** excessive,

frightful, horrified, nefarious **10** horrendous, tremendous, unpleasant
horrid: **4** grim, ugly **5** awful, rough **6** rugged,
   shaggy **7** hideous **8** dreadful, grewsome,
   gruesome, horrible, shocking, terrible **9**
   bristling, frightful, obnoxious, offensive,
   revolting **10** detestable, terrifying, unpleasant **13** objectionable
horrific: **5** awful **7** fearful **8** horrible **9** frightful **10** formidable
horrified: **6** aghast **7** ghastly
horrify: **5** shock **6** appall, dismay
horrifying: **8** horrific **9** execrable
horror: **4** fear **5** dread **6** terror **8** aversion **10**
   abhorrence, repugnance, shuddering **11**
   abomination, detestation **13** consternation
Horsa's brother: **7** Hengist
hors d'oeuvre: **4** tapa **6** canape, relish **7**
   zakuska **8** aperitif **9** antipasto, appetizer
horse: gee, nag, pad **4** barb, mare, plug, prad
   5 brock, caple, capul, draft, filly, hobby,
   hoist, mount, pacer, raise, shier, steed,
   waler **6** cheval, equine, geegee, ladino, pel-
   ter, rouncy **7** caballo (Sp.), cavallo (It.), cavalry, charger, clipper, courser, hackney,
   mustang, saddler, sheltie, sleeper, stepper,
   trestle **8** bathorse, cartaver (Sc.), footrope,
   jackstay **10** breastband
   Achilles': **7** Xanthus
   ankle: **4** hock
   breastplate: **7** peytrel, poitrel
   breed: **4** Barb **5** Shire **6** hunter, Morgan **7**
   Arabian, Belgian, harness, quarter, trotter **8**
   Galloway, Normandy, Shetland **9**
   Percheron **10** Clydesdale
   brown: bay **6** sorrel **8** chestnut
   buyer: **5** coper **6** trader **7** knacker
   calico: **5** pinto
   collar: **7** bargham (Sc.)
   color: bay **4** gray, pied, roan **5** pinto **6** calico, sorrel **8** chestnut, palomino, schimmel
   command: gee, haw, hup **4** whoa **6** giddap
   covering: **9** caparison
   cry: nie **5** neigh **6** whinny
   dappled: **4** roan **5** pinto **7** piebald
   dark: **4** zain
   dealer: **7** chanter, scorser
   disease: **5** surra **6** heaves, lampas **7** lam-
   pers, quittor, spavins **9** distemper
   docked-tail: **6** curtal **8** cocktail
   draft: **4** aver **5** aiver, hairy
   dressage: **15** movement control
   driver: **6** jockey **7** sumpter **8** coachman
   farm: **6** dobbin
   feeding box: **6** manger
   female: **4** mare, yaud **5** filly
   foot: **4** frog, hoof **7** coronet, fetlock, pastern
   forehead: **8** chanfrin
   gait: run **4** lope, pace, rack, trot, vott, walk

6 canter, gallop
genus: **5** equus
goddess of: **5** Epona
golden: **8** palomino
gray: **8** schimmel
guide: **4** rein **5** longe
harness: **5** pacer **7** trotter
hired: **4** hack **7** hackney
horned: **7** unicorn **9** monoceros
hybrid: **4** mule
leg: **6** instep **7** fetlock
lover: **10** hippophile
male: **4** stud **6** entire **7** gelding **8** stallion
measure: **4** hand
menage: **6** school **7** academy
pace: **4** lope, trot **5** amble **6** canter
pack: **5** bidet **7** sumpter
pair: **4** span, team
pert. to: **6** hippic
piebald: **5** pinto
prehistoric: **8** Eohippus
races: **8** claiming
racing: **4** turf
rearing: **6** pesade
relay: **6** remuda
round-up: **5** rodeo
saddle: cob **5** mount **7** palfrey
small: cob, nag, tit **4** pony **5** bidet, genet **6** cayuse, jennet **8** galloway, Shetland
sorrel: **4** roan **8** chestnut
spirited: **4** Arab **5** steed **6** rearer **7** courser
stable of: **6** string
talking: **5** Arion
track slope: **6** calade
trainer: **5** valet
trapping: **6** tackle **7** harness **9** caparison
trotting: **6** Morgan
turn: **7** passade
war: **5** steed **7** charger, courser **8** destrier
white-streaked face: **4** shim **5** blaze, reach
wild: **6** bronco, brumby, tarpan **7** mustang **8** warragal, warrigal **10** Przewalski
winged: **7** Pegasus
working: **4** aver **5** aiver **6** dobbin
worn-out: nag **4** hack, jade, moke, plug **5** crock, skate **6** garran, garron, gleyde **7** knacker **8** harridan **9** Rosinante
horse-and-buggy: rig **12** old-fashioned
horsefly: **4** cleg **5** clegg **6** botfly, gadfly
horsehair: **4** mane **9** haircloth
horsehide: **8** cordovan
horsekeeper: **5** groom **7** hostler
horselaugh: **5** snort **6** guffaw, heehaw
horse mackerel: **4** fish, scad, tuna **5** atule, tunny **6** bonita, saurel
horseman: **5** rider **6** carter, cowboy **7** centaur, courier, vaquero **8** buckaroo **9** chevalier **10** cavalryman, equestrian **12** broncobuster
horseman goad: **4** spur

horsemanship: **5** skill **6** manege, riding **10** equitation
rearing: **6** pesade
sidewalk: **4** volt
turn: **8** caracole
horseradish: **4** root **5** plant **6** relish
horseshoe: *point:* **6** sponge
rim: web
spur: **4** calk
horseshoer: **6** smithy **7** farrier **10** blacksmith
horsewhip: **4** flog **5** quirt **7** chabouk
horsewoman: **12** equestrienne
horticulturist: **7** gardener
Horus: **6** Sun God
brother: **6** Anubis
father: **6** Osiris
mother: **4** Isis
hose: **4** sock, tube, vamp **5** water **6** drench **7** hosiery **8** stocking
Hosea: **7** prophet
father: **5** Beeri
wife: **5** Gomer
hospice: inn **5** house **6** asylum, imaret
hospitable: **5** douce **6** cheery, social **7** cordial **8** friendly **9** convivial, receptive, welcoming
hospital: **6** clinic, creche, refuge, spital **9** infirmary **10** sanatorium **11** xenodochium **12** ambulatorium
attendant: **4** aide **5** nurse **6** intern **7** orderly **10** technician
mobile: **9** ambulance
user: **7** patient
hospitality: **7** welcome **10** cordiality
to strangers: **10** xendodochy
host: inn **4** army, here **5** crowd, guest, swarm **6** housel, legion, myriad, throng **7** company, lodging **8** landlord, harbinger, moderator, multitude, sacrifice **10** assemblage **11** entertainer, interviewer
receptacle for: pyx **5** paten **8** ciborium
hostage: **4** pawn **5** token **6** pledge **8** security **9** guarantee
hostel: inn **5** hotel, lodge **6** tavern **11** caravansary **12** lodginghouse
hostile: foe **5** black, enemy, fremd **7** adverse, opposed, warlike **8** contrary, inimical **9** resisting **10** malevolent, unfriendly **11** belligerent **12** antagonistic **13** unsympathetic
hostility: **4** feid, feud **6** animus, enmity, hatred, rancor **7** ill-will, warfare **9** animosity, antipathy **10** antagonism, bitterness, opposition, resistance **12** disaffection **14** unfriendliness, vindictiveness
hostler: **5** groom **6** ostler **9** stableman
hot: **5** acrid, angry, calid, eager, fiery, spicy **6** ardent, biting, fervid, recent, strong, sultry, torrid, urgent **7** burning, excited, fervent, flaming, glowing, intense, lustful, peppery,

pungent, thermal **8** sizzling, vehement, very warm **9** excitable, impatient, impetuous **10** passionate

hotbed: 4 nest

hot cakes: 5 crepe **7** pancake **11** flannel cake, griddle cake

hot dog: 5 frank **6** wiener **7** sausage, show off **11** frankfurter

hotchpotch: 4 stew **6** jumble **9** tripotage (F.) **10** hodgepodge

hotel: inn, spa **5** fonda, haven, house, lodge **6** hostel, imaret, tavern **7** auberge, gasthof, hostage **8** building, dwelling, gasthaus **11** caravansary, public house **12** caravanserai, lodginghouse

  airport: **6** airtel
  auto: **5** motel
  keeper: **4** host **7** padrone **8** boniface, hotelier

hotheaded: 5 fiery, hasty **8** reckless **9** impetuous

hothouse: 6 bagnio **10** greenhouse

hot line: 14 emergency phone

hotspur: 4 rash **5** Percy **6** madcap **7** violent **8** reckless **9** impetuous **10** headstrong

hot-tempered: 7 iracund **8** choleric **9** irascible

Hottentot: *dialect:* **4** Gona, Kora, Nama
  garment: **6** kaross
  instrument: **4** gora **5** gorah, goura
  tribe: **4** Gona, Kora, Nama **6** Damara, Griqua **7** Sandawe, Sandawi
  war club: **10** knobkerrie

hot-water bottle: pad, pig

hound: dog **4** bait, hunt **5** harry **6** addict, talbot **7** devotee, harrier **9** persecute
  tail: **5** stern

hour: *canonical:* **4** none, sext **5** lauds, nones, prime **6** matins, tierce **7** vespers **8** compline
  class: **6** period
  lights out: **4** taps **6** curfew

hourglass: 5 clock **7** shapely

hourly: 4 soon, brief **5** horal **6** horary, recent **7** quickly **8** frequent **9** continual **10** frequently **11** continually

house: cot, hut, log, row **4** casa (It., Sp.), cote, dorm, dump, firm, flat, flet, haus (G.), home, live, nest, town **5** abode, bahay, booth, cabin, cover, dacha, domus (L.), hovel, lodge, manor, ranch, shack, villa **6** biggin, billet, bottle, camara, casino, duplex, family, grange, harbor, maison (F.), palace, pre-fab, reside, shanty **7** cabildo, Cape Cod, chateau, cottage, enclose, mansion, quarter, salt box, shelter, theater **8** ancestry, audience, building, bungalow, colonial, domicile, dwelling, tenement **9** dormitory, playhouse, residence, Victorian

10 enterprise, habitation, split-level **11** post and beam
  cluster: **4** dorp **6** hamlet **7** village
  commercial: **4** firm **5** store **8** emporium
  dog: **6** kennel
  eating: inn **4** cafe **6** bistro, tavern **9** chophouse **10** restaurant
  English royal: **4** York **5** Tudor **6** Stuart **7** Hanover, Windsor **9** Lancaster
  guest: inn **5** b and b, hotel **11** caravansary
  Newfoundland: **4** tilt
  Oriental: **5** serai
  pert. to: **5** domal
  public: bar, inn, pub **5** hotel, motel **6** hostel, tavern **7** hospice **8** hostelry
  religious: **4** kirk **6** chapel, church, priory, mosque, temple **9** cathedral, synagogue **10** tabernacle
  Russian: **4** isba **5** dacha
  summer: **6** gazebo **9** belvedere
  Upper: **6** Senate

houseboat: 5 barge **6** wangan, wangun **7** waniga **8** dahabeah, wannigan

housefly: 4 pest **5** musca **6** insect

household: 5 meiny **6** common, family, housal, menage **8** domestic, familiar, ordinary **9** belonging
  gods: **5** Lares **7** Penates
  regulation: **6** thrift **7** economy **9** husbandry

housekeeper: 4 maid **6** matron **7** cleaner, janitor **8** janitrix **9** caretaker, janitress

houseleek: 8 sengreen **9** succulent **11** liveforever

house organ: 8 magazine **10** periodical

houseplant: ivy **4** fern **5** calla **6** cactus, coleus **7** begonia, violets **8** dracaena, **10** aspidistra **12** philodendron

house servant: 4 maid **6** butler **8** domestic **11** housekeeper

housewarming: 6 infare

housewife: 8 hausfrau (G.) **9** sewing kit

housework: 5 chore **8** drudgery

housing: box, pad **4** cowl **5** cover, niche **6** garage **7** lodging, shelter **8** covering **10** protection

Houston:
  stadium: **9** Astrodome
  team: **6** Astros, Oilers **7** Rockets

hove: See **heave**

hovel: hut, sty **4** crib, hole, hulk, hull, shed **5** cabin, hutch, lodge, shack **6** cruive, favela, hemmel, pigpen, pigsty, shanty **7** shelter **10** tabernacle

hover: 4 flit **5** float, pause, waver **7** flitter, flutter

howdy, howdie: 7 midwife **8** greeting **10** salutation

however: but, tho, yet **5** still **6** though **8** after all, although **10** all the same, howsomever

12 nevertheless 15 notwithstanding

howitzer: 6 cannon 9 artillery

howl: bay, cry, wow 4 bawl, gowl, gurl, hurl, wail, wawl, yawl, yell, yowl, yowt 5 whewl 6 lament, scream, squeal, steven 7 ululate 9 complaint 12 side-splitter

howling: 4 wild 5 great 6 baying, dreary, savage 7 extreme, ululant 10 pronounced

howling monkey: 5 araba 7 guereba, stentor

howsoever: 8 although

howsomever: 8 although 12 nevertheless

hox: 4 hock 5 annoy, worry 6 harass, pester 7 trample 9 hamstring

hoyden, hoiden: 4 romp, rude 6 blowze, tomboy 7 ill-bred 10 roistering

Hreidmar's son: 5 Otter, Regin 6 Fafnir, Reginn

huaca: 4 holy, idol, tomb 6 fetish, sacred, shrine, temple

hub: 4 core, nave 6 center, centre 10 focal point 11 nerve center

Hub: 6 Boston

hubbub: ado, din 4 stir 5 noise 6 clamor, hubble, racket, rumpus, tumult, uproar 7 bobbery 9 commotion, confusion 11 disturbance

hubristic: 4 vain 5 proud 7 haughty 8 arrogant, insolent 12 contemptuous, supercilious 13 high-and-mighty

huckleberry: 9 blueberry, buckberry 11 dangleberry, tangleberry
family: 9 ericaceae

Huckleberry Finn: *author:* 9 Mark Twain 13 Samuel Clemens
character: Jim, Tom 7 Dauphin, The Duke, The King
river: 11 Mississippi

huckster: 4 sell, vend 5 adman, cheap 6 badger, broker, cadger, cagier (F.), hawker 7 haggler, peddler 8 regrater, retailer 9 middleman

huddle: hug 4 hide, raff 5 crowd, hurry 6 bustle, fumble, jumble, mingle 7 conceal, embrace, meeting, scrunch 8 assemble, disorder 9 confusion 10 conference, discussion 14 conglomeration

Hudibras author: 6 Butler

hue: 4 balk, blee, form, tint 5 color, guise, shade, shout, tinge 6 aspect, clamor, depict, figure, outcry 7 clamour 8 shouting 10 appearance, complexion

hueless: 4 gray 9 colorless

huff: dod, pet 4 blow, brag, puff 5 bully, peeve, swell 6 hector 7 bluster, enlarge 8 boasting, offended 11 take offense

huffy: 4 airy 5 fuffy, puffy, windy 6 touchy 7 pettish 8 arrogant 9 conceited 10 swaggering

hug: lug 4 clip, coll, hold 5 carry, clasp, cling, creem, halse, press 6 cuddle, huddle, hug-

gle 7 cherish, embrace, squeeze 9 hold close

huge: big 4 stor (Sc.), vast 5 enorm, giant, humongous, great, jumbo, large 6 heroic 7 banging, bumping, immense, massive, monster 8 colossal, enormous, gigantic, titanic 9 monstrous, pyramidal, very large 10 gargantuan, prodigious, tremendous, unmeasured 11 elephantine

hugger-mugger: sly 6 jumble, muddle, secret 7 secrecy 8 confused, hush-hush, in camera, secretly 9 confusion 10 disorderly 11 clandestine 13 clandestinely

hui: 4 firm 5 guild 7 society 8 assembly 11 partnership

huisache: 4 wabe, wabi 5 aromo, plant, shrub, spiny 6 cassie 7 popinac

huitain: 6 octave, stanza

huke: 4 cape 5 cloak, dress

hulk: 4 bulk, hull, loom, ship 5 hovel 10 disembowel

hulking: 5 bulky, hulky, husky, large 7 loutish, massive 8 unwieldy

hull: hud, hut, pod 4 bulk, hulk, husk, shed 5 shell, strip 6 casing 8 covering 11 decorticate
grain: 4 bran

hullabaloo: ado, din 5 noise 6 clamor, hubbub, racket, tumult, uproar 7 clamour 9 confusion

hum: 4 blur, buzz, huss, huzz, sing, whiz 5 croon, drink, drone, feign, whizz 6 murmur 7 vibrate 9 bombinate 11 bombilation, bombination

human: 6 humane, mortal, person 7 hominid 9 enigmatic

human being: man 6 mortal, person 7 Homo sapiens, woman, Adamite 8 creature

humane: 4 good, kind 6 kindly, tender 8 merciful 9 forgiving 10 charitable, civilising 11 sympathetic 13 compassionate, tenderhearted

humanitarian: 10 altruistic, benevolent, charitable 14 philanthropist

humanity: 5 flesh, mercy 6 lenity, people 7 mankind 8 kindness 9 mortality 11 human nature

humanize: 6 refine 8 civilize

humble: low 4 mean, meek, mild, poor 5 abase, abash, lower, lowly, plain, stoop 6 debase, deject, demean, demiss, modest, reduce, simple 7 afflict, conquer, degrade, depress, ignoble, mortify 8 contrite, deferent, disgrace, reverent 9 humiliate 10 submissive, unassuming

humbug: gum, kid, pah 4 bosh, flam, guff, hoax, sham 5 cheat, faker, fraud, fudge, guile, trick 6 barney, blague, bunkum, cafard, cajole, gammon 7 deceive, flummer,

mislead 8 flimflam, flummery, huckmuck, nonsense, pretense **9** bamboozle, deception, imposture, stratagem **10** flumdiddle **11** flumadiddle

humdinger: 4 oner **5** dandy, doozy, nifty **6** corker **8** jimdandy **11** crackerjack

humdrum: 4 dull **6** boring **7** irksome, prosaic **10** monotonous **11** commonplace, indifferent **13** uninteresting

humerus: 4 bone **8** shoulder, upper arm

humid: wet **4** damp, dank **5** close, moist, muggy, soggy **6** clammy, sticky, sultry **8** humorous, vaporous

humidity: 8 dampness **9** moistness

humiliate: 5 abase, abash, shame **6** debase, humble **7** degrade, mortify **8** belittle, disgrace

humility: 7 modesty **8** meekness, mildness **9** lowliness **10** diffidence

humming: big **4** busy **5** brisk, brool **6** lively, strong **7** buzzing, droning **8** frothing, seething **13** extraordinary

hummingbird: ava **5** carib **6** hummer **8** froufrou **9** sheartail
genus of: **6** sappho

hummock: 4 hump **5** knoll **7** hillock

humor, humour: pet, pun, tid, wit **4** baby, mood, whim **5** fancy, farce, fluid, freak, vapor **6** levity, megrim, parody, please, satire, temper **7** caprice, cater to, gratify, indulge **8** drollery, moisture **9** burlesque, slapstick **11** inclination, temperament

humorist: wag, wit **4** card **5** cutup, joker **6** jester **7** punster **8** comedian

humorous, humourous: 5 comic, droll, funny, humid, moist, witty **6** watery **7** amusive, comical, jocular, playful **8** pleasant **9** facetious, laughable, whimsical **10** capricious

hump: 4 bile, hunk, lump **5** bouge, bulge, bunch, crump, hunch, mound, ridge **6** gibber, gibbus, hummie **7** hummock **12** protuberance

humpback: 5 whale **9** hunchback **10** huckleback

Humperdinck opera: 15 Hansel and Gretel

humus: mor **4** mull, soil

Hun: 6 vandal **9** barbarian
leader: **4** Atli **5** Etzel **6** Attila

Hunan river: 4 Yuan, Yuen

hunch: 4 balk, bend, hump, hunk, idea, lump, push **5** chunk, fudge, shove **6** chilly, frosty, thrust **7** feeling **9** intuition **11** premonition **12** protuberance

Hunchback of Notre Dame: 9 Quasimodo
author: **4** Hugo

hundred: 7 cantred, cantref, century **11** ten times ten
division into: **12** centuriation

hundred-eyed being: 5 Argus

hundredfold: 8 centuple **12** centuplicate

hundred percent: 6 entire **7** genuine, perfect **9** unalloyed **13** thoroughgoing **14** unquestionable

hundredweight: cwt **6** cental **7** quintal

hundred years: 7 century **9** centenary

hung: See **hang**

Hungary: *army:* **6** Honved **9** Honvedseg
capital: **8** Budapest
cavalryman: **6** Hussar
city: **4** Pecs **5** Erlau **6** Szeged **7** Miskolc **8** Debrecen **9** Debreczin, Kecskemet
composer: **5** Lehar, Liszt **6** Bartok **7** Romberg
currency: **6** filler, forint
dance: **7** czardas
gypsy: **7** tzigane
measure: ako **4** hold, joch, yoke **5** antal, itcze, marok, metze **7** huvelyk, merfold
mountain: **10** Carpathian
playwright: **6** Molnar (Ferenc)
poet: **5** Arany
river: **4** Raab **5** Drave, Maros, Tisza **6** Danube, Poprad **7** Vistula
weight: **7** vamfont **8** vammazsa

Hung Wu: 4 Ming

hunger: 4 long, want **5** belly, covet, crave, greed, yearn **6** desire, famine, starve **7** craving **8** appetite, need food, voracity **9** esurience **10** starvation
abnormal: **7** bulimia **10** polyphagia

hungry: 4 avid, howe, poor **5** eager **6** barren, hollow, jejune **7** craving, uneaten **8** esurient, hungered **10** avaricious

hunk: dad, gob, wad **4** daud, hump, lump, slab **5** chunk, hunch, piece **6** nugget

hunt: dig **4** drag, seek **5** chase, chevy, chivy, delve, drive, hound, probe, quest, stalk, track, trail **6** chivvy, ferret, follow, forage, hunter, pursue, search, shikar **9** persecute, try to find **11** inquisition
god of: **5** Ninip **6** Apollo
goddess of: **5** Diana **7** Artemis, Cynthia

hunted: 4 game, prey

hunter: 5 jager, yager **6** chaser, nimrod **7** catcher, stalker, venerer **8** chasseur **9** sportsman
assistant: **5** gilly, jager
attendant: **5** gilly (Sc.) **6** gillie
constellation: **5** Orion
Golden Fleece: **5** Jason
mythological: **5** Orion
patron saint: **6** Hubert

hunting: *bird:* **6** falcon

cry: yoi **4** toho **5** chevy, chivy, hoick **6** chivvy, hoicks, yoicks **7** tally ho
expedition: **6** safari
game: **6** shikar, venery
horn note: **4** mort
pert. to: **7** venatic
hunting dog: **5** hound **6** basset, beagle, setter **7** pointer, spaniel **9** retriever
huntress: **5** Diana **7** Artemis **8** Atalanta
huntsman: See **hunter**
hurdle: pen **4** clew, fold, leap **5** bound, cover, crate, frith, hedge **6** raddle **7** barrier, confine **8** obstacle, surmount **9** enclosure **10** impediment **11** obstruction
hurdy-gurdy: **4** lira, rota
hurl: **4** cast, dash, haul, howl, hurl, pelt, roar, send, toss, turn **5** fling, heave, pitch, sling, smite, throw, twist, whang **6** elance **9** overthrow
hurly-burly: **6** hubbub, tumult, uproar **7** turmoil **8** confused **9** confusion
huron: **6** grison
hurrah: joy **5** bravo, cheer, huzza, shout **6** tumult **7** triumph **8** applause **10** commotion **14** encouragement
hurricane: **4** gale, wind **5** storm **7** cyclone, prester, tempest, typhoon **8** chubasco **9** hurricano, whirlwind, windstorm **13** tropical storm
center of: eye
hurried: See **hurry**
hurry: ado, hie, run **4** pass, pell, race, rese, rush, scud, stir, trot, urge, whir **5** drive, fight, haste, impel, slide, speed, worry **6** convey, harass, hasten, hustle, scurry, tumult, urge on **7** agitato (It.), dispute, quarrel, quicken **8** dispatch, expedite **9** agitation, commotion **10** expedition **11** disturbance, festination, precipitate
hurst: **4** hill, wood **5** copse, grove, knoll **7** hillock **8** sandbank **11** wooded mound
hurt: **4** harm, maim, pain **5** abuse, blame, grief, sorry, wound **6** damage, grieve, impair, injure, injury, mittle, offend, scathe, strike, suffer **7** afflict, collide, hurting **8** be bad for, distress, mischief, nuisance **9** detriment **12** disadvantage
hurtful: bad **4** evil **6** nocent **7** baneful, harmful, malefic, noisome, noxious **10** pernicious **11** deleterious, destructive, detrimental, prejudicial
hurtle: **4** dash **5** clash, fling, whirl **6** assail, jostle **7** collide **8** brandish
husband: eke, man, rom **4** bond, buck, chap, keep, mate, save **5** churl, hoard, marry, store **6** manage, spouse, tiller **7** consort, espouse, partner, plowman, steward **8** conserve, helpmate **9** cultivate, economize, other half **10** cultivator, husbandman

more than one: **9** polyandry
property right: **7** curtesy
husbandman: **4** bond, boor, carl **5** colon **6** farmer, tiller **7** acre-man **8** agricole **10** cultivator
husbandry: **6** thrift **7** economy **8** managery **9** frugality **11** cultivation **12** conservation
god: **6** Faunus
hush: tut **4** calm, clam, hist, lull **5** allay, quiet, still **6** soothe **7** appease, repress, silence
husk: cod, hud **4** bark, bran, coat, hulk, hull, leam, peel, rind, skin **5** lemma, scale, shack, shell, shuck, straw, strip **6** colder **7** envelop, epicarp **8** covering, envelope **11** decorticate
Husky: dog **6** Eskimo
huss: **7** dogfish
hussar: **7** soldier **8** European **10** cavalryman
headdress: **5** busby
uniform cape: **6** dolman
hussy: **4** jade, minx **5** besom (Sc.), gipsy, gypsy, madam, quean **11** housekeeper
hustle: **4** push **5** crowd, hurry, shove **6** bustle, jostle, thrust **8** activity
hustler: **6** peeler **8** go-getter
hut: cot **4** bari, cote, crib, hulk, shed **5** benab, bohio, bothy, cabin, choza, house, hovel, humpy, hutch, kraal, lodge, scale, shack, toldo, wurly **6** bohawn, canaba, chalet, gunyah, gunyeh, lean-to, rancho, shanty **7** balagan, bourock, camalig, cottage, edifice, huddock, wickiup **8** barabara, building, chantier
fisherman's: **4** skeo
hermit's: **4** cell
military: **6** Nissen **7** quonset
mining: coe
shepherd's: **5** bothy
hutch: ark, bin, box, car, hut, pen **4** coop **5** chest, hoard, hotch, hovel **6** coffer, humped, shanty **7** hunched, shelter **9** inclosure
hutzpah: **4** gall **5** nerve **7** chutzpa **10** effrontery
huzza: **5** cheer, shout **6** hurrah
hyacinth: **4** bulb **7** greggle **8** bluebell, harebell
hyalite: **4** opal
hybrid: **4** mule **5** blend, cross **7** mongrel **9** composite **10** crossbreed
cow and buffalo: **7** cattalo
dog: **4** mutt **7** mongrel
horse and ass: **4** mule **5** hinny
horse and zebra: **7** zebrula, zebrule **8** zebrinny
zebra and donkey: **7** zebrass
hydrant: **4** plug **6** faucet **8** fireplug
hydraulic engine: ram
hydrazoate: **4** azid **5** azide
hydrocarbon: **6** butane, carane, nonane,

retene **7** benzene, methane, olefine, pentane
gaseous: **6** ethane, ethene
liver oil: **8** pristane
tree: **7** terpene
hydrocyanic acid: 6 prussic
hydrogen: gas **5** arsin **6** arsine
hydroid: 5 polyp **6** obelia **7** aceleph
hydromel: 4 mead **5** aloja **10** melicratum
hydrometer: 9 aerometer
hydromica: 4 mica **9** muscovite
hydrophobia: 5 lyssa **6** rabies
hydrophyte: See **aquatic plant**
hygienic: 4 good **7** healthy **8** sanitary
hymenopteron: ant, bee **4** wasp **6** sawfly **7** gallfly **9** ichneumon
hymn: ode **4** sing, song **5** psalm **6** himene, himine, hirmos, hirmus **7** introit **8** canticle **11** recessional **12** processional
following psalm: **9** sticheron
funeral: **5** dirge
praising: **4** pean **5** paean
ritual: **8** encomium
sing in unison: **6** choral **7** chorale **9** plainsong
tune: **6** choral **7** chorale
victory: **9** epinicion, epinikion
hyoscyamus: 8 narcotic
hype: 5 boost, put on **6** jack up **7** deceive, mislead, promote
hyperbole: 12 exaggeration **13** overstatement
Hyperborean sage: 6 Abaris
hypercritical: 7 carping **8** captious **10** censori-

ous **12** faultfinding, overcritical, supercilious
Hyperion: *daughter:* Eos **6** Selene
father: **6** Uranus
son: **6** Helios
hyphen: 4 band, dash
hypnotic: 6 opiate **8** narcotic **9** soporific **12** somnifacient
hypnotic condition: **4** coma **6** trance **8** lethargy
hypnotize: 5 charm **9** mesmerize, spellbind
hypnum: 4 moss
hypochondria: hyp **6** megrim
hypocrisy: 4 cant, sham **6** deceit **8** pretense **9** duplicity **10** simulation **11** insincerity **13** dissimulation
hypocrite: 4 sham **5** faker, phony, quack **6** humbug, poseur **8** Tartuffe **9** charlatan, lip server
hypocritical: 5 false **7** bigoted, canting **8** captious, specious **9** deceptive, insincere **11** dissembling, pharisaical **13** sanctimonious, self-righteous
hypostatic: 5 basic **9** elemental
hypotenuse: 5 slant
hypothesis: ism **6** system, theory **7** theorum **9** postulate **10** assumption **11** supposition
hypothetical being: ens **6** entity
hydrax: 4 cony **5** coney **8** procavia
hyssop: 4 mint **5** plant **9** evergreen **11** aspergillum
hysteria: 6 nerves
hysterical: 9 emotional **12** uncontrolled

I

I, Claudius author: **6** Graves
Iago's wife: **6** Emilia
Iberian: **4** Pict
ibex: tur, zac
Ibidite: See **Abadite**
ibis: **5** guara, stork **9** gourdhead
Ibsen (Henrik): *character:* Ase **4** Gynt, Nora **5** Hedda
  play: **6** Ghosts **8** Peer Gynt **10** Doll's House **11** Hedda Gabler
Icarian: **4** rash **6** daring **9** foolhardy
Icarius' daughter: **7** Erigone **8** Penelope
Icarus' father: **8** Daedalus
ICBM: **5** Atlas **6** missle, weapon
ice: **4** cool, geal, grue (Sc.), rime **5** chill, frost, glace (F.) **6** freeze, payola **7** congeal, hauteur **8** diamonds **10** confection **11** refrigerant, refrigerate
  crystals: **4** rime, snow **5** frost
  floating: **4** berg, floe
  fragment: **5** brash
  mass: **7** glacier
  pendant: **6** icicle
  pinnacle of glacier: **5** serac
  sea: **6** sludge
ice cream dish: **4** soda **6** frappe, sundae **7** parfait **9** milk shake **11** baked Alaska, banana split
icebox: **6** cooler, fridge **12** refrigerator
icecap: **7** calotte

Iceland: *capital:* **9** Reykjavik
  city: **8** Akureyri, Keflavik **9** Kopavogur
  epic: **4** edda **10** Grettisaga
  measure: fet **4** alin, lina **5** almud, turma **6** almenn, almude, ferfet, pottur **7** fathmur, feralin, fermila, oltunna, sjomila **9** korntunna **10** ferfathmur, kornskeppa, thumlungur
  milk product: **4** skyr
  sport: **5** glima

---

ichneumon: fly **8** mongoose **11** hymenoptera (pl.)
ichnography: map **9** floor plan
ichnolite: **6** fossil **9** footprint

---

icicle: **10** ice pendent
  limestone: **10** stalactite, stalagmite
icing: **7** topping **8** frosting
icky: **6** sticky **7** cloying **10** disgusting **11** distasteful, sentimental
icon, ikon: **5** image **6** eidola (pl.), idolon, symbol **7** eidolon, picture **8** portrait **12** illustration
iconoclast: **5** rebel **7** radical **9** dissenter **13** nonconformist
icterus: **8** jaundice
ictus: fit **4** blow **6** attack, stress, stroke
ICU: **17** intensive care unit
icy: **4** cold **5** gelid **6** arctic, frigid, frosty **8** chilling, freezing

---

Idaho: *capital:* **5** Boise
  city: **5** Nampa **6** Burley, Moscow, Rupert **8** Caldwell, Lewiston **9** Blackfoot, Pocatello, Twin Falls **10** Idaho Falls **11** Coeur d'Alene
  lake: **4** Bear **5** Grays **6** Priest **8** Flathead **11** Coeur d'Alene, Pend Oreille
  mountain range: **5** Lemhi **7** Cabinet **8** Sawtooth **9** Lost River **10** Bitterroot
  river: **4** Bear **5** Boise, Lemhi, Snake **6** Lochsa, Salmon **7** Big Wood, Payette **10** Clearwater
  state bird: **8** bluebird
  state flower: **7** syringa
  state horse: **9** Appaloosa
  state motto: **12** Esto perpetua (It Is Forever)
  state tree: **9** white pine

Idas' consort: **8** Marpessa
ide: **4** orfe **8** foodfish
idea: **4** idee (F.) **5** fancy, guess, ideal, image **6** design, figure, notion, theory **7** conceit, concept, fantasy, inkling, opinion, project, thought **8** gimcrack **9** archetype **10** appearance, cogitation, conception, impression, reflection
  impracticable: **7** chimera **8** chimaera
  prompting action: **6** motive
ideal: **5** dream, model **6** mental **7** paragon,

perfect, Utopian **8** abstract, fanciful, standard **9** imaginary, visionary **10** aspiration, conceptual

ideal state: **4** Eden **6** Utopia

ideate: **5** fancy **7** imagine **8** conceive

idée fixe: **9** fixed idea, obsession

identical: one **4** like, same, self, twin, very **5** alike, equal, samen (Sc.) **8** selfsame **10** equivalent, tantamount

identify: tag **4** mark, name **5** brand, prove **7** earmark, pick out **9** designate, establish, recognize

identity: **4** name **5** unity **7** oneness **8** sameness **9** exactness **11** homogeneity
 false: **5** alias

ideologist: **7** dreamer **8** theorist **9** visionary

ideology: ism **5** credo, creed, tenet, dogma **7** beliefs **8** doctrine **10** philosophy

idiasm: **9** mannerism **11** peculiarity **12** idiosyncrasy

idiocy: **7** anoesia, fatuity

idiograph: **9** signature, trademark

idiom: **5** style **6** phrase **7** dialect

idiosyncrasy: way **6** idiasm, manner **11** peculiarity

idiot: oaf **4** dolt, fool **5** ament, booby, dunce, moron **6** cretin, hobbil, nidget **7** dullard, omadawn **8** imbecile, omadhuan **9** blockhead, simpleton **10** changeling

idiotic: **4** daft, zany **5** barmy, inane **7** asinine, fatuous, foolish **9** senseless

idle: **4** lazy, loaf, vain **5** dally, empty **6** dawdle, futile, loiter, otiose, vacant **7** aimless **8** baseless, inactive, indolent, slothful, trifling **9** desultory, worthless **10** groundless, unemployed, unoccupied **11** ineffectual

idle talk: **5** rumor **6** gossip

idleness: **5** sloth **7** inertia **8** inaction **9** indolence

idler: bum **5** drone **6** loafer **8** faineant, loiterer, sluggard **9** do-nothing, goldbrick, lazybones

Idmon: *father:* **6** Apollo
 killer: **4** boar
 mother: **6** Cyrene
 ship: **4** Argo

idol: god **4** Baal, hero, icon **5** image **6** effigy, fetish
 matinee: **4** star

idolater: **5** pagan **6** adorer **7** Baalite **9** worshiper

idolize: **5** adore **6** admire, revere **7** worship **8** venerate

I do not wish to contend: **14** nolo contendere (L.)

idyl, idyll: **4** poem **7** eclogue **8** pastoral

idyllic: **7** bucolic **8** pastoral **9** unspoiled

if: **8** granting, provided **9** supposing

iffy: **6** chancy **8** doubtful **9** uncertain

igneous rock: **4** lava **5** magma **6** basalt, gab-

bro, pumice, scoria **8** porphyry

ignis fatuus: **8** delusion **9** pipe dream **12** will-o'-the-wisp

ignite: **4** burn, fire **5** light **6** kindle **7** inflame

ignoble: low **4** base, mean, vile **6** abject, sordid **8** shameful, wretched

ignominious: **4** base **5** sorry **6** odious **8** infamous, shameful **9** degrading **10** despicable, inglorious, mortifying **11** disgraceful, humiliating

ignoramus: **4** dolt **5** dunce **6** nitwit

ignorant: **5** green, naive, young **6** stupid **7** artless, unaware, uncouth **8** nescient, untaught **9** in the dark, unlearned, unskilled, untutored **10** illiterate, unlettered

ignore: cut **4** omit, snub **5** blink, elide **6** slight **7** neglect **8** overlook **9** disregard, eliminate

iguana: **6** lizard **7** tuatara

Iguvine: **7** Umbrian **8** Eugubine

I have found it: **6** eureka

ihi: **4** fish **7** skipper **8** halfbeak **9** stichbird

ijolite: **7** apatite, calcite **8** titanite

ilex: **5** holly

Iliad: **4** epic, poem
 attributed to: **5** Homer
 character: **4** Ajax **5** Helen, Paris, Priam **6** Aeneas, Hector **8** Achilles, Diomedes, Menelaus, Odysseus **9** Agamemnon, Cassandra, Patroclus **10** Andromache
 war: **6** Trojan

ilium: hip **4** bone

Ilium, Ilion: **4** Troy

ilk: **4** kind, sort, type **5** breed, class **6** family, nature, stripe

ill: bad **4** evil, harm, poor, sick **5** amiss, badly, wrong **6** ailing, faulty, wicked **7** adverse, ailment, baneful, noxious, trouble, unlucky **8** improper **9** adversity, defective **10** indisposed, iniquitous, misfortune **11** unfortunate

ill-advised: **4** rash **5** hasty **6** unwise **8** reckless **9** imprudent **10** indiscreet **11** thoughtless

ill at ease: **7** awkward **13** uncomfortable

ill-boding: **4** dire **7** ominous, unlucky **12** inauspicious

ill-bred: **4** rude **7** boorish, plebian, uncivil **8** churlish, impolite, malapert **9** bourgeois **11** impertinent **12** discourteous

ill-defined: dim **5** faint, fuzzy, vague **7** unclear **10** indistinct

illegitimate: **6** by-blow **7** bastard, bootleg **8** baseborn, improper, spurious, unlawful, wrongful **9** illogical

ill-favored: **4** ugly **9** offensive **10** unpleasant **12** disagreeable

illiberal: **6** stingy **7** bigoted **8** partisan **9** hidebound **10** intolerant

illicit: **7** bootleg, illegal **8** criminal, improper, unlawful **10** contraband, prohibited

illimitable: 4 vast 8 infinite 9 boundless 11 measureless 12 immeasurable

showing: 7 hostile 8 choleric 9 bellicose, irascible, litigious, wrangling 10 pugnacious 11 belligerent, contentious, quarrelsome 12 disputatious

Illinois: *capital:* 11 Springfield
city: 5 Cairo, Pekin 6 Aurora, Galena, Geneva, Joliet, Moline, Peoria, Urbana 7 Chicago, Decatur, Wheaton 8 Carthage, Danville, Kankakee, Rockford, Waukegan 9 Champaign 10 Belleville, Rock Island 11 East St. Louis
lake: 8 Michigan
river: 4 Ohio, Rock 6 Wabash 8 Big Muddy, Illinois, Kankakee, Mackinaw, Sangamon 9 Kaskaskia, Vermilion 10 Des Plaines 11 Mississippi
state bird: 8 cardinal
state flower: 6 violet
state insect: 9 butterfly (Monarch)
state mineral: 8 fluorite
state motto: 29 State Sovereignty, National Union
state tree: 8 white oak

illiterate: 6 unread 8 ignorant, untaught 9 barbarous, unlearned, untutored 10 unlettered

illness: 5 colic 6 malady, morbus 7 ailment, cachexy, disease 8 cachexia, disorder, sickness 9 complaint, distemper 10 affliction, wickedness
feign: 8 malinger

illogical: 7 invalid, unsound 8 specious 9 senseless 10 irrational, unreasoned

ill-suited: 5 inapt, unfit 8 improper 10 unbecoming 13 inappropriate

ill-tempered: 5 cross, moody, surly 6 crusty 7 bilious, grouchy, peevish 8 choleric, snappish 9 dyspeptic, irritable

ill-treat: 5 abuse 6 misuse

illuminate: 4 fire 5 adorn, clear, edify, flare, light 6 inform, kindle 7 clarify, emblaze, explain 8 brighten 9 enlighten, irradiate, make clear 10 illustrate

illumination: *device:* 4 lamp 5 torch 7 lantern 10 flashlight
in eclipse: 8 penumbra
measure: 4 phot 5 lumen 6 candle

illusion: 5 dream, fancy 6 mirage 7 chimera, fallacy, fantasy, mockery, phantom 8 delusion 9 deception 10 appearance

illusive: 4 sham 5 false 6 unreal 7 seeming 8

apparent, illusory 9 deceitful, deceptive, imaginary 10 fallacious, phantasmal

illustrate: 4 show 5 adorn 7 clarify, explain, draw, sketch, picture, point up, portray 9 elucidate, exemplify, make clear, represent 10 illuminate

illustration: 4 case 6 sample 7 example 8 instance, vignette

illustrator: 6 artist

illustrious: 5 famed, grand, noble, noted 6 bright, candid, heroic 7 eminent, exalted 8 glorious, renowned 9 honorable 10 celebrated 11 conspicuous

ill will: 4 hate 5 spite, venom 6 animus, enmity, malice, rancor 7 dislike 9 hostility 10 bad feeling

ilvaite: 8 silicate

image: god 4 copy, form, icon, idol, ikon 5 eikon 6 double, effigy, emblem, fetish, figure, statue, symbol 7 phantom, picture 8 likeness 9 depiction, semblance 10 conception, impression, reflection, similitude, simulacrum
attacker: 10 iconoclast
pert. to televised: 5 video
stone: 5 herma 6 hermae (pl.)
wooden: 4 tiki 6 xoanon 7 kachina

imaginary: 5 ideal 6 unreal 7 fancied, feigned 8 illusory, mythical, notional 9 dreamed up, fantastic, visionary 10 artificial, chimerical, fictitious 11 make believe

imagination: 7 fantasy, thought 9 ingenuity

imaginative: 6 dreamy, poetic 8 original

imagine: 5 dream, fancy, feign, think 6 gather 7 picture, suppose, surmise 8 conceive, envision 9 apprehend 10 comprehend, conjecture

imam: 5 mahdi, mufti, ruler 6 caliph

imaret: inn 7 hospice 11 caravansary

imbecile: 4 dolt, jerk 5 anile, daffy, idiot, moron 6 cranky, dotard, nitwit 7 fatuous 8 dumbbell 9 driveling 10 changeling, half-witted

imbed: fix 5 embed, inset 6 cement

imbibe: sip 4 soak 5 drink, imbue, steep 6 absorb 7 swallow 8 saturate

imbricate: 5 tiled 6 scaled 7 overlap

imbroglio: row 4 spat 7 dispute 8 squabble 11 altercation

imbrue: wet 4 soak 5 stain 6 drench

imbue: dye 4 soak 5 steep, tinge 6 imbibe, infuse, leaven 7 animate, ingrain, inspire, instill, pervade 8 permeate, saturate 9 inoculate 10 impregnate

imitate: ape 4 copy, echo, mime, mock 5 mimic 6 follow, repeat 7 copycat, emulate 8 resemble, simulate 9 dissemble 11 counterfeit

imitation: 4 fake, sham 5 dummy, phony 6

ersatz **7** replica **8** likeness **9** emulation, fac-simile

derisive: **6** parody **7** mockery **9** burlesque

fantastic: **8** travesty

imitation gem: **5** glass, paste

imitation pearl: **6** olivet

immaculate: **4** pure **5** clean **6** candid, chaste **7** correct, perfect **8** innocent, spotless, unsoiled **9** faultless, undefiled, unspotted, unstained, unsullied

immalleable: **5** rigid **10** unyielding

immanent: **8** inherent **9** intrinsic **10** indwelling, subjective

immaterial: **6** slight **8** trifling **9** asomatous, spiritual, unearthly **10** impalpable, intangible, irrelevant **11** unimportant **12** not pertinent

immature: **5** crude, green, young **6** callow, unripe **7** puerile, untried **8** childish, youthful **10** incomplete, unfinished **11** undeveloped

immaturity: **5** youth **6** nonage

immeasurable: **7** immense **8** infinite **9** boundless, unlimited **10** indefinite

immediate: **4** next **6** direct **7** instant **8** adjacent **9** proximate **10** contiguous, succeeding

immediately: now **4** anon **6** presto **8** directly **9** extempore, forthwith, presently

immemorial: **7** ageless, ancient **8** dateless **11** prehistoric, traditional

immense: **4** huge, vast **5** grand, great, large **7** titanic **8** colossal, enormous, gigantic, infinite **9** extensive, monstrous **10** prodigious, tremendous

immerse: dip **4** bury, duck **5** bathe, douse, souse **6** absorb, drench, occupy, plunge **7** engross **8** submerge

immigrant: **5** alien **6** emigré **8** newcomer

Israel: **6** halutz **7** chalutz

imminent: **9** expecting, impending **11** approaching, threatening

immitigable: **10** implacable

immobile: set **4** firm **5** fixed, inert **6** frozen, laid up, stable **9** immovable **10** motionless, stationary, stock-still

immoderate: **5** undue **7** extreme **9** boundless, excessive, voracious **10** exorbitant, inordinate **11** intemperate

immodest: **4** bold, lewd **6** brazen, coarse **7** forward, obscene **8** indecent, unchaste **9** shameless **10** indecorous

immolation: **7** burning **8** offering **9** sacrifice

immoral: bad **4** evil **5** loose, wrong **6** impure, sinful, wanton, wicked **7** corrupt, vicious **8** culpable, depraved, indecent **9** dissolute **10** licentious

immortal: **6** divine **7** endless, eternal, godlike, undying **8** enduring **9** ceaseless, deathless **11** amaranthine, everlasting

immortality: **8** athanasy **9** athanasia **11** endless life

Hindu: **6** amrita

immovable: pat, set **4** fast, firm **5** fixed, rigid **7** adamant **8** constant, immobile, obdurate **9** steadfast **10** adamantine, stationary

immunity: **7** freedom **9** exemption **12** resistance to

immunize: **8** make safe **9** inoculate

immunizer: **5** serum **7** vaccine

immure: **4** wall **7** confine **8** cloister, imprison **11** incarcerate

immutable: **4** firm **7** eternal **10** invariable, unchanging **11** unalterable

Imogen's father: **9** Cymbeline

imp: bud, elf **4** brat, cion, slip **5** child, demon, devil, graft, rogue, scamp **6** sprite, urchin **7** gremlin, progeny **8** devilkin, folletto **9** hobgoblin, offspring

impact: **4** blow, jolt, pack, slam **5** brunt, crash, force, shock, wedge **6** effect, stroke **7** impulse **9** collision **11** implication

impair: mar **4** harm, hurt **5** spoil, waste **6** damage, debase, hinder, injure, lessen, reduce, sicken, weaken **7** blemish, cripple, vitiate **8** decrease, enfeeble

impaired: **9** afflicted

impala: **7** rooibok **8** antelope

impale: **4** spit **5** spear, spike **6** pierce, skewer **8** transfix **10** run through

impalpable: **7** elusive **10** immaterial, intangible

impart: **4** give, lend, tell **5** share, yield **6** bestow, confer, convey, direct, impute, reveal **7** divulge, inspire, instill **8** disclose, discover **10** distribute **11** communicate

impartial: **4** even, fair, just **7** neutral **8** unbiased **9** colorless, equitable, objective

imparting motion: **7** kinetic

impassable: **5** solid **10** impervious

impasse: box **7** dead end **8** cul-de-sac (F.), deadlock, standoff **9** stalemate

impassible: **9** impassive, unfeeling **12** invulnerable

impassioned: **5** fiery **6** ardent, fervid **7** blazing, fervent, intense, zealous **8** eloquent, feverish, vehement

impassive: **4** calm **5** stoic **6** serene, stolid, wooden **9** apathetic **10** impassible, insensible, phlegmatic

impatient: hot **4** avid, edgy, keen **5** eager, hasty, testy **7** anxious, chafing, fidgety, fretful, peevish **8** choleric, petulant, restless **9** irascible, irritable

impeach: **6** accuse, charge, indict **7** arraign, censure **9** challenge, discredit

impeccable: **5** right **7** correct, perfect **8** flawless **9** exquisite, faultless **11** unblemished

impecunious: 4 poor 5 needy 8 indigent 9 destitute, penniless

impede: 4 clog 5 block, check, choke, delay 6 hamper, harass, hinder, retard, stymie 7 disrupt 8 encumber, handicap, hold back, obstruct
legally: bar 5 debar, estop

impediment: bar, rub 4 clog, flaw, snag 5 hitch 6 defect, malady, remora 8 obstacle 9 detriment, hindrance 10 difficulty

impedimenta: 4 gear 7 baggage, luggage

impel: pat 4 blow, goad, move, send, spur, urge 5 drive, force, hurry 6 compel, excite, incite, induce 7 actuate 8 motivate 9 constrain, encourage, influence, instigate, stimulate

impelling force: 7 impetus 8 momentum

impending: 7 looming 8 imminent, menacing, oncoming 11 approaching

impenetrable: 4 hard 5 dense, solid 8 airtight 10 impassable, impervious 11 impermeable, inscrutable

impenitent: 8 hardened, obdurate 11 remorseless, unrepentant

imperative: 4 duty, rule 5 order, vital 6 urgent 7 crucial 8 pressing, verb form 9 essential, mandatory, necessary 10 commanding, compelling, compulsory, peremptory

imperator: 6 leader 7 emperor, general

imperceptible: 10 insensible, intangible 13 indiscernible

imperfect: 4 cull, poor 5 rough 6 faulty, flawed, second 9 blemished, defective 10 inadequate, incomplete, unfinished

imperfection: 4 flaw, vice 5 fault 6 defect, foible 7 blemish, failing, frailty 8 weakness 10 deficiency 11 shortcoming

imperfectly: 4 half 5 badly

imperial: 5 regal, royal 6 kingly 8 majestic
cap: 5 crown
domain: 6 empire
officer: 8 palatine

imperial woodpecker: 9 ivorybill

imperil: 4 risk 6 expose, hazard 8 endanger 10 jeopardize

imperious: 6 lordly 7 haughty 8 arrogant, despotic, dominant, pressing 10 commanding, imperative, tyrannical 11 dictatorial, domineering, magisterial

imperishable: 7 eternal, lasting, undying 8 enduring, immortal 9 continual, deathless, perpetual

impermanent: 8 fleeting 9 ephemeral, temporary, tentative, transient 10 evanescent

impersonal: 4 cold 7 general 8 detached 9 objective

impersonate: act, ape 4 pose 5 mimic 6 typify

impersonator: 5 actor, mimic 8 imitator,

imposter, impostor 11 entertainer

impertinence: 4 sass 8 audacity 9 insolence 10 incivility

impertinent: 4 rude 5 sassy, saucy 7 illbred 8 arrogant, impudent 9 audacious 13 disrespectful

imperturbability: 8 ataraxia, calmness 9 composure, sangfroid 10 equanimity

imperturbable: 4 cool 6 placid, serene, stable 8 tranquil 9 impassive

impervious: 5 tight 8 hardened 10 impassable 11 impermeable 12 impenetrable

impetrate: 7 beseech, entreat, procure

impetuous: hot 4 rash 5 eager, fiery, hasty, heady, sharp 6 abrupt, ardent, fervid, fierce, flashy, sudden 7 furious, rushing, violent 8 forcible, headlong, vehement 9 impulsive, hot-headed 11 precipitate

impetus: 4 goad, prod, push, spur 5 drive, force 6 motive 7 impulse 8 momentum, stimulus 9 incentive

imphee: 5 plant 7 sorghum

impi: 4 Zulu 8 soldiers, warriors

impiety: 9 blasphemy 10 disrespect 11 irreverence, ungodliness

impignorate: 4 pawn 6 pledge 8 mortgage

impinge: 6 strike 7 intrude, touch on 8 encroach, trespass

impious: 6 unholy 7 godless, profane, ungodly 9 atheistic, undutiful 10 irreverent

impish: 6 elfish 7 naughty, puckish

implacable: 6 deadly 10 relentless 11 immitigable 12 unappeasable

implant: sow 4 root 5 embed, infix, inset 6 enroot, infuse 7 impress, inspire, instill 9 inculcate, inoculate, insinuate, introduce 10 impregnate

implausible: 4 weak 5 fishy 6 flimsy 7 dubious, suspect 8 unlikely 9 illogical 10 improbable 11 problematic 12 unbelievable

implement: 4 gear 6 device, gadget 7 enforce, fulfill, realize, utensil 8 complete, material 9 apparatus, appliance 10 accomplish, instrument
ancient: 4 celt 6 amgarn, eolith 9 paleolith
baker's: 4 peel
barbed: 7 harpoon
cleaning: mop 4 swab 5 broom, brush 6 sponge, vacuum 7 sweeper 9 steel wool
cutting: 5 blade, knife, mower, razor 6 reaper, scythe, shears, sickle 7 loppers 8 scissors 9 jackknife, secateurs 11 pocketknife
enlarging: 6 reamer 7 dilator
farm: 4 disc, disk, plow, rake 6 seeder, tiller 7 tractor
furcate: 4 fork
garden: hoe 4 rake 5 mower, spade 6

shovel, sickle, trowel, weeder
grasping: 5 tongs 6 pliers 8 tweezers
hand printing: 6 brayer, roller
hide cleaning: 6 slater
kitchen: 5 corer 6 kettle 7 skillet, spatula
lifting: pry 5 lever, tongs
logging: 6 peavey
nap-raising: 6 teasel
pounding: 4 maul 6 hammer, pestle, sledge
shovel-like: 5 scoop, spoon 6 trowel
surgical: 7 scalpel 9 tenaculum
threshing: 5 flail

implicate: 5 imply 7 concern, embroil, involve

implicit: 5 tacit 6 unsaid 7 implied 8 absolute, complete, inherent 9 suggested 10 unshakable

implied: 5 tacit 6 hinted 10 understood

implore: ask, beg 4 coax, pray 5 crave, plead 6 appeal 7 beseech, entreat, solicit 8 petition 10 supplicate

imply: 4 hint 7 connote, involve, presume, signify, suggest 8 comprise, intimate 9 insinuate 10 presuppose

impolite: 4 rude 5 bluff, crude, rough 7 ill-bred, uncivil 10 indecorous, ungracious, unmannerly, unpolished

impolitic: 6 unwise 10 indiscreet 11 inexpedient, injudicious 12 undiplomatic

import: 5 sense, value 6 convey, denote 7 betoken, bring in, meaning, signify 8 indicate 9 introduce, substance

importance: 4 rank 5 worth 6 moment, weight 7 account, gravity, stature 8 prestige, standing 9 dimension, influence 11 consequence 13 consideration
to be of: 6 matter

important: 4 dear, high 5 grave, great 6 famous, urgent 7 pompous, serious 8 eventful, material 9 momentous, ponderous 10 noteworthy, preeminent 11 influential, significant

important person: VIP 5 mogul, wheel 6 bigwig, tycoon 7 bigshot, magnate, notable

importunate: 6 urgent 7 teasing 8 pressing 9 demanding, imploring 10 burdensome, persistent

importune: beg, dun, nag, ply, woo 4 urge 5 plead 6 appeal 7 beseech, entreat, solicit 10 supplicate

impose: 4 levy 5 apply, exact, foist, order, visit 6 burden, create, slap on 7 command, dictate, inflict, obtrude 8 generate 9 institute
upon: 4 dupe 5 cheat 7 exploit

imposing: big 5 burly, proud 6 august 7 stately 9 grandiose, pyramidal 10 commanding, impressive 11 outstanding

imposition: tax 4 duty, fine, levy 5 fraud, gouge, trick 6 burden 7 penalty 9 deception

impossible: 9 insoluble 12 beyond reason, unattainable

impost: tax 4 duty, levy, task, toll 6 annale, avania, custom, excise, surtax, tariff, weight 7 tribute 8 chaptrel

impostor: 4 sham 5 cheat, faker, fraud, phony, quack 8 deceiver 9 charlatan, pretender 10 mountebank

imposture: gag 5 fraud, trick 6 deceit, humbug 8 artifice, delusion, quackery 9 deception, falsehood, imitation 10 imposition, simulacrum

impotence: 7 acratia 8 weakness 10 feebleness

impotent: 6 barren 7 sterile 8 helpless 9 powerless 11 ineffective

impound: 5 seize, store 6 freeze 7 collect 11 appropriate

impoverish: 4 ruin 6 beggar, weaken 7 deplete, exhaust

impoverished: 4 poor 5 needy 6 bereft 7 drained 8 bankrupt, indigent 9 destitute

impractical: 9 visionary 10 idealistic, starry-eyed, unfeasible 11 unrealistic

imprecation: 4 oath 5 curse 8 anathema 9 blasphemy, profanity 10 execration

impregnable: 4 firm, hard 10 invincible, unshakable, unyielding

impregnate: 4 soak 6 charge, infuse, leaven 8 fructify, permeate, saturate 9 fecundate, fertilize

impresario: 7 manager 8 director 9 conductor

impress: fix 4 etch, levy, mark, move, seal, sway 5 affix, brand, delve, print, seize, stamp 6 affect, enlist 7 engrave, implant, imprint 9 inculcate, influence

impressed: 4 awed 8 affected 10 shanghaied

impression: 4 dent, dint, idea, mark 5 fancy, print, stamp 6 affect, signet 7 opinion 8 reaction 10 conception

impressionable: 7 plastic 9 sensitive 10 responsive 11 susceptible

impressionist painter: 5 Manet, Monet, Degas, Sisley, 6 Renoir 8 Pissarro

impressive: 5 grand 6 august, moving, solemn 8 forcible, imposing, majestic, striking 9 arresting, memorable

imprimatur: 7 license 8 approval, sanction

imprint: fix 4 mark 5 press, stamp 6 effect 7 engrave, impress

imprison: 4 cage, jail 5 limit 6 arrest, commit, detain, immure, intern 7 confine, enclose 8 restrain 11 incarcerate

imprisonment: 6 duress 7 durance 9 captivity 11 confinement

improbable: 5 fishy 8 doubtful, unlikely

impromptu: 7 offhand 9 extempore 10 off the cuff 11 unrehearsed

improper: ill 4 evil 5 amiss, undue, unfit, wrong 6 unjust, naught 7 illegal, illicit, non-U, 8 indecent, infra dig, shameful, unseemly 9 incorrect 10 inaccurate, indecorous, indelicate

impropriety: 5 gaffe, shame 7 faux pas 8 solecism 9 barbarism 12 impertinence

improve: 4 grow, help, mend 5 amend, edify, emend 6 better, enrich 7 advance, augment, benefit, correct, enhance, perfect, promote, rectify, retouch 9 cultivate, intensify 10 ameliorate

improvident: 8 prodigal, wasteful 9 negligent 10 thriftless 11 extravagant

improvise: 5 ad-lib 6 devise, invent 8 contrive 11 extemporize

music: 4 vamp

imprudent: 4 rash 6 unwary, unwise 7 foolish 8 reckless 10 incautious, indiscreet

impudence: lip 4 gall 5 brass, cheek, folly 8 audacity 9 arrogance, assurance, hardihood, insolence 10 confidence, effrontery 11 presumption

impudent: 4 bold, pert, rude 5 brash, sassy, saucy 6 brazen 7 forward 8 insolent 9 barefaced, officious 11 impertinent 13 disrespectful

impugn: 4 deny 5 fight 6 assail, resist 7 gainsay 9 challenge, insinuate 10 contradict

impulse: 4 urge 5 drift, drive, force 6 impact, motive, thrust 7 impetus 8 instinct, stimulus 9 incentive 11 instigation

blind: ate

divine: 8 afflatus

traveling: 10 wanderlust

impulsive: 5 hasty, quick 6 fitful, sudden 8 headlong 9 impellent, impetuous

impure: 4 foul, lewd, vile 5 dirty, gross, mixed 6 coarse, filthy, unholy 7 bastard, defiled, obscene, unclean, vicious 8 indecent, inferior, unchaste 10 unhallowed 11 adulterated, incongruous, unwholesome

impurity: 5 dross, filth, taint 8 foulness 9 pollution 10 corruption 11 contaminant

impute: 4 give 5 count 6 assign, charge, credit, impart, reckon 7 arraign, ascribe 8 consider 9 attribute

in: 4 amid 5 among 6 at home, corner, entree 7 arrived, popular 9 incumbent

a bad way: 4 sick 5 upset 9 on the spot

a row: 6 alined, serial 7 aligned

abeyance: 7 pending

abundance: 6 galore, plenty

addition: too, yet 4 also, more, plus 7 besides, further 8 moreover

advance: 5 ahead 6 before

any case: 7 however 11 nonetheless

any event: 15 notwithstanding

arrears: 5 owing 6 behind 7 overdue

as much: 5 since 7 because

camera: 7 sub rosa 8 secretly 9 furtively

capacity of: qua

case: 4 lest

common: 5 alike

concert: 8 together

due course: 4 anon, soon 11 opportunely

Dutch: 9 disgraced, in trouble 10 out of favor

every way: 5 fully 6 wholly 7 totally 8 entirely 10 completely, thoroughly

excess: too 4 over 6 overly

existence: 6 extant

fact: 5 truly 6 indeed 7 de facto (L.)

favor of: for, pro

few cases: 6 rarely, seldom

great need: 7 straits

name only: 7 nominal 10 supposedly

place of: for 5 stead 7 instead

reality: 8 actually

regard to: 4 in re 5 anent 10 concerning

same place: 4 ibid

shape: fit 4 neat, trim 5 ready

spite of: 10 regardless

store: 8 awaiting

that case: 4 then

the case of: 4 in re (L.)

the center of: 4 amid

the interim: 9 meanwhile

the know: hep, hip 9 au courant

the manner of: a la

the mood: 5 eager 7 willing

the raw: 4 bare, nude 9 undressed 10 dishabille

the red: 5 broke 8 bankrupt, strapped

the same period: 15 contemporaneous

this: 6 herein

this way: 4 thus

toto: all 5 whole 8 complete 10 completely

truth: 6 certes, indeed, verily 8 forsooth

what way: how 7 quomodo (L.)

year of: 4 anno

inability: 9 impotence, ineptness 10 incapacity 12 incompetence

to articulate: 7 anaudia

to chew: 8 amasesis

to comprehend: 11 acatalepsia

to name correctly: 9 paranomia

to read: 6 alexia 10 illiteracy

to remember: 7 amnesia

to speak: 6 anepia

to stand erect: 7 astasia

to swallow: 7 aphagia

to understand speech: 7 aphasia

inaccessible: 6 closed 11 unreachable 12 unattainable

inaccuracy: 5 error 7 mistake

inaccurate: 5 false, wrong 6 faulty 7 inexact 8 specious 9 defective, erroneous, incorrect, off target

Inachus's daughter: Io

inaction: 8 idleness 9 inertness
temporary: 5 pause 6 recess 7 respite

inactive: lax 4 dead, idle, slow 5 heavy, inert, prone, slack, still 6 asleep, latent, otiose, supine 7 dormant, passive 8 dilatory, faineant, indolent, sleeping, slothful, sluggish 9 quiescent, sedentary

inadequate: 5 short 6 scanty 7 wanting 8 below par 9 deficient, imperfect 12 insufficient

inadvertence: 7 neglect 10 negligence 12 carelessness, heedlessness

inadvisable: 4 rash 6 unwise 9 imprudent 10 indiscreet

inalienable: 6 sacred 8 absolute, inherent 10 inviolable

inalterable: 9 steadfast 12 unchangeable

inamorata: 5 lover 7 beloved 8 mistress 10 sweetheart

inane: 5 empty, silly, vapid 6 absurd, stupid, vacant 7 fatuous, foolish, idiotic, vacuous 8 trifling 9 doddering, frivolous, pointless, senseless, worthless 11 nonsensical

inanimate: 4 dead, dull, flat 5 inert 6 stolid 8 lifeless 10 insensible, spiritless 11 unconscious

inanition: 7 fasting 8 lethargy 9 emptiness

inanity: 7 vacuity 9 emptiness, frivolity, silliness 10 flimsiness, triviality 11 foolishness

inapposite: 10 irrelevant

inappreciable: 4 thin 7 tenuous 10 impalpable 11 microscopic

inappropriate: 5 inapt 8 improper 9 unfitting 10 out of place, unsuitable

inapt: 5 inept 6 clumsy 7 awkward 8 backward 10 amateurish, unsuitable

inarch: 5 graft

inarticulate: shy 4 dumb, mute 7 blurred 10 tongue-tied

inartistic: 4 ugly 9 tasteless

inasmuch as: for 5 since 7 because 11 considering

inattention: 7 neglect 9 disregard 10 negligence 11 daydreaming

inattentive: lax 6 absent, remiss 8 careless, heedless 9 forgetful, negligent, unheeding, unmindful 10 abstracted, neglectful

inaugurate: 4 open 5 begin, start 6 induct, launch 7 install, usher in 8 initiate 9 auspicate, introduce 10 consecrate

inauspicious: bad 4 foul 7 adverse, ominous 8 sinister

inauthentic: 4 fake 5 false 6 mythic, unreal 8 doubtful, spurious 10 apocryphal, fictitious

inborn desire: 7 conatus

inbreak: 6 inroad 8 invasion 9 incursion

inbred: 6 inborn, innate, native 7 natural 10 congenital

Inca: *ancient city:* 11 Machu Picchu
beer: 6 chicha
capital: 5 Cusco, Cuzco
clan: 5 ayllu
conqueror: 7 Pizarro
counting cord: 5 quipu
land: 4 Peru
language: 7 Quechua
priest: 6 Amauta
ruler's sister-wife: 5 Ccoya
sacred: 5 huaca

incalculable: 6 untold 8 infinite 9 boundless, countless, uncertain 11 illimitable 12 immeasurable

incandescence: 4 glow, heat

incandescent: 6 bright 7 beaming, burning, fulgent, glowing, lambent, radiant, shining 8 luminous 9 brilliant

incantation: 5 chant, charm, magic, spell 6 carmen (L.) 7 sorcery 11 conjuration, enchantment

incapable: 5 inept, unfit 6 unable 9 untrained 11 inefficient, unqualified

incapacitate: 4 lame 7 cripple, disable 10 disqualify

incarcerate: 4 jail 6 immure, shut up 7 confine 8 imprison

incarnate: 6 embody 8 make real 10 give form to 11 personified

incarnation: 6 avatar, Christ 10 embodiment
of Vishnu: 4 Rama

incase: 5 cover 7 enclose 8 surround

incautious: 4 rash 6 unwary 8 careless, heedless, reckless 9 impolitic, imprudent, unguarded 10 indiscreet

incendiarism: 5 arson 9 pyromania

incendiary: 7 firebug 8 agitator 10 pyromaniac 12 inflammatory

incense: 5 anger, aroma 6 arouse, enrage, incite 7 perfume, provoke 8 enkindle, irritate
burner: 6 censer 8 thurible
user: 8 thurifer

incentive: 4 goad, spur 5 spark 6 motive 7 impetus, impulse 8 stimulus 9 influence 10 incitement, inducement

inception: 4 root 5 start 6 origin 9 beginning 10 initiation

incertitude: 5 doubt 9 suspicion 10 skepticism, insecurity

incessant: 6 steady 7 endless, eternal 8 constant 9 ceaseless, continual 11 everlasting, unremitting

incessantly: 7 forever 11 continually, unceasingly

inch: 5 creep 7 measure 10 move slowly

along: **9** worm ahead

inches: *forty-five:* ell
  four: **4** hand
  nine: **4** span
  39.37: **5** meter

inchmeal: 9 gradually

inchoate: 7 chaotic **8** formless, unformed, unshaped **9** incipient, shapeless **10** disordered, incomplete

incident: 5 event **7** episode **8** accident, casualty, occasion **9** happening **10** occurrence

incidental: 5 minor **6** casual **8** episodic **9** accessory, extrinsic, secondary **10** accidental, contingent, fortuitous, occasional

incidentally: 6 obiter **7** apropos **8** by the way

incinerate: 4 burn **7** combust, consume, cremate

incinerator: 7 furnace **9** crematory

incipient: 7 budding, initial, nascent **8** inchoate **9** beginning **10** commencing

incise: cut **4** chop, etch, rase **5** carve **7** engrave

incision: cut **4** gash, slit **5** notch, slash

incisive: 5 acute, sharp **6** biting **7** cutting, probing **9** sarcastic, trenchant **10** perceptive **11** penetrating

incisor: 6 cutter **9** foretooth

incite: egg, hie **4** abet, fire, goad, move, prod, spur, urge **5** impel **6** arouse, compel, entice, excite, exhort, foment, induce **7** actuate, agitate, animate, commove, provoke **8** motivate **9** encourage, instigate, stimulate

incitement: 6 motive **7** impetus **8** stimulus **9** incentive

incivility: 8 rudeness **9** surliness **10** disrespect, effrontery **11** discourtesy **12** churlishness, impertinence

inclemency: 8 asperity

inclement: bad, raw **4** cold, hard, rude **5** harsh, rough **6** severe, stormy **8** rigorous **10** unmerciful

inclination: 4 bent, bias, hang, urge, will **5** fancy, slant, slope, tenor **6** affect, animus, ascent, liking **7** descent, leaning **8** fondness, gradient, penchant, tendency **9** acclivity, affection, direction, proneness **10** attachment, proclivity **11** disposition**incline:** bow, dip, tip **4** bend, cant, heel, lean, list, ramp, tend, tilt **5** be apt, grade, pitch, shape, slant, slide, slope, trend **6** prefer **7** upgrade

inclined: apt **4** fain, wont **5** alist, atilt, prone **6** biased, likely, minded **7** hanging **8** addicted

inclose: 5 hem in, pen in **6** encase **7** contain **8** surround

inclosure: ree (Sc.) **4** wall **5** fence **8** sepiment
  animal: pen, sty **4** barn, cage, cote, fold **5** hutch, kraal **6** corral, stable

include: 5 cover **6** entail, take in **7** contain, embrace, involve **8** comprise **9** encompass

incognito: 5 alias **6** veiled **7** unknown **9** disguised

incoherent: 6 broken **8** rambling **9** illogical **10** disjointed **11** incongruous **12** disconnected

income: pay **4** gain **5** rente (F.) **6** profit, return, salary **7** produce, revenue **8** interest, proceeds, receipts **9** emolument

incommensurate: 7 unequal **10** dissimilar **12** inconsistent, insufficient

incommode: vex **5** annoy **6** molest, plague **7** trouble **8** disquiet **9** disoblige **10** discommode

incomparable: 8 peerless **9** matchless, nonpareil, unequaled, unrivaled **10** surpassing **11** superlative

incompatible: 8 contrary **9** unmixable **10** discordant **11** conflicting, incongruous **12** inharmonious **13** contradictory, unsympathetic

incompetence: 9 inability, unfitness

incompetent: 5 inept, unfit **8** helpless **9** incapable, unskilled **10** untalented **11** inefficient, unqualified

incomplete: 5 rough, short **6** broken, undone **7** divided, lacking, partial, wanting **8** immature, inchoate **9** defective, imperfect **10** unfinished **11** fragmentary

incomprehensible: 8 abstruse **9** graspless **10** fathomless, mysterious, unreadable **11** unthinkable **12** unimaginable **13** inconceivable

inconceivable: 7 strange **10** improbable, incredible **11** unthinkable

inconclusive: 4 open **9** uncertain, undecided **10** indefinite, up in the air

incondite: 5 crude **9** unrefined **10** unpolished **11** unorganized

incongruity: 9 inharmony **10** dissonance **11** incoherence **12** disagreement

incongruous: 5 alien **6** absurd, impure **9** grotesque **10** discordant, unsuitable **12** disagreeable, inconsistent, inharmonious

inconsequential: 5 petty, small **6** paltry **7** trivial **8** picayune, piddling, trifling **10** irrelevant **11** unimportant

inconsiderable: 5 petty **7** trivial **8** careless, unworthy **10** negligible

inconsiderate: 4 rash, rude **6** unkind **8** careless **9** imprudent, negligent **10** incautious, indiscreet, neglectful **11** improvident, injudicious, thoughtless

inconsistent: 6 fickle **8** unstable **9** dissonant **10** capricious, discordant, discrepant, inconstant **11** vacillating **13** contradictory

inconsolable: 11 comfortless, heartbroken

inconstant: 6 fickle **7** elusive, erratic **8** disloyal, variable **9** desultory, faithless **10**

capricious, changeable **12** inconsistent

incontestable: **4** sure **5** valid **7** certain **10** undeniable **11** indubitable, irrefutable

incontrovertible: **7** certain **10** undeniable

inconvenience: **5** annoy **6** bother **7** trouble **8** disquiet **9** aggravate, annoyance **10** discomfort, discommode, uneasiness **11** awkwardness, disturbance **12** discomfiture

inconvenient: **7** awkward, unhandy **8** annoying **10** unsuitable **11** troublesome **12** unreasonable

incorporate: mix **4** fuse, join **5** blend, merge, unite **6** absorb, embody **7** combine **9** integrate **10** assimilate

incorporation: **10** absorption **11** combination

incorporeal: **4** airy **8** bodiless **9** asomatous, spiritual, sprightly **10** immaterial

incorrect: bad **5** false, wrong **6** faulty, untrue **9** erroneous

incorrigible: bad **8** hardened, hopeless **10** beyond help **11** intractable **12** unmanageable

incorruptible: **4** just, pure **6** honest **7** upright

increase: add, eke, wax **4** eche, gain, grow, rise, rist **5** boost, raise, swell **6** accrue, amount, better, dilate, expand, extend, gather, growth **7** amplify, augment, enhance, enlarge, greaten, inflate, magnify **8** addition, flourish, heighten, multiply **9** accession, advantage, aggravate, expansion, extension, increment, intensify **10** accelerate, accumulate, aggrandize, appreciate **11** aggravation, development, enlargement *in sound:* **9** crescendo

incredible: **6** absurd **7** awesome **10** astounding, far-fetched, impossible **12** preposterous, unbelievable

incredulous: **7** dubious **8** doubting **9** faithless, skeptical **10** mistrustful

increment: **4** gain **6** growth, income **8** increase **12** augmentation

increscent: **6** waxing **7** growing **9** enlarging **10** increasing

incriminate: **6** accuse **7** impeach, involve **9** implicate

incrust: **4** coat **5** glaze **6** barkle

incubate: **5** brood, hatch **7** develop

incubus: **4** load **5** demon **6** burden, spirit **9** hindrance, nightmare **10** impediment

inculcate: **5** infix **6** infuse, instil **7** implant, impress, instill

inculpate: **5** blame **11** incriminate

incumbent: **7** binding **8** occupant **9** overlying **11** leaning upon

incunabula: **7** infancy, origins **10** beginnings **11** first stages

incur: **8** contract **9** encounter

incurable: **8** hopeless **11** irreparable **12** irremediable

incurious: **8** detached **9** apathetic **11** indifferent, unconcerned, uninquiring

incursion: **4** rade (Sc.), raid **5** foray **6** inroad **7** assault, descent, hosting **8** invasion **10** dragonnade

incurved: **7** concave

incus: ear **5** ambos, anvil

indebted: **8** beholden **9** obligated

indecency: **8** impurity **9** immodesty, indecorum, obscenity **10** indelicacy

indecent: **4** foul **5** gross, nasty **6** coarse, greasy **7** immoral **8** improper, unseemly **9** dishonest **10** scurrilous

indecipherable: **9** illegible

indecision: **5** doubt **9** hesitancy **10** hesitation **11** uncertainty, vacillation **12** irresolution

indecorous: **4** rude **6** coarse **7** uncivil **8** immodest, impolite, improper, indecent, unseemly **10** unbecoming **11** distasteful

indeed: yea **5** truly **6** really **7** honestly, in faith, in truth **8** actually, forsooth **9** certainly **10** positively

indefatigable: **4** busy **8** tireless, untiring **9** assiduous **10** persistent, unwearying **11** persevering

indefensible: **11** inexcusable **12** unpardonable

indefinite: **5** loose, vague **7** inexact, neutral **8** aoristic **9** ambiguous, equivocal, uncertain, unlimited **10** inexplicit **12** inconclusive

indehiscent fruit: uva **5** grape, melon

indelible: **4** fast **5** fixed **9** permanent **10** inerasable

indelicate: raw **5** broad, gross **6** coarse, greasy **7** fulsome **8** impolite, improper, unseemly **9** offensive, unrefined **10** indecorous, unbecoming

indemnification: **10** reparation **11** restitution

indemnify: pay **6** recoup **9** reimburse **10** compensate, recompense

indemnity: **7** amnesty **9** exemption **10** protection, reparation **12** compensation

indent: jag **4** dent, gimp **5** chase, delve, inlay, notch, press, stamp, tooth **6** bruise, emboss **7** depress

indentation: bay **4** dent, nick **5** notch **6** dimple, recess **10** impression

indenture: **8** contract **9** agreement, inventory

independence: **7** freedom, liberty **8** autonomy **10** competency **11** sovereignty

independent: **4** free **5** proud **9** sovereign, uncoerced **11** self-reliant

independently: **5** apart **10** absolutely

indestructible: **7** durable, lasting **9** permanent **10** inviolable **12** imperishable

indeterminate: **5** vague **7** obscure **8** formless **9** uncertain, unlimited

index: **4** file, list **5** table **7** catalog **9** catalogue, repertory

India: 6 Bharat
 capital: 8 New Delhi
 city: 4 Agra 5 Delhi, Patna, Poona,
  Simla 6 Baroda, Bombay, Guntur,
  Howrah, Imphal, Indore, Jaipur, Kan-
  pur, Madras, Nagpur, Ranchi 7 Lucknow 8 Calcutta, Shillong, Sholapur 9
  Ahmadabad, Allahabad, Bangalore,
  Huderabad
 clothing: 4 sari 5 dhoti 6 turban
 currency: lac, pie 4 anna, dawm, fels,
  hoon, lakh, pice, tara 5 abidi, crore,
  paisa, rupee
 forehead mark: 6 kumkum
 landmark: 8 Taj Mahal
 measure: ady, dha, gaz, gez, guz, jow,
  kos, lan, ser 4 byee, coss, dain, dhan,
  hath, jaob, koss, kunk, moot, para, raik,
  rati, seit, taun, teng, tola 5 bigha, cahar,
  covid, crosa, danda, denda, drona,
  garce, gireh, hasta, krosa, pally, parah,
  ratti, salay, yojan 6 adhaka, amunam,
  angula, covido, cudava, cumbha,
  geerah, lamany, moolum, mushti, palgat, parrah, ropani, tipree, unglee,
  yojana 7 adoulie, dhanush, gavyuti,
  khahoon, niranga, prastha, vitasti 8
  okthabah
 mountain: 5 Ghats 6 Zaskar 7 Satpura,
  Siwalik 8 Aravalli, Himalaya 9 Hindu
  Kush 12 Kanchenjunga
 mountain pass: 5 Bolan, Gumal 6 Khyber
 musical instrument: 5 sitar, tabla
 oven, clay: 7 tandoor
 poet: 6 Tagore (Rabindranath)
 river: 4 Beas, Kosi, Luni, Ravi, Sind 5
  Bhima, Indus, Rapti, Tapti, Tista 6
  Chenab, Ganges, Gomati, Jhelum, Sut-
  lej, Yamuna 7 Cauvery, Krishna, Nar-
  mada 8 Ghaghara, Godavari, Mahanadi
  9 Indravati 11 Brahmaputra
 strait: 4 Palk
 weight: moo, pai, ser, vis 4 bhar, dhan,
  drum, kona, myat, pala, pank, pice,
  raik, rati, ruay, seer, tank, tola, yava 5
  adpao, bahar, candy, catty, hubba,
  masha, maund, pally, pouah, ratti, retti,
  tical, ticul, tikal 6 abucco, dhurra, kar-
  sha, ruttee 7 chittak, peiktha 8 chittack

Indian (see also **Hindu**): *abuse:* 4 gali 5 galee
 acrobat: nat
 agent: 4 amin 5 ameen
 alphabet: 10 Devanagari

ambassador: 5 vakil 6 vakeel
ancestor: 4 Manu 5 Pitri
apartment: 6 zenana
army officer: 4 naig, naik 6 naique 7
 jemadar, jemidar
astrologer: 5 joshi
attorney: 6 muktar
awning: 9 shamianah
baby: 4 baba
bandit: 6 dacoit
bard: 4 bhat
bathing place: 4 ghat 5 ghaut
bazaar: 5 chawk, chowk
bean: urd
bear: 4 balu 5 baloo
bearer: 6 sirdar
bed: 7 charpai, charpoy
bed cover: 9 palampore
bill of exchange: 5 hundi
blight: 4 soka
boat: 7 masoola
bodice: 5 choli
body servant: 6 sirdar
boy: 6 chokra, Mowgli
bracelet: 6 sankha
bread: 5 poori 6 kulcha 7 chapati, pâratha
 8 chapatti
breakfast: 5 hazri
brick: 6 soorki, soorky 7 soorkee
bulbul: 4 kala
butter: ghi 4 ghee
cabinet: 7 almirah
calico: 5 saloo 6 salloo
cannabis: 5 ganja
canoe: 5 tanee
cape: 4 divi
carpet: 4 agra
carriage: 4 ekka 5 bandy, tonga 6 gharri,
 gharry
cashmere: 5 ulwan
cavalryman: 5 sowar 6 risala
cedar: 6 deodar
charm: 6 mantra
chief: mir 4 raja, rana 5 rajah 6 sirdar
church: 5 samaj
cigarette: 4 biri
clarinet: 4 been
clerk: 4 babu 5 baboo
cloak: 5 choga
cloth: 7 dhurrie
colonialist: 5 Clive
cook: 8 bawarchi
corn: zea
coronation: 8 abhiseka
court official: 5 nazir
cowrie: 5 zimbi
crop: 4 rabi
cymbal: tal
dagger: 5 katar

dais: **8** chabutra
dance: **6** nautch **7** cantico
dancer: nat **8** bayadere
demon: **4** bhut **5** asura
deputy: **5** nabob, nawab
dignitary: **5** rajah
dill: **4** soya
disease: **5** agrom
drama: **6** nataka
drink: **4** soma **6** arrack
drinking pot: **5** lotah
drought: **4** soka
dust storm: **7** shaitan, sheitan
earth: **5** regur
educated man: **4** babu **6** pundit
educated woman: **7** pundita
elephant: **5** hathi
elephant driver: **6** mahout
epic: **8** Ramayana **11** Mahabharata
falcon: **6** shahin **7** shaheen
fan: **5** punka **6** punkah
father: **4** babu
festival: **4** Holi, Mela
fiber: **6** ambary
fish: **5** dorab
flower: **5** lotus
fruit: bel
garment: **4** sari **5** burqa, saree
god/goddess: **4** Amma, Deva, Yama **5** Amman, Shiva
gossip: gup
government: **6** sircar
governor: **5** nazim
grass: **4** kusa **5** kusha **6** bhabar, darbha
grinding stone: **4** mano **6** metate
grove: **5** Sarna
guard: **7** daloyet
guide: **7** shikari **8** shikaree
hall: **6** durbar
handkerchief: **7** malabar
harem: **6** zenana
harvest: **4** rabi
hemp: **4** bang **5** bhang, ramie
herb: **6** sesame **7** curcuma, turmeric
hero: **4** Rama
holy: sri **4** shri **5** shree
holy man: **5** fakir, sadhu **6** saddhu
house: **5** mahal **8** bungalow
impost: **5** abwab
instrument: **4** vina **5** sarod, sitar **7** sarinda
intoxicant: **4** soma
jungle: **5** shola
justice: **7** adawlut
knife: dah
laborer: **4** toty **7** totyman
lady: **7** sahibah
law opinion: **5** futwa
legal claim: hak **4** hakh
loincloth: **5** dhoti

lord: **4** mian
mail: dak **4** dawk
mangrove: **5** goran
master: **5** saheb, sahib
matting: **5** tatta
meal: ata **4** atta
merchant: **5** banya **6** banian **8** soudagur **9** brinjaree
millet: **4** joar
mulberry: **6** alroot
muslin: **5** doria **6** gurrah
narcotic: **4** bang **5** bhang **7** hashish
nonviolence: **6** ahimsa
nurse: **4** amah, ayah, dhai
old money: **5** mohur
ox: **4** zebu
peasant: **4** ryot
pipe: **6** hookah
policeman: **4** peon **5** sepoy
priest: **5** mobed, mulla **6** mullah
prince: **4** bana, rana **5** rajah
princess: **4** rani **5** begum, ranee
property: **4** dhan
queen: **4** rani **5** begum, ranee **8** maharani
rainy season: **6** varsha **7** monsoon
religious sect: **4** Sikh
rice: **4** boro
rule: raj
sacred grove: **5** Sarna
saffron: **7** zedoary **8** turmeric
sage: **6** pandit, pundit
servant: **4** maty **6** bearer **10** mussalchee
sheep: **5** urial **6** oorial
shirt: **6** banian
shrine: **6** dagaba, dagoba
silk: **4** muga **6** cabeca
silkworm: eri
snake: **5** krait
soldier: **4** peon **5** sepoy
song: **4** raga
spinning wheel: **6** charka **7** charkha
storm: **5** tufan
sun worshiper: **5** Parsi **6** Parsee
tariff: **6** zabeta
tax: **10** chaukidari
teacher: **4** guru **5** akhun, mulla **6** akhund, mullah, pandit, pundit **7** akhoond
tenant: **4** ryot
title: sri **5** sahib **6** sirdar **7** sahibah
tower: **5** minar
turban: **8** seerband
vessel: **4** doni **6** shibar
viceroy: **5** nabob, nawab
village: **5** abadi **6** mouzah
wheat: **4** suji **5** sujee
widow's cremation: **6** suttee
wine: **5** shrab
wood: eng, sal **4** toon **5** kokra

Indian (Americas) (see also **Eskimo**): **6** red

man **7** Amerind **14** native American
blanket: **6** stroud **9** strouding
Bolivia: Uro **4** Iten, Moxo **6** Aymara **10** Chiriguano
Brazil: **5** Bravo **7** Tariana
Canadian: **4** Cree, Dene **5** Tinne **6** Micmac, Tinneh **7** Sanetch **9** Athabasca **10** Athabascan
Caribbean: **4** Cuna, Yaos **5** Arara, Trios **6** Caribs, Oyanas **7** Akawais, Aparais, Chaymas, Macusis, San Blas **8** Arawakan
carrier: **7** travois
ceremonial chamber: **4** kiva
chief: **6** sachem **8** sagamore
child: **7** papoose
Colombia: **7** Chibcha
corn: zea **4** samp **5** maize
council: **6** powwow
craft: **5** canoe, kayak **6** dugout **8** bullboat
curer: **6** shaman
dwelling: **5** hogan, tepee, toldo **6** wigwam, wikiup **7** wickiup **9** long house
female: **5** squaw **6** mahala, mahaly
festival: **7** potlach
fighter: **5** Boone, Miles **6** Custer
flathead: **7** Chinook
food: **8** pemmican
game: **6** canute, shinny, shinty **7** chunkey **8** lacrosse
Great Spirit: **6** manito
guardian spirit: **5** totem
hatchet: **8** tomahawk
headdress: **7** topknot
Iroquois League: **6** Cayuga, Mohawk, Oneida, Seneca **8** Onondaga
language of trade: **7** chinook
man: **4** buck **5** brave, chief **6** sannup
meal bread: **8** corncake
memorial post: xat **5** totem
Mexican: **4** Maya **5** Aztec
moccasin: pac
money: **6** seawan, shells, wampum **7** seawant **13** chocolate bean
pack strap: **8** tumpline
Paraguay: **7** Guarani
peace pipe: **7** calumet
Peru: **4** Ande, Inca, Peba, Yutu **5** Boros, Campa, Panos **6** Aymara, Jibaro, Lamano **7** Quechua
pillar: lat, xat
pony: **6** cayuse
porridge: **4** samp
potato: **4** yamp **9** breadroot
prayer stick: **4** paho
Rio Grande: Tao
snake dancer: **4** Hopi
sorcery: ob, obe, obi
spirit: **5** totem **7** Manitou

spirit power: **6** manito, orenda **7** wakonda
tent: **5** tepee **6** wigwam
Tierra del Fuego: Ona **4** Agni
Tropical Forest: **4** Mojo **5** Yagua **6** Arawak, Jivaro **7** Guarani **9** Amahuacan
U.S.: Kaw, Oto, Sac, Ute **4** Cree, Dene, Erie, Hopi, Iowa, Otoe, Pima, Sauk, Seri, Tana, Taos, Yuma, Zuni **5** Caddo, Creek, Huron, Kansa, Kiowa, Miami, Omaha, Osage, Piute, Sioux **6** Abnaki, Apache, Dakota, Kansas, Lenape, Mohave, Mojave, Navaho, Navajo, Ojibwa, Oneida, Ottawa, Paiute, Pawnee, Seneca, Sonora **7** Abenaki, Anasazi, Arapaho, Arikara, Choctaw, Keresan, Luiseno, Mohegan, Natchez, Shawnee, Tlingit **8** Apalachi, Cherokee, Cheyenne, Chippewa, Comanche, Delaware, Illinois, Iroquois, Kickapoo, Onondaga, Sagamore, Seminole, Shoshone **9** Algonquin, Apalachee, Blackfoot, Chickasaw, Tuscarora, Winnebago **12** Narragansett
village: **6** pueblo
wampum: **4** peag **5** peage
warrior: **5** brave
weapon: bow **5** arrow **7** blowgun **8** tomahawk
woman: **5** squaw
Indian Ocean: *bay:* **6** Bengal
deepest trench: **4** Java
gulf: **4** Aden, Oman
island: **5** Cocos, Sunda **6** Bouvet, Comoro, Crozet, St. Paul **7** Andaman, Maldive, Nicobar, Reunion **8** Sri Lanka **9** Amsterdam, Christmas, Kerguelen, Laccadive, Mauritius **10** Madagascar, Seychelles **12** Prince Edward
sea: **4** Java **5** Timor **7** Andaman, Arabian
strait: **5** Sunda **7** Malacca

Indiana: *capital:* **12** Indianapolis
city: **4** Gary, Peru **5** Paoli **6** Brazil, Delphi, Goshen, Kokomo, Marion, Muncie, Warsaw **7** Hammond, La Porte **8** Danville **9** Fort Wayne, Lafayette, South Bend **10** Evansville, Huntington, Terre Haute, Valparaiso
lake: **8** Michigan
river: Eel **4** Ohio **5** White **6** Maumee, Pigeon, Wabash **7** Big Blue, St. Marys **8** Kankakee, St. Joseph **9** Salamonie **10** Tippecanoe **12** Mississinewa
state bird: **8** cardinal
state flower: **5** peony
state tree: **5** tulip

indicate: say **4** bode, cite, mark, read, show **5** argue, augur, point **6** allude, denote, evince, import, reveal **7** bespeak, betoken, connote, declare, display, signify, specify **8** decipher, disclose, evidence, manifest, register **9** designate **10** denominate

indication: **4** clue, hint, mark, note, omen, sign **5** proof, token, trace **6** augury, signal **7** auspice, symptom **8** argument, evidence **10** intimation **11** designation

indicative: **10** expressive, suggestive

indicator: **4** dial, hand, sign, vane **5** arrow, clock, gauge, index **6** gnomon, marker **7** indices (pl.), pointer **11** annunciator

indict: **6** accuse, charge **7** impeach

indifference: **6** apathy **8** coldness, lethargy **9** aloofness, disregard **10** negligence **11** disinterest

indifferent: **4** cold, cool, soso **5** aloof, blase, stoic **6** casual **7** neutral, uneager **8** careless, listless, lukewarm, mediocre **9** apathetic, Laodicean **10** nonchalant

indigene: **6** native

indigenous: **5** natal **6** inborn, innate, native **7** endemic, natural **8** homeborn, inherent **10** aboriginal

indigent: **4** free, poor, void **5** needy **6** beggar, pauper **7** lacking, wanting **8** beggarly **9** destitute, penniless **11** impecunious, necessitous

indigestion: **9** dyspepsia, heartburn

indignant: **5** angry, irate, worth **7** annoyed **8** incensed, wrathful, **11** exasperated

indignation: ire **4** fury **5** anger, wrath **7** disdain **8** contempt **11** displeasure

indignity: cut **5** abuse, wrong **6** insult, slight **7** affront, outrage, **9** injustice

indigo: **4** anil, blue
  artificial source: **6** isatin
  bale of: **6** seroon
  derivative: **5** indol **6** indole
  natural source: **4** anil **7** indican

indigo bunting: **4** bird **5** finch

indirect: **4** side **5** vague **6** shifty, zigzag **7** devious, evasive, oblique **8** circular, rambling **9** dishonest **10** circuitous, collateral, meandering, misleading, roundabout

indiscreet: **4** rash **5** hasty, silly **6** unwise **7** foolish, witless **8** careless, heedless **9** impolitic, imprudent **10** ill-advised, incautious **11** injudicious

indiscretion: **4** slip **5** error, folly

indiscriminate: **5** mixed **6** motley, random, varied **7** aimless, jumbled, mingled **8** confused, slap-dash **9** haphazard, hit-or-miss, wholesale **10** uncritical

indispensable: **5** basic, vital **7** exigent **9** essential, necessary, requisite **10** imperative

indisposed: ill **4** sick **6** ailing, averse, unwell **7** opposed **8** hesitant **9** reluctant **11** disinclined

indisposition: **6** malady **7** ailment, illness, malaise **8** disorder, sickness **9** distemper **10** discomfort, reluctance **12** disaffection

indisputable: **4** sure **7** certain, evident **8** positive **10** undeniable **11** indubitable **12** irrefragable **13** incontestable

indissoluble: **4** firm **6** stable **7** lasting

indistinct: dim **4** dark, hazy **5** faint, misty, vague **6** cloudy, feeble **7** blurred, obscure, shadowy **9** ambiguous, unrefined

indite: pen **5** write **7** compose **8** inscribe

individual: one **4** oner, self, sole, unit **6** person, single, unique **7** private, special **8** distinct, selfsame, solitary **9** identical
  selfish: **6** egoist

individuality: **5** seity **7** oneness **9** character **10** uniqueness **11** distinction, personality

individually: **4** each **6** singly **9** severally **10** personally

Indo-Aryan: Jat **6** khatri, Rajput
  deity: **5** Indic, Indra

Indo-European: **5** Aryan
  language: **5** Greek, Hindi, Indic, Latin, **6** Baltic, Celtic, German, Italic, Slavic **7** English, Hittite, Iranian, Persian, Russian, Spanish **8** Albanian, Armenian, Germanic, Hellenic, Sanskrit **10** Lithuanian

indoctrinate: **5** imbue, teach, tutor **7** educate **8** instruct

indolence: **5** scorn, sloth **7** inertia, languor **8** laziness

---

Indonesia: *capital:* **7** Jakarta **8** Djakarta
  city: **5** Medan **6** Malang, Manado, Padang **7** Bandung **8** Semarang **9** Pontianak, Samarinda, Surakarta
  cloth: **5** batik
  dagger: **4** kris
  dance: **6** legong
  feast, ceremonial: **9** selametan
  lizard: **12** Komodo dragon
  musical instrument: **5** rebab **7** gambang
  orchestra: **7** gamelan
  river: **4** Deli, Hari, Musi, Solo **6** Asahan, Barito, Kampar, Kapuas, Liwung **7** Brantas, Kahajan, Kali Mas, Mahakam **9** Indragiri
  sport: **11** pencak silat
  Sunda Islands, Greater: **4** Java **6** Borneo **7** Sumatra **8** Sulawesi (Celebes)
  Sunda Islands, Lesser: **4** Bali **5** Sumba, Timor **6** Flores **7** Sumbawa
  volcano: **8** Krakatoa

indolent: 4 idle, lazy 5 inert 6 otiose, supine 7 dronish 8 inactive, slothful, sluggish

indomitable: 6 dogged 8 resolute 9 steadfast 10 invincible 11 intractable

Indonesia: (see box)

indorse: See **endorse**

Indra: 5 Hindu, Sakka, Sakra, Vedic
dragon: 6 Vritra
elephant: 8 Airavata
father: 8 Tvashtri
food: 4 soma
god of: 4 rain 7 thunder
heaven capital: 9 Amaravati

indubitable: 4 sure 7 assured, certain, evident 8 apparent 10 infallible, undeniable

induce: get 4 coax, draw, lure, urge 5 infer, tempt 6 advise, elicit, suborn 7 actuate, bring on 8 conclude, convince, persuade 9 encourage, influence

inducement: 4 bait, lure 5 prize 6 motive, reason 9 incentive, influence 10 enticement

induct: 5 enrol 6 enlist, enroll 7 install 8 initiate 9 introduce 10 inaugurate

inductance unit: 5 henry

induction: 8 entrance 9 accession, deduction 10 initiation

indue: 5 endow 6 assume, clothe, invest 7 furnish

indulge: pet 4 baby, feed 5 favor, humor, spoil 6 coddle, cosset, foster, pamper, please 7 cherish, gratify
in antics: 7 skylark
in fault finding: 5 cavil
to excess: 7 debauch

indulgence: 5 spree 8 clemency, lenience 9 tolerance 12 dispensation

indulgent: 4 easy, fond, good, kind, mild 9 compliant 10 charitable

indurate: 5 inure 6 harden 7 callous, scleral 8 obdurate, stubborn

industrial magnate: 6 tycoon

industrious: 4 busy 6 active 7 zealous 8 diligent, sedulous 9 assiduous 11 hardworking, painstaking

industry: 4 toil, zeal 5 labor, skill 6 energy 8 business, commerce, hard work 9 assiduity, diligence, ingenuity 10 occupation

indwell: 6 inhere 9 be present

indwelling: 8 immanent, inherent 9 intrinsic

inebriacy: 11 drunkenness 12 intemperance

inebriate: sot 4 lush, soak 6 boozer 7 tippler, tosspot 8 drunkard 11 intoxicated

ineffable: 4 holy 5 ideal 6 divine 11 unspeakable, unutterable

ineffaceable: 9 indelible 12 ineradicable

ineffectively: 6 feebly 9 uselessly

ineffectual: 4 dead, idle, vain, weak 6 futile 7 useless 8 hopeless, impotent, nugatory 9 fruitless 10 inadequate, unavailing 11 inefficient

inefficient: 4 poor 5 inept 8 slipshod 9 unskilled 11 incompetent

inelastic: 5 rigid, stiff 9 unbending 10 inflexible, unyielding

inelegant: 5 crass, crude, rough 6 coarse, vulgar 7 awkward, blatant 9 graceless

ineluctable: 4 sure 6 fated 7 doomed 7 certain 10 inevitable 11 inescapable

inept: 4 dull, slow 5 unfit 6 absurd, clumsy 7 awkward, foolish 8 backward, unsuited 11 incompetent

inequal: 5 rough 6 uneven

inequality: 4 odds 9 disparity, diversity 10 unevenness

inequity: 9 injustice 10 unfairness

ineradicable: 7 lasting 9 indelible, permanent 12 ineffaceable

inerrant: 8 unerring 10 infallible

inerratic: 5 fixed 7 settled 11 established

inert: 4 dead, lazy, slow 5 still 6 supine, torpid 8 immobile, indolent, lifeless, sluggish 9 apathetic, lethargic 10 motionless

inertia: 5 sloth 8 idleness 9 indolence

inesculant: 8 inedible

in essence: 9 basically 11 practically

inessential: 9 extrinsic 11 unimportant

inestimable: 9 priceless 10 invaluable 12 immeasurable, incalculable

inevitable: due 4 sure 5 fated 7 certain, fateful 8 destined 11 ineluctable, inescapable, unavoidable

inexact: 4 free 5 rough 10 inaccurate

inexhaustible: 8 tireless 9 unfailing, unlimited

inexorable: 4 grim 5 stony 6 strict 7 ominous 8 rigorous 9 unbending 10 inflexible, relentless, unyielding 11 unrelenting

inexpedient: 6 unwise 9 impolitic, imprudent 10 indiscreet 11 inadvisable, injudicious 12 unprofitable

inexpensive: 5 cheap 6 frugal 9 low-priced 10 reasonable

inexperienced: raw 5 crude, green, naive, young 6 callow 7 untried 8 inexpert 10 amateurish

inexpert: 5 green 9 unskilled

inexplicable: odd 7 uncanny 8 abstruse, peculiar, puzzling 9 ambiguous, enigmatic 10 mysterious 12 supernatural

inexpressible: 8 nameless 9 ineffable 11 unutterable

inexpressive: 4 dull, dumb 13 unintelligent

infallible: 4 sure 7 certain 8 inerrant, unerring 9 faultless, foolproof, unfailing 11 indubitable

infamous: 4 base 6 bloody, odious 8 shameful 9 nefarious, notorious 10 detestable

infamy: 5 odium, shame, stain 8 disgrace, dishonor, reproach **10** opprobrium

infancy: **8** babyhood **10** immaturity **11** incunabulum

infant: **4** baby **5** bairn, child, minor **7** bambino, chrisom **8** bantling **9** foundling
in law: **5** minor
Indian: **7** papoose
murder: **11** infanticide

infantile: **7** babyish, puerile **8** childish **10** sophomoric

infantryman: **6** doggie **7** dogface, dragoon **8** doughboy

infatuated: mad **4** fond **6** engoue (F.) **7** fatuous **8** enamored, obsessed **9** enamoured **10** captivated

infect: **5** taint **6** canker, defile, poison **7** pollute **11** contaminate

infection: **6** malady, plague **7** disease, illness **9** contagion
freedom from: **7** asepsis

infectious: **8** catching **9** vitiating **12** demoralizing, pestilential

infelicitous: **7** unhappy **11** unfortunate

infelicity: **6** misery **10** misfortune **11** unhappiness **12** wretchedness

infer: **4** hint **5** drive, educe, guess **6** adduce, deduce, derive, gather **7** surmise **8** conclude, construe

inference: **9** corollary, deduction **10** assumption, conclusion, derivation **11** consequence

inferential: **7** implied **8** illative **9** deductive

inferior: bad **4** base, cull, less, poor **5** baser, below, lower, minor, petit, petty, snide, worst **6** cagmag, common, feeble, impure, lesser, nether **7** cheaper, humbler, unequal **8** mediocre **9** underling **10** inadequate **11** subordinate

infernal: **7** avernal, hellish, satanic, stygian **8** all-fired, damnable, devilish, diabolic **9** tartarean **10** acherontic, demoniacal, diabolical

inferno: **4** fire, hell **9** holocaust

Inferno author: **5** Dante

infertile: **4** poor **6** barren **7** sterile

infest: **5** beset, haunt **6** plague **7** overrun **9** swarm over

infidel: **5** pagan **7** atheist, heathen **8** agnostic **10** unbeliever

infiltrate: **4** leak, seep

infinite: **4** vast **6** Ananta **7** endless, eternal, immense **9** boundless, countless, limitless, unlimited **11** everlasting, illimitable, measureless

infinitesimal: **4** tiny **5** small **6** minute **10** negligible **11** microscopic

infirm: old **4** lame, weak **5** anile, frail **6** cranky, feeble, senile, sickly **7** brittle, failing, fragile **8** decrepit, disabled **9** doddering **10** irresolute **11** debilitated

infirmary: **6** clinic **8** hospital

infirmity: **4** vice **7** ailment, disease, failing **8** debility, sickness

infix: **5** inset **6** insert **7** engrave, implant, impress, ingrain, instill **9** inculcate

inflame: **4** boil, fire, goad, heat, stir **5** anger, chafe **6** anneal, arouse, enrage, excite, rankle, redden **7** incense, provoke **8** enkindle, irritate **10** exasperate
with love: **6** enamor
with rage: **6** madden

inflamed: red **5** angry, fiery **6** ablaze

inflammable: **5** fiery **6** ardent, tinder **7** bitumen, piceous **9** excitable, irascible, irritable **10** accendible **11** combustible

inflammation: **4** fire **8** swelling **10** combustion, phlegmasia **13** conflagration

inflate: **4** blow, fill **5** bloat, swell **6** aerify, dilate, emboss, expand, tumefy **7** amplify, distend **8** increase

inflated: **5** wordy **6** turgid **7** fustian, pompous, swollen **9** bombastic, flatulent, plethoric

inflect: bow **4** bend **5** curve **8** modulate

inflection: **4** tone **6** accent, timbre
of words: **8** paradigm

inflexibility: **8** acampsia

inflexible: **4** dour, hard **5** eager, rigid, stiff, stony **6** strict **7** adamant **8** granitic, obdurate, rigorous **9** immovable, inelastic, unbending **10** implacable, inexorable, relentless

inflict: **4** dump **5** wreak **6** impose, unload **7** put upon **10** make suffer, perpetrate

infliction: **7** scourge

inflorescence: **4** cyme, head **5** spike, umbel **6** corymb, raceme **7** panicle

inflow: **6** influx, inrush

influence: **4** egis, hank, heft, lead, move, pull, rule, sway **5** clout, force, impel **6** affect, aspect, compel, effect, govern, induce, infuse, leaven, motive, weight **7** attract, bearing, command, control, gravity, impress, inspire, mastery **8** hegemony, persuade, pressure, prestige, reaction **9** authority **10** ascendancy, attraction, inducement **13** consideration

influenced: **6** biased **8** affected
easily: **7** pliable

influential: **5** grave **6** potent **8** powerful **9** effective, important, momentous

influenza: flu **5** virus **6** grippe **10** coqueluche

influx: **4** tide **6** inflow **7** arrival, illapse **8** increase **9** inpouring

inform: **4** post, tell **5** train **6** advise, notify, preach **7** apprise, apprize, educate, lighten **8** acquaint, instruct **9** advertise **11** communicate

informal: **6** casual, simple **7** relaxed **8** sociable **9** easygoing **10** colloquial

information: 4 data (pl.), dope, fact, news, word 5 aviso, datum 6 notice 7 tidings 9 direction, knowledge 11 instruction
condensed: 6 digest, precis 7 summary
detailed: 7 dossier

informative: 11 instructive 12 enlightening

informed: hep, hip 4 told, wise 5 aware 6 posted 7 knowing 8 apprised, notified 11 enlightened

informer: 4 fink, tout 6 canary, gossip, pigeon, snitch, teller 7 stoolie, tipster 8 observer, squealer, telltale 9 informant 10 discoverer, talebearer 11 stool-pigeon

infraction: 6 breach 8 trespass 9 violation 12 encroachment, infringement

infrequent: few 4 rare 6 scarce, seldom, sparse 8 sporadic, uncommon, unwonted 10 occasional

infringe: 6 refute 7 impinge, intrude 8 encroach, overstep, trespass 10 contravene

infringement: 6 breach 8 trespass 9 violation

infuriate: vex 6 enrage, madden 7 incense, outrage

infuscate: 6 darken 7 obscure

infuse: 4 soak 5 imbue, steep 6 aerify 7 engrain, implant, inspire, instill 9 inculcate, influence, insinuate, introduce

infusion: 7 extract 8 tincture 9 admixture, decoction
malt: 4 wort

Inge play: 6 Picnic 7 Bus Stop

ingeminate: 6 repeat 9 reiterate

ingenious: 4 cute, fine 5 acute, sharp, smart, witty 6 adroit, clever, crafty, daedal, gifted, subtle 7 artless, cunning 8 original, skillful, talented 9 daedalian, deviceful, inventive 11 intelligent, resourceful

ingenuity: art 7 address, cunning 8 artifice 10 adroitness, cleverness 11 originality

ingenuous: 4 naif 5 frank, naive, noble, plain 6 candid, honest, simple 7 artless, sincere 8 innocent 9 childlike, guileless 10 unaffected, unreserved

ingenuousness: 7 naivete 9 innocence

ingest: eat 6 absorb 7 consume, swallow

inglorious: 6 shoddy 8 shameful 11 disgraceful, ignominious 12 dishonorable

ingot: bar, pig 4 mold

ingrained: 6 imbued, inborn, inbred, innate, native 7 built-in, chronic 8 inherent 9 confirmed 10 congenital, deep-seated, inveterate

ingratiating: 4 oily 5 sweet 6 genial, smarmy 7 gushing, likable 8 unctuous 9 appealing 10 flattering, personable 11 sycophantic

ingredient: 7 element 9 component 11 constituent
incense: 6 stacte
ink: 6 tannin

varnish: lac, lax 5 drier, resin, rosin

ingress: 4 adit 5 entry 8 entrance

inhabit: 6 live in, occupy, people, settle 7 dwell in, possess 8 populate

inhabitant: 6 inmate, native, tenant 7 citizen, denizen, dweller 8 resident

inhale: 5 sniff 7 respire 9 breathe in

inharmonious: 6 absurd, atonal 7 jarring 9 dissonant, unmusical 10 discordant 11 conflicting

inherent: 5 basic 6 inborn, innate 7 infixed 8 immanent 9 essential, ingrained, intrinsic 10 congenital, deep-rooted, indwelling

inheritance: 6 estate, legacy 7 bequest 8 heredity, heritage 9 patrimony 10 birthright
by first-born: 13 primogeniture
partial: 6 moiety
portion: 8 legitime
restricted: 10 entailment
Scotch law: 5 annat

inherited: 6 inborn, native 7 connate, genetic, natural 10 handed down

inheritor: 4 heir 7 heiress, legatee

inhibit: ban, bar 4 curb 5 check 6 forbid, hinder 8 prohibit, restrain 9 interdict

inhuman: 4 fell 6 brutal, savage 7 beastly, bestial, brutish 8 devilish

inhumanity: 7 cruelty 9 barbarity

inhume: 4 bury 5 inter 6 entomb 7 deposit

inimical: 6 averse, frosty 7 hostile 8 contrary 9 repugnant 10 unfriendly 11 unfavorable

iniquitous: bad, ill 5 wrong 6 sinful, unjust, wicked 9 nefarious

iniquity: sin 4 evil, vice 5 crime, guilt 8 darkness 9 injustice 10 wickedness

initial: 5 first 6 letter, maiden 7 opening 8 earliest, monogram, original 9 beginning, incipient 10 commencing, elementary

initial payment: 4 ante 7 deposit

initiate: 4 head, open 5 enrol, found, start 6 enroll, induct, launch 7 install, kick off 8 commence 9 introduce, originate 10 inaugurate

initiation: 7 baptism 8 entrance 9 admission, beginning, induction

initiative: 4 lead, push 6 energy 8 aptitude, gumption 9 first move 10 creativity, enterprise, get-up-and-go, leadership

inject: put 4 pump 5 force 6 insert, instill 11 interpolate

injection: 4 hypo 5 enema

injudicious: 6 unwise 9 impolitic, imprudent 10 indiscreet 11 inexpedient

injunction: 4 hest, writ 5 order 6 behest, charge 7 mandate, precept, process 9 direction

injure: mar 4 harm, hurt, maim 5 abuse, spoil, sully, wound, wrong 6 impair, insult, sprain

7 affront, cripple **8** aggrieve, maltreat **9** disfigure

by bruising: **7** contuse **9** contusion

by friction: **7** blister

by scorching: **4** burn, char **5** singe

injury: cut, ill **4** bane, blow, evil, harm, hurt, loss, risk, stab **5** wound, wrong **6** damage, lesion, trauma **7** scratch **8** hardship **9** contusion, detriment, injustice **10** affliction, aggression, disservice, impairment, laceration, mutilation

causing: **7** malefic **9** traumatic

sense of: **7** umbrage

injustice: **5** wrong **6** injury **8** hardship, inequity, iniquity **9** grievance **10** imposition, unfairness

ink: **4** sign **9** autograph

ink fish: **5** squid **6** cuttle

inkling: **4** hint, idea **5** rumor, scent **6** desire, report **7** glimpse **10** glimmering, intimation

inky: **4** dark **5** black **9** cimmerian

inland: **7** central **8** domestic (Br.), interior

sea: **4** Aral **5** Black **7** Caspian

inlay: **5** adorn, couch, set in **6** insert **7** enchase **8** ornament

related: **9** marquetry

work: **6** mosaic **9** certosina, certosino, champleve

inlet: arm, bay, cay, ria **4** cove, gulf, rias (pl.), slew, sloo, slue **5** admit, bayou, bight, creek, fiord, firth, fjord, inlay, sound **6** estero, slough, strait **7** estuary, narrows, orifice, passage **8** entrance

coastline: **5** bight **6** strait

in loco parentis: **8** guardian

inmate: **5** guest, lifer **6** termer **7** convict **8** domestic, occupant, prisoner **10** inhabitant

harem: **9** odalisque

inn: pub **4** host, khan **5** fonda, hotel, lodge, serai, tambo, venta **6** fonduk, hostel, imaret, tavern **7** albergo, auberge, boliche, fondouk, hospice **8** choultry, gasthaus, hostelry, wayhouse **11** caravansary

innamorato (It.): **5** lover **10** sweetheart

innards: **4** guts **7** viscera **8** entrails

innate: **4** born **6** inborn, inbred, native **7** connate, natural **8** inherent **9** ingrained, intrinsic **10** congenital, hereditary

inner: ben **5** ental **6** inside, inward, secret **7** central, private **8** esoteric, interior, internal, personal

Innisfail: **4** Eire, Erin **7** Ireland

innkeeper: **4** host **8** boniface, hosteler, publican

innocence: **6** purity **7** naivete **9** ignorance

innocent: **4** free, naif **5** naive **6** chaste, dovish, simple **7** artless, upright **9** blameless, childlike, guileless, guiltless, ingenuous, stainless **10** immaculate, unblamable

innocent one: **4** babe, lamb **5** child **6** infant

innocuous: **8** harmless, innocent **9** innoxious **11** inoffensive, unoffending

innominate: **7** unnamed **9** anonymous

innovation: **6** change **7** novelty **9** departure **10** new wrinkle

innuendo: **4** clue, hint, slur **8** allusion **10** intimation **11** implication, insinuation

innumerable: **4** many **6** legion, myriad **10** numberless

inoculate: **5** imbue **6** infect **7** implant **8** immunize

inoffensive: **8** harmless **9** innocuous

inoperative: **4** dead, idle **10** out of order, unworkable

inopportune: **6** clumsy **8** ill-timed, untimely **10** malapropos **11** importunate **12** inconvenient

inordinate: **5** undue **6** wanton **7** extreme, surplus **8** needless, overmuch **9** excessive **10** disorderly, immoderate **11** unregulated **12** unrestrained

inorganic: **7** mineral

in perpetuum: **4** ever **6** always **7** forever **9** eternally

inquest: **6** search **7** inquiry **11** examination

inquire: ask, esk (Sc.) **4** quiz, seek **5** query **6** demand, search **7** dig into **8** question **11** interrogate, investigate

inquiring: **7** curious

inquiry: **4** hunt **5** audit, check, probe, query **7** inquest **8** question, research, scrutiny **9** catechism **11** examination

inquisition: **5** trial **8** grilling, tribunal **11** third-degree

director: **10** Torquemada

inquisitive: **4** nosy **5** nosey **6** prying **7** curious **8** meddling **10** meddlesome

in re (L.): **5** about, anent **9** regarding **10** concerning

inroad: **4** raid **5** foray **6** breach **8** invasion **9** incursion, irruption **12** encroachment

ins and outs: **5** ropes **7** details **11** particulars

insane: mad **4** daft **5** balmy, crazy, daffy, loony, manic **6** cranky, crazed **7** frantic, furious **8** bughouse, demented, deranged, frenetic **9** delirious, psychotic **10** distracted

house for: **6** asylum, bedlam **10** booby hatch, sanitarium

insanity: **5** folie, mania **6** frenzy, lunacy **7** madness, vesania **8** delirium, dementia **9** psychosis **10** aberration, alienation **11** derangement

insatiable: **6** greedy **9** voracious **11** unsatisfied

inscribe, enscribe: **4** etch **5** delve, enter, stamp, write **6** blazon, enroll, indite, scroll **7** ascribe, engrave **8** dedicate, describe

inscribed: **8** lettered **9** dedicated

on stone: **10** lapidarian

with Teutonic characters: **5** runed

inscription: **6** legend **7** epigram, writing **8** epigraph
end of book: **8** colophon
explanatory: **6** tituli (pl.) **7** titulus
on coins: **5** sigla
tomb: **7** epitaph

inscrutable: **6** secret **10** mysterious **12** impenetrable, unfathomable

insect: ant, bee, bug, fly **4** flea, gnat, lice, mite, moth, tick, wasp **5** emmet, roach **6** beetle, earwig, mantis, spider, weevil **7** cricket, katydid, termite **9** bumblebee, butterfly, centipede
adult: **5** imago
antenna: **4** palp **6** feeler
back surface: **5** notum
chirping: **7** cricket
destructive: **4** grub **5** scale **6** locust **7** cricket, termite **8** predator **9** cockroach **10** silverfish
dipterous: **8** mosquito
eye: **6** ocelli (pl.), stemma **7** ocellus
female: **4** gyne
hard covering: **6** chitin
hymenopterous: ant, bee **4** wasp **6** sawfly **7** gallfly **10** ichneumons
immature: **4** grub, pupa **5** larva, nymph **6** larvae (pl.) **9** chrysalis **11** caterpillar
long-legged: **5** emesa
molting of: **7** ecdysis
organ: **8** plantula **9** plantulae (pl.)
parasitic: **4** lice **5** louse
part of: **4** nota **5** chirr, media, palps **7** antenna **8** pronotum, tentacle
pert. to: **11** entomologic
plate: **6** scutum
resin: lac
science: **10** entomology
secretion: lac
small: **4** flea, gnat, mite, tick **5** aphid, aphis, micro, midge **6** garfly **8** bullhead
stage: **4** pupa **5** imago, larva **6** instar **9** chrysalis
stinging: ant, bee **4** wasp **6** hornet **7** sciniph **12** yellowjacket

insecticide: DDT **6** endrin, ethion **9** hellebore, Malathion, parathion **10** endosulfan

insecure: **5** loose, risky, shaky **6** infirm, unsafe, unsure **7** rickety, unsound **8** doubtful, perilous, unstable **9** dangerous, hazardous **10** precarious

inseminate: sow **7** implant, instill **9** fertilize **10** impregnate

insensate: **4** surd **5** blind, harsh **6** brutal, stupid **7** fatuous, foolish **9** senseless, unfeeling, untouched

insensibility: **4** coma **6** apathy, torpor, trance **8** lethargy **9** analgesia

insensible: **4** dull **7** unaware **8** obdurate **9** inanimate, insensate, unfeeling **10** insentient **11** indifferent, unconscious

insensitive: **4** cold, dead, numb **5** blase **7** boorish, callous **9** unfeeling

insert: **5** foist, infix, inlay, inset **9** interpose **11** intercalate, interpolate

inset: **4** gore **5** imbed, infix, panel **6** gusset, insert **7** appoint, engraft, implant **9** insertion

inside: **5** inner **6** lining, within **7** private **8** interior
toward: **5** entad **6** inward
track: **9** advantage

inside out: **7** everted **8** reversed **10** completely, thoroughly

insidious: sly **6** covert, crafty, subtle, tricky **7** cunning **8** guileful **9** concealed, deceitful **10** fallacious, fraudulent **11** treacherous

insight: ken **6** acumen, wisdom **9** intuition **10** perception **11** discernment **12** clairvoyance

insignia: **4** mark **5** badge **6** emblem
kind of: tie **7** caducei (pl.), regalia **8** caduceus

insignificant: **4** puny **5** dinky, petit, petty **6** paltry **7** trivial **8** inferior, small-fry, trifling **9** minuscule, senseless **10** immaterial **11** minor-league, unimportant
part: bit **4** iota **5** tithe **8** molehill

insincere: **5** false, phony **7** feigned **8** guileful, two-faced **9** deceitful, deceptive **11** duplicitous

insinuate: **5** imply **6** allude, infuse **7** implant, instill **9** introduce, penetrate **10** ingratiate, serpentine

insinuation: **4** hint **8** innuendo

insipid: dry **4** dead, dull, flat, pale, tame **5** bland, prosy, stale, tepid, vapid, waugh **6** jejune **7** prosaic **8** lifeless **9** pointless. tasteless **10** monotonous, spiritless

insist: **4** aver **5** claim **6** assert, demand **7** contend **8** maintain **9** reiterate

insistence: **7** command, urgency

insolence: **4** gall **5** nerve **6** insult **8** audacity **9** contumely **10** effrontery **11** haughtiness, presumption

insolent: **4** pert, rude **5** sassy, saucy **6** brazen, cheeky **7** abusive, defiant **8** arrogant, impudent **9** audacious, hubristic **11** overbearing **12** contemptuous, contumelious

insolvency: **7** failure **10** bankruptcy

insolvent: **5** broke **6** busted, ruined **9** destitute **12** impoverished

insomnia: **7** ahypnia **8** agrypnia **13** sleeplessness

insouciant: **4** calm **8** carefree, heedless **10** unbothered **11** indifferent, unconcerned

inspect: **4** pore, scan, view **5** check, study **6** peruse **7** examine, observe **8** consider, look over **9** supervise

inspection: **4** oyer **6** parade, review **8** scrutiny **11** examination

inspiration: 4 muse, spur 5 flash 6 motive, vision 7 impulse 8 afflatus, stimulus 9 incentive, influence 10 brainstorm
poetic: 7 pierian
pretender to: 6 eolist

inspire: 4 fire, move, stir 5 exalt, imbue 6 arouse, excite, inhale, prompt 7 actuate, animate, enliven, implant 8 motivate 9 encourage, influence, stimulate

inspirit: 4 stir 5 cheer, elate, rouse 7 animate, cherish, comfort, hearten, quicken 10 invigorate

inspissate: 7 thicken 8 condense 10 incrassate

instability: 8 fluidity 9 shakiness 10 insecurity 12 irresolution, unsteadiness

install: lay 4 seat, vest 6 induct, locate 7 instate 8 initiate 9 establish 10 inaugurate, set in place

installation: 11 investiture

instance: 4 case, cite, time 7 example, request, symptom 8 occasion 9 exemplify 10 suggestion

instancy: 7 urgency 8 pressure 9 imminence 10 insistence

instant: 4 urge 5 clink, flash, gliff, glisk, trice 6 breath, minute, moment, second, urgent 7 solicit 8 pressing 9 handwhile, immediate 11 importunate

instantly: now 4 just

instate: set 6 bestow, confer 7 install 8 initiate 9 establish 10 inaugurate

instead: 4 else 6 in lieu 10 equivalent, substitute

instigate: egg 4 abet, goad, move, prod, sick, spur, urge 5 impel 6 compel, excite, foment, incite, prompt, suborn 7 provoke 8 motivate 9 encourage, stimulate

instigator: 6 author, source 8 agitator 10 ringleader

instill: 5 imbue, infix 6 impart, infuse 7 implant, pervade 9 inculcate, insinuate

instinct: 4 bent, gift, urge 5 knack 7 impulse 8 aptitude

instinctive: 6 innate 7 natural 8 inherent, original 9 automatic, intuitive

institute: 5 begin, found 6 asylum 7 academy 8 initiate, organize 9 establish, originate 10 inaugurate

institution: 6 clinic, school 7 academy, college 8 hospital, seminary 10 university

instruct: 4 lead, show 5 breed, coach, drill, edify, guide, train, tutor 6 direct, inform, preach 7 counsel, educate 8 document 9 enlighten

instruction: 6 advice, charge, lesson 7 precept 8 teaching, training, tutelage 9 education, knowledge, schooling 10 directions
art of: 8 pedagogy

instructive: 8 didactic, sermonic

instructor: don 5 coach, tutor 6 docent, master, mentor 7 acharya, teacher, trainer 9 preceptor, professor

instrument (see also **apparatus, device, tool**): 4 deed, writ 5 agent, clock, means 6 medium 7 utensil, writing 9 appliance, implement
altitude: aba 9 altimeter 10 altazimuth
atmospheric pressure: 9 barometer
blood pressure: 16 sphygmomanometer
calculating: 6 abacus 8 computer 9 slide rule 10 calculator
copying: 10 hectograph, pantograph
current: 7 ammeter
depth: 10 fathometer
direction: 7 compass
earthquake: 11 seismograph
listening: 11 stethoscope
measuring: 5 gauge, radar, ruler, scale 7 caliper 10 micrometer 11 chronometer, speedometer, thermometer
motion: 11 stroboscope
radiant energy: 9 bolometer
scientific: EEG, EKG 4 X-ray 11 fluoroscope 12 Geissler tube, oscilloscope, spectrometer 13 bubble chamber, Geiger counter
sealed: 4 deed 6 escrow
ship's position: 7 sextant 11 chronometer
viewing: 5 loupe 9 telescope 10 microscope
wind: 10 anemometer

instrumental: 6 useful 7 helpful 9 conducive, effective

instrumentalist: 6 oboist, player 7 flutist, harpist, pianist 9 cornetist, violinist 10 trombonist

instrumentality: 5 means 6 agency, medium

insubordinate (see also **insurgent**): 6 unruly 7 defiant, riotous 8 insolent, mutinous, perverse 9 fractious, seditious 10 headstrong, rebellious, refractory, unyielding 11 disobedient, intractable

insubstantial: 4 airy, thin 5 frail 6 flimsy 10 intangible 12 apparitional

insufferable: 7 hateful, painful 10 unbearable 11 intolerable

insufficient: 4 bare, poor 5 short 6 feeble, scanty, scarce 7 unequal, wanting 9 deficient 10 inadequate

insular: 6 biased, narrow 8 isolated 9 parochial, separated 10 provincial

insulate: 4 line 5 cover 6 enisle 7 isolate 9 segregate 10 quarantine
material to: 4 cork, foam 5 paper 6 Kerite, rubber 8 asbestos 10 fiberglass

insulator: 4 tape 5 cleat 12 nonconductor

insult: 4 slap, slur 5 abuse, flout, scorn, shame 6 offend, revile 7 affront, offense, outrage 9 contumely, indignity, insolence

insulting: 4 rude 8 arrogant, derisive 9 offensive 10 scurrilous 11 opprobrious

insurance: 8 guaranty, warranty 9 assurance 10 protection
computer: 7 actuary 8 adjuster
payee: 11 beneficiary
system: 7 tontine

insurgent: 5 rebel 8 maverick, mutinous, revolter 9 dissident

insurmountable: 8 hopeless, too great 10 impassable, invincible 11 insuperable

insurrection: 6 mutiny, revolt 8 outbreak, uprising 9 rebellion

insusceptible: 6 immune 9 unfeeling

intact: 5 sound, whole 8 complete, unbroken 9 undefiled, undivided, uninjured, untouched 10 unimpaired

intaglio: cut, gem 9 engraving

intake: net 4 gain, gate 6 profit 8 receipts 11 contraction

intangible: 5 vague 8 abstract 10 immaterial, impalpable

integer: 5 digit 6 figure, number 7 numeral 11 whole number

integral: 4 full 5 basic, total, whole 8 complete 9 component, essential, requisite

integrate: mix 4 join 5 unite 7 combine

integrity: 5 honor 7 honesty, probity 9 chariness, constancy

integument: 4 aril, coat, skin 5 shell, testa, 7 cuticle 8 covering, envelope

intellect: wit 4 mind 5 brain 6 genius, reason 9 mentality 12 intelligence
limited in: 8 retarded

intellection: 6 notion 9 cognition, knowledge 12 apprehension

intellectual: 5 ideal 6 mental, noetic, savant 7 egghead, learned 8 cerebral, highbrow 9 scholarly

intelligence: 4 chit, mind, news, word 5 sense 6 esprit, notice, wisdom 8 learning 11 information 13 understanding
used alone: 6 noesis

intelligencer: spy 9 informant, messenger 10 newsmonger

intelligent: 5 acute, aware, sharp, smart 6 bright, clever, mental 7 knowing 8 rational, sensible 9 brilliant, cognizant

intelligentsia: 8 thinkers 13 intellectuals

intelligible: 5 clear, lucid, plain 10 conceptual

intemperate: 6 severe 7 extreme, violent 9 excessive, inclement 10 immoderate, inordinate 12 ungovernable, unrestrained

intend: aim 4 mean, plan 6 design 7 destine, propose 9 calculate 10 have in mind 11 contemplate

intended: 5 meant 6 fiance 7 fiancee 9 betrothed

intense: hot 4 deep, hard, keen 5 acute, great, heavy, vivid 6 ardent, severe, strong 7 chronic, earnest, extreme, fervent, violent, zealous 8 grievous, powerful, strained, vehement 9 assiduous, excessive, strenuous 11 far-reaching

intensify: 5 exalt 6 deepen 7 enhance, magnify, quicken, sharpen 8 condense, heighten, increase 9 aggravate 10 accentuate 11 concentrate

intensity: 5 depth, force, power, vigor 6 degree, energy, fervor 7 potency 8 severity, strength
of color: 6 chroma

intent: aim 4 rapt 5 eager, fixed 6 design, effect 7 earnest, meaning, purpose 8 absorbed, diligent, sedulous 9 attentive, engrossed, steadfast

intention: end 4 goal, plan, will 6 animus, motive, object 11 designation

intentional: 5 meant 9 voluntary 10 deliberate 12 premeditated

inter: 4 bury 6 entomb, inhume

interagent: 6 medium 12 intermediary

intercalary month: 4 Adar 6 Veadar

intercalate: 7 insert 9 insinuate, interpose 11 interpolate

intercede: 6 step in 7 mediate 9 arbitrate, interpose, intervene

intercept: nab 4 grab, stop 5 block, catch, seize 6 waylay 7 head off 9 forestall, interrupt

intercessor: 8 advocate, mediator

interchange: 4 vary 7 commute, permute 8 converse, exchange 9 alternate 10 transposal 11 reciprocate 12 conversation

interchangeable: 10 reciprocal, reversible 11 convertible

interconnection: 5 nexus 8 junction

intercourse: 7 dealing 8 business, commerce, converse 9 communion, relations 10 connection, fellowship

interdict: ban 4 veto 5 debar, fence 6 forbid 7 inhibit 8 prohibit 9 proscribe

interdiction: 4 tabu 5 taboo 11 prohibition

interest: 4 good, part 5 hobby, share, stake 6 behalf, engage, excite, notice 7 benefit, concern, involve, service, welfare 8 sympathy 9 advantage, attention, fascinate
exorbitant: 5 usury
rate: 5 yield

interested: 4 rapt 6 caring

interfere: 5 barge, clash 6 meddle, tamper 7 collide, disturb, intrude 8 obstruct, sabotage 9 interpose, intervene

interference: 6 static

interim: 5 break 6 hiatus 7 stopgap 8 interval, meantime 9 interlude 10 pro tempore

interior: ben 5 ental, inner 6 inland, inside 8 midlands 9 heartland

interject: 5 put in 6 insert, slip in 7 intrude 9 introduce

interjection: boo, hic, rah 4 ahem, alas, amen, egad, ouch, well 6 aroint 7 criminy 11 exclamation

interlace: mat **5** braid, twine, weave **7** entwine **9** interfret, interlink **10** intertwine, interweave **11** interpolate

interlaced: **7** complex

interlock: **4** knit **5** unite **6** clench, engage **9** interlace

interlocution: **12** conversation **13** communication

interlocutory: **9** mediatory **12** intermediate **14** conversational

interlope: **6** horn in, meddle **7** intrude **8** trespass **9** interfere

interlude: **4** lull **5** idyll, let up, pause **6** recess **7** respite

intermediary: **5** agent **6** medium **7** referee **8** mediator **9** go-between, middleman

intermediate: **5** mense **6** median, middle **7** average, between **8** middling, moderate **10** interposed **11** intervening

interminable: **7** endless, eternal **8** infinite, timeless, unending **9** boundless, limitless, unlimited **10** long-winded

interminably: **7** forever

intermingle: **8** intermix **9** socialize

intermission: **4** rest, stop **5** break, dwell, pause **6** recess **7** respite **8** entr'acte, vacation **9** cessation **10** suspension

intermittent: **6** broken, fitful **8** on and off, periodic, sporadic **9** recurrent, spasmodic **10** occasional

intermix: **6** mingle **10** interweave

intern: **6** detain, doctor **7** confine, impound, trainee **8** imprison

internal: **5** inner **6** inward, mental **8** domestic, enclosed **9** spiritual

international: **9** universal, world-wide

international organization: UN, ILO, IMF, IRO, OAS, WHO **4** NATO **5** SEATO **6** UNESCO, UNICEF

internecine: **6** deadly

interpolate: **5** alter **6** insert **9** introduce **11** intercalate

interpose: **6** thrust **7** intrude, mediate **9** intercede, interfere, intervene

interpret: **4** read **6** decode, define, render **7** explain, expound **8** construe **9** elucidate, explicate, make clear, translate **10** paraphrase

interpretation: **5** sense **7** meaning, version **8** exegesis **9** rendering
mystical: **7** anagoge
science of: **12** hermeneutics

interpretive: **10** expository **11** explanatory

interrogate: ask **4** quiz **5** grill, query **7** examine, inquire **8** question

interrogation: **5** probe **7** inquest **9** catechism

interrogation mark: **7** eroteme

interrogative: how, who, why **4** what, when **5** where **8** question

interrupt: **4** stop **5** break, burst, cease, check, cut in **6** arrest, hinder, thwart **7** disturb, sus-

pend **8** obstruct **9** intercept **11** discontinue

interruption: gap **5** pause **6** breach, hiatus **7** caesura

intersect: cut **4** meet **5** cross **6** divide, pierce **9** decussate

intersection: **6** corner **7** crossing, junction **10** crossroads

interstice: **4** mesh, pore, seam **5** chink, crack, space **6** areola, areole, cranny **7** crevice **8** interval

intertwine: **4** knit, lace **5** plait, weave, twist **9** interlace

interval: gap **4** rest, span **5** break, space **6** breach, hiatus, recess

intervene: **6** step in **7** mediate **9** intercede, interpose

intervening: **5** mesne (law) **12** intermediate

interview: see **7** consult, hearing **8** audience, question **9** encounter **10** conference

intervolve: **4** coil, roll, wind **5** twist

interweave: mat **5** braid, plait **6** splice **8** intermix **9** interlace

intestinal fortitude: **4** grit, guts **5** nerve, pluck, spunk **7** courage **8** backbone

intimate: pal **4** chum, dear, near **5** bosom, buddy, close, crony, homey, imply **6** allude, chummy, friend, homely, inmost, secret **7** signify, suggest **8** announce, domestic, familiar, friendly, informal, personal **9** associate, confidant

intimation: cue **4** clue, hint, wind **5** scent **6** notice **7** inkling **10** suggestion **11** declaration

intimidate: awe, cow **5** abash, bully, daunt, deter, scare **6** hector **7** overawe, terrify **8** browbeat, dispirit, frighten **9** blackmail, terrorize

into: **4** unto **5** among, until **6** inside

intolerance: **4** bias **6** racism **7** bigotry **9** misoneism, prejudice **10** chauvinism

intolerant: **6** narrow, stuffy **7** bigoted **8** dogmatic **9** hidebound, illiberal, impatient **10** prejudiced

intonation: **5** pitch, sound **7** sonance

intonational: **7** tonetic

intone: **4** cant, sing **5** chant **8** modulate **10** cantillate

in toto: **8** as a whole **10** altogether

intoxicant: gin, rum **4** wine **5** booze, drink **6** liquor **7** alcohol, whiskey

intoxicated: **4** high **5** drunk, tight, tipsy **6** boiled, soused, stewed, stoned, zonked **7** excited **8** besotted, glorious, polluted, squiffed **9** crapulous **10** inebriated

intracellular: **8** histonal

intractable: **6** mulish, unruly **7** willful **8** indocile, mutinous, obdurate, perverse, stubborn **9** obstinate **10** headstrong, refractory **11** disobedient, unteachable

intrada: **7** prelude **12** introduction

intranquillity: ado **12** restlessness

intransigent: **7** willful **8** obdurate, stubborn **9** unmovable **10** iron-willed, unyielding

intrepid: **4** bold **5** brave, hardy, nervy **6** daring, heroic **7** assured, doughty, gallant, valiant **8** fearless, resolute, valorous **9** dauntless, dreadless, nerveless **10** courageous

intricate: **4** hard **5** dedal **6** daedal, knotty **7** complex, Gordian, sinuous **8** involved **9** Daedalian, difficult, involuted **10** perplexing **11** complicated **12** labyrinthine

intrigue: **4** plot **5** cabal **6** deceit, design, scheme **8** artifice **9** fascinate **10** concoction, conspiracy

intrinsic: **4** real, true **6** inborn, inbred, innate, native **7** genuine, natural **8** immanent, inherent, intimate **9** essential, necessary

intrinsically: **5** per se **6** as such

introduce: **5** begin, enter, start, usher **6** broach, herald, infuse, insert **7** forerun, implant, precede, preface, present, sponsor **8** approach, initiate **9** insinuate, institute, originate

introduction: **5** debut, proem **7** intrada, introit, isagoge, preface, prelude **8** entrance, exordium, foreword, overture, preamble *of new word:* **7** neology

introductory: **7** initial **8** exordial **9** prefatory, prelusive **11** preliminary

introductory cry: **4** hear, oyes, oyez, heads up, attention

introit: **4** hymn **5** psalm **12** introduction

introverted: shy **8** brooding **9** withdrawn

intrude: **6** invade, meddle **8** encroach, infringe, muscle in, trespass **9** interfere, interlope, interpose

intruder: **8** outsider **11** gate crasher

intrusion: **10** aggression, infraction

intrusive: **7** curious

intuit: 4 feel **5** sense **8** perceive **9** apprehend

intuition: **5** hunch **7** feeling, insight **8** instinct **10** perception, sixth sense

inunction: **7** unguent **8** ointment **9** anointing

inundate: **4** flow **5** drown, flood **6** deluge **8** overflow, submerge **9** overwhelm **10** overspread

inundation: **8** alluvi:

inure, enure: **5** steel **6** harden, season **7** toughen **8** accustom **9** habituate **10** discipline **11** acclimatize

inurn: **4** bury **6** entomb

inutile: bad **7** useless **8** unusable **9** worthless **12** unprofitable

invade: **4** raid **6** attack, engulf, infest **7** assault, intrude, overrun **8** encroach, trespass **9** march into, penetrate

invalid: **4** null **6** feeble, infirm, sickly **8** nugatory **11** ineffective

invalidate: **4** undo **5** annul, break **7** abolish, nullify

invaluable: **8** precious **9** priceless **11** inestimable

invariable: **4** same **6** steady **7** uniform **8** constant **9** continual, immutable **10** unchanging **11** determinate **12** unchangeable

invariably: **6** always **7** forever **9** regularly **11** without fail **13** like clockwork

invasion: **6** inroad **8** trespass **9** incursion **10** aggression

invective: **5** abuse, venom **6** tirade **7** railing **8** diatribe, reproach

inveigh: **9** fulminate

inveigle: **4** coax, lure **5** snare **6** allure, entice, entrap **8** persuade

invent: **4** coin, form, make, vamp **5** feign, forge, frame **6** create, design, devise, patent **7** concoct, fashion **8** contrive, discover, engineer **9** fabricate, improvise, originate **11** manufacture

invention: **7** fiction, figment

inventive: **6** adroit **7** fertile **9** ingenious

inventor: **6** author, coiner **7** creator **8** engineer **10** discoverer, originator
airplane: **6** Fokker, Wright
barometer: **10** Torricelli
baseball: **9** Doubleday
condensing steam engine: **4** Watt
cotton gin: **7** Whitney
diode: **7** Fleming
dynamite: **5** Nobel
electric light: **6** Edison
elevator: **4** Otis
gun: **4** Colt **9** Remington
internal combustion engine: **4** Benz **6** Lenoir **7** Daimler
linotype: **12** Mergenthaler
motion-picture camera: **6** Edison
movable type: **7** Bi Sheng **9** Gutenberg
phonograph: **6** Edison
photography: **6** Niepce, Talbot **8** Daguerre
Polaroid camera: **4** Land
printing press: Hoe
radio: **7** Marconi **8** de Forest
sewing machine: **4** Howe **6** Lester
steam locomotive: **4** Watt **10** Stephenson
steamboat: **5** Fitch **6** Fulton, Rumsey
telegraph, electric: **5** Cooke, Morse
telephone: **4** Bell
telescope: **10** Lippershey
television: **6** Nipkow
transistor: **7** Bardeen **8** Brattain, Shockley
wireless: **7** Marconi

inventor's right: **6** patent

inventory: **4** list **5** stock, store, tally **7** account, backlog, reserve **8** register, schedule **9** catalogue, stockpile

inveracity: fib, lie **7** falsehood, falseness

inverse: **8** backward, contrary, opposite

invert: **4** turn **7** reverse

invertebrate: **4** worm **5** coral, hydra, polyp, squid **6** insect, spider, sponge **7** anemone, mollusk, octopus **8** arachnid, cray fish, nematode, starfish **9** jellyfish, sea urchin

invest: don **4** belt, gird, gown, robe, vest, wrap **5** allot, array, crown, dress, endow, endue, imbue **6** clothe, confer, embark, ordain **7** envelop, install, instate **8** accredit, enthrone, surround

investigate: pry **4** nose **5** probe, study, trace **6** search **7** examine, explore, inquire **8** research **10** scrutinize

investigator: **6** prober, tracer **9** detective

investiture: **8** clothing **9** induction **10** initiation **12** installation

investment: **4** ante **5** share, stake, stock **7** venture **9** contribution
list: **9** portfolio

investor: **10** capitalist, shareowner **11** stockholder

inveterate: **6** rooted **7** chronic **8** habitual, hardened **9** confirmed, ingrained

invidious: **6** odious **7** envious, hateful **8** spiteful **9** malignant **12** disagreeable

invigorate: **5** cheer, pep up, renew **6** vivify **7** animate, enliven, fortify, refresh **8** energize **9** stimulate **10** exhilarate, strengthen

invigorating: **7** bracing **9** healthful **10** energizing **12** rejuvenating

invincible: **10** unbeatable **11** indomitable

inviolate: **4** holy **6** sacred **9** undefiled, unstained **10** sacrosanct

invisible: hid **6** hidden, unseen **9** concealed **10** indistinct, unapparent

invitation: bid **4** call, lure **7** request, summons **8** entreaty **9** challenge
initials: **4** BYOB, RSVP

invite: ask, bid **4** call **5** court **6** allure, entice **7** attract, provoke, request, solicit

invocation: **4** plea **6** prayer, sermon **7** benison **8** entreaty **11** benediction

invoice: **4** bill **5** brief **7** account **8** manifest **9** statement

invoke: **4** call, pray **6** appeal, attest **7** conjure, entreat, provoke, solicit **9** imprecate **10** supplicate

involuntary: **6** forced **9** automatic, unwitting **10** compulsory **11** inadvertent, instinctive, spontaneous

involute: **6** curled, rolled **7** complex **8** involved **9** intricate

involve: **4** wrap **5** imply, snare **6** bemist, employ, engage, entail **7** concern, embrace, embroil, ensnare, include **8** comprise, encumber, entangle **9** implicate

involved: **7** complex **12** labyrinthine

inward: **5** entad, inner **6** inside **8** interior **10** internally

Io: *father:* **7** Inachus
son: **7** Epaphus

iodine: *source:* **4** kelp

Iolcus king: **6** Pelias

ion: *negative:* **5** anion

positive: **6** cation, kation

Ion: *father:* **6** Apollo
mother: **6** Creusa

iota: bit, jot **4** atom, whit **6** tittle **8** particle

Iowa: *artist:* **4** Wood
capital: **9** Des Moines
city: **4** Ames **5** Anita **7** Dubuque, Ottumwa **8** Iowa City, Waterloo **9** Davenport, Oskaloosa, Sioux City **11** Cedar Rapids **13** Council Bluffs
river: **4** Iowa, Rock **5** Boyer, Cedar, Skunk **6** Turkey **7** Nodaway **8** Big Sioux, Missouri **9** Des Moines **11** Mississippi
state bird: **9** goldfinch
state flower: **8** wild rose
state tree: oak

---

ipecac: **4** evea **6** emetic
substance: **7** emetine

Iphicles: *brother:* **8** Heracles, Hercules
mother: **7** Alcmene
son: **6** Iolaus

Iphis' daughter: **6** Evadne

irade: **5** edict **6** decree

Iran (see also Persia): *capital:* **7** Teheran
city: Qom, Qum **5** Ahvaz **6** Abadan, Kashan, Shiraz, Tabriz **7** Esfahan, Hamadan, Mashhad
currency: pul **4** asar, cran, kran, lari, rial, sahi **5** bisti, daric, dinar, larin, toman **6** shahee, stater **7** ashrafi, kasbeke, pahlavi
gulf: **4** Oman **7** Arabian, Persian
language: **5** Farsi **7** Kurdish, Pahlavi, Persian
measure: guz, mou, zar, zer **4** cane, foot **5** gareh, jerib, kafiz, makuk, qasab **6** artaba, charac, chebel, gariba, ghalva, ouroub **7** capicha, chenica, farsakh, farsang, mansion, mishara **8** parasang, piamaneh, sabbitha, stathmos **9** collothun, colluthun
mountain range: **9** Hindu Kush
river: **4** Mand **5** Atrek, Karun, Safid **7** Karkheh **9** Kizil Uzen
sea: **7** Arabian, Caspian
strait: **6** Hormuz
weight: ser **4** dram, dung, rotl, sang, seer **5** abbas, artal, artel, maund, pinar, ratel **6** batman, dirhem, gandum, karwar, miscal, miskal, nakhod **7** abbassi **8** tcheirek **9** saddirham

Irani, Iranian: **7** Persian
  almond: **5** badam
  angel: Mah
  athletic club: **9** zurkhaneh
  bazaar: **9** bezooteen
  bird: **6** bulbul
  cap: taj
  hat: fez **6** turban
  Islamic sect: **4** Shia **5** Sunni **6** Shiite
  javelin: **6** jereed
  Koran student: **5** hafiz
  moon: **4** Mahi
  New Year's Day: **6** Nawruz, Nowruz **7**
  Nawroze
  screen: **6** purdah
  tapestry: **7** susanee
  throne room: **5** aiwan
  tiara: **7** cidaris
  title: mir **4** azam **5** mirza **9** ayatollah
  tobacco: **6** tumbak, tumbek **7** tumbaki,
  tumbeki
  traders: **4** sart
  trumpet: **6** kerana **7** kerrana
  vessel: **6** aftaba
  water-pipe: **5** hooka **6** calean, hookah **8**
  narghile
  water wheel: **5** noria

Iraq: *capital:* **7** Baghdad
  city: **5** Basra, Erbil, Mosul **6** Kirkuk
  7 An Najaf, Karbala
  currency: **4** fils **5** dinar
  gulf: **7** Arabian, Persian
  lake: **6** Dalmaj, Saniya **8** Al Hammar
  9 Habbaniya
  mountain: **8** Poshtkuh
  river: **6** Tigris **9** Euphrates

---

irascible: **5** angry, cross, irate, testy **6** cranky,
  ornery, snappy, touchy **7** fretful, peevish **8**
  captious, choleric, petulant, snappish **9**
  impatient, irritable, splenetic **11** bad-tempered, Belligerent, hot-tempered **12** cantankerous
irate: mad **5** angry, het up, wroth **6** bitter **7**
  angered, enraged, furious, teed off **8**
  incensed, provoked, up in arms, wrathful **9**
  indignant, irascible
ire: vex **4** fury, heat, rage **5** anger, annoy,
  wrath **6** choler, dander, temper **8** asperity,
  vexation **9** vehemence **10** exasperate,
  resentment

Ireland (see also Irish, Northern Ireland): **4** Eire, Erin **5** Ierne **8** Hibernia
  9 Innisfail **11** Emerald Isle
  capital: **6** Dublin
  city: **4** Cobh, Cork **5** Ennis **6** Galway **7**
  Dundalk **8** Limerick **9** Killarney, Tipperary, Waterford **12** Dun Laoghaire
  cross: **6** Celtic
  currency: rap **4** real **5** penny, pound
  island: **4** Aran **5** Clare, Clear, Great **6**
  Achill, Dursey, Saltee **7** Elasket **8** Scarriff, Valentia
  mountain: **4** Mayo **7** Donegal, Wicklow
  9 Connemara
  political organization: IRA **8** Sinn Fein
  river: Lee **4** Erne, Nore, Suir **5** Avoca,
  Boyne, Foyle **6** Barrow, Liffey, Slaney
  7 Shannon **10** Blackwater

---

irenic: **4** calm **8** pacifist, peaceful **10** non-violent **12** conciliatory
iridescent: **6** nacred, pearly **9** prismatic **10**
  opalescent
iris: **4** flag **5** orris **7** eye part, rainbow **9** perennial
  family: **4** irid, ixia **6** crocus **9** gladiolus
  inflammation of: **6** iritis
Irish (see also **Gaelic**, **Ireland**): **4** Erse **6**
  Celtic, Gaelic
  accent: **6** brogue
  ancestor: Mil **6** Miledh **8** Milesius
  author: **4** Shaw **5** Joyce **7** O'Connor **9**
  O'Flaherty
  basket: **7** skeough
  battle cry: abu
  boat: **7** pookaun **8** pookhaun
  cabstand: **6** hazard
  cap: **6** barrad
  cattle: **5** Kerry
  chieftan: **6** Tanist
  church: kil
  church steward: **7** erenach
  clan: **4** sept **5** Cinel
  club: **8** shillala **9** shillalah, shillelah **10** shillelagh
  cordial: **10** usquebaugh
  coronation stone: **7** Lia Fail
  dagger: **5** skean
  dirge: **4** keen
  epic tales: **4** tain, tana (pl.)
  exclamation: och **4** arra **5** arrah, ohone
  fair: **6** aenach, aonach
  fairy: **4** shee **5** sidhe **7** banshee, banshie **10**
  leprechaun

festival: **4** feis
fort: Lis **4** rath
freebooter: **8** rapparee
freeman: **4** aire
fuel: **4** peat
garment: **4** inar
goblin: **5** pooka
goddess: **4** Badb, Bodb, Dana
god of love: **5** Dagda **6** Aengus, Oengus
god of sea: Ler
god's mother: Ana, Anu
good-for-nothing: **8** spalpeen
groggery: **7** shebeen
herring: **8** scud-dawn
infantryman: **4** kern
king: Rig **5** Ardri
kingdom: **6** tuatha
king's home: **4** Tara
lamentation: **6** ochone
landholding system: **7** rundale
lawyer: **6** brehon
liquor: **6** poteen **7** potheen **12** Irish
whiskey
lord: **6** tanist
luck: **4** cess
measure: **4** mile **6** bandle
melody: **7** planxty
moccasin: **9** pampootee, pampootie
monk: **6** culdee
monk's cell: kil **4** kill
musical festival: **4** feis
musical instrument: **4** harp, lyre
nationalist society: **8** Sinn Fein
negative: **5** sorra
oath: **5** bedad
patriot: **5** Emmet **6** Oakboy **7** Parnell
peasant: **4** kern **5** kerne
peat: gor
person: **4** aire, kern **5** kerne, paddy **7** shoneen **8** spalpeen **10** Eireannach
pig: **5** bonav
playwright: **4** Shaw **5** Behan, Synge, Wilde,
Yeats **6** Colvin, O'Casey **7** Beckett, Gregory
10 Boucicault
poem: **6** amhran
priest: **5** druid
princess: **6** Iseult
proprietor: **6** tanist
Protestant: **9** Sassenach
revolutionist: **6** Fenian
robber: **8** woodkern
saint: **5** Aidan **7** Patrick
salutation: **6** a chara
servant: **5** biddy **7** gossoon
slogan: **11** Erin go bragh
society: **4** aire
soldier: **6** bonagh **8** rapparee
song: **4** rann

sport: **7** camogie, hurling
steward: **7** erenach **8** herenach
stock: **4** daer
straw load: **5** barth
surgeon: **6** Colles
sweetheart: gra
symbol: **4** harp **8** shamrock
tax: **7** bonaght **8** bonaught
tenant: **4** saer
tenure: **6** sorren **7** sorehon
term of endearment: **5** aroon, aruin **7**
acushla, alannah, asthore **9** avourneen,
mavourneen
theatre: **5** Abbey
trout: **7** gilaroo
verse: **4** rann
white: **4** bawn
womanhood: **4** emer
writing system: **4** ogam **5** ogham
irk (see also **ire**): vex **4** bore **5** anger, annoy,
chafe, peeve, tease, upset, weary **6** nettle **7**
trouble **8** irritate **10** exasperate
irksome: **4** dull **7** humdrum, painful, tedious
8 tiresome **9** fatiguing, wearisome **10** burdensome, monotonous, unpleasant **11** displeasing
iron: fer (F.) **4** gyve, hard **5** metal, power,
press **6** fetter, robust, smooth, strong **7**
manacle, shackle **8** firmness, handcuff,
hematite, siderite **10** unyielding
compound: **5** steel
curtain: **7** barrier **8** frontier
dross: **6** sinter
lump: pig
lung: **10** respirator
meteoric: **8** siderite
pert. to: **6** ferric
tailor's: **5** goose
Iron City: **10** Pittsburgh
ironclad: **6** strict **7** armored **9** immutable
ship: **7** Monitor **8** Merrimac
ironer: **6** mangle **7** presser
ironhanded: **4** firm **6** strict **8** despotic **11** dictatorial
ironic: **7** satiric **9** sarcastic
irons: **6** chains **7** fetters **8** shackles
irony: wit **6** satire **7** asteism, mockery, sarcasm
8 ridicule
Iroquois tribes: **6** Cayuga, Mohawk, Oneida,
Seneca **8** Onondaga **9** Tuscarora
irradiate: ray **4** beam, emit **6** bright **7** diffuse
8 brighten **9** enlighten **10** illuminate
irrational: **4** surd **5** brute **6** absurd, insane,
stupid, unwise **7** bestial, brutish, foolish **9**
fanatical, illogical, senseless **10** ridiculous
12 unreasonable
irreclaimable: **4** lost **8** hopeless **9** abandoned
11 irrevocable **12** irredeemable

irreconcilable: 11 conflicting 12 incompatible, inconsistent, intransigent

irrefutable: 10 conclusive, undeniable

irregular: 4 wild 5 erose, false 6 ataxic, fitful, rugged, spotty, uneven, unlike 7 atactic, crabbed, crooked, cursory, devious, erratic, snatchy, unequal, wayward 8 abnormal, atypical, sporadic, unlawful, unstable, unsteady, variable 9 anomalous, desultory, eccentric, unsettled 10 changeable, disorderly, immoderate 11 intemperate

irregularity: 4 flaw 5 error 7 anomaly 8 disorder 9 variation 10 unevenness

irrelevant: 9 unrelated 10 extraneous, immaterial, inapposite 11 unessential

irreligious: 5 pagan 6 wicked 7 godless, heathen, impious, profane

irremediable: 6 ruined 8 helpless, hopeless 9 desperate, incurable

irreproachable: 8 spotless 9 blameless, exemplary, faultless 10 impeccable

irresistible: 10 superhuman 11 fascinating, unopposable 12 overpowering, spellbinding

irresolute: 6 fickle, infirm, unsure 8 doubtful, unstable, wavering 9 uncertain, undecided 10 changeable, inconstant 11 fluctuating 12 undetermined

irresponsible: 8 carefree 10 fly-by-night, unreliable 11 harum-scarum

irreverence: 7 impiety 8 dishonor 9 blasphemy, impudence, profanity

irrevocable: 4 firm 5 final 9 immutable 10 conclusive 11 unalterable

irrigate: wet 5 water 6 sluice 7 moisten

irritable: 4 edgy 5 cross, fiery, testy 6 cranky, ornery, tetchy, touchy 7 fretful, peevish, pettish 8 snappish 9 excitable, fractious, impatient, querulous

irritate: irk, nag, rub, vex 4 gall, goad, rile, roil 5 anger, annoy, chafe, cross, grate, peeve, pique, spite, sting, tease 6 abrade, badger, bother, burn up, enrage, excite, harass, hector, madden, needle, nettle, put out, ruffle 7 affront, incense, inflame, provoke 8 acerbate, make sore 9 aggravate, displease, stimulate 10 exacerbate, exasperate

irritating: 5 acrid 8 rankling, stinging

irritation: 4 itch, rash, sore 9 annoyance

Isaac's kin: 4 Esau 5 Jacob 7 Abraham

isagoge: 12 introduction

Iseult: *beloved:* 7 Tristan
   husband: 4 Mark

Ishmael: 5 rover 6 pariah 7 outcast
   kin: 5 Hagar 7 Abraham 8 Nebaioth

Ishtar's lover: 6 Tammuz

isinglass: 4 mica

Isis: 7 goddess 8 Egyptian
   kin: 5 Horus 6 Osiris
   mother: Nut

son: Set 4 Seth 5 Horus

Islam: *emigration:* 6 hegira
   fast: 7 Ramadan
   founder: 7 Mahomet 8 Mohammed, Muhammad
   god: 5 Allah
   holy city: 5 Mecca 6 Medina
   law: 4 adat 5 sheri 6 sharia, sheria
   New Year: 6 Naw Roz
   paradise: 5 jenna
   pilgrimage: 4 hadj, hajj
   priest: 4 imam
   scriptures: 5 Koran
   sect: 5 Sunni 6 Shiism 7 Sevener, Sufisan, Twelves
   shrine at Mecca: 5 Kaaba

island: ait, cay, ile (F.), key 4 holm, inch (Sc.), isle 5 atoll, holme, islet 6 cut off 7 isolate 8 insulate
   group: 11 archipelago
   kind: 5 coral 7 barrier 8 volcanic 11 continental

ism: 5 ology, tenet 6 belief 8 doctrine 10 hypothesis

isolate: 6 detach, enisle, island 7 seclude 8 insulate, separate 9 segregate, sequester 10 quarantine

isolated: 4 sole 5 alone 6 lonely 7 insular 8 singular, solitary

Isolde's lover: 7 Tristan

Israel (see also Hebrew, Judaism, Palestine): *author:* Oz 5 Agnon
   capital: 9 Jerusalem
   city: Lod 4 Gaza 5 Haifa, Holon, Ramla 6 Bat Yam 7 Natanya, Rehovot, Tel Aviv 8 Ashkelon, Nazareth, Ramat Gan 9 Beersheba
   collective community: 6 moshav 7 kibbutz
   currency: 6 agorot, prutah, shekel
   desert: 5 Negev
   former name: 5 Judea 9 Palestine
   gulf: 5 Aqaba
   lake: 4 Hule 7 Dead Sea 8 Kinneret
   mountain: 6 Carmel
   nationalist movement: 7 Zionism
   native-born Israeli: 5 sabra
   plain: 6 Sharon
   river: 5 Besor 6 Jordan, Qishon
   sea: 4 Dead 7 Galilee 13 Mediterranean

---

issuance: 5 issue 6 sortie 9 emanation

issue: 4 emit, flow, gush, pour, send 5 arise, child, sally, spout, topic, yield 6 accrue, emerge, source, upshot 7 descent, dispute, edition, emanate, fortune, outcome, prob-

lem, proceed, progeny **8** question **9** effluence, offspring **10** distribute
Istanbul: 9 Byzantium **14** Constantinople
  museum: **7** Topkapi
  strait: **8** Bosporus
  suburb: **7** Uskudar
isthmus: 4 neck **6** strait **9** peninsula
istle fiber: 4 pita, pito
it may be: 5 haply **8** possibly
Ita: Ata **4** Aeta **7** Negrito
Italian: *astronomer:* **6** Secchi **7** Galileo
  bell town: **5** Adano
  bowling game: **5** bocce
  carriage: **7** vettura
  cathedral: **5** duomo
  cereal: **5** arzun
  cheese: **6** Romano **7** riccota **8** Bel paese, Parmesan **10** gorgonzola
  chest: **7** cassone
  dance: **5** volta **8** courante **9** rigoletto **10** tarantella
  entertainment: **5** festa
  gentleman: ser **6** signor **7** signore
  goldsmith: **7** Cellini
  goodbye: **4** ciao
  grape: uva **6** verdea
  guessing game: **4** mora
  guitar: **8** chitarra
  hamlet: **5** casal **6** casale
  hello: **4** ciao
  holiday: **5** festa
  house: **4** casa **6** casino
  ice cream: **6** gelato
  inlay work: **6** tarsia
  inn: **7** albergo, locanda, osteria
  innkeeper: **4** oste **7** padrone
  lady: **5** donna **7** signora
  land: **5** paese, terra
  lover: **6** amante **7** amoroso
  magistrate: **4** doge **7** podesta
  marble: **7** Carrara
  master: **7** padrone
  mayor: **7** sindaco
  medieval faction: **4** Neri
  millet: **4** buda, moha **5** mohar, tenai
  monk: **5** padre **6** abbate
  musician: **5** Guido
  needlework: **6** Assisi, ricamo **8** trapunto
  noblewoman: **8** contessa, marchesa
  omelet: **8** frittata
  opera house: **5** Scala
  painting: **9** tenebrosi
  patriot: **6** Cavour, Rienzi **7** Mazzini **9** Garibaldi
  patron saint: **7** Francis
  peasant: **7** paesano **9** contadino
  philosopher: **5** Croce **7** Aquinas, Rosmini
  plays: **7** Vangeli
  poet: **4** Redi, Rota **5** Boito, Dante, Tasso **7**

Ariosto, Guarini **8** Petrarch
  poetic name: **7** Ausonia
  police officer: **6** sbirri, sbirro
  policeman: **11** carabiniere, carabinieri
  porridge: **7** polenta
  pottery: **8** majolica
  priest: **5** padre, prete
  printer: **6** Bodoni
  procession: **5** corso **7** trionfi, trionfo
  pronoun: che, chi, lei, mia **4** egli, ella, essa, esse, essi, esso, loro
  resort: **4** Como, Lido **5** Capri **6** Ischia, Stresa **7** San Remo **8** Positano, Sorrento, Taormina
  rice: **7** risotto
  road: **6** strada
  rock: **7** scaglia
  sausage: **6** salami
  scientist: **5** Fermi, Volta **7** Galileo, Galvani, Marconi
  secret society: **5** Mafia **7** Camorra **9** Carbonari
  shore: **4** riva
  soldier: **7** soldato **11** bersagliere
  song: **5** canto **7** canzone
  soup: **8** minestra **10** minestrone
  stream: **4** rivo
  theme: **4** tema
  theologian: **7** Aquinas, Peronne
  vessel: **9** trabacolo **10** trabascolo
  violin maker: **5** Amati **7** Guarneri **10** Stradivari
  violinist: **7** Corelli, Tartini **8** Paganini
  wine: **4** Asti **5** Corvo, Soave **6** Barolo, Massic **7** Barbera, Chianti, Marsala **8** Frascati **9** Bardolino, lambrusco, Vernaccia **12** Valpolicella
italicize: 6 set off **9** emphasize, underline **10** underscore

Italy: *actor/actress:* **4** Duse **5** Loren **7** Magnani **11** Mastroianni **12** Lollobrigida
  architect: **6** Giotto **7** Bernini **8** Bramante, Palladio **12** Brunelleschi **15** Leonardo da Vinci **22** Michelangelo Buonarroti
  artist: **4** Reni, Tisi **5** Colle, Lippi, Lotto **6** Crespi, Giotto, Guardi, Monaco, Sacchi, Titian **7** Amigoni, Bellini Bernini, Cellini, Chirico, Raphael, Robusti, Strozzi, Tiepolo, Uccello **8** Bronzino, Cagliari, Mainardi, Sassetta **9** Correggio, del Piombo, Donatello, Giorgione, Veneziano **10** Botticelli, Caracciolo, Caravaggio, Modigliani, *(cont.)*

Italy *(cont.)*

Tintoretto **11** della Robbia, Fra Angelico **15** Leonardo da Vinci **19** Piero della Francesca **22** Michelangelo Buonarroti

author: **5** Dante **6** Silone **7** Moravia **9** Boccaccio

bay: **6** Naples

boat: **7** gondola

capital: **4** Rome

city: **4** Bari, Pisa **5** Genoa, Milan, Parma, Siena **6** Ancona, Foggie, Modena, Naples, Venice **7** Bologna, Catania, Ferrara, Leghorn, Livorno, Messina, Palermo, Perugia, Ravenna, Trieste **8** Brindisi, Cagliari, Florence

composer: **5** Verdi **7** Bellini, Puccini, Rossini, Vivaldi **8** Mascagni, Paganini, Respighi **9** Donizetti, Scarlatti **10** Monteverdi **11** Leoncavallo

currency: **4** lira **5** grano, paoli, soldo **6** ducato, sequin, teston, zequin **8** sudo tari, zecchino **9** centesimo

dance: **10** tarantella

dramatist: **7** Ariosto, Goldoni **10** Pirandello

glassmaking center: **6** Murano

greeting: **4** ciao

hero: **9** Garibaldi

island: **4** Elba **5** Capri, Egadi, Ponza **6** Giglio, Ischia, Lipari, Salina, Sicily,

Ustica **7** Capraia, Pontine **8** Sardinia **9** Stromboli

lake: **4** Como **5** Garda **6** Albano, Lugano **7** Bolsena **8** Maggiore **9** Bracciano, Trasimeno

measure: pie **4** orna **5** canna, carat, palma, piede, punto, salma, staio, stero **6** barile, miglio, moggio, rubbio, tavola, tomolo **7** boccale, braccio, secchio **8** giornata, polonick, quadrato

mountain: **4** Alps **9** Apennines

mountain peak: **9** Mont Blanc **10** Matterhorn

opera site: **7** La Scala **16** Baths of Caracalla

opera star: **5** Gigli, Pinza **6** Caruso **7** Tebaldi **9** Pavarotti

poet: **5** Tasso **8** Petrarch **9** D'Annunzio **14** Dante Alighieri

pre-Roman nation: **7** Etruria

region at "heel": **6** Apulia

region at "toe": **8** Calabria

river: Po **4** Adda, Arno, Liri **5** Adige, Oglio, Piave, Tiber **6** Aterno, Isonzo, Mincio, Panaro, Ticino **7** Pescara **8** Volturno

school: **5** liceo

sport: **5** bocci

volcano: **4** Etna **8** Vesuvius **9** Stromboli

weight: **5** carat, libra, oncia, pound **6** denaro, libbra, ottava **11** chilogrammo

---

itch: **4** long, reef, urge, yeuk (Sc.) **5** chafe, mange, sting, yearn **6** desire, eczema, hanker **7** prickle, scabies **9** cacoethes, hankering, psoriasis **10** irritation

item (see also **object**): bit **5** entry, scrap, thing, topic **6** detail **7** account, article, product **8** personal **9** paragraph **10** particular **12** circumstance

itemize: **4** list **9** enumerate

Ithaca king: **8** Odysseus

Ithunn's husband: **5** Brage, Bragi

itinerant: **6** errant, roving **7** migrant, nomadic **8** traveler, wanderer **9** migratory, transient, traveling, unsettled, wandering **11** peripatetic

itinerary: **4** plan, tour **5** guide, route **6** record **8** roadbook **9** guidebook

Ivan the Terrible: **4** Tsar

wife: **9** Anastasia

Ivanhoe: *author:* **5** Scott

character: **4** Tuck **5** Isaac **6** Cedric, Rowena **7** Rebecca, Wilfred **9** Robin Hood

ivory: die **4** tusk **5** tooth **6** creamy **7** dentine

Ivory Coast, Cote d'Ivoire: *capital:* **7** Abidjan **12** Yamoussoukro

city: Man **5** Daloa **6** Bouake **7** Korhogo

currency: **5** franc **7** centime

mountain peak: **5** Nimba

river: **5** Komoe **7** Bandama, Cavally **9** Sassandra

ivory tower: **6** dreamy, unreal **7** retreat **8** escapist **9** visionary **11** impractical

ivy: **4** vine **6** hedera

poison: **5** sumac

Ixion's descendants: **8** Centaurs

ixtle: **4** pita **5** fiber, istle

izzat: **5** honor **6** credit **8** prestige **10** reputation

J

jaal: 4 goat, ibex 5 beden
jab: hit, jag 4 poke, prod, stab 5 nudge, prick, punch 6 thrust
Jabal's father: 6 Lamech
jabber: 4 chat 6 burble, gabble 7 chatter 9 gibberish
jabberwocky: 8 nonsense 9 gibberish, rigmarole
jabiru: 4 ibis 5 stork
jabot: 5 frill 6 ruffle
jacare: 6 caiman 9 crocodile
jack: nob 4 card, lift 5 knave, money 6 sailor
  group of: 8 quatorze
jack-in-the-pulpit: 4 arum, herb 5 plant 7 figwort 8 bog onion 12 Indian turnip
jack-of-all-trades: 6 tinker 8 handyman
jack tree: 4 jaca
jackal: 5 diebs 6 howler
jackanapes: ape, fop 4 beau 5 dandy 6 monkey 7 coxcomb
jackass: 4 dolt, fool 5 dunce 6 donkey, nitwit 9 blockhead
jackdaw: coe 6 caddow 9 blackbird
jacket: 4 bajo, coat, Eton 5 acton, grego, parka, wamus 6 anorak, banian (Ind.), bietle, blazer, bolero, dolman, reefer, sliver, wammus, wampus 7 cassock, doublet, pea coat, ristori, spencer 8 camisole, chaqueta (Sp.), hanselin 9 habergeon 10 carmagnole (F.), roundabout 11 nightingale
  knitted: 5 gansy 6 gansey, sontag 7 sweater 8 cardigan, penelope
  sleeveless: 4 vest 5 tunic 6 bolero, jerkin
Jack of clubs: pam
jackass: *laughing:* 10 koo ka burra
jackknife: 4 dive 6 barlow
jackpot: all 4 pool 5 award 8 windfall
jackrabbit: 4 hare
jackstay: 4 rope 5 staff
jackstones: 4 dibs 5 jacks 9 game
Jacob: *brother:* 4 Edom, Esau
  daughter: 5 Dinah
  descendant: 6 Levite 9 Israelite
  father-in-law: 5 Laban
  father: 5 Isaac
  new name: 6 Israel
  parent: 5 Issac 7 Rebekah
  retreat: 5 Haran
  son: Dan, Gad 4 Aser, Levi 5 Asher, Judah 6 Bononi, Joseph, Reuben, Simeon 7 Ger-

shon, Zebulum 8 Benjamin, Issachar, Naphtali
  vision (scene): 6 Bethel, ladder
  wife: 4 Leah 6 Rachel
jade: fag, nag 4 hack, minx, plug, tire 5 green, hussy, weary, wench 6 harass 7 exhaust, fatigue, hilding, pounamu 8 nephrite 10 greenstone
jaded: 4 worn 5 blase, tired, weary 6 dulled 7 wearied 9 exhausted, forjaskit, forjesket
jaeger: 4 bird, gull, skua 6 hunter 7 diamond 8 huntsman
jag: dag, jab, rag 4 barb, hair, load, mess, stab 5 carry, notch, prick, scrap, shred, slash, souse, spree, tooth 6 indent, tatter 7 bristle, pendant, portion 8 quantity 13 denticulation
jagged: 5 erose, rough, sharp 6 hackly, ragged 7 cutting
jaguar: 5 ounce 8 large cat
jai alai: 4 game 6 pelota
  court: 6 cancha 7 fronton
  racket: 5 cesta
jail (see also **prison**): can, jug 4 brig, dump, gaol, keep, stir 5 clink, pokey 6 asylum, carcel, cooler, lockup, prison 7 hoosgow 8 bastille, hoosegaw, hoosegow, imprison 9 calaboose 11 incarcerate
jailer, jailor: 4 caid 5 guard, screw 6 gaoler, keeper, warden 7 alcaide, turnkey
Jairite: Ira
jake: 4 fine, hick, rube 5 dandy 6 rustic 9 first-rate, greenhorn
jako: 6 parrot
jalousie: 5 blind 7 shutter
jam: 4 bind 5 crowd, crush, jelly, sweet 6 spread 7 squeeze 9 marmalade 10 congestion
Jamaica: *capital:* 8 Kingston
  city: 6 May Pen 10 Mandeville, Montego Bay 11 Spanish Town
  currency: 4 cent 6 dollar
  mountain: 4 Blue 5 Mocho
Jamaica dogwood: 8 barbasco
  ginger alcohol: 4 jake
James' father: 7 Zebedee
jangle: 4 ring 5 clang, upset 6 bicker, racket 7 quarrel, wrangle 8 irritate 11 altercation
jangling: 5 harsh 7 grating 9 dissonant 10 discordant 11 cacophonous
janitor: 6 porter 9 caretaker, custodian 10 doorkeeper 11 housekeeper

Japan: 5 Nihon 6 Nippon
 architect: 5 Tange
 bay: Ise 5 Mutzu, Osaka 6 Suruga, Toyama, Wakasa 8 Ishikari 9 Kagoshima, Shimabara
 capital: 5 Tokyo
 city: Ome, Usa 4 Kobe, Nara, Ueda 5 Kyoto, Osaka, Otaru, Sakai 6 Nagoya, Sendai 7 Okayama, Okazaki, Sapporo 8 Kawasaki, Nagasaki, Yokohama, Yokosuka 9 Hiroshima
 currency: sen, yen
 emperor: 7 Akihito 8 Hirohito
 island: 6 Honshu (mainland), Kyushu 7 Shikoku 8 Hokkaido
 measure: bu, jo, boo, cho 4 hiro 5 tsubo 11 kujira-shaku
 measure of distance: ri
 measure of land: se, tan
 measure of weight: mo, fun, kin, kon, rin, shi 4 kati, kwan, niyo 5 carat, carry, momme, picul 6 kwamme 8 hiyak-kin 11 komma-ichida
 mountain peak: 4 Fuji, Kuju 5 Iwaki 6 Ontake 7 Shirane 9 Asahi Dake
 opened to trade by: 5 Perry
 outcast: eta 9 burakumin
 river: 4 Kiso, Tone 5 Iwaki, Shire 6 Sumida, Tashio 7 Shinano
 sea: Suo 6 Harima, Inland, Kumano, Sagami 7 Okhotsk 9 East China
 strait: 5 Bungo, Korea 7 Tsugaru
 tidal wave: 7 tsunami
 volcano: Aso 4 Fuji 5 Asama, Iwate 6 Daisen, On-take

japan: 7 lacquer, varnish
Japanese: *abacus:* 7 soroban
 abalone: 5 awabi
 aborigine: 4 Ainu
 alcoholic beverage: 4 sake, saki
 alloy: 5 mokum
 allspice: 12 chimonanthus
 apricot: ume 4 ansu
 art design: 5 notan
 baron: 6 daimio, daimyo
 battle cry: 6 banzai
 biwa: 6 loquat
 boxes: 4 inro
 brake: 6 warabi
 brazier: 7 hibachi
 brocade: 7 nishiki
 Buddha: 5 Amida
 Buddhist festival: Bon
 Buddhist sect: Zen 4 Jodo, Shin

 bush clover: 4 hagi
 button: 7 netsuke
 calculator: 6 abacus 7 soroban
 calisthenics: 4 judo
 cape: 4 mino
 cherry: 4 fuji
 chess: 5 shogi
 chevrotain: 4 napu
 church: 4 tera
 circle: 4 maru
 clan: 7 Satsuma
 class: eta, roi 6 heimin 7 kwazoku, samurai, shizoku
 clogs: 4 geta
 clover: 4 hagi
 combine: 8 zaibatsu
 composition: 6 haikai
 costume: 7 netsuke
 court: 5 dairi
 crepe: 8 chirimen
 crest: mon 7 kikumon
 culture, early: 5 Jomon, Yayoi
 dancing girl: 6 geisha
 deer: 4 sika
 deity: 9 Amaterasu
 dextrose: ame
 district: 5 Ginza
 dog: 6 tanate
 door: 6 fusuma
 drama: no, noh 6 kabuki
 drink: 4 sake, saki
 drum: 5 tarko
 dwarf tree: 6 bonsai
 dye process: 5 yuzen
 earthenware: 5 banko 7 Satsuma 8 rakuware
 emperor's title of old: 6 mikado
 entertainer: 6 geisha
 ethics: 7 Bushido
 explosive: 7 shimose
 fabric: 6 birodi 7 habutai, nishiki 8 chirimen, habutaye
 family concern: 8 zaibatsu
 fan: ogi
 festival: Bon 7 Matsuri
 fish: ayu, tai, tho 4 fugu, funa
 flag: 7 sunflag
 flower: 9 nelumbium
 flute: 4 fuye
 food: 4 miso, tofu 5 sushi 7 sashimi, tempura 8 sukiyaki, teriyaki, yakitori
 founder of imperial line: 10 Jimmu Tenno
 game: 5 goban 6 gobang 8 pachinko
 garment: 5 haori 6 hakama, kimono, mompei
 gateway: 5 torii
 general: 6 shogun
 girdle receptacle: 4 inro
 girdle: obi

god: **5** Ebisu, Hotei **6** Benten **7** Daikoku **8** Bishamon **10** Fukurokuju **11** Kami Jurojin
goddess: **9** Amaterasu
governor's title: **6** shogun, taikun, tycoon
hanging: **8** kakemono
harp: **4** koto
herb: udo
kelp: **4** kome
lacquer: **6** urushi
legislature: **4** Diet
loquat: **4** biwa
lyric: **5** haiku, hokku
martial art: **4** judo **6** aikido, karate
mat: **6** tatami
metalwork: **5** zogan
military ruler: **6** shogun
monastery: **4** tera
music and dancing: **6** gagaku **7** san-gaku, sarugku
musical instrument: **4** biwa, fuye, koto **5** tarko **7** samisen, truyume **8** shamisen
nautical mile: **5** kairi
news service: **5** Domei
niche: **8** tokonoma
nobility: **7** kwazoku
original inhabitant: **4** Ainu
ornament: **4** inro
outcast: eta **5** ronin
overcoat: **4** mino
pagoda: taa
painting style: **4** kano **7** ukiyoye
palanquin: **4** kago **5** cango **7** norimon
paper mulberry: **4** kozo
paper-folding art: **7** origami
persimmon: **4** kaki **7** Hyakume
pine: **5** matsu
plant: udo **5** kudzu **6** sugamo
plum: **6** kelsey
poetry: **5** haiku, renga, tanka
porcelain: **5** Hizen, Imari **6** Hirado **9** Nabeshima, Sanda ware
porter: **5** akabo
potato: imo
quilt: **5** futon **10** shikibuton
quince: **8** japonica
radish: **6** daikon
receptacle: **4** inro
religion: **6** Shinto **8** Buddhism **9** Shintoism
rice cake: ame
rice wine: **4** sake
robe: **6** kimono
salad plant: udo
salmon: **4** masu
sash: obi
screen: **5** shoji
sculpture: **6** haniwa
seaweed: **4** nori
self-defense: **4** judo **6** karate **7** jujitsu, jujutsu

Shinto temple: Sha **5** Jinja **6** Jinsha **7** Yashiro
ship: **4** maro, maru
shoe: **4** geta, zori
shrub: **4** fuji **5** goumi **8** japonica
silk: **7** habutai **8** chirimen, habutaye
silkworm disease: uji
silkworm: **7** yamamai
sock: **4** tabi
song: uta
sport: **4** sumo **5** kendo
storm: **7** tsunami
suicide: **7** seppuku **8** hara-kari, hara-kiri, hari-kari, kamikaze
suntree: **7** hinokis
sword guard: **5** tsuba
sword: **5** catan **6** cattan **7** samurai **8** wacadash
tea ceremony: **7** chanoyu
tea girl: **7** mousmee, mousmee
temple: **4** tera
throne: **6** shinza
title: **4** kami **6** shogun
tortoise shell: **5** bekko
tree: **4** kozo, sugi **5** akeki, kiaki, yeddo **6** urushi **7** camphor **8** akamatsu **10** shirakashi
untouchable: eta **9** burakumin
vehicle: **7** ricksha **8** rickshaw **10** jinricksha, jinrikisha
velvet: **6** birodi
verse: **5** tanka
vine: **5** kudzu
wall: **5** shoji
warrior: **7** samurai
windstorm: **5** taifu
winged being: **5** tengu
wrestling: **4** sumo
writing: **4** kana
zitherharp: **4** koto
Japanese-American: **5** Issei, Kibei, Nisei **6** Sansei
jape: **4** fool, gibe, jeer, jest, joke, mock **5** fraud, taunt, trick **6** deride
japery: **10** buffoonery
Japheth: *brother:* Ham **4** Shem
    father: **4** Noah
    son: **5** Magog, Tubal **7** Meshech
japonica: **4** bush **5** shrub **8** camellia
jar: jug, ola, urn **4** jolt, olla, vase **5** banga, clash, cruse, shake, shock **6** croppa, hydria, krater, tinaja **7** agitate, amphora, clatter, concuss, discord **10** jardiniere
    fruit: **5** mason
    rubber: **4** lute
    top: lid
    two-handled: **7** amphora
    wide-mouthed: **4** ewer
jardiniere: jar, jug, urn **4** vase **5** stand **7** garnish **9** flowerpot

jargon: 4 cant 5 argot, idiom, lingo, slang 6 pidgin 9 baragouin, gibberish 10 balderdash, vernacular 12 gobbledygook
   lawyer's: 8 legalese
   scholar's: 9 academese
jarl: 4 earl 7 headman 9 chieftain
jarring: 5 rough 9 dissonant 10 discordant
jasmine: 4 vine 6 flower 7 perfume
Jason: *father:* 5 Aeson
   love: 6 Creusa
   men: 9 Argonauts
   ship: 4 Argo
   teacher: 7 Cheiron
   uncle: 6 Pelias
   wife: 5 Medea 6 Creusa, Glauce
jasper: 6 morlop, quartz 10 bloodstone, chalcedony
jaundice: 4 bias, bile, envy 7 gulsach, icterus 8 jealousy 9 hepatitis, prejudice
jaunt: 4 ride, trip 5 sally, tramp 6 ramble 7 journey 9 excursion
jaunty: 4 airy 5 cocky, perky, showy, smart 7 finical, stylish 8 debonair 9 debonaire, sprightly
java: 6 coffee
Java: See **Indonesia**
Javanese: *almond:* 7 talisay
   arrow poison: 4 upas
   badger: 5 ratel 6 teledu
   berry: 5 cubeb
   carriage: 4 sado 5 sadoo
   civet: 5 rasse
   cotton: 5 kapok
   dancers: 6 bedoyo
   drama: 6 topeng
   Dutchman: 6 blanda
   fabric: 4 ikat
   fig tree: 7 gondang
   grackle: beo
   measure: 4 paal 5 palen
   musical instrument: 5 saron 6 bonang, gender 7 gambang, gamelan 8 gamelang
   orchestra: 7 gamelan 8 gamelang
   ox: 7 bantens
   pepper: 5 cubeb
   plum: 5 duhal 6 jambul, lomboy 7 jambool
   puppet show: 6 wajang, wayang
   rice field: 5 sawah
   skunk: 6 teledu
   speech: 5 krama, ngoko
   squirrel: 8 jelerang
   straw: 6 peanit
   sumac: 6 fuyang
   temple: 5 candi 6 chandi, tjandi
   tree: 4 upas 6 antiar 7 gondang
   village: 5 dessa
   weight: 4 amat, pond, tali 5 pound
   wild dog: 5 adjag
javelin: 4 dart 5 lance, spear 7 assagai, assegai, harpoon

   cord: 7 amentum
jaw: maw 4 chaw, chop, talk 5 scold 6 berate, jabber 7 chatter, prattle
   lumpy: 13 actinomycosis
   muscle: 8 masseter
   part: 4 chin
   pert. to: 5 malar 7 gnathic
jawbone: 7 maxilla 8 mandible 13 apply pressure
Jayhawker: 6 Kansan 8 guerilla, marander
jazz: bop, hot 4 cool, scat 5 bebop, funky, swing 6 fusion 7 ragtime 9 Dixieland 11 barrelhouse, progressive 12 boogie-woogie
   cradle of: 10 New Orleans
   musicians: 4 Getz, Monk 5 Baker, Basie, Davis, Handy, Hines, Krupa, Lewis, Tatum 6 Dorsey, Herman, Joplin, Kenton, Miller, Parker, Waller 7 Brubeck, Goodman, Hampton 8 Coltrane, Marsalis, Mulligan, Shearing, Whiteman 9 Armstrong, Ellington, Gillespie, Teagarden 11 Beiderbecke
   singer: 4 Cole 5 McRae, Rawls, Smith 6 Bailey 7 Holiday, Vaughan 8 Eckstine 9 Armstrong 10 Fitzgerald, Washington
jealous: 7 envious 8 covetous, watchful 9 greeneyed 10 suspicious 11 mistrustful
jeer: bob, boo 4 gibe, hoot, jape, mock 5 fleer, flout, scoff, scout, sneer, taunt 6 deride 8 ridicule
Jeffersonian: 7 liberal 10 democratic
Jefferson's home: 10 Monticello
Jehiada's wife: 9 Jehosheba 12 Jehoshabeath
Jehoahaz's mother: 7 Hamutal
Jehoiachin's successor: 9 Salathiel
Jehoshaphat: *father:* Asa
   son: 4 Jehu
Jehovah: God 5 Jahve, Yahwe 6 Elohim, Jahveh, Yahweh
Jehu: 4 king 6 driver
jejune: dry 4 arid, dull, flat 5 empty, inane, prosy, trite, vapid 6 barren, hungry, meager 7 insipid, sterile 8 foodless, lifeless 9 innocuous
jell: 7 thicken 9 coagulate 11 crystallize
jelly: gel, jam 6 spread 7 gelatin 8 gelatine
   meat: 5 aspic
   vegetable: 6 pectin
jellyfish: 6 medusa 7 acaleph, milksop 8 weakling
   group: 10 discophora
   part: 10 exumbrella
jellylike: 10 gelatinous
je ne sais quoi: 13 I don't know what 14 elusive quality
jennet: ass 5 horse 6 donkey
jeopardize: 6 expose 7 imperil 8 endanger 10 compromise
jeopardy: 4 risk 5 peril 6 danger, hazard, menace
   show host: 6 Trebek

Jerahmeel's son: 4 Oren 5 Achia
jeremiad: 6 lament, tirade 9 complaint
jerez: 6 sherry
Jericho: *publican:* 8 Zaccheus 9 Zacchaeus
   woman: 5 Rahab
jerk: ass, bob, tic 4 fool, yank 5 idiot, pluck,
   twist 6 twitch, wrench
jerkin: 4 coat 6 jacket, salmon 9 blackjack,
   waistcoat
jerky: 4 meat 5 wagon 7 charqui 8 saccadic,
   staccato 9 irregular, twitching 10 paroxys-
   mal
jeroboam: 4 bowl 6 bottle, goblet
jerry-built: 5 tacky 6 sleazy 13 unsubstantial
jersey: 6 gansey 7 sweater
Jersey tea: 11 wintergreen 12 checkerberry
Jerusalem: 4 Sion, Zion 5 Salem
   captor: 4 Omar
   garden: 10 Gethsemane
   mosque: 4 Omar
   mountain: 4 Sion, Zion 6 Moriah, Olivet
   oak: 7 ambrose
   pool: 6 Siloam 8 Bethesda
   priest: 5 Zadoc, Zadok
   prophetess: 4 Anna, Anne
   region: 5 Perea
   spring: 5 Gihon 6 Siloam
   temple treasury: 6 Corban
   thorn: 6 retama
Jerusalem artichoke: 5 tuber 7 girasol 8
   girasole 10 topinambou
Jerusalem corn: 5 durra
Jerusalem haddock: 4 opah
jess: 5 strap, thong 7 binding
jessamy: fop 5 dandy
Jesse: *father:* 4 Obed
   son: 5 David
jest: fun, gag, kid 4 bull, fool, jape, joke,
   mime, quip 5 chaff, prank, sport, tease 6
   banter, japery, trifle 8 drollery 9 burlesque
   10 jocularity
jester: 4 fool, mime, zany 5 clown, droll 6
   motley 7 buffoon 8 comedian, humorist 9
   prankster 11 merry-andrew
Jesuit: *founder:* 6 Loyola (Ignatius)
   motto: 4 A.M.D.G.
   official name: 14 Society of Jesus
   saint: 5 Regis 13 Francis Xavier
Jesuits' bark: 8 cinchona
Jesus Christ (see also **apostle, Christian**): 7
   Messiah 8 Agnus Dei, Emmanuel, Son of
   God, Son of Man 9 Lamb of God
   betrayer: 13 Judas Iscariot
   birth: 8 Nativity 9 Christmas
   cousin: 14 John the Baptist
   crucifixion site: 7 Calvary 8 Golgotha
   death: 10 Good Friday, Holy Friday 11
   crucifixion
   first miracle: 4 Cana
   foster father: 6 Joseph

   mother: BVM 4 Mary 9 Theotokos 10 Virgin Mary
   path to crucifixion: 11 Via Dolorosa
   prisoner released in his stead: 8 Barabbas
   rising from dead: 6 Easter 12 Resurrection
   rising to heaven: 9 Ascension
   river baptized in: 6 Jordan
jet: 4 ebon, gush 5 black, raven, spout, spurt 6
   nozzle 7 lignite 8 aircraft
   lag: 7 fatigue
   set: 11 social group
jet-assisted takeoff: 4 JATO
Jethro's daughter: 8 Zipporah
jettison: 5 eject, scrap 7 abandon, discard 9
   throw away
jetty: 4 dock, mole, pier 5 groin, wharf 6
   groyne
jeu: 4 game, play 9 diversion
jeune fille: 4 girl, miss
Jew (see also **Hebrew, Judaism**): 6 Essene,
   Hebrew, Semite 9 Israelite
jewel: gem 5 bijou (F.), ideal, stone 6 bauble
   7 paragon, trinket 8 ornament
   box: 6 casket 7 casquet
   case: tye
   connoisseur: 10 lapidarist
   magnifying lens: 5 loupe
   set: 6 parure
   weight: 5 carat
jewelry: 10 bijouterie
   alloy: 6 oreide, oroide
   artificial: 5 paste 6 strass 7 costume
   cutting device: dop
   piece: pin 4 ring 5 tiara 6 brooch, diadem 7
   earring 8 bracelet, lavalier, necklace
   setting: 4 pave 5 mount
jezebel: 4 slut 5 hussy, wench 6 virago 7 trollop 8 strumpet
Jezebel: *father:* 7 Ethbaal
   husband: 4 Ahab
   slayer: 4 Jehu
   victim: 6 Naboth
jib: 4 balk, boom, sail 8 crane arm
jibe: 5 agree, shift 6 accord
jiffy: 5 flash, hurry, trice 6 moment, second 7
   instant
jig: 4 tool 5 dance, drill 8 fishhook
jigger: cup 4 boat 5 glass 6 gadget 7 measure
jiggle: jar 5 dance, shake 6 diddle, fidget,
   teeter 7 agitate
jihad, jehad: war 6 strife 7 contest, crusade,
   holy war 8 campaign
jill: 4 girl 5 woman 10 sweetheart
jilt: 4 dump 5 leave 6 betray, desert, reject 7
   abandon, discard, forsake, let down
jimmy: bar, pry 5 lever 7 crowbar, pry open
Jimsonweed: 6 datura 10 thorn apple
jingle: 4 ring 5 clank, clink, rhyme, verse 6
   tinkle 7 chinkle
jingoist: 10 chauvinist

jinni: **5** genie **6** afreet, Alukah, jinnee, Yaksha, Yakshi (fem.)

jinx: hex **5** jonah **6** hoodoo, whammy **7** evil eye, nemesis

jitters: **5** panic **6** dither, shakes **7** willies

jittery: **5** jumpy **7** fidgety, nervous

jive: kid **5** dance, swing **6** jargon, phoney **7** hot jazz **9** deceitful, jitterbug

Joan of Arc: **5** saint **7** Pucelle **10** Jeanne d Arc **13** Maid of Orleans
birthplace: **7** Domremy
counselors: **6** voices
killed at: **5** Rouen
victory: **7** Orleans

Joan's spouse: **5** Darby

job: **4** duty, task **5** chare, cheat, chore, stint, trick **7** farm out **8** position, vocation **10** employment

Job: *daughter:* **5** Kezia **6** Jemima
friend: **5** Elihu **6** Bildad, Zophar **7** Eliphaz

Job's tears: **4** coix **5** adlai, adlay, grass, plant

jobber: **6** dealer **10** wholesaler

Jocasta: *daughter:* **6** Ismene **8** Antigone
husband: **5** Laius **7** Oedipus
son: **7** Oedipus **8** Eteocles **9** Polynices **10** Polyneices

jock: **7** athlete

jockey: **4** gull **5** rider, trick **6** driver, outwit **8** maneuver, operator **10** manipulate
kind of: **4** disc

jocose: dry **6** joking **7** playful **9** full of fun

jocular: gay **4** airy **5** droll, funny, jolly, merry, silly, witty **6** blithe, elated, jovial, joyous, lively, ribald **7** comical, festive, gleeful, jesting, playful, waggish **8** animated, cheerful, gladsome, humorous, mirthful, sportive **9** burlesque, convivial, facetious, hilarious, vivacious **10** frolicsome

joculator: **4** mime **6** jester **7** juggler **8** conjurer, jongleur, minstrel **11** entertainer

jocund: gay **5** merry **6** genial, jovial **8** cheerful

jog: run **4** jerk, lope, poke, prod, trot **5** nudge **6** canter **7** refresh **9** stimulate

John: Ian **4** Ivan, Juan, Sean, Johan, Johannes, Jan

John Brown's Body author: **5** Benet

John of Gaunt: **9** Lancaster

John the Baptist: *cousin:* **5** Jesus
father: **7** Zachary **9** Zachariah, Zacharias
mother: **9** Elizabeth

johnnycake: **4** pone **9** corn bread

Johnson comedy: Fox **7** Epicene, Volpone **9** Alchemist

Johnson grass: **7** sorghum

join: add, mix, tie, wed **4** ally, fuse, knit, knot, link, mate, meet, seam, team, weld, yoke **5** annex, blend, enrol, enter, graft, hitch, marry, merge, miter, piece, unite **6** attach, cantle, cement, cocket, concur, couple,

engage, enlist, enroll, mingle, solder, splice, suture **7** combine, connect, consort, mortise **8** coalesce **9** associate **10** amalgamate **11** consolidate, participate

joint: ell, hip, tee **4** butt, dive, jail, knee, node, seam **5** ankle, cross, elbow, hinge, scarf, wrist **6** arthra (pl.), mutual, prison, rabbet, resort **7** arthron, brothel, calepin, hangout, knuckle, pastern **8** coupling **12** articulation
pert. to: **5** nodal **9** articular
plant stem: **6** phyton **8** phytomer
put out of: **5** upset **9** dislocate
right angle: ell, tee
turned outward: **6** valgus
without: **10** acondylose, acondylous
wooden: **5** tenon

joist: **4** beam **7** sleeper **8** studding

joke: fun, gag, kid, pun **4** fool, gibe, hoax, jape, jest, quip **5** flirt, prank, sally, sport, tease **6** banter **9** wisecrack
old: **6** wheeze **8** chestnut

joker: wag, wit **4** card **5** clown, cutup **6** gagman, jester **7** farceur **11** hidden catch

Joktan: *father:* **4** Eber
son: **5** Ophir

jollity: fun **5** cheer, mirth, revel **6** gaiety, gayety **7** revelry **8** hilarity **9** amusement, festivity, joviality, merriment **11** merrymaking **12** cheerfulness, exhilaration

jolly: **5** buxom, rally **6** cajole, jovial, mellow **7** jocular **9** convivial **11** intoxicated

jolly boat: **4** yawl

jolt: jar **4** blow, bump, butt **5** knock, shake, shock **6** jostle, jounce **7** startle

Jonah: **4** jinx **7** prophet
deliverer: **5** whale

jonquil: **8** daffodil **9** narcissus

Jordan: *ancient city:* **5** Petra **6** Jarash
capital: **5** Amman
city: **5** Irbid, Zarqa **6** Nablus
currency: **4** fils **5** dinar
king: **7** Hussein
people: **4** Arab, Kurd **7** Bedouin **9** Hashemite

Joseph: *brother:* Dan, Gad **4** Levi **5** Asher, Judah **6** Reuben, Simeon **7** Zebulun **8** Benjamin, Issachar, Naphtali
buyer: **8** Potiphar
father: **5** Jacob
mother: **6** Rachel
son: **4** Igal **7** Ephraim **8** Manasseh

josh: guy, kid, rib **4** joke **5** chaff, spoof, tease **6** banter **9** poke fun at

Joshua: *associate:* **5** Caleb
burial place: **5** Gaash
father: Nun
place of importance: **7** Aijalon

Joshua tree: **5** yucca

Josiah: *father:* **4** Amon

mother: **7** Jedidah
son: **8** Jehoahaz **9** Jehoiakim

joss: **4** fate, idol, luck **5** image **6** chance **8** divinity

jostle: jar, jog **4** jolt, push **5** crowd, elbow, shove **6** hurtle, hustle

jot: ace, bit **4** atom, iota, whit **5** grain, minim, point **6** tittle **7** smidgen **8** particle

jotting: **4** memo **9** short note

jounce: **4** jolt **5** shake **6** bounce

journal: log **5** diary, paper **6** record **7** daybook, gazette, logbook **8** magazine **10** periodical
keeper: **5** Pepys **7** diarist

journalist: **6** author, editor, writer **8** reporter **9** columnist

journey: run **4** eyre, fare, iter (L.), ride, sail, tour, trek, trip **5** jaunt, route **6** junket, safari, travel, voyage **7** circuit, odyssey, passage **8** navigate **9** excursion **10** expedition, pilgrimage **13** peregrination
course of: **9** itinerary
division of: lap, leg
pert. to: **6** viatic **11** peripatetic

joust: **4** tilt **6** combat **7** tourney **10** tournament
field: **4** list
ready to: **5** atilt

jovial: gay **5** bully, jolly, merry **6** elated, genial, jocose, jocund, joyous **7** jocular **9** convivial, hilarious

jowl: jaw **4** chop **5** cheek **6** dewlap, wattle **7** jawbone

joy: **4** glee **5** bliss, mirth **6** gaiety, gayety **7** delight, ecstasy, elation, rapture, revelry **8** felicity, gladness, hilarity, pleasure **9** beatitude, festivity, happiness, rejoicing **10** exultation **12** cheerfulness, exhilaration
Muse: **4** Tara

Joyce (James): *character:* **5** Bloom, Rowan **7** Dedalus **9** Earwicker
work: **6** Exiles **7** Ulysses **9** Dubliners **12** Chamber Music **13** Finnegan's Wake, Pomes Penyeach

joyless: **4** glum **6** dismal **7** unhappy **9** cheerless

joyous: gay **4** glad **5** merry **6** blithe, festal **7** blessed, festive, gleeful, jocular **8** cheerful, mirthful **9** blitheful, delighted

Jubal's father: **6** Lamech

jubilant: **6** elated **8** exulting **9** rejoicing **10** triumphant

Judah: *brother:* **4** Levi **6** Joseph, Reuben, Simeon
daughter-in-law: **5** Tamar
descendant: **4** Anub, Boaz **5** David, Jesse **9** Jerahmeel
father: **5** Jacob
mother: **4** Leah

queen: **8** Athaliah
son: Er **4** Onan

Judaism: *abode of the dead:* **5** Sheol
ascetic: **6** Essene
Bible, parts of: **5** Torah **8** Prophets, Writings
Bible text: **5** miqra
Book of Psalms: **8** Tehillim
bread: **5** echem, matzo **6** hallah, matzos **7** challah, matzoth **8** afikomen
butcher: **6** shohet **8** shochtim
cabalistic book: **5** Zohar
ceremony: **8** habdalah
community: **6** aljama **8** kehillah
confession of sins: **5** Alhet **7** Ashamnu
convert: ger
correct: **6** kosher
Day of Atonement: **9** Yom Kippur
devil: **6** Belial
dietary regulations: **7** kashrut
dispersion: **5** golah **8** diaspora
doctor of law: **6** scribe
doctrine: **6** Mishna **7** Mishnah **8** Kodashim
drum: **4** toph
garment: **5** shawl, talis **7** tallith
harp: **5** nebel
healer: Asa
heretical doctrine: **7** Karaism
holiday: **5** Pesah, Purim **6** Pesach, Succos, Sukkos, Yom Tov **7** Sukkoth **8** Chanukah, Hanukkah, Lagbomer, Shabouth **9** Tishahbab, Yom Kippur **11** Rosh Hashana **12** Simhath Torah
horn: **6** shofar **7** shophar
immigrant: **4** oleh **6** halutz **7** chalutz
instrument: **4** asor **5** nebel
instrument player: **9** psalterer, psaltress
judge: **7** shophet
land: **4** Zion
law: **4** Chok, Tora **5** Torah **6** Chukah, Talmud **7** Halacha, Halakah **8** Kashruth
lawgiver: **5** Moses
liturgy: **6** Maarib, Minhah **9** Shaharith
lyre: **4** asor
marriage broker: **8** shadchen
marriage custom: **8** levirate
meat inspection: **7** bedikah
miter: **7** petalon
month: **4** Adar, Elul, Iyar **5** Nisan, Sivan, Tebet **6** Beadar, Kislev, Shebat, Tammuz, Tishri **7** Heshvan
mourning period: **6** Shivah
New Year: **11** Rosh Hashana
Old Testament division: **11** Hagiographa
patriarch: **5** Isaac, Jacob **7** Abraham
patriot family: **8** Maccabee
pioneer: **6** halutz **7** chalutz
poems: **6** yigdal **8** Azharoth
prayer: **5** Alenu, Shema **7** Geullah

prayer book: 6 mahzor, siddur
priest: 4 Ezra 5 Aaron, Cohen 6 Levite
priestly caste: 7 Cohanim, Levites
prophet: 4 Amos, Ezra 5 Elias, Hosea, Jonah, Micah, Moses, Nahum 6 Daniel, Elijah, Elisha, Haggai 8 Habakkuk, Jeremiah 9 Zechariah
prophetess: 6 Huldah
proselyte: ger
psalm of praise: 6 hallel
redeemer: 4 goel
revelation: 5 Torah
sabbath: 8 Saturday
sacred objects: 4 urim
sage: 4 Agur
scarf: 5 abnet 7 tallith
scroll: 11 Sepher Torah
sect member: 6 Essene, Hassid
skullcap: 6 kippah 7 yamilke 8 yarmulka
song: 8 hatikvah 9 hattikvah
spirit: 8 Asmodeus
synagogue: 5 schul
tassel: 6 zizith
teacher: 5 amora, rabbi, tanna
temple precentor: 6 cantor
trumpet: 6 shofar 7 shophar
vestment: 5 ephod
women's organization: 8 Hadassah
Judas: 7 traitor 8 betrayer, Iscariot
place of suicide: 8 Aceldama, Akeldama
Judea: *ancient name:* 5 Judah
capital: 9 Jerusalem
governor: 6 Pilate
king: Asa 4 Ahaz, Amon 5 Herod 7 Jehoram 8 Manesseh 10 Jehoiachin 11 Jehoshaphat
place: 5 Berea
judge: try 4 deem, gage, rank, rate 5 court, gauge, opine 6 assess, critic, decide, reckon, umpire 7 arbiter, believe, justice, referee, suppose 8 consider, estimate, mediator, sentence 9 criticize, determine 10 adjudicate, arbitrator, chancellor, magistrate
bench: 4 banc 6 bancus
chamber: 6 camera
circuit: 4 iter
entry of, after verdict: 6 postea
group: 5 bench
junior or subordinate: 6 puisne
mallet: 5 gavel
of Hades: 5 Minos
of the dead: 6 Osiris
robe: 4 toga
judgment: 5 arret, award, sense, taste 7 censure, insight, insight, opinion, verdict 8 decision, sentence 9 criticism 10 astuteness, discretion, horse sense 11 sensibility
left to one's: 13 discretionary

judicable: 12 determinable
judicial assembly: 5 court
judiciary: 5 bench
document: 4 writ 8 decision
judicious: 4 wise 7 prudent 8 rational, sensible 9 sagacious 10 discerning
Judith: *husband:* 8 Manasses
victim: 10 Holofernes
judo: 7 jujitsu 10 martial art
rel. of: 9 wrestling
jug: jar 4 ewer, jail, olla 5 crock, cruse 6 carafe, flagon, lockup, prison, tinaja, urceus 7 pitcher 9 container 10 bellarmine, jardiniere
shaped like a man: 4 Toby
Juggernaut: 6 Vishnu
juggle: 7 falsify, shuffle 10 manipulate
jugglery: 8 trickery 9 deception 10 escamotage (F.), hanky-panky 11 legerdemain 13 sleight-of-hand
juice: jus (F.), oil, sap 4 broo 6 cremor 8 gasoline 10 succulence 11 electricity
apple: 5 cider
fermented apple: 9 apple jack
fruit: rob 4 must, stum, wine 5 cider 6 casiri 7 vinegar
plant: sap 4 aloe, milk 5 latex 6 achete
juicy: 4 frim, racy 5 spicy 6 lively 7 piquant 9 succulent
juju: 5 charm 6 amulet, fetish
juke: 4 fake 5 cheat 7 deceive
julep: 5 drink 8 beverage
Juliet: *betrothed:* 5 Paris
father: 7 Capulet
lover: 5 Romeo
Julius Caesar: *character:* 6 Brutus, Portia 7 Cassius 8 Lucilius 9 Calpurnia 10 Mark Antony
dramatist: 11 Shakespeare
jumble: 4 hash, heap, mess 5 mix up 6 huddle, medley, muddle 7 clutter, mixture 8 disorder, mishmash 9 confusion 10 hodgepodge
jump: hop 4 leap 5 bound, caper, vault 6 hurdle, prance, spring 7 saltate 8 increase
stick for: 4 pogo, pole
jumper: 5 dress, smock 6 blouse, jacket 8 pullover (Br.)
jumpsuit: 8 coverall
jumpy: 7 jittery, nervous 12 apprehensive
junco: 5 finch 8 snowbird
junction: 4 axil, seam 5 joint, union 6 suture 7 contact, meeting 8 crossing 10 confluence, connection, crossroads
juncture: 4 pass 5 union 6 choice, crisis 8 exigency 9 emergency 10 crossroads 12 turning point
June bug: 6 beetle 8 figeater
June grass: poa

Jungfrau: 4 peak 8 mountain
  site of: 4 Alps 11 Switzerland
jungle: 4 maze 6 tangle 9 labyrinth 10 wilderness
junior: 7 student, younger 8 namesake 11 subordinate
juniper: 4 cade, ezel 5 cedar, grose, retem, savin 6 sabine, savine
  family: 7 cypress
junk: 4 boat, dope, drug 5 scrap, trash, waste 6 heroin, refuse 7 discard, rubbish 8 jettison 9 narcotics
junker: 5 crate, noble, wreck 6 German 8 Prussian 10 aristocrat
junket: 4 trip 5 feast 6 picnic 9 excursion 13 entertainment
Juno: 4 Hera
  consort: 7 Jupiter
  special messenger: 4 Iris
junta/junto: 5 cabal 6 clique 7 council, faction 8 tribunal 9 committee 10 government
Jupiter: 4 Jove, Zeus 6 planet
  angel: 7 Zadkiel
  consort: 4 Juno
  daughter: 4 Bura 5 Diana, Muses 7 Minerva
  epithet: 6 Stator
  Roman temple: 7 Capitol
  satellite: Io, Pan 4 Hera, Leda 5 Carme, Elara, Hades, Metis, Thebe 6 Ananke, Europa, Hestia, Sinope 7 Demeter, Himalia 8 Adrastea, Amalthea, Callisto, Ganymede, Lysithea, Pasiphae, Poseidon
  son: 4 Mars 6 Apollo, Castor, Pollux, Vulcan 7 Bacchus, Mercury 8 Hercules
  space probe to: Pioneer X, Voyager
Jupiter Pluvius: 4 rain

jural: 5 legal 8 juristic
Jurassic division: 4 Lias
jurisdiction: law 5 venue 6 county, domain, sphere 8 dominion, province 9 authority, bailiwick, territory
  ecclesiastical: see 6 parish 7 deanery, diocese, mission 12 archdeaconry
jurisprudence: law 14 court decisions
juror: 4 peer 7 assizer, juryman 8 talesman
  group: 4 jury 5 panel
  selection list: 6 venire
just: due, fit 4 even, fair, only, true 5 equal, exact, legal, valid 6 candid, honest, merely, normal, purely, simply 7 correct, equable, upright 8 accurate, unbiased 9 equitable, impartial 10 legitimate
justice: law 5 judge 6 equity 7 honesty
  god: 7 Forsete, Forseti, Forsite
  goddess: 4 Maat
justification: 6 excuse, reason 7 apology, defense 9 authority, rationale
justify: 4 avow 6 adjust, defend, excuse 7 support, warrant 8 maintain, sanction 9 authorize, exculpate, vindicate
jut: 4 butt 5 bulge 6 beetle 7 project 8 overhang, protrude, stick out 10 projection
jute: 4 desi 5 gunny 6 burlap 7 sacking
Jutlander: 4 Dane
jutting: 7 salient 10 protruding 11 overhanging
Juvenal: 4 poet 5 Roman
  work: 7 satires
juvenile: 5 actor, young 6 callow 8 immature, youthful 10 adolescent 11 undeveloped
Juventas: 4 Hebe
juxtaposition: 7 contact 8 nearness 9 adjacence, adjacency, proximity 10 contiguity

K

kaama: **10** hartebeest
kaddish: **6** prayer **8** doxology
kae: **7** jackdaw
kaffeeklatsch: **6** social **9** gathering **11** get-together
Kaffir, Kafir: **5** Bantu
   language: **4** Xosa
   warriors: **4** Impi
Kafka character: **4** Olga
kaiser: **5** ruler **7** emperor
kaka: **6** parrot
   genus: **6** nestor
kakapo: **6** parrot
kaki: **4** bird **5** stilt **9** persimmon
kakkak: **7** bittern
kale: **4** cole **5** green **7** cabbage, collard **8** cole-wort
kali: **5** plant **6** carpet **8** saltwort
Kali's husband: **4** Siva **5** Shiva
kalinite: **4** alum **7** mineral
Kalmuck, Kalmuk: **6** Mongol
kamias: **7** bilimbi
Kampuchea: See **Cambodia**
Kanaka: **8** Hawaiian **10** Melanesian, Polynesian **11** Micronesian
kanari: **6** almond
kaba, kaaba, kabah, kaabah: **6** shrine
kangaroo: roo **4** euro **5** bilbi, bilby **6** turatt **7** bettong **8** bettonga, boongary, forester, wallaroo **9** marsupial **11** macropodian
   female: doe, gin, roo
   group: mob
   male: **6** boomer
   small: rat **4** tree **7** potoroo, wallaby **9** pademelon
   young: **4** joey
kangaroo rat: **7** potoroo

Kant's category: **7** quality **8** modality, quantity, relation
kaolin: **4** clay
kaput: **6** broken, ruined **8** defeated **9** destroyed
karakul: **5** sheep
karate: **10** martial art **14** self-defense art
karma: **4** fate **7** destiny **10** vibrations
karyotin: **9** chromatin
kasha: **4** mush **5** grain **6** cereal **9** buckwheat
katchung: **6** peanut
kava: ava, awa **5** drink, shrub **6** pepper
   bowl: **5** tanoa
kayak: **5** canoe
kayo: **8** knockout
Kazakhstan: *capital:* **6** Almaty **7** Alma-Ata
   currency: **5** ruble
Kazantzakis hero: **5** Zorba
kea: **6** parrot
Keats poem: **5** Lamia **8** Endymion, Hyperion
   odes: **8** To Autumn **13** On a Grecian Urn **14** To a Nightingale
kebbie: **4** club **5** stick **6** cudgel
ked: **4** tick
kedge: **6** anchor
keel: vat **4** ship **5** upset **6** careen, carina **7** capsize, carinae (pl.) **8** flounder, navigate
   part: **4** skag, skeg
   right angle to: **5** abeam
   without: **9** ecarinate
keelbill: ani
keeling: **7** codfish
keel over: **5** faint, upset **7** capsize
keel-shaped: **8** carinate
keen: cry **4** avid, fell (Sc.), nice, wide **5** acute, awake, eager, sharp **6** ardent, astute, bewail, biting, clever, hearty, lament, severe, shrewd

---

Kansas: *capital:* **6** Topeka
   city: **4** Iola **5** Lyons, Paola **6** Salina **7** Abilene, Wichita **8** Lawrence **9** Dodge City **10** Garden City, Hutchinson, Kansas City
   early explorer: **8** Coronado
   fort: **5** Riley **6** Larned **11** Leavenworth
   Indian: Kaw **5** Kiowa, Osage **6** Pawnee **7** Wichita **8** Comanche, Kickapoo
   lawmen: **4** Earp **6** Hickok **9** Masterson
   President Eisenhower's Library: **7** Abilene

   product: **5** wheat
   river: **5** Osage **6** Kansas (Kaw), Saline **7** Solomon **8** Arkansas, Cimarron **9** Smoky Hill **10** Republican
   state animal: **7** buffalo
   state bird: **10** meadow lark
   state flower: **9** sunflower
   state motto: **16** Ad astra per aspera (To the stars through difficulties)
   state song: **14** "Home on the Range"
   state tree: **10** cottonwood

7 cunning, fervent, intense, parlous, pungent, ululate **9** trenchant **10** hardheaded **12** enthusiastic **13** perspicacious

keenly: 6 dearly

keenness: 4 edge **6** acumen, genius, talent

keep: 4 fend, hold **5** board, guard, lodge, place **6** arrest, behold, living, stable **7** confine, contain, husband **8** fortress, maintain, preserve, restrain, withhold **9** celebrate **10** livelihood
going: **7** sustain

keep back: bar, dam **4** save **6** detain **7** reserve **8** withhold **10** stay behind

keep in: 6 retain

keep on: 7 persist **8** continue **9** persevere

keep out: 4 save **5** debar **7** exclude, reserve **8** hold back

keeper: 5 guard **6** pastor, warden **7** curator, janitor **8** guardian, watchdog **9** caretaker, constable, custodian **10** maintainer
of golden apple: **5** Ithun
of marches: **8** margrave
of park: **6** ranger

keeping: 4 care **5** award, guard, trust **6** charge **7** custody **10** caretaking, possession **11** maintenance **12** guardianship

keepsake: 5 token **7** memento **8** giftbook, souvenir

keest: sap **6** marrow **9** substance

keeve: tub, vat **5** basin

kef: 7 languor, tobacco **8** euphoria **10** dreaminess **12** tranquillity

keg: cag **4** cade, cask **6** barrel **7** barrico
open: **6** unhead

kegler: 6 bowler

keister, keester: 4 rump **7** satchel **8** suitcase

keitloa: 5 rhino

kelly: hat **5** color, derby, green

kelp: 5 algae, varec **6** varech **7** seaweed **8** bellware (Sc.)

kempt: 4 neat, tidy **11** well-groomed

ken: 4 know (Sc.), view **5** admit, sight **7** discern, insight **9** knowledge **10** cognizance **11** recognition **13** understanding

Kenilworth author: 5 Scott

kennel: 5 drain, sewer **6** cannel, gutter, stable **7** shelter **8** doghouse **9** enclosure

kentledge: 5 metal **7** ballast, pig iron

Kentucky bluegrass: poa

Kentucky coffee tree: 6 bonduc, chicot

Kenya: *capital:* **7** Nairobi
city: **5** Nyeri **6** Kisumu, Nakuru **7** Mombasa **8** Kakamega
currency: **4** cent **8** shilling
lake: **6** Rudolf **7** Turkana **8** Victoria
mountain: **5** Elgon
people: Luo **5** Bantu, Kamba, Kisii, Masai, Nandi **6** Kikuyu **7** Swahili, Turkana **8** Kipsigis
river: **4** Athi, Tana **5** Ewaso, Tsavo **6** Galana, Sabaki
secret society: **6** Mau Mau
valley: **9** Great Rift

---

kepi: cap

keratosis: 4 wart **6** growth

kerchief: 5 curch (Sc.) **6** hankie **7** panuelo **8** bandanna, headrail

kerchoo: 6 sneeze
answer to: **10** gesundheit **11** God bless you

Keresan Indian: Sia

kerf: cut **4** slit **5** notch **6** groove **7** cutting

kermis, kermess: 4 fair **8** carnival **11** celebration

kernel: nut **4** bunt, core, germ, meat, pith, seed **5** acini (pl.), grain **6** acinus, nuclei (pl.) **7** nucleus

kersenneh: ers **5** vetch

kestrel: 6 falcon, fanner **7** stannel **9** windhover
genus: **5** Falco

ketch: 4 boat **8** sailboat

ketone: 5 irone **7** acetone, camphor, muscone, shogaol **8** acridone, civetone, deguelin **9** heptanone **14** cyclopentanone

kettle: pot, vat **4** cazo (Sp.) **5** lebes **6** hollow **7** caldron **8** billy can, cauldron, flambeau **9** teakettle **10** kettledrum
nose: **5** spout

kettledrum: 5 naker, tabor **6** atabal, nagara

Kentucky: *capital:* **9** Frankfort
city: **5** Paris **6** Hazard **7** Paducah **8** Richmond **9** Covington, Lexington, Owensboro **10** Louisville
gold depository: **8** Fort Knox
horse race: **5** Derby
Indian: **7** Shawnee **8** Cherokee, Iroquois
music: **9** bluegrass
plateau: **10** Cumberland, Pennyroyal
President Lincoln's birthplace: **11** Hodgenville
river: **4** Ohio, Salt **5** Green, Rough **6** Barren **7** Licking, Rolling, Tug Fork **8** Big Sandy **9** Tennessee **10** Cumberland, Tradewater **11** Mississippi
state bird: **8** cardinal
state flower: **9** goldenrod
state song: **17** "My Old Kentucky Home"
state tree: **10** coffee tree
war: **10** Black Patch

(Ind.), timbal **7** attabal, timbale, timpani (pl.), timpano, tympani (pl.)

kevel: bar, bit, peg **4** bolt **5** cleat, staff **6** cudgel **7** bollard

key: cay, fin **4** clef, isle, quay, reef **5** dital, islet, pitch **6** claves (pl.), clavis, island, opener, spline, tapper **7** digital **8** clavecin, solution, tonality **11** explanation
notch: **4** ward
part: bit
pert. to: **5** tonal, tonic
skeleton: **4** gilt **5** screw **7** twirler

keyboard: **6** manual **7** clavier **8** pedalier **10** claviature

key chain: **10** chatelaine

keyed up: **4** agog **5** eager **7** excited **10** stimulated

keynote: **5** theme, tonic, topic **7** feature

keynoter: **6** orator **11** main speaker

keystone: **7** support **8** main part **9** principle

Keystone State: **12** Pennsylvania

khan: inn **5** ruler **9** sovereign **11** caravansary

khedive's estate: **5** daira

Khnemu's consort: **6** Anukit

kiang: ass

kibbutz: **4** farm **7** commune **10** collective, settlement
country: **6** Israel

kibble: **5** grind **7** dog food **10** coarse bits

kibitzer: **7** adviser, meddler **9** spectator

kick: **4** boot, funk (Sc.), punt **5** gripe, growl **6** fitter (Sc.), object, recoil, thrill **7** grumble **8** complain **10** calcitrate, enthusiasm
off: **5** begin, start **6** launch **8** commence
out: **4** fire, sack **5** evict **6** bounce **7** dismiss **9** discharge

kicker: **8** odd twist, surprise **11** hidden point

kickshaw: toy **6** bauble, gewgaw, tidbit, trifle **7** trinket **8** delicacy

kid: guy **4** goat, hoax, joke **5** child, suede, tease **6** banter **7** fatling, leather **8** cheverel, cheveril **9** youngster

kidcote: **6** prison

kidnap: **6** abduct **8** shanghai **10** spirit away

kidney: **4** neer (Sc.) **5** organ
pert. to: **5** renal

kidney-shaped: **8** reniform

kidney stone: **4** jade **8** calculus, nephrite **10** nephrolith

kier: vat

Kilauea goddess: **4** Pele

kilderkin: **4** cask **6** barrel **7** measure

Kilimanjaro peak: **4** Kibo **7** Mawenzi

kill: **4** hang, slay, veto **5** croak **6** deaden, murder **7** achieve, destroy, execute **8** dispatch, lapidate **9** finish off, slaughter **11** assassinate
by stoning: **8** lapidate
by strangling: **7** garotte, garrote

killdeer: **6** plover

killed: **4** slew **5** slain **9** immolated **12** assassinated

killer: **6** gunman, hit man, slayer **7** torpedo **8** assassin, murderer **10** triggerman

killer whale: orc **4** orca **7** grampus

killing: **6** murder **7** slaying **8** homicide **9** martyrdom, slaughter **10** euthanasia
of brother or sister: **10** fratricide
of father: **9** patricide
of king: **8** regicide
of mother: **9** matricide
of race: **8** genocide
of self: **7** suicide
of small child: **11** infanticide

killjoy: **8** hinderer **9** pessimist **10** spoil-sport

Kilmer poem: **5** Trees

kiln: **4** oast, oven **5** clamp, stove, tiler **6** cockle **7** furnace

kiloliter: **5** stere

kilt: **4** hang **5** pleat **6** fasten **7** filibag
pouch for: **7** sporran

kilter: **5** order **9** condition

kimono sash: obi

kin: ilk **4** boon, clan, folk, gest, good, kind, kith, mild, race, sept, soft, sort, type **5** breed, class, flesh, genre, genus, geste, order, tribe **6** benign, blithe, family, gender, genera (pl.), genial, gentle, goodly, humane, tender **7** amiable, clement, related, species, variety **8** affinity, amicable, benedict, cousinry, friendly, generous, gracious, merciful, relation, relative **9** benignant, brotherly, favorable, indulgent **10** benevolent, charitable **11** considerate, description, kindhearted, sympathetic **12** relationship **13** compassionate
same: **10** homogeneal

kindle: **4** fire, move **5** brood, light, young **6** arouse, decoct, excite, ignite, illume, incite **7** animate, emblaze, inflame, inspire, provoke

kindling: **5** fagot **6** faggot, sticks, tinder

kindness: **5** aloha **6** bounty **8** benefice **9** benignity **11** beneficence

kindred: kin, sib **5** blood, flesh **6** allied, family **7** cognate, kinsmen **8** affinity, kinsfolk **9** congenial **12** relationship

kine: **4** cows **6** cattle

kinetic: **6** active **7** dynamic **9** energetic

king: rex (L.), rey (Sp.), roi (F.) **4** czar, tsar, tzar **5** ruler **6** caesar, kaiser **7** emperor, monarch **9** sovereign
title of address: Sir **4** Sire **7** Majesty **8** Highness

King Arthur: *abode:* **6** Avalon
birthplace: **8** Tintagel
court site: **7** Camelot **8** Caerleon
crowner: **6** Dubric

death place: **6** Camlan
father: **5** Uther **9** Pendragon
fool: **7** Dagonet
forest: **7** Calydon
foster brother: Kay
hound: **6** Cavall
jester: **7** Dagonet
knight: Kay **5** Balan, Balin **6** Gareth, Gawain, Modred **7** Galahad, Geraint, Pelleas, Tristan **8** Lancelot, Parsifal, Percival, Tristram **9** Percivale
lady: **4** Enid **6** Elaine
lance: Ron
magician: **6** Merlin
mother: **7** Igraine
nephew: **6** Gareth **7** Mordred
queen: **8** Guinever **9** Guinevere
shield: **7** Pridwin
sister: **7** Morgain **11** Morgan le Fay
sword: **9** Excalibur
wife: **9** Guinevere
King Canute's consort: 4 Emma
king clover: 7 melilot
king crab: 7 limulus
kingdom: 5 realm **6** domain, empire **8** dominion
kingfish: 4 barb, haku, opah **6** bagara
kingfisher: 7 halycon
King Henry IV character: Hal **5** Blunt, Henry, Percy, Poins **6** Scroop **8** Falstaff
dramatist: **11** Shakespeare
kingly: 5 regal, royal **6** regnal **7** basilic, leonine **8** imperial, majestic
king of beasts: 4 lion
king's evil: 8 scrofula
king's yellow: 8 orpiment
kinin: 7 adenine, hormone
kink: 4 bend, curl, loop **5** bunch, chink, cramp, quirk, snarl, twist **6** buckle, tangle **7** caprice **11** peculiarity
kinkajou: 5 potto **6** mammal
kinky: odd **6** far-out **7** bizarre, strange **10** outlandish
kinship: 5 blood, nasab **8** nearness **9** cognation **10** connection **11** propinquity **13** consanguinity
father's side: **8** agnation
mother's side: **7** enation
kinsman: 4 ally **6** friend **8** bandhava, relative **9** rishtadar
kiosk: 5 booth **8** pavilion **9** newsstand
kip: 4 hide, pelt, skin **5** sleep
Kipling: *poem:* **6** L'Envoi
story: Kim
Kiribati: *capital:* **6** Tarawa
currency: **6** dollar
people: **11** Micronesian
kirtle: 4 coat, gown **5** dress, skirt, tunic **7** garment **9** petticoat

Kish: *father:* Ner
son: **4** Saul
kismet: 4 fate **7** destiny
kiss: 4 bass, buss, peck **5** smack **6** caress, salute, smooch **8** osculate
kiss-me-quick: 6 bonnet
kiss of peace: pax
Kiss sculptor: 5 Rodin
kist: box **4** cist **5** chest **6** locker
kit: bag, box, lot, set **4** gear **6** outfit **9** container **10** collection
and caboodle: all **10** everything
kitchen: ben (Sc.) **4** chil (Ind.) **5** calan (P.I.) **6** chilla (Ind.) **7** cuisine **8** scullery
pert. to: **8** culinary
ship's: **6** galley
tool or utensil: **5** corer, mixer, ricer **6** beater, grater, opener, sifter **7** spatula **8** colander, strainer
kite: 4 bird, hawk, sail, soar **5** check, fraud **6** decamp
kith: 5 group **6** friend **7** kindred **10** associates **12** acquaintance
kittenish: coy **6** frisky **7** playful **8** childish
kittiwake: 4 gull **5** annet
kitty: cat **4** bowl, pool **6** stakes
kiwi: 5 fruit **7** Apteryx **14** flightless bird
kleptomaniac: 5 thief **7** filcher **8** pilferer **10** shoplifter
kloof: 4 glen **5** gorge **6** ravine, valley
klutz: oaf **4** lout **6** lummox **9** schlemiel
knack: art **4** ease, gift, hang **5** catch, skill, trick **8** facility **9** dexterity **10** adroitness
knap: cut, rap, top **4** bite, blow, chip, crop, hill, snap **5** break, crest, knock, knoll **6** nibble, strike, summit **7** hillock, hilltop
knapsack: bag **4** case, pack
knarred: 6 knotty **7** gnarled
knave: boy, nob, pam **4** fool, jack **5** cheat, churl, losel, rogue, scamp **6** harlot, rascal, varlet **7** villain **9** miscreant, scoundrel, trickster
knavery: 5 fraud **8** mischief, villainy **10** dishonesty **12** sportiveness
knead: elt (Sc.), mix **5** malax **7** massage **8** malaxate **9** masticate **10** manipulate **11** incorporate
knee: bow **5** joint **10** supplicate
armor: **11** genouillere
bend: **5** kneel **6** curtsy **9** genuflect
kneecap: 7 patella
knee-jerk: 9 automatic **11** predictable
kneeling desk: 8 prie-dieu
knell: 4 bell, omen, ring, toll **6** stroke, summon **7** warning **8** proclaim
knickers: 7 panties **8** bloomers **9** plus fours **12** knee breeches, small clothes
knickknack: toy **6** bauble, bawble, gadget, gewgaw, trifle **7** novelty, trinket **8** gimcrack, kickshaw

knife: cut **4** bolo, dirk, draw, kris, shiv, snee, stab **5** bowie, bread, gully, scout, slash, sword **6** barong, boning, colter, coutel, dagger, paring, pocket, sickle, worker **7** carving, fishing, hunting, machete, spatula, whittle **8** linoleum, stiletto, yataghan **11** cutting tool, switchblade
artist's: **7** palette
case: **6** sheath
extension: **4** tang
maker: **6** cutler
one-bladed: **6** barlow
plaster and paint: **5** putty **7** filling, spatula
sharpener: **4** hone **5** steel, stone
surgical: **6** catlin **7** catling, scalpel

knight: dub, sir **5** eques **6** equite, Ritter **7** esquire, gallant, paladin, templar **8** banneret, cavalier, champion, horseman **9** caballero, chevalier
attendant: **6** squire
banner: **8** gonfanon
cloak: **6** tabard
famous: **6** Bayard **7** Caradoc, Cradock, Galahad **9** Lohengrin
fight: **5** joust
horse: **7** charger, palfrey
rank above: **7** baronet
servant: **4** page **6** varlet
title: sir
wife: **4** lady
wreath: **4** orle

knight-errant: **7** paladin
knighthood: **8** chivalry
confer: dub
knightly: **5** brave **7** courtly, gallant **9** courteous **10** chivalrous
knight of the road: **4** hobo **5** tramp **8** vagabond
knit: **4** bind, heal, join, mend, purl **5** plait, unite, woven **6** cement, fasten **7** conjoin, connect, crochet, wrinkle **8** contract, entangle **10** intertwine **11** compaginate, consolidate
knitted blanket: **6** afghan
knitter: **6** legger
knitting: **5** craft **9** handiwork
rod: **6** needle
term: **4** purl **7** castoff
knob: bob, bur, nub **4** boss, buhr, burr, club, heel, lump, node, tore, umbo **5** bulge **6** button, croche, emboss, handle, pommel **12** protuberance
pointed: **6** finial
knobby: **5** gouty, hilly **6** knotty
knobkerrie: **4** club **5** stick
knobstick: **4** cane, club **5** stick **8** blackleg
knock: hit, rap, tap **4** beat, blow, bolt, bump, chop, dash, jolt, rout, slay **5** abuse, pound, thump **6** bounce **7** hillock (Sc.) **8** belittle **9**

criticize **12** fault-finding
down: **4** fell **5** floor **9** prostrate
off: rob **4** copy, kill, stop **6** deduct **8** overcome **11** assassinate, discontinue
out: **4** daze, stun **6** defeat **7** exhaust **8** paralyze
knockabout: **5** actor, sloop, yacht
knock-kneed: **6** valgus
knockout: **4** kayo **5** facer **6** eyeful, looker **7** stunner
blow: **8** haymaker
knoll: **4** knap, knob, lump **5** mound **7** hillock
knop: **5** knosp **6** button **8** ornament
knot: bow, nep, tie **4** bond, burl, burr, harl, knag, knar, knob, knur, loop, lump, node, snag **5** gnarl, hitch, knurl, nodus, snarl **6** finial, granny, nodule, puzzle, splice, square, tangle **7** angler's, bowline, chignon, cockade, laniard, lanyard, rosette **8** cow hitch, entangle **9** lark's head **11** monkey's fist **12** entanglement, protuberance
joining: **9** sheet bend **11** carrick bend **13** weaver's, barrel
lifting: **7** cat's paw **11** timber hitch
pert. to: **5** nodal
running: **4** slip **5** noose
knotted: **5** noded **7** crabbed, nodated **9** intricate
knotted lace: **7** tatting
knotty: **4** hard **5** bumpy, gouty **6** craggy **7** complex, gnarled **9** difficult, intricate **10** perplexing
knout: **4** flog, lash, whip
know: can, con, ken (Sc.) **6** fathom, intuit **7** discern, realize **8** perceive **9** recognize **10** comprehend, experience, understand
know-how: **5** knack, skill **7** ability **9** expertise
knowing: **4** able, gash, wise **5** cagey, downy, leery, smart, witty **6** scient, shrewd **7** gnostic, sapient, stylish **8** informed **9** cognitive, conscious, gnostical, wide-awake **10** experience, perceptive **11** intelligent **13** comprehension
know-it-all: **6** smarty **8** wiseacre
knowledge: ken **4** lore **5** wisdom **7** cunning, hearing, science **8** learning, sapience **9** cognition, erudition **10** cognizance, experience **11** information, instruction **12** acquaintance **13** enlightenment, understanding
instrument: **7** organon
lack of: **9** ignorance, nescience
object of: **7** cognita (pl.), scibile **8** cognitum
pert. to: **7** gnostic
seeker: **9** philonist
slight: **7** inkling, smatter **8** sciolism **10** smattering
summary: **13** encyclopedia
systematized: **7** science
universal: **9** pantology

known: **5** couth, famed, noted **6** common, famous **7** notable **8** familiar, renowned **9** notorious

know-nothing: **8** agnostic **9** ignoramus **11** scissorbill

knuckle: **5** joint
 head: **5** dunce **9** numbskull
 under: bow **4** cave **5** defer, yield **6** submit **7** succumb **10** capitulate

kobird: **6** cuckoo

kobold: nis **5** gnome **6** goblin **7** Hodeken (G.) **10** nissespire

koel: **4** bird **6** cuckoo

kohl: **4** soot **5** horse **8** antimony, cosmetic

kohlrabi: **6** turnip **7** mustard

kokoon: gnu

kokopu: **4** fish, para **5** trout **10** galaxiidae

kola: nut **4** cola, guru **5** goora **6** jackal

kooky: **5** crazy, weird **6** far out, insane **7** offbeat **9** fantastic

kopecks (100): **5** ruble

kopje: **4** hill **5** mound **7** hillock

Koran: **8** holy book **9** scripture
 division: **4** Sura
 interpreter: **5** ulema **7** alfaqui **8** alfaquin
 register: **5** sijil **6** sijill
 religion: **5** Islam

kosher: fit **4** pure **5** clean **6** proper **8** Kashruth **9** undefiled
 meat maker: **6** porger
 opposite of: **4** tref

kowtow: **4** fawn **5** cower, toady **6** cringe, grovel **8** butter up **11** apple polish

kra: ape **7** macaque

kraal: pen **5** crawl **6** corral **9** enclosure

krimmer: fur **4** skin **8** lambskin

Krishna: **6** Vishnu **10** Juggernaut
 grandson: **9** Aniruddha
 mother: **6** Devaki
 paradise: **6** Goloka

kudos: **4** fame **5** award, glory, honor **6** praise, renown **7** laurels **8** accolade, prestige **9** extolling

kudu: **8** antelope

kulak: **6** farmer **7** peasant

kumiss: **4** milk **5** drink **8** beverage

kumquat: **5** fruit **6** citrus
 family: rue
 relative: **6** orange **8** mandarin

kung fu: **10** martial art **14** Chinese defense
 kin of: **6** karate

Kurile island: **6** Iturup

Kurland Peninsula inhabitant: **4** Lett

kurrajong: **4** tree **5** shrub **6** calool

kurtosis: arc **9** curvature

Kuwait: *capital:* **8** Al Kuwait
 city: **5** Magwa **7** Hawalli **8** Al Bahrah
 currency: **4** fils **5** dinar

kvetch (Yid.): **5** gripe, whine **8** complain

kyphosis: **8** humpback **9** curvature, hunchback

Kyrgyzstan: *capital:* **6** Frunze **7** Bishkek
 city: Chu, Osh **5** Naryn, Talas
 currency: **5** ruble
 former name: **7** Kirghiz

L

L: 5 fifty

laagte: 6 bottom, valley

La Boheme: *composer:* 7 Puccini
heroine: 4 Mimi

Laban's daughter: 4 Leah 6 Rachel

label: tab, tag 4 band, call, mark 5 brand 6 docket, lappet, tassel 7 epithet 8 classify 9 designate, dripstone 10 definition 11 appellation

labellum: lip 5 petal

labile: 8 shifting, unstable 9 adaptable 10 changeable

labium: lip

labor: 4 moil, task, toil, work 5 sweat, yakka 6 effort, labour, stress, strive 7 travail 8 business, drudgery, exertion, industry, struggle 11 lucubration, parturition

labor organization: AFL, CIO, UAW, UMW 5 ILGWU, union 6 AFSCME

labored: 5 heavy 6 forced 8 strained 9 difficult, elaborate

laborer: man 4 hand, hind, peon, prol 5 cooly, plebe 6 coolie, toiler, worker 7 bracero, dvornik, hobbler, wetback, workman 10 bluecollar

laborious: 4 hard 5 heavy 6 uphill 7 arduous, operose, tedious 8 diligent 9 assiduous, difficult 11 displeasing, hardworking, painstaking

Labrador retriever: dog 12 Newfoundland

Labrador tea: 5 heath, ledum 8 gowiddie 9 evergreen

labyrinth: web 4 knot, maze, mesh 6 jungle, morass, tangle 8 inner ear
builder: 8 Daedalus
monster: 8 Minotaur

labyrinthine: 7 complex 8 involved, puzzling, tortuous 9 intricate 10 perplexing 11 complicated

lac: 4 milk 5 resin 6 veneer 10 sealing wax

lace: gin, net, tat 4 band, beat, cord, lash, line 5 braid, lairs, noose, plait, snare, twine, unite 6 fasten, ribbon, string 7 ensnare, entwine, laniard, lanyard 8 biliment, openwork 9 embroider, interlace 10 embroidery, intertwine, shoestring
barred: 6 grille
edge: 5 picot
frilled: 5 jabot, ruche
front: 5 jabot
into: 5 abuse 6 attack 7 condemn
kind: 5 lisle, orris, tulle 7 alencon, allover, guipure, macrame, potlace 9 Alostlace 10 colberteen, colbertine 12 Valenciennes
knotted: 7 tatting
loop in: 5 picot
make: tat 7 crochet
opening: 6 eyelet

lacerate: cut, rip 4 bite, rend, rive, tear 6 harrow, mangle 8 distress

laceration: rip 4 tear 5 wound

lachrymose: sad 5 teary, weepy 7 tearful

lack: 4 need, void, want 5 fault, minus 6 dearth, in need 7 absence, failure, paucity, poverty 8 scarcity, shortage 9 indigence 10 deficiency 11 destitution

lackadaisical: 4 blah 7 languid 8 listless 10 spiritless 11 sentimental

lackaday: 4 alas

lackey: 5 toady, valet 6 flunky, menial 7 footman, servant

lacking: shy 5 short 6 absent, barren 7 wanting 8 desolate 9 deficient, destitute

lackluster: 4 dull 6 cloudy 8 dullness

Laconia: *capital:* 6 Sparta
people: Obe

laconic: 5 brief, pithy, short, terse 7 concise, pointed, summary, 8 succinct, taciturn

lacquer: 5 gloss, 7 shellac, varnish

lactate: 4 salt 5 actol, ester

lacteal: 5 milky

lacuna: gap 4 hole 5 break 7 opening 8 interval 10 depression

lacy: 7 weblike 8 delicate

lad: boy, tad 4 carl, dick, hind 5 caddy, youth 6 caddie, shaver 9 stripling 10 adolescent
on call: 4 page 7 bellboy 9 messenger
serving: 7 gossoon 8 coistrel, coistril

ladder: run, sty 4 stee 5 scale, steps 6 series 7 scalade
on fortification: 8 escalade
step between shrouds: 7 ratline

ladderlike: 6 scalar

lade: dip 4 bail, draw, lave, load, ship 5 drain, scoop 6 burden, charge, weight 7 fraught, freight

ladies' man: 4 beau 5 dandy 7 Don Juan 8 Casanova 11 philanderer

lading: 4 load 5 cargo 6 burden 7 freight 10 freightage

ladle: dip **4** bail **5** scoop, serve, spoon **6** dipper

ladrone: 5 thief **6** bandit, robber **7** brigand **9**
mercenary **10** highwayman

Ladrone island: 4 Guam **6** Saipan **7** Wan-
Shan **8** Marianas

lady (see also **woman**): **4** burd, dame, dona
(Sp.), rani (Ind.) **5** begum (Ind.), donna (It.),
madam, ranee (Ind.) **6** domina (L.), female,
senora (Sp.) **7** signora (It.) **11** gentlewoman
noble: **5** queen **7** duchess **8** countess,
princess
young: **7** damozel **10** demoiselle, jeune
fille (F.)

ladybird: bug **6** beetle **10** coleoptera
genus: **9** epilachna

ladyfish: oio **6** tarpon, wrasse

lady-killer: 4 wolf **5** sheik **7** Don Juan **8**
Casanova

ladylike: 6 dainty, demure, female, polite **7**
genteel **8** charming, feminine, mannerly **9**
courteous

ladylove: 4 wife **5** amour, lover **8** mistress **10**
sweetheart

Lady of the Lake: 5 Ellen, Nimue **6** Vivian,
Vivien
author: **5** Scott

lady's slipper: 6 orchid **14** moccasin flower

lady's thumb: 5 plant **9** peachwort, persicary

Laertes: *father:* **8** Acrisius, Polonius
sister: **7** Ophelia
son: **7** Ulysses **8** Odysseus
wife: **8** Anticlea

lag: 4 flag, rift, tire **5** delay, stave, tarry, trail,
weary **6** dawdle, linger, loiter, retard **8** fall
back **9** drawlatch **10** dillydally

lagan: See **ligan**

lager: ale **4** beer, brew **5** drink **8** beverage

laggard: 4 slow **6** remiss **8** backward, loiterer,
sluggish **9** straggler **10** slow person

lagging: 5 tardy **8** backward

lagniappe: tip **4** gift **5** bonus, pilon **7** present
8 gratuity

lagomorph: 4 hare, pika **5** coney **6** rabbit

lagoon: 4 cove, haff, pond, pool **5** liman **6**
laguna (Sp.)

Lagoon Islands: 6 Ellice

laic: 6 layman **7** secular **15** nonprofessional

laid-down: 5 posed **6** thetic **8** academic **10**
prescribed **11** traditional

lair: den, lie, mud (Br.) **4** cave, holt, mire
(Br.), nest **5** haunt **6** cavern **7** hideout,
retreat, showoff (Austrl.) **8** learning (Sc.),
quagmire

Lais: 7 Burmese

laissez-faire: 8 inactive, tolerant **9** donothing,
unconcern **11** philosophic **12** indifference,
mercantilism **15** individualistic, noninter-
ference

laity: 6 laymen

Laius' son: 7 Oedipus

lake: dye **4** loch, mere, pond, pool, shat, shot,
tarn **5** bayou, chott, color, lough, shott **6**
lagoon **7** pigment
deposit: **5** trona
highest: **8** Titicaca
Indian: **4** Erie
marshy: **5** liman

Lake State: 8 Michigan

lam: hit **4** bash, beat, flee, flog **6** escape,
thrash **7** getaway

Lamaism: *dignitary:* **8** hutukhtu
priest: **6** Getsul
stupa: **7** Chorten

lamasery: 9 monastery

lamb: ean **4** yean **5** agnus (L.) **6** agneau (F.),
cosset **7** chilver, fatling, hogling
hand-raised: hob
leg of: **5** gigot
pert. to: **5** ovine
pet: **4** cade **6** cosset

lambaste: 4 drub, flay **5** paste, poynd **6** thrash
7 clobber **8** lash into **10** tonguelash

Lamb of God: 8 Agnus Dei

Lamb's penname: 4 Elia

lambskin: 4 case **5** suede **6** bagdad **7** baghdad

lambent: 6 bright, lucent **7** glowing, radiant **8**
luminous, wavering **9** brilliant **10** flickering

lame: 4 game, halt **5** gammy **6** feeble **7** halting
8 crippled, decrepit, disabled **9** defective,
hamstring **11** handicapped **12** incapacitate

Lamech: *father:* **10** Methuselah
son: **4** Noah **5** Jabal, Jubal **9** Tubalcain
wife: **4** Adah **6** Zillah

lament: cry, rue **4** care, howl, keen, moan,
pine, sigh, wail, weep **5** croon, dirge, dolor,
elegy, greet, grief, mourn **6** bemoan,
bewail, beweep, dolour, grieve, lament,
ochone, outcry, plaint, regret, repent,
repine, yammer **7** condole, deplore, ele-
gize, wailing **8** jeremiad, mourn for, mourning **9** complaint

lamentable: sad **6** tragic, woeful **8** grievous,
pitiable, wretched **10** deplorable **11** distressing, unfortunate

lamia: hag, hex **5** witch **7** vampire **9** sorceress

lamina: 5 blade, flake, hinge, layer

laminated: 5 flaky **6** scaled **7** fissile, spathic,
tabular **8** foliated, lamellar

lamp: arc, eye, orb **4** davy, etna **5** Betty, light
7 lantern **8** kerosene, lanthorn **9** veilleuse
11 Argand torch
hanging: **10** chandelier
safety: **4** davy

lampblack: 4 soot

lamplighter: 5 match, spill, torch

lampoon: 5 squib **6** satire **8** ridicule, satirize
10 caricature, pasquinade

lamprey: eel **6** ramper
  migration: **7** eelfare
lanai: 5 patio, porch **7** terrace, veranda
lanate: 5 hairy, wooly **6** woolly
Lancashire section: 6 Eccles
lance: cut **4** dart, hurl **5** joust, spear **6** faucre,
  lancet, launch, pierce, weapon **7** javelin
  head: **5** morne
Lancelot: *lover:* **6** Elaine **9** Guinevere
  son: **7** Galahad
  victim: **6** Gawain
lancer: 4 ulan **5** uhlan **7** soldier, spearer **10**
  cavalryman
lancet: 5 fleam, knife
lancinate: 4 stab, tear **5** gouge **6** pierce **8** lacerate
land: erd **4** ager (L.), soil **5** catch, earth, end
  up, glebe, realm, shore, terra (L.) **6** alight,
  arrive, debark, estate, ground **7** acreage,
  capture, country, terrene **9** disembark, territory
  alluvial: **5** delta
  ancestral: **5** ethel
  arid: See **desert**
  barren: See **wasteland**
  body: **6** island **9** continent
  church: **5** glebe **8** abadengo
  cultivated: **4** farm **5** arada, arado, ranch,
  tilth **7** orchard, tillage
  dealer: **7** realtor
  depressed: **6** graben
  elevated: alp **4** hill, mesa **5** mound, ridge **7**
  plateau **8** mountain
  grazing: lea **5** field, plain, range **6** meadow
  7 pasture
  heritable: **4** alod, fief, odal **5** allod **7**
  alodium **8** allodium
  hilly: **4** down
  householder's: **6** barton, casate **7** demesne
  in foreign territory: **7** enclave
  living on: **11** terrestrial
  low: **4** vale **5** carse (Sc.) **6** polder, valley **9**
  intervale
  measure: are, rod **4** acre, mile, rood **5**
  meter, perch **6** decare **7** hectare
  mythical: **4** Eden **6** Utopia **7** Erewhon,
  Lemuria **9** Shangri-La
  narrow: **4** neck **6** strake **7** isthmus **9** peninsula
  open: **4** moor, vega, wold **5** field, heath,
  slash, weald
  pasture: ham, lea **5** grass **6** meadow
  pert. to: **11** continental
  piece: lot **4** acre, farm, plot **5** laine, ranch,
  range, solum (law), spong **6** estate, parcel
  plowed: **5** arada, arado, field **6** arable, fallow, furrow **7** thwaite
  point of: **4** cape, ness, spit
  profit: **4** crop, rent **7** esplees

  public: **4** parc, park
  reclaimed: **6** polder **7** novalia (Sc.)
  river drained: **5** basin
  sandy: **4** dene
  treeless: **5** llano **6** steppe, tundra **7** prairie,
  savanna **8** savannah
  triangular: **4** gore
  uncultivated: **5** heath, waste **6** desert, forest
  uplifted: **5** horst
  waterlocked: ile (F.) **4** isle **6** island
  watery: bog **4** flow, moor **5** marsh, swamp
  6 morass **7** maremma (It.)
landed: See **estate, land**
landholder: 5 laird **6** coscet, yeoman
landholding: 6 tenure
landing: 7 arrival **9** touch down
  kind: **5** crash **10** three-point
  place: **4** dock, pier **5** wharf **6** runway, stairs,
  tarmac **7** airport
landlady: 5 duena, owner **7** hostess **8** mistress
  9 concierge
landlord: 4 host **5** laird (Sc.), owner **6** lessor
landmark: 8 monument **9** milestone **10** guide
  point **11** classic case
Land of Cakes: 8 Scotland
Land of Nod: 5 sleep
Land of Plenty: 6 Goshen
Land of Promise: 6 Canaan **9** Palestine
Land of Rising Sun: 5 Japan
Land of the Midnight Sun: 6 Alaska, Norway **7** Lapland
landscape: 4 plan **5** plant, scene **7** paysage,
  picture, scenery **8** decorate, painting
land's end guardian: 8 Bellerus
landslide: 9 avalanche **10** eboulement
  debris: **5** scree, talus
landsman: 6 lubber, sailor **10** compatriot
lane: way **4** char, path, race **5** aisle, alley,
  byway, chare, tewer **6** boreen, bypath, gullet, street, throat, vennel **7** pathway **8** footpath **10** passageway
language: 4 chib **5** argot, idiom, lingo, slang **6**
  jargon, speech, tongue **7** dialect, diction **10**
  vernacular, vocabulary
  ancient: **4** Pali **5** Aryan, Greek, Latin **6**
  Hebrew **7** Chinese **8** Sanskrit **12** Indo-
  European
  artificial: **9** Esperanto
  change: **8** misquote **9** interpret, translate
  10 paraphrase
  classical: **5** Greek, Latin
  common: **6** Arabic, French, German **7** Chinese, English, Italian, Russian, Spanish
  Cretan: **6** Minoan
  expert: **8** linguist, polyglot
  figurative: **7** imagery
  international: od, ro, ido **7** Volapuk **9**
  Esperanto

meaningless: **9** gibberish
nonmetrical: **5** prose
pert. to: **8** semantic
pompous: **4** bull, wind **6** hot air **7** bombast, oratory **8** rhetoric
principles: **7** grammar
Romance: **5** Latin **6** French **7** Catalan, Italian, Spanish **8** Rumanian **10** Portuguese
sacred: **4** Pali
secret: **4** cant, code **5** argot
Semitic: **6** Arabic, Hebrew
spoken: **7** diction **13** pronunciation

languid: **4** dull, slow, weak **6** dreamy, sleepy, tender, torpid **8** drooping, indolent, listless, love-sick, sluggish **9** enervated, lethargic **11** indifferent

languish: die **4** fade, fail, flag, long, pine, wilt **5** droop, dwine, faint, swoon **6** linger, repine **7** decline **12** fail in health

languor: kef **4** kaif, keef, kief **5** ennui **7** boredom **8** debility **9** lassitude **10** stagnation

langur: **6** monkey **8** wanderoo

lanky: **4** lean, slim, tall, thin **5** gaunt, rangy, spare **6** gangly, meager, meagre, skinny **7** haggard, slender **8** gangling, ungainly **9** elongated **12** loose-jointed

lantern: **4** lamp **5** bouet

lanyard, laniard: **4** cord, knot, line, rope

Laocoon: **12** Trojan priest
killer: **7** serpent

Laodamia's father: **7** Acastus

Laodicean: **8** lukewarm **9** apathetic **10** uninvolved **11** indifferent

Laomedon: *father:* **4** Ilus
kingdom: **4** Troy
mother: **8** Eurydice
slayer: **8** Hercules
son: **5** Priam

Laos: *capital:* **9** Vientiane
city: **5** Pakxe **7** Ban Nape
Communist group: **9** Pathet Lao
currency: at, kip
Plain: **6** of Jars
river: **6** Kading, Mekong, Sabang
supply line: **14** Ho Chi Minh Trail

lap: sip **4** fold, lick, wash **5** bathe, drink, slurp **6** circle, cuddle, enfold, infold **7** circuit

lapactic: **8** laxative **9** cathartic

lapel: **5** rever **6** revers

lapidary: **7** jeweler **8** engraver **9** gem cutter
instrument: dop **4** dial

lapidate: **4** pelt **5** stone

lapin: **6** rabbit

Lapland: *animal:* **8** reindeer
city or town: **4** Kola **6** Kiruna
sled: **4** pulk **5** pulka

lappet: **4** flap, fold, lobe, moth **5** lapel **6** fabric, revers

lap robe: rug **5** throw **6** afghan **7** blanket

lapse: err **5** break, error, fault **6** expire **7** delapse, escheat, failure, relapse **8** caducity, slipping **9** backslide

lapsed: **4** dead, null, void

laputan: **6** absurd, dreamy **7** utopian **9** visionary **10** unfeasible **11** impractical

lapwing: **5** pewit **6** peewit, plover

Lar: god **6** gibbon, spirit

larboard: **4** left, port

larceny: **5** theft **7** looting, robbery **8** burglary, stealage, stealing
kind: **5** grand, petty

lard: fat, oil **4** mort **5** add to, adeps (L.), baste, enarm, inarm **6** enrich, fatten, grease, shmalz **7** garnish **8** schmaltz **9** embellish

larder: **4** cave **6** pantry, spence, spense **8** cupboard

large: big **4** bold, free, huge, main, vast, waly **5** ample, broad, bulky, burly, enorm, giant, great, hulky, massy, wally **6** goodly, heroic **7** copious, immense, liberal, massive, pompous, titanic, weighty **8** colossal, enormous, generous, gigantic **9** capacious, extensive, plentiful **11** exaggerated, far-reaching **12** considerable **13** comprehensive

largess, largesse: **4** gift **6** bounty **7** charity, present **10** generosity, liberality **11** beneficence

lariat: **5** noose, reata (Sp.), riata (Sp.) **10** rope,lasso
loop: **5** honda, hondo **6** hondoo, hondou

lark: **4** bird, dido **5** pipit, spree **6** frolic **8** carousal **9** make merry **10** meadowlark

larkspur: **8** crowfoot **10** delphinium

larrigan: **8** moccasin

larrup: **4** beat, blow, flog, whip

larry: hoe **5** grout, noise **6** mortar **7** mine car **9** confusion **10** excitement

larva: **4** bot, fly, loa **4** bott, grub, worm **5** eruca **6** botfly, woubit **7** atrocha, oestrid **8** cercaria, horsefly **11** caterpillar
aquatic: **7** tadpole **8** polliwog **12** hellgrammite
beetle: **4** grub

larvate: **6** masked **7** covered **9** concealed

lascar: **6** sailor **12** artilleryman

lascivious: **6** wanton **7** blissom **9** lecherous, salacious, seductive **10** libidinous, licentious

lash: **4** beat, bind, blow, flog, lace, whip, yerk **5** slash **6** berate, fasten, strike, stroke, swinge **7** belabor, eyelash, scourge

lasket: **8** latching

lass: gal **4** gill, girl, maid, miss **5** trull, woman **6** cummer, kimmer, lassie, maiden **7** colleen **10** sweetheart **11** maidservant

lassitude: **5** ennui **7** languor **8** debility, lethargy **10** exhaustion

lasso

lasso: See **lariat**

last: **4** dure, tail **5** abide, final, omega **6** endure, latest, newest, utmost **7** dernier, extreme, tail-end **8** at the end, continue, eventual, hindmost, rearmost, ultimate **9** aftermost **10** concluding, most recent
but one: **6** penult **11** penultimate
long: **7** outwear **9** perendure
word: **8** up-to-date **10** dernier cri (F.)

Last of the Mohicans: **5** Uncas
author: **6** Cooper

Last Supper: *painter:* **7** da Vinci
representation: **4** cena
room: **7** cenacle

lasting: **6** eterne, stable **7** chronic, eternal **8** constant, enduring **9** perennial, permanent, steadfast **11** everlasting
briefly: **9** ephemeral, temporary

latch: **5** catch, sneck **6** fasten **8** fastener

latchet: tab **4** lace **5** thong

late: new **4** dead, sere **5** tardy **6** former, recent **7** belated, overdue **8** neoteric, serotine **10** behindhand

latent: **6** hidden **7** dormant **9** concealed, potential, quiescent, suspended **11** undeveloped

later: **4** anon, soon **5** after, newer **6** behind, future, puisne **7** elderly, neozoic **9** hereafter, posterior, presently **10** subsequent **12** subsequently

lateral: **4** pass, side **8** indirect, sideward, sideways

latest: **4** last **6** newest

latex: **5** juice **6** rubber **9** secretion

lath: **4** slat **5** spale, stave, stick **8** forepole
attachment: **7** setover
operator: **6** turner
part: **7** mandrel

lather: **4** flog, foam, soap, suds **5** froth **6** bustle, freath **10** foamy sweat

Latin: **5** Roman **7** Italian, Romanic
always: **6** semper
barracks: **6** canaba
bath, bathhouse: **7** balneum
booth: **7** taberna
bowl: **6** patina
boxing glove: **6** ceston, cestus
boy: **4** puer
breath: **7** halitus
bronze: aes
building: **5** aedes
cape: **5** sagum **6** byrrus
cistern: **9** impluvium
connective: et
contract: **5** nexum
couch: **9** accubitum
deity: dea **4** deus
dish: **4** lanx **6** lances, patina **7** pateral
food: **5** cibus
foot: pes

force: vis
for example: **4** vide
friend: **6** amicus
garland: **6** corona
ghosts: **7** lemures
grammar: **5** donat, donet
grammatical case: **6** dative **8** ablative, genitive, vocative **10** accusative, nominative
hope: **4** spes
hour: **4** hora
javelin: **4** pile **5** aclys, pilum
life: **4** vita
ornament: **5** bulla
post: **4** meta
pronoun: tu, ego, hic **4** ille, ipse, iste
ram: **5** aries
rite: **4** orgy **5** sacra
roof opening: **10** compluvium
seat: **5** sella
shelter: **7** taberna
towel: **5** mappa
trumpet: **4** tuba **6** buccin **7** buccina

Latin America: See **Central America, South America**

Latinus's daughter: **7** Lavinia

latite: **4** lava

latitude: **4** room **5** scope, width **6** extent, leeway, margin **7** breadth, freedom **8** distance **9** elbowroom
complement: **10** colatitude
measure: **6** degree **8** parallel
zero degrees: **7** equator

latke: **7** pancake **11** griddle cake

latrant: **7** barking **8** snarling **11** complaining

latrine: **5** privy **6** toilet

latter: **4** last **5** final **6** latest **10** more recent

Latter Day Saints: **7** Mormons

latterly: **4** anew **6** lately **8** recently

lattice: **4** door, gate **6** pinjra (Ind.) **7** trellis **8** espalier

latticework: **5** arbor, grate **6** arbour **7** grating, tracery

Latvia: *capital:* **4** Riga
city: **5** Libau **6** Dvinsk, Libava **8** Dunaburg **10** Daugavpils
currency: lat **6** rublis **7** kapeika **8** santimas
measure: **4** stof **5** kanne, stoff, verst **6** kulmet, sagene, vechoc, versta, verste **7** verchok **8** krouchka, kroushka, pourvete **9** deciatine, lofstelle **10** tonnstelle
people: **4** Lett
river: **4** Ogre **5** Dvina, Gauga **6** Salaca
weight: **9** liespfund

laud: 4 lute 5 extol 6 extoll, praise 7 adulate, applaud, cittern, commend, glorify, magnify 8 emblazon, eulogize 9 panegyric 10 compliment

laudable: 9 allowable, exemplary 11 commendable 12 praiseworthy

laugh: 4 gaff, haha 5 fleer, snort 6 cackle, giggle, guffaw, hawhaw, nicker, titter 7 chortle, grizzle, snicker 9 cachinate
disposed to: 7 risible
incipient: 4 grin 5 smile
pert. to: 8 gelastic

laughable: odd 5 comic, droll, funny, merry, queer, witty 7 amusing, comical, risible, strange, waggish 8 gelastic, humorous, sportive 9 burlesque, diverting, facetious, grotesque, ludicrous 10 ridiculous

laughing: 5 riant

laughing bird: 4 gull, loon 5 pewit 10 kookaburra, woodpecker

laughing owl: 5 wekau

laughing stock: 4 butt, jest, joke 5 sport 7 mockery 8 derision, ridicule

laughter: 5 mirth, risus (L.) 8 hilarity
pert. to: 7 risible

launch: 4 open, toss 5 begin, fling, leave, set up, start, throw 6 get off 7 propose 9 motorboat 10 inaugurate

launder: tye 4 wash

laundry: 4 wash 10 laundromat 13 blanchisserie (F.)

laureate: 13 distinguished

laurel: bay 4 fame 5 honor 6 daphne, myrtle, tarata, trophy 7 cajuput, garland, taratah 9 spoonwood 11 distinction

ava: 4 slag 5 ashes 6 coulee, latite, scoria, verite 7 clinker 8 pahoehoe
fragment of: 8 lapillus
sheet of: 6 coulee

lavabo: 5 basin 8 washbowl 9 cleansing 11 wall planter

lavaliere, lavalier: 7 pendant 8 necklace

lavation: 4 bath 6 lavage 7 washing 9 cleansing

lavatory: 5 basin 6 toilet 8 washbowl, washroom

lave: 4 bail, lade, pour, soak, wash 5 bathe, rinse

lavender: 5 lilac 6 pastel, purple, violet

laver: 5 basin 6 trough, vessel 7 cistern, seaweed

Lavinia: *father:* 7 Latinus
husband: 6 Aeneas
mother: 5 Amata

lavish: 4 free, lash, rank, wild 5 flush, spend, waste 7 opulent, profuse 8 prodigal, reckless, splendid, squander 9 bountiful, expensive, exuberant, impetuous, luxuriant, sumptuous, unstinted 10 immoderate 11 extravagant, magnificent 12 unrestrained 13 superabundant

law: act, bar, ius (L.), jus (L.), lex (L.) 4 code, doom, rule, Tora 5 canon, edict, mesne, sutra, Torah 6 custom, decree, equity, noetic, sutrah, suttah 7 derecho, justice, precept, statute 8 handicap 9 enactment, ordinance, principle 10 regulation 11 commandment, legislation 12 constitution, jurisdiction 13 jurisprudence
action: res 4 suit 5 actus 8 replevin 9 gravamina
body of: 4 code 12 constitution
claim: 4 lien
contrary to: 7 illegal, illicit 8 criminal, unlawful 16 unconstitutional
decree: 4 nisi 5 edict
degree: JD, JCB, LLB, LLD
delay: 4 mora
document: 4 deed, writ 5 title 6 capias, elegit 7 warrant 8 contract, subpoena
expounder of: 6 jurist
goddess: 4 Maat
male succession: 5 Salic
offender: 5 felon 6 sinner 7 convict 8 criminal, gangster 9 desperado, wrongdoer
offense: 4 tort 5 crime, malum 6 delict
oral: 5 parol 11 nuncupative
order: 4 writ
permitted by: See **lawful**
person of: 5 judge 6 jurist, lawyer 7 counsel, justice 8 attorney 9 barrister
pert. to: 5 legal 7 canonic 9 canonical, judiciary 11 legislative
philosophy of: 13 jurisprudence
prevent by: 5 estop
violation of: sin 4 tort 5 crime, malum 6 felony
warning: 6 caveat

lawful: due 5 legal, licit, valid 7 canonic, ennomic 10 legitimate

lawgiver: 5 Moses, Solon 10 legislator

lawless: 4 lewd 6 unruly 7 illegal 8 anarchic 9 dissolute 10 anarchical, disorderly, tumultuous

lawlessness: 4 riot 5 chaos 6 mutiny, strife 7 anarchy, license 9 mobocracy 10 illegality

lawmaker: 5 solon 7 senator 10 legislator

lawn: lea 5 arbor, glade, grass, sward 6 arbour 7 batiste 9 grassland, grassplot, grasswork

lawsuit: 4 case 6 action 10 litigation
one engaged in: 8 litigant
subject: res

lawyer: 6 avocat (F.) 7 abogado (Sp.), counsel 8 attorney, commoner 9 barrister, counselor, solicitor 10 counsellor
bad: 7 shyster 11 pettifogger

lax: 4 dull, free, limp, open, pave, slow 5 loose, slack, tardy 6 remiss 7 lenient 8 backward, careless, inactive 9 dissolute, negligent 10 unconfined 11 inattentive 12 unrestrained

lay: bet, put, set 4 bury, cast, cite, hymn,

poem, rest, song **5** allay, carol, ditty, place, quiet, stake, still, wager **6** ballad, entomb, hazard, impose, impute, melody **7** appease, ascribe, deposit, secular, work out **8** suppress **9** knock down, short poem **14** unprofessional **15** nonprofessional

aside: **5** table **6** shelve **7** abandon, discard, neglect

away: See **lay by**

bare: **4** show **5** strip **6** denude, expose, reveal **7** uncover

by: **4** hive, save **5** amass, cache, hoard, store **7** deposit, husband, reposit **8** salt away, treasure **10** accumulate

down: set **5** posit **6** affirm, give up **9** establish, surrender

hold of: **4** grab, grip **5** grasp, gripe, seize **9** apprehend

out: **4** plan **5** set up, spend **6** design, expend, extend, invest, make-up **7** arrange **9** residence

up: See **lay by**

waste: **4** raze, ruin **6** harass, ravage **7** destroy **8** desolate **9** depredate, devastate

layer: bed, hen, ply **4** coat, film, fold, seam, tier, zona **5** paver **6** folium, lamina, patina, strata, veneer **7** bedding, provine, stratum **8** laminate **10** substratum

of coal: **4** seam

of stones: **4** dess

of wood: **4** core **6** veneer

pert. to: **7** stratal

layered: **7** laminal, laminar **8** tunicate

laymen: **4** laic **5** laity

lazar: **5** leper

lazy: **4** idle, laze **5** inert **6** otiose **8** indolent, slothful, sluggard

lea: **6** meadow **7** pasture **9** grassland

leach: wet **4** soak **7** draw out, moisten **9** lixiviate, percolate **11** bloodsucker

lead: con, van, wad **4** head, lode, star, wadd **5** carry, first, guide, krems, metal, pilot, steer, usher **6** bullet, ceruse, convey, deduce, direct, escort, induce, manage **7** command, conduct, pioneer, plumbum, precede **8** graphite, instruct, outstrip **9** influence **10** show the way

astray: **4** lure **6** allure, delude, entice, seduce **7** deceive, mislead, pervert **8** inveigle

color: **4** dull, gray **5** livid, olive

ore: **6** galena **9** anglesite, cerrusite

paste: **6** strass

pig: **6** fother

sounding: **7** plummet

sulfide: **6** galena

leaden: **4** dull, gray **5** heavy, inert **7** lanquid, stilted **8** plumbous, sluggish **9** colorless

leader: bo, boh, cob, dux **4** cock, duce, duke,

head, line, wire **5** chief, coach, pilot, sinew, snell **6** cantor, Fuhrer (G.), tendon **7** captain, demagog, foreman, Fuehrer (G.) **8** caudillo, choragus, headsman, preceder **9** chieftain, demagogue, drainpipe, principal **10** bellwether **11** condottiere, gymnasiarch

ecclesiastical: fra **4** abbe, pope **5** abbot, rabbi **6** abbess, bishop, father, pastor, priest **8** cardinal, minister, preacher **9** patriarch **10** evangelist

leadership: **8** guidance, hegemony **9** authority

leading: big **4** duct, head, main **5** ahead, chief, first **6** banner **7** capital, central, guiding, premier, stellar **8** foremost **9** conducive, directing, governing, hegemonic, inductive, principal **11** controlling

leaf: ola, ole, pan **4** foil, olay, olla, page **5** blade, bract, folio, frond, palet, scale, sepal, spine **6** areola, insert, spathe **7** tendril

angle with branch: **4** axil

aperture: **5** stoma

appendage: **6** ligula, stipel **7** stipule

aromatic: See **herb**

circle: **7** corolla

division: **4** lobe

edge: **9** crenation

fern: **5** frond

floating: pad

kind: **5** calxy, petal, sepal **7** corolla

part: pen **4** axil, vein **5** costa, stoma **6** pagina **7** petiole, stomate, tendril

secretion on: **4** lerp

set: **5** calyx **7** corolla

vein: rib **5** costa

leafage: **7** foliage, umbrage, verdure **8** greenery

leaflet: **5** pinna, tract **6** folder **7** booklet **8** pamphlet

leafy: **4** lush **5** green, shady **6** foliar **7** layered, sepaled

league: **4** bond **5** union **7** compact **8** alliance, covenant **9** coalition **10** federation **11** association, combination, confederacy **13** confederation

Leah: *father:* **5** Laban

husband: **5** Jacob

sister: **6** Rachel

son: **6** Simeon

leak: **4** drip, hole, loss, ooze, seep **5** crack **6** escape **7** channel, crevice, fissure

leaky: **6** porous

leal: **4** just, real, true **5** legal, loyal **6** lawful **7** correct, genuine **8** accurate, faithful

leam: **4** husk

lean: **4** bend, cant, lank, mean, poor, rely, slim, tend, thin, tilt **5** gaunt, lanky, scant, spare **6** depend, hollow, meager, meagre, skinny **7** conform, deviate, haggard, incline, recline, scrawny, slender **8** rawboned, scragged **9** deficient, emaciated **10** inadequate **12** unproductive

lean-to: hut **4** shed **5** shack

Leander's sweetheart: **4** Hera, Hero

leaning: **6** desire **7** pronate **8** aptitude, penchant, tendency **9** accumbent, prejudice **10** preference

leap: fly, hop **4** dart, dive, jump, loup, skip **5** bound, caper, exult, frisk, lunge, salto, vault **6** bounce, breach, cavort, curvet, gallop, gambol, hurdle, hurtle, spring **7** saltate **8** capriole **9** ballotade, entrechat

leap year: **10** bissextile

leaping: **7** jumping, salient, saltant **9** caprizant, saltation

lear: **4** lore **6** lesson **8** learning

Lear, King: *daughter:* **5** Regan **7** Goneril **8** Cordelia
dog: **4** Tray
dramatist: **11** Shakespeare
follower: **4** Kent

learn: con, get **4** find, here, lere **6** master, pick up **7** acquire, apprise, apprize, realize **8** memorize **9** ascertain

learned: wot **4** blue, read, sage, wise **6** astute, doctus **7** clerkly, cunning, erudite **8** lettered, literary, literose **9** scholarly **10** omniscient **12** well-informed

learner: **5** pupil **7** scholar, trainee **8** disciple, opsimath **10** apprentice

learning: art **4** lear, lore **6** wisdom **7** cunning **8** pedantry **9** education, erudition, knowledge **10** discipline, experience **11** information, scholarship
disability: **8** dyslexia **9** dysphasia
display of: **8** pedantry
love of: **9** philology
man of: **4** sage **6** pundit, savant **7** scholar, teacher **9** philomath, professor **12** intellectual

leary: See **leery**

lease: let **4** hire, rent **6** demise, engage, rental, tenure **7** charter **8** contract **10** concession

leash: **4** bind, cord, curb, harl, jess, lune **5** strap **6** couple, tether **7** control **8** restrain

least: **6** fewest, little, lowest **7** minimal, minimum **8** shortest, smallest **9** slightest

leather: tan **4** hide, napa, whip, yuft (Russ.) **5** balat, leder, strap **6** thrash
artificial: **7** keratol
drying: sam **4** samm **5** sammy
fine: kid **6** vellum
finish: **4** buff
inspector: **6** sealer
kind: elk, kid, kip **4** bock, buff, calf, doze, napa, roan, seal, vici **5** aluta, basil, glove, mocha, suede, trank **6** castor, levant, oxhide, skiver **7** belting, buffalo, canepin,

chamois, cowhide, morocco, saffian **8** buckskin, cheverel, cheveril, Cordovan
napped: **5** suede
pare: **5** skive
piece of: **4** rand, welt **5** clout, strap, thong **6** latigo
prepare: tan, taw **4** bate, cure, mull **5** curry, flesh, sammy
sheepskin: **4** roan **6** skiver
shiny: **6** patent
soft: **5** aluta, mocha, suede **8** cabretta
tool: **6** skiver
waste: **6** tanite
worker: **6** chamar, tanner **8** chuckler

leatherback: **6** turtle

leatherneck: **6** marine

leave: go, let **4** bunk, exit, quit **5** favor, forgo, grace, scram **6** beleve, decamp, depart, desert, entail, favour, forego, forlet, go away, permit, retire, vacate **7** abandon, beleave, forsake, getaway, liberty, license **8** bequeath, emigrate, furlough, vacation **9** allowance **10** permission, relinquish
behind: **11** outdistance
in the lurch: **6** desert, maroon, strand
off: **4** halt, quit, stop **6** desist **8** knock off
out: **4** omit, skip **5** elide **7** exclude

leaven: **5** imbue, yeast **7** lighten **10** impregnate

leave of absence: **5** exeat **8** furlough **10** sabbatical

leaves: **7** foliage
having: See **leafy**
medicinal: **5** senna

leave-taking: **5** adieu, conge **6** congee **7** parting **8** farewell **9** departure

leavings: See **lees, rubbish**

Lebanon: *capital:* **6** Beirut
city: **4** Tyre **5** Sidon, Zahle **7** Tripoli
currency: **5** pound **7** piaster
mountain: **4** Mzar **5** Aruba **6** Hermon **7** Lebanon, Sannine **11** Anti-Lebanon
river: **5** Kebir **6** Litani **7** Orontes **11** Nahr Ibrahim
tree: **5** cedar
valley: **6** El Bika

lech: **4** slab **8** capstone, monument

lecher: **4** rake, roué **7** glutton **8** gourmand, parasite **9** debauchee, libertine

lecherous: **4** lewd **7** boarish, goatish, lustful **9** salacious

lectern: **4** ambo, desk **5** stand **6** podium **10** escritoire

lecture: **5** scold **6** lesson, preach, rebuke, sermon, speech **7** address, hearing, lection, oration, prelect **8** scolding **9** discourse, sermonize **12** dissertation

lecturer: **6** docent, reader **9** prelector, professor

led: See **lead**

Leda: *daughter:* **5** Helen **12** Clytemnestra
lover: **4** swan, Zeus
son: **6** Castor, Pollux

ledge: **4** berm, sill **5** bench, berme, shelf **7** retable

ledger: **4** book, tome **6** record

lee: **5** haven **7** shelter **10** protection
oposite of: **5** stoss **8** windward

leech: **8** parasite **11** blackmailer, bloodsucker

leek: **4** ramp **5** onion **8** biennial
family: **9** Amaryllis

leer: **4** face, lear, lehr, loin, look, lust, ogle, void **5** empty, flank, fleer, smirk **6** entice, unlade **7** grimace

leery, leary: **4** wary **7** knowing **10** suspicious **11** distrustful, on one's guard

lees: **5** draff, dregs, dross, grout **6** bottom, dunder, refuse, ullage **7** grounds **8** leavings, sediment, settling **9** emptyings, excrement, left-overs

leeward: **4** alee
drift: **4** crab

Leeward group island: **5** Nevis **7** Antigua, Barbuda, St. Kitts **8** Anguilla, Dominica, Windward **10** Montserrat

leeway: **4** room **5** space **9** elbowroom

left: **4** port **8** larboard
toward: **4** haw **5** aport **9** sinistrad

left-handed: car **6** clumsy, gauche **7** awkward **8** southpaw **9** portsided, sinistral

leftist: red **7** liberal, radical **13** revolutionary

leg: gam, run **4** gamb, hoof, limb, prop, walk **5** bough, brace, gambe, jambe, shank **6** bender, gammon **8** cabriole
armor: **4** jamb **6** greave
bone: **4** shin **5** femur, ilium, tibia **6** fibula
in heraldry: **4** gamb
muscle: **8** peroneus **9** hamstring, peronaeus, sartorius **10** quadriceps
ornament: **6** anklet
part: **4** calf, crus, knee, shin **5** ankle, thigh **11** anticnemion
pert. to: **6** crural

legacy: **4** gift **6** legate **7** bequest **8** windfall **10** foundation
inheritor: **4** heir **7** legatee **11** beneficiary

legal (see also **law**): **5** licit, valid **6** lawful **7** juridic **9** juridical **10** authorized, legitimate

legal matter: res

legal right, by: **6** ex jure

legal tender: **4** cash, coin **5** money **6** dollar, specie

legalize: **9** authorize

legate: **5** envoy **6** deputy, legacy, nuncio **8** bequeath, delegate **9** messenger **10** ambassador **14** representative

legatee: **4** heir **11** beneficiary

joint: **6** coheir

legend: **4** edda, lore, myth, saga, tale **5** fable, story **6** record **7** fiction, proverb **9** tradition

legerdemain: **5** magic **6** deceit **8** trickery **9** conjuring **13** sleight of hand

legging: **4** spat **5** chaps **6** cnemis, cocker, puttee, puttie **7** bottine, gambado **8** bootikin, chivarra, chivarro, gamashes **11** galligaskin, spatterdash **12** antigropelos

legible: **8** distinct, readable **14** understandable

legion: **4** army, host **9** multitude

legislate: act **5** elect, enact

legislation: act, law **4** bill **7** statute

legislative body: Dail, diet, rada **5** house, junta **6** senate **7** althing **8** assembly, congress **9** Reichstag **10** parliament

legislator: **5** solon **7** enactor, senator **8** lawmaker **9** statesman **14** representative

legitimate: **4** fair, just, real, true **5** legal, licit, valid **6** cogent, lawful **7** genuine **11** efficacious

legman: **6** worker **8** reporter

legume: pea, pod, uva **4** bean, soya **5** pulse, vetch **6** clover, lentil, loment, peanut **7** alfalfa **9** vegetable

lei: **6** wreath **7** flowers, garland

leisure: **4** case, free, idle, time **5** otium (L.), spare **6** otiose **7** freedom **10** relaxation, unemployed, unoccupied **11** convenience, opportunity **12** unproductive

leisurely: **4** slow **7** gradual **12** deliberately

leitmotiv: **5** theme **6** motive **7** pattern

leman: **5** lover **8** mistress, paramour **10** sweetheart

lemma: **5** bract, theme **7** premise, theorem **8** membrane

lemon: **4** dud **5** fruit **6** citrus **7** failure **9** sour thing

lemonade: **5** drink **6** cooler **8** beverage

lemur: **4** maki, vari **5** avahi, indri, loris, potto **6** aye-aye, colugo, galago, macaco, maholi **7** half-ape, semiape, tarsier **8** kinkajou **9** babacoote **10** angwantibo

lend: **4** give, loan **5** grant, lease, prest **6** afford, impart, settle **7** advance, furnish **11** accommodate

length: **4** pace, term **6** extent **7** yardage **8** duration **9** dimension
measure: mil, rod **4** foot, inch, mile, yard **7** furlong

lengthen: eke **6** dilate, expand, extend **7** amplify, produce, prolong, stretch **8** elongate, increase, protract

lengthwise: **5** along **7** endlong, endways **14** longitudinally

lengthy: **4** long **6** prolix **8** drawn-out, extended **10** protracted

lenient: lax **4** easy, kind, mild **6** facile, gentle, humane **7** clement **8** lenitive, merciful, mitigant, relaxing, soothing, tolerant **9** assuasive, emollient, softening **10** charitable, forbearing, palliative

Leningrad: 9 Petrograd **12** St. Petersburg

lens: 5 glass, optic **7** bifocal, monocle **8** meniscus **10** anastigmat

Lent: 4 fast **6** Careme (F.) **9** forty days

Lenten: 5 plain **6** meager, meagre, somber, sombre **7** austere **8** meatless, rigorous **9** cheerless **14** unostentatious

lentigo: 7 freckle

lentil: 6 legume

Leo: 4 lion **6** zodiac **13** constellation
star: **7** Regulus

leonine: 8 lionlike, powerful

leopard: cat **4** pard **5** ounce **7** cheetah, panther

lepidopter: 4 moth **9** butterfly

leprechaun: elf **5** fairy **6** sprite **7** brownie

leprosy: 5 lepra **14** Hansen's disease

lerot: 8 dormouse

lese majesty: 7 treason **10** iconoclasm

Les Miserables author: 4 Hugo

lesion: cut **4** sore **5** ulcer, wound **6** injury **7** fissure

less: 5 fewer, minus, under **7** smaller **8** inferior

lessee: 6 leaser, renter, tenant **7** huurder (D.)

lessen: 4 bate, ease, wane **5** abase, abate, decry, lower, peter **6** impair, reduce, shrink, soften, weaken **7** amenuse, assuage, curtail, depress, relieve **8** belittle, condense, contract, decrease, derogate, diminish, minimize, mitigate, palliate, retrench, truncate **9** alleviate, attenuate, disparage, extenuate **10** depreciate **11** deteriorate

lesser: 5 fewer, minor **7** reduced, smaller **8** inferior **9** small-time **11** minor-league

lesson: 4 lear, task **5** moral, study **6** rebuke **7** example, lecture, precept, reading, reproof, warning **8** exercise **10** assignment **11** composition, instruction

lessor: 8 landlord

lest: 6 in case **11** for fear that

let: 4 hire, rent **5** allow, lease, leave **6** hinder, impede, permit, suffer **7** prevent **8** obstacle **9** hindrance
fall: **4** drop, slip **5** lower, spill **7** mention
forth: **4** emit
in: **5** admit, enter **6** insert
out: **4** free **7** enlarge, release

let it stand: sta **4** stet

letdown: 5 slump **8** comedown, drawback **10** anticlimax, relaxation, slackening

lethal: 5 fatal, toxic **6** deadly, mortal, poison **9** poisonous **12** death-dealing

lethargic: 4 dull **5** heavy, inert **6** drowsy, sleepy, torpid **7** languid **8** comatose, listless, sluggish **9** apathetic

lethargy: 5 sopor **6** stupor, torpor **8** hebetude

Lethe: 8 oblivion **13** forgetfulness

Leto: 6 Latona
daughter: **7** Artemis
father: **5** Coeus
mother: **6** Phoebe
son: **6** Apollo

Lett: 4 Balt **7** Latvian

letter: 4 bull, chit, line, memo, note, rune **5** breve, brief, chain, favor, vowel **6** billet, cartel, charta, favour, screed, symbol **7** collins, courant, epistle, initial, message, missile, missive **8** encyclic **9** consonant, precisely, semivowel **12** exact wording **13** communication, semiconsonant
Anglo-Saxon: edh, eth, wen, wyn **4** wynn
carrier: **6** correo (Sp.) **7** mailman, postman **9** messenger
decorated: fac
large: **7** capital **9** majuscule, upper case
sloping: **6** italic
small: **9** lower case, miniscule

lettered: 7 learned, stamped **8** educated, literate **9** inscribed

lettuce: *kind of:* cos **4** head, leaf **6** butter **7** romaine, simpson
sea: **4** alga **5** laver

letup: 7 respite **9** abatement, cessation

leucite: 5 lenad **9** amphigene

levant: 5 waver **6** decamp **7** abscond

Levant: 4 East **6** Orient **13** Mediterranean
garment: **6** caftan
river: **4** wadi, wady
ship: **4** jerm, saic
valley: **4** wady

levee: 4 bank, dike, dyke, pier, quay **6** durbar **9** reception **10** embankment

level: aim, par **4** even, flat, rase, raze, true **5** equal, flush, grade, peavy, plane, point, scalp **6** evenly, peavey, peavie, smooth **7** flatten, mow down, planate, uniform **8** demolish **10** horizontal **12** standardized
social: **5** caste, class
tool: **5** plane **6** gimbal

level-headed: 8 sensible

lever: bar, lam, pry **5** helve, jemmy, jimmy, peavy, pedal, prise, swipe **6** binder, garrot, peavey, peavie, tappet, tiller **7** crowbar, treadle **9** rockshaft
part: **7** fulcrum

leverage: 5 power **9** advantage, influence

leveret: 4 hare **8** mistress

Levi: *descendant:* **6** Levite **7** Gershon
father: **5** Jacob

son: **6** Kohath
leviathan: **4** ship **5** titan, whale **6** dragon
levigate: **5** grind **6** polish, smooth **9** pulverize
levin: **9** lightning
levitate: **4** rise **5** float
levity: **5** humor **6** gaiety, humour **8** buoyancy **9** frivolity, lightness, silliness **10** fickleness **11** foolishness, instability
levy: tax **4** cess, duty, fine, wage **5** exact, stent **6** assess, extent, impose, impost **7** collect **10** assessment, imposition
lewd: **4** base, rude **5** bawdy, dirty **6** carnal, coarse **7** lustful, obscene, rammish, sensual **8** unchaste **9** debauched, dissolute, lecherous, salacious **10** lascivious, libidinous, licentious **12** pornographic
lexicographer: **6** author, editor **8** compiler
product: **10** dictionary
lexicon: **6** record **7** calepin **8** glossary, wordbook **9** thesaurus **10** dictionary **11** concordance, onomasticon
Leyte capital: **8** Tacloban
liability: **4** debt, loan **5** debit **6** burden **10** obligation
liable: apt **6** likely **8** amenable **10** answerable **11** accountable, responsible **12** legally bound
liaison: **4** bond **5** agent **6** affair **8** intimacy, intrigue **12** relationship
liana: **4** cipo, vine **5** plant
kind: ivy **5** Kudzu **10** grapevines, greenbrier **11** bittersweet, honeysuckle, vanilla vine
liang: **4** tael
liar: **5** cheat **6** fibber **7** Ananias, cracker **8** deceiver, fabulist **10** fabricator **11** pseudologue **12** prevaricator, pseudologist **14** misrepresenter
lias: **4** rock **9** limestone
libation: **5** drink **8** potation
libel: **4** bill **6** defame, malign, vilify **7** calumny, lampoon, request, scandal, slander **8** circular, handbill, roorback **10** caluminate, defamation **11** certificate, declaration **12** supplication
libelant: **7** accuser
liberal: **4** free, good, open **5** ample, broad, frank, noble **6** honest **7** electic, profuse **8** abundant, eclectic, generous, handsome **9** benignant, bounteous, bountiful, expansive, expensive, plenteous, plentiful **10** benevolent, charitable, ecumenical, munificent **11** broad-minded, progressive
Liberal: **4** Whig
liberate: rid **4** flee, free **5** clear, loose, remit **6** acquit, redeem, rescue **7** deliver, manumit, release **8** unfetter **9** discharge, disengage, extricate **10** emancipate

Liberia: *animal:* **6** duiker
boatman: Kru
capital: **8** Monrovia
city: **8** Buchanan, Marshall **10** Greenville
currency: **4** cent **6** dollar
measure: **4** kuba
mountain: **4** Bomi, Bong **5** Nimba
people: Kru, Kwa, Vai, Vei **4** Loma, Toma **5** Bassa, Gibbi, Greba **6** Kpelle
river: **5** Manna **8** San Pedro

libertine: **4** rake, roue, wolf **6** lecher **7** sceptic **9** debauchee, dissolute, womanizer **10** lascivious, licentious
liberty: may **4** ease, play **5** leave, right **7** freedom, leisure, license **8** furlough **9** privilege **11** presumption **12** emancipation
Libra: **6** scales, zodiac **7** balance **13** constellation
library: **7** archive, bhander **8** atheneum **9** athenaeum **10** biblioteca (Sp.) **11** bibliotecha, reading room **12** bibliotheque (F.)
libretto: **4** book **5** words

Libya: *capital:* **7** Tripoli
city: **8** Benghasi
currency: **5** dinar **6** dirham
desert: **6** Sahara
export: **9** petroleum
measure: **4** drah **5** bozze, donum, jabia, teman **6** barile **7** mattaro

Libya's child: **5** Belus **6** Agenor
lice: See **louse**
license: tax **5** allow, exeat, grant, leave **6** patent, permit **7** dismiss, freedom, liberty **8** escambio, passport, sanction **9** approbate, authority, authorize, franchise **10** permission **11** imprimateur, unrestraint
licentious: gay, lax **4** free, lewd **5** frank, loose **6** unruly **7** immoral, obscene **9** dissolute **10** lascivious, profligate **12** pornographic, uncontrolled, unrestrained
lichen: **4** moss **6** fungus
derivative: **6** archil, litmus
genus: **5** usnea **7** evernia **10** pertusaria
kind: **6** azetic, script **7** oakmoss **8** parmelia, pyxie cup, reindeer **9** yellow map **10** canary weed **12** old man's beard

lich-house: 8 mortuary
licit: 5 legal 6 lawful 9 permitted
lick: bit, dab, hit, lap, win 4 beat, flog 5 slake, spank, taste 6 defeat, thrash 7 clobber, conquer, shellac 8 overcome, vanquish
lickety-split: 4 fast 5 apace 7 quickly, rapidly, swiftly 8 pell-mell 9 posthaste
licorice: 5 abrin, anise 8 absinthe 9 jequirity
pill: 6 cachou
seed: 9 jequirity
lid: cap, hat, top 4 curb 5 cover 7 shutter 9 operculum, restraint
lie: cog, fib, gab 4 bask, cram, flaw, hide, loll, rest 5 covet, exist 6 extend, grovel, patter, remain, repose 7 cracker, crammer, deceive, falsify, falsity, pronate, untruth 8 position, roorback 9 deception, fabricate, falsehood, fish story, mendacity, prostrate 10 equivocate, inveracity, taradiddle 11 fabrication, prevaricate, tarradiddle 12 song and dance
in ambush: 4 lurk 6 hugger 9 insidiate
Liebestraum composer: 5 Liszt
Liechtenstein: *capital:* 5 Vaduz
city: 4 Mals 7 Bendern, Ruggell, Triesen
currency: 5 franc, rappe 7 centime
lief: 4 fain, soon 5 leave 6 freely, gladly 7 happily 9 willingly 10 permission
liege: 5 loyal 6 vassal 7 devoted, subject 8 faithful, overlord 9 sovereign
lien: 5 claim 6 charge 8 mortgage 9 trust deed 11 encumbrance, garnishment
lieu: 5 place, stead 7 instead
lieutenant: 7 officer 10 aide-de-camp
life: vie (F.) 4 vida (Sp.) 5 blood, vigor 6 biosis, energy, spirit 8 vitality, vivacity 9 animation, biography, existence 11 anilopyrine
animal: 4 bios 5 biota, fauna
god of: 6 Faunus
pert. to: 5 vital 6 biotic, mortal 8 biotical
plant: 4 bios 5 biota, flora
principle: 5 atman, prana, tenet
professional: 6 career
science: 7 anatomy, biology, ecology, zoology 10 exobiology 12 paleontology
sea: 5 coral 8 halibios, plankton
simple form: 5 ameba 6 amebic, amoeba 7 amoebae (pl.), amoebic
staff of: 5 bread
without: 4 dead 5 azoic 9 inanimate
life jacket: 7 Mae West
lifeless: 4 arid, cold, dead, dull, flat 5 amort, heavy, inert, vapid 6 anemic, boring, jejune, torpid 7 anaemic 8 inactive, listless 9 bloodless, examinate, inanimate, powerless, tasteless 10 spiritless, unanimated
life-like: 9 realistic
lifer: 7 convict 13 career soldier
lifetime: age, day, eon 4 aeon 5 being 8 duration

lift: pry 4 help, jack, perk, rear 5 boost, crane, exalt, heave, hoick, hoist, hoosh, raise, scend 6 cleach, cleech 7 derrick, elevate, enhance 8 elevator, heighten
ligament: 4 band, bind, bond, cord 6 artery 7 bandage
ligan, lagan: 6 debris
ligate: 4 bind 5 tie up 7 bandage
ligature: tie 4 band, bond 6 taenia 7 bandage
light: dey, gay 4 airy, deft, easy, fair, fire, glim, lamp, mild, moon, neon, soft 5 agile, blond, fanal, filmy, flaky, flame, flare, happy, merry, torch 6 alight, beacon, bright, candle, floaty, gentle, ignite, kindle, lively, lumine, nimble, pastel, volant 7 animate, buoyant, cresset, flyaway, fragile, trivial, whitish 8 brighten, cheerful, delicate, ethereal, gossamer, graceful, illumine, luminary, luminous, trifling 9 frivolous, knowledge, touch down 10 capricious, illuminate 12 luminescence 15 phosphorescence
circle: 4 halo 7 aureola, aureole
cloud: 6 nimbus
faint: 7 glimmer, shimmer 9 starlight 10 glimmering, shimmering
globe: 4 bulb
god: 5 Baldr 6 Balder
kind of: arc 4 lamp 5 klieg, laser, torch 7 halogen, lantern 9 headlight 10 flashlight 11 fluorescent 12 incandescent
measure: lux, pyr, rad 5 lumen 6 Hefner 7 candela
overpower with: 6 dazzle
portable: 4 lamp 5 flare, taper, torch 6 candle 7 lantern 10 flashlight
reflector: 4 lens 6 mirror
refractor: 5 prism
science: 6 optics
source: sun 4 fire 11 electricity
unit: lux, pyr 4 phot 5 lumen
without: 4 dark 5 blind 7 aphotic
lighten: 4 ease, fade 5 allay, clear 6 alight, allege, bleach, illume, leaven 7 gladden, relieve 8 brighten 9 alleviate 10 illuminate
lighter (see also light): 5 barge, spill 7 pontoon 8 chopboat
lightheaded: 5 dizzy, giddy 6 fickle 7 flighty, glaiket, glaikit 8 flippant, heedless, unstable, unsteady 9 delirious, frivolous 10 disordered, inconstant 11 thoughtless
lighthearted: gay 4 glad 5 happy, merry 6 blithe, joyful, joyous 7 buoyant 8 carefree, cheerful, gleesome, volatile 9 vivacious 12 free from care
lighthouse: 5 phare 6 beacon, pharos 7 seamark, warning
lightness: 6 levity 8 delicacy, mildness 12 cheerfulness

lightning: 4 bolt 5 levin
  defier of: 4 Ajax
  pert. to: 8 fulgural
  protective device: rod 8 arrester
lightning bug: 6 beetle 7 firefly
lightning stone: 9 fulgurite
lights out: 4 taps
ligneous: 5 woody
lignite: 4 coal
ligulate: 11 strap-shaped
likable: 6 genial 7 winning 8 charming, pleasant 10 attractive
like: 4 akin, love, same, twin 5 alike, enjoy, equal, match 6 admire, prefer, regard, relish 7 similar 9 analogous, semblance 10 preference, synonymous 11 counterpart, homogeneous
likelihood: 6 chance 8 prospect 10 appearance 11 probability 14 verisimilitude
likely: apt 5 prone 6 liable 7 tending 8 credible, feasible, probable, suitable 9 promising 11 verisimilar
liken: 5 apply 7 compare 10 assimilate
likeness: 4 copy, form, twin 5 guise, image 6 effigy, figure, statue 7 analogy, parable, picture, replica 8 parallel, portrait 9 duplicate, facsimile, imitation, semblance, simulacre 10 comparison, photograph, similarity, similitude, simulacrum 11 counterfeit 12 reproduction 14 representation
likewise: and, nor, not, too 4 also 5 ditto 7 besides 8 moreover
lilac: 5 mauve, shrub 6 flower, purple 7 syringa 8 lavender
Lilith's successor: Eve
lilliputian: 4 tiny 5 small 6 midget, pretty 7 dwarfed 10 diminutive, teeny-weeny
lilt: air 4 sing, song, tune 7 cadence
lily: 4 aloe, ixia, sego, wood 5 calla, niobe, tiger, water, yucca 6 Easter, titree 7 leopard, Madonna 8 asphodel, hyacinth, mariposa, trillium 9 asparagus
  family: 9 liliaceae
  genus: 7 bessera
  sea: 7 crinoid
lily iron: 7 harpoon
lily-livered: 5 timid 6 coward 7 gutless 9 spunkless
Lily Maid of Astolat: 6 Elaine
lily of France: 10 fleur-de-lis
lily of the valley: 6 mugget, mugwet 7 maybell 10 convallily
  family: 11 convallaria
lima: 4 bean, seed 7 mollusk
liman: bay 5 marsh 6 lagoon 7 estuary
limation: 6 filing 9 polishing
limb: arm, fin, leg 4 edge, wing 5 bough 6 branch, member, rascal, switch 7 flipper, pleopod, support 9 appendage

  adapted for swimming: 8 nectopod
  flexion: 9 anaclasis
limber: 4 bain, flip, limp 5 agile, lithe 6 pliant, supple, swanky 7 elastic 8 flexible, flippant, handsome, yielding
limbo: 4 hell 5 dance 9 purgatory
lime: 5 color, fruit, green 6 cement, citrus
  pendent: 10 stalactite
  phosphate: 7 apatite
  tree: 4 teil 6 linden, tupelo
limen: 9 threshold
limestone: 4 calp, cauk, malm 5 chalk, ganil, poros (Gr.) 6 clunch, marble, oolite 7 hurlock 8 peastone, pisolite
limey: 6 sailor 7 soldier 10 Englishman
limit: end, fix 4 curb, mete 5 ambit, bound, bourn, check, fence, hedge, scant, stint, verge 6 border, bourne, curfew, define, extent, finish 7 astrict, barrier, closure, confine, environ, extreme 8 boundary, conclude, contract, deadline, restrain, restrict, terminal, terminus 9 condition, constrain, extremity 10 limitation 11 restriction, termination 12 boundary line, circumscribe 13 determination, qualification
limited: few, ltd 5 local, scant 6 finite, meager, narrow, scanty, strait 7 cramped 8 reserved 9 parochial 10 restricted 11 topopolitan
limiting: 5 final 9 bordering, enclosing 10 qualifying, relational
limitless: 4 vast 8 infinite 9 boundless, unbounded, unlimited 11 measureless
limn: 4 draw 5 paint 6 depict, sketch 7 portray 8 describe 9 delineate
limp: hop, lax 4 himp, soft 5 hilch, hitch, loose 6 flabby, flimsy, hirple, hobble, limber, wilted 7 flaccid 8 drooping, flexible, hang down 9 inelastic 13 unsubstantial
limpid: 4 pure 5 clear, lucid 6 bright 7 crystal 8 pellucid 11 translucent, transparent
limping: 4 halt, lame 10 claudicant
limy: 6 sticky 7 viscous
lin: See **linn**
Lincoln, Abraham:: *assassin:* 5 Booth
  debater: 7 Douglas
  nickname: 9 Honest Abe 12 Railsplitter
  secretary of state: 6 Seward
  secretary of war: 7 Stanton
  son: Tad 6 Edward, Robert 7 William
  wife: 8 Mary Todd
linden: lin 4 lime, teil 8 basswood
  genus of: 5 tilia
line: job, pad, ray, row, wad 4 axis, ceil, cord, dash, etch, face, file, mark, mere, race, rein, rope, rule, seam, wire 5 curve, front, leger, queue, route, serif, snell, steen, stich, stria, swath 6 border, ceriph, cordon, fettle, hawser, isobar, metier, nettle, streak, string, stripe, suture 7 barrier, carrier, contour,

outline, radiant, scratch **8** boundary, crossbar, isotherm, wainscot **9** delineate

bottom: **7** net loss **9** net profit

conceptual: **6** agonic, tropic **7** equator, isother **8** latitude, meridian **9** longitude

curved: arc

diagonal: **4** bias **5** slash **7** virgule

geometrical: arc, ess **4** cant, sine **6** secant **7** tangent **8** parallel **9** asymptote

mathematical: **6** vector

nautical: **6** earing, hawser, ratlin **7** marline, painter, ratline

of soldiers: **4** file, rank **6** column

pert. to: **5** filar **6** linear

raised: **4** weal, welt **5** ridge

with boards: **8** wainscot

lineage: **4** race **5** birth, blood, caste, tribe **6** family, havage, stirps **7** descent, stirpes (pl.) **8** ancestry, heredity, pedigree **9** genealogy **10** progenitor

lineal: **6** direct, racial **9** ancestral **10** hereditary

lineament: **5** trait **7** feature **14** characteristic

linear: **9** elongated

lineate: **7** striped **8** streaked

lined: **5** ruled **6** notate **7** creased, striate **8** careworn, wrinkled **9** lineolate

lineman: end **5** guard **6** center, tackle **7** wireman

linen: **4** brin, crea (Sp.), lawn **5** toile **6** barras, damask, dowlas, forfar **7** brabant, cambric, dornick **13** linsey-woolsey

fabric: **7** taffeta

household: **6** napery, sheets **10** tablecloth

source: **4** flax

yarn: lea

liner: **4** boat, ship **6** facing, vessel **7** backing, steamer **9** steamship

wrecked: **7** Titanic

lines: net **4** part, role **5** looks **6** script **7** harness, network **8** reticule

ling: **4** fish, hake **5** heath **6** burbot **7** heather **8** chestnut

linger: lag **4** drag, stay, wait **5** dally, delay, dwell, hover, tarry **6** dawdle, loiter, remain, stay on

lingerie: **9** sleepwear, underwear **11** underthings

lingering: **4** slow **7** chronic

lingo: **4** cant **5** argot **6** jargon, patter, tongue **7** dialect **8** language **10** vernacular

lingual: **7** glossal **10** linguistic, tonguelike

linguist: **8** polyglot **9** pantoglot **10** vocabulist **11** interpreter, philologist

linguistics: **7** grammar **9** philology

lingy: **5** agile **6** active, limber, nimble **7** healthy **8** heathery

liniment: oil **4** balm **6** lotion **8** ointment **11** embrocation

lining: **5** steen **6** facing, insert **7** backing, ceiling **8** wainscot

link: tie **4** join, joke **5** cleek, nexus, torch, unite **6** braced, catena, copula, couple, course, faster **7** conjoin, connect **8** catenate **10** connection, golf course **11** concatenate

series: **5** chain **13** concatenation

linn, lin: **4** pool **6** linden, ravine **8** cataract **9** precipice, waterfall

linnet: **5** finch, twite **9** gorsebird

linseed: oil **4** flax

lint: **4** fuzz, pile **5** fluff **7** charpie **8** raveling

lintel: **5** hance **6** clavel **7** transom

lion: **4** puma, star **5** simba **6** cougar, roarer **9** carnivore, celebrity

group: **5** pride

hair: **4** mane

winged, with woman's head: **6** sphinx

young: cub **6** lionet

lionlike: **7** leonine

Lion of God: Ali

lion's share: **8** best part **10** whole thing

lip: rim **4** brim, edge, kiss **5** brink, labia (pl.) **6** labium, margin **7** labella **8** labellum

ornament: **6** labret

part: **8** philtrum

pert. to: **6** labial **11** labiodental

lipoma: **5** tumor

lipid: fat, wax

liquefy: **4** fuse, melt **6** fusile **7** liquate **8** dissolve, eliquate **10** colliquate, deliquesce, make molten

liqueur: **5** creme, noyau **6** genepi **7** cordial, ratafee **8** anisette, beverage **9** Cointreau **10** pousse cafe **11** Benedictine

liquid: **5** fluid **6** fluent, watery **8** beverage

colorless: **5** vodka, water **7** alcohol

container: cup, jar, jug, mug, pan, pot **4** etna, ewer, vase, vial **5** cruse, glass, phial **6** boiler, bottle, bucket, goblet, kettle **7** creamer, pitcher, tumbler **8** decanter, demijohn

gasified: **5** steam, vapor

inflammable: see *volatile* below

measure: **4** dram, pint **5** fifth, liter, ounce **6** gallon, tierce

oily: **6** cresol, octane **7** aniline, picamar

particle form: **4** mist **5** spray

sweet: **5** sirup, syrup **7** treacle **8** molasses

volatile: gas **5** ether **6** butane **7** alcohol, ligroin **8** gasolene, gasoline, ligroine

liquidate: **4** kill, sell **5** pay up **6** murder, settle **8** amortize **9** discharge

liquor: ale, bub, dew, gin, rum, rye **4** arak, bang, beer, beno, brew, grog, nipa, raki, sake, saki, soma **5** bhang, booze, budge, drink, hooch, lager, pisco, stout **6** arrack, brandy, porter, pottle, scotch, stingo, strunt, tipple **7** bitters, whiskey **8** beverage **9** aqua

vitae, moonshine **10** intoxicant
bad: **5** smoke **6** rotgut **10** balderdash
cabinet: **8** cellaret
crude: **5** hooch **6** rotgut **9** hoochinoo,
moonshine
drugged: **5** hocus **6** mickey **10** mickeyfinn
manufacturer: **6** abkari **9** distiller
measure: **4** dram **5** rouse **7** snifter
mix with: **4** lace
mixture: **5** bogus **7** bragget
residue: **4** must **5** dregs **8** heeltaps
server: **6** barman **7** barmaid, skinker, tapster **9** barkeeper, bartender
shop: bar **6** saloon, tavern **7** shebeen
vessel: ama, keg **4** bowl **5** amula, flask **6**
barrel, bottle, flagon **7** bombard, psykter,
stamnos **8** cruisken, decanter **9** cruiskeen
lira (one-twentieth): **5** soldo
liripipe, liripoop: **4** hood **5** scarf **6** tippet
lirk: **6** crease **7** wrinkle
lish: **5** agile, quick **6** active, nimble
lisk: **4** loin **5** flank, groin
lisp: **7** prattle
lissome, lissom: **5** agile, lithe **6** limber, nimble, supple **8** flexible
list: tip **4** bill, cant, cast, file, item, keel, leet,
memo, ordo, roll, rota, rote, tilt **5** brief,
canon, index, panel, scrip, slate **6** careen,
docket, roster **7** catalog, incline **8** manifest,
register, schedule, tabulate **9** catalogue,
inventory, portfolio, repertory **10** reper-
toire **11** enumeration
listen: ear **4** hark, hear, heed, note **5** audit **6**
attend, harken **7** hearken **8** give heed, over-
hear **9** eavesdrop **10** auscultate, take advice
lister: **4** plow **8** assessor **9** appraiser **10** cata-
loguer
listing: **5** atilt **7** tilting, tipping **8** register **10**
enlistment, enrollment
individual: **4** item **5** entry
listless: **4** dull **5** faint, inert **6** abject, drowsy,
supine **7** languid **8** careless, heedless, sluggish **9** apathetic, heartless, lethargic **10**
spiritless **11** indifferent **13** uninteresting
listlessness: **8** doldrums
litany: **6** ectene, ektene, prayer **8** rogation **11**
orapronobis
liter: kan (D.) **7** measure
literal: **4** bald, dull, real **5** exact **7** factual, precise, prosaic **8** accurate, verbatim **11** word
for word **13** unimaginative
literary: **6** versed **7** bookish, erudite, learned
8 lettered **9** scholarly
literate: **6** reader, writer **8** educated, lettered
literati: **12** men of letters **13** intellectuals **14**
intelligentsia
literator: **6** critic
literature: **7** fine art, letters **13** belles-lettres

extracts: **9** anthology
form: **5** drama, essay, novel, prose **6** poetry
7 fiction **9** technical **10** nonfiction, scientific **11** pornography
lithe: **4** bain, slim **6** clever, limber, lissom, pliant, supple, svelte **7** lissome, slender **8** flexible
lithograph: **5** print **6** chromo

Lithuania: *capital:* **7** Vilnius
city: **6** Kaunas **8** Klaipeda
currency: lit **5** fenig, litas, marka **6** cen-
tas **7** ostmark **8** auksinas, skatikas
people: **4** Balt, Lett **5** Zhmud **6** Litvak
7 Yatvyag

litigant: **4** suer **6** suitor **7** accuser
litigation: **4** case, moot, suit **6** action **7** contest, dispute, lawsuit **10** contention, discussion
one involved in: **8** barrater, barrator, litigant
litigious: **10** disputable **11** belligerent, contentious, quarrelsome **14** controvertible
litter: bed, hay **4** bier, mess, raff **5** cabin,
couch, dooly, mulch, straw, trash, young **6**
doolie, refuse **7** cacolet, clutter, mullock,
rubbish, rummage **8** brancard (F.), disorder
9 offspring, stretcher **10** untidiness
litterateur: **6** author, writer **7** bookman
little: sma (Sc.), wee **4** mean, poco (It.), puny,
thin, tiny **5** brief, crumb, dwarf, minor,
petit, petty, short, small **6** bantam, meager,
minute, paltry, petite, scanty, seldom, slight
7 trivial **8** fraction, piddling, trifling **9**
miniature, miniscule **10** diminutive
by little: **8** bit by bit, inchmeal **9** gradually,
piecemeal
Little Dipper: **7** Polaris **9** North Star **13** constellation
little finger: **5** pinky **6** pinkie **7** minimus
little toe: **7** minimus
Little Women: Jo, Amy, Meg **4** Beth
author: **6** Alcott
surname: **5** March
littoral: **7** coastal
lituite: **6** fossil
liturate: **7** spotted
liturgy: **4** Mass, rite **6** ritual **7** service, worship
9 Communion, sacrament
livable: **8** bearable **9** endurable, habitable,
tolerable
live: **4** fare, room **5** abide, alive, dwell, exist,
green, vital, vivid **6** active, reside **7** animate, blazing, breathe, dynamic, subsist **8**

animated, continue, converse **9** energetic **10** experience, unexploded

in: **7** inhabit

in the country: **9** rusticate

passively: **8** vegetate

permit to: **5** spare **8** reprieve

with: **7** cohabit

livelihood: **4** keep **5** being **6** living **11** subsistence

liveliness: **6** spirit **8** vitality

lively: gay, vif (F.) **4** airy, cant, fast, pert, racy, vive, yare **5** agile, alert, alive, brisk, canty, chirk, cobby, desto (It.), fresh, peart, peppy **6** active, blithe, bright, cheery, chirpy, cocket, crouse, dapper, frisky, nimble, snappy **7** allegro (It.), animate, animato (It.), buoyant, chipper **8** animated, galliard, spirited, vigorous **9** energetic, sprightly, vivacious

liven: **5** cheer, pep up **7** animate **8** brighten

liver: **4** foie **5** hepar **8** tomalley

disease: **9** cirrhosis, hepatitis

fluid: **4** bile

pert. to: **7** hepatic

liverwort: **4** moss **8** agrimony, hepatica **9** bryophyte

genus: **6** riccia

livery: **7** uniform **8** clothing

livestock: yak **4** goat, hogs, mule, oxen **5** horse, llama, sheep **6** cattle, donkey **7** chattel, poultry **12** water buffalo

livid: **4** gray **5** bleak **6** purple **7** deathly **9** colorless **10** discolored **12** black and blue

living: **4** keep **5** alive, being, bread, vivid **6** extant **7** animate **8** animated, benefice **10** livelihood, sustenance **11** subsistence

again: **6** reborn **9** redivivus

correct: **7** regimen **11** orthobiosis

off others: **8** entozoic **9** parasitic, raptorial

together: **11** contubernal

lixiviate: **5** leach

lixivium: lye

lizard: dab, eft **4** adda, dabb, dhab, evet, gila, ibid, newt, seps, uran **5** agama, anole, dhabb, gecko, gekko, goana, scink, skink, varan, waran **6** ameiva, anolis, dragon, goanna, iguana, komodo, lacert, moloch, worral, worrel **7** cheecha, geitjie, monitor, saurian, tuatera **8** basilisk **9** chameleon, galliwasp **10** chuckwalla, horned toad **12** scheltopusik

family: **12** xenosauridae

genus: uta **5** agama **6** ameiva, anolis

mammal similar to: **10** salamander

lizard-like: **8** iguanoid

llama: **6** alpaca, vicuna **7** guanaco

family: **5** camel

habitat: **5** Andes

llanero: **6** cowboy, gaucho **8** herdsman

llano: **5** pampa, plain **7** lowland, prairie

Llyr's son: **4** Bran **7** Branwen

load: jag **4** clog, jagg, lade, onus, pack, stow, tote **5** cargo, weigh **6** burden, charge, hamper, lading, steeve, weight **7** fraught, freight, oppress **8** carriage, encumber **9** aggravate, exonerate **10** adulterate **11** encumbrance

small: jag **4** jagg **5** hurry

loader: **9** stevedore

loadstone: See **lodestone**

loaf: **4** idle, laze **5** bread **6** dawdle, loiter, lounge **10** dilly-dally

loafer: bum **4** hood, shoe **5** idler **7** flaneur, hoodlum, lounger, vagrant **8** hooligan, larrikin, vagabond **11** chairwarmer

loam: rab **4** silt **5** loess, regur (Ind.) **6** cledge **8** dark soil

constituent: **4** clay, lime **5** chalk

deposit: **4** silt **5** loess

loan: **4** dhan (Ind.), lend **5** prest **6** borrow, credit **7** advance **10** obligation, provisions **13** accommodation

loan shark: **6** usurer **11** money-lender

loath, loth: **6** averse, odious **7** hateful **8** backward, hesitant **9** reluctant, repulsive, unwilling

loathe: **4** hate **5** abhor **6** detest **7** adverse, condemn, despise, dislike **9** abominate

loathsome: **4** foul, ugly, vile **7** carrion, cloying, hateful **8** abhorent, deformed **9** offensive, repellent, repugnant **10** abominable, detestable, disgusting **11** distasteful

lob: hit **4** bowl, lots, lout, lump, step, till, toss, vein **5** droop, stair, throw **6** propel **7** pollack **9** chandelle

lobby: **4** hall, room, urge **5** foyer **7** solicit **8** advocate, anteroom, coulisse, persuade, pressure **9** enclosure, influence, vestibule

lobbyist: **8** promoter **12** propagandist

lobe: **4** flap **5** alula **6** alular, earlap, lappet, lobule

lobelike: **6** lobate

loblolly: **4** mush, pine, tree **5** gruel **6** puddle **7** mudhole

lobo: **4** wolf **10** timber wolf

lobster: **10** crustacean

claw: **5** chela **6** nipper

female: hen

part: **4** claw **6** pincer, telson, thorax

roe: **5** coral

trap: pot **5** creel **6** bownet

local: pub **5** narrow, native **7** bucolic, endemic, limited, topical **8** regional, specific **10** provincial, restricted

locale: **4** loci (pl.), site **5** locus (L.), place, scene **6** region **9** situation

locality: **4** loci (pl.), seat, site, spot **5** locus, place, situs **6** region **7** habitat **8** district, position **12** neighborhood

localize: **7** situate **8** pinpoint

locate (see also **place**): sat **4** espy, find, seat, show, site, spot **5** stand, trace **6** settle **7** situate, station **8** discover, pinpoint **9** establish

locatio: **7** leasing, letting

locating device: **5** lidar, radar, sonar

location: **4** area, seat, site, spot **5** place, scene, situs **6** ubiety **7** habitat **8** position **9** situation

loch: bay **4** lake, pond, pool **5** inlet, lough

loci: See **locus**

lock: **4** bolt, curl, frib, hank, hasp, wisp **5** latch, sasse, tress **6** fasten **7** confine, cowlick, ringlet **8** fastener
part: **4** bolt **5** stump **8** cylinder

locker: **5** hutch **6** ascham

locket: **7** jewelry, pendant **8** ornament

lockjaw: **7** tetanus, trismus **11** ankylostoma
remedy: **11** antitetanic, antitetanus

lockman: **11** executioner

lockup: jug **4** jail **5** clink **6** cooler **7** hoosgow **8** hoosegaw, hoosegow **9** calaboose

loco: mad **5** crazy **6** insane **8** demented

locomotive: **5** dolly, mogul **6** diesel, dinkey, engine, mallet **8** electric
inventor: **10** Stephenson
part: cab **5** pilot
service car: **6** tender **7** coalcar
type: **5** steam **6** diesel **8** electric

Locrine: *daughter:* **7** Sabrina
father: **4** Brut

locus: **4** area, loci (pl.), site **5** place **8** locality

locust: **5** bruke, carob, cicad **6** cicada, cicala, cigala, insect **11** grasshopper
wingless: **4** weta

locustberry: **5** drupe, nance **9** glamberry

locust bird: **7** grackle **8** starling

locust plant: **5** senna

locust tree: **5** carob **6** acacia

lode: **4** path, road, vein **5** canal, drain, ledge **6** course **7** deposit, fissure **8** waterway
cavity: vug **4** vugg, vugh

lodestone, loadstone: **6** magnet **7** adamant **8** terrella **9** magnetite

lodge: dig, lie **4** camp, club **5** board, cabin, couch, dwell, embed, hogan, motel, put up **6** alight, bestow, encamp, hostel **7** deposit, quarter **8** domicile, harbinge **11** brotherhood

lodger: **5** guest **6** roomer, tenant

lodging: bed, hut, inn **4** camp, gite (F.), host, howf, nest, room, tent **5** abode, cabin, hotel, house, hovel, howff **6** billet, tavern, teepee, wigwam **7** mansion **8** barracks, dwelling, hostelry, quarters **9** dormitory, harborage, residence **10** habitation, harbourage

cost: **4** rent **11** maintenance

loess: **4** loam, silt **7** deposit

loft: bin **4** balk **5** attic, raise **6** garret

lofty: **4** aery, epic, high, tall **5** aerie, elate, grand, noble, proud, steep **6** aerial, Andean, andine **7** Andesic, arduous, eminent, haughty, sublime **8** arrogant, assuming, elevated, eloquent, majestic **9** cockhorse, dignified, overproud **11** magisterial, mountainous

log: **4** clog, wood **5** diary **6** billet, loggat, logget, record, timber **7** journal
kind: **4** slab **5** splat **8** puncheon
mass: **5** drive
revolve: **4** birl **7** logroll

log gin: **6** jammer

logarithm: *inventor:* **6** Napier
unit: bel

loge: box **4** room **5** booth, stall

logger: **6** sniper **9** lumberman **10** lumberjack, woodcutter **11** woodchopper
boot: pac **4** pack

loggerhead: **6** turtle **9** blockhead

loggerheads: **4** odds, outs **7** stymied **10** quarreling

loggia: **5** lanai, porch **6** arcade, piazza **7** balcony, gallery, portico

logging: *sled:* **4** tode **7** travois **8** travoise
tool: **4** pevy **5** peavy, peevy **6** nigger, peavey

logic: **9** reasoning
inductive: **7** epagoge
specious: **7** sophism
term: **5** ferio, lemma **7** ferison, premise **8** argument **9** syllogism **10** conclusion

logical: **4** sane **5** sound, valid **8** coherent, rational **10** consistent, reasonable

logion: **5** maxim, motto **6** saying **11** observation

logograph: **5** rebus **6** puzzle, riddle **7** anagram

logotype: **8** colophon **9** nameplate, signature, trademark

logroll: **4** birl

logy: **4** dull **5** heavy **6** drowsy, groggy **8** sluggish

Lohengrin: *character:* **4** Elsa **8** Parsifal
composer: **6** Wagner

loincloth: **5** pagne

loir: **8** dormouse

loiter: lag **4** idle, loaf **5** dally, delay, drawl, shool, tarry **6** cooter, dawdle, linger **7** saunter **8** hesitate

loiterer: **4** slug **5** drone, idler **7** laggard **8** sluggard

Loki: *child:* Hel **4** Hela, Nare, Nari
mother: **9** Angrbodha
victim: **6** Balder
wife: **5** Sigyn

loll: **4** hang **5** droop, tarry **6** dangle, froust, frowst, lounge, sprawl **7** recline

loma: 4 hill
lombard: 6 banker, cannon
Lombardy: *king:* 6 Alboin
  lake: 4 Como
lomilomi: rub 7 massage, shampoo
lomita: 4 hill
London: *bus conductor:* 6 clippy
  district: 4 Soho 5 Acton 7 Adelphi, Alsatia,
  Chelsea, Mayfair, the City, West End
  fish market: 12 Billingsgate
  landmark: 6 Big Ben 11 Tower Bridge 13
  Tower of London 16 St. Paul's Cathedral,
  Westminster Abbey
  monument: Gog 4 Eros 5 Magog 6 Nelson
  8 Cenotaph, Victoria
  museums and galleries: 4 Tate 7 British,
  Hayward, Wallace 8 National 13 Madame
  Tussaud 17 Victoria and Albert
  parks: 4 Hyde 5 Green 7 Holland, Regen-
  t's, St. James 9 Battersea 10 Kew Gardens
  promenade: 4 Mall
  river: 6 Thames
  roisterer: mun
  society: 7 Mayfair
  square: 9 Leicester, Trafalgar
  stables: 4 mews
  street: 4 Bond 5 Fleet 6 Savile, Strand 7
  Downing, Wardour 9 Cheapside, Haymar-
  ket, Whitehall 10 Piccadilly
  suburb: Kew 8 Finchley
  subway: 4 tube 11 underground
  timepiece: 6 Big Ben
Londoner: 7 Cockney
lone: 4 sole 5 alone, apart 6 single 7 retired 8
  isolated, separate, solitary 9 unmarried 12
  unfrequented
Lone Ranger: *companion:* 5 Tonto
  horse: 6 Silver
Lone Star State: 5 Texas
loneliness: 8 solitude 9 dejection, isolation 10
  depression, desolation 12 lonesomeness
lonely: 4 lorn, sole 5 alone, apart 6 dismal,
  dreary 7 deavely, forlorn 8 deserted, desolate, lonesome, secluded, solitary 11
  sequestered 12 unfrequented
long: far 4 hone, hope, pine 6 aspire, hanker, hunger, prolix, thirst 7 lengthy,
  tedious 8 drawn-out, extended, tiresome
  9 elongated, prolonged, wearisome 10
  protracted
  and slender: 5 lanky, lathy, reedy 6 linear 9
  elongated
  for: 4 miss, want, wish 5 covet, crave, yearn
  6 aspire, desire
long ago: 4 yore
long dozen: 8 thirteen
Longfellow hero: 8 Hiawatha
longheaded: 4 wise 6 shrewd 9 sagacious 10
  hardheaded 11 foresighted

longing: yen 4 envy, itch 6 desire 7 athirst,
  craving, wistful 8 appetite, cupidity, home-
  sick, prurient, yearning 9 nostalgia 10
  desiderium
longitudinally: 7 endlong 10 lengthwise
longshoreman: 8 dockhand 9 stevedore
long-suffering: 4 meek 7 patient 8 patience
  9 endurance 10 forbearing
long-winded: 6 prolix 7 prosaic, verbose 9
  garrulous
loo: pam 6 toilet 8 card game 11 water closet
look: con, pry, see 4 gaze, leer, ogle, peek,
  peep, peer, pore, scan, seem, skew 5 blush,
  dekko, fleer, glare, gliff, glime, gloat,
  gloom, glout, lower, sight, smile, snoop,
  stare, watch 6 aspect, behold, gander,
  glance, glower, glunch, notice, regard,
  search, squint, visage 7 observe 8
  demeanor 10 appearance, get a load of
  after: 4 tend 6 attend 7 care for
  at: eye, see 4 glom, ogle, view 6 behold,
  regard 7 examine, observe
  back: 6 recall, relive, review 7 rethink 8
  remember 10 retrospect
  down on: 7 despise
  for: 4 seek 5 await 6 expect 10 anticipate
  forward to: 5 await 6 expect 10 anticipate
  into: 5 study 6 search 7 examine, inspect 8
  sound out 11 investigate
  like: 8 resemble
  over: 4 scan 6 ignore, survey 7 examine 8
  overlook 9 disregard 11 reconnoiter, recon-
  noitre
  toward: 4 face
looker-on: 8 audience, beholder 9 bystander,
  spectator 12 rubber-necker
lookout: 5 scout, watch, worry 6 conner, sentry 7 concern, palaver 8 observer 9 crow's
  nest 10 watchtower, widow's walk
looks (see also **look**): 4 face 8 features 10
  attraction
loom: 4 brew, hulk, tool 5 dobby, weave 6
  appear, emerge, gather, gentle, impend,
  vessel 7 machine 9 implement 10 receptacle
  part: bar, lam 4 caam, leaf, reed, sley, warp,
  weft 5 easer, lathe 6 batten, hanger, heddle
  7 harness, shuttle, treadle
loon: auk, nut, sap 4 bird, dolt, lout 5 diver,
  rogue, scamp, wabby 6 cobble, puffin, rascal 9 guillemot
loony: 5 crazy, kooky 8 demented 11 harebrained
loop: eye, tab 4 ansa, coil, fold, hank, kink,
  knot, oese, ring 5 bight, bride, coque,
  curve, honda, hondo, noose, picot, terry
loophole: out 4 muse 5 meuse, oilet 6 escape,
  eyelet, outlet 7 opening 8 aperture, weakness

loose: gay, lax **4** fast, floa, free, open **5** baggy, bulgy, crank, let up, loose, relax, slack, vague **6** coarse, dangly, random, unlash, wobbly **7** ease off, immoral, movable, relaxed, unbound, unleash **8** insecure, unstable, withdraw **9** desultory, dissolute, unbridled, unchecked **10** incoherent, indefinite, licentious, unattached, unconfined, unfastened **11** untrammeled **12** disconnected, uncontrolled, unrestrained **14** unconventional

loose ends: 4 dags **5** bored **7** details, tagrags **8** restless **9** fragments

loose-jointed: 5 lanky, rangy **6** clumsy, wobbly **7** rickety **10** ramshackle

loosen: pry **4** ease, free, undo **5** relax, untie **7** slacken **8** liberate, unfasten **9** disengage, extricate **10** talk freely **11** disentangle

loot: rob, sum **4** sack, swag **5** booty, money, spoil, steal, strip **6** pilfer, ravage, spoils **7** pillage, plunder, ransack
receipt of: **9** theftbote

lop: bob, cut, dod **4** clip, crop, flop, hang, sned (Sc.), snip, trim **5** droop, prune, slice **6** dangle **7** pendant, pendent **8** truncate

lope: job **4** gait **6** canter **7** dogtrot

lopper: 4 clot **6** curdle **7** clabber **9** coagulate

lopsided: 4 alop **5** askew **6** uneven **7** crooked **10** unbalanced

loquacious: 5 gabby **6** verbal **7** prating, verbose **8** cackling **9** garrulous, talkative **10** babblative, chattering

loquacity: 9 garrulity **13** talkativeness

lord: aga, god **4** agha, duke, earl, khan, peer, rule, tsar **5** baron, laird, liege, noble, ruler **6** domine, knight, master, prince **7** grandee, marquis, paladin, vavasor **8** domineer, governor, nobleman, seigneur, suzerain, vavasour, viscount **9** dominator
attendant: **5** thane

Lord have mercy upon us: 8 response **10** invocation **12** Kyrie eleison **14** miserere domine

Lord High Executioner: 4 Koko

Lord Jim author: 6 Conrad

lordly: 5 grand, noble, proud **6** uppish **7** haughty **8** arrogant, despotic **9** imperious, masterful **10** tyrannical **11** dictatorial, domineering, magisterial, overbearing

lordship: 4 rule **7** dynasty **8** dominion **10** allegiance

Lord's Prayer: 9 Our Father **11** Paternoster

lore: 4 lear, myth **6** advice, legend, wisdom **7** counsel **8** learning **9** erudition, knowledge, tradition **11** instruction

Lorelei: 5 siren **9** temptress **11** femme fatale
poet: **5** Heine

lorgnette: 8 eyeglass **10** opera glass

lorica: 5 shell **7** cuirass **8** corselet

lorikeet: 6 parrot

loriot: 6 oriole

loris: 5 lemur

lorn: 5 alone **6** bereft **7** forlorn **8** desolate, forsaken, lonesome **9** abandoned

Lorna Doone: 5 novel
author: **9** Blackmore

Lorraine: *capital:* **4** Metz
river: **4** Saar

Los Angeles: *baseball team:* **6** Angels **7** Dodgers
basketball team: **5** Kings **6** Lakers **8** Clippers
football team: **4** Rams **7** Raiders
landmark: **8** Grauman's **13** Farmers Market, Hollywood Bowl, La Brea Tar Pits
valley: **11** San Fernando

lose: 4 amit, fail, miss **5** waste **6** defeat, mislay **7** forfeit **8** misplace **9** dissipate, fail to win

losel: bum **6** loafer **10** ne'er-do-well

loss: 4 cost, leak, ruin, toll **5** price, waste **6** damage, damnum, defeat, injury, ullage **7** expense, failure **8** amission, casualty, decrease **9** decrement, detriment, privation **10** affliction, bankruptcy **11** bereavement, deperdition, deprivation, destruction

lost: 4 gone, lorn **5** perdu (F.) **6** absent, hidden, ruined, wasted **7** forlorn, mislaid, strayed **8** absorbed, confused, defeated, estrayed, obscured, prodigal **9** abandoned, forfeited, perplexed, reprobate, subverted **10** abstracted, bewildered, dissipated, overthrown **11** preoccupied **13** irreclaimable

Lost Horizon: *author:* **6** Hilton
land: **9** Shangri-La

lot: hap **4** dole, doom, fate, land, luck, much, plat, plot **5** batch, field, grist, group, share, weird **6** amount, bundle, chance, divide, hazard, parcel **7** destiny, fortune, portion **8** caboodle, quantity **9** allotment, apportion, great deal **13** apportionment
appointment by: **9** sortition
miscellaneous: **6** fardel, job lot

Lot: *father:* **5** Haran
place of flight: **5** Sodom
sister: **6** Milcah
son/grandson: **4** Moab **5** Ammon
uncle: **7** Abraham

loth: 8 See **loath**

lotion: 4 balm, wash **5** salve **8** ablution, liniment, ointment

lots: 4 gobs **5** scads **6** plenty

lottery: 6 gamble, raffle **7** drawing **10** sweepstake

lotto: 4 keno **5** bingo, keeno

lotus, lotos: 7 nelumbo **9** water lily **10** chinquapin

lotus bird: 6 jacana

lotus-eater: 7 dreamer **10** Lotophagus

423

lower

lotus tree: 4 sadr 9 persimmon

loud: 5 gaudy, heavy, noisy, showy, vivid 6 coarse, flashy, vulgar 7 blatant, clamant, obvious, raucous 8 emphatic, strepent, vehement 9 clamorous, insistent, turbulent, unrefined 10 blustering, boisterous, stentorian, tumultuous, vociferous 11 ear-piercing, thersitical 12 obstreperous

lough: sea 4 lake, loch, pool 5 water

Louisiana: *arena:* 9 Superdome
capital: 10 Baton Rouge
city: 7 Augusta 8 Metairie 9 Lafayette 10 New Orleans, Shreveport 11 Lake Charles
early explorer: 6 de Soto 7 la Salle
festival: 8 Carnival 9 Mardi Gras
flood wall: 5 levee
lake: 13 Pontchartrain
motto: 25 Union, Justice, and Confidence
people: 5 Cajun 6 Creole 7 Acadian
river: 11 Mississippi
state bird: 7 pelican
state flower: 8 magnolia
state tree: 11 bald cypress
university: LSU 6 Tulane 9 Grambling

---

lounge: bar 4 idle, loaf, loll, sofa 5 bange, couch, divan, relax 6 froust, frowst, loiter, sprawl

loup: 4 flee, jump, leap

louse: nit 4 lice (pl.) 5 aphid, aphis 6 cootie, slater

lousy: 5 dirty 6 rotten 9 pedicular 10 pediculous

lout: bow, oaf 4 bend, boor, clod, coof, dolt, fool, gaum, gawk, hulk 5 clown, cuddy, stoop, yahoo, yokel 6 curtsy, lubber 7 bumpkin, grobian, palooka 10 clodhopper

loutish: 4 rude 5 crude 6 clumsy, gauche (F.), stupid 7 awkward

lovable, loveable: 4 dear 7 amative, amiable, winning 8 adorable, dovelike 9 endearing 11 captivating, enthralling

love: gra (Ir.), loe (Sc.) 4 amor (Sp.), dear, dote, like 5 adore, aloha, amore (It.), amour (F.), Cupid, fancy, liebe (G.), lover 6 enamor 7 charity, embrace, idolize 8 fondness, goodwill, idolatry 9 adoration, affection 10 attachment, sweetheart 11 inclination
apple: 6 tomato
feast: 5 agape 7 banquet 9 gathering

god of: 4 Amor, Ares, Eros, Frey, Kama 5 Bhaga, Cupid
goddess of: 5 Athor, Freya, Venus 6 Freyja, Hathor, Ishtar 9 Aphrodite
knot: 6 amoret
potion: 5 charm 7 philter, philtre 11 aphrodisiac
science of: 9 erotology
story: 7 romance
token of: 6 amoret

lovebird: 6 parrot

loveliness: 6 beauty 10 prettiness 11 pulchritude

lovelock: 4 curl 5 tress 12 heartbreaker

lovely: 4 fair 5 sweet 6 loving, pretty, tender 7 amiable, amorous, angelic 8 adorable, alluring, angelina, charming, graceful 9 beautiful 10 attractive

lover: ami (F.), gra (Ir.) 4 beau, chap 5 amado (Sp.), amada (Sp.), amant (F.), leman, Romeo 6 adorer, amadis, amante (F.), bon ami (F.) 7 admirer, amorist, amoroso (It.), Don Juan, gallant 8 belamour, Lothario 9 bonne amie (F.), enamorata (It.) 10 dilettante, innamorata (It.), innamorato (It.), sweetheart, amateur (F.) 11 philanderer
meeting place: 5 tryst
patron saint: 9 Valentine
rustic: 7 Celadon

lovesick: 6 pining 7 longing 11 languishing

loving: 4 fond 6 ardent, erotic, lovely 7 adorant, adoring, amative, amatory, amorous, devoted 9 affecting 12 affectionate

loving cup: tyg 5 prize 6 trophy

low: bas (F.), moo 4 base, bass, blue, deep, hill, mean, neap, weak 5 dirty, gross, snide 6 bellow, coarse, common, earthy, feeble, filthy, humble, humbly, slight, sordid, vulgar 7 bestial, cut-rate, ignoble, plebian, shallow, slavish 8 dejected, off-color 9 depressed, earthbred 10 melancholy 11 undignified, unfavorable 12 contemptible, disreputable

lowan: 4 bird 6 leipoa, mallee

Low Country: 7 Belgium, Holland 10 Luxembourg 11 Netherlands

low-lived: 4 mean 10 despicable 12 contemptible

low-necked: 9 decollete

low tide: ebb 4 neap

lowbred: 5 crude 6 coarse, vulgar 11 ill-mannered

lower: dip 4 alow, bate, drop, sink, vail 5 abase, abate, baser, below, decry, demit, frown, glare, scowl, under 6 bemean, debase, deepen, demean, derate, glower, humble, lessen, meaner, nether, reduce 7 beneath, degrade, depress, descend, subside 8 diminish, downward, inferior, mark down 9 disparage **10** depreciate, nethermore

lowering: **4** dark **5** heavy **6** beetle, cloudy, gloomy, lowery, sullen **8** overcast **11** threatening

lowest: **5** least, nadir **6** bottom **7** bedrock, deepest **10** nethermost

lowing (see also **low**): **6** mooing **7** mugient **9** bellowing

lowland: **4** flat, holm, spit, vale **5** terai (Ind.) **6** valley **7** bottoms

Lowlander (see also **Scotland**): **4** Scot **9** Sassenach
language: **6** Lallan **7** Lalland

lowly: **4** base, mean, meek **6** humble, modest **7** ignoble **8** ordinary **11** commonplace **12** unpretending **13** unpretentious

lox: **6** salmon

loy: **4** tool **5** slick, spade

loyal: **4** feal, firm, leal, true **5** liege, pious **6** stanch **7** devoted, staunch **8** constant, faithful

loyalty: **6** fealty, homage **8** devotion, fidelity **10** allegiance **12** faithfulness

Loyalty island: Uea **4** Lifu, Uvea

Loyolite: **6** Jesuit

lozenge: **4** pill **5** candy **6** jujube, pastil, tablet, troche **7** diamond **8** pastille **9** cough drop

lubber: oaf **4** boor, gawk, lout **5** churl, drone, idler **6** sailor **8** landsman **10** landlubber

lubricate: oil **4** dope **6** grease **7** moisten

lubricious: **4** lewd **6** shifty, tricky, wanton **7** elusive **8** slippery, unstable **9** lecherous, salacious **10** lascivious

luce: **4** fish, pike

lucent: **5** clear, lucid **6** bright **7** shining **11** translucent, transparent

lucerne, lucern: **7** alfalfa

lucid: **4** sane **5** clear **6** bright, lucent **7** crystal, shining **8** luminous, pellucid, rational **11** clear-headed, resplendent, translucent

lucidity: **6** sanity **7** clarity

Lucifer: **5** devil, Satan

luck: hap, lot, ure **4** cess, eure, fate **5** deuce **6** chance, hansel **7** ambsace, fortune, handsel, success **8** fortuity **9** advantage, mischance **10** prosperity **11** good fortune
bringer: **5** Jonah **6** clover, mascot **9** horseshoe **10** rabbit-foot
stroke of: **5** fluke **11** serendipity
token for: **5** charm **6** amulet, mascot **7** periapt **8** talisman **9** horseshoe

lucky: **5** canny, happy, sonsy **6** sonsie **7** blessed **8** gracious **9** favorable, fortunate **10** auspicious, propitious, prosperous, successful **12** providential **13** serendipitous

lucrative: **6** paying **7** gainful **10** beneficial, productive, profitable **11** money-making **12** remunerative

lucre: **4** gain, gelt, loot, pelf **5** booty, money **6** profit, riches, wealth

ludicrous: **5** antic, awful, comic, droll, funny **6** absurd **7** comical, foolish, risible **8** farcical **9** burlesque, laughable **10** ridiculous

lug: box, ear **4** drag, draw, haul, lout, pull, tote, worm **5** carry **10** projection

luggage: **4** bags **7** baggage **9** suitcases

lugubrious: sad **4** dour **6** dismal, gloomy, morose **7** doleful **8** mournful

lukewarm: **5** tepid **11** indifferent

lull: **4** calm, hush, rock **5** allay, quiet, still **6** pacify, soothe **7** compose **8** calmness, mitigate **9** cessation **11** tranquilize

lullaby: **4** song **5** baloo, balow (Sc.) **10** cradlesong

lumber: **4** raff, wood **6** refuse, timber

lumbering: **7** awkward **11** heavy footed

lumberman: **6** logger, sawyer, scorer **10** lumberjack
boot: pac
hook: **5** peavy **6** peavey
sled: **4** tode **7** travois **8** travoise

luminary: sun, VIP **4** lion, name, star **5** light **7** notable **12** illumination, intellectual

luminous: **5** clear, light, lucid **6** bright **7** glowing, lambent, radiant, shining **8** gleaming **9** brilliant **11** illuminated, transparent **12** incandescent **14** phosphorescent

lummox: **4** boor, lout **5** yahoo **7** bumpkin, bungler

lump: bat, cob, dab, dad, dot, gob, nub, wad **4** beat, blob, burl, cake, clog, clot, daud, heap, hump, hunk, knob, knot, mass **5** bulge, claut, clump, clunk, hunch, wedge **6** dollop, gobbet, nodule, nugget **8** swelling **12** protuberance

lumpfish: **6** paddle **10** cockpaddle (Br.)

lumpish: **4** dull **5** heavy, inert **6** stodgy, stupid **8** sluggish **9** shapeless

lumpy: **5** bumpy, heavy, rough **6** choppy, clumsy

lunacy: **5** folly, mania **7** madness **8** delirium, insanity **9** craziness **11** derangement

lunar (see also **moon**): **6** lunate **8** crescent **9** satellite

lunatic: mad **6** insane, madman, maniac **7** frantic **8** demoniac **9** bedlamite, psychotic **10** moonstruck

lune: **5** leash **8** crescent

lung: **5** organ
disease: **9** emphysema **11** anthracosis **12** tuberculosis
having: **9** pulmonate
sound: **4** rale

lunge: jab **4** foin, leap, stab **5** barge, longe, lurch, pitch **6** plunge, thrust

lupine: **6** fierce **7** wolfish **8** ravenous, wolflike **9** perennial **10** blue bonnet

lurch: rob 4 jolt, reel, roll 5 barge, cheat, fraud, lunge, pitch, steal, trick 6 careen, career, swerve 7 stagger, stumble

lure: 4 bait, draw, trap 5 decoy, snare, tempt 6 allure, entice, seduce 7 attract, beguile, pitfall 8 inveigle 10 allurement, attraction, enticement

lurer: 4 bait 5 siren 7 trapper

lurid: wan 4 pale 5 gaudy, livid 6 dismal, gloomy 7 ghastly, hideous 8 gruesome, shocking, terrible 9 startling 11 sensational

lurk: 4 hide 5 skulk, slink, sneak 6 ambush 9 lie in wait

luscious: 4 rich, ripe 5 sweet 6 creamy 7 cloying 8 delicate 9 delicious 10 voluptuous

lush: sot 4 rich, soft 5 drunk 6 limber, mellow 7 profuse 9 alcoholic, luxuriant, succulent 11 intoxicated

lusory: 7 playful 8 sportive

lust: 4 long, urge 5 crave, yearn 6 desire, fervor, hunger, libido, liking 7 craving, lechery, passion 8 appetite, cupidity 11 inclination 12 sexual desire

luster, lustre: 4 cave, naif 5 sheen, shine, water 6 polish 7 glister 8 radiance, schiller, splendor 10 brightness, brilliance 11 distinction, iridescence

lusterless: mat, wan 4 dead, drab, dull 5 faded, fishy, matte 6 gloomy 9 tarnished

lustful: hot 4 gamy, lewd 5 cadgy 7 fulsome, rammish 9 lecherous, salacious

lustrous: 5 nitid 6 bright, glossy, orient 7 radiant 8 gleaming, nitidous 9 brilliant 11 illustrious, transparent

lusty: 4 cant, hale 5 crank, frack, frank, freck, hardy 6 cranky, gawsie, hearty, robust, strong, sturdy 8 bouncing, vigorous

lute: tar 4 clay, ring 6 cement 7 dyphone 10 instrument
  relative of: 8 mandolin

luxe: 8 elegance, richness

Luxembourg: *capital:* 10 Luxembourg
  city: 4 Hamm 7 Rosport 9 Dudelange
  currency: 5 franc 7 centime
  measure: 5 fuder
  river: 7 Moselle

luxuriant: 4 lush, rank, rich 5 frank 6 lavish 7 fertile, opulent, profuse, teeming 8 prolific 9 exuberant 10 voluptuous

luxuriate: 4 bask, riot 5 revel 6 wallow 7 delight

luxurious: 4 posh, rich 5 gaudy, plush 6 costly, lavish 7 elegant, opulent 8 gorgeous, sensuous 9 sumptuous 11 comfortable, extravagant

luxury: 6 frills 7 amenity, comfort 8 delicacy, grandeur
  lover of: 8 Sybarite

Luzon: *city:* 5 Gapan 6 Ilagan, Manila 10 Cabanatuan
  dialect: 6 Itaves
  mountain: Iba
  people: Ata, Ita 4 Aeta, Atta 5 Tagal 6 Aripas, Arupas, Igorot, Isinay, Itaneg 7 Igorote, Italone, Kalinga, Kankana, Tagalog
  seaport: 6 Aparri, Manila
  volcano: 5 Mayon

lyam: 5 leash 10 bloodhound

lycanthrope: 8 werewolf

lycee: 6 lyceum, school

lyceum: 11 meeting hall

Lydia: *capital:* 6 Sardis
  king: 5 Gyges 7 Croesus
  river: 8 Pactolus

lye: 6 potash 7 caustic 8 lixivium

lying: 4 flat 5 awald, awalt, false, prone 6 supine 8 couchant 9 deceitful, deceptive, dishonest, mendacity 10 pseudology, untruthful

lying-in: 8 birthing 11 confinement 12 accouchement

lymph: sap 5 chyle, water 6 plasma, spring

lynch: 4 hang 6 murder 7 execute

Lynette's knight: 6 Gareth

lynx: cat 5 pishu 6 bobcat, lucern 7 caracal 8 carcajou 9 catamount

Lyra star: 4 Vega

lyrate: 9 spatulate

lyre: 4 asor, harp 6 kissar, trigon 7 cithara, kithara, testudo
  symbol of: 6 Apollo

lye turtle: 11 leatherback

lyric: lai, lay, ode 4 alba, odic, poem 5 epode, gazel, melic, verse 6 ghazel, poetic, rondel 7 cancion, canzone (It.)
  descort: 7 rondeau 8 madrigal 9 dithyramb
  Muse: 5 Erato 8 Polymnia 10 Polyhymnia

lyrical: 6 epodic, poetic 7 musical, sestina

lyrichord: 11 harpsichord

lysogenic: 9 temperate 11 not virulent

lyssa: 6 rabies 11 hydrophobia

M

Maacah: *father:* **6** Talmai **7** Absalom
   husband: **5** David **8** Rehoboam
   son: Asa **5** Hanan **6** Abijah **7** Absalom
mabolo: **4** plum **7** camagon
macabre: **4** eery, grim **5** eerie **7** ghastly **8**
   grewsome, gruesome, horrible **9** death-like
macaca: **5** lemur **6** monkey
macadam: tar **8** pavement
macaroni: **5** dandy, pasta **6** noodle
macaque: **4** bruh **6** monkey, rhesus
macaw: ara **4** arra, bird **5** arara **6** parrot **7**
   maracan **8** aracanga, ararauna, cockatoo
Macbeth: *author:* **11** Shakespeare
   character: **5** Angus **6** Banquo
   slayer: **7** Macduff
   title: **5** Thane
   victim: **6** Banquo, Duncan
maccaboy: **5** snuff
mace: dod, rod **4** club, maul, rush **5** spice,
   staff **6** mallet **7** swindle
   bearer: **6** beadle
   royal: **7** scepter, sceptre
Macedonia: *ancient king:* **6** Philip **7** Perseus
   9 Alexander
   capital: **6** Skopje
   city: **4** Stip **6** Bitola **8** Gostivar
   currency: **5** denar
macerate: ret **4** fade, soak **5** steep **6** shrink,
   wither **7** shrivel **8** grow thin
machete: **4** bolo, fish **5** blade, knife **6** guitar,
   tarpon
Machiavellian: **4** wily **6** crafty **7** cunning **8**
   guileful **9** deceitful **11** treacherous **12**
   unscrupulous
Machiavelli's book: **6** Prince **8** Art of War,
   Mandrake
machila: **7** hammock
machination: **4** plan, plot **5** cabal **6** device,
   scheme **8** artifice, intrigue **9** stratagem **10**
   conspiracy **11** contrivance
machine: car **4** auto **5** motor, robot **6** device,
   engine **7** vehicle **9** apparatus, appliance,
   automatic, automaton, mechanism **10** automobile **11** contrivance, machination,
   stereotyped **12** organization, standardized
   hydraulic: **9** telemotor
   kind: **4** pump **5** crane, lever, screw, wedge **6**
   pulley **7** turbine **8** catapult, windlass, windmill **9** jackscrew, treadmill **12** wheel and axle
   13 inclined plane **14** block and tackle

   part: cam **5** rotor, wheel **6** piston, stator,
   tappet **8** flywheel **10** crankshaft
machine gun: **4** Sten **5** Maxim **7** Gatling **8**
   Thompson **9** Hotchkiss **10** chatterbox
   place: **4** nest
machismo: **7** manhood **8** virility **9** manliness
   14 masculine pride
macilent: **4** lean, thin **9** emaciated
mackerel: **4** scad **5** akule, atule, tunny **7** escolar, tassard **8** hardhead
   genus: **7** scomber
   net: **7** spiller
   young: **5** spike **6** tinker **7** blinker
mackerel bird: **7** wryneck **9** kittiwake
mackle: See **macula**
macle: **7** crystal **11** chiastolite
macrobiotic: **4** diet **9** long-lived
macula: **4** blot, blur, spot **5** stain **6** blotch,
   mackle, macule **7** blemish
maculate: **6** impure **7** defiled, spotted,
   stained **8** speckled, unchaste **10**
   besmirched
mad: **4** gite, gyte, hute (Sc.), loco, nuts **5** angry,
   crazy, folle, irate, rabid, vexed **6** frenzy,
   insane, unwise **7** enraged, foolish, frantic,
   furious **8** demented, frenetic, incensed,
   maniacal **9** desperate, fanatical, hilarious,
   phrenetic, psychotic **10** distracted, distraught, infatuated, infuriated **11** fantastical,
   mentally ill **12** arreptitious, unreasonable
Madagascar: *animal:* **6** aye-aye, tanrec, tenrec **7** tendrac
   capital: **12** Antananarivo
   city: **7** Mojanga **8** Tamatave
   civet: **7** fossane
   currency: **5** franc **7** centime
   language: **8** Malagasy
   lemur: **5** avahi, indri **6** aye-aye **9** babacoote
   measure: **7** gantang
   palm: **6** riffia
   people: **4** Hova
   tree: **11** antankarana
madam, madame: Mme., Mrs., Sra. (Sp.) **4**
   bawd, dame, doña, lady, wife **5** donna,
   hussy, title, wench, woman **6** senora **8** mistress **9** courtesan
Madame Bovary: **4** Emma
   author: **8** Flaubert
madcap: **4** wild **7** hotspur **8** reckless **9** impulsive

madder: aal 7 munjeet 8 dyestuff
  family: 9 rubiaceae
made: 8 prepared 10 artificial
  to-order: 6 custom 7 bespoke 11 custom
  built
  up: 8 invented 10 fabricated
Madeira: *capital:* 7 Funchal
  wine: 4 bual 5 tinta, tinto 7 malmsey, ser-
  cial 8 verdelho
mademoiselle: 4 miss 8 senorita
madhouse: 5 chaos 6 asylum, bedlam 8 bughouse 12 insane asylum
madid: wet 5 moist
madman: 6 maniac 7 furioso, lunatic 8 frenetic 9 phrenetic, psychotic
madness: ire 4 fury 5 folly, furor, mania 6
  bedlam, frenzy, lunacy, rabies 7 dewanee,
  ecstasy, widdrim 8 delirium, dementia,
  insanity 9 amazement, furiosity, phrenetic
  10 great folly, nonsomania 11 derangement
Madras: *present name:* 9 Tamil Nadu
madrepore: 5 coral 6 fossil
Madrid promenade: 5 Prado
madrigal: ode 4 glee, poem 5 lyric 6 verses 8
  part-song
Maecenas: 6 patron 10 benefactor
maelstrom: 4 eddy 5 swirl 7 current, turmoil
  9 whirlpool
maenad: 9 bacchante
maestro (see also individual countries, *conductor, composer*): 6 master 7 teacher 8
  composer 9 conductor 10 bandleader 11
  choir-master 13 kapellmeister
  di-cappela: 11 choirmaster 13 kapellmeister
maffle: 6 muddle, mumble 7 confuse, stammer 8 bewilder, squander
mafia: mob 8 brigands 9 syndicate 10 cosa
  nostra, underworld
Magadha king: 9 Bimbisara 10 Ajatasatru
magadis: 5 flute 9 monochord
magazine: 4 pulp 5 depot, store 7 almacen,
  arsenal, chamber, journal 9 ephemeris,
  reservoir, warehouse 10 periodical, repository, storehouse 11 armamentary
magenta: dye 7 fuchsia
maggot: bug 4 grub, mawk, whim 5 larva,
  mathe 6 gentle, notion 7 caprice 12 eccentricity
magi: 5 Sages 6 Gaspar 7 wise men 8 Melchior 9 Balthasar
  gift of: 4 gold 5 myrrh 12 frankincense
magic: art 4 rune 5 fairy, obeah, spell, turgy 6
  glamor, voodoo 7 alchemy, glamour, gramary, sorcery, theurgy 8 brujeria (Sp.), gramarye, illusion, witchery, wizardry 9 deception, diablerie, sortilege 10 hocus pocus,
  necromancy, witchcraft 11 conjuration,
  enchantment, legerdemain, thaumaturgy

12 invultuation 13 sleight of hand
  act of: 11 conjuration 13 sleight of hand 16
  prestidigitation
  lantern: 11 epidiascope 12 stereopticon
  perform: hex 6 sorcer 7 conjure 9 cast spell
  pert. to: 6 goetic
  staff: 4 wand 7 rhabdos 8 caduceus
  symbol: 5 charm 6 caract 8 pentacle
  tree: 13 polemoniaceae
  word: 5 selah 6 presto, sesame, shelah 11
  abracadabra
magical: 6 occult 8 charming 10 bewitching
  11 necromantic
magician: 4 mage, magi 5 magus 6 Merlin,
  wabeno, wizard 7 juggler 8 conjurer, conjuror, mandrake, sorcerer 9 archimage,
  charlatan, enchanter 11 entertainer,
  medicine man, necromancer, thaumaturge
  13 thaumaturgist 15 prestidigitator
  assistant: 6 famuli (pl.) 7 famulus
  manual: 8 grimoire
  motion: 4 pass
Magic Mountain: *author:* 4 Mann
  character: 7 Castorp
magirist: 4 cook
magisterial: 5 lofty, proud 6 august, lordly 7
  haughty, stately 8 arrogant, dogmatic 9 dignified, imperious, masterful 11 dictatorial,
  domineering, overbearing 13 authoritative
magistrate: 4 beak, doge 5 edile, judge 6
  alcade, alcaid, archon, bailie, bailli, syndic 7
  alcaide, alcalde, bailiff, burgess, podesta
  (It.) 8 alderman, governor, mittimus, official 11 burgomaster
  orders: 4 acta (pl.) 5 actum
magma: 5 dregs 8 sediment
  basalt: 10 limburgite, molten rock
magnanimous: big 4 free 5 lofty, noble 6
  heroic 7 exalted, liberal 8 generous 9 honorable, unselfish, unstinted 10 high-
  minded, high-souled 13 disinterested
magnate: 4 lord 5 baron, mogul, noble 6
  bashaw, tycoon 7 grandee, rich man 10
  clarissimo 11 millionaire
magnesian limestone: 8 dolomite
magnesium: *silicate:* 4 talc
  sulfate: 7 loweite
magnet: 7 terella 8 solenoid, terrella 9 loadstone, lodestone
  end: 4 pole
  pole: red
  type of: bar 9 horseshoe
magnetic: 5 polar 8 charming 10 attractive,
  electrical 11 charismatic
  unit: 5 weber
magnetize: 4 lure 5 charm 7 attract 9 captivate
magnificence: 4 pomp 6 luxury 8 grandeur,
  splendor 13 sumptuousness

magnificent: **4** rial, rich **5** grand, great, noble, regal **6** august, lavish **7** exalted, stately, sublime **8** glorious, gorgeous, palatial, splendid, striking **9** beautiful, excellent, sumptuous **10** munificent

magnify: **4** laud **5** exalt **7** amplify, enhance, enlarge, greaten **8** increase **9** aggravate, overstate **10** exaggerate

magniloquent: **6** turgid **8** boastful **9** bombastic **12** ostentatious **13** grandiloquent

magnitude: **4** bulk, mass, size **6** extent **7** bigness **9** dimension, greatness **10** importance

magnolia: **5** yulan **6** saucer **7** big-leaf **8** sweetbay **12** umbrella tree

Magnolia State: **11** Mississippi

magnum: **6** bottle

magnum opus: **4** work **11** achievement, masterpiece

magot: ape **6** figure

magpie: **4** bird, pica, piet, piot, pyat **6** gabber, prater **9** chatterer, haggister
diver: **4** smew
shrike: **7** tanager

magsman: **8** swindler

maguari: **5** stork

maguey: **4** aloe **5** agave, fiber, plant **7** cantala

magus: **4** mage, magi **6** wizard **7** charmer **8** magician

Magyar: **6** Ugrian **9** Hungarian

maha: **4** deer **6** langur, sambar

mahajan: **11** moneylender

mahala: **5** squaw

mahogany: **4** toon **6** acajou, totara **7** albarco, gunnung **8** bangalay **9** cailcedra **12** reddish brown

maholi: **5** lemur

Mahomet: See **Mohammed**

Mahometan: See **Muslim**

Mahound: **5** devil

mahout: **6** driver, keeper **14** elephant driver

Maia: **12** Earth Goddess
father: **5** Atlas
sisters: **8** Pleiades
son: **6** Hermes **7** Mercury

maid: **4** ayah, girl, help, lass **5** bonne, woman **6** damsel, maiden, virgin **7** Abigail, ancilla, colleen, servant, slavery **8** domestic, suivante **9** attendant, cameriera, tirewoman
mythical: **5** nymph
nurse: **4** amah

maiden: deb, new **4** girl, jill, lass **5** first, nymph, sylph **6** damsel **7** damosel, damozel, untried **8** damozell **9** damosella, damoysell, debutante

maiden duck: **8** shoveler

maidenhair: **4** fern **8** adiantum
tree: **6** ginkgo

maidenly: shy **6** gentle, modest, virgin

maiden name: nee

Maid of Astolat: **6** Elaine

Maid of Orleans: **7** Pucelle **9** Joan of Arc

mail: bag **4** post, send, ship **5** armor **6** wallet **8** dispatch
boat: **6** packet

maim: **4** hurt **6** mangle **7** cripple, disable **8** mutilate **9** dismember

main: sea **4** duct, high, pipe **5** chief, first, grand, ocean, prime **7** capital, conduct, conduit, leading, purpose **8** foremost **9** principal

Maine: *capital:* **7** Augusta
city: **4** Bath **6** Bangor **8** Lewiston, Portland **9** Biddeford, Skowhegan
Indian: **7** Abenaki **9** Penobscot
lake: **5** Moose **6** Sebago **8** Rangeley **9** Flagstaff, Moosehead **12** Androscoggin
motto: **6** Dirigo (I direct)
mountain: **8** Cadillac, Katahdin **10** Saddleback
nickname: **8** Down East
product: **7** lobster
river: **4** Saco **8** Kennebec
state bird: **9** chickadee
state flower: **8** pine cone
state tree: **4** pine

mainland: **8** fastland **9** continent

mainsheet: **4** rope

mainstay: key **4** prop **7** support

Main Street author: **5** Lewis

maintain: **4** avow, bear, fend, hold, keep **5** argue, claim **6** affirm, allege, assert, avouch, defend, retain, uphold **7** bolster, contend, declare, espouse, justify, support, sustain **8** conserve, preserve **9** vindicate **10** provide for
again: **8** reassert

maintainable: **7** tenable

maintenance: **5** batta **6** upkeep **7** alimony, prebend **10** livelihood

maison: **5** house
de sante: **6** asylum **8** hospital **10** sanatorium

maize: **4** corn, samp **5** grain **7** mealies
bread: **4** piki
genus: Zea

majestic: **5** grand, lofty, noble, regal, royal **6** august, kingly **7** leonine, stately, sublime **8** elevated, imperial, splendid **9** dignified, sovereign **11** magnificent

major: big **4** main **5** chief **7** capital, greater, officer **8** superior **9** principal
music: dur

Majorca: *city:* **5** Palma

group: **15** Balearic Islands
part of: **5** Spain
majordomo: **6** butler **7** bailiff, manager, servant, steward **9** seneschal
majority: age **4** body, more, most **6** quorum **7** greater
make: cut, gar (Sc.) **4** coin, form **5** brand, build, force, frame, shape **6** compel, create, invent, render **7** compose, confect, fashion, prepare, produce **8** contrive, generate **9** construct, fabricate **11** manufacture
   do: eke **6** manage **9** improvise
   fun of: rib **5** scoff, tease **8** ridicule
   known: **6** impart, reveal **7** divulge, publish, uncover **8** disclose, discover, proclaim **9** advertise, publicize
   off: fly, run **4** bolt, flee **7** abscond, run away
   out: see **4** fare, kiss **6** deduce, gather **7** discern, succeed **8** copulate
   over: **4** redo **6** revamp **9** refashion
   up for: **5** atone **10** compensate
   up: **6** create, devise **7** arrange, compose, typeset **8** assemble, complete, cosmetic **9** fabricate, improvise **11** grease paint
make-believe: **4** sham **5** feign, magic **7** charade, feigned, fiction, pretend **8** pretense
maker: god **4** doer **6** author, factor **7** creator **8** declarer, inventor **9** architect **10** originator **12** manufacturer
makeshift: **4** rude **8** resource **9** temporary
mal (F.): bad **4** evil
   de mer: **11** seasickness
   du pays: **12** homesickness
Malabar (see also **India**): *black:* **5** ochna
   canoe: **5** tonee
   monkey: **8** wanderoo
   palm: **7** talipot
   people: **4** Nair
malacca: **4** cane **5** stick
malachite: **4** bice **7** azurite, mineral
maladive: ill **4** sick **6** feeble, sickly, unwell **9** unhealthy
maladroit: **6** clumsy **7** awkward, unhandy **8** bungling, inexpert **10** left-handed
malady (see also **disease**): **7** ailment, illness **8** disorder, sickness **9** affection, complaint, distemper **10** affliction **13** indisposition
malanders: **6** eczema
malapropism: **8** solecism, word play **13** error in speech
malapropos: **8** untimely **10** irrelevant **11** inexpedient, inopportune
malar: **6** zygoma **9** cheek-bone
malaria: **4** agie, ague **5** chill, fever, miasm **6** miasma
   antidote: **7** quinine
   carrier: **8** mosquito **9** anopheles
malarkey: **6** drivel **8** nonsense
Malawi: *capital:* **8** Lilongwe

city: **5** Mzuzu, Zomba **8** Blantyre
currency: **6** kwacha **7** tambala
language: **7** Tumbuku **8** Chichewa
mountain: **7** Sapitwa
river: **5** Shire **7** Zambezi
malaxate: **5** knead

Malaysia: *almond:* **6** kanari
   animal: lar **5** tapir **10** chevrotain
   ape: lar
   boat: **4** proa **5** praam, prahu **6** praham **7** cougnar
   buffalo: **7** carabao **8** seladang
   capital: **11** Kuala Lumpur
   Christian: **7** Ilokano
   city: **4** Ipoh **6** Kelang, Melaka **7** Begawan, Malacca **10** George Town
   clothing: **4** baju **6** sarong
   condiment: **6** sambal, sambei **7** semball
   crane: **5** sarus
   currency: sen **7** ringgit
   disease: **4** amok, lata **5** amuck, latah
   food: **5** satay
   former part: **9** Singapore
   fruit: **8** rambutan
   island: Aru, Goa, Kei, Oma **4** Bali, Buru, Gaga, Java, Sulu **5** Ambon, Arroe, Arrou, Banca, Banda, Buton, Ceram, Misol, Sangi, Sumba, Timor **6** Boefon, Boeroe, Borneo, Flores, Jilolo, Lombik, Madura, Musool, Sangir, Soemba, Talaur, Waigeu
   isthmus: Kra
   knife: **4** cris, kris **5** crise **6** crease, creese, kreese, parang
   language: **5** Hakka, Malay, Tamil **6** Bahasa **7** Tagalog
   mammal: **10** chevrotain
   measure: **4** tael, wang
   mountain: **6** Gunong, Gunung **8** Kinabalu
   musical instrument: **7** anklong
   ox: **5** tsine **7** banteng
   palm: **4** ejoo, sago **5** areng **6** arenga, gebang, gomuti, nibong, nibung **7** talipot
   parrot: **4** lori, lory **6** lories
   people: Ata **4** Dyak **5** Bajau, Malay, Tagal **6** Aripas, Semang **7** Bisayan, Kadazan, Tagalog, Visayan
   pepper: **4** siri **5** sirih
   pewter: **4** trah
   rice field: **5** sawah
   settlement: **7** kampong
   skirt: **6** sarong
   title: **4** tuan
   tree: **4** upas **5** kapur, niepa, terap **6** durian, durion
   ungulate: **5** tapir

malconformation: 9 imperfect 16 disproportionate

malcontent: reb 5 rebel 6 uneasy 8 agitator, Frondeur 10 complainer, discontent, rebellious 12 discontented, dissatisfied

male: boy, lad, man, mas 4 gent 5 manly 7 mankind, manlike, mannish 9 masculine
animal: tom 4 buck, bull, hart, jack, stag, stud 8 stallion
figure: 5 atlas 7 telamon
gelded: ox 4 galt 5 steer 6 eunuch 7 gelding

malediction: ban 5 curse, spell 7 malison, slander 8 anathema, evil talk 9 blasphemy 11 imprecation 12 denunciation

malefactor: 5 felon 7 convict, culprit 8 criminal, evildoer, offender 9 wrongdoer

malefic: 4 evil 6 malign, wicked 7 harmful, hurtful 8 devilish 11 mischievous

malevolence: 4 evil, hate 5 pique, spite 6 enmity, hatred, malice, rancor 8 ferocity 9 animosity, hostility, malicious, malignity 10 bitterness

malfeasance: 5 crime, wrong 8 trespass 10 misconduct 11 delinquency

malheur: 10 misfortune

Mali: *capital:* 6 Bamako
city: 8 Timbuktu 10 Tombouctou (F.)
currency: 5 franc 7 centime
former name: 11 French Sudan
holy man: 8 marabout
mountain: 9 Timetrine 12 Hombori Tondo

malice: 5 pique, spite 6 enmity 7 ill will 9 animosity 13 maliciousness

malicious: 4 evil 5 catty, cruel, depit, nasty 6 bitter 7 heinous 8 sinister, spiteful 9 felonious, green-eyed, malignant, rancorous, resentful 10 calumnious, despiteful, despiteous, malevolent 11 ill-disposed 12 cantankerous, unpropitious
action: 5 arson, crime 8 sabotage 9 vandalism
intention: 6 animus

malign: 4 evil, foul 5 abuse, curse, libel, smear 6 bewray, defame, revile, vilify 7 asperse, baleful, blacken, deprave, hurtful, slander 8 sinister, virulent 10 calumniate, pernicious

malignant: 4 evil 6 wicked 7 hateful, heinous, hellish, noxious, vicious 8 spiteful, venomous, virulent 9 cancerous, felonious, ferocious, invidious, malicious, poisonous, rancorous 10 rebellious 11 deleterious

malikana: fee 4 duty 7 payment

maline: net 4 lace

malinger: 5 dodge, evade, shirk, skulk

malkin: cat, mop 4 drab, hare 6 sponge 8 slattern 9 scarecrow

mall: 4 walk 5 allee, alley, shops 6 arcade, mallet, stores 7 meeting 9 promenade

mallard: 4 duck

genus: 4 anas

malleable: 4 soft 6 docile 7 ductile, pliable 8 amenable, yielding

mallemuck: 6 fulmar, petrel 9 albatross

mallet: tup 4 club, mace, mall, maul, mell (Sc.) 5 gavel, madge 6 beater, beetle, driver, hammer
game using: 7 croquet
hatter's: 6 beater
presiding officer's: 5 gavel
wooden: 4 maul 6 beetle

Mallorca: See **Majorca**

mallow: 4 okra 5 plant 6 cotton, escoba 8 hibiscus 9 holly-hock

malm: 4 loam 5 brick 9 limestone

malmsey: 4 wine 5 grape 7 madeira

malnutrition: 7 cachexy, wasting 8 cachexia
disease: 6 anemia, scurvy 7 rickets 8 beriberi, marasmus, pellagra 11 kwachiorkor

malodorous: 4 gamy, high, rank 5 fetid 6 putrid, smelly 7 noisome 8 stinking 11 odoriferous

malt: 8 diastase
beverage: ale 4 beer, brew 5 lager, stout 6 zythem
froth: 4 barm
ground: 5 grist
infusion: 4 wort
vinegar: 6 alegar
worm: 5 toper 7 tippler

Malta: *award:* 11 George Cross
capital: 7 Valetta 8 Valletta
city: 5 Gharb, Gzira 8 Victoria 10 Paolaaghra
currency: 4 lira, liri 5 cents, pound
former defenders: 12 Hospitallers
hamlet: 5 casal 6 casale
measure: 4 salm 5 canna, salma 7 caffiso
weight: 4 rotl, salm 5 artal, artel, parto, ratel, salma 6 kantar
wind: 7 gregale 8 levanter

---

maltreat: 5 abuse 6 defile, defoul, demean, misuse 9 humiliate

malum: 4 evil 5 wrong 7 offense

malvaceous plant: 4 okra 6 cotton, escoba, mallow 7 althaea

malvasia: 5 grape

mameluke: 5 slave 7 servant

mammal (see also **animal**): cat, dog 5 beast, canid, horse, ovine, swine 6 bovine, equine, feline, monkey, rodent 7 primate 8 edentate, ruminant, ungulant 9 carnivore, marsupial
amphibious: 5 otter

antlered: elk **4** deer **5** moose **7** caribou **8** reindeer

aquatic: **4** seal **5** otter, shark, whale **6** desman, dugong, manati, rytina, walrus **7** dolphin, manatee, sea lion **8** sirenian **12** hippopotamus

aquatic order: **4** cete **7** cetacea

arboreal: ai **5** lemur, sloth **6** fisher, monkey **7** glutton, opossum, raccoon **8** banxring, kinkajou **9** orangutan

armored: **9** armadillo

badgerlike: **5** ratel **8** balisaur

bearlike: **5** panda

bovine: ox, bos, cow **4** bull, calf, zebu **5** bison, steer **7** taurine **8** longhorn

burrowing: **4** mole **6** badger, gopher, wombat **8** squirrel **9** armadillo, groundhog, wood chuck

camellike: **7** guanaco

caprine: **4** goat

carnivorous: **9** carnivore

cetacean: see *aquatic* above

civetlike: **5** genet

coat: fur **4** hide, skin **6** pelage

cud-chewing: **8** ruminant

deerlike: **10** chevrotain

desert: **5** camel **9** dromedary

doglike: **6** jackal

dolphinlike: **4** inia

domestic: cat, cow, dog, pig **4** goat **5** horse, sheep **6** cattle

donkeylike: **6** onager

edentate: **7** ant bear, tamadau **8** anteater, pangolin

egg-laying: **7** echidna **8** platypus

equine: **4** colt, foal, mare **5** filly, horse, zebra **8** stallion

extinct: **6** rytina **8** mastodon

feline: cat **4** lion, lynx, puma **5** ounce, tiger **6** bobcat, cougar, jaguar, ocelot, serval **7** cheetah, leopard, panther

fish-eating: **5** otter

fleet: **4** deer, hare **7** cheetah **8** antelope

flying: bat

fur-bearing: **4** coon, mink **5** coypu, otter, sheep, skunk **6** badger, ermine, marten, martin, nutria, rabbit **7** genette, raccoon **8** squirrel

giraffelike: **5** okapi

gnawing: **6** rodent

hands different from feet: **6** bimana

hedgehog-like: **6** tenrec

herbivorous: **5** daman, tapir **6** bovine, dugong, equine **7** manatee **8** ruminant **9** orangutan **10** rhinoceros **12** hippopotamus

highest order: **7** primate

horned: ox, cow **4** boar, gaur, goat, reem **5** bison, takin **7** buffalo, unicorn **8** antelope, reindeer, seladang **10** rhinoceros

insectivorous: bat **4** mole **6** tenrec **7** tendrac **8** hedgehog

large: **5** whale **7** mammoth **8** behemoth, elephant, mastodon **10** rhinoceros **12** hippopotamus

largest: **5** whale

lemurine: **5** potto

leopardlike: **4** lion, lynx, pard, puma **5** tiger **6** cougar, jaguar, ocelot **7** polecat, wildcat

llamalike: **6** alpaca, vicuna **7** guanaco

lowest order: **9** marsupial **11** marsupialia

marsupial: **4** tait **5** koala **7** opossum **8** kangaroo **9** bandicoot

meat-eating: **9** carnivore

molelike: **6** desman

monkey-like: **5** lemur, loris

mouselike: **5** shrew

musteline: **5** otter, ratel

nocturnal: bat **5** hyena, lemur, ratel, tapir **6** macaco, racoon **7** raccoon, tarsier **8** kinkajou, platypus

omnivorous: hog, pig **4** goat **5** swine

ovine: **5** sheep

plantigrade: **6** racoon **7** raccoon

porcine: hog, pig, sow **4** boar **5** swine **7** peccary

pouched: **9** marsupial

raccoon-like: **5** coati **6** olingo

retentive: **8** elephant

rhinoceros-like: **5** tapir **14** baluchitherium

ring-tailed: **4** coon **5** lemur **7** raccoon

ruminant: ox, yak **4** deer, goat **5** bison, camel, llama, moose, okapi, sheep, steer **6** alpaca, cattle, chewer, vicuna **7** buffalo, giraffe **8** antelope

scaled: **8** pangolin

shelled: **9** armadillo

short-tailed: **7** bobtail

skunk-like: **5** zoril

slow-moving: **5** loris, sloth

smallest: **5** shrew

snake-eating: **8** mongoose

spiny: **6** tenrec **9** porcupine

thick-skinned: **8** elephant **9** pachyderm **10** rhinoceros

toothless: **8** edentate

tropical: **5** coati, rhino **7** peccary **9** coatimodi **10** coati-mundi, rhinoceros

tusked: **4** boar **6** walrus **7** mammoth **8** elephant, mastodon

ursine: **4** bear **5** panda

viverrine: **8** falanaka

vulpine: fox **4** wolf

web-footed: **5** otter

winged: bat **5** lemur **6** colugo

wing-footed: **6** aliped

zebra-like: **6** quagga

mammock: **4** tear **5** break, scrap **6** mangle **8** fragment

mammogram: **10** breast X ray

mammon: **6** riches, wealth

mammoth: **4** huge **5** large **6** animal, fossil **8**

gigantic **10** gargantuan **11** elephantine

man (see also **fellow, person**): boy, guy, vir (L.) **4** aner (Gr.), chal, chap, homo (L.), male, mann (G.), uomo (It.), work **5** bloke, chiel, guard, homme (F.), human, valet **6** andros (Gr.), chield, fellow, hombre (Sp.), mensch (Yid.) **7** counter, fortify, homines (L.pl.), husband, laborer, mankind, operate **8** creature, humanity **9** anthropos (Gr.)

aged: vet **4** cuff, sire **5** elder, senex (L.), uncle **6** gaffer, geezer, stager **7** grandpa, starets (Russ.) **8** grandpop, old-timer **9** grandsire, graybeard, patriarch **10** goldenager, Methuselah **11** grandfather **12** nonagenarian, octogenarian

bad-tempered: **6** bodach, grouch **10** curmudgeon

bald: **9** pilgarlic **10** pillgarlic

big: cob

brass: **5** Talos

brave: **4** hero, lion

castrated: **6** eunuch

coarse: **5** churl, knave **7** ruffian

conceited: **7** coxcomb

cruel: **4** ogre **6** tyrant **7** monster, ruffian, villain

cunning: **5** rogue **7** shyster **9** trickster **10** mountebank

dissolute: **4** rake, roue

eccentric: **6** codger

effeminate: **5** fairy, sissy **7** milksop **9** androgyne

elderly: see *aged* above

enlisted: **6** rating, sailor **7** private, soldier **8** sergeant

fashionable: fop **4** dude **5** dandy **10** Corinthian **11** Beau Brummel **12** boulevardier

handsome: **6** Adonis

hardheaded: **5** boche

hard-pressed: Job

henpecked: **10** hoddy-doddy **11** milquetoast

impetuous: **7** hotspur

important: VIP **4** hero, name **5** nabob **6** big wig **7** grandee

ladies': **4** beau **5** beaux (pl.) **7** gallant

learned: PhD **4** bhat **6** doctor, pundit, savant **7** erudite, scholar, teacher **8** literati **9** literatus, professor **11** philologist

little: **6** mankin, shrimp, squirt **8** homuncio **10** homunculus

mechanical: **5** robot **7** android **9** automaton

medicine: **6** doctor, priest, shaman

money: **9** paymaster

mother of: Eve **6** Cybele

newspaper: **6** editor **8** reporter **9** columnist, publisher **10** journalist

objectionable: oaf **4** boor **5** bully **8** wiseacre

of all work: **4** joey, mozo **8** factotum, handyman

of letters: **6** savant **11** litterateur

of straw: **6** figure **9** nonentity

of the world: **6** layman **10** secularist **11** cosmopolite **12** sophisticate

old: see *aged* above

old-clothes: **4** poco **6** ragman

outdoor: **6** camper, hunter **7** athlete **9** fisherman

personifying: **15** anthropomorphic

pert. to: **5** human **6** humane, mortal

political: **7** senator **8** diplomat **9** statesman **10** ambassador, legislator **11** assemblyman **14** representative

poor: **6** pauper **7** peasant **8** beadsman, bedesman

primitive: **6** savage **8** urmensch (Yid.) **11** Neanderthal

resembling: **7** android **10** anthropoid

rich: **5** Midas, nabob, Trump **6** tycoon **7** Croesus, magnate **9** plutocrat **10** capitalist, Rothschild **11** billionaire, millionaire, Rockefeller

science: **9** ethnology **12** anthropology

self-important: **6** egoist **10** cockalorum

shadowless: **6** ascian

single: **4** stag **7** widower **8** bachelor, celibate

unattractive: **4** clod, goon, jerk, lout, rube, slob **5** yokel **6** lummox **7** fathead **11** clodhoppper

undercover: spy **5** agent **9** detective **12** investigator

unemployed: **6** batlan, batlon (Yid.)

white: **6** buckra **7** cachila (P.I.) **8** paleface

wicked: **7** villain

wise: **4** sage, seer **5** Solon **6** Nestor **7** Solomon

worthless: bum **4** hobo **5** idler, tramp

young: boy **5** youth **6** varlet

manacle: **4** bond, cuff, iron **5** chain, darby **6** fetter, hamper **7** confine, shackle **8** handcuff **9** restraint

manada: **4** herd **5** drove, flock

manage: man, run **4** boss, fare, head, lead, rule **5** dight, frame, get by, guide, order, steer, wield **6** convoy, demean, direct, govern, handle **7** achieve, conduct, control, dispose, execute, husband, operate, oversee **8** contrive, dispense, engineer, maneuver **9** supervise **10** accomplish, administer, manipulate

frugally: **6** eke out **7** husband **9** economize

hard to: **6** ornery

manageable: **4** easy, tame, yare **6** docile, wieldy **7** ductile, pliable **8** flexible, maniable, workable **9** compliant, tractable **10** governable

management: 4 care 6 agency, charge, menage 7 address, economy, gestion 8 carriage, demeanor 9 demeanour, governail, ordinance 10 enterprise, governance 11 generalship, supervision
  good: 6 eutaxy

manager: 4 doer 5 agent 6 gerent 7 captain, curator, foreman, handler, steward 8 director, governor 10 supervisor 12 entrepreneur

Manasseh: *father:* 6 Joseph
  grandfather: 5 Jacob
  son: 4 Amon, Jair 6 Machir

manatee: 6 dugong, seacow 8 sirenian

Manchuria (see also **China**): *city:* 5 Hulan, Kirin 6 Harbin, Mukden 8 Shenyang 9 Changchun, Niuchwang
  lake: 6 Khanka
  province: 5 Jehol, Jilin
  river: 4 Amur, Liao, Yalu 7 Songhua

manciple: 7 steward 8 purveyor

mandarin: 4 duck, tree 6 orange 7 Chinese 8 official 9 tangerine
  residence: 5 yamen

mandate: 4 writ 5 brief, edict, order 6 behest, charge, decree, demand, firman 7 bidding, command, precept 8 warranty 9 authority, direction 10 commission, injunction, referendum

mandatory: 7 binding 8 required 9 necessary 10 imperative, obligatory

mandible: jaw 4 beak 9 chelicera
  part: 5 molar

mandrel: bar, rod 4 axle, ball, beam, pick 5 arbor, winch 7 spindle

mandrill: 6 baboon, monkey

manducate: eat 4 chew 9 masticate

mane: 4 hair 5 brush 6 grivna 8 encolure

manege: 4 lope, trot 6 riding 8 training 13 riding academy

maneuver: 4 plot, ploy 5 trick 6 deploy, jockey, scheme, tactic 7 echelon 8 artifice, contrive, engineer 9 evolution, stratagem 10 manipulate
  aviation: 4 bank, loop, spin 7 echelon, flathat 9 chandelle, Immelmann 10 barrel loop
  military: 6 tactic

manful: See **manly**

mange: 4 itch, meal, scab 6 fodder, scurvy
  cause of: 4 mite 6 acarid

manger: bin, box 4 crib, meal 5 stall 6 creche, trough 7 banquet

mangle: cut, mar 4 hack, maim 5 botch, spoil 6 bruise, garble, ironer, smooth 8 calender, lacerate, mutilate 9 dismember

mango: 4 tree 5 bauno, fruit
  bird: 6 oriole 11 hummingbird
  fish: 9 threadfin
  tree: 4 tope

mangrove: 4 tree 5 goran, shrub

mangy: 4 mean 5 seedy 6 scurvy, shabby 7 squalid 10 despicable 12 contemptible

manhandle: 4 maul 5 abuse 7 rough up 10 knock about, slap around

Manhattan: See **New York City**

mani: 6 peanut

mania: 4 fad 4 rage 5 craze, furor 6 frenzy, furore, hangup 7 madness, passion 8 delirium, idée fixe (F.) 9 cacoethes, obsession 11 derangement
  burning: 9 pyromania
  buying: 9 oniomania
  stealing: 11 kleptomania

maniac: 6 crazed, insane, madman 7 lunatic 8 demented, deranged 9 psychotic 10 hysterical

manicure: cut 4 clip, pare, trim 6 polish

manifest: 4 open, show 5 argue, clear, index, overt 6 attest, evince, extant, graith, patent, reveal 7 approve, confess, declare, develop, display, evident, exhibit, explain, express, glaring, invoice, obvious, signify, visible 8 apparent, develope, disclose, discover, evidence, indicate, palpable 11 conspicuous, demonstrate, discernible, indubitable, perspicuous 12 indisputable, unmistakable

manifestation: 4 sign 5 phase 6 avatar, effect, ostent 7 display 8 epiphany 10 appearance, revelation

manifesto: 5 edict 7 placard 8 evidence 9 statement 11 declaration 13 demonstration

manifold: 4 many 7 various 8 multiple, numerous 9 different, multifold, multiplex, replicate 12 multifarious

manikin: 4 puny 5 dwarf, model, pygmy 7 phantom 9 mannequin 10 diminutive, homunculus

Manila: *creek:* 6 estero
  hemp: 5 abaca, abaka 6 banana
  river: 5 Pasig

Manila Bay boat: 6 bilalo

manioc: 7 cassava, tapioca

manipulate: rig, use 4 work 5 treat, wield 6 handle, manage 7 control, operate

manipulator: 9 osteopath 12 chiropractor

Manitoba: *capital:* 8 Winnipeg
  city: 7 Brandon, Portage, St. James 8 Flin Flon 10 St. Boniface
  lake: 8 Winnipeg 12 Winnipegosis
  mountain: 4 Duck 5 Baldy 6 Riding 9 Porcupine
  provincial flower: 6 crocus 12 pasqueflower
  river: Red 8 Winnipeg 9 Churchill 12 Saskatchewan

mankind: man 4 Adam, male 5 flesh, world 6 humans, people 8 humanity

division: sex **4** race **5** color, tribe **6** gender, people
hater: **11** misanthrope

manly: **4** bold, male **5** brave, hardy, noble **6** daring, strong, virile **7** manlike, mannish **8** resolute **9** dignified, honorable, masculine, undaunted **10** courageous

manna: **4** food, gift **7** Godsend, support **8** delicacy

Mann character: **7** Castorp

mannequin: See **manikin**

manner: air, way **4** cost, form, mien, mode, more, thew **5** guise, trick **6** aspect, course, method **7** address, bearing, fashion, quomodo **8** attitude, behavior **9** behaviour, technique **10** appearance, deportment
law: **4** modi (pl.) **5** modus

mannered: **8** affected, stylized **10** artificial **13** self-conscious

mannerism: **4** mode, pose **5** trait **7** bearing **11** affectation, peculiarity

mannerly: **4** nice **5** civil, moral **6** decent, polite, seemly **8** decorous **9** courteous **11** well-behaved

manners: **5** lates, mores **6** custom **7** conduct, decorum **8** behavior, courtesy **9** amenities, etiquette **10** deportment

Mannus' father: **6** Tuisto

Man of Destiny: **17** Napoleon Bonaparte

Man of Galilee: **11** Jesus Christ

man of God: **5** rabbi, saint **6** pastor, priest **7** ascetic, prelate **8** minister **12** ecclesiastic

man-of-war: **4** ship **7** frigate, soldier, warrior
deck: **5** orlop

manor: **4** hall **5** abode, house **6** estate **7** mansion
land: **6** barton **7** demesne

Man O'War: **5** horse **6** winner **9** racehorse

manse: **7** rectory **8** vicarage **9** parsonage

manservant: **4** help, mozo, syce **5** gilly (Sc.), groom, valet **6** Andrew, butler, garcon, gillie, Jeeves **8** factotum

manship: **5** honor **6** homage **7** courage, manhood **8** courtesy, humanity **9** manliness

mansion: **4** hall, home **5** abode, house, manor, siege **7** chateau, lodging **8** chateaux (pl.), dwelling **9** residence
papal: **7** Lateran

manslaughter: **6** murder **7** killing, slaying **8** butchery, homicide

mansuete: **4** kind, tame **6** gentle

manta: ray **4** wrap **5** cloak, cloth **7** blanket, bulwark, shelter **8** mantelet **9** devilfish

mantegar: ape

mantel: **4** arch, beam **5** brace (Sc.), ledge, shelf, stone **6** clavel, lintel **10** mantel-tree

mantilla: **4** cape **5** cloak, scarf

mantle: **4** brat, capa, cape, coat, cope, hood, mant, robe **5** blush, brain, cloak, cover **6** capote, pinken, redden **7** encloak, envelop **8** insignia, mantilla, vestment

mantra: **4** hymn **5** charm, spell

mantua: **4** gown, robe **5** cloak **9** overdress

manual: **4** book, text **7** clavier, didache **8** grimoire, handbook **9** catechism **11** enchiridion
art: **5** craft
religious: **9** catechism

manufacture: **4** fake, make **5** build, forge **6** invent, make up **7** confect, produce **9** fabricate

manufacturer: **5** maker **7** builder **8** employer **9** fabricant, operative **10** fabricator **12** entrepreneur **13** industrialist

manumission: **7** freedom, freeing, release **10** liberation **11** deliverance **12** emancipation

manure: **4** dung **5** addle **6** ordure **7** compost **10** compusture, fertilizer

manuscript: **4** copy, text **5** codex **7** papyrus, writing **8** document, original **9** archetype, minuscule **11** composition, handwriting
back: **5** dorso
copier: **4** monk **6** scribe
decorated: **11** illuminated
mark: **5** obeli (pl.) **6** obelus
space: **6** lacuna
writing instrument: **6** stylus
written on: **4** bark **6** copper, vellum **7** leather, papyrus **8** palm leaf **9** wax tablet

Man Without a Country: *author:* **4** Hale
character: **5** Nolan

many: **4** fele, raff **6** legion, myriad **7** diverse, several, various **8** manifold, multiple, numerous **9** multifold, multitude, plurality **10** multiplied **11** large number

many-footed: **8** multiped

many-sided: **9** versatile **12** multilateral

mao: **7** peacock

Maori: *bird:* poe, tue, tui
canoe: **4** waka
charm: **7** heitiki
chief: **5** ariki
clan: ati **4** hapu
club: **4** mere, patu, rata
compensation: utu
dance: **4** haka
food: kai
fort: **6** pa, pah
gathering: hui
god: **4** tiki
hen: **4** weka
hero: **4** Maui
house: **5** whare **8** wharekai **9** wherekura **12** wharewananga
over: umu
people: **10** Polynesian
priest: **7** tuhunga
raft: **4** moki **6** moguey

sect: **7** Ringatu
social center: **5** marae
store: **6** pataka
tatooing: **4** moko
tree: **5** mapau **6** manuka **9** tanehakas
tribe: Ati **4** Hapu
village: pah **4** kaik **5** kaika **6** kainga
wages: utu
weapon: **4** mere, patu, rata
map: **4** card, plan, plat, plot **5** carte, chard, chart, image **6** design, set out, sketch, survey **7** diagram, epitome, explore, outline, picture **8** roadbook **9** delineate **10** cartograph, embodiment **14** representation
book: **5** atlas
copier: **10** pantograph
grid: **8** latitude, meridian, parallel **9** longitude
land surface: **11** topographic
maker: **7** charter **8** Mercator **12** cartographer
townsite: **4** plat
weather line: **6** isobar
maple: **4** acer **5** mazer **7** dogwood **8** sycamore
cup: **5** mazer
derived from: **6** aceric
family: **9** aceraceae
fruit: key
kind: **4** rock **5** sugar **6** Norway, Oregon, silver **8** box elder, Japanese
sap: **5** humbo
scale: **10** pulvinaria
seed: **6** samara
spout: **5** spile
mar: **4** amar, blot, ruin, scar **5** botch, spoil **6** damage, deface, deform, impair, injure, mangle **7** blemish **8** obstruct **9** disfigure
marabou: **4** bird, silk **5** stork **6** argala, fabric **8** adjutant **11** feather trim
maral: **4** deer
Marapessa's abductor: **4** Idas
marasca: **6** cherry **10** maraschino
marasmus: **5** waste **10** emaciation **13** contabescence
marathon: **4** race **7** therapy **10** protracted **13** endurance test
maraud: **4** loot, raid, rove **7** pillage, plunder
marauder: **5** thief **6** bandit, pirate, robber **7** cateran (Sc.)
marble: **4** cold, hard **5** agate, rance, stone **6** basalt **7** cipolin **8** brocatel, dolomite **9** unfeeling **10** brocatelle
game: taw
mosaic: **7** tessera
playing: mib, pea, taw **4** doby **5** agate, aggie, alley, dobie **6** glassy **7** shooter
slab: **5** dalle (F.)
marbled: **6** veined **7** striped **10** variegated
Marble Faun: *author:* **9** Hawthorne

character: **5** Hilda **6** Kenyon, Miriam **9** Donatello
marc: **6** pomace, refuse **7** residue
march: **4** hike, slog, trek **5** route, troop **6** border, defile, parade **8** boundary, frontier, smallage **9** cavalcade **10** procession
day's: **5** etape
horsemen: **9** cavalcade
running: **10** double time
spirited: **9** quickstep
March 15: **4** ides
March King: **5** Sousa
marchland: **8** frontier **10** borderland
March sisters: Jo, Amy, Meg **4** Beth
marcid: **4** weak **7** decayed, tabetic **8** withered **9** exhausted **10** emaciating
marcor: **5** decay **7** maramus
Mardi Gras: **8** carnival **10** Fat Tuesday
king: Rex
site: **10** New Orleans
mare: yad **4** jade, yade, yaud (Sc.) **5** gilot, horse, meare **6** dobbin, equine, grasni
young: **5** filly
mare's nest: **4** hoax, mess **5** trick **8** disorder **9** confusion
mare's tail: **5** cloud **6** cirrus
margarine: **4** oleo **6** spread **9** butterine
margin: hem, lip, ori, rim **4** bank, brim, edge, orae (L.), rand, side **5** brink, shore, verge **6** border, fringe, leeway **7** minimum **8** latitude
narrow: **4** hair
note: **7** apostil **8** scholium **10** annotation
set in: **6** indent
marginal: **9** bordering **11** unimportant
Marianas: **4** Guam, Rota **5** Pagan **6** Saipan, Tinian **7** Agrihan **8** Anatahan
people: **8** Chamorro
marigold: **5** boots, caper, gools **6** buddle **7** cowslip, elkslip, golland
genus: **7** tagetes
marijuana: boo, hay, pot, tea **4** hash, hemp, weed **5** grass, joint **7** hashish **8** cannabis
cigarette holder: **4** clip **5** stone **6** crutch
cigarette: **5** joint, stick **6** greefa, griffo, moocah, reefer **7** mohasky **8** joy-smoke, loco weed, Mary Jane **9** Indian hay **10** bambalacha, Mary Warner, Mary Weaver **11** giggle-smoke
user: **7** pothead
marina: **4** dock **5** basin **6** harbor **9** esplanade, promenade
marinade: **5** brine **6** pickle **8** marinate
marinal: **6** marine, sailor, saline **7** mariner **8** nautical
marinara: **11** garlic sauce, tomato sauce
marine: gob, tar **5** jolly, naval, water **7** aquatic, marinal, mariner, oceanic, pelagic **8** halimous, maritime, nautical **9** aequoreal **11** leatherneck

crustacean: **4** crab **6** shrimp **7** lobster **8** barnacle

instrument: aba **5** loran, radar, sonar **7** pelorus, sextant

plant: **4** alga **5** algae **6** enalid **7** seaweed

science: **10** oceanology **12** oceanography **13** marine biology

skeleton: **5** coral

marine animal: orc **4** salp **5** coral, polyp **9** jellyfish

mariner: gob, tar **5** Jacky **6** galoot, lascar, sailor, seadog, seaman **7** buscarl, old salt **8** buscarle, seafarer, waterman **9** aequoreal

card: **5** chart

compass card: **4** rose

compass points: **6** rhumbs

marionette: **6** puppet **10** bufflehead

marital: **6** wedded **7** nuptial **9** connubial **11** matrimonial

marjoram: **4** herb, mint **6** origan

mark: dot, hob, tag, tee **4** belt, goal, heed, line, note, rate, rist, scar, sign, wale **5** badge, brand, grade, label, score, stamp, track, watch **6** accent, beacon, caract, denote, notice, target **7** betoken, blemish, earmark, impress, imprint, insigne, observe **8** identify, insignia (pl.), manifest, standard **9** character, designate, influence **10** impression, indication **11** distinguish **14** characteristic

bad: **7** demerit

diacritical: **5** breve, hacek, tilde **6** accent, macron, umlaut **7** cedilla **8** dieresis **10** circumflex **11** acute accent, grave accent

down: **5** lower

out: **6** cancel, define, delete **7** measure **10** obliterate

possessive: **10** apostrophe

printer's: **4** dele, fist, stet **5** caret, obeli, slash **6** dagger, diesis, obelus **7** obelisk, virgule

punctuation: **4** dash **5** colon, comma **6** hyphen, period **8** dieresis **9** diaeresis, semicolon **11** parentheses (pl.), parenthesis **16** exclamation point

question: **7** erotema, eroteme

reference: **4** star **6** dagger **8** asterisk

tiny: dot

under letter: **7** cedilla

white: **5** rache, ratch

with critical notes: **8** annotate

Mark Antony's wife: **7** Octavia

markaz: **8** district **11** subdivision

marked: **5** fated, noted **6** scored **7** eminent, pointed, scarred **9** prominent **10** emphasized, noticeable **11** conspicuous, outstanding

with lines: **5** ruled **6** gyrose, linear, notate

marker: peg **5** arrow **6** scorer, signal **7** brander, counter, monitor **8** bookmark, recorder **9** indicator, milestone, tombstone **10** gravestone

air course: **5** pylon

floating: **4** buoy

market: **4** gunj (Ind.), mall, mart, sale, sell, shop, sook, vend **5** agora (Gr.), bazar, gunge, halle, plaza, store, tryst (Sc.) **6** bazaar, outlet, rialto, shoppe **7** grocery **8** boutique, debouche (F.), emporium

marketable: **7** salable **8** vendible **10** commercial

markhor: **4** goat

marksman: **4** shot **6** sniper **12** sharpshooter

Mark Twain's name: **7** Clemens (Samuel Langhorne)

marl: **4** clay, loam, malm, sand, silt **5** earth **6** manure **10** fertilizer, overspread

marli: **4** lace **5** gauze, tulle

marlin: **6** curlew, godwit **9** spearfish

marlinspike: fid **4** skua, tool **6** Jaeger

marmalade: jam **5** jelly **6** sapote **8** preserve

tree: **6** mammee

marmite: pot **4** soup **6** kettle **9** casserole

marmoset: **4** mico **6** monkey, pinche, sagoin, wistit **7** tamarin, wistiti

marmot: **5** bobac **6** rodent **8** burrower, whistler **9** groundhog, woodchuck

maroon: **6** enisle, strand **7** abandon, cast off, forsake, isolate, reddish **8** cimarron, purplish

marooner: **6** pirate **9** buccaneer

marplot: **7** meddler, snooper **8** busybody

Marquand character: **4** Moto **5** Apley, Wayde **6** Pulham **7** Goodwin

marquee: **4** sign, tent **6** awning, canopy

marquetry: **5** inlay

kind of: **8** intarsia

marriage: **5** match, union **6** bridal, splice **7** nuptial, wedding, wedlock **8** nuptials **9** matrimony

absence of: **5** agamy

broker: **9** schatchen (Yid.)

forswearer: **8** celibate

fourth: **9** tetragamy

god: **5** Hymen

goddess: **4** Hera

hater of: **10** misogamist

more than one husband: **9** polyandry

more than one wife: **6** bigamy **8** polygamy

notice: **5** banns

of aged: **8** opsigamy

of gods: **8** theogamy

outside tribe: **7** exogamy

pert. to: **7** marital, nuptial, spousal **8** conjugal, hymeneal **9** connubial, endogamic

portion: dot **5** dowry

second: **6** digamy
secret: **9** elopement
single: **8** monogamy
to promise: **7** betroth **8** affiance
to two people: **6** bigamy
marriageable: 6 nubile **8** eligible
married person: 4 wife **6** spouse **7** husband **8** benedict
marrow: 4 best, pith **5** reest (Sc.) **6** inmost **7** essence, medulla
bones: **5** knees
marry: wed **4** join, mate, wive, yoke **5** cleek, hitch, unite **6** buckle, couple **7** espouse, husband **10** tie the knot
Mars: 4 Ares **6** planet, war god
consort: **10** Rhea Silvia
day: **7** Tuesday
discoverer of satellites: **4** Hall
lover: **5** Venus
month: **5** March
pert. to: **5** Arean **7** Martian
planet belt: **5** Libya
planet spot: **5** oases (pl.), oasis
priests of: **5** Salii
region (dark): **4** mare
satellites: **6** Deimos, Phobos
space-craft: **6** Viking **7** Mariner **8** Observer
twin sons: **5** Remus **7** Romulus
Marseillaise author: 13 Rouget de Lisle
marsh: bog, fen, hag **4** jeel, mire, moor, slew, sloo, slue **5** flash, liman, slash, swale, swamp **6** morass, palude, slough **7** cienaga, maremma (It.) **8** quagmire **9** everglade
animal: **4** frog **6** turtle **7** muskrat, raccoon
bird: **4** duck, rail, sora **5** snipe, stilt **7** bittern
crocodile: goa **6** mugger
elder: iva
fever: **7** helodes, malaria
gas: **7** methane **8** firedamp
grass: **4** tule **5** sedge, spart **7** cattail **10** phragmites
hawk: **7** harrier
marigold: **5** boots **7** cowslip
salt: **6** salina **7** corcass
shrub: **4** reed **7** bulrush, cattail **8** buckbean, moorwort
marsh plant genus: 4 sium **5** calla **6** caltha **7** elatine
marshal: 4 lead **5** align, aline, array, guide, usher **6** direct, parade **7** arrange, general, officer **8** official **9** commander
marshwort: 9 cranberry
marshy: wet **4** miry, oozy **5** boggy, fenny **6** callow, quaggy **7** helodes, paludal **8** paludous
lake: **5** liman

marsupial: 4 tait **5** coala, koala, tapoa **6** possum, wombat **7** dasyure, opossum **9** bandicoot
Australian: **4** tait **6** cuscus, possum **7** dasyure, wallaby **8** kangaroo **9** bandicoot, phalanger
bearlike: **5** coala, koala **6** wombat
feature: **5** pouch
mart: 4 fair **5** bazar **6** bazaar, market, rialto **8** emporium
martel: 6 hammer
marten: fur **5** sable **6** animal, fisher
beech: **4** foin
genus: **7** mustela
stone: **4** foin
martial: 7 warlike **8** military
martial art: 4 budo, judo **6** aikido, karate, kung fu, tai chi **7** Shaolin **8** jiujitsu, ninjutsu **9** tae kwan do
Martial's writing: 7 epigram
Martian: 5 Arean
martin: 7 swallow
martinet: 6 tyrant **14** disciplinarian
Martinique: *capital:* **12** Fort-de-France
clothing: **4** jupe
volcano: **5** Pelee
martyr: 5 saint **6** victim **8** sufferer **10** sacrificer
first Christian: **7** Stephen
royal: **7** Charles
martyrdom: 7 killing, passion, torment, torture **8** butchery, distress **10** affliction
place of: **8** Golgotha
marvel: 5 ferly **6** admire, rarity, wonder **7** miracle, portent **8** astonish, rara avis **9** horehound **12** astonishment
marvelous: 7 strange **8** splendid, wondrous **9** excellent **10** improbable, incredible

Maryland: *bay:* **10** Chesapeake
capital: **9** Annapolis
city: **5** Bowie **9** Baltimore, Frederick **10** Hagerstown **12** Havre de Grace
fort: **7** McHenry
founder: **7** Calvert
mountain: **8** Catoctin
nickname: **4** Free **7** Cockade, Old Line
racetrack: **5** Bowie
river: **7** Potomac **8** Patuxent, Pokomoke
state bird: **6** oriole
state flower: **14** black-eyed Susan
state tree: **8** white oak
university: **12** Johns Hopkins

masa: 8 cornmeal
Masada: 8 fortress
   builder: 5 Herod 8 Jonathan
   defender: 6 zealot
   enemy: 4 Rome
   historian: 8 Josephus
   patriot: 6 Sicari
   site: 5 Judea 6 Israel
masculine: 4 male 5 manly 6 strong, virile 7
   manlike, mannish
mash: 4 chap, feed, mess, ogle 5 champ,
   cream, crush, flirt, smash 6 cereal, muddle
   7 farrago, mixture, trouble
mashal: 7 parable, proverb
masher: 4 chap 5 flirt, ricer 6 lecher
masjid: 6 mosque
mask: 4 hide, veil 5 cloak, cover, guise, visor 6
   screen 7 conceal, curtain 8 defilade, disguise 9 dissemble
   half: 4 loup (Fr.) 6 domino (Fr.)
   top knot on: 5 onkos
masked: 6 covert 7 larvate, obscure 8 larvated
   9 concealed, disguised
masker: 6 domino, mummer
maslin: 5 brass 7 mixture 9 potpourri
mason: 7 builder 10 bricklayer 11
   stoneworker
   mixing rod: rab
masonary: 6 ashlar 7 backing, blocage 9
   stonework
masquerade: 4 ball, pose, sham 5 dance,
   guise, party 7 costume, pass for 8 carnival,
   disguise, pretense 13 impersonation
mass, Mass: bat, gob 4 blob, body, bulk,
   clot, heap, lump, size, swad 5 amass,
   batch, gross, group, Missa (L.), store 6
   gather, gobbet, prayer 7 liturgy, phalanx,
   service 8 assemble, majority 9 aggregate,
   Eucharist, magnitude 10 accumulate,
   assemblage, congregate, large-scale 11
   agglomerate, composition, compositure,
   concentrate, consolidate 16 congregation
   rite
   book: 6 missal
   cloudlike: 6 nebula 7 nebulae (pl.)
   confused: cot 5 chaos 6 welter 9 imbroglio
   10 hotchpotch
   directory: 4 ordo
   for dead: 7 requiem
   musical prayer: 5 Credo, Kyrie 6 Gloria 7
   Sanctus 8 Agnus Dei
   pert. to: 5 molar
   service: 7 liturgy 9 Eucharist 11 Lord's
   Supper 13 Holy Communion
   small: dab, pat, wad 4 floc
   tangled: mop 4 shag
mass meeting: 5 rally

Massachusetts: 12 commonwealth
   cape: Ann, Cod
   capital: 6 Boston
   city: 5 Salem 6 Lowell 8 Brockton,
   Lawrence 9 Cambridge, Fall River,
   Worcester 10 New Bedford, Pittsfield
   11 Springfield
   island: 9 Nantucket 14 Chappaquiddick
   15 Martha's Vineyard
   mountain: Tom 6 Brodie 8 Greylock
   mountain range: 10 Berkshires
   music festival: 9 Berkshire 10 Tangle-
   wood
   nickname: Bay 6 Old Bay 9 Old Colony
   peninsula: 7 Cape Cod
   pond: 6 Walden
   reservoir: 7 Quabbin
   river: 6 Nashua 7 Charles, Concord 9
   Merrimack 11 Connecticut
   state bird: 9 chickadee
   state fish: cod
   state flower: 9 mayflower
   state tree: elm
   president: 4 Bush 5 Adams 7 Kennedy

massacre: 6 pogrom 7 carnage 8 butchery 9
   slaughter
massage: rub 5 knead
massager: 7 masseur 8 masseuse
massed: 7 serried
Massenet's opera: 5 Manon, Thais 7 Werther
   12 Don Quichotte
massive: big 4 bold, huge 5 beamy, bulky,
   gross, heavy, large, massy 7 hulking,
   weighty 8 enormous, gigantic 9 cyclopean,
   ponderous 10 boisterous
mast: cue 4 spar 5 stick 6 forage 8 beechnut
   against: 5 aback
   crosspiece: fid
   inclination from perpendicular: 4 rake
   middle: 8 mainmast
   wood for: ash 4 poon
mastaba: 4 tomb 8 platform
master: get, man, rab 4 baas, best, boss, guru,
   head, lord, mian, rule, sire, tame 5 chief,
   learn, rabbi, sahib (Ind.), tutor 6 artist, bridle, buckra, defeat, doctor, domine, expert,
   govern, humble, subdue 7 captain, conquer, maestro, padrone (It.) 8 educator,
   overcome, regulate, surmount, vanquish 9
   commander, overpower, preceptor, subjugate 10 proprietor

Eton: **4** beak
fencing: **7** lanista
harbor: **7** havener, havenor
hard: **6** despot, Legree
of ceremonies: MC **5** emcee
of house: **13** paterfamilias
pert. to: **6** herile
ship's: **7** captain, skipper
masterful: 4 deft **6** expert, lordly **7** haughty, skilled **8** arrogant, masterly **9** arbitrary, imperious **10** commanding **11** dictatorial, domineering, magisterial, overbearing **13** authoritative
mastermind: 4 plan **6** expert **8** wiseacre
masterpiece: 4 coup **7** classic, triumph **9** objet d'art **10** magnum opus, masterwork **11** chef d'oeuvre
mastery: 4 gree **5** gripe, skill **7** control, victory **8** conquest, facility **9** influence, supremacy **13** understanding
mastic: 4 tree **5** gummy, resin **8** adhesive
masticate: 4 chaw, chew **5** crush, gnash, grind **6** crunch **9** manducate
mastiff: dog **5** burly **7** massive
mastodon: 5 giant **7** mammoth **9** pachyderm
mat: cot, rug **4** felt **5** doily, platt, snarl **6** carpet, cotter, petate (Sp.), tangle **7** cushion, drugget, gardnap **8** entangle **10** interweave, lusterless
Mataco: 4 apar **6** Indian **9** armadillo
matador: 6 torero **8** toreador **11** bullfighter
adversary: **4** bull, toro
garment: **4** cape **12** traje de luces
staff: **6** muleta
sword: **7** estoque **8** estocada
matagasse: 11 butcherbird
Mata Hari: spy **5** agent
match: go, cap, pit, tir (F.) **4** bout, cope, even, game, mate, pair, peer, side, spar, suit, team, twin, wife **5** amate, equal, fusee (F.), marry, rival, tally, torch, vesta **6** fellow, spouse **7** compare, compeer, contest, husband, lucifer (Br.) **8** equalize, lampwick, marriage **9** allumette (F.) **10** candlewick, correspond **11** counterpart, countervail, parallelize
matched: 6 paired, teamed
matchless: 5 alone **6** unlike **8** peerless **9** exquisite, non pareil, unequaled **10** inimitable **12** incomparable
mate: cap, pal, wed **4** fear, fere, join, pair, peer, wife **5** billy, buddy, bully, cully, feere, marry, match **6** bunkle, cobber, couple, fellow, spouse **7** brother, compeer, comrade, consort, espouse, husband, partner **9** associate, companion **10** yokefellow
matelot: 6 sailor

mater: mom **4** mama **6** mother
material (see also **cloth, fabric, substance**): **4** data, gear **5** goods, stuff **6** bodily, carnal, matter **7** apropos, weighty **8** physical, tangible **9** corporeal, essential, important **12** nonspiritual
discard: **4** junk, slag **5** scrap, trash, waste **6** refuse **7** rubbish
raw: ore **6** staple
materialism: 9 carnality, physicism
materialize: 4 loom, rise **6** appear, embody, emerge, show up, **8** manifest
materiel: 4 gear **6** tackle **8** supplies **9** apparatus, equipment
maternal: 8 motherly
relation: **7** enation
matey: 6 chummy **13** companionable
matezite: 7 pinitol **10** caoutchouc
mat grass: 4 nard **8** fogfruit
mathe: 4 grub **6** maggot
mathematician: 5 adder **7** figurer
Arab: **6** al-Tusi **7** Alhazen, Khayyam **10** Khowarizmi
European: **5** Boole **6** Cantor, Napier, Newton **7** Leibniz, Russell **9** Descartes, Whitehead
Greek: **6** Euclid **7** Eudoxus, Ptolemy **10** Archimedes, Pythagoras
mathematics: *abbreviation:* Q.E.D. (quod erat demonstrandum)
branch: **7** algebra, geodesy **8** calculus, geometry **9** logarithm **10** arithmetic **12** trigonometry
constant (arbitrary): **9** parameter
deduction: **8** analysis
diagram: **5** graph
equation: **4** surd
exercise: **7** problem
factor: **10** quaternion
instrument: **6** abacus, sector **7** compass **8** arbalest **10** calculator
irrational number: **4** surd
line: **6** vector **7** tangent
number: **5** digit **12** multiplicand
operation: **7** operand
operator: **5** nabla **10** quaternion
proposition: **7** theorem
quantity: **6** scalar
ratio: pi **4** sine **8** derivate
symbol: **7** faciend, operand **12** multiplicand
term: **4** cube, root, sine **6** cosine, square **7** tangent **9** cotangent, factorial
mathemeg: 7 catfish
matie: 7 herring
matin: 4 call, song **6** prayer **9** matutinal
song: **6** aubade
matinee: 4 play, show **5** party **6** soiree **8** neg-

ligee **9** afternoon, reception **13** entertainment

matinee idol: **4** lion, star **5** actor

matka: **4** seal

matrass: **4** tube **5** flask **6** bottle **8** bolthead

matriculate: **5** adopt, enter **6** enroll **8** register **10** naturalize **13** immatriculate

matrimonial: **6** wedded **7** marital, married, nuptial, spousal **8** conjugal, hymeneal **9** connubial

matrimony: **7** wedlock **8** marriage

matrix: bed, die, mat **4** form, mold, womb **5** plasm **6** gangue **7** pattern
plate: **6** stereo

matron: **4** dame, wife **5** widow **6** jailer **7** dowager **11** housekeeper

matte: **10** dull finish

matter: pus **4** gear, malm, mass **5** solid, topic **6** affair, behalf **7** article, concern, problem, signify, trouble **8** business, material **11** constituent
law: res
particle: **4** atom
pert. to: **5** hylic
property: **4** mass **7** inertia
rarefied: fog, gas **4** mist **5** vapor **6** miasma

matter of fact: **4** dull **7** literal, prosaic **9** practical, pragmatic **11** utilitarian **12** in plain style

mattock: axe, hoe **4** bill **5** tubal **6** twibil **7** twibill

mattress: pad **4** sack **6** pallet **7** bedding
cover: **4** tick **7** ticking

mature: age, old **4** aged, form, gray, grow, ripe **5** adult, grown, ripen **6** accrue, autumn, decoct, digest, grow up, mellow, season **7** develop **8** complete **9** come of age

matutinal: **5** early, matin **10** before noon

maud: **5** plaid, shawl **7** blanket

maudlin: **5** beery, corny, soppy, tipsy **7** mawkish, tearful, weeping **10** lachrymose **11** sentimental

mauger: **5** spite **7** ill-will **9** unwilling **15** notwithstanding

Maugham: **6** author
heroine: **5** Sadie
novel: **11** Cakes and Ale **14** Of Human Bondage **15** Moon and Sixpence
play: **4** Rain **9** The Circle

maul: paw **4** beat, bung, club, mace, mall, mell, moth **5** abuse, gavel, staff **6** beater, beetle, bruise, hammer, mallet **7** rough up **9** manhandle

Mau Mau land: **5** Kenya

maumet: god, guy **4** doll, idol **5** image **6** puppet

maund: beg **6** basket, hamper

maunder: **5** growl, haver **6** beggar, drivel, ramble **7** grumble

Maupassant character: **4** Fifi **6** Yvette

Maurois subject: **4** Hugo, Sand **5** Byron, Dumas **6** Proust **8** Disraeli

Mauser: arm, gun **5** rifle **6** weapon **7** firearm

mausoleum: **4** tomb **8** baradari (Ind.)

mauve: **5** lilac **6** purple, violet

maux: **8** slattern, slipshod **10** prostitute

maven: **6** expert **11** connoisseur

mavis: **6** thrush **8** thrasher

maw: **4** craw, crop **6** gullet, mallow **7** stomach

mawk: **6** maggot

mawkish: **5** banal, mushy, vapid **6** sickly **7** maudlin **8** nauseous **9** squeamish **10** disgusting, nauseating **11** sentimental

maxilla: jaw **4** bone

maxim: saw **4** dict, rule, word **5** adage, axiom, gnome, logia (pl.), moral, motto **6** logion, saying **7** brocard, precept, proverb **8** aphorism, apothegm, doctrine, moralism **9** erudition, principle **10** apophthegm

maximum: **4** most, peak **5** limit **7** highest, largest **8** greatest

may: can **4** mote **5** might, shall, shrub **8** hawthorn, possible

Maya: *city:* **5** Tikal **11** Chichen Itza **13** Piedras Negras
day: **5** uayeb
god: **4** Chac **6** Ix Chel **10** Kinich Ahau
month: **5** uinal
people: Mam **8** Pokonchi
year: **4** haab

maybe: **6** happen, mayhap **7** perhaps **8** possibly **9** not surely, perchance **10** indecision **11** possibility, uncertainty

maybird: **4** knot **6** thrush **8** bobolink

maycock: **5** melon **6** maypop, plover

mayfish: **9** killifish

mayflower: **7** arbutus **8** hawthorn, marigold **10** stitchwort **12** cuckooflower

Mayflower's sister ship: **9** Speedwell

mayfly: dun **6** insect

mayor: **5** maire (F.) **7** alcalde (Sp.) **8** official **10** magistrate **12** burgomeister (G.)

maze: **4** daze **5** amaze, fancy **7** confuse, perplex, stupefy **8** bewilder, confound, delirium, delusion **9** amazement, deception, labyrinth **10** hodgepodge **12** bewilderment

mazer: **4** bowl **6** goblet

mazy: **7** complex **9** intricate **10** circuitous, perplexing **11** bewildering

mea culpa: **7** my fault **10** I am to blame

mead: **5** drink **6** meadow **8** hydromel **9** metheglin

meadow: lea **4** mead, vega, wish, wong **5** field, haugh, marsh **6** saeter **7** pasture **9** grassland, grassplot
piece of: **5** swale

meadowlark: **5** acorn **6** medlar

meadowmouse: **4** vole

meadowsweet: 4 rose 7 spiraea

meager: 4 arid, bare, lank, lean, poor, slim, thin 5 gaunt, scant, spare 6 barren, jejune, lenten, meagre, narrow, pilled, scanty, scarce, skinny, sparse 7 scranny, starved, sterile, tenuous 9 emaciated 10 inadequate

meal: tub 4 bite, dune, feed, menu 5 feast, flour, grain, lunch, padar, salep, snack 6 brunch, bucket, dinner, morsel, nocake, powder, repast, supper 7 banquet, blowout, potluck, rations 8 sandbank 9 breakfast, collation, pulverize

army: 4 chow, mess 7 C-ration, K-ration

coarse: 5 grout 7 cribble 8 gurgeons

last course: 7 dessert

light: tea 5 lunch, snack 6 supper, tiffin

main dish: 6 entree

wheat: 4 atta (Ind.)

meals: 5 board

mealy: 4 pale 6 floury, spotty, uneven 7 friable, powdery, starchy 8 farinose 9 colorless, personate 11 farinaceous

mean: low 4 base, clam, hard, lean, norm, poor, show 5 argue, augur, footy, nasty, petty, ratty, snide, snivy, sorry 6 abject, chetif, coarse, common, denote, design, dirten, feeble, humble, intend, medial, median, medium, middle, narrow, paltry, pilled, snivey, sordid 7 average, caitiff, ignoble, pitiful, purport, purpose, signify 8 baseborn, beggarly, churlish, recreant, shameful 9 irascible, malicious, niggardly, penurious, truculent 11 disgraceful, hardhearted 12 contemptible, dishonorable, intermediate, narrow-minded, parsimonious

meander: 4 roam, rove, turn, wind 5 amble, curve, stray, twist 6 ramble, wander 7 complex 8 straggle 9 labyrinth

meaning: 5 drift, point, sense 6 import, intent, spirit 7 anagoge, bearing, essence, message, purport, purpose 9 intending, intention, knowledge 10 definition, indication 11 designation, implication 12 apprehension, significance 13 signification, understanding

without: 4 null

mean line: 9 bisectrix

meanly: 6 humbly, poorly 8 beggarly, shabbily

means: 4 cost, tool 5 agent, funds, money 6 agency, assets, method 7 quomodo 8 averages 9 resources 10 instrument 11 wherewithal 12 intermediary

of livelihood: 4 work 5 labor, trade 8 vocation 10 profession

support: 4 hold 6 income 7 aliment 11 maintenance

meantime: 7 interim 8 interval

meanwhile: 9 adinterim

mear: 8 boundary

measles: 7 rubella, rubeola

measly: 4 mean 6 skimpy, slight 9 worthless 12 contemptible

measure: act, law 4 area, gage, mete, rule, span, tape, time 5 clock, gauge, girth, meter, ruler, scale 6 amount, assize, degree, length, stadia 7 battuta, caliper 8 odometer, tapeline 9 admeasure, calculate, criterion, rotameter

area: are, rod 4 acre 6 decare 7 hectare

astronomical: 7 azimuth

Biblical: cab, hin, kor, log 4 epha 5 aphah, cubit, homer

cable: 4 naut

capacity: 4 cask, gill, orna, peck, pint 5 liter, quart 6 barrel, bushel, gallon

cloth: ell 4 yard

cubic: 4 cord 5 stere 10 hectostere

degree of angle: arc

depth: 6 fathom

dry: 4 bale, peck 6 bushel

energy: erg 5 ergon, joule

established: 8 standard

firewood: 4 cord 5 stere

fish: vog 4 cran (Sc.) 5 crane, crans

flexible: 4 tape 8 tapeline

heat: 4 term 6 calory, Kelvin, therme 7 calorie, Celsius 10 centigrade, Fahrenheit

horse: 4 hand

land: ar, are, rod 4 acre, area, mile, rood 6 decare 7 hectare, kiliare

length: dra, ell, pik, rod 4 foot, inch, knot, mile, nail, pace, pole, yard 5 cubit, digit, meter, metre, perch, toise (F.) 6 league, micron, mikron 7 furlong 9 decimeter, kilometer 10 centimeter, hectometer, millimeter

liquid: aam, keg 4 gill, pint 5 lagen, liter, quart 6 barrel, gallon, magnum, minims, runlet, tierce 7 rundlet 8 hogshead 9 hectolite, kiloliter

loudness: 4 phon

medicinal: 4 dram 5 minim, ounce 7 scruple

nautical: 4 knot 6 fathom

paper: 4 page, ream 5 quire, sheet

printer's: 4 pica 5 agate, empen, point

short: 6 ullage

sound: bel 7 decibel

space: 6 parsec

time: day 4 hour, week, year 5 month 6 decade, minute, moment, second 7 century 10 millennium

water depth: 5 sound

weight: ton 4 bale 5 carat, liter, ounce, pound, stone 9 kiloliter 10 hectoliter

wheat: 4 trug

wine: tun 4 butt, pipe

wire: mil **5** stone
work: erg **5** ergon
yarn: lea **4** heer, typp **6** denier **7** spindle
measured: 7 careful, guarded, regular, uniform **10** deliberate
Measure for Measure: *author:* **11** Shakespeare
character: **5** Elbow, Froth, Lucio **6** Angelo, Juliet
measureless: 4 vast **7** endless, immense **8** infinite **9** boundless, limitless, unbounded, unlimited **11** illimitable **12** immeasurable
measurement: 6 amount **8** quantity **9** dimension **11** mensuration
pert. to: **6** metric **11** dimensional
measuring instrument: 4 gage, tape **5** chain, gauge, meter, ruler, scale **7** alidade **8** measurer, tapeline **9** container, yardstick **13** saccharimeter
acidity: **10** acidimeter
heat: **11** calorimeter
lumber: **6** scaler
surveying: **11** stratameter
thickness: **7** caliper
measuring wheel: 8 odometer **12** perambulator
meat: ham **4** beef, food, gist, lamb, pork, veal **5** flesh **6** chevon, mutton **7** chilver, poultry, venison **9** nutriment
and-potatoes: **5** basic
ball: **7** rissole **9** croquette, fricandel **11** fricandelle
bony: **5** scrag **9** spareribs
cured: ham **5** bacon **6** flitch, salame, salami **7** biltong, bultong, sausage **8** pastrami, pastroma **9** biltongue
cut: ham, rib **4** chop, loin, rack, rump **5** baron, filet, flank, roast, shank, steak **6** breast, cutlet, rasher, saddle **7** brisket, icebone, sirloin **8** shoulder **9** aitchbone, club steak, rump roast, short ribs **10** tenderloin
dish: **5** pasty **6** potpie, ragout **7** goulash, haricot, ravioli **8** fricando **10** fricandeau
dish with vegetables: **4** olla, stew **8** mulligan **10** lobscouse **10** lobscourse
dried: **5** jerky **7** biltong, bultong, pemican **8** pemmican **9** biltongue
frozen: **5** frigo
ground: **7** rissole, roulade, sausage **9** hamburger
jelly: **5** aspic
pie: **5** pasty **7** rissole **8** empanada **9** shepherd's
pin: **6** skewer
potted: **7** rillett **8** rillette
roasted: **5** brede, cabob, kabob
sauce: **4** A-One **5** caper, gravy **14** Worcestershire

slice: **6** collop
smoking place: **5** bucan
unwholesome: **6** cagmag
meatless: 6 lenten, maigre **10** vegetarian
meatus: 4 butt, duct **5** canal **7** foramen, passage
meatworks: 8 abattoir **14** slaughterhouse
meaty: 5 heavy, pithy, solid **11** substantial
Mecca (see also **Muslim**): *deity:* **5** Hobal, Hubal
mosque: **5** Caaba, Kaaba **6** Kaabeh
pilgrimage: **4** hadj
mechanic: erk (F.) **7** artisan, workman **8** operator **9** artificer, craftsman, machinist, operative
mechanical: 9 automatic **10** uninspired **11** automatical, involuntary, perfunctory, stereotyped
mechanical man: 5 robot **7** android **9** automaton
mechanical part: 5 rotor **6** stator, tappet
mechanics branch: 7 statics **8** dynamics
mechanism: 4 gear, tool **5** apron, catch, slide **7** ratchet, tripper **8** selector, signaler **9** apparatus, machinery
driving: **9** propeller
eccentric: cam
self-moving: **8** automata (pl.) **9** automaton
medal: 4 disk **5** award, badge, honor **6** plaque **7** medalet **10** decoration
medallion: 4 coin **6** tablet **8** ornament **10** taxi permit **11** contorniate, contorniato
Medb's consort: 6 Ailill
meddle: 4 nose **5** snoop **6** butt in, dabble, finger, kibitz, monkey, potter, tamper **7** intrude **9** interfere
meddler: 5 snoop **7** marplot **8** busybody, kibitzer **14** polypragmatist
meddlesome: 4 busy **5** fresh **6** prying **7** curious **9** intrusive, officious
Mede: 5 Aryan, Mesne **6** Median
caste: **4** magi
king: Evi
Medea: *brother:* Apsyrtos
father: **5** Aites **6** Aeetes
husband: **5** Jason
lover: **6** Aegeus
rival: **6** Creusa, Glauce, Glauke
son: **5** Medus **6** Medeus
media: See **medium**
medial: 6 middle **8** ordinary
median: 4 mean **6** medial, middle **7** average, central **12** intermediate
mediate: 7 referee **8** ruminate **9** arbitrate, intercede, interpose
mediator: 5 judge **6** broker **7** daysman **9** go-between, middleman **10** ambocepter, interagent **12** intermediary
medic: 6 clover, doctor, intern, medico **7**

alfalfa, luterne, student, surgeon **8** resident
9 physician
false: **5** quack **9** charlatan **10** medicaster
medical: **6** iatric **11** aesculapian
medical officer: **7** coroner
medical student: **6** extern, intern **7** externe,
interne **8** resident
medicinal: **6** curing **7** healing **8** salutary **9**
relieving **11** aesculapian **12** pharmaceutic
  bark: yew **6** cartex
  berry: **5** cubeb
  capsule: **6** cachet
  compound: **4** pill, sera **5** hepar, iodin,
  serum **6** iodine **7** turpeth
  nut: **4** cola
  plant (see also *root* below): rue **4** aloe **5**
  ergot, senna, tansy **6** arnica, cohosh, ipecac
  7 chirata **8** valerian
  remedy: **5** serum **8** antidote
  root (see also *plant* above): **5** artar, jalap,
  orris **6** seneca, senega **8** licorice
  solution: **8** tincture
  tablet: **4** pill **6** caplet, troche **7** lozenge
medicine: **4** cure, drug **5** tonic **6** physic, remedy **7** anodyne, nostrum, placebo **10** abirri-
tant, alterative
  amount: **4** dose **6** dosage
  god of: **11** Aesculapius
  institution: **6** clinic **7** surgery **8** hospital
  instrument (see also **surgery:** *instrument*):
  8 otoscope **11** stethoscope, thermometer
  14 ophthalmoscope **15** tongue depressor
  mild: **6** tisane
  noncuring: **6** ptisan **7** placebo
  patent: **7** nostrum **14** over-the-counter
  vessel: **4** vial **5** ampul, phial **6** ampule **7**
  ampoule **8** gallipot
medicine dropper: **7** pipette
medicine man: **4** piay **6** doctor, shaman **8**
magician, sorcerer **9** physician
mediety: **4** half, part **6** moiety
medieval: old **6** Gothic **10** Middle Ages **12**
old-fashioned
  battle: **4** Acre **5** Crecy **9** Agincourt
  coin: **9** bracteate
  dagger: **6** anlace
  estate: **4** fief
  fiddle: **4** giga
  fort: **11** Carcassonne
  gown: **6** cyclas
  guild: **5** Hanse
  helmet: **5** armet **6** heaume
  holy war: **7** Crusade
  lyric: **4** alba
  prayer book: **7** portass
  shield: ecu
  union: **5** guild
  weapon: **5** lance, oncin, sword **7** gisarme **8**
  crossbow

Medina (see also **Muslim**): **8** holy city
  citizen: **5** Ansar
  former name: **7** Yathrib
mediocre: **4** mean, so-so **6** common, medium
7 average, of a sort **8** inferior, middling, not
so hot, ordinary, passable **11** commonplace,
indifferent
meditate: **4** chew, mull, muse, pore **5** brook,
study, think, watch, weigh **6** ponder, reason **7**
reflect, revolve **8** cogitate, consider, ruminate
10 deliberate **11** contemplate, premeditate
meditation: **4** yoga **6** prayer **8** inaction **11**
engrossment   **13**   consideration   **14**
omphaloskepsis
meditative: **7** pensive
mediterranean: **6** inland **7** midland **10** land-
locked
Mediterranean: sea **11** mare nostrum
  boat: nef **4** saic **5** setee, xebec, zebec **6**
  galiot, mistic, settee, tartan, zebeck **7**
  felucca, mistico, polacre
  canal: **4** Suez
  coast: **7** Riviera **11** Costa del Sol
  country: **5** Egypt, Italy, Libya, Spain **6**
  France, Greece, Israel, Turkey **7** Algeria,
  Lebanon, Morocco, Tunisia
  Eastern: **6** Levant
  falcon: **6** lanner
  fish: aco **6** remora
  fruit: **5** olive **7** azarole
  galley: **6** galiot
  grass: **4** diss
  island: **4** Elba **5** Capri, Crete, Ibiza, Iviza,
  Malta **6** Candia, Cyprus, Ebusus, Lesbos,
  Lipari, Rhodes, Sicily **7** Corsica, Knossos,
  Majorca, Panaria **8** Balearic, Cyclades, Sardinia, Sporades **9** Stromboli **10** Dodecanese
  shrub: **7** azarole
  storm: **7** borasca, borasco
  tree: **5** carob **6** mastic **7** azarole
  wind: **6** otesan, solano **7** gregale, mistral,
  sirocco **8** levanter **10** euroclyden
medium: **4** mean, seer **5** media (pl.), midst,
organ **6** agency, degree, medial **7** average,
channel, psychic, vehicle **8** mediator **10**
instrument, interagent **11** environment **12**
intermediary, intermediate
  communication: fax **4** note **5** cable,
  modem, phone, radio **6** letter **9** telegraph,
  telephone **10** television
  culture: **4** agar
  news: **5** radio **7** journal **8** magazine **9** newspaper **10** periodical, television
medlar: **4** lark, tree **5** fruit **6** loquat
medley: **4** olio **6** jumble **7** farrago, melange,
mixture **8** mingling **9** patchwork, potpourri
10 hodgepodge, miscellany, variagated **11**
gallimaufry **12** mingle-mangle

musical: **8** fantasia
medrick: **4** gull, tern
medulla: **4** pith **6** marrow **7** essence, summary **10** compendium **12** adrenal gland
Medusa: **6** Gorgon **7** blubber **9** jellyfish
father: **7** Phorcys
offspring: **7** Pegasus **8** Chrysaor
representation: **9** Gorgoneum
sister: **6** Stheno **7** Euryale
slayer: **7** Perseus
meed: due **4** gift **5** award, bribe, merit, repay, worth **6** desert, reward **7** bribery **10** excellence, recompense
meek: **4** deft, kind, mild **5** lowly **6** docile, gentle, humble, modest **7** pacific, patient **8** moderate, resigned, sheepish, yielding **9** childlike, spineless **10** spiritless, submissive
meerkat: **6** monkey **8** mongoose, suricate
meerschaum: **4** clay, pipe **7** seafoam **9** sepiolite
meet: fit, kep (Sc.), sit **4** duel, face, join, tidy **5** equal, occur, right, touch, tryst **6** battle, combat, confer, gather, proper **7** contact, contend, convene, fitting, fulfill, satisfy **8** assemble, assembly, confront, deal with, moderate, suitable **9** encounter, forgather, gathering, intersect **10** congregate, experience, foregather **11** appropriate, contend with
athletic: **4** game **5** match **8** gymkhana **10** tournament
meeting: **4** mall, moot **5** gemot, rally, union **6** caucus, gemote, huddle, parley **7** coition, consult, session **8** adjacent, assembly, conclave, congress, junction **10** concurrent, conference, confluence, rendezvous **11** convocation
meg: **6** guinea **9** halfpenny
megalithic chamber: **6** dolmen
megaphone: **8** bullhorn, vamphorn **11** loudspeaker
megapod: **4** bird **5** maleo **6** leipoa **11** large-footed
Megara king: **5** Nisus
megrim: **4** whim **5** blues, fancy, freak, humor, whiff **7** caprice, stagger, vertigo **8** flounder, headache, migraine **9** dizziness **10** low spirits **12** hypochondria
Meg's sisters: Jo, Amy **4** Beth
Mehitabel: cat
companion: **6** Archie **9** cockroach
creator: **7** Marquis
Mekong River: *site:* **4** Asia
tribe: Moi
mel: **5** honey
melancholia: **6** athymy **7** athymia **10** depression
melancholy: sad **4** blue, dram, dull, dump, glum **5** dolar (L.), drear, dusky, gloom **6** dismal, somber, sombre, sorrow, yellow **7** chagrin, doleful, pensive, sadness, unhappy **8** atrabile, downcast, tristful **9** cheerless, dejection, plaintive **10** allicholly, depression, desolation **11** despondency, downhearted **12** disconsolate, heavy-hearted, hypochondria, mournfulness
Melanesia: *island:* **4** Fiji **7** Vanuatu **9** New Guinea **10** New Britain **12** New Caledonia
language: **5** Santo **6** pidgin
melange: **4** olio **6** medley **7** mixture **10** hodgepodge
melanic: **5** black
melanous: **4** dark **6** brunet **8** brunette
meld: **4** fuse, join, play **5** blend, merge, unite
mele: **4** poem, song **5** chant, lyric **6** ballad
melee: row **4** fray, riot **5** brawl, fight, foray, mix-up **6** affray, fracas, ruckus **7** ruction, scuffle **8** dogfight, skirmish **9** commotion **10** free-for-all
melilotus: **6** clover
meliorate: **6** better, change, soften **7** improve **9** get better **10** ameliorate
Melkarth: **4** Baal **6** Moloch
mell: mix **4** maul **5** fight, honey **6** beetle, hammer, mallet, meddle, mingle
mellifluous: **5** sweet **7** honeyed, sugared **8** pleasant **9** melodious
mellow: age **4** aged, rich, ripe, soft **5** loamy, ripen **6** mature, tender **7** matured **8** patinate
melodeon: **5** organ **9** seraphine
melodious: **6** ariose, arioso, dulcet **7** lyrical, melodic, musical, tunable, tuneful **8** canorous **10** harmonious
melodist: **6** singer **8** composer **9** harmonist
melodramatic: **8** dramatic **9** emotional **10** histrionic, theatrical **11** sensational
melody: air, lay **4** aria, lilt, note, raga (Ind.), solo, song, tune **5** charm, dirge, music, theme **6** strain **7** arietta, harmony, rosalia, sortita **9** cantilena **11** tunefulness
characterization: **6** ariose, arioso
counter: **7** descant
outline: **5** melos
pert. to: **6** plagal
unaccompanied: **4** solo **6** monody
meloid: **6** beetle **9** oil beetle
melon: **4** musk, pepo **5** gourd, water **6** casaba, papaya, spoils **7** Persian **8** honeydew **10** cantaloupe, paddymelon
melongena: **7** mollusk **8** eggplant
melon pear: **6** pepino
melos: **4** song **6** melody
melt: rin (Sc.), run **4** flow, flux, fuse, thaw, warm **5** blend, smelt, sweal **6** render, soften **7** dwindle, liquefy **8** discandy, dissolve, eliquate **10** colliquate, deliquesce **12** disintegrate
down: **6** render **7** liquefy
partly: **4** frit
Melville: *character:* Pip **4** Ahab **5** whale **8**

Queequeg, Starbuck
novel: **4** Omoo **5** Mardi, Typee **7** Redburn
8 Moby Dick **11** White-Jacket
member: **4** limb, part **5** organ **6** branch, fellow **7** section **8** district **11** communicant
new: **6** novice, pledge **7** entrant **8** initiate,
neophyte **10** apprentice
oldest: **4** dean
membership: **4** seat **10** fellowship
membrane: web **4** caul, coat, skin, tela **5** layer
6 amnion, amnios, retina, tissue **7** cuticle,
eardrum, stiffen, velamen
diffusion through: **7** osmosis
fold of: **5** plica
fringe: **4** loma
of bird: **4** cere
spore: **6** intine
weblike: **4** tela
memento: **5** relic, token **6** trophy **8** keepsake,
memorial, reminder, souvenir **11** remem-
brance
memoir: **4** note **5** eloge **6** record, report **7**
history **8** memorial **9** biography, narrative
10 commentary **13** autobiography
memorabilia: ana **7** history **8** archives,
mementos **9** souvenirs
memorable: **7** namable, notable, special **9**
reminding **10** remarkable **11** reminiscent
13 distinguished, extraordinary
memorandum (see also **memo**): **4** bill, chit,
note, stub **5** brief **6** agenda (pl.) **7** agendum, memento, minutes, notanda (pl.),
proctol **8** notandum, notation, reminder **9**
directive **11** aide-memoire
book: **5** diary **6** agenda **7** tickler **8** calendar
legal: **5** jurat
memorial: ahu **5** facta (pl.), relic **6** factum,
marker, memoir, record, trophy **7** memento
8 mnemonic, monument **11** remembrance
12 recollection **13** commemorative
carved: **5** totem
stone: **5** cairn **6** statue **9** mausoleum
memorist: **8** prompter
memory: **4** mind, rote **8** memorial, mind's eye
9 retention **11** remembrance **12** recollection, reminiscence **13** retrospection
aid: **8** mnemonic, reminder **10** anamnestic
goddess: **9** Mnemosyne
loss: **5** blank, lethe **7** amnesia, aphasia **13**
forgetfulness
pattern: **6** engram
pert. to: **6** mnesic **7** mnestic **8** mnemonic
vivid: **7** eidetic
memory book: **5** album, diary **9** scrapbook
Memphis (see also **Egypt**): *chief:* Evi
god: Ra **4** Ptah
men: **4** crew **6** people, troops **9** work force
armed body: **4** army **5** posse, troop
party: **4** stag **6** smoker

section of Greek church: **6** andron
wise: **4** Magi **6** Gaspar **8** Melchior **9**
Balthasar, Balthazar
menace: **5** boast, peril **6** danger, impend,
threat **8** denounce, forebode, jeopardy,
threaten, work evil **9** fulminate
menacing: **10** formidable
menage: **4** club, home **6** family **7** society **8**
domicile **9** household, residence **10** management **12** housekeeping
menagerie: zoo **10** collection
mend: fix, sew **4** beet, darn, heal, help, knit **5**
amend, botch, clout, emend, moise, patch **6**
better, cobble, repair, solder **7** improve,
restore **9** get better **10** ameliorate, convalesce
mendacity: lie **5** lying **6** deceit **7** falsity,
untruth **9** falsehood
mender: **6** tinker **7** cobbler **9** repairman
mendicant: **4** monk **5** fakir **6** beggar, fakeer,
frater
Menelaus: **12** king of Sparta
brother: **9** Agamemnon
daughter: **8** Hermione
father: **6** Atreus
rival: **5** Paris
steersman: **7** Canopus
wife: **5** Helen
meng: mix **5** blend **6** mingle
menhaden: **4** fish, pogy **5** pogie, porgy **8**
bonyfish **10** mossbunker
young: **7** sardine
menial: fag, low **4** base, mean **6** drivel, harlot,
sordid, stocah, varlet **7** servant, servile,
slavish **8** coistrel, coistril, servitor **9** degrading, underling
meniscus: **4** lens **8** crescent **12** crescent moon
Mennonite: **5** Amish **10** Anabaptist **13** Swiss
Brethren
meno: **4** less
menopause: **12** change of life
Menotti character: **5** Amahl
mental: **5** ideal **6** insane **7** phrenic **8** cerebral
9 cognitive **11** intelligent **12** intellectual **13**
psychological, temperamental
mental aberration: fog **4** daze, haze **5** lapse
6 stupor **7** doldrum, madness **8** insanity
mental defective: **5** idiot, moron **8** imbecile
9 retardate
mental disorder: **6** ataxia **7** aphasia **8** insanity, neuritis, neurosis, paranoia **9** melomania, paranomia, psychosis **11** megalomania
12 hypochondria **13** schizophrenia
specialist: **12** psychiatrist, psychologist
mental faculties: **4** mind, wits
mental image: **4** idea **5** dream **6** idolum **7**
fantasy **8** phantasm **10** conception
mentality: **4** mind **5** sense **6** acumen, reason
9 endowment, intellect **11** rationality **12**
intelligence

mental state: 5 blues 6 morale 7 doldrum 8 euphoria

mention: 4 cite, hint, mind, name 5 clepe, honor, refer, speak, trace 6 allude, denote, inform, notice, record, remark 7 specify, vestige 8 allusion, citation 9 statement 10 indication

mentor: 4 guru 5 guide, rabbi 6 friend, helper 7 monitor, teacher 9 counselor 10 instructor

menu: 4 card, meal 5 carte 10 bill of fare
part of: 4 soup 5 salad 6 entree 7 dessert, special 8 beverage, side dish 9 appetizer

Mephistophelean: sly 4 evil 6 crafty 7 satanic 8 devilish

mephitic: 4 foul 6 deadly, smelly 7 noxious 8 stinking

mercantile: 7 trading 10 commercial

mercenary: 4 hack 5 venal 6 greedy, sordid 7 Hessian, soldier 8 covetous, hireling, vendible 10 galloglass (Sc.) 11 corruptible, gallowglass 13 stipendiarian

merchandise: 4 sell, ware 5 goods, stock, wares 6 deal in 7 chaffer
cheap: 5 borax 7 camelot, schlock
pert. to: 10 emporeutic

merchant: 4 Seth (Ind.) 5 buyer 6 dealer, seller, sutler, trader, vendor 7 chapman, goladar, howadji, vintner 8 purveyor 9 tradesman 10 shopkeeper 11 storekeeper
group: 5 guild, hansa 6 cartel
ship: 5 oiler 6 argosy, coaler, packet, tanker, trader 7 collier, steamer 8 bilander, Indiaman 9 freighter
wholesale: 6 packer

Merchant of Venice: 7 Antonio
author: 11 Shakespeare
character: 6 Portia 7 Lorenzo, Shylock 8 Bassanio

merciful: 6 benign 7 clement, lenient, sparing 9 benignant, forgiving 10 charitable 13 compassionate

merciless: 4 grim 5 cruel 6 savage 8 pitiless 9 ferocious, graceless, heartless 10 despiteous, implacable, relentless

mercurial: 6 clever, lively, shrewd 8 changing, thievish 9 faithless 10 capricious, changeable, inconstant

mercury: 5 azoth, guide, metal, thief 6 hawker 9 messenger 11 quicksilver
derivative: 11 quicksilver
ore: 8 cinnabar

Mercury: 6 Hermes, planet 11 evening star
father: 7 Jupiter
mother: 4 Maia
son: 5 Cupid
staff: 8 caduceus 9 kerykeion
winged cap: 7 petasos, petasus
winged shoes: 7 talaria

mercury chloride: 7 calomel

mercy: law 4 pity, ruth 5 grace, grith 6 lenity 7 charity 8 clemency, humanity, kindness, lenience, leniency, mildness 9 tolerance 10 compassion, indulgence, tenderness 11 forbearance, forgiveness
show: 5 spare 6 pardon 7 forgive 8 reprieve

mercy killing: 10 euthanasia

mere: but, sea 4 bare, club, lake, mear, only, pond, pool, pure, sole 5 bound, limit, plain, sheer, utter 6 divide, entire, famous, scarce, simple 7 unmixed 8 absolute, boundary, glorious, landmark, trifling 9 beautiful, undiluted 11 unqualified

merely: 4 also 5 quite 6 anerly 8 just only

meretricious: 5 gaudy 6 paltry, vulgar 9 deceptive 10 misleading

merganser: 4 smee, smew 5 harle, robin 7 becscie, bracket, garbill 9 goosander

merge: mix 4 fuse, join, meld 5 blend, unify, unite 6 absorb, mingle 7 combine, conjoin 8 coalesce 9 commingle 10 amalgamate 11 consolidate, incorporate

merger: 5 union 9 coalition 12 amalgamation

mericarp: 8 hemicarp

meridian: 4 apex, noon 6 midday 11 culmination

meringue: 5 icing 9 egg whites

merino: 4 wool 5 sheep 6 fabric 7 Delaine

merit: 4 earn, meed 5 worth 6 desert, reward 7 deserve, warrant 10 condignity, excellence

merited: due, fit 7 fitting 8 adequate, suitable

meritorious: 6 worthy 8 laudable, valorous 9 honorable

merkin: mop

merlin: 6 falcon 10 pigeon hawk

Merlin: 4 poem, seer 8 magician 9 alchemist
king: 6 Arthur

Merlin's grass: 9 quillwort

mermaid: 5 nymph, siren 6 merrow 7 Lorelei

meropia: 9 blindness

meros: 5 thigh

merriment: fun, joy 4 glee 5 deray, mirth 6 gaiety 7 revelry 9 amusement, diversion, rejoicing, wittiness 11 galliardise 12 cheerfulness, conviviality

merrow: 7 mermaid

merry: gai (F.), gay 4 agog, airy, boon, cant, glad 5 bonny, droll, happy, jolly, sunny 6 blithe, bonnie, cocket, hilary, jocose, jocund, jovial, joyous, lively 7 festive, gleeful, jocular 8 cheerful, chirping, gamesome, gleesome, mirthful, pleasant, sportive 9 hilarious, sprightly 10 blithesome, frolicsome 11 exhilarated 12 lighthearted

merry andrew: 4 zany 5 antic, clown, joker 6

jester **7** buffoon **8** merryman **10** mountebank

merry-go-round: **8** carousel **9** carrousel

merrymaking: **5** jolly, revel **6** splore **7** festive, revelry, wassail **8** carnival **9** festivity, merriment **12** conviviality

merrythought: **8** wishbone

Merry Widow composer: **5** Lehar

merrywing: **4** duck **9** goldeneye **10** bufflehead

Merry Wives of Windsor: *author:* **11** Shakespeare

character: Nym **4** Ford **5** Robin **6** Fenton, Pistol **8** Falstaff

merse: dip **5** marsh **6** plunge **7** immerse

merycism: **10** rumination

mesa: **7** plateau **8** plateaux (pl.) **9** tableland

mescal: **5** cacti (pl.), drink **6** cactus, maguey, peyote, peyotl

mesel: **5** leper **7** leprosy

mesh: net **4** moke **5** snare **6** areola, engage, macula, tangle **7** areolae, ensnare, maculae (pl.), netting, network **8** entangle **9** interlock **10** reticulate

mesial: **6** median, middle

mesmerize: **8** enthrall, entrance **9** fascinate, hypnotize, spellbind

mesne: **6** middle **11** intervening **12** intermediate

Mesopotamia: **4** Irak, Iraq

ancient city or town: **6** Nippur **7** Babylon

Biblical name: **10** Paddan Aram

capital: **6** Bagdad **7** Baghdad

captives' place: **5** Halah

city: **5** Mosul **7** Edessan, Kerbela

river: **6** Tigris **9** Euphrates

wind: **6** shamal

mesquite: **4** tree **5** plant, shrub **9** algarroba

genus: **8** prosopis

mess: jag, row **4** clat, jagg, meal, much, mull, muss, soil **5** batch, botch, cauch, chaos, dirty, lelee **6** bungle, dabble, jumble, litter, muddle, rumple, tousle **7** crumple, mixture, rations, wrinkle **8** disarray, dishevel, disorder, scramble, slaister, squabble **9** commotion, confusion, mares nest, ugly thing **10** hodgepodge, picklement

message: **4** bode, line, memo, news, note, wire, word **5** cable **6** brevet, letter **7** bodword, depeche, epistle, mission, missive, tidings **9** memoranda **10** communique, memorandum **13** communication

coded: **10** cryptogram

good news: **6** gospel **7** evangel

Messalina: **6** wanton **10** prostitute

husband: **8** Claudius

messenger: **4** bode, page, sand, toty **5** angel, envoy, miler **6** beadle, chiaus, herald, legate, nuncio **7** apostle, carrier, courant, courier, hi-carra, mercury, prophet, toty-

man **8** hi-carrah, minister, nunciate, portator **9** harbinger **10** ambassador, evangelist, forerunner **11** internuncio

mounted: **6** cossid (Ind.) **7** courier, estafet **9** estafette

of the gods: **6** Hermes **7** Mercury

Messiah: **5** Jesus **6** Christ, Savior **7** prophet, Saviour

Messina Strait: *rock:* **6** Scilla, Scylla

whirlpool: **9** Charybdis

messy: **5** dirty **6** sloppy, sticky, untidy

mestizo: **5** cross, metis **7** mixture **9** half-breed

metad: rat

metagnomy: **10** divination

metagnostic: **10** unknowable

metal: ore, tin **4** gold, iron, lead, zinc **6** cobalt, copper, oroide, pewter, radium, silver, sodium, spirit **7** bullion, gallium, mercury **9** potassium, substance

alloy: **5** brass, steel

bar: gad **5** ingot

base: **5** dross, sprue

cake: **4** slag

clippings: **7** scissel

containing: **13** metalliferous

crude: ore **4** slug **5** matte

decorate: **4** etch **6** emboss **7** engrave **9** damascene, damaskeen

decorative: **6** chrome, niello

deposit: **4** lode

disc: **5** paten **6** patten

fastener: pin **4** bold, brad, nail **5** rivet, screw **6** cotter, solder

filings: **5** lemel

heavy: **6** osmium **7** uranium

impure mass: **7** regulus

layer: **4** seam **5** stope

leaf: **4** foil

lightest known: **7** lithium

liquid: **7** mercury

lump: pig **4** slug **6** nugget

mixture: **5** alloy

nonexpanding: **5** invar

oblong piece: sow

patch: **6** solder

plate: gib

rare: **4** zinc **6** cerium, erbium **7** iridium, terbium, uranium, yttrium **8** lutecium, platinum

refuse: **4** slag **5** dross **6** scoria

science: **10** metallurgy

scrap: **6** filing

shaper: **5** swage

sheet: **4** foil **5** lames, plate **6** lamina, latten, tagger

spike: gad

stannic: tin

strip: **6** spline

suit: 4 mail 5 armor
test: 5 assay
tin-like: 7 cadmium
unrefined: ore
vein: 4 lode
waste: 4 slag 5 dross, sprue 6 scoria 9 recrement
worker: 5 smith 6 barman, welder 7 riveter 8 tinsmith 9 goldsmith 11 coppersmith, silversmith 12 metallurgist

metallic: 4 hard 5 tinny 6 brazen 13 metalliferous
content: ory

metamere: 6 somite 8 somatome

metamerism: 12 segmentation

metamorphose: 6 change 9 transform, transmute 16 transubstantiate

metamorphosis: 4 pupa 6 change 8 mutation 14 transformation

metaphor: 5 image, trope 6 figure, simile 8 allegory 10 comparison 11 tralatition
faulty or mixed use of: 11 catachresis

metaphorical: 10 figurative

metaphysical: 10 immaterial 12 supernatural, transcendent
poet: 5 Donne 6 Cowley, Marvel, Vaughn 7 Crashaw, Herbert 9 Cleveland

metastrophe: 11 interchange

metayer: 6 farmer

mete: 4 dole, give, goal, post 5 allot, award, bound, limit, stake 7 measure 8 allocate, boundary 9 apportion 10 distribute

meteor: 5 bolis, Cetid, comet, Lyrid 6 Antlid, bolide, Lyraid 8 aerolite, fireball 9 Andromede, meteorite, meteoroid 10 Andromedid 12 heavenly body
August: 8 Perseids
November: 6 Leonid

meteoric: 8 flashing 9 celestial, transient

meteorite: 8 aerolite, aerolith, siderite

meteorological instrument: 6 bolide 9 barometer 11 thermometer

meteorologist: 10 forecaster, weatherman

meteorology: 14 study of weather

meter: 4 beat, time 5 metre, swing, verse 6 rhythm 7 cadence, measure 8 measurer
cubic: 5 stere
one-billionth: 9 nanometer
one-hundredth: 10 centimeter
one-millionth: 6 micron
one-tenth: 9 decimeter
one-thousandth: 10 millimeter
square: 7 centare
unit: 4 mora 5 morae (pl.)

meterist: 10 verse-maker

meters: *10:* 9 decameter
100: 10 hectometer
100 square: ar, are

1,000: 9 kilometer
10,000: 10 myriameter

methane hydrocarbon: 8 paraffin 9 paraffine

metheglin: 4 mead 8 beverage

method: way 4 dart, form, garb, mode, rule 5 means, order, style, usage 6 course, manner, system 7 fashion, formula, process 8 approach 9 procedure, technique 11 orderliness
customary: rut 5 habit 7 routine

methodical: 5 exact 6 severe 7 orderly, precise

methodize: 8 regulate 11 systematize

Methuselah: *father:* 5 Enoch
grandson: 4 Noah
son: 6 Lamech

methyl: *cyanide:* 7 nitrile
ethyl ketone: 8 butanone
ketol: 6 acetol

meticulous: 4 neat, nice, prim 5 fussy, timid 7 careful, fearful, finical, precise 8 exacting 10 fastidious, scrupulous 11 painstaking

metier: 4 line 5 field, forte, trade 7 calling 8 business 10 occupation, profession

metis: 8 octoroon 9 halfbreed

metric: 8 criteria (pl.) 9 criterion
measure: are 5 carat, liter, litre, meter, stere, tonne 6 decare, hectar, micron, miglio 7 centare, deciare, dekiare, hectare, kiliare, manzana, myriare 8 centiare, dekagram, milliare 9 decaliter, decameter, decastere, deciliter, decimeter, decistere, dekaliter, dekameter, dekistere, kiloliter, kilometer, kilostere, megameter 10 centiliter, centimeter, centistere, dekadrachm, hectoliter, hectometer, hectostere, microliter, milliliter, millimeter, millistere, myrialiter, myriameter 15 micromillimeter

metrical beat: 5 ictus

metrical foot: 4 iamb 6 dactyl, iambic, iambus 7 anapest
accented syllable: 5 arsis
four syllables: 6 syzygy
three short syllables: 8 tribrach
two syllables: 7 spondee, trochee
two together: 6 dipody

metrist: 4 poet 9 metrician

metronome: 5 timer

metropolis: see 4 city, seat 6 center

metropolitan: 4 city 5 chief, urban 6 bishop 7 leading 9 principal 10 archbishop

mettle: 4 fire 5 ardor, nerve, pluck, spunk 6 ginger, spirit 7 bravery, courage 9 fortitude

mettlesome: 5 brave, fiery, proud 6 ardent 8 skittish, spirited

Metz's river: 7 Moselle

meuse: gap 4 hole, lurk 7 conceal, opening 8 loophole

mew: den 4 cage, cast, coop, gull, maas (Sp.),

molt, shed 5 miaow, miaul 6 change 7 conceal, confine, enclose, garages, stables 8 spicknel 9 enclosure 11 concealment, confinement

mewl: cry 5 whine 6 squall 7 whimper

Mexico, Mexican: *agave:* 5 datil 6 zapupe
 alcoholic beverage: 6 mescal, pulque 7 tepache, tequila
 annuity: 5 censo
 antelope: 9 pronghorn
 artist: 6 Rivera
 bean: 5 fejol 6 frijol 7 frijole
 bedbug: 8 conenose
 beverage: 4 chia
 bird: 6 jacana, towhee 7 jacamar, tinamou 8 zopilote
 blanket: 6 serape
 bread: pan 8 tortilla
 brigand: 6 ladron
 bull: 4 toro
 cactus: 6 bavoso, chaute, chende, mescal 8 alicoche, chichipe 11 alfilerillo
 candlewood: 8 ocotillo
 capital: 10 Mexico City
 cat: 4 gato 6 margay
 chaps (leather): 10 chaparajos, chaparejos
 city: 4 Leon, Tula 5 Tepic 6 Colima, Jalapa, Juarez, Merida, Oaxaca, Potosi, Puebla 7 Durango, Orizaba, San Luis, Tampico, Tijuana, Torreon 8 Culiacan, Mazatlan, Mexicali, Saltillo, Vera Cruz, Victoria 9 Chihuahua, Monterrey 10 Hermosillo 11 Guadalajara
 cloak: 5 manta 6 poncho, serape
 cockroach: 9 cucaracha
 conqueror: 6 Cortes, Cortez
 cottonwood: 5 alamo
 cowboy: 7 vaquero
 currency: 4 peso 5 adobe 6 azteca 7 centavo, piaster
 dance: hat 13 jarabe tapatio
 dish: 4 mole, taco 5 atole, tamal 6 tamale 7 tostada 8 tortilla 9 enchilada, guacamole
 dollar: peso
 drug: 7 damiana
 early dweller: 4 Maya 5 Aztec
 fiber: 4 pita 5 istle, sisal 6 catena
 fish: 6 salema 7 totuava
 garment: 5 manga 6 serape 7 chiripa
 gopher: 4 tuza 7 quachil
 grapefruit: 7 toronja
 grass: 5 otate 7 sacaton, zacaton 8 hanequen, hanequin
 guardian spirit: 6 nagual
 hat: 8 sombrero

 headdress, lacy: 6 huipil
 hero: 4 Diaz 6 Juarez
 hog: 7 peccary
 holiday: 6 fiesta
 house: 4 casa 5 jacal
 ivy: 6 cobaea
 laborer: 4 peon 7 bracero, wetback
 lake: 7 Chapala
 land owner: 8 ranchero
 language: 7 Nahuatl, Spanish
 laurel: 7 madrona
 leader: 4 Diaz 6 Alemán, Juarez 7 Salinas 11 Pancho Villa
 masonry: 5 adobe
 mat: 6 petate
 measure: pie 4 alma, vara 5 almud, baril, jarra, labor, legua, linea, sitio 6 almude, fanega 7 pulgada 8 curtillo 9 cuarteron 10 caballeria
 measure of weight: bag 4 onza 5 carga, libra, marco 6 adarme, arroba, ochava, tercio 7 quintal
 mixed blood: 7 mestizo
 mountain: 7 Orizaba 12 Citlaltepetl, Ixtaccihuatl, Popocatepetl
 musical group: 8 mariachi
 musical instrument: 6 clarin, guiros 7 cabacas, maracas, marimba 11 chiapanecas
 nap: 6 siesta
 onyx: 6 tecali
 orange: 7 choisya, naranja
 pancake: 5 arepa
 park: 11 Chapultepec
 peasant: 4 peon
 peninsula: 7 Yucatan 14 Baja California
 people: Mam 4 Cora, Maya, Seri, Xova 5 Aztec, Hauve, Lipan, Nahau, Opata, Otomi, Yaqui, Zoque 6 Indian, Mixtec, Otonia, Toltec 7 Haustec, Mestizo, Nahuatl, Tepanec, Zacatec, Zapotec 8 Tarascan, Totonaco, Zaceteco 9 Campesino 10 Cuitlateca, Cuitlateco
 plant: 4 chia 5 agave, amole, datil, jalap, sotol 6 chaute, maguey, slavia 7 tequila 8 acapulco 9 sabadilla
 plantation: 8 hacienda
 porridge: 5 atole
 porter: 5 tamen
 resort: 6 Cancun 8 Acapulco 14 Puerto Vallarta *(cont.)*

Mexico *(cont.)*
  river: **6** Balsas, Penuco, Urique **7** Tabasco
    8 Rio Bravo **9** Rio Grande
  rubber tree: ule
  sandal: **8** gauracha, guarache, guaracho,
    huarache, huaracho
  sandwich: **4** taco
  scarf: **4** chal **6** rebozo, tapalo **8** mantilla
  shawl: **6** rebozo, serape
  shrub: **6** anagua, anaqua, colima **7** choisya
  state: **6** Colima, Oaxaca, Puebla, Sonora **7**
    Chiapas, Durango, Hidalgo, Jalisco,
    Morelos, Nayarit, Sinaloa, Tabasco,
    Yucatan **8** Campeche, Coahuila, Guer-
    rero, Tlaxcala, Vera Cruz **9** Chihuahua,
    Michoacan, Nuevo Leon, Querétaro,
    Zacatecas **10** Guanajuato, Tamaulipas **11**
    Quintana Rao **13** San Luis Potosi **14**
    Aguascalientes, Baja California
  sugar: **6** azucar **7** panocha
  tea: **6** basote **7** apasote **9** alpasotes
  thong: **5** romal
  toy: **6** pinata
  tree: ule **4** sero **5** abeto, amapa, ebano,
    ocote **6** chacte, colima, mezcal, sabino **7**
    capulin, colorin **8** chaparro, ulmaceae **9**
    ahuehuete, canadulce **10** anacahuita
  village: **6** ejidos, tecali
  volcano: **6** Colima **7** Jorullo **9** Paricutin
    12 Popocatepetl
  yucca: **5** isote

mezereum: **5** shrub **6** daphne **8** camillia
mezzanine: **5** floor, story **7** balcony **8** entresol
Miami (see also **Florida**): *basketball team:* **4**
  Heat
  Bowl Game: **6** Orange
  football team: **7** Dolphins
mias: **9** orangutan
miasma: **4** reek **6** stench **7** malaria **9** contagion, infection
miaul: mew **4** meow, wraw **5** miaou, miaow **9**
  caterwaul
mib: **6** marble
mica: **4** talc **5** glist **7** biotite **8** silicate **9**
  damourite, hydromica, isinglass, muscovite
  10 lepidolite
micaceous: **7** talcose
Micah: **7** prophet
  son: **5** Abdon
miche: **4** lurk **5** skulk, sneak **6** pilfer **7** conceal, spy upon
Michelangelo work: **5** David, Pieta **12** Last
  Judgment, Medici Chapel **13** Sistine Chapel
micher: **5** cheat, thief **6** truant **8** panderer

Michigan: *capital:* **7** Lansing
  city: **5** Flint, Ionia **6** Warren **7** Detroit,
    Pontiac, Saginaw **8** Ann Arbor, Dear-
    born, Muskegon **9** Kalamazoo, Mar-
    quette **11** Battle Creek, Grand Rapids
  early explorer: **7** La Salle **9** Marquette
  Indian: **5** Miami **6** Ottawa **7** Wyandot **8**
    Chippewa
  lake: **4** Burt, Erie **5** Huron, Torch **8**
    Houghton, Michigan, Superior **9** Win-
    nebago
  mountain peak: **7** Curwood
  nickname: **9** Wolverine
  president: **4** Ford
  product: **5** autos
  river: **5** Grand, Huron **7** Au Sable, Clin-
    ton, Saginaw **8** Escanaba, Manistee,
    Muskegan **9** Menominee
  state bird: **5** robin
  state fish: **10** brook trout
  state flower: **12** apple blossom
  state tree: **9** white pine

mickle: **4** much **5** great
mico: **8** marmoset
micraner: ant
micro: **4** moth
microbe: **4** germ **8** bacillus, organism
microcosm: **4** atom, cell **5** world **7** village **8**
  universe **9** community, miniature
microfilm sheet: **5** fiche
microorganism: **4** germ **5** virus **6** aerobe,
  amoeba **7** aerobia **8** aerobium **9** autoblast,
  spirillum **10** spirochete **11** spirochaete
microphone: bug **4** mike **8** parabola
microscope: **5** glass **9** magnifier
microscopic: **5** small **6** minute **9** engyscope
microspore: **6** pollen
microsporophyll: **6** stamen
mid: See **midst**
midday: **4** **noon** **8** **noontide**
  intermission: **5** lunch **7** nooning **8** noon
    hour
  nap: **6** siesta
middle: **4** mean, part **5** mesne, midst, waist **6**
  center, centre, centry, median, mesial **7**
  average, central, centric, midriff **9** in
  between **11** equidistant, intervening **12**
  intermediate **13** intermediator
  combining form: mes **4** medi, meso
  way: **6** midway **7** halfway **10** moderation
Middle Ages: See **medieval**
Middle East: **6** Levant
  canal: **4** Suez
  country: **4** Iran, Iraq, Oman **5** Egypt,

Qatar, Sudan, Syria, Yemen **6** Cyprus, Israel, Jordan, Kuwait, Turkey **7** Bahrain, Lebanon **11** Saudi Arabia **18** United Arab Emirates
export: oil
gulf: **4** Aden, Oman **7** Arabian, Persian
people: **4** Arab **7** Iranian, Turkish

middleman: 5 agent, butty **6** dealer, trader **8** huckster, retailer **9** go-between **12** interlocutor, intermediary

middling: 4 fair, so-so **6** fairly, medium **7** average **8** mediocre, moderate, ordinary, somewhat **10** moderately **11** indifferent

midge: fly **4** fish, gnat, runt **5** dwarf, stout **6** insect, midget, punkie **8** carriage

midget: 5 dwarf, small **9** miniature

midi (see also **mini**): **11** skirt length

Midianite: *king:* Hur **4** Reba
prince: Evi, Zur

midshipman: 5 cadet, middy, plebe **6** reefer

midst: 4 amid, mean **5** among, depth **6** amidst, center, centre, medium, middle, mongst **7** amongst, between, halfway, setting **11** surrounding

Midsummer Night's Dream: *author:* **11** Shakespeare
character: **4** Puck **6** Oberon **7** Theseus, Titania **9** Hippolyta

midwife: 4 baba, dhai (Ind.) **5** nurse **6** cummer, kimmer **9** gracewife **10** accoucheur (F.) **11** accoucheuse (F.), finger-smith

mien: air, eye **4** brow, vult **5** guise **6** aspect, manner, ostent **7** bearing, conduct **8** attitude, behavior, carriage, demeanor **9** behaviour, demeanour **10** appearance, deportment **11** countenance

miffed: 5 sulky, vexed **8** offended **10** displeased

mig: 6 marble **11** sitting duck

migale: 5 mouse, shrew

migeloid fish: 4 bobo

might: arm **4** mote **5** power **7** ability **8** strength

mighty: big **4** bulk, fell, vast, very **5** felon, great **6** potent, strong **7** violent **8** enormous, forceful, forcible, powerful, puissant, vigorous **9** extensive, extremely, gigantean **10** omnipotent **11** efficacious

migniard: 6 dainty, minion **7** mincing **8** delicate, mistress

mignon/mignonne: 5 small **6** dainty, petite **8** delicate, graceful

mignonette: 4 herb **6** reseda
vine: **7** Madeira, tarweed

migraine: 4 whim **6** megrim **8** headache **10** hemicrania

migrant: See **migratory**

migrate: 4 flee, flit, move, pass, trek **8** colonize, transfer

migration: 5 exode **6** exodus, flight **8** diaspora, movement
of top experts: **10** brain drain

migratory: 5 gypsy **6** roving **7** nomadic **8** vagabond **9** peregrine, wandering
farm worker: **4** Okie

Mikado: 7 emperor **8** operetta **9** sovereign
court: **5** dairi
first: **5** Jimmu
office: **9** mikadoate

mike: 10 microphone

milady: 4 dame **5** madam **10** noblewoman **11** gentlewoman

Milan opera house: 7 La Scala

milarite: 8 silicate

mild: moy **4** calm, easy, kind, meek, soft, tame, warm **5** balmy, bland, claro **6** benign, gentle, humble **7** clement, lenient **8** benedict, favonian, gracious, lenitive, merciful, moderate, soothing, tranquil **9** assuasive, forgiving, indulgent, temperate **10** forbearing, mollifying **11** considerate

mildew: 4 mold, rust **5** mould **6** blight, fungus **8** honeydew
genus of: **7** erysibe **8** erysiphe

mildness: 6 comity **8** leniency, meekness **10** good nature, moderation

mile: *5000 feet:* **5** Roman
nautical: **4** knot, naut
one-eighth: **7** furlong

mileage: 8 distance

milepost: 4 mark **5** stela, stele **6** marker, stelae

miler: 6 runner

milestone: 5 event **8** landmark, occasion

milfoil: 6 yarrow **9** ahartalav

milieu: 6 sphere **7** climate, setting **11** environment **12** surroundings

militant: 7 martial, soldier, warlike **8** fighting **9** combating, combative **10** aggressive

military (see also **army, navy, troop**): **7** martial, warlike
advance: **5** drive **8** anabasis **11** penetration **12** breakthrough
adventurer: **10** filibuster
assistant: **4** aide **8** adjutant
base: **4** camp, fort, post **5** depot, field **7** billets **8** barracks, garrison, presidio, quarters **10** encampment
call: **6** tattoo
cloak: **5** sagum
command: **4** halt **6** at ease **9** attention
commander: **7** marshal
commission: **6** brevet
encampment: **7** bivouac
engine: ram **6** cannon, onager **7** robinet **8** catapult, mangonel
force: **5** guard **6** legion, troops **7** reserve
formation: **4** file, line **7** echelon

front: **5** lines **6** sector
guard: **6** patrol
hat: **4** kepi **5** shako **6** helmet **8** overseas
hat covering: **8** havelock
horsemen: **7** cavalry, Hussars
inspection: **5** drill **6** parade, review
landing point: **9** beachhead
machine: LST **4** jeep, tank
maneuver: **6** tactic
messenger: **7** estafet
obstruction: **6** abatis **7** abattis
officer: **5** major **7** captain, colonel, general **9** brigadier, subaltern **10** lieutenant
operations: **8** campaign, strategy
order: **7** command
organization: **5** cadre
pit: **10** trou-de-loup
police: M.P.
prisoner: POW
punishment: **9** strappado
quarters: **4** camp **7** billets **8** barracks
rank (see also *officer* above): PFC **6** brevet **7** private **8** banneret, corporal, sergeant
salute: **5** salvo
signal: **7** chamade
special forces: **4** SEAL **8** commando **10** Green Beret
staff officer: **4** aide
storage place: **4** dump **5** depot, étape **6** armory **7** arsenal
supplies: **8** materiel, ordnance
survey: **11** reconnoiter
unit: van **4** army, rear **5** cadre, corps, squad, troop **7** company, platoon **8** division, regiment **9** battalion
vehicle: **4** jeep, tank **6** camion, humvee **7** caisson **9** half-track
weapon: **4** croc, mine **5** rifle **6** mortar, napalm, onager, rocket **7** bazooka, grenade, robinet **8** ballista **9** catapult **10** machine gun
work: **4** fort
militate: **5** fight, weigh **6** debate **7** contend **8** conflict
milk: lac **4** draw, lait (F.) **5** drain, latte (It.), leche (Sp.), nurse **6** elicit, suckle **7** exploit
coagulator: **6** rennet
curdled: **6** yogurt **7** clabber, yoghurt, yogourt **8** yoghourt
curdler: **4** ruen **6** rennet
deodorizer: **7** aerator
derived from: **6** lactic
fermented: **5** kefir, kumys **6** koumis, koumys, kumiss **7** koumiss, matzoon
first after delivery: **9** beestings, biestings, colostrum
food: **10** lacticinia
mouse: **6** spurge
pail: soa, soe **5** bowie

pert. to: **6** lactic **7** lactary, lacteal
preparation: **9** lactarene, lactarine
protein: **6** casein
sap: **5** latex
selling place: **5** dairy **9** lactarium
separator: **7** creamer
sour: **4** whig **6** blinky
sugar: **7** lactose
thickened part: **4** curd
watery: **8** blue John
watery part: **4** whey
with: **6** au lait (F.)
milk and honey: **10** prosperity
milk-and-water: **4** weak **7** insipid **10** namby-pamby, wishy-washy
milk leg: **9** phlebitis
milkfish: awa **6** sabolo
milksop: **4** fool **5** sissy **6** coward **7** cockney **8** weakling **11** milquetoast, mollycoddle
milkweed: *down:* **4** silk **5** floss
family: **14** asclepiadaceae
fluid: **5** latex
milkwood: **4** tree **5** shrub **9** paperbark
milky: **4** meek, milk, pale, tame **5** timid, white **6** chalky, gentle, pearly **7** lacteal, opaline **8** timorous **10** effeminate
Milky Way: **6** galaxy
black spaces in: **9** coalsacks
mill: box **4** beat, nurl **5** crush, dress, fight, grind, knurl, shape, thief **6** finish, powder, thrash **7** factory, machine **8** snuff-box, vanquish **9** comminute, transform **12** housebreaker
end: **7** remnant
run of the: **7** average **8** ordinary
millennium: **6** utopia **8** paradise **13** thousand years
millepore: **5** coral
miller: ray **4** moth **5** boxer **7** harrier **8** pugilist **10** flycatcher
millerite: **7** sulfide
miller's thumb: **4** bird, fish **7** warbler **8** cottidae, titmouse **9** goldcrest
millesimal: **10** thousandth
millet: **5** grain **6** cereal
millimeter: *one millionth:* **15** micromillimeter
one thousandth: **6** micron
milliner: **6** hatter
millions of millions: **9** trillions
millpond: dam
millrace: **4** lade (Sc.) **10** millcourse
below wheel: **8** tailrace
millrind: **6** moline
millstone: **6** burden **7** grinder **9** albatross **10** affliction, deadweight
support: **4** rind, rynd
millstream: **5** fleam
milo: **5** grain **7** sorghum
milpa: **5** field **6** chacra **8** clearing

milt: 6 spleen

mim: shy 4 prim 5 quiet 6 demure, modest

mime: ape 4 aper, copy, jest 5 actor, clown, drama, farce, mimer, mimic 6 comedy, jester 7 buffoon, gesture, imitate, Marceau 9 represent 11 impersonate
chief: 9 archi-mime

mimeograph: 4 copy 7 stencil

mimesis: 7 mimicry 9 imitation

mimic (see also **mime**): 4 mima, mimo (G.), mock 6 parrot 7 copy-cat, copying, imitate, mimetic 9 burlesque 11 counterfeit

mimicry: 4 echo 5 apery, apism 7 mimesis 8 parrotry 9 imitation 10 camouflage

mimic thrush: 11 mockingbird

mimidae: 7 catbird 8 thrasher 11 mockingbird

mimmock: 6 dainty 10 fastidious

mimosa: 4 tree 6 acacia 8 turmeric

mimsey: 4 prim 7 prudish

minaret: 5 spire, tower 6 turret

minatory: 8 menacing 11 threatening

minaway: 6 minuet

mince: cut 4 chop, gait, hash, meat 5 grind 6 affect 7 finnick 9 subdivide 11 affectation

mincemeat: 5 gigot 10 pie filling

minchiate: 5 tarot

mincing: 5 fussy 6 dainty, la-di-da, too-too 7 finical 8 affected 9 11 persnickety

mincingly: 8 gingerly

mind: min (Sc.) 4 care, chit, heed, obey, reck, tend, will 5 besee, brain, manas (Ind.), watch 6 animus, burrow, memory, notice, psyche, regard 7 dislike, dispose 9 intellect, mentality 11 inclination, remembrance 12 intelligence, recollection
keep in: 8 remember 9 entertain
origin and development: 13 psychogenesis
pert. to: 6 mental, noetic 7 phrenic 13 psychological
state of: 4 mood, tune

Mindanao: *gulf:* 4 Moro 5 Davao
island: 5 Samal
language: Ata
people: Ata 5 Lutao 6 Bagobo, Illano, Lutayo
town: 4 Dapa 6 Butuan
volcano: Apo

mind-blowing: 7 awesome 11 psychedelic 12 overwhelming

mindful: 5 aware 7 heedful 9 attentive, observant, regardful

mine: bal, dig, pit, sap 4 delf, hole, lode, meum (It.), vein, work 5 bargh, delft, delve 6 cavity, gopher, quarry, threat 7 gallery, passage 8 colliery 10 excavation 13 treasure trove
basket: 4 corf
ceiling: 5 astel
chisel: gad

coal: rob
deposit: 4 lode, vein
entrance: 4 adit 5 stulm
excavation: 5 stope
extraction: ore, tin 4 gold, lead 6 silver 8 diamonds
kind: 5 strip 6 placer 8 dredging
partition: 8 brattice
passage: 4 sill 5 stope
platform: 6 sollar, soller
prop: 5 sprag
refuse: 4 dead 5 attle
reservoir: 4 sump 8 standage
rich: 4 lode 7 bonanza 8 golconda
roof support: nog
shaft: 4 sump
surface: 6 placer
sweeping device: 8 paravane
tunnel: 4 adit 5 stulm
vein: 4 lode
vertical passage: 5 shaft
wagon: 4 tram
waste: gob 4 goaf 5 attle 7 rubbish
worker: 5 cager, miner 6 canary 7 cageman, trapper 8 onsetter
worthless material: 6 gangue

miner: 6 dammer (Sc.), digger, sapper 7 collier 9 sourdough 10 forty-niner

mineral (see also **metal, ore**): cal, tin 5 irite 6 barite, iolite 7 alumite, ataxite, uralite 9 celestite, galactite, inorganic, uraninite 10 gadolinite, retinalite
amorphous: 6 pinite
black: jet 4 coal 5 irite 6 cerine, yenite 7 knopite, niobite 8 graphite 10 minguetite
blue: 7 azurite
blue-green: 5 beryl
brittle: 7 euclase
brown: 6 cerine, egeran, rutile 8 lederite 9 elaterite
calcium and magnesium: 8 diopside
calcium carbonate: 7 calcite 8 calcspar
crystalline: 4 spar 6 yenite 7 apatite, felsite, felspar, knopite 8 boracite, elaterin, felspath
deposit: 4 lode, nest, vein 6 placer
deposit cavity: vug 4 voog, vugg, vugh
earth like: 5 glebe
fibrous: 8 asbestos, oakenite
flaky: 4 mica
gray-green: 7 edenite
gray-white: 5 trona 6 galena 14 chromiumptrona
green: 4 talc 7 alalite, apatite, epidote, erinite, prasine, uralian 9 demantoid, malachite
gunpowder: 5 niter
hard: 6 spinel 7 adamant 8 corundum, spinelle

lustrous: **4** spar **7** blendes **8** smaltine, smaltite

magnetic: **9** lodestone

mixture: **5** magma

native: ore

non-combustible: **8** asbestos

non-metallic: **4** spar **5** boron **6** gangue, iodine

plaster of paris: **6** gypsum

potash: **4** alum

potassium sulfate: **8** misenite

quartz-like: **4** opal

rare: **7** euclase, thorite

red: **5** balas **6** garnet, rutile **7** bornite **8** cinnabar

salt: **4** alum

seam: **4** vein

silicate: **4** mica

smelting: ore

soft: **4** talc **6** gypsum

spot: **5** macle

tallow: **11** hatchettine

tar: **4** brea **6** maltha

transparent: **4** mica **5** fluor

vitreous: **4** spar **7** apatite

wax-like: **9** ozocerite

white: **6** barite **8** smaltine, smaltite

yellow: **4** iron **5** topaz **6** pyrite **7** sulphur

yellowish green: **7** apidote

mineral jelly: **8** Vaseline **10** petrolatum

mineral oil: **5** colza **9** petroleum

mineral spring: spa **4** well

mineral water: **6** selter **7** seltzer

miner's consumption: **8** phthisis **9** black lung

mine run: **6** common **7** average **11** unsorted ore

Minerva: **6** Athena, Athene

shield: **5** aegis

minestrone: **4** soup

ming: **6** remind **7** mention, recount **8** remember

minge: **5** midge

mingle: mix **4** amix, fuse, join, meng, mool **5** admix, blend, merge, unite **6** huddle **7** blender, combine, compost **8** coalesce, compound, intermix **9** associate, commingle, socialize **10** amalgamate, be sociable **11** consolidate

mingle-mangle: **6** medley **7** mixture **10** hodgepodge

mingwort: **8** wormwood

mingy: **4** mean **6** stingy

mini: **8** small car **9** miniature **10** short skirt

miniate: **8** decorate, luminate, paint red **9** rubricate

miniature: **4** copy, tiny **5** model, small, teeny **6** little, minute **8** painting, portrait **9** lineament, miniating **10** diminutive **11** little thing, rubrication **12** illumination **14** representation

minikin: **6** dainty **7** darling, elegant, mincing **8** affected, delicate **10** diminutive

minim: jot **4** drop, fish **6** minnow, minute **7** tiniest **8** smallest **9** miniature **10** diminutive

minimize: **6** reduce **7** detract **8** belittle **9** disparage **10** depreciate

minimum: **5** least **6** lowest

minion: **4** idol, neat **5** lover, toady **6** dainty, pretty **7** darling, elegant **8** creature, delicate, favorite, ladylove, mistress, paramour **9** sycophant, underling

minister (see also **priest**): **4** tend **5** angel, serve **6** afford, attend, cleric, curate, divine, pander, parson, pastor, supply **7** furnish, provide, servant **8** executor, preacher, reverend **9** attendant, clergyman, upstander **10** administer, ambassador

home: **5** manse **9** parsonage

minitant: **11** threatening

Minnesota: *capital:* **6** St. Paul

city: Ely **5** Edina **6** Duluth, Winona **7** Mancato, St. Cloud **9** Rochester **11** Bloomington, Minneapolis

early explorer: **4** Pike **6** Duluth **7** La Salle **8** Hennepin

Indian: **5** Sioux **6** Ojibwa **8** Chippewa

lake: Red **7** Bemidji **8** Superior

motto: **13** L'Etoile du Nord (North Star)

mountain peak: **5** Eagle **7** Misquah

mountain range: **6** Cuyuna, Mesabi **10** Vermillion

nickname: **6** Gopher **9** North Star

river: Rum **4** Sauk **5** Rainy **7** St. Croix **11** Mississippi

state bird: **4** loon

state flower: **11** lady slipper

state tree: **7** red pine **10** Norway pine

waterfall: Minnehaha

---

minnow: **4** chub **5** guppy **6** baggie, shiner **9** squawfish

minor: **4** less **5** petit, petty, youth **6** infant, lesser, slight **7** smaller **8** inferior, underage **11** subordinate **15** inconsequential

minorate: **7** curtail **8** diminish

minority: few **6** nonage **10** immaturity **11** inferiority

Minos: *brother:* **12** Rhadamanthus

child: **7** Ariadne, Phaedra **9** Androgeus

country: **5** Crete

father: **4** Zeus

lover: **6** Scylla

monster: **8** Minotaur

mother: **6** Europa
palace: **7** Knossos
slayer: **7** Cocalus
wife: **8** Pasiphae
Minotaur: *father:* **4** bull
home: **9** labyrinth
mother: **8** Pasiphae
owner: **5** Minos
slayer: **7** Theseus
minster: **6** church **9** cathedral, monastery
minstrel: **4** bard, bhat (Ind.), moke, poet **6** harper, jockey, singer **7** gleeman, goliard, Pierrot **8** jongleur, musician **9** blackface, troubador **10** gleemaiden, mountebank, troubadour **11** entertainer
accompanist: **7** harpist
minstrel show: *endman:* **7** Mr. Bones, Mr. Tambo
middleman: **12** interlocutor
part: **4** olio
mint: aim, iva **4** blow, coin, sage **5** basil, feint, money, thyme **6** catnip, hyssop, intend, mentha, ramona **7** attempt, dittany, potherb, purpose, venture **8** bergamot, brand-new, calamint, endeavor, lavender, marjoram **9** fabricate, horehound, spearmint **11** manufacture, wintergreen **12** spick-and-span
charge: see *levy* below
family: **8** labiatae **9** lamiaceae
genus of: **7** melissa **10** moluccella
geranium: **8** costmary
herb family: **4** balm **5** basil **6** catnip, hyssop **8** rosemary
levy: **8** brassage **11** seigniorage
mintage: **5** stamp **7** coinage
minuet: **5** dance
movement: **7** scherzo
minus: **4** lack, less **6** defect, devoid **7** lacking, without **8** negative, subtract, take away **10** deficiency
minuscule: **4** tiny **5** petty, small **6** minute **9** very small **10** diminutive, manuscript **13** insignificant
minute: jot, wee **4** mite, nice, note, time, tiny **5** draft, exact, petty, small **6** atomic, little, moment, record, slight, tittle **7** instant, minutia, precise **8** detailed, trifling **9** memoranda (pl.) **10** blow-by-blow, memorandum **13** imperceptible **14** circumstantial
glass: **9** hourglass
minutely: **7** exactly **9** continual, unceasing
minutes: **4** acta **5** actum **6** record
minutiae: **7** details, trifles **11** particulars
minx: dog **4** girl, jade **5** hussy, woman **7** baggage
Minyae king: **7** Athamas
minyan: **6** quorum
mir: **4** head **5** chief **6** leader **9** community

Mira: **4** star
constellation: **5** Cetus
mirabile dictu: **9** wonderful **12** strange to say
mirabilia: **7** marvels, wonders **8** miracles
miracle: **4** feat **5** anomy **6** marvel, wonder **8** act of God **10** occurrence, phenomenon
scene of: **4** Cana
worker of: **6** Christ **8** magician **11** thaumaturge
miraculous: **9** marvelous, unnatural, wonderful **12** supernatural
mirador: **5** oriel **6** loggia, turret **7** balcony **10** watchtower
mirage: **5** serab **7** chimera **8** delusion, illusion **10** phenomenon, refraction
Miranda's father: **8** Prospero
mire: bog, mud, wet **4** glar, moil, ooze, slew, slob, sloo, slud, slue **5** addle, embog, glaur (Sc.), marsh, sluig, slush, stall, swamp **6** defile, slough, sludge **7** clabber, sludder **8** entangle, slow down
mire duck: **7** mallard
Miriam: *brother:* **5** Aaron, Moses
father: **5** Amram
mother: **8** Jochebed
mirific: **9** marvelous, wonderful
mirror: **5** glass, model **7** reflect **8** speculum **9** girandole **12** looking glass
pert. to: **9** catoptric **11** catoptrical
mirth: fun, joy **4** glee **5** cheer **6** bawdry, gaiety, levity, spleen **7** delight, jollity **8** gladness, hilarity, laughter **9** festivity, happiness, merriment **10** jocularity, joyousness **12** cheerfulness
god: **5** Comus
mirthful: **5** cadgy, merry
miry: **5** boggy, muddy **6** filthy, swampy **7** guttery
misadventure: **4** slip **5** boner, lapse **6** mishap **7** faux pas **8** accident **9** cataclysm **11** catastrophe
misanthrope: **5** cynic, hater, loner, Timon **7** Alceste
author: **7** Moliere
misanthropic: **7** cynical **10** antisocial
misapplication: **5** abuse **6** disuse **10** perversion
misappropriate: **5** steal **8** embezzle
misbegotten: **7** bastard **8** spurious **10** fatherless **12** illegitimate
misbehave: **5** act up **7** disobey, misbear, mislead
misbeliever: **7** heretic, infidel **9** miscreant
misbirth: **8** abortion
miscalculate: err **9** overshoot
miscall: **5** abuse **6** revile **7** misname, slander
miscarriage: **5** lapse **6** mishap **7** failure, misdeed, mistake **8** abortion **9** mischance **11** misdemeanor **13** mismanagement

miscarry: err 4 fail 5 abort, misgo 7 founder 8 backfire 9 fall short

miscegenation: 13 interbreeding

miscellaneous: 5 mixed 6 sundry, varied 8 assorted 12 heterogenous 14 indiscriminate

miscellany: 4 olio 10 adversaria, hodgepodge

mischance: See **misfortune**

mischief: ate, hob, ill 4 bane, evil, harm, hurt 5 prank, wrack 6 cantip, damage, injury 7 devilry, trouble 8 deviltry 9 devilment, diablerie 10 disservice
  god: 4 Loki
  goddess: Ate 4 Eris

mischiefmaker: elf, imp, wag 5 knave, rogue

mischievous: sly 4 arch, impy 5 elfin, hempy 6 elfish, elvish, impish 7 harmful, knavish, malefic, mocking, naughty, parlous, roguish, teasing, waggish 8 prankish, sportive, venomous 9 injurious

mischievous child: imp 4 brat, limb 5 devil, scamp 6 monkey 7 hellion

miscible: 7 mixable

misconception: 7 mistake 8 abortion 16 misunderstanding

misconduct: 7 offense 8 disorder 9 mismanage 11 delinquency, malfeasance, misbehavior, misdemeanor
  mark of: 7 demerit

miscreant: 5 knave 6 rascal, wretch 7 heretic, infidel, villain 8 criminal 9 heretical, scoundrel 10 unbeliever 11 misbeliever, unbelieving 12 unscrupulous

miscue: 4 miss, slip 5 error 7 mistake

misdeed: sin 4 slip 5 crime, wrong 7 forfeit, offense 8 disorder 11 delinquency 13 transgression

misdemeanor: sin 5 crime, error, fault, wrong 6 delict 7 misdeed, offense 8 disorder 11 delinquency 12 misdemeanant 13 transgression

misdirect: 7 distort, pervert

mise: 4 levy, pact 5 grant 6 layout, treaty 8 immunity 9 agreement, privilege

misease: 7 poverty 8 distress 10 discomfort

mise-en-scène: set 4 site 7 setting 12 stage setting

miser: 4 cuff 5 churl, flint, hayne, hunks, Nabal 6 codger, huddle, nipper, snudge, wretch 7 hoarder, niggard, Scrooge 8 holdfast, tightwad 9 collector, skinflint 10 curmudgeon
  actor: 9 Jack Benny

miserable: bad 4 dawy 6 abject, chetif, elenge, feeble 7 forlorn, pitiful 8 pitiable 10 despicable, discomfort, inadequate 12 disconsolate 13 commiserative

misericord: 4 hall 6 dagger 9 refectory 10 compassion

miserly: 4 mean 5 close, gnede 6 greedy, grippy, stingy 8 covetous, grasping 9 penurious, scrimping 10 avaricious 12 parsimonious

misery: woe 4 ache, pain, ruth 5 agony, grief 6 sorrow 7 anguish, avarice, poverty, sadness, squalor 8 calamity, distress 9 adversity, privation, suffering 10 affliction, depression, melancholy, misfortune 11 despondency, unhappiness 12 covetousness, wretchedness 13 niggardliness 14 unpleasantness

misfeasance: See **malfeasance**

misfortune: woe 4 dole, evil, harm, slip 5 grief 6 misery, mishap, scathe 7 ill-luck, misfare, reverse, trouble 8 accident, calamity, casualty, disaster 9 adversity, holocaust, infortune, mischance 10 affliction, ill-fortune 11 catastrophe, contretemps, miscarriage 12 misadventure

misgiving: 5 doubt, qualm 7 anxiety 12 apprehension

misguide: 5 abuse 6 injure 7 mislead 8 misteach 9 misbehave, misdirect, misgovern, mismanage

mishandle: 6 bungle 7 rough up

mishap: See **misfortune**

mishmash: 4 hash, mess, olio 6 jumble, medley 10 hodge-podge

Mishnah: 6 Talmud 9 scripture
  pert. to: 7 tannaic 8 Mishnaic
  section: 4 Moed 5 Aboth
  supplement: 8 Toseftas

misinterpret: err 4 warp 7 misread

misjudge: err 12 miscalculate, misinterpret

misky: 5 foggy, misty

mislay: 4 lose 8 misplace

mislead: 4 dupe, fool 5 blear, cheat 6 betray, delude, humbug 7 beguile, debauch, deceive 8 hoodwink, inveigle, misguide 9 duplicate, mismanage

misleading: 5 false 7 crooked 10 fallacious, fraudulent

mismanage: 5 blunk 6 bungle

misplace: 4 lose 6 mislay

misplay: err 5 error 6 renege

mispronunciation: 8 cacology, solecism 12 speech defect 13 error in speech

misrepresent: lie 5 belie 6 garble 7 deceive, falsify

miss: err, fau, hip 4 balk, chit, fail, girl, lack, lass, lose, muff, omit, skip, slip, snab, want 5 lapse, title 6 escape, lassie, miscue 7 deviate, failure, neglect 8 fraulein (G.), miscarry, mistress, overlook, senorita (Sp.), spinster 9 signorina (It.) 10 desiderate, jeune fille (F.), prostitute 12 mademoiselle (F.) 13 misunderstand

missay: 5 abuse 6 vilify 7 slander

misshapen: 4 ugly 6 clumsy 8 deformed 9

distorted, misformed, monstrous **11** counterfeit

missile (see also **guided missile**): **4** bola, bolt, dart, shot **5** arrow, lance, shaft, spear **6** bullet, rocket, weapon **7** missive, outcast **8** brickbat **9** boomerang **10** projectile
pert. to: **9** ballistic

missing: out **4** lost **6** absent

mission: **6** charge, errand **7** calling, embassy, message **10** commission, delegation, deputation

missionary: **6** Marist **7** apostle **10** evangelist

Mississippi: *capital:* **7** Jackson
  city: **6** Biloxi, Laurel, Oxford **8** Columbus, Gulfport, Meridian **10** Clarksdale, Greenville
  early explorer: **6** De Soto **7** le Moyne
  Indian: **5** Osage, Yazoo **7** Choctaw, Natchez **9** Chickasaw, Merrimack
  motto: **14** Virtute et armis (By valor and arms)
  nickname: **8** Magnolia
  state bird: **11** mockingbird
  state flower, tree: **8** magnolia

Mississippian: **15** Eocarboniferous

Mississippi River: *mouth:* **4** pass
  source: **6** Itasca

missive: **4** note **6** billet, letter **7** epistle, message, missile **8** document
  love: **9** valentine **10** billet-doux

Missouri: *capital:* **13** Jefferson City
  city: **6** Joplin **7** St. Louis **8** Columbia **10** Kansas City **11** Springfield **12** Independence **13** Cape Girardeau
  early explorer: **6** De Soto **7** La Salle
  Indian: Fox **4** Sauk **5** Osage
  native: **5** Piker
  nickname: **6** Show Me **7** Bullion
  plateau: **5** Ozark
  president: **6** Truman
  river: **5** Osage **9** Merrimack **11** Mississippi
  state bird: **8** bluebird
  state flower: **8** hawthorn
  state tree: **7** dogwood
  symbol: **11** Gateway Arch

---

misspelling: **10** cacography

misspend: **4** lose **5** waste **8** squander

misstep: **4** slip, trip **5** error **7** faux pas

miss the mark: **4** fail **9** fall short

mist: dag, dim, fog, hag, rag **4** blur, damp, drow (Sc.), film, haze, scud, smog, soup **5** bedim, brume, cloud, smurr, vapor **6** mizzle, shadow, spirit **7** drizzle, mystery **9** confusion, obscurity **13** precipitation

mistake: err **4** balk, bull, slip **5** amiss, boner, error, fault, folly **6** astray, erring, escape, miscue, renege **7** blunder, default, erratum, rhubarb **10** inaccuracy **12** inadvertence **13** misconception **15** misapprehension

mistaken: **5** wrong **9** erroneous, incorrect **13** misunderstood

mister: don, man, sir **4** herr (G.) **5** senor (Sp.), title **6** signor (It.) **8** monsieur (F.)

mistletoe: **7** allheal, gadbush
  family: **12** loranthaceae

mistreat: **5** abuse **6** ill-use **7** violate

mistress: **4** amie, doll, dozy **5** amiga, dolly, donna, duena, leman, lover, woman **7** hostess **8** gudewife (Sc.), ladylove **9** chamberer, concubine, courtesan, courtezan, governess, kept woman **10** chatelaine, proprietor, sweetheart

mistrust: **5** doubt **8** distrust **9** suspicion **12** apprehension

misty: dim **5** foggy, musky, vague **6** vapory **7** obscure **10** indistinct **13** unilluminated **14** unintelligible

misunderstanding: **6** breach **7** mistake, quarrel **9** imbroglio **12** disagreement

misuse: **5** abuse **6** disuse **7** abusion, pervert **8** maltreat, mistreat **9** misemploy

mite: bit **4** atom, dite, dram, tick **5** acari (pl.), atomy, speck **6** acarid, acarus, minute, smidge **7** acarina, chigger, smidgen, smidgin **8** acaridan, arachnid, particle, smidgeon, smitchin

miter: **4** belt **5** frank, mitre, tiara **6** fillet, girdle, gusset, tavern **7** tall hat **8** headband **9** headdress
  flower: **8** cyclamen
  Jewish part: **7** Petalon

mithridate: **8** antidote **9** electuary **12** alexipharmic

mitigate: **4** balm, bate, cool, ease, tone **5** abate, allay, delay, mease (Sc.), relax, remit, slake **6** lessen, pacify, soften, temper **7** appease, assuage, mollify, qualify, relieve, sweeten **8** diminish, lenitive, moderate, palliate **9** alleviate, meliorate

mitten: **4** cuff, jilt, mitt **5** glove, hands

mittimus: **4** writ **6** notice **7** quietus, warrant **9** discharge, dismissal **10** magistrate

mittle: **4** hurt **8** mutilate

mix: pug **4** amix, fuse, join, link, meng, stir **5** admix, alloy, blend, cross, knead, merge, unite **6** jumble, mingle, muddle, wuzzle **7** blunder, combine, confect, confuse, shuffle

8 coalesce, compound, confound **9** associate, commingle, hybridize **10** amalgamate **11** incorporate, intermingle
up: **7** confuse, mistake **8** disorder
with water: **5** slake **6** dilute, weaken

mixable: **8** miscible

mixed: **6** impure, motley **7** piebald, various **11** farraginous **13** heterogeneous **14** indiscriminate

mixed blood (see also **hybrid**): *person of:* **5** metis **6** Baluga, Ladino, mestee, mustee **7** mestizo, metisse, mulatto

mixed metaphor: **11** catachresis

mixed-up: **7** complex, tangled **8** confused **10** disordered

mixer: **5** dance, party, paver **9** bartender

mixture: **4** hash, mash, olio **5** batch, blend **6** medley **7** amalgam, compost, farrage, farrago, melange **8** blendure **9** admixture, potpourri **10** concoction, hodgepodge **11** composition **12** mingle-mangle

mizmaze: web **4** knot, mesh **5** skein **6** tangle **9** confusion **12** bewilderment

mizzle: **4** mist, rain **5** misle **6** decamp **7** confuse, drizzle, speckle **9** disappear, misinform

mnemonic: **12** recollective **14** memory training

Mnemosyne: **6** Memory
daughters: **5** Muses
father: **6** Uranus
lover: **4** Zeus
mother: **4** Gaea

moa: **4** bird **6** ratite **8** dinornis

Moab: *city:* Kir
descendant: **7** Moabite
famous woman: **4** Ruth
god: **7** Chemosh
king: **5** Eglon, Mesha
mountain: **4** Nebo
people: **5** Emims

moan: cry **4** sigh, wail, weep **5** groan **6** bemoan, bewail, grieve, lament **7** deplore, whimper **8** complain **9** complaint **11** lamentation
as the wind: **5** sough

moat: gap **4** foss, lake, pond **5** ditch, fossa, fosse **6** trench **7** barrier

mob: set **4** crew, gang, herd, rout **5** cohue, crowd, drove, flock, group, horde, press, swarm, volge **6** clique, masses, rabble, throng **9** multitude **10** prostitute
member: **6** rioter **8** gangster
rule: **7** anarchy **8** violence **9** mobocracy

mobbish: **7** lawless **10** disorderly

mobile: **5** fluid **6** fickle, moving, vision **7** movable **8** populace **9** wandering **10** changeable
home: RV, van **6** camper **7** caravan (Br.), trailer

mobsman: **10** pickpocket

mobster: **7** hoodlum, Mafioso **8** gangster

Moby Dick: **5** whale **10** white whale
author: **8** Melville
character: Pip **6** Daggoo, Parsee **7** Ishmael **8** Queequeg, Starbuck
pursuer: **4** Ahab
ship: **6** Pequod

moccasin: pac **4** pack, shoe **5** snake, tegua **6** loafer **7** slipper **8** larrigan **11** cottonmouth

moch: **4** moth

mocha: **6** coffee **7** leather
stone: **5** agate

mochy: **4** damp **5** misty, moist, muggy

mock: ape, bob, dor, gab **4** gibe, gird, jape, jeer, jibe, leer, sham **5** bourd, elude, false, fleer, flirt, flout, frump, hoker, mimic, scoff, sneer, taunt **6** banter, deride **7** deceive, grimace, imitate **8** ridicule **9** burlesque, imitation **10** disappoint **11** counterfeit
brawn: **10** headcheese
cucumber: **5** apple
nightingale: **7** warbler **8** blackcap
orange: **7** seringa, syringa, syringe
ore: **10** sphalerite
plane: **8** sycamore

mocker: **4** bird **7** flauter **11** mockingbird
nut: **7** hickory

mockery: **5** bourd, farce, glaik, irony, scorn **6** satire, trifle **7** hething, sarcasm **8** derision, futility, illusion, ridicule, travesty **9** burlesque, imitation, indignity **11** insincerity **13** laughingstock

mocking: **8** fleering

mockingbird: **8** imitator, songster
genus: **5** mimus

mod: **4** bold, free **6** modern **7** offbeat **11** fashionable

mode: cut, fad **4** form, thew **5** modus, order, state, style, vogue **6** course, custom, fangle, manner, method, regime, system **7** fashion **10** convention

model: act, sit **4** form, mold, norm, plan, plot, pose, type **5** canon, ideal, shape **6** design, sitter **7** example, fashion, manikin, paragon, pattern, perfect, templet, typical **8** ensample, exemplar, formular, fugleman, mannikin, paradigm, specimen, standard, template **9** archetype, construct, exemplary, facsimile, flugelman, mannequin, miniature, precedent, prototype

moderate: **4** bate, calm, ease, easy, even, meek, mild, soft **5** abate, bland, lower, slake, sober **6** ease up, frugal, gentle, lessen, slight, soften, temper **7** average, control **8** attemper, decrease, diminish, tone down **9** abstinent, alleviate, temperate **10** abstemious, reasonable **12** conservative **13** dispassionate

moderating: 9 remissive

moderation: 7 control 9 restraint 10 abstinence, diminution, governance, limitation, mitigation, sedateness, temperance 11 restriction 12 middle course 13 temperateness

moderator: 6 umpire 7 arbiter 8 mediator 9 anchorman 10 arbitrator, negotiator

modern: new 4 late 6 latest, latter, recent 8 neoteric

modernize: 6 update 8 renovate

modest: coy, mim (Sc.), shy 4 deft, prim 5 douce, lowly, plain 6 chaste, decent, demure, humble 7 bashful 8 decorous, maidenly, moderate, reserved, retiring, verecund, virtuous 9 diffident 10 unassuming 13 unpretentious

modicum: bit 6 amount 7 portion, soupcon

modify: 4 edit, tone, vary 5 alter, limit 6 change, master, temper 7 assuage, qualify 8 attemper, mitigate, moderate, modulate 9 influence

modish: 4 chic 7 stylish

modiste: 7 stylist 8 milliner 9 couturier 10 dressmaker

modulated: 5 toned 7 changed, intoned 8 softened, tempered 9 inflected, moderated, regulated

modulation: 9 inflexion 10 inflection

modus: way 5 means 6 manner, method

modus operandi: 12 way of working

mog: jog 4 move, plod, walk 6 depart

moggan: leg 6 sleeve 8 stocking

moggy: cat, cow 4 calf 8 slattern 9 scarecrow

moguey: 4 moki, raft 5 mokhi

mogul: 4 lord, snow 5 nabob, ruler, Tatar 6 Tartar 7 magnate 8 autocrat 9 Mongolian, personage 10 locomotive

Mohammed, Muhammed: 7 Mahomet, Mahound
  birthplace: 5 Mecca
  daughter: 6 Fatima
  descendant: Ali 5 Hasan 6 Hosein, Husain, She-rif 7 Ibrahim, She-reef
  disciple: 7 Abu Bakr
  father: 8 Abdallah
  flight from Mecca: 6 hegira, hejira
  follower: 6 Moslem, Muslim, Wahabi 7 Wahabee, Wahabit, Wahhabi 8 Wahabite
  horse: 5 Buraq 7 Alborak
  nephew: Ali
  religion: 5 Islam
  son-in-law: Ali
  successor: 5 Calif 6 Caliph 7 Abu Bakr
  title: 4 Iman 7 Prophet
  tomb: 6 Medina
  uncle: 8 Abu-Talib
  wife: 5 Aisha 6 Avesha, Ayesha 7 Khadija

moho: 4 bird, rail 9 gallinule

mohock: 6 attack 8 maltreat

mohr: 7 gazelle

moider: 4 toil 5 worry 6 bother, wander 7 perplex, smother 8 distract, encumber

moiety: 4 half, part 5 piece, share 7 portion 9 community

moil: bar 4 mire, soil, spot, tire, toil, work 5 labor, taint, weary 6 defile, drudge 7 torment, trouble, turmoil 8 drudgery, vexation 9 agitation, confusion 10 defilement

moira: 4 fate 7 destiny

moire: 7 watered

moist: wet 4 damp, dank 5 humid, rainy 6 clammy 7 maudlin 8 humorous

moisten: dew, dip, ret, wet 4 moil 5 bedew, leach 6 anoint, dabble, dampen, humect, humify, imbrue, sparge 8 irrigate, sprinkle 9 humectate

moisture: fog, wet 4 bree (Sc.), drip, drop 5 humor, vapor, water 6 humour, liquid 8 aquosity, humidity 13 precipitation
  excess: 5 edema
  remove: dry 4 blot, wipe 5 wring 9 dehydrate

moisture-laden: 5 soggy 6 sodden

moistureless: dry 4 arid, sere 6 burned, desert 7 parched 8 scorched 10 desiccated

mojo: 4 Moxo 5 charm, spell 6 amulet 7 majagua

mokaddam: 5 chief 7 headman

moke: fog, net 4 dolt, mesh, mist 5 horse 6 donkey 7 network 8 minstrel 9 performer

moki: 4 fish, raft 9 trumpeter

moko: 9 tattooing

moko-moko: 6 lizard

mokum: 5 alloy

molar: 5 tooth 7 chopper, grinder

molarimeter: 11 thermometer

molasses: 5 syrup 7 claggum, sorghum, treacle 8 adherent, theriaca 10 blackstrap, sweetening

molaye: 4 tree, wood 5 vitex

mold, mould: die, fen 4 calm, cast, copy, core, form, mull, must, soil 5 decay, frame, humus, knead, model, shape 6 blight, matrix, mildew 7 fashion, matrice, moulage, pattern 9 ceroplast, character, sculpture
  opening: 6 ingate
  part: 5 nowel, sprue
  pert. to: 5 humic
  pouring hole: 5 sprue

moldable: 7 fictile

Moldavia: See **Moldova**

molder: rot 5 decay 7 crumble, molding 8 sculptor 9 become old, waste away 12 disintegrate

molding, moulding: ess 4 bead, beak, cima, cove, cyma, gula, ogee, reed, tore 5 angle, arris, conge, ogive, ovolo, splay, talon, thumb, torus **6** baguet, baston, fascia, fillet, listel, nebule, reglet, scotia **7** annulet, beading, cavetto, cornice, fingent, reeding, shaping **8** astragal, bageette, bezantee **9** trochilus

case: **5** chape

combination: **9** ledgement

concave: **4** gula **5** oxeye **7** cavetto

convex: **5** torus

curved: **4** ogee **6** nebule

flat: **6** fillet

ogee: **5** talon

pedestal: **7** surbase

rounded: **5** ovolo, torus **6** billet

rule for: **6** screed

Moldova, Moldavia: *capital:* **8** Chisinau, Kishinev

city: **5** Kagul **6** Beltsy **7** Bendery

moldy: **5** fusty, hoary, mucid, musty, stale **7** foughty **8** mildewed **12** old-fashioned

mole: cob, spy **4** cobb, pier, pile, quay **5** fault, jetty **6** anicut, burrow, rodent **7** annicut, barrier **8** excavate, starnose, tunneler **9** birthmark **10** breakwater **12** imperfection

cricket: **9** churrworm

genus: **5** talpa

molecule: **4** iota **5** speck **7** modicum **8** particle

component: **4** atom

gram: mol **4** mole

mole-like animal: **4** tape **6** desman

moleskin: fur **6** fabric

color: **5** taupe

molest: vex **5** annoy, tease **6** assail, attack, bother, harass, heckle, pester **7** disturb, torment, trouble **9** incommode, interfere **10** discommode

moliminous: **7** massive, weighty **9** laborious, momentous **10** cumbersome

moline: **8** millrind

moll: gal **5** wench **8** mistress **9** companion **10** prostitute

mollescent: **9** softening

mollify: **4** bate, calm, ease **5** abate, allay, relax, sleek **6** lessen, pacify, relent, soften, soothe, temper **7** amolish, appease, placate, relieve, sweeten **8** mitigate **9** attempter **10** conciliate **11** tranquilize

mollusk: **5** snail, whelk **6** chiton, limpet **7** abalone **10** cuttlefish

bivalve: **4** clam, leda, spat **5** chama **6** cockle, mussel, oyster **7** scallop

cephalopod: **8** argonaut

conical-shaped: **6** limpet

eight-armed: **7** octopus

fresh water: **8** etheria

gastropod: **4** slug **5** snail, whelk **7** abalone **12** taenioglossa

genus: **4** arca, leda (pl.) **5** eolis, ledum

group: **8** pteropod

large: **5** chama

larval: **7** veliger

marine: asi **4** welk **5** murex **7** abalone, scallop **8** nautilus

one shell: **5** snail **8** univalve

shell: **4** test **5** cowry, testa **6** cowrie, testae

shell concretion: **5** pearl

shell-less: **4** slug

teeth: **6** radula

ten-armed: **5** squid

used for bait: **5** squid **6** limpet

wrinkled shell: **6** cockle

young: **4** spat

mollycoddle: **4** baby **5** humor, spoil **6** coddle, pamper **7** indulge **8** weakling **12** spoiled child

moloch: **6** lizard

molt, moult: mew **4** cast, mute, shed **8** exuviate

molten rock: **4** lava **5** magma

molting, moulting: **7** ecdysis

Molucca islands (see also **Indonesia**): Aru, Kai, Obi **4** Buru **5** Ambon, Banda, Ceram, Spice **6** Maluku **7** Amboina, Ternate **15** Tidore Halmahera

moly: **4** herb **6** garlic

momble: **6** jumble, tangle

moment: sec, use **4** gird, hint, tick, tide, time **5** avail, braid, clink, filip, gliff, point, stage, trice, value **6** fillip, import, minute, second, weight **7** instant **8** occasion **9** short time, twinkling **10** importance **11** consequence

critical: **4** inch, nick **6** crises, crisis

momentary: **5** brief, quick, short **8** fleeting **9** ephemeral, impulsive, transient **10** evanescent, transitory **13** instantaneous

momentous: **4** fell **5** grave **7** epochal, fateful, serious, weighty **8** eventful **9** important, ponderous **10** chargeable **11** influential

momentum: **5** force, power **7** impetus

mommy: mom **4** duck, mama **5** mammy **6** mother

momus: **6** critic **11** fault-finder

monachist: **7** monkish

Monaco: *casino:* **10** Monte Carlo

currency: **5** franc **7** centime

dynasty: **8** Grimaldi

neighbor: **5** Italy **6** France

people: **10** Monegasque

prince: **6** Albert **7** Rainier

princess: **5** Grace **8** Caroline **9** Stephanie

monad: one **4** atom, unit **5** deity, henad **6** person **7** element **8** particle, zoospore

monarch: **4** csar, czar, king, shah, tsar, tzar **5** queen, ruler **6** caesar, despot, kaiser, prince, sultan **7** dynasty, emperor, empress **8** autocrat, princeps **9** butterfly, potentate, sovereign

461

Mongolia

monarchal: **5** regal, royal **6** kingly **8** imperial
monarda: tea **4** mint **5** plant **8** bergamot
monastery: **5** abbey, badia **6** friary, mandra, priory **7** convent, hospice, minster, nunnery **8** cloister, lamasery **9** sanctuary
Carthusian: **7** certosa
haircut: **7** tonsure
head: **5** abbot, prior **7** hegumen
Hindu: **4** math
room: **4** cell
superior: **5** prior
title: dom
monastic: **4** monk **5** friar **6** oblate **7** ascetic, monkish, recluse **8** abbatial, cenobite **9** cenobitic **10** conventual
monde (F.): **5** globe, mound, world **6** circle, people **7** coterie, society
monetary: **9** financial, pecuniary
money (see also **bill, coin**): oof, tin, wad **4** bill, cash, coin, cush, dubs, dump, gelt, gilt, grig, jack, jake, kale, loot, lour, mina, moss, pelf **5** blunt, brass, bread, bunce, chink, clink, dough, funds, livre, lucre, maneh, rhino **6** argent, boodle, change, flimsy, hansel, mazuma, moolah, siller (Sc.), spense, steven, tender, wampum, wealth **7** chattel, handsel, lettuce, ooftish **8** currency **9** spondulix **10** greenbacks, spondulics
ancient: aes
bag: **4** fels **6** follis, wealth **8** follicle
blood: cro **7** breaghe
box: **4** arca, safe, till **5** chest **6** drawer **8** register
bribe: **4** soap **6** boodle, grease
broker: **7** changer
certificate: **5** scrip
changer: **5** saraf, seraf **6** shroff
chest for: **7** brazier
coinage: **4** mint
coined: **6** specie
counterfeit: **5** bogus, queer **6** boodle
cowrie: **6** shells
dealer: **6** broker
depreciation: **4** agio **9** inflation
earnest: **5** arles (Sc.), arrha **6** hansel **7** deposit, handsel **8** handgeld
found: **5** trove **8** treasure
gambler's: **6** barato
gate: **9** admission
gift: **4** alms **7** bequest, charity **9** endowment **12** philanthropy
given to lord: **6** farleu, farley
hearth: **6** fumage
held: **6** escrow
hole for: **4** slot
hood: **4** lari **5** larin **6** larree
lender: **6** banker, usurer **7** shylock **9** loanshark **10** pawnbroker
lots of: pot **4** heap, mint, pile **5** loads

maker: **4** mint **7** moneyer
manual of exchange values: **7** cambist
metal: **4** coin **6** change, specie **7** coinage
of account: ora
overdue: **7** arrears
oversupply: **9** inflation
paid down: **4** cash **7** deposit **11** downpayment
paper: **4** bill, kale, note **5** green **6** flimsy **7** cabbage, lettuce
premium: **4** agio
ready: **4** cash **5** asset, darby **9** alcontado (Sp.)
roll of coin: **7** rouleau
sent: **10** remittance
shell: **4** peag **5** cowry, peage, sewan, uhllo **6** cowrie, seawan, wampum
small amount: **4** mite **7** peanuts **11** chickenfeed **12** pocket change
sorter: **6** teller **7** cashier
standard bank: **5** banco
transactions: **7** banking, finance
unit: ora, yen **4** lira, mark, mina, peso, real, tael **5** franc, krona, krone, maneh, pound, ruble, rupee **6** dollar, piatre, talent **7** drachma, guilder, milreis, piaster **8** cruzeiro
without: **4** poor **5** broke **11** impecunious
moneyed: **4** rich **6** heeled **7** opulent, wealthy **8** affluent, well-to-do **10** well-heeled
moneylender: **6** banker, usurer **10** pawnbroker
mong: mix **5** crowd **6** barter, mingle **7** mixture, traffic **8** mingling **11** intercourse
monger: **6** dealer, hawker, trader **7** peddler **8** huckster, merchant

Mongolia: *ass:* **8** chigetai
capital: **9** Ulan Bator
caravan leader: **5** bashi
city: **4** Urga **5** Kobdo **7** Kirghiz
conquerer: **9** Tamerlane **10** Kublai Khan **11** Genghis Khan
currency: **5** mungo **6** tugrik
desert: **4** Gobi
dynasty: **4** Yuan
fuel: **5** argal, argol, argul
measure: lan
monk: **4** lama
mountain: **5** Altai **7** Hangayn, Hentiyn **8** Tannu-Ola
people: Lai, Rai **4** Garo, Shan **5** Eleut, Tatar **6** Buriat, Tartar **7** Kalmuck, Khalkha **8** Annamese
river: Pei **4** Onon **5** Peiho **7** Kerulen, Selenga **8** Hobdo Gol
tent: ger **4** yurt
weight: lan

mongoose: 4 urva 5 lemur 7 meerkat 9 ichneumon
Kipling's Jungle Book: 14 Rikki-Tikki-Tavi
mongrel: cur, dog, mut 4 mutt 6 hybrid 7 bastard, piebald 9 crossbred, half-breed, sandpiper 10 mixed-breed
whitefish: 8 tullibee
monial: nun
moniker: 4 name 5 alias 8 nickname
monition: 5 order 6 advice, caveat, notice 7 caution, summons, warning 8 citation 10 admonition, indication, intimation 11 forewarning, instruction 13 animadversion
monitor: 6 mentor, nozzle 7 inciter 8 ironclad, reminder 9 catamaran 10 instigator
bug: 8 conenose
lizard: 4 ibid, uran 5 varan
monk: dom, fra 4 saki 5 clerk, friar, padre (Sp.) 7 brother, devotee 8 anchoret, cenobite, monastic 9 anchorite, baldicoot, bullfinch, hieronach
Buddhist: 4 lama 5 arhat, bonze, yahan 6 bhikku 7 bhikshu, poongee 8 poonghee, poonghie, talapoin
cap: 5 kulah 6 kullah
Eastern Church: 7 caloyer, starets
haircut: 7 tonsure
Hindu order founder: 7 Saukara
hood: 4 cowl
Muslim: 7 dervish
room: 4 cell
time in monastery: 9 monachate
monkey (see also *ape*): lar 4 fool, sime 5 burro 6 howler, meddle, nisnas, simian, tamper, trifle, urchin 7 colobin 9 catarhina, catarhine 10 catarrhina, catarrhine
African: 4 waag 5 jocko, patas, potto 6 baboon, grivet, guenon, langur, vervet 7 colobus, macaque
American: 4 saki 5 acari 6 grison, miriki, spider 7 ouakari, tamarin 8 capuchin, marmoset, orabassu, squirrel 9 beelzebub 11 douroucouli
Asiatic: 4 douc 5 toque 6 langur, rhesus 7 macaque
bearded: 8 entellus
beautiful: 7 guereza
big-nosed: 9 proboscis
bonnet: 4 zati
Callicebus: 5 yapok 6 yapock
capuchin: sai 7 sapajou
cebine: sai
Diana: 7 roloway
entellus: 7 hanuman 10 hoonoo-maun
genus of: 5 cebus 8 alouatta
god: 7 Hanuman
grivet: 4 tota
handsome: 4 mona

howling: 4 mono 5 araba 7 gauriba, stentor 8 alouatta
large: 5 sajou
long-tailed: sai 4 maha 5 patas 6 guenon, langur 7 hanuman, kalasie 8 entellus, telapoin, wanderoo
macaque: 6 rhesus
proboscis: 4 kaha 7 noseape
purple-faced: 8 wanderoo
rhesus: 6 bandar
saki: 6 couxia, couxio
small: 4 titi 6 apelet, teetee 7 apeling 8 marmoset
spider: 6 ateles, coaita 9 belzebuth
squirrel: 6 samiri
tailless: ape
monkey bear: 5 koala
monkey bread: 4 tree 6 baobab
monkey business: 6 pranks, tricks 7 foolish 11 mischievous
monkey flower: 7 figwort, mimulus 8 toadflax
monkey-nut: 6 peanut
monkey pot: 5 fruit
monkeyshines: 6 antics, pranks, tricks 7 aperies 12 clownishness
monkey with: 6 meddle 9 interfere
monkey wrench: 7 spanner
monkish: 7 ascetic 8 monastic
monkshood: 4 atis 5 atees 7 aconite 8 napellus
monoceros: 7 sawfish, unicorn 9 swordfish
monocle: 8 eyeglass
monocleid: 4 desk 7 cabinet
monocracy: 9 autocracy
monodist: 6 singer, writer 8 composer
monody: ode 4 poem, song 5 dirge 7 oration
monogram: 6 cipher, letter, sketch 7 outline 8 initials 9 character
monolith: 6 column, menhir, pillar, statue 7 obelisk 8 colossus, monument
monologue: 6 speech 9 soliloquy
monomachy: 4 duel 6 combat
monomaniac: 5 crank 11 derangement 12 single-minded
monophone: 9 homophone
Monophysite: 4 Copt 8 Jacobite
monoplane: 5 Taube
monopolize: 5 sew up 6 absorb, corner 7 consume, engross
monopoly: 5 grant, right, trust 6 cartel, corner 7 appalto, charter, control 9 privilege, syndicate 10 consortium
monosaccharide: ose 5 sugar
monostele: 4 root, stem
monotonous: 4 dead, drab, dull, flat, same 6 dreary 7 humdrum, jogtrot, tedious, uniform 8 unvaried 9 wearisome 10 repetitive
monotony: 4 drab 6 tedium 8 dullness, sameness 9 treadmill 10 continuity, regularity

monoxylon: 4 boat 5 canoe

monster (see also **beast**): 4 gowl, huge, ogre 5 bilsh, demon, devil, fiend, freak, giant, teras 6 geryon, sphinx 7 centaur, chimera, warlock 12 bandersnatch

   fabled: 4 Yeti 5 Argus, harpy 6 gorgon, medusa, Scylla, sphinx 7 cyclops, griffin 8 basilisk, Minotaur 9 bucentaur, sasquatch

   female: 5 harpy 6 gorgon, scylla

   fire-breathing: 6 dragon 7 chimera

   handless: 8 acheirus

   headless: 9 acephalus

   human: 5 teras 6 terata

   medical: 5 teras

   nine-headed: 5 hydra

   short-limbed: 9 nanomelus

   study of: 10 teratology

   two-bodied: 7 disomus

   two-headed: 10 dicephalus

   winged: 5 harpy

   without hind limbs: api 4 apus

monster-like: 8 teratoid

monstrous: 4 huge, vast 5 enorm, large 6 mortal 7 hideous, immense, massive, strange, titanic 8 colossal, cracking, deformed, enormous, flagrant, gigantic, horrible, shocking 9 atrocious, fantastic, unnatural 10 outrageous, prodigious, stupendous, tremendous 12 overpowering, overwhelming 13 extraordinary

---

Montana: *capital:* 6 Helena

   city: 5 Butte 7 Bozeman 8 Billings, Missoula 9 Kalispell 10 Great Falls 12 Virginia City

   early explorer: 5 Clark, Lewis

   highest point: 11 Granite Peak

   Indian: 4 Crow 5 Sioux 6 Atsina, Salish 8 Cheyenne, Nez Perce, Shoshone

   lake: 8 Flathead

   motto: 9 Oro y Plata (Gold and Silver)

   mountain range: 5 Rocky 11 Bittersweet

   nickname: 6 Big Sky 8 Mountain, Treasure

   river: 8 Kootenai, Missouri 11 Yellowstone

   state bird: 10 meadowlark

   state fish: 5 trout

   state flower: 10 bitterroot

   state tree: 13 Ponderosa pine

Monte Cristo: *author:* 5 Dumas

   hero: 6 Dantes

monteith: 9 punch bowl

Montenegro: *capital:* 8 Titograd

montero: cap 6 ranger 8 forester, huntsman

Montezuma's revenge: 8 diarrhea

month: *excess of calendar over lunar:* 5 epact

   following: 7 proximo

   half: 9 fortnight

   preceding: 6 ultimo

   present: 7 instant

monticule: 4 hill, rise 5 mount 7 hillock

montilla: 6 sherry

Montmorency: 6 sherry

Montrachet: 8 Burgundy

Montreal: *baseball team:* 5 Expos

   hockey team: 9 Canadiens

   province: 6 Quebec

monument: 4 tomb 5 cairn, relic, vault 6 effigy, record, shrine, statue, trophy 8 cenotaph, cromlech, memorial, reminder 9 antiquity, sepulcher, testament 10 gravestone 11 remembrance

   pillar-like: 5 stela, stele 6 stelae

monumental: big 4 huge 5 fatal, heavy 7 epochal, massive 8 enduring, historic

moo: low 6 bellow

mooch: beg, bum 4 loaf 5 cadge, skulk, sneak, steal 6 loiter, pilfer, sponge

moocha: 9 loincloth

mood: tid (Sc.) 4 tune, vein, whim 5 freak, humor 6 strain, temper 7 caprice, feeling 10 atmosphere 11 disposition

moody: sad 4 glum 6 gloomy, grumpy, sullen 7 pensive 8 brooding 9 depressed 10 capricious 11 ill-tempered

mools: 10 chilblains

moon: orb 4 Dian, Luna, lune (F.) 5 Diana, lunar 6 Phoebe 7 Cynthia, selenic 8 day dream, satelles, selenian 9 satellite

   above: 10 superlunar

   apogee: 5 apsis

   area on: 4 mare

   aspect: 5 phase

   beam: ray

   crater, largest: 12 Imbrium Basin

   crescent: 7 menisci 8 meniscus

   crescent point: 4 cusp, horn 6 apogee 7 perigee

   festival: 8 neomenia

   first man on: 9 Armstrong

   first quarter: 8 crescent

   geographer: 13 selenographer

   god: Sin 6 Nannar

   goddess: 4 Luna 5 Diana, Tanit 6 Hecate, Hekate, Salena, Selene, Tanith 7 Artemis, Astarte

   inhabitant: 8 Selenite

   instrument: 11 selenoscope

   Jupiter's: 6 Europa 8 Amalthea, Callisto, Ganymede

mock: **10** paraselene
new: **6** phasis
perigee: **5** apsis
pert. to: **5** lunar **7** selenic
phase: new **4** full **11** last quarter **12** first quarter
picture: **11** selenograph
position: **6** octant
Saturn's: **4** Rhea **5** Dione, Mimas, Titan **6** Phoebe, Tethys, Themis **7** Iapetus, Japetus **8** Hyperion **9** Enceladus
spacecraft: **6** Apollo
Uranus's: **5** Ariel
valley: **4** rill **5** cleft, rille
vehicle: LEM
moonack: **9** woodchuck
moonbill: **4** duck
mooncalf: **4** dolt, mole **7** lunatic, monster **11** monstrosity
mooned: **8** crescent
moonery: **7** madness
moonfish: **4** opah **7** sunfish **9** spadefish
moonflower: **5** daisy, oxeye **6** achete **12** morning glory
moonglow: **9** moonlight
moonish: **7** flighty **10** capricious
moonlighting: **4** raid **9** adventure, second job **10** expedition **11** moonshining
moon-mad: **7** lunatic
moonman: **5** gipsy **6** robber
moonraking: **13** woolgathering
moon-shaped: **6** lunate
half: **10** semilunate
moonshine: **4** idle **5** empty, month, sauce **6** liquor **7** bootleg, eyewash, trivial, whiskey **8** nonsense **10** balsamweed, bathtub gin
moonsick: **7** lunatic
moonstone: **8** feldspar
moony: **5** round, silly **6** dreamy **8** listless
moor: bog, fen, fix **4** fell **5** heath, lande, marsh, swale, swamp **6** anchor, fasten, secure **9** wasteland
Moor: **4** Moro **6** Berber, Moslem, Muslim **7** Bedouin, Othello, Saracen **8** Moroccan
moorage: **8** berthage **9** anchorage
moorburn: **7** quarrel **9** ill temper
moorcock: **6** grouse **9** blackcock
moor game: **6** grouse
moor hawk: **7** harrier
moorhen: **4** coot **9** gallinule
Moorish: **8** Moresque
alcazar: **8** Alhambra
garment: **5** jupon **7** burnous **8** albornoz, burnoose
horse: **4** barb
judge: **4** cadi
kettledrum: **5** tabor **6** atabal
king of Granada: **7** Boabdil

opiate: **4** kief
palace in Spain: **7** alcazar **8** Alhambra
moose: elk **4** alce, deer **5** eland
female: cow
genus: **5** alces
male: **4** bull
young: **4** calf
mooseberry: **10** hobblebush **13** cranberry bush
moot: dig **4** grub, plea, root, tell **5** argue, plead, speak **6** debate **7** discuss, meeting **8** argument, assembly, complain, disputed **9** debatable, encounter, gathering, uncertain, undecided **10** discussion, litigation
mop: **4** pout, swab, wash, wipe **5** bunch, clean **6** merkin, moppet, scovel **7** cleanse, grimace
mope: **4** pout, sulk **5** brood, idler
moped: **9** motorbike
moppet: tot **4** baby, doll, tike **5** child **7** darling, toddler **9** youngster
mopsy: son **6** moppet **8** slattern
moquette: **6** carpet, fabric **10** upholstery
mora: **5** delay, stool **7** default **9** footstool **12** postponement
moral: **4** good, pure, rule **5** axiom, ethic, maxim, noble, right **6** chaste, decent **7** dutiful, epimyth, ethical, upright **8** priggish, virtuous **9** honorable, righteous **10** principled **11** rightminded
fable: **8** apologue
failure: sin
law: **9** Decalogue
teaching: **5** maxim **7** precept **8** apologue **9** preaching **10** preachment **11** edification
morale: **4** hope, mood, zeal **6** spirit **8** morality **9** condition **10** confidence **13** esprit de corps
morals: **6** ethics **9** standards
morass: bog, fen **4** flow, maze, quag **5** flush, marsh, swamp **8** quagmire
morass weed: **8** hornwort
moratorium: ban **5** delay **10** suspension
Moravian city: **4** Brno, Zlin **5** Brunn
moray: eel **6** conger, hamlet **7** muraena
morbid: **4** sick **6** gloomy, grisly, morose, sullen **7** macabre **8** diseased, gruesome, horrible **9** debatable, saturnine, unhealthy **11** unwholesome **12** apprehensive, pathological
morbilli: **7** measles
morbus: **7** disease, illness
mordant: **4** keen **5** sharp **6** biting **7** burning, caustic, pungent **8** chemical, fixative, scathing **9** corrosive, sarcastic
more: piu **4** also, mair, plus **5** again, extra **6**

better, custom, manner **7** folkway, further, greater **10** additional, convention

or less: **4** so-so, some **6** nearly

than: **4** over **5** above

than enough: too **9** excessive

than one: few **4** many **6** couple, plural **7** several

morel: 8 mushroom **10** nightshade

More opus: 6 Utopia

moreover: and **4** also, then **5** again **7** besides, further **8** likewise **11** furthermore

morepork: 4 peho, ruru **7** boobook **9** frogmouth

mores: 6 ethics **7** manners **9** amenities **10** civilities

morgue: 7 library **8** mortuary **9** dead-house, stolidity **11** haughtiness, impassivity

moribund: 4 sick **5** dying **6** effete **8** decadent, decaying **10** acherontic, terminated **12** at death's door **13** deteriorating

morion: 6 helmet, quartz **8** cabasset

Mormon: 6 Danite

congregation: **4** ward

diocese: **5** stake

emblem: bee

founder: **5** Smith

leader: **5** Young

officer: **5** elder

official name: **14** Latter-day Saint

priesthood: **7** Aaronic **11** Melchizedek

prophet: **6** Moroni

state: **4** Utah

Mormonweed: 6 flower, mallow

morning: 4 dawn, morn **5** matin, sunup **6** aurora **7** sunrise **8** daybreak, forenoon

coat: **7** cutaway

concert: **6** aubade

moisture: dew

pert. to: **5** matin, wight **7** matinal **9** matutinal

prayer: **5** matin **6** matins

reception: **5** levee

morning glory: nil **7** gaybine, ipomoea

family: **14** convolvulaceae

morning star: 4 Mars **5** Venus **6** Saturn **7** Daystar, Jupiter, Lucifer, Mercury **8** Bartonia

moro: 5 finch

Moro: *chief:* **4** Dato **5** Datto

dialect: **4** Sulu

island: **8** Mindanao

knife: **6** barong

people: **4** Sulu **5** Lanao, Yakan

priest: **4** atli **5** sarip

sailboat: **5** sapit

morocco: 7 leather

imitation: **4** roan

Morocco: *cape:* Nun

capital: **5** Rabat

city: Fez **4** Assa **5** Oujda **9** Marrakech **10** Casablanca

currency: **6** dirham **7** centime

hat: fez

Jewish quarter: **8** El Millah

measure: **4** sahh **6** fanega, tomini

military expedition: **5** harka

mountain: Rif **5** Atlas **12** Jebel Toubkal

outdoor market: **4** souk

people: **4** Moor **6** Berber, Kabyle **7** Maghzen, Makhzan

soldier: **5** askar

strait: **9** Gibraltar

tree: **4** arar **5** argan **6** alerse **8** sandarac

weight: **4** rotl **5** artal, artel, gerbe, ratel **6** kintar **7** quintal

---

morology: 5 folly **8** nonsense

moron: 4 dull, fool **5** ament, idiot **6** stupid **7** dullard **8** imbecile, sluggish

moronic: 4 dull, slow **6** stupid **7** idiotic **8** retarded, sluggish

morose: 4 blue, dour, glum, grum, sour **5** gruff, moody, sulky, surly **6** crusty, gloomy, sullen **7** clumpse, clumpst, crabbed, crooked, unhappy **8** choleric, strounge **9** splenetic **10** embittered, ill-humored

morphine derivative: 6 heroin

morro: 4 hill **5** bluff, point **6** castle **8** headland

Morse code signal: dah, dit, dot **4** dash

morsel: bit, ort **4** bite, snap **5** crumb, piece, scrap, snack **6** tidbit, titbit **7** morceau, rarebit **8** delicacy, fragment, mouthful

mort: 4 dead, lard **5** death, fatal **6** deadly, grease, salmon

mortacious: 4 very **9** extremely

mortal: 4 dire, grim **5** being, fatal, human **6** deadly, lethal **7** capital, deathly, fleshly **8** grievous **9** extremely **10** implacable **11** destructive

mortality: 5 flesh **8** fatality

mortar: 5 compo, putty **6** cannon, cement, holmos, petard **7** perrier

carrier: hod

mixer: rab

mortarboard: cap **4** hawk

Morte d'Arthur author: 6 Malory

mortgage: 4 bond, deed, hock, lien, pawn **5** trust **6** pledge, wadset (Sc.) **11** encumbrance

giver: **6** lienee

receiver: **6** lienor

mortician: 10 undertaker

mortification: 5 shame 7 chagrin 8 gangrene, necrosis, vexation 11 humiliation 13 embarrassment

mortified: 7 ashamed, decayed 10 distressed, humiliated

mortify: 5 abase, abash, shame, spite 6 humble, offend 7 crucify 9 humiliate

mortifying: 8 humbling 11 humiliating, ignominious

mortise: 5 joint 6 cocket
complement of: 5 tenon
law: 8 amortize
machine: 7 slotter

mortuary: 6 morgue 9 dead-house, lich-house, sepulcher 11 funeral home
car: 6 hearse

mosaic: 5 inlay 7 chimera, picture 8 intarsia
formed like a: 10 tesselated
tile: 8 abaculus

mosaic gold: 6 ormolu
piece: 7 tessera

Moscow: 6 Moskva
ballet: 7 Bolshoi
cathedral: 8 St. Basil's
citadel: 7 Kremlin
department store: GUM
park: 5 Gorki
plaza: 9 Red Square
river: 5 Yauza

Moses: 5 judge 6 leader 7 prophet 8 lawgiver
brother: 5 Aaron
emissary: 5 Caleb
father: 5 Amram
father-in-law: 6 Jethro
flight from Egypt: 6 Exodus
law: 4 Tora 5 Torah 10 Pentateuch
led people to: 6 Canaan
mother: 8 Jochebed
mountain: 4 Nebo 5 Sinai
sister: 6 Miriam
son: 7 Eliezer, Gershom
wife: 8 Zipporah

mosey: 5 amble, drift 6 depart, ramble, stroll, wander 7 shuffle

Moslem: See **Muslim**

mosque: 4 jami, mosk 5 Caaba, Kaaba 6 church, dargah, durgah, Kaabeh, Kiblah, masjid, shrine, temple
crier: 7 muezzin
hall: 4 iwan
niche: 4 slab 6 mihrab
official: 4 imam 5 imaum
pulpit: 6 mimbar
student: 5 softa
tower: 7 manarat, minaret 8 minarete
warden: 5 nazir

mosquito: 5 aedes 7 culicid 11 gallinipper
genus of: 5 aedes, Culex 9 Anopheles

killer: 8 culicide
larvae: 8 wigglers

mosquito bee: 5 karbi 8 angelito

mosquito fish: 8 gambusia

mosquito hawk: 9 dragonfly, nighthawk

mosquito plant: 4 mint 10 pennyroyal

Mosquito State: 6 Jersey 9 New Jersey

moss: bog, fog, rag 5 swamp, usnea 6 lichen, morass 9 bryophyte, treebeard
cheeper: 5 pipit
club: 7 lycoped
coral: 8 bryozoan
duck: 7 mallard
edible: 4 agar 8 agaragar
fruit: 11 sporogonium
hammer: 7 bittern
peat: 8 sphagnum
polyp: 8 bryozoan

mossback: 4 fogy 5 fogey 6 rustic 13 stick-in-the-mud

mossberry: 9 cranberry

mossbunker: 8 menhaden

moss-grown: 10 antiquated 12 old-fashioned

mosshead: 9 merganser

moss-trouper: 6 raider 8 marauder

mosswort: 9 bryophyte

mossy: 4 dull 5 boggy, downy, green, hoary 6 marshy, stupid 7 covered 9 abounding, overgrown

most: 4 best 5 chief 6 utmost 7 maximum 8 majority, ultimate 9 principal

mostly: 7 chiefly, largely 8 normally 9 generally 10 on the whole

mot: 4 word 5 maxim 9 witticism

mote: dot, may 4 atom, hill, iota 5 atomy, match, might, speck, squib, straw 6 barrow, fescue, height, trifle 7 tumulus 8 eminence, impurity, particle 9 lightness 10 stronghold 11 small amount

motel: inn 5 hotel, lodge

motet: 4 song 6 anthem 11 composition

moth: 5 tinea 6 bogong, lappet, mallet, miller, tineah, tinean, tineid 7 tineina 8 chloasma, forester 11 yellowshell
clothes: 6 tineid
family: 7 tineina 9 arctiidae
genus of: 5 sesia
hawk: 10 goatsucker
hunter: 10 goatsucker
larva: 11 caterpillar
spot: 8 chloasma, fenestra
suborder: 10 heterocera
type: Io 4 hawk, luna 5 gypsy, owlet 6 looper, sphinx 7 tussock 8 silkworm 9 underwing 10 great tiger 11 royal walnut 13 giant Hercules

moth-eaten: 4 worn 7 decayed, worn-out 8 decrepit, out-dated

mother: dam, mom 4 dame, mama, womb 5

adopt, dregs, maman (F.), mamma, mater (L.), mommy, nurse **6** foster, matron, parent, source **7** old lady **8** genetrix **9** matriarch **10** ancestress
of believers: **5** Aisha **6** Ayesha
of gods: **4** Rhea **9** Brigantia
of Gracchi: **8** Cornelia
of Graces: **5** Aegle
of man: Eve **6** Cybele
of months: **4** moon
of presidents: **4** Ohio **8** Virginia
of sorrows: **4** Mary **6** Virgin
of states: **8** Virginia
one delivery: **7** unipara
related on side of: **6** enatic
spiritual: **4** amma
three deliveries: **7** tripara
two deliveries: **6** bipara
Mother Carey's chicken: **6** petrel
Mother Hubbard: **4** gown **5** dress
mother-in-law: **9** belle mere (F.)
motherland: **4** home **7** country **10** fatherland
motherly: **8** maternal
mother-of-pearl: **5** nacre
mother's mark: **9** birthmark
mother superior: **6** abbess
motion (see also **bodily motion**): **4** fard, idea, move, stir **5** faird **6** action, signal, unrest **7** gesture, impulse, kinesis, propose, request, suggest **8** movement, petition, proposal **9** agitation **10** suggestion **11** application, inclination **13** gesticulation
circular: **4** gyre **10** revolution
convulsive: **11** vellication
due to: **7** kinetic
expressive: **7** gesture
impetuous: **6** bensel, bensil **7** bensail, bensall, bensell
pert. to: **7** kinetic **9** kinematic **11** kinematical
producing: **6** motile
quality: **8** momentum
quivering: **6** tremor
rate: R.P.M. **4** time **5** speed, tempo **11** steerageway
science: **8** kinetics **10** ballistics, kinematics
transmitter: cog **4** belt, gear
upward: **5** scend **8** upthrust
motionless: **4** calm, dead **5** fixed, inert, quiet, rigid, still **6** asleep **8** becalmed, immobile, stagnant, stagnate, stirless **9** quiescent, sedentary **10** breathless, stock-still
motion picture: **4** film, show **5** flick, movie, talky **6** cinema, talkie **7** feature, flicker **9** photoplay **11** documentary
arc lamp: **5** kleig, klieg
award: **5** Oscar
building: **7** back lot **10** sound stage
camera mount: **5** dolly

cowboy and Indian: **5** oater **7** Western **10** horse opera
machine: **9** projector **11** kinetoscope **12** animatograph, theatrograph **13** cinematograph **14** cinematographe
outline: **6** script **8** scenario
personnel: **4** grip, star **5** actor, extra, mixer **6** cutter, editor, gaffer **7** actress **8** composer, designer, director, producer **15** cinematographer
pert. to: **9** cinematic
short: **4** clip **8** newsreel
story: **8** property
term: pan **4** shot, take **6** retake **7** reverse
motivate: **4** move **5** impel **6** incite, induce **7** inspire, provoke **9** encourage, influence, instigate, stimulate
motive: aim **4** sake, spur **5** cause **6** object, reason, spring **7** impulse, purpose **8** pressure, stimulus **9** incentive, objective **13** consideration
ostensible: **7** pretext
motley: **4** fool **5** mixed **6** jester, varied **7** diverse, mottled, piebald **9** checkered **10** variegated **11** incongruous **13** heterogeneous, miscellaneous
motmot: **4** bird
motor: car **4** auto, ride **5** drive **6** engine **7** kinetic, machine **8** motorcar **10** automobile
electric: **6** dynamo
hand-powered: **9** baromotor
part: cam **4** coil **5** rotor **6** piston, stator **9** capacitor **10** carburetor
rotary: **7** turbine
motorbike: **5** moped, vespa **7** scooter **9** trailbike **10** motorcycle
motorboat: **6** launch **7** cruiser **8** palander, runabout **9** cigarette
motor court: inn **5** motel
motorcycle: **6** Harley **7** chopper
motorman: **8** engineer, operator
motor speed control: **8** rheocrat
motte: **5** copse, grove
mottled: **4** pied, roed **5** pinto **6** motley **7** brocked, clouded, dappled, piebald, spotted **8** blotched **9** splotched **10** variegated **11** varicolored
motto: mot **4** word **5** adage, axiom, gnome, maxim **6** device, saying, slogan **7** empresa, epigram, precept, proverb **8** aphorism, apothegm **9** battle cry **10** shibboleth
mouche: **5** patch
mouchoir: **12** handkerchief
moue: **4** face, pout **7** grimace
mouflon, moufflon: **4** wool **5** sheep
moulding: See **molding**
moulting: See **molting**
mound: ahu, cop, dam, tee **4** balk, bank, butt, dene, dher, doon, dune, heap, hill, hump,

pile, terp **5** agger, berry, cairn, dheri, globe, huaca, knoll, stack, toman (Sc.) **6** barrow, bounds, burrow, causey **7** bourock, bulwark, hornito, rampart, tumulus **8** boundary **9** elevation **10** embankment
building people: **5** Adena **8** Hopewell **13** Mississippian
of sand: **4** dune
of stones: **5** cairn
pert. to: **7** tumular
prehistoric: **4** terp
mound bird: 8 megapode
Mound City: 7 St. Louis
mound of light: 8 kohinoor
mount: 4 glue, hill, peak, pile, pony, rise, seat **5** arise, climb, horse, paste, stage, steed **6** ascend, aspire **8** escalate, increase, mountain **9** intensify **10** promontory **13** fortification
by ladder: **8** escalade
horizontal bar: kip
two-legged: **5** bipod
mountain (see also **peak**): alp, ben (Sc.), kop, tor **4** berg, dagh, fell, heap, mesa, mont (F.) **5** crest, monte (Sp., It.) onlay **6** barrow, bundoc, sierra **7** montana (Sp.) mesa **8** bundocks, montagna (It.)
base of: **8** piedmont
beyond: **10** tramontane **11** transalpine
burning: **7** volcano
crest: tor
depression: col
formation: **7** orogeny **9** orogenesy **10** orogenesis
highest: **7** Everest
lake: **4** tarn
low: **5** butte
mythical: Kaf, Qaf **4** Meru **5** candy, glass **7** Helicon, Olympus **9** Parnassus
nymph: **5** dryad, oread
pass: col, gap **4** cove, duar, gate, ghat **5** ghaut, gorge, kotal **6** defile
pasture: alp **6** saeter
pert. to: **7** montane **10** orological
range: **4** Alps, Ural **5** Andes, Ozark, Rocky, Teton, White **6** Alatau **7** Rockies, Sierras **8** Cascades, Catskill, Caucasus, Pyrenees **9** Allegheny, Blue Ridge, Himalayas **11** Appalachian
ridge: **4** aret, peak, spur **5** arete, crest **6** sierra, summit **7** sawbuck
rocky: **7** nunatak
science: **7** orology
sickness: **4** veta **7** soroche
snow: **5** jokul
study: **7** orology **9** orography
sunset reflection: **9** alpenglow
trail marker: **5** cairn
mountain andromeda: 10 fetterbush

mountain ash: 4 sorb **5** rowan, rowen **8** dogberry, winetree
mountain badger: 6 marmot
mountain balsam: fir
mountain banana: fei
mountain barometer: 8 orometer
mountain beaver: 8 sewellel
mountain bluet: 8 centaury
mountain cat: 4 lynx **6** bobcat, cougar **10** cacomistle
mountain climber: 10 alpestrian
mountain climbing: 8 alpinism
equipment: axe **5** piton **7** crampon
mountain cock: 12 capercaillie
mountain curassow: 10 oreophasis
mountain dew: 7 bootleg, whiskey **9** moonshine
mountain duck: 9 harlequin, sheldrake
mountaineer: 5 Aaron **6** rustic **7** climber, hillman **9** hillbilly
song: **5** yodel
mountain finch: 9 brambling
mountain flax: 8 centaury
mountain fringe: 8 fumitory, wormwood
mountain goat: 4 ibex **6** mazame
mountain ivy: 6 laurel
mountain leather: 12 palygorskite
mountainlike: 7 etiolin
mountain lion: 4 puma **6** cougar
mountain magpie: 10 woodpecker **11** butcher-bird
mountain mint: 5 basil **8** calamint
mountain oak: 8 chestnut
mountainous: 4 high, huge **5** alpen **6** alpine, rugged **8** elevated **10** alpestrine, monumental, prodigious
mountain panther: 5 ounce **6** cougar **7** leopard
mountain parrot: kea
mountain partridge: 4 dove **5** quail
mountain pheasant: 6 grouse
mountain raspberry: 10 cloudberry
mountain rose: 6 laurel
mountain snow: 4 neve **5** jokul
mountain spinach: 5 orach **6** orache
mountain tea: 11 wintergreen
Mountain State: 7 Montana
Mountain States: 4 Utah **5** Idaho **6** Nevada **7** Arizona, Montana, Wyoming **8** Colorado **9** New Mexico
mountaintop: 4 acme, apex, cone, peak **6** summit
mountebank: 4 gull **5** cheat, quack **7** empiric **8** impostor, minstrel, swindler **9** charlatan, pretender
aid: **4** zany
Mount Etna city: 7 Catania
Mount Everest peak: 6 Lhotse
Mount Helicon fountain: 8 Aganippe

Mount Ida nymph: 6 Oenone
mounting: 7 setting 9 equipment 13 embellishment
Mount of Olives: 6 Olivet
Mount Parnassus fountain: 8 Castalia
Mount Rainier: 6 Tacoma
moup: 6 nibble 9 associate
mourn: cry, rue 4 dole, erme, long, pine, sigh, wail, weep 6 bemoan, bewail, grieve, lament, murmur, sorrow 7 deplore 8 mourning
mournful: sad 5 black 6 rueful, woeful 7 doleful, elegiac, pitiful 8 dejected, dirgeful, funereal 9 elegiacal, plaintive, sorrowful, threnodic, woebegone 10 deplorable, lamentable, lugubrious, melancholy 11 distressing 12 heavy-hearted
mourning: 4 garb 5 dolor, shiva 6 dolour 7 drapery
   bride: 5 plant 8 scabious
   dress: 5 black, crape, crepe, weeds 6 sables
   group: 7 cortege
   song: 5 dirge
mouse: erd, pry 4 girl, hunt, knot 5 snoop, steal 6 bruise, rodent 8 black eye
   deer: 7 plandok 10 chevrotain
   field: 4 vole 7 harvest
   hare: 4 pika
   leaping: 6 jerboa
   male: 4 buck
   milk: 6 spurge
   pert. to: 6 murine
mousebird: 4 coly 6 shrike
mouse-ear: 8 hawkweed 9 chickweed
mouselike: shy 4 drab 5 quiet, timid 6 murine 8 retiring
mouser: cat 9 detective
mouseweb: 6 cobweb 8 gossamer
mousing: 6 prying 7 binding 8 prowling 9 rapacious 11 inquisitive
mousle: 6 rumple
mousse: 7 dessert, messboy
mousy: shy 4 drab 5 quiet, timid 9 colorless
moutan: 5 peony, plant 6 flower
mouth: gab, gan, gob, mow, mug, mun, ora 4 boca (Sp.), dupe, guff, sass, talk, tell, trap 5 boast, front, orate, speak, spill, stoma 6 cavity, gebbie (Sc.), mumble, rictus 7 flummer, grimace, opening, stomata 8 back talk, entrance 9 impudence, spokesman
   away from: 6 aborad, aboral
   deformity: 7 harelip
   disease: 4 noma 6 canker 10 stomatitis 11 trench mouth
   muscle: 7 caninus
   of furnace: 5 bocca
   of river: 5 delta, firth
   part: lip 5 uvula 6 palate, tongue 7 pharynx
   pert. to: 4 oral 6 rictal 7 oscular, palatal 8 stomatic

   projecting: 5 spout
   roof: 6 palate
   tissue: gum
   toward: 4 orad
   with open: 5 agape
mouthful: lot, sup 4 bite, gulp 6 gobbet
mouth organ: 9 harmonica
mouthpiece: 5 bocal 6 lawyer 8 attorney
mouthwash: 6 gargle 9 collutory 10 antiseptic 11 collutorium
mouth-watering: 5 tasty 6 savory 8 alluring 9 delicious, palatable
mouthy: 5 talky 9 bombastic, talkative
mouton: fur, spy 4 wool 8 lambskin 9 sheepskin
movable: 5 loose 6 fickle, mobile, motile 8 exorable, floating, unstable, unsteady 10 changeable, inconstant 11 ephelcystic 12 figuratively
move (see also go): go, act, gee, mog 4 goad, pass, play, spur, stir 5 budge, cause, clink, impel, rouse, shift, start, sweep 6 affect, arouse, behave, bestir, betake, excite, incite, induce, kindle, motion, prompt, quetch, remble, remove 7 actuate, advance, agitate, animate, attempt, inspire, migrate, propose, provoke, suggest 8 converse, emigrate, maneuver, motivate, transfer 9 influence, instigate, stimulate, stratagem
   along: mog 5 mosey, scram 7 maunder
   away: shy 8 emigrate
   back: ebb 6 recede 7 retreat
   back and forth: wag 4 flap, rock, tack 5 dodge, weave 6 falter, seesaw, teeter, wabble, wiggle, wigwag, zigzag 7 shuttle 9 oscillate
   false: 4 balk 5 feint 7 misstep
   first: 10 initiative
   forward: 4 edge 5 drive, forge, surge 7 advance 8 progress
   furtively: 5 skulk, slink, sneak
   heaven and earth: try 6 strive
   heavily: lug 6 lumber, trudge
   noiselessly: 4 slip 5 creep, glide, skulk, slink, sneak, steal 6 tiptoe 9 pussyfoot
   noisily: 6 bustle 7 clatter, rollick
   obliquely: 4 edge, joll, skew, slue 5 sidle
   quickly: fly 4 dart, dash, flit, jump, leap, race, scud, scur, whir 5 bound, hurry, scoot, skirr, spank, start, sweep 6 career, gallop, hurtle, scurry, spring
   restlessly: 6 kelter, twitch
   rhythmically: bob, jig, jog 5 dance, march
   round and round: 4 eddy 5 swirl, twirl
   sinuously: 5 snake 6 writhe
   slowly: lag, mog 4 edge, inch, worm 5 crawl 6 trudge 7 crowhop
   smoothly: 4 slip 5 glide, skate, slide
movement: act 5 cause, tempo, trend 6

motion, rhythm **7** crusade, gesture **8** activity **9** mechanism
biological: **5** taxis
capable of: **6** mobile, motile
music: **4** moto
surface: **6** seiche

movie: See **motion picture**

moving: **7** current **8** ambulant, pathetic, poignant, touching **9** affecting, transient **10** ambulatory, impressive

moving about: **8** ambulant **10** ambulatory

moving part: cam, cog **5** rotor, wheel

moving staircase: **9** escalator

mow: bin, cut, lay, mew **4** barb, clip, crop, heap, hill, mass, pile, rick **5** mouth, scowl, stack **6** scythe, sickle **7** grimace, shorten **8** haystack **9** cornfield

mowana: **6** baobab

Mowgli: *elephant:* **5** Hathi
friend: **5** Akela, Baloo

Mozambique: *capital:* **6** Maputo
city: **4** Tete **7** Nampula **8** Lichinga
currency: **7** centavo, metical

Mozart: *opera:* **6** Figaro **8** Idomeneo **10** Magic Flute **11** Don Giovanni **12** Cosi fan Tutte
symphony: Jupiter

much: **4** fele, high, lots, many **5** great, heaps, scads **6** mickle **7** gaylies, geylies, greatly **8** abundant, uncommon **9** great deal, multitude **10** all kinds of
music: **5** molto

Much Ado About Nothing: *author:* Shakespeare
character: **4** Hero **6** Ursula **7** Antonio, Claudio, Leonato

mucid: **5** moldy, musty, slimy **6** mucous

mucilage: gum **4** glue **5** paste **6** arabin, mucago **8** adhesive

mucilaginous: **5** gluey, slimy **6** sticky, viscid **8** adhesive

muck: goo **4** dirt, dung, mess **5** botch, filth, money, slime, waste **6** manure, refuse, wealth **7** saunter **10** complicate

mucous: **5** moist, slimy **7** viscous **8** blennoid

mud: fen **4** dirt, gore, mire, ooze, roil **5** slime, slush **6** sludge **7** clabber
dab: **8** flounder
dabbler: **8** killfish
dauber: **4** wasp
deposit: **4** silt
devil: **10** hellbender
eel: **5** siren
hole: pan **6** puddle, wallow **8** quagmire
lark: **5** gamin **6** magpie, urchin
living in: **10** limicolous
mark: **7** mudflow
peep: **9** sandpiper
pert. to: **7** luteous

puppy: **7** dogfish **10** hellbender, salamander
snipe: **8** woodcock
sunfish: **4** bass

Mudcat State: **11** Mississippi

muddle: mix **4** ball, daze, doze, mess, roil **5** addle, besot, chaos, snafu **6** bemuse, burble, fuddle, jumble, pother **7** bedevil, blunder, confuse, fluster, mystify, perplex, stumble, stupefy **8** befuddle, bemuddle, bewilder, confound, disorder, flounder **9** confusion **10** complicate, intoxicate **12** huggermugger

muddled: ree **4** asea **5** beery, crazy, drunk, foggy, tipsy **10** incoherent

muddy: **4** miry, roil, soil **5** dirty, drovy, druvy, slaky, vague **6** claggy, clarty, clashy, cloudy, drubly, lutose, sludgy, slushy, turbid **7** clouded, guttery, obscure, sensual, squalid **8** confused, feculent **9** besmeared, spattered **11** bespattered

mudfish: **6** bowfin **9** killifish

mudhold: **4** slew, sloo, slue **6** slough

mudworm: ipo **9** earthworm

mudwort: **7** mudweed

muezzin's call to prayer: **4** adan, azan

muff: fur, vex **4** flub **5** botch, crest, error **6** bollix, bungle, goof up, warmer **8** irritate

muffin: bun, cob, gem **5** bread, scone **7** crumpet, popover

muffle: gag **4** damp, dull, mute, wrap **6** bumble, dampen, deaden, shroud, stifle **7** silence **8** envelope, suppress **10** camouflage

muffled: **6** hollow

muffler: **4** mask, mute **5** scarf **6** tippet **8** silencer

mufflin: **8** titmouse

mufti: **4** alim **8** assessor, civilian, clothing, official **9** expounder

mug: cup **4** cram, dupe, face, fool, toby **5** mouth, mungo, pulse, sheep, stein, study **6** attack, noggin, seidel **7** assault, canette, drizzle, goddard, grimace, tankard **8** schooner **10** photograph

muga: **4** silk **11** caterpillar

mugger: ham **4** thug **6** emoter **7** puncher **9** assailant, crocodile

muggy: **4** damp **5** humid, moist, moldy **6** sticky, sultry

mugwet: **4** rose **8** woodruff

Muhammed: See **Mohammed**

muir: **4** moor

mulatto: **5** metis **10** crossbreed, high yellow

mulberry bird: **8** starling

mulberry fig: **8** sycamore

mulch: **5** cover, straw **6** litter **7** compost, sawdust

mulct: **4** balk, fine, scot **5** cheat **6** amerce,

defect, fleece, punish **7** blemish, deceive, defraud, forfeit, penalty **8** penalize **10** amercement, forfeiture

mule (see also **hinny**): **4** mewl, mool, mute **5** coble, hinny **6** hybrid **7** bat-mule, slipper, spinner, tractor **9** chilblain **10** locomotive
cry: **4** bray **6** heehaw
dam: **4** mare **5** horse
group: **5** atajo, drove
leader in pack train: **6** donkey **8** cencerro
sire: **4** jack
spinning: **7** ironman
untrained: **9** shavetail

mule killer: **4** wasp **6** mantis **8** scorpion

muleteer: **4** peon **6** driver **7** arriero (Sp.), skinner **9** almocrebe

mulga: **6** acacia

mulish: **5** balky **6** hybrid, sullen **7** sterile **8** perverse, stubborn, pig-headed **9** obstinate, **10** determined

mull: cow **4** crag, dust, heat, mess, mold, muse **5** cloth, crush, grind, snout, spice, think **6** fettle, muslin, muzzle, ponder, powder **7** crumble, failure, rubbish, squeeze, sweeten **8** cogitate, consider, ointment, snuffbox **9** pulverize **10** promontory

mulligan: **4** stew

mulligatawny: **4** soup

mulligrubs: **5** blahs, blues, colic, sulks **8** doldrums **10** depression, melancholy

mulloway: **6** maigre **7** jewfish

multicolored: **4** pied **6** calico **7** dappled, spotted **10** variegated

multifarious: **7** diverse **8** manifold

multifold: **4** many **8** manifold, numerous

multiform: **7** diverse

multiple: **4** many **6** plural **8** numerous

multiplier: **7** facient

multiply: **5** breed **6** spread **7** amplify, augment, magnify **8** increase **9** procreate, reproduce
by eight: **11** octuplicate
by ten: **7** decuple

multitude: mob **4** army, bevy, heap, herd, hive, host, many, mass, much, ruck **5** cloud, crowd, drove, flock, group, horde, score, shoal, swarm **6** legion, myriad, nation, throng

multitudinous: **4** many **8** manifold, numerous **9** countless **10** numberless

mum: ale **4** beer, dark, mute **5** quiet, still **6** mother, silent **7** silence **9** voiceless **10** speechless **13** chrysanthemum

mumble: **4** chew, mump **5** mouth **6** chavel, chavle, faffle, fumble, haffle, murmur, mutter, palter, patter **7** flummer, grumble

mumbo-jumbo: **4** idol **6** fetich, fetish **7** bugaboo, mummery **8** nonsense **9** gibberish **10** hocus pocus

mummer: **4** mime **5** actor **6** guiser, player **7** buffoon **9** performer, puppeteer

mummery: **6** acting **8** puppetry **9** hypocrisy **10** hocus pocus **11** abracadabra

mummy: **5** relic **6** corpse, mother **7** cadaver, carcass

mummy apple: **6** papaya

mump: **5** cheat, sulks **6** mumble, mutter **7** grimace **10** sullenness **11** displeasure

mumper: **6** beggar **8** impostor

mumps: **9** parotitis

munch: eat **4** bite, chew **5** champ **6** growse, growze

mundane: **6** cosmic **7** earthly, prosaic, secular, terrene, worldly **8** temporal **11** terrestrial

municipality: **4** city, town **7** cabildo
pert. to: **5** civic

munificent: **4** free **5** ample **6** lavish **7** liberal **8** generous **9** bounteous, bountiful **10** benevolent

munitions: **7** baggage, weapons **8** armament **10** ammunition

munity: **9** privilege

Munro's penname: **4** Saki

muntjac, muntjak: **4** deer **6** kidang

muraena: eel **5** moray

mural: **6** fresco **12** wall painting

murder: **4** bane, kill, slay **5** death **6** finish, rub out **7** bump off, butcher, carnage, killing, murther **8** foul play, homicide **9** liquidate, slaughter **11** assassinate **12** manslaughter
brother: **10** fratricide
father: **9** patricide
fine: cro **7** wergild **9** bloodfine
infant: **11** infanticide
king: **8** regicide
mother: **9** matricide
own child: **9** prolicide
parent: **9** parricide
prophet: **8** vaticide
sister: **10** sororicide
son or daughter: **8** filicide
spouse: **10** mariticide
wife: **9** uxoricide
woman: **8** femicide

murderous: **4** gory **5** felon **6** bloody, brutal, deadly, savage **7** ruinous **9** ferocious, homicidal **10** sanguinary **12** bloodthirsty

mure: **4** wall **6** shut up, thrust **7** squeeze **8** imprison

murid: rat **5** mouse **6** rodent

murky: dim **4** dark **5** black, dense, foggy, mirky, misty, mucky, thick **6** cloudy, gloomy **7** obscure **12** impenetrable

murmur: coo, hum, pur **4** curr, fret, huzz, purl, purr, sigh, sugh **5** brool, drone, grank, sough **6** babble, grutch, hummer, mumble, mutter, repine, report **7** grumble, whisper **8** complain **9** grumbling

murphy: 6 potato
murre: auk 4 Uria 7 sea bird
Musa: 6 banana
muscadine: 5 grape
muscle: 4 beef, thew 5 brawn, flesh, force, might, power, sinew, teres 6 lacert 8 strength
  affliction: 5 crick 6 abasia, ataxia
  buttock: 7 gluteus
  column: 10 sarcostyle
  contracting: 7 agonist
  curve: 7 myogram
  expansion: 7 dilator
  lifting: 7 levator
  limb-straightening: 8 extensor
  round: 5 teres
  segment: 8 myocomma
  spasm: 5 tonus
  straight: 6 rectus
  stretching: 6 tensor
  sugar: 7 inosite 8 inositol
  trapezius: 10 cucullaris
  triangular: 7 deltoid
  turning: 7 evertor, rotator
  two-headed: 6 biceps
muscovado: 8 raw sugar
Muscovite: Red 4 mica, Russ 6 Moscow 7 Russian
  mica: 4 talc
  prince: 4 Ivan
muscular: 4 ropy, wiry 5 thewy 6 brawny, robust, sinewy, strong, torose, torous 7 fibrous, stringy 8 athletic, vigorous
muse: 4 dump, mull, poet 5 dream, think 6 loiter, ponder, trifle, wonder 7 reflect, reverie 8 cogitate, consider, meditate, ruminate 9 amusement 10 meditation 11 contemplate
Muse: *birthplace:* 6 Pieria
  epithet: 7 Pierian
  father: 4 Zeus 7 Jupiter
  fountain: 8 Aganippe
  home: 5 Aonia 7 Helicon 12 Mount Olympus
  leader: 6 Apollo
  mother: 9 Mnemosyne
  mountain: 9 Parnassus
  of astronomy: 6 Urania
  of comedy: 6 Thalia
  of dancing: 11 Terpsichore
  of eloquence: 8 Calliope
  of epic poetry: 8 Calliope
  of history: 4 Clio
  of love poetry: 5 Erato
  of lyric poetry: 7 Euterpe
  of music: 7 Euterpe
  of pastoral poetry: 6 Thalia
  of sacred poetry: 8 Polymnia 10 Polyhymnia
  of tragedy: 9 Melpomene
museful: 6 silent 10 meditative, thoughtful
musery: 4 play 9 amusement
musette: air 4 oboe 7 bagpipe, gavotte
museum: 7 gallery 8 archives, atheneum, preserve, treasury 10 collection, repository
  custodian: 7 curator
  director: 7 curator
mush: cut 5 atole, crush, gruel, march, notch, sepon 6 indent, sepawn, supawn, travel 7 confuse, journey, pudding, suppawn 8 flattery, porridge, sagamite, umbrella 14 sentimentality
mushroom: 4 grow 6 agaric, fungus, spread 7 explode, parvenu, upstart
  cap: 6 pileus
  disease: 5 flock
  edible: 5 morel 10 champignon 11 chanterelle
  like: 7 fungous
  part of: 4 gill 5 stipe, trama 6 pileus 7 annulus 8 basidium, hymenium, sterigma 12 basidiospore
  poisoning: 8 mycetism
  poisonous: 7 amanita 9 toadstool
  stem: 5 stipe
mushy: 4 hazy, soft, weak 5 gushy, soppy, thick 8 effusive, yielding 11 sentimental
music (see also **melody, song,** and entries under **musical**): air, art 4 tune 7 harmony
  aftersong: 5 epode
  beat: 5 ictus, pulse, tempo 6 rhythm
  change to another key: 10 modulation 13 transposition
  chord: 5 tonic, triad 8 dominant 11 subdominant
  ending chord: 7 cadence
  flourish: 7 roulade
  for eight: 5 octet
  for five: 7 quintet
  for four: 7 quartet
  for nine: 5 nonet
  for one: 4 soli, solo
  for seven: 6 septet
  for six: 6 sextet 7 sestole 8 sestolet
  for three: 4 trio
  for two: duo 4 duet
  god: 6 Apollo
  half tone: 8 semitone
  Japanese: 6 gagaku
  machine for: 5 radio 6 stereo 7 boom box, juke-box, pianola, walkman 8 musicbox 10 gramophone, phonograph
  major scale: 5 gamut
  major third: 6 ditone
  mania for: 9 melomania
  melodic phrase: 9 leitmotif, leitmotiv
  morning song: 6 aubade
  muse: 7 Euterpe

notation system: **5** neume
outdoor: **6** aubade **8** serenade
patron saint: **7** Cecilia
pert. to chance elements: **9** aleatoric
pitch: **4** tone
scale: **8** diatonic **9** chromatic
simple song: air, lay **4** tune
symbol: bar, key, tie **4** clef, flat, note, rest, slur **5** brace, sharp, staff
theme: **4** tema
timing device: **9** metronome
musical: **4** show **5** lyric, revue **7** lyrical, melodic **8** harmonic, rhythmic **9** melodious **10** harmonious
musical composition: **4** glee, opus **5** cento, fugue, opera, rondo, suite **6** ballad, sonata **7** ballade, boutade, cantata, chanson, prelude, requiem, scherzo, virelai **8** berceuse, concerto, nocturne, operetta, oratorio, serenade, serenata, sonatina, symphony **9** cabaletta, interlude **10** intermezzo
aria-like: **6** arioso
choral: **5** motet **7** chorale **9** plainsong
dancer's: **10** gymnopedie
dawn: **6** aubade
declamatory: **10** recitative
ending: **4** coda, fine **6** finale
exercise: **5** etude, study
feature: **5** motif, theme
folk song: **4** lied
Gregorian: **5** chant **9** plainsong
interlude: **6** verset
jazz: bop **4** cool, jive **5** bebop, swing **6** fusion **12** boogie-woogie
opera: **4** aria, duet **5** scena
poetic: ode
prelude: **6** verset
religious: **4** hymn **5** motet **7** cantata, requiem **8** oratorio
round: **5** canon, fugue, troll
suite: **7** partita
musical direction: *above:* **5** sopra
accented: **7** marcato **8** sforzato **9** sforzando
again: DC, DS, bis **6** da capo **8** dal segno
all: **5** tutti
always: **6** sempre
animated: **7** animato **9** spiritoso
ardent: **7** ardente **12** appassionato
as written: sta
begin now: **7** attacca
below: **5** sotto
bold: **6** audace
bowed: **4** arco
bright: **5** anime
cold: **6** freddo
continue: va
devout: **6** divoto
dignified: **8** maestoso
disconnected: **8** staccato

dying away: **7** calando
emotional: **12** appassionato
evenly: **10** eugalmente
everyone: **5** tutti
excited: **7** agitato **9** spiritoso
fast: **4** vivo **5** tosto **6** presto, veloce, vivace **7** allegro **10** tostamente
faster: **7** stretto
fastest: **11** prestissimo
freely: **9** ad libitum
furious: **7** furioso
gay: **7** giocoso
gentle: **5** dolce
gradually increasing tempo: **11** accelerando
great feeling: **12** appassionato
half: **5** mezzo
heavy: **7** pesante
held: **6** tenuto
hurried: **7** agitato
in the style of: **4** alla
joyous: **7** giocoso
leap: **5** salto
less: **4** meno
little: **4** poco
little by little: **9** poco a poco
lively: **6** vivace **7** allegro, animato, giocoso
loud: **5** forte **10** fortissimo
louder: **9** crescendo
lovingly: **7** amabile, amoroso
lyric: **5** erato
majestic: **8** maestoso
marked: **7** marcato
medium: **5** mezzo
moderate: **7** andante **8** moderato
more: piu
more rapid: **7** stretta, stretto
much: **5** molto
muted: **5** sorda
passionless: **6** freddo
plaintive: **7** dolente
playful: **7** giocoso **10** scherzando
plucked: **9** pizzicato
proceed: va
quick: **4** vite **5** tosto **6** presto **7** schnell
quickening: **11** affrettando
quick time: **9** alla breve
repeat: bis **6** ancoro **7** ripresa
restless: **7** agitato
sadly: **7** dolente **8** doloroso
sharp: **8** staccato **9** sforzando
silent: **5** tacet
singing: **9** cantabile
sliding: **9** glissando
slow: **5** grave, largo, lento, tardo **6** adagio **7** andante **9** larghetto
slower: rit **6** ritard **10** ritardando
slowing: **11** rallentando
smooth: **6** legato **7** andante **8** grazioso
smoothly connected: **6** legato

soft: **5** dolce, piano **10** pianissimo
softer: **10** diminuendo **11** decrescendo
solemn: **5** grave
somewhat: **4** poco
so much: **5** tanto
songlike: **9** cantabile
spirited: **7** animato **9** spiritoso
stately: **7** pomposo **8** maestoso
strong: **5** forte **10** fortissimo
sudden strong accent: **9** sforzando
sustained: **6** tenuto **9** sostenuto, sustenuto
sweet: **5** dolce
tempo irregular: **6** rubato
tender: **7** amabile
thrice: ter
throughout: **6** sempre
together: **8** ensemble
too much: **6** troppo
tranquil: **7** calmato
trembling: **7** tremolo
turn: **9** gruppetto
twice: bis
very: tre **4** tres **5** assai, molto **7** dimolto
with: con
musical disc: 33, 45, 78, CD, LP **5** album **6** cymbal, platter, record **9** recording **11** compact disc
musical drama: **5** opera **8** operetta, oratorio **9** singspiel
musical event: **5** opera **6** ballet **7** concert, recital **8** musicale, oratorio
musical instrument: **4** drum, fife, gong, harp, horn, lute, lyre, oboe, reed, tuba **5** banjo, flute, organ, piano, viola **6** cornet, guitar, spinet, violin, zither **7** bassoon, ocarina, piccolo, saxhorn, trumpet, ukelele **8** castanet, clarinet, dulcimer, mandolin, trombone **9** euphonium, flageolet, saxophone **11** synthesizer, violoncello
aid: **4** pick **8** diapason, plectrum **9** metronome, pitch pipe
ancient: **4** asor **5** rocta **6** rappel, sebaca **7** cithera, serpent **9** pantaleon
bass: **5** cello **11** violoncello
brass: **4** horn, tuba **5** bugle **6** cornet, tromba **7** althorn, cymbals, helicon, saxhorn, trumpet **8** altohorn, trombone **9** saxophone **10** flugelhorn, French horn, sousaphone
China: jin, kin **4** pipa
East Indies: **4** bina
Egypt: **7** sistrum
electronic: **11** synthesizer
for text: **7** setting
helicon: **4** tuba
Indian: **4** vina **5** sitar **7** tambura
Java: **7** gamelon **8** gamelang
keyboard: **5** organ, piano **6** spinet **7** celesta, clavier **8** melodeon **9** accordion **10** clavi-

chord, concertina, pianoforte **11** harpsichord
lute-like: **7** angelot, bandore, cithern, cittern **9** bandurria **10** colascione
lyre-like: **4** asor **6** cither, zither **7** cithara, kithara
medieval: **5** rebab, rocta **7** chrotta **10** clavichord, hurdy-gurdy
Mexico: **5** guiro **6** clarin **7** cabacas, maracas **11** chiapanecas
mouthpiece: **4** reed **6** fipple
oboe-like: **5** shawm **7** musette
old: **4** lute, lyre **5** rebec **7** cittern, gittern **8** dulcimer
percussion: **4** drum, gong **5** bells, snare, traps **6** chimes, maraca **7** cymbals, marimba, timpani, tympani **8** bass drum, qaraquib, triangle **9** castanets, snare drum, xylophone **10** kettledrum, tambourine, vibraphone **12** glockenspiel
piano-like: see *keyboard* above
reed: **4** oboe **7** bagpipe, bassoon **8** clarinet **9** harmonica, saxophone **11** English horn
stringed: oud, uke **4** asor, bass, harp, lute, lyre, vina, viol **5** banjo, cello, qanun, rebec, ruana, sitar, viola **6** citole, fiddle, guitar, rebeck, violin, zither **7** bandore, cythara, gittern, pandura, samisen, theorbo, ukelele **8** autoharp, dulcimer, mandolin **9** bala laika **11** harpsichord, violoncello
supplementary: **7** theorbo
two-necked: **7** ripieno
viol-like: **5** rebec, ruana **6** rebeck **7** claviol **8** claviole
wind: jub, sax **4** fife, horn, oboe, reed, tuba **5** brass, bugle, flute, organ **6** cornet **7** althorn, bagpipe, bassoon, clarion, ocarina, panpipe, piccolo, saxhorn, serpent, trumpet **8** altohorn, clarinet, recorder, trombone, zampogna **9** flageolet, harmonica, saxophone **10** French horn **11** sarrusphone
xylophone-like: **7** marimba
musical interval: **5** fifth, major, minor, sixth, third **6** ditone, fourth, octave, second, unison **7** perfect, seventh, tritone **9** augmented **10** diminished
musical medley: **4** olio **5** cento
musical note (see also **musical syllable**): **5** breve, minim, neume **6** quaver **9** semibreve
musical rhythm: **4** beat, time **5** ictus, meter, pulse, swing, tempo
measuring device: **9** metronome
musical scale: **5** gamut
musical sign: **5** segno
entrance: **5** presa
hold: **7** fermata, formata
key: **4** flat **5** sharp **7** natural
pitch level: **4** clef

silence: **4** rest
slur: **8** ligature
smooth: **4** slur
staff: bar
musical syllable: do, fa, la, mi, re, ti, doh, Ela, sol **7** alamire
musical term: *arrangement:* **7** ridotto
ballad style: **8** a ballata
between acts: **8** entracte
cadence: **4** half **6** plagal **7** perfect **9** authentic, deceptive, imperfect
chapel-style: **9** a cappella
dance-style: **7** da ballo
embellishment: **8** ornament **9** fioritura **12** appoggiatura
ending: **4** coda
florid: **7** bravura
flourish: **7** cadenza
half note: **5** minim
half tone: **8** semitone
major key: dur
melodic phrase: **5** motif **9** leitmotif, leitmotiv
melos: **4** song **6** melody
minor key: **4** moll
movement: **4** moto
note: **5** breve, neume
refrain: **5** epode **8** repetend
repeat: **5** rondo **7** reprise
run: **6** volata **9** glissando
shake: **5** trill **7** tremolo, vibrato
soft pedal: VC **7** celeste
third: **6** tierce
thirty-second note: **14** demisemiquaver
three-note chord: **5** triad
tones: **5** chord
tremble: **5** trill **7** tremolo, vibrato
triplet: **6** tercet, triole
two notes: **5** duole
unaccompanied: **9** a cappella
upbeat: **5** arsis
vocal part: **5** canto
musical theme: **4** tema **5** motif **9** leitmotif, leitmotiv
music hall: **4** gaff, odea (pl.) **5** odeon, odeum **7** theater, theatre
musician: **4** bard **5** piper **6** player, rocker, singer **7** drummer, flutist, gleeman, Orpheus, pianist **8** bandsman, composer, flautist, minstrel, organist, virtuoso **9** cornetist, performer, serenader, violinist **10** trombonist **11** clarinetist, saxophonist
group: **4** band, duet, trio **5** choir, nonet **6** chorus, septet, sextet **7** nonetto, quartet **8** ensemble, septette, sextette **9** orchestra, quartette
patron saint: **7** Cecelia
musing: **6** dreamy **7** pensive, reverie **10** meditation, meditative **13** contemplation

musk: **4** deer **7** perfume
beaver: **7** muskrat
cat: **5** civet
cavy: **5** hutia
cucumber: **11** cassabanana
deer: **6** cervid **10** chevrotain
mallow: **8** abelmosk
shrew: **6** desman
muskeg: bog **5** marsh
muskellunge: **4** pike
musket: gun **4** hawk **5** fusil, rifle **6** falcon **7** bundock, bundook, dragoon, firearm **8** biscayen **9** flintlock **11** blunderbuss
Musketeers: See **Three Musketeers**
muskmelon: **6** atimon, casaba **8** honeydew **10** cantaloupe
muskrat: **5** shrew **6** desman, rodent
fur: **10** Hudson seal
meat: **11** marsh rabbit
Muslim, Moslem (see also **Islam, Mohammed**): **4** Moro **6** Paynim **7** abadite, Islamic, Saracen **9** Mahometan, Moslemite, Mussulman **10** Mohammedan
Alexandria sect: **6** Senusi
angel: **6** Azrael **7** israfil, isrefel **8** israfeel
antenuptial settlement: **4** mahr
ascetic: **4** sufi **5** fakir **6** fakeer
bazaar: **4** sook, souk
beads: **6** tasbih
belt: **5** zonar **6** zonnar
bier: **5** tabut
blood relationship: **5** nasab
calendar: **5** Rabia, Rajab, Safar **6** Jumada, Shaban **7** al-Awwal, Ramadan, Shawwal **8** ath-Thani, Muharram, Zu'lhijah, Zu'lkadah
caliph: Ali **4** Omar **6** Uthman **7** Abu Bakr
call to prayer: **4** adan, azan
caravansary: **6** imaret
caste: **5** mopla **6** moplah
chief: **4** rais, sidi, syid **5** datto, sheik
convert: **5** ansar
council: **5** Ulema
creed: **5** Sunna **9** Fiqh Akbar
decree: **5** irade
demon: **5** afrit, eblis, jinni **6** jinnee
dervish: **6** Sadite, Santon
divorce: **5** ahsan, talak **7** mubarat
fast days: **7** Ramadan
festival: Eed **6** Bairam
freethinker: **7** Saracen **9** Aladinist
garment: **4** izar **6** jubbah
god: **5** Allah
guide (spiritual): pir
headdress: fez, taj **5** kulah **6** kullah, turban
hermit: **8** marabout
holy book: **5** Coran, Koran **7** Alcoran
holy city: **5** Mecca **6** Medina
holy war: **5** jehad, jihad
infidel: **5** kafir **6** kaffir

judge: **4** cadi, cazi, imam, kazi, qadi **5** hakim, imaum

kinship: **5** nasab

lady: **5** begum

law: **5** halal **7** sheriat

lawyer: **5** mufti

leader: **4** amir, emir **5** ameer, emeer **6** caliph

men's quarters: **8** selamlik

messiah: **5** Mahdi

minaret crier: **7** muezzin

minister of state: **6** vizier

monastery: **5** tekke

month: see *calendar* above

mosque: **6** masjid

mystic: **4** Sufi

nymph: **5** houri

officer: aga

official: **5** hajib, mufti

orthodox: **5** hanif **7** Sunnite

patriarch: **7** Abraham

people: Laz **4** Lazi, Moro, Sufi, Swat **5** Hanif, Isawa, Salar, Samal, Sunni, Swati **6** Dehgan, Senusi **7** Bazigar, Senousi, Senussi **8** Senusite **9** Senussian

physician: **5** hakim **6** hakeem

pilgrim: **4** haji **5** hadji, hajji

pilgrimage: **4** hadj

pilgrim's dress: **5** ihram

prayer: **5** namaz, salat

prayer call: **4** adan, azan

prayer leader: **4** imam **5** imaum

prince: **4** amir, emir, seid **5** ameer, emeer, nawab, sayid

princess: **4** tola **5** begum

prophet: Hud **4** nabi **5** Salih **6** Shuaub **8** Muhammad

religion: **5** Islam

religious authority: **5** ulama, ulema

ruler: aga **4** amir, emir **5** ameer, emeer, hakim, nawah **6** hakeem, sultan

saber: **7** yatagan **8** scimitar, scimiter, yataghan

saint: **4** qutb, wali **5** Abdal, tahir **6** marbut, Santon **8** Marabout **9** Abu Madyan **10** Mulay Idris

salutation: **5** salam **6** salaam

sect: **4** Shia **5** Isawa **6** Wahabi **7** Abadite, dervish, Sevener, Sunnite, Twelver **8** Ahmadiya, Sifatite

shrine: **5** Kaaba **6** Kaabeh

spirit: **4** jinn (pl.) **5** genie, jinni **7** jinnyeh

spiritual adviser: pir **5** sheik **6** shaykh

student: **5** softa

teacher: **4** alim, imam **8** mujtahid

title: sid **4** said, sidi **5** nawab, sayid **6** sayyid

tomb: **5** tabut

warrior: **7** Saracen

washing: **4** widu, wudu, wuzu

women's quarters: **5** harem **8** seraglio

muslin: **4** mull **5** cloth **6** cotton, fabric **7** organdy **8** nainsook, seerhand, sheeting

mussel: **4** unio **5** naiad **6** mucket, nerita **8** deerhorn

genus of: **8** modiolus

larva: **9** blackhead

part: **6** byssus

mussitate: **6** mutter

Mussolini: **7** Fascist **8** dictator

title: **6** Il Duce

Mussulman: See **Muslim**

must: **4** bood, duty, mold, musk, need, sapa, stum, want **5** juice, ought, shall **6** refuse **8** required **9** essential, have got to, necessary **10** obligation

mustang: **4** wild **5** horse, pinto **6** bronco **7** broncho

mustard: **5** nigra, senvy **6** senapi **7** cadlock **8** charlock

chemical: **5** allyl

family: **10** cruciferae **12** brassicaceae

genus of: **7** sinapis

pod: **7** silicle

mustard plaster: **8** poultice, sinapism

musteline animal: **6** weasel

muster: **4** call **5** erect **6** enroll, gather, roster, sample, summon **7** collect, convene, marshal, pattern **8** assemble, generate, mobilize **10** accumulate, congregate

mustiness: **4** fust, mold

musty: **4** dull, sour **5** dirty, fusty, hoary, moldy, rafty, stale, trite **6** filthy, rancid **7** foughty, spoiled, squalid **10** antiquated

Mut: *child of:* **5** Chons

husband: **4** Amen, Amon

mutable: **6** fickle **8** unstable, variable **9** alterable **10** changeable, inconstant **11** fluctuating, vacillating

mutate: **4** vary **5** alter **6** change, modify **9** transform

mutation: **6** change, revolt **9** posthouse, variation **10** revolution, succession **11** vicissitude

mute: mum **4** dumb, lene, surd **5** quiet **6** deaden, muffle, silent **7** mourner, muffler **8** deadener, silencer **9** voiceless **10** speechless **12** inarticulate

mutilate: mar **4** hack, hurt, maim **6** damage, deface, garble, injure, mangle, mittle (Sc.) **7** cripple, destroy **9** disfigure, dismember, sterilize

mutinous: **6** unruly **9** alienated, insurgent, seditious, turbulent **10** rebellious, refractory, tumultuous **11** disaffected, disobedient, intractable **12** contumacious **13** insubordinate

mutiny: **4** coup **6** revolt, strife **8** uprising **9** commotion, rebellion **12** insurrection

mutt: cur, dog **5** dunce **7** mongrel **9** block-head

mutter: **5** growl, rumor **6** mumble, murmur, patter **7** channer, grumble, maunder **9** mussitate

mutton: **4** meat **5** sheep **6** candle **10** prostitute
dried: **5** vifda, vivda
leg: **5** cabob, gigot **7** wabbler, wobbler

muttonbird: oii **6** petrel **10** shearwater

muttonchop: **7** whisker **8** burnside, sideburn

muttonfish: **4** sama **5** pargo, porgy **7** eelpout, mojarra

muttonhead: **5** dunce **9** blockhead, screwball

mutual: **5** joint **6** common, shared **7** related **10** associated, reciprocal, responsive

mutuality: **13** interrelation

mux: **4** mess **5** botch

muzhik: **7** peasant

muzzle: gag **4** face, grub, nose, root **5** snout **6** clevis, muffle **7** sheathe **8** restrain **10** respirator

muzzy: **4** dull **5** fuzzy **7** blurred, muddled **8** confused **9** befuddled **10** depressive

Mycenae: *founder:* **7** Perseus
king: **6** Atreus **9** Agamemnon

Myanmar: See **Burma**

mycoid: **7** fungoid

My Last Duchess author: **8** Browning

myna: **4** bird **7** grackle

myomorph: rat **5** mouse **6** rodent

myopic: **8** purblind **10** astigmatic **11** nearsighted **12** shortsighted

myriad: **4** host, many **9** countless **11** innumerable **13** multitudinous

myriapod: **9** centipede

myrmicid: ant

myrmidon: **8** adherent, follower, henchman **9** attendant, underling

myrrh: gum **4** tree **5** resin

myrtle: **6** laurel **8** ramarama **10** periwinkle **11** candleberry

myself: **5** masel (Sc.)

mysterious: dim **4** dark **5** runic **6** arcane, mystic, occult, secret **7** cryptic, strange, uncanny **8** abstruse **9** enigmatic, equivocal, recondite, sphinxine **12** inexplicable, unfathomable

mystery: **4** rune **5** craft, trade **6** cabala, enigma, puzzle, riddle, secret **7** arcanum, esotery, stumper **8** thriller, whodunit **9** conundrum **10** closed book **12** brain twister

mystery novel award: **5** Edgar

mystic: **4** seer **5** epopt, magic, runic **6** occult, orphic, secret **7** cryptic, epoptic, obscure **8** anagogic, esoteric, symbolic **9** enigmatic, recondite **10** cabalistic, mysterious
art: **6** cabala
initiate: **5** epopt
Muslim: **4** Sufi
secret sect: **5** cabal
word: **4** evoe **7** abraxas **10** hocus pocus, open sesame **11** abracadabra

mystical: **4** dark **6** occult, secret **7** magical **8** anagogic, hush-hush, symbolic, telestic **9** spiritual
significance: **7** anagoge

mysticism: **6** cabala **8** cabalism

mystify: **5** befog **6** muddle, puzzle **7** becloud, confuse, perplex **8** befuddle, bewilder **9** bamboozle, obfuscate

myth: **4** saga, tale **5** fable, fancy, story **6** legend **7** fiction, parable **8** allegory **9** apocrypha

mythical: **6** fabled, famous, unreal **9** imaginary, legendary **10** fabricated, fictitious

N

nab: 4 grab 5 catch, seize 6 arrest, clutch, snatch 7 capture 9 apprehend

Nabal: *home:* 4 Maon
  wife: 7 Abigail

nabob: 5 nawab 6 bigwig, deputy 7 rich man, viceroy 8 governor 9 personage, plutocrat 10 viceregent 11 billionaire

Nabokov novel: Ada 4 Pnin 6 Lolita

nacelle: 7 shelter 11 compartment

nacket: boy 4 cake 5 lunch

nacre: 8 lustrous 9 shellfish 10 conchiolin, iridescent 13 mother-of-pearl

nadir's opposite: 6 zenith

nag: tit 4 carp, frab, fret, gnaw, jade, plug, pony, twit 5 annoy, cobra, hobby, horse, scold, shrew, snake, tease 6 badger, berate, bother, carp at, harass, heckle, hector, padnag, pester, wanton 7 hackney, henpeck 8 complain, harangue, irritate 9 aggravate, criticize

naga, nag: 5 cobra, snake

nagor: 8 antelope, reedbuck

Nahor: *father:* 5 Serug
  grandson: 7 Abraham
  son: 5 Terah
  wife: 6 Milcah

Nahuatlan: 5 Aztec

naiad: 5 nymph 6 mussel

naif: See **naive**

nail: cut, fix, hit, hob 4 brad, brag, brod, claw, cloy, dump, spad, stub, stud, tack, trap 5 affix, catch, clout, grope, seize, spike, sprig, steal 6 arrest, clinch, detain, fasten, hammer, secure, strike, unguis, ungula 7 capture 8 fastener, sparable, spikelet 9 finishing, intercept
  drive at a slant: toe
  headless: 5 sprig
  ingrowing: 7 acronyx
  kind: bex 4 brad 5 screw 6 anchor, casing, common, staple 7 roofing 9 finishing
  marking on: 6 lunule
  perforated: 4 spad
  shoemaker's: 4 brad 8 sparable

nais: 5 naiad, nymph

naissance: 5 birth

naive: 6 candid, simple 7 artless, foolish, natural 8 childish, gullible, innocent, trusting, untaught 9 childlike, guileless, ingenuous, untutored, unworldly 13 inexperienced 15 unsophisticated

naked: 4 bare, nude, open 6 cuerpo 7 evident, exposed, obvious 8 manifest 9 au naturel, disclosed, unadorned, unclothed, uncovered 10 discovered 11 defenseless, unprotected

namaycush: 5 lunge, togue, trout

namby-pamby: 7 insipid 8 weakling 10 wishy-washy 11 sentimental

name: dub, nom (F.) 4 call, cite, fame, idol, term 5 claim, clepe, count, label, nemme, nemne, neven, nomen, style, title 6 adduce, appeal, choose, eponym, monica, renown, select 7 appoint, baptize, entitle, epithet, mention, moniker 8 christen, delegate, identify, identity, nominate 9 celebrity, designate, personage 10 denominate, denotation, reputation 11 appellation, designation
  added: 6 agname 7 agnomen
  assumed: 5 alias, stage 6 anonym 9 incognito, pseudonym, sobriquet 10 nom de plume, soubriquet 11 nom de guerre
  backwards: 6 ananym
  based on location: 7 toponym
  derivation: 7 eponymy
  family: 7 eponymy, sirname, surname 8 cognomen
  fictitious: 9 pseudonym
  first: 5 given 9 baptismal, Christian, praenomen
  list: 11 onomasticon
  maiden: nee
  objectionable: 7 caconym
  pet: 8 nickname 9 sobriquet
  tablet: 5 facia

nameable: 6 famous 7 notable 9 memorable 10 noteworthy

named: 6 yclept

nameless: 7 bastard, obscure 9 anonymous, unnamable 12 illegitimate

namely: viz 5 id est, noted, to wit 6 famous 8 scilicet 9 expressly, videlicet 10 especially 12 specifically

namesake: 6 junior

Namibia: (see box)

nandu: 4 rhea 6 nandow

nanny: 4 goat 5 nurse

nanny plum: 10 sheepberry

Naomi: 4 Mara
  daughter-in-law: 4 Ruth 5 Orpah

husband: **9** Elimelech
son: **6** Mahlon **7** Chilion

Namibia: *capital:* **8** Windhoek
city: **7** Gobabis **8** Rehoboth
desert: **5** Namib **8** Kalahari
park: **6** Etosha
river: **6** Kunene, Kwando, Orange **7**
Zambezi **8** Okavango

---

naos: **5** cella **6** shrine, temple
nap: nod **4** calk, doze, fuzz, lint, pile, rest,
shag, wink **5** fluff, grasp, let up, seize,
sleep, steal **6** siesta, snooze **7** respite **10**
forty winks
nape: nod **4** neck **5** nucha, nuque **6** scruff **7**
niddick
napery: **5** linen
Naphtali: *census taker:* **4** Enan
mother: **6** Bilhah
son: **4** Guni **5** Jezer **7** Jahziel, Shallum
naphtha: **9** petroleum
napkin: **5** cloth, doily, towel **6** diaper, napery
8 kerchief **9** handcloth, serviette
Naples (see also **Italy**): *biscuit:* **10** ladyfinger
coin: **6** carlin **7** carline
king: **5** Murat
secret society: **7** Camorra
napless: **10** threadbare
napoleon: **4** coin **6** pastry
Napoleon: *battle:* Ulm **4** Acre, Jena, Lodi **5**
Ligny **6** Toulon **7** Dresden, Marengo **8**
Borodino, Pyramids, Waterloo **10** Auster-
litz
birthplace: **7** Corsica
brother: **5** Louis **6** Jerome, Joseph, Lucien
brother-in-law: **5** Murat
exile: **4** Elba **8** St. Helena
marshal: Ney **5** Murat, Soult **6** Suchet **10**
Bernadotte
nickname: **5** Boney **14** Little Corporal
sister: **5** Elisa, Maria **7** Pauline **8** Carlotta,
Carolina
surname: **9** Bonaparte **10** Buonaparte
wife: **9** Josephine **11** Marie Louise
nappy: ale **4** dish **5** downy, heady, wooly **6** diaper, liquor, strong **7** foaming **8** textured **11**
intoxicated
napu: **7** deerlet **10** chevrotain
narcissistic: **4** vain **7** stuck-up **9** conceited **12**
vainglorious
narcotic (see also **drug**): kat **4** bang, dope,
junk, snow **5** bhang, dagga, ether, horse,
opium **6** heroin, opiate **7** alcohol, anodyne,
hashish **8** hasheesh, hypnotic, morphine,
takrouri **9** soporific **10** belladonna,
hyoscyamus, stramonium

agent: **4** narc
dose: **5** locus
package: **4** deck **6** bindle
plant: kat **4** coca, cuca, hemp, kaat, khat **5**
dutra, poppy **8** cannabis **9** marijuana
seller: **6** pusher **7** peddler
nard: **5** spice **6** anoint **7** rhizome **9** spikenard
nardoo: **5** plant **6** clover
nargileh: **4** pipe **5** hooka **6** hookah
nark: spy, vex **5** annoy **8** informer, irritate **11**
stool pigeon
narrate: **4** tell **5** state **6** detail, recite, relate,
report **7** descant, discuss, recount **8** describe,
rehearse **9** chronicle, discourse, expatiate
narrative: **4** epic, myth, saga, tale, yarn **5**
conte, drama, fable, novel, story **6** legend **7**
account, episode, history, parable **8** allegory, anecdote **9** narration
narrator: **9** raconteur
narrow: **4** fine, lean, mean, slim, thin **5** close,
scant, sound, taper **6** biased, linear, little,
meager, meagre, strait, strict **7** bigoted,
limited **8** condense, contract **9** constrict,
hide-bound, illiberal, niggardly, parochial
10 inflexible, prejudiced, restricted,
straighten **11** reactionary **12** parsimonious
13 circumscribed
narrowminded: **6** biased **7** bigoted
narsinga: **7** trumpet
narthex: **5** porch **7** portico **9** vestibule **10**
antetemple
nary: **5** never **6** not any
nasal: **6** narine, rhinal, twangy
nascency: **5** birth **6** origin **7** genesis **9** beginning
naseberry: **9** sapodilla
nasi: **9** patriarch
nasicorn: **10** rhinoceros
nasty: bad **4** foul, mean, ugly, vile **5** dirty, gross,
snide **6** filthy **7** harmful, obscene, squalid **8**
indecent **9** dangerous, malicious, offensive
10 disgusting, ill-natured, nauseating,
unpleasant **12** disagreeable, dishonorable
natal: **6** inborn, innate, native **7** gluteal **10**
congenital
natant: **6** afloat **8** floating, swimming
natator: **7** swimmer
natatorium: **4** bath, pool
natchbone: **7** hipbone **9** aitchbone
nation: **4** host, land, race **5** caste, class, realm,
state **6** people **7** country, kingdom **9** community, multitude **12** commonwealth
symbol: **4** flag **5** crest
national: **7** citizen, federal, subject **11** gentili-
tian
National Guard member: **10** militiaman
native: raw **4** home, wild **5** local, natal **6**
genial, inborn, innate, normal **7** citizen,
denizen, endemic, natural **8** domestic,

inherent, original, resident **9** aborigine, congenial, ingrained, unbranded, unrefined **10** congenital, indigenous, inhabitant

nativity: 5 birth **8** geniture **9** horoscope

natrium: 6 sodium

natty: 4 chic, neat, tidy, trig, trim **5** smart **6** dapper, spruce **10** fastidious

natural: 4 born, easy, fool, open, wild **5** usual **6** candid, common, cretin, inborn, inbred, innate, native, normal **7** general, regular **8** inherent, ordinary, physical **9** primitive, unassumed, unfeigned **10** congenital **13** unenlightened
dice: **5** seven

naturalize: 5 adopt **8** accustom **9** acclimate **11** acclimatize, domesticate, familiarize

nature: way **4** bent, cast, kind, mood, sort, type **5** shape **6** cosmos, figure **7** essence, quality **8** creation, universe **9** character, framework, structure **11** disposition, personality, temperament
divinity: **5** nymph
god: Pan
goddess: **6** Cybele **7** Artemis
same: **10** homogeneal

naught: 4 evil, zero **5** aught, ought **6** cipher, nought, wicked **7** nothing, useless **9** worthless

naughty: bad **4** evil **5** wrong **6** unruly, wicked **7** obscene, wayward, willful **8** contrary, improper, perverse **10** indelicate **11** disobedient, mischievous

naupathia: 11 seasickness

nausea: 4 pall **7** disgust **8** loathing, mal de mer, sickness **10** queasiness

nauseating: 5 nasty, waugh **7** fulsome **8** brackish **9** loathsome, offensive, sickening **10** disgusting **11** distasteful

nautical (see also **boat; navigation**): **5** naval **6** marine **7** oceanic **8** maritime
cry: **4** ahoy
flag: **6** cornet, pennon
instrument: aba **7** compass, sextant
mile: **4** knot
term: **4** atry **5** abaft, abeam, alist, avast

nautilus: 7 mollusk **9** argonauta

Navaho hut: 5 hogan

Naval Academy: 9 Annapolis

naval stores: tar **5** pitch, rosin **8** supplies **10** turpentine

nave: hob, hub, nef **4** apse, axle, body, fist **5** aisle, nieve **6** center **10** church part

navel: 6 orange **9** umbilicus **11** belly button

navigate: 4 keel, sail **5** guide, steer **6** direct, manage, travel **7** journey, operate

navigation (see also **boat; nautical**): **6** voyage **7** nautics **8** cabotage, piloting, seacraft **10** seamanship
hazard: fog, sub **4** mine, reef, rock **5** shoal, shore **7** sandbar **9** submarine

instrument: aba, log, RDF **5** loran, omega, radar **7** compass, pelorus, sextant **9** astrolabe **11** chronometer
kind: **6** NAVSAT **8** inertial, piloting **9** celestial, satellite **10** electronic **13** dead reckoning
measure: ton **4** knot, seam **6** fathom **7** renning, sea mile **12** cable's length
signal: **4** bell, flag

navigator: 5 flyer, pilot **6** airman **7** aviator, copilot, laborer **8** aeronaut, seafarer, spaceman

navite: 6 basalt

navvy: 4 hand **6** worker **7** laborer **9** navigator

navy: 5 fleet **6** armada **8** flotilla
battles: **6** Actium, Armada, Midway **7** Jutland, Lepanto, Salamis, Spanish **8** Coral Sea, Port Said **9** Falklands, Leyte Gulf, Trafalgar **12** Hampton Roads
board: **9** admiralty
depot: **4** base
force: **5** fleet **6** armada **8** squadron
jail: **4** brig
officer: **4** aide, bosh, mate **5** bosun **6** ensign **7** admiral, armorer, captain **8** armourer **9** commander, commodore **10** lieutenant
U.S. ships: **7** Monitor **8** Merrimac, Nautilus **12** Constitution **15** Bonhomme Richard
vessel: PT, sub **6** galley **7** carrier, cruiser, flattop, frigate, gun boat **9** destroyer, submarine, transport **10** battleship **11** minesweeper
wireless operator: **6** sparks

nawab: See **nabob**

nay: nai, not **4** deny, nyet (Russ.) **5** flute, never **6** denial, refuse **7** refusal **8** negative **11** prohibition

naysay: 6 denial **7** refusal

nayword: 6 signal **9** watchword

naze: 8 headland **10** promontory

Nazi (see also **Germany**): **9** Hitlerite **10** brownshirt
air force: **9** Luftwaffe
armed forces: **9** Wehrmacht
concentration camp: **6** Belsen, Dachau **9** Auschwitz, Treblinka **10** Buchenwald
leader: **4** Hess **6** Fuhrer, Hitler **7** Goering, Himmler **8** Goebbels, Heydrich
police: **7** Gestapo
symbol: **6** fylfot **8** swastika

nazim: 7 viceroy **8** governor

neal: 6 anneal, temper

neanic: 8 immature, youthful

neap: 4 tide

near: gin, kin, nar (Sc.) **4** bain, dear, hend, nigh **5** anear, anent, aside, close, equal, handy, hende, match, rival, touch **6** almost, around, beside, climax, narrow, stingy **7** advance, similar, thrifty, vicinal **8** adjacent, approach, intimate **9** niggardly, thriftily **10** contiguous, juxtaposed **11** approximate, closefisted

nearest: 4 next 5 ewest (Sc.) 7 closest 9 proximate

nearsighted: 6 myopic 12 shortsighted

neat: gim 4 cosh (Sc.), deft, dink, feil (Sc.), nice, prim, pure, snod (Sc.), snug, tidy, tosh, trig, trim 5 clean, compt, dinky, douce, natty 6 adroit, cattle, clever, dapper 7 concise, orderly, precise, refined, unmixed 8 skillful, straight, tasteful 9 dexterous, ship-shape, undiluted 10 concinnous, meticulous

neath: 5 below 7 beneath

neatherd: 7 cowherd 8 herdsman

neb: nib, tip 4 beak, bill, nose 5 snout

nebbish: 4 meek 5 timid 11 ineffectual

Nebraska: *capital:* 7 Lincoln
　　city: 5 Omaha 8 Bellevue, Hastings 11 Grand Island, North Platte
　　dune: 9 Sand Hills
　　lake: 10 McConaughy
　　river: 4 Loup 6 Platte 7 Elkhorn 8 Missouri, Niobrara 10 Republican
　　state bird: 10 meadowlark
　　state flower: 9 goldenrod
　　state tree: 10 cottonwood

---

nebris: 8 fawnskin

nebula: sky 4 Crab, Lyra 5 Orion, vapor 6 galaxy 9 Andromeda 10 atmosphere

nebulize: 7 atomize

nebulous: 4 hazy 5 foggy, misty, vague 6 cloudy 7 obscure, unclear 9 celestial 10 indefinite, indistinct

necessarily: 8 perforce 10 inevitably 12 consequently

necessary: 5 privy, vital 6 needed 7 needful 8 forcible, integral 9 essential, mandatory, requisite 10 inevitable, undeniable 11 unavoidable, water-closet

necessitate: 5 force, impel 6 compel, entail, oblige 7 require 9 constrain

necessity: 4 food, must, need, want 5 drink 7 ailment, poverty, urgency 8 distress 9 emergency, essential 11 destitution

neck: pet 4 cape, crag, crop, hals, kiss 5 halse 6 caress, cervix, collum, fondle, strait 7 channel, embrace, isthmus, make out
　　armor: 6 gorget
　　artery: 7 carotid
　　back of: 4 nape 5 nucha, nuque 6 scruff
　　muscle: 8 scalenus
　　part: 4 gula 7 withers
　　pert. to: 7 jugular 8 cervical
　　piece: bib, boa, tie 4 ruff 5 amice, ascot, jabot, nuche, rabat, scarf, stole 6 choker, collar, cravat, dickie 8 kerchief

neck and neck: tie 4 even 5 close

neckband: 6 collar, collet 10 collar-band

neckerchief: 4 gimp 5 ascot, scarf 7 belcher 8 kerchief, neckatee 12 handkerchief

necklace: 4 rope, torc 5 beads, chain, noose 6 choker, collar, grivna, locket, torque 7 baldric, chaplet, haltern, necktie, pendant, riviere 8 baldrick, carcanet, lavalier 9 esclavage, lavaliere 10 lavalliere

necktie: bow, tie 4 band 5 ascot, scarf, stock 6 cravat 10 four-in-hand

necktie party: 7 hanging 8 lynching

necrology: 8 obituary

necromancy: art 5 goety, magic 7 sorcery 8 gramarye, grammary, wizardry 10 divination 11 conjuration, enchantment

necropolis: 8 cemetery

necropsy: 7 autopsy

nectar: 5 honey 8 ambrosia

nee: 4 born 5 named 8 formerly

need: 4 lack, must, want 5 crave 6 behove, demand, desire, hanker, hunger 7 behoove, poverty, require, urgency 8 distress, exigency 9 emergency, extremity, indigence, necessity, requisite 10 compulsion, dependence, obligation, retirement 11 destitution, requirement

needful: 5 vital 8 integral, required 9 essential 13 indispensable

needle: sew 4 acus (L.), darn 5 annoy, worry 7 acicula, provoke, spicule 10 strengthen
　　hole: eye
　　treatment with: 11 acupuncture
　　type: 4 sail 5 blunt, style 6 bodkin, stylus 7 darning, obelisk 8 knitting, surgical 10 hypodermic, phonograph, upholstery 11 crochet hook

needlefish: gar 8 pipefish

needlelike: 6 acuate 7 acerate, acerose, acerous, aciform 8 acicular, belonoid

needless: 7 useless 10 gratuitous 11 superfluous, unnecessary

needlework: 4 lace 6 Assisi, sewing 7 sampler, seaming, tatting 8 knitting, quilting 9 Hardanger, hemstitch 10 canvaswork, crocheting, embroidery 11 cross-stitch, needlepoint

needy: 4 poor 8 indigent 9 destitute, penniless

neep: 6 turnip

ne'er-do-well: bum 5 losel, loser 9 no account, schlemiel, shiftless, worthless

nef: 5 clock

nefarious: 4 evil, rank 5 gross 6 wicked 7 heinous, impious, vicious 8 flagrant, horrible, infamous 9 atrocious 10 detestable, iniquitous, villainous

nefast: 6 wicked

negate: 4 deny, veto, void 5 annul 6 refute 7 abolish, nullify 10 neutralize

negation: not 5 empty 6 denial 7 refusal 9 annulment, blankness, nonentity 10 refutation**negative:** nae (Sc.), nay, non (F.), nor, not 4 film, veto 5 minus, never 7 neutral

neglect: 4 fail, omit, slip 5 fault, forgo, shirk 6 forego, forget, ignore, slight 7 blink at, default, failure 8 omission 9 disregard, oversight, pay no heed, pretermit 10 negligence 11 inattention 12 inadvertence, indifference

neglectful: lax 6 remiss 8 careless, derelict, heedless 9 dissolute, negligent

negligee: 4 robe 7 undress 8 peignoir 9 nightgown 10 dishabille

negligence: 7 laxness 9 disregard, oversight

negligent: lax 5 slack 6 remiss 8 careless, heedless, slipshod 10 delinquent 11 indifferent, thoughtless, unconcerned

negotiate: 4 deal 5 treat 6 dicker, settle 7 arrange, bargain, chaffer, discuss 8 transact 10 accomplish

negotiation: 6 treaty 8 entreaty

negus: 4 king 5 drink 8 beverage

neigh: 6 whinny

neighbor: 4 abut, line 5 touch, verge 6 adjoin, border 8 border on

neighborhood: 4 area 5 venue 6 locale, region 7 section 8 district, locality, vicinage, vicinity 9 community, proximity, territory 11 propinquity

neighboring: 4 nigh 5 close 6 near-by 7 vicinal 8 adjacent 10 contiguous

neither: not

nema: 7 eelworm 9 roundworm

nemesis: 4 bane, fate 5 enemy 7 avenger

nemoral: 6 sylvan, wooded

neophyte: 4 tyro 5 epopt 6 novice 7 amateur, convert 8 beginner 9 proselyte 10 catechumen

neoteric: new 4 late 6 modern, recent

Nepal: *capital:* 8 Katmandu 9 Kathmandu
city: 5 Palan 8 Bhatgaon 9 Bhaktapur
dynasty: Dev 6 Rajput
king: 8 Birendra
mountain: 7 Everest 8 Himalaya
mountain climber: 6 Sherpa 7 Hillary, Tenzing
mythical creature: 4 yeti
ox: yak
river: 4 Kusi 5 Bheri, Tamur 6 Gandak 7 Karnali
sheep: 6 bharal, nahoor, nayaur
tree: sal 4 toon 5 sisoo

---

nepenthe: 4 drug 6 opiate 7 anodyne 8 narcotic

nephew: 6 nepote (Sc.)

nephrite: 4 jade 6 pounam 10 greenstone

ne plus ultra: 4 acme 6 summit 9 nth degree

nepotism: 9 patronage 10 favoritism

Neptune: sea 5 ocean 6 planet, seagod 8 Poseidon
consort: 7 Salacia
emblem: 7 trident
father: 6 Cronus, Saturn
mother: Ops 4 Rhea
satellite: 6 Nereid, Triton
son: 6 Triton
wife: 10 Amphitrite

Ner's son: 5 Abner

Nereids: 6 Thetis 7 Galatea 8 Psamathe
father: 6 Nereus
mother: 5 Doris
steed: 8 seahorse

Nero: 6 tyrant 7 emperor, fiddler
mother: 9 Agrippina
stepfather: 8 Claudius
successor: 5 Galba
victim: 5 Lucan 6 Seneca
wife: 7 Octavia, Poppaea

Nero Wolfe creator: 5 Stout

nerve: 4 grit, guts 5 cheek, pluck, sinew, spunk, vigor 6 aplomb, daring, energy, tendon 7 courage 8 audacity, boldness, coolness, embolden, strength, temerity 9 encourage, fortitude 10 brazenness, effrontery, invigorate, resolution
apparatus: 6 sensor
cell: 6 neuron
center: 5 brain 8 ganglion
cranial: 5 optic, vagus
inflammation: 8 neuritis
malady: tic 8 neuritis
network: 4 rete 6 plexus
operation: 10 neurolysis
pathway: 4 rete 5 hilum 8 ganglion
pert. to: 5 neuro 6 neural
root: 5 radix
sensory: 8 afferent
tissue: 7 cinerea
tumor: 7 neuroma 9 neurinoma 11 neurocytoma 12 neuromatosis

nerveless: 4 dead, weak 5 brave, inert 8 unnerved 9 foolhardy, powerless 10 courageous

nervous: 4 edgy 5 jumpy, timid 6 on edge, sinewy, tenser, touchy 7 anxious, fearful, fidgety, fretful, jittery, restive, waspish 8 skittish, spirited, timorous 9 excitable, flustered, irritable, querulous, sensitive 10 highstrung 11 overwrought 12 apprehensive

nervous system: *center:* 5 brain
description of: 11 neurography
nomenclature: 9 neuronymy
science: 9 neurology

nervy: 4 bold 5 jerky, pushy, tense 6 brazen, sinewy, strong 7 jittery, nervous 8 impudent, vigorous 9 excitable

nescient: 7 infidel 8 agnostic, ignorant

ness: 4 cape 8 headland 10 promontory

nest: den, nid, web 4 aery, bike, dray, drey,

Netherlands: **7** Holland **10** Low Country
artist: Lis **4** Hals, Kalf, Neer **5** Bosch, Helst, Steen **6** Leyden **7** De Hoogh, Hobbema, Seghers, Van Gogh, Vermeer **8** Guysdael, Kroninck, Mondrian, Mostaert, Ter Borch **9** Rembrandt **10** Van de Velde **11** Van Ruisdael
capital: **9** Amsterdam
cheese: **4** Edam **5** Gouda **6** Leyden
city: Ede **5** Asten, Breda, Hague **6** Aalten, Arnhem, Leiden **7** Commune, Haarlem, Utrecht **8** Aalsmeer, The Hague **9** Groningen, Rotterdam **10** Gravenhage
fishing boat: **4** tode **6** hooker
gin: **7** genever **8** schnapps
inlet (former): **9** Zuider Zee
island: **5** Texel **7** Ameland **8** Vlieland **9** Schelling
island group: Aru **5** Arroe **12** Arrou Frisian
lake: **7** Haarlem **10** Ijsselmeer
measure: aam, ahm, aum, ell, kan, kop(pl.), mud, vat, zak **4** duim, jijl, lood, rood, rope, voet **5** anker, carat, roede, stoop, wisse **6** bunder, koppen, legger, maatje, muddle, mutsje, streep **7** leaguer, schepel **8** mimgelen, okshoofd, steekkan **10** vingerhoed
possession: **4** Saba **7** Bonaire, Curacao **8** Antilles **11** Dutch Guiana, Sint Maartin, St. Eustacius
pottery: **4** Delf **5** Delft
queen: **7** Beatrix, Juliana **10** Wilhelmina
reclaimed land: **6** polder
river: Eem **4** Leck, Maas, Rijn, Waal, Ysel **5** Meuse, Rhine, Yssel **6** Ijssel, Kromme **7** Scheldt
scholar: **7** Erasmus
seat of government: **7** den Haag **8** The Hague
sheriff: **6** schout
symbol: **5** tulip **8** windmill **10** wooden shoe
town hall: **9** stadhouse
uncle: eme, oom
vessel: **4** koff **5** yanky **6** schuit, schuyt
weight: ons **4** last, lood, pond **5** bahar, grein, pound **6** korrel **7** wichtje **8** esterlin **9** esterling
woman: **4** frau, frow
wooden shoe: **5** klomp

eyry, home, nidi (pl.) **5** abode, aerie, eyrie, haunt, nidus, swarm **6** cuddle, hotbed **7** lodging, retreat **9** residence **10** nidificate
builder of: ant, bee **4** bird, wasp
eagle's: **4** aery **5** aerie
insect's: **5** nidus
squirrel's: **4** drey
nest egg: **5** hoard, stock **7** reserve, savings **9** reservoir
nester: **7** settler **8** squatter **11** homesteader
nestle: pet **4** nest **6** cuddle, pettle (Sc.) **7** cherish, shelter, snuggle
nestling: **4** baby, bird, eyas **9** fledgling
nestor: **4** sage **6** parrot **7** adviser, advisor **9** counselor **10** counsellor
net: bag, gin, web **4** caul, flan, gain, lace, lawn, mesh, moke, neat, pure, rete, toil, trap, trim, weir **5** clean, clear, gauze, lacis, seize, snare, tulle, yield **6** bright, cobweb, entrap, maline, profit **7** dragnet, ensnare, network, protect, rinsing, shelter **8** meshwork **9** reticulum **10** reticulate **13** unadulterated
fishing: lam **4** flew, flue, fyke **5** seine, trawl **6** sagene **7** trammel
hair: **5** snood
interstice: **4** hole, mesh
nether: **5** lower, under **8** downward, inferior
Netherlands: (see box)
Netherlands Antilles (see also **Curacao**):
capital: **10** Willemstad
former part: **5** Aruba
islands: **4** Saba **7** Bonaire, Curacao **11** Sint Maarten **13** Sint Eustatius
netlike: **9** reticular
netop: **5** crony **6** friend **9** companion
netting: **4** lace, lint, mesh **7** network
nettle: vex **4** fret, line, rile **5** annoy, cnida, peeve, pique, sting **6** arouse, bother, henbit, ruffle, splice, stir up **7** affront, blubber, provoke **8** irritant, irritate **9** Urticacea **10** exasperate

Nevada: *capital* **10** Carson City
city: **4** Elko, Reno **8** Las Vegas
desert: **8** Amargosa
lake: Mud **4** Mead **5** Tahoe **6** Mohave, Walker **7** Pyramid
mountain range: **4** Ruby **5** Butte **6** Carson **7** Toiyabe **12** Sierra Nevada
plateau: **10** Great Basin
river: **6** Carson, Owyhee **7** Truckee **8** Colorado, Humboldt
state bird: **8** bluebird
state flower: **9** sagebrush
state tree: **5** pinon

nettle cell: **10** nematocyst
  family: **10** Urticaceae
  genus of: **10** parietaria
network: (see also **net**): ABC, CBS, CNN, FOX, NBC, PBS, TBS, TNT, USA **4** mesh, rete **5** retia **6** plexus, reseau
neural: **6** dorsal
neurite: **4** axon **5** axone
neurotic: **6** phobic **7** nervous **8** unstable **10** compulsive
neuter: **6** gender **7** neither, neutral, sexless **9** impartial, sterilize
neutral: **4** gray **8** middling, negative, unbiased **9** colorless, impartial **10** achromatic, indefinite, poker-faced **11** adiaphorous, indifferent, nonpartisan **12** noncombatant
neutralize: **5** annul **7** abolish, balance, destroy, nullify, vitiate **9** cancel out, frustrate **10** counteract **11** countervail
neutralizer: **6** alkali
Nevada: (see box)
neve: **4** firn, snow **7** glacier
never: nay, nie (G.), not **4** nary, ne'er **7** not ever
nevertheless: but, yet **5** still **6** even so **7** how-be-it, however **9** howsoever, natheless **10** howsomever
nevus: **4** mole **5** tumor **7** spiloma **9** birthmark
new: neu (G.) **4** late, nova (L.) **5** fresh, green, novel **6** latest, modern, recent, unused **7** foreign, strange, untried **8** neoteric, original, untested **9** first-hand **10** additional, promethean, unfamiliar **11** fashionable, modernistic **12** unaccustomed **13** inexperienced
New Brunswick: *bay:* **5** Fundy
  capital: **11** Fredericton
  city: **6** St. John **7** Moncton
  former name: **6** Acadia
  island: **10** Campobello
  province of: **6** Canada
  provincial flower: **6** violet
  river: **6** St. John **7** St. Croix **9** Miramicki
New Caledonia: *bird:* **4** kagu
  capital: **6** Noumea
  city: We **4** Kone
  sea: **5** Coral
newcomer: **6** novice **7** settler **8** beginner, comeling, neophyte **9** immigrant
New Deal agency: CCC, FHA, NRA, TVA, WPA **4** FDIC, NLRB
newel: **4** post **6** pillar **7** upright
New England (see also individual states):
  aristocrat: **7** Brahmin
  chair: **6** Carver **7** Windsor
  inhabitant: **6** Yankee
  of the West: **9** Minnesota
  settler: **7** Pilgrim, Puritan
  states: **5** Maine **7** Vermont **11** Connecticut,

Rhode Island **12** New Hampshire **13** Massachusetts
newfangled: **5** novel **6** latest, modern
Newfoundland: *airport:* **6** Gander
  bay: **4** Hare **5** White **9** Bonavista, Placentia
  cape: Ray **4** Race **5** Bauld
  capital: **7** St. John's
  city: **6** Gander **9** Grand Bank **10** Mount Pearl **11** Corner Brook **12** Stephenville
  island: **4** Bell, Fogo
  mainland part: **8** Labrador
  river: **6** Gander, Humber **8** Exploits
  strait: **5** Cabot **9** Belle Isle
New Guinea (see also **Indonesia**): *bay:* Oro
  capital: **11** Port Moresby
  city: Lae **4** Daru **5** Soron **6** Rabaul
  gulf: **4** Huon **5** Papua
  hog: **4** bene
  island: Aru **4** Buka **5** Ceram, Papua **6** Mussau
  island group: **7** Solomon
  parrot: **4** lory
  river: Fly **5** Sepik **7** Amberno **10** Strickland **15** Kaiserin Augusta

---

New Hampshire: *capital:* **7** Concord
  city: **5** Dover, Keene **6** Nashua **9** Rochester **10** Manchester, Portsmouth
  explorer: **5** Pring
  island: **4** Star **5** White **6** Seavey **7** Lunging **13** Isles of Shoals
  lake: **5** Squam **7** Ossipee, Sunapee **13** Winnipesaukee
  mountain: **5** White **7** Profile **9** Monadnock **10** Washington
  river: **4** Saco **9** Merrimack **10** Piscataqua **11** Connecticut, Salmon Falls
  state bird: finch
  state flower: **5** lilac
  state tree: **5** birch

New Jersey: (see box)
newly: **4** anew **5** again **6** afresh, lately **8** recently
New Mexico (see box)
New Orleans: *football team:* **6** Saints
  lake: **13** Pontchartrain
  street: **5** Canal, Royal **7** Bourbon
news: **4** word **6** notice **7** tidings **11** information, instruction **12** intelligence
  agency: AP, DNB, PAP (Pol.), UPI **4** Tass (Russ.) **5** Domei **6** Xinhua (Ch.) **7** Reuters **13** International

New Mexico: *capital:* **7** Santa Fe
   cavern: **8** Carlsbad
   city: **5** Hobbs **6** Clovis, Deming,
   Gallup **7** Artesia, Boswell, Roswell,
   Socorro **8** Carlsbad, Portales **9** Las
   Cruces, Los Alamos **10** Alamogordo,
   Farmington **11** Albuquerque
   explorer: **8** Coronado
   highest peak: **7** Wheeler
   lake: **10** Bottomless
   mountain range: **5** Jemez, Organ **6**
   Chuska **7** Caballo, Rockies **8** Mogollon,
   San Mateo **9** Guadalupe, San Andres
   10 Nacimiento
   resort: **4** Taos
   river: **4** Gila **5** Pecos **7** San Juan **8**
   Canadian **9** Rio Grande
   state bird: **10** roadrunner
   state flower: **5** yucca
   state tree: **5** pinon

New Jersey: *bay:* **6** Newark **7** Raritan **8**
   Barnegat, Delaware, Great Egg **9**
   Sandy Hook
   cape: May
   capital: **7** Trenton
   city: **6** Camden, Newark **7** Clifton **8**
   Paterson **9** Elizabeth **10** Jersey City **12**
   Atlantic City
   cliffs: **9** Palisades
   early explorer: **6** Hudson **9** Verrazano
   highest peak: **9** High Point
   inventor: **5** Morse **6** Edison
   lake: **9** Hopatcong
   lighthouse: **8** Barnegat
   mountain: **6** Ramapo **10** Kittatinny
   peninsula: **9** Sandy Hook
   resort: **7** Cape May **9** Ocean City **10**
   Asbury Park **12** Atlantic City
   river: **6** Hudson, Ramapo **7** Maurice,
   Mullica, Passaic, Raritan **8** Delaware,
   Tuckahoe
   state bird: **9** goldfinch
   state flower: **6** violet
   state tree: oak
   university: **7** Rutgers **9** Princeton,
   Seton Hall

gatherer: **8** reporter **13** correspondent
media: **5** radio **7** journal **8** magazine **9**

newspaper **10** periodical, television
   statement: **8** bulletin
newsboy: **7** carrier
newsmonger: **6** gossip **7** tattler **8** reporter
newspaper: **5** daily, organ **7** gazette, journal,
   tabloid **10** periodical **11** publication
   article: **4** item
   collectively: **5** press
   employee: **6** editor **7** printer **8** engraver,
   pressman, reporter **9** columnist, linotyper,

New York (see also **New York City**):
   academy: **4** USMA **9** West Point **10**
   Kings Point
   canal: **4** Erie
   capital: **6** Albany
   cavern: **4** Howe
   city: Rye **4** Erie, Rome, Troy **5** Utica **6**
   Elmira, Ithaca, Malone **7** Buffalo,
   Yonkers **8** Saratoga, Syracuse **9**
   Rochester **10** Binghamton
   explorer: **6** Hudson **9** Champlain, Verrazano
   island: **4** Fire, Long **6** Staten **7** Fishers,
   Shelter **9** Manhattan
   island group: **8** Thousand
   lake: **4** Erie **5** Keuka **6** Cayuga, Croton,
   Geneva, George, Oneida, Otsego,
   Placid, Seneca **7** Ontario, Saranac **8**
   Onondago **9** Champlain **11**
   Canandaigua, Skaneateles
   lake group: **6** Finger
   mountain: **5** Marcy **7** Poconos **9**
   Catskills **11** Adirondacks
   racetrack: **7** Belmont, Yonkers **8** Aqueduct, Saratoga
   river: **5** Tioga **6** Harlem, Hudson,
   Mohawk **7** Genesee, Niagara **8**
   Delaware **10** St. Lawrence
   state bird: **8** bluebird
   state flower: **4** rose
   state tree: **5** maple

publisher **10** cartoonist, compositor, journalist, plate maker **12** photographer **13**
correspondent
file: **6** morgue
hoax: **6** canard
part of: ads, ear **4** arts **6** banner, comics,
sports **7** feature **8** dateline, magazine, masthead, obituary **9** editorial, financial **11**
rotogravure
writer's name: **6** by-line
newsstand: **5** booth, kiosk, stall

newt: ask, eft **4** evet **6** lizard, triton **7** axolotl **10** salamander

New Testament (see also **Bible**): *book:* **4** Acts, John, Jude, Luke, Mark **5** James, Peter, Titus **6** Romans **7** Hebrews, Matthew, Timothy **8** Philemon **9** Ephesians, Galatians **10** Colossians, Revelation **11** Corinthians, Philippians **13** Thessalonians *gospel:* **4** John, Luke, Mark **7** Matthew *letter:* **7** epistle

New York (see box)

New York City (see also **New York**): *airport:* JFK **6** Newark **7** Kennedy **9** LaGuardia *area:* **4** Soho **6** Bowery, Harlem **7** Kips Bay, Tribeca **8** Broadway, East Side, Flatbush, West Side **9** Chinatown, Turtle Bay **10** Wall Street **11** Coney Island, East Village, Fifth Avenue, Little Italy, Off-Broadway, Sutton Place, Times Square *baseball team:* **4** Mets **7** Yankees *basketball team:* **6** Knicks **14** Knickerbockers *borough:* **5** Bronx **6** Queens **8** Brooklyn **9** Manhattan **12** Staten Island *football team:* **4** Jets **6** Giants *island:* **5** Ellis, Ward's **6** Rikers, Staten **7** Bedloes, Liberty, Welfare **8** Randalls **9** Governors, Manhattan, Roosevelt **10** Blackwells *museum:* **4** MOMA **5** Frick **7** Whitney **9** Cloisters **10** Guggenheim **12** Cooper Hewitt, Metropolitan *prison:* **5** Tombs *river:* **4** East **6** Harlem, Hudson

---

New Zealand: **7** Oceania **9** Polynesia *anteater:* **7** echidna *artist:* **8** Hodgkins *author:* **5** Frame, Hulme, Marsh **9** Mansfield **12** Ashton-Warner *bay:* **5** Hawke **6** Awarua, Plenty **7** Islands **8** Rangaunu, Ta Waewae *bird:* kea, moa, oii, poe, roa **4** kaka, kiwi, koko, kulu, ruru, titi, weka **6** kakapo **7** apteryx, wrybill **8** morepork, notornis *capital:* **10** Wellington *city:* **5** Levin, Otaki, Taupo **6** Foxton, Napier, Nelson, Oamaru, Picton, Timaru **7** Dunedin, Raetihi, Rotorua **8** Auckland, Gisborne, Hamilton, Hastings, Tauranga, Wanganui **9** Ashburton, Greymouth, Masterton, Whangarei **10** Dannenirke, Palmerston, Queenstown **11** Invercargil **12** Christchurch *clay:* **4** papa *currency:* **4** cent **6** dollar *dance:* **4** haka *dependency:* **4** Niue **7** Tokelau **11** Cook Islands *fern:* **4** weki **5** pitau, wheki *fish:* ihi **5** hikus *flax:* **8** harakeke *flightless bird:* **4** weka **7** apteryx *fort:* pa, pah, pau *fruit:* **4** kiwi *grass:* **6** toetoe *gun:* **6** tupara *heron:* **6** kotuku *hut:* **5** whare *island:* **5** North, South **7** Chatham, Stewart *island group:* **6** Bounty **7** Chatham **8** Auckland, Campbell, Kermadec **9** Antipodes *kiwi:* moa, roa **7** apteryx

lake: Ada **4** Gunn, Ohau, Rere **5** Hawea, Okara, Taupo **6** Fergus, Pukaki, Rotoma, Sylvan, Teanau, Tekapo, Wanaka **7** Brunner, Diamond, Kanieri, Okareka, Rotoiti, Rotoroa, Rotorua **8** Okataina, Paradise, Rotoaira, Tarawera, Wakatipu *mahogany:* **6** totara *mountain:* **4** Cook **5** Ohope **6** Egmont **7** Aorangi, Pihanga, Raupehu, Tauhara **8** Aspiring, Tarawera, Tauranga *national bird:* **4** kiwi *ostrich, extinct:* moa *owl:* **4** ruru *palm:* **5** nikau *parrot:* kea **4** kaka **6** kakapo *pine:* **4** rima **6** totara **9** kahikatea *plain:* **10** Canterbury *reptile:* **7** tuatara *river:* **7** Waikato **8** Wanganui *settlement:* pah, pau *shark:* **4** mako *shrub:* **4** tutu *song:* **6** waiata *spa:* **5** Aroha **7** Rotorua, Tearoha *storehouse:* **5** whata *strait:* **4** Cook **7** Foveaux *sweet potato:* **6** kumara *tree:* ake **4** hino, kopi, mako, miro, pelu, puka, rata, rimu, tawa, toro, toru, whau **5** hinau, hinou, karui, mahoe, maire, mapau, ngaio **6** ake-ake, karaka, kowhai, manuka, puriri, tarata, titoki **7** akepiro, taratah, wahahen **8** hiropito, makomako *vine:* aka *volcano:* **6** Egmont **7** Ruapehu **9** Ngauruhoe *wages:* utu *welcome:* **8** haeremai *white man:* **6** pakeha

square: **5** Times, Union **6** Herald **10** Washington
subway: BMT, IND, IRT
tunnel: **7** Holland, Lincoln **13** Queens Midtown **15** Brooklyn-Battery
New Zealand: (see box)
next: **4** then **5** after, ewest (Sc.), neist (Sc.) **6** coming **7** closest, ensuing, nearest **9** adjoining, following, immediate, proximate **10** contiguous, succeeding **12** conterminous
next to: **6** almost, beside, nearly **8** adjacent
nexus: tie **4** bond, link **10** connection
nib: pen **4** beak, bill **5** point, prong **8** pen point
nibble: eat, nab **4** bite, chew, gnaw, knap, peck, pick **5** graze **6** browse **7** chimble, gnabble, gnatter
Nicaragua: *capital:* **7** Managua
city: **4** Leon **6** Esteli, Masaya **7** Granada **8** Jinotepe **9** Matagalpa **10** Chinandega
coast: **8** Mosquito
lake: **7** Managua **9** Nicaragua
measure: **4** vara **5** cahiz, milla **6** suerte, tercia **7** cajuela, estadal, manzana
mountain: **6** Darien, Madera **8** Isabella **9** Momotombo **10** cordillera
revolutionary group: **7** contras **11** Sandinistas
river: **4** Coco **5** Wanks **7** San Juan **9** Tipitapa
volcano: **10** Concepcion
weight: bag **4** caja **8** tonelada
nice: **4** fine, good **5** exact, picky **6** bonita, dainty, minute, peachy, queasy, subtle **7** correct, elegant, finical, genteel, precise, prudish, refined **8** decorous, delicate, exacting, pleasant, pleasing **9** agreeable, appealing, exquisite, squeamish **10** appetizing, delightful, discerning, fastidious, oldmaidish, particular, puntilious, scrupulous **11** considerate, scrumptious
niche: **4** apse, nook **6** alcove, covert, cranny, recess **7** edicule, retreat **9** habitacle
nick: cut, nob **4** chip, slit **5** cheat, notch, tally, trick **6** arrest, record **7** defraud **9** indenture
nickle compound: **4** zinc **6** copper
nickelodeon: **5** movie **7** jukebox
nickname (see also **pen name; pseudonym**): tag **6** agname, byword **7** misname, moniker **8** cognomen, monicker **9** sobriquet **10** soubriquet
Thomas Hart Benton: **10** Old Bullion
James Boswell: **5** Bozzy
Winston Churchill: **6** Winnie
Henry Clay: **16** Great Pacificator
Bill Clinton: **10** Slick Willy
Georges Clemenceau: **5** Tiger
Joe DiMaggio: **9** Joltin Joe
Benjamin Disraeli: **5** Dizzy
Thomas Edison: **17** Wizard of Menlo Park
Dwight Eisenhower: Ike
Elizabeth I: **11** Virgin Queen
Frederick I: **10** Barbarossa
Ernest Hemingway: **4** Papa
Andrew Jackson: **10** Old Hickory
Thomas Jackson: **9** Stonewall
Abraham Lincoln: **9** Honest Abe
Louis XIV: **7** Sun King
Joe Louis: **11** Brown Bomber
Francis Marion: **8** Swamp Fox
Mary I: **10** Bloody Mary
Napoleon I: **5** Boney **14** Little Corporal
Napoleon II: **7** L'Aiglon
Richard Nixon: **10** Tricky Dick
Henry Percy: **7** Hotspur
William Pitt: **13** Great Commoner
Ronald Reagan: **15** Teflon President
Richard I: **11** Lion-Hearted
Richard III: **10** Crouchback
Babe Ruth: **7** Bambino **12** Sultan of Swat
Winfield Scott: **15** Fuss and Feathers
Joseph Stilwell: **10** Vinegar Joe
Charles Stratton: **8** Tom Thumb
Thomas Sumter: **8** Gamecock (of the Revolution)
Anthony Wayne: **10** Mad Anthony
John Wayne: **4** Duke
nicknaming: **12** prosonomasia
nictate: **4** wink **5** blink **7** twinkle
nide: **5** brood
nidge: **5** shake **6** quiver
nidget: **4** fool **5** idiot
nidification: **7** nesting
nidor: **4** reek **5** aroma, savor, scent, smell
nidus: **4** nest
nifty: **4** good **5** smart **7** stylish
Niger: *capital:* **6** Niamey
city: **6** Agadez, Maradi, Tahoua, Zinder
desert: **6** Sahara
lake: **4** Chad
mountain: Air **7** Greboun
river: **5** Niger, Tarka **6** Dillia
Nigeria: (see box)
niggard: **5** miser **8** scrimper **9** skinflint **10** curmudgeon

Nigeria: *ancient civilization:* Nok
bight: **5** Benin **6** Biafra
capital: **5** Abuja
capital, former: **5** Lagos
city: **4** Kano **6** Ibadan **9** Ogbomosho
gulf: **6** Guinea
lake: **4** Chad **6** Kainji
mountain: **7** Dimlang, Shebshi
river: Oli **5** Benue, Niger **6** Kaduna, Sokoto **7** Gongola
tree: **5** afara

niggardly: 4 mean 5 cheap, close 6 narrow, scanty, stingy 7 miserly 8 churlish, wretched 10 avaricious 11 closefisted 12 parsimonious

niggle: 6 potter, putter, trifle

nigh: 4 near 5 about, close 6 almost, nearly 8 adjacent, approach 10 contiguous 11 neighboring

night: 4 nuit (F.) 5 nacht (G.), noche (Sp.), notte (It.) 7 evening 8 darkness
goddess of: Nox, Nyx 6 Hecate
pert. to: 9 nocturnal

night bird: 10 shearwater 11 nightingale

night blindness: 10 nyctalopia

nightcap: 6 biggin

nightchurr: 10 goatsucker

nightclub: bar 4 cafe 5 boite 7 cabaret

nightfall: eve 4 dusk, even 6 sunset 7 evening 8 twilight

nightingale: 6 thrush 8 philomel 9 philomela

nightjar: 5 potoo 9 nighthawk 10 goatsucker, nightchurr

nightmare: 5 dream, fancy, fiend 7 incubus 9 cauchemar (F.), ephialtes 12 apprehension

nightshade: 5 morel 6 potato, tomato 7 henbane, morelle, petunia 8 capsicum, eggplant 10 belladonna, jimson weed 11 bittersweet

nightstick: bat 4 club 5 baton, billy 6 cudgel 8 bludgeon

night-wandering: 11 noctivagant

nihil: 7 nothing

nihilist: 9 anarchist, Nietzsche

nil: 4 zero 7 nothing

Nile: 4 Blue 5 White 6 Al-Bahr
bird: 4 ibis 7 wryneck
boat: 5 baris 6 nuggar 8 dahabeah
captain: 4 rais, reis
dam: 6 Makwar 9 Aswan High 10 Gebel Aulia
falls: 5 Ripon 9 Murchison
fish: 5 saide 8 mormyrid 9 mormyroid
historic ruins: 4 Giza 5 Luxor 6 Karnak 7 Memphis
houseboat: 8 dahabeah
island: 4 Roda
people: 4 Madi 5 Nilot
plant: 4 sudd 5 lotus
reptile: 9 crocodile
source: 6 Atbara 12 Lake Victoria
town: 5 Cairo, Rejaf 7 Rosetta 8 Khartoum
tributary: 6 Atbara, Kagera

nilgai: 8 antelope, blue bull

nimb: 4 halo 6 nimbus 7 aureole

nimble: 4 deft, lish, spry 5 agile, alert, fleet, quick 6 active, adroit, clever, feirie, lissom, lively, prompt, supple, volant 9 dexterous, wide-awake 11 quick-witted

nimbose: 6 cloudy, stormy

nimbus: 4 halo, nimb 5 cloud, vapor 6 gloria 7 aureole 10 atmosphere

nimiety: 4 glut 6 excess 10 redundancy

nimmer: 5 thief

nimrod: 5 ruler 6 hunter, tyrant

nincompoop: 4 dolt, fool 5 dunce, idiot, moron, ninny 9 simpleton

nine: 6 ennead 8 ninefold
based on: 8 novenary
days' devotion: 6 novena
group of: 5 nonet 6 ennead
inches: 4 span

nine-eyes: 7 lamprey

nine-headed monster: 5 Hydra

nine-killer: 6 shrike

ninepins: 6 kayles 7 bowling, skittle 8 skittles

ninth: 5 nonus (L.)

Niobe: *brother:* 6 Pelops
father: 8 Tantalus
husband: 7 Amphion
mother: 5 Dione
sister-in-law: 5 Aedon

nip: cut, sip 4 bite, clip, dram, tang 5 blast, check, clamp, draft, drink, frost, hurry, pinch, seize, sever, steal, sting 6 blight, catnip, snatch, tipple, twitch 7 squeeze 8 compress 10 pickpocket

nipa: 4 atap, palm 5 attap, drink 6 liquor

nipcheese: 5 miser 6 purser

nipper: boy, lad 4 claw, grab 5 biter, child 6 cunner, pliers, urchin 7 forceps, incisor, pincers 8 pincenez 9 handcuffs 10 eyeglasses

Nippon: See **Japan**

nippy: 4 cold 5 brisk, quick, sharp 6 active, biting, chilly, nimble, snappy 7 caustic, pungent 8 vigorous

nisse: 6 goblin, kobold, sprite 7 brownie

nisus: 6 effort 7 impulse 8 endeavor, striving 11 inclination

Nisus' daughter: 6 Scylla

nit: egg, nut 5 speck 6 insect 8 hazelnut

niter, nitre: 5 peter, petre 6 potash 9 saltpeter

nither: 5 blast 6 debase, shiver 7 tremble 9 humiliate

nitid: 6 bright, glossy 7 glowing, radiant 8 lustrous, nitidous

nitpick: 4 carp 6 niggle

nitrate: 4 salt 5 ester
sodium: 5 niter, nitre

nitrocotton: 9 guncotton

nitrogen: 5 azote 9 quinoline
compound: 7 ammonia

niveau: 5 level 7 plateau

nivellate: 5 equal, level

nivenite: 7 uranite

niveous: 7 snowy 8 snowlike

nix: 6 goblin, nobody, sprite 7 nothing, refusal 8 negation

Njorth: *daughter:* 5 Freya 6 Freyja
son: 4 Frey 5 Freyr
wife: 6 Skathi

Nobel Prizes: *Chemistry:* 1901 8 Van't Hoff; 1902 7 Fischer; 1903 9 Arrhenius; 1904 6 Ramsay; 1905 9 von Baeyer; 1906 7 Moissan; 1907 Buchner; 1908 10 Rutherford; 1909 7 Ostwald; 1910 7 Wallach; 1911 5 Curie; 1912 8 Grignard, Sabatier; 1913 6 Werner; 1914 8 Richards; 1915 11 Willstatter; 1918 5 Haber; 1920 6 Nernst; 1921 5 Soddy; 1922 5 Aston; 1923 5 Pregl; 1925 9 Zsigmondy; 1926 8 Svedberg; 1927 7 Wieland; 1928 7 Windaus; 1929 6 Harden 15 von Euler-Chelpin; 1930 7 Fischer; 1931 5 Bosch 7 Bergius; 1932 8 Langmuir; 1934 4 Urey; 1935 11 Joliot-Curie (Frederic; Irene); 1936 5 Debye; 1937 6 Karrer 7 Haworth; 1938 4 Kuhn; 1939 7 Ruzicka 9 Butenandt; 1943 9 von Hevesy; 1944 4 Hahn; 1945 8 Virtanen; 1946 6 Sumner 7 Stanley 8 Northrop; 1947 8 Robinson; 1948 8 Tiselius; 1949 7 Giauque; 1950 5 Alder, Diels; 1951 7 Seaborg 8 McMillan; 1952 5 Synge 6 Martin; 1953 10 Staudinger; 1954 7 Pauling; 1955 10 Du Vigneaud; 1956 7 Semenov 11 Hinshelwood; 1957 4 Todd; 1958 6 Sanger; 1959 9 Heyrovsky; 1960 5 Libby; 1961 6 Calvin; 1962 6 Perutz 7 Kendrew; 1963 5 Natta 7 Ziegler; 1964 7 Hodgkin; 1965 8 Woodward; 1966 8 Muliken; 1967 5 Eigen 6 Porter 7 Norrish; 1968 7 Onsager; 1969 6 Barton, Hasel 1970 6 Leloir; 1971 8 Herzberg; 1972 5 Moore, Stein 8 Anfinsen; 1973 7 Fischer; 9 Wilkinson; **1974** 5 Flory; 1975 6 Prelog 9 Cornforth; 1976 8 Lipscomb; 1977 9 Prigogine; 1978 8 Mitchell; 1979 5 Brown 6 Wittig; 1980 4 Berg 6 Sanger; 7 Gilbert; 1981 5 Fukui 8 Hoffmann; 1982 4 Klug; 1983 5 Taube; 1984 10 Merrifield; 1985 5 Karle 8 Hauptman; 1986 Lee 7 Polanyi 10 Herschbach; 1987 4 Cram, Lehn 8 Pederson; 1988 5 Huber 6 Michel 11 Deisenhofer; 1989 4 Cech 6 Altman; 1990 5 Corey; 1991 5 Ernst; 1992 6 Marcus; 1993 5 Smith 6 Mullis

Economics: 1969 6 Frisch 9 Tinbergen; 1970 9 Samuelson; 1971 7 Kuznets; 1972 5 Arrow, Hicks; 1973 8 Leontief; 1974 6 Myrdal 8 von Hayek; 1975 8 Koomans 11 Kantorovich; 1976 8 Friedman; 1977 5 Meade, Ohlin; 1978 5 Simon; 1979 5 Lewis 7 Schultz; 1980 5 Klein; 1981 5 Tobin; 1982 7 Stigler; 1983 6 Debreu; 1984 5 Stone; 1985 10 Modigliani; 1986 8 Buchanan; 1987 5 Solow; 1988 Allais; 1989 8 Haavelmo; 1990 6 Miller, Sharpe 9 Markowitz; 1991 5 Coase; 1992 Becker; 1993 5 Fogel, North

Literature: 1901 14 Sully-Prudhomme; 1902 7 Mommsen; 1903 8 Bjornson; 1904 7 Mistral 9 Echegaray; 1905 11 Sienkiewicz; 1906 8 Carducci; 1907 7 Kipling; 1908 6 Eucken; 1909 8 Lagerlof; 1910 8 von Heyse; 1911 11 Maeterlinck; 1912 9 Hauptmann; 1913 6 Tagore; 1915 7 Rolland; 1916 13 von Heidenstam; 1917 9 Gjellerup 11 Pontoppidan; 1919 9 Spitteler; 1920 6 Hamsun; 1921 6 France; 1922 6 Benavente; 1923 5 Yeats; 1924 7 Reymont; 1925 4 Shaw; 1926 7 Deledda; 1927 7 Bergson; 1928 6 Undset; 1929 4 Mann; 1930 5 Lewis; 1931 9 Karlfeldt; 1932 10 Galsworthy; 1933 5 Bunin; 1934 10 Pirandello; 1936 6 O'Neill; 1937 6 du Gard; 1938 4 Buck; 1939 9 Sillanpaa; 1944 6 Jensen; 1945 7 Mistral; 1946 5 Hesse; 1947 4 Gide; 1948 5 Eliot; 1949 8 Faulkner; 1950 7 Russell; 1951 10 Lagerkvist; 1952 7 Mauriac; 1953 9 Churchill; 1954 9 Hemingway; 1955 7 Laxness; 1956 Jimenez; 1957 5 Camus; 1958 9 Pasternak; 1959 9 Quasimodo; 1960 5 Perse; 1961 Andric; 1962 9 Steinbeck; 1963 7 Seferis; 1964 6 Sartre; 1965 9 Sholokhov; 1966 5 Agnon, Sachs; 1967 8 Asturias; 1968 8 Kawabata; 1969 7 Beckett; 1970 12 Solzhenitsyn; 1971 6 Neruda; 1972 4 Boll; 1973 5 White; 1974 7 Johnson 9 Martinson; 1975 7 Montale; 1976 6 Bellow; 1977 10 Aleixandre; 1978 6 Singer; 1979 6 Elytis; 1980 6 Milosz; 1981 7 Canetti; 1982 13 Garcia Marquez; 1983 7 Golding; 1984 7 Siefert; 1985 5 Simon; 1986 7 Soyinka; 1987 7 Brodsky; 1988 7 Mahfouz; 1989 4 Cela; 1990 Paz; 1991 8 Gordimer; 1992 7 Walcott; 1993 8 Morrison

Peace: 1901 5 Passy 6 Dunant; 1902 5 Gobat 8 Ducommun; 1903 6 Cremer; 1905 10 von Suttner; 1906 9 Roosevelt (Theodore); 1907 6 Moneta 7 Renault; 1908 5 Bajer 9 Arnoldson; 1909 9 Beernaert 13 d'Estournelles; 1911 5 Asser, Fried; 1912 4 Root; 1913 10 La Fontaine; 1919 6 Wilson; 1920 9 Bourgeois; 1921 5 Lange 8 Branting; 1922 6 Nansen; 1925 5 Dawes 11 Chamberlain; 1926 6 Briand 10 Stresemann; 1927 6 Quidde 7 Buisson; 1929 7 Kellogg; 1930 9 Soderblom; 1931 6 Addams, Butler; 1933 6 Angell; 1934 9 Henderson; 1935 12 von Ossietzky; 1936 3 Saavedra Lamas; 1937 5 Cecil; 1945 4 Hull; 1946 4 Mott 5 Balch; 1949 Orr; 1950 6 Bunche; 1951 7 Jouhaux; 1952 10 Schweitzer; 1953 8 Marshall; 1957 7 Pearson; 1958 4 Pire; 1959 9 Noel-Baker; 1960 7 Luthuli; *(cont.)*

Nobel Prizes *(cont.)*

1961 **12** Hammarskjold; *1962* **7** Pauling; *1964* **4** King; *1968* **6** Cassin; *1970* **7** Borlaug; *1971* **6** Brandt; *1973* **6** Duc Tho; **9** Kissinger; *1974* **4** Sato **8** MacBride; *1975* **8** Sakharov; *1976* **8** Corrigan, Williams; *1978* **5** Begin, Sadat; *1979* **12** Mother Teresa; *1980* **13** Perez Esquivel; *1982* **6** Myrdal, Robles; *1983* **6** Walesa; *1984* **4** Tutu; *1986* **6** Wiesel; *1987* **12** Arias Sanchez; *1989* **4** Lama; *1990* **9** Gorbachev; *1991* **13** Aung San Suu Kyi; *1992* **6** Menchu; *1993* **7** de Klerk, Mandela

Physics: 1901 **8** Roentgen; *1902* **6** Zeeman **7** Lorentz; *1903* **5** Curie (Pierre; Marie) **9** Bequerel; *1904* **8** Rayleigh; *1905* **6** Lenard; *1906* **7** Thomson; *1907* **9** Michelson; *1908* Lippmann; *1909* **5** Braun **7** Marconi; *1910* **11** van der Waals; *1911* **4** Wien; *1912* **5** Dalen; *1913* **15** Kamerlingh-Onnes; *1914* **7** von Laue; *1915* **5** Bragg (William H.; William L.); *1917* **6** Barkla; *1918* **6** Planck; *1919* **5** Stark; *1920* **9** Guillaume; *1921* **8** Einstein; *1922* **4** Bohr; *1923* **8** Millikan; *1924* **8** Siegbahn; *1925* **5** Hertz **6** Franck; *1926* **6** Perrin; *1927* **6** Wilson **7** Compton; *1928* **10** Richardson; *1929* **9** de Broglie; *1930* **5** Raman; *1932* **10** Heisenberg; *1933* **5** Dirac **11** Schrodinger; *1935* **8** Chadwick; *1936* **4** Hess **8** Anderson; *1937* **7** Thomson **8** Davisson; *1938* **5** Fermi; *1939* **8** Lawrence; *1943* **5** Stern; *1944* **4** Rabi; *1945* **5** Pauli; *1946* **8** Bridgman; *1947* **8** Appleton; *1948* **8** Blackett; *1949* **6** Yukawa; *1950* **6** Powell; *1951* **6** Walton **8** Cockroft; *1952* **5** Bloch **7** Purcell; *1953* **7** Zernike; *1954* **4** Born **5** Bothe; *1955* Lamb **5** Kusch; *1956* **7** Bardeen **8** Brattain, Shockley; *1957* *Lee* **4** Yang; *1958* **4** Tamm **5** Frank **9** Cherenkov; *1959* **5** Segre **11** Chamberlain; *1960* **6** Glaser; *1961* **9** Mossbauer **10** Hofstadter; *1962* **6** Landau; *1963* **5** Mayer **6** Jensen, Wigner; *1964* **5** Basov **6** Townes **9** Prokhorov; *1965* **7** Feynman **8** Tomonaga **9** Schwinger; *1966* **7** Kastler; *1967* **5** Bethe; *1968* **7** Alvarez; *1969* **8** Gell-Mann; *1970* **4** Neel **6** Alfven; *1971* **9** Gabor; *1972* **6** Cooper **7** Bardeen **10** Schrieffer; *1973* **5** Esaki **7** Giaever **9** Josephson; *1974* **4** Ryle **6** Hewish; *1975* **4** Bohr **9** Mottelson, Rainwater; *1976* **4** Ting **7** Richter; *1977* **4** Mott **8** Anderson, Van Vleck; *1978* **6** Wilson **7** Kapitsa, Penzias; *1979* **5** Salam **7** Glashow **8** Weinberg; *1980* **5** Fitch **6**

Cronin; *1981* **8** Schawlow, Siegbahn **11** Bloembergen; *1982* **6** Wilson; *1983* **6** Fowler **13** Chandrasehar; *1984* **6** Rubbia **10** van der Meer; *1985* **11** von Klitzing; *1986* **5** Ruska **6** Binnig, Rohrer; *1987* **6** Muller **7** Bednorz; *1988* **8** Lederman, Schwartz **11** Steinberger; *1989* **4** Paul **6** Ramsey **7** Dehmelt; *1990* **6** Taylor **7** Kendall **8** Friedman; *1991* **8** de Gennes; *1992* **7** Charpak; *1993* **5** Hulse **6** Taylor

Physiology or Medicine: 1901 **10** von Behring; *1902* **4** Ross; *1903* **6** Finsen; *1904* **6** Pavlov; *1905* **4** Koch; *1906* **5** Golgi **11** Ramon y Cajal; *1907* **7** Laveran; *1908* **7** Ehrlich **11** Metchnikoff; *1909* **6** Kocher; *1910* **6** Kossel; *1911* **10** Gullstrand; *1912* **6** Carrel; *1913* **6** Richet; *1914* **6** Barany; *1919* **6** Bordet; *1920* **5** Krogh; *1922* **4** Hill **8** Meyerhof; *1923* **7** Banting, Macleod; *1924* **9** Einthoven; *1926* **7** Fibiger; *1927* **10** von Jauregg; *1928* **7** Nicolle; *1929* **7** Eijkman, Hopkins; *1930* **11** Landsteiner; *1931* **7** Warburg; *1932* **6** Adrian **11** Sherrington; *1933* **6** Morgan; *1934* **5** Minot **6** Murphy **7** Whipple; *1935* **7** Spemann; *1936* **4** Dale **5** Loewi; *1937* **12** Szent-Gyorgyi; *1938* **7** Heymans; *1939* **6** Domagk; *1943* **5** Dam **5** Doisy; *1944* **6** Gasser **8** Erlanger; *1945* **5** Chain **6** Florey **7** Fleming; *1946* **6** Muller; *1947* **4** Cori **6** Houssay; *1948* **6** Muller; *1949* **4** Hess **5** Moniz; *1950* **5** Hench **7** Kendall **10** Reichstein; *1951* **7** Theiler; *1952* **7** Waksman; *1953* **5** Krebs **7** Lipmann; *1954* **6** Enders, Weller **7** Robbins; *1955* **5** Theorell; *1956* **8** Cournand, Richards **9** Forssmann; *1957* **5** Bovet; *1958* **5** Tatum **6** Beadle **9** Lederberg; *1959* **5** Ochoa **8** Kornberg; *1960* **6** Burnet **7** Medawar; *1961* **9** von Bekesy; *1962* **5** Crick **6** Watson **7** Wilkins; *1963* **6** Eccles, Huxley **7** Hodgkin; *1964* **5** Bloch, Lynen; *1965* **5** Jacob, Lwoff, Monod; *1966* **4** Rous **7** Huggins; *1967* **4** Wald **6** Granit **8** Hartline; *1968* **6** Holley **7** Khorana **9** Nirenberg; *1969* **5** Luria **7** Hershey **8** Delbruck; *1970* **4** Katz **5** Euler **7** Axelrod; *1971* **10** Sutherland; *1972* **6** Porter **7** Edelman; *1973* **6** Lorenz **9** Tinbergen, von Frisch; *1974* **6** de Duve, Palade (Albert; George); *1975* **5** Temin **7** Dulbecco **9** Baltimore; *1976* **8** Blumberg, Gajdusek; *1977* **5** Yalow **7** Schally **9** Guillemin; *1978* **5** Arber, Smith **7** Nathans; *1979* **7** Cormack *(cont.)*

Nobel Prizes *(cont.)*
10 Hounsfield; *1980* 5 Snell 7 Dausset
10 Benacerraf; *1981* 5 Hubel 6 Sperry,
Wiesel; *1982* 4 Vane 9 Bergstrom 10
Samuelsson; *1983* 10 McClintock; *1984*
5 Jerne 7 Koehler 8 Milstein; *1985* 5
Brown 9 Goldstein; *1986* Cohen 14
Levi-Montalcini; *1987* 8 Tonegawa;
1988 5 Black, Elion 9 Hitchings; *1989* 6
Bishop, Varmus; *1990* 6 Murray,
Thomas; *1991* 5 Neher 7 Sakmann;
1992 5 Krebs 7 Fischer; *1993* 5 Sharp 7
Roberts

no: nae (Sc.), naw, nay, nea (Sc.), nit, nix, non (F.), oxi (Gr.) 4 nein (G.), nyet (Russ.), play 5 drama 6 denial 7 refusal 9 by no means

no-account: 9 worthless

Noah: *dove:* 7 Columba
  father: 6 Lamech
  grandson: 4 Aram
  great-grandson: Hul
  place of debarkation: 6 Ararat
  raven: 6 Corvus
  ship: ark
  son: Ham, Sem 4 Shem 7 Japheth
  wine cup: 6 Crater

nob: 4 head, jack, toff 5 swell

nobby: 4 chic 5 swell 7 stylish 9 excellent, first-rate 11 fashionable

Nobel Prizes: (see box)

noble: 4 epic, fine, free, gent, good, peer, pure, rial 5 burly, ducal, grand, ideal, lofty, manly, moral, proud 6 august, epical, famous, heroic, lordly 7 eminent, exalted, gallant, liberal, soulful, stately, sublime 8 elevated, generous, glorious, highborn, nobleman, precious, renowned, splendid 9 chevalier, dignified, excellent, honorable 10 high-minded, idealistic, noblewoman 11 illustrious, magnanimous, magnificent

nobleman: don 4 duke, earl, lord, peer 5 barin (Russ.), baron, count 6 knight, prince, varlet 7 baronet, grandee (Sp.), hidalgo, marquis 8 marquess, viscount 10 aristocrat
  pert. to: 5 ducal 6 lordly

noble pine: 10 pipsissewa

noblewoman: 4 lady 7 duchess, peeress 8 baroness, countess, marquise, princess 10 marquisess 11 marchioness, viscountess

nobody: 4 none 9 nonentity

nocent: 6 guilty 7 harmful, hurtful, noxious 8 criminal

noctambulism: 11 sleep walker

noctuad: 4 moth, worm

noctule: bat, owl 9 pipistrel 11 pipistrelle

nocturnal: 5 night 7 nightly 11 nightwalker

nocturne: 7 lullaby 8 serenade 11 composition

nocuous: 7 harmful 8 damaging

nod: bow 4 beck, bend, doze, wink 5 droop 6 assent, beckon, drowse, nutate, salute 7 signify 8 approval, nutation

nodding: 6 drowsy, nutant, sleepy 8 cernuous 9 pendulous

noddy: auk 4 fool 5 dunce, ninny 7 hackney 9 simpleton

node: bow 4 bump, knob, knot, lump 5 joint, nodus, tumor 6 nodule 7 dilemma, granule 8 swelling, tubercle 10 difficulty

noel: 4 song 5 carol 9 Christmas

noetic: 8 abstract 12 intellectual

nog: ale, peg, pin 5 block 6 eggnog, noggin 8 beverage, treenail

noggin: cup, mug, nog 4 head, pate

no-good: 6 wretch 7 wastrel

noir (F.): 5 black

noise: air, din 5 bruit, rumor, sound 6 gossip, norate, report 11 pandemonium

noiseless: 5 quiet, still, tacit 6 silent 7 catlike 9 soundless

noisemaker: 4 bell, horn 6 rattle 7 clapper

noisette: 5 hazel

noisome (see also **noxious**): bad 4 foul 5 fetid 7 harmful, hurtful 8 stinking, unsavory 9 offensive 10 disgusting, malodorous, pernicious 11 destructive, unwholesome

noisy: 4 loud 6 clashy 7 blatant, rackety 8 brawling, clattery, strepent, strident 9 clamorous, hilarious, turbulent 10 boisterous, tumultuous, vociferous 12 obstreperous

noma: 5 ulcer

nomad: 4 Arab, hobo, Luri, Moor 5 Alani, gypsy, rover 6 roamer, roving 7 Bedouin, Saracen, scenite 8 vagabond, wanderer

nomadic: 9 itinerant

nomadism: 8 vagrancy 10 wanderlust

nom de plume: 5 alias 7 pen name 9 pseudonym 11 nom de guerre

nome: 4 Elis 5 nomos 8 nomarchy, province 10 department, prefecture

nomen: 4 gens, name

nomenclature: 4 list, name 8 glossary, register 9 catalogue, designate, recounter 10 dictionary, vocabulary 11 appellation, designation, terminology

nomic: 5 valid 8 ordinary 9 customary 12 conventional

nominal: 4 noun 5 cheap, token 6 slight, unreal 7 titular, trivial 8 platonic, so-called 11 theoretical 13 unsubstantial

nominate: tap 4 call, leet (Sc.), name 5 enter, put up, slate 7 appoint, entitle, propose, specify 9 designate 10 denominate

nominee: 9 candidate

nonage: 7 infancy 8 minority 10 immaturity 12 youthfulness

nonaspirate: 4 lene

nonbeliever: 5 pagan 7 atheist 8 agnostic

nonce: 7 present 8 occasion

nonchalant: 4 calm, cool, easy 5 blase 6 casual 8 careless 10 insouciant 11 indifferent 12 lighthearted 13 imperturbable

noncleric: lay 4 laic

noncombatant: 5 medic 8 chaplain, civilian, observer, pacifist

noncommittal: 7 neutral 8 reserved

noncompliance: 7 refusal 10 obstinance

non compos mentis: 6 insane 14 not of sound mind

nonconcurrence: 7 dissent

nonconductor: 5 resin

nonconforming: 9 anomalous

nonconformist: 5 rebel 6 hippie 7 beatnik, heretic 8 bohemian 9 dissenter

nonconformity: 6 heresy 7 dissent 9 recusance, recusancy 10 dissidence

nondescript: 4 dull 5 usual 7 insipid 8 ordinary 13 indescribable, unexceptional, uninteresting

none: 4 nane (Sc.), neen, noon 5 nones 6 not any, not one

nonentity: 4 zero 5 zilch 6 cipher, nobody 7 nothing, sad sack 9 small beer

nonessential: 5 extra 9 extrinsic 10 adiaphoron, extraneous 11 dispensable, unnecessary 12 adventitious 14 circumstantial

nonesuch: 5 apple, model 7 paragon 8 paradigm 9 matchless, nonpareil, unequaled, unrivaled 13 one in a million

nonexistent: 4 null 8 nonbeing

nonfestal: 6 ferial

nonfulfillment: 6 breach 12 infringement

nongrata: 9 unwelcome

nongypsy: 4 gajo

non-kosher: 4 tref

non-Mahometan: 5 Kafir

no-no: 4 tabu 5 taboo 9 forbidden 12 unacceptable

nonobjective: 8 abstract

nonobservance: 9 violation

nonpareil: 4 best 5 ideal 7 paragon, perfect, unequal 8 nonesuch, peerless 9 unrivaled

nonpartisan: 4 fair, just 7 neutral 9 impartial, objective

nonpasserine bird: 4 tody 6 hoopoe, motmot 8 hornbill 10 kingfisher 11 nonperching

nonphysical: 6 mental 7 psychic 9 psychical

nonplus: 5 blank, stump, trump 6 baffle, puzzle 7 confuse, perplex, stagger 8 confound 9 embarrass, frustrate

nonpositive: 8 negative

nonproductive: 6 barren 7 sterile 10 unfruitful 12 unbeneficial

nonprofessional: lay 4 laic 7 amateur

nonsense: bah, pah, rot 4 blah, bosh, buff, bull, bunk, flam, tosh 5 blash, folly, fudge, haver, hooey, stite (Sc.) 6 bunkum, drivel, faddle, folder 7 blarney, blather, buncome, inanity, twaddle 8 blahblah, blathery, falderal, flimflam, folderol, trumpery 9 absurdity, fandangle, frivolity, gibberish, moonshine, poppycock, silliness 10 balderdash, flapdoodle, flumdiddle, galimatias, triviality 11 flumadiddle, foolishness, monkeyshine 12 fiddle-dee-dee, flummadiddle

non sequitur: 15 it does not follow

nonsolid: 5 fluid 6 liquid

noodle: 4 bean, fool, head, nizy, noll, pate 5 brain, ninny, nizey, noddy, pasta 6 boodle, noddle, noggin 8 macaroni 9 blockhead, simpleton

nook: out, wro 4 cant, cove, glen, hole 5 angle, herne, niche 6 cantle, corner, cranny, recess 7 byplace, crevice, retreat

noon: 4 apex 6 midday 8 meridian 11 culmination

noose: tie 4 bond, dull, grin, hang, loop, trap 5 bight, grane, honda, snare, widdy 6 entrap, halter, lariat 7 ensnare, execute, laniard, lanyard, springe 8 slip-knot 9 headstall
armed with: 10 laquearian

nor: ner 7 neither 8 negative 10 connective

nori: 4 alga 7 amanori, seaweed

noria: 5 wheel 10 water wheel

norite: 4 rock 6 gabbro

norm: 4 rule, type 5 gauge, model, norma 7 average, pattern 8 standard, template

normal: 4 sane 5 usual 7 average, general, natural, regular, typical 8 habitual 11 commonplace

Normandy: *beach:* 4 Gold, Juno, Utah 5 Omaha, Sword
capital: 5 Rollo
conqueror: 5 Rollo
duke: 5 Rollo
town: 4 Caen 5 Rouen 7 Le Havre, Saint-Lo 9 Cherbourg
World War II battle: 4 D-Day

Norn: 4 fate, Urth, Wyrd 5 Skuld 9 Verthandi

Norse (see also **Odin**): 4 mink 8 Teutonic 9 Icelandic, Norwegian 12 Scandinavian
abode of gods: 6 Asgard 8 Valhalla
alphabet: 5 runic
bard: 5 scald, skald 7 sagaman
chieftain: 4 jarl, Rolf 5 Rollo
demigoddess of destiny: Urd

demon: **4** Mara, Surt, Wode **5** Surtr
epic: **4** Edda, saga
explorer: **4** Eric **7** Ericson
fate: **4** Norn
first being: **4** Ymir
first man: **4** Askr
first woman: **5** Embla
giant: **4** Atli, Loke, Loki, Natt, Norn, Nott, Wate, Ymer, Ymir **5** Jotun, Mimer, Mimir, Thrym **6** Fafnir, Jotunn
god: Asa, Ase, Ran, Tiu, Tyr, Ull, Zio **4** Frey, Hler, Hoth, Loke, Loki, Odin, Surt, Thor, Vali **5** Aeger, Aegir, Aesir (pl.), Baldr, Brage, Bragi, Donar, Freyr, Gymir, Othin, Surtr, Vanir (pl.), Wodan, Woden, Wotan **6** Balder, Hoenir, Njorth **7** Forsete, Forseti, Heimdal, Vitharr **9** Heimdallr, Hlorrithi
goddess: Eir, Hel **4** Frea, Hela, Nora, Saga, Urth, Wyrd **5** Freya, Frigg, Nanna **6** Freyja, Frigga **7** Asynjur
goddess of earth: **4** Erda
hall of heroes: **8** Valhalla
king: **4** Atli, Olaf
night: **4** Natt, Nott
nobleman: **4** jarl, yarl
poem: **4** rune
poet: **5** scald, skald
saint: **4** Olaf **5** Olaus
sea serpent: **6** Kraken **7** Midgard
tale: **4** saga
toast: **5** skoal
Viking: **5** Rollo
watchdog: **4** Garm **5** Garmr
wolf: **6** Fenrir
world tree: **8** Ygdrasil **9** Yggdrasil

North Africa: *antelope:* **5** addax **7** gazelle
country: **5** Egypt, Libya **7** Algeria, Morocco, Tunisia
desert: **6** Libyan, Sahara
lyre: **6** kissar
measure: **4** rotl
mountains: **9** Haut Atlas
native quarter: **6** casbah, kasbah
oasis: **4** wadi, wady
people: **4** Moor **5** Nilot **6** Berber, Hamite
port: **4** Oran **7** Tangier **10** Casablanca
sheep: **4** drui **6** aoudad

North America: (see box)
North Atlantic: *island:* Man **4** Long **6** Azores, Canary, Faeroe, Orkney **7** Bermuda, Britain, Iceland, Ireland, Madeira **8** Hebrides **9** Cape Verde, Greenland, Manhattan, Shetlands **12** Newfoundland

North Britain: **8** Scotland **9** Caledonia
North Carolina: (see box)
North Dakota: (see box)
northeaster: **4** blow, gale, wind **5** storm
northern: **6** boreal **13** septentrional
Northern Bear: **6** Russia
North Korea: *capital:* **9** Pyongyang
city: **7** Hamhung, Kaesong
currency: won **4** chon
river: Nam **4** Yalu **5** Tumen **7** Taedong **8** Changjin
North Pole discoverer: **5** Peary
North Sea: *arm:* **9** Skagerrak
canal: **4** Kiel
river: **5** Weser
North Star: **7** polaris **8** loadstar, lodestar, polestar **10** tramontane
North Vietnam: See **Vietnam**
Northwest Territories: *capital:* **11** Yellowknife
flower: **13** mountain avens
Indian: **10** Athabascan
people: **5** Inuit **6** Eskimo
north wind: **6** boreas, norther
Norway: (see box)
nose: neb, nez (F.), pry, spy **4** beak, conk, gift, lora (pl.) **5** lorum, scent, smell, sniff, snoop, snout **6** detect, muffle, muzzle, nozzle, schnoz, search, socket **7** advance, perfume **8** busybody, discover, informer, perceive **9** proboscis **11** investigate
cartilage: **6** septum
glasses: pince nez
inflammation: **6** coryza **8** rhinitis
kind: pug **5** Roman **8** aquiline, snub
large: **6** nasute
medicine: **7** errhine
muscle: **7** nasalio
nerve: **9** olfactory
opening: **4** nare **7** nostril
partition: **5** vomer
pert. to: **5** nasal **6** narial, rhinal
snub: **6** simous
surgery: **11** rhinoplasty
nosebleed: **9** epistaxis
nose-dive: dip **6** plunge **7** plummet
nosegay: **4** posy **7** bouquet, perfume
nosegay tree: **10** frangipani
nosepiece: **5** nasal **6** nozzle, noseband
nosh: **4** chew **5** munch, snack
nostalgia: **7** longing **10** melancholy
Nostradamus: **4** seer **7** prophet **10** forecaster
nostril: **4** nare **5** nares (pl.), naris (pl.) **6** thrill
pert. to: **5** naric **6** narial, narine
nostril-shaped: **8** nariform
nosy, nosey: **6** prying **7** curious **8** fragrant **10** malodorous **11** inquisitive
not: nae (Sc.), nay, nor **4** baal, bail, bale, nott **5** shorn **6** nought, polled, shaven **7** neither **8** hornless, negation, negative **11** nothingness

North America: *bay:* **6** Baffin, Hudson
  desert: **4** Yuma **6** Mojave **7** Painted,
  Sonoran **8** Colorado, Vizcaino **10** Chi-
  huahuan, Great Basin
  explorer: **5** Cabot **8** Columbus
  gulf: **6** Alaska, Mexico **10** California
  highest peak: **8** McKinley
  island: **5** Parry **6** Baffin **7** Bahamas,
  Bermuda **8** Aleutian, Antilles, Victoria
  9 Greenland **12** Newfoundland **14**
  Queen Elizabeth
  lake: **4** Erie **5** Huron **7** Ontario **8**
  Michigan, Superior, Winnipeg **9**
  Athabasca, Great Bear, Great Salt,
  Nicaragua **10** Great Slave
  lowest point: **8** Badwater **11** Death Val-
  ley
  mountain range: **5** Coast, Rocky **6**
  Alaska, Brooks **7** Cascade **11**
  Appalachian, Sierra Madre **12** Sierra
  Nevada
  nations: **4** Cuba **5** Haiti **6** Belize,
  Canada, Mexico, Panama **7** Bahamas,
  Grenada, Jamaica, St. Lucia **8** Anguilla,
  Dominica, Honduras **9** Costa Rica,
  Guatemala, Nicaragua **10** El Salvador
  12 United States **17** Dominican
  Republic, Trinidad and Tobago **18**
  Antigua and Barbados **25** St. Vincent
  and the Grenadines
  river: **4** Ohio **5** Yukon **6** Fraser, Nelson
  8 Arkansas, Colorado, Columbia, Mis-
  souri **9** Mackenzie, Rio Grande **10** St.
  Lawrence **11** Mississippi
  waterfall: **7** Niagara **8** Yosemite

all there: **6** insane, crazy
any: nul **4** nane (Sc.), nary, none
at all: **5** never **6** noways, nowise
either: **7** neither
final: **13** interlocutory
otherwise than: **6** merely
the same: **5** other **7** another **9** different
notable: **6** fabled, famous, fat cat **7** eminent,

North Dakota: *capital:* **8** Bismarck
  city: **5** Fargo, Minot **9** Dickinson,
  Jamestown **10** Grand Forks
  highest peak: **10** White Butte
  Indian: **6** Mandan **7** Arikara **8**
  Cheyenne
  motto: **45** Liberty and Union, Now and
  Forever, One and Inseparable
  region: **8** Badlands
  river: Red **5** James **8** Missouri
  state bird: **10** meadowlark
  state flower: **11** prairie rose

  storied **8** big wheel, eventful, historic **9**
  celebrity, memorable, notorious, personage
  10 noteworthy, remarkable **12** considerable
notal: **6** dorsal
notandum: **4** note **5** entry **9** memoranda (pl.)
  10 memorandum
notarize: **6** attest **7** certify
notary: **5** clerk **8** endorser, observer, official,
  recorder **9** notorious, scrivener
  chief: **11** protonotary **12** prothonotary
notation: **4** memo, note **5** entry **7** marking **10**
  annotation **14** representation
  phonetic: **5** Romic
notator: **5** noter **8** recorder **9** annotator
notch: cut, dag, gap, hag, jag **4** cope, dent, dint,
  gash, gimp, hila (pl.), kerf, nick, pock, step **5**
  crena, grade, hilum, score, tally **6** crenae
  (pl.), crotch, defile, degree, indent, record,
  scotch **7** crenate, serrate **8** undercut **9**
  indenture **10** depression **11** indentation
notched: **5** erose **7** crenate, serrate **8** cre-
  nated, serrated
  irregularly: **5** erose
note: I.O.U., jot, see **4** bill, call, chit, fame,
  heed, line, mark, memo, name, sign, sole,
  song, tone, tune **5** label, sound, token **6** billet, letter, minute, notice, record, regard,
  remark, renown, report **7** betoken, comment, message, missive, notanda (pl.),
  observe **8** annotate, breviate, dispatch, eminence, notandum, perceive, reminder **9**

North Carolina: *cape:* **4** Fear **8** Hatteras
  capital: **7** Raleigh
  city: **6** Durham **9** Asheville, Charlotte **10**
  Greensboro **12** Winston-Salem
  Indian: **7** Catawba **8** Cherokee, Hatteras
  island: **7** Roanoke **10** Outer Banks
  motto: **14** Esse Quam Videri (To Be,
  Rather Than to Seem)
  mountain: **8** Mitchell **9** Blue Ridge **10**

  Great Smoky **11** Grandfather
  mountain range: **11** Appalachian
  river: Haw, Tar **5** Neuse **6** Pee Dee, Yad-
  kin **7** Roanoke **8** Cape Fear
  sound: **7** Pamlico **9** Albemarle
  state bird: **8** cardinal
  state flower: **7** dogwood
  state tree: **4** pine

Norway: *artist:* **5** Munch **8** Vigeland
  bird: **4** rype
  boat: **4** pram **5** praam **6** praham
  capital: **4** Oslo
  cart: **11** stolkjaerre
  chieftain: **4** jarl
  city: Nes **4** Voss **5** Bjort, Hamar, Skein,
    Skjak **6** Bergen, Horten, Larvik, Narvik
    7 Alesund, Drammen **9** Stavanger,
    Trondhjem **11** Lillehammer
  composer: **5** Grieg
  currency: ore **5** krone
  current: **9** maelstrom
  dance: **7** halling
  dramatist: **5** Ibsen
  embroidery: **9** hardanger
  ethnologist: **9** Heyerdahl
  explorer: **8** Amundsen (Roald) **10** Eric
    the Red **11** Leif Ericson
  former capital: **10** Christiana
  goblin: **5** nisse **6** kobolk
  governor: **6** amtman
  haddock: **8** rosefish
  inlet: **5** fiord, fjord
  island group: **7** Lofoten **10** Vesteralen
  measure: fot, mal, pot **4** alen, maal **5**
    kande **6** fathom **7** skieppe **9** korntonde
  mountain: **5** Dovre, Sogne **6** Kjolen **7**
    Numedal **8** Telemark, Ustetind **9** Blod-
    fjell, Harteigen, Ramnanosi **12** Gald-
    hoppigen
  pirate: **6** Viking
  reef: **6** skerry
  river: Ena **4** Tana **5** Glama **6** Lougen
  ruler: **6** hersir
  saint: **4** Olaf **5** Olaus
  sport: **5** bandy
  traitor: **8** Quisling
  weight: lod **4** mark, pund **9** skaalpund
    10 bismerpund

character **10** indication, memorandum,
prominence, reputation **11** distinction,
observation
accompanying: **8** overtone
bank: **6** finnip, flimsy **8** frogskin, promissory
bugle: mot
explanatory: **8** scholium **10** annotation
highest: ela
marginal: **6** postil **7** apostil **9** apostille
middle: **4** mese
musical: **4** half **5** breve, gamut, sharp,
whole **6** eighth **7** punctus, quarter **8**
paramese **9** semibreve
prisoner's: **4** kite
promissory: **11** pledge to pay

writer: **9** annotator
notebook: log **5** diary **6** street **7** journal **10**
adversaria
notecase: **10** pocketbook, wallet
noted: **6** famous **7** eminent **8** renowned **9** distingue, well-known **10** celebrated **11** illustrious, distinguished
notes: *literary:* ana
  miscellaneous: **10** adversaria
note well: **8** nota bene (L.)
noteworthy: **6** rubric **7** eminent, notable **9**
memorable, red-letter **10** remarkable **11**
outstanding **12** considerable
nothing: nil **4** free, luke, nill, zero **5** aught,
nihil **6** naught, nought, trifle **7** useless **10**
triviality **12** nonexistence
nothing but: all **4** mere, only
notice: ban, see **4** espy, heed, idea, mark,
memo, mind, news, note, sign **5** await,
favor, quote **6** advice, billet, espial, notion,
regard, remark, review **7** affiche, article,
discern, mention, observe, warning **8**
apprisal, citation, civility, critique **9** attention, criticism **10** cognizance, intimation,
memorandum **11** garnishment **12**
announcement, intelligence, notification **13**
consideration
  advance: **8** heraldry
  book: **5** blurb
  death: **4** obit **8** obituary
  favorable: **4** rave
  honorable: **8** citation
  leave of: **8** mittimus
  legal: **6** caveat
  marriage: ban **4** bans **5** banns
  official: **5** edict **8** bulletin **12** proclamation
  paid: **13** advertisement
  Patent Office: **6** caveat
  public: **5** edict **8** bulletin
  refuse: cut **4** snub **6** ignore
noticeable: **7** evident, notable, obvious, salient
8 striking **9** prominent **10** noteworthy,
remarkable **11** conspicuous, eye-catching,
outstanding, significant
notification: **6** notice
notify: bid **4** cite, page, tell, warn **6** inform **7**
apprise, declare, frutify, publish **8** acquaint
9 broadcast **10** promulgate
notion: bee **4** buzz, hint, idea, idee, view,
whim **5** fancy, image **6** belief, desire, maggot, notice, theory, vagary **7** caprice, conceit, inkling, opinion, thought **9** intention
10 conception **11** inclination
notoriety: **5** eclat **9** publicity
notorious: bad, big **5** known **6** arrant, famous
7 evident **8** apparent, flagrant, infamous **9**
acclaimed, well-known **10** scandalous **11**
conspicuous **12** disreputable
notwithstanding: yet **4** even **6** algate, mauger,
maugre **7** against, algates, despite, however

8 although 12 nevertheless

nougat: 5 candy, shell 10 confection

nought: bad, nil 4 zero 5 wrong 7 nothing, useless 9 worthless 10 wickedness

noun: 4 name, word 11 substantive
form: 4 case 6 gender
indeclinable: 6 aptote
kind of: 6 common, proper
verbal: 6 gerund

nourish: 4 feed, grow, rear 5 breed, nurse 6 foison, foster, suckle, supply 7 cherish, nurture, support, sustain, develop 9 cultivate, stimulate

nourishing: 4 alma 6 alible, hearty 8 nutrient 9 alimental, healthful, nutritive 10 alimentary, nutritious

nourishment: 4 food, keep, meat 5 manna 6 foison, living 7 aliment, pabulum, support 9 nutriment 10 sustenance

nous: 4 mind 6 reason 9 intellect, common sense (Br.), gumption (Br.)

nova: new 4 star

Nova Scotia: *bay:* 5 Fundy
capital: 7 Halifax
city: 6 Sydney 8 Glace Bay 9 Dartmouth
native name: 6 Acadia
people: 7 Acadian 8 bluenose
provincial flower: 7 arbutus 9 mayflower

novel: new, odd 4 book, tale 5 fresh, prose, story 6 recent, unique 7 fiction, romance, strange, unusual 8 original, uncommon 9 different 10 newfangled
cut: 11 abridgement 12 condensation

novelette: 5 conte

novelty: fad 6 change 10 innovation, knick-knack

novice: cub 4 boot, punk, tyro 5 rooky 6 rookie, tyrone 7 amateur, convert, learner 8 beginner, freshman, initiate, neophyte 9 greenhorn 10 apprentice 11 abecedarian

novitiate: 9 postulant 14 apprenticeship

now: noo (Sc.) 4 here 5 today 7 because, present 9 forthwith 11 immediately

nowise: 5 navis

Nox: See **Nyx**

noxious: ill 4 evil 5 fetid 6 nocent, putrid 7 baneful, harmful, hurtful, nocuous, noisome, vicious 8 stinking, virulent 9 injurious, miasmatic, poisonous 10 pernicious 11 deleterious, destructive, unwholesome 12 insalubrious

nozzle: 4 nose, vent 5 snout

nuance: 5 shade 6 nicety 7 shading, soupcon 8 subtlety 9 variation 10 difference, suggestion

nub: 4 core, crux, gist, hang, knob, knot, knub, lump, neck, snag 9 substance 12 protuberance

nubia: 4 wrap 5 cloud, scarf

nubile: 12 marriageable

nubilous: 5 foggy, misty, vague 6 cloudy 7 obscure 8 overcast 10 indefinite

nuclear particle: 6 proton 7 neutron

nucleus: 4 core, seed 5 focus, umbra 6 kernel, fusion 7 fission
pert. to: 8 nucleate
starch: 4 hila (pl.) 5 hilum

nude: 4 bare 5 model, naked 6 statue, unclad 7 denuded, picture 8 buff-bare, painting, stripped 9 au naturel, unclothed, uncovered, undressed

nudge: jog, nog 4 knub, lump, poke, prod, push 5 block, elbow

nudibranch: 7 mollusk

nudie: 9 skin flick

nudist: 7 Adamite 12 gymnosophist

nugatory: 4 vain 5 empty 7 invalid, trivial 8 trifling 9 frustrate, worthless 11 ineffectual

nugget: 4 hunk, lump, mass, slug

nuisance: 4 harm, hurt, pest 6 bother, injury 9 annoyance 12 exasperation

null: nil 6 devoid 7 nullify 11 nonexistent

nullah: 5 gorge, gully 6 ravine

nullifidian: 7 skeptic 10 unbeliever

nullify: 4 flaw, null, undo, void 5 abate, annul, elide 6 cancel, negate, offset, repeal 7 abolish, destroy 8 abrogate, evacuate 9 frustrate 10 counteract, disappoint, invalidate, neutralize

numb: 4 dead, drug, dull 6 asleep, benumb, deaden, stupid, torpid 7 stupefy 8 enfeeble, helpless 9 incapable 10 indifferent, insensible 12 anesthetized

number: sum 4 curn (Sc.), data (pl.), herd, host, many, mort, slew 5 count, datum, digit, scads, score, total 6 amount, bundle, encore, figure, hirsel, myriad, reckon 7 chiffer, compute, decimal, several 8 fraction, numerate, quantity 9 aggregate, calculate, enumerate, multitude 10 collection, complement, percentage
cardinal: one, two 4 four 5 three
dice: 4 sise
indeterminate: 7 umpteen, zillion, gazillion
irrational: 4 surd
ordinal: 5 first, third 6 second, fourth
prime: one, two 4 five 5 seven, three 6 eleven 8 thirteen
pure: 6 scalar
third power: 4 cube
under ten: 5 digit
whole: 7 integer

numbles: 7 giblets, innards 8 entrails

numen: 5 deity 6 genius, spirit 8 divinity

numerable: 11 enumerative

numeral: 4 word 5 digit 6 figure, letter, number
style: 5 Roman 6 Arabic

numerate: 4 list, tell 5 count, tally 7 tick off, enumerate

numerical group: duo **4** trio **5** octet **6** septet, sextet **7** octette, quartet, quintet, twosome **8** foursome, sextette **9** threesome

numerous: 4 lots, many **6** legion, myriad **7** copious, crowded **8** abundant, multiple, thronged **9** multifold, plentiful

Numidia: *bird:* **10** demoiselle
  city: **5** Hippo
  king: **8** Jugurtha

numskull: 4 dolt, fool **5** dunce **9** blockhead

nun: 4 bird, snew **5** clerk **6** pigeon, sister, vestal **7** confine, devotee **8** titmouse, votaress **9** priestess **10** cloistress, anchoress
  chief: **6** abbess, Mother Superior
  Franciscan: **9** Poor Clare
  headdress: **6** wimple, coif, veil
  Latin: **5** Vesta
  order: **6** Marist **8** Trappist, Ursaline **9** Dominican, Lorettine **11** Sacred Heart, Maryknoll

nunbird: 6 monase

nuncio: 6 legate **8** delegate **9** messenger **14** representative

nuncupate: 7 declare **8** dedicate, inscribe, proclaim **9** designate

nuncupative: 4 oral **9** unwritten

nun moth: 7 tussock

nunnery: 5 abbey **7** convent **8** cloister **10** sisterhood

nunni: 7 blesbok **8** antelope

Nun's son: 6 Joshua

nuphar: 9 water lily

nuptial: 6 bridal, genial **7** marital, wedding **11** matrimonial

nurse: 4 amah, ayah, baba, care, feed, rear, tend **5** bonne (F.), mammy, nanny **6** attend, cradle, foster, norice, suckle **7** cherish, nource, nourish, nurture, promote **10** breast-feed, minister to

nursery: 6 creche **7** brooder **9** arboretum **10** greenhouse

nurse shark: 4 gata

nursling: 4 baby **9** foundling

nurture: 4 diet, feed, food, rear **5** nurse, raise, train **6** cocker, foster **7** bring up, cherish, educate **8** breeding, training **9** education, nutriment

nut: bur, guy, nit **4** burr, cola, core, head, kola, nute, pili, task **5** acorn, betel, crank, hazel, pecan **6** almond, Brazil, jojoba, walnut, butter, cashew, fellow, peanut, pyrene **7** filbert, hickory, lunatic, problem **8** beechnut, chestnut, crackpot **9** eccentric **10** pistachio, crackbrain, enthusiast **11** undertaking
  collective: **4** mast **5** shack
  edible part: **6** kernel
  Hawaiian: macadamia
  ivory: **4** anta

  kola: **5** bichy **8** gourou-nut
  medicinal: **4** cola, kola
  palm: **5** betel, lichi **8** cocoanut
  pert. to.: **5** nucal
  tropical: ben **4** cola, kola

nutant: 7 nodding **8** drooping

nut-brown: 5 hazel **6** walnut **8** chestnut

nut coal: 10 anthracite

nut grass: 5 sedge

nutmeg: *covering:* **4** mace

Nutmeg State: 11 Connecticut

nutramin: 7 vitamin

nutria: fur **5** coypu, rodent

nutriment: pap **10** sustenance **11** nourishment

nutrition: 11 nourishment **12** alimentation, food

nutritious: 9 healthful, wholesome **10** nourishing, salubrious

nutritive: 10 nourishing

nuts-and-bolts: 7 details **12** working parts

nutty: 4 gaga, zany **5** buggy, queer, spicy **7** amorous, piquant **8** demented, pleasant **10** unbalanced **12** crackbrained, enthusiastic

nuzzle: 5 nurse **6** cuddle, fondle, foster, nestle **7** snuggle

nye: 4 eyas, nest, nide **5** brood

nylon: 5 crepe, fiber, ninon, tulle **6** fabric **8** stocking

nymph: 5 Aegle, naiad, oread, siren, sylph **6** nereid **7** Corycia **9** hamadryad
  Arcadian: **6** Syrinx
  beloved of Narcissus: **4** Echo
  Cretan: **8** Cynosura
  laurel tree: **6** Daphne
  Messina Strait: **6** Scylla
  mountain: **5** Oread
  Mount Ida: **6** Oenone
  Muslim: **5** houri
  ocean: **5** siren **6** Nereid **7** Galatea, Oceanid **10** Callirrhoe
  pursued by Apollo: **6** Daphne, Syrinx **8** Arethusa
  queen: Mab
  sea: **6** Nereid **7** Calypso
  water: **4** Nais **5** Naiad **6** Egeria, Lurlei, Undine **7** Apsaras, Hydriad, Lorelei **8** Arethusa
  wood: **5** Dryad **6** Nereid **9** Hamadryad

nymphaea: 8 Castalia **9** water lily

nyssa: 6 tupelo **8** black gum

Nyx, Nox: 5 night
  brother: **6** Erebus
  daughter: Day **4** Eris **5** Light **10** Hesperides
  father: **5** Chaos
  husband: **5** Chaos **6** Erebus
  son: **6** Charon, Hypnos

O

oaf: **4** boor, dolt, fool, lout, yoke **5** clown, dunce, idiot **6** lummox **8** dumbbell **9** blockhead, foundling, schlemiel, schlemihl, simpleton **10** changeling

oak: **5** roble **6** barren, cerris, encina **7** ambrose, durmast, turtosa **8** chaparro **9** blackjack
bark: **4** cork, crut
bitter: **6** cerris
black: **10** quercitron
blight: **5** louse
evergreen: **4** holm
family: **5** beech **8** fagaceae
fruit: **5** acron **6** camata
gall: **8** oakapple
genus: **7** Quercus
holm: **4** ilex **5** holly
immature fruit: **6** camata
seed: **5** acorn
tannin: **6** queric **9** quercinic
white: **5** roble
young: **8** flittern

oak beauty: **4** moth
oak fern: **8** polypody
oam: **5** steam
oar: row **4** pole, pull **5** aloof, rower, scull **6** paddle, propel **7** oarsman **9** propeller
blade: **4** palm, peel
part: **4** loom
short: **5** scull
steering: **5** swape, swipe

oarlock: **5** thole **7** fulcrum, rowlock
oarsman: **5** rower **6** stroke **7** sculler
oasis: ojo, spa **4** merv, wadi, wady **6** refuge, relief **9** waterhole
oast: **4** kiln, oven **6** cockle
oat: ait (Sc.) **5** grain **6** angora, cereal **7** egilops
genus: **5** avena
head: **7** panicle

oater: **7** western **10** horse opera
oath: vow **4** aith **5** aithe, curse, haith, swear **6** appeal, pledge **7** serment **8** anathema **9** affidavit, expletive, profanity, swearword **10** adjuration, obligation **11** affirmation, imprecation
mild: **4** darn, drat, ecod, egad, gosh, jeez **5** golly, sugar **6** shucks **7** gee-wizz **8** gee-whizz

oatmeal: **6** cereal **7** granola **8** porridge
obbligato, obligato: **13** accompaniment, indispensable

obclude: **4** hide **7** conceal
obdurate: **4** firm, hard **5** rough, stony **6** inured, rugged **7** adamant **8** hardened, stubborn **9** calloused, immovable, obstinate, unbending, unfeeling **10** impenitent, inflexible, insensible, persistent, unyielding **11** hardhearted, intractable, stiff-necked, unrepenting

obeah: obi **5** charm **6** fetish, voodoo
Obed: *father:* **4** Boaz
grandson: **5** David
mother: **4** Ruth
son: **4** Jehu **5** Jesse **7** Azariah

obedience: **5** order **7** control **8** docility **10** compliance, conformity, submission **12** jurisdiction

obedient: **7** duteous, dutiful, heedful, mindful, obeying, slavish **8** amenable, biddable, yielding **9** attentive, compliant, observing, tractable

obedient plant: **10** dragonhead
obeisance: bow **5** binge, conge, honor, salam **6** congee, curtsy, fealty, homage, salaam **7** curtsey, loyalty **9** abaisance, deference, reference **10** submission

obelisk: **4** mark **5** pylon, shaft, tower **6** column, dagger, guglia, guglio, needle, obelus, pillar **8** monument

Oberon: **4** king, poem **5** fairy, opera
wife: **7** Titania

obese: fat **5** plump, pudgy, pursy, stout **6** fleshy, pyknic, rotund **8** blubbery, liparous **9** corpulent

obesity: **7** fatness **10** corpulence **11** avoirdupois

obey: ear **4** hear, mind **5** yield **6** accept, behave, submit **7** execute **9** acquiesce

obfuscate: dim **6** darken **7** becloud, confuse, mystify, obscure, perplex, stupefy **8** bewilder **9** obfuscous

obi: **4** sash **6** girdle
obiter dictum: **6** remark **7** comment **11** observation

obituary: **9** necrology **11** death notice
object: aim, end **4** goal, item **5** argue, cavil, demur, thing **6** design, entity, motive, oppose, target **7** dislike, protest, purpose, quarrel **9** challenge, intention, interpose **10** disapprove
lesson: **7** example

rare: **5** *curio* **7** *antique*
sacred: **4** urim
to: **4** mind **7** dislike **8** be averse **10** disapprove

objection: but **7** defense, protest **8** demurral **9** challenge, exception
legal: **5** demur

objectionable: **4** vile **6** horrid **9** obnoxious, offensive **11** exceptional

objective: aim, end **4** fair, goal **6** motive, target **7** purpose, reality **8** detached, unbiased **9** impartial, intention **10** impersonal

objet d'art: **4** vase **5** curio, virtu **6** bauble, gewgaw **7** bibelot **8** figurine

objurgate: **5** abuse, chide, decry **6** berate, rebuke **7** reprove, upbraid **8** execrate **9** castigate

oblate: **4** monk **8** dedicate, monastic **9** lay member
opposite of: **7** prolate

oblation: **4** gift **6** corban **7** charity **8** devotion, offering **9** Eucharist, sacrifice

obligate: **4** bind **6** fasten, hold to **7** promise

obligation: vow **4** band, bond, debt, duty, loan, must, onus **6** devoir, pledge **7** promise **8** contract **9** agreement, liability **10** allegiance, commitment, compulsion **11** obstruction **12** indebtedness

obligatory: **7** binding, bounden **8** forcible, imposing **9** mandatory

oblige: **4** pawn **5** favor, force **6** coerce, compel, engage, please **7** gratify, require **8** mortgage, required **9** constrain

obliged: **8** beholden, grateful, indebted

obliging: **4** kind **5** buxom, civil **6** clever **7** amiable **9** agreeable, courteous

oblique: **4** awry, bias, skew **5** askew, bevel, cross, slant **6** aslant, aswash **7** askance, crooked, evasive, scalene **8** inclined, indirect, sidelong, sideways, sidewise, slanting **9** slantways, slantwise, underhand **10** circuitous
render: **5** splay

obliterate: **4** blot, dele, rase, raze **5** annul, erase **6** cancel, delete, efface, remove, sponge **7** expunge **10** annihilate, extinguish

obliteration: **7** erasure, removal **10** extinction

oblivion: **5** Lethe, limbo **6** pardon **7** amnesty, nirvana **13** forgetfulness
producer of: **8** nepenthe

oblong: **8** avelonge **9** elongated **11** rectangular
rounded: **7** ellipse

obloquy: **5** abuse, odium **6** infamy **7** calumny, censure **8** disgrace, dishonor

obnoxious: **4** foul, vile **6** horrid, liable, odious, rancid **7** hateful **9** offensive, repugnant, verminous

oboe: **4** reed **5** shawm **6** surnai, surnay **7** hautboy, musette **8** szopelka

obscene: **4** blue, foul, lewd, nast **5** bawdy, crude, dirty, gross, nasty **6** coarse, filthy, impure, ribald, risqué, smutty, vulgar **7** profane **8** immodest, indecent **9** loathsome, offensive, repulsive **10** disgusting, fescennine, licentious **11** foul-mouthed

obscure: dim **4** blot, blur, dark, hazy, hide **5** bedim, befog, blind, faint, foggy, inner, murky, vague **6** bemist, cloudy, darken, darkle, gloomy, mystic, remote **7** becloud, conceal, confuse, cryptic, eclipse, shadowy, unknown, unnoted **8** darkling, disguise, mystical, nameless, obstruse, oversile **9** ambiguous, difficult, enigmatic, equivocal, mystical, recondite, undefined **10** caliginous, extinguish, indistinct, overshadow **14** uncomprehended

obsecrate: **4** pray **7** beseech, entreat **8** petition **10** supplicate

obsequious: **5** slick **7** devoted, dutiful, fawning, servile, slavish **8** obedient, toadying, toadyish, unctuous **9** attentive, compliant, parasitic **10** submissive **11** deferential, subservient

obsequy: **4** rite **6** exequy, ritual **7** funeral **8** ceremony

observance: act **4** form, rite, rule **6** custom, notice, regard **8** ceremony, practice **9** attention, deference **11** obser.ation **12** constitution

observant: **5** alert **7** careful, mindful **8** watchful **9** attentive **10** perceptive **11** considerate

observation: **4** heed, note **5** watch **6** notice, remark **7** auspice, autopsy, comment, descant
preliminary: **5** proem

observatory: **4** Bank, Lick **5** Naval, tower **6** Yerkes **7** Arecibo, Jodrell, lookout, Palomar, voyager **9** astronomy **11** Mount Wilson **14** Royal Greenwich

observe: eye, see, spy **4** espy, heed, keep, look, nark, note, obey, tout, wait, yeme **5** study, watch **6** behold, descry, follow, notice, regard, remark **7** comment, discern, respect, witness **8** perceive, preserve **9** advertise, celebrate, solemnize **10** animadvert, scrutinize

observer: spy **7** witness **8** audience, informer, onlooker **9** bystander, spectator

obsess: **5** beset, haunt **6** harass **9** preoccupy

obsession: **5** craze, mania **6** fetish, hang-up **7** passion **8** fixation, idee fixe (F.)

obsidian: **5** glass, lapis

obsolescence: **9** desuetude

obsolete: old **4** dead **5** passe **7** ancient, archaic, extinct, outworn **8** out-dated, outmoded **9** discarded, out-of-date **10** antiquated **12** old-fashioned

obstacle: bar, dam, let **4** snag **5** block, hitch **6** bunker, hocket, hurdle **7** barrier **9** hindrance **10** difficulty, impediment **11** Chinese wall, obstruction **12** entanglement
insurmountable: **7** impasse

obstetrician: **7** midwife **10** accoucheur

obstetrics: **8** tocology **9** maieutics, pregnancy **10** childbirth

obstinate: set **4** dour **5** balky, sulky, tough **6** assish, dogged, mulish, sullen, unruly **7** froward, willful **8** crotched, obdurate, perverse, stubborn **9** foreright, pigheaded **10** bullheaded, determined, headstrong, inflexible, persistent, refractory, selfwilled **11** intractable, opinionated **12** closedminded, contumacious, pertinacious, recalcitrant

obstreperous: **5** noisy **6** unruly **9** clamorous **10** boisterous, vociferous **11** disobedient

obstruct: bar, dam, dit, gag, mar **4** clog, ditt, fell, stop **5** beset, block, check, choke, delay, hedge **6** arrest, cumber, forbar, hamper, hinder, impede, oppose, retard, screen **7** barrier, forelay, occlude **8** blockade, encumber, incumber **9** barricade, embarrass, interfere, interrupt

obstruction: bar, dam, rub **4** snag **5** gorce, hitch **6** abatis **7** barrace, barrage, barrier, blinder **8** embolism, obstacle **9** hindrance **10** difficulty, impediment **11** impeachment

obtain: beg, bum, eke, get, win **4** earn, fang, gain, hent, reap **5** apply, cadge, ettle, reach **6** attain, derive, secure, sponge **7** achieve, acquire, capture, chevise, prevail, procure, receive, succeed
by threat: **6** extort **9** blackmail

obtainable: **9** available

obtest: **6** beg for **7** beseech **10** supplicate

obtrude: **5** eject, expel **6** butt in, impose

obtruncate: lop **6** behead **7** shorten **8** retrench **10** decapitate

obtrusive: **5** fresh, pushy **7** blatant, forward, pushing **9** intrusive **10** aggressive **11** impertinent

obtund: **4** dull **5** blunt, quell **6** deaden

obtuse: dim **4** dull **5** blink, blunt, crass, dense, thick **6** stupid **8** boeotian, hebetate, purblind **11** insensitive

obvelation: **7** veiling **10** concealing

obverse: **4** face, head **5** front **8** converse **10** complement **11** counterpart

obviate: **7** prevent, ward off **8** preclude **9** forestall, interfere, intervene

obvious: **4** open **5** broad, clear, gross, overt, plain **6** patent **7** evident, glaring, visible **8** apparent, distinct, manifest, palpable **11** conspicuous

obvolute: **9** contorted, convolute **11** overlapping

oca, oka: **5** tuber **6** oxalis, sorrel

occasion: **4** hint, sele, time **5** casus, cause, event, nonce, slant **6** excuse, moment **7** instant, pretext **8** ceremony, engender, exigency, function, incident **9** condition, happening
festive: **4** fete, gala **5** levee, party **7** holiday **9** reception **11** celebration

occasional: odd **4** orra **5** stray **6** daimen, random **8** sporadic **10** infrequent

occasionally: **7** betimes **9** sometimes **10** now and then

Occidental: **4** West **6** ponent **7** Western **9** Hesperian, Westerner
opposite: **8** Oriental

occlude: **4** clog, plug **5** block, close **6** absorb, take in **7** shut out **8** obstruct

occult: **4** hide **5** eerie, magic, weird **6** arcane, hidden, mystic, secret, voodoo **7** alchemy, cryptic **8** esoteric, mystical **9** concealed, recondite **10** mysterious, necromancy **11** supernormal **12** supernatural

occultation: **7** eclipse **13** disappearance

occultism: **5** magic **6** cabala **7** mystery

occupant: **6** inmate, tenant **7** citizen, dweller **10** inhabitant

occupation: job **4** note, toil, work **5** graft, trade **6** career, metier, tenure **7** calling, pursuit **8** business, function, industry, vocation **10** employment, habitation, profession

occupied: **4** busy, rapt **7** peopled, settled **9** engrossed, inhabited

occupy: sit, use **4** busy, fill, hold, take **6** absorb, employ, engage, expend, fulfil, live in, tenant **7** cohabit, engross, fulfill, inhabit, oversit, pervade, possess **8** interest

occur: be **4** come, meet, pass **5** clash, exist **6** appear, arrive, befall, betide, happen, strike **9** take place
again: **5** recur **6** repeat

occurrence: hap **4** case **5** event, thing **7** episode **8** incident, occasion **9** encounter, happening **12** circumstance
supernatural: **7** miracle

ocean: **4** blue, brim, deep, main **5** brine, briny **6** Arctic, Indian **7** expanse, Pacific **8** Atlantic, vastness **9** Antarctic
approach: **7** seagate
floating matter: **5** algae, lagan **7** flotsam
periodic motion: **4** tide
swell: sea **4** wave **6** roller

Oceania: **6** Malaya **9** Australia, Melanesia, Polynesia **10** Micronesia, New Zealand

Oceanid: **5** nymph

Oceanus: *daughter:* **5** Doris **7** Oceanid **8** Eurynome
father: **6** Uranus
mother: **4** Gaea
sister: **6** Tethys

wife: **6** Tethys
ocellus: 6 stemma **7** eyespot
ocelot: cat **7** leopard
ocher: 5 color **7** pigment
ocrea: 6 greave, sheath **7** legging
octave: 4 cask, note, utas **5** eight **8** interval **9** harmonics, organ stop
Octavia: *brother:* **8** Augustus
husband: **10** Mark Antony
octet: 5 group **7** huitain **8** electron
octopus: 5 polyp, poulp **6** poulpe **7** mollusk, polypus **9** devilfish **10** cephalopod
arm: **8** tentacle
kin: **5** squid **10** cuttlefish
secretion: ink
ten arms: **7** decapod
octoroon: 5 metis **7** metisse, mulatto
octose: 5 sugar
octroi: tax **5** grant **9** privilege **10** concession
octuple: 9 eightfold
ocular: eye **5** optic **6** visual
odd: awk **4** fell, left, lone, orra (Sc.), rare **5** eerie, droll, extra, funny, impar, outre (F.), queer, weird **6** quaint, uneven **7** azygous, bizarre, curious, strange, unusual **8** fanciful, freakish, peculiar, singular, unpaired **9** burlesque, eccentric, fantastic, grotesque, unmatched, whimsical **10** accidental, occasional
oddity: 5 quirk **8** crotchet, quiddity **9** curiosity **12** eccentricity, idiosyncrasy
odds: 4 line **6** chance **7** dispute, quarrel **8** handicap, variance **9** advantage **10** dissension **13** probabilities
odds and ends: 4 orts **6** refuse, scraps **7** mixture, seconds **8** remnants, sundries **9** leftovers **10** miscellany, remainders, potpourri
ode: 4 hymn, poem **5** lyric, paean, psalm, verse **7** epicede **8** canticle **9** epicedium
kind of: **8** pindaric
part: **5** epode **7** strophe **11** antistrophe
victory: **9** epinicion, epinikion
author: **5** Keats **6** Horace, Pindar **7** Shelley **8** Tennyson **10** Wordsworth
odeon: 4 hall **5** odeum **7** gallery, theater
Oder, Odra tributary: 5 Warta **6** Neisse
odic: 5 lyric
Odin (see also **Norse**): **5** Wodan, Woden, Wotan **8** Norse god
brother: Ve **4** Vili
daughter-in-law: **5** Nanna
descendant: **5** Scyld
father: Bor
frost giant: **4** Ymir
hall: **7** Valhall **8** Valhalla
horse: **8** Sleipner
maiden: **8** Valkyrie
mother: **6** Bestla
raven: **5** Hugin, Munin

ring: **8** Draupnir
ship: **7** Naglfar **11** Skidbladnir
son: Tyr **4** Thor, Vali **5** Baldr **6** Balder
spear: **7** Gungnir
sword: **4** Gram
throne: **10** Hlidskjalf
wife: **4** Fria, Rind **5** Freya, Frigg, Rindr **6** Frigga
wolf: **4** Gere, Geri **5** Freki
odious: **4** foul, loth, vile **5** loath **7** hateful, heinous, hideous **8** damnable, flagrant, infamous **9** abhorrent, invidious, obnoxious, offensive, repugnant **10** abominable, detestable, disgusting, forbidding **11** ignominious, opprobrious
odium: 6 stigma **7** dislike, scandal **8** aversion, disfavor, disgrace **9** antipathy **10** abhorrence, opprobrium
odontalgia: 9 toothache
odor: 4 fume, funk, nose, olid, tang **5** aroma, ewder, fetor, flair, fumet, nidor, scent, smell, stink **6** breath, flavor, foetor, repute, stench **7** bouquet, essence, flavour, fumette, perfume **9** fragrance, redolence **10** estimation, reputation
odoriferous: 4 gamy **5** balmy **6** smelly **8** fragrant **9** odiferous
Odysseus: See **Ulysses**
Odyssey author: 5 Homer
oeconomus: 7 manager, steward **9** majordomo
Oedipus: *brother-in-law:* **5** Creon
daughter: **6** Ismene **8** Antigone
father: **5** Laius
foster parent: **7** Polybus **8** Periboea
kingdom: **6** Thebes
riddler: **6** Sphinx
mother: **7** Jocasta
son: **8** Eteocles **9** Polynices **10** Polyneices
victim: **5** Laius **6** Sphinx
wife: **7** Jocasta
oeillade: 4 ogle **6** glance
Oeneus: *father:* **8** Porthaon
kingdom: **7** Claydon, Pleuron
mother: **6** Euryte
wife: **7** Althaea
Oenomaus: *charioteer:* **8** Myrtilus
daughter: **10** Hippodamia
father: **4** Ares
kingdom: **4** Pisa
slayer: **6** Pelops
oeuvre: 4 opus, work
of: 4 from **5** about **10** concerning
off: 4 away, doff, gone **5** aside, crazy, wrong **6** absent, cuckoo, remote **7** distant, further, removed **8** launched, postpone
and on: **8** fitfully **10** in snatches, now and then **11** irregularly
base: bad **5** wrong **7** illegal **9** incorrect, out-of-line **10** unsuitable

beat: odd **5** kinky, kooky **6** far out **7** unusual **9** different **10** unorthodox

color: **4** blue, racy **5** salty, spicy **6** risqué, unwell **10** discordant, out-of-sorts, suggestive

key: **4** flat **10** discordant

offal: **5** gurry, waste **6** refuse **7** carrion, garbage, hogwash, leaving, rubbish **8** gralloch

offend: sin, vex **4** hurt, miff **5** abuse, anger, annoy, grate, grill, pique, shock, wrong **6** attack, grieve, insult, revolt **7** affront, default, mortify, outrage, violate **8** trespass **9** disoblige, displease **10** transgress

offended: **4** sore **7** injured **8** insulted

offender: **6** sinner **7** culprit **8** criminal **10** malefactor

offense: sin **5** crime, error, fault, guilt, malum, pique **6** attack, felony, pritch **7** misdeed, umbrage **8** peccancy, trespass **9** indignity **10** aggression, peccadillo, resentment **11** delinquency, misdemeanor

civil: **4** tort **11** stellionate

law: **5** delit **6** delict **8** delictum

moral: **4** evil

offensive: bad **4** foul, rank, vile **5** fetid **6** attack, coarse, horrid **7** assault, beastly, fulsome, hateful, noisome **8** invading **9** loathsome, obnoxious, repugnant **10** aggressive, disgusting, forbidding, ill-favored, scurrilous, ungracious, unpleasant **11** distasteful **12** disagreeable

offer: bid, try **4** bode, show **6** adduce, allege, tender **7** advance, commend, hold out, present, proffer, propine, propose, suggest **8** bequeath, overture, proposal **9** avertment, volunteer

last: **9** ultimatum

solemn: **6** pledge

offering: **4** gift **6** corban, victim **7** present **9** sacrifice

religious: **5** tithe **7** deodate **8** anathema, oblation **12** contribution

sacrificial: **5** hiera **7** sphagia (pl.) **8** sphagion

offhand: **6** casual **7** brusque **8** cavalier, informal **9** impromptu **10** improvised **11** extempory **14** extemporaneous, unpremeditated **16** extemporaneously

office: job **4** post, wike **5** place, wiken **6** bureau **7** camarin, station **8** function, high sign, position **9** bailiwick, situation **10** commission **11** appointment

chief: **4** boss **7** manager

deprive of: **6** depose, unseat **7** impeach

help: **5** clerk **6** typist **9** secretary **12** receptionist, stenographer

machine: fax **5** modem, Xerox **6** copier **8** computer **9** stenotype **10** calculator, mimeograph, typewriter **11** comptometer

paid without work: **8** sinecure

purchase or sale: **8** barratry

put in again: **7** re-elect **9** re-instate

officeholder: **6** winner **8** official, placeman **9** incumbent **10** bureaucrat

officer: cop **4** aide **5** usher **6** direct, ensign, manage, police, tindal **7** command, conduct, general **8** adjutant **9** executive

army: **5** major **7** captain, colonel, general **10** lieutenant

assistant: **4** aide

college: **4** dean **6** bursar **7** provost **10** chancellor

future: **5** cadet, plebe **10** midshipman

law: cop **7** bailiff, marshal, sheriff **9** constable, detective, patrolman, policeman **11** policewoman

naval: **4** mate **5** bosun **6** ensign, yeoman **7** admiral, captain, striper **9** boatswain, commander, commodore **10** lieutenant

noncommissioned: **4** mate **5** chief **8** corporal, sergeant

presiding: **6** archon **7** speaker **8** chairman **9** moderator, president

prison: **5** guard **6** warden

warrant: **5** bosun **9** boatswain

officers: **5** staff

official: **6** formal **9** escribano (Sp.), ex officio, executive **10** authorized, bureaucrat, ex cathedra, magistrate **11** ceremonious **13** authoritative

administrative: **5** reeve **9** executive

city or town: **5** mayor **7** manager, marshal **8** alderman **9** selectman **10** councilman

civil: **5** judge, mayor **7** bailiff, marshal, sheriff **9** governor **9** constable, patrolman, policeman, president

corrupt: **7** grafter

despotic: **6** satrap

government: **6** syndic

judicial: **8** assessor, recorder **9** treasurer

local: **6** bailie (Sc.), grieve **7** burgess

public: **6** notary

state: **5** envoy **6** consul **8** minister **9** secretary **10** ambassador

officiate: act **5** chair **6** supply, umpire **7** perform, preside, referee **9** celebrate

officious: **4** busy, cool, pert **6** formal **7** pompous **8** arrogant, impudent, informal, official **10** impersonal, meddlesome **11** efficacious, impertinent, pragmatical **12** contemptuous

offing: **6** future **7** by-and-by, picture **10** background

offset: **6** contra **7** balance **10** compensate, complement **12** counterpoise

offshoot: rod **5** bough, scion **6** branch, sprout **7** spin-off **9** by-product, out-growth **10** descendant

offspring: fry, imp, kid, son **4** brat, chit, seed **5** brood, child, fruit, issue, scion **6** foster, result **7** outcome, produce, product, progeny **8** children, daughter, geniture **9** genealogy, youngster **10** descendant, generation

off the rack: 9 ready-made **11** ready-to-wear

oflete: 5 wafer **8** oblation, offering

often: 4 much **6** common **8** frequent, repeated **10** frequently **11** continually, over and over

ogdoad: 5 eight

ogee: See **molding**

Ogier: 4 Dane, hero **6** prince **8** Norseman

ogle: eye **4** gaze, leer, look **5** flirt, stare **7** examine **10** rubberneck

ogre: 5 demon, giant **6** tyrant, yaksha, yakshi **7** bugaboo, monster

ogress: 5 harpy, vixen **6** virago

ogygian: 7 ancient **8** primeval

oh: ay (Sp.), ach (G.) **4** ouch

O. Henry: 6 Porter

Ohio: *capital:* **8** Columbus
　city: Ada **5** Akron, Berea, Cadiz, Niles, Xenia **6** Canton, Dayton, Lorain, Toledo **8** Sandusky **9** Cleveland **10** Cincinnati, Youngstown
　Indian: **4** Erie **7** Wyandot
　lake: **4** Erie
　motto: **27** With God, All Things Are Possible
　mountain range: **9** Allegheny
　river: **4** Ohio **5** Miami **6** Maumee, Scioto **7** Portage **8** Cuyahoga **9** Olentangy
　state bird: **8** cardinal
　state flower: **9** carnation
　state tree: **7** buckeye
　U.S. president: **4** Taft **5** Grant, Hayes **7** Harding **8** Garfield, Harrison, McKinley

---

oil: ben, fat, ile **4** balm, fuel, lard, suet **5** bribe, crude, oleum **6** aceite, anoint, chrism, grease, petrol **7** lanolin **8** flattery, soft soap **9** lubricate, petroleum
　blasting: **14** nitroglycerine
　bone: **6** olanin
　butter: **4** ghee, oleo
　coal: **8** kerosene, paraffin, photogen
　derived from: **5** elaic, oleic
　exporting group: **4** OPEC
　in skin: **5** sebum
　linseed: **6** carron
　liquid compound: **5** olein
　mineral: **7** naphtha
　orange-blossom: **6** neroli
　pert. to: **5** oleic
　plant: **4** corn **5** olive **6** peanut, sesame **8** rapeseed **9** sunflower
　prospector: **10** wildcatter

rapeseed: **6** canola
salt: **7** bittern
ship: **6** tanker
torch: **7** lucigen
vessel: **4** drum, olpe **5** cruet, cruse **6** tanker **7** cresset
well: **6** gusher
whale: **5** sperm

oil beetle: 5 meloe

oilbird: 8 guacharo

oilcloth: 8 linoleum

oiler: 6 oilcan, tanker

oil fish: 7 escolar

oil lamp: 7 coal-oil **8** kerosene

oil rock: 5 shale **9** limestone

oilskin: 5 squam **7** slicker **8** raincoat

oilstone: 4 hone **5** shale **9** whetstone

oil tree: 4 eboe, tung **5** mahwa

oily: fat **4** glib **5** bland, fatty, soapy, suave **6** greasy, oleose, supple **7** fulsome, pinguid **8** slippery, unctuous **9** compliant, plausible **10** oleaginous **11** subservient

ointment: 4 balm, mull, nard **5** cream, salve **6** balsam, cerate **7** unguent **8** linament **9** spikenard
　application: **7** massage **11** embrocation
　Biblical: **9** spikenard
　dry: **9** xeromyron, xeromyrum
　hair: **6** pomade **7** pomatum
　veterinary: **8** remolade **9** remoulade
　wax: **6** cerate

Oise tributary: 5 Aisne

Oisin's father: 4 Finn

ojo: 5 oasis

oka: See **oca**

okay: yes **6** ratify **7** approve, consent, correct **8** all right **10** acceptable

Okie: 7 migrant

Okinawa capital: 4 Naha

Oklahoma: *capital:* **12** Oklahoma City
　city: Ada **4** Enid **5** Tulsa **6** Lawton, Norman **8** Muskogee
　Indian: **4** Otoe, Waco **5** Caddo, Kiowa, Osage **6** Pawnee **7** Arapaho, Tawkoni, Wichita **8** Cheyenne, Comanche **9** Chickasaw
　motto: **16** Labor Omnia Vincit (Labor Conquers All Things)
　mountain: **5** Ozark **6** Boston **7** Wichita **8** Arbuckle, Ouachita
　river: Red **4** Blue **5** Grand **6** Neosho **7** Washita **8** Arkansas, Canadian, Cimarron, Salt Fork **9** Verdigris
　state bird: **10** flycatcher
　state flower: **9** mistletoe
　state tree: **6** redbud

okra: 4 soup 5 bendy, gumbo 8 hibiscus

old: agy, ald, eld 4 aged, auld, past 5 anile, dated, hoary, stale 6 bygone, former, infirm, mature, senile, shabby 7 ancient, antique, archaic, elderly 8 lifelong, medieval, obsolete 9 doddering, hackneyed, long-lived, senescent, venerable 10 antiquated 11 experienced 12 antediluvian

old age: 10 senescence 11 senectitude
  science of: 10 geriatrics

Old Bailey: 4 gaol, jail 6 prison

Old Bay State: 13 Massachusetts

old boy: man, pal 6 alumni (pl.) 7 alumnus

Old Dominion State: 8 Virginia

olden: 4 past 6 bygone 7 ancient

older: 5 elder 6 senior 8 ancestor 11 forefathers 12 predecessors

oldest: 4 dean 6 eldest 9 first-born

Old Faithful: 6 geyser

old-fashioned: 5 dated, drink, glass, passe 6 fogram, fogrum, quaint 7 ancient, antique, archaic 8 cocktail, obsolete 9 primitive 10 antiquated

Old Franklin State: 9 Tennessee

Old Guard: 13 establishment

old hat: 5 dated, stale, trite 6 cliché 7 vintage 8 shopworn 9 hackneyed

Old Line State: 8 Maryland

old maid: 8 cardgame, spinster

Old Noll: 14 Oliver Cromwell

Old Rough and Ready: 6 Taylor

Old Sod: 4 Eire, Erin 7 Ireland

Old Testament: See **Bible**

old-womanish: 5 anile

Old World: 4 Asia 6 Africa, Europe 9 Australia
  opposite: 8 New World 17 Western Hemisphere

olea: 5 olive

oleaginous: 4 oily 5 fatty 7 fulsome

oleander: 5 shrub 9 evergreen 12 rhododendron
  family: 7 dogbane

olecranon: 5 ancon 9 funny bone

oleo: 9 margarine

oleoresin: 5 anime, elemi, tolus 7 copaiba 10 turpentine

oleum: oil

olfaction: 7 osmesis 8 smelling

olid: 4 gamy 5 fetid 6 smelly

olinda bug: 6 weevil

olio: 4 hash, stew 6 medley 7 melange, mixture 8 mishmash 9 potpourri 10 collection, hodgepodge, miscellany 11 olla podrida, variety show

oliphant: 7 horn 8 elephant

olive: 4 olea 9 appetizer
  enzyme: 6 olease
  fruit: 5 drupe

  pert. to: 9 oleaceous
  stuffed: 6 pimola
  wild: 8 oleaster

oliver: 6 hammer

olivet: 5 pearl

olla: jar, jug, pot

olivine: 10 chrysolite

olla podrida: 4 hash, olio, olla, stew 6 medley 9 potpourri

olm: 7 proteus 10 salamander

ology: ism 7 science

oloroso: 6 sherry

olpe: 5 flask 6 vessel 7 pitcher

Olympic cupbearer: 4 Hebe 8 Ganymede

Olympus: 8 mountain
  deity: See **Greek:** *god*
  pert. to: 7 exalted, godlike, Olympic 8 heavenly, majestic 9 celestial

Omar Khayyam: *quatrain:* 5 rubai
  translator: 10 Fitzgerald
  work: 8 Rubaiyat

omber: 8 cardgame

ombudsman: 5 judge 8 mediator

omega: end 4 last 6 letter

omelet: 4 eggs 7 fooyung

omen: 4 bode, sign 5 augur, boder, freet, freit, token 6 augury, handel, hansel 7 auspice, portent, presage, warning 8 bodement, forebode, foresign 9 foretoken 10 foreboding, forerunner, indication, prediction 11 premonition

ominous: 4 dire, dour, grim 5 fatal 6 dismal 7 fateful, fearful 8 menacing, sinister 9 prophetic 10 inexorable, portentous 11 threatening

omission: cut 5 blank, chasm, error 6 lacuna 7 default, failure 9 exclusion, oversight
  mark of: 5 caret 7 ellipse 8 ellipsis 10 apostrophe
  of vowel: 7 elision
  tacit: 7 silence

omit: cut 4 balk, dele, drop, miss, skip, slip 5 abate, elide, spare 6 beleve, cancel, delete, except, forget, ignore 7 beleave, discard, neglect 8 leave out, overlook 9 disregard

omneity: 7 allness 13 comprehensive

omnibus: 5 barge, whole 11 compilation

omnipotent: God 4 able 5 deity, great 6 arrant, mighty 8 almighty, powerful 9 unequaled, unlimited 11 all-powerful

omnipresent: 7 allover 10 everywhere, ubiquitous

omniscient: 4 wise 7 learned 8 powerful 10 all-knowing, allwitting

omnitude: 7 allness 8 totality 12 universality

omoplate: 7 scapula

omphalos: hub 4 boss, knob 5 navel, novel 6 center 9 umbilical 10 focal point

Omri: *daughter:* 8 Athaliah

successor: **4** Ahab

on: **4** atop, upon **5** about, above, ahead, along, anent **6** anenst, within **7** forward **10** concerning
account of: for **7** because
all sides: **5** about **6** around **10** surrounded
and on: **4** ever **7** endless, forever, tedious
other side: **4** over **6** across
the other hand: but **7** however **8** although **11** nonetheless **12** contrariwise, nevertheless

Ona: **7** Fuegian

onager: ass **5** kiang **6** donkey **8** catapult

Onam's son: **4** Jada **7** Shammai

once: ane (Sc.) **4** erst, past **5** aince (Sc.) **6** before, bygone, former **7** one time, quondam **8** formerly, whenever
in a while: **9** sometimes **12** occasionally
more: bis **4** anew, echo **5** again **6** encore, repeat
over: **6** glance, survey **10** inspection
upon a time: **8** formerly

oncorhynchus: **6** salmon

one: ain (Sc.), ein (G.), tae (Sc.), una, une (F.), yae (Sc.) **4** lone, same, sole, some, unal, unit **5** alone, unity **6** person, single, unique, united **7** numeral, pronoun **8** separate, singular, unbroken **9** singleton, undivided, unmarried **10** individual
after another: **8** serially, seriatim **11** consecutive **12** successively
by one: **6** apiece, singly **10** separately

one-chambered: **10** unicameral

one-colored: **13** monochromatic

one-footed: **6** uniped

onegite: **8** amethyst

one-horse: **5** petty **6** little

O'Neill, Eugene: **9** dramatist **10** playwright
character: **4** Anna, Nina, Orin, Yank **5** Brant **7** Lavinia **9** Christine
play: Ile **11** The Hairy Ape **12** Ah Wilderness, Anna Christie, Emperor Jones **15** The Iceman Cometh

---

oneism: **6** egoism, monism

oneness: **5** unity **7** concord **8** entirety, identity, sameness, totality **9** agreement, wholeness **11** singularity

onerous: **4** hard **5** heavy **7** arduous, onerose **8** exacting **9** laborious **10** burdensome, cumbersome, oppressive

one-sided: **6** biased, uneven, unfair, unjust **7** bigoted, partial **8** lopsided, partisan **10** prejudiced, unilateral

one-spot: **4** buck **6** dollar

one tenth: **5** tithe

one thousand: mil

onetime: **7** quondam **8** formerly, erst

one-upmanship: **7** cunning **11** competition, superiority

onfall: **5** onset **6** attack

ongoing: **6** course **9** improving, operating **10** continuing **11** progressive

onion: **4** boll, cepa, leek **5** cibol, peral **7** Bermuda, onionet, shallot **8** eschalot, rareripe, scallion
genus: **6** allium

onlooker: **5** gazer **7** witness **8** audience, beholder **9** bystander, spectator **12** rubbernecker

only: **4** just, lone, mere, sole **5** afald **6** anerly, barely, merely, simple, single, singly, solely **8** peerless, solitary **9** allenarly, excepting **11** exclusively

onomasticon: **7** lexicon **8** glossary **10** dictionary

onomatopoeic: **5** mimic **6** echoic **9** imitative

onset: **4** dash, dint, fard, rese, rush **5** braid, brunt, faird, frush, start **6** attack, charge **7** assault, attempt, brattle **9** beginning, encounter, onslaught **12** commencement

onslaught: **5** blitz, onset **6** attack **7** assault, descent

Ontario: *capital:* **7** Toronto
city: **6** London, Ottawa **7** Windsor **8** Hamilton **9** Kitchener
provincial flower: **8** trillium

onto: **4** atop **6** aboard

onus: **4** duty, load **6** burden, charge, stigma **10** obligation

onward: **4** away **5** ahead, along, forth **7** forward

onyx: **5** black **10** chalcedony

oodles: **4** heap **5** scads **8** lashings **9** abundance

oolong: tea

oomph: vim **5** drive, verve, vigor **6** energy, pizazz, spirit **8** strength, vitality

oopak: tea

oorial, urial: sha **5** sheep

ooze: bog, mud **4** drip, leak, mire, seep, slob **5** exude, gleet, marsh, slime, weeze **6** sludge **8** transude **9** percolate

opah: **4** fish **5** cravo

opal: gem **5** noble, resin **7** girasol, hyalite **8** girasole **10** chalcedony
girasole: **10** chalcedony
variety: **8** menilite **9** cacholong

opalescent: **7** opaline **8** irisated **10** iridescent

opaque: **4** dark **5** dense, vague **6** cloudy, obtuse, stupid **7** obscure **8** eyeshade **10** lightproof

open: dup, ope **4** ajar, flue, free, undo **5** agape, apert, begin, clear, frank, lance,

naked, overt, plain, start, untie **6** candid,
direct, expand, expose, honest, liable,
patent, unbolt, unfold, unfurl, unlock,
unseal, unstop **7** artless, dispart, obvious,
sincere, unclose **8** apparent, commence,
disclose, dispread, explicit, extended, initiate, manifest, patulous, unfasten **9** dis-
spread, originate, uncovered **10** accessible,
forthright, inaugurate, unreserved **11** susceptible, unconcealed, within reach **13**
undissembling
bursting: **10** dehiscence
fully: **4** wide **5** agape **7** yawning **9** dehis-
cent, full-blown
partly: mid **4** ajar
open air: **8** al fresco
open-and-shut: **5** clear, plain **7** evident, obvious **10** guaranteed
open door: **6** entree **7** welcome **11** hospitality
opener: key **4** knob **5** latch **6** sesame **8** aperitif **9** corkscrew
open-eyed: **5** alert, awake **8** vigilant, watchful
9 receptive **10** astonished, discerning
openhanded: **4** free **7** liberal **8** generous **9**
receptive **10** munificent
opening: os, gap, ora (pl.) **4** bore, door, fent,
gate, hole, pass, rift, rima, slit, slot, span,
vent **5** brack, cleft, debut, mouth, start,
width **6** avenue, breach, cavity, chance, hiatus, lacuna, outlet, portal, spread **7** crevice,
fissure, orifice **8** aperture, overture **11**
opportunity
enlarge: **4** ream
escape: **4** muse **5** batch, meuse
in chess: **6** gambit
mouth-like: **5** stoma **7** stomata (pl.)
slitlike: **4** rima
small: **4** pore **5** chink **6** cranny, eyelet **7**
foramen, pinhole **8** foramina (pl.)
openmouthed: **5** agape **6** amazed, gaping,
greedy **8** ravenous **9** clamorous **10** vociferous
openwork: **7** tracery
opera: **4** Aida **5** Faust, Tosca **6** Boheme, Carmen, Mikado, Otello **7** Fidelio **8** Falstaff,
Parsifal, Traviata, Walkyrie **9** Lohengrin,
Pagliacci, Rigoletto, Trovatore **10** Freischutz, Magic Flute, Tannhauser, Three-
penny **11** Don Giovanni **12** Boris
Godunov, Cosi Fan Tutte, Manon Lescaut,
Porgy and Bess **13** Meistersinger,
Rosenkavalier **15** Barber of Seville,
Madame Butterfly **16** Marriage of Figaro,
Tristan and Isolde
comic: **5** buffa
division: **5** scena
glasses: **9** lorgnette **10** binoculars
horse: **7** Western
kind: **4** soap **5** comic, grand, horse **8**
burletta

rock: **5** Tommy
serious: **5** seria
soap: **6** serial **9** melodrama
song: **4** aria **7** sortita **8** cavatina **9** cabaletta
star: **4** diva **5** tenor **7** soprano
opera house: **7** La Scala, theater **12**
Metropolitan
operate: act, man, run, use **4** work **5** pilot,
steer **6** affect, direct, effect, manage, open
up **7** conduct **8** function **10** accomplish
by hand: **10** manipulate
operation: use **4** deed **6** agency **7** process,
surgery **8** creation, exercise, function **9**
actuation, influence, procedure **10** production **11** maintenance, transaction
operative: **4** hand, open **5** agent **6** active,
artist **7** artisan **8** mechanic **9** detective
beyond itself: **9** transeunt
for past: **11** retroactive
operator: **5** agent, quack **6** dealer, driver **7**
manager, operant, surgeon **8** motorist **9**
conductor, operative **10** mountebank
operculum: lid **4** flap **8** covering
operose: **4** busy, hard **8** diligent **9** assiduous,
laborious **11** industrious
ophidian: asp, eel **5** snake **6** conger **7** reptile,
serpent
ophthalmic: **6** ocular
opiate: **4** dope, drug, hemp **5** dwale, opium **6**
deaden **7** anodine, anodyne **8** hypnotic,
narcotic **9** paregoric
opine: say **4** deem, hold **5** allow, guess, judge,
think **6** ponder **7** believe, imagine, suggest,
suppose
opinion: **4** idea, view, ween **5** dicta (pl.),
guess, tenet **6** advice, belief, dictum,
esteem, notion, repute **7** concept, feeling,
thought **8** decision, doctrine, estimate,
judgment **9** sentiment **10** conjecture, conviction, deposition, estimation, evaluation,
expression, impression, persuasion **11** point
of view
erroneous: **13** misconception
expression: **4** vote
preconceived: **9** prejudice
united: **9** unanimous
unorthodox: **6** heresy
opinionated: **6** biased **8** dogmatic, obdurate **9**
conceited, obstinate **11** dictatorial
opinions: *collected:* **9** anthology, symposium
professed: **5** credo
opium: **4** dope, drug **10** intoxicant
addiction: **8** thebaism
alkaloid: **7** codeine **8** morphine **9** narco-
tine, papaverin **10** papaverine
camphorate tincture: **9** paregoric
concentrated form: **6** heroin
derivative: **7** meconic
Egyptian: **8** thebaine

poppy seed: maw
prepared: **6** chandu **7** chandoo
source: **5** poppy
opossum: 6 mammal **9** marsupial
kind: **6** common, murine, woolly
water: **5** yapok **6** yapock
oppidan: 5 civic, urban **8** townsman
opponent: foe **5** enemy, rival **7** opposer **9** adversary, assailant **10** antagonist
opportune: apt, fit, pat **5** ready **6** timely **7** apropos **8** suitable **9** favorable, well-timed **10** auspicious, convenient, favourable, seasonable **11** appropriate
opportunely: 7 apropos, happily
opportunity: 4 hent, turn **5** break, slant **6** chance, look-in **7** opening **8** occasion **9** advantage **12** circumstance
oppose: pit, vie **4** buck, cope, face, meet, stem, wear **5** argue, block, check, cross, fight, front, match, rebel, rebut, repel **6** breast, combat, object, oppugn, resist **7** contest, counter, gainsay **8** conflict, confront, contrast, frontier, obstruct **9** encounter, withstand **10** calcitrate, contradict, contravene, controvert
opposed: 4 anti **5** alien **6** averse **7** adverse, against, counter, hostile **8** contrary, opposite **11** contrariant
opposite: 5 anent, polar **6** across, anenst, averse, contra, facing **7** adverse, antonym, counter, inverse, obverse, reverse **8** antipode, antipole, contrary, contrast, converse **9** antipodal, different, repugnant **10** antipodean **12** antagonistic **13** contradictory
opposition: 5 atilt, enemy **9** animosity, collision, hostility, renitency **10** antagonism, resistance **11** contrariety
oppress: 4 load, rape, thew **5** crush, grind, weigh, wrong **6** burden, defoil, defoul, extort, harass, harrow, ravish, subdue **7** afflict, depress, overlay, repress, trample **8** distress, encumber, pressure, suppress **9** constrain, overpower, overthrow, overwhelm, subjugate, weigh down
oppressed: 5 laden **7** servile **9** debruised **10** heavy-laden **11** downtrodden
oppression: 8 dullness **9** grievance, lassitude **10** affliction **11** obscuration
oppressive: 4 dire, hard **5** black, bleak, close, harsh, heavy **6** gloomy, severe **7** onerous **8** rigorous **10** hardhanded **11** gravaminous, heavyhanded, overbearing
oppressor: 4 csar, czar, Nero, tsar, tzar **6** despot, tyrant **8** dictator
opprobrium: 5 abuse, odium, scorn **6** infamy, insult **7** calumny, contempt, offense, scandal **8** disgrace, dishonor, reproach **9** contumely **10** disrespect, scurrility

oppugn: 6 oppose **7** contend **10** contradict
oppugnacy: 9 hostility **10** antagonism
Ops (see also **Rhea**): *associate:* **6** Consus
consort: **6** Saturn
daughter: **5** Ceres
son: **4** Zeus **8** Poseidon
opt: 4 cull, pick **5** elect **6** choose, decide, select
optical: 6 ocular, visual **9** opthalmic
instrument: **4** lens **5** laser **7** alidade **9** eriometer, magnifier, optometer, periscope, telescope **10** microscope **11** stereoscope
optimist: 5 hoper **7** dreamer **8** idealist **9** Pollyanna **10** positivist
optimistic: 4 rosy **6** joyous **7** hopeful, roseate **8** sanguine
option: 5 right **6** choice **9** privilege **10** free choice **11** alternative
optional: 4 free **8** elective **9** voluntary **10** permissive **13** discretionary
opulent: fat **4** lush, rich **5** ample, plush, showy **6** lavish **7** profuse, wealthy **8** abundant, affluent **9** luxuriant, plentiful, sumptuous **11** extravagant
opus: 4 book, work **5** etude, study **11** composition
oquassa: 5 trout
or: aut (L.), ere **6** either **11** alternative
heraldry: **4** gold **6** yellow
oracle: 4 seer **5** augur, maxim, sibyl **6** Pythia **7** prophet, wise man **10** soothsayer
pert. to: **8** pythonic **9** prophetic
oracular: 4 otic **5** vatic **7** vatical **9** prophetic **10** mysterious **11** dictatorial
orage: 5 storm **7** tempest
oral: 4 exam **5** aloud, parol, vocal **6** sonant, spoken, verbal **7** uttered **9** unwritten **10** acroamatic **11** word-of-mouth
orange: 5 blood, navel, Osage **7** Seville
family: rue **8** Rutaceae
genus: **6** citrus
heraldry: **5** tenne
membrance: **4** zest
mock: **7** seringa, syringa, syringe
piece: **4** lith (Sc.) **7** segment
red: **7** saffron
seed: pip
seedless: **5** navel
orangeberry: 9 cranberry
orangebird: 6 oriole **7** tanager
Orange Bowl site: 5 Miami
orange-flower oil: 6 neroli
orangutan: ape **4** mias **5** pongo, satyr **7** primate
orate: 5 plead, speak, spiel, spout **7** address, declaim, lecture **8** bloviate, harangue **9** discourse, speechify **10** filibuster **11** expostulate
oration: 6 sermon **7** address, concion **9** discourse, panegyric

funeral: **5** eloge **6** eulogy **7** elogium, encomia (pl.) **8** encomium

orator: **6** rhetor **7** demagog, speaker **8** cicerone, ciceroni (pl.) **9** demagogue, plaintiff **10** petitioner **11** rhetorician, spellbinder

oratorian: **6** priest

oratorical: **8** eloquent **10** articulate, rhetorical

oratorio: **7** Messiah, Seasons
coda in: **7** stretto

oratory: **6** chapel **8** rhetoric **9** elocution, eloquence

orb: eye, sun **4** ball, moon, star **5** earth, globe **6** circle, planet, sphere **7** circuit, enclose

orbed: **5** lunar, round

orbit: **4** path **5** range, scope, track **6** circle, domain, socket **7** circuit, ellipse, revolve
point: **5** apsis **6** apogee, epigee, syzygy **7** perigee

orc: **4** orca **5** whale **6** dragon **7** grampus

orchard: **4** farm **5** arbor, copse, grove **6** garden, huerta **8** arbustum **9** enclosure **10** plantation

orchestra: **4** band **5** group **8** ensemble, symphony **12** philharmonic
section: **4** wind, wood **5** brass **6** string **7** timpany **8** woodwind **10** percussion

orchestra bells: **12** glockenspiel

orchestra circle: **7** parquet **8** parterre

orchestrate: **5** score **7** arrange, compose **9** harmonize

orchid: **5** faham, petal, vanda **6** flower, praise, purple **7** aerides, calypso, lycaste, pogonia, vanilla **8** arethusa, labellum **9** perennial **10** compliment
appendage: **8** caudicle
dried tubers: **5** salep
genus of: **5** vanda **6** laelia **10** gymnadenia **14** gymnadeniopsis
leaves: **5** faham
meal: **5** salep
petal: lip **5** sepal **8** labellum
tuber: **5** salep **7** cullion

Orcus: See **Hades**

ordain: **4** deem **5** allot, enact, order **6** confer, decree, invest **7** adjudge, appoint, arrange, behight, command, conduct, destine, install, prepare **9** determine, establish, prescribe **10** adjudicate, commission, consecrate, constitute, predestine

ordeal: **4** gaff, test **5** trial **10** experience **11** tribulation

order: ban, bid **4** boon, fiat, form, ordo, rank, rule, sect, type, will **5** align, array, class, dight, edict, genus, grade, guide **6** billet, charge, cosmos, decree, degree, demand, direct, enjoin, extent, genera (pl.), graith, kilter, manage, method, ordain, police, series, system **7** adjudge, arrange, bespeak, bidding, command, compose, dispose, embargo, mandate, ordines (pl.), precept, process, society **8** decision, neatness, organize, regulate **9** direction, directive, magnitude, procedure **10** injunction, put in shape, succession **11** appointment, arrangement, association, instruction
back: **6** remand **8** recommit
connected: **8** seriatim
cosmic: tao **4** rita
grammar: **5** taxis
lacking: **5** amiss, chaos, messy, mussy **7** anarchy, chaotic, clutter, unkempt **8** confused **10** disarrayed
law: **4** writ **7** summons **8** subpoena
of preference: **8** priority
parliamentary: **9** procedure **12** Roberts Rules
writ: **7** precipe

orderly: **4** aide, neat, tidy, trim **5** trig, **6** batman **7** regular, servant **8** decorous, obedient **9** peaceable, regulated, shipshape **10** law-abiding, methodical, systematic **11** well-behaved

ordinal: **4** book **6** number **7** regular

ordinance: law **4** doom, fiat, rite, rule **5** bylaw, edict **6** assize, decree **7** control, decreta (pl.), statute **8** decretum **9** direction, prescript, sacrament **10** management, regulation **11** appointment

ordinary: **4** lala, ruck, so-so **5** nomic, plain, prose, usual **6** bishop, common, normal **7** average, natural, primate, prosaic, regular, trivial, vulgate **8** everyday, familiar, frequent, habitual, mediocre **9** customary, plain Jane, quotidian **11** commonplace

ordnance: **4** guns **5** armor, orgue **6** petard **7** weapons **8** basilisk, supplies **9** artillery, torpedoes **10** ammunition, serpentine

ordo: **7** almanac **8** calendar

ore: tin **4** gold, iron, lead **5** metal **6** copper, silver **7** mineral **8** platinum
compound: **5** oxide **7** sulfide
crusher: **5** dolly
deposit: **4** lode, vein **5** scrin **7** bonanza
fusing: **8** smelting
horizontal layer: **5** stope
impure: **6** speiss **7** halvana
iron: **5** ocher, ochre **8** hematite **9** magnetite
layer: **4** seam **5** stope
lead: **6** galena
mercury: **8** cinnabar
refuse: **4** slag **5** dross **6** scoria **8** tailings
separator: **6** vanner
silver: **10** stephanite
sluice: **5** trunk
tin: **5** scove
tungsten: **4** cals

washing trough: **6** strake
worthless: **5** matte
oread: **4** peri **5** nymph

Oregon: *bay:* **4** Coos **5** Alsea **7** Yaquina **9** Tillamook **10** Winchester
capital: **5** Salem
city: **6** Eugene **7** Medford **8** Portland **9** Corvallis **11** Springfield
early explorer: **5** Clark, Lewis **8** Coronado
highest peak: **6** Mt. Hood
Indian: **4** Coos **8** Cherokee
motto: **8** The Union
mountain range: **4** Blue **5** Coast **7** Cascade, Klamath, Wallowa
river: **4** Hood **5** Snake **7** John Day **8** Columbia **9** Deschutes **10** Willamette
state bird: **10** meadowlark
state flower: **5** grape
state tree: fir

oreortyx: **5** quail
Orestes: *father:* **9** Agamemnon
friend: **7** Pylades
mother: **12** Clytemnestra
sister: **7** Electra **9** Iphigenia
victim: **9** Aegisthus **12** Clytemnestra
wife: **8** Hermione
orfe: ide **4** fish **5** dusky
orfevrerie: **7** jewelry
organ: **6** medium **7** channel, journal, vehicle **8** magazine **9** equipment **10** instrument, periodical **11** publication
auricular: ear
barrel: **4** hand **8** autophon **10** hurdy-gurdy
desk: **7** console
elongated: **8** tentacle
essential: **5** brain, heart, liver, lungs **6** kidney, viscus **7** viscera (pl.)
fish: **8** drumfish
flutter device: **7** tremolo
footlike: pes
gallery: **4** loft
keyboard: **6** manual **10** pedalboard
lymphoid: **6** tonsil
mouth: **6** tongue **7** ocarina **9** harmonica
note: **9** tremolant
of insect: **7** stinger
of motion: **6** muscle
olfactory: **4** nare, nose
opening: os, ora (pl.)
optical: eye
part: **4** pipe, reed, stop **6** slider **7** bellows **8** keyboard **9** wind chest **10** pedalboard
piano: **9** melopiano

pipe: **4** reed **5** flute **7** mixture
portable: **5** regal
reed: **9** harmonium
respiratory: **4** lung
sawlike: **5** serra
secreting: **5** gland
sensory: ear, eye **4** nose **6** finger, tongue
speech: lip **6** throat, tongue
tactile: **6** feeler
organ stop: **5** quint, viola **7** aeoline, celesta, tertian **8** diapason, dulciana, gemshorn, register **9** philomela, rohrflute **10** quindecima
adjust: **10** registrate
bell-like: **8** carillon
labial: **7** melodia
reed: **4** oboe **7** bassoon **8** possaune
storm-imitating: **5** orage
string: **5** gamba
two banks of pipes: **7** tertian
organbird: **4** wren **6** magpie
organdy: **5** sheer **6** cotton, muslin
organic: **5** vital **6** inborn **7** natural **8** inherent **9** organlike **11** fundamental
body: **5** zooid
compound: **5** amine, ketol
organism: **5** being, plant **6** aerobe, animal, entity
bacterial: **4** germ **7** microbe
body: **4** soma **6** somata (pl.)
elementary: **5** monad
minute: **5** ameba, monad, spore **6** amoeba
pelagic: **6** nekton **7** benthos **8** plankton
process: **6** miosis **7** meiosis
organization: **4** club, firm **5** group, lodge, setup **6** agency **7** company, society **11** association, disposition **12** constitution
business: **4** firm **5** guild **6** Rotary **7** Jaycees, Kiwanis **11** cooperative, corporation, partnership **13** establishment
lack of: **5** chaos **7** anarchy
political: **4** bloc, ward **5** party **7** machine
skeleton: **5** cadre
social: **4** club **5** forum
veterans: A.V.C., D.A.V., G.A.R., S.A.R., V.F.W. **5** Fidac **6** AMVETS **14** American Legion
women's: D.A.R., N.O.W., W.A.F., W.R.C. **8** sorority
organize: **4** form, plan **5** edify, set up **6** embody **7** arrange **8** regiment
organized: **7** planned **8** arranged **10** systematic
orgy: **4** lark, romp **5** binge, revel, spree **6** frolic, shindy **7** rampage, revelry, wassail **8** carousal, ceremony **9** bacchanal **10** observance **11** celebration, merrymaking
Oriana: *father:* **8** Lisuarte
lover: **6** Amadis

oribi: 8 antelope, bleekbok
oriel: bay 6 recess, window 7 balcony, gallery, portico 8 corridor
orient: 4 dawn 5 adapt, place 6 adjust, locate 7 sunrise 11 accommodate
Orient: 4 Asia, East 6 Levant 7 Far East 8 Near East
Oriental: *archangel:* 5 Uriel
  bearer: 5 hamal
  beverage: 6 arrack
  bow: 6 salaam
  calculator: 6 abacus
  cap: 7 calpack
  caravansary: 4 khan 5 serai 6 imaret
  carriage: 4 sado 10 jinricksha 11 jinrickshaw
  cart: 5 araba
  chief: 4 khan
  currency: sen, yen 4 para, yuan 5 dinar, sapek
  commander: ras 4 amir, emir, rais, reis 5 ameer, emeer
  corn: 4 para
  cosmetic: 4 kohl
  council: 5 Divan
  cymbal: tal, zel
  deity: Bel
  destiny: 6 Kismet
  drug: 4 hemp 5 opium 6 heroin 7 hashish
  drum: 7 anacara
  dulcimer: 6 santir
  dwelling: dar
  emperor: 6 sultan
  exercise: 4 judo, yoga 6 tai chi 8 jiujitsu 11 tai chi chuan
  fan: ogi 5 punka
  fish: koi, tai
  garment: aba
  gate: dar
  guitar: 5 sitar
  inn: 5 serai 11 caravansary
  liquor: 4 sake, saki
  litter: 5 dooli, dooly 6 dooley, doolie
  lute: tar
  manservant: 5 hamal
  mansion: 5 yamen
  market: 4 souk 5 bazar 6 bazaar
  measure: dra, mao
  measure of weight: 4 kati, rotl, tael 5 abbas, bhaar, catty, picul 6 cantar, kantar, miskal
  musical instrument: tar 5 sitar, suray, surna, tabla 6 santir 7 anacara, samisen
  nomad: 5 Tatar 6 Tartar 7 Bedouin
  nurse: 4 amah, ayah
  oboe: 5 suray, surna
  pagoda: taa
  pine: 5 matsu
  pipe: 5 hooka 6 hookah 7 nargile 8 harghile, narghile, nargileh

plane-tree: 7 cheenar
porter: 5 hamal
rest house: 4 khan 5 serai
rice paste: ame
ruler: 4 amir, emir, khan, shah 5 ameer, calif, emeer 6 caliph, sultan
sailor: 6 calash, lascar
salutation: 5 saheb, salam 6 kowtow, salaam
sash: obi
sauce: soy
sea captain: ras 4 rais, reis
shrub: tea 5 henna 9 wineberry
silkworm: 6 tussah, tusseh, tusser 7 tussore
slipper: 7 baboosh 8 babouche
sword: 6 tulwar 7 samurai, tulwaur 8 scimitar
tamarisk: 4 atle 5 atlee
tambourine: 5 daira
taxi: 7 ricksha 8 rickshaw
tea: cha
title: aga 4 amir, baba 5 pasha 6 huzoor
tower: 6 pagoda
vessel: 4 dhow, junk, saic 6 sampan
wagon: 5 araba
weight: 4 mann, tael 5 artal (pl.), catty, liang
whip: 6 chabuk 7 chabouk
worker: 5 cooly 6 coolie
oriental: 5 pearl 6 bright, ortive, rising 7 eastern, shining 8 lustrous, pellucid, precious 9 ascending, brilliant 11 resplendent
Oriental rug: 4 Baku, Kali 5 Herez, Mahal, Saruk, Senna, Sumak 6 Kashan, Kerman, Kirman, Meshed, Pamiri, Sarouk, Shiraz, Soumak, Tabriz 7 Bokhara, Bukhara, Chinese, Hamadan, Isfahan, Ispahan, Karajas, Meshhed 8 Lerestan, Sedjadeh 9 Kurdistan
  pattern: 7 ainaleh
orifice: 4 hole, vent 5 inlet, mouth 6 cavity, outlet 7 chimney, opening, ostiole 8 aperture
  in brain: 4 lura
origin: nee 4 dawn, germ, rise, root, seed 5 birth, cause, start 6 nature, parent, source 7 genesis, lineage 8 ancestry, nascence, nascency 9 beginning, inception, naissance, parentage, paternity 10 extraction, incunabula (pl.), provenance 11 incunabulum, provenience 12 commencement, fountainhead
  foreign: 7 ecdemic
  of words: 9 etymology
  on earth: 7 epigene
original: new 5 first, fresh, model, novel 6 fontal, native, primal, primer 7 initial, primary 8 pristine 9 authentic, eccentric, inventive, primitive, prototype 10 aboriginal, innovative 11 fundamental, primigenial
originally: 5 first 9 initially, primarily 10 inherently

originate: 4 coin, make, open, rise 5 arise, begin, breed, cause, found, start 6 create, derive, devise, invent, spring 7 causate, emanate, produce 8 come from, commence, contrive, discover, generate, initiate 9 construct, establish, institute, introduce

originator: 6 author 7 creator 8 composer, inventor 9 architect, innovator

oriole: *golden:* 5 pirol 6 loriot

Orion: 5 Rigel 6 hunter 13 constellation
  hound: 6 Aratus
  slayer: 5 Diana 7 Artemis

orison: 6 prayer 7 request 8 entreaty

Orkney Islands (see also **Scotland**): *bay:* 9 Scapa Flow
  capital: 8 Kirkwall
  fishing ground: 4 haaf
  hut: 4 skio
  inlet: voe
  island: Hoy 4 Eday 6 Pomona, Rousay, Sanday 7 Westray 8 Mainland, Stronsay 9 Ronaldsay, Shapinsay

orle: 6 border, fillet, wreath 7 bearing, chaplet

orlean: 7 annatto

orlop: 4 deck

ormer: 7 abalone

ormolu: 4 gilt, gold 5 alloy 6 mosaic 7 varnish

ornament: dub, fob, pin 4 etch, gaud, gear, gild, tool, trim, waly 5 adorn, braid, chase, decor, gutta, inlay, wally 6 amulet, attire, bedaub, bedeck, billet, brooch, edging, emboss, enrich, finery, flower 7 agremen, engrave, garnish, spangle, trinket 8 agrement, applique, decorate, flourish, lavalier 9 arabesque, billiment, embellish, embroider, lavaliere 10 decoration, furnishing, habiliment, lavalliere
  apex: 6 finial
  bell-shaped: 9 clochette
  boat-shaped: 6 nef
  claw-like: 6 griffe
  crescent-shaped: 6 lunula 7 lunette
  delicate: 7 tracery
  dress: 4 frog, lace 5 braid, jabot 6 bar-pin, sequin, zequin 7 spangle 8 chequeen, zecchino 10 embroidery
  flower-like: 6 anadem 7 rosette
  hanging: 6 bangle, fringe, tassel 7 pendant
  magical: 6 amulet
  mantel: 7 bibelot
  neck: 4 ruff 5 chain 6 choker, gorget 8 necklace
  pagoda: tee
  protuberant: 4 boss
  scroll-like: 6 volute
  shoulder: 7 epaulet, lanyard
  silver: 6 tinsel
  spiral: 5 helix 7 helices (pl.)
  tufted: 6 pompon, tassel 7 rosette

ornamental: 5 fancy 6 chichi, frilly 7 elegant 8 fanciful 10 decorative

ornamented: 6 figury, ornate, tawdry 9 elaborate

ornate: gay 4 fine, lush, rich 5 fancy, showy 6 florid, garish, gilded, lavish, rococo 7 aureate, baroque, flowery, opulent 8 overdone 9 elaborate, unnatural 10 flamboyant 11 overadorned

ornery: 4 mean 7 crabbed 8 contrary, stubborn 9 irritable 12 cantankerous

ornithologist: 7 Audubon, birdman 11 birdwatcher

ornithon: 6 aviary

orogeny: 8 upheaval

orotund: 4 full, loud 5 clear, showy 6 mellow, strong 7 pompous 8 resonant 9 bombastic 10 stentorian

Orozco specialty: 5 mural

orphan: 4 waif 5 Annie 7 cast-off 9 foundling 10 parentless

orpheum: 7 theater

Orpheus: *birthplace:* 6 Pieria
  father: 6 Apollo 7 Oeagrus
  instrument: 4 lyre
  mother: 8 Calliope
  wife: 8 Eurydice

---

orphrey: 4 band 6 border 10 embroidery

orpiment: 7 arsenic

orpit: 7 fretful

orris: 4 gimp, iris, lace 5 braid 7 galloon

ort: bit 5 crumb, scrap 6 morsel, refuse 7 leaving, remnant 8 fragment, leftover

orthodox: 4 good 6 proper 7 canonic, correct 8 accepted, approved, standard 9 canonical, customary 12 conservative, conventional

orthographer: 7 speller

ortolan: 4 bird, rail 7 bunting 8 bobolink, wheatear

ortstein: 7 bedrock, hardpan

oryx: 7 gazelle, gemsbok 8 antelope

os: 4 bone 5 eskar, esker, mouth 7 opening, orifice

Osaka Bay port: 4 Kobe

Oscar: See **Academy Award**

oscillate: bob, wag 4 rock, roll, sway, vary 5 swing, waver, weave 7 vibrate 9 fluctuate, vacillate

oscitant: 4 dull 6 drowsy, gaping, sleepy, stupid 7 yawning 8 careless, sluggish 9 apathetic

osculate: 4 buss, kiss

osier: rod 4 wand 5 skein 6 basket, sallow, willow 7 dogwood, wilgers

Osiris: *brother:* Set **4** Seth
   father: Geb, Keb, Seb
   mother: Nut
   sister: **4** Isis
   son: **5** Horus **6** Anubis
   wife: **4** Isis

Osmanli: **4** Turk

osmesis: **8** smelling **9** olfaction

osmosis: **9** diffusion **10** absorption **12** assimilation

osprey: **4** hawk **8** fish hawk **9** ossifrage

osseous: **4** bony **6** osteal, spring

ossicle: **4** bone **5** incus **6** stapes **7** bonelet, malleus

ossify: set **6** harden

ossuary: urn **4** tomb **5** vault **9** mausoleum **10** depository, receptacle

ostend: **4** show **6** reveal **7** exhibit **8** manifest **11** demonstrate

ostensible: **7** alleged, feigned, seeming **8** apparent, declared, specious **9** pretended, professed

ostensorium: pix, pyx **10** monstrance

ostentation: **4** airs, pomp, show **5** eclat, flare **6** parade **7** display, flutter, pageant, portent, presage **8** flourish, pretense **9** showiness, spectacle **10** exhibition **11** fanfaronade

ostentatious: **4** arty, loud **5** gaudy, showy **6** flashy, sporty **7** blatant, obvious, pompous, splashy **8** fastuous **9** elaborate, flaunting **10** flamboyant **11** pretentious

osteoma: **5** tumor

osteria: inn **6** tavern **10** restaurant

ostiole: **4** pore **5** stoma **7** opening, orifice **8** aperture

ostracize: bar, cut **4** snub **5** exile **6** banish, reject **7** exclude **9** blackball, proscribe **10** expatriate

ostracon: **5** shell **8** fragment, potsherd

ostrich: **4** rhea **5** nandu
   extinct: moa

ostrichlike bird: emu **4** emeu

otalgia: **7** earache

otary: **4** seal

Othello: **4** Moor
   author: **11** Shakespeare
   friend: **4** Iago
   wife: **9** Desdemona

other: **4** else, more, otro (Sp.) **5** autre (F.), ither (Sc.) **6** former, second **7** further **8** distinct **9** different, remaining **10** additional

otherness: **8** alterity **9** diversity

others: **4** rest
   and: **4** et al **6** et alii

otherwise: **4** else **5** alias **6** aliter **11** differently

other-worldly: fey **9** imaginary, spiritual **12** supernatural, transmundane

otic: **5** aural **8** auditory **9** auricular

otiose: **4** idle, lazy, vain **6** futile, otiant **7** sterile, surplus, useless **8** inactive, indolent, reposing **10** unemployed **11** ineffective

otologist: **6** aurist

ottavino: **7** piccolo

otter: fur **4** fish **6** tackle, weasel **7** annatto **8** paravane
   genus: **5** aonyx, lutra
   sea: **5** kalan

ottoman: **4** pouf, seat **5** couch, divan, stool **6** fabric **9** footstool

Ottoman: **4** Turk **5** Osman
   court: **5** porte
   governor: **5** pasha
   imperial standard: **4** alem
   leader of: **5** Osman **7** Ataturk **8** Suleiman
   religious judge: **5** mufti
   ruler: **6** sultan
   soldier: **9** janissary

ouakari: **6** monkey

oubliette: **4** jail **6** prison **7** dungeon

ouch: **5** adorn, bezel, clasp **6** brooch, fibula **7** fibulae (pl.) **8** ornament **11** exclamation

ought: **4** bood, must, want, zero **6** cipher, naught, nought, should **7** behoove **9** obigation

ouija board part: **10** planchette

ounce: ure **6** weight **7** measure
   sixteenth of: **4** dram

ouph, ouphe: elf **6** goblin

our: wir (Sc.) **5** notre (F.), unser (G.) **6** nostra (It.) **7** nuestro (Sp.), pronoun **10** possessive

ousia: **6** entity, nature **7** essence **9** substance

oust: bar **5** eject, evict, expel **6** banish, remove **7** deprive, dismiss **9** forejudge **10** dispossess

out: **4** away, exit **5** forth, wrong **6** absent, begone, expose, issued, public, reveal **8** external, in the red, on strike, revealed **9** published **10** extinguish, make public
   at elbows: **4** poor **5** seedy
   of control: **4** amok, wild **7** chaotic
   of date: old **5** passe **10** antiquated
   of kilter: **4** alop, awry **6** broken
   of line: **4** awry **5** askew, fresh, wrong **8** improper
   of order: **5** amiss, kaput **6** faulty **9** deficient
   of place: **5** inept **13** inappropriate
   of sight: **5** great **6** hidden **7** extreme
   of sorts: **5** cross **7** peevish **9** irritable
   of the ordinary: odd **5** novel **6** unique **7** strange, unusual **8** peculiar, uncommon **9** different
   of the way: **5** aside **6** afield, remote **10** farfetched
   of this world: **4** fine **6** superb
   on a limb: **6** in a fix **7** stumped, up a tree

outage: **4** vent **6** outlet **7** failure **8** blackout **10** suspension

out-and-out: **5** sheer, utter **6** arrant, wholly **8** absolute, complete

outback: 4 bush 7 country 10 wilderness, boon docks

outbreak: fit 4 riot 5 burst 6 bust-up, emeute (F.), revolt, ruckus, tumult 7 boutade, ruction 8 eruption, uprising
widespread: 8 epidemic
worldwide: 8 pandemic

outbreeding: 7 exogamy

outbuilding: 4 barn, shed, shop, silo 5 privy 6 barton, garage, hemmel 8 henhouse, outhouse 9 backhouse

outburst: 4 fume, gale, gust, rage, tiff 5 blast, brunt, flare 6 blow-up, blower, tirade 7 tantrum, torrent 8 eruption 9 explosion 10 ebullition

outcast: 5 exile, leper, ronin 6 outlet, pariah 7 refugee 8 banished, castaway, derelict, rejected, vagabond 10 expatriate 11 untouchable

outclass: 4 best 5 excel 6 outwit 7 surpass

outcome: 4 fate 5 issue 6 effect, exitus, pay-off, result, sequel, upshot 9 aftermath 10 conclusion, denouement 11 consequence

outcrop: 5 ledge 10 break forth

outcry: hue, yip 4 bawl, bray, yell 5 alarm, noise, shout 6 clamor, hubbub, racket, shriek 7 protest, screech, shilloo 9 objection 11 lamentation

outdate: 7 outmode 8 obsolete 9 antiquate

outdistance: 7 surpass 11 leave behind, pull ahead of

outdo: cap, cow, top, win 4 beat 5 excel 6 defeat, exceed 7 nonplus, surpass 8 overcome

outdoors: 8 al fresco 9 in the open

outer: 5 alien, ectad, ectal 6 remote 7 farther, foreign 8 exterior, external 10 extraneous

outermost: 4 last 5 final, utter 6 utmost 7 extreme 8 farthest, remotest

outface: 4 defy 6 resist, subdue 8 overcome 9 stare down

outfit: kit, rig 4 gang, gear, suit, team, unit 5 dress, equip 6 attire 7 clothes, costume, furnish 8 equipage 9 equipment, furniture, grubstake 10 enterprise 12 organization

outflow: 4 flux 6 efflux, run-off 8 drainage

outgoing: 4 warm 6 genial 7 exiting, leaving 8 friendly, sociable 9 departing

outgrowth: 4 node 5 issue, shoot 6 result, sequel, sprout 8 offshoot 9 emergence 11 excrescence

outhouse: 4 shed 5 privy 6 toilet 7 latrine

outing: 4 stay, trip 6 junket, picnic 7 holiday 8 vacation 9 excursion

outlandish: 5 alien, queer, weird 6 exotic, remote 7 bizarre, foreign, strange, uncouth 8 peculiar 9 barbarous, fantastic, grotesque, tasteless 10 unorthodox

outlaw: ban 5 exile 6 bandit, banish, forbid 8 criminal, fugitive, prohibit, renegade 9 desperado, proscribe 10 disqualify

outlawed: 7 illegal, illicit

outlay: 4 cost 5 spend 7 expense 11 expenditure

outlet: 4 exit, vent 5 store 6 egress, escape, exitus, market 7 opening, release 8 aperture

outline: map 4 form, plan 5 brief, chart, draft, frame, shape, trace 6 border, design, figure, sketch 7 contour, profile, summary 8 describe, skeleton, synopsis 9 delineate, perimeter 10 compendium

outlive: 7 survive

outlook: 4 view 5 vista 6 aspect 7 purview 8 attitude, frontage, prospect 9 viewpoint 10 perception 11 expectation
medical: 9 prognosis

outlying district: 5 exurb 6 suburb 7 purlieu 8 environs 9 boondocks

outmoded: 5 dated, passe 6 demode 7 antique 8 obsolete, outdated

outpost: 4 fort 7 station, bastion 8 frontier 10 settlement 11 advance base

outpouring: 4 gale, gush 5 flood 6 stream 9 fusillade

output: 5 power, yield 6 energy 7 harvest 10 production

outrage: 4 evil, rape 5 abuse 6 insult, offend, ravish 7 affront, offense, violate

outrageous: 4 base, vile 5 gross 6 brutal, far-out 7 heinous, obscene, ungodly 8 flagrant, shocking 9 atrocious, desperate, execrable, fantastic, monstrous 10 exorbitant

outre: odd 5 weird 7 bizarre, strange 9 eccentric 11 exaggerated

outreach: 6 exceed, extend 7 project, surpass 8 protrude

outright: 5 total, utter, whole 6 direct, openly, wholly 8 complete, entirely 9 forthwith, instantly 10 thoroughly

outrival: 5 excel 7 eclipse

outroot: 6 pull up 7 extract 9 eradicate, extirpate

outrun: 4 beat 6 exceed 7 ski area 10 escape from

outset: 5 first, start 9 beginning

outside: 5 faint 6 facade, remote, slight 7 surface 8 al fresco, exterior, external 9 apart from 10 unfamiliar

outsider: 5 alien, loner 8 stranger 9 foreigner

outspoken: 4 bold, free 5 bluff, blunt, broad, frank 6 candid, direct 7 artless 8 explicit 10 unreserved

outstanding: big 4 arch, rare 5 famed, noted 6 famous, heroic, marked, unpaid 7 eminent 9 principal, prominent, unsettled 10 noticeable, pre-eminent, projecting 11 conspicuous, exceptional, uncollected, unfulfilled

outstretched: 5 stent (Sc.) 8 extended

outstrip: cap, top, win 4 best, lead, pass 5 excel 6 exceed 7 surpass 8 distance 9 transcend

outward: 5 ectad, overt 6 exodic, formal 7 extreme, visible 8 apparent, exterior, external 9 extrinsic 10 ostensible 11 superficial

outweighing: 8 dominant 12 preponderant

outwit: fox 4 balk, best, foil 5 block, check, cross 6 baffle, defeat, jockey, thwart 9 checkmate, frustrate 10 circumvent, disappoint

ouzel: 4 piet 5 colly 6 thrush 8 whistler 9 blackbird

ouzo: 7 cordial

oval: 7 ellipse, stadium 8 avelonge 10 elliptical 11 ellipsoidal

ovate: 9 egg-shaped

ovation: 4 hand 7 acclaim, tribute 8 applause

oven: 4 kiln, oast 5 baker, range, stove 6 calcar 7 furnace
annealing glass: 4 leer, lehr

over: oer, sur (F.), too 4 also, anew, done, uber (G.), upon 5 above, again, clear, ended, extra, vault 6 across, beyond, excess, on high 7 surplus, through 8 finished 9 completed, excessive 10 terminated 11 consummated, superfluous

overabundance: 4 glut 6 excess 7 surfeit, surplus 8 plethora

overact: mug 5 emote 7 ham it up 9 burlesque 10 exaggerate

overage: 6 excess 7 surplus

overall: 6 mostly 9 generally 10 throughout 13 comprehensive

overbalance: 8 dominate, outweigh

overbearing: 5 proud 6 lordly 7 haughty 8 arrogant, bullying, insolent, snobbish, subduing 9 imperious 10 disdainful, highhanded 11 dictatorial, domineering, magisterial 12 overpowering, supercilious

overburden: 7 oppress 8 encumber, overload 9 surcharge

overcast: dim, sew 4 bind, dark, dull, gray 5 cloud, heavy 6 cloudy, darken, gloomy, lowery 7 accloud, becloud, clouded, obscure

overcharge: gyp, pad 6 excise, fleece 9 extortion

overcoat: 5 benny 6 capote, slipon (Sc.), ulster 7 topcoat 9 balmacaan, greatcoat, macintosh 12 chesterfield
close fitting: 7 surtout
loose: 6 raglan 7 paletot
sleeveless: 9 inverness

overcome: awe, get, win 4 beat, best, lick 5 charm, crush, daunt, fordo 6 appall, beaten, craven, defeat, exceed, foredo, master 7 confute, conquer 8 convince, encumber, outstrip, overbear, overturn,

suppress, surmount, vanquish 9 overpower, overthrow, overwhelm, prostrate

overcrowded: 6 jammed 9 congested

overdo: 6 exceed 7 exhaust, fatigue 8 go too far, overcook, overwork 9 burlesque 10 caricature, exaggerate

overdue: 4 late 5 tardy 6 behind 7 arrears, belated, delayed 8 expected 10 unpunctual

overeager: 8 feverish

overeat: 5 gorge, stuff 7 satiate 8 gourmand 10 gluttonize

overflow: 4 slop, swim, teem, vent 5 float, flood, spate, spill 6 abound, debord, deluge, excess, outlet 7 overrun, surplus 8 alluvion, inundate 9 abundance, cataclysm, ebullient, exuberant

overflowing: 5 awash 7 copious, profuse, teeming

overgrown: 4 lush, rank 6 jungly 7 fulsome

overhang: jut 5 eaves, jetty 6 beetle 7 project, suspend 8 threaten

overhasty: 4 rash 6 daring 8 headlong 11 precipitate

overhaul: 6 repair 7 examine, restore 8 renovate 9 forereach

overhead: 4 cost 5 above, aloft 7 expense

overjoyed: 6 elated 8 jubilant 9 delighted

overkill: 9 excessive

overlapping: 5 cover 8 obvolute 9 imbricate

overlay: cap, lap 4 ceil, coat 5 couch, cover, glaze, plate 6 cravat, spread, veneer 7 encrust, oppress, overlie 8 covering 10 overburden 11 superimpose

overload: 4 glut 6 burden, charge 8 encumber

overlook: 4 balk, miss, omit, skip 5 forgo 6 acquit, excuse, forego, forget, ignore, manage, survey 7 absolve, condone, inspect, neglect 9 disregard, supervise

overlord: 5 liege, ruler 6 despot, satrap, tyrant 8 suzerain

overlying: 8 brochant, superior 9 incumbent

overmatch: 4 best 6 defeat, exceed 7 surpass 8 vanquish

overmodest: 4 prim 7 prudish

overmuch: too 6 excess 7 surplus 9 excessive

overnice: 5 fussy 7 precise 8 dentical, fawning, precious 10 fastidious

overpower: awe 4 rout 5 crush, whelm 6 compel, defeat, deluge, master, subdue 7 conquer 8 convince, entrance, overbear, overcome, vanquish 9 enrapture, overthrow, overwhelm

overpowering: 4 dire 6 fierce 8 dazzling, stunning

overreach: do 5 cheat 6 grease, nobble, outwit 8 go too far 10 circumvent

override: 4 veto 6 defeat 7 nullify 8 vanquish

overrule: 4 veto 7 reverse 8 abrogate

overrun: 5 crush 6 infest, invade, ravage, spread 7 destroy 9 overwhelm

overseas: 5 alien 6 abroad, exotic 7 foreign, strange 8 outre mer (F.) 11 ultramarine

oversee: 5 watch 6 manage, survey 7 examine, inspect 9 supervise 11 superintend

overseer: 4 boss 5 chief, ephor(Gk.), grave, reeve 6 bishop, censor, driver, gaffer, grieve 7 bailiff, caporal, curator, foreman, manager 8 banksman, martinet 9 inspector 10 supervisor
spiritual: 6 pastor, priest

overshadow: dim 5 cover, dwarf 6 darken 7 eclipse, obscure 8 dominate 9 adumbrate

overshoe: gum 4 boot 6 arctic, galosh, golosh, patten, rubber 7 flapper

overshoot: 6 exceed 8 go beyond

oversight: 4 care 5 error, lapse, watch 6 charge 7 blunder, control, custody, mistake 8 omission 9 direction 10 inspection, management, negligence 11 supervision 12 surveillance

overskirt: 6 peplum 7 pannier

overspread: 4 deck, pall 5 brede, cloud, cover 6 deluge, infest 7 blanket

overstate: 7 magnify 10 exaggerate

overstep: 6 exceed 8 trespass 10 transgress

overt: 4 open 6 patent, public 7 obvious 8 apparent, manifest

overtake: 5 catch 6 attain, detect 7 ensnare 9 apprehend, captivate

overtax: 6 burden, exceed, strain 8 overload

overthrow: tip 4 dash, down, fell, foil, fold, hurl, raze, rout, ruin, rush 5 allay, evert, fling, upset, worst, wrack 6 defeat, topple, tumble, unseat 7 afflict, conquer, destroy, dismiss, ruinate, unhorse 8 confound, demolish, overcome, overturn, reversal, supplant, vanquish 9 discomfit, overpower, overwhelm, prostrate

overtone: 4 hint 7 meaning 9 harmonics 11 implication

overture: 5 offer, proem 7 advance, opening, prelude 8 aperture, approach, proposal

overturn: tip 4 cave, coup, tilt 5 throw, upset 6 topple 7 capsize, destroy, pervert, reverse, subvert 8 overcome 9 overthrow, overwhelm

overweening: 4 rash, vain 8 arrogant, insolent 9 confident, excessive

overwhelm: 4 bury, whip 5 amaze, cover, crush, drouk, swamp 6 defeat, deluge, engulf, quench 7 confute, conquer, engross, oppress 8 astonish, inundate, overturn, submerge 9 overpower, overthrow

overword: 7 refrain

Ovid: *birthplace:* 5 Italy 7 Sulmona
burial place: 4 Tomi 5 Tomis
work: 5 Fasti 7 Tristia 8 Heroides 9 Art of

Love 13 Metamorphoses

ovine: 5 sheep 9 sheeplike
female: ewe

ovoid: 5 ovate 7 egglike 8 globular

ovule: egg 4 seed 6 embryo, gamete 7 seedlet
integument: 7 primine

ovum: egg 4 seed 5 spore

owala tree: 4 bobo

owe: due 7 possess 9 attribute

ower: 6 debtor

owl: ule 4 bubo, lulu, momo 5 wekau 7 boobook, harfang, woolert 8 billy-wix, moreport 10 gillhooter, hob-houchin
barn: 5 madge 11 monkey-faced
call: 4 hoot
genus of: 5 ninox
light: 7 evening
pert. to: 8 strigine
plumed eye area of: 4 disk
short-eared: 4 momo
small: elf 4 utum 6 howlet
young: 4 utum 5 owlet

Owl and Pussycat author: 4 Lear

own: ain (Sc.), owe 4 avow, have, hold, nain (Sc.) 5 admit 7 concede, confess, possess 9 recognize 11 acknowledge

ownership: 5 title 7 tenancy 8 dominium 11 condominium 14 proprietorship

own up: 7 confess 11 acknowledge

ox: yak 4 anoa, aver, beef, buff, gaur, musk, reem, zebu 5 bison, bugle, gayal, steer, takin, tsine 6 bovine 7 banteng, buffalo 8 seladang 9 quadruped
extinct: 4 urus
harness: 4 yoke
pert. to: 5 bovid 6 bovine 7 taurine
stall: 5 boose
wild: 4 gaur 8 seladang

oxalis: oca 5 plant 6 sorrel 10 wood sorrel

oxen: 6 cattle
yoke: 4 span

oxeye: 5 daisy

oxford: 4 shoe 5 cloth 10 saddleshoe

Oxford: 10 university
examination: 6 greats
library: 8 Bodleian
officer: 5 bedel 6 beadle
scholar: 4 demy
scholarship: 6 Rhodes 8 Marshall

oxhead: 4 dolt 9 blockhead

oxidation: 4 rust

oxide: *aluminum:* 7 alumina
barium: 6 baryta
calcium: 4 lime
hydrocarbon radical: 5 ether
iron: 4 rust
sodium: 4 soda
strontium: 8 strontia

oxidize: 4 heat, rust 7 calcine, corrode

oxlip: **8** primrose
oxtongue: **7** alkanet, bugloss
oxyacantha: **8** hawthorn
oxygen: gas
   allotropic: **5** ozone
oxygenate: **6** aerate
oyez: **4** hear **6** attend **9** attention
oyster: **5** porte **6** huitre **7** bivalve, mollusk
   bed: **4** park, stew **5** clair, group, layer
   eggs: **5** spawn
   fossil: **9** ostracite
   gatherer: **7** tongman
   genus: **6** ostrea
   phylum: **8** mollusca

   product: **5** pearl
   rake: **5** tongs
   shell: **4** husk, test **5** shuck, valve
   spawn: **5** culch **6** cultch
   tree: **8** mangrove
   young: **4** seed, spat **7** veliger
oyster catcher: **4** bird **5** tirma
oysterfish: **6** tautog **8** toadfish
oyster grass: **4** kelp **10** sea lettuce
oyster plant: **7** salsify
Ozark State: **8** Missouri
Oz books author: **4** Baum
ozone: air, gas **4** hole **5** layer **6** oxygen

P

pa, pah: dad, paw **4** fort, papa **5** daddy **6** father **7** village **8** stockade **10** settlement

pablum, pabulum: **4** food **6** cereal **7** aliment, support **9** nutriment **10** sustenance **11** nourishment

pac, pack: **4** boot **8** moccasin

paca: **4** cavy, lava **5** agout, labba **6** rodent

pace: way **4** clip, gait, lope, pass, rack, rate, step, trot, walk **5** amble, canto, speed, tempo, tread **6** canter, gallop, strait, timing **7** channel, chapter, dogtrot, measure, passage **8** platform **10** passageway

pacer: **5** horse **9** pacemaker

pachisi: **4** game, ludo **9** parcheesi

pachyderm: **6** mammal **8** elephant, ungulate **10** rhinoceros **12** hippopotamus

pacific: **4** calm, meek, mild **5** irene **6** irenic, placid, serene **7** amiable **8** peaceful, tranquil **9** appeasing, peaceable **12** conciliatory

Pacific coast state: **6** Oregon **10** California, Washington

Pacific Islands: *bird:* **4** kagu **8** whistler
cloth: **4** tapa
collective name: **7** Oceania
grass: **4** neti
tree: kou **4** ipil, taro **7** dasheen, madrona, madrono **8** eddyroot

Pacific Ocean: *archipelago:* Aru **4** Cook, Sulu **5** Colon, Malay, Samoa **6** Hawaii, Tulagi **7** Solomon **8** Kiribati **9** Galapagos
canal: **6** Panama
current: **4** Peru **5** Japan
deepest point: **13** Mariana Trench
European discoverer: **6** Balboa
island: Lae, Yap **4** Guam, Truk, Wake **5** Leyte, Samoa **6** Tahiti **8** Tasmania
island group: **7** Solomon **8** Aleutian, Caroline, Hawaiian, arquesa, Marshall **9** Galapagos **11** Philippines
named by: **8** Magellan
port: **5** Pusan **6** Manila, Sydney **7** Bangkok, Seattle **8** Hong Kong, Shanghai, Yokohama **9** Singapore **10** Los Angeles, Wellington **11** Vladivostok **12** San Francisco
"stepping stones": **9** Aleutians
volcanic zone: **10** Ring of Fire
winds: **7** typhoon **14** Roaring Forties

pacifier: sop **4** ring **6** nipple **8** sugartit **9** comforter **12** tranquilizer

pacifist: **4** dove **8** appeaser, peacenik

pacify: **4** calm, ease, lull **5** abate, allay, quiet,

still **6** serene, soften, soothe **7** appease, assuage, mollify, placate, sweeten **8** mitigate **9** alleviate, reconcile **10** conciliate, propitiate **11** tranquilize

pack: jam, wad **4** bale, cram, gang, load, stow, tamp **5** carry, crowd, flock, horde, steve, store, truss **6** barrel, bundle, duffle, embale, encase, fardel, impact, wallet **8** knapsack
back: **8** knapsack
of cards: **4** deck

package: bag, box, pad **4** bale **6** bundle, carton, packet, parcel

pack animal: ass **4** mule **5** burro, camel, horse, llama **6** donkey

packer: **5** baler, roper **6** canner

packet: **4** boat **6** bundle, parcel **7** fortune

packing: **4** rags **5** gauze, paper, straw, waste **7** stowage
box: **5** crate
clay: **4** lute
material: **6** baline, gasket **7** peanuts **9** excelsior **10** bubble wrap
water-tight: **5** oakum **6** gasket

packing plant: **7** cannery

Pacolet: **5** dwarf, horse

pact: **4** deal **6** cartel, treaty **7** bargain, compact **8** alliance, contract, covenant **9** agreement **10** settlement

Pactolian: **6** golden

pad: mat, wad, way **4** boss, foot, path, road, walk **5** quilt, stuff, tramp **6** basket, buffer, jockey, pillow, tablet, trudge **7** bolster, bombast, cushion **8** footfall **9** embroider **10** highwayman, protection

padding: **7** packing, robbery, wadding **8** stuffing

paddle: oar, row **4** spud, wade **5** aloof **6** dabble, toddle **8** lumpfish

paddock: lot **4** frog, park **5** field **6** corral, sledge **7** pasture **9** enclosure **10** saddle area

Paddy: **5** Irishman

paddywhack: **4** beat, blow **5** spank **9** thrashing

Paderewski opera: **5** Manru

padlock: **4** lock **6** fasten **7** closing, shackle **8** fastener

padre: **4** monk **6** cleric, father, priest **8** chaplain

padrona: **8** landlady, mistress

padrone: **4** boss **5** chief **6** master, padron,

patron **8** landlord **9** innkeeper

paean, pean: ode **4** hymn, song **6** praise

pagan: 6 ethnic, paynim **7** heathen, infidel **8** idolator **10** idolatrous, unbeliever **11** nonbeliever

god: **4** Baal, idol

page: boy **4** call, leaf **5** child, folio, sheet **6** donzel, summon, varlet **7** footboy, servant **8** henchboy, henchman **9** attendant, messenger

beginning: **4** leaf **7** flyleaf **9** title page

book: **5** folio **6** cahier

lady: **8** escudero

left-hand: **5** verso

number: **5** folio **10** pagination

paper: **5** sheet

reverse: **5** verso

right-hand: **5** recto

title: **5** unwan **6** rubric

pageant: 4 pomp, show **5** drama **6** parade **7** tableau **8** aquacade, pretense **9** spectacle **10** exhibition, procession

pageantry: 4 pomp **7** display **8** splendor **11** ostentation

Pagliacci: *character:* **5** Nedda, Tonio

composer: **11** Leoncavallo

pagoda: taa **6** alcove, gazebo, temple **10** kryailteyo **11** summerhouse

finial or ornament: tee

pagurian: 4 crab

pah: 5 nasty **6** humbug **8** improper

paha: 4 hill **5** ridge

paideutics: 8 pedagogy

pail: can, cog (Sc.), pan, soa, soe **4** beat, bowk, gawn, meal, trug **5** bowie, cogue (Sc.), eshin, skeel **6** bucket, coggie (Sc.), harass, piggin, situla (L.), thrash, vessel **7** collock, situlae (pl.) **8** cannikin

paillette: 7 spangle **8** ornament

pain: try, woe **4** ache, agra, care, cark, gall, harm, hurt, pang **5** agony, cramp, grief, sting, thraw (Sc.), throe, upset, wound **6** aching, bother, grieve, injury, misery, pierce, sorrow, suffer, twinge **7** afflict, agonzie, algesis, anguish, malaise, penalty, scourge, torment, torture, travail, trouble **8** disquiet, distress **9** suffering **10** affliction, algophilia, discomfort, punishment

abdominal: **5** colic

back: **7** lumbago **8** sciatica

dull: **4** ache

pert. to: **6** asonal **7** algetic

relayer: **5** nerve

sensitiveness to: **7** algesia

painful: raw **4** sore **5** angry **6** bitter **7** algetic, hurting, irksome **8** exacting **9** difficult, laborious

painkiller: 4 drug **6** opiate **7** anodyne, aspirin **8** morphine, reliever **9** analgesic, paregoric

pains: 4 care, work **5** labor **6** effort **7** trouble **8** exertion

painstaking: 5 exact, fussy **6** loving **7** careful **8** diligent, exacting **9** assiduous, elaborate, laborious **10** meticulous, scrupulous

paint: 4 coat, daub, gaud, limn **5** color, feign, fucus, rouge, stain **6** bedaub, depict, enamel, makeup **7** besmear, portray, pretend **8** decorate, disguise

dull: **5** matte

glossy: **6** enamel

painted: 5 pinto **6** fucate **10** artificial, variegated

painter: 6 artist **7** artiste, workman **9** decorator

painting: oil **5** mural **6** canvas **7** acrylic, picture **10** watercolor

equipment: **5** brush, easel, paint **6** canvas, pallet **7** palette

medium: oil **5** alkyd, vinyl **7** acrylic, gouache, tempera **10** watercolor

of objects: **9** still life

one-color: **8** monotint **10** monochrome

plaster: **5** secco **6** fresco

sacred: **5** pieta **7** madonna

scenic: **5** scape **8** seascape **9** cityscape, landscape

small: **9** miniature

studio: **7** atelier

three panels: **8** triptych

wall: **5** mural, panel, secco **6** fresco

pair: duo, two **4** case, diad, duad, dyad, mate, span, team, yoke **5** brace, match, twain, unite **6** couple

paisano: pal **7** comrade, peasant **8** landsman **10** compatriot, countryman

Paisley: 5 shawl **6** design, fabric **7** pattern

Pakistan: 9 South Asia

capital: **9** Islamabad

city: Dir **6** Lahore, Multan, Quetta **7** Karachi **9** Hyderabad **10** Rawalpindi

clothing: **5** burqa, lungi **7** dupatta **12** shalwar-qamiz

currency: **5** paisa, rupee

language: **4** Urdu **6** Sindhi **7** Bengali, Punjabi

mountain pass: **6** Khyber

mountain peak: **9** Tirich Mir

mountain range: **8** Himalaya **9** Karakoram

people: **6** Pathan, Sindhi **7** Baluchi, Bengali, Muhajir, Punjabi

plain: **4** Sind **6** Punjab

river: **4** Swat **5** Indus **6** Chenab, Kundar

valley: **5** Indus

weight: **4** seer, tola **5** maund

pal: 4 ally, chum, pard 5 buddy, crony 6 cobber, cohort, digger, friend 7 comrade, partner 9 associate, companion 10 accomplice 11 confederate

palace: 5 court, serai 6 castle, palais (F.) 7 alcazar, chateau, edifice, mansion, palazzo 8 Alcalzar 9 luxurious, pretorium 10 praetorium
officer: 7 paladin 8 palatine
papal: 7 Lateran, Vatican

paladin: 4 hero, peer 6 knight 8 champion, douzeper 11 protagonist

palaestra: 6 school 9 gymnasium

palamate: 9 web-footed

Palamedes: *enemy:* 7 Ulysses
father: 8 Nauplius
mother: 7 Clymene
war: 6 Trojan

Palamon: *rival:* 6 Arcite
wife: 6 Emelye

palanquin, palankeen: 4 kago 5 chair, dooli, dooly, palki, sedan 6 doolee, dooley, doolie, litter, palkee 9 stretcher 10 conveyance

palatable: 5 sapid, tasty 6 savory 8 delicate, pleasing 9 agreeable, delicious, toothsome 10 acceptable, appetizing

palatal: 5 front, velar 8 gutteral 9 consonant

palate: 5 taste 6 relish 7 gourmet 8 appetite
hard: 11 roof of mouth
pert. to: 6 uranic
soft: 4 cion, vela (pl.) 5 uvula, velum

palatial: 5 large, regal 6 ornate 7 stately 9 luxurious 11 magnificent

palaver: gab 4 chat, talk 6 confer, debate, glaver, parley, speech 7 chatter, flatter, wheedle 8 business, cajolery, flattery 10 conference 11 terminology 12 conversation

pale: dim, wan 4 ashy, fade, grey, gull, lily, pall, sick 5 ashen, blake, blate, bleak, faint, fence, livid, lurid, stake, stick, white 6 anemic, blanch, chalky, feeble, pallid, pastel, picket, region, sallow, sickly, whiten 7 anaemic, enclose, ghastly, haggard, insipid, obscure, whitish 8 encircle, etiolate 9 colorless 10 pasty-faced

paleness: 6 pallor

Palestine (see also **Israel, Philistine**): 5 Judea 7 Samaria 8 Holy Land
early name: 6 Canaan
early people: 11 Philistines
group: PLO 7 Al Fatah 8 Fedayeen
land: 6 Israel, Jordan 8 West Bank 9 Gaza Strip

paletot: 8 overcoat 9 greatcoat

palfrey: 5 horse

palimpsest: 6 tablet 9 parchment

palindrome: 5 verse 7 sotadic

paling: 4 pale 5 fence, flake, limit, stake 6 picket 7 fencing 9 enclosure

palinode: 6 abjure 8 take back 10 retraction 11 recantation

Palinurus: 9 steersman

palisade: 5 cliff, fence, stake 6 picket 7 barrier, enclose, fortify, furnish 8 espalier, stockade, surround 9 enclosure, implement

pall: 4 bore, cloy, glut, pale, sate 5 cloak, cloth, faint, stale, weary 6 casket, coffin, mantle, pairle, shadow, shroud 7 disgust, garment, pallium, satiate, surfeit 8 animetta, corporal, covering 10 melancholy, oppression 11 counterpane

pallet: bed, cot, pad 5 couch, quilt 7 blanket 8 mattress, plancher 9 headpiece

palliasse: 6 pallet 8 mattress

palliate: 4 ease, hide 5 cloak, cover, gloss, gloze 6 lessen, soften 7 conceal, shelter 8 disguise, mitigate 9 alleviate, exculpate, extenuate, gloss over, sugarcoat, whitewash

pallid: wan 4 ashy, dull, pale, paly 5 ashen, bleak, white 7 ghastly 9 colorless

pallion: bit 5 piece 6 pellet

pallium: 4 band, pall 5 cloak 6 mantle 8 himation, vestment

Pall Mall site: 6 London 7 West End

palm: 4 hide, tree 5 shrub 6 palmus (L.), thenar, trophy 7 conceal
betel nut: 5 areca, bonga
beverage: 5 assai
cabbage: 8 palmetto
climbing: 6 rattan
coconut: 4 coco
fan-leafed: 7 talipat, talipot, taliput 8 palmetto
feather: 5 howea 6 gomuti 7 urucuri, urucury
fiber: tal 4 buri 6 raffia
food: nut 4 sago 5 fruit
juice: 4 nipa, sura 5 taree, toddy
kind: ti 4 jara 5 assai, royal, tucum 6 bacaba, tucuma 7 babassu, jaggery, tokopat 8 bangalow
leaf: ola, ole 4 olay, olla 5 frond
low: 5 bussu 6 trooly, trouie, ubussu
palmyra: ola, ole, tal 4 brab, olla 6 ronier
pert. to: 6 palmar 8 frondous 10 palmaceous
pith: 4 sago
reader: 7 palmist
sap: 5 toddy
seeds: 4 nipa
spiny: 6 grigri, grugru
starch: 4 sago
stem: 4 cane 5 ratan 6 rattan
stemless: 5 curua
thatch: 4 nipa 9 barriguda
wax: 8 carnauba
wing-leaved: 6 cohune

palma: 5 fiber, yucca

palmary: 5 chief, palmy 6 palmar 8 superior 9 principal 10 pre-eminent, victorious

palmate: 4 flat 5 broad, lobed 6 palmed, webbed 10 hand-shaped

palmer: 4 monk 5 louse 6 stroll, travel, votary 7 pilgrim 8 wanderer 15 prestidigitator

Palmetto State: 13 South Carolina

palmistry: 10 chirognomy, chiromancy
practicer: 7 palmist 11 chiromancer

palm-leaf mat: 4 yapa

palmodic: 5 jerky

palm off: 5 foist

palms down: 7 pronate

palmy: 10 prosperous, triumphant 11 flourishing

Palmyra's queen: 7 Zenobia

palmyra tree: 4 brab, palm 7 talipot

palooka: oaf 4 fool

palp: 6 feeler 7 antenna, flatter 8 tentacle

palpable: 4 rank 5 plain 6 patent 7 audible, evident, obvious, tactile 8 apparent, distinct, manifest, tangible 10 noticeable 11 perceptible 12 recognizable

palpebra: 6 eyelid

palpebrate: 4 wink

palpitation: 4 beat, pant 7 flicker, flutter 9 pulsation, quivering, throbbing, trembling

palsied: 5 shaky 7 shaking 9 paralyzed, tottering, trembling

palsy-walsy: 8 friendly, intimate

palter: fib, lie 5 trick 6 babble, haggle, mumble, trifle 7 chatter, deceive, quibble 10 equivocate 11 prevaricate

paltock: 5 tunic 6 jacket 7 doublet

paltry: 4 bald, bare, base, mean, poor, puny, vile 5 cheap, footy, petty, trash 6 chetif, flimsy, measly, trashy 7 low-down, pitiful, rubbish, trivial 8 picayune, trifling 9 worthless 10 despicable 11 unimportant 12 contemptible 13 insignificant

paludal: 6 marshy

pampas: 6 plains
cat: 6 kodkod, pajero

pamper: pet 4 baby, cram, delt (Sc.), glut 5 humor, spoil 6 caress, cocker, coddle, cosher, cosset, cuddle, dandle, fondle, posset 7 cherish, cockney, forwean, gratify, indulge, satiate

pamphagous: 10 omnivorous

pamphlet: 5 flyer, tract 6 folder 7 booklet, catalog, leaflet 8 brochure 9 catalogue

pan (see also **pot**): ape, rap, tab 4 face, part, wash 5 basin 6 frache (F.), lappet, vessel 7 portion, subsoil, utensil 8 ridicule 9 container, criticize 10 acetabulum, receptacle
coal burner: 5 grill 7 brazier
frying: 6 spider 7 skillet
gold-washing: 4 tina 5 batea

Pan: 6 Faunus
father: 6 Hermes
instrument: 4 pipe, reed 6 syrinx 7 panpipe
place of worship: 7 Arcadia
son: 7 Silenus 8 Seilenos

panacea: 4 cure 6 elixir, remedy 7 allheal, cure-all, heal-all, nostrum 8 nepenthe 10 catholicon 11 panchreston

panache: 5 flare, plume, style, verve

panachure: 8 mottling

Panama: hat 7 isthmus
capital: 6 Panama
city: 5 Colon, David 8 Santiago 9 Aspinwall, Cristobal
clothing: 7 montuna, montuno, pollera 9 camisilla
currency: 6 balboa 9 centesimo
explorer: 6 Balboa
food: 6 guacho
Indian: 4 Cuna 5 Choco 6 Guaymi
language: 7 Spanish
measure: 7 celemin

Panama Canal: *cut:* 7 Culebra 8 Gaillard
dam and locks: 5 Gatun 10 Miraflores 11 Pedro Miguel
engineer: 9 de Lesseps
lake: 5 Gatun
nickname: 8 Big Ditch

panatela: 5 cigar

panax: 4 herb 7 ginseng

pancake: 5 arepa (Sp.), flawn 6 blintz, fraise, froise 7 blintze, fritter, hotcake 8 flapjack 11 griddlecake
delicate: 5 crepe

panda: wah 6 animal 7 bearcat

pandemonium: din 4 hell, riot, sink 5 chaos, noise 6 hubbub, racket, tumult, uproar 8 disorder 9 confusion

pander: 4 bawd, pimp 5 cater 7 whiskin 8 procurer 9 go-between, procuress

Pandora: *brother:* 10 Prometheus
daughter: 6 Pyrrha
husband: 10 Epimetheus

pandurina: 4 lute

pane: 5 glass 7 section

panegyric: 5 eloge, elogy 6 eulogy, praise 7 acclaim, encomia (pl.), oration, tribute, writing 8 encomium 9 discourse, laudation

panel: 4 jury 5 board, group 6 tympan 8 decorate

paneling: 4 wall 7 ceiling 8 covering

panfish: 4 crab, king 5 perch 7 sunfish 9 horseshoe

pan fry: 5 saute

pang: 4 ache, gird, pain, stab, tang 5 agony, cramp, spasm, throe 6 twinge, twitch, wrench 7 anguish, travail 8 paroxysm 9 heartache

Pangim native: 4 Goan

pangolin: 5 manis 8 anteater, edentate

order: **9** pholidota
panhandle: beg **5** cadge
Panhandle State: **12** West Virginia
panic: **4** fear, fray, funk, wild **5** alarm, chaos, crash, scare **6** frenzy, fright, terror **8** stampede **13** consternation
panjandrum: **7** magnate **8** official **9** personage
pannier, panier: bag, ped **5** seron **6** basket, dorsel, dorser, dosser, pantry **9** overskirt
panoply: **4** pomp **5** armor, array **6** armour **7** display
panorama: **4** view **5** range, scene, sweep, vista **7** picture, scenery **9** cyclorama
pan out: **7** succeed
panpipe: **6** syrinx **8** zampogna **10** mouth organ
pansy: **6** violet **9** heartease **10** heartsease
pant: **4** ache, beat, blow, gasp, puff, want, wish **5** crave, heave, throb, yearn **6** aspire, desire **7** breathe, pulsate **9** palpitate **11** palpitation
Pantagruel: **5** giant
companion: **7** Panurge
father: **9** Gargantua
mother: **7** Badebec
Panthea's husband: **9** Abradatus
pantheon: **4** gods **6** temple **7** deities
panther: cat **4** pard, puma **6** cougar, jaguar **7** leopard, painter
pantile: **7** biscuit **8** hardtack
pantomimist: **4** mime, Tati **5** actor **7** Marceau
pantry: **4** cave **5** ambry **6** closet, larder **7** buttery, pannier, pantler **8** cupboard **9** storeroom
pants: **5** jeans, Levis **6** slacks **7** drawers **8** britches, knickers, trousers **9** plus fours
leather: **5** chaps **10** chaparajos, chapareras, chaperejos, lederhosen (G.) **11** chaparreras
pantywaist: **8** weakling **13** characterless
panuelo: **6** collar, ruffle **8** kerchief **9** neckcloth
pap: **4** teat **5** trash **6** drivel, nipple **7** garbage, rubbish, twaddle **8** emulsion, mammilla
papa: dad, paw, pop **4** pope **6** baboon, father, potato, priest **7** vulture
papal (see also **pope**): **9** apostolic **10** pontifical
papal court: **5** curia
papaya: **5** melon, papaw **6** pawpaw
enzyme: **6** papain **10** tenderizer
genus: **6** Carica
paper (see also **parchment**): **5** cover, essay, theme, tract **6** cartel, report **7** journal, writing **8** document, treatise **9** monograph, newspaper, wallpaper **10** periodical, stationery **11** credentials
absorbent: **7** blotter **9** toweling
ancient: **7** papyrus **9** parchment
case: **4** file **5** folio **6** binder

collection: **4** file **7** archive, dossier
currency: **4** bill **5** scrip
damaged: **5** broke, casse, salle **6** cassie
design: **9** watermark
detachable: tab **4** stub **6** coupon
fine: **5** linen **6** vellum
folded once: **5** folio
gummed: **5** label, stamp **6** paster **7** sticker
hard: **6** pelure
kind: rag **4** bond **5** crepe, Kraft, sized **6** copier, lining **8** wrapping **9** cardboard, newsprint **12** Bristol board
large-size: **5** atlas
legal: **4** writ
medicinal: **6** charta
official: **5** targe **8** document
pad: **5** block **6** tablet
piece: **5** scrap, scrip, sheet
postage-stamp: **6** pelure
pulp: **4** ulla **9** waterleaf
quantity: **4** page, ream **5** quire, sheet **6** bundle
scroll: **9** parchment
size: cap **4** copy, demi, demy, pott **5** atlas, crown, folio, legal **7** bastard, emperor **8** foolscap, imperial **9** colombier
thin: **6** flimsy, pelure, tissue **9** onionskin
untrimmed edge: **6** deckle
writing-size: cap **8** foolscap
paper money: **4** bill, cash **7** lettuce **8** frogskin **9** greenback
papier-mache: **7** collage
papilla: bud **6** pimple
papist: **8** Catholic
papoose: **4** baby
pappy: dad, paw **4** papa, soft **5** mushy **6** father, spongy **7** squishy **8** yielding **9** succulent
Papua New Guinea: *capital:* **11** Port Moresby
city: Lae **4** Daru **5** Wewak **6** Rabaul
currency: **4** kina, toea
island: **4** Buka **8** Woodlark **12** Bougainville
papule: **6** pimple
papyrus: **4** reed **5** sedge **6** biblos, biblus, scroll **7** bulrush **9** parchment
respository: **5** capsa
par: by **5** equal **6** normal **7** average **8** equality, standard **9** enclosure **11** equivalence
1 stroke over: **5** bogey
1 stroke under: **6** birdie
2 strokes under: **5** eagle
parable: **4** myth, tale **5** fable, story **6** apolog, byword **7** byspell **8** allegory, apologue, forbysen **10** comparison, similitude
parabola: arc **5** curve **7** antenna
parachute: *material:* **4** silk **5** nylon
part: **4** pack **5** riser **6** canopy **7** harness, ripcord

soldier: **11** paratrooper

paraclete: 5 aider **6** helper **7** pleader **8** advocate, consoler **9** comforter, supporter **11** intercessor

parade: 4 pomp, show, walk **5** march, strut **6** flaunt, review, stroll **7** cortege, display, exhibit, marshal **8** ceremony, flourish, grandeur, splendor **9** advertise, pageantry, promenade, strollers **10** callithump, exhibition, pretension, procession **12** magnificence

paradigm: 5 ideal, model **7** example, pattern

Paradise: 4 Eden **5** bliss **6** Aidenn, Avalon, heaven, Utopia **7** Elysium, Nirvana **9** Shangri-la **12** promised land
Buddhist: **4** Jodo
fool's: **5** limbo
Muslim: **5** Jenna
river: **5** Gihon

Paradise Lost angel: 5 Ariel, Uriel

paraffin: 6 alkane **8** kerosene

paragon: gem **4** type **5** ideal, jewel, model **7** pattern **8** last word **9** nonpariel **10** perfection

paragram: pun

paragraph: 4 item, note, sign **5** caput **8** material

Paraguay: *capital:* **8** Asuncion
city: Ita **9** Paraguari, Villa Rica **10** Concepcion **11** Encarnacion
clothing: **6** rebozo **9** bombachas
currency: **7** centimo, guarani
food: **5** chipa **7** puchero
Indian: **7** Guarani
lace: **7** nanduti
language: **7** Guarani, Spanish
measure: pie **4** line, lino, vara **5** legua, linea **6** cordel, cuadra, cuarta, fanega
tea: **4** mate **9** yerba mate

parakeet: 6 budgie, parrot, wellat **8** lovebird, paraquet, paroquet, popinjay **10** budgerigas, budgerygay **11** budgereegah

parallel: 4 even, same **5** alike, along, equal, match **6** equate, line up **8** analogue **10** collateral **11** counterpart
render: **9** collimate

parallelism: 6 simile **10** similarity **11** resemblance **14** correspondence

parallelogram: 5 rhomb **6** oblong, square **9** rectangle

paralogist: 7 sophist

paralysis: 5 cramp, palsy **7** paresis **9** impotence **10** holoplexia, paraplegia **11** monoparesis **12** quadriplegia
with: **7** paretic **9** paralytic

paralyzed: 4 numb **7** palsied **8** benumbed, crippled, immobile

paramnesia: 6 déjàvu

paramount: 5 above, chief, ruler **7** capital, supreme **8** crowning, dominant, superior, suzerain **10** pre-eminent
lord: **5** liege

paramour: 5 leman, lover, wooer **6** amoret, friend, suitor **7** gallant, hetaera **8** mistress **9** concubine, kept woman **10** sweetheart

paranymph: 7 best man **8** advocate **10** bridesmaid

parapet: 4 butt, wall **5** redan **7** bulwark, railing, rampart **10** breastwork **12** embattlement **13** fortification
part of: **5** crete
V-shaped: **5** redan

paraphernalia: 4 gear **6** outfit, tackle **9** apparatus, equipment, trappings **10** belongings **11** furnishings **13** appurtenances

paraphrase: 6 reword **7** restate, version **9** interpret, translate **10** transcribe **11** translation

parasite: bug, bur **4** burr, moss **5** leech, toady, virus **6** fungus, sponge **7** sponger **8** hanger-on **9** dependent, mistletoe, sycophant **10** freeloader
animal: **4** flea, mite, tick **8** entozoan
blood: **4** tryp **5** fluke, leech
disease: **4** Lyme **6** typhus **7** malaria **11** trichinosis, yellow fever
marine: **6** remora, sponge
plant: **5** scale **9** entophyte, mistletoe **10** threadworm
trout: sug

parasol: 8 sunshade, umbrella **11** bumbershoot

paratrooper cry: 8 Geronimo

paravane: 5 otter

Parcae: See **Fates**

parcel: lot **4** deal, mete, pack, part, wrap **5** bulse, bunch, group, piece **6** bundle, divide, packet **7** package, portion **8** fragment **9** apportion **10** collection, distribute

parch: dry **4** burn, sear **5** roast, toast **6** dry out, scorch **7** bristle, burstle, graddan, shrivel

parched: 4 arid, sere **5** fiery **6** gizzen, torrid

parcheesi: 4 game, ludo **7** pachisi

parchment (see also **paper, scroll**): **6** charta **7** diploma **9** sheepskin
book cover: **5** forel **6** forrel
fine: vel **6** vellum
manuscript: **10** palimpsest
piece: **8** membrane
roll: **4** pell **6** scroll

pard: cob, pal **4** chum **6** cobber **7** leopard, partner **9** companion

pardesi: 9 foreigner, outlander

pardo: 7 mulatto

pardon: 4 free **5** mercy, remit, spare, waive **6** assoil, excuse **7** absolve, amnesty, condone, forgive **8** liberate, reprieve, tolerate **9**

exculpate, remission **10** absolution, indulgence **11** forgiveness
general: **7** amnesty
stall: **12** confessional
pardonable: **6** venial **9** excusable
pare: cut **4** chip, peel, skin **5** shave **6** reduce, remove, resect **7** curtail, cut back, cut down, whittle **8** diminish, trim back **11** decorticate
paregoric: **7** anodyne **8** sedative
parella, parelle: **6** lichen
parent: dad, dam, mom **4** mama, papa, sire **5** cause, daddy, mater (L.), mommy, pater (L.) **6** author, father, mother, origin **7** forbear, genitor **8** ancestor, begetter, forebear, generate, guardian, producer **10** forefather, progenitor
parentage: **5** birth **6** family, origin **7** lineage, progeny **8** ancestry **10** extraction, parenthood
parget: **4** coat **6** gypsum **7** plaster **8** decorate **9** whitewash
pariah: **7** Ishmael, outcast
parian: **5** china **6** marble, market **9** porcelain
Paris: *beloved:* **5** Helen
father: **5** Priam
killed: **8** Achilles
kin: **7** Troilus **9** Cassandra
mother: **6** Hecuba
sister: **9** Cassandra
slayer: **11** Philoctetes
wife: **6** Oenone
Paris: *airport:* **4** Orly **6** Roissy **8** DeGaulle **9** Le Bourget
avenue: **13** Champs Elysees
bishop: **5** Denis **7** Lombard
boulevard: **8** Rue Royal, St. Honore **11** Rue de la Paix, Rue de Rivoli **13** Champs Elysees
capital of: **6** France
cathedral: **9** Notre Dame **10** Sacre Coeur
cemetery: **12** Pere-Lachaise
city planner: **8** Hausmann
former food market: **9** Les Halles
garden: **9** Tuileries **11** Champ de Mars
museum: **4** Army **5** Cluny **6** Louvre **10** Carnavalet, Luxembourg
nickname: **11** City of Light
palace: **6** Elysee, Louvre **9** Tuileries **10** Luxembourg
park: **10** Luxembourg **14** Bois de Boulogne
place: **12** de la Concorde
river: **5** Seine
Roman name: **7** Lutetia
section: **8** Left Bank **9** Right Bank **10** Montmartre, Rive Gauche **12** Isle de la Cite, Montparnasse **16** St. Germain-des-Pres
site: **13** Arc de Triomphe **14** Pompidou Center

subway: **5** metro
tower: **6** Eiffel
university: **8** Sorbonne
parish: **4** fold **5** flock **7** diocese **12** congregation
head: **5** vicar **6** pastor, priest **8** minister
official: **6** beadle, verger **9** vestryman **10** borsholder, councilman
paristhmion: **6** tonsil
parity: **7** analogy **8** equality **10** similarity **11** equivalence, resemblance
park: **4** stop **5** field, green, grove **6** refuge **7** commons, paddock **8** preserve **10** playground
parlance: **4** talk **5** idiom **6** speech **7** diction **9** discourse **11** phraseology **12** conversation
parlay: **5** wager **6** double, paroli **7** build up **8** increase
parley: **4** talk **5** speak, treat, utter **6** confer **7** discuss, palaver **9** discourse **10** conference, discussion **12** conversation
parliament: **4** diet **5** senat (F.) **6** Senate **7** council **8** assembly, congress **9** gathering **10** conference **11** legislature
parlous: **4** keen **5** risky **6** clever, shrewd **7** cunning **8** critical, perilous **9** dangerous, hazardous **11** exceedingly, excessively, mischievous **13** disconcerting
Parnassian: **4** poet
parochial: **5** petty **6** narrow **7** bigoted, limited **9** of a parish, small-town **10** provincial
parody: **4** skit **5** spoof **6** satire **7** travesty **9** burlesque, imitation **10** caricature
paroemia: **7** proverb
parole: **4** word **6** pledge **7** promise
paronomasia: pun **8** word play **12** agnomination
paroxysm: fit **4** pang **5** agony, spasm, throe **6** access, attack, orgasm **8** epitasis, outburst **9** agitation **10** convulsion **12** exacerbation
parrot: ape, ara **4** copy, echo, jako, kaka, lory **5** arara, mimic, polly **6** repeat, tiriba **7** corella, imitate **8** cockatoo, lorikeet, lovebird, parakeet **9** cockateel, cockatiel
Australian: **4** lory **8** cockatoo, lorikeet
disease: **10** ornithosis **11** psittacosis
genus: **9** psittacus
gray: **4** jako
green: **5** cagit
hawk: hia
like: **5** arine **11** psittaceous
long-tailed: **5** macaw
monk: **4** loro
New Zealand: kea, owl **4** kaka
owl: **4** kaka **6** kakapo
part of bill: **4** cere
sheep-killing: kea
small: **5** pygmy **7** hanging **8** lovebird, parakeet

parrot fish 524

South American: **5** macaw **9** guacamayo
parrot fish: **4** scar **5** lania **6** scarus **8** bluefish **9** labroidea
parry: **4** fend, ward **5** avoid, block, evade **6** thwart **7** counter, deflect, evasion
parse: **7** analyse, analyze, diagram, dissect **8** construe **9** anatomize
Parsi, Parsee: **11** Zoroastrian
god: **10** Ahura Mazda
holy book: **6** Avesta
priest: **5** mobed **6** dastur **7** destour, dustoor
parsimonious: **4** mean, near **5** cheap, close, scant, spare, tight **6** frugal, meager, narrow, skimpy, sordid, stingy **7** miserly, sparing **8** covetous, grasping, wretched **9** illiberal, mercenary, niggardly, penurious **10** avaricious, economical, ungenerous **13** penny-pinching **17** narrowheartedness
parsley: **4** herb **5** cumin **6** eltrot **7** garnish **8** biennial
derivative: **5** apiol **6** apiole
genus: **12** petroselinum
relative: **6** celery **7** caraway
parsley camphor: **6** apiole
parson: **6** pastor, rector **8** minister, preacher **9** clergyman, guidepost
parsonage: **5** manse **6** parish **7** rectory **9** pastorium
parson bird: poe, tui **4** rook
parson-in-the-pulpit: **4** arum **10** cuckoopint **14** lords-and-ladies
part (see also **parts**): **4** deal, dole, half, role, rove, side, some, twin **5** chunk, piece, quota, sever, share **6** behalf, canton, cleave, depart, detail, divide, member, parcel, ration, sunder **7** disjoin, element, portion, section, segment **8** alienate, disperse, dissever, disunite, division, estrange, fraction, fragment, separate **9** abteilung (G.), apportion, dismember **10** department, incomplete **11** constituent
baglike: sac
basic: **4** core, pith **7** essence
central: **4** core **5** focus, solar **6** nuclei (pl.) **7** nucleus
choice: **5** cream, elite **6** marrow **7** essence
distinct: **4** unit **7** article
essential: **4** core, gist, pith **6** factor
final: **5** shank **6** epilog, upshot **8** solution **10** conclusion, denouement
hardest: **5** brunt
highest: top **4** apex **5** crest **6** summit
inmost: **4** core **5** heart **6** center
main: **4** body **5** trunk
minor: bit, cog
missing: **6** lacuna
moving: **5** rotor
narrow: **4** neck
revolving: **5** rotor **7** rotator

root-like: **7** radicle
rounded: **4** bulb
small: bit, jot **4** atom, iota, mite **5** tithe **6** detail, moiety **7** snippet
suddenly: **4** rend, snap
uppermost: top **4** peak **6** upside **7** topside
partage: **4** part **5** share **7** portion **8** division
partake: **4** bite **5** eat of, share **6** divide, join in **11** participate
of: use
partan: **4** crab
parted: **5** cleft **7** divided, partite **9** separated
Parthian ruler: **7** Arsaces
partial: **4** half, part **6** biased, unfair **7** colored, halfway **8** coloured, inclined, one-sided, partisan **10** fractional, incomplete, prejudiced **11** predilected, predisposed
participant: **6** member **8** partisan **10** accomplice
participate: **4** join, side **5** enter, share **6** be in on **7** compete, partake **9** cooperate **11** get in the act
particle: ace, bit, dot, gru, jot **4** atom, grue, iota, mite, mote, whit **5** fleck, grain, shred, speck **6** morsel, smidge, tittle **7** driblet, smidgen, smidgin **8** smidgeon, smitchin
affirmative: yes
burnt: **6** cinder
coordinating: or
cosmic: **5** meson
electrified: ion **5** anion **6** cation, proton **8** electron
incandescent: **5** spark
minute: jot, ort, ray **4** atom, iota, mite, mote **5** grain, speck **7** granule, ramenta (pl.) **8** molecule, ramentum **9** scintilla
negative: nor, not
negative-charged: ion **8** electron
pluvial: **4** drop
positive-charged: ion **6** proton **8** positron
subatomic: tan **4** mnon **5** boson, glnon, quark **6** hadron, lepton, photon, proton, weakon **7** neutron **8** electron, neutrino
parti-colored: **4** pied **7** piebald **9** checkered **10** variegated
particular: **4** item, nice **5** fussy, point, thing **6** detail, minute **7** article, careful, correct, precise, special, unusual **8** accurate, concrete, detailed, especial, exacting, itemized, specific **10** fastidious, individual, noteworthy, scrupulous **11** scrumptious **12** circumstance **13** extraordinary **14** circumstantial
opposite: **7** general
particularly: **9** expressly, unusually **10** especially
parting: **5** death **8** farewell **11** leavetaking
parting shot: **5** taunt **8** last word
partisan: **4** pike **5** staff **6** biased, fautor, friend **7** devotee **8** adherent, follower **9** truncheon

10 factionary, factioneer, interested
unwavering: **6** zealot **8** stalwart
partite: 6 parted **7** divided **9** separated
partition: 4 wall **5** septa (pl.) **6** divide, screen, septum **7** enclose, portion, scantle **8** cleavage, close off, division **9** severance **10** distribute, enterclose, separation **11** compartment **13** apportionment
partitioned: 6 walled **7** septate
partlet: hen **5** woman
partner: pal **4** ally, half, mate, wife **5** butty, crony **6** cohort, fellow, sharer **7** comrade, consort, husband **8** camarada, sidekick **9** associate, coadjutor, colleague, companion **10** accomplice **11** confederate, participant
comedian's: **6** stooge **11** straight-man
paid: **6** escort, gigolo, walker
partnership: hui **4** firm **5** tie-up **7** cahoots, company **8** alliance **11** association **14** compagnieschap (D.)
partridge: 4 yutu **5** quail, titar **6** chukar, chukor, grouse, seesee **7** tinamou **8** bobwhite **9** francolin
flock: **5** covey
young: **7** cheeper **8** squealer
parts (see also **part**): **9** genitalia
innermost: **10** penetralia
together: **9** adhesions
totality: **5** unity
two: **6** binary
parturition: 5 birth, labor **7** travail **8** delivery **10** childbirth
part with: 4 give, lose, sell **5** leave **6** donate **7** abandon
party (see also **political party**): bal (F.) **4** bash, clan, drum, fete, gala, orgy, sect, side **5** cabal, dance, group **6** affair, comite, fiesta, person, social **7** company, faction **9** gathering **10** detachment **11** association, combination **12** participator
afternoon: tea **9** reception
evening: **4** ball, fete, gala **6** soiree
gift: **5** favor
guilty: **7** culprit
men's: **4** stag **6** smoker
reconnaissance: **6** patrol
seashore: **6** picnic **8** clambake
party girl: 4 doxy **10** prostitute
party man: 8 adherent, partisan
parure: 5 adorn **6** paring **7** apparel, jewelry, peeling **8** ornament **11** matching set
par value: 4 face **7** nominal
parvenu: 4 snob **6** arrive **7** upstart **9** arriviste **11** pig in clover **12** nouveau riche
Pascal work: 7 Pensees
Pasch, Pascha: 6 Easter, Pâques (F.), Pasqua (Sp.) **8** Passover
paschal: 4 lamb **6** Easter, supper **8** Passover **11** celebration

pasear (Sp.): 4 walk **6** airing **9** excursion, promenade
pasha: dey **4** emir
territory: **8** pachalic, pashalic, pashalik
Pashur: *father:* **5** Immer **8** Malchiah
son: **8** Gedaliah
Pasiphae: *children:* **7** Ariadne, Phaedra **8** Minotaur
husband: **5** Minos
pasqueflower: 6 badger **7** anemone, gosling **9** april-fool **10** badgerweed **12** ranunculacea
pasquinade: 5 squib **6** satire **7** lampoon, pasquil
pass: col, end, gap **4** abra, beal (Sc.), comp, cove, fare, ghat, hand, lane, pace, step, wend **5** canto, enact, ghaut, gorge, hurry, kotal, lapse, lunge, occur, relay, smite, spend, utter, yodel **6** billet, convey, defile, elapse, exceed, expire, happen, passus, permit, ticket, twofer **7** advance, allonge, approve, devolve, passage, surpass, undergo **8** beallach, hand down, surmount **10** adjudicate, permission **11** Annie Oakley, leave behind **13** complimentary
slowly: **4** drag
without touching: **5** clear
passable: fit **4** fair, soso **7** genuine **8** adequate, mediocre, moderate **9** navigable, tolerable **10** admissable, negotiable **11** traversable
passage: gat, gut, wro **4** adit, belt, door, duct, exit, fare, flue, ford, gang, gate, hall, iter, lane, pass, path, pawn, race, ramp, road, slip **5** aisle, allee, alley, alure, atria (pl.), entry, going, gorge, meuse **6** access, arcade, atrium, avenue, burrow, course, defile, egress, strait, travel, tunnel, voyage **7** channel, couloir, estuary, gangway, itinera (pl.), journey, transit **8** aqueduct, corridor, crossing **9** enactment, ventiduct **10** bottleneck, transition **12** thoroughfare **13** accommodation
air: **4** flue **7** nostril **9** ventiduct
between two walls: **5** slype
covered: **6** arcade **8** cloister **9** breezeway
literary: **4** text **7** excerpt **9** quotation
mine: **5** stope
musical: bar, cue **4** link **5** break, stave **7** cadenza **8** flourish, spicatto
one outlet: **7** dead-end, impasse **8** cul-de-sac
roofed: see *covered* above
scripture: **4** text **5** verse
subterranean: **4** mine **6** tunnel **8** cuniculi (pl.) **9** cuniculus
passant: 4 past **7** current, cursory, walking **9** ephemeral, excelling **10** proceeding, surpassing, transitory

pass around: 5 skirt 6 detour

pass away: die 6 expire, perish, vanish 8 transfer 9 disappear, surrender

pass by: 4 cote, omit, skip 6 forego, forget, ignore 8 overlook 9 disregard

passe: 4 aged, past, worn 5 faded 6 old hat 7 demoded 8 obsolete, outmoded 9 out-of-date 10 antiquated 12 old-fashioned 13 superannuated

passel: 4 body 5 bunch, group 6 bundle 7 cluster

passementerie: 6 edging 8 trimming

passenger: 4 fare 5 rider 7 standby 8 ferryman, traveler, wayfarer

passe-partout: 9 master key 10 picture mat 11 skeleton key

passerby: 9 saunterer 10 pedestrian

passerine bird: 6 oscine 7 percher, sparrow

passing: 5 death 7 cursory 8 elapsing, fleeting 9 departing, ephemeral, exceeding 10 preeminent, surpassing, transitory

passion (see also **mania**): ire 4 fire, fury, heat, love, lust, raga, rage, zeal 5 anger, ardor 6 affect, choler, desire, fervor, temper 7 emotion, feeling, fervour 8 appetite, distress 9 calenture, martyrdom 10 affliction, enthusiasm, heart-throb

passionate: 4 fond 5 afire 6 fervid, fierce, sultry, torrid 7 amorous, flaming, peppery 8 desirous, frenetic 9 hot-headed, irascible, phrenetic 11 hot-tempered, impassioned 12 affectionate, concupiscent 13 quick-tempered

passion flower: 4 vine 6 maypop 8 bullhoof
family: 14 passifloraceae

passionless: 4 calm, cold 6 freddo (It.) 8 detached 11 emotionless

passive: 4 meek 5 inert, stoic 6 latent, stolid 7 patient 8 inactive, yielding 9 apathetic, impassive, lethargic, quiescent 10 phlegmatic, submissive

pass off: con 4 pose 5 foist

pass on: die 4 leak 6 convey, impart 7 decease 8 transmit 11 communicate

pass over: die 4 omit, skip 5 cross 6 elapse, excuse, expire, ignore 7 neglect 8 overlook, permeate, transfer, traverse 9 disregard
lightly: 4 skim
quickly: 4 scan, scud
smoothly: 5 elide

Passover: 5 Pesah 6 Pesach
bread: 5 matzo 6 matzos 7 matzoth 8 afikomen 10 unleavened
festival: 5 Sedar, Seder
month: 5 Nisan
pert. to: 7 paschal
songs of praise: 6 hallel
story: 7 Haggada 8 Haggadah

passport: key 5 conge 6 dustuk, permit, ticket

7 dustuck 8 furlough 9 safeguard 10 open sesame 11 safe conduct 13 laissez-passer
endorsement: 4 visa

pass through: 5 cross 6 divide, pierce 7 pervade 8 permeate, traverse 9 penetrate

pass up: 6 reject 7 decline 9 disregard

passus: 4 pace, part, step 5 canto 8 division

password: 11 countersign

past: ago 4 gone, over, yore 5 after, agone, ended, since 6 behind, beyond, bygone 8 foregone, previous 9 completed, foregoing 11 antecedents
immediate: 9 yesterday
pert. to: 8 historic
tense: 11 perteritive

pasta: 4 orzo, ziti 7 lasagne, noodles, ravioli 8 linguine, macaroni, rigatoni 9 fettucini, manicotti, spaghetti 10 tortellini, vermicelli

paste: hit, pap 4 beat, blow, cuff, duff, glue, pate 5 cream, dough, false, punch, stick 6 attach, batter, fasten, strass 7 filling 8 adhesive, mucilage 9 imitation
aromatic: 6 pastil 7 pastile 8 pastille
dried: 7 guarana

pasteboard: 4 card, sham 6 flimsy

pastel: 4 pale 6 crayon 7 picture

pastern: 6 hobble, hopple, tether 7 shackle

Pasternak novel: 13 Doctor Zhivago
heroine: 4 Lara

pastiche: 4 olio 6 jumble, medley 9 patchwork, potpourri 10 hodgepodge

pastime: 4 game 5 hobby, sport 9 amusement, diversion 10 recreation 13 entertainment

past master: 6 expert

pastor: 4 herd 5 angel, rabbi 6 curate, keeper, priest, rector 7 dominie 8 guardian, minister, shepherd 9 clergyman

pastoral: 4 poem 5 drama, rural 7 bucolic, idyllic, romance 8 agrarian, shepherd
god: Pan
pert. to: 8 agrestic, geoponic
pipe: 4 reed
place: 7 Arcadia
poem: 5 idyll 7 eclogue, georgic

pastry (see also **cake, pie**): pie 4 baba, cake, flan, huff, puff, tart 5 torte 6 eclair, phyllo 7 baklava, carcake (Sc.), strudel 8 napoleon, turnover 9 cream puff, vol-au-vent 11 petits fours
garnish: 5 cream, fruit 8 meringue
shell: 7 dariole, timbale

pasturage: 4 gang 6 eatage, forage 7 herbage

pasture: lea 5 agist, drift, field, grass, graze, veldt 6 meadow, saeter 7 grazing, vaccary 9 grassland 10 agostadero
god: Pan

pasty: pie 6 doughy, pallid, sickly 7 meat pie 9 unhealthy

pat: apt, dab, tap **4** blow, glib **5** fitly, fixed, impel, throw **6** caress, soothe, strike, stroke, timely **7** apropos, fitting, readily **8** suitable **9** immovable, opportune, pertinent **10** seasonable **12** commendation

Patagonia: *deity:* **7** Setebos
part of: **5** Chile **9** Argentina
rodent: **4** cavy, mara
tree: **6** alerce, alerse

patch: bit **4** mend, vamp **5** bodge, clout, clump, cover, piece, scrap **6** blotch, cobble, dollop, emblem, parcel, repair, revamp, solder **7** clobber, remnant
of woods: **5** motte
up: **4** heal, mend

patchwork: **5** cento, quilt **6** jumble, scraps **9** fragments **10** hodgepodge, miscellany

pate: pie, top **4** head **5** crown, paste, pasty, patty **6** badger, noggin, spread

patella: pan **4** dish, vase **6** limpet **7** kneecap, kneepan

paten: **4** arca, disc, dish, disk **5** plate **6** vessel

patent: **4** arca, open **5** clear, gross, overt, plain **7** evident, license, obvious **8** apparent, archives, enduring, flagrant, manifest **9** available, franchise **12** unobstructed
medicine: **7** nostrum
notice: **6** caveat

pater (L.): **6** father, priest

paternal: **8** fatherly **10** benevolent
kinsman: **6** agnate

paternity: **6** father, origin **10** authorship, fatherhood **12** fatherliness

path: pad, rut, way **4** fare, lane, line, road, walk **5** alley, byway, going, orbit, piste, route, track, trail **6** camino, casaun, comino, course, groove **7** footway, highway, tow-path **9** direction
hill: **4** berm **5** berme **6** roddin **7** rodding (Sc.)
math: **5** locus

pathetic: sad **5** sorry, teary **6** moving **7** forlorn, pitiful **8** stirring **9** affecting

pathic: **6** victim **7** passive, subject **8** catamite **9** suffering

pathological: **4** sick **6** morbid

pathos: **4** pity **9** poignancy

patience: **4** calm **8** stoicism **9** composure, endurance, fortitude **10** submission **11** forbearance, resignation, self-control **12** acquiescence **13** long-suffering

patient: **4** case, meek **6** bovine **7** invalid **13** long-suffering

patina: **4** film **5** gloss **6** finish, polish **9** oxidation

patio: **5** court, lanai, porch **6** piazza **7** terrace, veranda **9** courtyard

patisserie: **4** shop **6** bakery, pastry

patois: **4** cant **6** Creole, jargon **7** dialect

patriarch: **4** Enos, Levi, Nasi, Noah **5** elder, Isaac, Jacob, ruler **6** father, leader **7** Abraham, ancient, veteran **9** venerable

patrician: **5** noble **9** gentleman **10** aristocrat **12** aristocratic

patrimony: **6** legacy **8** ancestry, heritage **10** birthright **11** inheritance

patriot: **8** loyalist, partisan **9** flag-waver **10** chauvinist, countryman **11** compatriate, nationalist
song: **6** anthem **7** America

patrol: **5** guard, scout, watch **6** picket **7** lookout, protect **10** detachment

patrolman: cop **5** guard **9** inspector, policeman

patron: **5** buyer, guest **6** client, fautor **7** sponsor **8** advocate, champion, customer, defender, guardian **9** protector, supporter **10** benefactor
stock exchange: **5** buyer **6** seller, trader

patronage: **5** aegis, favor **6** custom, favour **7** auspice, fomento **8** business **10** assistance **13** encouragement

patronize: use **5** deign **8** frequent **10** condescend

patron saint: *of beggars:* **5** Giles
of Bohemia: **10** Wenceslaus
of carpenters: **6** Joseph
of children: **8** Nicholas
of cripples: **5** Giles
of England: **6** George
of fishermen: **5** Peter
of France: **5** Denis **9** Joan of Arc
of Greece: **4** Paul
of Hungary: **7** Stephen
of Ireland: **7** Patrick
of lawyers: **4** Ives, Yves
of medical profession: **4** Luke
of musicians: **7** Cecilia
of Norway: **4** Olaf
of philosophers: **13** Thomas Aquinas
of Poland: **10** Stanislaus
of Russia: **5** Basil **6** Andrew
of sailors: **4** Elmo **8** Nicholas
of Scotland: **6** Andrew
of shoemakers: **7** Crispin
of Spain: **15** James the Greater
of Wales: **5** David
of winegrowers: **7** Vincent
of workers: **6** Joseph

patsy: sap **4** dupe, fool **5** chump **6** sucker, victim **7** fall guy **9** scapegoat

patten: **4** base, clogfoot, shoe **5** skate, stand, stilt **6** sandal **7** support **8** overshoe, snowshoe

patter: **4** cant, jive, talk **5** lingo **6** jargon **7** blatter, chatter

pattern: **4** form, norm, plan **5** bysen, draft, epure, guide, ideal, model, order, plaid **6**

checks, design, figure, format, former, sample, stripe **7** example, project, stencil, templet **8** exemplar, forbysen, paradigm, specimen, template **9** archetype, ensampler, precedent **11** arrangement

patulous: **4** open **8** expanded **9** distended, spreading

paucity: **4** lack **5** saint **6** dearth **7** fewness **8** exiguity, scarcity **13** insufficiency

Paul: **7** apostle
birthplace: **6** Tarsus
companion: **5** Silas, Titus **7** Artemas, Timothy **8** Barnabas
original name: **4** Saul
place of conversion: **8** Damascus
prosecutor: **9** Tertullus
teacher: **8** Gamaliel
tribe: **8** Benjamin
work: **6** letter **7** epistle

pauldron: **5** armor **6** splint

paunch: gut **5** belly, rumen **7** abdomen, stomach **8** potbelly **10** disembowel, eviscerate

pauper: **6** beggar **8** bankrupt, indigent **10** down-and-out

pause: **4** halt, lull, rest, stop, wait **5** abide, break, cease, comma, delay, demur, dwell, hover, letup, selah, tarry **6** breach, breath, falter, stance **7** caesura, respite **8** breather, caesurae (pl.), hesitate, intermit **9** cessation **10** hesitation **12** intermission, interruption

paut: paw **4** poke **5** stamp **6** finger

pavane: **5** dance

pave: lay **4** path, stud, tile **5** cover, floor **6** causey, cobble, smooth **7** overlay, prepare **10** facilitate, macadamize

pavid: **5** timid **6** afraid **7** fearful

pavilion: **4** flag, tent **5** kiosk **6** canopy, ensign, litter **7** marquee **8** covering **9** gloriette

paving: **4** flag, sett **5** block, brick, dalle, paver, stone **6** cobble, Tarmac **7** asphalt **9** flagstone

pavis: **5** cover **6** screen, shield **10** protection

pavo: **7** peacock **13** constellation

paw: pud, toe **4** foot, gaum, hand, maul, paty **5** patte, touch **6** fumble, handle, pattee **7** crubeen, flipper **8** forefoot

pawky: sly **4** arch, bold **5** canny, saucy **6** crafty, lively, shrewd **7** cunning, forward **9** squeamish

pawl: cog, dog **4** bolt, sear, tent, trip **5** catch, click **6** detent, pallet, tongue **7** ratchet

pawn: **4** gage, hock, soak, tool **6** lumber, pledge, puppet **7** counter, hostage **8** chessman, guaranty **11** impignorate

pawnbroker: **11** moneylender

Pawnee: **6** Indian
rite: **4** hako

pawpaw: **4** tree **5** fruit, papaw, shrub **6** papaya **7** Asimina, immoral, naughty **8**

indecent **11** bushwhacker **12** custard apple

pax: **5** board, peace **6** friend, tablet **10** friendship, osculatory

pay: fee, tip **4** ante, foot, meet, rent, wage **5** clear, repay, spend, yield **6** defray, pony up, reward, salary **7** imburse, requite, satisfy, stipend, tribute **9** indemnify, make up for, reimburse **10** compensate, recompense, remunerate **11** retribution **12** compensation
attention: **4** heed **6** listen **9** give ear to
back: **6** rebate, refund **9** reimburse, retaliate, tit for tat
extra: tip **5** batta, bonus **8** kickback **9** baksheesh, lagniappe
for: buy **4** rent **7** finance **8** purchase
homage: **5** adore, honor **6** salaam
out: **5** spend **6** expend **8** disburse **10** distribute
up: **4** ante, quit **6** settle **9** liquidate

payable: due **5** owing **11** outstanding

paying: **5** sound **7** solvent **10** profitable **12** advantageous

paymaster: **6** bakshi, bukshi, purser **7** bukshee (Ind.) **8** buckshee **9** treasurer

payment: cro, fee, tax **4** bill, dole, dues, duty, feal, fine, gale, levy, toll **5** gavel, price **6** pledge, rebate, return, reward, tariff **7** alimony, annuity, customs, pension, stipend, trewage, tuition **8** defrayal, requital **9** acquittal, allowance, discharge, honoraria (pl.) **10** honorarium, recompense, remittance **12** compensation, contribution
demand: dun **4** bill
evade: **4** bilk **7** default
failure: **13** nonredemption
illegal: **5** bribe **6** payola **8** kickback
immediate: **4** cash **9** alcontado (Sp.)
on delivery: COD
without: **4** free **6** gratis

payoff: fix **5** bribe **6** climax, profit, return, reward **9** reckoning **10** settlement

payola: **5** bribe

payong: **8** umbrella

paysage: **7** picture **9** landscape

pea: dal **4** gram, seed, snow **5** arhar, chick, cicer, field, pease, split **6** gandul, garden, legume, pigeon **7** carmele, catjang **8** garvanro **9** black-eyed **12** peavetchling
dove: **7** zenaida
early: **8** hastings
family: **8** fabaceae **11** leguminosae
finch: **9** chaffinch
flour: **9** Erbswurst
pod: **5** quash
sausage: **9** Erbswurst
seeds: **5** pulse
shaped: **8** pisiform

peabird: 6 oriole 7 wryneck

peace: pax (L.), paz (Sp.) 4 calm, ease, liss, pace (It.), paix (F.), rest 5 amity, grith, lisse, quiet 6 Friede (G.), repose, shalom 7 concord, harmony, requiem 8 ataraxia, security, serenity 9 armistice, heartease 10 heartsease 11 tranquility
goddess: 5 Irene
symbol: 4 dove, toga 5 olive

peaceable: 6 gentle, placid 7 amiable, pacific, solomon 8 amicable 11 undisturbed

peaceful: 4 calm 5 still 6 irenic, placid, steady 7 halcyon, serenic 8 irenical 9 unruffled 11 undisturbed

peace pipe: 7 calumet

peach: 4 blab 5 dilly 6 accuse, beauty, betray, indict, inform 7 impeach, whittle 8 jim-dandy 11 crackerjack
grafted on quince: 9 melocoton
kind: 4 Sims 5 Gaume, Hiley 6 Carman, Crosby, Salwey 7 Elberta, Fortuna 8 Crawford, quandang, quandong, quantong 9 freestone, nectarine 10 clingstone
origin: 5 China
stone: 7 putamen

Peach State: 7 Georgia

peachwort: 9 persicary

peachy: 4 fine, nice 5 dandy 9 beautiful, excellent

peacock: mao 4 pavo, pawn 5 strut 7 peafowl, swagger
fan: 5 train 9 flabellum
feather fiber: 4 marl
female: 6 peahen
pert. to: 8 pavonine
tail spot: eye

peacock bittern: sun

peacock fish: 6 wrasse

peacock flower: 8 flambeau 9 poinciana

peacock heron: 7 bittern

peacock ore: 7 bornite 12 chalcopyrite

peag, peage: tax 4 toll 5 beads 6 pedage, wampum

pea jacket: 7 peacoat 11 seaman's coat 13 hiplength coat

peak: (see also **mountain**): Alp, ben, pic (F.), top, tor 4 acme, apex, cima, cusp, dent, dolt, pico (Sp.) 5 crest, crown, point, slink, sneak, steal, visor 6 shrink, summit, zenith 7 epitome, maximum 8 aiguille, headland, mountain, pinnacle 9 ascendant, ascendent, simpleton 10 promontory
ice: 4 berg 5 serac
ornament: epi 6 finial
rock: alp 4 crag
snow-capped: 7 calotte

peaked: wan 4 pale, thin 5 drawn, sharp 6 picked, sickly 7 pointed 9 emaciated

peal: 4 clap, ring, toll 5 chime 6 appeal, shovel 7 resound, summons, thunder 8 carillon

Peale Island: 4 Habe

pean: See **paean**

peanut: 4 mani, mean 5 petty, pinda 6 goober, pindal, pinder 7 beennut 8 earthnut, earthpea, grassnut, katchung 9 arachides, groundnut

peanuts: 8 trifling 15 inconsequential

pear: 4 bosc 5 Anjou, melon 6 beurre, burrel, Comice, Garber, Seckel, warden, winter 7 kieffer, LeConte, prickly 8 ambrette, Bartlett, bergamot, Endicott 9 alligator 10 chaumontel
cider: 5 perry
squash: 5 perry 7 chayote

pearl: gem 4 seed, tear 5 nacre, onion 6 bouton, orient 9 margarite
artificial: 4 blay 6 olivet
irregular shape: 7 baroque
of great luster: 8 oriental
seed: 7 aliofar

pearlbird: 6 barbet 10 guinea-fowl

pearl blush: 7 rosetan

pearl moss: 9 carrageen

Pearl of Antilles: 4 Cuba

pearl opal: 9 cacholong

pearlweed: 6 sagina 8 sealwort

pearlwort: 6 sagina 7 poverty

pearly: 5 milky 8 nacreous, precious 10 iridescent, opalescent

pear-shaped: 7 bulbous, rounded 8 pyriform

peasant: 4 bond, boor, hind, kopi, peon, ryot, serf 5 churl, knave, kulak, swain 6 cotman, cottar, cotter, farmer, fellah, rascal, rustic 7 bondman, laborer, paisano (Sp.) 9 chopstick, contadino (It.) 10 countryman
Arab: 6 fellah
class: 9 jacquerie
crop sharing: 7 metayer
dress: 7 dirndle
Irish: 4 kern 5 kerne
Russian: 5 kulak 6 muzhik

peashooter: 6 blower, pistol 7 blowgun 9 slingshot 11 beanshooter

peat: gor (Ir.), pet 4 fuel, turf 6 lawyer, minion 7 darling 8 favorite 11 combustible
bog: 4 cess, moss 6 yarpha
cutter: 5 piner (Sc.)
spade: 5 slane 6 tuscar

peatwood: 11 loosestrife

peau d'ange: 6 fabric, finish 9 angelskin

peavey, peavy: 4 hook 5 lever

peba: 9 armadillo

pebble: 5 scree, stone 6 gravel, quartz, sycite 7 chuckie, crystal 10 chuckstone

pebble-shaped: 9 calciform 11 calculiform

peccadillo: sin 5 error, fault 7 offense 8 mischief

peccant: 6 morbid 7 corrupt, sinning 8 diseased 9 incorrect, unhealthy

peccary: 6 warree **7** musk-hog, tagassu, tayassu **8** javelina

pech: 4 pant, sigh **6** breath **7** breathe

pecht: 4 pict **5** fairy, gnome, pygmy

peck: dab, dot, nag, nip **4** beak, bill, carp, food, hole, jerk, kiss, nose **5** pitch, prick, throw **6** nibble, stroke **7** chimble, measure **9** great deal
  at: nag **4** twit **5** tease **6** attack, harass
  four: **6** bushel

pectase: 6 enzyme

peculate: 5 steal **6** misuse **8** embezzle **11** appropriate

peculiar: odd **5** queer, weird **6** unique **7** curious, oddball, special, strange, unusual **8** especial, singular **9** eccentric, exclusive **10** particular **11** distinctive **14** characteristic

peculiarity: 4 kink **5** quirk, trait, twist **6** idiasm, oddity **7** feature **8** property **9** attribute **12** idiosyncracy
  of expression: **5** idiom **6** idioma, idiome

pecuniary: 8 monetary **9** financial

ped: 6 basket, hamper, panier **7** pannier

pedagogue: 5 tutor **6** pedant **7** dominie, teacher **12** schoolmaster

pedal: 5 lever **7** treadle
  coupler: **7** tirasse
  piano: **7** celeste

pedant: 4 prig **5** dunce, tutor **6** dorbel, purist, tassel **7** scholar **9** pedagogue **12** blue-stocking, schoolmaster

pedantic: 7 bookish, erudite, learned **8** academic, teaching **9** scholarly **10** didascalic, moralistic
  writing: **9** academese

peddle: 4 hawk, sell **5** cadge, cycle, trant **6** higgle, meddle, piddle, retail **7** colport

peddler: 5 faker **6** broker, coster, duffer, hawker, seller, vendor **7** camelot, chapman **8** huckster, pitchman **10** colporteur **12** carpetbagger, costermonger

pedestal: 4 anta, base **5** stand **6** pillar, podium **7** support **10** foundation
  part: die **4** dado **5** socle **6** plinth, quadra
  put on: **7** idolize **8** enshrine

pedestrian: ped **4** dull, slow **5** banal, inane **6** hoofer, walker **7** footman, plodder, prosaic **8** ordinary **11** commonplace **13** unimaginative

pedicel: ray **4** stem **5** scape, stalk **8** peduncle **9** footstalk
  umbel: ray

pedigree: 6 origin, stemma **7** descent, lineage **8** ancestry, purebred, stemmata **9** genealogy

pedometer: 8 odograph, waywiser **12** perambulator

pedum: 5 crook, staff

peek: 4 look, peep **6** glance **7** glimpse

peekaboo: 4 game **6** bopeep, peep-bo **7** peepeye

peel: 4 bark, harl, hull, pare, rind, skin **5** flipe, scale, slipe, stake, strip **6** shovel **7** undress **8** palisade, stockade **11** decorticate

peeler: 4 crab **5** bobby, corer **7** hustler **8** pillager, stripper **9** ecdysiast, policeman **11** stripteaser

peeling: 4 rind, skin **6** paring

peep: pry, spy **4** look, peek, peer, pule, skeg **5** cheep, chirp, dekko, glint, snoop, tweet **6** glance, squeak **9** sandpiper
  hawk: **7** kestrel
  show: **5** raree

peeper: eye, Tom **4** frog **6** voyeur

peepeye: 8 peekaboo

peephole: 4 hole **6** eyelet **7** crevice, eyehole, opening

peeping: 4 nosy **5** nosey **11** inquisitive

peer: pry **4** duke, earl, fear, fere, gaze, look, lord, mate, peep **5** baron, equal, feere, gloze, noble, snoop, stare, stime (Sc.), styme (Sc.), thane (Sc.) **7** comrade, marquis **8** nobleman, superior, viscount **9** associate **10** rubberneck **12** contemporary
  residence: **6** barony

Peer Gynt: *author:* **5** Ibsen
  character: **4** King **6** Anitra
  composer: **5** Grieg
  mother: Ase **4** Aase

peerage: 4 rank **7** dignity **8** nobility

peerdom: 8 equality

peerless: 9 matchless, nonpareil, unrivaled **11** superlative

peetweet: 9 sandpiper

peeve: irk **5** annoy **6** bother, grudge, nettle **8** irritate

peevish: 5 cross, techy, testy, wemod **6** crusty, hipped, snarly, sullen, touchy **7** carping, crabbed, frecket, fretful, forward, pettish, spleeny, waspish **8** captious, choleric, contrary, critical, crotched, frampoid, petulant, sawshach, snappish **9** fractious, impatient, irascible, irritable, plaintive, splenetic **10** illhumored **11** caper-noited, contentious, disgruntled

peewee: 4 bird, lark, tiny **5** dwarf **7** lapwing

peg: fix, hob, nob, nog, pin **4** plug, scob, step **5** cleat, dowel, drink, perch, piton, prong, spill, stake, throw, tooth **6** degree, dowell, marker, reason **7** pretext, support **8** fastener

pega, pegador: 6 remora

pegall: 6 basket

Pegasus: 11 winged horse **13** constellation
  rider: **11** Bellerophon
  source: **6** Medusa

Peggotty's niece: 5 Emily

peho: 6 morepork

peignoir: 4 gown **5** dress **6** kimono **7** wrapper **8** negligee **9** housecoat, nightgown **12** dressing-gown

pejorative: **10** derogatory **11** disparaging
Peking: See **Beijing**
pelage: fur **4** hair, pelt
pelagic: **6** marine **7** aquatic, oceanic **9** thalassic
Peleg: *father:* **4** Eber
   son: Reu

Peleus: *brother:* **7** Telamon
   father: **6** Aeacus
   son: **7** Pelides **8** Achilles
   wife: **6** Thetis

pelf: rob **4** gain **5** booty, lucre, money, spoil,
   trash **6** pilfer, refuse, riches, spoils, wealth
   7 despoil, rubbish
Pelican State: **9** Louisiana
pelike: jar **4** vase **7** amphora **8** amphorae
pellet: wad **4** ball, pill, shot **5** bolus, stone **6**
   bullet, pilule **7** granule
pellicle: **4** film, scum, skin **5** crust **7** coating,
   cuticle **8** membrane
pell-mell: **8** disorder, headlong, stampede **9**
   confusion **11** impetuously **13** helter skelter
pellock: **8** porpoise
pellucid: **5** clear, sheer **6** bright, limpid **7** crystal
   11 crystalline, translucent, transparent
pelmet: **7** cornice, valance
Peloponnesus (see also **Greece**): *ancient district:* **4** Elis **6** Achaea **7** Arcadia, Argolis,
   Laconia **8** Messenia
   city: **6** Sparta **7** Corinth
   former name: **5** Morea
   people: **7** Moreote
   river god: **7** Alpheus
Pelops: *father:* **8** Tantalus
   son: **6** Atreus **7** Troezen **8** Pittheus, Thyestes
   wife: **10** Hippodamia
pelota: **4** ball **7** jai-alai
pelt: fur **4** beat, blow, cast, dash, fell, hide,
   hurl, push, skin **5** fitch, flung, hurry, stone
   6 gallop, hasten, pelage, refuse, strike,
   thrust **7** rawhide, rubbish **8** woolfell
   dealer: **7** furrier
peludo: **9** armadillo
pelvis: *bone:* **4** ilia **5** ilium, pubis **6** coccyx,
   sacrum **7** ischium
   pert. to: **5** iliac
pen: cot, cub, get, mew, pin, sty **4** bolt, cage,
   coop, fold, jail, yard **5** bught, crawl, hutch,
   kraal, quill, write **6** bought, corral, cruive,
   fasten, hurdle, indite, prison, record, stylus,
   zareba **7** calamus, compose, confine,
   enclose, zareeba **9** enclosure **12** penitentiary
   kind: ink **7** felt tip **8** fountain **9** ball-point
   10 roller ball **12** stylographic
   point: neb, nib **4** stub

seller: **9** stationer
penal: **8** punitive, punitory
penalize: **4** fine **5** mulct **6** amerce, punish
penalty: **4** fine, loss, pain **5** mulct **6** amende,
   amerce **7** forfeit **8** hardship **10** forfeiture,
   punishment **12** disadvantage
   pay: aby **4** abye
penance: **6** sorrow **7** remorse **9** atonement,
   penitence, suffering **10** contrition, repentance **13** mortification
pencel: **4** flag **6** pennon **8** streamer **9** pennoncel
penchant: **4** bent **5** taste **6** liking **7** leaning **8**
   fondness **10** attraction, proclivity **11** inclination
pencil: red, wad **4** blue, lead, wadd **6** stylus **8**
   charcoal **9** eversharp **10** mechanical
   pert. to: **6** desmic
   worn-down: **4** stub
pendant, pendent: bob, jab **4** flag, jagg,
   pend, tail **5** aglet **6** aiglet, tassel **7** hanging,
   pensile, support **8** gamaliel, lavalier **9** lavaliere, pendulous, suspended, undecided **11**
   counterpart
pending: **6** during **8** awaiting
pendulous: lop **6** droopy **7** hanging **8** swinging
Penelope: *father-in-law:* **7** Laertes
   father: **7** Icarius
   husband: **7** Ulysses **8** Odysseus
   son: **10** Telemachus
   suitor: **8** Antinous
penetralia: **7** privacy **9** sanctuary
penetrate: **4** bore, dive, gore, stab **5** break,
   enter, imbue, steep **6** fathom, ficche, pierce
   7 discern, pervade **8** permeate **9** insinuate,
   perforate **10** infiltrate, understand
penetrating: **5** acute, sharp **6** astute, shrewd,
   shrill, subtle **7** knowing **8** incisive **9** sagacious **10** insightful **11** clairvoyant **14** discriminating
penetration: wit **6** acumen **13** understanding
penguin: auk **6** Johnny
   genus: **9** eudyptula
   home: **4** pole **7** rookery **10** penguinery
   large: **7** emperor
   small: **6** Adelie
peninsula: **4** neck **10** chersonese
penitence: rue **5** qualm **6** regret, sorrow **7**
   remorse, sadness, scruple **8** distress, humbling **10** contrition, repentance **11** compunction
   season of: **4** Lent
penitent: **4** ruer **5** sorry **6** humble **10**
   remorseful
penitentiary: jug, pen **4** jail, stir **5** tench **6**
   prison **8** big house
pen-like: **7** styloid
penman: **6** author, scribe, writer **10** amanu-
   enses, amanuensis **12** calligrapher
penmanship: **4** hand **6** script **7** writing **11** cal-

ligraphy, handwriting
poor: **10** cacography
pen name (see also **nickname, pseudonym**):
5 alias **6** anonym **9** pseudonym **10** nom de
plume
François Arouet: **8** Voltaire
Henri Beyle: **8** Stendhal
Isaac Bickerstaff: **9** Dean Swift
Eric Blair: **6** Orwell
Baroness Karen Blixen: **11** Isak Dinesen
Anne Bronte: **9** Acton Bell
Charlotte Bronte: **10** Currer Bell
Emily Bronte: **9** Ellis Bell
Samuel Clemens: **9** Mark Twain
Charles Dickens: Boz
Charles Dodgson: **12** Lewis Carroll
Amantine Dupin: **10** George Sand
Mary Ann Evans: **11** George Eliot
Benjamin Franklin: **11** Poor Richard
Theodore Seuss Geisel: **7** Dr. Seuss
Charles Lamb: **4** Elia
F. Danay and M.B. Lee: **11** Ellery Queen
H. H. Munro: **4** Saki
Alexei Peshkov: **10** Maxim Gorky
Jean Baptiste Poquelin: **7** Moliere
William S. Porter: **6** O. Henry
Jacques Thibault: **13** Anatole France
Louis Viaud: **10** Pierre Loti
pennant: **4** fane, flag, whip **5** roger **6** banner,
cornet, pennon, pinion **8** streamer **9** ban-
derole
yacht: **6** burgee
pennate: **6** winged **9** feathered, penniform
penniless: **4** poor **5** broke, needy **8** bankrupt
9 insolvent **11** impecunious
pennon: **4** flag, wing **6** banner, pinion **7**
feather, pennant

Pennsylvania: **12** commonwealth
battlefield: **10** Gettysburg
capital: **10** Harrisburg
city: **4** Erie **7** Reading **8** Scranton **9**
Allentown, Bethlehem **10** Pittsburgh
12 Philadelphia
Indian: **8** Delaware, Iroquois **9** Algonquin
mountain range: **6** Pocono **9** Allegheny
11 Appalachian
nickname: **6** Quaker **8** Keystone
plateau: **8** Piedmont
river: **4** Ohio **9** Allegheny **10** Schuylkill
11 Monongahela, Susquehanna
state bird: **6** grouse
state flower: **14** mountain laurel
state tree: **7** hemlock

penny: **4** cent **5** brown, pence **6** copper,
saltee, stiver
penny-pinching: **4** mean **5** tight **6** stingy **7**
miserly
penology: **11** criminology
Pensees author: **6** Pascal
pensile: **7** pendent **9** suspended **11** overhanging
pension: inn **5** hotel **6** retire **7** annuity, lodging, payment, stipend, subsidy, tribute **8**
gratuity **9** allowance **10** exhibition **13**
boardinghouse
pensive: **4** blue **5** sober **6** dreamy, musing **7**
wistful **10** meditative, melancholy, reflec-
tive, ruminating, thoughtful **13** contemplative
pent: **5** caged **6** shut up **8** confined, enclosed
pentacle: **4** star **8** hexagram
pentastitch: **4** poem **6** stanza **7** strophe
Pentateuch: law **4** Tora **5** Bible, Torah
books: **6** Exodus **7** Genesis, Numbers **9**
Leviticus **11** Deuteronomy
Pentheus: *grandfather:* **6** Cadmus
mother: **5** Agave
penthouse: **4** roof, shed **5** aerie **6** hangar **7**
pentice **8** dwelling **9** apartment, treehouse
pentyl: **4** amyl
penumbra: **5** shade **6** shadow **7** umbrage
penurious: **4** mean, poor **6** barren, frugal,
scanty, stingy **7** miserly, wanting **8** indigent
9 destitute **10** avaricious **12** parsimonious
penury: **7** beggary, poverty **9** indigence, privation **11** destitution
peon: **4** hand, pawn, serf **5** slave **6** thrall **7**
footman, laborer, peasant, soldier **9** atten-
dant, constable, messenger, policeman
peony: **4** piny **5** plant **6** flower, mouton
people (see also **person**): kin, men **4** folk,
gens, herd, pais (law), volk (G.) **5** demos,
gènte (It.), gente (Sp.), laity, stock, women
6 daonie, family, gentry, peuple (F.), popolo
(It.), settle **7** inhabit, persons, society,
tilikum (Ind.) **8** humanity, populate,
tillicum (Ind.) **11** inhabitants, rank and file
aggregation: **4** bloc **5** group, tribe
ancient: **4** Seba **5** Itali, Medes **6** Greeks,
Romans **7** Sabines **8** Grecians, Persians **9**
Assyrians, Egyptians, Etruscans, Sumerians
11 Babylonians
ape-shaped skull: **9** proghathi
body: **4** race **5** tribe **6** nation **7** society **8**
assembly, populace **9** citizenry, community
10 electorate, public Rais
group: mob **4** army, band, body, team **5**
corps, crowd, posse **6** chorus, throng,
troupe **7** company, coterie **8** assembly **9**
orchestra **11** association
headless: **8** Acephali

pert. to: **6** ethnic **7** demotic
present: **5** class, crowd **10** assemblage, attendance **12** congregation
well-bred: **6** gentry **9** gentility

pep: vim **4** dash, elan **5** verve, vigor **6** energy, ginger **7** animate, quicken **9** animation, briskness, encourage, stimulate **10** initiative, invigorate, liveliness

peplos: **5** scarf, shawl

peplum: **9** overskirt

pepo: **5** gourd, melon **6** squash **7** pumpkin **8** cucumber

pepper: ava, hot, red **4** kava, siri **5** betel, green, sirih, sweet **7** paprica, paprika, pimento, speckle **8** capsicum, kavakava, pimiento
beverage: **4** kava **8** kavakava
genus: **5** Piper
grass: **5** cress
hot: **5** chili **7** cayenne, tabasco **8** jalapeno
Jamaica: **8** allspice
package: **5** robin
shrub: **4** cava, kava
species: **5** betel **7** cayenne

peppermint camphor: **7** menthol

pepper picker: **5** Peter Piper

pepper plant: ava **5** chile, chili **6** chilli

peppery: hot **4** keen **5** alert, fiery **6** lively **7** piquant, pungent **8** choleric, spirited, stinging **9** irascible, irritable **10** passionate

peppy: **4** keen **5** alert **6** lively **8** spirited **9** vivacious

Pequod's captain: **4** Ahab

per: **4** each **6** apiece **7** through

peradventure: hap **5** doubt, maybe **6** chance, mayhap **7** happily, perhaps **8** possibly **11** uncertainty

perambulate: **4** walk **5** amble, mosey **6** ramble, stroll **7** meander, saunter **8** traverse **9** promenade

perambulator: **4** pram **5** buggy **8** odometer, stroller **12** baby-carriage, pushwainling

per capita: all **4** each **6** apiece

perceivable: **11** perceptible

perceive: see **4** feel, hear, know, note, take **5** grasp, scent, sense, smell, taste, touch **6** behold, descry, divine, notice **7** discern, observe, realize, sensate **8** comprise, comprize, identify **9** apprehend, recognize **10** articulate, comprehend, understand **11** distinguish **12** discriminate

perceiving: **5** acute

percentage: **4** agio, odds, part **5** share **6** profit **7** portion, rake-off **9** advantage **11** probability

perceptible: **5** clear, lucid **7** tactile, visible **8** palpable, sensible, tangible **10** cognizable, noticeable **11** appreciable, discernible, perceivable **12** intelligible, recognizable

perception: ken **4** idea **6** acumen **7** insight **9** sensation **13** animadversion, consciousness
capable of: **8** sentient
impaired: **13** acatamathesia

perch: bar, peg, rod, sit **4** dory, fish, jook, mado, okow, pike, pole, pope **5** barse, light, roost, ruffe, staff **6** alight, sauger, settle, weapon, zingel **7** walleye **8** blow fish, pickerel **9** trumpeter **10** jack salmon

perchance: **5** haply, maybe **7** perhaps **8** possibly

Percheron: **5** horse

percolate: **4** drip, ooze, seep, sift, silt **5** exude, leach **6** bubble, filter, strain **7** pervade **8** permeate

percolator: **6** biggin **9** coffeepot

percussion: **5** shock **6** impact **9** collision **10** detonation

percussion instrument: **4** drum, gong, trap **6** cymbal **7** marimba **8** triangle **9** xylophone **10** tambourine **12** glockenspiel

percylite: **7** boleite

perdition: **4** hell, loss, ruin **9** damnation **11** destruction

perdue, perdu: **4** lost **6** hidden **9** concealed

perdurable: **7** durable, eternal, lasting **8** enduring **9** permanent **11** everlasting

Pere Goriot author: **6** Balzac

peregrinate: **4** roam, walk **6** travel, wander **7** journey, sojourn **8** traverse

peregrine: **4** hawk **5** alien **6** exotic, falcon **7** foreign, pilgrim, strange

peremptory: **5** final, utter **7** decided, express **8** absolute, decisive, dogmatic, positive **9** arbitrary, imperious, masterful **10** conclusive, imperative **11** dictatorial **13** authoritative

perennial (see also **flower**): old, rue **4** tree **5** carex, liana, liane, peony, plant, sedum **6** banana **7** durable **8** enduring, geophyte, toadflax **9** continual, permanent, perpetual, recurrent, unceasing **12** neverfailing

perfect: all **4** fill, fine, holy, pure **5** exact, ideal, right, ripen, sheer, sound, utter, whole **6** entire, expert, finish **7** concoct, correct, improve, plenary, precise, sinless, spheral **8** absolute, accurate, circular, complete, finished, flawless, masterly, thorough **9** blameless, elaborate, exquisite, faultless, righteous **10** accomplish, consummate, immaculate, satisfying

perfecta: bet **6** exacta **11** betting pool

perfection: **4** acme, pink **5** ideal **6** purity **7** fulness, paragon **8** fullness, maturity **9** integrity **10** excellence **12** flawlessness
realm of: **6** Heaven, Utopia **8** Paradise

perfectly: **4** well **5** quite **10** altogether

perfecto: **5** cigar

perfervid: 6 ardent 7 zealous 11 impassioned

perfidious: 5 false, snaky, venal 8 disloyal, spiteful 9 deceitful, dishonest, faithless, felonious 10 traitorous, unfaithful 11 disaffected, treacherous

perfidy: 7 treason 8 apostasy, foul play 9 defection, Judas' kiss, treachery 10 disloyalty, infidelity 13 faithlessness

perforate: eat 4 bore, dock 5 drill, prick, punch 6 pierce, pounce, riddle 8 puncture 9 penetrate, torebrate 10 foraminate

perforation: 4 bore, hole 6 broach, eyelet, tresis 7 stencil 8 aperture

perform: act 4 char, fill, full, play 5 chare, dight, enact, exert, stage 6 effect, fulfil, render, wind up 7 achieve, execute, exhibit, exploit, fulfill, furnish, gesture 8 bring off, carry out, complete, transact 9 discharge, do up brown 10 accomplish, perpetrate
again: 7 re-enact
inadequately: 5 botch 6 bungle, mess up
with ceremony: 9 solemnise, solemnize

performance: act 4 deed, feat, play, show, test, work 5 stunt 6 acting, action, effect 7 benefit, concert, exploit, matinee 8 feasance, function 9 discharge, execution, rendition 10 completion, efficiency, fulfilment 11 fulfillment 12 consummation 14 accomplishment
daytime: 7 matinee
first: 5 debut 8 premiere
individual: 4 soli, solo
standard: 5 bogey

performer: 4 doer, mime, moke 5 actor, shine 6 artist, dancer, worker 7 actress, artiste 8 comedian, executor, musician, thespian
company: 6 troupe
diligent: 5 plier 6 drudge 7 plugger 10 workaholic
low-grade: 7 goof-off 9 hamfatter 11 goldbricker
supplementary: 7 ripieno
top-notch: ace 4 star

perfume: 4 atar, aura, balm, nose, otto 5 aroma, attar, cense, irone, myrrh, ottar, scent, smell 6 chypre, flavor, sachet 7 cologne, essence, extract, flavour, incense, odorize, sweeten 8 bergamot, fumigate 9 fragrance
base: 4 musk 5 civet 6 castor, neroli 8 bergamot 9 ambergris
container: 4 vial 5 phial 6 censer, flacon
medicated: 6 pastil, troche 7 pastile 8 pastille
oriental: 5 myrrh
pad: 6 sachet
powdery: 6 pulvil
shrub source: 8 abelmosk
source: 4 rose 7 jasmine 8 cinnamon, gera-

nium, lavender, rosemary, tuberose 9 patchouli 10 citronella, sandalwood
with burning spice: 5 cense

perfumed cherry: 7 mahaleb

perfumer: 6 censer, sachet 8 atomizer, pomander, thurible

perfunctory: 5 token, usual 7 cursory, routine 8 careless 9 automatic 10 mechanical 11 half-hearted, indifferent, superficial

pergola: 5 arbor, bower 6 arbour 7 balcony, trellis 9 colonnade

perhaps: 5 maybe 6 ablins, belike, theory 7 ablings 8 doubtful, possibly, probably 9 perchance 11 conceivably

peri: elf 5 dwarf, fairy, houri 6 sprite

periapt: 5 charm 6 amulet

pericarp: pod 4 boll 5 berry, shell

Pericles: *city:* 6 Athens
consort: 7 Aspasia
coworker: 9 Ephialtes
daughter: 6 Marina
disciple: 10 Alcibiades
father: 10 Xanthippus
great-uncle: 11 Cleisthenes
rival: 5 Cimon 10 Thucydides
ward: 10 Alcibiades

periculum: 4 risk 5 peril 6 danger

peril: 4 risk 6 crises, crisis, danger, hazard, menace 7 apperil, imperil 8 endanger, exposure, jeopardy 9 adventure 10 insecurity, subjection

perilous: 6 touchy 7 tottery 8 doubtful, unstable, unsteady 9 dangerous, desperate

perimeter: rim 6 border 7 outline 8 boundary 9 periphery 13 circumference

period: age, dot, end, eon, era 4 aeon, span, stop, term, time 5 avail, class, close, cycle, epact, epoch, spell, stage 6 season 8 duration, semester 10 conclusion 11 termination
critical: 6 crises, crisis
festive: 7 holiday 8 vacation
holding: 6 tenure
infinite: 8 eternity
penitential: 4 Lent
playing: 4 half, hand 5 frame, round 6 inning 7 chukkar, chukker, quarter
sleep: 6 godown 10 estivation 11 hibernation
tertiary: 6 eocene 7 neocene
time: day 4 hour, week, year 5 month 6 decade, minute, second 7 century 9 fortnight 10 millennium

periodic: 4 eral 6 annual 7 etesian, regular 8 frequent, seasonal 9 recurrent 10 occasional 12 intermittent

periodical: 5 daily, paper 6 annual, review 7 etesian, journal, tabloid 8 bulletin, magazine 9 ephemeris, newspaper

peripatetic: 6 roving 7 vagrant 8 rambling 9 itinerant, wandering
peripheral: 5 outer 6 distal 7 distant 8 confined, external, marginal
periphery: lip, rim 4 brim, edge 5 ambit, limit 6 areola, areole, border 7 areolae, outside 8 confines, environs 9 perimeter 13 circumference
periphrastic: 14 circumlocutory
perique: 7 tobacco
perish: die 4 fade, fall, ruin 5 decay 6 depart, expire 7 consume, crumble, forfare, go under, succumb 8 pass away
perishable: 6 caduke 7 brittle 9 ephemeral 10 transitory
peristyle: 6 arcade 7 portico 9 colonnade 10 peripteral
perite: 7 skilled
peritomy: 12 circumcision
peritoneum: 8 covering, membrane
    fold of: 7 omentum
peritroch: 5 larva 6 embryo
periwig: wig 6 peruke, toupee
periwinkle: 5 color, snail 6 mussel, myrtle 10 bluebutton
perjink: 4 neat, nice, trim 7 precise
perjure: lie 8 forswear 10 equivocate 11 prevaricate
perk (see also **perquisite**): 5 preen, prink 7 benefit, improve, smarten 8 animated, gratuity 9 percolate, privilege 10 perquisite
permanent: 4 wave 5 fixed 6 stable 7 abiding, durable, lasting 8 constant, enduring 9 continual, perennial 10 continuing, invariable 12 imperishable
permeable: 6 porous 9 saturable
permeate: 4 fill, seep 5 bathe, imbue 6 drench 7 pervade 8 saturate 9 penetrate
permission: 4 okay 5 leave 6 assent 7 consent, license 8 sanction 13 authorization
permit: let 4 leve, pass 5 admit, allow, conge, favor, grace, grant, leave 6 accord, beteem, dustuk, entree, favour, suffer 7 consent, dustuck, license, pompano, warrant 8 furlough, tolerate 9 authorize 10 permission
    travel: 4 visa 8 passport
permutation: 6 change 10 alteration 11 interchange 12 modification 13 rearrangement
pern: 7 buzzard
pernicious: bad 4 evil 5 fatal, toxic 6 deadly, malign, mortal, wicked 7 baleful, baneful, harmful, hurtful, malefic, noisome, noxious, ruinous 10 villainous 11 deleterious, destructive, detrimental
pernio: 9 chilblain
peronate: 5 mealy, wooly
perorate: 5 orate 7 address, declaim 8 harangue

perpendicular: 4 sine 5 erect, plumb, sheer 6 abrupt 7 apothem, stand-up, upright 8 binormal, straight, vertical 9 downright
perpetrate: 5 wreak 6 commit, effect 7 perform
perpetual: 7 abiding, endless, eternal 8 constant, unending 9 continual, incessant, perennial, permanent, unceasing 10 continuous 11 everlasting
perpetually: 4 ever 6 always 7 forever 11 ad infinitum
perpetuate: 4 keep 8 continue, eternize, maintain, preserve
perplex: cap 4 clog, doze 5 amaze, beset 6 baffle, boggle, bother, cumber, darken, gravel, hamper, harass, hobble, muddle, pother, puzzle, thwart, twitch 7 bedevil, confuse, diffuse, embroil, mystify, nonplus 8 astonish, babulyie, bewilder, confound, distract, distress, entangle 9 bamboozle, obfuscate 10 complicate
perplexed: 4 asea 5 upset 7 anxious, puzzled 8 confused, troubled 9 intricate 10 distraught
perplexing: 4 hard, mazy 6 crabby 7 carking, complex, crabbed 8 puzzling 9 equivocal 11 complicated
perplexity: fox 4 knot 6 puzzle, tangle 7 anxiety, problem, trouble 9 intricacy 11 encumbrance 13 embarrassment
perquisite (see also **perk**): fee, tip 5 right 6 income 7 adjunct, apanage 8 appanage, appenage, gratuity 9 accessory, privilege 11 appointment, prerogative 12 appurtenance 13 accompaniment
    congressional: 8 franking
    presidential: 4 veto
perquod: 7 whereby
Perry Mason: *character:* 9 Paul Drake 11 Della Street
    creator: 7 Gardner
per se: 5 alone 6 as such, solely 8 directly, in itself 11 essentially 13 intrinsically
Perse: *daughter:* 5 Circe 8 Pasiphae
    father: 7 Oceanus
    husband: 6 Helios
    son: 6 Aeetes, Perses
persecute: vex 4 bait 5 annoy, harry, hound, worry, wrack, wrong 6 harass, pester 7 afflict, oppress, torment, torture
Persephone: 4 Kore 8 Despoina 10 Proserpina
    daughter: 4 Cora, Kore
    father: 4 Zeus 7 Jupiter
    husband: 5 Hades, Pluto
    mother: 5 Ceres 7 Demeter
Perseus: *father:* 4 Zeus
    grandfather: 8 Acrisius
    mother: 5 Danae

rescuer: **6** Dictys
slayed: **6** Medusa
star of: **4** Atik **5** Algol
victim: **8** Acrisius
wife: **9** Andromeda

perseverance: **4** grit **7** stamina **8** patience, tenacity **9** assiduity, constancy, diligence, endurance **10** insistence **11** continuance, persistence, pertinacity **13** steadfastness

persevere: **4** go on **5** abide, stick **6** endure **7** persist **8** keep at it

persevering: **4** busy **6** dogged **8** tireless **10** persistent, unflagging **11** unremitting

Persia (see also **Iran**): *ancient inhabitant:* **4** Mede
apple: **6** citron
assembly: **6** majlis, meklis
bug: **5** miana
carpet: see *rug* below
cat: **6** Angora
chief officer: **5** dewan, diwan
city: **10** Persepolis
conqueror: **9** Alexander, Parthians, Sassanids
deer: **5** maral **6** fallow
dynasty: **8** Parthian, Sassanid, Seleucid
elf or fairy: **4** peri
first civilization: **7** Elamite
gate: bab
gazelle: **4** cora
god: **6** Ormazd **7** Mithras **9** Zoroaster **10** Ahura Mazda
goddess: **7** Anahita
king, ancient: **5** Cyrus **6** Darius, Xerxes **7** Jamshid, Jamshyd **9** Giamschid **10** Artaxerxes
lamb: **7** karakul **9** astrakhan
lynx: **7** caracal
measure: gaz, guz, zer
nightingale: **6** bulbul
oil center: **6** Abadan
old coin: **5** daric
poet: **4** Omar **5** Hafiz, Saadi **8** Firdausi
prophet: **9** Zoroaster **11** Zarathustra
province: **7** satrapy
robe: **6** caftan
rug: **4** Kali **5** Saruk, Senna **6** Sarouk **7** Isfahan, Ispahan, Teheran **8** Serabend
ruler: **4** shah
sungod: **7** Mithras

Persian Gulf: *country:* UAE **4** Iran, Iraq **5** Qatar **6** Kuwait **7** Bahrain, Chaldea **11** Saudi Arabia
port: **5** Dubai **6** Abaran, Basrah **7** Bushehr, Bushire, Dhahran **8** Abu Dhabi
province: **4** Fars
wind: **6** shamal, sharki **7** shurgee

persiennes: **6** blinds

persiflage: **6** banter **7** mockery **8** chaffing, raillery

persimmon: **4** kaki, tree **5** fruit **7** chapote
family: **5** ebony **9** ebenaceae

persist: **4** go on, last **6** endure, insist, remain **7** carry on, prevail **8** continue **9** persevere

persistent: **4** dree, hard **6** dogged, gritty **7** durable **8** constant, enduring, frequent, holdfast, obdurate, resolute, stubborn **9** assiduous, continued, steadfast, tenacious **10** consistent, continuing, determined, relentless **12** persevering **13** indefatigable

person (see also **people**): guy, man, one, urf **4** body, chap, coot, self, soul **5** being, child, human, wight, woman **6** entity, fellow, galoot **10** individual
admirable: **5** brick **6** mensch
amusing: wit **5** comic **8** comedian, comedien **10** comedienne **11** entertainer
backwoods: **7** cracker, redneck **9** hillbilly
bad-luck carrier: **4** jinx **5** jonah
baptized: **10** illuminato **11** illuminatus
base: cad **5** devil **6** rascal **7** caitiff, hangdog **8** criminal
bearing the blame: **4** butt, goat **9** scapegoat
beatified: **6** beatus
betrothed: **6** fiance **7** fiancee
brilliant: **6** genius **10** mastermind
callow: **6** gorlin, jejune, smarty **7** gosling, pevrile
canonized: **4** holy **5** saint
careless: **6** tassel **11** pococurante
charitable: **9** samaritan **14** philanthropist
cheery: **8** optimist
clumsy: **5** klutz
contemptible: cad, yap **4** heel, toad **7** bauchle
cunning: **8** slyboots **9** trickster
deranged: nut **7** lunatic **10** monomaniac, psychopath
despicable: **5** hound **6** rotter **10** blackguard
detested: **8** anathema
disgruntled: **8** sorehead
dull: **4** bore **5** dunce, moron **8** imbecile **9** blockhead, defective
eighty-year-old: **12** octogenarian
energetic: **10** ball of fire
enterprising: **8** go-getter
fearless: **10** fearnaught, fearnought **11** dreadnaught, dreadnought
fifty-year-old: **15** quinquagenarian
foolish: sop **4** zany **5** clown **6** dotard **7** halfwit **9** simpleton
forty-year-old: **14** quadragenarian
gloomy: **9** pessimist
good-luck carrier: **6** mascot
gray-headed: **7** grisard
guilty: **7** culprit
half-grown: **6** haflin **8** halfling **9** stripling
held as pledge: **7** hostage
holy: ste. (F.) **5** saint **7** blessed

horned: **7** cornute, cuckold

ill: **7** invalid, patient

indefinite: one **6** anyone **7** anybody, so and so, someone **8** somebody **11** whatsisname

indifferent to pleasure or pain: **5** stoic

injured: **6** victim **8** casualty

learned: **6** pundit, savant **7** scholar **9** professor **12** intellectual

left-handed: **9** portsider

loud-voiced: **7** stentor

married: **4** wife **6** spouse **7** husband

middle-class: **9** bourgeois **11** bourgeoisie

mischievous: imp **4** pest

named after another: **8** namesake

ninety-year-old: **12** nonagenarian

non-Jewish: goy **7** gentile

of distinction: VIP **4** star **7** notable

of mixed blood: **7** mestizo, mulatto **8** octoroon, quadroon **9** half-breed

one-hundred-year-old: **11** centenarian

overnice: **4** prig **5** priss

perfidious: **5** Judas, snake **7** serpent, traitor **8** betrayer

proposed for office: **7** nominee **9** candidate

rapacious: **4** wolf **5** harpy, shark

representing another: **5** mimic, proxy **6** lawyer **8** attorney **9** alternate

rude: **4** boor **7** caveman

scolding: hag, nag **5** shrew **8** harridan **9** catamaran

second: you **4** thee, thou

seventy-year-old: **14** septuagenarian

shiftless: bum **4** hobo **7** drifter, vagrant

sick: **5** ailer **7** invalid, patient **9** aegrotant

sixty-year-old: **12** sexagenarian

skilled: **5** adept **6** artist, master, talent **7** artisan **8** mechanic **9** craftsman **12** craftsperson

small: **4** runt **5** dwarf, sprat **6** midget, poppet

sponsored by another: **7** protege

studious: **5** grind, porer **7** egg head

stupid: ass **4** boob, clod, coot, dolt, fool, gump, moke **5** bucca, clout, moron, stirk, stock, stupe, sumph **6** boodle, duffer, gander, nitwit **7** dullard **8** bone-head, dumbbell, gamphrel **9** boeoetian, simpleton

timid: **11** milquetoast

trustworthy: **4** rock **7** standby

unmarried: **6** maiden **8** bachelor, celibate, spinster

unusual: **4** oner

wealthy: **5** nabob **6** tycoon **9** plutocrat **10** capitalist **11** millionaire **12** millionnaire

white: fay **4** ofay **5** haole, honky **6** albino, honkie **7** abiculi

young: kid **4** tyke **5** child **6** junior **8** chipling **9** stripling **14** whipper-snapper

personable: **6** comely **7** shapely **8** handsome **10** attractive **11** good-looking, well-favored

personage: VIP **5** celeb **6** shogun, tycoon **7** magnate, notable **9** celebrity

personal: own **7** private **8** intimate, news item

personality: ego **4** self **8** selfhood **11** disposition **13** individuality

dual: **13** Jekyll and Hyde

split: **13** schizophrenia (formerly)

persona non grata: **12** unacceptable

personification: **10** embodiment **11** incarnation **14** representation

of rumor: **4** Fama

of truth: Una

personify: **6** embody **9** incarnate, represent **11** impersonate

personnel: **5** staff **7** workers **9** employees

perspective: **5** vista **7** outlook **9** viewpoint

perspicacious: **4** keen **5** acute **6** shrewd **10** discerning, perceptive **11** penetrating, sharp-witted

perspicacity: wit **6** acumen **7** insight

perspicuous: **5** clear, lucid, plain **8** manifest **11** conspicuous, translucent, transparent **12** intelligible

perspiration: **5** sudor, sweat **9** exudation **10** ephidrosis

abnormal: **8** hidrosis

pert. to: **7** sudoric

sheep: **5** suint

persuade: get, win **4** coax, gain, sway, urge **5** argue **6** allure, assure, engage, entice, induce **7** convert, entreat, win over **8** convince, inveigle **9** influence

persuaded: **7** pliable **8** gullible **9** credulous

persuasion: **4** cult, mind, sect, view **6** belief, church **7** faction **8** judgment, religion **10** conviction

persuasive: **6** cogent **8** eloquent **9** impelling, inductive **10** convincing

pert: **4** bold **5** alert, alive, bardy, brisk, cocky, quick, sassy, saucy, smart **6** active, brazen, clever, cocket, comely, dapper, frisky, lively **7** forward, naughty **8** handsome, impudent, insolent, petulant **9** exquisite, officious, sprightly **11** flourishing

pertain: **5** belie **6** bear on, befall, belong, relate **7** concern **9** accessory, associate

pert girl: **4** minx **5** hussy

pertinacious: **4** firm **6** dogged **8** adhering, stubborn **9** obstinate, tenacious **10** determined, inflexible, persistent, unshakable, unyielding

pertinent: apt, fit, pat **6** proper, timely **7** adapted, apropos, germane, telling **8** apposite, relative, relevant **10** applicable, felicitous **11** appropriate **12** appurtenance

perturb: **5** upset, worry **7** agitate, confuse, derange, disturb, trouble **8** disorder, unsettle **10** discompose, disconcert

perturbation: **6** flight, pother **7** trouble, turmoil **9** agitation, commotion **10** uneasiness **12** irregularity

pertussis: **5** cough **13** whooping cough

Peru: *ancient ruler:* **4** Inca
  animal: **4** paco **5** llama **6** alpaca **7** guanaco
  bark: **8** cinchona
  capital: **4** Lima
  city: Ica **5** Cuzco, Paita **6** Callao **8** Arequipa, Chiclayo, Chimbote, Trujillo
  conqueror: **7** Pizarro
  cormorant: **6** guanay
  currency: sol **5** libra **6** dinero, peseta **7** centavo **8** nuevo sol
  dance: **5** cueca
  empire: **4** Inca
  fog: **5** garua
  goddess: **4** Mama
  hillock: **4** loma
  inn: **5** tambo
  king: rey **7** cacique
  lake: **8** Titicaca
  language: **6** Aymara **7** Quechua, Spanish
  measure: **4** topo, vara **5** galon **7** celemin **8** fanegada
  mountain: **5** Andes **9** Huascaran
  partridge: **4** yutu
  plant: oca **6** ulluco **7** rhatany
  relic: **5** huaco
  rodent: **10** chinchilla
  ruins: **8** Chanchan **11** Machu Picchu
  shrub: **6** chilca, matico, shansa
  tableland: **4** mesa, puna
  tavern: **5** tambo
  tinamou: **4** yutu
  tree: **6** bucare **8** cinchona
  tuber: oca
  volcano: **5** Misti
  weight: **5** libra **7** quintal

---

peruke: wig **6** toupee **7** periwig

peruse: con **4** read, scan **5** study **6** handle, search, survey **7** examine, inspect **9** supervise

pervade: **4** fill **5** bathe, imbue **6** infuse, occupy **8** permeate, traverse **9** penetrate

pervading: **8** profound **9** prevalent, universal **10** widespread

perverse: awk **4** awry, wogh, wraw **6** cranky, divers, wicked, wilful **7** awkward, distort, diverse, forward, froward, twisted, vicious, wayward, willful **8** backward, camshach, contrary, crotched, petulant, stubborn **9** camsteary, camsteery, difficult, fractious, obstinate **10** determined **11** contentious, contrarious, disobedient, intractable **12** cantankerous, contumacious

perversely: auk, awk **7** athwart **8** overwart

pervert: **4** ruin, skew, warp **5** abuse, twist, upset **6** debase, divert, garble, invert, misuse, poison **7** contort, corrupt, deprave, distort, outrage, vitiate **8** apostate, misapply, overturn, renegade **9** misdirect **10** demoralize **12** misinterpret, misrepresent

perverted: bad **6** warped, wicked **7** corrupt, twisted, vicious **9** unnatural

pervious: **4** open **6** leachy **9** permeable **10** accessible **11** transparent

pervulgate: **7** publish

Pescadores (see also **Taiwan**): *island:* **4** Hoko **6** Pengho
  town: **4** Mako

peshkar: **5** agent **7** steward **8** minister **10** accountant

peshkash: tax **7** present, tribute **8** offering

pesky: **6** plaguy **8** annoying **9** pestering, vexatious **11** troublesome **12** disagreeable

peso: **4** coin
  silver: **4** duro

pessimism: **5** gloom **7** despair **8** cynicism

pessimistic: **6** gloomy **7** alarmed, cynical **8** negative **9** depressed

pest: **4** bane, weed **5** hound, mouse, worry **6** insect, plague, vermin **7** trouble **8** epidemic, nuisance **9** annoyance **10** pestilence

pester: dun, nag, rib **4** ride **5** annoy, devil, tease, worry **6** badger, bother, harass, molest **7** torment, trouble **9** aggravate **10** drive crazy

pestiferous: **4** evil **10** pernicious **11** mischievous

pestilence: **4** pest **5** death **6** plague **7** disease, scourge **8** epidemic

pestilent: **6** deadly **7** noxious **9** poisonous **10** contagious, infectious

pestle: **4** bray **5** grind **6** beetle, muller
  vessel: **6** mortar **10** pulverizer

pet: cat, dog, hug **4** coax, daut (Sc.), dawt (Sc.), dear, duck, huff, neck, snit, sulk, tiff **5** drunt, humor, pique, quiet, spoil **6** animal, caress, coddle, cosher, cuddle, dautie (Sc.), dawtie (Sc.), faddle, fantad, fantod, fondle, pamper, stroke **7** darling **8** favorite **9** cherished

petal: ala **4** leaf **5** bract, sepal **8** labellum

petals: **7** corolla
  without: **9** apetalous

petard: **6** mortar **8** firework **11** firecracker

peteman: **5** thief **7** burglar **8** peterman **9** cracksman **10** safeblower **11** safecracker

peter: **4** fade, fail, wane **5** cease **7** dwindle, exhaust **8** decrease, diminish
  out: **6** fizzle

Peter: 4 czar, rock 5 saint, Simon
  brother: 6 Andrew
  father: 5 Jonas
Peter Pan: *author:* 6 Barrie
  character: 4 John 5 Wendy 7 Michael 9 Tiger Lily 10 Tinker Bell
  dog: 4 Nana
  pirate: 4 Smee
petiole: 4 stem 5 stalk 8 peduncle 9 leaf-stalk 10 mesopodium
petite: 4 size, trim 5 small 6 demure, little 10 diminutive
petition: ask, beg, sue 4 bill, boon, plea, pray, suit, wish 5 apply, orate, plead 6 appeal, prayer, steven, sue for 7 address, entreat, implore, oration, request, solicit 8 entreaty 10 supplicate 11 application, deprecation 12 supplication 13 contemplation
petitioner: 5 asker 6 beggar, seeker 8 appealer, beadsman, bedesman 9 applicant, suppliant
  chancery: 7 relator
peto: 5 wahoo
Petrarch's love: 5 Laura
petrel: 4 titi 5 mitty 7 assilag 8 allamoth 9 albatross, allamonti, allamotti, mallemuck
petrify: 4 daze, numb 5 alarm 6 appall, deaden 7 horrify, startle 9 fossilize 11 turn to stone
petrifying: 7 numbing 9 deadening, hardening 10 petrescent, terrifying 11 fossilizing, frightening
Petrograd: 9 Leningrad
petrol: gas 8 gasoline
petroleum: oil 6 octane 7 naphtha 10 illuminant
  by-product: 6 butane, diesel 7 benzine, propane 9 propylene
  product: wax 4 coke 5 ethyl 6 petrol 7 alcohol, ammonia, asphalt, canadol, naphtha 8 gasoline, hydrogen, kerosene, paraffin 9 righolene 10 fertilizer
petrosal: 4 hard 5 stony
petticoat: 4 kilt, slip 5 jupon, pagne 6 kirtle 7 placket, whittle 8 basquine, halfslip, vasquine 9 crinoline, undercoat, waistcoat 10 fustanella, underskirt 11 farthingale
  tails: 7 teacake 9 shortcake
pettifogger: 6 lawyer 7 shyster 8 attorney, quibbler 10 bush lawyer
pettle: 4 spud 5 spade 6 cuddle, nestle, potter 7 cherish, indulge
petty: 4 base, mean, orra, puny 5 minor, small 6 little, paltry, puisne 7 trivial 8 childish, inferior, nugatory, trifling 9 frivolous, jerkwater, minuscule 10 diminutive 11 Mickey Mouse, subordinate, unimportant 12 contemptible 13 insignificant 14 inconsiderable

  fault: 10 peccadillo
  matter: 6 fidfad
  morel: 9 spikenard 10 nightshade
  whin: 10 restharrow
petulant: 4 pert 5 cross, huffy, saucy, short, sulky, testy 6 sullen, wanton, wilful 7 forward, fretful, grouchy, peevish, pettish, wayward 8 contrary, immodest, insolent, perverse 9 impatient, irascible, irritable, plaintive, querulous 10 ill-humored
pew: 4 desk, seat, slip 5 bench, bught, stall 6 bought (Sc.) 10 amen corner
pewee: 10 flycatcher
pewter: tra 5 alloy, bidri, bidry 6 bidery, bidree 7 biddery
peyote: 5 plant 6 cactus, mescal, peyotl 9 mescaline
Phaedo's school: 5 Elian
Phaedra: *father:* 5 Minos
  husband: 7 Theseus
  stepson: 10 Hippolytus
Phaëthon: *created:* 8 Milky Way
  father: 6 Helios
  mother: 6 Aymene
phaeton: 8 carriage 10 automobile, touring car
phalacrocorax: 4 coot 9 cormorant
phalacrosis: 8 alopecia, baldness
phalanger: 5 ariel, tapoa 6 animal, possum 7 opossum 8 squirrel 9 marsupial
phalera: 4 boss, disk, moth, stud 5 cameo
phantasm: 5 dream, fancy, ghost, shade, vapor 6 mirage, shadow, vision 7 phantom 8 delusion
phantasmal: 6 unreal 10 transitory
phantom: 4 idol 5 bogie, ghost, idola, image, shade, umbra 6 eidola (pl.), idolon, idolum, shadow, spirit 7 bugbear, eidolon, fantasy, specter, spectre 8 illusion 10 apparition
Phaon's consort: 6 Sappho
Pharaoh: 4 king 5 ruler 6 tyrant
Pharaoh's chicken: 7 vulture
Pharaoh's fig: 8 sycamore
Pharaoh's mouse: 9 ichneumon
phare: 6 strait 10 lighthouse
pharisaical: 12 hypocritical
pharmaceutical: dia 7 mellite 9 medicinal
pharmacist: 8 druggist 9 dispenser 10 apothecary
pharmacy weight: 5 obole 6 obolus
pharos: 5 cloak 6 beacon 7 lantern 10 chandelier, lighthouse
phase: 4 hand, side 5 angle, facet, stage 6 aspect 8 passover 13 manifestation
pheasant: 5 argus, cheer, monal 6 monaul, moonal, pukras 7 kallege 8 fireback, tragopan
  breeding-place: 4 stew
  brood: nid, nye 4 nide
  kind: 6 golden, Reeves 10 ring-necked

nest: 4 nide
pheasant cuckoo: 6 coucal
pheasant duck: 7 pintail 9 merganser
pheasant finch: 7 waxbill
phenol: 6 orcine, thymol 9 germicide
   derivative: 4 anol 5 orcin 6 iresol, thymol
phenomenal: 7 unusual 9 marvelous 10 remarkable 11 exceptional 13 extraordinary
phenomenon: 4 fact 6 marvel, phenom 7 miracle, reality, stunner 9 actuality 10 experience
phenyl salicylate: 5 salol
phial: cup 4 bowl, vial 6 bottle, vessel
Philadelphia: *baseball team:* 8 Phillies

basketball team: 13 Seventy-Sixers
football team: 6 Eagles
landmarks: 11 Liberty Bell 16 Independence Hall
philander: 5 cheat, dally, flirt 7 opossum 10 flirtation, fool around, play around
philanthropic: 6 humane 10 altruistic, benevolent, charitable 11 civic-minded 12 eleemosynary, humanitarian
philanthropist: 5 donor 10 benefactor 12 humanitarian
philanthropy: 4 alms 10 almsgiving
   universal: 15 omnibenevolence
philippic: 6 screed, tirade 8 diatribe 9 invective

Philippines: *ant:* 4 anai, anay
   attendant: 5 alila
   banana: 7 lacatan, saguing
   barracks: 7 cuartel
   beer: 7 pangasi
   bird: 4 maya 6 abacay
   boat: 5 balsa, banca 8 balangay, barangay
   breadfruit: 4 rima 8 casmansi
   buffalo: 7 carabao, timarau, timerau
   canoe: 5 banca, vinta 6 baroto
   capital: 6 Manila
   carriage: 9 carretela, carromata
   chief: 4 dato 5 datto, Iloco 7 Ilocano, Ilokano
   Christianized tribe: 5 Bicol, Bikol, Tagal, Vicol 7 Bisayan, Tagalog, Visayan
   city: Iba 4 Agoa, Cebu, Naga 5 Albay, Davao 6 Aparri, Baguio, Cavite, Ilagan 7 Dagupan 9 Zamboanga 10 Quezon City
   clothing: 10 balintawak 13 barong tagalog
   currency: 4 peso 7 centavo
   cyclone: 6 baguio
   dagger: 4 itac 7 balarao
   deity: 5 Dagon
   dialect: 4 Moro 5 Bicol, Tagal 6 Ibanag 7 Ilocano, Visayan
   discoverer: 8 Magellan
   drink: 4 beno, tuba, vino 5 bubud 7 pangasi
   farmer: lao, tao
   fern: 4 nito
   fetish: 5 anito
   fiber: 4 eruc 6 buntal 9 pineapple
   fish: 7 tilapia 8 langaray
   forest: 5 gubat
   garment: 4 saya
   grass: 5 cogon
   guerrilla: Huk

   hardwood: 4 ipil 5 narra
   hat: 7 salacot
   hemp: 5 abaca 6 manila
   house: 5 bahay
   idol: 5 anito
   kitchen: 5 calan
   knife: 4 bolo, itac 7 balarao, machete
   language: 8 Pilipino
   lighthouse: 4 faro
   litter: 7 talabon
   lizard: 4 ibid
   mango: 5 bauno 7 pahutan
   market-day: 7 tiangue
   measure: 4 loan 5 braza, caban, cavan, chupa, ganta 6 apatan, balita, quinon
   measure of weight: 5 catty, fardo, picul, punto 6 lachsa 7 quilate 8 chinanta
   mother: ina
   mountain: Apo, Iba 5 Mayon, Pulog 7 Banahao 8 Zambales
   mountaineer: 8 mentesco
   mudfish: 5 dalag
   muskmelon: 6 atimon
   Muslim: 4 Moro
   nut: 4 pili
   oil: 5 cebur
   pagan: 6 Italon
   palm: 4 nipa 6 anahao, anahau
   parrot: 5 cagit
   peasant: tao
   plain: 6 Iloilo
   plant: aga 4 alem 5 abaca, baroi, batad 6 agamid
   plum: 6 sapote
   priest: 7 pandita
   raft: 5 balsa
   rice: 4 paga 5 barit, bigas, macan
   road: 4 daan
   rope tree: 4 nabo 5 anabo *(cont.)*

Philippines *(cont.)*
  sapodilla: **5** chico
  sarong: **8** padadion
  sentinel: **6** bantay
  servant: **4** bata **5** alila
  shirt: **4** baro **6** barong
  shrub: **4** alem, nabo **6** anilao
  silk: **10** alcaiceria
  skirt: **4** saya
  slave: **6** alipin
  slipper: **7** chinela
  soap vine: **4** gogo
  spirit: **5** anito
  stream: **4** ilog
  sword: **6** barong **8** campilan

  textile: **4** pina, saba **7** sina-may
  thatch: **4** nipa
  timber: **5** cahuy
  tree bark: aga **6** agamid
  vehicle: **7** jeepney
  vine: iyo
  volcano: Apo **5** Mayon **7** Canlaon **8** Pinatubo
  watchtower: **7** atalaya **8** bantayan
  water buffalo: **7** carabao
  water-jar: **5** bango
  white man: **7** cachila
  wine: **4** beno
  yam: ubi, uve

Philistine: **4** boor **6** Cretan **7** Babbitt **9** barbarian, bourgeois
  city: **4** Gath, Gaza **5** Ekron **6** Ashdod **8** Ashkelon
  foe: **5** David **6** Samson
  giant: **7** Goliath
  god: **4** Baal **5** Dagan, Dagon
Philomela: **11** nightingale
  father: **7** Pandion
  ravisher: **6** Tereus
  sister: **6** Procne
philosopher: wit **4** sage **5** cynic, stoic **7** scholar, thinker
  disciples: **4** sect **6** school
  famous: **4** Hume, Kant, Marx, Mill, More, Zeno **5** Bacon, Hegel, James, Locke, Occam, Plato, Solon **6** Hobbes, Pascal, Sartre, Seneca, Thales **7** Abelard, Aquinas, Emerson, Leibniz, Russell, Spinoza **8** Avicenna, Diogenes, Rousseau, Socrates, Spengler, Voltaire **9** Aristotle, Confucius, Descartes, Epictetus, Heidegger, Nietzsche **10** Democritus, Parmenides, Pythagoras **11** Kierkegaard **12** Schopenhauer, Wittgenstein
philosophical: **4** wise **8** composed, rational **9** temperate, unruffled **11** level-headed
philosophy: **4** yoga **7** dualism **8** stoicism **9** esoterics, esthetics **10** empiricism, pragmatism **17** transcendentalism
philter, philtre: **4** drug **5** charm **6** potion **7** amatory **9** fascinate
phlebotomize: **5** bleed **8** venesect
phlegm: **5** mucus **6** apathy **8** stoicism **9** composure **10** equanimity **12** indifference
phlegmasia: **12** inflammation
phlegmatic: **4** calm, cool, dull, slow **5** inert **6** watery **7** viscous **8** composed, sluggish **9** apathetic, impassive, lethargic **11** indifferent **13** imperturbable

phloem: **4** bast, flax **6** tissue
phobia: **4** fear **5** dread **12** apprehension
phoca: **4** seal
Phoebad: **7** seeress **9** priestess **10** prophetess
phoebe: **4** bird **5** pewee, pewit **6** peewee **10** flycatcher
Phoebe: **5** Diane **6** Selene **7** Artemis
Phoebus: Sol, sun **6** Apollo
Phoenicia: *city:* **4** Tyre **5** Sidon **6** Byblos, Ugarit **7** Berytus
  colony: **8** Carthage
  dialect: **5** Punic
  god: **4** Baal **6** Eshmun **7** Melgart
  goddess: **5** Tanit **6** Baalat, Baltis, Tanith **7** Astarte
  goddess of love: **7** Astarte
  king: **5** Hiram **6** Agenor
  queen: **4** Dido
  seaport: **5** Sidon
phoenix: **4** bird **7** paragon **8** rara avis
phonetic: **4** oral **5** vocal
  notation system: **5** romic
phonograph: **6** stereo **8** victrola **9** turntable **10** gramophone **12** record player
  inventor: **6** Edison
  record: LP **4** disc, disk **5** vinyl **7** platter
phony: **4** fake, sham **5** bogus, false **8** impostor, spurious **9** charlatan **10** fictitious **11** counterfeit
Phorcys: *child:* **5** Ladon **6** Gorgon, Graeae (pl.)
  father: **6** Pontus
  mother: **4** Gaea
phosphate: **6** ehlite **7** apatite, uranite **9** wavellite
photocopy: **4** stat **5** print, Xerox
photoengraving: **8** halftone **15** heliotypography
photograph: mug **4** film, snap, X ray **7** picture, tintype **8** likeness, portrait, snapshot **9**

ferrotype, pictorial **10** cheesecake, heliograph **13** daguerreotype
bath: **5** fixer, toner **7** reducer **9** developer
book: **5** album
developer: **5** ortol **6** amidol **9** revelator
facsimile: **9** Photostat
fixing agent: **4** hypo
instant: **8** Polaroid
instrument: **6** camera **8** enlarger
inventor: **4** Land **6** Niepce, Talbot **7** Eastman **8** Daguerre
kind: **5** panel, still **6** motion **7** boudoir, cabinet, diamond **8** imperial, passport, portrait **12** composograph
negative: **4** film
old-fashioned: **7** tintype **13** daguerreotype
printing: **7** ozotype
photographer: **9** cameraman **10** shutterbug
photology: **6** optics **7** photics
photometric unit: pyr, rad **5** lumen
phrase: mot **4** term, word **5** idiom, state **6** clause, cliche, saving, slogan **7** adjunct, diction, epigram, epithet, thought **8** acrostic, locution **9** catchword, leitmotif **10** expression
phraseology: **7** dialect, diction, wording **8** parlance
phratry: **4** clan **5** curia, tribe
phrenetic: See **frenetic**
phrenic: **6** mental
Phrixos: *father:* **7** Athamus
mother: **7** Nephele
sister: **5** Helle
Phrygia: *enthusiast:* **9** Montanist
god: **4** Atys **5** Attis **8** Sabazios
goddess: **6** Cybele
king: **5** Midas **7** Gordius
river: **7** Meander
town: **5** Ipsus
phylactery: **5** charm **6** amulet, scroll **8** talisman
phyletic: **6** lineal, racial
phyma: **5** tumor **6** nodule
physic: **5** purge **6** remedy **8** medicine **9** cathartic
physical: **5** lusty **6** bodily, carnal **7** check up, natural, somatic **8** material **9** corporeal, somatical
physician (see also **doctor**): asa, doc **5** curer, medic, quack **6** doctor, healer, intern, medico **7** interne **8** restorer, sawbones **10** consultant, medicaster **11** aesculapian, Hippocrates, philosopher **12** practitioner
association: AMA
symbol: **8** caduceus
physicist: **9** hylozoist **10** naturalist
physiognomy: mug **4** face, mien **5** looks **7** feature **8** portrait **10** expression **11** countenance

physique: **4** body **5** build, frame, shape **6** figure **7** anatomy **8** strength **10** appearance **12** constitution
physostigmine: **5** esere **6** eserin **7** eserine
pian: **4** yaws **5** tumor **9** frambesia **10** framboesia
piano: **5** grand **6** player, softly, spinet **7** clavial, quietly, upright **8** pianette **10** anemochord, electronic, pianoforte
dumb keyboard: **9** digitoria **10** digitorium **11** finger board
early: **6** spinet **8** dulcimer **10** clavichord, pianoforte **11** harpsichord
key: **7** digital
keyboard: **7** clavier
notes: **6** octave
pedal: **6** damper **7** celeste **9** sostenuto
pedal keyboard: **8** pedalier
piatti: **7** cymbals
piazza: **5** porch **6** loggia, square **7** balcony, gallery, portico, veranda
pic: **4** peak **5** lance **8** picayune
picacho: **4** hill **5** butte
picador: wit **6** jester **7** debater **11** bullfighter
picadura: **7** tobacco
picaro, picaroon: **5** knave, rogue, tramp **6** bandit, pirate, rascal **7** sharper **8** vagabond **9** hooka-roon **10** adventurer, freebooter
picayune: **4** mean **5** small **6** little, measly, paltry
pichiciago: **9** armadillo
pick: **4** best, gaff, pike, wale **5** adorn, beele, cavil, elect, elite, pluck **6** choice, choose, gather, pickax, select, twitch **7** bargain, diamond **8** plectrum
on: **5** abuse, annoy, tease **9** criticize
out: **4** cull, sort **5** glean **6** assort, choose, select, winnow
pickax: **4** bill, pick **6** tubber, twibil **7** mattock, twibill
picked: **5** spiny **8** selected, stripped **10** fastidious
picket: peg **4** pale, post **5** fence, guard, stake **6** fasten, paling, sentry, tether **7** enclose, fortify, lookout, outpost, postern
pickle: **4** alec, dill, mess, peck **5** achar, brine **6** capers, dawdle (Sc.), muddle, nibble, piddle, pilfer (Sc.), trifle (Sc.) **7** chutney, condite, confect, gherkin, trouble, vitriol **8** marinate **9** tight spot **11** predicament
mixed: **6** higdon **10** piccalilli
pickled: **5** drunk, soust **6** soused **9** preserved **11** intoxicated
pickling herb: **4** dill **7** mustard **10** celery seed
pickpocket: dip **4** bung, hook, wire **5** diver, filer, ganef, thief **6** buzzer, cannon, dipper, figboy, hooker, ratero (Sp.), robber **7** foister, mobsman, stealer **8** clyfaker, cutpurse **11** fingersmith

helper: 4 duke 5 shill, stall 6 bulker

pickup: 5 tonic, truck 6 arrest, bracer, chippy 8 recovery 9 stimulant 10 hitchhiker 11 improvement, stimulation 12 acquaintance

Pickwick Papers author: 7 Dickens

picky: 4 nice 5 fussy 6 choosy 7 finicky

picnic: 4 snap 6 junket, outing

picot: 4 loop 6 edging 8 notching

picotee: 9 carnation

pictograph: 5 glyph

picture: oil 4 copy, draw, icon, idea, ikon 5 ikono, image, photo, print, scene, vinet 6 chromo, crayon, depict, marine, pastel 7 diorama, etching, explain, imagine, paysage (F.), portray, porture, reflect, tableau 8 describe, likeness, makimono, painting, panorama, portrait, seascape, triptych, vignette 9 delineate, landscape, miniature, represent 10 illustrate, impression, photograph, watercolor
border: mat 5 frame
composite: 7 montage
drawn with heated instrument: 11 pyrogravure
gallery: 5 salon 6 museum
painted on wall: 5 mural 6 fresco
section: 7 gravure
small: 5 cameo 9 miniature
stand: 5 easel
viewer: 9 projector 11 alethoscope, stereoscope 12 stereopticon

pictured: 11 counterfeit

Picture of Dorian Gray author: 5 Wilde

picture puzzle: 5 rebus 6 jigsaw

picturesque: 5 vivid 6 quaint, scenic 7 graphic 8 informal, scenical, striking

picuda: 9 barracuda

piddle: toy 4 pick, play 6 dawdle, putter, trifle

piddling: 5 petty 6 paltry 7 trivial, useless 8 trifling 13 insignificant

pie (see also **cake, pastry**): 4 mess, snap, tart 5 chaos, flawn, graft, pasty, patty 6 jumble, pastry, tourte 7 cobbler, dessert, mixture 8 crustade, turnover 9 blackbird, confusion
meat: 5 pasty 7 rissole 8 empanada 9 shepherd's
with ice cream: 7 a la mode

piebald: 4 pied, piet, pyot 5 mixed, motly, pinto 6 bauson, calico 7 dappled, mongrel, mottled 10 variegated 12 multicolored 13 heterogeneous

piece: bat, bit, cob, eke, gun 4 chip, gare, hunk, join, mend, part, slab, slat, snip, stub, tate (Sc.) 5 crumb, flake, patch, pezzo (It.), scrap, sheet, shred, slice, snack, strip 6 cantle, gobbet, morsel, parcel, sliver 7 cantlet, driblet, flinder, flitter, morceau (F.), oddment, portion, section, segment, snippet 8 assemble, dribblet, fraction

tapering: 4 gore, shim 6 gusset

piece de resistance: 8 main dish 9 showpiece 11 centerpiece, chef d'oeuvre, masterpiece

piecemeal: 7 gradual 8 bit by bit 10 in snatches, step-by-step

piece of eight: 4 peso (Sp.), real 6 escudo (Sp.)

piece out: eke 8 assemble, complete 10 supplement

piece together: 4 form, make 5 unite

pied: 7 blotchy, dappled, mottled, piebald 10 variegated

pied antelope: 8 bontebok

pieplant: 7 rhubarb

pier: cob 4 cobb, dock, mole, pile, quai, quay 5 groin, jetty, stilt, wharf 6 bunder, pillar 7 landing, support 8 buttress, pilaster 10 breakwater
architectural: 4 anta
base: 5 socle

pierce: cut, dag, rit 4 bear, bite, bore, brod, cloy, dirl, gore, hole, stab, tang 5 break, drill, enter, gride, lance, probe, smite, spear, spike, stick, sting 6 broach, cleave, empale, ficche, impale, riddle, tunnel 7 discern, poniard 8 puncture 9 intersect, lancinate, penetrate, perforate 10 comprehend, run through
with horn: 4 gore
with stake: fix 6 impale

pierced: 5 ajour 8 cribrose 10 perforated

piercer: awl 6 gimlet

piercing: 4 fell, high, keen, loud, tart 5 acute, clear, sharp 6 shrill 7 cutting, pungent 8 poignant 9 searching 10 foraminate

Pierus: *consort:* 4 Clio
son: 10 Hyacinthus

piety: 4 zeal 5 faith 7 loyalty 8 devotion, fidelity, holiness, religion 9 godliness, reverence 10 compassion, devoutness

pig (see also **hog**): far, ham, hog, sow 4 boar, pork 5 bacon, chuck, crock (Sc.), ingot, shoat, shote, swine 6 farrow, gussie, porker 7 casting, dogboat, glutton, grumphy (Sc.) 8 grumphie (Sc.), pressman, sixpence
female: sow 4 gilt
lead: 6 fother
litter: far 6 farrow
male: hog 4 boar 6 barrow
metal: bar 5 ingot
pert. to: 7 porcine
pickled feet of: 5 souse
red variety: 5 Duroc
tender: 9 swineherd
young: elt 4 gilt, runt 5 grice (Sc.), piggy, shoat, shote, snork 6 bonham, farrow, piggie, piglet 7 teatman 9 gruntling

pig bed: sty 4 sand

pigboat

pigboat: sub **9** submarine

pig deer: **8** babirusa **9** babirussa **10** babiroussa

pigeon: **4** barb, bird, dodo, dove, dupe, fool, gull **5** decoy, pluck, squab, wonga **6** coward, culver, cushat, dodlet, fleece, homing, isabel, pouter, turbit **7** cropper, crowned, fantail, jacobin, namaqua, pintado, swallow, tumbler **8** rock dove, squealer **9** frillback, harlequin **10** sweetheart, turbitteen, turtle-dove, wongawonga **12** mourning dove
call: coo
carrier: **5** homer **6** homing **8** horseman **10** scandaroon
clay: **5** skeet **6** target
disease: **11** psittacosis
domestic: nun **4** barb, ruff, runt, spot **6** pouter, roller **7** tumbler **9** satinette, trumpeter
extinct: **4** dodo **9** passenger
feed: **7** saltcat
genus of: **5** goura **7** columba
hawk: **6** falcon, merlin
pert. to: **9** columboid **12** peristeronic
short-beaked: **4** barb
tooth-billed: **6** dodlet
young: **5** piper, squab **8** squealer

pigeonberry: **8** pokeweed **9** Juneberry **11** coffeeberry

pigeon blood: red **6** garnet

pigeon grass: **7** foxtail **9** crabgrass **12** bristle-grass

pigeon hawk: **6** merlin

pigeonhearted: **5** timid **8** cowardly **14** chicken-hearted

pigeonhole: **5** label **6** assort, shelve **7** arrange, catalog, cubicle **8** classify **9** cubbyhole

pigeon house: **7** dovecot **9** columbary

pigeon-livered: **4** meek, mild **6** gentle

pigeon pea: dal, tur **4** herb, seed **5** arhar **6** gandul **7** cajanus, catjang

pigeonry: **7** dovecot **8** dovecote

pigeon woodpecker: **7** flicker

piggery: **6** pigsty **8** crockery (Sc.)

piggish: **4** mean **6** filthy, greedy **7** selfish **8** stubborn **10** gluttonous

piggy bank: **6** pishke **7** knippel, pushkeh

pigheaded: **7** willful **8** perverse, stubborn **9** obstinate **10** determined

piglike animal: **7** peccary

pigment: **4** tint **5** color, paint **8** colorant
absence of: **8** achromia, alphosis **9** tacheture
applied to canvas: **7** impasto
black: tar **5** sepia **7** melanin **8** india ink
blood: **10** hemoglobin
blue: **4** bice **5** azure, smalt **7** cyanine **8** cerulean, verditer

blue-gray: **4** bice
blue-white: **4** zinc
brown: **5** sepia, umber **6** bister, bistre, sienna **7** melanin
green: **4** bice **7** veriter
kind: **7** aniline, rubiate **8** alizarin, massicot **9** alizarine
red: **7** amatito, realgar, turacin
toxic: **8** gassypol
yellow: **5** ocher, ochre **7** etiolin **8** orpiment

pigmy: See **pygmy**

pignus: **4** lien, pawn **6** pledge

pigpen: sty

pig potato: **7** cowbane

pig rat: **9** bandicoot

pigskin: **5** glove **6** saddle **7** leather **8** football

pigsney: eye **4** dear **7** darling **10** sweetheart

pigsticker: **4** sled **5** spear, sword **7** butcher **11** pocketknife

pigtail: **5** braid, plait, queue

pika: **4** cony, hare **5** mouse **6** rodent **11** calling hare

pike: gen (Sc.) **4** dore, fish, gedd (Sc.), luce, pick, road **5** cairn, point, spike, tower **6** beacon, pickax, summit **7** highway **8** poulaine **9** spearhead **11** muskallonge, muskallunge, muskellunge

pikel, pikle: **7** hayfork **9** pitchfork

pikelet: **7** crumpet

pike perch: **4** dory **6** sander, sauger

piker: **5** thief, tramp **6** coward **7** drifter, gambler, quitter, shirker, vagrant **8** pilferer, tightwad **9** skinflint **10** cheapskate, speculator

pilar: **5** downy, hairy

pilaster: **4** anta **5** antae **6** column, pillar

Pilate: **8** governor **10** procurator
prisoner: **5** Jesus **8** Barabbas
tribunal: **8** Gabbatha
wife: **6** Procla

pilchard: **7** herring, sardine
smoked: **6** fumado, kipper

pile: cop, mow, nap **4** bank, bing, cock, dass (Sc.), dess (Sc.), heap, mass, mole, much, pier, rick, sess, shag **5** amass, crowd, spile, stack, stake **6** boodle, bundle, pillar **7** edifice, fortune **8** buttress **10** accumulate, breakwater, coacervate
funeral: **4** pyre **5** mound
hay: **4** cock, rick **5** stack **6** doodle
rubbish: **4** dump
stone: **5** cairn, scree

pile driver: **6** beetle
weight: tup

pileup: **4** heap, mass **5** amass, stack **8** accident **9** collision

pilewort: **4** herb **6** ficary **8** fireweed

pilfer: rob **4** hook, loot, pelf, take **5** filch, sneak, steal, swipe **6** finger, snitch **7** purloin **8** scrounge

pilgrim: **5** hadji, ihram **6** palmer **7** Puritan **8** crusader, traveler, wanderer, wayfarer **9** sojourner **12** peregrinator
bottle: **7** ampulla, costrel
garb at Mecca: **5** ihram
ship: **9** Mayflower, Speedwell
to Ganges River: **5** Hindu
to Holy Land: **6** palmer
to Mecca: **6** Muslim
pilgrimage: **4** hadj, trip **7** journey
Pilgrim's Progress: **8** allegory
author: **6** Bunyan
character: **5** Demas **9** Christian
pill: **4** ball, dose, goli, pare, peel, pool **5** bolus, creek, strip **6** caplet, pellet, pilule, tablet **7** capsule, granule, lozenge, pitcher, placebo **9** billiards (Br.) **11** decorticate
pillage: **4** flay, loot, prey, sack **5** booty, foray, harry, rifle, spoil, steal, strip **6** maraud, rapine, ravage **7** despoil, plunder **8** expilate, spoliate, trespass **9** depredate, devastate **10** confiscate **11** appropriate
pillager: **6** looter, peeler, raider, robber, sacker **8** marauder **10** freebooter
of Rome: **6** Alaric
pillaging: **9** predatory
pillar: lat **4** pier, pile, post, prop **5** cippi (pl.), pylon, shaft, stela, stele **6** cippus, column, stelae (pl.), steles **7** obelisk, osiride, support **8** mainstay, pedestal, pilaster, pillaret **9** stanchion, totem pole
capital: **7** chapter
pert. to: **6** stelar
resembling: **6** stelar
series of: **9** colonnade
without: **7** astylar
pillar saint: **7** stylite
Pillars of Hercules: **5** Abila, Calpe **9** Gibraltar, Jebal Musa
pillar-stone: **8** monument **11** cornerstone
pillbox: cap, hat **7** shelter **8** brougham **11** emplacement **13** fortification
pill bug: **5** louse **6** isopod, slater
pilled: **4** bald, bare **6** barked, peeled, shaven **8** tonsured **12** decorticated
pillion: pad **6** saddle **7** cushion
pillory: **4** joug (Sc.) **5** stock, trone **6** cangue, punish
pillow: cod, pad **5** block **7** bolster, cushion, support
stuffing: **4** down **5** eider, kapok **6** dacron **8** feathers
pillowcase: **4** sham, slip **5** cover, linen **8** flanerie
pilm: **4** dust
pilon: **4** gift **5** bonus **7** present **8** gratuity, lagnappe **9** lagniappe
pilose: **5** hairy
pilot: ace, fly **4** lead **5** flyer, guide, steer **6** airman, leader **7** aviator, birdman, conduct, hobbler **8** chaplain, coxswain, director, governor, helmsman, preacher **9** clergyman, cockswain, steersman **10** cowcatcher
test for: **4** solo
pilot bird: **6** plover
pilot fish: **6** remora, romero **9** whitefish
pilot snake: **4** bull **10** copperhead
pilot whale: **9** blackfish
pilum: **6** pestle **7** javelin
Pima Indian: **5** Opata **7** Hohokam
pimento: **6** myrtle **7** paprika **8** allspice
pimple: zit **4** acne, blob, boil, burl, flaw **6** burble, papule **7** abscess, bubukle, pustule **8** eruption **9** blackhead
pin: fed, fix, hob, nog, peg, pen, tit **4** axle, bolt, coak, dart, join, lill, scob **5** affix, arrow, badge, dowel, preen, rivet, spile, stake, style **6** bobbin, broach, brooch, cotter, fasten, fibula, pintle, secure, skewer **7** clothes, confine, enclose, eyebolt, gudgeon, jewelry, skittle, spindle, trenail **8** fastener, kingbolt, linchpin, ornament, spilikin, straight, transfix **9** spillikin **10** chatelaine
for clothes: **6** safety
for hair: **4** hair **5** bobby
machine: **6** cotter
money: **4** cash **9** allowance
oar: **5** thole
rifle: **4** tige
wooden: **4** fid, peg **5** dowel, thole
pinafore: **4** slip **5** apron, dress, smock **6** daidly (Sc.) **8** sundress **9** gaberdine
Pinafore author: **7** Gilbert **8** Sullivan
pince-nez: **5** specs **7** glasses, lorgnon **9** lorgnette **10** eyeglasses, spectacles
pincers: tew **5** chela, tongs **6** pliers, tenail **7** forceps **8** tenaille, tweezers
pinch: nip, rob, wry **4** bite, nick, raid **5** cramp, gripe, hinch, steal, stint, theft, tweak **6** arrest, crisis, extort, snatch, snitch, twince **7** confine, squeeze **8** contract, hardship, juncture, straiten **9** emergency, vellicate
pinch bar: pry **5** lever
pinchbeck: **4** fake, sham **5** alloy, cheap **8** spurious **11** counterfeit
pinched: **6** wasted **7** haggard
pinch-hitter: sub **6** fill-in **7** stand-in **9** alternate **10** substitute, understudy
pinchpenny: **4** carl **5** miser, stint **9** niggardly
Pindaric: ode
pine: ara, fir, iva, lim **4** ache, flag, fret, hone, mope, tree **5** cedar, droop, dwine, kauri, kaury, larch, mourn, pinon, vacoa, waste, white, yearn **6** balsam, grieve, lament, pandan, repine, spruce, totara, vacona, vacoua, wither **7** agonize, dwindle **8** galagala, languish, Northern **9** evergreen, Norwegian
acid: **5** pinic

exudation: **5** resin, rosin
family: **12** bromeliaceae
fruit: **4** cone
genus of: **6** ananas
grove: **7** pinetum
kind: **4** jack **5** slash **6** Aleppo, Scotch **8** lob lolly, longleaf **9** lodgepole, ponderosa **11** bristlecone
leaf: **6** needle
mahogany: **6** totara
product: tar **5** resin **8** wood pulp **10** turpentine
segment: pip
pineapple: **4** bomb, nana, pina (Sp.) **5** anana (It.) **7** grenade **8** ornament **10** decoration
pineapple weed: **8** marigold
pine bark aphid: **10** phylloxera
pinecone: **4** clog **8** strobile
pine family: **8** pinaceae
pine gum: **8** sandarac **9** oleoresin
pine knot: **7** dovekie
pine siskin: **5** finch
pine tar: **6** retene
Pine Tree State: **5** Maine
pine tulip: **10** pipsissewa
pinfold: **4** jail **5** pound **7** confine
ping: **4** push, urge **5** prick
pin grass: **7** erodium **9** alfilaria
pinguid: fat **5** fatty, obese
pinguin: **7** aguamas
pinguitude: **7** fatness, obesity **8** oiliness **10** greasiness
pinhead: **4** dolt, fool **5** clown **6** minnow
pinion: pin, tie **4** bind, gear, wing **5** quill **7** confine, disable, feather, pennant, shackle, trundle **8** cogwheel, restrain
pink: cut **4** coat, deck, rose, rosy, stab, tint **5** adorn, blush, color, coral, prick **6** flower, minnow, pastel, pierce, salmon **7** blossom, radical **8** decorate, dianthus, grayling **9** embellish **12** Sweet William **14** clove carnation
eye: **14** conjunctivitis
family: **15** caryophyllaceae
genus of: **7** silence
pinkeen: **6** minnow
pinkeye: **14** conjunctivitis
pink needle: **9** alfilaria
pink pill: **7** cure-all
pinkster: See **pinxter flower**
pinnace: **4** boat, ship **5** woman **6** tender **8** mistress
pinnacle: epi, tee, top, tor **4** acme, apex, peak **5** crest, crown, serac **6** finial, needle, summit **8** gendarme
glacial: **5** serac
rocky: tor **8** aiguille
pinnate: **6** winged **9** feathered **11** featherlike
pinniped: **4** seal **6** walrus

pinnule: fin **4** barb **5** pinna, plate **6** finlet
Pinocchio author: **7** Collodi **9** Lorenzini
pinochle: **8** card game
term: bid, run, set **4** meld **5** widow **7** auction
two-handed: **7** goulash
pin point: **5** tacca
pinpoint: aim, dot, fix **5** exact, point **6** locate, trifle **7** precise **8** identify
pintado: **4** cero, fish, sier **6** chintz, pigeon, sierra **7** siering, spotted
pintail: **4** duck, smee **6** grouse
pintle: **4** bolt **5** dowel, hinge
pinto: **4** pied, pony **5** horse **6** calico **7** mottled, painted, piebald
pin-wing: **6** pinion
pinxter flower: **6** azalea **8** pinkster **11** honeysuckle **12** rhododendron
pioneer: **5** first, miner **6** digger, open up **7** settler **8** colonist, explorer **9** excavator **11** trailblazer
pious: **4** good, holy **5** froom, godly, loyal **6** devine, devout, pietic **7** canting, goddard, godlike, piteous **8** faithful, priestly **9** religious **11** reverential **13** sanctimonious
pip: dot **4** lulu, paip, peep, seed, spot **5** cheep, chirp, speck **7** ailment, disease **8** insignia **9** black ball (Br.)
pipe: oat **4** cask, duct, flue, lead, main, reed, snap, tube **5** briar, canal, drain, spout, stack **6** dudeen, leader, outlet, tubule **7** calumet, channel, conduit, corncob, fistula, larigot **8** mirliton (F.)
angle: **5** elbow
bender: **6** hickey
ceremonial: **7** calumet
clay: **4** tile **5** straw **10** meerschaum **12** churchwarden
closer: **5** valve
connection: ell, tee **5** cross, elbow **6** flange
end: **4** taft **6** nozzle
joint: ell, tee, wye **5** cross, elbow **7** calepin **8** coupling
musical instrument: **4** fife **5** flute, organ **7** panpipe, piccolo
Oriental: **5** hooka, water **6** hookah **7** nargile **8** narghile, nargileh **12** hubble-bubble
part: **4** bowl, stem
pastoral: oat **4** reed
pert. to: **6** tubate
player: **5** fifer **8** shepherd
smoke: **5** tewel
steam: **5** riser
stove: **4** flue **5** tewel **7** chimney
pipe dream: **4** hope **6** bubble **7** chimera, fantasy **8** illusion
piperly: **7** trivial **9** worthless
Piper's son: Tom
pipette: **4** tube **6** baster, taster **7** burette, dropper

measuring: **11** stactometer

pipe wrench: **8** Stillson

piping: **6** edging, tubing

pipistrel, pipistrelle: bat

pipit: **6** wekeen **7** titlark

pippin: **4** seed **5** apple

pipsqueak: **4** nerd **5** twerp **6** nobody **7** upstart

piquancy: **4** salt, zest **5** spice **6** flavor, ginger **7** flavour **8** tartness

piquant: **4** racy, tart **5** salty, sharp, spicy, tasty, zesty **6** biting, bitter **7** peppery, pungent, zestful **8** poignant, stinging **11** provocative, stimulating

pique: irk **4** fret, goad, huff, tick **5** annoy, pride, spite, sting **6** arouse, bother, excite, fabric, grudge, harass, malice, nettle, offend, pritch, strunt **7** chigger, dudgeon, offense, provoke, umbrage **8** irritate, vexation **9** annoyance, displease **10** irritation, resentment **11** displeasure

piqued: **5** pouty

piquet: **8** card game
score: pic
tricks: **5** capot

pirate: (see also **plunderer**): **4** Hook, Kidd **5** rover, thief **6** Dragut, ladron, Morgan, robber, seadog **7** brigand, corsair, omnibus, sea wolf **8** algerine, marauder, picaroon, predator, sea rover **9** buccaneer, pickaroon, privateer **10** Barbarossa, Blackbeard, filibuster, freebooter, plagiarize
flag: **10** Jolly Roger
gallows: **7** yardarm

piripiri: **4** weed **5** birch, mapau

pirl: **4** spin **5** twine, twist

pirn: **4** reel **5** spool **6** bobbin **7** spindle

pirogue: **4** boat **5** canoe **6** dugout

pirol: **6** oriole

piscation: **7** fishery, fishing

piscator: **6** angler **9** fisherman

Pisces: **4** fish **6** zodiac **13** constellation

piscina: **4** pool, tank **5** basin **8** fishpond, lavatory **9** reservoir

Pisgah summit: **4** Nebo

pishogue, pishoge: **5** charm, spell **7** sorcery **10** witchcraft

pismire: ant **5** emmet, twerp **9** nonentity

pismo: **4** clam

piste: **4** path **5** spoor, track, trail **8** ski trail

pistil: **6** carpel, umbone

pistle: **4** tale **5** story **7** epistle

pistol: dag, gat, gun, rod **4** Colt **5** Luger **6** barker, buffer, heater, weapon **7** dungeon, firearm, hand gun, sidearm **8** bulldoze, revolver **9** automatic, derringer
case: **7** holster
lock: **5** rowet

piston: **4** disk, knob, plug **5** valve **6** roller **7** plunger

pit: pip **4** butt, delf, foss, hell, hole, mine, pool, seed, sump, trap, weem, well **5** abyss, chasm, delft, delve, fossa, fosse, fovea, grave, shaft, snare, stone **6** cavern, cavity, fossae, hollow, oppose **7** abaddon, cockpit **8** downfall **9** barathron, waterhole **10** depression, excavation **11** indentation
bottomless: **5** abyss **7** Abaddon
of peach: **4** seed **7** putamen
of theater: **7** parquet
small: **6** areole, lacuna **7** foveola **8** alveolus

pitch: dip, key, tar **4** cant, cast, fall, hurl, line, roll, send, tone, toss **5** fling, heave, lunge, lurch, resin, rosin, spiel, throw **6** accent, encamp, patter, plunge, seesaw, totter **7** asphalt, bitumen **8** alkitran **9** alchitran
above: **5** sharp
apple: **5** copei, cupay
baseball: **5** curve **6** slider **8** changeup, fastball, fork ball, knuckler, palm ball, spitball **11** knuckleball
below: **4** flat
high in: alt
in: **4** help **5** set to **7** get busy **8** get going **10** contribute
pipe: **9** epitonion
relating to: **7** piceous

pitchblende: **6** radium **7** uranium

pitcher: jar, jug, urn **4** ewer, olla, olpe, toby **5** buire, crock, cruet, flask, gorge, gotch, ollae, olpae **6** beaker, carafe, heaver, hurler, tosser, urceus **7** canette, creamer **8** cruisken, oenochoe **9** container, cruiskeen **10** ballplayer
false move: **4** balk
handle: ear **4** ansa
left-handed: **8** southpaw
motions: **6** windup
place: **5** mound
relief: **7** fireman

pitchfork: **4** evil **5** pikel, pikle **8** sheppeck, sheppick

piteous: **5** pious **6** devout, moving, ruined, tender **7** doleful, pitiful, pitying **8** pitiable, touching **9** imploring **10** beseeching, entreating **13** compassionate

pitfall: **4** lure, trap **5** snare **6** danger **9** booby trap **10** difficulty

pith: jet, nub **4** core, crux, gist, meat, pulp **5** force, vigor **6** center, kernel, marrow **7** essence, medulla, nucleus **8** strength **9** substance
full of: **5** heady, meaty, terse **7** concise

pith helmet: **4** topi **5** topee

pith tree: **7** ambatch

pithy: **5** crisp, meaty, short, terse **7** compact, concise, laconic **11** sententious **12** apothegmatic **13** short and sweet
plant: **4** sola**

saying: mot **5** maxim **9** witticism

pitiful: sad **4** mean **6** rueful, woeful **7** forlorn, piteous **8** pathetic, pitiable **9** miserable, sorrowful **10** despicable, lamentable **12** contemptible

pitiless: **4** grim **5** cruel, stony **6** savage **8** ruthless **9** ferocious, merciless, unfeeling **10** despiteous, dispiteous, relentless **11** hardhearted

pitpit: **8** guitguit

pittance: bit **4** alms, dole, gift, mite, song **5** trace **6** trifle **7** bequest

pitted: **6** etched **7** foveate, opposed, scarred **9** alveolate **10** pockmarked **11** honeycombed

pit viper: **4** habu **8** lachesis **10** bushmaster, copperhead, fer-de-lance **11** rattlesnake

pity: **4** ruth **5** mercy, piety **6** pathos **8** clemency, sympathy **10** compassion, condolence, tenderness **11** commiserate **13** commiseration

pivot: toe **4** slew, slue, turn **5** hinge, swing **6** evener, swivel **7** gudgeon

pivotal: key **5** polar, vital **7** central, crucial **8** cardinal **9** essential

pivot pin: **6** pintle **8** kingbolt

pix: See **pyx**

pixie, pixy: elf **5** fairy **6** sprite **7** brownie **9** prankster

pixilated: **5** dotty, drunk **9** whimsical **10** inebriated **11** intoxicated

placable: **4** calm **8** tolerant **9** agreeable, forgiving, tractable

placard: **4** bill, post, sign **6** poster **7** affiche **9** manifesto **12** proclamation **13** advertisement

placate: **4** calm **5** quiet, sooth **6** pacify, please, soothe **7** appease, comfort **10** conciliate, lay the dust **11** tranquilize

place: (see also **position**): lay, put, set **4** area, calm, city, home, lieu, loci, post, room, seat, site, spot, town **5** being, court, estre, locus, plant, point, posit, siege, situs, space, stead, where **6** bestow, locale, locate, region, repose, square, status **7** allodge, bestead, demesne, deposit, dispose, situate, village **8** dwelling, estimate, identify, locality, location, position **9** collocate, residence, situation

again: **6** reseat **7** restore
apart: **6** enisle **7** isolate **8** separate
before: **6** appose, prefix
beneath: **9** infrapose
between: **6** insert **9** interpose
business: **5** plant, store **6** office **7** factory
by itself: **7** isolate **10** quarantine
camping: **4** site **5** etape
frequented: **4** dive **5** haunt **6** resort **7** hangout
hiding: mew **4** cave

holy: **6** shrine
in a row: **5** align, aline
intermediate: **5** limbo
in the sun: **5** glory **11** recognition
market: **4** mart, souk **5** agora
meeting: **5** tryst **10** rendezvous
one inside another: **4** nest
perfect: **6** heaven, utopia **8** paradise
safe: **9** sanctuary
side by side: **9** collocate, juxtapose
trial: **5** venue

placebo: **5** toady **7** vespers **8** medicine **11** preparation

placid: **4** calm, even, mild **5** downy, quiet, suant **6** gentle, irenic, serene **8** peaceful, tranquil **9** unruffled **11** undisturbed **13** imperturbable

placket: **4** slit **6** pocket **7** opening

plage: **4** zone **5** beach **6** region **7** country **8** transept

plagiarize: rob **4** copy, crib, lift **5** steal **6** borrow, pirate, thieve **7** purloin

plague: dun, pox, vex **4** fret, gall, pest, twit **5** annoy, chafe, harry, tease, worry **6** badger, bother, harass, hector, pester, wanion **7** bubonic, scourge, torment, trouble **8** calamity, epidemic, irritate, nuisance **9** annoyance **10** affliction, black death, pestilence **11** infestation

carrier: fly, rat
pert. to: **6** loimic

plaice: **5** fluke **8** flatfish, flounder

plaid: **4** maud **5** cloth **6** design, tartan **7** bracken, garment, pattern **9** checkered **11** crossbarred

plain: dry, lea **4** bald, bare, chol, down, even, fair, mead, mere, mesa, moor, open, vega, wold **5** blair, blunt, broad, camas, campo, clear, corah, frank, gross, heath, homey, llano, veldt **6** coarse, graith, homely, humble, lenten, meadow, pampas, simple, steppe, tundra, undyed **7** artless, certain, evident, genuine, glaring, legible, obvious, prairie, quamash, savanna **8** apparent, distinct, explicit, flatland, homemade, homespun, ordinary, straight, tailored **9** unaffected **11** perspicuous, transparent, undisguised **12** short on looks, unattractive **13** unembellished

depression: **5** swale
elevated: **4** mesa **7** plateau
Indian: Ute **4** Cree, Iowa **5** Caddo, Creek, Kiowa, Omaha, Sioux **6** Dakota, Oneida, Pawnee **7** Shawnee **8** Comanche **9** Algonquin **10** Athapascan
Olympic games: **4** Elis
salt-covered: **5** flats **6** salada
treeless: **5** llano, pampa, veldt **6** steppe, tundra **7** prairie, savanna **8** savannah

upland: **4** wold **5** weald

plaint: **4** wail **6** lament **7** protest **9** complaint **11** lamentation

plaintiff: **4** suer **7** accuser **8** litigant **9** recoverer **10** prosecutor **11** complainant
opposite: **9** defendant

plaintive: sad **5** cross **7** elegiac, fretful, peevish, pettish, piteous, pitiful, wailing, wistful **8** dolorous, mournful, petulant, repining **9** lamenting, sorrowful **10** melancholy **11** complaining **12** discontented

plait: cue **4** fold, knit **5** braid, crimp, pleat, weave **6** border, gather, goffer, pleach **7** gauffer, pigtail **9** gathering **10** interweave

plaited: **7** braided, browden **10** corrugated

plan: aim, map **4** card, dart, form, game, idea, plat, plot **5** draft, epure, ettle, frame **6** budget, decoct, design, devise, intend, layout, method, policy, scheme, sketch, system **7** arrange, concert, diagram, draught, drawing, outline, program, project, purpose **8** conspire, contrive, engineer, platform, prepense, schedule, strategy **9** blueprint, calculate, machinate, stratagem **10** concoction **11** arrangement, contemplate, contrivance, preconceive, precontrive, premeditate

planate: **5** level **9** flattened

plancher: bed **4** slab **5** board, floor, plank **6** pallet **7** ceiling **8** planking, platform

plane: **4** even, flat, soar **5** glide, level **6** aequor, chinar, smooth **7** surface **8** aircraft, sycamore
block: **5** stock
handle: **4** toat, tote
inclined: **4** ramp **5** chute, shute
kind of: **4** iron, jack **5** block **6** router **8** grooving, tounging
on same: **8** coplanar

plane figure (see also **geometry:** *figure*):
boundary: **9** perimeter
four angles: **8** tetragon
nine-sided: **7** nonagon

plane iron: bit **5** blade, knife

planer: **4** tool **6** shaper **8** surfacer

planet: orb **4** Mars, moon, star **5** Earth, Pluto, Venus **6** Saturn, sphere, Uranus **7** Jupiter, Mercury, Neptune **8** asteroid, terrella, wanderer **9** satellite
brightest: **5** Venus
cone: **8** strobile
course: **5** orbit
farthest from sun: **5** Pluto
nearest sun: **7** Mercury
orbit: **7** ellipse
orbit point: **5** apsis, nadir **6** apogee, zenith **7** perigee
period: **9** alfridary
red: **4** Mars

relation to another: **5** trine **7** sextile **10** opposition **11** conjunction
ringed: **6** Saturn, Uranus
ruling: **9** dominator
satellite: **4** moon
shadow: **5** umbra

planeta: **5** cloak

planetarian: **10** astrologer

planetarium: **6** orrery **11** observatory

planetary: **4** huge **7** earthly, erratic **9** universal, wandering, worldwide **10** astrologer **11** terrestrial

plane-tree: **8** plantain, sycamore

planisphere: **9** astrolabe **11** meteorscope

plank: **4** deal, slab **5** board, slate, stone **6** lumber, timber **8** plancher **9** two-by-four **10** gravestone
breadth: **6** strake
increasing bearing surface: **5** shole
lengthwise: **8** stringer

planking: **8** flooring

plankton: **4** alga **5** krill **8** organism, protozoa

planner: **9** architect

plant (see also **annual, flower, perennial**): fix, set, sow, spy **4** arum, bury, bush, fern, herb, hide, rape, root, seed, trap, tree, vine, weed, wort **5** berry, decoy, found, fruit, grain, place, put in, shoot, shrub, sotol, spice, trick, works **6** annual, clover, flower, legume, scheme, settle **7** conceal, creeper, factory, furnish, sapling **8** building, business, geophyte, radicate **9** equipment, establish, perennial, succulent, swindling, vegetable **10** prearrange
acid-juice: **5** ribes **6** nettle **8** knotweed **9** smartweed
aconite: **4** bikh
amaryllis family: **5** agave
ambrosia genus: **7** ragweed
ammoniac: **5** oshac
apiaceous: **4** ache
apoplexy: **4** esca
appendage: **7** stipule
arboreal: **4** tree
arrowroot-yielding: **7** curcuma
arum family: **4** arad, taro **5** aroid, calla
asteraceous: **5** daisy
aster family: **5** oxeye, tansy **8** fleabane
bayonet: **5** datil
bean family: **6** lupine **8** licorice **9** liquorice
benthonic: **6** enalid
bitter: ers, rue **9** colicroot
blue-blossomed: **6** lupine **8** ageratum
body: **6** cormus
bog genus: **5** abama **10** narthecium
bramble: **5** briar, furze, gorse, thorn
branched: **4** bush, tree **5** shrub
breathing organ: **5** stoma **7** stomata (pl.)
bulbous: **4** lily **5** camas, onion, tulip **7** jon-

quil, quamash **8** hyacinth **9** narcissus
cabbage family: **4** rape
cactus family: **5** dildo **6** cereus, mescal **7**
saguaro **11** prickly pear
cactus-like: **8** stapelia **9** xerophyte
capsule: pod
carrot-like: **7** parsnip
cassia genus: **5** senna
catnip family: nep **6** nepeta
celery family: **5** anise
celery-like: udo
cell: **6** gamete
chlorophyll-rich: **4** alga **5** algae (pl.)
class: **4** alga **5** algae (pl.)
climbing: ive, ivy **4** bine, vine **5** betel, liana,
vetch **6** byrony, smilax **7** creeper, jasmine **8**
wisteria **12** morning glory, philodendron
clover-like: **5** medic **7** calomba
coloring matter: **8** clorofil **10** endochrome
11 chlorophyll
corn lily: **4** ixia
crocus family: **4** irid
crossbred: **6** hybrid
crowfoot family: **5** peony **8** clematis
cruciferous: **5** cress **7** alyssum
cryptogamous: **4** moss
cuticle: **5** cutin
cyperaceous: **5** sedge
decorative: ivy **4** bush, fern **6** flower
desert: **5** agave **6** alhagi, cactus **8** mesquite
11 brittlebush
dipsacus genus: **6** teasel
disease: **4** gall, mold, rust, scab, smut **5**
ergot **6** blight, mildew **7** blister
dock-like: **6** sorrel
dry-climate: **5** xerad **9** xerophyte **10**
ombrophobe
dwarf: **5** cumin, stunt
dye: **4** anil, weld, woad, wold **5** henna,
woald, would **6** kamala, madder, wurras,
wurrus **7** alhenna, orselle
dye-yielding: **4** anil, woad **5** henna, sumac
6 madder **7** alkanet
ebony family: **6** ebenad
embryo: **8** plantule
environmentally modified: **4** ecad
erica genus: **5** heath **7** heather
Euphorbia genus: **6** spurge
exudation: gum, sap **4** milk **5** latex, resin,
rosin
fabaceous: pea **5** vetch **9** coronippa
family: **7** araceae
fernlike: **8** filicoid
flag-family: **4** irid
floating: **5** lotus **7** frogbit **9** water lily
flowerless: **4** fern, moss **6** fungus, lichen **7**
seaweed
forgetfulness-causing: **5** lotus
fragrant: **5** orris **8** angelica

garden: **4** geum, iris, ixia, rose **5** aster, calla,
canna, daisy, pansy, phlox, poppy, stock,
viola **6** bellis, bletia, celery, clivia, cosmos,
crocus, lupine, oxalis, zinnia **7** agathea,
alyssum, anchusa, anemone, begonia,
celosia, clarkia, gazania, gerbera, godetia,
lettuce, lobelia, muscari, petunia, primula,
statice, verbena **8** ageratum, arctotis, cyclamen, daffodil, dianthus, herebell, hyacinth,
larkspur, marigold, myosotis, scabiosa,
sparaxis, sweet pea, tithonia, watsonia **9**
amaryllis, calendula, campanula, candytuft,
carnation, centaurea, cinararia, coreopsis,
digitalis, gladiolus, hollyhock, linararia, narcissus, nicotiana, penstemon, portulaca **10**
delphinium, gaillardia, gypsophila, marguerite, ranunculus, snapdragon, sweet
basil, wallflower **11** dusty miller, forget-me-
not, helichrysum, hunnemannia, Madonna
Lily, shasta daisy **12** nierembergia, rhododendron, salpiglossis, Sweet William **13**
chrysanthemum, dimorphotheca, glory of
the sun **14** canterbury bell **15** Star of Bethlehem **16** spring snowflakes
geography: **14** phytogeography
grain: oat, rye **4** corn, teff **5** wheat **6** barley
grass: **5** avena
grass cloth: **5** ramee, ramie
grassland: **6** baccar **7** bacchar
grass-like: **5** sedge
growing from inside: **7** endogen **9** endoge-
nae (pl.)
growing from outside: **6** exogen
growth layer: **7** cambium
growth on: **4** gall
habitat: **4** ecad
hawthorn: **7** azarole **9** mayflower
head: bud, bur **4** burr **5** fruit **6** flower
healing: **7** sanicle
heather family: **4** ling **5** erica
hedge: **6** espino
honey-secreting organ: **7** nectary
interior chaff: **5** palea, palet
iridaceae: **4** irid
joined to another: **5** graft
joint: **4** node
juice: see *exudation* above
leafless: **4** ulex **6** dodder **7** restiad, triurid
liliaceous: **4** aloe, leek **5** onion **9** birthroot
lily family: **4** aloe, sego **5** lotos, lotus, yucca
6 camass
linen-producing: **4** flax
main axis: **4** stem **5** stalk, trunk
male: mas **16** androgametophore
mallow family: **5** altea **6** escoba
manufacturing: **4** mill
marsh: **4** fern, reed **6** juncus **7** bulrush, cattail
masculine: see *male* above

medicinal: hop, oak, yew **4** aloe, dill, flax, herb, lime, sage **5** buchu, elder, erica, guaco, jalap, peony, poppy, senna, tansy **6** arnica, carrot, catnep, catnip, fennel, garlic, ipecac, kousso, laurel, nettle, simple **7** aconite, boneset, calamus, camphor, caraway, catechu, copaiba, ephedra, gentian, hemlock, henbane, juniper, lobelia, mullein, mustard, parsley, rhubarb, saffron **8** barberry, camomile, crowfoot, foxglove, licorice, plantain, rosemary, valerian, wormwood **9** asparagus, bearberry, buckthorn, chamomile, colchicum, coltsfoot, dandelion, liquorice, monkshead **10** assafetida, pennyroyal, peppermint, stavesacre **11** assafoetida, bittersweet

microscopic: **5** spore **10** microphyte

millet: **5** hirse

mock orange: **7** syringa

moss-like: **6** orpine **7** hepatic

mottled leaf: **8** ratsbane

multicellular: **9** metaphyte

mushroom-type: **6** fungus

mustard family: **4** woad **5** cress **6** radish **7** alyssum

native: **8** indigene

nettle family: **4** hemp

nightshade family: **6** tomato

nursery: **8** seedling

oil-yielding: **4** odal **6** sesame

old-world: **5** lotus

one-seeded fruit: **9** olacaceae

onion family: **4** leek

onion-like: **5** chive **7** shallot

opening: **5** stoma **7** stomata (pl.)

packing: **7** cannery

part: **6** stamen, stipel **7** tendril

pert. to: **6** agamic **7** botanic, vegetal **9** botanical **10** vegetative

pigment-lacking: **6** albino

poaceae: **5** grass

pod: **4** boll

poisonous: **4** atis **6** datura **7** amanita, cowbane **8** oleander **10** belladonna

poisonous to cattle: **4** loco **8** calfkill, locoweed

poisonous to fowl: **7** henbane

pore: **8** lenticel

potted: **6** bonsai

preserving: **4** dill **7** cannery

prickly: **4** rose **5** briar, brier, cacti (pl.), thorn **6** cactus, nettle, teasel **7** thistle **9** tearthumb

rat poison: **8** oleander, ratsbane

reproductive organ: **5** spore

root: **5** radix

rope: **4** hemp

round-leaved: **9** pennywort

salad: **5** cress **6** celery, endive, greens **7** let-

tuce, romaine **8** purslane **10** watercress

scented: **4** mint **6** catnip **7** catmint

science: **6** botany

sedge family: **5** carex

seed: nut, pip **4** bulb **5** grain **6** button **7** putamen

seedless: **4** fern

seller: **7** florist

shoot: rod **4** cion **5** scion, sprig **6** stolon

silk: **5** floss

soap: **5** amole

sour-juice: **6** sorrel

starch: pia **4** arum, taro **7** cassava

stem: **4** bine **5** shaft **6** caulis

stem joint: **4** node

stem tissue: **4** pith **6** phloem

submerged: **6** enalid

succulent: **4** aloe, herb **8** gasteria **9** houseleek

tanning: **5** sumac

three-leaved: **9** trifolium

tissue: **4** pith **5** xylem **6** phloem **7** cambium

trailing: **7** arbutus

tropical: **4** arum, palm, taro **5** agave, altea, canna, liana, liane, yucca, zamia **6** pepino **7** dasheen, hamelia **8** mangrove, redwithe

tufted: **4** moss **5** dryas

urticaceous: **6** nettle

wall: ivy

waterside: **4** arum, iris **5** sedge

wild-growing: **9** agrestial

woody: **4** bush, tree, vine **5** shrub

woody-vine genus: **5** vitis

xyloid: **4** tree

young: **4** cion **5** scion, shoot **6** sprout **7** cutting, vinelet **8** seedling

Plantagenets: **7** Angevin

plantain: **4** weed **6** banana, wabron **8** balisier

plantain eater: **7** touraco **9** splitbeak

plantation: **4** farm **5** finca, ranch **6** estate **8** estancia, hacienda

cacti: **7** nopalry

coffee: **5** finca **7** cafetal, fazenda

coniferous tree: **7** pinetum

fictional: **4** Tara

oak tree: **9** quercetum

sugar: **8** trapiche

trees: **5** grove **6** forest **7** orchard

willow: **4** holt **6** osiery

planter: **5** sower **6** farmer, grower, seeder **7** pioneer, settler **8** colonist, gardener **13** agriculturist

government by: **11** plantocracy

wall: **6** lavabo

planting stick: **6** dibble

plant life: **5** flora **10** vegetation

plant louse: **5** aphid

secretion: **4** laap, lerp **5** laarp

plant raising: *pert. to:* **13** floricultural

plaque: pin **5** medal **6** broach, brooch **9** nameplate

plash: **4** pool **5** blash, hedge **6** pleach, puddle, splash **9** bespatter

plashy: wet **6** marshy

plasm: **4** mold **6** matrix

plasma: **5** blood, lymph, serum **11** trophoplasm

plaster: **4** coat, daub, harl **5** affix, cover, gatch, gesso, grout, salve, smear **6** cement, mortar, parget **9** slick down
adhesive: **4** tape **7** Band-Aid, bandage **8** dressing
coarse: **5** grout **6** parget, stucco
of paris: **5** gesso **6** gypsum
patch: **7** spackle
stone: **6** gypsum
support: **4** lath
tool: **7** spatula
wax: **6** cerate

plastered: **5** drunk **6** soused **11** intoxicated

plasterer: **5** mason **6** dauber

plastic: **4** soft **5** phony, vinyl **6** pliant, supple **7** ductile, fictile, pliable **8** flexible, unctuous **9** adaptable, formative **10** credit card **14** impressionable
cotton-sizing: **7** viscose
dentist's: **6** cement

plastron: **6** dickey **7** calipee **8** trimming **11** breastplate

plat: lot, map **4** boat, plan **5** braid, chart, plait **6** buffet **7** plateau **9** tableland **10** interweave

plate: cut, gib **4** coat, disc, dish, disk, lame, tile **5** aglet, armor, china, facia, layer, scute, stove **6** aiglet, discus, lamina, platen, tagger, veneer **7** denture, lamella, laminae, overlay **8** assiette, lamellae, laminate **9** silverize
communion: **5** paten **6** patina
from matrix: **6** stereo **10** stereotype
glass: **4** pane **5** slide **6** louver
horny: **5** scale, scute
perforated: dog **4** grid **7** stencil **8** hallmark **14** identification
pitcher's: **4** slab **6** rubber
ship-shaped: nef
stereotype: **6** cliche
thin: **6** lamina **7** lamella

plateau: **4** dish, mesa, puna, seir **5** fjeld, table **6** hamada, plaque, salver **7** uplands **9** altiplano, tableland **12** altiplanicie

plateholder: **8** cassette

platen: **6** roller

platform: map **4** bank, base, bema, dais, deck, plan **5** bench, chart, floor, forum, ledge, shelf, stage, stand **6** bemata (pl.), podium, pulpit **7** estrade, program, rostrum, tribune **8** chabutra, plancher **9** banquette, gangplank, vestibule

church: **5** solea **6** pulpit
fort: **8** barbette
mining: **6** sollar, soller
nautical: **7** maintop
reloading: **6** staith
salt-manufacturing: **6** hurdle
ship: **7** foretop, maintop **9** gangplank
sleeping: **4** kang
temple: **5** dukan
temporary: **8** scaffold
theater: **7** logeion
wheeled: **5** dolly, float
wooden: **9** boardwalk

platinum: *blond:* **7** towhead
crude: **7** platina
wire: **4** oese

platitude: **6** cliche, truism **7** bromide, proverb **8** banality, chestnut, dullness, flatness **9** rechauffé, staleness, triteness **10** triviality **11** commonplace **15** commonplaceness

---

Plato: **6** writer **8** educator **11** philosopher
father: **7** Ariston
idea: **5** eidos
knowledge: **6** noesis
literary form: **8** dialogue
mother: **10** Perictione
pupil: **9** Aristotle
real name: **10** Aristocles
school: **7** Academe, Academy
stepfather: **10** Pyrilampes
teacher: **8** Socrates
work: Ion **4** Laws, Meno **5** Crito **6** Laches, Phaedo **7** Apology, Gorgias, Sophist, Timaeus **8** Cratylus, Phaedrus, Republic **9** Symposium **10** Protagoras, Theaetetus

---

platoid: **4** flat **5** broad

platonic: **9** spiritual, visionary **10** idealistic **11** impractical, theoretical
body: **4** cube **10** hexahedron, octahedron **11** icosahedron, tetrahedron **12** dodecahedron
philosophy follower: **9** academist

platoon: set **4** team, unit **5** group, squad **6** volley **7** coterie **8** division **9** formation

platter: **4** dish, lanx (L.) **5** ashet (Sc.), grail, plate **6** record, salver **7** charger **8** trencher

platter-shaped: **10** scutellate

platyfish: **8** moonfish

platypus: **8** duckbill **9** mallagong

plaudit: **4** clap **5** kudos **6** praise **8** applause, approval, encomium **11** acclamation, approbation

plausible: 4 oily 6 glossy 7 colored 8 coloured, credible, specious 10 applausive, believable, creditable, ostensible, plauditory

Plautus: 5 Roman 10 playwright
forte: 6 comedy
language: 5 Latin
work: 6 Casina 9 Amphitruo

play: act, fun, hit, jeu (F.), toy 4 game, jeux (F.), move, romp 5 amuse, charm, dally, drama, enact, flirt, sport 6 cavort, divert, engage, fiddle, frolic, gamble, gambol, rollix 7 disport, execute, perform 9 amusement, dalliance, diversion, pantomime 10 manipulate, recreation 13 entertainment
around: 5 cheat 7 cuckold 9 philander
badly: err 4 miff 5 choke 6 bobble
ball: 5 begin 6 resume 9 cooperate
complication: 4 node
down: 9 soft-pedal
festival: 9 festspiel
kind: 4 auto 5 drama, farce 6 comedy, one-act 7 musical, tragedy 8 burletta 9 melodrama
musical: 5 opera 8 burletta, operetta
off: 4 game 6 oppose 8 showdown
on words: pun
outline: 8 scenario
part: act, bit 4 acte (F.), lead, role 5 exode, scene 7 prelude 8 epilogue, epitasis, prologue
possum: 4 sham 5 feign 7 pretend
put on: 5 stage 7 produce
seasonal: 11 summer stock
silent: 9 pantomime
small: 4 skit 8 one-acter
up: 6 stress 9 emphasize

playa: 4 lake 5 basin, beach 6 salina

playboy: 4 fool 5 clown, idler 6 madcap 7 buffoon, Don Juan, swinger

played out: 5 all in, ended, spent, tired 8 finished, unreeled 9 exhausted

player: man 4 cast, star 5 actor 6 leader 7 athlete, enactor, gambler 8 gamester, thespian 9 performer 10 competitor, contestant
card: 4 pone 6 dealer, eldest
leading: 4 star
poor: dub, dud, ham, sub 5 scrub 12 second-string
strolling: 8 mariachi 9 serenader, troubador 10 troubadour 11 barnstormer

playful: 5 elfin, merry 6 blithe, frisky, joking, lusory, wanton 7 jocular, larkish, puckish 8 gamesome, humorous, playsome, sportive 10 frolicsome

playground: 4 grid, park, yard 5 field 7 diamond

playhouse: 5 movie 6 casino, cinema 7 theater

playing cards: 4 deck 6 tarots
hand: cat 4 deal

playlet: 4 skit

playmate: pal 6 friend

playroom: bar, den, gym 7 nursery

plaything: die, toy 4 hoop 6 bauble, trifle

playtime: 6 recess

playwright (see also **dramatist**): 6 author, writer 9 dramatist

plaza: 4 park 5 green, platz 6 common, piazza, square 9 carrefour 11 marketplace

plea: sue 4 suit 6 abater, answer, appeal, excuse, prayer 7 apology, pretext, request, solicit 8 argument, entreaty, petition, pretense 12 supplication 14 nolo contendere
defendant's: 4 nolo 6 guilty 8 the fifth 9 not guilty 14 nolo contendere

pleach: 5 plait 9 interlace 10 interweave

plead: beg, sue 4 pray 5 orate 6 allege, assert 7 beseech, entreat, implore, solicit 8 advocate, appealed, petition 9 importune, intercede 10 supplicate

pleading: 4 oyer 6 answer 8 argument, demurrer 9 suppliant 10 litigation 12 supplication

pleasant: gay 4 bien (F.), fair, fine, good, hend, joli, mild, nice, waly 5 balmy, bigly, cushy, douce (F.), hende, hoddy, jolie, lepid, merry, sweet, wally 6 genial 7 amiable, amusing, cordial, farrand, farrant, jesting, jocular, leesome (Sc.), likable, playful, welcome, winsome 8 charming, delicate, friendly, gracious, grateful, humorous, pleasing, sportive 9 agreeable, appealing, congenial, diverting, enjoyable, laughable, sprightly 10 acceptable, delightful, gratifying

pleasantness: 7 amenity 8 goodness, niceness

pleasantry: fun 4 jest, joke 6 banter 7 jesting 10 jocularity 11 gauloiserie 13 facetiousness

please: 4 suit, will 5 agree, amuse, elate, humor 6 arride, humour, tickle 7 aggrate, appease, content, delight, gladden, gratify, indulge, placate, satisfy 9 delectate, titillate

pleased: 5 happy 8 gladsome

pleasing: 4 glad, lief 5 amene, sooth 6 comely, eesome (Sc.), liking 7 roseate 8 fetching, pleasant 9 desirable, favorable, palatable 10 attractive, delectable, delightful, enchanting, favourable

pleasure: fun, joy 4 ease, este, gree, will 5 bliss, mirth, sport, treat 6 gaiety, liking, relish 7 delight, jollity 8 delicacy, fruition, gladness, hilarity 9 amusement, diversion, enjoyment, happiness, merriment 10 beneplacit 11 beneplacity, contentment, delectation 12 cheerfulness 13 gratification

god: Bes
ground: 4 park 9 pleasance
insensitiveness to: 9 anhedonia
pert. to: 7 hedonic
philosophy of: 8 hedonism
seeker: 5 sport 7 epicure, playboy 8 hedonist

pleat: 4 fold, kilt, shir, tuck 5 braid, crimp, prank 7 plicate

plebe: 5 cadet 8 commoner, freshman 10 midshipman

plebeian: 5 crude 6 coarse, common, homely, vulgar 7 ignoble, illbred, lowborn 8 baseborn, everyday, ordinary

plebiscite: 4 vote 6 decree 7 mandate 10 referendum

plectrum: 4 pick 5 uvula 6 fescue, tongue 7 malleus

pledge: bet, vas (L.), vow 4 adhi, band, bond, gage, hand, hest, hock, oath, pawn, seal, wage, word 5 siker, skoal, toast, troth 6 arrest, assure, borrow, commit, engage, lumber, parole, plight 7 betroth, earnest, espouse, hostage, promise, warrant 8 affiance, contract, guaranty, mortgage, security 9 assurance, certainty, sacrament 11 association, impignorate
security for: IOU 4 bond, gage 6 marker 10 collateral

pledget: 4 swab 5 oakum 8 compress

Pleiades: 4 Maia 6 Merope 7 Alcyone, Celaeno, Electra, Sterope, Taygeta 8 Asterope
constellation: 6 Taurus
father: 5 Atlas
mother: 7 Pleione

Pleiad of Alexandria: 5 Homer 6 Aratus 8 Nicander 9 Lycophron 10 Apollonius, Theocritus 11 Callimachus

plenary: 4 full 6 entire 7 perfect, summary 8 absolute, complete 11 unqualified

plenipotentiary: 5 agent, envoy 8 minister 10 ambassador

plentiful: 4 full, rich, rife 5 ample, sonsy 6 galore, sonsie 7 copious, fertile, liberal, opulent, profuse 8 abundant, affluent, fruitful, generous, prolific 9 abounding, bounteous, bountiful, exuberant, plenteous 10 productive

plenty: 4 enow, heap, lots, much, raff 5 ample, cheap, fouth 6 enough, foison, scouth 7 copious 8 fullness, opulence 9 abundance, affluence, plenitude 10 exuberance, luxuriance, perfection, sufficient 11 copiousness, sufficiency 12 completeness
goddess: Ops
horn of: 10 cornucopia

plenum: 5 space 8 assembly, fullness, plethora

pleonasm: 8 fullness, verbiage 9 tautology 10 redundancy 11 superfluity

plethora: 4 glut 5 flood 6 deluge, excess 7 surfeit, surplus 8 fullness 9 profusion, repletion 13 overabundance 14 superabundance

plethoric: 6 turgid 7 swollen 8 inflated, overfull 9 bombastic 10 overloaded

pleurapophysis: rib

plexiform: 7 complex, netlike 9 intricate 11 complicated

plexus: 4 rete 5 retia (pl.) 6 tangle 7 network

pliable: 4 easy, limp, soft, waxy 5 lithe 6 docile, limber, pliant, supple 7 bending, ductile, flaccid, flexile, plastic, tensile, willowy 8 amenable, flexible, fluxible, informal, suitable, tractile, workable, yielding 9 adaptable, compliant, malleable, tractable 10 applicable 13 unconstrained

plicate: 4 fold 5 pleat

plight: fix, jam 4 fold, risk 5 array, braid, plait, state 6 engage, pickle, pledge, status 7 betroth, embrace, promise, trouble 8 position, quandary 9 betrothal, condition 10 difficulty 11 predicament

plinth: 4 base, orlo 5 block, couch, stone, table 6 course 7 subbase 8 skirting 9 baseboard
flat: 4 orlo

plod: dig, mog, peg 4 grub, plow, slog, toil, tore, vamp, work 5 tramp 6 drudge, trudge

plop: 4 fall 5 plump 8 drop down 10 sit heavily

plot: lot, map 4 land, plan, plat 5 cabal, chart, draft, story, tract 6 design, devise, scheme, secret 7 compact, connive, diagram, outline 8 conspire, contrive, engineer, intrigue, scenario 9 insidiate, machinate 10 conspiracy 11 machination
garden: bed 5 patch 8 parterre
ground: lot 5 grave 7 terrain
inventor: 8 schemist
play: 4 node

plover: 4 bird, crab, dupe 5 drome, kolea, oxeye, sandy 6 kildee, piping 7 collier, killdee, lapwing, maycock, Wilson's 8 dotterel, killdeer, squealer, toadhead 9 courtesan, turnstone 10 beetle-head, blacksmith
relative: 7 wrybill 9 sandpiper

plow, plough: dig, ear 4 farm, mole, rove, till, turn 5 break 6 cleave, digger, furrow 9 cultivate 10 cut through
handle: 5 stilt
kind of: 4 disc, gang, snow 5 sulky 6 chisel, gopher, lister, rotary, shovel 7 breaker, tractor, walking 8 stirring, turnplow 9 moldboard 14 prairie-breaker

knife: **6** colter **7** coulter

part: **4** beam, frog, hale **5** share, sheth, slade, stilt **6** bottom, sheath **7** pinhead **9** mold board, plowshare, sharebeam

plowhead: 4 beam **5** frame **6** clevis

plowing: 8 aeration

plowshare, ploughshare: lay **5** laver **6** colter **7** coulter

bone: **5** vomer

ploy: 4 joke, plan **5** sport, trick **6** frolic, gambit, tactic **7** pastime **8** escapade, maneuver, strategy **11** merrymaking

pluck: rob, tug **4** grit, guts, jerk, pick, pull, sand, tear **5** cheek, nerve, spunk, strip, strum, twang **6** daring, finger, fleece, gather, snatch, spirit, twitch **7** bravery, courage, deplume, plunder **8** decision, gameness **9** endurance, fortitude, hardihood **10** resolution

plug: peg, tap, tit **4** blow, bung, calk, cork, puff, push, slog **5** boost, caulk, estop, knock, punch, shoot, spile, spill **6** dottle, tampon **7** bouchon, pledget, promote, stopper, stopple **9** advertise, persevere

cannon muzzle: **7** tampion

clay: bod **4** bott

fire: **7** hydrant

medical: **4** clot **7** embolus

wall: **6** outlet

water: **6** spigot **7** hydrant

plug bib: 6 faucet, spigot

plugboard: 11 switchboard **12** control-panel

plug cock: 6 spigot

plug hat: 4 tile **5** gibus **6** topper

plug-in: 4 jack

plug-ugly: 4 thug **5** rowdy, tough **7** ruffian **8** criminal, gangster **9** roughneck

plum: hog **4** amra, coco, find, gage, sloe **5** catch, drupe, duhat, icaco, prune **6** damson, jambul, reward, sapote **7** bullace, jambool **8** dividend, windfall **9** greengage **10** amatungula

dried: **5** prune

seed: pit **7** putamen

wild: **4** skeg, sloe **5** islay

plumage: 4 down **5** dress **6** hackle **7** floccus **8** feathers **9** adornment

plumb: 4 bung, well **5** delve, probe, solve, sound **6** chunky, fathom, plunge **7** explore, plummet **8** absolute, complete, entirely, vertical **9** downright **10** absolutely, straighten, understand **13** perpendicular

plumbeous: 6 leaden

plum-colored: 4 puce **5** mauve **6** purple

plum duff: 7 pudding

plume: 4 tuft **5** crest, egret, preen, pride, prize, prune **6** aigret, plumet **7** feather, panache **8** aigrette **9** plumicorn

plummet: dip **4** drop, fall, lead **5** plumb **6** plunge, tumble, weight **8** nose-dive

plump: fat **4** back, drop, fall, plop, rich, sink, tidy **5** ample, bonny, buxom, obese, plunk, stout, tubby **6** bonnie, chubby, dilate, flatly, fleshy, portly, rotund, zaftig **7** bluntly, distend, fulsome, rounded, support **9** downright

plum weevil: 8 curculio

plunder: gut, rob **4** boot, loot, pelf, prey, raid, sack, swag **5** booty, cheat, harry, pluck, poach, raven, reave, rifle, spoil, steal, strip **6** bezzle, boodle, creach (Sc.), creagh (Sc.), dacoit, maraud, pilfer, pirate, rapine, ravage, ravish, spoils **7** despoil, pillage, ransack **8** spoliate **9** depredate, devastate

plunderer (see also **pirate**): **5** thief **6** bandit, looter, raider, sacker, vandal, Viking **8** marauder, predator **10** freebooter

plunge: bet, dig, dip **4** cave, dive, duck, dump, pool, rush, sink **5** douse, dowse, drive, fling, lunge, merse, pitch, plumb, souse **6** absorb, emerge, footer, gamble, thrust **7** immerge, immerse **8** submerge

plunger: ram **6** risker **10** speculator

plunk: 4 drop, flop, pull, push, sink, toss **5** drive, pluck, plump, sound, throw **6** dollar, strike

plunther: 4 plod **8** flounder

plurality: 4 most **8** majority **9** multitude

plus: add, too **4** also, more, over **5** extra **6** excess **8** addition, increase, moreover, positive

plush: 4 posh **6** deluxe **7** opulent **8** palatial **9** luxurious **11** upholstered

Plutarch work: 5 Lives **6** Morals

Pluto (see also **planet**): Dis **5** Hades, Orcus **8** Dis Pater

kingdom: **5** Hades

wife: **10** Persephone, Proserpina

plutocracy: 13 establishment, rule by wealthy

plutocrat: 5 nabob **6** fat cat **7** Croesus, rich man **9** moneybags **10** capitalist

Plutus: *father:* **6** Iasion

mother: **7** Demeter

ply: web **4** bend, fold, mold, sail, urge, work **5** beset, exert, layer, plait, wield **6** double, handle, travel **7** belabor, shuttle **8** belabour, exercise, function **9** importune, thickness

with drink: **5** birle

pneuma: 4 soul **5** neume **6** breath, spirit **8** ligature **9** breathing, life force

pneumonia: *kind:* **5** lobar, viral **9** bronchial

poach: 4 boil, cook **5** shirr, spear, steal, steam **6** pierce, thrust **7** trample **8** encroach, trespass

poacher: pan **5** thief **7** lurcher, stalker, widgeon **8** baldpate

salmon: **7** rebecca, rebekah

Pocahontas: *Christian name:* **7** Rebecca

  father: **8** Powhatan

  husband: **5** Rolfe

  saved: **9** John Smith

pochard: **4** duck **5** scaup **6** dunker

pochette: **6** violin **7** handbag **8** envelope

pock: pit **4** hole, scar **6** hollow **7** pustule

pocket: bin, cly, fob **4** hole, keep, poke, prat, sack **5** pouch **6** cavity **7** cantina, conceal, confine, enclose, isolate, put away **8** cul-de-sac **9** miniature, small area **10** blind alley **11** appropriate

  ore: **4** lode **7** bonanza

  water: **6** tinaja

pocketbook: bag, fob, lil **4** poke **5** burse, pouch, purse **6** clutch, wallet **8** billfold **12** portemonnaie

poco: **6** little **8** slightly, somewhat

pococurante: **9** apathetic **10** nonchalant **11** indifferent

pocosin, pocoson, pocosen: **5** marsh, swamp

pod: bag, bur, cod, kid, sac **4** aril, boll, hull, swad **5** belly, carob, pouch, shell, shuck **6** legume, loment **7** silicle **8** potbelly

podesta: **5** judge, mayor **8** executor, governor, official **10** magistrate

podgy: fat **5** pudgy, squat

podium: **4** base, dais, wall **7** lectern **8** pedestal, platform **12** substructure

Poe: *bird:* **5** raven

  house: **5** Usher

  poem: **5** Bells, Raven **6** Lenore **7** Ulalume **10** Annabel Lee

poem: ode **4** duan, epic, raff, rann (Ir.), rime, rune, song, vers (F.) **5** canto, ditty, elegy, ionic, lyric, poesy, raffe, rhyme, stave, verse **6** ballad, carmen, epopee, iambic, jingle, screed, sonnet, tercet **7** ballade, couplet, dimeter, sestina, triolet, virelay **8** acrostic, doggerel, hexapody, limerick, madrigal, senarius, trimeter **9** hexameter, hexastich, monometer, octameter **10** tetrameter **11** acatalectic

  accented foot: **5** arsis

  break in rhythm: **6** cesura **7** caesura

  bucolic: **8** pastoral

  closing: **5** envoi, envoy

  collection: **5** sylva

  comic: **8** doggerel, limerick

  eight-line: **7** triolet

  foot: **4** iamb **6** iambus **7** anapest, spondee, trochee

  four-line: **8** quatrain

  fourteen-line: **6** sonnet

  heroic: **4** epic

  line: **8** trimeter **9** hexameter **12** decasyl-labic

  love: **6** erotic **8** madrigal

  lyric: lay **4** alba **7** roundel

  medieval: lai **4** alba

  melodic: **5** lyric

  moral: dit

  mournful: **5** elegy

  narrative: **4** epos

  node: **4** plot

  part: fit **4** feet, foot, line **5** canto, epode, stich, verse **6** epilog, prolog, stanza **7** refrain **8** epilogue, prologue

  pastoral: **4** idyl **7** bucolic, eclogue, georgic

  religious: **4** hymn **5** psalm

  rural: **7** eclogue, georgic

  satirical: dit (F.) **6** iambic, kasada, parody

  seven-line: **10** heptastich

  six-line: **9** hexastich

  six-stanza: **7** sestina

  sort: dit (F.) **5** ditty **6** sonnet **7** epigram **8** rondelet

  ten-line: **6** dizain **7** dizaine **9** decastich

  two-line: **7** couplet

poesy: **4** poem **5** motto, verse **7** nosegay

poet: **4** bard, fili, muse, scop **5** odist, rishi **6** lyrist **7** dreamer, imagist, metrist **8** idyllist, minstrel **9** bucoliast **10** Parnassian **13** cinque-centist

  humorous: **4** Lear, Nash

  inferior: **5** rimer **6** rhymer **8** rimester **9** poetaster, poeticule, rhymester, versifier

  inspiration: **4** Muse

poetic: **4** odic **5** lyric **6** dreamy **8** romantic **9** beautiful, visionary **11** imaginative

poetical: **8** sonnetic

poet laureate: *American:* **4** Dove **6** Strand, Warren, Wilbur **7** Brodsky, Nemerov, Van Duyn

  British: Pye **4** Rowe, Tate **6** Austin, Cibber, Dryden, Eusden, Hughes, Warton **7** Bridges, Southey **8** Betjeman, Davenant, Day-Lewis, Shadwell, Tennyson **9** Masefield, Whitehead **10** Wordsworth

poetry (see also **poem**): **4** song **5** poesy, rhyme, verse

  god: **5** Bragi

  inspiring to: **7** helicon

  muse: **5** Erato **6** Thalia **7** Euterpe **8** Calliope

pogonip: fog

pogrom: **6** attack **7** pillage **8** genocide, massacre **9** slaughter

pogy: **5** perch, trout **8** menhaden

poi: **4** food **5** paste

  source: **4** taro

poietic: **8** creative

poignant: **4** keen, tart **5** acute, sharp **6** biting, bitter, moving **7** cutting, piquant, pointed, pungent **8** piercing, pricking, touching

poind: 4 sell **5** seize **7** impound

point: aim, dot, jag, jet, jot, neb, nib, tip **4** apex, barb, cape, crux, cusp, gist, horn, item, peak, pith, pole, show, spit, spot **5** angle, focus, issue, level, prong, punch, refer, sense, spire, taper **6** allude, degree, detail, direct, tip-off, tittle **7** apicula (L.), apiculi (L.), article, element, feature, meaning **8** apiculus (L.), emphasis, indicate, salience, validity **10** particular, promontory

cardinal: **4** east, west **5** north, south

final: dot, end **6** period **7** outcome **8** full stop (Br.)

finishing: **4** line, tape **7** end zone **9** home plate

highest: tip **4** acme, apex, noon, peak **6** apices, apogee, maxima, summit, zenith **7** maximum **8** meridian, pinnacle **11** ne plus ultra

land: **4** hook, spit

law: res

lowest: **4** zero **5** nadir **6** bottom, perigee **7** bedrock

pert. to: **6** apical

scoring: ace, run **5** punto **6** sponge

spear: **4** grad

strong: **5** forte

supporting: **5** pivot **7** fulcrum

to the: **5** terse **6** cogent, direct **8** relevant **9** pertinent

turning: **4** tide **5** cardo, epoch **6** crises, crisis

utmost: **7** extreme, sublime **9** extremity

vibration: **4** node

weak: **4** blot, flaw **5** fault **6** foible

point-blank: **6** direct, head-on, wholly **7** bluntly, exactly **8** directly **9** perfectly, precisely **10** completely **13** unqualifiedly

pointed: **5** acute, sharp, tangy, terse **6** acuate, marked, picked **7** actuate, capapie, concise **8** aculeate, piercing, poignant, spicated, stinging **9** acuminate, apiculate, fastigate **10** noticeable **11** conspicuous

pointer: arm, dog, tip **4** clue, hand, hint **5** index **6** advice, fescue, gnomon **7** indices **9** indicator

pointless: **4** dull **5** blunt, inane, silly, vapid **6** absurd, stupid **7** insipid **9** senseless **11** meaningless

point of view: eye **4** bras **5** angle, sight, slant **6** stance **7** opinion, outlook **8** attitude, position

pointsman: **7** flanker, trapper **9** switchman

poise: tee **4** tact **5** carry, grace, weigh **6** aplomb **7** balance, ballast, bearing, support, suspend **8** calmness, carriage, elegance, liberate, maintain **9** assurance, equipoise, stability **10** confidence, equanimity **11** equi-

librium **12** counterpoise **14** counterbalance

poison: fig **4** bane, drab, gall **5** atter, taint, venin, venom, virus **6** amarin, debase, infect, miasma **7** amarine, arsenic, botulin, corrupt, pervert, vitiate **8** empoison, ptomaine **11** contaminate

ant: **11** formicicide

arrow: **4** haya, inee, upas **5** urali, urare, urari **6** antiar, curare, curari **7** ouabain, woorlai

hexapod: **11** insecticide

kind: **4** bikh **5** abrin, nabee, ricin **6** antiar, datura, mescal **7** arsenic, cyanide, hemlock, henbane, tanghin **8** atropine **9** pesticide **10** belladonna, nightshade, strychnine

pert. to: **9** arsenious

tree: **4** upas

poison ash: **5** sumac **6** sumach **9** torchwood

poison fish: **4** fugu **6** weever **8** scorpion, toadfish

poison flag: **4** iris

poison flower: **8** oleander **11** bittersweet

poisoning: **6** pyemia **7** jimmies **9** ichthyism, lathyrism

food: **5** E. coli **8** botulism, ergotism

lead: **8** plumbism

poison ivy: **5** sumac **6** laurel

poisonous: **5** fatal, toxic **6** deadly, mortal, virose **7** baneful, noxious **8** mephatic, venomous, virulent **9** malignant **11** destructive

fish: **4** fugu

fungus: **7** amanita

gas: **6** arsine **8** chlorine, phosgene **14** carbon monoxide

herb: **8** aconitum

lizard: **4** gila

plant: **8** mandrake **10** nightshade

weed: **4** loco

poison tobacco: **7** henbane

poisonwood: **5** sumac **8** metopium **10** manchineel

poisson bleu: **7** blue cat, catfish **8** grayling

poitrel: **5** armor, plate **7** pectron **9** stomacher **11** breastplate

poke: bag, dig, hat, jab, jog **4** blow, bore, brod, cuff, prod, root, sack **5** bulge, delay, dunce, nudge, probe, punch, purse, snoop **6** bonnet, dawdle, loiter, meddle, pocket, potter, putter, sleeve, thrust, wallet **7** dawdler, intrude, tobacco

poker: rod **4** dart, game

drawing by: **10** pyrography

forerunner: **7** primero

form: **4** draw, stud

stake: pot **4** ante **5** chips, kitty

poker-faced: **7** neutral, serious **11** unemotional

pokeweed: **5** pocan **6** garget **8** inkberry

family: **14** phytolaccaceae

pokey, poky: 4 dull, jail, mean, slow 5 dowdy 6 narrow, shabby, stuffy 7 tedious 8 trifling

---

Poland: 6 Polska 7 Polonia 8 Sarmatia
astronomer: 10 Copernicus
cake: 4 baba
capital: 6 Warsaw
carriage: 7 britska
city: 4 Lodz 5 Brest, Posen, Vilna 6 Cracow, Gdansk, Gdynia, Grodno, Krakow, Lublin, Poznan, Tarnow 7 Beuthen, Lemberg, Litovsk, Wroclaw 8 Gleiwitz, Katowice, Szczecin, Tarnopol 9 Bialystok, Bielostok, Byelostok
composer: 6 Chopin 10 Paderewski
currency: 5 ducat, grosz, marka, zloty 6 fennig, halerz, korona
dance: 5 polka 7 mazurka 9 krakowiak, polonaise 11 cracovienne
dollar: 5 dalar
labor union: 10 Solidarity
measure: cal 4 mila, morg, pret 5 linja, morga, sazen, stopa, vloka, wloka 6 cwierc, korzec, kwarta, lokiec 7 garniec 9 kwarterka
nobility: 8 szlachta
nobleman: 7 starost
people: 4 Slav 5 Marur 8 Silesian
pope: 7 Wojtyla 10 John Paul II
river: Bug, San 4 Oder, Styr 5 Dwina, Seret, Warta 6 Neisse, Niemen, Pripet, Strypa 7 Vistula
scientist: 5 Curie
title of address: 4 Pani
weight: lut 4 funt 5 uncya 6 kamian 7 centner, skrupul

---

polar: 6 Arctic 7 pivotal 8 opposite
polar explorer: 4 Byrd 5 Peary 6 Wilkes 8 Amundsen
Polaris: 7 missile 9 North Star
pole: bar, pew, poy, rod, xat 4 axis, boom, brog, mast, palo (Sp.), pike, prop, punt, spar, wand 5 caber, guide, nader, perch, sprit, staff, stake, stick, stool, sweep, totem 6 crotch 7 barling
circle: 11 circumpolar
electric: 5 anode 7 cathode, kathode 9 electrode
fishing: rod
tribal: xat 5 totem
vehicle: 4 cope, neap 5 thill
polecat: 5 fitch, skunk, zoril 6 ferret, musang, weasel 7 fitchet, fitchew, foumart

pole fluke: 8 flounder
polehead: 7 tadpole
pole horse: 7 wheeler
polemic: 6 debate 7 dispute 8 argument 9 disputant 10 discussion 11 disputation 12 disputatious 13 argumentative, controversial
polenta: 4 mush 8 cornmeal, porridge
polestar: 5 guide 8 lodestar 10 tramontane
pole strip: 8 template
police: 4 cops, fuzz 5 guard, watch 6 govern, patrol 7 protect, rurales, trooper 8 officers 11 carabinieri (It.) 12 constabulary
British: 12 Scotland Yard
Canadian: 4 RCMP
federal: FBI
French: 6 Sûreté
headquarters: 4 tana 7 station 8 bargello, barracks, precinct 9 marshalcy
international: 8 Interpol
line: 6 cordon
officer: 5 chief, reeve 6 kotwal 7 sheriff 8 bargello 10 prefecture
organization: PAL
self-appointed: 10 vigilantes
special team: 4 SWAT
trap: 7 dragnet
vehicle: car, van 7 cruiser 8 prowl car, squad car
police officer: cop 4 bull 5 bobby, bulky, burly, rural, sepoy 6 bobbie, copper, peeler 7 crusher, gumshoe, officer, sheriff, trooper 8 flatfoot, gendarme (F.), marshall 9 burkundaz, constable, detective, patrolman, policeman 11 burkundauze, carabiniere (It.), policewoman
badge: 6 buzzer, shield
British: 5 bobby 9 constable
Canadian: 6 mounty
club: 5 billy 9 espantoon, truncheon 10 nightstick
federal: 4 G-man, T-man
French: 8 gendarme
policy: wit 4 plan, rule 6 course, wisdom 8 contract, prudence, sagacity 9 diplomacy, principle, procedure 10 artfulness, management, shrewdness 14 administration
polish: rub 4 buff 5 frush, glaze, gloss, grind, rabat, scour, scrub, sheen, shine, slick 6 finish, glance, luster, lustre, rabbat, refine, smooth 7 brush up, burnish, culture, furbish, perfect 8 brighten, civilize, elegance, lapidate, levigate, urbanity 10 refinement
polished: 4 fine 5 compt, shiny, suave 6 buffed, glossy, polite, urbane 7 gallant
polisher: 5 brush, emery, rabat (F.) 6 glazer, pumice 8 abrasive

polishing: 7 sanding 8 frottage, limation
polish off: end 4 kill 5 eat up 6 finish 7 consume
polite: 5 civil, suave 6 gentle, smooth, urbane 7 correct, courtly, cunning, gallant, genteel, refined 8 cultured, debonair, decorous, discreet, polished 9 attentive, courteous, debonaire 10 cultivated, debonnaire, thoughtful 11 complaisant, considerate 12 well-mannered
politesse: 8 courtesy 12 decorousness
politic: 4 wary, wise 5 suave 6 artful, astute, crafty, shrewd 7 prudent 8 discreet 9 expedient, politique, provident, sagacious 10 diplomatic 12 unscrupulous
political: *division:* 4 city, town, ward 5 shire, state 6 county 7 borough 8 province 9 community
  gathering: 5 rally 6 caucus 10 convention
  group: 4 bloc, cell, ring 5 cadre, junta, party 6 caucus 7 faction, machine
  hanger-on: 10 ward heeler
  incumbents: ins
  influence: 5 lobby
  list: 5 slate 6 ticket
political party: G.O.P. 4 Tory, Whig 5 Labor 8 Populist 9 Communist, Greenback, Socialist 10 Democratic, Federalist, Republican 11 Know-Nothing, Libertarian 12 Conservative
  principles: 8 platform
  program article: 5 plank
politician: pol 4 boss 7 schemer, senator, statist 8 lawmaker 9 intriguer, president, statesman 10 wirepuller 16 congressionalist
polka dot: 4 spot 6 circle
poll: cow 4 clip, coll, head, list, trim 5 count, shave, shear 6 ballot, cut off, dehorn, fleece, survey 7 canvass, despoil, listing 8 counting, register 9 enumerate
pollack: 4 fish, pool 6 billet, saithe 7 baddock (Sc.) 8 bluefish, coalfish
pollan: 9 whitefish
pollard: cow 4 bran, deer, goat, stag, tree 5 prune, sheep 8 truncate
polled: 8 hornless
pollen: 4 dust, meal 5 flour 6 powder, spores
pollen brush: 5 scopa 6 scopae
pollenization: 5 xenia
pollex: 4 inch 5 digit, thumb 6 finger 7 phlange
pollicitation: 7 promise 8 proposal
pollinate: 9 fecundate, fertilize
pollinosis: 8 hay fever
polliwog: 7 tadpole
pollute: 4 foul, soil 5 dirty, smear, stain, sully, taint 6 befoul, defile, ravish 7 corrupt, debauch, profane, violate, vitiate 9 desecrate 11 contaminate

pollution: 4 smog 5 filth 8 impurity 11 desecration, uncleanness
Pollux: *brother:* 6 Castor
  father: 4 Zeus
  mother: 4 Leda
polo: *division:* 7 chucker, chukker
  mount: 4 pony 5 horse
  stick: 6 mallet
  team: 4 four
Polonius (see also **Hamlet**): *daughter:* 7 Ophelia
  son: 7 Laertes
Polony: 6 Polish 7 sausage 9 polonaise
polt: 4 blow, club 5 knock, thump
poltergeist: 5 ghost, spook 6 spirit
poltfoot: 8 clubfoot
poltroon: cad 4 idle, lazy 6 coward, craven, wretch 7 dastard 8 cowardly, sluggard 9 dastardly
polverine: 6 potash 8 pearlash
polyandrium: 8 cemetery
polychromatic: 10 variegated 12 multicolored
polygamy: 6 bigamy
polygon: 4 ngon 6 square 7 decagon, hexagon, nonagon, octagon 8 pentagon, triangle
  equal sides: 6 isagon
  nine sides: 7 nonagon
  twelve sides: 9 dodecagon
Polynesia: *apple:* 4 hevi
  baking pit: umu
  banana: fei
  beverage: 4 kava, kawa
  breech cloth: 4 malo
  burial place: ahu
  butterfly: io
  chestnut: 4 rata
  cloth: 4 tapa
  clothing: 4 sulu 5 pareu 6 muumuu 8 lavalava
  dance: 4 hula, siva 6 tamure
  dragon: ati
  fern: 4 tara
  god: Oro 4 Tane, Tiki
  goddess: 4 Pele
  herb: pia
  homeland: 7 Havaiki
  island: 4 Nive 5 Tonga 6 Easter, Ellice, Midway, Tahiti, Tuvalu 7 Phoenix, Tokelau
  magical power: 4 mana
  memorial: ahu
  oven: umu
  people: Ati 5 Malay, Maori 6 Kanaka, Samoan, Tongan 8 Hawaiian, Tahitian 9 Marquesan
  pepper plant: 4 avas
  pigeon: 4 lupe
  pine: ara 4 hala

plant: **4** taro
ruler: **7** faipule
sky: **5** langi
sling: ma
spirit: **4** Atua
statue: **4** Tiki
tree: ti **4** ahia, rata
wages: utu
woman: **6** vahine
yam: ube, ubi, uve, uvi
polyp: **5** hydra, tumor **6** growth, seapen **7** anemone, hydroid, octopod
skeleton: **5** coral
polytrophic: **9** versatile
Polyxena: *father:* **5** Priam
lover: **8** Achilles
mother: **6** Hecuba
pomade: **4** balm **5** cream, salve **7** pomatum, unguent **8** cosmetic, ointment
pomander: **4** case **7** pouncet
pome: **4** ball, pear **5** apple, fruit, globe **6** quince, sphere **9** juneberry
pomegranate: **6** granet **7** grenade **8** balausta
syrup: **9** grenadine
pomelo: **8** shaddock **10** grapefruit
Pomerania: *capital:* **7** Stettin
city: **5** Thorn, Torun **6** Anklam
island: **5** Rugen **6** Usedom
river: **4** Oder
Pomeranian: dog
pomme de terre (F.): **6** potato
pommel: bat **4** beat, horn, knob **6** finial, handle **12** protuberance
bag: **7** cantina
pomp: **4** fare, form **5** boast, pride, state **6** estate, parade, ritual **7** cortege, display, liturgy, pageant **8** ceremony, grandeur, splendor **9** pageantry, spectacle **10** ceremonial **11** ostentation **12** magnificence
Pomp and Circumstance composer: **5** Elgar
pompano: **4** fish **7** alewife, cobbler **8** mackerel **9** poppy fish
Pompeii: *archeologist:* Mau
heroine: **4** Ione
mountain: **8** Vesuvius
pom-pom: gun **6** cannon **15** anti-aircraft gun
pompon: **4** ball, tuft **6** dahlia **8** ornament **13** chrysanthemum
pompous: big **4** vain **5** showy **6** stuffy **7** bloated, fustian, orotund, stately, stilted **8** arrogant **9** bombastic, flatulent, grandiose **10** altisonant, pontifical, rhetorical **11** altiloquent, dictatorial, magnificent, pretentious, stateliness **12** ostentatious **13** grandiloquent, self-important
Ponchielli opera: **8** Gioconda
pond: dam, lum **4** delf, dike, lake, mere, pool,

tarn **6** lagoon **7** lakelet, stalina
fish: **7** piscina, pisoina **8** aquarium
frog: **8** ranarium
oyster: **6** claire
pond dogwood: **10** buttonbush
pond duck: **7** mallard
ponder: **4** chaw, mull, muse, pore **5** brood, opine, study, think, weigh **6** reason **7** mediate, reflect, revolve **8** appraise, cogitate, consider, evaluate, meditate, ruminate, turn over **10** deliberate **11** contemplate
ponderous: dry **4** dull **5** bulky, grave, heavy, hefty, massy **7** awkward, massive, weighty **8** unwieldy **9** important, momentous **11** elephantine, heavy-footed
pondfish: **7** sunfish
pond hen: **4** coot **6** fulica
pondokkie: hut **5** hovel
pone: **4** cake, lump, turf **5** bread **8** swelling **9** cornbread **10** johnny-cake
pongee: **4** silk **5** cloth **6** fabric **7** paunche **8** shantung
pongy: **4** monk **6** priest **8** Buddhist
poniard: **4** dirk, kill, stab **6** bodkin, dagger, pierce, stylet **8** stiletto
pont: **5** ferry, float **6** bridge **7** caisson **9** ferryboat
pontiff: **4** pope **6** bishop **8** pontifex **11** chief priest
pert. to: **5** papal **7** sistine
pontifical: **5** papal **7** pompous **8** dogmatic
pontoon: **4** boat **5** barge, float **6** bridge, vessel **7** caisson
plank: **5** chess
pony: cab, cob, nag **4** crib, trot **5** glass, horse **6** garran, liquor **7** hackney, measure
kind: **5** pinto, tatoo **6** cayuse, Exmoor **8** Shetland
student's: **4** crib, trot
up: pay
pooch: dog **6** barbet **7** mongrel
pooh-pooh: **6** deride **7** dismiss, kiss off **8** ridicule **9** denigrate, raspberry
pook: **4** heap, pile, pull **5** pluck, stack
pooka: **6** goblin **7** specter
pool: car, dib (Sc.), dub (Sc.), lin, pit, pot **4** carr, dike, game, jeel, linn, loch, mear, meer, mere, pond, tank, tarn **5** flash, flush, funds, kitty, lough, plash, stake, trunk, trust **6** cartel, charco, flodge, lagoon, plunge, puddle, salina **7** alberca, carline, combine, jackpot, plashet **8** monopoly **9** billabong, billiards, reservoir, resources, syndicate **10** natatorium **11** combination
ball: cue **4** spot **6** ringer
poon: **4** dilo, tree **5** domba, keena **8** mastwood

poop: 4 deck, fool, gulp, seat 5 cheat, cozen, stern 7 exhaust 8 hinddeck 10 nincompoop 11 information

poor: bad, ill 4 bare, base, lean, mean 5 broke, cheap, dinky, naked, needy, seedy 6 abject, barren, feeble, hard up, humble, hungry, in need, meager, paltry, pilled, scanty, shabby, sparse 7 hapless, pitiful, squalid, sterile, unlucky 8 bankrupt, beggared, dirt poor, indigent, inferior 9 defective, destitute, emaciated, imperfect, infertile, insolvent, penurious 10 inadequate, ungenerous 11 impecunious, inefficient, unfortunate 12 contemptible, impoverished, insufficient 13 insignificant 14 unsatisfactory

Poor Clare: nun 6 sister 10 Franciscan

poorer: 5 worse 8 inferior

poorhouse: 6 asylum 9 almshouse, measondue, workhouse

poor joe: 4 bird 5 heron

poor John: cod 4 fish, food, hake

poorly: low 4 mean 5 badly 6 ailing, sickly, unwell 10 indisposed 13 disparagingly

poor man's pepper: 9 stonecrop 11 peppergrass

poor man's soap: 7 spiraea 8 hardhack

poor man's weatherglass: 9 pimpernel

poor soldier: 9 friarbird

poor-spirited: 4 base, mean 8 cowardly

pop: dad 4 blow, dart, pawn, soda 5 fling 6 father, strike 8 beverage 9 explosion

popadam: 4 cake 5 wafer 8 cookie

popdock: 8 foxglove

pope (see also **papal**): 4 ruff 6 bishop, priest, puffin, shrike 7 pontiff, primate 9 bullfinch, patriarch 10 holy father
cape: 5 fanon, orale 7 mozetta 8 mozzetta
collar: 7 pallium
court: 5 Curia
court office: 6 datary 7 dataria
court officer: 6 datary
crown: 5 tiara 9 triregnum
envoy: 6 legate, nuncio 7 nuntius 8 ablegate
epistle: 8 decretal
headdress: 5 miter, mitre, tiara
letter: 4 bull
name: Leo 4 John, Paul, Pius 5 Felix, Linus, Peter, Ratti, Urban 6 Adrian, Cletus, Martin, Sixtus, Victor 7 Clement, Gregory, Paschal, Stephen, Zachary 8 Agapitus, Benedict, Boniface, Calistus, Eusebius, Innocent, John Paul, Nicholas, Theodore 9 Alexander
palace: 7 Lateran, Vatican
seal: 5 bulla
secretary: 11 apocrisiary
veil: 5 orale 6 fannel

Popeye: *baby:* 7 Swee' Pea

creator: 5 Segar
food: 7 spinach
girlfriend: 8 Olive Oyl
moocher: 5 Wimpy
occupation: 6 sailor
rival: 5 Bluto

popinac: 8 huisache

popinjay: fop 6 parrot 7 coxcomb, papingo 8 parakeet 10 woodpecker

poplar: 4 liar 5 abele, alamo, aspen, bahan, bolle, garab 6 balsam 7 populus 9 tacamahac 10 cottonwood
white: 5 abele, aspen

Poppaea's husband: 4 Nero

poppy: 5 plant 6 blaver, canker, flower 7 coprose, papaver, ponceau 8 foxglove 10 coquelicot
genus: 7 Papaver
herb family: 9 celandine
seed: maw

poppycock: rot 4 bosh, bunk, dung 8 nonsense

populace: mob 4 mass 5 demos, plebs 6 people, public 9 hoi-polloi 11 commonality, proletariat, rank and file, third estate

popular: lay, pop 6 common, simple, vulgar 7 demotic, favored 8 accepted, favorite 9 prevalent, well-liked 10 democratic, prevailing 11 proletarian 12 nontechnical

popularity: 5 vogue 8 claptrap

populate: 6 occupy, people 7 inhabit

population: 8 universe 9 habitancy 11 inhabitants
count: 6 census
study: 10 demography, larithmics

populous: 7 crowded 9 abounding

porbeagle: 5 shark 7 lamnoid

porcelain: 4 frit 5 china 7 biscuit 9 bone china
ancient: 5 murra
clay: 6 kaolin 7 kaoline
furnace: 7 hovel
kind of: 5 Imari, Lenox, Spode 6 Lladro, Sevres 7 Belleek, Celadon, Dresden, Limoges, Meissen 8 Haviland, Noritake 9 Rosenthal, Wedgewood 12 Royal Doulton

porch: 4 door, stoa 5 lanai, plaza, stoae (pl.), stoop 6 harbor, loggia, piazza 7 balcony, galilee, gallery, portico, terrace, veranda 8 entrance 9 colonnade
church: 7 galilee 8 martliex
sun: 7 solaria (pl.) 8 solarium
swing: 6 glider

porcine: fat 7 piglike

porcupine: 5 urson 7 cawquaw 8 hedgehog
disease: 10 ichthyosis
genus of: 7 hystrix
spine: 5 quill

porcupine anteater: 7 echidna

porcupine fish: 6 atinga, diodon 11 spiny puffer

porcupine grass: 5 stipa 8 spinefex
 quill: pen

pore: con 4 gaze 5 gloze, stare, stoma, study 6 ponder 7 foramen, opening, orifice, ostiole, stomata (pl.) 8 lenticel, meditate
 plant: 7 ostiole 8 lenticel

porgy: tai (Jap.) 4 fish, scup 6 besugo, pagrus 7 margate, pinfish 8 menhaden 9 spadefish

pork: ham, pig 4 jowl 5 bacon, money, swine 6 hamhog 7 fatback, griskin, hamhock, sausage 8 chitlins, pig's feet, position, salt pork, sowbelly 9 chitlings 12 chitterlings, pig's knuckles 14 picnic shoulder

pork-barrelling: 9 patronage

porker: hog, pig 5 swine

porkfish: 4 sisi

porky: fat, pig 6 greasy

pornographic: 4 lewd 6 smutty 7 obscene 9 salacious 10 licentious

porous: 4 open 5 leaky, light 6 leachy 9 permeable 10 penetrable 13 insubstantial

porphyry: 4 rock

porpoise: 4 inia 6 seahog 7 dolphin, pellock (Sc.) 8 cetacean, gairfish

porrect: 6 extend, tender 7 present

porret: 4 leek 5 onion 6 garlic 8 scallion

porridge: 4 samp 5 atole, brose (Sc.), grout, gruel, pease 6 burgoo 7 brochan, burgout, oatmeal, polenta, pottage 9 stir-about 10 miscellany 11 skilligalee
 container: 6 bicker

port: 4 gate, goal, left, wine 6 carry, haven 6 apport, harbor, market, portal, refuge 7 bearing, harbour, meaning, purport, shelter 8 carriage, demeanor, larboard 9 demeanour, transport 10 deportment 11 destination

portable: 5 handy 6 mobile 7 movable 8 bearable 10 convenient, manageable
 bathtub: 4 tosh
 bed: cot 5 futon 8 rollaway 11 sleeping bag
 chair: 5 sedan
 computer: 6 lap top 7 palm top 8 notebook
 lamp: 7 lantern
 stove: 4 etna 7 Coleman

portal: 4 arch, door, gate 7 gateway 8 entrance

portance: 7 bearing, conduct 8 carriage, demeanor

portcullis: bar 4 door, gate, shut 5 grate, herse 7 grating, lattice

portefeuille: 9 portfolio

porte-monnaie: 5 purse 10 pocketbook

portend: 4 bode 5 augur 6 divine 7 betoken, forbode, predict, presage 8 forebode, foretell, prophesy 10 foreshadow

portent: 4 omen, sign 5 event 6 marvel, ostent, wonder 7 meaning, prodigy 8 ceremony 9 foretoken 10 foreboding, prognostic 11 forewarning

portentous: 4 dire 5 fatal, grave 6 solemn 7 fateful, ominous, pompous, weighty 10 impressive 11 significant

porter: ale 4 beer 5 carry, hamal, lager, stout 6 bearer, durwan, hamaul, hammal, khamal, redcap, suisse 7 bailiff, carrier, durwaun, dvornik (Russ.), gateman, hummaul, janitor, ostiary 8 beverage, cargador, janitrix 9 attendant, concierge, janitress, transport 10 doorkeeper

Portia (see also **Merchant of Venice**): *alias:* 9 Balthazar
 husband: 6 Brutus
 lover: 8 Bassanio
 maid: 7 Nerissa

portia tree: 4 maho 5 bendy

portico: 4 stoa (Gr.), xyst 5 porch, stoae (Gr., pl.) 6 atrium, piazza, xystus 7 narthex, pteroma, terrace, veranda 9 colonnade, pteromata (pl.), vestibule 10 ambulatory, antetemple
 enclosed: 9 peridrome
 long: 6 xystus 7 veranda

portiere: 5 drape 7 curtain

portion: bit, cut, dab, dot, jag, lot, nip 4 chaw, deal, dole, dunt, fate, jagg, part, some 5 allot, allow, divvy, dower, dowry, endow, piece, quota, ratio, share 6 canton, divide, dowery, gobbet, moiety, parcel, rasher, ration 7 destiny, helping, scruple, section, segment, serving 8 legitime, quantity 9 allotment, allowance, apportion 10 distribute 13 apportionment

portly: fat 5 ample, heavy, obese, stout 6 chubby, chunky 7 stately 8 imposing, majestic 9 corpulent, dignified

portmanteau: bag 4 case 6 valise 7 attache 8 suitcase 9 carpetbag, gladstone

Porto Rico: See **Puerto Rico**

portrait: 4 copy, icon, ikon 5 image 6 effigy 7 picture, profile 8 likeness, painting 9 miniature 10 silhouette, similitude
 pert. to: 6 iconic

portray: act 4 copy, draw, form, limn, mime, show 5 enact, frame, graph, image, paint 6 depict 7 fashion, picture 8 describe 9 delineate, duplicate, pantomime, represent, reproduce 11 demonstrate

portreeve: 5 mayor 7 bailiff, officer

portress, porteress: 6 porter 9 charwoman 10 doorkeeper

Portugal: (see box)

porwigle: 7 tadpole

posada: inn 5 hotel

Portugal: *art style:* **9** Manueline
brandy: **10** aguardente
capital: **6** Lisboa, Lisbon
city: **4** Ovar **5** Braga, Evora, Porto **6** Guarda **7** Coimbra **8** Braganca
currency: **5** dobra **6** escudo **7** centavo
dance music: **4** vira **5** chula
explorer: Cao **4** Diaz **6** Cabral, da Gama **8** Magellan
festival: **9** chamarita
guitar: **6** violao
harbor: **4** Faro, Ovar **5** Macao **6** Aveiro, Lisbon, Oporto, Vianna **7** Setubal **8** Figueira
liquid measure: **6** canada
measure: pe **4** alma, bota, meio, moio, pipa, vara **5** almud, braca, fanga, geira, legoa, linha, milha, palmo **6** almude, covado, quarto **7** alquier, estadio, ferrado, selamin **8** alqueire, tonelada
people: **7** Iberian
poet: **6** Camoes
port: **5** Porto, Sines, Velas **7** Leixoes, Setubal
river: **4** Sado **5** Douro, Duero, Minho, Tagus **7** Mondego **8** Guadiana
saint: sao
song: **4** fado
territory: **5** Macao **6** Azores **8** Madeiras
title: dom **4** dona **6** senhor **7** fidalgo, senhora **9** senhorita
vessel: **7** caravel
weight: **4** grao, onca, once **5** libra, marco **6** arroba, oitava **7** arratel, quintal
wine: **4** port **7** Madeira

posaune: **8** trombone
pose: ask, put, set, sit **4** airs, sham **5** feign, model, offer, place, strut **6** baffle, puzzle, stance **7** nonplus, posture, pretend **8** attitude, confound, position, propound, question **9** mannerism **10** disconcert, expression **11** affectation, impersonate **12** attitudinize
Poseidon: **7** Neptune (L.) **11** earthshaker
attendant: **6** Nereid **7** Proteus
brother: **4** Zeus **5** Hades, Pluto
father: **6** Cronus
mother: **4** Rhea
offspring: **5** Arion **6** Albion, Triton **7** Alebion, Antaeus, Antaios **10** Polyphemus
scepter: **7** trident
servant: **7** Proteus
wife: **10** Amphitrite
poser: **5** facer **6** puzzle **7** problem **8** question

posh: **4** chic **5** smart **6** spruce, swanky **7** elegant, stylish **9** luxurious **11** fashionable
posit: **6** affirm, assert, assume **9** postulate **10** presuppose
position (see also *place*): job, lie, set **4** loci (pl.), pose, post, rank, side, site, view **5** cense, coign, locus, place, situs, stand **6** billet, coigne, estate, locale, office, plight, stance, status **7** calling, posture **8** attitude, doctrine, location, sinecure, statuses (pl.) **9** condition, gradation, situation **10** standpoint **11** affirmation, appointment, disposition **12** circumstance
change: **4** move **5** shift
correct: **8** oriented
defensive: **4** fort **10** bridgehead
relative: **4** rank **5** grade **8** standing
troops: **6** deploy
positional: **6** situal
positive: set **4** plus, sure **6** actual, thetic **7** assured, certain, decided **8** absolute, complete, constant, definite, dogmatic, emphatic, explicit **9** assertive, confident, downright, empirical, practical **10** peremptory **11** affirmative, categorical, dictatorial, opinionated, right-handed, unqualified **13** authoritative, overconfident
positively: **5** truly **6** easily, really **8** actually **9** certainly, obviously **11** indubitably
positivism: **7** Comtism **9** certainty, dogmatism **11** materialism
founder: **5** Comte
positure: **7** posture **11** arrangement, disposition **13** configuration
poss: **4** beat, dash, push **5** drive, knock, pound, stamp **6** thrust
posse: **4** band **6** throng
possess: get, owe, own **4** bear, have, hold, keep **5** boast, reach, seize **6** occupy **7** inhabit **8** dominate, maintain
possessed: mad **4** calm **7** haunted **8** demoniac **10** spellbound
possession: **4** aver, hold **5** asset, aught **6** havior, seisin, wealth **7** control, dewanee, haviour, mastery **8** property **9** ownership
family: **8** heirloom
legal: **5** title **6** estate
of goods by finding: **6** trover
take: **5** seize
possessions: **5** goods **6** assets, graith **8** chattels, property
possessor: **5** owner **10** proprietor
posset: **4** turn **6** curdle, pamper **8** beverage **9** balductum, coagulate
possibility: **11** contingency, eventuality
possible: may **6** likely **8** feasible, probable **9** expedient, potential **10** contingent **11** practicable

possibly: may **5** maybe **7** perhaps
possum: **4** coon, tait **9** marsupial, phalanger
  comic strip: **4** Pogo
  play: **4** sham **5** feign **7** pretend
post: set **4** dole, dool, fort, mail, pole, ride, send **5** after, cippi (pl.), haste, later, newel, place, stake, stock **6** assign, cippus, column, inform, office, picket, pillar, poster, travel **7** courier, placard, station **8** announce, dispatch, garrison, position **9** advertise, situation
  airplane race: **5** pylon
  boat rope: **5** winch **7** bollard, capstan **8** windlass
  easy: **4** pipe, snap **8** sinecure
  middle: **8** kingpost
postage: **5** stamp
  free: **5** frank
  stamp design: **6** burele **8** burelage
postbox: **7** mailbox
postboy: **7** courier, yamshik (Russ.) **8** horseman, yemschik (Russ.) **9** messenger, postilion, yamstchik (Russ.)
post chaise: **4** jack **5** coach **8** carriage
poster: **4** bill, clap, sign **6** banner **7** affiche, courier, placard, sticker **8** handbill **9** broadside **10** billposter **12** announcement **13** advertisement
posterior: **4** back, hind, rear **6** behind, caudal, dorsal, hinder **7** adaxial **8** buttocks **10** subsequent
posterity: **6** sequel **9** offspring **10** generation **11** descendants
postern: **4** door, exit, gate, side **7** clocket, private **8** entrance **10** undercover
postfix: add **5** annex **6** append, suffix
postiche: wig **4** sham **5** false **6** switch, toupee **8** pretense, spurious **9** imitation **10** artificial **14** counterfeiting
postil: **6** homily **7** comment **10** commentary
postilion: **5** rider **7** courier, postboy
postpone: **4** stay, wait **5** defer, delay, remit, table **6** remand, retard, shelve **7** adjourn, prolong **8** reprieve **10** pigeonhole **11** subordinate **13** procrastinate
postponement: **4** mora, stay **5** delay, morae (pl.) **7** respite **8** reprieve **10** ampliation
postprandial: **11** after-dinner
postscript: **6** sequel **8** footnote
postulant: **6** novice **9** applicant, candidate **10** apprentice, petitioner
postulate: **5** claim, posit **6** assume, demand **7** premise, require **10** assumption, hypotheses (pl.), hypothesis, presuppose **11** proposition **12** prerequisite
posture: **4** mien, pose **5** stand, state **6** stance **7** bearing, gesture, stature **8** attitude, carriage, position **9** composure
  erect: **11** orthostatic

posy: **5** motto, verse **6** flower, legend **7** bouquet, nosegay **9** anthology, sentiment **11** composition
pot (see also **pan**): bag, pan, win **4** dixy, pool **5** abyss, crewe, dixie, drink, kitty, shoot **6** aludel, basket, cruset, posnet, secure, toilet, vessel **7** caldron, capture, cuvette, fortune, notable **8** cauldron, crucible, potation **9** marijuana **11** deteriorate
  arch: **4** kiln
  earthen: **4** olla **5** crock, cruse **6** chytra
  handle: **4** bool
  hat: **5** derby **6** bowler
  lead: **8** graphite
  wheel: **5** noria
potable: **4** pure **5** clean, drink, water **8** beverage **9** drinkable
potage: **4** soup **5** broth
potash: **4** kali **5** niter, nitre, salin **6** alkali, saline **8** pearlash
potassium: **6** kalium
  compound: **4** alum **6** chrome, potash
  sulphate: **4** alum **8** misenite
potation: **4** bout, dram **5** draft, drink **6** liquid, liquor **7** spirits **8** beverage, drinking, libation
potato: ima, oca, yam **4** chat, papa, spud **5** rural, tuber **6** murphy **7** manroot **12** pomme de terre (F.)
  beetle: **8** hardback
  bud: eye
  chip: **5** crisp (Br.) **8** Saratoga
  disease: pox **4** curl, scab **6** blight
  dish: **4** Anna **6** mashed **7** whipped **8** au gratin, Dauphine **9** lyonnaise, scalloped **11** French fried
  family: **10** nightshade, solanaceae
  kind: new, red **6** LaSoda **7** Norchip, Pontiac, russett **8** Katahdin, Kennebee **12** Irish cobbler
  planting ridge: **4** hill, ruck
  seed part: eye
  starch: **6** farina
  state: **5** Idaho, Maine
  sweet: yam **6** batata, comote, patata **7** batatas, ocarina
pot-au-feu: **4** soup, stew
potbank: **7** pottery
potbelly: gut **5** stove **6** paunch **9** bay window
potboiler: **4** book **7** painting **9** potwaller **10** manuscript, mediocrity
potboy: **8** Ganymede **9** cupbearer
pote: **4** kick, poke, push **5** nudge, shove **6** thrust
poteen, potheen: **6** whisky
potence: **5** cross **6** gibbet **7** gallows
potency: vis **5** force, might, power, vigor **6** energy **8** efficacy, strength, vitality **9** fertility

potent: 4 able 6 cogent, mighty, strong 7 dynamic 8 forceful, powerful, puissant, vigorous, virulent 9 effective, efficient 10 convincing 11 influential

potentate: 4 amir, czar, emir, king, shah, tsar 5 ameer, emeer, mogul, ruler 6 moghul, prince 7 monarch 9 sovereign

potential: 6 latent, mighty 8 inchoate, possible 10 unrealized 11 influential, possibility, undeveloped

potentiality: 5 power 8 capacity 9 pregnancy

potgun: 6 pistol, popgun 8 braggart

pothead: 9 blackfish

pother: ado, row, vex 4 fuss, stir, to-do 5 worry 6 bother, bustle, dither, harass, muddle, puzzle, uproar 7 fluster, perplex, trouble 9 annoyance, commotion, confusion 11 disturbance 12 perturbation

potherb: 4 kale, mint, wort 5 chard 6 greens 7 mustard, quelite, spinach
  pert. to: 7 olitory

pothole: pit 4 cave 5 cahot 6 kettle, tinaja

potholer: 9 spelunker

pothook: rod 4 hake, nine 5 crook 6 collar, scrawl

pothouse: bar 6 tavern 8 alehouse

potiche: jar 4 vase

potion: 4 brew, dose, drug 5 draft, drink 6 drench 7 draught, philter, philtre 8 nepenthe
  sleeping: 5 dwale 6 opiate 8 narcotic, sedative 9 soporific 10 belladonna

potlatch: 4 gift 5 feast

pot liquid: 6 brewis 9 pot likker, pot liquor

potomania: 10 dipsomania

potpie: 4 stew 9 fricassee

potpourri: jar 4 olio, stew 6 jumble, medley 7 mixture 9 anthology 10 hodge-podge, miscellany, salmagundi

potrero: 6 meadow 7 pasture

Po tributary: 4 Adda 5 Oglia 6 Trebba 9 Cispadane

pot-rustler: 4 chef, cook

potsherd: bit 4 chip 5 shard 8 fragment

potshot: 4 jeer, jibe 5 shoot 6 assail, attack, insult 9 aspersion, sideswipe

potstone: 8 steatite

pottage: 4 soup, stew 6 brewis 8 porridge

pottah: 4 deed 5 lease 11 certificate

potted: 5 drunk 7 planted, shallow (Br.) 9 condensed, preserved 11 intoxicated, superficial (Br.)

potter (Br.) (see also **putter**): fad, pry 4 fuss, mess, poke, push 6 cotter, dabble, dacker, daiker, dawdle, dodder, fiddle, footer, footle, loiter, meddle, putter, tamper, tinker, trifle 7 cloamer, fossick, saunter 8 ceramist 10 ceramicist, mess around

potter's clay: 5 argil

potter's field: 8 Aceldama, cemetery

potter's wheel: 4 disk 5 lathe, palet, throw 6 jigger, pallet

pottery: 4 bank, ware 5 china, delft 7 Keramos (F.) 8 ceramics, crockery 9 delftware, Keramikos (Gr.), porcelain, stoneware 11 earthenware
  cement: 4 slip
  civilization: 6 Minyan
  decorating paste: 9 barbotine
  decoration: 9 sgrafitto
  dish: 7 ramekin
  enameled: 8 majolica
  firing box: 6 saggar, sagger 7 saggard
  fragment: 5 shard, sherd
  kind: uda (Ind.) 4 delf 5 delft 6 basalt, jasper 7 aretine, bocraro, celadon, faience 8 bucchero, Majolica, Rookwood, vitreous 9 delftware, ironstone, sigillate 10 terracotta 12 buccheronero
  maker: 6 potter 8 ceramist
  mineral: 8 feldspar
  pert. to: 7 ceramic

pottle: 6 liquor 7 tankard 10 half-gallon

potty: 5 crazy, dotty, petty 6 little 7 foolish, haughty, trivial 8 snobbish 9 eccentric 12 supercilious

pouch: bag, cod, pod, sac 4 cyst, sack 5 bulge, bursa, purse 6 budget, gipser, pocket, sporan 7 alforja, gipsire, mailbag, saccule, silicle, sporran 9 spleuchan 10 pocketbook
  abdominal: 9 marsupium
  Highlander's: 7 sporran

pouch bone: 9 marsupial

pouched: 9 sacculate
  dog: 4 wolf
  marmot: 8 squirrel 11 spermophile

pouf: 4 puff 5 bangs, quilt 7 ottoman 9 hairdress

poule: 6 wanton 10 prostitute

poulp, poulpe: 7 octopus

poultice: 7 plaster 8 compress, dressing 9 cataplasm

poultry: 4 fowl, hens 5 ducks, geese, quail 7 peacock, pigeons, turkeys 8 chickens 9 partridge, pheasants 10 guinea fowl
  breed: 6 Ancona 7 Cornish, Dorking, Leghorn 9 White Rock 11 Rock Cornish 12 Plymouth Rock 14 Rhode-Island Red
  dealer: 6 eggler
  disease: pip 4 roup
  dish: 9 galantine
  farm: 7 hennery
  yard: 6 barton

pounamu: 4 jade 8 nephrite 10 greenstone

pounce: nab 4 jump, leap, pink, poke, stab 5 pound, prick, punch, stamp, swoop, talon 6 emboss, spring, thrust 8 ornament 9 comminute, perforate

pound: **4** bang, bash, beat, bray, club, ding, maul, pond, tamp, unit **5** knock, thump **6** batter, bruise, buffet, hammer, powder, pummel, wallop, weight **7** contuse, shelter **8** currency, malleate, sterling **9** enclosure, pulverize

poundage: **6** charge, weight **8** distrain **9** constrain, enclosure **11** confinement

pour: **4** emit, flow, gush, hale, lash, lave, pass, rain, teem, tide, toom (Sc.), vent, well **5** birle, drain, empty, flood, heald, hield, issue, spout, utter **6** affuse, decant, deluge, effuse, libate, sluice, stream **8** downpour **9** discharge

pourboire (F.): fee, tip **7** douceur **8** gratuity **9** buona-mani (pl.), buona-mano

pout: bib, mop **4** moue, sulk **5** boody, bulge, pique, scowl **7** catfish, eelpout **8** bullhead **9** sulkiness

poverty: **4** lack, need, want **6** dearth, penury **7** paucity, tenuity **8** scarcity **9** indigence **10** bankruptcy, insolvency **11** destitution
program: **5** VISTA
stricken: **9** penurious

powder: **4** abir (Ind.), dust, kish, mull, talc **5** boral, boron, chalk, flour, grind **6** empasm, pollen, pounce, yttria **7** araroba, aristol, malarin, saponin, tripoli **8** cosmetic, sprinkle, tannigen **9** pulverize **10** epiplastic
abrasive: **5** emery
case: **7** compact **9** bandolier
container: **4** horn **7** arsenal **8** magazine
make: **4** bray **5** grind **7** calcine **9** pulverize
poisonous: **4** antu **5** robin
sachet: **6** pulvil
smokeless: **6** filite, poudre **7** cordite **8** amberite

powdered: **4** seme **5** semee **6** floury

power: arm, art, vis **4** bulk, dint, gift, hand, iron, rial, sway, thew **5** force, might, state, steam, vigor, vires (pl.), wield **6** agency, effort, empire, energy, foison, muscle, throne, weight **7** ability, command, control, mastery, potence, potency, stamina, voltage **8** capacity, efficacy, function, momentum, prestige, strength, virility **9** authority, dominator, influence, intensity, puissance, supremacy **10** domination, efficiency **11** sovereignty **12** jurisdiction, potentiality
deprive of: **4** maim **6** depose, unseat **7** impeach **8** dethrone **12** departliament
lack: **5** atony
loss of electrical: **8** blackout
natural: **4** odyl **5** odyle
partnership: **9** champerty
provide with: **5** elect, endow, endue
reduction: **8** brownout
second: **6** square
superior: **10** prepotency **12** predominance
symbol: **5** sword **7** scepter, sceptre
third: **4** cube
unlimited: **11** omnipotence

powerboat: **5** yacht **6** launch **7** cruiser **9** motorboat

powerful: **4** able, bold, deep **5** great, stout **6** brawny, cogent, heroic, mighty, potent, strong **7** feckful, leonine, weighty **8** forceful, puissant, vigorous **9** effective, effectual **10** dominating, omnipotent **11** efficacious

powerless: **4** weak **6** feeble, supine, unable **7** passive **8** helpless, impotent, inactive, lifeless

power of attorney: **5** agent **8** document **10** procurator

Powhatan: *daughter:* **10** Pocahontas

powwow: **4** talk **6** confer, priest **7** meeting **8** assembly, ceremony, congress, conjurer **10** conference

poyou: **6** peludo **9** armadillo

prabble: **7** chatter, quarrel **8** squabble

prabhu: **4** lord **5** chief **6** writer

practic: **6** artful, shrewd **7** cunning, skilled **8** decision (Sc.) **9** practical, practiced

practical: **5** handy, utile **6** actual, beaten, usable, useful **7** working **8** feasible, possible, practice, workable **9** available, practiced, pragmatic, realistic **11** pragmatical, utilitarian
example: **6** praxis
joke: **4** hoax **5** prank, trick **7** waggery

practically: **6** almost, nearly **9** virtually **13** substantially

practice: do, ply, rut, try, use **4** mode, plot, rote **5** apply, canon, cause, drill, habit, trade, train, usage **6** custom, follow, praxic, system **7** perform, process **8** exercise, intrigue, rehearse **9** construct, negotiate, procedure **10** experience
pert. to: **9** pragmatic
sharp: **4** game **5** dodge, fraud, usury **6** deceit **9** chicanery

practiced: **5** adept **7** skilled, veteran **8** seasoned **10** conversant **11** experienced

practitioner: **5** agent **6** artist, doctor, healer, lawyer, novice **7** learner, plotter, schemer **8** civilian **9** assistant

prad: **5** horse

praenomen, prenomen: **4** name **5** Caius, Gaius, Titus **9** first name

pragmatic: **7** skilled **8** busybody, dogmatic, meddling **9** conceited, empirical, officious, practical, realistic **10** meddlesome, systematic **11** dictatorial, opinionated, pragmatical

Prague: **4** Prag **5** Praha
river: **6** Moldau, Vltava

prairie: bay **5** camas, llano, marsh, plain **6** camass, meadow, steppe **7** quamash **8** flatland **9** grassland

Argentine: **5** pampa
clump of trees in: **5** motte
mud: **5** gumbo
plant: **5** camas **6** camass
soil: **9** chernozem
South African: **4** veld
tropical: **7** savanna
prairie anemone: 12 pasqueflower
prairie antelope: 9 pronghorn
prairie apple: 9 breadroot
prairie berry: 9 trompillo **10** nightshade
prairie breaker: 4 plow
prairie chicken: 6 grouse
prairie crocus: 12 pasqueflower
prairie dog: 6 gopher, marmot **11** wish-ton-wish
prairie dog weed: 8 marigold
prairie pigeon: 6 plover **9** sandpiper
prairie potato: 9 breadroot
Prairie Province (Canada): 7 Alberta **8** Manitoba **12** Saskatchewan
prairie schooner: ark **12** covered wagon
Prairie State: 8 Illinois
prairieweed: 10 cinquefoil
prairie wolf: 6 coyote
praise: 4 hery, laud, tout **5** adore, allow, alose, bless, cry up, extol, glory, honor, kudos, roosa, roose **6** eulogy, extoll, kudize **7** acclaim, adulate, applaud, commend, encomia (pl.), glorify, hosanna, magnify, plaudit, tribute **8** applause, appraise, blessing, encomium, eulogize, macarism **9** adulation, celebrate, intensify, panegyric **10** compliment, panegyrize **11** approbation **12** commendation **13** glorification
ascription of: **6** Gloria
praiseworthy: 8 laudable **9** admirable, estimable, exemplary **11** commendable, meritorious **13** complimentary
Prakrit: 4 Pali **7** Bahlika **8** language **11** Dakshinatya
praline: 5 candy **10** confection
pram: 4 cart **5** barge **8** carriage, pushcart, sailboat, stroller **12** baby carriage, perambulator
prance: 4 step, walk **5** brank, caper, dance, strut **6** cavort, frolic, sashay **7** swagger
prank: jig **4** dido, fold, lark, prat, whim **5** adorn, antic, caper, freak, pleat, shine, trick **6** curvet, fegary, frolic, gambol **7** caprice, dress up **8** capricci (pl.), escapade, mischief **9** capriccio **11** monkeyshine **13** practical joke
prase: 6 quartz **10** chalcedony
prat: 4 push **5** nudge, prank, trick **8** buttocks
prate: gab 4 blab, buck, bukh, carp, chat, talk **5** blate, boast, clack, clash **6** babble, claver, tattle, tongue **7** blatter, chatter, deblate, prattle, twaddle **8** harangue **11** deblaterate

prattle: 4 gaff, lisp **5** prate **6** cackle **7** blather, blether, clatter **9** bavardage **11** confabulate
prawn: 6 shrimp **10** crustacean
praxis: 5 habit **6** action, custom **8** practice
pray: ask, beg, bid, sue **5** daven (Heb.), plead **6** appeal, invite, invoke **7** beseech, conjure, entreat, implore, request **8** petition **10** supplicate
praya: 4 bund, road **5** beach **6** strand **9** esplanade **10** waterfront
prayer: ave **4** bead, bede, bene, boon, hope, plea, suit **5** grace, matin **6** appeal, ectene, ektene, errand, orison **7** Angelus, bidding, collect, complin, gayatri, oration, request, savitri **8** Ave Maria, compline, entreaty, Hail Mary, petition **9** competory, Our Father, Pater Imon, precation, suppliant **10** paratheses (pl.), parathesis, requiescat **11** application, benediction, paternoster **12** intercession, supplication
beads: **6** rosary
call: **4** adan, azan, bell **5** chime **6** oremus **9** let us pray
chancery: **7** relator
day's first: **6** matins **7** mattins
day's last: **7** complin **8** compline
form of: **5** chant **6** litany **8** akathist **10** meditation **13** contemplation
for the dead: **7** kaddish, requiem
group: **12** comprecation
nine-day: **6** novena
set: **9** akoluthia
short: **5** grace **11** benediction
prayer book: 6 missal, portas, ritual **7** portass **8** breviary, porthors **9** porthouse **12** sacramentary
prayer desk: 8 prie-dieu
prayer rug: 5 asana
prayer shawl: 5 orale **7** tallith
prayer tower: 7 minaret
praying figure: 5 orant
preach: 4 sugh **5** sough, teach **6** exhort, inform **8** advocate, homilize, instruct, moralize, proclaim **9** discourse, predicate, sermonize **10** concionate, evangelize
preacher: 6 parson, rector **8** homilist, minister **9** clergyman, predicant, pulpiteer **10** evangelist
preachment: 6 homily, sermon **7** lecture **9** discourse **11** exhortation
preachy: 8 didactic **10** moralistic
preamble: 7 preface **8** foreword, prologue **12** introduction
prebend: 4 land **5** tithe **7** stipend **8** benefice **9** allowance
prebendary: 5 canon **9** clergyman
precarious: 5 risky **7** dubious **8** delicate, doubtful, insecure, perilous, unstable **9** dangerous, hazardous, uncertain, unsettled

10 touch-and-go

precative: 10 beseeching 12 supplicating

precaution: 4 care 6 cautel 7 caution 8 prudence 9 safeguard

precede: 4 lead, pace, rank 5 usher 6 forego, herald 7 forerun, outrank, predate, preface 8 antecede, antedate 9 introduce 10 foreshadow

precedence: pas 8 priority

precedent: 5 model, usage 7 example 8 decision, standard

preceding: 5 first 6 before, former 8 anterior

precentor: 6 cantor 7 chanter

precept: law 4 hest, rule, tora, writ 5 adage, axiom, breve, brief, dogma, maxim, order, sutra, tenet, torah 6 behest, lesson 7 caution, command, mandate 8 doctrine, document, teaching 9 direction, principle 10 injunction 11 commandment, fundamental, instruction

preceptive: 8 didactic 9 mandatory 11 instructive

preceptor: 5 tutor 6 master 7 teacher

precinct: 4 beat 5 ambit, bound 6 hieron 7 temenos 8 boundary, district, environs 9 enclosure

precious: 4 dear, nice, rare, very 5 chere (F.), loved 6 costly, valued 7 beloved, genteel 8 affected, esteemed, favorite, valuable 9 extremely 10 fastidious 11 inestimable, overrefined

precipice: lin 4 crag, drop, linn, pali, scar 5 bluff, brink, cliff, steep 7 clogwyn 8 downfall 9 declivity

precipitate: 4 fall, floc, hurl, rash 5 hasty, heady, hurry, speed, steep, throw 6 abrupt, effect, hasten, madcap, sudden, tumble, unwary 7 hurried, willful 8 headlong, sediment, settling, slapdash 9 desperate, impetuous, impulsive 11 precipitous

precipitation: dew 4 hail, mist, rain, snow 5 haste, sleet 8 downpour 9 hastening 10 deposition 11 impetuosity 12 acceleration

precipitous: 5 sheer, steep 6 steepy 7 prerupt
rock: 4 crag, scar 5 steep

precis: 6 digest, sketch 7 epitome, summary 8 abstract 10 compendium 11 abridgement 12 condensation

precise: 4 even, nice, prim 5 exact, rigid, stiff 6 formal, minute, strict 7 buckram, certain, correct, finicky, literal, starchy 8 accurate, definite, delicate, explicit, overnice, priggish, specific 9 faultless, stringent, veracious 10 fastidious, particular, scrupulous 11 ceremonious, on the button, painstaking, punctilious

preclude: bar 4 quit, stop 5 avert, close, debar, estop 6 forbid, hinder, impede 7 obviate, prevent 9 eliminate, foreclose, forestall 11 discontinue

precocious: 5 early 6 unripe 7 forward 8 advanced 9 premature

preconceive: 4 plan 5 dream 6 ideate, scheme 8 foreknow

precursor: 4 sign 5 usher 6 herald 8 ancestor, foregoer 9 harbinger, messenger 10 forefather, forerunner 11 predecessor

precursory: 11 preliminary, premonitory 12 introductory

predatory: 7 harmful, robbing 8 ravenous 9 pillaging, piratical, rapacious, raptorial 10 plundering, predacious
bird: owl 4 hawk 5 eagle
insect: 6 mantis, spider

predestine: 4 doom, fate 6 decree, ordain 7 destine, predoom 8 foredoom 9 determine, forepoint, preordain 10 foreordain 12 predetermine

predetermine: 4 bias 6 decree 7 destine, predict 8 forecast 9 prejudice 10 prepossess

predicament: box, fix, jam 4 hole, mess, spot, stew 5 state 6 pickle, plight, scrape 7 dilemma, in a bind, problem 8 hot water, quandary 9 condition, situation 10 difficulty

predicant: 5 friar 8 preacher 9 dominican

predicate: cry 4 aver, base 5 imply 6 affirm, assert, preach 7 commend, declare, foresee, involve, predict 8 foretell, proclaim

predict: 4 bode, call, dope, omen 5 augur, guess, weird 6 divine, halsen 7 forbode, foresee, presage, presume, suppose 8 forebode, forecast, foretell, prophesy, soothsay 9 auspicate, predicate 13 prognosticate

prediction: 5 weird 6 augury 7 bodword 8 prophesy 9 horoscope 10 divination 12 forespeaking, vaticination

predictor: 4 seer 7 prophet

predilection: 4 bent, bias 7 leaning 8 fondness, tendency 9 prejudice 10 partiality, preference, propensity 11 inclination 14 predisposition, susceptibility

predisposed: 5 prone 6 biased 7 partial, willing 8 inclined

predisposition: 7 leaning 12 predilection

predominant: 5 chief 6 ruling 8 dominant, reigning, superior 9 ascendant, ascendent, hegemonic, prevalent 10 dominating, noticeable, prevailing 11 controlling, outstanding 12 preponderant

predominate: 4 rule 6 domine, exceed 8 domineer, overrule

preeminent: big 4 star 5 chief, grand 7 capital, palmary, ranking, supreme 8 dominant, superior 9 excellent, prominent 10 surpassing 11 outstanding

preempt: 5 usurp 8 arrogate 9 establish 10 monopolize 11 appropriate

preen: pin, sew 4 perk, trim 5 adorn, clasp, dress, plume, press, pride, primp, prink, prune 6 bodkin, brooch, smooth, spruce, stitch

preface: 5 front, proem 6 herald 7 forerun, precede, prelude 8 exordium, foreword, overture, preamble, prologue 9 introduce 11 preliminary 12 forespeaking, introduction, introductory

prefect, praefect: 4 dean 7 monitor, officer 8 director, minister, official 9 president 10 magistrate

prefecture: 7 eparchy (Gr.) 8 district

prefer: opt 4 like 5 elect, favor 6 choose, desire, favour, rather, select 7 advance, propose

preferable: 6 better

preference: 6 choice, liking 8 appetite, priority 9 promotion 10 partiality 11 advancement, alternative 12 predilection

prefigure: 4 type 5 augur 6 ideate, typify 7 forerun 8 foretell 9 adumbrate 10 foreshadow

prefix: See list at back of book

pregnable: 10 assailable, expugnable, vulnerable 11 conquerable

pregnancy: 6 cyesis 9 fertility, gestation

pregnant: big 5 heavy 6 gravid 7 fertile, teeming, weighty 8 enceinte, fruitful, prolific 9 abounding, gestating, potential, with child 10 expressive, germinable

prehend: 5 catch, seize

prehistoric: 10 immemorial

preindicate: 7 presage 8 announce, prophesy

prejudice: 4 bent, bias, harm, hurt 6 damage, hatred, impair 7 bigotry, leaning 9 suspicion 10 partiality, prepossess 11 inclination, intolerance 12 disadvantage, jaundiced eye, predetermine, predilection, prejudgement 13 prejudication

prejudicial: 7 harmful 8 contrary 9 injurious 11 contrarious, detrimental 14 discriminatory

prelate: 4 head, pope 5 abbot, chief 6 abbess, bishop, priest 7 pontiff, primate 8 ordinary, superior 9 dignitary 10 archbishop 12 ecclesiastic

prelector: 6 reader 8 lecturer 9 professor 10 discourser

preliminary: 5 basic, prior 7 preface 8 entrance, previous, proemial 9 elemental, inductive, prefatory, threshold 10 antecedent 11 fundamental, preparatory

prelude: 6 verset 7 descant, intrada, opening, preface 8 overture, ritornel 10 ritornelle 12 introduction

premature: 5 early, hasty 6 unripe 8 immature, untimely 10 precocious 11 precipitate 12 unseasonable

premeditation: 11 forethought 12 aforethought

premier: 4 head 5 chief, first 7 leading 8 earliest, foremost 9 principal 13 prime minister

premise: 6 ground, theory, thesis 7 theorem 9 postulate 10 assumption 11 proposition, supposition

premium: fee 4 agio 5 award, bonus, prize, spiff 6 bounty, deport, reward 8 lagnappe, superior 9 lagniappe 10 recompense

premonition: 4 omen 5 hunch 6 notice 7 bodword, warning 9 forescent 10 foreboding 11 forewarning, information 12 apprehension, presentiment

prenomen: See **praenomen**

preoccupied: 4 lost, rapt 6 absent, filled 8 absorbed 9 engrossed

preordain: 10 predestine

preparation: 5 array 7 extract, product 8 cosmetic, training 9 condiment, decoction, make ready, rehearsal 10 confection 11 arrangement 12 introduction
place of: 5 stage 7 kitchen 10 laboratory, paratorium 12 dressing room
without: 5 ad lib 8 careless 9 extempore, impromptu 10 off-the-cuff

prepare: arm, fit, fix, get, set 4 bush, busk, gibe, gird, make, pave, suit, tibe 5 adapt, alert, coach, curry, dight, dower, equip, ettle, frame, groom, prime, ready, train 6 adjust, devise, graith, make up 7 address, affaite (F.), apparel, arrange, concoct, confect, dispose, furnish, provide, qualify 8 accustom, compound, instruct, rehearse 9 calculate, condition, construct 10 concinnate 11 set the stage
for the press: 4 edit 6 redact, revise

prepared: apt 4 yare 5 ready

prepaschal period: 4 Lent

prepense: 8 designed 11 forethought 12 aforethought, premeditated

preponderance: 6 weight 8 majority 9 dominance, supremacy 10 ascendancy, prevalence 12 predominance

preponderate: 4 rule, sink 7 incline, surpass

preposition: at, by, in, of, on, to, up, but, for, off, out 4 down, from, into, onto, over, upon, with 5 about, above, after, along, among, below, under, until 6 across, around, before, behind, beside, beyond, toward, within 7 beneath, between, through

prepossess: 4 bias 7 impress, prevent 12 predetermine

prepossessing: 10 attractive

prepossession: 4 bent, bias 9 prejudice 10 absorption 11 inclination 12 predilection 14 predisposition

preposterous: 4 wild 5 crazy 6 absurd, screwy 7 foolish 9 fantastic, grotesque, senseless **10** irrational, ridiculous **11** extravagant, nonsensical

preppy: **7** student **11** traditional

prerequisite: **4** must **9** essential, necessary, necessity, postulate

prerogative: **5** right **8** appanage, immunity, priority **9** exemption, privilege **10** precedence

eldest son's: **6** esnecy

prerupt: **5** steep **11** precipitous

presage: **4** bode, omen, osse, sign **5** augur, token **6** augury, betide, divine, import **7** bespeak, betoken, forbode, meaning, portend, portent, predict, warning **8** announce, forebode, foretell, indicate, prophecy, prophesy **9** foretoken, harbinger **10** foreboding, prediction, prognostic **11** foreknowing, preindicate **12** apprehension, presentiment **13** prognosticate

presbyter: **5** elder **6** priest **7** prester **8** minister **9** clergyman

presbytery: **5** court **7** council, rectory **9** residence

prescience: **9** foresight **11** omniscience **13** foreknowledge

prescind: **6** detach **7** isolate **8** abstract, separate

prescribe: fix, set **5** allot, guide, limit, order **6** assign, define, direct, ordain, outlaw **7** appoint, command, control, dictate, lay down **9** prescript **10** invalidate

prescribed: set **5** basic **6** thetic **9** formulary

prescript: law **7** command, mandate

prescription: **6** recipe **7** formula **8** medicine

presence: air **4** mien **5** being **6** aspect, spirit **7** bearing, company, dignity, seeming, spectre **8** assembly **9** influence **10** apparition, appearance, attendance, deportment

present: now, tip **4** boon, gift, give, here **5** adsum (L.), being, bonus, cuddy, favor, grant, nonce, offer, ready, today **6** adduce, allege, bestow, bounty, confer, donate, render, tender **7** cumshaw, display, exhibit, largess, perform **8** donation, gratuity, lagnappe **9** collected, introduce, lagniappe, personate **10** exhibition, here and now **11** benefaction, efficacious

again: **5** rerun

pert. to: **6** modern **7** current **12** contemporary

to guest or stranger: **6** xenium

with another: **8** collocal

presentable: fit **6** decent, proper **8** suitable **11** appropriate, respectable

present-day: **7** current **12** contemporary

presentiment: **4** fear **5** alarm, dread **10** foreboding **11** disquietude, premonition **12** apprehension

presently: **4** anon, enow, soon **7** by and by,

shortly **8** directly **9** forthwith **11** immediately

preservation: **6** saving **7** defense **11** safekeeping

preservative: **4** salt **5** borax, brine, spice, sugar **7** alcohol, vinegar **8** creosote **12** conservative

preserve: can, dry, jam, tin **4** corn, cure, keep, salt, save **5** bless, guard, jelly, store, uvate **6** athold, comfit, defend, govern, keep up, retain, secure, shield, uphold **7** compote, condite, confect, forfend, protect, succade, sustain **8** conserve, forefend, maintain **9** confiture, safeguard **11** freeze spare

preside: run **5** chair **6** direct **7** control, oversee **8** moderate, regulate **9** supervise

president: CEO, mir **4** head **5** ruler **8** governor **9** commander, executive, sovereign

successor: **9** designado (Mex.)

President (U.S.): (1, 1789–97) George Washington; (2, 1797–1801) John Adams; (3, 1801–09) Thomas Jefferson; (4, 1809–17) James Madison; (5, 1817–25) James Monroe; (6, 1825–29) John Quincy Adams; (7, 1829–37) Andrew Jackson; (8, 1837–41) Martin Van Buren; (9, 1841) William Henry Harrison; (10, 1841–45) John Tyler; (11, 1845–49) James K. Polk; (12, 1849–50) Zachary Taylor; (13, 1850–53) Millard Fillmore; (14, 1853–57) Franklin Pierce; (15, 1857–61) James Buchanan; (16, 1861–65) Abraham Lincoln; (17, 1865–69) Andrew Johnson; (18, 1869–77) Ulysses S. Grant; (19, 1877–81) Rutherford B. Hayes; (20, 1881) James A. Garfield; (21, 1881–85) Chester A. Arthur; (22, 1885–89) Grover Cleveland; (23, 1889–93) Benjamin Harrison; (24, 1893–97) Grover Cleveland; (25, 1897–1901) William McKinley; (26, 1901–09) Theodore Roosevelt; (27, 1909–13) William H. Taft; (28, 1913–21) Woodrow Wilson; (29; 1921–23) Warren G. Harding; (30, 1923–29) Calvin Coolidge; (31, 1929–33) Herbert Hoover; (32, 1933–45) Franklin D. Roosevelt; (33, 1945–53) Harry S. Truman; (34, 1953–61) Dwight D. Eisenhower; (35, 1961–63) John F. Kennedy; (36, 1963–69) Lyndon B. Johnson; (37, 1969–74) Richard M. Nixon; (38, 1974–77) Gerald R. Ford; (39, 1977–81) Jimmy Carter; (40, 1981–89) Ronald Reagan; (41, 1989–93) George H.W. Bush; (42, 1993–) William J. Clinton

last name: **4** Bush, Ford, Polk, Taft **5** Adams, Grant, Hayes, Nixon, Tyler **6** Arthur, Carter, Hoover, Monroe, Pierce, Reagan, Taylor, Truman, Wilson **7** Clinton, Harding, Jackson, Johnson, Kennedy, Lincoln, Madison **8** Buchanan, Coolidge, Fill-

more, Garfield, Harrison, McKinley, Van Buren **9** Cleveland, Jefferson, Roosevelt **10** Eisenhower, Washington
nickname: Abe, Cal, FDR, Ike, JFK, LBJ **5** Teddy

presignify: 7 presage **8** intimate **9** foretoken

press: hug, jam **4** bale, bear, bind, cram, dint, iron, mash, push, spur, tamp, thew, urge **5** brize, brizz, chest, chirt, clasp, crowd, crush, drive, force, knead, media, preen, serry, wring **6** compel, crunch, impact, insist, roller, smooth, squash, throng **7** armoire, embrace, entreat, express, flatten, impress, imprint, scrunge, smasher, squeeze **8** calender, compress, pressure, straiten, wardrobe **9** constrain, embarrass, emphasize, importune **10** constipate, newspapers

press agent: 5 flack **8** PR person **9** publicist

press down: 4 quat, tamp

pressed: 5 dense **6** ironed **7** compact, mangled, serried

presser: 5 baler **6** ironer, mangle
of skins: **7** sammier

pressing: 4 dire **5** acute **6** urgent **7** burning, crucial, exigent **8** exacting **9** imperious **10** imperative **11** importunate

pressman: pig **7** printer

pressure: 4 heat, push **5** force **6** burden, duress, stress **7** bearing, squeeze, tension **8** exigency, instancy **10** affliction, constraint, impression, oppression **11** compression
equal: **8** isobaric
gauge: **9** barometer, manometer, manoscope
law: **6** Boyle's **7** Pascal's
unit: **4** atmo, dyne **5** barad **7** mesobar
using: **11** arm-twisting

pressure group: 5 lobby

pressure measuring instrument: 9 barometer **10** piezometer

prester: 4 vein **5** snake **6** priest **7** serpent **9** hurricane, presbyter, whirlwind

prestidigitator: 6 palmer **7** juggler **8** conjurer, magician, pythonic

prestige: 4 rank, sway **5** power **6** renown, status **7** sorcery **8** eminence, illusion, position, standing **9** deception, influence **10** importance, prominence

presto: 4 fast **7** passing, quickly **8** suddenly **11** immediately **13** instantaneous

presumably: 6 likely **8** probably **9** assumably **10** ostensibly, supposedly

presume: 5 guess, infer **6** gather, impose **7** daresay, suppose, surmise, venture **8** arrogate **9** postulate **10** conjecture, presuppose

presumptuous: 4 bold, smug **5** brash, fresh, pushy **6** uppity **7** forward, haughty, icarian **8** arrogant, assuming, familiar, impudent, insolent **9** audacious, confident, foolhardy **11** adventurous, venturesome

presuppose: 5 posit **6** assume

pretend: act **4** fake, pose, seem, sham **5** bluff, claim, feign **6** affect, allege, assume, gammon **7** profess **8** disguise, simulate **10** conjecture **11** dissimulate, make-believe

pretended: 5 faked, false **7** alleged, colored, reputed **8** coloured, intended, proposed **10** fictitious, ostensible

pretender: fop **4** fake, idol, snob **5** cowan (Sc.), faker, quack **6** poseur, seemer **8** aspirant, claimant, deceiver, impostor **9** charlatan **10** mountebank **11** fourflusher **12** dissimulator

pretense, pretence: act, peg **4** brag, cant, flam, mask, plea, ruse, sham, show **5** claim, cloak, cover, feint, gloze, study, trick **6** excuse, humbug, tinsel **7** charade, fiction, grimace, pageant, potiche, pretext **8** artifice, disguise, occasion **9** deception, moonshine, semblance **10** appearance, assumption, pretension, subterfuge **11** affectation, fabrication, make-believe, ostentation **13** stalking-horse

pretentious: big **4** arty **5** gaudy, showy **6** turgid **7** pompous **8** affected, assuming **10** flamboyant **12** highfaluting, ostentatious

pretermit: 4 omit **6** ignore **7** neglect, suspend **8** intermit **9** disregard, interrupt

preternatural: 6 gousty **7** ghostly, goustie, strange **8** abnormal, uncommon **9** irregular **12** supernatural

pretext: 4 mask **6** excuse **8** pretense

pretty: gay, toy **4** cute, deft, fair, gent, joli **5** bonny, jolie, lindo (Sp.) **6** bonita, bonnie, clever, comely, lovely **7** cunning, dollish **8** betcheri, budgeree, handsome, skillful, somewhat **9** beautiful, ingenious **10** attractive, knickknack, moderately

prevail: win **4** rule **5** reign **6** induce, obtain **7** conquer, persist, succeed, triumph **8** dominate **11** predominate
upon: **4** urge **6** allure, induce **7** entreat **8** persuade **9** influence

prevalent: 4 rife **6** common, potent, wonted **7** current, general **8** dominant, epidemic, powerful **9** extensive **10** prevailing, successful, victorious, widespread **11** efficacious, influential, predominant

prevaricate: fib, lie **5** dodge, evade **6** garble **7** quibble, shuffle **10** equivocate **12** misrepresent

prevarication: lie **10** subterfuge

prevent: 4 bar, gag, let **4** balk, bind, save, stop, ward, warn **5** avert, avoid, debar, deter, estop **6** defend, forlet, hinder, impede, resist, thwart **7** forfend, impeach, obviate, rule out **8** antevert, forefend, preclude, prohibit, restrain, stave off **9** foreclose,

forestall, frustrate **10** anticipate, circumvent
by law: **5** estop
preventive: **12** prophylactic **13** precautionary
previous: ere **4** erst, fore, past **5** early, prior, supra **6** before, bygone, former **7** earlier **8** anterior, foregone, untimely **9** foregoing, preceding, premature **10** antecedent, beforehand, heretofore **11** unwarranted
prevision: **8** forecast **9** foresight **10** prediction, prescience, prevoyance **13** foreknowledge **15** prognostication
prewar: **10** antebellum
prey: **4** feed, game **5** booty, raven, ravin, seize, spoil **6** quarry, ravage, ravine, victim **7** capture, plunder **8** underdog **9** victimize
living on: **9** predatory
prey upon: **4** feed **5** seize **6** devour **9** depredate, victimize
Priam: **10** King of Troy
daughter: **6** Creusa **8** Polyxena **9** Cassandra
father: **8** Laomedon
grandfather: **4** Ilus
servant: **7** Agelaus
slayer: **7** Pyrrhus **11** Neoptolemus
son: **5** Paris **6** Hector **7** Helenus, Troilus
wife: **6** Hecuba
price: fee, sum, tab **4** bill, cost, fare, fiar (Sc.), fier (Sc.), hire, rate **5** cheap, value, worth **6** amount, assess, charge, figure, ransom, reward, tariff **7** expense **8** appraise, evaluate **10** estimation, excellence **12** preciousness **13** consideration
fixed: **8** prix fixe
maintain: peg
reduced: **4** sale **7** bargain
rising: **4** boom **9** inflation
priceless: **4** rare **6** absurd, costly, unique **7** amusing **8** valuable **9** unsalable **10** invaluable **11** inestimable
prick: dot, jag **4** brod, brog, cloy, drob, goad, jagg, ping, pink, prod, stab, tang, urge **5** briar, point, smart, spine, sting, thorn **6** broach, cactus, incite, nettle, pierce, skewer, tingle **7** bramble, pricker, prickle **8** puncture **9** perforate, stimulate
pricket: **4** buck **5** spike **11** candlestick
pricking: **8** poignant
prickle: **4** barb, seta **5** setae (pl.), sieve, spine **6** basket **7** acantha, aculeus, spicula (pl.) **8** spiculum **9** sensation
prickly: **5** burry **8** echinate
animal: **8** hedgehog **9** porcupine
heat: **4** rash **6** lichen **8** eruption
plant: **6** cactus, nettle
seed coat: bur **4** burr
shrub: **4** rose, tuna **5** nopal **6** cactus **7** opuntia **9** briar pear, Indian fig
prick song: **7** descant

pride: **5** glory, pique, plume, valor **6** egoism, esteem, hubris, spirit, vanity **7** conceit, dignity, egotism, elation, hauteur, respect **8** nobility, splendor, valiancy **9** arrogance, cockiness, insolence, loftiness, vainglory **10** lordliness, self-esteem **11** amour propre, haughtiness, self-conceit, self-respect **13** self-assurance **15** self-approbation **16** superciliousness
Pride and Prejudice: *author:* **6** Austen
character: **5** Darcy **7** Bingley, Collins, Wickham **9** Elizabeth
prier, pryer: **8** busybody **10** inquisitor, Nosy Parker
priest: (see also **minister**): fra **4** abbe, club, cura, cure (F.), imam, lama, papa (It.), pere (F.) **5** clerk, druid, hotar (Ind.), imaum, mulla, padre (Sp.), rabbi, sarip, vicar **6** bhikku, bishop, cleric, curate, dastur, divine, father, gallah (Heb.), mullah, oblate, rector, shaman, vestal, wahabi **7** cassock, destour, dustoor, prester, tuhunga, wahhabi **8** minister, reverend **9** clergyman, dignitary, oratorian, priesteen **10** chancellor, hierophant, priestling **12** ecclesiastic
army: **5** padre **8** chaplain, sky pilot
assistant: **6** curate, deacon, server **7** acolyte **8** altar boy **9** deaconess
cap: **7** biretta
garment: alb **4** cope, robe **5** ephod, habit **8** scapular **9** vestments
habit ornament: **4** urim
headdress: **7** biretta **9** saghavart
high: Eli **5** Aaron **7** pontiff, prelate, primate
neckpiece: **5** amice, stole
pert. to: **10** sacerdotal
scarf: **5** rabat **7** maniple
server: **7** acolyte
surplice: **5** ephod
voodoo: **5** mambu **6** hungan **7** gangang
priestly: **8** hieratic **10** sacerdotal
prig: beg, fop, pan **4** buck, prim **5** dandy, filch, plead, prink, prude, steal, thief **6** haggle, pilfer, purist, tinker **7** bargain, entreat, pitcher **8** pilferer **9** precision **10** pickpocket
priggish: **4** prim, smug **7** prudish **8** thievish **10** complacent **11** overprecise
prill: **4** rill **6** button, nugget, pellet, stream
prim: mim, set **4** neat, nice **5** stiff **6** demure, formal, proper, wooden **7** correct, genteel, precise, prudish **8** accurate, decorous **9** bluenosed **10** ceremonial
prima donna: **4** diva, lead, star **6** singer **7** actress
prima facie: **9** on its face **11** self-evident
primary: **4** main **5** chief, first, prime **6** primal **7** capital, central, initial **8** earliest, original, primeval, pristine **9** elemental, primitive,

principal **10** elementary, pre-eminent, primordial **11** fundamental

primate: ape, man **5** chimp, lemur, orang **6** bishop, monkey **7** gorilla **8** marmoset **9** orangutan, prosimian **10** anthropoid, archbishop, chimpanzee **11** orangoutang

prime: **4** best, main, size **5** coach, first, paint **6** finest **7** morning, prepare, primary, provoke **9** copacetic, excellent, undercoat
of life: **5** bloom **6** heyday

prime minister: **5** ruler **6** leader **7** premier

primer: **5** paint **6** reader **8** hornbook, textbook **9** first coat **11** abecedarium

primeval: **6** primal **7** ancient, ogygian **8** original, pristine **9** primitive

primitive: **5** basic, crude, first, rough **6** savage, simple **7** ancient, archaic, primary, priscan, radical **8** barbaric, original, pristine **9** elemental, underived **10** aboriginal, antiquated **11** uncivilized **12** old-fashioned

primordial: **5** early, first, prime **7** primary **8** primeval **9** elemental **11** fundamental

primordium: bud **6** embryo, origin **8** rudiment

primp: **5** adorn, preen, prink **7** dress up

primrose: **4** best **5** oxlip, spink (Sc.) **7** cowslip, primula **8** auricula
family: **11** primulaceae

primus: **5** first, stove

prince: bey, ras **4** amir, emir, raja, rial **5** alder, ameer, emeer, ruler **6** despot, dynast, satrap **7** dauphin, dynasty, monarch **8** archduke **9** potentate, princekin, princelet, sovereign **10** princeling, tsarevitch
allowance: **8** appanage
Black: **6** Edward
petty: **6** satrap **9** vergobret
pine: **10** pipsissewa
title: **6** serene

princedom: **4** rank **11** sovereignty **12** jurisdiction

Prince Edward Island: *capital:* **13** Charlottetown
city: **8** Sherwood **10** Summerside
province of: **6** Canada
provincial flower: **12** lady's slipper

princely: **5** grand, noble, regal, royal **6** kingly **7** liberal, stately **8** generous, splendid **9** sovereign **10** munificent **11** magnificent

Prince of: *Apostles:* **7** St. Peter
Darkness: **5** devil, Satan **7** Ahriman **9** Beelzebub
Destruction: **6** Timour **9** Tamerlane
Evil Spirits: **7** Sammael
Liars: **5** Pinto
Peace: **5** Jesus **7** Messiah
the Ode: **7** Ronsard
the Sonnet: **15** Joachim du Bellay

princeps: **4** head **5** first **7** headman **8** original

princess: **5** begum (Muslim), ranee (Muslim) **7** infanta
loved by Cupid: **6** Psyche
loved by Zeus: **6** Europa
mythological: **8** Atalanta

Princeton symbol: **5** tiger

principal: top **4** arch, head, high, main, star **5** chief, first, grand, major, prime **6** leader, staple **7** capital, captain, chattel, leading, palmary, primary, stellar **8** cardinal, dominant, foremost **9** important, preceptor **10** headmaster **11** outstanding

principle: law **4** rule **5** axiom, canon, dicta (pl.), maxim, prana, tenet **6** dictum **7** brocard, capital, essence, precept, theorum **8** doctrine **9** integrity **11** fundamental, uprightness
accepted: **4** norm **5** axiom
embodiment: **6** avatar
first: ABC **4** base, seed **5** basis **8** rudiment
general: **9** generalia **12** generalities
statement: **5** credo, creed, motto
vital: **4** soul **5** anima
without: **6** amoral

principles: **5** creed **6** ethics **8** alphabet

princox: fop **7** coxcomb

prink: **4** deck, perk, wink **5** adorn, dress, preen, primp, prune **6** bedeck, glance, sashay

print: **4** copy, film, mark **5** issue, proof, stamp **6** fabric **7** edition, engrave, etching, impress, picture, publish **8** negative, positive **9** engraving, newspaper **10** impression

printer: **4** type **8** letterer, pressman **9** linotyper **10** compositor **11** typographer **12** lithographer
aid: fly **5** devil
cross stroke: **5** serif
direction: cut **4** dele, stet **6** delete, insert **9** transpose
emblem: **8** colophon

printing: *block:* **4** wood **7** edition **8** linoleum
blurred appearance: **5** macul
color: **17** chromolithography
correction: **10** corrigenda (pl.) **11** corrigendum
error: pie **6** errata (pl.) **7** erratum
form: cut, die, mat **5** frame **6** matrix **7** matrice
implement: **5** burin **6** brayer, dabber, dauber
ink spreader: **6** brayer
mark: **4** dash, dele, list, stet **5** caret, obeli, tilde **6** dagger, diesis, obelus, umlaut **7** obelisk, virgule **8** asterisk, dieresis, ellipses
measure: em, en **4** pica **5** agate, empen, point
metal block: **4** quad
plate: **6** stereo **10** stereotype

press part: **6** platen, roller, rounce **7** frisket

process: **5** laser **6** inkjet, offset **7** braille, typeset **8** cerotype **9** dot-matrix **10** photolitho **11** letterpress, lithography, rotogravure **13** thermographic **14** photoengraving

second: **7** reissue, reprint

space block: **4** quad

type for spacing: **4** quad, slug

prion: **6** petrel

prionid: **6** beetle

prior: ere **4** fore, monk, past **5** ahead, elder, until **6** before, former **7** earlier, forward **8** anterior, previous **9** preceding **10** antecedent **11** retroactive

priority: **5** order **8** position **9** privilege **10** ascendancy, precedence, preference **11** superiority

priory: **5** abbey **7** nunnery **8** cloister **9** monastery, sanctuary

priscan: **4** rare **7** ancient **9** primitive

prism: **5** block, nicol **8** cylinder, spectrum, wernicke

prism device: **8** iriscope

prismatic: **5** showy **9** brilliant **10** iridescent **12** orthorhombic

prison: gib, jug, pen **4** brig, cell, gaol, hell, hold, hole, jail, keep, nick (Br.), quod, rock, stir **5** bagne, clink, grate, Tombs **6** Attica, bagnio, carcel, carcer, cooler, Folsom, lockup **7** Atlanta, Bocardo, college, dungeon, Gehenna, hoosgow, kidcote, Ludgate, Newgate, Spandau **8** Alcatraz, Bastille, Dartmoor, hoosegaw, hoosegow, Lubyanka, Sing Sing **9** Bridewell, calaboose, enclosure, Old Bailey **10** guardhouse, panopticon, San Quentin **11** Leavenworth **12** penitentiary

guard: **5** screw

keeper: **5** guard **6** gaoler, jailer, jailor, keeper, warden **7** turnkey

naval or ship: **4** brig

room: **4** cell, hole, tank **7** dungeon **8** solitary

sentence: rap

spy: **6** mouton

prisoner: con **5** felon, lifer **6** detenu (F.), inmate **7** caitiff, captive, convict, detenue (F.), parolee **8** jailbird **9** collegian **10** emancipist **11** probationer

exchange agreement: **6** cartel

Prisoner of the Vatican: **4** Pope

prisoner of war: PW, P.O.W. **7** kriegie

prissy: **4** prim **5** fussy **7** finicky, precise, prudish **9** sissified **10** effeminate **11** overrefined

pristine: new **4** pure **5** early, fresh **7** ancient, primary **8** original **9** primitive, unspoiled, untouched **11** uncorrupted

pritch: **5** prick, spike, staff **6** pierce **9** perforate

privacy: **7** privity, retreat, secrecy **8** darkness, solitude **9** seclusion **10** penetralia **12** hugger-mugger

privado: **6** friend **8** intimate **9** confidant

private: **5** alone, privy **6** closet, covert, hushed, inside, secret **7** soldier **8** esoteric, homefelt, intimate, personal, secluded, singular, solitary **10** unofficial **12** confidential, unpublicized

private eye: PI, tec **6** shamus, tailer **7** gumshoe **9** detective, operative **12** investigator

privateer: **4** Kidd, ship **5** caper **6** pirate **7** corsair, drumler **8** drumbler

commission: **14** letter of marque

privately: **5** aside **7** sub rosa **8** in camera, inwardly, secretly

privation: **4** loss, need, want **6** misery **7** absence, poverty **8** hardship **9** suffering **11** deprivation, destitution

privet: **5** hedge, ibota, shrub **7** alatern, ibolium **9** houseleek

privilege: law, soc, use **4** boon, soke **5** favor, grace, grant, right **6** favour, patent **7** charter, liberty **8** easement, immunity **9** advantage, allowance, exemption, franchise, vouchsafe **10** concession **11** prerogative

privy: **4** gong **5** biffy, jakes **6** cloaca, closet, hidden, secret, toilet **7** cloacae (pl.), furtive, private **8** familiar, intimate, out-house **9** backhouse, confidant, necessary **11** clandestine, water-closet **12** confidential **13** surreptitious

prix (F.): **4** fare **5** award, price, prize **6** charge

prize: cup, pry **4** best, gree (Sc.), prix (F.), tern **5** award, bacon, booty, lever, medal, plate, purse, spoil, stake, value **6** esteem, glaive, reward, trophy **7** capture, cherish, garland, guerdon, jackpot, premium, seizure **8** estimate, leverage, purchase, treasure **10** appreciate

lowest: **5** booby

prized: **4** dear **5** chary **9** treasured

prizefight: **4** bout, mill **5** match, scrap **7** contest **11** boxing match

ring: **5** arena

segment: **5** round

pro: for **4** whiz, with **6** expert **8** advocate, favoring **9** favouring, in favor of **12** professional

probability: **4** odds **6** chance **8** prospect **10** appearance, likelihood, likeliness **11** credibility

probable: **5** maybe **6** likely **8** apparent, credible, feasible

probably: **6** belike, likely **10** presumably

probation: **4** test **5** trial **6** parole **9** novitiate **11** examination

probe: **4** acus, tent, test **5** grope, query, sound **6** pierce, search, seeker, stylet, tracer **7** examine, explore, feel out, inquiry **9** catechize, delve into, penetrate **10** ankylomele, instrument, scrutinize **11** exploration, interrogate, investigate **13** investigation

probity: **6** virtue **7** honesty **8** goodness **9** integrity, rectitude **11** uprightness

problem: nut, sum **4** crux, knot **5** hydra, issue, poser **6** enigma, puzzle, riddle **7** dilemma **8** headache, quandary, question **9** situation

problematical: **4** moot, open **8** doubtful **9** ambiguous, equivocal, uncertain, unsettled **12** questionable

proboscis: **4** nose **5** snout, trunk

proboscis monkey: **4** kaha

procacious: **4** pert, wise **8** impudent, insolent, petulant

Procas' son: **7** Amulius, Numitor

procavia: **5** hyrax **10** hyracoidea

procedure: **6** course, method, policy, tactic **7** measure, process, program, routine

proceed: **4** come, fand, fare, flow, move, pass, stem, wend **5** arise, frame, issue **6** derive, spring **7** advance, emanate, forthgo **8** continue, progress **9** originate
  laboriously: mog **4** plod, plow, slog, wade **6** trudge
  rapidly: run **5** speed **6** gallop

proceeding: **4** acta (pl.), step **5** actum, doing **6** affair, afflux, course **7** conduct, measure, process **9** affluxion, procedure **11** transaction

proceeds: **4** gate, loot, take **5** booty, yield **6** income, profit, return **8** stealage

procerity: **6** height **8** tallness

process: **4** cook, writ **5** lapse, order **6** capias, course, manner, method, notice, system **7** advance, mandate, routine, summons **8** progress **9** operation, outgrowth, procedure, sterilize, technique **10** injunction

procession: **4** file **5** march, order **6** course, exequy, litany, parade, series **7** cortege, pageant **9** cavalcade, formation, recession

prochein: **4** next **7** nearest

proclaim: bid, cry **4** call, deem, show, toot, tout **5** blare, blast, blaze, claim, grede, knell, utter, voice **6** blazon, bounce, defame, herald, indict, outcry, preach **7** declare, divulge, enounce, publish **8** announce, denounce, forspeak **9** advertise, celebrate, enunciate, forespeak, ventilate **10** promulgate

proclamation: ban **4** bans, fiat **5** bando (Sp.), banns, blaze, edict, ukase **6** notice **7** bidding, placard **9** manifesto **11** declaration, publication **12** announcement, annunciation, denunciation, notification, promulgation

proclivity: **4** bent **6** talent **7** leaning **10** propensity **11** disposition, inclination

Procne: *father:* **7** Pandion
  husband: **6** Tereus
  sister: **9** Philomela
  son: **4** Itys

procrastination: **5** delay, stall **9** deferment **10** cunctation, inactivity **12** dilatoriness, postponement

procreant: **8** fruitful **9** producing **10** generating

procreate: **4** sire **5** beget, breed **6** father **7** produce **8** engender, generate **11** give birth to

procreation: **8** virility **9** offspring **10** generation, production

Procris: *father:* **10** Erechtheus
  husband and slayer: **8** Cephalus

proctor: **5** agent, proxy **7** monitor **8** advocate, attorney **9** supervise **10** supervisor

procumbent: **5** prone **9** prostrate

procurable: **7** parable **10** accessible, obtainable

procure: get **4** fang, find, gain **5** bring **6** effect, induce, obtain, secure, suborn **7** acquire, chevise, receive **8** contrive **9** impetrate

procurer: **4** bawd, pimp **6** pander **8** purveyor

procuress: **4** bawd, hack **5** madam **7** commode

prod: egg, jab **4** brog, goad, poke, urge **5** nudge, pique **6** excite, incite, thrust **9** instigate, stimulate

prodigal: **5** flush **6** lavish **7** copious, liberal, profuse, spender, wastrel **8** abundant, generous, wasteful **9** bounteous **10** profligate, squanderer **11** extravagant, spendthrift, squandering

prodigious: **4** huge **5** giant **7** amazing, immense **8** enormous, gigantic **9** marvelous, monstrous, wonderful **10** portentous, tremendous **11** astonishing **13** extraordinary

prodigy: **4** omen, sign **6** marvel, ostent, wonder **7** miracle, portent **8** ceremony

prodition: **7** treason **8** betrayal **9** treachery **15** treacherousness

prodrome: **7** symptom

produce: **4** bear, form, give, grow, make, show **5** breed, carry, cause, raise, shape, stage, yield **6** create, devise, effect, fruits **7** exhibit, product **8** engender, generate **9** fabricate, offspring, procreate **10** bring about, production, vegetables **11** manufacture
  new: **6** create, invent **9** originate

producer: **6** author, backer, farmer, grower, parent **7** creator **8** director **12** manufacturer

product: **4** item **5** fruit, yield **6** number, result **9** offspring, outgrowth

production: **4** film, play, work **5** fruit **6** output **11** performance

productive: 4 rich 6 active, fecund, parous 7 fertile 8 creative, fruitful, prolific, sonorous 10 generative 11 originative

proem: 7 preface, prelude 8 foreword, overture, preamble, prologue 12 introduction

profanation: 9 blasphemy, sacrilege, violation 11 desecration

profane: lay 4 foul 5 abuse 6 debase, defile, defoil, defoul, unholy, vulgar, wicked 7 godless, heathen, impious, obscene, secular, ungodly, violate, worldly 8 temporal 9 desecrate, vulgarize 10 irreverent, unhallowed 11 blasphemous 12 sacrilegious, unsanctified

profanity: 4 oath 5 curse 8 swearing 9 blasphemy

profess: own 4 avow 5 admit, claim 6 affect, affirm, allege, assert 7 confess, declare, pretend, protest 8 proclaim 11 acknowledge

profession: art, job 4 work 5 craft, faith, forte, trade 6 avowal, career, metier (F.) 7 calling 8 function, vocation 9 following 10 employment, occupation

professional: pro 4 paid 5 hired 6 expert 7 artiste, skilled, trained 8 finished

professor: don, fly 5 tutor 6 doctor 7 teacher 8 lecturer 10 instructor

proffer: bid 4 give, hand 5 offer 6 extend, tender 8 proposal 11 countenance

proficiency: 5 skill 7 ability, advance, aptness, mastery 9 adeptness 10 capability, competence, efficiency, expertness 14 accomplishment

proficient: 4 able 5 adept 6 actual, expert, master, versed 7 skilled 8 skillful 9 competent, effective, effectual 10 conversant 11 crackerjack, experienced 12 accomplished

profile: 4 form 6 figure 7 contour, drawing, outline 10 silhouette 14 representation

profit: net, pay, use 4 boot, gain, good, help, mend, nett 5 avail, frame, lucre, melon 6 behoof, return 7 account, benefit, bestead, revenue, utility 8 earnings, increase, interest, proceeds 9 advantage, emolument 10 bottom line 12 remuneration
receiver of: 6 pernor
undercover: 4 loot, skim 5 booty 6 payola
usurious: vig 8 vigorish

profitable: fat 8 repaying 9 expedient, lucrative 12 advantageous

profitless: 9 fruitless 12 unprofitable

profligate: 4 rake, roue, wild 6 rioter 7 corrupt, riotous, spender, vicious, wastrel 8 depraved, flagrant, prodigal, rakehell, wasteful 9 abandoned, dissolute, reprobate 10 licentious 11 extravagant, spendthrift

profound: low 4 deep, sage, wise 5 heavy 7 abysmal, intense 8 abstruse, unbroken 9 intensive, recondite, sagacious 10 acroamatic, exhaustive 11 farreaching 12 unfathomable

profuse: 4 lush 5 frank 6 galore, hearty, lavish 7 copious, liberal, opulent, riotous 8 abundant, generous, prodigal, wasteful 9 bountiful, excessive, exuberant, luxuriant, plentiful 10 munificent 11 extravagant, overflowing

prog: 4 food 5 prick, prowl, tramp 6 forage 7 vagrant 8 supplies 9 provender

progenitor: 4 sire 6 parent 8 ancestor 9 precursor 10 forefather, foreparent, forerunner 11 predecessor

progeny: imp, son 4 race, seed 5 breed, brood, brook, child, issue, scion, shoot 6 family, strain 8 children, daughter 9 genealogy, offspring 10 generation 11 descendants

prognostic: 4 omen, sign 5 token 6 augury 7 portent 8 forecast, prophesy 10 prediction

prognosticate: 4 bode 5 augur 6 divine 7 betoken, forbode, forerun, portend, predict, presage 8 forebode, forecast, foreshow, foretell, prophesy 9 foretoken, hariolate

prognosticator: 4 seer 5 augur 6 divine 7 augurer, diviner, palmist, prophet 9 predictor 10 soothsayer

program: 4 card, list, show, sked 5 draft, edict 6 agenda, course, notice 7 agendum, catalog, outline 8 bulletin, calendar, schedule, syllabus 9 broadcast 10 prospectus 12 proclamation
theater: 8 playbill

programma: 5 edict 6 decree 7 preface 12 prolegomenon

progress: 4 fare, flow, grow, tour, wend 5 march 6 course, growth, motion 7 advance, circuit, develop, headway, improve, journey, passage, proceed 10 betterment, expedition 11 development, furtherance, improvement
planned: 7 telesia, telesis

progression: 5 stage 6 growth, series 8 sequence 9 evolution, unfolding 10 succession 11 development

progressive: 6 active, onward 7 forward, liberal, radical 9 advancing, ascensive 12 enterprising

prohibit: ban, bar, bid 4 stop, veto 5 debar, estop, fence 6 defend, enjoin, forbid, hinder, outlaw 7 forfend, forwarn, prevent 8 disallow, forefend 9 interdict, proscribe 11 countermand

prohibited: hot 4 tabu 5 taboo 6 banned 7 illegal, illicit 8 unlawful, verboten (G.) 9 forbidden

prohibiting: 8 vetitive

prohibitionist: dry 4 WCTU

project: jet, jut, lap **4** abut, apse, barb, butt, game, idea, plan, send, task **5** bulge, filip, shoot, think **6** beetle, design, device, extend, fillip, scheme, wander **7** extrude, imagine, pattern, problem, prolong **8** contrive, lengthen, proposal, protrude **9** intention **10** enterprise **11** contrivance, proposition, undertaking

projectile (see also **guided missile, missile**): **4** bomb, dart, rock, shot **5** arrow, shell **6** bullet, rocket **7** missile, torpedo **8** shrapnel **9** cartridge
curve: **8** parabola
explosive part: **7** warhead, warnose
pert. to: **9** ballistic
submarine: **7** torpedo

projecting: **6** beetle **7** jutting, salient **10** protruding

projection: arm, cam, ell, hob, hub, jag, lee, lug, toe **4** apse, barb, croc, fang, lobe **5** bulge, crena, redan, socle, tenon, tooth **6** corbel, crenae (pl.), dormer, lobule, tappet **7** cornice, empathy **8** abutment, ejection, eminence, overhang **9** crenation **10** protrusion **12** protuberance

projector: **4** kino **8** bioscope **9** vitascope **12** magic lantern, stereopticon **13** cinematograph, kinematograph

prolapse: **7** falling

prolate: **9** elongated
opposite of: **6** oblate

proletarian: **4** mean, rude **6** coarse, vulgar, worker **7** laborer

proletariat: mob **4** mass **6** rabble **7** workers **9** hoi polloi **11** rank and file **12** working class

prolific: **6** birthy, fecund **7** fertile, teeming **8** fruitful, spawning, swarming **9** abounding, plentiful **10** generative, productive **11** propagative **12** reproductive

prolix: **5** wordy **6** boring **7** diffuse, irksome, prosaic, tedious, verbose **8** tiresome **9** prolonged, wearisome **10** longwinded, protracted **11** displeasing **13** uninteresting

prolocutor: **6** orator **7** speaker **8** advocate, chairman **9** spokesman **10** mouthpiece

prologue: **7** preface **8** foreword, preamble **12** introduction

prolong: **5** defer **6** endure, extend **7** drag out, persist **8** continue, lengthen

prolonged: **4** long **5** great **6** prolix **7** chronic, delayed, dilated **8** extended **9** continued, postponed, sostenuto, sustained **10** lengthened, protracted

prom: **4** ball **5** dance **9** promenade

promenade: **4** ball, deck, hall, mall, walk **5** march, prado (Sp.) **6** avenue, marina, parade, pasear (Sp.) **7** alameda, gallery **9** boardwalk, esplanade

Prometheus: **5** Titan
father: **7** Iapetus
gift to man: **4** fire
mother: **6** Themis **7** Clymene
rescuer: **8** Heracles, Hercules

prominence: **4** cusp, fame **5** agger **6** renown **8** eminence, prestige, salience **9** celebrity **10** colliculus, promontory **11** distinction

prominent: **5** chief, famed, noted **6** famous, marked, signal **7** capital, eminent, notable, obvious, salient **8** aquiline, manifest, renowned **9** egregious, well-known **10** celebrated, noticeable, projecting **11** conspicuous, distinctive **13** distinguished

promiscuous: **4** lewd **5** light, loose **6** random, wanton **7** immoral **8** careless **9** haphazard

promise: vow **4** band, bond, hest, hote, oath, pawn, word **5** agree, grant, swear **6** assure, behest, engage, parole, pledge, plight **7** behight, betroth **8** affiance, contract, covenant, financed **9** assurance, betrothal, foretoken, guarantee **10** convenable, engagement, obligation **11** declaration, word of honor

Promised Land: **6** Canaan, heaven

promissory note: I.O.U. **5** check **6** pledge, ticket

promontory: hoe **4** bill, cape, head, mull, nase, naze, ness, peak, scaw, skaw, spit **5** mount, point **8** headland **10** projection, prominence

promote: aid **4** help, plug, push **5** boost, exalt, nurse, raise, speed **6** better, foster, prefer **7** advance, build up, dignify, elevate, forward, further **9** advantage, advertise, encourage, patronize, publicize **10** aggrandize, make much of

promoter: **5** agent **7** abetter, abettor, booster, hustler **8** broacher, lobbyist **9** publicist

promotion: **6** brevet **7** advance **9** publicity **10** graduation, preferment **11** advancement, furtherance

prompt: apt, cue **4** fast, goad, move, urge, yare (Sc.) **5** alert, quick, rapid, ready, swift, yeder **6** active, assist, excite, induce, nimble, remind, timely **7** animate, forward **8** punctual, vigilant, watchful **11** expeditious

prompter: aid **4** cuer **7** readier

promptly: **4** soon, tite (Sc.) **8** directly

promptness: **8** alacrity, dispatch

promulgate: **7** declare, publish **8** announce, proclaim **9** advertise

prone: apt **4** bent, flat **5** buxom **6** agroof, agrufe, agruif, liable, likely, supine **7** passive, willing **8** addicted, disposed, inclined, pronated **9** declivous, groveling, lying down, prostrate, reclining, recumbent **10** decubitous

prong: nib, peg **4** fang, fork, horn, tine **5** point, tooth **6** branch

prongbuck: 9 pronghorn, springbok

pronghorn: 4 deer 6 cabree 8 antelope, berrendo

prong key: 7 spanner

pronoun: any, her, him, his, its, one, our, she, thy, you 4 mine, ours, that, thee, them, they, this, thou, your 5 their, these, thine, those 6 itself, myself 7 herself, himself, oneself, ourself 8 yourself 9 ourselves 10 themselves, yourselves
demonstrative: 4 that, this 5 these, those
interrogative: who 4 what, whom 5 which, whose
substantive: who 7 whoever 9 whosoever

pronounce: 4 pass 5 sound, speak, utter 6 affirm 7 behight, declare, deliver, enounce 8 announce 9 enunciate 10 articulate
free: 7 absolve
guilty: 7 condemn
indistinctly: 4 slur
slowly: 5 drawl

pronounced: 6 marked 7 decided, howling 12 unmistakable

pronouncement: 4 fiat 5 dicta (pl.) 6 dictum 9 manifesto, statement 11 declaration 12 announcement, proclamation, promulgation

pronto: 4 fast 5 quick 6 at once 7 quickly 8 promptly 11 immediately

pronunciation: 4 burr, lisp, slur 5 drawl, twang 6 accent
correct: 8 orthoepy 9 phonology
incorrect: 7 cacoepy 8 psellism

pronunciation mark: 5 breve, caron, hacek, tilde 6 accent, macron, ogonek, umlaut 7 cedilla 8 dieresis 9 diacritic 10 circumflex

proof: 4 test 5 trial 6 reason, result 7 approof, exhibit, outcome, probate 8 argument, evidence 9 testimony 10 indication, validation 11 approbation 12 confirmation, impenetrable, verification 13 certification, demonstration

proofreaders' mark: cap 4 dele, ital, stet 5 caret, space

prop: leg, nog 4 stay 5 appui, brace, shore, sprag, staff, stell (Sc.), stilt 6 scotch, shorer 7 fulcrum, shore up, support, sustain 8 buttress 10 strengthen

propaganda: 4 hype, plan 5 ideas 6 scheme, system 8 agitprop, doctrine 12 brainwashing

propagate: 4 grow 5 breed 6 spread 7 diffuse 8 engender, generate, increase, multiply 9 circulate, procreate 11 disseminate

propagation: 8 breeding 9 diffusion, spreading 10 dispersion 12 continuation

propel: gun, oar, row 4 flip, move, pole, push, send, urge 5 drive, egg on, flick, force, impel, shove 7 project

propeller: fan, fin, oar 4 vane 5 rotor, screw 6 driver, paddle 8 windmill
arm: 4 vane 5 blade

propensity: yen 4 bent, bias 6 liking 7 aptness, avidity, leaning 8 appetite, penchant, tendency 9 affection, proneness 10 proclivity, propension 11 disposition, inclination 12 predilection

proper: due, fit 4 able, fair, fine, good, meet, prim, true 5 right, stiff, utter 6 behove, chaste, comely, decent, honest, modest, sedate, seemly, strict 7 behoove, correct, fitting, genteel, precise, prudish, seeming 8 accurate, decorous, formular, suitable 9 advisable, allowable, befitting, beseeming, excellent 10 commodious, convenient, scrupulous 11 appropriate, respectable

properly: 6 featly, gladly 8 by rights

property: lot, res 4 acre, alod, aver, bona, dhan (Ind.), gear, land 5 addle, allod, asset, aught, glebe, goods, manor 6 domain, estate, havier, realty, wealth 7 acquest, alodium, capital, chattel, haviour, holding, quality 8 allodium, freehold 9 acensuada, attribute, homestead, ownership 10 real estate 11 appropriate, possessions 14 characteristic
act to regain: 8 replevin
bride's gift to husband: dos 5 dowry
charge against: 4 lien 8 mortgage
conveyor of: 7 alienor, grantor
deceased wife's gift to husband: 8 courtesy
destruction of: 5 arson 8 sabotage 9 vandalism
found on the thief: 6 mainor
personal: 5 goods 7 chattel
real: 4 land 7 acreage
receiver: 7 alienee
seller: 7 realtor
settle: 6 entail
stolen: 4 loot, pelf 5 booty, lucre 6 spoils
suit for: 6 trover
transferring party: 7 alienor

property right: 4 lien 5 title 8 easement

prophecy: 5 weird 6 augury, oracle, vision 8 bodement, forecast 9 utterance 10 prediction, revelation 11 declaration, foretelling 12 vaticination
pert. to: 9 vaticinal

prophesy: 4 dope, osse, spae 5 aread, areed, augur 6 divine 7 predict, presage 8 ariolate, forecast, foreshow, foretell 10 vaticinate 11 preindicate 13 prognosticate

prophet: 4 Amos, Joel, John, seer 5 augur, Elias, fatal, Hosea, Jonah, Micah, Moses, Nahum, sibyl, Syrus 6 divine, Elijah, Elisha, Haggai, Isaiah, Joshua, leader, mantis, oracle, Samuel 7 augurer, diviner, Ezekiel, Malachi, Obadiah, teacher 8

Habakkuk, Jeremiah, Mohammed, Muhammed, presager **9** predictor, Zephaniah **10** astrologer, soothsayer **11** Joseph Smith, Nostradamus, vaticinator

prophetess: **5** Sibyl **6** Miriam, Pythia **7** Deborah, seeress **9** Cassandra

prophetic: **5** vatic **6** mantic **7** fateful, fatidic, vatical **8** foretell, oracular **9** prescient, sibylline **10** divinatory, mysterious, predictive, presageful, signifying **11** apocalyptic, fatiloquent, foretelling, nostradamic **12** vaticinatory **14** interpretative

propine: **4** gift **5** offer **6** pledge **7** present, propose

propinquity: **7** kinship **8** affinity, nearness, vicinity **9** closeness, proximity **12** neighborhood, relationship

propitiate: **5** adapt, atone **6** adjust, pacify **7** appease, conform, expiate, mollify, satisfy **9** reconcile **10** conciliate

propitious: **4** good, rosy **5** happy, lucky **6** benign, timely **8** benedict **9** benignant, favorable, opportune, promising **10** auspicious, benevolent, prosperous **12** advantageous

proponent: **6** backer **8** advocate **9** supporter

proportion: **4** part, rate, size **5** quota, ratio, scale, share **6** amount, degree **7** analogy, portion, prorate **8** relation, symmetry **9** dimension

proportional: **5** equal **7** ratable **8** adequate, balanced, relative **10** answerable, equivalent, reciprocal **11** symmetrical **12** commensurate

proportionately: **6** fairly **7** prorata **10** adequately

proposal: bid **4** idea, plan **5** offer **6** design, feeler, motion, scheme **7** project **8** overture **10** invitation, nomination, suggestion **11** proposition

propose: ask, put **4** give, moot, move **5** offer, state **6** allege, design, submit, tender **7** suggest **8** propound **11** contemplate

proposition: ask **4** deal, plan **5** axiom, offer, point **6** affair, porism, theory, thesis **7** premise, project, theorem **8** offering, overture, proposal, question **9** corollary, postulate, situation, statement **10** hypothesis **11** affirmation, undertaking
antecedent: **7** premise
preliminary: **5** lemma **7** lemmata (pl.)

propound: **4** pose **5** posit, state **7** propose

proprietor: **5** owner **6** master, tanist **7** lairdie **8** landlord

propriety (see also **proper**): **4** code, rule **7** customs, decency, decorum, manners, quality **8** behavior, elegance, standard **9** attribute, etiquette **13** possessorship

propugnator: **8** defender **10** vindicator

propulsion: jet **5** drift **8** ejection **9** expulsion

prorate: **5** allot **6** assess, divide **9** apportion **10** distribute, proportion

prorogue: **5** defer **6** extend **7** adjourn, prolong **8** postpone, protract

prosaic: **4** drab, dull, flat **5** prosy **6** common, prolix, stolid, stupid **7** humdrum, insipid, tedious **8** everyday, tiresome, unpoetic **9** colorless **10** unexciting **11** commonplace **12** matter-of-fact **13** unimaginative, uninteresting

proscenium: **5** stage
front area: **5** apron

proscribe: ban **4** tabu **5** exile, taboo **6** banish, forbid, outlaw **7** condemn **8** prohibit, sentence **9** interdict, ostracize

prosecute: sue **4** urge **5** carry, chase, hound, press **6** accuse, charge, follow, indict, pursue **7** enforce **8** continue

prosecutor: **6** lawyer **7** accuser, relator **8** quaestor

prose form: **5** essay, novel, story, tract **7** fiction, romance **8** treatise **9** biography **10** nonfiction

proselyte: **5** alien **7** convert, recruit **8** neophyte, newcomer

Proserpine: See **Persephone**

perseuche: **7** oratory **9** synagogue

prosit: **5** toast **10** salutation

prosody: **5** meter

prospect: **4** hope, mine, view **5** buyer, scene, vista **6** aspect **7** explore, outlook **8** customer, exposure **9** applicant, candidate, foretaste **10** contestant

prospective: **5** lofty **6** future, likely **7** eminent **8** expected, prospect **9** provident **11** anticipated, perspective

prospector: **9** sourdough **10** forty-niner

prosper: dow, hie, wax **4** fare **5** cheve, edify, frame, speed **6** thrive **7** augment, blossom, succeed, turn out **8** flourish, increase

prosperity: hap, ups **4** fare **5** ikbal **6** thrift, wealth **7** fortune, success, welfare **9** abundance, happiness, well-being
god: **4** Frey
goddess: **5** Salus
symbol: **9** turquoise

Prospero (see also **Tempest**): *daughter:* **7** Miranda
servant: **5** Ariel
slave: **7** Caliban

prosperous: **4** bein, bien, boon, rich **5** flush, happy, lucky, palmy, sonsy **6** sonsie, timely **7** halcyon, wealthy, well-off **8** thriving, well-to-do **9** favorable, fortunate **10** auspicious, propitious, successful, well-heeled **11** comfortable, flourishing

prostitute: bat, cat **4** aunt, doxy, drab, hack, slut, tart, trug **5** abuse, broad, venal, whore **6** cal-

let, debase, harlot, hooker **7** baggage, brothel, corrupt, Cyprian, hackney, trollop **8** berdache, call girl, commoner, customer, infamous, occupant **9** courtesan, courtezan **10** crosha-bell, hobby-horse, licentious **12** camp follower, street-walker **13** commercialize
customer: **4** john
reformed: **8** Magdalen

prostitution, house of: 6 bordel **7** brothel **8** bordello, cathouse
district: **8** red light

prostrate: bow **4** fell, flat **5** prone **6** fallen, supine **7** exhaust **8** dejected, helpless, overcome, paralyze **9** collapsed, flattened, overthrow, overwhelm, recumbent **10** subjugated, submissive

prosy: dry **4** dull **6** boring, jejune **7** humdrum, prosaic, tedious **9** colorless **11** commonplace, displeasing **13** unimaginative

protagonist: foe **4** hero, star **5** actor, agent, enemy **6** leader **7** heroine **8** advocate, champion, defender **9** character, contender, principal, spokesman

protasis: 8 foreword **11** conditional, proposition **12** introduction

protean: 8 variable **9** many-sided **10** changeable

protect: arm **4** bind, hill, save, wear **5** bield, bless, fence, guard, hedge, shade, watch **6** assert, defend, harbor, insure, patent, police, screen, shield **7** bulwark, cherish, forfend, shelter, tuition **8** champion, conserve, forefend, preserve **9** copyright

protecting: 7 tutelar **8** tutelary

protection: bib, lee, pad **4** egis, fort, moat, pass **5** aegis, apron, armor, bribe, frith, graft, guard, shell, smock **6** amulet, armour, patent, safety, shield **7** auspice, defense, parapet, shelter, squeeze, tuition, umbrage **8** passport, security **9** shakedown **12** preservation

protector: 5 guard **6** fautor, patron, shield **8** defender, guardian **9** custodian
name meaning: **5** Edgar **9** Alexander

protectorate: 6 colony **9** territory **10** dependency, possession **11** condominium

protege: 4 ward **5** pupil

proteid: 6 alexin **7** albumin **9** legumelin

Proteida family: olm **7** proteus **8** necturus **11** salamanders, typhlomolge

protein: 6 avidin, casein, fibrin **7** albumin, edestin, mucedin **8** aleurone, creatine, prolamin
group: **8** globulin
poison: **5** abrin, ricin **6** ricine
source of: egg, soy **4** bean, fish, meat, milk, tofu **6** cheese, legume, lentil **12** dairy product

pro tem: 6 acting **7** interim **9** temporary

protest: 4 aver, beef, deny, kick **5** demur, fight **6** affirm, assert, assure, holler, object, oppose, plaint, resist **7** contest, declare, dispute, dissent, testify **8** complain **9** challenge, complaint, objection, stipulate **10** asseverate **11** expostulate, remonstrate **12** remonstrance

Protestant: 7 Baptist **8** Anglican, Lutheran, Reformed **9** Calvinist, dissenter, Methodist **10** Anabaptist **12** Presbyterian **14** Congregational

proteus: olm **5** ameba **6** amoeba

Proteus: 6 sea god
friend: **9** Valentine
love: **6** Silvia
wife: **5** Julia

protograph: 7 writing **9** holograph **12** illustration

protoplasm: 5 ameba, spore **6** amoeba **7** sarcode
outer layer: **9** ectoplasm
substance: gel

prototype: 5 model **6** emblem **7** example, pattern **8** antetype, original **9** archetype **10** forerunner

protozoan: 5 ameba **6** amoeba **7** stentor **8** rhizopod
genus of: **7** arcella
order: **6** lobosa
parasitic: **5** ameba **6** amoeba **8** amoebida

protract: 4 spin **5** defer, delay **6** dilate, extend **7** detract, prolong **8** continue, elongate, lengthen, protrude

protrude: jut **5** blear, bulge **7** extrude, project **8** stick out **9** interfere

protuberance: nub, wen **4** boll, boss, bulb, bump, heel, hump, knob, knot, lobe, lump, node, snag, umbo **5** bulge, bunch, caput, hunch, torus **8** eminence, swelling **9** gibbosity **10** projection, prominence, protrusion
rounded: **4** hump, umbo

protuberant: 5 bulgy **6** convex, extant **7** bottled, gibbous, jutting **8** blubbery **9** prominent

proud (see also **pride**): **4** ikey, smug, vain **5** brant, chuff **7** haughty, pompous, stately, valiant **8** arrogant, imposing, splendid **9** cock-horse, conceited, egotistic, hubristic **10** impressive **11** magisterial, overbearing **12** presumptuous, supercilious

prove: try **4** aver, fand, pree, show, test **5** argue, essay, nurse, prive (Sc.) **6** argify, argufy, attest, evince, verify **7** confirm, justify, probate **8** identify, indicate, manifest **9** ascertain, establish **11** corroborate, demonstrate

provenance: 6 origin, source **10** derivation

provender: hay **4** corn, feed, food, oats, prog

5 grain, straw **6** fodder, forage **7** prebend **10** provisions

proverb: saw **4** word **5** adage, axiom, maxim, motto **6** ballad, byword, enigma, saying **7** byspell, epigram, parable **8** allegory, aphorism, forbysen

proverbial: 6 common **9** well-known **11** sententious

provide: 4 give **5** cater, equip, stock, store, yield **6** afford, foison, purvey, ration, render, supply **7** chevise, furnish, support **8** accouter, accoutre **9** stipulate **10** contribute

provided: but **5** boden, found **6** if only, sobeit **8** afforded, equipped, supplied **9** furnished

providence: 4 fate **6** thrift **7** economy **8** function, guidance, prudence

provident: 4 wise **6** frugal, saving **7** careful, prudent, sparing, thrifty **8** cautious, discreet **9** farseeing **10** economical, farsighted **11** foresighted

providential: 4 kind **5** happy, lucky **6** timely **9** fortunate, opportune **10** auspicious

province: 4 area, nome, work **5** arena, range, realm, shire, tract **6** colony, domain, eparch, region, sphere **7** country, emirate, pursuit **8** district, division, function **9** bailiwick, territory **10** department, palatinate **12** jurisdiction
pert. to: **5** nomic

provincial: 4 rude **5** crude, local, rural **6** narrow, rustic **7** bigoted, insular, limited **9** hidebound, parochial **10** uncultured **11** countrified **15** unsophisticated

provision: 4 fare, food **5** board, cater, grist, stock, store **6** clause, outfit, supply, wraith **7** proviso **9** condition

provisional: 4 iffy **7** aeolian **9** makeshift, provisory, temporary, tentative **10** contingent **11** conditional

provisions: 4 cate, chow, fare, food **5** board, bouge, terms **6** forage, stocks, stores, viands **7** rations **8** victuals **9** groceries, provender **10** chevisance
search for: **6** forage
stock of: **6** larder, pantry **8** magazine

proviso: 4 term **5** salvo **6** clause **7** article, caution **9** condition **11** stipulation

provisory: 11 provisional

provocation: 6 appeal **7** offense **9** annoyance, incentive

provocative: 7 agacant **8** agacante, stimulus **9** desirable, provoking **10** aggressive **11** stimulating

provoke: ire, vex **4** bait, move, spur, stir **5** anger, annoy, cause, eager, evoke, frump, pique, start, tease **6** arouse, excite, harass, incite, insult, invite, invoke, madden, nettle, summon **7** affront, incense, outrage, perturb, quicken **8** generate, irritate **9**

aggravate, challenge, displease, forthcall, stimulate **10** exasperate

provost: 4 dean, head **5** chief **6** jailer, keeper **7** bailiff, prefect **8** director, official **10** magistrate **13** administrator **14** superintendent

prow: bow **4** beak, nose, stem **5** brave, prore **6** steven **7** gallant, rostrum, valiant **9** honorable **10** courageous

prowess: 5 skill, valor **6** valour **7** address, bravery, courage, heroism **8** strength **9** ingenuity **10** excellence

prowl: 4 lurk, roam **6** brevit, ramble, wander

proximate: 4 next **5** close **6** direct, nearby **7** nearest **8** imminent **9** immediate **10** near-at-hand

proximity: 8 nearness, nighness, vicinage, vicinity **9** adjacence, closeness, immediacy **10** contiguity **11** propinquity **13** approximation, juxtaposition

proxy: 4 vote **5** agent, power, vicar **6** agency, deputy **7** proctor **8** assignee, function **9** authority **10** procurator, substitute

prudence: wit **4** care **6** acumen, wisdom **7** economy **10** management **11** calculation

prudent: 4 sage, wary, wise **5** canny, chary, douce, siker **6** frugal, sicker **7** careful, politic **8** cautious, discreet, sensible **9** advisable, cautelous, expedient, provident, sagacious **10** economical, forehanded **11** circumspect, considerate, foresighted **14** forethoughtful

prudish: 4 nice, prim **5** stern **6** demure, severe **7** austere **8** priggish **10** overmodest **11** straitlaced

prune: cow, cut, lop **4** clip, coll, frog, geld, plum, sned (Sc.), thin, trim **5** brake, dress, dunce, fruit, plume, preen, purge, rasee, razee, shave **6** anoint **7** exclude, tonsure **8** castrate **9** eliminate, simpleton

pruning knife: 8 serpette

prurient: 4 lewd **5** bawdy **6** erotic **7** itching, longing, lustful **10** lascivious

pruritis: 4 itch

Prussia: 11 German state (former)
city: **4** Kiel **5** Essen **6** Aachen, Altena, Berlin, Tilsit **7** Breslau, Hanover, Munster, Stettin **9** Frankfurt, Magdeburg **10** Dusseldorf, Konigsberg **14** Charlottenburg
district: **7** Stettin
lagoon: **4** haff **7** Frische **8** Kurische **11** Pommerische
lancer: **4** Ulan **5** Uhlan
land-holding aristocracy: **6** Junker
legislature, upper house: **10** Herrenhaus
measure: **4** fuss, rute, zoll **5** fuder, meile **6** morgen, oxhoft **8** scheffel
mountain: **4** Harz **7** Sudeten **11** Schneekoppe **13** Riesengebirge
prime minister: **8** Bismarck

ruler: **8** margrave **12** Hohenzollern
spa: Ems
university town: **5** Halle
weight: **4** mark **9** quentchen
prussiate: **4** salt **7** cyanide **12** ferricyanide, ferrocyanide
pry: spy **4** gaze, lift, move, nose, peek, peep, peer **5** jemmy, jimmy, lever, mouse, prize, raise, snoop, twist **6** pick up, potter **7** crowbar **8** leverage, scrounge, separate **10** scrutinize
pryer: See **prier**
prying: **4** busy, nosy **5** nosey **7** curious **9** obtrusive, officious **11** inquisitive
psalm: ode **4** hymn, land, poem, song **6** praise **11** composition
collection of: **6** hallel **7** psalter
kind: **4** laud **6** hallel, Venite **7** Cantate, introit **8** Jubilate, Miserere **10** Benedictus
opening Communion: **7** introit
sign: **5** selah
word of punctuation: **5** selah
psalmist: **4** poet **5** David **6** cantor, writer **8** composer **9** precentor
psalterium: **4** bouk, lyra **6** omasum **7** stomach **9** manyplies
psammite: **9** sandstone
pseudo: **4** fake, mock, sham **5** bogus, false, wrong **7** feigned **8** spurious **9** pretended, simulated **11** counterfeit
pseudologist: **4** liar
pseudonym (see also **nickname, pen name**): **5** alias **6** anonym **7** anonyme **9** incognito
Lev Bronstein: **11** Leon Trotsky
Josip Broz: **4** Tito
Iosif Dzhugashvili: **12** Joseph Stalin
Adolf Schicklgruber: **11** Adolf Hitler
Vladimir Ulyanov: **13** Vladimir Lenin
Ehrich Weiss: **7** Houdini
psittaceous: **10** parrotlike
psyche: **4** mind, soul **6** spirit **12** subconscious
psychiatrist: **4** Jung **5** Adler, Freud **6** shrink **7** analyst **8** alienist **9** Rorschach
psychic: **6** medium, mental, occult **7** sensile **9** animistic, spiritual **10** responsive, telepathic **11** impressible
psychic power: ESP
psychotic: mad **5** crazy **6** insane **8** schizoid **10** disordered **12** unreasonable
Ptah's wife: **6** Sekhet
ptarmica: **10** sneezewort
ptarmigan: **4** bird, ripa, rype **6** grouse
PT boat: **11** torpedo boat
pteric: **4** alar **8** winglike
pteroid: **8** fernlike, winglike
ptisan: tea **5** drink **6** coddle, tisane **9** decoction
Ptolemy: **10** astronomer, geographer
astronomy work: **8** Almagest
wife: **12** Philadelphia

ptomaine: **8** chemical, compound **13** food poisoning
pub: bar, inn **5** hotel **6** tavern
pubble: fat **5** plump
public: **4** open **5** civic, civil, overt, state **6** common, vulgar **7** general, popular, society **8** national, open-door **9** community, following **10** widespread
discussion: **5** forum **11** town meeting
record office: **7** archion **8** archives
service: **7** railway, utility **9** telegraph, telephone **10** waterworks
way: **4** road **5** alley **6** avenue, bridge, street, tunnel **7** freeway, highway **8** turnpike **9** boulevard
publican: **6** farmer, keeper **9** catchpole, catchpoll, collector **12** saloon keeper, tax collector
publication: **4** book **5** paper **6** annals, blazon, digest **7** booklet **8** magazine, pamphlet **9** ephemeris **10** periodical **11** declaration **12** notification, proclamation, promulgation
examiner: **6** censor
list: **12** bibliography
make-up: **6** format
permit: **7** release
preliminary: **9** prodromus
prepare for: **4** edit
regular: **10** periodical
publicist: **5** agent, solon **6** writer **8** promoter **10** journalist, press agent
publicity: air **7** buildup, puffery, reclame, write-up **8** ballyhoo **9** promotion **11** advertising, information
publicize: **4** tout **5** extol **7** promote **9** advertise
publish: air **4** blow, edit, vent **5** issue, print **6** blazon, defame, delate, expose, get out, put out **7** declare, diffuse, divulge, release **8** announce, evulgate, forspeak, proclaim, promulge **9** advertise, forespeak **10** promulgate **11** disseminate
without authority: **6** pirate **10** plagiarize
publisher: **6** editor, issuer **7** printer **8** broacher **10** journalist
copy: **5** blurb **8** colophon **12** announcement
Puccini: *heroine:* **4** Mimi **6** Minnie **8** Lauretta **9** Cio-Cio-San
opera: **5** Manon, Tosca **7** Lescant **8** La Boheme, Turandot **10** Il Trittico **14** Gianni Schicchi, Madam Butterfly **16** Fanciulla del West
puck: elf, imp **4** disk **5** fairy **6** roller, sprite, strike **9** hobgoblin, prankster **10** goatsucker
pucker: **4** fold **5** bulge, purse, reeve, smock **6** cockle, cotter, lucken **7** wrinkle **8** contract
puckered: **7** bullate
puckfist: **8** braggart, puffball
puckish: **6** impish **7** playful **8** annoying **10** mysterious **11** mischievous

pud: paw **4** hand **7** pudding **8** forefoot

pudding: **4** duff, mush, sago **5** bread **6** burgoo, hackin, haggis (Sc.), Indian, junket, panada **7** burgout, custard, dessert, hacking, sausage, tapioca **8** roly-poly **9** stirabout **10** blancmange **14** floating island

puddle: dub **4** plud, pond, pool **5** plash, swamp **6** charco, fiddle, flodge **7** plashet **8** quagmire

pudency: **7** modesty, shyness **8** delicacy **11** bashfulness, prudishness **13** embarrassment **14** shamefacedness

pudgy: fat **5** dumpy, plump, squab, squat **6** rotund **7** bulging **8** roly-poly

pueblo: **4** town **7** village **8** dwelling

Pueblo: **4** Hopi, Zuni **6** Indian
  ancestor: **7** Anasazi
  assembly hall: **6** estufa
  ceremonial chamber: **4** kiva
  spirit: **7** Kachina
  village: **4** Taos

puerile: **4** weak **5** silly, young **6** jejune **7** babyish, foolish, trivial **8** childish, immature, juvenile, unworthy, youthful **10** unthinking

Puerto Rico: **12** commonwealth
  bark: **4** mavi
  beverage: **4** mavi
  bird: **4** rola **7** yeguita
  breadfruit: **7** castana
  capital: **7** San Juan
  city: **5** Ponce **6** Cagvas, Dorado **7** Arecibo, Bayamon **8** Mayaguez
  conqueror of: **5** Miles
  discoverer: **8** Columbus
  fish: **4** sama, sisi
  fortress: **7** El Morro
  measure: **6** cuerda **10** caballeria
  mountains: **10** Cordillera
  peak: **12** Cerro de Punta
  people: **11** borrinqueno
  person of mixed blood: **6** jibaro
  rain forest: **8** El Yunque
  tree: **4** mora **5** yagua, yaray **8** guayroto **9** guaraguao

puff: **4** blow, chug, flam (Sc.), flan, fuff, gust, huff, pant, pegh (Sc.), plug, pouf, waff, waft **5** fluff, quilt, whiff **6** praise

puffball: **4** fist, fuzz **5** smoke **8** fuzzball, snuffbox

puffbird: **6** barbet **8** barbacou
  genus: **6** monasa

puffed up: **5** large **6** astrut **7** souffle **8** arrogant, bouffant, imposing, inflated **9** bombastic, bouffante, conceited **11** pretentious

puffer: **6** blower **8** blowfish **9** globefish

puffin: auk **4** bird **9** sea parrot

puff up: **5** bloat, swell **6** tumefy **7** distend, inflate

puffy: **4** soft **5** pursy **6** flabby **7** pompous, swollen

pug: dog, elf **4** clay, plug, poke, puck **5** boxer, chaff, churn, dwarf, knead, track **6** harlot, refuse, sprite, thrust **7** trample **8** mistress, pugilist **9** footprint, hobgoblin

puggy: **6** monkey (Sc.), sweaty **10** sweetheart

pugilist: lug **5** boxer **7** battler, bruiser, fighter **12** prizefighter

pugnacious: **7** defiant, warlike **8** brawling, fighting **9** bellicose, combative **10** aggressive **11** belligerent, contentious, quarrelsome

pug-nosed: **5** camus

puisne: **4** puny **5** judge, later, petty **6** feeble, junior **9** associate **10** subsequent **11** subordinate **13** insignificant

puissance: **4** army, host, sway **5** clout, force, might, power, vigor **7** potency **8** strength **9** influence **12** forcefulness

puissant: **6** mighty, strong **8** powerful **10** commanding

puke: **4** snot, wool **5** vomit

pukka, pucka: **4** good, real **7** genuine **8** complete **9** authentic **11** substantial **13** thoroughgoing

pulchritude: **5** grace **6** beauty **10** comeliness, excellence, loveliness

pule: cry **4** mewl, peep **5** cheep, whine **6** repine, snivel **7** whimper **8** complain

Pulitzer Prize (see box)

pull: lug, row, tew, tit, tow, tug, wap **4** claw, drag, draw, duct, hale, haul, jerk, yank, yerk **5** bouse, heave, hitch, pluck, tweak **6** allure, arrest, twitch, wrench **7** attract, revulse, stretch **9** influence **10** persuasion **12** drawing power
  apart: rip **4** rend, tear **8** separate **9** criticize
  away: **5** wrest **6** remove **8** withdraw
  down: **4** raze **5** wreck **7** destroy **8** demolish
  off: pug **6** avulse, manage **7** achieve, succeed **10** accomplish
  one's leg: **4** fool, hoax, joke **7** deceive **8** hoodwink

Pulitzer Prize: *Biography:* *1917* **4** Hall **6** Elliot **8** Richards; *1918* **5** Bruce; *1919* **5** Adams; *1920* **9** Beveridge; *1921* Bok; *1922* **7** Garland; *1923* **8** Hendrick; *1924* **5** Pupin; *1925* **4** Howe; *1926* **7** Cushing; *1927;* **8** Holloway; *1928* **7** Russell; *1929* **8** Hendrick; *1930* **5** James; *1931* **5** James; *1932* **7** Pringle; *1933* **6** Nevins; *1934* **7** Dennett; *1935* **7** Freeman; *1936* **5** Perry; *1937* **6** Nevins; *1938* **5** James **7** Shepard; *1939* **8** Van Doren; *1940* **5** Baker; *1941* **7** Winslow; *1942* **6** Wilson; *1943* **7** Morison; *1944* **5** Mabee; *1945* Nye; *(cont.)*

Pulitzer Prize *(cont.)*

1946 **5** Wolfe; *1947* **5** White; *1948* **5** Clapp; *1949* **8** Sherwood; *1950* **5** Bemis; *1951* **4** Colt; *1952* **5** Pusey; *1953* **4** Mays; *1954* **9** Lindbergh; *1955* **5** White; *1956* **6** Hamlin; *1957* **7** Kennedy; *1958* **7** Carroll, Freeman **8** Ashworth; *1959* **8** Walworth; *1960* **7** Morison; *1961* **6** Donald; *1963* **4** Edel; *1964* **4** Bate; *1965* **7** Samuels; *1966* **11** Schlesinger; *1967* **6** Kaplan; *1968* **6** Kennan; *1969* **4** Reid; *1970* **8** Williams; *1971* **8** Thompson; *1972* **4** Lash; *1973* **8** Swanberg; *1974* **8** Sheaffer; *1975* **4** Caro; *1976* **5** Lewis; *1977* **4** Mack; *1978* **4** Bate; *1979* **5** Baker; *1980* **6** Morris; *1981* **6** Massie; *1982* **7** McFeely; *1983* **5** Baker; *1984* **6** Harlan; *1985* **9** Silverman; *1986* **5** Frank; *1987* **6** Garrow; *1988* **6** Donald; *1989* **7** Ellmann; *1990* **8** de Grazia; *1991* **5** Smith **6** Naifeh; *1992* **6** Puller; *1993* **10** McCullough

Drama: *1918* **8** Williams; *1920* **6** O'Neill; *1921* **4** Gale; *1922* **6** O'Neill; *1923* **5** Davis; *1924* **6** Hughes; *1925* **6** Howard; *1926* **5** Kelly; *1927* **5** Green; *1928* **6** O'Neill; *1929* **4** Rice; *1930* **8** Connelly; *1931* **8** Glaspell; *1932* **7** Kaufman, Ryskind **8** Gershwin; *1933* **8** Anderson; *1934* **8** Kingsley; *1935* **5** Akins; *1936* **8** Sherwood; *1937* **4** Hart **7** Kaufman; *1938* **6** Wilder; *1939* **8** Sherwood; *1940* **7** Saroyan; *1941* **8** Sherwood; *1943* **6** Wilder; *1945* **5** Chase; *1946* **6** Crouse **7** Lindsay; *1948* **8** Williams; *1949* **6** Miller; *1950* **5** Logan **7** Rodgers **11** Hammerstein; *1952* **5** Kramm; *1953* **4** Inge; *1954* **7** Patrick; *1955* **8** Williams; *1956* **7** Hackett **8** Goodrich; *1957* **6** O'Neill; *1958* **6** Frings; *1959* **8** Macleish; *1960* **4** Bock **6** Abbott **7** Harnick, Weidman; *1961* **5** Mosel; *1962* **7** Burrows, Loesser; *1965* **6** Gilroy; *1967* **5** Albee; *1969* **7** Sackler; *1970* **7** Gordone; *1971* **6** Zindel; *1973* **6** Miller; *1975* **5** Albee; *1976* **5** Dante **6** Kleban **7** Bennett **8** Hamlisch, Kirkwood; *1977* **9** Cristofer; *1978* **6** Coburn; *1979* **7** Shepard; *1980* **6** Wilson; *1981* **6** Henley; *1982* **6** Fuller; *1983* **6** Norman; *1984* **5** Mamet; *1985* **6** Lapine **8** Sondheim; *1987* **6** Wilson; *1988* **4** Uhry; *1989* **11** Wasserstein; *1990* **6** Wilson; *1991* **5** Simon; *1992* **9** Schenkkan; *1993* **7** Kushner

Fiction: *1918* **5** Poole; *1919* **10** Tarkington; *1921* **7** Wharton; *1922* **10** Tarkington;

1923 **6** Cather; *1924* **6** Wilson; *1925* **6** Ferber; *1926* **5** Lewis; *1927* **9** Bromfield; *1928* **6** Wilder; *1929* **8** Peterkin; *1930* **7** LaFarge; *1931* **6** Barnes; *1932* **4** Buck; *1933* **9** Stribling; *1934* **6** Miller; *1935* **7** Johnson; *1936* **5** Davis; *1937* **8** Mitchell; *1938* **8** Marquand; *1939* **8** Rawlings; *1940* **9** Steinbeck; *1942* **7** Glasgow; *1943* **8** Sinclair; *1944* **6** Flavin; *1945* **6** Hersey; *1947* **6** Warren; *1948* **8** Michener; *1949* **7** Cozzens; *1950* **7** Guthrie; *1951* **7** Richter; *1952* **4** Wouk; *1953* **9** Hemingway; *1955* **8** Faulkner; *1956* **6** Kantor; *1958* **4** Agee; *1959* **6** Taylor; *1960* **5** Drury; *1961* Lee; *1962* **7** O'Connor; *1963* **8** Faulkner; *1965* **4** Grau; *1966* **6** Porter; *1967* **7** Malamud; *1968* **6** Styron; *1969* **7** Momaday; *1970* **8** Stafford; *1972* **7** Stegner; *1973* **5** Welty; *1975* **6** Shaara; *1976* **6** Bellow; *1978* **9** McPherson; *1979* **7** Cheever; *1980* **6** Mailer; *1981* **5** Toole; *1982* **6** Updike; *1983* **6** Walker; *1984* **7** Kennedy; *1985* **5** Lurie; *1986* **8** McMurtry; *1987* **6** Taylor; *1988* **8** Morrison; *1989* **5** Tyler; *1990* **8** Hijuelos; *1991* **6** Updike; *1992* **6** Smiley; *1993* **8** Butler

General Non-Fiction: *1962* **5** White; *1963* **7** Tuchman; *1964* **10** Hofstadter; *1965* **5** Jones; *1966* **5** Teale; *1967* **5** Davis; *1968* **6** Durant; *1969* **6** Mailer; *1970* **7** Erikson; *1971* **6** Toland; *1972* **7** Tuchman; *1973* **5** Coles **10** FitzGerald; *1974* **6** Becker; *1975* **7** Dillard; *1976* **6** Butler; *1977* **6** Warner; *1978* **5** Sagan; *1979* **6** Wilson; *1980* **10** Hofstadter; *1981* **8** Schorske; *1982* **6** Kidder; *1983* **7** Sheehan; *1984* **5** Starr; *1985* **6** Terkel; *1986* **5** Lukas **8** Lelyveld; *1987* **7** Shipler; *1988* **6** Rhodes; *1989* **7** Sheehan; *1990* **9** Maharidge **10** Williamson; *1991* **6** Wilson **10** Holldobler; *1992* **6** Yergin; *1993* **5** Will

History: *1917* **9** Jusserand; *1918* **6** Rhodes; *1920* **5** Smith; *1921* **4** Sims; *1922* **5** Adams; *1923* **6** Warren; *1924* **8** McIlwain; *1925* **6** Paxton; *1926* **8** Channing; *1927* **5** Bemis; *1928* **10** Parrington; *1929* **7** Shannon; *1930* **7** Van Tyne; *1931* **7** Schmitt; *1932* **8** Persing; *1933* **6** Turner; *1934* **4** Agar; *1935* **7** Andrews; *1936* **10** McLaughlin; *1937* **6** Brooks; *1938* **4** Buck; *1939* **4** Mott; *1940* **8** Sandburg; *1941* **6** Hansen; *1942* **5** Leech; *1943* **6** Forbes; *1944* **5** Curti; *1945* **6** Bonsai; *1946* **11** Schlesinger; *1947* *(cont.)*

Pulitzer Prize *(cont.)*
6 Baxter; *1948* 6 De Voto; *1949* 7 Nichols; *1950* 6 Larkin; *1951* 5 Buley; *1952* 7 Handlin; *1953* 11 Dangerfield; *1954* 6 Catton; *1955* 6 Horgan; *1956* 10 Hofstadter; *1957* 6 Kennan; *1958* 7 Hammond; *1959* 5 White 9 Schneider; *1960* 5 Leech; *1961* 4 Feis; *1962* 6 Gibson; *1963* 5 Green; *1964* 6 Powell; *1965* 5 Unger; *1966* 6 Miller; *1967* 9 Goetzmann; *1968* 6 Bailyn; *1969* 4 Levy; *1970* 7 Acheson; *1971* 5 Burns; *1972* 6 Degler; *1973* 6 Kammen; *1974* 8 Boorstin; *1975* 6 Malone; *1976* 6 Horgan; *1977* 6 Potter; *1978* 8 Chandler; *1979* 12 Fehrenbacher; *1980* 7 Litwack; *1981* 6 Cremin; *1982* 8 Woodward; *1983* 5 Issac; *1985* 6 McCraw; *1986* 9 McDougall; *1987* 6 Bailyn; *1988* 5 Bruce; *1989* 6 Branch 9 McPherson; *1990* 6 Karnow; *1991* 6 Ulrich; *1992* 5 Neely; *1993* 4 Wood

Music: 1943 7 Schuman; *1944* 6 Hanson; *1945* 7 Copland; *1946* 7 Sowerby; *1947* 4 Ives; *1948* 6 Piston; *1949* 7 Thomson; *1950* 7 Menotti; *1951* 5 Moore; *1952* 5 Kubik; *1954* 6 Porter; *1955* 7 Menotti; *1956* 4 Toch; *1957* 4 Joio; *1958* 6 Barber; *1959* 10 La Montaine; *1960* 6 Carter; *1961* 6 Piston; *1962* 4 Ward; *1963* 6 Barber; *1966* 7 Bassett; *1967* 8 Kirchner; *1968* 5 Crumb; *1969* 4 Husa; *1970* 8 Wuorinen; *1971* 10 Davidovsky; *1972* 8 Druckman; *1973* 6 Carter; *1974* 7 Martino 8 Sessions; *1975* 7 Argento; *1976* 5 Rorem; *1977* 7 Wernick; *1978* 8 Colgrass; *1979* 10 Schwantner; *1980* 10 Del

Tredici; *1982* 7 Babbitt 8 Sessions; *1983* 7 Zwilich; *1984* 5 Rands; *1985* 6 Albert; *1986* 5 Perle; *1987* 8 Harbison; *1988* 6 Bolcom; *1989* 8 Reynolds; *1990* 6 Powell; *1991* Ran; *1992* 8 Peterson; *1993* 5 Rouse

Poetry: 1922 8 Robinson; *1923* 6 Millay; *1924* 5 Frost; *1925* 8 Robinson; *1926* 6 Lowell; *1927* 6 Speyer; *1928* 8 Robinson; *1929* 5 Benet; *1930* 5 Aiken; *1931* 5 Frost; *1932* 6 Dillon; *1933* 8 MacLeish; *1934* 7 Hillyer; *1935* 9 Wurdemann; *1936* 6 Coffin; *1937* 5 Frost; *1938* 10 Zaturenska; *1939* 8 Fletcher; *1940* 8 Van Doren; *1941* 5 Bacon; *1942* 5 Benet; *1943* 5 Frost; *1944* 5 Benet; *1945* 7 Shapiro; *1947* 6 Lowell; *1948* 5 Auden; *1949* 7 Viereck; *1950* 6 Brooks; *1951* 8 Sandburg; *1952* 5 Moore; *1953* 8 MacLeish; *1954* 7 Roethke; *1955* 7 Stevens; *1956* 6 Bishop; *1957* 6 Wilbur; *1958* 5 Warren; *1959* 6 Kunitz; *1960* 9 Snodgrass; *1961* 8 McGinley; *1962* 5 Dugan; *1963* 8 Williams; *1964* 7 Simpson; *1965* 8 Berryman; *1966* 8 Eberhart; *1967* 6 Sexton; *1968* 5 Hecht; *1969* 5 Oppen; *1970* 6 Howard; *1971* 6 Merwin; *1972* 6 Wright; *1973* 5 Kumin; *1975* 6 Snyder; *1976* 7 Ashbery; *1977* 7 Merrill; *1978* 7 Nemerov; *1979* 6 Warren; *1980* 7 Justice; *1981* 8 Schuyler; *1982* 5 Plath; *1983* 7 Kinnell; *1984* 6 Oliver; *1985* 5 Kizer; *1986* 6 Taylor; *1987* 4 Dove; *1988* 8 Meredith; *1989* 6 Wilbur; *1990* 5 Simic; *1991* 7 Van Duyn; *1992* 4 Tate; *1993* 5 Gluck

---

out: 7 extract 8 withdraw 9 extirpate 10 deracinate
through: 7 recover, succeed, survive
up: 4 halt, stop 5 elate, trice
pullet: hen 4 fowl 5 frier 6 earock (Sc.) 7 pollard 8 poullard
pulley: 4 ring 5 fusee, fuzee, wheel 6 sheave
part: 4 arse, drum 6 rigger
Pullman: car 5 berth, coach 7 sleeper
pullulate: bud 4 teem 5 swarm 9 germinate
pulp: pap 4 marc, mash, mass, pith 5 chyme, crush, magma 6 pomace 7 bagasse
machine: 9 macerater
pulpit: 4 ambo, bema, desk 5 chair, stage 7 lectern, rostrum 8 ministry, platform, scaffold
pulpy: 6 flabby, fleshy

pulque: 5 drink 6 liquor, mescal 9 stimulant
pulsate: 4 beat, move, pant 5 pound, throb 6 quiver, strike, thrill 7 vibrate
pulsatory: 8 rhythmic 9 systaltic, throbbing
pulse: mug, pea 4 bean, beat 6 lentil, rhythm 7 battuta 8 sphygmus
pulverize: 4 bray, meal, mull, ruin 5 crush, grind, pound, smash 6 bruise 7 atomize, destroy, shatter 8 demolish, levigate 9 comminute, triturate 12 contriturate
pulverized: 4 fine 5 dusty
pulverizer: 6 pestle 7 blender, grinder 13 disintegrator
pulverulent: 5 dusty 7 crumbly, powdery 8 powdered
puma: cat 6 cougar 7 panther 9 carnivore 12 mountain lion

pumice: 4 lava 5 glass, stone 8 abrasive
powdered: 4 talc
pummel: fib, hit 4 beat, maul, slug 5 thump 6
batter, hammer
pump: gin, ram 4 jack, lift 5 drain 6 racker 7
draw off, inflate, stirrup, syringe 10 pulsometer
handle: 5 sweep, swipe
pumpernickel: 5 bread 8 rye bread
pumpkin: 4 pepo 5 clump, gourd 6 citrul,
squash
head: 4 dolt 5 dunce 7 Puritan 9 blockhead
species: 9 Cucurbita
pumpkinseed: 7 sunfish 8 bluegill, flatfish,
flounder 10 butterfish
pun: mot 4 beat, joke, quip 5 knock, pound 7
quibble 8 paragram, wordplay 9 calembour,
conundrum, witticism 11 paronomasia,
play on words
punch: ade, hit, jab 4 cuff, glog, poke, prod,
slug 5 douse, dowse, drink, negus, paste,
point, vigor 6 pierce, strike 7 mattoir 8
beverage, puncture 9 perforate
Punch: 5 clown 6 puppet 7 buffoon, journal 8
magazine 10 periodical, Pulcinella
first editor of: 5 Lemon
wife: 4 Judy
puncheon: die 4 cask, post, snap, stud, tool 5
punch, stamp 6 timber
puncher: 6 cowboy 7 cowpoke 10 cowpuncher, perforator
Punchinello: 5 clown 7 buffoon
punctilious: 4 nice 5 exact 6 formal, proper 7
careful, correct, precise 8 exacting 9 observant 10 ceremonial, scrupulous 11 ceremonious 13 conscientious
punctual: 6 on time, prompt, timely 7 careful
punctuate: 4 mark 5 break, point 6 divide 8
separate 9 emphasize 11 distinguish
punctuation mark: dot 4 dash, stop 5 colon,
comma, quote, slash 6 hyphen, period 7
bracket, virgule 8 ellipsis, full stop 9 semicolon 10 apostrophe 11 parenthesis 12
question mark 15 exclamation mark
puncture: 4 bite, hole, stab, vent 5 prick,
wound 6 pierce, riddle 7 blowout, deflate 9
penetrate, perforate 11 perforation
pundit: 4 sage 5 swami 6 nestor 7 Brahman,
scholar, teacher
pung: 4 sled 6 sleigh
pungent: hot 4 fell, keen, racy, rich, tart 5
acrid, acute, cress, minty, salty, sharp,
smart, spicy, tangy 6 biting, bitter, pepper,
snappy 7 caustic, cutting, peppery, piquant
8 aromatic, incisive, piercing, poignant,
stinging 9 trenchant 10 expressive, irritating 11 acrimonious, stimulating
pungi: bin 4 pipe 5 flute
pungled: 8 shrunken 9 shriveled

Punic: 9 faithless 10 perfidious 11 treacherous 12 Carthaginian
punish: 4 beat, fine, whip 5 abuse, mulct,
scold, slate, smite, spank, strap, wreak 6
amerce, strike 7 chasten, consume, correct,
corrige, revenge, scourge, torment, torture
8 chastise, penalize 9 castigate 10 discipline 13 excommunicate
punishing: 8 grueling
punishment: 4 loss, pain 5 peine (law), wrack
6 desert, dirdum, ferule 7 penalty, penance
9 suffering 10 correction, discipline 11 castigation 12 chastisement 13 animadversion
device: rod 4 lash 6 stocks 7 pillary
freedom from: 8 impunity
spare: 6 acquit 7 absolve 9 exculpate, exonerate
punitive: 5 penal 9 punishing 10 vindictive
Punjab: *East:* 5 India
West: 8 Pakistan
punk: bad, ill 4 fuel, poor, sick 5 conch, tough,
tramp 6 amadou, novice, rookie, tinder 8
beginner, elephant, inferior, nonsense,
strumpet 9 beginning, miserable, touchwood, worthless 10 prostitute
punt: 4 boat, kick 6 gamble
punter: 5 poler 6 bettor 7 gambler, scalper
puny: 4 weak 5 dawny, frail, petty, small 6 feeble, puisne, sickly, slight 8 droghlin, inferior 9 unskilled 13 inexperienced, insignificant
pupa: 9 chrysalis
case: 5 theca
pupil: 4 tyro 5 cadet, eleve (F.), minor, plebe,
youth 6 junior, senior 7 ecolier (F.), learner,
scholar, student 8 disciple, freshman, neophyte 9 sophomore
pupilage: 6 nonage 10 immaturity
puppet: 4 baby, doll, dupe, pawn, tool 5
dummy, image, slave 6 muppet, stooge 8
drollery 9 neuropast 10 marionette
show: 6 wajang, wayang 7 buaraku 10
shadow-play 12 Punch and Judy
puppy: dog, fop 5 twerp, whelp
purblind: 5 blind 6 bisson, myopic, obtuse 12
shortsighted
purchasable: 5 venal 7 corrupt, for sale, salable, to be had 9 available 10 marketable
purchase: buy 4 hire 5 cheap, yield 6 emptio,
income, obtain, return 7 acquire, bargain,
emption 11 acquisition
purchaser: 4 user 5 buyer 6 emptor, patron,
vendee 7 shopper 8 co-emptor, customer 9
acquereur 13 adjudicataire
purdah: 6 screen 7 curtain 9 seclusion
pure: 4 fine, good, mear, meer, mere, neat,
nice, pute, true 5 clean, clear, fresh, moral,
sheer, utter 6 candid, chaste, simple, vestal,
virgin 7 genuine, perfect, refined, sincere,

sinless, unmixed **8** absolute, complete, innocent, straight, virtuous, zaccheus (Heb.) **9** authentic, blameless, downright, elemental, faultless, guiltless, out-and-out, stainless, unalloyed, undefiled, unsullied **10** immaculate **11** crystalline, unblemished, uncorrupted, unqualified **13** unadulterated

puree: **4** mush, soup **5** paste **8** porridge

purely: all **4** just, only **5** quite **6** solely, wholly

purfle: hem **6** border **7** outline **8** decorate, ornament, trimming

purgative: **5** jalap **6** physic **8** cleanser, evacuant **9** cathartic **10** alviducous

purgatory: **5** limbo, swamp **6** misery **7** torment

purge: rid **5** clear **6** physic, purify, remove, seethe **7** cleanse, deterge, shut out **8** absterge **9** exculpate, expurgate, liquidate **11** exterminate

purification: **7** baptism **9** catharsis

purify: **5** clean, clear, purge **6** bleach, filter, refine **7** baptize, clarify, cleanse, distill, epurate **8** depurate, lustrate, renovate **9** elutriate

Puritan: **7** Pilgrim **9** Roundhead **10** Separatist
leader: **8** Cromwell

puritanical: **4** prim **6** strict **7** genteel, prudish **8** rigorous **9** blue-nosed

purl: rib **4** eddy, knit, spin **5** frill, swirl **6** murmur, purfle, stitch

purlieu: **4** area **5** haunt **6** resort **7** environ **8** district **12** neighborhood

purloin: **4** crib **5** filch, steal, swipe **6** finger, pilfer, pirate **7** cabbage **8** abstract **10** plagiarize **11** appropriate

purple: **4** plum, puce **5** grape, lilac, mauve, royal **6** blatta, emblem, maroon, ornate, risqué, tyrian, violet **7** cassius **8** amaranth, imperial, lavender **9** cathedral, elaborate **10** rhetorical
delicate: **5** mauve
dye: **7** cassius

purple copper ore: **7** bornite

Purple Heart: **5** award, medal, order

purple ragwort: **4** herb **6** jacoby

purport: **4** feck, gist, mean **5** drift, imply, sense, tenor **6** allege, effect, import, intent, object **7** bearing, meaning, purpose **9** intention, substance **11** connotation, implication

purpose: aim, end, use **4** bent, goal, main, mean, plan, sake **5** avail, point **6** design, intend, intent, motive, object, reason **7** mission **8** ambition, proposal **9** intention, objective, predesign **10** aspiration, cogitation, conception, employment, resolution **13** determination
alleged: **6** excuse **7** pretext
lacking: **9** driftless

purposive: **5** telic **6** hormic **12** teleological

purpure: **6** purple **7** mercury

purr: hum **5** noise, sound, thrum, whurl **6** murmur

purse: bag, cly **4** bung, poke **5** bulse, burse, money, pouch, prize, stake **6** pucker, wallet **7** almoner, handbag **8** coco-wort, finances, treasury **9** exchequer **10** pocketbook **12** portemonnaie

purse crab: **5** ayuyu **7** pagurid

purser: **6** bursar **7** boucher, cashier **8** pinchgut **9** paymaster, treasurer

pursue: run **4** bait, hunt, seek **5** chase, chevy, chivy, hound, stalk **6** badger, follow, gallop **7** address, persist, proceed **8** continue **9** prosecute

pursuer: **5** lover **6** chaser, hunter **8** huntress **9** plaintiff

pursuit: **4** hunt, work **5** chase, hobby, quest, scent **6** search **7** calling **10** occupation
means: **7** dragnet

pursy: fat **5** obese, puffy **7** swollen, wealthy **9** asthmatic

purulent: **4** foul, pyic **5** pussy

purvey: tax **5** cater **6** supply **7** foresee, furnish, procure, provide **10** assessment

purveyor: **6** seller, sutler **7** caterer **9** victualer

push: go, pop, por, ram **4** birr, bore, bunt, butt, ding, dush, goad, move, pelt, ping, pole, porr, poss, prod, spur, urge **5** bevel (Sc.), boost, crowd, drive, elbow, force, heave, hunch, impel, nudge, press, shove, vigor **6** clique, effort, energy, expand, extend, hustle, jostle, launch, potter, propel, thrust **7** advance, promote **8** ambition, bulldoze, increase, persuade, pressure, stimulus **10** enterprise **14** aggressiveness
along: **4** prod **5** nudge
around: **4** bait **5** bully **6** heckle
down: **7** detrude
in: **5** stove

pushy: **5** bossy **7** forward **9** assertive, officious **10** aggressive **12** presumptuous

pusillanimous: **4** tame **5** timid **6** afraid **8** cowardly **10** irresolute **12** fainthearted

puss: cat **4** face, girl, hare **5** child, mouth, woman **8** baudrons (Sc.)

pustule: **4** blob, burl **5** achor, blain **6** blotch, pimple **7** abscess, blister **8** eruption, swelling **9** carbuncle

put (see also **place**): lay, set **4** cast, push, urge, word **5** clink, drive, fixed, force, impel, place, state, throw **6** appose, attach, bestow, fasten, incite, thrust **7** deposit, express, propose **8** estimate **9** attribute, constrain, translate
away: eat **4** kill, save, stow **5** store **6** murder **7** consume
back: **6** demote **7** replace, restore
before: **5** offer **7** apposed, present
by: **4** save **5** store **6** reject **8** preserve

down: 6 humble, record 7 degrade, depress 8 suppress 9 deposited
forth: 4 show 5 exert, offer 7 extrude, propose, publish 9 circulate
forward: 7 prepose, propone
in: 4 ante 5 defer, delay, elude, plant 6 baffle, divert, insert 7 discard, enclose 8 postpone 9 frustrate
in for: 7 request
off: fob 4 doff, haft 5 defer, delay, evade, table 6 divert, remove, shelve 7 discard 8 deferred, postpone
on: act, don 5 apply, endue, indue, stage 6 employ 7 assumed, feigned, pretend 10 exaggerate
out: irk, vex 4 oust 5 anger, annoy, eject, evict, exert, exile, expel 6 banish, deport, retire 7 publish 8 displace, distress, irritate 9 ostracize 10 discompose, disconcert, expatriate, extinguish 14 discountenance
over: 4 bilk, hoax 5 cheat, defer, trick 7 deceive
together: add 4 join 5 piece, unite 6 gather, muster 7 collect 8 assemble 9 construct 10 congregate
up: can 4 post 5 build, erect
up with: 4 bear, take 5 brook, stand 6 endure 7 stomach 8 tolerate
putrefy: rot 5 decay 6 fester 7 corrupt 9 decompose 12 disintegrate
putrid: bad 4 foul 6 rotten 7 friable, noisome, vicious 8 depraved 10 malodorous, putrescent 11 displeasing 12 disagreeable
puttee: 4 spat 6 gaiter 7 legging
putter (see also **potter**): 6 dawdle, fiddle, tinker 8 golf club 10 boondoggle
putting area: 5 green
putty: 5 epoxy 6 cement
puxy: 5 swamp 8 quagmire
puzzle: cap, get 5 addle, amaze, glaik, griph, pinon, poser, rebus, stick 6 baffle, enigma, fickle, jigsaw, riddle 7 anagram, charade, confuse, foitter, griphus, mystery, mystify, nonplus, paradox, perplex 8 acrostic, bewilder, distract, entangle, intrigue 9 conundrum, dumbfound 10 difficulty, disconcert, palindrome
puzzled: 4 asea 8 confused
puzzling: 6 knotty 7 knotted 9 difficult, equivocal

pygarg: 5 addax 6 osprey
Pygmalion: *king of:* 6 Cyprus
offspring: 6 Paphos, Paphus
sister: 4 Dido
sister's husband: 8 Sichaeus
statue: 7 Galatea
victim of: 8 Sichaeus
pygmy, pigmy: elf 4 pixy, runt, tiny 5 atomy, dwarf, gnome, minim, short, small 6 midget 8 dwarfish 9 dandiprat 10 chimpanzee
pygmy musk deer: 10 chevrotain
pygostyle: 4 bone 5 vomer
pyknic: 5 solid, squat 6 stocky, sturdy 8 muscular 9 endomorph, squatness 11 endomorphic
pylon: 4 post 5 stake, tower 6 marker 7 gateway 8 monument
Pylos king: 6 Nestor
pyramid: 4 heap, pile, tomb 6 accrue 8 increase
inhabitant: 5 Khufu 6 Cheops
site: 4 Giza 7 Cholula
pyramidal: 4 huge 8 enormous, imposing
pyre: 4 bale, bier 6 suttee 7 bonfire
pyrene: pip 4 seed 5 stone
Pyrenees: *bandit:* 8 miquelet
border of: 5 Spain 6 France
chamois: 5 izard
mountain peak: 5 Aneto
people: 6 Basque
republic: 7 Andorra
resort: Pau
tunnel: 8 Canfranc
pyriform: 10 pear-shaped
pyromaniac: 7 firebug 8 arsonist
pyrosis: 9 heartburn
pyrotechnical device: 8 pinwheel
pyrotechnics: 9 fireworks
pyroxene: 6 augite 8 diopside 11 schefferite 12 hedenbergite
Pythagoras' birthplace: 5 Samos
Pythias' friend: 5 Damon
python: boa 5 snake 7 serpent
slayer: 6 Apollo
pythonic: 4 huge 8 inspired, oracular 9 monstrous
pyx, pix: box 4 case, test, vase 5 assay, capsa, carry, chest 6 casket, coffer, vessel 8 binnacle, ciborium, preserve 10 tabernacle

Q

Q: cue **5** queue

q.e.d.: **21** quod erat demonstrandum

quaalude: **4** drug **8** hypnotic, sedative

quabird: **5** heron

quack: cry **4** duck **5** faker, fraud **6** crocus **7** shammer **8** impostor **9** charlatan, pretender **10** mountebank, stimulator

quad: **4** quod, yard **5** block, court **6** campus, person **7** sibling **9** courtyard

quadra: **6** fillet, listel, plinth

quadragenarian: **8** fortyish

quadragesimal: **5** forty **6** Lenten

quadrangle: **5** court **6** campus, square **8** tetragon

quadrant: arc, bow **4** gill **6** fourth, radial **7** quarter, section **8** farthing **9** antimeter **10** instrument

quadrate: **4** suit **5** adapt, agree, ideal **6** adjust, square **7** perfect, squared **8** balanced **9** rectangle **10** correspond

quadriga: **4** cart **6** horses **7** chariot

quadrille: **5** cards, dance **9** cotillion

quadroon: **6** hybrid **7** mixture, mulatto **8** terceron

quadrumane: ape **6** monkey **7** gorilla **10** chimpanzee, four-handed

quadruped: **6** mammal **10** four-footed, four-legged

quaff: sip **5** draft, drink **6** tipple, waught

quag: **5** quake **6** quiver **8** quagmire

quagga: **7** wild ass
relative: **5** zebra

quaggy: **4** miry, soft **5** boggy **6** flabby, spongy **7** queachy **8** yielding

quagmire: bog, gog, hag **5** marsh, swamp **6** morass

quahog: **4** clam **10** little neck **11** cherry stone

quail: cow **4** bird **5** colin, cower, quake, shake **6** blench, cringe, curdle, flinch, recoil, shrink, tremor, turnix **7** Gambel, massena, tremble **8** bobwhite **9** montezuma, partridge
flock of: **4** bevy **5** covey
young: **7** cheeper **8** squealer

quail snipe: **9** dowitcher

quaint: odd **4** nice **6** crafty **7** antique, curious, strange, unusual **8** fanciful, graceful, peculiar, singular **9** whimsical

quake: **5** quail, shake, waver **6** quiver, shiver, tremor **7** shudder, tremble, vibrate **10** earthquake

Quaker: Fox **4** Penn **6** Friend **9** broadbrim

Quaker-ladies: **5** bluet **11** meadowsweet

quaking: **5** aspen, quaky **6** trepid **7** shaking **8** timorous **9** trembling, trepidity

qualification: **7** ability **8** aptitude **9** condition, endowment, knowledge, requisite **10** adaptation, capability, competence, experience, limitation **11** acquirement, designation, restriction

qualified: **4** able **5** ready **7** trained **8** eligible, licensed

qualify: fit **5** abate, adapt, equip, limit **6** enable, modify, soften, temper **7** ascribe, assuage, entitle, prepare **8** diminish, mitigate, moderate, restrain, restrict **9** predicate **10** habilitate **12** characterize

quality: **4** cost, kind, rank, rate, sort, thew, tone **5** class, grade, power, quale, taste, trait, worth **6** aspect, nature, status, strain, virtue **7** caliber, calibre, element, feature, stature **8** capacity, nobility, property **9** attribute, character **10** excellence **11** aristocracy, superiority
of tone: **6** timbre **9** resonance

qualm: **4** drow, fear, pall **5** doubt, spasm **6** attack, nausea, plight, puzzle, regret, twinge **7** anxiety, scruple **8** sickness **9** faintness, misgiving **10** hesitation, perplexity **11** compunction, uncertainty **12** apprehension

quandary: fix, jam **4** pass **6** pickle, plight, scrape **7** dilemma, nonplus **11** predicament **12** bewilderment

quantity (see also **amount**): ace, any, bit, jag, jot, lot, sea, sum **4** atom, body, bulk, dash, dose, dram, drop, feck, iota, lick, load, lots, many, mass, mort, much, pile, raff, raft, size, slew, some, unit **5** batch, bunch, grist, hoard, scads, stack, store **6** amount, capful, degree, extent, figure, hirsel, morsel, number, volume, weight **7** average, driblet, handful, modicum, portion, slather **9** allowance
excessive: **4** glut **5** flood, spate **10** inundation
full: **10** complement
irrational: **4** surd
prescribed: **4** dose **6** dosage
small: **4** dram, drop, gill, iota **5** scrap, shred **7** dribble, smidgen
without direction: **6** scalar

quantum: 4 unit 6 amount, photon 7 portion 8 quantity 9 aggregate

quarantine: ban 7 exclude, isolate 8 restrain, sanction 9 interdict, segregate

quaranty: 5 court

quarantene: 4 rood 7 furlong

quark: caw 5 croak, quawk 8 particle

quarl, quarle: 4 tile 5 brick

quarrel: row 4 feud, fuss, spat, tiff 5 arrow, brawl, broil, cavil, flite, flyte, scene, scrap, set to 6 affray, barney, bicker, breach, fracas, hassle, jangle, ruckus, strife 7 contend, dispute, faction, rhubarb, wrangle 8 argument, disagree, squabble 9 upscuddle 10 contention 11 altercation 12 disagreement

quarrelsome: 7 hostile, scrappy 8 brawling, choleric, petulant 9 bellicose, irascible, irritable, litigious 10 discordant, pugnacious 11 belligerent, contentious 12 disputatious

quarry: pit 4 game, mine, prey 6 object, ravine, victim

quart: 6 fourth 7 measure
  four: 6 gallon
  metric: 5 liter, litre
  one-eighth: 4 gill
  two: 6 flagon

quartan: 5 fever 7 malaria

quarter: aft 4 area, coin, digs 5 house, lodge, mercy, put up, tract 6 bestow, billet, canton, divide, fourth, harbor, region, supply 7 furnish, harbour, housing, shelter 8 clemency, district, division 9 direction, dismember 11 forbearance

quarters: 4 camp, room 7 billets, lodging, shelter 8 barracks, chambers 9 dormitory
  sleeping: 9 dormitory
  winter: den 10 hibernacle
  women's: 5 harem

quarter note: 8 crotchet

quartz: 4 onyx, sand, sard 5 agate, flint, prase, silex, topaz 6 jasper, silica 7 citrine, crystal, mineral, rubasse, sinople 8 amethyst, sardonyx 9 carnelian 10 calchedony

quartzite: 9 itabarite, sandstone

quash: 4 cass, drop, void 5 abate, annul, crush, quell 6 cancel, subdue 7 abolish, destroy, shatter 8 abrogate, suppress 9 overthrow

Quasimodo: 9 hunchback
  creator: 4 Hugo
  occupation: 10 bell ringer
  rescued: 9 Esmeralda
  residence: 9 Notre Dame

quaternion: 6 tetrad 7 quartet 8 quatrain

quaver: 5 shake, trill, waver 6 falter, quiver 7 tremble, tremolo, vibrate 9 vacillate, vibration

quawk: caw 5 heron 6 squall 7 screech

quay: key 4 bund, dock, mole, pier, wall 5 levee, wharf 7 landing 10 embankment

quean: 4 jade 5 hussy, wench 6 harlot 10 prostitute

queasy: 4 sick 5 timid 8 delicate, doubtful, qualmish, ticklish, troubled 9 hazardous, nauseated, squeamish, uncertain, unsettled 10 fastidious 11 embarrassed 13 uncomfortable

Quebec: *capital:* 10 Quebec City
  city: 4 Hull 5 Laval 6 Quebec, Verdun 8 Gatineau, Montreal 9 Longuevil
  provincial flower: 4 lily

quebrada: gap 5 brook, creek, gorge 6 ravine, stream 7 fissure 8 brooklet

Quechua: 4 Inca 6 Indian

queen: ant, bee 4 card, fers, rani (Ind.) 5 ranee (Ind.), reina (Sp.), reine (F.), ruler 6 regina 7 czarina, empress, monarch 9 sovereign 10 chess piece
  it: 8 domineer 9 put on airs, tyrannize
  widowed: 7 dowager

Queen Anne's lace: 10 wild carrot

Queen City: 10 Cincinnati

queenly: 5 noble, regal, royal 7 haughty, reginal 8 majestic

queen of fairies: Mab, Pam, Una 7 Argante, Titania 8 Gloriana

queen of gods: 4 Hera, Juno, Sati

Queen of Heaven: 4 Hera, Isis, Mary, moon 6 Ishtar 7 Astarte 9 Ashtoreth

Queen of Isles: 6 Albion

Queen of Sheba: 6 Balkis

queen of spades: 5 basta

Queen of the Adriatic: 6 Venice

Queen of Thebes: 5 Dirce

Queen of the East: 7 Antioch, Zenobia

queen of the underworld: Hel 4 Hela 10 Persephone

queen's arm: 6 musket

queen's-delight: oil 4 herb 9 perennial, queenroot

queen's-flower: 6 myrtle 9 bloodwood

queer: odd, rum 4 harm, sham 5 drunk, faint, funny, giddy, rally, spoil, weird 6 banter, insane 7 bizarre, curious, disrupt, erratic, oddball, strange, touched, unusual 8 abnormal, doubtful, fanciful, obsessed, peculiar, qualmish, singular, spurious 9 dishonest, eccentric, fantastic, squeamish 10 jeopardize, outlandish, suspicious 11 counterfeit, intoxicated

queest: 8 ringdove

queet: 4 coot

quell: end 4 calm, cool, dash, kill, quay, sate 5 allay, check, crush, quash, quiet, still 6 obtund, pacify, reduce, soothe, spring, stanch, stifle, subdue 7 assuage, destroy, put down, repress, satisfy **8** fountain, overcome, suppress **9** overpower, overwhelm, subjugate **10** extinguish

quelque-chose: **6** trifle

quench: **4** cool **5** allay, douse, quell, quiet, slake **6** put out, subdue **7** satisfy **8** mitigate **10** extinguish

quenelle: **8** dumpling, meatball **9** forcemeat

quercus: oak **4** tree **9** evergreen

querent: **8** inquirer **9** plaintiff **11** complainant

querist: **8** inquirer **10** questioner

quern: **4** mill **7** grinder **9** millstone

querulous: **6** cranky **7** fretful, peevish, whining **9** irritable, plaintive **11** complaining

query: ask **5** doubt **6** demand **7** examine, inquire, inquiry **8** question **9** challenge **11** interrogate, uncertainty

quest: ask, bay **4** hunt, seek **6** search **7** examine, inquest, journey, pursuit, seeking **9** adventure **10** enterprise, expedition **13** investigation

question: ask **4** crux, pump, quiz **5** demur, doubt, grill, poser, query, scout, targe (Sc.) **6** appose, cruces (pl.), debate, demand, quaere, riddle, shrive **7** dispute, inquire, inquiry, problem, scruple, stumper **9** catechise, catechize, challenge, interview **10** discussion **11** examination, interrogate, proposition **12** interpellate **13** interrogation
   denoting: **15** interrogational

question mark: **7** erotema, eroteme

questionable: **4** moot **7** dubious, suspect **9** ambiguous, equivocal, uncertain **10** improbable, suspicious, unreliable

questionnaire: **4** form, poll **7** canvass

quetzal: **4** bird, coin **5** dance **6** trogon

queue: cue **4** line **5** braid, plait **7** pigtail

quiaquia: **4** scad **9** cigarfish

quibble: **4** carp **5** cavil, cheat, dodge, evade, hedge **6** bicker **7** evasion, shuffle **8** pettifog, sidestep **9** find fault **10** equivocate, split hairs

quica: **7** opossum

quick: apt, yap **4** deft, fast, flit, lish, live, spry, vite (F.), yare **5** acute, agile, alert, alive, apace, brisk, fiery, fleet, hasty, heart, rapid, ready, sharp, smart, swift, tosto (It.), yeder **6** abrupt, active, bright, lively, living, moving, nimble, prompt, speedy, sudden, volant **7** intense **8** animated, dextrous, shifting, vigorous **9** dexterous, impatient, sensitive, sprightly **10** celeritous, perceptive **11** expeditious

quick bread: **6** scones **7** muffins, popover **8** biscuits **9** cornbread

quicken: **4** move, stir, whet **5** hurry, speed **6** arouse, excite, hasten, incite, revive, vivify **7** animate, enliven, provoke, refresh, sharpen **8** expedite, inspirit **9** reanimate, stimulate **10** accelerate **11** resuscitate **12** reinvigorate

quicker than: ere **6** before

quicklime: **5** rusma

quickly: **4** fast, rath, soon, vite (F.) **5** alive, apace **6** belive, hourly, presto, pronto **7** rapidly **8** promptly, speedily

quickness: **5** speed **6** acumen **7** acidity **8** celerity, dispatch, progress, pungency, rapidity, sagacity, velocity **9** acuteness, swiftness **10** expedition

quicksand: **4** flow, syrt, trap **6** danger, syrtis

quickset: **5** hedge **7** thicket **8** hawthorn

quicksilver: **7** mercury **9** heautarit

quid: cud, fid **4** chaw, chew **5** pound, trade **6** barter, guinea, return **8** exchange, quiddity

quidnunc: **5** frump, snoop **6** gossip, tatler **8** busybody

quiescent: **4** calm **5** quiet, still **6** latent, static **7** dormant, resting **8** inactive, sleeping

quid pro quo: **9** tit-for-tat **10** equivalent

quiet: coy, pet **4** calm, cosh, dead, ease, fair, hush, lull, meek, mild, mute, rest, tame **5** allay, downy, inert, peace, privy, sober, still, tasty **6** gentle, hushed, merely, modest, placid, repose, secret, sedate, serene, settle, silent, smooth, soothe, static, stilly **7** appease, compose, halcyon, restful, retired, silence, subdued **8** composed, decorous, inactive, peaceful, secluded, taciturn, tasteful, tranquil **9** alleviate, contented, noiseless, peaceable, placidity, quiescent, reposeful, soundless, unruffled **10** motionless, silentness, unmolested

quietus: **5** death **6** repose **8** mittimus **11** acquittance

quiff: **4** girl, puff **5** whiff **8** forelock

quill: cop, pen **5** remex, spina **6** bobbin, pinion **7** remiges (pl.), spindle
   porcupine: pen **5** spine

quilt: pad, sew **4** gulp **5** eider **6** caddow, pallet, stitch **7** blanket, comfort, swallow **8** coverlet **9** bedspread, comforter, eiderdown, patchwork

quink: **5** brant

quinoa: **5** seeds **7** pigweed

quintuplets: **6** Dionne **7** Fischer

quip: mot, pun **4** gibe, jest, joke **5** sally, taunt **6** bon mot, saying **7** quibble

quire: **4** fold **5** choir, paper

quirk: **4** bend, kink, quip, turn **5** clock, crook, knack, sally, trait, twist **6** groove, strike **7** caprice, evasion **8** flourish **9** deviation, mannerism **10** subterfuge **11** peculiarity **12** eccentricity

quirquincho: **5** pichi **6** peludo **9** armadillo

quirt: 4 whip 5 romal

quisling: rat 7 traitor 8 turncoat 12 collaborator

quit: rid 4 free, stop 5 avoid, cease, clear, forgo, leave, repay 6 acquit, depart, desist, forego, resign, vacate 7 abandon, forsake, release, relieve 8 abdicate, absolved, liberate, renounce 9 surrender

quitclaim: 5 grant 7 release 12 convey by deed

quite: all 4 very, well 5 stark, truly 6 really, wholly 7 totally, utterly 8 entirely 10 altogether, completely, positively

quite so: 7 exactly 9 precisely

quittance: 5 repay 6 return 8 requital 9 discharge, repayment 10 recompense, reparation

quitter: 4 seal, slag 5 piker 6 coward 7 dropout, shirker

quiver: 4 beat, case, quag, tirl (Sc.) 5 bever, quake, quick, shake, thirl (Sc.), throb, trill 6 active, arrows, bicker, cocker, dindle, lively, nimble, quaver, sheath, shiver, tremor 7 frisson, pulsate, tremble, vibrate 8 flichter 9 palpitate, vibration

quivering: 5 aspen 6 ashake, didder 7 aquiver 8 blubbery 9 tremulous

quixotic: mad 4 rash 6 unreal 7 utopian 9 fantastic, imaginary, visionary 10 chivalrous, idealistic 11 impractical, in the clouds

quiz: ask 4 exam, hiss, hoax, jest, joke, mock, test, whiz 5 chaff, probe 7 examine 8 instruct, question, ridicule 11 examination, questioning

quizzical: odd 7 amusing, comical, curious, probing, teasing 9 bantering, eccentric, perplexed 11 incredulous

quizzing glass: 7 monocle

quod: jug 4 jail 8 imprison

quodlibet: 6 debate, medley 8 fantasia, question, subtlety 11 composition

quod vide: 8 which see

quoin: 4 coin 5 angle, wedge 6 corner 8 keystone, voussoir

quoit: 4 disc, ring 5 throw 6 discus 8 cromlech
mark aimed at: tee
pin: hob

quomodo: 5 means 6 manner

quondam: 4 once 6 former 7 onetime 8 sometime

quonset hut: 6 prefab
British type: 6 Nissen

quorum: 5 group 7 council 8 majority

quota: 4 part 5 share 6 divide, ration 8 dividend 9 apportion 10 contingent

quote: 4 cite, cote, name, note 5 motto, price, refer 6 adduce, allege, allude, notice, repeat, select 7 excerpt, extract, passage 8 citation 9 quotation

quoth: 4 said 5 spoke

quotidian: 5 daily 7 trivial 8 everyday, ordinary 9 recurring 11 commonplace

quotient: 5 ratio 6 result 8 fraction

quotity: 5 group 10 collection

R

R: rho **6** letter

Ra, Re: Shu, Sun, Tem, Tum **4** Aten **5** Horus **7** Chepera, Khepera, Sokaris **9** Harmachis
bull form: **5** Bacis
child: Mat, Shu **4** Maat **5** Athor
parent: Geb, Keb, Nut, Seb **5** Neith
wife: **4** Mout

raad: **7** catfish

rab: **6** beater

rabato, rebato: **4** ruff **6** collar

rabban: **6** master **7** teacher

rabbet: **4** plow **5** check **6** groove, plough, recess **7** channel **9** fillister

rabbi: **4** lord **5** amora **6** master, mentor, rabbin **7** amoraim, tannaim, teacher **8** sabaraim, saboraim **9** clergyman
assistant: **6** cantor
school: **7** yeshiva **8** yeshibah, yeshivah **9** yeshiboth (pl.)
wife: **9** rebbetzin

rabbit: bun, doe **4** buck, cony, hare, tyro **5** bunny, capon, coney, lapin (F.) **6** coward, novice, rodent, tapeti
fictional: **4** Brer **5** Mopsy, Peter, Roger **6** Harvey **9** Bugs Bunny
fur: **4** cony, rack, scut **5** coney, lapin
genus: **5** lepus
relative: **4** pika
shelter: **5** hutch **6** burrow, warren **7** clapper
tail: fud (Sc.) **4** scut
young: **4** rack **6** gazabo, gazebo **7** starter

rabbit-ear: **6** aerial, cactus **7** antenna **8** toadflax

rabbit fever: **9** tularemia

rabbitfish: **8** chimaera

rabbit flower: **8** foxglove, toadflax

rabbit-foot: **5** charm **8** talisman

rabbit-meat: **5** lapin **9** archangel

rabbitmouth: **10** harelipped, snapdragon

rabbit tobacco: **10** balsamweed

rabbitry: **5** hutch **6** warren

rabbit's-root: **12** sarsaparilla

rabbit vine: **9** groundnut

rabble: mob **4** herd, raff, rout, scum **5** crowd, horde **6** polloi, ragtag **7** bobtail **8** canaglia, canaille, riffraff **9** confusion, hoi polloi, tag and rag **10** clamjamfry, hubble-shoo, hubble-show **11** commonality, rank and file

rabble-rouser: **6** ragtag **8** agitator **9** demagogue

Rabelaisian: **5** bawdy **6** earthy

rabid: mad **6** raging **7** extreme, frantic, furious, violent, zealous **8** demented, deranged, frenzied, virulent **9** fanatical **12** enthusiastic

rabies: **5** lyssa, lytta **7** madness **11** hydrophobia

raccoon: **5** guara, tejon **6** mapach **7** mapache **9** crabeater
related animal: **5** coati, panda **8** kinkajou, ringtail

race: cut, ilk, run **4** dash, gest, herd, kind, lane, line, root, rush, slit, sort, stem, stud, type **5** birth, blood, breed, brood, caste, chevy, chivy, class, corso, creek, flesh, geste, hurry, relay, speed, stock, track, tribe **6** arroyo, bicker, broose, chivvy, course, family, groove, hasten, hurdle, nation, people, slalom, sprint, stirps, strain **7** bombast, channel, contend, contest, dynasty, lineage, regatta, running, scamper, scratch, species **8** marathon **9** holethnos **10** free for all, generation, passageway **11** competition, descendants, nationality, watercourse
human: man **6** mortal **7** mankind
murder: **8** genocide
pert. to: **6** ethnic
science: **9** athletics, ethnology
series: **7** regatta
starting line: **7** scratch

raceabout: **5** sloop **8** roadster, sailboat

race board: **9** gangplank

race colors: **5** silks

racecourse: **4** heat, oval, ring, turf **5** track **6** career, circus, course **8** gymkhana **10** hippodrome
marker: **4** meta **5** pylon

racehorse: **4** pace **6** maiden, mantis, mudder, plater **7** sleeper, trotter **12** thoroughbred

racer: **4** crab **5** miler, snake **6** runner **7** courser, serpent **8** sprinter **9** turntable **10** blacksnake

racetrack: **5** Ascot **7** Belmont, Hialeah, Pimlico **8** Saratoga **9** Newmarket **10** Epsom Downs, Gulf Stream, Santa Anita

raceway: **5** canal **7** channel, fishway **8** millrace

Rachel: *children:* **6** Joseph **8** Benjamin
father: **5** Laban
husband: **5** Jacob

sister: 4 Leah
rachis: 4 stem 5 spine 7 spindle 8 backbone
rachitis: 7 rickets
racist: 5 bigot 9 sectarian 10 prejudiced
rack: bar, fly, gin, jib 4 bink, crib, gait, pace, path, scud, skin, tree 5 airer, brake, creel, flake, horse, stand, touse, trace, track, vapor 6 course, cratch, gantry, harass, strain, wrench 7 afflict, agonize, grating, oppress, pathway, stretch, torment, torture, vestige 9 framework, persecute 10 excruciate, foresaddle
up: 4 gain 5 score 7 achieve 10 accomplish
racket: bat, din 4 shoe 5 babel, bandy, dodge, noise, trick, work 6 bustle, clamor, crosse, hubbub, outcry, scheme, strike, tumult, uproar 7 clangor, clatter, pattern, revelry 8 business, snowshoe 10 battledore, turbulence 11 merrymaking, pandemonium
rackle: 5 clank 6 rattle 7 clatter 8 reckless 9 impetuous 10 headstrong
raconteur: 8 narrator 11 storyteller
racy: 5 brisk, fiery, fresh, smart, spicy, swift 6 lively, risque 7 piquant, pungent, zestful 8 indecent, spirited, stirring, vigorous 10 suggestive
rad: 5 eager, quick, ready 6 afraid, elated 7 radical
Radames' love: 4 Aida
radar: 5 loran 7 Doppler
image: 4 blip
screen: 5 scope
raddle: rod 4 beat 5 color, ocher, twist 6 branch, cudgel, thrash 9 separator 10 interweave
radial: ray 8 quadrant
radiance: 4 beam, glow 5 glare, gleam, glory, light, nitor, sheen, shine 6 luster 7 glitter, glowing, shining 8 lambency, splendor 9 brilliant 10 brightness, brilliancy, effulgence, refulgence
radiant: 5 aglow 6 bright 7 auroral, beaming, glowing, lambent, shining 8 luminous, lustrous 11 resplendent
radiate: 4 beam, emit 5 shine 6 spread 7 diffuse, emanate, project 9 coruscate 10 illuminate
radiating: 6 radial 8 stellate 11 centrifugal
radiation detector: 6 geiger
radiator: 6 heater
radical: red 4 left, root, surd 5 basal, basic, rebel, ultra 7 capital, drastic, extreme, forward, leftist, liberal, organic, support 8 cardinal, complete 9 extremist, fanatical 10 foundation, iconoclast 11 fundamental
chemical: ion 4 amyl, aryl 6 acetyl, adenyl, adipyl 7 nitrate, nitrite, sulfate, tartryl 8 aluminyl
political: 9 anarchist, extremist 13 revolutionary

radicate: fix 4 root 5 plant 9 establish
radicle: 7 rootlet 9 hypocotyl
radio: set 8 portable, wireless 9 broadcast, radiogram 10 transistor 12 walkie-talkie
detector: 5 radar
frequency: 5 audio
interference: 6 static
operator: ham 6 sparks 11 broadcaster
part: 5 diode 8 detector, selector
wave: 5 micro, short
radish: 5 radis (F.) 7 cadlock 9 crossweed
radium: *discoverer:* 5 Curie
emanation: 5 niton, radon
source: 7 uranite, uranium 11 pitchblende
radius: ken 5 orbit, range, spoke, sweep 6 circle, extent, length
radix: 4 root 6 etymon 7 radical
raffish: low 4 wild 5 cheap 6 flashy, frowsy, rakish, tawdry 7 unkempt 9 worthless 11 disgraceful 12 disreputable
raffle: 4 raff 6 chance, jumble, rabble, refuse, tangle 7 drawing, lottery, rubbish, serrate
raft: cow, lot, mat 4 crib, floe, heap, moki, raff, slew, spar 5 balsa, barge, float 6 dinghy, jangar 9 catamaran, transport 10 collection
part: 5 brail
rider: 8 Huck Finn
raft duck: 5 scaup 7 redhead 8 bluebill
rafter: 4 balk, beam, firm, viga 6 timber 7 carline, chevron
rag: jag, kid, rib 4 mock, rail, rate, tune 5 annoy, dance, scold, scrap, shred, tease 6 banter, harass, rumpus, tatter, uproar 7 quarrel, remnant, wrangle 9 newspaper
ragamuffin: bum 4 hobo, waif 5 tramp 6 loafer, orphan 9 scarecrow
rage: fad, ire 4 beef, fret, fume, funk, fury, heat, rant, rave, tear 5 anger, chafe, craze, furor, mania, storm, wrath 6 choler, fervor, frenzy, furore, temper 7 amentia, bluster, bombast, emotion, fashion, fervour, passion, thunder 8 acerbity, acrimony, insanity, violence 9 vehemence 10 enthusiasm
ragged: 4 worn 5 harsh, rough, seedy 6 jagged, shabby, shaggy, uneven 7 shreddy, unkempt, worn out 8 strident, tattered 9 defective, dissonant, imperfect, irregular 10 straggling, threadbare 11 dilapidated 14 tatterdemalion
ragged jacket: 4 seal
ragged lady: 5 guara 11 love-in-a-mist
ragged sailor: 10 bluebottle, cornflower
raggedy doll: Ann 4 Andy, Anne
raggle-taggle: 6 motley, ragtag
raging: 4 grim, wild 5 rabid 6 fierce 7 fervent, furious, violent 8 furibund 9 ferocious
raglan: 6 sleeve 8 overcoat
ragout: 4 hash, stew 5 salmi 6 salmis 7 goulash, haricot, terrine 8 salpicon 10 capilotade 11 gallimaufry

ragpicker: 6 bunter 10 chiffonier 11 chiffonnier (F.)

rags: 4 duds 6 shreds 7 clothes, tatters

ragwort: 5 plant 8 ambrosia 9 groundsel 10 butterweed

rah: 5 cheer 6 hurrah

raid: 4 bust, tala 5 foray, sally 6 attack, creach (Sc.), creagh (Sc.), forage, harass, inroad, invade, maraud, piracy, sortie 7 assault, chappow, despoil, hership, pillage 8 invasion 9 cavalcade, chevachie, incursion, onslaught, roadstead

rail: bar, jaw 4 coot, flow, gush, jest, rant, rate, slat, sora 5 abuse, array, chide, cloak, crake, dress, guard, heron, plank, scoff, scold, soree, track 6 banter, berate, callet, mudhen, revile, septum 7 arrange, bidcock, bilcock, clapper, clocker, garment, inveigh 8 decorate, footrest, Rallidae (pl.), reproach 9 corncrake, gallinule, spectator
genus of: 4 sora 6 rallus

railing: bar 5 fence 7 barrier, parapet 8 balconet, banister, espalier, rabulous 9 bannister, guardrail 10 balconette, balustrade 12 vituperation

raillery: 4 gaff, jest, play 5 chaff, irony, sport 6 banter, blague, satire 8 badinage, ridicule 10 persiflage

railroad: 4 herd, line, push, rush 5 hurry, track 7 railway (Br.) 8 ceinture, commuter, elevated, monorail 9 transport 11 underground
branch: 4 spur, stub 6 feeder
bridge: 7 trestle, viaduct
car: bar 4 flat, tank 5 coach, diner 6 boxcar, dining, parlor 7 caboose, coal-car, parlour, Pullman, sleeper
center: 4 yard 7 station 8 terminal, terminus 10 roundhouse
cross rail: tie 4 frog 8 crosstie
signal: 5 fusee 9 semaphore
station: 4 gare (F.) 5 depot
switch: 4 frog
tie: 6 timber 7 sleeper
worker: 6 boomer, porter 7 fireman 8 brakeman, engineer, strapper 9 conductor, signalman 11 gandy dancer

railway: 5 train 6 subway 8 elevated, jackstay, monorail 9 funicular

rain: dag, fog 4 mist, pour 5 blizz, blout, misle, plash, spate, storm 6 deluge, mizzle, serein, shower 7 drizzle 8 downpour, sprinkle 10 cloudburst 13 precipitation
check: 4 stub 12 postponement
fine: 4 mist 6 serein 7 drizzle
god: 8 Parjanya
icy: 4 hail, snow 5 sleet
pert. to: 7 pluvial

rain bird: 6 plover 7 tomfool

rainbow: arc, bow 4 iris

goddess: 4 Iris
measuring device: 12 spectrometer
pert. to: 6 iridal

rainbow chaser: 8 idealist 9 visionary 11 doctrinaire

rain cloud: 5 nimbi (pl.) 6 nimbus

raincoat: mac 4 mino 6 poncho, ulster 7 slicker 10 mackintosh, trenchcoat

rainfall: *pert. to:* 6 hyetal

rain forest: 5 selva

rainfowl: 6 cuckoo 10 woodpecker 11 channelbill

rain gauge: 8 udometer 10 hyetometer 11 pluviograph, pluviometer 15 hyetometrograph

rain glass: 9 barometer

rain leader: 9 downspout

rainspout: 4 rone (Sc.) 8 gargoyle

rain tree: 5 saman, zaman 6 zamang 8 genisaro 9 monkeypod

rainy: wet 4 damp 5 misty, moist 6 drippy 7 drizzly, flooded, pouring, showery 8 cluttery 9 drizzling
season: 7 monsoon

raise: end 4 buoy, grow, hain, heft, hike, levy, lift, rear, rise, stir 5 arear, boost, breed, build, crane, dight, elate, erect, exalt, hance, heave, heeze, hoist, horse, rouse, set-up, start, trice 6 arouse, ascend, assume, awaken, cantle, create, emboss, excite, gather, incite, leaven, muster, obtain, remove, uplift 7 address, advance, bring up, chevise, collect, elevate, enhance, ennoble, lighten, present, procure, produce, promote 8 addition, heighten, increase 9 cultivate, establish, institute, intensify, originate, propagate, resurrect 10 aggrandize

raised: 4 grew, hove 6 arrect, enleve (F.), reared, tended 8 elevated 10 cultivated

raisin: 5 lexia, zibeb 7 currant, sultana 8 muscatel

raison d'être: 14 reason for being

raiyat: See **ryot**

raj: 4 rule 5 reign 11 sovereignty

rajah: 4 king 5 chief, ruler 6 prince 9 dignitary
wife: 4 rani 5 ranee

Rajmahal creeper: 4 jiti, vine

rake: gad, rue, rut 4 comb, path, raff, roue, rove, trip, wolf 5 claut, glean, scour, track 6 gather, groove 7 collect, gleaner, scratch 8 enfilade, rakehell 9 debauchee 11 inclination
with gunfire: 8 enfilade

rakehell: 4 wild 7 immoral 9 debauched, debauchee, dissolute, libertine 10 profligate

rake-off: 4 skim, take 6 profit, rebate 10 commission, percentage

rakish: 4 lewd, pert 7 roguish 9 dissolute

rale: 6 rattle

rally: 4 drag, mock, stir 5 chaff, noise, rouse 6 arouse, attack, banter, deride, gather, revive 7 recover, restore, reunite 8 assemble, mobilize, raillery, ridicule 10 recuperate, strengthen 11 concentrate

rallying cry: 5 motto 6 slogan 9 battle cry

ram: hit, pun, tup, wad 4 buck, butt, cram, tamp, teap 5 Aries, crash, sheep, stuff 6 batter, beetle, chaser, rancid, strike, thrust, wether 7 collide, plunger 8 bulldoze
  cat: tom 4 male

Rama: *bride:* Sita
  enemy: 6 Ravana
  god: 6 Vishnu
  poem: 8 Ramayana 11 Mahabharata
  poet: 8 Tulsi Das

ramage: 4 wild 5 bough, rough 6 unruly 7 untamed 8 branches, frenzied, wildness

ramage hawk: 8 brancher

ramate: 8 branched

ramble: gad 4 roam, rove, walk 5 jaunt, prowl, range 6 sprawl, stroll, travel, wander 7 digress, meander, saunter 8 straggle 9 excursion

rambling: 7 aimless, cursory, devious 9 desultory, scattered, wandering 10 circuitous, discursive 11 peripatetic 12 disconnected

rambunctious: 4 wild 5 rough 6 unruly 9 turbulent 10 boisterous, disorderly, rampageous 12 obstreperous

ramekin: pan 4 dish 9 casserole

ramentum: 5 palea, palet 6 paleae (pl.), scales 7 shaving 8 particle

ramie, ramee: 4 hemp, rhea 5 fiber 6 ortiga 10 China grass
  family: 6 nettle

ramification: arm 4 rama, rami (pl.) 5 ramus 6 branch, spread 8 division, offshoot 9 branching 10 divergence 11 consequence

rammish: 4 lewd, rank 7 violent

Ramona author: 7 Jackson

ramose: 7 cladose 8 branched 9 branching

ramp: rob 4 bank, rage, walk 5 apron, crawl, creep, slope, storm 6 dupery, unruly 7 incline, swindle 8 gradient, platform 9 helicline 10 cuckoopint

rampage: 4 riot 5 binge, spree, storm 6 uproar 7 turmoil

rampant: 4 rife 6 fierce 7 violent 9 excessive, unchecked 10 immoderate, prevailing, rampageous, widespread 11 extravagant, flourishing, threatening

rampart: 4 wall 5 agger, mound, redan 6 vallum 7 barrier, bastion, bulwark, parapet, ravelin 10 breastwork, embankment
  part: 4 spur

ramper: 7 lamprey

rampire: dam 7 fortify, rampart 10 embankment, strengthen

Ramses' goddess: 4 Anta

ramshackle: 4 rude 5 loose, shaky 7 rickety 10 disorderly, dissipated, tumbledown

ramus: 6 branch 10 branchlike

rancel: 6 search 7 ransack

ranch: 4 casa, farm, tear 5 finca, pluck 7 acreage, scratch 8 estancia, hacienda 9 estacion
  worker: 4 hand 5 owner 6 cowboy, farmer, gaucho 7 cowpoke, rancher 8 herdsman, ranchero (Sp.), ranchman

rancid: 4 rank, sour 5 musty, stale 6 frowsy, putrid 7 spoiled 8 stinking 9 obnoxious, offensive, repulsive 10 malodorous, unpleasant

rancor, rancour: ire 4 gall, hate 5 spite 6 enmity, grudge, hatred, malice 8 rankling 9 animosity, antipathy, hostility, virulence 10 bitterness

randan: row 4 boat 5 spree 6 uproar 7 rampage

random: 5 loose, stray 6 casual, chance 7 aimless 9 desultory, haphazard, hit-or-miss 10 accidental, fortuitous 11 purposeless

randy: 4 lewd, wild 5 crude, revel, shrew 6 beggar, coarse, frolic, virago, vulgar 7 canvass 8 carousal 9 festivity 10 disorderly, licentious 12 unmanageable

range: ken, row 4 ally, area, farm, line, rank, roam, rove 5 align, aline, ambit, blank, class, field, gamut, orbit, order, reach, ridge, scope, space, stove, stray, sweep 6 extent, ramble, series, sphere, stroll, tether, wander 7 arrange, compass, explore, habitat, saunter 8 classify, distance 9 cookstove, grassland 11 systematize

range-finder: 6 stadia 9 mekometer, telemeter 10 trekometer

ranger: 4 seal 5 rover, sieve 6 keeper, warden 8 commando, wanderer

rangy: 4 lean, tall, thin 5 lanky, reedy, weedy 8 gangling, spacious

rank: row 4 army, file, foul, line, rate, sort, tier 5 array, caste, cense, class, fetid, frank, genus, grade, gross, order, proud, range, space, utter 6 barony, coarse, degree, estate, gentry, mighty, rancid, rating, series, status, strong 7 caliber, calibre, calling, compeer, copious, corrupt, dignity, extreme, fertile, froward, glaring, haughty, noisome, obscene, overfed, peerage, precede, quality, rammish, rampant, station, stratum, swollen, violent 8 absolute, abundant, classify, division, eminence, estimate, flagrant, gentrice, headlong, indecent, palpable, position, powerful, priority, vigorous 9 downright, egregious, formation, gradation, offensive, overgrown, plentiful **10** malodorous **11** arrangement, distinction

deprive of: **4** bust **5** break **6** depose **7** cashier

mark of: **6** stripe

military: NCO, PFC **5** major **6** ensign **7** admiral, captain, colonel, general, private **8** banneret, corporal, sergeant **9** commander **10** lieutenant

rank and file: **6** member, plebes **9** common man **11** commonality

rankle: irk, vex **4** fret, gall **6** fester, obsess, plague **7** inflame **8** irritate, ulcerate

rann: **5** verse **6** stanza, strain

ransack: **4** loot, rake, sack **5** rifle, steal **6** search **7** pillage, rummage

ransom: buy, fee **5** atone, price **6** redeem, rescue **7** deliver, expiate, release **8** liberate, retrieve

money: **10** redemptory

rant: **4** fume, huff, rage, rail, rand, rave, riot, song, tune **5** dance, orate, revel, scold, spout **6** frolic, speech, steven **7** bluster, bombast, carouse, declaim, fustian **9** discourse

rantipole: **4** wild **6** rakish, unruly **9** termagant

ranula: **4** cyst **8** swelling

rap: bob, box, con, hit, tap **4** blow, chap, chat, grab, knap, talk, tirl **5** blame, clink, clout, knock, music, seize, smite, steal, utter **6** rebuke, snatch, strike, thwack **7** deliver **8** sentence **9** criticism, criticize, enrapture, transport **10** conference, punishment

rapacious: **6** fierce, greedy **8** covetous, grasping, ravening, ravenous **9** ferocious, voracious **10** avaricious, predacious

rapacity: **5** claim, ravin **7** edacity **8** appetite, cupidity, exaction **9** extortion

Rapa Nui: **12** Easter Island

rape: **4** file, rasp, ruin **5** abuse, haste, hasty, hurry, quick, seize, spoil **6** defile, pomace, rapine, ravish, turnip **7** assault, despoil, hastily, outrage, pillage, plunder, robbery, scratch, violate **8** dishonor **9** violation **10** plundering, spoliation

rapeseed: **4** herb **5** colza **7** ravison

oil: **6** canola

Raphael: **5** angel **7** painter **9** archangel

raphe: **4** line, seam **5** joint **6** suture

rapid: **4** fast **5** agile, brisk, chute, fleet, quick, steep, swift **6** abrupt, moving, nimble, speedy **10** fastmoving **11** expeditious

rapidity: **5** haste, speed **8** celerity, velocity **9** quickness

rapidly: **4** fast **5** apace **6** pronto **7** quickly

rapier: **5** bilbo, sword **6** verdun **7** ricasso

blade heel: **7** ricasso

part of: **5** forte **6** foible

rapine: **7** pillage, plunder **10** spoliation

rapparee: **6** robber **8** vagabond **9** plunderer **10** freebooter

rappee: **5** snuff

rapport: **6** accord **7** harmony **8** affinity, relation **9** agreement **10** connection **12** relationship

rapscallion: **5** rogue, scamp **6** rascal, wretch **7** villain **8** vagabond

rapt: **4** deep **5** tense **6** intent **8** absorbed, ecstatic **9** comprised, enchanted, engrossed, entranced, transport **10** captivated, enraptured **11** preoccupied, transported

raptorial: **9** predatory, rapacious **11** accipitrine

raptorial bird: owl **4** hawk **5** eagle **7** vulture

rapture: joy **5** bliss **6** trance **7** delight, ecstasy **8** rhapsody **9** enrapture, happiness, transport **10** exultation

rara avis: **4** oner **6** rarity, wonder **7** phoenix **8** rare bird

rare: odd, raw **4** fine, good, nice, thin **6** choice, dainty, geason, scarce, seldom, unique **7** antique, capital, curious, extreme, special, tenuous, unusual **8** precious, uncommon, unwonted **9** beautiful, excellent, exclusive, exquisite, scattered, underdone **10** infrequent **11** distinctive, exceptional

rarefied: **4** thin **7** diluted, ethered, gaseous, refined **8** aethered **10** attenuated

rarely: **5** extra **6** seldom **10** hardly ever

rarity: **5** curio, relic **6** geason, oddity **7** antique

ras: **4** cape **6** fabric, prince **7** fascist **8** headland **9** commander

rascal: boy, cad, imp **4** file, loon **5** foist, gipsy, gypsy, knave, rogue, scamp **6** ablach, budzat, coquin, harlot **7** budzart, glutton, villain **8** hosebird, scalawag, sealpeen, widdifow **9** miscreant, reprobate, scallawag, scoundrel, trickster

rascally: **4** base, mean **6** arrant **9** dishonest, worthless **11** furciferous, mischievous

rash: mad **4** bold **5** brash, erase, hardy, hasty, heady, hives, scamp, shave, slash, uredo **6** daring, eczema, scrape, unwary **7** foolish, hotspur, icarian, scratch **8** careless, epidemic, eruption, headlong, heedless, reckless, temerous **9** desperate, foolhardy, foreright, hotheaded, impetuous, imprudent, overhasty, urticaria, venturous **10** headstrong, hotspurred, incautious, indiscreet, unthinking **11** adventurous, furthersome, harum-scarum, precipitate, precipitous, temerarious

rasher: **5** bacon, slice **6** collop **7** portion **8** rockfish

rashness: **4** rage, rese **5** folly **6** acrisy **8** temerity **9** headiness

rasorial: **7** gnawing **10** scratching

rasp: rub **4** file **5** belch, eruct, grate **6** abrade, scrape **8** irritate

rasping: **5** harsh, raspy, rough **6** hoarse, rasion **7** raspish, raucous **8** guttural **9** offensive

rasse: **5** civet **6** weasel

rat: pad **4** scab, snot **6** defect, inform, rodent, vermin **8** betrayer, deserter, informer, renegade, squealer **9** councilor, counselor **11** stool-pigeon
catcher: **9** pied piper
family: **7** Muridae
genus: **6** spalax
kind: kok **4** pack **5** metad, zemmi, zemni **6** tosher **7** hamster **8** kangaroo
poison: **7** arsenic **8** ratsbane

ratafia: **5** noyau **7** biscuit, cordial, liqueur **8** macaroon

rataplan: **8** drumbeat

ratch: bar **4** rend **7** stretch **8** distance

ratchet: **4** pawl **5** click **6** bobbin, detent

rate: fee, tax **4** cost, duty, earn, fare, gait, levy, pace, rail, rank **5** abuse, blame, chide, class, grade, price, ratio, scold, score, speed, tempo, value **6** amount, assess, assize, berate, charge, degree, figure, reckon, regard, tariff **7** account, analyze, censure, chasten, despise, quality, reprove **8** appraise, classify, consider, estimate, evaluate, handicap, quantify, velocity **9** quotation, reprimand, valuation **10** proportion
of exchange: **4** agio **5** batta

ratel: **6** badger, burier, weasel

ratfish: **8** chimaera

rathe, rath: **4** soon **5** eager, early, quick **6** prompt, speedy **7** betimes **8** promptly, speedily

rather: **5** prior **6** before, choice, enough, in lieu, prefer, pretty, sooner **7** earlier, instead, quickly **8** somewhat **9** assuredly (Br.) **10** preferably, preference **11** immediately

ratify: **4** amen, pass, seal **6** affirm, enseal, verify **7** approve, confirm, endorse, license **8** roborate, sanction **9** authorize, establish

rating: **4** rank **5** class, grade **6** rebuke **8** estimate, scolding, standing **9** reprimand **10** evaluation **14** classification

ratio: cos **4** rate, sine **5** quota, share **6** cosine, degree, ration **7** average, portion **8** relation **10** percentage, proportion **11** capacitance

ratiocination: **5** logic **7** thought **8** argument **9** inference, reasoning

ration: **4** dole, food, meed, mete **5** allot, quota, ratio, share **6** divide **7** portion **8** relation **9** allotment, allowance, apportion **10** distribute **11** calculation

rational: **4** sane **5** lucid, right, sober, sound **7** logical, prudent **8** sensible **10** reasonable **11** intelligent, level-headed
integer: **4** norm
principle: **5** logos

rationale: **6** reason **11** explanation

rations: **4** food **8** buckshee **10** provisions

ratite: emu, moa **4** bird, emeu, rhea **7** ostrich **9** cassowary
genus: **7** apteryx **8** dinornis

ratoon: **5** shoot, stalk **6** spring, sprout

rattail: **4** comb, file **5** braid **7** pigtail

rattan: **4** cane, lash, palm, sega, whip **5** noose, thong **6** punish, switch, wicker

ratter: cat, dog **8** betrayer

rattle: din, toy **4** birl, chat, rale, rick, stun, tirl **5** addle, annoy, clack, rouse, scold, upset **6** assail, bicker, maraca, racket, uproar **7** agitate, chatter, clapper, clatter, clitter, confuse, fluster, gnatter, shatter **9** crepitate, embarrass **10** disconcert

rattlebrained: **5** dizzy, giddy, silly **7** flighty **9** frivolous **11** empty-headed, harebrained

rattlepate: ass **4** dolt **9** chatterer

rattleroot: **7** bugbane

rattlesnake: **8** cascavel, crotalus **9** sistrurus **10** massasauga

rattlesnake fern: **9** sporangia

rattlesnake herb: **9** baneberry

rattlesnake pilot: **10** copperhead

rattle-top: **7** bugbane

rattletrap: **5** ratty **7** gewgaws, rickety **10** ramshackle **11** knickknacks

ratty: **4** mean **6** shabby **7** unkempt **11** dilapidated

ratwa: **7** muntjac

raucous: dry **4** loud **5** gruff, harsh, noisy, rough **6** coarse, hoarse **7** braying, brusque, grating, rasping **8** strident **9** turbulent **11** cacophonous

raun: roe **5** spawn

raupo: **7** cattail

ravage: eat **4** loot, prey, rape, raze, ruin, sack **5** foray, harry, havoc, spoil, waste, wreck **6** forage **7** despoil, destroy, overrun, pillage, plunder, scourge, violate **8** decimate, deflower, desolate, lay waste **9** devastate **10** depopulate

rave: **4** rage, rant **5** blurb, crush, orate, storm **7** bluster, bombast, declaim, enthuse **8** harangue **10** rhapsodize

ravel: run **4** comb, fray, rail **5** snarl **6** runner, sleave, tangle, unwind **7** crumble, involve, perplex, railing, untwist, unweave **8** entangle, separate **10** complicate **11** disentangle

ravelin: **8** demilune **13** fortification

raveling: **4** lint **6** thread

Ravel work: **6** Bolero

raven: **4** crow **5** black **9** blackbird
genus: **6** corvus
of Odin: **5** Hugin

Raven, The: *author:* Poe

character: **6** Lenore
refrain: **9** Nevermore

ravenous: **6** greedy, hungry, lupine, toothy **7** starved **8** edacious, famished, starving **9** cormorant, ferocious, rapacious, voracious **10** catawampus, gluttonous

ravine: cut, den, gap, lin **4** dell, ghyl, gill, gulf, linn, pass, sike, wadi, wady **5** abyss, canon, chasm, chine, clove, ditch, flume, glack, gorge, goyal, goyle, griff, grike, gulch, gully, kloof, notch, strid **6** arroyo, canyon, cleuch, clough, coulee, gulley, gutter, hollow, nullah **7** crevice, dry wash **8** barranca, barranco, quebrado **10** depression

raving: **8** frenzied **9** delirious **10** incoherent, irrational **12** arreptitious

ravish: rob **4** rape **5** abuse, charm, force, harry, seize **6** abduct, defile, snatch **7** afforce, corrupt, delight, despoil, enchant, plunder, violate **8** deflower, entrance **9** captivate, constrain, enrapture, transport

ravishment: **7** ecstasy, rapture **9** transport

raw: **4** cold, damp, dazy (Sc.), lash, nude, rare, rude **5** bawdy, bleak, chill, crude, green, harsh, naked **6** abrade, chilly, coarse, unfair **7** cutting, natural, obscene **8** immature, indecent, uncooked **9** inclement, unexposed, unrefined, unskilled, untrained **10** indelicate, unfinished, unprepared, unseasoned **11** unprocessed

rawboned: **4** lean **5** gaunt **7** angular, scrawny

rawhide: **4** pelt, skin, whip **5** knout, quirt, thong

ray: **4** beam, beta, dorn, fish, soil **5** array, dress, flair, gleam, gleed, light, manta, order, shaft, shine, sight, skate **6** defile, glance, obispo, radial, streak, stripe, vision **7** besmear, homelyn, radiate, raiment **9** irradiate, selachian **10** perception, vertebrate **11** arrangement, irradiation
kind: **4** dorn **5** manta, skate
penetrating: **5** gamma

rayon: **5** moire, ninon, tulle **6** faille, pongee **7** taffeta
yarn size: **6** denier

raze, rase: cut, rub **4** rage, ruin, tear **5** erase, graze, growl, level, shave, wreck **6** efface, incise, scrape **7** destroy, implode, scratch, subvert **8** demolish **9** deprecate, dismantle, overthrow, prostrate **10** obliterate

razee: cut **5** prune **6** reduce **7** abridge

razor: **4** clam **6** shaver
sharpen: **4** hone **5** strop

razorback: hog **5** ridge **10** roustabout

razorbill: auk **7** skimmer

razor stone: **10** novaculite

razz: **5** chaff, tease **6** banter, deride, heckle **8** ridicule

razzle-dazzle: **5** spree **7** confuse **8** hilarity **9** confusion

re: **5** about, anent **9** regarding **10** concerning

Re: See **Ra**

reach: ken, run, toe **4** come, gain, hawk, hent, ryke (Sc.), seek, span, spit **5** get to, grasp, orbit, range, retch, scope, vomit **6** advene, affect, amount, arrive, attain, extend, extent, strive **7** achieve, compass, contact, expanse, possess, stretch **8** approach, make up to **9** culminate, penetrate **10** accomplish

reachable: **10** accessible

reaching: **6** effort **8** profound

reaction: **4** kick **5** start **6** answer **7** tropism **8** response **9** influence **10** impression, opposition
adverse: **8** backlash

read: con **4** lire (F.), pore, scan, show, skim, tell **5** aread, areed, drone, guess, solve, study **6** advise, browse, peruse, record, relate **7** counsel, declare, dictate, discern, foresee, learned **8** decipher, describe, foretell, indicate, register **9** interpret, supervise
ability to: **8** literacy
inability to: **6** alexia **8** dyslexia **10** illiteracy
intently: **4** pore
metrically: **4** scan
superficially: **4** skim **6** glance

readable: **7** legible

reader: **6** lector, lister, primer **7** reciter, scanner **8** bookworm, lectrice, lecturer **9** anthology **10** instructor

readily: **4** well **6** easily, freely **7** lightly

readiness: art **4** ease, gift **6** graith **7** address, freedom **8** alacrity, facility, goodwill, volition **9** dexterity, eagerness, quickness **10** promptness, volubility **12** preparedness

reading: **6** lesson **7** lection, lecture, perusal, recital, version **9** collation, rendition **10** prelection

ready: apt, fit **4** done, free, game, gird, glib, here, pret (F.), ripe **5** alert, apert, bound, eager, handy, happy, point, quick **6** active, adroit, facile, fluent, prompt **7** forward, prepare, willing **8** cheerful, dextrous, handsome, prepared, skillful **9** agreeable, available, dexterous **10** convenient **11** expeditious **12** unhesitating

real: **4** true, very, vrai (F.) **5** being, loyal **6** actual, hearty **7** certain, cordial, factual, genuine, gradely, literal, sincere **8** concrete, existent, faithful, physical, tangible **9** authentic, effective, heartfelt, intrinsic, unfeigned, veritable **10** unaffected

real estate: **4** alod **5** allod, house, lands **6** domain, realty **7** holding **8** allodium, building, freehold, premises, property
claim: tax **4** lien **8** mortgage **9** trust deed **11** encumbrance

pert. to: **7** predial

realistic: **5** vivid **6** shrewd **7** prudent **8** lifelike **9** practical **11** down-to-earth

reality: **4** fact

realization: **8** fruition **9** awakening

realize: get **4** gain, know **5** sense, think **6** effect, obtain **7** achieve, acquire, convert, fulfill **8** complete, conceive **9** apprehend **10** accomplish, appreciate, understand

really: aru **4** very, well **5** quite, sooth, truly **6** indeed **8** actually

realm: **4** land **5** bourn, clime, range **6** bourne, circle, domain, empire, region, sphere **7** country, demesne, dynasty, kingdom, terrene **8** division, dominion, province **9** territory **10** department **11** sovereignty **12** jurisdiction

realty: **7** honesty, loyalty, royalty **8** fidelity, property **10** possession

ream: **4** bore, draw, foam, scum **5** bevel, cheat, cream, froth, widen **7** enlarge, stretch

reamer: **4** tool **5** borer, drift **6** broach

reanimate: **5** rally, renew **6** revive **11** resuscitate **12** reinvigorate

reap: cut **4** crop, rake **5** glean **6** garner, gather **7** acquire, collect, harvest, receive

rear: aft, end, fix **4** back, buck, cave, grow, last, lift, rere, tail **5** abaft, breed, build, erect, nurse, raise, stern, train **6** astern, behind, foster, nursle **7** arriere (F.), bring up, educate, elevate, nurture **8** buttocks **9** construct, establish, posterior **10** background, forthbring

rearing by horse: **5** stend **6** pesade

rearhorse: **6** insect, mantis

rearward: **7** retreat **8** backward **9** posterior **10** retrograde

reason: aim, peg, why, wit **4** mind, nous **5** argue, brain, cause, logic, sense, think **6** debate, ground, motive, object, ponder, sanity **7** meaning **8** argument, converse **9** discourse, intellect, rationale, wherefore **10** moderation, understand **11** explanation, expostulate, ratiocinate, rationality, rationalize

alleged: **6** excuse **7** pretext

deprived of: **8** demented

pert. to: **6** noetic

want of: **5** folie **7** amentia, madness **8** insanity

reasonable: **4** fair, just **5** cheap **7** logical **8** feasible, moderate, rational, sensible **9** equitable, plausible **11** inexpensive

reasoning: **5** logic **8** argument, thinking **10** conclusion **13** argumentation

basis of: **7** premise

reassure: **5** cheer **7** comfort, hearten **9** encourage

reata, riata: **4** rope **5** lasso **6** lariat

reave: rob **4** tear **5** burst, seize, split **7** bereave, pillage, plunder, unravel

rebate: **5** check **6** lessen, reduce, refund, weaken **8** diminish, discount, kickback **9** abatement, deduction, reduction, remission

rebato: See **rabato**

rebec: **4** lyre **5** rebab, sarod **6** fiddle, violin

Rebekah: *brother:* **5** Laban

father: **7** Bethuel

husband: **5** Isaac

mother: **6** Milcah

son: **4** Esau **5** Jacob

rebel: **4** rise **6** oppose, revolt, rise up **8** renegade **9** adversary, insurgent **10** antagonist

rebellion: **6** mutiny, putsch, revolt **8** defiance, sedition, uprising **10** resistance, revolution **12** disobedience, insurrection, renunciation

rebellious: **7** defiant **8** mutinous **9** estranged **10** refractory **11** disobedient **12** contumacious, recalcitrant

rebirth: **7** revival **10** conversion, renascence **11** renaissance **13** reincarnation

reboant: **7** echoing **13** reverberating

rebound: dap **4** echo, stot **5** bound, carom **6** bounce, carrom, re-echo, recoil, resile, return, spring **7** recover, reflect, resound **8** backlash, ricochet, snap back **9** boomerang **11** reverberate

rebuff: cow **4** scat, slap, snub **5** check, chide, fling, repel, scold, spurn **6** lesson **7** censure, fend off, refusal, reprove, repulse **9** rejection, reprimand

rebuke: nip, rap, tsk, tut, wig **4** beat, snub, tush **5** barge, blame, check, chide, scold **6** berate, dirdum, lesson, rating **7** censure, downset, lecture, repress, reproof, reprove **8** admonish, chastise, reproach, restrain **9** criticism, criticize, reprehend, reprimand, talking-to **10** correction **11** comeuppance, reprobation

rebus: **6** enigma, puzzle, riddle

rebut: **5** reply **6** oppose, rebuff, refute, revile **7** fend off, repulse **8** disprove **10** contradict

recalcitrant: **5** rebel **6** unruly **7** defiant **8** perverse, stubborn **9** obstinate, resisting **10** rebellious, refractory **11** intractable

recall: **5** annul **6** abjure, cancel, encore, memory, remind, repeal, revoke **7** abolish, bethink, rescind, restore, retrace, retract, summons **8** remember, withdraw **9** recollect, reminisce

recant: **6** abjure, revoke **7** abandon, disavow, retract **8** renounce, take back, withdraw **9** repudiate **10** contradict

recapitulate: **5** essay, sum up **6** repeat, review **7** restate **8** argument **9** enumerate, reiterate, summarize

recapture: 6 recall, regain, retake 7 recover 8 remember 9 reacquire

recede: ebb 4 fade, sink, wane 6 depart, retire 7 deviate, regress, retreat 8 decrease, fall back, withdraw 10 retrograde

receipt: 4 chit, stub, take 6 acquit, apocha, binder, recipe 7 formula 9 reception 11 acquittance

receipts: 4 take 5 sales 6 income 7 revenue 8 payments

receive: get 4 take 5 admit, adopt, greet 6 accept, assume, derive, obtain, take in 7 acquire, procure

receiver: 4 host 5 donee, fence, radio 6 pernor, porter 7 breaker, catcher, hostess, rentier 8 cymaphen, receptor 9 collector, condenser, treasurer
of property in trust: 6 bailee 7 trustee

recension: 6 review 8 revision 9 reviewing 11 enumeration, examination

recent: neo, new 4 late 5 fresh 6 latest, modern 7 current 8 neoteric

recently: 4 anew 6 lately 8 latterly

receptacle: bin, box, can, cup, fat, pan, pot, tub, urn, vat 4 bowl, case, cell, cist, crib, dish, etui, ewer, font, pail, tank, tray, vase, well 5 basin, chest, torus 6 basket, bottle, bucket, carton, holder, hopper, trough 7 cistern, humidor, pitcher 8 canister, receiver, trash can 9 container, reservoir

reception: tea 5 levee, party 6 accoil, durbar, soiree 7 accueil, ovation, receipt, welcome 8 greeting 9 admission, collation 10 admittance
morning: 5 levee
place: 4 hall 5 atria (pl.), foyer, salon 6 atrium, parlor 7 parlour 9 vestibule

receptive: 8 amenable 9 acceptant 10 hospitable, open-minded 11 sympathetic

receptor: 5 basin 8 receiver 10 dispositor, sense organ 11 nerve ending

recess: ala, bay 4 apse, cave, cove, grot, halt, hole, nook 5 ambry, cleft, crypt, niche, sinus 6 alcove, closet, cranny, grotto, rabbet, retire 7 adjourn, conceal, crevice, retreat, seclude, time out 8 dissolve, interval, vacation 9 cessation, embrasure 10 suspension

recessive: 8 backward, receding 13 retrogressive

Rechab's son: 7 Jonadab

recherché: new 4 rare 5 fresh, novel 6 choice, exotic 7 unusual 8 uncommon 9 exquisite 10 farfetched

recidivation: 7 relapse 8 apostasy 10 repetition 11 backsliding

recipe: 4 dish 7 formula, pattern, receipt 12 prescription

recipient: 4 heir 5 donee 7 alienee, devisee, legatee 8 receiver 9 receiving, receptive

reciprocal: 4 mate, twin 6 mutual 9 alternate 11 convertible, correlative

reciprocate: 5 bandy, repay 6 return 7 requite 8 exchange, give back 9 alternate 10 recompense 11 countervail, interchange

recital: 4 saga, tale 5 story 6 report 7 account, concert, program 8 relation 9 narration, narrative, rehearsal, statement 10 recitation, repetition 11 declamation, description, enumeration

recitation: 7 reading

recitative: 5 scena 9 narrative

recite: say 4 carp, read, scan, tell 5 chant, quote, speak, spout 6 intone, parrot, relate 7 declaim, recount 9 cantilate, enumerate 12 recapitulate

reciter: 6 anteri, diseur (F.) 7 diseuse (F.) 8 narrator 12 elocutionist

reck: 4 care, deem, heed, mind 7 concern 8 consider, estimate

reckless: 4 bold, rash 5 blind, folle, perdu 6 madcap, perdue 7 hotspur 8 careless, headlong, heedless 9 blindfold, bodacious, daredevil, desperate, dissolute, hotheaded, imprudent 10 neglectful, regardless 11 adventurous, extravagant, harum-scarum, indifferent, thoughtless

reckon: 4 aret, date, deem, rate, rely, tell 5 audit, count, guess, think 6 arette, figure, impute, number, regard, repute 7 account, ascribe, compute, imagine, include, suppose, surmise 8 consider, estimate, numerate 9 calculate, enumerate 10 adjudicate, understand 11 connumerate

reckoner: 5 abaci, brain 6 abacus 9 tabulator 10 calculator 11 comptometer

reckoning: 4 bill, rate, scot, shot 5 chalk, score 6 compot, esteem 11 computation

reclaim: 4 save, tame 5 train 6 ransom, recall, redeem, reform, repair, rescue, revoke 7 recover, restore, salvage 8 civilize, empolder, retrieve

reclaimed land: 6 polder

reclining: 5 lying, prone 6 supine 7 leaning, lolling, passive, resting 8 reposing 9 accumbent, recumbent

recluse: nun 4 monk 6 hermit, hidden, secret 7 eremite, incluse 8 anchoret, secluded, solitary 9 anchoress, anchorite, cloistral 10 cloistered 11 sequestered

recognition: 4 fame 6 credit 9 awareness

recognize: ken, own, see 4 avow, know, note, spot 5 admit, greet 6 accept, acknow, agnize, beknow, notice, recall, remark, review, revise, salute 7 consent, correct, recover 8 identify, perceive 9 apprehend 10 appreciate

recoil: shy 4 balk, kick 5 quail, wince 6

blanch, flinch, shrink 7 rebound, retreat, reverse, squinch 8 backlash, withdraw

recollect: 4 cite 5 waken 6 recall 7 bethink 8 remember 11 remininisce

recollection: 4 mind 6 memory 8 memorial 9 anamnesis 11 remembrance

recommence: 5 renew 6 resume 7 reprise

recommend: 4 tout 5 refer 6 advise, commit, denote 7 commend, consign, counsel, entrust 8 advocate

recommit: 6 remand

recompense: fee, pay 5 repay 6 amends, bounty, reward, salary 7 premium, requite 8 requital 9 gratulate, indemnify, reimburse, repayment 10 compensate, remunerate, reparation 11 reciprocate, restitution, retribution 12 compensation, remuneration 13 consideration, gratification

without: 4 free 6 gratis 7 pro bono

reconcile: 4 mend, wean 5 adapt, agree, atone, patch 6 accord, adjust, pacify, regain, settle, shrive, square 7 absolve, conform, expiate, explain, restore, reunite, satisfy 9 harmonize, make peace 10 conciliate, propitiate

recondite: 4 dark, deep 5 heavy 6 hidden, mystic, occult, secret 7 cryptic, learned, obscure 8 abstract, abstruse, esoteric, profound 9 concealed 10 mysterious

reconnaissance: 5 recce 6 survey

reconnoiter: spy 5 scout 6 recall, survey 7 examine, explore, inquire 8 discover

record: log, tab 4 acta (pl.), book, copy, disc, disk, dope, file, memo, note, past, roll, show, tape 5 actum, album, annal, chart, diary, enrol, enter, entry, graph, score, video 6 agenda, enroll, legend, memoir, postea, report 7 account, archive, blotter, calends, catalog, dossier, estreat, history, journal, kalends, platter, rotulet 8 calendar, document, memorial, register 9 catalogue, chronicle, itinerary, narration, videotape 10 chronology, transcribe

historical: 6 annals

keeper: 8 Guinness, recorder 9 registrar

of arrest: 7 blotter

of proceedings: 4 acta (pl.) 7 minutes

of ship: log

personal: 5 diary 7 journal

recorder: 5 flute, judge 8 greffier, register 9 cartulary, registrar 10 chartulary

recording: 5 album, label 7 cutting

recording device: 4 tape 5 meter 6 camera 8 tape deck

recount: 4 deem, tell 5 count 6 recite, reckon, relate, repeat, retail 7 account, include, narrate 8 describe, rehearse 9 enumerate

recoup: 7 recover 9 indemnify, reimburse 10 compensate, recuperate

recover: get 5 amend, rally, upset 6 obtain, recoup, reform, regain, rescue, resume, retake 7 balance, get back, reclaim, recruit, restore, salvage 8 overcome, retrieve, snap back 9 repossess 10 bounce back, compensate, convalesce, recuperate

recovery: 4 cure 8 comeback 13 convalescence

law: 6 trover

recreant: 5 false, knave 6 coward, craven, crying, wretch, yellow 7 traitor 8 apostate, betrayer, cowardly, deserter, disloyal, renegade, yielding 9 faithless, reprobate 10 traitorous, unfaithful 11 disaffected

recreation: 4 meal, play 5 dance, hobby, sport 6 picnic 7 renewal 9 amusement, avocation, diversion 10 relaxation 11 delassement, refreshment

time: 6 recess 7 holiday, weekend 8 vacation

recrement: 4 scum, slag 5 dregs, dross, spume 6 refuse, scoria

recruit: 4 bleu (F.), boot 5 raise, renew, rooky 6 gather, muster, novice, revive, rookie, supply 7 draftee, private, recover, refresh, restore, soldier 8 assemble, bezonian, inductee, renovate 9 reinforce, replenish 10 recuperate, strengthen

rectangle: 6 oblong, square 13 parallelogram

rectifier: 5 diode

rectify: fix 4 mend 5 amend, emend, right 6 adjust, better, purify, refine, reform, remedy, repair 7 correct, distill, rebuild 8 emendate, regulate 10 straighten

rectitude: 6 equity, virtue 7 fitness, honesty 8 goodness, morality 10 straitness 11 uprightness 12 straightness

rector: 4 head 5 chief, ruler 6 leader, priest 7 proctor 8 director, governor, minister 9 clergyman, corrector 10 headmaster, proproctor

rectory: 5 manse 8 benefice 9 parsonage

recumbent: 4 idle 5 lying, prone 6 supine 7 leaning, resting 8 inactive, reposing 9 reclining

recuperate: 4 heal, rest 5 rally 6 perk up, regain 7 get well, improve, recover 9 get better 10 convalesce

recur: 6 advert, repeat, resort, return 7 iterate, rearise 8 reappear

recurrent, recurring: 6 cyclic 7 chronic 8 repeated 9 returning 10 isochronal 11 reappearing 12 intermittent

recusant: 8 apostate 9 dissenter 11 dissentient 12 non-conformer

red: 4 lake, puce, rosy, ruby 5 canna, color, coral, fiery, gules, peony, roset, rouge, ruddy 6 cerise, cherry, claret, florid, garnet, maroon, rubric, sienna, titian 7 carmine, crimson, glowing, leftist, magenta, nacarat, radical, roseate, scarlet 8 amaranth, blushing, inflamed, rubicund 9 anarchist, bloodshot, Bolshevik, communist, vermilion 10 erubescent 11 incarnadine

antique: 5 canna

brown: 5 sepia 6 russet, sorrel 8 chestnut 10 terra cotta

dye: aal, lac 4 chay, choy 5 aurin, eosin, henna 6 aurine 8 morindin 9 cochineal

marked with: 6 rubric

purplish: 4 lake 6 claret 7 fuschia, magenta

Venetian: 5 siena 6 sienna

yellow: 4 lama 5 aloma, brass, coral, ochre, peach, tenne 6 alesan, orange 7 saffron 9 alabaster, peachblow, vermilion 10 Chinese red

redact: 4 edit 5 draft, frame 6 reduce, revise

redan: 7 rampart 8 fortress 10 breastwork 13 fortification

red ape: 9 orangutan

red arsenic: 7 realgar

red bell: 9 columbine

red-bellied snipe: 9 dowitcher

redbelly: 4 char 7 grouper 8 terrapin

red benjamin: 9 birthroot

redbird: 7 tanager 8 cardinal 9 bullfinch

redbird cactus: 7 jewbush

red-blooded: 5 vital 6 virile 8 vigorous

red blotch: 10 adustiosis

red box: 8 official 12 bureaucratic

redbreast: 5 robin

redbud tree: 5 judas

red bug: 7 chigger

redcap: 6 porter 7 carrier, specter, spectre 8 tarboosh 9 goldfinch

red cedar: 5 savin 6 sabine, savine 7 juniper 8 flindosa

red cell: 11 erythrocyte

red chalk: 4 bole 6 ruddle

red cobalt: 9 erythrite

red copper ore: 7 cuprite

red corpuscle deficiency: 6 anemia

Red Cross founder: 6 Barton, Dunant

Red Cross Knight: 6 George

    wife: Una

red deer: roe 4 hart, hind, spay, stag

redden: 4 burn 5 blush, color, flush, rouge

Red Desert: 5 Nefud

redeem: buy 4 free, save 5 atone 6 ransom, regain, rescue 7 deliver, fulfill, reclaim, recover, release, restore 8 liberate

redeye: 4 rudd 5 plane, vireo 6 whisky 7 sunfish, whiskey 8 rock bass 10 copperhead 11 night flight

red-faced: 5 ruddy 6 florid 7 blowzed, flushed 8 blushing 9 chagrined 11 embarrassed

red fever: 10 erysipelas

red fir: 4 pine 6 spruce 7 Douglas

red gum: 10 eucalyptus, strophulus

redhead: 5 finch 7 pochard 10 woodpecker

red honeysuckle: 5 sulla

red lead ore: 8 corcoite

red-letter: 9 important 10 noteworthy

red man: 6 Indian

redmouth: 4 fish 5 grunt

red-neck: 4 hick, rube 5 yokel 6 rustic

redolence: 4 balm, odor 5 aroma, odour, scent, smell 7 bouquet, perfume 9 fragrance, sweetness

redouble: 6 reecho, repeat 7 reprise, retrace 9 intensify 10 ingeminate

redoubt: 4 fort 6 schanz 10 breastwork, stronghold 13 fortification

redoubtable: 5 brave, dread 6 famous, strong 7 fearful, valiant 8 fearsome 10 formidable

redound: 5 react 6 accrue, recoil 7 conduce, resound 10 contribute

red pepper: 5 chile, chili 6 chilli

red perch: 8 rosefish

Red Planet: 4 Mars

redress: 5 amend, emend 6 adjust, relief, remedy 7 correct, relieve 9 indemnity 10 compensate, reparation

Red Sea: 9 Erythrean

    gulf: 4 Aden, Suez 5 Aqaba

    peninsula: 5 Sinai 7 Arabian

redshank: 4 bird, clee 9 sandpiper

redshirt: 9 anarchist 11 Garibaldian 13 revolutionist

reduce: cut 4 bant, bate, bust, diet, ease, pare, raze, thin 5 abase, abate, annul, break, level, lower, scale, slash, smelt 6 appall, change, debase, demote, depose, derate, dilute, equate, humble, impair, lessen, rebate, refine, subdue, weaken 7 abridge, assuage, commute, conquer, curtail, cut back, degrade, deplete, whittle 8 attemper, condense, contract, decrease, diminish, discount, emaciate, minimize, retrench, slim down 9 evaporate, subjugate 10 annihilate, bantingize

    to half: 9 dimidiate

    sail: 4 furl, reef 7 shorten

reduction: cut 5 slice 6 rebate 7 cut back, cutting, meiosis 8 analysis, discount 9 attrition 11 contraction, degradation

redundancy: 7 nimiety 8 pleonasm, plethora, verbiage 9 verbosity 10 flatulence 11 periphrasis, superfluity

redundant: 5 wordy 6 lavish, prolix 7 copious, diffuse, verbose 9 excessive, exuberant 10 pleonastic, repetitive 11 overflowing, superfluous

red viper: 10 copperhead

red willow: 5 osier 6 cornel

redwing: 6 thrush 7 gadwall 9 blackbird, francolin

redwood: 4 tree 7 Sequoia 9 evergreen

Ree: 7 Arikara

re-echo: 7 rebound, resound 8 resonate 11 reverberate

reed: sag 4 dart, junk, pipe, sley, stem 5 arrow, grass, spear, stalk 7 bulrush, calamus, fistula

reedbird: 7 warbler 8 bobolink

reedbuck: kob 4 koba 5 bohor, nagor 7 reitbok 8 antelope 9 waterbuck

reeder: 8 thatcher

reed organ: 8 melodeon 9 harmonium

reedy: 4 thin, weak 11 arundineous

reef: bar, cay, key 4 cayo, itch, lode, vein 5 atoll, coral, ledge, mange, shoal 6 boiler 7 bioherm, sandbar, shorten 8 eruption
mining: 4 lode, vein

reefer: 4 coat, eton 5 miner 6 jacket, oyster 9 cigarette, marijuana 10 midshipman

reek: rig 4 emit, fume, heap, pile, vent 5 equip, exude, smell, smoke, steam, stink, vapor 6 exhale, stench 7 seaweed 8 mountain 10 exhalation

reel: 4 drum, pirn (Sc.), roll, spin, sway, swim, wind 5 dance, lurch, spool, swift, swing, waver, whirl, wince 6 bobbin, careen, hammer, teeter, totter, wintle 7 stagger, stumble 8 titubate, windlass

reem: 4 moan, uris 7 unicorn

reeve: pen 4 pass, wind 5 twist 6 pucker, thread 7 bailiff, provost, steward, wrinkle 8 overseer 9 enclosure, sheepfold

refection: 4 food, meal 5 drink, lunch 6 repast 11 refreshment

refectory: 4 mess 10 dining hall
monastery: 6 frater

refer: 4 cite, harp, send 5 recur 6 advert, allude, appeal, assign, charge, commit, direct, impute, regard, relate, return, submit 7 ascribe, bring up, consult, mention, specify 8 identify 9 affiliate, appertain, attribute

referee: 5 judge 6 decide, umpire 7 arbiter 8 mediator 10 arbitrator

reference: 5 quote 6 aspect 7 respect 8 allusion, citation 9 relevance 10 connection, pertinence 11 credentials
mark: 4 star 6 dagger 8 asterisk

reference book: 5 atlas 7 almanac, lexicon 8 handbook, syllabus, yearbook 9 gazetteer, thesaurus 10 dictionary 12 encyclopedia

referendum: 4 poll, vote 7 mandate 10 plebiscite

refine: 4 edit 5 exalt, smelt 6 decoct, filter, finish, polish, purify 7 clarify, cleanse, concoct, elevate, improve, perfect 8 chastise, separate 9 cultivate, elaborate, subtilize

refined: 4 nice 5 civil 6 artful, chaste, polite, urbane 7 courtly, elegant, genteel 8 delicate, graceful, highbred, purified 9 courteous, exquisite 10 fastidious

refinement: 5 grace 6 polish 7 culture, dignity, finesse

refining cup: 5 cupel

reflect: 4 echo, muse, pore 5 glass, image, study, think, weigh 6 divert, mirror, ponder 7 bethink, deflect 8 cogitate, consider, meditate, ruminate 9 reproduce 10 deliberate 11 contemplate, reverberate

reflected: 7 derived 8 mirrored, specular

reflection: 4 idea 5 image 6 musing 7 thought 8 likeness 10 cogitation, meditation, rumination 12 deliberation
measuring device: 11 albedograph

reflective: 7 pensive 10 thoughtful

reflex: 4 bend, fold, turn 11 involuntary

reflux: ebb 6 ebbing, euripi (pl.), reflow 7 euripus 9 refluence, returning

reform: 4 mend, trim 5 amend, emend, prune, renew 6 better, direct, punish, remass, repair, revise 7 censure, correct, improve, rebuild, reclaim, rectify, redress, reprove, reshape, restore 8 instruct 10 regenerate 11 reformation

refract: 6 impair 7 deflect, reflect 8 diminish 9 break down

refraction: *device:* 4 lens 5 prism 9 telescope
pert. to: 10 anaclastic

refractory: 6 immune, unruly 7 froward, restive, willful 8 contrary, perverse, stubborn 9 camsteary, camsteery, obstinate 10 headstrong, rebellious, unyielding 11 contrarious, disobedient, intractable, stiff-necked 12 contumacious

refrain: bob 4 curb, deny, shun 5 avoid, cease, check, epode, forgo 6 chorus, forego, govern 7 abstain, forbear, inhibit 8 response, restrain, withhold
music: air 4 aria, song 5 ditty 6 chorus, melody

refresh: 4 rest 5 bathe, cheer, renew, slake 6 caudle, revise, revive, vivify 7 comfort, enliven, freshen, hearten, quicken, restore 8 recreate, renovate 9 reanimate, replenish 10 invigorate, rejuvenate, strengthen 12 reinvigorate

refreshing: 4 dewy 5 balmy, tonic 11 refectorial, refrigerant 12 invigorating

refreshment: 4 food, meal 5 drink, lunch 8 beverage, refresco 9 collation

refrigerant: ice 5 freon 6 cooler 7 ammonia, coolant

refrigerate: ice 4 cool 5 chill 6 freeze 8 preserve

refuge: ark 4 fort, home, port, rock 5 haven, oasis 6 asylum, bilbie, covert, harbor, resort, shield 7 crannog (Sc.), harbour, retreat, shelter 8 crannoge (Sc.), hospital, immunity, resource **9** sanctuary **10** protection, rendezvous, subterfuge

refugee: **5** exile **6** emigre **8** fugitive

refulgent: **6** bright **7** glowing, radiant, shining **8** flashing, gleaming, splendid **9** brilliant **11** resplendent

refund: **5** repay **6** rebate **8** kickback **9** reimburse, repayment

refurbish: **5** renew, shine **6** polish, revamp **7** freshen, restore **8** brighten, renovate **11** recondition

refusal: no, nay **4** nope **6** denial

refuse: nay, ort **4** balk, coom, culm, deny, dirt, dreg, junk, marc, nite, pelf, pelt, veto **5** chaff, coomb, crawm, debar, drast, drest, dross, grith, offal, renig, repel, scrap, trash, waste, wrack **6** debris, forbid, garble, litter, lumber, reject, renege **7** backing, baggage, decline, disavow, forsake, garbage, gubbins, leaving, mullock, repulse, rubbish **8** disclaim, renounce, withhold **9** excrement, repudiate

grape: **4** marc

metal: **4** slag **5** dross **6** scoria

table: ort **5** scrap

wine: **4** lees

refute: **4** deny, meet **5** avoid, rebut, refel **6** assoil **7** confute **8** disprove, infringe, redargue **9** overthrow **10** contradict

regain: **4** save **6** recoup **7** get back, recover **8** retrieve

regal: **5** jewel, noble, royal **6** august, kingly **7** channel, queenly, stately **8** imperial, imposing, majestic, splendid

regale: **4** dine, fete **5** amuse, feast, treat **6** dinner, divert, spread **7** delight, gratify **9** entertain

regalia: **5** crown, dress **6** finery **7** emblems, ensigns, scepter, symbols **8** costumes, insignia **9** full dress **11** decorations

Regan: *father:* **4** Lear
sister: **7** Goneril **8** Cordelia

regard: air, awe, con, eye **4** care, deem, gaze, heed, hold, look, mind, note, rate, sake, view, yeme **5** assay, honor, think, treat, value, watch **6** admire, aspect, assess, attend, behold, esteem, glance, homage, notice, remark, repute, revere **7** adjudge, concern, observe, respect **8** consider, estimate, interest, relation **9** adoration, affection, attention, deference, reference **10** admiration, appearance, attendance, estimation, veneration **11** contemplate

regarding: **4** as to, in re **5** about, anent **6** anenst **7** apropos

regardless: **8** heedless **9** negligent **10** neglectful **12** nevertheless

regatta: **4** race **7** contest **8** boat race

regency: **4** rule **8** dominion **10** government

regenerate: **4** grow **5** renew **6** reborn, redeem, reform, revive, sprout **7** convert, newborn, reclaim, refresh, restore **8** gracious, recreate, renovate **9** reproduce

regent: **5** ruler **6** ruling **7** regnant, teacher **8** governor **9** governing
of sun: **5** Uriel

regimen: **4** diet, rule **6** system **7** control, hygiene **10** government, regulation

regiment: **4** alai, unit **5** cadre, order **7** company **11** systematize **12** military unit
flag: **6** pennon
member: **9** grenadier
nucleus: **5** cadre
officer: **5** boots **7** colonel

regina: **5** queen

region: des, erd, gay **4** area, belt, part, zone **5** clime, field, place, realm, space, tract **6** locale, sector, sphere **7** climate, country, demesne, kingdom **8** district, division, latitude, province, vicinity **9** territory **12** neighborhood
elevated: **4** mesa **8** highland
infernal: **5** Hades **7** Avernus **8** Tartarus **10** underworld
inhabited by one group: **6** ghetto
pert. to: **5** areal
surrounded by alien power: **7** enclave
upper: **5** ether
warm: **7** tropics
wooded: **5** taiga **6** forest
woodless: **4** wold **5** llano, plain, weald **6** desert, meadow, steppe **7** pasture, savanna **8** savannah

regional: **5** local **9** parochial, sectional **10** provincial

register: lid **4** book, list, roll, rota, show **5** album, annal, diary, enter, entry, slate **6** agenda, docket, enlist, enroll, record, roster **7** ascribe, calends, catalog, certify, coucher, kalends, license, stopper **8** archives, bookmark, calendar, indicate, recorder, registry, schedule **9** catalogue, chronical, inventory, registrar
cash: **6** damper
legal: **6** docket
of deaths: **9** necrology

registrar: **5** clerk **7** actuary **8** greffier, recorder, register

reglet: **5** strip **7** molding

regnal: **5** royal **6** kingly

regnant: **6** regent, ruling **8** dominant, reigning **9** prevalent **10** widespread **11** predominant

regorge: **5** vomit **8** disgorge

regress: **6** egress, return, revert **9** backslide, throwback **10** retrograde, withdrawal

regret: rew, rue, woe **4** miss, ruth **5** demur, grief, mourn, qualm, sorry, spurn **6**

bemoan, bewail, lament, repent, repine, sorrow **7** anguish, apology, bethink, deplore, dislike, remorse, scruple **8** aversion, distress, forthink **9** penitence **10** misgivings **11** compunction

regular: **4** even **5** exact, sober, usual, utter **6** formal, normal, proper, serial, stated, steady **7** amiable, correct, general, habitué, ordered, orderly, typical, uniform **8** complete, constant, decorous, formular, habitual, ordinary, ordinate, periodic, pleasant, rhythmic, rotative, standard, thorough **9** continual, customary, isometric **10** consistent, dependable, methodical, systematic **11** symmetrical

regulate: set **4** pace, rule, time **5** frame, guide, order **6** adjust, behave, direct, govern, police, settle **7** arrange, compose, conduct, control, correct, dispose, rectify **8** attemper, modulate **9** establish **10** discipline **11** standardize

regulation: law **4** rule **5** bylaw, canon, regle **6** assize, normal **7** precept, regimen, repulse, statute **8** ordinary **9** ordinance

regulator: **5** valve **8** rheostat **10** thermostat

regulus: **4** king, star **5** matte, ruler

rehabilitate: **7** reclaim, recover, restore, salvage **9** reinstate

rehash: **6** go over, repeat **7** restate **9** rechauffe

rehearse: say **4** cite, tell **5** drill, quote, speak, train **6** detail, recite, relate, repeat **7** mention, narrate, prepare, recount **8** describe, instruct, practice **9** enumerate **12** recapitulate

Rehoboam: hat **4** king **6** bottle, flagon
father: **7** Solomon
kingdom: **5** Judah **6** Israel
son: **6** Abijah

reign: raj **4** rule, sway **5** guide, power, realm **6** empire, govern **7** dynasty, kingdom, prevail **8** dominate **9** authority, dominance **10** prevalence **11** predominate
pert. to: **6** regnal

reimburse: pay **5** repay **6** defray, offset, recoup, refund **7** recover, replace **9** indemnify **10** compensate, recompense, remunerate

rein: **4** curb, slow, stop, turn **5** check, guide, leash, strap **6** bridle, direct, govern, haunch, kidney **7** compose, control, repress **8** restrain **9** hindrance

reindeer: **6** tarand **7** caribou, cervine
family: **8** cervidae
genus: **8** rangifer
Santa's: See **Santa Claus's reindeer**

reinforce: **4** back **5** brace, reman **6** second **7** afforce, augment, bolster, stiffen, support **8** buttress, multiply **10** strengthen

reinforcement: **4** sput **9** accession

reinstate: **6** recall, revest **7** put back

reinvigorate: **7** quicken, refresh

reiterate: **4** drum, echo, harp **6** repeat, resume **7** restate **8** rehearse **10** ingeminate **12** recapitulate

reject: **4** defy, snub **5** eject, repel, scorn, scout, spurn, vomit **6** abjure, disown, rebuff, recuse, refuse **7** cashier, decline, discard, dismiss, disobey, forsake, shut out **8** abnegate, castaway, disallow, forswear, relegate, renounce **9** blackball, eliminate, ostracize, reprobate, repudiate **10** disapprove

rejoice: **5** cheer, elate, exult, glory, revel **6** please **7** delight, gladden **8** jubilate **9** celebrate **10** exhilarate, tripudiate

rejoin: **5** reply **6** answer **7** respond, reunite

rekindle: **6** revive **7** relight

relapse: **4** fall, sink, slip **7** setback, subside **9** backslide **10** recurrence

relate: **4** ally, tell **5** apply, refer, state **6** allude, detail, recite, report **7** connect, declare, narrate, pertain, recount, restore **8** describe, rehearse **9** appertain, associate, correlate, enumerate **10** make public

related: kin **4** akin **7** cognate, connate, germane, kindred **9** affiliate, connected **10** becousined **11** appropriate
on father's side: **6** agnate
on mother's side: **5** enate **6** enatic **7** cognate

relation: kin, sib **4** link **5** blood, ratio **6** degree, family, status **7** account, bearing, history, kinship, sibling **8** affinity, standing **10** connection, friendship
mutual: **11** correlation

relative: eme, kin, sib **4** aunt, mama, papa, twin **5** aunty, niece, uncle **6** auntie, cousin, father, friend, mother, nephew, parent, sister **7** brother, kindred, kinsman, sibling **8** ancestor, apposite, relation, relevant **9** connected, kinswoman, pertinent **10** pertaining **11** comparative, grandfather, grandmother, grandparent
distant: **10** kissing kin

relative amount: **5** ratio **6** ration

relatives: **6** family **7** kinfolk **8** cousinry, kinsfolk
favoritism to: **8** nepotism

relax: **4** ease, open, rest **5** abate, loose, remit **6** divert, lessen, loosen, reduce, soften, unbend **7** cool off, mollify, release, relieve, slacken **8** be at ease, calm down, mitigate **10** feel at home

relaxation: **4** ease, rest **6** repose **7** detente (F.), relache **9** amusement, diversion **10** recreation **11** delassement

relaxed: **4** calm, lash **7** lenient **8** flexuous, informal

relay: **4** post, race **5** spell **6** remuda (Sp.), sup-

607

remainder

ply **7** forward, relieve, station **8** avantlay, transmit

release: **4** bail, drop, emit, free, liss, trip, undo, vent **5** let go, lisse, relay, remit, slake, untie, yield **6** acquit, assoil, demise, exempt, loosen, parole, remise, rescue, spring **7** absolve, deliver, disband, freedom, manumit, publish, relieve, unleash, unloose **8** cut loose, liberate, mitigate, unfasten **9** acquittal, discharge, disengage, eliminate, exculpate, extricate **10** emancipate, liberation, permission, relinquish **11** acquittance, deliverance **12** emancipation
in law: **9** remission, surrender **10** relinquish
in music: **6** bridge

relegate: **5** exile, refer **6** banish, charge, commit, deport, remove **7** consign, dismiss **8** accredit, turn over

relent: **4** melt **5** abate, let up, yield **6** soften **7** abandon, liquefy, mollify, slacken **8** dissolve, moderate **10** deliquesce

relentless: **4** grim, hard **5** cruel, harsh, stern, stony **6** fierce, strict **8** pitiless, rigorous, ruthless **10** inexorable, persistent **11** unremitting

relevant: apt **5** ad rem **6** timely **7** apropos, germain, germane **8** apposite **9** connected, pertinent **10** applicable, to the point **11** appropriate, referential

reliable: **4** safe, true **5** tried **6** dinkum, honest, secure, steady, trusty **7** certain **9** authentic, unfailing **10** believable, dependable, infallible **11** trustworthy

reliance: **4** hope **5** faith, trust **6** belief **8** affiance, credence **10** confidence, dependence

relic: **5** curio, mummy **6** corpse, hallow, remain **7** antique, leaving, memento, remnant, residue, vestige **8** memorial, souvenir **11** remembrance
of death: **11** memento mori
pert. to: **9** reliquary

relic cabinet: **6** etager **7** etagere, whatnot

relict: **5** widow **7** widower **8** residual, survivor

relief: aid, bot **4** alms, boot, bote, dole, ease, help **6** assist, succor **7** comfort **10** assistance, mitigation **11** alleviation
ornamental: **4** fret **7** relievo

relieve: aid **4** beet, ease, free, help, liss **5** abate, allay, beete, erase, lisse, raise, relay, slake, spare, spell **6** assist, lessen, remedy, remove, succor **7** assuage, comfort, console, deliver, lighten, redress, release, support, sustain, unloose **8** diminish, mitigate **9** alleviate, debarrass, disburden, discharge, exonerate

religieuse (F.): nun **6** sister **9** religious

religieux (F.): **5** pious **6** devout **9** religious

religion: **4** cult, sect **5** creed, faith, piety **6** belief, church **7** service, worship **8** devotion, doctrine, fidelity **9** adoration
sect: **5** alogi
study of: **8** theology
system of: **5** faith

religious (see also specific religions): **4** holy **5** exact, godly, pious **6** devout, divine **7** fervent, godlike, zealous **8** faithful, monastic **9** pietistic, spiritual **10** devotional, scrupulous
belief: **5** credo, creed
brotherhood: **8** sodality
directory: **4** ordo **7** ordines (pl.)
formally: **5** rigid **6** strict **8** orthodox **9** pharisaic
image: **4** icon, ikon **6** statue
military order member: **7** Templar
offering: **5** tithe **7** deodand **8** oblation
reformer: Hus **4** Huss, Knox **6** Luther, Wesley **7** Zwingli
sayings: **5** logia

relinquish: **4** cede, drop, quit **5** demit, forgo, grant, leave, waive, yield **6** desert, forego, give up, remise, resign **7** abandon, dispose, forsake, lay down **8** abdicate, abnegate, disgorge, renounce **9** surrender

reliquary: box **4** apse, arca **5** apsis, chest **6** casket, chasse, shrine **7** chorten

reliquiae: **6** relics **7** remains

relish: **4** dash, gust, like, tang, zest **5** achar, enjoy, gusto, sauce, savor, taste **6** admire, canape, degust, flavor, palate, savour **7** delight, flavour **8** appetite, hautgout **9** appetizer, condiment, degustate, enjoyment, seasoning **10** appreciate **11** inclination
kind: **5** achar, curry **6** catsup, caviar **7** botargo, chutney, mustard **8** tapenade

relucent: **6** bright **7** radiant, shining **9** refulgent

reluct: **5** fight **6** revolt **8** struggle

reluctance: **6** revolt **8** aversion **9** adversion, antipathy, hesitancy **10** opposition, repugnance, resistance **13** indisposition, unwillingness **14** disinclination

reluctant: **4** loth, wary **5** loath **6** averse, forced **7** adverse **8** backward, grudging, hesitant, opposing **9** resisting, unwilling **11** disinclined

rely: **4** bank, base, hold, hope, lean, rest **5** bet on, count, rally, trust **6** belong, cleave, depend, expect, lippen, reckon, repose **7** believe, confide, count on

Remagen's river: **5** Rhine

remain: lie **4** bide, last, rest, stay, wait **5** abide, dwell, hover, stand, tarry, thole **6** endure, linger, reside **7** persist, survive **8** continue **11** stick around

remainder: **4** lees, orts, rest, stub **5** dross, stump **6** excess, refuse, scraps **7** balance, grounds, remanet, remnant, residue, surplus **8** leavings, residual, residuum **9** leftovers

remains: **4** dust **5** ashes, relic, ruins, trace **6** corpse, fossil **7** vestige

remand: **6** commit **7** consign **8** recommit, send back

remanent: **7** further **8** enduring **10** additional **13** supplementary

remark: say, see **4** barb, heed, note, word **5** aside, gloss, state, write **6** notice, postil, regard **7** comment, descant, express, observe **8** indicate, perceive **9** aspersion, platitude **10** animadvert, annotation, commentary, expression **11** distinguish, observation

embarrassing: **5** boner, break **7** blooper, faux pas

incidental: **12** obiter dictum

witty: gag, mot **4** quip **5** sally **6** bon mot **7** sarcasm **9** witticism

remarkable: **7** strange, unusual **8** uncommon **9** egregious, wonderful **10** noteworthy, noticeable, phenomenal **11** exceptional

remble: **4** move, stir

remedy: aid, bot **4** balm, boot, bote, cure, drug, gain, hale, heal, help **5** amend, salve, topic **6** arcana (pl.), elixir, physic, relief, repair **7** arcanum, correct, cure-all, nostrum, panacea, placebo, rectify, redress, relieve **8** antidote, curative, medicine **9** treatment **10** assistance, catholicon, chevisance, corrective

imaginary: **6** elixir **7** panacea, placebo

quack: **7** nostrum, placebo

remember: **4** cite **6** ideate, recall, record, remind, retain, reward **7** bethink, mention **8** memorize **9** recollect, reminisce **10** look back on **11** commemorate

remembrance: **4** gift, mind **5** relic, token **6** memory, minnie, notice, trophy **7** memento, mention **8** allusion, keepsake, memorial, souvenir **12** recollection

remex: **5** quill **7** feather

remind: jog **4** hint, prod **5** nudge **6** recall **7** suggest

reminder: cue **4** hint, memo, note, prod, twit **7** memento, monitor **10** admonition, expression

reminiscence: act **4** fact, tale **5** power **6** memoir, memory **9** anamnesis, recalling **10** experience **11** memorabilia, remembering, remembrance **12** recollection

remiss: lax **4** lazy, mild, pale **5** slack, tardy **6** gentle **7** diluted, languid, lenient, relaxed **8** careless, derelict, dilatory, faineant, heedless, indolent, moderate, slothful **9** dissolved, liquefied, negligent **10** neglectful **11** inattentive, thoughtless **13** irresponsible

remission: **6** hiatus, rebate **7** respite **9** abolition, cessation, lessening **10** diminution

remit: pay **4** send **5** abate, defer, enter, refer, relax, spend **6** cancel, excuse, insert, pardon, resign, return, submit **7** abandon, absolve, forgive, forward, readmit, release, restore, slacken, suspend **8** abrogate, liberate, mitigate, moderate, postpone, recommit, transmit **9** exculpate

remittance: **7** payment **9** allowance

remnant: bit, end, ort, rag **4** dreg, fent, left, part, rest, stub **5** crumb, piece, relic, scrap, trace, wrack **7** leaving, portion, remains, residue, vestige **8** fragment **9** remainder **10** suggestion

remodel: **6** change, recast **7** rebuild **8** renovate **11** reconstruct

remolade, remoulade: **5** sauce **8** dressing, ointment

remonstrance: **5** demur **7** protest **10** benedicite

remonstrate: **5** argue, fight **6** combat, object **7** declare, profess, protest **8** complain **11** demonstrate, expostulate

remora: **4** clog, drag, fish, pega **5** delay **7** pegador **9** hindrance **10** impediment

remorse: rue **4** pity, ruth **5** grief, qualm **6** regret, sorrow **7** penance **8** distress **9** penitence **10** compassion, contrition, repentance **11** compunction

remote: far, off **4** afar, back, cool **5** alien, aloof, faint, vague **6** forane, slight **7** distant, faraway, foreign, obscure, removed **8** isolated, secluded, separate, unlikely **9** backwater **10** abstracted, impersonal, unfriendly **11** out of the way

goal or end: **5** Thule

more: **7** endmost, farther **8** ulterior

most: **6** ultima **8** farthest **9** diametric **11** farthermost, ultima Thule

remove: rid **4** bate, dele, doff, fire, free, kill, move, oust, pare, raze, rend, sack, void, weed **5** amove, apart, avoid, elide, eloin, erase, evict, expel, strip **6** banish, betake, cancel, change, convey, deduct, delete, depose, disbar, distal, eloign, recall, remble, retire, uproot **7** cast off, deprive, despoil, dismiss, extract, take off, uncover, whittle **8** abstract, disclose, discover, dislodge, displace, relegate, separate, supplant, transfer **9** clear away, eliminate, eradicate, translate **10** disconnect **11** assassinate

by surgery: **6** ablate **8** amputate

clothing: **5** strip **7** disrobe, undress

from office: **4** oust **6** depose, recall **7** dismiss, impeach

hair: **5** shave **8** depilate

ice: **7** defrost

impurities: **5** smelt **6** filter, refine

seeds: **5** stone
skin: **4** hull, husk, pare, peel

removed: off **4** away, move **5** alone, aloof, apart **6** remote **7** distant, obscure **10** abstracted

remuneration: pay **5** wages **6** reward, salary **7** payment, stipend **8** requital **9** emolument, repayment **10** recompense **12** compensation, satisfaction **13** consideration, gratification, reimbursement

remunerative: **10** beneficial, profitable **12** advantageous

Remus: See **Romulus and Remus**

renaissance: **7** rebirth, revival

renal: **7** nephric **9** nephritic

Renard: See **Reynard**

rend: cut, rip **4** pull, rent, rive, slit, tear **5** break, burst, sever, split, wrest **6** breach, cleave, divide, enrive, pierce, remove, screed, sunder **7** abscind, dispart, disrupt, rupture **8** lacerate, separate **9** dismember

render: pay, put, try **4** emit, give, make, melt **5** treat, yield **6** depict, recite, repeat, return, submit **7** clarify, deliver, exhibit, extract, furnish, inflict, payment, perform, present, requite, restore **8** transmit **9** interpret, represent, surrender, translate **10** administer

rendezvous: **4** date, meet **5** place, tryst **6** affair, gather, refuge **7** hangout, meeting, retreat **8** assemble, mobilize **9** agreement, gathering **11** appointment

rendition: **8** delivery **9** surrender **11** deliverance, performance, translation

renegade: rat **5** rebel **6** bolter **7** traitor **8** apostate, deserter, fugitive, renegado, turncoat **10** changeling

renege, renig: **4** deny **5** cheat, welsh **6** desert, refuse, revoke **7** decline **8** back down, renounce

renew: **4** beet, mend **5** beete **6** extend, refill, repair, repeat, resume, revamp, revive, update **7** freshen, rebuild, refresh, remodel, replace, restore **8** make over, recreate, reassume, rekindle, renovate **9** modernize, refurbish, replenish **10** invigorate, recommence, regenerate, rejuvenate **11** re-establish, reintegrate

renitent: **7** opposed **8** opposing **9** obstinate, resistant **12** recalcitrant

rennet: lab **5** apple **6** curdle, keslop **7** earning (Sc.) **8** earnings (Sc.), membrane **9** cheeselip, coagulate
ferment: **6** enzyme, rennin

renounce: **4** cede, defy, deny, quit **5** cease, forgo, renay, renig, waive **6** abjure, defect, desert, disown, eschew, forego, forlet, forsay, give up, recant, reject, renege, repeal, resign **7** abandon, disavow, forbear, forfeit, forsake, retract **8** abdicate, abnegate, disclaim, forspeak, forswear, renounce **9** repudiate, surrender **10** abrenounce, relinquish

renovate: **4** mend, redo **5** alter, clean, renew **6** purify, repair, resume, revive **7** cleanse, furbish, refresh, replace, restore **10** invigorate, regenerate

renown: rap **4** fame, name, note **5** eclat, glory, kudos, rumor **6** report **7** acclaim **8** eminence **9** celebrity **10** reputation **11** celebration, distinction

renowned: **5** known **6** famous **10** celebrated **11** illustrious

rent (see also **rend**): let, pay **4** gape, hire, hole, rime, toll, torn **5** censo, chink, cleft, crack, cuddy, gavel, gorge, lease, split **6** breach, engage, schism **7** fissure, opening, revenue, tribute
high: **8** rackrent
transfer: **6** attorn

rental: **4** cost, flat, list **5** house **8** lodgings, schedule **9** apartment

rente (F.): **6** income **7** annuity, revenue

renter: **6** lessee, roomer, tenant **8** occupant

reopen: **6** resume **10** recommence

rep: **4** fame **5** cloth **6** fabric **10** reputation

repair: fix **4** darn, heal, help, mend **5** amend, order, patch, piece, refit, renew **6** remedy, return, revamp, revive **7** correct, rebuild, restore **8** overhaul, renovate

repairman: **6** tinker **7** cobbler **8** mechanic

repand: **4** bent, wavy **6** uneven

reparation: **4** bote **6** amende, amends, reward **7** damages, redress **8** requital **9** amendment, atonement, indemnity, quittance, repairing **10** recompense **11** restitution **12** compensation

repartee: wit **5** reply **6** banter, retort **7** riposte, sarcasm **8** badinage

repast: tea **4** bait, feed, food, meal **5** bever, feast, lunch, snack, treat **6** brunch, dinner **7** banquet **9** collation, refection **11** refreshment
pert. to: **8** prandial

repatriation: **6** return **8** send home **11** restoration

repay: pay **4** meed **5** appay, award **6** avenge, offset, profit, punish, refund, return, reward **7** balance, deserve, requite, restore **9** gratulate, reimburse, retaliate **10** compensate, recompense, remunerate **11** reciprocate

repeal: **4** lift, void **5** amend, annul, emend **6** appeal, cancel, recall, revoke **7** abolish, rescind, retract, reverse **8** abrogate, derogate, renounce, withdraw

repeat: bis (It.), din **4** burp, cite, echo, rame **5** ditto, quote, recap, recur **6** encore, parrot, resume, retell **7** iterate, recount, reprise,

restate **8** redouble **9** duplicate, reiterate **10** ingeminate **12** recapitulate
performance: **6** encore
sign in music: **5** segno

repeatedly: oft **5** again, often **10** frequently **11** continually, day after day

repeater: gun **5** rifle, watch **6** pistol **7** firearm **8** holdover **10** recidivist

repel: **4** beat, stop **5** check, debar, force **6** combat, defend, oppose, rebuff, refuse, reject, remove, resist **7** decline, disgust, fend off, repulse **8** vanquish **10** extinguish

repellent: **4** grim **5** harsh, nasty **9** offensive, repugnant, repulsive, revolting

repent: rue **5** atone, mourn **6** bewail, grieve, lament, regret **7** reptant **8** crawling, creeping, forthink, penitent

repentance: **4** pity, ruth **5** shame **7** penance, remorse **9** attrition, penitence **10** contrition **11** compunction

repentant: **8** contrite **9** regretful **10** remorseful **11** penitential

repercussion: **4** blow, echo **5** tenor **6** effect, impact, recoil **7** rebound **8** backwash, reaction

repertory: **4** list **5** index **7** theater, theatre **8** calendar, magazine, treasury **9** catalogue **10** collection, storehouse

repetition: bis **4** copy, echo, rote **5** rondo **6** dilogy, encore **7** replica, tremolo **8** iterance **9** duplicate, iteration, rehearsal **10** redundancy **12** reproduction
mechanical: **4** rote **8** anaphora
of homologous parts: **6** merism
of idea: **8** pleonasm **9** tautology
of others: **7** echolia, mimicry **9** echolalia

repine: **4** fail, fret, mope, wane **5** mourn **6** grieve, grouse, lament, regret, weaken **7** grumble, whimper **8** complain, languish

replace: **5** alter, reset, stead **6** change, follow, recoup **7** put back, relieve, restore, succeed **8** supplant **9** reimburse, supersede **10** substitute

replacement: **6** ersatz **9** successor **10** substitute

replenish: **4** feed, fill **5** renew, stock **6** refill **7** restore

replete: fat **4** full, rife **5** alive, sated, stout **6** filled, gorged **7** bloated, implete, stocked, stuffed **8** complete **9** abounding, surfeited

replica: **4** copy **5** image **6** carbon, ectype **8** likeness **9** facsimile, imitation **10** repetition

replicate: **4** bend, copy, fold **5** reply **6** repeat **8** manifold, repeated **9** duplicate

reply: **4** echo, fold, sass **5** rebut **6** answer, oracle, re-echo, rejoin, repeat, retort, return **7** respond, retract, riposte **8** repartee, response **9** rejoinder

report: pop **4** fame, tell, word **5** bruit, noise,

rumor, state, story **6** breeze, cahier (F.), delate, digest, recite, relate, repeat, return, rumour **7** account, crackle, hansard, hearing, hearsay, inkling, narrate, recital, summary **8** announce, describe **9** circulate, grapevine, narration, narrative **10** reputation
false: fib, lie **6** canard **7** slander **8** tall-tale

reporter: cub **6** legman, writer **7** newsman **9** columnist, newswoman **10** journalist
symbol: **6** thirty

repose: lie, set, sit **4** calm, ease, rely, rest, seat **5** peace, place, quiet, sleep **6** relief **7** compose, confide, deposit, dignity, recline, replace, restore, support **8** calmness, serenity **9** composure, quietness **10** relaxation, stretch out

repository: ark, box **4** bank, file, safe, shop **5** ambry, capsa, chest, depot, vault **6** closet, museum **7** archive, arsenal, capsule, granary, storage **8** magazine, treasury **9** confidant, reliquary, sepulcher, warehouse **10** depository, storehouse

reposoir: **5** altar

repossess: **6** regain **7** recover **8** retrieve

reprehend: **4** warn **5** blame, chide, scold **6** berate, rebuke **7** censure, reprove, upbraid **8** admonish, disprove **9** criticize

reprehensible: **8** criminal, culpable **11** blameworthy

represent: act **4** play, show **5** enact, image **6** clothe, denote, depict, embody, render, typify **7** exhibit, express, picture, portray, produce, profess **8** describe, simulate **9** delineate, designate, epitomize, exemplify, reproduce, symbolize **10** illustrate **11** impersonate

representation: map **4** icon, idol, ikon **5** chart, graph, image, model **6** avowal, blazon, sample, symbol **7** account, diagram, drawing, picture **8** likeness, notation **9** portrayal, statement **10** similitude **11** histrionics, performance, portraiture

representative: **4** heir **5** agent, envoy **6** consul, deputy, legate, nuncio **7** senator, tribune, typical **8** delegate, emissary, executor, exponent, instance, salesman **10** ambassador **12** illustrating, illustrative

repress: **4** bury, curb, hush, rein, stop **5** check, choke, crush, daunt, press, quell **6** bridle, censor, deaden, reduce, stifle, subdue **7** compose, depress, inhibit **8** compress, restrain, restrict, suppress, withhold **9** constrain

reprieve: **5** defer, delay, grace **6** escape **7** amnesty, respite, suspend **8** postpone

reprimand: rap, wig **4** call **5** check, chide, scold, slate **6** rebuff, rebuke **7** censure, chapter, chasten, condemn, repress, reproof, reprove **8** admonish, call down **9** criticize, reprehend

reprint: **4** copy

reprisal: **7** redress **8** requital **9** tit for tat **11** eye for an eye

reprise: **6** repeat **8** reassume **10** compensate, recommence, repetition

reproach: **4** blot, slur, twit **5** abuse, blame, braid, chide, shame, shend, sully, taunt **6** accuse, infamy, rebuke, revile, stigma, vilify **7** censure, condemn, reprove, traduce, upbraid **8** besmirch, disgrace, dishonor **9** bespatter, challenge, contumely, discredit, disrepute, invective **10** correction, exprobrate, opprobrium, scurrility **11** impeachment **12** vilification **13** animadversion
old word of: **4** raca

reprobate: cad, cur, dog, rat **4** hard, heel **5** knave, rogue, Satan, scamp, wrong **6** disown, rascal, reject **7** abandon, bounder, condemn, corrupt, decline, vicious **8** blamable, castaway, denounce, hardened **9** abandoned, blameable, condemned, criticize, dissolute, reprehend, scoundrel **10** censurable, disallowed **11** blameworthy, disapproved **12** unprincipled

reproduce: **4** copy, draw, sire **5** breed **6** repeat **7** imitate **8** multiply **9** duplicate, procreate, propagate, represent **11** reconstruct
asexually: bud **5** clone **11** sporulation

reproduction: **6** ectype **7** fission, replica **8** likeness **9** facsimile, photostat **10** carbon copy

reproductive: **8** prolific

reproductive cell: **6** gamete

reprove: **4** flay, rate, slam **5** blame, check, chide, roast, scold, shame **6** berate, rebuff, rebuke, refute, reject **7** censure, confute, correct, lecture, upbraid **8** admonish, carritch, chastise, disgrace, disprove, lambaste, redargue, reproach **9** castigate, challenge, criticize, objurgate, reprehend, reprimand, reprobate **10** administer, animadvert

reptant: **8** crawling, creeping

reptile: **4** croc, worm **5** skink, snake **6** cayman, gavial, lizard, turtle **7** tuatara **8** dinosaur, tortoise **9** alligator, crocodile, pterosaur **11** gila monster, pterodactyl
age: **8** Mesozoic
edible: **5** snake **6** iguana, turtle
group: **6** sauria
inactive state: **10** estivation
legless: **4** apod **5** snake
pert. to: **7** saurian **8** ophidian
scale: **5** plate, scute
shelled: **6** turtle **8** tortoise
study of: **11** herpetology

reptilian: low **4** mean **5** snaky **6** lizard, sneaky

7 reptant, saurian, serpent **8** crawling, creeping, herpetic, ophidian **9** groveling, malignant **10** despicable

republic: **5** state **6** nation **9** democracy **10** commonweal, government

Republic author: **5** Plato

repudiate: **4** defy, deny **5** spurn **6** abjure, defect, disown, recant, refuse, reject **7** abandon, decline, disavow, discard, divorce, forsake, retract **8** abrogate, disclaim, renounce **9** disaffirm

repugn: **5** fight **6** oppose, resist

repugnance: **5** odium **6** enmity, hatred **7** disgust, dislike **8** aversion, distaste, loathing **9** antipathy, hostility, repulsion **10** abhorrence, antagonism, opposition, reluctance **11** abomination

repugnant: **4** foul, vile **6** odious **8** inimical **9** offensive, repellent **10** refractory

repulse: **4** deny, foil, rout **5** check, fling, rebut, refel, repel **6** defeat, denial, rebuff, refuse, reject **7** disgust, exclude, fend off, refusal **9** rejection

repulsive: **4** dain, evil, loth, ugly, vile **5** loath, toady **6** odious **7** fulsome, hateful, loathly **9** loathsome, offensive, repellent, repugnant, revolting **10** disgusting, forbidding **11** distasteful, gorgonesque

repurchase: **6** redeem

reputable: **4** good **8** credible, esteemed **10** creditable **11** respectable, responsible

reputation: **4** fame, name, note, odor **5** eclat, glory, honor, izzat, odour, stamp **6** credit, honour, renown, repute **7** respect **8** standing **9** attribute, character **11** distinction
loss of: **5** shame **7** scandal

reputed: dit **8** putative, supposed **11** conjectural **12** hypothetical

request: ask, beg, sue **4** plea, pray, suit, wish **5** apply, crave, order **6** appeal, behest, demand, invite **7** entreat, implore, prithee, solicit **8** entreaty, petition, rogation **11** application **12** solicitation
for help: SOS
formal: **8** petition, rogation

requiem: **4** hymn, Mass, rest, song **5** chant, dirge, peace, quiet **7** service

requiescat: **4** wish **6** prayer
in pace: **11** rest in peace

requiescence: **4** rest **6** repose

requin: **5** shark **8** man-eater

require: ask **4** lack, need **5** claim, crave, exact, force **6** behove, compel, demand, enjoin, entail, expect, oblige **7** behoove **9** postulate **11** necessitate

requirement: **4** duty **9** essential, formality, necessity, requisite

requisite: **4** just, need **7** needful **9** condition, essential **11** requirement

requisition: 5 order 6 billet, demand 7 embargo, request

requital: 6 amends 7 guerdon 8 reprisal 9 repayment, vengeance 11 retaliation, retribution

requite: pay 5 atone, repay 6 acquit, avenge, defray, return, reward 7 content, deserve, gratify, revenge, satisfy 9 retaliate 10 compensate, recompense

reredos: 4 wall 6 screen 7 brazier, drapery 9 backplate, partition

rerun: 6 repeat, replay, reshow

res: 5 point, thing 6 matter 7 subject

rescind: 4 lift, void 5 annul 6 cancel, repeal, revoke 7 abolish, retract, reverse 8 abrogate 11 countermand

rescript: 5 edict, order 6 answer, decree, letter 9 rewriting 11 counterpart

rescue: 4 free, help, save 6 ransom, redeem, succor 7 deliver, reclaim, recover, release, salvage 8 delivery, liberate 9 extricate 11 deliverance

research: 4 test 5 study 7 inquiry 11 examination 13 investigation 15 experimentation

reseau: net 6 ground 7 network 10 foundation 12 filter screen

reseda: 5 plant 9 gray-green 10 mignonette

resemblance: 5 image 6 simile, symbol 7 analogy 8 affinity, likeness, parallel, vicinity 9 agreement, imitation, semblance 10 comparison, similarity, similitude

one bearing: 6 ringer 9 lookalike

resemble: 5 favor 8 look like 9 take after

resentment: ire 4 gall 5 anger, depit, pique, spite 6 animus, choler, enmity, grudge, hatred, malice, rancor, spleen 7 dudgeon, ill will, offense, umbrage 8 acrimony, bad blood 9 animosity, annoyance, hostility, malignity 10 irritation 11 displeasure, indignation

reserve: 4 book, cash, cave, fund, keep, save 5 spare, stock, store 6 assets, retain, supply 7 backlog, bespeak, caution, modesty, nest egg, shyness, silence, surplus 8 coldness, distance, forprise, preserve, withhold 9 exception, reservoir, restraint, retention, reticence 10 constraint, diffidence, discretion, substitute

reserved: coy, shy 4 cold 5 aloof, saved, staid, taken 6 sedate 7 bashful, distant 8 backward, cautious, withheld 9 qualified 10 unsociable

reservoir: vat 4 font, pond, pool, sump, tank 5 basin, fount, stope, store 6 cenote, supply 7 cistern, favissa, forebay, piscina 8 favissae (pl.)

reset: 4 boot, help 5 abode, alter 6 harbor, refuge, resort, succor 7 receipt, receive, replace, secrete, shelter 9 receiving

reside: lie 4 bigg, live, room, stay 5 abide, dwell, habit, lodge 6 remain, settle 7 consist, hang out, inhabit, sojourn, subside 8 habitate

residence: 4 digs, home, seat, shed 5 abode, house, villa 6 biding, castle, palace 7 habitat, mansion 8 domicile, residuum, sediment 9 apartment 10 habitation, villanette

resident: cit 6 lessee, tenant 7 burgess, citizen, denizen, dweller 8 inherent, occupant

residue: ask 4 dreg, lees, marc, orts, rest, silt, slag 5 ashes, dregs 6 cinder, excess, relics, sludge, sordes 7 balance, remains, remnant 8 leavings, remanent, residuum, sediment

residuum: 7 deposit 8 hangover 9 remainder

resign: 4 quit 5 demit, leave, remit, yield 6 devote, submit 7 abandon, consign, deliver 8 abdicate, renounce 9 surrender

resignation: 7 modesty 8 meekness, patience 9 endurance 12 acquiescence

resile: 6 recede, return 7 rebound, retract, retreat 8 back down, withdraw

resilient: 5 toned 7 buoyant, elastic, springy 8 bouncing, flexible, stretchy, volatile 9 recoiling 10 rebounding

resin, rosin: alk, gum, lac, tar 4 aloe, balm, tolu 5 amber, anime, animi, copal, damar, elemi, gugal, gugul, loban, myrrh, pitch, roset, syrup 6 balsam, charas, dammar, derrid, elemin, googul, salban, storax 7 acouchi, acrylic, ambrite, arioera, copaiba, copaiva, derride, exudate, fluavil, galipot, hartite, ladanum, retinol 8 alkitran, bdellium, fluavile, gedanite, glessite, guaiacum, labdanum, retinite, sandarac 9 alchitran, asafetida, colophony, elaterite 11 colophonium 12 frankincense

fossil: 5 amber 8 glessite, retinite

gum: 5 gugal, myrrh 6 mastic 8 bdellium

incense: 5 myrrh 8 sandarac 12 frankincense

purified: 7 shellac

varnish: 5 anime, copal

resinous tree: fir 4 pine 6 balsam

resist: 4 balk, buck, defy, fend 5 rebel, repel 6 baffle, combat, defeat, defend, impugn, oppose, wither 7 contest, counter, dispute, prevent 8 obstruct, traverse 9 frustrate, gainstand, withstand

resistance: 6 rebuff 7 defense 9 hostility, renitence 10 antagonism, oppugnance

resistant: 4 hard 8 obdurate, stubborn

resolute: 4 bold, firm 5 fixed 6 dogged 7 animose, animous, decided, earnest 8 constant, faithful, positive, resolved, stalwart, stubborn, unshaken 9 unbending 10 determined, unwavering

resolution: vow 4 grit, guts, thew 5 heart, nerve, pluck, spunk 6 mettle, spirit 7 courage, purpose, resolve, verdict **8** analysis, backbone, decision, firmness, proposal, strength **9** assurance, certainty, constancy, fortitude, hardihood, statement, sternness, stoutness **10** conviction, separation, steadiness **11** intrepidity, persevering **12** deliberation, faithfulness, perseverance **13** determination, inflexibility, steadfastness

resolve: **4** free, melt **5** relax, solve, untie **6** answer, assoil, decide, dispel, inform, loosen, reduce, remove, settle **7** analyze, appoint, dispose, explain, liquefy, scatter, unravel **8** conclude, decision, dissolve, enfeeble, persuade, separate

resonant: **4** deep, full, rich **5** round **6** mellow, rotund **7** ringing, vibrant **8** sonorous, sounding **10** resounding

resort: inn, spa, use **4** howf **5** crowd, haunt, haven, hotel, howff, joint, lodge, place, visit **6** betake, casino, refuge, return, revert, throng **7** company, retreat **8** frequent, habitual, recourse **10** assemblage, fall back on

resound: **4** echo, peal, ring **5** clang **6** re-echo **11** reverberate

resounding: **7** vibrant **8** emphatic

resource: **5** shift **6** device **7** stopgap

resourceful: apt **5** sharp **6** clever

resources: **5** funds, means, money **6** assets, riches, stocks, stores **7** capital, fortune, resorts **8** property, reserves, supplies, supports **10** expedients

guardian: **9** ecologist **11** conservancy **15** conservationist

respect: awe **4** heed **5** defer, honor, value **6** admire, esteem, homage, regard, revere **7** concern, observe, respite, tribute, worship **8** postpone, venerate **9** attention, deference, reference, reverence

act of: bow **6** devoir, salaam, salute **7** curtsey

pay: **5** greet, kneel, toast **6** salute **7** curtsey **9** genuflect

respectable: **4** good **6** decent, honest, proper **7** fausant **8** decorous **9** estimable, honorable, reputable

respectful: **5** civil **6** polite **7** careful, duteous, dutiful **8** gracious **9** courteous

respective: **4** each **6** sundry **7** partial, several **9** regardful **10** individual, particular

respiration: **6** breath **7** eupnoea **9** breathing

difficulty: **4** rale **5** cough **7** dyspnea **8** dyspnoea **9** emphysema, pneumonia

respire: **4** live, sigh **6** exhale, inhale **7** breathe

respite: **4** lull, rest **5** break, delay, pause **6** hiatus, recess **7** leisure **8** interval, reprieve, surcease **9** cessation **10** suspension **12** intermission, postponement

resplendent: **6** bright **7** aureate, blazing,

flaming, glowing, radiant, shining **8** dazzling, glorious, gorgeous, lustrous, splendid **9** brilliant, refulgent **10** epiphanous, flamboyant

respond: **4** echo, feel **5** react, reply, write **6** accord, answer, pillar, rejoin, retort, return **8** response **10** correspond

response: **4** word **5** reply, verse **6** anthem, chorus, letter, phrase **7** introit, refrain **8** sentence

involuntary: **6** reflex **7** tropism **8** knee-jerk

responsibility: **4** care, duty, onus **6** burden, charge **9** liability **10** obligation **11** reliability

responsible: **6** liable **8** amenable **9** accordant, reputable **10** answerable, dependable, sufficient **11** trustworthy

responsive: **5** aware **6** mutual, tender **8** amenable, sentient **9** sensitive **11** sympathetic

res publica (L.): **5** state **8** republic **10** commonweal **12** commonwealth

rest: lay, lie, set, sit **4** clam, ease, hang, lair, lean, liss, prop, rely, seat, slip, stay, stop **5** abide, cease, found, let up, lisse, pause, peace, quiet, relax, renew, repos (F.), sleep, stand **6** alight, cesura, depend, desist, ease up, remain, repose, settle **7** balance, caesura, comfort, leisure, lie down, refresh, remains, remnant, reposal, residue, respite, shelter, support, surplus **8** breather, interval, slack off, vacation **9** cessation, establish, quietness, remainder, stillness **10** immobility, inactivity, relaxation **11** refreshment **12** intermission

noonday: nap **6** siesta

poetic: **7** caesura

rest house: inn **4** chan, khan **5** hotel, motel, serai **6** abalam, hostel, tavern **7** chhatri **11** caravansery **12** caravanserai

restate: **6** repeat, reword **8** reassert, say again **10** paraphrase

restaurant: inn **4** cafe **5** diner, grill, hotel **6** bistro, tavern **7** automat, beanery, cabaret, tearoom **9** brasserie, cafeteria, chophouse, hashhouse, trattoria **10** rotisserie, steakhouse **11** rathskeller (G).

restful: **5** quiet **6** placid, serene **8** peaceful, tranquil

resting: **4** abed **6** asleep, latent **7** dormant

restitution: **6** amends, return **7** redress **8** recovery **10** recompense, reparation **11** restoration **12** compensation

restive: **5** balky, tense **6** uneasy, unruly **7** fidgety, nervous **8** contrary, perverse, restless, stubborn **9** impatient **10** refractory

restless: **5** itchy, jumpy **6** fidget, fitful, haunty, hectic, roving, uneasy **7** agitato (It.), fidgety, fretful, inquiet, jittery, nervous, restive, unquiet **8** agitated, feverish, stirring **9** disturbed, impatient, sleepless, unsettled, wandering **10** disquieted

restoration: **6** repair **7** renewal **10** reparation **11** restitution

restorative: **5** tonic **6** remedy **7** anodyne **8** salutary **9** analeptic

restore: **4** cure, heal, mend **5** amend, atone, renew, repay, right **6** redeem, refund, repair, return, revive **7** convert, get back, put back, rebuild, recover, replace **8** renovate **9** reinstate, resurrect **10** regenerate **11** re-establish, reconstruct, reintegrate, resuscitate

restrain: bar, dam, gag **4** bate, bind, calm, clog, curb, hold, rein, rule, stay, stop **5** chain, check, cramp, deter, guard, limit, still, stint **6** arrest, behave, bridle, coerce, detain, fetter, forbid, govern, halter, hamper, hinder, pinion, tether **7** abridge, abstain, chasten, command, compose, confine, contain, control, forbear, inhibit, prevent, repress, shackle, trammel **8** attemper, compesce, compress, conclude, imprison, moderate, prohibit, restrict, suppress, withhold

restrained: **5** quiet **6** severe **8** reserved **9** hidebound

restraint: bit **4** curb **5** check, force, leash **7** barrier, durance, reserve, shackle **9** avoidance, reticence
legal: **5** estop
of trade: **7** embargo

restrict: bar, tie **4** curb **5** bound, cramp, limit, scant, stint **6** censor, coerce, hamper, modify, ration, shrink **7** confine, repress, tighten **8** contract, derogate, prohibit, restrain, straiten

restricted: **5** local **6** closed, finite, narrow, strait **9** parochial **10** provincial

restriction: **5** cramp **9** condition, restraint **10** limitation, regulation **11** reservation

restrictive: **7** binding **8** limiting **9** confining, stringent

result: end, sum **4** leap, rise **5** close, ensue, event, fruit, issue, score, total **6** accrue, answer, effect, finish, follow, sequel, spring, upshot **7** outcome, proceed, redound **8** aftering, decision **9** aftermath, eventuate, terminate **10** conclusion **11** achievement, consequence

resume: **4** go on, vita **5** renew **6** pick up, reopen, repeat, review **7** dossier, epitome, summary **8** continue, reoccupy, return to, synopsis **9** biography, epitomize, reiterate, summarize **10** abridgment, recommence

resurrection: **6** Easter **7** rebirth, revival **11** restoration

resuscitate: **6** revive **7** quicken, restore **8** revivify

ret: rot, sop **4** soak **5** steep **6** dampen

retable: **5** ledge, shelf **6** gradin **9** framework

retail: **4** hawk, sell, vend **5** trade **6** barter, peddle, relate, repeat

retailer: **6** dealer **8** clothier, huckster, merchant, reseller

retain: **4** have, hire, hold, keep, save **6** adhere, athold, behold, employ **7** contain, prevent, reserve **8** maintain, preserve, remember, restrain, withhold **9** entertain, recollect

retainer: fee **4** cage **5** frame **6** lackey, menial, minion, vassal **7** hobbler, servant **8** employee, follower

retaining: **9** retentive

retaliate: **5** repay **6** avenge, punish, retort **7** requite, revenge

retaliation: **6** talion **7** revenge **8** reprisal, requital **9** vengeance **11** retribution

retard: **4** slow **5** brake, catch, defer, delay, deter, trash **6** belate, deaden, detain, fetter, hamper, hinder, impede **8** encumber, obstruct, postpone, restrain **10** decelerate

retardation: lag **4** drag **5** delay **8** slowness

retch: gag **4** hawk, keck, spit **5** heave, reach, vomit **6** expand, extend, strain **7** stretch

rete: **6** plexus **7** network

retention: **6** memory, recall **7** holding, keeping, storage **11** maintenance, remembering

retiary: **6** meshed, telary **7** netlike

reticent: shy **4** cool, dark **5** aloof, quiet **6** silent **7** distant, sparing **8** discreet, reserved, retiring, taciturn **9** secretive **10** mysterious

reticule: bag **4** etui **5** cabas, etwee **6** pocket, sachet **7** handbag, reticle, workbag **8** carryall

reticulum: net **7** network, stomach **8** meshwork

retinaculum: **6** frenum

retinue: **4** band, crew, ging, rout, suit, tail **5** harem, meiny, suite, train **6** attend, escort **7** cortege, service **8** equipage **9** entourage, following, retainers **10** attendants

retire: ebb **5** leave **6** depart, recede, recess, remove, turn in, vanish **7** pension, retreat **8** withdraw **9** sequester

retired: **4** abed, lone **5** quiet **6** secret **7** obscure, private, recluse **8** abstruse, emeritus, reserved, secluded, solitary **9** recondite

retiring: shy **5** timid **6** modest **7** bashful, fugient **8** reserved **9** diffident **11** introverted, unobtrusive

retort: mot **4** quip, turn **5** facer, repay, reply, sally **6** answer, recoil, return **7** alembic, cornute, respond, riposte **8** blizzard, comeback, repartee, take back **9** rejoinder, retaliate

retortion, retorsion: **7** bending **8** reprisal, twisting **10** reflection

retract: **4** bend **6** abjure, cancel, disown, recall, recant, remove, repeal, retire, revoke **7** disavow, prevent, rescind, retreat **8** restrain, withdraw **9** repudiate

retraction: **8** palinode

retral: **8** backward **9** posterior **10** retrograde

retreat: den, ebb, run **4** abri, cave, flee, holt, lair, nest, nook, quit, rout **5** arbor, bower, leave, yield **6** arbour, asylum, harbor, recede, recess, refuge, retire **7** harbour, privacy, pull out, retiral, shelter **8** fall back, solitude, withdraw **9** departure, hibernate, sanctuary, seclusion **10** retirement, withdrawal
religious: **5** asram **6** ashram
underground: **4** abri, cave **6** bunker

retrench: cut **4** bate, omit, pare **6** delete, excise, lessen, reduce, remove **7** abridge, curtail, cut back, repress, shorten **8** decrease, diminish **9** economize, intercept

retrenchment: **5** ditch **7** parapet, rampart **8** traverse **10** breastwork

retribution: pay **6** return, reward **7** nemesis, revenge, tribute **8** requital **9** vengeance **10** punishment, recompense
goddess of: Ate **4** Fury **7** Nemesis

retrieve: **6** recall, recoup, regain, revive **7** get back, reclaim, recover, restore, salvage **8** discover **10** recuperate

retrograde: **4** slow **5** lapse **6** recede, retral, worsen **7** decline, inverse, opposed, regress **8** backward, contrary, decadent, inverted, rearward, withdraw **9** backslide, catabolic, reversely **10** degenerate **11** deteriorate

retrogress: **4** sink **6** revert **9** backslide **10** degenerate

retrospective: **6** review **8** backward **11** retroactive **13** contemplative

return: lob **4** bend, turn **5** recur, remit, repay, yield **6** advert, answer, come in, profit, render, report, retort, revert **7** put back, regress, replace, reprise, requite, respond, restore, revenue, reverse **8** give back, requital, response, take back **9** repayment, repercuss, retaliate, reversion **10** recompense, recurrence **11** restoration **12** reappearance

Return of the Native author: **5** Hardy

Reuben: *brother:* **6** Joseph
father: **5** Jacob
mother: **4** Leah

Reuel's father: **4** Esau

reunite: **6** rejoin **9** reconcile

reus (L.): **9** defendant

revamp: **4** redo **5** renew **7** restyle, rewrite

reveal: bid **4** bare, blab, jamb, open, show, tell, wray **5** exert **6** betray, bewray, descry, detect, expose, impart, unveil **7** come out, confide, develop, display, divulge, exhibit, give out, let slip, publish, uncover **8** announce, decipher, develope, disclose, discover, evidence, manifest

reveille: **4** call, dian **5** diana, levet, rouse **6** signal

revel: joy **4** orgy, play, riot, wake **5** feast, let go, randy, spree, watch **6** bezzle, gavall, high-go **7** carouse, delight, revelry, roister **8** carnival, carousal, cut loose, domineer, festival **9** celebrate, festivity **11** celebration, merrymaking

revelation: **4** Tora **5** Torah **6** vision **8** epiphany, prophecy **9** discovery **10** apocalypse, disclosure

reveler, reveller: **6** ranter, rioter **8** bacchant **9** bacchanal, roisterer **10** merrymaker
cry: **4** evoe

revenant: **5** ghost **7** specter **9** recurring **10** apparition

revenge: **6** avenge, defend **7** redress, requite **8** reprisal, requital **9** retaliate, vengeance **11** retaliation, retribution

revenue: **4** rent **5** rente (F.), yield **6** income, profit, rental, return **7** finance **8** earnings, interest

reverberate: **4** echo, ring **6** return **7** reflect, resound

reverberating: **7** echoing, reboant, ringing **8** resonant **10** resounding

revere: **4** love **5** adore, honor, prize, value **6** admire, esteem, regard, repute **7** respect, worship **8** venerate

reverence: awe **4** fear **5** dread, honor, piety **6** homage **8** devotion **9** deference, obeisance, solemnity
gesture of: **8** kneeling **11** prostration **12** genuflection

reverend: sri **4** holy **5** abbot **6** clergy, priest, sacred **8** minister **9** clergyman, monsignor, venerable

reverent: **6** devout, humble **7** awesome, dutiful **10** worshipful

reverie: **5** dream, fancy **6** musing, trance, vision **7** fantasy **8** daydream **10** brown study

revers: **5** lapel

reverse: **5** annul, upset **6** defeat, invert, regard, repeal, revoke **7** abolish, backset, convert, subvert **8** backward, contrary, converse, disaster, opposite, overturn **9** about face, disaffirm, overthrow, transpose **10** misfortune **11** countermand

reversion: **6** return **7** relapse **9** throwback,

volte-face
to crime: **10** recidivism
to state: **7** escheat
to type: **7** atavism

revert: **5** lapse, react **6** advert, return, revive **7** escheat, recover **9** backslide, throw back **10** retrograde, retrogress **11** antistrophe

review: **4** edit **5** recap **6** notice, parade, resume, survey **7** account, journal **8** ceremony, critique, revision **9** criticise, criticism, criticize, re-examine **10** certiorari, commentary, inspection, periodical, reconsider, retrospect **11** examination

revile: **4** hate, rail **5** abuse, blame, brawl, libel, scold **6** debase, defame, malign, vilify **7** chew out, slander **8** reproach **9** blaspheme, denigrate **10** calumniate

revise: edit **5** alter, amend, emend **6** change, polish, redact **7** correct, improve, recense, rewrite **8** readjust, work over **9** castigate, reexamine, supervise **10** blue-pencil

reviser, revisor: **6** editor **8** redactor, reformer

revival: **6** recall **7** rebirth **8** wakening **11** renaissance

revive: daw **4** gain, wake **5** rally, renew, rouse **6** return **7** enliven, freshen, quicken, recover, refresh, restore **8** reawaken, recreate, rekindle, remember, revivify **9** reanimate, refreshen, resurrect **10** recuperate, regenerate, rejuvenate **11** resuscitate **12** reinvigorate

revoice: **4** echo, tune **5** refit **7** restore

revoke: **4** lift, void **5** adeem, annul, check, renig **6** cancel, recall, recant, renege, repeal **7** abolish, fenagle, finagle, prevent, repress, rescind, retract, reverse **8** abrogate, remember, restrain, withdraw **9** fainaigue **11** countermand

revolt: **5** rebel, repel **6** mutiny, offend **7** disgust, retreat **8** renounce, sedition, uprising **9** rebellion **12** insurrection

revolting: **4** ugly **5** nasty **6** horrid **7** hateful, hideous **8** shocking **9** loathsome, offensive, repellent, repulsive **10** disgusting, nauseating

revolution: **4** gyre, turn **5** cycle, epoch **7** circuit, shake-up **8** disorder, rotation, uprising **9** overthrow, rebellion **12** renunciation

revolutions per minute: RPM **4** revs

revolve: con **4** birl, roll, spin, turn, whir **5** recur, swing, trend, twirl, wheel, whirl, whirr **6** circle, gyrate, ponder, rotate **7** agitate, reflect, trundle **8** consider, meditate **10** deliberate

revolver: gat, gun **6** pistol **7** sidearm

revolving: **4** orby **6** rotary
part: **5** rotor **7** rotator

revue: **4** show **7** cabaret, follies **9** burlesque **13** entertainment

revulsion: **4** fear **6** change **8** distaste, loathing, reaction **9** reversion **10** withdrawal **11** abomination

reward: fee, pay, utu **4** heed, hire, meed, plum, rent **5** ameed, award, bonus, check, crown, medal, merit, prize, repay, wages, yield **6** bounty, carrot, gersum, notice, profit, regard, return, salary, trophy **7** guerdon, premium, success **8** requital **9** honoraria (pl.) **10** compensate, honorarium, recompense, remunerate **11** retribution **12** compensation, remuneration

rewarding: **7** helpful **10** beneficial, satisfying

rex: **4** king

Reynard, Renard: fox

rezai: **8** coverlet, mattress

rhapsodic: **8** ecstatic, effusive **9** emotional, rapturous

rhea: emu **4** emeu **5** nandu **6** ratite **7** ostrich **8** avestruz (Sp.)

Rhea (see also **Ops**): **6** Cybele
child: **4** Hera, Zeus **5** Hades **6** Hestia **7** Demeter **8** Poseidon
father: **6** Uranus
husband: **6** Cronus, Saturn
mother: **4** Gaea

rhema: **4** term, verb, word

rheoscope: **12** galvanoscope

rheostat: **6** dimmer **8** resistor **9** regulator

rheotome: **11** interrupter

rhesus: **6** monkey **7** macaque

rhetor: **6** master, orator **7** teacher

rhetoric: **6** speech **7** bombast, oratory **9** eloquence

rhetorical: **6** florid **8** forensic **9** highflown **10** figurative, oratorical

rhetorician: **6** master, orator, writer **7** speaker, teacher

rheum: **4** cold **7** catarrh **8** rhinitis

rhexis: **7** rupture

rhinal: **5** nasal **6** narial

Rhine: **5** river
city: **4** Bonn, Koln **5** Basel, Mainz **7** Cologne **8** Duisburg, Mannheim **9** Rotterdam, Wiesbaden **10** Strasbourg
magic hoard: **9** Rheingold, Rhinegold
nymph: **7** Lorelei
pert. to: **7** Rhenish
tributary: Aar, Ill **4** Aare, Lahn, Main, Nahe, Ruhr, Waal **5** Lippe **6** Neckar **7** Moselle

rhino: **4** cash **5** money **10** rhinoceros

rhinoceros: **5** abada, topan **6** borele, umhofo **7** keitloa, upeygan
black: **6** borele
cousin of: **5** horse, tapir
feature: **4** horn

> **Rhode Island:** *capital:* **10** Providence
>   *Indian:* **6** Pequot **7** Niantic, Nipmuck **9**
>   Wampanoag **11** Narraganset
>   *island:* **5** Block **8** Prudence **9** Aquid-
>   neck
>   *resort:* **7** Newport
>   *state bird:* **14** Rhode Island Red
>   *state flower:* **6** violet
>   *state tree:* **5** maple

rhinoceros beetle: **4** uang
rhinoceros bird: **9** beefeater
rhizoid: **7** rootlet **8** rootcell
rhoda: **4** rose
Rhode Island: (see box)
Rhodes: *ancient wonder:* **8** Colossus
  festival: **10** Chelidonia
Rhodesia: See **Zimbabwe**
rhoeadales: **5** poppy
rhomboid: **13** parallelogram
rhonchus: **4** rale **7** snoring **8** croaking **9**
  whistling
Rhone: *town:* **4** Lyon **5** Arles **7** Avignon
  tributary: **5** Isere, Saone **7** Durance
rhubarb: **5** error, fruit **6** hassle **7** mistake,
  quarrel, yaw-weed **8** argument, pieplant **9**
  butterbur, rhapontic, vegetable **10** discussion
  derived from: **5** rheic
  genus: **5** rheum
rhus tree: **5** sumac **6** sumach
rhyme: **4** poem **5** agree, verse **6** poetry **8** doggerel
rhymester: **4** bard, poet **6** rhymer **8** rimester
  9 poetaster
rhythm: **4** beat, lilt, time **5** clink, meter, pulse,
  swing, tempo **7** cadence, measure
  break in: **7** caesura **8** caesurae (pl.)
  instrument: **4** drum, gong **6** chimes **7** cymbals **8** triangle **9** xylophone **10** tambourine
  monotonous: rap **8** singsong
rhythmic: **5** paced **6** poetic **8** metrical **9**
  recurrent
ria: bay **5** creek, inlet
rialto: **4** mart **6** bridge, market **8** district,
  exchange
riant: gay **5** merry **6** bright **7** smiling **8** cheerful, laughing
riata: See **reata**
rib: **4** bone, hair, purl, stay, wale, wife **5** costa,
  ridge, tease **6** banter, costae (pl.), lierne **7**
  bristle, support **9** cotelette
  pert. to: **6** costal **7** costate
ribald: low **5** rogue, scamp **6** coarse, rascal,
  vulgar **7** obscene **8** indecent **9** offensive **10**

irreverent, scurrilous **11** blasphemous
ribband: bar **4** spar **5** plank, strip **6** bridge,
  timber **9** scantling
ribbed: **6** barred, corded **7** costate
  fabric: rep **5** twill **6** faille **8** corduroy
ribbon: bow **4** tape **5** braid, corse, padou,
  reins, shred, snood, strip, taste **6** cordon,
  fillet, riband, silver, taenia, tatter **7** bandeau, binding, taeniae (pl.) **8** banderol,
  decorate, tressour, tressure
ribbon-fish: **7** cutlass, oarfish **8** bandfish,
  dealfish
ribbon gum: **8** eucalypt
ribbon-like: **8** taeniate, taenioid
ribbon worm: **9** nemertean
ribless: **8** ecostate **9** decostate
ribwort: **8** hardhead, plantain
rice: **4** boro, chit, paga, twig **5** arroz (Sp.),
  bigas, canin, macan, pilaf, pilau, stick **6**
  branch **7** risotto **9** brushwood
  drink: **4** sake **5** bubud **7** pangasi
  field: **4** padi **5** paddy
  husk: **4** hull, shud **5** shood
  inferior: **4** chit
  long-stemmed: **4** aman
  paste: ame
  polishings: **5** darac
ricebird: **7** bunting, sparrow **8** bobolink **9**
  gallinule
rice rail: **4** sora
rich: fat **4** dear, oofy, posh **5** ample, flush,
  heavy, opime **6** absurd, costly, creamy,
  daedal, fruity, greasy, hearty, loaded, mellow, mighty, oofier, ornate, potent **7** copious, fertile, moneyed, opulent, orotund,
  pinguid, rolling, wealthy, well off **8** abundant, affluent, generous, luscious, powerful,
  valuable, well-to-do **9** abounding, bountiful, elaborate, expensive, laughable, luxuriant, plentiful, sumptuous **10** high-priced, in
  the money, productive
  man: **5** Midas, nabob **7** Croesus **9** plutocrat
  11 billionaire, millionaire
Richelieu's successor: **7** Mazarin
riches: **4** gold, pelf, weal **5** lucre, worth **6**
  wealth **7** fortune **8** treasure
  demon of: **6** Mammon
  region of: **8** Eldorado
  worship of: **10** plutomania
rick: **4** goaf, heap, pile **5** noise, scold, stack,
  twist **6** jingle, rattle, sprain, wrench **7** chatter
rickety: **4** weak **5** crazy, frail, shaky **6** feeble,
  senile **7** unsound **8** unstable **9** tottering **10**
  ramshackle, tumbledown
ricksha, rickshaw: **6** samlor **8** carriage
ricochet: **4** skip **5** carom **6** bounce, glance **7**
  rebound
rictus: **4** gape, grin, mask **7** grimace
rid: **4** free **5** clear, empty **6** assoil, remove, res-

cue, unload **7** deliver, relieve **8** dispatch, liberate, throw off **9** eradicate

ridder: 4 sift **5** sieve

riddle: ree **4** crux, sift **5** aread, areed, griph, poser, rebus, sieve **6** enigma, pierce, puzzle **7** griphus, mystery, perplex, problem **8** disprove, separate **9** conundrum, criticize, perforate

ride: 4 bait, dosa **5** drift, drive, float, motor, tease **6** harass **7** hagride, journey, torment **8** ridicule **9** excursion

rider: 6 clause, cowboy, jockey, knight **7** allonge **8** addition, appendix, bucaayro, buckaroo, cavalier, desultor, horseman **9** amendment, passenger, performer, straddler **10** equestrian, freebooter, highwayman, horsewoman **11** endorsement**ridge:** aas, rib, top **4** aret, asar, back, balk, bank, barb, bult, dene, dune, gold, kame, lira, loma, osar (pl.), rand, reef, ring, ruck, ruga, seam, spur, wale, wave, weal, welt **5** arete, arris, bargh, chine, costa, crest, eskar, esker, hause, oesar (pl.), rugae (pl.), serac, spine, stria, varix, wheal, whelk **6** costae (pl.), crista, rideau, striae (pl.) **7** annulet, costula, cristae (pl.), hogback, porcate, varices (pl.), wrinkle, yardang **8** costulae (pl.), headland, sastrugi, shoulder, zastrugi **9** elevation, razorback
cloth: rib **4** wale
glacial: **5** esker
shell: **5** varix **7** varices (pl.)
skin: **4** wale, welt

ridge oak: 9 blackjack

ridicule: guy, pan **4** gibe, haze, jape, jeer, lout, mock, quiz, razz, ride, twit **5** borak, chaff, irony, roast, scout, sneer, taunt **6** banter, deride, expose, satire **7** asteism, buffoon, lampoon, mockery, pillory, sarcasm **8** derision, raillery, satirize **9** burlesque, make fun of, poke fun at
deity: **5** Momus
object of: **4** butt **13** laughingstock

ridiculous: 5 droll **6** absurd **7** amusing, foolish **8** farcical **9** laughable, ludicrous **10** outrageous

riding: 8 shivaree **9** chevachie **10** equitation
art of: **6** manege
costume: **5** habit
pants: **8** breeches, jodhpurs
shoe: **4** boot **8** solleret

riding whip: 4 crop **5** quirt

ridotto: 6 resort **7** redoubt, retreat **8** festival **9** gathering **10** masquerade **11** abridgement, arrangement

riem: 5 strap, strip, thong

Rienzi composer: 6 Wagner

rife: 5 alive, brief **6** common **7** current, replete **8** abundant, numerous **9** abound-

ing, plentiful, prevalent, universal **10** prevailing, widespread

riff: 4 scan, skim **6** browse, riffle, ripple **7** midriff **9** diaphragm

Riff: 6 Berber

riffle: 4 plow, reef **5** rapid, shoal **6** rattle, ripple **7** shallow, shuffle

riffraff: mob **4** raff, scum **5** dregs, trash **6** rabble, refuse **7** rubbish **9** sweepings

rifle: arm, gun, rob **4** tige **5** reeve, steal **6** furrow, groove, weapon **7** bundock, carbine, despoil, escopet, firearm, pillage, plunder, ransack **8** bandhook **9** chassepot, escopette
accessory: **6** ramrod
ball: **5** minie
instrument: **7** bayonet
pin: **4** tige

rifleman: 5 jager, yager **6** sniper **8** marksman

rift: lag **4** flaw, rive **5** belch, break, chasm, cleft, crack, rapid, split **6** breach, cleave, divide **7** blemish, fissure, opening, shallow **8** crevasse, division

rig: fig, fit, fix **4** dupe, fool, gear, hoax, wind **5** dress, equip, prank, rifle, storm, trick **6** lateen, outfit, square, tackle **7** arrange, costume, derrick, furnish, ransack, swindle, turnout **8** accouter, accoutre, carriage, equipage **9** apparatu s, equipment, imposture **10** manipulate

riga: 6 balsam

Riga Gulf island: 5 Oesel

Riga native: 4 Lett **7** Latvian

rigadoon: 5 dance

rigescence: 8 numbness **9** stiffness

rigging: 4 gear, spar **5** ropes **6** chains, tackle **7** clothes

right: due, fit, gee, hak **4** fair, good, just, meet, mend, real, sane, soke, true **5** droit, moral, sound, truth **6** angary, decent, dexter, equity, excuse, lawful, normal, patent, proper **7** correct, diehard, fitting, genuine, liberty, rectify, redress **8** accurate, appanage, becoming, courtesy, directly, easement, interest, straight, suitable, usufruct, virtuous **9** authority, equitable, faultless, franchise, privilege **10** obligation, perquisite **11** appropriate, certificate, prerogative
angled: **10** orthogonal, rectangled **11** rectangular
exclusive: **6** patent **10** concession
hand: **6** dextra **9** assistant
hand page: **5** recto
handed: **6** righty **7** dextral **8** dextrous, positive
minded: **5** moral **7** ethical **10** principled
of way: **8** easement
on: **7** exactly **8** relevant **10** to the point
proprietary: **6** patent **8** interest

royal: **7** regalia
widow's: **5** terce

righteous: **4** fair, good, holy, just **5** godly, moral, pious, zadoc, zadok **6** devout, honest, worthy **7** perfect, sinless, upright **8** virtuous **9** blameless, equitable, guiltless

righteousness: **6** dharma **9** rectitude

rightful: due, fit **4** fair, just, true **5** legal **6** honest, lawful, proper **7** fitting, upright **9** equitable **11** appropriate

rightist: **4** Tory **11** reactionary **12** conservative

rigid: set **4** firm, hard, taut **5** fixed, stark, stern, stiff, stony, tense, tight **6** marbly, severe, strait, strict, wooden **7** austere, brittle **8** exacting, hard-line, rigorous **9** immovable, stringent, unbending **10** inflexible, ironhanded, motionless, unyielding

rigmaree: **4** coin **6** trifle

rigmarole: **8** nonsense **10** balderdash

Rigoletto: *composer:* **5** Verdi
role: **5** Gilda

rigor, rigour: **4** fury **5** trial **7** cruelty **8** asperity, hardship, rigidity, severity, violence **9** austerity, harshness, rigidness, sharpness, stiffness **10** difficulty, exactitude, puritanism, strictness

rigorous: **5** angry, rigid, stern, stiff **6** severe, strait, strict **7** ascetic, correct, drastic, onerous, precise, spartan **8** accurate **9** inclement, stringent **10** inexorable, oppressive

rikk: **10** tambourine

rile: vex **4** roil **5** anger, annoy, upset **7** agitate, disturb **8** irritate **9** turbidity

rill: **5** brook, creek, crick, ditch **6** course, furrow, groove, runnel, trench **7** rillock, rivulet **8** brooklet **9** arroyuelo (Sp.)

rim: lip **4** bank, brim, edge, orle, ring, tire **5** basil, bezel, bezil, brink, somma, verge **6** border, flange, margin, shield **7** enclose, horizon **8** boundary
external: **6** flange
horseshoe: web
wheel: **4** tire **5** felly **6** felloe

rima: **5** cleft, crack **7** fissure **8** aperture **10** breadfruit

rimate: **7** cracked **8** fissured

rime: ice **4** hoar, poem, rent, rung, step **5** chink, crack, frost, rhyme, verse **6** freeze **7** fissure, versify **8** aperture **9** cranreuch (Sc.), hoarfrost **10** incrustate

rimple: **4** fold **6** crease, ripple, rumple **7** wrinkle

rimption: lot **4** scad **9** abundance

Rinaldo's steed: **6** Bayard **7** Bajardo

rind: **4** bark, husk, melt, peel, skin **5** crust, waste **6** cortex **7** clarify, epicarp, peeling **8** cortices (pl.)

rindle: **5** brook, creek **6** runnel **7** rivulet

ring: bee, cut, orb, rim, set **4** bail, band, belt, cric, ding, dirl, echo, gird, gyre, halo, hank, hoop, link, loop, lute, peal, rink, toll, tore **5** anlet, arena, bague, bezel, chime, clang, group, knell, longe, ridge, rigol, sound **6** arenae, border, boxing, brough (Sc.), chaton, circle, circus, clique, collar, collet, corona, dindle, dingle, famble, gasket, girdle, nimbus, signet, spiral, terret, tingle, tinkle, toroid **7** annulet, annulus, aureole, circlet, coterie, curette, ferrule, grommet, resound, ringlet, tanbark, vibrate **8** bracelet, cincture, encircle, surround **9** archivolt, enclosure, encompass, telephone **10** racecourse **11** combination
gem setting: **5** bezel **6** chaton
of chain: **4** link
of rope: **7** grommet
pert. to: **7** annular
stone: gem
to hold reins: **6** terret

ringdove: **6** cushat, pigeon

ringed: **6** wedded **7** engaged, married **8** annulate, circular **9** annulated, decorated, encircled **10** surrounded

ringed worm: **7** annelid

ringent: **6** gaping

ringing: **4** clam **6** bright **7** orotund **8** resonant

ringleader: **4** boss **10** instigator

ringlet: **4** curl, lock, ring **5** tress

ring ouzel: **5** amsel **6** thrush **8** whistler

ring plover: **5** sandy

rings: *interlocking:* **6** gimmal

ring-shaped: **7** annular **8** annulate, circular **9** annulated

ring-worm: **5** tinea **6** kerion, tetter **7** serpigo **8** milleped **9** millepede

rink: man **4** hero, race, ring **5** arena, skate **9** encounter

rinse: **4** lave, sind (Sc.), wash **5** douse, swill **6** douche, gargle, sluice **7** cleanse

Rio de Janeiro: *beach:* **10** Copacabana
festival, pre-Lenten: **8** Carnival
mountain: **9** Corcovado, Sugarloaf **11** Pao de Azucar
slum: **6** favela

riot: din, row, wow **4** clem, howl **5** brawl, feast, fight, melee, revel **6** affray, bedlam, clamor, excess, pogrom (Russ.), tumult, uproar **7** dispute, quarrel, revelry **8** carousal, debauche, disorder, outburst, sedition, uprising **9** commotion, confusion, luxuriate **10** donnybrook **11** dissolution, disturbance, pandemonium

riotous: **4** loud, roid (Sc.), wild **5** loose **6** wanton **7** profuse **10** boisterous, profligate **11** saturnalian **12** contumacious

rip: hag, rit **4** rend, rent, rive, tear **6** sunder **7**

sputter **8** disunite, harridan, lacerate **9** debauchee **10** laceration

roaring: **5** noisy **6** lively **8** exciting **9** hilarious **10** boisterous, uproarious

ripa: **4** bank **5** beach, shore **6** strand

ripe: **4** fit, rob **4** aged, bank, rife **5** adult, ready **6** addled, august, mature, mellow **7** grown-up, matured, plunder **8** complete, finished, seashore **9** developed, full-grown, perfected, riverbank

early: **8** rareripe

ripen: age **4** grow **5** bloom **6** mature, mellow, season **7** blossom, develop, enhance, improve, perfect, prepare **8** heighten

ripost, riposte: **4** quip **5** reply **6** retort, return, thrust **8** repartee

ripper: **5** dilly, super **6** corker **7** bobsled **8** jimdandy **9** humdinger **11** crackerjack

rippet: **4** fuss, romp **6** uproar **7** quarrel

ripping: **4** fine **5** grand, great, swell **8** splendid **9** admirable, excellent, marvelous **10** remarkable

rippit: **5** fight

ripple: **4** cut, lap **4** curl, fret, purl, riff, tear, wave **5** acker, graze **6** cockle, dimple, riffle, rimple **7** crinkle, scratch, wavelet, wrinkle **8** undulate

ripple grass: **7** ribwort

rise: **4** flow, grow, hulk, loom, rare, rear, soar, stem, well **5** arise, begin, climb, get up, issue, mount, raise, reach, rebel, stand, start, surge, swell, tower **6** amount, appear, ascend, ascent, aspire, assume, attain, derive, emerge, growth, mature, revolt, spring, thrive **7** adjourn, advance, elevate, emanate, prosper, roll out, stand up, succeed **8** addition, eminence, flourish, increase, levitate **9** ascension, beginning, elevation, originate

above: **8** surmount

again: **7** resurge **8** comeback **9** resurrect

against: **5** rebel **6** mutiny **9** insurrect

and fall: **4** tide **5** heave **6** welter

up: **4** fume **5** tower **6** ascend

riser: **4** pipe, step

risible: **5** droll, funny **7** amusing **9** laughable, ludicrous

rising: **5** arise **6** orient, ortive, revolt **7** growing, montant, nearing, surging **8** gradient, uprising **9** ascendant, ascension **11** approaching

risk: **4** dare, defy, face, gage, wage **5** peril, stake **6** chance, danger, expose, gamble, hazard, injury, plight, plunge **7** imperil, venture **8** endanger, exposure, jeopardy **9** adventure, liability

risky: **5** dicey, hairy **6** chancy **7** parlous **8** ticklish **9** dangerous, hazardous

risqué: **4** racy **5** broad, salty, spicy **6** daring,

ribald **8** off-color **9** salacious **10** suggestive

rissle: **4** pole **5** staff, stick

rist: **4** mark **5** wound **6** ascent **7** engrave, scratch

risus: **5** laugh **8** laughter

ritardando: **9** retarding **11** rallentando

rite: **4** cult, form, orgy **5** sacra, usage **6** augury, exequy, novena, prayer, ritual **7** liturgy, obsequy **8** accolade, ceremony, occasion **9** formality, ordinance, procedure, sacrament, solemnity **10** ceremonial, initiation, observance

ritter: **6** knight

ritual: **4** cult, form, rite **7** liturgy, obsequy, service **8** ceremony **9** obsequies (pl.) **10** ceremonial

ritus: **5** usage **6** custom

ritzy: **4** posh **6** modish, swanky **7** elegant, haughty **9** expensive, luxurious **11** fashionable

rivage: **4** bank, duty **5** coast, shore

rival: try, vie **4** even, peer **5** equal, match **6** amount **7** compete, emulate, feuding **8** corrival, emulator, opponent, struggle **9** adversary, competing **10** antagonist, competitor, contending **11** comparative

rivalry: **7** contest **11** competition

rive: rip, rob **4** bank, chop, plow, pull, rend, rent, rift, tear **5** break, cleft, shore, split, steal **6** arrive, cleave, pierce, sunder, thieve, thrust **7** dispart, shatter **8** lacerate **9** disembark

rivel: **6** shrink **7** shrivel, wrinkle

river: ree, ria (Sp.), rio (Sp.), run **4** flow, wadi, wady **5** bayou, brook, creek, fiume (It.), flood, waddy **6** fleuve (F.), stream **7** channel, riviere (F.), torrent **8** effluent **9** abundance **11** watercourse

arm: **4** fork **6** branch **7** estuary **9** tributary

bank: **4** rand, ripa **5** levee

bends: **8** meanders

channel: bed **4** rill **6** alveus, canyon

current: **4** eddy **6** rapids

dam: **4** weir

gauge: **9** nilometer

horse: **5** hippo **12** hippopotamus

ice: **7** glacier

inlet: **5** bayou **6** slough

island: ait **4** holm

Kubla Khan's: **4** Alph

land: **5** carse (Sc.), flats **7** bottoms

living in: **9** amphibian, rheophile

longest: **4** Nile

long run: **9** sluiceway

mouth: **4** beal (Sc.), lade **5** delta **7** estuary

nymph: **4** nais **5** naiad

obstruction: **4** snag **5** gorce

of oblivion: **5** Lethe

passage: **4** ford **7** estuary

pert. to: **5** amnic **7** fluvial, potamic **8** riverine **9** fluminose, fluminous

sacred: **4** Nile **5** Ganga **6** Ganges

siren: **7** Lorelei

small: **4** rill **5** brook, creek, tchai **6** stream **7** rivulet **8** riverlet **9** streamlet

thief: **6** ackman

underworld: **4** Styx **5** Lethe **7** Acheron, Cocytus

winding part: ess

riverbed: **4** wadi **5** waddy **7** batture

riverboat: **4** punt **5** barge **6** pulwar **8** flatboat **11** paddlewheel

river dog: **10** hellbender

river duck: **4** teal **7** mallard, widgeon

river mussel: **4** unio

River of Forgetfulness: **5** Lethe

River of Hate: **4** Styx

River of Sorrows: **7** Acheron

riverweed family: **13** podostemaceae

rivet: fix **4** bolt, brad **6** clinch, fasten **8** fastener

riviere: **8** necklace

rivulet: **4** burn, rill **5** bache, bayou, bourn, brook, creek **6** bourne, rindle (Sc.), runlet, runnel, stream **7** channel **9** streamlet

rixatrix: **5** scold **6** virago

rixy: **4** tern

roach: bug, cut **4** butt, fish, hill, rock, roll, soil, spot **6** braise **7** sunfish **9** cockroach

road: rue (F.), via (It.), way **4** fare, gang, iter, path, raid, ride **5** agger, bargh, going, itero (pl.), route **6** avenue, camino, career, causey, chemin, course, street **7** calzada (Sp.), estrada, gangway, highway, itinera (pl.), journey, passage, railway, strasse (G.) **8** beallach, causeway, chaussee (F.), cul-de-sac, pavement, railroad **9** direction, incursion, roadstead **10** expedition

around city: **6** bypass **7** beltway

bend: **7** hairpin

character: **4** hobo **5** tramp **10** hitchhiker

country: **4** lane **6** boreen (Ir.)

edge: **4** berm **8** shoulder

interchange: **10** cloverleaf

machine: **4** harl **5** paver **6** grader **9** bulldozer

menace: **7** pothole, speeder

military: **5** agger

surface: tar **6** bricks, gravel, stones **7** asphalt, macadam **8** concrete, pavement

roadblock: bar **7** barrier **8** blockade

road book: map **5** atlas **9** gazetteer, itinerary

roadhouse: bar, inn **5** hotel, lodge, motel **6** tavern

roadman: **7** drummer, peddler **8** salesman **9** canvasser

road runner: **6** cuckoo **7** paisano (Sp.)

roam: err, gad **4** roil, rove **5** prowl, range, stray **6** bangle, ramble, stroll, travel, wander **7** meander **8** straggle **9** gallivant

roamer: **5** gipsy, gypsy, nomad, rover **7** Bedouin, drifter **8** fugitive **12** peregrinator

roan: bay **5** color, horse **6** sorrel **8** chestnut **9** sheepskin

Roanoke bell: **7** cowslip

roar: cry, din **4** bawl, beal, bell, bere, boom, bray, clap, hurl, rote, rout, yell **5** blart, brool, fream, laugh, shout **6** bellow, buller, clamor, outcry, steven **7** bluster, thunder **8** shouting

roaring: **4** loud **5** aroar, brisk, noisy **7** howling **10** boisterous, stentorian

roaring game: **7** curling

roast: fry **4** bake, burn, cook, heat, razz, roti (F.) **5** asado (Sp.), bar-b-q, brede, broil, grill, parch **6** assate, banter **7** torrefy, torrify **8** barbecue, lambaste, ridicule **9** criticize

meat on stick: **5** cabob, kabob

prepare: **4** lard **5** truss

roasting stick: **4** spit **6** skewer

rob: cop **4** fake, flap, loot, pelf, roll, take **5** bribe, filch, harry, heist, pilch, pinch, pluck, raven, reave, rifle, spoil, steal, strip, touch **6** burgle, hold up, pilfer, pirate, ravish, shrive, snatch, snitch, thieve **7** bereave, defraud, deprive, despoil, pillage, plunder, purloin **10** burglarize, housebreak, plagiarize

robber: **4** goul, yegg **5** ghoul, thief **6** arrant, bandit, cat-man, dacoit, pirate **7** brigand, corsair, footpad, ladrone, yeggman **8** marauder **9** bandolero, buccaneer, privateer **10** depredator, highwayman

robe (see also **dress, gown**): aba **4** skin, vest, wrap **5** array, camis, camus, cloak, cover, cymar, habit, simar, talar, tunic **6** caftan, chimer, clothe, dolman, invest, kimono, mantle, revest **7** chimere, costume, garment, manteau, vesture **8** clothing, covering, vestment

robin: **4** lout, tody **6** oriole, thrush **7** bumpkin, chewink, warbler **8** trimming **9** redbreast **10** cuckoopint, toxalbumin

robinet: **6** cannon **9** chaffinch

Robin Goodfellow: elf **4** Puck **5** fairy **6** sprite **9** hobgoblin

Robin Hood: *chaplain:* **9** Friar Tuck

follower: **4** John **8** Merry Men **10** Allan-a-dale, Little John **11** Will Scarlet

sweetheart: **6** Marian **10** Maid Marian

robin sandpiper: **4** knot **9** dowitcher

Robinson Crusoe: *author:* **5** Defoe

companion: **9** Man Friday

roborant: **4** drug **5** tonic **13** strengthening

roborean: **5** oaken, stout **6** strong

robot: **5** droid, golem **7** android **9** androides, automaton

drama about: RUR

Rob Roy: **5** canoe, drink **8** cocktail

robust: 4 hale, hard, iron, rude 5 hardy, lusty, rough, sound, stout, wally 6 brawny, coarse, hearty, rugged, sinewy, strong, sturdy 7 healthy 8 athletic, muscular, vigorous 10 boisterous 11 flourishing

roc: 4 bird 6 simurg 7 simurgh, soldier

rocca: 4 hold, keep 6 donjon 8 fortress

rochet: 5 cloak, frock 7 camisia, garment, gurnard 8 vestment
relative: alb

rock: dag, ore, tor 4 clay, crag, lull, peak, reef, reel, roll, scar, shog, spar, sway, toss, trap, tufa, tuff, wash 5 agate, brack, candy, chert, cliff, earth, flint, geest, hurry, lytta, prase, scree, shake, shale, shaul, slate, stane (Sc.), stone, swing, wacke 6 aplite, basalt, dacite, egeran, gneiss, gravel, issite, oolite, pebble, refuge, rognon, schist, silica, sinter, teeter, totter 7 adinole, akerite, alunite, defense, diamond, gondite, granite, griesen, support, tremble, vibrate 8 andesite, banakite, dolomite, laterite, obsidian, porphyry, psephite, rhyolite, undulate 9 epidosite, flagstone, oscillate, phanerite 10 greenstone, promontory
Australian: 5 Ayers
boring tool: 6 trepan
cavity: vug 4 vugg 5 druse, geode
clay: 8 ganister
debris: 5 talus 8 detritus, xenolith
decomposed: 6 gossan
discarded: 5 attle
fissile: 5 shale
flintlike: 5 chert 6 quartz
floating: 6 pumice
fold: 8 syncline 9 anticline
glacier deposit: 7 moraine
glacier-transported: 7 erratic
igneous: 4 boss, sial, sima, trap, tufa 5 trass 6 basalt, domite, latite, pumice 7 diabase, diorite, felsite, granite, ijolite, peridot 8 extaxite, ijussite, obsidian, porphyry 11 agglomerate
laminated: 4 mica 5 shale, slate
liquid: 4 lava
nodule: 5 geode
pert. to: 6 petric 7 petrean
point: 4 crag, peak
science: 7 geology 9 petrology
volcanic: 4 lava, tufa, tuff
wall of broken: 6 riprap

rockaway: 8 carriage

rock badger: 4 cony 5 hyrax

rock bass: 6 red-eye 8 cabrilla

rockbell: 9 columbine

rockbird: 5 murre 9 sandpiper

rock bottom: 6 lowest 7 essence 8 cheapest

rock dove: 6 pigeon 9 guillemot

rocker: 5 chair, skate 6 cradle 7 shoofly

rocket: 4 weld, wold 5 slate, woald, would 7 missile 9 satellite, spaceship 11 firecracker
end of combustion: 7 burnout
landing: 7 reentry 10 splashdown
launcher: 7 bazooka
launching: 4 shot 8 blastoff

rock falcon: 6 merlin

rockfish: 4 bass, rena 5 perch, reina, viuva 6 gopher, tambor 7 grouper 9 killifish 10 priestfish

rock grouse: 9 ptarmigan

rock hind: 7 grouper

rock kangaroo: 7 wallaby

rockling: 4 fish, gade

rock oak: 8 chestnut 10 California, chinquapin

rock oil: 9 petroleum

rock plant: 4 moss 6 lichen

rock starling: 5 ouzel

rock tripe: 6 lichen

rocky: 4 hard, weak 5 dizzy, shaky, stony 6 cliffy 7 obscene, petrean 8 obdurate, unsteady 9 unfeeling 10 insensible

Rocky Mountain: *goat:* 6 mazame
park: 5 Banff, Estes 11 Yellowstone
peak: 5 Logan, Pikes 6 Elbert
range: 5 Teton 7 Wasatch
sheep: 7 bighorn

rococo: 4 arty 6 ornate 7 baroque 9 fantastic

rod: bar, gad, gun, guy, rab, rib 4 axle, bolt, came, cane, crop, goad, I-bar, lath, pole, prod, race, scob, spit, wand, wire 5 arrow, baton, board, lytta, osier, perch, power, scion, spoke, staff, stick, stock, strip, tribe 6 baculi (pl.), batten, broach, carbon, etalon, eyebar, ferule, needle, pistol, piston, pontil, raddle, skewer, switch, toggle 7 baculus, caliper, crowbar, distaff, measure, scepter, sceptre, spindle, stemmer, support, tringle, tyranny 8 arrester, offshoot, revolver 9 authority 10 oppression, punishment
bundle: 6 fasces
divination by: 7 dowsing
movable: 6 piston
square: 5 perch

rodd: 8 crossbow, stonebow

rodent: rat 4 cavy, cony, cypu, hare, mole, paca, pika, utia, vole 5 aguti, hutia, jutia, lerot, mouse, ratel, zokor 6 agouti, agouty, beaver, biting, cururo, gerbil, gopher, gundie, jerboa, marmot, murine, rabbit, weasel 7 chincha, hamster, leveret, muskrat, pack rat 8 capibara, capybara, dormouse, gerbille, leporide, sewellel, squirrel, viscacha, vizcacha 9 porcupine 10 chinchilla
genus: Mus 5 Lepus
pert. to: 8 rosorial

rodeo: 7 roundup 9 enclosure

rodge: 7 gadwall

rod-like: **6** rhabdo **7** virgate

rodman: **4** thug **10** highwaymen

rodomontade: **4** brag, rant **5** boast, empty, pride **6** vanity **7** bluster, bombast **8** boastful, boasting, braggart

roe: ova, pea **4** deer, eggs, hart, hind **5** coral, spawn **6** caviar

roebuck: **4** girl **9** chevreuil

Roentgen's discovery: **4** X-ray

roestone: **6** oolite

rogation: law **6** appeal, decree, litany, prayer **7** inquiry, request **8** petition **12** supplication

rogue: boy, cad, gue, imp, wag **4** hemp, kite **5** catso, cheat, crank, decry, gipsy, gypsy, hempy, knave, scamp, shark, tramp **6** beggar, canter, coquin, harlot, pirate, rascal, wander **7** corsair, culprit, erratic, hellion, sharper, vagrant, villain, waggish **8** picaroon, swindler, vagabond **9** scoundrel, trickster **10** delinquent, frolicsome, stigmatize **11** rapscallion
  pert. to: **10** picaresque

roguery: **5** fraud **8** mischief, trickery

roguish: coy, sly **4** arch **5** pawky **6** wanton **7** playful, puckish **8** espiegle, sportive **9** dishonest, fun-loving

roid: **5** rough **6** severe **7** riotous, roguish **10** frolicsome **12** unmanageable

roil: mud, vex **4** foul, rile, roam, romp, rust, stir **5** anger, annoy, muddy, rouse **6** cloudy, fidget, ruffle, wander **7** blunder, disturb, pollute **8** irritate, unsettle **9** displease **10** exasperate

roily: **6** turbid

roister: **4** brag, play, rude **5** bully, revel, spree **7** bluster, boorish, carouse, reveler, swagger, violent **9** gilravage

roistering: **6** hoiden, hoyden

rojo (Sp.): red **6** Indian **7** redskin

roke: fog **4** mist, stir **5** smoke, steam, vapor **8** moisture

roker: ray **8** rockling **9** thornback

roky: **4** damp **5** foggy, misty, smoky **6** hoarse

Roland: **7** Orlando
  beloved: **4** Aude
  enemy: **4** Gano **7** Ganelon **8** Saracens
  friend: **6** Oliver
  horn: **7** Olivant
  horse: **10** Veillantif
  sword: **8** Durendal
  uncle: **11** Charlemagne

role: bit **4** cast, duty, lead, part **5** cameo, heavy **6** office **8** business, function **9** character, soubrette **13** impersonation
  leading: **4** star

roll: bun, gad, rob **4** bolt, coil, file, flow, furl, list, pell, pour, roam, rota, seel, sway, toss, turn, wind, wrap **5** bagel, cadre, frisk, lurch, shift, surge, swing, trill, troll, wheel **6** bundle, enroll, enwrap, goggle, grovel, ponder, roster, rotate, rumble, scroll, spiral, swathe, tumble, wallow, wander, welter, whelve, wintle **7** biscuit, brioche, fortune, revolve, rissole, stagger, swagger, trundle **8** cylinder, flounder, register, undulate
  roll mop: **7** herring **9** appetizer
  of hair: bun **7** chignon
  sweet: **6** danish **9** schnecken

roll back: **5** lower **6** reduce **7** repulse

roller: **4** band, wave **5** finer, inker, swath, winch **6** barrel, canary, caster, fascia, fillet, pigeon, platen, rowlet, sponge **7** bandage, breaker, presser, sirgang, tumbler **8** cylinder **9** surcingle

rolleyway: **4** road **5** track **7** gangway, tramway

rollick: **4** romp **5** sport **6** frolic, gambol, wallow **8** escapade

rollicking: gay **5** antic, happy **6** jovial, lively **8** careless **9** hilarious

roll in: **4** flow **6** arrive, wallow, welter

rolling stock: **4** cars **6** trucks **7** coaches, engines **8** cabooses **9** traincars **11** locomotives

rolling stone: **5** rover **7** drifter **8** wanderer

rolling weed: **10** tumbleweed

rolltop: **4** desk

roll up: **4** furl **5** amass **6** arrive, gather

roly-poly: **5** dumpy, pudgy, round **6** portly, rotund **7** pudding

rom: **5** gipsy, gypsy

romaine: cos **5** plant **7** lettuce

romal: **5** thong

Roman: **5** brave, Latin **6** frugal, honest, simple **7** Italian

Roman Catholic: *administration:* **5** Curia
  cassock: **7** soutane, zimarra
  head: **4** pope
  palace: **7** Vatican
  skullcap: **9** zucchetto

romance: woo **4** gest, love, tale **5** amour, court, dream, fable, fancy, feign, geste, novel, story **6** affair **7** chimera, fantasy, fiction, romanza **9** falsehood, sentiment **10** exaggerate, flirtation, love affair **12** exaggeration

Romance language: **6** French **7** Catalan, Italian, Romansh, Spanish **8** Romanian **9** Provencal **10** Portuguese

romantic: **5** mushy **6** exotic, poetic, unreal **8** quixotic **9** imaginary, visionary **10** idealistic, passionate **11** extravagant, sentimental

Romania, Rumania: **5** Dacia
  brandy: **6** tzuica
  capital: **9** Bucharest
  city: **4** Arad, Iasi **5** Bacau, Jassy, Neamt, Turnu **6** Braila, Brasov, Galati, Galatz **7** Craiova, Focsani, Ploesti, Severin **8** Cer-

Rome (see also **Latin**): **4** Roma
  adviser to king: **6** Egeria
  amphitheater: **9** Colosseum
  apostle: **4** Neri, Paul
  army wing: ala
  assembly: **5** forum **6** senate **7** comitia
  augur: **6** auspex
  authority symbol: **6** fasces
  basilica: **7** Lateran
  battle array: **5** acies
  biographer: **5** Nepos **9** Suetonius
  brothers: **5** Remus **7** Romulus
  burial site: **9** catacombs
  Caesar's title: **9** imperator
  captain: **9** centurion
  chapel: **7** Sistine
  chief god: **4** Jove **7** Jupiter
  citadel: arx
  city within: **7** Vatican
  clans: **4** gens
  cloak: **4** toga
  coin: aes **5** assis (pl.), aurei (pl.), semis **6** aureus, dinder, triens **7** denarii (pl.), siliqua **8** decussis, denarius, sesterce **10** sestertius
  comedy writer: **7** Plautus, Terence
  concert hall: **5** odeum
  conqueror: **6** Alaric
  conspirator: **8** Catiline
  court: **5** atria (pl.) **6** atrium
  custodian: **10** neocorates
  date: **4** Ides **5** Nones **7** Kalends
  diviner: **5** augur **6** auspex
  earthwork: **5** agger
  emperor: **4** Nero, Otho, Otto **5** Galba, Nerva, Titus **6** Caesar, Julian, Trajan **7** Hadrian **8** Augustus, Claudius, Domitian, Tiberius **9** Vespasian **10** Elagabalus **11** Constantine
  empress: **7** Eudocia
  encampment: **7** castrum
  epic: **6** Aeneid
  farmer: **7** colonus **8** agricola
  Fate: **4** Mors, Nona **5** Parca **6** Decuma, Parcae (pl.)
  fighter: **9** gladiator
  fortress: **7** castrum
  founder: **5** Remus **7** Romulus
  fountain: **5** Trevi
  galley: **6** bireme **7** trireme
  garment: **4** toga **5** palla, sagum, stola, stole, togae (pl.), tunic
  general: **5** Sulla, Titus **6** Antony, Fabius, Marius, Scipio **8** Agricola
  god: Lar **4** Jove **5** Cupid, Janus, Lares, manes **6** Faunus **7** Jupiter, lemures, penates, Phoebus **8** Dispater, Quirinus

11 Aesculapius
  god of dead: **5** Orcus
  god of death: **4** Mors
  god of fire: **6** Vulcan
  god of love: **4** Amor
  god of mirth: **5** Comus
  god of sea: **7** Neptune
  god of sleep: **8** Morpheus
  god of sun: Sol
  god of underworld: Dis **5** Pluto
  god of war: **4** Mars
  god of wind: **5** Eurus **6** Boreas
  god of wine: **7** Bacchus
  goddess: dea (L.), Lua **4** Caca, Maia, Paca **5** Epona, Terra **6** Aestas, Annona, Aurora, Lucina, Rumina, Tellus **7** Fortuna **8** Libitina **9** Abudantia, Discordia, Felicitas
  goddess of agriculture: Ops **5** Ceres
  goddess of beauty: **5** Venus
  goddess of flowers: **5** Flora
  goddess of hearth: **5** Vesta
  goddess of hope: **4** Spes
  goddess of hunting: **5** Diana
  goddess of love: **5** Venus
  goddess of marriage: **4** Juno
  goddess of moon: **4** Luna
  goddess of night: Nox
  goddess of peace: Pax
  goddess of plenty: Ops
  goddess of underworld: **10** Proserpina
  goddess of victory: **6** Vacuna
  goddess of war: **7** Bellona, Minerva
  goddess of wisdom: **7** Minerva
  greeting: ave
  guard: **6** lictor
  hall: **5** atria (pl.) **6** atrium
  helmet: **5** galea **6** galeae (pl.)
  highway: via **4** iter **6** Appian **8** itineres (pl.)
  hill: **7** Caelian, Viminal **8** Aventine, Palatine, Quirinal **9** Esquiline **10** Capitoline
  historian: **4** Livy **5** Nepos **7** Sallust, Tacitus
  holiday: **5** feria **6** feriae (pl.)
  jurist: **5** Gaius
  king: **7** Romulus, Servius, Tullius **12** Ancus Martius **13** Numa Pompilius **15** Tullus Hostilius
  law: fas, lex **4** cern
  leader: dux
  magistrate: **5** edile **6** aedile, censor, pretor **7** praetor, tribune
  marble: **7** cipolin
  measure: pes, urn **4** mile, pace, urna **5** actus, clima, cubit, juger **6** culeus, dolium, gradus, hemina, modius, *(cont.)*

Rome *(cont.)*
  palmus, passus, saltus, versus **7** amphora, congius, cyathus, digitus, stadium **8** centuria, hereduim, quadrant **9** decempeda, millarium, sextarius **10** acetabulum, quartarius
  measure of weight: bes **5** assis (pl.), libra, uncia **6** duella **7** dodrans, sextula, solidus **8** sicilium **9** scrupulum, scrupulus
  military formation: ala **6** alares (pl.) **7** phalanx
  military machine: **7** terebra
  military unit: **6** cohort, legion **7** century, maniple
  naturalist: **5** Pliny
  nymph: **6** Egeria
  official: **5** augur, edile **6** aedile, censor, consul, lictor **7** prefect, tribune
  people: **5** Laeti **7** Sabines **8** plebians **10** patricians
  philosopher: **4** Cato **6** Seneca
  pin: **4** acus
  poet: **4** Ovid **5** Cinna, Lucan **6** Horace, Vergil, Virgil **7** Juvenal, Terence **8** Catullus, Tibullus **10** Propertius
  port: **5** Ostia
  praenomen: **5** Aulus, Caius, Gaius, Titus **6** Appius, Lucius, Marcus, Sextus **7** Publius, Quintus, Spurius **8** Tiberius
  priest: **5** epulo **6** flamen **7** luperci
  priestess: **6** vestal
  procurator: **5** Felix **6** Pilate
  racecourse: **6** circus
  river: **5** Tiber
  road: **4** iter
  room: ala **5** atria (pl.) **6** atrium **7** tablina (pl.) **8** fumarium, tablinum
  saint: **4** Neri
  senate emblem: **9** laticlave
  senate house: **5** curia
  shield: **5** scuta (pl.) **6** ancile, scutum **7** ancilia (pl.), clypeus
  slave: **9** Spartacus
  spirits of dead: **5** manes
  standard: **7** labarum, vexilla (pl.) **8** vexillum
  standard-bearer: **9** vexillary
  statesman: **4** Cato **5** Pliny **6** Caesar, Cicero, Seneca **7** Agrippa **8** Maecenas
  temple: **4** naos **5** cella **8** pantheon
  treasurer: **8** quaestor
  veteran: **7** emeriti (pl.) **8** emeritus

nauti, Irongate, Kishenef, Kolsovar, Temesvar **9** Timisoara
  conservative: **5** boyar
  currency: ban, lei, leu, ley **4** bani(pl.)
  gymnast: **8** Comaneci (Nadia)
  playwright: **7** Ionesco
  river: Alt, Jiu **4** Prut **5** Aluta, Schyl, Siret **6** Danube, Sereth **7** Argesul
Romany, Rommany: rom **5** gipsy, gypsy
  tongue: **7** Romanes
romanza: **7** fiction, romance
Rome: (see box)
Romeo: **7** gallant
  author: **11** Shakespeare
  beloved: **6** Juliet
  city: **6** Verona
  enemy: **6** Tybalt
  father: **8** Montague
  friend: **8** Benvolio, Mercutio
  rival: **5** Paris
romp: **4** hoit, play, roil **5** caper **6** cavort, frolic, gambol, hoiden, hoyden **7** carouse, courant, gammock **8** carousal, courante **9** cut capers
Romulus and Remus: **5** twins **8** brothers
  father: **4** Mars
  foster mother: **4** wolf
  founded: **4** Rome
  mother: **10** Rhea Silvia
  Remus' slayer: **7** Romulus

rondure: orb **4** ball **5** globe, round **6** circle, sphere **9** plumpness, roundness
rood: **5** cross **7** measure **8** crucifix
roodebok: **6** impala
roof: top **5** cover, crown, haven, house **6** harbor, palate **7** shelter **8** covering, housetop
  border: **4** eave
  of mouth: **6** palate
  style: hip **4** dome, flat, nave, sark **5** gable, spire **6** cupola, lean-to **7** cricket, gambrel, mansard **9** butterfly, penthouse, pyramidal **10** jerkin-head
  support: **6** rafter
  window: **6** dormer
roofing material: tar, tin **4** tile **5** paper, slate, straw, terne **6** copper, gravel, shakes, thatch **7** pantile **8** shingles
rook: **4** bird, crow **5** cheat, raven, steal **6** castle, fleece **7** defraud, sharper, swindle **8** swindler
rookery: **5** roost **8** building
rookie: **4** tyro **6** novice **7** recruit, trainee **8** beginner **10** apprentice
rooky: **5** foggy **6** untidy **10** disheveled
room: ala, ben, den **4** aula, cell, digs, hall, loge, play, sala (Sp.), seat **5** atria (pl.), aulae (pl.), cubby, divan, kiosk, lodge, place, salle (F.), salon, scope, space **6** atrium, casino, harbor, leeway, margin, reside, saloon, scouth **7** boudoir, cabinet, chamber, cubi-

cle, expanse, gallery, lodging, rotunda, theater **9** apartment, garderobe **10** auditorium

conversation: **6** exedra, parlor **7** exedrae (pl.)

eating: **4** nook **7** cenacle, kitchen **8** cenacula (pl.), mess hall **9** cafeteria, cenaculum, refectory

group of: **5** suite

on a ship: **5** cabin **6** galley

private: **7** boudoir

provision: **4** ewry **5** ewery **6** larder, pantry **8** cupboard

reading: den **5** study **7** library

sleeping: **5** lodge **6** dormer **7** barrack, bedroom **8** roomette **9** dormitory

storage: **4** loft, shed **5** attic **6** cellar **8** basement

room and board: **7** lodging **14** accommodations

roomer: **5** guest **6** lodger, tenant **7** boarder

rooms: **4** flat **5** suite **9** apartment

roomy: **5** ample, broad, spacy **8** spacious **9** capacious **10** commodious

roorback, roorbach: lie **4** hoax **6** canard **7** fiction **9** falsehood

roose: **5** boast, extol, vaunt **6** praise

Roosevelt, F. D.: *dog:* **4** Fala

radio report: **12** fireside chat

wife: **7** Eleanor

roost: sit **4** nest, pole, rest **5** abode, perch, sleep **6** alight, garret **7** lodging, support

rooster: **4** cock **5** gallo (Sp.) **11** chanticleer

root: dig **4** base, bulb, core, grub, moot, rout, stem **5** basis, cheer, grout, plant, radix, shout, tuber **6** bottom, center, etymon, ground, origin, search, settle **7** applaud, essence, radical, radices (pl.), rootlet, support **8** entrench **9** beginning, establish **10** foundation

dyeing: **6** madder

edible: oca, roi, rue, uva, yam **4** beet, eddo, taro **5** orris, tania **6** carrot, ginger, orrice, potato, radish, turnip **7** cassava, parsnip **8** rutabaga **9** sassafras

fragrant: **4** khus **5** orris

medicinal: **5** jalap, lappa **7** ginseng

pert. to: **7** radical

principal: **7** taproot

starch: **4** arum

root out: **4** stub **6** evulse **7** destroy **8** demolish **9** eradicate, extirpate **10** annihilate, deracinate

rooted: **5** fixed **7** chronic **10** deep-seated, inveterate **11** established, traditional

rooter: fan **10** enthusiast

rootlet: **7** radicle, rhizoid

rootstock: **5** orris **6** ginger, pannum, stolon **7** rhizome

rope: gad, guy, tie, tow **4** bind, cord, hemp, line, stay **5** cable, longe, riata, sheet, widdy **6** binder, fasten, halter, hawser, lariat, shroud, tether **7** aweband, binding, bobstay, bollard, cordage, halyard, marline, painter **8** inveigle, prolonge

animal's: **5** leash **6** halter, tether

fiber: **4** coir, flax, jute **5** istle, sisal **6** cotton, Manila

holder: **6** becket

loop: **5** bight, noose **6** becket, parral

ship's: tye **4** colt, lift, rode, stay, vang **5** brace, braid, sheet **6** hawser, inhaul, parral, parrel, ratlin, shroud **7** halyard, lanyard, painter, ratline

splice pin: fid

throwing: **5** lasso, reata, riata **6** lariat

ropedancer: **7** acrobat **9** funambulo **11** funambulist

roper: **6** cowboy, packer

ropery: **6** banter **7** roguery

roque: **7** croquet

roric: **4** dewy

rosary: **4** bede **5** beads **6** prayer **7** chaplet, garland **8** beadroll

section: **6** decade

rose: ris **5** blush, delta, flush **6** flower, nozzle **7** rambler, rosette **9** hellebore

family: **8** rosaceae

kind of: dog, tea **4** moss, musk

oil: **4** atar, otto **5** attar, ottar

rosebay: **8** oleander

Rose City: **8** Pasadena, Portland

rosemary: **4** herb, mint **8** moorwort

rose of Sharon: **6** althea **8** hibiscus **12** shrubby plant

rose pogonia: **10** snakemouth

rosette: **4** chou, knot **7** cockade **8** ornament

rosilla: **9** rockbrush **10** sneezeweed

rosin: See **resin**

Rosinante: nag **4** jade, plug **5** horse, steed

owner: **10** Don Quixote

rosiness: **5** blush, flush

ross: **4** bark, peel **5** waste **8** exterior

roster: **4** list, roll, rota **5** slate **6** muster **7** catalog

rostrum: **4** beak, dais **5** snout, stage **6** pulpit **7** lectern, tribune **8** platform

rosy: red **4** pink **5** ruddy **6** bright, florid **7** auroral, flushed, hopeful, roseate **8** blooming, blushing, cheerful, rubicund **9** promising, rosaceous **10** favourable, optimistic

rot: ret **4** bosh, dote, doze, joke **5** chaff, decay, spoil, tease, trash **6** banter, fester, perish **7** corrupt, putrefy, rubbish, twaddle **8** nonsense **9** decompose, poppycock **10** degenerate

rota: **4** list, roll **5** court, round **6** course, roster **8** register

rotate: **4** pass, roll, spin, turn **5** pivot, twirl, wheel, whirl **6** circle, gyrate **7** perform, revolve, trundle **8** rotiform **9** alternate, pirouette, take turns

rotation: **4** eddy **6** torque, vortex **9** pirouette **10** revolution
part: cam **4** axle **5** rotor, wheel

rote: **4** list **5** learn **6** course, custom, memory, repeat, system **7** routine **8** practice **9** automatic **10** memorizing, repetition

rotiform: **6** rotate **11** wheel-shaped

rotor: **7** spinner **8** impeller

rotten: bad **4** evil, foul **5** fetid, nasty **6** putrid **7** carrion, corrupt, decayed, spoiled, tainted, unsound, vicious **8** depraved, unstable **9** offensive, putrefied **10** decomposed, putrescent

rotter: cad **7** shirker, slacker **10** blackguard

rotula: **5** round **6** troche **7** kneepan, lozenge, patella

rotund: **5** beefy, obese, plump, round, stout **6** chubby, chunky, portly **7** rounded **8** roly-poly, sonorant, sonorous **9** spherical

roturier: **7** freeman, upstart **8** commoner

roué: rip **4** rake **9** debauchee, libertine

rouge: red **5** blush, color, flush, paint, score **6** redden, ruddle **8** cosmetic

rough: **4** hard, rude, wild **5** acrid, brute, crude, gross, hairy, harsh, husky, lumpy, raggy, rowdy, seamy, stern, surly, tight, tough, uncut **6** abrupt, broken, choppy, coarse, crabby, craggy, hoarse, jagged, rugged, severe, shaggy, uneven **7** boorish, bristly, brusque, grating, hirsute, inexact, jarring, raucous, ruffian, ruffled, uncivil **8** churlish, clownish, gangster, impolite, obdurate, unplaned **9** imperfect, inclement, turbulent, unrefined **10** boisterous, indecorous, tumultuous, unpolished

rough-and-ready: **5** crude **9** makeshift **10** unpolished

roughen: **4** chap, fret, shag **5** feaze **7** engrail **10** exasperate

roughneck: **4** boor **5** rowdy, tough **7** hoodlum **10** roustabout

roughness: **7** crudity **8** acrimony, asperity **10** inequality, unevenness

rough out: **5** draft **6** sketch

roulade: **8** arpeggio, division, flourish

roulette: **9** epicyloid **11** epitrochoid **12** hypotrochoid
bet: bas **4** noir **5** carre, rouge **6** milieu **7** dernier, encarre, enplein
dealer: **8** croupier

rounceval: **5** giant, large **6** virago **7** monster **8** gigantic **9** termagant

round: **4** ball, beat, bout, full, ring, rung, song **5** cycle, dance, globe, group, large, orbed, plump, salvo, whirl **6** circle, curved, nearly, period, polish, rotund **7** bulbous, circuit **8** circular, encircle, globular, rolypoly **9**

spherical **10** revolution **11** cylindrical
clam: **6** quahog
dance: hay, ray **5** polka, waltz **7** roundel **9** roundelay, schottish
robin: **6** letter, series **7** contest **8** document, petition, sequence **9** cigarfish **10** tournament

roundabout: **4** tour **5** dance **6** detour **7** devious **8** circular, indirect, tortuous, verbiage **9** excursion **10** circuitous, farfetched **13** approximately

rounded: **4** oval **5** bombe, ovate **6** convex, curved, rotund **7** arrondi, bunting, gibbous **8** circular **10** curvaceous, labialized

roundel: **4** guze, hurt **5** plate **6** circle, pellet, shield

rounder: **4** roue **5** sport **7** wastrel **8** criminal, drunkard, preacher **11** spendthrift

roundhead: **5** Swede **7** Puritan **11** Cromwellian

Round Table: *empty seat:* **13** Siege Perilous
knight: Ban, Kay **4** Bors, Owen **5** Ector, Ywain **6** Gareth, Gawain, Modred **7** Caradoc, Cradock, Gaheris, Galahad, Geraint, Launfal, Mordred, Paladin, Tristan **8** Bedevere, Lancelot, Parsifal, Tristram **9** Palomides, Percivale, Sagramore

roundup: **5** rodeo **7** summary **9** gathering

roundworm: **4** nema **7** ascaris **8** nematode

roup: **4** sale **6** clamor **7** auction **8** shouting

rouse: daw, hie **4** call, goad, move, stir, wake, whet **5** alarm, anger, awake, raise, rally, start, toast, upset, waken **6** arouse, awaken, bestir, excite, foment, frolic, incite, revive, stir up **7** actuate, agitate, animate, disturb, enliven, provoke, startle **8** inspirit, Rousseau **9** intensify, stimulate

roussette: **5** shark **7** dogfish

roust: **4** roar, stir, tide **5** rouse **6** bellow, tumult **7** current, provoke, roaring **9** bellowing

roustabout: **4** hand **6** worker **7** laborer **8** deckhand, floorman

rout: mob **4** band, beat, bray, dart, fuss, roar, root **5** crowd, drive, expel, knock, noise, scoop, shout, snore, snort, troop **6** bellow, clamor, defeat, furrow, rabble, search, strike, throng, tumult, uproar **7** company, confuse, debacle, repulse, retinue, retreat, rummage, slumber, trouble **8** assemble, assembly, confound, disperse, reversal, shouting, stampede, vanquish **9** discomfit, multitude, overpower, overthrow, overwhelm **11** put to flight

route: way **4** gest, lane, line, path, road, send **5** gauge, guide, march, trail **6** course, skyway **7** circuit, journey **9** direction, itinerary
circuitous: **6** detour
straight: **7** beeline

routh: 6 plenty 8 abundant 9 abundance, plentiful

routine: rut 4 pace, rote, wont 5 grind, habit, round, troll, usual 6 course, groove, system 7 humdrum, regular 8 everyday, habitual, ordinary 9 customary, treadmill

rove: gad 4 move, part, pass, plow, roam, turn 5 prowl, range, stray 6 maraud, pierce, ramble, stroll, wander 8 straggle

rover: 5 gipsy, gypsy, nomad 6 pirate 7 corsair, drifter, floater, Ishmael, migrant, vagrant 8 gadabout 9 itinerant

roving: 6 errant 7 cursory, devious 9 desultory, itinerant, wandering 10 discursive

row: air, oar 4 bank, dust, file, fuss, line, list, pull, rank, sail, scud, spat, tier 5 align, aline, brawl, broil, garry, mouth, noise, scold, scull, swath 6 barney, clamor, paddle, pother, propel, rumpus, swathe 7 dispute, quarrel, ruction 8 argument, squabble 9 catalogue, commotion, excursion 11 disturbance 13 collieshangie

rowan tree: ash 4 sorb

rowboat: cog, gig 4 bark, dory, skif 5 canoe, cobil, coble, scull, skiff, skift 6 barque, caique, dinghy, galley, randan, wherry
stern: 7 transom

rowdy: 4 b'hoy, punk, rude 5 rough, tough 6 roarer 7 hoodlum, trickly, vicious 8 hooligan, larrikin, plug-ugly 9 obstinate, roughneck 10 boisterous

rowel: 4 spur 5 wheel 6 circle

rowen: 4 crop 5 field 9 aftermath

rower: oar 6 punter 7 oarsman, sculler

rowing: 6 randan 8 sculling

royal: 4 easy, real (Sp.), rial, stag, true 5 basil, grand, noble, regal 6 august, kingly, superb 7 queenly, stately 8 imperial, imposing, majestic, princely, splendid 9 excellent, sovereign 11 magnificent, monarchical

royal agaric: 8 mushroom

Royal Canadian Mounted Police: 7 Mountie

royalist: 4 Tory 8 Cavalier 10 monarchist 11 reactionary

royal standard: 4 flag 6 banner, emblem

royalty: fee 4 share 6 emblem, income 7 kingdom 8 dividend, kingship, nobility 10 kingliness, percentage 11 sovereignty
denoting: 5 crown 6 purple 7 scepter
symbol: 6 ermine

rub: irk, vex 4 bark, bray, buff, fret, rasp, wear, wipe 5 chafe, dight, feeze, grind, peeve, scour, smear 6 abrade, anoint, fridge, nettle, polish, scrape, smooth, stroke 7 burnish, massage 8 friction, irritate, obstacle 9 hindrance, triturate 10 difficulty, impediment
down: 4 comb, wipe 5 curry, groom 7 massage

elbows: 6 jostle 9 associate 10 fraternize
out: 4 kill 5 elide, erase 6 cancel, delete, efface, murder 7 expunge 10 obliterate

rubber: 4 band 5 brick 6 caucho, condom, cutter, eraser 7 ebonite, masseur 8 busybody, masseuse, overshoe, polisher 9 vulcanite 10 caoutchouc
juice: 5 latex 6 achete
substitute: 7 factice
synthetic: 4 buna 5 butyl
tree: ule 7 cahucho, seringa

rubberneck: 4 gape, gawk, gaze 5 stare 6 butt-in 7 meddler, tourist 8 busybody, kibitzer, quidnunc

rubber tree: ule 4 para 6 caucho 7 seringa 10 caoutchouc

rubbish: ket (Sc.), pap 4 flam, gear, junk, mull, pelf, pelt, raff, rose 5 crawm, dross, offal, trash, waste, wrack 6 colder, debris, garble, litter, refuse, rubble, trashy 7 baggage, beggary, mullock, rummage 8 nonsense, trumpery 9 worthless 10 clamjamfry 11 foolishness

rube: 4 hick, jake 5 yokel 6 rustic 7 bumpkin, hayseed 9 hillbilly 10 countryman

rubellite: 10 tourmaline

rubeola: 7 measles, rubella

rubescent: red 4 pink 8 blushing, flushing 9 reddening 10 erubescent

rubicund: red 4 rosy, ruby 5 ruddy 6 florid 7 flushed, reddish, redness 8 sanguine 11 fullblooded

rubor: 9 hyperemia

rubric: red 4 name 5 gloss, title 6 redden 7 concept, heading 8 category, protocol 11 explanation
book: 4 ordo 7 ordines (pl.)

ruby: gem, red 5 balas, jewel, stone 6 spinel 7 rubasse
mineral: 8 corundum

ruck: rut, sit 4 fold, heap, mass, pile, rake, rick 5 cower, crowd, squat, stack 6 crease, crouch, furrow, pucker 7 crumple, wrinkle 9 gathering, multitude

ruckus: ado, row 4 to-do 5 noise 6 rumpus, uproar 7 ruction 9 confusion 11 disturbance

ruction: 4 fray 5 fight, melee 6 uproar 7 quarrel 8 fraction, outbreak 11 disturbance

rudder: *control:* 4 helm 5 wheel 6 tiller
edge: 8 bearding
part: 4 yoke

ruddle: 5 flush, rouge 6 redden

ruddy: red 4 rosy 5 fresh 6 florid, tanned 7 reddish 8 blushing

rude: 4 bold, curt, lewd 5 bluff, crass, crude, harsh, rough, rowdy, surly 6 bloody, borrel, brutal, clumsy, coarse, crusty, fierce, rugged, rustic, savage, severe, vulgar 7 artless, boorish, brutish, country, jarring, loutish, uncivil, uncouth, violent **8** churlish, clownish, homespun, ignorant, impolite, impudent, insolent, ungentle, untaught **9** barbarian, barbarous, dissonant, ferocious, imperfect, impetuous, inclement, inelegant, insulting, make-shift, truculent, turbulent, unskilled, untrained **10** uncultured, unmannerly, unpolished **11** acrimonious, impertinent, uncivilized **12** contumelious, discourteous

rudeness: 4 gaff **6** ferity

rudiment: 4 base, germ **7** vestige **9** beginning

rudimentary: 4 ABCs **5** basic **7** initial **9** elemental, vestigial **10** elementary **11** abecedarian, fundamental

rue: rew **4** herb, pity, rake **5** dolor, grief, mourn **6** bewail, grieve, lament, regret, repent, sorrow, street, suffer **7** afflict, deplore, remorse **8** penitent **10** bitterness, compassion, repentance

rueful: 5 sorry **6** woeful **8** penitent, wretched **10** despondent, melancholy

ruff: ree **4** bird, fish **5** frill, perch, plait, reeve, stamp, trump **6** collar, fraise, hackle, pigeon, rabato, rebato, ruffle, tippet **7** applaud, sunfish **8** disorder, drumbeat **9** sandpiper

ruffian: 4 hood, pimp, rage, thug **5** bully, cruel, rowdy, tough **6** brutal, cutter, cuttle, ismene, pander, roarer, stormy **7** hoodlum, lawless, lustful, violent **8** assassin, gangster, hooligan, paramour **9** cutthroat, desperado

ruffle: irk, vex **4** beat, blow, fret, roil, rool **5** annoy, crimp, frill, jabot, ruche, shake **6** abrade, bother, nettle, riffle, ripple, tousel, tousle, tumult **7** agitate, derange, disturb, flounce, flutter, panuelo, roughen, shuffle, swagger, wrinkle **8** brandish, disheveled, disorder, drumbeat, furbelow, irritate, undulate **9** balayeuse, carfuffle, commotion, confusion **10** disarrange, discompose, intimidate

ruffler: 5 bully, tramp **6** beggar **7** boaster, ruffian **8** braggart, shuffler **9** swaggerer

rufous: 5 color, rusty, tawny **7** reddish

rug: dog, mat, tug **4** Agra, cozy, haul, pull, snug, tear, wrap **5** Herat **6** afghan, carpet, frieze, kaross, liquor, runner, wrench **7** bargain, blanket, drugget, laprobe **8** Akhissar, Amritsar, covering, portiere **9** Samarkand **11** comfortable

ruga: 4 fold **6** crease **7** wrinkle **8** membrane

rugby: 8 football
formation: **5** scrum **9** scrummage
player: **6** center, hooker, winger **8** standoff **9** scrum half
score: try **4** goal **10** conversion

rugged: 4 hard, rude, sour **5** asper, hardy, harsh, rough, stern, surly, tough **6** craggy, fierce, horrid, robust, seamed, severe, shaggy, stormy, strong, sturdy, uneven **7** arduous, austere, crabbed, gnarled, uncivil, unkempt **8** obdurate, vigorous, wrinkled

rugose: 6 ridged **8** wrinkled **10** corrugated

ruin: gin **4** bane, bust, dash, do in, doom, fall, fate, fell, harm, loss, undo **5** blast, break, decay, exile, fordo, havoc, spoil, waste, wrack, wreck **6** beggar, blight, damage, deface, defeat, diddle, dismay, foredo, impair, injure, perish, ravage **7** decayed, despoil, destroy, pervert, ruinate, subvert **8** bankrupt, calamity, demolish, desolate, disaster, downfall **9** confusion, crumbling, decadence, desecrate, disfigure, overthrow, perdition, ruination **10** bankruptcy, desolation, subversion **11** destruction, devastation, dissolution, ecroulement

ruined: 4 dead **5** kaput **6** shabby **7** forlorn **8** bankrupt, desolate **10** tumbledown

ruinous: 5 fatal **10** calamitous, disastrous, pernicious **11** destructive

rule: law **4** code, lead, lord, norm, sway **5** adage, axiom, by-law, canon, guide, judge, logos, maxim, order, regle, reign, tenet **6** course, decide, decree, direct, domine, empire, govern, manage, method, regime, screed **7** alidade, brocard, command, conduct, control, counsel, formula, mastery, precept, prevail, regency, regimen, theorem **8** behavior, decision, doctrine, domineer, dominion, persuade, practice, regulate, standard **9** authority, criterion, direction, enactment, influence, principle **10** convention, government, regulation **11** aristocracy, be number one, commandment, predominate
pert. to: **5** rutic

rule out: bar **5** debar **6** forbid, refuse **7** exclude, prevent, scratch **8** preclude, prohibit

ruler: dey, min **4** amir, czar, doge, duce, emir, Khan, king, lord, raja, shah, tsar, tzar **5** alder, ameer, emeer, chief, mogul, nabob, nawab, prior, queen, rajah, sheik **6** archon, author, caesar, caliph, despot, dynast, ferule, gerent, kaiser, leader, sachem, shogun, prince, regent, satrap, sultan, tyrant **7** emperor, empress, infanta, khedive, pharaoh, monarch, regulus, viceroy **8** autocrat, dictator, governor, hierarch, interrex, mandarin, padishah, premier, suzerain **9** dominator, governail, imperator, matriarch, potentate, president, sovereign, yardstick **10** interreges (pl.) **12** straightedge
family: **7** dynasty
one of three: **7** triarch **8** triumvir
one of two: **6** duarch

wife: **4** rani **5** queen, ranee **7** consort, czarina, empress, tsarina

rules: **4** code

infraction: **4** foul **8** cheating **ruling:** law **4** fiat **5** edict **6** decree **7** average, central, current, inkling, regnant, statute **8** decision, dominant **9** ascendant, ascendent, hegemonic, prevalent **10** prevailing **11** predominant

rum: bad, odd (Br.) **4** good, grog, poor **5** queer (Br.), tafia **6** liquor **7** Bacardi, cachaca, strange **8** beverage, Jamaican, peculiar **9** excellent

Rumania: See **Romania**

rumble: **4** clap, peal, roll, seat **5** crack, crash, growl, rumor **6** murmur, polish, ramble, report, ripple, uproar **7** grumble, thunder **9** complaint **11** disturbance

rumbo: **4** grog **6** liquor

rumen: cud **6** paunch **7** stomach

ruminant: yak **4** deer, goat **5** bison, camel, llama, moose, okapi, sheep, steer **6** alpaca, cattle, vicuna **7** buffalo, chewing, giraffe **8** antelope **10** meditative, thoughtful

female: cow, doe, ewe **5** nanny

genus: bos **5** capra

male: ram **4** buck, bull

stomach: **4** read, reed **5** rumen **6** omasum **8** abomasum, abomasus, roddikin **9** reticulum

ruminate: **4** chaw, chew, mull, muse **5** munch, think, weigh **6** ponder **7** reflect **8** cogitate, consider, meditate **9** masticate

rummage: **4** grub, rout, stow **6** gather, litter, search **7** clutter, collect, derange, examine, fossick, ransack, rubbish, stowage, turmoil **8** disorder, upheaval **9** confusion, ferret out, searching **10** disarrange **11** derangement

rummer: cup **5** glass

rummy: **4** chap, game **5** drunk **7** bizarre, strange **8** drunkard

rumor: **4** buzz, fame, sugh, talk, tell, word **5** bruit, noise, on-dit, sough, story, voice **6** clamor, furphy, gossip, murmur, norate, report, spread, uproar **7** hearsay, message, tidings, whisper **9** grapevine, statement **10** reputation **11** scuttlebutt

personification: **4** Fama

rump: **4** dock **6** behind, insult **7** hurdies, plunder, remnant **8** bankrupt, buttocks **11** legislature

rump bone: **6** sacrum **8** edgebone **9** aitchbone

rumple: **4** fold, muss, rool, rump, tail **5** plait, touse **6** crease, frowse, tousle **7** crinkle, crumple, wrinkle

rumpus: row **4** to-do **5** brawl **6** barney, fracas, hubbub, ruckus, tumult, uproar **8** argument, brouhaha **9** commotion, confusion **11** disturbance

rumshop: bar **6** saloon, tavern **7** barroom, taproom

run: fly, gad, hie, jog, ply, rin (Sc.), sew **4** bolt, butt, cast, dart, dash, emit, flee, flow, fuse, gait, grow, hare, hunt, lope, melt, mold, move, pass, pour, race, roam, rove, rush, sail, scud, tear, tend, trip, trot, turn, work **5** blend, brook, carry, climb, cover, creek, creep, dog it, drive, enter, going, hurry, range, ravel, reach, recur, river, route, scoot, score, scour, speed, stand, trace, treat **6** ascend, become, bicker, canter, career, charge, course, elapse, extend, gallop, govern, hasten, ladder, manage, output, pursue, refine, resort, rotate, scurry, spread, spring, sprint, stream, thrust **7** conduct, contend, descend, develop, diffuse, journey, liquefy, make off, migrate, operate, proceed, process, roulade, scamper, scutter, scuttle, smuggle, stretch, trickle, vamoose **8** continue, dissolve, duration, function, sequence, stampede, traverse **9** discharge, suppurate, transport **10** take flight

across: **4** meet **8** discover **9** encounter **10** transverse

aground: **5** beach **6** strand **7** founder

away: **4** bolt, flee **5** elope **6** decamp, desert, escape, maroon

down: hit **4** kill, sink, stop **5** crush, decry, seedy **6** pursue **7** capture, decline, traduce **8** overbear **9** disparage, exhausted, overthrow **11** dilapidated

for office: **5** stand **8** campaign

-in: **4** tiff **5** fight **7** quarrel **11** altercation

of-the-mill: **4** so-so **6** common, medium **7** average, general **8** ordinary

off: **5** drain, print, waste **7** impress **9** effluence

out: **4** fail, flow **5** expel, lapse, peter, spill, spilt, waste **6** banish, elapse, expire, spread **8** squander

over: **6** exceed, review, strike **8** overflow, rehearse **9** knock down

through: **4** stab **5** use up **6** browse, pierce, review **7** examine, inspect, pervade **8** rehearse, transfix

up: **4** grow, rise **5** erect **7** enlarge, throw up **8** increase **9** construct **10** accumulate

runagate: **7** runaway **8** apostate, deserter, fugitive, renegade, vagabond, wanderer

runaway: **7** escapee **8** fugitive, runagate

rundle: **4** ball, drum, rung, step **5** orbit, round **6** circle, sphere

rundlet: keg, tun **4** cask **6** barrel

rune: wen **4** poem, song **5** charm, magic, rhyme, spell, verse **6** poetry, secret **7** mystery **9** character

Russia: 7 Muscovy

   alcoholic beverage: 5 kvass, quass, vodka 9 slivovitz

   alphabet: 8 Cyrillic

   antelope: 5 saiga

   apple: 9 astrachan

   aristocrat: 5 Boyar 6 Boyard

   artist: 7 Chagall 9 Kandinsky

   automobile: Zil, Zis

   ballet: 7 Bolshoi 9 Leningrad

   bondman: 4 serf

   braid: 8 soutache

   cactus: 7 thistle

   cap: 4 aska

   capital: 6 Moscow

   carriage: 6 drosky, troika 8 tarantas

   cathedral: 5 sobor

   caviar: 4 ikra 5 ikary

   citadel: 7 Kremlin

   city: 4 Omsk, Orel, Perm 5 Gorki, Kasan, Kazan, Pensa, Pskov 6 Moskva, Nizhni, Rostov, Sartov 7 Bataisk, Ivanovo, Kalinin, Rybinsk 8 Kostroma, Orenburg, Smolensk, Taganrog, Vladimir, Voronezh, Yaroslaf 9 Archangel, Kuibishev 11 Novosibirsk, Vladivostok

   coal area: 6 Donets

   commune: 6 kolhoz 7 kolkhos, kolkhoz

   Communist institution: 6 soviet 9 Comintern, Politburo, Presidium 10 Praesidium 11 Politbureau 13 Supreme Soviet

   Communist youth group: 8 Comsomol, Komsomol

   composer: Cui 5 Glink 7 Borodin 8 Scriabin 9 Prokofiev 10 Stravinsky 11 Moussorgsky 12 Rachmaninoff, Tschaikovsky 13 Shostakovitch 14 Rimsky-Korsakov

   cooperative: 5 artel

   cossack: 6 Tartar

   council: 4 Duma

   country house: 5 dacha

   currency: 5 altin, copec, kopek, ruble, ruble 6 copeck, grivna, kopeck 9 altininck, poltinnik 10 chervonets

   dance: 7 ziganka

   despot: 4 czar, tsar

   devil: 5 chort

   dog: 4 alan 6 borzoi 7 owtchah 9 wolfhound

   dramatist: 5 Gogol, Gorki 7 Chekhov, Tolstoy 8 Karamzin, Turgenev 9 Pasternak 10 Dostoevsky 12 Solzhenitsyn

   dress: 7 sarafan

   exclamation: 7 nichevo 8 nitchevo

   farmer: 5 kulak

   fish: 6 beluga 8 sturgeon

   flax: 6 bobbin

   folk song: 6 bylina

   gambling game: 6 coocoo

   government farm: 7 sovkhos, sovkhoz

   government group: 4 duma, rada, tsik 6 soviet 7 zemstvo

   grandmother: 8 babushka

   hood: 7 bashlik, bashlyk

   horse: 6 tarpan

   house: 4 isba 5 dacha

   image: 4 icon, ikon 5 ikono

   imperial order: 5 ukase

   kerchief: 6 analav

   labor association: 5 artel

   lagoon: 5 liman

   lake: 4 Aral, Neva, Sego 5 Elton, Ilmen, Onega 6 Baikal

   measure: fut, lof 4 duim, fass, loof, stof 5 duime, foute, korec, ligne, osmin, pajak, stoff, vedro, verst 6 arshin, charka, liniya, osmina, paletz, sagene, tchast, versta, verste 7 arsheen, botchka, chkalik, garnetz, verchoc, verchok 8 boutylka, chetvert, krouchka, kroushka 9 chetverik 10 dessiatine 11 polugarnetz

   mile: 5 verst

   monk: 7 starets, Tikhon 8 Rasputin

   mountain range: 4 Ural 5 Altai 6 Pamirs 8 Caucasus

   museum: 9 Hermitage

   musical instrument: 5 gudok, gusla, gusle 9 balalaika

   naval academy: 6 Frunze

   negative: 4 nyet

   news agency: 4 Tass

   newspaper: 6 Pravda 8 Izvestia

   noble: 5 boyar

   novelist: 5 Gorki 7 Chekhov, Tolstoy 10 Dostoevsky

   peasant: 5 kulak 6 muzhik, muzjik

   plain: 6 steppe

   poet: 5 Bunin 6 Jehuda 7 Pushkin 9 Aleksandr, Pasternak, Sholokhov 11 Sergyeevich, Voznesensky, Yevtushenko

   prince: 4 knez 5 knais, knyaz

   revolutionist: 5 Lenin, Rykov 6 Stalin, Tomsky 7 Trotsky

   river: Don, Ili, Ner, Oka, Ros, Ufa 4 Amur, Duna, Kara, Lena, Neva, Orel, Sura, Svir, Ural 5 Dnepr, Dvina, Onega, Terek, Tobol, Volga 6 Donets, Irtish, Irtysh 7 Dnieper

   satellite: 7 sputnik

   secretary of government: 11 apparatchik

   soup: 5 shchi 6 borsch 7 borscht *(cont.)*

rung: rod **4** spar, step **5** round, spoke, staff, stair, stake, stave, tread **6** cudgel, degree, rundle **7** girdled

runnel: **4** rill **5** brook, creek, rhine **6** runlet, stream **7** channel, rivulet **9** streamlet **11** watercourse

runner: rug, ski **5** agent, miler, racer, ravel, scarf **6** carpet, cursor, stolon **8** operator, smuggler, sprinter **9** collector, detective, messenger, solicitor

running: **4** care, easy, race, trip **6** active, attack **7** contest, current, cursive, flowing, journey **8** skirmish, together **9** oversight **10** management, successive

running knot: **5** noose

runt: **4** chit, wrig **5** dwarf, pygmy **6** durgan, durgen, peewee, titman **8** smallest

runty: **4** puny **5** small **7** stunted **8** dwarfish **10** diminutive, undersized

runway: **4** file, path, ramp, road **5** chute, strip, track, trail **6** bridge, groove, trough **7** channel **8** airstrip, platform **10** passageway

rupia: **8** eruption

rupture: **4** open, part, rend, rent **5** break, burst, split **6** breach, hernia, rhexis **7** divorce, parting, ruction, ruption **8** division, fraction, fracture **10** disruption

rural: **6** rustic **7** bucolic, country, idyllic, natural, outland **8** agrestic, Arcadian, geoponic, pastoral **10** provincial **11** countrified

ruse: **4** fall, hoax, slip, wile **5** dodge, feint, fraud, shift, trick **6** deceit, gambit **8** artifice **9** stratagem **10** subterfuge

rush: run, sag **4** birr, bolt, dart, dash, flow, junk, race, rout, scud, tear **5** break, brook, chute, feeze, haste, hurry, onset, press, sally, scoot, spate, sprat, sprot, straw, surge **6** attack, bustle, charge, combat, course, defeat, fescue, hasten, hurtle, hustle, plunge, runlet, sortie, trifle **7** assault, bulrush, cattail, destroy, rampage, repulse, tantivy **8** eruption, stampede, vanquish

rusk: **4** cake **5** bread, crisp, toast **7** biscuit **8** zweiback

Russia: (see box)

russud: **5** grain **6** forage

rust: eat **5** erode **6** aerugo, blight, canker, patina **7** corrode, erosion, oxidize **9** corrosion, oxidation, verdigris

rustic: hob **4** boor, carl, dull, hick, hind, jake, rube, rude **5** bacon, carle, chuff, churl, clown, doric, hodge, plain, rough, rural, swain, yokel **6** coarse, farmer, gaffer, honest, simple, sturdy, sylvan **7** artless, awkward, boorish, bucolic, bumpkin, bushman, Corydon, country, georgic, hayseed, peasant, plowboy, plowman, uncouth **8** agrestic, churlish, clownish, pastoral **9** agrestian, campesino, chaw-bacon, greenhorn, hillbilly, unadorned **10** clod-hopper, countryman, unaffected

rustle: **5** haste, steal **6** fissle, fistle, forage, hustle, scroop **7** crinkle

Rustum: *father:* Zal
son: **6** Sohrab

rut: rat, rit **4** brim, heat **5** ditch, grind, track **6** estrus, furrow, groove, strake **7** channel, routine, wrinkle

rutabaga: **5** swede **6** turnip

ruth: rue, woe **4** pity **5** grief, mercy **6** regret, sorrow **7** remorse, sadness **9** penitence **10** compassion, repentance, tenderness

Ruth: *husband:* Boaz
mother-in-law: **5** Naomi
son: **4** Obed

ruthless: **4** grim **5** cruel **6** savage **8** pitiless **9** cutthroat, ferocious, merciless **10** implacable, relentless

rutter: **4** plow **5** guide **7** trooper **8** horseman

ruttle: **6** gurgle, rattle

rye: ree, rie **5** grain, grass **6** whisky **7** whiskey **9** gentleman
disease: **5** ergot

ryot, raiyat (Ind.): **6** farmer, tenant **7** peasant **10** cultivator

S

sabbat: 8 assembly 14 witches' sabbath

sabbath: 6 Friday, Sunday 7 sabaoth, shabbat, shabbos 8 first day, Saturday 10 seventh day

saber, sabre: 5 sword 7 cutlass 8 scimitar, scimiter, yataghan

Sabine: *goddess:* 6 Vacuna
people: 7 Vestini

sable: sad 4 dark, ebon 5 black, brush, saber 6 dismal, gloomy, marten, pellet 8 antelope, darkened 10 mysterious 11 threatening
genus of: 7 mustela
pert. to: 8 zibeline 9 zibelline

sablefish: cod 6 beshow 10 candlefish

sabot: 4 clog, shoe

sabotage: 5 block, wreck 6 damage 7 destroy, subvert 9 undermine 10 impairment 11 destruction

Sabrina River: 6 Severn

sabulous: 5 dusty, sandy 6 floury, gritty 10 arenaceous

sabutan: 5 fiber, straw

sac: bag, pod 4 cyst, sack 5 ascus, bursa, pouch, theca 6 cavity 7 cistern, utricle, vesicle

Sacar's son: 5 Ahiam

sacaton: 5 grass

saccadic: 5 jerky 9 twitching

saccharine: 5 sweet 6 sugary, syrupy 7 cloying, gluside, honeyed 10 sweetening 12 ingratiating

saccos: See **sakkos**

sacculated: 7 pouched

sacerdotal: 8 clerical, hieratic, priestly

sachem: 4 boss 5 chief, ruler 8 sagamore 15 political leader

sachet: bat, pad 5 orris, pouch, scent 8 reticule

sack: bag, bed 4 base, fire, loot, poke, ruin 5 bursa, gunny, harry, pouch, purse, waste 6 budget, burlap, jacket, ravage, wallet 7 boucher, dismiss, musette, pillage, plunder, ransack 8 desolate 9 container, discharge, dismissal
fiber: 4 jute 5 gunny 6 burlap

sackbut: 8 trombone

sackless: 4 weak 7 bashful 8 harmless, innocent 9 guiltless, peaceable 10 dispirited, unmolested

sacque: 6 jacket

sacrament: 4 host, Mass, rite, sign 5 token 6 pledge, symbol 7 baptism, mystery, penance, promise, unction 8 ceremony, covenant 9 communion, Eucharist, matrimony 10 confession, holy orders 12 confirmation

sacrarium: 5 ambry 6 chapel, shrine 7 oratory 9 sanctuary 10 tabernacle

sacred: 4 holy 5 godly, huaca, santo 6 divine 7 blessed, saintly 8 hallowed, reverend 9 cherished, inviolate, venerated 10 sacrosanct, sanctified 11 consecrated
make: 8 enshrine

sacred bean: 5 lotus

sacred beetle: 10 scarabaeus

sacred fig: 5 pipal

sacred place: 5 altar 6 chapel, church, shrine, temple 7 sanctum 9 sanctuary

sacred weed: 7 vervain

sacrifice: 4 host, loss 5 forgo, yield 6 corban, homage, korban, martyr, victim 8 hecatomb, immolate, oblation, offering, part with 9 holocaust, martyrdom, privation, surrender 10 immolation

sacrilege: 7 profane, ungodly 9 blasphemy 11 desecration, profanation

sacristy: 6 vestry

sacrosanct: 6 sacred 8 esteemed, regarded 9 inviolate, respected

sad: bad 4 blue, dark, dram (Sc.), dull 5 dusky, grave, sober, sorry, trist 6 dismal, dreary, gloomy, rueful, solemn, somber, sombre, tragic, triste (F.), wicked, woeful 7 doleful, dolente (It.), forlorn, painful, pensive, serious, unhappy 8 dejected, desolate, dolorous, downcast, grievous, mournful, pathetic, pitiable, wretched 9 afflicted, cheerless, depressed, plaintive, sorrowful 10 calamitous, deplorable, despondent, lamentable, lugubrious, melancholy 11 distressing, melancholic 12 disconsolate, heavyhearted

sadden: 7 attrist, depress 8 make blue

saddle: 4 load 5 ridge 6 burden, howdah 7 aparejo, pillion 8 encumber, restrict
blanket: 6 corona, tilpah
bow: 6 pommel
kind: 7 English, western
maker: 7 knacker, saddler
pad: 5 panel 7 housing

part: **4** horn, tore **5** cinch, croup, girth, panel, pilch, skirt **6** corona, crutch, pommel **7** stirrup **8** sudadero

saddleback: 4 hill **5** ridge

saddlebag: sag (Sc.) **4** jagg (Sc.) **7** alforja, pannier, sumpter

saddlecloth: 5 panel **7** blanket, housing **8** shabrack **9** shabraque

saddle horse: 4 pony **5** mount **7** palfrey

saddler: 4 seal **5** horse **7** cobbler, knacker, lorimer, loriner **9** shoemaker **11** saddlemaker

saddle rock: 6 oyster

saddle strip: 5 cinch, cindi, girth, strap **6** latigo **7** harness

sadness: woe **4** funk **5** blues, dolor, dumps, grief **6** sorrow **7** anguish, despair, megrims **9** heartache **10** depression, melancholy **11** unhappiness

saeter: 6 meadow **7** pasture

safari: 4 hunt, trek **7** caravan, journey **9** excursion **10** expedition

safe: box **4** sure **5** chest, siker, sound, vault **6** armory, closet, coffer, holder, secure, sicker, unhurt **8** cautious, cupboard, harmless, unharmed **9** strongbox, untouched **10** depository **11** gardeviance, trustworthy

safe-conduct: 4 pass **5** cowle, guard **6** convoy **10** permission, protection

safecracker: 4 yegg **7** burglar, peteman, Raffles

safeguard: 4 pass **5** guard **6** convoy, escort, safety **7** defense, protect **10** protection

safekeeping: 4 care **7** custody, storage **10** protection **12** preservation

safety: 8 security **9** assurance, touchback
place of: ark **4** port **5** haven **6** asylum, refuge **7** retreat, sanctum, shelter

safety lamp: 4 Davy

safety pin: 5 clasp **6** fibula

safety rail: 9 guardrail

safety zone: 5 islet **6** island, refuge

saffron: dye **6** crocus, yellow **9** flavoring, safflower
source: **12** Crocus sativa

sag: 4 bend, flag, reed, rush, sink, wilt **5** drift, droop, sedge, slump **6** settle, weaken **7** deflate

saga: 4 edda, epic, gest, myth, tale **5** story **6** legend **7** history, recital **9** narrative

sagaciate: 4 fare **6** thrive

sagacious: 4 sage, wise **5** acute, quick **6** argute, astute, shrewd **7** knowing, politic, prudent, sapient **9** far-seeing, judicious **10** discerning, farsighted, hardheaded **11** clairvoyant, penetrating, wise as an owl **13** perspicacious

sagacity: 6 acumen, wisdom **8** sapience

sagamore: 5 chief, ruler **6** sachem

sage: 4 herb, mint, seer, wise **5** clary, grave, rishi (Ind.), solon, spice **6** pundit, salvia, savant, shrewd, solemn **7** learned, prudent, sapient, wise man **8** sagebush **9** counselor, judicious, venerable **10** counsellor, discerning, perceptive **11** philosopher

Sage: *of Chelsea:* **13** Thomas Carlyle
of Concord: **17** Ralph Waldo Emerson
of Emporia: **17** William Allen White
of Ferney: **8** Voltaire
of Monticello: **15** Thomas Jefferson
of Pylos: **6** Nestor

Sagebrush State: 6 Nevada

sage cheese: 7 cheddar

sage cock: 6 grouse

sage hen: 6 grouse **7** Nevadan

saginate: 6 fatten, pamper

Sagittarius: 6 archer, bowman, zodiac **13** constellation

sago: 5 flour **6** starch

sagoin: 8 marmoset

sago palm: 7 coontie

saguaro: 6 cactus

sagum: 5 cloak

Sahara: 6 desert
people: **4** Arab, Moor **5** nomad **6** Berber, Tuareg
plateau: **6** hamada **7** hammada
wind: **5** leste **6** gibleh

saic: 4 boat **5** ketch

said: dit (F.) **4** such **5** quoth **6** spoken, stated **7** reputed, uttered **8** supposed

saiga: 4 coin **8** antelope

sail: awe, awn, fly, rig, van **4** dart, duck, haul, keel, luff, scud, skim, soar, swim, trip **5** fleet, float, glide, sheet **6** canvas, depart, embark, voyage **7** journey **8** navigate
kind of: jib **5** royal **6** lateen, mizzen, square **7** balloon, lugsail, skysail, spanker, topsail, trysail **8** foresail, mainsail, staysail, studding **9** crossjack, foreroyal, spinnaker **10** topgallant **12** forestaysail
nearer wind: **4** luff
part: **4** bunt, clew, yard **5** leach, leech, sheet **6** earing **7** earring, yardarm
pert. to: **5** velic
prepare to: **4** trim

sailboat: cat **4** bark, dhow, junk, pram, yawl **5** ketch, praam, skiff, sloop, yacht **7** caravel, lakatoi **9** caravelle
large: cog **4** bark, brig, proa, saic, yawl **5** prahu **6** barque, cutter, galley, packet, sampan, vessel **7** carrack, clipper, frigate, galleon **8** lateener, schooner **10** barkentine, brigantine

sailcloth: 4 duck **6** canvas

sailfish: 6 woohoo **8** billfish

sailing: 4 asea **6** afloat **7** boating **8** cruising, yachting *terms:* run, yar **4** beat, jibe, luff, tack, trim **5** abeam, plane, reach **8** downwind **9** come about

sailor: gob, hat, tar, tot **4** salt, swab **5** Jacky **6** hearty, lascar, ratiny, seaman **7** mariner **8** coxswain, seafarer, waterman **10** bluejacket, lobscouser

assent: aye

associate: **4** mate **8** messmate, shipmate

British: tar **5** limey

call: **4** ahoy

carving: **9** scrimshaw

chapel: **6** bethel

fictional: **6** Sinbad

group: **4** crew **5** hands

jacket: **6** reefer

mess tub: kid

patron saint: **4** Elmo

patroness: **11** Mother Carey

potion: rum **4** grog

song: **6** chanty **7** chantey **9** barcarole

saint: Sao (Port.), Ste. (F.) **4** holy **5** santa (Sp.), santo (Sp.) **6** hallow **7** beatify **8** canonize, enshrine

biography: **11** hagiography

image: **4** icon **5** santo

worship: **10** hagiolatry, hierolatry

Saint Andrew's cross: **7** saltier, saltire

Saint Anthony's cross: tau **4** ankh

Saint Catherine's home: **5** Siena

Saint Elmo's fire: **5** flame **6** furole **9** corposant

Saint John's bread: **5** carob

saintly: **4** holy **5** godly, pious **6** devout **7** angelic **8** beatific **9** angelical **10** God-fearing **13** sanctimonious

Saint Paul: *birthplace:* **6** Tarsus

companion: **4** Luke

Saint Peter: **5** Simon **7** apostle

Saint-Saens opera: **16** Samson and Delilah

Saint Vitus' dance: **6** chorea

sake: end **4** good **5** cause, drink **6** behalf, motive, regard **7** account, benefit, concern, purpose **8** beverage, rice wine **9** advantage, intention **13** consideration

saker: **6** falcon

saki: **5** drink, yarke **6** monkey, yarkee **8** beverage, rice wine **9** cup bearer

sakkos, saccos: **7** tunicle **8** vestment

sal: **4** salt

sala: **4** hall, room **10** living room

salaam, salam: bow **4** bend **5** kneel **6** kowtow, salute **8** greeting **9** obeisance, prostrate **10** compliment, salutation

salacious: **4** lewd **7** lustful, obscene **8** scabrous **9** lecherous **10** licentious **12** pornographic

salad: **4** slaw **5** aspic, green, mixed **6** Caesar, tossed **7** melange **8** cole slaw

ingredient: **5** cress **6** celery, endive, greens, tomato **7** cabbage, lettuce, parsley, romaine **8** scallion **9** dandelion **10** watercress

meal-size: **5** chef's **7** Nicoise **10** salmagundi

Saladin's foes: **9** Crusaders

salamander: eft, olm **4** evet, newt **6** spirit, triton **7** axoloti, axolotl, caudata, urodela, urodele **9** amphibian, fireplace **10** hellbender

order: **7** caudata, urodela

salami: **7** sausage

Salammbo author: **8** Flaubert

salary: fee, pay **5** wages **6** reward **7** stipend **8** pittance **9** allowance, emolument **10** recompense **12** compensation, remuneration

sale: net **4** deal, hall, vend **5** bower **6** market, palace, vendue, willow **7** auction, bargain, rummage **8** contract, transfer **9** utterance, vendition **10** conveyance **11** transaction

kind: **4** yard **5** white **6** garage, moving

salesperson: **5** agent, clerk **6** hawker, pedlar, sutler, vendor **7** chapman, drummer, hustler, peddler **8** pitchman, retailer, vendeuse (fem.)

sales talk: **4** line **5** pitch, spiel **6** patter

salience: **5** point **7** agility **8** emphasis **9** highlight **10** notability, prominence **12** protuberance

salient: **4** line **5** redan **6** marked, moving, signal, trench **7** germane, jumping, leaping **8** bounding, extended, striking **9** arresting, important **10** noticeable **11** conspicuous

salient angle: **5** arris

salientia: **5** anura, frogs, toads **7** aglossa, costata **8** Amphibia, linguata

salient point: **5** heart **6** detail, source **7** feature

salina: **4** lake, pond **5** marsh **9** saltworks

saline: **4** tear **5** briny, salty **8** brackish **10** saliferous

Salisbury steak: **9** hamburger

saliva: **4** spit **5** water **7** spittle

salix: **5** genus **6** osiers **7** sallows, willows

salle (F.): **4** room, sala (Sp.)

sallet: **6** helmet, salade

sallow: wan **4** pale, twig **5** muddy, osier, shoot **6** pallid, willow **9** colorless, yellowish

sally: **4** jest, joke, leap, quip, rush, trip **5** dance, issue, jaunt, start **6** attack, emerge, escape, retort, sortie, spring **7** darting, journey, rushing **8** escapade, outbreak, outburst **9** excursion, witticism **10** liveliness

salmagundi: **4** hash, olio **5** salad **6** medley **7** mixture **9** potpourri **10** hodgepodge

salmi: **6** ragout **8** game stew

salmon: gib **4** chum, kelt, keta, pike, pink **5** color, haddo, holia, smolt, tecon **6** jumper, laurel, sauqui, taimen **7** gilling, saumont, shedder **8** schoodic, springer, weakfish **9**

ceratodus **10** barramunda
enclosure: **4** weir, yair
female: **4** raun **6** baggit
male: **6** kipper
pool: **5** stell
smoked: lox
trap: **4** slap
young: **4** parr
salmon trout: **5** sewen **9** steelhead
Salome: *mother:* **8** Herodias
stepfather: **5** Herod
salon: **4** hall, room **5** group, party **6** museum **7** gallery **9** apartment, reception **10** assemblage, exhibition **11** drawing room
saloon: bar, pub **4** hall, room **5** cabin, coach, cuddy, divan, sedan **6** tavern **7** barroom, cantina (Sp.) **8** alehouse, groggery
salpa, salp: **8** tunicate
salse: **7** volcano
salsify: **9** vegetable **11** oyster plant
salt: sal, tar, wit **4** alum, corn, cure **5** brine, briny, ester, salic, sharp, witty **6** alkali, flavor, halite, harden, lively, sailor, saline, seaman, season **7** bromate, piquant, pungent, seadust **8** brackish, halinous **9** seasoning
deposit: **6** saline
oleic acid: **6** oleate
resembling: **5** halid **6** halide, haloid
rock: pig
working: **7** halurgy
saltate: **4** jump, leap **5** bound, dance
saltcellar: **5** saler **6** shaker
salted: **4** alat **5** cured **6** corned
salt-like: **6** haloid
salt marsh: **6** salina **9** grassland
saltpeter, saltpetre: **5** niter, nitre
salt pit: vat
salt tree: **4** atle **8** tamarisk
salt water: **5** brine
saltworks: **7** saltern, saltery
salty: **4** racy **5** briny, witty **6** ribald, risque, saline **8** brackish, indecent, nautical
salubrious: **4** good **7** bracing, healthy **8** salutary **9** benignant, healthful, wholesome **10** beneficial
salutary: **4** good **6** benign **7** healthy, helpful **8** curative **9** desirable, healthful, medicinal, wholesome **10** beneficial **11** restorative
salutation: ave, bow **4** beck, g'day, hail **5** aloha, hello, howdy, skoal **6** curtsy, kowtow, Mizpah, Mizpeh, prosit, salaam, salute **7** address, slainte (Ir.), welcome **8** accolade, chin-chin, encomium, farewell, greeting
salute: nod **4** hail **5** greet, halse, salvo **6** accost, praise, signal **7** address **9** obeisance **11** pay homage to
salvage: **4** save **6** redeem, rescue **7** reclaim, recover

salvation: **6** rescue **10** redemption **12** conservation, preservation
pert. to: **8** soterial **9** soterical
salve: **4** balm, nard **6** anoint, cerate, soothe **7** assuage, unguent **8** flattery, gratuity, ointment, palliate **9** alleviate
salver: **4** tray
salvo: **4** hail, shot **5** burst, spray **6** excuse, salute, shower, volley **7** barrage, gunfire, pretext, proviso, quibble **9** exception **11** reservation, testimonial
samadh: **4** tomb **6** shrine
samaj: **6** church **7** society **12** congregation
samaritan: **6** helper **8** welldoer **10** benefactor
Samaritan: *god:* **6** Tartak
people: **8** Assyrian **9** Israelite
sambar, sambur: elk **4** deer, maha, rusa
same: ilk, one **4** ibid, idem, like, meme (F.), self, very **5** alike, ditto, equal, exact **7** identic **8** constant **9** identical, unchanged **10** invariable
sameness: **8** identity, monotony **10** similarity **11** equivalence, resemblance
Samhain Eve: **9** Halloween
Samian philosopher: **10** Pythagoras
samisen: **5** banjo
samlet: **4** parr **6** salmon **10** fingerling
Samoa: See **Western Samoa**
samovar: urn **6** teapot
samp: **4** meal, mush, soup **6** cereal, hominy **8** porridge
sampaloc: **8** tamarind
sampan: **4** boat **5** skiff
sample: **4** case, test **5** piece, taste **6** swatch **7** example, pattern **8** instance, specimen **10** experiment **12** illustration
sampleman: **6** taster **12** demonstrator
sampler: **5** model **6** taster **7** example, hanging, pattern **8** original, specimen **9** archetype **10** embroidery, needlework
Samson: *betrayer:* **7** Delilah
deathplace: **4** Gaza
vulnerable part: **4** hair
Samuel: *home:* **5** Ramah
mentor: Eli
parent: **6** Hannah **7** Elkanah
son: **5** Abiah
victim: **4** Agag, Agog
samurai: **7** soldier, warrior
sanative: **6** curing **7** healing **8** curative **9** healthful
sanatorium, sanitarium: spa **8** hospital, rest home **16** convalescent home
Sancho Panza: *island:* **9** Barataria
master: **10** Don Quixote
mule: **6** Dapple
sanctify: **5** bless, exalt **6** anoint, hallow, purify **8** dedicate, enshrine **10** consecrate
sanctimonious: **4** holy **5** pious **6** devout,

sacred **7** canting, prudish, saintly, zealous **10** sanctified **12** hypocritical

sanction: 4 amen, fiat, okay **5** allow **6** assent, avouch, permit, placet, ratify **7** approve, confirm, consent, endorse, license, support **8** accredit, approval, legalize **9** allowance, approbate, authority, authorize, encourage, subscribe **10** imprimatur, permission **11** approbation, countenance, countersign, endorsement **12** ratification **13** authorization

sanctity: 5 piety, rites **6** purity **7** halidom **8** halidome, holiness, recesses **9** godliness, solemnity **10** sacredness **11** obligations, saintliness **13** inviolability
place of: **4** fane **5** altar, hiera **6** chapel, church, hieron, shrine, temple **7** chaitya **9** synagogue

sanctuary: ark **4** bema, fane, holy, naos, port **5** abbey, adyta (pl.), bamah, grith, haven, oasis **6** adytum, asylum, bemata, chapel, church, haikal, harbor, priory, refuge, shrine, temple **7** alsatia, chancel, convent, halidom, retreat, sanctum, shelter **8** cloister, halidome, holiness, preserve **9** monastery **10** penetralia, protection, tabernacle **11** hiding place, reservation

sanctum: den **5** study **6** adytum, office **7** retreat **9** sanctuary

sand: rub **4** grit **5** nerve **6** abrade, desert, gravel, smooth **7** courage **8** alluvium, asbestic
particle: **5** grain
particles: **4** silt
resembling: **7** arenoid

sandal: 4 clog, shoe, zori **6** buskin, caliga, charuk **7** rullion, slipper, talaria **8** huarache **9** alpargata **10** espadrille
winged: **7** talaria (pl.)
wooden: **6** patten

sandalwood: 5 algum, almug, maire
Sandalwood Island: 5 Sumba

sandarac: 4 tree **5** resin **7** realgar
tree: **4** arar
wood: **6** alerce, alerse

sandbank: 4 dune, meal

sandbar: 4 dene, dune, reef, spit **5** beach, shelf, shoal

sand dune: 4 areg, hill, sand, seif **5** towan

sand eel: 4 grig **5** lance **6** launce

sand flea: 6 chigoe **7** chigger

sand flounder: 5 fluke **10** windowpane

sandpiper: ree **4** bird, knot, ruff **5** reeve, terek **6** dunlin, teeter, tiltup **7** brownie, chorook, fiddler, haybird **8** redshank, triddler **10** canderling

sandstone: 4 grit **5** hazel **6** arkose **8** ganister **9** gritstone
block: **6** sarsen
pert. to: **10** arenilitic

sandy: dry **6** gritty **7** arenose **8** granular, sabuline, shifting
pert. to: **6** eremic

sane: 4 wise **5** lucid, sober, sound **6** cogent, normal **7** healthy, sapient **8** all there, rational, sensible **10** reasonable

San Francisco: *baseball team:* **6** Giants
district: **7** Nob Hill **8** Presidio **9** Chinatown **11** Embarcadero **13** Haight-Ashbury
football team: **11** Forty-Niners
former district: **12** Barbary Coast
hill: Nob **7** Russian **9** Telegraph
trolley: **8** cable car

sangfroid: 8 calmness, coolness **9** composure, stability **10** equanimity

Sangraal: See **Holy Grail**

sanguinaria: 6 yarrow **9** bloodroot

sanguine: red **4** fond, gory, warm **5** cruel, ruddy **6** ardent, bloody, crayon, savage, yarrow **7** buoyant, hopeful **8** cheerful, hematite **9** confident, expectant, ferocious, murderous **10** bloodstone, ensanguine, optimistic, sanguinary

sanitarium: See **sanatorium**

sanitary: 5 clean **8** hygienic

sanitize: 8 clean out

sanity: 6 reason **7** balance **8** lucidity, normalcy, saneness **9** soundness

San Marino: *capital:* **9** San Marino
city: **6** Dogana **7** Faetano **10** Fiorentino
currency: **4** lira **9** centesimo

sans (F.): 7 without

San Simeon name: 6 Hearst

Sanskrit: *dialect:* **4** Pali
dictionary: **10** amara-kosha
epic character: **4** Sita
epic poem: **5** Kavya **8** Ramayana

sans souci: 12 free from care

Santa Barbara island: 8 Catalina

Santa Claus's reindeer: 5 Comet, Cupid, Vixen **6** Dancer, Dasher, Donder, Donner **7** Blitzen, Prancer, Rudolph

santon: 4 monk **5** image, saint **6** hermit **7** dervish

sap: lac **4** dupe, fool, milk, mine, seve (F.), upas **5** drain, fluid, juice, latex, lymph, vigor **6** energy, impair, trench, weaken **7** exhaust, saphead **8** enervate, knock out, vitality, weakling **9** exudation, schlemiel, schlemihl, screwball, undermine **10** debilitate, devitalize
dried: gum
spout: **5** spile

sapajou: 6 monkey

sapanwood, sappanwood: 4 tree **10** brazilwood

saphie: 5 charm **6** amulet **8** talisman

sapid: 5 tasty **6** savory **7** savoury **8** engaging **9** palatable **10** flavorable **11** fit for a king

sapient: 4 sage, sane, wise 6 shrewd 7 erudite, knowing, learned 9 sagacious 10 discerning

sapiutan: 4 anoa

sapless: dry 7 insipid 8 withered 9 exsuccous 11 devitalized

sapling: 5 plant, youth

sapo: 4 soap 8 toadfish

sapodilla: 5 chico, fruit 7 nispero 9 naseberry
sap: 5 latex 6 chicle

saponaceous: 5 soapy 7 elusive 8 slippery

sapor: 5 gusto, savor, taste 6 flavor, relish

sapper: 5 miner 6 digger

Sappho: 7 poetess
consort: 5 Phaon
home: 6 Lesbos

sappy: 5 juicy, moist, pithy, plump, silly 6 sodden 7 fatuous, foolish 8 vigorous 9 energetic, succulent 11 sentimental

sapsago: 6 cheese

sapsucker: 10 woodpecker

sapwood: 8 alburnum

Saracen: 4 Arab 5 nomad 6 Moslem, Muslim 7 corsair
knight: 6 Rogero 8 Ruggiero
leader: 7 Saladin

Sarah: *husband:* 7 Abraham
slave: 5 Hagar
son: 5 Isaac

sarcasm: wit 4 gibe, jeer 5 fling, humor, irony, taunt 6 attack, rebuke, satire 7 mockery 8 acerbity, acridity, derision, reproach, ridicule 9 criticism
pert. to: 8 ironical

sarcastic: dry 6 biting, ironic 7 acerbic, caustic, cutting, cynical, mordant 8 derisive, incisive, sardonic, sneering 9 corrosive, trenchant

sarcenet, sarsenet: 4 silk, soft 6 gentle, smooth 8 tempered

sarcina: 8 bacteria

sarcle: hoe

sarcophagus: 4 tomb 6 casket, coffin, cooler

sardine: 4 bang, sild 8 pilchard

Sardinia: *capital:* 8 Cagliari
language: 7 Catalan

sardonic: 8 derisive 9 sarcastic

sargo: 5 grunt 7 pinfish 10 sheepshead

sarkinite: 9 arsenate

sarong: 5 skirt 6 comboy 7 garment

sarrazin: 9 buckwheat

sarsen: 5 block 8 monument 9 sandstone

sartor: 6 tailor

sash: obi 4 band, belt, benn (Sc.) 5 scarf 6 fascia, girdle 8 casement, ceinture, cincture 9 waistband 10 cummerbund

sasin: 8 antelope 9 black buck

Saskatchewan: *capital:* 6 Regina
city: 7 Yorkton 8 Moose Jaw 9 Saskatoon

provincial bird: 6 grouse
provincial flower: 11 prairie lily

sasquatch: 4 omah 7 big foot

sassaby: 8 antelope

sassafras: tea 6 saloop

Satan (see also **devil**): 4 liar, Nick 5 demon, devil, eblis, fiend 6 Belial 7 Lucifer, Old Nick, tempter 8 diabolus 9 archfiend 14 Mephistopheles
associate: 9 Beelzebub

satanic: 4 evil 5 cruel 6 wicked 7 demonic 8 devilish, diabolic, infernal, terrible 10 diabolical

satchel: bag 4 case, grip 5 cabas 6 valise

sate: 4 cloy, cram, fill, glut, jade, pall 5 gorge, stuff 7 gratify, surfeit

satellite (see also **Jupiter, Saturn, Uranus**): 4 luna, moon, vein 6 minion, planet 7 Iapetus, Japetus 8 follower, hanger-on 9 attendant, dependent
man-made: ESA, Oso 4 Anik, Anna, Echo, Luna 5 Ariel, Samos, Soyuz, Tiros 6 Cosmos, Ranger, Skylab, Syncom, Viking, Vostok 7 Comstar, Mariner, NAVSTAR, Pioneer, Sputnik, Telstar, Voyager 8 Alouette, Explorer, Intelsat, Telestar 10 Discoverer
space telescope: 6 Hubble
weather: 4 Goes 5 Tiros

satiny: 5 sleek 6 glossy, smooth 8 lustrous

satire: 5 grind, irony, spoof 6 banter, parody 7 lampoon, mockery, sarcasm 8 ridicule, travesty

satiric: dry 6 bitter, ironic 7 abusive, atellan, caustic, cutting, mocking 8 ironical, poignant, spoofing 10 censorious, lampooning 11 reproachful

satirize: 4 lash, mock 5 grind, spoof 6 attack, expose 7 lampoon 8 denounce, ridicule 9 criticize

satisfaction: 4 ease, gree 6 amends 7 content, payment 8 pleasure 9 atonement, enjoyment 10 bloodmoney, recompense, reparation, settlement 11 complacence, contentment, restitution 12 compensation, propitiation, remuneration 13 gratification

satisfactory: pat 4 fair, good, okay 5 valid 6 decent, enough 8 adequate, passable 9 allowable, expiatory, tolerable 10 acceptable, sufficient

satisfied: fed 4 paid, smug 5 proud 9 contented, gratified 10 complacent

satisfy: pay 4 cloy, feed, fill, free, meet, sate, suit 5 appay, atone, clear, repay, serve, slake 6 assure, defray, please, settle, square, supply 7 appease, assuage, content, expiate, fulfill, gratify, requite, satiate, suffice, surfeit 8 convince, make good, reparate 9 discharge 10 compensate, remunerate

satrap: 5 ruler 6 prince, tyrant 7 viceroy 8 governor, official, overlord

sattva: 5 truth 6 purity, wisdom 8 goodness 12 tranquillity

saturate: ret, sog, sop, wet 4 fill, glut, soak 5 imbue, souse, steep 6 dampen, drench, imbibe, imbrue, infuse, seethe, sodden 7 ingrain, pervade, satiate, satisfy 8 permeate 9 penetrate 10 impregnate

Saturday: 7 Sabbath
pert. to: 9 sabbatine

Saturday night special: 7 handgun

Saturn: 6 Cronus, planet
in alchemy: 4 lead
ring part: 4 ansa 5 ansae (pl.)
satellite: 4 Rhea 5 Dione, Janus, Mimas, Titan 6 Phoebe, Tethys 7 Iapetus, Japetus 8 Hyperion 9 Enceladus
wife: Ops

saturnalia: 4 orgy 5 feast 7 revelry 8 carnival, festival

saturnine: 4 dour, dull 5 grave, heavy, staid 6 gloomy, morose, silent, somber, sullen 8 sluggish, taciturn

satyr: 4 faun, idol 5 deity 7 centaur, demigod 9 butterfly, libertine

sauce: dip 5 gravy 6 flavor, liquor, relish 8 back talk, dressing, matelote 9 condiment
kind: soy 4 alec, hard, lear 5 garum 6 catsup 7 catchup, gascony, ketchup, mustard 8 chawdron, remolade 9 genevoise, remoulade 10 Bordelaise, mayonnaise 11 Hollandaise, vinaigrette

saucy: 4 bold, coxy, pert, rude 5 brash, fresh 6 bantam, cocket 7 defiant, forward 8 impudent, malapert 9 audacious, sprightly 11 impertinent

Saudi Arabia: *capital:* 6 Riyadh 7 Ar Riyad
city: 5 Mecca 6 Makkah, Medina 7 Dhahran
currency: 5 qursh, riyal 6 halala
gulf: 5 Aqaba 7 Arabian, Persian
religious center: 5 Mecca 6 Medina

sauger: 4 fish 5 perch

Saul: *concubine:* 6 Rizpah
daughter: 6 Michal
father: 4 Kish
son: 8 Jonathan
successor: 5 David
wife: 7 Ahinoam

Saul of Tarsus: 9 Saint Paul

Sault Sainte Marie: Soo

saumont: 6 salmon

sauna: 4 bath 9 bathhouse, steam room

saunter: lag 4 idle, roam, rove, walk 5 amble, mosey, range, shool, stray 6 dander, dawdle, go slow, loiter, lounge, potter, ramble, stroll, wander 8 ruminate

saurel: 4 fish, scad 5 xurel

saurian: 6 lizard 8 dinosaur

saury: 4 fish

sausage: 5 gigot, wurst 6 salami, wiener 7 balloon, baloney, bologna, saveloy 8 drisheen, rollejee, rolliche 9 andouille, bratwurst, cervelate, pepperoni, rollichie 11 frankfurter 12 andouillette
casing: 4 bung
poisoning: 11 allantiasis

sausage-shaped: 9 allantoid 10 botuliform

savage: 4 fell, grim, rude, wild 5 brute, crude, cruel, feral, rabid, rough 6 bloody, brutal, ferine, fierce 7 brutish, furious, howling, inhuman, untamed, vicious 8 barbaric, pitiless, ruthless, work evil 9 aborigine, atrocious, barbarian, barbarous, ferocious, merciless, murderous, primitive, truculent

Savage Island people: 5 Niuan

savanna, savannah: 5 plain 9 grassland

savant: 4 sage 5 Solon 6 expert, pedant 7 scholar, wise man 9 scientist

savarin: 7 brioche 10 coffeecake

save: aid, bar, but 4 bank, hain, keep, only, stow 5 amass, catch, guard, hoard, salve, spare, store 6 defend, except, redeem, rescue, retain, scrimp, unless 7 deliver, deposit, husband, protect, reclaim, reserve, salvage 8 conserve, maintain, preserve 9 economize, excepting 10 accumulate

savin, savine: 7 juniper 9 evergreen

saving: 6 frugal, rescue, thrift 7 thrifty 9 frugality 10 economical

savings: 5 asset 7 account, addlins, nest egg 8 addlings

savoir faire: 4 tact 6 aplomb 7 know-how 8 elegance 10 adroitness 11 worldliness 14 sophistication

savor, savour: eat 4 odor, zest 5 sapor, scent, smack, smell, taste, tinge 6 degust, fervor, flavor, relish, season 9 degustate

savory: 5 gusty, salty, sapid, tasty 7 piquant 8 aromatic, delicacy, flavored, fragrant, pleasing 9 agreeable, palatable 10 appetizing, delightful

saw: cut, hew 4 talk, word 5 adage, axiom, maxim, motto, rumor, sever 6 cliche, saying 7 proverb 8 aphorism, apothegm 9 platitude 10 apophthegm
kind: bow, rip 4 back, band, hack 5 briar, chain, edger, saber, serra 6 coping, jigsaw, stadda, trapan, trepan 7 keyhole 8 circular, crosscut, trephine
part: 4 tine 5 redan, tooth

sawbelly: 7 alewife

sawbones: 7 surgeon

sawbuck: 7 ten spot 13 ten-dollar bill

sawder: 7 flatter

sawfish: ray

sawhorse: 4 buck 7 sawbuck

saw-like: 8 serrated

sawyer: 6 beetle, logman 9 lumberman 10 woodcutter

saxhorn: 4 alto, tuba
Saxon: 9 Sassenach
  chief: 5 Horsa
  city: Ave
  king: Ine 6 Harold
  lady: 6 Godiva, Rowena
  serf: 4 esne
  swineherd: 5 Gurth
  warrior: 5 Thane
say: 4 aver, call, deem, show, silk, talk, tell 5 put it, speak, state, utter, voice 6 advise, allege, answer, assert, bucket, direct, fabric, nearly, recite, relate, remark, repeat, report 7 comment, declare, deliver, dictate, express, iterate, testify 8 announce, indicate, proclaim 9 pronounce 10 asseverate
  again: 6 repeat 9 reiterate
saying: mot, saw 4 quip, word 5 adage, axiom, logia, maxim, motto 6 byword, phrase 7 epigram, proverb 8 aphorism, apothegm 9 statement 11 declaration
  apt: 6 bon mot
  collection: ana 9 gnomology
scab: 4 sore 5 crust, mange 6 eschar, ratter 7 blemish 8 blackleg 9 scoundrel 13 strikebreaker
scabbard: 4 case 6 sheath, tsubas 7 holster
  put in: 7 sheathe
  tip: 7 crampit
scabby: low 4 base, mean 5 flaky, mangy 6 scurvy, shabby, stingy 7 blotchy 9 blemished 12 contemptible
scabies: 4 itch 5 mange 11 skin disease
scads: 4 lots 5 loads 6 oodles
scaffold: 4 cage, dais, loft 5 easel, stage 6 gibbet 7 gallery, gallows, support 8 platform
scalar: 10 ladderlike
scalawag, scallawag: imp 4 pony, runt 5 scamp 6 rascal 10 scapegrace
scald: vex 4 burn 5 worry 6 blanch, excite, scorch 7 inflame, torment
scale: cup, hut 4 bowl, film, husk, peel, rate, rule, scut, shed, size, skin 5 climb, flake, gamut, palea, plate, scute, shive, weigh 6 ascend, degree, lamina, rament, series, spread, vessel, weight 7 balance, clamber, coating, compare, lamella, measure, scatter, vernier 8 covering, disperse, flake off, separate 9 gradation, steelyard 12 incrustation
  bony: 6 scutum
  earthquake: 7 Richter
  graduated: 7 Vernier
  having: 7 leprose, scutate 8 squamate, squamous 10 squamulose
  musical: 5 major, minor 8 diatonic 9 chromatic
  temperature: 6 Kelvin 7 Celsius 10 centigrade, Fahrenheit
scale-like: 6 scurfy 7 leprose

scallion: 4 leek 5 onion 7 shallot
scallop: 4 quin 5 crena, notch, twist 7 crenate, mollusk
scalp: rob 4 head, peel, skin 5 cheat, skull 6 defeat, denude, profit, resell, trophy 9 speculate
  disease: 5 favus, scurf 8 dandruff
scalpel: 5 blade, knife 6 lancet 8 bistoury
scalper: 6 punter, trader 10 speculator
scaly: low 4 mean 5 flaky 6 stingy 7 powdery 8 squamous 10 despicable
scam: con 7 swindle
scamble: 6 sprawl 7 collect, shamble, trample 8 scramble
scamp: imp 5 cheat, knave, rogue 6 rascal 8 scalawag, spalpeen, widdifow 9 scallawag, scoundrel 10 highwayman 11 rapscallion
scamper: run 4 race 5 speed 6 frolic, hasten, scurry 7 brattle, skitter 9 hurry away, skedaddle
scan: eye 5 study, watch 6 behold, browse, peruse, review, survey 7 examine, observe, poetize 8 skim over 10 scrutinize 11 contemplate
scandal: 5 eclat, odium, shame 6 gossip, malign 7 calumny, outrage, slander 8 disgrace, ignominy, iniquity 9 discredit 10 defamation, detraction, opprobrium
scandalize: 5 shock 6 malign, offend, vilify
scandalous: 6 unholy 8 libelous, shocking 9 offensive 10 flagitious, outrageous 11 furciferous
Scandinavian: 4 Dane, Lapp 5 Norse, Swede 7 Suigoth 8 Norseman 9 Icelandic, Norwegian
  alphabetical character: 4 rune
  bard: 5 scald 7 sagaman
  country: 6 Norway, Sweden 7 Denmark, Finland, Iceland
  division: amt
  drink: 4 glog 7 aquavit
  explorer: 4 Eric
  hero's place: 8 Valhalla
  king: 4 Atli
  land: 4 odal
  legend: 4 edda, saga
  legendary creature: nis 5 nisse, troll 6 Kraken
  measure: ass, lod, ort, vog 4 last, mark, pund, sten, untz 5 carat 6 nylast 7 centner, lispund 8 lispound, skalpund, skeppund, skippund 9 shippound, skaalpund, skibslast 10 bismerpund
  money: 5 krone
  navigator: 4 Eric
  nobleman: 4 jarl
  plateau: 5 fjeld
  rulers: Ros 10 Varangians
  ship: 4 aesc

small bay: **5** fjord

trumpet: **4** lure

scant: few **4** lean, poor **5** chary, short, spare, stint **6** geason, meager, meagre, narrow, scarce, scrimp, slight, sparse **7** limited, sparing, wanting **9** not enough **12** parsimonious

scantling: **4** beam, size, stud **5** grade **6** timber **7** caliber **8** standard

scape: **4** slip, stem, view **5** fault, shaft **7** picture **8** escapade, peduncle

scapegoat: **4** dupe **5** patsy **6** target, victim **7** fall guy **9** sacrifice **10** substitute **11** whipping boy

scapegrace: **5** rogue, scamp **6** madcap, rascal **7** wastrel **8** scalawag **9** reprobate, scallawag **10** profligate

scar: arr, cut, mar, shy **4** flaw, mark, rock, seam, slit, wild **5** chink, cliff, crack, score, wound **6** cinder, damage, deface, scared **7** blemish, catface, clinker **8** cicatrix, mountain, pockmark **9** disfigure, precipice **13** disfigurement

pert. to: **5** uloid

tissue: **6** keloid

scarab: **5** charm **6** beetle **7** June bug

scaramouch: **4** fool **5** scamp **6** rascal **7** buffoon **8** braggart, poltroon

scarce: few, shy **4** dear, just, rare **5** scant, short **6** geason, meager, meagre, scanty, sparse **8** uncommon **9** deficient **10** infrequent **12** insufficient

scarcely: **6** barely, hardly, merely

scarcity: **4** lack, need, want **6** dearth, famine, penury, rarity **7** failure, paucity, poverty **8** rareness, sparsity **9** parsimony **10** deficiency **11** infrequency, sparingness **13** insufficiency

scare: awe, shy **4** fear, fleg **5** alarm, dread, gliff, gloff, panic, spook **6** fright **7** scarify, startle, terrify **8** affright, frighten

scarecrow: **5** bogle **6** figure **9** jackstraw **10** frightener

scarf: boa, tie **4** gand, sash, wrap **5** adorn, ascot, barbe, cloud, cover, orale, shawl, stole, unite **6** cravat, groove, rebozo, runner, tapalo, tippet **7** dopatta (Ind.), foulard, muffler, necktie **8** liripipe, neckwear **9** comforter, cormorant **10** fascinator **11** comfortable, neckerchief

feathered: boa

head: **8** babushka, kerchief

scarfskin: **7** cuticle **9** epidermis

scarify: See **scare**

scarlet: red **4** lewd **5** bawdy **8** flagrant **10** prostitute

Scarlet Pimpernel author: **5** Orczy

Scarlett O'Hara: *beloved:* **6** Ashley

home: **4** Tara

husband: **5** Frank, Rhett **7** Charles

scarp: cut **5** cliff, slope **7** descent, incline **8** fragment **9** declivity, precipice

scary: **4** eery **5** eerie, timid, weird **6** spooky **7** fearful, ghostly, uncanny **8** alarming **11** frightening

scat: bop, tax **4** beat, riff, shoo **5** smash **6** begone, go away, rebuff, shower **7** getaway, scatter, tribute, vamoose **8** nonsense

scathe: **4** harm, hurt, sear **5** blast **6** assail, damage, injure, scorch, wither **8** denounce, lash into, work evil **9** castigate

scathing: **6** biting, severe **7** acerbic, caustic, cutting, mordant **8** blasting, incisive, injuring, wounding **9** scorching, truculent, withering **10** blistering

scatological: **5** fecal **7** obscene, raunchy

scatter: sow, ted **4** cast, deal, rout **5** fling, spray, strew, waste **6** dispel, shower, splash, spread **7** bestrew, confuse, diffuse, disband, fritter, radiate **8** dishevel, disperse, distract, separate, sprinkle, squander **9** bespatter, circulate, discomfit, dissipate **10** disconnect, distribute **11** disseminate

scatterbrained: **5** giddy **7** flighty **9** frivolous

scattered: **6** sparse **7** diffuse, divided, erratic, strawed **8** rambling, sporadic **9** irregular **10** straggling

scatter-gun: **7** shotgun

scatula: **7** pill box

scaup: **4** duck **8** grayback **10** canvasback

scavage: tax **4** duty, toll

scavenger: rat **7** sweeper, vulture

scenario: **4** plot **6** script **7** outline **10** continuity, screenplay

scend: **4** lift **5** heave, pitch

scene: act **4** site, view **5** arena, place, sight, vista **6** blow-up, locale, milieu **7** diorama, display, episode, picture, quarrel, setting, tableau **8** backdrop, location, prospect **9** landscape, spectacle, way of life **10** background **11** environment

last: **6** finale

scenery: set **4** view **5** decor, props **8** stage set **9** landscape

sceneshifter: **4** grip **9** stagehand

scenic: **8** dramatic **9** panoramic **10** theatrical **11** picturesque

scent (see also **smell**): **4** clue, nose, odor **5** aroma, odour, savor, smell, sniff, spoor, track, whiff **6** breath, flavor **7** bouquet, essence, flavour, inkling, perfume **8** effluvia **9** emanation, fragrance

scented: **5** olent **8** perfumed

scepter, sceptre: rod **4** mace **5** baton, staff **6** emblem **7** trident **8** caduceus **9** authority **11** sovereignty

sceptic: See **skeptic**

schedule: **4** card, list, plan, time **5** slate, table **6** agenda, docket, tariff **7** catalog, program, routine, writing 8 calendar, document, register, tabulate 9 catalogue, inventory, timetable

schefferite: 8 pyroxene

schelm: 5 rogue 6 rascal

schema: 4 plan 6 figure 7 diagram, outline

scheme: aim, gin, web 4 dart, list, plan, plot 5 angle, cabal, draft, drift, table, trick 6 design, device, devise, figure 7 concoct, diagram, epitome, outline, program, project, purpose 8 conspire, contrive, gimcrack, intrigue, maneuver 9 stratagem 10 conspiracy 11 contrivance, machination

schemer: 7 plotter, traitor 9 con artist

scheming: 6 artful, crafty, tricky 8 fetching 9 designing 10 intriguing

schism: 4 rent, rift 5 break, chasm, cleft, split 6 breach, heresy 7 dissent, rupture 8 division 10 separation

schist: 5 slate

schizocarp: 5 fruit, regma

schizophrenia: 8 catatony, insanity 9 psychosis

schlemiel: dub, oaf 4 clod, goof 5 chump 7 saphead

schlepp: lug 4 drag, jerk, pull, tote 5 carry

schmaltz: 4 corn, lard 14 sentimentality

scholar: 4 sage 5 clerk, pupil 6 master, pedant, savant 7 bookman, learner, student 8 disciple 11 academician, philologist
day: 6 extern
servant: 7 famulus, femulus

scholarly: 7 erudite, learned 8 studious 10 scholastic

scholarship: aid 5 award, grant 7 bursary, stipend 8 learning 9 allowance, education, erudition, knowledge 10 fellowship 11 instruction

scholiast: 6 critic 9 annotator 10 glossarist 11 commentator 13 glossographer

school: gam, pod 4 cult, sect 5 drill, ecole (F.), flock, group, lycee (F.), shoal, teach, train, tutor 6 lyceum, manege 7 academy, advance, college, company, convent, educate, seminar 8 atheneum, document, exercise, instruct, seminary 9 cultivate 10 university
grounds: 6 campus
group: PTA, PTO
kind: 4 high, prep 5 grade 7 primary 8 business, graduate, military 9 finishing, secondary 10 elementary, vocational 11 preparatory
official: 9 principal, scholarch 10 headmaster 14 superintendent
of fish: 5 shoal
of whales: gam
pert. to: 8 academic
religious: 7 yeshiva 8 seminary

riding: 6 manege
task: 6 lesson 7 problem 10 assignment 11 composition 12 dissertation
term: 7 quarter 8 semester 9 trimester

schoolbook: 4 text 5 atlas 6 primer, reader 7 speller 9 geography

schoolmaster: 4 caji, head 7 dominie, manager, pedagog, teacher 9 pedagogue

schooner: 4 boat, brig, tern 5 glass 6 vessel 7 measure
prairie: 12 covered wagon

schottische: 5 dance, polka

schout: 7 bailiff, sheriff

schrik: 5 panic 6 fright

science: art, sci 5 ology 9 education, knowledge 10 technology
of agriculture: 8 agronomy
of animals: 7 zoology
of crop production: 8 agronomy
of environment: 7 ecology
of healing: 9 iatrology
of heredity: 8 genetics
of human behavior: 6 ethics 10 psychology
of motion: 8 kinetics
of mountains: 7 orology
of plants: 6 botany
of projectiles: 10 ballistics
of robotics: 11 cybernetics
of words: 9 semantics 11 linguistics

sciential: 4 able 7 capable 9 competent

scientific: 5 exact 8 skillful 9 objective, practical, technical

scilicet: 5 to wit 6 namely 9 videlicet

scimitar, scimiter: 4 snee 5 saber, sword 8 billhook

scintilla: 4 atom, iota 5 spark, trace 8 particle 10 least trace

scintillate: 5 flash, gleam, spark 7 glitter, sparkle, twinkle 9 coruscate

scion: bud, son 4 heir, twig 5 shoot, sprig 6 sprout 8 offshoot 9 offspring 10 descendant

scissor: cut 4 clip, trim 5 shear

scleroid: 4 hard 8 hardened 9 indurated

scoff: 4 food, gibe, gird, jeer, leer, meal, mock, rail 5 fleer, flout, gleek, scorn, scout, sneer, steal, taunt 6 deride 7 disdain, mockery, plunder 8 ridicule 9 indignity

scoffer: 5 clown, cynic 6 jester, mocker 10 unbeliever

scold: nag, yap 4 haze, jump, rail, rant, rate 5 abuse, barge, blame, boast, brawl, chide, harpy, hound, score, shrew, slate 6 berate, bounce, rebuff, rebuke, revile, virago 7 bawl out, censure, chew out, reprove, upbraid 8 admonish, chastise, fishwife, lambaste, reproach 9 criticize, objurgate 10 vituperate

scolding: 6 dirdum, rating, rebuke 7 combing,

hearing, reproof **8** dressing **9** complaint

scombroid fish: **4** tuna **6** bonito **8** mackerel

sconce: **4** fine, fort, head **5** cover, skull **7** bracket, bulwark, lantern, penalty, protect, shelter **10** protection **11** candlestick

scone: **4** farl **7** biscuit **10** quickbread

scoop: dig **4** bail, beat, lade, news **5** didle, empty, gouge, ladle, skeet, spoon **6** bucket, chisel, dipper, dredge, gather, hollow, shovel, vessel **7** curette **8** excavate **9** exclusive

scoot: run **4** bolt, dart, dray, scud **5** hurry, scram, shoot, slide **6** begone, decamp, scurry **9** skedaddle

scooter: toy **4** boat, plow **6** glider

scop: **4** bard, poet **5** scald **10** troubadour

scope: **4** area, goal, room **5** field, range, reach, theme, tract **6** domain, extent, import, intent, length, object, sphere, target **7** breadth, liberty **8** distance, latitude **9** dimension, extension, intention **13** comprehensive
large: **7** general

scopic: **6** visual **9** extensive

scorch: cut, dry **4** bake, burn, char, cook, flay, sear, skin **5** adust, be hot, broil, parch, roast, score, singe, slash, speed, sting, toast **6** birsle, scathe, wither **7** blister, scratch, shrivel **8** lambaste

score: cut, run, tab, taw, win **4** goal, line, mark, rate **5** chalk, chase, corge, count, judge, notch, scold, slash, tally, total **6** abrade, barter, berate, furrow, grudge, number, reason, record, scotch, twenty, weight **7** account, achieve, arrange, scratch, upbraid **8** incision **9** criticize, grievance, reckoning **10** obligation **11** enumeration, orchestrate **12** indebtedness

scoria: **4** lava, rock, slag **5** ashes, dross **6** cinder, refuse **7** residue

scoring point: ace, hit, run **4** down, goal **5** tally **6** basket **7** home run **9** touchdown

scorn: **4** geck, jeer, mock **5** flout, scoff **6** deride, reject, slight **7** condemn, despise, despite, disdain **8** contempt, derision **9** contumely

scornful: **5** aloof **7** haughty, stuckup **8** arrogant, insolent **9** rejecting **10** disdainful, fastidious

Scorpio: **6** zodiac **8** scorpion **13** constellation

scorpion: **4** nepa **6** onager, weapon **7** scourge, stinger **8** arachnid, catapult **10** vinegaroon
stinger: **6** telson

Scorpion's Heart: **7** Antares

scot: tax **4** levy **6** assess **7** payment **9** reckoning **10** assessment **12** contribution

Scot: **4** Gael, Pict **10** Caledonian, Highlander

scotch (see also **Scotland**): cut **4** foil, stop **5** check, chock, crush, notch, score, wedge **6** hinder, stingy, whisky **7** scratch, scruple, sparing **8** hesitate, stamp out **9** frustrate

scoter: **4** coot, duck, fowl
genus: **7** oidemia **9** melanitta

scot-free: **4** safe **5** clear **6** unhurt **7** untaxed

Scotland: (see box)

Scotsman: Mac **4** Gael, Scot **7** bluecap, Scottie **10** Highlander

Scott: *character:* **5** Norma **7** Ivanhoe **9** Lochinvar
novel: **6** Rob Roy **7** Ivanhoe **8** Talisman **10** Kenilworth
poem: **7** Marmion

Scottish: See **Scotland**

scoundrel: cad **4** scab **5** cheat, filth, knave, rogue, scamp **6** rascal, rotter, varlet **7** glutton, villain, warlock **8** bezonian **9** miscreant, reprobate **10** blackguard

scour: eat, rub, run **4** beat, rake, rush, wash **5** clean, hurry, purge, scrub, sweep **6** decamp, polish, punish, remove **7** cleanse, roister **8** brighten, traverse

scourge: **4** bane, flay, flog, lash, whip **5** harry, shoot, slash **6** plague, punish, ravage, swinge, switch **7** afflict, torment **8** chastise, epidemic, lambaste **9** devastate **10** affliction, discipline, flagellate, infliction, punishment

Scourge of God: **6** Attila

scout: guy, spy **4** chap, jeer, look, seek **5** agent, guide, scoff, spurn, watch **6** fellow, ferret, patrol, search **7** explore, lookout, observe **8** emissary, informer, ridicule, watchman **9** search out **11** reconnoiter
unit: den **4** pack **5** troop

scouth: **4** room **5** range, scope **6** plenty

scow: tub **4** acon (F.), boat, hulk, punt **5** barge, float **6** garvey **7** lighter

scowl: **5** frown, glare, glout, lower **6** glower

scraggly: **6** jagged, ragged **7** unkempt **9** irregular **10** splintered

scraggy: **4** bony, lean, thin **5** rough, weedy **6** meager, rugged, skinny **7** knotted, scrawny **8** slovenly

scram: **4** flee, raus (G.), scat, shoo **5** leave, scoot **6** beat it, benumb, depart, go away **7** vamoose **8** paralyze, withdraw, withered

scramble: mix **4** push, rush **5** climb, crowd, crush, fight, haste **6** hustle, jostle, sprawl, spread, strive **7** clamber, pushing, scatter **8** struggle

scrambled: **4** pied **5** mixed **7** jumbled **11** meaningless

scrap: bit, end, jag, jot, ort, rag **4** chip, item, junk **5** brawl, fight, grain, piece, shred, waste **6** cullet, morsel, refuse **7** cutting, discard, extract, oddment, quarrel, remnant **8** fraction, fragment **11** small amount

Scotland: *accent:* **4** birr, burr
askew or awry: **4** agee **5** agley
at all: ava
beg: **4** sorn
bird: gae **4** hern **6** grouse, snabby **7** snabbie **8** throstle **9** swinepipe
blessing: **6** rebuke **8** scolding
blood money: cro
boat: **4** zulu **6** scaffy, sexern **7** coracle, skaffie
bonfire: **6** tandle
brain: **4** harn
bread: **5** briar **6** tammie **7** bannock
bread dish: **4** saps
brook: **4** sike
bucket: **5** stoop, stoup
bull: **4** stot
bushel: fou
buxom: **6** sonsie
cake: **5** scone
camp follower: **6** gudget
cap: tam **6** bonnet, tassel, toorie **8** Balmoral **9** Glengarry **11** tam o' shanter
capital: **9** Edinburgh
cap tassel: **6** toorie
cascade: lin **4** linn **5** force
cat: **6** malkin
cattle: **8** Ayrshire
celebration: **4** kirn
chafing dish: **7** choffer
chief: **5** thegn
child: **4** dalt **5** bairn **6** scuddy **8** smatchet
church: **4** kirk
city: Ayr **5** Alloa, Leith, Perth, Troon **6** Dundee **7** Glasgow, Grunock, Paisley **8** Aberdeen, Stirling **9** Edinburgh, Inverness, St. Andrews **10** Kilmarnock
cloth: **4** kelt **6** tartan
colt: **4** stag
congress: Mod
corner: **4** neuk
court officer: **5** macer
cross: **8** crantara **9** crostarie
cuddy: **6** draper **7** peddler
cup: **4** tass
curlies: **4** kale
currency: **4** demy **5** bodle, groat, pence, pound **6** baubee, bawbee, siller
dagger: **5** skean
dance: bob **4** reel **7** walloch **9** ecossaise **10** strathspey, sword dance **13** Highland-fling
destiny: **5** weird
devil: **4** deil
donkey: **5** cuddy
drapery: **4** pand

drinking bout: **6** screed
drinking vessel: **4** tass **6** quaich, quaigh
duck: **10** bufflehead
elm: **4** wych
ember: **5** aizle
endure: **4** dree
excuse: **6** sunyie
explorer: Rae
eye: ee
fairy: **4** fane
family group: **4** clan
farmer: **6** cottar, cotter **7** crofter
fashion: **7** Scotice
festival: Mod **7** Uphelya
fiddle: **4** itch
fingering: **4** wool, yarn
fireplace: **5** ingle
firth: Tay **4** Loch, Lorn **5** Clyde, Forth, Moray **6** Linnhe **8** Cromarty
fish: **4** sile **7** sillock **8** spalding
fishing expedition: **5** drave
fish trap: **4** yare **5** yaire
fog: **4** haar
fool: **4** gype
fort: **4** dune **10** roundabout
game: **6** shinty
garment: tam **4** kilt, maud **5** toosh **6** fecket, tartan **7** arisard **8** Balmoral **11** tam o'shanter
garter: **8** wooer-bab
ghost: **6** taisch
girl: **4** jill, lass **5** quean **6** lassie, towdie **7** winklot
give: gie
grandchild: oe, oy, oye
grandfather: **8** gudesire
grandmother: **6** gudame
granite: **5** gowan
guess: **4** rede
gutter: **5** siver
hands: **8** paddling
have: hae
hazelnut: nit
heater: **7** choffer
heavy: **5** tharf
hero: **11** Robert Bruce
hill: **4** brae **6** strone
historian: **4** Hume **5** Skene
hoppers: **9** hopscotch
icicle: **7** shoggle
inlet: gio
island: **4** Iona **5** Arran **6** Orkney **8** Hebrides, Shetland
kale: **8** borecole
kelp: **8** bellware
king: **6** Robert *(cont.)*

Scotland *(cont.)*
- *kiss:* **8** smoorich
- *lake:* dee **4** loch, Ness **6** Lomond
- *lament:* **6** ochone
- *land:* **6** carses
- *landholder:* **5** laird, thane
- *land tax:* **4** cess
- *language:* **4** Erse **6** Gaelic, Lallan **7** Lalland
- *liquor:* **5** scour **6** athole **8** whittier **12** Scotch whisky
- *lord:* **5** laird
- *loyal:* **4** leal
- *marauder:* **7** cateran
- *measure:* cop **4** cran, fall, mile, peck, pint, rood, rope **5** crane, crans, lippy **6** firlot, lippie **7** auchlet, chalder, choppin **8** mutchkin, stimpart, stimpert **9** particate, shaftment, shaftmont
- *mist:* ure
- *monk:* **6** culdee
- *mountain:* **8** Ben Nevis **9** Grampians
- *muddled:* ree
- *musical instrument:* **5** pipes **7** bagpipe
- *music festival:* Mod
- *musician:* **5** piper
- *must:* **4** maun
- *native:* **4** Gael, Pict, Scot
- *naval base:* **9** Scapa Flow
- *negative:* nae
- *oath:* **4** aith
- *odd:* **4** orra
- *pastry:* **5** scone **7** carcake
- *patron saint:* **6** Andrew
- *peasant:* **6** cottar, cotter
- *peninsula:* **5** Rinns
- *people:* **8** Dammonii **9** Dammonian
- *physicist:* **4** Watt
- *plaid:* **4** maud **6** tartan
- *playwright:* **5** Scott **6** Barrie **7** Boswell, Carlyle **8** Lockhart **9** Stevenson
- *poet:* **4** Hogg, Moir **5** Burns
- *pole:* **5** caber
- *pool:* lin **4** linn
- *porridge:* **5** brose
- *pouch:* **6** sporan **7** sporran
- *proprietor:* **5** laird
- *pudding:* **6** haggis
- *refuge:* **6** bilbie
- *ridge:* run
- *river:* Ayr, Dee, Don, Esk, Tay **4** Doon, Find, Nith, Norn, Spey **5** Afton, Annan, Clyde, North, Tweed **6** Teviot **7** Deveron
- *sausage:* **9** whitehass **10** whitehawse
- *schoolmaster:* dux
- *scurvy grass:* **8** seabells
- *sect:* **9** Buchanite
- *self:* sel
- *servant:* **5** gilly **6** gillie
- *sheepfold:* ree
- *small:* sma
- *snow:* sna **4** snaw
- *soldier:* **7** cateran
- *song:* **6** strowd **7** pibroch
- *student:* **5** bejan **6** nejant
- *sweetheart:* **4** jill
- *tenure:* **6** sorren **7** sorehon
- *tinker:* **5** caird
- *tithe:* **5** teind
- *title:* **5** laird
- *to:* tae
- *toad:* ted **4** taed
- *tobacco:* **5** elder
- *toe:* tae
- *toil:* **4** darg
- *topaz:* **6** tassel **9** cairngorm
- *tourist resort:* **4** Oban
- *tower:* **7** toorock
- *town hall:* **8** tolbooth **9** tollbooth
- *tree:* arm
- *treeless area:* **4** moor **5** heath
- *trousers:* **5** trews
- *uncle:* eme
- *unit:* ane
- *valley:* **4** glen **6** strath
- *vigor:* vir
- *warrior:* **4** kemp
- *waterfall:* lin **4** linn **5** force
- *water spirit:* **5** kelpy **6** kelpie
- *weakling:* **4** ribe **5** shilp **7** shilpit
- *weapon:* **5** skean **8** claymore, skeandhu
- *weight:* **4** boll, drop **5** trone **6** bushel
- *whine:* **4** yirn
- *whirlpool:* **7** swilkie **8** swelchie
- *whisky:* **6** athole **9** Glenlivet **10** Usquebaugh
- *whitefish:* **7** vendace
- *window:* **7** winnock
- *woman:* **4** burd
- *woodcock:* **4** eggs
- *world:* **4** warl
- *yell:* **4** gowl
- *youth:* **5** chiel **7** callant

scrape: bow, hoe, row, rub, saw **4** claw, grit, harl, rake, rasp, scud, trap **5** claut, erase, grate, graze, gride, hoard, order, shave **6** abrade, dredge, fiddle, gather, harass, refine, remove, sclaff **7** collect, corrode, scratch **9** situation **10** difficulty **11** predicament **12** touch lightly

scraper: **4** tool **6** barber, rasper, xyster **7** fiddler, strigil **8** grattoir

scraping: 6 rasion, rasure

scrapper: 5 boxer 7 fighter 8 pugilist 9 combatant

scratch: dig, mar, rat, rit, rub, wig 4 claw, draw, feed, heap, line, mark, race, rake, rist, tear 5 break, claut, clawk, erase, expel, fluke, frush, money, score, wound 6 cancel, furrow, gather, injury, rasure, scotch, scrape, scrawl 7 expunge, roughen, scarify 8 abrasion, incision, scribble, scrobble, withdraw

scratchy: 6 uneven 10 irritating

scrawl: 4 teem 5 crawl 7 scratch, writing 8 scribble

scrawny: 4 bony, lank, lean, poor, thin 5 gaunt, lanky, spare 6 meager, skinny 7 scraggy, scranny, scrubby 8 rawboned

screak: 4 rasp 5 creak, grate

scream: cry 4 howl, roar, wail, yarm, yaup, yawl, yell, yowt 5 shout 6 bellow, shriek, squall, yammer 7 screech

screamer: 5 chaja, error 7 caption

scree: 5 stone, talus 6 pebble 7 deposit

screech: cry 4 yell 5 quawk 6 outcry, scream, shriek 7 ululate

screed: say 4 land, rend, rent, tear 5 board, shred, strip 6 scrape, smooth, tirade 7 leveler 8 diatribe, fragment, harangue 9 discourse

screen: 4 cage, hide, mask, mesh, reja, sept, sift, veil 5 arras, blind, chick (Ind.), cloak, cover, grill, guard, purda, scarf, shade, sieve, speer, spier 6 defend, filter, grille, purdah, settle, shield 7 conceal, curtain, protect, reredos, shelter, shut out 8 block out, covering, separate 9 breakwind, partition
architectural: 5 spier
chancel: 4 jube 7 reredos
chimney: 6 bonnet
Japanese: 5 shoji
mesh: 4 laun 5 sieve
wind: 8 paravent

screw: key, pay 4 turn, wind, worm 5 cheat, guard, horse, miser, twist 6 extort, gimlet, keeper, salary, scrimp, spiral 7 contort, crumple, distort, panhead, robbery, squeeze, tighten, turnkey 8 flathead 9 bargainer, propeller, skinflint 10 contortion, crustacean, instructor

screwball: nut, sap 5 crank, crazy, dippy, goose 6 galoot 7 fanatic, saphead 8 crackpot, dumbbell 9 blockhead, eccentric 10 crackbrain, muttonhead

screwed: 5 drunk 11 intoxicated

screw pine: 5 vacoa 6 vacona, vacoua 8 pandanus

screw-pine family: 11 pandanaceae

screw up: 5 spoil 6 fasten, mess up, tangle 7 blunder

screwy: 5 crazy, kooky, wacky 6 absurd, insane, whacky 7 winding 8 freakish, peculiar 9 eccentric, fantastic 10 irrational, misleading, unbalanced

scribble: 5 write 6 doodle, scrawl 7 jot down, scratch 8 scrabble

scribe: 5 clerk, write 6 author, copier, doctor, notary, penman, writer 7 copyist, graffer, teacher 9 scrivener, secretary 10 amanuensis, journalist 11 transcriber

scriggle: 5 twist 6 squirm, wiggle 7 wriggle 8 curlicue

scrimmage: 4 play 5 fight 6 battle, splore, tussle 8 football, practice, skirmish 10 free-for-all

scrimp: 4 save 5 stint 6 meager, save up, scanty 9 economize 12 pinch pennies

scrimping: 7 miserly, sparing 9 niggardly

scrip: 4 list 5 token 7 writing 8 currency, schedule 10 paper money 11 certificate

script: 4 text 5 ronde 8 dialogue, libretto, scenario 10 penmanship, screenplay 11 chirography, handwriting
Arabic: 5 neski
round: 5 ronde
Syriac: 5 serta

scriptural: 8 Biblical

scrivello: 4 tusk

scrivener: 6 notary, scribe, writer 7 copyist 8 recorder 9 secretary 10 amanuensis

scrofula: 4 evil 6 struma 9 king's evil 12 tuberculosis

scrofulous: 7 corrupt 10 degenerate 12 contaminated

scroll: 4 curl, list, roll 5 draft, Torah 6 amulet, legend, record, scrawl, spiral, volute 7 outline, papyrus, writing 8 document, enscribe, inscribe, schedule, streamer
Hebrew: 5 Torah 6 mezuza 7 mezuzah
writing: 8 makimono

scrouge: 5 crowd, press 7 squeeze

scrounge: beg 5 cadge, steal 6 pilfer, search, sponge

scrub: mop, rub 4 mean, poor, runt, stop, wash 5 clean, dwarf, scour, small 6 drudge, paltry, shabby 7 call off, cleanse 8 inferior 9 brushwood, shrubbery

scrubby: 5 runty, small 6 shabby 7 stunted 8 inferior

scrub turkey: 6 leipoa 8 megapode

scruff: 4 film, nape, scum 5 crust, dross 6 refuse 7 coating 8 covering, dandruff

scrumptious: 4 fine, nice 5 dandy, tasty 6 savory 7 capital, elegant 8 splendid 9 delicious, excellent

scrunch: 5 crush 6 crunch, huddle 7 squeeze

scruple: 4 balk, part 5 blink, demur, doubt, qualm 6 amount, boggle, weight 7 anxiety, portion 8 hesitate, question 9 disbelief, misgiving, principle **10** conscience, hesitation, uneasiness **11** compunction

scrupulous: **4** nice **5** chary, exact **6** honest, proper, strict **7** careful, correct, precise, upright **8** accurate, cautious **9** honorable **11** punctilious
to excess: **7** finicky, prudish **10** fastidious

scrutinize: eye, pry **4** scan, sift **5** probe, study **6** survey **7** examine, inspect, observe **8** look over

scrutiny: **4** gaze, look **8** overview

scryer: **4** seer

scuba diver: **4** SEAL **7** frogman **8** aquanaut

scud: ale, fly, run **4** beer, gust, mist, move, skim **5** cloud, hurry, spray **6** scrape, shower **7** missile **10** crustacean

scuff: **4** blow, cuff, drag, gust, toss, wipe **5** brush, evade, graze, rowdy, slare, touch, tread **6** buffet, rabble, scrape, scruff, shower, slight **7** scatter, shuffle, slipper **8** scramble **9** roughened, scratched

scuffle: row **4** cuff, fray **5** amble, fight, melee, set-to **6** affray, bustle, clinch, combat, sclaff, strive, tussle **7** contend, shamble, shuffle **8** struggle

scug: **5** shade **6** shadow **7** protect, shelter **8** pretense, squirrel **9** schoolboy

scull: oar, row **4** boat **6** basket, propel, wherry **7** rowboat **8** scullion

scullion: **6** menial **7** servant

sculptor: **6** artist, carver, graver, imager **8** chiseler
famous: Arp **4** Gabo **5** Moore, Rodin, Smith **6** Calder, Robbia, Zorach **7** Cellini, daVinci, Epstein, Maillol, Noguchi, Pevsner, Phidias, Picasso, Zadkine **8** Brancusi, Hepworth, Nevelson **9** Donatello, Lipschitz, Mestrovic **10** Giacometti, Praxiteles **11** Polycleitus **12** Michelangelo
tool: **6** chisel, graver, mallet

sculpture: **4** bust, form, head **5** carve, grave, torso **6** clusel, emboss, relief, statue **7** engrave, relievo
framework: **8** armature
pert. to: **7** glyphic, glyptic **9** glyptical
slab: **6** metope

scum: **4** brat, foam, scud, silt, skim **5** dregs, dross, froth, range, scour, slime, sperm, spume, sweep **6** rabble, refuse, scoria

scumfish: **5** choke **9** discomfit, overpower, suffocate

scup: **4** fish **5** bream, porgy

scuppernong: **4** wine **5** grape **9** muscadine

scurrilous: low **4** foul, vile **5** gross **6** coarse, ribald, vulgar **7** abusive, obscene **8** indecent **9** insulting, offensive **11** disparaging, foulmouthed, opprobrious

scurry: hie, run **4** race, rush **5** harry, hurry, scoot, scour, skirr, speed **6** flurry, hasten **7**

scamper, scuttle, skelter **9** skedaddle

scurvy: bad, low **4** base, mean **6** shabby, vulgar **7** disease **8** scorbute **12** contemptible
preventative: **6** citrus **13** antiscorbutic

scutage: fee, tax **4** fine, levy **6** impost **7** penalty

scuttle: hod, run **4** dish, ruin, rush, sink, veto **5** scoot **6** basket, bucket, scotch, scurry, shovel **7** octopus, platter **8** bankrupt, hatchway **10** cuttlefish

scuttlebutt: **5** rumor **6** gossip **7** hearsay

scutum: **5** plate, scute **6** shield

Scylla: **4** rock
father: **5** Nisus
lover: **5** Minos

scythe: cut, mow **6** sickle
handle: **5** snath, thole **6** snathe
sweep: **5** swath

sea: mar (Sp.), mer (F.), Red **4** Azov, blue, deep, Kara, main, mare (It.), meer (G.) **5** Black, briny, China, Coral, Irish, Japan, North, White **6** Baltic, Bering, Laptev, Tasman, Yellow **7** Andaman, Arabian, Barents, Chukchi **8** Beaufort, Bismarck **9** Caribbean, Laccadive, Norwegian **10** Philippine **13** Mediterranean
anemone: **5** polyp **7** actinia
approach: **7** seagate
arm: bay **4** gulf, loch **5** bayou, bight, firth, fjord, frith, inlet, lough **7** estuary
at: **4** asea
bottom: bed
current: **4** tide **8** undertow
delicacy: roe **4** nori
description: **11** haliography
god/goddess: Ler, Ran **4** Nina **5** Aegir, Doris **6** Nereus, Thetis, Triton **7** Neptune, Phorcus, Phorcyn, Phorcys, Phorkys, Proteus **8** Eurynome, Palaemon, Poseidon **9** Leucothea **10** Amphitrite
Homer's description: **8** wine-dark
king: Ler **5** chief **6** pirate, Viking
life of: **8** halibios
little: **6** sealet
open: **6** midsea
pert. to: **4** vast **5** naval **6** marine **7** oceanic, pelagic **8** maritime, nautical **9** aequoreal, thalassic
plant: **6** enalid **7** seaweed
roughness: **5** swell, waves **6** lipper
route: **4** lane
spray: **9** spindrift **10** spoondrift
swell: **4** surf

sea cow: **4** dugong, rytina, walrus **7** manatee **8** sirenian **12** hippopotamus

sea cucumber: **6** pedata **7** trepang **11** holothurian

sea dog: gob, tar **4** seal **6** pirate, sailor, seaman **7** breaker, dogfish **9** privateer

sea duck: **5** eider **6** scoter

sea eagle: ern **4** erne, tern **6** osprey

sea-ear: **7** abalone

seafarer: gob, tar **4** salt **6** sailor, seaman **7** mariner **9** navigator

sea-foam: **5** froth, spume **9** sepiolite **10** meerschaum

seagoing: **8** maritime, nautical **9** seafaring

sea hog: **8** porpoise

sea horse: **6** walrus **8** pipefish, whitecap **11** hippocampus

sea kale: **4** cole **7** potherb

seal: cap, fix, hem, set, wax **4** bind, bull, cere, lute, rope, shut, sign **5** bulla, chain, close, sigil, stamp, token, wafer **6** attest, cachet, clinch, fasten, pledge, ranger, ratify, scarab, secure, signet **7** closure, confine, confirm, leather, sticker **8** breloque, document, guaranty, imprison, sealskin, validate, wax wafer **9** assurance, carnivore, guarantee, sigillate **10** obligation **12** authenticate

  bearded: **5** ursuk **6** makluk

  decorated with: **9** sigillate

  eared: **5** otary

  eared genus: **8** zalophus

  female fur: cow **5** matka

  letter: **6** cachet

  limb: **7** flipper

  pert. to: **7** phocine

  place: **7** rookery

  polar: fur **5** otary, phoca, Ross's, ursal, ursuk **6** makluk **8** bedlamer, seecatch **9** sterrinck

  school: pod

  young: pup **4** calf **5** whelp **6** beater, hopper **7** quitter, saddler **11** flipperling, holluschick

sea lettuce: **5** algae, laver **7** seaweed

sealing wax: lac **5** resin

seam: sew **4** bond, fash, fold, line, load, mark, scar **5** cleft, joint, layer, raphe, ridge, strip, unite **6** groove, streak, suture **7** crevice, fissure, joining, stratum, wrinkle **8** cicatrix, coupling, junction, juncture **10** packsaddle

  pert. to: **7** sutural, suturic

seamark: **4** buoy **6** beacon, pharos **8** landmark **10** lighthouse

seamer: **5** sewer **8** stitcher **10** dressmaker

seamless: **5** whole **7** unsewed **12** araphorostic

seamy: **5** rough **6** sordid **8** degraded, wrinkled **12** disreputable

seance: **7** meeting, session, sitting

  holder: **6** medium **12** spiritualist

sea nettle: **6** medusa **9** jellyfish

sea nymph: **5** siren **6** Nereid, Ondine, Scylla, Undine **7** Calypso, Galatea, mermaid, Oceanid **10** Callirrhoe

seaport: **6** harbor

sear (see also **sere**): dry **4** burn, cook, mark,

scar **5** brand, brown, catch, parch, singe **6** braise, deaden, scorch, sizzle, wither **9** cauterize

sea raven: **7** sculpin **9** cormorant **10** squaretail

search: **4** comb, grub, hunt, look, nose, rout, seek **5** delve, frisk, probe, quest, scour **6** brevit, ferret, forage, pierce, sphere, survey **7** canvass, examine, explore, inquire, inquiry, inspect, ransack, rummage **8** research, scrounge, scrutiny **9** penetrate, shake down **10** scrutinize **11** exploration, investigate

searching: **4** hard, keen **5** acute, sharp **6** shrewd **7** groping **8** piercing **10** discerning

sea robber: **6** jaeger, pirate **7** corsair **9** buccaneer, privateer

sea rover: **6** pirate, viking **7** scummer

seashell: **4** clam **5** conch, snail **7** scallop

seashore: **4** sand **5** beach, coast, plage (F.), playa, shore **6** strand **7** seaside **8** seabeach, seacoast

  pert. to: **8** littoral

sea slug: **6** trepan **8** cucumber **10** nudibranch

sea soldier: **6** marine

season: age, dry, tid, ver **4** beek, fall, salt, sele, term, tide, time **5** devil, imbue, inure, ripen, savor, spice, taste, tinge, train **6** autumn, embalm, flavor, harden, mature, pepper, period, school, soften, spring, summer, temper, winter **7** condite, flavour, prepare, toughen, weather **8** accustom, marinate **9** habituate **10** impregnate **11** acclimatize, opportunity

seasonable: apt, pat **4** ripe **6** timely **7** apropos **8** suitable **9** opportune **11** appropriate

seasonal: **8** periodic

seasoned: **7** veteran **8** finished, flavored **11** experienced

seasoning: **4** herb, mace, sage, salt **5** cumin, onion, spice, thyme **6** celery, cloves, garlic, nutmeg, pepper, relish **7** caraway, mustard, oregano, paprika, vinegar **8** allspice, cardamom, marjoram, rosemary, turmeric **9** condiment, coriander **10** experience

sea squirt: **5** salpa **8** ascidian, tunicate

sea swallow: **4** tern **6** petrel

seat: fix, pew, put, see **4** apse, bank, base, form, hold, home, loge, rear, room, rump, site, sofa **5** asana, bench, chair, couch, divan, floor, house, perch, place, roost, sella (L.), siege, stool, usher **6** behind, bottom, center, exedra, grange, howdah, locate, rocker, saddle, sedile, settee, settle, throne **7** capital, install, ottoman, situate, station, taboret, tendoor, tendour **8** bleacher, buttocks, derriere, dwelling, locality, location, tabouret **9** banquette, establish, posterior, residence, situation **10** foundation

chancel: **6** sedile
of judgment: **8** tribunal
of justice: **4** banc
on elephant: **6** houdah, howdah
tier of: **6** gradin
seat bone: **7** ischium
seat worm: **7** pinworm
sea unicorn: **7** narwhal
sea urchin: **6** repkie **7** echinid, echinus **8** echinoid **10** echinoderm
sea wall: **7** bulwark **8** buttress **10** embankment
seaweed: ore **4** agar, alga, kelp, nori **5** algae, dulse, laver, varec, vraic, wrack **6** delisk, desmid, fucoid, varech **7** oreweek **8** agaragar, gulfweed, hempweed, sargasso **9** desmidian
edible: **4** limu, ulva **5** dulse
extract: **4** agar
genus of: **6** alaria
pert. to: **6** algous
purple: **4** nori **5** laver **9** carrageen, Irish moss
red: **5** dulse **6** delisk
study: **8** algology
sea wolf: **4** seal **6** pirate **9** privateer, submarine
sebaceous: **4** oily **5** fatty
sec: dry **8** not sweet
secant: **5** chord **7** cutting **12** intersecting
secede: **5** leave **6** desert **7** dissent **8** withdraw
secern: **11** distinguish **12** discriminate
seckel: **4** pear
seclude: bar **4** deny, hide **5** debar, expel **6** recess, remove, retire, screen **7** exclude, isolate, protect, retreat **8** cloister, prohibit, separate, withdraw **9** segregate, sequester **10** quarantine
secluded: **5** alone, aloof, apart **6** hidden, remote, secret **7** private, retired **8** excepted, isolated, solitary **9** quiescent
second: aid **4** abet, back, echo, time **5** loser, other, vouch **6** assist, attend, backer, handle, moment, repeat **7** another, confirm, endorse, forward, further, instant, succeed, support, sustain **8** inferior **9** assistant, duplicate, encourage, imperfect, reinforce, secondary, supporter **10** additional **11** corroborate, subordinate
secondary: bye **5** minor **6** deputy, lesser **8** delegate, inferior **9** accessory, auxiliary, satellite **10** accidental, incidental **11** subordinate, unessential
color: **5** green **6** orange, purple
proposition: **5** lemma
secondary school: **4** high, prep **5** lycee (F.) **7** academy **10** realschule (G.), vocational
second childhood: **6** dotage **8** senility
secondhand: old **4** used, worn **6** resold **7**

derived **8** borrowed **10** hand-me-down
dealer: **6** ragman **7** junkman
girl in song: **4** Rose
second-rate: **6** shabby, shoddy **8** inferior, mediocre
second sight: ESP **9** foresight, intuition **12** clairvoyance
second-story man: **5** thief **7** burglar **10** cat burglar
second team: **6** scrubs **8** reserves **9** yannigans **11** substitutes
secret: **4** dark, dern, hide, rune **5** blind, cabal, close, inner, privy **6** arcana, arcane, closet, covert, hidden, occult, remote, stolen **7** arcanum, cryptic, devious, furtive, mystery, obscure, privacy, private, privity, retired, sub-rosa, unknown **8** abstruse, discreet, esoteric, eyes-only, hush-hush, intimate, mystical, reticent, secluded, stealthy **9** clancular, concealed, intrinsic, recondite, seclusion, secretive, underhand **10** classified, confidence **11** clandestine, concealment **12** confidential, hugger-mugger
secret agent: spy **4** mole **8** emissary, saboteur **10** counterspy
secretaire: **4** desk **10** escritoire
secretary: **4** aide, desk **5** clerk **6** typist **8** recorder **9** assistant, confidant **10** amanuensis
secrete: **4** bury, hide, ooze, stow **5** exude **7** conceal, store up
secretion: gum, sap **4** bile, laap, lerp, milk **5** juice, latex, mucus, resin, sudor, sweat **6** saliva **9** exudation
secret place: **4** lair **6** adytum **7** retreat, sanctum
sect: **4** clan, cult **5** class, creed, faith, group, order, party **6** schism, school **7** faction **8** religion **9** following **10** persuasion, philosophy **12** denomination
sectarian: **7** bigoted, heretic **8** apostate **9** dissenter **12** narrow-minded **13** nonconformist **17** denominationalist
section: **4** area, pane, part, zone **5** field, piece, slice, tract **6** canton, divide, member, parcel, region, sector **7** portion, quarter, segment **8** division **9** signature, territory **11** subdivision
concluding: **8** epilogue
section hand: **6** worker **7** crewman, laborer **9** roughneck **10** roustabout
sector: **4** area, part **8** division **10** semicircle
secular: lay **4** laic **5** civil **6** carnal, laique (F.), vulgar **7** earthly, profane, worldly **8** temporal **9** temporary
secure: buy, fix, get, pot, tie **4** bail, bind, bolt, easy, fast, firm, gain, gird, lock, moor, nail, safe, sure, tape **5** chain, guard, siker, solid, sound, spike, tight, trice, truss **6** anchor,

assure, cement, clinch, defend, ensure, fasten, insure, obtain, pinion, sicker, stable, strong **7** acquire, assured, certain, procure, protect, tie down **8** à couvert, conserve **9** confident, constrain, guarantee **10** batten down, dependable **11** trustworthy

security: 4 bail, bond, ease, gage **5** guard **6** pledge, safety, surety **7** defense, hostage, shelter **8** guaranty, warranty **9** assurance, certainty, guarantee, insurance, stability **10** confidence, protection

sedan: car **4** auto, limo **5** chair **6** litter **9** palanquin **10** automobile

sedate: 4 calm, cool, dope, drug **5** douce, grave, quiet, sober, staid **6** demure, proper, serene, solemn **7** earnest, serious, settled **8** composed, decorous **9** dignified, unruffled **10** put to sleep **12** tranquillize

sedative: 6 opiate, remedy, Valium **7** aconite, bromide, chloral, Demerol, nervine, Seconal **8** barbital, lenitive, Nembutal, pacifier **9** paregoric **10** anesthetic, palliative **11** barbiturate **12** sleeping pill

sedent: 6 seated **7** sitting
opposite: **9** analeptic

sedentary: 5 inert **7** settled, sitting **8** inactive, slothful, tranquil **10** deliberate, motionless, stationary

sederunt: 7 session, sitting **8** assembly

sedge: sag **5** brood, flock **7** bulrush, hassock
genus of: **5** carex **7** scirpus

sediment: lee **4** crap, lees, silt **5** dregs, magma, waste **6** bottom, refuse **7** deposit, grounds, residue **8** settling

sedition: 4 coup **6** revolt, strife, tumult, unrest **7** treason **9** coup d'etat, rebellion **10** dissension, dissention, turbulence **12** insurrection

seduce: 4 lure **5** charm, decoy, tempt **6** allure, betray, enamor, entice, ravish **7** beguile, corrupt, debauch, mislead **8** inveigle, persuade

seducer: 4 beau, rake, wolf **7** Don Juan **8** Casanova, Lothario **11** philanderer

sedulous: 4 busy **8** diligent, untiring **9** assiduous, laborious, unwearied **10** persistent **11** industrious, painstaking, persevering, unremitting

see: spy **4** date, espy, gaze, hear, ibid, look, mark, meet, note, peek, peer, rank, scry, seat, vide, view **5** chair, grasp, power, visit **6** accept, attend, behold, descry, detect, divine, escort, notice, office, throne **7** diocese, discern, examine, glimpse, inspect, observe, realize, undergo, witness **8** cathedra, consider, discover, envisage, perceive **9** accompany, apprehend, authority, bishopric, encounter, interview, visualize **10** anticipate, comprehend, experience, scrutinize, understand

seed: ben, bud, egg, pea, pip, pit, sow **4** core, germ, milt, tare **5** acorn, drupe, grain, ovule, plant, sperm, spore, stock **6** acinus, bubble, kernel, origin, samara, source **7** capsule, progeny, seedlet **8** ancestry **9** beginning, inoculate, offspring, posterity **10** descendant
cell: **4** cyst
coat: pod **4** aril, bran, burr **5** testa
container: bur, pod **6** carpel, legume, loment
immature: **5** ovule
organ: **6** pistil
part: pod **4** aril **5** testa **6** tegman, tunica **9** endosperm
poisonous: **7** calabar **9** jequirity **10** belladonna, castor bean
remove: gin, pit **5** picul
scar: **4** hila (pl.) **5** hilum

seed leaf: 9 cotyledon

seedless: 7 agamous

seedy: 4 worn **5** dingy, tacky **6** shabby **7** rundown, scruffy **8** slovenly **11** debilitated

seek: beg, sue, try, woo **4** busk, fand, hunt, look, sick **5** court, crave, essay, probe, quest, scout, trace **6** aspire, follow, fraist, pursue, search **7** attempt, beseech, entreat, examine, explore, inquire, request, solicit **8** endeavor **9** cast about, importune, search out **11** investigate

seeker: 6 hunter, prober, tracer **7** pursuer, zetetic **9** applicant **10** petitioner

seel: 5 blind **8** hoodwink

seem: 4 look **5** feign **6** appear **7** pretend **8** manifest

seeming: 5 false **8** apparent, illusory **10** ostensible

seemingly: 5 quasi **10** apparently, supposedly

seemly: fit **5** right **6** comely, decent, proper, rather, suited **7** fitting **8** decently, decorous, graceful, handsome, suitable, suitably **10** becomingly

seen: 7 visible

seep: run **4** leak, ooze **5** exude **7** trickle **8** transude **9** percolate **10** infiltrate

seer: 4 sage **5** augur, sybil **6** mystic, oracle, scryer **7** diviner, prophet **8** haruspex **9** predictor, spectator **10** forecaster, foreteller, soothsayer **11** clairvoyant, Nostradamus **14** prognosticator

seesaw: 6 teeter, tilter, totter **9** alternate, crossruff, vacillate **10** reciprocal

seethe: hum **4** boil, fume, soak, stew, teem **5** steep **6** bubble, buller, decoct **7** blubber **8** saturate

segment: arc **4** part **5** piece, tmema **6** cantle, divide, set off, somite **7** isomere, portion, section **8** division, fragment, metamere, separate
body: **8** somatome

of crustacean: **6** telson

segregate: **4** part **5** sever **6** divide, select **7** exclude, isolate, seclude **8** classify, separate **9** sequester **10** quarantine

seine: net **5** trawl

Seine tributary: **4** Aube, Eure, Oise **5** Marne, Yonne

seism: **10** earthquake

seity: **8** selfhood **13** individuality

seize: bag, cap, cly, cop, hap, nab, net **4** bind, bite, claw, fang, grab, grip, hent, hook, prey, take, trap **5** annex, catch, clink, grasp, ravin, reave, usurp, wrest **6** affect, arrest, attach, attack, betake, clinch, clutch, collar, fasten, kidnap, ravene, snatch, strike **7** afflict, capture, grabble, grapnel, possess, prehend **8** arrogate **9** apprehend, deprehend, lay hold of, raptorize **10** comprehend, confiscate, understand **11** appropriate
for debt: **6** attach **8** distrain **9** garnishee, repossess

seizure: fit **4** turn **5** spell **6** attack, stroke **10** androlepsy, convulsion **11** androlepsia, manucapture

Sekhet's husband: **4** Ptah

seladang: **4** gaur **6** animal **7** buffalo

seldom: **4** rare **6** rarely **10** infrequent **12** infrequently

select: opt **4** best, cull, draw, name, pick, rare, wale **5** allot, elect, elite **6** assign, choice, choose, chosen, exempt, picked, prefer **7** favored, the best **8** eximious **9** excellent, exclusive, segregate **10** fastidious, particular **11** outstanding

selection: **5** piece **7** analect, excerpt, passage **10** collection

selective: **5** fussy, picky **6** choosy **8** eclectic **9** demanding

Selene: **4** Luna, moon

selenium: *compound:* **7** selenid **8** selenide
soft acid: **8** selenate

self: ego, own, sel (Sc.), soi (F.) **4** same, very **5** being **6** myself **7** himself **9** identical **10** particular **11** personality
killing of: **7** suicide **8** felo-de-se

self-acting: **9** automatic

self-assertion: **6** egoism, vanity

self-centered: **4** vain **6** stable **7** selfish **9** egotistic **10** egocentric

self-confidence: **5** poise **6** aplomb **8** presence **9** composure, sang froid

self-contained: **4** calm, cool **8** composed, reserved **9** collected **11** independent **15** uncommunicative

self-control: **4** will **8** calmness **9** willpower **10** equanimity **11** forbearance, moderation

self-defense: **4** judo **6** aikido, boxing, karate, Kung fu **7** fencing, jujitsu **8** fighting

self-denial: **9** restraint, sacrifice **10** abstinence, asceticism, puritanism, temperance **11** forbearance

self-esteem: **5** pride **6** egoism, vanity **7** egotism **9** assurance

self-evident: **5** clear **7** certain, obvious **8** truistic **9** axiomatic

self-examination: **13** introspection

self-generated: **11** spontaneous

self-government: **8** autonomy **11** self-control **12** independence

self-important: **7** pompous **10** egocentric

selfish: **6** stingy **7** hoggish **9** dissocial, egotistic **10** egocentric **11** egomaniacal **12** self-centered

self-love: **6** vanity **7** conceit, egotism **10** narcissism

self-possessed: **4** calm, cool **6** cooler, poised **8** composed **11** undisturbed **12** strongwilled

self-reproach: rue **5** guilt **6** regret **7** remorse **9** penitence **10** contrition

self-respect: **5** pride **6** vanity

self-righteous: **11** pharisaical **12** hypocritical

selfsame: **9** identical

self-satisfied: **4** smug, vain **6** jaunty **10** complacent

self-subsistence: **12** independence

sell: **4** bilk, cant, deal, dump, dupe, give, gull, hand, hawk, hoax, vend **5** cheat, trade, trick, yield **6** barter, betray, impose, market, peddle, retail **7** auction, bargain, deceive, deliver, dispose **8** convince, persuade, transfer **9** negotiate, wholesale
out: **6** betray, desert **8** inform on
over official rate: **5** gouge, scalp

seller: **6** dealer, factor, seller, sutler, trader, vender, vendor **7** peddler **8** merchant, retailer, salesman **9** tradesman **10** auctioneer, saleswoman, saltcellar, wholesaler **11** salesperson

selvage: **4** edge, list **5** gouge **6** border, margin **8** sticking

semblance: air **4** copy, face, form, look, mask **5** guise, image **6** aspect, figure **7** pretext **8** likeness, pretense **10** apparition, appearance, conformity, likelihood, similarity, similitude, simulacrum **11** countenance, presumption, resemblance **14** representation

Semele: *brother:* **9** Polydorus
father: **6** Cadmus
sister: Ino **5** Agave
son: **7** Bacchus **8** Dionysos **9** Dionysius

semester: **4** half, term **6** course, period

semi: **4** half, part

semiape: **5** lemur

semidiameter: **6** radius

seminar: **6** course, school **7** meeting **8** workshop **10** conference, discussion

seminary: **6** school **7** academy, college **11** institution **14** divinity school

Seminole Indian chief: **7** Osceola

Semiramis: *husband:* **5** Ninus
kingdom: **7** Babylon

Semite: Jew **4** Arab **6** Hebrew **7** Eblaite, Moabite **8** Aramaean, Assyrian **9** Canaanite **10** Babylonian, Phoenician
god: **4** Baal **5** Anath, Hadad **6** Moloch **7** Shamash
language: **4** Geez **6** Arabic, Hebrew, Syrian **7** Hebraic, Maltese
people: **6** Shagia **7** Shaigia **9** Shaikiyeh

semolina: **4** meal, suji **5** flour, grain, sujee **6** groats

semper (L.): **6** always

semper fidelis: **14** always faithful

sempiternal: **4** ever **7** endless, eternal **11** everlasting

senate: **5** boule, divan **7** council **8** assembly **11** legislature

senator: **5** solon **8** lawmaker **10** legislator **11** congressman

send: **4** haul, mail, post, ship **5** drive, grant, impel, issue, relay, speed **6** bestow, commit, convey, depute, export, launch, ordain, propel, thrill **7** address, consign, delight, deliver, dismiss, forward, inflict, project **8** delegate, dispatch, transmit **9** broadcast, discharge, vouchsafe **10** commission
back: **5** remit **6** remand, return
down: **5** demit
for: **4** call **5** order **6** summon
forth: **4** emit **6** effuse **7** emanate
out: **4** beam, emit **5** depot, exile **6** export
packing: **7** dismiss **9** discharge
up: **4** jail **6** parody, satire **7** take-off **8** imprison

Senegal: *capital:* **5** Dakar
currency: **5** franc **7** centime
gazelle: **5** korin
people: **5** Serer, Wolof **6** Fulani

senescent: **5** aging

senile: old **4** aged, weak **5** aging **6** daffle, dotard, infirm **7** ancient, elderly, rickety **8** decrepit **9** doddering **12** feeble-minded **13** deteriorating

senility: **6** dotage **8** caducity **10** senescence

senior: **4** aine, dean **5** doyen, elder, older **7** ancient, student **8** alderman, superior

senior citizen: **8** Old Guard, old-timer **10** golden-ager

seniority: age **5** state **6** status **7** quality **8** priority **9** authority **10** precedence
by birth: **13** primogeniture

Sennacherib: *father:* **6** Sargon
son: **8** Sharezer **10** Esarhaddon

sensation: **5** sense **6** marvel, thrill **7** emotion, feeling **8** interest **10** appearance, experi-ence, impression, perception **11** sensibility
lacking: **4** numb **6** asleep

sensational: **5** lurid **6** superb, yellow **8** eloquent, exciting **9** emotional, startling, thrilling **12** melodramatic

sense: wit **4** feel, mind, pith **5** smell, think, touch **6** import, intuit, reason, sanity, wisdom **7** believe, feeling, meaning **8** judgment, perceive, prudence **9** apprehend, awareness, sensation, sentience, soundness, substance **10** appreciate, brainpower, cognizance, comprehend, perception **12** intelligence **13** consciousness, understanding

Sense and Sensibility author: **6** Austen

senseless: mad **4** cold, dumb, numb **5** blind, inane **6** asleep, simple, stupid, unwise **7** foolish, idiotic, unaware, witless **9** insensate, unfeeling **10** half-witted, insensible, irrational **11** meaningless, nonsensical, purposeless, unconscious **12** unreasonable

sense organ: ear, eye **4** nose, skin **5** nerve **6** finger, tongue **8** receptor

sensible: **4** wise **5** aware, privy, solid, sound **7** prudent **8** rational **10** reasonable, responsive **11** cognizant of

sensitive: raw **4** nice, sore **5** acute, alive **6** pliant, tender, touchy, tricky **8** delicate **9** emotional, receptive **10** compatible, responsive **11** susceptible **14** impressionable
plant: **6** mimosa

sensual: **4** lewd **5** alive, gross **6** carnal, coarse, earthy, fleshy, sexual **7** bestial, brutish, fleshly, lustful, worldly **9** seductive **10** lascivious, licentious, voluptuous

sentence: rap **4** doom **5** award, axiom, maxim, motto **6** decide, decree, saying **7** adjudge, condemn, opinion, passage, proverb **8** aphorism, decision, judgment **9** destinate, proscribe, statement **12** adjudication, pass judgment
consisting of one word: **7** monepic
construction: **6** syntax
describe: **5** parse
part: **6** clause, object, phrase **7** subject **9** predicate
type: **6** simple **7** complex **8** compound

sententious: **5** pithy, short, terse **7** compact, concise, laconic **10** meaningful, moralistic, proverbial

sentient: **5** alive, aware **6** living **7** feeling **8** sensible **9** conscious

sentiment: **4** idea, love **5** maxim, toast **6** lyrics, saying **7** emotion, feeling, leaning, meaning, opinion, schmalz **8** schmaltz **9** sensation, substance **10** perception **11** sensibility

sentimental: **5** gushy, mushy, sappy, sweet **6** jejune, loving, syrupy, tender **7** maudlin, mawkish **8** romantic **9** fantastic, schmaltzy

10 idealistic, lovey-dovey, moonstruck **11** susceptible, tear-jerking

sentinel: **5** guard, vedet (Sp.), videt (Sp.), watch **6** bantay (P.I.), sentry, warder **7** soldier **8** watchman **10** factionary

sepal: **4** leaf

separate: **4** bolt, cull, deal, free, know, lone, only, part, rend, rift, shed, sift, slay, sley, sole, sort **5** alone, aloof, apart, aside, break, halve, hedge, ravel, sever, space, split, strip **6** assort, breach, cleave, decide, deduct, depart, detach, divide, refine, remove, secede, single, sleave, sleeve, sunder, winnow **7** break up, disjoin, dispart, dissect, diverse, divorce, expanse, isolate, segment, split up, various **8** abstract, alienate, detached, discrete, disperse, dissolve, distinct, disunite, estrange, secluded, solitary, uncouple, withdraw **9** demarcate, different, discharge, disengage, dismember, disparate, eliminate, segregate, withdrawn **10** disconnect, dispossess, dissociate, distribute, individual, quarantine, sejunctive **11** disembodied, distinctive, distinguish, fractionate, independent, part company, precipitate, unconnected **12** disassociate

separation: **4** gulf **6** schism, tmesis **7** diacope, divorce **8** distance **9** apartheid, cessation, partition **12** estrangement

separatist: **8** apostate **9** dissenter

separatists: **8** Pilgrims, Puritans, Zoarites **9** Bimmelers

Sephardim: **4** Jews
country of origin: **5** Spain **8** Portugal
dialect: **6** Ladino

sepia: dun **5** brown, color **7** pigment **9** red-yellow **10** cuttlebone, cuttlefish

sepiment: **5** hedge **7** defense **9** enclosure

sepiolite: **10** meerschaum

sepoy: **7** soldier **9** policeman **11** infantryman

seps: **5** snake **6** lizard **7** serpent

sept: **4** clan, fine **5** seven, tribe **8** ancestry

septic: **6** putrid, rotten **8** diseased, infected

septum: **4** wall **9** partition

sepulcher: **4** bury, tomb **5** grave, inter, vault **6** coffin, entomb **8** monument **10** repository
subterranean vault: **8** catacomb

sepulchral: low, sad **4** deep **6** gloomy, hollow **7** charnel **8** funereal

sequacious: **6** pliant **7** ductile, servile **9** attendant, compliant, dependent, following, malleable

sequel: **4** next **5** issue **6** effect, result, upshot **7** outcome **8** follow up, follower, sequitur **9** aftermath, following, inference **10** conclusion **11** consequence, continuance **12** continuation

sequence: run, set **5** chain, gamut, order, suite, train **6** course, series, tenace **8** straight **10** succession **11** progression

sequential: **6** serial **9** following **10** continuous, processive, succeeding **11** consecutive

sequester: **5** seize **6** cut off, enisle **7** isolate, seclude **8** cloister, separate **9** segregate **10** confiscate **11** appropriate

sequestered: **5** alone **6** lonely, seized **7** private, recluse, removed, retired **8** confined, isolated, secluded, solitary, withdrew **9** concealed, renounced, separated, withdrawn **10** cloistered, disclaimed, segregated **11** confiscated **12** appropriated

sequin: **4** disk **7** spangle

sequoia: **7** conifer, redwood **9** evergreen

serac: **5** block **11** ice pinnacle

seraglio: oda **5** harem **6** serail, zenana **7** brothel **8** lodgings **9** enclosure, warehouse

serai: **8** lodgings, seraglio **9** rest house **11** caravansary **12** caravanserai

serape: **5** cloak, shawl **7** blanket

seraph: **5** angel **6** cherub

seraphic: **4** pure **5** pious **7** angelic, lovable, refined, sublime **8** beatific, cherubic **9** unworldly

Serb: **4** Slav

Serbia: *capital:* **7** Beograd **8** Belgrade
river: **6** Danube

sere, sear: dry, wax **4** worn **5** dried, talon **6** yellow **7** parched, several, various **8** scorched, separate, withered **10** desiccated, threadbare

serenade: woo **4** sing, song **5** court **6** aubade, ballad **8** nocturne, serenata
burlesque: **8** shivaree **9** charivari **10** callithump

serene: **4** calm, cool, damp **5** clear, light, quiet **6** bright, irenic, placid, sedate, serein, steady **7** pacific **8** composed, decorous, peaceful, tranquil **9** collected, impassive, unruffled **10** unobscured **11** undisturbed **13** dispassionate

serenity: **4** calm **5** peace, quiet **6** repose **7** balance **10** equanimity **11** tranquility

serf: **4** esne, peon **5** churl, helot, slave **6** servus, thrall, vassal **7** bondman, peasant, villein **8** bondsman, hireling
female: **5** neife **6** colona

serge: **7** worsted

sergeant: **4** rank **6** chiaus, noncom **7** officer, soldier, topkick **9** attendant

sergeant fish: **5** cobia **6** robalo

series: row, set **4** list **5** chain, gamut, suite, train **6** catena, course **8** beadroll, category, sequence, seriatim **9** gradation **10** continuity, succession
arranged in: **6** serial **7** seriate **11** installment

serious: **4** deep, grim, hard, keen **5** grave, heavy, sober, staid **6** demure, intent, sedate, severe, solemn, somber, steady **7** austere, capital, earnest, weighty **9** humorless, important, momentous, unamusing **10** no-nonsense, poker-faced, thoughtful **11** considerate

serment: **4** oath **9** sacrament

sermon: **4** talk **5** psalm, speak **6** homily **7** address, lecture **8** harangue **9** collation, discourse, preaching **10** admonition
study of: **10** homiletics
subject: **4** text **5** Bible **6** Gospel

sermonic: **5** grave **8** didactic

sermonize: **6** advise, preach **8** admonish, homilize, moralize **9** discourse

seroon: **4** bale **7** package

serotine: bat

serous: **4** thin **6** watery

serow: **5** goral, jagla **8** antelope

serpent: **5** devil, fiend **7** entwine, reptile
elapine: **4** naia, naja
mythological: Ahi **5** Apepi, Dahak, Hydra **6** dragon, ellops **8** basilisk **11** Amphisbaena
pert. to: **7** anguine
thousand-headed: **5** Sesha **6** Ananta
victim: **7** Laocoon
worship of: **6** ophism

serpentine: **4** file, wily, worm **5** snaky **7** devious, sinuous, turning, winding **8** fiendish, tempting **10** circuitous, convoluted, meandering

serpigo: **5** tinea **6** herpes, tetter **8** ringworm

serrated: **6** scored **7** notched, toothed **11** denticulate

serried: **5** dense **6** massed, packed **7** compact, concise, crowded **10** continuous

serum: **4** whey **5** fluid **9** antitoxin

servable: **6** usable **10** functional

serval: **7** wildcat

servant: **4** amah, bata, cook, dasi, esne, girl, help, hewe, hind, maid, maty, mozo, syce **5** alila, biddy, boots, chela, gilly, groom, hamal, nurse, scout, slave, usher, valet **6** batman, bearer, bildar, butler, chakar, ewerer, flunky, garcon, gillie, hamaul, hammal, harlot, helper, khamal, menial, tenant, varlet, vassal **7** bondman, famulus, flunkey, footman, hummaul **8** chasseur, domestic, retainer, scullion, sergeant, servitor **9** atriensis, attendant **11** chamberlain, subordinate
female: **4** amah, maid **5** wench **6** slavey
garment: **5** apron **6** livery **7** uniform
head: **6** butler
male: **5** valet **6** butler, lackey
of God: **4** monk, pope **5** friar, rabbi **6** bishop, priest **8** chaplain, minister, preacher **10** Holy Father, missionary
of nobleman: **7** equerry
pert. to: **8** famulary

serve: act, aid **4** abet, give, help, mess, pass, suit, tend, wait, work **5** avail, cater, frame, ladle, treat **6** answer, assist, attend, do good, succor, wait on **7** advance, be of use, benefit, bestead, deliver, forward, further **8** do a hitch, function, minister **9** officiate **10** distribute

server: urn **4** tray **6** salver, waiter **7** caterer **9** assistant, lazy-Susan

service: use **4** Mass, rite **5** favor, lauds, throw **6** employ, matins, repair, ritual, supply **7** chakari, liturgy, requiem, retinue, utility, vespers **8** ceremony, compline, kindness, ministry **11** maintenance
military: **4** duty **5** hitch **7** stretch **10** enlistment **12** conscription
public: **7** utility

serviceable: **4** kind **6** useful **7** durable, helpful, lasting **8** obliging **9** available, practical **10** beneficial, commodious

service charge: fee, tip **8** gratuity

serviette: **6** napkin

servile: **4** base, bond, mean **6** abject, menial, sordid **7** fawning, slavish **8** cringing, enslaved, obedient, obeisant **9** dependent, groveling, parasitic, truckling **10** obsequious, sequacious, submissive **11** subservient, sycophantic

Servite: **5** friar **9** mendicant

servitor: **6** beadle, menial, squire **7** servant, soldier **8** adherent, follower **9** assistant, attendant **10** apprentice **12** exhibitioner

servitude: **4** yoke **7** bondage, peonage, serfdom, service, slavery **8** sentence **9** captivity, vassalage **10** subjection

sesame: til **4** herb, teel **5** benne **7** passkey **8** ajonjoli, password
seed: **7** gingili, tilseed

session: **4** term **6** assize **7** meeting, sitting **8** assembly, sederunt **10** assemblage, conference

set: fix, gel, lay, put, sit **4** bent, clan, club, cock, crew, gang, jell, laid, park, port, pose, prim, ring, seat, stud, suit **5** align, aline, brood, elect, elite, embed, fixed, group, imbed, place, plant, posit, range, ready, rigid, scene, staid, stake, stand, suite **6** adjust, assign, cement, circle, clique, define, direct, formal, harden, impose, impost, ordain, series, settle **7** appoint, arrange, bearing, company, confirm, congeal, coterie, decline, deposit, dispose, instate, platoon, station, stiffen **8** attitude, decorate, exchange, immobile, moveless, regulate, solidify **9** coagulate, collocate, designate, determine, establish, immovable, obstinate, prescribe, stabilize **10** assortment, collection, constitute, stationary *afloat:* **6** launch

apart: **5** elect **6** exempt **7** isolate, reserve, seclude **8** allocate, dedicate, separate **9** segregate, sequester

aside: **4** keep, save, void **5** annul, store, table **6** except, reject **7** discard, dismiss, earmark, exclude, reserve **8** overrule, separate

at naught: **4** defy **7** despise **9** disregard

back: **4** loss **5** check, delay **6** defeat, hinder **7** relapse, reverse, setback

down: fix **4** alit, land, seat **5** abase, enter, place, write **6** alight, depose, encamp, ordain, reckon, record, regard, relate **7** appoint, descend, resolve, slacken **8** consider, estimate, register **9** attribute, determine, establish, humiliate

forth: **5** adorn, offer, state **6** expone, expose **7** arrange, commend, display, enounce, espouse, exhibit, explain, expound, present, promote, propone, propose, publish **8** announce, decorate, manifest **9** interpret, translate **10** promulgate

fresh: **5** relay

in motion: **5** begin, start **6** excite, launch **7** kick off **8** activate, initiate **9** originate **10** inaugurate

in order: **4** file, tidy **5** align, aline **6** adjust **7** arrange **8** organize

off: **5** start **8** mobilize **10** compensate

of rules: **4** code

on end: **5** upend **10** topsyturvy

on fire: **4** tind **5** light **6** ignite, kindle

out: **4** head, plan **5** adorn, allot, equip, extol, issue, leave, limit, start **6** design, embark, escort, outfit, recite **7** display, present, publish **8** describe, proclaim **9** embellish **10** promulgate

right: fix **4** file **5** align, aline, amend, order **6** adjust, repair, square **7** arrange, correct, redress, take off **11** systematize

to: **4** bout **5** fight **6** fracas **7** contest **8** skirmish, struggle

up: **4** plan, post **5** build, erect, exalt, found, hoist, raise, treat **7** appoint, arrange, elevate, install, prepare **8** organize **9** establish

Set: **5** deity **9** god of evil

brother: **6** Osiris

father: Geb

mother: Nut

victim: **6** Osiris

wife: **8** Nephthys

seta: **6** chaeta **7** bristle

setaceous: **7** bristly

seth: **6** banker **8** merchant

Seth: *brother:* **4** Abel, Cain

descendant: **4** Enos **7** Sethite

father: **4** Adam

son: **4** Enos

seton: **6** suture

setout: **4** fuss **5** get-up **6** outfit **7** costume, display, exhibit **9** beginning

settee: **4** seat, sofa **5** bench, couch, divan **6** settle

setter: dog **5** Irish **6** Gordon **7** English **10** compositor

setting: **4** eggs, pave, trap **5** decor, scena (It.), scene, snare **6** locale, milieu **7** scenery **8** backdrop, mounting **9** hardening **10** background, thickening **11** environment, mise-en-scene **12** surroundings

settle: fix, pay, sag, set **4** calm, firm, lend, nest, root, rule, seat, sink, toit **5** affix, agree, audit, bench, clear, couch, lodge, order, perch, plant, quiet, serve, solve **6** accord, adjust, alight, assign, clinch, decide, locate, purify, reduce, render, reside, secure, soothe, square, wind up **7** appoint, arrange, clarify, compone, compose, confirm, conform, deposit, depress, dispose, inhabit, provide, resolve, satisfy, silence, subside **8** colonize, compound, conclude, ensconce, regulate **9** arbitrate, designate, determine, discharge, establish, habituate, liquidate, touch down **10** adjudicate, administer, strengthen **11** accommodate

strike: **7** mediate **9** arbitrate, negotiate

settled: **4** alit, fast, firm **5** ended, fixed, staid **6** formed, sedate **7** certain, decided, peopled, statary, testate **8** decorous **9** inerratic, sedentary, steadfast **10** consistent, contracted, determined, inveterate, unchanging **11** established

settlement: dos **4** camp, lees **5** abode, dowry, dregs **6** colony, hamlet **7** payment, village **8** decision, disposal, fixation, sediment **9** agreement, aldeament, community, residence **10** adjustment, compromise, conclusion, habitation, occupation, regulation, resolution **11** arrangement **12** colonization, satisfaction **13** clarification

arrange: **9** negotiate

study of: **8** ekistics

settler: **6** Sooner, vessel **7** pioneer, planter **8** colonist, emigrant, squatter **9** colonizer, immigrant **10** forehearth, receptacle

seven: **4** zeta

days and nights: **8** sennight

deadly sins: **4** envy, lust **5** anger, pride, sloth **8** gluttony **12** covetousness

dice roll: **7** natural

group of: **6** heptad, septet **8** hebdomad

Seven Against Thebes: **6** Tydeus **8** Adrastus, Capaneus, Eteocles **10** Amphiaraus, Hippomedon, Polyneices **13** Parthenopaeus

Seven Churches: **6** Sardis, Smyrna **7** Ephesus **8** Laodicea, Pergamum, Thyatira **12** Philadelphia

Seven Dwarfs: Doc 5 Dopey, Happy 6 Grumpy, Sleepy, Sneezy 7 Bashful

seven-fold: 8 septuple

seven-sided: 10 heptagonal

seventh heaven: 5 bliss 7 ecstasy, rapture

sever: cut 4 chop, deal, know, part, rend, slit 5 break, split 6 breach, cleave, depart, detach, divide, sunder 7 dispart, divorce 8 disunite, separate 9 dismember 10 disconnect, dissociate 12 disassociate
from neck: 6 behead 9 decollate 10 decapitate

several: few 4 many, some 6 divers, single, sundry 7 diverse, not a few, various 8 distinct, peculiar 9 different 10 individual, respective

severe: bad 4 cold, dear, dere, dour, dure, grim, hard, keen, sore, tart 5 acute, cruel, grave, gruff, harsh, rethe, rigid, rough, sharp, sober, stark, stern, stiff 6 biting, bitter, chaste, coarse, sedate, simple, solemn, strict, trying, unkind 7 arduous, ascetic, austere, caustic, chronic, condign, crucial, cutting, drastic, extreme, intense, painful, serious, spartan, violent 8 captious, exacting, grievous, rigorous, scathing 9 difficult, draconian, inclement, strenuous, stringent, unsparing 10 afflictive, censorious, forbidding, methodical, oppressive, restrained

severity: 8 acerbity, acrimony, asperity 10 simplicity, unkindness

Seville cathedral tower: 7 Giralda

sew: hem, hog, sow 4 bind, darn, join, mend, seam, tack 5 baste, broth, drain, patch, quilt, sewer, shirr, smock, unite 6 fasten, needle, stitch, suture 7 pottage
up: end 5 cinch 6 secure, settle 7 exhaust 8 conclude 10 monopolize
with gathers: 4 full 5 shirr, smock

sewan: 5 beads, money 6 wampum

Seward's Folly: 6 Alaska

sewer: 4 sump 5 drain 6 tunnel 7 channel, conduit 8 cesspool 10 seamstress
opening: 5 drain 7 manhole

sewing machine: *inventor:* 9 Elias Howe
part: 8 plicator 10 zipperfoot

sex: 6 gender 10 copulation
hormone: 7 steroid

sexless: 6 neuter 7 epicene

sexton: 6 beadle, shamus, verger, warden 7 sacrist 9 sacristan 12 underofficer

sextuplet: 7 sestole 8 sestolet

sexual: 5 gamic 6 carnal, erotic, loving 7 amatory 8 intimate 10 lascivious
continence: 8 chastity
inclination: 4 urge 6 libido

sexy: 4 racy 5 spicy 6 carnal, earthy, erotic, risqué 7 amatory 8 off-color

sha: 5 sheep, urial 6 nahoor, oorial

shabby: old 4 base, mean, worn 5 dowdy, faded, seedy 6 paltry, ragged, scurvy 7 outworn, unkempt 8 beggarly, dogeared, shameful, tattered, unworthy 10 despicable, gone to seed, threadbare 11 disgraceful

shack: coe, cot, hut 4 dump, plug 5 cabin, catch, chase, hovel 6 lean-to, refuse, shanty, wander

shackle: tie 4 band, bind, bolt, bond, curb, gird, gyve, idle, iron, loaf, ring 5 chain, gyves 6 fetter, hamper, hinder, hobble, pinion, secure, unfree 7 confine, manacle, trammel 8 coupling, restrain 10 fetterlock

shad: 4 fish 5 alose 6 allice 7 crappie, herring, mojarra

shaddock: 5 fruit 6 pomelo 10 grapefruit

shade: bar, dim, hue 4 dark, dull, hint, tint, tone, veil 5 color, cover, ghost, hatch, tinge, trace, umbra, vault 6 awning, canopy, darken, degree, nuance, screen, shadow, shield, spirit, sprite 7 curtain, eclipse, foliage, obscure, parasol, phantom, protect, shelter, shutter, specter, umbrage, vestige 8 clearing, darkness, ornament, penumbra 9 adumbrate, gradation, variation 10 apparition, difference, overshadow, protection
light: 6 pastel
lines: 5 hatch
of cap: 5 visor
of meaning: 6 nuance
provider: 6 canopy 7 parasol 8 umbrella

shaded: 7 shadowy 8 screened 10 umbrageous

shaded walk: 4 mall 6 arcade 8 cloister

shadetail: 8 squirrel

shadow: dog 4 blot, haze, lurk, omen, tail 5 cleek, cloud, shade, shady, tinge, touch, trace, umbra 6 attend, follow, shroud, symbol 7 remnant, suggest, vestige 8 penumbra 9 adumbrate 10 apparition, indication
dark cone of: 5 umbra
dispelling: 9 scialytic
light: 8 penumbra
of death: 5 gloom, Sheol
outline: 10 silhouette
person without: 6 ascian

shadowbox: 4 spar

shadowy: dim 5 faint, vague 6 opaque, umbral, unreal 7 ghostly, obscure, retired 8 adumbral 9 imaginary 10 impalpable, indistinct, transitory

Shadrach: *companion:* 7 Meshach 8 Abednego
persecutor: 14 Nebuchadnezzar

shady: 5 fishy 6 risque 7 shadowy, suspect, umbrous 8 doubtful 9 dishonest 11 underhanded 12 disreputable, questionable

shaffle: 4 limp 5 shirk 6 hobble, loiter 7 shuffle

shaft: bar, pit, ray, rod **4** axle, beam, bolt, cone, dart, fust, hole, pole, stem, tige, tole **5** arbor, arrow, helve, heuch, heugh, irony, lance, scape, shank, spear, spire, staff, stalk, stave, stele, thill, tower, trunk **6** arbour, column, dagger, groove, handle, pillar, tongue, upcast **7** chamber, chimney, Maypole, missile, obelisk, spindle **8** flagpole, gatepost **9** flagstaff
  column: **4** fust **5** scape, verge
  feather: **5** scape
  part: **4** orlo
  plant: **4** axis
  vehicle: **5** thill

shag: mat, nap, rug **4** hair, mane, mass, pile, toss, wool **5** chase, fetch, fiber, shake **6** carpet, follow, rascal, refuse **7** garment, thicket, tobacco **9** cormorant **10** blackguard

shaggy: **5** bushy, furry, hairy, nappy, rough **7** bearded, hirsute, scrubby, unkempt, villous **8** straggly, textured **10** unpolished

shagreen: **4** skin **7** leather, rawhide **8** galuchat

shaitan, sheitan: **5** devil, fiend

shake: bob, jar, jog, wag **4** ague, bump, deal, free, jerk, jolt, move, pass, rese, rock, shog, stir, sway, toss, wave **5** agree, churn, drink, eject, evade, greet, quake, shock, steal, swing, trill **6** bounce, depart, dither, dodder, goggle, hustle, jiggle, joggle, quaver, quiver, rattle, shiver, totter, tremor, weaken, wiggle **7** agitate, chatter, concuss, disturb, fluster, flutter, shudder, tremble, unnerve, vibrate **8** brandish, convulse, dislodge, enfeeble, flourish **10** convulsion, earthquake
  down: bed, con **5** dance **6** extort, search, settle, try out **9** blackmail
  off: **4** shed **6** excuss **8** disagree
  up: **6** jumble **7** agitate **10** clean-sweep

Shaker: **4** sect
  founder: Lee

Shakespeare (see also play names): *actor:* **4** Kean, Ward **5** Booth **6** Burton, Kemble **7** Burbage, Garrick, Gielgud, Olivier, Siddons, Sothern **8** Modjeska **9** Barrymore
  alternate author: **5** Bacon
  elf: **4** Puck
  forest: **5** Arden
  home: **17** Stratford-upon-Avon
  theater: **5** Globe
  wife: **4** Anne

shaking: **4** ague **7** jittery **9** tremulant, tremulous **10** concussion

shako: cap **9** headdress
  decoration: **5** plume **6** pompon

shakti: **5** force, power

shaky: **4** weak **6** groggy, infirm, wabbly, wobbly **7** rickety, unsound **8** insecure **9** tottering, trembling, tremulous, uncertain **10** unreliable **12** questionable

shale: **4** bone, husk, rock **5** metal, slate **8** impurity

shall: may **4** must, will **5** would **7** obliged

shallop: **4** boat **6** dinghy, vessel

shallot: **4** herb, tube **5** onion **8** eschalot

shallow: hat **4** cart, flat, idle, tray, vain, weak **5** inane, light, shoal **6** basket, flimsy, slight **7** cursory, surface, trivial **9** depthless, frivolous **11** superficial

shalom (Heb.): **5** peace **8** farewell, greeting

sham: act **4** fake, hoax, mock, play **5** bogus, cheat, dummy, false, farce, feign, fraud, phony, spoof, trick **6** assume, bunyip, chouse, deceit, delude, device, duffer, ersatz, facade, fakery, humbug, pseudo, shoddy **7** deceive, feigned, forgery, grimace, imitate, mockery, pretend **8** imposter, pretense, spurious, travesty, trickery **9** brummagem, deception, hypocrisy, imitation, imposture, pretended, trickster **10** artificial, fictitious, simulacrum, substitute **11** counterfeit, make-believe

shamal: **4** wind

shaman: **4** monk **6** beggar, priest **8** conjurer **11** medicine man

Shamash: **6** sun god
  consort: Aya
  messenger: **6** Bunene
  worship center: **5** Larsa **6** Sippar

shamble: **5** stall, table **7** bauchle, butcher, shuffle **9** malformed, slaughter

shambles: **4** mess **5** mix-up **8** wreckage **9** confusion

shame: **5** abase, abash, guilt **6** assume, bemean, bismer, infamy **7** chagrin, degrade, mortify **8** contempt, disgrace, dishonor, ignominy **9** disrepute, embarrass, humiliate **10** repentance **11** degradation, shortcoming **12** self-reproach **13** embarrassment, mortification

shamefaced: shy **6** humble, modest **7** bashful **9** diffident, regretful

shameful: **4** base, mean **5** gross, wrong **7** ignoble **8** flagrant, improper, indecent, infamous **9** degrading, dishonest **10** outrageous, scandalous, slanderous **11** disgraceful, ignominious, opprobrious **12** contumelious

shameless: **4** bold, lewd **6** arrant, brazen, cheeky **7** blatant **8** immodest, impudent **9** abandoned, audacious, barefaced, unabashed **10** unblushing

shampoo: **4** lave, wash **5** clean

shamrock land: **4** Eire, Erin **5** Irena **7** Ireland

Shang dynasty: Yin

shanghai: **4** drug, ship **5** seize **6** abduct, coerce, kidnap

Shangri-la: 6 utopia 8 paradise

shank: leg 4 gamb, meat, shin, stem, tang 5 gambe, knife, ladle, ridge, tibia
pert. to: 6 crural

shantung: 4 silk 6 fabric, pongee, tussah

Shantung's capital: 6 Tsinan

shanty: cot, hut 5 cabin, hovel, hutch, lodge, shack 6 lean-to 7 cottage 8 chantier, dwelling

shape: fit, hew 4 bend, cast, form, knap, make, mold, plan, tool, trim 5 block, boast, build, carve, feign, forge, frame, guise, image, model, mould, order, state, torus 6 aspect, create, decree, design, devise, figure, format, happen, ordain 7 appoint, arrange, conform, contour, fashion, fitness, incline, phantom, posture, whittle 8 attitude, contrive 9 condition, determine, semblance, structure 10 apparition, appearance, figuration 11 arrangement
different: 8 variform
garden: 7 topiary
in: fit 4 trim 5 ready 7 healthy
up: 9 get better 13 straighten out

shapeless: 6 deform 8 deformed, formless, inchoate 9 amorphous, contorted, distorted, misshapen, unshapely

shapely: fit 4 neat, trim 5 buxom 6 comely, decent, gainly 7 rounded 8 suitable 9 beautiful 10 curvaceous 11 symmetrical

shaping machine: 5 edger, lathe, plane 6 router, shaper

shard: 5 scale, shell, sherd 8 fragment, potsherd

share: cut, lot 4 cant, deal, dole, hand, part, rent 5 claim, divvy, enter, quota, ratio, shear, slice, split, stake 6 cleave, divide, impart, moiety, parcel, ration 7 measure, mete out, partake, portion 8 dividend, division, interest 9 allotment, allowance, apportion, communion, plowshare 10 distribute, percentage 11 participate
widow's: 5 dower, dowry, terce, third 6 dowery

sharecropper: 7 metayer 12 tenant farmer

shark: 4 gata, haye, mako, tope 5 adept 6 expert, lawyer, usurer 7 sharper 8 drunkard, hybodont, man-eater, parasite, predator, swindler, thrasher, thresher 9 porbeagle, selachian, trickster
blue pointer: 4 mako
dried skin: 8 shagreen 9 sandpaper
family: 12 elasmobranch
genus of: 11 carcharodon
largest: 10 whale shark
nurse: 4 gata
pilot: 6 remora
small: 4 tope 5 lamia
young: pup 8 sharklet

sharp: sly 4 acid, cold, cute, edgy, fell, gash, gnib, high, keen, nice, sour, tart, wise 5 acrid, acute, adept, alert, brisk, canny, crisp, eager, edged, fiery, harsh, honed, quick, salty, short, slick, smart, steep, tangy, witty 6 abrupt, active, acuate, astute, barbed, biting, bitter, bright, clever, crafty, crispy, expert, peaked, severe, shrewd, shrill, snelly (Sc.) 7 angular, austere, caustic, cunning, cutting, gingery, grating, intense, knowing, lyncean, nipping, painful, piquant, pointed, prickly, pungent, rasping, violent, waspish 8 aculeate, distinct, handsome, incisive, piercing, poignant, stabbing, stinging, vigilant, vigorous 9 attentive, beautiful, brilliant, designing, impetuous, merciless, penetrant, sagacious, sarcastic, trenchant, unethical 10 astringent, discerning, perceptive, ungracious 11 acrimonious, intelligent, penetrating, quick-witted, underhanded
to taste: 4 acid 5 acrid

sharpen: nib, ted 4 edge, file, hone, whet 5 grind, point, reset, strop 6 acuate 7 enhance, quicken 9 aggravate, intensify, stimulate 10 cacuminate

sharper: gyp 4 bite 5 cheat, rogue 6 cogger, con man, keener 7 cheater, gambler 8 deceiver, swindler 9 trickster 12 double-dealer

sharpness: 4 edge 6 acumen 8 acrimony, keenness

sharpshooter: 6 sniper 8 marksman

sharp-sighted: 6 astute

shatter: 4 blow, dash 5 blast, break, burst, crash, smash, split, wreck 6 batter, damage, impair 7 clatter, derange, destroy, disable, scatter 8 demolish, disorder, disperse, splinter 9 dissipate

shattered: 6 broken 7 damaged 8 broozled, doddered

shave: ace, cut 4 pare, poll, trim 5 cheat, graze, skive 6 glance, rasure, reduce, scrape 7 tonsure, whittle

shaveling: boy 4 monk 5 youth 6 priest 9 hypocrite, stripling 10 cut it close

shaving: 5 flake, piece 8 ramentum

shawl: 4 maud, wrap 5 cloak, manta, orale, stole 6 chadar, chador, mantle, serape 7 amlikar, paisley 8 epiblema

Shawnee Indian chief: 8 Tecumseh, Tecumtha

sheaf: 5 bunch 6 bundle 7 cluster

Shea player: Met

shear: cut 4 clip, crop, gnaw, reap, rend, snip, trim 5 carve, force, mince, prune, sever, shave, strip 6 barber, cleave, divest, fleece, nibble, pierce, remove

shearing machine: 7 cropper

shears: 6 forfex 7 pinking 8 scissors, secateur

sheartail: 4 tern 11 hummingbird

shearwater: 4 crew 6 hagdon, haglet, petrel, puffin

sheatfish: 4 wels 7 catfish

sheath: cot 4 boot, case, skin, wrap 5 dress, ocrea, stall, theca 6 forrel, quiver, sleeve, spathe 7 capsule, holster 8 covering, envelope, scabbard

sheathe: 4 bury, case, ceil, dull, hide 5 blunt, cover, glove 6 clothe, encase 7 conceal, enclose, envelop

sheave: 4 bind 5 wheel 6 gather, pulley 7 collect 9 back water

sheaves: See **sheaf**

shebang: hut 4 deal 5 shack 6 affair, outfit, shanty 7 concern 8 business 11 contrivance

shed: cut, hut 4 abri (F.), byre, cast, cote, doff, drop, emit, hull, lair, molt, nest, part, pour 5 booth, cabin, hovel, repel, scale, scrap, spill, tease 6 belfry, dingle, divest, divide, effuse, hangar, hemmel, impart, lean-to, slough 7 cast off, cottage, diffuse, discard, emanate, fall off, radiate, scatter, shelter, take off, testudo 8 disperse, jettison, outhouse, separate, sprinkle, throw out, workshop 9 irradiate, penthouse, slough off 11 intersperse, out-building
skin: 7 ecdysis

shedder: 4 crab 6 peeler, salmon 7 lobster
of clothes: 9 ecdysiast

sheen: 4 fair 5 gleam, gloss, shine, shoes 6 bright, finish, glossy, luster, polish 7 burnish, exalted, glisten, glitter, radiant, shimmer, shining 8 lustrous, splendid, splendor 9 beautiful, shininess 10 brightness

sheep: mug, sha 5 argal, dumba, ovine, urial 6 aoudad, argali, wether 7 bighorn, bleater, karakul, mouflon 8 karakule, moufflon, ruminant 9 blackface
breed: 4 Horn 6 Dorset, Exmoor, Merino, Romney 7 Cheviot, Delaine, Lincoln, Suffolk 8 Cotswold, Dartmoor 9 Leicester, Southdown, Teeswater 10 Corriedale, Oxford Down, Shropshire
caretaker: 8 shepherd
coat: 4 wool 6 fleece
cry: maa 5 bleat
disease: coe, gid, rot 5 braxy 6 sturdy
feed: 5 graze 7 pasture
female: ewe
male: ram, tup 6 wether 10 bellwether
mark: 4 smit 5 brand
meat: 4 lamb 6 mutton
pathway: 6 roddin 7 rodding
pen: 5 bught (Sc.) 6 bought (Sc.)
pert. to: 5 ovine
wild: sha 4 arui, udad 5 argal, audad, urial 6 aoudad, argali, bharal, nahoor, nayaur 7 mouflon 8 moufflon

young: hog, teg 4 lamb, tegg 5 heder 6 bident, gimmer, hogget, sheder 7 twinter 8 hoggerel, shearhog 9 four-tooth, shearling

sheepheaded: 5 silly 6 stupid 12 simpleminded

sheepish: shy 4 meek 5 blate, silly, timid 7 abashed, awkward, bashful, daffish 9 diffident

sheep-like: 4 meek 5 ovine 6 docile

sheepskin: 4 bond, cape 5 basil 6 mouton 7 diploma 9 parchment
leather: 4 roan

sheepwalk: run 5 range, slait 7 pasture

sheer: 4 fine, mere, pure, thin, turn, veer 5 brant, clear, filmy, gauzy, steep, utter 6 abrupt, bright, flimsy, swerve 7 deviate, shining, unmixed, utterly 8 absolute, gossamer, outright 9 deviation, downright, undiluted 10 diaphanous 11 precipitous, transparent, unmitigated, unqualified 12 change course 13 perpendicular

sheet: air 4 fine, leaf, page, rope, sail 5 chain, daily, linen, paper, plate, white 6 expand, lamina, shroud 7 tabloid 8 handbill, pamphlet 9 baking tin, newspaper
of stamps: 4 pane
twelvemo: 9 duodecimo

sheeting: 5 linen 6 cotton 7 percale

sheitan: See **shaitan**

shelf: 4 bank, berm, bink, reef, sill 5 altar, berme, layer, ledge, shoal 6 gradin, mantel 7 bedrock, bracket, gradine, retable, sandbar, stratum 8 credence, credenza, sandbank 9 banquette 10 pigeonhole

shell: hud, pod 4 boat, bomb, case, coin, hull, husk, lyre, shot, skin, swad, test 5 balat, cameo, conch, cover, cowry, crust, frame, money, murex, scale, shuck, spoon, testa, troca 6 coffin, concha, cowrie, ˙crusta, dolite, dugout, lamina, lorica, strafe 7 abalone, admiral, bombard, capsule, caracol, dariole 8 caracole, carapace, exterior, frustule 9 cartridge 10 open fire on, projectile
beads: 4 peag 6 wampum
casing: 5 gaine
defective: dud
explosive: 4 bomb 7 grenade
hole: 6 crater
money: 4 peag 5 cowry, peage, sewan, uhllo 6 cowrie, seawan, wampum
protected with: 8 loricate
ridge: 4 lira 5 varix 7 varices (pl.)

shellac: lac 4 whip 5 resin 6 defeat 7 lacquer, trounce

shellacking: 6 defeat 7 beating 8 flogging, whipping

Shelley: 4 poet
alias: 5 Ariel

poem: **7** Adonais, Alastor **8** Queen Mab **10** Ozymandias, To a Skylark

shellfire: 6 strafe, volley **7** barrage

shellfish (see also **mollusk**): **5** nacre **6** limpet **7** mollusk **10** crustacean

shell out: pay **4** give **5** spend **8** disburse

shelter: cot, hut, lee **4** abri, barn, camp, cote, fold, gite (F.), herd, howf, port, roof, shed, skug, tent **5** benab, bield, boist, bower, cloak, cover, embay, haven, house, hovel, howff, hutch, shack **6** asylum, burrow, covert, defend, garage, hangar, harbor, hostel, refuge, sconce, sconse, screen, shield, trench **7** carport, cottage, defense, embosom, foxhole, harbour, hideout, hospice, housing, imbosom, lodging, nacelle, pillbox, protect, retreat, trailer, umbrage **8** bescreen, ensconce, mantelet, quarters, security **9** coverture, harbinger, harborage, sanctuary **10** harbourage, protection

shelve: tip **4** tilt **5** defer, ledge, shelf, table **6** mantel, retire **7** dismiss, project, put away **8** overhang, platform, postpone **10** pigeonhole

Shem: *brother:* Ham **7** Japheth
father: **4** Noah
son: Lud **4** Aram, Elam **6** Asshur

shenanigan: 4 game, lark, play, ploy, ruse **5** caper, prank, stunt, trick **6** frolic **7** evasion, foolery **8** goings-on, mischief, nonsense, trickery **10** tomfoolery **11** monkeyshine **12** clownishness

Sheol: 4 hell **5** grave, Hades **10** underworld

shepherd: 4 herd, lead, tend **5** drive, guard, guide, watch **6** attend, escort, feeder, gather, herder, leader, pastor, shadow **7** care for **8** guardian, minister
band of: **10** pastoureau
dog: **6** Collie **8** Cebalrai
god: Pan **5** Pales
pert. to: **8** pastoral
pipe: **4** reed **7** musette, panpipe **11** flageolette
purse: **4** herb **9** blindweed
staff: **4** kent **5** crook

shepherdess: 7 bergere **9** Amarillis, Amaryllis

sherbet: ice **5** glace **6** sorbet

sherd: See **shard**

Sheridan play: 6 Critic, Rivals **16** School for Scandal

sheriff: 6 grieve **7** bailiff, marshal, officer **9** constable
aides: **5** posse
deputy: **6** elisor **7** bailiff
jurisdiction: **9** bailiwick

Sherlock Holmes: *companion:* **6** Watson
creator: **5** Doyle

sherry: 4 wine **5** tokay **6** Solera **7** oloroso **11** amontillado

Shetland Islands: *capital:* **7** Lerwick
musical instrument: gue
tax: **4** scat

shibboleth: 4 test **6** phrase, slogan **8** password **9** criterion, watchword

shield: ecu (F.), rim **4** egis, hide, umbo **5** aegis, armor, avert, badge, board, cloak, cover, guard, pavis, shade, targe **6** blazon, brooch, canopy, defend, forbid, screen, target **7** buckler, clypeus, conceal, defense, lirelle, prevent, protect, rotella, shelter, testudo **8** conserve, rondache **9** protector, safeguard **10** escutcheon, protection
band across: **4** fess
boss: **4** umbo
Minerva's: **4** egis **5** aegis
part of: **4** boss, ente, orle, umbo **6** pointe **7** bordure, impresa
rim: **4** orle
Roman: **6** scutum
small: ecu
strap: **6** enarme

shield-bearer: 8 escudero

shield-shaped: 7 peltate, scutate **9** clypeate

shift: yaw **4** deal, eddy, fend, jibe, move, quit, ruse, slip, stir, tour, turn, veer **5** avoid, dodge, dress, evade, feint, hours, order, shunt, slide, smock, spell **6** assign, bestir, change, device, divide, period **7** arrange, chemise, convert, dispose, evasion, replace, shuffle **8** artifice, clothing, exchange, mutation, transfer **9** apportion, expedient, vacillate **10** equivocate, subterfuge, transition, transplant **11** contrivance

shifting: 8 ambulant, changing, drifting, floating **9** deviation

shiftless: 4 lazy **8** feckless, indolent, slothful **10** thriftless **11** inefficient

shifty: sly **4** haft **6** fickle, tricky **7** cunning, devious, evasive, hangdog **8** sneaking **9** faithless, underhand **10** changeable

shikar: 4 hunt **5** sport **7** hunting

shikari, shikaree: 5 guide **6** hunter **9** sportsman

shill: 4 dupe, foil **5** decoy **10** accomplice **11** confederate

shillelagh: 4 club **6** cudgel **7** sapling

shillibeer: 6 hearse **7** omnibus

shilly-shally: 5 hedge, waver **6** dawdle, trifle **8** hesitate **9** fluctuate, vacillate

shim: hoe **5** image, knife, level, wedge **6** streak, washer **7** glimpse, shingle

Shimeil's father: 4 Gera

Shimel's father: Ela

shimmer: 5 flash, light **7** glimmer, glisten

shimmy: 5 dance, shake **6** quiver **7** chemise, tremble, vibrate

shin: run **4** kick, walk **5** climb, ridge, shank, tibia **6** ascend *pert. to:* **7** cnemial

shindig: **4** fete **5** basli, party **6** shiono **7** she-bang

shindy: row **4** jump, lark, orgy, romp **5** brawl, dance, noise, party, revel, spree **6** fracas, frolic, rumpus, uproar **7** quarrel, wassail **8** carousal **9** commotion **11** disturbance, merrymaking

shine: ray, rub **4** beam, beek (Sc.), buff, glow, star **5** black, blaze, blink, excel, flash, glaik, glare, gleam, glent, glint, gloss, gloze, light, prank, sheen **6** liking, luster, polish **7** burnish, glimpse, glisten, glister, glitter, radiate, sparkle, touch up, twinkle **8** fondness, illumine **9** coruscate, irradiate

shiner: hat **4** chub **6** bruise, minnow **8** black-eye **9** bootblack

shingle: **4** sign, whip, wood **5** shake, slate **7** haircut **9** clapboard, hair style, signboard

splitting tool: **6** prower

shingles: **4** zona **6** herpes, zoster

shining: **4** glad, gold **5** aglow, glary, lucid, nitid, sleek **6** ardent, argent, bright, fulgid, glossy, lucent **7** beaming, eminent, fulgent, glowing, radiant **8** flashing, gleaming, gorgeous, luminous, lustrous, radiance, splendid **9** brilliant, effulgent, refulgent, sparkling, unclouded **10** glistening, glittering, remarkable **11** illustrious, irradiating, resplendent

shinplaster: **5** scrip

Shinto: *deity:* **4** kami **8** Hachiman

gateway: **5** torii

temple: **4** sha **5** Jinja **6** Jinsha **7** Yashiro

ship: **4** boat, pink, send **5** shift **7** hagboat **8** balinger

abandoned: **8** derelict

above the water: **9** hydrofoil **10** hovercraft

ancient: **4** long **5** knorr **6** dugout, galley **7** galleon, trireme

Arabian: **6** boutre

arctic: **6** sealer

Argonaut's: **4** Argo

ascent: **5** scend

auxiliary: **6** tender

back: aft **4** stem **5** abaft, stern

beam: **7** carling, keelson

berth: **4** dock, slip

boarding device: **6** ladder **9** gangplank

boat: **4** dory, life **5** barge, dingy **6** dingey, dinghy, tender **7** pinnace

body: **4** hull

breadth of: **4** beam

burden: **5** cargo

cabin: **9** stateroom

canvas: **4** sail

capacity: **7** tonnage

capacity unit: ton

cargo: **7** gaiassa

cargo invoice: **8** manifest

cargo storage: **4** hold

carpenter: **5** Chips

channel: gat **5** canal **6** narrow, strait

clean: **6** careen

clock: nef

coastal: hoy **4** dhow, grab **6** droger, trader **7** drogher

Coast Guard: **6** cutter

codfishing: **6** banker **8** walloper

commercial: **6** trader

company: **4** crew **5** fleet, hands

compass housing: **8** binnacle

cook: **6** slushy

course: **7** sealane

crane: **5** davit

crew member: **4** hand, mate **5** bosun, oiler **6** purser, sailor **7** steward **8** deckhand, engineer, helmsman, steerman **9** navigator

curved planking: sny

deck: **4** poop **10** forecastle

deserter: rat

drain: **7** scupper

enemy watching: **7** vedette

fishing: **5** smack **6** hooker, lugger **7** trawler

flat-bottom: **4** keel **5** barge

fleet of: **6** armada, convoy

floor: **4** deck

front part: bow, ram **4** prow, stem **7** forward

fuel: **5** barge, oiler **6** coaler, tanker **7** collier

fur-hunting: **6** sealer

group: **4** navy **5** fleet **6** armada, convoy **8** flotilla, squadron

hoist: **4** boom **5** crane, davit **7** capstan, derrick

jail: **4** brig

kitchen: **6** galley

left side: **4** port

line: **7** marline, ratline

lookout platform: **9** crow's nest

merchant: **6** argosy

middle: **9** amidships

mortgage: **8** bottomry

movement: **6** leeway

navigation area: **6** bridge **10** chart house, pilot house

oar: **6** bireme, galley, sampan **7** pinnace, rowboat, trireme

officer: **4** mate **5** bosun **6** master, purser **7** captain, steward **9** boatswain

part: bow **4** beam, brig, deck, helm, hold, hull, keel, mast, prow **5** bilge, hatch, stern, waist, wheel **6** bridge, fo'c'sle, galley, rudder, steven, tiller **7** lazaret, scupper, yardarm **8** binnacle, bowsprit, bulkhead, porthole, steerage **9** lazarette, lazaretto, sternpost **10** forecastle

partition: **7** bulwark **8** bulkhead

pirate: **8** gallivat
planking: sny **6** strake
privateer: **10** brigantine
prow: **4** stem **5** prore
quarters: **5** cabin **6** fo'c'sle **8** steerage **10** forecastle
record: log
repair: **6** careen
rightside: **9** starboard
room: **4** brig **5** cabin, salon **6** galley, saloon **7** caboose **10** forecastle
rope: **4** line **6** hawser **7** halyard, lanyard, painter, ratline
shovel: **5** skeet
side: **5** abeam
smokestack: **6** funnel
steps: **12** companion way
structure frame: **7** carcass
table frame: **6** fiddle
tender: **7** collier, pinnace
tiller: **4** helm
timber: rib **4** bitt, keel, mast, spar **5** stick **7** bollard
triple-hulled: **8** trimaran
twin-hulled: **9** catamaran
upward movement: **5** scend
Venetian: **9** frigatoon
wheel: **4** helm
widest point: **4** beam
windlass: **7** capstan
window: **4** port **8** porthole
worm: **5** borer **6** teredo
shipment: **5** cargo **7** carload, freight **8** delivery
Ship of Fools author: **5** Brant **6** Porter
ship out: **4** send **6** enlist, export
shipshape: **4** neat, taut, tidy, trim **7** orderly
shipwright: **6** fairer, plater, shorer, wayman **10** woodworker
shire: **5** derby, horse **6** county, region **8** district, province **11** subdivision
shirk: **4** duck, funk **5** avoid, dodge, evade, slack **6** desert **7** neglect **9** fainaigue **11** leave undone
shirker: **6** loafer, truant **7** slacker **8** embusque **11** gold bricker
shirr: **4** cook **5** smock **6** gather **7** wrinkle
shirt: tee, top **4** hair, jupe, polo, sark **5** dress, kamis, middy, parka, sport **6** blouse, boiled, camisa, camise, cilice, parkee
  button: **4** stud
  hair: **6** cilice
shirtfront: **5** dicky **6** dickey
shirtwaist: **5** dress **6** blouse **9** garibaldi
Shiva: See **Siva**
shiver: **4** grue **5** chill, quake, shake **6** dither, quiver, tremor, twitch **7** flicker, frisson, shatter, shudder, tremble, vibrate **8** fragment, splinter
  fit: **4** ague **6** chills **10** goosebumps

shoal: bar **4** bank, fish, mass, reef **5** barra, crowd, flock **6** school, throng **7** shallow **9** coral reef, multitude
shoat: hog, pig
shock: jar, lot **4** blow, bump, jolt, pile, stun **5** appal, brunt, bunch, bushy, gliff, gloff, quake, scare, shake **6** excite, fright, impact, offend, shaggy, stroke, trauma **7** astound, collect, disgust, horrify, outrage, startle, terrify **8** astonish, paralyze, surprise **10** concussion
  mental: **6** trauma
  to reality: **5** sober
shocking: **5** awful, lurid **6** horrid, unholy **7** fearful, ghastly, hideous **8** dreadful, horrible, shameful, terrible **9** appalling, atrocious, egregious, monstrous, revolting **10** disgusting, outrageous, scandalous
shod: **5** shoed, soled **6** booted **7** ensoled
shoddy: bad **4** poor **5** cheap **6** paltry, shabby **8** inferior, slovenly
shoe: pac **4** boot, clog, flat, pump **5** gilly, sabot, scuff **6** brogan, brogue, buskin, caliga, crakow, gaiter, galosh, gillie, loafer, oxford, patten, sandal **7** blucher, flattie, mocasin, slipper, sneaker **8** colonial, Congress, mocassin, solleret **9** brodequin **10** clodhopper
  aid: **4** horn
  baby: **6** bootee, bootie
  form: **4** last, tree
  gym: **7** sneaker **8** high tops, plimsoll (Br.)
  house: **4** mule **7** slipper
  mule's: **6** planch
  part: box, cap, tip, toe, top **4** heel, lace, lift, pull, rand, vamp, welt **5** shank, strap **6** insole, tongue **7** counter, outsole **8** backstay, slipsole
  paste: **7** clobber
  piked: **6** cleats, crakow
  repair: tap **5** retap **6** reheel, resole, stitch
  rolling: **5** skate **12** Rollerblades
  rubber: **4** boot **6** arctic, galosh **8** overshoe
  winged: **7** talaria
  wooden: **5** sabot **6** patten
  worker: **6** laster **7** cobbler
  worn: **7** bauchle
shoelace: tie **5** lacet **7** latchet
  tip: **5** aglet **6** aiglet
shoemaker: **5** soler, sutor (L.) **7** cobbler, crispin, farrier **10** cordonnier (F.)
  apprentice: **4** snob
  patron saint: **7** Crispin
  tool: **4** butt **5** elsin **6** elshin
shoeshine: **9** bootblack
shofar, shophar: **4** horn
shog: jog **4** jerk, jolt, push, rock **5** shake **6** jostle
shole: **5** plank, plate

shoneen: 4 snob 5 toady

shoo: 4 scat 5 scram 7 vamoose
in: 6 victor 9 sure thing

shooi: 4 bird, skua 6 jaeger

shoot: bud, pot, zap 4 bang, bine, bolt, cast, chit, cion, dart, emit, film, fire, grow, hunt, limb, move, plug, push, rush, twig 5 blast, blaze, bough, chute, drive, eject, frond, lance, plant, scion, snipe, spear, spout, spray, sprig, spurt, throw, tuber, utter, wound 6 branch, extend, flower, inject, launch, propel, sprout, stolon, strike, thrust, twinge 7 burgeon, project, tendril 8 protrude 9 discharge, offspring 10 photograph

shooting match: tir (F.) 5 skeet 6 affair

shooting star: 5 comet 6 meteor 8 fireball

shop: buy 4 firm, mart 5 store 6 botega, market, office, prison (Br.), tienda 7 factory 8 boutique, emporium, workshop 9 workplace
bakery: 9 panaderia (Sp.) 10 patisserie
coffee: 4 cafe 6 bistro 9 estaminet
dairy: 8 cremerie
meat: 7 butcher, shamble 10 rotisserie 11 charcuterie
wine: 4 cafe 6 bistro, tavern

shopkeeper: cit 8 merchant, retailer 11 storekeeper

shoplift: cop 4 take 5 boost, pinch, steal, swipe 6 rip off

shopper: 5 buyer 8 customer

shopworn: 4 used 5 trite 6 cliche 8 overused 9 hackneyed

shore: 4 bank, edge, land, prop, sand, side 5 beach, brink, coast, drain, offer, scold, sewer 6 border, rivage, strand 7 seaside, support 8 buttress, threaten 9 foreshore 10 embankment
pert to: 8 littoral
poetic: 6 strand
recess: bay 4 cove 5 bayou, inlet

shorebird: ree 4 ruff 5 snipe 6 curlew, plover 9 sandpiper

shore up: 4 prop 7 bolster, fortify, support 10 strengthen

shorn: See **shear**

short: 4 curt, rude 5 bluff, blunt, brief, brusk, crisp, gruff, harsh, scant, spare, terse 6 abrupt, scanty, scarce 7 briefly, brusque, concise, crisply, curtail, friable, summary, wanting 8 abridged, abruptly, succinct, unawares 9 deficient 10 to the point 11 compendious

shortage: 4 lack, need 5 pinch 6 dearth 7 deficit, failure 10 deficiency 13 insufficiency

short-breathed: 5 pursy 6 winded 7 puffing

shortcoming: 4 flaw 5 fault 6 defect, foible 7 failure 9 weak point 10 deficiency, inadequacy 12 imperfection

shortcut: 5 alley, route 6 bypass, byroad, cutoff 8 diagonal

shorten: bob, cut, lop 4 clip, dock, furl, reef 5 check 6 lessen, reduce 7 abridge, curtail, curtate, deprive 8 compress, condense, contract, decrease, diminish, truncate 9 apocopate, decurtate 10 abbreviate 11 encapsulate

short fuse: 11 quick temper

shorthand: 11 stenography, stenotyping 12 brachygraphy, speedwriting
system: 5 Gregg 6 Pitman

short-lived: 9 ephemeral, transient

shortly: 4 anon, soon 7 quickly 8 directly 9 presently

shortness: 7 brevity

shortsighted: 4 dull 6 myopic, obtuse 11 nearsighted 12 narrow-minded 13 opportunistic

short-spoken: 4 curt 5 gruff 7 laconic

Shoshone Indian: Ute 4 Hopi, Otoe, Utah 5 Piute 6 Paiute 8 Comanche

shot (see also **shoot**): pop, try 4 dram 5 blank, carom, drink, fling, guess, masse, photo, range, reach, sally, snort, tired, weary 6 bullet, chance, pellet, stroke 7 attempt, missile 8 marksman, snapshot 9 exhausted, reckoning 10 conjecture, projectile 11 intoxicated, opportunity

should: 4 must, want 5 ought, would

shoulder: 4 berm, edge, push, side 5 bough, elbow, raise, shove 6 axilla, hustle, jostle 7 bulwark, support
angle: 6 epaule
belt: 4 sash 7 baldric
bone: 7 scapula 8 clavicle
muscle: 7 deltoid
ornament: tab 7 lanyard 9 epaulette
pain: 7 omalgia
pert to: 4 alar 7 humeral 8 scapular
protection for: 8 pauldron
to shoulder: 5 as one 7 serried 8 together

shoulder blade: 7 scapula 8 acromion

shout: boo, cry, hoy, hue 4 bark, bawl, call, crow, hoot, howl, roar, root, scry, yell, yelp 5 cheer, huzza, noise, whoop, yodel, yodle 6 clamor, halloo, hurrah, outcry, yammer 7 acclaim 10 vociferate 11 acclamation
hunting: 5 hallo, holla 6 yoicks 7 tallyho 9 view-haloo

shove: 4 cast, prod, push 5 drive, eject, elbow, hunch, press, shunt 6 hustle, jostle, propel, thrust

shovel: dig 4 pale, peel 5 scoop, skeet, spade 7 shuffle 8 excavate

shoveler: 9 broadbill, river duck

shovelfish: 9 spadefish 10 paddlefish

shovelhead: 5 shark 7 catfish 8 flathead, sturgeon

show: 4 bosh, come, dash, fair, film, lead, look, mask, pomp 5 coach, farce, gloss, guide, movie, plead, prove, raree, revue, stage, teach, train 6 accuse, afford, allege, appear, assign, bestow, blazon, cinema, circus, confer, denote, detect, escort, evince, expose, flaunt, gaiety, gayety, inform, locate, parade, reveal, tinsel, turn up, unveil, veneer 7 bespeak, betoken, bravura, cabaret, declare, display, divulge, exhibit, explain, perform, picture, present, produce, trot out 8 brandish, ceremony, disclose, evidence, flourish, indicate, instruct, manifest 9 barnstorm, burlesque, designate, establish, rareeshow, represent, semblance 10 appearance, exhibition, exposition, expression 11 countenance, demonstrate, opportunity, performance 13 demonstration
forth: 7 publish 8 manifest, proclaim 9 publicize
stylized: 4 mime 6 parade 7 pageant 9 cavalcade, pantomime
way: 5 guide, usher 6 direct, escort 7 conduct

showcase: 7 cabinet, exhibit, vitrine

shower: tub, wet 4 bath, hail, rain, sump, wash 5 bathe, party, salvo, spray, storm, water 6 bestow, deluge 7 barrage, drizzle, scatter 8 downpour, rainfall, revealer, sprinkle 9 exhibitor 10 cloudburst

showery: wet 4 damp 5 moist 7 drizzly, tearful

showing: 4 sign 6 aspect 7 account 10 apocalypse, appearance 11 performance
first: 8 premiere

show up: 5 strip 6 appear, arrive, expose 7 display

showy: gay 4 arty, loud 5 dashy, gaudy, grand, tacky 6 flashy, garish, ornate, swanky 7 dashing, gallant, opulent, pompous, splashy 8 gorgeous, splendid, striking 9 brilliant, flaunting, sumptuous 10 flamboyant 11 pretentious 12 ostentatious

shrapnel: 5 shard, shell 8 fragment 10 projectile

shred: bit, cut, hew, jag, rag 4 fell, iota, jagg, snip, tear, twig, wisp 5 blype, crumb, grate, ounce, piece, prune, rip up, scrap, sever, shard, speck, strip 6 divide, screed, sliver, tailor, tatter 7 fritter, parings, smidgen, vestige 8 fragment, particle 9 pulverize, tear apart 12 make confetti

shrew: 5 curse, harpy, scold, vixen 6 mammal, rodent, tartar, virago 7 muskrat, villain 8 harridan 9 scoundrel, termagant, Xanthippe

shrewd: bad, sly 4 cagy, cute, evil, foxy, hard, keen, sage, wily, wise 5 acute, cagey, canny, harsh, sharp, slick, smart, stern 6 argute,

artful, astute, biting, clever, crafty, subtle, wicked 7 abusive, cunning, gnostic, hurtful, knowing, parlous, politic, prudent, sapient 8 piercing, sensible 9 gnostical, ingenious, sagacious 10 discerning, farsighted, hardheaded 11 intelligent, mischievous, penetrating, sharpwitted

shrewish: 7 nagging 8 vixenish 9 termagant 10 ill-humored 11 quarrelsome

shriek: cry, yip 4 yell 5 shout 6 holler, outcry, scream, squeal 7 screech

shrift (see also *shrive*): 10 absolution, confession, disclosure 12 confessional

shrike: 10 loggerhead 11 butcherbird

shrill: 4 high, keen 5 acute, sharp 6 argute, biting, piping, shriek, squeak, squeal 7 screech 8 piercing, poignant, strident 9 dissonant 11 highpitched, penetrating

shrimp: kid 5 dwarf 6 shaver 7 seafood 9 stripling 10 crustacean
large: 5 prawn
small: 6 seabob

shrine: box 4 case, naos, tomb 5 altar, caaba, chest, huaca, kaaba 6 abaton, adytum, chapel, chasse, dagaba (Ind.), dagoba (Ind.), entomb, hallow, temple 7 chaitya, enclose, memoria 8 canonize, enshrine, memorial 9 container, holy place, reliquary, sanctuary
visitor: 7 pilgrim

shrink: shy 4 fawn, funk, shun, wane 5 cling, cower, demur, quail, rivel, shrug, wince, wizen 6 blench, boggle, cotter, cringe, flinch, gizzen, huddle, humble, lessen, recoil, retire, wither 7 atrophy, dwindle, retract, scruple, shrivel 8 condense, contract, decrease, pull back, withdraw 9 constrict 10 depreciate 15 psychotherapist

shrinking: shy 5 timid 6 afraid, modest 8 receding, reticent, retiring 9 diffident 10 decreasing

shrive: rob 4 free 5 purge 6 acquit, pardon 7 absolve, confess 8 disclose 9 reconcile

shrivel: age 4 wilt 5 blast, crine, parch, rivel, wizen 6 cotter, scrump, shrink, weazen, wither 11 deteriorate

shroff: 6 banker, expert 7 changer, inspect 8 separate 12 moneychanger

shroud: lop 4 hide, trim, veil, wrap 5 array, cloak, cover, crypt, drape, dress, shade, sheet, vault 6 branch, clothe, enfold, screen, shadow 7 conceal, curtain, envelop, foliage, garment, plumage, protect, shelter 8 cerement, clothing, covering, envelope 9 cerecloth 10 protection

shrub: lop, tea, tod 4 bago, bush, cade, coca, gumi, majo, nabo, olea, sida, sola 5 elder, lilac, prune, punch, salal 6 cudgel, frutex 7 arboret, buckeye, cassava, chamise,

chamiso, heather, scratch, tarbush **8** abelmosk, barberry, beverage, huisache **9** chaparral, manzanita
aromatic: tea **4** mint, sage **5** batis, thyme **8**
rosemary
bean family: **4** ulex
collection: **10** fruticetum
desert: **5** retem **6** alhagi, raetam
evergreen: box **4** ilex, moss, titi **5** furze,
heath, holly, salal, savin **6** laurel, myrtle **7**
jasmine, juniper **8** oleander **9** mistletoe
fence: box **5** hedge
flowering: **5** lilac, tiara, wahoo **6** azalea, laurel, myrtle, spirea **7** lantana, rhodora, spiraea, syringa **8** japonica, oleander, oleaster
9 mistletoe **10** mignonette
fruit: **5** salal
genus of: **4** inga **5** erica, ledum **6** aralia
hardy: **7** althaea, heather
indigo: **4** anil
myrtle-like: **7** cajeput, cajuput
ornamental: **6** privet
parasitic: **9** mistletoe
pert. to: **9** fruticose, fruticous
poisonous: **5** sumac **6** sumach **8** oleander
prickly: **4** whin **5** briar, brier, caper, gorse **7**
bramble **8** allthorn, hawthorn
rubber: **7** guayule
stunted: **5** scrag, scrub
tea-like: kat **4** coca
tropical: **5** henna **6** olacad **7** lantana **8**
hibiscus, oleander **10** frangipani
shruff: **5** dross **7** rubbish
shrug: don, tug **5** hitch **6** fidget, shiver, shrink
7 gesture, shudder **8** contract
off: **6** ignore **7** dismiss, not care
shrunken (see also **shrink**): **4** lank **7** wizened
9 atrophied, shriveled
Shu: *parent:* Ra **6** Hathor
sister: **6** Tefnut
wife: **6** Tefnut
shuck: pod **4** husk, sham **5** fraud, shell, strip **6**
recoil, remove **7** discard, mislead, swindle
shudder: **4** ague, grue **5** quake, shake **6**
quiver, shiver, tremor **7** frisson, tremble
shuffle: mix **4** gait, plod, walk **5** dance, scuff **6**
huddle, juggle, jumble, mingle, remove, sclaff
7 evasion, quibble, scuffle, shamble **8** artifice
9 confusion **10** equivocate **11** prevaricate
shuffling: **6** shifty **7** evasive **9** deceitful
shun: **4** balk, flee, hide, snub **5** avert, avoid,
evade, evite **6** eschew **7** abstain, forbear,
forsake, refrain **8** forebear
shunt: **4** move, push **5** shift, shove **6** divert,
remove, switch **7** shuttle **9** conductor,
rechannel, sidetrack, turn aside
shut: bar, rid **4** free **5** close **6** climax, fasten,
forbid **7** confine, exclude, turn off **8** prohibit **10** portcullis

in: hem, pen **4** cage, coop, pent, wall **5**
embar, embay, fence **6** bottle, hemmed,
immure **7** bottled, confine, enclose, impound
8 imprison **10** quarantine, surrounded
shut-in: **7** invalid, recluse **12** convalescent
shut out: bar **6** screen **7** exclude **8** preclude
shutter: **5** blind, cover **6** screen **7** buckler **8**
jalousie
shuttle: **4** loom **5** shunt, train **6** looper **9** air
travel
shuttlecock: **4** bird **6** birdie
shut up: end, gag **4** hush **7** seclude **8** be
silent, conclude **9** terminate
shy: coy, mim **4** balk, jump, meek, shun, wary
5 aloof, avoid, chary, dodge, scant, start,
throw, timid **6** boggle, demure, escape,
modest, recoil, shrink **7** bashful, fearful,
lacking, nervous, potshot **8** farouche, hesitant, reserved, retiring, secluded, sheepish,
skittish, timorous **9** diffident, reluctant,
shrinking **10** incomplete, unassuming **11**
distrustful, introverted, unobtrusive
Shylock: **6** usurer **9** loan shark **11** money
lender
coin: **5** ducat
daughter: **7** Jessica
friend: **5** Tubal
shyster: **11** pettifogger
si (Sp.): if, yes
Siam: See **Thailand**
Siamese twin: Eng **5** Chang
sib: kin **4** akin **5** ayllu **6** allied, sister **7** brother,
kindred, kinship, kinsman, related **8**
friendly, relation, relative **9** congenial,
kinswoman **12** well-disposed
Sibelius: **8** composer
work: **9** Finlandia **11** Valse Triste **13** Swan
of Tuonela
Siberia: (see box)
sibilant: ess **7** hissing
sibling (see also **sib**): **6** sister **7** brother
sibyl, sybil: **4** seer **5** witch **6** Libyan, Samian,
Trojan **7** Cumaean, prophet, seeress **8** Del-
phian, Phrygian **9** Cimmerian, Erythrean,
sorceress, Tiburtine **10** prophetess
sibylline: **6** occult **7** cryptic, obscure **8** oracular **9** ambiguous, equivocal, prophetic **10**
exorbitant, mysterious **11** prophetical
sic: set **4** seek, thus, urge **5** chase, egg on **6**
attack, incite **7** exactly
Sicilian: **10** Trinacrian
Sicily: *capital:* **7** Palermo
city: **4** Gela **5** Aetna, Bidis, Nakos **6**
Alcamo, Modica, Ragusa **7** Catania,
Marsala, Messina **8** Taormina **9** Agrigento
code of honor: **6** omerta
composer: **7** Bellini
crime society: **5** Mafia
god: **7** Adranus

king: **4** Eryx
measure: **5** salma **7** caffiso
people: **5** Elymi, Sicel
river: **5** Salso **6** Belice, Simeto **7** Platani
volcano: **4** Etna
whirlpool: **9** Charybdis
youth: **4** Acis

Siberia: *antelope:* **5** saiga
carnivore: **5** sable
city: **4** Enna, Omsk **5** Chita, Tomsk **7** Barnaul, Irkutsk **11** Novosibirsk
dog: **7** Samoyed **8** Samoyede
Eskimo: **4** Yuit
fish: **5** nelma
forest: **5** taiga, Urman
fur: **7** calabar
hunters and fishers: **6** Giliak, Gilyak **7** Samoyed **8** Samoyede
hut: **8** barabara, barabora
leopard: **5** ounce
mountains: **4** Ural **5** Altai
people: **5** Sagai, Tatar, Yakut **6** Kirgiz, Tartar **7** Kirghis, Kirghiz, Yukagir **8** Yukaghir **9** Mongolian
plain: **6** steppe, tundra
river: **2** Ob, Ili, Tom **4** Amur, Lena, Maya, Onon, Yana **5** Sobol, Tobol **6** Anadyr, Olenek **7** Yenisei
squirrel: **7** miniver
squirrel-skin: **7** calabar
storm: **5** buran
tanning plant: **5** badan
tent: **4** yurt **5** yurta
wild cat: **5** manul
wild sheep: **6** argali

---

sick: bad, ill, set, wan **4** abed, pale, seek, urge, weak **5** badly, chase, crank, cronk, fed-up, unfit, weary **6** ailing, attack, incite, insane, unwell **7** unsound **8** diseased, impaired **9** crapulous, depressed, disgusted, disturbed, nauseated, surfeited, unhealthy **10** indisposed **12** disconsolate
deathly: **5** amort **7** alamort **8** terminal
person: **7** invalid, patient
sickbay: **6** clinic **8** hospital **9** infirmary **10** dispensary
sicken: **5** upset **6** affect **8** get worse, languish, nauseate
sickening: **7** fulsome **9** offensive, revolting **10** disgusting, nauseating
sickle: **5** blade **6** scythe
sickly: ill, wan **4** flue, pale, puny, weak **5** cothy, faint, frail **6** ailing, cranky, feeble, infirm, morbid, peaked, unwell, weakly **7** cothish, insipid, invalid, languid, mawkish **8**

diseased **9** unhealthy **11** unwholesome
sickness: **6** malady, nausea **7** ailment, disease, disgust, illness **8** insanity **9** complaint, condition, distemper, infirmity, weariness **10** affliction **12** qualmishness **13** indisposition
feign: **8** malinger
side: far **4** edge, face, line, part, team, wall, wide **5** agree, ample, costa, facet, flank, latus, party, phase, place, proud, shore, slope, space, width **6** aspect, behalf, border, margin, region, severe **7** conceit, distant, faction, lateral, sheathe, support, surface **8** district, position, spacious **9** declivity, direction, outskirts, viewpoint **10** collateral, occasional
left: **4** port
pain in: **6** stitch
pert. to: **7** lateral
piece: rib **5** stave
right: **9** starboard
sheltered: lee **4** alee
side arm: gun **5** sword **6** pistol, weapon **7** bayonet, hand gun **8** revolver, small arm
sideboard: **6** buffet **8** credence, credenza, cupboard
side by side: **6** next to **8** abutting, parallel, together **12** cheek to cheek
sidekick: pal **4** chum **6** friend **7** partner **8** follower **9** assistant, companion, satellite **11** confederate
sideline: **5** bench, hobby **7** put away **9** avocation
sidepiece: rib **6** border
sidereal: **6** astral, starry **7** stellar **8** starlike
siderite: ore
sideroad: **5** byway **6** detour **10** digression
siderolite: **9** meteorite
sideslip: yaw **4** skid **5** slide **10** digression
sidestep: **4** duck **5** avoid, dodge, evade
sidetrack: **4** spur **5** shunt **6** divert, switch
side view: **7** profile
sidewalk: **6** causey **7** walkway **8** pavement **9** banquette, boardwalk
part: **4** curb, kerb **5** crack **6** paving
sideways: **5** aside **6** askant **7** askance, athwart, lateral **8** indirect **9** laterally, obliquely
Sidi's wife: **5** Amine
sidle: **4** edge **6** loiter **7** saunter
Sidon's modern name: **5** Saida, Sayda
siege: see **4** bout, rank **5** bench, beset, flock, place, privy **6** attack **7** sitting **8** blockade
Siegfried: *mother:* **9** Sieglinde
slayer: **5** Hagen
sword: **7** Balmung
vulnerable spot: **4** back **8** shoulder
wife: **9** Kriemhild
sierra: **4** fish **5** range, ridge
Sierra Leone: *capital:* **8** Freetown
city: Bo **6** Makeni
currency: **4** cent **5** leone

Sierra Nevada: *fog:* **7** pogonip
   peak: **4** Dana **7** Whitney
siesta: nap **4** lull, rest **5** sleep **6** catnap **10** forty winks
sieve: **4** lawn, sift **5** tamis, temse **6** basket, bolter, filter, gossip, ranger, riddle, screen, sifter, strain **7** chaffer, cribble, measure **8** colander, separate, strainer
   for clay: **4** laun
sift: **4** bolt, cull, scry, sort **5** sieve, temse **6** dredge, filter, refine, riddle, screen, search, strain, winnow **7** analyze, canvass, examine, inspect, scatter **8** look into, separate **10** scrutinize
sifter: **5** sieve **6** bolter **8** strainer
sigh: sob **4** moan, wail **5** mourn, sough, yearn **6** bemoan, grieve, lament **7** breathe, deplore **11** respiration
sight: aim, ken, see **4** espy, gaze, look, mess, show, vane, view **5** scene **6** behold, descry, glance, vision **7** discern, display, eyesore, glimpse **9** spectacle **10** exhibition, inspection, perception **11** examination, observation
   defect: **6** myopia **7** anopsia
   loss: **9** amaurosis, blindness
   obscurity: **6** caligo
   offending: **7** eyesore
   out of: **4** gone **9** forgotten **11** disappeared
   pert. to: **6** ocular, visual
   second: ESP, fey **7** psychic
sightless: **5** blind **6** unseen **9** invisible
sightseer: **7** tourist **12** rubbernecker
sigil: **4** seal, sign, word **6** device, signet **9** signature
sigmoid: cee, ess
Sigmund: *father:* **7** Volsung
   son: **6** Sigurd **9** Sinfjotli
   sword: **4** Gram
   wife: **7** Hiordis **8** Borghild
sign: cue, nod **4** hint, hire, mark, note, omen **5** badge, image, segno (It.), sigil, spoor, token, trace **6** banner, beacon, beckon, effigy, emblem, engage, ensign, figure, motion, notice, poster, signal, signet, symbol, wigwag **7** auspice, endorse, gesture, initial, message, picture, portent, prodigy, vestige, warning **8** evidence, password, pretense, standard **9** autograph, character, semaphore, semblance, subscribe, watchword **10** denotation, expression, forerunner, indication, prognostic, suggestion, underwrite **11** countersign **13** constellation
   direction: **5** arrow **6** finger
   illuminated: **4** neon **6** lights
   liturgical: **5** selah **6** shelah
   magic: **5** sigil
   music: **4** clef, flat **5** presa, segno, sharp
   pert. to: **5** semic **8** semantic
signal: **4** flag **5** alarm, light, siren **6** buzzer,

ensign, marked, notify, sennet, tocsin **7** betoken, eminent, lantern, notable, presage, signify **9** memorable, prominent, semaphore, symbolize **10** noticeable, remarkable **11** communicate, conspicuous **13** extraordinary
   distress: PAN, SOS **6** mayday
   system: **4** code
   warning: **5** alarm, alert, flare, siren **6** alarum, beacon, tocsin **7** blinker
signature: ink **4** hand, mark, name, sign, visa, vise **5** sigil, stamp **9** allograph, autograph **10** directions, impression **11** bookbinding, countersign, John Hancock
signet: **4** mark, ring, seal, sign **5** sigil, stamp **10** impression **12** authenticate
significance: **6** import, repute, weight **7** bearing, meaning, purport **9** magnitude **10** importance **11** consequence
significant: **4** sign **5** grave, token **6** symbol **7** ominous, weighty **8** eloquent, sinister **9** important, momentous, prominent **10** compelling, expressive, indicative, meaningful, portentous, suggestive **12** considerable
signify: nod **4** mean, show, sign **5** augur, count, imply, spell, utter, weigh **6** amount, convey, denote, import, inform, matter, signal **7** add up to, betoken, compare, connote, declare **8** announce, foreshow, indicate, intimate, manifest **11** communicate
sign language: **11** dactylology
sign off: end, out **6** thirty
sign on: **4** hire, ship **6** engage, enlist, enroll **8** register
signor: man **4** lord **5** title **9** gentleman
signpost: **5** guide **6** beacon **7** pointer **9** guidepost
signum: **4** bell, mark, sign **9** signature
Sigurd: *father:* **7** Sigmund
   foster father: **5** Regin **6** Reginn
   horse: **5** Grani
   slayer: **5** Hogni
   victim: **6** Fafnir
   wife: **6** Gudrun
Sigyn's husband: **4** Loki
silage: **4** feed **6** fodder
Silas Marner author: **5** Eliot
silence: gag **4** calm, hush, mute, rest, stun **5** choke, death, floor, quell, quiet, still, tacet **6** muffle, muzzle, refute, squash **7** destroy, repress, secrecy, squelch **8** muteness, suppress **9** obscurity, reticence, stillness
   goddess: **8** Angerona
   music: **5** tacet
silencer: **4** mute **5** gavel **7** muffler **8** sourdine
silene: **7** campion **8** catchfly
silent: mum **4** dumb, flat, mute **5** muted, quiet, still, tacit **8** inactive, overcome, reserved, reticent, taciturn, unspoken,

wordless **9** noiseless, secretive, unuttered **10** flavorless, speechless, unrecorded **11** unexpressed, unmentioned

silex: **5** flint **6** quartz, silica **7** mineral

silhouette: **6** shadow **7** outline, profile **9** lineation **10** figuration

silicate: **4** mica **6** cerite, iolite **7** epidote **8** calamine, severite, wellsite

silk: **5** pekin, surah, tulle **6** fabric **7** foulard **8** florence, sarcenet, sarsenet

corded: **6** faille

embroidery thread: **5** floss **8** arrasene

fabric: **4** gros **5** caffa, China, crepe, moire, ninon, pekin, satin, surah, tabby, tulle **6** cendal, faille, mantua, pongee, samite, sendal, tussah, tusser, tussur **7** alamode, marabou, sarsnet, taffeta, tsatlee, tussore **8** sarcenet, sarsenet

fishline: **4** gimp

hat: **6** topper

Indian moth: **4** muga

raw: **5** grege **8** marabout

refuse: **6** strass

rough weave: **8** shantung **9** duoppioni

source: **6** cocoon

thread: **4** filo

unspun: **6** sleave

waste: **4** noil **5** floss **6** frison

watered: **5** moire

wild: **6** tussah **7** tussore

worker: **7** thrower **9** throwster

yarn: **4** tram **7** schappe

yarn size: **6** denier

silken: **4** fine, soft **5** quiet, silky, sleek, suave, sweet **6** gentle, glossy, smooth, tender **7** elegant **8** delicate, lustrous, silklike **9** luxurious, sericeous **10** effeminate **12** ingratiating

silk-stocking: **5** elite **7** elegant, wealthy **9** blue-blood, exclusive, luxurious **10** Federalist **12** aristocratic

silkworm: eri **4** eria **6** bombyx, tussah **8** bombycid

silkworm rot: **7** calcino

sill: **4** base, beam, edge, seat, sile **5** bench, frame, ledge, shelf, stone **6** timber **9** threshold **10** foundation

silliness: **5** folly **6** betise (F.) **9** absurdity **11** foolishness

silly: **4** bete, daft, fond, fool, simp, weak **5** anile, apish, barmy, crazy, daffy, dazed, dense, dizzy, frail, funny, giddy, goofy, goose, inane, plain, wacky **6** absurd, cranky, cuckoo, dotard, dottle (Sc.), feeble, footle, humble, infirm, paltry, rustic, sickly, simple, stupid, unwise **7** asinine, fatuous, flighty, foolish, foppish, shallow, trivial, vacuous, witless **8** childish, fopperly, ignorant, imbecile, innocent **9** brainless, childlike, ludicrous, pointless, senseless, simpleton **10**

half-witted, indiscreet **11** empty-headed **12** simple-minded

silt: **4** scum **5** dregs **7** deposit, moraine, residue **8** sediment **9** percolate

silver: **4** coin, pale **5** money, plate, sweet **6** argent, gentle **7** bullion **8** argentum, eloquent, flatware, lustrous, sterling **9** holloware, tableware **11** resplendent

containing: **5** lunar

lace: **8** filigree

pert. to: **9** argentine, argentous

reducing kettle: **4** cazo (Sp.)

silverfish: **6** insect, tarpon

silversmith: **5** sonar **6** Revere **9** artificer

silver thistle: **8** acanthus

silver-tongued: **4** glib **8** eloquent **10** persuasive

silverware: **5** vases **6** dishes **8** flatware, platters **9** ornaments, tableware

ornament: **7** gadroon

silverweed: rue **5** tansy **9** jewelweed **10** cinquefoil, potentilla

silvery: **7** frosted, shining **9** argentine **10** argenteous, shimmering

silviculture: **8** forestry

s'il vous plait (F.): **6** please

simar: **4** robe **6** jacket **7** garment **12** undergarment

Simeon: *father:* **5** Jacob

mother: **4** Leah

son: **4** Ohad **6** Nemuel

simian: ape **6** monkey **7** apelike **10** anthropoid

similar: sib **4** akin, like, such **5** alike **6** evenly **7** uniform **8** analogic, parallel **9** analogous, semblance **10** resembling **11** approximate, counterpart, homogeneous, resemblance

simile: **10** comparison

similitude: **4** form **5** image **6** simile, symbol **7** analogy, parable, replica **8** allegory, likeness **9** facsimile, semblance **10** similarity **11** counterpart, resemblance

similize: **5** liken **7** compare

simmer: **4** boil, stew **5** anger **6** braise, bubble, seethe

simnel: **5** bread **7** biscuit **8** cracknel **9** fruitcake

Simon: **5** Peter **7** apostle

Simon Legree: **10** taskmaster **11** slave driver

simon-pure: **4** real, true **6** simple **7** genuine **9** authentic **11** unqualified

simony: **8** barratry **11** indulgences

simoom, simoon: **4** wind **5** storm **6** tebbad **9** dust storm, sandstorm

simper: **5** mince, smile, smirk **7** whimper

simple: **4** bald, bare, dull, easy, fond, mere, open, poor, pure, real, true, weak **5** basic, clear, dense, folly, lowly, naive, naked, plain, Roman, silly, stark **6** common, Dorian, facile, homely, humble, oafish, rustic, severe, single, stupid **7** artless, ascetic, austere, babyish, evident, foolish, genuine, idyllic, natural, obvious, onefold, sincere, Spartan, unmixed **8** absolute, arcadian, childish, complete, gullible, homemade, homespun, ignorant, informal, innocent, modestly, ordinary, retarded, tailored, trifling **9** childlike, elemental, guileless, ingenuous, primitive, unadorned, unalloyed **10** effortless, elementary, unaffected, unassuming, uninvolved **11** homogeneous, undesigning, unimportant **12** inartificial, uncompounded, unpretending **13** insignificant, plain speaking, uncomplicated, unconstrained, unembellished

simple-minded: **6** simple, stupid **7** artless, moronic **12** feeble-minded, unsuspecting

simpleton: ass, daw **4** boob, dolt, fool, gaby, gawk, gawp, gowk, lout, simp, tony, zany **5** dunce, goose, idiot, moron, ninny, noddy, sammy **6** dawkin, gander, gawney, gulpin, nincom, nincum, nitwit, noodle, stupid **7** dullard, gomeral, gomerel, gomeril, half-wit, muggins, widgeon **8** Abderite, dumbbell, fondling, imbecile, numskull, omadhaun **10** changeling, nincompoop **11** ninnyhammer

simplify: **6** reduce **7** clarify, clean up, cut down, expound **8** boil down **9** elucidate, interpret **10** streamline

simulacrum: **4** copy, fake, sham **5** image **6** aspect **7** phantom **8** likeness, pretense, travesty **9** imposture, semblance **11** assemblance, counterfeit

simulate: act, ape **4** fake, mock, sham **5** feign, feint, mimic **6** affect, assume **7** feigned, imitate, pretend **8** make like, resemble **9** dissemble, personate, pretended **10** fictitious **11** counterfeit

simulation: **4** copy **9** hypocrisy **10** sanctimony

sin: **4** debt, envy, evil, lust, vice **5** anger, blame, crime, error, fault, folly, guilt, pride, sloth, wrong **6** acedia, felony, offend **7** do wrong, offense, violate **8** gluttony, iniquity, peccancy, trespass **9** deviation **10** immorality, peccadillo, transgress, wickedness, wrongdoing **11** misdemeanor, ungodliness, viciousness **12** covetousness, imperfection **13** transgression

Sinai mountain: **5** Horeb

sinapis: **4** herb **7** mustard

Sinbad's bird: roc

since: ago, for, fro, now **4** ergo, gone, past, sith, syne (Sc.) **5** after, hence, later **7** already, because, whereas **8** inasmuch, until now **9** afterward, therefore, thereupon **11** considering

sincere: **4** open, pure, real, true **5** frank, whole **6** candid, devout, hearty, honest **7** artless, cordial, correct, earnest, genuine, unmixed,

upright **8** faithful, truthful, virtuous **9** authentic, blameless, heartfelt, unfeigned, veracious **10** aboveboard, forthright, unaffected **11** unvarnished **12** wholehearted

sinciput: **8** forehead

sind: **5** rinse **6** drench, quench

sinecure: **4** pipe, snap **5** cinch, gravy

sine qua non: **9** essential **13** indispensable

sinew: **5** power, snare **6** tendon **7** potency

sinewy: **4** firm, ropy, wiry **5** thewy, tough **6** brawny, robust, strong **7** fibrose, nervous, stringy **8** forceful, muscular, powerful, vigorous **9** tendinous

sinful: bad **4** evil **5** wrong **6** wicked **7** immoral, ungodly, vicious **10** iniquitous **11** blameworthy

sing: hum **4** cant, lilt, pipe, ring, talk **5** carol, chant, chirl, croon, ditty, yodel, yodle **6** betray, inform, intone, warble **7** chortle, confess, descant, divulge, rejoice, roulade, tweedle **8** serenade, vocalize
 as a round: **5** troll
 softly: hum **5** croon

singable: **7** lyrical, melodic, tuneful **9** cantabile

Singapore: *city:* **6** Changi, Jurong
 currency: **4** cent **6** dollar
 hotel: **7** Raffles

singe: **4** burn, char, sear **6** scorch **7** blemish
 fiber: **6** genapp

singer: **4** alto, bard, bass, diva **5** basso, buffa, buffo, lyric, mezzo, tenor **6** artist, cantor **7** artiste, chanter, crooner, soloist, songman, soprano **8** baritone, minstrel, vocalist **9** chanteuse, chorister, contralto, descanter **10** cantatrice, coloratura **11** entertainer, heldentenor **12** countertenor, mezzo-soprano
 comic opera: **5** buffa
 female: **9** chanteuse **10** cantatrice
 opera: **4** diva

singerie: **6** design **7** picture **10** decoration **11** monkeyshine

singing: **4** cant **5** charm **9** cantation
 group: **4** duet, trio **5** choir, octet **6** chorus, sextet **7** octette, quartet **8** chanters, sextette **9** quartette
 pert. to: **6** choral **9** cantative
 style: **4** scat **6** doowop **7** melisma **8** vocalise **9** solfeggio
 trio: **9** tricinium

single: one **4** lone, only, part, sole, song, unit **5** alone, unwed **6** record, unique **7** base hit, one-fold, unusual **8** celibate, separate, singular, solitary, withdraw **9** sequester, unmarried **10** individual, particular, unattached **11** unsupported

single out: **4** pick **6** choose, select

singlet: **5** shirt **6** jersey **9** waistcoat **10** undershirt

singly: 4 once 5 alone, apart 6 merely, solely 7 unaided 8 honestly 9 severally, sincerely 12 individually, particularly, single-handed

singsong: rap 5 chime 7 tedious 11 repetitious

singular: odd, one 4 each, lone, oner, only, rare, sole, solo 5 queer, weird 6 single, unique 7 bizarre, curious, eminent, oddball, private, several, strange, unusual 8 isolated, peculiar, rara avis, separate, superior, uncommon 9 eccentric, fantastic, whimsical 10 individual, one and only, remarkable, unexampled 11 exceptional 12 unparalleled

singultus: 7 hiccups

sinister: car (Sc.) 4 dark, dire, evil, grim, left 6 malign 7 adverse, baleful, corrupt, malefic, ominous 8 menacing 9 dishonest, injurious, malicious, underhand 10 disastrous, portentous 11 apocalyptic, prejudicial, threatening, unfortunate

sink (see also **sunk**): bog, dip, ebb, pet, sag 4 bowl, cave, drop, fail, fall, hole, pool, ruin, sump, wane 5 avale, basin, drain, droop, drown, embog, heald, hield, lower, plump, sewer, slope, stoop, swamp 6 cavity, debase, dolina, doline, drench, extend, finish, gutter, hollow, humble, plunge, recede, settle, thrust 7 capsize, decline, degrade, depress, descend, destroy, founder, immerse, relapse, subside 8 decrease, diminish, submerge, suppress 9 penetrate 10 depression
below horizon: set

sinker: 5 pitch 6 weight 8 doughnut

Sinkiang: 8 Xinjiang
capital: 6 Urumqi 7 Urumchi
river: 5 Tarim

sinking: 7 descent 10 depression

sinless: 4 pure 7 perfect 8 innocent 9 righteous

sinner: 5 rogue, scamp 8 evildoer, offender, penitent 9 bad person, reprobate, wrongdoer 10 backslider, trespasser

sinning: 6 erring 7 peccant

sinuous: 4 wavy 5 snaky 7 bending, crooked, curving, devious, winding 9 deviating, intricate 10 circuitous, serpentine 11 anfractuous

sinus: bay 4 bend, fold 5 bosom, curve 6 cavity, hollow, recess 7 channel, opening 10 depression
pert. to: 5 sinal 7 sinusal

Sioux: Kaw, Oto 4 Crow, Iowa, Otoe 5 Brule, Omaha, Osage, Teton 6 Dakota, Lakota, Oglala, Santee, Tutelo 7 Catawba 9 Winnebago

sip: bib, lap, nip, sup 5 draft, drink, quaff, taste 6 tipple 8 toothful 11 small amount

sipper: 4 tube 5 straw

sir: 4 lord 5 title 6 knight, master 7 baronet 9 gentleman

sirdar: 5 chief, noble 6 bearer 7 officer, servant

sire: 4 king, lord, stud 5 title 6 father, master, parent 8 ancestor, begetter, generate 10 forefather, procreator, progenitor

siren: 5 alarm, lurer 7 charmer, foghorn, Lorelei, mermaid 8 water god 9 Cleopatra, temptress 10 attractive, bewitching, seductress 11 fascinating, femme fatale

Siren: 5 Ligea 8 Leucosia 10 Parthenope

siriasis: 9 sunstroke

Sirius' master: 5 Orion

sirocco: 4 wind

sisal: 4 hemp 5 fiber
source: 8 henequen, sisalana

Sisera: *enemy:* 5 Barak
murderer: 4 Jael

siskin: 5 finch, tarin 9 small bird

sissy: 6 coward 7 girlish, milksop, unmanly 8 weakling 10 effeminate 11 mollycoddle

sister: nun, sis 4 girl 5 soror (L.) 7 sibling
murder: 10 sororicide
pert. to: 5 soral 8 sororate, sororial

Sister Carrie author: 7 Dreiser

sisterhood: 8 sorority

Sister Superior: 6 abbess

sistrum: 6 rattle 10 noisemaker

sit: lie, set 4 meet, pose, rest, seat 5 brood, dwell, model, perch, press, roost, squat 6 occupy, remain, repose, settle 7 convene 8 incubate
carelessly: 4 loll 6 sprawl

site: dig 4 ruin, seat, spot 5 arena, locus (L.), place, scene, venue 6 locale, locate 8 location, position 9 situation

sitfast: 5 fixed, stone 8 crowfoot 9 immovable 10 stationary

sithe: lot 6 chance, mishap

sit in: 5 audit 6 attend, object 7 protest 11 participate

sit on: 6 confer, hush up, rebuke 7 repress, squelch 8 suppress 9 reprimand

Sitsang: 5 Tibet

sitting: 4 seat 5 abode, place 6 clutch, posing, seance, sedent, sejaul 7 meeting, sejeant, session 8 brooding, sederunt
court: 6 assize 7 session

Sitting Bull: *enemy:* 6 Custer
tribe: 5 Sioux

sitting duck: 4 dupe, mark 5 decoy 6 target

situated: 4 seat 5 basal 6 nether, placed, plight 7 located, station
between folds: 11 interplical
in the middle: 6 medial, median
on left: 9 sinistral
on right: 6 dexter
toward rear: 6 astern 7 postern 9 posterior

situation: job **4** case, need, post, seat, site **5** berth, place, siege, situs (L.), state **6** estate, locale, morass, plight, scrape, strait **7** bargain, dilemma, station, vantage **8** locality, location, position, quandary **9** condition, emergency, imbroglio, pregnancy **11** predicament, whereabouts **12** circumstance

situla: **4** pail, vase **6** bucket **10** receptacle

situs: **5** place **8** location, position **9** situation

Siva, Shiva: **8** Hindu god **9** Destroyer
consort: Uma **4** Devi
son: **6** Skanda
trident: **6** trisul **7** trisula
wife: **4** Sati

six: **6** senary, sestet **7** digamma, sestole **8** senarius
group: **5** hexad **6** hexade, senary, sextet **8** sextette **9** sextuplet
pert. to: **6** senary
series of: **5** hexad **6** hexade

six-eyed: **9** senocular

sixfold: **8** sextuple

six-footed: **7** hexaped **9** hexapodal, hexapodan

six-line stanza: **6** sestet

six on dice: **4** sice

six sheets: **7** sextern

six-shooter: gun **6** pistol, weapon **8** revolver

size: **4** area, bore, bulk, mass **5** cover, glaze, grade, width **6** adjust, amount, candle, extent, format, height, length, spread, volume **7** arrange, breadth, examine, expanse, measure, stiffen **8** classify, standard **9** dimension, magnitude **10** dimensions **11** measurement
book: **5** folio **6** octavo, quarto **8** twelvemo **9** duodecimo
paper: cap **4** copy, demi, demy, pott **5** atlas, crown, felic, folio, legal **6** bagcap **7** bastard, emperor **8** foolscap, imperial **9** colombier
separation device: **6** grader
yarn: lea **5** forty **6** denier

sizing: **4** glue **6** starch **9** allotment

sizy: **7** viscous **9** glutinous

sizzle: fry **4** burn, sear, siss **7** shrivel

sizzling: hot **6** torrid

sjambok: **4** flog, whip

skate: jag, man, ray **4** fish, plug, shoe, skid **5** flair, glide, horse
kind: **6** figure, hockey, roller **11** Rollerblade

skate blade: **6** runner

skating arena: **4** rink

skean: **4** dirk **5** sword **6** dagger

skedaddle: run **4** bunk, flee **5** leave, scoot, scram **6** go away, scurry **7** scamper, vamoose **8** clear out, hightail

skeesicks: **6** rascal **9** skeezicks, skinflint

skeet: **12** trapshooting

skegger: **4** fish, parr **6** salmon

skein: rap **4** hank, maze, wind, yarn **5** flock **6** flight, hurdle, sleeve **7** spireme, thimble **8** filament, wild fowl

skelder: **5** cheat **7** vagrant **9** panhandle

skeletal: **4** bony **9** emaciated

skeleton: **4** past **5** atomy, bones, coral, frame, ilium, mummy **6** sketch **7** outline, remains **9** framework
disease: **7** rickets
hiding place: **6** closet
organization: **5** cadre
sea animal: **5** coral, shell **6** sponge

skeleton key: **4** gilt **5** screw **6** master **7** twirler

skelly: **4** chub **6** squint **9** chaffinch

skelp: say **4** beat, blow, kick, pare, push, rain, slap, walk **5** write **6** basket, colony, squall, stride, strike **7** beehive, measure, perform, quickly, scratch, scuttle **8** splinter, suddenly

skeppist: **8** apiarist **9** beekeeper

skeptic, sceptic: **5** cynic **7** doubter, infidel, scoffer **8** agnostic **10** pyrrhonist, unbeliever **11** disbeliever, freethinker, nullifidian

skeptical, sceptical: **7** cynical **8** doubting **9** faithless, quizzical **10** suspicious **11** incredulous, questioning

skerry: **4** isle, punt, reef, rock **6** potato

sketch: dot, jot, map **4** draw, limn, plan, play, skit **5** draft, paint, skate, story, trace **6** apercu, design, layout, pastel **7** cartoon, croquis, diagram, drawing, outline, schizzo (It.) **8** describe, rough out **9** delineate, summarize **10** compendium **11** composition, delineation, description

sketchy: **5** rough, vague **7** cursory **10** inadequate, unfinished **11** superficial

skew: cup, cut, set **4** awry, bias, fail, make, shun, slip, turn, veer **5** askew, avoid, flunk, slant, stone, throw, twist **6** coping, escape, eschew, gauche, glance, offset, squint, swerve **7** blunder, distort, drizzle, oblique, pervert **8** slanting **9** deviating, distorted **12** misrepresent

skewer: pin, rod **4** spit **5** prick, truss **6** fasten, impale, pierce **7** hairpin **8** puncture **9** brochette

ski: **5** glide, slide
fall marker: **8** sitzmark
lift: **4** j-bar, t-bar **5** chair **7** gondola
race: **6** alpine, slalom **8** downhill
run: **6** schuss

skid: bar **4** clog, curb, drag, hook, rail, scud, shoe, slip, trig, veer **5** brake, check, slide **6** fender, runner, timber, twitch **7** plummet, protect, skidpan, support **8** fishtail, platform, sideslip

skid row: **4** slum **6** bowery

skiff: **4** boat, skim **5** canoe, glide, graze, touch

6 caique, flurry **7** currane, rowboat

skill: art, can **5** craft, haunt, knack, virtu **7** ability, address, aptness, command, cunning, finesse, justice, know-how, mastery, prowess, science **8** artifice, capacity, deftness, facility, industry, training **9** adeptness, dexterity, expertise, knowledge, readiness **10** adroitness, artfulness, astuteness, capability, cleverness, competence, efficiency, experience, expertness **11** proficiency

skillet: **6** spider **9** frying pan

skillful: apt **4** able, deft, fine, good, hend **5** adept, handy **6** adroit, artful, aufait, clever, crafty, daedal, expert, habile **7** capable, cleanly, cunning **8** dextrous, masterly, tactical **9** daedalian, dexterous, ingenious, righteous **10** proficient **11** intelligent **12** accomplished

skim: cut **4** film, flit, sail, scud, scum, skip **5** clear, cover, fleet, float, glide, graze, ready, study, throw **6** browse, glance, refuse **7** examine

off: **5** cheat, steal

over: **5** skirr **6** passim

skimp: **6** meager, scanty, scrimp **7** neglect **9** economize

skimpy: **5** chary, scant, spare **6** meager, scanty, sparse, stingy **9** niggardly **12** parsimonious

skin: **4** bark, best, derm, dole, fell, film, flay, hide, pare, peel, pell, pelt, rack, rind, scum **5** balat, cheat, cover, cutis, derma, fraud, layer, plica, purse, scalp, shell, strip, sweep **6** abrade, callus, dermis, escape, fleece, scrape, spoils **7** callous, coating, cuticle, defraud, plating, profits, sharper, sheathe, surface, swindle **8** covering, exterior, membrane, pellicle, planking **9** epidermis **10** integument, overcharge, pocketbook **11** decorticate

animal: fur **4** coat, hide, pelt, plew, rack, robe, vair **5** coney, sculp **6** hackle, peltry

beaver: **4** plew

blemish: wen **4** mole, wart **6** pimple **7** freckle

burning sensation: **5** uredo

decoration: **6** tattoo

deeper layer: **5** cutis **6** dermis

depression: **5** cleft **6** dimple

disease: **4** acne **5** hives, mange, psora, rupia, tinea **6** eczema, tetter **9** psoriasis

dryness: **7** xerosis

excessive pigment: **8** melanism

exudation: **5** sudor, sweat **12** perspiration

fold: **5** plica **7** dewlaps

fruit: **7** epicarp

layer: **4** derm **5** cutis, derma **7** cuticle **9** epidermis

oil: **5** sebum

opening: **4** pore

pert. to: **5** deric **6** dermal **9** cuticular, epidermal

piece: **5** blype

presser: **7** sammier

protuberance: wen **4** mole, wart **6** goiter, pimple

remover: **5** parer

resembling: **7** dermoid

sensitive layer: **5** cutis **7** enderon

spot: **7** freckle

tan: taw

tumor: wen

unsheared pelt: **8** woolfell

without: **8** apellous

skin-deep: **7** shallow **9** cutaneous

skinflint: **5** miser **6** huddle **7** niggard **8** tightwad **10** cheapskate

skin game: **5** bunco, bunko, fraud **7** swindle

skink: **4** adda, draw, hock, shin **5** drink, serve **6** liquor, lizard

skinker: **7** tapster

skinned: *dark:* **7** melanic, swarthy

thick: **9** pachyderm **11** pachydermic

thin: **9** sensitive

skinner: bet, gyp **5** cheat **6** driver **8** swindler

skinny: **4** bony, lank, lean, thin **5** gaunt, lanky, scant, spare **6** meanly, stingy **7** scrawny **9** emaciated, niggardly **10** membranous

dip: **8** nude swim

skip: dap, hip, hop **4** balk, flee, gait, jump, leap, miss, omit, trip **5** bound, caper, elide, frisk, leave, scout, vault **6** basket, bucket, escape, gambol, glance, lackey, spring **7** abscond, captain, footman, servant **8** be absent, ricochet

along a surface: **4** skip **7** skitter

school: tib **9** play hooky

skipjack: **6** bonito, elater **7** upstart **8** sailboat **9** stripling **10** butterfish

skip over: **5** elide

lightly: **4** skim

water: dap

skipper: ihi **5** saury **6** leader, master **7** captain **9** butterfly, commander

East Indian: **6** serang

skippet: box **4** boat **5** skiff **8** envelope

skirl: fly **4** pipe, rain, snow **5** sweep, whirl **6** scream, shriek

skirling: **5** trout **6** salmon

skirmish: **4** fray **5** brush, clash, fence, fight, melee **6** action, battle, bicker, combat, effort **7** contend, contest **8** conflict, flourish **9** encounter **10** velitation

skirr: fly, run **4** move, skim, tern **5** scour, whirr **6** scurry

skirt: lie, rim **4** edge, flap, girl, maxi, mini, slit **5** avoid, dodge, dress, evade, trend, woman **6** border, fringe **7** garment **8** envelope, environs, go around, sidestep **9** outskirts, periphery, petticoat **10** circumvent, wraparound

ballet: **4** tutu

coat: **6** lappet
divided: **7** culotte
hoop: **6** peplum **9** crinoline, krinoline **11** farthingale
section: **4** gore **5** panel
short: **4** kilt, mini
steel: **5** tasse **7** lamboys
velvet: **4** base

skit: act **4** gibe, girl, gust, hoax, jeer, jest, slap **5** caper, pound, revue, story, taunt, trick **6** parody, shower, sketch, splash **7** asperse, flounce **8** ridicule **9** enclosure, stage show

skitter: hop **4** pass, skim, skip **5** glide **7** scamper, scatter **8** sprinkle

skittish: coy, shy **4** edgy **5** jumpy **6** fickle, frisky, lively **7** nervous, playful, restive **8** spirited, unstable, volatile **9** excitable, frivolous, sensitive

skittle: **4** play **5** trash **7** ninepin **8** nonsense, squander **9** enjoyment

skive: **4** dart, pare, skim **5** shave, wheel

skiver: **6** impale, skewer **7** leather, scatter

skivvy, skivvies: **9** underwear

skoal: **5** drink, toast **10** salutation

skua: **4** gull **5** jager **6** jaeger

skulduggery: **8** foul play, trickery **10** craftiness, wickedness

skulk: **4** hide, lurk **5** dodge, evade, hedge, shirk, slink, sneak **8** malinger

skull: **4** bean, bone, head, mind **5** brain **6** cobbra, crania (pl.) **7** cranium, harnpan
back part: **7** occiput **9** occipital
bone: **5** vomer **6** facial, zygoma **7** ethmoid, frontal, maxilla **8** mandible, parietal, sphenoid, temporal **9** occipital
cavity: **5** fossa **7** foramen
pert. to: **5** inial **7** cranial
protuberance: **5** inion
soft spot: **8** fontanel

skullcap: **5** calot **6** beanie **8** capeline
Arabian: **7** chechia
cardinal's: **10** berrettino
defensive: **4** coif **9** coiffette
ecclesiastical: **6** callot **7** calotte **9** zucchetto
felt: **6** pileus
Jewish: **8** yarmelke, yarmulke

skunk: **5** snipe **6** putois (F.) **7** polecat, stinker **8** betrayer **9** overwhelm
family: **6** weasel
spray: **4** musk

skunk-like animal: **5** civet **7** zorillo

sky: **4** blue **5** azure, ether **6** welkin **7** heavens **9** firmament
highest point: **6** zenith
pert. to: **9** coelar **9** celestial

sky-blue: **5** azure **7** celeste **8** cerulean

skylark: run **4** bird, jump, lark, play, skip, yerk **5** pipit **6** frolic
genus: **6** alauda

skylight: **6** dormer, window **8** abatjour (F.)

skyline: **7** horizon

sky pilot: **5** padre **6** cleric, divine, parson **8** chaplain, minister **9** clergyman

skyscraper: **5** tower **8** building

slab: **4** tile, wood **5** dalle, ingot, plate, slice, stela, stele **6** tablet

slab-like: **6** stelar **7** stelene

slack: lax **4** dull, idle, lazy, lull, slow, soft **5** chaff, evade, loose, relax, shirk, slake, tardy **6** abated, ease up, loosen, remiss **8** careless, dilatory, inactive, indolent, listless, slothful, sluggish, unsteady **9** dissolute, impudence, looseness, negligent

slacken: **4** ease, slow **5** abate, delay, relax **6** loosen, reduce, relent, retard **7** subside **8** decrease, moderate

slackening: **6** easing **7** detente (F.), slowing

slacker: **4** spiv **5** idler **6** loafer **7** coucher, shirker **8** embusque **9** goldbrick

slacks: **5** pants **8** trousers

slade: den **4** cave, glen **5** glade, glide, slide **6** ravine, valley **7** peat bog **8** hillside

slag: **4** lava **5** ashes, dross, waste **6** cinder, debris, refuse, scoria **7** residue, scoriae (pl.) **9** recrement **11** agglomerate

slain: **4** dead **6** fallen, killed **8** murdered **11** slaughtered **12** assassinated

slainte (Ir.): **5** toast **6** health **8** greeting **10** salutation

slake: mud, wet **4** cool, daub, flag, free, lick, mire, sate **5** abate, algae, allay, gully, loose, relax, slack, slime, smear, yield **6** aslake, deaden, lessen, quench, reduce **7** appease, assuage, crumble, gratify, refresh, relieve, satisfy, slacken **8** decrease, mitigate, moderate **10** extinguish

slam: hit **4** bang, beat, blow, cuff, dash, gibe, push, shut, vole **5** abuse, clash, close, noise, throw **6** impact **7** collide, flounce **9** criticize
in cards: **4** vole **5** grand **6** little

slammer: pen **4** jail, nick **6** prison

slander: **4** tale **5** belie, libel, shame, smear **6** defame, malign, report, vilify **7** asperse, blacken, calumny, distort, scandal, traduce **8** derogate, disgrace, dishonor, reproach, tear down **9** denigrate **10** defamation, depreciate, detraction, scandalize **12** misrepresent

slang: **4** cant **5** abuse, argot, lingo **6** jargon, rakish, vulgar **7** dialect, license, swindle **10** vernacular

slant: tip **4** bend, bias, cant, heel, list, skew, slab, tilt, turn, view **5** angle, aside, bevel, focus, point, slope **6** biased, breeze, glance, sklent **7** falsify, incline, opinion **8** attitude, diagonal, occasion **9** prejudice, viewpoint **10** hypotenuse **11** inclination

slap: box, hit, lap **4** blow, clap, cuff, nick, scud, snub, spat **5** break, click, clink, cluff, plump, skelp, smack **6** buffet, insult, rebuff, slight, strike **7** attempt **8** haymaker **9** castigate

slapdash: **5** abuse, hasty, messy **6** random, sloppy, untidy **8** careless, reckless **9** impetuous, roughcast **11** haphazardly

slapjack: **4** game **5** cards **7** pancake **8** flapjack **11** griddlecake

slapstick: **4** joke **5** farce, humor **6** comedy

slash: cut **4** dash, gash, lash, slit **5** crack, slosh, wound **6** attack, defeat, lessen, reduce, splash, strike, stripe **7** censure, scourge, slitter, solidus, virgule **8** diagonal, mark down **9** criticize, light into

slasher: **5** knife, sword **6** dagger, knifer **8** billhook **9** swordsman **12** swashbuckler

slashing: **7** dashing, immense **8** spirited **9** merciless **11** criticizing

slat: bar, dab, rib **4** blow, flap, hide, hurl, lath, slap **5** board, strip, throw **6** louver **8** fragment, splinter

slate: rag **4** gray, list, rock, tile **5** board, color, flesh, hound, plank, scold **6** ballot, berate, pummel, punish, pursue, record, roster, tablet, thrash, ticket **7** censure, roofing **8** nominate, register, schedule **9** criticize, reprimand, thrashing
clean: **10** tabula rasa

slater: **6** critic **9** wood louse

slath: **6** basket

slattern: daw **4** drab, frow, slut **5** dolly, idler, moggy, waste **6** blowze, faggot, sloppy, sloven **7** trifler, trollop **8** careless

slatternly: **5** dirty, dowdy **6** blowzy, sordid, untidy **8** slovenly

slaty: **6** clayey **7** grayish **9** argillous **12** argillaceous

slaughter: **4** gash, kill, slay **6** battue, murder, pogrom, reduce **7** butcher, carnage, destroy, killing **8** butchery, decimate, hecatomb, massacre, violence **9** bloodbath, bloodshed, reduction **10** annihilate, butchering **11** destruction
of one group: **8** genocide **15** ethnic cleansing

slaughterhouse: **8** abattoir, butchery

Slav: **4** Pole, Serb, Sorb, Wend **5** Croat, Czech **6** Slovak **7** Russian, Serbian, Servian **8** Bohemian, Croatian, Moravian, Silesian **9** Bulgarian, Ukrainian **12** Czechoslovak

slave: **4** bond, esne, neif, peon, serf, toil **5** chela, helot, thane **6** addict, cumhal, drudge, penest (Gr.), thrall, toiler, vassal, wretch **7** bondman, captive, chattel, enslave, odalisk, servant **8** work hard **9** gallerian, hierodule, odalisque
block: **7** catasta
comedy: **5** Davus (L.)
dealer: **5** bichy
freedom: **11** manumission **12** emancipation
fugitive: **6** maroon

The Tempest: **7** Caliban
traveling group: **6** coffle

slave driver: **6** despot, tyrant **8** martinet **11** Simon Legree

slaver: **5** drool, smear **6** drivel, saliva **7** flatter, slabber, slobber **8** be insane

slavery: **6** thrall **7** bondage, service **8** drudgery **9** captivity, servitude, thralldom, vassalage **10** subjection **11** enslavement
release from: **7** manumit **8** liberate **10** emancipate **11** affranchise, enfranchise

Slave States: **5** Texas **7** Alabama, Florida, Georgia **8** Arkansas, Delaware, Kentucky, Maryland, Missouri, Virginia **9** Carolinas, Louisiana, Tennessee **11** Mississippi **13** North Carolina, South Carolina

slavish: low **4** base, bond, hard, vile **6** abject, menial **7** servile **8** despotic, enslaved **9** barbarous, dependent, imitative **10** oppressive, tyrannical **11** downtrodden, subservient

slay: **4** do in, kill **5** amuse, smite **6** murder, strike **7** butcher, delight, destroy, execute **9** slaughter **10** annihilate **11** assassinate, exterminate
by strangling: **7** garotte
by suffocation: **5** burke
legally: **7** execute

slayer: **4** bane **6** killer **8** criminal, genocide, murderer, regicide, vaticide **9** matricide, patricide **10** fratricide, sororicide

sleazy: **4** mean, thin **5** cheap, seedy, tacky **6** common, flimsy, shabby, trashy **11** promiscuous

sled: **4** luge, pung **6** jumper, sleigh **7** clipper, coaster, travois, vehicle **8** toboggan **10** conveyance
Russian: **6** troika

sledge: **4** dray, sled **5** break **6** hammer, hurdle, sleigh, strike

sleek: nap **4** chic, oily **5** gloss, preen, shiny, slick, smart, suave **6** finish, glossy, polish, smooth, soigne **7** flatter, mollify, soignee **8** polished, unctuous

sleep: nap **4** doss, doze, rest **5** death, sopor **6** drowse, repose, snooze, stupor **7** bed down, slumber **8** lethargy **10** somnipathy **11** hibernation
after dinner: **12** postprandial
deep: **4** coma **5** sopor **6** stupor
god: **4** Soma **6** Hypnos **8** Morpheus
inability to: **8** insomnia
inducer of: **6** opiate **7** sandman, sopient **8** sedative **13** counting sheep
midday: **6** siesta
pert. to: **7** somnial

sleeper: bet, tie **4** beam **5** horse, shark **6** rafter, rester, timber **7** dormant, earmark, Pullman, reposer **8** dormouse, long shot **9** dowitcher, slumberer

sleepiness: 10 drowsiness, somnolence

sleeping: 4 abed 6 asleep, latent 7 dormant 8 inactive 9 quiescent
  place: bed 4 bunk, cell, doss 5 berth, couch 6 pallet 7 bedroom, cubicle 9 cubiculum, dormitory

sleepless: 5 alert 7 unquiet, wakeful 8 restless, vigilant, watchful 9 ceaseless 11 industrious, presevering

sleepwalker: 12 noctambulist, somnambulist

sleepy: 4 dull 5 tired 6 drowsy, groggy 7 languid 8 sluggish, soporose, soporous 9 lethargic, somnolent 10 phlegmatic, slumberous

Sleepy Hollow author: 6 Irving

sleeve: 6 armlet, dolman, moggan, raglan 7 bushing, cathead
  bar on: 7 chevron
  leg-of-mutton: 5 gigot

sleigh: 4 pung, sled 6 cutter, sledge 7 cariole 8 carriole, toboggan
  runner: 4 shoe

sleight: sly 5 craft, knack, skill, trick 6 crafty, wisdom 7 address, agility, conjure, cunning 8 artifice, deftness, prudence, trickery 9 chicanery, deception, dexterity, dexterous, quickness, stratagem 10 nimbleness

sleight-of-hand: 5 magic 11 legerdemain
  performer: 4 mage 8 conjurer, magician 15 prestidigitator

slender: 4 lean, slim, thin, weak 5 exile, frail, gaunt, lanky, lithe, petit, reedy, short, small, sylph, wispy 6 feeble, lissom, little, meager, narrow, slight, svelte 7 gracile, lissome, tenuous, trivial, willowy 8 ethereal 9 attenuate, elongated

slenderize: 4 diet, slim 6 reduce

slenderness: 7 exility, tenuity

sleuth: PI, tec 4 dick 6 ferret, tracer 7 gumshoe, tracker, trailer 9 detective 10 private eye 12 investigator

slew (see also **slough**): lot 4 many, much, slue, turn 5 bunch, twist 6 slough

sley: 4 reed 8 guideway

slice: cut, saw 4 jerk, part 5 carve, piece, sever, share, shave, slash, wedge, whang 6 cantle, divide, rasher, shiver, sliver 7 portion 8 separate, splinter
  of meat: 6 collop

slick: mag 4 fine, neat, oily, tidy 5 alert, preen, sleek, slide 6 adroit, chisel, clever, crafty, glossy, paddle, polish, smooth 7 cunning, dress up, smarten, thicket 8 slippery 9 ingenious 10 attractive, glistening

slicker: 4 dude 5 cheat 6 gypper 7 gambler 8 raincoat, swindler 9 trickster

slide: 4 fall, skid, sled, slew, slip, slue 5 chute, coast, creep, glide, hurry, scoot, steal 6 sledge 7 decline, incline, relapse, slither,

sluther 8 glissade, ornament 9 avalanche, backslide, landslide
  fastener: 6 zipper

slight: cut 4 fine, slap, snub, thin 5 flout, frail, leger (L.), light, minor, scant, scorn, sleek, small 6 flimsy, ignore, meager, remote, scanty, simple, slight, smooth 7 distain, fragile, gracile, neglect, nominal, shallow, slender, trivial 8 careless, delicate, overlook 9 disesteem, disparage, disregard, indignity 10 immaterial, negligible 11 discourtesy, superficial, unimportant 12 contemptuous
  sound: 4 peep 7 whisper

slightest: 5 least

slighting remark: 4 slur

slim: sly 4 lean, slur, thin 5 gaunt, small, spare 6 adroit, crafty, meager, meagre, scanty, skinny, slight, sparse, svelte 7 cunning, slender, tenuous 9 worthless 10 slenderize

slime: mud 4 gore, ooze, slop 5 cover, filth, gleet, smear 6 mucous

slimer: 8 toadfish

slimy: 4 vile 6 filthy, vulgar 7 viscous 9 glutinous, offensive, repulsive 10 disgusting

sling: 4 cast, hurl, toss 5 drink, fling, throw 6 weapon 7 bandage 9 slingshot

slink: 4 lurk 5 cower, crawl, sneak, steal

slip: err, imp 4 balk, clay, dock, fall, omit, pier, quay, shed, skid, slue, trip 5 berth, chute, elude, error, fault, gaffe, glide, lapse, leash, scion, shift, shoot, slide 6 elapse, harbor, miscue 7 blunder, chemise, cutting, delapse, descend, faux pas, illapse, misstep, mistake, neglect, slither, sluther 8 lingerie, pinafore 9 anchorage, crinoline, gaucherie 12 undergarment

slip away: die 4 pass 5 elude, steal 6 elapse, escape

slip back: 6 revert 7 relapse 8 get worse

slip by: 4 pass 6 elapse

slipknot: 5 noose

slipper: 4 mule, pump, shoe 5 moyle, scuff 6 juliet, pliant, sandal 7 bauchle, scuffer, shuffle, willowy 8 babouche, slippery

slippery: 4 eely, glib, oily 5 slick 6 crafty, shifty, tricky, wanton 7 elusive, evasive, glidder 8 glibbery, unstable 9 deceitful, uncertain 10 unreliable 11 treacherous

slipshod: lax 5 slack 6 sloppy 8 careless, slommack, slovenly, slummock 10 disorderly

slip-up: 5 error 6 miscue 7 failure 9 oversight

slit: cut, rit 4 fent, gash, kerf, nick, open, race, rent, tear 5 break, crack, sever, slash, split, unrip 6 cleave 7 fissure, opening 8 aperture, incision

slither: 4 slip 5 glide, slide 6 rubble 7 rubbish 8 slippery

sliver: cut **5** shred, slice, slops, split **6** strand **7** slobber **8** fragment, splinter

slob: ice, mud **4** boor, mire, ooze, snow **5** slime **6** sloven, sludge **7** bungler

slobber: **4** gush, kiss **5** drool, slime, smarm **6** drivel, slaver, sloven **7** blubber, moisten, slabber

sloe: haw **4** plum **10** blackthorn

slog: hit **4** blow, plod, plug, slam, slug, toil, work **5** drive **6** drudge, strike **9** persevere

slogan: cry **4** word **5** maxim, motto **6** byword, phrase **9** catchword **10** shibboleth

sloop: **4** boat, dray **8** sailboat

slop: mud **4** gulp, gush, mash, plod **5** slush, smock, spill, swill, waste **6** puddle, refuse, splash **7** cassock, clothes, garment, slobber **8** breeches, clothing, trousers

slope: dip, lie **4** bank, brae (Sc.), brow, cant, hang, ramp, rise, tilt **5** bevel, cliff, grade, scarp, slant, talus **6** ascent, aslant, aslope, bajada, depart, escarp, glacis **7** descent, incline, terrace, versant **8** gradient, hillside **9** acclivity, declivity, obliquely **10** declension **11** inclination

angle-measuring device: **10** clinometer

sloping: **6** aslant **7** oblique **8** downhill, inclined, slanting **9** declivous, inclining

sloppy: **5** messy **6** slushy, untidy **7** splashy **8** careless, effusive, slipshod, slovenly

slosh: mud **4** blow, gulp **5** slime, slush, spill, throw **6** splash, wallow **8** flounder

slot: bar, cut **4** bolt, slat, slit, stab **5** crack, track, trail **6** groove, hollow, keyway, spline **7** keyhole, opening **8** aperture, guideway **10** depression

sloth: ai **4** idle, lazy, pack, slow, unau **5** delay **6** acedia, animal, apathy, torpor **7** accidie, inertia, neglect **8** edentate, idleness, laziness, slowness **9** indolence, tardiness

two-toed: **4** anau

slothful: **4** argh, idle, lazy **5** inert **8** inactive, indolent, sluggish **9** sedentary

slouch: hat **4** gait, idle, loll, lout, pipe **5** droop **6** bonnet, loafer, lubber **7** posture **8** drooping, laziness **9** pendulous

slough, slew, slue: bog, mud **4** fall, hull, husk, mire, molt, ooze, plod, road, shed, skin, turn, veer **5** bayou, inlet, pivot, swamp, swing, twist **6** sheath, strike, swerve **7** cast off, channel, discard, mudhole **8** imprison

of despond: **7** despair **10** depression

sloughing: **7** ecdysis

Slovak Republic: *capital:* **10** Bratislava

city: **6** Kosice

currency: **6** koruna

sloven: **4** slob **5** besom, clart **6** loafer **7** hallion **8** slattern **9** scoundrel **11** undeveloped

slovenly: **4** lazy **5** dirty, dowdy, messy **6** blowzy, frouzy, frowsy, frowzy, grubby, sloppy, untidy **7** unkempt **8** careless, slattern, slipshod, sluttish **9** negligent **10** disorderly, slatternly

slow: lax **4** dull, late, poky **5** brosy, delay, grave, hooly, inert, pokey, slack, tardy **6** boring, hamper, hinder, retard, stolid, strike, stupid **7** dronish, gradual, halting, laggard, slacken **8** boresome, dawdling, dilatory, diminish, inactive, plodding, retarded, sluggard, sluggish **9** leisurely, lingering, slowgoing, unhurried **10** decelerate, deliberate, phlegmatic, retrograde

music: **5** largo, lento, tardo **6** adagio

slow down: lap **4** idle **5** delay, relax **6** retard **7** decline **10** decelerate, deliberate

slow loris: **5** kokam

slowness: **5** delay **6** lentor

slowpoke: **5** snail **7** dawdler **9** straggler

slow-witted: **4** bull **6** stupid

sludge: ice, mud **4** mire, ooze, slob **5** slime, waste **7** deposit, mixture **8** sediment **9** settlings

slue: See **slough**

sluff: **4** molt **6** slough **7** cast off, discard

slug: bat, hit **4** blow, dose, dram, slam, slow, snag, stud **5** delay, drink, limax, punch, snail **6** bullet, hinder, loiter, nugget, strike **7** draught, mollusk, trepang **9** gastropod

genus of: **4** doto **5** limax **6** elysia

pert. to: **8** limacine

sea: **7** trepang **10** nudibranch

sluggard: daw **4** idle, lazy, slug **5** drone, idler **7** dawdler, lie-abed, shirker **8** faineant **9** goldbrick, lazybones

slugger: bat **4** goon **5** boxer **6** batter, hitter, mauler **7** batsman **8** operator

sluggish: **4** dull, lazy, logy, slow **5** brosy, faint, heavy, inert **6** bovine, drowsy, leaden, supine, torpid **7** dronish, languor, lumpish **8** dilatory, inactive, indolent, slothful, sluggard, stagnant **9** apathetic, lethargic

sluice: **4** flow, gash, gote, gout, pipe, pour, race, wash **5** flume, flush, swill, valve **6** breach, stream, trough **7** channel, launder, opening, passage **8** irrigate **9** floodgate

sluit: **5** ditch, gulch, gully

slum: **4** dump, junk, room **5** alley **6** barrio, ghetto **7** skid row

slumber: **4** coma, doze **5** sleep **6** drowse, repose **8** lethargy

slumberous: **4** calm **5** quiet **6** drowsy, sleepy **8** peaceful, tranquil **9** lethargic, somnolent, soporific

slump: sag **4** drop, fall, loll, sink, slip **5** droop **6** cave in, slouch **7** decline **8** collapse, downturn **9** downslide, recession **10** depreciate, depression

slur: **4** blot, blur, slip, soil **5** cheat, decry,

elide, glide, slare, slide, smear, stain, sully, trick **6** defame, insult, macule, malign, slight, smirch, stigma **7** blacken, blemish, calumny, dimness, traduce **8** besmirch, disgrace, innuendo, reproach **9** aspersion, criticize, denigrate, discredit, disparage, indignity **10** calumniate

slush: mud, wet **4** gush, mire, muck, pulp, slud, wash **5** grout **6** drench, drivel, sluice, splash **7** mixture, sludder

slut: **4** jade, minx, tart **5** bitch, filth, quean **6** harlot, wanton **8** slattern, strumpet **9** dratchell **10** prostitute

sluttish: **4** lewd **5** gross **6** filthy, sordid **8** slovenly **10** disorderly

sly: **4** arch, cagy, foxy, ruse, slee, wily **5** cagey, canny, coony, snaky, sneak **6** artful, clever, crafty, feline, secret, shrewd, slinky, sneaky, subtle, tricky **7** cunning, evasive, furtive, roguish **8** skillful, sneaking **9** cautelous, deceitful, secretive, underhand **10** fallacious **11** clandestine, dissembling, mischievous, underhanded

slyly spiteful: 5 catty

smack: bit, hit **4** bash, belt, blow, boat, buss, drug, kiss, slap, tang **5** crack, savor, sloop, taste, touch, trace **6** cutter, flavor, heroin, strike, vessel **7** vestige **8** mouthful, sailboat **10** suggestion

smacking: **5** brisk, sharp **6** lively **8** spanking, vigorous

small: dab, sma (Sc.), tot, wad, wee (Sc.) **4** base, cute, lite, mean, puny, thin, tiny, whit, wisp **5** dwarf, minim, minor, petty, scant **6** atomic, dapper, grubby, humble, little, mignon, minute, modest, paltry, petite (F.), remote, slight **7** minimal, selfish, slender, trivial **8** atomical, picayune, trifling **9** miniature, minuscule, thumbnail **10** diminutive

amount: mot **4** atom, chip, drop, iota, mote, tate **5** speck **6** detail, morsel **7** driblet, handful, modicum, morceau (F.), snippet **8** molecule

smallage: 6 celery **7** parsley

small-fry: 4 kids, tots **8** children **10** youngsters

small-minded: 4 mean **5** petty **6** narrow **7** bigoted, selfish **10** prejudiced, ungenerous, vindictive

smallness: 7 elixity, paucity

smallpox: 7 variola

small talk: 4 chat **6** babble, gossip **7** prattle **8** badinage, chitchat

smaragd: 7 emerald

smarm: 4 gush **7** flatter, slobber

smarmy: 8 unctuous

smart: **4** bite, braw, chic, hurt, neat, pain, posh, smug, tidy, tony, trig, wily, wise **5**

acute, alert, brisk, clean, fresh, natty, nifty, quick, sharp, sting, witty **6** active, adroit, astute, bright, cheesy, clever, dapper, dressy, jaunty, lively, modish, shrewd, spruce, suffer, swanky **7** capable, elegant, knowing, pungent, stylish **8** spirited, talented, vigorous **9** competent, dexterous **10** precocious, suffer pain **11** fashionable, intelligent

smarten: **6** spruce **7** improve **8** brighten, spruce up, titivate

smash: hit **4** bash, blow, bung, dash, ruin **5** break, crash, crush, stave, wreck **6** defeat, impact **7** destroy, shatter, smash-up, success **8** collapse, demolish, stramash (Sc.) **9** collision, pulverize **10** bankruptcy

smashed: 5 drunk **11** intoxicated

smashup: **4** ruin **5** wreck **6** defeat, impact **7** failure **8** collapse **9** collision **10** bankruptcy **11** destruction

smatter: **5** break **6** babble, dabble **7** chatter, clatter, crackle, shatter **9** fragments, small bits

smatterer: 7 dabbler **8** sciolist

smear: dab, rub **4** blot, blur, daub, gaum, soil, spot, stop, whip **5** clart, cleam, slake, slare, stain, sully, taint **6** anoint, bedaub, blotch, defame, defeat, defile, grease, malign, smirch, smudge, spread, stigma, thwart **7** besmear, plaster, pollute, slander, splatch **8** besmirch, ointment, slaister **9** overwhelm **10** overspread

smearcase: 6 cheese

smectic: 9 detergent, purifying

smell: **4** funk, fust, odor, olid, reek **5** aroma, flair, scent, sniff, stink, trace **6** breath, stench **7** hircine, noisome, perfume **9** fragrance, redolence **10** suggestion **11** get a whiff of

having a disagreeable: bad **4** foul, olid, rank **5** fetid **6** putrid, rancid **7** noisome, reeking **10** malodorous

loss of sense: **7** anosmia

offensive: **4** reek **5** fetor, nidor, stink **6** stench

pert. to: **9** olfactory

pleasant: **5** aroma, scent **7** perfume

stale: **5** fusty, musty

smeller: 4 nose **6** feeler **7** antenna, bristle

smell-feast: 7 sponger **8** parasite

smelling salts: 9 hartshorn

smelt: 4 fish, flux, fuse, melt, prim **6** iuanga, reduce, refine **7** process, scorify

smelting: *by-product:* **4** slag

smew: 4 duck **9** merganser

smidge, smidgen: bit **4** mite **8** particle

smile: **4** beam, grin **5** smirk, sneer **6** arride, simper

smirch: **4** blot, soil **5** smear, stain, sully, taint **6** blotch, smudge, smutch **7** begrime, blacken, blemish, tarnish **8** besmirch, discolor, dishonor

smirk: **4** grin, leer, trim, yirn **5** quick, smart, smile, sneer **6** simper, spruce **7** grimace, smiling

smite: hit **4** blow, clap, cuff, dash, gird, hurl, kill, pass, slap, slay, swat **5** blast, knock, skite **6** attack, buffet, defeat, hammer, pierce, punish, strike **7** afflict, chasten, clobber, collide, destroy, disease, impress, inspire **8** distress

smith: **6** forger, Vulcan **7** farrier **10** blacksmith, Hephaestus **11** metalworker

smithereens: **4** bits **5** atoms **6** pieces **8** flinders **9** fragments, particles

smithy: **6** forger **7** farrier **10** blacksmith

smitten: **6** fond of **8** affected, enamored, stricken **9** afflicted, enamoured **10** infatuated

smock: **5** kamis, shift, shirt, tunic **6** camise **7** chemise **11** overgarment

smog: fog **4** haze, mist **5** smoke

smoke: **4** floc, fume, funk, haze, mist, pipe, smog **5** cigar, cubeb, segar, **smokejack: 4** flue **6** funnel

smoke out: **5** flush **6** reveal **8** discover

smoker: car **4** stag **5** party

smokestack: **4** pipe **6** funnel **7** chimney

smoky: **4** hazy **5** dingy, fumid **6** fumish, smudgy **9** fumacious

smolder, smoulder: **4** burn **5** choke, smoke **6** smudge **7** smother **9** fulminate, suffocate

smooth: **4** calm, ease, easy, even, flat, glib, iron, lene, mild, oily, pave, sand **5** bland, brent, furry, glace, glary, gloze, level, plane, preen, press, quiet, silky, sleek, slick, soapy, suave **6** creamy, evenly, fluent, gentle, glassy, glossy, mangle, placid, serene, silken, sleeky, urbane **7** amiable, equable, erugate, flatten, plaster, uniform **8** explicit, friendly, glabrous, hairless, levigate, palliate, pleasant, polished, soothing, unbroken **9** courteous, unruffled **10** diplomatic, flattering **11** alabastrine **12** frictionless, ingratiating
phonetically: **4** lene

smoother: **6** sander **7** abraser

smorgasbord: **6** buffet **8** mishmash **9** appetizer **10** assortment, restaurant **12** hors d'oeuvres

smother: **5** choke **6** stifle, welter **7** overlie, repress, smolder, turmoil **8** suppress **9** suffocate

smudge: **4** blot, blur, smug, smut, soil, soot **5** laugh, prink, smear, smile, stain **6** smutch **7** begrime, chuckle, smolder **10** blackening

smug: dig **4** neat, prig, tidy, trim, vain **5** clean, grind, smart, steal, suave **6** pilfer, spruce **7** correct **9** confident **10** blacksmith, complacent **13** sanctimonious, selfsatisfied

smuggler: **6** runner **9** rum runner **10** bootlegger

smurr, smur: **4** mist **5** cloud **7** drizzle

smut: **4** bunt, coom, dirt, mark, soil, soot, spot **5** coomb, fungi, grime, stain, sully, taint **6** blight, defile, smudge **8** besmirch, discolor **9** obscenity **11** pornography

smutch: **4** blot, dirt, smut, soot, spot **5** grime, stain, sully, taint, tinge, touch, trace **6** defile, smudge **7** blacken

smutty: **5** dirty, dusky, sooty **6** soiled, sordid **7** obscene, spoiled, tainted

Smyrna: **5** Izmir
fig: **5** eleme, elemi

snack: bit, sip **4** ball, bite, jibe, nosh, part, snap, tapa (Sp.) **5** acute, alert, chack, lunch, quick, seize, share, smack, taste **6** adroit, canape, morsel, repast, snatch **7** portion, quickly, sharply, teatime **8** grasping, snappish **9** light meal

snaffle: bit **4** curb, loot **5** check, steal **6** pilfer **7** saunter, snuffle **8** restrain **9** bridle bit, restraint

snafu: **4** awry **5** chaos, mix-up **6** muddle **8** disorder, entangle **9** confusion

snag: cut, hew, nag, nub **4** base, carp, knot, part, slug, tear, tine, tree, trim, unit **5** break, catch, fault, point, snail, stump, tooth **6** branch, damage, hazard, tongue **8** obstacle **9** hindrance **10** difficulty, impediment **11** obstruction

snagger: **8** billhook

snail: **4** slug, snag, wilk **5** drone, mitra **6** dodman, tritou, winkle **7** driller, mollusk, testudo **8** escargot, neritine, sluggard **9** gastropod **10** hoddy-doddy
clam-killing: **6** winkle
edible: **5** Helix **8** escargot
genus of: **5** fusus **6** nerita **9** clausilla
poisonous: **4** cone
pond: **5** coret
shell: **7** cochlea **9** operculum

snailflower: **7** caracol

snake (see also **serpent**): asp, boa, nag, rat, sea **4** bind, bull, corn, curl, drag, draw, king, naga, skid, snot, tail, tree, turn, wind, worm **5** aboma, adder, arrow, braid, cobra, coral, crawl, creep, cribo, filch, green, krait, mamba, racer, sneak, steal, viper **6** garter, katuka, python, taipan **7** bokadam, camoodi, elapine, hagworm, ingrate, meander, rattler, reptile, serpent, slither **8** anaconda, bungarum, camoodie, moccasin, ophidian, ringhals **9** boomslang, coachwhip, whipsnake **10** blacksnake, bushmaster, copperhead, massasauga, sidewinder **11** cottonmouth, rattlesnake **12** schaapsteker
big: boa **6** python **8** anaconda
expert: **13** herpetologist
genus of: boa **7** ophidia

horned: **8** cerastes
marine: **6** chital
movement: **7** slither
resembling: **8** viperine
sea: **6** kerril
sound: **4** hiss **6** rattle

snakeberry: **6** byrony **9** baneberry **11** bittersweet **14** partridge-berry

snakebird: **6** darter **7** anhinga, wryneck

snakebite antidote: **5** guaco, serum

snake charmer's flute: **5** pungi

snake dancers: **4** Hopi, Taos **5** Moqui

snakeflower: **7** campion **8** blueweed **10** starflower, stitchwort

snake-haired woman: **6** Gorgon, Medusa, Stheno **7** Euryale

snakehead: **7** figwort **10** turtlehead

snake in the grass: **4** evil **7** traitor **12** hidden danger

snake killer: **8** mongoose **10** road runner

snakelike: **8** ophidian **9** colubrine **10** anguineous
fish: eel, gar **5** moray

snakemouth: **6** orchid **7** pogonia

snakeroot: **6** seneca, senega **7** bugbane, sangrel **9** birthwort **10** bitter-bush

snake-shaped: **9** anguiform

snakeskin: **6** exuvia

snaky: **4** cold, evil, wavy **5** angry **6** touchy **7** anguine, sinuous, winding, wriggly **8** spiteful, twisting, venomous **9** snakelike **10** perfidious, serpentine

snap: rod **4** bark, easy, knap, pass, shut **5** break, catch, chack, cheat, cinch, close, crack, filip, flask, flick, ganch, grasp, hanch, quick, seize, sever, smart, snack, spell, stamp, steal, vigor, wafer **6** biting, breeze, cookie, energy, fillip, report, retort, snatch **7** capture, crackle, project, sharper, sparkle **8** interval, particle, puncheon, sinecure, snapshot **9** crackling, crispness, fastening, handcuffs, interrupt, smartness, snatching **10** elasticity, photograph **11** scintillate
with finger: **6** fillip

snap back: **6** retort **7** rebound, recover

snape: nip **4** snub **5** bevel, check, stint, taper **6** rebuke **8** beveling **10** disappoint

snapper: **4** bean **5** error **6** beetle, bonbon, turtle **7** cosoque, stumble, whopper **8** cachucho, fastener **9** castanets **10** stitchwort, woodpecker **11** firecracker, glassworker, phainopepla

snappish: **4** curt, edgy, tart **5** angry, cross, short, testy **6** cranky, touchy **7** cutting, peevish, uncivil **8** petulant **9** fractious, irascible, irritable **12** sharp-tongued

snappy: **4** cold **5** brisk, quick, sharp, smart **6** lively, spiffy, strong, sudden **7** pungent, stylish **9** copacetic, energetic

snapshot: **5** photo, print **7** picture, tintype **8** polaroid **10** photograph

snare: bag, gin, net, pit, web **4** drum, fang, grin, lure, mesh, toil, trap **5** benet, brake, catch, grasp, noose, steal **6** ambush, cobweb, entice, entoil, entrap, gilder, tangle, trapan, trepan **7** involve, overnet, pitfall **8** entangle, inveigle **9** booby trap, deception **12** entanglement

snark: **5** snore **6** boojum

snarl: arr **4** bark, carl, girn, gnar, harl, hurr, knot, maze, snap, yarr, yirr **5** anvil, catch, ganch, gnarl, gnarr, growl, scold **6** hamper, tangle **7** confuse, grizzle, grumble, involve, quarrel **8** complain, entangle **9** confusion **10** complicate

snarly: **5** cross, surly **7** peevish, snarled, tangled **8** confused

snash: **5** abuse **6** gibing **9** insolence

snatch: bit, get, hap, nab **4** grab, snap, take, trap, yerk **5** braid, catch, clawk, cleek, erept, grasp, gripe, nip up, pluck, seize, snare, spell, stint, swipe, wrest **6** abduct, clutch, kidnap, remove, twitch **7** excerpt, grabble **8** fragment

snatchy: **9** irregular, spasmodic **11** interrupted **12** disconnected

snath, snathe: lop **5** prune, shaft, snead **6** handle

sneak: **4** lurk **5** cower, creep, filch, miche, peach, prowl, rogue, skulk, slink, snoop, steal, thief **6** coward, cringe, pilfer, rascal, secret, snudge, tattle **9** fefnicute

sneaking: sly **4** mean, poor **6** craven, hidden, paltry, secret **7** furtive, hangdog **8** cowardly, stealthy **9** dastardly, niggardly, underhand **12** contemptible **13** surreptitious

sneap: spy **5** sneak **7** reprove

sneb: bar **4** bolt, snub **6** fasten, rebuke **9** reprimand

sneer: **4** gibe, gird, grin, jeer, mock, snub **5** fleer, fling, flird, flout, flurn, scoff, slare, snirl, snort, taunt **7** disdain, grimace, snicker **8** belittle, ridicule

sneeze: **5** neese (Sc.) **7** kerchoo **12** sternutation
pert. to: **7** errhine **12** sternutatory

sneezewort: **8** achillea, ptarmica, ptarmite

snell: **4** hard, keen **5** acute, eager, harsh, sharp, smart, snood, swift **6** active, biting, clever, leader, severe **7** caustic, extreme, pungent, quickly, swiftly **8** piercing **10** vigorously

snick: cut, hit **4** blow, draw, kink, knot, move, nick, snip **5** click, notch, share, shoot, snack **6** pierce, strike

snicker: **5** knife, laugh, neigh, sneer, snirl **6** giggle, hee-haw, titter, whinny **7** chortle, chuckle

snide: low, sly **4** base, mean **6** tricky **7** crooked

8 inferior, spurious **9** malicious

sniff: 4 nose **5** scent, smell, snuff **6** detect, inhale **7** sniffle **8** perceive, sibilate **9** recognize

sniffy: 8 scornful **10** disdainful **12** contemptuous, supercilious

snifter: 4 blow, dram, good **5** drink, sniff, snort, storm **6** goblet, moment, snivel **7** dilemma, reverse **9** excellent

snig: eel, lop **4** chop, drag, jerk **5** snake, sneak **6** pilfer

sniggle: 4 trap **5** catch, eeled **7** broggle

snip: bit, cut **4** clip, curb, minx, snap **5** check, filch, notch, piece, shred, snack **6** snatch, stripe, stroke, tailor **8** fragment, incision, particle **9** disfigure

snipe: 4 bird, butt, fool **5** skunk **8** fire upon **9** criticize **10** sharp-shoot

snipe hawk: 7 harrier

sniper: 6 gunman **7** shooter **8** ambusher **10** bushwacker

snippy: 4 curt, mean, tart **5** bluff, brief, gruff, sassy, saucy, sharp **6** sniffy, stingy **8** snappish, snippety

snit: 5 hissy, pique, tissy **8** angry fit

snitch: 4 nose, tell **5** catch, peach, pinch, steal, thief **6** betray, inform, pilfer, smitch, snatch **8** inform on, informer, particle **9** informant

snivel: cry **4** cant, fret, weep **5** sniff, whine **6** pathos **7** emotion, sniffle, snuffle **8** complain

snob: cut, sob **4** aper, scab **5** toady **6** flunky, poseur **7** cobbler, cricket, flunkey, parvenu, plebian, shoneen, upstart **8** blackleg, bluenose, commoner, parvenue, townsman **9** pretender

snobbish: 7 high-hat **8** scornful **11** overbearing

snood: hat, tie **4** bind **5** braid **6** fasten, fillet, ribbon **7** hairnet

snook: pry **4** bass **5** smell, sneak, sniff **6** follow, robalo, search **7** snuffle **9** barracuda

snooker: 4 dupe, pool **5** cheat **7** deceive

snoop: pry **4** look, nose, peek, peep **5** sneak **6** search **8** busybody **10** Nosy Parker

snooper: 7 marplot, meddler **8** busybody

snoot: 4 face, nose, snub **7** grimace

snooty: 7 haughty, upstage **8** arrogant, snobbish **10** hoity-toity

snooze: nap **4** doze **5** sleep **6** drowse, siesta **7** snoozle

snoozle: 4 doze **5** sleep **6** cuddle, nuzzle **7** snuggle

snore: 4 rout **5** snork, snort **7** saw wood

snoring: 5 stiff **7** roaring, stertor **10** stertorous

snork: pig **5** grunt, snore, snort

snort: 4 rout, slug **5** drink, grunt, laugh, snirl, snore, snork **11** inhale a drug

snotty: 5 dirty, nasty, slimy **6** offish, snooty **7** haughty, viscous **8** impudent, snotlike **9** offensive **12** contemptible

snout: neb **4** mull, nose **5** groin, spout, trunk **6** nozzle **7** conduit, rostrum, tobacco **9** proboscis

snout-nose: 7 gruntle **9** proboscis

snow: con, ice, sna **4** grue, snaw (Sc.) **5** blizz, cover, flake, opium **6** heroin **7** cocaine, deceive **8** obstruct **9** overwhelm, whiteness
  glacial: 4 firn, neve
  granular: 4 corn
  half-melted: 4 slob **5** slush
  house: 4 iglu **5** igloo
  living in: 5 neval
  pellet: 7 graupel
  resembling: 7 niveous
  slide: 8 glissade **9** avalanche
  vehicle: 4 luge, pung, sled **6** sledge, sleigh **8** toboggan **10** snowmobile
  wedding: 4 rice

snow ball: 8 viburnum **11** guelder rose

snow drop: 9 galanthus

snowflake: 4 bird **5** finch **7** bunting, crystal

snow flurry: 5 skirl

snow goose: 4 chen **5** brant, wavey

snow grouse: 9 ptarmigan

snow leopard: cat **5** ounce **7** panther

snow mass: 9 avalanche

snow ridges: 8 sastrugi, zastrugi

snow runner: ski **4** skee

snowshoe: pac, ski **4** skee

snowstorm: 8 blizzard

snowy: 4 pure **5** nival, white **6** chaste **8** spotless, unsoiled

snub: cut, nip **4** chip, curb, slap, stop **5** check, frump, quell, scold, snool, snoot **6** hinder, ignore, rebuff, rebuke, remark, retort, slight, tauten **7** affront, disdain, neglect, repress, setdown, upbraid **8** restrain, send away **9** interrupt, ostracize, reprimand

snuff: 4 odor **5** pinch, pique, scent, smell, sniff, snort **6** detect, inhale **7** offense, tobacco, umbrage **8** sibilate **10** extinguish
  kind of: 5 musty **6** rappee **8** bergamot, Maccaboy **10** blackguard, Copenhagen

snuffbox: 4 mill, mull **9** tabatiere

snuffy: 5 dirty, sulky, vexed **6** horrid **7** annoyed **10** displeased **12** disagreeable, unattractive

snug: 4 bein, bien, cosh, cozy, neat, safe, tidy, trim, warm **5** close, comfy, quiet, tight **6** modest, secure, silent **7** compact, snuggle **8** reticent, secreted, taciturn **9** concealed, seaworthy, secretive **10** prosperous **11** comfortable

snuggery: den **4** nook **7** cottage

snuggle: 4 nest **6** cuddle, nestle

so: sae, sic, sua **4** ergo, thus, true, very **5** hence

7 because **8** likewise **9** in this way, similarly, therefore **11** accordingly **12** consequently

soak: dip, hit, ret, sog, sop, sot, wet **4** bate, blow, bowk, buck, hurl, ooze, pawn, sock **5** binge, drink, drouk, imbue, punch, souse, spree, steep **6** drench, engage, imbibe, imbrue, seethe, tipple **8** drunkard, macerate, permeate, saturate **9** distemper, percolate **10** impregnate, instructor, overcharge
flax: ret
in brine: **4** corn, salt **8** marinate

soaked: wet **6** sodden **8** drenched

soap: **4** sape, sapo, wash **5** money, savon **6** lather **7** cleanse, flatter **8** flattery **9** detergent
convert into: **8** saponify
frame bar: **4** sess
ingredient: lye
mottled: **7** castile **8** eschwege

soap plant: **5** amole

soapstone: **4** talc **8** steatite
full of: **7** talcose

soapy: **4** oily, soft **5** suave, sudsy **6** smooth **7** saponic **8** lathered, unctuous **11** saponaceous

soar: fly **4** lift, rise, sail **5** float, glide, hover, mount, plane **6** ascend, aspire **7** take off **9** transcend

Soave: **12** dry white wine

sob: cry **4** sigh, wail, weep **6** boohoo **7** blubber, whimper **8** frighten

so be it: **4** amen

sober: **4** calm, cool, dark, gray, poor, sane **5** douce, grave, quiet, staid **6** ailing, feeble, gentle, humble, sedate, severe, simple, solemn, somber, steady, subdue, temper **7** chasten, earnest, regular, serious, subdued, weighty **8** composed, decorous, moderate, peaceful, rational **9** abstinent, collected, realistic, temperate **10** abstemious

sobol: **5** sable **6** marten

soboles: **5** shoot **6** stolen, sucker

sobriety: **7** gravity **9** restraint, soberness, solemnity, soundness **10** abstinence, moderation, sedateness, temperance **11** seriousness

sobriquet, soubriquet: **4** name **5** alias, chuck, title **6** byname **7** affront, epithet **8** nickname **9** pseudonym **11** appellation

so-called: **7** alleged, nominal **8** supposed **10** ostensible

soccer player: **4** Pele **6** booter, goalie, kicker, winger **7** striker

sociability: **10** affability

sociable: **4** cozy, sofa **6** chummy, social **7** affable **8** carriage, familiar, friendly, informal, tricycle **9** aeroplane, agreeable, reception, talkative **10** accessible, gregarious

social: tea **4** stag **5** party **6** genial, smoker **9** agreeable, convivial, gathering

affair: tea **4** ball **6** soiree **9** reception
career beginning: **5** debut
climber: **4** snob **7** parvenu, upstart **12** nouveau riche
gathering: bee, tea **4** club, stag **5** dance, party **6** smoker **7** reunion **9** reception
group: **4** clan, club **5** caste, class, lodge, tribe **6** estate, family, jet set **7** coterie **8** sorority **10** fraternity
insect: ant, bee
outcast: **5** leper **6** pariah
person: **4** host **5** mixer **7** hostess
system: **6** feudal, modern, regime, tribal
worker: **7** almoner, analyst **8** do-gooder **9** clinician, deaconess

socialism: **7** etatism **9** Communism **10** utopianism

socialist: Red **6** Fabian **7** Marxist **9** anarchist, Bolshevik, communist

socialize: mix **6** mingle **9** associate

society (see also **organization**): **4** bund, clan, club **5** guild, order, union **6** gentry, jet set, menage **7** academy, company, hetaera, hetaira **8** academie, alliance **9** accademie, community **10** connection, upper crust **11** aristocracy, association, cooperation, intercourse, partnership **12** denomination, relationship **13** companionship, confederation, confraternity
girl: deb
high: **9** beau monde, haut monde
low (member): **4** raff **8** riff-raff
kind of: **4** frat, SPCA, tong **5** choir, elite, order **8** sorority **10** fraternity
secret: Hui **4** egbo, tong **5** lodge, mafia **6** ogboni **7** Camorra **9** Carbonari

Society Islands: **5** Tahaa **6** Moorea, Tahiti **7** Huahine, Maupiti, Raiatea **8** Bora Bora

Society of Friends: **7** Quakers
founder: Fox

sociology: **8** demotics

sock: hit, sew **4** beat, blow, hurl, shoe, sigh, tabi, vamp **5** drive **6** anklet, bootie, buskin, comedy, sandal, strike **7** hosiery, slipper, socking **8** drainage, stocking **9** plowshare

sockdolager: **4** oner **8** clincher, finisher

socket: **5** lance, spear **6** cavity, collet, hollow **7** opening **9** plowshare
kind of: pan **4** birn **5** orbit **8** alveolus

Socrates: *biographer:* **5** Plato **8** Xenophon
birthplace: **6** Athens
love: **10** Alcibiades, philosophy
method: **8** maieutic
poison: **7** hemlock
wife: **8** Xantippe **9** Xanthippe

sod: **4** delf, dove, flag, land, peat, soak, soil, turf **5** delft, divot, glebe, soggy, sward **6** saddle, sodden **7** stratum **9** fermented
pert. to: **8** alkaline

soda: pop, sal **8** beverage **9** saleratus **11** bicarbonate

sodalite: **5** lenad **7** mineral

sodality: **5** union, unity **6** chapel **10** fellowship, fraternity **11** association, brotherhood **13** companionship

sodden: wet **5** drunk, heavy, moist, sammy, soggy **6** boiled, dulled, soaked, stewed, stupid **7** bloated, drunken, steeped **8** spirited **9** saturated **11** intoxicated

sodium: **4** salt **6** alkali **7** natrium
carbonate: **4** soda **5** borax, trona **6** natron **7** salsoda, soda ash
chloride: sal, tar **4** NaCl, salt **7** saltcat
compound: **4** soda
nitrate: **5** niter **9** saltpeter
tetraborate: **5** borax

Sodom: *king:* **4** Bera
neighbor: **8** Gomorrah

sodomite: **6** bugger **8** catamite

sofa: **5** boist, couch, divan **6** daybed, lounge, settee, settle **7** bergere, dosados, ottoman **8** causeuse **9** banquette, davenport **12** chesterfield

so far: yet **4** thus

soft: coy, low **4** easy, feil, fine, limp, mild, waxy, weak **5** bland, cushy, dolce, downy, dulce, faint, givey, hooly, light, mushy, piano, sooth **6** clammy, dreamy, dulcet, flabby, fluffy, gentle, gently, placid, silken, simple, smooth, tender **7** clement, ductile, lenient, lightly, quietly, squashy, subdued, velvety **8** delicate, feminine, flexible, tranquil **9** temperate, tractable, untrained **10** effeminate, peacefully **11** comfortable, sympathetic **12** nonalcoholic
food: pap
mass: **4** pulp
music: **5** dulce, piano
palate: **4** cion **5** uvula, velum
pedal: **6** hush-up **7** silence **8** play down
soap: **4** gush **7** blarney, flatter, wheedle **8** flattery **9** sweet-talk, wheedling

softa: **7** student **8** beginner

soft drink: ade, pop **4** cola, soda **5** tonic

soften: **4** ease, melt **5** allay, malax, relax, yield **6** affect, anneal, gentle, pacify, relent, subdue, temper, weaken **7** amolish, appease, assuage, mollify, soother **8** attemper, enervate, enfeeble, lenitive, macerate, mitigate, modulate **9** alleviate, emolliate, meliorate **10** depreciate, emasculate, intenerate **11** tranquilize

softening: **7** lenient **8** emulsive **9** demulcent **10** moderation **11** melioration
of brain: **8** dementia
of decayed fruit: **4** blet

softhearted: **6** tender

soft-spoken: **4** mild **5** bland, suave **6** gentle, smooth **12** ingratiating

soft touch: **4** snap **6** sucker **8** easy mark, pushover

sog: **4** doze, soak **6** drowse **8** saturate

soggy: wet **4** damp **5** heavy, humid, moist **6** soaked, sodden, watery **9** saturated

soigne, soignee: **4** chic, neat, tidy **5** sleek **7** elegant, stylish **9** dressed up **11** well-groomed

soil: mud, sod **4** blot, blur, daub, dirt, foil, grit, land, loam, moil, mool, muck, slur, spot **5** dirty, earth, filth, glebe, grime, smear, solum, stain, sully, taint **6** assoil, bedaub, befile, befoul, bemire, defile, grease, ground, refuse, sewage, smirch, smudge, vilify **7** begrime, benasty, besmear, corrupt, country, pollute, tarnish **8** alluvium, besmirch, disgrace **9** bedraggle, bespatter, droppings, excrement **11** contaminate
claylike: **4** marl
goddess of: **7** Demeter
kind of: **4** clay, lair, loam, malm, marl, moss **5** adobe, groot, humus, loess **7** topsoil
organic: **5** humus

soiled: **4** foul **5** dingy, dirty, grimy **6** smeary **7** sullied **8** unchaste **9** blemished

soilure: **5** satin **6** smirch

soiree: **4** ball, fete **5** party **6** affair

sojourn: **4** bide, howf, rest, stay, stop **5** abide, abode, delay, dwell, howff, lodge, tarry, visit **6** reside, travel **7** allodge, mansion **8** abidance, vacation **9** residence, tarriance **11** peregrinate

sojourner: **7** boarder, visitor **8** comeling, resident **9** transient **10** vacationer

sol: sun **4** gold **6** Helios, sun god **7** Phoebus

solace: **4** ease **5** allay, amuse, cheer **6** lessen, relief, soothe **7** assuage, comfort, console **9** alleviate, diversion, entertain **10** condolence, recreation, relaxation **11** alleviation, consolation

solan: **4** fowl **5** goose **6** gannet

solar, soler, sollar: **4** loft, roof, room **5** floor, story **6** garret, heliac, tropic **7** chamber **8** heliacal **9** apartment
disk: **4** aten, aton
excess over lunar year: **5** epact

solar system: *member:* sun **4** moon **5** comet **6** planet **8** asteroid **9** meteoroid, satellite
beyond: **9** deep space
model: **6** orrery

solder: **4** fuse, heat, join, mend, weld **5** braze, patch, unite **6** cement **9** sculpture

soldering: *flux:* **5** resin, rosin
piece: lug

soldier (see also **army**): GI, man, vet **4** fogy, swad **5** fogey, GI Joe, guffy, poilu, sammy, shirk **6** galoot, marine, Zouave **7** brigand,

feedman, fighter, hobbler, hotspur, palikar, private, regular, trooper, veteran, warrior **8** bear arms, buffcoat, cavalier, gendarme, malinger, partisan, rifleman, servitor, shackman, tolpatch **9** grenadier, guerrilla, mercenary, musketeer **10** serviceman
cavalry: **6** hussar **8** chasseur
detachment: **4** file
drinking flask: **7** canteen
foreign: **4** kern, peon **5** kerne, nezam, poilu, sepoy, spahi **6** askari, lascar, sapper **7** Billjim, cateran, hoplite **8** grognard, miquelet **10** base wallah, carabineer, carmagnole
group of: **4** army, band, file **5** corps, force, squad, troop **6** legion **7** brigade, caterva, company, platoon **8** division **9** battalion
irregular: **9** guerrilla
mercenary: **7** Hessian, Swisser, Switzer
newly trained: **5** cadet, plebe, rooky **6** rookie **7** chicken, recruit, trainee **8** bezonian **11** replacement
of fortune: **10** adventurer
old: vet **7** veteran **8** grognard
overcoat: **6** capote
quarters: **7** billets **8** barracks **9** Nissen hut **10** Quonset hut
special functions: **6** lancer, sapper **7** dragoon, trooper, velites **8** fencible, fugleman **9** fantassin, flugelman, targeteer **10** carabineer, carabinier, cuirassier, velitation **12** antesignanus
trenching tools: **8** burgoyne
vacation: **4** pass **5** leave, R and R **8** furlough

soldierly: **5** brave **6** heroic **7** martial

sole: one **4** dish, fish, foot, lone, mere, only, yoke **5** afald, alone, floor, plate, slade **6** bottom, entire, furrow, halter, hearth, lonely, single, unique, valley **7** outsole, subsoil **8** desolate, flatfish, isolated, solitary, unshared **9** exclusive, threshold, unmarried, unmatched **10** foundation, one and only, underframe, unsharable, windowsill
foot: **4** vola **5** pelma
part: **5** shank
pert. to: **7** plantar

solecism: **5** error, gaffe **7** faux pas **9** barbarism, deviation **11** impropriety

solely: all **4** only **5** alone **6** merely, simply, singly, wholly **8** entirely **9** allenarly **11** exclusively

solemn: sad **5** budge, grave, sober, usual **6** august, devout, formal, gloomy, ritual, sacred, severe, somber **7** earnest, serious, stately, weighty **8** eloquent, funereal, splendid **9** dignified **10** ceremonial, devotional **11** reverential

solemnize: **5** exalt, marry **7** dignify, glorify, observe **9** celebrate **11** commemorate

soler: **7** cobbler **9** shoemaker

solicit: ask, beg, woo **4** bark, plea, seek, tout **5** court, crave, mooch, tempt **6** accost, arouse, demand, entice, excite, incite, invite, manage **7** beseech, canvass, entreat, forward, implore, provoke, request **8** campaign, disquiet, petition **9** importune, panhandle, prosecute **10** supplicate **12** make advances

solicitor: **4** tout **6** barker, lawyer **8** advocate, attorney **9** barrister **10** counsellor, petitioner

solicitous: **5** eager **7** anxious, careful, worried **8** desirous, troubled **9** attentive, concerned **10** thoughtful **11** considerate **12** apprehensive

solicitude: **4** care, coda, ease, fear, heed, yeme **7** anxiety, concern **8** business **9** attention **11** carefulness **12** apprehension **13** consideration

solid: **4** cone, cube, firm, full, hard **5** cubic, dense, level, sound, stiff, valid **6** bodily, cogent, secure, sphere, stable, strong **7** bedrock, compact, uniform, weighty **8** constant, reliable, sterling, unbroken **9** estimable, unanimous **10** consistent, convincing, dependable, inflexible **11** homogeneous, responsible, substantial, trustworthy
geometrical: **4** cone, cube **5** prism **7** pyramid **8** cylinder **11** heptahedron, pentahedron **12** dodecahedron

solidify: gel, set **4** cake, jell **6** cement, cohere, harden **7** compact, congeal **8** concrete, condense, contract **9** coagulate **11** consolidate, crystallize

solidity: **5** unity **8** firmness, hardness **9** solidness, soundness, stability **11** compactness, consistency **13** dependability

solidum: sum **4** dado

soliloquy: **4** poem **6** speech **9** discourse, monologue, utterance

solitaire: **4** game **6** hermit **7** diamond, recluse **8** Canfield, patience **9** neckcloth

solitary: one **4** hole, lone, monk, only, sole **5** alone, aloof **6** hermit, lonely, remote, simple, single, unique **7** dungeon, eremite, recluse **8** derelict, desolate, lonesome, separate **9** withdrawn **10** antisocial, individual **12** unfrequented

solitude: **6** dearth, desert **7** expanse, privacy, retreat **8** soleness **9** isolation, seclusion **10** loneliness, remoteness, retirement, wilderness ness

sollar: See **solar**

solo: air **4** aria **5** alone, radel, scena **6** flight, strain **9** a cappella, monologue **13** unaccompanied

accompaniment: **8** obligato **9** obbligato
soloist: **6** cantor, singer **7** aviator
Solomon: **7** wise man
  ally: **5** Hiram
  father: **5** David
  gold obtained from: **5** Ophir
  mother: **9** Bathsheba
  son: **8** Rehoboam
  song: **8** canticle
  temple: **6** shamir
Solon: **4** sage **7** senator **8** lawmaker **9** publicist, statesman **10** legislator
soluble: **4** frim **6** solute **11** liquefiable
solus: **5** alone
solute: **4** free **5** loose, solve **7** arrange, soluble **8** dissolve, separate **9** dissolved **13** disintegrated
solution: key **6** answer, result **8** analysis **9** discharge, releasing **10** denouement, resolution **11** deliverance, explanation
  kind of: lye **5** brine, eusol, iodin, sirup, syrup, titer **6** iodine, phenol, saline
  strength of: **5** titer
solve: **4** free, undo **5** break, crack **6** assoil, decode, fathom, have it, unfold **7** dope out, explain, resolve, unravel, work out **8** decipher, dissolve **9** interpret **11** disentangle
solvent: **8** dilution, solution **9** able to pay, detergent
Somalia: *capital:* **9** Mogadishu
  city: **5** Marka **7** Berbera **8** Hargeysa
  currency: **8** shilling **9** centesimo
  measure: top **4** caba **5** chela, darat, tabla **6** cubito
somatic: **6** bodily, carnal **8** parietal, physical **9** corporeal
somber, sombre: sad **4** dark, dern, dull, gray **5** dusky, gloom, grave, sober **6** dismal, gloomy, lenten, severe, solemn **7** austere, ominous **8** funereal **9** depressed **10** depressing, lackluster, melancholy
sombrero: hat **8** headgear, sunshade
some: any, few, one **4** part **5** about **6** nearly **7** certain, portion, several **13** approximately
somersault: **4** flip
something: **5** drink **6** entity, liquor **7** aliquid, whatnot **8** beverage, somewhat
sometime: **4** late, once **6** former, whilom **7** quondam **8** formerly **12** occasionally
somewhat: **6** rather **7** aliquid **9** something, to a degree **10** moderately
Somme city: **6** Amiens **9** Abbeville
sommelier: **6** butler **9** cellarman **11** wine steward
somnambulism: **12** noctambulism, sleepwalking
somnolent: **6** drowsy, sleepy **7** languid
son: ben, boy **4** fils, heir **5** child, scion **6** filius, Jesuit, junior, native **8** disciple, follower,

relative **9** offspring **10** descendant
  pert. to: **6** filial
  youngest: **5** cadet
sonance: **4** tune **5** sound
sonant: **4** oral **5** tonic, vocal **6** voiced **8** sounding **9** intonated
sonata: *closing:* **4** coda
  part: **5** rondo **7** scherzo
song: air, dit, lay, uta **4** aria, call, cant, dite, duan, fuss, glee, hymn, lied, lilt, noel, pean, poem, tune **5** blues, canto, carol, chant, charm, ditty, lyric, melos, music, paean, psalm, rondo, round, verse, vocal **6** anthem, ballad, cantic, cantus, canzon, carmen, chanty, clamor, himene, himine, melody, poetry, shanty, sonnet, strain, trifle **7** cancion, cantion, canzone, chanson, chantey, descant, lullaby, shantey **8** canticle, pittance, serenade **9** cabaletta **11** composition
  baby's: **7** lullaby
  Christmas: **4** noel **5** carol
  collection: **9** anthology **10** cancionero
  college: **4** glee **9** alma mater
  evening: **6** vesper **8** serenade
  funeral: **5** dirge, elegy, elogy **6** elegie, lament, threne **7** elogium, epicede **8** epicedia, threnody **9** epicedium
  German: **4** lied **6** lieder (pl.)
  gypsy: **10** zingaresca
  love: **6** amoret, ballad, serena **8** serenade
  mountaineer's: **5** yodel
  of joy: **5** paean
  operatic: **4** aria
  part: **5** canon, round **8** madrigal
  pert. to: **5** melic
  sacred: **4** hymn **5** carol, chant, motet, psalm **6** anthem **7** polymny
  simple: **5** ditty
  wedding: **6** ariose, arioso **8** hymeneal
songbird: **4** lark, wren **5** mavie, mavis, robin, veery, vireo **6** canary, linnet, mocker, oriole, oscine, thrush **7** mocking, warbler **8** redstart, vocalist
song-like: **7** lyrical
songman: **6** singer **7** crooner, gleeman **8** minstrel **9** balladeer, chorister
songwriter: **8** composer, lyricist
son-in-law: **5** gener **8** beau fils
sonnet: **4** poem, song **5** octet, verse **6** sestet
  conclusion: **6** sestet
Son of God: **5** Jesus **6** Christ, Savior **7** Saviour
sonority: **8** loudness **9** resonance
sonorous: **4** deep, full, loud, rich **7** ringing **8** imposing, resonant **10** impressive, rhetorical
sook (Austr.): **6** coward **7** crybaby
soon: ere **4** anon, fast, yern **5** early, later,

quick, yerne **6** belive, pronto, rather, speedy **7** betimes, by-and-by, erelong, quickly, readily, shortly **8** directly, promptly, speedily **9** presently, willingly **10** beforetime **11** immediately, in the future

sooner: **4** erst **6** before **9** Oklahoman **10** preferably

Sooner State: **8** Oklahoma

soot: **4** coom, smut, stup **5** black, colly, coomb, grime, smoke, sweet **6** carbon, gentle, smudge **7** blacken, residue **9** melodious *particle:* **4** isel, izle *pert. to:* **10** fuliginous

sooth: **4** fact, real, soft, true **5** being, sweet, truly, truth **6** augury, in fact, smooth **7** comfort, genuine, present, proverb **8** pleasing, pleasure, soothing, truthful **10** delightful **11** soothsaying, trustworthy

soothe: coy, pat, pet **4** balm, calm, dill, ease, lull **5** accoy, allay, charm, dulce, quiet, salve **6** pacify, soften, solace, stroke **7** appease, assuage, comfort, compose, console, demulce, flatter, mollify, placate, relieve **8** mitigate, palliate **9** alleviate, attempter **10** demulceate **11** tranquilize

soother: **4** balm, nard **5** salve **7** anodyne **8** ointment **9** emollient, flatterer

soothing: **4** mild **5** balmy, downy, dulce **6** dreamy, dulcet, gentle **7** anodyne, calming **8** lenitive, sedative **9** appeasing, assuasive, demulcent **13** tranquilizing

soothsay: **4** omen **5** augur **7** portent, predict, proverb **8** foretell

soothsayer: **4** seer **5** vates, weird **6** ariole, mantis **7** augurer, diviner, prophet, seeress **8** chaldean, haruspex **10** forecaster, hariolizer **14** prognosticator

sooty: **4** dark **5** black, colly, dingy, dirty, dusky **6** brokie **9** blackened **10** fuliginous

sop: mop, tip, wet **4** blot, dunk, gift, heap, lump, mass, mess, soak, tuft **5** bribe, cloud, clump, steep **6** drench, pay-off **7** advance, milksop **8** gratuity, saturate, weakling

sophist: **7** casuist, teacher, thinker **8** reasoner **10** paralogist **11** philosopher

sophistical: **7** cunning **8** captious, specious **9** deceptive, insincere **10** fallacious **11** adulterated

sophisticated: **4** chic, wise **7** amended, complex, refined, worldly **8** tasteful **9** deceptive, intricate **10** cultivated, misleading **11** adulterated, experienced, worldly-wise **12** cosmopolitan

sophistry: **5** error **6** deceit **7** fallacy, quibble **8** argument, trickery **9** deception **11** insincerity

Sophocles play: **4** Ajax **7** Electra **8** Antigone **10** Oedipus Rex

sopor: **5** sleep **6** apathy, stupor

soporific: **5** dwale **6** drowsy, opiate, sleepy **8** hypnotic, narcotic **9** apathetic **11** somniferous **12** somnifacient, somnivolency

soppy: wet **5** mushy, rainy **6** soaked **7** mawkish **8** drenched **11** sentimental

soprano: **6** singer, treble **9** high voice **12** mezzo-soprano
operatic: **4** Lind, Pons **5** Freni, Melba, Moffo, Patti, Price, Sills **6** Arroyo, Battle, Callas, Norman, Peters, Resnik, Scotto **7** Crespin, Farrell, Kirsten, Lehmann, Nilsson, Stevens, Tebaldi, Traubel **8** Flagstad, Ponselle, te Kanawa **10** Sutherland, Tetrazzini **11** Schwarzkopf **12** de los Angeles

sora: **4** bird, rail

sorcerer: **4** mage, magi **5** boyla, brujo, Goeta **6** boolya, wizard **7** charmer, warlock **8** conjurer, magician **9** occultist **11** necromancer, thaumaturge

sorceress: hag, hex **5** Circe, Lamia, sibyl, witch **6** Gorgon **11** enchantress

sorcery: **5** magic, obeah, spell **6** fetich, fetish, voodoo **7** alchemy **8** pishogue, prestige **9** diablerie, diabolism **10** necromancy, witchcraft **11** enchantment

sordid: low **4** base, mean, vile **5** dirty, gross **6** chetif, filthy, greedy, menial **7** ignoble, selfish, servile, squalid **8** churlish, covetous, grasping, grewsome, gruesome, sluttish, wretched **9** mercenary, niggardly **10** avaricious, despicable, slatternly **12** contemptible

sordor: **4** lees **5** dregs **6** refuse **10** sordidness

sore: raw **4** boil, buck, evil, harm, hurt, kibe, pain, sair **5** angry, blain, botch, grief, ulcer, vexed, wound, wrong **6** bitter, bruise, fester, peeved, severe, sorrel, sorrow, tender, touchy **7** angered, annoyed, disease, extreme, grieved, hostile, painful, penance, trouble, violent **8** abrasion, grievous, inflamed, offended, sickness **9** detriment, irritated, sensitive, suffering, ulcerated, vexatious **10** affliction, afflictive, contrition, difficulty, distressed, unpleasant **11** disgruntled

sorehead: **5** loser **6** griper, grouch **10** malcontent

sorely: **7** greatly **8** severely, urgently **9** extremely, painfully, violently **10** grievously **12** unpleasantly **13** distressingly

soreness: **4** ache, pain **8** severity, vexation, violence **10** bitterness **11** painfulness **12** irritability

sorghum: **4** cush, dura, milo **5** batad, darso, durra, sorgo, syrup **6** shallu **8** feterita, molasses

sorite: **4** heap **10** collection

sorority: **4** club **7** society **10** sisterhood

sorrel: oca **5** brown, color, horse, plant **6** oxalis **7** roselle

sorrow: rue, woe **4** ache, bale, care, dole, harm, hurt, loss, sigh, teen, weal **5** devil, dolor, grief, mourn, rogue, scamp **6** grieve, lament, misery, plague, regret **7** sadness, trouble, waeness **8** calamity, distress, egrimony, mourning **9** adversity, penitence, suffering **10** affliction, compassion, contrition, discomfort, melancholy **11** lamentation, tribulation, unhappiness **12** wretchedness

over: rue **6** bemoan, bewail, lament **7** deplore **9** feel guilt

sorrowful: sad **4** blue, teen **5** drear, sadly **6** dismal, dolent, dreary, rueful, woeful **7** doleful, grieved, unhappy **8** contrite, dolesome, dolorous, grievous, mournful **9** afflicted, plaintive **10** lamentable, melancholy **11** distressing **12** disconsolate

sorry: bad, sad **4** hurt, mean, poor **5** vexed **6** dismal, gloomy, paltry, regret, repent, rueful, vulgar **7** chagrin, doleful, painful, pitiful, unhappy **8** contrite, grievous, mournful, penitent, wretched **9** afflicted, chagrined, miserable, mortified, regretful, worthless **10** apologetic, melancholy, remorseful **12** contemptible, disappointed

sort: ilk, set, way **4** cull, gere, kind, part, race, rank, sift, suit, type **5** adapt, allot, batch, befit, breed, class, genus, grade, group, order **6** adjust, assign, garble, gender, manner, nature, punish, screen, select **7** arrange, conform, fashion, quality, species, stripes, variety **8** classify, separate **9** character **10** collection, distribute **11** accommodate, description

sorted: **6** chosen **8** assorted, selected **9** separated **10** classified

sortie: **4** knot, raid **5** foray, sally **6** attack

sortilege: **7** sorcery **8** witchery **11** enchantment

so-so: bad **4** poor **6** medium, unwell **8** mediocre, middling, passable **9** tolerable **11** indifferent

sot: **4** fool, lush **5** drunk, fixed, toper, waste **6** befool, tipple **7** dastard, guzzler, stupefy, tippler, tosspot **8** drunkard, squander, stubborn **9** alcoholic, immovable, inebriate

sottish: **4** dull **6** stupid **7** doltish, drunken, foolish **9** senseless

sotto: **5** below, under

sotto voce: **5** aside **6** weakly **7** faintly **9** privately

soubise: **5** sauce

soubrette: **4** maid, role **7** actress **11** entertainer, maidservant

soubriquet: See **sobriquet**

soucar: **6** banker **8** merchant, straight **9** honorable

souce: See **souse**

souchong: tea

sough: die, sob **4** moan, sigh, whiz **5** chant, ditch, drain, rumor, whizz **6** murmur, report **7** breathe, moaning, whistle **8** singsong **9** murmuring

soul: ame (F.), God, ker **4** alma (Sp.) **5** atman, being, force, heart, human, saint **6** dibbuk, esprit, fervor, leader, person, pneuma, psyche, spirit **7** courage, essence **8** inspirer **10** embodiment, heartiness, individual

personification: **6** Psyche

soulless: **5** brute

sound: cry, din **4** birr, blow, bray, firm, good, hail, hale, rime, safe, sane, seem, test, tone, true, well **5** alarm, audio, blare, bruit (F.), chang, clang, fresh, grope, hoddy, inlet, legal, loyal, noise, plumb, probe, rhyme, solid, valid, whole **6** bedlam, bratte, clamor, entire, fathom, hearty, honest, hubbub, intact, outcry, racket, report, robust, secure, stable, steven, strong, sturdy, tumult, uproar **7** bluster, clamour, clangor, clatter, clitter, clutter, declare, earshot, examine, explore, feel out, healthy, hearing, measure, perfect, sonance, sputter **8** complete, flawless, orthodox, profound, rational, reliable, shouting, splutter, thorough **9** honorable, undamaged **10** dependable, hullabaloo, scrutinize **11** arm of the sea, trustworthy, undisturbed

amorous: coo

atonic: **4** surd

beating drum: **8** rataplan

bell-like: **4** ding **5** clang, knell **6** tinkle

breathing: **4** rale **5** snore

bullet: zip **4** ping

buzzing: **4** whiz **5** whirr, whizz

cat's: mew **4** meow, mewl, purr

contemptuous: **5** snort

contented: **4** purr

derisive: bah, boo **4** hiss **7** catcall **9** razzberry

discordant: **6** jangle **9** cacophony

donkey's: **4** bray **6** heehaw

dove's murmuring: **4** curr

drum: **4** roll, tuck **8** rataplan

dry leaves: **6** rustle

dull: **4** thud **5** clonk

engine: **4** chug, ping

explosive: pop **4** bang, boom, clap, roar **5** blast **6** report

guttural: **4** burr **5** grunt

harsh: **4** bray **5** creak, twang **9** cacophony

high-pitched: **4** ping, ting

hissing: zip **4** siss

hoarse: caw **4** bray

in doctrine: **8** orthodox

in mind: **4** sane

insect's: **5** chirr

jingling: **16** tintinnabulation
light: **4** peep **5** swish **7** pitapat
loud: **4** bang, boom, peal, roar **5** blare, clang, crash
magnifying device: **9** megaphone **11** loudspeaker
measurement of: bel **4** phon **7** decibel
measure of frequency: **5** hertz
menacing: **5** growl, snarl
mentally: **4** sane **5** lucid **6** normal
metallic: **4** ping, ting **5** clang, clank **6** tinkle
monotonous: hum **4** moan **5** drone
mournful: sob **4** keen, wail
murmuring: **4** purr **5** groan
musical: **4** note
nasal: **5** snore, whine **7** stridor
of bell: **4** ding, dong
of hoofbeat: **4** clop
of horn: **7** tantara
of pain: **4** moan, ouch, yell **5** groan **6** scream **7** screech
of surf: **4** rote
pert. to: **5** tonal **6** sonant **10** acoustical
pleasing in: **8** euphonic
quality of: **6** timbre
repeated: **4** echo
ringing: **5** clang **8** tinnitus
rustling: **8** froufrou
science: **9** acoustics
shallow: **6** lagoon, laguna, lagune
shrill: **5** reedy, skirl
sibilant: **4** hiss, siss
small: **4** peep
solemn: **4** peal
syllabic: **6** sonant
throat: **8** guttural
trumpet: **5** blare **7** clarion
tuning instrument: **4** fork
unvaried: **8** monotone
vibrant: **4** birr
warning: **5** alarm **6** alarum, tocsin
water: **4** klop, rote **5** plash, swish **6** splash
whispering: **8** susurrus
whizzing: **4** ping **5** swish
word imitating a sound: **12** onomatopoeia
yelping: yip
sounded: **4** blew, rang, rung **5** oaten **6** tooted **7** clanged **8** syllabic
sounding: **6** sonant **8** plangent, resonant, sonorous, strident **9** bombastic **11** mellisonant **12** grandisonant, grandisonous
soundless: **4** deep **5** quiet, still **6** silent **9** noiseless **10** bottomless **12** unfathomable
soundly: **6** deeply **7** healthy **8** securely **9** violently **10** completely, forcefully, profoundly, thoroughly
soundness: wit **5** truth **6** sanity **8** lucidity, solidity, strength **9** integrity, rectitude, stability **10** heartiness **11** healthiness

sound off: **7** speak up **8** speak out
sound out: **5** study **7** explore **11** investigate
sounds: *succession of:* **4** peal
vocal symbols: **6** sonant
soup: **5** broth, gumbo, puree, slash **6** bisque, borsch, borsht, oxtail **7** chowder, garbure, shtchee **8** consomme, gazpacho **11** predicament, vichyssoise **12** mulligatawny **13** bouillabaisse
dish: **6** tureen
spoon: **5** ladle
thick: **4** bisk **5** hoosh, puree **6** bisque, burgoo **7** burgout, pottage **8** minestra **10** minestrone
thickener: **6** potato **7** tapioca
thin: **5** broth **8** bouillon, consomme
soupcon: **4** dash, hint **5** taste, trace **7** modicum, portion **8** particle **9** suspicion **10** suggestion
sour: bad, wry **4** acid, dour, grim, hard, tart **5** acerb, acrid, cross, eager, gruff **6** acetic, bitter, cruety, morose, sullen **7** acetose, acetous, acidify, austere, crabbed, painful, peevish **8** acerbate, acescent, embitter, vinegary **9** acidulate, acidulent, acidulous, fermented **10** afflictive, astringent, ill humored, unpleasant **11** distasteful **12** disagreeable
source: **4** base, fons, font, germ, head, rise, root, seed **5** cause, fount **6** ascent, origin, parent, spring **7** edition **8** fountain, wellhead **9** beginning **10** wellspring **12** fountainhead
of contrary action: **7** reagent
of income: **4** wage **6** salary **7** revenue **10** investment
of indigo: **4** anil
of inspiration: **4** Muse
of knowledge: **7** organon
of metal: ore
primary: **4** root **5** radix
sourdine: **5** muted **7** subdued
sourdough: **5** bread **6** leaven **7** settler **10** prospector
sourness: **7** acidity **8** acerbity, acrimony, asperity, tartness **10** moroseness **16** disagreeableness
sourpuss: **5** crank **6** grouch **8** sorehead **10** complainer
soursop: **4** tree **9** guanabana
souse, souce, sowce, sowse: ear, jag, sot, wet **4** blow, cuff, duck, fall, prop, soak, wash **5** bathe, brine, douse, drink, drunk, swoop, thump **6** drench, pickle, plunge, pounce, strike, thwack **7** heavily, immerse, tippler **8** clumsily, drunkard, saturate, steeping, submerge **9** drenching
soutache: **5** braid **8** trimming
soutane: **5** cloak **7** cassock, zimarra

South Africa: *animal:* das **5** nenta **8** suricate
antelope: gnu **5** eland, leche, oribi, peele **6** lechee, lechwe, rhebok **7** blaubok, blesbok, boshbok, grysbok, rheeboc, rheebok, sassaby **8** blesbuck, bontebok, boschbok
armadillo: **4** para
ass: **6** quagga
assembly: **4** raad **9** Volksraad
aunt: **5** tanta
bay: **5** Algoa, False
blaubok: **5** etaac
breastwork: **6** scherm
bushman: **4** Qung
camp: **5** lager **6** laager
cape: **7** Agulhas **8** Good Hope
capital: **8** Cape Town, Pretoria
caterpillar: **6** risper
cattle enclosure: **5** kraal
city: **6** Durban, Soweto **9** Germiston **12** Bloemfontein, Johannesburg **13** Port Elizabeth
cliff: **4** klip
club: **10** knobkerrie
colonist: **4** Boer
conference: **6** indaba
cony: das
corn: **5** mealy **6** mealie
criminal: **8** amalaita
currency: **4** cent, rand **5** pound **6** florin
dialect: **4** Taal
diamond: **5** jager **9** schlenter
Dutch: **4** Boer, Taal
Dutch speech: **9** Afrikaans
farmer: **4** Boer
ferry: **4** pont
foreigner: **9** uitlander
fox: **4** asse **5** caama
garment: **6** caross, kaross
gazelle: **9** springbok
goldfield: **4** rand
grass country: **4** veld **5** veldt

greenhorn: **5** ikona
gully: **5** donga
gun: **4** roer
hill: kop **8** spitzkop
hillock: **5** kopje
hippopotamus: **6** zeekoe
hog: **9** boschvark
hut: **8** rondavel, rondawel
javelin: **7** assagai
laborer: **4** togt
lowland: **4** vlei, vley
monkey: **6** vervet **8** talapoin
mountain: kop **9** Swartberg
pass: nek
people: **4** Xosa, Zulu **5** Bantu, Namas, Pondo, Sotho, Xhosa **6** Tswana **8** Bechuana **9** Hottentot
plain: **5** veldt
plant: **4** aloe
plateau: **6** Karroo
plot: erf
polecat: **6** musang
policeman: **4** zarp
political group: ANC **7** Inkatha
river: **4** Vaal **6** Molopo, Orange **7** Limpopo
rodent: **5** ratel
segregation policy: **9** apartheid
shrub: **6** protea
simpleton: **5** ikona
snake: **5** elaps **8** eggeater
spirit: **8** tikolosh
starling: **5** sprew **7** spreeuw
stream: aar
sumac: **6** karree
throng: **4** reim **7** riempie
tick: **6** tampan
tract: **9** zuurveldt
tree: **5** tenio **7** assagai **8** gamdeboo
village: **5** kraal
warrior: **4** impi
weaverbird: **4** taha
whip: **7** sjambok

South America: *animal:* **4** paca **5** coati, coypu, llama, sloth, tapir **6** alpaca, caiman, jaguar, nutria, vicuna **7** guanaco **8** anteater, capybara **9** armadillo
ant: **5** sauba, sauva **7** hormiga
anteater: **7** tamandu

arbor: **6** ramada
armadillo: **4** apar **7** tatouay **10** pichiciago
arrow poison: **6** curara, curare
balsam: **4** tolu
beast of burden: **5** llama
beef: **6** tasajo (*cont.*)

South America *(cont.)*
> *beverage:* **4** mate
> *bird:* **4** aura, guan, mitu, myna, rara, taha **5** agami, arara, chaja, egret, macaw, mynah **6** barber, barbet, parrot, toucan **7** aracari, jacamar, oil-bird, seriema, tinamou **8** bellbird, boat-bill, curassow, flamingo, guacharo, puffbird, rhea yeni, screamer, terutero **9** guaca-mayo
> *blanket:* **6** serape
> *boat:* **6** cayuco
> *cactus:* **7** airampo
> *catfish:* **5** dorad
> *cattle ranch:* **6** rancho **8** estacion, estancia
> *country:* **4** Peru **5** Chile **6** Brazil, Guyana **7** Bolivia, Ecuador, Uruguay **8** Colombia, Paraguay, Suriname **9** Argentina, Venezuela
> *cowboy:* **6** gaucho **7** llanero, planero
> *cowboy's weapon:* **5** bolas
> *dance:* **5** mambo, samba **6** cha-cha
> *deer:* **6** guemal, guemul
> *dove:* **9** talpacoti
> *duck:* **7** muscovy
> *estuary:* **4** Para **5** Plata
> *farm:* **5** finca
> *fish:* **4** paru **6** aimara, carbie **7** piranha, scalare **8** arapaima, pirarucu
> *fox:* **4** asse
> *game:* **6** pelota
> *grassland:* **5** llano, pampa
> *griddle cake:* **5** arepa
> *hare:* **6** tapeti
> *hawk:* **8** caracara
> *herb:* **9** romerillo
> *herdsman:* **7** llanero
> *Indian:* Ges, Ona **4** Auca, Inca, Tama **5** Carib, Tapas **6** Arawak, Jivaro **7** Caya-pos, Goyanas, Guatoan, Pampero, Tapuyan **8** Camacans, Coroados, Tim-biras **9** Caingangs, Chavantes **10** Patag-onian
> *Indian hut:* **5** toldo
> *island:* **5** Aruba **6** Staten, Tobago **7** Bonaire, Curacao **8** Malvinas, Trinidad **9** Falklands, Galapagos, Margarita **14** Tierra del Fuego
> *language:* Ona **7** Spanish **9** Portuguese
> *lapwing:* **8** terutero
> *liberator:* **7** Bolivar
> *limestone:* **5** tosca
> *liquor:* ron **6** chicha

> *lizard:* **4** teju **5** coati
> *lowlands:* **6** llanos, pampas, selvas
> *mammal:* ai **4** paca **5** coati, llama, tapir **6** alpaca, guanco **8** kinkajou, pacarana **10** coati-mondi, coati-mundi
> *marmoset:* **7** tamarin
> *measure:* **4** vara **7** manzana
> *mineral:* **4** urso
> *monkey:* sai **4** saki, titi **5** acari, araba **6** grison, teetee **7** ouakari, sapajou **8** mar-moset, orabassu **9** barrigudo, beelze-bub
> *mountains:* **5** Andes **6** Acarai, Parima
> *opossum:* **5** quica **7** sarigue
> *ostrich:* **4** rhea
> *palm:* **5** assai, bussu, datil, troly **6** tooroo, ubussu **7** troolie
> *parrot:* **5** macaw
> *plant:* **6** ipecac **8** crassula **10** tillandsia
> *plateau:* **10** Mato Grosso
> *porridge:* **5** atole
> *rabbit:* **6** tapeti
> *rain forest:* **5** selva
> *rancher:* **8** ranchero **10** estanciero
> *river:* **4** Para **5** Plata **6** Amazon **7** Orinoco
> *rodent:* **4** degu, mara, paca **5** coypu **6** agouti, agouty **8** viscacha, vizcacha **10** chinchilla
> *root:* oca
> *rubber tree:* **4** para
> *scarf:* **5** manta
> *shrub:* **4** coca
> *silver:* **5** plata
> *slaughterhouse:* **11** frigorifico
> *snake:* bom **4** lora **5** aboma **8** anaconda **10** bushmaster
> *sorrel:* oca
> *strait:* **8** estrecho, Magellan
> *tapir:* **5** danta
> *tiger cat:* **5** chati, tigre
> *toucan:* **4** toco **7** aracari
> *tree:* **4** fotu, lana, mora, para, vera **5** balsa, cacao, cebil, couma, pekea **6** chicha, simaba, yachan **7** bebeeru, quayabi **9** balaustre, chinchona, cou-vatari, quebracho **11** chichicaste
> *trumpeter:* **5** agami
> *tuber:* oca
> *vulture:* **6** condor
> *walnut:* **9** conacaste
> *weapon:* **4** bola **5** bolas
> *wild cat:* **4** eyra
> *wind:* **7** pampero

South: **5** Dixie
  crop: **6** cotton **7** tobacco
  dish: **4** okra **5** gumbo **7** hoecake **9** hush
  puppy
  inlet: **5** bayou
South Africa: (see box)
South American: **5** Latin **6** Latino

South Carolina: *capital:* **8** Columbia
  city: **8** Rock Hill **10** Charleston,
  Greenville **11** Spartanburg
  fort: **6** Sumter **8** Moultrie
  Indian: **7** Catawba, Yamasee **8** Cherokee
  mountain: **9** Blue Ridge, Sassafras
  resort: **10** Hilton Head **11** Myrtle
  Beach
  river: **6** Peedee, Saluda, Santee **8**
  Savannah
  state bird: **4** wren
  state flower: **7** jasmine **9** jessamine
  state tree: **8** palmetto

South Dakota: *capital:* **6** Pierre
  city: **8** Aberdeen **9** Rapid City **10** Sioux
  Falls
  Indian: **5** Brule, Sioux **6** Dakota,
  Lakota **7** Arikara **8** Cheyenne
  mountain: **10** Black Hills
  region: **8** Badlands
  river: **5** James **7** Big Bend, Randall **8**
  Cheyenne, Missouri
  state animal: **6** coyote
  state bird: **8** pheasant
  state flower: **12** pasqueflower
  state tree: **6** spruce

Southeast Asia: **4** Laos, Siam **5** Burma **6**
  Brunei, Ceylon **7** Myanmar, Vietnam **8**
  Cambodia, Malaysia, Pakistan, Thailand **9**
  Indonesia, Kampuchea, Singapore **10**
  Bangladesh **11** Philippines
southeast wind: **5** eurus
southern: **7** austral
Southern France: **4** Midi **7** Riviera
South Korea: *capital:* **5** Seoul
  city: **5** Pusan, Taegu **6** Inchon
  currency: won **4** chon
South Pacific: See **South Sea**
South Pole: See **Antarctica**
South Sea: *canoe:* **4** proa
  island: **4** Bali, Fiji, Sulu **5** Samoa, Tonga **6**

Tahiti **7** Society **8** Pitcairn **9** New Guinea
  island currency: **6** wakiki
  island drink: ava
  islander: **5** Maori **6** Kanaka, Samoan **10**
  Melanesian, Polynesian **11** Micronesian
  plant: **4** taro
Southwest: *cowboy:* **7** llanero
  Indian: **4** Cree, Zuni **6** Navaho, Navajo
southwester: hat **4** gale **5** squam, storm **7** oilskin, rain hat
southwest wind: **8** libeccio
south wind: **5** notus **6** auster
South Wind author: **7** Douglas
souvenir: **5** curio, relic **6** memory **7** memento
  8 keepsake, reminder **11** remembrance **12**
  recollection
sovereign: **4** coin, czar, free, king, tsar, tzar **5**
  chief, liege, queen, royal, ruler **6** couter,
  Kaiser, Mikado, prince **7** emperor,
  empress, highest, monarch, supreme **8**
  absolute, autocrat, greatest, princely,
  reigning, superior, suzerain **9** governing,
  potentate **10** omnipotent **11** controlling,
  independent
  petty: **6** satrap **8** tetrarch
sovereign prerogative claim: **11** seigniorage
sovereignty: **4** rule, sway **5** realm **6** diadem,
  empery, empire, status, throne **7** dynasty,
  majesty, scepter, sceptre **8** dominion **9**
  authority, supremacy **10** ascendancy, ascendency, domination
  absolute: **8** autarchy
  joint: **11** condominium
soviet: **7** council, Russian **8** assembly **9** committee
Soviet Union: **4** CCCP, USSR
  administrative committee: **9** presidium
  currency: **5** ruble
  founder: **5** Lenin
  government farm: **7** sovkhos, sovkhoz **8**
  sovkhose
  hero: **5** Lenin **6** Stalin
  news agency: **4** Tass
  newspaper: **6** Pravda **8** Izvestia
  secret police: KGB **4** NKVD, OGPU
sow: hog, pig **4** heap, seed, shed **5** ditch,
  drain, drill, plant, stack, strew, swine **6** runner, sluice, spread **7** channel, furnish,
  grumphy, implant, scatter **8** disperse,
  grumphie **9** broadcast, inoculate **10** salamander **11** disseminate
  wild: **8** javelina
  young: elt **4** gilt
sower: **7** seedman
  of dragon's teeth: **6** Cadmus
sowse: See **souse**
soya: **4** dill **6** fennel **7** soybean
soy bean: **4** soja, soya
  bean curd: **4** tofu

spa: **5** oases, oasis **6** resort, spring **10** sanatorium
  place: Ems **4** Bath **5** Baden **8** Karlsbad,
  Saratoga **14** Sulphur Springs
space: gap **4** area, path, rank, roam, room,
rove, void, walk **5** ambit, plena (pl.), range,
track **6** course, divide, extent, plenum,
region **7** areolae, arrange, expanse **8** capacity, distance, duration, interval, quantity **11**
reservation
  agency: **4** NASA
  architectural: **8** pediment
  between eyes: **4** lore
  between two points: **8** distance
  blank: **6** lacuna **7** lacunae (pl.)
  breathing: **6** recess **7** respite
  cleared: **5** glade
  coin: **7** exergue
  docking: **6** linkup
  empty: **4** void **5** blank, inane **6** vacuum
  forest: **4** glen **5** glade
  hollowed: **7** mortice, mortise
  included: **8** contents
  limitless: **8** infinite
  occupied: **6** volume
  of time: **8** interval
  on surface: **4** area
  partitioned: **4** room **11** compartment
  pert. to: **5** areal
  portion of: **5** place
  safekeeping: **4** bank **7** storage **9** strong box

  secluded: **5** niche **6** alcove
  small: **6** areola, areole **7** aerolae
  storage: **4** shed **5** attic **6** cellar, closet **8**
  basement **9** storeroom, warehouse
  telescope: **6** Hubble
  void: **5** abyss, chasm **7** inanity
  wall: **5** niche
  white: **6** margin
spacecraft: **6** rocket **7** shuttle **9** satellite
  first: **7** Sputnik
  part: **6** module **7** capsule
  to moon: **6** Apollo
spaced out: **4** high **5** doped **6** spacey, stoned,
zonked **7** drugged
space full of matter: **6** plenum
spaceman: **9** astronaut, cosmonaut
spacer: bar
space theory: **7** plenism
spacious: **4** vast **5** ample, broad, great, large,
rangy, roomy **9** capacious, expansive, extensive
spad: **4** nail
spadassin: **5** bravo **7** duelist **9** swordsman
spade: dig **4** pick, suit **5** graft **6** shovel, trowel
11 playing card
  Irish: **5** slane
  kind of: **6** scavel
  narrow: loy
  plasterer's: **6** server
  sharp: **4** spud
  triangular: **5** didle
  turf: **5** slane

Spain: **6** Espana, Iberia
  adventurer: **9** almogaver
  ancient name: **8** Hispania
  article: el, la, las, los, una, uno **4** unos
  aunt: tia
  avocado pear: **8** aguacate
  bay: **5** bahia **6** Biscay
  bayonet plant: **5** yucca
  beach: **5** playa
  belle: **4** maja
  blanket: **5** manta **6** serape
  boat: **5** aviso
  brandy: **11** aguardiente
  bull: **4** toro
  capital: **6** Madrid
  cart: **7** carreta **8** carretta
  cedar: **6** acajou
  celery: **4** apio
  cellist: **6** Casals
  chaperone: **5** duena **6** duenna
  cheer: ole
  chili: aji
  city: **4** Vigo **6** Bilbao, Malaga **7** Granada,

  Seville **8** Valencia **9** Barcelona, Saragossa
  clerk: **11** escribiente
  cloak: **4** capa **5** manta **6** mantle
  coat: **6** abrigo **7** zamarra, zamarro
  conqueror: Cid **7** Pizarro **12** conquistador
  contract: **7** asiento **8** assiento
  council: **5** junta
  count: **5** conde
  currency: **5** dobla **6** cuarto, doblon,
  peseta **7** Alfonso, centimo, piaster **8**
  cuartino **9** cuartillo
  dance: **4** jota **5** baile, danza, tango **6**
  bolero, gitano **8** fandango, flamenco,
  saraband **9** paso doble, zapateado **10**
  seguidilla
  dish: **6** posole
  dollar: **4** duro, peso, pezo **7** piaster, piastre
  dumpling: **6** tamale
  earth: **6** tierra
  east: **4** este **7** oriente
  exclamation: **7** caramba, carrajo (*cont.*)

Spain (*cont.*)
execution: **7** garotte, garrote **8** garrotte
explorer: **7** Mendoza **8** Coronado
fabric: **5** tiraz
festival: **6** fiesta
fleet: **6** armada
friend: **5** amiga, amigo
frigate: **5** zabra
game: **5** omber **6** pelota **7** jai-alai
gentleman: don **5** senor **9** caballero
god: **4** dios
goddess: **5** diosa
gold: oro
governor: **10** gobernador, idelantado
grass: **5** spart **7** esparto
greeting: **4** hola
griddlecake: **5** arepa
guitarist: **7** Segovia
gunboat: **5** barca
gypsy: **7** zincalo
hall: **4** sala
head covering: **8** mantilla
herdsman: **8** ranchero
hero: Cid **8** Palmerin
hill: **5** cerro, morro
holiday: **6** fiesta
horse: **7** caballo
hotel: **5** venta **6** posada
house: **4** casa
instrument: **8** castanet, zambomba
judge: **7** alcalde
kettle: **4** cazo
lady: **4** dona **6** senora
lagoon: **6** laguna
lake: **4** lago
lariat: **5** reata, riata
leather: **5** cuero **8** cordovan
legislature: **6** cortes
letter: **5** carta
linen cloth: **4** crea
lute: **7** vihuela
magic: **8** brujeria
mail: **6** correo
man: don **5** senor **6** hombre
mausoleum: **8** Escorial
mayor: **6** alcade **7** alcalde
measure: pie **4** codo, copa, dedo, moyo, paso, vara **5** aroba, braza, cafiz, cahiz, legua, linea, medio, milla, palmo, sesma **6** cordel, cuarta, estado, fanega, league, racion, yugada **7** azumbre, cantara, celemin, estadel, pulgada **8** aranzada, fanegada **9** cuarteron, cuartilla, cuartillo **10** caballeria
miss: **8** senorita
monk: **5** monje, padre

mountain range: **8** Asturian, Pyrenees **9** Mulahacem **10** Cantabrian, Pic de Netou **11** Guardarrama, La Maladetta **12** Sierra Morena, Sierra Nevada **14** Sierra de Toledo
mouth: **4** boca
muleteer: **7** arriero
native: **7** Catalan, Iberian
nobleman: don **7** grandee, hidalgo
north: **5** norte
now: **5** ahora
nun: **5** monja **6** Teresa
officer: **8** alguacil, alguazil
operetta: **8** zarzuela
other: **4** otro
oyster: **5** pinna
painter: **4** Cano, Dali, Goya, Miro, Sert **6** Ribera **7** El Greco, Murillo, Picasso, Zuloaga **9** Velasquez
palace: **7** alcazar **8** Escorial
peasant: **4** peon **7** paisano
peninsula: **7** Iberian
pepper: **5** chili **7** pimento
pickpocket: **6** ratero
plateau: **6** meseta
poet: **6** Encina **7** Jimenez, Unamuno **11** Garcia Lorca
porridge: **5** atole
pot: **4** olla
priest: **4** cura **5** padre
promenade: **5** paseo
pronunciation mark: **5** tilde
raisin: **4** pasa **7** uva pasa
rice: **5** arroz
rider: **8** herisson
river: ria, rio **4** Ebro **5** Douro, Tagus **8** Guadiana **12** Guadalquivir
road: **6** camino
room: **4** sala
sentinel: **5** vedet, videt **7** vedette, vidette
shawl: **5** manta **6** serape
sherry: **5** Xeres **11** Amontillado
silk: **5** tiraz
sorcerer: **5** brujo
south: sur
stanza: **10** seguidilla
street: **5** calle
sword: **5** bilbo
tax: **8** alcabala
title: don **4** dona **5** senor **6** senora **7** hidalgo **8** senorita
tomorrow: **6** manana
trefoil: **7** alfalfa, lucerne
uncle: tio
vase: **4** urna (*cont.*)

Spain *(cont.)*
> *vehicle:* **7** tartana
> *very:* muy
> *watchword:* **6** alerta
> *water:* **4** agua
> *watercourse:* **6** arroyo
> *weight:* **4** onza **5** frail, grano, libra, marco, tomin **6** adarme, arroba, dinero, dracma, ochava **7** arienzo, quilate, quintal **8** caracter, tonelada **9** escrupulo **10** castellano
> *west:* **5** oeste **9** occidente
> *white:* **6** blanco
> *wind:* **6** solano
> *window:* **7** ventana
> *witchcraft:* **8** brujeria
> *woman:* **4** dona **5** mujer **6** senora

spaghetti: **5** pasta **8** linguine **10** vermicelli

spahi, spahee: **7** cavalry, soldier

Spain: (see box)

spall: **4** chip, fall **5** break **6** reduce **7** breakup, crumble **8** fragment, shoulder

spalpeen: boy, fop, lad **5** rogue, scamp **6** rascal **7** laborer, workman **8** braggart **9** youngster

spalt: **4** chip, tear **5** crisp, split **7** brittle

span: **4** arch, cock, pair, rope, swim, team, time **5** cover, grasp, range, reach, seize, vault **6** attach, bridge, extend, fasten, fetter, hobble, length, period, spread **7** confine, matched, measure, stretch **8** distance, duration, encircle **9** encompass, perfectly **10** completely

spancel: tie **4** clog **6** fetter, hobble

spang: **4** bang, hurl, jump, kick, leap, yoke **5** clasp, crack **6** stride **7** spangle **8** abruptly, directly, ornament, straight

spangle: set **4** boss **5** adorn, aglet, gleam, plate **6** aiglet, sequin, zequin **7** glisten, glitter, sparkle **8** ornament, sprinkle, zecchino

spaniel: **5** trasy **6** cocker, punish **7** clumber **8** Brittany, springer **9** sycophant **11** King Charles

spank: **4** beat, blow, cane, prat, slap, whip **6** strike **7** reprove **8** chastise

spanker: **4** sail

spanking: new **4** fine **5** brisk, fresh, large, stout **6** lively, strong **7** dashing **8** vigorous

spanner: **6** wrench

spar: bar, box, rod **4** beam, bolt, boom, gaff, mast, pole, raft, rung, shut, yard **5** bandy, close, fight, lever, lunge, sprit, steve **6** barite, bicker, charge, fasten, rafter, strike,

thrust, timber **7** contend, contest, dispute, enclose, quarrel, wrangle, yardarm **8** dolomite, lazulite
> *end:* **7** yardarm

spare: **4** bare, bear, free, gain, hain, lean, part, save, slim, slit, slow, stop, thin **5** avoid, chary, extra, favor, gaunt, grant, lanky, stint **6** desist, endure, exempt, favour, frugal, let off, meager, scanty, scrimp **7** deprive, forbear, forgive, haggard, leisure, opening, placket, refrain, relieve, reserve, sparing **8** dilatory, forebear, preserve, tolerate **9** duplicate, parsimony **10** substitute **11** replacement, superfluous **12** parsimonious

spare time: **7** leisure

sparge: **6** splash **7** moisten **8** sprinkle **9** bespatter

sparing: **5** chary, gnede, scant **6** frugal, meager, saving, scanty **7** careful, limited, thrifty **8** merciful, reticent, stinting **9** scrimping **11** tightfisted

spark: arc, woo **4** beau, funk, soil **5** aizle, belle, blade, court, dandy, flash, gleam, glint, grain, light, lover **6** escort, glance **7** diamond, gallant, shimmer, sparkle, spatter **8** motivate, sparklet **9** scintilla **10** sweetheart **11** scintillate

sparked: **5** arced **7** courted, spotted **8** streaked **10** variegated

sparker: **5** lover **7** gallant **8** firework

sparkle: **5** blaze, blink, flash, gleam, glent, glint, shine, spark, strew, trace **6** bubble **7** diffuse, glisten, glitter, reflect, scatter, showing, spangle, twinkle **8** sprinkle, vivacity **9** coruscate **10** effervesce, liveliness **11** coruscation, scintillate

sparkling: **4** dewy **5** crisp, witty **6** bright, lively, starry **7** shining **8** animated, eloquent, flashing, gleaming **9** brillante, brilliant, twinkling **10** glittering, reflecting **12** effervescent, effervescing

sparoid fish: **4** scup **5** porgy **10** sheepshead

sparrer: **5** boxer **7** sparrow

sparrow: **7** chanter

sparse: few **4** thin **5** scant **6** meager, meagre, scanty **7** scatter **8** disperse **9** scattered **10** distribute, infrequent

Sparta: **9** city-state **10** Lacedaemon
> *army:* **4** mora
> *bondman:* **5** helot
> *commander:* **7** lochage
> *country:* **7** Laconia
> *dog:* **10** bloodhound
> *enemy:* **6** Athens
> *festival:* **6** Carnea **7** Carneia
> *governor:* **7** harmost
> *king:* **8** Leonidas, Menelaus **9** Tyndareus
> *lawgiver:* **8** Lycurgus

magistrate: **5** ephor
method of cipher writing: **7** scytale
native: **8** Laconian
queen: **4** Leda **5** Helen
serf: **5** helot
tyrant: **5** Nabis

spartan: **5** brave, hardy, stoic **6** frugal, heroic, severe **7** austere, laconic **9** undaunted **10** courageous

spasm: fit, tic **4** grip **5** cramp, crick **6** frenzy **7** seizure **8** paroxysm **10** convulsion **11** contraction
muscle: **5** cramp
of pain: **5** throe

spasmodic: **6** fitful, sudden **7** snatchy, violent **9** excitable **12** intermittent
disease: **7** tetanus

spat: row **4** blow, clap, fuss, slap, tiff **5** eject, fight **6** gaiter, oyster, splash, strike **7** dispute, legging, quarrel **8** squabble

spate: **4** gush, rain **5** flood **6** throng **7** freshet, outflow, torrent **8** cataract **9** overwhelm, rainstorm **10** waterspout

spatial: **5** areal **6** steric **8** sterical

spatter: jet **4** dash, drop, soil, spot **5** slart, smear, spray, spurt **6** dabble, defame, injure, splash, spread, squirt **7** scatter, spatule, sputter **8** splutter, sprinkle

spatterdash: **6** gaiter, puttee **7** legging

spatula: **4** tool **5** spade **6** thible, turner

spatulate: **6** lyrate **11** spoon-shaped

spawn: roe **4** eggs, germ, seed, sire, spot **5** fungi **6** bulbis, source **7** cormels, deposit, produce **8** generate, mycelium **9** procreate
ascending river to: **10** anadromous

spay: **4** geld **6** neuter **8** castrate **9** sterilize

speak: say **4** carp, chat, hail, talk, tell **5** extol, honor, mouth, orate, state, utter **6** remark, reveal **7** address, bespeak, chatter, declaim, declare, deliver, express, mention, publish **8** converse, harangue, manifest, proclaim **9** celebrate, discourse, enunciate, pronounce **10** articulate
affectedly: **4** mimp **5** mince
against: **6** oppose
at length: **7** dissert **9** expatiate
curtly: **4** bark, birk, snap
evasively: **5** hedge, stall **9** obfuscate
foolishly: **5** prate **6** drivel **7** blather
for: **5** claim **6** defend **7** testify
from memory: **6** recite
hesitantly: **7** stammer, stutter
imperfectly: **4** lisp **7** stutter
impulsively: **5** blurt
inability to: **4** mute **6** alalia, mutism **7** aphasia **8** aglossia
incoherently: **6** gabble, gibber
in undertone: **6** mumble, murmur **9** sotto voce

of: **4** call **6** recall **7** mention
offhand: **11** extemporize
oracularly: **11** pontificate
out: **6** affirm, assert
profusely: **6** dilate **7** palaver
rapidly: **5** troll **6** patter **8** splutter
rhetorically: **5** orate **7** declaim
slightingly: **5** sneer **6** gossip **8** backbite **9** disparage
slowly: **5** drawl
softly: **7** whisper
thoughtlessly: **4** blat **8** splutter
through nose: **9** nasillate
to: **5** greet **6** accost, answer **7** address **11** acknowledge
under breath: **6** mumble, mutter
with interruption: haw, hem

speaker: **5** drone, sayer **6** lisper, orator, proser, ranter, talker **7** utterer **8** lecturer **9** spokesman **10** mouthpiece, prolocutor **11** entertainer
inspired: **7** prophet
of many languages: **8** linguist, polyglot

speaker's hammer: **5** gavel

speaking: *style:* **8** fluently, staccato
without preparation: **13** extemporizing

spear: gad, rod **4** dart, fram, pike, reed, shut, spar, stab **5** apine, blade, lance, shoot, stalk **6** aprout, glaive, impale, pierce, strike **7** bayonet, feather, harpoon, javelin, missile, trident **9** penetrate
grass: **5** blade
kind of: **4** gaff, pole **5** gidia, gidya, sling **6** bident, fizgig, gidgea, gidgee, gidjee, gidyea **7** assagai, assegai, bourdon, harpoon, leister, trident
three-pronged: **7** trident

spearfish: **8** billfish **9** swordfish

spearhead: **4** gaff, lead **6** direct **7** advance, precede

spear-shaped: **7** hastate

spearwort: **8** crowfoot

special: **4** dear, rare, sale **5** chief, extra, local **6** unique **7** express, limited, notable, unusual **8** favorite, paramour, peculiar, personal, specific, standout, uncommon **10** individual, noteworthy, particular, restricted **11** distinctive, exceptional **12** particularly **13** distinguished
ability: **6** talent

specialty: **5** forte, major, skill **6** talent **8** aptitude, strength

specie: **4** cash, coin **5** money **8** currency

species: **4** kind, race, sort, type **5** breed, brood, class, genre, genus, image **7** mankind, variety **8** category, humanity **9** spectacle **10** exhibition, reflection
various: **5** genus **6** genera

specific: **5** exact **6** remedy **7** express, precise,

special 8 clearcut, concrete, definite, detailed, explicit, peculiar 10 particular, restricted, specifying 11 determinate

specifically: 6 namely 9 expressly, specially

specify: 4 cite, name, tell 5 allot, state 6 assign, define, detail, select 7 itemize, mention 8 describe, indicate, nominate 9 designate, enumerate, stipulate 10 articulate

specimen: 4 mark 5 model, relic, token 6 cotype, sample, swatch 7 example, pattern 8 instance 11 examination 12 illustration

specious: gay 4 fair, fake, sham 5 false, showy 6 glossy, hollow 7 colored 8 coloured, illusory, spurious 9 colorable, plausible 10 ostensible 12 hypocritical

speck: bit, dot, nit 4 blot, iota, mark, mite, mote, spot, whit 5 glebe, stain 7 blemish, blubber 8 impurity, particle

speckle: dot 5 fleck 7 stipple

speckled: 4 pied 6 dotted, menald 7 bracket, mottled, spotted 8 stippled

specs: 10 eyeglasses, spectacles

spectacle: 5 bysen, drama, model, scene, sight 6 marvel, mirror 7 diorama, display, example, pageant, pattern 8 panorama 10 exhibition

structure for: 5 arena 7 stadium, theater, theatre 8 coliseum

spectacles: 6 lenses 7 glasses

part of: 6 bridge, temple

spectator: 4 eyer 6 espier, voyeur 7 watcher, witness 8 beholder, kibitzer, looker-on, observer, onlooker

specter: 4 bogy 5 bogey, bogie, bogle, demon, ghost, haunt, shade, spook 6 boggle, spirit, wraith 7 boggard, boggart, bugaboo, bugbear, phantom 8 boggle-bo, guytrash, illusion, phantasm, revenant 10 apparition

spectral: 5 eerie 6 ghosty, spooky 7 ghostly, phantom 12 apparitional 13 insubstantial

spectrum: 5 range 8 infrared 11 ultraviolet 15 electromagnetic

colors: red 4 blue 5 green 6 indigo, orange, violet, yellow

speculate: 4 muse, risk 5 guess, think 6 gamble, hazard, mirror, plunge, ponder, reason, wonder 7 predict, venture 8 consider, meditate, ruminate, theorize 10 conjecture, deliberate, philosophy 11 contemplate

speculation: 4 risk 6 bubble, vision 7 surmise 8 decision 9 guesswork, intuition 10 conclusion, conjecture

speculative: 5 risky 9 uncertain 11 theoretical

speculator: 7 gambler, lookout, scalper 8 explorer, observer, theorist 12 contemplator, investigator

speculum: 6 mirror 7 diopter

speech: gab 4 talk 5 idiom, lingo, slang, spiel,

voice 6 accent, dilogy, epilog, orison, steven, tongue 7 address, dialect, oration, oratory, palaver, vinegar 8 colloquy, epilogue, harangue, language 9 utterance

abusive: 6 tirade

art: 8 rhetoric

bitter: 8 diatribe

blunder: 8 solecism

boastful: 7 bluster 11 rodomontade

bombastic: 8 harangue

conclusion: 10 peroration

defect: 4 lisp 6 alogia 7 stammer, stutter

denunciation: 5 frump 6 tirade 8 filippic 9 philippic

difficulty: 9 baryphony 10 baryphonia

element: 4 surd

expert: 9 phonetist

figure of: 5 irony, trope 6 aporia, simile 7 imagery 8 metaphor

hesitation: haw 7 stammer, stutter

impassioned: 6 tirade 8 harangue 9 dithyramb

insane: 9 bedlamism

local: 6 patois 7 dialect

long: 5 spiel

loss: 6 alalia 7 aphasia 8 muteness

part: 4 noun, verb 6 adverb 7 pronoun 9 adjective 11 conjunction, preposition 12 interjection

peculiar: 5 idiom

readiness: 8 glibness 9 fecundity

religious: 6 homily, sermon 9 preaching

violent: 6 tirade

voiceless element: 4 surd 7 spirate

speechless: mum 4 dumb, mute 6 silent 9 voiceless 12 inarticulate

speed: hie, rip 4 dash, drug, fare, flee, help, race, rate 5 haste, hurry, tempo 6 assist, career, gallop, hasten, hustle, profit, succor 7 execute, prosper 8 celerity, dispatch, expedite, rapidity, velocity 9 advantage, discharge, quickness, swiftness 10 accelerate, expedition, facilitate 11 amphetamine

full: 5 amain

great: 4 zoom 5 amain, haste, spurt 6 career 9 posthaste

measuring device: 5 radar 8 odometer 10 tachymeter 11 speedometer, velocimeter

rate of: RPM 4 pace 5 tempo

ratio: 4 Mach

up: 6 hasten 8 catalyze

speeder: 5 racer 6 driver 11 accelerator

speedily: 4 fast, soon 5 apace 6 presto 7 betimes, hastily, quickly, rapidly 8 promptly 13 expeditiously

speedy: 4 fast 5 fleet, hasty, quick, rapid, swift 6 active, prompt, sudden 7 express, helpful 11 expeditious

spell: bar, peg 4 chip, form, lath, mean, rest,

rung, save, snap, tale, talk, tell, trap, turn **5** brief, charm, curse, magic, relay, shift, spare, speak, spell, story, utter, weird, while **6** glamor, gospel, import, period, relate, relief, splint, trance, voodoo **7** bewitch, cantrip, compose, drought, glamour, relieve, shaving, signify, sorcery, syncope **8** pishogue, splinter **9** discourse **10** constitute, demonifuge **11** abracadabra, conjuration, enchantment, fascination **12** entrancement **13** orthographize, prognosticate

in another alphabet: **13** transliterate

out: **7** clarify, develop, explain **9** interpret

spellbind: **5** charm, orate **7** enchant, engross **8** enthrall, transfix **9** fascinate

speller: *according to pronunciation:* **9** phonetist **11** phoneticist

poor: **11** cacographer

spelt: **5** grain, wheat **6** cereal

spelter: **4** zinc

spencer: wig **4** coat **6** butler, jacket, pantry **7** buttery, steward, trysail

spend: pay, run, use **4** blow, dash, flow, give, jump, lose, pass, shop, span **5** beset, exert, grasp, waste **6** attach, bestow, beware, devote, elapse, expend, fasten, lavish, lay out, manage, spread, spring, weaken **7** consume, exhaust, fatigue, perform **8** confound, disburse, shell out, squander **9** dissipate, sacrifice **10** distribute

wisely: **6** manage **7** husband

spend the summer: **8** estivate

spendthrift: **6** waster **7** wastrel **8** prodigal, wasteful **10** dingthrift, profligate, squanderer

Spenserian character: Una **8** Gloriana **12** Faerie Queene

spent: **4** beat, paid, used **5** all in, weary **6** bushed, effete, wasted **7** drained, worn out **8** lavished **9** exhausted **10** squandered

speos: **4** cave, tomb **6** grotto, temple

sperm: **4** germ, seed **5** semen

sperm whale: **8** cachalot

spet: **9** barracuda

spew, spue: bog **4** gush, ooze, spit **5** belch, eject, exude, retch, strew, vomit **7** extrude, flow out, scatter **8** disgorge

sphacelate: **7** decayed **8** withered **9** mortified

sphenic: **11** wedge-shaped

spheral: **7** perfect **10** harmonious **11** symmetrical

sphere: orb, sky **4** ball, rank, star, zone **5** ambit, arena, class, field, globe, orbit, order, range, reach, realm, round, scope **6** circle, domain, orblet, planet, region **7** circuit, compass, heavens, station, stratum, terella, theatre **8** dominion, function, idiosome, position, province **9** idioblast **10**

atmosphere, department, occupation **12** jurisdiction

of action: **4** ring, site, zone **5** arena, field **7** theater

of influence: **5** orbit

perforated: **4** bead

spheric: **8** globular **11** globe-shaped

spherical: **5** orbic, round **6** rotund **7** globate, globose, spatial **8** globated, globular, obrotund **9** globulous, orbicular

spheroid: **4** ball **5** earth

spherule: **7** globule, variole

sphinx: **6** enigma **7** monster, prophet **8** colossus, hawkmoth

land of: **5** Egypt

mother: **7** Echidna

query of: **6** riddle

site of: **4** Giza **5** Luxor

sphinxian: **10** mysterious **11** enigmatical, inscrutable

sphygmus: **5** pulse

spica: **4** star **7** bandage

spice: **4** dash, hint, kind, mace, mull, nard, odor, sort, vein **5** aroma, taste, touch **6** embalm, flavor, relish, season **7** modicum, perfume, portion, species, variety **8** quantity, specimen **9** admixture, condiment, fragrance, seasoning

kind of: **4** mace, mull, sage **5** anise, cumin, curry, thyme **6** cloves, fennel, ginger, nutmeg, pepper, stacte, tamara **7** caraway, cayenne, mustard, oregano, paprika, pimento **8** allspice, cinnamon, marjoram, pimiento, turmeric **9** coriander

mill: **5** quern

package for: **6** robbin

spick-and-span: **4** neat, trim **5** clean, fresh **6** spruce **7** band box **8** brand-new, spotless **11** well-groomed

spicknel: mew **8** bearwort

spicule: rod **4** dart, nail, toxa **5** aster, spine **6** actine **7** prickle, rhabdus **8** sclerite, spikelet

sponge: **5** cymba

spicy: hot **4** keen, racy **5** balmy, natty, showy, smart, sweet, tangy **6** active, risque **7** gingery, peppery, piquant, pungent, zestful **8** aromatic, fragrant, spirited **11** interesting

spider: bug, cob, cop, hub, pan **5** arain **6** epeira, eresid, snarer, tripod, trivet **7** pokomoo, retiary, skillet **8** arachnid, attercop, telarian **9** frying pan, tarantula **12** candleholder

family of: **7** attidae **9** drassidae **10** citigradae

genus of: **6** aranea, epeira

three-legged: **6** trivet

venomous: sac **9** tarantula **10** black widow, brown widow **11** varied widow **12** brown recluse **14** red-legged widow

web-spinning organ: **9** spinneret
spider bug: **5** emesa
spider crab: **4** maia
spider monkey: **9** belzebuth
spider nest: web **5** nidus
spider web: **8** attercop
   resembling: **9** arachnoid
spiel: **5** pitch **6** speech
spieler: **5** crier **6** barker, talker **7** sharper, showman, speaker **8** lecturer, swindler **9** announcer **11** spellbinder
spiffy: **4** chic, neat **5** smart **6** spruce
spifflicate, spifflicate: **4** beat, kill **6** stifle **8** astonish, bewilder, confound
spigot: peg, pin, tap **4** cock, plug **5** spile, spout **6** dossil, faucet, nozzle, pierce **7** stopper
spike: cob, cut, ear, gad **4** barb, brob, chat, nail, pike, stab, tine, umbo **5** ament, block, prong, thorn **6** antler, cereal, earlet, fasten, finish, impale, needle, pierce, secure, thwart **7** bayonet, disable, fortify, trenail **8** mackerel, puncture **9** frustrate, merganser
spikenard: **4** nard **8** ointment
spile: pin, rod, tap **4** bung, heap, pile, plug, rule, tube **5** spill, spout, stake **6** spigot **7** stopper **8** forepole, splinter
spill: die, mar, peg, pin, rod **4** disk, fail, fall, flow, kill, roll, ruin, shed, slip, slop, tell **5** flosh, spile, spoil, spool, waste **6** betray, injure, perish, punish, reveal, sheath, tumble, wasted **7** confess, correct, destroy, divulge, scatter **8** chastise, downpour, gratuity, overflow, spillway, splinter, squander **11** deteriorate
Spillane's detective: **10** Mike Hammer
spiloma: **5** nevus **9** birthmark
spin: **4** birl, burl, gyre, pirl, reel, ride, turn **5** drive, spurt, swirl, twirl, twist, wheel, whirl **6** gyrate, rotate **7** prolong, revolve **8** protract
spina: **4** wall **8** backbone
spinach: **7** epinard, potherb
   family: **9** goosefoot
spinal: **5** balas
   area: **4** dorsal, lumbar, sacral **8** cervical, thoracic **9** coccygeal
   column: **6** rachis **8** backbone **9** vertebrae
   cord: **4** alba **6** myelon
   disease: **5** polio **8** myelitis
   layer: **4** dura
   muscle: **5** psoas
spin a yarn: **7** narrate
spindle: pin, rod **4** axis, axle, hasp, roll, stem **5** arbor, fusee, shaft, spool, stalk, xeres **6** arbour, bobbin, broach, fuseau, rachis **7** mandrel
spindling: **4** weak **5** leggy **7** slender **11** ineffectual
spine: awn **4** back, seta **5** chine, ridge, thorn **6**

chaeta, needle, spirit **7** acantha, acicula, courage, prickle, spicule **8** backbone, spiculum **9** vertebrae
spine bone: **6** sacrum **8** vertebra
spineless: **4** weak **7** slavish **11** ineffectual **12** invertebrate
spinet: **5** piano **7** giraffe **8** virginal **11** harpsichord
spine-tingling: **4** eery **5** eerie, scary **7** ghostly **8** exciting
spinnaker: **4** sail
spinner: cap, top **5** spoon **6** spider, weaver **8** narrator **10** goatsucker
spinney: **5** copse, grove **7** thicket
spinning: **5** areel **6** rotary **8** whirling **9** revolving
   device: **7** distaff
   machine: **4** mule **5** jenny **8** throstle
spinning wheel: **6** charka **7** charkha
spin-off: **9** byproduct, outgrowth
Spinoza work: **6** Ethics
spinster: **7** old maid **10** maiden lady **12** bachelorette
spiny: **6** picked, thorny **7** prickly **9** acanthoid, difficult
spiny-footed: **10** acanthopod
spiny shrub: **4** ulex
spiracle: **4** hole, pore, vent **6** breath **7** orifice **8** aperture, blowhole
spiral: **4** coil, curl **5** curve, helix **7** coiling, curving, helical, winding **8** circling, helicoid **9** corkscrew **11** anfractuous
spire: **4** coil, curl **5** blade, stalk, tower, twist, whorl **6** fleche, sprout **7** sapling, steeple
   finial: epi **4** epis
   ornament: **6** finial
spirit: hag, pep, vim **4** aitu, alma, brio, dash, dook, elan, fire, gimp, kami, life, mood, soul, wind, zeal **5** angel, ardor, bugan, dhoul, ethos, fairy, fling, ghost, haunt, heart, lares, manes, metal, pluck, shade, spook, spunk, verve, vigor **6** animus, ardour, asuang, breeze, daring, elixir, energy, esprit, ginger, mettle, morale, pneuma, psyche, shadow, temper, wraith, yaksha (mas.), yakshi (fem.) **7** animate, bravery, courage, entrain, hearten, loyalty, phantom, specter **8** folletto, phantasm, vivacity **9** animation, encourage **10** apparition, enterprise, enthusiasm, get-up-and-go **11** disposition, inspiration, poltergeist
   air: **5** Ariel
   animating: **6** animus
   avenging: Ate **6** alecto, erinys **7** megaera, nemesis **9** tisiphine
   away: **6** abduct, kidnap, snatch
   evil: Ate, imp, Ker **4** baka, beng, boko, drow, gyre **5** bugan, demon, devil **6** animus, asuang, daemon, daitya, dibbuk,

Erynes, Lilith **9** cacodemon
female: **6** undine **7** banshee, banshie **8** succubus
fire: **4** Agni
good: **5** genie, genus **7** eudemon
heralding death: **7** banshee, banshie
kinds of: akh, imp, lar, nat **4** arac, gimp, Kuei, Kwei, soul **5** angel, Ariel, duffy, duppy, dusio, ethos, genie, jinni, manes, rakee, shade **6** animus, fulgja, jinnee, mammon, tangie, Undine **7** banshee
lose: **7** despond
male: **7** incubus
mischievous: imp **4** Puck **6** goblin **7** brownie, gremlin **10** leprechaun **11** poltergeist
of censure: **5** Momus
of people: **5** ethos
spirited: gay **4** bold, fell, gamy **5** brisk, eager, fiery **6** active, audace, birkie, feisty, ginger, lively, spunky **7** animato, dashing, zealous **8** animated, desirous, eloquent, frampoid, generous, vigorous **9** audacious, energetic, spiritoso, sprightly, vivacious
horse: **5** steed **7** charger
spirit-land: **9** fairyland
spirit-leaf: **8** manyroot
spiritless: **4** cold, dead, meek **5** amort, blate, vapid **6** flashy **7** daviely, hilding, languid **8** dejected, feckless, flagging, lifeless, listless, thewless **9** apathetic, depressed, exanimate, heartless **10** dispirited
spiritlike: **8** ethereal
spirits (see also **alcoholic drink**): **4** grog, mood **5** booze **6** liquor **7** alcohol
dash of: **5** lacer
dead: **5** manes
dwelling place of: Po **5** Hades **7** Elysium
kinds of: **6** furies, uplift **7** elation, Sammael **9** firewater **13** aquacaelestis
lift: **5** elate **7** gladden
low: **5** blues, dumps, gloom **6** gloomy **8** doldrums
spiritual: **4** holy, hymn, pure, song **6** devout, divine, sacred **7** ghostly **8** churchly, internal, platonic, spirited **9** animastic, geistlich, unworldly **10** devotional, immaterial **11** animastical, disembodied, incorporeal
apathy: **6** acedia
being: ens **5** angel, entia (pl.) **6** seraph
darkness: **4** Hell **5** tamas
spiritualistic meeting: **6** seance
spiritualize: **5** endow **6** purify, refine **7** animate **8** idealize **11** etherealize
spirituous: gay **4** airy, hard **5** vivid **6** active, ardent, lively **7** tenuous **8** ethereal **9** alcoholic **10** immaterial
spiry: **4** tall **6** coiled, curled, spiral **7** slender **8** tapering, wreathed **10** serpentine

spit: dig, fix, rod **4** emit, hang, rain, reef, snow **5** eject, image, light, plant, reach, retch, shoal, spade, stick, sword, utter **6** broach, dagger, impale, saliva, skewer, sputum, thrust **7** spindle, spittle, sputter **8** barbecue, broacher, likeness, sandbank, spadeful, sprinkle **9** brochette, secretion **11** counterpart, expectorate
spital: den **6** refuge, resort **7** shelter **8** hospital **9** lazaretto
spite: vex **4** hate, mood **5** annoy, depit, pique, shame, venom **6** enmity, grudge, hatred, injury, malice, mauger, maugre, rancor, spleen, thwart **7** chagrin, despite, dislike, ill-will, mortify **8** disgrace, dishonor **9** animosity, antipathy, frustrate, hostility, humiliate **10** resentment **11** malevolence
spiteful: **4** mean **5** catty, cruel, snaky **6** sullen **7** hostile, vicious, waspish **8** annoying, venomous **9** malicious, malignant **10** dispiteous, irritating, malevolent, vindictive **11** troublesome
spitfire: **6** virago **7** sulphur **8** aircraft **9** brimstone
spitter: **4** deer **5** spade **7** brocket **8** spitball
spitting: **6** saliva **10** exspuition **13** expectoration
spitting image: **4** twin **6** double, ringer
spittle: **4** peel, spit **6** saliva, sputum
spittle insect: **10** froghopper
spittoon: **8** crachoir, cuspidor
spiv (Br.): **4** tout **7** slacker **8** parasite **10** petty thief
splash: lap **4** dash, daub, gout, lave, mark, plop, pond, pool, spot **5** bathe, blash, slart, slash, spray **6** blotch, dabble, flouse, floush, strike **7** display, feature, scatter, spatter **8** splatter **10** appearance, excitement
splashboard: **4** gate, trap **5** board, plank **6** fender, screen **8** mudguard
splashy: wet **5** muddy, showy **6** blashy, slushy, watery **8** striking **11** sensational, spectacular **12** ostentatious
splat: **4** open, plot, spot **5** patch **6** blotch **7** flatten
splatter: dab **4** dash, rush **6** hubbub, splash **7** cluster
splay: hem **4** awry, turn **5** adorn, bevel, carve, slant, slope **6** clumsy, expand, spread **7** awkward, display, diverge, sloping **8** ungainly **9** dislocate, expansion, obliquely, slopingly, spreading **10** slantingly **11** enlargement
spleen: ire **4** fire, milt **5** anger, ardor, freak, mirth, organ, spite **6** choler, enmity, malice, temper **7** dislike, ill-will, impulse **8** ill-humor, laughter **9** lienculus, merriment **10** melancholy **11** impetuosity
pert. to: **6** lienal

spleeny: 5 angry 7 fretful, peevish 9 irritable 10 melancholy

splendent: 6 glossy 7 beaming, shining 8 lustrous, splendid 9 brilliant 11 conspicuous, illustrious, magnificent, resplendent

splendid: gay 4 braw, fine, good, rial 5 grand, regal, showy, tinny 6 bright, candid, costly, superb 7 gallant, ripping, shining, sublime 8 glorious, gorgeous, imposing, palatial 9 brilliant, elaborate, excellent, grandiose, important, sumptuous, wonderful 10 impressive 11 illustrious, magnificent, resplendent

splendor: 4 gite, pomp 5 blaze, eclat, gleam, glory, sheen 6 bright, fulgor, luster, parade 7 display 8 elegance, grandeur, radiance, richness 9 pageantry, showiness 10 brightness, brilliance, brilliancy, effulgence 12 gorgeousness, magnificence, resplendence

splenetic: 6 sullen, vapory 7 fretful, peevish, splenic 8 choleric, spiteful 9 depressed, irascible, irritable, malicious, spleenful 10 melancholy

splice: 4 join 5 marry, unite 6 fasten 7 wedding 8 marriage 10 interweave

splint: 4 coal, lath, scob, tace 5 brace, plate, split, strip, tasse 6 fasten 7 confine, support

splinter: 4 chip, rend 5 break, broom, piece, slice, smash, spale, split 6 fasten, shiver, sliver 7 confine, flinder, shatter 8 fragment

split: cut, rit 4 chap, reft, rend, rent, rive, ruin, tear 5 break, burst, clave, cleft, crack, peach, reave, riven, share, wedge 6 betray, bisect, bottle, breach, broken, cleave, cloven, dilute, divide, rifted, schism, sliver, sunder 7 destroy, dispart, divided, fissure, portion, rupture, shatter 8 fragment, informer, separate, splinter 9 fractured, separated 10 separation

in two parts: 5 bifid 6 cloven, halved 8 bisected 9 bipartite

up: 5 sever 7 break-up, divorce 10 separation

split pea: dal

splitting: 5 funny 6 severe 7 comical, fission, rending 8 piercing

splotch: dab 4 blob, blot, dash, daub, mark, spot 5 smear, stain 6 blotch, mottle, splash 7 blemish

splurge: 5 spend 6 effort, splash 7 display, indulge 8 squander 11 ostentation

splutter: 4 fuff 5 hurry, noise, stuff 6 bustle, splash 7 bluster, dispute, glutter, quarrel, scatter, spatter, stammer 8 nonsense 9 confusion

Spode: 5 china 9 porcelain

Spohr opera: 8 Jessonda

spoil: mar, rob, rot 4 baby, blad, boot, loot, pelf, prey, rape, ruin, swag 5 bitch, blend, booty, carve, cheat, decay, harry, prize, seize, strip, taint, waste 6 coddle, damage, deface, divest, forage, impair, infuse, injure, pamper, perish, ravage, thwart 7 connach, corrupt, deprive, despoil, destroy, estrepe, indulge, pillage, plunder, violate, vitiate 8 confound, unclothe 10 chevisance, corruption, impairment

eggs: 5 addle

spoiled: bad 4 sour 5 dazed, moldy, musty 6 addled, marred, molded, petted, preyed, rancid, rotted, ruined, turned 7 botched, damaged, decayed, tainted 8 pampered, pillaged 9 plundered

spoiler: 6 robber 7 marplot 8 marauder, pillager 9 despoiler, plunderer 10 depredator

spoilsport: 7 killjoy 10 wet blanket

spoke: bar 4 clog, grip, pole, rung, tale, talk 5 block, check, drone, round, spake, stake, stick 6 radius 7 uttered 8 handhold 10 impediment

spoken: 4 oral, said 5 parol, vocal 6 verbal 7 uttered 9 declaimed

spoliate: rob 6 ravage 7 despoil, pillage, plunder

spoliation: 4 loss 6 rapine 7 pillage, plunder, robbery 8 pillaged 11 destruction

spondyl: 8 vertebra

sponge: bum, wet 4 form, swab, wipe 5 ascon, cadge, dough, erase, mooch 6 absorb, ascula, efface, rhagon 7 badiaga, cleanse, destroy, drinker, scrunge, zimocca 8 drunkard, parasite, scrounge

calcareous: 6 leucon

orifice: 6 oscula (pl.) 7 osculum

pen: 5 kraal

pert. to: 9 poriferal

spicle: 4 toxa

vegetable: 5 loofa, luffa 6 loofah

sponger: 5 leech 6 cadger 7 moocher 8 parasite

sponge tree: 8 huisache

spongewood: 4 sola

spongy: 4 fozy, soft 5 rainy 6 porous, quaggy 9 absorbent

sponsor: 4 back 5 angel, rabbi 6 backer, gossip, mentor, patron 8 champion, endorser, promoter 9 godfather, godmother, introduce, supporter

sponsorship: 4 egis 5 aegis 7 backing 8 auspices

spontaneous: 4 free, wild 6 native 8 careless, untaught 9 automatic, impetuous, impromptu, impulsive 10 indigenous, self-acting 11 instinctive, involuntary

spontoon: 4 club, pike 6 cudgel 7 halberd, pantoon 9 truncheon

spoof: guy 4 fool, hoax, joke 5 trick 7 deceive, swindle 8 nonsense 9 deception

spook: spy 5 annoy, ghost, haunt, scare 6

spirit, wraith **7** specter, startle **8** frighten **9** hobgoblin **10** apparition **11** make nervous

spooky: **4** eery **5** eerie, weird **6** creepy **7** ghostly, haunted, uncanny **8** spectral

spool: **4** reel, wind **6** bobbin, broach, holder **7** spindle **8** cylinder

spoon: pet, woo **4** neck **5** court, labis, ladle, lover, ninny **6** nestle, shovel, spoony **7** student **8** cochlear, golf club **9** simpleton **10** bill and coo

spoonbill: **5** ajaja **8** shoveler **10** paddlefish

spoon-fed: **7** coddled **8** pampered

Spoon River poet: **7** Masters

spoon-shaped: **8** cochlear, spatular

spoor: **4** clue, hint, odor **5** piste, scent, trace, track, trail

spore: **4** cyst, germ, seed

spore sac: **5** ascus **7** capsule

sport: bet, fun, gig, toy **4** game, gaud, glee, jest, joke, mock, play, polo, romp **5** dally, freak, mirth, scoff, wager **6** frolic, gamble, gambol, racing, shikar **7** bowling, contest, deviant, gambler, hunting, jesting, mockery, pastime, show off **8** derision, mutation, raillery, ridicule **9** amusement, bon vivant, diversion, plaything, wrestling **10** pleasantry, recreation, trifle with

attendance: **4** gate

event: **4** game, meet, race **5** match

shirt: tee **4** polo **5** sweat

shoe: **6** cleats, spikes, tennis **7** high top, sneaker **8** plimsoll

site: gym **4** grid, lane, lawn, oval, park, pool, ring, rink **5** arena, court, field, links, track **6** course **7** diamond, stadium **8** coliseum, gridiron **9** gymnasium

summer: **6** diving, hiking, quoits, rowing **7** croquet, fishing, sailing **8** swimming

water: **4** polo **6** diving, rowing **7** sailing, surfing **8** canoeing, swimming, yachting

winter: **6** hockey, luging, skiing **7** curling, skating **8** sledding **11** tobogganing

sportive: gay **5** merry **6** frisky, lusory, wanton **7** amorous, festive, jocular, playful **8** frolicky, gamesome, playsome, pleasant **9** lecherous **10** frolicsome

sportiveness: **7** devilry, roguery, waggery

sportsman: **6** hunter **7** shikari **8** shikaree

sportula: **4** gift **7** largess, present

sporty: **4** loud **5** showy **6** casual, flashy

spot: bit, dab, dot, job, see **4** blot, blur, find, fish, flaw, mark, mole, site, soil **5** blaze, fault, fleck, nevus, patch, place, point, ready, speck, stain, sully, tache, taint **6** blotch, defect, detect, locate, macula, macule, naevus, pimple, random, remove, stigma **7** asperse, blemish, freckle, splotch **8** discolor, disgrace, handicap, identify,

locality, location, maculate, particle, position, quantity, reproach **9** bespatter, birthmark, recognize **10** beauty mark **11** predicament

kinds of: ace, dot, pip, tee **4** blet, fret, gall, rone, spil, wems **5** macle, oasis **6** alcove, bethel, mascle, mottle, mouche **7** freckle **8** bethesda, fenestra, fontanel

on animal's face: **4** star **5** blaze

on playing card: pip

spotless: **5** clean, snowy **6** chaste **7** sinless **9** blameless, stainless, unspotted, unsullied **10** immaculate **11** unblemished, untarnished

spotlight: arc **4** beam **9** emphasize, publicity **10** illuminate

spotted: **4** pied **5** pinto **6** bauson, calico, dotted, espied, marked, notate, sanded, ticked **7** bracket, dappled, guttate, mottled, noticed, stained, sullied **8** blotched, freckled, speckled, stippled **9** blemished, suspected, tarnished

animal: **4** paco, part **6** chital, ocelot **7** cheetah, leopard

fever: **6** typhus

spotter: **7** watcher **9** detective

spotty: few **5** dotty **6** uneven **9** irregular

spousal: **6** wedded **7** marital, wedlock **8** ceremony, marriage, nuptials

spouse: **4** mate, wife **5** bride **6** fiance **7** consort, fiancee, husband, partner **9** companion **10** bridegroom

spout: jet, jut, lip **4** dale, flow, geat, gush, lift, pawn, pipe, rant **5** chute, eject, issue, orate, shoot, speak, spile, spurt, utter **6** pledge, recite, spigot, spring, squirt, stream, trough **7** conduit, declaim **8** downpour, gargoyle **9** discharge, waterfall **10** waterspout

sprack: **4** deft **5** alert **6** active, lively, nimble, shrewd

sprag: **4** prop **6** billet

sprain: **4** pull, tear, turn **5** chink **6** weaken, wrench **10** overstrain

sprat: **5** bleak **6** garvie **7** herring **8** sixpence (Br.)

sprattle: **6** sprawl **8** scramble, struggle

sprawl: **4** loll **5** slump **6** lounge, spread **7** grabble, recline **8** struggle **9** sprauchie

spray: jet **4** chap, hose, twig **5** bough, shoot, spree, sprig, water **6** branch, sparge, spread, spritz, volley **7** atomize, bouquet, flowers, scatter **8** sprinkle **9** aspersion, discharge **10** sprindrift

spread: fan, jam, ted **4** emit, meal, oleo, open, span, taft **5** apply, cover, feast, flare, jelly, reach, scope, smear, splay, strew, widen **6** anoint, dilate, dinner, expand, extend, extent, ramify, sprawl, unfold, unfurl **7** blanket, broaden, compass, diffuse, display, distend, diverge, divulge, enlarge, exhibit, expanse, overlay, overrun, prolong, protect, publish, radiate, scatter, slather, stretch **8** bedcover, coverlet, diffused, dispense, disperse, expanded, extended, increase, multiply, permeate, straddle **9** broadcast, circulate, dispersed, displayed, expansion, expatiate, propagate **10** distribute, generalize **11** disseminate

as plaster: **4** teer

for drying: ted

loosely: **5** strew **7** scatter

on: **5** apply

out: fan, lap, ted **4** bray, open, span **5** flare, widen **6** deploy, flange, sprawl, unfold

spreader: **5** knife **6** tedder **7** spatula

spreading of light: **8** halation **9** radiation

spreading out: **6** radial

spree: bat, jag **4** bout, bust, gell, jagg, lark, orgy, romp, toot **5** beano, binge, booze, revel **6** bender, bust-up, buster, frolic, high-go, shindy **7** carouse, debauch, wassail **8** carousal **10** indulgence

sprig: **4** brad, nail, trim, twig **5** bough, scion, shoot, smart, spray, youth **6** active, branch, sprout, spruce **7** tendril **9** stripling, youngster

sprightly: gay, tid **4** airy, pert **5** agile, alive, antic, brisk, canty, crank, desto, elfin, peart **6** active, blithe, clever, lively **7** briskly, buoyant, chipper, ghostly, quickly **8** animated, vigorous **10** enlivening, spiritedly, spiritlike **11** incorporeal, quick-witted

spring: ain, fly, hop, spa **4** bend, dart, font, head, jump, leap, lilt, rise, warp, well **5** arise, begin, bound, flirt, issue, lymph, shoot, spurt, start, therm, tower, vault **6** accrue, bounce, emerge, season, therme, venero **7** estuary, thermae **8** fountain

back: **6** recoil, resile **7** rebound

hot: spa **7** balneum, gipsies, thermae

kind of: ain, cee, hop, hot, ojo, spa, ver **4** font **5** lymph **6** charco, geyser, saline, source **7** gambado, mineral **9** Castalian

pert. to: **6** vernal

up: **5** arise **6** sprout

springboard: **5** wagon **6** batule **8** tremplin **10** trampoline

springbok: **7** gazelle

springe: gin, set **4** trap **5** agile, catch, noose, snare **6** supple **7** pitfall **9** booby trap

springer: **5** fryer **7** grampus, spaniel **9** springbok

springing back: **7** elastic **9** renascent

springtime: May **5** youth **8** germinal **9** primavera (It., Sp.), printemps (F.)

springy: wet **6** pliant, spongy **7** elastic **8** flexible **9** resilient

sprinkle: deg, dot, wet **4** dart, rain, spot **5** color, flour, spray, strew, twist, water **6** affuse, bedrop, dabble, dredge, sparge **7** asperge, asperse, baptize, drizzle, moisten, scatter, spairge, sparkle, spatter, speckle **8** disperse **9** bespangle, bespatter **10** besprinkle, intoxicate

with flour: **6** dredge

with grit: **4** sand

with moisture: **5** bedew **6** spritz

with mud: **9** bespatter

with powder: **4** dust

with water: deg

sprinkler: **7** dredger **11** aspergillum, watering pot

sprinkling: **4** seme **7** baptism **9** aspersion

sprint: run **4** dash, race **5** snare, speed **6** bicker **7** springe

sprit: bud **4** dart, rush, spar **5** shoot, speck, sprat **6** sprint, sprout, squirt **8** bowsprit **9** germinate

sprite: elf, fay, hob, imp **4** elve, life, mind, mood, peri, puck, soul **5** Ariel, bucca, fairy, genie, ghost, gnome, nisse, pixie, shade, vital **6** goblin, person, spirit **7** brownie, essence **9** germinate, hobgoblin **10** apparition, woodpecker **11** disposition, inspiration

kind of: nix **5** ariel, demon, Holda, naiad, nixie **6** Kelpie **8** coltpixy **9** coltpixie **10** leprechaun, shoopiltie

sprocket: **5** tooth, whelp **7** cam gear

sproil: **6** active, energy **7** agility **8** activity

sprout: bud, eye, son **4** brod, chit, chun, cion, germ, malt **5** achar, brode, chine, shoot, spire, spout, sprig, spurt **6** braird, expand, germen, growth, ratoon **7** burgeon **8** offshoot, seedling

spruce: gim **4** chic, deft, neat, posh, smug, tidy, trig, trim **5** compt, fussy, natty, Picea, smart, sprig **6** dapper, picked **7** dandify, dress up, finical, smarten **8** overnice, titivate **11** well-groomed

tree: **5** larch **8** epinette

sprue: **4** hole **5** dross **7** opening **8** psilosis **9** asparagus

sprunt: **4** hill, leap **5** steep **6** spring **8** struggle

spry: **5** agile, brisk, quick, smart **6** active, clever, lively, nimble, spruce **7** knowing **8** vigorous **9** sprightly

spud: dig, man **4** hand **5** child, dough, drill, money, spade, tater **6** paddle, potato, reamer, remove, shovel **10** projection

spue: See **spew**

spume: **4** foam, scum **5** froth **6** lather

spunk, sponk: vim **4** fire, gall, grit, punk **5** anger, flame, gleam, match, nerve, pluck, spark **6** kindle, mettle, spirit, sponge, tinder **7** courage, passion **9** fortitude, touchwood **10** doggedness

spunky

spunky: 4 game 5 brave, quick 6 plucky, touchy 8 spirited 9 irritable 10 courageous, mettlesome

spur: egg 4 calk, gaff, goad, move, peak, prod, prop, urge 5 arete, brace, drive, hurry, impel, press, prick, range, ridge, rowel, spine, spoor, strut, tower 6 arouse, broach, calcar, digger, excite, foment, griffe, hasten, incite, motive, urge on 7 gablock, provoke, publish 8 buttress, stimulus 9 incentive, instigate, stimulate 10 blockhouse 11 publication

having: 7 spicate
of mountain: 5 arete
on gamecock: 4 gaff
railroad: 6 siding
wheel: 5 rowel

spurge: 4 weed 6 balsam, croton, purify 8 milk-weed 9 euphorbia 10 castor bean, poinsettia

spurious: 4 fake, sham 5 bogus, false, phony, snide 6 forced 7 bastard 10 adulterate, apocryphal, artificial, fictitious, fraudulent 11 counterfeit, superficial 12 illegitimate

spurn: hit 4 blow, dash, kick, rush, snub, spur 5 flout, haste, scorn 6 affray, incite, pillar, rebuff, refuse, reject, scrape, strike 7 contemn, decline, despise, disdain, scratch, stumble 10 engagement

spurt: jet, jut 4 dart, gush 5 expel, spell, spout 6 sprout, squirt 8 increase

spur wheel: 5 rowel

Sputnik: 9 satellite
dog: 5 Laika

sputter: ado 4 fuss, spit 7 bluster

sputum: 4 spit 6 saliva 7 spittle

spy: pry, see 4 case, espy, keek, note, tout 5 agent, scout, sneak, snoop, spook, watch 6 behold, descry, detect, espial, gaycat, mouton, search 7 discern, examine, hicarra, inspect, observe, snooper 8 discover, hicarrah, informer, perceive, stake out 10 scrutinize 11 secret agent

spying: 9 espionage 12 surveillance

Spyri's heroine: 5 Heidi

squab: coy, fat, shy 4 drop, sofa 5 couch, piper, plump, press, short, spill, thick 6 callow, pigeon, stocky 7 cushion, ottoman 8 nestling 9 fledgling, unfledged, upholster

squabble: row 4 spat 5 argue, brawl 6 bicker, jangle 7 bobbery, contend, dispute, quarrel, wrangle 13 collie-shangie

squad: 4 team 5 force, group, troop

squadron: 6 armada 10 escadrille

squalid: 4 base, foul, mean, poor, ugly, vile 5 dirty, nasty 6 filthy, shabby, sordid 7 unclean 8 wretched 9 miserable, repellant, repellent, repulsive 10 broken-down

squall: cry, pet 4 bawl, dear, drow, gale, gush, gust, wawl 5 storm 6 flurry, scream, shower, squawk, wretch 7 borasca, borasco, dispute, quarrel, trouble 8 borasque 9 windstorm 11 disturbance

squalor: mud 4 dirt, mire 5 filth

squander: 4 burn, lash 5 spend, waste 6 befool, lavish, wander 7 consume, debauch, dispend, scatter 8 disperse, embezzle, misspend 9 dissipate 10 trifle away

squanderer: 5 loser 7 wastrel

square: pay 4 even, fair, parc, park, true 5 agora, carre, clear, exact, hunky, plaza 6 dinkum, direct, honest, settle 7 commons, quarrel, upright 8 justness, quadrate 9 carre-four, criterion, principle 11 unequivocal 12 conventional 13 parallelogram

square dance: 4 reel 7 hoedown, lancers 9 quadrille

squared circle: 4 ring 5 arena

squarehead: 4 dolt 5 dunce, Dutch, Swede 6 German 8 numskull 9 screwball 12 Scandinavian

squarish: 4 boxy

squarrose: 5 rough, scaly

squash: 4 beat, fall, ooze, pepo, stop 5 crowd, crush, press 6 stifle 7 cymling, flatten, pumpkin, squeeze, squelch 8 suppress 9 discomfit 10 disconcert
kind of: 5 acorn 6 banana, cushaw, simnel, summer, turban, yellow 7 cymling, Hubbard, Italian, pumpkin, scallop 8 cymbling, patty pan, zucchini 9 crookneck, spaghetti

squashy: wet 4 soft 5 boggy, muddy, mushy, pulpy 8 overripe

squat: sit 5 cower, dumpy, pudgy, stoop 6 bruise, crouch, fodgel, hurkle, settle, splash, stocky, stubby 8 thickset

squatter: 4 flap 5 squat 6 crouch, nester, plunge 7 bywoner, confuse, flutter, nestler, scatter, settler 8 bewilder, squander 9 sandpiper

Squatter State: 6 Kansas

squaw: 4 wife 5 woman 6 coween, mahala 10 klootchman
husband: 4 buck 5 brave 6 sannup

squawbush: 5 sumac 6 shoval

squawfish: 4 chub 8 chappaul 9 surfperch

squeak: cry, wee 4 peep, talk 5 cheep, creak, noise, speak 6 betray, escape, inform, shrill 7 confess, disturb 11 opportunity

squeal: yip 4 blab, sing 5 broil, frail, weary 6 betray, inform, scream, tattle 7 dispute, protest, quarrel 8 complain

squealer: 4 duck, fink 5 quail, swift 6 grouse, pigeon, plover 7 traitor 8 informer 9 partridge

squeamish: shy 4 helo, nice, stir 5 dizzy,

heloe **6** bustle, dainty, dauncy, modest, queasy **7** finical, prudish **8** overnice, qualmish **9** dizziness, giddiness, nauseated, reluctant, sensitive **10** fastidious, scrupulous **13** oversensitive

squeeze: eke, hug, jam **4** gain, mull, neck, silk **5** chirt, creem, crowd, crush, force, pinch, press, wring **6** corner, eke out, escape, extort, scrump, scruze, thrust, twitch **7** embrace, extract, oppress, procure, scrunch, scrunge **8** compress, condense, pressing, pressure, scrounge **9** constrict, influence **10** commission, constraint **11** compression

squeezer: **5** drier, noose **6** juicer, reamer **7** wringer **8** squeegee **9** extractor

squelch: **4** blow, fall **5** crush, quash, quell, stamp **6** rebuke, subdue **7** silence **8** suppress **9** discomfit **10** disconcert

squib: jet **4** ball, bomb, mote, pipe, skit, tube **5** candy, match, throw **6** filler, squirt, writer **7** dispute, explode, lampoon, pasquil, torpedo, writing **9** bespatter **10** pasquinade **11** firecracker

squid: **6** loligo **7** mollusk, octopus **8** calamare, calamari, nautilus, sea arrow **10** cuttlefish
arm: **8** tentacle
pen: **5** quill
secretion: ink
shell: pen
tongue: **6** radula

squiffer (Br.): **10** concertina

squiggle: **4** curl, line **5** shake, twist **6** doodle, squirm, writhe **7** wriggle **8** curlicue, scribble

squill: **4** bulb **6** scilla **8** sea onion

squilla: **5** prawn **6** shrimp **8** sea onion

squinch: **4** arch **5** twist **6** lintel, quince, recoil, squint, wrench **7** squeeze, squench **9** corbeling

squint: **4** bent, cast, glee, gleg, look, peer, scan, skew **5** glent, trend **6** gledge, goggle **7** deviate **10** hagioscope, strabismus

squint-eyed: **5** gleed, gleyd

squire: **4** beau **5** lover, title **6** donzel, escort **7** equerry, gallant **8** henchman, servitor **9** accompany, attendant, gentleman, landowner

squirrel: bun **5** hoard, sisel, stash, xerus **6** chippy, gyrate, rodent **7** assapan **8** archilla, jelerang **9** assapanic, chickaree, shadetail
genus of: **7** sciurus
nest: **4** dray, drey
shrew: **4** tana
skin: **4** vair
tassel-eared: **6** kaibab

squirrellike: **8** sciuroid
animal: **6** marmot **8** chipmunk, dormouse **10** prairie dog

squirt: jet **5** chirt, eject, skite, slirt, spout, spurt **14** whippersnapper

sri: **4** holy **7** Lakshmi **8** glorious, reverend **9** fortunate

Sri Lanka: *boat:* **4** done, doni **5** balsa, dhoni, doney **10** wakamoowee
capital: **7** Colombo
currency: **4** cent **5** rupee
Dravidian: **5** Tamil
export: tea
measure: **4** para **5** parah **6** amunam, parrah
monkey: **4** maha **5** toque **6** langur, rilawa, rillow **10** wanderoock
moss: **4** agar, alga **5** jaffa **7** gulaman
oak: **5** kusam
palm: **7** talipat, talipot
people: **5** Tamil, Vedda **6** Veddah **9** Sinhalese
rat: **9** bandicoot
resthouse: **6** abalam
rice field: **4** padi **5** paddy
rose: **8** cleander
sedan: **6** tomjon, tonjon
snake: **7** adjiger
tea: **5** pekoe
tree: **4** doon, hara, palu, tala **7** talipot

S-shaped: **4** ogee **7** sigmate, sigmoid

stab: dab, jab, jag, try **4** gore, jagg, pink, yerk **5** chive, drive, knife, knive, lance, lunge, prick, sound, stake, stick, stool, stump, wound **6** attack, broach, dagger, pierce, strike, stroke, thrust **7** attempt, poniard, roughen **8** puncture **9** penetrate
in fencing: **4** pink **8** stoccado

stability: **5** poise **6** anchor **7** balance **8** firmance, firmness, security, strength **9** constancy, fixedness **10** permanence, stableness, steadiness **12** immutability

stabilize: fix, set **4** calm **5** poise **6** steady **7** balance **8** regulate

stabilizer: **7** ballast

stable: **4** barn, fast, firm, mews, shed, sure **5** fixed, set-up, solid, sound, stall **6** hangar, secure, steady, strong, sturdy **7** durable, equerry, lasting, staunch **8** constant, enduring, immobile, reliable **9** confirmed, establish, permanent, resistant, steadfast, unabashed, unvarying **10** stationary, unwavering **11** established, trustworthy

stableman: **5** groom **6** ostler **7** hostler

stack: set **4** bike, flue, heap, pike, pile, rick, stow, tier **5** group, hovel, mound, scroo, shock **7** chimney, conduit **9** fireplace

stacked: **7** piled up **10** curvaceous

stad: **4** town **7** village

staddle: row **4** tree **5** stain, swath **7** sapling, support

stadium: **4** oval **5** arena, stade, stage **7** furlong **8** coliseum **10** hippodrome

staff: bar, gad, rod **4** cane, club, line, mace, maul, pole, prod, rung, wand **5** aides, baton, crook, equip, lance, pedum, perch, spear, stave, stick, suite **6** baston, cudgel, stanza **7** attache, bailiff, caducei (pl.), scepter, sceptre, support **8** caduceus **9** constable, entourage, personnel
bearer: **5** macer
kinds of: **4** kent, wand **5** filch **6** croche, muleta **7** baculus, bourdon, cambuca, crosier, crozier, distaff, rhabdos **10** alpenstock
officers: **5** aides, cadre

staff of life: **5** bread

stag: **4** colt, deer, hart **5** party **7** pollard, shorten **8** informer
horn: **4** rial **9** bezantler

stage: era **4** dais, gest, step, tier **5** arena, board, coach, floor, grade, level, phase, scene, shelf, stair, story **6** boards, degree, pulpit, stadia **7** display, exhibit, produce, rostrum, stadium, theater **8** platform, scaffold **9** condition, dramatize, gradation **10** proscenium, stagecoach **11** subdivision
extra: **4** supe **5** super
hanging: **7** scenery **8** backdrop
on: **7** en scene
part: **4** role
pert. to: **6** scenic
raised: **4** dais **7** estrade
signal: cue

stage direction: **4** exit, sola **5** aside, enter, manet, omnes, solus **6** exeunt, sennet **8** loquitur

stage whisper: **5** aside

stagger: **4** reel, rock, stun, sway **5** lurch, shake, waver **6** falter, hobble, totter, wintle (Sc.), wobble **7** startle, stumble, tremble, vibrate **8** flounder, hesitate, titubate, unsettle

stagnant: **4** foul **5** inert, stale, still **7** languid **8** sluggish, standing **10** motionless

stagnate: **4** dull **5** inert **8** vegetate

stagnation: **6** stases, stasis, torpor **8** dormancy **10** depression

stagy: **8** affected **10** theatrical **12** ostentatious

staid: set **5** fixed, grave, sober **6** demure, sedate, solemn, steady **7** earnest, serious, settled **8** decorous, sensible **9** dignified, steadfast

stain: dye **4** blot, blur, daub, soil, spot, tint **5** cloud, color, paint, smear, sully, tache, taint, tinge, trace **6** blotch, debase, infamy, macula, smirch, smudge, stigma, vilify **7** blem-

ish, corrupt, tarnish, varnish **8** discolor, disgrace, dishonor, maculate, tincture **9** bespatter, pollution **10** attainture **11** contaminate

stainless: **4** pure **6** chaste, honest **10** immaculate

stair: **4** step **5** stage, stile **6** degree
face: **5** riser
post: **5** newel
series of: **6** flight
step: **5** tread

staircase: **5** grece, grice **6** griece, ladder
handrail: **8** banister **9** bannister
moving: **9** escalator
on ship: **12** companionway
outdoor: **6** perron
part of: **4** rung **5** newel, riser, tread
portable: **6** ladder **9** step stool
spiral: **8** caracole

stake: bet, peg, pin, pot, set **4** ante, back, gage, pale, pile, pole, pool, post, risk, spit, stob **5** anvil, kitty, money, prize, purse, spile, spoke, staff, stick, teest, wager **6** chance, gamble, hazard, picket **7** venture **8** interest **9** horse race **10** capitalize
driver: **4** maul
pert. to: **5** palar

stale: old **4** flat, hoar, lure, rung, worn **5** banal, blown, corny, decoy, frowy, moldy, musty, shaft, tired, trite, vapid, waugh (Sc.) **7** insipid, tainted **9** hackneyed, tasteless **10** flavorless, prostitute **11** commonplace, overtrained **13** uninteresting

stalemate: tie **4** draw **5** check **7** impasse **8** deadlock, standoff **10** standstill

stalk: bun **4** axis, halm, hunt, mote, prey, risp, seta, stem **5** chase, haulm, shaft, spear, stipe, straw **6** follow, pursue, ratoon, stride **7** pedicel, petiole **8** peduncle
having: **9** petiolate
remove: **5** strig

stalker: **6** hunter

stalking-horse: **4** mask **5** blind, decoy **7** pretext **8** pretense

stalkless: **7** sessile

stall: bin, cot, pew **4** barn, crib, loge, mire, seat, stop **5** boose, boosy, booth, check, crame, decoy, delay, stand **6** manger, stable **7** cubicle, pretext, station **8** hesitate **9** enclosure **10** dilly-dally **11** compartment, confederate **13** procrastinate

stallion: **5** horse **6** cooser (Sc.)

stalwart: **4** bold, firm, hero **5** brave, stout **6** brawny, robust, strong, sturdy **7** valiant **8** partisan, resolute **10** unyielding

stamina: gut **4** grit **5** force, vigor **7** courage, essence **8** backbone, capacity, strength, vitality **9** endurance, fortitude

stammer: **6** falter, hacker, jabber **7** stumble, stutter **8** hesitate

stamp: die **4** beat, chop, coin, form, kind, mark, mold, seal, sort, tool, type **5** brand, class, crush, drive, label, pound, press, print, stomp **6** signet, strike, thresh **7** impress, imprint, postage, sticker, trample **8** inscribe **9** character **10** impression **11** distinguish
  collecting: **9** philately
  fencing: **5** appel
  madness for: **11** timbromania
  paper: **6** pelure
  space: **8** spandrel
stampede: **4** bolt, rout, rush **5** blitz, panic **6** charge, flight **7** debacle
stamping plate: die
stance: **4** pose **7** posture, station **8** attitude, position
stanch, staunch: dam **4** firm, stem, stop, true, weir **5** allay, check, close, loyal, quell, sound **6** hearty, quench, steady, strong, trusty **7** zealous **8** constant, faithful, resolute, suppress **9** steadfast **10** extinguish, unswerving, unwavering, watertight **11** substantial, trustworthy
stanchion: bar **4** beam, post, prop **5** brace, piton **6** confine, support, upright
stand: set **4** bear, dais, ease, halt, hold, last, rack, stop **5** abide, arise, booth, cease, erect, kiosk, pause, stall, table **6** afford, endure, hack it, podium, remain, resist, tripod, trivet **7** etagere, station, support, sustain, taboret, undergo **8** attitude, continue, hesitate, maintain, position, tabouret, tolerate **9** withstand **10** resistance
  candle: **6** sconce **7** epergne **10** candelabra **11** candlestick
  cuplike: **4** zarf
  for: **4** mean **8** tolerate **9** represent
  for election: run
  in awe of: **4** fear **5** dread **7** respect
  on end: **5** upend
  on hind legs: **4** ramp, rear
  opposite: **4** face
  ornamental: **7** atagere, etagere
  out: jut **6** beetle **7** project **8** overhang, protrude
  painter's: **5** easel
  three-legged: **6** tripod, trivet
standard: cup, par, set **4** fiar (Sc.), flag, mark, norm, suit, type, unit **5** canon, gauge, grade, ideal, level, model, usual **6** assize, banner, beacon, common, ensign, goblet, normal, sample, signal **7** classic, example, labarum (L.), pattern, support, upright **8** accepted, brattach (Sc.), gonfalon, ordinary, orthodox, vexillum **9** criterion, oriflamme, yardstick **10** touchstone **11** candlestick, rule of thumb
  bearer: **11** gonfalonier
  of measurement: **4** troy **6** metric **11** avoirdupois
standardize: **9** calibrate, normalize
stand-in: **6** deputy **9** surrogate **10** substitute
standing: **4** rank, term **5** being, erect, fixed **6** credit, estate, stable, stance, status **7** lasting, settled, statant, station, upright **8** constant, duration, location, position, stagnant, vertical **9** permanent, situation **10** reputation, stationary
  upright: **5** erect **11** orthostatic
standing room only: S.R.O. **7** sold out **9** full house
standoff: tie **4** draw **10** unsociable
standstill: tie **4** halt, rest, stop **5** check, state **8** deadlock **9** cessation, stalemate
stanhope: **5** buggy
stank: **4** pond, pool **5** ditch **9** reservoir
stanza: **5** envoi, stave, verse **7** strophe **8** division **9** apartment
  eight line: **6** huitain, octave **7** triolet
  five line: **8** cinquain
  four line: **8** quatrain
  irregular: **13** alloeostropha
  six line: **6** sestet
  ten line: **6** dizain **7** dizaine
  three line: **8** tristich
  two line: **7** couplet
staple: **4** city, town **5** chief, fiber, goods, shaft **6** fasten **7** chaplet, support **8** fastener **9** commodity, principal **10** foundation
star (see also **constellation, planet**): ace, orb, sun **4** diva, hero, lead **5** actor, badge, chief, shine **6** etoile **7** actress, estoile, heroine, ingenue, stellar **8** asterisk, luminary, pentacle, twinkler **9** bespangle, headliner, principal **10** preeminent, topnotcher
  apple: **7** caimito
  brightest: **6** Sirius
  brightest in constellation: **5** alpha
  divination: **9** astrology
  evening: **5** Venus **6** Hesper, Vesper **7** Evestar **8** Hesperus
  evil: **8** sidereal
  exploding: **4** nova **9** supernova
  five-pointed: **8** pentacle
  group: **6** galaxy **13** constellation
  in Aquila: **5** Deneb **6** Altair
  in Bootes: **8** Arcturus
  in Canis Major: **6** Sirius
  in Carina: **7** Canopus
  in Centaurus: **5** Agena, Rigil
  in Cetus: **4** Mira
  in Cygnus: **5** Deneb **7** Albireo
  in Draco: **6** Alsafi **7** Al Rakis, Eltanin
  in Gemini: **5** Pollux, Wasat **6** Alhena, Castor
  in Leo: **7** Regulus
  in Lyra: **4** Vega

in Orion: **5** Rigel, Saiph **10** Betelgeuse
in Perseus: **5** Algol
in Scorpius: **7** Antares
in Taurus: **8** Pleiades
in Ursa Major: **5** Alcor, Mizar **6** Alkaid
in Ursa Minor: **7** Polaris
in Virgo: **5** Spica
morning: **5** Venus
north: **7** Polaris **8** loadstar, lodestar, polestar
pert. to: **6** astral **7** astrean, stellar **8** sidereal, stellate
representation: **6** etoile
shooting: **5** comet **6** Leonid, meteor
six-pointed: **8** hexagram
smallest: **7** neutron
two: **9** bistellar
variable: **4** Mira
worshiper: **7** sabaist
starch: vim **4** arum, sago, size **5** salep, tikor, vigor **6** amylum, energy, farina, potato, strong **7** cassava, precise, stiffen, tapioca **8** activity, glycogen, strength, vitality **9** arrowroot, formality, stiffness **12** carbohydrate
starchy: **5** rigid, stiff **6** formal **7** precise **9** unbending
star cluster: **6** nebula
star-crossed: **6** doomed **7** unlucky **11** unfortunate
stare: **4** bore, gape, gaup, gawk, gawp, gaze, gouk, gowk, gype, leer, look, ogle, peer, pore **5** glare, glaze, glore **6** glower, goggle **7** bristle **8** starling
star facet: **4** pane
starfish: **7** sun star **8** asteroid
limb: ray
stargazer: **4** fish **10** astrologer, astronomer
staring: **5** agape **6** gazing **7** glaring **8** wide-eyed
stark: **4** bare, firm, hard, nude, pure **5** bleak, harsh, plain, quite, rigid, rough, sheer, stern, stiff, tense, utter **6** barren, severe, strong, wholly **7** violent **8** absolute, complete, desolate, entirely, metallic, obdurate, powerful, stalwart, stripped, vigorous **9** downright, unadorned **10** absolutely, unyielding **11** intractable
starnose: **4** mole
Star of David: **10** Magen David
starry: **6** astral, bright **7** shining, stellar **8** luminous, sidereal, starlike, stellate **9** celestial, sparkling
Star-Spangled Banner author: **15** Francis Scott Key
start: fit, run, shy **4** dart, head, jerk, jump, lead, rush **5** alarm, begin, birth, debut, dodge, enter, flush, found, glent, lever, onset, rouse, sally, shock, wince **6** boggle, broach, flinch, fright, loosen, origin, outset,

recoil, spring, twitch **7** disturb, get away, impulse, kickoff, provoke, retreat, startle **8** commence, displace, draw back, embark on, handicap, initiate, outburst **9** advantage, beginning, dislocate, introduce, originate **10** inaugurate
starter: **5** drill, punch **7** entrant **8** ignition, official **10** controller
startle: **5** alarm, rouse, scare, shock, start **6** excite **8** affright, frighten, surprise **9** electrify
startling: **7** rousing **8** alarming, restless, skittish **10** surprising **11** astonishing
starvation: **4** lack, want **6** famine
starve: **4** fast **6** famish, hunger
starveling: **4** lean **6** hungry, pining, wasted
Star Wars: **5** force
characters: Han **4** C3PO, Ewok, Jedi, Leia, Luke, R2D2, Solo, Yoda **5** Jabba **7** Han Solo **8** Boba Fett **9** Chewbacca **10** Darth Vader **12** Obi-Wan Kenobi, Princess Leia **13** Luke Skywalker
starwort: **5** aster **9** chickweed, colicroot
stash: end **4** hide, stop **5** cache, hoard, store **7** secrete
state: say **4** acme, aver, etat (F.), form, land, mode, mood, pomp, rank, seat, tell, term, weal **5** chair, phase, posit, realm, style, utter, voice **6** affirm, allege, aspect, assert, avouch, degree, empire, estate, height, nation, plight, polity, recite, relate, report, status, temper, throne **7** account, country, declare, dignity, enounce, express, narrate **8** ceremony, eminence, grandeur, position, property, propound, province, set forth, standing **9** community, condition, enunciate, pronounce, situation, territory **10** asseverate, government, possession **11** body politic, stateliness **12** commonwealth
based on honor: **9** timocracy
bound by treaty: **4** ally
emotional: **5** fever **7** feeling
explicitly: **6** define **7** itemize, specify
ideal: **6** Utopia
member: **7** citizen
of balance: **9** equipoise
of excitement: **7** ferment
of mind: **4** mood **5** humor **6** fettle, morale
relating to: **6** statal
subdivision: **4** city, town **6** county **7** village **8** township
under foreign control: **9** territory **12** protectorate
stated: **4** firm **5** fixed, given **6** avowed **7** express, regular **8** declared **10** formulated **11** established
State Fair author: **5** Stong
statehouse: **7** capitol
stately: **5** grand, lofty **6** august, formal, superb **7** courtly, gallant, haughty **8** imperial,

imposing, majestic **9** dignified **10** deliberate **11** ceremonious, magisterial, magnificent

music: **5** largo

statement: **4** bill, word **5** audit, brief, dicta **6** dictum, precis, record, remark, report, resume, thesis **7** account, address, article, bromide, epitome, invoice, premise, recital, summary **8** abstract, averment (law), relation, schedule, sentence **9** affidavit, agreement, manifesto, narrative, testimony **10** abridgment, allegation, deposition, expression **11** abridgement, affirmation, assertation, certificate, declaration **12** presentation

assumed true: **7** premise

authoritative: **6** dictum

defamatory: **5** libel

false: lie

financial: **6** budget **12** balance sheet

formal: **9** affidavit **10** deposition

introductory: **5** proem **7** preface, prelude **8** foreword, prologue

mathematical: **7** theorem

of belief: **5** credo, creed

self-contradictory: **7** paradox

self-evident: **6** truism

stateroom: **5** cabin

statesman: **7** statist **8** diplomat, minister **10** ambassador, politician

static: **5** fixed, inert, noise **7** resting **8** inactive **9** quiescent **10** stationary **11** electricity

station: fix, run, set **4** base, camp, halt, post, rank, seat, site, spot, stop **5** berth, depot, field, place, serai, siege **6** assign, church, degree, region, stance, status **7** appoint, calling, cuartel (Sp.), dignity, habitat, posture **8** attitude, garrison, location, position, terminal **9** condition, homestead, situation **10** constitute **11** equilibrium, institution

stationary: set **4** fast **5** fixed **6** stable, static **8** immobile, inactive, moveless **9** immovable, permanent, sedentary **10** motionless, stockstill, unchanging

stationer: **10** bookseller

stationery: ink, pen **5** blank, paper **6** pencil **9** blank book **10** papeteries

statist: **9** statesman **10** politician

statistician: **7** analyst, statist

statue: **4** bust, icon, ikon, nude **5** atlas, image, orant **6** bronze **7** Madonna **8** caryatid, Colossus, figurine, likeness, monument **9** sculpture

base: **6** plinth

gigantic: **8** colossus

in London Guildhall: Gog **5** Magog

praying: **5** orant

primitive: **6** xoanon

small: **8** figurine

that came to life: **7** Galatea

upper part of: **4** bust **5** torso

weeping: **5** Niobe

Statue of Liberty: *poet:* **7** Lazarus

sculptor: **9** Bartholdi

statuesque: **4** tall **7** shapely, stately **8** graceful

statuette: **8** figurine

stature: **6** height **8** eminence, prestige

status: **4** rank **5** state **6** aspect, classe (F.) **8** position, prestige, relation, standing **9** condition

statute: act, law **4** rule **5** edict **6** assize, decree **9** enactment, ordinance **10** regulation **11** legislation

heading of: **5** title

volume of: **4** code **5** codex **7** codices

staunch (see also **stanch**): **4** firm, true **5** loyal **8** constant, faithful **9** steadfast **10** watertight **11** substantial

stave: bar **4** pole, rung, slat, stap (Sc.) **5** break, lathi, smash, staff, stick, verse **6** cudgel, stanza **7** baculus **8** puncture

bundle of: **5** shook

off: **7** fend off, ward off **8** postpone **9** drive away

stavesacre: **8** larkspur

stay: dam, guy, lie, rib **4** base, bide, calm, curb, halt, hold, last, live, prop, rely, rest, rope, stem, stop, tack, wait **5** abide, allay, avast, await, brace, cable, cease, check, defer, delay, demur, dwell, pause, quell, stand, stare, tarry, visit **6** arrest, corset, depend, detain, endure, fasten, linger, pacify, remain, reside, resist, secure, shroud, status **7** appease, control, incline, refrain, satisfy, sojourn, support, sustain, triatic **8** continue, postpone, restrain **9** anchorage, cessation, hindrance, residence **10** impediment

staying power: **7** stamina **9** endurance

stead: **4** farm, help, lieu, site, spot **5** avail, beset, place, trace, track **6** assist, behalf **7** benefit, bestead, impress, involve, replace, service, support **8** bedstead, locality, position **9** advantage, farmstead, situation, successor **10** substitute

steadfast, stedfast: **4** fast, firm, sure, true **5** fixed, staid, tried **6** stable, stanch, steady **7** certain, settled, staunch **8** constant, enduring, faithful, reliable, resolute **9** immovable **10** inflexible, unchanging, unswerving **11** established, unalterable

steadiness: **5** nerve **7** balance **8** firmness **9** constancy, stability

steading: **4** site **9** farmhouse, homestead

steady: **4** beau, calm, even, firm, girl, safe, sane, sure **5** fixed, sober, solid, staid **6** direct, stable, sturdy **7** assured, equable, regular, uniform **8** constant, diligent, faithful, reliable, resolute **9** boyfriend, impassive, incessant, stabilize, steadfast **10** continuous, controlled, girlfriend, invariable, sweetheart

steak: **4** club, rump **5** chuck, filet, round, shell, strip, swiss, t-bone **6** minute **7** griskin, New York, sirloin **9** cube, flank, entrecote **10** tenderloin **11** porterhouse

steal: bag, cly, cop, gyp, nim, rap, rob **4** crib, gain, glom, hook, lift, loot, nick, palm, stem, take **5** bribe, creep, fetch, filch, harry, pinch, poach, shaft, sneak, stalk, swipe, theft **6** abduct, burgle, convey, divert, extend, handle, hijack, kidnap, pilfer, pirate, rustle, snatch, snitch, thieve **7** bargain, plunder, purloin **8** embezzle, peculate **9** condiddle **10** plagiarize

stealer: **5** thief **6** robber **7** burglar **10** plagiarist **11** biblioklept
cattle: **7** abactor, rustler

stealthy: sly **6** artful, covert, secret, sneaky **7** catlike, cunning, furtive **11** clandestine
walk: **5** stalk **6** tiptoe

steam: **4** boil, cook, fume, heat, reek **5** force, power, smoke, vapor, water **6** energy **8** vaporize, vexation **10** exhalation, irritation
bath: **5** sauna
jet: **5** stufa **8** soffione
pipe: **5** riser

steamer: **4** boat, clam, ship **5** liner **6** vessel **9** steamship
cabin: **5** texas

steamroller: **4** whip **5** crush **8** override

steamship: **5** liner **7** steamer
route: **4** lane
smokestack: **6** funnel

steatite: **4** talc **9** soapstone

steed: **4** Arab **5** horse, mount **7** charger, courser

steel: **4** gird, rail **5** acier (F.), inure, metal, press, sword **6** damask, harden, smooth, toledo **8** Bessemer, Damascus **9** encourage **10** strengthen
process: **8** Bessemer **11** cementation

steelhead: **5** trout

steely: **10** unyielding

steelyard: **7** balance

steep: ret **4** bate, bath, bold, bowk, brew, buck, high, soak, stew, tall **5** bathe, brant, brent, heavy, hilly, imbue, lofty, proud, sharp, sheer **6** abrupt, bright, clifty, decoct, drench, imbibe, imbrue, infuse, seethe **7** arduous, extract, extreme, immerse **8** elevated, headlong, macerate, saturate, solution **9** difficult, distemper, excessive, expensive, precipice **10** exorbitant, impregnate

steeper: vat **6** teapot, vessel **7** cistern

steeple: **5** spire, tower **6** cupola **7** minaret **8** pinnacle **9** campanile

steeplechase: **9** horse race, track race

steer: con, tip **4** bull, conn, helm, lead, stot **5** guide, pilot **6** advise, bovine, direct, govern, manage **7** bullock, control, operate, oversee

steerage: **8** guidance **9** direction **10** management, regulation

steering: aim **9** direction **10** government, management
apparatus: **4** helm **5** wheel **6** rudder, tiller
superintend: con **4** conn

steeve: **4** pack, stow **5** store, stuff

stein: mug **4** pint, toby **6** flagon **8** schooner

steinbock: **8** antelope

stela, stele: **4** slab **5** stone **6** pillar **8** memorial, monument **10** gravestone

stelar: **10** columnlike

stellar: **5** chief, major **6** astral, starry **7** leading **8** starlike, stellate **9** principal **10** preeminent **11** outstanding

Steller's sea cow: **6** rytina

stem: bow, bun, dam, leg, ram **4** axis, base, body, bole, cane, culm, halt, load, prow, race, reed, risp, root, stop, tamp **5** check, haulm, orise, shaft, stalk, stipe, stock, trunk **6** branch, derive, oppose, spring, stanch **7** contain, lineage, pedicel, petiole, spindle **8** ancestry, contract, peduncle, restrain **9** originate, petiolule
bulblike: **4** corm **5** tuber **7** rhizome
climbing: **4** bine, vine **7** tendril
fungus: **5** stipe
joint: **4** node
part: **4** bark, pith **5** stele
pert. to: **7** cauline **8** stipular
sheath: **5** ocrea

stemma: **7** descent, lineage **8** ancestry, pedigree **9** genealogy

stemmer: bar

stench: **4** fogo, funk, odor, reek **5** fetor, smell, stink **6** foetor

stenographer: **8** recorder

stenography: **9** shorthand

stent (see also **stint**): **5** tight **6** extend, extent **7** stretch **12** outstretched

stentorian: **4** loud **6** strong **10** resounding

step: act, pas, sty, way **4** gait, pace, rank, rest, rung, trip, trot, walk **5** break, crush, dance, grade, ledge, level, plane, round, shelf, space, stage, stair, stalk, strut, stufe (G.), tread **6** action, degree, ladder, manner, squash, stride, tiptoe **7** advance, deprive, measure **8** distance, footfall, foothold, footrest, footstep, movement **9** footprint, gradation, procedure, promotion **10** proceeding
dance: pas **5** coule **6** chasse **8** glissade
introductory: **8** rudiment **10** initiative
measuring device: **9** pedometer **10** passimeter

over fence: **5** stile
part: **5** riser, tread **6** nosing
recording device: **8** odograph
rope ladder: **7** ratline
series of raised: **6** gradin **7** gradine
step-by-step: **7** gradual, in order
stepdame: **10** stepmother
step-in: **4** mule, shoe **6** loafer **7** slipper **8** mocassin
step-ins: **10** underpants
steppe: **5** plain, space **7** prairie **9** grassland, wasteland
storm: **5** buran
stepper: **5** horse **6** dancer
step up: rev **8** increase **10** accelerate
stere: **9** kiloliter
stereotyped: **5** banal, tired, trite **7** cliched, routine **9** hackneyed
sterile: dry **4** arid, dead, geld **6** barren, meager, meagre, otiose **7** aseptic, useless **8** impotent, sanitary **9** fruitless, infertile **10** unfruitful, unoriginal **11** ineffective **12** unproductive
sterilize: fix **4** boil, geld, spay **5** unsex **6** change, neuter **9** disinfect
sterling: **5** penny **6** silver **7** genuine **9** excellent
stern: **4** back, dour, firm, grim, hard, helm, rear **5** harsh, rough, steer, stout **6** fierce, gloomy, mighty, rudder, savage, severe, strict, strong, sturdy, sullen, tiller, unkind **7** austere, massive, spartan, tail end **8** buttocks, exacting, resolute, rigorous **9** unbending, unfeeling **10** astringent, forbidding, inexorable, inflexible, relentless
toward: aft **5** abaft **6** astern
Sterne character: **4** Slop, Toby, Trim **6** Shandy, Yorick **8** Tristram
sternforemost: **7** awkward **8** backward **9** hind end to
sternness: **5** rigor **7** cruelty **8** hardness, severity **9** austerity, harshness, rigidness, stiffness **10** strictness
sternum: **8** skeleton **10** breastbone
sternutation: **6** sneeze **8** sneezing
sterol: **7** alcohol **11** cholesterol
stertor: **5** snore
stevedore: **6** loader, stower **8** cargador, dockhand **12** longshoreman
Stevenson: *character:* **4** Hyde **6** Jekyll **10** Jim Hawkins **14** Long John Silver
home: **5** Samoa
novel: **9** Kidnapped **14** Treasure Island
stew: **4** boil, cook, dive, fret, mess, olio, slum, snit **5** anger, cloud, imbue, steep, study, sweat, worry **6** burgoo, dither, ragout, seethe, simmer **7** brothel, goulash, haricot, swelter **8** hothouse **9** Brunswick, commotion, confusion **10** capilotade, excitement,

hodgepodge, hotchpotch, miscellany **11** predicament
game for: **5** civet
steward: **5** dewan, diwan, graff, grave, reeve **6** factor, grieve, waiter **7** bailiff, curator, foreman, granger, manager, officer, proctor **8** bhandari, dispense, employee, guardian **9** caretaker, custodian, seneschal **10** magistrate **11** chamberlain
monastery: **8** cellarer
ship: **6** flunky **7** flunkey **8** cabin boy
stewed: **5** drunk **10** inebriated **11** intoxicated
sthenic: **6** active, strong
stib: **6** dunlin **9** sandpiper
stich: **4** line **5** verse
stick: bar, bat, bow, cue, gad, gum, put, rod, set **4** bind, cane, clag, clam, club, fife, glue, kill, mast, poke, pole, push, spit, stab, stem, stop, twig, wand **5** affix, baton, cheat, cleam, cling, decoy, delay, demur, flute, mount, paste, place, prick, shoot, shove, staff, stalk, stall, stave, trunk **6** adhere, attach, baffle, ballow, billet, branch, cement, cleave, cohere, cudgel, endure, ferule, fescue, fleece, impale, mallet, pierce, puzzle, rammer, strike, thrust **7** defraud, drummer, nonplus **8** bludgeon, puncture **10** overcharge
bamboo: **5** lathi **6** lathee
bundle of: **5** fagot **6** fasces **7** fascine
conductor's: **5** baton
crooked: **5** caman **7** cammock, gambrel
jumping: **4** pogo
measuring: **5** ruler **7** ellwand **8** yardwand **9** yardstick
mountain climbing: **10** alpenstock
walking: **4** cane
sticker: bur **4** burr, seal **5** knife, label, poser, stamp, thorn **6** paster, puzzle, weapon **7** bramble
sticking: **6** viscid **8** adhering, cohesive
stick-in-the-mud: **4** fogy **6** square **10** fuddy-duddy **12** conservative
stickleback: **4** fish **6** bandie (Sc.)
stickler: **6** purist, second, umpire **7** arbiter, fanatic, meddler
stick out: **5** bulge **6** beetle **7** extrude **8** protrude
stick up: rob **6** hold up **7** plunder, ransack
sticky: **4** clit, hard **5** gluey, gooey, humid, messy **6** claggy, clammy, clarty, slushy, viscid, wooden **7** viscous **8** adhesive **9** difficult, glutinous **10** saccharine **11** sentimental
stiff: bum **4** body, dead, deep, firm, hard, high, hobo, taut **5** brave, budge, clung, dense, drunk, fixed, grave, harsh, horse, miser, rigid, steep, tense, thick, tramp, woody **6** clumsy, corpse, formal, loafer, proper, robust, severe, stanch, strong, sturdy **7** awkward, buckram, cadaver, precise, starchy **8** absorbed, drunkard, exact-

ing, resolute, rigorous, stalwart, starched, stubborn **9** difficult, excessive, laborious, obstinate, unbending **10** ceremonial, consistent **11** intoxicated

stiffen: set **5** brace **6** benumb, harden, starch **10** inspissate

stiff-necked: **5** proud, rigid **6** mulish **8** stubborn **9** obstinate **12** contumacious

stiffness: **5** rigor **8** rigidity **10** constraint **11** rigor mortis, starchiness

stifle: gag **4** stop **5** check, choke **6** muffle, quench **7** repress, silence, smother, squelch **8** restrain, strangle, stultify, suppress, throttle **9** suffocate **10** extinguish

stigma: **4** blot, mark, scar, spot **5** brand, cloud, odium, shame, stain, taint **6** defect **7** blemish **8** disgrace, dishonor

stigmatize: **5** brand **7** censure **8** denounce

stile: **4** post, step **8** entrance **9** turnstile

stiletto: **4** kill, stab **6** bodkin, dagger, stylet **9** eyeleteer

still: but, een, low, mum, tho, yet **4** also, calm, cosh, drip, even, ever, hush, lull, stop **5** allay, check, inert, quiet **6** always, distil, gentle, hushed, pacify, serene, soothe **7** appease, however, silence, subdued **8** habitual, inactive, restrain, suppress, tranquil **9** noiseless, uniformly **10** constantly, distillery, motionless, photograph, stationary, uneventful **11** continually **12** nevertheless

stillicide: **4** drip, drop **9** eavesdrop

stilt: **4** bird, limp, pile, pole, post **5** shaft **6** crutch **8** longlegs

stilted: **5** stiff **6** formal, wooden **7** awkward, pompous **8** affected **9** bombastic, dignified **10** rhetorical **11** sententious

Stilton: **6** cheese
 feature: **4** mold

stimulant: kat **4** drug **5** drink, speed, tonic, upper **6** bracer, pickup **7** impetus **8** beverage **9** incentive, sassafras **11** amphetamine
 heart: **8** cardiant, thialdin **9** digitalis, thialdine **10** adrenaline, epinephrin **11** epinephrine
 in coffee: **7** caffein **8** caffeine
 in tea: **5** thein

stimulate: fan, jog, pep **4** goad, move, spur, stir, urge, whet **5** brace, elate, filip, impel, rouse, sting **6** affect, arouse, excite, fillip, incite **7** animate, enliven, inspire, provoke, quicken **8** irritate, motivate **9** encourage, galvanize, instigate **10** exhilarate, invigorate

stimulating: **5** brisk **7** bracing, pungent **8** exciting **9** innerving **12** invigorating

stimulus: **4** goad, spur **5** cause, filip, sting **6** fillip, motive **7** impetus **9** incentive

sting: con, gyp **4** bite, dupe, goad, mast, pain, pike, pole, post, tang, urge **5** cheat, prick,

shaft, smart, wound **6** impale, incite, needle, nettle, pierce, tingle **7** stimuli **8** irritate, stimulus **9** stimulate **10** incitement **11** double cross

stinger: **4** blow **5** drink **8** cocktail

stinginess: **9** closeness, frugality, parsimony **13** niggardliness

stinging: **6** biting, bitter **7** caustic, piquant, pungent **8** piercing **10** irritating **11** acrimonious

stingo: ale, vim, zip **4** beer, zest **6** energy

stingy: **4** dree (Sc.), hard, mean **5** cheap, close, light, sharp, stint, tight **6** biting, greedy, meager, scanty **7** chintzy, miserly, niggard, nipping, selfish **8** covetous **9** illiberal, penurious **10** avaricious **11** closefisted **12** parsimonious

stinking: bad **4** foul, rank **5** drunk, fetid **6** putrid, rancid **7** noisome **8** unsavory **9** offensive **10** malodorous

stint, stent: **4** duty, stay, stop, task **5** bound, cease, check, chore, limit, scant, serve, spare, spell, stunt **6** assign, desist, divide, scrimp **7** confine **8** quantity, restrain, restrict **9** economize, restraint **10** assignment, limitation, proportion **11** restriction

stipe: **4** stem **5** stalk **6** caudex **7** petiole

stipend: ann, fee, pay **4** hire, wage **5** annal **6** income, salary **7** payment, prebend **9** allowance, emolument **12** compensation, remuneration

stipendiary: **4** beak **7** soldier, teacher **9** clergyman, mercenary **10** magistrate **11** beneficiary

stipple: dot **5** fleck **6** dapple, render **7** engrave, speckle

stipulate: **4** name **5** agree **7** bargain, provide, specify **8** contract, covenant

stipulation: **4** bond, item, term **6** clause, demand, detail **7** article, bargain, compact, proviso **8** contract, covenant **9** agreement, condition, situation **11** arrangement, undertaking

stir: ado, fan, gog, jog, mix, sir **4** busk, fuss, jail, move, plow, poke, roil, to-do **5** awake, budge, churn, doing, hurry, rally, rouse, shake, shift, shove, stoke, waken **6** arouse, awaken, bestir, bustle, excite, flurry, foment, hubbub, incite, motion, muddle, pother, prison, quetch, seethe, tumult **7** agitate, animate, blunder, disturb, flutter, inflame, provoke, trouble **8** activity **9** commotion, stimulate **10** manipulate

stirabout: **8** porridge

stirk: cow **4** bull **6** heifer **7** bullock

stirless: **10** motionless

stirps: **4** race **5** stock **6** branch, family

stirring: **5** afoot, astir **6** moving, tumult, uproar **7** rousing **8** activity, eloquent, exciting, movement **9** agitation, animating, inspiring, thrilling **10** incitement **11** stimulating

stirrup: bar **4** ring, rope **5** clamp, strap **6** stapes **7** support **8** footrest
hood: **8** tapadera (Sp.)
straps: **8** chapelet

stitch: bit, hem, sew **4** ache, join, pain, purl, seam **5** baste, picot, ridge, unite **6** feston, suture, tailor **8** distance, tack loop **9** embroider
knitting: **4** purl **6** feston
zigzag: **8** bargello

stitchbird: ihi

stitcher: **5** sewer **6** seamer **10** dressmaker

stitchwort: **9** chickweed

stithy: **5** anvil, forge **6** smithy **8** smithery

stive: **5** pen up **6** stifle **9** suffocate

stiver: **4** coin **5** money **7** bristle, stagger **8** struggle

stivy: **5** close **8** stifling

stoa: **5** porch **7** portico **9** colonnade

stoat: **6** ermine, weasel **8** clubster **9** clubstart

stob: **4** post, stab **5** stake **6** pierce

stock: cop, log **4** band, bond, butt, fund, hive, line, post, race, rail, soup, stem **5** banal, block, blood, brace, breed, broth, flesh, frame, hoard, stake, stick, store, stump, swell, trite, trunk, trust **6** budget, common, cravat, family, handle, holder, pillar, strain, supply **7** capital, descent, extract, lineage, provide, reserve, rhizome, support **8** ancestry, bitstock, colewort, material, ordinary **9** hackneyed, livestock, provision, replenish **10** estimation, foundation **11** commonplace
of food: **5** foray **6** larder, pantry
racial: **6** family **8** ancestry, pedigree

stockade: pen **4** jail **5** etape, pound **6** corral, kennel, prison **7** barrier, fortify, protect **8** hoosegow, poundage **9** enclosure

stocked: **7** replete

stock exchange: **4** NYSE **6** bourse (F.), NASDAQ
business: **9** arbitrage
patron: **5** buyer **6** seller, trader

stockfish: cod **4** hake, ling **5** torsk **7** haddock

stockholder: **8** investor

stocking: bas (F.) **4** hose **5** nylon **6** tights **7** hosiery **9** pantyhose
bishop's: **6** buskin, caliga
cotton: **5** lisle
footless: **7** hushion
ornament: **5** clock
run: **6** ladder
soleless: **7** traheen
worsted: **7** scogger

stock-in-trade: **4** tool, ware **5** goods **7** capital **8** material **9** equipment **11** merchandise

stockjobbing: **8** agiotage

stockman: **5** groom **6** cowboy, gaucho, herder **7** rancher **8** beastman, wrangler

stockpile: **5** amass, hoard, lay up **7** backlog, reserve **9** inventory, reservoir

stocky: fat **4** stub **5** cobby, solid, squat, stout **6** chumpy, chunky, stubby, sturdy **7** bunting, defiant **8** thickset **9** corpulent **10** boisterous, headstrong

stodge: **4** plod **6** trudge **7** satiate, satisfy

stodgy: **4** dull **5** bulky, heavy, tacky, thick **6** packed, sticky **7** crammed, lumpish, stuffed, tedious **8** thickset **9** out-of-date

stogy: **4** boot, shoe **5** cigar **6** brogan, clumsy, coarse

stoic: **5** porch **6** stolid **7** ascetic, passive, patient **9** impassive **10** phlegmatic **11** unconcerned

stoicism: **6** apathy **8** patience **9** stolidity **11** impassivity **13** impassiveness
founder: **4** Zeno

stoke: **4** feed, fire, fuel, poke, tend **5** stick **6** supply

stoker: **5** firer **7** fireman, greaser

stole: boa, fur **4** wrap **5** scarf **7** garment, orarion **8** vestment **13** epitrachelion

stolen property: **4** loot, pelf
buyer of: **5** fence

stolid: **4** dull, firm, slow **5** beefy, inert **6** stupid **7** brutish, clumpse, clumpst, passive **9** impassive, unfeeling **10** impassable, phlegmatic

stolon: **4** stem **5** shoot **6** branch, runner **7** rhizome

stoma: **4** pore **5** mouth **7** opening, orifice

stomach: gut, maw **4** bear, craw, crop, kyte, vell **5** belly, bingy, brook, pride, rumen, stand **6** bingey, desire, endure, gebbie (Sc.), resent, spirit **7** abdomen, gizzard, gizzern **8** appetite, tolerate **9** arrogance **11** inclination
acidity: **4** acor
enzyme: **6** pepsin, rennin
lower opening of: **7** pylorus
muscle: **7** pylorus
pert. to: **7** gastric
ruminant's first: **5** rumen
ruminant's fourth: **4** read, reed **8** abomasum, roddikin (Sc.)
ruminant's second: **6** bonnet **9** reticulum
ruminant's third: **6** omasum **9** manyplies **10** psalterium
used as food: **5** tripe

stomach-ache: **5** colic **6** nausea **7** gullion **12** collywobbles

stomacher: **4** gimp **7** echelle, garment **8** forepart

stomachy: **5** proud **8** paunched, spirited **9** irascible, irritable, obstinate, resentful **10** potbellied

stone: gem, pit, rub **4** bone, buhr, pelt, rock **5** block, brick, lapis (L.), scour, scrub **6** chaton, cobble, domino, marble **7** diamond, dornick, scruple, sharpen **8** lapidate, memorial, monolith, testicle **9** hailstone, hemachate, milestone, millstone, whetstone **10** gravestone, grindstone

abrasive: **5** emery

artificial: **8** albolite, albolith **9** granolith

base: **6** plinth

Biblical: **4** ezel

broken: **6** rubble

carved: **5** cameo

chip of: **5** spall **6** gallet

convert into: **7** petrify

druid: **6** sarsen

drupe: **6** nutlet

eagle: **5** etite

engraving: **8** intaglio

famous: **4** Hope, Pitt **5** Ayers, Green, Mogul, Sancy, Scone **6** Jonker, Nassak, Orloff, Regent, Vargas **7** Blarney, Dresden, Jubilee, Kohinur, Rosetta, Stewart, Tiffany **8** Braganza, Cullinan, Kohinoor **9** Excelsior, Polar Star **10** Florentine, Great Mogul **12** Star of Africa

fruit: pit **4** paip **5** drupe **6** pyrene **7** putamen

gem cutting: **6** adamas

granitic: **6** gneiss

grave: **5** stela, stele **6** marker, stelae, steles **8** memorial, monument

grinding: **6** metate

hammering: **8** lapstone

hand grinding: **4** mano

hard: **5** flint **6** quartz **7** adamant **9** chatoyant

heap: **4** karn **5** cairn

hoist: **5** lewis

hollow: **5** druse, geode

hurling device: **9** trebucket

implement: **4** celt **5** arrow **7** neolith

kidney: **8** calculus

loose: **6** gibber

meteoric: **8** aerolite, aerolith

monumental: **4** lech **6** menhir **8** megalith

paving: **4** flag, slab, slat **5** slate **6** cobble

pert. to: **7** lithoid

philosopher's: **6** carmot, elixir

precious: gem **4** ruby **5** beryl, pearl **7** diamond, emerald **8** sapphire

pyramid-shape: **6** benben

sharpening: oil **4** hone, whet

seam: dry

semiprecious: **4** jade, keas, onyx, opal, sard **5** agate, lapis, topaz **6** garnet, jasper, lazule, lazuli, ligure **7** olivine, peridot **8** amethyst, murrhine, tigereye **9** aromatite **11** lapis lazuli

small: **6** pebble

squared: **6** ashlar

to death: **8** lapidate

uncut: **4** naif

upright: **5** bauta **6** menhir

used for cameos: **4** onyx **5** ivory

woman turned into: **5** Niobe

worker: **5** mason **6** slater

writing: **5** slate

Stone Age tool: **4** celt **6** eolith **7** neolith **10** palaeolith

stonecrop: **5** orpin, sedum **6** orpine

stonecutter: **6** jadder

chisel: **5** drove

disease: **9** silicosis

wooden receptacle of: **7** sebilla

stoned: **4** high **5** doped, drunk **6** zonked **7** drugged **8** turned on **9** spaced-out **11** intoxicated

stonelike: **7** lithoid

stoneman: **5** cairn

stonewall: **5** evade, stall **8** obstruct, stubborn **9** obstinate **10** determined, filibuster

stoneware: **4** gres **7** ceramic, pottery **11** earthenware

stonework: **7** masonry

stoneworker: **5** mason

stonewort: **5** algae

stony: **4** card, cold, poor **5** fixed, rigid, rocky, rough, still **7** adamant **8** obdurate, pitiless **9** petrified, unfeeling **10** inexorable, inflexible, petrifying, relentless, stupefying

stood: **5** arose **7** endured

stooge: **4** foil, tool

stookie: **4** fool

stool: **4** base, mora, pole, seat, thew **5** bench, decoy, morae, stand, stump **6** buffet, growth, tiller, tripod **7** commode, creepie, taboret, trestle **8** kingship, platform, standard, tabouret

stoolpigeon: spy **4** fink, sing **5** decoy, narks, shill **6** inform, snitch **7** peacher **8** betrayer, informer, observer, squealer

stoop: bow, lay **4** bend, bode, duck, lean, post, sink, tilt **5** deign, lower, porch, slant, souse, stake, steps, stump, swoop, yield **6** alight, boggle, coorie, crouch, debase, gamble, huckle, humble, patron, pillar, pounce, submit **7** decline, degrade, descend, subject, succumb, veranda **8** overcome, platform, stairway **9** prostrate, supporter **10** condescend

stop: bar, dam, end, inn, pug **4** bait, balk, bode, bung, calk, call, clog, cork, drop, fill, halt, hold, mend, pawl, plug, quit, stay, stem, stum, wear, weir, whoa **5** avast, basta, belay, block, brake, break, catch, caulk, cease, check, choke, close, daunt, delay, embar, estop, holla, hollo, parry, pause, point, quell, repel, stall, tarry **6** alight, anchor, arrest, behold, boggle, defeat, desist, detain, draw up, finish, gravel, hinder, period, reside, scotch, stanch, stench **7** caesura, counter, prevent, shut off, sojourn, station, staunch, stopper, suspend **8** blockade, caesurae (pl.), obstacle, obstruct, obturate, pinblock, preclude, prohibit, restrain, stoppage, suppress, withhold **9** barricade, cessation, hindrance, intercept, interrupt, punctuate **11** countermand, discontinue, obstruction **12** intermission, interruption, lodginghouse

blood: **6** stanch

legally: **5** estop

organ: **5** orage, viola **7** posaune **8** dulciana, gemshorn **9** rohrflote

up: dam **4** cork, plug **7** occlude

stopcock: **5** valve **6** faucet

stope: **8** excavate **10** excavation

stopgap: **4** plug **5** shift **6** resort **9** expedient, makeshift, temporary **10** substitute

stoppage: end **4** halt **5** block, choke, hitch **6** arrest, devall, strike **7** embargo, seizure **9** cessation, detention **10** arrestment, congestion **11** obstruction

body fluid: **6** stasis

debate: **7** cloture

temporary: **5** delay, pause **6** arrest, recess **10** arrestment **12** interception, intermission, interruption

stopper: wad **4** bung, cork, fill, plug **7** bouchon, stopple

stopping: **4** halt **5** block, check **7** seizure **9** detention **11** obstruction, punctuation

device: **5** brake

stop watch: **5** timer

storage: **4** dump **11** safekeeping

battery plate: **4** grid

bin: mow **4** loft, silo **7** granary **8** elevator

charge: **7** yardage **9** demurrage

place: bin **4** bank, barn, shed, silo **5** attic, depot **6** armory, cellar, closet **7** arsenal, freezer, granary **8** cupboard, elevator, magazine **9** blood bank, reservoir, warehouse

prepare for: can **6** freeze

room: **6** closet, larder, pantry **7** lastage, lazaret **9** lazarette, lazaretto

storax: **5** resin **6** balsam

store: bin **4** cave, deck, deep, dose, fond, fund, hold, mass, save, shop, stow **5** amass, breed, cache, chain, depot, hoard, stash, stock **6** amount, budget, garner, market, repair, shoppe, supply **7** arsenal, bhandar, collect, deposit, furnish, grocery, husband, provide, put away, reserve, restore **8** boutique, emporium, magazine, quantity, reserves, supplies, treasure **9** abundance, chandlery, livestock, replenish, reservoir,

resources, warehouse **10** accumulate, collection, provisions **11** supermarket **12** accumulation

candle: **9** chandlery

fodder: **6** ensile **8** ensilate

fruit: **12** greengrocery

hidden: **5** cache

in ground: **5** cache

in silo: **6** ensile

military: **7** canteen **10** commissary

shoe: **7** bootery

up: **4** hive **6** garner **8** squirrel

storehouse: **4** barn, bike, crib, shed, silo **5** cache, depot, etape **7** arsenal, bhandar, camalig, camarin, granary **8** building, magazine, treasury **9** repertory, warehouse **10** commissary **11** chalkotheke

rural: mow **4** barn, crib, shed, silo **7** granary

wool: **6** lanary

storekeeper: **6** grocer **8** bhandari, merchant, storeman **10** shopkeeper **11** almacenista, haberdasher, stockkeeper

storeroom: **4** cave, gola, loft **5** attic **6** bodega, cellar, larder, pantry **7** buttery, genizah, granary **8** basement **10** repository

stork: **4** ibis **6** jabiru, simbil **7** maguari, marabou

kin of: **4** ibis **5** heron **10** hammerhead

storken: **6** thrive **7** congeal, stiffen

storklike: **8** pelargic

storm: wap **4** birr, blow, bura, fume, gale, gust, hail, rage, raid, rain, rand, rant, rave, snow, wind **5** anger, blizz, brash, buran, orage **6** attack, expugn, shamal, shower, simoom, simoon, squall, tumult, Wester **7** assault, barrage, bluster, borasca, borasco, bravado, cyclone, monsoon, rampage, tempest, tornado, trouble **8** blizzard, calamity, eruption, outburst, upheaval, violence **9** agitation, bourasque, commotion, hurricane **10** hurly-burly **11** disturbance

dust: **6** simoom

revolving: **7** cyclone, tornado **9** hurricane

sand: **6** tebbad

snow: **5** buran **8** blizzard

stormcock: **6** petrel, thrush **9** fieldfare **10** woodpecker

stormy: **4** dark, foul, wild **5** angry, dirty, gusty, rainy **6** cloudy, raging **7** furious, riotous, violent **8** agitated, cluttery **9** inclement, turbulent **10** blustering, passionate, tumultuous **11** tempestuous

story: fib, lie **4** hoax, myth, news, plot, saga, tale, tier, yarn **5** etage, fable, floor, rumor, solar, soler **6** canard, fabula, gossip, legend, record, report **7** account, article, episode, fiction, history, narrate, parable, recital, romance, untruth **8** anecdote, intrigue **9**

falsehood, happening, narration, narrative, statement, tradition **11** description
complication in: **4** node **5** nodus
continued: **6** sequel, serial
exclusive: **4** beat **5** scoop
heroic: **4** epic, gest, saga **5** geste
involved: **8** megillah
kind of: **4** epic, saga, tale, yarn **5** conte, fable, novel **6** canard, legend, script **7** fantasy, mystery, novella, parable, romance **8** allegory, scenario, whodunit **10** historical
short: **5** conte **8** anecdote
traditional: **4** myth **6** legend **8** folk tale
upper: **5** attic **6** garret
storyteller: **4** liar **5** Aesop **6** author, disour, fibber, writer **8** narrator, novelist **9** raconteur
stot: **4** bull **5** bound, lurch, steer **6** bounce **7** rebound, stagger, stammer, stumble, stutter
stound: **4** ache, beat, blow, pain, pang, stun, time **5** grief, shock, sight, smart, swoon, throb **6** attack, benumb, bruise, moment, period, season, sorrow, thrill, twinge **7** assault, instant, stupefy **8** astonish, occasion **10** apparition **12** astonishment, stupefaction
stoup: cup **4** cask, font, pail **5** basin **6** bucket, flagon, vessel **7** measure, tankard **10** aspersoria **11** aspersorium
holy water: **8** benitier, canthari (pl.) **9** cantharus, kantharoi (pl.), kantharos
stoush: **4** beat, blow **6** attack, strike, tirade **7** assault
stout: ale, fat **4** beer, bold, firm, gnat, hard **5** brave, bulky, burly, cobby, frack, freck, hardy, heavy, obese, plump, proud, shock, solid, tough **6** active, fierce, flagon, fleshy, liquor, porter, portly, robust, rotund, stable, stanch, stocky, stouty, strong, sturdy **7** defiant, haughty, valiant, violent, weighty **8** arrogant, bouncing, enduring, forceful, forcible, horsefly, insolent, intrepid, powerful, resolute, stalwart, stubborn, thickset, vigorous **9** corpulent, energetic, obstinate, strapping **10** courageous, overweight **11** substantial
stout-hearted: **4** bold, good **5** brave **7** doughty, valiant **8** unafraid **9** dauntless **10** courageous
stove: **4** dent, etna, kiln, oven **5** grate, plate, range, stave **6** cockle, cooker, galley, heater **7** furnace **8** Franklin, hotplate, potbelly **10** calefactor, glasshouse
alcohol: **4** etna
charcoal: hod
grated: **8** chauffer
part: **4** oven **6** burner **7** broiler, firebox, griddle
stovepipe: hat **4** flue **7** silk hat

stow: box, cut **4** cram, crop, hide, hold, mass, pack, stop, trim **5** cease, crowd, douse, dowse, lodge, place, shoot, slice, stack, store, stump **7** arrange, contain, secrete
cargo: **5** steve **6** steeve
stowage: **6** charge **7** packing
Stowe novel: **14** Uncle Tom's Cabin
character: **5** Topsy **8** Uncle Tom **9** Little Eva **11** Simon Legree
stower: **9** stevedore
strabismus: **6** squint **7** cock-eye **8** cross-eye
Strad, Stradivarius: **6** violin
straddle: **5** hedge, perch **6** option, sprawl **7** astride, bracket **8** bestride **11** noncommital, spread-eagle
strafe: **4** bomb **5** shell **6** punish **7** bombard **8** fire upon **9** castigate
straggle: lag **4** rove **5** stray **6** ramble, sprawl, wander **7** meander
straight: **4** neat **5** brant, erect, euthy, frank, ortho, plain, recti, rigid, sober, stern **6** aright, candid, direct, graith, honest, severe **7** rightly, sincere, stretch, through, unmixed, upright **8** accurate, directly, honestly, reliable, rigorous, sequence, unbroken, virtuous **9** correctly, honorably, undiluted **10** continuous, methodical, unmodified **11** immediately, straightway, undeviating, unqualified **12** continuously, conventional, heterosexual
straightaway: **4** anon **6** aright, bedene **8** directly **9** downright, forthwith **10** forthright **11** immediately
straight course: **7** beeline
straight edge: **5** ruler
straighten: **5** align, aline, level, order, plumb **7** compose, rectify, unravel **11** disentangle
up: **4** tidy **6** neaten
straight-faced: **7** deadpan **9** impassive
straightforward: **4** even, open **5** apert, frank **6** aright, candid, dexter, direct, honest, simple **7** sincere **8** directly, outright, straight **9** foreright, outspoken **10** forthright
straight-haired: **12** leiotrichous **13** lissotrichous
straight man: **4** foil **6** stooge
partner: **8** comedian
straight-out: **5** utter **6** direct **8** outright **11** unqualified
straight up and down: **8** vertical **13** perpendicular
strain: air, hug, sie, sye, tax, try **4** balk, barb, bend, bind, curb, dash, gain, heft, kind, line, mood, note, ooze, race, sift, solo, sort, tone, tune, turn, urge, vein **5** breed, clasp, class, demur, exert, force, music, press, raise, shade, sieve, stock, style, tenor, touch, trace, track, trail, wield **6** burden, colate, effort, extend, extort, family, fasten,

filter, injure, manner, melody, obtain, sprain, strand, streak, stress, strive, temper, thread, weaken, wrench **7** anxiety, confine, descent, element, embrace, lineage, overtax, progeny, quality, squeeze, stretch, strophe, tension, trickle, variety **8** ancestry, brandish, compress, eliquate, exertion, restrain, tendency **9** begetting, character, constrain, constrict, percolate **10** distortion, generation **11** deformation, disposition
blood: **4** race **5** breed, stock **6** family **7** lineage
chief: **5** brunt
great: tax, tug **5** tense **6** stress **7** tension **8** exertion, overbear **11** tenterhooks
measuring device: **9** telemeter

strained: **4** taut **5** tense, tight **6** forced **7** intense **8** weakened, wrenched **9** distorted, laborious **10** farfetched

strainer: **4** cage, sile **5** sieve, strum, tamis **6** filter, milsey, milsie, sifter **8** colander, colature, huckmuck **10** colatorium

strait: **4** area, bind, neck, pass **6** crisis, narrow **7** channel, isthmus

straiten: **5** hem in, limit, pinch **6** hamper **7** confine, enclose **8** contract, distress, restrict **9** embarrass

strait-jacket: **8** camisole **9** restraint

strait-laced: **4** prim **5** stiff **6** proper, severe **7** prudish **8** stubborn **9** obstinate, puritanic **10** restricted **11** constrained

Strait of Messina rock: **6** Scylla

straits: **4** need **5** pinch, rigor **7** narrows, poverty **8** extremes **10** difficulty

Straits Settlement: **6** Melaka, Penang **7** Malacca **9** Singapore
district: **8** Dindings
island: **5** Cocos **6** Labuan **9** Christmas
native state: **5** Perak **6** Johore, Pahang **8** Selangor **11** Sungei Ujong **13** Negri Sembilan

strake: rut **4** band **5** crack **6** loiter, streak, stripe, stroll, trough, wander **7** stretch

strand: sea **4** bank, quay, sand, wire **5** beach, coast, fiber, shore, wharf **6** gutter, maroon, region, stream, thread **7** channel, current **8** filament **9** shipwreck

stranded: **5** stuck **6** ashore **7** aground, beached **8** castaway, marooned **10** high and dry

strange: neo, new, odd **4** fell, rare, unco **5** alien, droll, eerie, fremd, fresh, novel, queer **6** exotic, quaint **7** bizarre, curious, distant, erratic, foreign, oddball, uncanny, unknown, unusual **8** abnormal, estrange, fanciful, peculiar, reserved, singular, uncommon **9** couthless, different, eccentric, unnatural, wonderful **10** mysterious, outlandish, unfamiliar, unfriendly **11**
exceptional **12** unaccustomed **13** extraordinary

stranger: **5** alien, guest, odder **6** ganger, novice **7** comical, visitor **8** emigrant, estrange, intruder, newcomer, outsider **9** auslander, foreigner, outlander **10** tramontane **12** intermeddler

strangle: **4** kill, slay **5** choke, grane **6** stifle **7** garrote, repress **8** garrotte, suppress, throttle **9** constrict, suffocate

stranglehold: **4** grip **8** chancery, monopoly

strangulate: **5** choke **8** compress, obstruct **9** constrict

strap: bar, fit, tie **4** band, beat, belt, bind, cord, flog, gird, hang, rein, riem, whip **5** girth, groom, strip, strop, thong **6** billet, chaser, credit, enarme, fillet, halter, latigo, ligule, punish, secure, string **7** furnish, laniard, lanyard, sharpen **8** chastise
kind of: **4** jess, taws **5** guige, leash, strop, tawse, thong **6** chaser, enarme **8** bretelle **10** boondoggle

strapping: **5** lusty, stout **6** robust, strong, sturdy **7** beating **9** thrashing

strap-shaped: **6** lorate **7** ligular **8** ligulate

strass: **5** glass, paste

strata: *geological:* **4** lias
later: **7** neozoic
social: **7** classes

stratagem: **4** coup, plot, ruse, wile **5** cheat, dodge, feint, fetch, fraud, trick **6** blench, device, humbug, scheme **7** finesse **8** artifice, intrigue, maneuver **9** chicanery, deception, execution, expedient, slaughter **10** artfulness **11** machination
smart: **8** liripipe, liripoop

strategy: **4** plan **7** tactics **8** artifice, game plan, intrigue, maneuver

stratification: **5** layer **7** bedding

stratum: bed **5** class, layer, level, table **6** couche **7** section **8** division
thin: **4** seam

Strauss opera: **6** Salome **7** Electra **10** Fledermaus **13** Rosenkavalier **14** Ariadne on Naxos

Stravinsky work: **8** Firebird **10** Petrouchka **12** Rite of Spring

straw: hat, wap **4** gloy, mote, pipe, rush **5** chaff **6** fescue, litter, trifle **9** worthless, yellowish **11** meaningless **12** churchwarden
bed: **6** pallet
bundle of: **6** batten **8** windling
coat: **4** mino
color: **6** flaxen
colored: **11** stramineous
for hats: **6** sennit **7** leghorn, sabutan **8** jipijapa
half rotten: **5** mulch
load of: **5** barth

man: **9** scarecrow
plaited: **6** sennit
threshing floor: **6** bhossa
to protect plants: **5** mulch
waxed: **6** strass
weaving: **5** rafia

strawberry: **6** fraise, runner **8** fragaria

straw in the wind: **4** clue, omen, sign **7** portent, warning

strawlike: **11** stramineous

straw vote: **4** poll

stray: err, gad, odd **4** cavy, roam, rove, waif **5** range **6** casual, course, errant, random, stroll, swerve, wander **7** decline, deviate, digress, forlorn, go wrong, habitat, runaway, saunter **8** detached, distract, divagate, isolated, maverick, straggle **9** straggler, unrelated **10** incidental, occasional
calf: **4** dogy **5** dogie

straying: **6** astray, errant **7** erratic **8** aberrant **9** deviation, erroneous **10** adulterous, unfaithful

streak: **4** hint, line, mark, vein, wale **5** fleck, freak, garle, hurry, layer, lined, round, smear, spell, trace, trait **6** period, smooth, strain, strake, stripe, stroke **7** stratum, striped **8** discolor, run naked **10** suggestion
mottled: roe
narrow: **5** stria **6** striae

streaked: **4** liny **6** marked **7** alarmed, brindle, striped, worried **8** brindled **10** variegated

streaking: **11** frosted hair

streaky: **4** liny **5** liney, mixed **6** uneven **8** variable

stream: run **4** burn, flow, flux, ford, gote, gush, pour, rill, rush **5** bache, bayou, bourn, brook, creek, fleam, floss, flume, fluor, force, issue, river, speed, trend **6** amount, bourne, course, fluent, runnel **7** channel, current, rivulet **8** affluent **9** anabranch **11** watercourse
dry bed: **6** arroyo
lava: **6** coulee
living in: **7** aquatic **9** amphibian, rheophile
ravine: **4** ghyl, gill
rushing: jet **7** torrent
small: run **4** race **5** brook **6** rillet, runlet **7** rivulet **9** streamlet
sound: **4** purl **6** murmur
underground: aar
upper part of: **6** source **9** headwater

streamer: jet **4** flag **5** strip **6** guidon, ribbon **7** feather, pendant, pennant **8** banderol, headline **9** banderole

streamlet: **4** rill **5** brook **6** rillet, runlet, runnel **7** freshet, rivulet

streamlined: **5** clean, sleek **6** modern **8** straight **10** simplified

street: rew (Sc.), rue (F.), via (It.), way **4** lane, road **5** calle (Sp.), chare, route **6** avenue, causey, ruelle, spread **7** highway, roadway, strasse (G.) **8** chaussee, contrada **9** boulevard
ditch: **6** gutter
narrow: **4** wynd **5** alley, place

streetcar: **4** tram **7** trolley
driver: **8** motorman

street urchin: **4** arab **5** gamin

streetwalker: **5** whore **6** hooker, wanton **7** cruiser **10** prostitute

strength: arm **4** beef, iron, main, thew **5** brawn, force, might, power, sinew, vigor **6** energy, foison, muscle **7** ability, potency, stamina, sthenia **8** capacity, firmness, solidity, validity **9** coherence, endurance, fortitude, intensity, lustiness, puissance, stability, stoutness, substance, toughness, vehemence **10** heartiness, robustness
deprive of: **7** unnerve **8** diminish, enervate
diminish: **6** dilute, weaken **9** water down
electric current: **8** amperage
liquor: **5** proof
loss: **8** asthenia
of character: **4** grit, guts, sand **8** backbone **9** fortitude
of will: **8** backbone
regain: **5** rally
solution: **5** titer, titre

strengthen: add **4** back, bind, frap, gird, help, prop **5** brace, nerve, steel **6** clench, deepen, endure **7** afforce, comfort, confirm, educate, fortify, nourish, stiffen, support, sustain, toughen **8** buttress, roborate **9** encourage, reinforce **10** invigorate **11** consolidate
with alcohol: **5** spike **7** fortify

strenuous: **4** hard **5** eager **6** active, ardent, severe **7** arduous, zealous **8** vigorous **9** energetic

strepitant: **5** noisy **9** clamorous

stress: try **4** pain **5** brunt, force, labor, press **6** accent, strain **7** afflict, amplify, overtax, tension, urgency **8** ampliate, distrain, distress, emphasis, exertion, pressure **9** emphasize, intensity **10** constraint, importance, overstrain, resistance **12** significance
free from: **4** calm **6** anneal **7** relaxed
mechanical: **8** erossure
metrical: **5** ictus
music: **6** accent
voice: **5** arsis **6** accent

stretch: run **4** span, walk **5** crane, range, reach, retch, space, tract, while, widen **6** course, dilate, effort, eke out, expand, extend, period, spread, strain **7** distend, elastic, enlarge, expanse, tension **8** distance, elongate, sentence **9** direction, embroider, extension **10** exaggerate

injuriously: **6** sprain
out: lie **4** rest **6** repose **7** recline
the neck: **5** crane
the truth: lie **10** exaggerate
stretched: **6** craned **7** porrect **8** extended, prolated **9** elongated
tight: **4** taut **5** tense
while drying: **8** tentered
stretcher: **5** dooly **6** gurney, litter, racker, tenter **8** ringhead
neck: **6** craner
strew: **4** cast **6** litter, spread **7** diffuse, scatter **8** disperse, sprinkle **9** bespatter, broadcast **10** besprinkle **11** disseminate
strewing: **4** seme
stria: **4** band, line, vein **5** ridge **6** fillet, furrow, groove, hollow, streak, stripe **7** channel
stricken (see also **strike**): ill **5** upset **7** smitten, worn out, wounded **9** afflicted **13** incapacitated
strickle: **5** rifle **7** pattern **8** template
strict: **4** blue, hard, true **5** close, exact, harsh, rigid, stern, tense, tight **6** entire, narrow, severe **7** ascetic, austere, binding, correct, literal, perfect, precise **8** absolute, accurate, intimate, limiting, rigorous, straight **9** confining, puritanic, stringent **10** compressed, forbidding, hardboiled, inexorable, inflexible, iron-handed, relentless, scrupulous **11** punctilious, puritanical, restricting, straitlaced
disciplinarian: **8** martinet
discipline: **13** regimentation
strictness: **5** rigor **9** closeness
in law: **8** legalism
stricture: **4** sign **5** spark, touch, trace **7** binding, censure, closing **9** criticism **11** contraction **13** animadversion
strid: **5** gorge **6** ravine
stride: **4** pace, step, walk **5** stalk **7** advance **8** bestride, progress, straddle **11** advancement
strident: **5** harsh, noisy, rough **6** shrill **7** grating, raucous, yelling **11** acrimonious, cacophonous
stridulate: **5** cheep, chirk, chirp, creak, crick **7** clitter
strife: war **4** bait, bate, feud **5** clash, fight, flite, flyte, noise, strow **6** combat, debate, estrif, fracas **7** contest, discord, hurling, quarrel **8** conflict, endeavor, exertion, struggle **9** emulation **10** contention **11** altercation, competition, controversy
about mere words: **9** logomachy
civil: **6** stasis
striffen: **8** membrane, thin skin
strigil: **7** scraper
strigose, strigous: **5** rough, sharp **6** hispid **7** bristly

strike: bat, bob, box, cob, cop, dab, dad, hew, hit, lam, pat, ram, rap, wap **4** baff, bang, bash, bean, beat, biff, bill, bump, bunt, chap, cope, coup, cuff, dash, daub, daud, dint, dunt, fist, flap, flog, frap, gird, give, gowf, hurl, hurt, knap, lash, pelt, rout, slam, slap, slay, swat **5** clash, clink, clout, douse, dowse, dunch, filch, gowff, impel, knock, occur, punch, skelp, skite, slash, smear, smite, spank, swipe, trend, whang **6** assail, attack, attain, bounce, buffet, cancel, fettle, hammer, hartal, picket, pommel, punish, wallop **7** afflict, boycott, clobber, collide, impress, walkout **8** discover, shutdown, slowdown, struggle
a balance: **5** agree **6** settle **10** compromise
against: ram **4** bump **5** crash **7** assault, collide
demonstrator: **6** picket
down: **4** fell, kill **5** floor **7** disable, nullify
dumb: **4** stun
feature: **7** lockout **10** picket line
gently: dab, pat **4** bump, putt
heavily: lam, ram **4** bash, slog, slug
obliquely: **5** carom
on head: **4** bean
out: fan **4** dele, head **5** elide, erase **6** cancel, delete, set out **7** venture **9** eliminate
prepare to: **4** coil
series of blows: **4** pelt
settler: **8** mediator
together: **5** clash, crash **7** collide
up: **5** begin, start **8** commence
violently: ram **4** bash, slam
with fist: jab **4** plug **5** pound, punch
with head: **4** butt
with wonder: awe **7** astound **8** surprise
strikebreaker: rat **4** fink, goon, scab **8** blackleg (Br.)
striker: **4** tern **6** batman, batter, helper, hitter, smiter **7** batsman, clapper, mobster **9** assistant, harpooner
striking: **4** dint **5** showy, vivid **6** cogent, signal **7** salient, telling **8** dramatic, stunning **9** arresting, effective **10** noticeable, pronounced, remarkable, surprising **11** conspicuous
effect: **5** eclat
string: **4** band, cord, hoax, josh, lace, line **5** bound, braid, chain, fiber, jolly, strip, twine **6** series, thread **8** resource **10** conditions, succession
course: **6** guidon
kinds of: **4** wire **5** lacet, snare **6** amenta, hypate, lachet **7** amentum, langate
of beads: **6** rosary **8** necklace
up: **4** hang, lace **5** lynch, scrab **6** gibbet
string along: toy **4** fool **5** dally **6** follow, lead on **7** deceive, flatter

stringent: 4 grim, hard, ropy 5 harsh, rigid, tense, tight 6 cogent, severe, strict 7 binding, extreme 8 exacting, rigorous 10 convincing 11 restrictive

stringer: tie 4 rope, vein 6 timber 8 filament 13 correspondent

string instrument: uke 4 harp, lute, lyre 5 banjo, cello, piano, viola 6 fiddle, guitar, spinet, violin, zither 7 ukelele, ukulele 8 mandolin 11 harpsichord
old: 4 lute, lyre 6 spinet 8 psaltery 11 harpsichord

stringy: 4 ropy 5 gluey 6 sinewy, viscid 7 fibrous, viscous 8 muscular 11 filamentous

strip: bar, rob, tab, tag, top 4 band, bare, bark, belt, doff, flay, hull, husk, peel, pull, skin, tear 5 clear, flake, fleck, pluck, shred, spoil, swath, unrig 6 border, denude, devest, divest, expose, flense, length, ravage, reduce, remove, runway, swathe 7 bandage, bandeau, bereave, degrade, deprive, despoil, disrobe, pillage, plunder, uncloak, uncover, undress, unleave 8 bandeaux (pl.), denudate, disarray, headland, separate 9 dismantle, excoriate 10 disfurnish, dispossess 11 debenzolize, decorticate
blubber: 6 flense
kinds of: 4 came, cove, lead, rand, riem, tirr 5 cleat, ridge, stave 6 inwale, reglet 7 gunwale
leather: 4 welt 5 thong 6 latigo 7 belting
narrow: 4 slat, tape 5 reeve, strap 7 bandeau 8 bandeaux (pl.)
wooden: rib 4 lath, slat 5 stave 6 reglet

stripe: bar, ilk, roe 4 band, beat, belt, blow, kind, lash, line, mark, sort, type, wale, weal, welt, zone 5 chest, stria 6 border, frenum, streak, strike, stroke 7 chevron, lineate, pattern, rivulet 8 division 9 character

striped: 5 bandy, tabby 6 banded, barred 7 lineate, vittate 8 bayadere, streaked
animal: 5 bongo, zebra
cloth: 6 madras 7 ticking 10 seersucker

stripling: boy, lad 5 chiel, youth 6 chield

stripped: 4 bare, nude 5 naked 6 picked 10 deprived of 11 defenseless
by trickery: 7 buncoed, bunkoed, fleeced

strip tease dancer: 9 ecdysiast

strive: aim, hie, tew, try, tug, vie 4 seek, toil 5 assay, bandy, ensue, fight, labor, rival 6 battle, buffet, resist, strain 7 attempt, compete, contend, contest, emulate 8 contrast, endeavor, struggle

striving: 5 nisus 7 attempt, contest

strobile: 4 chat 8 pine cone

strockle: 6 shovel

stroke: bat, coy, fit, hew, hit, pat, pet, rub 4 baff, beat, blow, chap, coup, dash, ding, dint, feat, flip, gowf, hurt, lash, lick, line, mark, milk, oner, peal, shot, walk, whet 5 chare, douse, dowse, flack, fluke, gowff, ictus, knell, knock, palsy, power, pulse, rower, strut, throb, trait 6 attack, caress, effort, fondle, ictuse, impact, injury, soothe, stride 7 massage, seizure, sharpen, whample 8 apoplexy, disaster 9 influence
brilliant: ace 4 coup
cutting: 4 chop 5 slice
kinds of: 5 cerif, eagle, serif, wedge 6 birdie 7 virgule
of luck: hit 5 fluke 6 strike 8 windfall
short: 4 flip, putt 5 whisk

stroll: 4 gait, mosy, roam, rove, walk 5 amble, mosey, range, stray, tramp 6 dacker, daiker, dander, ramble, soodle, wander 7 saunter

stroller: 4 cart, pram 5 actor, sulky, tramp 6 beggar, gocart, pedler, player, shuler 7 peddlar, shuiler, vagrant 8 bohemian, carriage, wanderer 9 saunterer

Stromboli: 6 island 7 volcano

stromming: 7 herring

strong: fit, hot 4 able, bold, dure, elon, fere, firm, fort, hale, hard, rank, sure, warm, wiry 5 bonny, clear, eager, frack, freck, fresh, great, gross, hardy, heavy, large, lusty, solid, sound, stout, tough, valid, vivid, yauld 6 active, ardent, bonnie, brawny, cogent, feckle, fierce, mighty, potent, robust, rugged, sinewy, stable, sturdy 7 buirdly, durable, fertile, greatly, humming, intense, sthenic, violent, zealous 8 accented, athletic, distinct, flagrant, forceful, forcible, muscular, powerful, puissant, resonant, rigorous, severely, stalwart, striking, strongly, superior, vehement, vigorous 9 Atlantean, difficult, effective, herculean, impetuous, important, strapping, tenacious, violently 10 boisterous, formidable, forthright, malodorous, nourishing, outrageous, passionate, persuasive, productive, pronounced, remarkable, spirituous

strong-arm: rob 4 beat, thug 5 force, power 7 assault 8 violence 9 terrorize 10 intimidate
man: 4 goon 7 bouncer

strongbox: 4 case, safe 5 chest, vault 6 coffer

stronghold: 4 fort, hold, keep 5 tower 6 castle 7 bulwark, citadel, fortify, redoubt 8 fasthold, fastness, fortress 13 fortification

strong man: 6 tyrant 10 powerhouse
Biblical: 6 Samson 7 Sampson
legendary: 5 Atlas 8 Herakles, Hercules

strong point: 5 forte

strong-smelling: 4 foul, rank 5 fetid 8 mephitic, stinking

strop: 4 hone, whet 5 strap 7 sharpen

strophe: 6 stanza 10 heptastich

stroygood: 7 wastrel 11 spendthrift

struck: 4 smit 5 smote 7 shocked, smitten 8 punished 9 impressed

with amazement: **6** aghast **9** astounded
with sudden fear: **7** alarmed **10** terrorized
with terror: **6** aghast **7** shocked
struck out: **5** deled **6** elided, erased, fanned **7** deleted
structural quality: **7** texture
structure: dam **4** form **5** frame, house **6** bridge, fabric, format, make-up, syntax **7** edifice, texture **8** building, bulkhead **9** formation, framework **11** arrangement, composition, fabricature
abnormal: **12** malformation
calcareous: **5** coral
conical: **7** pyramid
crown-like: **6** corona
curved: **4** arch
floating: **4** roar
funeral: **10** catafalque
grammatical: **6** syntax
hallowed: **6** bethel, chapel, church, temple **8** basilica **9** cathedral, synagogue **10** tabernacle
high: **5** tower **7** steeple **9** campanile **10** skyscraper
human: **8** physique, skeleton
keel-like: **6** carina
latticework: **7** trellis
looplike: **4** ansa
monumental: **5** pylon **7** pyramid
on roof: **6** cupola, dormer **7** chimney **9** penthouse **10** widow's walk
Oriental: **6** pagoda
original: **6** isogen
osseous: **4** bone
pergola-like: **6** ramada
pert. to: **8** tectonic
projecting into water: **4** dock, jiti, pier, quay **5** jetty, wharf **6** jettee **10** breakwater
raised: **4** dais **5** altar, stage **8** platform
sacrificial: **5** altar
sheltering: cot **4** cote
supporting: **4** pier
tent-like: **10** tabernacle
white: **6** albedo
strudel: **6** pastry **10** puff pastry
struggle: try, tug, vie **4** agon, cope, fend, frab, toil, wade **5** fight, heave, labor **6** battle, buckle, bustle, combat, effort, Peniel, strife, strike, strive, throes, tussle, widdle **7** attempt, bargain, barrace, contend, contest, flounce, grapple, scuffle, warfare, wrestle **8** conflict, endeavor, exertion, flounder, scraffle, scramble **10** contention, difficulty
a deux: **4** duel
helplessly: **8** flounder
struma: **6** goiter, goitre
strummed: **8** thrummed
strumpet: **4** brim, tart **5** belie, wench **6** blowen, harlot, wanton **7** cocotte, debauch,

slander, trollop **8** harridan **10** prostitute
strung: **6** beaded
highly: **4** taut **5** tense **7** nervous
strut: **4** brag, cock, gait, step, walk **5** brace, bulge, swell **6** flaunt, parade, sashay, stride, strife, strunt, thrust **7** distend, peacock, provide, stiffen, stretch, support, swagger, wrangle **8** protrude **10** contention **11** protuberant
struthious: **4** emus **5** rheas **6** ratite **9** ostriches
stub: pen **4** beat, dolt, snag **5** crush, drive, guard, hinge, squat, stumb **6** coupon, nubbin, stocky, strike **7** feather, remnant **8** thickset **9** blockhead, extirpate **11** counterfoil
stubble: bun **6** strunt **8** eelgrass
field: **5** rowen
stubborn: set **4** rude **5** fixed, hardy, harsh, rough, tough **6** coarse, dogged, mulish, sturdy **7** restive, willful **8** obdurate, perverse, resolute, starkish, vigorous **9** camsteary, camsteery, difficult, obstinate, pigheaded **10** bullheaded, calcitrant, determined, hardheaded, headstrong, inflexible, refractory, unyielding **11** intractable, persevering **12** pertinacious
stubby: **5** squat **6** stocky, stumpy **8** thickset
stuck: See **stick**
stuck in the mud: **7** bemired
stuck-up: **4** vain **6** snooty **7** haughty **8** arrogant, snobbish **9** conceited **12** supercilious
stud: dot, pin, rod **4** boss, knob, male, nail, spot, stub **5** adorn, aglet, beset, brace, haras, horse, study, stump **6** aiglet, button, pillar **7** chaplet, support **8** sprinkle **9** studhorse
farm: **5** haras
for shoe: **7** hobnail
with jewels: **5** engem
with radiating bodies: **6** enstar
student: **5** eleve (F.), pupil **6** bursar **7** educand, learner **8** disciple, observer
according to grade: **6** termer
agricultural college: **5** Aggie
college: **4** coed, soph **6** junior, senior **7** protege, scholar **8** freshman **9** sophomore **13** undergraduate
divinity: **9** theologue **10** seminarian, theologian
fellow: **9** classmate
first-year: **5** Fuchs (G.) **8** freshman
former: **4** alum **6** alumna **7** alumnus, dropout **8** graduate
fourth-year: **6** senior
female: **4** coed
group: **5** class
hall: **5** burse **9** dormitory
in charge: **7** monitor
law: **8** stagiary

medical: **6** intern **7** interne
military: **5** cadet, plebe
naval academy: **5** cadet **10** midshipman
of birds: **13** ornithologist
of crime: **10** penologist
of heavens: **13** uranographist
of proverbs: **14** paroemiologist
of punishment: **10** penologist
of reptiles: **13** herpetologist
of spiders: **13** arachnologist
Oxford: **8** commoner
probationary: **8** stibbler
residence: **4** dorm **5** house **6** hostel **9** dormitory
second-year: **9** sophomore
stipend paid: **6** bursar
talmudic: **5** bahur
third-year: **6** junior
West Point: **5** cadet, plebe
studied: **5** pored **6** intent **7** learned, planned **8** affected, designed, inclined, measured, reasoned **10** calculated, ceremonial, deliberate **12** premeditated
studies: *academic:* **4** arts **7** science **10** humanities
   advanced: **7** seminar **8** doctoral, graduate **12** post-graduate
   chosen by students: **9** electives
   series of: **6** course
studio: **7** atelier, bottega **8** workshop **11** ergasterion
studious: **5** booky **7** bookish, devoted, studied **8** diligent, sedulous **9** assiduous, scholarly
study: con, den, mug **4** bone, cram, muse, muzz, pore, read, scan **5** grind, learn **6** lesson, peruse, ponder **7** analyse, analyze, canvass, croquis, examine, reverie **8** consider, exercise, meditate **9** attention **10** scrutinize **11** contemplate **13** consideration, contemplation
animals: **9** zoography
bees: **8** apiology
Bible: **9** isagogics
closely: con **4** pore **7** examine
course: **7** seminar
fingerprints: **13** dactylography
fixed course: **4** rote
flowers: **12** anthoecology
group: **7** seminar
handwriting: **10** graphology
horses: **9** hippology
human generations: **15** anthropogenesis
insect's habits: **10** entomology
laborious: **11** lucubration
mountains: **7** orology
musical: **5** etude
optional: **8** elective
population: **10** demography, larithmics
preliminary: **6** sketch

punishment: **8** penology
sacred edifices: **7** naology
sacred images: **9** iconology
sermons: **10** homiletics
wines: **7** enology **8** oenology
words: **9** etymology **10** lexicology
stuff: eat, jam, pad, ram, wad **4** copy, cram, fill, gaum, junk, pang, sate **5** crowd, farce, force, grain, pulse, steve **6** fabric, graith, matter, refuse, stifle **7** bombast, element, essence, filling, mixture, portion **8** material, medicine, nonsense, overload **9** character, principle, substance, suffocate
full: **4** glut, sate **5** gorge **6** stodge **7** satiate
stuffed: **4** full **6** bourre, stodgy **7** bombast, replete **8** farctate
stuffing: **7** padding, viscera **8** dressing **9** forcemeat
stuffy: fat **4** dull, prim **5** angry, close, fubsy, fuggy, humid, stout, sulky **6** froust, frowst, stodgy **7** airless, pompous **8** resolute, stifling **9** obstinate **10** mettlesome, old-fogyish **11** strait-laced **12** conservative, old-fashioned
Stuka: **6** bomber **10** dive-bomber
stulm: **4** adit **8** entrance **10** passageway
stultiloquy: **6** babble **11** foolish talk
stumble: err **4** fall, slip, trip **5** lurch **6** boggle, chance, faffle, falter, happen, offend, puzzle, teeter, wallow **7** blunder, failure, founder, perplex, stagger, stammer **8** confound, flounder, scrupple
stumbling block: **8** obstacle **9** hindrance **10** impediment **11** obstruction
stump: cob, end, lop **4** butt, dare, foil, grub, plod, snag, stab, stub **5** block, clump **6** baffle, corner, hobble, lumber, pillar, puzzle, strunt, thwart, travel **7** blunted, canvass, nonplus, perplex, rostrum, stumble **8** defiance, platform **9** challenge **11** electioneer
stumps: **4** legs **5** stubs
stumpy: **5** bunty, money **6** stubby **8** thickset
stun: **4** bowl, daze, tear **5** amaze, daunt, daver, dizzy, dover, shock **6** appall, benumb, bruise, crease, deaden, deafen **7** astound, dammish, scratch, startle, stupefy **8** astonish, bewilder, surprise **9** dumbfound, overpower, overwhelm **10** strike dumb
stunning: **7** stylish **8** dazzling, gorgeous **9** beautiful, excellent **10** foudroyant
stunt: act **4** feat **5** angry, blast, blunt, check, cramp, crowl, dwarf, stamp, trick, whale **6** abrupt, hinder **7** curtail, exploit, shorten **8** stubborn, suppress **10** undersized **11** performance
stunty: **5** short **6** flashy, stocky **7** dwarfed
stupa: **4** tomb **5** mound, tower **6** shrine
lamaism: **7** chorten
stupefacient: **4** drug **8** narcotic

stupefy: fox, sot **4** baze, daze, dope, doze, drug, dull, dunt, numb, stun **5** amaze, aston, besot, blunt, daunt, daver, deave, shock **6** astone, bedaze, bemuse, benumb, muddle **7** astound, confuse **8** astonish, bewilder, confound **10** incrassate
with drink: **6** fuddle

stupendous: **4** huge, vast **5** great, large **7** amazing, immense **8** enormous **9** humongous, marvelous, monstrous **10** astounding **11** astonishing **12** overpowering, overwhelming

stupid: **4** bete, clod, dull, dumb, dunt, guam, lewd, slow **5** besot, blunt, booby, crass, dazed, dense, dizzy, dunce, goosy, heavy, inane, sumph **6** assish, barren, beetle, boring, bovine, dawkin, doiled, doited, drowsy, goosey, hebete, lurdan, oafish, obtuse, simple, stolid, torpid **7** asinine, brutish, buzzard, calvish, daffish, doldrum, doltish, duffing, dullard, fatuous, foolish, foppish, glaiket, glaikit, gomerel, goosish, gullish, lurdane, prosaic, stunned, vacuous, witless **8** anserine, anserous, backward, bayardly, blockish, boeotian, cloddish, deadened, footless, headless, retarded, sluggish **9** blocklike, bourgeois, brainless, codheaded, inanimate, insensate, insipient, lethargic, plumbeous, pointless, senseless, stupefied **10** hardwitted, hulverhead, slow-witted **11** claybrained
person: ass, sap **4** clod, clot, coot, dolt, dope, fool, jerk, loon **5** dummy, dunce, goose, idiot, moron, ninny **6** dimwit **7** dullard, fathead **8** numskull **9** blockhead, simpleton

stupor: fog **4** coma, damp, daze, dote **5** sleep, sopor **6** apathy, trance **7** languor **8** lethargy
pert. to: **7** carotic, narcose

sturdy: gid, set **4** buff, firm **5** felon, hardy, harsh, lusty, sound, stern, stiff, stout **6** brawny, robust, rugged, rustic, stable, steady, strong **7** violent **8** obdurate, resolute, stalwart, stubborn, vigorous **9** obstinate, rigidness, strapping **10** courageous, determined, unyielding **11** substantial

sturgeon: **6** beluga
roe: **6** caviar
small: **7** sterlet

Sturm und Drang (G.): **6** tumult, unrest **7** ferment, turmoil **8** upheaval

stutter: **7** stammer

stuttering: **8** psellism

sty, stye: pen **4** boil, dump, sink **5** lodge, stair, steps, stile **6** ladder, pigpen **8** swelling **9** enclosure

stygian: **4** dark **5** black **6** gloomy **7** hellish **8** infernal

style: air, dub, fad, pen, pin, ton, way **4** call, garb, gere, kind, mode, name, rage, sort, term, tone, type **5** craze, taste, usage, vogue **6** format, gnomon, graver, manner, method, needle, phrase, stylus **7** alamode, diction, entitle, fashion, variety **8** demeanor **9** designate, execution **10** denominate **12** characterize, construction
architecture: **5** Doric, Greek, Ionic, Roman, Saxon **6** Gothic, Norman **7** Italian **8** Colonial, Georgian, Monterey **9** Byzantine **10** Art Nouveau, Corinthian, Romanesque **11** Elizabethan, Renaissance **13** Mediterranean
art: **5** genre
artistic: **5** gusto
fantastic: **6** rococo **7** baroque
hair: **4** Afro, coif **6** Mohawk **7** buzzcut, crewcut, pageboy **8** coiffure
lofty: **4** epic
oratorical: **10** rhetorical
out of: **5** dated, passe **6** old hat
performance: **9** execution

stylet: pro **5** organ, probe **6** dagger **7** poniard **8** stiletto **9** appendage
surgical: **6** trocar

stylish: **4** chic, posh, tony **5** dashy, nifty, smart, swell **6** chichi, classy, dressy, jaunty, modish, spiffy, swanky **7** alamode, dashing, doggish, genteel, knowing, swagger **11** fashionable

stylist: **7** modiste **10** hair cutter

stylites: **7** hermits **8** ascetics

styloid: **8** belonoid

stymie, stymy: **4** foil, stop **5** block, check **6** hinder, impede **8** obstruct **9** frustrate

styptic: **4** alum **10** astringent, tannic acid

Styx: **5** nymph, river
father: **7** Oceanus
ferryman: **6** Charon
locale: **5** Hades
mother: **6** Tethys
pert. to: **7** stygian

suant: **4** even **5** grave, quiet **6** demure, placid, smooth, steady **7** equable, regular **9** agreeable, following

suave: **4** easy, oily, smug **5** bland, civil, soapy, sweet **6** polite, smooth, urbane **7** fulsome, tactful **8** gracious, mannered, pleasant, polished, unctuous **9** agreeable, debonaire **12** ingratiating

suavity: **6** comity **7** amenity **8** urbanity **10** politeness **12** complaisance

sub: **6** fill-in **9** alternate, auxiliary, submarine **10** substitute **11** replacement

subbase: **6** plinth

subdivide: **5** carve, mince **8** separate

subdivision: **4** part **5** tract **6** sector, suburb **8** category **10** department **11** development

subdue: cow **4** bend, quay, tame **5** accoy,

allay, amate, atill, break, charm, crush,
daunt, dompt, lower, quell, sober **6** adaunt,
bridle, disarm, dismay, evince, master, mellow, reduce, soften, steady, subact **7** affaite,
chasten, conquer, control, put down,
repress, squelch **8** convince, diminish,
overcome, suppress, surmount, vanquish **9**
captivate, castigate, overpower, subjugate

suber: **4** cork

subjacent: **8** inferior **10** underlying

subject: try **4** text **5** basis, cause, prone,
theme, topic **6** course, liable, motive,
phrase, reason, submit, vassal **7** article, citizen, conquer, exposed, reality **8** disposed,
incident, inferior, obedient **9** dependent,
leitmotif, subjugate **10** contingent, predis-
pose, submissive, substratum **11** conditional, subordinate
of discourse: **5** theme, topic
of disease: **4** case **7** patient
of lawsuit: res
of verb: **4** noun
to abuse: **6** revile
to argument: **4** moot
to authority: **6** master
to be taught: **10** didascalic
to change: **7** mutable
to choice: **8** elective
to control: **7** rulable
to death: **6** mortal
to depression: **5** moody
to discussion: **4** moot **9** debatable
to ill treatment: **6** misuse
to taxation: **8** rateable

subjection: **7** bondage, slavery **8** thirling **9**
captivity

subjoin: add **5** affix, annex **6** append, attach

subjugate: **6** compel, master, reduce, subdue
7 conquer, depress, overawe **8** overcome

sublate: **4** deny **5** annul **6** cancel, lift up,
negate, remove **8** take away **9** eliminate

sublime: **5** exalt, grand, great, lofty, noble,
proud **6** purify, refine **7** emotion, exalted,
haughty, supreme **8** elevated, empyreal,
heavenly, heighten, majestic, splendid,
upraised

sublimity: **4** apex **7** majesty **8** grandeur **12**
magnificence

submarine: **4** boat **5** diver, U-boat **11**
bathyscaphe, submersible
detector: **5** sonar
"father" of nuclear: **8** Rickover
first: **6** Turtle
first nuclear: **8** Nautilus
group: **8** wolf-pack
part: fin **4** sail **7** ballast **9** periscope **12** con-
ning tower
projectile: **7** missile, torpedo

submerge: dip **4** bury, dive, hide, sink **5** souse
6 deluge, drench, engulf, plunge **7**
immerse **8** inundate, suppress

submerged: **4** sunk **5** awash **6** latent, sunken
10 underwater
continent: **8** Atlantis

submission: **5** offer **8** docility, meekness,
offering **9** deference, obedience, surrender
10 compliance, confession **11** resignation
act of: bow **5** kneel **6** curtsy, kowtow **7** curtsey **9** obeisance
to destiny: **8** fatalism

submissive: **4** meek, tame **5** buxom **6** abject,
docile, humble, menial, pliant **7** dutiful,
passive, servile, subdued **8** obedient,
resigned, yielding **9** childlike, compliant
to wife: **8** uxorious

submit: bow **4** bend, fall, obey **5** abide, agree,
avale, defer, heald, hield, lower, stoop, yield
6 assent, comply, delate, hand in, resign,
soften, subdue, suffer, temper **7** exhibit,
knuckle, propose, succumb, suggest **8** moderate **9** acquiesce, surrender **10** condescend
for consideration: **5** remit
proposal to: **4** move
to: **4** obey **5** defer **6** suffer

subordinate: **4** aide **5** lower, minor, under **6**
junior, puisne, subdue **7** control, subject **8**
inferior, obedient, servient **9** ancillary,
assistant, auxiliary, dependent, secondary,
underling **10** accidental, collateral, incidental, submissive **11** subservient
activity: **8** parergon
adjunct: **9** appendage
officer: **4** exon

suborn: **5** bribe, foist **6** father, incite, induce **7**
procure **9** instigate

subpoena: **4** writ **6** summon **7** summons

subrogate: **10** substitute

sub rosa: **8** covertly, secretly

subscribe: **5** agree, favor **6** adhere, assent,
attest **7** ascribe, consent, support **8** sanction **10** contribute, underwrite

subscription to newspaper: **10** abonnement

subsequent: **5** after, later **6** puisne **7** ensuing
8 retainer **9** attendant, companion, following **10** succeeding **11** consecutive
to birth: **9** postnatal

subsequently: **5** after, later, since **10** afterwards, thereafter

subservient: **6** abject, menial, vassal **7**
duteous, servile **8** obeisant **9** accessory,
ancillary, auxiliary, truckling **10** obsequious,
submissive **11** subordinate

subside: ebb **4** bate, fall, lull, sink, wane **5**
abate, cease, lower, quiet **6** settle **7** decline,
descend, flatten, relapse **8** decrease, withdraw

subsidiary: **6** back-up, branch **7** reserve **8**

division 9 accessory, assistant, auxiliary, tributary **10** collateral **12** nonessential

subsidy: aid **4** gift, help **5** bonus, grant **6** bounty **7** pension, reserve, stipend, support, tribute **10** assistance, subvention

subsist: 4 feed, hold, live, stay **5** abide, exist, stand **6** obtain, remain **7** support, survive **8** continue, maintain

subsistence: 4 keep **6** living **9** allowance, inherency, substance **10** livelihood, provisions **11** persistence

subsoil: bed, pan **4** sole **7** stratum
animal: **4** mole **8** chipmunk

substance: sum **4** body, core, drug, form, gist, mass, meat **5** basis, metal, stuff, tenor, thing **6** estate, ground, import, matter, realty, spirit, supply, wealth **7** aliment, content, essence, meaning, purport **8** hardness, majority, material, property, solidity, sum total **9** actuality, affluence, resources, solidness **11** consistency
amorphous: **5** resin, rosin **7** ferrite
animal: **7** gelatin
bitter: **4** acid, gall **5** aloes, aloin, linin **6** ilicin **7** amarine, emetine **8** elaterin
dissolving: **9** resolvent
drying: **9** desiccant
reaction-inducing: **7** reagent
rubber-like: **5** gutta **11** gutta percha
sour: **4** acid **7** vinegar
starch-like: **6** inulin, olivil **8** alantine
sticky: goo, gum, tar **4** glue **5** paste
transparent: **6** hyalin **7** hyaline **9** celluloid
unctuous: oil **6** grease
vegetable: **4** peat **5** resin, rosin
white: **4** alba **6** inulin **7** alanine, albumin **8** elaterin

substantial: big **4** firm, real, true, vast **5** ample, large, meaty, solid, sound, stout **6** actual, bodily, hearty, stable, strong, sturdy **7** genuine, wealthy **8** material, tangible **9** corporeal, important **10** meaningful **11** significant **12** considerable

substantiate: try **4** test **5** prove **6** assure, embody, verify **7** confirm **9** establish **11** corroborate

substantive: 4 firm, noun **5** solid, vital **6** actual, entity **7** pronoun **9** essential

substitute: sub **5** extra, fudge, proxy, vicar **6** backup, deputy, ersatz (G.), fill-in, relief, ringer **7** commute, replace, stand-in **8** exchange, nominate, resource **9** alternate, makeshift, surrogate **10** understudy, viceregent **11** pinch hitter, succedaneum **13** succenturiate
for a name: **6** dingus, doodad, widget **9** doohickey **11** thingamabob
temporary: **7** stopgap **9** expedient

substructure: 4 base **6** podium **10** foundation

subsume: 7 contain, include **8** classify **9** encompass

subterfuge: 4 plan, ruse **5** blind, fraud, trick **6** device, escape, refuge **7** evasion, secrecy **8** artifice, pretense **9** chicanery, deception, strategem

subterranean: 4 cave **6** cavern, grotto, hidden, secret **11** underground

subtile: See **subtle**

subtilize: 5 exalt **6** rarefy, refine **9** sublimate

subtle: sly **4** deft, fine, keen, nice, thin, wily, wise **5** acute **6** artful, clever, crafty, expert, shrewd **7** cunning, elusive, logical, refined, subtile, tenuous **8** abstruse, analytic, delicate, rarefied, skillful **9** beguiling, designing, ingenious, intricate **10** mysterious, perceptive **11** penetrating **14** discriminating
emanation: **4** aura
variation: **6** nuance

subtlety: 7 exility, finesse **8** delicacy

subtract: 5 minus **6** deduct, remove **7** detract **8** withdraw, withhold

suburb: 5 exurb **7** purlieu **8** environs **9** outskirts, periphery

subvention: aid **4** help **5** grant **7** subsidy, support **9** endowment, provision **10** assistance **11** maintenance

subvert: sap **4** ruin **5** evert, upset **6** change, uproot **7** corrupt, deceive, destroy, pervert **8** alienate, overturn, sabotage **9** overthrow, undermine

subway: 4 tube **5** metro, train **6** tunnel **11** underground

succeed: win **4** fare, gain, rise **5** fadge **6** attain, follow, make it, thrive **7** achieve, catch on, come off, inherit, prevail, prosper, replace **8** approach, flourish, make good **10** accomplish

succeeding: 7 ensuing, sequent **10** subsequent, successful **11** consecutive

success: hit, SRO, wow **4** luck **7** arrival, fortune, sell-out, triumph, victory **8** accolade **9** happiness **11** consequence

succession: row, run **4** line **5** cycle, order, train **6** course, series **7** dynasty **8** sequence **9** gradation

succin: 5 amber

succinct: 4 curt **5** blunt, brief, pithy, short, terse **6** direct, girded **7** compact, concise, laconic, summary **10** compressed

succor: aid **4** abet, cure, help **5** serve **6** assist, refuge, relief, rescue **7** comfort, deliver, provide, sustain **8** befriend, mitigate **9** alleviate **10** strengthen

succory: 7 chicory

succubus: 5 demon **8** strumpet **10** evil spirit, prostitute

succulent: 4 aloe, lush **5** fresh, juicy, sappy, sedum, tasty, vital **6** cactus, spurge, tender

9 impatiens, jade plant 11 sempervivum
fruit: uva

succumb: die 4 fall 5 yield 6 perish, submit 8 pass away 10 capitulate

succursal: 6 branch 8 offshoot 9 auxiliary 10 subsidiary

such: sic (L.) 4 kind, like, some 7 certain, similar

suck: rob, sip 4 draw, lick, swig 5 bleed, draft, drain, drink, nurse 6 absorb, imbibe, inhale, take in 7 consume, extract, suction

sucker: 4 dupe, fish, fool, gull 5 leech 6 victim 7 fall guy 8 lollipop, parasite, pushover 9 simpleton

sucking fish: 6 remora 7 buffalo, lamprey

suckle: 4 feed, rear, suck 5 nurse 6 foster 7 nourish 10 breast feed

sucrose: 5 sugar 10 saccharose

suction: 6 intake 7 drawing, lifting

Sudan: *animal:* 4 dama 6 oterop
beer: 4 dolo
capital: 8 Khartoum
city: 4 Juba 7 Kassala 8 Omdurman 9 Port Sudan
currency: 5 pound 7 piaster
desert: 6 Nubian
language: Ewe, Ibo, Kru 4 Efik, Mole, Tshi 5 Dinka 6 Arabic, Yoruba 8 Mandingo 10 Kordofaman
river: 4 Nile
stockade: 6 zareba 7 zareeba
stretcher: 7 angareb
weapon: 8 trombash, trumbash
weight: 5 habba

---

sudarium: 6 napkin 8 veronica 10 sweat cloth 12 handkerchief

sudden: 4 rash, soon 5 early, ferly, hasty, short, swift 6 abrupt, speedy 7 prerupt, violent 8 headlong, meteoric, unawares 9 alertness, impetuous, impromptu 10 unexpected, unforeseen, unprepared 11 precipitate, precipitous

suddenly: 6 presto 8 abruptly

Sudra caste member: 5 palli

suds: bog 4 beer, foam, soap 5 dregs, filth, froth 6 lather, refuse 7 bubbles, sadness

sue: beg, woo 4 seek, urge 5 chase, court, ensue, plead 6 appeal, guided 7 address, beseech, contest, entreat, proceed, request, solicit 8 litigate, petition, practice 9 prosecute

suer: 9 plaintiff

suet: fat 6 tallow

Suez Canal: *builder:* 9 de Lesseps
port: 4 Said 7 Ismalia

suffer: get, let 4 ache, bear, bide, dree (Sc.),

hurt 5 admit, allow, groan, thole 6 endure, grieve, permit, submit 7 agonize, undergo 8 tolerate 10 experience

sufferance: 4 pain 6 misery 7 consent 8 patience, sanction 9 endurance, tolerance 10 permission 11 forbearance

sufferer: 6 martyr, victim

suffering: ill 4 bale, dree (Sc.), loss, pain 5 agony 6 ailing, injury, misery, sorrow 7 anguish, passion 8 distress, hardship, sickness 9 adversity 10 affliction 11 tribulation

suffice: 5 serve 6 answer 7 appease, content, satisfy

sufficiency: 4 fill 6 enough 7 ability, conceit 8 adequacy, capacity 9 abundance 10 capability, competency

sufficient: due, fit 4 able, enow, good 5 ample, valid 6 decent, enough, plenty 7 suffice 8 abundant, adequate 9 competent, effectual, efficient, qualified 11 responsible, substantial 12 satisfactory 13 well-qualified

suffix: See list at back

suffocate: 4 kill 5 burke, choke, stive 6 stifle 7 destroy, smother 8 compress, strangle, suppress, throttle 10 asphyxiate, extinguish

suffrage: aid 4 help, vote 5 right, voice 6 assent, ballot, prayer 7 witness 8 petition 9 franchise, testimony 10 assistance 12 intercession, supplication

suffuse: 4 fill, pour 5 embay, imbue 6 infuse 7 diffuse 8 permeate 9 interject, introduce 10 overspread

sugar: gur, ose 4 cane, kiss 5 biose, candy, maple, money, oside 6 acrose, aldose, fucose, gulose, hexose, ketose, talose, triose, xylose 7 caramel, chitose, glucide, glucose, maltose, sucrose, sweeten, tetrose, threose 8 fructose, rhodeose 9 muscovado, raffinose, sweetness 10 digitoxose, endearment, piloncillo, saccharose, sweetening 12 carbohydrate
artificial: 6 allose 9 aspartame, saccharin
boiling kettle: 8 flambeau
burnt: 7 caramel
crystals: 5 candy
daddy: 4 beau 6 patron
fruit: 8 fructose, levulose
liquid: 5 sirup, syrup
lump: 4 cube, loaf
measure: 13 saccharimeter
milk: 7 lactose
mixture: 5 syrup
preparation device: 10 granulator
raw: 9 cassonade
source: sap 4 beet, cane, corn 5 maple
syrup: 7 treacle 8 molasses

sugar apple: 6 biriba 8 sweetsop

sugarcane: *disease:* 5 sereh

pulp: **4** marc **6** megass **7** bagasse
  stalk: **6** ratoon
sugarloaf: 4 hill **8** conoidal, mountain
sugarplum: sop **6** bonbon **9** juneberry, sweetmeat
sugary: 5 sweet **7** honeyed **8** pleasant **10** flattering, saccharine **11** mellifluous
suggest: 4 hint, move **5** imply **6** advise,
  allude, broach, prompt **7** connote, inspire,
  mention, propose **8** indicate, intimate **9**
  adumbrate, insinuate **11** bring to mind
suggestion: 4 clue, hint, idea **5** tinge, touch,
  trace **6** advice **7** inkling, remnant, soupcon,
  thought **8** proposal **9** complaint **10** accusation, incitement, intimation, temptation **11**
  information
suicidal: 4 rash **5** fatal **6** deadly, lethal **8**
  dejected, wretched **9** depressed
suidae: hog **5** swine
sui generis: 4 oner **6** unique **8** peculiar
sui juris: 5 adult **11** responsible
suing: 6 wooing **11** prosecution
suint: 5 sweat **6** grease **12** perspiration
suit: fit **4** case (law), plea **5** adapt, agree,
  apply, cards, dress, fadge, group, habit,
  match, serve, tally **6** accord, adjust, answer,
  appeal, attire, behove, outfit, please, prayer,
  series, trover, wooing **7** arrange, behoove,
  clothes, comport, conform, costume, flatter, request, satisfy, uniform **8** courting,
  entreaty, petition **9** harmonize **10** correspond, litigation **11** accommodate **12** solicitation
  maker: **6** sartor, tailor
  type: law **4** zoot **6** monkey **9** paternity **10**
  pinstriped, three-piece **11** class action,
  malpractice **14** double-breasted
suitable: apt, due, fit, pat **4** able, fair, good,
  just, meet **5** happy, ideal, right **6** comely,
  gainly, proper, seemly **7** a propos, seeming
  8 adequate, apposite, becoming, coherent,
  eligible, feasible, idoneous, matching **9**
  competent, congruent, congruous, consonant, expedient **10** commodious, compatible, consistent, convenient, equivalent **11**
  appropriate **12** commensurate
suitcase: bag **4** grip **6** duffle, valise **7** luggage,
  satchel **9** gladstone
suite: set **4** band **5** abode, group, music,
  rooms, staff, train **6** series **7** retinue **8**
  equipage **9** apartment, entourage **10** collection
  member of: **7** attache
suiting: 4 silk, wool **5** serge, tweed **6** fabric **9**
  gabardine, gaberdine
suitor: 4 beau **5** flame, lover, wooer **7** gallant
  8 follower, litigant **10** petitioner, sweetheart
suk, sug, souk: 5 booth **6** bazaar, market

sulcate: 4 plow **6** fluted **7** grooved **8** furrowed
sulfate: 5 treat **7** convert, sulphur **9** brimstone **10** impregnate
  kind: **4** alum **5** hepar, matte **6** barite,
  blende **7** ilesite, loweite
sulfur: 9 brimstone
  substance containing: **5** hepar
sulfuric acid: 7 vitriol
sulk: pet **4** dort (Sc.), fret, mope, pout **5**
  brood, frown, grump **6** glower, grouch
sulky: 4 cart, dull, weak **5** chuff, dorty, inert **6**
  gloomy, gocart, grouty, sullen, touchy **7**
  doggish, fretful, peevish **8** carriage, inactive, perverse **9** querulous **10** unyielding
sullage: mud **4** silt **5** filth **6** refuse, scoria,
  sewage **8** drainage **9** pollution **10** filthiness
sullen: sad **4** dour, dull, glum, grim, sour **5**
  alone, black, cross, felon, gruff, heavy,
  moody, pouty, stern, sulky, surly, testy **6**
  cranky, crusty, dismal, dogged, gloomy,
  grouty, morose, silent, somber **7** baleful,
  boorish, crabbed, fretful, hostile, peevish,
  serious **8** churlish, lowering, petulant, solitary **9** obstinate, saturnine **10** depressing,
  ill-humored, ill-natured, refractory, unsociable **11** intractable, threatening **12**
  unpropitious
Sullivan's collaborator: 7 Gilbert
sully: See **soil**
sulphate: See **sulfate, sulfur**
sultan: 5 ruler **6** caliph **8** padishah **9**
  sovereign
  decree: **5** irade
sultry: hot **5** close, fiery, humid, lurid **6**
  coarse, erotic, smutty, torrid **7** obscene,
  sensual **8** stifling **10** oppressive, sweltering
sum: add, end, tot **4** gist, host, mass **5** count,
  gross, issue, total, whole **6** amount, degree,
  extent, figure, height, number, result, summit **7** integer, numeral, problem, summary
  8 addition, assembly, entirety, perorate,
  quantity, totality **9** aggregate, calculate,
  epitomize, gathering, magnitude, substance, summarize, summation **11** epiloga-
  tion **12** recapitulate
  forfeited: **5** dedit (F.)
  large: gob, pot
  small: **4** drab **7** driblet, peanuts **8** pittance
  11 chickenfeed
  subtracted: **9** deduction
  unexpended: **7** savings
  up: add **5** total **9** summarize **12** recapitulate
sumac: 4 rhus **7** shoemak **11** balinghasay
Sumatra: 6 island
  animal: **4** balu, tanu **5** orang
  ape: **5** orang **6** ourang **9** orangutan
  city: **5** Achin, Jambi, Medan **6** Padang **8**
  Bonkulin **9** Bencoolen, Indrapoor, Palem-

bang
deer: **4** napu
fiber: **6** caloee
measure: **4** paal
raft: **5** rakit
river: **4** Musi **5** Jambi, Rokan **9** Indragiri
wildcat: **4** balu
summarize: sum **5** recap **6** digest, review **7** abridge, outline, shorten **8** abstract **9** epito-mize
summary: sum **4** gist **5** brief, recap, short **6** digest, precis, resume, review, summit **7** concise, epitome, extract, general, medulla **8** abstract, argument, breviate, succinct, synopsis **9** condensed, inventory **10** com-pendium, run-through **11** abridgement
summer: ete (F.) **6** lintel **8** estivate
ailment: **8** hay fever, heat rash **11** prickly heat
beverage: ade **7** iced tea **8** spritzer **10** Tom Collins, wine cooler
pass: **8** estivate
pert. to: **7** estival
summerhouse: **5** kiosk **6** alcove, casino, gazebo, pagoda **7** cottage **8** pavilion **9** belvedere
summery: **4** warm **5** light **7** estival **8** delicate
summit: bow, cap, tip, top, van **4** acme, apex, knap, roof **5** crest, crown, pitch, point, ridge, spire **6** apogee, climax, comble, height, vertex, zenith **8** pinnacle **9** fastigium (L.) **10** conference **11** culmination
pert. to: **6** apical
summon: ban, bid **4** buzz, call, page **5** charm, evoke, rally, rouse **6** accite, appeal, arouse, compel, demand, gather, muster **7** call for, collect, command, convene, convoke, pro-voke, send for
to court: **4** cite, sist **8** subpoena
summoner: **6** beadle **9** apparitor
summons: **4** beck, call, writ **6** venire **7** com-mand, warning **8** citation, subpoena **9** chal-lenge **12** notification
sump: mud, pit **4** dirt, pool, pump, tank, well **5** drain, march, marsh, sewer, swamp **6** puddle, slough **7** cistern, depress **8** cesspool **9** reservoir **10** depression, excava-tion, receptacle
sumpter: **4** pack **6** burden **7** baggage
sumptuous: **4** rich **5** grand **6** costly, lavish, superb **7** opulent **8** splendid **9** expensive, grandiose, luxurious **11** magnificent
sun: orb, sol **4** bask, star **5** Titan **6** bleach **7** daystar, Phoebus **8** luminary **9** Harmachis
crossing equator: **7** equinox
god: Re, Tem, Utu **4** Amen, Baal, Lleu, Llew, Utug **5** Horus **6** Apollo, Helios, Osiris, Vishnu **7** Chepera, Khepara, Shamash, Sokaris **8** Hyperion
measuring device: **13** pyrheliometer

mock: **9** parhelion
near: **6** heliac
outer layer: **6** corona
path: **8** ecliptic
pert. to: **5** solar **6** heliac
protective devices: hat **4** brim **5** visor **6** shades **7** parasol **8** blindage, havelock **10** sunglasses
satellite: **6** planet
worshiper: **5** Parsi **6** Parsee **10** heliolater
sunburn: tan **8** heliosis
sunburst: **6** brooch, ensign
sun-clock: **7** sundial
Sunda Island: **4** Bali, Java, Nias **6** Borneo, Lombok **7** Celebes, Sumatra
Sunday: *following Easter:* Low **9** Quasimodo
mid-Lent: **7** Laetare
pert. to: **9** dominical
special: **4** Palm **6** Easter **9** Pentecost
sunder: cut, rip **4** part, rend, rive **5** break, sever, split **6** cleave, divide **7** disjoin, dis-rupt, divorce **8** demolish, dissever, disunite, separate
sundial part: **6** gnomon
sun disk: **4** Aten
sun dog: **4** halo **7** rainbow **9** parhelion
sundown: See **sunset**
sundowner: **5** drink, tramp **7** captain **8** night-cap
sundry: **4** many **5** apart **6** divers **7** asunder, diverse, several, various **8** distinct, fre-quent, manifold, numerous, separate, sun-dered **9** different, disunited **10** all sorts of
companion of: all
sunfish: **4** opah **5** bream **8** bluegill, pondfish
genus of: **4** mola
sunflower: **8** marigold, rockrose **10** balsam-root, helianthus, heliotrope
maid turned into: **6** Clytie
Sunflower State: **6** Kansas
sunk: pad **4** bank, seat, turf **5** couch **6** abject, hollow **8** absorbed, downcast, overcome **9** depressed
sunken: **6** hollow **9** depressed
fence: **4** ha-ha
Sun King: **8** Louis XIV
sunless: **4** dark, gray **6** cloudy **8** overcast
sunny: gay **4** fair, warm **5** clear, happy, merry **6** bright, cheery, golden, sunlit **8** cheerful, luminous **9** sparkling, vivacious
sunrise: **4** dawn, east **6** aurora **8** daybreak
song: **6** aubade
sun room: **7** solaria (pl.) **8** solarium
sunset: e'en, eve **4** dusk **7** evening **8** twilight **9** nightfall
pert. to: **9** acronical
reflection: **9** alpenglow
Sunset State: **6** Oregon **7** Arizona
sunshade: **5** visor **6** awning, canopy **7** parasol **8** umbrella

sunshine: 5 cheer, light 6 warmth 8 daylight, sunburst 9 happiness, sunniness

Sunshine State: 9 New Mexico 11 South Dakota

sunspot: 4 flaw 6 facula 7 blemish, freckle

sunstroke: 8 siriasis 9 calenture

sun watch: 7 sundial 9 timepiece

sunwise: 6 deasil 9 clockwise

Suomi: 7 Finland

sup: eat, sip 4 dine, feed 5 drink, feast, taste 6 tipple 7 swallow 8 mouthful, quantity, spoonful

supawn: 4 mush 12 hasty pudding

super: 5 actor, watch 6 square 7 janitor 9 excellent, first-rate, marvelous

superable: 12 surmountable

superabundance: 4 lots 5 flood 6 excess, plenty 8 plethora, quantity 10 exuberance 11 diffuseness, superfluity

superabundant: 4 rank 6 lavish 9 luxuriant, redundant 11 overflowing

superannuate: 6 retire 7 outdate, outlast 8 obsolete 9 antiquate, out-of-date 10 disqualify

superb: 4 fine, rich 5 grand, noble, proud 6 lordly 7 elegant, haughty, opulent, stately 8 enormous, majestic, splendid, very best 9 excellent, grandiose, luxurious, sumptuous 13 extraordinary

superbity: 5 pride 9 arrogance 11 haughtiness

supercilious: 5 lofty, proud 6 lordly, snooty, uppish 7 haughty 8 arrogant, cavalier, insolent, snobbish 9 arbitrary 10 disdainful 11 overbearing

superficial: 4 glib 5 hasty 6 casual, flimsy, slight 7 cursory, outward, shallow, surface, trivial 8 apparent, external

superfine: 4 luxe, nice, rich 5 extra, plush, prime 6 choice, deluxe, subtle, superb 8 delicate, overnice 9 excellent, grandiose

superfluity: 6 excess, luxury 7 surfeit, surplus 9 abundance, profusion 11 prodigality

superfluous: 4 over 5 extra, spare 6 de trop (F.) 7 surplus, useless 8 abnormal, needless, wasteful 9 excessive, redundant, worthless 10 gratuitous, inordinate 11 extravagant, unnecessary 12 nonessential

superhuman: 6 divine 7 demigod, uncanny 9 herculean

superhumeral: 5 amice, stole

superimpose: 5 cover 7 overlay

superintend: 4 boss, lead 5 guide 6 direct, manage 7 conduct, control, inspect, oversee 8 engineer 9 supervise 10 administer

superintendence: 4 care 8 guidance 9 authority, oversight 14 responsibility

superintendent: 4 boss 5 super 6 bishop 7 captain, curator, foreman, manager 8 director, minister, overseer 9 inspector 10 supervisor 11 chamberlain

superior: 4 boss, fine, head, lord, over, peer 5 abbot, above, chief, eigne, extra, liege, upper 6 abbess, better, choice, higher, leader, senior 7 exalted, greater, haughty, palmary, prelate, ranking 8 alderman, arrogant, assuming, cardinal, dominant, elevated, masterly 9 ascendant, ascendent, excellent, marvelous, paramount, spiritual 10 preeminent, surpassing 11 predominant 12 supercilious

superiority: 4 edge, gree (Sc.), rank 8 priority 9 advantage, meliority, seniority
position of: 10 domination

superlative: 4 acme, best, peak 6 utmost 7 supreme 8 peerless 9 excessive 10 consummate 11 exaggerated
absolute: 7 elative

Superman's friend: 8 Lois Lane 10 Jimmy Olsen

supernal: 4 high 6 divine 8 ethereal, heavenly 9 celestial

supernatural: 5 magic 6 divine, occult 7 ghostly 9 marvelous 10 miraculous

supernatural being: elf, god 4 atua 5 angel, deity, demon, fairy, gnome, nymph, troll 6 cherub, seraph, spirit 7 banshee, goddess 10 leprechaun
Moslem: 4 jinn
Persian: 4 peri

supernatural happening: 6 vision 7 miracle

supernumerary: 5 actor, extra

superscribe: 5 write 6 direct 7 address, engrave

superscription: 5 title 7 caption 9 direction 11 description, inscription

supersede: 7 replace, succeed 8 displace, override, set aside, supplant

supersonic noise: 4 boom

superstition: 5 freet, freit, magic 6 fetish, voodoo 8 idolatry

supervene: 5 ensue 6 follow, happen 7 succeed

supervise: 4 boss, edit, read, scan 5 check 6 direct, govern, manage, peruse, revise 7 conduct, correct, inspect, oversee 11 superintend

supervisor: 4 boss, head 7 foreman, manager 8 alytarch (G.), director 9 spectator 10 roadmaster

supine: 4 flat 5 inert, prone 6 abject, drowsy 7 languid, leaning, passive, sloping, unalert 8 inactive, inclined, indolent, listless, sluggish 9 apathetic, negligent, prostrate, reclining 10 face upward, submissive 11 inattentive, indifferent

supper: tea 4 meal 6 dinner

supplant: 4 oust 5 usurp 6 follow, remove, uproot 7 replace, succeed 8 displace 9 extirpate, supersede, undermine

supple: sly 4 bain, oily 5 agile, lithe 6 limber,

lissom, nimble, pliant, swanky **7** cunning, elastic, fawning, lissome, plastic, pliable, servile **8** flexible, yielding **9** adaptable, compliant, resilient, versatile **10** obsequious, responsive **11** complaisant

supplement: add, eke **5** annex **7** adjunct **8** addendum, addition, appendix **9** accessory **10** complement

supplemental: **7** special **12** adscititious

suppliant: **5** asker **6** beggar, suitor **10** beseeching, entreating, petitioner

supplicate: beg, sue **4** pray **5** crave, plead **6** appeal, invoke, obtest **7** beseech, conjure, entreat, implore, request, solicit **8** petition **9** importune, obsecrate

supplication: **6** litany, prayer **8** entreaty, petition, rogative

supply: aid, fit **4** feed, fill, fund, give, help, load **5** cache, cater, equip, hoard, relay, stock, store, yield **6** afford, employ, foison, purvey, relief, succor **7** fraught, furnish, granary, nourish, plenish, provide, replace, reserve, satisfy **8** minister, ordnance, turn over **9** profusion, provision, reinforce, replenish, reservoir, temporary **10** administer, assistance, compensate, contribute **12** accumulation

support: aid, arm, guy, leg, peg, rib **4** arch, back, base, beam, bear, bibb, fend, help, hold, keep, limb, pier, prop, stay **5** boost, brace, carry, cheer, cleat, easel, favor, found, frame, hinge, shore, sling, staff, strut, truss, vouch **6** anchor, assent, assist, behalf, better, bridge, cradle, crutch, defend, endure, lintel, living, pillar, second, shield, splint, spring, steady, suffer, tripod, trivet, uphold, upkeep, verify **7** backing, bolster, cherish, comfort, confirm, console, endorse, espouse, finance, fulcrum, nourish, nurture, protect, provide, reserve, shore up, subsidy, sustain, trestle **8** advocate, approval, baluster, befriend, buttress, champion, evidence, maintain, pedestal, sanction, tolerate, underlie **9** adminicle, encourage, financing, patronize, reinforce, stanchion, vindicate **10** assistance, foundation, strengthen, sustenance **11** corroborate, countenance
for statue: **5** socle **8** pedestal

supporter: fan **4** ally, knee **5** brace **6** bearer, patron, rooter **7** abetter, abettor, booster, founder **8** adherent, advocate, assertor, champion, exponent, follower, henchman, partisan **9** auxiliary, suspender

suppose: **4** deem, trow, ween **5** allow, guess, imply, infer, judge, opine, think **6** assume, expect, gather, reckon, repute, theory **7** believe, imagine, incline, opinion, presume, suspect **8** conceive, conclude, consider, obligate, supposal, theorize **9** apprehend, intention **10** conjecture, presuppose, substitute, understand

supposed: **7** alleged, assumed **8** presumed, surmised

supposition: **4** idea **6** notion, theory **7** forgery, surmise **9** postulate **10** alteration, assumption, conjecture, estimation, hypothesis **11** expectation, implication, proposition, uncertainty

supposititious: **7** assumed, feigned **8** fabulous, putative, spurious, supposed **9** imaginary, pretended **10** artificial, chimerical, fictitious **11** counterfeit **12** hypothetical, illegitimate

suppress: ban **4** hide, keep, kill, stop **5** check, choke, crush, elide, quash, quell, stunt **6** arrest, bridle, censor, harass, hush up, ravish, retard, stifle, subdue **7** abolish, compose, conceal, conquer, destroy, exclude, inhibit, oppress, prevent, put down, refrain, repress, silence, smother, squelch **8** compress, prohibit, restrain, withhold **9** interdict, overpower, overthrow **10** dissolving, extinguish

suprarenal: **7** adrenal

supremacy: **4** sway **5** power **7** control, mastery **8** dominion **9** authority, autocracy, dominance, influence **10** ascendancy, domination **11** sovereignty **12** predominance

supreme: **4** acme, best, last **5** alone, chief, final, first **6** superb, utmost **7** crucial, highest, maximum **8** foremost, greatest, loftiest, peerless, ultimate **9** excellent, paramount **10** preeminent

supreme being: God **5** Allah, deity, monad **7** creator, Jehovah

suq: See **suk**

surcease: end **4** lull, rest, stay, stop **5** abate, defer, delay **6** desist, relief **7** refrain, respite, suspend **8** postpone **9** cessation

surcharge: tax **4** cost, fill, load **6** burden, impost **7** surfeit **8** overload, surprint **9** overcrowd, overprint, overstock **10** impregnate, overburden, overcharge

surcingle: **4** band, belt **6** girdle **8** cincture

surcoat: **5** jupon **6** cyclas **7** garment

surd: **4** deaf, mute **7** radical **9** insensate, voiceless **10** irrational

sure: **4** fast, firm, safe, true **5** siker (Sc.) **6** indeed, secure, sicker (Sc.), stable, steady, strong **7** assured, certain **8** enduring, positive, reliable, unerring **9** authentic, betrothed, confident, convinced, steadfast, undoubted, unfailing **10** dependable, inevitable, infallible **11** indubitable, trustworthy **12** indisputable

surely: **6** atweel (Sc.), indeed, really **8** of course **9** certainly

sureness: **9** certitude

sure thing: **6** shoo-in, winner **7** safe bet **9** certainty

surety: **4** bail **6** backer, pledge **7** engager, sponsor **8** bailsman, bondsman, security **9**

- assurance, certainty, guarantee, guarantor **10** confidence
post: **4** bond

surf: **4** foam, wave **5** spray, swell **7** breaker
sound of: **4** roar, rote

surface: top **4** area, face, pave, side, skin **5** facet, plane **6** come up, facing, finish, patina **7** outside **8** boundary, exterior **11** superficial
flat: **4** area **5** plane, sheet **7** lateral
geometrical: **5** nappe **6** sphere, toroid
inclined: **4** cant, ramp **7** descent
pert. to: **6** facial
rounded: **9** concavity, convexity
toward: **5** ectad

surfacing: tar **6** gravel, paving **7** asphalt, macadam **8** blacktop, emerging

surfboard: **5** paipo **9** kneeboard **10** belly board **11** knee machine

surfeit: **4** cloy, feed, glut, pall, sate **6** excess, nausea, sicken, supply **7** disgust, replete, satiate, satiety, satisfy **8** disorder **9** satiation **10** discomfort **11** extravagant, overindulge, superfluity

surge: **4** flow, gush, pour, rise, rush, tide, wave **5** gurge, swell **6** billow **7** estuate, rolling **8** sweeping, swelling

surgeon: **6** doctor **8** sawbones **9** physician **10** chirurgeon

surgeonfish: **4** tang

surgery: **9** operation, resection
appliance: **4** brace **6** crutch, splint
compress: **5** stupe
instrument: **5** clamp, fleam, lance, probe, scala **6** bilabe, gorget, lancet, splint, stylet, trapan, trepan, trocar, vectis **7** forceps, levator, ligator, rongeur, scalpel, trilabe, trochar **8** bistoury, ecraseur, hemostat, trephine, tweezers **9** goosebill, tenaculum, vulsellum **10** abaptiston, adaptistum, terebellum, tourniquet
perform: **7** operate
plug: **6** tampon
puncture: **8** centesis
roller: **6** fascia **7** fasciae
stitch: **5** seton **6** suture
thread: **6** catgut

surly: **4** glum, grum, rude **5** bluff, chuff, cross, gruff, gurly **6** abrupt, grumpy, morose, sullen **7** boorish, crabbed, haughty, uncivil, waspish **8** arrogant, churlish, growling **9** fractious **10** illnatured **11** intractable

surmise: **4** deem **5** guess, infer, think, trace **6** assume, charge, theory **7** believe, imagine, presume, suppose **8** conclude **9** suspicion **10** allegation, assumption, conclusion, conjecture **11** supposition

surmount: top **4** beat, lick, pass, rise, tide **5** clear, climb, crown, excel, outdo, total **6** ascend, defeat, exceed, hurdle, subdue **7** conquer, surpass **8** overcome **9** negotiate, transcend

surmountable: **8** possible **9** superable

surmounting: **4** atop

surname: **6** byname **7** agnomen **8** cognomen, patronym **10** patronymic **11** appellation

surpass: cap, cob, top **4** beat, best, flog **5** amend, excel, outdo **6** better, exceed, outvie **7** eclipse, outrank, outsoar **8** outclass, outreach, outstrip, surmount **9** transcend

surpassing: **4** fine **6** banner **7** supreme **9** excellent **10** inimitable, preeminent

surplice: **5** cotta, ephod **8** vestment

surplus: **4** glut, over, rest **5** extra, spare **6** excess, plenty **7** backlog, reserve, surfeit **8** leftover, overplus **9** remainder **10** additional, redundancy

surprise: awe, cap **5** alarm, amaze, catch, seize, shock **6** ambush, dazzle, detect, strike, waylay, wonder **7** astound, capture, gloppen, nonplus, perplex, startle, stupefy, uncover **8** astonish, bewilder, confound, dumfound, overcome **9** amazement, overwhelm **11** flabbergast

surprised: **5** agape

surprising: **6** sudden **9** startling **10** unexpected

surrender: **4** cede, fall, give **5** remit, yield **6** give up, remise, resign, submit, tender, waiver **7** abandon, cession, concede, deliver, forsake **8** back down, dedition, remittal **9** rendition **10** abdication, capitulate, compromise, relinquish **11** divestiture **12** cancellation

surreptitious: sly **6** covert, secret **7** bootleg, furtive **8** sneaking, stealthy **9** deceitful, deceptive, underhand **11** clandestine

surrey: **8** carriage

surrogate: **6** deputy **8** delegate, resource **9** subrogate **10** substitute

surround: bar, hem **4** belt, fold, gird, ring, span, wrap **5** beset, embay, flood, hedge **6** border, circle, corral, encase, enfold, enring, invest **7** besiege, embosom, enclose, envelop, environ, imbosom **8** encircle, envelope, inundate, overflow **9** beleaguer, encompass

surrounded: **4** amid, girt **5** among **6** amidst **7** between, bounded

surrounding: **5** about, midst **7** context, setting **8** ambiance **9** entourage

surtax: **4** agio, levy **5** extra

surtout: **4** coat, hood **5** cloak **7** garment **8** overcoat

survey: map **4** look, note, plan, plot, poll, pool, scan, view **5** study **6** behold, digest, precis, regard, review, search **7** canvass, examine, history, inspect, outline, oversee **8** consider, estimate, traverse **9** delineate, determine, supervise, treatment **10** compendium, exposition, scrutinize **11** description, examination, reconnoiter, superintend

surveyor: **6** gauger **9** arpenteur, inspector
helper: **6** rodman **7** lineman, poleman **8** chainman
instrument: **11** stratameter
nail: **4** spad
tool: **6** alidad **7** alidade, transit **10** theodolite **12** perambulator

survival: **5** relic

survive: **4** last, live **6** endure, make it **7** outlast, outlive **11** live through, pull through

Susanna: *accusers:* **6** elders
husband: **7** Joachim

susceptibility: **5** sense **7** emotion, feeling

susceptible: **4** easy, open **5** prone **6** liable **7** exposed, subject **8** allergic, sensible, sentient **9** receptive, sensitive **10** responsive, vulnerable **11** predisposed, softhearted, unresistant **13** tenderhearted
to error: **8** fallible

suscitate: **5** rouse **6** excite **7** animate, provoke **9** stimulate

suslik: **5** sisel **8** squirrel **11** spermophile

suspect: **4** fear **5** doubt, guess **7** accused, believe, dubious, imagine, inkling, presume, suppose, surmise **8** conceive, distrust, doubtful, mistrust **9** discredit **10** disbelieve

suspend: bar **4** halt, hang, hold, oust, stop **5** cease, debar, defer, demur, expel, swing **6** dangle, recess, repeal **7** adjourn, exclude **8** intermit, postpone, withhold **9** pretermit

suspended: **4** hung **5** inert **6** halted, latent **7** abeyant, hanging, pendent, pensile **8** dangling, inactive **11** inoperative

suspender: **5** brace **6** gallus, garter, hanger **9** supporter

suspense: **5** worry **6** unease **7** anxiety **8** cautious, hesitant, withheld **11** tenterhooks, uncertainty **12** apprehension
in: **7** pending **13** on tenterhooks

suspension: **4** stop **5** delay, pause **7** failure **8** abeyance, buoyancy, stoppage **9** remission **11** withholding
in air: **5** vapor
of court sentence: **9** probation
of hostilities: **5** truce **9** armistice, ceasefire
of tension: **7** detente

suspicion: **4** hint, idea **5** doubt, hunch, touch, trace **7** askance, caution, inkling, surmise **8** distrust, jealousy, mistrust **9** misgiving **10** diffidence, intimation, suggestion, uneasiness **11** expectation, uncertainty **12** apprehension

suspicious: **4** wary **5** fishy, leery, shady **7** suspect **8** doubtful **9** equivocal, skeptical **11** mistrustful **12** questionable

suspire: **4** sigh **7** long for, respire

sustain: **4** abet, back, bear, buoy, dure, feed, help, prop **5** abide, carry **6** assist, endure, foster, second, succor, suffer, supply, uphold **7** comfort, confirm, console, contain, nourish, prolong, provide, stand by, support, undergo **8** befriend, continue, maintain **9** encourage, withstand **10** experience, strengthen **11** corroborate

sustenance: **4** food, keep, meat **5** bread, viand **6** living, upkeep **7** aliment, support **9** nutrition, provision **10** exhibition **11** maintenance, nourishment, subsistence

susurrus: **6** murmur, rustle **7** whisper

sutler: **7** provant **9** vivandier **10** vivandiere

suttee: **7** suicide **10** immolation

suture: sew **4** line, seam **6** stitch **9** arthrosis

suzerain: **4** lord **5** liege **8** overlord **9** paramount, sovereign **10** feudal lord

svelte: **4** slim, thin, trim **5** lithe **6** lissom **7** lissome, slender **8** graceful

swab: gob, mop, tar **4** lout, wash, wipe **5** brush, clean **6** sailor **7** epaulet, officer, plunger, swabbie **8** medicate

swack: **4** blow, cuff **5** whack **6** nimble, pliant, supple

swaddle: **4** beat, bind, wrap **6** clothe, cudgel, swathe **7** bandage **8** restrict, surround

swag: pit, sag, tip **4** list, loot, sway **5** booty, lurch, money, spoil, swing, tramp **6** bundle, hollow, wreath **7** festoon, hanging, plunder **10** decoration

swagger: **4** brag **5** bluff, boast, bully, lurch, strut, swank, swell **6** cuttle, hector, prance **7** bluster, bravado, gauster, panache, quarrel, roister, ruffler, stagger, stylish **8** flourish, vagabond **11** braggadocio, fanfaronade

swaggering: **6** gascon **7** huffcap

swagman: **5** fence **7** bushman **9** sundowner
bundle: **5** bluey

swain: boy **5** lover, youth **6** escort, rustic, suitor **7** admirer, gallant, peasant, servant **8** shepherd **9** attendant, boyfriend **10** countryman

swale: fen **4** moor, sway **5** marsh, shade, slash, sweal, swing, swirl **6** hollow, meadow, valley **8** coolness **10** depression

swallow: eat, sip, sup **4** bear, bird, bolt, down, gaup, gawp, glut, gulp, take, tern **5** drink, merge, quilt, swift **6** absorb, accept, englut, engulf, go-down, gullet, imbibe, ingest, martin, mumble, recant, resorb, throat, vanish **7** believe, consume, engorge, fall for, retract **8** aperture, suppress, tolerate, withdraw

swamp: bog, fen **4** mire, moor, muck, ruin, sink, slew, sloo, slue, thin, wham **5** clear, empty, flood, marsh **6** deluge, Dismal, engulf, hollow, morass, slough **7** cienaga, pocosin, pocoson, slender **8** overcome, quagmire, submerge **9** marshland, overwhelm **10** Everglades, Okefenokee

gas: **6** miasma **7** methane
grass: **5** sedge
pert. to: **7** miasmal, paludal
swan: cob, elk, pen **5** swear **6** cygnet **7** declare, whooper **8** surprise **9** trumpeter
female: pen
genus: **6** cygnus
male: cob
young: **6** cygnet
swank: **5** showy **6** active, lively **7** stylish, swagger **12** ostentatious
swanky: **4** chic, rich **9** grandiose, luxurious **11** pretentious
Swann's Way author: **6** Proust
Swan river: **4** Avon
swap: **5** bandy, trade **6** barter, dicker **7** bargain **8** exchange
sward: sod **4** lawn, skin, turf **5** grass **8** covering
swarm: **4** bike (Sc.), byke (Sc.), herd, hive, host, move, pack, shin, swim, teem **5** climb, cloud, crowd, flock, group, horde, mount, press **6** abound, flight, rabble, throng **7** migrate **8** assemble **9** multitude **10** congregate
swarming: **6** aswarm **10** emigration
swarthy: dun **4** dark **5** dusky **8** blackish
swash: bar **4** blow, move **5** noise, slosh, sound **6** splash, strike **7** bluster, channel, dashing, swagger **9** splashing
swashbuckler: **5** bravo **6** gascon **7** ruffian, slasher, soldier **9** combatant, dare-devil, swaggerer
swashy: **4** weak **6** watery **7** insipid
swastika: **5** cross **6** fylfot **8** insignia **9** Gammadion
swat (see also **swot**): bat, hit **4** blow, slap **5** clout, smack **6** strike
swatch: **5** swash **6** fabric, sample **7** channel
swath, swathe: row **4** band, bind, crop, wrap **5** strip, sweep **6** clothe, enfold, stroke **7** swaddle, windrow **8** surround
sway: **4** bend, bias, lean, move, reel, rock, rule, veer **5** force, grace, guide, lurch, power, shake, swing, waver, wield **6** affect, direct, divert, govern, induce, swerve, totter, waddle **7** command, control, deflect, incline, shoggie **8** convince, dominion, persuade, rotation **9** authority, dominance, influence, oscillate, vacillate **10** ascendancy, ascendency **11** fluctuation, inclination, sovereignty **13** lithesomeness
Swaziland: *capital, administrative:* **7** Mbabane
capital, royal: **7** Lobamba
currency: **4** cent **9** lilangeni
swear: vow **4** avow, bind **5** curse, utter **6** adjure, affirm, assert, attest, depose, pledge, plight, threat **7** declare, promise, testify **8** execrate **9** blaspheme **10** administer, asseverate, vituperate

falsely: lie **7** perjure, slander
to secrecy: **4** tile
sweat: dry **4** emit, ooze, toil, work **5** bleed, exude, hoist, labor, sudor (L.) **6** drudge, fleece **7** excrete, extract, ferment, glisten, putrefy, soldier, swelter **8** condense, overwork, perspire, transude
sweater: **5** shell **6** jersey **8** cardigan, pullover, slipover

---

Sweden: *actress:* **5** Garbo **6** Ullman **7** Bergman
adventurer: **6** Viking **11** Leif Ericson
bread: **10** knackebrod
capital: **9** Stockholm
city and town: **5** Boras, Edane, Falun, Gavle, Malmo, Ystad **6** Orebro, Upsala **7** Uppsala **8** Goteborg, Nykoping **9** Falkoping, Jonkoping **10** Eskilstuna, Gothenburg, Norrkoping **11** Halsingborg
clover: **6** alsike
currency: ore **5** krona **8** skilling
dynasty: **4** Vasa
explorer: **5** Hedin
farm: **4** torp
island: **5** Aland, Oland **7** Gotland
king: **4** Eric, Wasa **5** Oscar **10** Bernadotte, Carl Gustaf
manual training: **5** sloyd
match: **12** taendstikker
measure: aln, fot, mil, ref, tum **4** famn, last, stop **5** carat, foder, kanna, kappe, linje, nymil, spann, stang, tunna **6** fathom, jumfru **7** kollast, oxhuvud, tunland **8** fjarding, kappland, koltunna, tunnland
motion-picture director: **7** Bergman
noble title: **4** graf
opera star: **4** Lind **7** Nilsson **9** Bjoerling
physicist: **5** Dalen
river: Dal **4** Gota, Klar, Umea **5** Indal, Kalix, Lagen, Lulea, Pitea, Ranea, Torne **6** Lainio, Ljusne, Tornea, Windel **7** Ljungan **8** Osterdal
saint: **6** Anskar
sour milk: **8** tatmjolk
tribe: **6** Geatas
weight: ass, lod, ort **4** last, mark, pund, sten, untz **5** carat **6** nylast **7** centner, lispund **8** lispound, skalpund, skeppund **9** ship pound
writer: **6** Carlen **7** Bellman **8** Lagerlof **10** Strindberg

Swedish Nightingale: 4 Lind (Jenny)

sweep: fly, oar 4 line 5 besom, broom, brush, clean, clear, drive, range, scope, scour, strip, surge, swath 6 extend, remove 7 contour, stretch 8 traverse

sweeping: 4 vast, wide 5 broad 6 all-out 8 complete 9 extensive, out-and-out, wholesale 13 comprehensive

sweepings: 6 fulyie (Sc.), fulzie (Sc.), refuse

sweet: 4 dear, easy, fair, rich, soft 5 bonny, candy, dolce (It.), douce (F.), dulce (Sp.), fresh, soave 6 dulcet, gentle, lovely, mellow, pretty, sugary, syrupy 7 beloved, caramel, darling, honeyed, musical, winning 8 aromatic, fetching, fragrant, pleasant, pleasing, preserve 9 agreeable, ambrosial, melodious 10 attractive, confection, harmonious 11 good-natured, mellisonant

sweetbread: 4 meat, veal 6 thymus 9 ris de veau

sweetbrier: 4 rose 9 eglantine

sweeten: 4 mull 5 sugar 6 pacify, purify, refine, soften, solace 7 appease, cleanse, freshen, mollify, perfume, relieve 9 disinfect, sugarcoat 10 edulcorate

sweetfish: ayu

sweet flag: 4 arum 7 calamus

sweetheart: gra 4 agra, beau, dear, doll, doxy, gill, girl, jill, lass, love 5 bully, court, flame, honey, leman, lover, swain 6 adorer, fellow, orpine 7 beloved, darling 8 paramour, true-love 9 good thing

sweetmeat: 4 cake 5 candy, goody 6 comfit, dragee, pastry 7 caramel, dessert 8 confetti, conserve, hardbake, marzipan, preserve 9 marchpane, sugarplum 10 confection

sweet potato: yam 6 batata 7 ocarina

sweetsop: 4 ates

swell: nob, sea 4 bell, bulb, bulk, grow, huff, lord, rise, surf, toff, wave 5 bloat, bulge, grand, surge 6 billow, dilate, expand, extend, roller, tiptop, tumefy 7 amplify, augment, distend, enlarge, inflate, seagate, stylish 8 increase 9 elevation, excellent, first-rate, intumesce, marvelous, wonderful

swelled head: 6 egoist 7 conceit

swellfish: 6 puffer 8 puff-fish

swelling: sty 4 bleb, bubo, bump, lump, node 5 blain, botch, bouge, bulge, bunch, edema, tumor 6 aswell, gather, goiter, growth 7 blister, gibbous, turgent 8 windgall 9 gibbosity 10 rhetorical, tumescence
on plants: 4 gall
pert. to: 5 nodal 9 edematose, edematous

swelter: 4 burn, fret, heat, rush 5 exude, faint, roast, sweat 6 wallow, welter 8 perspire

swerve: bow, shy 4 skew, tack, turn, veer 5 dodge, shift, stray, swing, yield 6 totter 7 deflect, deviate, digress 8 sidestep

swift: 4 bird, cran (Sc.), fast, reel 5 alert, fleet, hasty, quick, rapid, ready 6 abrupt, lizard, prompt, speedy, sudden, winged 8 headlong

Swift: 8 Jonathan, satirist
brute: 5 Yahoo
flying island: 6 Laputa
hero: 8 Gulliver
lady friend: 6 Stella
pen name: 11 Bickerstaff

swig: 4 gulp, rock, sway 5 booze, draft, drink, hoist, snort, swash, swill 6 guzzle, imbibe, tackle

swile: 4 seal

swill: 4 fill, swig, wash 5 drink, flood, rinse, swash, waste 6 basket, drench, guzzle, refuse 7 garbage, hogwash

swim: 4 reel, spin 5 bathe, float, swoon, whirl 9 dizziness 13 forgetfulness
pert. to: 8 natatory

swimmer: 6 bather 7 natator
of the English Channel: 6 Ederle
of the Hellespont: 7 Leander
of the Tiber River: 7 Cloelia

swimming: 6 filled, naiant, natant 7 flooded, vertigo 8 aquatics 9 dizziness

swimming pool: 4 tank 10 natatorium

swimming stroke: 4 back, side 5 crawl 6 breast 7 trudgen 9 butterfly, dogpaddle, freestyle

swindle: con, gyp 4 bilk, dupe, fake, gull, hoax, mace, rook, scam 5 bunco, bunko, cheat, foist, fraud, spoof, trick 6 diddle, extort, trepan 7 defraud 8 embezzle, flimflam 10 overcharge

swindler: fob 5 biter, cheat, crook, knave, rogue, shark, thief 6 chiaus, chouse, shaver 7 sharper 8 blackleg

swine: hog, pig, sow 4 boar 7 peccary
feeding of: 7 pannage 8 slopping
female: sow 4 gilt
fever: 6 rouget 7 cholera
flesh: 4 pork
litter of: 6 farrow
male: 4 boar
pert. to: 7 porcine
young: pig 5 shoat 6 piglet

swing: 4 beat, bent, blow, hang, hurl, lilt, slew, slue, sway, turn, whip 5 fling, lurch, power, shake, throw, trend, waver, wield 6 dangle, gyrate, handle, manage, rhythm, stroke, totter 7 flutter, shoggie (Sc.), suspend, trapeze, vibrate 8 brandish, undulate 9 fluctuate, oscillate

swing around: jib 4 jibe, slue

swinger: 8 party man 9 bon vivant

swinish: 5 gross 6 coarse 7 beastly, boarish, brutish, piggish, sensual

swipe: cut, hit 4 blow, glom 5 draft, drink, lever, steal, swape, sweep 6 pilfer, snatch, strike

swirl: ess 4 curl, eddy, purl 5 curve, gurge, twist, whirl, whorl 9 pirouette

swish: 4 cane, flog, hiss, lash, whip 5 birch, smart, sound 6 rustle, strike 9 exclusive

switch: gad, rod, wag 4 beat, flog, lash, turn, twig, wand, whip 5 shift, shunt, swing 6 change, divert, strike 7 scourge 8 exchange, transfer 10 disconnect, substitute

switchboard: pbx 5 panel 9 telephone

switchman: 7 shunter

Switzerland: (see box)

swivel: 4 turn 5 pivot, swing

swollen: 4 blub 5 blown, proud, puffy, pursy, tumid 6 turgid 7 bloated, blubber, bulbous, bulging, pompous 8 enlarged, inflated, varicose 9 bombastic, distended, increased, tumescent 10 rhetorical

swoon: fit 4 coma, dwam 5 dwalm (Sc.), faint, sleep, spell 6 attack, stupor 7 ecstasy, pass out, succumb, syncope 8 black out, languish

swoop: cut 4 dive 5 seize, sweep 6 pounce 7 descend

sword: sax 4 dirk, epee, foil, pata 5 bilbo, brand, estoc, glawe, gully, kukri, saber, sabre 6 barong, creese, cutlas, Damask, dusack, espada, floret, katana, parang, rapier, spatha, Toledo 7 ascalon, askelon, baslard, curtana, curtein, cutlass, espadon, estoque, shabble, simitar 8 acinaces, camplian, claymore, Damascus, falchion, flamberg, schlager, scimitar, whinyard 9 achiavone, flamberge

blade of: 5 forte

cross guard: 7 quillon

curved: 5 saber, sabre 8 scimitar

fencing: 4 epee, foil 6 rapier

handle: 4 haft, hilt

of the Cid: 6 Colada

shaped: 6 ensate 8 ensiform

short: 4 dirk 5 skean 6 bodkin, dagger 8 stiletto

two-edged: 4 pata

two-handed: 7 espadon 8 claymore 10 broadsword

swordfish: 6 espada 7 espadon 9 broadbill

swordlike: 5 xypho 6 ensate 8 ensiform, gladiate

sword lily: 9 gladiolus

swordsman: 6 fencer 7 epeeist, soldier 8 thruster

Switzerland: 6 Suisse (F.) 7 Schweiz (G.) 8 Helvetia (L.), Svizzera (It.)

archer: 11 William Tell

architect: 11 Le Corbusier

artist: 4 Klee 10 Giacometti

ax: 6 piolet

capital: 4 Bern

card game: 4 jass

cheese: 7 Gruyere, sapsago 9 schweizer 10 Emmentaler 13 schweizer-kase

city: 4 Bale, Chur, Genf, Sion 5 Basel, Basle, Berne 6 Geneva, Schwyz, Zurich 7 Fyzabad, Ginevra, Locarno, Lucerne 8 Faizabad, Lausanne, Montreux, St. Gallen 9 Constance, Neuchatel 10 Farukhabad, Winterthur

currency: 5 franc, rappe 6 rappen 7 angster, centime, duplone 8 blaffert 9 centesimi

herdsman: 4 senn

lake: Uri, Zug 4 Joux, Thon 5 Leman 6 Bienne, Brienz, Geneva, Lugano, Sarnen, Wallen, Zurich 7 Lucerne, Lungern 8 Viervald 9 Constance, Neuchatel, Sarnersee, Thunersee 10 Stattersee 11 Brienzersee

measure: imi, pot 4 aune, elle, fuss, immi, muid, pied, saum, zoll 5 lieue, ligne, linie, maass, moule, pouce, schuh, staab, toise 6 perche, setier, strich 7 juchart, klafter, viertel 9 quarteron 11 holzklafter

mountain: 4 Alps, Jura, Rigi, Rosa 5 Blanc, Cenis, Genis 7 Bernese, Pennine, Pilatus 8 Jungfrau, Rhaetian 9 Lepontine 10 Matterhorn, St. Gotthard 11 Burgenstock 12 Dufourspitze

mountain pass: 5 Furka 7 Grimsel, Simplon 8 Gotthard, Lotschen 13 Saint Gotthard

officer: 5 amman

orchestra: 13 Suisse Romande

pine: 6 arolla

psychologist: 4 Jung

river: Aar, Inn 4 Aare 5 Doubs, Reuss, Rhine, Rhone 6 Ticino

sled: 4 luge 5 luger

song: 5 yodel

tunnel: 5 Cenis 7 Simplon 8 Gotthard 11 Loetschberg

weight: 5 pfund 7 centner, quintal

wind: 4 bise 5 foehn

wine: 7 Dezaley

sworn: 5 bound 6 avowed 7 devoted 8 affirmed, attested 9 confirmed 10 determined, inveterate

swot (see also **swat**): 4 cram 5 grind, labor, sweat

syagush: 7 caracal

sybarite: 7 epicure 8 hedonist 10 voluptuary

Sybil: See **sibyl**

sycophant: 5 toady 6 flunky, lackey, stooge, yes-man 7 fawning, spaniel 8 informer, parasite 9 charlatan, flatterer 10 bootlicker, footlicker, talebearer

syllable: bit 4 whit 5 shred 7 modicum 8 particle
  added: 6 prefix, suffix
  deletion: 7 apocope
  final: 6 ultima
  lacking at end: 10 catalectic
  next to last: 6 penult
  second before last: 10 antepenult
  short: 4 mora 5 breve
  shortening: 7 apocope, elision, systole
  stressed: 5 arsis
  unaccented: 6 atonic

syllabus: 4 list 5 brief 6 digest, precis, sketch 7 outline, program, summary 8 abstract, headnote, synopsis 9 statement 10 compendium

sylloge: 10 collection, compendium

syllogism: 5 logic 7 Sorites 8 argument 9 reasoning 10 epichirema

sylph: elf, fay 5 fairy 6 spirit, undine

sylphlike: 4 thin 7 lissome, slender 8 graceful

sylvan: 5 woody 6 rustic, wooded 8 woodsman 10 forestlike

sylvan deity: Pan 4 faun 5 satyr 6 Faunus

symbol (see also **element**): 4 flag, icon, ikon, seal, sign, type, word 5 badge, creed, crest, cross, image, token, totem 6 caract, device, emblem, ensign, fetish, figure, letter 7 diagram, regalia 8 talisman 9 character, hierogram, trademark 10 indication, substitute 12 abbreviation
  achievement: 5 medal 6 ribbon
  comedy: 4 sock
  early Christian church: 4 fish 5 orant 6 chi rho
  immortality: 6 phenix 7 phoenix
  mourning: 5 crepe 7 cypress
  peace: 4 dove
  put into: 6 notate
  saintliness: 4 halo
  servitude: 4 yoke
  victory: 4 palm 6 laurel
  wisdom: owl

symbolical: 7 typical 8 mystical 11 allegorical 12 emblematical

symbolize: 5 agree 6 concur, mirror, typify 7 betoken, combine, express, signify 9 harmonize, represent 10 illustrate

symmetrical: 4 even 5 equal 7 regular, spheral, uniform 8 balanced 13 commensurable

symmetry: 7 balance, harmony 9 congruity 10 conformity, proportion 11 consistency

sympathetic: 4 soft, warm 6 humane, tender 7 pietoso, piteous 8 affected 9 condolent, congenial, consonant, expansive, sensitive, simpatico 10 responsive 13 compassionate, understanding

sympathize: 4 pity 6 bemoan 7 condole, feel for 11 commiserate

sympathy: 4 pity 6 accord, liking 7 empathy, harmony 8 affinity, interest, kindness 9 agreement 10 compassion, condolence, kindliness, tenderness
  expression of: 8 clemency 10 condolence
  lack of: 8 dyspathy

symphony: 5 music 7 concord, harmony 9 orchestra 11 composition
  division: 8 movement
  form: 6 sonata
  for Napoleon: 6 Eroica

symposium: 4 talk 7 banquet 8 dialogue, potation 10 conference, discussion 11 compotation

symptom: 4 mark, note, sign 5 token 7 warning 8 evidence 10 indication

synagogue: 4 shul 5 group 6 temple 8 assembly, building, religion 9 communion, community 12 congregation
  officer: 6 parnas
  platform: 7 almemar
  pointer: yad
  Sephardic: 5 snoga
  singer: 6 cantor, chazan 7 chazzan

synaxis: 4 rite 7 meeting, service 12 congregation

synchronize: 4 mesh 6 concur 7 arrange 8 coincide, regulate 12 contemporize

synchronous: 8 existing 10 concurrent 11 concomitant 12 contemporary

syndetic: 10 connective

syndic: 5 agent, judge, mayor 7 manager, officer, trustee 8 advocate, official 10 magistrate

syndicate: 4 gang, pool, sell 5 chain, group, mafia, trust, union, unite 6 cartel 7 censure, combine, council 8 monopoly 9 committee 10 underworld 11 association 12 conglomerate

syndrome: 6 malady 7 ailment, disease 8 disorder

synod: 4 body 5 court 7 council, meeting 8 assembly, congress 10 convention

synonymous: 4 like 5 alike, equal 10 equivalent

synopsis: 4 plan 5 brief 6 digest 7 outline, summary 8 abstract, syllabus 9 statement, synthesis 10 compendium, conspectus 11 abridgement

syntax: **5** order **6** system **7** grammar **9** structure **11** arrangement
analyze: **5** parse
mistake: **8** solecism

synthesis: **5** blend, summa **7** complex **8** abstract **11** combination, composition **13** incorporation

synthetic: **6** ersatz **7** man-made **10** artificial, fabricated

syphilis: pox **4** lues **7** disease
lesion: **7** chancre
old remedy: **9** Salvarsan

Syracuse: *conqueror:* **4** Rome
founder: **7** Archias
tyrant: **5** Gelon **9** Dionysius

Syria: (see box)

syringa: **5** lilac, shrub **10** mock orange

syrup: **4** karo, sapa **5** honey, maple **6** orgeat **7** glucose, sorghum

system: ism **4** code, plan **5** credo, group, setup, whole **6** circle, method, regime, theory **7** regimen **8** religion, treatise, universe **9** procedure **10** assemblage, hypothesis, philosophy, regularity **11** aggregation, arrangement, bureaucracy, orderliness
of rules: **4** code
of weights: **4** troy **11** avoirdupois **12** apothecaries
of writing: **7** braille **8** alphabet **9** cuneiform, ideograph **10** pictograph

systematic: **4** neat **7** logical, orderly, regular **9** organized **10** methodical

systematics: **8** taxonomy

systematize: **5** order **6** adjust **7** arrange, catalog, marshal **8** organize, regiment **9** catalogue

---

Syria: *ancient name:* **4** Aram
bear: **4** dubb
bishop: **4** abba
capital: **8** Damascus
city: **4** Hama, Homs **5** Calno, Derra **6** Aleppo, Balbec, Calneh **7** Antioch, Latakia **8** Seleucia
currency: **5** pound **6** talent **7** piaster
dynasty: **8** Mameluke
god: **4** Baal **5** Allat **6** Mammon **7** Resheph
gypsy: **5** Aptal
measure: **5** makuk **6** garava

mountain: **6** Carmel, Hermon **7** Lebanon, Libanus
peasant: **6** fellah
people: **5** Druse **7** Ansarie, Saracen
political party: **5** Baath
religious sect: **5** Druse **7** Alawite
river: Asi **6** Barada, Jordan **7** Orontes **9** Euphrates
script: **5** serta
silk: **4** acca
tetrarchy: **7** abilene
weight: oke **4** cola, rotl **5** artal, artel, ratel **6** talent

T

taa: 6 pagoda

Taal: 4 Boer **7** volcano **9** Afrikaans

tab: eye, pan, tag **4** bill, drop, flap, loop **5** aglet, check, index, label, price, score, strap, strip **6** aiglet, eartab, record **7** account, latchet, officer **9** appendage, reckoning **10** accounting

tabac: 5 snuff **7** tobacco

tabanid: 6 gadfly **8** horsefly

tabard: inn **4** cape, coat **5** cloak, tunic **6** chimer, jacket, mantle **7** pendant

Tabasco: 5 sauce

tabatiere: 8 snuffbox

tabby: cat, pad **4** gown, silk **5** dress **6** fabric, gossip, moreen **7** old maid, padding, taffeta **8** brindled, spinster

tabella: 6 tablet **7** lozenge

tabernacle: 4 tent **5** abode, altar, dwell, hovel, niche **6** church, recess, reside, temple **7** deposit, shelter, support **8** enshrine **9** sanctuary, structure **10** habitation, house of God, receptacle **13** house of prayer
part: Ark **5** altar **9** Holy Place **11** candlestick **12** Holy of Holies

table: bar, hem **4** fare, feed, food, list, slab, wash **5** bench, board, canon, chart, delay, index, panel, plate, treat **6** buffet, indius, lamina, record, repast, tablet **7** console, counter, plateau, surface **8** credence, feasting, postpone, schedule, synopsis, tabulate **9** sideboard **10** collection **11** concentrate **12** string-course
centerpiece: **7** epergne
communion: **5** altar **8** credence, credenza
cover: **5** baize, cloth, doily, tapis **8** place mat
decorative cloth: **6** runner
d'hote: **6** dinner **8** prix fixe **12** complete meal
dish: **6** tureen **7** platter **12** service plate
dressing: **6** toilet, vanity
game: **4** pool **7** snooker **8** foosball, Ping-Pong **9** billiards
linen: **6** napery **7** napkins **11** tablecloths
philosophers: **14** deipnosophists
small: **5** stand, wagon **6** teapoy **7** taboret, tendoor, tendour
working: **5** bench
writing: **4** desk **10** escritoire

tableau: 5 scene **7** picture **8** register, schedule **14** representation

tableland: 4 mesa **5** karoo **6** karroo **7** plateau **8** balaghat, plateaus, plateaux (pl.) **9** balaghaut **12** altiplanicie

tablet: pad **4** bred, pill, slab **5** facia, panel, slate **6** plague, troche **7** lozenge **8** cartouch, memorial, monument **9** cartouche **10** receptacle cartouch
medicine: **4** disc **6** troche
sculptured: **5** stela, stele
stone: **4** slab **5** stele
three-leaved: **8** triptych
two-leaved: **7** diptych
writing: pad **5** slate

tableware: cup **4** bowl, dish, fork **5** china, glass, knife, plate, spoon **6** saucer, silver **7** crystal, tumbler **8** flatware, utensils

tabloid: 5 paper, short **9** condensed, newspaper **10** periodical **11** sensational **12** concentrated

taboo, tabu: ban **5** debar **6** forbid **8** prohibit **9** forbidden, ineffable **12** interdiction
opposed to: noa

tabor, tabour: 4 drum **6** atabal **7** attabal, eardrum, timbrel **10** tambourine

taboret, tabouret: 4 drum, seat **5** stand, stool, tabor **6** tabour **7** cabinet

tabulate: 4 list, rank, sort **5** group, order **7** arrange, tabular **8** classify, schedule

tabulation: 5 table, tally
grammatical: **8** paradigm
of the year: **8** calendar

tache: tie **5** clasp **6** attach, buckle

tacit: 6 silent **7** implied **8** implicit, unspoken, wordless **9** noiseless **10** understood

taciturn: 5 close, quiet, terse **6** silent **7** laconic **8** reserved, reticent **9** saturnine **15** uncommunicative

tack: 4 beat, busk, clap, gear, gibe, gybe, haul, jibe, join, link, nail, rope, slap, trim, turn, veer **5** baste, catch, fetch, rider, shift, spell, strip, tying, unite **6** attach, course, fasten, handle, method, secure, tackle **7** clothes, connect, payment **8** contract, saddlery **9** agreement, endurance, fastening **10** deflection, digression, stickiness, supplement **12** adhesiveness
glazier: **4** brad
nautical: **5** board
to windward: **4** trip
two pointed: **6** staple

tackle: rig **4** arms, food, gear, tack **5** angle, drink, seize, stuff **6** attack, collar, secure, take on **7** grapple, harness, rigging, weapons **8** mistress, windlass **9** apparatus, encounter, equipment, undertake
fishing: tew
football: **4** sack, stop
single and double block: **6** burton
strong: cat

tacky: **5** cheap, crude, dowdy, gaudy, seedy **6** frowsy, frumpy, shabby, sticky, untidy **8** adhesive, slovenly

tact: **5** grace, poise, touch **6** stroke **7** address, feeling, finesse **8** delicacy **9** appendage, diplomacy **10** adroitness, cleverness, discretion, perception **11** discernment, sensitivity

tactful: **8** discreet, graceful **10** diplomatic

tactical: **9** expedient

tactics: **4** plan **6** method, system **9** procedure, stratagem

tactless: **5** blunt, brash **11** heavy-handed

tactlessness: **9** gaucherie

tad: bit, boy, lad, son **5** child **6** urchin

tadpole: **8** polliwog

taenia: **4** band **6** fillet **8** headband

taffy: **5** candy, gundy **7** glaggum **8** flattery

Taffy: **8** Welshman

tag: dog, end, tab **4** flap, game, join, lock, name **5** aglet, label, shred, strip, touch **6** aiglet, append, attach, eartab, fasten, follow, rabble, ticket **7** refrain, taglock **9** appendage, catchword **10** shibboleth **11** aiguillette, commonplace
metal: **5** aglet **6** aiglet **12** license plate

Tagalog: **8** Filipino, Pilipino

taha: **4** baya **10** weaverbird

Tahiti: *canoe:* **4** pahi
capital: **7** Papeete
centipede: **4** veri
food plant: **4** taro
god: Oro **6** Taaroa
loincloth: **4** malo, maro
mountain: **7** Orohena
mulberry: **4** aute
old name: **8** Otaheite
resident painter: **7** Gauguin
woman: **6** vahine, wahine

tail: bun, cue, end, eye **4** arse, back, bunt, coda, last, rear **5** cauda **6** behind, follow, pursue, shadow, switch **7** limited, pendant, reduced **8** abridged, buttocks, encumber, entailed **9** appendage, curtailed, extremity, fundament
kinds of: bob, bun, fud **4** bunt, scut **5** cauda, plume, stern, twist **6** strunt, wreath **8** streamer **9** empennage
pert. to: **6** caudal
plane: **10** stabilizer

short: bun **4** scut

tailed: **7** caudate

tailing: **5** chaff, waste **6** refuse **9** following

tailless: **7** acaudal, anurous **8** acaudate, ecaudate **9** excaudate

tailor: fit, sew **4** make, snip **5** adapt, alter, style **6** darzee, draper, sartor **7** cabbage, fashion **8** clothier **9** bushelman **11** bushelwoman
goose: **8** flatiron
iron: **5** goose
lap board: **5** panel
made by: **7** bespoke (for men) **8** tailleur (for women)
pert. to: **9** sartorial

tailspin: **7** flicker **8** downturn

taint: dip, dye, hit, hue **4** blot, blow, blur, evil, flaw, hogo, hurt, mark, spot, tint, vice **5** cloud, color, imbue, prove, spoil, stain, sully, tinge, touch, trace, wound **6** accuse, damage, defile, infect, poison, stigma **7** attaint, blemish, convict, corrupt, debauch, deprave, pollute, vitiate **8** disgrace, empoison, hautgout, tincture **10** conviction, corruption, impregnate **11** contaminate

tainted: bad **5** blown **6** rancid **7** corrupt, spoiled

taipo: **5** demon, devil **10** theodolite

tait: **9** marsupial

Taiwan: **7** Formosa
capital: **6** Taipei
city: **7** Chilung **8** Taichung
currency: **4** yuan **6** dollar
island: **5** Matsu **6** Penghu, Quemoy **10** Pescadores
river: **5** Wuchi **6** Tachia **7** Choshui, Tanshui
seat of: **10** Kuomintang (Chinese Nationalists)

Taj Mahal site: **4** Agra

Tajikistan: *animal:* **7** karakul
capital: **8** Dushanbe
city: **9** Khudzhand
currency: **5** ruble
river: **8** Amu Darya, Syr Darya

take: act, bag, buy, eat, get, hit, nab, net, win **4** bear, doff, fang, glom, grab, haul, lead, loot, trap **5** adopt, atone, avail, booty, carry, catch, charm, cheat, check, fetch, glaum, grasp, infer, pluck, seize, snare, spell, steal, study, swear, touch, treat, trick, wrest **6** absorb, accept, affirm, amount, arrest, assume, attach, attack, borrow, choose, clutch, convey, deduce, deduct, derive, employ, endure, engage, gather, income, number, obtain, profit, remove, secure, select, snatch, strike, submit, tenure **7** acquire, attract, capture, conduct, detract, extract, procure, promise, receive, swallow, swindle, undergo **8** abstract, contract, proceeds, quantity, receipts, subtract, swag grip **9** apprehend, interrupt **10** confiscate, photograph **11** appropriate

aback: **5** check **7** startle **8** astonish, confound, surprise

account of: **6** notice, regard **8** consider

advantage of: use **5** abuse **6** misuse **7** exploit

advice: **4** hear, heed, mind **6** listen

after: **6** follow **8** resemble

aim: **4** bead **5** level **13** set one's sights

another's place: sub **9** alternate **10** substitute

apart: **4** ruin **7** analyze, destroy, dissect **9** dismantle

as one's own: **5** adopt **6** borrow

away: **5** decry, reave **6** adempt, deduct, divest, recant, remove **7** deprive, detract, retract **8** derogate, diminish, subtract

back: **6** abjure, recall, recant **7** retract **8** withdraw **9** repossess

beforehand: **7** pre-empt

by force: **5** erept, seize **8** ereption

by storm: **5** seize **6** attack

by stratagem: **4** trap **7** ensnare

care: **4** mind, reck **5** nurse, watch **6** beware **7** cuidado (Sp.)

care of: fix **4** mind, tend **5** nurse

chair: sit **7** conduct, preside

cognizance of: **4** note **6** notice

comb from beehive: **4** geld

delight: **5** revel

direction: **4** obey **5** steer

down: **4** note **5** abase, lower, write **6** escort, humble, lay low, record, reduce **7** swallow **8** dismount, emaciate, withdraw **10** distribute

exception: **5** demur **6** object

first: **7** preempt

five: **4** rest

for a ride: **4** kill **7** execute

forcibly: **5** seize **6** kidnap

for granted: **6** assume **7** presume

from: **5** wrest **6** deduct, divest **7** deprive, derived, detract **8** derogate, subtract

heed: **4** mind, reck, ware **6** beware, listen, notice

hold: **5** grasp **6** obtain **7** control

in: **4** furl, open **5** admit, annex, brail, cheat, fence, trick, visit **6** absorb, attend, escort **7** deceive, embrace, enclose, explore, include, observe, receive **8** commence, comprise, contract **9** apprehend, encompass **10** comprehend, understand

in hand: **5** seize **7** attempt **9** undertake

in sail: **4** furl, reef

into custody: **6** arrest **9** apprehend

it easy: **4** rest **5** relax **8** calm down

leave: **6** decamp, depart

legal possession of: **5** seise, seize **6** attach **7** garnish **9** garnishee

liberties: **7** presume **8** overstep

no notice of: **6** ignore **9** disregard

notice: see **4** heed **7** witness

off: **4** copy, doff, flee, lift, soar **5** abate, begin, deter, leave, mimic, start, strip **6** deduct, depart, get out, lessen, remove **7** detract, discount, distract, subtract, withdraw **9** burlesque, calculate, determine, reproduce

offense at: **6** resent

on: add, don **4** hire **5** start **6** accept, assume, employ, engage, oppose, tackle **7** consort, receive **8** arrogate **9** associate, undertake

on cargo: **4** lade

orders: **4** obey **5** yield

out: **4** copy, dele, kill, omit, food, to go **5** elide **6** deduct, delete, efface, escort, except, remove **7** excerpt, extract, overall, scratch, unhitch **8** airbrush, omit food, separate **9** eliminate

out by roots: **4** weed **5** pluck **9** eradicate, extirpate

out of pawn: **6** redeem

over: **5** seize, usurp **6** assume, convey **7** relieve

part: **4** join **5** share **11** participate

part in contest: **7** compete

part of: **4** side **5** enact

place: **5** occur **6** happen

place again: **5** recur

place of: **4** else **8** supplant **9** supersede **10** substitute

pleasure in: **5** enjoy, fancy **6** admire

root: **4** grow **6** settle

shape: **4** form, jell **11** crystallize

shelter: **6** nestle, shroud

some of: **5** share **7** partake

stock: **5** count **6** survey **8** appraise, estimate **9** inventory

to court: sue

turns: **9** alternate

umbrage at: **6** resent

unawares: **5** seize **7** astound, capture, startle **8** astonish, confound, overcome, surprise **9** overwhelm

unlawfully: rob **5** steal, usurp **6** pilfer, thieve **8** embezzle

up: buy **4** fill, lift **5** adopt, allow, begin, check, enter, exact, mount, raise, seize, set to **6** absorb, accept, arrest, assume, borrow, employ, gather, occupy, remove, resume **7** collect, dissent, elevate, engross, receive **8** commence, initiate **9** extirpate, reprimand **10** comprehend, understand

up again: **5** renew **6** reopen, resume

up weapons: arm, war **4** rise **5** rebel

with: **4** like **5** brook **6** accept **7** confess **11** acknowledge
  without authority: **5** usurp
taken: **8** occupied
  in all: **7** overall **9** inclusive
taker: **5** thief **6** captor **7** catcher **8** pilferer, purveyor **10** plagiarist
  of court action: **4** suer
  of income or profits: **6** pernor
takin: **5** bovid **6** mammal **7** gazelle **8** antelope, ruminant
  rel. of: **6** musk ox
taking: **4** take **5** catch, palsy **6** arrest, attack, blight, plight **7** capture, malefic, seizing, seizure, winning **8** alluring, captious, catching, charming, engaging, grasping **9** accepting, rapacious, receiving, reception **10** attachment, attractive, contagious, infectious **11** captivating
  different form: **7** protean **11** metamorphic
  precedence: **7** ranking
takt: **4** beat **5** beats, pulse, tempo **7** measure
talapoin: **6** monkey
talc: **4** mica **6** powder, talcum **7** agalite **8** steatite **9** soapstone
tale: lie **4** gest, myth, saga, talk, tell, yarn **5** conte, count, fable, geste, novel, speak, story, tally, total, whole **6** esteem, gossip, legend, reckon, report, speech **7** account, fiction, history, parable, recital **8** anecdote, category, consider, counting, relation **9** discourse, falsehood, narration, narrative, numbering, reckoning **10** detraction, fairy story **11** declaration, enumeration, information **12** conversation
  adventure: **4** epic, gest **5** geste
  kind of: lai **4** epic, gest, saga, tall, yarn **5** bourd, geste, roman **6** legend **7** romance **8** allegory, jeremiad **9** storiette
  medieval: lai, lay
Tale of Two Cities: *author:* **7** Dickens
  characters: **5** Lucie **6** Carton, Darnay
talebearer: **6** buzzer, gossip **7** tattler **8** busybody, informer, talepyet, telltale **10** newsmonger, tattletale **11** rumormonger **13** scandalmonger
talent: **4** bent, gift, turn **5** anger, dowry, flair, gifts, knack, money, skill, talon **6** custom, desire, flavor, genius, powers, riches, weight, wealth **7** ability, faculty, feature **8** appetite, aptitude, capacity, charisma, property **9** abilities, abundance, expertise **10** endowments **11** disposition, inclination
  special: **5** forte
talented: **4** able **5** smart **6** clever, gifted
talesman: **5** juror **8** narrator
taletelling: **4** blab
tali (see also **talus**): **6** ankles
taliation: **5** tally **10** adjustment

taliera: **4** tara
talion: **11** retaliation
talipot: **4** palm
talisman: **4** tara **5** charm, saffi, safie **6** amulet, fetich, fetish, grigri, saphie, scarab, symbol, telesm **8** greegree **10** lucky piece
talk: gab, jaw, rap, yak, yap **4** blab, buck, bukh, carp, chat, chin, gaff, knap, talk, tell, word **5** bazoo, drawl, drone, lingo, noise, orate, parle, prate, rumor, scold, speak, spout, state, theme, utter **6** banter, confab, confer, debate, drivel, gabble, gossip, intone, parley, reason, report, speech, steven, tongue **7** address, chatter, confess, consult, council, dialect, discuss, express, meeting, mention, oration, palabra, palaver **8** badinage, causerie, chitchat, collogue, colloquy, converse, dialogue, parlance, repartee, verbiage **9** dalliance, discourse **10** conference, discussion **11** communicate **12** conversation
  about: **6** gossip **7** discuss
  back: **4** sass **6** retort, ripost **7** riposte **8** repartee
  big: **4** brag **5** boast **11** rodomontade
  boastful: **4** gaff, rant **11** braggadocio
  ceremonious: **8** chin-chin
  chatty: gab **6** gossip
  common: **7** hearsay
  complaining: **4** carp **7** whining
  confused: **10** galimatias
  deliriously: **4** rave
  desultorily: **6** ramble
  down: **7** outtalk, silence **8** belittle **9** disparage
  down to: **9** patronize **10** condescend
  effusively: **4** gush, rave
  familiar: **6** confab
  flattering: **7** palaver
  flippant: **10** persiflage
  fluent: **6** prolix **7** verbose, voluble
  foolish: gab, gas **4** bosh, buff, bunk, gash **5** spiel **6** babble, bunkum, claver, fraise, patter **7** blabber, blather, palaver, twaddle **8** buncombe, wishwash **9** poppycock, rigmarole **11** goosecackle, stultiloquy
  formal: **6** speech **7** address, lecture, oration
  from pulpit: **6** homily, sermon **7** address
  glib: **6** patter **7** palaver
  idly: gab, gas **5** prate **6** tattle **7** chatter, twaddle
  imperfectly: **4** lisp **7** stutter
  indiscreetly: **4** blab
  indistinctly: **6** mumble, mutter **7** sputter
  into: **6** induce **8** convince
  light: **5** chaff **6** banter **8** raillery
  over: **7** discuss
  persuasively: **6** reason
  pert: lip **4** sass

profuse: 4 chat 6 patter 7 palaver 10 persiflage
slowly: 5 drawl
small: gab 4 chat, chin 7 prattle 8 chit-chat
table: ana 9 symposiac
together: 4 chat 8 converse
to no purpose: 4 blat
turgid: 4 cant, rant
unintelligible: 6 drivel, jargon, patter 9 gibberish
wildly: 4 rant, rave

talkative: 4 cozy, gash, glib 5 gabby 6 chatty,
clashy, fluent 7 verbose, voluble 8 flippant
9 garrulous 10 babblative, loquacious

talker: 6 proser, ranter, rhetor 7 babbler,
spieler
incessant: 6 gasbag, magpie 10 chatterbox
12 blabbermouth

talkfest: 6 confab 9 gathering 10 discussion
11 bull session

talking iron: gun 5 rifle

tall: big 4 bold, deft, fine, high, lank, long 5
brave, grand, great, lanky, large, lofty, rangy
6 seemly 7 doughty, skyhigh, unusual 8
obedient, towering, vaulting 10 courageous, incredible 11 exaggerated

tallow: fat 4 suet 5 sevum, smear 6 candle,
fatten, grease
pert. to: 7 stearic
pot: 7 fireman
refuse: 9 crackling
sediment: 7 greaves

tally: run, tab, tag 4 deal, goal, jibe, mark,
mate, suit 5 agree, check, count, grade,
label, match, notch, score, total 6 accord,
reckon, record 7 account, compare, loftily 8
coincide, estimate, numerate 9 agreement,
reckoning 10 correspond 11 counterpart

tallyho: cry 5 coach
crier of: 6 hunter

talma: 4 cape, coat 5 cloak

Talmud: 7 debates 9 Jewish law
commentary: 6 Gemara
text: 6 Mishna 7 Mishnah

Talmudic academy: 7 Yeshiva 8 Yeshibah,
Yeshivah 9 Yeshiboth
student: 5 bahur

talon: 4 claw, fang, heel, nail, sere 6 clutch,
hallux 7 molding 11 certificate

Talos' slayer: 8 Daedalus

talus: 4 tali (pl.) 5 ankle, scree, slope 6 debris
8 clubfoot 9 anklebone 11 knucklebone

tam: cap, hat 5 beret 8 headgear

tamarack: 5 larch

tamarin: 6 monkey 8 marmoset

tamarind: 8 sampaloc 9 evergreen

tamarisk: sal 4 atle, jhow, weed 5 atlee, shrub

tambo: inn 6 corral, stable, tavern 7 station

tambour: cup 4 desk, drum 5 frame 7 drum-

mer 8 buttress, ornament 9 embroider 10
embroidery, projection

tambourin: 4 drum 5 dance, tabor

tambourine: 4 dove, drum, taar 5 daira 7
travale, timbrel 10 instrument

tame: cut 4 bust, dead, dull, meek, mild 5
accoy, begin, break, daunt, prune, timid 6
crushed, insipid, servile 8 amenable, cicu-
rate, civilize, familiar, harmless 9 deficient,
subjugate, tractable 10 accustomed, submissive 11 domesticate, housebroken 12
domesticated
animal: pet 4 cade 6 cosset

tamed: 6 broken, gentle

tameness: 10 mansuetude

Tamil: 8 language
caste member: 7 Vellala
race: 9 Dravidian

Taming of the Shrew: *author:* 11 Shakespeare
character: Sly, 4 Kate 6 Bianca, Tranio 8
Baptista

tamis: 5 sieve, tammy 8 strainer

Tammany Society: *boss:* 5 Tweed
leader: 6 sachem
officer: 8 Wiskinky 9 Wiskinkie

Tammuz: *love:* 6 Ishtar
sister: 6 Belili

tamp: ram 4 cram, pack 5 drive, press 6 plug
up 11 concentrate

tamper: fix 4 fool, plot, tool 5 alter, bribe 6
dabble, meddle, potter, scheme, tinker 7
machine 9 influence, interfere

Tampico fiber: 5 istle

tampon: 4 plug 6 tympan 9 drumstick
nasal: 9 rhinobyon

tan: dun, sun, taw 4 beat, camp, cure, ecru,
flog, tent, whip 5 brown, color, toast 6
almond, bronze, switch, tannin, thrash 7
embrown, imbrown, sunburn, tanbark

tanager: 4 bird, yeni 8 cardinal, firebird
genus of: 7 piranga

tang: nip 4 bite, butt, capt, fang, foil, hint,
odor, pang, pike, ring, root, spur, tine, zest
5 aroma, knife, prick, prong, savor, shank,
smack, sting, taste, tinge, trace, twang 6
branch, flavor, pierce, relish, tangle, tongue
7 flavour, seatang, seaweed 8 piquancy,
pungency, rockweed 10 suggestion 11 surgeonfish

Tanganyika: See **Tanzania**

tangelo: 4 ugli 8 mandarin, Minneola

tangent: 5 slope 8 adjacent, touching

tangible: 4 real 5 solid 6 actual 7 tactile 8
definite, manifest, material, palpable, physical 9 objective touchable 11 perceptible,
substantial

Tangier(s): *feature:* 6 casbah
measure: 4 kula, mudd

tangle: bar, cot, mat 4 fank, harl, kink, knot,

mesh, trap **5** catch, frame, gnarl, ravel, snare, snarl, twine **6** balter, entrap, icicle, medley, muddle, puzzle, sleave **7** ensnare, involve **8** obstruct, quandary, scrobble **9** confusion, embarrass **10** complicate, intertwine, perplexity

tangled: 11 complicated

tangle-foot: 5 drink **6** liquor, whisky

tango: 5 bingo, dance **7** milonga

tangor: 6 citrus **8** mandarin

tania: 4 taro **6** yautia

Tanis: 4 Zoan

tank: hit, vat **4** bang, lake, pond, pool **5** basin, knock, Tiger, trunk **6** Abrams, pancer **7** cistern, cuvette, drinker, pachuca, piscina, Sherman, stomach **8** aquarium **9** container, reservoir
  part: **5** hatch, track, tread **6** cannon, turret

tankard: mug **5** facer, hanap, stein, stoup **6** flagon, pottle, vessel **7** goddard

tanked: 5 drunk **11** intoxicated

tanker: 4 ship **5** oiler

tanned: 5 brown, tawny **7** bronzed **8** sixpence, sunburnt

tanner: 6 barker **8** sixpence

Tannhauser composer: 6 Wagner

tannic acid salt: 7 tannate

tannin: 7 mordant **10** astringent

tanning: 6 curing **7** pasting, sunning **8** browning, flogging, spanking, whipping
  extract: **5** cutch **7** amaltas, catechu
  material: **5** sumac **6** sumach **7** oak gall
  method: **4** napa
  pert. to: **11** scytodepsic
  plant: **5** alder, sumac **6** sumach

tansy: 4 weed **9** tanacetum

tantalize: 4 bait, grig **5** taunt, tease, tempt **6** excite, harass **7** torment

Tantalus: *children:* **5** Niobe **6** Pelops
  father: **4** Zeus

tantamount: 4 same **5** equal **9** identical **10** equivalent

tantara, tantarara: 5 blare **7** fanfare

tantieme: 5 bonus, share **10** percentage

tantrum: fit, pet **4** rage **6** temper **8** outburst, paroxysm

tantum: 5 stint **9** allowance

Tanzania: (see box)

Taoism: way **4** road **8** religion **12** cosmic reason
  basic force: yin **4** yang
  founder: **6** Lao Tzu

tap: bar, bob, cut, hit, hob, pat, rap, tit, vat **4** beat, blow, cock, flip, heat, hole, open, pipe, plug **5** break, dance, fever, flirt, knock, leach, spile, touch, valve **6** broach, faucet, nozzle, pierce, repair, signal, spigot, strike, tapnet **7** censure, connect, penance, reprove **8** nominate **9** designate
  down: **4** tamp

tape: gin, tie **4** band, bind, mole **5** scale, strip **6** fasten, liquor, ribbon, secure **7** bandage, binding **10** seal fillet
  kind of: **4** duct, lear, wick **5** inkle **6** ferret, Scotch **7** masking **8** adhesive, magnetic **9** measuring, recording
  machine: VCR **8** recorder
  needle: **6** bodkin

Tanzania: *capital:* **11** Dar es Salaam
  city: **5** Moshi **6** Arusha, Tabora
  currency: **4** cent **8** shilling
  formed by union of: **8** Zanzibar **10** Tanganyika
  lake: **5** Nyasa, Rukwa **8** Victoria **10** Tanganyika
  mountain: **4** Meru **8** Usambara **11** Kilimanjaro
  people: **4** Goma **5** Bantu **6** Sukuma, Wagogo, Wagoma **7** Swahili, Wabinga
  river: **6** Kagera, Rufija **7** Pangane
  weight: **8** farsalah

taper: 4 ream, wick **5** light, point, snape **6** candle, cierge, lessen, narrow, reduce, trowel **7** conical, dwindle, trindle **8** decrease, diminish, slack off **9** acuminate **11** pyramidical

tapering: 5 conic **6** terete **7** conical **9** acuminate
  blades: **6** spires
  four-sided pillar: **7** obelisk
  piece: **4** gore, shim **5** miter **6** gusset

tapestry: 5 arras **6** Bayeux, dorser, dosser **7** dossier, Gobelin, hanging **8** dossiere
  design: **11** millefleurs
  hanging: **5** tapis
  kind: **5** Arras **7** Gobelin **8** Aubusson
  pattern: **7** cartoon
  warp thread: **5** lisse

tapeworm: 6 taenia **8** parasite
  embryonic form: **10** oncosphere
  head: **6** scolex
  segments: **8** strobila

taphouse: bar, inn **6** saloon, tavern **7** taproom

tapioca-like food: 5 salep
  source: **7** cassava

tapir: 4 anta **5** danta **8** anteater, ungulate

taproom: bar, pub **6** saloon, tavern

tapster: 7 barmaid, skinker **9** barkeeper, bartender

Tapuyan: 8 S.A. Indian
  tribe: Ges **5** Gesan **6** Cayapo, Goyana, Timbra **7** Camacan, Coroado **8** Botocudo, Caingang, Chavante

tar: gob **4** brea, salt **5** black, pitch, taint, tease **6** cresol, incite, sailor, seaman **7** asphalt, blacken, mariner, provoke **8** alkitran, irritate, pavement, seafarer, telegram **9** alchitran **10** bluejacket

taradiddle: fib, lie **8** nonsense

Taranaki volcano: **6** Egmont

tar and feathers: **12** plumeopicean

tarantula: **6** spider

tarboosh: cap, fez **6** turban

tardigrade: **8** sluggish **9** slow-paced

tardy: lag, lax **4** late, slow **5** delay, slack **6** behind, remiss, retard **7** belated, lagging, overdue **8** backward, dilatory **10** behindhand, unprepared **11** cunctatious

tare: **4** weed **5** vetch, weigh **6** darnel **7** leakage **9** allowance **13** counterweight

target: aim, cut, tee, use **4** butt, coin, goal, mark, vane **5** shred, sight, slice **6** cymbal, object, shield, tassel, tatter **7** buckler, pendant **8** ambition, bullseye, ornament, quintain, ridicule **9** criticism, indicator, objective
center: eye **5** clout **8** bull's-eye
shooting gallery: **4** duck

target finder: **5** radar, sonar

Tarheel State: **13** North Carolina

tariff: tax **4** duty, list, rate, toll **5** price, scale **6** charge, excise, impost, scheme, system **7** average, revenue, tribute **8** schedule
favorer: **13** protectionist

Tarkington title: **6** Penrod **9** Seventeen

tarn: **4** lake, pool

tarnish: dim **4** blot, dull, fade, soil, spot **5** cloud, dirty, spoil, stain, sully, taint **6** canker, darken, defile, injure, smirch **7** asperse, blemish, destroy, distain, obscure **8** besmirch, diminish, discolor

taro: **4** coco, eddo, gabi, root **5** aroid, cocgo, eddoe, tania **7** dasheen **8** caladium
paste: poi

tarpaulin: hat, tar **4** coat **5** cover **6** canvas, sailor **7** sea-bred **10** sailorlike

tarpon: **6** sabalo **9** savanilla **10** silverfish
rel. of: **5** chiro

tarriance: **5** delay **7** sojourn **8** awaiting, tarrying **9** hindrance, lingering

tarrock: **4** gull, tern

tarry: lag, vex **4** bide, idle, loll, rest, stay, stop, wait **5** abide, await, black, dally, defer, delay, demur, dwell, lodge, pause, visit, weary **6** arrest, bundle, dawdle, hinder, linger, loiter, remain, retard, soiled, tarred, tarrow **7** fatigue, outstay, sojourn, unclean **8** irritate

tarrying: **6** arrest

tarsus: **5** ankle
fore: **4** pala

tart: pie **4** acid, curt, doxy, flan, girl, keen, slut, sour **5** acerb, acrid, acute, bowla, hussy, sharp **6** pastry, pielet, severe, tender, tourte,

wanton **7** brusque, caustic, cutting, painful, piquant, pungent, trollop, waspish **8** piercing, poignant, turnover **9** acidulous, endearing, sensitive **10** astringent, prostitute

tartan: **4** sett, ship **5** plaid **6** fabric

tartar: **5** argol **8** calculus **12** incrustation

Tartar: See **Tatar**

tartarean: **8** infernal

Tartarus: **4** hell **5** Hades

Tartary prince: **4** Agib

Tartuffe: **9** hypocrite, pretender
author: **7** Moliere

tarweed: **5** Madia

Tarzan's mate: **4** Jane

task: job, tax **4** busk, char, darg, duty, feat, lade, load, test, toil, work **5** blame, chare, chore, labor, stent, stint, study **6** amount, burden, dargue, devoir, effort, impost, lesson, strain **7** aufgabe, censure, oppress, overtax **8** drudgery, quantity **10** accounting, assignment, employment **11** undertaking
easy: **4** pipe, snap **5** cinch **8** sinecure

taskmaster: **6** driver, tyrant **8** overseer **11** slave driver
harsh: **11** Simon Legree

Tasmania: **5** state **6** island
animal: **6** wombat
capital: **6** Hobart
devil: **7** dasyure **9** marsupial
mountain: **4** Grey **5** Brown, Drome, Nevis **6** Barrow **8** Humboldt **9** Ben Lomond **10** Wellington
phalanger: **5** tapoa

tass, tasse: cup, mow **4** bowl, heap **5** draft **6** goblet **10** small draft

tassel: **4** tuft **5** adorn, label **6** fringe, toorie, zizith **7** pendant **8** ornament

taste: bit, eat, gab, goo, nip, sip, try **4** bent, dash, feel, gout, gust, heed, hint, lick, rasa, tang, test, zest **5** drink, flair, gusto, prove, sapor, savor, scent, sense, shade, smack, smell, spice, tinge, touch, trace **6** degust, flavor, liking, little, morsel, palate, relish, relush, ribbon, sample, savour **7** flavour, soupcon, thought **8** appetite, delicacy, elegance, fondness, judgment **9** attention, degustate, judgement **10** experience, suggestion **11** discernment, inclination
absence of: **7** ageusia
fundamental: **4** acid, salt, sour **5** sweet **6** bitter
kind of: nip, sip **4** tang **5** prose, sapor, savor, smack **8** penchant
lacking in: **4** rude **5** bland **8** ungentle **9** inelegant **10** unpolished, unseasoned **11** inaesthetic
pert. to: **5** sapid **7** palatal **9** gustative, gustatory
perversion: **7** malacia

refined: **7** elegant
strong: **4** tang

tasteful: **4** neat **5** tasty **6** savory **7** elegant, refined **9** aesthetic

tasteless: **4** dull, flat, rude **5** crude, vapid **6** vulgar **7** insipid, uncouth **8** barbaric, lifeless **9** savorless **10** flavorless, inartistic **11** unpalatable

tasty: **5** quiet, sapid **6** savory **7** palatal **9** flavorful, palatable, toothsome **10** delectable

tat: rag, tap **4** knot, pony **5** touch **6** tangle **7** crochet **8** absolute

tatami material: **5** straw

Tatar, Tartar: Hun **4** Turk **6** ataman, hetman **7** Cossack
dynasty: Kin, Wei
horseman: **7** Cossack
king: **4** khan
militiaman: **4** Ulan **5** Uhlan
mounted band: **4** ulan **5** horde, uhlan **7** chambul
nobleman: **5** murza
principality: **7** Khanate
tribe: Hun **5** Alani, Alans **7** Shortzy

tatou, tatu: **9** armadillo

tatter: jag, rag, rip **4** jagg, rend, stir, tear **5** hurry, scold, scrap, shred, testy **6** bustle, gabble, ribbon, tattle **7** chatter, flitter, peevish **8** guenille **14** tatterdemalion

tatterdemalion: **8** vagabond **10** ragamuffin

tattered: **4** rent, torn **6** broken, jagged, ragged, shabby, shaggy **7** slashed **9** disrupted **10** disheveled **11** dilapidated

tattle: **4** blab, chat, gash, talk, tell **5** cheep, clash, clype, prate, sneak **6** betray, gossip, report, snitch, squeal **7** chatter, clatter, divulge, prattle, stammer

tattler: **6** gossip **8** informer, telltale **9** sandpiper **10** talebearer

taunt: bob **4** dare, gibe, jeer, jibe, mock, quip, tall, twit **5** chaff, check, crack, fleer, flout, glaik, reply, scoff, slare, slart, sneer, tease, tempt **6** banter, deride, flaunt, insult, offend, rejoin, revile **7** provoke, upbraid **8** reproach, ridicule **9** aggravate

taurine: **4** bull **6** bovine

Taurus: **4** bull **6** zodiac **13** constellation

taut: **4** firm, neat, snug, tidy, trim **5** rigid, stiff, tense, tight, tough **6** severe, strict **9** distended, shipshape

tauten: **5** tense **7** stiffen, tighten

tautog: **9** blackfish **10** oysterfish

tautology: **8** pleonasm, verbiage **10** redundancy

tavern: bar, hut, inn, pub **4** bush, cafe, howf **5** booth, hotel, house, howff **6** bistro, saloon **7** cabaret, cantina, gasthof, taproom **8** alehouse, gasthaus, hostelry, ordinary, taphouse **9** roadhouse **11** public house

tavert (Sc.): **5** tired **6** stupid **8** confused

taw: tan, tew **4** beat, whip **5** agate, stake **6** harass, marble **7** scourge, shooter, torment, toughen

tawdry: **4** loud **5** cheap, gaudy, showy **6** coarse, flashy, sleazy, tinsel, vulgar

tawny, tawney: tan **5** brown, dusky, olive, swart, tenne **6** Indian, tanned **7** fulvous, tigrine **8** brindled **9** bullfinch

tawse, taws: **4** whip **5** strap

tax: fee, try **4** cess, duty, feel, fine, levy, load, rate, scat, scot, task, toll **5** abuse, agist, exact, order, scatt, stent, stint, tithe, touch, value **6** accuse, assess, avania, burden, charge, demand, excise, extent, handle, hidage, impose, impost, settle, strain, tariff **7** censure, dispute, finance, gabelle, license, oppress, revenue, tailage, tallage, tollage, tribute **8** estimate, exaction, overtire, overwork, reproach **9** prescribe **10** assessment, imposition **12** contribution
agency: IRS
assessment: **7** doomage
church: **5** tithe
feudal: **7** scutage, tailage, tallage
gatherer: IRS **8** publican **9** catchpole, catchpoll, collector, exciseman
hide: **6** hidage
kind of: cro, soc, VAT **4** cess, geld, gift, head, poll, salt, scat, toll **5** finta, sales, tithe **6** abkari, estate, excise, export, import, income, luxury, pavage, surtax, taille, vinage **7** boscage, chevage, customs, license, patente, prisage, scewing, scutage, tailage **8** auxilium, carucage, property **9** surcharge **10** chaukidari **11** inheritance **12** capital gains
rate: **10** assessment
salt: **7** gabelle

taxable: **10** assessable, censurable

taxation: tax **6** charge **7** finance, reproof, revenue **9** valuation **10** accusation, assessment
degree of: **5** ratal

taxi: cab **4** hack **5** jixie **6** fiacre (F.), litter **7** vehicle
parking place: **5** stand

taximeter: **5** clock

taxing: **5** tough **6** tiring, trying **7** onerous **9** demanding **10** accusation, exhausting

taxman: **8** publican

tazza (It.): cup **4** bowl, vase

tea: **5** party **6** repast, social, supper **8** beverage, function **9** collation, decoction, marijuana, reception
black: **5** bohea, oopak, pekoe **8** souchong
cake: **5** scone **6** cookie **7** biscuit
ceremony: **7** chanoyu
constituent: **6** theine **8** caffeine
container: **5** chest **8** canister
expert: **6** taster
family: **8** Theaceae

genus: **4** thea
Indian: **10** Darjeeling
kind of: cha **4** chaa, chia, herb, tsia **5** assam,
black, bohea, chias, congo, Emesa, green,
hyson, Ledum, oopak, pekoe, salop **6**
congue, oolong, saloop **7** cambric **8** bouillon, go-widdie **9** gunpowder
plant: **4** thea
serve: **4** pour
stimulant: **5** thein **6** theine
table: **5** tepoy **6** teapoy
urn: **7** samovar
weak: **5** blash

teach: **4** show **5** coach, drill, edify, endue,
guide, point, train, tutor **6** commit, direct,
inform, lesson, preach, school **7** apprise,
apprize, beteach, conduct, educate, lecture
8 accustom, amaister, document, instruct **9**
enlighten **10** discipline **11** demonstrate **12**
indoctrinate

teachable: apt **6** docile, pliant **7** fitting **8**
amenable

teacher: don **4** guru, prof **5** coach, guide, Plato,
tutor **6** docent, doctor, master, mentor,
pedant, pundit, reader, regent **7** adjunct, edi-
fier, maestro, sophist, trainer **8** civilian, director, educator, gamaliel, lecturer, moralist,
preacher **9** pedagogue, preceptor, professor
10 instructor **12** schoolmaster
Alexandria: **6** Origen
association: AFT, NEA
fee: **8** minerval
Hindu: **4** guru **5** swami
Jewish: **5** rabbi
Muslim: pir **5** molla, mulla **6** mollah, mullah **7** alfaqui **8** alfaquin
of the deaf: **7** oralist
Russia: **7** starets

teaching: **5** moral **6** docent **7** precept, tuition
8 guidance, pedagogy, tutelage **9** education
10 discipline **11** instruction
of a fable: **5** moral
of the Twelve: **7** Didache
pert. to: **9** pedagogic

Tea House location: **4** Naha **7** Okinawa

teak: **4** wood **5** djati

teakettle: **4** suke, suky **5** sukey, sukie

teal: **4** blue, duck **8** garganey

team: two **4** crew, gang, join, pair, race, span,
yoke **5** brace, brood, chain, flock, group,
squad, wagon **6** convey, couple, number,
string **7** lineage, progeny, vehicle **8** carriage
9 associate
baseball: **4** nine
basketball: **4** five
football: **6** eleven
kinds of: duo **4** crew **6** jayvee, scrubs **7** varsity
soccer: **6** eleven

supporter: fan **6** rooter
two animals: **4** pair, yoke

teamster: **6** carter, driver **7** carrier

tear: ram, rip, rit, run **4** claw, drag, fine, pull,
rage, rend, rent, rive, rush, skag, snag,
weep **5** binge, break, claut, larme, reave,
shred, slash, split, spree, touse, unrip, waste
6 cleave, course, dainty, damage, divide,
flurry, lament, pierce, remove, screed, sunder, tatter, wrench **7** agitate, chatter, consume, destroy, disrupt, extract, fritter, passion, shatter, torment **8** carousal, delicate,
lacerate, lachryma, separate
apart: **4** rend **9** criticize, dismember
down: **4** rase, raze **6** malign **7** destroy **8**
demolish **10** scandalize **11** disassemble
into: rip **6** attack
limb from limb: **9** dismember
off: rip, run **4** rush **5** start
to pieces: **5** shred **6** tatter **10** dilacerate
up by the roots: **6** arache **9** eradicate, extirpate

teardrop design: **5** larme

tearful: sad **5** weepy **6** crying, watery, woeful
7 flebile, maudlin, snively, weeping **8**
lacrimal **10** lachrymose
mother: **5** Niobe

tearing: **4** rage **5** hasty, hurry **7** furious, violent **8** splendid **9** harrowing, impetuous **10**
impressive **12** excruciating

tear-jerking: sad **5** mushy **6** sticky, tragic **7**
maudlin **8** bathetic

tearpit: **7** larmier

tears: **5** grief
inducing: **9** rheumatic
pert. to: **8** lacrimal **9** lachrymal
poetic: **5** rheum

tease: beg, guy, irk, nag, rag, rib, tew, vex **4**
bait, card, coax, comb, drag, fret, hare, josh,
razz, ride, stir, tear, twit **5** annoy, chafe,
chevy, chivy, devil, taunt, worry, wrack **6**
badger, bother, caddle, chivvy, harass,
heckle, hector, molest, pester, pick on,
plague, teasel **7** disturb, hatchel, provoke,
scratch, torment **8** irritate, separate **9**
aggravate, importune, tantalize **11** disentangle
wool: tum **4** comb, toom

teasel: **4** comb **5** plant

teaser: **4** gull **5** joker **6** carder, curler, sniper,
stoker, willow **7** curtain, fireman, problem
8 operator, pesterer, willower

teasing: **5** chaff **6** banter **8** badinage **11**
importune

teaty: **5** cross **7** fretful, peevish

tebbad: **6** simoom **9** sandstorm

tebeldi: **6** baobab

teched: **4** daft **5** batty **6** insane **7** cracked **8**
demented

techy: **4** spot **5** habit **6** touchy, vexing **7** blemish, fretful, peevish, quality **9** irascible, irritable, splenetic

teck: tie **6** cravat **10** four-in-hand

tectonic: **7** builder **9** carpenter **10** structural

ted: **4** toad, turn **5** waste **6** spread **7** scatter

tedge: **6** ingate, runner

tedious: dry **4** arid, dead, dree, dull, long, slow **5** bored, prosy **6** boring, borish, dreary, elenge, prolix **7** irksome, noxious, peevish, prosaic **8** dilatory, slowness, tiresome **9** exhausted, irritable, laborious, prolixity, wearisome **10** monotonous **11** displeasing, everlasting **13** uninteresting

tedium: **5** ennui **7** boredom, doldrum **8** monotony **11** irksomeness, tediousness **13** wearisomeness

tee: **5** mound, shirt
   off: **5** drive, scold **9** reprimand

teem: **4** bear, fill, gush, lead, pour, rain, swim **5** bring, burst, drain, empty, fetch, swarm **6** abound, resort, seethe, summon, throng **7** produce **8** abundant, conceive, generate, prolific

teeming: **4** full **5** agush, alive **7** pouring, replete **8** crowding, prolific, swarming **9** abounding, bristling **11** overflowing **13** overabounding

teeny: wee **4** tiny **5** small **7** fretful, peevish **9** malicious

teeny-weeny: **4** tiny **5** small **6** minute

teeter: **4** rock, sway **5** lurch, waver **6** jiggle, quiver, seesaw **7** rocking, rolling, tremble **9** sandpiper, vacillate

teeter board: **6** seesaw

teeth (see also **tooth**): **5** tines **6** molars **7** canines **8** bicuspid, choppers, crackers, grinders, incisors
   child's: **4** baby, milk **7** primary
   decay of: **6** caries
   false: **5** plate **8** dentures
   grinding of: **7** bruxism
   hard tissue: **7** dentine
   incrustation on: **6** plaque, tartar
   large: **4** buck **5** snags
   long: **5** fangs **6** tushes
   outer covering of: **6** enamel
   pert. to: **5** molar **6** dental
   serpent: **5** fangs
   socket: **7** alveoli (pl.) **8** alveolus
   sower of dragon's: **6** Cadmus
   space between: **8** diastema
   without: **10** edentulate, edentulous

teethy (Sc.): **5** cross **6** biting **7** crabbed **9** irritable

teeting: **7** titlark

teetotal: dry **6** entire **7** abstain **8** complete

teetotaller: dry **7** nonuser **9** abstainer, rechabite, refrainer **10** non-drinker

teetotum: top, toy **9** whirligig

teg: doe **4** deer **5** sheep, woman **6** fleece

tegmen: **5** cover, plate **6** elytra **7** tympani **8** covering, fore-wing

tegua: **6** sandal

tegula: **4** tile

tegument: **4** coat **5** cover, testa **6** thatch

tegurium: hut **5** cabin **6** shrine

teehee: **5** laugh **6** giggle, titter **7** snicker

Tehuantepec Gulf Indian: **5** Huave

teiidae: **4** teju **7** lizards

teju: **6** lizard **8** teguexin

tekke: rug **6** carpet **7** convent **9** monastery

tela: web **6** tissue **7** bristle **8** membrane

telamon: **5** atlas **6** column **8** atlantes, caryatid

Telamon: **5** Atlas
   brother: **6** Peleus
   father: **6** Aeacus
   friend: **8** Heracles, Hercules
   son: **4** Ajax **6** Teucer

teledu: **6** badger

telega: **4** cart **5** wagon

telegraph: **4** wire **5** cable **8** telegram
   code: **5** Morse
   inventor: **5** Morse
   key: **6** tapper
   signal: dit, dot **4** dash **9** semaphore

telegraphic communication: **4** wire **5** cable **8** mailgram **10** lettergram

Telemachus: *father:* **7** Ulysses **8** Odysseus
   mother: **8** Penelope

teleost fish: eel **5** apoda

telephone: **4** buzz, call, dial, horn, ring **5** phone **6** ring up
   book: **9** directory
   inventor: **4** Bell

Telephus: *father:* **8** Hercules
   mother: **4** Auge

telescope: jam **4** lens **5** glass **7** shorten **8** collapse, condense, simplify **9** magnifier **10** instrument
   kind: **5** radio **7** optical **8** infrared **10** reflecting, refracting
   object seen with: **11** debilissima
   site: **7** Arecibo, Palomar **8** Mt. Wilson **11** Jodrell Bank
   space: **6** Hubble

telescopic: **9** farseeing

television: TV **4** tube **5** telly, video **8** boob tube, idiot box
   award: **5** Emmy
   broadcast: **8** telecast
   cable: **7** coaxial
   camera platform: **5** dolly
   commercial: **4** spot **7** message
   device: **5** tuner **6** remote, zapper **7** antenna **10** rabbit ears
   frequency: UHF, VHF
   interference: **4** snow **5** ghost

network: ABC, CBS, CNN, FOX, HBO, MTV, NBC, NET, PBS, TBS, TNN, TNT, USA **4** ESPN **5** C-Span

picture tube: CRT **9** kinescope **10** cathode-ray

type of show: **4** game, live, news, quiz, soap, talk **5** crime, drama, movie, panel, rerun **6** comedy, serial, sitcom, sudser **7** cartoon, reality, variety, western **9** docudrama, soap opera **10** miniseries **11** documentary

telic: **9** purposive **10** purposeful **12** teleological

tell: bid, say **4** blab, chat, deem, hill, know, tale, talk, tole, toll **5** aread, areed, breve, count, mound, order, speak, state, utter, value, weigh **6** betray, decide, direct, impart, inform, notify, number, recite, reckon, regard, relate, repeat, report, reveal, tattle **7** account, apprise, command, confess, declare, dictate, discern, divulge, explain, express, mention, narrate, publish, recount, request **8** acquaint, announce, disclose, rehearse **9** broadcast, calculate, discourse, enumerate, recognize **11** communicate **12** discriminate

confidentially: **7** confide

in advance: **4** warn **7** caution

on: **4** sing **5** peach **6** snitch, squeal, tattle

secrets: **5** elype

stories: lie **4** yarn **6** tattle

thoughtlessly: **4** blab, blat

without authority: **5** rumor **6** gossip

teller: **4** blow **5** shoot **6** banker, remark, sprout **7** cashier **8** informer, narrator **9** bank clerk, describer **11** annunciator

telling: **5** valid **6** cogent **8** forceful, relation, striking **9** effective, pertinent **10** convincing, satisfying

Tell's home: Uri

telltale: **4** blab, clue, hint **6** gossip **7** tattler **8** betrayer, informer **9** betraying, indicator **10** indication, talebearer

telltruth: **7** honesty **9** frankness

telluride: **7** altaite

telson: **6** somite **7** segment

of king crab: **5** pleon

temblor: **5** shake, shock **6** tremor **10** earthquake

temerarious: **4** bold, rash **6** chance **8** heedless, reckless **9** foolhardy, venturous **10** fortuitous, headstrong **11** adventurous, venturesome

temerity: **4** gall **5** brass, cheek, nerve **6** daring **8** audacity, boldness, rashness **9** assurance, hardihood **10** effrontery **12** recklessness **13** foolhardiness **15** venturesomeness

temper: fit, ire, mix **4** bait, bate, coll, cool, curb, cure, ease, heal, heat, mean, mood,

neal, rage, tone **5** adapt, anger, birse, blend, delay, humor **6** adjust, animus, anneal, attune, church, dander, dilute, direct, govern, harden, manage, medium, mettle, mingle, modify, puddle, reduce, season, soften, soothe, spleen, steady **7** assuage, chasten, control, hackles, lighten, moisten, mollify, passion, qualify, restore, tantrum, toughen **8** chastise, compound, mitigate, moderate, modulate, regulate, restrain **9** composure **10** equanimity, irritation **11** accommodate, disposition, state of mind

display: fit **5** scene **7** tantrum

even: **4** calm **5** staid **6** sedate

kind of: ire **4** huff, mood **6** choler, spleen

temperament: **4** mood **5** gemut, humor **6** crasis, nature **7** caprice, climate, emotion **10** adjustment **11** disposition, personality, temperature **12** constitution

temperance: **7** measure **8** sobriety **10** abstinence, continence, moderation **11** self-control

temperate: **4** calm, cool, even, fair, just, mild, warm **5** balmy, sober **6** gentle, soften **8** moderate **9** continent **10** abstemious, restrained **12** conservative

temperature: **4** heat **5** fever, state **6** temper, warmth **7** mixture **8** compound, mildness **9** intensity **10** moderation, proportion **11** disposition, temperament **12** constitution

tempest: **4** gale, rage, wind **5** blast, orage, storm **6** squall, tumult **7** agitate, borasca, borasco, turmoil **9** agitation, bourasque, commotion, hurricane **12** thunderstorm

Tempest: *author:* **11** Shakespeare

characters: **5** Ariel **7** Caliban, Miranda **8** Prospero

tempestuous: **4** wild **5** galey, gusty **6** stormy **7** violent **9** turbulent

template, templet: **4** beam, lute, mold **5** bezel, bezil, gauge **7** cartoon, pattern

temple: **4** fane, naos, rath **5** candi, cella, edile, huaca, kovil, ratha, speos **6** aedile, chandi, church, haffet, haffit, hieron, mosque, shrine **9** cathedral, sanctuary **10** house of God, tabernacle

basin: **5** laver

for all gods: **8** pantheon

kind of: sha, taj, wat **4** deul, Rath **5** Ratha **6** church, jinjua, jinsha, pagoda **7** capitol **8** pantheon **9** Parthenon

part: **5** cella

sanctuary: **10** penetralia

tempo: **4** beat, pace, rate, time **5** meter, pulse, speed **6** rhythm, timing **7** cadence

pert. to: **6** agogic

rapid: **6** presto **7** allegro

slow: **5** lento **6** adagio

very slow: **5** grave

temporal: 4 laic **5** civil, scale **6** carnal, muscle **7** earthly, profane, secular, worldly **9** ephemeral, political, temporary **10** transitory **11** impermanent **13** chronological, materialistic

temporary: 5 brief **6** acting, pro tem, timely **7** interim, passing, secular, topical **8** fleeting, temporal **9** ad interim, ephemeral, makeshift, transient **10** transitory **11** provisional

contrivance: **9** makeshift

temporize: 5 delay, humor, stall, yield **6** demand, parley, soothe **9** negotiate **13** procrastinate

tempt: try **4** defy, fand, lead, lure, test **5** decoy, probe, prove, taunt **6** allure, assail, entice, incite, induce, seduce **7** assault, attempt, attract, provoke **8** endeavor, persuade **9** endeavour, seduction **10** inducement

temptation: 4 bait, lure **5** trial **7** testing **9** seduction **10** allurement, enticement, inducement

tempter: 5 devil, Satan **6** baiter

tempting: 8 alluring, enticing, inviting **9** seductive **10** attractive

temptress: 4 vamp **5** Circe, siren **7** Delilah, Lorelei, mermaid **10** Parthenope **11** enchantress

tempus fugit: 9 time flies

ten: dix (F.) **4** diez (Sp.), iota (Gr.) **5** decad, decem (L.) **6** decade, denary

ares: **6** decare

decibels: bel

dollars: **7** sawbuck

group of: **6** decade

prefix: dec **4** deca

tenable: 8 credible **9** plausible **10** defensible **11** justifiable **12** maintainable

tenacious: 4 fast, firm **5** tough **6** cledgy, dogged, grippy, sticky, strong **7** gripple, miserly, viscous **8** adhesive, cohesive, grasping, holdfast, resolute, sticking, stubborn **9** glutinous, niggardly, retentive **10** persistent **11** closefisted, persevering **12** pertinacious

tenacity: 4 grit, guts **7** courage **8** firmness **9** toughness **11** miserliness, persistence **12** adhesiveness, cohesiveness, perseverance

tenancy: 6 estate, tenure **7** holding **9** occupancy **10** possession

tenant: 4 leud **5** ceile, dreng **6** border, drengh, geneat, holder, leaser, lessee, lodger, occupy, renter, vassal **7** chakdar, cottier, dweller, inhabit **8** occupant **9** bordarius, collibert **10** inhabitant

feudal: **4** leud **6** vassal **7** socager

Ten Commandments: 9 Decalogue

tend: 4 burn, care, feed, lead, lean, mind, move, till, wait, work **5** apply, await, groom, guard, nurse, offer, reach, see to, serve, swing, treat, verge, watch **6** attend, direct, expect, extend, foster, intend, kindle, listen, manage, supply **7** care for, conduce, hearken, incline, nurture, oversee, provide, purpose, stretch, tending **8** minister, tendency **9** accompany, attentive, co-operate, cultivate, gravitate, look after **10** contribute

a fire: **5** stoke

to rise: **8** levitate

toward one point: **8** converge

tendency: run, set **4** bent, bias, tide **5** drift, drive, tenor, trend **6** course, effect, object, result **7** aptness, bearing, current, impulse, leaning **8** appetite, movement, penchant, relation **9** affection, direction, proneness, readiness **10** proclivity, propension, propensity **11** disposition, inclination

structural: **7** peloria

tender: bid, tid **4** boat, dear, fond, gift, give, keen, kind, mild, nice, soft, sore, thin, warm, weak **5** chary, frail, light, offer, young **6** delate, extend, feeble, gentle, humane, loving, submit, touchy, vessel, waiter **7** amabile, amatory, amorous, careful, fragile, hold out, painful, pitiful, present, proffer, propose, slender, sparing, steamer, subdued, suggest, tenuous, vehicle **8** delicate, feminine, immature, merciful, overture, precious, proposal, ticklish, tolerant, yielding **9** brotherly, forgiving, sensitive, succulent **10** charitable, effeminate, scrupulous **11** considerate, kindhearted, softhearted, susceptible, sympathetic, warmhearted **12** affectionate **13** compassionate **14** impressionable

for cloth: **9** stenterer

music: **7** amoroso

of animals: **6** herder **8** shepherd **10** husbandman

of cattle: **6** cowboy, herder **7** byreman **8** neatherd **9** byrewoman

of horse: **5** groom **6** ostler, walker **7** hostler, stabler

ship: gig **5** aviso, barge **6** dingey, dinghy **7** collier, pinnace

tenderfoot: 4 tyro **6** novice, rookie **7** greenie **8** beginner, neophyte, newcomer **9** cheechaco, cheechako, greenhorn

tenderhearted: 4 kind, soft **6** humane **11** sympathetic

tenderloin: 5 steak **11** filet mignon

tenderness: 4 love, pity **6** cherte **8** kindness, softness, sympathy, weakness **9** affection **10** compassion, gentleness **13** sensitiveness

tendon: 4 band, cord, thew **5** chord, nerve, sinew **11** aponeurosis

tendril 748

Achilles: **9** hamstring

tendril: **4** curl **5** clasp, sprig **6** branch, cirrus **7** ringlet, stipule

tenebrous: **4** dark **5** dusky, murky, vague **6** gloomy **7** obscure **8** darkness

tenement: **4** flat, slum **5** abode, rooms **8** building, dwelling **9** apartment **10** habitation

tenet: ism **4** view **5** adoxy, axiom, canon, creed, dogma, maxim **6** belief, decree **7** opinion, paradox **8** doctrine **9** principle

tenfold: **6** denary **7** decuple

ten-footed: **7** decapod

ten-gallon hat: **7** Stetson **8** sombrero

tengere: sky **7** heavens

teniente: **6** deputy **7** headman **10** lieutenant

tenne: **5** brown, color, tawny

Tennessee: *capital:* **9** Nashville
city: **7** Jackson, Memphis **9** Knoxville **11** Chattanooga
federal agency: TVA
horse: **7** Walking
Indian: **8** Cherokee **9** Chickasaw **11** Chickamauga
mountain: **5** Unaka **7** Lookout **8** Blue Ridge **11** Appalachian **12** Great Smokies **13** Clingman's Dome
pioneer: **12** Davy Crockett
river: **9** Tennessee **10** Cumberland **11** French Broad
state bird: **11** mockingbird
state flower: **4** iris
state tree: **11** tulip poplar
U.S. president: **4** Polk **7** Jackson, Johnson (Andrew)

---

tennis: *between four persons:* **7** doubles
between two persons: **7** singles
champion: **4** Ashe, Betz, Borg, Graf, King, Noah, Wade **5** Budge, Bueno, Chang, Court, Evert, Laver, Lendl, Lloyd, Perry, Riggs, Seles, Vilas, Wills **6** Agassi, Austin, Becker, Edberg, Fraser, Gibson, Kramer, Marble, Tilden **7** Connors, Courier, Lacoste, McEnroe, Nastase, Sampras, Sanchez, Sedgman **8** Capriati, Connolly, Gonzalez, Newcombe, Rosewall, Sabatini, Wilander **10** Mandlikova **11** Navratilova
game series: set
no score: **4** love
old form: **5** bandy
prize cup: **5** Davis
related game: **6** squash **8** handball, ping pong **9** badminton **11** racquetball

score: ace **4** game, love **5** deuce, point
shot: cut, let, lob **4** chop, dink **5** smash **6** volley **8** backhand, forehand
term: net **5** fault, serve **6** volley **7** receive, service **9** advantage

Tennyson: *character:* **4** Enid **5** Arden, Enoch **6** Elaine, Hallam
poem: **4** Maud **7** Ulysses **10** In Memoriam **11** The Princess **12** Locksley Hall

tenon: cog **4** coak **8** dovetail **10** projection

tenor: **4** body, copy, feck, gist, mood, tone **5** drift, stamp, trend **6** course, import, intent, nature, singer **7** holding, meaning, purport, writing **8** tendency **9** character, condition, direction, discourse, procedure, substance **10** transcript
falsetto: **8** tenorino
famous: **5** Lanza **6** Caruso, Tucker **7** Domingo **8** Carreras **9** Bjoerling, Pavarotti

tense: **4** edgy, rapt, taut, time **5** brace, rigid, stiff, tight **6** intent, queasy, tauten **7** intense, uptight **8** strained **9** stretched **10** breathless
past: **9** preterite
verb: **4** past **6** aorist, future **7** perfect, present **9** preterite **10** pluperfect **11** conditional

ten-sided figure: **7** decagon

tensile: **6** pliant **7** ductile, elastic

tension: **4** bent **6** nerves, strain, stress, unrest **7** anxiety, closure **8** pressure

ten-stringed: **9** decachord

tent: hut **4** camp, care, heed, show, stop, tend, test, wine **5** cover, crame, frame, lodge, probe, teach, tempt **6** attend, beware, encamp, hinder, intent, pulpit, tender **7** observe, prevent, proffer, shelter **9** attention, attentive **10** habitation
circus: **6** big top
dweller: **4** Arab **5** nomad **6** camper, Indian **7** scenite, tourist
flap: fly
kind: pup **4** pawl, tipi, wall, yurt **5** cabin, darry, shool, tepee, toldo, yurta **6** abbacy, A-frame, lean-to, teepee, tienda, wigwam **7** balagan, kibitka, marquee, sparver **8** pavilion **9** pretorium **10** praetorium
large: **8** pavilion
maker: **4** Omar

tentacle: **4** palp **6** feeler **7** antenna, tendril
animal with: **5** squid **7** octopus **10** cuttlefish
without: **7** acerous

tentage: **5** camps

tentamen: **5** trial **7** attempt

tentative: **6** unsure **9** temporary, uncertain **11** conditional, impermanent, provisional, vacillating **12** experimental

tenter: **5** frame **9** stretcher

tenterhooks: 4 nail 6 strain 8 suspense

tenth: 5 tithe 6 decima 7 decimae 8 decimate
part: 5 tithe

tenuity: 6 rarity 7 exility, poverty 8 delicacy, fineness, rareness, thinness 9 faintness, indigence 10 meagerness, slightness 11 slenderness

tenuous: 4 airy, fine, rare, slim, thin, weak 6 flimsy, slight, subtle 7 gaseous, slender, subtile 8 delicate, ethereal 11 implausible 13 insignificant, unsubstantial

tenure: 4 hold, term 5 lease 6 manner 8 courtesy 9 condition 10 incumbency

ten-year period: 6 decade 9 decenniad, decennium

tepee, teepee: 4 tent, tip; 6 wigwam

tepid: 4 mild, warm 8 lukewarm 11 halfhearted

tequila: 5 drink 6 liquor, mescal

tera: 6 church 9 monastery

Terah: *father:* 5 Nahor
son: 5 Haran 7 Abraham

teraph: 4 idol 5 image 8 talisman

teras: 7 monster

tercet: 5 rhyme 7 triplet

terebene: 9 deodorant 10 antiseptic 11 expectorant 12 disinfectant

terebra: 5 auger, drill

terebrate: 4 bore 9 perforate

teredo: 7 mollusk 8 shipworm

terete: 7 centric, tapered 8 columnar 11 cylindrical

Tereus: *sister-in-law:* 9 Philomela
son: 4 Itys 6 Itylus
wife: 6 Procne

tergal: 4 back 6 dorsal

tergiversate: lie 5 evade, shift 6 defect, weasel 7 shuffle 10 apostatize, equivocate

tergiversation: 6 deceit 7 evasion 8 apostasy, reversal 10 subterfuge

tergum: 4 back

term: end 4 call, date, half, name, span, time, word 5 bound, limit, state 6 extent, period, tenure 7 article, entitle, epithet, session 8 boundary, duration, semester 9 condition, extremity 10 definition, expression 11 appellation, termination
jail: lag 4 jolt 7 stretch 8 sentence
of address: sir 4 ma'am, sire 6 milady, milord, sirrah
of life: age 5 sands
of office: 6 regime, tenure

termagant: 5 scold, shrew 6 Amazon, tartar, virago 7 furious 8 scolding 9 turbulent 10 boisterous, tumultuous 11 quarrelsome

termed: 5 named 6 called, styled, yclept

terminable: 6 finite 9 limitable 12 determinable 13 discontinuing

terminal: end 4 last 5 anode, depot, final, limit 6 finish 7 cathode, closing, limital, station 8 desinent, railhead, ultimate 9 electrode, extremity 10 concluding
negative: 7 cathode, kathode
positive: 5 anode

terminate: end 4 call, fire, halt, kill, quit, stop 5 abort, bound, cease, close, limit 6 define, direct, expire, finish, result 7 achieve, adjourn, confine, destine, dismiss, perfect 8 complete, conclude, restrict

terminating: 5 final 6 ending
distinct point: 9 apiculate
trefoil: 6 botone

termination: end 4 amen 5 bound, close, event, limit 6 ending, expiry, finale, finish, period, result, upshot 7 outcome, purpose 8 boundary, decision, finality, terminus 9 extremity 10 completion, concluding, conclusion, expiration 13 determination
malady: 5 lysis

terminative: 8 absolute, bounding, definite 10 concluding 11 determining

termite: ant 4 anai, anay 8 white ant

termless: 8 infinite, nameless, unending 9 boundless, limitless 13 indescribable, inexpressible, unconditional

terms: 7 footing 8 standing 9 agreement 10 conditions, provisions 11 limitations 12 propositions, stipulations 13 circumstances
come to: 5 agree
make: 5 treat 9 negotiate, stipulate

tern: 4 darr, gull 10 sea swallow
genus: 5 anous 6 sterna

ternary: 6 treble, triple 7 ternion, trinity 9 threefold

ternate: 12 trifoliolate

terra: 4 Gaea, land 5 earth

terra alba: 4 clay 6 gypsum, kaolin 9 magnesium

terra cotta: 4 clay 6 statue 7 pottery 11 earthenware

terra firma: 5 earth 6 estate, ground 7 dry land 8 mainland 11 solid ground

terrace: 4 bank, dais, mesa, step 5 bench, patio 6 piazza 7 balcony, gallery, portico 8 chabutra, platform 9 colonnade
in series: 8 parterre
wall: 6 podium

terrain: 4 form, turf 5 field, tract 6 milieu, region, sphere 7 contour, demesne 9 territory 11 environment

terrapin: 4 emyd, emys 6 coodle, heifer, potter, slider, turtle 11 diamond back

terrestrial: 6 earthy, layman, mortal 7 earthly, mundane, terrene, worldly 9 planetary 10 earth bound

terret: 4 ring 7 cringle

terrible: bad 4 dire, gast, grim, hard 5 awful, lurid 6 fierce, horrid, severe, tragic 7 direful, extreme, fearful, ghastly, hideous, intense, painful, very bad, violent **8** almighty, dreadful, horrible, terrific **9** appalling, atrocious, excessive, frightful **10** formidable, horrifying, terrifying, tremendous, unpleasant **12** disagreeable

Terrible one: **4** Ivan

terrier: dog, fox **4** Bull, Skye **5** cairn, Irish, Welsh **6** Boston **8** Airedale, Scottish, Sealyham **9** Yorkshire **10** Bedlington, Clydesdale

terrific: **4** good **5** great **6** superb **7** extreme, fearful **8** dreadful, exciting, terrible **9** appalling, excessive, frightful, marvelous, wonderful **10** terrifying, tremendous

terrified: **4** awed **6** afraid, aghast, frozen **7** ghastly **9** petrified **10** struck dumb

terrify: awe, cow, hag **4** bree, fray, stun **5** alarm, annoy, appal, daunt, deter, drive, haunt, impel, scare, shock, tease **6** affirm, afread, agrise, appall, bother, dismay, injure **7** horrify, stupefy, torment **8** affright, frighten **9** importune

terrifying: **6** horrid **7** ghastly, hideous **8** terrible **11** frightening

terrigenous: **9** earthborn **13** autochthonous

terrine: jar **4** dish, stew **6** ragout

territorial division: amt **6** canton **7** commune **10** department **14** arrondissement

territory: **4** area, city, land, town **5** field, scope, state, tract **6** county, extent, ground, region, sphere **7** country, portion, terrain **8** district, environs, province **9** bailiwick **10** possession **12** neighborhood

kind of: **5** banat **6** canton **7** banliue, enclave **8** banlieue, Pashalic **10** palatinate

terror: awe **4** fear, fray, pest **5** alarm, dread, panic **6** affray, dismay, fright, horror **8** dreddour **11** trepidation **12** terribleness **13** consternation

terrorism: **11** subjugation **12** intimidation

terrorist: **5** rebel **6** bomber, killer **8** alarmist **11** scaremonger

terrorize: awe **5** abash, alarm, appal, bully, scare **6** appall, coerce **8** frighten **9** embarrass **10** intimidate

terry: **4** loop **5** cloth **8** toweling

terse: **4** curt, neat **5** brief, pithy, short **6** abrupt, claret, rubbed, smooth **7** compact, concise, laconic, pointed, refined **8** clearcut, incisive, polished, succinct, unprolix **11** sententious, tightlipped **12** accomplished

tertiary period: **5** third **7** Neocene **8** Cenozoic

tertulia: **4** club **5** party **7** meeting

terzina: **6** tercet **7** triplet

tessellated: **5** tiled **6** mosaic **9** checkered

tessera: **4** cube, tile **5** glass, label, token **6** abacus, billet, marble, pledge, tablet, ticket **7** voucher **8** password **9** rectangle **11** certificate

test: pot, try **4** exam, fand, feel, quiz, will **5** assay, check, cupel, essay, final, grope, proof, prove, shell, taste, testa, trial, weave **6** ordeal, refine, sample, verify **7** approof, approve, examine, measure, witness **8** analysis, cupeling, evidence, potsherd, standard **9** construct, criterion, determine, testament, testimony **10** experience, experiment, touchstone **11** examination, investigate, performance **12** authenticate

in fineness and weight: pyx

kind: IQ, GRE, SAT **4** acid, LSAT, PSAT **5** blood **7** regents **8** aptitude **9** Rorschach

ore: **5** assay

testa: **5** shell **7** coating **8** covering, episperm, tegument **10** integument

testament: Job **4** will **5** Bible **8** covenant, landbook **9** scripture, testimony **12** confirmation

testator, testatrix: **7** legator, witness **9** willmaker

beneficiary of: **4** heir **7** heiress, heritor **9** inheritor

tester: bed **5** crown, frame **6** canopy, conner, helmet, prover, teston **7** assayer, candler, sparver **8** denierer **9** chauffeur, headpiece

testicle: cob **5** gonad **6** testes (pl.), testis **7** genitor

deer: **6** doucet, dowcet, dowset

testifier: **7** witness **8** deponent

testify: **5** state, swear, vouch **6** affirm, attest, avouch, depone, depose **7** certify, declare, express, profess, protest, witness **8** indicate, manifest, proclaim

testimonial: **4** sign **5** salvo, token **7** tribute, warrant, writing **8** evidence **9** testimony **10** credential **11** certificate

testimony: say **6** attest, avowal **7** witness **8** evidence **10** deposition, profession **11** affirmation, attestation, certificate, declaration

testudo: **4** lyre, shed **5** cover, talpa, tumor, vault **6** screen **7** ceiling, shelter

testy: **4** edgy **5** cross **6** touchy **7** crabbed, fretful, grouchy, peevish, waspish **8** petulant, snappish **9** impatient, irascible, irritable, obstinate **10** headstrong

tetanus: **7** lockjaw **9** holotonia

Tethys: **5** Titan **8** Titaness
brother: **6** Cronus
father: **6** Uranus
husband: **7** Oceanus

---

tetchy: **6** touchy **7** peevish **9** irascible, irritable, sensitive

tête-a-tête: **4** chat, seat, sofa, talk **7** meeting, private, vis-a-vis **8** causeuse, intimate **12** conversation

tetel: 5 torah
tether: tie 4 band, rope 5 cable, chain, leash, limit, noose 6 fasten, picket 7 confine 8 restrain
Tethys: (see box)
tetrad: 4 four 7 quartet 8 fourfold
tetragon: 6 square 7 rhombus 10 quadrangle
tetraodont: 4 fish
tetric: 5 harsh 6 gloomy, sullen 7 austere
tetter: 4 fret 6 eczema, herpes, lichen
Teutonic: 5 Dutch 6 German, Gothic 7 English 12 Scandinavian
  alphabet character: 4 rune
  barbarian: 4 Goth
  deity: Eir, Hel, Tiu, Tyr, Ull 4 Erda, Frea, Frig, Norn, Odin, Thor 5 Aesir, Baldr, Brage, Bragl, Donar, Othin, Tiwaz, Wodin, Wotan 6 Balder, Frigga, Saeter 7 Forseti 8 Heimdall
  homicide: 5 morth
  Knights: 9 crusaders
  land: 4 odal
  law: 5 Salic
  legendary hero: 4 Offa
  race: 4 Ubii 5 Danes, Goths, Jutes 6 Angles, Franks, Saxons 7 Germans, Vandals 8 Lombards 10 Norwegians 11 Burgundians 13 Scandinavians
  water nymph: nis
tew: taw, tow, vex 4 beat, fuss, pull, work 5 knead, tease, tools 6 incite, strive, tackle, tuyere 7 fatigue 8 struggle
tewit: 7 lapwing

text: 4 book, copy 5 theme, topic 7 content, passage, subject 11 handwriting 13 subject matter
  operatic: 8 libretto
  pen: 5 ronde
  pert. to: 7 textual
  revision: 9 recension
  set to music: 5 opera 6 lieder 8 oratorio
  variation: 7 lection
textbook: 6 manual, primer
textile: 5 cloth, stuff 6 fabric 8 material
  dealer: 6 mercer
  finish: 11 mercerizing, Sanforizing
  goods: 7 mercery
  ornament: 4 lace 5 braid 8 fagoting
  plant refuse: 5 hurds
  ring device: 6 poteye
  unfinished: 6 greige 9 gray goods
  worker: 4 dyer 6 reeder, weaver
texture: web 4 feel, pile, wale 5 fiber, grain 6 cobweb, fabric, tissue 7 essence, textile 9 structure 11 composition, fabrication
tez: 7 pungent, violent
tezkirah: 7 license 8 passport 11 certificate
Thackeray: *character:* 10 Becky Sharp 12 Amelia Sedley, Ethel Newcome
  novels: 9 Pendennis 10 Vanity Fair, Virginians 11 Barry Lyndon, Henry Esmond

Texas: *battle:* 5 Alamo 10 San Jacinto
  bronco, broncho: 7 mustang
  capital: 6 Austin
  city: 4 Waco 6 Dallas, El Paso, Laredo, Odessa 7 Abilene, Denison, Houston, Lubbock 8 Amarillo 9 Fort Worth 10 San Antonio
  fortress: 5 Alamo
  founder: 6 Austin
  hero: 5 Bowie 6 Travis 7 Houston 8 Crockett
  plain: 6 Staked 13 Llano Estacado
  river: Red 5 Pecos 6 Brazos, Neches, Nueces, Sabine 7 Trinity 9 Rio Grande
  shrub: 6 anagua, anaqua
  state bird: 11 mockingbird
  state flower: 10 bluebonnet
  state police: 6 Ranger
  state tree: 5 pecan
  U.S. president: Ike, LBJ 7 Johnson (Lyndon B.) 10 Eisenhower

Thailand: 4 Siam
  cab: 5 samlo 6 samlaw, samlor
  canal: 5 klong
  capital: 7 Bangkok
  currency: att 4 baht 5 fuang, tical 6 pynung, salung, satang
  demon: nag
  measure: ken, niu, nmu, rai, sat, sen, sok, wah, yot 4 keup, ngan, tang, yote 5 kwien, laang, sesti, tanan 6 kabiet, kammeu, kanahn 7 chai meu, roeneng 8 chang awn 9 anukabiet
  peninsula: 5 Malay
  people: Lao, Tai 4 Thai 7 Siamese
  river: 6 Makong, Mekong, Meping 10 Chaophraya
  spirit: nat
  sport: 6 takraw
  temple: wat
  tree: 4 teak

Thais composer: 8 Massenet
thalassic: 6 marine 7 oceanic, pelagic 8 maritime
thalidomide: 8 sedative 12 hypnotic drug
Thames: 4 Isis 5 river
  city and town: 4 Eton 6 Henley, London, Oxford 7 Reading

tributary: **6** Tyburn
Thanatopsis author: 6 Bryant
Thanatos: 5 death
  brother: **6** Hypnos
  mother: Nyx
thane: 5 baron, chief, churl **7** servant, warrior
  8 follower **9** attendant
  estate: **5** manor
  of Cawdor: **7** Macbeth
thank: 5 blame **11** acknowledge
thankful: 8 grateful **11** meritorious **12** appreciative
thankless: 10 ungrateful, unrewarded **13** unappreciated
  person: **7** ingrate
thanks: 5 danke (G.), grace, merci (F.) **6** grazie (It.) **7** cumshaw, gracias (Sp.) **8** gramercy **9** because of, gratitude **11** gratulation **12** appreciation **15** acknowledgement
that: yon **4** such **6** yonder **7** because
that is: 5 id est, to wit **6** namely
that not: 4 lest
thatch: 4 nipa, roof **5** cover
  peg: **4** scob
  support: **6** wattle
thatcher: 6 reeder **7** crowder, hellier
thaumaturgists: 5 mages **6** Goetae **7** wizards **9** magicians, sorcerers
thaumaturgy: 5 magic **7** alchemy, sorcery **11** legerdemain
thaw: 4 melt **5** relax **6** unbend **7** liquefy **8** dissolve
the: 7 article
  French: la, le, les
  German: das, der, die
  Italian: il, la, le, lo, gli **4** egli, ella
  Spanish: el, la, las, los
theater, theatre: 4 film, hall, play **5** arena, drama, house, movie, odeon, odeum, opera, stage **8** coliseum **9** playhouse
  audience: **5** house
  award: **4** Tony
  curtain: **4** drop **6** teaser
  district: **6** Rialto **8** Broadway **11** Off-Broadway
  Elizabethan: **5** Globe
  entrance hall: **5** foyer, lobby
  full: SRO
  Greek: **5** odeon, odeum
  motion-picture: **5** movie **6** cinema **8** bioscope
  outdoor: **5** arena **7** drive-in, open-air
  part: box, pit **4** loge, wing **5** apron, foyer, stage **7** balcony, gallery, parquet **8** parterre **9** back stage, orchestra **10** auditorium, proscenium **12** dressing room
  pit: **6** circle **7** parquet **8** parterre
  scenery: **5** drops, flats **9** cyclorama
  ticket booth: **9** box office

theater-in-the-round: 5 arena
theatrical: 5 showy, stagy **6** scenic **7** pompous **8** affected, dramatic **10** artificial, histrionic **11** declamation **12** melodramatic
  company: **6** troupe
  extra: **4** supe **5** super **13** supernumerary
  profession: **5** stage **6** acting
  spectacle: **7** pageant
  star: **4** hero, lead **7** heroine
  valet: **7** dresser
Thebes (Egypt): *deity:* **4** Amon **5** Ament **6** Amon Re
  river: **4** Nile
  site of ruins: **5** Luxor **6** Karnak
  statue: **6** Memnon
Thebes (Greece): *acropolis:* **6** Cadmea
  blind soothsayer: **8** Tiresias
  district: **7** Thebiad
  founder: **6** Cadmus
  king: **5** Laius **7** Amphion, Oedipus **8** Eteocles, Pentheus
  poet: **6** Pindar
  queen: **5** Aedon, Niobe **7** Jocasta
  wicked queen: **5** Dirce
theca: 5 sac, sad **4** case **7** capsule
theft: job **5** caper, filch, heist, pinch, steal **6** furtum, holdup, piracy, ripoff **7** bribery, larceny, robbery **8** burglary, stealing, thievery **9** pilferage **10** conveyance, plagiarism **12** embezzlement
theft-like: 7 piratic
thelium: 6 nipple **7** papilla
them: 5 hemen, those **6** people
theme: 4 base, idea, text **5** ditty, essay, motif, paper, point, topic **6** matter, theses, thesis **7** article, subject **9** discourse **11** composition, proposition **12** dissertation **13** subject matter
  hackneyed: **6** cliche
  literary: **5** motif **9** leitmotif
  musical: **4** tema
  title: **5** lemma
Themis: *concern of:* law **7** harmony
  father: **6** Uranus
  mother: **4** Gaea
then: 4 also, anon, next, soon **5** after, again, alors (F.) **6** before **7** besides **8** formerly, moreover **9** therefore **11** accordingly
thence: 4 away **9** elsewhere, therefore, therefrom **10** henceforth **11** thenceforth
theodolite: 7 alidade, transit
theologian: 6 cleric, divine **9** churchman
  famous: **4** Küng **5** Arius, Barth, Buber **6** Calvin, Luther, Newman, Rahner, Wesley **7** Erasmus, Tillich, Zwingli **9** Augustine **11** Melanchthon **13** Thomas Aquinas
  Islamic authority: **4** imam **5** ulema
theorbo: 4 lute
theorem: 4 rule **5** axiom **6** theory, thesis **9**

753   **thigh**

principle **10** hypothesis

theoretical: **5** ideal **8** abstract, platonic **11** speculation, speculative, unpractical **12** hypothetical

theorist: **10** ideologist

theorize: **7** suggest **9** postulate, speculate **11** hypothesize

theory: ism **4** idea, plan **5** guess **6** notion, scheme, thesis **7** formula, opinion, premise **8** analysis, doctrine **9** postulate, principle **10** assumption, conjecture, hypothesis **11** explanation, speculation **13** contemplation
kind of: **9** evolution, Platonism **10** relativity

therapy: **9** treatment **10** psychiatry

there: ibi (L.), yon **4** able **5** ready, voila **6** yonder **7** thither **8** equipped, reliable **10** dependable

thereafter: **9** afterward **11** accordingly **12** subsequently

therefore: **4** ergo, then, thus **5** hence, since **6** frothy, thence **9** wherefore **11** accordingly **12** consequently

therewith: mit **6** withal **7** besides, thereat **8** moreover **9** forthwith, thereupon

therm, therme: spa **4** bath, pool **7** calorie

thermal: hot **4** warm

thermal unit: BTU **6** degree **7** calorie

thermometer: **7** Celsius, Reaumur **8** pyrostat **9** pyrometer **10** Centigrade, Fahrenheit

thesaurus: **5** Roget **7** lexicon **8** treasury **10** repository, storehouse

Theseus: **12** King of Athens
father: **6** Aegeus **8** Poseidon
lover: **7** Ariadne
mother: **6** Aethra
slayer of: **8** Minotaur
son: **10** Hippolytus
wife: **7** Antiope, Phaedra **9** Hippolyte

thesis: **5** essay, point, theme **6** theory **7** premise **8** treatise **9** discourse, monograph, postulate, statement **10** assumption, conception, hypothesis **11** affirmation, proposition **12** dissertation
opposed to: **5** arsis

thespian: **5** actor **6** player **7** actress **8** dramatic **9** performer, tragedian

Thessaly: *king:* **7** Admetus
mountain: Ida, Osa **4** Ossa **6** Othrys, Pelion, Pindus **7** Olympus **9** Psiloriti

thetic: **8** positive **9** arbitrary **10** prescribed

Thetis: **6** Nereid **8** sea nymph
husband: **6** Peleus
son: **8** Achilles

theurgy: **5** magic **7** miracle, sorcery **9** occultism

thew: **4** form, mode **5** habit, power, press, sinew, stool, trait **6** custom, manner, muscle, virtue **7** oppress, pillory, quality **8** strength **10** discipline, resolution

thewless: **4** lazy **6** feeble **10** spiritless

thick: fat **4** dull, dumb, hazy, wide **5** broad, brosy, bulky, burly, close, crass, dense, gross, heavy, husky, midst, plump, solid **6** coarse, filled, greasy, hoarse, obtuse, stocky, stodgy, stupid **7** compact, crowded, doltish, grumous, massive, thicket, viscous **8** abundant, familiar, friendly, guttural, intimate, profound **9** excessive, luxuriant **10** indistinct **11** inspissated, marticulate **12** impenetrable

thicken: gel **4** clot, crud, curd **5** cloud, crowd, flock **6** curdle, deepen, harden **7** confirm, congeal, stiffen **8** condense **9** coagulate, intensify **10** incrassate, inspissate, strengthen

thicket: **4** bosk, bush, rone, shaw **5** brake, clump, copse, grove, hedge, shola **6** bosket, covert, greave **7** boscage, boskage, bosquet, coppice, spinney **9** brushwood **10** underbrush **11** undergrowth
kind: **7** chamise, chamiso **8** chamisal **9** chaparral

thickheaded: **4** dull, dumb, slow **5** dense **6** stupid **7** doltish **11** blockheaded

thickness: ply **5** layer, sheet **7** density **8** diameter **9** curdiness, denseness, dimension, heaviness, viscosity **10** corpulence **11** consistency

thickset: **4** stub **5** beefy, squat, stout **6** chumpy, chunky, fleshy, portly, stocky, stodgy, stubby

thick-skinned: **4** cold **6** obtuse **7** callous **9** pachyderm **11** pachydermic

thickskulled: **4** dull, slow **5** heavy **6** obtuse, stupid **11** thickheaded

thief (see also **stealer**): **4** chor, gilt, prig **5** budge, crook, rogue, scamp **6** ackman, arrant, bandit, cannon, cloyer, hooker, klepto, looter, nimmer, pirate, rascal, robber, sucker, waster **7** bramble, brigand, burglar, filcher, footpad, grifter, hoodlum, poacher, prowler, rustler, sneaker, stealer **8** criminal, cutpurse, gangster, larcener, swindler **9** larcenist, scoundrel **10** cat burglar, depredator, freebooter, highwayman, plagiarist, shoplifter **11** safecracker **12** kleptomaniac
crucified beside Christ: **6** Desmas, Dismas, Dysmas
kind of: gun **5** ganef, ganof, gonof, snoop **6** ackman, angler, gonoph, pirate, swiper **7** gorilla, mercury, rustler **9** drawlatch **10** cat burglar, pickpocket **14** secondstory man

thieveless (Sc.): **4** cold **5** bleak **6** frigid **7** aimless **8** bootless, listless **10** forbidding

thievish: sly **7** furtive, kleptic **8** stealthy **9** dishonest, larcenous

thigh: ham **4** hock **5** carve, femur, flank, meros, merus **6** femora (pl.), gammon

armor: **5** cuish
bone: **5** femur, ilium
muscle: **8** gracilis **9** hamstring, sartorius **10** quadriceps
pains: **8** sciatica
pert. to: **6** crural

thill: **4** sill **5** plank, shaft **6** thwart **8** planking, wainscot

thimble: cap, cup **5** cover
conjurer: **6** goblet
machine: **6** sleeve

thimblerigger: **5** cheat **8** imposter, swindler

thin: dim **4** bony, fine, flue, lank, lean, pale, poor, puny, rare, slim, weak **5** acute, exile, faint, gaunt, lanky, lathy, reedy, scant, sharp, sheer, spare, washy, wispy, wizen **6** dilute, flimsy, hollow, meager, meagre, papery, piping, rarefy, reduce, scanty, scarce, shrill, skinny, slight, slinky, sparse, watery, weaken, weazen **7** gracile, haggard, scrawny, slender, tenuous **8** araneous, gossamer, piercing, rarefied, scantily, skeletal **9** attenuate, emaciated, extenuate, infertile, subtilize **10** cadaverous, inadequate **11** high-pitched, implausible, transparent, watered down **12** unbelievable, unconvincing **13** unsubstantial
and delicate: **8** araneous
and haggard: **5** gaunt
and slender: **4** lean **5** lanky
and withered: **5** wizen **6** weezen **7** wizened
plate: **4** leaf, shim **5** wedge **6** lamina, tegmen
scale: **5** flake **6** lamina **7** lamella

thing: act, fad, res **4** deed, idea, item, mode, rage **5** cause, chose, court, craze, event, point, stuff, style, vogue **6** action, affair, detail, entity, matter, notion, object, reason, wealth **7** article, council, fashion **8** assembly, incident, property, vocation **9** happening, substance **10** occurrence **11** transaction **12** circumstance
accomplished: **4** acta, deed **5** actum, actus
added: ell **6** insert **7** addenda (pl.) **8** addendum, addition, appendix **9** insertion **10** additament, complement, supplement
admitted: **4** fact **5** datum **7** element **9** principle
assumed: **7** premise, premiss **9** postulate **11** implication, stipulation **14** presupposition
capable of spontaneous motion: **8** automata **9** automaton
cursed: **8** anathema
extra: **5** bonus **6** bounty, lanyap **7** premium **8** lagnappe **9** lagniappe
following: **6** sequel
forfeited to crown: **7** deodand
found: **5** trove
given as security: **4** gage **6** pledge **10** collateral

indefinite, unnamed: **7** so and so, whatsis, whatsit **11** nondescript **15** whatchamacallit
known by reasoning: **7** noumena **8** noumenon
known by senses: **9** phenomena **10** phenomenon
of no value: **4** bean, junk **5** nihil, waste **6** fillip, nought, stiver, trifle **7** bauchle, nothing, pinhead, trinket **8** picayune **9** nonentity, resnihili **10** resnullius
of remembrance: **5** token **7** memento
precious: **4** oner **5** curio, relic **6** pippin, rarity **8** treasure
small: dot, jot **4** atom, iota, whit **6** tittle **8** particle, scuddick
to be done: **5** chore **6** agenda **7** agendum

thingamajig: **6** device, doodad, gadget, widget **9** doohickey, doohickus, doohinkey, doohinkus, thingummy **10** thingumbob

things: res **4** duds, gear, togs **5** goods **7** clothes, effects **8** clothing, property **10** belongings **11** possessions
done: **9** res gestae
for sale: **5** goods, wares **8** services **11** merchandise
gained by purchase: **10** acquirenda **12** acquisitions
hidden: **10** penetralia
movable: **8** chattels **10** resmobiles
worth remembering: **11** memorabilia

think: wis **4** deem, feel, mull, muse, seem, trow, ween **5** brood, guess, judge, opine, study, weigh **6** appear, assume, esteem, expect, gather, intend, noodle, ponder, reason, repute, scheme **7** believe, bethink, concoct, imagine, presume, purpose, realize, reflect, resolve, suppose, surmise, suspect **8** cogitate, conceive, consider, meditate, ruminate **9** calculate, determine, speculate **10** conjecture, deliberate, reconsider, understand **11** contemplate
alike: **5** agree
logically: **6** reason **11** ratiocinate
out: **4** plan **5** solve **6** devise **7** develop, perfect **8** cogitate, contrive, discover **10** excogitate
over: **4** mull **5** brood **6** ponder **10** reconsider

thinker: **4** mind **5** brain **7** sophist, student **9** meditator **11** philosopher **12** intellectual

Thinker sculptor: **5** Rodin

thinking: **7** opinion **8** judgment **9** judgement **10** cogitation, reflection **13** ratiocination

thinly: **6** airily **8** sparsely **14** insufficiently
metallic: **5** tinny
scattered: **6** sparse

Thin Man: **9** detective **11** Nick Charles
dog: **4** Asta
wife: **4** Nora

thinner: 5 rarer 7 sheerer 10 turpentine

thinness: 6 rarity 7 exility, tenuity 11 attenuation

thin-skinned: 6 tender, touchy 9 sensitive

third: *figure mood:* 7 ferison
in number: 8 tertiary
music: 6 tierce

third estate: 6 people, plebes 8 plebians, populace 10 commonalty 11 bourgeoisie, rank and file

Third Man author: 6 Greene

thirlage: fee, pay 4 dues 5 right 7 multure, service 8 mortgage 9 servitude, thralldom

thirling: 7 bondage 10 subjection

thirst: 4 long, want, wish 5 covet, crave, dryth 6 desire 7 aridity, craving, dryness, longing
absence of: 7 adipsia
excessive: 9 anadipsia

thirsty: dry 4 adry, arid, avid, keen 5 eager 6 desire, drouth 7 athirst, craving, drought, longing, parched, wild for 8 droughty

thirty: end 6 lambda (Gr.), trente (F.)

this: ces (F.), cet (F.), hic, hoc (L.), yis 4 ceci (F.), esta (Sp.), este (Sp.), esto (Sp.), haec (L.), 5 cette (F.), 6 dieser (G.), questo (It.), questa (It.), questi (It.)
and that: 8 sundries 11 odds and ends
way: so 4 here

Thisbe's love: 7 Pyramus

thistle: 4 weed 7 bedegar, caltrop 8 bedeguar 10 acanaceous, tumbleweed
genus of: 5 layia

thistledown: 6 pappus

thistle-like plants: 7 carlina

thither: end, yon 5 hence, there 6 yonder 7 farther, thereat 8 ulterior

thole: peg, pin 4 bear 5 allow 6 endure, remain, suffer 7 fulcrum, oarlock, undergo 8 tolerate

Thomas' opera: 6 Mignon

thong: 4 cord, lace, lash, rein, riem, whip 5 lasso, leash, quirt, romal, strap, strip, whang 6 twitch 7 amentum, laniard, lanyard, latchet 8 whiplash

thong-shaped: 6 lorate

Thor: *father:* 4 Odin
giant: 8 Hrungnir
god of: 7 thunder 9 lightning
hammer: 8 Mjollnir
stepson: Ull
wife: Sif

thorax: 5 chest, trunk 6 breast

thorn: 4 brod, goad 5 briar, brier, spine, worry 7 acantha 8 vexation 9 annoyance 10 irritation
apple: 5 metel 6 datura 10 Jimson weed
Egyptian: 5 babul 6 gonake 7 gonakie
full of: 6 briery
small: 7 spinule

thorny: 5 sharp, spiny 6 spinal 7 brambly, bristly, complex, prickly 8 spinated 9 acanthoid, difficult, vexatious 10 nettlesome 11 contentious, troublesome

thorough: 4 deep, full 5 total 6 arrant 8 absolute, accurate, complete, detailed, finished, sweeping 9 downright 10 exhaustive, throughout 11 painstaking 13 comprehensive

thoroughbred: 5 horse 7 trained 8 cultured, educated, pedigree, purebred, well-bred 9 race horse 11 full-blooded

thoroughfare: way 4 road 5 alley 6 artery, avenue, street 7 highway, passage, transit 8 waterway 9 boulevard

thoroughgoing: 6 arrant 7 radical 8 complete 13 dyed-in-the-wool

thoroughly: all 4 inly, well 6 deeply 7 roundly 9 downright, intensive 10 absolutely, altogether, completely

thoroughwort: 7 boneset 9 hoarhound

thorp, thorpe: 4 dorp, town 6 hamlet 7 village 9 community

Thoth: god 6 Tehuti
head: dog 4 ibis

though: tho 4 when 5 still, while 6 albeit, even if 7 however, whereas 12 nevertheless

thought: 4 care, hope, idea, mind, view 5 trace 6 deemed, musing, notion, opined 7 anxiety, concept, judging, opinion 9 brainwork, cogitated, reasoning 10 cogitation, conception, meditation, reflection, rumination 11 cerebration, expectation, imagination, speculation 12 deliberation, recollection 13 concentration, consideration, contemplation, ratiocination
form: 6 ideate
inability to express: 6 asemia
reader: 8 telepath
transference: ESP 9 telepathy

thoughtful: 4 kind 5 moody 6 polite 7 careful, earnest, heedful, mindful, pensive, prudent, serious 8 rational 9 attentive, courteous, designing, regardful 10 meditative, melancholy, reflective, ruminative 11 circumspect, considerate

thoughtless: 4 dull, rash, rude 5 brash, hasty, short 6 remiss, stupid 7 glaiket, glaikit, selfish 8 careless, heedless, reckless, tactless 9 brainless, impulsive 10 unthinking 11 harum-scarum, inadvertent, inattentive, lightheaded 13 inconsiderate

thousand: *dollars:* 5 grand
one: mil 5 grand 7 chiliad
years: 10 millennium

thousand-headed snake: 5 Sesha 6 Shesha

thousandth: 10 millesimal
of an inch: mil

Thrace: *gladiator:* 9 Spartacus

goddess: **6** Bendis
king: **6** Tereus
musician: **7** Orpheus

thrall: **4** esne, serf, thew **5** slave **7** bondage, bondman, captive, enslave, slavery, subject **8** enslaved, enthrall **9** servitude, suffering **10** oppression, subjugated

thrash: lam, tan **4** bang, beat, bray, ding, drub, flax, flog, lash, maul, pelt, rush, sail, whip, yerk **5** array, baste, bless, flail, pound, swing, threp, whale, whang **6** anoint, batter, buffet, defeat, fettle, pummel, raddle, strike, threap, threep, threip, threpe, thresh, thwack, wallop **7** trounce **8** belabour, blathery, vanquish **9** pulverize, triturate **10** flagellate
out: **5** argue **6** debate **7** discuss **10** kick around

thrashing: **4** bean, loss **6** defeat **7** beating, milling **8** drubbing, flogging, whipping

thrave: **4** bind **5** crowd **6** bundle, number, throng **8** quantity

thread: ray **4** cord, filo, line, vein, wind, yarn **5** fiber, reeve, stand, twine, weave **6** strata, stream, string **7** quality, stratum **8** filament, fineness, raveling **9** ravelling **11** composition
a needle: **5** reeve
ball of: **4** clew, clue
bits of: **4** lint **9** ravelings
cell: **5** cnida
dental: **5** floss
division of: **4** beer
holder: **6** bobbin
inserted beneath skin: **5** seton
in weaving shuttle: **4** weft
kind of: **4** bast, bave, yarn **5** floss, seton, trame **6** lingel, lingle **8** arrasene, surgical
knot in: **4** burl
like: **6** filose
on spindle: cop
pert. to: **5** filar
raveled: **6** sleave
silk: bur **4** bave, burr **5** floss, trame **9** filoselle
skein of: **4** hasp
surgical: **5** seton **6** catgut, suture
tape: **5** inkle
tester: **9** serimeter

threadbare: **4** bare, poor, sere, thin, worn **5** banal, corny, stale, trite **6** frayed, pilled, shabby **7** napless **9** hackneyed

threads: **4** beer, suit, togs, weft, woof **6** filler **7** clothes **8** clothing

threadworm: **7** filaria **8** nematode

threat: vex **4** fail, lack, urge, want, warn **5** chide, crowd, peril, press, troop **6** coerce, compel, menace, misery, throng **6** oppress, reprove, trouble, warning **8** maltreat, threaten **10** compulsion **12** intimidation

threaten: cow **4** brag, loom **5** augur, boast, bully, lower, utter **6** charge, harass, menace **7** portend, promise **8** denounce **10** intimidate

threatening: big **5** scary **6** greasy, lowery **7** ominous **8** lowering, menacing **9** impending **10** formidable

three: tre (It.) **4** drei (G.), tres (Sp.) **5** crowd, gamma (Gr.), trias, trois (F.) **7** Trinity
combination of: **7** ternary, triplet
consisting of: **7** ternate
group of: tre **4** trio **5** triad, trine **7** ternion **8** triumvir
months: **7** quarter **9** trimester

Three B's (in music): **4** Bach **6** Brahms **9** Beethoven

three-card monte: **9** montebank

three-cleft: **6** trifid

three-dimensional: 3D **5** cubic **6** stereo **7** cubical, spatial
picture: **8** hologram

threefold: **4** tern **5** trine **6** ternal, thrice, treble, trinal, triple, triply

Three Graces: joy **5** bloom **6** Aglaia, Thalia **10** brilliance, Euphrosyne

three-headed goddess: **6** Hecate

three-hundredth anniversary: **12** tercentenary **13** tercentennial, tricentennial

three in one: **6** triune **7** trinity

Three Kingdoms: Wu, Shu, Wei

three-layered: **10** trilaminar

three L's: **4** lead **7** lookout **8** latitude

three-masted vessel: **5** xebec **8** schooner

Three Musketeers: **5** Athos **6** Aramis **7** Porthos
author: **5** Dumas
friend: **9** D'Artagnan

three-piled: **4** best **6** costly **11** extravagant

three-pointed: **11** tricuspidal

three Rs: **6** readin', writin', **9** 'rithmetic

three-seeded: **11** trispermous

three-sided figure: **6** trigon **8** triangle

threesome: **4** trio **5** triad **11** triumvirate

three-spot: **4** trey

three-square: **5** cross **9** irritable, three-fold

three-styled: **10** trystylous

Three Wise Men: **4** Magi **6** Gaspar **8** Melchior **9** Balthasar

threnody: **4** song **5** dirge **6** hearse, lament

thresh (see also **thrash**): cob **4** beat, flog, lump, rush **5** berry, flail, pound **9** winnow

thresher: **5** flail, shark **6** beater **7** combine

thresher shark: **6** sea fox **7** foxfish **8** whiptail
genus: **7** alopias

threshold: eve **4** gate, sill **5** limen, start, verge **6** outset **8** doorsill, entrance **9** beginning

thresh out: **5** argue **6** debate, settle **7** discuss

thribble: **6** triple **9** threefold

thrice: **9** three-fold

thrift: 4 work 5 labor 7 economy 8 prudence 9 austerity, frugality, husbandry, parsimony

thriftless: 6 lavish 8 prodigal, wasteful 11 extravagant, improvident

thrifty: 4 near 5 canny, fendy, small 6 frugal, narrow, proper, saving, worthy 7 careful, prudent, sparing 8 thriving 9 befitting, estimable, provident 10 economical, fore-handed, prospering

thrill: 4 bang, bore, cast, dirl, girl, hurl, kick 5 drill, elate, flush, thirl, throw 6 arouse, dindle, excite, pierce, quiver, tingle, tremor, wallop 7 delight, frisson, tremble, vibrate 8 fremitus, transfix 9 electrify, galvanize, penetrate, per-forate, throbbing, vibration 10 excitement

thrilling: 8 stirring 11 sensational

thrive: dow 4 boom, gain, grow 5 addle, moise 6 batten, fatten 7 burgeon, improve, prosper, succeed 8 flourish, increase
in shade: 11 sciophilous

thrivingly: 5 gaily, gayly 7 bravely

throat: maw 4 crag, crop, gowl, hals, lane, neck, tube 5 gorge, halse 6 groove, gullet, guzzle, weason 7 channel, jugular, orifice, weasand 8 guttural
armor: 6 gorget
covering: 4 barb
infection: 5 croup 6 angina, quinsy 8 cynanche 9 squinancy 10 laryngitis 11 strep throat, tonsillitis
irritation: 4 frog 6 tickle
lozenge: 6 pastil, troche 7 pastile 8 pastille
part: 7 glottis
pert. to: 5 gular 7 jugular 8 guttural
protector: 5 brace, scarf 7 muffler
swelling: 6 goiter
to clear: hem 4 hawk
upper: 4 gula

throat skin: 6 dewlap

throaty: 5 husky 6 hoarse 8 guttural

throb: 4 ache, beat, drum, pant 5 flack, pound, pulse, thump 7 flacker, pulsate, vibrate 8 resonate 9 palpitate, pulsation

throbbing: 4 beat 7 pitapat 9 splitting

throe: 4 ache, pain, pang 5 agony 6 attack, effort 7 anguish 8 struggle 10 convulsion

thrombus: 4 clot 6 fibrin

throne: see 4 apse, seat 5 asana, chair, exalt, gaddi, gadhi, power, siege 6 toilet 7 anguish, dignity 8 cathedra, enthrone 11 sovereignty
remove from: 6 depose

throng: mob 4 army, busy, crew, heap, host, pack, push, rout, teem 5 bunch, close, crowd, crush, flock, group, horde, peril, press, swarm, troop 6 busily, bustle, strain, stress 7 company, hurried 8 distress, famili-iar, hardship, intimate 9 confusion, fre-quency, multitude 10 assemblage

thronged: 5 alive 7 peopled 8 crawling 10 celebrious

throttle: gun 5 check, choke 6 throat 7 smother 8 compress, garrotte, strangle, sup-press, windpipe 9 suffocate 11 accelerator

through, thru: per, via 4 done, over, past 5 about, athro, ended 6 across, coffin, direct 7 by way of, owing to, perpend 8 athrough, complete, finished, straight, washed-up 9 because of, by means of, completed, con-cluded, tombstone 10 terminated 11 sar-cophagus 12 thoroughfare, unobstructed
the agency of: per
the mouth: 7 peroral

throughgan (Sc.): 5 labor 6 energy 11 over-hauling 12 thoroughfare

throughgoing: 9 reprimand 11 examination, overhauling 12 thoroughfare

throughout: 5 about 6 bedene, during, sem-pre 7 perfect 8 thorough 10 completely, everywhere

throw: boa, cob, don, hit, lob, pat, peg, put, shy, wap 4 bail, bear, blow, bowl, bung, cast, dash, fall, flip, form, hike, hove, hurl, pass, pelt, rack, risk, shed, time, toss, turn, yerk 5 check, chuck, chunk, crank, drive, eject, exert, flick, fling, flirt, force, frame, heave, impel, pitch, place, scarf, shoot, sling, start, strip, trice, twist, whang, while, whirl 6 change, defeat, divest, hinder, launch, propel, retard, sprain, spread, spring, strike, stroke, thrust, thwart, unseat, wrench, writhe 7 address, advance, discard, fashion, present, produce, project, revolve, unhorse, venture 8 catapult, coverlet, dis-tance, obstruct 9 prostrate 10 flagellate
a fit: 4 rage 5 angry 6 scream 7 excited 9 disturbed, irritated
at quoits: 6 leaner, ringer
away: 5 waste 6 refuse, reject 7 discard, leaflet 8 handbill, squander
back: 5 check, delay, repel 6 refuse, reject, retort, revert 8 reversal 9 reversion
dice: 4 cast, main, roll
double one at dice: 7 ambsace
down: 4 cast, fell 5 fling 6 defeat, reject 7 refusal, subvert 9 overthrow, rejection 11 precipitate
down the gauntlet: 4 defy 9 challenge
from saddle: 6 unseat 7 unhorse
in: add 4 join 6 inject 9 introduce 10 con-tribute
in the towel: 4 cede, quit 5 yield 6 give up 9 surrender
into confusion: 4 riot 5 snafu 7 disturb 8 stampede 10 demoralize
into disorder: pif 4 pied 7 clutter, derange
lazily: lob 4 toss
off: rid 4 cast, emit, free, molt, shed 5 abate,

expel, moult, shake **6** reject **7** abandon, deflect, discard **8** discount **10** disconnect

off the track: **6** derail **7** mislead

one's weight around: **4** push, urge **5** bully **8** domineer

out: say **4** emit, lade **5** egest, eject, evict, expel, utter **6** extend, reject **7** clean up, confuse, discard, excrete, project **8** distance **9** eliminate

over: **4** jilt **7** abandon

overboard: **8** jettison

six at dice: **4** sise **5** sises

together: **7** collect **8** assemble

underhand: lob

water upon: **5** douse

throwing rope: **5** lasso, reata, riata **6** lariat

throwing-stick: **6** atlatl **7** wommara, woomara **9** boomerang

thrown: **4** cast **6** hurled **7** twisted **8** confused, unseated **9** surprised

thrum: bit **4** birr, drum, lout, purr, tuft **5** strum, waste **6** fringe, recite, repeat, tangle, thatch **8** particle **10** threepence

thrush: **5** mavie, mavis, ouzel, robin, veery **6** missel, oriole, shrike **7** bearing **8** bluebird, throstle **9** blackbird

disease: **4** soor **5** aptha **6** aphtha

European: **4** osel **5** ossel, ousel

ground: **5** pitta

thrust: dig, jab, ram, run **4** bear, birr, bore, butt, core, cram, dush, gird, gist, jerk, meat, pelt, pith, poke, prop, push, stab **5** barge, clash, crowd, drive, force, hunch, impel, longe, lunge, onset, press, sense, shove **6** attack, detude, extend, hustle, pierce, plunge, propel, repost, ripost, spread, stress, throng **7** allonge, assault, collide, extrude, intrude, riposte **8** estocade, pressure, protrude **9** interject, interpose, substance

aside: **5** elbow, shove, shunt

thud: **4** baff, blow, gust, move, push **5** clonk, clunk, press, thump **6** strike **7** tempest **9** windstorm

thug: **4** goon, hood **5** rough, tough **6** attack, cuttle, gunman **7** gorilla, hoodlum, ruffian **8** assassin, gangster, hooligan **9** cutthroat

thumb: **5** digit, hitch **6** pollex, thenar **9** hitchhike, peachwort

part: **6** thenar

through: **4** scan **6** browse **7** dip into **8** glance at

Thummim's partner: **4** Urim

thump: cob, dad, dub, hit **4** bang, beat, blow, bump, daud, ding, dird, drub, dunt, polt, whip, yerk **5** blaff, bunch, clour, crump, knock, pound, throb **6** bounce, cudgel, hammer, pummel, strike, thrash, thunge

thumping: big **4** huge **5** large **6** tattoo **7**

bumping **8** whopping

thunder: **4** bang, boom, clap, peal, rage, rant, roar, roll **6** bronte **7** fouldre **9** fulminate

god: **4** Thor, Zeus

witch: **4** baba

thunderbolt: **5** shock **6** fulmen **7** fouldre **8** surprise **9** fulminant, lightning

thunderhead: **4** omen **5** cloud **7** warning

thundering: **5** large, noisy **8** thumping, whopping **10** foudroyant

thunder-smitten goddess: **6** Semele

thunge: **4** bang **5** sound, thump

thurible: **6** censer

Thuringia: *castle:* **8** Wartburg

city: **4** Gera, Jena **5** Gotha **6** Erfurt, Weimar

Thursday: *god of:* **4** Thor

Holy: **5** Skire **6** Maundy

thus: so, sae, sic **4** ergo, fiat **5** hence **9** therefore **11** accordingly **12** consequently

thwack: rap **4** bang, blow, pack **5** crump, crush, drive, force, knock, whack **6** defeat, strike, thrash **7** belabor **8** belabour

thwart: **4** balk, beat, curb, dash, foil, pert, ruin, seat **5** bench, block, brace, clash, cross, parry, saucy, spite, spoil, upset, zygon **6** across, arrest, baffle, defeat, hinder, impede, oppose, outwit, resist, scotch, stymie **7** athwart, flummoy, oblique, prevent, quarrel **8** contrair, obstruct, perverse, stubborn, thwartly **9** frustrate, interpose **10** circumvent, contravene

Thyestes: *brother:* **6** Atreus

father: **6** Pelops

mother: **10** Hippodamia

son: **9** Aegisthus

thylacine: **4** wolf **5** tiger, yabbi

thyme: **4** herb **8** hillwort

thymus: **5** gland, organ

thyroid enlargement: **6** goiter

thyrsus: **5** staff, stick

tiara: **5** crown, miter **6** diadem, fillet **7** cidares, cidaris, coronet **8** frontlet **9** headdress

Tibet: (see box)

Tibetan: **6** Tangut

tibia: **4** bone **5** flute, shank **6** cnemis **8** shinbone

pert. to: **7** cnemial

tiburon: **5** shark

Tiburon Island Indian: **4** Seri

tic: **4** jerk, jump **5** spasm **6** twitch **8** fixation **9** twitching **11** vellication

tick: dot, fag, ked, pat, tag, tap **4** beat, case, dash, kade, mark, mite, note, pest **5** acari, chalk, click, count, cover, flirt, speck, touch, trust **6** acarid, acarus, credit, fondle, insect, moment, pallet, record, second, talaje, tampon **7** acarina, account, instant **8** acaridan, arachnid, garapata, indicate, mattress, para-

site **10** pajahuello, pajaroello **11** bloodsucker
genus of: **5** argas

Tibet: **7** Sitsang
  animal: yak **5** panda
  antelope: goa, sus
  ass: **5** kiang
  banner: **5** tanka
  beer: **5** chang
  butter: **4** ghee
  capital: **5** Lassa, Lhasa
  city: **6** Xigaze, Yadong **7** Gyangze
  currency: **5** tanga
  deer: **4** shou
  ecclesiastic: **4** lama **5** dalai
  food: **6** tsamba
  goat fleece: **5** pashm
  leopard: **5** ounce
  monastery: **8** lamasery
  mountain: **7** Everest
  nickname: **14** Roof of the World
  oxlike animal: **4** zebu
  pony: **6** tangum, tangun **7** tanghan
  river: **5** Indus **6** Mekong **7** Salween,
    Yangtze **11** Brahmaputra
  ruminant: **5** takin
  sheep: sha **6** bharal, nahoor, nayaur
  wildcat: **5** manul

---

ticker: **4** bomb **5** clock, heart, watch
ticket: bid, tag **4** book, card, list, note, pass,
  slip, tick **5** check, ducat, fiche, label, score,
  sight, slate, token **6** ballot, billet, docket,
  notice, permit, record **7** license, placard,
  voucher, warrant **8** document, passport **9**
  cardboard, discharge, etiquette **10** memorandum **11** certificate
  complimentary: **4** comp, pass **11** Annie
    Oakley
  of leave: **6** parole
  receiver of free: **8** deadhead
  sell above cost: **5** scalp
tickle: **4** beat, nice, play, stir, take, whip **5**
  amuse, annoy, chuck, frail, tease, touch **6**
  arouse, cuitle, divert, excite, kittle, please,
  stroke, thrill, tingle, touchy, wanton **7** capture, cuittle, delight, gratify **9** stimulate, titillate, vellicate
tickled: **4** glad **6** amused **7** pleased **9** gratified
tickler: pad, sip **4** book, cane, file **5** flask,
  knife, prong, strap **6** pistol, puzzle, record,
  weapon **7** problem **8** reminder
tickling: **7** craving **13** gratification
ticklish: **4** nice **5** risky **6** fickle, queasy, touchy,
  tricky **7** awkward, comical **8** critical, delicate, unstable, unsteady **9** difficult, sensitive, uncertain **10** changeable, inconstant,

precarious, unreliable **13** oversensitive
tick off: **4** list, mark **5** check **6** rebuke **8**
  reproach **9** make angry
tidal: *current:* **8** tiderace
  flow: **4** bore **5** eagre
  stream: run **5** firth **6** estero **7** estuary
tidbit, titbit: **5** goody **6** morsel **7** saynete **8**
  beatille, delicacy
tide: sea **4** fair, flow, flux, hour, pass, time **5**
  carry, drift, drive, flood, point, space, spate,
  surge, tidal **6** befall, betide, chance,
  endure, happen, moment, period, season,
  stream **7** current, freshet, proceed **8** continue, festival, occasion, surmount, tendency **11** anniversary, opportunity
  lowest: **4** neap
  type: ebb, low **4** high **5** flood **6** spring
tidewater: **5** shore **6** strand **8** seaboard
tidily: **5** fitly **7** smartly **8** cleverly, suitable **9**
  shipshape
tiding, tidings: ebb **4** flow, news, word **5**
  event **6** advice, gospel **7** account, message
tidy: **4** fair, good, meet, neat, redd, snug, tosh,
  trig, trim **5** clean, douce, great, groom,
  kempt, large, natty, plump, sleek **6** comely,
  fettle, sleeky, spruce, timely, worthy **7**
  healthy, orderly, upright **8** diligent,
  pinafore, skillful **9** shipshape **10** seasonable
  11 uncluttered **12** considerable
tie: rod, sag, wed **4** band, beam, beat, bind,
  bond, cord, draw, duty, even, join, knot,
  lace, lash, link, mate, post, rope, teck, yoke
  5 angle, ascot, brace, cadge, chain, equal,
  hitch, jabot, marry, nexus, sheaf, trice,
  union, unite **6** attach, cement, connex, couple, cravat, enlace, fasten, fetter, hamper,
  hobble, pledge, secure, string, tether,
  tiewig **7** confine, connect, necktie, oxfords,
  shackle, sleeper, truss up **8** alligate, deadlock, restrain, restrict, shoelace, standoff **9**
  constrain, constrict, influence, stalemate **10**
  allegiance, attachment, obligation
  down: **6** hobble **7** confine, shackle **8**
    restrain, restrict
  off: **4** snub **5** belay
  ornament: pin **4** clip, tack **5** clasp
  securely: **4** lash **5** truss **7** shackle, trammel
  up: **4** bind, moor, stop **5** truss **6** hinder,
    tether **8** obstruct
tied: **4** even **5** bound **7** knotted, married
  up: **4** busy **8** occupied **10** encumbered
tier: row **4** bank, deck, line, rank **5** class,
  grade, layer, level, place, stack, story **6**
  degree **7** antenna, arrange **8** pinafore
tierce: **4** cask **5** lunge, parry, third **7** measure
  8 sequence
Tierra del Fuego Indian: Ona **4** Agni
tie-up: **5** delay **6** strike **7** mooring **10** connection

tiff: fit, pet, row, sip **4** huff, mood, spat **5** draft, dress, drink, fight, humor, lunch, order, run-in, scent, smell, sniff, spell, state, taste **6** bicker, liquor **7** discord, quarrel, wrangle **8** outburst, squabble **9** condition **11** altercation

tiffin (Br.): 5 lunch **6** eating, repast **8** drinking

tiger: cat, cub **4** howl, rake, yell **5** bully, groom **6** feline, jaguar **7** leopard **9** carnivore, swaggerer, thylacine **12** organization
family: **7** felidae

tiger finch: 8 amadavat

tiger-hunting dog: 5 dhole

tigerish: 5 cruel **6** fierce, flashy **9** ferocious **10** swaggering **12** bloodthirsty

tigers-mouth: 8 foxglove, toadflax **10** snapdragon

tight: 4 fast, firm, hard, held, neat, snug, taut, tidy, trim **5** alert, bound, cheap, close, dense, drawn, drunk, fixed, ready, smart, solid, tense, tipsy **6** climax, comely, firmly, packed, secure, severe, steady, stingy, strait, strict **7** capable, compact, concise, crowded, drunken, miserly, quickly, shapely, soundly, unmoved **8** constant, exacting, faithful **9** competent, condensed, energetic, mercenary, niggardly, penurious **10** impervious, inebriated, vigorously **11** close-fisted, constricted, intoxicated, restraining **12** parsimonious **13** penny-pinching

tighten: 5 tense **6** tauten **9** constrict
ropes: **4** frap

tight-fisted: 6 stingy **12** parsimonious

tight-laced: 4 prim

tight-lipped: 5 terse **6** silent **8** taciturn **9** secretive

tightwad: 4 fist **5** miser, piker **7** niggard, scrooge **9** skinflint **10** cheapskate

Tigris River city: Kut **5** Ashur, Calah **7** Baghdad, Nineveh

til: 5 plant **6** sesame

tile: hat **5** brick, drain, plate, slate **6** tegula **7** carreau, quarrel
composed of: **7** tegular **9** tessellar
curved: **7** pantile
malting floor: **6** pament **7** pamment
mosaic: **7** tessera **8** abaculus
used in game: **6** domino

tiler: cat **4** kiln, oven **5** field, thief **7** hellier **10** doorkeeper

tilery: 4 kiln

till: box, far, for, get, hoe, sow **4** cash, draw, earn, farm, gain, plow, seed, tend, tray, up to, work **5** charm, dress, labor, train, until, while **6** casket, drawer, entice, plough, strive, whilst **7** develop, prepare **9** cultivate **10** concerning **12** cash register

tillable: 6 arable **7** earable

tillage: 4 farm, land **7** aration, culture **11** cultivation

tilled land: 5 arada

tiller: bar, bow **4** helm, hoer **5** lever, stalk, stick **6** farmer, handle, rudder, sprout **7** husband, rancher **10** cultivator, husbandman

tilt: tip, yaw **4** cant, duel, heel, lean, list, rush, tent **5** argue, fight, forge, grade, heald, hield, joust, lurch, pitch, poise, slant, slope, speed, upend, upset **6** awning, canopy, careen, combat, hammer, oppose, seesaw, stroke, thrust, topple **7** contest, dispute, incline **8** covering, gradient, tiltyard **10** tournament **11** altercation, inclination
hammer: **6** oliver
skyward: **5** upend

tilter: 5 sword **6** avocet, seesaw **7** jouster **9** sandpiper

tilting: 5 alist **7** swaying **8** inclined, jousting, slanting

timbal: 10 kettledrum

timber: log, rib **4** balk, beam, fuel, gate, land, raff, stay, tree, wood **5** board, build, cahuy, cover, fence, frame, gripe, joist, plank, spile, stile, trees, woods **6** forest, girder, lumber, rafter **7** support **8** building, contrive, woodland **9** construct, structure, underpier
bend: sny **6** camber, rafter
central portion: **7** duramen **9** heartwood
decay: **4** conk, dote, doze
estimator: **6** scaler **7** cruiser
joining peg: **7** trenail, trunnel **8** treenail
ship: bao, rib **4** bibb, bitt, keel, mast, spar, wale **5** snape, spale **7** stemson **8** sternson
standing: **4** stud **5** spile **6** forest, purlin **8** puncheon, studding, stumpage
wolf: **4** lobo

timberman: 6 logger, sawyer **7** cruiser **8** woodsman **9** carpenter, lumberman

timbre: 4 mood, ting, tone **5** crest, miter **6** spirit, temper **7** coronet, quality, timbrel **9** character, resonance

timbrel: 4 drum **5** tabor **10** tambourine

time: age, day, eld, era, tid **4** beat, book, date, fuss, hint, hour, sele, term, week, year **5** clock, epoch, limit, month, set up, spell, tempo, tense, watch **6** during, indeed, minute, moment, period, season, second, steven **7** cadence, measure **8** duration, occasion, regulate, schedule **11** opportunity
ahead of: **5** early **9** premature
allowed for payment: **6** usance
and again: **5** often **10** frequently, repeatedly **11** over and over
another: **5** again
at no: **5** never **9** nevermore
before: ere, eve
break in: **6** hiatus
brief: **4** span **6** moment, second
error in order of: **11** anachronism

gone by: ago **4** past, yore **10** yesteryear

granted: **4** stay **5** delay, frist **8** reprieve

happy: **4** bust, lark **5** party, revel, spree **6** soiree **8** jamboree

intervening: **7** interim **8** meantime **9** meanwhile

long ago: **4** yore

of great depression: **5** nadir

of highest strength: **6** heyday

olden: eld **4** auld, syne (Sc.), yore

period of: age, day, eon, era **4** aeon, date, hour, span, term, week, year **5** epoch, month, spell, trice **6** decade, ghurry, minute, moment, recess, season, second **7** century, instant **8** azoic age **9** fortnight **10** millennium

pert. to: **4** eral **8** temporal

waste: **4** idle, loaf **5** dally **6** dawdle, diddle, loiter, putter, tinker **7** goof off **8** flanerie

time being: **5** nonce

time clock: **8** recorder

timeless: **4** true **5** valid **6** eterne **7** ageless, endless, eternal, undated **8** dateless, unending, untimely **9** ceaseless, co-eternal, continual, perpetual, premature **11** everlasting **12** interminable

timely: apt, fit, pat **4** meet, soon **5** early **6** prompt, proper **7** fitting **8** punctual, relevant, suitable, temporal **9** favorable, opportune, pertinent **10** auspicious, forehanded, seasonable **11** appropriate

Time Machine author: **5** Wells

time out: **5** break **6** recess **10** rest period

timepiece: **4** dial **5** clock, watch **7** horlage, sundial **8** sunwatch **9** horologue, hourglass, sandglass **11** chronometer **17** chronothermometer

water: **9** clepsydra

times: *many:* oft **5** often **10** frequently

olden: eld **9** yesterday **10** yesteryear

timetable: **7** program **8** schedule

timid: shy **4** argh, eery **5** arghe, bauch, blate, chary, eerie, faint, jumpy, mousy, pavid, scary **6** afraid **7** bashful, fearful, gastful, nervous **8** cautious, cowardly, fearsome, ghastful, hesitant, retiring, skittish, timorous, undaring **9** diffident, shrinking **11** vacillating **12** apprehensive, fainthearted **13** pusillanimous **14** chicken-hearted

timor: **5** dread

Timor: *capital:* **4** Dili

coin: avo **6** pataca

island: **4** Leti

timorous: **5** faint, timid **6** afraid, cowish, sheepy **7** fearful **8** fearsome, hesitant, quailing, terrible **9** shrinking **10** shuddering **12** apprehensive, fainthearted

timpani: **11** kettledrums

tin: box, can, pan **5** metal, money, plate, terne

6 latten **7** element, stannic, stannum **8** preserve, prillion **9** container

pert. to: **7** stannic, stranic

rubbish: **5** stent

sheet: **6** latten

symbol: Sn

tinamou: **4** bird, yutu **6** ynambu **7** ostrich

tin and copper alloy: **6** pewter

tincal: **5** borax

Tin Can Island: **7** Niuafoo

tincture: or, dye **4** cast, tint **5** color, gules, imbue, myrrh, shade, smack, stain, taint, tenne, tinge, touch, trace **6** elixir, imbrue, streak **7** pigment, vestige **8** coloring **9** admixture, suspicion **10** extraction **12** modification

of opium: **9** paregoric

tinder: **4** punk **6** amadou **8** kindling

tine: tub, vat **4** fork, lose, pain, teen **5** grief, point, prong, spike, tooth **6** harrow, perish **7** destroy, trouble

tinea: **8** ringworm **11** skin disease

tinean: **4** moth

tineoidea: **5** moths

tin foil: **4** tain

tinge: dye, hue **4** cast, hint, odor, tint **5** color, imbue, paint, savor, shade, smack, stain, taint, touch, trace **6** affect, flavor **7** glimpse, quality **8** coloring, discolor, tincture **9** influence **10** suggestion

tinged with purple: **10** violaceous

tingle: **4** burn, dirl, girl, nail, ring, tack **5** alive, chime, creep, patch, smart, sting **6** dindle, jingle, thrill, tickle, tinkle **7** support, tremble, vibrant **9** fastening, sensation, stimulate

tinker: auk **4** fuss, mend, work **5** caird, gypsy, murre, patch, rogue, skate, tramp **6** fiddle, mender, mugger, potter, putter, rascal, repair, wander **7** botcher, bungler, vagrant **8** mackerel **10** play around **11** silversides

tinkle: **5** clink **6** dindle, dingle, tingle

tinner: **6** canner **8** tinsmith

tinny: **4** hard, rich, thin **5** cheap, harsh **6** bright **7** brittle, wealthy **8** metallic, tinsmith

Tin Pan Alley group: **5** ASCAP

tin-pot: **4** poor **6** paltry **8** inferior, wretched

tinsel: **4** fake, sham **5** gaudy, showy **6** tawdry **8** specious, splendor **9** clinquant **10** forfeiture, glittering

tinstone: **11** cassiterite

tint: dye, hue **5** blush, color, shade, stain, taste, tinge, trace **6** nuance **9** foretaste **10** complexion

cheeks: **5** rouge

tinter: **4** dyer

tintinnabulum: **4** bell **5** rhyme **6** rhythm **8** rhymster

tintype: **9** ferrotype **10** photograph **13** daguerreotype

tiny: wee **4** fine **5** small, teeny **6** atomic, bantam, infant, minute, petite **9** miniature **10** diminutive, pocket-size **11** lilliputian, microscopic **13** infinitesimal

tip: cap, cue, end, fee, neb, tap, toe, top **4** apex, barb, blow, cant, cave, clue, dump, fall, heel, hint, keel, lean, list, peak, pile, tilt, vail **5** aglet, alist, chape, crown, drink, empty, point, slant, slope, snick, spire, steer, touch, upset **6** advice, aiglet, apices, arista, careen, corona, nozzle, summit, topple, unload **7** crampit, ferrule, incline **8** bakshish, bonamano, crumshaw, gratuity, overturn **9** baksheesh, buona-mani, buona-mano, extremity, lagniappe, overthrow, pourboire
near to: **6** apical
off: **4** hint, tell, warn **5** alarm **8** forewarn **10** indication

tippet: boa, fur **4** barb, cape, hood, rope, ruff **5** amice, scarf, snell **6** almuce, sindon **7** hanging, muffler, patagia (pl.) **8** liripipe, liripoop, palatine, patagium **9** comforter, victorine

tipping: **5** alist **7** ripping, topping

tipple: bib, nip, sip, tip **4** drip, gill, grog, lose, suck, swig, whet **5** booze, drink, spend, swill, upset **6** fuddle, guzzle, imbibe, liquor, spirit, sipple, tumble **8** overturn

tippler: sot **4** lush, soak **5** drunk, souse, toper, winer **6** boozer, bubber **7** drinker, whetter **8** drunkard **9** draftsman, inebriate **11** draughtsman

tippy: **5** smart **6** wobbly **7** stylish **8** unsteady

tipstaff: **7** bailiff **9** attendant, constable

tipster: **4** tout **8** dopester, informer **10** forecaster

tipsy: ree **4** awry **5** bosky, drunk, shaky, tight **6** bungfu, groggy **7** crooked, drunken, ebriose, ebrious, foolish, fuddled, muddled, puddled **8** unsteady **10** inebriated, staggering **11** intoxicated

tiptoe: **5** alert, eager, steal **6** roused, warily **7** eagerly, exalted, gumshoe, quietly **8** cautious, stealthy **9** pussyfoot **10** cautiously **11** expectantly

tiptop: ace **4** best, fine, good **5** great, prime, sound, swell **9** first-rate **11** galumptious

tirade: **4** rant **5** abuse **6** screed, speech **7** censure **8** diatribe, harangue, jeremiad **9** philippic

tirailleur: **5** tease **8** skirmish **12** sharpshooter

tire: fag, lag, rim, sap **4** band, bore, gnaw, hoop, jade, pall, prey, pull, shoe, tear, tier, wear **5** drain, recap, seize, spare, weary, wheel **6** casing, harass, tucker **7** exhaust, fatigue, frazzle, satiate, vesture, wearout **8** decorate, enervate, enfeeble, enginery, overwork, pinafore, wear down **10** debilitate
kind: mud **4** bias, snow, tube **5** recap **6** radial **7** retread, studded **8** tubeless **9** whitewall **11** steel-belted
saver: **5** recap **7** retread

tired: **4** beat **5** all in, blown, spent, weary **6** aweary, fagged, sleepy **7** wearied **8** fatigued **9** exhausted, hackneyed **11** tuckered out

tireless: **4** busy **6** active **8** untiring **10** unflagging, unwearying **12** enthusiastic **13** indefatigable

Tiresias: **4** seer **10** soothsayer
blinded by: **6** Athena, Athene
home: **6** Thebes

tiresome: dry **4** dull, tame **6** boring, borish, dreary, prolix **7** irksome, onerous, prosaic, tedious **8** annoying, ennuyant **9** fatiguing, wearisome **10** irritating, monotonous **13** uninteresting

tiro: See **tyro**

tissue: gum, web **4** mesh, tela **5** cloth, fiber, gauze, sheer, telae, weave **6** fabric, girdle, ribbon **7** network **8** meshwork **9** embroider, gauzelike **10** interweave
animal: fat, gum **4** bone, seur, suet **5** sinew **6** muscle, paxwax **7** keratin **8** gelatine
connective: **6** stroma, tendon **9** cartilage
human: fat, gum **4** bone, suet, tela **5** fiber **6** albedo, diploe, keloid, stroma, tendon **7** tonsils **8** ligament, stromata **9** cartilage **10** aerenchyma
layer of: **6** dermis, strata **7** stratum
nerve: **8** ganglion
pert. to: **5** telar
resembling: **7** histoid
vegetable: **4** bast **5** xylem **6** lignin, phloem **7** endarch **8** meristem **9** epidermis
wasting away of: **8** phthisis

tit: nag, pap, pin, tap, tee, tug **4** bird, blow, draw, girl, hade, jerk, plug, pull, teat, tite, twit **5** horse, woman **6** nipple, twitch

Titan: **4** Bana, Leto, Maia, Rhea **5** Atlas, Coeus, Creus, Dione, giant, Theia **6** Cronus, Kronos, Pallas, Phoebe, Tethys, Themis **7** Iapetus, Oceanus **8** gigantic, Hyperion **9** extensive, Mnemosyne
father: **6** Uranus
mother: **4** Gaia

Titania's husband: **6** Oberon

titanic: big **4** huge, vast **5** great **7** immense **8** colossal, enormous, gigantic

titanite: **6** sphene **7** ijolite

tite: **4** soon **7** quickly **8** promptly **11** immediately

tithe: tax **4** levy, rate, toll **5** tenth **6** decima, tariff **7** tribute
pert. to: **7** decimal

titi: **6** monkey **8** marmoset

titillate: **6** excite, thrill, tickle **9** stimulate, vellicate

titlark: **4** bird **5** pipit

title: bey, dub, sir, tag **4** call, czar, dame, deed, duke, earl, emir, head, khan, king, lien, name, raja, rank, shah **5** baron, claim, count, friar, major, mayor, noble, right, style **6** assign, ensign, kaiser, knight, legend, madame, mikado, milady, milord, notice, prince, record, squire, sultan **7** address, admiral, ascribe, baronet, captain, caption, emperor, epithet, esquire, general, heading, justice, khedive, marquis, placard, viceroy **8** archduke, cognomen, document, governor, masthead, viscount **9** commander, commodore **10** appellation **11** designation **12** championship
   ecclesiastic: dom, fra **4** abba **8** reverend **10** excellency **11** monseigneur
   feminine: **4** dame, lady, ma'am **5** hanum, madam **6** hanoum, milady, missis, missus **8** mistress
   foreign: aga, aya, dan, don, mir, sha, sri **4** baba, dona, frau, herr, lars, shri, sidi **5** basha, mirza, mpret, pasha, rajah, sayid, senor, shree, sieur **6** bashaw, madame, senora, shogun, squire **7** dominus, effendi, mynheer, signora **8** Fräulein, maharaja, maharini, monsieur, senorita **9** ayatollah, signorina
   holder: **4** peer **5** noble **8** champion
titmouse: mag, nun, tit **4** bird **6** fuffit, puffer, titmal, tomtit, verdin **7** jacksaw, titmall, tomnoup **8** heckimal **9** chickadee, mumruffin
   pert. to: **6** parine
titter: **5** laugh **6** giggle, rather, seesaw, sooner, totter, wobble **7** tremble
tittle: dot, jot **4** atom, iota, mark, mite, sign, whit **5** fleck, point, speck, tilde **6** accent, gossip, tattle **7** cedilla, smidgen, snippet, whisper **8** particle
tittup: **5** caper, frisk
titubate: **4** reel **6** totter **7** stagger **8** unsteady **11** vacillating
titular: **7** nominal **8** honorary, so-called
Titus Andronicus: *author:* **11** Shakespeare
   daughter: **7** Lavinia
   queen: **6** Tamora
tizzy: **4** snit **6** dither **7** anxiety
TNT: **6** trotyl **8** dynamite **14** trinitrotoluol **15** trinitrotoluene
to: tae **4** till, unto **5** until **6** before, toward **7** against, ahead of, forward
   a conclusion: out **6** finish
   an end: out **6** finish **8** conclude
   be: ser (Sp.) **4** esse (L.), etre (F.), sein (G.) **5** einai (Gr.), estar (Sp.) **6** essere (It.)
   be sure: **4** even **6** indeed **8** of course **9** certainly
   one side: **5** abeam
   sheltered side: **4** alee

   that place: **5** there **7** thither
   the left: haw **5** aport
   the point that: **5** until
   the rear: aft **5** abaft **6** astern
   the right: gee **9** starboard
   this place: **4** here **6** hither
   which: **7** whereto
   wit: viz. **6** namely **8** scilicet **9** videlicet
   your health: **5** salud, skoal **6** cheers, prosit, salute **7** wassail **11** a votre sante
toa: **7** warrior
toad: ted **4** agua, bufo, hyla, pipa, scum, snot, tade **6** anuran, peeper **7** crapaud, paddock, quilkin **9** amphibian, spadefoot, sycophant
   genus of: **4** bufo, hyla **6** alytes
   larva: **7** tadpole **8** polliwog
   tongueless suborder: **7** aglossa
toadfish: **4** sapo **6** angler, grubby, puffer, slimer **8** frogfish **10** midshipman
toadflax: **8** gallwort, ramstead **13** butter-and-eggs
toady: **4** fawn, snob, ugly, zany **6** flunky, lackey, sponge, yes-man **7** flunkey, hideous, shoneen, truckle **8** bootlick, hanger-on, parasite, truckler **9** dependent, flatterer, repulsive, sycophant, toadeater
toast: dry, tan **4** soak, warm **5** brede, brown, drink, melba, parch, roast, skoal, worst **6** birsle, pledge, prosit, salute **7** bristle, carouse, drinker, propose, swindle, tippler, wassail **8** cinnamon **9** celebrate
   kind of: **4** rusk **8** zwieback
toastmaster: **5** emcee
tobacco: **4** leaf, weed
   chewing: **4** chaw, quid
   coarse: **7** caporal
   disease: **6** calico **7** walloon **10** black shank
   flavor mixture: **6** petune
   hookah smoking: **7** goracco
   ingredient: tar **8** nicotine
   in pipe-bowl: **6** dottel, dottle
   juice: **6** ambeer, ambier
   kind of: **4** capa, shag **5** bogie, fogus, tabac **6** burley, cowpen **7** caporal, henbane, Latakia, perique, Turkish **8** domestic, Virginia **9** salvadora
   leaf moistener: **5** caser
   paste: **7** goracco
   pile: **4** bulk
   pulverized: **5** snuff
   receptacle: **4** pipe **7** humidor
   roll: **5** cigar, segar **7** carotte **9** cigarette
   small portion: cud, fid, fig **4** quid **6** dottel, dottle **7** carotte
Tobacco Road: *author:* **8** Caldwell
   character: **5** Pearl **6** Jeeter
tobacco smoke hater: **11** misocapnist
Tobias: *father:* **5** Tobit
   wife: **4** Sara

toboggan: 4 sled 7 coaster, decline

toby: cup, jug, mug, way 4 road 5 cigar, stein 6 street 7 highway, pitcher, robbery

toby-man: 6 robber 10 highwayman

tocology: 9 midwifery 10 obstetrics

tocsin: 4 bell, sign 5 alarm 6 alarum, signal 7 warning

tod: fox, mat 4 bush, load, pack 5 clump, shrub 6 bundle, weight

today: now 4 here, oggi (It.) 7 present 8 nowadays
pert. to: 7 diurnal 9 hodiernal

toddle: 4 walk 5 dance 6 daddle, diddle, stroll, totter, waddle 7 saunter

toddler: kid, tot 4 trot 5 child 6 infant 9 youngster

to-do: ado 4 fuss, stir 6 bustle 9 commotion

toe: paw, tip 5 digit, pivot, reach, touch 7 journal 10 projection
great: 6 hallux
little: 7 minimus
pert. to: 7 digital
thickening of skin: 4 corn 6 callus
without: 10 adactylous

toehold: 7 footing

toga: 4 gown, robe 5 tunic 7 garment

togated: 7 stately 9 dignified

together: mix 4 with 5 along, as one, chain, on end, union 6 at once, bedene, couple, fasten, joined, unison 7 alongst, concert, contact, en masse, harmony, jointly 8 ensemble 9 cojointly, collision, courtship 11 association 12 cohabitation

toggle, toggel: pin, rod 4 bolt, mend 5 screw 6 cotter 10 crosspiece

togs: 6 attire 7 clothes, raiment 8 clothing

togue: 9 namaycush

toil: fag, net, tug 4 drag, mesh, moil, plod, pull, rend, roll, task, trap, work 5 broil, chore, cloth, graft, labor, pains, slave, snare, sweat 6 battle, drudge, effort, entrap, harass, strife 7 contend, ensnare, travail, turmoil 8 distress, drudgery, industry, overwork, struggle 10 accomplish, contention, employment, occupation

toiler: 5 slave 6 drudge 7 laborer, plodder, workman

toilet: can, loo, pot 4 head, john 5 cloth, dress, privy 6 attire 7 costume, latrine 8 bathroom, grooming, lavatory, outhouse, restroom, toilette 9 cleansing 10 facilities
case: 4 etui 5 etwee

toilsome: 4 hard 7 arduous 9 difficult, laborious, wearisome

toise: eye 4 extend 6 extend 7 stretch

toit: 6 dawdle, settle, totter 7 saunter

Tokay: 4 wine 5 grape

token: 4 gift, mark, omen, sign 5 badge, check, medal, merit, proof 6 amulet, emblem, hansel, ostent, pledge, signal, symbol 7 betoken, betroth, earnest, feature, gesture, handsel, memento, minimal, portent, presage, promise, signify 8 accolade, evidence, forbysen, keepsake, reminder, souvenir, tessella 9 character, symbolize 10 denotation, expression, indication, prognostic 11 remembrance
affection: 6 amoret, mascot 7 handsel 8 accolade
officer: 5 badge
servitude: 4 yoke
victory: 4 palm 6 laurel

Tokyo: Edo 4 Yedo
district: 5 Ginza
island: 6 Honshu
river: Edo 4 Tama
Shinto shrine: 5 Meiji

tolbooth, tollbooth: 4 city, hall, jail, town 5 burgh 6 prison 9 tollhouse 11 customhouse

toldo: hut 4 tent

tole: 5 decoy 6 allure, entice

tolerable: gey 4 fair, so-so 6 decent 8 bearable, mediocre, middling, moderate, passable 9 allowance, endurable 10 good enough, sufferable 11 comportable, respectable, supportable

tolerance: 5 grace 6 leeway 7 stamina 8 leniency, patience 9 allowance, endurance, variation 10 indulgence 11 forbearance 13 understanding

tolerant: 5 broad 7 lenient, liberal, patient 8 enduring 9 indulgent 10 ecumenical, open-minded 11 forebearing

tolerate: 4 bear, bide 5 abide, allow, broad, brook, stand 6 accept, endure, permit, resist, suffer

Tolkien creature: Ent 6 Hobbit

toll: due, tax 4 bell, chum, cost, drag, draw, duty, lure, peal, pull, rent, ring 5 annul, chime, decoy, knell, price, sound 6 allure, charge, custom, entice, excise, impost, invite, vacate 7 expense, scatter, trewage 8 announce, exaction 10 assessment 12 compensation
gatherer: 8 customer, publican 9 collector
kind of: 6 caphar 7 tronage 9 chiminage 10 ballastage

tolly: 4 cane 5 spire 6 candle

Toltec: 7 Nahuatl 9 Nahuatlan

tolu: 6 balsam

tolypeutine: 4 apar 9 armadillo

tomahawk: ax, axe, cut 4 kill 6 assail, attack, strike 7 hatchet, missile 9 criticize

toman: 4 coin 6 weight 8 division
tomato: 9 loveapple 10 prostitute
   sauce: 6 catsup 7 ketchup 8 marinara
   soup: 6 bisque 8 gazpacho
tomb: 4 bury 5 crypt, grave, house, huaca, mound, speos, vault 6 burial, hearse, shrine, tholos 7 chamber, ossuary, pyramid, tumulus 8 catacomb, cenotaph 9 mausoleum, sepulcher
   Buddhist: 4 tape
   empty: 8 cenotaph
   for bones: 7 ossuary 9 reliquary
   kind of: 4 cist 7 tritaph 8 cistvaen, kistvaen 9 mausoleum 11 sarcophagus
   saint's: 6 shrine
tombe: 4 drum
tomboy: meg 5 rowdy 6 gamine, harlot, hoyden 8 strumpet
tombstone: 5 cairn, cross, stele 8 cenotaph, memorial, monument 9 headstone 11 grave marker
Tombstone marshal: 4 Earp 5 Wyatt
tomcat: gib 9 womanizer
tome: 4 book 5 atlas 6 ledger, letter, volume 12 encyclopedia
tomfool: ass 5 clown 6 stupid 7 buffoon, doltish, foolish, half-wit 8 rainbird 9 blockhead 10 flycatcher, nincompoop 11 harebrained
tomfoolery: 5 prank 8 nonsense 9 silliness
tommyrot: rot 4 bosh 7 hogwash, rubbish 8 nonsense 9 silliness 10 balderdash
tomorrow: 4 cras (L.) 6 demain (Fr.), domani (It.), manana (Sp.)
Tom Sawyer: *aunt:* 5 Polly
   author: 5 Twain 7 Clemens
   brother: Sid
   girl friend: 5 Becky
   pal: 15 Huckleberry Finn
Tom Thumb: 4 runt 5 dwarf 6 midget, peewee 8 Stratton (Charles) 10 locomotive
Tom Tulliver's river: 5 Floss
ton: 4 lots, mode 5 heaps, style, tunny, vogue 6 weight 7 fashion
tonant: 7 blatant 10 boisterous
tone: 4 beep, feel, mood, note, tint, vein 5 color, pitch, shade, sound, trend, vigor, voice 6 accent, effect, intone, modify, temper, timbre 7 cadence, quality 8 coloring, mitigate, modulate, strength 9 character, harmonize 10 atmosphere, elasticity, expression, inflection, intonation, modulation 12 modification
   deafness: 6 asonia
   down: 4 mute, tame 6 soften, subdue 8 modulate
   of cord: 8 concento
   rapid: 7 tremolo
   sharp: 4 tang
   single: 8 monotone

   singsong: 4 sugh 5 sough
   succession: 5 melos
   system of: 6 tonart
   thin: 7 sfogato
toneless: 5 atony 6 atonal
tones: *combination of:* 5 chord
   series of: 5 scale
Tonga: 15 Friendly Islands
   capital: 9 Nukualofa
   city: 6 Neiafu
   currency: 6 paanga
tongs: 6 tenail 7 forceps, pincers, tueiron 8 scissors, tenaille, tweezers 10 clamp gangs
tongue: gab 4 bark, chib, fame, flap, howl, lick, pole, sole, talk, vote 5 chide, clack, lingo, prate, scold, speak, taste, utter, voice 6 report 7 beeweed, clapper, dialect, feather, lingula 8 language, lingulae, parlance, reproach 9 pronounce
   bone: 5 hyoid
   classical: 5 Greek, Latin 6 Hebrew
   click of: tch, tsk
   disease: 5 agrom 9 lichenoid
   insect's: 6 glossa
   mother: 10 vernacular
   of land: 4 spit 5 reach
   oxcart: 4 cope
   pert. to: 7 glossal, lingual
   projection: 7 papilla 8 papillae (pl.)
   seam: 5 raphe
   tied: 4 dumb, mute 5 quiet 8 taciturn 10 speechless 12 inarticulate
   tip of: 6 corona
   wagon: 4 neap, pole 5 shaft
tongued: 6 licked, prated, tasted
tongue-lash: 5 baste, scold 6 berate 7 tell off
tongueless: 4 dumb, mute 10 speechless
tonic: 5 aloes 6 bracer, elixir 7 bracing, quinine 8 medicine, pick-me-up, roborant 9 sassafras, stimulant 10 astringent, refreshing 11 corroborant 12 invigorating
   kind of: 4 dope, soda 6 catnip 7 bitters, boneset, nervine
tonsil: 5 gland 8 amygdala
   inflammation: 6 quinsy
   kind: 7 adenoid, faucial, lingual 8 palatine 10 pharyngeal
tonsorialist: 6 barber
tonsure: 5 crown, shave 7 haircut
tonsured: 4 bald 5 shorn 6 pilled, shaven 7 clipped
tony: 4 chic, posh 5 smart 7 stylish
too: and, tae 4 also, else, ever, over, trop (F.), very 6 as well, overly 7 besides 8 likewise 9 extremely 11 exceedingly, excessively, furthermore 13 superfluously
   bad: 4 alas 5 alack
   late: 5 tardy 7 belated 8 untimely
   little: 6 scanty, skimpy 12 insufficient

much: **7** nimiety

small to matter: **13** inappreciable

soon: **9** premature

tool (see also **instrument**): adz, axe, saw, zax **4** adze, draw, dupe, file, form, pawn, ride **5** agent, drive, means, plane, shape, sword **6** convey, device, finish, gadget, hammer, manage, puppet, weapon **7** cat's-paw, hatchet, utensil **8** creature, ornament **9** appliance, implement **10** manipulate

abrading: **4** file, rasp

biting edge: bit

bookbinding: **5** gouge

boring: awl, bit **5** auger, drill **6** gimlet, reamer **7** bradawl

bricklayer: **4** hock **5** float, level **6** hammer, trowel

butcher: saw **5** knife, steel **6** skewer, skiver **7** cleaver

carpenter: bit, saw **4** file, rasp **5** auger, level, plane, punch **6** chisel, gimlet, hammer, pliers, router, square **7** crow bar, handsaw, hatchet, scriber **8** miter box

chest: kit

chopping: **7** dolabra

cobbler's: awl **6** hammer

cooper's: **5** croze

cultivating: hoe **4** plow **6** harrow, plough **7** leveler

cutting: adz, axe, bit, hob, saw **4** adze **5** bezel, bezil, burin, gouge, knife, plane, razor **6** chisel, graver, reamer, shears

engraver's: **5** burin **7** scouper

excavating: **4** pick **6** pickax, shovel **7** mattock

flat: **7** spatula **10** putty knife

garden: hoe **4** fork, rake **5** edger, mower, spade **6** shovel, sickle, trowel, weeder

gripping: **4** vise **5** clamp, tongs **6** pliers **7** pincers **8** tweezers

hole-making: awl **6** dibble

marble worker's: **6** fraise

mason's: hod **6** chisel

mining: gad **4** pick

molding: die

pointed: awl, fid, gad **4** barb, brod, brog, pick **6** gimlet, stylet

pounding: **6** hammer, mallet, pestle, sledge

prehistoric: **4** celt **5** flint **6** eolith **9** paleolith **10** palaeolith

shaping: **5** lathe, swage

slate-measuring: **7** scantle

smoothing: **4** file **5** plane **7** sleeker

splitting: axe **4** frow **7** hatchet

trimming: ax, axe, saw **5** knife **6** shears **8** clippers, scissors

woodworking: adz **4** adze **7** edgeman, grainer, scauper, scriber **10** spokeshave

tool handle: *end:* **4** butt

fitted part: **4** tang

tools: tew **4** gear **7** gibbles (Sc.)

toot: pry, spy **4** beep, blow, fool, gaze, honk, peep, tear **5** binge, blast, draft, drink, drunk, shout, sound, spree **6** bender, spread, sprout **7** carouse, declare, trumpet, whistle **8** carousal, eminence, proclaim **9** elevation

tooter: spy **7** lookout **8** watchman **9** trumpeter

tooth (see also **teeth**): cog, jag **4** bite, dent, fang, jagg, snag, tine, tusk **5** molar, point, prong **6** cuspid, indent, wisdom **7** consume, grinder, incisor, snaggle **8** bicuspid, sprocket **10** projection

canine: **4** tush **6** cuspid, holder **7** laniary

cap: **5** crown

diminutive: **8** denticle **13** denticulation

doctor: **7** dentist **12** orthodontist, periodontist

edge: **7** dentate

fore: **5** biter **6** cutter

gear wheel: cog **4** dent, tine

grinding surface: **5** mensa

having but one: **8** monodont

toothache: **4** worm (Sc.) **8** dentagra **10** odontalgia

tooth decay: **6** caries **8** cavities **12** saprondontia

toothed: *irregularly:* **5** erose

on edge: **8** serrated

tooth for tooth: **6** talion

toothless: **4** weak **5** gummy **6** futile **7** edental **8** decrepit, edentate **9** infantile **10** agomphious, edentulate

toothsome: **5** sapid, tasty **6** dainty, savory **8** pleasing **9** agreeable, delicious, desirable, palatable **10** appetizing, delectable

top: ace, cap, fid, lid, tip, toy **4** acme, apex, beat, best, crop, head, knap, lead, peak, pick, roof, tent, tilt, tuft **5** caput, cream, crest, crown, drain, drink, elite, equal, excel, outdo, point, prime, prize, prune, ridge, upset **6** apices (pl.), better, capote, choice, climax, culmen, exceed, finial, summit, swells, topple, tumble, upside, utmost, vertex, zenith **7** gyrator, highest, maximum, surface, surpass, topmost **8** covering, dominate, forelock, foremost, loftiest, pinnacle, superior, surmount, vertexes (pl.), vertices (pl.) **9** excellent, uppermost **10** pre-eminent **11** aristocrats

altar: **5** mensa

head: **4** pate **5** scalp

of wave: **5** crest

toy: **8** teetotum

wooden stand: **5** criss

topaz: gem **5** stone **7** pycnite **11** hummingbird

symbol of: **8** fidelity

topcoat: **6** reefer **8** overcoat, siphonia **12** chesterfield

tope: 4 butt, wren 5 clump, drink, grove, shark, stupa 6 guzzle 7 dogfish, orchard

topee, topi: cap, hat 6 helmet 10 pith-helmet

toper: sot 5 drunk, shark 6 boozer, bouser 7 tippler, tosspot 8 drunkard

tophaceous: 5 rough, sandy, stony 6 gritty

tophet, topheth: 4 hell 5 chaos 8 darkness 9 confusion

top-hole: 6 tiptop 9 excellent, first-rate 10 first-class

topic: 4 item, text 5 issue, motif, theme 6 reason, remedy, thesis 7 heading, subject, themata

topical: 5 local 6 timely 9 temporary

top kick: 8 sergeant

topknot: bun 4 hair, head, tuft 5 crest, onkos 7 chignon, commode 8 flounder, pony tail 9 headdress

toplofty: 5 proud 7 haughty 8 arrogant, inflated 9 egotistic 10 disdainful 12 contemptuous, supercilious

topmost: 6 apical 7 highest, maximum 9 uppermost

top-notch: 4 best 6 tiptop 7 highest 9 excellent, first-rate 11 unsurpassed

topnotcher: ace 4 hero, star 8 jimdandy, knockout

topography: 7 terrain

topper: hat 5 cover, float 6 stower 7 cheater, snuffer, topcoat 10 high-rigger 11 high-climber

toppiece: 4 head 6 toupee 11 masterpiece

topping: 4 bran, fine, good 5 icing, proud 6 refuse, tiptop 7 forlock, gallant, highest, topknot, topmost 8 superior 9 excellent, first-rate, skimmings

topple: tip 4 fall, tilt 5 pitch, upset 6 teeter, totter, tumble 7 overset 8 collapse, overhang, overturn 9 overthrow 10 somersault 11 overbalance

tops: 4 A-one, aces, best 7 supreme 8 topnotch

topsman: 5 chief 6 drover 7 hangman, headman

topsy-turvy: 4 awry 5 upset 7 chaotic 8 cockeyed, confused, inverted 10 disordered, upside-down 11 withershins

toque: hat 6 bonnet 9 headdress

tor: taw 4 crag, hill, peak 5 mound 8 pinnacle

tora: 10 hartebeest

Tora, Torah: law 5 tetel 6 scroll 7 precept 10 Pentateuch, revelation 11 instruction 12 Old Testament

torch: 4 lamp 5 blaze, brand, flare, fusee, light 7 lucigen 8 flambeau 9 flambeaux (pl.) 10 flashlight, incendiary

tore: 4 knob, plod 5 grass 6 pommel

toreador: 6 torero 7 matador 11 bullfighter

torii: 7 gateway

torment: rib, vex 4 bait, bane, hurt, pain, rack 5 agony, annoy, chevy, chivy, devil, force, grill, harry, tease, worry, wrack 6 badger, bother, burden, chivvy, harass, harrow, hector, misery, molest, ordeal, pester, plague, strain 7 afflict, agitate, anguish, bedevil, crucify, distort, hagride, hatchel, tempest, torture, travail, trouble 8 distress, vexation 9 martyrdom, persecute, suffering, tantalize 10 cruciation 11 persecution

tormenting: 12 excruciating

tormina: 5 colic, pains 6 cramps, gripes

torn: 4 rent 5 riven 6 broken, ripped 7 mangled 9 lacerated, undecided

tornado: 4 wind 5 storm 7 cyclone, twister 9 whirlwind

Tornado Junction: 8 Trinidad

toro: 4 bull, tree 7 cavalla, cowfish

Toronto: *baseball team:* 8 Blue Jays
hockey team: 10 Maple Leafs

torous, torose: 6 brawny 7 bulging, knobbed, swollen 8 muscular 11 protuberant

torpedinous: 9 benumbing 10 stupefying

torpedo: 4 bomb, mine, ruin 5 shell, wreck 6 attack, benumb, damage, gunman 7 destroy, explode, missile, shatter 8 assassin, firework, gangster, numbfish, paralyze 9 crampfish, detonator

torpedo fish: ray

torpid: 4 boat, dull, numb 5 inert 6 leaden, static, stupid 7 dormant 8 benumbed, inactive, lifeless, sluggish 9 apathetic, lethargic

torpor: 4 coma 5 sleep 6 acedia, apathy, stupor 7 accidie, inertia 8 dormancy, dullness, lethargy 10 inactivity, stagnation 12 sluggishness 13 insensibility

torque: bee 5 chain, sarpe, twist 6 collar 8 necklace

torrefy, torrify: dry 5 parch 6 scorch

torrent: 4 flow, rush 5 flood, parch, roast, spate 6 deluge, shower, stream 7 burning, channel, consume, current, niagara, roaring, rushing 8 downpour 9 impetuous

torrid: hot 4 arid 5 dried, fiery 6 ardent, sultry 7 burning, parched, zealous 8 inflamed, parching, scorched 9 scorching 10 oppressive, passionate 11 impassioned

tort: 4 evil 5 libel, wrong 6 damage, injury 7 offense 8 iniquity 9 grievance

tortoise: 6 turtle 8 terrapin 9 chelonian
genus: 4 emys
kind: 4 emyd 5 giant, Texas 6 desert 9 Galapagos
marsh: 6 gopher 7 elodian
shell: 8 carapace

tortuous: 4 bent, mazy 5 snaky 6 cranky, spiral 7 crooked, devious, immoral, sinuate, sinuous, winding, wriggly 8 twisting, wrongful 9 deceitful, injurious 10 circuitous, roundabout, serpentine **11** anfractuous **12** labyrinthine

torture: **4** hurt, maim, pain, rack **5** agony, twist, wheel **6** deform, impale, injure, punish, wrench **7** afflict, agonize, anguish, crucify, cruelty, distort, torment **8** distress, mutilate, twisting **9** martyrdom **10** affliction, cruciation, distortion, excruciate, perversion, punishment
device: **4** rack **10** Iron Maiden, thumbscrew

torus: **4** tore **6** baston **7** molding **9** elevation **10** anchor ring, receptacle **12** protuberance

torvous: **4** grim **5** stern **6** severe

Tory: **6** Papist **8** loyalist, marauder, Royalist **11** reactionary **12** conservative

Tosca's love: **5** Mario

tosh: **4** bath, bosh, neat, tidy **5** souse, trash **6** drench, neatly **7** bathtub **8** familiar, intimate, nonsense **10** intimately

toss: cob, cup, lob **4** cast, cave, flip, hike, hurl, rear, roll **5** bandy, chuck, drink, flick, fling, flirt, heave, pitch, quaff, raise, serve, sling, throw, wager **6** buffet, chance, fillip, harass, tossup, totter, uplift, writhe **7** agitate, disturb **8** disquiet **9** agitation, commotion **10** excitement
about: **5** bandy **6** thrash, thresh **7** discuss
side to side: **6** career

tosspot: sot **5** drunk, souse, toper **7** drinker **8** drunkard

tosticate: **6** harass **8** distract **10** intoxicate

tosto: **4** fast **5** quick

tot: add, cup **4** dram, item, note **5** add up, child, count, drink, total, totum **6** amount, toddle, totter **7** jotting, toddler **9** calculate

tota: **6** grivet, monkey

total: add, all, sum, tot **4** full **5** count, gross, run to, tally, utter, whole **6** abrupt, all-out, amount, entire, figure, number **7** concise, overall, perfect, plenary, summary **8** absolute, complete, entirety, thorough **9** aggregate, calculate, full-scale, undivided **10** accumulate

totalitarian: **7** fascist **8** absolute, despotic **9** arbitrary **10** tyrannical **11** dictatorial **13** authoritarian

tote: all, bag, lug, tot **4** bear, haul, lead, load **5** carry, count, purse, shlep, total **6** handle, reckon, schlep **7** conduct **9** abstainer, transport

totem: **4** pole **5** shaft **6** emblem, fetich, fetish, figure, pillar

totem pole: xat

toto: all **4** baby **5** young

totter: **4** fall, hang, reel, rock, sway, toss **5** lurch, pitch, shake, swing, waver **6** dodder, falter, quiver, seesaw, staver (Sc.), toddle, wobble **7** fribble, stagger, tremble **8** flounder, titubate, unstable, unsteady **9** vacillate

tottle: **4** boil, purl **5** count, total **6** reckon, simmer, toddle, topple

toty (Ind.): **7** laborer **9** messenger

toucan: **4** bird, toco **7** aracari **8** hornbill, toucanet **13** constellation

touch: dab, hit, paw, rap, rob, tag, tap, tig, toe, use **4** abut, blow, feel, hint, meet, rape **5** brush, equal, graze, reach, refer, rival, shade, steal, taste, trait, verge **6** accuse, adjoin, affect, amount, attain, border, borrow, caress, extend, finger, handle, molest, rebuke, strike, stroke, twinge **7** attinge, censure, contact, feeling, impinge, palpate *clumsily:* paw
for medical diagnosis: **7** palpate
lightly: **5** brush, graze **7** attinge, twiddle
measuring device: **10** haptometer
off: **4** fire **5** start
organ of: **4** palp **6** feeler, finger **7** antenna
perceptible by: **7** tactile **8** palpable
pert. to: **6** haptic **7** tactile, tactual

touching: **4** upon **5** about **6** moving, tender **7** against, apropos, contact, meeting, piteous, tangent **8** adjacent, pathetic, poignant **9** affecting, attingent, bordering, conjoined, impinging **10** concerning, contacting, contiguous, contingent

touchstone: **4** test **8** basanite, standard **9** barometer, criterion

touchwood: **4** funk, punk **5** sponk, spunk **6** amadou, tinder **8** punkwood

touchy: **4** sore **5** cross, risky, snaky, techy, testy **6** cranky, tricky **7** peevish **8** choleric, delicate, ticklish, volatile **9** irascible, irritable, sensitive **10** precarious **11** inflammable **13** over-sensitive

tough: **4** goon, hard, hood, punk, thug, wiry **5** bully, hardy, harsh, rigid, rough, rowdy, stiff **6** brutal, flinty, robust, rugged, severe, sinewy, sticky, strong, sturdy, taxing, trying, uphill **7** arduous, drastic, hickory, hoodlum, onerous, ruffian, violent, viscous **8** cohesive, enduring, hard-line, hardened, leathery, obdurate, rigorous, rowdyish, stalwart, stubborn, sturdily, toilsome, vigorous **9** demanding, difficult, glutinous, obstinate, ruffianly **10** aggressive, unyielding

toughen: **5** inure **6** anneal, endure, harden, temper

tough-minded: **6** shrewd **7** willful **8** stubborn **9** practical, realistic **10** hardheaded **13** unsentimental

toupee: rug, wig **5** doily **6** peruke **7** periwig

tour: **4** trip, turn **5** cover, drive, range, round, shift, spell, trick, watch **6** course, travel **7** circuit, compass, journey, proceed **9** barnstorm, excursion **10** appearance, revolution

tourbillion: **5** whirl **6** vortex **8** firework, karrusel **9** whirlwind

tour de force: 4 feat 7 classic, exploit 11 masterpiece

tourelle: 5 tower 6 turret

tourist: 8 traveler 9 sightseer 12 rubber-necker

tourmaline: 6 schorl 7 mineral 8 achroite, siberite 9 rubellite

tournament: 4 meet, tilt 5 joust, match, sport, trial 6 battle 7 contest, tourney 9 encounter

tournure: pad 5 poise 6 bustle 7 contour, outline

touse: 4 pull, rack, tear 5 worry 6 handle, rumple 8 dishevel

tousle, tousel: 4 drag, muss, pull, tear 5 touse 6 ruffle, rumple, tussle 7 rummage 8 dishevel, disorder 9 mop of hair

tout: spy, vex 4 peep, peer, puff, toot 5 tease, thief, watch 6 herald, praise 7 canvass, lookout, scalper (Br.), solicit, tipster, touting, trumpet 8 ballyhoo, informer, proclaim, smuggler 9 importune, recommend

tout a fait (F.): 5 quite 8 entirely 10 altogether, completely

tout de suite (F.): now 6 at once 11 immediately

tow: tew, tug 4 drag, draw, flax, haul, jute, lead, pull, rope, yarn 5 barge, chain 6 hawser, propel 7 towboat, towrope, tugboat 8 cordelle

tow-row: 4 to-do 6 rumpus, uproar 9 racketing

toward: tae (Sc.) 4 near 5 anent 6 coming, facing, future, onward 7 apropos, forward, willing 8 imminent, obliging 9 compliant, promising, regarding, tractable 10 concerning 11 approaching
  center: 5 entad
  exterior: 5 ectad
  mouth: 4 orad
  stern: aft 5 abaft 6 astern
  the front: 7 advance, forward

towardly: 6 docile, gentle, kindly 7 affable 8 friendly 9 compliant, favorable, tractable 10 propitious

towel: dry, rub 4 swab 5 cloth 6 lavabo, napkin 8 vesperal 9 handcloth
  fabric: 4 huck 5 linen, terry

tower: 4 rise, silo, soar 5 broch, exalt, mount, pylon, raise, reach, shaft, sikar, spire, stupa 6 ascend, belfry, castle, column, cupola, donjon, pagoda, pillar, prison, turret 7 antenna, bastile, bulwark, citadel, clocher, defense, derrick, elevate, mansion, minaret, mirador, obelisk, overtop, pyramid, shikara, steeple, surpass, zikurat 8 bastille, domineer, fortress, look down, overlook, pilaster, ziggurat, zikkurat 9 campanile 10 protection, skyscraper, stronghold

bell: 6 belfry 8 carillon 9 campanile
Buddhist: 6 pagoda
castle: 6 donjon
famous: 4 Pisa 5 Babel, Minar, Sears 6 Eiffel, London
glacier ice: 5 serac
mosque: 7 minaret
of silence: 6 dakhma
over: 4 loom 5 dwarf 7 command 8 dominate
signal: 6 beacon 10 lighthouse

towering: 4 high, tall 5 great, lofty, steep 7 eminent, intense, supreme, violent 9 monstrous 11 overweening

towhee: 5 finch 7 bunting, chewink

town: 4 burg, city, dorp, farm, stad, vill, yard 5 bourg, burgh, court, derby, house, manor, ville (F.), voter 6 ciudad (Sp.), garden, hamlet, parish, podunk, staple 7 borough, village 8 bourgade 9 enclosure, farmstead
Attica: 4 deme
official: 5 mayor 6 grieve 8 alderman
pert. to: 5 civic, urban 7 oppidon
plan: 4 plat
small: 6 podunk 8 one-horse 10 dullsville, hicksville 11 whistle-stop

townsman: cit 7 burgher, citizen, oppidan 8 urbanite

township: 4 area, dorp 8 district

toxic: 9 poisonous

toxophilite: 6 archer

toy: pet, top 4 ball, daff, doll, fool, game, hoop, kite, play, whim, yoyo 5 antic, dally, fancy, flirt, jacks, panda, small, tease 6 bauble, cosset, finger, frolic, gewgaw, hoople, puzzle, rattle, trifle 7 caprice, conceit, disport, frisbee, marbles, pastime, trinket 8 aversion, flirting, gimcrack, interest, mistress, ornament, teetotum, weakling 9 bandalore, dalliance, headdress, plaything, rattlebox, teddybear 10 knick-knack 11 puppet sport 12 kaleidoscope

toyish: 6 wanton 7 playful, trivial, useless 8 sportive, trifling 9 fantastic, frivolous, whimsical 13 unsubstantial

trabant: 9 attendant, bodyguard

trabea: 4 toga

trabeation: 6 beamed 9 with beams 11 entablature

trabuco: 5 cigar 11 blunderbuss

trace: 4 clew, clue, copy, draw, fall, file, hint, line, mark, nose, path, road, seek, sign, step, tang, tint, walk 5 grain, march, probe, route, shade, spoor, tinge, token, track, trail, tread, whiff 6 amount, deduce, derive, detect, follow, locate, nuance, ramble, shadow, sketch, streak, trudge 7 conduct, glimpse, impress, imprint, inquire, outline, remnant, soupcon, uncover, vestige 8 discover, evidence, quantity, traverse **9** ascertain, attribute, delineate, establish, footprint, scintilla, suspicion **10** indication, intimation, procession **11** investigate

tracer: **5** horse **6** bullet, gilder, seeker, stylus **7** stainer **8** outliner, searcher **9** draftsman

trachea: **4** duct **8** windpipe

trachyte: **4** rock **6** domite

tracing: **4** copy **6** record **7** outline

track: rut, way **4** drag, draw, hunt, line, mark, oval, path, rail, road, sign, wake **5** march, orbit, route, scent, sight, spoor, stalk, trace, trail, tread **6** course, follow, infuse, pursue, shadow, teapot, travel **7** circuit, conduct, vestige **8** guideway, sequence, speedway, trackage, traverse **9** ascertain, footprint, spectacle **10** beaten path, cinder path, succession
animal: run **4** slot **5** spoor
official: **5** judge, timer **7** referee, starter
race: **4** dash, mile **5** relay **6** hurdle, sprint **7** walking **12** steeplechase
running: **4** flat **7** cinders
train: **4** rail, spur **6** siding

tracker: **5** guide, tower **7** tugboat

tract: lot **4** area, book, path, plot, zone **5** block, campo, clime, essay, field, lapse, range, trace, track **6** course, estate, extent, region, spread **7** article, country, expanse, housing, leaflet, portion, quarter, section, stretch, terrain **8** brochure, district, duration, pamphlet, treatise **9** lineament, narrative, territory **10** exposition **11** development, subdivision

tractable: **4** easy, meek, tame **5** buxom **6** docile, gentle, pliant **7** ductile, flexile, pliable **8** amenable, flexible, obedient, workable **9** adaptable, complaint, malleable **10** governable, submissive

tractate: **5** essay, tract **8** handling, treatise **9** discourse, treatment **10** discussion **12** dissertation

tractile: **6** pliant **7** ductile, tensile

traction: **5** power **7** drawing, utility **8** friction **9** influence **10** attraction

tractor: rig **7** vehicle **9** agrimotor

trade: buy, way **4** chap, chop, deal, fuss, path, sell, swap, work **5** bandy, cheap, craft, habit, track, trail, tread **6** action, barter, bother, course, employ, manner, market, method, metier, peddle, scorse, switch **7** bargain, calling, dealing, pursuit, traffic **8** activity, business, commerce, exchange, industry, practice, purchase, vocation **9** patronage **10** employment, handicraft, occupation, profession **11** intercourse, nundination
association: NAM **5** hansa, hanse
combination: **4** gild **5** guild, hanse **6** cartel, merger

pert. to: **10** emporeutic
unlawful: **10** contraband **11** black market

trademark: **4** logo **5** brand **8** logotype

trader: **4** ship **6** broker, dealer, monger, seller, slaver, sutler **7** chapman **8** barterer, merchant **9** tradesman **10** shopkeeper **11** stockbroker

tradesman: **5** buyer **6** dealer **7** artisan, workman **8** merchant, retailer **9** craftsman **10** shopkeeper **11** storekeeper
supply: **4** line **5** stock **9** inventory

tradition: **4** code, lore **5** usage **6** belief, custom, legend **8** heritage, practice **9** surrender **10** convention

traduce: **4** slur **5** abuse, belie **6** debase, defame, malign, vilify **7** asperse, blacken, detract, pervert, slander **8** disgrace **10** calumniate

traffic: buy **4** coup, deal, sell **5** trade **6** barter, market **7** chaffer, dealing **8** business, commerce, exchange, movement **9** patronage **11** intercourse
in holy offices: **6** simony

tragacanth: gum **4** tree **5** shrub

tragedy: lot, woe **6** buskin, misery **8** calamity, disaster **10** misfortune
Muse: **9** Melpomene

tragic: sad **4** dire **5** fatal **7** doleful **8** dreadful, mournful, pathetic, terrible

tragopan: **8** pheasant

tragule: **4** deer **10** chevrotain

trail: lad **4** drag, draw, halt, hang, hunt, mark, path, plod, slot, tail, wake **5** blaze, chase, delay, drail, piste, route, scent, spoor, trace, track, train, tramp, troll **6** camino (Sp.), course, dawdle, follow, linger, loiter, pursue, shadow, trapse, trudge **7** draggle, dwindle, pathway, traipse, trellis **8** footpath, straggle
blazer: **7** pioneer
marker: **5** blaze, cairn

trailer: RV **4** vine **5** coach, truck **7** flatbed
truck: **4** semi

train: row **4** bait, drag, draw, file, form, gait, lead, line, lure, rack, rank, rear, tail, tame, trap **5** break, breed, coach, decoy, drawl, drill, flier, guide, local, seine, shape, snare, suite, teach, trace, trail **6** allure, coffle, convoy, cradle, direct, entice, gentle, ground, harden, scheme, school, season, series, shaped **7** caravan, conduct, cortege, educate, prepare, retinue **8** accustom, artifice, equipage, instruct, protract, rehearse, sequence, trickery **9** condition, cultivate, entourage, following, stratagem, treachery **10** attendants, conveyance, discipline, procession, succession
end car of: **7** caboose
engine: **10** locomotive

fast: **7** express, limited
horses: **6** manege
of attendants: **5** suite **7** cortege, retinue **9** entourage
overhead: **8** elevated, monorail
slow: **5** local

trained: **4** bred **5** aimed **8** educated

trainee: **4** boot **5** cadet, pupil **6** novice **10** apprentice

trainer: **5** coach, tamer **7** handler, lanista **11** gymnasiarch

training: **4** diet **5** drill **8** breeding, exercise **9** education **10** background, discipline **11** supervision
lack of: **11** inappetence
manual: **5** sloid, sloyd

traipse, trapes: gad **4** drag, walk **5** trail, tramp, tread **6** stroll, trudge, wander **8** gadabout, slattern **9** gallivant

trait: **4** line, mark, note, thew **5** touch **6** streak, stroke **7** feature, quality **9** attribute, lineament, mannerism **11** peculiarity **14** characteristic

traitor: **5** Brown, Judas **6** Arnold **7** Dreyfus **8** betrayer, Iscariot, Quisling, renegade

traitorous: **5** false **8** disloyal **9** faithless, felonious **11** disaffected, treacherous, treasonable

traject: way **4** cast **5** ferry, route, throw **6** course, trajet **7** conduct, passage **8** transmit

tralatitious: **10** handed down **12** metaphorical

tram: car, leg **4** beam, haul, limb **5** bench, shaft, wagon **6** thread **7** tramcar, trammel, tramway, trolley **9** streetcar **10** conveyance

trammel: net, tie **4** clog, hold, lock **5** check, gauge, limit **6** braids, fasten, fetter, hamper, hobble, impede **7** compass, confine, inhibit, pothook, prevent, shackle, tresses **8** entangle, restrain, restrict, stultify **9** intercept, plaitings **10** instrument

tramontane: **4** boor, wind **5** alien **7** foreign **8** stranger **9** barbarous, outlander **10** outlandish **11** transalpine

tramp: bo, boe, bum, vag **4** hike, hobo, hoof, plod, prog, slut, step, tart, vamp, walk **5** bimbo, caird, gypsy, jaunt, nomad, rover, tread **6** gaycat, trapes, travel, trudge, waffie, wander, wanton **7** steamer, traipse, vagrant **8** vagabond **9** excursion **10** prostitute **11** bindle stiff
baggage: **6** bindle
offering to: **7** handout

trample: **4** foil, hurt **5** crush, stamp, stomp, tread **6** injure **7** destroy, tread on, violate

trance: **4** coma, daze **5** dream, spell, swoon **6** prance, raptus, stupor **7** ecstasy, enchant, passage, reverie **8** entrance, hypnosis **9** catalepsy, enrapture, transport

tranquil: **4** calm, cool, easy, even, mild **5** equal, quiet, still **6** gentle, placid, serene, steady **7** equable, pacific, restful **8** composed, peaceful **9** sedentary **10** motionless **11** undisturbed **13** imperturbable

tranquility, tranquillity: kef, kif **5** peace, quiet **8** ataraxia, serenity **10** equanimity **12** peacefulness

tranquilize: **4** calm, lull **5** allay, quiet, relax **6** sedate, settle, soften, soothe, subdue **7** appease, assuage **9** alleviate

transact: **5** treat **7** conduct, perform **8** complete, transfer **9** negotiate

transaction: **4** deal, sale **6** affair **7** bargain **8** business, contract, covenant **10** proceeding **11** negotiation, proposition
unlawful: **10** chevisance

Transcaucasia: **7** Armenia, Georgia **10** Azerbaijan

transcend: **4** pass, soar **5** climb, excel, mount, raise **6** ascend, exceed **7** elevate, surpass **8** outstrip, overstep, surmount **9** rise above

transcendent: **5** ideal **7** perfect, supreme **8** superior **10** consummate, preeminent, surpassing **12** incomparable **13** extraordinary

transcendental: **5** ideal **7** eternal, supreme **8** abstract, ethereal **10** superhuman **12** metaphysical, otherworldly, supersensual, supranatural

Transcendentalist: **4** Kant **6** Alcott **7** Emerson, Thoreau

transcribe: **4** copy **5** write **6** impute, record **7** ascribe, imitate **9** reproduce, translate **10** paraphrase

transcript: **6** record **8** apograph **9** duplicate **12** reproduction

transfer: **4** cede, deed, give, move, pass, sale, send **5** carry, grant, shift **6** assign, attorn, change, convey, decant, demise, depute, remove **7** convert, dispose **8** alienate, delegate, make over, relocate, sign over, transmit **9** transform, translate, transport **10** abalienate **12** transmission **13** transposition
bus or train: **6** ticket **8** add-a-ride
design: **5** decal
of court suit: **7** remover
property: **4** deed **5** grant **6** convey

transference: **7** passage **10** conveyance **12** displacement

transfigure: **5** exalt **7** glorify **8** idealize **9** transform **12** metamorphose

transfix: fix, pin **5** spear, stick **6** fasten, impale, pierce, skewer, thrill **11** transpierce

transform: **4** turn **5** alter **6** change, mutate **7** convert **9** transmute **11** transfigure **12** metamorphose, transmogrify
into human form: **16** anthropomorphize

transfuse: **5** imbue **6** infuse **7** instill **8** permeate, transfer, transmit

transgress: err, sin **5** break, cross **6** offend **7** disobey, violate **8** overstep, trespass

transgression: sin **4** slip, vice **5** crime, error, fault, lapse **6** breach **7** misdeed, offense **8** trespass **9** violation **10** infraction **12** infringement **13** contravention

transient: **6** lodger, renter, roomer **7** flighty, passing **8** fleeting, fugitive **9** ephemeral, itinerant, migratory, momentary, temporary, transeunt **10** evanescent, shortlived, transitory **11** impermanent

transit: **6** change, travel **7** passage **9** transport **10** conveyance, pass across, theodolite, transition **12** thoroughfare

transition: **4** flux, turn **5** phase, shift **6** bridge, change **7** passage **9** metabasis **10** alteration, conversion

transitive: **7** flowing **12** transitional

transitory: **5** brief, fleet **8** caducous, temporal **9** ephemeral, short-term, temporary **10** evanescent

translate: put **4** read, rede **6** change, decode, remove, render **7** convert **8** construe, decipher, entrance, transfer **9** enrapture, interpret **10** paraphrase

translation: key **4** pony, trot **7** version **9** rendition **10** paraphrase **14** interpretation **15** transliteration

translucent: **5** clear **6** limpid **7** obvious **8** pellucid **9** alabaster **11** perspicuous, transparent

transmigration: **7** samsara **13** reincarnation

transmit: **4** emit, hand, mail, post, send, wire **5** cable, carry, relay **6** convey, render **7** conduct, devolve, forward **8** bequeath, dispatch **9** pass along, telegraph **11** communicate

transmutation: **9** evolution

transom: **5** trave **6** lintel, louver, window

transparent: **4** open **5** clear, filmy, frank, gauzy, lucid, plain, sheer **6** candid, limpid, lucent **7** obvious, pelucid **8** luminous, lustrous **9** colorless **10** diaphanous **11** crystalline, perspicuous, translucent **12** clear as glass

transpierce: **6** impale **8** transfix **9** penetrate

transpire: **5** occur **6** get out, happen, result **7** develop **9** eventuate

transport: bus, car, dak, tug **4** bear, boat, buss, haul, move, send, ship, tote **5** barge, bring, carry, ferry, flute, truck **6** banish, convey, deport, ravish **7** bicycle, emotion, fraught, freight, passion, portage, rapture, transit, vehicle **8** enthrall, entrance, overcome, palander, transfer **9** captivate, enrapture

transportation: *business:* **4** mail **7** air-line, express **8** shipping, trucking **9** steamship **11** railroading

transpose: **5** shift **6** change, remove, switch **7** convert, disturb, reverse **8** exchange, transfer **9** rearrange, transform, translate, transmute **11** interchange

transposition: **5** shift **7** anagram **10** spoonerism **11** permutation

Transvaal: *capital:* **8** Pretoria

city: **12** Johannesburg

goldfield: **13** Witwatersrand

native: **4** Zulu **7** Bushman **9** Hottentot

transverse: bar, way **4** bank, over, pass, rung, turn **5** argue, cross, pivot, route, shift, trace **6** across, denial, stripe, survey, swivel, thwart, travel **7** athwart, barrier, discuss, examine, impeach, oblique, pervade, quarrel **8** diagonal **9** alternate, crossbeam, crosswise **10** crosspiece

Transylvania: *city:* **4** Cluj

fabled resident: **7** Dracula, vampire

trap: bag, get, gin, net, pit **4** cage, lure, nail, snag **5** brake, buggy, catch, goods, mouth, rocks, snare, steps, trick **6** ambush, corner, detect, enmesh **7** capture, cunning, ensnare, luggage, pitfall, springe **8** carriage, confound, covering, deadfall, separate, trapball **9** caparison, detective, policeman, stratagem **10** belongings, stepladder

animal: pot, web **4** weir **5** creel **6** bownet, eelpot **8** deadfall

police: **7** dragnet **9** roadblock

trapdoor: **4** drop, slot

trapeze: bar

trapping: **4** gear **5** cloth **6** finery **7** harness, housing **8** catching, covering, ornament **9** adornment, caparison, coverture **10** decoration **12** accouterment, accoutrement **13** embellishment, paraphernelia

theatrical: **4** prop **7** scenery **8** property

Trappist: **4** monk **10** Cistercian

cheese: oka

writer: **6** Merton

traps: **5** bells, drums **7** cymbals

trapshooting: **5** skeet

target: **10** clay pigeon

trash: jog, lop **4** bosh, clog, crop, dirt, jade, pelf, plod, raff, tosh **5** leash, money, tramp, waste, wrack **6** bushwa, debris, halter, hinder, rabble, refuse, retard, rubble, trudge **7** baggage, beggary, blather, garbage, rubbish **8** encumber, flummery, nonsense, restrain, riffraff, trumpery **9** vandalize **10** balderdash **11** sleuth-hound

trashy: **4** mean **5** cheap, tacky, tatty **6** common, shoddy, sleazy **9** worthless

trauma: **4** blow **5** shock, wound **6** injury, stress **8** collapse

travail: **4** pain, pang, task, toil, work **5** agony, drive, labor **6** effort, travel **7** journey, torment, trouble **8** exertion, struggle **9** suffering **10** birth throe **11** parturition

trave: 9 crossbeam

travel: run 4 fare, move, mush, pass, post, ride, roam, tour, trek, trip, walk, wend 5 coast, jaunt 6 motion, voyage 7 commute, journey, migrate, passage, proceed, sojourn, travail 8 traverse 9 gallivant, itinerate 10 locomotion 11 peregrinate
pert. to: 6 viatic
schedule: 9 itinerary
yen for: 10 wanderlust

traveler: 5 farer, nomad, tramp 6 viator 7 drummer, pilgrim, swagman, tourist, voyager 8 explorer, salesman, vagabond, wanderer, wayfarer 9 sightseer 10 intinerant 12 globe-trotter
aid of: 5 guide 7 courier 8 cicerone
commercial: 5 agent 6 bagman 7 drummer 8 salesman
refuge: inn 5 motel, oasis 6 imaret 7 hospice

travels: 7 journey, odyssey

traverse: 4 deny, ford, pass, walk 5 cross, range, rebut 6 oppose, patrol, refute, swivel, thwart, travel

travesty: 5 farce, mimic 6 parody, satire 7 mockery 8 disguise 9 burlesque, imitation 10 caricature
writer: 8 parodist, satirist

trawl: net 4 fish, line 5 seine, troll 7 boulter, dragnet

tray: hod 4 font 6 hurdle, salver, server 7 coaster, platter

treacherous: 5 false, punic, snaky 6 fickle, hollow, tricky 8 disloyal, insecure, plotting, unstable 9 dangerous, deceptive, faithless, hazardous, insidious 10 fraudulent, perfidious, precarious, traitorous, unfaithful, unreliable 13 Machiavellian, untrustworthy

treachery: 5 guile 6 deceit 7 perfidy, treason, untruth 8 betrayal 9 dirty pool 10 infidelity

treacle: 4 cure 5 syrup 6 remedy 7 claggum 8 molasses

treaclewort: 4 herb 10 pennycress

tread: rut 4 gait, mark, pace, rung, step, volt, walk 5 clump, crush, dance, labor, march, press, stair, stamp, trace, track, trail, tramp 6 balter, course, quench, stride, subdue, trapes 7 conquer, repress, traipse, trample 8 copulate, footfall 9 footprint 10 employment, occupation

treadle: 5 pedal 7 chalaza

treason: 6 deceit, revolt 7 perfidy 8 betrayal, sedition 9 treachery

treasure: 4 find, plum, roon 5 cache, hoard, pearl, prize, store, trove, value 6 gersum, revere, riches, supply, wealth 7 cherish, finance, respect 8 hold dear 9 thesaurus (L.) 10 appreciate, collection 12 accumulation

treasured: 4 dear 5 chary 8 precious

treasurer: 6 banker, purser 7 cashier, curator 8 bhandari, cofferer, deftedar, guardian, receiver 11 chamberlain
college: 6 bursar

Treasure State: 7 Montana

treasury: 4 bank, fisc, fund, mine, safe 5 chest, hoard, vault 6 coffer, museum 7 bonanza, bursary, revenue 8 archives, gold mine 9 exchequer 10 depository, repository, storehouse
Roman: 6 fiscus

treat: use 4 blow, deal, dose, lead, urge 5 argue, besee, Dutch, feast, goody, guide, nurse, serve, stand, touch 6 attend, confer, demean, doctor, govern, handle, morsel, parley, physic, pow wow, regale, regard, repast, tidbit 7 address, bargain, control, discuss, entreat, expound, prepare 8 consider, deal with, delicacy, transact, treatise 9 discourse, entertain, negotiate 10 manipulate
improperly: 4 snub 5 flout, scout, spite 6 ill-use, misuse 8 dishonor
leather: tan, taw 7 chamois
tenderly: 5 spare 6 coddle, pamper

treatise: 4 book 5 essay, study, tract 6 thesis, treaty 7 account, grammar 8 argument, brochure 9 discourse, monograph, narration, treatment 10 commentary, discussion, exposition 11 description 12 dissertation
elementary: 6 primer 7 grammar
opening part: 8 exordium
preface: 7 isagoge

treatment: 4 care, cure 5 usage 7 regimen, therapy 8 analysis, antidote, demeanor, entreaty, handling 10 management, medication 13 entertainment
before doctor's arrival: 8 first aid
compassionate: 5 mercy
harsh: 5 abuse 8 misusage, severity

treaty: 4 pact 5 truce 7 article, compact, concord, entente 8 alliance, contract 9 agreement 10 convention, discussion 11 arrangement

treaty-bound: 6 allied

treble: 4 high 5 acute 6 shrill, triple 7 soprano 9 threefold 11 high-pitched

tree: ach, ber, dal, dao, ebo, elm, fir, hur, iba, kou, lin, mee, oak 4 acle, alan, alof, anam, asak, asok, ates, ausu, bael, biti, bogo, bola, dali, dhak, dita, ipil, mabi, mora, odal, palm, pole, post, ship, toon, trap, wood, yaya 5 areca, asoka, betis, bongo, bulak, bumbo, cacao, carob, catch, cebil, couma, dadap, dalli, fulwa, genip, ligas, mahua, neeba, nepal, niepa, nitta, oodal, rohan, roman, salai, sassy, shaft, shift, siman, sissu, spade, staff, stake, stick, tikur, yacca 6

bahera, banyan, barbas, bariba, brauna, bucare, cativo, cedron, chalta, chogak, chupon, cocuyo, colima, corner, cudgel, design, gibbet, gomart, illupi, jarrah, locust, marane, marara, ramoon, sabino, simaba, sissoo, stemma, tikoor, timber **7** anubing, araraba, arboret, assagai, assegai, azarole, capture, champac, champak, cocullo, dhamnoo, diagram, gallows, guaraba, gumihan, hautboy, hollong, madrona, madrono, malpaho, mambong **8** ahueuete, cockspur, gamdeboo, ironbark, magnolia, mangrove, mokihana, phulwara, seedling, tamarack **9** bandoline, betel-palm, bitanhole, canadulce, couratari, currajong, genealogy, sassywood **10** bunyabunya, chaulmugra, chinaberry **11** balinghasay, chaulmaugra, chaulmoogra, guachipilin, hursinghair
alder: arn **5** alnus, birch **12** ament-bearing
algarroba: **5** carob **6** calden
allspice: **7** pimento
apple: **4** sorb
aromatic: **9** sassafras
balsam: fir **9** torchwood
bark: **4** ross, tapa
basswood: **6** linden
bead: nim
bean: **5** sapan
bearing samara: ash
beefwood: **5** belah, belar
betel: **5** areca
bignoniacious: **7** catalpa
blinding sap: **7** alipata
boxwood: **5** seron
breadnut: **6** capomo
buckthorn: **7** cascara
buckwheat: **4** titi **6** teetee
burned, broken: **7** rampick, rampike
buttonball: **5** plane **8** sycamore
cabbage: **7** angelin
camphor: **5** kapur
candlenut: ama
caoutchouc: ule **6** rubber
caucho-yielding: ule
cemetery: yew
chestnut: **8** chinkapin **10** chinquapin
chocolate: **5** cacao
cinchona: **7** quinine **9** quinidine
cinnamon family: **6** cassia
citrus: **4** lime **5** lemon **6** orange **8** bergamot **10** calamondin
clump: **4** tump **5** motte
coffee: **6** chicot
conebearing: fir, yew **4** pine **5** alder, cedar, cycad, larch **6** spruce **7** conifer, cypress, hemlock, juniper, redwood **8** gnetales **10** podocarpus
coral: **6** gabgab
cottonwood: **5** abele, alamo

covering: **4** bark
cranberry: **7** pembina
derivative: **5** pinic
devil: **4** dita
drumstick: **11** canafistolo, canafistula, canafistulo
drupe bearing: **4** bito
dwarf: **5** scrub **7** abuscle **10** chinquapin
dwelling: **4** nest
dye yielding: tua, tui **4** mora **7** annatto **10** hursinghar
ebony: **9** diospyros
elder: **7** trammon
eucalyptus: **4** yati **6** mallee
evergreen: fir, yew **4** pine, tawa, titi **5** carob, cedar, holly, larch, ocote, olive **6** balsam, carobe, cazaba, coigue, tarata **7** bebeery, juniper, madrona, madrono, taratah
exudation: gum, lac, sap, tar **5** amber, resin, rosin, xylan
fabacious: **5** agati
fiber: **5** bulak, simal, terap **7** bentang
fig family: **4** upas **5** pipal **6** botree **7** gondang
flowering: **5** agati, apple, elder, sumac, titis **6** cherry, mimosa, redbud **7** dogwood **8** cleaster, oleaster
fodder: **5** mahoe **9** tagasaste
food: **4** akee
fruit: bel, fig, gab **4** gaub, lime **5** apple, araca, lemon, mahis, olive, papaw, peach, topes **6** annona, banana, bearer, biriba, cherry, litchi, medlar, orange, pawpaw, sapota **7** avocado, capulin, genipap, tangelo **8** bakupari, tamarind **9** tangerine **12** custard apple
group: **4** bosk **5** copse, grove, woods **6** forest **7** coppice, orchard
grower: **8** arborist
gum: **5** babul, balta **6** balata, sapota, sapote, tupelo, zapote **8** banildad **9** sapodilla, sapotilha, sapotilla **10** bansalague, eucalyptus
hardwood: oak **4** poon **5** aalii, apple, gidia, gidya, mabee, maple, narra, ngaio **6** gidgea, gidgee, gidjee, gidyea, walnut **7** hickory, tindalo **8** macaasin, mahogany **9** quebracho
health: **5** briar, brier
heartwood: **7** duramen
hickory: **5** pecan
holly: **4** ilex
honeberry: **5** genip
horseradish: **4** behn **5** behen
jobber: **10** woodpecker
juniper: **4** cade **5** cedar
kino: **4** bija
koranic: **6** zaggum
largest: **12** giant sequoia
laurel: bay **7** tarairi

limb: **5** bough **6** branch

lime: lin **4** linn, teil **6** linden **9** tilicetum

linden: **4** lime, teil **8** basswood

locust: **6** acacia **9** courbaril

lotus: sad **6** jujube

mafurra: **6** elcaja

magnolia: **5** yulan

mahogany: **4** toon

maple: **4** acer

margosa: **4** neem

marmalade: **6** mammee, mammey, sapote

medicinal: **5** sumac, yucca **6** sumach, wahahe

mimosaceous: **5** siris

monkeybread: **6** baobob

mountain ash: **4** sorb **5** rowan **7** service

mulberry: **5** osage **8** sycamine

nut: **4** cola **5** hazel, pecan, pinon **6** akhrot, almond, chicha, walnut **9** almendron, pistachio

nymph turned into: **6** Daphne

oil: **5** mahua, mahwa **9** candlenut

oil-yielding: bel, ben **4** eboe, shea

old: **6** ginkgo **7** redwood **10** maidenhair **15** bristlecone pine

olive: **4** olea

olive family: ash

palm: tal **4** coco, date, nipa **5** ratan, sabal **6** arengs **9** coco-de-mer

paradise: **8** aceituna

part: **4** bark, bole, knot, leaf, root, twig **5** trunk **6** branch

pert. to: **8** arboreal

plane: **8** sycamore **10** buttonwood

plantain: **4** pala

pod-bearing: **7** catalpa

poisonous: **4** upas **5** ligas **7** tanquen

poon: **4** dilo **5** keena

poplar: **5** abele, alamo, aspen, tulip **10** cottonwood

pottery: **7** caraipe, caraipi

rain: **5** saman, zaman **6** zamang **8** genisaro **9** algarroba

rare: **6** Joshua

resin: **4** arar

ribbon: **6** akaroa **7** houhere

rubber: ule **4** para **6** caucho **7** seringa **10** caoutchouc

rutaceous: **4** lime

salt: **4** atle **5** atlee **8** tamarisk

sandarac: **4** arar

sandbox: **6** assacu

science: **7** silvics

shade: ash, elm, oak **5** guama, maple **6** linden, poplar **7** catalpa **8** sycamore

smoke: **6** fustet **9** zante-wood

soft-wood: lin **5** ambay, balsa, linde

sour gum: **5** nyssa **6** tupelo

sprout: **5** sprig **7** sapling

streaked wood: **5** baria

stunted: **5** scrub

sugar: **5** maple

tallest: **7** redwood **10** eucalyptus

tallow: **4** cera

tamarisk: see *salt* above

tea: **6** manuka

teak: **4** teca

thorny: bel **4** bael, bito, brea **7** colorin **9** barriguda **11** chichicaste

timber: ash, dar, eng, koa, saj, sal, yew **4** coco, cuya, ipil, pelu, pine, poon, rata, tala, teak, toon, ulmo **5** acana, almon, amate, balao, balau, bayok, beech, birch, cedar, culla, dalli, ebano, fotui, guijo, icica, kauri, kaury, maple, narra, pekea, penda, rauli, tenio, timbo, uadal, yacal, zorro **6** alerce, alerse, alfaje, ausubo, bacury, banaba, banago, banaki, bancal, banuyo, bataan, batino, dagame, dungon, lanete, molave, satine, totara, walnut **7** batulin, becuiba, billian, camagon, capulin, cypress, gateado, gomavel, guacimo, hapiton, redwood **8** flindosa, flindosy, mahogany, zapetero **9** balaustre, guaraguao **10** batikuling

treatise: **5** silva

tropical genus: **8** bauhinia

trunk: **4** bole **5** shaft

tulip: **6** poplar

Turkey oak: **6** cerris

turpentine: **6** tarata **7** taratah **9** terebinth

walnut: (see also *nut* above): **6** akhrot

wattle: **5** boree

wide-spreading: **5** cedar **7** juniper

willow: **5** osier, saugh **6** poplar

worship: **11** dendrolatry

yellow alder: **8** sagerose

young: **7** sapling

yucca: **6** Joshua

tree bear: **7** raccoon

treeless: **6** barren

plain: **5** llano, pampa **6** steppe **7** prairie, savanna **8** savannah

treelike: **8** arboreal **11** arborescent

treen: **6** wooden

treenail: nog, peg, pin **5** spike **7** trunnel

tree runner: **8** nuthatch

tree toad: **4** hyla **6** peeper

trefoil: **4** leaf **6** clover

treillage: **5** grill **7** trellis **8** espalier **11** latticework

trek: **4** draw, pull, trip, wade **5** march, tramp **6** safari, travel **7** journey, migrate **10** expedition

trellis: **5** arbor, bower, cross **7** lattice, pergola **8** espalier **9** treillage **10** interweave **11** latticework

trematode: **8** cercaria, flatworm, parasite

tremble: **5** aspen, bever, quake, shake **6** didder, dither, dodder, falter, quaver, quiver, shiver, totter, tremor **7** flacker, flicker, shudder, vibrate **9** trepidate

trembling: shy **5** shaky, timid **7** aquiver, fearful, twitter **9** tremulous

tremendous: big **4** huge **5** awful, giant, great, large **6** mighty **7** amazing, fearful, immense **8** colossal, dreadful, enormous, great big, horrible, powerful, terrific **9** frightful, momentous, monstrous **10** monumental, prodigious, terrifying **13** extraordinary

tremolo: **6** quaver **7** vibrato

tremor: **5** quake, shake **6** quaver, quiver, shiver, thrill **7** shudder, tremble **9** vibration **10** earthquake

tremplin: **10** trampoline **11** springboard

tremulous: **5** aspen, timid **7** aquiver, fearful, nervous, palsied, quaking, quivery, shaking, shivery **8** timorous, unsteady, wavering **9** quavering, quivering, sensitive, shivering, trembling **11** palpitating

trench: cut, gaw **4** bury, gash, moat, sike, sink **5** canal, carve, ditch, drain, fossa (L.), fosse, graff, graft, gully, slash, slice, verge **6** border, furrow, groove, gutter, trough **7** acequia, channel **8** encroach, entrench, infringe **10** excavation

digger: **6** sapper

trenchant: **4** keen **5** acrid, acute, sharp **6** biting **7** caustic, cutting, mordant, probing, satiric **8** clear-cut, distinct, forceful, incisive, sardonic, scathing, vigorous **9** energetic, sarcastic **11** penetrating

trencher: **4** food, tray **5** board, plate **7** platter **9** parasitic **11** sycophantic

trencherman: **5** eater **7** glutton, gormand, sponger **8** gourmand, hanger-on, parasite **11** gormandizer **12** gourmandizer

trend: fad, run **4** bend, bent, mode, rage, tone, turn, vein, wind **5** craze, drift, style, swing, tenor, vogue **6** extend, strike **7** fashion, incline **8** movement, tendency **9** direction **11** inclination

trepan: cut, saw **4** lure, tool, trap **5** cheat, snare, trick **6** entrap **7** deceive, ensnare, swindle **9** perforate, stratagem

trepang: **8** teatfish **10** beche-de-mer

trepid: **7** quaking **8** timorous **9** trembling

trepidation: **4** fear **5** alarm, dread, worry **6** dismay, tremor **7** anxiety, quaking **9** agitation, confusion **10** excitement **11** disturbance **12** perturbation **13** consternation

trespass: err, sin **5** poach **6** breach, invade, offend **7** intrude **8** encroach, entrench, infringe, invasion **9** do wrong by, interlope, intrusion **10** infraction, transgress **11** misfeasance

tress: **4** curl, hair, lock, mane **5** braid, plait **7** ringlet, wimpler

tressure: **4** band, caul **6** border, fillet, ribbon **9** headdress

trestle: leg **5** bench, horse, stand, stool **6** tripod, trivet **7** support, viaduct **8** sawhorse **9** framework

tret: **9** allowance

trews: **8** breeches, trousers **9** stockings

triad: **4** trio **5** three, trine **6** triune **7** trinity **9** threesome, trivalent **11** triumvirate

trial: try **4** bout, case, pain, suit, test **5** assay, cross, essay, grief, proof, rigor **6** assize, effort, ordeal, sample **7** approof, attempt, calvary, contest, hearing, inquiry, lawsuit, trouble **8** crucible, endeavor, evidence, hardship, striving, struggle **9** adversity, nightmare, suffering **10** affliction, difficulty, experience, experiment, misfortune, tournament, visitation **11** examination, tribulation **12** experimental **13** investigation

and error: **10** experiment

inconclusive: **8** hung jury, mistrial

pert. to: **7** empiric

trial balloon: **4** kite, test **6** feeler

triangle: **5** delta **6** obtuse, trigon **7** scalene, trigone **9** isosceles **10** instrument **11** equilateral

draw circle touching: **7** escribe

in heraldry: **5** giron

side: leg **10** hypotenuse

triangular: **6** cunate **7** deltoid, hastate **9** cuneiform **10** trilateral **13** three-cornered

piece: **4** gore **5** miter, mitre, wedge **6** gusset

sail: jib **6** lateen **9** spinnaker

triangular muscle: **7** deltoid

triarchy: **11** triumvirate

tribe: rod **4** band, clan, kind, race, sept **5** class, firca (Ind.), group **6** family **9** community

head: **5** chief **9** patriarch

tribulation: **5** agony, cross, trial **6** misery, ordeal, sorrow **8** distress **9** suffering **10** affliction, oppression, wrongdoing **11** persecution

tribunal: bar **4** banc, seat **5** bench, court, forum **7** tribune **8** assembly **10** consistory

tribune: **4** dais **5** chief **6** throne **8** platform **10** magistrate

tributary: **5** ruler, state **6** feeder **7** subject **9** auxiliary, confluent, dependent, satellite, secondary **10** subsidiary **11** subordinate **12** contributory

tribute: fee, tax **4** cain, dues, duty, gift, levy, rent, scat **5** grant, tithe **6** assign, eulogy, excise, heriot, homage, impost, praise, tariff **7** chevage, ovation, payment, respect **8** encomium, heregeld **9** attribute, gratitude, laudation, panegyric **10** obligation **11** testimonial

trice: 4 bind, gird, haul, lash, pull 5 flash, jiffy 6 moment, secure 7 instant 9 twinkling

trichome: 4 hair 7 bristle, prickle

trichord: 4 lyre

trick: bob, boy, cog, dor, fob, fox, fub, gag, gum, toy 4 bilk, dupe, feat, flam, fool, gaff, gaud, girl, gull, hoax, jest, joke, prat, ruse, trap, turn, wile 5 antic, bluff, caper, catch, cheat, child, craft, cully, dodge, feint, fraud, gleek, guile, hocus, knack, magic, prank, shift, skite, spell, stunt 6 begunk, chouse, delude, humbug, palter, trepan, trifle 7 beguile, cantrip, deceive, defraud, finesse, gimmick, pretext, sleight, swindle 8 artifice, flimflam, illusion, maneuver 9 bamboozle, capriccio, chicanery, deception, diablerie, imposture, mannerism, shell game, stratagem 10 subterfuge 11 hornswoggle, legerdemain

trickery: art 4 sham 5 fraud, hocus 6 cautel, deceit, japery 7 knavery, roguery, slyness 8 artifice, cheating, trumpery 9 chicanery, deception, duplicity 10 hanky-panky 11 double-cross

trickle: 4 drip, drop, flow, leak, seep, sipe (Sc.) 5 exude 6 distil 7 distill, dripple

trickster: 5 cheat, joker 6 rascal 7 slicker 8 swindler 9 gyp artist, prankster

tricksy: 5 smart, tight 6 spruce 7 evasive, playful, quirksy, roguish 8 prankish, sportive 9 deceiving, deceptive, uncertain 11 embellished, mischievous

tricky: sly 4 foxy, wily 5 dodgy 6 artful, catchy, crafty, touchy 7 cunning, devious 8 delicate, gimmicky, guileful, ticklish, unstable 9 deceitful, deceptive, difficult, dishonest, intricate

tricycle: 6 tricar

trident: 4 fork 5 spear 7 scepter
bearer: 7 Neptune 8 Poseidon

tried: 6 ettled (Sc.), proved, select, tested 7 staunch 8 faithful, reliable, rendered 9 steadfast 10 dependable 11 trustworthy

trier: 5 judge 7 refiner 8 examiner, renderer 12 experimenter, investigator

trifle: bit, fig, rap, sou, toy 4 bean, doit, fike, fool, hint, jest, mash, mock, mote, play 5 curio, dally, flirt, straw, trick, use up, waste 6 bauble, burn up, coquet, dabble, dawdle, delude, dibble, doodle, fiddle, fidget, footer, footle, frivol, gewgaw, misuse, potter 7 bibelot, deceive, dessert, fribble, nothing, novelty, traneen, trinket, whatnot 8 flimflam, gimcrack, raillery 9 bagatelle, philander 10 equivocate, knick-knack, triviality

trifling: 4 airy, idle, mere 5 banal, inane, petty 6 futile, slight 7 foolish, shallow, wasting 8 badinage, frippery, picayune, piddling 9 dalliance, frivolous, small talk 10 immate-

rial 11 unimportant 12 little paltry 13 insignificant

trifolium: 6 clover 7 trefoil 8 shamrock

trig: run 4 chic, cram, deck, fill, firm, full, line, neat, prim, prop, snug, stop, tidy, trim, trot 5 brisk, dandy, natty, smart, sound, stiff, stone, stuff, wedge 6 active, classy, lively, snappy, spruce, steady, strong, trench 7 distend, foppish, orderly, precise, stylish, support 9 shipshape 10 methodical

triggerman: gun 6 gun man, gunsel, hit man 8 assassin

trigo: 5 wheat

trigon: 4 harp, lyre 5 trine 8 triangle

trigonometry function: 4 sine 6 cosine, secant 7 tangent

Trilby: *author:* 9 du Maurier
character: 8 Svengali

trill: 4 drip, flow, move, sing, turn 5 shake, twirl 6 gruppo, quaver, quiver, warble 7 mordent, trickle, vibrate

trim: bob, cut, gay, lop 4 beat, chic, clip, crop, deft, dink, edge, fine, firm, neat, nice, pare, snod (Sc.), snug, tidy, trig, whip 5 adorn, braid, cheat, chide, dress, equip, fitty, natty, nifty, order, preen, prune, ready, shape, shave, shear, whack 6 adjust, barber, bedeck, dapper, defeat, modify, petite, punish, spruce, thrash 7 balance, compact, defraud, furnish, garnish, orderly, shapely 8 chastise, decorate, ornament, pleasant, tailored 9 condition, embellish, excellent, shipshape 10 commission, compromise 11 disposition
a tree: 5 prune 7 pollard
coin: nig
lace: 5 jabot 6 ruffle

trimmer: 5 finer 6 barber

trimming: 4 gimp, lace 5 braid, ruche 6 frieze, fringe, piping, ribbon, ruffle, sequin 7 beading, falbala, flounce, garnish, ruching 8 froufrou, furbelow, ornament, rickrack 9 garniture 10 decoration 13 passementerie

trindle: 4 roll 5 wheel 7 trundle

trine: 4 hang, trio 5 march, triad 6 trigon, trinal, triple, triune 7 Trinity 9 favorable, threefold 10 auspicious

Trinidad and Tobago: *capital:* 11 Port of Spain
dance: 5 limbo

trinitrotoluene: TNT 6 trotyl 13 high explosive

trinity: 5 three, triad 6 triune 9 threeness 10 spiderwort

trinket: toy 4 bead, gaud, ring 5 bijou, jewel 6 bangle, bauble, gewgaw, tinsel, trifle 7 bibelot 8 intrigue, gimcrack, ornament 9 plaything, showpiece 10 knick-knack

trio

trio: 5 triad 9 threesome

trip: run 4 fall, gait, halt, hike, pawl, skip, slip, spin, tour, trek 5 brood, caper, catch, danse, drive, error, flock, jaunt, lapse, tread, wedge 6 cruise, falter, flight, junket, voyage 7 blunder, failure, journey, misstep, mistake, release, stumble 8 obstruct 9 excursion 10 expedition

tripe: 5 trash 7 rubbish 8 entrails, nonsense

triple: hit 5 triad, trine 6 treble 9 threefold 11 three-bagger

triplet: 4 trin, trio 5 trine 6 triune

tripletail: 9 berrugate, spadefish

triplicate: 6 treble, triple 9 threefold

tripod: cat 5 easel, stand 6 trivet

Tripoli ruler: dey

trippet: cam

tripping: 5 quick 6 nimble 7 walking

triptych: 7 picture 10 altarpiece
  wing: 5 volet

trismus: 7 lockjaw, tetanus

Tristram, Tristan: *beloved:* 5 Isolt 6 Iseult, Isolde
  uncle: 4 Mark
  villain: 5 Melot

Tristram Shandy author: 6 Sterne

triste (F.): sad 4 blue, dull 6 dismal 8 mournful 9 sorrowful 10 depressing, melancholy

trite: 4 dull, flat, hack, worn 5 banal, corny, stale, stock, tired, vapid 6 cliché, common, jejune, old hat 7 bromide, clichéd, prosaic, trivial 8 ordinary 9 hackneyed 10 threadbare, unoriginal, warmed-over 11 commonplace, stereotyped 12 conventional 13 platitudinous

triton: eft 4 newt 7 demigod 10 salamander

triturate: rub 5 crush, grind 6 bruise 9 comminute, pulverize

triumph: win 4 beat, best, gain 5 exult, glory 6 defeat, hurrah 7 conquer, prevail, rejoice, succeed, success, victory 8 flourish 10 exultation 11 achievement, celebration

triumvirate: 5 junta, triad 6 troika
  first: 6 Caesar, Pompey 7 Crassus
  second: 6 Antony 7 Lepidus 8 Octavian

trivet: 4 rack 5 stand 6 tripod 7 support

trivial: 5 banal, fluff, inane, minor, petty, small, trite 6 common, little, paltry, slight 7 nominal 8 ordinary, picayune, trifling 9 frivolous 10 negligible 11 unimportant 13 insignificant

troche: 4 pill 6 pastil, rotula, tablet 7 lozenge, pastile 8 pastille 9 small ball

trochilus: 7 warbler 9 goldcrest 11 hummingbird

trod: 4 path, walk 5 trace, track, tread 8 footpath, footstep

trogon: 4 bird 7 quetzal

troika: 5 triad 6 sleigh 8 carriage 11 triumvirate

Troilus: *beloved:* 8 Cressida
  father: 5 Priam
  mother: 6 Hecuba
  slayer: 8 Achilles

Trojan (see also **Troy**): 9 Dardanian
  epic: 5 Iliad
  king: 5 Priam
  prince: 5 Eneas, Paris 6 Aeneas, Hector
  prisoner: 5 Sinon
  river: 9 Scamander
  serpent victim: 7 Laocoon
  soothsayer: 7 Helenus 9 Cassandra

Trojan horse: 4 ruse, trap 6 ambush 8 saboteur 10 subversive
  builder: 5 Epeus

Trojan War: *cause:* 5 Helen
  hero: 4 Ajax 5 Eneas 6 Aeneas, Agenor, Hector, Nestor 7 Ulysses 8 Achilles, Diomedes, Odysseus 9 Agamemnon, Palamedes

troll: run, wag 4 bowl, fish, lure, pull, reel, roll, sing, song, turn 5 angle, catch, chant, dwarf, giant, gnome, round, spoon, trawl 6 trolly 7 revolve, trolley, trollop 9 circulate

trolley: car 4 cart, tram 5 block 6 barrow, sledge 8 carriage, handcart 9 streetcar

trollop: 4 doxy, drab, hang, slut 5 slump, whore 6 dangle, slouch, wanton 8 slattern 10 bedraggled, prostitute

trombone: 4 horn 7 sackbut

trommel: 5 sieve 6 screen

troop: lot 4 army, band, ging, host, line, pace, rout, step, walk, wave 5 corps, crowd, group 6 forces, legion, number, outfit, troupe 7 battery, cavalry, company, echelon, militia, phalanx 8 assembly, quantity, soldiers 9 associate, gathering, multitude 10 combatants, congregate 11 armed forces
  Anglo-Indian: 6 risala 7 ressala, risalah
  assembling: 6 muster
  quarters: 4 camp 5 etape 7 bivouac 8 barracks
  raise: 4 levy 5 draft 9 conscript
  seller to: 6 sutler 10 vivandiere

trooper: 6 hussar 7 soldier 9 policeman, troopship 10 cavalryman

trop: too 4 many

trope: 5 irony 6 simile 8 metaphor

trophy: cup 4 Emmy, palm, Tony 5 award, crown, Edgar, honor, medal, Oscar, prize 6 laurel, reward 7 memento 8 memorial, ornament 11 remembrance

tropic: 5 limit 8 boundary

tropical: hot 6 steamy, torrid
  animal: 4 alco, eyra 5 agama, coati, potto 6 agouti, iguana 7 peccary
  bird: ani 4 tody 5 jalap 6 toucan 7 jacamar
  fish: 4 toro 6 salema 7 piranha, squetee
  fruit: 4 date 5 guava, mango, papaw 6

banana, papaya **8** tamarind **9** pineapple
genus of herb: **4** evea, sida **5** tacca, urena **8** laportea
helmet: topi
plant: dal **4** aloe, arum, sida, taro **5** agave **6** alacad **7** cowhage, lantana **8** gardenia
plant genus: **5** rhoeo **6** cannas **7** bomarea, geonoma, hamelia
storm: cyclone, typhoon **9** hurricane
tree: ebo **4** ceba, coco, dali, eboe, etua, guao, mabi, palm **5** acapu, amate, artar, assai, balsa, banak, bongo, cacao, dalli, guama, guava, icica, nepal, nitta, njave, papaw, seron, zorro **6** baboen, bacury, banana, barbas, cazaba, chupon, dagame, espave, mammee, pawpaw, sapota **7** anubing, gateado, guacimo **8** amarillo, mangrove, sweetsop, tamarind **9** huamuchli, quebracho, sapodilla, sapotilha, sapotilla **10** frangipane, frangipani, manchineel **11** guachipilin

trot: hag, jog, run, tot **4** gait, pony **5** child, hurry **6** canter, hasten **7** toddler **11** translation

troth: **5** certy, faith, truth **6** certie, pledge **7** promise **8** fidelity **9** betrothal **10** engagement

trot out: **4** show **6** expose **7** display, show off

trottoir: **8** footpath, pavement, sidewalk

troubadour, troubador: **4** bard, poet, scop **5** scald **6** rhymer, singer **8** jongleur, minstrel, musician

trouble: ado, ail, irk, try, vex, woe **4** busy, care, cark, fike, fuss, harm, pain, sore, stir **5** anger, annoy, grief, labor, pains, tease, upset, worry **6** bother, burble, caddle, cumber, dither, effort, harass, impair, matter, mishap, molest, pester, plague, pother, sorrow, unrest **7** afflict, agitate, anxiety, chagrin, concern, disease, disturb, embroil, illness, perturb, torment, travail **8** aggrieve, calamity, disorder, disquiet, distress, exertion, hardship, mischief, vexation **9** adversity, incommode, interfere **10** difficulty, disarrange, discomfort, discommode, misfortune, perplexity, uneasiness **11** catastrophe, displeasure, encumbrance **13** inconvenience

troubled: **6** queasy **7** anxious, worried **9** disturbed, perturbed **10** distraught

troublemaker: **6** gossip **8** agitator, bad actor, nuisance

troublesome: **4** mean, ugly **5** pesky **6** wicked **8** annoying, fashious **9** difficult, pestilent, turbulent, vexatious, wearisome **10** bothersome, burdensome, oppressive

troublous: **6** stormy, turbid **7** unquiet **8** restless, troubled **9** unsettled **10** distraught

trough: bin **4** bosh, bowl, dale, moat, tank, tomb **5** bakie, basin, chute **6** buddle, coffin, dugout, gutter, sluice **7** channel, conduit
between waves: **6** valley
inclined: **5** chute

trounce: sue **4** beat, flog, roat, whip **5** scold, tramp, whomp **6** cudgel, defeat, indict, punish, ramble, thrash, wallop **7** censure, clobber, journey

troupe: **4** band **5** group **7** company **9** cuadrilla (Sp.)

trouper: **5** actor **11** entertainer

troupial: **6** oriole **7** cacique, cowbird **9** blackbird **10** meadowlark

trousers: **5** cords, jeans, pants, trews **6** denims, skilts, slacks **8** breeches, britches, culottes, jodphurs, knickers **9** dungarees, pantalets, shintiyan **10** pantaloons
foreign: **7** shalwar **9** shaksheer, shulwaurs **10** calzoneras (Sp.)

trout: sea **4** char, peal **5** brook, brown, river, sewen **6** finnac, grilse **7** gilaroo, rainbow **8** finnacle, speckled **9** steelhead **10** squeteague
lake: **9** namaycush

trovatore (It.): **10** troubadour

trove: **8** treasure **9** discovery **10** collection **12** accumulation

trow: **4** boat, hope **5** barge, faith, fancy, smack, think, troll, trust **6** belief, expect **7** believe, imagine, suppose **8** covenant **9** catamaran

Troy (see also **Trojan, Trojan horse, Trojan War**): **5** Iliac, Ilian, Ilion, Ilium, Troad, Troas **8** Teucrian
defender: **6** Aeneas, Hector
epic: **5** Iliad **6** Aeneid **7** Odyssey
excavator: **6** Blegen **8** Dorpfeld **10** Schliemann
founder: **4** Ilus, Tros
king: **5** Priam
mountain: Ida
pert. to: **5** Iliac **6** Trojan
strait: **10** Hellespont **11** Dardanelles

troy weight: **5** grain, ounce, pound **11** pennyweight

truant: **4** idle **5** stray **6** beggar, errant **7** shirker, vagrant **8** straying, vagabond, wanderer **9** shiftless
play: **4** skip **5** ditch, miche

truce: **4** halt, lull, pact **5** break, pause, peace, treve (F.) **7** respite **9** armistice, cease-fire, cessation **12** intermission

truck: van **4** cart, deal, dray, jeep, move **5** lorry, trade, trash **6** barrow, barter, camion, peddle, potter **7** bargain, produce, rubbish, traffic, trolley, trundle **8** business, commerce, exchange, handcart **9** negotiate, transport, vegetable **10** handbarrow **11** association, intercourse
with trailer: **4** semi

truckle: 4 deal, fawn 5 toady, wheel 6 caster, cheese, cringe, submit 7 trundle 8 bootlick 11 apple-polish 12 knuckle under

truckling: 7 servile

truculent: 4 mean, rude 5 cruel, harsh 6 brutal, fierce, savage 7 abusive 8 ruthless, scathing 9 barbarous, ferocious 11 belligerent, destructive

trudge: pad 4 hike, pace, plod, slog, trek, wade, walk 5 march, stoge, tramp 6 trapes 7 traipse

true: 4 just, leal (Sc.), pure, real, vera (L.), very, vrai (F.) 5 align, aline, exact, level, loyal, plumb, right, sooth, valid 6 actual, adjust, honest, lawful, proper, steady 7 certain, correct, devoted, factual, genuine, germane, precise, sincere, staunch, upright 8 accurate, bonafide, constant, faithful, reliable, rightful, unerring, virtuous 9 authentic, steadfast, truepenny, unfeigned, veracious, veritable 10 legitimate 11 trustworthy, unfaltering

truelove: 10 sweetheart

truffle: 5 candy, tuber 6 fungus 8 earthnut

truism: 5 adage, axiom, maxim 6 cliché 8 veracity 9 platitude 11 commonplace

Truk island: Tol 4 Moen, Udot, Uman 6 Dublon

trull: 4 dell, girl, lass 5 demon, fiend, giant, wench 6 blowze, callet, wanton 7 trollop 8 strumpet 10 prostitute

truly: 4 iwis, very, well 6 atwee, dinkum, indeed, really, verily 9 certainly, sincerely

trump: cap, pam 4 beat, ruff 5 outdo, pedro 7 nonplus, surpass 8 jew's-harp

trumpery: 5 fraud, showy, trash, weeds 6 deceit, paltry 7 rubbish 8 gimcrack, nonsense, trickery 9 deception, worthless

trumpet: 4 horn, tout 5 blare, bugle 6 blazon, bucina (L.), cornet, funnel, kerana, summon 7 begonia, clarion, publish 8 denounce, proclaim
belt: 7 baldric
blare: 6 sennet 7 fanfare, tantara
caller: 7 Gabriel
muffler: 4 mute
ram's horn: 6 shofar
stage direction: 6 sennet

trumpet creeper: 5 plant 6 tecoma 7 campsis 8 bignonia

trumpeter: 4 bird, swan 6 herald, pigeon, tooter 7 yakamik

trumpet shell: 6 triton

truncate: cut, lop, top 4 dock 6 lessen 7 shorten 10 abbreviate

truncheon: 4 club, stem 5 baton, staff 6 cudgel 8 fragment, splinter 9 billy club 10 nightstick

trundle: bed 4 bowl, cart, hoop, roll 5 truck, twirl, wheel, whirl 6 barrow, caster, pinion, rotate 7 revolve 11 wheelbarrow

trunk: box 4 body, bole, boot, pipe, runt, stem, tank, tube 5 chest, shaft, snout, stock, torso 6 caudex, coffer, corpse, locker, thorax 7 baggage, carcass 9 proboscis
animal: 4 soma 5 snout, torso

truss: tie, wap 4 bind, furl, gird, hang, lade, pack 6 bundle, fasten 7 arrange, bracket, enclose, package, support, tighten 10 strengthen

trust: 4 affy, care, duty, hope, rely, task, ward 5 faith 6 belief, cartel, charge, credit, depend, merger, rely on 7 believe, combine, confide, consign, count on, custody, keeping, loyalty, presume 8 affiance, commenda, credence, depend on, reliance, security 9 assurance, certainty, certitude, coalition, fiduciary, syndicate 10 commission, confidence, conviction, dependence 11 combination 12 conglomerate

trustee: 6 bailee 7 sindico 8 director, guardian 9 fiduciary, garnishee 13 administrator

trustful: 7 devoted 9 confiding 13 unquestioning

trustworthy: 4 safe, true 5 siker, solid, tried 6 honest, secure, sicker 7 certain, upright 8 accurate, credible, faithful, fiducial, reliable 9 authentic, confiding 10 dependable 12 confidential

truth: 4 fact 5 maxim, sooth, troth 6 candor, certes, gospel, verity 7 honesty, loyalty, veritas 8 accuracy, fidelity, veracity 9 agreement, constancy, integrity, principle, sincerity 11 correctness, genuineness, uprightness 12 authenticity, faithfulness 14 verisimilitude
goddess: 4 Maat
personification of: Una
self-evident: 5 axiom 6 truism

truthful: 5 frank 6 candid, honest 7 correct, factual, sincere 9 veracious, veridical

try: aim, bid, irk, vex 4 cull, sift, test 5 annoy, assay, essay, ettle (Sc.), fling, found, judge, prove, taste, tempt, trial 6 aspire, choose, effort, hansel, harass, plague, purify, refine, render, sample, screen, select, strain, strive 7 adjudge, afflict, approve, attempt, contest, extract, handsel, subject, torment, venture 8 audition, endeavor, irritate, separate, struggle 9 ascertain, undertake 10 experience, experiment 11 demonstrate, investigate

trying: 5 rough, tight, tough 6 severe, taxing, vexing 7 exigent, irksome, onerous, painful 8 annoying 9 demanding 10 irritating 12 exasperating

tryst: 4 date, fair, meet 5 visit 6 affair, market

7 bespeak, meeting **9** agreement, gathering **10** engagement, rendezvous **11** appointment, assignation

tsar: 4 czar, Ivan, king, tzar **5** Peter **6** caesar, despot **7** emperor **8** autocrat, Nicholas

tsetse fly: 4 kivu **6** muscid **8** glossina
    disease: **6** nagana **16** sleeping sickness

t-shaped: tau

tsine: 6 wild ox **7** banteng

tuatara, tuatera: 6 iguana, lizard

tub: box, kid, pan, pot, soe, vat **4** bath, boat, bowl, cask, cool, ship, tram **5** barge, basin, bathe, bowie (Sc.), eshin, fatty, keeve, skeel **6** bucket, pulpit, vessel **7** bathtub, cistern, tubfish **9** container

tuba: 7 helicon
    mouthpiece: **5** bocal

tubal: 8 pipelike

Tubalcain's father: 6 Lamech

Tubal's father: 7 Japheth

tubber: 6 cooper, pickax

tubby: 5 obese, plump, round, squat **6** chubby, portly, rotund

tube: 4 bore, duct, hose, lull, pipe, reed **5** chute, diode, straw **6** ampule, cannon, siphon, subway, tremie, triode, tunnel **7** cannula, conduit, fistula, pipette, tetrode **8** adjutage, bombilla (Sp.), cylinder **9** telescope **10** television
    anatomical: **7** salpinx
    for winding silk: cop
    glass: **6** sipper **7** pipette
    remove by: **6** siphon, syphon
    system of: **6** pipage

tuber: oca, yam **4** beet, bulb, clog, eddo, root, taro, yamp **5** jalap, salep **6** potato **8** swelling **9** tubercule **10** tuberosity **12** protuberance

tubercle: 6 nodule **10** prominence

tuberculosis: 8 phthisis **11** consumption

Tubuai island: 4 Rapa **6** Rurutu **8** Rimatara

tubular: 4 pipy **5** round **11** cylindrical

tuck: eat, nip **4** draw, fold, food, gird, hang, hide, poke, wrap **5** cover, cramp, feast, pinch, pleat, scold, stuff, sword **6** energy, gather, hamper, rapier **7** consume, shorten, tighten

tucked up: 7 cramped, worn out **8** fatigued, hampered **9** exhausted

tucker: bib **4** food, meal, tire, wilt **5** board, weary **6** collar, ration **7** exhaust, fatigue **10** chemisette

Tuesday: 5 mardi (F.) **6** martes (Sp.) **7** martedi (It.), **8** Dienstag (G.)
    god of: Tiu, Tyr
    Shrove: **9** Mardi Gras

tuft: 4 beat, coma, disk, wisp **5** beard, bunch, clump, crest, mound, shock **6** button, comose, dollop, goatee, pompon, tassel **7** cluster, cowlick, fetlock, scopula, topknot **8** imperial
    of feathers: **7** panache
    of hair: **4** tate
    vascular: **6** glomus

tuft-hunter: 4 snob

tug: lug, tit, tow **4** boat, drag, draw, haul, maul, pull, rope, toil, yank **5** chain, exert, hitch, labor, strap, trace **6** drudge, effort, strain, strife, strive, tussle **7** contend, contest, tugboat, wrestle **8** struggle **11** counterpull

tuition: 4 care, fees **5** watch **6** charge **7** custody, payment **8** teaching **9** education **10** protection **11** instruction **12** guardianship

tule: 7 bulrush

tumble: 4 drop, fall, flop, leap, mess, roll, slip, trip, veer **5** pitch, sault, slope, spill, whirl **6** happen, rumple, spring, tousle **7** clutter, plummet, stumble **8** collapse, discover, dishevel, disorder **9** confusion, overthrow **10** disarrange, handspring, somersault **11** precipitate
    down: **11** dilapidated

tumbler: dog **4** cart, pupa **5** glass **6** dunker, pigeon, roller, vessel **7** acrobat, gymnast, tippler, tumbrel

tumbrel, tumbril: 4 cart **5** wagon **8** dumpcart

tumefy: 4 puff **5** swell **7** inflate

tumid: 6 turgid **7** bloated, bulging, fustian, pompous, swollen, teeming **8** bursting, enlarged, inflated **9** bombastic, distended, plethoric **10** rhetorical **11** protuberant

tumor: wen **4** beal, cyst, wart **5** edema, gumma **6** ambury, anbury, glioma, growth, lipoma **7** bombast, sarcoma **8** blastoma, ganglion, hepatoma, neoplasm, papiloma, sarocele, swelling **12** protuberance
    benign: **7** fibroid, fibroma
    hard: **8** scirrhus
    operation: **8** ancotomy
    small: wen **7** papilla
    study of: **8** oncology

tumult: 4 din, mob **4** flap, fray, fuss, riot, to-do **5** babel, brawl, broil, noise **6** affray, babble, bedlam, bustle, clamor, dirdum (Sc.), emeute, hubbub, jangle, racket, uproar **7** bluster, bobbery, ferment, tempest, turmoil **8** disorder, outbreak, outburst, paroxysm, upheaval, uprising **9** agitation, commotion, confusion, distemper, hurlement, maelstrom **10** convulsion, excitement, hullabaloo, hurly burly, turbulence **11** disturbance, pandemonium

tumultuous: 4 high, wild **5** rough, rowdy **6** stormy **7** furious, raucous, violent **9** termagant, turbulent **10** boisterous, hurly-burly

tumulus: 4 hill, tump **5** mound **6** barrow **7** hillock

tun: cup, jar, keg, tub, vat **4** butt, cask **5** drink **6** barrel, guzzle, vessel **7** chimney **8** hogshead

tuna: **8** albacore, skipjack **11** prickly pear

tune: air, fix, key, lay, pat **4** lilt, port, song, sync, tone **5** carol, dirge, drant, sound, synch **6** accord, choral, draunt, melody, strain, string **7** chorale, concert, concord, harmony, sonance **8** anglaise, regulate **9** agreement **10** adjustment

tuneful: **7** lyrical, melodic, musical, tunable **9** melodious **10** concordant, euphonious, harmonious

tungsten: **7** wolfram **8** scheelin
alloy: **8** carboloy

tunic: **4** coat, jupe, robe, toga, vest **5** acton, frock, gippo, jamah, jamah, jamah, smock **6** blouse, caftan, chiton, kirtle **8** colobium **10** cote-hardie, sticharion **11** houppelande

tunicate: **4** salp **5** salpa **12** marine animal

Tunisia: *capital:* **5** Tunis
  city: **4** Sfax **6** Sousse **7** Bizerte **8** Kairouan
  currency: **5** dinar **7** millime
  leader: **9** Bourguiba
  measure: saa, sah **4** saah **5** cafiz, whiba **6** mettar **9** millerole
  mountain: **5** Atlas **7** Shanabi **8** Tabassah
  people: **4** Arab **6** Berber
  ruins: **8** Carthage
  weight: saa **4** rotl **5** artal, artel, ratel, uckia **6** kantar

tunk: rap, tap **5** thump

tunnel: net **4** adit, bore, flue, tube **6** burrow, funnel **7** conduit **8** excavate **9** underpass **10** passageway, smokestack

tunny: **4** tuna **7** bluefin **8** albacore

tupelo: gum **4** tree **5** nyssa

tur: pea **4** goat

turban: cap, fez, hat **4** pata **5** scarf **6** fillet, mandil **7** bandana **9** headdress

turbid: **4** dark, dull, foul **5** dense, dirty, gumly (Sc.), muddy, murky, riley, roily, thick **6** cloudy, grumly (Sc.), impure, opaque **7** muddled, obscure **8** confused, polluted **9** perplexed
render: **4** roil

turbine: **6** engine
part: **6** stator
wheel: **5** rotor

turbot: **5** brill **8** flatfish

turbulence: **4** fury **5** babel, fight **6** fracas, furore, pother, tumult, uproar **7** bluster, ferment, rioting, turmoil **8** disorder **9** agitation, commotion, confusion **11** disturbance, pandemonium

turbulent: **4** wild **5** rough **6** raging, stormy, unruly **7** furious, violent **8** agitated, swirling **9** clamorous **10** boisterous, rip-roaring, tumultuous **11** tempestuous

turdine bird: **6** thrush

turf: sod **4** area, flag, peat, vell **5** divot, grass, sward, track **6** region, sphere **7** terrain **9** racetrack **12** neighborhood

turgid: **5** tumid **7** bloated, pompous, swollen, turgent **8** inflated, swelling **9** bombastic, distended, flatulent, grandiose, tumescent **10** rhetorical **12** magniloquent **13** grandiloquent

Turk: aga **5** Tatar **7** Osmanli, Ottoman **9** Kizilbash

Turkestan: See **Turkistan**

turkey: tom **4** flop **5** poult **7** bustard, failure, gobbler
buzzard: **7** vulture
young: **5** poult

Turkey: *agent:* **6** Kehaya
  army corps: **4** ordu **8** seraglio
  army regiment: **4** alai
  bath: **6** hamman
  boat: **4** sail **6** mahone
  cabinet: **5** divan
  camp: **7** palanka
  cap: **6** calpac
  capital: **6** Ankara
  cavalryman: **5** spahi **6** spahee
  city: bir **4** Homs, Sert, Urfa **5** Adana, Bursa, Izmir, Konya, Siirt, Sivas **6** Aintab, Edessa, Edirne, Elaziz, Marash, Samsun, Smyrna **7** Broussa, Erzurum, Kayseri, Scutari, Skutari, Uskudar **8** Istanbul, Stamboul **9** Eskisehir **10** Adrianople, Diyarbekir
  commander: **4** amir, emir **5** ameer, emeer, pacha, pasha **6** sirdar **9** seraskier
  council: **5** divan, diwan
  court: **5** porte
  currency: **4** atun, kuru, lira, lire, para **5** akcha, asper, pound, rebia **6** akcheh, sequin, zequin **7** altilik, beshlik, chequin, chiquin, pataque, piaster **8** medjidie, zecchino **9** medjidieh
  decree: **5** irade **11** hatti-sherif **12** hatti-humaiun, hatti-humayum
  deputy: **6** kahaya
  dignitary: **5** pasha *(cont.)*

Turkey *(cont.)*
  division: **4** caza **5** adana **6** eyalet **7** vilayet **8** villayet
  drink: **5** airan
  dynasty: **6** Seljuk
  empire: **7** Ottoman
  fig: **5** eleme, elemi
  flag: **4** alem, toug **9** horsetail
  general: **5** kamal
  gold coin: **4** lira **6** mahbub
  hat: fez **6** calpac
  infidel: **6** giaour
  inn: **6** imaret **7** cafenet
  javelin: **5** jerid **6** jeered
  judge: **4** cadi
  liquor: **4** raki **5** rakee **6** mastic
  man-of-war: **6** carvel **7** caravel **9** caravelle
  measures: dra, oka, oke, pic, pik **4** alma, draa, hatt, khat, kile, zira **5** almud, berri, donum, fotin, kileh, zirai **6** almude, arshin, chinik, djerib, halebi, parmak **7** arsheen, arshine, nocktat, parmack **9** pik halebi
  military camp: **4** ordu
  military rank: **6** chiaus **7** chaoush **8** bimbashi, binbashi
  minister: **5** vizir **6** vizier
  mosque: **4** jami
  mountain: **6** Ararat
  musical instrument: **5** canum, kanum **7** kussier
  musket: **8** tophaike
  oak: **6** cerris
  official: **4** amir, emir **5** ameer, emeer **6** vizier **7** osmanli, subashi **8** subbassa
  palace: **5** serai
  policeman: **7** zaptiah, zaptieh
  prayer rug: **5** kulah, melas, meles
  religious war: **11** crescentade
  reservist: **5** redif
  river: Gok **5** Mesta, Sarus **6** Delice, Seihun, Seyhan, Tigris **7** Maritsa **9** Euphrates
  saber: **6** odolus
  sailor: **8** galionji **9** galiongee
  slave: **8** mameluke
  soldier: **6** nizami **8** janizary **9** janissary **11** bashi-bazouk
  statue: **8** tanzimat
  storage place: **5** ambar
  strait: **8** Bosporus **11** Dardanelles
  sword: **7** yatagan **8** yataghan
  tambourine: **5** daira
  tax: **5** vergi **6** avania, caphar
  title: ali **4** amir, baba **5** ameer, basha, pasha **6** bashaw **7** effendi
  tobacco: **7** chibouk, Latakia **9** chibouque
  treasurer: **8** deftedar
  veil: **7** yashmac, yashmak **8** maharmah
  weight: oka, oke **4** dram, kile, ocha, rotl **5** artal, artel, cequi, cheke, kerat, kileh, maund, obolu, ratel **6** batman, dirhem, kantar, miskal **7** drachma, quintal, yusdrum
  wheat: **6** bulgar

turkey buzzard: **4** aura **9** gallinazo
Turkish: **7** Osmanli
  toweling: **10** terrycloth
Turkistan: *cities:* **6** Frunze, Kokand **7** Alma-Ata, Andijan, Bukhara **8** Tashkent **9** Samarkand
  highland: **6** Pamirs
  mountain: **4** Alai **6** Kunlun **8** Tian Shan
  regiment: **4** alai
Turkmenistan: *capital:* **8** Ashgabat **9** Ashkhabad
  carpet: **5** Tekke, Yomud **6** Afghan **7** Boghara, Bokhara
  city: **4** Mary **5** Kerki **6** Kushka
  desert: **7** Karakum
  fur: **9** astrakhan **11** Persian lamb
turmeric: rea **4** herb **5** spice **7** curcuma **9** bloodroot
turmoil: ado, din **4** hurl, toil, toss **5** chaos, hurly, labor, touse, upset, worry **6** harass, tumult, unrest, uproar, welter **7** ferment, quarrel, tempest, trouble **8** brouhaha, disorder, disquiet, drudgery **9** agitation, commotion, confusion **10** turbulence **11** disturbance, pandemonium **12** perturbation

turn: bow, lap, rev, yaw **4** airt, bend, bent, bout, cant, char, head, plow, roll, skew, slew, slue, sour, spin, tack, veer, vert **5** alter, angle, avert, cramp, crank, crook, curve, flair, hinge, knack, pivot, quirk, scare, screw, sheer, shift, shock, shunt, spell, swing, swirl, tarve, twirl, twist, upset, wheel, whirl, whorl **6** bought, change, circle, curdle, detour, direct, divert, gyrate, invert, ponder, rotate, sprain, swerve, swivel, talent, wimple (Sc.), zigzag **7** circuit, convert, deflect, derange, deviate, digress, diverge, ferment, meander, rebound, reverse, revolve **8** exchange, nauseate, persuade **9** cinclamen, deviation, influence, pirouette, transform, translate **11** disposition **12** metamorphose *about:* 6 rotate 7 revolve 9 alternate

inside out: 5 evert 6 invert

inward: 9 introvert

left: haw 4 port, wynd, wyne

outward: 5 evert, splay 8 extrorse 9 extrovert

right: gee 9 starboard

sour: 5 blink, spoil 8 acescent

to stone: 7 petrify 8 lapidify

turnabout: 8 reversal 9 about-face, volte-face

turn around: 4 gyre, slew, slue, spin 5 pivot, twirl 9 about-face, volte-face

turn aside: 4 skew, veer 5 avert, sheer, shunt 6 detour, divert, swerve 7 deflect, deviate, digress

turn away: shy 5 avert, avoid, deter, evade, repel, shunt 6 depart, desert, divert, swerve 7 abandon, decline, deflect, deviate, dismiss, diverge

turn back: 4 fold 5 repel 6 return, revert 7 evolute, retrace 9 inversion 10 recrudesce, retroverse

turncoat: 7 traitor 8 apostate, quisling, renegade 10 changeling

turn down: 4 fold, veto 6 invert, refuse, reject 7 decline 9 blackball, repudiate

turned up: 4 snub 9 retrousse

turner: 7 gymnast, tumbler

turn in: 5 rat on 6 betray, retire 7 deliver, produce 8 hand over, inform on

turning point: 6 crisis 8 decision, juncture, landmark

turnip: 4 neep (Sc.) 5 dunce, watch 8 rutabaga 9 blockhead

turnip-shaped: 8 napiform

turnkey: 5 screw 6 jailer, warder

turn off: 4 hang 5 marry, repel, shunt 6 detour, divert 7 consign, deflect, disgust, dismiss, putrefy 9 discharge

turn out: 4 bear, oust, trig 5 array, evert, evict, expel, prove 6 outfit, output, siding 7 abandon, costume, dismiss, produce, reverse, striker 8 equipage, withdraw 9 discharge, equipment, eventuate 10 attendance

turn over: 4 keel 5 spill, upend, upset 6 invert, ponder, reform 7 capsize, evolute, examine 8 consider, delegate, overturn, transfer 10 relinquish, somersault

turnover: 4 tart 7 shake-up 8 empanada (Sp.), flapjack

turnpike: 4 road 7 highway 8 toll road, tollgate

gatekeeper: 7 pikeman

turnstile: 4 tirl 5 stile

turnstone: 4 bird 5 pover 6 redleg

turn up: 6 appear, arrive, crop up, show up

turpentine: 4 thus 5 resin, rosin 7 galipot, thinner 9 oleoresin

tree: 4 pine 6 tarata 9 terebinth

turpitude: 6 fedity 8 baseness, vileness 9 decadence, depravity 10 corruption 11 dissolution 12 degeneration

turquoise: 4 blue 5 color, stone 10 chalchuite 12 greenish-blue

turret: 5 tower 6 belfry, cupola 7 minaret, steeple 8 gunhouse, turricle

turtle: 5 arrau, caret, torup 6 cooter, emydea, jurara 7 reptile, snapper 8 chelonia, matamata, shagtail, terrapin, tortoise 10 loggerhead, thalassian 11 leatherback

genus of: 4 emys 7 caretta, testudo 9 chelodina

lower shell: 8 plastron

Tuscany: *ancient people:* 8 Etruscan

city: 4 Pisa 5 Siena 7 Firenze, Leghorn, Livorno 8 Florence

river: 4 Arno

tusk: 4 fang, horn 5 ivory, tooth 9 scrivello

tussis: 5 cough

tussle: 4 spar 5 fight 6 tousel, tousle 7 contend, contest, grapple, scuffle, wrestle 8 argument, conflict, skirmish, struggle 9 scrimmage

tussock: 4 tuft 5 bunch, clump 7 hassock

tut: 4 hush 5 scold 6 rebuke

tutelage: 7 nurture 8 guidance, teaching 9 tutorship 11 instruction 12 guardianship

tutelary: 10 protecting

gods: 5 Lares 7 penates

tutor: don 5 coach, drill, guide, teach, train, watch 6 docent, ground, master, mentor, school 7 educate, grinder, pedagog, teacher 8 guardian, instruct 9 pedagogue, preceptor 10 discipline

tutta, tutti, tutto (It.): all 5 whole 6 entire

tuyere: tew 4 pipe 5 tewel 6 nozzle

twaddle: rot 4 bosh, bunk, chat 5 haver, prate 6 babble, drivel, fottle, gabble, piffle 7 prattle 8 nonsense 9 poppycock 10 balderdash

twangy: 5 nasal

tweak: 4 jerk, pull 5 pinch, twist 6 twitch

tweet: 4 peep 5 cheep, chirp 7 chirrup

tweezers: 7 pincers, pincher 9 merganser

Twelfth Night: *author:* 11 Shakespeare

character: 6 Olivia, Orsino 8 Malvolio 9 Toby Belch 15 Andrew Aguecheek

twenty: 5 corge, kappa, score

twenty-faced: 11 icosahedral

twerp: 4 brat, jerk 5 sprat 6 squirt 7 big shot 9 pipsqueak

twibil: axe 6 chisel 7 mattock

twice: bis (L.) 6 doubly, encore 7 replica, twofold

twig: see 4 beat, mode, pull, stem 5 birch, bough, scion, shoot, spray, sprig, stick, style, tweak, withe 6 branch, detect, fescue, notice, sallow, switch, twitch, wattle 7 fash-

ion, observe **8** discover, off shoot, perceive **9** apprehend **10** comprehend, understand
bundle: **5** besom, fagot **6** barsom

twiggy: **4** thin **6** slight **7** slender **8** delicate

twilight: **4** dusk **5** gloam **6** dimmet **7** decline, evening, obscure **8** eventide, gloaming, glooming **9** cocklight, nightfall **10** crepuscule *of the Gods:* **8** Ragnarok **15** Gotterdämmerung **17** Goetterdaemmerung

twill: rib **5** chino, cloth, quill, weave

twin: two **4** dual, mate, pair, part **5** gemel, match, sever, twain **6** couple, double, fellow, sunder **7** sibling, two-fold **8** didymous **9** duplicate **11** counterpart
crystal: **5** macle
kind of: **9** fraternal, identical
one: **5** gemel
Siamese: Eng **5** Chang
stars: **6** Castor, Gemini, Pollux

twinge: tic **4** ache, pain, pang **5** pinch, qualm, tweak **6** stitch, twitch **7** scruple

twine: ran **4** bend, coil, cord, hemp, rope, turn, vine, warp, wind, wrap **5** braid, sisal, snarl, twist **6** encurl, enfold, enlace, infold, mingle, string, tangle, thread **7** anamite, embrace, wreathe **8** encircle, undulate **9** interlace **10** interweave **11** convolution, intermingle

twink: **6** punish, thrash **9** chaffinch

twinkle: **4** wink **5** blink, flash, gleam, glint, shine **7** flicker, flutter, glimmer, glisten, glitter, instant, light up, shimmer **9** coruscate **11** scintillate **16** sparkle nictitate

twinkler: **4** star **8** sparkler

twirl: **4** coil, curl, gyre, move, spin, turn, wind **5** querl, swirl, twist, wheel, whirl **6** gyrate, rotate **7** revolve, twizzle **8** flourish, rotation **9** pirouette, whirligig **11** convolution

twist: **4** bend, bias, coil, cord, curl, kink, knot, skew, slew, slue, spin, tirl (Sc.), turn, wind, yarn **5** braid, crink, crook, curve, dance, gnarl, hinge, quirk, screw, snake, tweak, twine, whirl, wring **6** hankle, spiral, sprain, squirm, thread, torque, wrench, writhe, zigzag **7** confuse, contort, deviate, distort, entwine, flexure, meander, perplex, pervert, revolve, scatter, tendril, torment, torsion, torture, wreathe **8** appetite, squiggle **9** constrain, corkscrew, deviation, insinuate **10** intertwine, interweave **11** convolution, peculiarity **12** misrepresent

twisted: cam, wry **4** awry **5** askew, crazy **6** warped **7** complex, tortile

twister: **4** roll, turn **7** cruller, cyclone, mallard, tornado **8** doughnut **9** whirlwind **10** somersault, waterspout

twit: guy, kid, tax **4** gibe, jive, josh, mock **5** blame, chirp, taunt, tease **6** deride, needle **7** upbraid **8** reproach, ridicule

twitch: nip, tic, tie, tug **4** draw, jerk, jump, pick, pull, skid, yank **5** grasp, pluck, shake, start, thong, tweak **6** clutch, fasten, snatch **8** convulse **9** vellicate **11** contraction

twitter: **4** chat **5** chirp, run on, shake **6** giggle, titter, tremor **7** chatter, chitter, flutter, tremble **9** agitation

two: dos (Sp.), duo, twa (Sc.) **4** beta (Gr.), both, deux (F.), dual, duet, dyad, pair, team, zwei (Gr.) **5** brace, deuce, twain, twins **6** binary, binate, couple, double **7** company, twosome
chambered: **9** bicameral
edged: **9** ancipital
headed: **11** dicephalous
languages: **9** bilingual
metrical feet: **6** dipody
parts: **6** bident **9** bifurcate **11** dichotomous
pert. to: **4** dual **6** dyadic
weeks: **9** fortnight
winged: **7** bialate **8** dipteral **9** dipterous

two-bit: **5** cheap

two bits: **7** quarter

two-faced: **5** false **9** deceitful, insincere **11** treacherous **12** hypocritical
god: **5** Janus

two-fisted: **6** virile **8** vigorous

two-foot: **5** biped **7** bipedal

two-pronged: **6** bident

two-sided: **9** bilateral

two-spot: **5** deuce

two-time: **5** cheat **6** betray **7** deceive **11** double-cross

two-tone: **7** bicolor

twofold: **4** dual, twin **5** duple **6** bifold, binary, double, duplex **7** diploid **9** bifarious, duplicate

twopenny: ale **4** mean **5** cheap **8** tuppenny **9** worthless

twosome: duo **4** duet, pair **6** couple

tycoon: VIP **5** baron, mogul, nabob **7** magnate **9** executive, financier **12** entrepreneur **13** industrialist

tydie: **4** bird, wren **8** titmouse

tyee: **5** chief

tyke, tike: cur, dog, imp, tot **5** child **6** moppet, shaver **7** bumpkin

tylopod: **5** camel

tympan: **4** drum **8** membrane

tympanum: **6** tympan **7** eardrum **10** kettledrum

tympany: **7** bombast, conceit **9** inflation **10** distention, turgidness

Tyndareus: *kingdom:* **6** Sparta
wife: **4** Leda

type: gem, ilk, lot **4** font, form, kern, kind, mark, mold, norm, pica, sign, slug, sort **5** agate, brand, class, doric, elite, genre, genus, group, ideal, ionic, metal, model,

mould, order, pearl, print, roman, stamp, token, write **6** emblem, italic, minion, nature, rubric, stripe, symbol **7** brevier, example, impress, paragon, pattern, species **8** boldface, classify, original, standard **9** bourgeois, character, condensed, nonpareil, represent **10** persuasion **11** Baskerville
block: **4** quad **7** quadrat
frame: **5** chase
line: **4** slug
mold: **6** matrix
size: **4** pica, ruby **5** agate, elite, pearl **6** cicero, minion, primer **7** brevier, diamond **9** excelsior, nonpareil
slanting: **6** italic
stroke: **5** serif
tray: **6** galley
typeset: 7 compose
typesetter: 7 printer **8** linotype, monotype **10** compositor **11** typographer
typewriter part: key **4** bail, bale **6** platen, ribbon, spacer **8** carriage **9** tabulator
typhoon: 4 blow, gale, gust, wind **5** storm **7** cyclone **9** hurricane
typical: 5 ideal, model, stock, typal, usual **6** common, normal **7** average, classic, regular **9** exemplary, schematic **10** emblematic, figurative **14** characteristic, representative

typify: 6 embody **9** epitomize, exemplify, prefigure, represent, symbolize
tyrannical: 5 cruel, harsh **6** brutal, lordly, unjust **7** slavish **8** absolute, despotic **9** arbitrary, imperious **10** autocratic, oppressive **11** dictatorial, domineering **13** authoritarian
tyrannosaurus: 8 dinosaur
tyranny: 5 rigor **7** fascism **8** iron heel, severity **9** autocracy, despotism, harshness **10** oppression
tyrant: 4 czar, tsar, tzar **6** caesar, despot **7** fuehrer, monarch, usurper **8** autocrat, dictator, martinet, oligarch **9** oppressor, strong man **11** slave driver
murder: **11** tyrannicide
Tyre: *king:* **5** Belus, Hiram
noble: **7** Acerbas
prince: **8** Pericles
princess: **4** Dido
tyro: 4 tiro **5** pupil **6** novice, rookie **7** amateur, learner **8** beginner, neophyte, newcomer **9** commencer **10** apprentice **11** abecedarian
Tyrol: *mountains:* **4** Alps **6** Ortler, Otztal **9** Kitzbuhel **10** Hohe Tavern
tzar, czar, tsar: 4 king **5** ruler **6** tyrant **7** emperor
tzigane: 5 gypsy

U

ubermensch (G.): 8 superman
uberous: 7 copious 8 abundant, fruitful
ubiety: 8 location, position, relation 9 whereness
ubiquitous: 10 everywhere 11 omnipresent
U-boat: sub 7 pigboat 9 submarine
uca: 4 crab
udder: bag 4 dugs 5 gland
Uffizi site: 8 Florence
Uganda: *capital:* 7 Kampala
   city: 5 Jinja, Mbale 7 Entebbe
   currency: 4 cent 8 shilling
   lake: 8 Victoria
   leader: 7 Idi Amin
   valley: 9 Great Rift
ughten: 4 dawn, dusk 7 evening, morning 8 twilight
ugli: 5 fruit 6 citrus 7 tangelo
ugliness symbol: 4 toad
ugly: bad 4 base, evil, foul, mean, vile 5 awful, cross, grave, nasty, snivy, surly, toady 6 cranky, gorgon, homely, snivey, sullen 7 crabbed, hideous, ominous 8 grewsome, gruesome, horrible, terrible, unlovely 9 dangerous, fractious, frightful, graceless, grotesque, loathsome, monstrous, offensive, repulsive, revolting, unsightly 10 ill-favored, ill-natured, unpleasant 11 ill-tempered, quarrelsome, threatening, troublesome 12 cross-grained, disagreeable
Ugrian: *language:* 5 Mansi 6 Khanty, Ostyak 9 Hungarian
   people: 4 Avar 6 Magyar
ugsome: 6 horrid 9 abhorrent, frightful, loathsome
uhlan: 5 scout 6 lancer 7 soldier 10 cavalryman
uitlander: 5 alien 9 foreigner, outlander
ukase: 5 edict, order 6 decree 7 command 12 proclamation
ukelele, ukulele: uke

Ulalume author: Poe
ulcer: 4 noma, sore 6 canker, lesion 7 abscess, chancre, egilops 8 aegilops, fossette 9 cacoethes
   kind of: 6 peptic 8 duodenal
ulceration: 7 bedsore 8 helcosis
ule: 4 tree 6 caucho 10 rubber ball
uliginous: wet 4 oozy 5 moist, muddy 6 swampy
ullage: 4 lees 5 dregs 7 wantage 8 shortage 10 deficiency
ulna: 4 bone 5 elbow 7 cubitus, forearm
   end of: 5 ancon
ulster: 8 overcoat
ulterior: 5 later, privy 6 future 7 further, guarded, remoter 9 concealed 10 subsequent, succeeding, under wraps 11 undisclosed
ultimate: end 4 acme, best, dire, last 5 final, telos (Gr.), total 6 latest, remote 7 extreme, maximum, primary 8 absolute, eventful, eventual, farthest 9 elemental, uttermost 10 apotheosis, concluding, conclusive 11 fundamental
ultimatum: 5 order 6 demand, threat
ultra: top 5 kinky, outré 6 beyond 7 extreme, forward, radical 8 superior 9 excessive, extremist, fanatical 10 outlandish 11 extravagant
ulu: 5 knife
ululate: bay, cry, sob 4 hoot, howl, keen, wail, yelp 6 lament 7 screech
Ulysses: 8 Odysseus
   antagonist: 4 Irus
   author: 5 Joyce
   character: 5 Bloom, Molly 7 Dedalus
   dog: 5 Argos
   enchantress of: 5 Circe
   enemy: 8 Poseidon
   epic: 7 Odyssey

Ukraine: *capital:* 4 Kiev 5 Kiyev, Kyyiv
   city: 7 Donetsk, Kharkov
   currency: 6 grivna 7 hryvnia, schagiv
   Easter egg: 7 pysanky
   nuclear disaster site: 9 Chernobyl
   peninsula: 6 Crimea
   resort: 5 Yalta
   river: 5 Dnepr 6 Dnestr, Odessa 7 Pripyat
   soldier: 7 Cossack

father: **7** Laertes
friend: **6** Mentor
kingdom: **6** Ithaca
mother: **8** Anticlea
rescuer: Ino
son: **9** Telegonus **10** Telemachus
swineherd: **7** Eumaeus
temptress: **5** Circe
voyage: **7** odyssey
wife: **8** Penelope

umber: **5** brown, shade, visor **6** darken, shadow **7** protect, umbrere **8** grayling, umbrette

umbilicus: **4** cord, core **5** heart, navel

umbra: **4** fish **5** ghost, shade **6** shadow **7** phantom, vestige **10** apparition

umbrage: **4** fury, huff, rage **5** anger, cloak, doubt, pique, shade, trace, wrath **6** offend, shadow **7** dudgeon, foliage, offense, pretext, shelter **8** disfavor, disgrace, disguise **9** disesteem, semblance, suspicion **10** overshadow, protection

umbrageous: **5** shady **6** shaded **7** dubious **10** suspicious

umbrella: **4** gamp **5** blind, chute, guard, shade **6** brolly, chatta, payong, pileus, screen **7** parasol, protect, shelter **8** disguise, sunblind, sunshade **9** parachute **10** protection

umbrella tree: **8** magnolia

umbrette: **9** hammerkop **10** hammerhead

umbrous: **5** shady

umiak: **4** boat **6** oomiac, oomiak

umpire: **5** judge **6** decide, oddman **7** arbiter, daysman, oddsman, referee **9** supervise **10** arbitrator

Una boat: **7** catboat

unable: **6** cannot **8** disabled, helpless, impotent **9** incapable **11** incompetent, inefficient, unqualified

unaccented: **4** lene **6** atonic

unaccompanied: **4** bare, solo **5** alone

unaccountable: **7** strange **9** countless **10** mysterious **12** inexplicable, unfathomable **13** irresponsible

unaccustomed: new **7** strange **8** uncommon, unwonted **10** unfamiliar

unacquainted: **5** alien **7** strange, unusual **8** ignorant **9** unknowing **10** unfamiliar **13** inexperienced

unadorned: **4** bald, bare **5** naked, plain, stark **6** rustic, simple **7** austere

unadulterated: **4** neat, pure, true **5** clean, frank **6** honest **7** genuine, sincere, unmixed **8** straight **9** immutable, unalloyed

unaffected: **4** easy, naif, real **5** naive, plain **6** rustic, simple **7** artless, genuine, natural, sincere, unmoved **8** unbiased **9** ingenuous, unaltered, unfeigned, untouched

unalleviated: **4** hard **10** unrelieved

unalloyed: **4** pure **7** genuine, unmixed

unambiguous: **5** clear **7** decided **8** explicit

unanchored: **6** adrift

unanimous: **5** solid **6** mutual, united **8** agreeing **9** of one mind **10** concordant **11** consentient

unanimously: **5** as one **7** una voce

unanswerable: **5** final **10** conclusive **11** irrefutable

unappeasable: **10** implacable

unapproachable: **5** aloof **6** remote **7** distant **10** unsociable **11** standoffish **12** inaccessible

unarmed: **4** bare **5** inerm **11** defenseless

unaspirated: **4** lene

unassailable: **10** invincible **11** impregnable **12** invulnerable

unassuming: shy **6** humble, modest **7** natural **8** retiring **9** diffident **10** unaffected

unattached: **4** free **5** loose **6** single **9** unmarried **11** independent

unattractive: **4** rude, ugly **5** plain **6** homely **10** ungracious **11** unappealing

unau: **5** sloth

unavailing: **6** futile **8** bootless, gainless **9** fruitless

unavowed: **6** secret **8** ulterior

unaware: **6** unwary **8** heedless, ignorant

unbalanced: mad **6** insane, uneven **8** deranged, lopsided, one-sided

unbecoming: **4** rude **5** inept **6** clumsy, gauche **8** improper, unseemly, unworthy **10** indecorous, unsuitable **11** disgraceful **12** unattractive

unbefitting: **5** below **8** improper

unbelief: **7** atheism **8** paganism **10** skepticism **11** agnosticism, incredulity

unbelievable: **5** thick **6** absurd **8** fabulous **9** fantastic **10** incredible, ridiculous **11** implausible

unbeliever: **5** pagan **7** atheist, doubter, heretic, infidel, scoffer, skeptic **8** agnostic **11** freethinker

unbend: **4** rest, thaw **5** relax, untie, yield **6** loosen, uncock **7** slacken **8** unfasten

unbending: **5** rigid, stern, stiff **8** obdurate, resolute **10** inexorable, inflexible

unbiased: **4** fair, just **8** detached **9** impartial **12** unprejudiced

unbind: **4** free, undo **5** let go, untie **6** detach, loosen **7** absolve, deliver, release, unleash **8** dissolve, unfasten **9** unshackle

unbleached: **4** blae, ecru **5** beige **7** natural

unblemished: **4** pure **5** whole **6** chaste **8** flawless, spotless

unblushing: **6** brazen **8** immodest **9** shameless

unbolt: **4** open **5** unbar, unpin **6** unlock **8** unfasten

unbosom: **4** tell **6** reveal **7** confess, confide **8** disclose

unbound: 4 free 5 loose 10 unconfined

unbounded: 4 open 8 infinite 9 limitless, unchecked, unlimited 11 measureless

unbrace: 4 free, undo 5 carve, relax 6 loosen, reveal, weaken 8 disjoint, enfeeble

unbridled: 4 free 5 loose 7 violent 8 uncurbed 9 dissolute, unchecked 10 immoderate, licentious, ungoverned 11 intemperate 12 uncontrolled, unrestrained

unbroken: one 4 flat 5 undug, whole 6 entire, intact 7 untamed 8 unplowed 9 continual, undivided, unsubdued

unburden: rid 4 ease 5 empty, untax 6 unload 7 disload, relieve

uncanny: 4 eery 5 eerie, scary, weird 6 spooky 7 awkward, ghostly, strange 8 careless 9 dangerous, unnatural 10 mysterious

uncanonical: 10 apocryphal

unceasing: 6 eterne 7 endless, eternal 8 constant, unending 9 continual, incessant, perennial 11 everlasting

unceremonious: 4 curt 5 bluff, blunt, short 6 abrupt 8 familiar, informal

uncertain: 4 asea, dark, hazy, moot 5 fluky, vague 6 chancy, fitful, queasy, unsure 7 at a loss, dubious 8 aleatory, confused, doubtful, insecure, unsteady, variable, wavering 9 ambiguous, equivocal, hazardous, undecided 10 changeable, inconstant, indefinite, irresolute, precarious 11 vacillating

uncertainty: 4 were 5 doubt, query 6 gamble, wonder 7 dubiety 8 suspense 9 dubiosity 10 skepticism 11 vacillation

unchanging: 4 same 6 steady 7 eternal, forever, settled, uniform 9 immutable, permanent, steadfast, unvarying 10 invariable, stationary

unchaste: 4 lewd 5 bawdy 6 coarse, impure 7 haggard, obscene 8 immodest

unchecked: 4 free, rife 5 loose 7 rampant 9 unbounded, unbridled

uncia: 4 coin, inch 5 ounce 7 twelfth

uncivil: 4 rude 5 bluff, crass, crude 7 ill-bred 8 clownish, impolite 9 barbarous 10 indecorous, ungracious, unsuitable 11 ill-mannered, uncivilized 12 discourteous

uncivilized: 4 rude, wild 5 feral 6 brutal, ferine, savage 7 boorish 8 barbaric 9 barbarian, barbarous, primitive 10 outrageous, unmannerly

uncle: eme (Sc.), oom (Sc.) 10 pawnbroker
pert. to: 9 avuncular

Uncle Remus: *author:* 6 Harris
rabbit: 4 Brer

Uncle Tom's Cabin: *author:* 5 Stowe
character: 5 Eliza, Topsy 6 Legree 9 Little Eva 11 Simon Legree

unclean: 4 foul, tref, vile 5 black, dirty 6 common, filthy, impure, soiled 7 defiled, obscene, sullied 8 polluted, unchaste

unclose: ope 4 open 6 reveal 10 unreserved

unclothe: 5 spoil, strip 6 divest, expose 7 despoil, uncover, undress

unclothed: 4 bare, nude 5 naked

unclouded: 4 fair, open 5 clear, sunny

uncoil: 6 unlink, unwind

uncombined: 4 free 5 frank, loose 8 solitary 10 elementary

uncomfortable: 5 harsh 6 uneasy 7 awkward, prickly 8 scratchy

uncommon: odd 4 rare 5 extra, novel 6 choice, scarce, unique 7 special, strange, unusual 8 especial, unwonted 10 infrequent, remarkable 11 exceptional 12 unaccustomed

uncommunicative: 4 dumb 6 silent 8 reserved, reticent, taciturn 10 unsociable

uncompassionate: 5 stony 9 unfeeling

uncomplaining: 5 stoic 7 patient, stoical

uncomplicated: 5 plain 6 honest, simple

uncompromising: 4 firm 5 rigid, stern, tough 6 strict 9 unbending 10 determined, inflexible, unyielding

unconcealed: 4 bare, open 5 frank, overt

unconcerned: 4 cool, easy 5 aloof 6 casual, serene, stolid 7 passive 8 careless, composed, detached 9 apathetic, impassive, unworried 10 insouciant, nonchalant 11 indifferent

unconditional: 4 free 5 frank 8 absolute, explicit 11 categorical

unconfined: lax 4 free 5 loose 7 braless 9 boundless, limitless, ungirdled, unlimited 10 uncorseted

unconfused: 4 calm, sure 5 clear 6 steady

unconnected: 6 abrupt 8 detached, rambling, separate 10 incoherent

unconscionable: 5 undue 6 wanton 7 corrupt, extreme 9 excessive 10 outrageous

unconscious: out 6 asleep, torpid 7 stunned, unaware 8 comatose, ignorant, mindless 9 inanimate, lethargic, oblivious
render: 4 dope, stun 8 knock out
state: 4 coma 5 faint, sleep, swoon 6 stupor

unconsciousness: 6 torpor

unconstrained: 4 easy, free 7 natural 8 familiar 9 easygoing 11 spontaneous 12 unrestrained

uncontrollable: 4 wild 6 unruly 11 intractable

uncontrolled: 4 free, wild 5 loose 9 abandoned, irregular, unbounded, unchecked, unmanaged 10 capricious, hysterical, licentious, ungoverned 11 unregulated 12 obstreperous

unconventional: 5 loose, outre, queer 6 casual, daring 7 devious, offbeat 8 Bohemian, informal 9 eccentric 10 unorthodox

uncorrupted: 4 pure 5 naive 6 virgin 8 pristine 9 unspoiled

uncouple: 5 loose 6 detach 8 separate, unfasten 10 disconnect

uncouth: odd 4 rare, rude 5 crude 6 clumsy, coarse, dismal, rugged 7 awkward, boorish, loutish, strange, uncanny, unknown 8 derelict, desolate, dreadful, ignorant, uncommon, ungainly, yokelish 9 offensive, unrefined 10 mysterious, outlandish, uncultured, unpolished 11 comfortless

uncouth person: oaf 4 boor, lout, rube 5 yahoo, yokel 6 bumkin, galoot, rustic 7 bumpkin

uncover: 4 bare, open, tirl (Sc.), tirr (Sc.) 6 denude, detect, divest, expose, remove, reveal, unveil 7 display, divulge, undrape, unearth 8 disclose, discover

uncovered: 4 bald, nude, open 5 naked 7 exposed 9 developed 10 bareheaded

unction: oil 4 balm 7 suavity, unguent 8 ointment
give extreme: 5 anele 6 anoint 9 chrismate

unctuous: fat 4 oily 5 bland, fatty, soapy, suave 6 fervid, greasy 7 fulsome, gushing, pinguid, plastic 10 obsequious, oleaginous

uncultivated: 4 arid, wild 5 feral 6 coarse, desert, fallow 7 deserty

uncultured: 4 rude 6 coarse, vulgar 7 artless, boorish 8 ignorant 9 unrefined

uncurbed: 9 audacious 12 uncontrolled

undamaged: 5 whole 6 intact, unhurt

undaunted: 4 bold 5 brave 7 spartan, valiant 8 fearless, intrepid, unafraid, undashed 9 confident, turbulent, unbridled, unchecked 10 courageous, undismayed

undecayed: 5 fresh, green 6 edible

undeceive: 8 disabuse 11 disillusion

undecided: 4 moot, pend 7 dubious, pending 8 doubtful, hesitant, wavering 9 unsettled 10 inconstant, indefinite, irresolute, unresolved, up in the air

undefiled: 4 pure 6 chaste 8 innocent, pristine, virtuous 9 unlimited 10 immaculate

undemonstrative: 4 calm, cold, cool 7 aseptic, laconic 8 reserved

undeniable: 4 true 7 certain, evident 11 irrefutable 12 indisputable

undependable: 5 trick 6 unsafe 7 erratic 10 fly-by-night, unreliable 13 irresponsible

under: 4 alow 5 below, lower, neath, sotto (It.) 6 nether 7 beneath 8 inferior 10 underneath 11 subordinate
the weather: 4 sick 5 drunk 6 ailing

undercover: 6 covert, hidden, secret 7 sub rosa 11 clandestine 13 surreptitious
man: spy 4 mole 5 agent 9 detective 10 counterspy

underdog: 6 victim 9 dark horse

underestimate: 8 minimize 9 underrate 10 undervalue

undergarment (see also **underwear**): bra 4 slip 5 teddy 6 bodice, briefs, cilice, corset, flimsy, girdle, shorts, stepin 7 chemise, panties, step-ins 8 camisole, lingerie 9 brassiere, chemilonn, hairshirt, petticoat, teddybear, underwear 10 foundation 11 camiknicker, combination

undergo: 4 bear, pass 5 carry, defer, yield 6 endure, suffer 7 sustain 8 tolerate

undergraduate: 4 coed 6 junior, senior 7 student 8 freshman 9 sophomore

underground: 5 train 6 cellar, hidden, secret, subway 7 beneath 8 basement, railroad 10 undercover 12 subterranean
burial place: 5 crypt 8 catacomb
dweller: 5 dwarf, gnome, troll
fighter: 5 rebel 6 marquis 8 partisan 9 guerrilla
fungus: 7 truffle 8 earthnut
worker: 5 miner 6 mucker, pitman, sapper

undergrowth: 4 rush 5 brush 10 hypotrophy, underbrush

underhanded: sly 4 dern, mean 5 shady 6 byhand, secret, sneaky, unfair 7 furtive 8 sneaking, stealthy, unfairly 9 deceitful 10 circuitous, fraudulent 11 clandestine, shorthanded, unobtrusive 13 unobtrusively

underlie: 4 bear 7 support

underline: 4 mark 6 stress 9 emphasize

underling: 6 menial, minion 8 inferior 11 subordinate

underlying: 5 basic, inate 7 obscure 8 cardinal 9 elemental 11 fundamental

undermine: sap 4 cave 5 drain, erode 6 impair, weaken 7 corrupt, founder, subvert 8 discover, enfeeble, excavate, sabotage 10 demoralize

underneath: 5 below, under 6 bottom, secret 7 beneath

underpin: 7 justify, support 8 maintain 9 vindicate

underprop: 6 uphold 7 support

underrate: 5 decry 7 devalue 8 discount 9 extenuate 10 depreciate, undervalue

underscore: 6 stress 9 emphasize, italicize

undersea boat: sub 5 U-boat, wreck 9 submarine 11 submersible
eye: 9 periscope

under-set: 4 prop 6 sublet 7 provide, support 8 maintain, underlet 10 strengthen

undershirt: 4 vest 6 T-shirt 7 chemise

undersized: 4 puny 5 runty, small 7 scrubby

underskirt: 4 slip 9 crinoline, petticoat

understand: con, dig, get, ken, see 4 know, sabe, twig 5 grasp, infer, sabby, savey, savvy, sense 6 follow, reason, savvey 7 discern, realize 8 conceive, perceive 9 apprehend, interpret, penetrate 10 comprehend, conjecture

understandable: 5 clear, lucid 6 simple

understanding: ken 4 feet, idea, news 5 amity,

brain 6 humane, kindly, reason, treaty 7 compact, concept, empathy, entente, knowing, meaning 8 attitude, contract, footwear, judgment, skillful, sympathy 9 agreement, diagnosis, knowledge, tolerance 10 acceptance 11 intelligent, sympathetic 12 intelligence

understatement: 7 litotes

understood: 5 clear, lucid, tacit 7 implied 8 implicit

undertake: try 4 dare, fand, fang 5 chide, grant, seize 6 accept, assume, engage, incept, take on 7 attempt, emprise, emprize, execute, perform, promise, receive, reprove 8 contract, covenant, endeavor, overtake 9 guarantee

undertaker: 5 cerer 6 surety 7 rebuker, sponsor 8 embalmer 9 mortician

undertaking: 4 task 5 chore 6 charge, pledge, scheme 7 attempt, calling, project, promise, venture 8 business, covenant, endeavor 9 adventure, guarantee 10 enterprise 11 proposition

undertone: 5 aside 6 murmur 11 association

undertow: 4 eddy 6 vortex 7 current, riptide

undervalue: 5 decry 8 disprize, disvalue 10 depreciate

underwater: *apparatus:* 6 tremie 7 caisson
breathing equipment: 5 scuba
captain: 4 Nemo
chamber: 4 cave 7 caisson
missile: 7 torpedo
sound detector: 5 sofar, sonar

underwear (see also **undergarment**): 6 skivvy 7 dessous (F.), stepins 8 lingerie, skivvies 12 underclothes

underwood: 5 frith 7 boscage, coppice 10 underbrush

underworld: mob 4 hell 5 Hades, mafia, Orcus, Sheol 6 Amenti, Erebus 7 xibalba 8 gangland 9 antipodes, syndicate
boatman: 6 Charon
deity: Dis 4 Bran 5 Hades, Pluto 6 Osiris 8 Dispater 9 Enmeshara 11 Ningishzida
goddess: 6 Allatu, Belili, Hecate, Trivia
pert. to: 8 chthonic 9 chthonian
river: 4 Styx 5 Lethe 7 Acheron
watchdog: 8 Cerberus

underwrite: 4 sign 6 assure, insure 7 endorse, finance, sponsor, support 9 guarantee, subscribe

undesigning: 6 simple 7 artless, genuine, sincere

undetermined: 5 vague 7 dubious, pending 8 aoristic, doubtful 9 equivocal

undeveloped: 5 crude 6 latent 8 backward, immature 9 primitive

undeviating: 4 even 6 direct 8 straight

undiluted: 4 neat, pure 8 straight

undine: nix 4 wave 5 nymph 11 water spirit

undisciplined: 4 wild 6 unruly, wanton 9 untrained

undisclosed: 6 covert, hidden, sealed, secret 8 ulterior 10 unrevealed

undisguised: 4 bald, open 5 frank, overt, plain 9 barefaced

undisturbed: 4 calm 5 quiet, sound 6 placid, secure, serene 8 peaceful, tranquil

undivided: one 5 total, whole 6 entire, intact 8 complete, unbroken

undo: 4 open, ruin 5 annul, erase, fordo, loose, solve, untie 6 betray, cancel, defeat, diddle, foredo, outwit, unlash, unwrap 7 abolish, defease, destroy, disjoin, explain, nullify, release, uncover, unravel 8 unfasten 9 bring down 10 disappoint, disconnect, invalidate

undoing: 8 downfall 9 overthrow

undomesticated: 4 wild 5 feral 6 ferine 7 untamed

undone: raw 6 ruined 9 disgraced, neglected 10 defeasible

undoubted: 4 sure 7 certain 8 accepted, admitted 9 authentic 11 indubitable

undraped: 4 bare, nude

undress: 4 bare, doff 5 strip 6 devest, divest, expose, unveil 7 disrobe 8 unclothe

undressed skin: kip 4 pelt

undue: 8 improper 9 excessive 10 exorbitant, immoderate, inordinate, unsuitable 11 unwarranted 12 unreasonable

undulant: 7 aripple, sinuous
fever: 11 brucellosis

undulate: 4 roll, sway, wave 5 swell, swing 6 billow, gyrate 9 fluctuate

undying: 6 eterne 7 ageless, endless, eternal 8 immortal, unending 9 continual, deathless, perpetual 10 continuing, persistent

unearth: dig 4 show 5 learn 6 exhume, expose 7 uncover 8 disclose, discover

unearthly: 4 eery 5 eerie, weird 7 awesome, foolish, uncanny, ungodly 8 terrific 9 appalling, fantastic 10 mysterious, outlandish 12 preposterous

uneasiness: 4 care 5 worry 6 qualms, unrest 7 anxiety, disease, malaise, trouble 8 disquiet 10 constraint, discomfort, discontent 11 displeasure, disturbance 12 apprehension

uneasy: 5 jumpy, stiff, tense 7 anxious, awkward, fidgety, jittery, nervous, restive, unquiet, worried 8 agitated, doubtful, restless, skittish 9 difficult, perturbed, unsettled 11 constrained

uneducated: 8 ignorant 9 unlearned 10 illiterate, unlettered, unschooled

unemotional: 4 cold 5 stoic, stony 7 passive, stoical 9 apathetic 10 phlegmatic, unfeeling 11 indifferent

unemployed: 4 idle 6 otiant, otiose 7 jobless, laid off 8 inactive, leisured 9 at liberty

unencumbered: 4 free

unending: 7 endless, eternal, undying 8 time-less 9 ceaseless, continual 11 everlasting 12 interminable

unendurable: 10 impassible, unbearable 11 intolerable 12 insufferable

unenthusiastic: 4 cool 5 tepid 9 apathetic 12 uninterested

unequal: 6 uneven, unfair, unjust 8 lopsided, variable 9 different, disparate, irregular 11 fluctuating

unequaled: 5 alone 7 supreme 9 matchless, unmatched, unrivaled 10 surpassing

unequivocal: 5 clear, plain 7 sincere 8 defi-nite, explicit, positive 9 certainly

unerring: 4 sure, true 5 exact 6 deadly 7 cer-tain, perfect 8 accurate, flawless, inerrant 9 inerrancy, unfailing 10 infallible

unethical: 5 wrong 6 amoral 7 corrupt, immoral

uneven: odd 5 erose, gobby, haggy, rough 6 hobbly, rugged, spotty, unfair, unjust, unlike 7 unequal, varying 8 lopsided 9 dis-parate, irregular 10 ill-matched

unexamined: 7 a priori 11 nonanalytic

unexcelled: 8 champion, superior, topnotch, unbeaten 11 unsurpassed

unexceptional: 5 usual 6 common, decent 7 regular 8 ordinary

unexcited: 4 calm 5 level 7 stoical

unexciting: 4 dead, dull, tame 6 boring 7 pro-saic

unexpected: 5 eerie 6 abrupt, chance, sud-den 9 inopinate, unguarded 10 accidental, surprising, unforeseen

unexpended: 6 saving 7 reserve, surplus 8 left over

unexpired: 5 alive, valid 9 operative, remain-ing

unexpressed: 5 tacit 6 silent 8 implicit

unfadable: 4 fast 9 memorable

unfaded: 5 fresh 6 bright

unfading flower: 8 amaranth 11 everlasting

unfailing: 4 same, sure 7 certain 8 constant, reliable, unerring 10 infallible, unflagging

unfair: 4 foul, hard 5 wrong 6 biased, uneven, unjust 7 partial 8 unseemly, wrongful 9 dis-honest, unethical 10 prejudiced 11 inequitable, underhanded, unfavorable

unfaithful: 7 infidel, traitor 8 derelict, dis-loyal, recreant, turncoat 9 dishonest, faith-less 10 adulterous, inaccurate

unfaltering: 4 sure, true 5 brave 6 steady

unfamed: 5 lowly 6 humble 7 obscure

unfamiliar: new 5 alien, fresh, novel 7 strange, unknown 8 ignorant 12 unaccustomed

unfashionable: 5 dated, passe 9 distorted, unshapely

unfasten: 4 free, open, undo 5 loose, unbar, unfix, unpin, untie 6 detach, loosen, unbind, unlace, unlock 7 release, unhitch 8 untether

unfathomable: 8 abstruse 10 bottomless 12 impenetrable

unfavorable: bad, ill 4 evil, foul 6 averse 7 adverse 8 contrary

unfeeling: 4 dull, hard, numb 5 cruel, harsh, stern, stony 6 brutal, marble, stolid 7 cal-lous 8 numbness, obdurate, pitiless 9 apa-thetic, bloodless, heartless, insensate, senseless 10 impassible, insensible 11 cold-blooded, hardhearted

unfeigned: 4 real, true 6 hearty 7 genuine, natural, sincere

unfermented grape juice: 4 stum

unfertile: 4 arid 6 barren

unfettered: 4 free 5 broad, loose

unfilled: 5 blank, empty 6 vacant 7 vacuous

unfilled cavity: 4 vugg

unfinished: raw 4 rude 5 crude, rough 7 sketchy 8 immature 9 imperfect 10 ama-teurish, incomplete

unfit: bad 4 sick 5 inept, pasul (Heb.) 6 faulty 8 disabled, improper 9 ill-suited, maladroit 10 out of place, unsuitable 11 incompe-tent, unqualified 12 disqualified

unfix: 6 detach, loosen 8 dissolve, unfasten, unsettle

unflagging: 6 steady 8 constant, tireless

unflappable: 4 calm, cool 6 steady 7 relaxed

unflattering: 4 open 5 blunt, frank 6 candid 10 derogatory, unbecoming

unfledged: 5 green, young 6 callow 8 imma-ture 11 undeveloped, unfeathered
bird: 4 eyas 8 nestling

unflinching: 4 calm, firm, grim 6 stanch 8 resolute 9 steadfast 10 unwavering

unfold: ope 4 open 5 break, solve 6 deploy, evolve, expand, explat, flower, reveal, spread, unfurl, unwrap 7 develop, display, divulge, evolute, explain, explate, release 8 disclose 9 explicate

unforced: 4 easy 7 natural, willing 9 voluntary

unforeseen: 6 casual, chance, sudden 10 accidental, unexpected

unformed: 4 rude 6 callow 9 shapeless, uncreated 11 undeveloped

unfortunate: bad, ill, sad 4 poor 5 worst 6 dismal, tragic, wretch 7 hapless, malefic, unhappy, unlucky 8 luckless, wretched 9 graceless, miserable 10 calamitous, deplor-able, lamentable, prostitute, ungracious

unfounded: 4 idle, vain 5 false 6 untrue 8 baseless 10 chimerical, groundless

unfrequented: 6 lonely 8 isolated, solitary

unfriendly: 4 cool 5 aloof 6 remote 7 asocial, hostile 8 inimical, unsocial 9 dissocial 10 unsociable

unfruitful: 5 blunt 6 barren, wasted 7 sterile, useless 8 impotent, infecund 9 fruitless, infertile 12 unproductive

unfurl: 4 open 5 enrol 6 enroll, expand,

spread, unfold, unroll **7** develop

unfurnished: 4 bare **6** vacant

ungainly: 5 lanky **6** clumsy **7** awkward, boorish, uncouth **8** clownish, slammock, slummock **9** maladroit **11** elephantine

ungenerous: 4 mean **5** harsh, nasty, petty **6** stingy **7** miserly **8** grudging **9** illiberal

ungirt: 5 loose, slack **7** unbound

ungodly: 6 impure, sinful, unholy, wicked **7** impious, profane **8** dreadful **9** atheistic, atrocious, unearthly **10** indecorous, outrageous **11** blasphemous, unbelieving

ungovernable: 4 wild **6** unruly **7** froward, willful **8** contrary **9** unbridled **10** disorderly, headstrong, licentious, rebellious **11** intractable

ungraceful: 6 clumsy **7** angular, awkward **8** ungainly **9** inelegant

ungracious: 4 hard, rude **5** short, surly **8** churlish, impolite **9** offensive **10** unmannerly, unpleasant **11** unfortunate

ungrateful: 9 offensive, thankless

ungrounded: 8 baseless **9** unfounded **10** uninformed **12** uninstructed

ungrudging: 7 willing **8** cheerful

unguarded: 4 open, weak **6** unwary **8** careless **9** imprudent **10** incautious **11** defenseless, thoughtless, unprotected

unguent: 4 balm **5** salve **6** cerate, ceroma, chrism **8** ointment **9** lubricant

ungula: 4 claw, hoof, nail

unhallowed: 6 impure, unholy, wicked **7** impious, profane **10** desecrated

unhandsome: 4 mean, rude **5** plain **6** homely, stingy **10** unbecoming

unhandy: 6 clumsy **7** awkward

unhappiness: woe **5** blues, dolor, grief, worry **6** misery, unrest **7** sadness **9** tristesse **10** depression, melancholy

unhappy: sad **4** blue, evil, glum **6** dismal **7** joyless, unlucky **8** dejected, desolate, ill-fated, wretched **9** miserable, sorrowful, woebegone **10** calamitous, melancholy **11** melancholic, mischievous, unfavorable, unfortunate **12** inauspicious

unharmed: 4 safe **6** unhurt **8** harmless **10** scatheless

unharmonious: 6 atonal **9** dissonant **11** cacophanous

unharness: 6 disarm, divest, ungear **7** unhitch, unhorse

unhealthy: ill **4** sick **6** ailing, sickly **7** vicious **8** delicate, diseased **9** dangerous **11** unwholesome

unheard of: 7 obscure, strange, unknown

unheeded: 4 cold

unheeding: 4 deaf **8** careless **11** inattentive **12** disregarding

unhesitating: 5 ready

unhidden: 5 overt

unholy: See **ungodly**

unhorse: 5 throw **6** unseat **8** dislodge, dismount **9** overthrow, unharness

unhurried: 4 easy, slow **7** languid **9** leisurely **10** deliberate

unhurt: 4 safe **5** whole **8** unharmed **9** uninjured

unicellular animal: 5 ameba **6** amoeba **9** protozoan **10** paramecium

unicellular plant: 5 spore

unicorn: 4 reem **9** monoceros

unicorn fish: 4 unie **7** narwhal **8** filefish

uniform: 4 even, flat, like, same, suit **5** alike, equal, level, plain **6** livery, outfit, steady **7** similar **8** constant, equiform **9** continual, equitable, unvarying **10** compatible, consistent, equiformal, invariable, monotonous, unchanging **11** homogeneous

cord: **11** aiguillette

in color: **13** monochromatic

prisoner's: **7** stripes

servant's: **6** livery

shoulder ornament: **7** epaulet **9** epaulette

uniformly: 6 always, evenly

unify: 5 merge, unite **7** combine **8** coalesce **9** correlate, harmonize, integrate **11** consolidate

unimaginative: 4 dull **5** banal, tri*te* **7** literal, prosaic **9** hackneyed **10** pedestrian

unimpaired: 4 free **5** fresh, sound, whole **6** entire, intact

unimpassioned: 6 steady **7** prosaic **10** phlegmatic

unimpeachable: 6 decent **9** blameless, faultless **12** unassailable **14** irreproachable

unimpeded: 4 free **8** expedite

unimportant: 5 minor, petty, small **6** little, paltry **7** trivial **8** picayune, piddling, trifling **9** frivolous **10** negligible

uninformed: 7 unaware **8** ignorant

uninhabited: 5 empty **6** vacant **8** deserted, desolate

uninspired: 4 dull **6** stodgy **9** ponderous

unintelligent: 4 dumb **5** brute **6** obtuse, simple, stupid, unwise **7** asinine, foolish, vacuous **8** ignorant **9** senseless **10** irrational

unintentional: 9 haphazard, unwitting **10** accidental **11** inadvertent

uninteresting: dry **4** arid, drab, dull, flat **5** stale **6** boring, jejune, prolix, stupid **7** humdrum, insipid, prosaic, tedious **8** tiresome **9** colorless **10** unexciting

uninterrupted: 6 direct **7** endless, eternal **8** constant, unbroken **9** continual, perpetual **10** continuous

union: AFL, CIO, one, UAW **4** bloc, club **5** artel, group, guild, hansa, ILGWU, joint, local, trust, unity **6** accord, copula, fusion, fusion, gremio (Sp.), league, merger, unicum **7** amalgam, combine, concord, contact, entente, harmony, liaison, meeting, oneness, society, wedlock **8** alliance, junction, marriage **9** coalition, coherence, composure, matrimony **10** connection, copulation, federation, fellowship **11** association, coalescence, combination, concurrence, confederacy

political: **4** bloc **9** coalition

trade: **5** guild, hanse

Union Jack: 4 flag **7** British

Union of Soviet Socialist Republics: 4 CCCP, USSR **6** Russia, Soviet

unique: odd, one **4** only, rare, sole **5** alone, queer **6** single **7** notable, special, unequal, unusual **8** peculiar, rara avis, singular **9** matchless **11** exceptional

unison: 5 union **6** accord **7** concord, harmony **9** agreement, consonant, homophony, identical, unanimity, unisonous **10** concordant, consonance

unit: ace, one **4** item, part **5** digit, group, monad, piece, squad, whole **6** branch, entity **10** individual

conductivity: mho

fluidity: rhe

flux density: **5** gauss

force: **4** dyne, volt **5** kinit, tonal **6** newton **7** poundal

heat: BTU

hypothetical: **5** idant **6** pangen **7** pangene

illumination: **4** phot

inductance: **5** henry

light: lux, pyr **5** lumen

magnetic: **7** weber

measure: are, mil, rod, ton **4** foot, mile, pint, yard **5** meter, quart, stere **6** barrel, bushel, fathom, league **7** furlong, scruple **8** hogshead

measuring sound: *bel* **7** decibel

metrical: **4** dyne, gram, mora **5** liter, liter, morae **9** kilometer **10** centimeter

military: **4** army **5** corps, squad, troop **7** brigade, company, platoon **8** division, regiment **9** battalion

physical: erg **7** atomerg

power: bel **4** watt **5** dynam, horse

pressure: **5** barad, barye **10** atmosphere

reluctance: rel

resistance: ohm

social: **4** clan, club, sect **5** tribe **6** family **7** chapter

sound: bel **7** decibel

speed: **4** velo

stellar: **6** parsec

telegraphic: **4** baud

thermal: BTU **6** calory **7** calorie

time: day **4** bell, hour, week, year **5** month **6** decade, minute, season, second **7** century **9** fortnight **10** millennium

ultimate: **5** monad

velocity: kin **4** kine, velo

volume: cwt, ton **5** ounce, pound **13** hundredweight

weight: ton **4** dram, gram, tael **5** carat, grain, ounce, pound, stone

work: erg **5** ergon, joule **6** kilerg

unite: add, ass, fay, mix, pan, sew, tie, wed **4** ally, band, bind, bond, club, fuse, hasp, join, knit, link, meld, pair, seam, weld **5** affix, annex, blend, graft, hitch, marry, merge, piece, rally, unify **6** adhere, adjoin, attach, cement, cohere, concur, couple, embody, gather, mingle, solder, splice **7** combine, conjoin, connect, consort, convene **8** assemble, coalesce, compound, concrete, condense, conspire, continue, federate, regulate **9** affiliate, aggregate, associate, integrate, reconcile **10** amalgamate, articulate, consociate, federalize, hook up with, join forces **11** concentrate, consolidate, incorporate **12** conglutinate

united: one **9** concerted, conjugate, corporate

United Arab Emirates: *capital:* **8** Abu Dhabi

city: **6** Dubbai

currency: fil **6** dirham

export: **9** petroleum

strait: **6** Hormuz

United Kingdom (see also **British, England, Northern Ireland, Scotland, Wales**): **7** Britain **12** Great Britain

capital: **6** London

currency: **5** pence, pound

highest peak: **8** Ben Nevis

hills: **8** Pennines

industrial center: **8** Midlands

invader: **4** Celt **5** Angle, Roman, Saxon **6** Norman, Viking

island: Man **4** Jura, Mull, Skye **5** Arran, Islay, Wight **6** Jersey **8** Guernsey

island group: **6** Orkney **7** Channel **8** Hebrides, Shetland

king: **5** Henry, James **6** Edward, George **7** Richard, William

national anthem: **15** God Save the Queen

prime minister: **4** Eden **5** Heath, Major **6** Attlee, Wilson **7** Baldwin, Balfour **8** Disraeli, Thatcher **9** Churchill, Gladstone, Macmillan **11** Chamberlain, Lloyd George

queen: **4** Anne **8** Victoria **9** Elizabeth

royal house: **6** Stuart **7** Hanover, Windsor **15** Saxe-Coburg-Gotha

strait: **5** Dover

United Nations Organization: UNO
United Provinces: 7 Holland, Utrecht, Zeeland 9 Friesland, Groningen 10 Gelderland, Overijssel 12 Uttar Pradesh

unity: one 5 union, whole 6 accord, unison 7 concert, concord, harmony, oneness 8 alliance, identity, integral 9 agreement, communion, congruity, integrity, unanimity

---

United States of America (see also individual states): 7 America
actor/actress: 4 Bara, Dean, Gish, Kaye, Lunt, Peck 5 Adams, Booth, Brice, Davis, Dunne, Fiske, Fonda, Gable, Garbo, Grant, Hardy, Hayes, Lloyd, Quinn, Scott, Tracy, Wayne 6 Bogart, Brando, Cagney, Cooper, Crosby, De Niro, Duvall, Foster, Heston, Hirsch, Keaton, Laurel, Lemmon, Martin, Monroe, Newman, Pacino, Streep, Taylor, Temple, Welles 7 Bergman, Chaplin, Douglas, Garland, Hackman, Hepburn, Hoffman, Karloff, Pickens, Poitier, Redford, Robards, Robeson, Russell, Stewart 8 Crawford, Dietrich, Eastwood, Gillette, Laughton, Robinson, Stallone, Woodward 9 Barrymore, Fairbanks, Lancaster, Nicholson, Valentino 10 Lanchester
architect: Pei 4 Cram, Hunt 5 Jenny, Mills, Stone, White 6 Fuller, Wright 7 Johnson, Latrobe, Olmsted 8 Bulfinch 10 Richardson, Strickland
artist: 4 Kent, Wood 5 Homer, Johns, Moses, Segal, Shahn, Wyeth 6 Albers, Calder, Hopper, Stella, Warhol 7 O'Keeffe, Parrish, Pollock, Sargent 8 Nevelson, Rockwell 9 de Kooning, Oldenburg, Remington 10 Motherwell 12 Lichtenstein, Rauschenberg 13 Frankenthaler
capital: D.C. 10 Washington
commonwealth states: 8 Kentucky, Virginia 12 Pennsylvania 13 Massachusetts
composer: 4 Cage, Ives 5 Bloch, Grofe 6 Barber 7 Copland, Menotti, Schuman, Thomson 8 Billings, Gershwin, Williams 9 Bernstein, Hindemith, MacDowell 10 Blitzstein, Schoenberg
conductor: 5 Ozawa, Szell 6 Levine, Previn, Thomas 7 Fiedler, Ormandy, Quellar 8 Caldwell, Damrosch 9 Bernstein, Stokowski
currency: bit 4 cent, dime 5 eagle, penny 6 dollar, nickel 7 quarter 10 half dollar
desert: 6 Mojave, Sonora 7 Painted
dramatist: 4 Inge, Rabe 5 Albee, Barry, Mamet, Odets, Simon 6 Baraka, Miller, O'Neill, Wilder 7 Behrman, Saroyan,

Shepard 8 Anderson, Hellmann, Williams 9 Hansberry
frontiersman: 4 Cody 5 Boone, Clark, Lewis 8 Crockett
measure: lea, mil, rod, ton, tub, vat 4 acre, bolt, cord, drum, foot, gill, hand, hank, heer, inch, iron, last, line, link, mile, nail, pace, palm, peck, pint, pipe, pole, pool, roll, sack, span, typp, vara, yard 5 block, carat, chain, labor, minim, perch, point, prime, quart, skein, stran 6 barrel, basket, bushel, fathom, gallon, league, pottle, square, strand, thread 7 quarter, section, spindle 8 hogshead, quadrant, standard 9 board foot, decillion, fluid dram 10 fluid ounce 11 teaspoonful 13 tablespoonful 16 Winchester bushel
mountain: 4 Hood 5 Rocky 6 Cumbre, Elbert, Helena, Shasta 7 Massive, Rainier, Whitney 8 Katahdin, McKinley 10 Laurentian 11 Appalachian
poet (see also **poet laureate**): Poe 4 Nash 5 Aiken, Frost, Guest, Moore, Plath, Pound, Riley 6 Ciardi, Dickey, Lanier, Lowell, Millay, Parker 7 Lazarus, Lindsay, Stevens, Whitman 8 cummings, Ginsberg, MacLeish, Sandburg, Whittier 9 Dickinson, Lindbergh 10 Longfellow
songwriter: 4 Kern 5 Cohan, David, Loewe, Styne 6 Berlin, Porter 7 Rodgers 8 Gershwin, Loessser, Sondheim 9 Bacharach 10 Carmichael 11 Hammerstein
state: 4 Iowa, Ohio, Utah 5 Idaho, Maine, Texas 6 Alaska, Hawaii, Kansas, Nevada, Oregon 7 Alabama, Arizona, Florida, Georgia, Indiana, Montana, New York, Vermont, Wyoming 8 Arkansas, Colorado, Delaware, Illinois, Kentucky, Maryland, Michigan, Missouri, Nebraska, Oklahoma, Virginia 9 Louisiana, Minnesota, New Jersey, New Mexico, Tennessee, Wisconsin 10 California, Washington 11 Connecticut, Mississippi, North Dakota, Rhode Island, South Dakota 12 New Hampshire, Pennsylvania, West Virginia 13 Massachusetts, North Carolina, South Carolina
volcano: 8 Mauna Loa 10 Mt. St. Helens

10 singleness, solidarity, uniformity

universal: all 5 local, total, whole 6 common, cosmic, entire, global, public 7 general 8 catholic, constant 9 continual, unlimited 11 omnipresent
language: ido 9 Esperanto
military training: SSS 5 draft

universe: 5 earth, monad, world 6 cosmos, nature, sphere, system 7 mankind 8 creation, megacosm, totality
controlling principle: 4 tien 5 logos
pert. to: 6 cosmic

university: 7 academy, college 8 academie, seminary 9 accademie, institute
division: 6 school 7 college
grounds: 6 campus
Ivy League: 4 Yale 5 Brown 7 Cornell, Harvard 8 Columbia 9 Dartmouth, Princeton 12 Pennsylvania
official: 4 dean 6 bursar, regent 7 provost
team: 7 varsity

univocal: 5 clear 7 uniform 9 unanimous, unisonous 11 indubitable

unjust: 5 cruel 6 biased, unfair 8 improper, wrongful 9 dishonest, faithless 10 inaccurate, iniquitous, prejudiced, unfaithful 11 inequitable

unkempt: 5 crude, messy, rough 6 frouzy, frowsy, frowzy, shaggy, untidy 7 ruffled, squalid, tousled, unclean 8 slovenly 9 unrefined 10 disarrayed, disheveled, slatternly, unpolished

unkind: bad, ill 4 mean, vile 5 cruel, harsh, rough, stern 6 brutal, severe, wicked 7 foreign, strange 8 inhumane, ungenial 9 heartless, inclement, undutiful, unnatural 10 degenerate, ungenerous, ungracious, ungrateful, unsuitable 11 unfavorable

unknit: 4 undo 5 ravel, relax, untie 6 unknot 7 unravel 8 disperse, dissolve, disunite

unknowable: 6 sealed 8 mystical 9 enigmatic

unknown: 4 unco 6 secret 7 inconnu (F.), obscure, strange 9 anonymous, incognito 10 unfamiliar 12 incalculable

unlace: 4 undo 5 loose, untie 6 carver 7 undress, unravel 8 unfasten, untangle

unlawful: 7 bastard, bootleg, illegal, illicit 8 criminal, wrongful 9 irregular 10 contraband
hunting: 8 poaching
intrusion: 8 trespass

unlearned: 4 lewd 5 gross 6 borrel 7 natural 8 ignorant, untaught 9 untutored 10 illiterate, uneducated 11 instinctive, instinctual, unscholarly

unleashed: 4 free 5 loose 8 released

unleavened: 4 flat 7 azymous
bread: 4 azym 5 azyme, matzo 7 matzoth (pl.)

unless: but 4 lest, nisi (L.), save 6 except 7 without 9 excepting

unlettered: 4 lewd 8 ignorant 9 barbarian, unlearned 10 illiterate, uneducated

unlike: 6 uneven 7 difform, diverse 8 unlikely 9 different, irregular 10 dissimilar

unlikely: 4 rare 5 unfit 6 remote 7 dubious 10 improbable, unsuitable 11 unpromising 12 disagreeable

unlikeness: 8 contrast 12 disagreement 13 dissimilarity

unlimited: 4 free, vast 5 total 9 boundless, limitless, unbounded, undefined, universal 10 indefinite, unconfined 11 illimitable, untrammeled 12 immeasurable, unrestricted

unload: 4 dump, land, sell 5 eject, empty, trash 6 decant, remove 7 deplete, discard, lighten, relieve 8 jettison, unburden 9 disburden, discharge, liquidate, sacrifice

unlock: ope 4 open 5 solve 6 reveal, unbolt

unlooked for: 6 chance 10 unexpected, unforeseen 13 serendipitous

unlucky: bad, fey, ill 7 hapless 8 ill-fated 9 ill-omened 11 apocalyptic, starcrossed, unfortunate

unman: 5 crush 7 monster, unnerve 8 castrate 10 emasculate

unmanageable: 4 wild 5 randy 6 unruly 8 churlish 10 disorderly 14 uncontrollable

unmanly: 4 weak 5 sissy 8 childish 10 effeminate

unmannerly: 4 rude 7 boorish, uncivil 8 impolite 10 ungracious 12 discourteous

unmarried: one 4 lone 5 unwed 6 chaste, single 8 celibate, divorced
man: 8 bachelor
woman: 7 old maid 8 spinster 12 bachelorette

unmask: 6 expose, reveal, unface 7 uncloak 8 disclose 9 dismantle

unmatched: odd 5 alone 6 single 8 peerless 9 matchless, nonpareil

unmeasured: 4 huge, vast 7 immense 8 infinite 9 boundless 12 incalculable, unrestrained

unmelodious: 9 dissonant 11 cacophonous

unmerciful: 5 cruel 7 callous 8 pitiless, ruthless 9 inclement 10 relentless

unmethodical: 7 cursory, erratic 9 desultory, haphazard

unmindful: 6 remiss 8 careless, heedless 9 forgetful, negligent 10 neglectful 11 unconscious

unmistakable: 4 open 5 clear, plain 6 patent 7 evident, obvious 8 apparent, definite, manifest

unmitigated: 4 mere, pure 5 sheer, utter 6 arrant 8 absolute, clearcut 10 unmodified

unmixed: 4 deep, mear, mere, pure 5 blank, sheer, utter 7 sincere 8 straight

unmoved: 4 calm, cool, firm 5 inert, stony 6 serene, stolid 7 adamant 8 obdurate, stubborn, unshaken 9 apathetic, obstinate

unmoving: 5 inert 6 static

unnatural: 4 eery 5 eerie 7 strange, uncanny 8 abnormal, affected, farcical 9 irregular, perverted, synthetic 10 artificial, factitious 11 counterfeit

unnecessary: 6 excess 7 useless 8 needless, prodigal 9 redundant 10 gratuitous 11 superfluous, uncalled-for

unnerve: 5 unman 6 weaken 8 castrate, enervate 10 dishearten, emasculate

unobservant: 8 heedless 11 inattentive

unobstructed: 4 free, open 9 panoramic

unobtrusive: 5 quiet 6 modest 8 retiring

unobtrusively: 7 quietly 9 underhand

unoccupied: 4 free, idle, void 5 empty 6 vacant 9 at leisure 10 unemployed 11 uninhabited

unofficial: 7 private 8 informal

unorganized: 5 messy 7 chaotic 8 inchoate 10 disorderly, incoherent

unoriginal: 4 arid, copy 5 trite 6 cliché 7 sterile 9 hackneyed 10 secondhand 11 plagiarized, stereotyped

unorthodox: 9 heretical

unostentatious: 5 plain, quiet 6 lenten, modest, simple 10 restrained

unpaid: due 5 owing 6 arrear 10 unrevenged 11 outstanding

unpaired: odd 6 single

unpalatable: 4 flat, thin, weak 8 inedible, nauseous 10 unpleasant 11 distasteful

unparalleled: 5 alone 6 unique 7 unequal 8 peerless 9 matchless, unmatched 10 inimitable

unpleasant: bad 7 irksome 8 unsavory 9 offensive 10 abominable, forbidding, illfavored, ungracious 11 displeasing, distasteful

unplowed: lea 6 fallow 8 untilled

unpolished: 4 dull, rude 5 bruit, crude, rough 6 coarse, rugged 7 boorish, unwaxed 8 agrestic, impolite 9 barbarous 10 agrestical

unprecedented: new 5 novel 9 unheard-of 10 unexampled

unprejudiced: 4 fair 8 unbiased 9 impartial

unpremeditated: 6 casual 9 extempore, impromptu, unplanned 10 accidental 11 spontaneous

unprepared: raw 5 unfit 6 asleep 11 unorganized

unprepossessing: 4 ugly 5 plain 6 homely 11 unappealing 12 unattractive

unpretentious: 5 plain 6 homely, humble, modest, simple 10 unaffected

unprincipled: 4 lewd 7 corrupt 9 abandoned, unethical 10 perfidious 12 unscrupulous

unprocessed: raw 5 crude

unproductive: 4 arid, dead, lean 6 barren, fallow, futile, geason 7 sterile 8 impotent 9 fruitless

unprofessional: lay 6 laical 7 amateur 9 unskilled 15 nonprofessional

unprofitable: dry 4 dead 6 barren 7 inutile, useless 8 bootless, gainless 9 fruitless, frustrate 10 unfruitful

unpropitious: 4 evil 6 malign 7 adverse, counter, ominous, opposed 12 antagonistic

unprotected: 6 unsafe 7 exposed 8 helpless, insecure 9 unguarded 10 undefended, vulnerable

unqualified: 4 bare, mear, meer, mere, sure 5 final, fixed, sheer, unfit, utter 6 entire, unable 7 decided, plenary 8 absolute, complete, definite 9 categoric, downright, incapable 11 categorical, incompetent

unquestionable: 7 certain, decided, evident 8 absolute, implicit, positive 9 authentic, downright 11 irrefutable

unravel: 4 undo 5 feaze, ravel, solve 6 unfold, unlace 7 resolve 8 disorder, disunite, separate, untangle 9 disengage, extricate, figure out 11 disentangle

unready: 4 slow 5 unfit 6 clumsy 7 awkward 8 hesitant 9 undressed 10 unprepared

unreal: 5 false, ideal 6 aerial 7 fancied, fatuous, nominal, phantom 8 aeriform, fanciful, illusive, illusory, spurious 9 deceptive, fantastic, imaginary, pretended, visionary 10 apocryphal, artificial, barmecidal, fictitious, mendacious 11 counterfeit, imaginative, theoretical

unreasonable: mad 5 blind 6 absurd 9 excessive, illogical, senseless 10 exorbitant, immoderate, irrational 11 extravagant

unrecognized: 6 unsung 7 unknown 13 unappreciated

unrefined: raw 4 base, dark, loud, rude 5 broad, crass, crude, gross 6 coarse, common, earthy, native, vulgar 7 uncouth 8 ungraded 10 unpurified

unregenerate: 6 carnal, sinful 9 obstinate, reprobate, shameless 10 impenitent

unrelated: 5 fremd 8 separate 9 disjoined 11 independent

unrelaxed: 4 taut 5 tense

unrelenting: 4 firm, grim, hard, iron 5 cruel, stern 6 severe 7 adamant 8 obdurate, pitiless, rigorous, ruthless 9 merciless, obstinate, tenacious 10 implacable, inexorable, inflexible, relentless, unyielding

unreliable: 5 fishy 6 fickle, shifty, unsafe 7 casalty 10 capricious, fly-by-night 12 undependable 13 irresponsible

unremitting: 4 busy, hard 9 assiduous, continual, incessant 10 persistent 11 persevering

unrepentant: 11 remorseless

unreserved: 4 free, open 5 frank 6 candid 9 guileless, outspoken, unlimited

unresponsive: 4 cold, cool 6 frigid 9 unfeeling

unrest: 5 alarm 6 bustle, motion 7 anarchy, ferment 8 disquiet, sedition 9 agitation, commotion 10 uneasiness

unrestrained: lax 4 free, wild 5 bluff, blunt, broad, loose 6 wanton 7 riotous 9 abandoned, audacious, dissolute, excessive, expansive, unbounded, unbridled, unlimited 10 licentious, unmeasured 11 extravagant 12 uncontrolled

unrestraint: 7 abandon, license 8 immunity 11 spontaneity

unrevealed: 6 hidden, latent, masked, untold 7 covered 9 concealed

unripe: raw 5 crude, green, young 6 callow 7 uncured, unready 8 immature 9 premature 10 precocious, unseasoned

unroll: 6 evolve, uncoil, unfold, unfurl, unwind 7 develop, display, open out 8 disclose

unruffled: 4 calm, cool 5 quiet 6 placid, poised, sedate, serene, smooth 8 decorous 10 nonchalant 11 undisturbed

unruly: 4 wild 5 rowdy 6 haunty, ramage 7 froward, lawless, restive 8 contrary 9 fractious, obstinate, out of hand, turbulent, unbridled 10 disorderly, headstrong, licentious, refractory 11 disobedient, intractable 12 obstreperous, recalcitrant, ungovernable, unmanageable

unsafe: 5 risky, shaky 7 exposed 8 insecure, perilous 9 dangerous, hazardous

unsatisfactory: bad 4 poor 9 defective, imperfect 10 inadequate 11 inefficient

unsavory: 4 flat, rank, sour 6 rancid 7 insipid 9 offensive, tasteless 10 unpleasant 11 distasteful, unpalatable 12 disagreeable, unappetizing

unscrupulous: 5 shady, venal 6 crafty 7 corrupt, devious 8 rascally 9 dishonest, miscreant, unethical 12 unprincipled

unseal: 4 open 8 disclose

unseasonable: 6 unripe 8 ill-timed, improper, untimely 9 premature

unseasoned: raw 5 bland, green 6 unripe 8 immature, untimely 9 tasteless

unseat: 6 depose, remove 7 unhorse 9 overthrow

unseemly: 5 crude, inept 6 coarse 8 improper, indecent, unworthy 10 indecorous, unbecoming

unseen: 9 invisible, unnoticed 10 unobserved 11 unperceived 12 undiscovered

unselfish: 6 heroic 8 generous 10 altruistic, benevolent 13 philanthropic

unserviceable: 6 no good 7 useless 11 impractical

unsettle: 5 upset 7 agitate, commove, derange, disturb, perturb, trouble, unnerve 8 disorder, displace, disquiet 10 disarrange, discompose

unsettled: 4 back, moot 6 fickle, queasy, unpaid 7 dubious, erratic, pending 8 restless, unstable 9 ambiguous, desultory, itinerant, uncertain, unquieted 10 changeable, precarious, unoccupied 11 unpopulated 12 undetermined

unshaken: 4 firm, sure 6 steady

unsheathe: 4 draw 6 expose, remove 7 pull out 8 withdraw

unsightly: 4 drab, ugly 5 messy 6 homely

unskilled: 4 rude 5 green 6 puisne 7 artless 8 ignorant, malapert 10 amateurish

unskillful: 5 inept 6 bungly, clumsy 7 awkward 8 inexpert

unskillfully: 5 badly 7 ineptly

unsociable: shy 4 cool 5 aloof 6 sullen 8 reserved, retiring 9 withdrawn 11 standoffish

unsoiled: 5 clean 10 immaculate

unsophisticated: 4 naif, pure 5 frank, green, naive 6 callow, simple 7 artless, genuine, natural 8 bona fide, innocent 9 guileless, ingenious, untutored, unworldly

unsound: bad 4 evil, sick, weak 5 crazy, dotty, false, frail, risky, shaky 6 addled, fickle, flawed, hollow, insane, rotten, weakly 7 decayed, wracked 8 diseased, impaired, insecure, weakened 9 dangerous, defective, imperfect, tottering

unspeakable: bad 4 vile 6 wicked 7 heinous 9 ineffable, loathsome 10 abominable, outrageous

unspoiled: 4 racy 5 fresh 6 virgin

unspoken: 4 mute 5 tacit 6 silent, unsaid 7 implied 8 implicit 9 ineffable, unuttered

unspotted: 5 clear 7 sinless 8 spotless 10 immaculate

unstable: 5 loose, sandy 6 fickle, fitful, flitty, labile 7 astatic, dwaible, dwaibly, erratic, mutable, plastic 8 doubtful, flightly, insecure, ticklish, unhinged, unsteady, variable 9 eccentric, faithless, irregular, mercurial, unsettled 10 changeable, inconstant, precarious, unreliable

unsteady: 5 dizzy, fluky, shaky, tippy 6 flicky, fluffy, groggy, wabbly, wobbly 7 movable, quavery, rickety, unsound, wayward 8 titubate, unstable, variable, wavering 9 desultory, uncertain 10 capricious, flickering 11 lightheaded

unstinted: 5 ample 6 lavish 7 endless 8 generous 10 open-handed

unstudied: 7 natural 8 careless, unforced, unversed 9 unlearned 10 colloquial, unaffected 11 extempory, spontaneous

unsubstantial: 4 airy, slim, thin, weak 5 filmy, light, paper 6 aerial, flimsy, papery, slight, unreal **7** folious, fragile, gaseous, nominal, shadowy, tenuous **8** filigree, footless **9** visionary **10** immaterial

unsuccessful: **4** vain **6** losing **7** failing, unlucky **8** abortive **9** fruitless **10** disastrous **11** ineffectual, unfortunate

unsuitable: bad **5** inapt, inept, undue, unfit **6** unmete **8** improper **10** unbecoming

unsullied: **4** fair, pure **5** clean **6** chaste **8** innocent, pristine, spotless **10** immaculate

unsure: **4** weak **5** timid **6** infirm **8** doubtful **9** dangerous, hazardous **10** precarious, unreliable **11** vacillating

unsusceptible: **6** immune **8** obdurate

unsweetened: dry, sec **4** sour

unswerving: **4** firm, true **5** fixed, loyal **6** steady **7** staunch **8** straight **9** steadfast

unsymmetrical: **8** lopsided **9** irregular **12** asymmetrical

unsympathetic: **4** cold, cool, hard **5** stony **6** frozen **7** hostile **9** heartless, unfeeling, unlikable **11** hardhearted

untainted: **4** free, good, pure **8** innocent **9** unsullied

untalented: **8** mediocre **11** incompetent

untamed: **4** wild **5** feral **6** ferine, ramage, ramish, savage **9** unsubdued

untangle: **4** free **6** sleave, unlace **7** release, unravel, unsnarl **9** extricate **11** disentangle

untanned skin: kip **4** hide, pelt **8** shagreen

untarnished: **5** clean **8** spotless

untaught: **5** naive **7** natural **8** ignorant **9** unlearned **10** illiterate, uneducated **11** spontaneous

untenanted: **5** empty **6** vacant

untended: **7** run-down **9** neglected

untested: new **5** green **7** untried

unthinking: **4** rash **5** brute **6** casual **8** careless, feckless, heedless, tactless **9** automatic, impetuous, impulsive **10** mechanical **11** thoughtless

unthrifty: **6** wanton **7** foolish, profuse **8** prodigal **10** profitless, profligate **11** extravagant, improvident

untidy: **5** dirty, dowdy, messy **6** sloppy **7** bunting, unkempt **8** careless, littered, slipshod, slovenly **10** disheveled, disordered, slatternly

untidy person: pig **4** slob **6** sloven **8** slattern

untie: **4** free, undo **5** loose **6** loosen, unbind, unlash **8** disunite, unfasten **9** disengage, extricate

untimely: **5** early **8** immature **9** premature **11** inopportune

untiring: **4** busy **8** sedulous, tireless **10** unflagging

untold: **4** huge, vast **6** secret **8** infinite **9** boundless, unrelated **10** suppressed, uninformed, unrevealed **11** innumerable

untouchable: **6** pariah **7** outcast **8** chandala, déclassé **10** intangible

untouched: **5** whole **6** intact, virgin **9** insensate

untoward: **6** unruly **7** awkward, froward, unlucky **8** improper, perverse, stubborn, unseemly **9** vexatious **10** indecorous, ungraceful **11** troublesome, unfavorable, unfortunate **12** inconvenient

untrained: raw **4** wild **5** green **7** awkward, untamed **8** undocile **9** unskilled **10** amateurish, unprepared

untrammeled: **4** free **5** loose **9** audacious, unlimited **10** unhampered

untried: new **4** tyro **5** fresh, green **6** maiden **7** amateur **8** immature, untested **13** inexperienced

untrue: **4** flam **5** false, wrong **8** disloyal, perjured **9** erroneous, faithless, incorrect **10** fallacious, fictitious, perfidious, unfaithful

untrustworthy: **6** tricky, unsafe **8** slippery **9** dishonest, uncertain **10** perfidious, unreliable **11** treacherous **12** undependable

untruth: lie **5** fable, story **7** fallacy, falsity, fiction **9** falsehood, mendacity, treachery **11** fabrication, tarradiddle

untutored: **5** naive **6** simple **7** artless, natural **8** clownish, ignorant, untaught **9** barbarian, unlearned **10** illiterate

untwine: **4** free, undo **5** frese, untie **6** unwind **9** extricate **11** disentangle

unused: new **4** idle **5** fresh **6** vacant **8** unwonted **12** unaccustomed

unusual: odd **4** rare **5** novel, outre, queer, weird **6** exotic, quaint, unique **7** bizarre, curious, foreign, strange **8** abnormal, singular, uncommon, unwonted **9** anomalous, different, eccentric, recherche **10** remarkable **11** exceptional **12** illegitimate

unusual person or thing: **4** oner **8** rara avis **10** sui generis

unutterable, inutterable: **9** ineffable **11** unspeakable **13** inexpressible

unvaried: **5** alike **7** uniform **10** monotonous

unvarnished: **4** bald **5** clear, frank, plain **6** simple **8** unglazed **9** unadorned, unglossed

unveil: **4** open **6** reveal **7** uncover **8** disclose

unvoiced: **4** surd **5** tacit **6** secret **8** devoiced, unspoken **9** unuttered

unwarranted: **5** undue **8** baseless **11** unjustified **12** unreasonable

unwary: **4** rash **7** unaware **8** careless, heedless **9** credulous, unguarded **10** groundless, incautious **11** precipitate

unwavering: **4** firm, pure **5** solid **6** stable, steady **7** staunch **8** constant **9** steadfast

unwearied: **4** busy **8** tireless **9** assiduous **13** indefatigable

unweave: **4** undo **5** ravel **6** unfold

unwed: **6** single

unwelcome: 8 non grata, unwanted 9 intruding, intrusive

unwell: ill 4 evil, sick 5 badly 6 ailing 8 off-color 9 squeamish 10 out-of-sorts

unwholesome: 4 evil 6 impure, sickly 7 corrupt, harmful, immoral, noisome, noxious, tainted, unclean 9 offensive, pestilent, unhygenic 11 unhealthful

unwieldy: 5 bulky, heavy 6 clumsy 7 awkward, hulking 8 cumbrous, ungainly 9 ponderous 10 cumbersome

unwilling: 4 loth 5 loath 6 averse, mauger, maugre 7 loathly 8 backward 9 eschewing, reluctant 11 disinclined

unwind: 5 ravel, relax 6 uncoil 8 untangle 10 straighten 11 disentangle

unwise: 5 inane, naive, silly 6 simple 7 foolish, witless 9 brainless, impolitic, imprudent, senseless 10 indiscreet, irrational 11 injudicious 12 undiplomatic

unwonted: 4 rare 6 unused 7 unusual 8 uncommon 10 infrequent 11 exceptional 12 unaccustomed

unworldly: 4 eery 5 eerie, naive, weird 6 dreamy 7 natural 8 innocent 9 spiritual, unearthly

unworthy: 4 base 5 unfit 7 beneath 8 shameful, unseemly, wretched 9 no-account, worthless 10 despicable, unbecoming 12 contemptible

unwrinkled: 5 brent (Sc.) 6 smooth

unwritten: 4 oral 5 blank, vocal 6 spoken, verbal 11 word-of-mouth

unyielding: set 4 fast, firm, grim, hard, iron 5 fixed, rigid, stern, stiff, stith, stony, tough 6 frozen, steely 7 adamant 8 obdurate, stubborn 9 inelastic, obstinate, unbending 10 determined, inexorable, inflexible, relentless 11 immalleable 12 contumacious, unsubmissive

unyoke: 4 free, part 5 loose 6 remove 7 disjoin, release 8 separate

up: 4 busy, rise 5 about, aloft, astir, awake, raise 6 active 7 expired, success 8 familiar 9 according
and down: 5 erect 6 direct, uneven 7 upright 8 vertical 9 downright, irregular 10 thoroughly, undulating 13 perpendicular
to date: new 4 chic 6 modern 7 current, stylish 11 fashionable
to this time: 5 so far 6 hereto 8 hitherto

upbeat: 5 arsis, happy 10 optimistic

upbraid: 4 draw, rail, twit 5 abuse, blame, braid, chide, scold, score, taunt, twist 6 accuse, charge, rebuke 7 censure, reprove 8 denounce, reproach 9 exprobate

upbuilding: 8 increase 11 edification

update: 5 renew 7 restore 9 modernize

upgrade: 5 raise, slope 6 ascent 7 incline

upheaval: 5 storm 6 revolt 7 rummage 9 agita-tion, cataclysm, commotion 10 convulsion

upheave: 4 lift, rear, rise

uphill: 4 hard 6 rising, tiring 7 arduous, labored 9 ascending, difficult, laborious

uphold: 4 abet, back, bear, buoy, lift 5 favor, raise 6 assert, defend, favour, second 7 bolster, confirm, support, sustain 8 conserve, maintain 9 encourage, vindicate

upholder: 6 dealer 8 adherent 9 tradesman 10 undertaker 11 upholsterer

upholstered: fat 9 cushioned, luxurious

upkeep: 4 cost 6 repair 7 support 8 overhead 11 maintenance

upland: 4 mesa, wold 5 downs 6 coteau 7 plateau

uplift: 4 buoy, head, lift, rock 5 erect, raise, tower 7 collect, elevate, ennoble, improve 8 upheaval 9 elevation 10 illuminate

Upolu: *city:* 4 Apia
island group: 5 Samoa

upon: oer, sur (law) 4 atop, over 5 about, above 8 touching 10 concerning

upper: 4 bunk, drug, over, vamp 5 above, berth 8 superior 9 stimulant
case: 7 capital
crust: 5 elite 7 segment, society

upperclassman: 6 junior, senior

uppermost: top 5 first 6 apical 7 highest, topmost 8 farthest, foremost, loftiest 9 outermost 11 predominant

uppish: 5 brash, proud 6 elated 7 haughty, peevish 8 arrogant, assuming, snobbish 12 presumptuous, supercilious

upraised: 5 atilt 6 lifted, raised 7 erected 8 elevated, extolled, improved, vertical 10 encouraged

uprear: 5 build, erect, exalt, raise

upright: 4 good, just, true 5 erect, moral, piano, right, stela, stele, stile 6 honest, square, worthy 7 endwise, sincere 8 straight, vertical, virtuous 9 elevation, equitable, honorable, righteous 10 aboveboard, pianoforte, scrupulous 11 unambiguous
support: 4 jamb, stud

uprightness: 5 honor 6 equity 7 honesty, probity 9 rectitude

uprising: 4 coup, riot 6 ascent, mutiny, putsch, revolt, tumult 7 ensuing 8 reaction 9 ascending, commotion, rebellion 10 increasing, insurgency, revolution

uproar: ado, din 4 fuss, riot, rout, stir, to-do 5 brawl, chaos, hurly, melee, noise 6 bedlam, bustle, clamor, dirdum, fracas, habble, hoopla, hubble, hubbub, racket, rattle, ruckus, rumpus, squall, strife, tumult 7 clamour, ferment, trouble, turmoil 8 brouhaha, outbreak 9 commotion, confusion 10 convulsion, donnybrook, hurly-burly, rumbullion, tintamarre

uproot: 4 move 5 shift 7 destroy 8 supplant 9

801   **usage**

eradicate, extirpate **10** annihilate, transplant **11** exterminate

upset: irk **4** cave, coup, keel, rile, turn **5** alarm, anger, angry **6** defeat, dismay, refund, thwart, topple, uneasy **7** agitate, anxious, capsize, confuse, derange, disturb, fluster, nervous, outcome, perturb, pervert, quarrel, reverse, subvert, unnerve **8** capsized, disorder, distress, overturn, vanquish **9** discomfit, embarrass, overthrow, perturbed **10** debilitate, discompose, disconcert, disordered, distressed, overturned **11** disorganize

upshot: end **5** issue, limit **6** effect, finish, result, sequel **7** outcome **9** aftermath, substance **10** conclusion

upside-down: **7** chaotic, jumbled **8** inverted **10** topsy-turvy

upstage: shy **5** aloof, outdo **6** offish **8** backward, outshine, snobbish **9** conceited

upstart: **4** snob **6** origin **7** dalteen, parvenu, saffron **8** arrivist, parvenue **9** arriviste, cockhorse

upstir: **6** incite **7** agitate **9** stimulate

upsurge: **4** boom, rise **9** inflation

uptake: **4** flue, tube **5** shaft **6** upcast **10** collection, comprehend **13** comprehension, understanding

uptight: **4** edgy **5** tense **6** uneasy

up-to-date: **6** modern **7** abreast, current **9** au courant

upward: **4** more, over **5** above, aloft, lofty **7** airward, skyward **8** airwards **9** ascending

uraeus: **6** symbol **8** ornament **9** sacred asp **10** decoration

uralite: **9** amphibole

uranian: **8** heavenly **9** celestial **10** homosexual **12** astronomical

Urania's son: **5** Hymen

uranium: **15** chemical element
    source: **11** pitchblende

Uranus: *children:* **4** Rhea **5** Titan **6** Cronus, Furies **7** Cyclops
    mother: **4** Gaea, Gaia
    satellite: **5** Ariel **6** Oberon **7** Miranda, Titania, Umbriel
    wife: **4** Gaea, Gaia

urban: **5** civic **7** oppidan **8** citified **9** inner city, municipal

urban division: **4** ward **7** borough

urbane: **5** bland, civil, suave **6** poised, polite, smooth **7** affable, elegant, genteel, refined **8** polished **9** courteous **12** cosmopolitan **13** sophisticated

urchin: boy, cub, elf, imp, tad **4** arab, brat **5** child, elfin, gamin **8** cylinder, hedgehog, hurcheon **9** hunchback, youngster **10** ragamuffin, street arab

urease: **6** enzyme

uredo: **5** hives **9** urticaria **11** burning itch

urge: dun, egg, ert (Sc.), hie, ply, sic, sue **4** brod, coax, goad, itch, lust, prod, push, spur **5** broad, drive, egg on, filip, force, hurry, impel, plead, press, shove **6** allege, cajole, compel, demand, desire, excite, exhort, fillip, incite, induce, insist, motive, needle, prompt, propel **7** animate, augment, craving, entreat, impulse, passion, provoke, solicit, wheedle **8** advocate, appetite, blandish, persuade, pressure **9** encourage, flagitate, importune, incentive, influence, stimulate **10** exasperate

urgency: **4** need **5** haste, hurry **6** crisis, stress **8** exigency, pressure **10** insistence **11** importunity

urgent: hot **5** grave **6** crying **7** burning, clamant, driving, exigent **8** critical, pressing **9** clamorous, demanding, impelling, important, insistent **10** imperative, solicitous **11** importunate

Uriah's wife: **9** Bathsheba

urial, oorial: sha **5** sheep

Uriel: **5** angel **9** archangel

Urim's partner: **7** Thummim

Uris novel: **5** QBVII **6** Exodus **7** Trinity

urisk: **7** brownie

urn: jar, run **4** bury, ewer, urna, vase **5** grave, inurn, steen, theca **6** spring **7** amphora, capsule, cistern, pitcher, samovar, vaselet **8** fountain **9** container **10** jardiniere
    for bones: **7** ossuary
    tea: **7** samovar

urn-shaped: **9** urceolate

Ursa: **4** Bear
    Major: **9** Great Bear
    Minor: **10** Little Bear

ursine: **7** arctoid **8** bearlike

urticaria: See **uredo**

urubu: **7** vulture

Uruguay: *capital:* **10** Montevideo
    city: **4** Melo **5** Minas **6** Rivera **8** Mercedes
    currency: **4** peso **9** centesimo
    estuary: **5** Plata
    Indian: **7** Charrua
    measure: **4** vara **6** cuadra, suerte
    terrorist group: **8** Tupumaro
    weight: **7** quintal

urus: tur **7** aurochs

us: ci (It.), noi (It.), nos (Sp.), uns (G.) **4** nous (Fr.) **8** nosotros (Sp.)

usable: **4** fit **8** open **8** servable **9** available, practical **10** convenient, functional

usage: use **4** form, wont **5** habit, haunt, idiom **6** custom, manner, method **7** conduct, manners, utility **8** behavior, interest, practice **9** treatment **10** convention, employment, experience, preference

use: try **4** duty, hire, need, wont, work **5** apply, avail, guide, habit, right, serve, spend, stead, treat, trope, value, wield, worth **6** custom, employ, expend, handle, hansel, manage, manner, occupy, profit, target **7** benefit, consume, exhaust, exploit, fitness, operate, purpose, service, utility, utilize **8** accustom, deal with, exercise, frequent, function, handling, practice **9** habituate, privilege, treatment **10** employment, manipulate **11** application, consumption
as example: **4** cite
refrain from: **7** boycott
up: eat **4** tire **5** drain, spend **7** consume, deplete, exhaust, outwear
wastefully: **5** spill **7** fritter **8** squander **9** dissipate

used: **8** shopworn **10** secondhand **11** experienced

useful: **4** good, meet **5** handy, utile **7** helpful, thrifty **8** suitable **9** practical **10** beneficial, commodious, convenient, functional, profitable **11** serviceable

usefulness: **5** avail, value **6** profit **7** utility

useless: **4** idle, null, vain **6** futile, otiose **7** inutile **8** bootless, hopeless **9** fruitless, worthless **11** ineffectual, inefficient, superfluous **12** unprofitable **13** impracticable

user: **6** addict **7** pothead **8** consumer

usher: **4** lead, page **5** guide **6** beadle, escort, herald **7** chobdar, conduct, officer, precede, preface, servant, teacher **9** announcer, assistant, attendant, harbinger, introduce, precursor **10** doorkeeper, forerunner, inaugurate
in: **6** launch **8** initiate **9** introduce **10** inaugurate

usual: **4** rife **6** common, normal, wonted **7** average, chronic, general, natural, regular, routine, typical **8** accepted, familiar, frequent, habitual, ordinary, orthodox, workaday **9** customary, prevalent **10** accustomed, prevailing **11** commonplace, stereotyped

usurer: **5** shark **7** Shylock **9** loan shark

Utah: *capital:* **12** Salt Lake City
city: **4** Orem **5** Logan, Ogden, Provo **6** Murray
Indian: Ute **7** Anasazi
lake: **9** Great Salt
Mormon leader: **12** Brigham Young
motto: **8** Industry
river: **5** Grand, Green, Snake, Weber **6** Jordan, Sevier **8** Colorado
state bird: **7** seagull
state flower: **8** sego lily
state tree: **6** spruce

---

usurp: **4** take **5** seize, wrest **6** assume **7** preempt **8** accroach, arrogate, displace, supplant

usury: vig **7** gombeen **8** vigorish

Utah (see box)

utensil: pan, pot, wok **4** bowl, fork, tool **5** knife, mixer, sieve, spoon **6** beater, grater, peeler, sifter, vessel **7** chopper, scraper, skillet, spatula **8** colander, strainer **9** corkscrew, implement **10** instrument
cleaning: mop **5** broom, brush **6** Hoover, sponge, vacuum **7** sweeper

Uther's son: **10** King Arthur

utile: **5** handy **6** useful **9** practical **10** functional, profitable

utilitarian: **5** plain **6** useful **8** economic **9** practical, realistic **10** functional

utility: use **5** avail **6** profit **7** benefit, service

utilize: **6** employ **7** consume, harness, husband

utmost: end **4** best, last **5** final **7** extreme, maximum **8** farthest, greatest

Uto-Aztecan Indian: Ute **4** Hopi, Pima **6** Papago **7** Nahuatl **8** Comanche, Shoshone

Utopia: **4** Eden **6** heaven **8** Paradise **9** Shangri La
author: **4** More
Harrington's: **6** Oceana

utopian: **5** ideal **8** idealist, quixotic **9** visionary **10** chimerical

utricle: sac **7** vesicle

Uttar Pradesh: *capital:* **7** Lucknow

utter: add, say **4** blat, bray, emit, gasp, pipe, pray, rail, roar, tell, vent **5** blurt, clack, croak, drawl, final, gross, issue, sheer, speak, spill, spout, stark, state, total, trill, voice **6** arrant, assert, direct, entire, mumble, reveal **7** bluster, declare, deliver, divulge, enounce, express, extreme, iterate, publish **8** abnormal, absolute, complete, disclose, vocalize **9** downright, enunciate, pronounce, verbalize **10** articulate, consummate, peremptory **11** unqualified

utterance: gab **4** osse, word **5** aside, dicta, ditty **6** dictum, oracle, speech **7** calling **8** effusion, monotone, phonesis, rhapsody **9** phonation, statement **10** expression, forthgoing
voiced: **6** sonant
voiceless: **4** surd **7** spirate

uttered: **4** oral **6** spoken

utterly: all **4** well **5** fully, quite, stark **6** in toto, merely, purely, wholly **7** totally **8** entirely **10** absolutely, completely **11** diametrally

uttermost: **5** final **6** utmost **7** extreme, outmost **8** farthest, furthest, remotest

utu: **6** reward **12** compensation, satisfaction

uva: **5** fruit, grape

uxorial: **6** wifely

Uzbekistan: *capital:* **8** Tashkent
city: **9** Samarkand

V

V: vee **5** five
  symbol of: **5** peace **7** victory
vacancy: gap **4** void **5** break, chasm, space **6** cavity, hollow, vacuum **7** interim, opening, vacuity **10** hollowness, interstice **11** vacuousness
vacant: **4** free, idle, open, void **5** blank, empty, fishy, inane, silly **6** barren, devoid, hollow, lonely **7** foolish, lacking, leisure, vacuous, wanting **8** unfilled **9** destitute **10** disengaged, unemployed, unoccupied, untenanted
vacate: **4** move, quit, void **5** annul, avoid, clear, empty, leave **6** repeal **7** abandon, abolish, rescind **8** abdicate, abrogate, evacuate
vacation: **4** rest, trip **5** break, leave, spell **6** outing, recess **7** holiday, leisure, nonterm, respite, time off **8** furlough **9** justitium **10** sabbatical **12** intermission
  place: spa **4** city, lake, park **5** beach, ocean **6** forest, resort **7** country, seaside **9** mountains
vaccinate: **9** inoculate
vaccine: **4** sera, shot **5** serum
  discoverer of: **4** Salk **5** Sabin **6** Jenner
vacillate: **4** sway **5** dally, waver **6** dacker, daiker, dawdle, dither, falter, seesaw, teeter, totter, wobble **7** flutter, stagger **8** hesitate, titubate **9** alternate, fluctuate, hem and haw, oscillate
vacillation: **5** doubt **7** halting **8** demurral, stalling, wavering **9** infirmity **10** fickleness, indecision, unsureness **11** uncertainty **12** irresolution
vacuity: **4** hole, void **6** cavity, hollow **7** inanity, vacancy **9** blankness, emptiness **11** nothingness
vacuous: **4** dull, idle **5** blank, empty, inane, silly **6** stupid **7** foolish, shallow **8** unfilled **9** evacuated, senseless **11** purposeless
vacuum: **4** void **5** space **9** emptiness
  opposite of: **6** plenum
vacuum pump: **10** pulsometer
vacuum tube: **5** diode **7** tetrode **9** electrode
vade mecum: **5** guide **6** manual **8** handbook **9** guidebook
vadimonium: **4** bond **6** pledge **8** bailment, contract, security
vadium: **4** bail, pawn **6** pledge

vagabond: bum **4** hobo, rove **5** gypsy, rogue, rover, scamp, stray, tramp **6** beggar, canter, jockey, rascal, wander **7** drifter, erratic, gadling, migrant, nomadic, vagrant, wayward **8** bohemian, brodyaga, derelict, drifting, fugitive, wanderer **9** itinerant, shiftless, straggler, transient, wandering, worthless **10** blackguard, ne'er-do-well **11** bindle stiff
vagarious: **5** kinky **7** erratic **9** arbitrary, eccentric, whimsical **13** unpredictable
vagary: **4** kink, roam, whim **5** caper, fancy, freak, humor, jaunt, prank, quirk, stray, trick, waver **6** action, breach, megrim, notion, oddity, ramble, totter, whimsy **7** caprice, conceit **8** crotchet, flagarie, rambling **9** departure, excursion, procedure, wandering **10** digression, divergence **12** passing fancy **13** manifestation
vagrant: See **vagabond**
vague: dim **4** dark, hazy **5** faint, fuzzy, loose, misty, stray **6** bleary, blurry, cloudy, dreamy, vagary **7** cryptic, evasive, obscure, shadowy, sketchy, tenuous, unclear, unfixed, vagrant **8** confused, nebulous, vagabond, wanderer **9** ambiguous, enigmatic, imprecise, uncertain, undefined, unsettled, wandering **10** ill-defined, indefinite, indistinct, intangible **11** unspecified **13** indeterminate
vail: tip, use **4** doff, dole **5** bribe, lower, yield **6** humble, submit **7** benefit, subside **8** gratuity **9** advantage **10** beneficial
vain: **4** idle **5** empty, flory, petty, proud, silly **6** flimsy, futile, hollow, otiose, snooty **7** foolish, foppish, stuckup, trivial, useless **8** arrogant, bootless, delusory, gorgeous, hopeless, ignorant, nugatory, peacocky, trifling **9** conceited, egotistic, fruitless, worthless **10** chimerical, egocentric, evanescent, unavailing, unrewarded **11** empty-headed, ineffectual, overweening, unimportant **12** narcissistic, unprofitable, vainglorious
  boasting: **11** fanfaronade
  person: fop **5** dandy **7** coxcomb
vainglorious: **8** boastful, bragging, insolent **9** conceited
vair: fur
Vaishnava: *deity:* **6** Vishnu
Vaisya caste: **6** Aroras
valance: **5** drape **6** pelmet **7** curtain, drapery, hanging

vale: 4 dale, dean, dell, dene, glen 5 bache, combe, glade 6 dingle, valley 8 farewell

valediction: 5 adieu 7 address, good-bye 8 farewell

valence: 5 power, value 7 atomism 10 importance

Valence's river: 5 Rhone

valentine: 4 card, gift, love 7 beloved 8 greeting 10 sweetheart

valerian: 4 drug, herb 5 plant 7 allheal, panacea, setwall 9 corn salad 10 heliotrope

valet: man 4 goad 5 stick 6 andrew, Jeeves, tartar 7 dresser, servant 9 attendant, cameriere, chamberer 10 manservant

Vali's parents: 4 Odin, Rind 5 Rindr

valiant: 4 bold, prow 5 aught, brave, proud, stout 6 heroic, robust, strong, sturdy 7 doughty 8 galliard, intrepid, powerful, stalwart, vigorous, virtuous 9 bounteous, excellent, steadfast 10 chivalrous, courageous

valid: 4 good, just, true 5 legal, solid, sound 6 cogent, lawful, robust, strong 7 binding, healthy, telling, weighty 8 attested, forcible, powerful, verified 9 authentic, confirmed, effective, efficient 10 conclusive, convincing, sufficient 11 efficacious 12 satisfactory, well-grounded

opposite of: 4 null, void 7 invalid

validate: 7 approve, confirm, endorse 8 sanction 9 establish 11 rubber-stamp

valise: bag 4 case, grip 7 baggage, luggage, satchel 8 suitcase

valium: 4 drug 12 tranquilizer

Valjean: *friend:* 6 Marius

pursuer: 6 Javert

story: 13 Les Misérables

Valkyrie: 6 maiden 8 Brynhild 10 Brunnhilde

vallecula: 6 furrow, groove 7 channel 10 depression

valley: dip 4 brae, comb, coom, cove, dale, dean, dell, dene, ghyl, gill, glen, rill, vale, wadi, wady 5 atrio, basin, combe, coomb, dhoon, glack, gorge, goyal, goyle, gully, kloof, swale, waddy 6 bolson, canada, canyon, clough, coombe, coulee, dingle, gutter, hollow, ravine, rincon, strath, trough 7 blowout 10 depression

bottom: 5 floor

deep: 4 rift 5 canon 6 canyon

vallum: 4 wall 7 rampart

valor, valour: 4 grit, guts, sand 5 arete, merit, value, worth 6 bounty, mettle, spirit, virtue 7 bravery, courage, heroism, prowess 8 backbone, position 9 fortitude, gallantry, valuation 10 importance 11 distinction 12 fearlessness

valuable: 4 dear 5 asset 6 costly, prized, useful, worthy 8 esteemed, precious 9

estimable, excellent, expensive, priceless, respected, treasured 10 worthwhile 11 serviceable

value: use 4 cost, feck (Sc.), rate 5 assay, avail, cheap, gauge, merit, price, prize, worth 6 assess, assize, esteem, extend, figure, moment, reckon 7 account, apprise, apprize, care for, cherish, compute, expense, opinion, quality, respect, utility 8 appraise, estimate, evaluate, treasure 9 appraisal, inventory, valuation 10 appreciate, estimation, importance

anything of little: 5 plack (Sc.) 6 trifle 7 trinket

equal: 6 parity

full: 11 money's worth

mean: 7 average

nominal: par

reduction: 12 depreciation

relative: 9 ad valorem

without: 5 waste 6 trashy 7 useless 9 worthless

valve: tap 4 cock, gate 6 faucet, outlet, piston, spigot 7 petcock

heart: 6 mitral 8 bicuspid

sliding: 6 piston

vamoose: go, lam 4 scat 5 leave, scram 6 decamp, depart, get out 8 hightail 9 skedaddle

vamp: 4 hose, mend, plod, sock 5 fix up, flirt, patch, siren, tramp 6 invent, repair, seduce 7 beguile, concoct, fireman 8 contrive, coquette 9 fabricate, improvise, temptress 10 gold digger, seductress 11 enchantress, femme fatale

vampire: bat 5 lamia 6 alukah, corpse, usurer 7 seducer 11 blackmailer, blood-sucker

famous: 7 Dracula 9 Nosferatu

van: fan 4 fore, lead, wing 5 front, truck, wagon 6 leader, shovel, summit, winnow 7 fourgon, vehicle 9 forefront

Van Gogh town: 5 Arles

vandal: hun 6 looter 7 hoodlum, ruffian, wrecker 8 hooligan 9 plunderer

vandalize: mar 5 trash, wreck 6 deface, rip off 7 destroy

Vandyke: 5 beard 6 artist 7 picture

vane: arm 5 blade 7 feather 9 indicator 11 weathercock

feather: web 8 vexillum

vanguard: 9 forefront 10 avant-garde

vanilla: 4 bean, vine 5 bland 6 orchid 7 extract

vanilla substance: 8 coumarin

vanish: 4 fade, melt 5 clear 8 disperse, dissolve, evanesce 9 disappear, evaporate

vanity: 4 airs 5 pride 6 egoism 7 compact, conceit, egotism, falsity, foppery 8 futility,

idleness **9** dizziness, emptiness **10** hollowness
symbol of: **7** peacock

vanity case: **4** etui **7** compact

Vanity Fair: *author:* **9** Thackeray
character: **10** Becky Sharp

vanquish: get, win **4** beat, best, rout **5** expel, floor **6** defeat, expugn, humble, master, subdue **7** confute, conquer, subvert **8** confound, overcome, suppress, surmount **9** overpower, overthrow

vanquisher: **6** victor **8** champion **9** conquerer

vantage: See **advantage**

vapid: dry **4** dull, flat, pall, weak **5** inane, stale, trite **6** jejune **7** insipid, mawkish **8** lifeless **9** milk-toast, pointless, tasteless **10** flavorless, namby-pamby, spiritless, unanimated, unexciting, wishy-washy **13** uninteresting

vapor: fog, gas **4** fume, haze, idea, mist, smog **5** boast, brume, cloud, ewder, fancy, humor, smoke, steam **6** breath, bubble, humour, nimbus, notion **7** halitus **8** contrail, humidity, phantasm **9** evaporate **10** blustering
frozen: **4** hail, rime, snow **5** frost, sleet

vaporize: **5** steam **7** boil off **9** evaporate

vaporous: **4** airy, hazy **5** foggy, gassy, misty, vague **6** unreal **7** gaseous **8** ethereal, fleeting, illusory, volatile

vaquero: **6** cowboy **8** herdsman, horseman **10** equestrian

varec, varech: **4** kelp **5** ashes, wrack **7** seaweed

variable (see also **vary**): **5** fluid **6** fickle, fitful **7** mutable, protean, unequal, variant, varying **8** floating, unstable, unsteady, volatile **9** mercurial, irregular, uncertain **10** capricious, changeable, inconstant

variance: **7** discord, dispute **8** conflict, disunity, division **9** deviation **10** difference

variation (see also **vary**): **5** shift **6** change **8** heterism, mutation **9** disparity, tolerance **10** aberration, alteration, deflection, divergence **11** discrepancy, distinction

varicose: **7** dilated, swollen **8** enlarged

varied: **5** mixed **6** daedal **7** several **13** miscellaneous

variegated: **4** pied, shot **5** lyard (Sc.), lyart (Sc.) **6** daedal, menald, motley, varied **7** dappled, flecked, mottled, painted, piebald, tissued **8** speckled **9** different, enamelled **11** diversified

variety: ilk **4** kind, sort, type **5** breed, class, grade **7** species **9** diversity, variation **10** assortment, difference, miscellany

variola: **6** cowpox **8** horsepox, smallpox

various: **4** many **6** divers, sundry **7** certain, diverse, several **8** assorted, distinct, manifold, variable **9** different, disparate, divergent, uncertain, versatile **10** changeable, inconstant, individual

varlet: boy **4** page **5** gippo, knave, noble, youth **6** menial, rabble, rascal, vassal **7** bailiff, footman, servant **8** coistrel, coistril **9** attendant, scoundrel

varnish: **4** coat, spar **5** glaze, japan **7** lacquer, shellac **8** brighten, palliate **9** embellish
ingredient: lac **5** copal, elemi, resin, rosin **6** dammar **8** urethane

vary: **4** part **5** alter, range, shift **6** change, depart, differ, divide, modify, swerve **7** deviate, dispute, dissent, diverge, qualify, quarrel, variate **8** disagree, modulate, separate **9** alternate, diversify, fluctuate, oscillate

vas: **4** duct **6** pledge, surety, vessel

vase: jar, urn **4** asci, ewer, olla, vaso **5** ascus, askos, echea, tazza **6** crater, deinoi, deinos, krater, vessel **7** amphora, urceole **9** lekythose **10** cassolette, jardiniere
handle: **4** ansa

vassal: man **4** bond, esne, lend, rule, serf **5** ceile, helot, liege, slave **6** geneat, tenant, varlet **7** bondman, feedman, feodary, homager, peasant, servant, servile, subject **8** dominate, liegeman **9** dependent, feudatory, underling **11** beneficiary, subordinate
pert. to: **6** feudal

vast: big **4** huge **5** ample, broad, giant, great, large, vasty **6** cosmic, lonely, mighty, untold **7** immense **8** colossal, enormous, far-flung, gigantic, spacious **9** boundless, capacious, cyclopean, expansive, extensive **10** tremendous, wide-spread **11** far-reaching, illimitable

vastness: **7** expanse **8** enormity, grandeur **9** immensity, magnitude

vat: fat, pit, tub, tun, wit **4** back, beck, cask, coom, gyle, keel, kier, tank **5** coomb, keeve, kieve, press **6** barrel, kettle, vessel **7** caldron, chessel, cistern **8** cauldron

vatic: **8** inspired, oracular **9** prophetic

Vatican City: **5** state **7** Holy See
basilica: **8** St. Peter's
chapel: **7** Sistine
guards' nationality: **5** Swiss
includes: **14** Castel Gandolfo
leader: **4** pope
official: **6** datary
palace: **7** Lateran
publication: **4** bull **10** encyclical

vaticinate: **5** augur **7** predict **8** foretell

vaudeville: **5** revue **7** variety **9** burlesque
act: **4** skit, song, turn **5** dance

vaudevillian: **5** actor, comic **6** dancer, hoofer, singer **7** acrobat, juggler **9** performer

vaudy: gay **5** gaudy, showy **6** elated, sturdy **8** cheerful

vault: box, pit **4** arch, bend, cave, cope, dome, jump, leap, over, roof, room, safe, soar, tomb **5** bound, clear, croft, crypt, curve, floor, groin, mount, shade **6** cavern, cellar, crater, cupola, curvet, flaunt, grotto, hurdle, spring, welkin **7** ceiling, chamber, dungeon, glorify, testudo **8** catacomb, flourish, overjump, overleap, surmount **9** concavity, staircase **10** depository, repository, testudines (pl.)

vaunt: van **4** brag, font **5** boast, roose **6** avaunt **7** display, exhibit, show off **8** brandish **11** ostentation

veal: **4** calf, meat, veau (F.)
cutlet: **9** schnitzel (G.)
shank: **8** osso buco

vector: **4** host **7** carrier **8** gradient
opposite of: **6** scalar

vedette: **5** vigil, watch **8** sentinel

Vedas: **11** sacred books
god: **4** Agni **6** Aditya **7** Savitar
hymn: **6** mantra
language: **4** Pali **8** Sanskrit
religion: **8** Hinduism
sky serpent: ahi
supreme being: **7** Brahman
text: **5** Sakha, Shaka

veer: yaw **4** skew, slue, sway, turn **5** alter, avert, pivot, sheer, twist **6** broach, careen, change, depart, swerve **7** deviate, digress, diverge **8** angle off **9** fluctuate

veery: **6** thrush

vega: **5** tract **6** meadow

Vega's constellation: **4** Lyra

vegetable: pea, yam **4** bean, beet, corn, kale, leek, lima, ocra, okra, soya, taro **5** chard, melon, onion, plant **6** carrot, celery, lentil, peanut, pepper, potato, radish, squash, tomato, turnip **7** bok choy, brocoli, cabbage, chayote, lettuce, parsley, parsnip, peascod, pumpkin, rhubarb, salsiby, soybean, spinach **8** broccoli, collards, cucumber, eggplant, kohlrabi, peasecod, rutabaga, zucchini **9** artichoke, asparagus **11** cauliflower, horseradish, sweet potato **13** mustard greens **14** Brussels sprout
dealer: **8** huckster **11** greengrocer **12** costermonger
decayed: **4** duff **5** humus
green: **5** sabzi
pepsin: **6** caroid
pod: **4** hull **8** peasecod
salad: **5** cress **6** endive, garlic, sorrel **7** romaine, shallot **8** scallion
sponge: **5** loofa, luffa **6** loofah
spread: **4** oleo **9** margarine

vegetable caterpillar: **5** aweto

vegetable pear: **7** chayote

vegetate: **4** idle **8** languish, stagnate **9** hibernate

vegetation: **5** flora **6** growth **7** verdure **8** greenery
god: **4** Atys, Esus **5** Attis

vegete: **6** lively **7** healthy **11** flourishing

vehement: hot **4** wild **5** angry, eager, fiery, hefty, irked, rabid, yeder **6** ardent, fervid, fierce, flashy, heated, raging, urgent **7** animose, animous, fervent, furioso, furious, intense, violent, zealous **8** emphatic, forceful, vigorous **9** impetuous **10** boisterous, passionate, pronounced **11** impassioned

vehicle (see also **aircraft, automobile, car, ship**): ark, bus, car, van **4** auto, shay, taxi, tool, wain **5** araba, brake, break, buggy, dilly, means, sedan, sulky, wagon **6** agency, barrow, charet, device, hansom, landau, medium, troika, vector **7** carrier, chariot, kibitka (Russ.), tallyho **8** carriage, charette **9** buckboard, implement, velociman **10** automobile, conveyance
army: **4** jeep, tank **9** ambulance
child's: **4** pram **5** buggy **6** walker **7** scooter **8** carriage, stroller, tricycle **10** velocipede **12** perambulator
hauling: van **4** dray, semi, sled **5** lorry, truck **7** tractor, trailer
parade: **5** float
passenger: bus, cab **4** hack, ship, taxi, tram **5** liner, train **6** hansom, subway **7** minibus, omnibus, taxicab, tramcar, trolley **8** airplane, cablecar **9** charabanc
public: bus, cab, car **4** taxi, tram **5** train **7** omnibus, ricksha **8** rickshaw **10** jinricksha
snow: **4** pung, sled **6** sleigh **8** toboggan
two-wheeled: **4** cart **5** sulky, tonga **6** cisium **7** bicycle, caleche **9** carromata (P.I.) **11** vinaigrette
wheelless: **4** ship, sled **6** cutter, sledge, sleigh

veil: dim **4** caul, film, hide, mask **5** cloak, cover, orale, velum, volet **6** bumble, enfold, facade, fannel, mantle, masque, screen, shroud, soften **7** conceal, cover up, curtain, secrete, watcher **8** calyptra, disguise, headrail
Moslem: **7** yashmak

veiling: **5** tulle, voile **6** purdah **7** curtain **10** obvelation

vein: bed, rib **4** dash, hilo, hint, lode, mind, mode, mood, seam, tang, tone, tube, vena, wave **5** costa, crack, humor, scrin, shade, smack, spice, style, tenor, tinge, touch, trend, venae **6** cavity, costae, manner, nature, strain, streak **7** bonanza, channel, crevice, fashion, fissure, stratum **8** tendency **9** character **11** inclination, variegation

enlarged: **5** varix **8** varicose
fluid: **4** icor **5** blood, ichor
inflammation: **9** phlebitis
large: **8** vena cava
leaf: rib **5** costa
mining: **4** lode
pert. to: **6** veinal, venous
throat: **7** jugular
veinstone: **6** gangue, matrix **9** lodestuff
velamen: **5** velum **8** membrane
velar: **7** palatal **8** guttural
velarium: **6** awning **8** covering
veldt, veld: **6** meadow, plains **9** grassland
velitation: **5** brush, run-in **7** contest, dispute
    8 skirmish **9** encounter
velleity: **4** hope, will, wish **5** fancy **6** desire,
    liking **8** volition **11** inclination
vellicate: nip **4** jerk, pull, snap, yank **5** pinch,
    pluck **6** fidget, tickle, twitch **9** titillate
velocious: **4** fast **6** speedy
velocipede: **4** bike **6** tandem **7** bicycle, dicy-
    cle **8** tricycle **11** quadricycle
velocity: **4** pace **5** haste, hurry, speed **7** head-
    way, impetus **8** celerity, dispatch, momen-
    tum, rapidity **9** quickness, swiftness
velum: **4** veil **6** awning, palate **8** membrane
velutinous: **7** velvety
velvet: **4** gain **5** cloth, drink **6** birodo (Jap.),
    profit **7** surplus **8** winnings
    fabric like: **5** panne **6** velour, velure
velvetbreast: **9** merganser
velvet dock: **6** mullen **7** mullein **10** elecam-
    pane
venal: **6** venous **7** corrupt, crooked, for sale,
    salable **8** bribable, infamous, saleable,
    vendible **9** mercenary
vend: **4** hawk, sell **5** utter **6** market, peddle **7**
    declare, publish **8** transfer **9** advertise
vendetta: **4** feud **9** blood feud
vendeuse: **9** salesgirl **10** saleswoman
vendible: **5** venal **7** salable **8** saleable **9** mer-
    cenary **10** marketable
vendition: **4** sale
vendor, vender: **6** seller **7** alienor, butcher,
    peddler **8** merchant, salesman
vendue: **4** sale **7** auction
veneer: lac **4** coat, face, mask, show **5** cover,
    front, glaze, gloss, layer, plate **6** enamel,
    facade, facing **7** coating, overlay, varnish **8**
    palliate
venerable: old **4** aged, hoar, sage **5** hoary **6**
    august **7** ancient, antique, classic, elderly,
    honored, revered, stately **8** imposing, time-
    worn **9** honorable
veneration: awe **4** fear **5** honor **6** esteem,
    homage **7** respect, worship **8** devotion,
    idolatry **9** adoration, reverence
venerer: **6** hunter **8** huntsman
venery: **5** chase **7** coition, hunting

Venezuela: *bird:* **8** guacharo
    capital: **7** Caracas
    city: **4** Aroa, Coro **6** Merida **7** Barinas,
    Cabimas **8** Valencia **9** Maracaibo
    currency: **4** real **5** medio **6** fuerte **7** boli-
    var, centimo **8** morocota **10** venezolano
    dance: **5** salsa **6** joropo **8** guaracha,
    merengue
    export: **9** petroleum
    Indian: **6** Timote
    lake: **8** Valencia **9** Maracaibo, Tacariga
    language: **4** Pume
    measure: **5** galon, milla **6** fanega **7**
    estadel
    mountain: **5** Andes
    musical instrument: **6** cuatro, maraca
    people: **5** Carib **6** Timote **7** Timotex **8**
    Guarauno
    river: **4** Meta **5** Apure, Caura **6** Arausa,
    Caroni **7** Orinoco, Ventuar
    waterfall: **5** Angel
    weight: bag **5** libra

vengeance: **5** wrack **6** wanion **7** revenge **8**
    reprisal, requital **9** repayment **10** punish-
    ment **11** retaliation
    god of: **6** Erinys **7** Alastor
    goddess of: Ara, Ate **7** Nemesis
venial: **5** minor **7** trivial **8** harmless, trifling **9**
    allowable, excusable, tolerable **10** forgiv-
    able, pardonable

Venice: *beach:* **4** Lido
    bell tower: **9** Campanile
    boat: **7** gondola **9** bucentaur
    bridge: **6** Rialto **7** of Sighs
    district: **6** Rialto
    magistrate: **4** doge
    old silver coin: **5** betso
    painter: **6** Titian **7** Bellini **8** Veronese **9**
    Giorgione **10** Tintoretto
    palace: **5** Doges
    product: **4** lace **7** crystal **9** glassware
    square: **7** St. Mark's

Venice of the North: **9** Stockholm
venin: **6** poison
venireman: **5** juror
venison: **8** deer meat
venomous: **5** snaky, toxic **6** attern, deadly,
    malign, poison **7** baleful, baneful, noxious **8**
    poisoned, spiteful, virulent **9** malicious,

malignant, poisonous, rancorous **10** malevolent

vent: air **4** draw, emit, exit, hole, slit, slot **5** brand, eject, loose, state, utter, voice **6** go into, outlet **7** cast out, declare, exhaust, express, fissure, opening, orifice, release, unleash **8** aperture, disgorge, emission **9** discharge, embrasure **10** escapement, expression

ventilate: air, fan **6** aerate, aerify, broach, winnow **7** bring up, discuss, express, publish **8** talk over **9** broadcast, oxygenate

ventilation: **6** aerage **9** breathing **10** conference

ventilator: **6** blinds, funnel, louver **8** airshaft

ventral: **7** sternal

ventriloquist: **12** engastrimyth **13** gastriloquist

venture: bet, hap, try **4** dare, face, luck, risk, wage **5** brave, essay, stake, wager **6** chance, danger, feeler, gamble, hazard **7** attempt, courage, flutter, fortune, risking **8** trespass **9** adventure, speculate **10** enterprise **11** contingency, presumption, speculation, undertaking

venturesome: **4** bold, rash **5** brave, hardy, risky **6** daring, heroic **8** fearless, heedless, reckless, stalwart **9** audacious, dangerous, daredevil, foolhardy, hazardous, venturous **11** adventurous, furthersome

venue: hit **4** bout, site **5** lunge, match, onset, place **6** coming, ground, locale, thrust **7** arrival, assault **9** encounter

Venus (see also **Aphrodite**): **6** Hesper, planet, Vesper **8** Hesperus **11** Evening Star, Morning Star
as morning star: **7** Lucifer
girdle: **6** cestus
husband: **6** Vulcan
lover: **4** Mars **6** Adonis
mother: **5** Dione
son: **5** Cupid **6** Aeneas
sweetheart: **6** Adonis
tree sacred to: **6** myrtle

Venus flytrap: **5** plant **7** dionaea **9** carnivore **10** swamp plant

venust: **6** comely **7** elegant **8** graceful **9** beautiful

veracious: **4** true **6** direct **8** accurate, faithful, truthful **9** measuring, veridical

veracity: **4** fact **6** gospel, truism **7** honesty **8** accuracy **9** frankness, judgement, precision, sincerity **11** correctness

veranda: **5** lanai, porch, stoop **6** loggia, piazza **7** gallery, portico

verb: *auxiliary:* be, are, can, did, had, has, may, was **4** hast, have, must, will **5** could, might, shall, shalt, would **6** should
table: **8** paradigm

tense: **4** past **6** aorist, future **7** perfect, present **9** imperfect **10** pluperfect **11** conditional, past perfect

verbal: **4** oral **5** wordy **6** spoken **7** verbose **9** talkative **10** articulate

verbatim: **5** close, exact **6** direct, orally, strict **7** literal **8** verbally **11** word for word

verbena: **4** tree **5** plant **7** aloysia, lantana, verrain

verbiage: **4** talk **7** chatter, diction, fustian, wording **9** verbosity, wordiness

verbose: **5** windy, wordy **6** prolix **7** diffuse, flowery **9** redundant **10** long-winded **11** tautologous

verboten: **4** tabu **5** taboo **6** banned **9** forbidden **10** prohibited

verdant: raw **5** fresh, green **6** grassy **8** immature, innocent

Verdi: *opera:* **4** Aida **6** Ernani, Otello **7** Nabucco, Othello **8** Falstaff, Traviata **9** Don Carlos, I Lombardi, Rigoletto, Trovatore

verdict: **4** word **6** ruling **7** finding, opinion **8** decision, judgment

verdigris: **4** rust **6** aerugo, patina

Verdun river: **5** Meuse

verdure: **4** odor **5** scent, smell **6** flavor **7** foliage **8** greenery, strength, tapestry, tartness **9** freshness, greenness **10** vegetation

verecund: shy **6** modest **7** bashful

Verein (G.): **7** society **11** association **12** organization

verge: lip, rim, rod **4** brim, edge, tend, twig, wand **5** bound, brink, limit, march, marge, point, range, scope, shaft, skirt, staff, stick, touch, watch **6** border, fringe, margin **7** incline, selvage, touch on, virgate **8** approach, boundary, yardland **9** extremity, threshold, timepiece

verger: **4** dean **6** garden **7** justice, orchard **8** official **9** attendant

Vergil: See **Virgil**

veridical: **4** real, true **7** genuine **8** accurate, truthful **9** veracious **12** truthtelling

verification: **5** proof **7** checkup **8** averment **12** confirmation

verify: **4** aver, back, test **5** audit, check, prove **6** affirm, ratify, second, settle **7** certify, collate, confirm, support **8** document, maintain, validate **9** establish **11** certificate, corroborate

verily: yea **4** amen, even **5** parde, pardi, pardy, truly **6** certes, indeed, pardie, really **9** certainly **11** confidently

verisimilitude: **5** color, truth **10** likelihood **11** probability, resemblance

veritable: **4** real, true **6** actual, gospel, honest **7** factual, genuine **9** authentic, undoubted, veracious

verity: 5 truth 8 veracity 12 faithfulness
verjuice: 7 acidity 8 sourness, tartness
vermiform: 4 long, thin 7 sinuous, slender 8 wormlike 10 vermicular
vermilion: red 7 scarlet 8 cinnabar
vermin: 4 lice, mice, rats 5 filth, fleas, flies 7 bedbugs, rodents, weasels
verminous: 5 dirty 6 filthy 7 noxious 9 offensive

Vermont: *capital:* **10** Montpelier
city: **5** Barre **7** Rutland **10** Bennington, Burlington **11** Brattleboro
hero: **10** Ethan Allen
Indian: **9** Algonquin
lake: **9** Champlain
motto: **15** Freedom and Unity
mountain range: **5** Green **7** Taconic
product: **10** maple syrup
river: **8** Lamoille, Poultney, Winooski **10** Otter Creek **11** Connecticut
state bird: **6** thrush
state flower: **6** clover
state tree: **5** maple
U.S. president: **6** Arthur **8** Coolidge

---

vernacular: 4 cant 5 argot, idiom, lingo, slang 6 jargon, patois 7 dialect 10 colloquial
vernal: 4 mild, warm 5 fresh, young 6 spring 8 youthful 10 springlike
Verne: *character:* 4 Fogg, Nemo 12 Passepartout
submarine: 8 Nautilus
verneuk: 5 cheat 6 humbug 7 swindle
versatile: 5 handy 6 adroit, facile, gifted, mobile 7 elastic, flexile, pliable, skilled 8 flexible, talented, variable 9 adaptable, all-around, many-sided 10 changeable, reversible
verse: lay, ode 4 epic, poem, rune, song, turn 5 haiku, lyric, meter, poesy, rhyme, stave, stich 6 ballad, poetry, stanza 7 stichos
foot: 4 iamb 6 dactyl 7 anapest, spondee, trochee
pert. to: 6 poetic
stress: 5 ictus
versed: 5 adept 6 au fait, beseen 7 abreast, erudite, learned, skilled 8 familiar 9 au courant, competent, practiced 10 acquainted, conversant, proficient
versifier: 4 bard, poet 5 rimer 6 rhymer, verser 7 poetess 8 lyricist 9 poetaster
versify: 6 berime 7 berhyme
version: 5 story 6 report 7 account, edition,

reading, turning 9 rendition 10 conversion, paraphrase 11 translation
versipel: 8 werewolf
versus: con 6 contra 7 against, vis-a-vis
vertebra: 4 axis, bone 7 spondyl
vertebrae: 4 back 5 spine
vertebrate: ray 6 animal 9 backbone
class: 5 birds, shark 7 hagfish, lamprey, mammals, reptile 8 bony fish 9 amphibian
vertex: top 4 apex, peak 5 crest, crown 6 apogee, summit, tip-top, zenith 11 culmination
vertical: 4 acme 5 apeak, erect, plumb, sheer 6 abrupt, height, summit, vertex 7 upright 9 up-and-down 10 straight-up 13 perpendicular
verticil: 5 whorl
vertiginous: 5 dizzy, giddy 6 rotary 8 rotating, spinning, swimming, unstable, whirling 9 dizziness, giddiness, revolving 10 inconstant 11 light-headed, vacillating
vertigo: 6 megrim 9 dizziness, giddiness
verve: pep, vim, zip 4 brio, dash, elan, fire, life, zest 5 ardor, gusto, vigor 6 bounce, spirit, talent 7 ability 8 aptitude, vivacity 9 animation 10 enthusiasm, resiliency
vervet: 6 monkey
very: muy, too 4 bare, fell, mere, most, much, real, same, sehr, tres (F.), true, unco (Sc.) 5 assai (It.), molto (It.), quite, super, truly, utter 6 actual, lawful, mighty, really 7 awfully, dimolto (It.), exactly, genuine, precise 8 absolute, actually, complete, especial, peculiar, rightful, terribly, truthful 9 authentic, extremely, identical, precisely, veracious, veritable 10 legitimate, mortacious 11 exceedingly
vesicle: sac 4 bleb, cell, cyst 5 bulla 6 cavity, vessel 7 bladder, blister, utricle
air: 8 aerocyst
Vesper: 4 star 5 Venus 8 Hesperus 11 evening star
vespers: 6 prayer 7 service 8 ceremony, evensong
vessel: can, cog, cup, jar, pan, tub, urn, vas 4 bell, boat, bowl, cadi, drum, duct, ewer, olla, olpe, pail, ship, tank, tube, vase, vein 5 bocal, cadus, canoe, cogue, craft, cruse, laver, liner, paten 6 aftaba, aludel, artery, barrel, bottle, bucket, cootie, crater, cutter, firkin, flagon, funnel, goblet, goulah, holmos, kettle, krater, patera, situla, yetlin 7 aleyard, blickey, blickie, cistern, cresset, gabbard, gabbart, paterae, pinnace, pitcher, situlae, steamer, utensil, yetling 8 aiguiere, ciborium, crucible 9 alcarraza 10 receptacle
anatomical: vas 4 vasa (pl.), vein 6 artery

assaying: **5** cupel

drinking: cup, mug **4** toby **5** flask, glass, gourd, jorum, stein, stoup **6** dipper, flagon, goblet, seidel **7** tankard, tumbler **8** schooner

earthen: **5** crock

oil: **5** cruet, cruse

pert. to: **5** vasal

sacred: ama, pix, pyx

small: nog **4** pony, shot **6** dinghy, jigger, noggin

wooden: soe **5** cogue, skeel **6** barrel, piggin

vest: **4** coat, robe **5** dress, endow, gilet **6** accrue, belong, clothe, jacket, jerkin, linder, weskit **7** furnish, garment **9** waistcoat **10** undershirt

Vesta: **5** match **6** Hestia

brother: **7** Jupiter

father: **6** Saturn

mother: Ops

symbol: **10** hearth fire

vestal: nun **4** pure **6** chaste, virgin

vestibule: **4** hall **5** entry, foyer, lobby, porch **6** portal **7** chamber, narthex, passage, portico **8** anteroom, entrance, entryway, vestibule **10** antechapel

vestige: bit **4** mark, path, sign **5** relic, scrap, shred, smack, trace, track, trail, umbra **7** remains, remnant **8** footstep, tincture

vestiture: **4** garb **5** dress **8** clothing

vestment (see also **dress**): **4** garb, gear, gown, hood, robe **5** cotta, dress, orale **6** chimer, chimre, gloves, rochet, tippet **7** cassock, garment, sandals **8** cincture, clothing, covering **10** habiliment

ecclesiastical: alb, cap **4** alba, cope **5** albae, amice, ephod, fanon, miter, orale, stole **6** lappet, palium, rochet, saccos, tippet **7** cassock, maniple, tunicle **8** chasuble, dalmatic, surplice

vestry: **4** room **7** meeting **8** sacristy

vesture: **4** corn **5** cover, crops, grass **6** clothe, seizin **7** apparel, costume, envelop, garment, raiment, stubble, wrapper **8** clothing, garments, vestment **9** underwood **11** investiture

vesuvian: **5** fusee, match **8** volcanic

vetch: ers **4** akra, tare, vine, weed **5** fetch **6** legume **7** arvejon **10** fertilizer

veteran: old **6** expert, master, versed **7** oldster **8** old-timer, seasoned **9** practiced **10** past master **11** experienced

veterinarian: **7** farrier **12** animal doctor

vetiver: **5** grass **6** cuscus **8** aromatic, khuskhus

veto: nix **4** deny, kill **5** say no **6** defeat, forbid, refuse, reject **7** decline, message **8** disallow, document, negative, overrule, prohibit **9** blackball **11** disapproval, forbiddance, prohibition

vettura: **5** coach **8** carriage

veuve: **4** bird **5** widow **6** whydah

vex: ire, irk, tew **4** cark, chaw, fret, fuss, gall, miff, rile, roil, toss **5** anger, annoy, chafe, harry, shake, spite, tease, worry, wrack **6** bother, cumber, harass, madden, molest, nettle, offend, plague, pother, ruffle **7** afflict, agitate, discuss, dispute, disturb, perplex, provoke, torment, trouble **8** disquiet, irritate, vexation **9** annoyance, displease, infuriate **11** disturbance

vexation: **5** pique, thorn **7** fatigue **9** annoyance, weariness **10** irritation **11** aggravation, bedevilment

vexatious: **4** chaw, sore **5** pesky **8** annoying, cumbrous, frampoid, untoward **9** disturbed, pestilent, troublous **10** afflictive **11** contrarious, troublesome

vexed: **5** sorry **7** grieved

vexillum: web **4** flag, vane **6** banner **8** standard

via: way **4** road, with **5** right **7** by way of, passage, through **9** by means of

viable: **6** doable **8** feasible, possible, workable **11** practicable

viaduct: **6** bridge **7** trestle

vial: **5** ampul, cruet, flask, glass, phial **6** ampule, beaker, bottle, caster, vessel **7** ampoule

viand: **4** fare, food, grub **6** edible **7** aliment **8** victuals **9** provender **10** provisions

viaticum: **5** money **8** last rite, supplies **9** allowance **10** provisions

viator: **8** traveler, wayfarer

Viaud's pen name: **4** Loti

vibrant: **5** alive, ringy, vital **7** ringing **8** resonant, sonorous, vigorous

vibrate: jar, wag **4** beat, cast, dirl, rock, whir **5** pulse, quake, shake, swing, throb, throw, trill, waver, whirr **6** dindle, launch, quaver, quiver, shimmy, shiver, thrill, tremor **7** agitate, resound, shudder, tremble **8** brandish, flichter (Sc.), resonate **9** fluctuate, oscillate, vacillate

vibration: **4** dirl (Sc.), tirl (Sc.) **5** quake, shake, thirl (Sc.) **6** dingle, quaver, quiver, thrill, tremor **7** flutter **8** fremitus, stirring **9** trembling **11** oscillation, vacillation

musical: **5** trill **7** sonance, tremolo, vibrato **8** overtone

vicar: **5** proxy **6** deputy, priest **8** minister **9** clergyman **10** substitute, vicegerent

assistant: **6** curate

of Christ: **4** pope

Vicar of Wakefield author: **9** Goldsmith

vicarage: **4** dues **5** house **6** salary, tithes **8** benefice **9** household, pastorate, rectorate, residence

vice: sin **4** evil, flaw, grip, hold, turn **5** crime, fault, force, grasp, place, proxy, stead, taint, wrong **6** defect **7** blemish, failing, frailty, squeeze, stopper **8** iniquity, stairway **9** deformity, depravity **10** corruption, debauchery, immorality, perversion, wickedness

Vice President (U.S.): **4** Burr, Bush, Ford, Gore, King **5** Adams, Agnew, Dawes, Gerry, Nixon, Tyler **6** Arthur, Colfax, Curtis, Dallas, Garner, Hamlin, Hobart, Morton, Quayle, Truman, Wilson **7** Barkley, Calhoun, Clinton, Johnson, Mondale, Sherman, Wallace, Wheeler **8** Coolidge, Fillmore, Humphrey, Marshall, Tompkins, Van Buren **9** Fairbanks, Hendricks, Jefferson, Roosevelt, Stevenson **11** Rockefeller **12** Breckinridge

Adams J.: **9** Jefferson
Adams J.Q.: **7** Calhoun
Arthur: **4** none
Buchanan: **12** Breckinridge
Bush: **6** Quayle
Carter: **7** Mondale
Cleveland: **9** Hendricks (1), Stevenson (2)
Clinton: **4** Gore
Coolidge: **5** Dawes
Eisenhower: **5** Nixon
Fillmore: **4** none
Ford: **11** Rockefeller
Garfield: **6** Arthur
Grant: **6** Colfax (1), Wilson (2)
Harding: **8** Coolidge
Harrison B.: **6** Morton
Harrison W.H.: **5** Tyler
Hayes: **7** Wheeler
Hoover: **6** Curtis
Jackson: **7** Calhoun (1) **8** Van Buren (2)
Jefferson: **4** Burr (1) **7** Clinton (2)
Johnson A.: **4** none
Johnson L.B.: **8** Humphrey
Kennedy: **7** Johnson
Lincoln: **6** Hamlin (1) **7** Johnson (2)
Madison: **5** Gerry (2) **7** Clinton (1)
McKinley: **6** Hobart (1) **9** Roosevelt (2)
Monroe: **8** Tompkins
Nixon: **4** Ford (2) **5** Agnew (1)
Pierce: **4** King
Polk: **6** Dallas
Reagan: **4** Bush
Roosevelt F.D.: **6** Garner (1), Truman (3) **7** Wallace (2)
Roosevelt T.: **9** Fairbanks
Taft: **7** Sherman
Taylor: **8** Fillmore
Truman: **7** Barkley
Tyler: **4** none
Van Buren: **7** Johnson
Washington: **5** Adams
Wilson: **8** Marshall

viceroy: **5** nabob, nazim, ruler **6** exarch, satrap **7** khedive, provost **8** governor **9** butterfly

vice versa: **5** again **10** conversely

vicinity: **4** area **5** range **6** region **8** district, locality, nearness **9** proximity **11** propinquity

vicious: bad, ill **4** evil, foul, lewd, mean, vile, wild **5** feral, wrong **6** faulty, savage, severe, wicked **7** corrupt, immoral, intense, noxious, violent **8** debasing, depraved, infamous, spiteful **9** dangerous, defective, dissolute, malicious, malignant, nefarious, perverted **10** corrupting, iniquitous, villainous

vicissitude: **6** change **8** hardship, mutation, reversal **9** adversity, mischance **10** affliction, difficulty, misfortune, revolution, succession **11** alternation, interchange, permutation, tribulation

victim: **4** dupe, fool, goat, gull, prey **6** pigeon, quarry, sucker **8** casualty, easy mark, offering, underdog **9** sacrifice

victor: **5** champ **6** captor, master, winner **7** conquer **8** bangster, champion, unbeaten **9** conqueror **10** vanquisher

victory: win **7** mastery, success, triumph **8** conquest, dominion **9** landslide, supremacy **11** superiority
crown: bay **6** laurel
easy: **4** snap **6** breeze **7** runaway
ruinous: **7** Pyrrhic
sign: vee
song: **9** epinicion
symbol: **4** palm **5** scalp **6** ribbon, trophy

Victory heroine: **4** Lena

victrola: **9** turntable **10** phonograph **12** record player

victualler: **6** sutler **9** innkeeper (Br.)

victuals: bit **4** bite, chow, eats, food, grub, meat **6** viands **7** edibles, vittles **9** provender **10** provisions

videlicet: viz **5** to wit **6** namely **8** scilicet **11** that is to say

vie: bet, run **4** cope **5** bandy, match, rival, stake, wager **6** endure, hazard, oppose, strive **7** compete, contend, contest, emu-

Vietnam: *bay:* **7** Cam Ranh
capital: **5** Hanoi
city: Hue **8** Nha Trang **13** Ho Chi Minh City (formerly Saigon)
clothing: **5** ao dai
Communist leader: **9** Ho Chi Minh
currency: xu **4** dong **7** piastre
gulf: **6** Tonkin
holiday: Tet
people: **5** Khmer **10** Montagnard, Vietnamese
river: Red **6** Mekong

late **8** panorama, prospect, struggle **9** challenge

Vienna: 4 Wien
horses: **10** Lippizaner
palace: **7** Hofburg **10** Schonbrunn
river: **6** Danube

Vietnam: (see box)

view: aim, eye, ken, see, vue (F.) **4** deem, espy, goal, look, mark, scan **5** aview, scape, scene, sight, slant, tenet, vista, watch **6** admire, apercu (F.), aspect, behold, belief, design, notice, notion, object, regard, sketch, survey, vision **7** concept, examine, feeling, inspect, observe, opinion, outlook, picture, profile, scenery, summary, thought, witness **8** attitude, consider, panorama, prospect, scrutiny, synopsis **9** apprehend, objective, sentiment **10** appearance, conviction, inspection, perception, photograph, scrutinize, standpoint **11** contemplate
extended: **5** vista **8** panorama
mentally: **8** envision

viewer: 9 spectator **10** eyewitness **11** stereoscope

viewing instrument: 5 scope **9** telescope **10** binoculars, microscope

viewy: 5 showy **8** fanciful **9** visionary **11** spectacular, unpractical

vigil: eve **4** wake **5** guard, watch **7** lookout, prayers, service **8** devotion, watchman

vigilant: 4 agog, wary **5** alert, awake, aware **7** careful, wakeful **8** cautious, watchful **9** attentive, observant, sharp-eyed, sleepless, wide-awake

vigilantes: 5 posse

vigilant one: 5 Argus

vigneron: 10 winegrower **13** viticulturist

vignette: 5 scene **6** sketch **7** picture

vigor, vigour: pep, vim, vir (Sc.), vis **4** bang, birr, dash, fire, zeal **5** drive, flush, force, getup, might, nerve, power, punch, steam **6** energy, foison, growth, health, muscle, spirit **7** impetus, potency, stamina **8** activity, boldness, strength, virility, vitality **9** animation, fraicheur, hardihood, intensity, vehemence **10** get-up-and-go, invigorate
deprive of: sap **6** deaden **8** enervate

vigoroso (It.): 8 vigorous **9** direction, energetic

vigorous: yep **4** able, cant, fell, hale, spry, yepe **5** brisk, eager, frank, hardy, hefty, husky, lusty, tough, vital **6** florid, hearty, lively, potent, robust, rugged, strong, sturdy **7** cordial, dashing, dynamic, healthy **8** athletic, muscular, spirited **9** effective, energetic, strenuous **10** red-blooded **11** efficacious, hard-hitting

Viking: 4 Dane, Eric **5** rover **6** pirate **7** warrior **8** Norseman, Northman **12** Scandinavian

vile: bad, low **4** base, evil, foul, mean, ugly **5** cheap, lowly, nasty **6** abject, coarse, drasty, filthy, horrid, impure, odious, sinful, sordid, vulgar, wicked **7** bestial, carrion, corrupt, debased, ignoble, noisome, obscene, squalid, unclean, vicious **8** baseborn, befouled, depraved, wretched **9** abandoned, abhorrent, corrupted, degrading, loathsome, nefarious, obnoxious, offensive, perverted, repugnant, repulsive, revolting, worthless **10** abominable, despicable, disgusting, flagitious

vileness: 6 fedity **9** turpitude

vilify: 5 abuse, avile, libel **6** assail, attack, bemean, berate, debase, defame, malign, revile, slight **7** asperse, blacken, cheapen, debauch, degrade, despise, detract, slander, traduce **8** belittle, denounce, disgrace, dishonor, mistreat, reproach, vilipend **9** blaspheme, denigrate, disparage **10** calumniate, depreciate

villa: 5 aldea, dacha (Russ.), house, manor **6** castle, estate **7** chateau, mansion **9** residence

village: gav, mir (Russ.), rew (Sc.) **4** burg, dorp, home, stad (Afr.), town, vici **5** aldea, bourg, kraal, thorp, vicus **6** bustee, castle, hamlet, pueblo, thorpe **7** borough, caserio (Sp.), endship **8** bourgade **9** aldeament **10** settlement

villain: 4 boor, heel, Iago, lout, serf **5** churl, demon, devil, heavy, knave, rogue, scamp **6** rascal **8** criminal, evildoer, offender, scalawag, scelerat **9** miscreant, scoundrel **10** blackguard, malefactor, reprobate, villainous
mythological: **4** ogre **5** giant **6** dragon

villainous: bad, low **4** base, evil, mean, vile **6** common, rotten, slight, vulgar, wicked **7** boorish, corrupt, debased, heinous, vicious **8** clownish, criminal, depraved, flagrant, infamous, perverse, wretched **9** atrocious, dastardly, dissolute, felonious, nefarious **10** degenerate, detestable, flagitious, iniquitous, outrageous

villainy: 5 crime **7** knavery **9** depravity

villatic: 5 rural **6** rustic

villein: 4 carl, serf **5** ceorl, churl, helot **7** cottier, peasant **8** bondsman

vim: zip **4** brio, dash, élan, gimp, kick, life, push, zing **5** force, verve, vigor **6** energy, esprit, ginger, pepper, spirit **8** strength

vinaigrette: box **5** sauce **6** bottle, flacon **7** vehicle **8** carriage

vincible: 11 conquerable

vinculum: tie **4** band, bond, link **5** brace, union **6** frenum

vindicate: 4 free **5** clear **6** acquit, assert, avenge, defend, excuse, uphold **7** absolve, bear out, deliver, justify, propugn, revenge, support, sustain **8** advocate, maintain, plead for **9** exculpate, exonerate

vindication: **7** apology

vindictive: **5** nasty **6** malign **7** hostile **8** punitive, spiteful, vengeful **9** malicious, malignant, merciless **10** implacable, relentless, revengeful **11** retaliatory, retributive, unrelenting

vine: hop, ivy **4** akas, bine, gogo, odal, soma **5** betel, buaze, bwazi, guaco, liana, liane **6** maypop **7** creeper, cupseed, trailer **8** clematis **9** grapevine **10** chilicothe
covered with: **5** ivied **7** lianaed
fruit-bearing: **5** grape **7** chayote, cupseed **9** cranberry
twining: **4** bine **11** bittersweet
vegetable-bearing: pea **4** bean **5** gourd **6** cowpea, squash **8** cucumber

vinegar: vim **4** acid **5** eisel **6** acetum, alegar, eisell **8** vinaigre (F.)
bottle: **5** cruet
dregs: **6** mother
ester: **7** acetate
preserve in: **6** pickle

vinegary: **4** sour **7** acetose, crabbed **9** unamiable **11** ill-tempered

vineyard: cru **7** grapery
protector: **7** Priapus

vinous: **4** winy **9** vinaceous

vintage: old **4** crop, wine **5** cuvee, dated, yield **6** demode **7** antique, classic

vintner: **8** merchant

viol: **5** gigue, rebec **6** fiddle, rebeck, vielle **7** quinton **9** viola alta

violate: err, sin **4** flaw, rape **5** abuse, break, force, harry, spoil, wrong **6** betray, breach, broach, defile, defoil, defoul, injure, insult, invade, offend, ravage, ravish **7** corrupt, debauch, disturb, falsify, outrage, pollute, profane **8** deflower, dishonor, infringe, mistreat, trespass **9** constrain, desecrate, disregard **10** contravene, transgress

violation: **5** crime, error, wrong **6** breach **7** offense **8** trespass **9** sacrilege **10** infraction **11** delinquency, desecration, profanation

violence: **4** fury, riot **5** ardor, force **6** bensel, bensil, duress, fervor, frenzy, hubris, hybris **7** assault, bensail, bensall, bensell, outrage **8** coercion, ferocity, foul play, savagery **9** bloodshed **11** desecration

violent: **4** high, loud **5** acute, fiery, great, harsh, heady, heavy, hefty, rabid, rough, sharp, vivid **6** fierce, mighty, raging, savage, severe, stormy, strong **7** extreme, furious, hotspur, intense, rammish, vicious **8** flagrant, forceful, forcible, frenetic, powerful, terrible, vehement **9** atrocious, explosive, impetuous, phrenetic, turbulent **10** headstrong, hotspurred, immoderate, inordi-

nate, passionate, tumultuous **11** destructive, tempestuous

violently: **4** hard **5** amain, madly **6** wildly **8** fiercely, like fury, slambang **9** furiously

violet: **5** mauve, viola **6** blaver, flower, purple

violet root: **5** orris **6** iridin

violet tip: **9** butterfly

violin: kit **4** alto, bass **5** Amati, cello, Rocta, Strad **6** fiddle **7** Cremona, quinton **8** Guarneri **10** Guadagnini, Guarnerius, Stradivari **11** violincello **12** Stradivarius
city: **7** Cremona
forerunner: **5** gigue, rebec **6** vielle **9** kemantche **16** viola d'amore rabab
rare: **5** Amati, Strad

violin-shaped: **7** waisted

violinist: *comic:* **5** Benny
fabled: **4** Nero
famous: **4** Auer **5** Elman, Stern, Ysaye **7** Heifetz, Menuhin, Perlman, Vivaldi **8** Kreisler, Milstein, Oistrakh, Paganini, Spalding, Zukerman **9** Zimbalist
first: **13** concertmaster

V.I.P.: **4** lion **5** titan **6** bigwig, fat cat, leader **7** big shot, notable

viper: asp **5** adder, snake **8** cerastes **10** bushmaster, copperhead, fer-de-lance **11** rattlesnake
genus of: **5** echis

viperish: **8** spiteful, venomous **9** malicious

virago: **5** harpy, randy, scold, shrew, vixen, woman **6** Amazon, beldam, callet **7** beldame **8** fishwife **9** brimstone, termagant, Xanthippe

vireo: **7** grasset **8** greenlet, songbird

Virgil (Vergil): **9** Roman poet
birthplace: **6** Mantua
family name: **4** Maro
friend: **8** Maecenas
hero: **6** Aeneas
language: **5** Latin
poem: **4** epic **6** Aeneid **8** Bucolics, Eclogues, Georgics
queen: **4** Dido

virgin: new **4** maid, pure **5** first, fresh, unwed **6** chaste, intact, maiden, modest, vestal **7** initial **8** celibate, innocent, maidenly, primeval, pristine, spinster **9** unalloyed, undefiled, unmarried, unspoiled, unsubdued, unsullied, untouched **10** uncaptured **11** undisturbed

Virgin Islands (of U.S.): **6** St. John **7** St. Croix **8** St. Thomas
capital: **15** Charlotte Amalie

Virgin Mary: BVM **9** Theotokos **11** Mother of God
image: **5** Pieta

Virgin Queen: **10** Elizabeth I

virginal: **4** pure **6** chaste, intact, maiden, spinet **11** harpsichord

Virginia: 12 commonwealth
aristocracy: FFV
bay: **10** Chesapeake
capital: **8** Richmond
city: **7** Hampton, Norfolk, Roanoke **9** Arlington **10** Chesapeake **11** Newport News **13** Virginia Beach
gap: **10** Cumberland
Indian: **8** Powhatan
motto: **17** Sic semper tyrannis (Thus Always to Tyrants)
mountain: **9** Allegheny, Blue Ridge
mountain range: **11** Appalachian
peninsula: **8** Delmarva
river: Dan **5** James **7** Potomac, Rapidan, Roanoke **9** Elizabeth **10** Shenandoah **12** Rappahannock
state bird: **8** cardinal
state flower: **7** dogwood
state tree: **7** dogwood
U.S. President: **5** Tyler **6** Monroe, Taylor, Wilson **7** Madison **8** Harrison **9** Jefferson **10** Washington

Virginia creeper: ivy **5** plant **8** woodbine **10** ampelopsis
Virginia snakeroot: **7** sangrel **9** birthwort **11** sangree-root
Virginia willow: iva **4** itea
Virginian author: **6** Wister
Virgo: **6** virgin, zodiac **13** constellation
virdity: **5** youth **7** verdure **8** verdance **9** freshness, greenness **10** liveliness
virile: **4** male **5** macho, manly **6** potent, robust, strong **7** lustful **8** forceful, powerful, vigorous **9** masculine, masterful
virose: **5** fetid **8** virulent **9** poisonous **10** malodorous
virtu: **5** curio **7** antique
virtually: **6** almost, nearly **7** morally, totally **8** actually, in effect **9** basically, in essence **11** practically
virtue: **4** dint, thew **5** arete, grace, merit, piety, power, trait, value, worth **6** bounty, purity **7** probity, quality **8** chastity, efficacy, goodness, morality **9** rectitude **10** excellence, perfection
cardinal: **4** hope **5** faith **7** charity, justice **8** prudence **9** fortitude **10** temperance
virtuoso: **4** whiz **6** expert, savant **7** scholar **8** aesthete, esthete, musician **10** dilettante, empiricist **11** connoisseur, philosopher
virtuous: **4** good, pure **5** brave, moral, noble **6** chaste, honest, potent, worthy **7** ethical, goddard, sinless, thrifty, upright, valiant **8**

innocent, spotless, valorous **9** blameless, effective, faultless, guiltless, righteous, unsullied
virulent: **5** acrid, rabid, toxic **6** biting, bitter, deadly, malign, poison, potent **7** cutting, hateful, hostile, noxious **8** spiteful, venomous **9** festering, injurious, malignant, poisonous **10** infectious
virus: **4** bane, germ **5** taint, venom **6** poison **8** acrimony **9** contagion, infection **10** corruption
vis: **5** force, might, power, vigor **7** potency **8** strength
vis-a-vis: **4** seat, sofa **6** contra, facing, toward, versus **7** against **8** carriage, opposite **9** tete-a-tete **10** face to face
visage: **4** face, look, phiz, show **5** image **6** aspect **8** features, portrait **9** semblance **10** appearance, expression **11** countenance
viscera: **4** guts **6** vitals **7** innards, insides **8** entrails **10** intestines
visceral: gut **5** inner **9** intuitive **11** instinctive, instinctual
viscid: **7** viscous
viscount: **4** peer **6** deputy **7** sheriff **8** nobleman
viscous: **4** limy, ropy, sizy **5** gobby, gummy, slimy, tarry, thick, tough **6** mucous, sirupy, sticky, viscid **7** stringy **8** adhering, sticking **9** glutinous, semifluid, semisolid, tenacious
vise: **4** grip, tool **5** clamp, winch
part: jaw
Vishnu: *consort:* Sri **7** Lakshmi
incarnation: **4** Rama **6** avatar **7** Krishna **8** Balarama **11** Ramachandra
religion: **8** Hinduism
visible: **4** seen **6** extant **7** evident, glaring, obvious **8** apparent, manifest **9** available **11** conspicuous, discernible
Visigoth king: **6** Alaric
vision: eye **5** dream, fancy, image, sight, think **6** beauty, oracle, seeing **7** fantasy, imagine **8** daydream, eyesight, phantasm, phantasy, prophecy **9** nightmare **10** apparition, revelation
doctor: **11** optometrist **15** ophthalmologist
double: **8** diplopia
illusory: **6** mirage
instrument of: **6** retina
measuring device: **9** optometer
pert. to: **5** optic **6** ocular, visual
visionary: fey **4** aery, airy, wild **5** ideal, lofty, noble **6** unreal **7** dreamer, fantast, laputan, utopian **8** delusive, idealist, quixotic, romantic **9** ambitious, fantastic, grandiose, ideologue, imaginary, unworldly **10** chimerical, idealistic, ideologist **11** imaginative, impractical, speculative
visit: gam, see, vis **4** call, chat, hawk, slum,

stay, talk **5** apply, haunt, tarry **6** assail, attend, avenge, come by, drop by, look in, look up, stop by, stop in **7** afflict, ceilidh (Sc.), inflict, sojourn **8** converse **10** inspection

visitation: **5** trial **6** ordeal **7** calvary **8** disaster **9** migration **10** affliction

visitor: **5** guest **6** caller **7** company

vison: **4** mink

visor: **4** bill, peak **8** eyeshade

vista: **4** view **5** range, scene, scope, sight **7** outlook **8** long view, panorama, prospect

Vistula tributary: Bug, San **5** Nogat

visual: **5** optic **6** ocular, scopic **7** optical, visible **11** perceptible

visualize: **4** view **5** fancy, think **6** ideate **7** foresee, imagine, picture **8** conceive, envisage

vita: **4** life **9** biography

Vita Nuova author: **5** Dante

vital: **4** live **5** alive, basic, chief, fatal, lusty **6** deadly, lively, living, needed, souled, viable **7** animate, capital, dynamic, exigent, supreme **8** animated, integral, required, vigorous **9** breathing, elemental, energetic, essential, important, necessary, requisite **10** imperative, red-blooded **11** fundamental
fluid: sap **5** blood, lymph
signs: **5** pulse **11** respiration, temperature

vitality: sap, vim **5** vigor **6** foison

vitalize: **5** pep up **7** animate **8** activate

vitals: **7** viscera

vitamin: **6** biotin, citrin, niacin **7** choline, retinol **8** ascorbic, carotene, inositol, thiamine **9** folic acid **10** calciferol, pyridoxine, riboflavin, tocopherol

vitellus: **4** yolk **7** egg yolk

vitiate: mar **4** harm, hurt, soil, undo **5** abate, annul, pical, quash, spoil, sully, taint **6** damage, debase, defile, faulty, impair, impure, injure, negate, poison, weaken **7** abolish, corrupt, deprave, envenom, nullify, pervert, pollute **8** abrogate, depraved **9** defective **10** adulterate, invalidate, neutralize **11** contaminate

viticulturist: **8** vigneron **9** winemaker **10** vinegrower **11** grape-grower

vitrify: **5** glaze

vitrine: **8** showcase

vitriol: **4** acid, sory **5** venom **7** caustic

vitriolic: **5** sharp **6** acidic, biting, bitter **7** caustic, hostile **8** scathing, virulent **9** sarcastic

vituperate: **4** lash, rail, rate **5** abuse, curse, scold **6** berate, revile **7** censure, chew out, condemn, rip into, upbraid **8** lambaste

vituperative: **6** severe **7** abusive **8** critical, scolding **10** scurrilous **11** opprobrious

vivacious: gay **4** airy **5** alert, brash, brisk, merry **6** active, breezy, lively, vivace (It.) **7** buoyant, vibrant, zestful **8** animated, cheerful, spirited, sportive **9** exuberant, sprightly

vivacity: **4** fire, zeal **5** ardor, force, verve, vigor **6** esprit, gaiety, gayety **7** gayness, sparkle **9** longevity **10** liveliness

vivarium: box, zoo **4** cage **6** warren **9** enclosure

viva voce: **5** vocal **6** orally **8** oral exam (Br.)

vive: **5** brisk, vivid **6** lively, living **8** forcible, lifelike **9** perceived

vivid: gay **4** keen, live, rich **5** alive, clear, fresh, sharp **6** active, bright, lively, living, strong **7** eidetic, flaming, glaring, glowing, graphic, intense **8** animated, colorful, distinct, dramatic, spirited, striking, vigorous **9** brilliant

vivify: **5** endue **6** revive **7** animate, enliven, quicken **10** give life to, invigorate

vivres: **9** foodstuff **10** provisions

vixen: fox, nag **4** fury **5** scold, shrew, woman **6** virago **9** termagant

viz: **5** to wit **6** namely **9** videlicet

vizard: **4** mask **5** guise, visor **8** disguise

vizcacha, viscacha: **6** rodent

vocabulary: **4** cant **5** words **6** jargon **7** diction, lexicon **8** glossary, language, verbiage, wordbook **10** dictionary **11** terminology

vocal: **4** oral **5** vowel **6** fluent, spoken, voiced **7** uttered **8** eloquent **9** outspoken, unwritten **10** articulate

vocalist: **4** alto **5** basso, tenor **6** artist, singer **7** soprano **8** baritone, songster **9** performer **10** coloratura

vocalization: **4** word **5** sound, vowel **6** speech **7** diction **9** utterance

vocation: art, job **4** call, work **5** craft, trade **6** career, metier **7** calling, mission, summons **8** business, lifework **9** following **10** employment, occupation, profession

vociferate: cry **4** bawl, call, roar, yell **5** shout, utter **6** assert, bellow, clamor, holler **7** clamour

vociferous: **4** loud **5** noisy **6** shrill **7** blatant **8** brawling, strident **9** clamorous, turbulent **10** boisterous

voe: bay **5** creek, inlet

vogue: cry, cut, fad, ton (F.) **4** chic, mode, rage **5** craze, style, trend **6** bon ton, custom **7** fashion **8** practice **10** dernier cri, popularity

voice: say, vox (L.), voz (Sp.) **4** emit, talk, voce (It.), vote, wish **5** rumor, say-so, speak, utter **6** choice, report, speech, steven, tongue **7** divulge, express, opinion **8** announce, falsetto, proclaim, vocalize **9** enunciate, formulate, pronounce, utterance, verbalize
handicap: **4** lisp **7** stutter

loss of: **7** anaudia, aphonia **10** laryngitis
loud: **12** megalophonic **13** megalophonous
natural singing: **7** dipetto
pert. to: **5** vocal **8** phonetic
quality: **5** pitch **6** timbre
quiet: **5** sotto **7** whisper **9** sotto voce
sound: **5** vowel **6** symbol
stop: **9** affricate
stress: **5** arsis

voice box: 6 larynx

voiced: 4 oral **5** aloud, vocal **6** sonant, spoken **11** articulated

voiceless: mum **4** dumb, mute, surd **6** atonic, flated, silent **7** aphonic, spirate **8** aphonous **10** speechless **12** inarticulate

void: gap **4** free, hole, idle, lack, null, vain, want **5** abyss, annul, blank, drain, egest, eject, empty, leave, space **6** bereft, cavity, devoid, hollow, remove, vacant, vacate, vacuum **7** invalid, lacking, leisure, nullify, opening, useless, vacuity, wanting **8** evacuate, throw out **9** destitute, discharge, emptiness, frustrate **10** unemployed, unoccupied **11** ineffective, ineffectual

voile: 5 ninon **6** fabric

voir dire: 10 juror's oath

voiture: car **5** wagon **8** carriage

volage: 5 dizzy, giddy **6** fickle **7** flighty **8** fleeting

volant: 4 spry, yare **5** agile, light, quick **6** active, flying, nimble **7** flounce **8** volitant

volary: 4 cage **6** aviary **8** bird cage

volatile: 4 airy, bird **5** ether **6** fickle, figent, flying, lively, volage, volant **7** alcohol, ammonia, buoyant, elastic, essence, flighty, gaseous, volatic **8** fleeting, fugitive, unstable, vaporous **9** excitable, explosive, fugacious, mercurial, transient **10** capricious, changeable, evanescent, inconstant, transitory **11** hair-brained

volcano: Apo, Aso **4** Etna **5** Askja, Pelee **6** Katmai, Ranier, Shasta **7** Kilauea, Surtsey **8** Cotopaxi, Krakatau, Krakatoa, Mauna Loa, Pinatubo, Vesuvius **9** Stromboli **10** Mt. St. Helens **12** Popocatepetl
matter: ash **4** lava, tufa **5** magma **6** pumice, scoria, tephra
mud from: **5** salse
opening: **5** mouth **6** crater **7** caldera **8** fumarole
rock: **5** trass **6** dacite **8** tephrite
steam from: gas **5** stufa **10** geothermal

vole: 6 craber, rodent

Volga: Rha
city: **5** Gorki, Kazan **9** Volgograd **10** Stalingrad
tributary: Oka **4** Kama, Sura **7** Vetluga

volition: 4 will **6** choice, desire, option **8** election **13** determination

volley: 4 hail, shot **5** blast, burst, round, salvo **6** shower **7** barrage **8** blizzard, drumfire

volplane: 5 coast, glide

Volsunga Saga: *characters:* **4** Atli **6** Sigurd **7** Gunther **8** Brunhild **9** Siegfried
dragon: **6** Fafnir

Voltaire: *real name:* **6** Arouet
work: **5** Zadig, Zaire **6** Oedipe **7** Candide

volte face: 4 turn, veer **5** pivot, sheer, wheel **8** reversal **9** about-face

voluble: 4 glib **5** wordy **6** fickle, fluent **8** rotating, unstable **9** garrulous, revolving, talkative **10** changeable, loquacious

volume: 4 body, book, bulk, coil, mass, roll, tome, turn **6** amount, cubage, scroll **7** content **8** capacity, document, fullness, loudness, quantity, strength **9** aggregate **10** crassitude **11** convolution
large: **4** tome

voluminous: 4 full, many **5** bulky, large

Volund's brother: 4 Egil **5** Egill

voluntary: 4 free **6** chosen, freely **7** elected, willful, willing **8** elective, optional, unforced **9** volunteer, willingly **10** deliberate, unimpelled **11** intentional

volunteer: 5 offer **6** enlist, worker **7** proffer

Volunteer State: 9 Tennessee

voluptuous: 4 lush **6** wanton **7** sensual **8** sensuous **9** luxurious **11** pleasurable

volute: 4 turn **5** whorl **6** cilery, scroll, spiral **7** cillery

volution: 4 coil, turn **5** twist, whorl **7** rolling **9** revolving **11** convolution

vomit: gag **4** barf, boke, bolk, puke, spew **5** braid, brake, eject, expel, reach, retch **6** emetic **7** throw up, vomitus **8** disgorge **10** egurgitate **11** regurgitate

voodoo: hex, obe, obi **5** charm, Jonah, magic, obeah, spell, witch **6** fetish **7** bewitch **8** magician, sorcerer
charm: **4** mojo

voracious: 4 avid **5** eager **6** greedy, hungry **8** covetous, esurient, grasping, ravening, ravenous **9** cormorant, devouring, rapacious **10** gargantuan, gluttonous, immoderate, insatiable

voracity: 7 edacity

vorago: 4 gulf **5** abyss, chasm

vortex: 4 apex, eddy, gyre **5** spout, whirl **6** spiral **7** tornado **9** maelstrom, waterpool, whirlpool, whirlwind **10** waterspout

votary: fan **4** buff **5** freak, hound, lover **6** addict, zealot **7** amateur, devoted, devotee, fancier, habitué **8** adherent, disciple, follower, promised **10** enthusiast

vote: aye, con, nay, pro, vow, yes **4** anti, poll, wish **5** elect, grant **6** assign, ballot, choice, confer, decide, prayer, ratify, ticket **7** declare, opinion **8** dedicate, suffrage **9**

franchise **10** plebiscite, referendum
group: **4** bloc
method: **4** hand **5** proxy, straw, voice **6** ballot, secret **7** write-in **8** roll-call **10** plebiscite, referendum
of assent: aye, nod, yea **6** placet
of dissent: nay
right to: **8** suffrage **9** franchise
voter: **6** poller **7** chooser, elector **8** balloter **11** constituent
kind: **8** absentee
voters (body of): **10** electorate
vouch: vow **4** aver, back, bail, call, pray **5** prove **6** affirm, allege, assure, attest, second, summon, uphold, verify **7** certify, confirm, declare, resolve, support, warrant, witness **8** accredit, maintain, sanction **9** assertion, establish, guarantee **11** attestation, corroborate
voucher: **4** chit **7** receipt **9** debenture, statement **10** credential
vouchsafe: **4** give **5** grant, yield **6** assure, bestow, beteem, design **7** concede **9** guarantee **10** condescend
voussoir: **5** wedge **8** keystone
projection: ear
vow: vum **4** bind, hote, oath, wish **5** swear **6** behest, devote, pledge, plight, prayer **7** behight, declare, promise **8** covenant, dedicate **9** assertion **10** consecrate, obligation
vowel: **5** sound, vocal, voice **6** letter
contraction: **6** crases, crasis **9** diphthong
group of two: **6** digram **7** digraph **8** ligature
mark: **5** breve, caron, grave, tilde **6** macron, ogonek, umlaut **8** dieresis **10** circumflex **11** diacritical
omission: **7** aphesis **11** contraction
sound: **6** dental, labial **7** palatal
unaspirated: **4** lene

vox: **5** voice
voyage: **4** tour, trek, trip **6** cruise, travel **7** journey, passage, passing, project **8** proceeds **9** excursion **10** enterprise, expedition, pilgrimage **11** undertaking
voyageur: **5** guide **7** boatman, trapper **8** traveler, woodsman
voyaging: **4** asea
vrouw (D.): Mrs. **4** frau, frow, lady, wife **5** woman **8** mistress **9** housewife
v-shaped piece: **5** wedge
vug, vugg, vugh: **6** cavity, hollow
Vulcan: **5** smith **8** Roman god **10** blacksmith, Hephaestus
consort: **4** Maia **5** Venus
parents: **4** Juno **7** Jupiter
son: **5** Cacus **8** Caeculus
workshop: **4** Etna
vulcanite: **7** ebonite
vulcanize: **4** burn, cure **10** strengthen
vulgar: low, raw **4** base, lewd, rude **5** crass, crude, dirty, gross, nasty **6** coarse, common, public, ribald, slangy, smutty, spoken **7** boorish, general, obscene, popular, profane, uncouth **8** barbaric, churlish, ordinary **9** customary, earthbred, inelegant, unrefined
vulgarism: **4** cant **9** barbarism
vulgate: **6** common, patois **10** colloquial, vernacular
vulnerable: **4** open, weak **6** liable **7** exposed **9** pregnable, untenable **10** assailable
point: **12** Achilles heel
vulpine: fox, sly **4** foxy, wily **6** artful, clever, crafty, tricky **7** cunning **9** alopecoid
vulture: **4** papa **5** arend, grape, gripe, griph, urubu **6** condor, griphe **8** aasvogel, zopilote **9** gallinazo

W

waag: 6 grivet, monkey

wabby: 4 loon

wabeno: 6 shaman 8 magician

wachna: cod 7 codfish

wacky, whacky: mad 4 nuts 5 crazy, loony, silly 6 absurd, insane, screwy 7 erratic, foolish 9 eccentric 10 irrational

wad: bat, gag, pad, ram 4 cram, heap, lead, line, lump, mass, plug, roll, tuft 5 crowd, money, stuff, trace, track, would 6 bundle, insert, packet, pledge, wealth 7 fortune, stopper 8 bankroll, compress, graphite

Wadai Muslim: 4 Maba

wadding: 4 hemp 5 kapok 6 cotton

waddle: 5 tread 6 hoddle, toddle, widdle 7 trample

waddy: peg 4 beat, cane, club 5 stick 6 attack, cowboy 7 rustler

wade: 4 ford, pass, plod 6 paddle 7 proceed 8 struggle

wader: 4 boot, coot, hern, ibis, rail 5 crane, heron, snipe, stork 6 jacana 8 flamingo, shoebill 9 sandpiper

wadi, wady: bed 4 wash 5 gully, oasis, river 6 ravine, stream, valley 7 channel 11 watercourse

wadset: 4 pawn 6 pledge 8 mortgage

wafer: 4 cake, disk, Host, ring, seal, snap 5 close 6 fasten, matzoh 7 biscuit, cracker
container for: pix, pyx

waffle: 4 cake 6 babble 10 equivocate

waft: 4 blow, buoy, flag, gust, odor, puff, turn, wave, weft 5 carry, drift, float, gleam, sound, taste, whiff 6 beckon, breath, direct, propel, signal, wraith 7 glimpse, pennant 9 transport

wag: wit 4 card, move, stir, sway, wave, zany 5 clown, comic, joker, leave, nudge, rogue, shake, swing 6 beckon, depart, jester, kidder, signal, twitch, wiggle 7 farceur, vibrate 8 brandish, comedian, flourish, humorist, jokester 9 oscillate, prankster

wage: fee, pay, utu 4 hire, levy, pawn 5 bribe, fight, incur 6 employ, engage, income, reward, salary 7 attempt, conduct, contend, stipend 9 emolument 10 recompense 12 compensation, remuneration

wage earner: 6 worker 7 laborer 8 employee, mechanic 11 proletarian

wager: bet, bid, lay, pot, vie 4 ante, gage, game, play, risk 5 prize, sport, stake 6 chance, gamble, hazard, parlay, pledge 7 venture
made in bad faith: 6 levant

waggery: gag 4 jest, joke, quip 7 foolery 10 pleasantry

waggish: 4 arch, pert 5 droll, merry, saucy 7 jesting, jocular, parlous, playful, roguish 8 humorous, sportive 10 frolicsome 11 mischievous

waggle: 4 sway, wave 6 switch, waddle, wobble

Wagner, Richard: *character:* Eva 4 Elsa, Erda 5 Hagen, Senta, Wotan 8 Parsifal
father-in-law: 5 Liszt
opera: 6 Rienzi 7 Fairies 8 Parsifal 9 Lohengrin 10 Tannhauser 12 Das Rheingold 14 Flying Dutchman 15 Gotterdammerung
wife: 5 Minna 6 Cosima

wagon: bin, car, van 4 cart, dray, tram, wain 5 araba, aroba, dilly, gilly, lorry, lurry, tonga 6 camion, telega 7 caisson, chariot, fourgon, vehicle 8 carryall 9 buckboard, Conestoga 12 perambulator
maker: 10 wainwright
part: 4 neap, pole, rave 5 thill 6 tongue

wagon-lit: 7 Pullman, sleeper 11 railroad car

wagonload: 5 cargo 6 fother

wah: 5 panda

wahine: 4 wife 5 woman 8 mistress 10 girl surfer, sweetheart

wahoo: elm 4 fish, peto, tree 8 mackerel, nonsense, tommyrot 9 buckthorn, guarapucu 11 burning bush

waif: 4 flag 5 stray 7 pennant, vagrant, wastrel 8 castaway, homeless, wanderer 9 foundling

wail: cry, sob, wow 4 bawl, howl, keen, moan, waul, weep, yarm, yowl 5 croon, mourn 6 bemoan, bewail, boohoo, grieve, lament, plaint, repine 7 blubber, deplore, ululate 8 complain 9 complaint 11 lamentation

wain: 4 cart 5 fetch, wagon 6 convey 7 chariot, vehicle

wainscot: 4 ceil, dado, line 6 lining 7 ceiling 8 paneling 10 wall lining

waist: 4 belt, wasp 5 shirt 6 basque, blouse, bodice, camisa, girdle 7 corsage 8 camisole 10 mid-section
circumference: 5 girth

waistband: obi 4 sash 6 girdle 8 ceinture, cincture

waistcoat: 4 vest 5 benjy, gilet 6 fecket, jacket, jerkin, weskit

wait: 4 bide, rest, stay, stop, tend 5 abide, await, cater, court, dally, defer, delay, guard, serve, tarry, watch 6 ambush, attend, escort, expect, follow, harken, linger, remain 7 hautboy, hearken, observe 8 hesitate 9 accompany 10 anticipate 11 stick around

waiter: spy 4 tray 6 garcon, salver, server, vessel 7 messboy, messman, servant, steward, watcher 8 servitor, watchman, waylayer 9 attendant

waive: put 4 cast, cede, turn 5 allow, cease, defer, forgo, grant, leave, swing, yield 6 desert, forego, give up, refuse, reject, shelve, vacate 7 abandon, concede, forbear, forsake, neglect, suspend 8 postpone 9 disregard 10 relinquish

waka: 5 canoe

wake: 4 call, stir, wauk (Sc.) 5 arise, get up, guard, revel, rouse, track, trail, vigil, waken, watch 6 arouse, awaken, excite, kindle, revive 7 passage

wakeful: 5 alert 8 restless, vigilant 9 sleepless

Walden author: 7 Thoreau

Waldensian: 7 Leonist

wale: rib 4 best, flog, mark, pick, weal, welt 5 ridge, strip, wheal 6 choice, choose, select, streak, timber 8 choicest

Wales: (see box)

walk: mog, pad, wag 4 foot, gait, hike, hoof, limp, mall, pace, path, plod, ramp, reel, roam, roll, slog, step, turn, wade 5 allee, amble, field, haunt, march, mince, scuff, stalk, stram, stray, strut, stump, trail, tramp, tread, troop 6 airing, arcade, foot it, hobble, loiter, lumber, parade, pasear, prance, ramble, resort, stride, stroll, toddle, totter, trapes, trudge, wander 7 alameda, saunter, shuffle, stretch, traipse 8 ambulate, frescade, traverse 9 esplanade, promenade,

tilicetum 11 perambulate

a beat: 6 patrol

affectedly: 5 mince

inability to: 6 abasia 9 paralysis

lamely: 4 limp

off: 5 leave 6 depart

off with: win 5 steal

-out: 6 strike

out on: 5 leave 6 desert 7 abandon

reeling: 5 lurch

walkaway: 4 rout 7 victory

walker: 5 hiker 6 ganger 7 footman 8 stroller 10 pedestrian

walking: 7 passant (her.) 8 ambulant 10 ambulation 11 peripatetic

walking meter: 9 pedometer

walking stick: 4 cane 5 kebby, staff, stilt, waddy 6 kebbie

walkway: 4 path 7 catwalk, passage 8 sidewalk 9 promenade

wall: bar 4 cage, coop, dike, ha-ha 5 block, fence, hedge, levee, redan, scarp 6 bailey, cashel, escarp, haw-haw, paries, podium, septum 7 barrier, bastion, curtain, defense, enclose, parapet, rampart 8 blockade 9 barricade, enclosure, encompass, partition, revetment 13 fortification

bracket: 6 corbel, sconce

covering: 4 tile 5 cloth, paint, paper 8 paneling 9 calcimine, draperies, kalsomine

dividing: 5 septa (pl.) 6 septum 9 partition

enclose within: 4 mure 6 immure

hanging: 5 arras 8 tapestry

lining: 8 wainscot

masonry: 9 revetment

material: 4 lath, stud 6 gypsum 7 plaster 9 sheetrock 12 plasterboard

opening: 4 bole, door 6 window 7 archway, scupper

ornament: 4 dado 6 mirror, plaque 7 art-

Wales: Cymru 7 Cambria

bard: 5 ovate

boat: 7 coracle

capital: 7 Cardiff

cheese: 10 Caerphilly

city: 6 Amlweh, Bangor 7 Rhondda, Swansea 8 Hereford, Holyhead, Pembroke 9 Carnarvon, Worcester

currency: 5 pence, pound

dog: 5 corgi

emblem: 4 leek

fine: 6 saraad

food: 4 cawl 10 laver bread

god: 4 Bran 5 Dylan

lake: 4 Bala

language: 5 Welsh 6 Cymric, Kymric 7

Cymraeg

law: 7 galanas

legendary prince: 5 Madoc

marriage fee: 6 amober

measure: 5 cover 7 cantred, cantref, lestrad, listred 8 crannock

mountain: 5 Eryri 6 Berwyn 7 Snowdon 8 Cambrian

musical festival: 10 eisteddfod

musical instrument: 7 pibcorn

patron saint: 5 David

people: 5 Cymry, Kymry

person: 5 Taffy 8 Welshman

poet: 6 Thomas (Dylan)

river: Dee, Wye 4 Teme 5 Teifi 6 Conway, Severn

work, hanging, molding, picture, placque **8** moulding, painting, tapestry
painting on: **5** mural **6** fresco
part: **4** dado, pier **5** bahut, gable **6** coping, plinth **7** cornice
pert. to: **5** mural **8** parietal
plug: **6** outlet
protective: **7** parapet

wallah, walla: **5** agent, owner **6** fellow, master, person, worker **7** servant

wallet: bag, jag **4** jagg, pack, poke, sack **5** purse, scrip **6** budget **8** billfold, knapsack **10** pocketbook

wallop: **4** bang, bash, beat, belt, blow, drub, flog, lick, pelt, slam, slug, whip, whop **5** baste, paste, pound, smash **6** defeat, impact, pummel, strike, thrash, thrill

walloping: **5** large **6** strong **7** beating **8** enormous

wallow: pit **4** bask, fade, mire, roll **5** enjoy, revel, surge **6** billow, grovel, hollow, trough, welter, wither **7** founder, indulge, stumble **8** flounder, kommetje **9** delight in, luxuriate **10** depression

wallowish: **4** flat **7** insipid

wallpaper measure: **4** bolt, roll

walnut: **6** bannut
skin: **4** hull, zest **5** shell

walrus: **4** seal **5** morse **6** mammal, seacat **8** mustache **9** rosmarine
flock: pod
limb: **7** flipper
order: **5** bruta
tooth: **4** tusk

waltz: zip **5** dance, valse **6** breeze **7** two-step **9** three-step
kind of: **6** Boston, Vienna
king: **7** Strauss

wampum: **4** peag **5** beads, money **6** shells **7** roanoke

wamus: **6** jacket **7** doublet **8** cardigan

wan: dim, one, sad **4** ashy, dark, fade, pale, sick, weak, worn **5** dusky, faint, livid, waxen **6** anemic, dismal, feeble, gloomy, pallid, pallor, peaked, sickly **7** ghastly, haggard, languid, wanness **8** blanched, bleached, paleness **9** bloodless, colorless, sorrowful, washed out **10** lusterless

wand: rod **4** pole, tube, twig **5** baton, shoot, staff, stick **6** switch **7** pointer, rhabdos, scepter, sceptre **8** caduceus **9** horsewhip
royal: **4** mace **7** scepter

wand-shaped: **7** virgate

wander: bat, err, gad **4** haik, hake, prog, rave, roam, roil, rove, wind **5** amble, drift, mooch, prowl, range, shift, stray, tramp **6** cruise, dander, depart, ramble, stroll, trapes, travel **7** deviate, digress, diverge, maunder, meander, saunter, traipse **8** divagate, strag-

gle, traverse **9** gallivant **11** peregrinate
aimlessly: gad **5** slosh, stray **7** meander, traipse

wanderer: vag **4** Arab, waif **5** gypsy, nomad, rover **6** truant **7** drifter, migrant, pilgrim, vagrant **9** itinerant, meanderer **11** extravagant **12** rolling stone
religious: **6** palmer

wandering: **5** vagus (anat.) **6** astray, errant **7** devious, erratic, journey, odyssey **8** aberrant **9** aberrance, delirious, planetary **10** circuitous, incoherent **11** noctivigant, perambulant

wandering Jew: ivy **5** plant **7** Zebrina **10** spiderwort **12** Tradescantia

wanderlust: **8** nomadism **9** itchy-foot **12** restlessness

wane: ebb **4** fail, fall, lack, sink, want **5** abate, decay, let up, peter **6** absent, defect, repine, shrink, weaken **7** decline, die away, die down, dwindle, slacken, subside **8** decrease, diminish **10** defervesce
opposite of: wax

wang: **4** king **5** ruler **6** prince

wanga: **5** charm, spell **6** voodoo **7** philter, sorcery

wanghee: See **whangee**

wangle: **4** fake **5** shake **6** adjust, change, juggle, totter, wiggle **7** falsify, finagle, wriggle **8** contrive, engineer, maneuver **9** extricate **10** manipulate

want: gap **4** hole, lack, lose, miss, mole, must, need, void, wish **5** covet, crave, fault, ought **6** besoin, choose, dearth, defect, demand, desire, forget, hunger, penury **7** absence, beggary, blemish, craving, default, lacking, missing, poverty, require, straits, vacancy **8** exigency, scarcity, shortage **9** deficient, fall short, indigence, necessary, necessity, privation **10** deficiency, inadequacy **11** deprivation, destitution

wanting: shy **4** less **5** minus, short **6** absent, devoid **7** without, witless **9** deficient **10** inadequate

wanton: gay **4** doxy, easy, fast, jade, lewd, slut **5** cadgy, dally, flirt, frisk, hussy, light, loose, merry, revel, tramp, wench **6** frisky, frolic, giglet, harlot, lavish, trifle, unruly **7** baggage, fulsome, haggard, ill-bred, immoral, jezebel, lustful, playful, sensual, trollop, wayward **8** arrogant, flagrant, inhumane, insolent, perverse, prodigal, spiteful, sportive, strumpet, unchaste **9** dissolute, lecherous, luxuriant, luxurious, malicious, merciless **10** capricious, frolicsome, gratuitous, lascivious, licentious, prostitute, refractory, voluptuous **11** extravagant, mollycoddle **12** supererogant, unrestrained

wantwit: **4** fool **5** dunce

wap: 4 beat, bind, blow, whop, wrap 5 blast, fight, knock, storm, truss 6 bundle, strike 8 wrapping

wapiti: elk 4 deer, stag 8 wampoose

war (see also **weapon**): 4 feud 5 blitz, fight 6 battle, combat, strife 7 contend, crusade 8 struggle
alarm: 4 flap
club: 4 mace 5 nulla 6 nullah
fleet: 6 armada
god of: Ira, Tyr 4 Ares, Coel, Mars, Odin, Thor 5 Woden 6 Nergal
goddess: 4 Alea 5 Anath, Bella 6 Anunit, Ishtar 7 Bellona
instrument: 4 mine 7 caltrap, caltrop 9 relocator
machine: 4 ram 4 bomb, tank 6 rocket 7 missile 8 catapult
religious: 5 jehad, jihad 7 crusade
restriction: 7 embargo 8 blockade
trophy: 4 star 5 booty, medal, scalp 6 ribbon, spoils
vehicle: 4 jeep, tank 6 humvee

War and Peace author: 7 Tolstoy

warbird: 7 aviator, tanager 8 airplane

warble: 4 sing, tune 5 carol, chant, chirl, shake, trill, yodel 6 melody, strain 7 descant, twitter, vibrate

warbler: 4 wren 5 pipit, robin 6 singer, thrush 8 blackcap, grosbeak, redstart, songbird, songster 9 beccafico 10 bluethroat 11 whitethroat

war chest: 8 treasury 13 campaign money

ward: 4 care, fend, foil, halt, jail, rule, stay, turn, warn 5 avert, block, check, deter, guard, parry, repel, watch 6 charge, defend, divert, govern, picket, prison, rebuff, sentry, shield, stymie, thwart, warden, warder 7 counsel, custody, defense, deflect, enclose, fend off, forfend, fortify, hold off, keeping, prevent, protege, repulse 8 armament, district, garrison, guardian, preclude, security, sentinel, watchman 9 forestall, frustrate, interrupt, safeguard 10 protection 11 confinement 12 guardianship
off: end 4 fend 5 avert, guard, parry, repel 7 forfend, prevent
pert. to: 9 pupillary

warden: 4 caid 5 guard, nazir 6 disdar, dizdar, jailer, jailor, keeper, ranger, regent, sexton, warder (Br.) director 7 alcaide, alcayde, turnkey, viceroy 8 cerberus, governor, guardian, overseer, watchdog, watchman 9 castellan, concierge, constable, custodian 10 doorkeeper, gatekeeper, supervisor

warder: 5 staff 7 bulwark 8 sentinel 9 caretaker, truncheon 10 doorkeeper, stronghold

wardrobe: 4 room 5 dress, privy, trunk 6 closet 7 apparel, armoire, bedroom, cabinet, chamber, clothes 8 clothing, costumes 9 garderobe 12 clothespress

ware: 4 host, sage, shun, wary, wise 5 avoid, aware, china, cloth, goods, ready, spend, stuff, waste 6 people, shrewd 7 careful, chaffer, fabrics, heedful, knowing, pottery, prudent, seaweed 8 cautious, products, sensible, squander, vigilant 9 cognizant, commodity, conscious, porcelain

warehouse: 4 silo, stow 5 depot, etape, guard, store 6 bestow, fonduk, godown 7 almacen, fondouk, funduck, protect, shelter, storage 8 elevator, entrepot, magazine 10 storehouse 11 accommodate

war hawk: 5 jingo

war-horse: 5 steed 6 leader 7 charger, standby, veteran 8 partisan 10 campaigner, politician

warily (see also **wary**): 6 tiptoe 8 gingerly

warlike: 7 hawkish, hostile, martial, warring 8 militant, military 9 bellicose, Bellonian, combative, soldierly, truculent 10 battailous, contending, pugnacious 11 belligerent, contentious, quarrelsome

warlock: 4 mage 5 magus 6 wizard 8 conjuror, magician, sorcerer 9 enchanter

warm: 4 avid, beek, heat, keen, kind, mild 5 angry, brisk, calid, chafe, eager, fiery, fresh, tepid, toast 6 ardent, devout, genial, hearty, heated, kindly, lively, loving, strong, tender, toasty 7 affable, amorous, clement, cordial, earnest, enliven, excited, fervent, glowing, irksome, sincere, thermal, zealous 8 animated, friendly, generous, gracious, grateful, vehement, vigorous 9 harassing, heartfelt, irascible, irritated, sprightly, strenuous 10 responsive 11 kindhearted, softhearted, sympathetic 12 affectionate, disagreeable, enthusiastic

warmth: 4 elan, glow, heat, zeal, zest 6 spirit 7 feeling, passion
pert. to: 7 thermal

warn: tip 4 clew, clue, post, rede, tell 5 alarm, alert 6 advise, beacon, charge, enjoin, exhort, inform, notify 7 apprise, apprize, caution, command, counsel 8 admonish, threaten 9 reprehend

warning: tip 4 hint, omen 5 knell 6 advice, alarum, beware, caveat, lesson, signal 7 caution, counsel, sematic 8 guidance 10 admonition, suggestion 13 animadversion
sound of: 4 bell 5 alarm, siren 6 alarum, tocsin

warp: abb, end, hit, mud, wry 4 beat, bend, bias, cast, emit, hurl, kink, line, rope, silt, sway, turn, warf 5 eject, expel, fling, quirk, throw, twist 6 buckle, debase, deform, devise, fasten, garble, swerve, wrench 7 confuse, contort, corrupt, deflect, distort,

falsify, pervert **8** misshape, sediment **9** fabricate **10** aberration, intertwine **12** misinterpret, misrepresent
thread for loom: **6** stamen

warragal, warrigal: 5 dingo, horse

warrant: act **4** earn, save **5** basis, berat, claim, guard, merit, order, right, write **6** affirm, assert, assure, defend, ensure, ground, insure, permit, pledge, reason, refuge, safety, secure **7** behight, call for, certify, command, contend, defense, earnest, justify, precept, protect, require, sponsor, voucher, writing **8** document, guaranty, maintain, mittimus, sanction, security **9** assurance, authority, authorize, guarantee, protector, safeguard, stipulate, vindicate **10** commission, foundation, instrument, obligation, protection **11** certificate, stand behind **13** authorization, justification

warranty: 4 bail, bond **6** surety **8** guaranty, sanction, security **9** assurance, guarantee **13** authorization, justification

warren: 5 hutch **6** rabbitry, tenement

warrior: toa **4** hero, impi **5** brave **6** Amazon **7** fighter, martial, soldier **10** serviceman
group: **4** army
mythical: **6** Amazon **7** Aslauga
professional: **7** Hessian **9** gladiator, mercenary

warship: LST, sub **4** long **5** razee **6** bireme **7** cruiser, dromond, flattop, frigate, galleon, onebank, trireme **8** corvette **9** destroyer, submarine **10** battleship **11** dreadnaught, minesweeper
deck: **4** poop **5** orlop
famous: **4** Hood **5** Maine **7** Arizona, Monitor **8** Bismarck, Graf Spee, Merrimac, Missouri **12** Constitution, Old Ironsides
fleet: **6** armada **8** squadron
quarters: **7** gunroom
squadron: **10** escadrille
three-bank: **7** trireme
two-bank: **6** bireme

wart: 5 tumor **6** lesion **7** verruca **9** subaltern **10** midshipman

wary: shy **5** alert, cagey, canny, chary, leery **6** frugal **7** careful, guarded, knowing, prudent, sceptic, skeptic, sparing, thrifty **8** cautious, discreet, doubting, stealthy, vigilant, watchful **9** cautelous, provident **10** economical, suspicious **11** circumspect, distrustful, on one's guard

wase: pad **4** wisp **6** bundle

wash: lap, mud, pan **4** lave, silt, soap, suds **5** bathe, clean, creek, drift, float, leach, rinse, scour, scrub, slosh **6** bubble, debris, purify, shower, sluice, sperge **7** cleanse, launder, shampoo **8** ablution, alluvium **9** lixiviate
away: **5** erode, purge

out: **4** fail **5** elute, erase, flush **7** discard, launder

washbowl: 4 sink **5** basin **6** lavabo **8** lavatory **9** aljofaina

washed-out: wan **4** pale **5** all in, faded, tired **6** effete **7** drained **8** depleted **9** exhausted **10** dispirited, spiritless

washer: 4 rove **5** clove

washing: 7 laundry **8** ablution, lavation
chemical: **6** eluate

Washington, George: *home:* **11** Mount Vernon
portraitist: **6** Stuart
wife: **6** Martha

Washington, State of: *capital:* **7** Olympia
city: **6** Tacoma, Yakima **7** Everett, Seattle, Spokane **8** Bellevue **10** Walla Walla
dam: **11** Grand Coulee
explorer: **4** Gray **6** Heceta **9** Vancouver **13** Lewis and Clark
fish: **6** salmon **8** sturgeon
Indian: **6** Yakima **7** Chinook **8** Sahaptin
mountain peak: **5** Adams, Baker **7** Glacier, Rainier **8** St. Helens
mountain range: **4** Blue **5** Rocky **6** Kettle **7** Cascade, Olympic, Rockies
nickname: **7** Chinook **9** Evergreen
river: **5** Snake **6** Yakima **8** Columbia
sound: **5** Puget
state bird: **9** goldfinch
state flower: **12** rhododendron
state tree: **7** hemlock
volcano: **10** Mt. St. Helens

Washington D.C.: *art gallery:* **5** Freer **8** Corcoran, National, Phillips
basketball team: **7** Bullets
designer: **7** L'Enfant (Pierre)
district: **8** Columbia
football team: **8** Redskins
hill: **7** Capitol
landmark: **4** Mall **7** Capitol, Ellipse **10** Tidal Basin, White House
memorial: **7** Lincoln **9** Jefferson **15** Vietnam Veterans
neighbors: **8** Maryland, Virginia
nickname: **11** Foggy Bottom
river: **7** Potomac
section: **9** Anacostia **10** Georgetown **11** Adams-Morgan, Capitol Hill

washout: 4 fail, flop 5 gulch, gully 6 fiasco, reject 7 erosion, failure

washy: 4 oozy, thin, weak 5 loose 6 feeble, watery 7 diluted, insipid 8 slippery 9 frivolous, worthless

wasp: 5 whamp 6 cuckoo, dauber, digger, hornet, insect, vespid 12 hymenopteron, yellow jacket
genus of: 5 sphex
pert. to: 6 vespal 7 vespine

waspish: 5 huffy, sharp, testy 6 cranky, ornery 7 crabbed, fretful, peevish, slender 8 choleric, contrary, crochety, perverse, petulant, snappish, spiteful 9 fractious, impatient, irascible, irritable, querulous 11 bad-tempered 12 cantankerous

wassail: 4 lark, orgy, romp 5 binge, drink, revel, spree 6 frolic, shindy 7 carouse 8 carousal 9 festivity, high jinks, merriment 10 salutation 11 celebration

waste: 4 bush, fail, idle, loss, pine, ruin, sack 5 decay, dwine, havoc, offal, trash 6 barren, bezzle, debris, desert, devour, litter, molder, ravage, refuse, sewage, weaken 7 atrophy, badland, consume, corrode, destroy, dwindle, exhaust, fritter, garbage, rubbish 8 confound, decrease, demolish, desolate, emaciate, enfeeble, misspend, squander 9 condiddle, devastate, dissipate 11 consumption, destruction, devastation, dissipation, fritter away, prodigality 12 extravagance, improvidence
allowance: 4 tret
away: age, rot 4 fail, pine, wane, wilt 5 decay 6 molder 7 atrophy, decline
lay: 4 ruin, sack 5 havoc, spoil 6 ravage 7 destroy 9 devastate
matter: 5 ashes, dregs, dross 6 debris 7 garbage

wasted: 4 worn 5 gaunt 7 haggard, wizened 8 impaired, phthisic, skeletal, withered 9 emaciated, shriveled 10 cadaverous

wasteful: 6 lavish 8 prodigal 10 thriftless 11 extravagant, improvident

wasteland: fen 4 burn, moor 5 heath, marsh, swamp, wilds 6 barren, desert, morass 8 badlands

Waste Land author: 5 Eliot

wastrel: 4 rake, roué, waif 5 idler, knave, rogue 6 waster 8 prodigal, vagabond 10 profligate 11 spendthrift

wat: 6 temple

watch: eye, see, spy 4 espy, glom, heed, look, mark, mind, tend, view, wait, ward 5 await, clock, guard, stare, timer, vigil 6 ambush, behold, defend, patrol, picket, police, regard, sentry 7 bivouac, lookout, monitor, observe, oversee 8 horologe, meditate, sentinel 9 ambuscade, timepiece 11 keep an eye on, observation 13 sleeplessness
maker: 10 horologist
part: fob 7 battery, crystal 10 mainspring

watchdog: 6 keeper, warden 8 guardian 9 custodian
Hel's: 4 Garm 5 Garmr
underworld: 8 Cerberus

watcher: spy 5 scout 7 lookout, witness 8 observer, watchman 9 bystander, spectator

watchful: 4 wary 5 alert, aware 7 careful, wakeful 8 cautious, open-eyed, vigilant 9 attentive, wide-awake 10 unsleeping 11 circumspect

watchman: 5 guard, scout 6 picket, sentry, warder 7 lookout 8 sentinel 10 gatekeeper

watchtower: 6 beacon, garret 7 lookout, mirador 8 bantayan 10 lighthouse, widow's walk 11 observatory

watchword: 5 motto 6 ensign, parole, signal, slogan 8 consigne, password 10 shibboleth 11 countersign

watchworks: 8 movement
arrangement: 7 caliper
mechanism: 10 escapement

water: eau (F.), wet 4 agua (Sp.), aqua (L.), brim, broo, burn, hose, pani 5 abyss, acqua (It.), brine, fluid, flume, laver, lough, lymph, spray 6 dilute, liquid, wasser (G.) 7 moisten 8 beverage, calender, irrigate, moisture, sprinkle 10 citronelle
body: bay, sea 4 deep, gulf, lake, loch, mear, mere, pind, pond, pool, tank, well 5 oasis, ocean 6 lagoon, strait 7 springs 9 reservoir
carrier: 4 duct, main, pipe 5 barge, canal, flume, zanja 7 aguador 8 aqueduct
congealed: ice 4 hail 5 glace, sleet 6 icicle 7 glacier, iceberg
covered by: 5 awash 7 flooded 9 inundated
down: 4 thin 6 dilute
draw: 4 lade, pump
element: 6 oxygen 8 hydrogen
goddess: 4 Nina 5 naiad 6 nereid 7 Anahita, Anaitis
hog: 8 capybara
hole: 4 lake, pond, pool, tarn 5 oasis 7 alberca, caldera
lack of: 6 desert 7 drought
mineral: 5 Vichy 6 selter, Shasta 7 seltzer
obstruction: bar, dam 4 reef 7 sandbar
pert. to: 6 marine 7 aquatic
pure: 8 aqua pura (L.)
raising apparatus: 4 pump 5 sweep 6 siphon 7 shadoof 10 water wheel
rough: rip, sea 4 eddy 5 waves 6 rapids 8 breakers
search for: 5 dowse
soapy: 4 suds 6 graith
sound: 4 drip 5 plash 6 babble, murmur, splash

still: **6** lagoon
surface: **4** ryme
vessel: jug **4** cowl, ewer, lota, pail **5** cruse, flask, lotah **6** bottle, bucket, goblet **7** pitcher, stamnos **8** decanter
Water Bearer: 8 Aquarius
water bird (see also **bird**): **4** coot, loon **5** diver **8** alcatras **9** waterfowl
water bottle: 4 lota, olla **6** carafe, tinaja **7** canteen
water buffalo: ox **7** carabao, tamarau
water carrier: 4 pipe **7** aguador (Sp.), bheesty (Ind.), channel **8** bheestie (Ind.)
water chicken: 9 gallinule
water clock: 6 ghurry **9** clepsydra
water cooler: 4 icer, olla, tank **7** bubbler **8** fountain **11** refrigerant
watercourse (see also **water**: *body*): run **4** dike, dyke, race, wadi, wady **5** brook, canal, chute, creek, drain, gully, river **6** arroyo (Sp.), course, gutter, nullah, ravine, sluice, stream **7** channel, trinket **8** barranca (Sp.)
water cow: 6 dugong **7** manatee
watercraft: See **boat, sailboat, ship**
watercress: 9 brooklime **10** nasturtium
water crow: 4 coot **9** snakebird
water cure: 10 hydropathy **12** hydrotherapy **17** hydrotherapeutics
water deer: 5 chevrotain
water eagle: 6 osprey
watered: 4 silk **5** moire
water elephant: 12 hippopotamus
waterfall: lin **4** linn **5** chute, force, rapid, sault, spout **6** rapids **7** cascade, Niagara **8** cataract, Victoria, Yosemite **9** Multnomah
waterfowl (see also **bird**): **4** coot, loon **5** diver
waterfront worker: 5 navvy **9** stevedore **12** longshoreman
water gate: 6 sluice **9** floodgate **11** watercourse
Watergate judge: 6 Sirica
water germander: 4 mint
water glass: 6 goblet **7** tumbler **8** compound **9** clepsydra
waterhead: sap **5** booby **6** source **9** headwater **12** fountainhead **13** hydrocephalus
water hog: 7 bushpig **8** capybara
water hole: pit **4** lake, pond, pool **5** oasis **7** alberca
water horse: 6 kelpie **11** hippocampus **12** hippopotamus
water ice: 6 sorbet **7** sherbet
watering device: can **4** hose, pump **5** spray **6** nozzle **7** hydrant
watering place: bar, pub, spa **4** café, pool **5** oasis **6** aguada (Sp.), battis, lounge, resort, saloon, spring, tavern **7** barroom, hangout **9** nightclub
waterless: dry **4** arid

water lily: 5 lotos, lotus **6** bobbin, nuphar **7** nelumbo, nymphia **8** nenuphar, pond lily
waterlog: 4 soak **5** swamp **8** saturate
watermelon: 5 fruit, gourd **6** citrul, sandia **7** anguria
water meter: 7 orifice, venturi
water moccasin: 5 snake, viper **11** cottonmouth
water mole: 6 desman **8** duckbill, platypus
water nymph: nix **4** lily **5** Ariel, naiad, nixie **6** flower, kelpie, nereid, Undine **7** goddess, hydriad, Oceanid **9** dragonfly
water on the brain: 12 hydrocephaly
water ouzel: 4 bird **6** dipper, thrush
water pig: 7 gourami **8** capybara
water pipe: 4 bong, duct, hose, tube **6** hookah **8** narghile, nargileh
water plant: 5 cress, lotus **7** aquatic, bulrush, cattail, papyrus, seaweed **9** water lily **10** hydrophyte
water plug: tap **6** spigot **7** hydrant
water pocket: 6 tinaja
water rat: 4 vole **6** rodent **7** muskrat
watershed: 5 ridge **6** divide
waterspout: 5 canal, spate **7** tornado **8** gargoyle **9** hurricane, whirlwind
water sprite: See **water nymph**
water thief: 6 pirate **9** buccaneer
waterwheel: 5 noria, sakia **6** sakieh **7** sakiyeh **8** tympanum
watery: wet **4** pale, soft, thin, weak **5** fluid, sammy, soggy **6** anemic, blashy, dilute, jejune, serous, soaked, sweaty **7** aqueous, insipid, tearful, weeping **8** humorous **11** transparent
wattle: rod **4** beat, bind, flog, gill, jowl, twig, wand **5** cooba, fence, stick, twist, withe **6** acacia, coobah, dewlap, hurdle, lappet **9** boobyalla, framework, hackthorn, intertwine **10** interweave
wave: ola (Sp.), sea, set, wag **4** bore, chop, curl, flap, surf, sway, tide, vein **5** bless, crimp, curve, eager, eagre, float, flood, ridge, shake, surge, swell, swing, tilde, vague (F.), water, waver **6** beckon, billow, comber, fickle, flaunt, marcel, ripple, roller, signal, waggle **7** breaker, flutter, ripplet, seagate, tsunami, vibrate, wavelet **8** brandish, flourish, undulate, whitecap **9** fluctuate, permanent, vibration **10** undulation, unevenness
largest: **7** decuman
top: **5** crest
upward motion: **5** scend
valley: **6** trough
waver: 4 reel, sway, trim, twig **5** hedge, quake, shift, swing **6** change, dither, falter, seesaw, teeter, totter, wiggle **7** flicker, flitter, flutter, sapling, stagger, tremble, vibrate **8** hesitate

9 fluctuate, hem and haw, oscillate, vacillate **11** back and fill **12** shilly-shally

wavering: **4** weak **5** shaky **6** fickle, unsure, wobbly **7** lambent **8** doubtful, flexuous, unsteady **9** desultory, faltering, hesitancy **10** hesitating, irresolute **11** vacillating

wavy: **4** ente (her.), onde (her.), unde (her.), undy (her.) **5** crisp, curly, snaky, undee (her.) **6** flying **7** billowy, sinuate, sinuous **8** squiggly, undulant **9** undulated **10** undulating

wax: **4** cere, grow, pela, rise **5** lipid, putty **6** become, expand **7** cerumen, enlarge, suberin **8** adhesive, increase, paraffin **11** zietriskite

   animal: **4** wool **7** beeswax, lanolin **10** spermaceti
   candle: **5** taper **6** cierge
   cobbler's: **4** code
   figure: **9** ceroplast
   match: **5** vesta
   mineral: **6** montan **7** peat wax **8** paraffin **10** petrolatum
   myrtle: **6** Myrica **8** bayberry
   opposite of: **4** wane
   pert. to: **5** ceral
   preparation: **6** cerate
   substance: **5** cerin
   used for skis: **7** klister
   vegetable: **8** bayberry, carnauba **10** candelilla
   yellow: **7** ceresin

waxbill: **7** astrild

waxen: **4** ashy, pale **5** ashen **6** pallid, viscid **7** cerated, pliable **8** yielding **11** impressible

waxwing: **9** cedarbird **10** weaverbird

waxy: **5** angry, vexed **7** pliable **8** yielding

way: via **4** cost, door, drag, fore, gait, lane, mode, pass, path, plan, plot, rite, road, room, rule, tack, wont **5** alley, calle, going, habit, means, milky, route, space, style, track, trail, usage **6** ambage, arcade, artery, avenue, career, causey, chemin, course, custom, detour, device, manner, method, scheme, street, system **7** advance, channel, fashion, highway, opening, passage **8** behavior, causeway, contrada, distance, doctrine, progress **9** banquette, boulevard, direction, procedure, technique
   in: **4** door **5** entry **7** contact **8** entrance
   out: **4** exit **6** egress, escape

waybill: **8** manifest **9** itinerary

wayfarer: **5** nomad **6** viator **8** traveler **9** itinerant

waygate: **4** path **9** departure **10** passageway

waylay: **5** await, belay, beset, prowl, skulk, slink **6** ambush **7** forelay **8** surprise **9** ambuscade

waymark: ahu **5** arrow, blaze **9** guidepost, milestone

wayward: **6** errant, fickle, unruly **7** erratic, froward, naughty, willful **8** contrary, perverse, stubborn, unsteady, untoward **9** arbitrary, irregular **10** capricious, headstrong, inconstant, refractory, selfwilled **11** disobedient, fluctuating, intractable

we: us, noi (It.), nos (L.), wir (G.) **4** nous (F.) **8** nosotros (Sp.) **9** ourselves

weak: wan **4** puny, soft, thin, worn **5** anile, bauch, chirp, crank, crimp, dicky, faint, frail, seely, shaky, washy, waugh, young **6** caduke, debile, dickey, dilute, dotish, faulty, feeble, flabby, flaggy, flimsy, foible, infirm, sickly, squeak, tender, unwise, watery, wobbly **7** brittle, diluted, dwaibly, fragile, pliable, rickety, spindly, unsound **8** asthenic, childish, decrepit, feckless, flagging, helpless, impotent, wavering **9** childlike, dissolute, enfeebled, nerveless, powerless, spineless **10** effeminate, inadequate **11** debilitated, implausible, ineffective

weaken: sap **4** fade, fail, flag, thin, tire, wane **5** blunt, break, craze, delay **6** appall, damage, deaden, defeat, dilute, impair, lessen, reduce, soften **7** cripple, decline, depress, disable, exhaust, unnerve **8** enervate, paralyze **9** attenuate, undermine

weakling: sop **4** baby **5** puler, sissy **6** softie, sucker **7** crybaby, milksop, sad sack **8** mama's boy, pushover

weakness: **4** flaw **5** taste **6** defect, foible, liking **7** acratia, ailment, failing, frailty **8** appetite, debility, fondness **9** inability **11** attenuation

weal: **4** line, mark, pomp, wale, welt **5** ridge, state, whelk **6** choice, choose, riches, stripe, wealth **7** welfare **9** happiness, wellbeing **10** commonweal, prosperity

wealth: **4** dhan, gear, gold, good, mean, pelf, weal **5** goods, money, worth **6** assets, estate, graith, mammon, riches **7** capital, fortune, welfare **8** big bucks, holdings, opulence, property, treasure **9** abundance, affluence, resources, substance, wellbeing **10** prosperity
   gained: **8** chevance **9** chievance
   person of: **5** Midas, nabob **7** Croesus, magnate **9** moneybags, plutocrat

wealthy: **4** full, rich **5** ample, pursy **8** affluent

wean: **4** baby **5** child **6** detach, infant **8** alienate, estrange **9** reconcile

weapon: arm, dag, gun **4** beak, bola, bolo, celt, claw, club, dart, dirk, epee, foil, mace, pike **5** arrow, bolas, glave, knife, lance, rifle, saber, sabre, shaft, sling, spear, sword, talon, vouge **6** bomber, cannon, dagger, eolith, glaive, mortar, musket, pistol, poleax, rapier **7** bayonet, bazooka, carbine, cutlass, firearm, gisarme, halberd, halbert,

machete, missile, poleaxe, shotgun, trident
8 battleax, catapult, claymore, crossbow,
fauchard, leeangle, revolver, scimitar,
stiletto, tomahawk **9** artillery, boomerang,
derringer **10** machine gun **11** blunderbuss
lay down: **6** disarm **9** surrender
storage place: **6** armory **7** arsenal
without: **7** unarmed

wear: don, rub **4** fray, gall, jade, tire **5** chafe,
erode, grind, sport, weary **6** abrade, attire,
batter, endure, impair **7** apparel, clothes,
consume, corrode, display, exhaust, exhibit,
fatigue, frazzle **8** diminish **11** deteriorate
away: eat **5** erode **6** abrade **7** corrode
out: **6** tucker **7** exhaust **8** knock out

weariness: **4** arid **5** ennui **6** tedium **7** fatigue
8 vexation **9** lassitude

weary: bad, fag, irk, sad **4** bore, jade, pall,
puny, sick, tire, weak, worn **5** annoy, bored,
curse, jaded, spent, timid, tired **6** harass,
plague, sickly **7** exhaust, fatigue, irksome,
tedious **8** fatigued, grievous, tiresome **9**
forjaskit, forjesket, surfeited **10** defatigate,
disastrous **11** unfortunate

Weary Willie: **5** tramp **7** shirker, vagrant **8**
vagabond

weasand: **6** gullet, throat **7** trachea **8** windpipe **9** esophagus

weasel: **4** cane, stot, vare **5** ratel, sneak, stoat
6 ermine, ferret **9** pussyfoot **10** equivocate
family: **6** marten **9** musteline

weather: dry **4** hail, rain, snow, wind **5** clime,
erode, sleet **7** climate **8** discolor, elements,
windward **12** disintegrate

weather map line: **6** isobar

weather satellite: **4** UARS **5** Tiros

weathercock: **4** fane, vane

weathered: **5** faded **6** tanned **7** bronzed,
stained **8** bleached, hardened, wrinkled **9**
roughened, toughened

weatherman: **13** meteorologist

weave: **4** darn, knit, lace, spin **5** braid, drape,
lurch, plait, swing, twill, unite **6** devise,
enlace, wattle **7** canille, crochet, entwine,
fashion, stagger **8** cannelle, contrive **9** fabricate, interlace, interwind **10** intertwine,
intertwist
kind: **4** pile, silk **5** fancy, gauze, plain,
tabby, twill
twigs: **6** wattle

weaverbird: **4** baya, taha **5** finch **6** whidah **7**
sparrow

weaver's tool: **4** loom, reed, sley

weaving: *crosswise thread:* **4** weft, woof **7** filling
beam
goddess: **6** Ergane
lengthwise thread: **4** warp
machine: **4** loom **6** carder **8** jacquard
rug **5** cloth **7** textile **8** tapestry

weazen: See **wizen**

web: mat, net, ply **4** caul, maze, mesh, trap,
veil, warp **5** cloth, fiber, skein, snare, toils **6**
fabric, morass, tangle, tissue **7** ensnare,
network, texture, webbing **8** entangle, gossamer, membrane, vexillum **9** labyrinth
footed: **7** palmate **11** totipalmate
half: **11** semi-palmate
pert. to: **6** telary **7** retiary

webbing: **7** binding

Weber opera: **6** Oberon **9** Euryanthe **13** Der
Freischutz

wed: tie **4** bind, join, link, mate, yoke **5** elope,
hitch, marry, mated, unite **6** joined,
pawned **7** espouse, pledged, spliced **9**
mortgaged
pert. to: **7** marital, nuptial

wedding: **6** bridal, splice **8** ceremony,
espousal, marriage, nuptials
attendant: **5** usher **7** best man **9** grooms-
man **10** bridesmaid, flower girl, ring bearer
11 maid of honor **13** matron of honor
canopy: **5** chupa **6** huppah **7** chuppah
celebration: **8** shivaree **9** charivari
party: **4** stag **6** shower **8** bachelor **9** reception
proclamation: **5** banns

wedding anniversary: *fifteenth:* **7** crystal
fifth: **4** wood
fiftieth: **6** golden
first: **5** paper
kind of: tin **4** ruby **5** candy, china, coral,
linen, paper, pearl, straw **6** floral, golden,
silver, wooden **7** crystal, diamond, emerald,
leather
seventy-fifth: **7** diamond
tenth: tin
thirtieth: **5** pearl
twentieth: **5** china
twenty-fifth: **6** silver

wedge: jam **4** club, heel, lump, shim, shoe **5**
cleat, crowd, ingot, piece, split **6** cleave,
sector, wedgie **7** niblick **8** separate, triangle, voussoir **9** formation

wedge-shaped: **6** cuneal **7** cuneate, sphenic **8**
cuneated, cuniform **9** cuneiform

wedgie: **4** shoe

wedlock: **4** wife **8** marriage **9** matrimony

Wednesday (source of name)**:** **5** Woden

wee: **4** tiny **5** bitty, small, teeny **6** little,
minute **9** miniature **10** diminutive

weed: **4** band, garb, loco, milk, sida, tare **5**
armor, cheat, dress, horse, vetch **6** darnel,
datura, nettle, remove, sarcle, spurge **7**
allseed, clothes, costume, garment, illness,
mallows, purloin, ragweed, relapse, thistle,
tobacco **8** clothing, plantain, purslane, sealwort, toadflax, trumpery **9** alfilaria, dandelion, eradicate, marijuana

weed killer: 8 paraquat 9 herbicide

weeds: 8 mourning

weedy: 4 foul, lean 5 lanky 7 scraggy 8 ungainly 9 overgrown

weekday: 5 feria

weekly: 5 aweek 10 hebdomadal, periodical 11 hebdomadary, publication

weeks (two): 9 fortnight

weel: 4 eddy, pool, trap 6 basket 9 whirlpool

ween: 4 hope 5 fancy, think 6 expect 7 believe, imagine, suppose 8 conceive

weep: cry, sob 4 drip, leak, moan, ooze, tear, wail 5 exude, greet, mourn 6 bewail, beweep, boohoo, grieve, lament 7 blubber, deplore

Weeping Philosopher: 10 Heraclitus

weeping statue: 5 Niobe

weepy: 5 moist, seepy, teary 6 oozing 7 maudlin, tearful, weeping 8 mournful 10 lachrymose

weevil: 4 boll, lota 7 billbug 8 circulio

weft: web 4 film, woof, yarn 5 shoot, shute 6 fabric, thread 7 filling

weigh: tax 4 bear, lift, tare, test 5 carry, count, hoist, poise, study 6 burden, esteem, matter, ponder, regard 7 balance, examine, measure, portion, support 8 appraise, consider, dispense, evaluate, meditate, militate 9 apportion

weigh down: sit 4 lade, load, sway 5 beset 6 sadden 7 depress, oppress 8 encumber

weigher: 5 trone 6 potdar, scaler 7 balance, trutine 8 computer 9 steelyard

weighing machine: 5 scale, trone 7 balance 9 steelyard

weight: bob, CWT, keg, lot, mol, tod, tom, ton, tup 4 beef, dram, gram, heft, lade, last, load, mina, onus, pari, rati, shot, tola 5 carat, clove, flask, grain, ounce, pfund, poise, pound, power, ratti, rider, scale, stein 6 barrel, burden, cental, charge, denier, fother, fotmal, gramme, grivna, import, moment 7 centner, drachma, gravity, oppress, plummet, quarter, quintal, scruple, tonnage 8 decagram, encumber, kilogram, pressure, vamfront, vammazsa, vierling 9 authority, centigram, heaviness, hectogram, influence, liespfund, microgram, milligram, myriagram, quentchen, zollpfund 10 importance 11 consequence 12 significance 13 hundred-weight

allowance: 4 tare, tret 7 scalage

gem: 5 carat

inspector: 6 sealer

of 100 pounds: 6 cental

official: 6 metage

pert. to: 5 baric 8 ponderal

system of: net 4 troy 5 avoir 6 metric 8 jeweler's 11 avoirdupois 12 apothecaries

weighted: 5 laden 6 biased, loaded 8 burdened 9 evaluated, oppressed

weightiness: 4 pith, pomp 6 import, moment 7 dignity, gravity 9 magnitude, solemnity 10 importance

weighty: fat 5 bulky, grave, heavy, hefty, large, massy, obese, sober, solid 6 severe, solemn, taxing 7 capital, massive, onerous, serious, telling 8 forcible, grievous, powerful 9 corpulent, important, momentous, ponderous 10 burdensome, chargeable, cumbersome, impressive, oppressive

weir: dam 4 bank 5 fence, garth, levee 7 barrier, milldam 11 obstruction

weird: lot, odd 4 eery, fate, unco, wild 5 charm, eerie, queer, scary, spell 6 creepy, kismet, spooky 7 awesome, bizarre, curious, destiny, eldrich, fortune, ghostly, macabre, oddball, strange, uncanny, unusual 8 haunting, peculiar, prophecy 9 eccentric, unearthly, unnatural 10 mysterious

weka: 4 bird, rail

welcome: 4 hail 5 adopt, greet 7 acclaim, cordial, embrace 8 greeting, pleasant 9 agreeable, bienvenue, desirable 10 acceptable, gratifying, salutation, satisfying

weld: 5 unite 6 solder 11 consolidate

welding gas: 9 acetylene

welfare: aid 4 dole, good, sele, weal 7 benefit 10 assistance, prosperity

welkin: air, sky 10 atmosphere

well: fit, pit 4 bene (It., L.), bien (F., Sp.), fair, flow, gush, hale, hole, sane, sump 5 aweel (Sc.), fitly, fount, happy, lucky, sound, truly 6 gusher, hearty, indeed, justly, nicely, origin, rather, really, source, spring, wholly 7 cistern, gaylies, geylies, gradely, healthy, perhaps 8 artesian, expertly, fountain 9 correctly 10 gratifying, prosperous 11 excellently

drill device: jar

lining: 5 steen

Welland: 4 city 5 canal, river

wellaway: woe 4 alas 5 alack 6 regret 9 alackaday

well-behaved: 4 good

well-being: 4 good, weal 6 health 7 comfort, welfare 8 eucrasia, felicity 9 eudaemony, happiness 10 prosperity

wellborn: 4 rich 5 noble 7 eugenic

well-bred: 5 civil 6 polite 7 genteel, refined 8 cultured, polished, wellborn 9 pedigreed 10 cultivated 11 gentlemanly

well-defined: 8 distinct 11 distinctive

well-developed: 5 curvy 7 rounded 10 curvaceous

well-founded: 4 firm, good, just 5 sound, valid 6 cogent

well-groomed: 4 neat, trig, trim 5 clean, natty, sleek 6 dapper, soigne 7 soignee

wellhead: 6 source, spring 8 fountain 12 fountainhead

well-heeled: 4 rich 7 moneyed 8 affluent 10 prosperous

well-known: 5 noted 6 famous 7 eminent, leading, popular 8 familiar 9 notorious, prominent

well-liked: 7 popular 8 favorite 9 preferred

well-made: 5 solid 6 sturdy 9 affabrous

well-nigh: 6 almost, nearly

well-off: 5 lucky 8 thriving 10 prosperous 11 comfortable

well-timed: 6 timely 9 opportune 10 auspicious, propitious

well-versed: 7 erudite 13 knowledgeable

welsh, welch: 5 cheat, evade, renig 6 renege 7 swindle 8 back down

welsh drake: 7 gadwall

Welsh onion: 4 leek 5 cibol

Welsh Rabbit: 7 rarebit

welt: 4 blow, mark, turn, wale 5 ridge, upset, wheal, whelk 6 stripe, thrash 8 overturn

welter: 4 reel, roll, toss, wilt 5 upset 6 grovel, tumble, wallow, wither 7 stagger, turmoil 8 overturn 9 confusion

wem: 4 flaw, scar, spot 5 stain

wen: 4 cyst, rune 5 tumor 6 growth 7 blemish 11 excrescence

wench: 4 dell, doxy, drab, gill, girl, jade, lass, maid, miss 5 child, gouge, hussy, tramp, trull, woman 6 blowen, blowze, damsel, maiden, wanton 7 consort, servant, trollop 8 strumpet 11 maidservant

wend: bow, hie 4 fare, pass 5 alter, shift 6 depart, push on, travel 7 circuit, journey, proceed

Wend: 4 Slav, Sorb 7 Sorbian

wenzel: 4 jack 5 knave

werewolf: 8 turnskin, versipal 11 lycanthrope

West: 8 frontier, Occident

West Indies: 7 Bahamas 8 Antilles
   dance: 5 limbo
   Indian: 5 Carib 6 Arawak 7 Ciboney
   island: 4 Cuba 5 Aruba, Haiti, Nevis 6 Bahama, Cayman 7 Bonaire, Curacao, Grenada, Jamaica 8 Anguilla, Barbados, Dominica, Trinidad 10 Hispaniola, Martinique, Puerto Rico, Santa Lucia 17 Dominican Republic
   island group: 7 Bahamas 8 Antilles 13 Cayman Islands, Virgin Islands 14 Leeward Islands 15 Windward Islands
   liquor: 5 mobby, tafia 6 mobbie, taffia
   mistletoe: 7 gadbush
   mountain: 5 Pelee 9 Soufriere
   palm: 5 yagua, yaray 6 grigri, grugru

   people: Ebo 4 Eboe 5 Carib, Cuban 6 Creole
   religion: 6 voodoo 14 Rastafarianism
   sorcery: obe, obi 6 voodoo
   volcano: 5 Pelee

West Point: 4 USMA 11 army academy
   mascot: 4 mule
   student: 4 pleb 5 cadet, plebe 8 yearling

West Virginia: *capital:* 10 Charleston
   city: 7 Weirton 8 Wheeling 10 Huntington 11 Parkersburg
   Indian: 7 Shawnee 8 Cherokee, Iroquois
   motto: 20 Montani Semper Liberi (Mountaineers Are Always Free)
   mountain: 9 Allegheny, Blue Ridge 11 Appalachian
   product: 4 coal 9 glassware
   river: Elk, New 4 Ohio 7 Kanawha, Potomac
   state bird: 8 cardinal
   state flower: 12 rhododendron
   state tree: 5 maple

---

western: 5 oater 10 horse opera

Western Samoa: *capital:* 4 Apia
   currency: 4 tala
   island: 5 Upolu 6 Savaii
   people: 10 Polynesian

Western treaty alliance: 4 NATO

Westminster clock: 6 Big Ben

wet: lax, off, sop 4 damp, dank, dewy, dram, lash, mire, rain, soak, wash 5 bedew, bewet, dabby, douse, foggy, humid, leach, misty, moist, mushy, rainy, soggy, soppy, sweat, wrong 6 clashy, dampen, drench, humect, imbrue, jarble, liquor, shower, soaked, sodden, watery 7 flotter, moisten, soaking, splashy, squashy 8 dampened, drenched, dripping, irrigate, moisture, saturate, sprinkle 9 misguided 11 intoxicated
   blanket: 6 dampen 7 depress, killjoy 8 deadhead, dispirit 10 discourage, spoilsport 11 party pooper
   flax: ret

weta: 6 insect, locust

wetbird: 9 chaffinch

wether: ram 4 wool 5 sheep 6 eunuch 7 dinmont

whack: hit, try 4 bang, beat, belt, blow 5 fling, share, thump, trial, whang 6 chance, strike, stroke, thwack 7 attempt, portion 8 division 9 allowance, condition

whacking: **4** huge, very **5** large **8** whopping **10** tremendous

whacky: See **wacky**

whale: fin, hit, orc, sei **4** beat, cete, drub, gray, lash, orca, wale, whip, whop **5** giant, minke, pilot, poggy, right, sperm, whack **6** baleen, beluga, blower, killer, mammal, strike, thrash **7** bowhead, Cetacea, dolphin, grampus, narwhal, ripsack, rorqual **8** cachalot, hardhead, humpback, narwheel, porpoise **9** blackfish, Greenland, mysticete, mysticeti, zeuglodon **10** bottlehead
   blue: **9** sibbaldus
   carcass: **5** kreng
   constellation: **5** Cetus
   fat: **7** blubber
   female: cow
   food: **4** brit **8** plankton
   male: **4** bull
   order: **4** cete **7** Cetacea
   pert. to: **5** cetic
   school: gam, pod
   secretion: **9** ambergris
   strip blubber from: **6** flense
   tail part: **5** fluke
   young: **4** calf **5** stunt **9** shorthead

whaleback: **9** steamship **10** turtleback **12** grain-carrier

whalebird: **4** gull **6** petrel **9** phalarope, turnstone

whalebone: *carving:* **9** scrimshaw

whalehead: **8** shoebill

whaler: **4** ship **7** bushman, swagman, whopper **8** whaleman **9** sundowner, whaleboat

whale oil: **10** spermaceti

whaling: **4** huge **8** whopping
   cask: **4** rier **6** cardel
   spear: **7** harpoon

whaling ship: **6** Pequod, whaler

wham: **4** bang **5** crack, smash

whammy: hex **5** jinks **6** hoodoo, voodoo **10** Indian sign

whang: **4** bang, blow, chop **5** chunk, slice, thong, throw, whack **6** assail, strike **7** leather, rawhide

whangee, wanghee: **4** cane **5** stick **6** bamboo

wharf: **4** dock, pier, quai (F.), quay, slip **5** berth, jetty, levee **7** landing
   space: **7** quayage
   worker: **9** stevedore **12** longshoreman

whatnot: **4** curio **6** bauble, gewgaw, trifle **7** etagere **10** knickknack

wheal: **4** mark, mine, wale, weal, welt **5** whelk **6** strake, streak, stripe **7** pustule **9** suppurate

wheat: **5** durum, spelt, trigo **6** imphee **7** einkorn, semoule
   beard: awn
   chaff: **4** bran

   disease: **4** bunt, rust, smut **5** ergot **6** aecium, fungus
   gritty part: **8** semolina
   head: ear **5** spike
   outer coat: **4** bran
   processed: **4** suji **5** grits **6** bulgur **9** middlings
   repository: bin **4** silo **8** elevator
   stubble: **6** arrish

wheatbird: **4** lark **9** chaffinch

wheat duck: **7** widgeon **8** baldpate

wheater: **4** bird **5** chack **8** chickell **10** gorsehatch

wheat smut: **4** bunt **8** colbrand

wheedle: cog, con **4** cant, coax **5** carny, tease, whine **6** banter, butter, cajole, carney, fleech, whilly **7** blarney, cuittle, flatter **8** blandish, persuade, soft-soap **9** influence, sweet-talk

wheel (see also **gear**): cam, cog **4** auto, bike, disk, gyre, helm, loop, reel, roll, tire, turn **5** cycle, drive, pilot, pivot, rotor, round, rowel, sheer, skeif, skive **6** caster, circle, league, roller, rotate, sheave **7** bicycle, chukkar, chukker, pedrail, revolve **10** revolution, waterwheel
   furniture: **6** caster
   part: cam, cog, hub, rim **4** tire **5** felly, spoke, sprag **6** felloe **8** sprocket
   pert. to: **5** rotal
   shaft: **4** axle
   spoke: **6** radius
   spurred: **5** rowel
   stopper: **5** brake
   toothed: cog **4** gear

wheelbarrow: hod **10** hurlbarrow

wheeler: **7** cyclist, vulture **11** wheelwright

wheeler-dealer: **7** shrewdy **8** go-getter, operator, promoter

wheelman: **5** pilot **6** driver **7** cyclist, steerer, wheeler **8** helmsman, pedalist **9** bicyclist

wheel-shaped: **6** rotate **8** circular, rotiform

wheeze: gag **4** hint, hiss, joke **5** adage, dodge, hoose, hooze, prank, trick **6** cliche, coghle (Sc.), device, saying **9** witticism
   relative of: **4** rale

wheezy: **9** asthmatic

whelk: **4** acne, wale, weal, welt **5** snail **6** papule, pimple, winkle **7** pustule

whelm (see also **overwhelm**): **5** cover, crush, drown, flood, swamp **6** deluge **9** drainpipe

whelp: cub, dog, pup **4** bear, fawn, lion, wale, welt, wolf **5** child, puppy, tiger, youth **7** leopard

when: **5** until **6** though **7** whereas **8** although, whenever

where: **4** site, spot **5** locus, place, point **7** whither

whereas: 5 since 7 because

wherefore: why 5 cause, proof 6 reason 9 therefore 11 accordingly

wherewithal: 5 funds, means, money 9 resources

wherry: 4 boat 5 barge, carry, scull 7 lighter, rowboat, vehicle 9 transport

whet: 4 hone, stir 5 grind, rouse, strop 6 arouse, awaken, bestir, excite, kindle 7 quicken, sharpen 9 appetizer, stimulate

whetstone: bur 4 buhr, burr, hone 8 strickle 9 sharpener

whey: 4 pale 5 serum 6 plasma, watery

whicker: 5 neigh 6 whinny

whiff: fan 4 flag, fuff, guff, gust, hint, odor, puff, waft, wave 5 expel, fluff, jiffy, smell, tinge, trace 6 breath, exhale, inhale, stench 7 instant 10 inhalation

whiffle: 4 blow, emit, idle, turn, veer, wave 5 expel, shake, shift, waver 6 change, trifle 7 flicker, flutter, scatter 8 disperse, hesitate 9 vacillate

while: yet 5 until 6 albeit, effort 7 whereas 8 although, occasion

whilom: 4 erst, once, past 6 former 8 erewhile

whim: fad, fit, gig 4 idea, mood 5 fancy, freak, humor, winch 6 desire, megrim, notion, trifle, vagary, vision, whimsy 7 boutade, caprice, capstan, conceit, fantasy, thought, whimsey 8 crotchet

whimper: cry, sob 4 mewl, moan, pule, weep 5 whine 6 murmur, yammer 7 grizzle, sniffle

whimsical: odd 5 droll, queer 6 cockle, quaint 7 bizarre, comical, strange 8 fanciful, freakish, notional 9 arbitrary, conceited, eccentric, fantastic, grotesque, uncertain 10 capricious 11 fantastical

whin: 4 rock 5 furze, gorse

whinchat: 8 songbird 9 gorsechat, grasschat

whine: wow 4 cant, fuss, girn, moan, pule, wail 5 croon, whewl 6 snivel, yammer 7 whimper 8 complain

whinny: 4 bray 5 hinny, neigh 6 nicker

whinyard: 5 sword

whip: cat, gad, tan 4 beat, cane, crop, drub, flay, flog, hide, jerk, lace, lash, urge, wind, wrap 5 birch, flick, knout, outdo, quirt, spank, strap, swish 6 defeat, foment, incite, punish, stir up, stitch, strike, swinge, switch, thrash 7 belabor, chicote, conquer, overlay, rawhide, scourge, sjambok 8 chawbuck, coachman, huntsman 9 bullwhack, flagellum 10 discipline, flagellate
mark: 4 *wale, weal, welt*

whippersnapper: 6 squirt 9 nonentity

whir, whirr: bur, fly 4 birl, burr, move, whiz, zizz 5 hurry, skirr, swirl, whizz 6 bustle, hurtle 7 revolve, vibrate 9 commotion

whirl: try 4 eddy, fuss, gyre, reel, shot, spin, stab, stir, tirl, turn 5 drill, fling, hurry, pivot, swirl, twirl 6 bustle, circle, flurry, gyrate, hubbub, pother, rotate, swinge, tumult, uproar, vortex 7 revolve 9 commotion, pirouette

whirlbone: 7 kneepan, patella 10 hucklebone

whirlpool: 4 eddy 5 gorce, swirl 6 gurges, vortex 9 Charybdis, maelstrom

whirlwind: 4 dust, fuss, stir 6 bustle, flurry, furore 7 cyclone, tornado 9 hurricane, maelstrom

whisk: 4 tuft, whip, wisp 5 flisk, hurry

whiskers (see also **beard**): 6 growth 7 stubble 9 sideburns, vibrissae 11 muttonchops
fish: 7 barbels

whiskey, whisky: rye 4 corn 5 hooch 6 poteen, redeye, rotgut, Scotch 7 bourbon 8 blockade, busthead 9 moonshine 10 usquebaugh
maker: 9 distiller
punch: 5 facer

whisper: 4 buzz, hint 5 rumor, shade, tinge, touch, trace, whiff 6 breath, breeze, murmur 7 confide

whisperer: 7 tattler 9 backbiter, slanderer 10 talebearer

whist: 4 game, hush, mute 5 cards, quiet, still 6 silent 7 silence 8 silently
dummy: 4 mort
hand: 6 tenace 10 Yarborough

whistle: 4 hiss, pipe, sugh, toot 5 flute, siren, sough 6 signal

whistlewing: 9 goldeneye

whit: bit, jot 4 atom, damn, doit, haet, hate, hoot, iota 5 speck 8 particle

white: wan 4 ashy, bawn, hoar, pale, pure 5 ashen, happy, hoary, ivory 6 albino, argent, blanch, bleach, blench, bright, chalky, grayed, honest, pallid, pearly 7 ivorine, silvery 8 harmless, innocent, palliate, spotless 9 colorless, fortunate, honorable 10 auspicious
becoming: 9 canescent
egg: 5 glair 7 albumen
with age: 4 hoar 5 hoary

white ant: 4 anai, anay 7 termite

whitebelly: 6 grouse, pigeon

whitecap: 4 wave 5 crest

white cell: 9 leucocyte

White Cliffs' site: 5 Dover

white-collar: 5 clerk 6 typist 9 executive, secretary 10 accountant, bookkeeper, management 11 salesperson

white elephant (land of): 4 Siam 5 Burma, India 6 Ceylon 8 Thailand

white feather: 4 fear 9 cowardice

whitefish: 5 cisco 6 beluga 8 menhaden

white flag: 5 truce 9 surrender

white-haired: old **4** aged **8** favorite

white heat: **13** incandescence

White House: *designer:* **5** Hoban
first resident: **5** Adams

white iron pyrites: **9** marcasite

white jade: **9** alabaster

white lead: **6** ceruse

white-lightning: **7** bootleg **9** moonshine

white livered: **8** cowardly **11** lily-livered **13**
pusillanimous

white merganser: **4** smew

white mica: **9** muscovite

White Monk: **10** Cistercian

white mule: gin **6** liquor, whisky **7** bootleg,
whiskey **9** moonshine **10** bathtub gin

whiten: **4** pale **5** chalk **6** blanch, bleach **8** etiolate, palliate

white plague: **8** phthisis **11** consumption **12**
tuberculosis

white plantain: **9** pussytoes

white pyrite: **9** marcasite

white snipe: **6** avocet **10** sanderling

whitetail: **4** deer

white walnut: **8** shagbark, sycamore **9** butter-
nut

whitewash: **6** blanch, defeat, parget, veneer **7**
absolve, conceal **8** palliate **9** sugarcoat,
gloss over

white whale: **6** beluga **8** Moby Dick

whitewing: **4** sail **6** scoter **7** sweeper **9**
chaffinch

whither: **5** where **8** wherever

whiting: **4** fish, hake **5** chalk

whitlow: **4** sore **5** felon **6** fetlow **12** inflammation

Whitsunday: **9** Pentecost

whitterick: **6** curlew

whittle: cut **4** pare, whet **5** carve, knife, shape,
shave **6** reduce, remove

whiz: hum **4** buzz, hiss, pirr, whir **5** hurry **6**
corker, expert, rotate **7** bargain

who: quo (L.), wer (G.), wha (Sc.) **4** what **5**
which **13** interrogative

whoa: **4** halt, stop

whole: all, sum **4** full, hail, hale, sane, sole,
unit **5** gross, sound, total **6** entire, healed,
intact, wholly **7** perfect **8** absolute, complete, ensemble, entirely, entirety, flawless,
integral, thorough, totality, unbroken **9**
aggregate, unanimous, undamaged, undivided **10** unimpaired
note: **9** semibreve
number: **7** integer

wholehearted: **6** hearty **7** abiding, devoted,
earnest, fervent, genuine, sincere **8** bona
fide, complete **9** heartfelt, unfeigned **10**
unreserved

wholesale: **4** bulk, lots **7** massive **8** abundant,
sweeping **9** extensive

wholesome: **4** good, hale, safe, well **5** sound **6**
benign, hearty, robust **7** healthy **8** benedict,
clean cut, curative, halesome, salutary, vigorous **9** favorable, healthful **10** beneficial,
healthsome, propitious, salubrious

wholly: all **4** well **5** fully, quite **7** algates

whoop: **4** hoot, urge, yell **5** cheer, shout **6**
halloo

whooping cough: **9** pertussis

whop: **4** beat, blow, bump, flop **5** knock,
throw **6** strike, stroke

whopper: lie **5** story **6** bender, bumper **7**
bouncer **8** tall tale

whopping: **4** huge, much, very **5** great, large
7 banging, immense **8** colossal, enormous,
gigantic

whore: **4** drab **5** wench **6** harlot **8** strumpet **9**
courtesan **10** prostitute

whorl: **5** spire, swirl

why: **5** proof **6** enigma, puzzle, reason **7** mystery **8** argument **9** wherefore

whyo: **6** robber **7** footpad **8** gangster

wick: bay **4** bend, town **5** creek, inlet, taper **6**
corner, hamlet **7** borough **9** farmstead

wicked: bad **4** evil, vile **5** wrong **6** guilty, horrid, malign, risqué, sinful, unjust **7** beastly,
harmful, hateful, heinous, hellish, immoral,
painful, playful, profane, vicious **8** criminal,
depraved, devilish, diabolic, fiendish, flagrant, indecent, skillful, spiteful **9** atrocious, dangerous, difficult, felonious, malicious, nefarious, perverted **10** diabolical,
flagitious, impassable, iniquitous, outrageous, villainous

wicker: **4** twig **5** osier, withe

wicket: **4** arch, door, gate, hoop **5** hatch **6**
window **7** guichet, opening

wickiup: hut **5** lodge, tepee **7** shelter

wide: **5** ample, broad, loose, roomy **6** opened
7 liberal **8** expanded, spacious **9** capacious,
distended, expansive, extensive **12** far-
spreading **13** comprehensive

wide-awake: hat **4** keen, tern **5** alert, aware **7**
knowing **8** watchful **10** interested

widely: far **4** afar **6** abroad

widen: **4** ream **6** dilate, expand, extend,
spread **7** amplify, broaden, enlarge **10** generalize

widespread: **4** rife **6** ruling **7** allover, current,
diffuse, general, popular, rampant **8** dif-
fused, sweeping **9** extensive, pervasive,
prevalent, universal

widgeon: **4** duck **5** goose **8** baldpate **9** simpleton
genus: **6** mareca

widget: **4** part

widow: **5** widdy **6** relict **7** dowager **8** bereaved
right: **5** dower **10** quarantine
suicide: **6** suttee

widowhood: **7** viduage

widowman: **7** widower

widow monkey: **4** titi

width: **5** girth, range **6** length, radius **7** breadth, compass **8** diameter, latitude, wideness

wield: ply **4** bear, cope, deal, rule **5** exert, power, swing **6** direct, employ, handle, manage, ordain **7** conduct, control **8** brandish **9** determine **10** manipulate

wife: hen, Mrs. **4** frau (G.), frow, mate, uxor (L.) **5** bride, donna, femme (F.), mujer (Sp.), squaw **6** esposa (Sp.), gammer, matron, missus, moglie (It.), spouse **7** consort **8** helpmate, helpmeet

bequest to: dot **5** dowry

clergyman's: **8** curatess **10** presbytera

killer: **9** uxoricide

lord's: **4** lady

pert. to: **7** uxorial

rajah's: **4** rani **5** ranee

slave's: **9** broadwife

wig: rug **4** gizz **5** busby, caxon, jasey, judge, scold **6** baguio, peruke, rebuke, toupee **7** censure, periwig, spencer **8** Chedreux, reproach **9** dignitary, Gregorian, reprimand

wiggle: **5** shake **6** waggle, wobble **7** stagger, wriggle

wight: man **4** loud **5** being, brave, human, swift, witch **6** active, mortal, nimble, person, strong **7** swiftly, valiant **8** creature, powerful, strongly

wigwag: **6** signal

wigwam: hut **4** home, tipi **5** lodge, tepee

wild: mad, ree **4** daft, fast, wowf (Sc.) **5** crazy, feral, rough, waste, weird **6** desert, ferine, native, ramage, savage, stormy, unruly **7** badland, bestial, frantic, furious, haggard, natural, riotous, untamed, wilsome **8** aberrant, agrestal, barbaric, desolate, dramatic, farouche, frenetic, reckless, untilled **9** agrestial, barbarian, barbarous, dissolute, disturbed, fantastic, ferocious, hellicate, imprudent, primitive, turbulent, unbridled, visionary **10** chimerical, dissipated, irrational, licentious, tumultuous, wilderness **11** extravagant, harumscarum, uncivilized, uninhabited **12** obstreperous, uncontrolled, uncultivated

arum: **10** cuckoopint

ass: **5** kiang **6** onager

banana: **5** papaw **6** pawpaw

coffee: **9** buckthorn, feverroot

crocus: **12** pasqueflower

dog: **5** dhole, dingo

goat: **4** ibex

goose: **7** greylag **8** Jacobite

hog: **4** boar

horse: **7** mustang

kale: **6** radish **8** charlock

masterwort: **8** goutweed

musk: **9** alfilaria

mustard: **8** charlock

passionflower: **6** maypop

pineapple: **7** pinguin

plum: **4** sloe

pumpkin: **11** calabazilla

sage: **5** clary **6** salvia **7** eyeseed, vervain

sago: **7** coontie

succory: **7** chicory

sweet potato: **7** manroot **8** sand vine

turnip: **6** radish **8** rutabaga **9** breadroot

wildcat: cat **4** balu, eyra, lynx **6** ocelot, serval, unsafe **7** panther **9** promotion **10** unreliable

wildebeest: gnu

wilderness: **5** waste **6** barren, desert, forest **9** wasteland **10** hinterland

wildfowl: **4** duck **5** goose, quail **8** pheasant **9** partridge

flock: **5** skein

wildness: **5** waste **6** ramage **8** ferocity

wile: art **4** lure, ploy, ruse **5** charm, fraud, guile, trick **6** allure, deceit, entice **7** attract, beguile, cunning **8** artifice, trickery **9** stratagem

will: **4** lust, wish **5** elect, fancy **6** animus, choose, decree, desire, devise, prefer, see fit **7** command, longing **8** appetite, bequeath, pleasure, volition **9** intention, testament **11** disposition, inclination, self-control

appendix: **7** codicil

having no: **9** intestate

proof of: **7** probate

willful: mad **4** rash **5** heady **7** wayward **8** stubborn **9** camsteary, camsteery, impetuous, obstinate, voluntary **10** hardheaded **11** intentional

willies: **6** creeps **7** jitters

William Tell: *composer:* **7** Rossini

William the Conqueror's burial place: **4** Caen

willing: apt **4** fair, game, open **5** prone, ready **6** minded **7** tending **8** desirous, disposed, unforced **9** agreeable, voluntary **10** volitional

willingly: **4** fain, lief **5** lieve **6** freely, gladly

willingness: **7** consent **8** alacrity

willow: iva **4** itea **5** osier, salix **6** teaser

twig: **5** withe

willow wren: **10** chiffchaff

willowy: **5** lithe **6** pliant, supple **7** slender **8** flexible, graceful

willpower: **7** purpose **10** resolution **11** self-control **12** resoluteness

willy-nilly: **8** perforce **11** whether or no

Wilson's thrush: **5** veery

wilt: sag **4** fade, flag **5** droop, dry up, quail **6** wither **7** anguish **8** collapse

wily: sly **4** deep, foxy **5** canny, smart **6** artful, astute, clever, crafty, shrewd, subtle, tricky **7** cunning, subtile **9** cautelous, sagacious

wimble: awl **4** bore **5** auger, brace, scoop, twist **6** active, gimlet, pierce **9** penetrate, sprightly, whimsical

wimple: **4** bend, flag, fold, turn, veil, wind **5** curve **6** ripple **7** confuse, deceive, meander, wriggle **8** hoodwink **9** headdress

win: get, pot **4** b eat, earn, gain, take **5** charm, reach, score, yield **6** allure, attain, defeat, entice, obtain, secure **7** achieve, acquire, capture, conquer, prevail, succeed, triumph, victory **8** vanquish **9** captivate, influence **10** accomplish, conciliate
all tricks: **4** slam
over: **6** defeat, disarm, induce **8** persuade, talk into

wince: **4** crab, reel **5** cower, quail, start **6** cringe, flinch, recoil, shrink **8** windlass

wind: air **4** birr, bise, blow, bora, coil, curl, flaw, gale, gust, hint, kona, reel, wend, wrap **5** belay, blast, buran, crank, curve, foehn, noser, reeve, samum, siroc, spool, storm, trade, twine, twist, weave, wield **6** boreas, bought, breath, breeze, buster, deform, gibleh, simoom, simoon, solano, squall, writhe, zephyr **7** chamsin, chinook, cyclone, entwine, entwist, etesian, gregale, khamsin, meander, monsoon, nothing, pampero, revolve, sirocco, tempest, tornado, typhoon, wreathe, wriggle, wulliwa **8** blizzard, encircle, entangle, khamseen, libeccio, williwaw, willywaw **9** corkscrew, harmattan, hurricane, libecchio, noreaster **10** euroclydon, tramontana, tramontane
desert: **6** simoon **7** sirocco
down: **5** relax **10** deescalate
instrument: sax **4** fife, horn, oboe, tuba **5** flute, organ **6** cornet **7** bassoon, hautboy, trumpet **8** clarinet, trombone
periodic: **7** etesian, monsoon
pert. to: **6** eolian **7** aeolian
scale: **8** Beaufort
summer: **6** breeze, zephyr
up: end **4** coil **5** close **6** finish, settle **8** conclude

windbreaker: **6** jacket

windfall: **4** boon, vail **5** manna **7** bonanza, fortune **8** buckshee

windflower: **7** anemone

windhover: **7** kestrel

windiness: **7** conceit **9** puffiness, verbosity

winding: **4** wily **6** screwy, spiral, tricky **7** coiling, crinkle, devious, pliable, sinuous, twining, wriggly **8** flexible, rambling, tortuous, twisting **9** deceitful, intricate, meandrous, sinuosity **10** anfracture, circuitous, convoluted, meandering, serpentine

winding device: **4** reel **7** capstan **8** windlass

winding sheet: **6** shroud

windjammer: **4** ship **6** bugler, sailor, talker **8** musician **9** trumpeter

windlass: **4** crab, reel **5** hoist, winch **7** capstan

windle: **7** measure, redwing

windmill: *blade:* **4** vane
fighter of: **7** Quixote
pump: gin
sail: awe, ban

window: bay, bow, eye **4** pane **5** gable, glaze, oriel **6** dormer **7** balcone, fenetre, lucarne, mirador, opening, winnock (Sc.) **8** aperture, casement, fenestra, jalousie **10** double-hung
bay: **5** oriel
frame: **4** sash
leading: **4** came
ledge: **4** sill
pane holder: **6** muntin **7** mullion
recess: **6** exedra
roof: **6** dormer **8** skylight
round stained glass: **4** rose
sash weight: **5** mouse
ship's: **4** port **8** porthole
tall, pointed stained glass: **6** lancet
ticket: **6** wicket **7** guichet
worker: **7** glazier

windpipe: **6** artery, gullet, throat, weason **7** trachea, weasand, weazand **9** esophagus

windrow: **4** pile **5** swath **6** furrow, swathe

windshake: **8** anemosis

windstorm: **4** gale **7** cyclone, typhoon **9** hurricane

windward: **5** aloof **8** aweather

Windward Island: **7** Grenada, St. Lucia **9** St. Vincent **10** Grenadines, Martinique

windy: **4** airy **5** blowy, brisk, empty, gusty, huffy, swift, wordy **6** breezy, drafty, prolix, stormy **7** gustful, pompous, verbose **8** blustery, boastful, inflated, skittish **9** aeolistic, bombastic **10** boisterous, changeable, intangible

Windy City: **7** Chicago

wine: vin (F.) **4** alac, Asti, Bual, cote, deal, Gavi, port, tent, vino (It., Sp.), wein (G.) **5** Baden, Casel, drink, juice, liane, Medoc, merum (L.), Rhine, Rioja, Soave, tinta, tokay, Yquem **6** Barolo, Barsac, Beaune, canary, claret, Malaga, Massic, Muscat, Saumur, sherry **7** Alicant, Banyals, Bastard, Chablis, chacoli, Chateau, Chianti, Conthey, Dezaley, Falerno, hollock, Madeira, Margaux, Marsala, Moselle, Orvieto **8** Alicante, Ambonnay, beverage, Bordeaux, Bucellas, Burgundy, Cabernet, Florence, Marsalla, muscadel, Muscatel, Riesling,

Ruchelle, sauterne, Sylvaner **9** champagne, Gladstone, hermitage, Lambrusco, Pinot Noir, teneriffe, Zeltinger, zinfandel **10** Barbaresco, Beaujolais, Calon-Segur, chardonnay, Hockheimer, Roussillon **11** Niersteiner, scuppernong

apple: **5** cider **6** brandy **9** applejack

bag: **8** wineskin

bottle: **5** split **6** fiasco, magnum **8** decanter, jeroboam

cask deposit: **6** tartar

cask: tun, vat **4** pipe

cellar: **6** bodega

comb. form: oen **4** oeno

cruet: **7** burette

cup: ama **5** amula **6** goblet **7** chalice

deposit: **6** tartar

disorder: **5** casse

drink: kir **5** clary, mulse, negus, punch **7** sangria **8** spritzer

dry: sec **4** brut

film: **8** beeswing

fragrance: **7** bouquet

list: **4** card

lover: **11** oenophilist

maker: **6** abkari, abkary **7** vintner

measure: aam, aum **4** orna, orne

merchant: **6** bistro (F.) **7** vintner **8** gourmand

mixed with soda: **8** spritzer

new: **4** must

pert. to: **5** vinic **6** vinous

pitcher: **4** olpe **5** olpae **8** oenochoe

punch: **7** sangria

residue: **4** marc

rice: **4** sake

scene of miracle: **4** Cana

shop: **6** bistro, bodega

spiced: **9** hippocras

steward: **9** sommelier

stock: **6** cellar

strength: **4** seve

year: **7** vintage

wine and dine: **4** fete **6** regale

wineberry: **5** grape **7** currant **8** makomako **9** billberry, raspberry **10** gooseberry

winegrower: **8** vigneron **13** viticulturist

Winesburg Ohio author: **8** Anderson

wineskin: **5** askos

wing: ala, arm, ell, fin, fly, van **4** limb **5** aisle, alula, annex, pinna, shard, speed, volet, wound **6** hasten, pennon, pinion **7** flutter **9** extension

building: ell

pert. to: **4** alar **6** pteric

under: **8** subalary

vestigial: **5** alula

wing cover: **7** elytron

winged: **4** aile, alar **5** alary, alate, lofty, rapid,

swift **6** alated **7** bialate, pennate, sublime, wounded **9** aliferous, aligerous, feathered

in heraldry: **4** aile

Winged Horse: **7** Pegasus

wing-footed: **5** fleet, swift **6** aliped **9** mercurial

wingless: **7** apteral **8** apterous

wingless locust: **4** weta

wing-like: **4** alar **5** alary, alate **6** pteric **7** aliform, pteroid

wings: *being with:* **5** angel, putti (pl.), putto **6** cherub, seraph **7** Mercury

conjoined: vol (her.)

wink: bat, nap, nod **4** hint **5** blink, flash, gleam, prink, shake, sleep, trice **6** signal **7** connive, flicker, instant, nictate, slumber, sparkle, twinkle **9** nictation, nictitate, twinkling **10** periwinkle

winks (forty): nap **6** catnap

winner: **6** earner, reaper, victor **7** faceman, sleeper **8** bangster, champion **9** conqueror

bread: **6** earner **9** supporter

Winnie-the-Pooh: *author:* **5** Milne

character: Owl, Roo **5** Kanga **6** Piglet, Rabbit, Tigger **16** Christopher Robin

winning: **5** shaft, sweet **6** profit **7** victory **8** engaging

winnow: fan, van **4** beat, blow, comb, flap, sift, sort **5** dight **6** assort, select **7** analyze, examine, scatter **8** brandish, disperse, separate **9** eliminate, screen out

winsome: gay **5** bonny, merry, sweet **6** blithe, bonnie **7** likable, lovable, winning **8** adorable, charming, cheerful, engaging, pleasant **9** agreeable **10** attractive **11** captivating

winter: *French:* **5** hiver

pear: **6** seckel, warden

pert. to: **6** brumal, hiemal

Spanish: **8** invierno

winterbloom: **6** azalea **10** witch hazel

wintergreen: **10** pipsissewa

winter quarters: **5** saith **10** hibernacle **12** hibernaculum

Winter's Tale: *author:* **11** Shakespeare

character: **4** Dion **5** Mopsa **6** Dorcas **7** Camillo, Leontes, Perdita

wintle: **4** reel, roll **7** stagger, wriggle

wintry: icy **4** aged, cold **5** hoary, snowy, white **6** frigid, hiemal, stormy **8** chilling, hibernal, wintered **9** cheerless

wipe: dry, hit, mop, rub **4** beat, blow, draw, gibe, jeer, pass **5** annul, brand, cheat, clean, dight, erase, stain, swipe, towel, trick **6** cancel, defeat, delete, efface, remove, sponge, strike, stroke **7** abolish, defraud, exhaust, sarcasm **8** disgrace **9** eradicate **10** annihilate, obliterate **11** exterminate

out: **5** erase, scrub **6** cancel **7** destroy, kill off **11** exterminate *up:* mop **4** swab, swob

wire: **4** coil **5** cable **6** fasten **8** telegram **9** cablegram, telegraph
for teeth: **6** braces
measure: mil **5** stone
system: **7** network, reticle

wire cutter: **6** pliers **8** secateur

wiredraw: **4** thin **5** wrest **7** distort, prolong, spin out **8** protract **9** attenuate **10** over-refine

wireless: **5** radio

wirework: **7** netting **8** filigree

wireworm: **8** myriapod **9** millepede

wiry: **4** lean, ropy, thin **5** hardy, stiff, tough **6** sinewy, strong **8** muscular

wis: **4** deem, know **5** think **7** believe, imagine, suppose

---

Wisconsin: *capital:* **7** Madison
city: **6** Racine **7** Kenosha **8** Green Bay **9** Milwaukee
Indian: **6** Dakota **9** Menominee, Winnebago
lake: **7** Mendota **8** Michigan, Superior **9** Winnebago
motto: **7** Forward
peninsula: **4** Door
product: **5** dairy
river: **4** Wolf **5** Black **7** St. Croix **8** Chippewa **9** Wisconsin **11** Mississippi
state bird: **5** robin
state flower: **6** violet
state tree: **5** maple

---

wisdom: **4** lore **5** sense **7** insight **8** judgment, sagacity **9** knowledge
man of: **6** Nestor

wisdom tooth: **5** molar

wise: hep **4** mode, sage, sane, show, wary **5** acute, aware, cagey, canny, quick, sharp, smart, sound, witty **6** advise, astute, bright, cheeky, crafty, direct, inform, manner, method, shrewd, subtle, versed, witful **7** beguile, cunning, erudite, explain, fashion, gnostic, heedful, know all, knowing, learned, politic, prudent, sapient, skilled **8** discreet, flippant, impudent, informed, insolent, instruct, persuade, profound, sensible, skillful **9** advisable, cognizant, dexterous, expedient, judicious, on the beam, provident, sagacious **10** discerning, omniscient **11** calculating, circumspect, enlightened, intelligent
infinitely: **10** omniscient
up: **5** learn **6** advise, inform

wiseacre: **5** dunce **7** prophet **9** simpleton **10** mastermind, smart aleck

wisecrack: gag **4** joke, quip **9** witticism

wiselike: **6** decent **7** fitting **8** becoming, sensible **9** judicious **11** appropriate

wise man: **4** sage **5** magus, solon **6** Casper, Gasper, Nestor, savant, wizard **7** scholar **8** magician, Melchior **9** Balthasar, Balthazar, councilor

Wise Men: **4** Magi

wise saying: saw **5** adage, maxim **7** proverb

wish: **4** hope, like, long, want, will **5** covet, crave, elect, fancy, yearn **6** behest, desire, expect, impose, invoke **7** longing, propose, request **8** petition, yearning **10** aspiration

wishbone: **8** furculum **10** fourchette

wishful: **5** eager **7** longing **8** desirous **9** desirable **10** attractive

wishy-washy: **4** pale, sick, thin, weak **5** banal, bland, tepid, vapid **6** feeble, trashy, watery **7** insipid

wisp: **4** band, lock, ring, wase **5** broom, brush, bunch, clean, flock, shred, torch, whisk **6** bundle, parcel, rumple, strand, wreath **7** crumple, handful **8** fragment

wispy: **5** filmy, frail **6** slight **7** slender **8** gossamer, nebulous

wisteria: **4** bush, fuji, vine **6** purple, violet

wistful: sad **6** intent **7** longing, pensive **8** yearning **9** attentive, nostalgic **10** melancholy

wistfulness: rue **6** regret

wit: wag **4** know, mind **5** comic, humor, irony, learn, sense **6** acumen, esprit (F.), namely, reason, satire, wisdom **7** cunning, faculty, punster **8** comedian, drollery, funnyman, prudence, repartee **9** intellect **12** intelligence
low form of: pun

witch: hag, hex **4** baba **5** biddy, bruja, charm, crone, lamia, woman **6** cummer, kimmer, wizard **7** beldame **8** magician, sorcerer **9** fascinate, sorceress **11** enchantress
cat: **9** grimalkin
city: **5** Endor, Salem
famous: **5** Circe **6** Lilith
gathering: **5** coven
male: **7** warlock

witch hazel: **4** tree **5** shrub **6** lotion **8** hornbeam **10** astringent

witchcraft: **5** charm, magic **6** voodoo **7** cunning, hexerei, sorcery **8** brujeria (Sp.), pishogue, witchery, wizardry **9** sortilege **11** enchantment, fascination
practice: hex **7** bewitch

witchman: **6** shaman, wizard **8** sorcerer

with: wi (Sc.); con (It, Sp.), cum (L.), mit (G.) **4** avec (F.), near **5** along **7** against **9** alongside *respect to:* **4** as to **5** as for **7** apropos

withdraw: **4** exit, quit, void **5** avoid, leave, unsay **6** abjure, absent, depart, detach, divert, recall, recant, recede, remove, retire, secede, shrink **7** abscond, decline, detract, extract, forbear, forsake, give way, refrain, retract, retreat, subduce, subside **8** abstract, alienate, derogate, distract, evacuate, fall back, renounce, restrain, withhold **9** disengage, sequester **10** relinquish, retrograde

from reality: **6** autism

withdrawn: shy **5** aloof **6** remote **8** detached **10** unsociable **11** indifferent

withe: **4** band, bind, herb, rope, twig **5** osier, snare, withy **6** branch, fasten, halter, wattle, willow

wither: age, die, dry **4** fade, pine, sear, sere, wane, wilt **5** blast, cling, daver, decay, wizen **6** blight, cotter, shrink, weaken **7** shrivel, wrinkle **8** languish

withered: **4** arid, sere **7** sapless, wizened **8** shrunken

withershins: **10** topsy-turvy **12** contrariwise

withhold: **4** curb, deny, hide, keep **5** check **6** desist, detain, refuse, retain **7** abstain, forbear, prevent, refrain, repress, reserve **8** maintain, postpone, restrain

within: in, on, ben **4** inly, into **5** among **6** during, herein, inside **7** indoors **8** interior, inwardly **10** underneath

without: sin (Sp.) **4** bout, sans (F.), sine (L.) **5** minus, senza (It.) **6** beyond **7** lacking, outside **9** outwardly **10** externally, out-of-doors

without this: **7** sine hoc (L.)

withstand: **4** bear, bide, defy **5** abide, fight, repel **6** combat, endure, oppose, resist, suffer **7** gainsay **8** confront, tolerate **9** gainstand **10** contradict, controvert

withy: **4** turn, twig, wind, wiry **5** agile, braid, tough, widdy **6** branch, willow **7** pliable **8** flexible

witless: mad **4** daft **5** crazy, gross **6** insane, simple, stupid **7** foolish, unaware **8** heedless, mindless **9** brainless, pointless, unknowing **10** dullwitted, indiscreet

witness: eye, see, wit **4** know, view **5** teste, vouch **6** attest, beheld, behold, martyr **7** certify, endorse, observe, sponsor, testify **8** beholder, evidence, indicate, observer, onlooker **9** bystander, spectator, subscribe, testifier, testimony

witticism: gag, mot, pun **4** gibe, jeer, jest, joke, quip **5** sally **8** drollery **9** wisecrack

witting: **5** aware **7** knowing, tidings **8** judgment, sentient **9** knowledge, voluntary **10** deliberate **11** information, intentional **12** intelligence

witty: **4** gash, wise **5** comic, funny **6** bright, clever, facete, jocose, jocund, versed **7** amusing, comical, jocular, knowing **8** humorous, informed **9** facetious

witty reply: **6** bon mot **7** riposte **8** repartee

wizard: **4** mage, sage **5** fiend, magus **6** expert, genius, Merlin **7** magical, prodigy, warlock **8** charming, conjurer, magician, sorcerer **10** enchanting **11** necromancer, thaumaturge

wizardry: art **5** magic **7** sorcery **10** witchcraft

wizen, weazen: dry **7** shrivel, whither

woad: **6** indigo **8** dyestuff

wobble, wabble: **4** boil **5** lurch, shake, waver **6** quaver, teeter **7** tremble **9** vacillate

wobbly: **4** weak **5** loose, shaky **7** rickety

woe: rue **4** bale, bane, care **5** grief **6** misery, sorrow **7** anguish, sadness, trouble **8** calamity, disaster **9** dejection **10** affliction, desolation, melancholy, misfortune

tale of: **8** jeremiad **11** lamentation

woebegone: **4** worn **6** gloomy, shabby **8** dejected, downcast **10** lugubrious

woeful: sad **4** dire **6** paltry **7** direful, pitiful, unhappy **8** mournful, wretched **9** miserable, sorrowful, woebegone **10** deplorable, dispirited

wold: lea **5** plain **6** meadow

wolf: **4** lobo **6** canine, chanco, coyote **7** Don Juan **8** Casanova **9** thylacine **10** ladykiller **11** philanderer

genus: **5** canis

timber: **4** lobo

young: pup **5** whelp

wolfhound: **4** alan **6** borzoi **9** deerhound

wolf-like: **6** lupine **9** rapacious

wolfsbane: **7** aconite **9** monkshood

Wolsey's birthplace: **7** Ipswich

wolverine: **7** glutton **8** carcajou

genus of: **4** gulo

Wolverine State: **8** Michigan

woman: gin, hen **4** bint, dame, dona, lady, maid, rani, wife **5** begum, broad, chick, donna, femme, madam, mujer, ranee, skirt, squaw **6** calico, cummer, domina, female, heifer, kimmer, maness, matron, senora **7** alewife, servant, signora **8** mistress, senorita **10** klootchman, sweetheart

attractive: **4** doll, peri **5** belle, filly, pin-up, siren, sylph, Venus **6** beauty, looker **7** charmer, Zenobia **8** Musidora

beloved: **9** inamorata

celibate: **7** agapeta

domain: **7** distaff

dowdy: **5** frump

kept: **8** mistress **9** concubine **12** demimondaine

learned: **4** blue **7** basbleu (F.), seeress **12** bluestocking

little: Mrs. **4** wife **6** spouse **7** ladykin

loose: tib **4** drab, flap, jilt, slut **5** hussy, quean, queen **6** chippy, giglet, giglot, harlot, wanton **7** cocotte, Jezebel, trollop **9** courtesan, courtezen, dratchell

married: Mrs. **4** frau, frow, wife **5** vrouw **6** matron, senora **7** signora

mythical: **6** Amazon, Gorgon, Medusa

objectionable: hag **5** fagot, shrew, witch **6** faggot, gorgon, virago **8** harridan **9** grimalkin, termagant

old: gib, hag **4** baba, dame, trot **5** crone, frump **6** carlin, gammer, granny **7** carline, dowager, grandam **8** grandame, spinster **9** cailleach, cailliach

patient: **8** Griselda

pert. to: **6** female **7** gynecic **8** feminine, gynaecic **9** muliebral

pregnant: **7** gravida

sailor: **4** SPAR, WAVE

single: **6** virgin **8** mistress, spinster **12** bachelor girl

soldier: WAC **4** WAAC

staid: **4** lady **6** beldam, matron **7** beldame **10** grande dame

state of: **10** muliebrity

strong: **6** Amazon, virago **8** titaness

suffragist: **4** Mott **5** Stone **7** Anthony, Stanton

talkative: cat, gad, hen **5** dolly, flirt, scold, shrew, vixen **6** fizgig, virago **7** hellcat **9** termagant

unattractive: bag, dog **4** drab **5** crone, dowdy, witch **8** slattern

young: tib **4** burd, dell, drab, lass **5** filly, trull, wench **6** lassie **7** damozel **10** demoiselle

woman chaser: **4** wolf **7** Don Juan **8** lothario **10** sheepbiter **11** philanderer

woman hater: **10** misogynist

womanish: **5** anile **6** effete, female **8** feminine **10** effeminate

womb: bag **5** belly **6** uterus

wombat: **6** badger **9** marsupial

won: **4** live, stay **5** abide, dwell **7** inhabit **8** trounced

wonder: awe **4** evil, fear, harm, sign **5** amaze, doubt, grief, shock, wrong **6** esteem, marvel **7** curious, miracle, portent, prodigy **8** surprise **9** amazement, reverence, speculate, uncertain **10** admiration, wonderment **11** destruction, uncertainty **12** astonishment

of the world: **6** Pharos **8** Colossus, pyramids **9** Mausoleum **14** Hanging Gardens

Wonder State: **8** Arkansas

wonderful: **4** fine, good **5** great, super **6** lovely **7** amazing, amusing, corking, mirific, strange **8** terrific, wondrous **9** admirable, excellent, marvelous **10** miraculous, surprising **11** astonishing, interesting

wonky: off **4** awry **5** shaky **6** boring, feeble, stupid, groggy **7** tottery **8** unsteady **9** tottering **10** unreliable

wont: apt, use **5** dwell, habit, usage, usual **6** custom, manner, reside **8** inclined, practice **10** accustomed

woo: beg, sue **4** coax, seek **5** court, spark **6** assail, invite, pursue, splunt (Sc.) **7** address, beseech, entreat, solicit **9** importune **10** bill and coo

wood: hag, keg, mad **4** bois (F.), bosk, bowl, cask, holt, wold **5** angry, cahuy, grove, hurst, trees, xylem **6** forest, insane, lumber, timber **7** enraged, furious, violent **8** woodland

ash: **6** potash

black: **5** ebony

bundle of: **5** fagot

burned: ash **4** brae **8** charcoal

dealer: **10** xylopolist

decayed: **4** punk

derivative: tar **5** turps **6** balsam **10** turpentine

eater: **7** termite

edge: **8** woodrime, woodside

fine-grained: yew **6** brauna

firing easily: **4** punk **5** sponk, spunk **6** tinder **7** fatwood **8** kindling, punkwood, softwood **9** touchwood

flexible: **5** edder, osier **6** willow

fragrant: **5** aloes, cedar **8** agalloch **9** eaglewood

growth: **5** grove, weald **6** forest, jungle **7** coppice

gum: **5** resin, xylan

hard: ash, elm, eng, oak **4** lana, pear, poon, rata, teak **5** apple, beech, birch, ebony, maple, zante **6** cherry, red gum, walnut **7** hickory **8** mahogany, rosewood, sycamore **9** deciduous

juice: sap

knot: nur **4** burl, knag, knar **5** gnarl

light: **4** cork **5** balsa

machine: saw **5** drill, edger, lathe, miter **6** planer, router, sander, shaper **7** sticker

overlaying: **6** veneer

part: fid, nog, peg, rib **4** lath, shim, slat **5** dowel, spile, sprag, stave, tenon **6** batten, billet, reglet, splint **7** dingbat

pert. to: **5** treen **6** xyloid

softwood: fir **4** pine **5** cedar **7** conifer, hemlock, redwood

steward: **8** forester **9** woodreeve

strip: **4** lath, slat **6** batten, spline

striped: roe

supporting: **5** cleat

tool: adz, saw **4** adze, file **5** clamp, drill, plane **6** chisel, hammer, square

valuable: sal **4** teak

worker: **6** joiner, sawyer, turner **7** paneler **9** carpenter **12** cabinetmaker

wood alcohol: 6 methyl **8** methanol

woodbine: 8 lonicera **11** honeysuckle **15** Virginia creeper

woodchuck: 6 marmot, rodent **9** groundhog

woodcock: 4 dupe, fool **5** pewee **7** becasse (F.) **8** game bird **9** simpleton **10** woodpecker

woodcutter: 6 axeman, logger, sawyer **7** chopper **8** woodsman **9** lumberman

wooded: 5 bosky **6** sylvan

wooden: dry **4** dull, wood **5** heavy, oaken, stiff, treen **6** clumsy, stolid **7** awkward, stilted **8** lifeless **9** ponderous **10** spiritless **11** insensitive **14** expressionless

wooden-headed: 4 dull **6** stupid **8** blockish

Wooden Horse: See **Trojan Horse**

wooden shoe: 4 clog, geta **5** sabot **6** patten

woodland: 5 weald **6** forest **10** timberland

burnt over: **6** brulee

landscape: **7** boscage

wood nymph: 4 moth **5** dryad **8** grayling **11** hummingbird

woodpecker: 4 chab **5** picus **6** picule, yaffle, yockel, yuckle, yukkel **7** flicker, piculet, whetile, wryneck, yaffler **8** hickwall, woodcock, woodhack **9** sapsucker, woodchuck, woodspite **10** carpintero, woodhacker, woodjobber **11** hickoryhead, woodknacker

genus: **5** picus

type: **5** acorn, downy, green, hairy **7** flicker **8** imperial, pileated **9** redheaded, sapsucker **11** ivory-billed

wood pigeon: 4 dove **6** cushat **8** ringdove

wood pussy: 5 skunk

woodsman: 5 guide, scout **6** hunter, ranger **7** bushman, trapper **8** forester

wood sorrel: oca **6** oxalis **7** begonia **8** haremeat, shamrock

wood stork: 4 ibis

woodwind: 4 oboe **5** flute **7** bassoon, piccolo **8** clarinet **9** saxophone

woody: 5 bosky **6** sylvan, xyloid **8** ligneous

woody fiber: 4 bast, hemp **5** xylem

wooer: 4 beau **5** lover, spark, swain **6** suitor **8** courtier, paramour

woof: abb **4** weft, yarn **5** cloth, weave **6** fabric **7** filling, texture **9** essential

wool: fur **4** coat, hair, lamb **5** llama, sheep **6** fleece, mohair **8** barragan, barragon **9** cordillas

blemish: **4** mote

clean: **7** garnett

cloth: **4** felt **5** baize, crepe, duroy, serge, tweed **6** alpaca, angora, baline, duffel, frieze, hodden, kersey, melton, merino, mohair, vicuna **7** flannel, ratteen, stammel, worsted **9** cassimere, gabardine, hauberget **10** broadcloth, fearnaught, fearnought

dirty fleece: **7** tag lock **10** stain piece (Austr., Br.)

fat: **5** suint **7** lanolin **8** lanoline

fibers: nep **4** noil

finishing process: **7** fulling **8** crabbing

implement: **6** carder, shears, teaser **7** distaff, spindle

inferior: **7** cleamer

kind: **4** noil, shag **8** mortling **9** downright, shearling

lock: **5** flock

measure: **6** micron

mixed hues: tum

nap-raising plant: **6** teasel

package: **5** fadge

piece: **4** frib, tate (Sc.) **7** cleamer

pulled: **4** skin **5** slipe

reclaimed: **5** mungo **6** shoddy

refuse: **6** pinion **7** backing

rope: **6** sliver

sheet: web

source: **4** goat, lamb **5** camel, llama, sheep **6** alpaca, vicuna

tease: tum **4** card

texture: nap

twisted roll: **4** slub

unravel: **5** tease

waste: fud

weight: tod **5** clove

yarn: abb, eis **7** eiswool

wool-colored: 4 ecru **5** beige, camel

wool-dryer: 5 fugal

woolly: 5 hairy **6** fleecy, lanate, lanose **7** lanated **8** peronate

woozy: 4 sick, weak **5** dazed, dizzy, drunk, shaky **7** muddled, sickish, strange, trembly **9** befuddled

word: say, vow **4** fame, news, oath, talk, tell, term **5** adage, couch, honor, maxim, motto, order, parol, rumor, state, voice **6** assent, avowal, phrase, pledge, remark, report, repute, saying, signal, speech **7** account, adjunct, bidding, command, comment, dispute, express, message, promise, proverb, tidings **8** acrostic, language, password **9** direction, discourse, statement, watchword **10** expression **11** affirmation, declaration, information

battle: **9** logomachy

colorful: **5** slang

connective: **11** conjunction

containing all vowels: **6** oiseau (F.) **7** eulogia, miaoued, sequoia **9** facetious **11** facetiously **12** ambidextrous **14** undiscoverably **15** uncopyrightable

containing all vowels in reverse sequence: **10** duoliteral

containing all vowels in sequence: **8** caesious **9** facetious

containing four letters: **9** tetragram
containing no vowels: cwm, nth **5** crwth
containing three double letters: **10** book-keeper **11** bookkeeping
containing uu: **6** mutuum, vacuum **7** duumvir, triduum **8** residuum **9** continuum, menstruum, perpetuum, zuurveldt **10** duumvirate
figurative use: **5** trope **7** metonym
group: **6** clause, phrase **8** sentence
hard to pronounce: **10** jawbreaker **13** tongue-twister
imitative: **9** onomatope **12** onomatopoeia
inventor: **6** coiner **9** neologist
last sound omitted: **7** apocope
magical: **6** presto, sesame **10** hocus pocus **11** abracadabra
meaning: **9** semantics
misuse of: **8** solecism **11** catachresis, malapropism
mystical: **7** anagoge
new: **9** neologism, neoterism
of action: **4** verb
of naming: **4** noun
of opposite meaning: **7** antonym
of same meaning: **7** synonym
pretentious: **10** lexiphanic **14** sesquipedalian
root: **6** etymon
sacred: **5** selah **6** sesame, shelah
same backward and forward: **10** palindrome
same sound: **7** homonym **9** homophone
same spelling: **9** homograph
scrambled: **7** anagram
square: **10** palindrome
substituted: **5** trope **7** metonym
use of unnecessary: **8** pleonasm
word blindness: **6** alexia
wordbook: **5** index **7** lexicon, speller **8** glossary, libretto **9** thesaurus **10** cyclopedia, dictionary, vocabulary
word for word: **7** exactly **8** verbatim **9** literally
wordiness: **8** verbiage **9** prolixity, verbosity
wording: **8** phrasing **9** wrangling **10** expression
wordless: **4** mute **5** tacit **6** silent **8** unspoken
Word of God: **5** Logos
word of honor: **4** oath **6** parole **7** promise
word puzzle: **5** rebus **7** anagram, charade **8** acrostic **9** crossword
words: **4** text **6** lyrics, script **7** quarrel **8** libretto
depiction in: **8** vignette
meaningless: **6** drivel **9** gibberish
misuse: **11** catachresis, heterophemy
put into: **5** state **6** phrase **7** express
written: **4** copy, text **6** script

word-sign: **6** symbol **8** ideogram, logogram **9** cuneiform **10** hieroglyph, pictograph
wordy: **6** prolix **7** diffuse, verbose **9** garrulous, redundant, talkative **10** long-winded, loquacious
work: act, job, tew **4** beat, book, deed, duty, feat, move, opus, plan, task, till, toil, worm **5** chore, craft, draft, ergon, exert, graft, grind, knead, labor, pains, solve, stint, sweat, trade **6** arbeit (G.), career, design, drudge, effort, puddle, strive **7** belabor, ferment, operate, pattern, perform, travail **8** activity, belabour, business, drudgery, endeavor, exertion, function, industry, struggle **10** accomplish, employment, manipulate, manuscript, occupation, profession **11** achievement, performance, undertaking
agreement: **4** code, pact **8** contract
aimlessly: **6** fiddle, potter, putter
aversion to: **10** ergophobia
by day: **4** char **5** chare
divine: **7** theurgy
evade: **4** snib **9** goldbrick
excess: **6** overdo
hard: peg, ply **4** char, moil, plod, plug, toil **5** chare, delve, drill, labor, sweat **6** drudge **7** travail **8** scrabble **9** lucubrate
lover of: **9** ergophile **10** workaholic
period: day **4** hour, turn, week **5** month, shift, spell, trick, watch **8** schedule
steadily: ply
together: **4** team **5** co-act **9** co-operate **11** collaborate
traditional women's: **7** distaff
unit: erg **4** dyne, watt **5** ergon, joule **6** newton **7** calorie
workable: **4** ripe **6** doable, mellow, pliant **8** feasible, possible **9** practical
work-a-day: **7** humdrum, prosaic **8** everyday, ordinary **11** commonplace
workaholic: **5** grind
workbag: **8** reticule
worker: **4** arry, doer, hand, hind **5** navvy **6** earner, menial, toiler **7** artisan, laborer **8** employee, operator **9** artificer, craftsman, operative, performer **11** breadwinner, proletarian
fellow: **5** buddy **7** comrade **8** confrere **9** colleague
group: **4** crew, gang, team **5** corps, shift, staff, union **9** personnel
head: **4** boss **5** super **6** ganger **7** foreman, manager **8** employer, overseer **10** supervisor **14** superintendent
kind: **5** diver, mason, miner, smith, tuner **6** barman, cocker, hopper, joiner, laster, sapper, sawyer, slater, smithy, tanner, warper, welder, wright **7** analyst, cobbler, collier,

geordie, glazier, paneler, plumber, reed-
man, riveter, sandhog, spinner **8** chaffman,
chuckler, enameler, mechanic, shedhand,
strapper **9** carpenter, groundhog, machinist, stevedore **10** blue collar **11** white collar
12 long shoreman
migrant: **4** hobo, Okie **5** Arkie **6** boomer **7**
floater, wetback
objectionable: **4** scab **7** botcher, bungler **11**
scissorbill **13** featherbedder
skilled: **7** artisan **12** professional
unskilled: **4** peon, tyro **6** coolie **7** laborer
10 apprentice

work for: **4** earn **5** serve **7** benefit

workhorse: **4** peon, serf **5** slave **6** drudge,
toiler **7** trestle **8** sawhorse

workhouse: **6** prison **8** workshop **9**
almshouse, poorhouse

working: up **4** busy **5** alert **6** active, decree,
effort **7** halurgy, running **8** employed,
endeavor **9** ordinance, practical **10** contortion
not: off **4** down, idle **5** kaput **6** broken,
otiose **10** unemployed

working class: **7** laborer **10** blue collar **11**
proletariat

workman-like: **4** deft **5** adept **8** skillful **10**
proficient

work of art: **4** song **6** fresco, statue **7** carving,
classic, etching, picture **8** painting **9** sculpture

work on: **6** affect **9** influence

work out: fix **5** erase, solve **6** efface **7** arrange,
develop, exhaust **8** exercise **9** calculate,
elaborate **10** accomplish

work over: **4** redo **6** recast, rehash, revamp,
revise **8** persuade **9** brainwash, elaborate,
influence

workroom: den, lab **4** mill, shop **5** plant,
study **6** studio **7** atelier, bottega, factory,.
library **10** laboratory **11** ergasterion

works: **5** plant **7** factory

worktable: **5** bench

work up: irk **4** stir **5** raise, rouse **6** arouse,
excite, expend **7** advance, develop **8** generate **9** elaborate **10** manipulate

world: **5** earth, globe, realm, terra **6** cosmos,
domain, people, public, sphere **7** kingdom,
mankind **8** creation, humanity, universe
antedating creation of: **10** premundane
bearer of: **5** Atlas
miniature: **9** microcosm
pert. to: **7** earthly, mundane, secular **11** terrestrial

World War I: *battle:* **5** Marne, Somme, Ypres
6 Amiens, Verdun **7** Argonne, Jutland **8**
Ardennes **9** Gallipoli
general: **8** Pershing
hero: **4** York **8** Mitchell **9** Kitchener **12**
Rickenbacker

marshal: **4** Foch
spy: **8** Mata Hari
treaty: **10** Versailles

World War II: *admiral:* **6** Halsey, Nimitz
alliance: **4** Axis **6** Allies
battle: **4** Guam, Orel, Wake **5** Anzio, Bulge
6 Bataan, Midway, Sicily, Tarawa, Warsaw **7**
Cassino, Dunkirk, Iwo Jima, Okinawa **8**
Normandy **10** Corregidor, Stalingrad **11**
Guadalcanal
collaborator: **6** Petain
general: **6** Patton, Rommel **7** Bradley **9**
Doolittle, MacArthur **10** Eisenhower,
Montgomery
hero: **6** Murphy
landing: **4** D-Day
traitor: **8** Quisling

worldly: **6** carnal, laical **7** earthen, earthly,
mundane, secular, sensual, terrene **8** temporal **11** terrestrial

worldwide: **6** global **8** ecumenic, pandemic **9**
planetary, universal **10** ecumenical

worm: bob, eel, eri, ess, ipo, loa, lug, pin **4**
grub, nais, nema **5** borer, larva, tinea **6**
looper, maggot, palolo, teredo, wretch **7**
annelid, ascarid, ipomoea, reptile, sagitta,
serpent, tagtail, wriggle **8** cercaria,
helminth **9** angleworm, earthworm, insinuate, nemertina, nemertine, trematode
aquatic: sao **4** nais, nema **5** cadew, leech **6**
nereis, ribbon **7** achaeta, annelid **8** bootlace
eye-infecting: loa
genus of: **6** nereis **8** geoplana
parasitic: **5** fluke, leech **7** ascarid, cestode,
filaria, pinworm **8** flatworm, hookworm,
tapeworm, trichina **9** roundworm
threadlike: **7** filaria

worm-eaten: old **6** pitted, ragged, shabby **7**
decayed, worn-out **8** decrepit

worm-eating mammal: **4** mole

wormlike: **7** vermian **11** helminthoid

wormwood: **4** moxa **7** cudweed, mugwort **8**
mingwort **9** artemisia, sagebrush

wormy: **6** earthy, rotten **8** crawling, diseased

worn down: **5** erose, tired **6** eroded **7**
abraded, attrite **8** attrited

worn-out: **4** sere, used **5** jaded, passe, seedy,
spent, stale, trite **6** effete, frayed, shabby **7**
haggard **8** consumed, decrepit, impaired,
weakened **9** enfeebled, exhausted, hackneyed **10** bedraggled, threadbare

worry: dun, hox, nag, vex **4** bait, care, cark,
faze, fear, fike, fret, fuss, gnaw, hare, stew
5 annoy, brood, chafe, choke, gally, harry,
hurry, tease, touse, trial, upset **6** badger,
bother, caddle, fidget, harass, hatter, hector, pester, plague, pother **7** anxiety,
bedevil, chagrin, concern, despair, disturb,
perturb, torment, trouble **8** distress, stran-

gle **9** worriment **10** disconcert, uneasiness
without: **8** carefree

worsen: **5** decay **7** decline, descend **8** pejorate **9** aggravate **10** retrogress **11** deteriorate

worship: **4** cult, fame, love **5** adore, dulia, exalt, honor, worth **6** credit, esteem, homage, latria, praise, renown, repute, revere, ritual **7** dignity, idolism, idolize, liturgy, magnify, respect **8** blessing, devotion, hierurgy, idolatry, venerate **9** adoration, deference, monolatry, reverence, theolatry **10** admiration, allotheism, hagiolatry, hierolatry, hyperdulia, reputation, veneration, worthiness
form of: **4** hymn, Mass, rite **6** ritual **7** liturgy
house of: dom **6** chapel, church, mosque, shrine, temple **8** basilica **9** cathedral, synagogue **10** tabernacle
nature: **11** physiolatry
object of: God **4** icon, idol **5** totem **6** fetich, fetish
place of: **5** altar

worshiper: **6** adorer, bhakta, votary **7** devotee **8** disciple, idolater

worshipful: **4** good **5** proud **6** devout **7** adoring, notable **8** esteemed **9** honorable, respected **10** venerating **11** worshipping

worst: bad **4** beat, best **5** outdo **6** defeat **9** discomfit, overthrow

worsted: **4** garn, yarn **5** serge **6** fabric, tamine **8** whipcord **9** gabardine
yarn: **4** wool **6** caddis, crewel, sports **7** caddice, genappe, Persian **9** fingering

wort: **4** herb, root **8** fleabane

worth: **4** cost, mark, note **5** merit, price, value **6** bounty, desert, esteem, riches, virtue, wealth **7** account, benefit, caliber, dignity, fitting, quality, stature, utility **8** eminence **9** deserving, desirable, substance **10** excellence, importance, possession, usefulness
sense of: **5** pride **7** dignity, respect **10** self-esteem
thing of little: rap **6** stiver, trifle

worthless: bad, rap **4** base, evil, idle, vain, vile **5** inane **6** cheesy, drossy, futile, hollow, nogood, paltry, putrid, rotten, trashy **7** fustian, inutile, useless **8** feckless, unworthy **9** frivolous, no-account, valueless **11** undeserving

worthy: **4** dear, good **5** noble, pious **7** condign **8** deserved, eligible, laudable, meriting, valuable **9** competent, deserving, estimable, excellent, honorable, qualified **11** appropriate, meritorious

wound: cut **4** gore, harm, hurt, pain, stab, wing **5** break, ganch, sting **6** breach, damage, grieve, harrow, injure, injury, trauma **7** afflict, attaint, outrage **8** distress, incision, lacerate, puncture
discharge from: pus **5** ichor, serum
in heraldry: **4** vuln
mark: **4** scab, scar, welt **7** blister

woundwort: **6** betony **7** allheal

woven (see also **weave**): **4** lacy **7** damasse
raised figures: **6** broche **7** brocade

wow: hit, mew **4** howl, rave, wail **5** smash, whine **7** delight, success

wrack: **4** kelp, rack, raze, ruin **5** goods, trash, weeds, wreck **6** avenge, defeat, injury **7** destroy, seaweed, torment, unsound **8** calamity, mischief, wreckage **9** overthrow, shipwreck, vengeance **10** punishment **11** destruction, persecution

wraith: **5** ghost, spook **6** shadow, spirit **7** phantom, specter **10** apparition

wrangle: **4** spar **5** argue, brawl, chide, fight **6** bicker, debate, haggle **7** contend, contest, dispute, quarrel **11** altercation, controversy

wrangler: **6** cowboy, hafter **7** student **8** herdsman, opponent, stockman **9** disputant **10** antagonist

wrap: hap, rug, wap **4** cere, coat, coil, fold, furl, hide, mask, roll, wind **5** cloak, cover, nubia, twine **6** afghan, encowl, enfold, infold, invest, mantle, muffle, swathe **7** blanket, conceal, enclose, envelop, package **8** enshroud, enswathe, overcoat, surround **9** encompass **10** camouflage

wrapper: **4** gown, robe **5** cover **6** fardel **8** galabeah, negligee, peignoir

wrapping: wap **8** cerement, covering

wrasse: **4** fish **6** ballan

wrath: ire **4** fury, rage **5** anger **6** choler, felony **7** offense, passion **8** acerbity, violence **10** turbulence **11** indignation

wrathful: **5** angry, wroth **8** choleric, incensed **9** malignant

wreak: **5** exact **6** avenge, punish **7** gratify, indulge, inflict, revenge **9** vengeance

wreath, wreathe: lei **4** bank, coil, orle, roll, turn **5** crown, drift, torse (her.), twine, twist, whorl **6** anadem, corona, crants, crease, laurel, spirea, wrench **7** bouquet, chaplet, contort, coronet, crownal, entwine, festoon, garland, spiraea, wrinkle **8** encircle, surround
in heraldry: **5** torse

wreck: **4** hulk, raze, ruin, undo **5** crash, ruins, smash, total, wrack **6** damage, defeat, jalopy, thwart **7** destroy, disable, founder, shatter **8** collapse, demolish, derelict, sabotage **9** overthrow, shipwreck, vandalize **11** destruction

wreckage: **5** ruins **6** jetsam **7** flotsam **8** driftage **9** driftwood

wrench: wry **4** jerk, pipe, pull, rack, tear, tool,

turn **5** force, lever, twist, wring **6** injury, monkey, socket, sprain, strain, twinge **7** distort, spanner **8** Stillson **9** alligator, epitonion **10** distortion

wrest: 4 rend, ruse **5** exact, fraud, seize, trick, usurp **6** elicit, extort, snatch **7** pervert, wrestle

wrestle: tug **6** squirm, strive, tussle, wraxle **7** contend, grapple, wriggle 8 struggle

wrestler: 6 mauler

wrestling: *ceremonial:* **4** sumo
  hold: **4** ride **5** tie-up **6** nelson **8** headlock, scissors
  place: **4** ring **5** arena **8** palestra **9** palaestra
  term: pin **6** escape **8** reversal, takedown
  throw: hip

wretch: bum, cur, dog **4** worm **5** exile, loser **6** beggar, pauper **7** hilding, ingrate, sad sack, scroyle **8** derelict, recreant **9** miscreant

wretched: 4 base, foul, lewd, mean, poor **5** dawny **6** abject, dismal, paltry, pilled, woeful **7** baleful, caitiff, forlorn, pitiful, unhappy **8** dejected, grievous, inferior, pathetic, pitiable **9** afflicted, execrable, miserable, niggardly **10** calamitous, deplorable, depressing, despicable, distressed, melancholy **11** unfortunate

wriggle: 4 frig, turn, wind **5** dodge, evade, snake, twist **6** fitter, squirm, widdle, wintle, writhe **7** meander **10** equivocate

wring: 4 fret, rack **5** choke, clasp, exact, press, screw, twist, wrest **6** elicit, extort, squirm, wrench **7** afflict, extract, squeeze, wrestle **8** compress, strangle, struggle

wrinkle: 4 fad, rut **4** fold, idea, knit, line, lirk, ruck, ruga, seam **5** crimp, fancy, knack, reeve, ridge, rivel **6** cockle, crease, device, furrow, notion, pucker, rimple, rumple **7** crimple, crinkle, crumple, frumple, novelty, winding **8** contract **9** corrugate, crow's foot **10** prominence

wrinkled: 6 crepey, rugate, rugose, rugous **7** savoyed **8** furrowed, rugulose
  free from being: **6** smooth **7** erugate

wrist: 5 joint **6** carpus
  bone: **4** ulna **6** carpal, radius **7** carpale
  mark: **7** rasceta
  ornament: **4** band **8** bracelet

wristlet: 4 band **5** strap **8** bracelet, handcuff **9** wristband

writ: 5 breve, brief, order, tales **6** capias, elegit, extent, venire **7** exigent, process, writing **8** detainer, document, mittimus, replevin, subpoena **10** certiorari, distringas, injunction, instrument

write: pen **4** copy, note, type **5** chalk, clerk, enrol **6** author, direct, enface, enroll, indite, record, scrawl, scribe **7** compose, engross, scratch **8** inscribe, scribble **9** character

letters: **10** correspond

write down: 4 list, note **6** record **10** depreciate

write off: 4 drop **5** decry **6** cancel, deduct, remove

writer: 4 bard, hack, poet **5** clerk, odist **6** author, critic, glozer, lawyer, penman, scribe **7** copyist, diarist, glosser, hymnist, penster, realist, tropist **8** annalist, composer, essayist, gazeteer, literate, lyricist, narrator, novelist, parodist, prefacer, reviewer, scriptor **9** annotater, columnist, craftsman, dramatist, glossator, scrivener, solicitor **10** amanuensis, chronicler, glossarist, journalist
  inferior: **4** hack **8** rhymster **9** poetaster, scribbler
  unscrupulous: **10** plagiarist

writhe: 4 bend, bind, curl, toss, turn **5** twist, weave, wrest, wring **6** squirm **7** agonize, contort, distort, shrivel, wriggle **8** encircle, enswathe **9** convolute, insinuate **10** contortion, intertwine

writhing: 4 eely **9** wriggling

writing: 4 ola **4** book, deed, olla, poem, writ **5** diary, essay, print, prose, verse **6** script **7** epistle, pothook **8** contract, covenant, document, makimono, pleading, spelling **9** allograph, cerograph, enrolment, esoterics **10** enrollment, instrument, literature, penmanship **11** chirography, composition, handwriting, inscription, orthography, publication
  ancient manuscript: **6** uncial
  character: **4** sign **6** letter, symbol **9** cuneiform, ideograph, logograph **10** hieroglyph, pictograph
  desk: **9** secretary **10** escritoire
  inferior: **9** potboiler
  material: pad **5** board, paper, slate **6** tablet **7** papyrus **9** parchment **10** stationery
  on the wall: **4** mene **5** tekel **8** upharsin
  sacred: **5** Bible, Koran **6** psalms, Talmud **7** Gospels **8** epistles **9** hagiology, testament **10** scriptures
  secret: **4** code **6** cipher **10** cryptogram **12** cryptography
  tool: pen **5** chalk, stick **6** pencil, stylus **8** computer **9** ballpoint **10** typewriter, word processor

wrong: bad, car, ill, off, out, sin **4** awry, evil, harm, hurt, tort **5** abuse, agley, amiss, crime, error, false, grief, malum, shame, unfit **6** astray, faulty, injure, injury, malign, seduce, sinful, unfair, unjust, wicked **7** crooked, defraud, immoral, misdeed, twisted, vicious, violate **8** dishonor, improper, iniquity, mistaken, tortuous, wrongful, wrongous **9** erroneous, incorrect,

injurious, injustice, reprobate, violation **10**
dispossess, inaccurate, iniquitous,
transgress, unsuitable **11** impropriety,
malfeasance, misfeasance
civil: **4** tort

wrongdoer: **5** crook, felon **6** sinner **7** convict
8 criminal, violator **9** miscreant **10** malefactor, tort-feasor, trespasser **12** transgres-
sor

wroth: **5** angry, irate, upset **7** violent **8**
incensed, wrathful **9** turbulent

wrought: **4** agog, made **5** eager **6** beaten,
formed, shaped, worked **7** created, excited,
operose **9** decorated, disturbed, fashioned,
processed **10** elaborated, ornamented,
stimulated
up: **7** excited, stirred

wry: **4** awry, bend, bias, sour, tend, turn **5**
avert, pinch, twist, wring **6** swerve, warped,
wrench **7** contort, crooked, cynical, deflect,
deviate, distort, incline **8** contrary, perverse, sardonic

wryneck: **5** loxia **9** snakebird **10** woodpecker
11 torticollis
genus: **4** jynx

Wurttemberg: *capital:* **9** Stuttgart
city: Ulm **9** Esslingen, Heilbronn
river: **6** Danube, Neckar
Wuthering Heights author: **6** Bronte
Wycliffe disciple: **7** Lollard

Wyoming: *capital:* **8** Cheyenne
city: **6** Casper **7** Laramie **8** Sheridan
11 Rock Springs
highest point: **11** Gannett Peak
Indian: Ute **4** Crow **7** Arapaho **8**
Shoshone
motto: **11** Equal Rights
mountain range: **5** Rocky, Teton **7**
Bighorn, Granite, Laramie, Rockies **8**
Absaroka **9** Wind River **11** Sierra
Madre
river: **5** Green, Snake **6** Powder **7**
Bighorn **11** North Platte
state bird: **10** meadowlark
state flower: **16** Indian paintbrush
state tree: **10** cottonwood
trail: **6** Oregon **7** Bozeman

X

X: chi, ten **4** mark **5** cross, error **7** mistake **9** signature
Xanadu's river: **4** Alph
xanthic: **6** yellow **9** yellowish
Xanthippe: **5** scold, shrew **6** nagger, virago **9** termagant
  husband: **8** Socrates
xanthous: **6** yellow **9** Mongolian
xebec: **4** boat, ship **6** vessel
xema: **4** gull
xenium: **4** gift **6** dainty **7** present **8** delicacy
xenogamy: **11** pollination
xenon: **7** element
Xenophanean: **7** eleatic
Xenophon: **14** Greek historian
  subject: **8** Socrates
Xeres: **4** wine **5** Jerez **6** sherry
xerophyte: **6** cactus
xerosis: **7** dryness
xerotic: dry, sec
xerus: **8** squirrel
Xerxes: *composer:* **6** Handel
  kingdom: **6** Persia
  parent: **6** Atossa, Darius
  wife: **6** Esther
Xhosa, Xosa: **5** Bantu, tribe **8** language
Xinjiang: See **Sinkiang**
xiphoid: **8** ensiform **9** sword-like
Xmas: **4** Noel, Yule **9** Christmas
X-ray: *inventor:* **8** Roentgen
  science: **9** radiology **13** roentgenology
  type: **8** grenzray **11** fluoroscope
X-shaped: **8** cruciate
xurel: **4** scad **6** saurel
xylem: **6** hadrom **7** hadrome, xylogen
xylograph: **5** print **7** woodcut **9** engraving **10** impression
xyloid: **5** woody **8** ligneous
xylophone: **5** saron **6** gender **7** gambang, gamelan, marimba **8** gamalang, gigelira, sticcado
xyrid: **4** iris
xyst, xystos, xystus: **4** stoa, walk **5** porch **7** portico, terrace

Y

yabber: 4 talk 6 jabber 8 language 12 conversation

yabby, yabbie: 8 crayfish

yacht: 4 boat, race, sail, ship 5 craft 6 cruise, dinghy, sonder

yacht basin: 6 marina

yacht flag: 6 burgee

yaffle: 10 woodpecker

yahoo: 4 lout 5 brute, tough 6 savage 7 bumpkin 9 roughneck
creator: 5 Swift

Yahweh: God 4 YHVH, YHWH 5 Yahwe 7 Jehovah

yak: ox 4 joke, zobo 5 bison 6 sarlak, sarlyk 7 buffalo, chatter 10 grunting ox

yakamik: 4 bird 5 agami 9 trumpeter

yaksha: god 4 jinn, ogre 5 angel, demon, dryad, fairy, gnome 6 spirit

Yakut's river: 4 Lena

Yale: Eli 4 lock 5 bulldog 10 university

Yalta: *conference member:* 6 Stalin 9 Churchill, Roosevelt

yamp: ube, ubi 5 tugui 6 buckra, igname, potato, uviyam 7 boniata 8 cush-cush 9 posthouse 11 sweet potato

yamen (Ch.): 5 court 6 office 7 mansion 9 residence 12 headquarters

yammer: cry 4 chat, yell 5 crave, gripe, shout, whine, yearn 6 clamor, desire, lament, scream 7 chatter, grumble, stammer, whimper 8 complain

yam: 5 tuber 12 Indian potato

yang (see also **yin**)**:** cry 4 honk, male 5 light 8 positive

yang-kin (Ch.): 8 dulcimer

yank: tug 4 blow, draw, jerk, pull 5 hoick 6 snatch, twitch 7 extract

Yank, Yankee: 8 American 10 Northerner 12 New Englander

yap: apt, cur, dog, gab 4 bark, keen, talk, yelp 5 cheep, clown, eager, mouth, quick, ready, rowdy, scold 6 active, hungry, jabber, rustic 7 bumpkin, chatter, hoodlum 9 greenhorn

yapock, yapok: 6 monkey 7 opossum

Yaqui: 5 river 6 Indian

yard: rod 4 area, lawn, quad, rule, spar, wand 5 close, court, field, garth, patio, staff, stick 6 campus, garden 7 confine, grounds, measure, terrace 8 compound 9 courtyard, curtilage, enclosure 10 correction, playground, quadrangle
enclosed: 5 garth, patio 9 courtyard
part of: 4 foot, inch

yards: *five and one-half:* rod
600: 4 heer
two hundred twenty: 7 furlong

yardage: 6 length 8 distance

yardland: 7 virgate

yardstick: 5 gauge 7 measure 8 standard

yarn: abb, eis, fib, lie, tow 4 chat, flax, garn, saga, silk, sley, slub, tale, wool 5 fiber, story 6 caddis, crewel, strand, thread 7 caddice, eiswool, genappe, schappe 8 anecdote, converse 9 fingering, narrative
ball: 4 clew
holder: cop
quantity: cop, lea 4 clew, clue, hank, hasp 5 skein 7 spangle
reel: 4 pirn
size: 6 denier
waste: 5 thrum

yarr: 5 growl, snarl 7 spurrey

yarrow: 4 herb 7 allheal, milfoil 8 Achillea

yashmak, yasmak: 4 veil

yataghan: 5 knife, saber 8 scimitar

yaupon: 4 ilex 5 holly, yapon 7 cassena, cassina 9 evergreen

yaw: 4 bend, gape, tack, turn, veer 5 lurch, steer 6 seesaw, swerve 7 deviate

yawl: 4 boat, howl 6 scream, vessel

yawn: nap 4 galp, gant (Sc.), gape, open, yaup, yawp 5 chasm 6 tedium 7 opening, stretch 8 oscitate

yawp: bay, cry, yap 4 bawl, call, gape, yelp 5 gripe 6 bellow, scream, squall 8 complain

yaws: 7 disease 9 frambesia

yawweed: 7 rhubarb

yclept: 5 named 6 called, styled

ye: you 4 thee, thou

yea: aye, yes 4 also, even 5 truly 6 assent, indeed, verily 11 affirmative

yean: ean 4 bear, lamb 7 produce

yeanling: kid 4 lamb 7 newborn

year: año (Sp.) 4 anno (L., It.), haab, jahr (G.) 5 annee (F.), annus (L.)
designation: 4 leap 5 lunar, solar 6 fiscal 7 natural 8 calendar, sidereal, tropical 11 equinoctial 12 astronomical

of plenary indulgence: **7** jubilee
record: **5** annal **8** calendar
yearbook: **6** annual **7** almanac
yearling: **4** colt **9** hornotine
Yearling: *author:* **8** Rawlings
   boy: **4** Jody
yearly: **6** annual **7** etesian **8** annually **9** perennial
yearn: beg, vex, yen **4** ache, long, pine, sigh, wish **5** covet, crave **6** aspire, desire, grieve, hanker, hunger, yammer **7** request
yearning: **4** wish **5** eager **6** desire **7** anxious **8** ambition **10** aspiration
years: age, eon, era **4** time
   eight: **9** octennial
   fifteen: **9** indiction
   five: **6** pentad **7** lustrum
   four: **11** quadrennial
   hundred: **9** centenary **10** centennial
   ninety: **10** nonagenary
   seventy: **12** septuagenary
   ten: **6** decade **8** decenary **9** decennary, decenniad, decennium
   thousand: **7** chiliad **10** millennium
   two: **8** biennium
yeast: bee **4** barm, foam, rise **5** froth **6** fungus, leaven **7** ferment **9** agitation
yeasty: **5** giddy, light **6** bubbly **7** foaming, gaseous **9** restless, frivolous, unsettled **11** superficial
yegg: **5** thief **6** robber **7** burglar **8** criminal **11** safebreaker, safecracker
yell: cry **4** bawl, call, gowl, howl, roar, yarm, yowl **5** cheer, shout, whoop **6** outcry, scream, shriek, yammer **7** yelloch
yelling: **8** strident **9** clamorous
yellow: **4** gull, mean, sere, turn, yolk **5** amber, blake, color, favel, lemon, ochre, tinge **6** butter, canary, citron, fallow, flavic, flavid, flaxen, golden, sallow **7** unmanly, xanthic **8** cowardly, recreant **9** flavicant, jaundiced, lutescent **10** flavescent, melancholy **11** lily-livered, sensational, treacherous **12** contemptible, dishonorable
   brown: dun **4** bran **5** aloma, amber, khaki, pablo, straw **6** manila **7** mustard
   dyestuff: **5** morin **6** orlean **7** annatto, annotto, arnatto
   egg's: **4** yolk
   gray: **4** drab
   green: **5** olive **6** acacia, privet **7** sulphur **8** glaucous, tarragon **10** chartreuse
   lemon: **8** generall
   orange: **9** grenadine
   red: **4** lava, roan **5** sandy **6** orange **7** nacarat
yellow alloy: **5** brass
yellowback: **9** dime novel
yellowbelly: rat **4** funk **6** coward **11** treacherous **12** contemptible

yellow bird: **6** canary **7** warbler **9** goldfinch
yellow copperas: **9** copiapite
yellowhammer: **4** bird, yite **5** ammer, finch, skite **6** gladdy **7** flicker, yeldrin **8** yeldrine, yeldring, yeldrock, yoldring **10** flycatcher, woodpecker
Yellowhammer State: **7** Alabama
yellow jacket: **4** wasp **6** hornet **8** eucalypt
yellowlegs: **4** bird **7** tattler **8** redshank **9** sandpiper
yellow mustard: **8** charlock
yellow ocher: sil
yellow pigment: **7** etiolin **8** orpiment
Yellow River: **7** Hwang Ho
yellow starwort: **10** elecampane
Yellowstone Park: *geyser:* **11** Old Faithful
   state: **5** Idaho **7** Montana, Wyoming
Yemen: *capital, commercial:* **4** Aden
   capital, political: **5** Sanaa
   city: **5** Damar, Taizz **6** Dhamar **7** Mukalla
   currency: fil **4** rial **5** dinar
yelp: cry, yip **4** bark, brag, howl **5** boast, cheep, shout **6** greedy, outcry, shriek, squeal **7** ululate **8** complain **9** criticize
yen: **4** coin, long, urge, want **5** yearn **6** desire, hanker **7** craving, longing **10** propensity
   one-hundredth: sen
yenta (Yid.): **6** gossip
yeoman: **5** clerk **6** butler, tenant **8** retainer **9** assistant, attendant **10** freeholder, journeyman, manservant **11** subordinate
   of guard officer: **4** exon
yes: ja (G.) yeah, si (It., Sp.), aye, iss, oui (F.), yeh, yep **4** okay, true **5** agree, quite, right, roger **6** assent, indeed **7** exactly **8** all right **9** assuredly **11** affirmation, affirmative
yet: but **4** also **5** again, still **6** even so, though **7** algates, besides, further, however **8** after all, sometime **10** eventually **11** nonetheless
yeti: **7** monster, snowman
yew: **4** tree **5** shrub **7** conifer **9** evergreen **13** ground hemlock
   genus: **5** taxus
Yiddish: **6** Jewish **8** language
   writer: **6** Singer
yield: bow, net, pay, sag **4** bear, bend, cave, cede, cess, crop, elde, fold, give, obey, quit, vail **5** addle, admit, agree, allow, avale, bring, defer, fruit, grant, heald, hield, repay, stoop, waive **6** accede, afford, comply, impart, income, output, profit, relent, render, return, reward, soften, submit, supply, swerve **7** abandon, bring in, concede, consent, crumple, deliver, forfeit, furnish, harvest, produce, product, revenue, succumb **8** back down, collapse, dividend, generate **9** acquiesce, surrender **10** capitulate, recompense, relinquish
yielding: **4** meek, soft, waxy **5** buxom **6** fee-

ble, flabby, pliant, supple **7** flaccid, passive **8** flexible, recreant **9** tractable **10** manageable

yin (see also **yang**): one **4** dark **6** female, shadow **8** negative

yip: 4 yell, yelp

Ymer, Ymir: 5 chaos, giant
slayer: **4** Odin, Vili

yodel: 4 call, sing **5** carol, shout **6** warble **7** refrain

yogi: 5 fakir, yogin **6** fakeer **7** ascetic
sitting posture: **5** asana, lotus
teacher: **4** guru

yoke: tie **4** bail, bond, join, link, pair, span, team **5** bangy, fight (Sc.), hitch, marry, seize (Sc.) **6** attack (Sc.), banghy, couple, inspan, tackle (Sc.) **7** bondage, carrier, enslave, harness, oppress, service, slavery **8** restrain **9** associate, servitude

yoked: 9 conjugate

yokefellow: 4 mate, wife **6** spouse **7** husband, partner **8** coworker **9** associate, companion

yokel: oaf **4** boor, clod, lout, rube **6** obtuse, rustic **7** bumpkin, hayseed, plowboy **8** Abderite, gullible **10** countryman, slowwitted

yolk: 6 center, yellow **7** essence **8** vitellus

yon, yonder: 4 away **5** there **6** beyond **7** distant, farther, further, thither

yore: 4 past **7** long ago

Yorkshire: *river:* Ure
town: **5** Leeds

you: lei (It.), sie (G.), toi (F.) yez, voi (It.) **4** loro (It.), thee, thou, vous (F.,pl.) **5** usted (Sp.) **7** ustedes (Sp.,pl.)

young: fry, new, raw **4** tyro, weak **5** brood, fetus, fresh, green **6** active, callow, clutch, foetus, litter, strong, tender **7** pliable **8** childish, ignorant, immature, juvenile, newcomer, vigorous, workable, youthful **9** offspring, succulent
bring forth: ean **4** yean **5** birth, calve, whelp
with: **6** gravid **8** pregnant

young animal: cub, kid, pup **4** calf, colt, fawn, joey **5** chick, puppy **6** kitten **7** tadpole

young hare: 7 leveret

young herring: 4 brit

younger: 6 junior

younger son: 5 cadet

youngster: boy, cub, lad, tad, tot **4** baby, calf, colt, girl, lass, tike **5** chick, child, filly, minor, sprig, youth **6** moppet, shaver, urchin **9** stripling **10** midshipman

youth: bud **4** chap **5** chabo, chiel (Sc.) **6** hoiden, hoyden **7** callant (Sc.), ephebos, ephebus, gossoon, puberty **8** juvenile, minority, teenager **9** stripling, youngster **10** adolescent **11** adolescence
time of: **5** teens **9** salad days

youth shelter: 6 hostel

youthful: new **5** early, fresh, green, young **6** active, boyish, callow **7** girlish, puerile **8** immature, juvenile, vigorous, virginal

yowl: cry **4** bawl, howl, wail, yell

yo-yo: top **9** fluctuate, vacillate

Yucatan: 12 Mexican state
capital: **6** Merida
people: **4** Maya **5** Mayan

yucca: 5 palma

Yugoslavia (see also **Bosnia and Herzegovina, Croatia, Slovenia, Macedonia, Serbia, Montenegro**): *capital:* **7** Beograd **8** Belgrade
city: Nis, Pec **8** Titograd
currency: **4** para **5** dinar
leader: **4** Broz, Tito
measure: rif **4** akov, ralo **5** donum, khvat, lanaz, stopa **6** motyka, palaze, ralico
river: **5** Drina, Timok
weight: oka, oke **5** dramm, tovar, wagon **7** satlijk

Yukon Territory: *capital:* **10** Whitehorse
flower: **8** fireweed
gold rush region: **8** Klondike
mountain range: **5** Rocky **7** Ogilvie, St. Elias, Stikine **9** Mackenzie
river: **5** Lewes, Liard, Pelly, White, Yukon **8** Klondike

yule: 9 Christmas **13** Christmastide

Z

Z: zed **6** izzard
zac: **4** goat, ibex
zacate: hay **5** grass **6** forage
Zacchaeus, Zaccheus: **4** pure **8** innocent
Zadok: **4** just **9** righteous
   son: **7** Ahimaaz
zaftig: **5** buxom, juicy, plump **10** full-bodied
zaguan: **4** gate **8** entrance **11** entranceway
Zaire: *capital:* **8** Kinshasa (Leopoldville)
   city: **7** Kananga **10** Luluabourg
   currency: **5** zaire **6** makuta
   lake: **10** Tanganyika
   leader: **6** Mobutu **7** Lumumba **8** Kasavubu
   river: **4** Uele **5** Congo, Dengi, Zaire **6** Likati **7** Aruwimi, Lualaba
Zimbabwe: *capital:* **6** Harare (Salisbury)
   city: **8** Bulawayo
   currency: **4** cent **6** dollar
   leader: **5** Nkomo **6** Mugabe
Zambia: *capital:* **6** Lusaka
   city: **5** Kitwe, Ndola **8** Chingola
   currency: **5** ngwee **6** kwacha
   waterfalls: **8** Victoria
zamia: **4** tree **5** cycad, shrub
zampogna: **7** bagpipe, panpipe
zanja: **5** canal, ditch, gully **6** arroyo
zanni: **5** clown
zany: mad, nut, wag, wit **4** dolt, fool **5** clown, comic, crazy, dotty, nutty, toady **6** jester **7** acrobat, buffoon, idiotic **8** clownish, follower, imitator **9** simpleton
Zanzibar: See **Tanzania**
zap: hit, pep **4** kill **5** shoot, verve **6** defeat, energy
zarf: cup **5** stand **6** holder
zarzuela: **5** opera **6** comedy **8** operetta **11** seafood stew
zati: **6** monkey **7** ascetic, devotee
zeal: **4** fire **5** ardor, force, gusto, heart **6** desire, fervor, relish, spirit **7** passion **8** devotion, interest **9** eagerness, intensity, vehemence **10** enthusiasm, fanatacism
Zealand: *city:* **10** Copenhagen
zealot: bug, nut **5** bigot **6** votary **7** devotee, fanatic **8** disciple, partisan, votaress **10** enthusiast
zealous: **4** avid, warm **5** eager, rabid **6** ardent, fervid, hearty **7** devoted, earnest, fervent, intense, serious, sincere **8** frenetic, vigorous, wild-eyed **9** phrenetic, strenuous

Zebedee's son: **4** John **5** James
zebra: **4** dauw **6** animal **9** butterfly
   extinct: **6** quagga
zebrawood: **7** arariba **9** nakedwood **10** marblewood
Zebulon, Zebulun: *brother:* **4** Levi **5** Judah **6** Simeon
   father: **5** Jacob
   mother: **4** Leah
Zelus: *brother:* Bia **6** Cratus
   father: **6** Pallas
   mother: **4** Styx
   sister: **4** Nike
zemi: **5** charm
zenana: **5** harem **8** seraglio
zenith: top **4** acme, apex, peak **5** prime **6** apogee, climax, height, heyday, summit **8** pinnacle **11** culmination
   opposite of: **5** nadir
Zeno: *city:* **4** Elea
   follower: **5** Stoic
Zenobia: *husband:* **9** Odenathus
zephyr: **4** aura, wind **6** breeze
zeppelin: **5** blimp **7** airship, balloon **9** dirigible
zero: nil **4** hour, love, none **5** aught, zilch **6** cipher, naught, nought **7** nothing **9** nonentity

Zeus: **7** Alastor, Jupiter
   beloved of: Io **6** Europa
   brother: **5** Hades **8** Poseidon
   daughter: Ate **4** Hebe, Kore **5** Fates, Horae, Irene, Muses **6** Athena, Athene, Graces, Hecate **7** Artemis, Astraea, Electra **8** Atalanta, Despoina **9** Aphrodite **10** Persephone, Hephaestus, Proserpina, Proserpine **11** Persephassa
   form assumed by: **4** bull, swan
   mount: **7** Olympus
   parent: **4** Rhea **6** Cronus, Kronos
   sister: **4** Hera **6** Hestia **7** Demeter
   son: Gad **4** Ares **5** Arcas, Argus **6** Aeacus, Apollo, Castor, Hermes, Pollux, Tityus, Vulcan **7** Perseus **8** Dardanus, Dionysos, Dionysus, Heracles, Herakles, Hercules, Tantalus **10** Hephaestus
   wife: **4** Hera, Juno **5** Danae, Metis **6** Semele

Zeruiah's son: 7 Abishai

zest: 4 kick, lust, peel, tang 5 gusto, savor, taste 6 flavor, relish 7 delight 8 appetite, piquancy 9 enjoyment 10 enthusiasm

zestful: 4 racy 6 hearty 7 pungent

Zeus: (see box)

ziarat, ziara: 4 tomb

ziggurat: 5 tower 6 temple 7 pyramid

zigzag: 4 tack, turn 5 angle, crank, weave 8 flexuous

zilch: 4 zero 7 nothing 8 goose egg

Zillah: *husband:* 6 Lamech
    son: 9 Tubal-cain

Zilpah's son: Gad 5 Asher

zimarra: 5 cloak 7 cassock, soutane

zimb: bug, fly 6 insect

zinc: 7 adamine, adamite, spelter, tutenag 9 galvanize, tutenague
    ore: 6 blende 11 splialerite
    sulphate: 7 ilesite

zing: pep, vim, zip 4 dash, snap 5 force, vigor 6 energy, spirit, stingo 9 animation, eagerness

zingaro: 5 gypsy, nomad 7 tsigane

zingel: 4 fish 5 perch

zinger: 6 retort 9 punch line

Zion: 4 hill 6 heaven, Utopia 9 Palestine

Zionism founder: 5 Herzl

zip: 4 zing 5 hurry 6 breeze

zipper: 8 fastener

Zipporah's kin: 5 Moses, Reuel 6 Jethro 7 Eliezer, Gershom

zippy: 5 agile, brisk 6 snappy

zizith: 7 fringes, tassels

zizz: 4 whir, whiz

Zoan: 5 Tanis

zodiac sign: Leo (lion), Ram 4 Bull, Crab, Fish, Goat, Lion 5 Aries (ram), decan, Libra (scale), Scale, Twins, Virgo (virgin) 6 Archer, Cancer (crab), Fishes, Gemini (twins), Pisces (fishes), Taurus (bull), Virgin 7 Balance, Scorpio 8 Aquarius (waterbearer), Scorpion 9 Capricorn (goat) 11 Capricornus, Sagittarius (archer), Waterbearer

Zola: *defended:* 7 Dreyfus

work: 4 Nana 5 Crash 6 Verite 7 J'accuse 8 Germinal, Grog Shop

zombie: 5 drink, dunce, snake 6 corpse 8 snake god 9 eccentric 10 automaton

zone: 4 area, band, belt, path, ward, zona (L.) 5 layer, tract 6 course, girdle, region, sector, stripe 7 circuit, climate, segment 8 cincture, encircle, engirdle
    geological succession: 6 assise

zonked: 4 high 5 doped 6 stoned, wasted 7 drugged 8 turned on 9 spaced-out 11 intoxicated

zoom: 4 lens 5 climb, speed 9 chandelle 11 move quickly

zoo: 8 vivarium 9 menagerie

zoophyte: 5 coral 9 ectoproct

zoril: 5 skunk 6 weasel 7 polecat

Zoroaster's works: 6 Avesta

Zoroastrian: 5 Parsi 6 gheber, ghebre, Mazdan, Parsee
    demon: 4 deva
    founder: 9 Zoroaster 11 Zarathustra
    god: 5 Ahura, Mazda 10 Ahura-Mazda

zoster: 4 belt 6 girdle 8 shingles

Zouave: 4 Zuzu 7 soldier

zounds: 4 egad 8 mild oath

zoysia: 5 grass

zucchetto: 7 calotte 8 skullcap

zucchini: 5 gourd 6 squash

zufolo: 5 flute 9 flageolet

zuisin: 4 duck 7 widgeon 9 baldplate

Zulu: *king:* 5 Shaka
    language: 5 Bantu
    spear: 7 assegai

Zuni: 6 Indian, Pueblo
    ancestor: 7 Anasazi

zwieback: 4 rusk 5 toast 7 biscuit

zygomatic bone: 5 malar 9 cheekbone

zygote: 7 oosperm

zymase: 6 enzyme
    source: 5 yeast

zymogen activating substance: 6 kinase

zymosis: 7 disease 12 fermentation

zythum: 4 beer

Prefixes, Suffixes, and Combining Forms

Prefixes, suffixes and combining forms are listed alphabetically under their meaning rather than by number of letters. The endings given in parentheses may be added on to the affix given, or the affix may be used on its own. For example, the prefix for **accessory** may be either *par* or *para*.

PREFIXES

abnormal: dys
about: ambi
above: hyper, super, supra, sur
accessory: par(a)
across: di(a), trans
additional: super
advocating: pro
afar: tele
after: meta, post
again: an(a), re
against: ant(h) (i), cat(a) (h) (o), contra, kat(a) (h) (o)
ahead: pre
all: pan
almost: pen(e)
alongside: par(a)
alternate: counter
among: inter
anew: an(a)
apart: di(s) (f)
around: ambi, circum, peri
asunder: dis
at the front: pre
away from: ab(s), ap(h) (o)
back: an(a), re, retro
before: ante, pre, pro
beforehand: pre
below: hypo, infra
beside: par(a)
between: inter, intra
beyond: extra, praeter, preter, sur, trans, ultra
billion: giga
both: ambi
changed: meta
chemical: ox(a)
chief: arch(i)
close to: juxta
combating: ant(h) (i)
complementary: counter
completely: con(m) (l), per
corresponding: counter

deprived of: dis
detached: ap(h) (o)
different: ap(h) (o)
difficult: dys
diseased: dys
down: cat(a) (h) (o), de, kat(a) (h) (o)
dwarf: nan(o)
earlier: ante
excess: hyper
excessive: sur
extreme: arch(i)
faulty: par(a)
forward: ante, pro
front: pro
good: eu
great: arch(i)
half: hemi, semi
higher: super, supra
hundred: centi
improper: mis
in advance: pre
incorrect: mis
inner, inside: endo, ento
large, very: maxi
later: meta
less than: hypo
low-pitched: contra
lower: hypo
million: mega
mistaken: mis
near: pros
nearer: cis
near to: ep(h) (i)
negative: dis
not: a(n), in(l) (m) (r), non
on: in(l) (m) (r)
one: uni
opposed: dis
opposing: ant(h) (i)
opposite: counter
out: ec, ex

outer: ep(h) (i)
outside: ecto, exo, extra (o)
over: ep(h) (i), extra, hyper, super, supra, sur
painful: dys
partial: demi, semi
poor: dys
prime: arch(i)
principal: arch(i)
prior: ante, pro
resembling: par(a)
retaliatory: counter
reverse: dis, dys
rival: ant(h) (i)
round: peri
ruler: arch
secondary: sub
single: uni
small: mini
subsequent: post
substituting: pro
succeeding: meta

surrounding: circum, peri
ten: deci
thousand: kilo
through: di(a), per
throughout: per
together: co(l) (m) (n) (r), sym (n) (l)
toward: ad, pros
transcending: meta, supra
transformation: meta
trillion: tera
two: twi
under: hypo, sub (c) (p)
underneath: intra
unfavorable: dys
up: an(a), sur
upon: ep(h) (i)
upward: ano
well: eu
with: co(l) (m) (n) (r), sym(n) (l)
within: intra (o)
wrong: mis

SUFFIXES

able to be: able, ible, ile
abundance: ose
accomplishing: ive
act: ade, ance, ion, ure
act (upon): ate
action: age, ance, ence, ing, ization
adherent: ist, ite
adjective: ular
agency: ator, eer
agent: ator, eer, facient, fic, ier
alcohol: itol
approximately: ish
art: ery
becoming: escence, escent
beginning: escent
being: ant, ent, ical, ure
belief: ism
belonging to: an, ean, ian, ish
capable of: ile
capable: able, ible
caused by: ical
causing: able, facient, fic, ible
character: ery
characteristic: ism
characteristic of: ical, ish, ist, istic(al)
characterized by: ful, ial, ical, in(a) (e), ory, ous
chemical: ane, ein(e), ene, idin, ile, ine, ite, ole, olic, ose, ylene
citizen: ese, ian, ist, ite
city: polis
collection: ery
collection of: age
compound: ate

condition: ance, ate, ence, ency, hood, ile, ism, ment, sia, (o)sis
cult: ism
degree: ity
descendant: ite
diminutive: cle, cular, ette, ole, ule
direction: ling
disease: itis, oma, pathy
doctrine: ism
doer: ast, ator, eer, er, facient, ier, ist, or, ster
existing: ent
expert: ician, ist
fear of: phobia
female: ine
feminine: ette
fit: able, ible
form: ify
formation: osis
full of: olent, ose, ous, ulent
function: ate, ure
group: ery, ome
group of: ette
hater: phobe
having: ate
imitation: ette
inferior: ling
inflammation: itis
inhabitant: ese, ite
instrument: tron
language: ese
like: oid, ose ,
little: cle, cule, ellum, ette, ole, ule
little one: el, elle, ium, kin(s), ock

madness: mania
make: ate, (i)fy, (i)gate, ize
making: (i)fic
marked by: ling
mineral: ite
musical instrument: in(a) (e)
native: ite
object: ment
office: ate, dom, ship, ure
offspring: id(e)s, ite
old: ster
one who: ist
ordinal: eth, th
participant: ster
pertaining to: ac, al, ar(y), eal, ese, ic, ile, ine, ose, tic, (u)ous
place: arium, ary, ery, orium
place for: ory
place of: age
places: aria
plant: acea
plants: aceae, ales
practice: ery, ics, ism
practitioner: ician
process: age, ence, ing, ion, ization, ment, osis, ure
product: ade
profession: ship
quality: ance, ancy, ence, ency, hood, ice, itude, ity, ness, ship
rank: ate
realm: dom
reflecting: escent
regulation: nomy
related to: in(a) (e)
relating to: ative, ean, ese, ial, ical, ile, ine, ist, istic(al), itious, ory

resembling: ular
result: ization, ment
rule by: archy, cracy
serving for: ory
skill: ics, ship
small: ling
small one: ula, ule, ulum, ulus
specialists: ician
specialized in: an, ean, ian
state: age, ance, ancy, ate, ation, dom, ence, ency, ery, hood, ion, ism, ity, ization, ment, ness, or, osis, our, ship
stem: ome
study: ics
style: esque
substitute: ette
sugar: ose, ulose
superlative: est
supporter: ite
sweet drink: ade
system: ism
tendency: itis
tending toward: acious, id, itious, ive
theory: ism
thing: ant, orium
things: oria
trace of: ish
trade: ery
trait: ism
tumor: oma
user: ster
vacuum tube: tron
vision: opia
worthy: able, ible
young: ster
youngster: ling

COMBINING FORMS

abdomen: ventr(i) (o)
abounding: poly
above: super(o)
accelerating: aux(o)
acid: acet(o), oxy
acorn: balan(o)
action: praxia
adhesion: anchyl(o), ancyl(o), ankyl(o)
affinity: phily
again: pali
against: cat(h) (a), kat(a)
agricultural: agro
air: atm(o), pneumo
aldehyde: ald(o)
alike: hom(o), is(o)
all: omn(i), pan(o)
alone: mon(o), soli
alternative: allel(o)

amber: succin(o)
ancient: archae(o), arche(o), palae(o), pale(o)
angle: angul(i) (o), gon
animal: zo(ic)
ankle: tars(o)
ant: myrmec(o)
antimony: stib(i) (o)
ape: pithec(o) (us)
apex: apic(i) (o)
appear: phan, phaner(o)
appearance: phany
appetite: orexia
archetypal: prot(o)
arising: genous
arm: brachi(o)
armed: hoplo
around: amph(i)
arrangement: tax(i) (o) (y)

art: techn(o)
ass: on(o)
asunder: dich(o)
atlas: atlant(o), atl(o)
aviation: aer(o)
avoidance: phob(o)
back: dors(i) (o), not(o) (us), opisth(o)
bad: cac(o), mal
balance: stat(o)
bearing: ferous
beautiful: cali(o), calli(o)
bed: clin(o)
bee: api, avi
beginning: acr(o), akr(o)
berry: bacci, cocc(i) (o)
best: arist(o)
billionth: nano
bird: ornith
bitter: picr(o)
black: atro, mel(a) (o), melan(o)
blind: typhl(o)
blood: haem(o), hem(a) (i) (o), sangu(i) (in)
blue: cyan(o)
boat: scaph(o)
body: corp(or), dema, soma, somat(o)
bone: oste(o)
book: bibli(o)
both: amph(i) (o), bis
brain: cerebr(i) (o), encephal(o)
branched: cladous
breast: mamm(i) (o), mast(o)
brief: brevi
bright: lampro
bristle: chaet(o), seti
broad: lati
broom: scopi
brush: scopi
bud: blast(o)
bulk: onc(h) (o)
bulky: hadr(o)
bull: taur(i) (o)
burn: cau(s)
butter: butyr(o)
buttocks: glut, pygia
cancer: carcin(o)
cat: aelur(o), ailur(o)
cattle: bovi
caudal: ur(o)
cause: aetio, aitio, etio
cavity: antr(o)
cecum: typhl(o)
cell: blast, cyt(e) (o), gamet(o), phag(e)
cement: lith
chain: strept(o)
chamber: thalam(o)
cheek: bucco, mel(o)
cheese: case(o), tyr(o)
chemical: amid(o), amin(o)
chest: stern(o), steth(o), thorac(i) (o)

chief: prot(o)
child: paed(o), ped(o)
chin: genio, mento
China: sino
Chinese: sinic(o)
church: ecclesi(o)
clay: argill(i) (o), argillaceo, pel(o)
cleft: fissi, schist(o), schiz(o)
climate: meteor(o)
close: sten(o)
closed: cleist(o), clist(o)
closure: cleisis, clisis
clot: thromb(o)
cloud: cirr(hi) (i) (o) (ho), nephel(o), neph(o), nimb(o)
cluster: cym(o), kym(o)
coal: anthrac(o)
cold: cry(o), frigo, psychro
color: chromat(o), chrom(o)
colorless: leuc(o), leuk(o)
combination: hapt(o)
compact: pycn(o)
complete: hol(o), tel(e) (o)
concealed: adel(o)
condition: ance, ancy, blasty
contact: hapt(o)
contemporary: ne(o)
contest: machy
contraction: stole, stalsis
copper: chalc(o), chalk(o), cupr(o)
correct: orth(o)
cough: tuss
counterfeit: pseud(o)
counterpart: pseud(o)
covered: crypt(o), krypt(o)
craft: techn(o)
creeping: herpet(o)
crooked: anchyl(o), ancyl(o), ankyl(o)
crown: coron(o), stephan(o)
crystal: hedron
cup: cotyl(i) (o), cyath(o), scyph(i) (o)
current: rheo
cut: sect
cutting instrument: tome
dark: melan(o), nyct(i) (o)
dead: abio
death: thanat
decomposition: lysis
deep: bathy
deer: cervi
defective: atel(o)
deficiency: penia
deficient: privic
dense: pycn(o)
depth: bath(o)
descendant: ite
desire: orexia
development: plasia, trophia, trophy
devouring: vorous

diaphragm: phren(i) (o)
difficult: mogi
discharge: rrhea
disease: agra, pathia, pathic, pathy
diseased: cac(o)
disintegration: lysis
dislike: mis(o)
distant: tel(e) (o)
distinct: idio
diver: dyt(a) (es)
diverse: vari(o)
divided: fid, fissi, schist(o)
doctrine: logy
doer: ist
dog: cyn(o)
donkey: on(o)
double: bi(s), dipl
down: cat(h) (a), kat(a)
dream: oneir(o), onir(o)
drug: pharmac(o)
dry: sicc, xer(o)
dull: ambly(o), brady
dwarf: nan(o)
eagle: aet(o)
ear: aur(i), ot(o)
earnest: serio
earth: ge(o)
earthquake: seism(o)
eat: phag(o), vor
eating: vor(e)
egg: ov(i) (o)
eight: oct(i) (o)
embryonic: blast(o)
empty: ken(o)
end: acr(o), akr(o), tel(e) (o)
enlargement: megaly
entire: hol(o), integr(i), tot(i)
environment: ec(o), oec(o), oik(o)
equal: aequ(i), equ(i), is(o), par(i)
era: zoic
eruption: anthema
even: homal(o)
everywhere: omni
evil: mal
examination: opsy, scopy
examining instrument: scope
excrement: copr(o), fec(al)
existence: ont(o)
external: ect(o), ex(o)
extremity: acr(o), akr(o)
eye: irid(o), ocul(o), ophthalm(o), opt(o), opy
eyelid: blephar(o)
false: pseud(o)
fast: tach(y)
fat: adip(o), lip(o), seb(i) (o), steat(o)
fatty: lipar(o)
fear: phob(o)
fearful: din(o)
feather: penn(i) (o), pinn(i), pter(o)
feeling: pathia, pathy

feigned: pseud(o)
female: gyn(e) (o)
few: olig(o), pauci
fewer: mei(o), mi(o)
fictitious: pseud(o)
fifth: quint(i)
fight: machy
fin: pinn(i)
fine: lept(o)
finger: dactyl(o), digit(i)
fire: ign(i), pyr(o)
first: prim(i), prot(o)
fish: ichthy(o), pisc(i)
five: pent(a), quinqu(e)
fixed: aplano, stato
flagellum: mastig(o)
flat: homal(o), plan(i)
flesh: carn(i)
flow: rrhea
flute: aul(o)
fondness: phily
food: bromat, sit(o), troph(o)
foot: ped(i) (o), pod(e) (o)
footprint: ichn(o)
foreign: xen(o)
forest: hyl(o)
form: morph(o)
four: quadr(i) (u), tessar(a), tesser(a), tetr(a)
freezing: cry(o)
front: anter(o)
fruit: carp(ia) (ium) (us), fructi
fungus: myc(o), mycete(e) (o)
gas: aer(o), pneum(o)
gate: pyl(e) (o)
genital: inguin
ghost: sci(a) (o), skia
giant: megal(o)
gill: branch
gilled: branchia
gland: aden(o), adren(o)
glandular: aden(o)
glass: hyal(o), vitr(o)
glue: coll(o)
gnat: culic(i)
goat: capri
gold: aur(i) (o), chrys
good: agath(o)
goose: chen(o)
government: archy, cracy
grain: cocc(i) (o), sito
grape: botry(o)
grave: serio
grease: seb(i) (o)
great: macr(o), meg(a), megal(o)
green: chlor
growth: auxo, phyte
guest: xen(o)
guiding: agogue
gums: gingiv, ulo
habitat: ec(o), oec(o), oik(o)

hair: capill, trich
half: hemi, semi
hand: cheir(o), chir(o), man(i) (u)
hard: scler(a) (o), stere(o)
hardening: scler(a) (o)
hare: lag(o)
hatred: mis(o), phobia
head: capit, cephal(o) (us), cipit, crani(o)
healing: iatric(s), iatro(y)
heap: cumul(i) (o)
hearing: acou(o), acousia, audi(o) (t), oto
heart: cardi(a) (o), kardi(a) (o)
heat: therm(o)
heavens: uran(o)
heavy: bary, gravi, hadr(o)
heel: calcaneo
height: acr(o), akr(o), alt, hyps(i) (o)
hidden: adel(o), crypt(o), krypt(o)
hide: derm(a) (o)
high: alti
hollow: cel(o), coel(o)
holy: hagi(o), hier(o), sacr(o)
homogeneous: is(o)
honey: meli, mell(i)
horn: cerat(o), corn(i) (u), kerat(o)
horned: cera
horse: equi, hipp(o)
human: anthrop(o)
hundred: cent(i), hect(o)
hundredth: cent(i)
idea: ide(o)
illness: agra
image: eidolo, idolo, typ(o)
imperfect: atel(o)
incision: tomy
incomplete: atel(o)
increase: auxo
individual: idio
infection: sepsis
inner: ent(o)
insect: entom(o)
instrument: labe
intermediate: mes(o)
intestine: enter(o)
iris: irid(o)
iron: ferr(i) (o), sider(o)
irregular: anom(o), anomal(i) (o)
irregularly: mal
ivory: elephant(o)
jackass: ono
jaw: gnath(o)
joint: arthr(o), condyl(o)
juice: opo
kernel: cary(o), kary(o)
key: cleid(o)
kidney: nephr(o), ren(i) (o)
killer: cide
kind: gen(o)
knee: gon
knob: tyl(o)

knowledge: gnosia, gnosis, gnosy, ics
lake: limn(i) (o)
land: chor(o), gaea, geo
language: gloss(o), glott(o), lexi(co), lingu(a) (i) (o)
large: macr(o), magn(i), meg(a), megal(o)
law: nom(o)
layer: cline
lead: molybd(o), plumb(o)
leaf: foli, phyll(o)
left: sinistr
leg: crur
level: plan(i) (o)
lifeless: abio
ligament: desm(o)
light: luc(i), lumin(i) (o), phos, phot(o)
like: home(o), homoe(o), homoi(o)
lily: crinus
line: line(o), stich
lip: labi(o)
listening: acou(o)
liver: hepat
living: ont(o), vivi
lizard: saur(o)
local: top(o)
love: erot(o), phil(ia)
loving: phil(e) (o)
lung: pneum(o), pulm(on)
maiden: partheno
male: andr(o)
man: anthrop(o)
manifest: phaner(o)
many: mult(i), pluri, poly
marriage: gam(y)
marrying: gamous
mass: onc(h) (o)
master: arch
matter: hyl(o)
measurement, science: metry
medical treatment: iatric(s), iatro(y)
memory: mnem(o)
middle: medi, mes(i) (o)
milk: galact, lact(i) (o)
million: meg(a)
millionth: micr(o)
mind: menti, noo, phren(i) (o), psych(o)
mineral: lite, lyte
mite: acar(i) (o)
modern: ne(o)
moisture: hygr(o)
monster: terat(o)
moon: lun(i), selen(i) (o)
mosquito: culic(i)
mother: matr(i) (o)
motley: part(i) (y)
mouse: my(o) (s)
mouth: or(i) (o), stom(a) (e) (o)
mouths: stomat(a) (o)
movement: kinesis
much: mult(i), poly

mud: pel(o)
muscle: my(o)
name: nom(in), omato, onym
naked: gymn(o)
narrow: sten(o)
native: ite
navel: omphal(o)
near: juxta, proxim
neck: cervic(i) (o)
nerve: neur(o), nerv(i)
nerve tissue: gangli(o)
new: ne(o)
night: nyct(i) (o)
nine: enne(a), non(i)
ninth: non(a)
nipple: mast(o), papilli(o)
nitrogen: az(a) (o)
none: null(i)
nose: nas(i) (o), rhin(o) (us)
novel: caen(o), cen(o)
nucleus: cary(o), kary(o)
number: arithmo
nut: cary(o), kary(o)
nutrition: troph(o)
occult: crypt(o), krypt(o)
odd: azygo
offspring: gen(o), ped(o)
oil: elaeo, elaio, eleo, ole(i) (o)
oily: lipar(o)
old: pal(a)e(o)
old age: ger, geront(o)
one: mon(o), un(i)
opening: pora, pore, pyle, stom(a) (o)
organ (internal): viscer(i) (o)
organism: ont(o)
other: all(o), heter(o)
out of: ect(o)
outside: ect(o), exo
ox: bovi
oyster: ostre(i) (o)
pain: agra, alg(o), algia
paralysis: plegia, plegy
part: mer(o)
particle: plast
parturition: toky
path: ode
peak: acr(o), akr(o)
peculiar: idio
penis: pen(i), phall
people: dem(o), ethn(o)
perfect: tel(e) (o)
person: idio
phenomena: ics
physician: iatrist, iatro(y)
picture: picto, pinac(o)
pig: choerus
pillar: styl(o)
pipe: aul(o), siphon(i) (o), solen(o)
pit: bothr(o)
place: chor(o), gaea, gea, loc(o), top(o)

plant: chore, phyt(a)
pleasant: hedy
poem: stich
poison: tox(i), toxic(o)
pond: limn(i) (o)
pool: limn(i) (o)
pouch: cyst(i) (is) (o)
poverty: penia
power: dyn, dynam(o)
practice: ics
practitioner: path
pressure: baro, piezo, tono
prickly: echin(o)
primary: prot(o)
producer: gen(e)
producing: genetic
qualities: ics
quinine: chin(o)
race: ethn(o), gen(o), phyl(o)
radiating: actin(i) (o)
rain: hyet(o), ombro, pluvi(a) (o)
rainbow: irid(o)
raven: corax
ray: actin(i) (o)
recent: caen(o), cen(o), ne(o)
reciprocal: allelo
recital: logue
recognition: gnosia, gnosis, gnosy
record: gram, graph
recording: graphy
recurring: ennial
red: erythr(o), pyrrh(o), rhod(o), rub(r)
reduction: lysis
remote: dist(i) (o), palae(o), pale(o), tel(e) (o)
repetition: pali
representation: graphy
reptile: herpet(o)
resembling: form
respiration: pneumo
resting: stato
rib: cost(i) (o), pleur(i) (o)
ribbon: taen(i) (o)
rice: oryz(i) (o)
right: dextr(o), orth(o), rect(i)
river: potam(o)
rock: clast, ite, lite, lith, lyte, petr(i) (o), phyre
rod: rhabd(o)
roof: steg(o)
root: rhiz(o)
rose: rhod(o)
rotten: sapr(o)
rough: trachy
round: globo, troch(o), ventr(i) (o)
rule: archy
ruler: arch
running: drom(o), dromous
sac: cyst(i) (o)
sacred: hagi(o), sacr(o)
saints: hagi(o)
salt: hal(o), ite, sali

same: hom(o), is(o)
saw: serri
science: ics, logy, ology, onomy, sophy
sea: mer, pelag(o)
second: deuter(o), deut(o)
seed: sperm(a) (i) (o), spermat(o)
seizure: agra
self: aut(o)
separate: idio
serpent: ophi(o)
seven: hept(a), sept(i)
sex: gen(o)
shadow: sci(a) (o), skia
shaggy: dasy
shape: form, morph(o)
sharp: oxy
sheet: pallio
shell: conch(o), oeco, ostrac(o)
shield: aspid(o), aspis, scut(i)
shoot: blast(o), thall(i) (o)
short: brachy, brevi
shoulder: om(o)
shrub: thamn(o)
side: ali, later(i) (o), pleur(i) (o)
sides: ali
sight: opsia, opsy
silver: argent(i) (o), argyr(o)
similar: hol(o), home(o), hom(o), homoe(o), homoi(o)
simple: apl(o), hapl(o)
single: apl(o), hapl(o), mon(o)
six: hex(a), sex(i), sexti
skill: ics, techn(o)
skin: derm(a) (o), dermat(o), dermis
skull: crani
slant: clin(o)
sleep: dorm(i), hypn(o)
slope: cline
slow: brady
small: lept(o), micr(o), olig(o), parv(i) (o)
smaller: meio, mi(o)
smell: brom(o)
smooth: leio, lio, liss(o)
snake: ophi(o)
snow: chio, chion(o)
sodium: natr(o)
soil: agro, geo
solid: stere(o)
solitary: erem(o)
song: melo
soul: psych(o), thym(o)
sound: audio, phon(e) (o) (y), phonia
south: austr(o), not(o)
sow: choerus
speak: pha(s), phem
specialist: ician, ist, logue
speech: lalo, log(o), phon(o)
spherical: globo
spider: arachn(o)
spiral: helic(o)

spirit: psych(o), thym(o)
spot: macul(i) (o)
spring: cren(o)
sprout: blast(o), clad(o)
sprouting: blastic
stain: macul(i) (o)
star: astr(o), stell
starch: amyl(o)
steam: atmid(o)
stem: caul(i) (o)
stick: rhabd(o)
stomach: gaster(o), gastr(i) (o)
stone: lith(o)
stoppage: stasis
straight: lineo, orth(o), rect(i)
strain: tono
strange: xen(o)
stranger: xen(o)
stream: fluvio
stroke: plegia
structure: morph(o)
study: (o)logy
stupor: narc(o)
substance: hyl(o), phane, state
suffering: path(o), pathia, pathy
sugar: gluc(o), glyc(o), sacchar(i) (o), sucr(o)
sulfur: thi(o)
summit: acr(o), akr(o), apic(i) (o)
sun: heli(o), sol
supporter: crat, ist, ite
surface: hedron
surgery on: tomy
surgical crushing: tripsy
surgical instrument: tome
surgical removal: ectomy
surgical repair: plasty
sweat: hidr(o)
sweet: glyc(o)
swelling: edema
swine: hyo
swollen: phys(o)
tablet: pinac(o), plac(o)
tail: caud
talk: logue
tallow: seb(i) (o), stear(o), steat(o)
tapeworm: taen(i) (o)
taste: geusia
tear: lacrim
teeth: odontia
ten: dec(a) (i), decem, dek(a)
tendency: philia, phily
tendon: teno
tenth: deci
terrible: din(o)
theft: klept(o)
theory: logy
therapy: pathia, pathic, pathy
thick: dasy, hadr(o), pachy
thigh: mer(o), merus
thin: lept(o)

third: terti, tri, trit(o)
thorn: acanth(o) (us), spini(o)
thought: ideo, log(o)
thousand: kilo
thread: fil, nem(a) (o), nemat(o)
three: ter, tri
throat: bronch(o)
thunder: bront(o), ceraun(o), kerauno
tick: acar(i) (o)
time: chron(o), chronous
tin: stann(i) (o)
tip: acr(o), akr(o), apic(i)(o)
tissue: hist(o), hypho
toe: dactyl(o), digit(o)
tone: phon(o)
tongue: gloss(o), lingu(a) (i) (o)
tooth: dent(i) (o), odont(o)
top: acr(o), akr(o), apic(i)(o)
total: hol(o)
touch: hapt(o), thigmo
track: ichn(o)
translucent: hyal(o)
transmission: phoresis
transparent: hyal(o)
treatise: logy
treatment: therapy
tree: dendr(o), dendron
trench: bothr(o)
triangular: trigon(o)
tribe: phyl(o)
trillion: treg(a)
trillionth: pico
trough: bothr(o)
true: orth(o)
tube: siphon(i) (o), solen(o), syring(o)
tumor: cele, gangli(o), myom(o), onc(h) (o)
turn: trop
twice: bis
twin: didym(o)
twist: spir(i) (o)
twisted: strept(o)
two: bi(n), du(o) (i)
twofold: diphy(o), dipl(o)
type: morph(o)
umbilicus: omphal(o)
unarmed: anopl(o)
unequal: anis(o)
uniform: is(o)
union: gamous, gamy, zyg(o)
united: gam(o)
universal: cosm(o), omni
universe: cosm(o)
unpleasant: cac(o)
unreal: pseud(o)
untrue: pseud(o)
unusual: anom(o)
upright: orth(o)
urchin: echin(o)
usage: nom(o)

vapor: atm(o)
variation: all(o)
various: part(i) (y)
vehicle: mobile
vein: phleb(o), ven(i) (o)
vertebra: spondyl(o) (us)
vessel: angi(o), arteri(o), vas(i) (o), vascul(o)
viewing instrument: scope
vine: ampel(o), viti
vinegar: acet(o)
virgin: parthen(o)
viscera: splanchn(o)
visible: phaner(o)
vision: opia, opsy, opto, opy
voice: phon(e) (o) (y)
war: machy
water: aqu(a) (e), hydr(o)
wave: cym(o), kym(o)
wax: cer(o)
way: ode
weak: asthen(o), lept(o)
wealth: plut(o)
weather: meteor(o)
web: hypho
weight: bar(o)
well: agath(o)
wet: hygr(o)
whale: cet(o)
wheel: troch(o)
whip: mastig(o), mastix
white: alb(o), cali(o), calli(o), leuc(o), leuk(o)
whole: hol(o), integri, pan(o), toti
wholly: toti
wide: eury, lati
wild: agrio
wild beast: ther(o)
wind: anem(o), venti, vento
windpipe: bronchi(o), trache(o)
wing: ali, pter(o)
within: end(o), ent(o), eso
wolf: lyc(o)
woman: gyn(e) (o), gynaec(o), gynec(o)
womb: hyster(o), metr(a) (o), uter(o)
wood: hyl(o), lign(i) (o), xyl(o)
wool: erio, lan(i) (o)
word: log(o), verb(i)
work: erg(o) (y)
worker: ergat(o)
world: cosm(o)
worm: helminth(o), vermi
worship: latry
wound: traumat(o)
wrist: carp(o)
writer: grapher
writing: grapho
year: ennial
yellow: chrys(o), flav(o), lute(o), xanth(o)
yoke: zyg(o)
yolk: vitell(o)